Koren Talmud Bavli

THE NOÉ EDITION

KETUBOT · PART ONE

Shefa

KOREN

תלמוד בבלי

KOREN TALMUD BAVLI

THE NOÉ EDITION

כתובות א

KETUBOT · PART ONE

COMMENTARY BY
Rabbi Adin Even-Israel
Steinsaltz

EDITOR-IN-CHIEF
Rabbi Dr Tzvi Hersh Weinreb

EXECUTIVE EDITOR
Rabbi Joshua Schreier

•

SHEFA FOUNDATION
KOREN PUBLISHERS JERUSALEM

Supported by the Matanel Foundation

Koren Talmud Bavli, The Noé Edition
Volume 16: Tractate Ketubot, Part One

Standard Size Color Edition, ISBN 978 965 301 577 7
Daf Yomi Size B&W Edition, ISBN 978 965 301 622 4

First Hebrew/English Edition, 2015

Koren Publishers Jerusalem Ltd.
PO Box 4044, Jerusalem 91040, ISRAEL
PO Box 8531, New Milford, CT 06776, USA
www.korenpub.com

Shefa Foundation

Shefa Foundation is the parent organization of institutions established by Rabbi Adin Even-Israel Steinsaltz

PO Box 45187, Jerusalem 91450 ISRAEL
Telephone: +972 2 646 0900, Fax +972 2 624 9454
www.hashefa.co.il

Hardcover design by Ben Gasner

הִנֵּה יָמִים בָּאִים, נְאֻם אֲדֹנָי יֱהֹוִה, וְהִשְׁלַחְתִּי רָעָב בָּאָרֶץ,
לֹא־רָעָב לַלֶּחֶם וְלֹא־צָמָא לַמַּיִם, כִּי אִם־לִשְׁמֹעַ אֵת דִּבְרֵי יהוה.

Behold, days are coming – says the Lord God –
I will send a hunger to the land, not a hunger for bread
nor a thirst for water, but to hear the words of the Lord.

(AMOS 8:11)

The Noé edition of the Koren Talmud Bavli
with the commentary of Rabbi Adin Even-Israel Steinsaltz
is dedicated to all those who open its cover
to quench their thirst for Jewish knowledge,
in our generation of Torah renaissance.

This beautiful edition is for the young, the aged,
the novice and the savant alike,
as it unites the depth of Torah knowledge
with the best of academic scholarship.

Within its exquisite and vibrant pages,
words become worlds.

It will claim its place in the library of classics,
in the bookcases of the Beit Midrash,
the classrooms of our schools,
and in the offices of professionals and businesspeople
who carve out precious time to grapple with its timeless wisdom.

For the Student and the Scholar

DEDICATED BY LEO AND SUE NOÉ

Once upon a time, under pressure of censorship,
printers would inscribe in the flyleaves
of volumes of the Talmud:

Whatever may be written herein about gentiles
does not refer to the gentiles of today,
but to gentiles of times past.

Today, the flyleaves of our books bear a similar inscription,
albeit an invisible one:

Whatever may be written herein about Jews
does not refer to the Jews of today,
but to Jews who lived in other times.

So we are able to sit down and study Torah, Talmud,
books of ethics, or books of faith
without considering their relevance to our lives.

Whatever is written there
does not apply to us or to our generation,
but only to other people, other times.

We must expunge from those invisible prologues
the notion that the words are written about someone else,
about others, about anyone but us.

Whether the book is a volume of Torah,
a tractate of the Talmud, or a tract of faith,
the opposite must be inscribed:

Whatever is written herein refers only to me;
is written for me and obligates me.

First and foremost, the content is addressed to me.

– From a public address by Rabbi Adin Even-Israel Steinsaltz
as quoted in חיי עולם (*Talks on Parashat HaShavua*)
Maggid Books, 2011

Contents

For the vocalized Vilna Shas layout, please open as a Hebrew book.

Haskama

Rabbi Moshe Feinstein

RABBI MOSES FEINSTEIN
455 F. D. R. DRIVE
New York, N. Y. 10002

OREgon 7-1222

משה פיינשטיין
ר״ם תפארת ירושלים
בנוא יארק

בע״ה

הנה ראיתי הפירוש החשוב של הרב הגאון מוהר״ר עדין שטיינזלץ שליט״א מעיה״ק ירושלים, על מסכתות ביצה ור״ה. באמת כבר ידוע לי פירושו של הרה״ג הנ״ל על מסכתות מתלמוד בבלי, וכבר כתבתי מכתב הסכמה עליהם. ובאתי בזה רק להדגיש מחדש איך שהפירושים של הרה״ג הנ״ל, שכולל פירוש חדש על הגמרא עצמו וגם פירוש שיש בו סיכום להלכה מהנידונים שבגמרא, נוסף לעוד כמה חלקים, הם באמת עבודה גדולה, שיכולים להיות לתועלת לא רק לאלו שכבר מורגלים בלמוד הגמרא, ורוצים להעמק יותר, אלא גם לאלו שמתחילים ללמוד, להדריכם בדרכי התורה איך להבין ולהעמיק בים התלמוד.

והריני מברך להרה״ג הנ״ל שיצליחהו השי״ת בספריו אלו ושיזכה לחבר עוד ספרים, להגדיל תורה ולהאדירה, לתפארת השם ותורתו.

ועל זה באתי על החתום לכבוד התורה ביום ז׳ לחודש אייר תשמ״ג.

משה פיינשטיין

משה פיינשטיין

…These new commentaries – which include a new interpretation of the Talmud, a halakhic summary of the debated issues, and various other sections – are a truly outstanding work; they can be of great benefit not only to those familiar with talmudic study who seek to deepen their understanding, but also to those who are just beginning to learn, guiding them through the pathways of the Torah and teaching them how to delve into the sea of the Talmud.

I would like to offer my blessing to this learned scholar. May the Holy One grant him success with these volumes and may he merit to write many more, to enhance the greatness of Torah, and bring glory to God and His word…

Rabbi Moshe Feinstein
New York, 7 Adar 5743

ר׳ משה פיינשטיין שליט״א

הנה ראיתי את מסכת אחת מהש״ס שנקד אותה וגם צייר צורות הצמחים וכדומה מדברים שלא ידוע לכמה אנשים הרה״ג ר׳ עדין שטיינזלץ מירושלים שליט״א וגם הוסיף שם בגליון פירושים וחידושים וניכר שהוא ת״ח וראויין לעיין בהם ת״ח ובני הישיבה וטוב גם לקניתם בבתי כנסיות ובבתי מדרשות שיש שיהיו להם לתועלת. — ועל זה באתי עה״ח ג׳ אדר ב׳ תש״ל.

נאם משה פיינשטיין
ר״מ תפארת ירושלים, ניו־יורק, ארה״ב

I have seen one tractate from the Talmud to which the great scholar Rabbi Adin Steinsaltz שליט״א has added *nikkud* (vowels) and illustrations to explain that which is unknown to many people; he has also added interpretations and innovations, and is evidently a *talmid ḥakham*. *Talmidei ḥakhamim* and yeshiva students ought to study these volumes, and synagogues and *batei midrash* would do well to purchase them, as they may find them useful.

Rabbi Moshe Feinstein
New York, Adar 5730

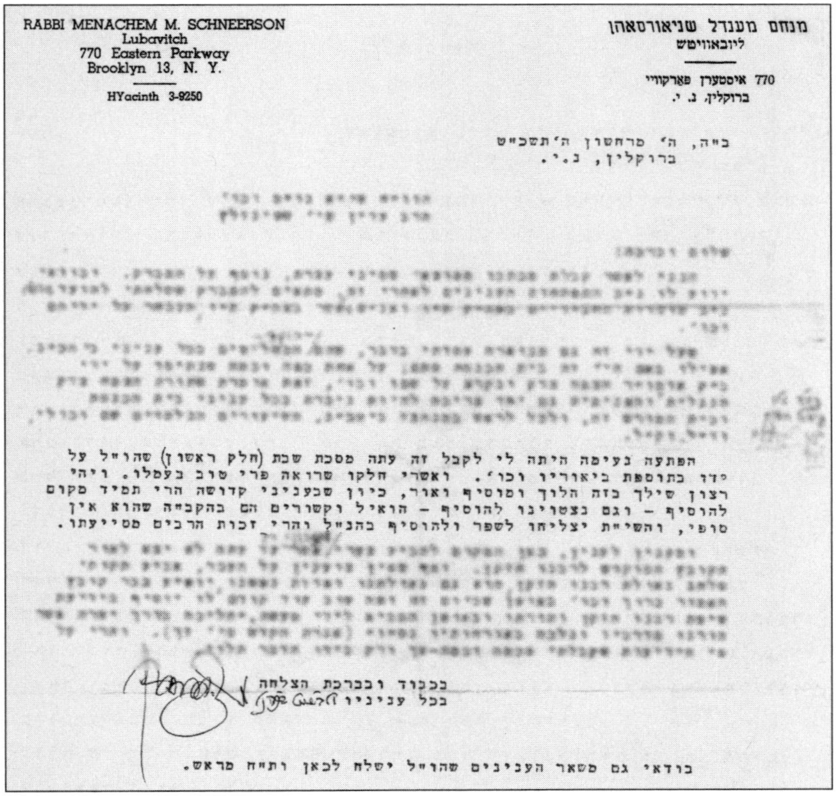
RABBI MENACHEM M. SCHNEERSON
Lubavitch
770 Eastern Parkway
Brooklyn 13, N. Y.
HYacinth 3-9250

מנחם מענדל שניאורסאהן
ליובאוויטש
770 איסטערן פּארקוויי
ברוקלין, נ. י.

ב״ה, ה׳ מרחשון ה׳תשכ״ט
ברוקלין, נ.י.

הפתעה נעימה היתה לי לקבל זה עתה מסכת שבת (חלק ראשון) שהו״ל על ידו בתוספת ביאוריו וכו׳. ואשרי חלקו שרואה פרי טוב בעמלו. ויהי רצון שילך בזה הלוך ומוסיף ואור, כיון שבעניני קדושה הרי תמיד מקום להוסיף – וגם נצטוינו להוסיף – הואיל וקשורים הם בהקב״ה שהוא אין סופי, והשי״ת יצליחו לשפר ולהוסיף בהנ״ל והרי זכות הרבים מסייעתו.

בכבוד ובברכת הצלחה
בכל עניניו

בודאי גם משאר הענינים שהו״ל ישלח לכאן ותח״ח מראש.

Haskama
Rabbi Menachem Mendel Schneerson

…I have just had the pleasant surprise of receiving tractate *Shabbat* (part one), which has been published by [Rabbi Steinsaltz] along with his explanations, etc. Happy is the man who sees good fruits from his labors. May he continue in this path and increase light, for in the matters of holiness there is always room to add – and we have been commanded to add – for they are linked to the Holy One, Blessed be He, Who is infinite. And may the Holy One grant him success to improve and enhance this work, since the greater good strengthens his hand…

Rabbi Menachem Mendel Schneerson
The Lubavitcher Rebbe
Brooklyn, 5 Marḥeshvan 5729

Haskama

Rabbi Moshe Zvi Neria

העתק של הרב משה צבי נריה

ב"ה

"ושמעו ביום ההוא החרשים דברי ספר"
(ישעי' כט' יח')

תרגום ספרי קדמונים לשפת דורות אחרונים – היא משימתם של חכמי דור ודור. ובישראל שמצוות "ושננתם לבניך" מקיפה את כל חלקי האומה, ודאי שהיתה זאת המשימה בכל עידן ועידן.

בכל דור כך, ובדורנו אשר רבים בו הקרובים שנתרחקו וחוזרים ומתקרבים – לא כל שכן. כי רבים היום האומרים "מי ישקנו מים מבאר" התלמוד, ומועטים הם הדולים ומשקים.

ראוי אפוא להערכה מיוחדת נסיונו המבורך של הצעיר המופלא, הרב עדין שטיינזלץ, לפרש פרקי-תלמוד בהסברה מורחבת-תמציתית, אשר נוסף על הפרוש המלולי והעניני הוא מעלה גם את ההגיון של הדברים ומתרגמת אותם לשפת-המושגים של בן-דורנו.

דומה שכל הנגשים אל חומר למודי מתוך רצון להבינו – התלמיד החרוץ והמבוגר המשכיל – לא יתקלו בשום קושי בבואם ללמוד סוגיא תלמודית לפי פרוש זה. ולא עוד אלא שיש לקוות כי ההסברה הגיונית תעמידם מיד על טוב-הטעם [illegible] של דף-הגמרא, והם ימשכו יותר ויותר אל הלמוד העיוני הזה אשר טובי המוחות בישראל לנו בעומקו, ואשר ממנו פינה, ממנו יתד לבנין חיינו.

נועם ד' על המפרש הנמרץ להמשיך במפעלו, וברוכים כל העוזרים להוצאתו לאור-עולם.

ביקר אורייתא

(חתימה)

The translation of the books of our past into the language of the present – this was the task of the sages of every generation. And in Israel, where the command to "teach them repeatedly to your children" applies to all parts of the nation, it was certainly the task of every era. This is true for every generation, and in our time – when many of those who have strayed far are once again drawing near – all the more so. For many today say, "Who will let us drink from the well" of Talmud, and few are those who offer up the waters to drink.

We must, therefore, particularly commend the blessed endeavor of Rabbi Adin Steinsaltz to explain the chapters of the Talmud in this extensive yet succinct commentary, which, in addition to its literal interpretation of the text, also explicates the latter's underlying logic and translates it into the language of our generation.

It appears that all those who seek to study Talmud – the diligent student and the learned adult – will have no difficulty understanding when using this commentary. Moreover, we may hope that the logical explanation will reveal to them the beauty of the talmudic page, and they will be drawn deeper and deeper into the intellectual pursuit which has engaged the best Jewish minds, and which serves as the cornerstone of our very lives…

Rabbi Moshe Zvi Neria

 This haskama refers to the original Hebrew edition of the Steinsaltz Talmud, upon which this volume is based

ב"ה

MORDECHAI ELIAHU
FORMER CHIEF RABBI OF ISRAEL & RICHON LEZION

מרדכי אליהו
הראשון לציון והרב הראשי לישראל לשעבר

ז' בתשרי תשנ"ד
נד.5-137

מכתב ברכה

הגמרא בעירובין כ"א: אומרת: דרש רבא מאי דכתיב ויותר שהיה קהלת חכם, עוד לימד דעת את העם - ואזן וחקר תקן משלים הרבה". לימד דעת את העם - קבע כיצד לקרוא פסוק וסימנים בין תיבות המקרא וממשיכה הגמרא ואומרת: אמר עולא אמר ר' אליעזר בתחילה היתה תורה דומה לכפיפה שאין לה אזנים עד שבא שלמה ועשה לה אזנים". וכדברי רש"י שם: "וע"י כך אוחזין ישראל במצות שנתרחקו מן העבירה כדרך שנוח לאחוז בכלי שיש לו בית יד וכו' (ערובין כ"א, י').

דברים מעין אלו אפשר לאמר על האי גברא יקירא, על איש מורם מעם, משכמו ומעלה בתורה ובמידות. ויותר ממה שעשה בתורה שבע"פ עושה בתורה שבכתב - מלמד דעת את העם. ולא זו בלבד אלא גם עושה אזנים לתורה, היא תורת התלמוד שהוא חתום וסתום בפני רבים. ורק מעט מזער מבני עליה שהם מועטים ומי שלומד בישיבה יכל כיום ללמוד בש"ס ולהבין מה שלפניו, ואף שיש לנו פירוש רש"י, עדין לא הכל ממשמשין בו. עד שקם הרב הגדול מעוז ומגדול הרה"ג ר' **עדין שטיינזלץ** שליט"א ועשה אזנים לתורה, שאפשר לאחוז גמרא ביד וללמוד, ואפי' לפשוטי העם ועשה פרושים ושם אותם בצד הארון, פרושים נאים בשפה ברורה ונעימה דבר דבור על אופניו. ועם הסברים וציורים להבין ולהשכיל, כדי שמי שרוצה לקרבה אל מלאכת ה' ללמוד יכל לעשות זאת.

ועיני ראו ולא זר שבשיעורי תורה בגמרא הרבה באים עם גמרות בידם ואלה שבאים עם "פירוש הרב שטיינזלץ לתלמוד הבבלי" הם מוכנים ומבינים טוב יותר. כי כבר יש להם הקדמה מפרושיו ומבאוריו.
ואמינא לפועלו יישר ומן שמיא זכו ליה ללמד דעת את העם .

ויהי רצון שחפץ בידו יצלח, וכל אשר יפנה ישכיל ויצליח, ויזכה להגדיל תורה ולהאדירה, ויוסיף לנו עוד גמרות מבוארות כהנה וכהנה עד לסיומו , "וישראל עושה חיל".

ובזכות לימוד תורה ואני זאת בריתי וכו', ובא לציון גואל, בב"א.

מרדכי אליהו
ראשון לציון הרב הראשי לישראל לשעבר

Haskama

Rabbi Mordechai Eliyahu

The Talmud in *Eruvin* 21b states: Rava continued to interpret verses homiletically. What is the meaning of the verse: "And besides being wise, Kohelet also taught the people knowledge; and he weighed, and sought out, and set in order many proverbs" (Ecclesiastes 12:9)? He explains: He taught the people knowledge; he taught it with the accentuation marks in the Torah, and explained each matter by means of another matter similar to it. And he weighed [*izen*], and sought out, and set in order many proverbs; Ulla said that Rabbi Eliezer said: At first the Torah was like a basket without handles [*oznayim*] until Solomon came and made handles for it. And as Rashi there explains: And thus were Israel able to grasp the mitzvot and distance themselves from transgressions – just as a vessel with handles is easily held, etc.

Such things may be said of this beloved and eminent man, a great sage of Torah and of virtue. And far more than he has done with the Oral Torah, he does with the Written Torah – teaching the people knowledge. And beyond that, he also affixes handles to the Torah, i.e., to the Talmud, which is obscure and difficult for many. Only the intellectual elite, which are a precious few, and those who study in yeshiva, can today learn the Talmud and understand what it says – and even though we have Rashi, still not everyone uses him. But now the great scholar Rabbi Adin Steinsaltz שליט"א has come and affixed handles to the Torah, allowing the Talmud to be held and studied, even by simple men. And he has composed a commentary alongside the text, a fine commentary in clear, comprehensible language, "a word fitly spoken" with explanations and illustrations, so that all those who seek to study the work of God can do so.

Rabbi Mordechai Eliyahu
Former Chief Rabbi of Israel, 7 Tishrei 5754

Message from Rabbi Adin Even-Israel Steinsaltz

The Talmud is the cornerstone of Jewish culture. True, our culture originated in the Bible and has branched out in directions besides the Talmud, yet the latter's influence on Jewish culture is fundamental. Perhaps because it was composed not by a single individual, but rather by hundreds and thousands of Sages in *batei midrash* in an ongoing, millennium-long process, the Talmud expresses the deepest themes and values not only of the Jewish people, but also of the Jewish spirit. As the basic study text for young and old, laymen and learned, the Talmud may be said to embody the historical trajectory of the Jewish soul. It is, therefore, best studied interactively, its subject matter coming together with the student's questions, perplexities, and innovations to form a single intricate weave. In the entire scope of Jewish culture, there is not one area that does not draw from or converse with the Talmud. The study of Talmud is thus the gate through which a Jew enters his life's path.

The *Koren Talmud Bavli* seeks to render the Talmud accessible to the millions of Jews whose mother tongue is English, allowing them to study it, approach it, and perhaps even become one with it.

This project has been carried out and assisted by several people, all of whom have worked tirelessly to turn this vision into an actual set of books to be studied. It is a joyful duty to thank the many partners in this enterprise for their various contributions. Thanks to Koren Publishers Jerusalem, both for the publication of this set and for the design of its very complex graphic layout. Thanks of a different sort are owed to the Shefa Foundation and its director, Rabbi Menachem Even-Israel, for their determination and persistence in setting this goal and reaching it. Many thanks to the translators, editors, and proofreaders for their hard and meticulous work. Thanks to the individuals and organizations that supported this project, chief among them the Matanel Foundation and the Noé family of London. And thanks in advance to all those who will invest their time, hearts, and minds in studying these volumes – to learn, to teach, and to practice.

Rabbi Adin Even-Israel Steinsaltz
Jerusalem 5773

Acknowledgments

We are indeed privileged to dedicate this edition of the *Koren Talmud Bavli* in honor of the generous support of Leo and Sue Noé of London.

The name Noé is synonymous with philanthropy. The family's charitable endeavors span a vast range of educational projects, welfare institutions, and outreach organizations across the globe, with a particular emphasis on the "nurturing of each individual." Among so many other charitable activities, the Noés have been deeply involved with Kisharon, which provides the British Jewish community with vital support for hundreds of people with learning difficulties and their families; they provide steadfast support of SEED, which stands at the forefront of adult Jewish education in the UK, and Kemach, an organization in Israel that "helps Haredi students sustain themselves in dignity," providing both professional and vocational training for the Haredi community in Israel.

The Noés are not simply donors to institutions. They are partners. Donors think of a sum. Partners think of a cause, becoming rigorously and keenly involved, and giving of their time and energy. We are honored that they have chosen to partner with our two organizations, Shefa and Koren Publishers Jerusalem, enabling us to further and deepen learning among all Jews.

Leo and Sue are the proud parents and grandparents of five children and their families. The next generation has been taught by example that with life's gifts come the responsibilities to be active within and contribute to society – both Jewish and non-Jewish – as is consistent with the noblest of Jewish values.

Rabbi Adin Even-Israel Steinsaltz
Matthew Miller, Publisher
Jerusalem 5773

Introduction by the Editor-in-Chief

The vastly expanded audience of Talmud study in our generation is a phenomenon of historical proportions. The reasons for this phenomenon are many, and include the availability of a wide array of translations, commentaries, and study aids.

One outstanding example of such a work is the translation of the Talmud into modern Hebrew by Rabbi Adin Even-Israel Steinsaltz. The product of a lifetime of intense intellectual labor, this translation stands out in its uniqueness.

But what can the interested student do if he or she does not comprehend the Hebrew, even in its modern form? Where is the English speaker who wishes to access this instructive material to turn? The *Koren Talmud Bavli* that you hold in your hand is designed to be the answer to those questions.

This work is the joint effort of Rabbi Steinsaltz himself, his closest advisory staff, and Koren Publishers Jerusalem. It is my privilege to have been designated editor-in-chief of this important project, and to have worked in close collaboration with a team of translators and copy editors, artists and graphic designers, scholars and editors.

Together we are presenting to the English-speaking world a translation that possesses all the merits of the original Hebrew work by Rabbi Steinsaltz and provides assistance for the beginner of any age who seeks to obtain the necessary skills to become an adept talmudist.

To date we have completed the orders of *Zera'im* and *Moed*. Our work has been enthusiastically received by a broad and diverse audience. Particularly gratifying is the fact that many have chosen to use our text as the basis for the group study of Talmud. We appreciate the comments and suggestions from our readers the world over and are committed to improving future editions of the *Koren Talmud Bavli* on the basis of that input. Indeed, a second edition of our first volume, *Berakhot*, has already been released, incorporating much of the advice brought to our attention by our readers. We encourage you to continue to advise us of your experience with our work.

Ketubot, Part I, is the sixteenth volume of this project. It includes the entire original text, in the traditional configuration and pagination of the famed Vilna edition of the Talmud. This enables the student to follow the core text with the commentaries of Rashi, *Tosafot*, and the customary marginalia. It also provides a clear English translation in contemporary idiom, faithfully based upon the modern Hebrew edition.

At least equal to the linguistic virtues of this edition are the qualities of its graphic design. Rather than intimidate students by confronting them with a page-size block of text, we have divided the page into smaller thematic units. Thus, readers can focus their attention and absorb each discrete discussion before proceeding to the next unit. The design of each page allows for sufficient white space to ease the visual task of reading. The illustrations, one of the most innovative features of the Hebrew edition, have been substantially enhanced and reproduced in color.

The end result is a literary and artistic masterpiece. This has been achieved through the dedicated work of a large team of translators, headed by Rabbi Joshua Schreier, and through the unparalleled creative efforts of Raphaël Freeman and the gifted staff at Koren.

The group of individuals who surround Rabbi Steinsaltz and support his work deserve our thanks as well. I have come to appreciate their energy, initiative, and persistence. And I thank the indefatigable Rabbi Menachem Even-Israel, whom I cannot praise highly enough. The quality of his guidance and good counsel is surpassed only by his commitment to the dissemination and perpetuation of his father's precious teachings.

Finally, in humility, awe, and great respect, I acknowledge Rabbi Adin Even-Israel Steinsaltz. I thank him for the inspirational opportunity he has granted me to work with one of the outstanding sages of our time.

Rabbi Tzvi Hersh Weinreb
Jerusalem 5775

Preface by the Executive Editor

Toward the beginning of tractate *Pesaḥim* (3a), the Gemara questions the Mishna's use of the term *or* rather than the standard term *leil* when referring to the evening of the fourteenth of Nisan. The Gemara introduces a discussion of the value of euphemism and refraining from the use of crude language. It concludes that despite the importance of euphemism, if the euphemism comes at the expense of clarity and requires a less succinct formulation, it is preferable to speak concisely. Only when the choice is between equally concise phrases is the euphemism preferred.

In his *peirush*, Rabbi Steinsaltz's language is both concise and aesthetic. While explaining often difficult passages, he avoids the temptation to over-explain, inviting the reader to study the Talmud with him rather than doing all the thinking in the reader's place. We have attempted to follow his path in translating and editing the *Koren Talmud Bavli*.

My involvement in the production of the *Koren Talmud Bavli* has been both a privilege and a pleasure. The Shefa Foundation, headed by Rabbi Menachem Even-Israel and devoted to the dissemination of the wide-ranging, monumental works of Rabbi Adin Even-Israel Steinsaltz, constitutes the Steinsaltz side of this partnership; Koren Publishers Jerusalem, headed by Matthew Miller, with the day-to-day management of the project in the able hands of Dena Landowne Bailey, constitutes the publishing side of this partnership. The combination of the inspiration, which is the hallmark of Shefa, with the creativity and professionalism for which Koren is renowned and which I experience on a daily basis, has lent the *Koren Talmud Bavli* its outstanding quality in terms of both content and form.

I would like to express my appreciation for Rabbi Dr. Tzvi Hersh Weinreb, the editor-in-chief, whose insight and guidance have been invaluable. The contribution of my friend and colleague, Rabbi Dr. Shalom Z. Berger, the senior content editor, cannot be overstated; his title does not begin to convey the excellent direction he has provided in all aspects of this project. In addition, I would like to thank Rabbi Jason Rappoport, managing editor; Rabbi Joshua Amaru, coordinating editor; and Rabbi Avishai Magence, content curator, whose tireless devotion to this project has been and continues to be crucial to its continued success. The erudite and articulate men and women who serve as translators, editors, and copy editors have ensured that this project adheres to the highest standards.

There are several others whose contributions to this project cannot be overlooked. On the Steinsaltz side: Meir HaNegbi, Yacov Elbert, and Tsipora Ifrah. On the Koren side, my colleagues at Koren: Rabbi David Fuchs, Rabbi Hanan Benayahu, Efrat Gross, Rachel Hanstater Meghnagi, Rabbi Eliahu Misgav, and Rabbi Yinon Chen. Their assistance in all matters, large and small, is appreciated.

At the risk of being repetitious, I would like to thank Rabbi Dr. Berger for introducing me to the world of Steinsaltz. Finally, I would like to thank Rabbi Menachem Even-Israel, with whom it continues to be a pleasure to move forward in this great enterprise.

Rabbi Joshua Schreier
Jerusalem 5773

Introduction by the Publisher

The Talmud has sustained and inspired Jews for thousands of years. Throughout Jewish history, an elite cadre of scholars has absorbed its learning and passed it on to succeeding generations. The Talmud has been the fundamental text of our people.

Beginning in the 1960s, Rabbi Adin Even-Israel Steinsaltz שליט״א created a revolution in the history of Talmud study. His translation of the Talmud, first into modern Hebrew and then into other languages, as well the practical learning aids he added to the text, have enabled millions of people around the world to access and master the complexity and context of the world of Talmud.

It is thus a privilege to present the *Koren Talmud Bavli*, an English translation of the talmudic text with the brilliant elucidation of Rabbi Steinsaltz. The depth and breadth of his knowledge are unique in our time. His rootedness in the tradition and his reach into the world beyond it are inspirational.

Working with Rabbi Steinsaltz on this remarkable project has been not only an honor, but a great pleasure. Never shy to express an opinion, with wisdom and humor, Rabbi Steinsaltz sparkles in conversation, demonstrating his knowledge (both sacred and worldly), sharing his wide-ranging interests, and, above all, radiating his passion. I am grateful for the unique opportunity to work closely with him, and I wish him many more years of writing and teaching.

Our intentions in publishing this new edition of the Talmud are threefold. First, we seek to fully clarify the talmudic page to the reader – textually, intellectually, and graphically. Second, we seek to utilize today's most sophisticated technologies, both in print and electronic formats, to provide the reader with a comprehensive set of study tools. And third, we seek to help readers advance in their process of Talmud study.

To achieve these goals, the *Koren Talmud Bavli* is unique in a number of ways:

- The classic *tzurat hadaf* of Vilna, used by scholars since the 1800s, has been reset for greater clarity, and opens from the Hebrew "front" of the book. Full *nikkud* has been added to both the talmudic text and Rashi's commentary, allowing for a more fluent reading with the correct pronunciation; the commentaries of *Tosafot* have been punctuated. Upon the advice of many English-speaking teachers of Talmud, we have separated these core pages from the translation, thereby enabling the advanced student to approach the text without the distraction of the translation. This also reduces the number of volumes in the set. At the bottom of each *daf*, there is a reference to the corresponding English pages. In addition, the Vilna edition was read against other manuscripts and older print editions, so that texts which had been removed by non-Jewish censors have been restored to their rightful place.

- The English translation, which starts on the English "front" of the book, reproduces the *menukad* Talmud text alongside the English translation (in bold) and commentary and explanation (in a lighter font). The Hebrew and Aramaic text is presented in logical paragraphs. This allows for a fluent reading of the text for the non-Hebrew or non-Aramaic reader. It also allows for the Hebrew reader to refer easily to the text alongside. Where the original text features dialogue or poetry, the English text is laid out in a manner appropriate to the genre. Each page refers to the relevant *daf*.
- Critical contextual tools surround the text and translation: personality notes, providing short biographies of the Sages; language notes, explaining foreign terms borrowed from Greek, Latin, Persian, or Arabic; and background notes, giving information essential to the understanding of the text, including history, geography, botany, archaeology, zoology, astronomy, and aspects of daily life in the talmudic era.
- Halakhic summaries provide references to the authoritative legal decisions made over the centuries by the rabbis. They explain the reasons behind each halakhic decision as well as the ruling's close connection to the Talmud and its various interpreters.
- Photographs, drawings, and other illustrations have been added throughout the text – in full color in the Standard and Electronic editions, and in black and white in the Daf Yomi edition – to visually elucidate the text.

This is not an exhaustive list of features of this edition; it merely presents an overview for the English-speaking reader who may not be familiar with the "total approach" to Talmud pioneered by Rabbi Steinsaltz.

Several professionals have helped bring this vast collaborative project to fruition. My many colleagues are noted on the Acknowledgments page, and the leadership of this project has been exceptional.

RABBI MENACHEM EVEN-ISRAEL, DIRECTOR OF THE SHEFA FOUNDATION, was the driving force behind this enterprise. With enthusiasm and energy, he formed the happy alliance with Koren and established close relationships among all involved in the work.

RABBI DR. TZVI HERSH WEINREB שליט״א, EDITOR-IN-CHIEF, brought to this project his profound knowledge of Torah, intellectual literacy of Talmud, and erudition of Western literature. It is to him that the text owes its very high standard, both in form and content, and the logical manner in which the beauty of the Talmud is presented.

RABBI JOSHUA SCHREIER, EXECUTIVE EDITOR, assembled an outstanding group of scholars, translators, editors, and copy editors, whose standards and discipline enabled this project to proceed in a timely and highly professional manner.

RABBI MEIR HANEGBI, EDITOR OF THE HEBREW EDITION OF THE STEINSALTZ TALMUD, lent his invaluable assistance throughout the work process, supervising the reproduction of the Vilna pages.

RAPHAËL FREEMAN created this Talmud's unique typographic design which, true to the Koren approach, is both elegant and user-friendly.

It has been an enriching experience for all of us at Koren Publishers Jerusalem to work with the Shefa Foundation and the Steinsaltz Center to develop and produce the *Koren Talmud Bavli*. We pray that this publication will be a source of great learning and, ultimately, greater *avodat Hashem* for all Jews.

Matthew Miller, Publisher
Koren Publishers Jerusalem
Jerusalem 5773

Introduction to **Ketubot**

Ketubot is the central tractate in the order of *Nashim*. It provides clarification of most of the matters that constitute the relationship between husband and wife: Conjugal relations, mutual obligations, and monetary arrangements between them. In a general sense it addresses the entirety of marital life. Due to the abundance and variety of the topics, which branch out into many different areas of *halakha*, the early commentaries called tractate *Ketubot* the miniature Talmud or the key to the Talmud.

The marital bond is, from its inception, a sacred bond, which explains the fact that the term for betrothal is sanctification [*kiddushin*]. That bond can be terminated only by the death of one of the parties or by means of a special document, a scroll of severance. Violation of this bond by means of adultery engenders severe punishments administered both by man, i.e., execution by stoning or strangulation, and by Heaven, i.e., *karet*, besides fines and monetary penalties.

At the same time, according to *halakha*, the relationship between husband and wife within the framework of marriage is founded upon a system of mutual commitments fashioned on the basis of provisions and arrangements agreed upon by the parties. This system of arrangements is set out in a contract formulated between the husband and wife or their representatives, the marriage contract [*ketuba*]. This *ketuba* is fundamentally a written [*katuv*] contract, and is characterized in that manner because it is, for all intents and purposes, the only written document that every person requires. Since the provisions between husband and wife are articulated in the marriage contract, it is clear that the discussion in tractate *Ketubot* is fundamentally a comprehensive analysis of the marital rights and obligations.

The significance of the marriage contract is not merely as a practical apparatus regulating married life. The Sages established that marital ties not regulated by a marriage contract do not constitute marriage at all. The fundamental difference between a casual relationship, licentious relations, and marriage is contingent upon both the existence of an agreement between the parties articulating their mutual commitments for the duration of their relationship and the arrangements governing their potential separation. Any marital relationship that is not regulated by a marriage contract is tantamount to a licentious relationship.

The details of the agreement between husband and wife are like the details of any contract; both parties entering into marriage establish the provisions on the basis of which they intend to live their life together. Certain restrictions exist, as the marriage agreement, like any other agreement, cannot include stipulations that are against *halakha*, because of the principle: Anyone who stipulates a condition counter to what is written in the Torah, his condition is void. This includes stipulations that call for violation of a prohibition as well as those that abrogate obligations incumbent upon the parties by Torah law. Furthermore, over the generations, a system of permanent provisions was instituted, which constitute the standard formula of the marriage contract.

Although husband and wife can agree to abrogate certain details, or to add details and other arrangements, the standard marriage contract has a fixed configuration that establishes the guidelines for the marriage, unless additional provisions were stipulated. Analysis of these provisions, ranging from the commitments that stem from the marriage by Torah law to the various rabbinic ordinances, as well as the cases where the standard formula can be amended and the manner in which these changes are effected, constitute the primary topics of this tractate.

Most of the provisions and arrangements in the marriage contract are universally accepted. However, the Sages of the Mishna and the Gemara disputed the details: Which provisions and *halakhot* are by Torah law and which are by rabbinic law; which provisions are compulsory for all and which of them are merely customary and can be amended. Fundamentally, the conclusion reached is that there is a distinction between provisions that govern interpersonal relations, which cannot be abrogated, and monetary agreements, even those by Torah law, which can be amended or abrogated at the agreement of the two parties.

Based on Exodus 21:10, the obligations of a husband to his wife by Torah law are food, clothing, and conjugal rights. Food refers to the husband's obligation to provide sustenance to his wife according to her needs; clothing, his obligation to provide her with garments; and conjugal relations, his obligation to engage with her in sexual relations at regular intervals. Also by Torah law, the husband is entitled to nullify certain vows taken by his wife. After her death he inherits her property, although not everyone agrees that this is by Torah law. By rabbinic law, the husband is obligated to pay his wife's medical bills and to redeem her from captivity.

The Sages instituted that the wife will perform certain tasks in the home as well as contribute to supporting the family. Income that the wife earns from work, as well as any profits accrued from property belonging to her, and any lost item that she finds, belong to the husband. The Sages also instituted ordinances relating to the rights of the woman after the ties between them are severed by means of divorce or death.

One primary ordinance is the fixed sum of money identified as payment of the bill of divorce, which the husband is obligated pay his wife if he divorces her, or the heirs are obligated to pay the wife if she is widowed. For this payment, there is a distinction between a virgin, whose marriage contract is two hundred dinars, and one who is not a virgin, whose marriage contract is one hundred dinars. The husband is permitted to add to that sum any amount of money that he chooses, but he may not reduce the fixed sum. If he does, that is tantamount to nullification of the marriage contract, and the couple's relations are considered licentious and not marital relations.

The early Sages instituted that all the husband's property is liened to payment of the marriage contract. After the woman dies, the husband is obligated to bury her. After the death of the husband, the widow may continue to live in his house and be supported from his property for the duration of her widowhood. Likewise, there is a fixed condition that by the authority of the marriage contract, daughters born to the husband from this wife are supported from his property after his death, and sons born to this woman inherit the sum of her marriage contract in addition to their share in the inheritance.

This system of marital obligations and rights is typically in effect in every marriage, as even if a particular stipulation is omitted from the document, it is in effect as a stipulation of the court. However, the precise application of these provisions in different cases requires analysis. Similarly, the question arises: Which are the provisions that cannot be amended or abrogated, either due to their essence or because the Sages decreed that they cannot be changed or eliminated? And with regard to the provisions that can be amended, what is the legal way to effect this?

Marriage is based on agreement, and as such, conflict is apt to arise between the parties. Quarrels or incompatibility require intervention of the courts or halakhic authorities only if the couple decides to separate. However, there are additional conflicts that require halakhic resolution. One example is when husband and wife each accuse the other that he or she violated the provisions of the agreement. These claims can be with regard to the marriage itself, e.g., when one of the parties claims that he was misled to the extent that he would not have agreed to marry had he been privy to that information. Cases where this problem arises after betrothal and prior to marriage are discussed in tractate *Kiddushin*; cases where this problem arises after marriage belong in tractate *Ketubot*. There are additional claims with regard to fulfillment of the provisions of the agreement between the parties, where each accuses the other of failure to fulfill the obligations.

When these disputes come before the court, there are two stages to the halakhic deliberation. First, the court seeks to ascertain whether or not the claims are true. In this case, more than in any other agreement, there are various details that are difficult or impossible to ascertain. For example, if the husband claims that he discovered on the wedding night that his wife was not a virgin, there is rarely external testimony supporting either the husband's claim or the bride's counterclaim. In order to resolve the dispute, the court must rely on general determinations with regard to the credibility of the people and their claims.

The second stage involves ameliorating the situation. Based on the severity of the claims of the husband or wife, there are different manners of resolution, e.g., annulment of the marriage; mandating that the husband divorce his wife, paying her marriage contract if he was the guilty party and not paying it if she was the guilty party; or imposing fines and penalties to compel fulfillment of the terms of the *ketuba*.

All these topics, both in terms of whether certain actions are permitted or prohibited as well as with regard to the monetary ramifications of those actions, constitute the primary focus of tractate *Ketubot*. In addition, several related matters are discussed, e.g., the *halakhot* of lineage, victims of rape and seduction, and the *halakhot* of the slanderer. Typically, the Gemara addresses various tangential matters that arise in the course of discussion of these matters.

There are three general sections in this tractate: The first deals with the *halakhot* of a virgin; her marriage, as a victim of rape, and as a victim of slander. The second explores the details of the standard provisions of the marriage contract. The third discusses the *halakhot* of the wife's property and payment of the marriage contract. There are thirteen chapters in the tractate, the first five of which appear in the present volume. Typically, some address one defined issue and some address several, and some topics are discussed in several chapters.

Chapter One deals primarily with the marriage of a virgin and the credibility of the husband and the wife with regard to the claim concerning virginity.

Chapter Two deals with those cases where testimony is deemed credible from those whose testimony is typically not accepted, e.g., the testimony with regard to oneself or his relatives, or the testimony of one disqualified from testifying, such as a slave or a maidservant. The chapter also discusses the *halakhot* of a captive.

Chapter Three deals with the *halakhot* of a rapist and a seducer and analyzes the relationship between corporal and monetary punishment.

Chapter Four discusses in general the mutual rights of father and daughter, husband and wife, and specifically the *halakhot* of the slanderer. The primary provisions of the marriage contract are also explained.

Chapter Five discusses the details of the ordinances instituted with regard to the marriage contract and especially in cases where they alter the fixed provisions, either through mutual agreement or unilaterally.

Introduction to **Perek I**

This chapter deals primarily with the initial stages of marriage: The appropriate time, the marriage ceremony, and the monetary and ritual ramifications of the initial act of intercourse. Most of the questions analyzed are related to the *halakhot* of the marriage contract, specifically the marriage contract of the virgin.

The sum of the marriage contract of a virgin is two hundred dinars, and of a non-virgin, one hundred dinars. A fundamental question relates to the definition of a virgin for these purposes: Is this a medical-biological definition or is it merely a legal definition? Is a virgin a woman whose hymen is intact, a woman who never engaged in intercourse, or a woman who never married? On a related note, who are the women with the presumptive status of a virgin, and who are the women who have lost that presumptive status?

Various questions arise when a man marries a woman based on the assumption that she is a virgin and later discovers that she is not. His claim can be grounds for annulment, for reduction of the sum of the marriage contract, or for concern that the bride is forbidden to her husband as an adulteress. However, before these questions are analyzed, there is another fundamental problem: Was she or was she not a virgin when she married, and if she was not a virgin, how did she lose her virginity? Typically, there is no clear evidence or testimony in that case. There are instances where the woman admits that she was not a virgin, and there are instances where she explains the phenomenon in different ways. Therefore, it must be determined to what degree are the claims of the woman deemed credible. In what cases is the claim of the husband deemed credible, and in what cases is the claim of the wife deemed credible?

Stemming from these dilemmas, whose answers are largely dependent upon the credibility accorded to the husband's claim, another series of dilemmas is raised, not directly related to the *halakhot* of the marriage contract but related to matters of lineage. In the case of an unmarried woman who was suspected or proven to have engaged in intercourse with an unidentified man, to what degree is she deemed credible to claim that the man was of unflawed lineage and therefore she is not disqualified from marrying a priest? Likewise, if she was impregnated by an unidentified man, is she deemed credible if she says that the father of the fetus is of unflawed lineage?

These are the central issues raised in this chapter. However, in the course of clarifying them, difficulties with regard to the marriage ceremony are addressed. In addition, questions related to engaging in intercourse on Shabbat with one's virgin bride are discussed, as well as questions relating to other prohibitions.

מתני׳ בְּתוּלָה נִשֵּׂאת לְיוֹם הָרְבִיעִי, וְאַלְמָנָה לְיוֹם הַחֲמִישִׁי. שֶׁפַּעֲמַיִם בְּשַׁבָּת בָּתֵּי דִינִין יוֹשְׁבִין בָּעֲיָירוֹת: בַּיּוֹם הַשֵּׁנִי וּבַיּוֹם הַחֲמִישִׁי, שֶׁאִם הָיָה לוֹ טַעֲנַת בְּתוּלִים הָיָה מַשְׁכִּים לְבֵית דִּין.

MISHNA **A virgin**[N] **is married on Wednesday**[HN] **and a widow on Thursday.**[N] The reason for the former is **that twice a week**[N] **courts convene in the towns, on Monday and Thursday,** so **that if** the husband **had a claim concerning** the bride's **virginity**[N] when consummating the marriage on Wednesday night, **he would go early** the next day **to court** and make his claim.

גמ׳ אָמַר רַב יוֹסֵף אָמַר רַב יְהוּדָה אָמַר שְׁמוּאֵל: מִפְּנֵי מָה אָמְרוּ בְּתוּלָה נִשֵּׂאת לְיוֹם הָרְבִיעִי – לְפִי שֶׁשָּׁנִינוּ: הִגִּיעַ זְמַן וְלֹא נִישְּׂאוּ – אוֹכְלוֹת מִשֶּׁלּוֹ, וְאוֹכְלוֹת בִּתְרוּמָה.

GEMARA **Rav Yosef said** that **Rav Yehuda said** that **Shmuel said: Due to what** reason **did they say**[N] **that a virgin is married on Wednesday?** It is **because we learned** in a mishna elsewhere (57a): **If the time** that the groom designated for the wedding **arrived,** and the wedding was postponed, **and they were not married,** the brides are entitled to **eat from his** food **and,** if he is a priest, **eat *teruma*.**

יָכוֹל הִגִּיעַ זְמַן בְּאֶחָד בְּשַׁבָּת יְהֵא מַעֲלֶה לָהּ מְזוֹנוֹת – לְכָךְ שָׁנִינוּ: בְּתוּלָה נִשֵּׂאת לְיוֹם הָרְבִיעִי.

One might think that if the designated **time arrived on Sunday,** and the wedding was postponed, **he would provide her sustenance** beginning on Sunday. **Therefore, we learned: A virgin is married on Wednesday.** Until Wednesday, the designated time is not considered to have arrived, even if the original date was earlier in the week.

HALAKHA

A virgin is married on Wednesday – בְּתוּלָה נִשֵּׂאת לְיוֹם הָרְבִיעִי: In places where the courts convene only on Mondays and Thursdays, a virgin is married on Wednesday, so that if the groom has a claim concerning her virginity, he can go to court early the next day (Rambam *Sefer Nashim, Hilkhot Ishut* 10:15; *Shulḥan Arukh, Even HaEzer* 64:3).

NOTES

Virgin – בְּתוּלָה: *Tosafot* ask: Why doesn't the tractate begin with the definite article: The virgin, a style employed by the Mishna in other areas? The primary answer is that the definite article is employed only with regard to matters mentioned in the Torah, and the day set for the wedding of a virgin is a rabbinic ordinance.

Wednesday – יוֹם הָרְבִיעִי: *Tosafot* write that this indicates that the wedding is performed during the day and not on Wednesday night. This is because frequently lengthy negotiations precede the signing of the marriage contract between the parties. In addition, in the case of wedding performed at night, the wedding celebration and feast would likely extend deep into the night, (*Tiferet Yisrael*). Due to these factors, there is concern that if the wedding is performed at night, it will not be consummated that night.

The Ritva notes that use of the prefix *le*, meaning to, instead of *be*, meaning on, alludes to the fact cited later in the Gemara that the wedding is postponed to Wednesday even if the time designated for the marriage was earlier in the week. The prefix in the variant reading in the Jerusalem Talmud is the more conventional *be*.

And a widow on Thursday – וְאַלְמָנָה לְיוֹם הַחֲמִישִׁי: The mishna does not specify why a widow is married on Thursday. Some commentaries explain that the reasons cited in the Gemara for this ordinance do not apply in all cases. That the Sages were assiduous in seeing to the well-being of Jewish women (5a), ensuring that her groom will rejoice with her three days, applies only if the groom has a profession. The other reason cited there: Since the blessing of procreation was stated to man on the sixth day of Creation, is not obligatory (Ramban; Ritva).

The Ran writes that the main reason the Sages set a specific day for a wedding was for virgin brides, where there is concern that perhaps she committed adultery after betrothal and is therefore forbidden to the groom. Once that ordinance was instituted, additional reasons to establish a specific day for widows were suggested as well. However, since the primary ordinance was instituted for virgins, the Gemara does not elaborate on the ordinance instituted with regard to widows.

The Ran, in his commentary on the Rif, writes that the Sages obscured the reasons for establishing these specific days to prevent people from taking them lightly, as the reasons do not apply in all cases.

That twice a week – שֶׁפַּעֲמַיִם בְּשַׁבָּת: This ordinance that courts convene on Monday and Thursday is one of the ten ordinances instituted by Ezra (*Bava Kamma* 82a). Prior to the institution of that ordinance, no courts convened in the towns at all, and people would rely on the courts in the big cities, or convene a court ad hoc when necessary. No flexibility was displayed with regard to this ordinance in order to facilitate greater freedom in choosing a wedding day because of the significance accorded Ezra and his ordinances. There was concern that if one of his ordinances was revoked, others might follow (see Meiri).

If the husband had a claim concerning the bride's virginity – אִם הָיָה לוֹ טַעֲנַת בְּתוּלִים: The early commentaries question this reason from a variety of perspectives. For one, the Gemara in several places states that promiscuity is uncommon. Why then, did the Sages institute an ordinance due to an uncommon phenomenon?

They answer that when the Sages said that promiscuity was uncommon, they spoke with regard to specific cases, e.g., engaging in relations with one's sister's daughter or with a married woman. However, engaging in relations with a woman who is merely betrothed before marriage is sufficiently commonplace to warrant instituting the ordinance (see *Tosafot* and Rosh).

The commentaries raise an additional question with regard to the validity of the claim concerning virginity in terms of rendering the bride forbidden to him. Even if he discovered that she was not a virgin, there is a compound uncertainty with regard to whether his bride is forbidden: There is uncertainty whether she engaged in relations before betrothal, in which case she is not forbidden to him, or whether she did so after betrothal, in which case she is forbidden to him. There is additional uncertainty, as, even if she engaged in relations after betrothal, it is uncertain whether she engaged in relations of her own volition or whether she was raped, in which case she would be permitted to him. In cases of compound uncertainty with regard to a prohibition, the ruling is lenient. Therefore, the woman should be permitted in this case.

Therefore, *Tosafot* explain that the original ordinance setting the wedding of a virgin on Wednesday was instituted due to those women with regard to whom there is only one uncertainty, e.g., the wife of a priest, who is rendered forbidden to him even if she was raped, or a woman who was betrothed before she was three years and one day old, in which case it is clear that she engaged in relations after betrothal. Once the ordinance was in place, the Sages established it as the standard for all virgins.

Rashi explains that the groom's claim that the wife is not a virgin does not render her forbidden to her husband. Rather, the expectation is that once the matter is publicized in court, perhaps witnesses will come and testify that she committed volitional adultery after betrothal.

The Ritva explains that it is implausible that the Sages would institute an ordinance for the small minority of cases included in the explanation of *Tosafot*. However, if Rashi's reason is combined with theirs, that would provide sound basis for instituting the ordinance.

The Meiri cites an opinion shared by several commentaries. They explain that the hope is that when the woman stands before the court, if she is guilty, she will admit that she committed adultery. The Rashba rejects that opinion. The Meiri cites an additional consideration: There is a monetary aspect to the claim, as the groom is claiming that he agreed to a marriage contract of two hundred dinars based on the presumption that she was a virgin. After discovering that she is not a virgin, he claims that the marriage contract should be for the one hundred dinars to which a non-virgin is entitled, or even that the betrothal was a mistaken transaction and the bride is not entitled to a marriage contract at all.

Due to what reason did they say – מִפְּנֵי מָה אָמְרוּ: The commentaries go to great lengths to explain the first version of Shmuel's comments, which ties the ordinance that a virgin marry on Wednesday to the time from which the groom is duty bound to provide for his betrothed, in an attempt to explain why the Gemara thought to connect the two *halakhot*, although it was ultimately rejected.

According to the Rivash, Rav Yosef doesn't think that the claim concerning virginity is a sufficient reason to institute an ordinance, and so he wanted to explain Shmuel's position as follows: Since the Sages set a time after which the groom is obligated to provide for his betrothed, the wedding should take place on that day as well.

אֲמַר רַב יוֹסֵף: מָרֵיהּ דְּאַבְרָהָם! תָּלֵי תַּנְיָא בִּדְלָא תַּנְיָא. הֵי תַּנְיָא וְהֵי לָא תַּנְיָא? הָא תַּנְיָא וְהָא תַּנְיָא! אֶלָּא: תָּלֵי תַּנְיָא דִּמְפָרֵשׁ טַעֲמָא, בִּדְתַנְיָא דְּלָא מְפָרֵשׁ טַעֲמָא!

After citing the statements above, **Rav Yosef said** in astonishment: **Lord of Abraham,**[N] Shmuel **makes** that which **is taught dependent on** that which **is not taught,** using the latter to explain the former. The Gemara asks: **Which is taught and which is not taught?** Both **this** mishna **is taught** and **that** mishna **is taught.** The Gemara answers: **Rather,** Shmuel **makes** the *halakha* that **is taught** in the mishna here, **whose reason is explicit,**[N] **dependent on** a *halakha* that **is taught** in the later mishna, **whose reason is not explicit.** Citation of the later mishna contributed nothing to the understanding of the mishna here.

אֶלָּא, אִי אִיתְּמַר הָכִי אִיתְּמַר, אָמַר רַב יְהוּדָה אָמַר שְׁמוּאֵל: מִפְּנֵי מָה אָמְרוּ בְּתוּלָה נִשֵּׂאת לְיוֹם הָרְבִיעִי – שֶׁאִם הָיָה לוֹ טַעֲנַת בְּתוּלִים הָיָה מַשְׁכִּים לְבֵית דִּין. וְתִינָּשֵׂא בְּאֶחָד בְּשַׁבָּת, שֶׁאִם הָיָה לוֹ טַעֲנַת בְּתוּלִים הָיָה מַשְׁכִּים לְבֵית דִּין. שָׁקְדוּ חֲכָמִים עַל תַּקָּנַת בְּנוֹת יִשְׂרָאֵל, שֶׁיְּהֵא טוֹרֵחַ בִּסְעוּדָה שְׁלֹשָׁה יָמִים: אֶחָד בְּשַׁבָּת וְשֵׁנִי בְּשַׁבָּת וּשְׁלִישִׁי בְּשַׁבָּת, וּבָרְבִיעִי כּוֹנְסָהּ.

Rather, if it was stated, this is how **it was stated: Rav Yehuda said** that **Shmuel said: Due to what** reason **did** the Sages in the mishna **say** that **a virgin is married on Wednesday?**[N] It is so **that if** the husband **had a claim concerning** the bride's **virginity, he would go early** the next day **to court** and make his claim. The Gemara asks: **But** if that is the reason, **let her marry on Sunday, as** then too, **if** the husband **had a claim concerning** the bride's **virginity, he would go early** the next day **to court** and make his claim. The Gemara answers: The **Sages were assiduous in seeing to the well-being of Jewish women**[N] and instituted that the wedding take place on Wednesday, **so that** the groom **would exert** himself **in** arranging **the** wedding **feast for three days:**[H] **Sunday, Monday, and Tuesday, and on Wednesday, he marries her.**

וְעַכְשָׁו שֶׁשָּׁנִינוּ ״שָׁקְדוּ״, אוֹתָהּ שֶׁשָּׁנִינוּ הִגִּיעַ זְמַן וְלֹא נִישְּׂאוּ אוֹכְלוֹת מִשֶּׁלּוֹ וְאוֹכְלוֹת בִּתְרוּמָה, הִגִּיעַ זְמַן בְּאֶחָד בְּשַׁבָּת, מִתּוֹךְ שֶׁאֵינוֹ יָכוֹל לִכְנוֹס – אֵינוֹ מַעֲלֶה לָהּ מְזוֹנוֹת.

The Gemara continues: **And now that we learned** that the reason for the ruling in the mishna that a woman is married on Wednesday is that the Sages **were assiduous**[N] in this matter, then with regard to **that** *halakha,* **which we learned** in the later mishna: **If the time arrived and they were not married,** the brides are entitled to **eat from his** food **and eat** *teruma,* one may conclude: **If the time arrived on Sunday,**[H] **since** he is **unable to marry** her because he is busy preparing the wedding feast, **he is not obligated to provide her sustenance** until Wednesday.

לְפִיכָךְ, חָלָה הוּא, אוֹ שֶׁחָלְתָה הִיא, אוֹ שֶׁפֵּירְסָה נִדָּה – אֵינוֹ מַעֲלֶה לָהּ מְזוֹנוֹת.

Therefore, according to the same line of reasoning, if the husband **fell ill,**[H] **or if** the bride **fell ill, or** in a case **where she began to menstruate** [***peirsa nidda***][LN] and the wedding had to be postponed, he similarly need **not provide her sustenance** from the designated time, as he did not initiate the delay.

HALAKHA

So that the groom would exert himself in arranging the wedding feast for three days – שֶׁיְּהֵא טוֹרֵחַ בִּסְעוּדָה שְׁלֹשָׁה יָמִים: In places where the courts convene every day, a man and woman can marry on any day that he chooses, provided that he exerts himself for three days preparing the feast. Therefore, in many places it was customary for marriages to take place on Friday, after the groom had exerted himself sufficiently for the feast. However, if the bride and her family are willing to forgo the elaborate preparations, the three days apparently are not required, and that is in fact the custom (Rambam *Sefer Nashim, Hilkhot Ishut* 10:14, 19; *Shulḥan Arukh, Even HaEzer* 64:3).

If the time arrived on Sunday – הִגִּיעַ זְמַן בְּאֶחָד בְּשַׁבָּת: If a date several months after the betrothal was set for the wedding, and that date occurred, for example, on a Sunday or Friday, the groom is not required to provide for his wife from that day, since the wedding was postponed due to a rabbinic ordinance, as explained later in the Gemara (Rambam *Sefer Nashim, Hilkhot Ishut* 10:19; *Shulḥan Arukh, Even HaEzer* 56:3).

If the husband fell ill, etc. – חָלָה הוּא וכו׳: If a date was set for the wedding, and it was postponed due to unavoidable circumstances, e.g., the bride or groom fell ill or the bride began to menstruate, then the groom is not required to provide sustenance for his betrothed (Rambam *Sefer Nashim, Hilkhot Ishut* 10:19; *Shulḥan Arukh, Even HaEzer* 56:3).

LANGUAGE

Began to menstruate [*peirsa nidda*] – פֵּירְסָה נִדָּה: It is difficult to ascertain the meaning of the verb *peirsa* as it is employed here. There is a variant reading, *peirsha*, meaning separation or a discharge from the woman. Others suggest that it is taken from, or at least influenced by, the Greek ἀπόρρυσις, *aporrusis*, meaning flow or leak.

NOTES

Lord of Abraham – מָרֵיהּ דְּאַבְרָהָם: The commentaries explain Rav Yosef's powerful reaction to the statement of Shmuel in different ways. Some explain that he cited the statement as he originally heard it, and he wondered how to resolve the problem. Others explain that, as mentioned throughout the Talmud, due to illness, Rav Yosef lost his memory, and he was uncertain whether he cited the statement correctly.

The answer of the Gemara is understood in various ways, based on these explanations. According to the first explanation, the Gemara proceeds to answer Rav Yosef's question. According to the second explanation, Rav Yosef himself remembered that the statement that he cited was actually stated differently (see Rashba and Meiri).

He makes the *halakha* that is taught, whose reason is explicit – תָּלֵי תַּנְיָא דִּמְפָרֵשׁ טַעֲמָא: Although the reason isn't fully articulated in the mishna, as no explanation is provided why the marriage is on Wednesday and not Sunday, there is a reason cited: If the husband had a claim concerning the bride's virginity when consummating the marriage on Wednesday night, he would go early the next day to court and make his claim. No reason is cited in the other mishna (Ramban; Rashba).

Due to what reason did the Sages say that a virgin is married on Wednesday – מִפְּנֵי מָה אָמְרוּ בְּתוּלָה נִשֵּׂאת לְיוֹם הָרְבִיעִי: Most commentaries explain that the question is: Why did the ordinance designate Wednesday as opposed to Sunday? It is implausible to suggest that Wednesday is merely an example and the same is true for Sunday. Were that the case, the mishna should have mentioned Sunday, which is earlier in the week. According to this understanding, when the Gemara suggests: Let her marry on Sunday, it is not an additional question but rather the conclusion of the first question (Rabbi Aharon HaLevi). Others explain that the original question is: Why was Wednesday chosen and not any other day of the week? According to that explanation, there are two separate questions (Rivash; see *Shita Mekubbetzet*).

The Sages were assiduous in seeing to the well-being of Jewish women – שָׁקְדוּ חֲכָמִים עַל תַּקָּנַת בְּנוֹת יִשְׂרָאֵל: The Ramban asks: Why is this ordinance specifically attributed to the well-being of Jewish women? Don't the men rejoice as well? He explains that this ordinance is said to benefit the woman because if the husband did not prepare the feast in advance, he would be occupied with the preparations during the days of celebration, and the bride would be left alone.

The Ritva explains that the Sages sought to ensure that the groom would exert himself in arranging the wedding feast, since, as the Gemara later explains, he will be reluctant to make false accusations and have all his efforts go to waste. That is the reason his claim concerning virginity is accorded credibility.

And now that we learned that the Sages were assiduous – וְעַכְשָׁו שֶׁשָּׁנִינוּ שָׁקְדוּ: It appears that Shmuel was referring to the *baraita* where it is stated that the Sages were assiduous in seeing to the well-being of Jewish women and ensured that the groom would exert himself in arranging the wedding feast for three days prior to the wedding. He considered that to be the primary reason for the ordinance in the mishna, and he therefore explained the mishna to mean: If the time arrived and they did not marry. An opinion cited in the *Shita Mekubbetzet* suggests that Shmuel's statement itself is a primary halakhic source, as Shmuel was one of the first *amora'im*.

With regard to the connection between the assiduousness of the Sages and the fact that the groom need not provide for his betrothed until Wednesday, Rashi explains that once the Sages instituted that the wedding must be on Wednesday, it is tantamount to circumstances beyond his control preventing him from marrying earlier in the week. Therefore, he is exempt from the obligation to provide support for his betrothed.

The Ramban explains that were Wednesday designated merely to facilitate the groom's claim concerning virginity, the bride could contend that if that is the reason for waiting until Wednesday to marry, she should not have to forgo the support to which she is entitled. However, once there is an additional reason of which she is the beneficiary, that claim is baseless and the groom is exempt.

The Ramban provides another explanation. If not for the statement of Shmuel, it could have been understood that there is a dispute between the mishna and the *baraita*. The mishna here holds that the only reason for the ordinance was the claim concerning virginity. Therefore, although the mishna stated that a virgin marries on Wednesday, the same is true for Sunday. However, according to the *baraita* with regard to the assiduousness of the Sages, a virgin marries only on Wednesday. Taken together, the reasons cited in the two sources lead to the conclusion that the *tanna* of the mishna is also of the opinion that a virgin marries specifically on Wednesday.

She began to menstruate – פֵּירְסָה נִדָּה: Based on this and other sources, the Rambam and the *ge'onim* maintain that it is actually prohibited to conduct a wedding ceremony if the status of the bride is that of a menstruating woman. Others are of the opinion that it is not prohibited, but the custom is not to do so, so that he will not be in seclusion with her while she is forbidden to him. The Meiri and others discuss this at length and tie this dispute to the fundamental dispute with regard to the nature of the wedding canopy.

וְאִיכָּא דְּבָעֵי לַהּ מִיבַּעְיָא: חָלָה הוּא מַהוּ? הָתָם טַעְמָא מַאי – מִשּׁוּם דַּאֲנִיס, וְהָכָא נַמִּי – הָא אֲנִיס. אוֹ דִּלְמָא: הָתָם אֲנִיס בְּתַקַּנְתָּא דְּתַקִּינוּ לֵיהּ רַבָּנַן, הָכָא – לָא.

And there are those who raised it as a dilemma: If the groom **fell ill, what is** the ruling with regard to his obligation to provide her sustenance? **There,** in the case where the designated time arrived on Sunday, **what is the reason** that he is exempt? It is **due to** the fact **that he was forced** to postpone the wedding by circumstances beyond his control. **And here too, isn't he forced** by circumstances beyond his control, and he should therefore be exempt? **Or, perhaps** there is a distinction between the cases. **There, he was forced by an ordinance that was instituted by the Sages** that a virgin marries on Wednesday, and they exempted him from providing for her until then. **However, here,** that is **not** the case. Therefore, despite the existence of circumstances beyond his control, he is not exempt from providing her sustenance due to his illness.

וְאִם תִּמְצֵי לוֹמַר חָלָה הוּא מַעֲלֶה לָהּ מְזוֹנוֹת, חָלְתָה הִיא מַהוּ? מָצֵי אָמַר לַהּ: אֲנָא הָא קָאֵימְנָא, אוֹ דִּלְמָא, מָצְיָא אָמְרָה לֵיהּ ״נִסְתַּחֲפָה שָׂדֵהוּ״?

And if you say that if he fell ill, he provides her sustenance at the time designated for the wedding, then **if she fell ill, what is** the ruling? **Can he say to her: I am standing here** prepared to wed you, and if you are not prepared, it is not my fault? **Or perhaps she can say to him that his field was inundated,**[N] i.e., her illness is tantamount to a natural disaster that befell him, and he must nevertheless provide for her.

וְאִם תִּמְצֵי לוֹמַר אָמְרָה לֵיהּ ״נִסְתַּחֲפָה שָׂדֵהוּ״, פֵּירְסָה נִדָּה מַהוּ?

And if you say that if she fell ill **she** can **say to him that his field was inundated,** if **she became a menstruating woman** and the wedding was postponed, **what is** the ruling? Is this too considered an unavoidable circumstance, like illness, and he must provide for her, or was this predictable?

בִּשְׁעַת וִוסְתָּהּ – לָא תִּיבְּעֵי לָךְ,

If she began menstruating **at the time of her set period** [*vista*],[L] **do not raise the dilemma,**

NOTES

His field was inundated – נִסְתַּחֲפָה שָׂדֵהוּ: Based on Rashi's explanation that she is effectively saying to him that it is his misfortune that caused the postponement, the commentaries ask: Why not say when he falls ill that her misfortune caused the postponement? Some explain that since the mitzva of procreation is incumbent specifically on the husband, any delay in the wedding is attributable to his misfortune. The Ramban and others reject this.

Apparently, since he committed to marry her at a certain time, he incurs a monetary obligation. If the wedding is postponed, even due to circumstances beyond his control, it is like any case of monetary loss due to circumstances beyond one's control (Rabbi Aharon HaLevi).

LANGUAGE

Set period [*veset*] – וֶסֶת: This term is employed throughout the Talmud and midrash in the sense of anything that works on a fixed schedule. It is especially employed in reference to a woman's menstrual cycle. Many scholars attribute the word to the Greek ἔθος, *ethos*, whose principle meaning is custom or habit. However, others assert that the word, at least in its specific meaning with regard to the menstrual cycle, is connected to the Aramaic *vas*, to be sullied.

Perek **I**
Daf **2** Amud **b**

דְּלָא מָצְיָא אָמְרָה לֵיהּ ״נִסְתַּחֲפָה שָׂדֵהוּ״. כִּי תִּיבְּעֵי לָךְ – שֶׁלֹּא בִּשְׁעַת וִוסְתָּהּ מַאי? כֵּיוָן דְּלָא בִּשְׁעַת וִוסְתָּהּ הָוְיָא – מָצְיָא אָמְרָה לֵיהּ ״נִסְתַּחֲפָה שָׂדֵהוּ״, אוֹ דִּלְמָא, כֵּיוָן דְּאִיכָּא נָשֵׁי דְּקָא מְשַׁנְּיָא וִוסְתַּיְיהוּ, כִּבְשְׁעַת וִוסְתָּהּ דָּמֵי?

as it is clear that **she cannot say to him** that **his field was inundated.** Here, the circumstances were avoidable, and postponement of the wedding is attributable to her. **When you** should **raise a dilemma** is in a case where menstruation began **not at the time of her set period. What** is the ruling there? **Since it is not the time of her set period,** it is comparable to the case of her illness, and **she can say to him that his field was inundated. Or, perhaps since there are some women whose set period changes,** it is avoidable, and its legal status **is like** menstruation at **the time of her set period,** and postponement of the wedding is attributable to her.

פָּשֵׁיט רַב אַחַאי: הִגִּיעַ זְמַן וְלֹא נִישְּׂאוּ אוֹכְלוֹת מִשֶּׁלּוֹ וְאוֹכְלוֹת בִּתְרוּמָה. ״לֹא נָשְׂאוּ״ לָא קָתָנֵי, אֶלָּא ״לֹא נִישְּׂאוּ״,

Rav Aḥai resolved[N] these dilemmas through a careful reading of the mishna: **If the time arrived and they were not married,** the brides are entitled to **eat from his food and eat *teruma*. It doesn't teach: And** the grooms **didn't marry,** in the active form. **Rather,** it teaches: **And** the brides **were not married,**[N] in the passive form.

הֵיכִי דָּמֵי, אִי דְּקָא מְעַכְּבָן אִינְהִי – אַמַּאי אוֹכְלוֹת מִשֶּׁלּוֹ וְאוֹכְלוֹת בִּתְרוּמָה? אֶלָּא לָאו דְּאִיתְּנִיס כִּי הַאי גַּוְונָא, וְקָתָנֵי: אוֹכְלוֹת מִשֶּׁלּוֹ וְאוֹכְלוֹת בִּתְרוּמָה!

The Gemara asks: **What are the circumstances** described in the phrase: They were not married? **If the** brides **postpone** the marriage, **why do they eat from his** food **and eat *teruma*? Rather, is it not** referring to a case **where they were compelled** by circumstances beyond their control **in that manner,** e.g., the bride falling ill or beginning to menstruate, **and it teaches:** The brides **eat from his** food **and eat *teruma*,** and his bad fortune is responsible for his situation.

NOTES

Rav Aḥai resolved – פָּשֵׁיט רַב אַחַאי: *Tosafot* reject the Rashbam's opinion that this is referring to Rav Aḥai Gaon, the author of the *She'iltot*, as the *amora* Rav Ashi, who is cited in the Gemara as rejecting the resolution of Rav Aḥai, could not have rejected the statement of one who lived several centuries after his death. There are variant readings (see Meiri), who cite the rejection of the resolution of Rav Aḥai without attribution. Based on the Epistle of Rav Sherira Gaon, the reference is to Rav Aḥai of Bei Hittim, who was one of the *savora'im*, a member of the post-amoraic generation responsible for the redaction of the Talmud.

It doesn't teach: And the grooms didn't marry [*nasu*], rather: And the brides were not married [*nisu*] – לֹא נָשְׂאוּ לָא קָתָנֵי, אֶלָּא לֹא נִישְּׂאוּ: The early commentaries question how the Gemara determined that the term in the mishna is *nisu*, referring to the brides, and not *nasu*, referring to the grooms. After all, the mishna was written without vocalization. The Ritva answers, citing Rabbeinu Yitzḥak, that had the groom been the subject of the sentence, it should have said *nasa*, in the singular, as in the first clause of the mishna it says: One gives the man twelve months, in the singular. Others determined that the bride is the subject from the continuation of the mishna: The brides are entitled to eat from his food. Had the grooms been the subject, it would have continued: The brides are entitled to eat from their food. The Rashba and the Rosh explain simply that since the Gemara is a record of study conducted orally, they were aware of the correct reading.

אמר רב אשי: לעולם אימא לך: כל אונסא לא אכלה, ודקא מעכבי אינהו, ובדין הוא דאיבעי ליה למיתני "לא נשאו", ואיידי דתנא רישא בדידהי תנא נמי סיפא בדידהי.

Rav Ashi said: Actually, I will say to you:[N] **In any case of unavoidable circumstances,** whether they affect him or they affect her, **she doesn't eat** from his food, **and** the mishna is referring to a case **where** grooms **postpone the wedding. And by right,** the *tanna* **should have taught: They didn't marry,** which would have established that grooms caused the postponement. **And since** the *tanna* taught **the first clause** of the mishna cited above **in** terms of a bride: The Sages give a virgin twelve months, **it taught the latter clause in** terms of a bride. Therefore, no inference may be drawn from the formulation of the latter clause. Only if the groom postpones the wedding is he obligated to provide sustenance for the women when the time designated for the wedding arrives.

אמר רבא: ולענין גיטין אינו כן. אלמא קסבר רבא: אין אונס בגיטין.

Rava said: And although delays caused by circumstances beyond his control exempt the groom from providing support to his betrothed at the time originally designated for the wedding, with regard **to bills of divorce that is not so. Apparently, Rava maintains that unavoidable circumstances** have **no** legal standing with regard **to bills of divorce.**[NH] If one stipulated that the bill of divorce will take effect only with the fulfillment of a condition, even if that condition was fulfilled due to circumstances beyond his control, the bill of divorce takes effect.

מנא ליה לרבא הא? אילימא מהא דתנן: "הרי זה גיטיך אם לא באתי מכאן ועד שנים עשר חדש", ומת בתוך שנים עשר חדש, אינו גט. מת – הוא דאינו גט, הא חלה – הרי זה גט.

The Gemara asks: **From where does Rava learn this** principle? **If we say it is from that which we learned** in a mishna (*Gittin* 76b) with regard to one who said to his wife: **This is your bill of divorce, if I do not return from now until** the conclusion of **twelve months, and he died within** those **twelve months,**[H] the document **is not a bill of divorce.** Therefore, if she has no children from her deceased husband, the *halakhot* of levirate marriage would apply to her. The Gemara infers: If **he died,** that **is when it is not a bill of divorce,** since a divorce cannot take effect posthumously. By inference, in cases involving other circumstances beyond his control, e.g., if **he fell ill,** and therefore did not return, **it is a bill of divorce** and it takes effect. Apparently, if the reason for his failure to arrive is a circumstance beyond his control, the divorce takes effect.

ודלמא לעולם אימא לך: חלה נמי אינו גט, והיא גופא קא משמע לן: דאין גט לאחר מיתה?

The Gemara refutes that proof. **And perhaps, actually I will say to you** that in the case where **he falls ill it is also not a bill of divorce,** and the mishna cited the case of death merely as an example of circumstances beyond his control. **And** the reason **that** example **itself** was chosen is **to teach us that there is no bill of divorce posthumously.**[N] Even if the divorce is not conditional, and the husband simply states that it will take effect after he dies, it is not a valid bill of divorce.

אין גט לאחר מיתה – הא תנא ליה רישא: "הרי זה גיטיך אם מתי" "הרי זה גיטיך מחולי זה" "הרי זה גיטיך לאחר מיתה" – לא אמר כלום.

The Gemara asks: Does it come to teach that **there is no bill of divorce posthumously? Wasn't it** already **taught in the first clause** of the mishna (*Gittin* 72a) that if one on his deathbed said to his wife: **This is your bill of divorce if I die,**[H] or: **This is your bill of divorce** if I die **from this illness,** or: **This is your bill of divorce after I die, he said nothing.** The bill of divorce does not take effect after his death.

NOTES

Actually I will say to you, etc. – לְעוֹלָם אֵימָא לָךְ וכו׳: The Meiri has a variant reading. First, the Gemara cites an unattributed response: Actually, I will say to you that in a case of unavoidable circumstances, she is not entitled to eat from his food, meaning that in a case where the circumstance came about due to the woman, he need not provide for her until the wedding. The Gemara then cites the statement of Rav Ashi: In any case of unavoidable circumstances, whether they affect him or they affect her, she doesn't eat from his food. The only case where she eats from his food prior to the wedding is when the groom made a conscious decision to postpone the wedding.

Unavoidable circumstances have no legal standing with regard to bills of divorce – אֵין אוֹנֶס בְּגִיטִּין: The early commentaries broaden the scope of this discussion and ask a more general question: In what cases do unavoidable circumstances have legal standing, so that a condition that was violated due to those circumstances is considered not to have been violated?

With regard to stipulations in monetary agreements, some maintain that unavoidable circumstances have legal standing (Rashba). Others maintain that they do not (see Rabbi Aharon HaLevi).

Others distinguish between different cases. In the case of a mutual agreement between two parties, a claim of unavoidable circumstances is not accepted in favor of one of the parties at the expense of the other. However, in a unilateral action, e.g., a gift, that claim is effective. Based on that approach, a claim of unavoidable circumstances should be effective in the case of divorce as well, as delivery of the bill of divorce is a unilateral action on the part of the husband. However, there are other reasons that the claim is not accepted in those cases.

Others distinguish between conditions that require performance of an action and conditions stipulating failure to perform an action, e.g., if I do not return. In the former case, failure to perform the action negates the transaction, regardless of the reason for that failure. However, in the latter case, since one sought to fulfill the condition and prevent the transaction from taking effect, the claim of unavoidable circumstances is effective, and his failure to fulfill the condition does not activate the transaction (see Meiri).

That there is no bill of divorce posthumously – דְּאֵין גֵּט לְאַחַר מִיתָה: The question is raised: What proof is there that the reason it is not a divorce is that there is no bill of divorce posthumously and not that there are unavoidable circumstances?

Some explain that were the intention to teach that failure to fulfill the condition due to unavoidable circumstances is not considered failure, the *tanna* should have taught the case: This is your bill of divorce from now if I did not return from now until the conclusion of twelve months, where the bill of divorce would not be posthumous. The fact that the *tanna* did not teach that case indicates that the reason the bill of divorce is void is that there is no bill of divorce posthumously.

HALAKHA

Unavoidable circumstances have no legal standing with regard to bills of divorce – אֵין אוֹנֶס בְּגִיטִּין: With regard to one who gave his wife a bill of divorce and stipulated that it will take effect only if a condition is fulfilled, if the condition remains unfulfilled due to circumstances beyond his control, the divorce takes effect because unavoidable circumstances have no legal standing with regard to bills of divorce.

The early commentaries (Rosh) rule, based on the Gemara in tractate *Gittin*, that this is the ruling only in cases involving normal circumstances beyond one's control. However, in extremely rare circumstances of that kind, even Rava would agree that the bill of divorce would not take effect.

Although the Gemara here (3a) cites an alternative version of Rava's statement, and the *halakha* is typically ruled in accordance with the latter version, the *ge'onim* and Rabbeinu Ḥananel note that in this case there are reasons for ruling in accordance with the first version. For one, the Gemara cites several sources that support the first version and are difficult according to the second. Furthermore, the discussion in the parallel Gemara in *Gittin* (34a) is according to the first version (Rambam *Sefer Nashim*, *Hilkhot Geirushin* 9:8; *Shulḥan Arukh*, *Even HaEzer* 144:1).

This is your bill of divorce…and he died within those twelve months – הֲרֵי זֶה גִּיטֵּיךְ...וּמֵת בְּתוֹךְ שְׁנֵים עָשָׂר חֹדֶשׁ: The Rambam rules, in accordance with the unattributed mishna, that in the case of one who gave his wife a bill of divorce and stipulated that it would take effect only if he failed to return by a specified time, and he died within that period, the divorce does not take effect. The Ra'avad, cited by Rashba and the *Tur*, rules that the divorce takes effect, in accordance with the opinion of our Rabbis, who disagree with the unattributed mishna and in accordance with the opinion of Rav (*Gittin* 72a). Based on the dispute between authorities, the ruling in the *Shulḥan Arukh* is that there is uncertainty whether or not she is divorced. Therefore, if her husband dies without children, this woman must perform *ḥalitza* and may not enter into levirate marriage (Rambam *Sefer Nashim*, *Hilkhot Geirushin* 9:2; *Shulḥan Arukh*, *Even HaEzer* 144:2).

This is your bill of divorce if I die – הֲרֵי זֶה גִּיטֵּיךְ אִם מַתִּי: With regard to one who said to his wife: This is your bill of divorce if I die, the Rambam rules, in accordance with the unattributed mishna, that the divorce does not take effect. The Ra'avad rules that the divorce takes effect, in accordance with the opinion of our Rabbis. In the *Shulḥan Arukh*, the ruling of the Rambam is cited first, followed by a ruling introduced with the phrase: Some say, indicating that there is uncertainty whether or not the divorce takes effect (Rambam *Sefer Nashim*, *Hilkhot Geirushin* 9:12; *Shulḥan Arukh*, *Even HaEzer* 145:1).

דִּלְמָא לְאַפּוּקֵי מִדְּרַבּוֹתֵינוּ? דְּתַנְיָא: וְרַבּוֹתֵינוּ הִתִּירוּהָ לְהִנָּשֵׂא, וְאָמְרִינַן: מַאן רַבּוֹתֵינוּ? אֲמַר רַב יְהוּדָה אֲמַר שְׁמוּאֵל: בֵּי דִינָא דְּשָׁרוּ מִשְׁחָא. סָבְרִי לַהּ כְּרַבִּי יוֹסֵי, דְּאָמַר: זְמַנּוֹ שֶׁל שְׁטָר מוֹכִיחַ עָלָיו.

The Gemara answers: **Perhaps** it was necessary for the first clause to mention specifically the case of death, **to exclude that which our Rabbis**[N] said[N] and not to exclude the case of one who fell ill, **as it is taught** in a *baraita*: **And our Rabbis permitted her to remarry,** in a case where he died within the twelve months that he stipulated. **And we said: Who are our Rabbis** mentioned here? **Rav Yehuda said** that **Shmuel said:** It is **the court that permitted** the **oil**[B] of gentiles for consumption. In this regard, **they hold in accordance with** the opinion of **Rabbi Yosei, who said: The time** written **in a document proves** when **it** takes effect. The fact that a certain date is written in the bill of divorce indicates that one's intention was that the divorce take effect from the day that it was written and delivered, not after his death. In any event, there is proof neither for nor against Rava's opinion from this *baraita*.

וְאֶלָּא מִסֵּיפָא: "מֵעַכְשָׁיו אִם לֹא בָּאתִי מִכָּאן וְעַד שְׁנֵים עָשָׂר חֹדֶשׁ" וּמֵת בְּתוֹךְ שְׁנֵים עָשָׂר חֹדֶשׁ – הֲרֵי זֶה גֵּט. מֵת – וְהוּא הַדִּין לְחָלָה.

And rather, proof may be cited from the **latter clause** of the mishna. If a man says to his wife: This is your bill of divorce **from now**[N] **if I do not return**[H] **from now until** the conclusion of **twelve months, and he died within** those **twelve months, this** document **is a bill of divorce.** This is the *halakha* in a case where **he dies,** and **the same is true** if **he fell ill.** If the divorce takes effect when his failure to return is attributable to death, the ultimate circumstance beyond his control, all the more so should it take effect if it is attributable to a less extreme circumstance.

דִּלְמָא מֵת דַּוְקָא, דְּלָא נִיחָא לֵיהּ דְּתִפּוֹל קַמֵּי יָבָם!

The Gemara rejects that proof: **Perhaps** the divorce takes effect **specifically** in the case where **he died,** because **he is not amenable** to have his wife **happen before** her *yavam*, his brother, if he had no children. However, if other circumstances beyond his control caused the condition to be fulfilled, where levirate marriage is not a consideration, his intention is that the bill of divorce will not take effect.

אֶלָּא מֵהָא: דְּהַהוּא דַּאֲמַר לְהוּ "אִי לָא אָתֵינָא מִיכָּן וְעַד תְּלָתִין יוֹמִין לֶיהֱוֵי גִּיטָּא", אֲתָא בְּסוֹף תְּלָתִין יוֹמִין וּפַסְקֵיהּ מַבְרָא, אֲמַר לְהוּ: "חֲזוּ דַּאֲתַאי, חֲזוּ דַּאֲתַאי"! אֲמַר שְׁמוּאֵל: לָאו שְׁמֵיהּ מָתְיָא.

Rather, proof may be cited **from this** case, **where a certain** man **who said to** the agents with whom he entrusted the bill of divorce: **If I do not return from now until after thirty days** have passed, **let this be a bill of divorce. He came at the end of thirty days,** before the deadline passed, **but was prevented** from crossing the river **by the ferry**[H] that was located on the other side of the river, so he did not come within the designated time. **He said to the** people across the river: **See that I have come, see that I have come. Shmuel said:** This **is not considered** to be **a return.** Apparently, even if the condition was fulfilled due to circumstances beyond his control, the condition is considered fulfilled.

BACKGROUND

The court that permitted the oil – בֵּי דִינָא דְּשָׁרוּ מִשְׁחָא: The oil of gentiles was prohibited by an ancient decree. Some assert that the decree dates back to the time of Daniel, but everyone agrees that it is one of the eighteen decrees issued during the Second Temple period. Many generations later, when the Sages became aware that the decree was not observed by a majority of the people, it was repealed. Although initially the Sages were hesitant about instituting this leniency, it was eventually adopted as normative *halakha* (see *Avoda Zara* 35b). Apparently, it was the court of the grandson of Rabbi Yehuda HaNasi, Rabbi Yehuda Nesia, which judged during the first generation of *amora'im*, that repealed the decree prohibiting the use of the oil of gentiles (see Rashi on *Avoda Zara* 35b). That is the court referred to in the Gemara by the words: And our Rabbis permitted her to marry. Some explain that any time the term our Rabbis is used, the reference is to the court of Rabbi Yehuda Nesia.

HALAKHA

From now if I do not return – מֵעַכְשָׁיו אִם לֹא בָּאתִי: With regard to one who said to his wife: This is your bill of divorce from now if I do not return within twelve months, and he dies within the twelve months, the divorce takes effect. Therefore, if her husband dies without children and the *halakhot* of levirate marriage apply, she must wait twelve months for the condition to actually be fulfilled before remarrying (Rambam *Sefer Nashim, Hilkhot Geirushin* 9:11; *Shulḥan Arukh, Even HaEzer* 144:3).

But was prevented from crossing the river by the ferry – וּפַסְקֵיהּ מַבְרָא: With regard to one who said to his wife: This is your bill of divorce from now if I do not return within thirty days, and due to circumstances beyond his control he was unable to cross the river and complete his return, the divorce takes effect, because unavoidable circumstances have no legal standing with regard to bills of divorce (Rambam *Sefer Nashim, Hilkhot Geirushin* 9:8; *Shulḥan Arukh, Even HaEzer* 144:1).

NOTES

Our Rabbis – רַבּוֹתֵינוּ: Rabbeinu Ḥananel explains that this is an appellation for Rabbi Yehuda HaNasi, redactor of the mishna, while others explain that the reference is to his grandson, Rabbi Yehuda Nesia (Rashba).

To exclude that which our Rabbis said – לְאַפּוּקֵי מִדְּרַבּוֹתֵינוּ: The commentaries ask: The Gemara could have learned to exclude that which our Rabbis said from the first clause of the mishna, as in the first clause, the bill of divorce is valid only if the husband said: From now, contrary to the opinion of Rabbi Yosei and our Rabbis, who hold: The time written in a document proves when it takes effect.

The Ri Migash answers that the first clause is referring to a case where no specific date was written in the document. Rather, a more general time was written, e.g., the month or the year.

The Ramban suggests the possibility that there is a distinction between the opinion of Rabbi Yosei and the opinion of our Rabbis. According to Rabbi Yosei, even if the husband explicitly said: This is your bill of divorce after my death, which is the case in the first clause of the mishna, because of the time written in the document the bill of divorce takes effect. However, our Rabbis hold that in a case where one specifically stipulated that it will take effect after death, the bill of divorce does not take effect, as he merely wrote the document to ensure that she will not be subject to levirate marriage after his death. Only in a case where one stipulated that the bill of divorce will take effect if he does not return by a specific time, and he died and did not return would the bill of divorce take effect, as in that case our Rabbis concede: The time written in a document proves when it takes effect. Therefore, the first clause does not exclude the opinion of our Rabbis.

From now – מֵעַכְשָׁיו: There is a difference between a standard bill of divorce, in which the date is written, and one in which the man giving the bill of divorce to his wife stipulates that it will take effect from now. In the standard bill of divorce, the husband's intent is that the divorce will take effect only if the condition is fulfilled. However, in the latter case, where he specifies that it will take effect from now, his intent is that the divorce will take effect; he simply stipulated a condition to void it. Therefore, even if the condition remained unfulfilled due to circumstances beyond his control, the divorce takes effect.

NOTES

Due to virtuous women and due to licentious women – מִשּׁוּם צְנוּעוֹת וּמִשּׁוּם פְּרוּצוֹת: Most commentaries explain that a virtuous woman is one who is concerned that perhaps there was some extenuating circumstance and she will therefore remain unmarried indefinitely, despite the fact that the failure of the husband to return was obviously due to circumstances not beyond his control and clearly the courts would permit her to remarry. In contrast, licentious women are those who remarry despite the clear impression, although it falls short of actual testimony, that the husband's failure to arrive is attributable to circumstances beyond his control (*Tosafot*; Ritva).

The Rashba writes that a licentious woman is one who, without basis, resolutely concludes that her husband's failure to arrive was not due to unavoidable circumstances, and she marries without seeking to ascertain the truth.

Rabbi Aharon HaLevi and others explain that the term licentious is a misnomer, as the court permitted them to remarry. Relative to the virtuous women, who take special precautions to avoid any possible impropriety, these women are characterized as licentious.

וְדִלְמָא אוּנְסָא דִּשְׁכִיחַ שָׁאנֵי, דְּכֵיוָן דְּאִיבָּעֵי לֵיהּ לְאַתְנוּיֵי וְלָא אַתְנֵי – אִיהוּ דְּאַפְסֵיד אַנַּפְשֵׁיהּ!

The Gemara rejects that proof: **And perhaps unavoidable circumstances that are common** and could be anticipated, e.g., the ferry is located at the other side of the river, **are different, since he should have stipulated** that exception when establishing the condition, **and he did not stipulate** it, **he brought the failure** to arrive **upon himself.** Although he regrets it now, at the time his intent was that even if the condition were fulfilled due to that circumstance, the divorce would take effect. In contrast, however, if the condition is fulfilled due to an uncommon circumstance that could not have been anticipated, the divorce would not take effect.

אֶלָּא רָבָא סְבָרָא דְּנַפְשֵׁיהּ קָאָמַר, מִשּׁוּם צְנוּעוֹת וּמִשּׁוּם פְּרוּצוֹת; מִשּׁוּם צְנוּעוֹת, דְּאִי אָמְרַתְּ לָא לֶהֱוֵי גֵּט

Rather, Rava is stating a *halakha* based on **his own reasoning.** Circumstances beyond one's control are not a factor in determining whether or not a condition is fulfilled, and this is **due to virtuous women and due to licentious women.**[N] The Gemara articulates: There is concern **due to virtuous women** is, as, **if you said: Let it not be a bill of divorce,** if the reason that the condition was not fulfilled was due to circumstances beyond his control,

Perek **I**
Daf **3** Amud **a**

זִימְנִין דְּלָא אָנֵיס, וְסָבְרָה דְּאָנֵיס, וּמִיעַגְנָא וְיָתְבָה. וּמִשּׁוּם פְּרוּצוֹת, דְּאִי אָמְרַתְּ לָא לֶיהֱוֵי גִּיטָּא, זִימְנִין דְּאָנֵיס וְאָמְרָה לָא אָנֵיס, וְאָזְלָא וּמִינַּסְבָא, וְנִמְצָא גֵּט בָּטֵל וּבָנֶיהָ מַמְזֵרִים.

then **sometimes, where he was not** detained **unavoidably** but he fulfilled the condition willingly to effect the divorce, **and** the wife **thinks** that he was detained **unavoidably, she will sit deserted,** forever unable to remarry. **And** the concern **due to licentious women** is, as, **if you said: Let it not be a bill of divorce,** then **sometimes, when he was** detained **unavoidably and she thinks** that he was **not** detained **unavoidably,** she goes **and remarries. And** the result will be **that the bill of divorce is void, and her children** from the second marriage will be ***mamzerim***, products of an adulterous relationship.

וּמִי אִיכָּא מִידֵּי דְּמִדְּאוֹרָיְיתָא לָא לֶהֱוֵי גֵּט וּמִשּׁוּם צְנוּעוֹת וּמִשּׁוּם פְּרוּצוֹת שָׁרֵינַן אֵשֶׁת אִישׁ לְעָלְמָא?!

The Gemara questions the following premise: By Torah law, a condition that is unfulfilled due to circumstances beyond one's control is considered fulfilled, and it is merely by rabbinic ordinance that it is deemed unfulfilled: **And is there a matter**[N] **where by Torah** law **it is not a bill of divorce, but due to virtuous women and due to licentious women we permit a married woman to others?**

אִין, כׇּל דִּמְקַדֵּשׁ – אַדַּעְתָּא דְּרַבָּנַן מְקַדֵּשׁ, וְאַפְקְעִינְהוּ רַבָּנַן לְקִידּוּשֵׁי מִינֵּיהּ.

The Gemara answers: **Yes,** it is within the authority of the Sages to institute an ordinance freeing the woman from the marriage, as **anyone who betroths** a woman, **betroths** her contingent **upon the agreement of the Sages,** and in certain cases, such as those mentioned above, **the Sages invalidated his betrothal**[N] retroactively.

NOTES

And is there a matter – וּמִי אִיכָּא מִידֵּי: The commentaries ask: Why is this difficulty not raised earlier, before the reason for Rava's opinion is analyzed? Some suggest that at that stage the thinking was that although the fact that unavoidable circumstances are halakhically significant is derived from the passage in the Torah with regard to a betrothed young woman who was raped (Deuteronomy 22:25–26), perhaps Rava holds that the claim of unavoidable circumstances is not relevant in all cases, and it has no legal standing with regard to bills of divorce. However, once it became clear that Rava holds that it is only by rabbinic law that those circumstances are ignored, and the bill of divorce is ruled effective, the question is raised: How can the Sages rule that a woman married by Torah law is divorced?

The Sages invalidated his betrothal – אַפְקְעִינְהוּ רַבָּנַן לְקִידּוּשֵׁי מִינֵּיהּ: This *halakha* that the Sages retroactively invalidated the betrothal is applied only in a few specific cases throughout the Talmud, and is not a panacea to be applied in every case that a problem arises, even if the problem is a severe one, e.g., a deserted wife.

Many early commentaries state that this solution is applied only in cases where there is a bill of divorce of some kind (Ramban; Rashba; Rabbi Aharon HaLevi). The Meiri proves that in certain cases, when halakhic problems arise with regard to the betrothal itself, the Sages used this procedure to invalidate it.

The early and later commentaries discussed at length the precise mechanism through which the Sages invalidate the betrothal retroactively. Some explain that just as a man can betroth a woman and stipulate that it will take effect contingent on the approval of his father, so too, in every act of betrothal there is an implicit stipulation: This betrothal will take effect contingent upon the approval of the Sages, or on the condition that the Sages do not object to it (Ritva).

Rashi goes a step further and asserts that the betrothal takes effect only when the Sages actively ratify it. Apparently, that is the opinion of *Tosafot*, who explain that this is the reason that the groom adds, when reciting the formula of the betrothal: In accordance with the law of Moses and Israel, which acknowledges that the betrothal takes effect in accordance with the provisions of both Torah and rabbinic law.

The explanation in *Sefer Hafla'a* is that there are two complementary mechanisms mentioned in the Gemara that together resolve potential difficulties. On the one hand, it is difficult to explain how the Sages can invalidate the betrothal by rendering the money with which the man betrothed the woman, which is no longer in existence, ownerless retroactively. On the other hand, there is the concern that certain people will not make their betrothal contingent on rabbinic approval. The combination of both mechanisms facilitates invalidation of the betrothal in all cases.

אֲמַר לֵיהּ רָבִינָא לְרַב אַשִׁי: תֵּינַח קָדֵישׁ בְּכַסְפָּא, קָדֵישׁ בְּבִיאָה מַאי אִיכָּא לְמֵימַר? שַׁוְיוּהָ רַבָּנַן לִבְעִילָתוֹ בְּעִילַת זְנוּת.

Ravina said to Rav Ashi: That works out well if **he betrothed** her **with money,**[N] as in that case, the courts could declare the money ownerless, and one cannot betroth a woman with money that is not his. However, if **he betrothed** her **with intercourse, what can be said?** Rav Ashi answered: **The Sages rendered his intercourse licentious intercourse.**

אִיכָּא דְּאָמְרִי, אֲמַר רָבָא: וְכֵן לְעִנְיַן גִּיטִּין. אַלְמָא קָסָבַר רָבָא: יֵשׁ אוֹנֶס בְּגִיטִּין,

Some say, to the contrary, that **Rava said:** Just as with regard to postponement of a wedding due to circumstances beyond his control, the groom is not obligated to provide sustenance for his betrothed, **the same is true with regard to the matter of bills of divorce.** The Gemara concludes that **apparently Rava maintains: Unavoidable circumstances** have legal standing **with regard to bills of divorce.**[N]

מֵיתִיבֵי: ״הֲרֵי זֶה גִּיטֵּיךְ אִם לֹא בָּאתִי מִכָּאן וְעַד שְׁנֵים עָשָׂר חֹדֶשׁ וּמֵת בְּתוֹךְ שְׁנֵים עָשָׂר חֹדֶשׁ – אֵינוֹ גֵּט״. מֵת – הוּא דְּאֵינוֹ גֵּט, הָא חָלָה – הֲרֵי זֶה גֵּט!

The Gemara raises an objection from a mishna (*Gittin* 76b): With regard to one who said to his wife: **This is your bill of divorce if I do not return from now until** the conclusion of **twelve months, and he died within** those **twelve months,** the document **is not a bill of divorce.** The Gemara infers: If **he died,** that **is when it is not a bill of divorce,** since a divorce cannot take effect posthumously. However, in cases involving other circumstances beyond his control, e.g., if **he fell ill** and therefore did not return, **it is a bill of divorce** and it does take effect.

לְעוֹלָם אֵימָא לָךְ חָלָה נַמִי אֵינוֹ גֵּט, וְהִיא גּוּפָהּ קָא מַשְׁמַע לָן, דְּאֵין גֵּט לְאַחַר מִיתָה.

The Gemara answers: **Actually, I will say to you** that in the case where **one falls ill it is also not a bill of divorce,** and death is merely an example of circumstances beyond one's control. **And** the fact that the mishna cited **that** example **itself teaches us that there is no bill of divorce posthumously.**

אֵין גֵּט לְאַחַר מִיתָה – הָא תָּנָא לֵיהּ רֵישָׁא! דִּלְמָא לְאַפּוּקֵי מִדְּרַבּוֹתֵינוּ.

The Gemara asks: Does it come to teach that **there is no bill of divorce posthumously? Wasn't it already taught in the first clause** of that mishna? The Gemara answers: **Perhaps** it was necessary for the first clause to mention specifically the case of death, **to exclude** the opinion **of our Rabbis.**

תָּא שְׁמַע: ״מֵעַכְשָׁיו אִם לֹא בָּאתִי מִכָּאן וְעַד שְׁנֵים עָשָׂר חֹדֶשׁ״ וּמֵת בְּתוֹךְ שְׁנֵים עָשָׂר חֹדֶשׁ – הֲרֵי זֶה גֵּט. מַאי לָאו – הוּא הַדִּין לְחָלָה? לָא, מֵת דַּוְקָא, דְּלָא נִיחָא לֵיהּ דְּתִפּוֹל קַמֵּי יָבָם.

Come and hear an additional proof from the latter clause of that mishna: If one said: This is your bill of divorce **from now if I have not returned from now until** the conclusion of **twelve months, and he died within** those **twelve months,** then **this** document **is a bill of divorce. What, is it not that the same is true** if his failure to return is due to the fact that **he fell ill?** The Gemara rejects that proof. The divorce takes effect **specifically** in the case where **he died,** and he wrote the bill of divorce because **he was not amenable** to have his wife **happen before** her ***yavam***, his brother, for levirate marriage if he had no children. However, in cases where that is not a consideration, if other circumstances beyond his control caused the condition to be fulfilled, his intention is that the bill of divorce will not take effect.

תָּא שְׁמַע: מֵהַהוּא דַּאֲמַר לְהוּ: ״אִי לָא אָתֵינָא מִכָּאן וְעַד שְׁלֹשִׁים יוֹם לֶיהֱוֵי גִּיטָּא״, אֲתָא בְּסוֹף תְּלָתִין יוֹמִין וּפַסְקֵיהּ מַבְרָא, וַאֲמַר לְהוּ: ״חֲזוּ דַּאֲתַאי, חֲזוּ דַּאֲתַאי!״ וַאֲמַר שְׁמוּאֵל: לָא שְׁמֵיהּ מָתְיָא.

Come and hear an additional proof **from** the case of **a certain** man **who said to** the agents with whom he entrusted the bill of divorce: **If I do not return from now until thirty days** have passed, **let this be a bill of divorce. He came at the end of thirty days,** before the deadline passed, **but was prevented** from crossing the river **by the ferry** that was located on the other side of the river, so he did not come within the designated time. **He said to the** people across the river: **See that I have come, see that I have come. Shmuel said:** It **is not considered** to be **a return.** Apparently, even if the condition was fulfilled due to circumstances beyond his control, the condition is considered fulfilled.

אוֹנְסָא דִּשְׁכִיחַ שָׁאנֵי, דְּכֵיוָן דְּאִיבָּעֵי לֵיהּ לְאַתְנוּיֵי וְלָא אַתְנֵי – אִיהוּ הוּא דְּאַפְסִיד אַנַּפְשֵׁיהּ.

The Gemara rejects that proof: **Perhaps unavoidable circumstances that are common** and could be anticipated, e.g., the ferry being located at the other side of the river, **are different, since he should have stipulated** that exception when giving his wife the bill of divorce. **And** since he did not **stipulate** it, **he brought the failure upon himself.**

NOTES

That works out well if he betrothed her with money – תֵּינַח קָדֵישׁ בְּכַסְפָּא: Rashi rejects the explanation raised by several commentaries, that betrothal effected with money can be invalidated because this means of betrothal is not effective by Torah law. According to the Rambam, only betrothal effected by means of sexual intercourse or with a betrothal document is by Torah law. Rather, the simple explanation is that the courts have the power to declare the money ownerless, thereby retroactively invalidating the betrothal.

With regard to betrothal through sexual intercourse, many explain the difficulty raised by the Gemara as: How can the Sages retroactively transform an action performed as a mitzva into a transgression? (see *Tosafot*). With regard to invalidation of betrothal with a betrothal document, some explain that the Sages retroactively disqualify the witnesses who signed the document (*Tashbetz*).

Unavoidable circumstances have legal standing with regard to bills of divorce – יֵשׁ אוֹנֶס בְּגִיטִּין: A related dilemma is raised in the Jerusalem Talmud with regard to betrothal: If a man stipulated that his betrothal is contingent on fulfillment of a certain condition, and the condition was not fulfilled due to circumstances beyond his control, is the betrothal nevertheless valid? The dilemma remains unresolved.

אָמַר רַב שְׁמוּאֵל בַּר יִצְחָק: לֹא שָׁנוּ אֶלָּא מִתַּקָּנַת עֶזְרָא וָאֵילָךְ, שֶׁאֵין בָּתֵּי דִינִין קְבוּעִין אֶלָּא בְּשֵׁנִי וּבַחֲמִישִׁי. אֲבָל קוֹדֶם תַּקָּנַת עֶזְרָא, שֶׁבָּתֵּי דִינִין קְבוּעִין בְּכׇל יוֹם – אִשָּׁה נִשֵּׂאת בְּכׇל יוֹם.

§ **Rav Shmuel bar Yitzḥak said:** The Sages **teach** that this *halakha* that a virgin is married on Wednesday is in effect **only from** the institution of **the ordinance of Ezra**[NB] **that courts are in regular session only on Monday and Thursday. However, prior to** the institution of **the ordinance of Ezra, when courts** were in **regular** session **every day,**[NH] **a woman was married on any day** of the week.

קוֹדֶם תַּקָּנַת עֶזְרָא? מַאי דַּהֲוָה הֲוָה! הָכִי קָאָמַר: אִי אִיכָּא בָּתֵּי דִינִין דִּקְבוּעִין הָאִידָּנָא כְּקוֹדֶם תַּקָּנַת עֶזְרָא – אִשָּׁה נִשֵּׂאת בְּכׇל יוֹם.

The Gemara asks: **Prior to** the institution of **the ordinance of Ezra? What was** in the past **was** in the past. There are no halakhic ramifications to that statement. The Gemara answers: **This is** what Rav Shmuel bar Yitzḥak **is saying: If there are courts** in **regular** daily session **today, as** they were **prior to** the institution of **the ordinance of Ezra, a woman is married on any day** of the week.[N]

הָא בָּעֵינַן שָׁקְדוּ! דִּטְרַיחַ לֵיהּ.

The Gemara asks: **Don't we require** the additional reason that a virgin is married on Wednesday because the Sages **were assiduous** in seeing to the well-being of Jewish women and made certain that the groom would have several days to prepare for the wedding feast prior to the wedding? The Gemara answers: This is referring to a case **where he** already **exerted himself**[N] and prepared everything before Shabbat, so the feast will be prepared even if the wedding is Sunday or Monday.

NOTES

The ordinance of Ezra – **תַּקָּנַת עֶזְרָא**: The early commentaries ask: What was the objective of the ordinance? Did Ezra seek to limit the activity of the courts? They answer that prior to the ordinance, the court convened each day in a different city, or there were no fixed hours when the court was in session. Ezra instituted an ordinance to ensure that in each city, the courts would regularly convene in session at fixed hours (Ritva; *Shita Mekubbetzet*).

When courts are in regular session every day – **שֶׁבָּתֵּי דִינִין קְבוּעִין בְּכׇל יוֹם**: The early commentaries ask: Based on the principle that one court can abrogate ordinances instituted by another court only if the court is greater in wisdom and number, even if the reason for the ordinance is obsolete, how could a court abrogate the ordinance of the court of Ezra that determined Wednesday as the day for the marriage of a virgin, since no court was greater than the court of Ezra? Some suggest that in the original ordinance there was a provision that if the court schedule changed, the marriage day would change accordingly (Ritva). On a similar note, others explain that the essence of the original ordinance was that a wedding should take place on the day before the court is in session. If the court convenes daily, every day is suitable for a wedding (*Ḥatam Sofer*).

A woman is married on any day of the week – **אִשָּׁה נִשֵּׂאת בְּכׇל יוֹם**: Some hold that the phrase every day is not to be taken literally, as the courts do not convene on Friday or Shabbat, and there are other reasons precluding getting married on those days. They explain that although the courts do not convene on Friday on a regular basis, when the need arose, they would convene on that day as well. In addition, since today betrothal, marriage, and consummation of the marriage take place consecutively on the same day, the primary reason for limiting weddings to the day before the courts convene is no longer in effect, and weddings may be held any day of the week.

Where he already exerted himself – **דִּטְרַיחַ לֵיהּ**: Rav Aḥai writes that even today, when the reasons relating to the court convening on Thursday are no longer relevant, a distinction remains between Wednesday and other days. When the wedding is on Wednesday, the groom's claim that he exerted himself in preparing the wedding feast is accorded credibility. When the wedding is on other days, he must provide proof to support his claim. Some prove from here that although the Sages remain insistent with regard to ensuring that the groom exert himself in preparing the feast, even when the wedding takes place on a day other than Wednesday, there is no such insistence with regard to ensuring that the wedding take place on a day when the blessing for procreation was stated (Ritva).

BACKGROUND

The ordinance of Ezra – **תַּקָּנַת עֶזְרָא**: The Gemara (*Bava Kamma* 82a) cites a tradition that Ezra the Scribe instituted ten ordinances whose purpose was to promote fulfillment of Torah law and observance of ancient customs. The focus of these ordinances was to imbue the daily existence of the people with sanctity. For example, by Torah law, one who experiences a seminal emission is ritually impure, and it is prohibited for him to partake of consecrated foods. In his ordinance, Ezra instituted that the individual must immerse himself for purification before praying or engaging in Torah study. Although this ordinance was repealed several generations later, it remained the custom in many communities, as well as a custom of the pious throughout the generations.

HALAKHA

When courts are in regular session every day – **שֶׁבָּתֵּי דִינִין קְבוּעִין בְּכׇל יוֹם**: In places where the courts convene only on Monday and Thursday, a virgin is married on Wednesday. In places where the courts convene every day, or where they do not regularly convene on any particular day, she may marry on any day of the week, provided that the groom exerted himself in preparing the feast three days prior to the wedding.

Some early commentaries (Ran; Meiri) rule that since today betrothal, marriage, and consummation of the marriage take place consecutively on the same day, the primary reason for limiting weddings to the day before the courts convene, i.e., so that the groom can make a claim concerning virginity, is no longer in effect, and therefore weddings may be held on any day of the week (Rambam *Sefer Nashim*, *Hilkhot Ishut* 10:14–15; *Shulḥan Arukh*, *Even HaEzer* 64:3).

מַאי שָׁקְדוּ? דְּתַנְיָא: מִפְּנֵי מָה אָמְרוּ בְּתוּלָה נִשֵּׂאת לְיוֹם הָרְבִיעִי – שֶׁאִם הָיָה לוֹ טַעֲנַת בְּתוּלִים הָיָה מַשְׁכִּים לְבֵית דִּין. וְתִנָּשֵׂא בְּאֶחָד בְּשַׁבָּת, וְאִם הָיָה לוֹ טַעֲנַת בְּתוּלִים – הָיָה מַשְׁכִּים לְבֵית דִּין! שָׁקְדוּ חֲכָמִים עַל תַּקָּנַת בְּנוֹת יִשְׂרָאֵל, שֶׁיְּהֵא אָדָם טוֹרֵחַ בִּסְעוּדָה שְׁלֹשָׁה יָמִים: אֶחָד בְּשַׁבָּת, וְשֵׁנִי בְּשַׁבָּת, וּשְׁלִישִׁי בְּשַׁבָּת, וּבִרְבִיעִי כּוֹנְסָהּ.

The Gemara asks: **What is** the meaning of: The Sages **were assiduous?**[N] It is **as it is taught** in a *baraita*: **Due to what** reason **did** the Sages in the mishna **say** that **a virgin is married on Wednesday?** It is so **that if** the husband **had a claim concerning** the bride's **virginity, he would go early** the next day **to court** and make his claim. The *baraita* continues: **But** if that is the reason, **let her marry on Sunday, as** then too, **if** the husband **had a claim concerning** the bride's **virginity, he would go early** the next day **to court** and make his claim. The Gemara answers: The Sages **were assiduous in seeing to the well-being of Jewish women** and preferred Wednesday, **so that** the husband **would exert** himself **in** arranging **the** wedding **feast for three days, Sunday, Monday and Tuesday, and on Wednesday, he marries her.**

וּמִסַּכָּנָה וְאֵילָךְ נָהֲגוּ הָעָם לִכְנוֹס בִּשְׁלִישִׁי, וְלֹא מִיחוּ בְּיָדָם חֲכָמִים. וּבְשֵׁנִי לֹא יִכְנוֹס, וְאִם מֵחֲמַת הָאוֹנֶס – מוּתָּר. וּמַפְרִישִׁין אֶת הֶחָתָן מִן הַכַּלָּה לֵילֵי שַׁבָּת תְּחִלָּה, מִפְּנֵי שֶׁהוּא עוֹשֶׂה חַבּוּרָה.

The *baraita* continues: **And from** the time of **danger and onward, the people adopted the custom to marry on Tuesday** as well, **and the Sages did not reprimand them. And on Monday one may not marry** even in time of danger. **However, if it is due to the coercion,** it is **permitted.**[N] The *baraita* concludes: **One isolates the groom from the** virgin **bride,** so that he will not engage in intercourse with her for the **first** time **on Shabbat evening, because** by rupturing the hymen **he inflicts a wound,** which is a labor prohibited on Shabbat.

מַאי סַכָּנָה? אִילֵּימָא דְּאָמְרִי: בְּתוּלָה הַנִּשֵּׂאת לְיוֹם הָרְבִיעִי תֵּיהָרֵג, נָהֲגוּ?! לְגַמְרֵי נִיעַקְרֵיהּ!

The Gemara elaborates: **What is** the **danger** mentioned in the *baraita*? **If we say** it is referring to a situation where the government **said that a virgin who is married on Wednesday will be executed,** would the response be merely **that they adopted the custom** to marry on Tuesday? **Let them** totally **abolish** the ordinance[N] to marry on Wednesday in the face of life-threatening danger.

אֲמַר רַבָּה, דְּאָמְרִי: בְּתוּלָה הַנִּשֵּׂאת בְּיוֹם הָרְבִיעִי – תִּיבָּעֵל לַהֶגְמוֹן תְּחִלָּה הַאי סַכָּנָה?! אוֹנֶס הוּא! מִשּׁוּם דְּאִיכָּא צְנוּעוֹת דְּמָסְרָן נַפְשַׁיְיהוּ לְקַטְלָא, וְאָתְיָין לִידֵי סַכָּנָה.

Rabba said: The *baraita* is referring to a period where the government **said that a virgin who is married on Wednesday will** submit to **intercourse with the prefect** [*hegmon*][L] **first.**[B] The Gemara questions the formulation of the *baraita*: **Is that** characterized as **danger? It is coercion.** The Gemara answers: There is also danger involved, **as there are virtuous women who give their lives** rather than allow themselves to be violated, **and they will come to** mortal **danger.**

NOTES

What is the meaning of the Sages were assiduous – מַאי שָׁקְדוּ: Why is this question raised here when the assiduousness of the Sages was mentioned earlier? Rashi explains that the Gemara is not seeking to ascertain the meaning of their assiduousness but is attempting to determine its tannaitic source. An explanation more in keeping with the language of the Gemara is cited in the *Shita Mekubbetzet*: One of the reasons for the ordinance to marry on Wednesday is to ensure that the groom prepare the wedding feast. This was discussed extensively. However, the other reason cited, that the wedding take place on the day that the blessing of procreation was given, was not discussed at length. What was the significance of the former reason that led the Sages to devote so much discussion to it? The Gemara cites the *baraita* that indicates that the Sages were so insistent about preparations for the wedding feast that they enforced its observance even in the face of danger.

Others explain that the question is: Where in the mishna is there an allusion to the assiduousness of the Sages on this matter (*Sefer Hafla'a*)? Their answer, based on the Rosh, is that the Sages were particularly assiduous in ensuring that the groom exert himself for three days in preparing the wedding to prevent any possibility of making false allegations against his bride. That also answers the difficulty raised by the Ran: Why must the three days be consecutive? The answer is that the Sages wanted the groom to be busy preparing the wedding feast during the three days immediately prior to the wedding to prevent discord between the bride and the groom.

Adopted the custom…permitted – נָהֲגוּ...מוּתָּר: Rashi explains: They adopted the custom, means that most people accepted it as the norm. It is permitted, means that if one did so, it is acceptable after the fact.

Tosafot explain to the contrary: They adopted the custom, means that it is permitted after the fact, and: It is permitted, means that it is permitted even *ab initio*. Support for the opinion of Rashi appears in the Jerusalem Talmud, where it is stated that only in exigent circumstances may one marry on Monday. The reason for that statement is that the longer the break between consummating the marriage and convening the court, the greater the chance that the groom's resolve will cool.

They adopted the custom, let them totally abolish the ordinance – נָהֲגוּ, לְגַמְרֵי נִיעַקְרֵיהּ: Some explain this as an answer to the question: If it was a decree of religious persecution, why weren't they required to sacrifice their lives as martyrs rather than violate Jewish customs, and all the more so rabbinic ordinances? They answer that since the decree was directed at the women, the Sages, who were not directly affected by the decree, would have been free to repeal their ordinance, thereby negating the prohibition altogether (Rivash). A slight variation of that explanation is that although in that situation it is prohibited to violate a rabbinic ordinance, the court should initiate a repeal of the ordinance and create a situation where martyrdom would not be required (*Shita Mekubbetzet*).

LANGUAGE

Prefect [*hegmon*] – הֶגְמוֹן: From the Greek ἡγεμών, *heguemon*, meaning leader, in particular a military leader. In a later period, this served as the title for local Roman governors. In the Talmud it is a term meaning general or high government official.

BACKGROUND

Will submit to intercourse with the prefect first – תִּיבָּעֵל לַהֶגְמוֹן תְּחִלָּה: These decrees, which underscore the total domination by a ruler of his subjects, were in effect in several countries in the ancient world. Even in the Middle Ages, *jus primae noctis*, the right of the first night, was one of the rights the feudal lords held over their serfs and vassals. There are several sources of uncertain credibility indicating that a decree of this kind was in effect in the period prior to the Hasmonean revolt.

LANGUAGE

Decree of religious persecution [*shemada*] – שְׁמָדָא: The term: Decree of religious persecution was changed by the Christian censor to decree or royal decree. The term *shemada* is a pejorative term describing the act of a Jew adopting another religion in general, Christianity in particular. The *ge'onim* explain that the term is from the Aramaic term *amad*, meaning wash or immerse. However, there is also a secondary meaning, something disgusting, e.g., a container filled with urine. The term *meshumad*, apostate, literally means immersed. However, *shemada* is commonly used in reference to any law or punitive action designed to convert Jews to other religions. In addition, it is associated with the related Hebrew term *hashmada*, destruction.

וְלִידְרוֹשׁ לְהוּ דְּאוֹנֶס שָׁרֵי! אִיכָּא פְּרוּצוֹת, וְאִיכָּא נַמִי כֹּהֲנוֹת.

The Gemara asks: **And** if so, **let** the Sages **instruct** these women **that** in cases of **coercion** it is **permitted**[N] to submit to violation rather than sacrifice their lives, and they will not be forbidden to their husbands. The Gemara answers: The Sages cannot issue an instruction of that sort, because **there are licentious women**[N] who would exploit the situation to engage in intercourse willingly, rendering them forbidden to their husbands. **And** furthermore, **there are also** women married to **priests,**[N] who are rendered forbidden to their husbands even if they are raped.

וְלִיעַקְרֵיהּ! שְׁמָדָא עֲבִידָא דְּבָטְלָא, וְתַקַּנְתָּא דְּרַבָּנַן מִקַּמֵּי שְׁמָדָא לָא עָקְרִינַן. אִי הָכִי בִּשְׁלִישִׁי נַמִי אָתֵי וּבָעֵיל! מִסְּפֵיקָא לָא עָקַר נַפְשֵׁיהּ.

The Gemara asks: **And let** the Sages completely **abolish** the ordinance to marry on Wednesday and establish marriage on a different day. The Gemara answers: **A decree of religious persecution [*shemada*]**[L] **is likely to be abrogated, and we do not abolish a rabbinic ordinance in the face of a decree of religious persecution.**[N] Rather, a lenient ruling is issued instructing them not to follow the ordinance, as long as the decree of persecution is in effect. The Gemara asks: **If so,** what is accomplished by moving the marriage to Tuesday? The prefect **will come on Tuesday too,** to violate them. The Gemara answers: The date of the marriage is not fixed, and **for** a situation of **uncertainty** the prefect will not **uproot himself** to violate the bride.

וּבְשֵׁנִי לֹא יִכְנוֹס, וְאִם מֵחֲמַת הָאוֹנֶס – מוּתָּר. מַאי אוֹנֶס? אִילֵימָא הָא דַּאֲמָרַן – הָתָם קָרֵי לֵיהּ סַכָּנָה וְהָכָא קָא קָרֵי לֵיהּ אוֹנֶס? וְתוּ, הָתָם נָהֲגוּ, הָכָא – מוּתָּר!

The *baraita* continues: **And on Monday one may not marry** even in time of danger. **However, if it is due to the coercion, it is permitted.** The Gemara asks: **What is the coercion**[N] mentioned in the *baraita*? **If we say it is referring to that which we mentioned** with regard to the decree of *prima nocta* it is difficult, as **there** the *tanna* **calls it danger, and here he calls it coercion. Furthermore, there** it says that they **adopted the custom** to marry on Tuesday; **here** it states that it is **permitted.**

NOTES

That in cases of coercion it is permitted – דְּאוֹנֶס שָׁרֵי: Although one forced to perform a forbidden action under duress is not considered a transgressor, in this case, two difficulties arise. First, this is a case involving forbidden sexual relations, which is one of the three transgressions for which one is required to sacrifice his life rather than violate them. Second, this was a decree of religious persecution, for which one must be killed even if it involves a minor transgression.

Several solutions are suggested. *Tosafot* explain that one must give his life rather than perform a forbidden action. However, since the woman plays a passive role in intercourse, she need not submit to being killed.

Tosafot cite a second explanation in the name of Rabbeinu Tam: Intercourse with a gentile does not fall into the category of forbidden sexual relations that require martyrdom. The Ramban explains that there is a distinction between a decree intended to cause apostasy among the Jews, in which case one must be killed rather than violate the prohibition, and a decree motivated by self-gratification, for which martyrdom is not required. The Ra'avad disagrees.

There are licentious women – אִיכָּא פְּרוּצוֹת: The commentaries raise the question: Must virtuous women give their lives due to the concern that licentious women will engage in illicit relations? They answer that the existence of licentious women is not the reason that the Sages did not issue a ruling that a raped woman is permitted to her husband. Rather, it is the reason that the Sages allowed the ordinance to be changed. Because there are licentious women who are likely to be forbidden to their husbands by willingly engaging in intercourse, it is preferable to change the day designated for marriage and avoid that pitfall (*Shita Mekubbetzet*). The *Ḥatam Sofer* writes that there is an additional concern that once licentious women are aware that intercourse with the prefect is permitted, they will allow themselves to engage in forbidden intercourse with others, as once the woman is no longer a virgin, it is impossible to ascertain with whom they engaged in intercourse.

And there are also women married to priests – וְאִיכָּא נַמִי כֹּהֲנוֹת: Since women married to priests know they will be rendered forbidden to their husbands if raped, they will give their lives rather than submit to the rape. Therefore, there is mortal danger involved (Ritva).

And we do not abolish a rabbinic ordinance in the face of a decree of religious persecution – וְתַקַּנְתָּא דְּרַבָּנַן מִקַּמֵּי שְׁמָדָא לָא עָקְרִינַן: With regard to the decree that anyone who marries on Wednesday will be killed, the Sages explicitly abolished the ordinance to marry on Wednesday. However, in this case, where the decree would not necessarily lead to death, as it is permitted for women to submit to rape, the Sages did not want to abolish the ordinance, due to licentious women and the wives of priests who opted to give their lives rather than submit to rape (Ritva).

What is the coercion – מַאי אוֹנֶס: In the Jerusalem Talmud, the phrase: Due to the coercion, is explained to mean due to sorcery. Some explain that the concern is that the gentiles will attribute the fact that Jews insist on marrying on the same day as due to sorcery (*Penei Moshe*). Others explain that the concern is that if the sorcerers knew when the wedding was taking place, they would cast a spell on the bride and the groom (*Korban HaEda*).

אֲמַר רָבָא: דְּאָמְרִי שַׂר צָבָא בָּא לָעִיר. הֵיכִי דָּמֵי? אִי דְּאָתֵי וְחָלֵיף – לִיעַכֵּב! לָא צְרִיכָא, דְּאָתֵי וְקָבַע בִּשְׁלִישִׁי מִיהָא לִכְנוֹס! אַסְפַּרְוָוא דִּידֵיהּ בִּשְׁלִישִׁי קָאָתוּ.

Rava said: Coercion refers to a case **where they said: A general** and his army **are coming to the city** on Wednesday, and the concern is that the troops will appropriate the supplies for the feast. **What are the circumstances? If** it is a situation **where** the general **comes and passes** through, **let** them **postpone** the wedding until the following week. **Rather, it is necessary** to teach the *halakha* with regard to the general only in a case **where he comes and establishes** himself there. The Gemara asks: **In any case, let one marry on Tuesday.** Why does the *baraita* permit marrying on Monday? The Gemara answers: It was necessary to move the wedding to Monday because **his entourage** [*asperava*][L] **arrives on Tuesday.**

וְאִיבָּעֵית אֵימָא: מַאי מֵחֲמַת הָאוֹנֶס – כִּדְתַנְיָא: הֲרֵי שֶׁהָיָה פִּתּוֹ אָפוּי, וְטִבְחוֹ טָבוּחַ, וְיֵינוֹ מָזוּג, וּמֵת אָבִיו שֶׁל חָתָן אוֹ אִמָּהּ שֶׁל כַּלָּה – מַכְנִיסִין אֶת הַמֵּת לְחֶדֶר, וְאֶת הֶחָתָן וְאֶת הַכַּלָּה לַחוּפָּה,

And if you wish, say instead: **What is** the meaning of: **Due to the coercion?** It is **as it is taught** in a *baraita*: **If one's bread was baked, and his animal slaughtered, and his wine diluted,** and all preparations for the wedding feast were complete, **and the father of the groom or the mother of the bride died**[H] before the wedding, then before burying the deceased, which would trigger the onset of mourning, **one moves the corpse into a room, and the bride and groom** are ushered **to the wedding canopy** and they are married.

LANGUAGE

Entourage [*asperava*] – אַסְפַּרְוָוא: The source of this word and its precise meaning are unknown. Some claim that it is the Persian form of the Greek σπεῖρα, *speira*, meaning the garrison of a military unit, a group of people stationed around a temple, or an organization.

HALAKHA

If one's bread was baked…and the father of the groom or the mother of the bride died – הֲרֵי שֶׁהָיָה פִּתּוֹ אָפוּי...וּמֵת אָבִיו שֶׁל חָתָן אוֹ אִמָּהּ שֶׁל כַּלָּה: If the groom's father dies after the wedding preparations were completed, and it is a place where the prepared items cannot be sold and will be lost if the wedding is postponed, or similarly, if the bride's mother dies and it will be impossible to reproduce the preparation invested in the hair, clothing, and jewelry of the bride, the corpse is placed in a separate room, and the wedding proceeds as planned. The groom engages in intercourse with the bride to fulfill the mitzva, and this is followed by the seven-day period of rejoicing. During this period, mourning is observed in private. Therefore, the couple may not engage in conjugal relations, nor may they sleep in the same room. Afterward, the seven-day period of mourning is observed.

If, however, the bride and groom are in a place where the prepared items can be sold, and no loss will be incurred if the wedding is postponed, or if it was the groom's mother or the bride's father who died and the groom's father and the bride's mother will be able to assist in preparations for the postponed wedding (see 4a), then the deceased is buried immediately and the seven-day mourning period ensues. Afterward, the wedding takes place, followed by seven days of rejoicing (Rambam *Sefer Shofetim*, *Hilkhot Evel* 11:8; *Shulḥan Arukh*, *Yoreh De'a* 342:1).

Perek **I**
Daf **4** Amud **a**

וּבוֹעֵל בְּעִילַת מִצְוָה וּפוֹרֵשׁ, וְנוֹהֵג שִׁבְעַת יְמֵי הַמִּשְׁתֶּה, וְאַחַר כָּךְ נוֹהֵג שִׁבְעַת יְמֵי אֲבֵילוּת. וְכׇל אוֹתָן הַיָּמִים הוּא יָשֵׁן בֵּין הָאֲנָשִׁים וְהִיא יְשֵׁנָה בֵּין הַנָּשִׁים. וְאֵין מוֹנְעִין תַּכְשִׁיטִין מִן הַכַּלָּה כׇּל שְׁלֹשִׁים יוֹם.

And the groom then **engages in intercourse** with the bride to fulfill the **mitzva,**[N] **and** then he **withdraws**[N] from his wife, and the corpse is buried. **And** the groom then **observes the seven days of** the wedding **feast,** which are a personal festival for him, when the obligation of mourning rites does not take effect, **and thereafter he observes the seven days of mourning. And throughout those days** of rejoicing and mourning, the groom **sleeps among the men, and** the bride **sleeps among the women,** and they are not permitted to enter into seclusion. **And** in the event of mourning, **one does not withhold jewels from the bride**[HN] for the **entire thirty-day** period after the wedding, so that she not be undesirable to her husband.

HALAKHA

And one does not withhold jewels from the bride – וְאֵין מוֹנְעִין תַּכְשִׁיטִין מִן הַכַּלָּה: A bride whose close relative dies within thirty days after the marriage ceremony need not refrain from adorning herself, even during the seven-day mourning period (see Rashi; Rambam *Sefer Shofetim*, *Hilkhot Evel* 11:8; *Shulḥan Arukh Yoreh De'a* 342, 381:6).

NOTES

And the groom then engages in intercourse to fulfill the mitzva – וּבוֹעֵל בְּעִילַת מִצְוָה: Until the deceased is buried, the *halakhot* of mourning are not in effect. However, between the death and the burial, there is a period of acute mourning. During that period, various leniencies are in effect to allow the mourner to tend to the burial. Some maintain that, fundamentally, none of those matters forbidden to a mourner are forbidden to an acute mourner, and therefore the Rambam writes that he may bathe, smear himself with oil, eat meat, drink wine, and engage in sexual relations. Only eating consecrated foods and performing the Temple service are prohibited. According to that opinion, it is clear why the groom would be permitted to engage in the initial intercourse to fulfill the mitzva. According to the Ramban and others, it is prohibited by rabbinic law for an acute mourner to engage in sexual relations; however, the Sages permitted the groom to do so in order to fulfill a mitzva (Meiri).

With regard to the concept that the wedding celebration overrides mourning, some explain that even on the day of death and burial, there is no explicit mitzva of mourning by Torah law. The Sages derived this from the verse "And I will make it as the mourning for an only son, and the end thereof as a bitter day" (Amos 8:10). Similarly, the mitzva of the wedding celebration is not by Torah law, but according to Rabbi Meir HaLevi there is an allusion from the verse "On the day of his marriage and the day of the gladness of his heart" (Song of Songs 3:11). According to the Meiri, it is derived from the verse "The voice of mirth and the voice of gladness, the voice of the bridegroom and the voice of the bride" (Jeremiah 16:9). Since failure to perform the wedding would lead to financial loss, and there is concern that postponement would undermine the wedding celebration, the week of rejoicing is not postponed. The Radbaz adds that since the mourning is not completely annulled, but merely postponed, no Torah law or rabbinic law is actually being abrogated.

And engages in intercourse…and withdraws – וּבוֹעֵל...וּפוֹרֵשׁ: Rashi explains that after intercourse the husband withdraws and the deceased is immediately buried (see *Tosafot*). Others say that were they to bury the deceased immediately, that day would be the day of death and burial on which, according to many opinions, the mourning would be by Torah law. If so, it would be prohibited to engage in intercourse that day. Therefore, they maintain that the deceased is buried only the next day, at which point the mourning period begins. In this case, one is allowed to postpone the burial. Although postponing a burial is generally prohibited so as not to compromise the dignity of the deceased, doing so here is permitted, as it enhances the dignity of the deceased by preventing the humiliation his son would suffer by postponing his wedding (Meiri). The Ramban, however, prohibits postponing the burial, as doing so violates a Torah prohibition. Rather, once the groom consummates the marriage, the deceased is buried that same day.

And one does not withhold jewels from the bride – וְאֵין מוֹנְעִין תַּכְשִׁיטִין מִן הַכַּלָּה: Rashi explains that this refers to a bride whose mourning period was postponed due to the wedding. Most commentaries interpret it as referring to any bride in mourning.

וְדַוְקָא אָבִיו שֶׁל חָתָן אוֹ אִמָּהּ שֶׁל כַּלָּה, דְּלֵיכָּא אִינִישׁ דְּטָרַח לְהוּ, אֲבָל אִיפְּכָא – לָא.

And the wedding takes place and is followed by seven days of feasting and seven days of mourning, **specifically** if it is **the father of** the **groom or the mother of** the **bride**[N] who died, as in that case **there is no** other **person** who would **exert** themselves **for them.** They are the ones responsible for the wedding preparations, and therefore the preparations that were completed must be utilized. **However,** if **the opposite** takes place, i.e., the mother of the groom or the father of the bride dies, **no,** the practice is different. The corpse is buried immediately, the seven-day mourning period is observed, and only afterward is the couple married.

אָמַר רַפְרַם בַּר פַּפָּא אָמַר רַב חִסְדָּא: לֹא שָׁנוּ אֶלָּא שֶׁנָּתַן מַיִם עַל גַּבֵּי בָשָׂר. אֲבָל לֹא נָתַן מַיִם עַל גַּבֵּי בָשָׂר – מִזְדַּבַּן.

Rafram bar Pappa said that **Rav Ḥisda said:** The Sages **taught** that they are married immediately **only if one** already **placed water on the meat.** In that case, it will be impossible to sell it to others, and if it is not cooked immediately it will spoil and a significant loss will be incurred, potentially resulting in cancellation of the wedding feast. **However, if he did not place water on the meat, it** can be **sold.** No significant loss will be incurred, so the mourning period need not be postponed.

אָמַר רָבָא: וּבִכְרָךְ, אַף עַל פִּי שֶׁנָּתַן מַיִם עַל גַּבֵּי בָשָׂר – מִזְדַּבַּן. אָמַר רַב פַּפָּא: וּבִכְפָר, אַף עַל פִּי שֶׁלֹּא נָתַן מַיִם עַל גַּבֵּי בָשָׂר – לָא מִזְדַּבַּן. וְאֶלָּא, דְּרַב חִסְדָּא הֵיכִי מַשְׁכַּחַתְּ לָהּ? אֲמַר רַב אַשִׁי: כְּגוֹן מָתָא מְחַסְיָא, דְּמַפְּקָא מִכְּרָךְ וּמַפְּקָא מִכְּפָר,

Rava said: And in a city, where there are typically many buyers, **even if he placed water on the meat it** can be **sold,** and the mourning period need not be postponed. **Rav Pappa said: And in a village, even if he did not place water on the meat, it cannot** be **sold,** because no buyers can be found to purchase a quantity of meat that great. Based on the statements of Rava and Rav Pappa, whether or not water was placed on the meat is irrelevant both in a large city and in a village. The Gemara asks: **Where do you find** a case where the statement **of Rav Ḥisda** applies? **Rav Ashi says:** It can be found in a place **like** his city of **Mata Meḥasya,**[NB] **which is removed from** the category of **a city,** as it is too small, **and removed from** the category of **a village,** as it is too large.

תַּנְיָא כְּוָותֵיהּ דְּרַב חִסְדָּא: הֲרֵי שֶׁהָיָה פִּתּוֹ אֲפוּיָה וְטִבְחוֹ טָבוּחַ וְיֵינוֹ מָזוּג, וְנָתַן מַיִם עַל גַּבֵּי בָשָׂר, וּמֵת אָבִיו שֶׁל חָתָן אוֹ אִמָּהּ שֶׁל כַּלָּה – מַכְנִיסִין אֶת הַמֵּת לְחֶדֶר וְאֶת הֶחָתָן וְאֶת הַכַּלָּה לַחוּפָּה, וּבוֹעֵל בְּעִילַת מִצְוָה וּפוֹרֵשׁ, וְנוֹהֵג שִׁבְעַת יְמֵי הַמִּשְׁתֶּה, וְאַחַר כָּךְ נוֹהֵג שִׁבְעַת יְמֵי אֲבֵילוּת. וְכָל אוֹתָן הַיָּמִים הוּא יָשֵׁן בֵּין הָאֲנָשִׁים וְאִשְׁתּוֹ יְשֵׁנָה בֵּין הַנָּשִׁים.

The following *baraita* was **taught in accordance** with the opinion of **Rav Ḥisda: If one's bread was baked, and his animal slaughtered, and his wine diluted, and he placed water on the meat, and the father of the groom or the mother of the bride died,**[N] **one moves the corpse into a room, and the bride and groom** are ushered **to the wedding canopy,** and they are married. The groom then **engages in intercourse** with the bride **to fulfill the mitzva,**[N] and he then **withdraws** from his wife, and the corpse is buried. **And** the groom then **observes the seven days of** the wedding **feast, and thereafter observes the seven days of mourning. And throughout those days** of feast and mourning, the groom **sleeps among the men, and his wife sleeps among the women,** and they are not permitted to be alone together.

וְכֵן מִי שֶׁפֵּירְסָה אִשְׁתּוֹ נִדָּה – הוּא יָשֵׁן בֵּין הָאֲנָשִׁים וְהִיא יְשֵׁנָה בֵּין הַנָּשִׁים. וְאֵין מוֹנְעִין תַּכְשִׁיטִין מִן הַכַּלָּה כָּל שְׁלֹשִׁים יוֹם. בֵּין כָּךְ וּבֵין כָּךְ לֹא יִבְעוֹל לֹא בְּעֶרֶב שַׁבָּת וְלֹא בְּמוֹצָאֵי שַׁבָּת.

And likewise, a groom **whose wife began to menstruate**[H] at the time of the wedding, **he sleeps among the men and she sleeps among the women,** until she becomes ritually pure. **However,** the Sages **do not withhold jewels from the bride** while she is in mourning for the **entire thirty-day** period after the wedding. **In any event, the groom may not engage in intercourse** with his virgin bride, **neither on Shabbat evening,**[N] as he will thereby inflict a wound, **nor at the conclusion of Shabbat.**

NOTES

The mother of the bride – אִמָּהּ שֶׁל כַּלָּה: Some explain that the reason the wedding is not postponed is that the mother of the bride is the one who undertakes the wedding preparations in general (Rambam; see *Kesef Mishne* and *Talmidei Rabbeinu Yona*). Most early commentaries, beginning with Rav Hai Gaon, explain that the mother of the bride is involved with preparing the bride's jewelry. The Ramban asks why that is considered a major loss, as most jewelry will not be ruined in the course of an additional week. He explains that the concern is with regard to items that lose value over time. Furthermore, the term used in the Gemara, *takhshit*, refers not only to jewelry but also to makeup and body treatments. In the mother of the bride's absence, there will be no one to see to those details.

Like Mata Meḥasya – כְּגוֹן מָתָא מְחַסְיָא: *Tosafot* ask why Rav Ḥisda establishes this in so limited a case. They explain that this is prototypical of most places that are neither small villages nor large cities. Some explain that Rav Ḥisda himself does not accept the distinction of Rava and Rav Pappa but holds that even in a large city there would be financial loss, since it would not be possible to sell this meat in the market, but only in private homes. Therefore, the ruling is applicable everywhere (*Shita Mekubbetzet*). This explains the proof cited from the *baraita*, which establishes a general ruling without distinguishing between different places.

The father of the groom…died, etc. – מֵת אָבִיו שֶׁל חָתָן וכו׳: The early commentaries discuss the ruling in the case of the death of a relative of the bride or the groom not mentioned in the Gemara, e.g., a brother or sister.

Some authorities rule that in those cases, too, the couple engages in initial intercourse to fulfill the mitzva, after which the groom withdraws from his wife; however, the seven days of mourning precede the seven days of rejoicing (*Ba'al Halakhot Gedolot*). Others hold that the wedding is postponed until after the mourning period (Rosh). There are those who also make a distinction between the groom's mother and the bride's father and other relatives (see Meiri).

Intercourse to fulfill the mitzva – בְּעִילַת מִצְוָה: See *Tosafot* for an explanation why this is referred to as intercourse to fulfill the mitzva. Some early commentaries write that since conjugal relations are an essential component of marriage, the seven days of rejoicing begin only after the marriage is consummated.

In any event, the groom may not engage in intercourse, neither on Shabbat evening – בֵּין כָּךְ וּבֵין כָּךְ לֹא יִבְעוֹל לֹא בְּעֶרֶב שַׁבָּת: Some explain that this *halakha* is cited here because if one marries a virgin on Wednesday and waits until the thirty-day mourning period ends before consummating the marriage, the thirtieth day is Friday evening.

HALAKHA

And likewise, a groom whose wife began to menstruate – וְכֵן מִי שֶׁפֵּירְסָה אִשְׁתּוֹ נִדָּה: If the bride begins to menstruate before the couple engaged in conjugal relations for the first time, the couple may not enter into seclusion together. The groom sleeps among the men and the bride sleeps among the women (Rambam *Sefer Kedusha, Hilkhot Issurei Bia* 22:1; *Shulḥan Arukh, Even HaEzer* 22:1).

BACKGROUND

Mata Meḥasya – מָתָא מְחַסְיָא: Mata Meḥasya was a city adjacent to Sura in Babylonia. In its day, Sura was a large city and even served as the capital of the Parthian Empire. Mata Meḥasya was relatively small. Apparently, most of its inhabitants were Jews, and it is said to date back to the beginning of Jewish settlement in Babylonia. In the time of Rav Ashi, the yeshiva in Sura moved to Mata Meḥasya. Due to the proximity of the two cities, during the geonic period, the academy was sometimes called the Sura Yeshiva and sometimes called the Meḥasya Yeshiva. Throughout all these periods, the city of Meḥasya remained the same, larger than a village but never reaching the size of a large city.

אָמַר מָר: הוּא יָשֵׁן בֵּין הָאֲנָשִׁים וְהִיא יְשֵׁנָה בֵּין הַנָּשִׁים. מְסַיֵּיעַ לֵיהּ לְרַבִּי יוֹחָנָן. דְּאָמַר רַבִּי יוֹחָנָן: אַף עַל פִּי שֶׁאָמְרוּ אֵין אֲבֵילוּת בַּמּוֹעֵד – אֲבָל דְּבָרִים שֶׁל צִינְעָא נוֹהֵג.

The Gemara proceeds to analyze the *baraita*. **The Master said: He sleeps among the men and she sleeps among the women.** This **supports** the opinion **of Rabbi Yoḥanan, as Rabbi Yoḥanan said: Although they stated that there is no mourning** observed **on a Festival, yet one observes matters of privacy,**[NH] i.e., mourning practices not apparent to onlookers. Therefore, the groom and the bride may not engage in relations during the seven days of rejoicing, as the legal status of those days is like that of a Festival for them.

דָּרַשׁ רַב יוֹסֵף בְּרֵיהּ דְּרָבָא מִשְּׁמֵיהּ דְּרָבָא: לֹא שָׁנוּ אֶלָּא שֶׁלֹּא בָּעַל, אֲבָל בָּעַל – אִשְׁתּוֹ יְשֵׁנָה עִמּוֹ.

Rav Yosef, son of Rava, taught in the name of Rava: They taught the *halakha* that if the bride began menstruating, the bride and groom may not be alone together, **only if he did not engage in intercourse** with her. **However, if he engaged in intercourse** with her, and afterward she begins menstruating, **his wife sleeps with him,** and there is no concern that this will lead to their engaging in forbidden relations.

וְהָא הָכָא, דִּבְבָעַל עָסְקִינַן, וְקָתָנֵי: הוּא יָשֵׁן בֵּין הָאֲנָשִׁים וְהִיא יְשֵׁנָה בֵּין הַנָּשִׁים! כִּי קָאָמַר – אַפֵּירְסָה אִשְׁתּוֹ נִדָּה.

The Gemara asks: **But here,** with regard to mourning, **we are dealing** with a case **where he** already **engaged in intercourse** that was permitted prior to the funeral, **and** yet the *tanna* **teaches: He sleeps among the men and she sleeps among the women.** The Gemara answers: **When he states** the ruling that if they already engaged in intercourse she sleeps with him, it was **concerning** only a case where **his wife began menstruating,** and it is not a case of mourning.

הָא "וְכֵן" קָתָנֵי!

The Gemara asks: But **doesn't it state: And likewise,** indicating that the legal status of the mourner and the legal status of the groom whose wife is menstruating are the same?

Perek **I**
Daf **4** Amud **b**

הָכִי קָאָמַר: וְכֵן מִי שֶׁפֵּירְסָה אִשְׁתּוֹ נִדָּה וְלֹא בָּעַל – הוּא יָשֵׁן בֵּין הָאֲנָשִׁים, וְאִשְׁתּוֹ יְשֵׁנָה בֵּין הַנָּשִׁים.

This is what the *tanna* **is saying: And likewise,** with regard to a groom **whose wife began to menstruate, and he had not** yet **engaged in intercourse** with her, **he sleeps among the men, and his wife sleeps among the women.** However, in the case of a mourner, even if they already engaged in sexual relations, he sleeps among the men and she sleeps among the women.

לְמֵימְרָא דַּאֲבֵילוּת קִילָּא לֵיהּ מִנִּדָּה?

The Gemara asks: **Is that to say that** the prohibition against relations during **mourning is more lenient in his** opinion **than** the prohibition against relations with **a menstruating woman?**[N] That is apparently the case, as after engaging in the initial intercourse, he may enter into seclusion with his menstruating wife but not with his wife when either of them is in mourning.

NOTES

One observes matters of privacy – דְּבָרִים שֶׁל צִינְעָא נוֹהֵג: There is a difference of opinion among the early commentaries with regard to the meaning of: One observes. Some explain that it means that he must observe those matters. Others maintain that he may do so. However, that dispute is with regard to the intermediate days of the Festival. During the seven days of rejoicing after a wedding, whose legal status is like that of a Festival by rabbinic law, everyone agrees that it means one must observe these mourning practices.

HALAKHA

One observes matters of privacy – דְּבָרִים שֶׁל צִינְעָא נוֹהֵג: If the close relative of an individual dies during a Festival, although the seven-day period of mourning does not begin until the conclusion of the Festival, private mourning practices are still observed, and sexual relations are forbidden, in accordance with the opinion of Rabbi Yoḥanan. That is the ruling of most authorities, following the ruling of *Ba'al Halakhot Gedolot* and contrary to the ruling of the Rambam (Rambam *Sefer Shofetim*, *Hilkhot Evel* 10:3; *Shulḥan Arukh*, *Yoreh De'a* 399:2).

NOTES

Is that to say that mourning is more lenient in his opinion than a menstruating woman – לְמֵימְרָא דַּאֲבֵילוּת קִילָּא לֵיהּ מִנִּדָּה: The Meiri notes that the discussion here is clearly not with regard to their relative halakhic stringency, as intercourse with a menstruating woman is forbidden by Torah law and punishable by *karet*, while intercourse during the mourning period is forbidden by rabbinic law. However, since the discussion in the Gemara relates to the measures instituted by the Sages to distance one from transgression, this depends more on the way one subjectively relates to these matters. There are major prohibitions that one takes lightly and minor prohibitions with regard to which one is especially observant (see *Shita Mekubbetzet*).

וְהָאָמַר רַבִּי יִצְחָק בַּר חֲנִינָא אָמַר רַב הוּנָא: כָּל מְלָאכוֹת שֶׁאִשָּׁה עוֹשָׂה לְבַעְלָהּ, נִדָּה עוֹשָׂה לְבַעְלָהּ, חוּץ מִמְּזִיגַת הַכּוֹס וְהַצָּעַת הַמִּטָּה וְהַרְחָצַת פָּנָיו יָדָיו וְרַגְלָיו. וְאִלּוּ גַּבֵּי אֲבֵילוּת תַּנְיָא: אַף עַל פִּי שֶׁאָמְרוּ: אֵין אָדָם רַשַּׁאי לָכוֹף אֶת אִשְׁתּוֹ לִהְיוֹת כּוֹחֶלֶת וְלִהְיוֹת פּוֹקֶסֶת, בֶּאֱמֶת אָמְרוּ: מוֹזֶגֶת לוֹ הַכּוֹס, וּמַצַּעַת לוֹ הַמִּטָּה, וּמַרְחֶצֶת לוֹ פָּנָיו יָדָיו וְרַגְלָיו!

The Gemara continues: **But didn't Rav Yitzḥak bar Ḥanina say** that **Rav Huna said: All tasks that a woman** typically **performs for her husband, a menstruating woman performs for her husband,**[H] **except for pouring** his drink into the **cup;**[N] **arranging** his **bed; and washing his face, hands, and feet,** as these actions are particularly intimate. **Whereas with regard to mourning, it is taught** in a *baraita*: **Although they said that a man may not compel his** mourning **wife, to paint** her eyes **blue or to rouge** [*pokeset*][L] her face, **in truth they said that she may pour**[H] his drink into **the cup; arrange his bed; and wash his face, hands, and feet.** Apparently, the concern lest they come to engage in relations while in mourning is less pressing than the concern while she is menstruating.

לָא קַשְׁיָא, כָּאן – בַּאֲבֵילוּת דִּידֵיהּ, כָּאן – בַּאֲבֵילוּת דִּידַהּ.

The Gemara answers: This is **not difficult. Here,** where the Sages required them to sleep apart, it is **in** a case of the husband's **mourning; there,** where the Sages allowed her to pour his drink and perform other intimate activities, it is **in** a case of the wife's **mourning.**[N] The prohibition against relations when one is mourning is not perceived to be as severe as the prohibition against relations with a menstruating woman. However, when his wife is mourning, even were he unable to restrain himself, his wife would not be complicit. Therefore, the Sages did not restrict their interaction.

וְהָא אָבִיו שֶׁל חָתָן אוֹ אִמָּהּ שֶׁל כַּלָּה קָתָנֵי! כִּי קָתָנֵי – אַשְּׁאָרָא.

The Gemara asks: **But isn't it taught** in that *baraita*: **The father of the groom and the mother of the bride?** This indicates that it makes no difference which of them was in mourning. **When** the *tanna* **teaches** that there is no distinction between which of them was in mourning, it was **concerning the rest** of the mourning practices cited there, not with regard to prohibiting their seclusion.

HALAKHA

A menstruating woman performs for her husband – נִדָּה עוֹשָׂה לְבַעְלָהּ: A menstruating woman may perform all the tasks that a wife normally performs for her husband, except for washing his face, hands, or feet; serving him his drink; and arranging his bed (Rambam *Sefer Kedusha, Hilkhot Issurei Bia* 11:19; *Shulḥan Arukh, Yoreh De'a* 195:10–12).

In truth they said that she may pour – בֶּאֱמֶת אָמְרוּ מוֹזֶגֶת: It is prohibited for a mourner to engage in conjugal relations. However, if either the husband or the wife is in mourning, acts of intimacy are permitted. Therefore, the wife is permitted to serve a drink to her husband; wash his face, hands, or feet; and arrange his bed, whether it is he or she that is in mourning. This ruling is in accordance with the opinion of Rav Ashi, a later *amora*. In his opinion he does not distinguish whether it is the husband or the wife who is the mourner (Ran; *Shulḥan Arukh, Yoreh De'a* 383:1).

LANGUAGE

Rouge [*pokeset*] – פּוֹקֶסֶת: From the Greek φῦκος, *fukos*, meaning a red dye made of a kind of seaweed. Some claim that the origin of the Greek word is the Hebrew *pukh*, meaning eye shadow.

NOTES

Except for pouring his drink into the cup – חוּץ מִמְּזִיגַת הַכּוֹס: Following Rashi, the Ritva explains that the reference here is not to the actual pouring, but to serving the drink to her husband. Similarly, he explains that arranging the bed is prohibited only when she does so in his presence. He also cites the opinion of *Tosafot*, who explain that it is referring specifically to placing the sheets on the bed and not arranging the mattress or similar tasks. With regard to washing his face, the reference is not to actual washing, as contact is forbidden. Rather, the reference is to preparing water for him to wash himself. Common to all of these cases is a degree of intimacy unique to a man and his wife, and these actions could lead to conjugal relations.

His mourning…her mourning – בַּאֲבֵילוּת דִּידֵיהּ...בַּאֲבֵילוּת דִּידַהּ: Some cite a variant reading with the opposite meaning: His mourning is a greater deterrent to intimacy than hers. When he is in mourning, there is no concern that he will come to commit a transgression. However, her mourning does not have the same effect upon him, and he is more likely to be tempted and to commit a transgression. There is a variant reading in the continuation of the Gemara as well. However, most commentaries subscribe to Rashi's reading and explanation of the Gemara, that stringency is necessary when he is in mourning. Although he is in mourning, there is still concern that he will not be able to control his urges. In fact, the Sages say that even during the period of acute mourning, one's temptations are powerful. However, when a woman is in mourning, she would refuse her husband even if he were to approach her, as her urges are less powerful. The Rashash adds that women are more sensitive than men and therefore mourning affects them more than it does men.

וּמִי שָׁאנֵי בֵּין אֲבֵילוּת דִּידֵיהּ לַאֲבֵילוּת דִּידַהּ? וְהָתַנְיָא: מִי שֶׁמֵּת חָמִיו אוֹ חֲמוֹתוֹ אֵינוֹ יָכוֹל לָכוֹף אֶת אִשְׁתּוֹ לִהְיוֹת כּוֹחֶלֶת וְלִהְיוֹת פּוֹקֶסֶת, אֶלָּא כּוֹפֶה מִטָּתוֹ וְנוֹהֵג עִמָּהּ אֲבֵילוּת. וְכֵן הִיא שֶׁמֵּת חָמִיהָ אוֹ חֲמוֹתָהּ אֵינָהּ רַשָּׁאָה לִהְיוֹת כּוֹחֶלֶת וְלִהְיוֹת פּוֹקֶסֶת, אֶלָּא כּוֹפָה מִטָּתָהּ וְנוֹהֶגֶת עִמּוֹ אֲבֵילוּת!

The Gemara asks: **And do** the Sages **distinguish between his mourning and her mourning? But isn't it taught** in a *baraita*: With regard to **one whose father-in-law or mother-in-law died, he may not compel his wife to paint** her eyes **blue**[B] **or to rouge** her face.[H] **Rather, he overturns his bed,** as was the practice among mourners, **and observes** the **mourning** period **with her.**[N] **And likewise, if** a wife's **father-in-law or mother-in-law dies, she is not allowed to paint** her eyes **blue or to rouge** her face. **Rather, she overturns her bed and observes** the **mourning** period **with him.** There is no mention in the context of his mourning that he must not be alone with his wife.

תְּנֵי בַּאֲבֵילוּת דִּידֵיהּ: הוּא יָשֵׁן בֵּין הָאֲנָשִׁים וְאִשְׁתּוֹ יְשֵׁנָה בֵּין הַנָּשִׁים. הָא "וְכֵן" קָתָנֵי! כִּי קָתָנֵי – אַכִּיחוּל וְאַפִּירְכּוּס. וְהָא "עִמּוֹ" קָתָנֵי, מַאי לָאו עִמּוֹ בְּמִטָּה? לָא, עִמּוֹ בְּבַיִת. וּכְדַאֲמַר לֵיהּ רַב לְחִיָּיא בְּרֵיהּ: בְּאַפַּהּ – נְהוֹג אֲבֵילוּתָא, דְּלָא בְּאַפַּהּ – לָא תִּנְהוֹג אֲבֵילוּתָא.

The Gemara emends the *baraita*. **Teach with regard to his mourning: He sleeps among the men and his wife sleeps among the women.** The Gemara asks: But **doesn't** the *tanna* **teach: And likewise?** This indicates that there is no difference between the two cases. The Gemara answers: **When** the *tanna* **teaches** that there is no distinction between which of them is mourning, it is with regard to **painting and rouge.** The Gemara asks: But **doesn't** the *tanna* **teach: With him? What,** does **it not** mean **with him** together **in bed,** and there is no concern that it will lead to sexual relations? **No,** it means **with him at home, and** it is **as that which Rav said to Ḥiyya, his son,** when his wife's father died: **Before her, observe mourning** practices;[H] **not before her, do not observe mourning** practices. Understood in this context, the term: With him, means in his presence.

רַב אַשִׁי אָמַר: מִי קָמְדַמֵּית אֲבֵילוּתָא דְּהָכָא לַאֲבֵילוּתָא דְּעָלְמָא? אֲבֵילוּתָא דְּעָלְמָא – חָמִיר, וְלָא אָתֵי לְזַלְזוּלֵי בֵּיהּ. אֲבֵילוּת דְּהָכָא, כֵּיוָן דְּאַקִּילוּ רַבָּנַן – אָתֵי לְזַלְזוּלֵי בֵּיהּ.

Rav Ashi said that the question was based on a mistaken premise: **Can you compare the mourning here with mourning in general? Mourning in general is stringent, and one will not come to take it lightly.** However, with regard to **mourning here,** immediately following the wedding, **since the Sages were lenient, one will come to take it lightly.**[N]

BACKGROUND

To paint her eyes blue – לִהְיוֹת כּוֹחֶלֶת: The eye shadow described here is kohl, apparently a black-blue color that was derived from the mineral stibnite, Sb_2S_3. The stibnite crystals were ground into powder and women would color the area around their eyes to draw attention to them and create the impression that they were larger. It was apparently also utilized for medicinal purposes.

Stibnite

Ancient kohl tube

Ancient kohl applicator

HALAKHA

He may not compel his wife to paint her eyes blue or to rouge her face – אֵינוֹ יָכוֹל לָכוֹף אֶת אִשְׁתּוֹ לִהְיוֹת כּוֹחֶלֶת וְלִהְיוֹת פּוֹקֶסֶת: If a man's wife is in mourning for her father or mother, he may not compel her to apply makeup during her mourning period (Rambam *Sefer Shofetim*, *Hilkhot Evel* 2:5; *Shulḥan Arukh*, *Yoreh De'a* 381:6).

Before her, observe mourning practices – בְּאַפַּהּ, נְהוֹג אֲבֵילוּתָא: If a man's father-in-law or mother-in-law dies, he is not obligated to observe mourning practices together with his wife, but he should observe them when he is in his wife's presence. So too, a wife is obligated to observe mourning practices in her husband's presence when he is in mourning for his father or mother, in accordance with the opinion of Rav (Rambam *Sefer Shofetim*, *Hilkhot Evel* 2:5; *Shulḥan Arukh*, *Yoreh De'a* 374:6, 381:6).

NOTES

And observes the mourning period with her – וְנוֹהֵג עִמָּהּ אֲבֵילוּת: The Ritva cites two explanations. The first is a literal explanation: If he is actually in her presence, i.e., at home with her, he observes the mourning practices with her. The second explanation, which seems more reasonable in this context, says that he observes mourning practices in any place where she will be informed of his conduct, even if he is not actually in her presence. The Ramban rules that these mourning practices for the relative of a spouse are no longer observed. The reason for these practices is to show deference to one's spouse, not due to any obligation of mourning. The custom today is to forgo that deference.

Mourning here…one will come to take it lightly – אֲבֵילוּת דְּהָכָא...אָתֵי לְזַלְזוּלֵי בֵּיהּ: Some commentaries ask why this explanation wasn't already suggested earlier, seeing as it is the least complicated of those suggested (*Shita Mekubbetzet*). They explain that the case of death before a wedding was likened to death during a Festival, where the mourning is delayed until after the Festival and there is no concern that one will take it lightly.

Based on the Gemara here, the Rosh raises the possibility that even on a Festival the bride and groom must separate for similar reasons. However, he draws a distinction between the cases. Since the Festival predated the mourning, the mourning never takes effect and there is no active postponement of the mourning, the husband and wife engaging in conjugal relations will not lead them to take mourning lightly. However, in the case of a wedding there is concern that they will take mourning lightly, as even though they did not yet marry, the period of mourning is postponed, and they are allowed to engage in conjugal relations on the first night.

NOTES

That mourning has not yet taken effect upon him – דְּלָא חָל עָלָיו אֲבֵילוּתָא: The question is raised: Although mourning does not take effect before the burial, isn't he an acute mourner? The Rashba and the Ritva answer that there is a difference between the status of a mourner before his relative's burial and his status thereafter. Although both statuses are effected by the death of a relative, clearly the mourning that takes places before burial is more lenient.

BACKGROUND

Covering of the grave – גּוֹלֵל: This covering is a large stone that was rolled to seal the opening of a grave. In the burial caves of significant families, this stone is in the shape of a large wheel, which is not susceptible to ritual impurity and could be moved in order to gain access to the cave.

Stone covering of the grave of the royal house of Herod, from the end of the Second Temple period

מַאי קוּלָּא? אִילֵימָא דְּקָתָנֵי בּוֹעֵל בְּעִילַת מִצְוָה וּפוֹרֵשׁ – הָתָם מִשּׁוּם דְּלָא חָל עָלָיו אֲבֵילוּתָא; אִי לְרַבִּי אֱלִיעֶזֶר – עַד שֶׁיֵּצֵא מִפֶּתַח הַבַּיִת, אִי לְרַבִּי יְהוֹשֻׁעַ – עַד שֶׁיִּסָּתֵם הַגּוֹלֵל!

What leniency did the Sages enact in this case? If we say it is that which the *tanna* teaches: The groom engages in the initial intercourse with the bride to fulfill the mitzva and then he withdraws from his wife, then there, where the corpse is placed into a room in the house, it is due to the fact that mourning has not yet taken effect upon him.[N] Consequently, there is no leniency with regard to mourning practices. If it is according to the opinion of Rabbi Eliezer, mourning does not take effect until the corpse emerges from the entrance of the house for burial. If it is according to the opinion of Rabbi Yehoshua, mourning does not take effect until the covering of the grave[B] is sealed.

אֶלָּא דְּקָתָנֵי: נוֹהֵג שִׁבְעַת יְמֵי הַמִּשְׁתֶּה, וְאַחַר כָּךְ נוֹהֵג שִׁבְעַת יְמֵי אֲבֵילוּת.

Rather, the leniency is that which the *tanna* teaches: And the groom then observes the seven days of feast following the wedding, and thereafter he observes the seven days of mourning. Since the Sages were lenient and allowed him to observe the wedding feast, despite the fact that he is a mourner, they prohibited his being alone with his wife so he would be less likely to practice additional leniencies in his mourning.

אֲמַר מָר: בֵּין כָּךְ וּבֵין כָּךְ לֹא יִבְעוֹל לֹא בְּעֶרֶב שַׁבָּת וְלֹא בְּמוֹצָאֵי שַׁבָּת. בִּשְׁלָמָא בְּעֶרֶב שַׁבָּת – מִשּׁוּם חַבּוּרָה, אֶלָּא בְּמוֹצָאֵי שַׁבָּת אַמַּאי לֹא?

§ The Master said in the *baraita*: In any event, the groom may not engage in intercourse with his virgin bride, neither on Shabbat evening, nor at the conclusion of Shabbat.[H] Granted, on Shabbat evening he may not engage in intercourse due to the prohibition against inflicting a wound on Shabbat. However, at the conclusion of Shabbat, why may he not engage in intercourse with his virgin bride?

אֲמַר רַבִּי זֵירָא:

Rabbi Zeira said:

HALAKHA

In any event, the groom may not engage in intercourse with his virgin bride, neither on Shabbat evening nor at the conclusion of Shabbat – בֵּין כָּךְ וּבֵין כָּךְ לֹא יִבְעוֹל לֹא בְּעֶרֶב שַׁבָּת וְלֹא בְּמוֹצָאֵי שַׁבָּת: According to the Rambam, a wedding may not take place on Friday or at the conclusion of Shabbat, lest one desecrate Shabbat in the course of preparing the wedding feast. This ruling is in accordance with the conclusion of the Gemara, based on the *baraita* (Ramban). Other authorities maintain that this restriction was said only in places where courts convene on Monday and Thursday (Rosh; *Tur*). Furthermore, they rule based on the Gemara's conclusion that the initial intercourse with one's virgin wife is permitted on Shabbat evening, and there is no concern lest it lead to desecration of Shabbat. In fact, there were periods when the custom was to schedule weddings on Friday to benefit the poor, so that the wedding feast and the Shabbat meal would coincide (Mordekhai). However, there was no widespread custom to marry on Sunday, because that is the day when gentiles marry, and it is prohibited to follow the statutes of the gentiles (Rema in a responsum; Rambam *Sefer Nashim, Hilkhot Ishut* 10:14; *Shulḥan Arukh, Even HaEzer* 63:4).

Perek **I**
Daf **5** Amud **a**

NOTES

Calculations for a mitzva – חֶשְׁבּוֹנוֹת שֶׁל מִצְוָה: The source of the prohibition against speaking about mundane matters on Shabbat is the verse "And call Shabbat a delight…and you shall honor it…neither pursuing your business, nor speaking thereof" (Isaiah 58:13). However, the Gemara infers (*Shabbat* 140b): Your business is forbidden, but matters of Heaven are permitted. The question is raised: If matters of Heaven are permitted, why on Shabbat is it prohibited to consecrate an item? That is a matter of Heaven par excellence. Some early commentaries answer: Since consecration typically involves transfer of a clearly defined object into the treasury of God, so to speak, it resembles a transaction, which is prohibited on Shabbat.

מִשּׁוּם חֶשְׁבּוֹנוֹת.

It is due to calculations performed on Shabbat to prepare for the wedding. He would thereby engage in weekday matters on Shabbat.

אֲמַר לֵיהּ אַבַּיֵי: וְחֶשְׁבּוֹנוֹת שֶׁל מִצְוָה מִי אֲסִירִי? וְהָא רַב חִסְדָּא וְרַב הַמְנוּנָא דְּאָמְרִי תַּרְוַיְיהוּ: חֶשְׁבּוֹנוֹת שֶׁל מִצְוָה מוּתָּר לְחַשְּׁבָן בְּשַׁבָּת! וְאָמַר רַבִּי אֶלְעָזָר: פּוֹסְקִין צְדָקָה לַעֲנִיִּים בְּשַׁבָּת! וְאָמַר רַבִּי יַעֲקֹב אָמַר רַבִּי יוֹחָנָן: הוֹלְכִין לְבָתֵּי כְנֵסִיּוֹת וּלְבָתֵּי מִדְרָשׁוֹת לְפַקֵּחַ עַל עִסְקֵי רַבִּים בְּשַׁבָּת. וְאָמַר רַבִּי יַעֲקֹב בַּר אִידִי אָמַר רַבִּי יוֹחָנָן: מְפַקְּחִין פִּיקּוּחַ נֶפֶשׁ בְּשַׁבָּת.

Abaye said to him: And are calculations for a mitzva prohibited on Shabbat? But wasn't it Rav Ḥisda and Rav Hamnuna who both said: With regard to calculations for a mitzva,[NH] it is permitted to reckon them on Shabbat? And Rabbi Elazar said: One may allocate charity[H] to the poor on Shabbat. And Rabbi Ya'akov said that Rabbi Yoḥanan said: One goes to synagogues and study halls to supervise matters affecting the multitudes on Shabbat. And Rabbi Ya'akov bar Idi said that Rabbi Yoḥanan said: One supervises matters of saving a life on Shabbat.[H]

HALAKHA

Calculations for a mitzva – חֶשְׁבּוֹנוֹת שֶׁל מִצְוָה: One may engage in calculations with regard to a mitzva on Shabbat (Rambam *Sefer Zemanim, Hilkhot Shabbat* 24:5; *Shulḥan Arukh, Oraḥ Ḥayyim* 306:6).

One may allocate charity – פּוֹסְקִין צְדָקָה: One may allocate charity to the poor and pledge to donate money for the purpose of a mitzva on Shabbat (Rambam *Sefer Zemanim, Hilkhot Shabbat* 24:5; *Shulḥan Arukh, Oraḥ Ḥayyim* 306:6).

One supervises matters of saving a life on Shabbat – מְפַקְּחִין פִּיקּוּחַ נֶפֶשׁ בְּשַׁבָּת: One may violate all Shabbat prohibitions in order to save a life, and he need not seek permission from the courts before doing so. On the contrary, anyone who takes the initiative is praiseworthy (Rambam *Sefer Zemanim, Hilkhot Shabbat* 2:16; *Shulḥan Arukh, Oraḥ Ḥayyim* 328:13).

וְאָמַר רַב שְׁמוּאֵל בַּר נַחְמָנִי אָמַר רַבִּי יוֹנָתָן: הוֹלְכִין לְטַרְטִיָּיאוֹת וּלְקַרְקִיָּיאוֹת לְפַקֵּחַ עַל עִסְקֵי רַבִּים בְּשַׁבָּת. וְתָנָא דְּבֵי מְנַשְּׁיָא: מְשַׁדְּכִין עַל הַתִּינוֹקֶת לֵיאָרֵס בְּשַׁבָּת, וְעַל הַתִּינוֹק לְלַמְּדוֹ סֵפֶר וּלְלַמְּדוֹ אוּמָּנוּת!

And Rabbi Shmuel bar Naḥmani said that Rabbi Yoḥanan said: One goes to theaters [*tartiyyaot*][BL] **and circuses** [*karkiyyaot*][L] **to supervise matters** affecting the **multitudes on Shabbat,**[H] because the fate of the Jewish people or of individual Jews is often decided there and one's presence could prevent calamity. **And** the Sage **of the school of Menashya taught:** One **makes matches** [*meshadkhin*][L] among the families concerned **for a young girl to be betrothed on Shabbat,**[H] **and** similarly one may make arrangements **for a young boy to teach him Torah and to teach him a craft.** Apparently, calculations for a mitzva may be reckoned on Shabbat, including calculations for a wedding. Therefore, this cannot be the reason for the prohibition against marrying at the conclusion of Shabbat.

אֶלָּא אָמַר רַבִּי זֵירָא: גְּזֵירָה שֶׁמָּא יִשְׁחוֹט בֶּן עוֹף. אֲמַר לֵיהּ אַבַּיֵי: אֶלָּא מֵעַתָּה, יוֹם הַכִּפּוּרִים שֶׁחָל לִהְיוֹת בְּשֵׁנִי בְּשַׁבָּת יִדָּחֶה, גְּזֵירָה שֶׁמָּא יִשְׁחוֹט בֶּן עוֹף! הָתָם, דִּלְנַפְשֵׁיהּ, לָא טָרִיד, הָכָא דִּלַאֲחֵרִים – טָרִיד. אִי נַמִּי: הָתָם – אִית לֵיהּ רַוְוחָא, הָכָא – לֵית לֵיהּ רַוְוחָא.

Rather, Rabbi Zeira said: It is a decree lest one slaughter a young fowl[N] on Shabbat, due to his preoccupation with the preparations for that night's wedding feast. **Abaye said to him: If** that is so, **Yom Kippur that occurs on Monday should be postponed**[N] when fixing the calendar, due to **a decree lest one slaughter a young fowl** on Shabbat for the meal on Yom Kippur eve, which is a mitzva. The Gemara distinguishes between the cases. **There,** with regard to Yom Kippur eve, when one is preparing a meal **for himself, he is not preoccupied,** and he will not overlook the fact that it is Shabbat. **Here,** in the case of a wedding, one is preparing a meal **for others** and is **preoccupied. Alternatively, there,** on Yom Kippur eve, **he has an interval** of time during which he can slaughter the bird, as the mitzva is to eat the meal on Yom Kippur eve the next day. **Here, he does not have an interval** of time, because the wedding and the feast take place at night at the conclusion of Shabbat.

הַשְׁתָּא דְּאָתֵית לְהָכִי – עֶרֶב שַׁבָּת נַמִּי, גְּזֵירָה שֶׁמָּא יִשְׁחוֹט בֶּן עוֹף.

The Gemara says: **Now that we have come to this** understanding of the prohibition against marrying at the conclusion of Shabbat, the prohibition not to engage in sexual intercourse on **Shabbat evening, too,**[N] is not due to the intercourse. Rather, it is **a decree lest one slaughter a young fowl** for the wedding feast.

אִיבַּעְיָא לְהוּ: בְּתוּלָה נִשֵּׂאת בִּרְבִיעִי וְנִבְעֶלֶת בִּרְבִיעִי, וְלֹא חָיְישִׁינַן לְאִיקְּרוּרֵי דַּעְתָּא, אוֹ דִּלְמָא: בְּתוּלָה נִשֵּׂאת בִּרְבִיעִי וְנִבְעֶלֶת בַּחֲמִישִׁי, דְּחָיְישִׁינַן לְאִיקְּרוּרֵי דַּעְתָּא?

§ The Gemara **raises a dilemma: Is a virgin married on Wednesday and** does she **engage in intercourse on** that **Wednesday, and we are not concerned** lest **his resolve** to take his bride to court upon discovering that she was not a virgin **cool** overnight? Rather, he will certainly go to court the next morning. **Or perhaps, a virgin is married on Wednesday but engages in intercourse on Thursday,**[H] **as we are concerned that his resolve will cool.** [N]

BACKGROUND

One goes to theaters – הוֹלְכִין לְטַרְטִיָּיאוֹת: Theaters, circuses, and arenas occasionally served as venues for public gatherings. Furthermore, riots would erupt, often over the outcome of sporting events, and would escalate into large-scale riots that went beyond the walls of those structures. More often than not, this led to pogroms directed against the Jews. Some of the performances in the theaters, at least in Eretz Yisrael, were of a distinctly anti-Jewish nature and often incited riots. The presence of Jews at those events could be effective either in preventing the riots or in warning the Jews that a riot was developing. In addition, Jews were sometimes among the participants in the battles in the circuses as gladiators, and the presence of Jewish spectators would enable them to outshout the supporters of the gentile combatant and prevent the Jew from being thrown to the beasts.

LANGUAGE

Theaters [*tartiyyaot*] **– טַרְטִיָּיאוֹת:** One form of the Greek θέατρον, *theatron,* meaning theater, or place for seeing.

Circuses [*karkiyyaot*] **– קַרְקִיָּיאוֹת:** One form of the Latin word circus. Some claim that it derives from the Latin carcer, meaning an enclosed place.

Makes matches [*meshadkhin*] **– מְשַׁדְּכִין:** Apparently from Aramaic, the term's primary meaning is to quiet or to calm. Its additional related meaning in Hebrew is to appease both sides and reach an agreement, in particular, a marriage agreement.

HALAKHA

One goes…to supervise matters affecting the multitudes on Shabbat – הוֹלְכִין...לְפַקֵּחַ עַל עִסְקֵי רַבִּים בְּשַׁבָּת: One may go to the synagogues and study halls, and even to the theaters and palaces of gentiles, in order to supervise matters affecting the multitudes on Shabbat (Rambam *Sefer Zemanim, Hilkhot Shabbat* 24:5 *Shulḥan Arukh, Oraḥ Ḥayyim* 306:6).

One makes matches among the families concerned for a young girl to be betrothed on Shabbat – מְשַׁדְּכִין עַל הַתִּינוֹקֶת לֵיאָרֵס בְּשַׁבָּת: It is permitted to engage in matchmaking on Shabbat to arrange one's daughter's betrothal. Similarly, one may undertake arrangements necessary for his son's Torah education or vocational training on Shabbat (Rambam *Sefer Zemanim, Hilkhot Shabbat* 24:5; *Shulḥan Arukh, Oraḥ Ḥayyim* 306:6).

A virgin is married on Wednesday but engages in intercourse on Thursday – בְּתוּלָה נִשֵּׂאת בִּרְבִיעִי וְנִבְעֶלֶת בַּחֲמִישִׁי: The Rabbis instituted that a virgin is married on Wednesday during the day, and the marriage is consummated on Wednesday night, so that if the groom has a claim concerning the bride's virginity he can go to court on Thursday when the courts convene. In places where the courts are in session every day, the couple may marry any day of the week, provided that the groom completed the preparations for the wedding feast, because the blessing to the fish on the fifth day of Creation is not sufficient reason to fix a specific day for the wedding (*Tur, Even HaEzer* 64; *Beit Yosef*, citing Rosh).

NOTES

Lest one slaughter a young fowl – שֶׁמָּא יִשְׁחוֹט בֶּן עוֹף: The commentaries provide several explanations for use of the term young fowl, as opposed to another source of meat that requires slaughter. Some explain that since young fowl are typically available in the proximity of the house, the concern is that one will forget that it is Shabbat and slaughter one (*ge'onim*). Others explain that, contrary to slaughtering an animal, slaughtering a young fowl requires little effort. Due to that relative ease, one will slaughter the fowl without realizing that it is Shabbat (Ritva). The Meiri explains that it was customary to specifically slaughter young chickens for the wedding feast as a portent that the couple will procreate like chickens. This custom remains in effect in several places.

Yom Kippur…should be postponed – יוֹם הַכִּפּוּרִים...יִדָּחֶה: The *ge'onim* explain that the concern with regard to young fowl is due to the fact that it is customary to slaughter roosters and chickens for the meal preceding Yom Kippur. The early commentaries question the notion of postponing Yom Kippur for so insignificant a concern. They answer that the calendar is fixed to prevent Yom Kippur from occurring on Sunday or Friday for similar reasons.

An additional question is raised. If Yom Kippur is postponed until Tuesday, the seventh day of *Sukkot* will coincide with Shabbat. The very reason that the calendar is fixed to prevent Rosh HaShana from occurring on Sunday is to preclude that coincidence. The commentaries answer that the Gemara is not suggesting that Yom Kippur be postponed specifically until Tuesday. Rather, in a case where, based on calculations, Yom Kippur was going to occur on Sunday, it would be preferable to postpone it until Tuesday rather than Monday.

Shabbat evening too – עֶרֶב שַׁבָּת נַמִּי: This answer is difficult, as a *baraita* cited later in the Gemara prohibits intercourse on Friday night because it causes a wound. The Rashba explains that Rabbi Zeira sought to interpret the *baraita* in accordance with the *halakha*, that there is no concern lest one cause a wound during intercourse. In the *Shita Mekubbetzet* an explanation is cited that Rabbi Zeira preferred to explain the entire *baraita* according to the same reason. With regard to the actual concern that one will slaughter a young fowl, some explain that if one engages in relations on Shabbat, the groomsmen will need to remain with him, and in seeking to feed them, he will come to slaughter a young fowl (*Talmidei Rabbeinu Yona*). Others suggest that the wedding feast will not take place on Friday night in any case. Rather, the intention is that one will prepare the feast for the conclusion of Shabbat, and the concern is that he will slaughter the fowl on Shabbat for the purpose of this meal (Rabbi Meir HaLevi).

As we are concerned that his resolve will cool – דְּחָיְישִׁינַן לְאִיקְּרוּרֵי דַּעְתָּא: The Ramban and many other early commentaries following discuss the relationship between this problem and the adjacent *halakha*, that one may engage in intercourse with his virgin wife on Shabbat. Ostensibly, if the wedding was on Friday, the concern that his resolve will cool is even greater, as the court reconvenes only the following Monday. The Ramban explains that the Gemara is not discussing a wedding that took place on Friday. Rather, the Gemara is discussing a wedding that took place on Wednesday but was not consummated until Shabbat.

HALAKHA

A widow is married on Thursday and engages in intercourse on Friday – אַלְמָנָה נִשֵּׂאת בַּחֲמִישִׁי וְנִבְעֶלֶת בְּשִׁשִּׁי: The Sages instituted that a widow is married on Thursday during the day, and the couple consummates the marriage on Thursday night, so that the husband will celebrate with his wife for three days and not go to work the morning after the wedding. One who is unemployed may marry a widow any day of the week (*Tur, Even HaEzer* 64; *Beit Yosef*).

That he rejoice with her for three days – שֶׁיְּהֵא שָׂמֵחַ עִמָּהּ שְׁלֹשָׁה יָמִים: The Sages instituted that a man who marries a woman who is not a virgin is obligated to rejoice with her for three days. The Rema notes that since this ordinance was instituted for the bride's benefit, she may waive that benefit (Rambam *Sefer Nashim, Hilkhot Ishut* 10:12; *Shulḥan Arukh, Even HaEzer* 64:2).

תָּא שְׁמַע, דְּתָנֵי בַּר קַפָּרָא: בְּתוּלָה נִשֵּׂאת בִּרְבִיעִי וְנִבְעֶלֶת בַּחֲמִישִׁי, הוֹאִיל וְנֶאֶמְרָה בּוֹ בְּרָכָה לַדָּגִים. אַלְמָנָה נִשֵּׂאת בַּחֲמִישִׁי וְנִבְעֶלֶת בְּשִׁשִּׁי, הוֹאִיל וְנֶאֶמְרָה בּוֹ בְּרָכָה לָאָדָם. טַעֲמָא – מִשּׁוּם בְּרָכָה, אֲבָל מִשּׁוּם אִיקְרוּרֵי דַּעְתָּא – לָא חָיְישִׁינַן.

Come and hear proof, **as bar Kappara taught: A virgin is married on Wednesday and engages in intercourse on Thursday, since the blessing to the fish:**[N] Be fruitful and multiply, **was stated** on the fifth day of Creation. **A widow is married on Thursday and engages in intercourse on Friday,**[H] **since the blessing** of procreation **was stated to man** on the sixth day of Creation. It may be inferred that **the reason is due to the blessing, but with regard to** the possibility lest **his resolve cool, we are not concerned.**

אִי הָכִי, אַלְמָנָה נַמִי תִּיבָּעֵל בַּחֲמִישִׁי, הוֹאִיל וְנֶאֶמְרָה בּוֹ בְּרָכָה לַדָּגִים! בְּרָכָה דְּאָדָם עֲדִיפָא לֵיהּ.

The Gemara asks: **If so, a widow should also engage in intercourse on Thursday, since the blessing to the fish was stated then.**[N] The Gemara answers: Since there is the option to postpone engaging in relations to the day on which **the blessing of man** was stated, doing so **is preferable for him.**

וְאִי נַמִי – מִשּׁוּם שָׁקְדוּ. דְּתַנְיָא: מִפְּנֵי מָה אָמְרוּ אַלְמָנָה נִשֵּׂאת בַּחֲמִישִׁי וְנִבְעֶלֶת בְּשִׁשִּׁי? שֶׁאִם אַתָּה אוֹמֵר תִּיבָּעֵל בַּחֲמִישִׁי – לְמָחָר מַשְׁכִּים לְאוּמָנְתוֹ וְהוֹלֵךְ לוֹ, שָׁקְדוּ חֲכָמִים עַל תַּקָּנַת בְּנוֹת יִשְׂרָאֵל, שֶׁיְּהֵא שָׂמֵחַ עִמָּהּ שְׁלֹשָׁה יָמִים: חֲמִישִׁי בְּשַׁבָּת, וְעֶרֶב שַׁבָּת, וְשַׁבָּת.

Alternatively, that day was established as the day for a widow to engage in sexual relations **due to** the fact that the Sages **were assiduous**[N] in seeing to the well-being of Jewish women, **as it is taught** in a *baraita*: **Why did** the Sages **say that a widow is married on Thursday and engages in intercourse on Friday?** It is **because if you say that she should engage in intercourse on Thursday, on the next day** the groom will **go to** ply **his craft early**[N] and leave his wife alone. When a man marries a widow, there is no observance of the seven days of rejoicing, whose legal status is like that of a Festival, during which he does not go to work. Therefore, **the Sages were assiduous in seeing to the well-being of Jewish women** and ensured **that** the groom **rejoice with her** for **three days:**[H] **Thursday,** the day of the wedding; **and Shabbat eve,** the day when they engage in sexual relations; **and Shabbat.**

מַאי אִיכָּא בֵּין "בְּרָכָה" לְ"שָׁקְדוּ"? אִיכָּא בֵּינַיְיהוּ אָדָם בָּטֵל, אִי נַמִי יוֹם טוֹב שֶׁחָל לִהְיוֹת בְּעֶרֶב שַׁבָּת.

What practical difference **is there between** the two reasons given to engage in relations on Friday, i.e., the **blessing** of procreation for man **and** the fact that the Sages **were assiduous?**[N] The Gemara answers: **There is** a practical difference **between them** in the case of **an idle person,** who has no job, in which case the reason of blessing applies and the reason that the Sages were assiduous does not, as no matter what he will not go to work early. **Alternatively,** there is a practical difference in the case of **a Festival that occurs on Shabbat eve.** There too, the reason of blessing applies but the Sages' assiduousness does not apply, as one does not work on a Festival.

NOTES

The blessing to the fish – בְּרָכָה לַדָּגִים: Although there was a blessing of procreation for the birds as well, the Gemara mentions the fish because their blessing preceded the blessing of the birds: "Be fruitful, and multiply, and fill the waters in the seas, and let fowl multiply in the earth" (Genesis 1:22). Furthermore, the language of the blessing to the birds is similar to the blessing of procreation given to man (see Genesis 1:28; *Shita Mekubbetzet*). In certain respects, the blessing to the fish is superior to the blessing to man, as the fish are more numerous, and the evil eye has no dominion over them (Ritva; *HaBoneh*). Alternatively, with regard to man, the blessing could be interpreted as a mitzva more than a blessing. For the fish, it is clearly a blessing (*Penei Yehoshua*).

Since the blessing to the fish was stated then – הוֹאִיל וְנֶאֶמְרָה בּוֹ בְּרָכָה לַדָּגִים: The Ritva explains that the question is: If the blessing to the fish is a reason to hold the wedding on Wednesday, why is the wedding of a widow on Thursday? The Gemara then answers that if the content of the blessing is considered, the blessing to man is preferable.

Blessing, the Sages were assiduous – בְּרָכָה, שָׁקְדוּ: Some explain that even bar Kappara himself held that there are two reasons for the ordinance of the Sages: One, the Sages were assiduous or the claim concerning virginity; two, the blessing of procreation. Others say that bar Kappara considered the latter reason to be an auxiliary reason for the ordinance, not one that stands on its own (Ramban; Rabbi Aharon HaLevi). However, the Meiri says that bar Kappara considered the blessing of procreation as an independent and significant reason for the ordinance. That appears to be the conclusion of the Jerusalem Talmud, contrary to the conclusion of the Gemara here.

The groom will go to ply his craft early – מַשְׁכִּים לְאוּמָנְתוֹ וְהוֹלֵךְ לוֹ: Based on the Gemara here, it is fundamentally permitted for the groom to work, but the Sages prevented him from doing so by instituting ordinances seeing to the well-being of Jewish women. This line of reasoning is difficult, because several sources indicate that it is prohibited for a groom to work for seven days after marrying a virgin and for three days after marrying a widow. The Ritva suggests two solutions. Although it is prohibited for him to work, there is still concern that he might ignore the prohibition. Therefore, for the benefit of the bride, the Sages fixed the wedding on a day when the groom would be unable to go to work. Alternatively, the prohibition mentioned in the other sources ensued from the ordinance of the Sages that the widow marries on Thursday, so that the groom will remain with his wife and not work for three days.

What practical difference is there between the blessing and the Sages were assiduous – מַאי אִיכָּא בֵּין בְּרָכָה לְשָׁקְדוּ: This Gemara is asking: What element is added by the reason of the blessing of procreation? Clearly, the reason that the Sages were assiduous introduces the element of the authority of the Sages. Although one could assert that the groom can be indifferent with regard to the blessing, he cannot be indifferent to an ordinance instituted by the Sages.

דָּרַשׁ בַּר קַפָּרָא: גְּדוֹלִים מַעֲשֵׂה צַדִּיקִים יוֹתֵר מִמַּעֲשֵׂה שָׁמַיִם וָאָרֶץ, דְּאִילּוּ בְּמַעֲשֵׂה שָׁמַיִם וָאָרֶץ כְּתִיב: "אַף יָדִי יָסְדָה אֶרֶץ וִימִינִי טִפְּחָה שָׁמַיִם" וְאִלּוּ בְּמַעֲשֵׂה יְדֵיהֶם שֶׁל צַדִּיקִים כְּתִיב "מָכוֹן לְשִׁבְתְּךָ פָּעַלְתָּ ה׳ מִקְּדָשׁ אֲדֹנָי כּוֹנְנוּ יָדֶיךָ".

§ The Gemara cites additional aggadic statements of bar Kappara. **Bar Kappara taught: The handiwork of the righteous is greater**[N] **than the creation of heaven and earth, as with regard to the creation of heaven and earth it is written: "My hand also has laid the foundation of the earth, and My right hand has spanned the heavens"** (Isaiah 48:13). There, hand is written in the singular. **Whereas with regard to the handiwork of the righteous it is written: "The place which You have made for Yourself to dwell in, Lord, the Sanctuary, Lord, which your hands**[N] **have established" (Exodus 15:17).** The reference is to the Temple, which is the handiwork of man, and hand is written in the plural.

הֵשִׁיב בַּבְלִי אֶחָד, וְרַבִּי חִיָּיא שְׁמוֹ: "וְיַבֶּשֶׁת יָדָיו יָצָרוּ"! "יָדוֹ" כְּתִיב. וְהָכְתִיב "יָצָרוּ"! אָמַר רַב נַחְמָן בַּר יִצְחָק: יָצְרוּ אֶצְבְּעוֹתָיו, כִּדְכְתִיב "כִּי אֶרְאֶה שָׁמֶיךָ מַעֲשֵׂה אֶצְבְּעוֹתֶיךָ יָרֵחַ וְכוֹכָבִים אֲשֶׁר כּוֹנַנְתָּה".

A certain Babylonian, and his name is Rabbi Ḥiyya, responded[N] with a challenge. It is written with regard to creation of the earth: **"And His hands formed the dry land"** (Psalms 95:5). The Gemara answers: **"His hand"** is the way it **is written.** Although the word is vocalized in the plural, it is written in the singular, without the letter *yod*. **But isn't it written: "Formed,"** in the plural? Rav Naḥman bar Yitzḥak said: The plural is referring to **His fingers, as it is written: "When I see Your heavens, the work of Your fingers, the moon and stars, which You have established"** (Psalms 8:4).

מֵיתִיבֵי: "הַשָּׁמַיִם מְסַפְּרִים כְּבוֹד אֵל וּמַעֲשֵׂה יָדָיו מַגִּיד הָרָקִיעַ"! הָכִי קָאָמַר: מַעֲשֵׂה יְדֵיהֶם שֶׁל צַדִּיקִים מִי מַגִּיד – הָרָקִיעַ, וּמַאי נִיהוּ – מָטָר.

The Gemara raises an objection: "The heavens declare the glory of God, and the firmament proclaims the work of His hands" (Psalms 19:2). The heavens were created by His hands. The Gemara answers that **this** is what the verse **is saying: Who attests to the handiwork of the righteous,** that they are performing the will of God? It is **the heavens. And what is** the avenue through which the heavens do so? It is by means of **rain** that falls due to the prayers of the righteous.

דָּרַשׁ בַּר קַפָּרָא: מַאי דִּכְתִיב "וְיָתֵד תִּהְיֶה לְךָ עַל אֲזֵנֶךָ" – אַל תִּקְרֵי "אֲזֵנֶךָ" אֶלָּא "עַל אָזְנֶךָ", שֶׁאִם יִשְׁמַע אָדָם דָּבָר שֶׁאֵינוֹ הָגוּן,

Bar Kappara taught: What is the meaning of that which **is written: And you shall have a peg among your weapons** [***azenekha***]" (Deuteronomy 23:14)? **Do not read** it as: **Your weapons** [***azenekha***].[N] **Rather,** read it: **On your ear** [***oznekha***], meaning **that if a person hears an inappropriate matter,**

NOTES

The handiwork of the righteous is greater – גְּדוֹלִים מַעֲשֵׂה צַדִּיקִים: The obvious connection between this passage and those that precede it is that they are taught by the same Sage. Some add that this statement of bar Kappara comes to explain his preference for the blessing to man over the blessing to the fish. The actions of man are greater than God's Creation of the world (see *Shita Mekubbetzet* and *Ḥatam Sofer*).

One hand or two hands – יָד אַחַת שְׁתֵּי יָדַיִם: In the *Otzar HaKavod*, it is explained that there is a dichotomy between heaven and earth, between the spiritual and the corporeal, and symbolically each was created with a different hand. However, the handiwork of the righteous, i.e., the Temple, unites the heavenly and the earthly. This is represented by both hands.

Others explain that the world of creation is static and unchanging, whereas the actions of man are constantly developing. The question in the Gemara notes that even in the heavens there is change. The Gemara explains that those changes are minor changes within a fixed framework. They are characterized as: The work of Your fingers (*Leḥem Shlomo*).

A certain Babylonian…responded – הֵשִׁיב בַּבְלִי אֶחָד: In the *Shita Mekubbetzet*, there is an explanation why the Gemara mentioned that he was a Babylonian. The reason, as stated in tractate *Kiddushin*, is that the Babylonians were not expert enough in the spelling in the Bible to know whether a word is written with a *yod* or a *vav*. The answer to the question in the Gemara is based on that distinction.

Do not read it as: Your weapons – אַל תִּקְרֵי אֲזֵנֶךָ: The Maharal in *Be'er HaGola* explains this statement at great length according to the plain meaning of the verses. He writes that the verse says that there are certain matters that are best concealed. The term: Your weapons [*azenekha*], is redundant. It would have been sufficient to write that one should use the peg to obscure those matters. Where one suspends that peg is irrelevant (Rav Yoshiya Pinto; Maharal). Furthermore, the term for your weapons should have been [*zayinkha*]. The additional *alef* at the beginning of the word alludes to an additional meaning (*Shita Mekubbetzet*; Maharsha).

Perek **I**
Daf **5** Amud **b**

יַנִּיחַ אֶצְבָּעוֹ בְּאָזְנָיו. וְהַיְינוּ דְּאָמַר רַבִּי אֶלְעָזָר: מִפְּנֵי מָה אֶצְבְּעוֹתָיו שֶׁל אָדָם דּוֹמוֹת לְיִתֵידוֹת? מַאי טַעֲמָא? אִילֵימָא מִשּׁוּם דְּמִחַלְּקָן – כָּל חֲדָא וַחֲדָא לְמִילְּתֵיהּ עֲבִידָא, דְּאָמַר מָר: זוֹ זֶרֶת, זוֹ קְמִיצָה, זוֹ אַמָּה, זוֹ אֶצְבַּע, זֶה גּוּדָל!

he should place his finger, which is shaped like a peg, **into his ears. And that is what Rabbi Elazar said: Why are the fingers of a person similar to pegs?** The Gemara asks: **What is the reason** that Rabbi Elazar said that fingers are like pegs? **If we say** that it is **due to** the fact **that they are discrete**[N] from each other, **each and every** finger **was designated for its** own discrete, sacred **matter, as the Master said: This** small finger is for measuring **a span,** the distance between the little finger to the tip of the thumb used in measuring the breastplate of the High Priest; **this** next finger is used for taking **a fistful** of the meal-offering; **this** middle finger is used for measuring **a cubit,** the distance from the elbow to the tip of the middle finger; **this** one next to the thumb is the **finger** used to sprinkle the blood of offerings on the altar; **this** is the **thumb,** on which the blood and oil is placed in the purification ritual of a leper.

NOTES

Due to the fact that they are discrete – מִשּׁוּם דְּמִחַלְּקָן: See *Tosafot*, who explain the need for the thumb as also being related to the fistful of flour in a meal-offering. With regard to the question of *Tosafot*, that the thumb could have served its role even if it were not discrete, see *Shita Mekubbetzet*, where it is explained that the same question could have been asked with regard to the middle finger and fourth finger as well. However, since each has its own role, they must be discrete, and it is clear why they were separated.

BACKGROUND

They are the first of the limbs burned – הֵן נִכְווֹת תְּחִלָּה לְאֵיבָרִים: The surface area of the auricle of the ear is large relative to its volume, due to its thin, soft tissue and lack of bone. It is therefore more sensitive to changes in temperature than other parts of the body. That is why the ears are the first of the body parts burned.

The blood is pooled or flowing through vessels attached – דַּם מִיפְקַד פְּקִיד אוֹ חַבּוּרֵי מִיחַבַּר: The medical explanation for the blood that flows after the rupture of the hymen is that it occurs due to the bleeding from the blood vessels in the hymen. In that way, it is similar to bleeding from any other part of the body. However, there are cases, albeit uncommon ones, where the hymen creates an impermeable seal, and menstrual blood pools behind the hymen. In that case, the blood that results from intercourse with a virgin is halakhically characterized as pooled blood.

אֶלָּא: מָה טַעַם מְשׁוּפּוֹת כִּיתֵידוֹת? שֶׁאִם יִשְׁמַע אָדָם דָּבָר שֶׁאֵינוֹ הָגוּן יַנִּיחַ אֶצְבְּעוֹתָיו בְּאׇזְנָיו. תָּנָא דְּבֵי רַבִּי יִשְׁמָעֵאל: מִפְּנֵי מָה אוֹזֶן כּוּלָּהּ קָשָׁה וְהָאַלְיָה רַכָּה? שֶׁאִם יִשְׁמַע אָדָם דָּבָר שֶׁאֵינוֹ הָגוּן – יָכוֹף אַלְיָה לְתוֹכָהּ. תָּנוּ רַבָּנַן: אַל יַשְׁמִיעַ אָדָם לְאׇזְנָיו דְּבָרִים בְּטֵלִים מִפְּנֵי שֶׁהֵן נִכְווֹת תְּחִלָּה לְאֵיבָרִים.

Rather, the question is: **What is the reason that they are pointed like pegs?** It is so **that if a person hears an inappropriate matter, he will place his fingers in his ears.** Similarly, a Sage **of the school of Rabbi Yishmael taught: Why is the entire ear hard and the earlobe soft?** It is so **that if a person hears an inappropriate matter, he will bend his earlobe into** his ear to seal it. **The Sages taught: A person should not allow his ears to hear idle matters.**[N] **Because** of the fact **that** ears are very sensitive and **are the first of the limbs burned,**[B] one should make certain not to expose them to anything problematic.

אִיבַּעְיָא לְהוּ: מַהוּ לִבְעוֹל בְּתוּלָה בְּשַׁבָּת, דַּם מִיפְקַד פְּקִיד אוֹ חַבּוּרֵי מִיחַבַּר?

§ **A dilemma was raised** before the Sages: **What is the** *halakha* with regard **to engaging in intercourse** with one's virgin bride **for the first time on Shabbat?**[N] The dilemma is with regard to the nature of the blood that emerges as a result of the piercing of the hymen. Is it that the **blood is pooled,** and it is released once the hymen is pierced, so that no prohibition is violated? **Or,** is the blood flowing through vessels **attached**[B] to the body, and it emerges as a result of a wound, so that he does violate a prohibition?

וְאִם תִּימְצֵי לוֹמַר דַּם מִיפְקַד פְּקִיד, לְדָם הוּא צָרִיךְ – וְשָׁרֵי, אוֹ דִּלְמָא לְפֶתַח הוּא צָרִיךְ – וַאֲסִיר?

And if you say that **it is pooled** and the intercourse does not cause a wound, there is an additional dilemma: **Does the husband require the blood**[N] to flow, and that is his objective in performing the act, in which case it is **permitted?**[N] **Or, perhaps he requires the opening**[N] caused by the rupture of the hymen, **and** creating that opening is **prohibited** on Shabbat.

וְאִם תִּימְצֵי לוֹמַר לְדָם הוּא צָרִיךְ, וּפֶתַח מִמֵּילָא קָאָתֵי, הֲלָכָה כְּרַבִּי שִׁמְעוֹן דְּאָמַר: דָּבָר שֶׁאֵין מִתְכַּוֵּין מוּתָּר, אוֹ הֲלָכָה כְּרַבִּי יְהוּדָה דְּאָמַר: דָּבָר שֶׁאֵין מִתְכַּוֵּין אָסוּר?

And if you say that **he requires the blood, and the opening comes** about **incidentally**[N] as an unintended consequence, **is the** *halakha* **in accordance with** the opinion of **Rabbi Shimon, who said: An unintentional act,**[N] i.e., a permitted action from which a forbidden labor inadvertently ensued, **is permitted? Or, is the** *halakha* **in accordance with** the opinion of **Rabbi Yehuda, who said: An unintentional act is forbidden?**

NOTES

Idle matters – דְּבָרִים בְּטֵלִים: After prohibiting listening to inappropriate matters and suggesting the actions that one should take to avoid doing so, the Gemara adds that one should avoid idle matters as well. Although they are not inappropriate, one should refrain from hearing them, as one is influenced by what he hears. The characterization that one's ears are the first body parts that burn alludes to this idea (Maharal).

What is the *halakha* with regard to engaging in intercourse with one's virgin bride for the first time on Shabbat – מַהוּ לִבְעוֹל בְּתוּלָה בְּשַׁבָּת: Rashi, *Tosafot*, and other early commentaries discuss the connection between this passage in the Gemara and the *baraitot* in which it is explicitly taught, that one may not engage in intercourse with his virgin bride for the first time on Shabbat. Rashi suggests two solutions: First, the Sages of the Gemara were unaware of the *baraitot* (see *Tosafot* and Rabbi Aharon HaLevi). Second, they were aware of the *baraitot* and were either debating whether they were in accordance with the *halakha* or assumed that they were not in accordance with the *halakha* (see *Derush VeḤiddush*).

Those who consider this passage a continuation of the previous one discuss why the concern lest one slaughter a young fowl was not raised. The Ramban explains that the case here is one where the wedding took place the previous day, but it has not yet been consummated. The Ritva and others explain that it is referring to a case where the groom already completed the wedding preparations.

Does the husband require the blood – לְדָם הוּא צָרִיךְ: Two reasons were suggested as to why the husband would require the blood. First, he wants as much blood as possible to flow the first time, so that when they engage in relations on subsequent occasions there will be less blood. Second, he wants to see the blood flow to verify that she is a virgin (see *Tosafot* and Ritva). The phrase: The husband requires the blood, is more appropriate according to the latter explanation.

Does the husband require the blood and it is permitted – לְדָם הוּא צָרִיךְ וְשָׁרֵי: The term permitted is problematic, as even if he requires the blood, the question whether or not it is permitted hinges on the tannaitic dispute cited in the Gemara. The Rashba has a variant reading in which the words: And it is permitted, are omitted. According to that version, the legal status of the act in a case where one needs the blood is clarified in the subsequent discussion.

Others, based on Rashi, include the term: And it is permitted, and explain that it is not a decisive ruling but a conditional statement: Even if you say that it is permitted according to one tannaitic opinion, the question of its status remains according to the other opinion (Ritva).

He requires the opening – לְפֶתַח הוּא צָרִיךְ: With regard to the prohibition against creating an opening on Shabbat, Rashi explains that it is categorized under the rubric of the forbidden labor of building.

Others explain that it falls under the category of one who strikes a blow with a hammer, which includes all activities that complete production of a vessel. In this case, consummating the marriage completes the forging of the bond between the husband and wife.

The Rashba writes that if the husband requires the opening and that is his intention, although it is a fundamentally destructive action, it is not a full-fledged destructive action because it contains a constructive element.

And the opening comes about incidentally – וּפֶתַח מִמֵּילָא קָאָתֵי: Even Rabbi Shimon, who holds that it is permitted to perform an unintentional act, agrees that it is prohibited to do so when the forbidden result is inevitable.

Rashi discusses the question: Since rupturing the hymen during intercourse with a virgin is inevitable, why is intercourse permitted according to Rabbi Shimon? Rashi explains that the ruling in the Gemara is limited to one who is adept at engaging in intercourse without rupturing the hymen. Others explain that even if the groom in question is not capable of doing so, since there are those who are, that suffices to generally characterize this case as one where the consequences are not inevitable (Ritva; Meiri).

An unintentional act – דָּבָר שֶׁאֵין מִתְכַּוֵּין: The dispute between Rabbi Yehuda and Rabbi Shimon with regard to unintentional actions with forbidden results is discussed extensively in tractate *Shabbat*. Although this is an issue pertinent to other areas of *halakha* as well, in the context of the *halakhot* of Shabbat there is a unique aspect.

Labor is forbidden only if it is planned, thoughtful, constructive labor. Unintentional actions, with regard to which there is a dispute between Rabbi Yehuda and Rabbi Shimon, are not actions performed accidentally or unwittingly. Rather, they are permitted actions that one intends to perform, from which a forbidden action unintentionally ensues. Rabbi Shimon permits performing these actions and Rabbi Yehuda prohibits doing so.

וְאִם תִּימְצֵי לוֹמַר הֲלָכָה כְּרַבִּי יְהוּדָה – מְקַלְקֵל הוּא אֵצֶל הַפֶּתַח אוֹ מְתַקֵּן הוּא אֵצֶל הַפֶּתַח?

And even if you say that the *halakha* is in accordance with the opinion of **Rabbi Yehuda** in this regard, is this **a destructive** action **vis-à-vis the opening,** and is it consequently permitted on Shabbat because only constructive actions are forbidden? **Or, perhaps** it is **a constructive** action **vis-à-vis the opening.**

אִיכָּא דְּאָמְרִי: וְאִם תִּימְצֵי לוֹמַר דָּם חַבּוּרֵי מִיחַבַּר – לְדָם הוּא צָרִיךְ וְאָסוּר, אוֹ דִּלְמָא לַהֲנָאַת עַצְמוֹ הוּא צָרִיךְ וְשָׁרֵי?

Some say that the series of dilemmas is as follows: **And if you say** that **the blood is** flowing through vessels **attached** to the body and emerges as a result of a wound, **does** the husband **require the blood,** and engaging in intercourse is consequently **prohibited,** as his intent is to cause the wound? **Or, perhaps he requires** the act of intercourse solely **for his own pleasure, and** it is **permitted.**

וְאִם תִּימְצֵי לוֹמַר לַהֲנָאַת עַצְמוֹ הוּא צָרִיךְ, וְדָם מִמֵּילָא קָאָתֵי – הֲלָכָה כְּרַבִּי יְהוּדָה אוֹ הֲלָכָה כְּרַבִּי שִׁמְעוֹן?

And if you say that he requires the act of intercourse solely **for his own pleasure, and the blood comes incidentally,** as it was not his intent to draw blood, **is the *halakha* in accordance with** the opinion of **Rabbi Yehuda** with regard to an unintentional act, **or is it in accordance with** the opinion of **Rabbi Shimon?**

וְאִם תִּימְצֵי לוֹמַר הֲלָכָה כְּרַבִּי יְהוּדָה – מְקַלְקֵל בְּחַבּוּרָה אוֹ מְתַקֵּן בְּחַבּוּרָה הוּא?

And if you say that the ***halakha* is in accordance with** the opinion of **Rabbi Yehuda** and unintentional acts are forbidden, is one **destructive in** causing the **wound** or **constructive in** causing the **wound?**

וְאִם תִּימְצֵי לוֹמַר מְקַלְקֵל בְּחַבּוּרָה הוּא – בִּמְקַלְקֵל הֲלָכָה כְּרַבִּי יְהוּדָה

And if you say that he is **destructive in** causing the **wound,**[N] **in** cases involving **destructive** acts **is the *halakha* in accordance with** the opinion of **Rabbi Yehuda,**[N] who rules that one who performs any destructive act on Shabbat is exempt, even if he did so intentionally?

NOTES

Destructive in causing the wound – מְקַלְקֵל בְּחַבּוּרָה: The Ramban cites an explanation that he himself rejects, that the reference here is to the wound caused by slaughtering young fowl. In the *Shita Mekubbetzet*, a defense of that explanation is cited.

The Gemara seems to be saying that if the intercourse is considered destructive, it is permitted *ab initio* according to Rabbi Yehuda. The commentaries ask: Isn't performance of a destructive action prohibited by rabbinic law (see *Tosafot*)? They respond that there are two factors here dictating leniency: The action is destructive action and unintentional. Others add a third factor: It is in the course of performing a mitzva. The Rashba contends that the Sages issue decrees prohibiting certain actions, only due to the concern that otherwise one might come to perform a similar action prohibited by Torah law. Here, although creating the opening falls into the category of building, people do not consider it building and will not come to perform the forbidden labor of building as a result of the intercourse. Others explain that since the intercourse is a destructive action as far as the woman is concerned, it is in no way comparable to the forbidden labor of building, and no decree was issued (*Ha'amek She'ala*).

In cases involving destructive acts is the *halakha* in accordance with the opinion of Rabbi Yehuda – בִּמְקַלְקֵל הֲלָכָה כְּרַבִּי יְהוּדָה: Some ask why the ruling with regard to intercourse with his virgin bride, which is a mitzva, is not the same as the ruling with regard to circumcision, which is considered a constructive act due to the mitzva involved (*Sefer Hafla'a*). Some distinguish between circumcision, where creating the wound is the essence of the mitzva, and intercourse with a virgin, where the wound is ancillary to the mitzva.

Perek **I**
Daf **6** Amud **a**

אוֹ הֲלָכָה כְּרַבִּי שִׁמְעוֹן?

Or, is the *halakha* in accordance with the opinion of **Rabbi Shimon,** who ruled that one who is destructive in causing a wound on Shabbat is liable if he did so intentionally?

(אִיתְּמַר), בְּבֵי רַב אָמְרִי: רַב שָׁרֵי וּשְׁמוּאֵל אָסַר. בִּנְהַרְדְּעָא אָמְרִי: רַב אָסַר וּשְׁמוּאֵל שָׁרֵי. אָמַר רַב נַחְמָן בַּר יִצְחָק, וְסִימָנֵיךְ: אֵלּוּ מְקִילִין לְעַצְמָן וְאֵלּוּ מְקִילִין לְעַצְמָן.

With regard to the *halakha* of engaging in intercourse with one's virgin bride on Shabbat, **it was stated** that **in the school of Rav they say: Rav permitted** doing so **and Shmuel prohibited** doing so. **In Neharde'a,**[B] where Shmuel lived, **they say: Rav prohibited** doing so **and Shmuel permitted** doing so. **Rav Naḥman bar Yitzḥak said: And your mnemonic is: These are lenient** with regard **to themselves, and those are lenient** with regard **to themselves.** Each attributes the lenient ruling to the local halakhic authority, whose ruling is binding in that locale.

BACKGROUND

Neharde'a – נְהַרְדְּעָא: This city, located on the Euphrates near the Malka River, was one of the oldest Jewish communities in Babylonia. According to tradition, Jews lived in Neharde'a as early as the First Temple period, in the sixth century BCE, beginning with the exile of King Jehoiachin of Judea. Neharde'a was one of the most important Jewish communities in Babylonia. It was a center of Torah study from an early period, and its yeshiva was the oldest in Babylonia. Many of the greatest *tanna'im* visited Neharde'a, among them Rabbi Akiva, who intercalated the calendar there (*Yevamot* 122b). In Rav's time, the first half of the third century CE, the Neharde'a Yeshiva was headed by Rav Sheila and then by Shmuel. Since the city was located near the border between the Roman and Persian empires, it frequently suffered from wars between the two, and Pappa ben Nazer Odonathus, king of Tadmor, destroyed it completely in 259 CE. Later, however, Jews resettled there, and many Torah scholars remained in Neharde'a even after its yeshiva relocated to Meḥoza and Pumbedita.

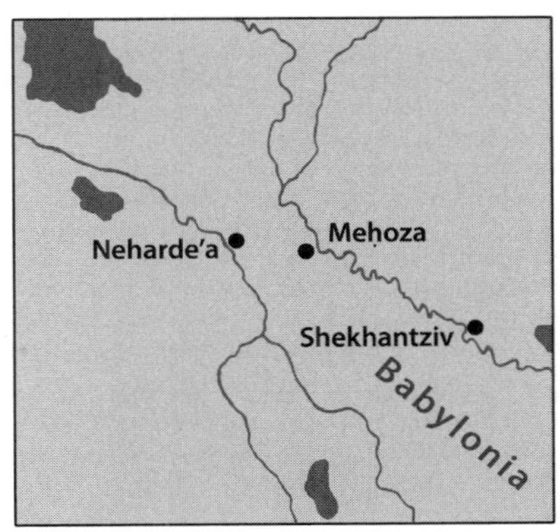

Location of Neharde'a

וְרַב שָׁרֵי?! וְהָאָמַר רַב שִׁימִי בַּר חִזְקִיָּה מִשְּׁמֵיהּ דְּרַב: הַאי מְסוֹכְרִיָּא דְּנַזְיָיתָא אָסוּר לְהַדּוּקָהּ בְּיוֹמָא טָבָא!

The Gemara asks: **And did Rav permit** engaging in intercourse in those circumstances? **But didn't Rav Shimi bar Ḥizkiyya say in the name of Rav:** In the case of **this** cloth **stopper of a barrel** [*nazyata*],[LHN] it is **prohibited to insert it tightly**[N] in the spout of the barrel **on a Festival,** because in the process liquid will be squeezed from the cloth, and squeezing liquids is prohibited on Shabbat and Festivals. Apparently, Rav prohibits even unintentional actions.

בְּהַהוּא אֲפִילּוּ רַבִּי שִׁמְעוֹן מוֹדֶה. דְּאַבַּיֵי וְרָבָא דְּאָמְרִי תַּרְוַיְיהוּ: מוֹדֶה רַבִּי שִׁמְעוֹן בִּפְסִיק רֵישֵׁיהּ וְלָא יָמוּת.

The Gemara answers: **In the case** of the barrel, **even Rabbi Shimon concedes, as it is Abaye and Rava who both say: Rabbi Shimon concedes in** the case of: **Cut off its head**[N] **and will it not die,** i.e., a case that involves inevitable consequences like the decapitation of an animal, that the action is forbidden. Here, the liquid will inevitably be squeezed from the cloth.

וְהָא אָמַר רַב חִיָּיא בַּר אַשִׁי אָמַר רַב: הֲלָכָה כְּרַבִּי יְהוּדָה, וְרַב חָנָן בַּר אַמִי אָמַר שְׁמוּאֵל: הֲלָכָה כְּרַבִּי שִׁמְעוֹן. וְרַב חִיָּיא בַּר אָבִין מַתְנֵי לָהּ בְּלָא גַּבְרֵי, רַב אָמַר: הֲלָכָה כְּרַבִּי יְהוּדָה, וּשְׁמוּאֵל אָמַר: הֲלָכָה כְּרַבִּי שִׁמְעוֹן!

The Gemara asks: **But didn't Rav Ḥiyya bar Ashi say** that **Rav said** with regard to unintentional acts: **The *halakha* is in accordance with** the opinion of **Rabbi Yehuda, and Rav Ḥanan bar Ami said** that **Shmuel said: The *halakha* is in accordance with** the opinion of **Rabbi Shimon. And Rav Ḥiyya bar Avin taught** these rulings directly, **without** citing additional **men** who transmitted them. **Rav said: The *halakha* is in accordance with** the opinion of **Rabbi Yehuda, and Shmuel said: The *halakha* is in accordance with** the opinion of **Rabbi Shimon.** How then did Rav permit intercourse with one's virgin bride on Shabbat?

לְעוֹלָם רַב כְּרַבִּי יְהוּדָה סְבִירָא לֵיהּ לְהָךְ לִישָּׁנָא דְּאָמַר דָּם מִיפְקַד פְּקִיד – מְקַלְקֵל הוּא אֵצֶל הַפֶּתַח. לְהָךְ לִישָּׁנָא דְּאָמַר דָּם חַבּוּרֵי מִיחַבַּר – מְקַלְקֵל בְּחַבּוּרָה הוּא.

The Gemara answers: **Actually, Rav holds in accordance with** the opinion of **Rabbi Yehuda.** According **to that version that said** that **the blood is pooled, he is destructive vis-à-vis the opening.** According **to that version that said** that blood is flowing through blood vessels **attached** to the body, **he is destructive in** causing **the wound,** and Rabbi Yehuda concedes that it is permitted.

מְתִיב רַב חִסְדָּא: תִּינוֹקֶת שֶׁלֹּא הִגִּיעַ זְמַנָּהּ לִרְאוֹת וְנִשֵּׂאת, בֵּית שַׁמַּאי אוֹמְרִים: נוֹתְנִין לָהּ אַרְבָּעָה לֵילוֹת, וּבֵית הִלֵּל אוֹמְרִים: עַד שֶׁתֶּחְיֶה הַמַּכָּה.

Rav Ḥisda raised an objection from a mishna (*Nidda* 64b). With regard to **a young girl whose time to see** the flow of menstrual blood **has not arrived,**[N] as she has not yet reached puberty, **and she married,**[H] **Beit Shammai say: One gives her four nights** during which she may engage in intercourse, as any blood is attributed to the ruptured hymen. **Beit Hillel say:** There is no limit. Rather, any blood she sees is attributed to the ruptured hymen **until the wound heals.**[BN]

BACKGROUND

Until the wound heals – **עַד שֶׁתֶּחְיֶה הַמַּכָּה**: The period of time in which a wound forms a scab and the bleeding ceases is determined by different variables and differs from person to person. Clearly, additional wounds irritating the affected area, e.g., by means of additional acts of intercourse, would extend that period of time. Therefore, no time limit is set, and the duration of the healing process varies based on the circumstances in each case.

LANGUAGE

Barrel [*nazyata*] – **נַזְיָיתָא**: From the ancient Syriac-Aramaic *nazanta* or *nazita*, meaning large barrel. Its source is the Akkadian namzitu, meaning vessel for fermenting alcoholic beverages.

HALAKHA

Stopper of a barrel – **מְסוֹכְרִיָּא דְּנַזְיָיתָא**: According to some authorities, it is permitted to remove and return the cloth stopper that is inserted into the opening in the side of the barrel, although it is inevitable that liquid will be squeezed out of the cloth, since that is an undesirable inevitable consequence (*Tur*, based on *Arukh*). Others prohibit performing a permitted action with an inevitable forbidden consequence in all circumstances (Ri). It is customary to adopt the lenient ruling, but one must be certain to avoid placing a vessel under the stopper to receive the dripping wine, as doing so renders the action permitted with an inevitable forbidden consequence that is desirable (*Shulḥan Arukh, Oraḥ Ḥayyim* 320:18).

A young girl whose time to see has not arrived and she married – **תִּינוֹקֶת שֶׁלֹּא הִגִּיעַ זְמַנָּהּ לִרְאוֹת וְנִשֵּׂאת**: If a man marries a young girl whose time to see the flow of menstrual blood has not yet arrived, she is permitted to her husband until the wound heals, as any blood that flows is from the ruptured hymen (Rambam; see Rif). Nevertheless, the accepted custom is that even in the case of a minor girl, they engage in intercourse to fulfill the mitzva, then the groom withdraws, and they refrain from further relations until the wound heals. This is the opinion of the Rambam and the Ra'avad, and most authorities, based on the conclusion of the Gemara (*Nidda* 65b; Rambam *Sefer Kedusha, Hilkhot Issurei Bia* 5:19, 11:8; *Shulḥan Arukh, Yoreh De'a* 193:1).

NOTES

Stopper of a barrel – **מְסוֹכְרִיָּא דְּנַזְיָיתָא**: There are various opinions with regard to the nature of this item, as well as with regard to the halakhic issue involved. According to Rashi and several of the *ge'onim*, the reference is to a cloth stopper or one covered in cloth that plugs a hole in the side of the barrel, and the halakhic problem relates to squeezing the liquid from the cloth. A similar explanation is that the reference is to a garment used to cover the top of the barrel, and there too the concern is with regard to squeezing the liquid from the garment (*Tosefot Rid*; Meiri). In both of those cases, one does not intend to squeeze the liquid, but that consequence is inevitable.

The *Arukh* cites a different opinion, based on a geonic tradition, that the reference is to a wooden covering used to seal the side of the barrel, and the concern is with regard to the prohibited labor of building. Although one's intention is merely to prevent the wine from leaking, by fixing the covering in place, he is essentially building the side of the barrel.

It it is prohibited to insert it tightly – **אָסוּר לְהַדּוּקָהּ**: According to most opinions, the halakhic issue under discussion is the prohibited labor of squeezing a liquid. The question arises: Under the rubric of which of the thirty-nine primary categories of prohibited labor does this action fall? The question is not merely academic, as each of the categories of labor is unique with regard to its objective, its typical method of performance, and the manner in which one incurs complete liability.

The Ritva summarizes the various opinions, enumerating three primary categories under whose rubric squeezing could fall: (1) Threshing, i.e., extracting a substance suitable for use from an outer covering unfit for use. This is prohibited by Torah law only with regard to substances that grow from the ground. (2) Whitening, i.e., laundering, cleaning, etc., as immersing the cloth in water is a form of laundering. (3) Dyeing, as the wine changes the color of the cloth (see *Tosafot*). An interesting proof that it cannot fall under extracting, a subcategory of threshing, is cited in *Shoel UMeshiv*. The Gemara states that this activity is forbidden on a Festival. Extracting, which is necessary for preparation of food, is permitted on a Festival.

Cut off its head – **פְּסִיק רֵישֵׁיהּ**: The opinion of Rava and Abaye is that in cases where the forbidden consequence is inevitable, even Rabbi Shimon concedes that there is no exemption based on lack of intent. However, there is an additional consideration, cited in the *Arukh*, which is whether the inevitable consequence is desirable to the one performing the permitted action, whether he is indifferent to it, or whether it is undesirable to him. Some authorities rule that in the latter cases, Rabbi Shimon holds that the action is permitted.

A young girl whose time to see has not arrived – **תִּינוֹקֶת שֶׁלֹּא הִגִּיעַ זְמַנָּהּ לִרְאוֹת**: These discussions are based on two fundamental principles. By Torah law, the blood from a ruptured hymen is not a source of ritual impurity, and its halakhic status is like that of blood from any other wound. In many cases, however, the concern is that during intercourse, or immediately thereafter, the bride began to menstruate, and there is no clear way to distinguish between menstrual blood and the blood from the hymen.

Furthermore, at one point, Jewish women adopted the stringency that any blood that emerges from the womb is treated as the blood of a *zava*, who is eligible for purification only after counting seven clean days without blood. The combination of these two factors forms the basis for the disputes of the *tanna'im* and later halakhic authorities on this matter.

Until the wound heals – **עַד שֶׁתֶּחְיֶה הַמַּכָּה**: In other words, even if the wound takes a long time to heal, they may engage in intercourse. Beit Hillel also permits relations for four nights even after the wound heals. There is no alternative to understanding the dispute in this manner, as otherwise, this would be a case where the opinion of Beit Shammai is more lenient than the opinion of Beit Hillel, and it is not enumerated among the leniencies of Beit Shammai in tractate *Eduyyot*.

הִגִּיעַ זְמַנָּהּ לִרְאוֹת וְנִשֵּׂאת. בֵּית שַׁמַּאי אוֹמְרִים: נוֹתְנִין לָהּ לַיְלָה הָרִאשׁוֹן. וּבֵית הִלֵּל אוֹמְרִים: עַד מוֹצָאֵי שַׁבָּת, אַרְבָּעָה לֵילוֹת.

If, however, **her time to see** the flow of menstrual blood **has arrived,**[H] as she has reached the age of puberty, even if she has not yet menstruated, **and she married, Beit Shammai say: One gives her the first night,** during which the blood is attributed to the wound. Thereafter, the blood is presumed to be menstrual blood, and she is forbidden to her husband. **Beit Hillel say: One gives her** from Wednesday, the day designated for marriage of a virgin, **until the conclusion of Shabbat, four nights.** During that period, any blood is attributed to the wound, and she is permitted to her husband.

HALAKHA

Her time to see has arrived – הִגִּיעַ זְמַנָּהּ לִרְאוֹת: A girl who reached the age of menstruation but has not yet menstruated is permitted to her husband for four days following the first act of intercourse, even if there is some bleeding, provided the wound has not healed. According to the Rosh, she is permitted even if the wound has healed. Today, however, Jewish women adopted the stringency that any blood that emerges from the womb is treated as the blood of a *zava*. Therefore, the accepted custom is to engage in intercourse and withdraw until the wound is completely healed and there is no bleeding (Rambam *Sefer Kedusha, Hilkhot Issurei Bia* 5:19, 11:8; *Shulḥan Arukh, Yoreh De'a* 193:1, *Even HaEzer* 63:1).

Perek **I**
Daf **6** Amud **b**

מַאי לָאו דְּאִי לָא בָּעַל מָצֵי בָּעֵיל אֲפִילּוּ בְּשַׁבָּת! אֲמַר רָבָא: לָא, לְבַר מִשַּׁבָּת. אֲמַר לֵיהּ אַבָּיֵי: וְהָא עַד מוֹצָאֵי שַׁבָּת אַרְבָּעָה לֵילוֹת קָתָנֵי! אֶלָּא אֲמַר רָבָא: כְּשֶׁבָּעַל.

What, is it not referring to a case **where if he did not** yet **engage in** full-fledged **intercourse,** i.e., rupturing the hymen, with his bride, **he may engage in** full-fledged **intercourse** with her **even on Shabbat?** Apparently, it is permitted to engage in intercourse with a virgin on Shabbat. **Rava said: No,** it is referring to any other day **except for Shabbat. Abaye said to him: But isn't it taught: Until the conclusion of Shabbat, four nights?** Four nights from Wednesday until the conclusion of Shabbat includes Shabbat. **Rather, Rava said:** It is referring to a case **where he engaged in** full-fledged **intercourse** with his bride before Shabbat. Therefore, there is no concern lest he cause a wound on Shabbat.

אִי כְּשֶׁבָּעַל – מַאי קָא מַשְׁמַע לַן? קָא מַשְׁמַע לַן דִּשְׁרֵי לְמִיבְעַל בְּשַׁבָּת, כִּדִשְׁמוּאֵל. דְּאָמַר שְׁמוּאֵל: פִּירְצָה דְּחוּקָה מוּתָּר לִיכָּנֵס בָּהּ בְּשַׁבָּת, וְאַף עַל פִּי שֶׁמַּשִּׁיר צְרוֹרוֹת.

However, **if** it is referring to a case where **he** already **engaged in intercourse, what is** the *tanna* **teaching us** when he says that it is permitted to have intercourse with her even on Shabbat? **He teaches us that** although it might cause bleeding, **it is permitted to engage in intercourse on Shabbat, in accordance with** the statement **of Shmuel, as Shmuel said:** It is **permitted to enter into a narrow opening** in a wall **on Shabbat, although** doing so **causes pebbles to fall** from the wall. Here too, although it might cause a wound and bleeding, intercourse is permitted on Shabbat.

מְתִיב רַב יוֹסֵף: חָתָן פָּטוּר מִקְּרִיאַת שְׁמַע לַיְלָה הָרִאשׁוֹן עַד מוֹצָאֵי שַׁבָּת אִם לֹא עָשָׂה מַעֲשֶׂה. מַאי לָאו – דִּטְרִיד, דְּבָעֵי לְמִיבְעַל? אֲמַר לֵיהּ אַבָּיֵי: לָא, דִּטְרִיד דְּלָא בְּעִיל.

Rav Yosef raised an objection from a mishna (*Berakhot* 16a): **A groom is exempt from the** mitzva **of reciting *Shema* on the first night**[H] of his marriage to a virgin on Wednesday night, **until Saturday night, if he has not taken action** and consummated the marriage. **What, is it not** that he is exempt due to the fact **that he is preoccupied because he wishes to engage in intercourse** with her and is concerned that he will fail to do so properly? Apparently, if he did not yet consummate the marriage, he is exempt from reciting *Shema* even on Shabbat, indicating that it is permitted to engage in intercourse on Shabbat. **Abaye said to him: No.** It can be explained **that he** is exempt from reciting *Shema* because he **is preoccupied** due to the fact **that** he did **not** yet **engage in intercourse** with her. No proof may be cited with regard to engaging in intercourse on Shabbat.

אֲמַר לֵיהּ רָבָא: וּמִשּׁוּם טִירְדָּא פָּטוּר?! אֶלָּא מֵעַתָּה טָבְעָה סְפִינָתוֹ בַּיָּם הָכִי נָמֵי דְּפָטוּר?! וְכִי תֵּימָא הָכִי נָמֵי – וְהָאָמַר רַבִּי אַבָּא בַּר זַבְדָּא אָמַר רַב: אָבֵל חַיָּיב בְּכָל הַמִּצְוֹת הָאֲמוּרוֹת בַּתּוֹרָה חוּץ מִן הַתְּפִילִּין, שֶׁנֶּאֱמַר בָּהֶן ״פְּאֵר״!

Rava said to Abaye: **And** is one **exempt due to preoccupation?**[N] **If that is so,** would **one whose ship sunk at sea also** be exempt? The Gemara reinforces its question: **And if you would say:** In fact, **that is so, didn't Rabbi Abba bar Zavda say** that **Rav said: A mourner is obligated in all the mitzvot**[N] **in the Torah except for** the mitzva to don **phylacteries,**[H] as the term **splendor is stated with regard to** phylacteries:[N] "Make no mourning for the dead; bind your splendor upon yourself" (Ezekiel 24:17). Splendor is antithetical to mourning. If a mourner, who is clearly pained and preoccupied, is obligated to recite *Shema*, then certainly all others who are preoccupied due to events that transpired in the past should be obligated. If the groom is exempt, it must be due to his preoccupation with a mitzva that remains incumbent upon him to perform in the future.

HALAKHA

A groom is exempt from the mitzva of reciting *Shema* on the first night – חָתָן פָּטוּר מִקְּרִיַּת שְׁמַע לַיְלָה הָרִאשׁוֹן: A groom who marries a virgin is exempt from reciting *Shema* until he consummates the marriage because he is preoccupied that he will discover that she is not a virgin. Since he is preoccupied with the performance of a mitzva, he is exempt from performing another. If he has not engaged in sexual relations three nights after the wedding, he is obligated to recite *Shema*, since he is more comfortable with his bride and no longer preoccupied. That exemption applied in earlier generations. However, today most people typically recite *Shema* without the proper intent, so a groom who marries a virgin recites *Shema* as well (Rambam *Sefer Ahava, Hilkhot Keriat Shema* 4:1; *Shulḥan Arukh, Oraḥ Ḥayyim* 70:3).

A mourner is obligated in all the mitzvot in the Torah except for the mitzva to don phylacteries – אָבֵל חַיָּיב בְּכָל הַמִּצְוֹת הָאֲמוּרוֹת בַּתּוֹרָה חוּץ מִן הַתְּפִילִּין: It is prohibited for a mourner to don phylacteries on the day of the burial (Rambam *Sefer Shofetim, Hilkhot Evel* 4:9; *Shulḥan Arukh, Oraḥ Ḥayyim* 38:5).

NOTES

Preoccupation – טִירְדָּא: Several explanations are provided for the preoccupation of one who marries a virgin. They must be taken together in order to understand the course of the Gemara's discussion here. In the Rambam's Commentary on the Mishna it is explained that he is anxious that he will discover that his bride is not a virgin. In the *Shita Mekubbetzet*, an opinion is cited that his concern is that he might falsely suspect his wife of not being a virgin. Apparently, he is also worried that he will be unable to engage properly in full-fledged intercourse.

Is obligated in all the mitzvot – חַיָּיב בְּכָל הַמִּצְוֹת: The Ritva notes that a mourner is also prohibited from studying Torah, which means that the statement here is not completely accurate. The Sages, in various formulations, stated that practical *halakha* cannot be learned from principles stated in the mishna, as there are no principles without exceptions.

As the term splendor is stated with regard to phylacteries – שֶׁנֶּאֱמַר בָּהֶן פְּאֵר: Rashi adds that since a mourner is downhearted and despondent, it is inappropriate for him to place splendor on his head. The Ritva explains that Rashi did not suffice with merely citing the verse from Ezekiel, from which it is derived that the mourner is exempt from the mitzva of phylacteries, because he wanted to explain, in passing, why all mitzvot are not derived from the mitzva of phylacteries by means of an analogy.

אֶלָּא אָמַר רָבָא: תַּנָּאֵי הִיא. דְּתָנְיָא חֲדָא: אִם לֹא עָשָׂה מַעֲשֶׂה בָּרִאשׁוֹן – פָּטוּר אַף בַּשֵּׁנִי, בַּשֵּׁנִי – פָּטוּר אַף בַּשְּׁלִישִׁי.

Rather, Rava said: This matter of intercourse with a virgin on Shabbat **is** subject to a dispute between ***tanna'im*, as one *tanna* taught: If he did not take action on the first** night **he is exempt** from reciting *Shema* **even on the second.** If he failed to consummate the marriage on the **second** night **he is exempt even on the third** night, which is Shabbat evening.

וְתַנְיָא אִידָּךְ: רִאשׁוֹן וְשֵׁנִי – פָּטוּר, שְׁלִישִׁי – חַיָּיב.

And another *baraita* is taught: On the **first and second** nights **he is exempt;** on the **third he is obligated** to recite *Shema*. He is obligated on the third night, even if he did not yet consummate the marriage, because the third night is Shabbat, when intercourse with his virgin wife is forbidden. The different rulings in the two *baraitot* indicate that there is a tannaitic dispute with regard to intercourse with a virgin on Shabbat.

וְאַבַּיֵי: הָתָם נַמִי בְּטִירְדָּא פְּלִיגִי.

And how does **Abaye** respond to this proof? He says that **there too,** it can be explained that it **is with regard to preoccupation** that the *tanna'im* **disagree.** Everyone agrees that it is prohibited to engage in intercourse with a virgin on Shabbat. The dispute is whether or not one's preoccupation with the fact that he has not yet performed the mitzva of consummating the marriage in the past is considered preoccupation with a mitzva, which would exempt him from reciting *Shema*?

וְהָנֵי תַּנָּאֵי כִּי הָנֵי תַּנָּאֵי; דְּתַנְיָא: הַכּוֹנֵס אֶת הַבְּתוּלָה לֹא יִבְעוֹל בַּתְּחִלָּה בְּשַׁבָּת, וַחֲכָמִים מַתִּירִין.

And the dispute between **these *tanna'im*** in the *baraitot* cited is **parallel** to the dispute between **these *tanna'im*, as it is taught** in another *baraita*: With regard to **one who marries a virgin, he may not engage in intercourse** with her for the **first** time on **Shabbat, and the Rabbis permit** doing so.

מַאן חֲכָמִים? אָמַר רַבָּה: רַבִּי שִׁמְעוֹן הִיא, דְּאָמַר: דָּבָר שֶׁאֵין מִתְכַּוֵּין מוּתָּר.

The Gemara asks: **Who are the Rabbis** that permit doing so? **Rabba said: It is** the opinion of **Rabbi Shimon, who said: An unintentional act is permitted** on Shabbat. Since one's intention is to perform a permitted action, i.e., the consummation of the marriage, and there is no intent to perform a forbidden action, any forbidden action that may ensue is not a source of concern.

אֲמַר לֵיהּ אַבַּיֵי: וְהָא מוֹדֶה רַבִּי שִׁמְעוֹן בִּפְסִיק רֵישֵׁיהּ וְלָא יָמוּת! אֲמַר לֵיהּ: לֹא כְּהַלָּלוּ בַּבְלִיִּים שֶׁאֵין בְּקִיאִין בְּהַטָּיָה, אֶלָּא יֵשׁ בְּקִיאִין בְּהַטָּיָה.

Abaye said to Rabba: **But doesn't Rabbi Shimon concede** that **in** the case of: **Cut off its head and will it not die,** i.e., inevitable consequences, one is not exempted by lack of intent. Since rupture of the hymen and the subsequent bleeding is inevitable, Rabbi Shimon would concede that intercourse with a virgin is forbidden. Rabba **said to him: Unlike these Babylonians, who are not experts in diverting**[B] during intercourse and are unable to engage in intercourse without rupturing the hymen, **there are** those who are **experts in diverting.** Therefore, rupture of the hymen is not an inevitable consequence.

אִם כֵּן טוֹרֶד לָמָּה? לְשֶׁאֵינוֹ בָּקִי. יֹאמְרוּ בָּקִי – מוּתָּר, שֶׁאֵינוֹ בָּקִי – אָסוּר! רוֹב בְּקִיאִין הֵן.

The Gemara asks: **If so,** and the groom is expert in diverting, **why** is there **preoccupation** that renders him exempt from reciting *Shema*? The Gemara answers: The exemption due to preoccupation is limited to **one who is not expert.** The Gemara asks: If so, the Sages **should say** explicitly: One who is **expert is permitted** to have intercourse with a virgin on Shabbat, and one **who is not expert**[N] **is prohibited** from doing so. The Gemara answers: The **majority** of men **are experts** in this matter. Therefore, rupture of the hymen is not an inevitable consequence, and intercourse is permitted on Shabbat.

BACKGROUND

Diverting – הַטָּיָה: Diverting can be accomplished in several manners. It can be a form of intercourse without penetrating the vagina, which is one of the possibilities raised by the Gemara with regard to the preliminary stage of intercourse. Here, it seems more likely that we are dealing with a case of complete penetration that avoids rupturing the hymen. This is possible when the hymen is naturally perforated sufficiently to allow entry. In the case of most mature grown women, the hymen is no longer intact and there is often an opening large enough to enable penetration at a certain angle without causing rupture.

NOTES

One who is expert…one who is not expert – בָּקִי...שֶׁאֵינוֹ בָּקִי: The early commentaries analyzed this brief passage very closely, since the different reasons cited are apparently contradictory (see *Tosafot*). They conclude that even those who are not expert at diverting are at times successful in doing so. However, due to their lack of expertise, they will not know in advance whether or not they will be successful. On the other hand, those who are expert may decide to engage in full-fledged intercourse. On that basis, the various statements can be reconciled.

אֲמַר לֵיהּ רָבָא בַּר רַב חָנָן לְאַבָּיֵי: אֶלָּא מֵעַתָּה שׁוֹשְׁבִינִין לָמָּה? מַפָּה לָמָּה? אֲמַר לֵיהּ: הָתָם שֶׁמָּא יִרְאֶה וְיִאַבֵּד.

Rava bar Rav Ḥanan said to Abaye: If that is so, and most people are able to engage in intercourse with a virgin without rupturing the hymen, **why are groomsmen** stationed to ensure that no deceit is employed by the groom with regard to the bride's virginity? And **why** is **a sheet** necessary to determine whether there was blood? The absence of blood proves nothing if intercourse is possible without blood. Abaye **said to him: There,** the groomsmen and the sheet are necessary **lest** the groom **see** blood **and** seek to **destroy** it intentionally. Certainly, if he seeks to engage in intercourse and keep the hymen intact he can do so. However, if he engages in full-fledged intercourse and the hymen is ruptured, the Sages sought to ensure that the facts are clear.

מְתִיב רַבִּי אַמִי: הַמֵּפִיס מוּרְסָא בְּשַׁבָּת, אִם לַעֲשׂוֹת לָהּ פֶּה – חַיָּיב. וְאִם לְהוֹצִיא מִמֶּנָּה לֵיחָה,

Rav Ami raised an objection from a mishna (*Eduyyot* 2:5): With regard to **one who drains an abscess**[NHB] **on Shabbat, if** his intent is **to create** a permanent **opening** so that the abscess will dry, **he is liable** to receive punishment for performing an action similar to the prohibited labor of building on Shabbat. **However, if** he created the opening **to remove pus,**

NOTES

One who drains an abscess – הַמֵּפִיס מוּרְסָא: Rashi explains that creating a permanent opening in the abscess falls under the rubric of the prohibited labor of building, which is applicable to human bodies as well. The Rambam explains that creating this opening is included in the category of striking with a hammer, i.e., completing production of a vessel. The purpose of this opening is to facilitate the exit of the pus and the entry of air (*Tosafot*). Others, citing *Tosafot*, explain that the opening facilitates exit of the pus and the introduction of medicine.

HALAKHA

One who drains an abscess – הַמֵּפִיס מוּרְסָא: One who lances a pus-filled abscess on Shabbat in order to create a permanent opening to facilitate healing is liable to receive punishment for performing the prohibited labor of striking with a hammer, i.e., completing production of a vessel. However, it is permitted for one to lance the abscess if his intention is to drain the pus (Rambam *Sefer Zemanim*, *Hilkhot Shabbat* 10:17; *Shulḥan Arukh*, *Oraḥ Ḥayyim* 328:28).

BACKGROUND

Drains an abscess – מֵפִיס מוּרְסָא: An abscess is a wound filled with pus that is drained by means of squeezing. The continued drainage of the pus is a necessary step in healing the abscess. The accumulation of pus in a closed abscess causes significant pain, and lancing the abscess and draining the pus temporarily relieves that pain.

Perek **I**
Daf **7** Amud **a**

פָּטוּר! הָתָם פְּקִיד וַעֲקִיר, הָכָא – פְּקִיד וְלָא עֲקִיר.

he is exempt. In this case, exempt means permitted *ab initio*. Ostensibly, intercourse with a virgin is comparable to creating an opening in an abscess. Why then, would intercourse with a virgin be forbidden on Shabbat? The Gemara rejects the proof: **There,** the pus in the abscess **is pooled** in one place **and** completely **removed** from the vessels in the flesh. In creating the opening, he creates nothing enduring. **Here,** however, in the case of the ruptured hymen, even according to the opinion that the blood **is pooled, it is not** completely **removed** from the blood vessels in the flesh. Through intercourse, the blood is removed from its place, which constitutes an aspect of a prohibited labor.

רַבִּי אַמִי שְׁרָא לְמִיבְעַל בַּתְּחִלָּה בְּשַׁבָּת. אָמְרִי לֵיהּ רַבָּנַן: וְהָא לָא כְּתִיבָא כְּתוּבָּתָהּ! אֲמַר לְהוּ: אַתְפְּסוּהָ מִטַּלְטְלִין.

The Gemara relates: **Rav Ami permitted** one **to engage in intercourse** with his virgin wife for the **first time on Shabbat. The Sages said to him: But her marriage contract is not** yet **written.** Engaging in conjugal relations with one's wife without a marriage contract is considered an act of promiscuity. **He said to them: Have her seize** a portion of her husband's **movable property**[H] equivalent to the value of her marriage contract, and that will serve as a deposit until he writes the marriage contract. He may then engage in sexual relations with her.

רַב זְבִיד שְׁרָא לְמִיבְעַל בַּתְּחִלָּה בְּשַׁבָּת. אִיכָּא דְּאָמְרִי: רַב זְבִיד גּוּפֵיהּ בָּעַל בַּתְּחִלָּה בְּשַׁבָּת.

The Gemara relates: **Rav Zevid permitted** one **to engage in intercourse** with his virgin wife for the **first** time **on Shabbat. There are** those **who say: Rav Zevid himself engaged in intercourse** with his virgin wife for the **first** time **on Shabbat.**

רַב יְהוּדָה שְׁרָא לְמִיבְעַל בַּתְּחִלָּה בְּיוֹם טוֹב. אֲמַר רַב פַּפֵּי מִשְּׁמֵיהּ דְּרָבָא: לָא תֵּימָא בְּיוֹם טוֹב דִּשְׁרֵי, הָא בְּשַׁבָּת אָסוּר – דְּהוּא הַדִּין דַּאֲפִילּוּ בְּשַׁבָּת נַמִי שְׁרֵי, וּמַעֲשֶׂה שֶׁהָיָה כָּךְ הָיָה.

It was further related: **Rav Yehuda permitted** one **to engage in intercourse** with his virgin wife for the **first** time **on a Festival. Rav Pappi said in the name of Rava: Do not** infer and **say:** It is **on a Festival that** it is **permitted,** but **on Shabbat** it is **prohibited,** similar to actions involving food preparation, which are permitted on Festivals and prohibited on Shabbat, **as the same is true that even on Shabbat it is permitted. And** the reason Rav Yehuda issued his ruling with regard to a Festival is due to the fact that **the incident that took place, took place in this way.**

HALAKHA

Have her seize her husband's movable property – אַתְפְּסוּהָ מִטַּלְטְלִין: If a man neglected to or is unable to write a marriage contract for his wife, e.g., on Shabbat, he may give her movable property corresponding to the value of the marriage contract accompanied by a guarantee that he will compensate her for any loss of value. He may then engage in intercourse with his wife until he has the opportunity to draft a marriage contract, at which point he is obligated to do so (Rambam *Sefer Nashim*, *Hilkhot Ishut* 10:9; *Shulḥan Arukh*, *Even HaEzer* 66:2).

רב פפא משמיה דרבא אמר: ביום טוב – שרי, בשבת – אסור. אמר ליה רב פפי לרב פפא: מאי דעתיך, מתוך שהותרה חבורה לצורך הותרה נמי שלא לצורך? אלא מעתה מותר לעשות מוגמר ביום טוב, דמתוך שהותרה הבערה לצורך – הותרה נמי שלא לצורך!

Rav Pappa said in the name of Rava: According to Rav Yehuda, **on a Festival** it is **permitted, on Shabbat** it is **prohibited. Rav Pappi said to Rav Pappa: What is your thinking?** Is it: **Since** causing **a wound was permitted**[N] on a Festival when performed **for the purpose** of food preparation, it **was also permitted** when **not** performed **for the purpose** of food preparation? **If that is so,** it would be **permitted to prepare incense** [*mugmar*][LB] **on a Festival** due to the following reason: **Since kindling** a fire **was permitted** on a Festival when performed **for the purpose** of food preparation, it **was also permitted** when **not** performed **for the purpose** of food preparation.

אמר ליה: עליך אמר קרא ״אך אשר יאכל לכל נפש״ דבר השוה לכל נפש.

Rav Pappa **said to him:** It is **about your** assertion that **the verse states** with regard to a Festival: **"Save that which every person must eat,** that alone may be done by you" (Exodus 12:16), indicating **a matter that is equal for every person.** Incense is burned only by those who are particularly delicate. It is not equally utilized by everyone, and therefore it is not permitted. Intercourse, on the other hand, is universally practiced.

אמר ליה רב אחא בריה דרבא לרב אשי: אלא מעתה, נזדמן לו צבי ביום טוב, הואיל ואינו שוה לכל נפש – הכי נמי דאסור למשחטיה?! אמר ליה: אנא דבר הצורך לכל נפש קאמינא, צבי צריך לכל נפש הוא.

Rav Aḥa, son of Rava, said to Rav Ashi: If that is so, if a deer happened to come into **his** possession **on a Festival, since** it is **not** a food that is **equal for every person,** would the ruling **also be that** it is **prohibited to slaughter it? Rav Ashi said to him: I said a matter that is a need for every person,** and **deer** meat **is a matter that** although difficult to acquire, is **a need for every person.** Incense, even when available, is not universally utilized.

אמר רבי יעקב בר אידי: הורה רבי יוחנן בציידן: אסור לבעול בתחלה בשבת. ומי איכא הוראה לאיסור?

Rabbi Ya'akov bar Idi said: Rabbi Yoḥanan issued a ruling in the city of **Tzaidan:**[B] **It is prohibited to engage in intercourse** with one's virgin wife for the **first** time **on Shabbat.** The Gemara asks: **And is there a ruling issued to prohibit**[N] an action? Typically, that language is utilized in reference to a firmly established ruling. A stringent ruling can be issued even based on uncertainty. In contrast, a lenient ruling can be issued only if the matter is clearly established by means of tradition or the reasoning of the Sage issuing the ruling.

NOTES

Since…was permitted – מתוך שהותרה: There is a dispute between Beit Shammai and Beit Hillel in tractate *Beitza* with regard to the principle: Since it was permitted for the purpose of food preparation, it was also permitted when not performed for the purpose of food preparation. According to Beit Hillel, since certain actions were permitted for the purpose of food preparation, they are permitted for other purposes as well. *Tosafot* and the Rashba note that this is not blanket permission to perform these activities for any purpose. These activities are permitted only when performed for the purpose of that day, even if it is not for food preparation.

And is there a ruling issued to prohibit – ומי איכא הוראה לאיסור: Apparently, the question arises from the use of the term: Issued a ruling, which typically connotes a novel element. A Sage may rule that a matter is prohibited merely to avoid entering a situation of uncertainty, not due to any novel understanding. However, in order to rule that a matter is permitted, it must be based on a clear-cut, often novel understanding (see Rashi). In the *Shita Mekubbetzet*, an explanation is cited that the question of the Gemara is: Perhaps Rabbi Ya'akov bar Idi was mistaken, and based on the fact that he heard that Rabbi Yoḥanan issued a ruling, he assumed that he had ruled that it is permitted.

LANGUAGE

Incense [*mugmar*] – מוגמר: From the Aramaic *gomra* or *gomarta*, meaning coal. Incense consisted of various spices placed on hot coals that would fill the home with a pleasant fragrance.

BACKGROUND

Incense – מוגמר: Incense vessels, also called censers, were at times fashioned with a perforated cover in order to allow the fragrance to diffuse. Others were sealed, and the cover was removed only when one wanted the fragrance to diffuse throughout the house or to perfume one's garments. The use of various types of incense was customary among well-to-do families.

Censer from Eretz Yisrael dating back to the period of the *ge'onim*

Ruins of Tzaidan

Tzaidan – ציידן: Tzaidan was a town on the northern bank of the Sea of Galilee, adjacent to the place where the Jordan River flows into the Sea of Galilee. It is also called Beit Tzaida in other sources, and Josephus used its Roman name, Julias. The Sages of Tiberias frequently visited there and issued various rulings.

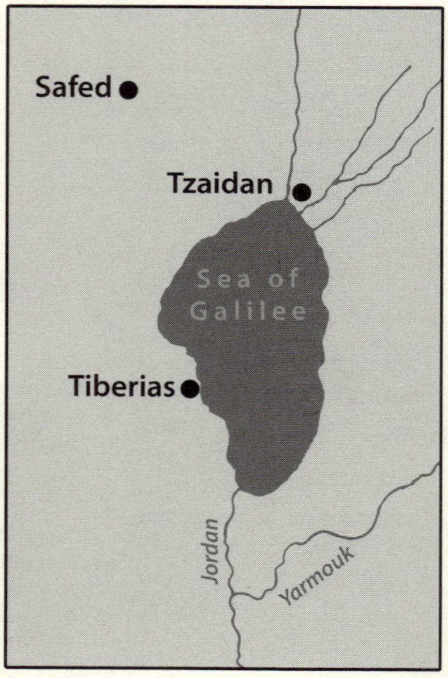

Location of Tzaidan

אִין. וְהָתְנַן: הוֹרוּהָ בֵּית הִלֵּל שֶׁתְּהֵא נְזִירָה עוֹד שֶׁבַע שָׁנִים אֲחֵרוֹת,

The Gemara answers: **Yes,** that language is used with regard to a stringent ruling, as **didn't we learn** the following in a mishna (*Nazir* 19b): When Queen Helene's son went to war, she took a vow to be a nazirite for seven years, and she fulfilled that vow for the duration of her stay in the Diaspora? When she immigrated to Eretz Yisrael, **Beit Hillel issued a ruling that she shall be a nazirite for seven additional years.**[HN] Apparently, rulings are issued to prohibit an action as well.

וְאִי נַמִי כִּי הָא, דְּתַנְיָא: חוּט הַשִּׁדְרָה שֶׁנִּפְסַק – בְּרוּבּוֹ, דִּבְרֵי רַבִּי. רַבִּי יַעֲקֹב אוֹמֵר: אֲפִילּוּ נִיקַּב. הוֹרָה רַבִּי כְּרַבִּי יַעֲקֹב. אָמַר רַב הוּנָא: אֵין הֲלָכָה כְּרַבִּי יַעֲקֹב.

And alternatively, this is **similar** to **that which is taught** in a *baraita*: **If a majority of the spinal cord** of an animal **is severed,**[H] the animal is a *tereifa*; **this is the statement of Rabbi** Yehuda HaNasi. **Rabbi Ya'akov says: Even** if the spinal cord is **perforated** but otherwise intact, the animal is a *tereifa*. The *baraita* continues: **Rabbi** Yehuda HaNasi **issued a ruling in accordance with** the opinion of **Rabbi Ya'akov.** Here too, the term: Issue a ruling, is employed with regard to a stringent ruling. **Rav Huna said:** Despite the fact that Rabbi Yehuda HaNasi ruled in accordance with his opinion, **the *halakha* is not in accordance with** the opinion of **Rabbi Ya'akov,** but rather it is in accordance with the opinion of Rabbi Yehuda HaNasi. This is one version of this discussion.

רַב נַחְמָן בַּר יִצְחָק מַתְנֵי הָכִי: אָמַר רַבִּי אַבָּהוּ שָׁאַל רַבִּי יִשְׁמָעֵאל בֶּן יַעֲקֹב דְּמִן צוֹר אֶת רַבִּי יוֹחָנָן בְּצַיְידָן, וַאֲנָא שְׁמָעִי: מַהוּ לִבְעוֹל בַּתְּחִלָּה בְּשַׁבָּת? וַאֲמַר לֵיהּ: אָסוּר. וְהִלְכְתָא: מוּתָּר לִבְעוֹל בַּתְּחִלָּה בְּשַׁבָּת.

Rav Naḥman bar Yitzḥak taught this alternative version of the ruling of Rabbi Yoḥanan. **Rav Abbahu said: Rabbi Yishmael ben Ya'akov, who is from Tyre, asked Rabbi Yoḥanan in Tzaidan, and I heard** the exchange: **What is** the *halakha* with regard **to engaging in intercourse** with one's virgin wife for the **first** time **on Shabbat? And he said to** him: It is **prohibited.** The Gemara concludes: **And the *halakha*** is that it is **permitted to engage in intercourse** with one's virgin wife for the **first** time **on Shabbat,**[H] and one need not be concerned lest he cause a wound, create an opening, or initiate bleeding.

אָמַר רַבִּי חֶלְבּוֹ אָמַר רַב הוּנָא אָמַר רַבִּי אַבָּא בַּר זַבְדָּא אָמַר רַב: אַחַת בְּתוּלָה וְאַחַת אַלְמָנָה טְעוּנָה בְּרָכָה. וּמִי אֲמַר רַב הוּנָא הָכִי? וְהָאָמַר רַב הוּנָא: אַלְמָנָה אֵינָהּ טְעוּנָה בְּרָכָה! לָא קַשְׁיָא; כָּאן – בְּבָחוּר שֶׁנָּשָׂא אַלְמָנָה, כָּאן – בְּאַלְמוֹן שֶׁנָּשָׂא אַלְמָנָה.

§ **Rabbi Ḥelbo said** that **Rav Huna said** that **Rabbi Abba bar Rav Zavda said** that **Rav said: Both a virgin and a widow** who marry **require** that the **benediction**[N] of the grooms be recited. The Gemara asks: **Did Rav Huna say that? But didn't Rav Huna say: A widow does not require** that a **benediction** be recited? The Gemara answers: This is **not difficult. Here,** where Rav Huna said that a widow requires a benediction, it is **with regard to a bachelor who married a widow. There,** where Rav Huna said she does not require a benediction, it is **with regard to a widower who married a widow.**[H]

וְאַלְמוֹן שֶׁנָּשָׂא אַלְמָנָה לָא? וְהָאָמַר רַב נַחְמָן, אֲמַר לִי הוּנָא בַּר נָתָן, תָּנָא: מִנַּיִן לְבִרְכַּת חֲתָנִים בַּעֲשָׂרָה? שֶׁנֶּאֱמַר ״וַיִּקַּח עֲשָׂרָה אֲנָשִׁים מִזִּקְנֵי הָעִיר וַיֹּאמֶר שְׁבוּ פֹה וַיֵּשֵׁבוּ״, וּבוֹעַז אַלְמוֹן שֶׁנָּשָׂא אַלְמָנָה הֲוָה!

The Gemara asks: **And does a widower who married a widow not** require a benediction to be recited? **But didn't Rav Naḥman say: Huna bar Natan said to me** that it was **taught: From where** is it derived **that the benediction of the grooms** is recited **in a** quorum of **ten** men?[H] It **is as it is stated** with regard to Boaz, who married Ruth: **"And he took ten men of the Elders of the city and said: Sit you here, and they sat"** (Ruth 4:2). **And** when **Boaz** married Ruth, **he was a widower marrying a widow.**[N] As that is the primary source for the obligation to recite the benediction, apparently the benediction is recited even in that case.

HALAKHA

Beit Hillel issued a ruling that she shall be a nazirite for seven additional years – הוֹרוּהָ בֵּית הִלֵּל שֶׁתְּהֵא נְזִירָה עוֹד שֶׁבַע שָׁנִים אֲחֵרוֹת: The vows of a nazirite can be fulfilled only in Eretz Yisrael. If one takes a nazirite vow outside of Eretz Israel, he is obligated to go to Eretz Yisrael and observe the entire period of the vow, and the period that he observed outside of Eretz Yisrael is discounted. According to the Rambam, even today he is obligated to go to Eretz Yisrael and observe the vow there until he dies or until the Temple is rebuilt, at which point he can sacrifice the requisite offerings and conclude his tenure as a nazirite. The Ra'avad disagrees, contending that today there is no point in the nazirite going to Eretz Yisrael, as there is no way for him to purify himself from impurity imparted by a corpse (Rambam *Sefer Hafla'a, Hilkhot Nezirut* 2:21; see Radbaz).

If a majority of the spinal cord of an animal is severed – חוּט הַשִּׁדְרָה שֶׁנִּפְסַק בְּרוּבּוֹ: If more than half the sheath enveloping an animal's spinal cord is severed, it is a *tereifa* and may not be eaten, in accordance with the ruling of Rabbi Yehuda HaNasi (Rambam *Sefer Kedusha, Hilkhot Sheḥita* 9:1; *Shulḥan Arukh, Yoreh De'a* 32:1).

It is permitted to engage in intercourse with one's virgin wife for the first time on Shabbat – מוּתָּר לִבְעוֹל בַּתְּחִלָּה בְּשַׁבָּת: It is permitted to engage in intercourse with one's virgin wife for the first time on Shabbat, and there is no concern that causing a wound or pain entail desecration of Shabbat. Some (Rosh) rule that in places where the custom is to rule stringently and to refrain from engaging in intercourse with a virgin for the first time on Shabbat, one may not rule leniently unless there are compelling circumstances (*Pitḥei Teshuva*; Rambam *Sefer Zemanim, Hilkhot Shabbat* 30:14; *Shulḥan Arukh, Even HaEzer* 63:1).

A widower who married a widow – אַלְמוֹן שֶׁנָּשָׂא אַלְמָנָה: If a widower marries a widow, the benediction of the grooms is recited only on the day of the wedding. However, whenever a virgin is married, whether the groom is marrying for the first time or has been married before, the benediction of the grooms is recited on all seven days of the wedding celebration (Rambam *Sefer Ahava, Hilkhot Berakhot* 2:9; *Shulḥan Arukh, Even HaEzer* 62:6).

The benediction of the grooms is recited in a quorum of ten men – בִּרְכַּת חֲתָנִים בַּעֲשָׂרָה: The benediction of the grooms is recited only if there is a quorum of ten adult, free males present. Therefore, the wedding should not be held without a quorum. However, if there is no alternative, the wedding may be held without the benediction, and the benediction is recited later (Rashba; *Ḥelkat Meḥokek*). Others maintain that the presence of ten men is not critical after the fact, and so in cases where assembling the quorum would require a major effort, one need not insist on the presence of the quorum (*Darkhei Moshe*; *Beit Shmuel*; *Be'er Heitev*; Rambam *Sefer Ahava, Hilkhot Berakhot* 2:10; *Shulḥan Arukh, Even HaEzer* 62:4).

NOTES

That she shall be a nazirite for seven additional years – שֶׁתְּהֵא נְזִירָה עוֹד שֶׁבַע שָׁנִים: The essential reason was that a decree of ritual impurity was issued with regard to the land of the gentiles, and since it is prohibited for a nazirite to become impure with impurity imparted by a corpse, the naziriteship observed outside of Eretz Yisrael is disregarded.

A bride requires the benediction – טְעוּנָה בְּרָכָה כַּלָּה: In tractate *Kalla*, it states more forcefully that a bride without a blessing is forbidden to her husband like a menstruating woman. See *Tosafot* and Rav Yoshiya Pinto, who note that an additional source for the wedding benediction is cited there, from the verse "And they blessed Rebecca, and said to her: Our sister, may you be the mother of thousands of ten thousands" (Genesis 24:60).

He was a widower marrying a widow – אַלְמוֹן שֶׁנָּשָׂא אַלְמָנָה הֲוָה: Some derive that Boaz was a widower from the fact that he is identified with Ibzan, one of the judges from Bethlehem, about whom it is written that he had many children. In the Jerusalem Talmud, a midrash is cited with regard to the verse that describes Naomi and Ruth's arrival: "All the city was astir" (Ruth 1:22). It wasn't astir due to their arrival; rather, it was astir due to the funeral of Boaz's wife.

מַאי אֵינָהּ טְעוּנָה בְּרָכָה דְּאָמַר רַב הוּנָא – אֵינָהּ טְעוּנָה בְּרָכָה כׇּל שִׁבְעָה – אֲבָל יוֹם אֶחָד טְעוּנָה בְּרָכָה.

The Gemara answers: **What is the meaning of: Does not require a benediction, that Rav Huna stated?** It means that **she does not require a benediction all seven** days of the wedding celebration, **but** everyone agrees that for **one day, she requires** that a **benediction** be recited.

אֶלָּא הָא דְּתַנְיָא: שָׁקְדוּ חֲכָמִים עַל תַּקָּנַת בְּנוֹת יִשְׂרָאֵל שֶׁיְּהֵא שָׂמֵחַ עִמָּהּ שְׁלֹשָׁה יָמִים, בְּמַאי? אִי בְּבָחוּר – הָאָמַרְתְּ שִׁבְעָה, אִי בְּאַלְמוֹן – הָאָמַרְתְּ יוֹם אֶחָד!

The Gemara asks: **However, that which is taught** in a *baraita*, that **the Sages were assiduous**[N] **in seeing to the well-being of Jewish women,** ensuring **that** the groom **will rejoice with her three days,** and that is why they established that a widow is married on Thursday, **with regard to what** circumstance is the *baraita* speaking? **If** it is **with regard to a bachelor** who marries a widow, **didn't you say** he celebrates **seven** days; why then did the Sages see to a mere three-day celebration? **If** it is **with regard to a widower** who marries a widow, **didn't you say** he celebrates for **one** day? Why then did the Sages see to a three-day celebration?

אִיבָּעֵית אֵימָא: בְּאַלְמוֹן – יוֹם אֶחָד לִבְרָכָה וּשְׁלֹשָׁה לְשִׂמְחָה, וְאִיבָּעֵית אֵימָא: בְּבָחוּר – שִׁבְעָה לִבְרָכָה וּשְׁלֹשָׁה לְשִׂמְחָה.

The Gemara answers that this can be resolved in several manners. **If you wish, say: In** the case of **a widower** marrying a widow, there is **one day for benediction and three days for celebration.** The wedding is scheduled on Thursday to facilitate a three-day celebration. **And if you wish, say** instead: **In** the case of **a bachelor** marrying a widow, there are **seven days for benediction and** there are **three days for celebration,** during which he must refrain from going to work.[H]

NOTES

However that which is taught in a *baraita* that the Sages were assiduous – אֶלָּא הָא דְּתַנְיָא שָׁקְדוּ: The connection between rejoicing at a wedding and the blessing is underscored by the *halakha* cited later in the Gemara, that the wedding benediction is recited at occasions celebrating the wedding and not specifically on the days of the wedding feast itself.

HALAKHA

The marriage celebration – שִׂמְחַת נִישּׂוּאִין: If a man marries a virgin, he must rejoice with her for a period of seven days. However, if he marries a woman who was previously married, he must rejoice with her for a period of three days. According to most authorities, who consider the two versions of the Gemara not mutually exclusive, this applies whether or not the groom was married before. However, the Rashba and others maintain that in the case of a widow marrying a man who was never married, he must also rejoice with her for seven days. In their opinion, the two versions are mutually exclusive, and the *halakha* is in accordance with the latter version, and that is the custom (*Be'er HaGola*; Rambam *Sefer Nashim*, *Hilkhot Ishut* 10:12; *Shulḥan Arukh*, *Even HaEzer* 64:2).

Perek **I**
Daf **7** Amud **b**

מֵיתִיבֵי: מְבָרְכִין לִבְתוּלָה שִׁבְעָה וּלְאַלְמָנָה יוֹם אֶחָד. מַאי לָאו – אֲפִילּוּ אַלְמָנָה שֶׁנִּשֵּׂאת לְבָחוּר! לָא, לְאַלְמוֹן. אֲבָל לְבָחוּר מַאי – שִׁבְעָה, אִי הָכִי לִיתְנֵי: מְבָרְכִין לִבְתוּלָה שִׁבְעָה, וּלְאַלְמָנָה שֶׁנִּשֵּׂאת לְבָחוּר שִׁבְעָה, וּלְאַלְמָנָה יוֹם אֶחָד!

The Gemara raises an objection from a *baraita*: **One recites a benediction for a virgin** who marries for **seven** days **and for a widow** who marries for **one** day. **What, is it not even** in the case **of a widow who is married to a bachelor,** that one recites the benediction for one day? The Gemara answers: **No,** it is only in the case of a widow who is married **to a widower** that the benediction is recited for one day. The Gemara asks: **However,** one may then infer that in the case of a widow who is married **to a bachelor, what** is the *halakha*? The blessing is recited **seven** days? **If so, let** the *tanna* **teach** the *baraita*: **One recites a benediction for a virgin** who marries for **seven** days, **and for a widow** who marries **a bachelor seven** days, **and for a widow** marrying a widower for **one day.** Why was the middle case omitted?

מִילְּתָא פְּסִיקְתָּא קָתָנֵי, דְּלֵיכָּא בְּתוּלָה דְּבָצְרָה מִשִּׁבְעָה, וְלֵיכָּא אַלְמָנָה דְּבָצְרָה מִיּוֹם אֶחָד.

Although the *tanna* could have included that case in the *baraita*, **he taught categorical matters.** He preferred to avoid entering into detail, **as there is no virgin for whom** the benediction is recited **fewer than seven** days, **and there is no widow** for **whom** the benediction is recited for **less than one day.** However, there are circumstances where even for a widow the benediction is recited for more than one day.

גּוּפָא, אֲמַר רַב נַחְמָן: אֲמַר לִי הוּנָא בַּר נָתָן, תָּנָא: מִנַּיִן לְבִרְכַּת חֲתָנִים בַּעֲשָׂרָה – שֶׁנֶּאֱמַר "וַיִּקַּח עֲשָׂרָה אֲנָשִׁים מִזִּקְנֵי הָעִיר וַיֹּאמֶר שְׁבוּ פֹה". וְרַבִּי אַבָּהוּ אֲמַר מֵהָכָא: "בְּמַקְהֵלוֹת בָּרְכוּ אֱלֹהִים ה׳ מִמְּקוֹר יִשְׂרָאֵל".

§ Apropos the source for the benediction of the grooms, the Gemara discusses **the matter itself. Rav Naḥman said: Huna bar Natan said to me** that it was **taught: From where** is it derived **that the benediction of the grooms** is recited **in** a quorum of **ten** men? It is **as it is stated: "And he took ten men of the Elders of the city and said: Sit you here,** and they sat" (Ruth 4:2). **And Rabbi Abbahu said** that the source is **from here: "In assemblies** [*mak'helot*], **bless God, the Lord, from the source of Israel"** (Psalms 68:27). This verse indicates that a congregation [*kahal*], which contains at least ten men, blesses God when reciting a benediction related to the source of Israel, i.e., conjugal relations, which will lead to the birth of Jewish children.

וְרַב נַחְמָן בְּהַאי קְרָא דְּרַבִּי אַבָּהוּ מַאי דָּרֵישׁ בֵּיהּ? מִיבָּעֵי לֵיהּ לְכִדְתַנְיָא: הָיָה רַבִּי מֵאִיר אוֹמֵר: מִנַּיִן שֶׁאֲפִילּוּ עוּבָּרִים שֶׁבִּמְעֵי אִמָּן אָמְרוּ שִׁירָה עַל הַיָּם? שֶׁנֶּאֱמַר "בְּמַקְהֵלוֹת בָּרְכוּ אֱלֹהִים ה׳ מִמְּקוֹר יִשְׂרָאֵל". וְאִידָּךְ – אִם כֵּן לֵימָא קְרָא "מִבֶּטֶן", מַאי "מִמְּקוֹר" עַל עִסְקֵי מָקוֹר.

And what does Rav Naḥman derive from this verse from which Rabbi Abbahu derived that *halakha*? **He requires** the verse **to** derive **that which is taught** in a *baraita*: **Rabbi Meir would say: From where** is it derived **that even fetuses in their mother's womb recited** the **song at the** Red **Sea?** It is **as it is stated** in the chapter of Psalms that describes the exodus from Egypt: **"In assemblies, bless God, the Lord, from the source of Israel."** Even those fetuses that were still in the source, i.e., the womb, joined the assemblies in blessing God. **And the other** Sage, Rabbi Abbahu says: **If that** is the meaning, **let the verse say: From the belly of Israel. What is** the meaning of the term **"source"?** Clearly, it is referring **to matters** related to **the source**[N] of Israel, i.e., the benediction of the grooms, which must be recited in a congregation, a quorum of ten.

וְרַבִּי אַבָּהוּ בְּהַאי קְרָא דְּרַב נַחְמָן מַאי דָּרֵישׁ בֵּיהּ? הַהוּא מִיבָּעֵי לֵיהּ לְמִידְרַשׁ: "עַמּוֹנִי וְלֹא עַמּוֹנִית, מוֹאָבִי וְלֹא מוֹאָבִית". דְּאִי סָלְקָא דַּעְתָּךְ לִבְרָכָה – לָא סַגְיָא דְּלָאו זְקֵנִים?

And what does Rabbi Abbahu derive from this verse from which **Rav Naḥman** derived his *halakha*? **He requires** the verse stating that Boaz assembled ten men in order **to teach** that the Torah prohibition with regard to marrying members of the nations of Ammon and Moab is limited to a male **Ammonite and not a female Ammonite,**[H] and to a male **Moabite and not a female Moabite, as, if it would enter your mind** that Boaz gathered the men only **to** recite **a benediction,** would it **not** have been **sufficient** if they **were not Elders?**[N] From the fact that he convened a quorum of Elders, apparently it was to engage in halakhic discourse and to issue a halakhic ruling.

וְאִידָּךְ: אִי סָלְקָא דַּעְתָּךְ לְמִידְרַשׁ – לָא סַגְיָא דְּלָאו עֲשָׂרָה? אִין, לְפַרְסוּמֵי מִילְּתָא. וּכְדַאֲמַר לֵיהּ שְׁמוּאֵל לְרַב חָנָא בַּגְדָּתָאָה: פּוֹק וְאַיְיתִי לִי בֵּי עֲשָׂרָה, וְאֵימָא לָךְ בְּאַנְפַּיְיהוּ: הַמְזַכֶּה לְעוּבָּר – קָנָה. וְהִלְכְתָא: הַמְזַכֶּה לְעוּבָּר – לֹא קָנָה.

And the other Sage, Rav Naḥman, would reject that proof. **If it would enter your mind** that he gathered the men **in order to teach** a *halakha*, would it **not** have been **sufficient** if they **were not ten?** The Gemara answers: **Yes,** in fact a quorum of ten is not necessary to issue a halakhic ruling. Nevertheless, Boaz convened ten Elders **to publicize the matter, as Shmuel said to Rav Ḥana of Baghdad: Go and bring me an assembly of ten** men **and I will say to you before them** a *halakha* that I seek to disseminate: With regard to **one who transfers ownership** of an object **to a fetus,** the fetus **acquires** it, although it has not yet entered the world. Boaz too assembled ten Elders to publicize the matter. Apropos the *halakha* that Shmuel publicized, the Gemara rules: **And the *halakha*** is: With regard to **one who transfers ownership** of an object **to a fetus,** the fetus **does not acquire** it.[NH]

תָּנוּ רַבָּנַן: מְבָרְכִין בִּרְכַּת חֲתָנִים בְּבֵית חֲתָנִים. רַבִּי יְהוּדָה אוֹמֵר: אַף בְּבֵית הָאֵרוּסִין מְבָרְכִין אוֹתָהּ.

The Sages taught in a *baraita*: **One recites the benediction of the grooms in the house of the grooms,** when the bride enters into the wedding canopy. **Rabbi Yehuda said: One recites it even in the house of the betrothal,** at the time of the betrothal.

אָמַר אַבַּיֵּי: וּבִיהוּדָה שָׁנוּ, מִפְּנֵי שֶׁמִּתְיַיחֵד עִמָּהּ.

Abaye said: And the Sages **taught** the statement of Rabbi Yehuda **in Judea because** there the custom was **that** the groom **be secluded with** his betrothed,[H] leading to the concern lest he engage in conjugal relations with her. Therefore, the blessing is recited already at that stage.

NOTES

To matters related to the source – עַל עִסְקֵי מָקוֹר: The early commentaries disagree whether a quorum of ten is required not only for the wedding blessing but for the betrothal blessing as well (see Rabbi Shmuel HaNagid and Rosh). Support for those who maintain that it is required can be cited from this Gemara, as betrothal is also a matter relating to the source of Israel.

Would it not have been sufficient if they were not Elders – לָא סַגְיָא דְּלָאו זְקֵנִים: The Ritva writes that although it is not derived from here that the quorum must be Elders, it is derived that the ten must have reached the age of majority, as the verse employs the term men.

And the *halakha* is: With regard to one who transfers ownership of an object to a fetus, the fetus does not acquire it – וְהִלְכְתָא, הַמְזַכֶּה לְעוּבָּר לֹא קָנָה: This ruling was stated explicitly to ensure that one does not rule in accordance with Shmuel, who issued his ruling publicly.

HALAKHA

A male Ammonite and not a female Ammonite – עַמּוֹנִי וְלֹא עַמּוֹנִית: An Ammonite or Moabite who converted to Judaism may not marry a Jewish woman, nor may male descendants of those converts marry Jewish women, regardless of the number of generations that have passed since the conversion of their ancestor. However, a female Ammonite or Moabite who converted to Judaism may marry a Jewish man, like any other convert (Rambam *Sefer Kedusha*, *Hilkhot Issurei Bia* 12:18; *Shulḥan Arukh*, *Even HaEzer* 4:2).

One who transfers ownership of an object to a fetus, the fetus does not acquire it – הַמְזַכֶּה לְעוּבָּר לֹא קָנָה: If one consigns a gift to a fetus, the latter does not acquire it. However, if one consigns a gift to a fetus that he fathered, the fetus does acquire it (*Bava Batra* 142b). Some maintain that the fetus acquires a gift from its father only if it is a gift bequeathed on his deathbed (*Sefer HaIttur*, citing Rav Hai Gaon), but most authorities disagree (see *Shakh*; Rambam *Sefer Kinyan*, *Hilkhot Mekhira* 22:10, *Hilkhot Zekhiya* 8:5; *Shulḥan Arukh*, *Ḥoshen Mishpat* 210:1).

Because the custom was that the groom be secluded with his betrothed – מִפְּנֵי שֶׁמִּתְיַיחֵד עִמָּהּ: In places where it is customary for a betrothed couple to be secluded together, the wedding benediction is recited at the betrothal, as in that case everyone agrees that it is permitted for the bride to engage in relations with the groom, in accordance with the statements of Rabbi Yehuda and Abaye. Even those authorities who do not rule in accordance with the statement of Rabbi Yehuda infer from this statement that if the groom does not enter into seclusion with his betrothed, the wedding benediction is not recited then (Rambam *Sefer Nashim*, *Hilkhot Ishut* 10:6; *Shulḥan Arukh*, *Even HaEzer* 55:1–2).

תַּנְיָא אִידָךְ: מְבָרְכִין בִּרְכַּת חֲתָנִים בְּבֵית חֲתָנִים, וּבִרְכַּת אֵרוּסִין בְּבֵית הָאֵרוּסִין, בִּרְכַּת הָאֵרוּסִין מַאי מְבָרֵךְ? רָבִין בַּר רַב אַדָּא וְרַבָּה בַּר רַב אַדָּא, תַּרְוַיְיהוּ מִשְּׁמֵיהּ דְּרַב יְהוּדָה אָמְרִי: בָּרוּךְ אַתָּה ה׳ אֱלֹהֵינוּ מֶלֶךְ הָעוֹלָם אֲשֶׁר קִדְּשָׁנוּ בְּמִצְוֹתָיו וְצִוָּנוּ עַל הָעֲרָיוֹת וְאָסַר לָנוּ אֶת הָאֲרוּסוֹת וְהִתִּיר לָנוּ אֶת הַנְּשׂוּאוֹת עַל יְדֵי חוּפָּה וְקִדּוּשִׁין. רַב אַחָא בְּרֵיהּ דְּרָבָא מְסַיֵּים בָּהּ מִשְּׁמֵיהּ דְּרַב יְהוּדָה: בָּרוּךְ אַתָּה ה׳ מְקַדֵּשׁ יִשְׂרָאֵל עַל יְדֵי חוּפָּה וְקִדּוּשִׁין.

It is taught in another *baraita*: **One recites the benediction of the grooms**[H] **in the house of the grooms, and the benediction of the betrothal in the house of the betrothal.** With regard to **the benediction of the betrothal,**[N] **what** formula **does one recite?**[H] **Ravin bar Rav Adda and Rabba bar Rav Adda both said in the name of Rav Yehuda: Blessed are You, Lord our God, King of the universe, Who sanctified us through His mitzvot, and commanded us concerning the forbidden relatives,**[N] **and prohibited to us those women who are betrothed,**[N] **and permitted to us** those **women who are married**[N] **by means of the wedding canopy and betrothal. Rav Aḥa, son of Rava, concludes** the blessing **in the name of Rav Yehuda: Blessed are You, Lord, Who sanctifies Israel by means of the wedding canopy and betrothal.**[HN]

מַאן דְּלָא חָתֵים – מִידֵי דַּהֲוָה אַבִּרְכַּת פֵּירוֹת וְאַבִּרְכַּת מִצְוֹת, וּמַאן דְּחָתֵים – מִידֵי דַּהֲוָה אַקִּידּוּשָׁא.

One who does not conclude the benediction of the betrothal in accordance with the opinion of Rav Aḥa, but instead recites it without a concluding blessing, deems the formula of this blessing **just as** the formula **is in the blessing** recited over **fruits and the blessing** recited over **mitzvot,** in which the words: Blessed are You, Lord, appear only at the beginning of the blessing. **And one who concludes** the benediction of the betrothal in accordance with the opinion of Rav Aḥa, deems the formula of this blessing **just as** the formula **is in** the blessing **of *kiddush*,** in which the words: Blessed are You, Lord, appears both at the beginning and the conclusion of the blessing.

HALAKHA

The time for reciting the benediction of the grooms – זְמַן בִּרְכַּת חֲתָנִים: The wedding benediction is recited for the first time when the bride enters the wedding canopy. It is subsequently recited at each of the wedding meals in the groom's house (Rambam *Sefer Ahava*, *Hilkhot Berakhot* 2:9 and *Sefer Nashim*, *Hilkhot Ishut* 10:3; *Shulḥan Arukh*, *Even HaEzer* 62:1).

The formula for the benediction of the betrothal – נוּסַח בִּרְכַּת הָאֵרוּסִין: Today the formula for the benediction of the betrothal is consistent with the formula that appears in the Gemara, with minor variations, based on variant readings and divergent halakhic rulings. The formula of the benediction according to the Ashkenazic custom is: Blessed are You, Lord our God, King of the universe, Who sanctified us through His mitzvot, and commanded us concerning the forbidden relations, and has prohibited to us those women who are betrothed, and has permitted to us those women who are married to us by the rite of the wedding canopy and betrothal. The added phrase: Married to us, is an emendation by Rabbeinu Tam. According to the Sephardic custom, the benediction concludes: By the rite of the wedding canopy with betrothal (*Beit Yosef*, based on *Sefer HaIttur*). The Yemenite custom, based on the Rambam, is: Who has sanctified us through His mitzvot, and distanced us from the forbidden relations, and prohibited to us those women who are betrothed, and permitted to us those women who are married by the rite of the wedding canopy and betrothal (see *Maggid Mishne*; Rambam *Sefer Nashim*, *Hilkhot Ishut* 3:24; *Shulḥan Arukh*, *Even HaEzer* 34:1).

The conclusion of the benediction of the grooms – חֲתִימַת בִּרְכַּת חֲתָנִים: The prevalent custom is to end the betrothal benediction with a concluding blessing, in accordance with the statement of Rav Aḥa. According to both the Ashkenazic and the Sephardic customs, based on the text in the Gemara and the prayer book of Rav Amram Gaon and the Maḥzor Vitri, the benediction concludes: Blessed are You, Lord, Who sanctifies Israel by means of the wedding canopy and betrothal. Alternatively, it concludes as follows: With betrothal, according to the Sephardic custom. The Yemenite custom concludes with: Who sanctifies Israel (Rav Hai Gaon; Rif; Rambam; Rambam *Sefer Nashim*, *Hilkhot Ishut* 3:24; *Shulḥan Arukh*, *Even HaEzer* 34:1).

NOTES

The benediction of the betrothal – בִּרְכַּת הָאֵרוּסִין: The early commentaries (Ramban) note that this blessing is anomalous, as there are no blessings on prohibitions, and the formula of this blessing refers to the prohibitions governing sexual relations between a man and woman. They explain that the blessing is not recited over observance of those prohibitions. Rather, it is a blessing of thanksgiving to God for sanctifying the Jewish people by commanding them to fulfill mitzvot. Analysis of Rashi's commentary reveals that he alluded to this as well. In the *Roke'aḥ*, it is explained that because these prohibitions are unique to the Jewish people, there is room to recite a blessing over them. The Meiri writes that the blessing is recited not over the prohibitions. Rather, it is recited over the mitzva of betrothal.

And commanded us concerning the forbidden relations – וְצִוָּנוּ עַל הָעֲרָיוֹת: The use of the term: And commanded us, is difficult in this context, as it does not indicate what the command is. The Rambam has a variant reading: And distanced us from the forbidden relatives (see *Maggid Mishne*). The term: Commanded us, is more easily understood in light of the explanation of the Ramban cited above, that this is not a blessing over performance of a mitzva, but a blessing of thanksgiving. Others write that in this context the term: Forbidden relatives, is referring not only to illicit sexual intercourse, but to sexual relations in the broader sense. Therefore, the blessing means: Who commanded us, both with regard to the prohibition against relations with those who are forbidden and with regard to the positive mitzva to betroth those who are permitted (*Ḥatam Sofer*).

And prohibited to us those women who are betrothed – וְאָסַר לָנוּ אֶת הָאֲרוּסוֹת: Rashi explains that although the prohibition against engaging in relations with one's betrothed is by rabbinic law, the expression: Who commanded us, is appropriate even for rabbinic mitzvot, e.g., kindling Hanukkah lights. Others write that since the Gemara proves that the obligation to enter into the wedding canopy is by Torah law, then the bride is forbidden to him by Torah law (see Rosh). With regard to the reason for the blessing, the Ramban explains that since it was customary for the betrothal to take place up to a year before the wedding, it was necessary to remind the groom that the betrothed woman was forbidden to him until marriage.

And permitted to us those women who are married – וְהִתִּיר לָנוּ אֶת הַנְּשׂוּאוֹת: The prevalent custom is in accordance with the opinion of Rabbeinu Tam, who says that although the intention is clear, the formula of a blessing must nevertheless be unambiguous. Therefore, he emended the blessing and added: Those women who are married to us. In the opinion of Rav Hai Gaon, the phrase: And permitted to us those who are married, is omitted. Rather, the formula is: And permitted them to us, referring to the aforementioned betrothed women. This was the custom in the Babylonian academies. The early commentaries approve of that formula. However, that custom never became prevalent elsewhere.

Who sanctifies Israel by means of the wedding canopy and betrothal – מְקַדֵּשׁ יִשְׂרָאֵל עַל יְדֵי חוּפָּה וְקִדּוּשִׁין: According to Rav Hai Gaon, the blessing concludes merely: Who sanctifies Israel, as it is inappropriate to attribute the sanctity of Israel to the wedding canopy and betrothal. However, according to the understanding that this is a blessing of thanksgiving, it can be explained as thanksgiving for this additional element of sanctity, similar to the Sages' interpretation of the verse "You shall be sacred" (Leviticus 19:2) as: You shall be separate.

תָּנוּ רַבָּנַן: מְבָרְכִין בִּרְכַּת חֲתָנִים בַּעֲשָׂרָה כׇּל שִׁבְעָה. אָמַר רַב יְהוּדָה: וְהוּא שֶׁבָּאוּ פָּנִים חֲדָשׁוֹת.

§ **The Sages taught: One recites the benediction of the grooms in** a quorum of **ten** men **all seven** days of the wedding celebration. **Rav Yehuda said: And that is** the case only **when new faces**[HN] who did not previously participate in the festivities **came** to join the celebration.

מַאי מְבָרֵךְ? אָמַר רַב יְהוּדָה: בָּרוּךְ אַתָּה ה׳ אֱלֹהֵינוּ מֶלֶךְ הָעוֹלָם

The Gemara asks: **What blessings does one recite?**[N] **Rav Yehuda said** that these are the seven blessings: **Blessed are You, Lord our God, King of the universe,**

HALAKHA

New faces – פָּנִים חֲדָשׁוֹת: For the seven days of the celebration following the wedding, the wedding benedictions are recited at each meal where new faces are present. There are various opinions as to who qualifies as a new face. Some maintain that people who did not hear the wedding benedictions at the wedding are considered new faces (Rambam). Others maintain that even people who attended the wedding may be considered new faces if they did not yet participate in one of the wedding meals. The *Shulḥan Arukh* notes that this is the prevalent custom. The Rema writes that even if the new guests do not actually partake of the meal that they attend, the wedding benedictions may be recited on that night and the following day. According to *Tosafot*, only new guests whose presence enhances the festive nature of the occasion qualify as new faces. Some maintain that Shabbat and Festivals are also considered new faces, so that the benedictions are recited on Friday and Festival nights and the following day. The Rema adds that the Ashkenazic custom is to recite the benediction even at the third Shabbat meal (Rambam *Sefer Ahava*, *Hilkhot Berakhot* 2:10; *Shulḥan Arukh*, *Even HaEzer* 62:7–8).

NOTES

New faces – פָּנִים חֲדָשׁוֹת: Some learn from the fact that this term is in the plural that at least two new people are required. In the *Shita Mekubbetzet*, that conclusion is rejected, as the plural refers to all the guests who will participate in the festivities throughout the seven days.

The order of the wedding blessings – סֵדֶר בִּרְכוֹת נִשּׂוּאִין: Rashi explains the order of the wedding blessings as follows: The first was instituted in deference to the congregation attending the wedding, followed by a blessing over the creation of man and his union with his spouse in the Garden of Eden. Before proceeding to blessing the couple upon their entry beneath the wedding canopy, there is a blessing over the solace of Jerusalem, to fulfill the verse "If I set not Jerusalem above my greatest joy" (Psalms 137:6). That is followed by the blessing wishing the couple happiness together for the rest of their lives, followed by the final blessing wishing them joy at the wedding. That is the approach adopted by most early commentaries (see Ritva).

The Maharsha explains the order as follows: First comes God, then the creation of man, followed by the creation of woman, and subsequently God's providence in the world, including celebration of the wedding.

Perek **I**
Daf **8** Amud **a**

שֶׁהַכֹּל בָּרָא לִכְבוֹדוֹ,

Who has created all for His glory.

וְ״יוֹצֵר הָאָדָם״,

And the second blessing is: Blessed are You… **Creator of mankind.**

וַ״אֲשֶׁר יָצַר אֶת הָאָדָם בְּצַלְמוֹ בְּצֶלֶם דְּמוּת תַּבְנִיתוֹ וְהִתְקִין לוֹ מִמֶּנּוּ בִּנְיַן עֲדֵי עַד. בָּרוּךְ אַתָּה ה׳ יוֹצֵר הָאָדָם״,

And the third blessing is: Blessed are You… **Who made humanity**[N] **in His image, in the image of the likeness of His form, and out of His very self formed a building** (see Genesis 2:22) **for eternity. Blessed are You, Lord, Creator of mankind.**

״שׂוֹשׂ תָּשִׂישׂ וְתָגֵל הָעֲקָרָה בְּקִבּוּץ בָּנֶיהָ לְתוֹכָהּ בְּשִׂמְחָה. בָּרוּךְ אַתָּה ה׳ מְשַׂמֵּחַ צִיּוֹן בְּבָנֶיהָ״,

The fourth blessing is: **May the barren** city of Jerusalem **greatly rejoice and delight**[N] **with the ingathering of her children within her in joy. Blessed are You, Lord, Who gladdens Zion through her children.**

״שַׂמֵּחַ תְּשַׂמַּח רֵיעִים הָאֲהוּבִים כְּשַׂמֵּחֲךָ יְצִירְךָ בְּגַן עֵדֶן מִקֶּדֶם. בָּרוּךְ אַתָּה ה׳ מְשַׂמֵּחַ חָתָן וְכַלָּה״,

The fifth blessing is: **Bring great joy to these loving friends, as You gave joy to Your creations**[N] **in Eden in ancient times. Blessed are You, Lord, Who brings joy to the groom and bride.**

״בָּרוּךְ אַתָּה ה׳ אֱלֹהֵינוּ מֶלֶךְ הָעוֹלָם אֲשֶׁר בָּרָא שָׂשׂוֹן וְשִׂמְחָה חָתָן וְכַלָּה גִּילָה רִינָּה דִּיצָה חֶדְוָה אַהֲבָה וְאַחֲוָה וְשָׁלוֹם וְרֵיעוּת, מְהֵרָה ה׳ אֱלֹהֵינוּ יִשָּׁמַע בְּעָרֵי יְהוּדָה וּבְחוּצוֹת יְרוּשָׁלַיִם קוֹל שָׂשׂוֹן וְקוֹל שִׂמְחָה קוֹל חָתָן וְקוֹל כַּלָּה קוֹל מִצְהֲלוֹת חֲתָנִים מֵחוּפָּתָם וּנְעָרִים מִמִּשְׁתֵּה נְגִינָתָם. בָּרוּךְ אַתָּה ה׳ מְשַׂמֵּחַ חָתָן עִם הַכַּלָּה״.

The sixth blessing is: **Blessed are You, Lord our God, King of the universe, Who has created joy and gladness, groom and bride, delight, exultation, happiness, jubilation, love and brotherhood, and peace and friendship. Soon, Lord our God, may there be heard in the cities of Judea and in the streets of Jerusalem the sound of joy and the sound of gladness, the sound of the groom and the sound of the bride, the joyous sound of grooms from their wedding canopy and of young people from their feast of song** (see Jeremiah 33:11). **Blessed are You, Lord, Who makes the groom rejoice with the bride.** Together with the blessing over the wine, these are the seven wedding blessings.

NOTES

Who made humanity – אֲשֶׁר יָצַר אֶת הָאָדָם: Many commentaries are of the opinion that the first blessing: Creator of mankind, refers to the creation of Adam, and the second refers to the creation of Eve. Despite the fact that the formula of the second blessing also employs the term *adam*, in the Bible that term refers to women as well (see Numbers 31:35 and Isaiah 44:13).

May the barren city of Jerusalem greatly rejoice and delight – שׂוֹשׂ תָּשִׂישׂ וְתָגֵל הָעֲקָרָה: In addition to the primary reason for this blessing, i.e., to fulfill the verse "If I set not Jerusalem above my greatest joy" (Psalms 137:6), the Meiri cites an additional reason: In many places in the Bible, the relationship between God and the Jewish people is likened to the relationship between a man and woman, or a bride and groom, e.g., "And as the bridegroom rejoices over the bride, so shall your God rejoice over you" (Isaiah 62:5). Therefore, while reciting blessings over the marriage of a man and a woman, it is appropriate to mention the relationship of God and His people.

As You gave joy to Your creations – כְּשַׂמֵּחֲךָ יְצִירְךָ: In the midrash there is a description of how God prepared the wedding celebration for Adam and Eve, and the angels were the wedding guests (see *Eiruvin* 18a).

לֵוִי אִיקְּלַע לְבֵי רַבִּי בְּהִלּוּלֵיהּ דְּרַבִּי שִׁמְעוֹן בְּרֵיהּ, בְּרִיךְ חָמֵשׁ. רַב אַסִּי אִיקְּלַע לְבֵי רַב אַשִׁי בְּהִלּוּלֵיהּ דְּמָר בְּרֵיהּ, בְּרִיךְ שִׁית.

The Gemara relates: **Levi happened** to come **to the house of** Rabbi Yehuda HaNasi **during the wedding celebration of Rabbi Shimon,**[P] **his son, and recited five** of these **blessings. Rav Asi happened** to come **to the house of Rav Ashi during the wedding celebration of Mar, his son, and recited six**[N] of these **blessings.**[H]

לֵימָא בְּהָא קָמִיפַּלְגִי, דְּמָר סָבַר חֲדָא יְצִירָה הֲוַאי, וּמָר סָבַר: שְׁתֵּי יְצִירוֹת הֲוַאי?

The Gemara suggests: **Let us say that they disagree about this:** One **Sage holds: It was one** act of **creation** with which man was created. **And one Sage holds: It was two** acts of **creation** with which man was created.[N] The first opinion, that there was one act of creation, is based on the concept that man was created with two sides, one male and one female. There was no additional act of creation. Man and woman were subsequently separated into two independent beings. Therefore, there is no need for the two blessings: Who created mankind, and: Who created mankind in His image. The second opinion is that there were in fact two separate acts of creation. Therefore, it is appropriate to recite two blessings with regard to the creation of mankind.

לָא, דְּכוּלֵּי עָלְמָא חֲדָא יְצִירָה הֲוַאי, מָר סָבַר: בָּתַר מַחֲשָׁבָה אָזְלִינַן, וּמָר סָבַר: בָּתַר מַעֲשֶׂה אָזְלִינַן. כִּי הָא דְּרַב יְהוּדָה רָמֵי: כְּתִיב ״וַיִּבְרָא אֱלֹהִים אֶת הָאָדָם בְּצַלְמוֹ״, וּכְתִיב ״זָכָר וּנְקֵבָה בְּרָאָם״, הָא כֵּיצַד? בַּתְּחִלָּה עָלָה בְּמַחֲשָׁבָה לִבְרֹאות שְׁנַיִם, וּלְבַסּוֹף נִבְרָא אֶחָד.

The Gemara rejects that suggestion: **No, everyone agrees** that it **was** only **one act of creation.** However, one **Sage holds:** It is **according to** the initial **thought** that **we proceed. And one Sage holds:** It is **according to** the **action** that **we proceed.** God's initial thought was to create man and woman as separate entities. Ultimately, they were created as one entity. That explanation is **like the following. Rav Yehuda raises a contradiction.** In one verse **it is written: "And God created man in His own image"** (Genesis 1:27), indicating one act of creation, **and** in another verse **it is written: "Male and female He created them"** (Genesis 5:2), indicating two acts. **How can this** apparent contradiction be resolved? **Initially, the thought entered** God's mind **to create two, but ultimately only one was** actually **created.**[N]

רַב אַשִׁי אִיקְּלַע לְבֵי רַב כָּהֲנָא, יוֹמָא קַמָּא בְּרִיךְ כּוּלְּהוּ, מִכָּאן וְאֵילָךְ, אִי אִיכָּא פָּנִים חֲדָשׁוֹת – בְּרִיךְ כּוּלְּהוּ, וְאִי לָא – אַפּוּשֵׁי שִׂמְחָה בְּעָלְמָא הוּא, מְבָרֵךְ ״שֶׁהַשִּׂמְחָה בִּמְעוֹנוֹ״ וַ״אֲשֶׁר בָּרָא״.

The Gemara relates: **Rav Ashi happened** to come **to the house of Rav Kahana** to attend a wedding. **The first day he recited all** seven **blessings.**[H] **From** that **point forward, if there were new faces** present,[H] **he recited all the blessings, and if not,**[H] he would say: **It is merely an extension of the** original **celebration, and he would recite the blessing: In Whose dwelling is joy,** in the *zimmun* prior to Grace after Meals, **and** the sixth blessing after Grace after Meals: **Who has created.**

PERSONALITIES

Rabbi Shimon – רַבִּי שִׁמְעוֹן: Rabbi Shimon was the youngest son of Rabbi Yehuda HaNasi and his foremost student. He was a member of the group of prominent students of Rabbi Yehuda HaNasi and discussed halakhic issues with them. He was especially close to Rabbi Ḥiyya, who was also his close friend and his partner in the silk business. In many sources, it is evident that Rabbi Shimon was very scrupulous with regard to his honor, which he considered to be related to the honor of the office of the *Nasi*. He was especially careful to ensure that nothing he did or said would reflect poorly on the reverence due his prominent father.

At least one of his statements is cited in the Mishna, although he a member of the transitional generation between *tanna'im* and *amora'im*. His statements are often introduced with the term: It was stated, characteristic of statements of *amora'im*.

Rabbi Yehuda HaNasi considered Rabbi Shimon a Torah luminary and before his death appointed him *Ḥakham*, the third-highest position in the Sanhedrin after the *Nasi* and the deputy *Nasi*. He appointed Rabbi Shimon's older brother, Rabban Gamliel, to succeed him as *Nasi*.

NOTES

Recited six blessings – בְּרִיךְ שִׁית: There is a dispute with regard to which blessing is the one omitted by Levi and Rav Asi. According to Rashi, it is the second blessing. According to the Ri Migash, it is the third blessing.

The Gemara is referring to either five or six blessings that are recited. However, the custom of referring to the wedding blessings as the seven blessings is an early one. The practice, originating with the *ge'onim*, is to recite the blessing over wine prior to the six wedding blessings. In other places, a blessing was recited over a myrtle branch (*Seder Rav Amram Gaon*), or even over wine and incense. Rabbeinu Tam adopted a different approach. Because today betrothal and marriage are held consecutively, the blessing of betrothal that precedes the six wedding blessings brings the total to seven.

One act of creation or two acts of creation – יְצִירָה אַחַת אוֹ שְׁתַּיִם: Most commentaries understand this question like the question raised in tractate *Eiruvin*: Were man and woman created separately, or was Adam created with two faces and subsequently separated into man and woman? Rabbeinu Ḥananel, however, explains it differently. The opinion that says that there were two separate creations holds that man and woman were created separately. However, the first woman fled and a second woman was created from man.

Initially, the thought entered God's mind to create two, but ultimately only one was actually created – בַּתְּחִלָּה עָלָה בְּמַחֲשָׁבָה לִבְרֹאות שְׁנַיִם, וּלְבַסּוֹף נִבְרָא אֶחָד: The Maharsha explains that initially God thought to create man and woman separately, as He had all the other species. However, anticipating potential discord, He ultimately created them together and then separated them, to enhance the potential of peaceful coexistence.

HALAKHA

Recited six blessings – בְּרִיךְ שִׁית: The six blessings recited at the wedding are (1) Blessed…Who has created all for His glory, (2) Blessed…Creator of man, (3) Blessed…Who created man… Creator of man, (4) May the barren city greatly rejoice…Blessed… Who gladdens Zion through her children, (5) Bring great joy to these loving friends…Blessed…Who makes groom and bride rejoice, (6) Blessed…Who has created…Blessed…Who makes the groom rejoice with the bride (Rambam *Sefer Ahava, Hilkhot Berakhot* 2:11, *Sefer Nashim, Hilkhot Ishut* 10:3; *Shulḥan Arukh, Even HaEzer* 62:7).

The first day he recited all seven blessings – יוֹמָא קַמָּא בְּרִיךְ כּוּלְּהוּ: Most authorities rule that all seven blessings, the six mentioned in the Gemara and the benediction over wine, are recited at the first wedding meal, even if there are no new faces who did not attend the wedding ceremony partaking of the meal (Rosh; *Tur*), and even in the marriage of a widower to a widow. According to the Rif, the Rambam, and *Tosafot*, when there are no new guests the six blessings are not recited, even at the first meal. However, if there are new faces, one recites the blessings at the conclusion of all meals throughout the day (see *Beit Shmuel*; *Arukh HaShulḥan*; Rambam *Sefer Ahava, Hilkhot Berakhot* 2:9–10; *Tur, Even HaEzer* 62, *Shulḥan Arukh, Even HaEzer* 62:1).

From this point forward if there were new faces present – מִכָּאן וְאֵילָךְ, אִי אִיכָּא פָּנִים חֲדָשׁוֹת: The seven blessings are recited at each of the meals during the seven days of the wedding feast, when new faces are in attendance (Rambam *Sefer Ahava, Hilkhot Berakhot* 2:9–10; *Shulḥan Arukh, Even HaEzer* 62:7).

And if not – וְאִי לָא: When there are no new faces at the meal during the seven days of the wedding feast, only the final marriage blessing: Who has created joy and gladness, is recited. The Rema writes that the prevalent custom is in accordance with those who maintain that this blessing is recited only when there are guests in attendance due to the wedding (Ramban; Ran). However, if they are dining with their family, even that blessing is not recited (Rambam *Sefer Ahava, Hilkhot Berakhot* 2:9–10; *Shulḥan Arukh, Even HaEzer* 62:7).

מִשִּׁבְעָה וְעַד שְׁלֹשִׁים, בֵּין אֲמַר לְהוּ מֵחֲמַת הִלּוּלָא וּבֵין לָא אֲמַר לְהוּ מֵחֲמַת הִלּוּלָא – מְבָרֵךְ ״שֶׁהַשִּׂמְחָה בִּמְעוֹנוֹ״. מִכָּאן וְאֵילָךְ, אִי אֲמַר לְהוּ מֵחֲמַת הִלּוּלָא – מְבָרֵךְ ״שֶׁהַשִּׂמְחָה בִּמְעוֹנוֹ״, וְאִי לָא – לָא.

§ Apropos the wedding blessings, the Gemara continues: **From seven** days after the wedding **until the thirtieth** day, **whether** the groom **said** to the guests that he is inviting them **due to the wedding celebration or whether he did not say to them** that he is inviting them **due to the wedding celebration, he recites the blessing: In Whose dwelling is joy.**[H] **From this** point, thirty days after the wedding, **forward, if he said to them** that he is inviting them **due to the wedding celebration** [*hillula*],[L] **he recites the blessing: In Whose dwelling is joy, and if not, he doesn't.**

וְכִי אֲמַר לְהוּ מֵחֲמַת הִלּוּלָא עַד אֵימַת? אֲמַר רַב פַּפִּי מִשְּׁמֵיהּ דְּרָבָא: עַד תְּרֵיסַר יַרְחֵי שַׁתָּא. וּמֵעִיקָּרָא מֵאֵימַת? אֲמַר רַב פַּפָּא: מִכִּי רָמוּ שַׂעֲרֵי בְּאָסִינְתָּא. אִינִי? וְהָא רַב פַּפָּא אִיעֲסַק לְאַבָּא מָר בְּרֵיהּ, וּבְרֵיךְ מִשְּׁעַת אֵירוּסִין! שָׁאנֵי רַב פַּפָּא דַּהֲוָה טְרִיחַ לֵיהּ.

The Gemara asks: **And when** the groom **said to them** that he is inviting them **due to the wedding celebration, until when** is this blessing recited? **Rav Pappi said in the name of Rava: Until twelve months of the year**[N] have passed since the wedding. Since his legal status remains that of a groom, the blessing: In Whose dwelling is joy, may be recited. The Gemara asks: **And initially,** prior to the wedding, **from when** is that blessing recited? **Rav Pappa**[P] **said: From when they cast barley into the mortar**[NB] to prepare beer for the wedding. The Gemara asks: **Is that so? But didn't Rav Pappa, involve** himself in preparations **for the wedding of his son, Abba Mar, and** begin **reciting the blessing from the time of betrothal? Rav Pappa is different, because** the wedding preparations had already been **prepared for him,** and it was merely a matter of waiting for the designated time to arrive. Therefore, the wedding celebration began for him from the time of betrothal.

רָבִינָא אִיעֲסַק לֵיהּ לִבְרֵיהּ בֵּי רַב חֲבִיבָא, וּבְרֵיךְ מִשְּׁעַת אֵירוּסִין. אֲמַר: קִים לִי בְּגַוַּיְיהוּ דְּלָא הָדְרִי בְּהוּ. לָא אִסְתַּיַּיע מִילְּתָא, וְהָדְרִי בְּהוּ. רַב תַּחְלִיפָא בַּר מַעַרְבָא אִיקְּלַע לְבָבֶל, בְּרֵיךְ שִׁית אֲרִיכָתָא. וְלֵית הִלְכְתָא כְּוָותֵיהּ.

The Gemara relates: **Ravina arranged for his son** to marry a woman from **the house of Rav Ḥaviva and recited the blessing from the time of betrothal. He said: I am certain with regard to them, that they will not retract** their commitment and terminate the betrothal, and the wedding will take place on time. Nevertheless, **the matter was not to be, and** ultimately **they retracted** their commitment, and the wedding was canceled. The Gemara relates: **Rav Taḥlifa, from the West,** i.e., Eretz Yisrael, **happened** to come **to Babylonia,** and he elaborated on the themes of the wedding blessings **and recited six long blessings.**[N] The Gemara concludes: **And the *halakha* is not in accordance with his** opinion. Rather, one must adhere to the formula coined by the Sages.

רַב חֲבִיבָא אִיקְּלַע לְבֵי מְהוּלָא, בְּרֵיךְ ״שֶׁהַשִּׂמְחָה בִּמְעוֹנוֹ״, וְלֵית הִלְכְתָא כְּוָותֵיהּ, מִשּׁוּם דִּטְרִידִי, דְּאִית לֵיהּ צַעֲרָא לְיָנוֹקָא.

It is further related: **Rav Ḥaviva happened** to come **to the house** where **a circumcision** was taking place. He **recited the blessing: In Whose dwelling is joy.**[N] The Gemara concludes: **And the *halakha* is not in accordance with his** opinion. **Since** the parents of the baby **are anxious, as the baby is** experiencing **pain,** it is not appropriate to recite the blessing under those circumstances.

HALAKHA

In Whose dwelling is joy – שֶׁהַשִּׂמְחָה בִּמְעוֹנוֹ: If one dines in the wedding house, he recites in the *zimmun* prior to the Grace after Meals: In Whose dwelling there is joy. According to Rav Pappa, this applies once the preparations for the wedding feast have begun. According to Rav Pappi, this applies within the thirty days after the wedding or at a meal celebrating the marriage throughout the first year of the marriage. If there is a quorum of ten men present, one recites: Our God, in Whose dwelling there is joy. That is the *halakha* as cited in the Gemara. In later times, in the wake of the numerous tragedies that befell the Jewish people, the prevalent custom is to recite: In Whose dwelling there is joy, only during the seven days of the wedding feast. In the case of a widower who married a widow, it is recited only during the first three days of marriage (Rambam *Sefer Ahava, Hilkhot Berakhot* 5:5; *Shulḥan Arukh, Even HaEzer* 62:13, citing *Tur*).

LANGUAGE

Wedding celebration [*hillula*] – הִלּוּלָא: From the Hebrew *hallel*, meaning praise. The Aramaic form, *hillula*, is used specifically for a wedding or a wedding celebration.

NOTES

Until twelve months of the year – עַד תְּרֵיסַר יַרְחֵי שַׁתָּא: The Ritva finds an allusion in the Torah to the fact that the marriage celebration lasts a year: "When a man takes a new wife…he shall be free for his house one year, and shall cheer his wife whom he has taken" (Deuteronomy 24:5).

From when they cast barley into the mortar – מִכִּי רָמוּ שַׂעֲרֵי בְּאָסִינְתָּא: Another explanation is that they would crush the shell of the barley to prepare from it sweet toasted grain, which they would eat at the wedding meal (*Shita Mekubbetzet*).

Recited six long blessings – בְּרֵיךְ שִׁית אֲרִיכָתָא: Rav Hai Gaon explains that the problem was not that Rav Taḥlifa emended or added to the formula of the blessing. Rather, he deviated from the formula coined by the Sages in blessings. He changed short blessings, which do not both begin and conclude with: Blessed, into long blessings, which both begin and conclude with: Blessed.

In Whose dwelling is joy – שֶׁהַשִּׂמְחָה בִּמְעוֹנוֹ: Rav Ḥaviva's reasoning for reciting this blessing was that circumcision is a joyous occasion for the parents of the baby. There are several *halakhot* that reflect that celebratory aspect, e.g., the *taḥanun* prayer is not recited that day. Some proposed reciting this formula at the redemption of the firstborn, where the baby does not experience pain. That was rejected, as it is only with regard to circumcision that there is an allusion in the Bible to special rejoicing (see *Megilla* 16b).

PERSONALITIES

Rav Pappa – רַב פַּפָּא: Rav Pappa was a fifth-generation Babylonian *amora*. He was a student of both Abaye and Rava in Pumbedita. Rav Pappa established an academy in Neresh, where he was joined by his close friend Rav Huna, son of Rav Yehoshua, who delivered the principal lecture. After Rava's death, many of his students came to study with Rav Pappa, and more than two hundred students attended his lectures.

Rav Pappa's father was a wealthy merchant who supported him throughout his many years of study. Rav Pappa became a wealthy businessman in his own right, successful as a brewer of date beer as well as in his other business ventures. The Talmud records that he engaged in trade with both Jews and gentiles and had a reputation for fairness and generosity in his business dealings. Rav Huna, son of Rav Yehoshua, was his partner in many of those and also became wealthy.

Rav Pappa was blessed with ten sons, all of whom were Torah scholars. Traditionally, the names of the ten sons of Rav Pappa are enumerated as part of the formula recited upon completion of the study of a tractate. While the source of this tradition is unclear and the identities of the sons are uncertain, the Rema suggests that it commemorates the celebrations of Rav Pappa and his sons upon completion of a tractate.

BACKGROUND

From when they cast barley into the mortar [*asinta*] – מִכִּי רָמוּ שַׂעֲרֵי בְּאָסִינְתָּא: *Asinta* is a synonym, or perhaps a diminutive, for *asita*, meaning mortar, which is a bowl used in crushing. Rashi cites two possible explanations that appear in geonic literature. One explanation is that the reference is to placing barley seeds into a vessel to soak them in preparation for brewing beer. There is a variant reading: Once the barley is soaked. *Tosafot* on *Avoda Zara* 8b question that explanation because in the talmudic period, beer was brewed from dates, not barley. Furthermore, *Tosafot* note that mortars are not used for soaking.

The second explanation in Rashi, which is also cited in the *Arukh*, is that there was a custom to sow barley seeds before the wedding and to bring the barley sprouts before the bride and groom as an auspicious sign for fertility. The *Arukh* cites an additional explanation: The reference is to crushing barley in the mortar to prepare sweet toasted grain.

אָמַר רַב נַחְמָן אָמַר רַב: חֲתָנִים מִן הַמִּנְיָן, וְאֵין אֲבֵלִים מִן הַמִּנְיָן. מֵיתִיבֵי: חֲתָנִים וַאֲבֵלִים מִן הַמִּנְיָן! מַתְנִיתָא קָא רָמֵית עֲלֵיהּ דְּרַב – רַב תַּנָּא הוּא, וּפָלֵיג. אִיתְּמַר, אָמַר רַבִּי יִצְחָק אָמַר רַבִּי יוֹחָנָן: חֲתָנִים מִן הַמִּנְיָן, וְאֵין אֲבֵלִים מִן הַמִּנְיָן. מֵיתִיבֵי: חֲתָנִים וַאֲבֵלִים מִן הַמִּנְיָן!

§ **Rav Naḥman said** that **Rav said:** With regard to the quorum of ten required to recite the wedding blessings, **grooms are included in the tally.**[NH] **And mourners are not included in the tally** for the blessing of the mourners. The Gemara **raises an objection** from a *baraita*: **Grooms and mourners are included in the tally.** The Gemara responds: **Are you raising a contradiction from a *baraita* against** the opinion of **Rav? Rav himself** had ***tanna*** status **and** therefore, unlike later *amora'im*, could **disagree**[N] with opinions of *tanna'im*. **It was stated: Rabbi Yitzḥak said that Rabbi Yoḥanan said: Grooms are included in the tally, but mourners are not included in the tally. The Gemara raises an objection** from the *baraita* cited above: **Grooms and mourners are included in the tally.**

NOTES

Grooms are included in the tally – **חֲתָנִים מִן הַמִּנְיָן**: The simple reason for this *halakha* is that at the wedding the groom participates in the celebration, and therefore he is included in the tally, as it is written: "And shall cheer his wife whom he has taken" (Deuteronomy 24:5). A mourner does not participate in the comforting of mourners, and therefore he is not included in the tally (*Talmidei Rabbeinu Yona*). An alternative explanation is that a mourner, who is in a state of despondency and sadness, cannot be included in the quorum of ten, where the Divine Presence rests, as the Divine Presence does not rest in an atmosphere of sadness (*Penei Yehoshua*).

Rav himself had *tanna* status and could disagree – **רַב תַּנָּא הוּא וּפָלֵיג**: Rav Hai Gaon writes that in at least three places in the Talmud (see, e.g., *Ketubot* 81a), a *tanna* by the name of Rav Abba is mentioned and the reference is to Rav, indicating that Rav was one of the last *tanna'im* cited in *baraitot*.

HALAKHA

Grooms are included in the tally – **חֲתָנִים מִן הַמִּנְיָן**: The benediction of the grooms is recited only in the presence of a quorum of ten adult males, and the groom himself is included in the tally (Rambam *Sefer Nashim*, *Hilkhot Ishut* 10:5; *Shulḥan Arukh*, *Even HaEzer* 62:4).

Perek **I**
Daf **8** Amud **b**

כִּי תַּנְיָא הַהִיא – בְּבִרְכַּת הַמָּזוֹן, כִּי קָאָמַר רַבִּי יוֹחָנָן – בְּשׁוּרָה.

The Gemara answers: **When that *baraita* is taught,** it is **with regard to** combining with others to form a quorum of three to recite **Grace after Meals,**[H] as a mourner is obligated to recite Grace after Meals. However, **when Rabbi Yoḥanan says** that mourners are not included in the tally, it is **with regard to** the quorum of ten men required to form **a line**[HN] to comfort the mourners following the burial.

וְאֶלָּא הָא דְּאָמַר רַבִּי יִצְחָק אָמַר רַבִּי יוֹחָנָן: מְבָרְכִים בִּרְכַּת חֲתָנִים בַּעֲשָׂרָה – וַחֲתָנִים מִן הַמִּנְיָן, וּבִרְכַּת אֲבֵלִים בַּעֲשָׂרָה – וְאֵין אֲבֵלִים מִן הַמִּנְיָן. בְּרָכָה בְּשׁוּרָה מִי אִיכָּא? אֶלָּא, כִּי קָאָמַר רַבִּי יוֹחָנָן – בִּרְחָבָה.

And the Gemara raises an objection: **However, that which Rabbi Yitzḥak said** that **Rabbi Yoḥanan said: One recites the blessing of the grooms in** a quorum of **ten, and the grooms are included in the tally, and one recites the blessing of the mourners in** a quorum of **ten, and the mourners are not included in the tally. Is there a blessing** recited **in the line** formed to comfort the mourners? Clearly, this statement of Rabbi Yoḥanan cannot be explained as referring to the line. **Rather, when Rabbi Yoḥanan said** that mourners are not included in the tally, it was **with regard to** the blessing recited **in the square**[N] adjacent to the cemetery, where the meal of comfort takes place and various blessings are recited to comfort the mourners. Mourners are not included in the requisite quorum of ten.

וְאֶלָּא הָא דְּאָמַר רַבִּי יִצְחָק אָמַר רַבִּי יוֹחָנָן: מְבָרְכִין בִּרְכַּת חֲתָנִים בַּעֲשָׂרָה כָּל שִׁבְעָה – וַחֲתָנִים מִן הַמִּנְיָן, וּבִרְכַּת אֲבֵלִים בַּעֲשָׂרָה כָּל שִׁבְעָה – וְאֵין אֲבֵלִים מִן הַמִּנְיָן, בִּרְכַּת רְחָבָה כָּל שִׁבְעָה מִי אִיכָּא? מַשְׁכַּחַתְּ לַהּ בְּפָנִים חֲדָשׁוֹת.

The Gemara asks: **However,** with regard to **that which Rabbi Yitzḥak said** that **Rabbi Yoḥanan said: One recites the blessing of the grooms in** a quorum of **ten all seven** days of celebration, **and the grooms are included in the tally; and one recites the blessing of the mourners all seven** days of mourning **in** a quorum of **ten, and the mourners are not included in the tally, is there a blessing** recited **in the square all seven** days? The meal of comfort and the associated blessings take place directly after the burial, not throughout the seven days of mourning. The Gemara answers: **You find** blessings recited throughout the seven-day mourning period **in** a case where **new faces** who did not attend the burial are present.[N] In that case, eulogies and words of comfort are repeated, and the blessing of the mourners is recited again.

HALAKHA

When that *baraita* is taught, it is with regard to Grace after Meals – **כִּי תַּנְיָא הַהִיא בְּבִרְכַּת הַמָּזוֹן**: A mourner is included in the tally of people required in order to recite the *zimmun*, the invitation to Grace After Meals, both for the quorum of three and for the quorum of ten, in accordance with the explanation of Rashi. Some authorities question whether this ruling applies even at the meal of comfort, the first meal eaten by the mourners upon returning from the cemetery after a funeral (see Mordekhai; *Shakh*; *Dagul MeRevava*; Rambam *Sefer Shofetim*, *Hilkhot Evel* 4:6; *Shulḥan Arukh*, *Yoreh De'a* 379:5).

With regard to a line – **בְּשׁוּרָה**: After the burial, only if there is a quorum of ten, not including the mourners, do those assembled stand in a line and offer the mourners words of consolation (Rambam *Sefer Shofetim*, *Hilkhot Evel* 13:1; *Tur*, *Yoreh De'a* 376).

NOTES

With regard to a line – **בְּשׁוּרָה**: Rav Hai Gaon writes that the custom was that after the burial, those comforting the mourners would stand in rows. In the first row, those with the closest ties to the mourner would stand; in the second row, those with ties that were not as close, etc. Each row would consist of at least ten of those providing comfort.

The blessing recited in the square – **בִּרְחָבָה**: During talmudic times, the practice was to perform the rite of standing and sitting in the square next to the cemetery. They would sit and then stand, and sit, and stand again. While they were sitting, and each time they sat, statements of comfort like those cited in the Gemara were said (*ge'onim*).

In a case where new faces are present – **בְּפָנִים חֲדָשׁוֹת**: During festive times, the joy is enhanced when people who did not yet participate in the celebration arrive, and it is therefore appropriate to recite the wedding blessing. So too, when new people come to comfort the mourner, the feelings of mourning are again aroused and statements of comfort are appropriate.

כִּי הָא דְּרַב חִיָּיא בַּר אַבָּא מַקְרֵי בְּנֵיהּ דְּרֵישׁ לָקִישׁ הֲוָה, וְאָמְרִי לַהּ מַתְנֵי בְּרֵיהּ דְּרֵישׁ לָקִישׁ הֲוָה. שְׁכֵיב לֵיהּ יָנוֹקָא. יוֹמָא קַמָּא לָא אֲזַל לְגַבֵּיהּ, לְמָחָר דַּבְרֵיהּ לִיהוּדָה בַּר נַחְמָנִי מְתוּרְגְּמָנֵיהּ, אֲמַר לֵיהּ: קוּם אֵימָא מִלְּתָא כָּל קְבֵיל יָנוֹקָא. פְּתַח וַאֲמַר: ״וַיַּרְא ה׳ וַיִּנְאָץ מִכַּעַס בָּנָיו וּבְנוֹתָיו״, דּוֹר שֶׁאָבוֹת מְנָאֲצִים לְהַקָּדוֹשׁ בָּרוּךְ הוּא – כּוֹעֵס עַל בְּנֵיהֶם וְעַל בְּנוֹתֵיהֶם, וּמֵתִים כְּשֶׁהֵם קְטַנִּים.

§ This is **similar** to **that** incident **involving Rav Ḥiyya bar Abba, who was the Bible teacher of the sons of Reish Lakish, and some say** that he was **the Mishna teacher of the son of Reish Lakish. His child died. On the first day,** Reish Lakish **did not go to** comfort **him. The next day, he took Yehuda bar Naḥmani,**[P] **his disseminator,** with him to comfort Rav Ḥiyya bar Abba. Reish Lakish **said to** his disseminator: **Stand and say a matter** of comfort **with regard to** the death of **the child.**[N] **He began and said: "And the Lord saw it and He abhorred them,**[N] **due to the provocation of His sons and His daughters"** (Deuteronomy 32:19). **A generation in which the fathers abhor the Holy One, Blessed be He, He is angered at their sons and their daughters, and they die when they are small.**

וְאִיכָּא דְּאָמְרִי: בָּחוּר הֲוָה, וְהָכִי קָאָמַר לֵיהּ: ״עַל כֵּן עַל בַּחוּרָיו לֹא יִשְׂמַח ה׳ וְאֶת יְתוֹמָיו וְאֶת אַלְמְנוֹתָיו לֹא יְרַחֵם כִּי כֻלּוֹ חָנֵף וּמֵרַע וְכָל פֶּה דֹּבֵר נְבָלָה בְּכָל זֹאת לֹא שָׁב אַפּוֹ וְעוֹד יָדוֹ נְטוּיָה״, מַאי ״וְעוֹד יָדוֹ נְטוּיָה״? אָמַר רַב חָנָן בַּר רַב: הַכֹּל יוֹדְעִין כַּלָּה לָמָּה נִכְנְסָה לַחוּפָּה, אֶלָּא כָּל הַמְנַבֵּל פִּיו וּמוֹצִיא דְּבַר נְבָלָה מִפִּיו, אֲפִילּוּ נֶחְתַּם לוֹ גְּזַר דִּינוֹ שֶׁל שִׁבְעִים שָׁנָה לְטוֹבָה – נֶהְפָּךְ עָלָיו לְרָעָה.

And there are those who **say** that the child who died **was** not a small child, but **a youth, and this is what** the disseminator **said to him: "Therefore the Lord shall have no joy in their young men, nor shall He have compassion on their orphans and widows, for everyone is a flatterer and an evildoer, and every mouth speaks obscenity. For all this His anger is not turned away, and His hand is still outstretched"** (Isaiah 9:16). **What** is the meaning of the phrase **"And His hand is still outstretched"? Rav Ḥanan bar Rav said: Everyone knows why a bride enters the wedding canopy.**[N] It is the step before consummation of the marriage. **However,** one should not speak about it unnecessarily, as **anyone who profanes his mouth and issues a matter of profanity from his mouth, even if a positive decree of seventy years was sealed for him,** nevertheless, **it is transformed for him into an evil** decree.

אֲתָא לְנַחוּמֵי, צַעוּרֵי קָמְצַעַר לֵיהּ?! הָכִי קָאָמַר לֵיהּ: חָשֵׁיב אַתְּ לְאִתְפּוּסֵי אַדָּרָא.

The Gemara asks about this incident: **He came** at the behest of Reish Lakish **to comfort** Rav Ḥiyya bar Abba **and** instead **he upset him** by attributing the death of his son to his transgressions. The Gemara answers: It was not his intention to upset Rav Ḥiyya bar Abba and to attribute the death of his son to his actions. Rather, **this is what he is saying to him: You are** sufficiently **significant to be seized,** i.e., to die or suffer, **for the** sins of the **generation,** as it is specifically the righteous few who are punished for the transgressions of a sinful generation.

אֲמַר לֵיהּ: קוּם אֵימָא מִלְּתָא כְּנֶגֶד שִׁבְחוֹ שֶׁל הַקָּדוֹשׁ בָּרוּךְ הוּא. פְּתַח וַאֲמַר: הָאֵל הַגָּדוֹל בְּרוֹב גָּדְלוֹ, אַדִּיר וְחָזָק בְּרוֹב נוֹרָאוֹת, מְחַיֶּה מֵתִים בְּמַאֲמָרוֹ, עוֹשֶׂה גְּדוֹלוֹת עַד אֵין חֵקֶר וְנִפְלָאוֹת עַד אֵין מִסְפָּר, בָּרוּךְ אַתָּה ה׳ מְחַיֶּה הַמֵּתִים.

Reish Lakish **said to his** disseminator: **Stand and say a statement with regard to the praiseworthiness of the Holy One, Blessed be He. He began and said: God, Who is great in the abundance of His greatness, mighty and strong in the abundance of His awesome** deeds, **Who revives the dead in** fulfillment of **His statement, Who does great deeds beyond comprehension, wondrous deeds without number. Blessed are You, Lord, Who revives the dead.**

אֲמַר לֵיהּ: קוּם אֵימָא מִלְּתָא כְּנֶגֶד אֲבֵלִים. פְּתַח וַאֲמַר: אַחֵינוּ הַמְיוּגָּעִים הַמְדוּכָּאִין בָּאֵבֶל הַזֶּה, תְּנוּ לְבַבְכֶם לַחֲקוֹר אֶת זֹאת. זֹאת הִיא עוֹמֶדֶת לָעַד, נָתִיב הוּא מִשֵּׁשֶׁת יְמֵי בְרֵאשִׁית, רַבִּים שָׁתוּ רַבִּים יִשְׁתּוּ, כְּמִשְׁתֵּה רִאשׁוֹנִים כָּךְ מִשְׁתֵּה אַחֲרוֹנִים. אַחֵינוּ, בַּעַל נֶחָמוֹת יְנַחֵם אֶתְכֶם, בָּרוּךְ מְנַחֵם אֲבֵלִים.

Reish Lakish **said to him: Stand and say a statement with regard to the mourners. He began and said: Our brothers, who are exhausted, who are overwhelmed by this mourning, set your heart to examine this: This is what stands forever. It is a path from the six days of Creation,** i.e., death exists since Creation, and it is well known that this is the fate of man. **Many have drunk** from the poisonous cup of death, **and many will drink. As** was the consequence of the **drink of the first** who have drunk, **so too** will be the consequence of the **drink of the last** who will drink. **Our brothers, may the Master of solace comfort you. Blessed** are You, Lord, **Who comforts the mourners.**

NOTES

With regard to the death of the child – כָּל קְבֵיל יָנוֹקָא: The Maharsha explains that this is mentioned here because ostensibly, young children are not subject to punishment at all, and those younger than twenty years old are not punished at the hand of Heaven. Therefore, when children suffer, one might have a grievance against God. Consequently, Reish Lakish asked his disseminator to explain that their deaths are attributable to the sins of others.

And the Lord saw it and He abhorred them – וַיַּרְא ה׳ וַיִּנְאָץ: Fundamentally, a minor is not considered an independent individual with personal responsibility who is subject to reward and punishment for his actions. Rather, minors are without sin. Their deaths are merely to torment their relatives.

Everyone knows why a bride enters the wedding canopy – הַכֹּל יוֹדְעִין כַּלָּה לָמָּה נִכְנְסָה לַחוּפָּה: The Maharsha writes that the punishment fits the crime in this case. Anyone who profanes his mouth with regard to the bride entering the wedding canopy will die young before entering the wedding canopy.

PERSONALITIES

Rabbi Yehuda bar Naḥmani – רַבִּי יְהוּדָה בַּר נַחְמָנִי: Rabbi Yehuda bar Naḥmani was also known as Rabbi Yudan, and his father was identified at times as bar Naḥman or bar Neḥemya. He was one of the great homiletic experts of his generation. In addition to his role as disseminator of the Torah of Reish Lakish, both he and his colleague Rabbi Levi would lecture on *aggada* before the congregation, as a prelude to the central lecture of Rabbi Yoḥanan. The Talmud and Midrash cite several homiletic interpretations attributed to him, and he often cited the statements of Reish Lakish.

אֲמַר אַבַּיֵי: ״רַבִּים שָׁתוּ״ – לֵימָא: ״רַבִּים יִשְׁתּוּ״ – לָא לֵימָא. ״מִשְׁתֵּה רִאשׁוֹנִים״ – לֵימָא: ״מִשְׁתֵּה אַחֲרוֹנִים״ – לָא לֵימָא. דְּאֲמַר רַבִּי שִׁמְעוֹן בֶּן לָקִישׁ, וְכֵן תָּנָא מִשְּׁמֵיהּ דְּרַבִּי יוֹסֵי: לְעוֹלָם אַל יִפְתַּח אָדָם פִּיו לַשָּׂטָן. אֲמַר רַב יוֹסֵף: מַאי קְרָא – ״כִּסְדוֹם הָיִינוּ לַעֲמוֹרָה דָּמִינוּ״ מַאי אַהֲדַר לֵיהּ – ״שִׁמְעוּ דְבַר ה׳ קְצִינֵי סְדוֹם״ וגו׳.

Abaye said with regard to the statement concerning the mourners: **Let him say: Many have drunk;**[N] **let him not say: Many will drink. Let him say: The drink of the first; let him not say: The drink of the last.** This is as **Rabbi Shimon ben Lakish said, and likewise it was taught in the name of Rabbi Yosei: A person should never open his mouth to Satan**[N] and speculate about potential disasters. **Rav Yosef said: What is the verse** from which it is derived? **"We should have almost been as Sodom, we should have been like unto Gomorrah"** (Isaiah 1:9), after which, **what did** the prophet **reply to them? "Hear the word of the Lord, rulers of Sodom;** give ear unto the law of our God, people of Gomorrah" (Isaiah 1:10). Isaiah drew the analogy and immediately it was realized.

אֲמַר לֵיהּ: קוּם אֵימָא מִלְּתָא כְּנֶגֶד מְנַחֲמֵי אֲבֵלִים. פְּתַח וַאֲמַר: אַחֵינוּ גּוֹמְלֵי חֲסָדִים בְּנֵי גּוֹמְלֵי חֲסָדִים, הַמַּחֲזִיקִים בִּבְרִיתוֹ שֶׁל אַבְרָהָם אָבִינוּ, (שֶׁנֶּאֱמַר ״כִּי יְדַעְתִּיו לְמַעַן אֲשֶׁר יְצַוֶּה אֶת בָּנָיו״ וגו׳). אַחֵינוּ, בַּעַל הַגְּמוּל יְשַׁלֵּם לָכֶם גְּמוּלְכֶם, בָּרוּךְ אַתָּה מְשַׁלֵּם הַגְּמוּל.

Reish Lakish **said to the disseminator: Stand and say a statement with regard to those who comfort the mourners. He began and said: Our brothers, bestowers of loving-kindness, sons of bestowers of loving-kindness, who embrace the covenant of Abraham our Patriarch, as it is stated: "For I know him, that he will command his children…** to do righteousness and justice" (Genesis 18:19). **Our brothers, may the Master of reward pay you your just deserts. Blessed are You,** Lord, **Who pays the just deserts.**

אֲמַר לֵיהּ: קוּם אֵימָא מִלְּתָא כְּנֶגֶד כָּל יִשְׂרָאֵל. פְּתַח וַאֲמַר: רִבּוֹן הָעוֹלָמִים, פְּדֵה וְהַצֵּל מַלֵּט הוֹשַׁע עַמְּךָ יִשְׂרָאֵל מִן הַדֶּבֶר, וּמִן הַחֶרֶב, וּמִן הַבִּיזָּה, וּמִן הַשִּׁדָּפוֹן, וּמִן הַיֵּרָקוֹן, וּמִכָּל מִינֵי פּוּרְעָנִיּוֹת הַמִּתְרַגְּשׁוֹת וּבָאוֹת לָעוֹלָם. טֶרֶם נִקְרָא וְאַתָּה תַּעֲנֶה, בָּרוּךְ אַתָּה עוֹצֵר הַמַּגֵּפָה.

Reish Lakish **said to the disseminator: Stand and say a statement with regard to the entire Jewish people. He began and said: Master of the worlds, redeem and save, rescue and deliver Your people, Israel, from the pestilence and from the sword, and from spoil, and from the blight, and from the mildew, and from all types of afflictions that suddenly erupt and come to the world. Before we call and You will respond. Blessed are You,** Lord, **Who halts the plague.** Apparently, several blessings are recited on the days following the burial.

אֲמַר עוּלָּא, וְאָמְרִי לָהּ בְּמַתְנִיתָא תָּנָא: עֲשָׂרָה כּוֹסוֹת תִּקְּנוּ חֲכָמִים בְּבֵית הָאָבֵל; שְׁלֹשָׁה קוֹדֶם אֲכִילָה – כְּדֵי לִפְתּוֹחַ אֶת בְּנֵי מֵעָיו, שְׁלֹשָׁה בְּתוֹךְ אֲכִילָה – כְּדֵי לִשְׁרוֹת אֲכִילָה שֶׁבְּמֵעָיו, וְאַרְבָּעָה לְאַחַר אֲכִילָה – אֶחָד כְּנֶגֶד ״הַזָּן״, וְאֶחָד כְּנֶגֶד בִּרְכַּת הָאָרֶץ, וְאֶחָד כְּנֶגֶד ״בּוֹנֵה יְרוּשָׁלַיִם״, וְאֶחָד כְּנֶגֶד ״הַטּוֹב וְהַמֵּטִיב״.

§ In connection with comforting mourners, **Ulla said, and some say that it was taught in a *baraita*: The Sages instituted ten cups of wine**[N] to be drunk **in the house of the mourner:**[H] **Three** cups **prior to the meal, in order to open his intestines,**[B] i.e., whet his appetite; **three during the meal, to soak the food in his intestines** in order to facilitate digestion; **and four** cups **after** the **meal,** each corresponding to a blessing in the Grace after Meals. **One corresponds to** the first blessing: **Who feeds all;**[N] **one corresponds to the** second blessing, the **blessing of the land; one corresponding to the third blessing: Who builds Jerusalem; and one corresponding to** the fourth blessing: **Who is good and does good.**

הוֹסִיפוּ עֲלֵיהֶם אַרְבָּעָה: אֶחָד כְּנֶגֶד חַזָּנֵי הָעִיר, וְאֶחָד כְּנֶגֶד פַּרְנָסֵי הָעִיר, וְאֶחָד כְּנֶגֶד בֵּית הַמִּקְדָּשׁ, וְאֶחָד כְּנֶגֶד רַבָּן גַּמְלִיאֵל. הִתְחִילוּ, הָיוּ שׁוֹתִין וּמִשְׁתַּכְּרִין. הֶחֱזִירוּ הַדָּבָר לְיוֹשְׁנָהּ.

Later, the Sages **added to those four** additional blessings: **One,** noting the actions **of the attendants of the city [*ḥazzanei ha'ir*],**[L] who tend to burials and other communal needs; **one,** noting the actions of **the leaders of the city,** who would provide funding for the burial of the poor; **one, noting the Temple,** commemorating its destruction; **and one,** noting the actions of **Rabban Gamliel.** The people **began** observing this ordinance instituted by the Sages, **and they would drink and become intoxicated.** Therefore, the Sages **restored the matter to its previous** status[N] and established that they drink no more than ten cups.

NOTES

Many have drunk – רַבִּים שָׁתוּ: Some explain that this dispute is dependent on the question of whether, at the end of days, when people will live much longer, death will still exist. Abaye was of the opinion that at that time death will no longer exist. Therefore, the expression that death is ubiquitous is inappropriate (*Iyyun Ya'akov*).

A person should never open his mouth to Satan – לְעוֹלָם אַל יִפְתַּח אָדָם פִּיו לַשָּׂטָן: When a person explicitly makes a statement about some event, he thereby prepares himself psychologically for its occurrence. He thereby renders it a genuine possibility, enhancing its potential for realization. Therefore, one should avoid speaking badly about himself (Maharsha).

Ten cups of wine – עֲשָׂרָה כּוֹסוֹת: It appears from the commentary of Rashi and the Meiri that the ten cups mentioned here are considered obligatory, to ease the pain of the mourner. However, from the comments of the Rambam and others, it appears that it was not required, although the custom was to drink one cup of wine.

One corresponding to the first blessing: Who feeds all – אֶחָד כְּנֶגֶד הַזָּן וכו׳: The Ritva writes that there is an inherent connection between each of the blessings and mourning. The first blessing: Who feeds all, states that God provides sustenance to all His creations. The request for sustenance is therefore a request for life. The second blessing, the blessing of the land, reflects the verse: "So that your days will be lengthened…upon the land which the Lord swore unto your fathers to give them" (Deuteronomy 11:21). The third blessing: Who builds Jerusalem, is connected to mourning because it written that with the restoration of Zion: "He will swallow up death forever" (Isaiah 25:8). The fourth blessing: Who is good and does good, was instituted in praise of God for the fact that those massacred in Beitar were ultimately buried. According to the variant reading of the Vilna Gaon, this passage is omitted. He explains that perhaps the four cups were instituted parallel to the four blessings of consolation spoken by the disseminator.

The Sages restored the matter to its previous status – הֶחֱזִירוּ הַדָּבָר לְיוֹשְׁנָהּ: According to Rashi and the Rambam, the explanation is that they restored the custom of drinking ten cups and no more. The Ramban, the Rashba, the Ritva, and Rabbi Aharon HaLevi explain that they restored the custom that the mourner drinks wine only during the meal, and they do not drink ten cups, and this is the prevalent custom.

HALAKHA

The Sages instituted ten cups of wine in the house of the mourner – עֲשָׂרָה כּוֹסוֹת תִּקְּנוּ חֲכָמִים בְּבֵית הָאָבֵל: According to the Rambam, mourners may not drink more than ten cups of wine each: Three prior to the meal, three during the meal, and four after the meal. They may drink no more than that lest they get drunk. The *Beit Yosef* notes that according to the Rambam there is no obligation to drink ten cups of wine. There is merely a prohibition against drinking more than that quantity. The *Shulḥan Arukh*, based on the Rambam (*Sefer Shofetim*, *Hilkhot Evel* 4:6), rules that after the burial, the mourner is permitted to drink a small amount of wine in order to facilitate digestion, but not enough to become drunk (Rambam *Sefer Shofetim*, *Hilkhot Evel* 13:8; *Shulḥan Arukh*, *Yoreh De'a* 378:8).

BACKGROUND

To open his intestines – לִפְתּוֹחַ אֶת בְּנֵי מֵעָיו: A small amount of wine stimulates secretion of stomach enzymes and thereby whets the appetite. That quality, along with its ability to ease inhibitions, makes wine an ideal drink for a mourner. Mourning often suppresses one's appetite, and eating and drinking help the mourner deal with the emotional strain of his mourning.

LANGUAGE

Attendants of the city [*ḥazzanei ha'ir*] – חַזָּנֵי הָעִיר: In the Talmud and the Mishna, the word *ḥazzan* means a caretaker, one responsible for upkeep and seeing to the needs of a particular place. In this vein, there is a *ḥazzan* in a synagogue, in the court, and in the city.

There are several opinions with regard to the source of the word. According to early authorities, it comes from the word *ḥaza*, meaning one who sees or oversees the particular needs of a certain place (*Dunash*). Others associate the word with the Akkadian ahazan, meaning officer, because the *ḥazzan* would fill the role of the local police and low-level government officials. Here too, the reference is to attendants, among whose tasks was dealing with the burial of the dead.

The use of the term *ḥazzan* in the exclusive sense of prayer leader in the synagogue is a later phenomenon, although it appears in medieval Jewish literature. Perhaps one of the duties of the *ḥazzan* in ancient times was that of prayer leader.

מַאי רַבָּן גַּמְלִיאֵל? דְּתַנְיָא: בָּרִאשׁוֹנָה הָיְתָה הוֹצָאַת הַמֵּת קָשָׁה לִקְרוֹבָיו יוֹתֵר מִמִּיתָתוֹ, עַד שֶׁהָיוּ מַנִּיחִים אוֹתוֹ וּבוֹרְחִין. עַד שֶׁבָּא רַבָּן גַּמְלִיאֵל וְנָהַג קַלּוּת בְּעַצְמוֹ, וְהוֹצִיאוּהוּ בִּכְלֵי פִשְׁתָּן. וְנָהֲגוּ כָּל הָעָם אַחֲרָיו לְהוֹצִיא בִּכְלֵי פִשְׁתָּן, אָמַר רַב פַּפָּא: וְהָאִידָּנָא נְהוּג עָלְמָא אֲפִילּוּ בְּצַרְדָּא בַּר זוּזָא.

What is the connection between **Rabban Gamliel** and a house of mourning? It is **as it is taught** in a *baraita*: **Initially, the funeral** expenditures **for the deceased were more taxing for his relatives than his death,** as the burials were opulent, **until** it reached a point where people **would abandon the deceased and flee.** This continued **until Rabbi Gamliel came and conducted himself in a self-deprecatory** manner, instructing the people that they were **to take him** for burial **in** plain **linen garments. And all the people conducted themselves following his** example, and instructed their families **to take** them for burial **in** plain **linen garments.**[H] **Rav Pappa said: And today, everyone is accustomed** to bury the dead in plain garments, **even in rough cloth** [*tzerada*][L] **worth one** *zuz*.

אָמַר רַבִּי אֶלְעָזָר:

Rabbi Elazar said:

HALAKHA

And all the people conducted themselves following his example and instructed to take them for burial in linen garments – וְנָהֲגוּ כָּל הָעָם אַחֲרָיו לְהוֹצִיא בִּכְלֵי פִשְׁתָּן: The prevalent custom is to bury the deceased in white linen shrouds, as per the allusion in the Gemara. The Rambam writes that according to the custom of the Sages, the shrouds should be worth no more than a dinar. However, if one wants to add to that sum, he is not reprimanded (Radbaz; Rambam *Sefer Shofetim, Hilkhot Evel* 4:1; *Shulḥan Arukh, Yoreh De'a* 352:2).

LANGUAGE

Rough cloth [*tzerada*] – צַרְדָּא: In the *Arukh*, this word is written *tzedara*. It is apparently related to the Middle Persian čādur, meaning a veil.

Perek **I**
Daf **9** Amud **a**

הָאוֹמֵר ״פֶּתַח פָּתוּחַ מָצָאתִי״ – נֶאֱמָן לְאוֹסְרָהּ עָלָיו.

A groom **who says: I encountered an unobstructed orifice,**[HN] claiming that when he consummated the marriage he discovered that his bride was not a virgin, **is credible**[N] **to render her forbidden to himself.** Although it is not always possible to corroborate his claim with testimony that his wife committed adultery after betrothal, he is credible to render her forbidden to him as though she had in fact committed adultery.

וְאַמַּאי? סְפֵק סְפֵיקָא הוּא: סָפֵק תַּחְתָּיו סָפֵק אֵין תַּחְתָּיו, וְאִם תִּמְצָא לוֹמַר תַּחְתָּיו – סָפֵק בְּאוֹנֶס סָפֵק בְּרָצוֹן!

The Gemara asks: **But why** is she forbidden to him? It **is** a case of **compound uncertainty.**[N] It is **uncertain** whether she engaged in intercourse while **under his** jurisdiction, after betrothal, in which case she would be forbidden to him, and it is **uncertain** whether she engaged in intercourse while **not under his** jurisdiction, in which case she would not be forbidden to him. **And if you say** that she engaged in intercourse while **under his** jurisdiction, it is **uncertain** whether she engaged in intercourse **by coercion,** in which case she would not be forbidden to him, and it is **uncertain** whether she engaged in intercourse **willingly,** in which case she would be forbidden to him. In cases of compound uncertainty, the ruling is lenient. Why, then, is his claim deemed credible?

HALAKHA

A groom who says: I encountered an unobstructed orifice – הָאוֹמֵר פֶּתַח פָּתוּחַ מָצָאתִי: If a priest betroths a woman, marries her after a period of time, and claims that he discovered that his wife was not a virgin when consummating the marriage, then the woman is forbidden to him, as there is only one uncertainty, whether she lost her virginity before or after she was betrothed to her husband. However, if the man is not a priest, the woman is permitted to her husband, as there is compound uncertainty: Did she lose her virginity before or after betrothal? And even if she lost her virginity after betrothal, it may have been by means of rape, in which case she is not forbidden to her non-priest husband (Rambam *Sefer Kedusha, Hilkhot Issurei Bia* 18:10; *Shulḥan Arukh, Even HaEzer* 68:7).

NOTES

I encountered an unobstructed orifice – פֶּתַח פָּתוּחַ מָצָאתִי: A fundamental question addressed by all the early commentaries is: What of the bleeding that accompanies rupture of the hymen? The presence or absence of blood clearly indicates whether or not a woman is a virgin. Rashi explains that perhaps the Gemara is referring to a woman from a family where the women do not bleed from a ruptured hymen, or perhaps the sheet was lost and it cannot be ascertained whether or not there was bleeding. Rabbeinu Ḥananel explains that the Gemara is dealing with a grown woman who does not bleed, although her hymen is intact (see *Tosafot*). The Ramban explains that even if there was bleeding, the groom could claim that it was the result of a wound or deceit. The Meiri adds that he could claim that it was menstrual blood.

With regard to the case itself, the groom is making a claim that cannot be corroborated by witnesses. Therefore, the matter is entirely dependent on the credibility of the husband and whether he is sufficiently knowledgeable to ascertain the matter.

Credible – נֶאֱמָן: The early commentaries write that the groom is accorded credibility specifically when the bride denies the matter, claiming that she is a virgin and the husband is falsely accusing her, or when she remains silent. However, if she can explain the lack of a hymen by claiming that she was raped or that she engaged in intercourse before betrothal, or that her hymen was ruptured by a foreign object, she is accorded credibility not only with regard to monetary claims, i.e., that she does not lose the right to payment of the marriage contract, but also with regard to the prohibition, i.e., she is not forbidden to her husband as an adulteress. This is because the husband's claim is not a certain one, as even if it is true that the orifice was unobstructed, he can only speculate how that came to be, while hers is a certain claim.

The early commentaries also question why the court doesn't make one of those effective claims on her behalf if she remains silent. They answer that the court does not do so because those occurrences are rare.

It is a case of compound uncertainty – סְפֵק סְפֵיקָא הוּא: This principle that the ruling is lenient in cases where there are multiple elements of uncertainty is unique to the Babylonian Talmud. According to the Jerusalem Talmud, she remains forbidden to him, just as she is in the case of *sota*, where he suspects that she committed adultery, although he is not accorded credibility to prohibit her to others or to void her marriage contract.

Various explanations were proposed with regard to the reason that the ruling is lenient in cases of compound uncertainty. The Rambam is of the opinion that in any case of uncertainty with regard to a Torah prohibition, the ruling is lenient by Torah law. The stringent ruling in those cases is by rabbinic law. Therefore, the second uncertainty is uncertainty with regard to a rabbinic prohibition, in which case the ruling is lenient.

According to *Tosafot*, who maintain that in any case of uncertainty with regard to a Torah prohibition the ruling is stringent by Torah law, the reason for leniency in the case of compound uncertainty is, according to the Rashba, based on the principle of majority. Since any uncertainty is essentially an equally balanced uncertainty, with each possibility carrying a probability of 50 percent, the second uncertainty, which is based on one of those possibilities, carries with it only a 25 percent probability of prohibition. The *Shakh*, in his summary of the principles of compound uncertainty (*Yoreh De'a* 110), writes that not every case of multiple uncertainties has the legal status of a compound uncertainty. In addition, based on the modern discipline of statistics and probability, there are cases where the elements of uncertainty are factored together and others where they are not. Later authorities greatly elaborate on this topic, conceptually and practically.

לָא צְרִיכָא בְּאֵשֶׁת כֹּהֵן. וְאִיבָּעֵית אֵימָא בְּאֵשֶׁת יִשְׂרָאֵל, וּכְגוֹן דְּקַבֵּיל בָּהּ אֲבוּהּ קִידּוּשִׁין פְּחוּתָה מִבַּת שָׁלֹשׁ שָׁנִים וְיוֹם אֶחָד.

No, it is necessary to teach this ruling only **in the case of the wife of a priest,**[N] who is rendered forbidden to her husband even if she engaged in intercourse by coercion. In that case, there is a single uncertainty. **And if you wish, say** instead that this ruling is relevant **even to the wife of an Israelite, and** it is in a case **where her father accepted** her **betrothal** when she was **less than three years and one day old.**[H] Intercourse with a girl less than three years old does not permanently rupture the hymen, and therefore there is no uncertainty whether she engaged in intercourse before or after betrothal. Clearly, it took place after betrothal, and there is only one uncertainty: Did she engage in intercourse by coercion or willingly?

מַאי קָא מַשְׁמַע לָן? תְּנֵינָא. הָאוֹמֵר לְאִשָּׁה ״קִדַּשְׁתִּיךְ״. וְהִיא אוֹמֶרֶת ״לֹא קִדַּשְׁתַּנִי״ – הִיא מוּתֶּרֶת בִּקְרוֹבָיו, וְהוּא אָסוּר בִּקְרוֹבוֹתֶיהָ!

The Gemara asks: If this is a case where there is only one uncertainty, **what is it teaching us? We** already **learned** this explicitly: With regard to **a man who says to a woman: I betrothed you,**[H] **and she says: You did not betroth me,** and there are no witnesses to corroborate either claim, **she is permitted to** marry any of **his relatives,** e.g., his brother, because based on her claim they are not related. **And** it is **prohibited** for **him to** marry **her relatives,** as based on his claim she is his betrothed. Apparently, one is capable of creating a prohibition for himself without corroborating witnesses.

מַהוּ דְּתֵימָא: הָתָם וַדַּאי קִים לֵיהּ, אֲבָל הָכָא – מִיקַּם הוּא דְּלָא קִים לֵיהּ, קָא מַשְׁמַע לָן.

The Gemara says that it was necessary to teach the case of the claim of virginity, **lest you say: There, where certainly** it is **clear to him** that he betrothed her, it is prohibited for him to marry her relatives. **However, here,** perhaps it is **not clear to him** that she was not a virgin, as he is not experienced in these matters and is mistaken. Therefore, Rabbi Elazar **teaches us** that his claim is nevertheless credible and she is forbidden to him.

וּמִי אָמַר רַבִּי אֶלְעָזָר הָכִי? וְהָאָמַר רַבִּי אֶלְעָזָר: אֵין הָאִשָּׁה נֶאֱסֶרֶת עַל בַּעְלָהּ: אֶלָּא עַל עִסְקֵי קִינּוּי וּסְתִירָה, וּכְמַעֲשֶׂה שֶׁהָיָה!

And did Rabbi Elazar say that? But didn't Rabbi Elazar say: A woman is forbidden to her husband due to adultery, **only over matters of jealous warning and seclusion,**[N] **and as** it was in **the incident that transpired**[N] involving David and Bathsheba? A wife is forbidden to her husband only in a case where he warns her not to seclude herself with a certain man and witnesses testify that she subsequently entered into seclusion with him.

וְתִסְבְּרָא, מַעֲשֶׂה שֶׁהָיָה בְּקִינּוּי וּסְתִירָה הֲוָה?! וְעוֹד: מִי אֲסָרוּהָ?

And how can **you understand** it in that manner? **Was the incident that transpired with jealous warning and seclusion? Furthermore, did** the Sages **render** Bathsheba **forbidden** to her husband? Had she been forbidden to her husband, she would have also been forbidden to David, based on the following principle: Just as an adulteress is forbidden to her husband, she is also forbidden to her paramour.

הָא לָא קַשְׁיָא; הָכִי קָאָמַר: אֵין הָאִשָּׁה נֶאֱסֶרֶת עַל בַּעְלָהּ אֶלָּא עַל עִסְקֵי קִינּוּי וּסְתִירָה, מִמַּעֲשֶׂה שֶׁהָיָה דְּלָא הֲוָה קִינּוּי וּסְתִירָה, וְלָא אִיתַּסְרָא. מִכָּל מָקוֹם קַשְׁיָא: קִינּוּי וּסְתִירָה – אִין, פֶּתַח פָּתוּחַ – לָא!

That is **not difficult,** as **this is** what Rabbi Elazar **is saying:** The fact that **a woman is forbidden to her husband** due to adultery **only over matters of jealous warning and seclusion** is derived **from the incident that transpired** involving David and Bathsheba, **as there was no jealous warning and seclusion,** and therefore **she was not forbidden** to her husband. **In any case,** it is **difficult,** as the statements of Rabbi Elazar are contradictory. It may be inferred: By means of **jealous warning and seclusion, yes,** a man renders his wife forbidden to him; by means of the claim that he encountered **an unobstructed orifice, no,** he does not render her forbidden.

וּלְטַעֲמִיךְ, קִינּוּי וּסְתִירָה – אִין, עֵדִים – לָא?!

The Gemara rejects that inference: **And** according **to your reasoning,** that the statement of Rabbi Elazar restricts to jealous warning and seclusion the manner in which a husband can render his wife forbidden, infer: By means of **jealous warning and seclusion, yes,** a man renders his wife forbidden to him; by means of the testimony of two **witnesses** that she engaged in adulterous relations, **no,** he does not render her forbidden. That cannot be so, as clearly two witnesses establish her as one who committed adultery and render her forbidden to her husband.

NOTES

In the case of the wife of a priest – בְּאֵשֶׁת כֹּהֵן: The Ramban asks: Why is there not a compound uncertainty in this case as well, as, even if the women's hymen were ruptured after betrothal, perhaps it was ruptured by a foreign object and she is permitted to her husband? He answers that there is an additional reason to rule stringently, as, even if the hymen were ruptured before betrothal, a woman who had relations with one disqualified from entering the congregation of Israel renders her forbidden to a priest. Others answer that, as cited previously, the possibility that her hymen was ruptured by a foreign object is uncommon and therefore cannot be classified as an uncertainty. The early commentaries discuss at length whether or not that circumstance is uncommon.

Only over matters of jealous warning and seclusion – אֶלָּא עַל עִסְקֵי קִינּוּי וּסְתִירָה: The Ritva proves at length that this statement is not to be taken literally. If it were to be taken literally, even if a man actually witnessed his wife committing adultery she would not be forbidden to him. He therefore explains that the Gemara means that in a case of uncertainty, where there is no full-fledged testimony that she committed adultery, a woman is rendered forbidden to her husband only through warning followed by seclusion. Others reject his proof and explain that perhaps Rabbi Elazar maintains that by Torah law a woman is rendered forbidden to her husband only by means of the testimony of witnesses, and the Gemara can be explained that in bringing his wife to court, the matter will be publicized and witnesses will come to testify against her (Rabbi Akiva Eiger).

And as it was in the incident that transpired – וּכְמַעֲשֶׂה שֶׁהָיָה: Rabbeinu Ḥananel explains that there is a tradition that the incident in question is the incident involving David and Bathsheba, and the reference is obscure in deference to David. He adds that the correct understanding of the Gemara is: Either over matters of jealous warning and seclusion or as it was in the incident that transpired.

HALAKHA

In a case where her father accepted her betrothal when she was less than three years and one day old – וּכְגוֹן דְּקַבֵּיל בָּהּ אֲבוּהּ קִידּוּשִׁין פְּחוּתָה מִבַּת שָׁלֹשׁ שָׁנִים וְיוֹם אֶחָד: If a man accepts betrothal on behalf of his daughter when she is less than three years and one day old, and if her husband claims that when consummating the marriage he discovered that his wife is not a virgin, she is forbidden to her husband. In that case, there is only one uncertainty: Whether or not she was raped. She could not have lost her virginity before betrothal, as the hymen of a girl younger than three years old does not rupture (Rambam *Sefer Kedusha, Hilkhot Issurei Bia* 18:11; *Shulḥan Arukh, Even HaEzer* 68:7).

A man who says to a woman: I betrothed you – הָאוֹמֵר לְאִשָּׁה קִדַּשְׁתִּיךְ: If a man says to a woman that he betrothed her in the presence of two witnesses who are currently unavailable to testify, e.g., they died or moved, and she claims that she had never been betrothed to him, it is prohibited for him to marry any of her relatives, e.g., her mother or sister, but it is permitted for her to marry any of his relatives (Rambam *Sefer Nashim, Hilkhot Ishut* 9:15–16; *Shulḥan Arukh, Even HaEzer* 48:5).

אֶלָּא הָכִי קָאָמַר: אֵין הָאִשָּׁה נֶאֱסֶרֶת עַל בַּעְלָהּ בְּעֵד אֶחָד אֶלָּא בִּשְׁנֵי עֵדִים, וְקִינּוּי וּסְתִירָה – אֲפִילּוּ בְּעֵד אֶחָד נַמִּי, וּפֶתַח פָּתוּחַ – כִּשְׁנֵי עֵדִים דָּמֵי.

The Gemara explains: **Rather, this is** what Rabbi Elazar **is saying: A woman is not rendered forbidden to her husband through** the testimony of **one witness. Rather,** she is rendered forbidden **only by means of** the testimony of **two witnesses**[H] who testify that she engaged in adulterous relations. **And** if there was **jealous warning and seclusion,** she is rendered forbidden **even by means of** the testimony of **one witness as well,**[H] if he comes after the husband warned his wife and testifies that she engaged in adulterous relations. **And** the legal status of the claim: I encountered **an unobstructed orifice,** is **like** that of **two witnesses,** and it renders her forbidden even without jealous warning and seclusion.

וְכִי תֵּימָא: מַעֲשֶׂה שֶׁהָיָה מִפְּנֵי מָה לֹא אֲסָרוּהָ – הָתָם אוֹנֶס הֲוָה. וְאִיבָּעֵית אֵימָא, כִּי הָא דְּאָמַר רַבִּי שְׁמוּאֵל בַּר נַחְמָנִי אָמַר רַבִּי יוֹנָתָן:

And if you would say with regard to **the incident that transpired** involving David and Bathsheba: **For what** reason did the Sages **not deem her forbidden,** when clearly David committed adultery with a married woman? The Gemara answers: **There it was rape,** and she did not engage in intercourse willingly. **And if you wish, say** instead[N] that the Sages did not deem her forbidden, **as that which Rabbi Shmuel bar Naḥmani said** that **Rabbi Yonatan said:**

HALAKHA

A woman is not rendered forbidden to her husband… Rather, only by means of the testimony of two witnesses – אֵין הָאִשָּׁה נֶאֱסֶרֶת עַל בַּעְלָהּ...אֶלָּא בִּשְׁנֵי עֵדִים: Although the Sages said that one who notices improper conduct in his wife, leading him to the conclusion that his wife committed adultery, is obligated to divorce her, the court compels him to divorce her only when there are two witnesses who testify that they saw the woman committing adultery of her own volition (Rambam *Sefer Nashim, Hilkhot Ishut* 24:18; *Tur, Even HaEzer* 115; *Shulḥan Arukh, Even HaEzer* 11:1).

And if there was jealous warning and seclusion, even by means of the testimony of one witness as well – וְקִינּוּי וּסְתִירָה אֲפִילּוּ בְּעֵד אֶחָד נַמִּי: If a man grows suspicious of his wife and warns her not to enter into seclusion with a specific man, then even if only a single witness testifies that she engaged in relations with that man, she does not drink the ritual water of a *sota*, but rather he divorces her immediately and she does not receive payment of her marriage contract. This is the case even if the witness is one who is ordinarily disqualified from giving testimony, e.g., a relative (Rambam *Sefer Nashim, Hilkhot Sota* 1:14–15; *Shulḥan Arukh, Even HaEzer* 178:14).

NOTES

And if you wish, say instead – וְאִיבָּעֵית אֵימָא: There is a practical halakhic difference between these two answers. According to the first, since a woman who is raped is not forbidden to her husband, after her husband dies she would be permitted to the rapist. Although the rapist raped her intentionally, the reason that a woman who commits adultery is forbidden to her paramour is based only on her being forbidden to her husband (*Beit Shmuel*). Others add that this is dependent on a tannaitic dispute (*Sota* 28a) with regard to the source of her prohibition to her paramour. If it is derived from an amplification in the verse that prohibits her to the husband, then she is not forbidden to the rapist since she is not forbidden to her husband. However, if there is an independent source for her prohibition to the paramour, it is entirely possible that she is forbidden to the rapist even in the absence of a prohibition to her husband, if he has died (*Ḥatam Sofer*).

Perek **I**
Daf **9** Amud **b**

כָּל הַיּוֹצֵא לְמִלְחֶמֶת בֵּית דָּוִד גֵּט כְּרִיתוּת כּוֹתֵב לְאִשְׁתּוֹ, דִּכְתִיב ״וְאֶת אַחֶיךָ תִּפְקֹד לְשָׁלוֹם וְאֶת עֲרֻבָּתָם תִּקָּח״. מַאי ״וְאֶת עֲרֻבָּתָם תִּקָּח״ – תָּנֵי רַב יוֹסֵף: דְּבָרִים הַמְעוֹרָבִין בֵּינוֹ לְבֵינָהּ.

Anyone who goes to a war waged by the royal **house of David writes a** conditional **bill of divorce to his wife.**[N] This was done to prevent a situation in which the wife of the soldier would be unable to remarry because her husband did not return from battle and there were no witnesses with regard to his fate. The conditional bill of divorce accorded the wife the status of a divorcée and freed her to remarry, **as it is written: "And to your brothers bring greetings and take their pledge [*arubatam*]"** (I Samuel 17:18).[N] **What is** the meaning of: **And take *arubatam*? Rav Yosef taught:** It is referring to **matters that are shared [*hame'oravin*] between** the husband **and** his wife, i.e., marriage. Since apparently it was customary for men at war to send their wives a conditional divorce, and since Uriah later died, Bathsheba assumed divorced status retroactively from the time that he set out to war. Therefore, she was not forbidden to David.

NOTES

Writes a conditional bill of divorce to his wife – גֵּט כְּרִיתוּת כּוֹתֵב לְאִשְׁתּוֹ: From Rashi's explanation, it appears that this was a bill of divorce that was given conditionally, to take effect if the husband dies at war, to spare his wife the obligation to enter into levirate marriage with her brother-in-law. The question is raised: If that is its purpose, it affects only a small segment of the population, i.e., men with a brother and no children. Rather, to prevent their wives from assuming the status of a deserted wife, all those going out to war would write a conditional bill of divorce that would take effect retroactively from the time the bill of divorce was written (*Tosafot*; Ramban).

Another problem discussed is with regard to the legal status of the wife between receipt of the bill of divorce and the husband's failure to return. *Tosafot* note that there is a tannaitic dispute whether during that interim period the woman is considered married or divorced. Apparently, according to the opinion in the Gemara that Uriah gave his wife a conditional bill of divorce, it is determined retroactively that she was not married in the interim. However, many authorities question that from the statement in *Bava Metzia* (59a), where Bathsheba is characterized, even according to that opinion, as a woman whose marital status is uncertain, not a woman who is considered divorced and permitted.

Tosafot explain simply that at the time that David had relations with Bathsheba, there was uncertainty with regard to whether or not Uriah would return. The Ramban explains that although the matter was ultimately resolved, David did not know what the resolution would be when he engaged in relations with Bathsheba. Therefore, ostensibly he engaged in relations with a woman whose marital status is uncertain.

Rabbeinu Tam (see *Tosafot*) explains the Gemara in its plain sense, as follows: Those going to war, who were uncertain about their fate, would write an unconditional bill of divorce and divorce their wives; upon their return, they betrothed and married them a second time. Therefore, David did not commit even an uncertain transgression; nevertheless, taking Uriah's wife before it became clear that Uriah died in battle was despicable.

As it is written…and take their pledge – דִּכְתִיב...וְאֶת עֲרֻבָּתָם תִּקָּח: Although this verse is written with regard to the wars of King Saul, apparently it was the custom of Yishai, David's father. When David assumed the throne, he taught this practice to all his troops (Ritva; see Rashi).

אֲמַר אַבַּיֵי: אַף אֲנַן נַמִּי תְּנֵינָא, בְּתוּלָה נִשֵּׂאת לְיוֹם הָרְבִיעִי. לְיוֹם רְבִיעִי – אִין, לְיוֹם חֲמִישִׁי – לָא, מַאי טַעֲמָא – מִשּׁוּם אִיקְּרוּרֵי דַּעְתָּא.

§ Apropos the credibility of the claim: I encountered an unobstructed orifice, **Abaye said: We, too, learn** in the mishna proof for the opinion of Rabbi Elazar: **A virgin is married on Wednesday.** Abaye infers: **On Wednesday, yes,** a virgin is married; **on Thursday, no,**[N] she is not married. **What is the reason** for this ruling? It is **due to** the fact **that** if the marriage were to be held on Thursday, several days would elapse before the court would next convene, and in the interim **his resolve will cool**[N] and his anger subside. The concern is that consequently he will fail to claim before the court that his bride was not a virgin.

וּלְמַאי? אִי לְמֵיתַב לָהּ כְּתוּבָּה – נֵיתִיב לָהּ, אֶלָּא לְאוֹסְרָהּ עָלָיו, וּדְקָא טָעֵין טַעֲנָה.

The Gemara asks: **And for what** matter is that a source of concern? **If** the concern is with regard **to giving her** payment for her **marriage contract,** i.e., if he fails to go to court, her legal status at the time of marriage will remain that of a virgin, and when the time comes she will receive payment for her marriage contract to which she is not entitled; then **let him give** it **to her** if he wishes. Why is that a concern? **Rather,** it is with regard **to rendering her forbidden to him, and** that would result in a case **where he makes a claim.**

מַאי לָאו דְּקָטָעֵין טַעֲנַת "פֶּתַח פָּתוּחַ"! לָא, דְּקָטָעֵין טַעֲנַת דָּמִים.

What, is it not referring to a case **where he makes the claim:** I encountered **an unobstructed orifice,** after engaging in intercourse with his bride, and his claim is accorded credibility to render her forbidden to him in accordance with the opinion of Rabbi Elazar? The Gemara rejects that proof: **No,** it can be explained that it is a case **where he makes the claim** that there was no **blood,**[NHB] which would have resulted from rupture of the hymen had she been a virgin. That is a claim based on objective, verifiable evidence and not merely dependent on his subjective sensation.

אָמַר רַב יְהוּדָה אָמַר שְׁמוּאֵל: הָאוֹמֵר "פֶּתַח פָּתוּחַ מָצָאתִי" נֶאֱמָן לְהַפְסִידָהּ כְּתוּבָּתָהּ. אֲמַר רַב יוֹסֵף: מַאי קָא מַשְׁמַע לַן? תְּנֵינָא: הָאוֹכֵל אֵצֶל חָמִיו בִּיהוּדָה שֶׁלֹּא בְּעֵדִים – אֵינוֹ יָכוֹל לִטְעוֹן טַעֲנַת בְּתוּלִים, מִפְּנֵי שֶׁמִּתְיַיחֵד עִמָּהּ. בִּיהוּדָה הוּא דְּלָא מָצֵי טָעֵין, הָא בַּגָּלִיל – מָצֵי טָעֵין.

§ **Rav Yehuda said** that **Shmuel said** that a groom **who says: I encountered an unobstructed orifice, is deemed credible** with regard **to causing her to lose her marriage contract.**[N] **Rav Yosef said: What is he teaching us? We** already **learned** explicitly in a mishna (12a): A man **who eats at** the house of **his father-in-law in Judea** after betrothal, **without witnesses** to attest to the fact that he was not alone with her, **cannot make a claim about** his bride's **virginity** after marriage, **because** in accordance with the custom in Judea, the assumption is **that he secluded himself with her** and it was he who engaged in intercourse with her. The Gemara infers: It is **in Judea that he cannot claim** that she is not a virgin, **but in the Galilee, he can claim** that this is the case.

NOTES

On Thursday, no – לְיוֹם חֲמִישִׁי לָא: Some ask: Why is this inference necessary, when the reason for this ordinance, i.e., to enable him to go to court the next day and make the claim concerning virginity, is articulated explicitly in the mishna? Rashi explains that if the groom marries on Thursday, he would need to wait several days until Monday.

The *Shita Mekubbetzet* cites an explanation why Thursday is emphasized rather than simply another day: The blessing to procreate, "Be fruitful, and multiply" (Genesis 1:22), was first stated on Thursday, and therefore one might think that marriage can be held on Thursday. Even so, the Sages insisted that a virgin should marry specifically on Wednesday. The inference was necessary to prove that the Sages were concerned that the groom's resolve will cool, and therefore it is clear that they were concerned due to the prohibition.

His resolve will cool – אִיקְּרוּרֵי דַּעְתָּא: The distinction between the claim of an unobstructed orifice and a claim that there was no blood from the rupture of the hymen is that in the former case the groom lacks confidence in his claim and is concerned that perhaps he is mistaken, either due to his lack of sexual experience or due to his lack of familiarity with a woman's body. Therefore, with the passage of time, if he grows fond of his bride, or as it is phrased in the Jerusalem Talmud, his acquisition is pleasant in his eyes, the feeling he had when he consummated the marriage and discovered an unobstructed orifice is forgotten. However, with regard to a claim of the lack of blood, there is no uncertainty or lack of confidence and the passage of time will not compromise that fact (see *Tosafot*; Ritva).

Where he makes the claim that there was no blood – דְּקָטָעֵין טַעֲנַת דָּמִים: The commentaries discuss the difference between these two claims at length, and there are different opinions with regard to both the explanation and the halakhic implications of that difference. Some say that in the claim of an unobstructed orifice, there is concern that he is lying, and there is no way to disprove his claim. In the claim that there was no blood, she could bring proof to refute that claim (Rabbeinu Ḥananel). Rashi explains that in a claim of an unobstructed orifice, there is uncertainty with regard to the degree of the husband's expertise in those matters. Accordingly, there would be a distinction between a bachelor and one who was previously married. The claim that there was no blood requires no expertise. Others explain on a similar note that the claim of an unobstructed orifice is based on feeling and the claim of blood is based on empirical evidence and can be verified (see Ramban; Rashba).

He is deemed credible with regard to causing her to lose her marriage contract – נֶאֱמָן לְהַפְסִידָהּ כְּתוּבָּתָהּ: There are numerous opinions among the early commentaries with regard to the relationship between the statements of Rav Yehuda in the name of Shmuel and the earlier statement of Rabbi Elazar that the groom is deemed credible with regard to rendering her forbidden to him. Some suggest that Shmuel agrees with Rabbi Elazar, i.e., that she is forbidden to the husband; he is merely adding that she loses her marriage contract. Others are of the opinion that Shmuel holds that the groom is accorded credibility only with regard to losing the marriage contract but not to rendering her forbidden to him (see *Tosafot*; Ramban).

Yet others claim that the Sages agree with each other, but that each formulates the ruling in a far-reaching and novel manner. Rabbi Elazar holds that the fact that she is forbidden is a more novel element, as despite her presumptive status of being permitted, she is rendered forbidden by his claim. In contrast, the fact that his claim is credible in monetary matters is clear, as the burden of proof is incumbent upon the claimant. On the other hand, Shmuel holds that he is accorded credibility with regard to the monetary issue, where there is room for leniency, as stringency for one party is leniency for the other. Once his claim is deemed credible with regard to the marriage contract, the result is that she is forbidden, as with regard to the prohibition there is certainly greater concern (Ritva).

HALAKHA

The claim of an unobstructed orifice and the claim that there was no blood – טַעֲנַת פֶּתַח פָּתוּחַ וְטַעֲנַת דָּמִים: If the groom claims after engaging in intercourse with his virgin bride for the first time that she is not a virgin, based on the absence of blood from the ruptured hymen, and that absence cannot be attributed to illness, malnutrition, or a genetic anomaly, his claim is accepted, whether the woman in question is an adult or a minor. If, however, his claim that she is not a virgin is based on encountering an unobstructed orifice and she is a grown woman, i.e., more than twelve and a half years old, his claim is not accepted and it is attributed to the fact that he did not sense that the hymen was intact. If she is a young woman, i.e., less than twelve and a half years old, his claim is accepted even if there is evidence of bleeding (Rambam). Others maintain that if there is blood, the claim of an unobstructed orifice is not accepted, even if the bride is less than twelve and half years old (Ri; Ramban; Rashba; Rambam *Sefer Nashim, Hilkhot Ishut* 11:12–13; *Shulḥan Arukh, Even HaEzer* 68:3, 6).

BACKGROUND

An unobstructed orifice and blood – פֶּתַח פָּתוּחַ וְדָמִים: Most women have some opening in the hymen, the size of which varies from woman to woman and is influenced by age. If the opening is relatively large it is conceivable that one could engage in intercourse with a virgin without encountering that membrane at all. Nevertheless, if the hymen is at all ruptured it bleeds. However, unlike bleeding, where there is a clear, objective criterion to determine the matter, his sensing that he encountered an unobstructed orifice is subjective. It is entirely possible that the hymen was intact, but it simply had a relatively large opening (see 36a).

וּלְמַאי? אִי לְאוֹסְרָהּ עָלָיו – בִּיהוּדָה אַמַּאי לָא? אֶלָּא לָאו – לְהַפְסִידָהּ כְּתוּבָּתָהּ, וּדְקָא טָעֵין טַעֲנָה, מַאי לָאו דְּקָא טָעֵין טַעֲנַת ״פֶּתַח פָּתוּחַ״! לָא, דְּקָא טָעֵין טַעֲנַת דָּמִים.

The Gemara asks: **And for what** matter is this claim directed? **If it is to render her forbidden to him,** then **in Judea why** is the claim **not** credible? If he is certain that he did not engage in intercourse with her, and finds that she is not a virgin, apparently she committed adultery and that claim should render her forbidden. **Rather, is it not** that he is seeking **to cause her to lose her marriage contract**[N] in a case **where he makes a claim?** And **what, is it not** referring to a case **where he makes the claim:** I encountered **an unobstructed orifice,** and apparently he is accorded credibility? The Gemara rejects that proof: **No,** it can be explained that it is a case **where he makes the claim** that there was no **blood.**[N]

NOTES

To cause her to lose her marriage contract – לְהַפְסִידָהּ כְּתוּבָּתָהּ: The Gemara later (13a) cites a dispute among the *amora'im* whether this means that she loses the marriage contract of two hundred dinars to which a virgin is entitled, and instead receives one hundred as a non-virgin, or whether she loses her entire marriage contract, since the entire marriage was based on false pretenses and is therefore a mistaken transaction. The early halakhic authorities (Rif, citing Rav Hai Gaon) write that the dispute is only with regard to the standard payment of the marriage contract. However, the groom is required to pay any sum that he committed to add to the marriage contract.

In Judea…where he makes the claim that there was no blood – בִּיהוּדָה...דְּקָא טָעֵין טַעֲנַת דָּמִים: Some explain that with regard to the claim of an unobstructed orifice, it is conceivable that they engaged in intercourse while betrothed and were both under the impression that it was not full-fledged intercourse. However, with regard to bleeding, had they engaged in intercourse in Judea, and she saw blood, she would have told both him and her parents, to avoid suspicion later. However, if she said nothing at the time, it is likely that she had engaged in intercourse with another man (*Tosefot Yeshanim*).

Perek **I**
Daf **10** Amud **a**

אִיתְּמַר, אָמַר רַב נַחְמָן אָמַר שְׁמוּאֵל מִשּׁוּם רַבִּי שִׁמְעוֹן בֶּן אֶלְעָזָר: חֲכָמִים תִּקְּנוּ לָהֶם לִבְנוֹת יִשְׂרָאֵל, לִבְתוּלָה מָאתַיִם, וּלְאַלְמָנָה מָנֶה. וְהֵם הֶאֱמִינוּהוּ, שֶׁאִם אָמַר ״פֶּתַח פָּתוּחַ מָצָאתִי״ נֶאֱמָן. אִם כֵּן מָה הוֹעִילוּ חֲכָמִים בְּתַקָּנָתָם?

§ **It was stated: Rav Naḥman said** that **Shmuel said in the name of Rabbi Shimon ben Elazar: The Sages instituted** the marriage contract **for Jewish women:**[N] **For a virgin two hundred** dinars[N] **and for a widow one hundred dinars.**[H] And they **deemed** the groom **credible** in **that if** he **says** with regard to his virgin bride: **I encountered an unobstructed orifice** and she is not a virgin, **he is deemed credible,** causing her to lose her marriage contract. The Gemara asks: **If so,** and the Sages deemed him credible, **what did the Sages accomplish in their ordinance** that the marriage contract of a virgin is two hundred dinars, if his claim that she is not a virgin is effective?

אָמַר רָבָא: חֲזָקָה, אֵין אָדָם טוֹרֵחַ בִּסְעוּדָה וּמַפְסִידָהּ.

Rava said: The ordinance is effective due to the **presumption** that **a person does not**[N] exert himself to prepare a wedding **feast and** then **cause it to be lost.**[N] Investing in the wedding preparations clearly indicates that the groom's intention is to marry the bride and rejoice with her. If, nevertheless, he claims that she is not a virgin, apparently he is telling the truth.

HALAKHA

For a virgin two hundred dinars and for a widow one hundred dinars – לִבְתוּלָה מָאתַיִם וּלְאַלְמָנָה מָנֶה: If a man marries a virgin, even if she was widowed or divorced after betrothal to another man, she is entitled to a marriage contract of two hundred dinars. However, if a man marries a woman who was widowed or divorced after marriage to another man, or who engaged in sexual relations while single, she is entitled to a marriage contract of only one hundred dinars (Rambam *Sefer Nashim, Hilkhot Ishut* 11:1; *Shulḥan Arukh, Even HaEzer* 66:6, 67:1–2).

NOTES

The Sages instituted the marriage contract for Jewish women – חֲכָמִים תִּקְּנוּ לָהֶם לִבְנוֹת יִשְׂרָאֵל: Rashi states that the Gemara explained the fact that the Sages accorded credibility to the claim of the groom to void the marriage contract, by stating that the marriage contract is an obligation by rabbinic law. The commentaries discuss why his claim would not be accepted if it was an obligation by Torah law.

For a virgin two hundred dinars – לִבְתוּלָה מָאתַיִם: According to Rabban Shimon ben Gamliel, who holds that the marriage contract is an obligation by Torah law, the source of two hundred dinars for a virgin is clear, as that is the sum of the dowry of a virgin in the Torah. According to the Rabbis, who hold that it is an obligation by rabbinic law, the reason that the Sages instituted two hundred dinars is that they concluded that one with that sum, which was approximately the basic annual wage, is not considered poor, and they sought to ensure that the divorcée or widow would not be dependent on the aid of society. For a widow, who already received a certain sum from the marriage contract of her first husband, one hundred dinars was sufficient (*Ramat Shmuel*).

The presumption that a person does not, etc. – חֲזָקָה אֵין אָדָם וכו׳: The early commentaries discuss the fundamental legal situation with regard to the woman's claim that she is entitled to payment of the marriage contract. On the one hand, since the husband is currently in possession of the disputed funds, the burden of proof is incumbent upon the woman, who is the claimant in this case. On the other hand, the woman's claim is supported by the presumptive status of her body, as most women marry as virgins. As a rule, the presumptive status of her body takes precedence over the possession of disputed property. Therefore, it was necessary to buttress the husband's claim with an additional presumption: A person does not exert himself to prepare a wedding feast and then cause it to be lost.

A person does not exert himself to prepare a wedding feast and then cause it to be lost – אֵין אָדָם טוֹרֵחַ בִּסְעוּדָה וּמַפְסִידָהּ: *Tosafot* infer that this presumption is relevant only in a case where he stands to lose his entire investment in the feast because the wedding is voided, e.g., where the groom is a priest and therefore there is only one uncertainty, or where he claims that the betrothal was a mistaken transaction. However, if his claim is merely to reduce the marriage contract payment to the one hundred dinars of a non-virgin, his claim is not accorded credibility. Similarly, the Rosh explains that in any case where his intention is for her to remain his wife, then since he doesn't actually lose the value of the entire feast, his claim is not credible. The Ramban writes that the primary reason is not that he will lose the money invested in the feast, but rather, in a broader sense, that a person does not get married in order to immediately cast aspersions upon the woman he just married. Or, as he phrased it: A person does not spit in the cup from which he is drinking. According to all of these explanations, the groom's credibility is based on the assumption that he will behave rationally.

תנא: הואיל וקנס חכמים הוא – לא תגבה אלא מן הזיבורית. קנסא?! מאי קנסא? אלא אימא: הואיל ותקנת חכמים הוא – לא תגבה אלא מן הזיבורית. רבן שמעון בן גמליאל אומר: כתובת אשה מן התורה.

§ A Sage **taught** in a *baraita*: **Since** payment of the marriage contract **is a penalty** instituted by the **Sages,**[N] **she may collect only from the** husband's **land of the most inferior quality.**[H] The Gemara asks: **A penalty? What penalty** is there in a marriage contract? **Rather,** emend the *baraita* and **say: Since it is a rabbinic ordinance**[H] and not a Torah obligation, **she may collect only from the husband's land of the most inferior quality. Rabban Shimon ben Gamliel says: The marriage contract of a woman is** an obligation **by Torah** law.

ומי אמר רבן שמעון בן גמליאל הכי? והתניא: "כסף ישקל כמהר הבתולות" שיהא זה כמוהר הבתולות, ומוהר הבתולות כזה. מכאן סמכו חכמים לכתובת אשה מן התורה. רבן שמעון בן גמליאל אומר: כתובת אשה אינה מדברי תורה אלא מדברי סופרים!

The Gemara asks: **And did Rabban Shimon ben Gamliel say that? But isn't it taught** in a *baraita* that it is written with regard to a seducer: **"He shall pay money according to the dowry of virgins"** (Exodus 22:16)? The Torah establishes that **this** fine **will be like the dowry of a virgin,** and that **the dowry of a virgin** will be **like this** fine, i.e., fifty silver *sela*, or two hundred dinars. **From here the Sages based**[N] their determination **that a woman's marriage contract is** an obligation **by Torah law. Rabban Shimon ben Gamliel says: The marriage contract of a woman is not** an obligation **by Torah law, but is by rabbinic law.**[N]

איפוך. ומאי חזית דאפכת בתרייתא? איפוך קמייתא!

The Gemara resolves the contradiction between the statements of Rabban Shimon ben Gamliel: **Reverse** the attribution of opinions in this *baraita*. The Gemara asks: **And what did you see that** led **you to reverse** the attribution of opinions **in the latter** *baraita*? **Reverse** the attribution of opinions in **the former,** in the *baraita*, and say that Rabban Shimon ben Gamliel is the one who holds that the marriage contract is a rabbinic ordinance.

הא שמעינא ליה לרבן שמעון בן גמליאל דאמר כתובת אשה מדאורייתא, דתנן: רבן שמעון בן גמליאל אומר: נותן לה ממעות קפוטקיא.

The Gemara answers: The reason is **that we learned that** it is **Rabban Shimon ben Gamliel who said** elsewhere **that the marriage contract of a woman is** an obligation **by Torah** law, **as we learned** in a mishna (110b) that **Rabban Shimon ben Gamliel says** that if a man marries a woman in Cappadocia, where the currency is more valuable, and he divorces her in Eretz Yisrael, **he gives her** payment for the marriage contract **from the money of Cappadocia.**[N] From the fact that he is obligated to pay the marriage contract in the currency of the place where he undertook the obligation, apparently the marriage contract of a woman is not an obligation by Torah law.

ואי בעית אימא: כולה רבן שמעון בן גמליאל היא, וחסורי מיחסרא והכי קתני: מכאן סמכו חכמים לכתובת אשה מן התורה. כתובת אלמנה אינה מדברי תורה אלא מדברי סופרים, שרבן שמעון בן גמליאל אומר כתובת אלמנה אינה מדברי תורה אלא מדברי סופרים.

And if you wish, say instead that the **entire** latter *baraita* **is** in accordance with the opinion of **Rabban Shimon ben Gamliel, but** the *baraita* **is incomplete and it is teaching the following:**[B] **From here, the Sages based** their determination **that a woman's marriage contract** in the case of a virgin **is** an obligation **by Torah** law. However, the **marriage contract of a widow is not** an obligation **by Torah law but** is an ordinance **by rabbinic law,** as **Rabban Shimon ben Gamliel says: The marriage contract of a widow is not** an obligation **by Torah law but** is an ordinance **by rabbinic law.**

NOTES

Since it is a penalty instituted by the Sages – הואיל וקנס חכמים הוא: The use of the term penalty in this context is questionable, even though it is ultimately abandoned. The Ya'avetz writes that fundamentally the marriage contract was instituted as a type of penalty to deter the husband from coveting another woman and divorcing his wife for no good reason. Even though the marriage contract applies in all cases, even where there is justification for the divorce, this was the initial motive for the ordinance.

From here the Sages based – מכאן סמכו חכמים: From a precise analysis of the language, the early commentaries conclude that even according to Rabban Shimon ben Gamliel, the sum written in the marriage contract is a rabbinic ordinance and not fixed by Torah law. However, the fundamental obligation to write a marriage contract is derived from the verse in the Torah: "He shall pay money according to the dowry of virgins" (Ritva).

The marriage contract of a woman…is an ordinance by rabbinic law – כתובת אשה...מדברי סופרים: There are various opinions as to whether the marriage contract is by Torah law or by rabbinic ordinance (see HALAKHA). The dispute dates back at least to the geonic period and may have been the subject of a dispute between the Sages in Babylonia, where the ruling is in accordance with the opinion of Shmuel and Rav Naḥman, and those in Eretz Yisrael, where the ruling is in accordance with the opinion of Rabban Shimon ben Gamliel. That could also explain some of the differences between the formulas of the marriage contract employed in those places.

With regard to the standard formula of the marriage contract, which includes the expression: Two hundred dinars to which you are entitled by Torah law, many authorities reprimanded those who included that phrase, and some ruled the marriage contract invalid. However, the Ritva and the Meiri explain that the wording is merely to enhance the authority of the marriage contract enabling the woman to collect payment as if it were a commitment by Torah law (see *Tosafot*).

He gives her payment from the money of Cappadocia – נותן לה ממעות קפוטקיא: The early commentaries discuss the significance of the coins used to pay the marriage contract if ultimately the amount of the payment is the same (see *Tosafot*). The Meiri writes that if the groom did not specify the coinage, his intention is to use the legal tender in the place where the contract was signed. Others explain that although the values are the same, currency that is universally accepted is preferable.

BACKGROUND

The *baraita* is incomplete and it is teaching the following – חסורי מיחסרא והכי קתני: This method of explanation appears throughout the Talmud. Generally speaking, it does not suggest an actual emendation of the text of the *baraita*. The addition introduced by the Gemara is a necessary elaboration upon that which is written in the *baraita*, which is insufficiently clear in its current form. The addition provides the necessary clarification.

HALAKHA

She may collect only from the land of the most inferior quality – לא תגבה אלא מן הזיבורית: A wife collects payment of her entire marriage contract, both the standard payment and any additional commitment assumed by the husband, from the land of the lowest quality belonging to the husband, in accordance with the *baraita*. The early commentaries disagree with regard to the ruling in a case where the husband expressly stipulates that his wife will collect payment of the marriage contract from his highest quality land. The *Shulḥan Arukh* (*Ḥoshen Mishpat* 108:18) rules that a condition of that kind takes effect. In the *Beit Shmuel* it is written that since today the prevalent custom is to include in the marriage contract the phrase: The choicest of properties, the wife collects payment of the marriage contract from land of the highest quality (Rambam *Sefer Nashim, Hilkhot Ishut* 16:3; *Shulḥan Arukh, Even HaEzer* 100:2).

Since it is a rabbinic ordinance – הואיל ותקנת חכמים הוא: Some authorities (Rabbeinu Tam) rule in accordance with the statement of Rabban Shimon Ben Gamliel, whose statements in the mishna are generally the basis for the halakhic ruling that the marriage contract is an obligation by Torah law. However, most authorities rule that the marriage contract is an ordinance by rabbinic law. This in accordance with the statement cited by Rav Naḥman in the name of Shmuel, as the halakhic ruling is generally in accordance with both Shmuel and Rav Naḥman in civil matters (Rambam *Sefer Nashim, Hilkhot Ishut* 10:7; *Shulḥan Arukh, Even HaEzer* 66:6).

הַהוּא דַּאֲתָא לְקַמֵּיהּ דְּרַב נַחְמָן, אֲמַר לֵיהּ: פֶּתַח פָּתוּחַ מָצָאתִי. אֲמַר לֵיהּ רַב נַחְמָן: אַסְבּוּהוּ כּוּפְרֵי, מְבָרַכְתָּא חֲבִיטָא לֵיהּ.

§ The Gemara relates: **A certain man who** had never been married **came before Rav Naḥman and said to him: I encountered an unobstructed orifice** when I consummated the marriage. Rav Naḥman **said in his regard: Flog him** with **palm branches** [*kufrei*];[L] **prostitutes** [*mevarakhta*][LN] **are common** around **him.**[N] As he was never previously married, how was he able to determine whether or not the orifice was unobstructed, if he did not gain experience with prostitutes?

וְהָא רַב נַחְמָן הוּא דַּאֲמַר מְהֵימָן! מְהֵימָן, וּמַסְבִּינַן לֵיהּ כּוּפְרֵי. רַב אַחַאי מְשַׁנֵּי: כָּאן – בְּבָחוּר, כָּאן – בְּנָשׂוּי.

The Gemara asks: **But isn't Rav Naḥman he who said that he is deemed credible** when he claims that he encountered an unobstructed orifice? The Gemara answers: Yes, **he is deemed credible,** and nevertheless, **we flog him** with **palm branches. Rav Aḥai answered: Here,** in the case where he is flogged, it is **with regard to a bachelor,** who is not accorded credibility, because he lacks experience. **There,** in the case where he is accorded credibility, it is **with regard to** one who has been **married.**[H]

הַהוּא דַּאֲתָא לְקַמֵּיהּ דְּרַבָּן גַּמְלִיאֵל, אֲמַר לֵיהּ: פֶּתַח פָּתוּחַ מָצָאתִי. אֲמַר לֵיהּ: שֶׁמָּא הִטִּיתָהּ? אֶמְשׁוֹל לְךָ מָשָׁל, לְמָה הַדָּבָר דּוֹמֶה – לְאָדָם שֶׁהָיָה מְהַלֵּךְ בְּאִישׁוֹן לַיְלָה וַאֲפֵילָה, הִיטָּה – מְצָאוֹ פָּתוּחַ, לֹא הִיטָּה – מְצָאוֹ נָעוּל.

The Gemara relates a similar incident from an earlier era: **A certain** man **who came before Rabban Gamliel said to him: I encountered an unobstructed orifice.** Rabban Gamliel **said to him: Perhaps you diverted** your approach[NH] and therefore, you encountered no obstruction? **I will tell you a parable to which this is similar.** It is similar **to a man who was walking in the blackness of night and darkness** and he arrived at the entrance to the house; if **he diverts** the object preventing the door from opening, **he finds it open;** if **he does not divert** it, **he finds it locked.** Perhaps you too diverted your approach and entered from a different angle and that is why you did not encounter an obstruction.

אִיכָּא דְּאָמְרִי, הָכִי אֲמַר לֵיהּ: שֶׁמָּא בְּמֵזִיד הִטִּיתָהּ וְעָקַרְתָּ לְדַשָּׁא וְעַבְרָא? אֶמְשׁוֹל לְךָ מָשָׁל לְמָה הַדָּבָר דּוֹמֶה – לְאָדָם שֶׁהוּא מְהַלֵּךְ בְּאִישׁוֹן לַיְלָה וַאֲפֵילָה; הִיטָּה בְּמֵזִיד – מְצָאוֹ פָּתוּחַ. לֹא הִיטָּה בְּמֵזִיד – מְצָאוֹ נָעוּל.

Some say this is what Rabban Gamliel **said to him: Maybe you diverted** your approach **intentionally and you displaced the door**[N] **and the bolt. I will tell you a parable to which this is similar.** It is similar **to a man who is walking in the blackness of night and darkness** and he arrives at his entrance. **If he diverts intentionally, he finds it open; if he does not divert intentionally, he finds it locked.**

הַהוּא דַּאֲתָא לְקַמֵּיהּ דְּרַבָּן גַּמְלִיאֵל בַּר רַבִּי, אֲמַר לֵיהּ: רַבִּי, בָּעַלְתִּי וְלֹא מָצָאתִי דָּם. אָמְרָה לוֹ: רַבִּי, בְּתוּלָה הָיִיתִי. אָמַר לָהֶם: הָבִיאוּ לִי אוֹתוֹ סוּדָר. הֵבִיאוּ לוֹ הַסּוּדָר וּשְׁרָאוֹ בְּמַיִם, וְכִבְּסוֹ, וּמָצָא עָלָיו כַּמָּה טִיפֵּי דָמִים. אָמַר לוֹ: לֵךְ זְכֵה בְּמִקָּחֲךָ.

The Gemara relates: **A certain** man **who came before Rabban Gamliel bar Rabbi** Yehuda HaNasi **said to him: My teacher, I engaged in intercourse and did not find blood.** The bride **said to him: My teacher, I was a virgin.** Rabban Gamliel bar Rabbi Yehuda HaNasi **said to them: Bring me that cloth** [*sudar*][L] on which you consummated the marriage. **They brought him the cloth, and he soaked it in water and laundered it and found upon it several drops of blood** from the rupture of the hymen. Rabban Gamliel bar Rabbi Yehuda HaNasi **said to** the groom: **Go take possession of your acquisition,** as she was a virgin and there is no need for concern.

אֲמַר לֵיהּ הוּנָא מָר בְּרֵיהּ דְּרָבָא מִפַּרְזָקְיָא לְרַב אַשִׁי: אֲנַן נַמִי נַעֲבֵיד הָכִי – אֲמַר לֵיהּ

Huna Mar, son of Rava, from Parzakya, said to Rav Ashi: Let us do so as well in similar cases and examine whether there is blood that is obscured by semen or another substance. Rav Ashi **said to him:**

LANGUAGE

Palm branches [*kufrei*] – כּוּפְרֵי: An Aramaic word, similar to the Arabic كفرى, *kafarrā*, meaning palm fronds and palm branches.

Prostitutes [*mevarakhta*] – מְבָרַכְתָּא: According to Rashi, this is the name of a village or town near Meḥoza whose name means caravan or convoy of camels. Therefore, it may have been a market town frequented by prostitutes. Some say that the word means convoy, and in this context, a group of prostitutes.

In Syriac, the term *mevarekh* is employed as a euphemism for debased or shameful. Therefore, it is possible that *mevarakhta* means prostitutes.

Cloth [*sudar*] – סוּדָר: From the Greek σουδάριον, *sudarion*, or the Latin sudarium, meaning towel or napkin. In the language of the Sages a *sudar* is apparently a cloth with a variety of functions, e.g., a scarf, a head covering, or a tablecloth.

NOTES

Prostitutes – מְבָרַכְתָּא: Rashi writes, and it is also cited in the *Arukh*, that this is the name of a place frequented by prostitutes. Rabbeinu Ḥananel explains, and it is also cited in the *Arukh* and elsewhere in the name of the *ge'onim*, that it means a small pool. In this context, it is a euphemism for the female genitalia. Others explain that because the word contains the Hebrew root for bless, it is a euphemism for prostitutes, substituting blessed for cursed.

Flog him with palm branches, prostitutes are common around him – אַסְבּוּהוּ כּוּפְרֵי מְבָרַכְתָּא חֲבִיטָא לֵיהּ: Rashi understands the expression: Prostitutes are common around him, as a statement. The Gemara is saying that he is accorded credibility and flogged because he is suspect of gaining experience through licentious relations. *Tosafot* understand the expression as a rhetorical question. The Gemara is saying that the bachelor is not accorded credibility because he is not expert in the matter.

Some explain that there are three distinct cases. If a bachelor makes the claim it is considered impertinent and slanderous; his claim is not accorded credibility and he is flogged for slander. If he is insistent and states that he is certain, his claim is accepted but he is flogged for licentiousness. If he was previously married, his claim is credible and there are no sanctions (see Meiri).

The Ritva asks: If a bachelor claiming that his bride is not a virgin is flogged, he will refrain from coming to court at all, and that undermines the whole purpose of the ordinance of marrying a virgin on Wednesday. He answers that there remains the claim that no bleeding resulted from the rupture of the hymen. Furthermore, once his claim is a certain one and he is angry, he will certainly not be deterred from making his claim in court even if as a result he will be flogged.

Perhaps you diverted your approach, etc. – שֶׁמָּא הִטִּיתָהּ וכו׳: The Ritva notes that there were no grounds to prohibit the woman here, e.g., she was the wife of a non-priest and therefore there was compound uncertainty. Rabban Gamliel simply sought to appease the husband, so that he would not be resentful toward his wife for no reason. Indeed, based on the questions that Rabban Gamliel asked and the groom's silence in response, it appears that he was appeased.

And you displaced the door – וְעָקַרְתָּ לְדַשָּׁא: The explanation is that in his passion, he engaged in intercourse so forcefully that he did not sense her hymen (Ritva; see Rambam and *Shulḥan Arukh*).

HALAKHA

Here it is with regard to a bachelor, there it is with regard to one who has been married – כָּאן בְּבָחוּר, כָּאן בְּנָשׂוּי: According to the Rambam, if a groom claims that he encountered an unobstructed orifice when consummating his marriage with his bride, whom he presumed was a virgin, his claim is accorded credibility, whether or not he was previously married, in accordance with the first answer cited in the Gemara and the second explanation of *Tosafot* (see Gra). However, if he is a bachelor, he is deserving of lashes because he is suspected of gaining experience through licentious relations (*Ḥelkat Meḥokek*). The Rema cites authorities (Rif; *Tur*) who rule that the groom's claim is credible only if he was previously married. If not, his claim is rejected and he is flogged for slandering his wife (Rambam *Sefer Nashim, Hilkhot Ishut* 11:12; *Shulḥan Arukh, Even HaEzer* 68:6).

Perhaps you diverted your approach – שֶׁמָּא הִטִּיתָהּ: If a groom claims that he encountered an unobstructed orifice when consummating his marriage with his bride, whom he presumed was a virgin, the court asks him whether he diverted his approach during intercourse or if perhaps he employed force and therefore did not sense when the hymen was ruptured. This is in accordance with the opinion of Rambam Gamliel (Rambam *Sefer Nashim, Hilkhot Ishut* 11:12; *Shulḥan Arukh, Even HaEzer* 68:6).

גִּיהוּץ שֶׁלָּנוּ כְּכִבּוּס שֶׁלָּהֶם. וְאִי אָמְרַתְּ נִיעֲבַד גִּיהוּץ – מַעַבְרָא לֵיהּ חוּמְרְתָא.

Our calendering in Babylonia, which includes passing an abrasive stone over the garments to scrape off dirt, **is like their laundering** in Eretz Israel, and only in that manner do the garments in Babylonia reach that level of cleanliness. **And if you say: Let us perform** the process of **calendering** on cloths brought as proof that she was not a virgin, **the stone removes** any trace of blood. Therefore, the process would be ineffective.

הַהוּא דַּאֲתָא לְקַמֵּיהּ דְּרַבָּן גַּמְלִיאֵל בַּר רַבִּי, אֲמַר לֵיהּ: רַבִּי, בָּעַלְתִּי וְלֹא מָצָאתִי דָּם. אָמְרָה לֵיהּ: רַבִּי, עֲדַיִין בְּתוּלָה אֲנִי. אָמַר לָהֶן: הָבִיאוּ לִי שְׁתֵּי שְׁפָחוֹת, אַחַת בְּתוּלָה וְאַחַת בְּעוּלָה. הֵבִיאוּ לוֹ, וְהוֹשִׁיבָן עַל פִּי חָבִית שֶׁל יַיִן. בְּעוּלָה – רֵיחָהּ נוֹדֵף, בְּתוּלָה – אֵין רֵיחָהּ נוֹדֵף, אַף זוֹ הוֹשִׁיבָהּ, וְלֹא הָיָה רֵיחָהּ נוֹדֵף, אָמַר לוֹ: לֵךְ זְכֵה בְּמִקָּחֲךָ.

The Gemara relates: **A certain** man **who came before Rabban Gamliel bar Rabbi** Yehuda HaNasi **said to him: My teacher, I engaged in intercourse and did not find blood.** The bride **said to him: My teacher, I am still a virgin.** Rabban Gamliel bar Rabbi Yehuda HaNasi **said to them: Bring me two maidservants,**[H] **one a virgin and one a non-virgin,** to conduct a trial. **They brought him** the two maidservants, **and he seated them on the opening of a barrel of wine.** From **the non-virgin,** he discovered that the **scent** of the wine in the barrel **diffuses** from her mouth; from **the virgin** he discovered that the **scent does not diffuse** from her mouth.[B] Then, **he also seated that** bride on the barrel, **and** the scent of the wine **did not diffuse** from her mouth. Rabban Gamliel bar Rabbi Yehuda HaNasi **said to** the groom: **Go take possession of your acquisition,** as she is a virgin.

וְנִבְדּוֹק מֵעִיקָּרָא בְּגַוַּהּ? גְּמָרָא הֲוָה שְׁמִיעַ לֵיהּ, מַעֲשֶׂה לָא הֲוָה חָזֵי, וְסָבַר דִּלְמָא לָא קִים לֵיהּ בְּגַוָּוהּ דְּמִלְּתָא שַׁפִּיר, וְלָאו אוֹרַח אַרְעָא לְזַלְזוֹלֵי בִּבְנוֹת יִשְׂרָאֵל.

The Gemara asks: Since Rabban Gamliel was familiar with this method of examination, **let him** use it to **examine her initially.** Why was the trial with the maidservants necessary? The Gemara answers: **He learned** that it was effective through **tradition;**[N] however, **he had never seen it in action, and he thought perhaps he was not sufficiently expert in** that **manner** of examination, **and it is improper conduct to demean Jewish women** by subjecting them to that indignity for naught. Once he established the effectiveness of that method, he proceeded to examine the bride to resolve the matter.

הַהוּא דַּאֲתָא לְקַמֵּיהּ דְּרַבָּן גַּמְלִיאֵל הַזָּקֵן, אָמַר לוֹ: רַבִּי, בָּעַלְתִּי וְלֹא מָצָאתִי דָּם. אָמְרָה לוֹ: רַבִּי, מִמִּשְׁפַּחַת דּוֹרְקְטִי אֲנִי, שֶׁאֵין לָהֶן לֹא דַּם נִדָּה וְלֹא דַּם בְּתוּלִים. בָּדַק רַבָּן גַּמְלִיאֵל בִּקְרוֹבוֹתֶיהָ וּמָצָא כִּדְבָרֶיהָ. אָמַר לוֹ: לֵךְ זְכֵה בְּמִקָּחֲךָ, אַשְׁרֶיךָ שֶׁזָּכִיתָ לְמִשְׁפַּחַת דּוֹרְקְטִי.

The Gemara relates: **A certain** man **who came before Rabban Gamliel the Elder said to him: My teacher, I engaged in intercourse and did not find blood.** The bride **said to him: My teacher, I am from the family of Dorketi,**[HLB] **who have neither menstrual blood nor blood** from the rupture of **the hymen. Rabban Gamliel investigated among her relatives** to determine whether the claim with regard to her family was true, **and discovered** that the truth was **in accordance with her statement. He said to him: Go take possession of your acquisition. Happy are you that you were privileged** to marry a member of **the Dorketi family,** as those forms of blood will never pose a problem for you.

HALAKHA

Bring me two maidservants – הָבִיאוּ לִי שְׁתֵּי שְׁפָחוֹת: If the groom claims he discovered that his bride was not a virgin, and she claims in response that she is still a virgin, she is examined. The *Maggid Mishne* explains that the Rambam did not specifically mention examination by means of a barrel of wine because any examination that is effective is appropriate (see *Taz*; Rambam *Sefer Nashim*, *Hilkhot Ishut* 11:12; *Shulḥan Arukh*, *Even HaEzer* 68:4).

I am from the family of Dorketi – מִמִּשְׁפַּחַת דּוֹרְקְטִי אֲנִי: In a case where the groom claims that he found no traces of blood upon consummating the marriage and the bride claims that the women in her family do not bleed, if the court determined the latter to be true, her presumptive status is that she was a virgin before the marriage was consummated (Rambam *Sefer Nashim*, *Hilkhot Ishut* 11:12; *Shulḥan Arukh*, *Even HaEzer* 68:5).

NOTES

He learned that it was effective through tradition, etc. – גְּמָרָא הֲוָה שְׁמִיעַ לֵיהּ וכו׳: The commentaries ask: If there was a tradition that this examination is effective, why didn't Rabban Gamliel examine the bride herself? They explain, based on the responsa of the *ge'onim*, that this examination requires extreme attention to detail, both in terms of the manner in which the woman is seated on the barrel and in terms of ascertaining the aroma of wine in her breath. His lack of expertise was with regard to those details, as he knew based on tradition that it was effective (*Tur*; *Maggid Mishne*).

LANGUAGE

Dorketi – דּוֹרְקְטִי: The source of this word is unclear. Some suggest, especially according to the variant reading *trokati*, that it is from the Greek τρυγᾶν, *trugan*, meaning to harvest or to rob.

BACKGROUND

The scent of the virgin does not diffuse – בְּתוּלָה אֵין רֵיחָהּ נוֹדֵף: Although there is no direct connection between the reproductive system and the lungs, different systems in the body are connected by means of the diffusion of volatile substances. An example of this is that although there is no direct connection between the digestive and respiratory systems, the fact is that alcohol that one drinks diffuses through the membranes of the lungs.

Apparently, the examination discussed in the Gemara is based on the phenomenon of diffusion through the vagina. Based on the assumption that there is a palpable difference between the diffusion of alcohol vapors between a virgin and a non-virgin, this difference would eventually be discernible in the air exhaled from the lungs.

The reliability of this examination is clearly dependent on the manner in which the woman is seated on the barrel, the percentage of alcohol in the wine, and the speed at which the alcohol fumes diffuse. Therefore, Rabban Gamliel performed a preliminary examination because he thought perhaps he was not sufficiently expert in that manner of examination.

The family of Dorketi – מִשְׁפַּחַת דּוֹרְקְטִי: Apparently, there is a genetic factor that influences the prevalence or lack of blood. As a rule, the assumption is that a woman with no menstrual blood is infertile and incapable of bearing children. In the case of the Dorketi family mentioned here, there was presumably a hereditary factor in the women that caused the absolute lack of menstrual blood. The women in the family who did not menstruate were barren, and the family was perpetuated by the women who menstruated at least somewhat. However, as even they were carriers of that same genetic factor, the result was that as many as half the women in the family were barren. For this reason they were called a truncated generation.

מַאי דּוֹרְקְטִי – דּוֹר קָטוּעַ. אָמַר רַבִּי חֲנִינָא: תַּנְחוּמִים שֶׁל הֶבֶל נִיחֲמוֹ רַבָּן גַּמְלִיאֵל לְאוֹתוֹ הָאִישׁ. דְּתָנֵי רַבִּי חִיָּיא: כְּשֵׁם שֶׁהַשְּׂאוֹר יָפֶה לְעִיסָּה כָּךְ דָּמִים יָפִים לְאִשָּׁה. וְתָנָא מִשּׁוּם רַבִּי מֵאִיר: כׇּל אִשָּׁה שֶׁדָּמֶיהָ מְרוּבִּין – בָּנֶיהָ מְרוּבִּים.

The Gemara elaborates: **What is the meaning of Dorketi?** It means **truncated generation** [*dor katua*].[N] **Rabbi Ḥanina said: Rabban Gamliel consoled that man with vain** words of **consolation,** because the absence of blood in this woman is a drawback. **As Rabbi Ḥiyya taught: Just as leaven is fortuitous for dough,** so too, **blood is fortuitous for a woman. And** it was **taught in the name of Rabbi Meir: Any woman whose blood is plentiful, her children are plentiful.**[B] This bride, who lacks blood, will not produce many children.

אִתְּמַר, רַבִּי יִרְמְיָה בַּר אַבָּא אֲמַר: ״זְכֵה בְּמִקָּחֲךָ״ אֲמַר לֵיהּ. וְרַבִּי יוֹסֵי בַּר אָבִין אֲמַר: ״נִתְחַיֵּיב בְּמִקָּחֲךָ״ אֲמַר לֵיהּ. בִּשְׁלָמָא לְמַאן דַּאֲמַר ״נִתְחַיֵּיב״ – הַיְינוּ דְּרַבִּי חֲנִינָא, אֶלָּא לְמַאן דַּאֲמַר ״זְכֵה״ – מַאי זְכוּתָא? דְּלָא אָתֵי לִידֵי סְפֵק נִדָּה.

It was stated that there is a dispute with regard to Rabban Gamliel's reply. **Rabbi Yirmeya bar Abba said** that Rabban Gamliel **said to** the groom: **Exercise your privilege** and take possession **of your acquisition.**[N] **And Rabbi Yosei bar Avin said** that Rabban Gamliel **said to him:** It is your **misfortune** to take possession **of your acquisition. Granted, according to the one who says:** It is your **misfortune, that is** in accordance with the opinion **of Rabbi Ḥanina,** who said the consolation was vain. **However, according to the one who says: Exercise your privilege, what is the privilege** to which he is referring? The Gemara answers: The privilege is **that** thanks to the condition of the women of this family, **he will not come to a situation of uncertainty** whether she has the halakhic status of a **menstruating woman.**

הַהוּא דַּאֲתָא לְקַמֵּיהּ דְּרַבִּי, אֲמַר לֵיהּ: רַבִּי, בָּעַלְתִּי וְלֹא מָצָאתִי דָּם. אָמְרָה לוֹ: רַבִּי, עֲדַיִין בְּתוּלָה הָיִיתִי, וּשְׁנֵי בַצּוֹרֶת הֲוָה. רָאָה רַבִּי שֶׁפְּנֵיהֶם שְׁחוֹרִים, צִוָּה עֲלֵיהֶן וְהִכְנִיסוּם לַמֶּרְחָץ, וְהֶאֱכִילוּם וְהִשְׁקוּם, וְהִכְנִיסוּם לְחֶדֶר, בָּעַל וּמָצָא דָּם. אֲמַר לוֹ: לֵךְ זְכֵה בְּמִקָּחֲךָ. קָרֵי רַבִּי עֲלֵיהֶם: ״צָפַד עוֹרָם עַל עַצְמָם יָבֵשׁ הָיָה כָעֵץ״.

The Gemara relates: **A certain** man **who came before Rabbi** Yehuda HaNasi **said to him: My teacher, I engaged in intercourse and did not find blood.** The bride **said to him: My teacher, I was still a virgin. And** the Gemara comments that this incident **was** during **years of drought.**[H] **Rabbi** Yehuda HaNasi **saw that their faces were black**[BN] due to hunger. **He instructed** his attendants to tend **to them and they took them into the bathhouse** and bathed them **and they fed them and gave them drink.** Then **they took them into a room,** and the groom **engaged in intercourse** with her **and found blood,** as it was due to the famine that there was no blood. Rabbi Yehuda HaNasi **said to him: Go take possession of your acquisition. Rabbi** Yehuda HaNasi **read** this verse **in their regard: "Their skin is shriveled upon their bones, it is withered, it has become like a stick"** (Lamentations 4:8), in the sense that no blood flows from them.

מתני׳ בְּתוּלָה כְּתוּבָּתָהּ מָאתַיִם וְאַלְמָנָה מָנֶה. בְּתוּלָה, אַלְמָנָה, גְּרוּשָׁה, וַחֲלוּצָה מִן הָאֵירוּסִין – כְּתוּבָּתָן מָאתַיִם, וְיֵשׁ לָהֶן טַעֲנַת בְּתוּלִים.

MISHNA With regard to **a virgin, her marriage contract is two hundred dinars,**[H] **and** with regard to **a widow,** her marriage contract **is one hundred** dinars. With regard to **a virgin** who is **a widow, a divorcée, or a *ḥalutza***[N] who achieved that status **from** a state of **betrothal,** before marriage and before consummation of the marriage, for all of these **their marriage contract is two hundred** dinars, **and they are subject to a claim concerning** their **virginity,** as their presumptive status of virginity is intact.

BACKGROUND

Her blood and her children – דָּמֶיהָ וּבָנֶיהָ: There is a connection between a woman's menstrual blood and the degree of her fertility. A woman who does not experience a monthly period but rather menstruates once every few months or even less frequently will tend to be less fertile, as the menstrual blood is an indicator of the ovulation that preceded it. Similarly, when the amount of menstrual blood is less than is typical, it can indicate a hormonal, nutritional, or physiological problem, which could also prevent conception.

He saw that their faces were black – רָאָה...שֶׁפְּנֵיהֶם שְׁחוֹרִים: Severe malnutrition could cause a simple wound, e.g., the rupture of the hymen, not to bleed. Similarly, starvation and exhaustion could have affected the husband, rendering him unable to engage in the full act of intercourse. Treatment that addresses this condition could alleviate the problem.

HALAKHA

Years of drought – שְׁנֵי בַצּוֹרֶת: If the groom claims that upon consummating the marriage he found no traces of blood, and it is a period of famine or the woman appears to be suffering from malnutrition, she is brought to the bathhouse and treated and given food and drink. Then the next time she engages in intercourse she is examined for bleeding (Rambam *Sefer Nashim, Hilkhot Ishut* 11:12; *Shulḥan Arukh, Even HaEzer* 68:5).

With regard to a virgin, her marriage contract is two hundred dinars – בְּתוּלָה כְּתוּבָּתָהּ מָאתַיִם: The marriage contract of a virgin is at least two hundred dinars, and that of a widow is at least one hundred dinars (Rambam *Sefer Nashim, Hilkhot Ishut* 11:12; *Shulḥan Arukh, Even HaEzer* 66:6).

NOTES

Truncated generation [*dor katua*] – דּוֹר קָטוּעַ: According to Rashi, the menstrual cycles of the female members of the family were truncated. Alternatively, the *Arukh* posits that the generations of that family were truncated, as their women were incapable of giving birth.

Exercise your privilege [*zekhe*] and take possession of your acquisition, etc. – זְכֵה בְּמִקָּחֲךָ וכו׳: The *Shita Mekubbetzet* explains that the dispute was not with regard to the language employed by Rabban Gamliel. Rather, the dispute is whether he employed the term *zekhe* in the positive sense of privilege, or whether it was in the neutral sense of taking possession. There is a similar dispute in the Jerusalem Talmud with regard to that which Rabbi Yishmael, son of Rabbi Yosei, said to a woman with the same condition: May there be many like you among the Jewish people. Some say he was implying that it was a positive phenomenon, as the potential for rendering ritually pure items impure was non-existent in those women. Others say that he was speaking euphemistically, and actually considered it a negative phenomenon.

That their faces were black – שֶׁפְּנֵיהֶם שְׁחוֹרִים: There is a variant reading: That her face grew pale. This would indicate that that the ruling was dependent on the physical condition of the woman, who due to hunger and weakness did not bleed (*Piskei Rid*; *Yam shel Shlomo*). This appears to be the position of the Rambam as well. According to that understanding, they fed the husband merely as an act of loving-kindness, not because his condition influenced hers. The halakhic authorities write that even if the woman does not claim that the failure to bleed was due to her weakness, nevertheless when it can be attributed to that condition, the matter is examined.

A widow, a divorcée, or a *ḥalutza* – אַלְמָנָה גְּרוּשָׁה וַחֲלוּצָה: See *Tosafot* for an explanation of the novel element with regard to a *ḥalutza*. *Shita Mekubbetzet* explains that the novelty for each of the women listed is greater than for the previous one. Not only does a widow from betrothal receive the marriage contract of a virgin, but even a divorcée receives two hundred dinars, although one might contend that divorce carries with it a stigma rendering her less desirable. Had only the widow and the divorcée been listed, one might have contended that the *ḥalutza*, who is not only a widow but has suffered the indignity of performing the *ḥalutza* ceremony in court and at times even in public, would not receive a marriage contract of two hundred dinars due to the stigma involved.

גמ׳ מַאי אַלְמָנָה? אָמַר רַב חָנָא בַּגְדָּתָאָה: אַלְמָנָה – עַל שֵׁם מָנֶה. אַלְמָנָה מִן הָאֵירוּסִין מַאי אִיכָּא לְמֵימַר? אַיְּידֵי דְּהָא קָרֵי לָהּ אַלְמָנָה – הָא נַמִי קָרֵי לָהּ אַלְמָנָה.

GEMARA **What is** the relationship between the term ***almana***[L] and its meaning, widow? **Rav Ḥana of Baghdad said:** A widow is called **an *almana* after** the ***maneh***,[N] one hundred dinars, which is the sum of her marriage contract. The Gemara asks: With regard to **a widow from betrothal,** whose marriage contract is two hundred dinars and not a *maneh*, **what is there to say?** The Gemara answers: **Since they called this** widow from marriage ***almana*, this** widow from betrothal **they also called *almana*.**

אַלְמָנָה דִּכְתִיבָא בְּאוֹרַיְיתָא מַאי אִיכָּא לְמֵימַר? דַּעֲתִידִין רַבָּנַן דִּמְתַקְּנִי לָהּ מָנֶה. וּמִי כָּתַב קְרָא לֶעָתִיד? אִין, דִּכְתִיב ״וְשֵׁם הַנָּהָר הַשְּׁלִישִׁי חִדֶּקֶל הוּא הַהוֹלֵךְ קִדְמַת אַשּׁוּר״, וְתָנָא רַב יוֹסֵף: אַשּׁוּר זוֹ סְלֵיקָא. וּמִי הֲוַאי? אֶלָּא דַּעֲתִידָה, הָכָא נַמִי – דַּעֲתִידָה.

The Gemara asks: That explains the use of *almana* in the terminology of the Sages. However, with regard to the term ***almana* that is written in the Torah, what is there to say?** The rabbinic ordinance that the marriage contract of a widow is a *maneh* was not yet instituted. The Gemara answers: The Torah employs the term *almana* **because the Sages are destined to institute** the sum of a ***maneh* for her** in her marriage contract. The Gemara asks: **And is a verse written for the future?** The Gemara answers: **Yes,** indeed it is, **as it is written: "And the name of the third river is Tigris; that is it which goes toward the east of Asshur"** (Genesis 2:14). **And Rav Yosef taught: Asshur, that is Seleucia.**[B] **And did** that city **exist** when the Torah was written? **Rather,** the Torah is referring to that city **because** it was **destined** to exist in the future. **Here too,** the Torah employs the term *almana* **because** a widow was **destined** to have a marriage contract of a *maneh* instituted for her.

וְאָמַר רַב חָנָא בַּגְדָּתָאָה: מָטָר מַשְׁקֶה, מַרְוֶה, וּמְזַבֵּל, וּמְעַדֵּן, וּמַמְשִׁיךְ. אֲמַר רָבָא בַּר רַבִּי יִשְׁמָעֵאל וְאִיתֵּימָא רַב יֵימַר בַּר שֶׁלֶמְיָא: מַאי קְרָא – ״תְּלָמֶיהָ רַוֵּה נַחֵת גְּדוּדֶיהָ בִּרְבִיבִים תְּמֹגְגֶנָּה צִמְחָהּ תְּבָרֵךְ״.

Apropos the statement of Rav Ḥana of Baghdad, the Gemara cites additional statements of his. **And Rav Ḥana of Baghdad said: Rain irrigates, saturates, and fertilizes** the land, **and refines** the fruit **and** causes it to **proliferate. Rava bar Rabbi Yishmael, and some say** it was **Rav Yeimar bar Shelamya** who **said: What is the verse** that alludes to this? **"Watering its ridges abundantly, settling its furrows, You make it soft with showers, You bless its growth"** (Psalms 65:11). "Watering its ridges abundantly" indicates that the rain irrigates and saturates the land, "You make it soft with showers" indicates that it fertilizes the land, and "You bless its growth" indicates that it refines the fruit and causes it to proliferate.

אָמַר רַבִּי אֶלְעָזָר: מִזְבֵּחַ – מֵזִיחַ, וּמֵזִין, מְחַבֵּב, מְכַפֵּר. הַיְינוּ מְכַפֵּר הַיְינוּ מֵזִיחַ! מֵזִיחַ גְּזֵירוֹת וּמְכַפֵּר עֲוֹנוֹת.

Rabbi Elazar said: The term ***mizbe'aḥ***, altar, is a rough acrostic representing its qualities. **It moves [*meziaḥ*]** sins **and sustains [*mezin*]**, because as a result of the offerings sacrificed on the altar, sustenance is provided to all. It **endears [*meḥabev*]**, and **atones [*mekhapper*]**. *Mizbe'aḥ* evokes the letters *mem* and *zayin* from the first two qualities, *bet* from *meḥabev* and the *kaf* from *mekhapper*. The Gemara asks: **This** quality, that the altar **atones, is** the same as **that** quality, that it **moves** sins. Why are they listed separately? The Gemara answers: The altar **moves** evil **decrees, and atones** for **sins.**

וַאֲמַר רַב חָנָא בַּגְדָּתָאָה: תַּמְרֵי מְשַׁחֲנָן, מַשְׂבְּעָן, מְשַׁלְשְׁלָן, מְאַשְּׁרָן וְלָא מְפַנְּקָן. אָמַר רַב: אָכַל תְּמָרִים אַל יוֹרֶה. מֵיתִיבֵי: תְּמָרִים, שַׁחֲרִית וְעַרְבִית – יָפוֹת, בְּמִנְחָה – רָעוֹת, בַּצָּהֳרַיִם – אֵין כְּמוֹתָן. וּמְבַטְּלוֹת שְׁלֹשָׁה דְּבָרִים: מַחֲשָׁבָה רָעָה, וְחוֹלִי מֵעַיִם, וְתַחְתּוֹנִיּוֹת!

And Rav Ḥana of Baghdad said: Dates warm and satiate, loosen the bowels, strengthen, but do not pamper. Rav said: If one ate dates[B] **he should not issue** halakhic **rulings,**[NH] as dates are intoxicating. The Gemara **raises an objection:** With regard to **dates,** in the **morning and evening** they have a **positive** effect on one who eats them; **in the afternoon,** they have a **negative** effect on one who eats them. **At noon, their** positive effect is **unparalleled, and they negate three matters: A troubling thought, intestinal illness, and hemorrhoids.** Apparently, the effect of dates is primarily a positive one.

LANGUAGE

Widow [*almana*] – אַלְמָנָה: The derivation of this word is not at all simple. The early grammarians claimed that it is from the Hebrew word for mute, *illem*, and the letter *nun* is a suffix. This is also the case in the Hebrew words for complacent [*sha'anan*] and fresh [*ra'anan*].

In similar Semitic languages there are various forms of the word *almana*, e.g., the Aramaic *armalta*, which is similar to the Hebrew. This would indicate that the word *almana* is an independent term and not an extension of a different Hebrew root. The word *armalta* underwent a not uncommon transposition of the letters *lamed* and *reish* and *nun* and *lamed*, respectively, creating the word *almana*. Due to this apparent difficulty in ascertaining the source of the term, the Gemara thought it appropriate to add a homiletic interpretation.

NOTES

A widow is called an *almana* after the *maneh* – אַלְמָנָה עַל שֵׁם מָנֶה: The Ritva writes that the source of the term *almana* stems from the Hebrew word for mute, *illem*, as she is alone and there is no one to fight her battles. This consigns her to silence, unable to defend herself. The interpretation in the Gemara is based on the suffix *na*. Rashi explains that the word *almana* is an abbreviation meaning: Merely a *maneh* [*ela maneh*], while the *ge'onim* interpret it as an abbreviation for: Not a *maneh* [*al maneh*], because she receives one hundred dinars less than her virgin counterpart.

If one ate dates he should not issue halakhic rulings – אָכַל תְּמָרִים אַל יוֹרֶה: The source of the *halakha* that it is prohibited for one who is intoxicated to issue halakhic rulings is the prohibition, punishable by death at the hand of Heaven, against priests performing the Temple service under the influence of alcohol or any other food or drink capable of causing intoxication or confusion (Leviticus 10:9). The next two verses state: "And that you may distinguish between the holy and the profane, and between the impure and the pure; and that you may teach the children of Israel all the statutes which the Lord has spoken unto them by the hand of Moses" (Leviticus 10:10–11), indicating that the prohibition goes beyond Temple service and applies to teaching the Jewish people as well.

BACKGROUND

Seleucia – סְלֵיקָא: This seems to be referring to the large city of Σελεύκεια, *Silukia*, on the Tigris River. The city was established by King Seleucus I in the beginning of the third century BCE on the ruins of an ancient city, and became the capital of the Seleucid Empire and one of the largest cities in the East. It had a large population as well, and was an important commercial center. It remained an important city during the Parthian Empire. Seleucia was destroyed in the year 153 CE, and the city of Ardashir was built on its ruins.

Eating dates – אֲכִילַת תְּמָרִים: Dates are high in calories, which are mostly delivered in the form of simple carbohydrates that are digested rapidly. Therefore, eating dates satiates, raises the body temperature, and due to their high level of fiber acts as a laxative. Satiation that is not accompanied by a sense of overeating creates a general sense of calm and thereby negates troubling thoughts.

Because dates satiate, it is recommended not to eat them before a meal. However, after a meal they are beneficial; first, because they satiate, and secondly, because their laxative property is beneficial for digestion. This latter property helps ease the pain of those suffering from hemorrhoids, and there could be an element in dates that aids in healing that ailment.

Eating a large quantity of a concentrated, sweet substance could create an excess of sugar in the blood, which could cause dizziness and drowsiness, similar to the effects of drinking alcohol. Therefore, the Sages said that one may not issue a halakhic ruling after eating dates.

HALAKHA

If one ate dates he should not issue halakhic rulings – אָכַל תְּמָרִים אַל יוֹרֶה: A rabbinic scholar may not render a halakhic decision while intoxicated. Even if he ate dates or drank milk, leading to slight lightheadedness, he may not issue a halakhic ruling, in accordance with the opinion of Rav (Rambam *Sefer Avoda, Hilkhot Biat HaMikdash* 1:3; *Shulḥan Arukh, Yoreh De'a* 242:13 and in the comment of Rema).

מִי אָמְרִינַן דְּלָא מַעֲלוּ? עַלּוּיֵי מַעֲלוּ, וּלְפִי שַׁעְתָּא טַרְדָּא. מִידֵּי דַּהֲוָה אַחַמְרָא, דְּאָמַר מָר הַשּׁוֹתֶה רְבִיעִית יַיִן אַל יוֹרֶה. וְאִיבָּעֵית אֵימָא: לָא קַשְׁיָא; הָא – מִקַּמֵּי נַהֲמָא, הָא – לְבָתַר נַהֲמָא. דְּאָמַר אַבָּיֵי, אָמְרָה לִי אֵם: תַּמְרֵי מִקַּמֵּי נַהֲמָא – כִּי נַרְגָּא לְדִיקוּלָא, בָּתַר נַהֲמָא – כִּי עַבְרָא לְדַשָּׁא.

The Gemara answers that there is no contradiction. **Did we say that they are not exemplary? They are exemplary, and** at the same time **cause temporary distraction** and **intoxication, just as it is** in the case **of wine, as the Master said: One who drinks a quarter-***log* **of wine should not issue** halakhic **rulings. And if you wish, say** instead: This apparent contradiction is **not difficult. This** statement, which prohibits issuing a ruling under the influence of dates, is referring to one eating dates **before** he eats **bread,** when eating them can lead to intoxication. **That** statement, which enumerates the salutary effects of dates, is referring **to** one eating dates **after** he eats **bread. As Abaye said: My mother told me** that **dates** eaten **before** eating **bread** are destructive **like an ax to a palm tree;** dates eaten **after** eating **bread** they are beneficial **like a bolt to a door,** which provides support.

דַּשָּׁא, אָמַר רָבָא: דֶּרֶךְ שָׁם. דַּרְגָּא, אָמַר רָבָא: דֶּרֶךְ גַּג. פּוּרְיָא, אָמַר רַב פַּפָּא: שֶׁפָּרִין וְרָבִין עָלֶיהָ. אָמַר רַב נַחְמָן בַּר יִצְחָק:

Apropos the term door [*dasha*], the Gemara cites statements referring to its etymology as well as that of several other Aramaic terms. With regard to the word *dasha*, door, **Rava said:** It is an acrostic for ***derekh sham***, meaning through there. With regard to the word ***darga***, ladder or stair, **Rava said:** It is an acrostic for ***derekh gag***, meaning way to the roof. With regard to the word ***purya***, bed, **Rav Pappa said:** It is an acrostic for ***parin veravin aleha***, meaning one procreates upon it. **Rav Naḥman bar Yitzḥak said:**

אַף אָנוּ נֹאמַר: אַיְילוֹנִית – דּוּכְרָנִית דְּלָא יָלְדָה.

We too will say: ***Ailonit***, a sexually underdeveloped woman,[B] is a term meaning: Like a **ram** [***dukhranit***],[L] **because** like a male sheep [*ayyil*] **she does not bear children.**

מַתְנִי׳ הַגִּיּוֹרֶת וְהַשְּׁבוּיָה וְהַשִּׁפְחָה, שֶׁנִּפְדּוּ וְשֶׁנִּתְגַּיְּירוּ וְשֶׁנִּשְׁתַּחְרְרוּ פְּחוּתוֹת מִבְּנוֹת שָׁלֹשׁ שָׁנִים וְיוֹם אֶחָד – כְּתוּבָּתָן מָאתַיִם, וְיֵשׁ לָהֶן טַעֲנַת בְּתוּלִין.

MISHNA With regard to **a female convert, or a captive woman,**[N] **or a maidservant,**[B] **who were ransomed** with regard to the captive, or **who converted** with regard to the convert, **or who were freed** with regard to the maidservant, when they were **less than three years and one day old,**[H] **their marriage contract is two hundred** dinars, as their presumptive status is that of a virgin. Even if they were subject to intercourse when they were younger than that age, the hymen remains intact. **And they are** subject to **a claim** concerning their **virginity.**

BACKGROUND

Sexually underdeveloped woman [*ailonit*] – אַיְילוֹנִית: From the detailed discussions in the Talmud, primarily in tractate *Yevamot*, an *ailonit* is apparently a woman suffering from a genetic condition that renders her unable to have children. This is not to be confused with sterility, which is a condition caused by certain secondary defects; the physical and sexual development of a sterile woman is standard. The *ailonit* is also characterized by different physical development in secondary sexual characteristics, e.g., growth of pubic hair. There are different theories as to the causes of this condition, ranging from those who attribute it to overproduction of male hormones to those who identify it as Turner's syndrome.

There are detailed halakhic discussions with regard to the legal status of an *ailonit*, primarily due to the total lack or delayed development of secondary sexual characteristics. As a result, various questions are raised with regard to determining when the *ailonit* assumes the status of a young woman and a grown woman.

Maidservant – שִׁפְחָה: This refers to a Canaanite maidservant, a female gentile purchased by a Jew as a slave. Like a male Canaanite slave, after she is purchased she must be immersed in a ritual bath and subsequently her personal status changes: She henceforth must observe all of the Torah's prohibitions and is obligated to observe positive mitzvot that apply to a Jewish woman. Nevertheless, she is not fully Jewish and may not marry a Jewish man, except under special circumstances, where her master arranges a marriage for her with a Hebrew slave for the purpose of producing children whose status is like her own. As with a male Canaanite slave, it is permitted to sell a maidservant to other Jews but not to non-Jews. Although the *halakha* is that her master is ordinarily prohibited from freeing her, if she receives a bill of manumission, it takes effect, and her status as a freed maidservant is similar to that of a convert.

LANGUAGE

Like a ram [*dukhranit*] – דּוּכְרָנִית: In Aramaic a ram [*ayyil*] is called *dikhra*, meaning male. Consequently, the term *ailonit* is derived from the Hebrew word for ram, whose Aramaic equivalent means male or masculine. An *ailonit*, therefore, is a woman incapable of having children, often masculine in appearance.

NOTES

A female convert, or a captive woman, etc. – הַגִּיּוֹרֶת וְהַשְּׁבוּיָה וכו׳: The Ritva points out that the order of the verbs: Ransomed, converted, and freed, does not correspond to the order of the subjects: Convert, captive, and maidservant. He explains that both the subjects and the verbs are listed in their respective order of importance. Converts, as people who consciously chose to join the Jewish people, are listed before victims of captivity and maidservants. Likewise, ransoming, i.e., fulfilling the mitzva of freeing captives, is the highest form of lovingkindness and takes precedence over conversion. Conversion, in turn, takes precedence over the freeing of slaves, as the latter is generally prohibited.

HALAKHA

A female convert…less than three years and one day old, etc. – הַגִּיּוֹרֶת...פְּחוּתוֹת מִבְּנוֹת שָׁלֹשׁ שָׁנִים וְיוֹם אֶחָד וכו׳: A female convert, redeemed captive, or freed slave who converted or was redeemed or freed when she was less than three years and one day old retains the presumptive status of a virgin. Therefore, she is entitled to a marriage contract of two hundred dinars and her husband may make a claim concerning her virginity (Rambam *Sefer Nashim*, *Hilkhot Ishut* 11:1; *Shulḥan Arukh*, *Even HaEzer* 67:3).

גמ׳ אָמַר רַב הוּנָא: גֵּר קָטָן מַטְבִּילִין אוֹתוֹ עַל דַּעַת בֵּית דִּין.

GEMARA **Rav Huna said:** With regard to **a convert who is a minor,**[N] **one immerses him**[N] in a ritual bath **with the consent of the court.**[H] As a minor lacks the capacity to make halakhic decisions, the court is authorized to make those decisions in his stead.

מַאי קָא מַשְׁמַע לָן – דִּזְכוּת הוּא לוֹ, וְזָכִין לְאָדָם שֶׁלֹּא בְּפָנָיו – תָּנֵינָא: זָכִין לְאָדָם שֶׁלֹּא בְּפָנָיו, וְאֵין חָבִין לְאָדָם שֶׁלֹּא בְּפָנָיו!

What is Rav Huna **coming to teach us?** Is he teaching **that it is a privilege for** the minor to convert,[N] **and one may act in a person's interests** even **in his absence?**[HN] **We** already **learned** that explicitly in a mishna (*Eiruvin* 81b): One **may act in a person's interests in his absence, but one may not act against a person's interests in his absence.**

מַהוּ דְּתֵימָא: גּוֹי בְּהֶפְקֵירָא נִיחָא לֵיהּ, דְּהָא קַיְימָא לָן דְּעֶבֶד וַדַּאי בְּהֶפְקֵירָא נִיחָא לֵיהּ,

Rav Huna's statement was necessary **lest you say:** With regard to **a gentile, licentiousness is preferable for him,** so conversion is contrary to his interests, just **as we maintain that** with regard to a **slave, licentiousness is certainly preferable.**[N] Just as a slave has no interest in assuming the restrictions that come with freedom, in that a freed Canaanite slave is a convert to Judaism, a gentile would have the same attitude toward conversion.

קָא מַשְׁמַע לָן: דְּהָנֵי מִילֵּי – גָּדוֹל, דְּטָעַם טַעַם דְּאִיסּוּרָא. אֲבָל קָטָן – זְכוּת הוּא לוֹ.

Therefore, Rav Huna **teaches us: That applies** only with regard to **an adult, who has experienced a taste of prohibition.** Therefore, presumably he prefers to remain a slave and indulge in licentiousness. **However,** with regard to a **minor,** who did not yet engage in those activities, **it is a privilege for him**[N] to convert.

לֵימָא מְסַיַּיע לֵיהּ: הַגִּיּוֹרֶת וְהַשְּׁבוּיָה וְהַשִּׁפְחָה שֶׁנִּפְדּוּ וְשֶׁנִּתְגַּיְּירוּ וְשֶׁנִּשְׁתַּחְרְרוּ פְּחוּתוֹת מִבְּנוֹת שָׁלֹשׁ שָׁנִים וְיוֹם אֶחָד. מַאי לָאו – דְּאַטְבְּלִינְהוּ עַל דַּעַת בֵּית דִּין?

The Gemara suggests: **Let us say** that the mishna **supports** Rav Huna's statement: With regard to **a female convert, or a captive woman, or a maidservant, who were ransomed** with regard to the captive, or **who converted** with regard to the convert, **or who were freed** with regard to the maidservant, when they were **less than three years and one day old; what, is it not** referring to a case where **they immersed** the minor converts and the maidservants **with the consent of the court?** Apparently, a conversion of that sort is valid.

HALAKHA

With regard to a convert who is a minor, one immerses him with the consent of the court – גֵּר קָטָן מַטְבִּילִין אוֹתוֹ עַל דַּעַת בֵּית דִּין: A gentile minor may be immersed in a ritual bath for the purpose of conversion with the consent of the court, because the conversion is considered to be to his benefit, in accordance with the opinion of Rav Huna (Rambam *Sefer Kedusha, Hilkhot Issurei Bia* 13:7; *Shulḥan Arukh, Yoreh De'a* 268:7).

One may act in a person's interests in his absence – זָכִין לְאָדָם שֶׁלֹּא בְּפָנָיו: One may accept a gift on another's behalf or perform actions that benefit him without his knowledge; however, one may not act on his behalf to his detriment without his agreement (Rambam *Sefer Kinyan, Hilkhot Zekhiya* 4:2; *Shulḥan Arukh, Ḥoshen Mishpat* 243:1).

NOTES

A convert who is a minor – גֵּר קָטָן: Rashi explains that this case is one of a fatherless, gentile child, whose mother is bringing him to be converted. The early commentaries seek to clarify: If the reference is to a case where the mother is converting with the child, then that is identical to the case cited later of a father converting his children; there is no distinction between the father and the mother in this matter (see Rashba). Some explain that this is a case where both the father and the mother want the child to convert, although they themselves are not converting (Ritva, citing Rashi). Others say that the child comes on his own initiative, as although he has not reached majority, he has the capacity, albeit limited, to make advised decisions.

Later commentaries explain, based on various sources, that the determination of majority as the age when one is halakhically capable of independent decision is a Torah law that applies uniquely to Jews. With regard to gentiles, that capacity is determined based on the ability of each individual, unrelated to age. According to all these opinions, the initiative for this conversion must originate either with the convert or with his parents; the court does not proselytize (see Mordekhai, citing Ra'avya). The Ran holds that if the court initiates conversion, the conversion is valid after the fact.

One immerses him – מַטְבִּילִין אוֹתוֹ: The early commentaries ask why Rav Huna did not mention the requirement of circumcision. They explain that he sought to address conversion that applies to all, not only to males (Ritva). The Meiri concurs, adding that the conversion process culminates with immersion even for males. The Rashba adds that there is a novel element with regard to immersion. Circumcision performed when one is a minor obviously remains into his adulthood. However, with regard to immersion, which leaves no lasting imprint, one might have thought that when he reaches majority he would require an additional immersion.

The *Shita Mekubbetzet* cites an opinion that since immersion is wholly beneficial, one may therefore act in the minor's interests and immerse him. However, circumcision is accompanied by pain, and therefore it is not an unadulterated privilege and cannot be performed for a minor convert. According to this explanation, Rav Huna is referring to a convert who is already circumcised.

It is a privilege for the minor to convert – זְכוּת הוּא לוֹ: *Tosafot* ask how the principle that one can act in another's interests even in his absence can be applied in this case. That principle is based on agency, and both a child and a gentile are halakhically incapable of appointing an agent. The *Shakh* explains in the book *Nekuddot HaKesef* that the conversion is not effected for the gentile child based on agency, but rather on the authority of the court to act on his behalf.

One may act in a person's interests in his absence – זָכִין לְאָדָם שֶׁלֹּא בְּפָנָיו: The *Shita Mekubbetzet* cites an opinion that provided an action is not completely to the detriment of another, it can be considered to be in his interests. That is why although converting to Judaism carries with it certain difficulties, e.g., the onus of the mitzvot, it is considered to be in his interests.

We maintain that with regard to a slave licentiousness is certainly preferable – הָא קַיְימָא לָן דְּעֶבֶד וַדַּאי בְּהֶפְקֵירָא נִיחָא לֵיהּ: *Tosafot* note that only according to Rabbi Meir is freeing a slave considered contrary to his interests, as he prefers his unrestricted lifestyle. According to the Rabbis, that is not the case. *Tosafot* ask why the Gemara cites that opinion as the consensus. For this reason, some early commentaries prefer a variant reading of the Gemara: With regard to a gentile, licentiousness is certainly preferable. The Ritva explains that even the Rabbis concede that the slave prefers his unrestricted lifestyle; however, they hold that the prospect of freedom outweighs that preference.

With regard to a minor, it is a privilege for him – קָטָן, זְכוּת הוּא לוֹ: Some maintain that until he reaches majority he is a convert by rabbinic law. Only upon reaching majority and accepting the mitzvot does he become a full-fledged convert by Torah law. The Ritva and others prove that he is considered a full-fledged convert by Torah law immediately, although he may renounce his conversion when reaching majority.

לָא, הָכָא בְּמַאי עָסְקִינַן, בְּגֵר שֶׁנִּתְגַּיְּירוּ בָּנָיו וּבְנוֹתָיו עִמּוֹ, דְּנִיחָא לְהוּ בְּמַאי דְּעָבֵיד אֲבוּהוֹן.

The Gemara rejects that proof: **No, with what are we dealing here?** It is **with a convert whose** minor **sons and daughters converted with him, as they are content with whatever their father does**[HN] in their regard. However, that does not apply to a child who is converting on his own.

אָמַר רַב יוֹסֵף: הִגְדִּילוּ יְכוֹלִין לִמְחוֹת. אֵיתִיבֵיהּ אַבָּיֵי: הַגִּיּוֹרֶת וְהַשְּׁבוּיָה וְהַשִּׁפְחָה שֶׁנִּפְדּוּ וְשֶׁנִּתְגַּיְּירוּ וְשֶׁנִּשְׁתַּחְרְרוּ פְּחוּתוֹת מִבְּנוֹת שָׁלֹשׁ שָׁנִים וְיוֹם אֶחָד – כְּתוּבָּתָן מָאתַיִם. וְאִי סָלְקָא דַּעְתָּךְ הִגְדִּילוּ יְכוֹלִין לִמְחוֹת – יָהֲבִינַן לַהּ כְּתוּבָּה דְּאָזְלָה וְאָכְלָה בְּגֵיוּתָהּ?!

Rav Yosef said: In any case where minors convert, when **they reach majority**[N] **they can protest**[HN] and annul their conversion.[N] **Abaye raised an objection to his** opinion from the mishna: With regard to **a female convert, or a captive woman, or a maidservant who were ransomed,** or **who converted, or who were freed** when they were **less than three years and one day old, their marriage contract is two hundred** dinars. **And if it enters your mind** to say that when **they reach majority they can protest** and annul their conversion, **do we give her** the payment of the **marriage contract that she** will **go and consume in her gentile** state?

לִכִי גָּדְלָה. לִכִי גָּדְלָה נַמִי, מִמַּחְיָא וְנָפְקָא! כֵּיוָן שֶׁהִגְדִּילָה שָׁעָה אַחַת וְלֹא מִיחֲתָה – שׁוּב אֵינָהּ יְכוֹלָה לִמְחוֹת.

The Gemara answers: She receives payment of her marriage contract **once she has reached majority**[H] and does not protest, but not while still a minor. The Gemara asks: **When she reaches majority too,** is there not the same concern that **she will protest and abandon** Judaism? The Gemara answers: **Once she reached majority** for even **one moment**[H] **and did not protest, she may no longer protest.** This mishna poses no difficulty to the opinion of Rav Yosef.

מְתִיב רָבָא: אֵלּוּ נְעָרוֹת שֶׁיֵּשׁ לָהֶן קְנָס: הַבָּא עַל הַמַּמְזֶרֶת, וְעַל הַנְּתִינָה, וְעַל הַכּוּתִית, וְעַל הַגִּיּוֹרֶת, וְעַל הַשְּׁבוּיָה, וְעַל הַשִּׁפְחָה שֶׁנִּפְדּוּ וְשֶׁנִּתְגַּיְּירוּ וְשֶׁנִּשְׁתַּחְרְרוּ פְּחוּתוֹת מִבְּנוֹת שָׁלֹשׁ שָׁנִים וְיוֹם אֶחָד – יֵשׁ לָהֶן קְנָס. וְאִי אָמְרַתְּ הִגְדִּילוּ יְכוֹלִין לִמְחוֹת – יָהֲבִינַן לַהּ קְנָס דְּאָזְלָה וְאָכְלָה בְּגֵיוּתָהּ?!

Rava raised an objection from a mishna (29a): **These** are the cases of **young women for whom there is a fine** paid to their fathers by one who rapes them: **One who engages in intercourse with a *mamzeret*; or with a Gibeonite woman [*netina*],** who are given [*netunim*] to the service of the people and the altar (see Joshua 9:27); **or with a Samaritan**[B] **woman [*kutit*].** In addition, the same applies to one who engages in intercourse **with a female convert, or with a captive woman, or with a maidservant,** provided **that** the captives **were ransomed or that** the converts **converted, or that** the maidservants **were freed** when they were **less than three years and one day old,** as only in that case do they maintain the presumptive status of a virgin. In all of these cases, **there is a fine** paid **to their** fathers if they are raped. **And if you say** that **when they reach majority they can protest** and annul their conversion, **do we give her** payment of the **fine that she** will **go and consume in her gentile** state?

לִכִי גָּדְלָה. לִכִי גָּדְלָה נַמִי, מִמַּחְיָא וְנָפְקָא! כֵּיוָן שֶׁהִגְדִּילָה שָׁעָה אַחַת וְלֹא מִיחֲתָה – שׁוּב אֵינָהּ יְכוֹלָה לִמְחוֹת.

The Gemara answers: Her father receives payment of the fine **once she has reached majority** and does not protest, but not while she is still a minor. The Gemara asks: **When she reaches majority too,** is there not the same concern that **she will protest and abandon** Judaism? The Gemara answers: **Once she reached majority** for even **one moment and did not protest, she may no longer protest.**

HALAKHA

They are content with whatever their father does – נִיחָא לְהוּ בְּמַאי דְּעָבֵיד אֲבוּהוֹן: A gentile child may be converted to Judaism by his father (*Shulḥan Arukh, Yoreh De'a* 268:7).

When they reach majority they can protest – הִגְדִּילוּ יְכוֹלִין לִמְחוֹת: A child who converted to Judaism, whether he converted alone with the consent of the court, or whether he converted with his father or mother, may protest and renounce the conversion once he reaches majority. According to some authorities, if the child converted together with his parents, he may not renounce his conversion when he comes of age (*Ba'al Halakhot Gedolot*; see Rambam; *Ḥatam Sofer*; *Pitḥei Teshuva*; Rambam *Sefer Shofetim, Hilkhot Melakhim* 10:3; *Shulḥan Arukh, Yoreh De'a* 268:7).

Once she has reached majority – לִכִי גָּדְלָה: If a female child who converted marries and is then widowed or divorced, her marriage contract remains in the hands of the court until she reaches majority. This is in order to prevent a situation where she will protest her conversion and renounce her Judaism upon reaching adulthood, and benefit from payment of the marriage contract as a gentile (Rambam *Sefer Shofetim, Hilkhot Melakhim* 10:3).

Once she reached majority for even one moment – כֵּיוָן שֶׁהִגְדִּילָה שָׁעָה אַחַת: If a child who converted reaches majority and continues to practice Jewish customs he is considered a full-fledged convert. He can no longer protest his conversion and abandon Judaism. This is in accordance with the opinion of Rav Yosef, as explained by *Tosafot* (Rambam *Sefer Shofetim, Hilkhot Melakhim* 10:3; *Shulḥan Arukh, Yoreh De'a* 268:8).

BACKGROUND

Samaritan – כּוּתִי: The Samaritans are the descendants of the nations displaced by Sennacherib, King of Assyria, and relocated to Eretz Yisrael. Eventually, they accepted upon themselves several mitzvot (II Kings 17). At the beginning of the Second Temple period, during the times of Ezra and Nehemiah, relations between the Samaritans and the Jews deteriorated. Later, the Samaritans established a center of worship on Mount Gerizim, as they claimed that the sanctity of that mountain was established by one of the Ten Commandments.

Some generations of Sages recognized Samaritans as half Jewish. They went so far as to say: In the mitzvot that the Samaritans adopted, they are extremely exacting in their fulfillment, even more than the Jews are. Ultimately, as the Samaritans continued to distance themselves from the Jewish people in virtually every regard, they were accorded the legal status of gentiles.

NOTES

As they are content with whatever their father does – דְּנִיחָא לְהוּ בְּמַאי דְּעָבֵיד אֲבוּהוֹן: According to the Rashba, there is no difference between a father and a mother in this regard. In fact, it is reasonable to assume that the child would tend more to follow his mother. The Meiri, however, suggests that the Sages stated this *halakha* only with regard to the father.

When they reach majority – הִגְדִּילוּ: *Talmidei Rabbeinu Yona* ask: As majority is reached at a given moment, just prior to that moment he is a minor and just after that moment he is an adult. How, then, is it possible to determine the precise moment when she may protest and renounce the conversion? *Tosafot* explain that reaching majority and conducting oneself as a Jew indicates that he is not protesting. The Rosh elaborates: If after reaching majority one performs an action unmistakably characteristic of Judaism, this would indicate he is not protesting. Others explain that the protest need not coincide precisely with reaching majority. Rather, when the convert comes of age he is informed of the onus of mitzvot. If he accepts, he is a full-fledged Jew (Ritva).

The Ra'avad and the Rashba require that the process of acceptance or rejection of Judaism must begin during the latter stages of a child's minority and continue into the beginning of majority. According to *Tosefot Rid*, the process must be completed during the final days of minority, when the minor has the intellectual capacity to make decisions but has not yet reached the age of legal capacity to accept the mitzvot as a Jew.

When they reach majority they can protest – הִגְדִּילוּ יְכוֹלִין לִמְחוֹת: The halakhic authorities disagree whether this applies only to a case where the child is converted with the consent of the court, or even in a case where he converted with his father. The Rashba and others cite the fact that Rav Yosef formulated his statement in the plural, indicating that it applies in the case of all child converts.

They can protest and annul their conversion – יְכוֹלִין לִמְחוֹת: The question is asked: Once the convert renounces Judaism, is he retroactively considered a gentile who never converted? There is a practical ramification to this question with regard to wine with which he came into contact prior to his protest. If he is retroactively considered a gentile, the wine is forbidden. The Ḥatam Sofer maintains that this is the ruling, although he was unaware of that which the Meiri cited in the name of the *ge'onim*, that the wine is not forbidden after the fact. Fundamentally, the prohibition of wine with which a gentile child came into contact is by rabbinic decree. As it is uncommon for converts to renounce their Judaism, the Sages do not issue decrees in uncommon cases.

אַבַּיֵי לָא אָמַר כְּרָבָא – הָתָם קְנָסָא, הַיְינוּ טַעְמָא שֶׁלֹּא יְהֵא חוֹטֵא נִשְׂכָּר.

Abaye did not state his objection from the same source **as** did **Rava,** because **there,** in the mishna cited by Rava, it is referring to **a fine,** and in that case **this is the reason: So that the sinner will not profit.** The Sages did not absolve the rapist from payment of the fine merely due to the concern that the woman he raped may ultimately negate the conversion.

רָבָא לָא אָמַר כְּאַבַּיֵי – כְּתוּבָּה הַיְינוּ טַעְמָא – שֶׁלֹּא תְּהֵא קַלָּה בְּעֵינָיו לְהוֹצִיאָהּ.

Rava did not state his objection from the same source **as** did **Abaye,** as with regard to **a marriage contract, this is the reason**[NH] that the Sages instituted it: **So that** his wife **will not be inconsequential in his eyes,** enabling him **to** easily **divorce her.** As long as this woman does not negate her conversion, she is a Jewish woman and the Sages saw to her interests.

מתני׳ הַגָּדוֹל שֶׁבָּא עַל הַקְּטַנָּה, וְקָטָן שֶׁבָּא עַל הַגְּדוֹלָה, וּמוּכַּת עֵץ – כְּתוּבָּתָן מָאתַיִם, דִּבְרֵי רַבִּי מֵאִיר. וַחֲכָמִים אוֹמְרִים: מוּכַּת עֵץ – כְּתוּבָּתָהּ מָנֶה.

MISHNA With regard to **an adult man who engaged in intercourse with a minor girl** less than three years old; **or a minor boy** less than nine years old **who engaged in intercourse with an adult woman;**[H] **or a** woman who had her hymen **ruptured by wood** or any other foreign object, for all these women **their marriage contract is two hundred** dinars, as their legal status is that of a virgin. This is **the statement of Rabbi Meir. And the Rabbis say: The marriage contract** of a woman whose hymen was **ruptured by wood is one hundred dinars,**[H] as physically, since her hymen is not intact, she is no longer a virgin.

בְּתוּלָה, אַלְמָנָה, גְּרוּשָׁה וַחֲלוּצָה מִן הַנִּשּׂוּאִין – כְּתוּבָּתָן מָנֶה,

With regard to **a virgin** who is either **a widow, a divorcée, or a *ḥalutza*** who achieved that status **from** a state of **marriage,**[NH] for all these women **their marriage contract is one hundred dinars,**

NOTES

With regard to a marriage contract this is the reason, etc. – **כְּתוּבָּה הַיְינוּ טַעְמָא וכו׳:** The Ritva explains this in a unique manner: If he doesn't give her a marriage contract at all the concern is that she will consider the lack of a marriage contract demeaning, as the lack will ease the way for her husband to divorce her. That itself may lead to her renunciation of Judaism.

A virgin…from a state of marriage – **בְּתוּלָה...מִן הַנִּשּׂוּאִין:** In explaining why a virgin who was married receives a marriage contract of only one hundred dinars, Rashi writes that upon entering the wedding canopy, she assumes the presumptive status of a non-virgin. The early commentaries add that this is the ruling even if she claims that she is still a virgin and brings proof to that effect. Nevertheless, the concern is that she is seeking to be valued more highly by her groom, and the witnesses share that objective.

Although there are certainly cases where it is clear that she did not engage in intercourse, the Sages did not distinguish between the cases. The Rashba explains the reason for this *halakha* based on the Jerusalem Talmud: A virgin receives a marriage contract of two hundred dinars from the groom because she finds favor in his eyes. The fact that she previously entered the wedding canopy with another man mitigates that favor. That is also the reason that according to one opinion, a woman whose hymen was ruptured by a foreign object receives a marriage contract of one hundred dinars.

HALAKHA

With regard to a marriage contract this is the reason – **כְּתוּבָּה הַיְינוּ טַעְמָא:** The Sages instituted payment of the marriage contract to the wife so that she will not be inconsequential in her husband's eyes, enabling him to easily divorce her (Rambam *Sefer Nashim, Hilkhot Ishut* 10:7; *Tur, Even HaEzer* 66).

With regard to an adult man who engaged in intercourse with a minor girl, or a minor boy who engaged in intercourse with an adult woman – **הַגָּדוֹל שֶׁבָּא עַל הַקְּטַנָּה וְקָטָן שֶׁבָּא עַל הַגְּדוֹלָה:** A girl who engaged in intercourse when she was less than three years and one day old, even if it was with an adult man, is entitled, when she marries, to a marriage contract of two hundred dinars. Similarly, an adult woman who engaged in intercourse with a boy less than nine years and one day old is entitled, when she marries, to a marriage contract of two hundred dinars (Rambam *Sefer Nashim, Hilkhot Ishut* 11:3; *Shulḥan Arukh, Even HaEzer* 67:4).

The marriage contract of a woman whose hymen was ruptured by wood is one hundred dinars – **מוּכַּת עֵץ כְּתוּבָּתָהּ מָנֶה:** A woman whose hymen was ruptured by means of a foreign object, not through intercourse, is entitled to a marriage contract of one hundred dinars, in accordance with the opinion of the Rabbis (Rambam *Sefer Nashim, Hilkhot Ishut* 11:3; *Shulḥan Arukh, Even HaEzer* 67:5).

A virgin…from a state of marriage – **בְּתוּלָה...מִן הַנִּשּׂוּאִין:** A woman who was widowed or divorced or who underwent *ḥalitza* after marriage, even if the marriage was not consummated, no longer has the legal status of a virgin, and is entitled to a marriage contract of one hundred dinars. In addition, her husband cannot later make a claim concerning her virginity (Rambam *Sefer Nashim, Hilkhot Ishut* 11:1; *Shulḥan Arukh, Even HaEzer* 67:2).

וְאֵין לָהֶן טַעֲנַת בְּתוּלִים.

and they are not subject to **a claim** concerning their **virginity.** Since they were married, even if they did not engage in intercourse with their husband, their presumptive status is that of non-virgins, and the second husband cannot claim that he was misled with regard to their status as virgins.

הַגִּיּוֹרֶת וְהַשְּׁבוּיָה וְהַשִּׁפְחָה שֶׁנִּפְדּוּ וְשֶׁנִּתְגַּיְּירוּ וְשֶׁנִּשְׁתַּחְרְרוּ יְתֵירוֹת עַל בְּנוֹת שָׁלֹשׁ שָׁנִים וְיוֹם אֶחָד – כְּתוּבָּתָן מָנֶה, וְאֵין לָהֶן טַעֲנַת בְּתוּלִין.

And similarly, with regard to **a female convert, or a captive woman, or a maidservant, who were ransomed** with regard to the captive, or **who converted** with regard to the convert, **or who were freed** with regard to the maidservant, when they were **more than three years and one day old,**[NH] **their marriage contract is one hundred dinars and they are not** subject to **a claim** concerning their **virginity.** When they married, their presumptive status was that of a non-virgin.

גְּמ׳ אָמַר רַב יְהוּדָה אָמַר רַב: קָטָן הַבָּא עַל הַגְּדוֹלָה עֲשָׂאָהּ מוּכַּת עֵץ. כִּי אָמְרִיתָהּ קַמֵּיהּ דִּשְׁמוּאֵל, אֲמַר: אֵין מוּכַּת עֵץ בְּבָשָׂר.

GEMARA **Rav Yehuda said** that **Rav said: A minor boy who engaged in intercourse with an adult woman**[N] **renders her** as one whose hymen was **ruptured by wood,** as the act is not considered full-fledged intercourse. Rav Yehuda continues: **When I said** this statement **before Shmuel,** he **said** to me: A woman does **not** achieve the status of one whose hymen was **ruptured by wood** by means of **flesh,**[H] i.e., intercourse.

אִיכָּא דְּמַתְנֵי לָהּ לְהָא שְׁמַעְתָּא בְּאַפֵּי נַפְשַׁהּ: קָטָן הַבָּא עַל הַגְּדוֹלָה, רַב אָמַר: עֲשָׂאָהּ מוּכַּת עֵץ, וּשְׁמוּאֵל אָמַר: אֵין מוּכַּת עֵץ בְּבָשָׂר.

Some teach this *halakha* independent of Rav Yehuda: With regard to **a minor boy who engaged in intercourse with an adult woman, Rav said: He renders her** as one whose hymen was **ruptured by wood. And Shmuel said:** A woman does **not** achieve the status of one whose hymen was **ruptured by wood** by means of **flesh.**

מְתִיב רַב אוֹשַׁעְיָא: גָּדוֹל שֶׁבָּא עַל הַקְּטַנָּה, וְקָטָן הַבָּא עַל הַגְּדוֹלָה, וּמוּכַּת עֵץ – כְּתוּבָּתָן מָאתַיִם, דִּבְרֵי רַבִּי מֵאִיר. וַחֲכָמִים אוֹמְרִים: מוּכַּת עֵץ כְּתוּבָּתָהּ מָנֶה!

Rav Oshaya raised an objection to the opinion of Rav from the mishna: With regard to **an adult man who engaged in intercourse with a minor girl** less than three years old, **or a minor boy** less than nine years old **who engaged in intercourse with an adult woman, or a** woman who had her hymen **ruptured by wood**[B] or any other foreign object, **the marriage contract** for each of these women **is two hundred** dinars. This is **the statement of Rabbi Meir. And the Rabbis say: The marriage contract** of a woman whose hymen was **ruptured by wood is one hundred dinars.** Contrary to Rav's opinion, the Rabbis distinguish between the *halakha* in the case of the intercourse of a minor boy and the *halakha* in the case of a woman whose hymen was ruptured by wood.

אָמַר רָבָא: הָכִי קָאָמַר גָּדוֹל הַבָּא עַל הַקְּטַנָּה – וְלֹא כְלוּם, דִּפְחוֹת מִכָּאן כְּנוֹתֵן אֶצְבַּע בָּעַיִן דָּמֵי. וְקָטָן הַבָּא עַל הַגְּדוֹלָה – עֲשָׂאָהּ מוּכַּת עֵץ, וּמוּכַּת עֵץ גּוּפָא – פְּלוּגְתָּא דְּרַבִּי מֵאִיר וְרַבָּנַן.

Rava said that **this is what** the mishna **is saying: An adult man who engaged in intercourse with a minor girl** less than three years old has done **nothing, as** intercourse with a girl **less than** three years old **is tantamount to poking a finger into the eye.** In the case of an eye, after a tear falls from it another tear forms to replace it. Similarly, the ruptured hymen of the girl younger than three is restored. **And a young boy who engaged in intercourse with an adult woman renders her** as one whose hymen **was ruptured by wood. And** with regard to the case of a woman whose hymen was **ruptured by wood itself,** there is a **dispute between Rabbi Meir and the Rabbis.** Rabbi Meir maintains that her marriage contract is two hundred dinars, and the Rabbis maintain that it is one hundred dinars.

NOTES

More than three years and one day old – יְתֵירוֹת עַל בְּנוֹת שָׁלֹשׁ שָׁנִים וְיוֹם אֶחָד: In all these cases, these women no longer have the presumptive status of a virgin either due to the fact that they are subject to the control of others or because chastity is not their concern. This is not age dependent; however, for a girl younger than three, intercourse is not considered intercourse at all.

A minor boy who engaged in intercourse with an adult woman – קָטָן הַבָּא עַל הַגְּדוֹלָה: With regard to the dispute between Rav and Shmuel, there are two primary approaches. According to *Tosafot*, they disagree with regard to a case where her hymen remained intact. The dispute is whether a woman who engaged in intercourse with a boy younger than nine is comparable to a woman whose hymen was ruptured by a foreign object according to the opinion of the Rabbis that her marriage contract is one hundred dinars, or whether that does not apply in this case as the intercourse of a boy less than nine is inconsequential.

Tosefot Rid, however, maintains that they disagree even in a case where the hymen was ruptured. Based on the understanding that the amount in the marriage contract is determined based on the degree that the woman finds favor in the eyes of the groom, the definition of virgin is not necessarily dependent on whether or not the hymen is intact. Rather, it is dependent on whether or not she engaged in intercourse. The Rid explicitly writes that if she herself ruptured her hymen, she is still considered a virgin. According to Rav, intercourse with a boy less than nine years old is considered intercourse in the sense that it mitigates the favor that she finds in the eyes of the groom. The same is true of a woman whose hymen was ruptured by a foreign object according to the Rabbis. According to Shmuel, intercourse with a minor is not considered intercourse at all, and it carries with it less of a stigma than a woman whose hymen was ruptured by a foreign object according to the Rabbis.

HALAKHA

A female convert…more than three years and one day old – הַגִּיּוֹרֶת...יְתֵירוֹת עַל בְּנוֹת שָׁלֹשׁ שָׁנִים וְיוֹם אֶחָד: A female gentile, captive, or slave who was converted, redeemed, or freed respectively when she was more than three years and one day old has lost her presumptive status of a virgin and is entitled to a marriage contract of only one hundred dinars. On the other hand, her husband cannot make a claim concerning her virginity (Rambam *Sefer Nashim, Hilkhot Ishut* 11:1; *Shulḥan Arukh, Even HaEzer* 67:3).

A woman does not achieve the status of one whose hymen was ruptured by wood by means of flesh – אֵין מוּכַּת עֵץ בְּבָשָׂר: If a grown woman engages in intercourse with a boy younger than nine years old, she is still entitled to a marriage contract of two hundred dinars in accordance with the opinion of Shmuel, as the *halakha* is ruled in accordance with his opinion in civil matters. This ruling applies only if the woman's hymen was not ruptured as a result of that intercourse; however, if the hymen was ruptured, she is entitled to a marriage contract of one hundred dinars, like a woman whose hymen was ruptured by a foreign object (*Tosafot*; Rambam *Sefer Nashim, Hilkhot Ishut* 11:3; *Shulḥan Arukh, Even HaEzer* 67:4).

BACKGROUND

A woman who had her hymen ruptured by wood – מוּכַּת עֵץ: Penetration of the vagina with a hard, foreign object can rupture the hymen, e.g., if a girl falls and a hard, protruding object comes into contact with the vagina (see 36b). This is an unlikely occurrence, as a typical fall would not lead to such a result (see *Tosafot* 9b).

אֲמַר רָמִי בַּר חָמָא: מַחֲלוֹקֶת כְּשֶׁהִכִּיר בָּהּ; דְּרַבִּי מֵאִיר מְדַמֵּי לָהּ לְבוֹגֶרֶת, וְרַבָּנַן מְדַמּוּ לָהּ לִבְעוּלָה. אֲבָל לֹא הִכִּיר בָּהּ – דִּבְרֵי הַכֹּל וְלֹא כְּלוּם.

Rami bar Ḥama said: This dispute is specifically in a case **where** the husband **was aware that her** hymen was ruptured by wood, **as** in that case **Rabbi Meir likens her to a grown woman,**[N] whose hymen does not completely obstruct the orifice as a result of the maturation process. Nevertheless, her marriage contract is that of a virgin, two hundred dinars. **And the Rabbis liken her to a non-virgin** who engaged in intercourse in the past. Her marriage contract is one hundred dinars. **However, if he was not aware that her** hymen was ruptured by wood and was under the impression that she was a full-fledged virgin, **everyone agrees** that she receives **no** marriage contract **at all** when he becomes aware of her condition, as the marriage was a mistaken transaction.

וְרַבִּי מֵאִיר אַמַּאי מְדַמֵּי לָהּ לְבוֹגֶרֶת? נְדַמְּיַיהּ לִבְעוּלָה! בְּעוּלָה אִיתְעֲבֵיד בָּהּ מַעֲשֶׂה בִּידֵי אָדָם. הָא – לָא אִיתְעֲבֵיד בָּהּ מַעֲשֶׂה בִּידֵי אָדָם. וְרַבָּנַן, אַדְּמַדְּמוּ לָהּ לִבְעוּלָה נְדַמְּיַיהּ לְבוֹגֶרֶת! בּוֹגֶרֶת לָא אִיתְעֲבֵיד בָּהּ מַעֲשֶׂה כְּלָל, הָא – אִיתְעֲבֵיד בָּהּ מַעֲשֶׂה,

The Gemara asks: **And why does Rabbi Meir liken her to a grown woman? Let him liken her to a non-virgin,** who engaged in intercourse in the past. The Gemara answers: In the case of **a non-virgin, an action was performed on her by a person;** but with regard to **this** woman, whose hymen was ruptured by wood, **an action was not performed on her by a person.** The Gemara asks: **And** with regard to **the Rabbis, rather than likening her to a non-virgin, let them liken her to a grown woman.** The Gemara answers: In the case of a **grown woman, no action was performed on her;** but with regard to **this** woman, whose hymen was ruptured by wood, **an action was performed on her.**

אֲבָל לֹא הִכִּיר בָּהּ – לְדִבְרֵי הַכֹּל וְלֹא כְּלוּם. מְתִיב רַב נַחְמָן: הִיא אוֹמֶרֶת "מוּכַּת עֵץ אֲנִי" וְהוּא אוֹמֵר "לֹא כִּי, אֶלָּא דְּרוּסַת אִישׁ אַתְּ". רַבָּן גַּמְלִיאֵל וְרַבִּי אֱלִיעֶזֶר אוֹמְרִים: נֶאֱמֶנֶת!

Rami bar Ḥama concluded his statement: **However, if he was not aware that her** hymen was ruptured by wood, **everyone agrees** that she receives **no** marriage contract **at all. Rav Naḥman raised an objection** from a mishna (13a): In a case where **she says: I** am one whose hymen was **ruptured by wood,**[N] i.e., she admits that her hymen is not intact but claims that it was not ruptured through intercourse, **and** the groom **says: No; rather, you are** one who **was violated by a man** and you are no longer a virgin, **Rabban Gamliel and Rabbi Eliezer say: She is deemed credible** and her claim is accepted. In that case, she is claiming that she is entitled to a marriage contract. Despite the fact that the groom had no prior awareness of her condition, Rabban Gamliel and Rabbi Eliezer maintain that she is deemed credible and receives a marriage contract of at least one hundred dinars. Apparently, not everyone agrees that in that case she receives nothing at all.

אֶלָּא אָמַר רָבָא: בֵּין הִכִּיר בָּהּ וּבֵין לֹא הִכִּיר בָּהּ, לְרַבִּי מֵאִיר – מָאתַיִם, לְרַבָּנַן; הִכִּיר בָּהּ – מָנֶה, לֹא הִכִּיר בָּהּ – וְלֹא כְּלוּם.

Rather, Rava said: This is what the mishna is saying: **Whether** the husband **was aware that her** hymen was ruptured by wood **and whether he was not aware of her** condition, according **to Rabbi Meir** she receives a marriage contract of **two hundred** dinars and it is not a mistaken transaction. According **to the Rabbis,** if **he was aware of her** condition she receives a marriage contract of **one hundred dinars** like a non-virgin; if **he was not aware of her** condition she receives **no** marriage contract **at all,** since it is a mistaken transaction, as when he married her he believed that her hymen was intact. According to this explanation, the mishna cited by Rav Naḥman is in accordance with the opinion of Rabbi Meir.

וַהֲדַר בֵּיהּ רָבָא, דְּתַנְיָא: כֵּיצַד הוֹצָאַת שֵׁם רַע? בָּא לְבֵית דִּין וְאָמַר: פְּלוֹנִי, לֹא מָצָאתִי לְבִתְּךָ בְּתוּלִים. אִם יֵשׁ עֵדִים שֶׁזִּינְּתָה תַּחְתָּיו – יֵשׁ לָהּ כְּתוּבָּה מָנֶה. אִם יֵשׁ עֵדִים שֶׁזִּינְּתָה תַּחְתָּיו?! בַּת סְקִילָה הִיא! הָכִי קָאָמַר: אִם יֵשׁ עֵדִים שֶׁזִּינְּתָה תַּחְתָּיו – בִּסְקִילָה, זִינְּתָה מֵעִיקָּרָא – יֵשׁ לָהּ כְּתוּבָּה מָנֶה.

And Rava retracted his opinion, **as it is taught** in a *baraita*: **How** does the **slander**[N] described in the Torah come about? If the groom **comes to court and says: So-and-so,** father of the bride, **I did not find in your daughter** an intact **hymen. If there are witnesses that she committed adultery** while **under** the husband's jurisdiction after betrothal, **she** receives **a marriage contract of one hundred dinars.** The Gemara asks: **If there are witnesses that she committed adultery** while **under his** jurisdiction after betrothal, **she is subject to** execution by **stoning.**[N] Obviously, she is in no position to receive a marriage contract. The Gemara answers that **this is what** the mishna **is saying: If there are witnesses that she committed adultery** while **under his** jurisdiction after betrothal, she is subject **to** execution by **stoning.** However, **if she engaged in intercourse initially,** prior to betrothal, **she receives a marriage contract of one hundred dinars,** like any non-virgin.

NOTES

Likens her to a grown woman – מְדַמֵּי לָהּ לְבוֹגֶרֶת: The commentaries agree that the comparison is not perfect, as in the case of a grown woman, whose hymen, as a result of the maturation process, does not completely obstruct the orifice, whether or not her husband was aware of that phenomenon her marriage contract is two hundred dinars (Rashba). In the Jerusalem Talmud this discussion is tied to the matter of a woman whose hymen was ruptured by a foreign object, in terms of the degree in which the woman finds favor in the eyes of the groom. Does a woman whose hymen was ruptured by a foreign object receive a marriage contract of two hundred dinars like a grown woman, who receives two hundred dinars, even though her hymen does not completely obstruct the orifice due to maturation?

She says I am one whose hymen was ruptured by wood – הִיא אוֹמֶרֶת מוּכַּת עֵץ אֲנִי: The early commentaries ask: Why doesn't the Gemara explain that the woman claims that her husband was aware of the fact that her hymen was ruptured; and he claims that he was unaware, and that he married her assuming that she was a virgin but she in fact engaged in intercourse with a man (Rashba; Ritva)? They add that this is the explanation in the Jerusalem Talmud. According to the Gemara here, apparently, in that case where there is a dispute between the groom and the bride with regard to the nature of the agreement between them, there is no reason why Rabban Gamliel would accord credibility specifically to the woman.

Slander – הוֹצָאַת שֵׁם רַע: This source of the *halakha* of a man who accuses his wife of adultery and claims that she was not a virgin is from the Torah (Deuteronomy 22:13–21), and is explained at length by the Gemara (44b–46b). The conclusion drawn from the verses is that it is not merely the claim of a suspicious groom but is a claim corroborated by witnesses. The difference between the various cases depends on the essence of the witnesses' testimony and an examination of their credibility.

She is subject to execution by stoning – בַּת סְקִילָה הִיא: The Rashba writes that it does not mean that she will actually be executed, as stoning is administered only after forewarning. It means that if there are witnesses that she committed adultery she does not receive payment of her marriage contract at all, as a *sota*, a woman suspected of adultery, also does not receive payment.

וְאָמַר רַב חִיָּיא בַּר אָבִין אָמַר רַב שֵׁשֶׁת: זֹאת אוֹמֶרֶת כְּנָסָהּ בְּחֶזְקַת בְּתוּלָה וְנִמְצֵאת בְּעוּלָה – יֵשׁ לָהּ כְּתוּבָּה מָנֶה. וּמְתִיב רַב נַחְמָן: הַנּוֹשֵׂא אֶת הָאִשָּׁה וְלֹא מָצָא לָהּ בְּתוּלִים, הִיא אוֹמֶרֶת ״מִשֶּׁאֵרַסְתַּנִי נֶאֱנַסְתִּי וְנִסְתַּחֲפָה שָׂדֵהוּ״ וְהוּא אוֹמֵר ״לֹא כִּי, אֶלָּא עַד שֶׁלֹּא אֵירַסְתִּיךְ, וְהָיָה מִקָּחִי מִקַּח טָעוּת״, וְלֵית לָהּ כְּלָל?

And Rav Ḥiyya bar Avin said that Rav Sheshet said: That is to say, if the groom married a woman with the presumptive status of a virgin and she is found to be a non-virgin, she receives a marriage contract of one hundred dinars. And Rav Naḥman raised an objection to the statement of Rav Sheshet from a mishna (12b): There is a case of one who marries a woman and did not find her hymen intact, and she says: After you betrothed me I was raped, and his, i.e., her husband's, field was inundated, meaning that it is his misfortune that she is not a virgin, as she was raped after betrothal. And he says: No; rather, you were raped before I betrothed you, and my transaction was a mistaken transaction. The betrothal was predicated on your presumptive status as a virgin and in fact, you were not a virgin then. In that case, she does not receive any marriage contract at all.

וְאָמַר לְהוּ רַב חִיָּיא בַּר אָבִין: אֶפְשָׁר רַב עַמְרָם וְכָל גְּדוֹלֵי הַדּוֹר יָתְבֵי כִּי אֲמַר רַב שֵׁשֶׁת לְהָא שְׁמַעְתָּא, וְקַשְׁיָא לְהוּ, וְשַׁנִּי: מַאי מִקַּח טָעוּת – נַמִי מִמָּאתַיִם, אֲבָל מָנֶה – אִית לָהּ. וְאַתְּ אָמַרְתְּ לֵית לָהּ כְּלָל?!

And Rav Ḥiyya bar Avin said to those present: Is it possible that Rav Amram and all the prominent Sages of the generation were sitting when Rav Sheshet said this *halakha*, and Rav Naḥman's question was difficult for them, and they answered: What is the meaning of mistaken transaction in this context? It too means that he is absolved from his commitment to pay the marriage contract of a virgin, two hundred dinars, because she is not entitled to that sum. However, she is entitled to one hundred dinars. And, contrary to that consensus, you say that she does not receive any marriage contract at all?

וַאֲמַר רָבָא: מַאן דְּקָא מוֹתִיב – שַׁפִּיר קָא מוֹתִיב, מִקַּח טָעוּת – לְגַמְרֵי מַשְׁמַע. וְאֶלָּא קַשְׁיָא הָךְ! תָּרֵיץ וְאֵימָא הָכִי: אִם יֵשׁ עֵדִים שֶׁזִּינְּתָה תַּחְתָּיו – בִּסְקִילָה, זִינְּתָה מֵעִיקָּרָא – וְלֹא כְּלוּם, נִמְצֵאת מוּכַּת עֵץ – יֵשׁ לָהּ כְּתוּבָּה מָנֶה.

And Rava said: The one who raised the objection, Rav Naḥman, raises the objection well, as the term: Mistaken transaction, indicates that the betrothal is dissolved totally.[H] The Gemara asks: But that *baraita* with regard to slander remains difficult, as in that case, if he discovered that she was not a virgin, she receives a marriage contract of one hundred dinars. The Gemara answers: Resolve the apparent contradiction and say this in the text of the *baraita*: If there are witnesses that she committed adultery while under his jurisdiction after betrothal, she is subject to execution by stoning. If she engaged in intercourse initially, prior to betrothal, she receives nothing at all. If she was discovered to be one whose hymen was ruptured by wood,[H] she is entitled to a marriage contract of one hundred dinars.

וְהָא רָבָא הוּא דַּאֲמַר לְרַבָּנַן לֹא הִכִּיר בָּהּ וְלֹא כְּלוּם! אֶלָּא שְׁמַע מִינַּהּ: הֲדַר בֵּיהּ רָבָא מֵהַהִיא.

But isn't it Rava himself who said that according to the Rabbis, in the case of a woman whose hymen was ruptured by wood, if he was not aware of her condition she receives no marriage contract at all? Rather, conclude from it that Rava retracted that statement, and he holds that even according to the Rabbis, even if he was unaware of her condition she receives a marriage contract of one hundred dinars.

תָּנוּ רַבָּנַן: כְּנָסָהּ רִאשׁוֹן לְשׁוּם נִישּׂוּאִין, וְיֵשׁ לָהּ עֵדִים שֶׁלֹּא נִסְתְּרָה. אִי נַמִי, נִסְתְּרָה וְלֹא שָׁהֲתָה כְּדֵי בִּיאָה – אֵין הַשֵּׁנִי יָכוֹל לִטְעוֹן טַעֲנַת בְּתוּלִים, שֶׁהֲרֵי כְּנָסָהּ רִאשׁוֹן.

§ The Sages taught: If her first husband brought her into his home for the purpose of marriage,[N] and she has witnesses who testified that she did not seclude herself with him,[N] or alternatively, they testified that she secluded herself with him and did not stay in seclusion with him for a period equivalent to the time required to engage in intercourse, if the first husband dies or divorces her and she remarries, despite the testimony of the witnesses, the second husband cannot make a claim concerning virginity,[H] and say the betrothal was predicated on the assumption that she was a virgin and she should lose her marriage contract. Since the first husband brought her into his home, the second husband should have considered that a woman who entered her husband's home is no longer a virgin.

HALAKHA

Mistaken transaction indicates that the betrothal is dissolved totally – מִקַּח טָעוּת לְגַמְרֵי מַשְׁמַע: If a man marries a woman under the assumption that she is a virgin and he discovers that she was not a virgin, even if it was due to rape, the marriage contract is voided and she receives no payment, in accordance with the ruling of Rav Sheshet (Rambam *Sefer Nashim*, *Hilkhot Ishut* 11:3; *Shulḥan Arukh*, *Even HaEzer* 67:5).

If she was discovered to be one whose hymen was ruptured by wood – נִמְצֵאת מוּכַּת עֵץ: A woman whose hymen was ruptured by a foreign object is entitled to a marriage contract of one hundred dinars. Even if the groom married her under the assumption that she was a virgin and he discovers that her hymen was ruptured by a foreign object, she is still entitled to a marriage contract of one hundred dinars, in accordance with the opinion of Rami bar Ḥama, as Rava eventually conceded to his opinion (Rambam *Sefer Nashim*, *Hilkhot Ishut* 11:3; *Shulḥan Arukh*, *Even HaEzer* 67:5).

The second husband cannot make a claim concerning virginity – אֵין הַשֵּׁנִי יָכוֹל לִטְעוֹן טַעֲנַת בְּתוּלִים: If a woman was widowed or divorced or underwent *ḥalitza*, she is entitled to a marriage contract of only one hundred dinars when she remarries. The second husband cannot make a claim with regard to her virginity, even if there are witnesses who testify that she never entered into seclusion with her first husband (*Shulḥan Arukh*, *Even HaEzer* 67:2).

NOTES

If her first husband brought her into his home for the purpose of marriage – כְּנָסָהּ רִאשׁוֹן לְשׁוּם נִישּׂוּאִין: Some conclude based on the mishna and other sources that once the woman enters the wedding canopy, which is a prelude to consummation of the marriage, she loses her presumptive status of virginity even though intercourse did not actually take place yet.

Witnesses that she did not seclude herself with him – עֵדִים שֶׁלֹּא נִסְתְּרָה: In the *Shita Mekubbetzet* an explanation appears why these two examples were cited. In the case where the witnesses testified that she did not seclude herself with him there is room for concern that she was indeed secluded, as perhaps they are attempting to have the husband value her more highly. However, in the case where the witnesses testify that she entered into seclusion but did not remain there long, since they testified that she entered the wedding canopy, they are clearly not seeking to praise her; therefore, one might have thought that their testimony is reliable. Furthermore, when they testify that she did not enter into seclusion, perhaps their testimony is not accurate, as their intention was not to observe in order to testify; however, when they testify that she entered into seclusion and they indicate that they had calculated its duration, one might have thought that their testimony is reliable.

NOTES

Because the first husband brought her into his house – **שֶׁהֲרֵי כְּנָסָהּ רִאשׁוֹן**: The commentaries ask: Ostensibly, the distinction suggested by the Gemara is obvious, as the reason for the *halakha* is written explicitly. Why did Rabba think otherwise? The Rivam, cited in *Tosefot*, explains that Rabba understood the phrase to mean that since the first husband brought her into his house and caused her to receive a marriage contract of one hundred dinars, the second husband can no longer make a claim with regard to the other hundred dinars, as a claim of virginity can affect only the hundred dinars to which a virgin is entitled. The Ramban explains that Rabba understood that the phrase adds a novel element, as although he could claim that he relied on the witnesses and did not pay the additional amount of the marriage contract, he would not have married her if he did not believe that she was a virgin. Therefore, even though he could say that he relied on the witnesses, and even though he did not add anything to the one hundred dinars of the marriage contract, he would not have married her had he not thought she was a virgin. Therefore, it states that since she entered the wedding canopy, he can no longer be said to be certain that she is a virgin.

Because she entered the wedding canopy – **שֶׁהֲרֵי נִכְנְסָה לַחוּפָּה**: Rabbeinu Ḥananel writes that since the groom should have determined whether or not the bride previously engaged in intercourse, as there were indications that this was the case, and he failed to investigate, he appears to have assumed that she was not a virgin. The Ramban and others explain that since she had entered the wedding canopy, she no longer finds favor in the eyes of the groom in the manner that a full-fledged virgin does.

אָמַר רַבָּה: זֹאת אוֹמֶרֶת; כְּנָסָהּ בְּחֶזְקַת בְּתוּלָה וְנִמְצֵאת בְּעוּלָה יֵשׁ לָהּ כְּתוּבָּה מָנֶה. רַב אַשִׁי אֲמַר: בְּעָלְמָא לְעוֹלָם אֵימָא לָךְ – לֵית לָהּ כְּלָל, וְשָׁאנֵי הָכָא – שֶׁהֲרֵי כְּנָסָהּ רִאשׁוֹן.

Rabba said: That is to say, if **one married** a woman **with the presumptive status of a virgin,** as there were witnesses that she did not engage in intercourse, **and she was found** to be **a non-virgin, she is** entitled to **a marriage contract of one hundred dinars.** The Gemara rejects the proof. **Rav Ashi said: In general, actually, I** would **say to you** that in that case **she does not** receive a marriage contract **at all,** as it is a mistaken transaction. **But here it is different,** and she does not totally lose her marriage contract, **because the first** husband **brought her into** his house.[N] Therefore, the second husband should have considered that a woman who entered her husband's home is no longer a virgin.

וְנֵיחוּשׁ שֶׁמָּא תַּחְתָּיו זִינְּתָה! אָמַר רַב שֵׁרֵבְיָא: כְּגוֹן שֶׁקִּידֵּשׁ וּבָעַל לְאַלְתַּר.

The Gemara asks: **And** since there are witnesses that she did not engage in intercourse with the first husband, **let us be concerned that perhaps she committed adultery** after betrothal, **while under** the jurisdiction of the second husband, and rule that she is forbidden to him due to suspicion of adultery and is not entitled to a marriage contract at all. **Rav Sherevya said:** The *baraita* is referring to a case **where he betrothed** her **and engaged in intercourse immediately.** Therefore, there was no opportunity to engage in adultery between her betrothal and her marriage to the second husband.

וְאִיכָּא דְּמַתְנֵי לָהּ אַמַּתְנִיתִין: בְּתוּלָה אַלְמָנָה, גְּרוּשָׁה, חֲלוּצָה, מִן הַנִּישּׂוּאִין – כְּתוּבָּתָן מָנֶה, וְאֵין לָהֶן טַעֲנַת בְּתוּלִין. בְּתוּלָה מִן הַנִּישּׂוּאִין הֵיכִי מַשְׁכַּחַתְּ לָהּ? כְּגוֹן שֶׁנִּכְנְסָה לַחוּפָּה וְלֹא נִבְעֲלָה.

Others taught this statement of Rabba **with regard to the mishna:** Concerning **a virgin** who is **a widow, a divorcée,** or **a** *ḥalutza* who achieved that status **from** a state of **marriage,** for all these women **their marriage contract is one hundred dinars, and they are not subject** to **a claim** concerning their **virginity.** The Gemara asks: **How can you find a virgin from** a state of **marriage?** It is in a case **where she entered the wedding canopy and did not engage in intercourse.**

אָמַר רַבָּה: זֹאת אוֹמֶרֶת; כְּנָסָהּ בְּחֶזְקַת בְּתוּלָה וְנִמְצֵאת בְּעוּלָה – כְּתוּבָּתָהּ מָנֶה. רַב אַשִׁי אֲמַר: בְּעָלְמָא לְעוֹלָם אֵימָא לָךְ – לֵית לָהּ כְּלָל, וְשָׁאנֵי הָכָא – שֶׁהֲרֵי נִכְנְסָה לַחוּפָּה.

Rabba said: That is to say, if **one married** a woman **with the presumptive status of a virgin and she was found** to be **a non-virgin, her marriage contract is one hundred dinars.** The Gemara rejects the proof. **Rav Ashi said: In general, actually, I** would **say to you** that **in general, she does not** receive a marriage contract **at all,** as it is a mistaken transaction. **But here it is different,** and she does not totally lose her marriage contract, **because she entered the wedding canopy.**[N] Therefore, the second husband should have considered that a woman who entered her husband's home is no longer a virgin.

וְנֵיחוּשׁ שֶׁמָּא תַּחְתָּיו זִינְּתָה! אָמַר רַב שֵׁרֵבְיָא: כְּגוֹן שֶׁקִּידֵּשׁ וּבָעַל לְאַלְתַּר.

The Gemara asks: **And let us be concerned that perhaps she committed adultery** after betrothal, **while under** the jurisdiction of the second husband. **Rav Sherevya said:** The *baraita* is referring to a case **where he betrothed** her **and engaged in intercourse immediately.** Therefore, there was no opportunity to engage in adultery between her betrothal and her marriage to the second husband.

מַאן דְּמַתְנֵי לָהּ אַבָּרַיְיתָא – כׇּל שֶׁכֵּן אַמַּתְנִיתִין, וּמַאן דְּמַתְנֵי לָהּ אַמַּתְנִיתִין – אֲבָל אַבָּרַיְיתָא לָא, מִשּׁוּם דְּמָצֵי אָמַר לָהּ: אֲנָא אַעֵדִים סָמְכִי.

The Gemara notes: **The one who taught** the exchange between Rabba and Rav Ashi **with regard to the** *baraita,* where there is explicit testimony that she did not engage in intercourse with the first husband and nevertheless no proof can be brought that if he discovers that she is not a virgin she receives a marriage contract of one hundred dinars, **all the more so** would he say that the same is true **with regard to the mishna.** And **the one who taught** the exchange **with regard to the mishna, however,** would **not** say the same **with regard to the** *baraita,* **due to** the fact **that** the husband could **say to her: I relied on witnesses.** Therefore, proof can be brought from the *baraita* that if he discovered that she is not a virgin, she receives a marriage contract of one hundred dinars.

מתני׳ הָאוֹכֵל אֵצֶל חָמִיו בִּיהוּדָה שֶׁלֹּא בְּעֵדִים – אֵינוֹ יָכוֹל לִטְעוֹן טַעֲנַת בְּתוּלִים, מִפְּנֵי שֶׁמִּתְיַיחֵד עִמָּהּ.

MISHNA A man **who eats at** the house of **his father-in-law**[HN] **in Judea** after betrothal and **without witnesses** to attest to the fact that he was not alone with his betrothed **is unable to make a claim concerning virginity** after marriage **because** in accordance with the custom in Judea, the assumption is **that he secluded himself with her,** and the concern is that it was he who engaged in intercourse with her.

גמ׳ מִדְּקָתָנֵי ״הָאוֹכֵל״ מִכְּלָל דְּאִיכָּא דּוּכְתָּא בִּיהוּדָה נַמִי דְּלָא אָכֵיל! אָמַר אַבַּיֵי: שְׁמַע מִינָּהּ בִּיהוּדָה נַמִי מְקוֹמוֹת מְקוֹמוֹת יֵשׁ. כִּדְתַנְיָא, אָמַר רַבִּי יְהוּדָה: בִּיהוּדָה, בָּרִאשׁוֹנָה הָיוּ מְיַיחֲדִין אֶת הֶחָתָן וְאֶת הַכַּלָּה שָׁעָה אַחַת קוֹדֶם כְּנִיסָתָן לַחוּפָּה, כְּדֵי שֶׁיְּהֵא לִבּוֹ גַּס בָּהּ. וּבַגָּלִיל לֹא הָיוּ עוֹשִׂין כֵּן.

GEMARA The Gemara infers: **From** the fact **that** the mishna **teaches** the *halakha* employing the phrase: A man **who eats, by inference** one may conclude **that there is also a place in Judea where** the groom **does not eat** at the house of his father-in-law, and does not enter into seclusion with his betrothed. **Abaye said: Conclude from it that in Judea too there are** different **places** with different customs, **as it is taught** in a *baraita* that **Rabbi Yehuda said: In Judea, at first they would seclude the groom and bride** together **for a brief period before their entry into the wedding canopy, so that he would** grow **accustomed to her** companionship in order to ease the awkwardness when they would consummate the marriage. **And in the Galilee they did not do so.**

בִּיהוּדָה, בָּרִאשׁוֹנָה הָיוּ מַעֲמִידִין לָהֶם שְׁנֵי שׁוֹשְׁבִינִין, אֶחָד לוֹ וְאֶחָד לָהּ, כְּדֵי לְמַשְׁמֵשׁ אֶת הֶחָתָן וְאֶת הַכַּלָּה בִּשְׁעַת כְּנִיסָתָן לַחוּפָּה, וּבַגָּלִיל לֹא הָיוּ עוֹשִׂין כֵּן.

The *baraita* continues. **In Judea, at first they would appoint for them two groomsmen** [*shushvinin*],[LN] **one for him and one for her, in order to examine**[N] **the groom and the bride at the time of their entry into the wedding canopy** and thereafter, to ensure that neither would engage in deception with regard to the presence or absence of blood from the rupture of the hymen. **And in the Galilee**[B] **they would not do so.**[N] As the custom of appointing groomsmen would be relevant only in a case where the groom and the bride had not been together in seclusion prior to marriage, this is apparently a custom in Judea different from the first custom cited in the mishna, where they would enter into seclusion prior to marriage.

בִּיהוּדָה, בָּרִאשׁוֹנָה הָיוּ שׁוֹשְׁבִינִין יְשֵׁנִים בְּבַיִת שֶׁחָתָן וְכַלָּה יְשֵׁנִים בָּהּ, וּבַגָּלִיל לֹא הָיוּ עוֹשִׂין כֵּן.

The *baraita* continues. **In Judea, at first the groomsmen would sleep in the house in which the groom and bride sleep,** in order to examine the sheet on which the marriage was consummated immediately following intercourse. This was in order to ensure that the groom would not attempt to obscure the blood of the rupture of the hymen and claim that the bride was not a virgin. **And in the Galilee they would not do so.**

NOTES

A man who eats at the house of his father-in-law – הָאוֹכֵל אֵצֶל חָמִיו: The reason for this custom in Judea is cited by several commentaries in the Jerusalem Talmud. It was related to the Roman decree that virgin brides submit to intercourse with the prefect first. To ensure that the woman would not submit to the prefect willingly, they sought in Judea to bolster the relationship between the bride and groom by cultivating a more intimate relationship between them. Rabbeinu Yehonatan adds that once the prefect discovered that the woman was not a virgin, he would not be insistent in exercising his right. From most commentaries it appears that this seclusion included physical intimacy and at times involved intercourse. The Meiri writes that when they entered into seclusion they would make a festive meal, and this is why it is referred to as: A man who eats in the house of his father-in-law. In the Jerusalem Talmud it is noted that the custom remained in effect in Judea even after the decree was revoked.

In Judea at first they would appoint for them two groomsmen – בִּיהוּדָה בָּרִאשׁוֹנָה הָיוּ מַעֲמִידִין לָהֶם שְׁנֵי שׁוֹשְׁבִינִין: The Rashba and the Ritva explain that this custom was prevalent specifically in Judea because the people of Judea were deceitful and required supervision. It appears from several sources that Judeans were educated and quick witted, in contrast to those in the Galilee who were simpler people.

The Meiri explains that there is a connection between this custom and the custom to enter into seclusion. Since it was common in Judea for the bride to enter the wedding canopy when no longer a virgin, there was naturally more suspicion as well as additional opportunity for deception by both the groom and the bride. Others explain that the examination by the groomsmen was effective only with regard to the claim of blood from the rupture of the hymen, but not with regard to the claim of an unobstructed orifice. The Meiri writes that in places where there was suspicion with regard to these matters, women would be enlisted to examine the bride and ensure that she was not seeking to deceive the groom with regard to her virginity.

Examination – מִשְׁמוּשׁ: The meaning of this term here and elsewhere (see Genesis 31:37), is examination. This examination was to ensure that the bride did not bring a bloodstained sheet and replace the sheet of the marriage bed with it, and also that the groom did not bring a clean sheet and replace the bloodstained sheet of the marriage bed with it in order to make a false claim against the bride. See the Meiri and other sources, who point out that there were other forms of deception employed by the bride on the wedding night in order to create an impression that she was indeed a virgin. The examination was designed to prevent all forms of deception.

And in the Galilee they would not do so – וּבַגָּלִיל לֹא הָיוּ עוֹשִׂין כֵּן: The Rashba writes that even though there were groomsmen in the Galilee, these would examine the bride to ensure that she did not bring a cloth already stained with blood, but they would not examine the groom.

HALAKHA

A man who eats at the house of his father-in-law – הָאוֹכֵל אֵצֶל חָמִיו: If the groom enters into seclusion with the bride before the wedding, he cannot then make a claim concerning her virginity. See, however, *Beit Shmuel*, which points out that according to *Tosafot*, this applies only in places where the seclusion is sanctioned according to local custom, not where it happened unsanctioned (Rambam *Sefer Nashim, Hilkhot Ishut* 11:8; *Shulḥan Arukh, Even HaEzer* 68:1).

LANGUAGE

Groomsmen [*shushvinin*] – שׁוֹשְׁבִינִין: This word, which appears in both Aramaic and Hebrew, apparently derives from Syriac. Some assert that it is from the root *yod, shin, beit*, meaning sit, indicating the one who seats the groom at the wedding. In Aramaic, *shushvinim* are the friends and those who accompany the groom. Apparently, during the mishnaic and talmudic eras the *shushvinim* did not merely fill the symbolic function of escorting the groom to the wedding; rather, they gave him gifts and assisted him at the wedding.

The role of *shushvin* was firmly established to the extent that it was considered a legal obligation for the groom, or his family, to reciprocate and serve as groomsman at the wedding of his groomsman or members of his family. This Gemara notes that the groomsman filled the additional role of ensuring that there was no deception on the part of the groom or the bride with regard to claims concerning virginity.

BACKGROUND

Judea and Galilee – יְהוּדָה וְגָלִיל:

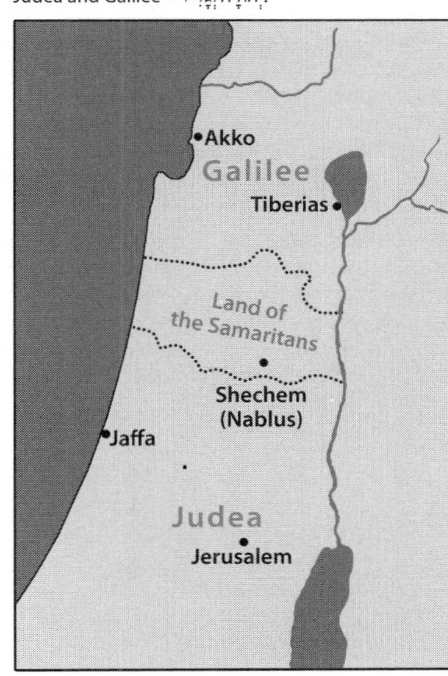

Location of Judea and Galilee

וְכָל שֶׁלֹּא נָהַג כְּמִנְהָג הַזֶּה אֵינוֹ יָכוֹל לִטְעוֹן טַעֲנַת בְּתוּלִים. אַהַיָּיא? אִילֵימָא אַרֵישָׁא – ״כָּל שֶׁנָּהַג״ מִיבְּעֵי לֵיהּ!

The *baraita* concludes: **And anyone who did not conduct** himself **in accordance with this custom cannot make a claim concerning virginity** against the bride. The Gemara asks: **Concerning which** case in the *baraita* was this principle stated? **If we say** it is **concerning the first clause** of the *baraita*, regarding the custom to seclude the couple prior to marriage, in that case, the phrase: **Anyone who conducted** himself in accordance with this custom cannot make a claim concerning virginity, is what **it needed to say,** due to the concern that perhaps they had sexual relations before the marriage.

אֶלָּא אַסֵּיפָא – ״כָּל שֶׁלֹּא מוּשְׁמָשׁ״ מִיבְּעֵי לֵיהּ!

Rather, it is **concerning the latter clause** of the *baraita*: They would appoint for them two groomsmen to examine them, that the principle was stated. In that case, the phrase: **Anyone who was not examined**[H] by the groomsmen, is what **it needed** to say, as it is dependent on the family of the bride, and not the phrase: Anyone who did not conduct himself in accordance with this custom, which indicates that it depends on him.

אָמַר אַבָּיֵי: לְעוֹלָם אַרֵישָׁא, וּתְנֵי: ״כָּל שֶׁנָּהַג״. אֲמַר לֵיהּ רָבָא: וְהָא ״כָּל שֶׁלֹּא נָהַג״ קָתָנֵי! אֶלָּא אָמַר רָבָא, הָכִי קָאָמַר: כָּל שֶׁלֹּא נָהַג מִנְהַג גָּלִיל בְּגָלִיל אֶלָּא מִנְהַג יְהוּדָה בְּגָלִיל אֵינוֹ יָכוֹל לִטְעוֹן טַעֲנַת בְּתוּלִים. רַב אַשִׁי אָמַר: לְעוֹלָם אַסֵּיפָא, וּתְנֵי: ״כָּל שֶׁלֹּא מוּשְׁמָשׁ״.

Abaye said: Actually, the principle is stated **concerning the first clause; and** emend the *baraita* **and teach: Anyone who conducted** himself in accordance with this custom. **Rava said to him: But isn't it teaching** explicitly: **Anyone who did not conduct** himself in accordance with this custom? One should not corrupt a *baraita* due to a difficulty that arose in understanding it. **Rather, Rava said** that **this is what** the *baraita* **is saying: Anyone who did not practice the custom of the Galilee in the Galilee, but** instead observed **the custom of Judea in the Galilee, cannot make a claim concerning virginity** against the bride. **Rav Ashi said: Actually,** this principle could be applied **concerning the latter clause, and teach: Anyone who was not examined.**[N] When it said in the *baraita*: Anyone who did not conduct himself in accordance with this custom, it is referring to the custom of being examined.

מתני׳ אַחַת אַלְמְנַת יִשְׂרָאֵל וְאַחַת אַלְמְנַת כֹּהֲנִים כְּתוּבָּתָהּ מָנֶה. בֵּית דִּין שֶׁל כֹּהֲנִים הָיוּ גּוֹבִין לִבְתוּלָה אַרְבַּע מֵאוֹת זוּז, וְלֹא מִיחוּ בְּיָדָם חֲכָמִים.

MISHNA For **both a widow** who is **an Israelite woman**[N] **and a widow** who is the daughter **of priests, her marriage contract is one hundred dinars. A court of priests**[NB] **would collect** a marriage contract of **four hundred dinars for a virgin** daughter of a priest, twice the sum of the standard marriage contract for a virgin, **and the Sages did not reprimand them.**[N]

גמ׳ תָּנָא: וְאַלְמְנַת כֹּהֲנִים כְּתוּבָּתָהּ מָאתַיִם. וְהָאֲנַן תְּנַן: אַחַת אַלְמְנַת יִשְׂרָאֵל וְאַחַת אַלְמְנַת כֹּהֲנִים כְּתוּבָּתָן מָנֶה!

GEMARA A Sage **taught** in a *baraita*: **And** for a **widow** who is the daughter **of priests, her marriage contract is two hundred** dinars. The Gemara asks: **But didn't we learn** in the mishna: For **both a widow** who is **an Israelite woman and a widow** who is the daughter **of priests, their marriage contract is one hundred dinars?**

אָמַר רַב אַשִׁי: שְׁתֵּי תַקָּנוֹת הָווּ; מֵעִיקָּרָא תַּקִּינוּ לִבְתוּלָה אַרְבַּע מֵאוֹת זוּז, וּלְאַלְמָנָה מָנֶה.

Rav Ashi said: There were two ordinances[N] instituted: **Initially, the** court of priests **instituted for a virgin** daughter of a priest a marriage contract of **four hundred dinars, and for a widow,** a marriage contract of **one hundred dinars.**

HALAKHA

Anyone who was not examined – כָּל שֶׁלֹּא מוּשְׁמָשׁ: If it is the local custom to appoint witnesses to examine the bride and groom to prevent deception with regard to the groom's claim concerning virginity, and none were appointed, the husband cannot make a claim. However, in places where this is not the custom, the husband's claim is accepted based on the presumption that a person does not exert himself to prepare a wedding feast and then cause it to be lost (*Ḥelkat Meḥokek*; *Shulḥan Arukh, Even HaEzer* 68:2).

NOTES

And teach: Anyone who was not examined – וּתְנֵי כָּל שֶׁלֹּא מוּשְׁמָשׁ: The Rivam explains that Rav Ashi disagrees with the presumption: A person does not exert himself to prepare a wedding feast and then cause it to be lost (10a), because in his opinion whether the groom can make a claim concerning virginity is dependent upon the examination. Rabbeinu Tam says that Rav Ashi does not disagree with the presumption, but that he adds that since in Judea the custom was to be examined and the groom failed to observe it, there is suspicion that the failure was not due to forgetfulness but rather it was intentional, in order to cast aspersions on the bride. Therefore, his claim is groundless (*Tosefot Yeshanim*; Rosh).

Both a widow who is an Israelite woman – אַחַת אַלְמְנַת יִשְׂרָאֵל: Rabbeinu Yehonatan writes that the basis for specifying this is that since this mishna is discussing even a woman marrying a priest, one might say that since she is improving her social status she would be satisfied with any amount, even less than one hundred dinars.

A court of priests – בֵּית דִּין שֶׁל כֹּהֲנִים: It is explained in the name of the *ge'onim* that these were courts that were in cities in which the majority of the population consisted of priests. Such cities existed during the second Temple period and thereafter.

And the Sages did not reprimand them – וְלֹא מִיחוּ בְּיָדָם חֲכָמִים: Some explain that the Sages approved of this practice, and that even if the sum was not explicitly written in the marriage contract they would collect this amount based on general agreement (Ritva). Others explains that despite the potential for jealousy caused by the inequality, the Sages did not reprimand them (Meiri).

Two ordinances – שְׁתֵּי תַקָּנוֹת: The early commentaries discuss: How did they arrive at a total of two ordinances, and how do they know that there were two ordinances? According to Rav Ashi it was only one ordinance, which was later revoked. Rashi explains that there were two steps taken for the benefit of the widows of priests, as both the original ordinance and its subsequent repeal were for their benefit.

BACKGROUND

A court of priests – בֵּית דִּין שֶׁל כֹּהֲנִים: Based on descriptions in various talmudic sources, there were apparently several courts under the jurisdiction of the Great Sanhedrin that convened in the Temple and that addressed different problems. One of those courts was the court of priests. This court addressed problems relating to the Temple and its service, e.g., examining the lineage of the priests who came to serve, as well as additional matters, and there are sources indicating that it was the responsibility of this court to establish the New Moon. The court, and the priests in general, had special traditions and customs. See later in the Gemara (14a), where it says that the priests would not always accept the rulings of other courts with regard to the lineage of the priests. Based on the Gemara here, this tribunal also served as the official court of the priests, establishing matters applicable to all priests.

כֵּיוָן דְּחָזוּ דְּמְזַלְזְלִי בְּהוּ – תַּקִּינוּ לְהוּ מָאתַן. כֵּיוָן דְּחָזוּ דְּקָא פָּרְשִׁין מִינַּיְיהוּ, דְּאָמְרִי: עַד דְּנַסְבִינַן אַלְמְנַת כֹּהֲנִים – נֵיזִיל נִסֵּיב בְּתוּלָה בַּת יִשְׂרָאֵל, אַהַדְרִינְהוּ לְמִלְּתַיְיהוּ.

Once the members of the court **saw that** the priests **were demeaning** the widows, **they instituted for them** a marriage contract of **two hundred** dinars, so that they would treat them with greater esteem. **Once they saw that** the grooms **were distancing** themselves **from them, as they said: Instead of marrying a widow** who is the daughter of **priests** and paying a marriage contract of two hundred, **let us go marry a virgin Israelite woman** for the same price. Since men would no longer marry widows from priestly families, **they restored** matters **to their** original **status.** This indicates that the mishna and the *baraita* are addressing different time periods and different ordinances.

״בֵּית דִּין שֶׁל כֹּהֲנִים״ כו׳. אָמַר רַב יְהוּדָה אָמַר שְׁמוּאֵל: לֹא בֵּית דִּין שֶׁל כֹּהֲנִים בִּלְבַד אָמְרוּ, אֶלָּא אֲפִילּוּ מִשְׁפָּחוֹת הַמְיוּחָסוֹת בְּיִשְׂרָאֵל, אִם רָצוּ לַעֲשׂוֹת כְּדֶרֶךְ שֶׁהַכֹּהֲנִים עוֹשִׂין – עוֹשִׂין.

§ It is stated in the mishna that **a court of priests** would collect a marriage contract of four hundred dinars for a virgin daughter of a priest. **Rav Yehuda said** that **Shmuel said: Not only with regard to a court of priests did** the Sages **say** that[H] they could collect a greater sum for the marriage contract of their daughters, **but even families of distinguished lineage**[N] **in Israel. If they wanted to act as the priests do, they may act** in that manner.

מֵיתִיבֵי: הָרוֹצֶה לַעֲשׂוֹת כְּדֶרֶךְ שֶׁהַכֹּהֲנִים עוֹשִׂין, כְּגוֹן בַּת יִשְׂרָאֵל לְכֹהֵן וּבַת כֹּהֵן לְיִשְׂרָאֵל – עוֹשִׂין. בַּת יִשְׂרָאֵל לְכֹהֵן, וּבַת כֹּהֵן לְיִשְׂרָאֵל הוּא דְּאִיכָּא צַד כְּהוּנָּה, אֲבָל בַּת יִשְׂרָאֵל לְיִשְׂרָאֵל – לָא!

The Gemara **raises an objection** from a *baraita*: **One who sought to act as the priests do,** as in cases **where an Israelite woman** is married **to a priest, or the daughter of a priest** is married **to an Israelite, may act** in that manner. The Gemara infers: This allowance is specifically in cases where **an Israelite woman** is married **to a priest, or the daughter of a priest** is married **to an Israelite, where there is an aspect of priesthood**[N] involved. **However,** apparently, in a case where **the daughter of an Israelite** is married **to an Israelite, no,** it is not allowed.

לָא מִבַּעְיָא קָאָמַר; לָא מִבַּעְיָא בַּת יִשְׂרָאֵל לְיִשְׂרָאֵל, דְּלָא מָצֵי אָמַר לַהּ עַלּוּיֵי קָא מְעַלֵּינַן לִיךְ, אֲבָל בַּת יִשְׂרָאֵל לְכֹהֵן, דְּמָצֵי אָמַר לַהּ עַלּוּיֵי קָא מְעַלֵּינַן לִיךְ, אֵימָא לָא – קָא מַשְׁמַע לַן.

The Gemara rejects that inference. The *baraita* **is stated** employing the style of: **It is not necessary. It is not necessary** to state a case where **the daughter of an Israelite** is married **to an Israelite, as** in that case the groom **cannot say to her:** By marrying you, **I am raising your** social status, and it is clear that women from distinguished families would demand a marriage contract with a greater sum. **However,** in a case where **an Israelite woman** is married **to a priest,**[N] **where he can say to her: I am raising your** social status, as you are marrying into the priesthood, you might think to **say no,** the woman cannot demand a marriage contract with a greater sum. Therefore, the *baraita* **teaches us** that even in the case of a woman from a distinguished family of Israelites marrying a priest, she may demand a marriage contract with a greater sum.

HALAKHA

Not only with regard to a court of priests did the Sages say that – לֹא בֵּית דִּין שֶׁל כֹּהֲנִים בִּלְבַד אָמְרוּ: If a family has a custom to write in their marriage contract a sum greater than the standard sum established by the Sages, they are not reprimanded. Furthermore, if a member of that family did not write a marriage contract for his wife, the court collects payment for her in the amount corresponding to the family custom (*Ḥelkat Meḥokek*; *Shulḥan Arukh*, *Even HaEzer* 66:7).

NOTES

But even families of distinguished lineage – אֶלָּא אֲפִילּוּ מִשְׁפָּחוֹת הַמְיוּחָסוֹת: The courts would support this practice and collect the greater sum for the women according to the family custom. It was necessary to state this in order to emphasize that this practice does not constitute violation of the rabbinic ordinance of two hundred dinars for a virgin and one hundred for a non-virgin (*Tosefot Rid*). The *ge'onim* note that despite the approval expressed in the Gemara, this practice was not adopted in Babylonia. The Meiri writes that this *halakha* applies only to families of distinguished lineage.

Where there is an aspect of priesthood – דְּאִיכָּא צַד כְּהוּנָּה: This explanation appears strange, since the reason for the greater sum is relevant only to the daughter of a priest but not to the daughter of a non-priest. Ritva explains that the priests did not want to flaunt their prominence conspicuously, so they instituted a marriage contract with a greater sum in any case involving a priestly family, even if the groom was the priest and the bride the daughter of a non-priest. Rashba explains the matter in terms of interpersonal relationships. Were the daughter of a non-priest marrying a priest to receive a standard marriage contract, lower than the one received by her mother-in-law and sister-in-law, she would be jealous and resentful of them.

An Israelite woman married to a priest – בַּת יִשְׂרָאֵל לְכֹהֵן: In the Jerusalem Talmud, explanations are cited supporting the payment of a greater sum in each of the cases. On the one hand, the daughter of a priest marrying a non-priest should receive a greater sum in her marriage contract, as in general priests receive gifts from non-priests, and in contrast, the daughter of a non-priest marrying a priest should suffice with her newly acquired elevated social status and no additional sum should be necessary.

On the other hand, the daughter of a non-priest marrying a priest should receive a greater sum in her marriage contract because she is now being elevated into the priesthood, i.e., she may now partake of *teruma*. Her marriage contract should reflect that elevated status. And in contrast, the daughter of a priest marrying a non-priest should receive a standard marriage contract since she thereby forfeits all rights of the priesthood.

The conclusion is that in both cases there is a marriage contract with a greater sum. In addition, in order to encourage people to marry within their own tribe, the Sages levied a fine penalizing the non-priest groom who marries the daughter of a priest.

מתני׳ הַנּוֹשֵׂא אֶת הָאִשָּׁה וְלֹא מָצָא לָהּ בְּתוּלִים, הִיא אוֹמֶרֶת: מִשֶּׁאֵרַסְתַּנִי נֶאֱנַסְתִּי, וְנִסְתַּחֲפָה שָׂדֵהוּ. וְהוּא אוֹמֵר: לֹא כִּי, אֶלָּא עַד שֶׁלֹּא אֵרַסְתִּיךְ, וְהָיָה מִקָּחִי מִקַּח טָעוּת. רַבָּן גַּמְלִיאֵל וְרַבִּי אֱלִיעֶזֶר אוֹמְרִים: נֶאֱמֶנֶת. רַבִּי יְהוֹשֻׁעַ אוֹמֵר: לֹא מִפִּיהָ אָנוּ חַיִּין, אֶלָּא הֲרֵי זוֹ בְּחֶזְקַת בְּעוּלָה עַד שֶׁלֹּא תִּתְאָרֵס וְהִטְעַתּוּ, עַד שֶׁתָּבִיא רְאָיָה לִדְבָרֶיהָ.

MISHNA There is a case of one **who marries a woman and did not find her hymen** intact, and **she says: After you betrothed me I was raped,**[H] **and his,** i.e., her husband's, **field was inundated,** meaning that it is his misfortune that she is not a virgin, as she was raped after betrothal. **And he says: No; rather,** you were raped **before I betrothed you, and my transaction was a mistaken transaction. Rabban Gamliel and Rabbi Eliezer say: She is deemed credible.**[N] **Rabbi Yehoshua says:** It is **not** based on the statement emerging **from her mouth** that **we conduct our lives;**[N] **rather, this** woman assumes **the presumptive status of one who engaged in intercourse when she was not yet betrothed and she misled him, until she brings proof** supporting **her statement.**

גמ׳ אִתְּמַר: ״מָנֶה לִי בְּיָדְךָ״ וְהַלָּה אוֹמֵר ״אֵינִי יוֹדֵעַ״. רַב יְהוּדָה וְרַב הוּנָא אָמְרִי: חַיָּיב, וְרַב נַחְמָן וְרַבִּי יוֹחָנָן אָמְרִי: פָּטוּר. רַב הוּנָא וְרַב יְהוּדָה אָמְרִי: חַיָּיב, בָּרִי וְשֶׁמָּא – בָּרִי עָדִיף. רַב נַחְמָן וְרַבִּי יוֹחָנָן אָמְרִי: פָּטוּר, אוֹקֵי מָמוֹנָא בְּחֶזְקַת מָרֵיהּ.

GEMARA **It was stated:** With regard to one who approaches another and says: **I have one hundred dinars in your possession, and the other says: I don't know,**[H] **Rav Yehuda and Rav Huna say:** The respondent is **obligated** to pay, because he did not deny the claim, **and Rav Naḥman and Rabbi Yoḥanan**[N] **say:** He is **exempt** from payment. The Gemara elaborates. **Rav Huna and Rav Yehuda say** that the respondent is **obligated** to pay based on the principle: When there is a **certain** claim, e.g., that of the claimant, **and an uncertain** claim,[N] e.g., that of the respondent, the **certain** claim **prevails.**[N] **Rav Naḥman and Rabbi Yoḥanan say:** The respondent is **exempt** based on the principle: **Establish the money in the possession of its owner,** and the burden of proof rests upon the claimant. Since the claimant does not support his claim with proof, the money remains in the possession of the respondent.

אֲמַר לֵיהּ אַבַּיֵּי לְרַב יוֹסֵף: הָא דְּרַב הוּנָא וְרַב יְהוּדָה – דִּשְׁמוּאֵל הִיא. דִּתְנַן: הָיְתָה מְעוּבֶּרֶת, וְאָמְרוּ לָהּ: מַה טִּיבוֹ שֶׁל עוּבָּר זֶה? מֵאִישׁ פְּלוֹנִי, וְכֹהֵן הוּא. רַבָּן גַּמְלִיאֵל וְרַבִּי אֱלִיעֶזֶר אוֹמְרִים: נֶאֱמֶנֶת. וְאָמַר רַב יְהוּדָה אָמַר שְׁמוּאֵל: הֲלָכָה כְּרַבָּן גַּמְלִיאֵל.

Abaye said to Rav Yosef: This ruling **of Rav Huna and Rav Yehuda is** essentially the statement **of Shmuel, as we learned** in a mishna (13a): In the case of an unmarried woman **who was pregnant, and** the Sages **said to her: What is the nature of this fetus,** i.e., who is the father. And she says: It is **from a man** called **so-and-so and he is a priest** and is certainly of valid lineage. **Rabban Gamliel and Rabbi Eliezer say: She is deemed credible,** and the fetus is deemed to be of valid lineage. **Rav Yehuda said** that **Shmuel said: The *halakha* is in accordance with** the opinion **of Rabban Gamliel.**

HALAKHA

She says: After you betrothed me I was raped – הִיא אוֹמֶרֶת מִשֶּׁאֵרַסְתַּנִי נֶאֱנַסְתִּי: A woman who married with the presumptive status of a virgin, whose husband discovered that she was not, and she admits that she is not a virgin but claims that she was raped after the betrothal, is accorded credibility and is entitled to a marriage contract of two hundred dinars in accordance with the opinions of Rabban Gamliel and Rabbi Eliezer. However, in an effort to ensure that the woman is telling the truth, the *ge'onim* instituted that the husband may request that the court excommunicate her if it is discovered that she made a false claim in order to obligate him to pay money (Rambam *Sefer Nashim, Hilkhot Ishut* 11:11; *Shulḥan Arukh, Even HaEzer* 68:9).

One says I have one hundred dinars in your possession and the other says I don't know – מָנֶה לִי בְּיָדְךָ וְהַלָּה אוֹמֵר אֵינִי יוֹדֵעַ: If one claims that another owes him money that he loaned him or deposited with him, and the other person asserts that he is uncertain whether he borrowed money or received the deposit from the claimant, the respondent is exempt from payment in accordance with the opinions of Rav Naḥman and Rabbi Yoḥanan. However, he is required by rabbinic law to take an oath of inducement, instituted to induce him to tell the truth, that he does not know. Furthermore, one may request the court to excommunicate anyone making false claims to collect money from him (Rambam *Sefer Mishpatim, Hilkhot To'en VeNitan* 1:9; *Shulḥan Arukh, Ḥoshen Mishpat* 75:9).

NOTES

She is deemed credible – נֶאֱמֶנֶת: In the Jerusalem Talmud the question is raised: If she is accorded credibility then there is no case where the groom's claim concerning virginity would be accepted. It would be far-fetched to explain that all the discussions concerning that claim up to this point were exclusively according to the opinion of Rabbi Yehoshua. The explanation there is that there is a distinction between a case where the bride denies the groom's claim and asserts that she was a virgin, in which case the groom's certain claim that she was not is accorded credibility; and a case where she admits that she was not a virgin but provides an alternative explanation for the situation (see *Tosefot Rid*).

It is not based on the statement emerging from her mouth that we conduct our lives – לֹא מִפִּיהָ אָנוּ חַיִּין: This unique formulation contains an allusion to a mishna in tractate *Avot* (1:18), which states: On three matters does the world stand, on truth, on justice, and on peace. Since Rabbi Yehoshua maintains that she is not deemed credible and that she is not telling the truth, then based on that mishna he says: It is not based on her statement that we conduct our lives; it is based on truth (Ritva; Radbaz; *Melekhet Shlomo*, citing the Ari).

Rav Naḥman and Rabbi Yoḥanan – רַב נַחְמָן וְרַבִּי יוֹחָנָן: It is unusual that Rav Naḥman is cited before Rabbi Yoḥanan, as not only was Rabbi Yoḥanan greater than Rav Naḥman, he preceded him chronologically as well. The Rosh explains that this *halakha* was formulated in Babylonia, where Rav Naḥman's opinion was the only one known. Later, when the Sages discovered that Rabbi Yoḥanan shared his opinion, they appended his name to the statement.

A certain claim and an uncertain claim – בָּרִי וְשֶׁמָּא: *Tosafot* and many early commentaries analyze at length the various issues concerning the subject of certain and uncertain claims as it relates to different areas of *halakha*, and in terms of how the various opinions can be reconciled with the sources. They explain that although in general a certain claim prevails over an uncertain claim, there are distinctions drawn between different types of claims. Some claims have lesser certainty, due to additional factors and considerations that oppose them, e.g., presumptions, majorities, or logic. Similarly, there are uncertain claims that are enhanced in a situation where there is no way for the claimant to ascertain the facts, and all the more so where there are elements supporting his contention. When one claims: I don't know, in the case of a loan, this would be an inferior uncertain claim, because he should know whether or not there was a loan. However, the uncertain claim of the husband is enhanced by the fact that the rape never became public, even though rape is usually publicized.

The certain claim prevails – בָּרִי עָדִיף: In the *Penei Yehoshua* the question is raised: Why is this principle not applied to lost articles? The finder can make only an uncertain claim, as he does not know whether he is the owner, and the owner can claim with certainty that it belongs to him. Why must the owner provide identifying indicators that the item belongs to him? He answers that since the article could have belonged to anyone and the majority of the world is not the one claiming ownership, the claim of the finder is supported by that majority. Others explain that even one making an uncertain claim can request time to clarify the matter, and in this case the finder could say that he prefers waiting before returning the article, as someone else may claim it and provide indicators or witnesses (*Ḥatam Sofer*).

Rav Ḥayyim Soloveitchik explains that with regard to returning lost articles there is another consideration, since the verse states: "And it shall be with you until your brother demands it" (Deuteronomy 22:2), meaning that it is incumbent upon the finder to investigate whether the claimant is indeed the one who lost it. Therefore, even a certain claim does not suffice.

וְאָמַר לֵיהּ רַב שְׁמוּאֵל בַּר יְהוּדָה לְרַב יְהוּדָה: שִׁינָּנָא, אָמְרַתְּ לָן מִשְּׁמֵיהּ דִּשְׁמוּאֵל הֲלָכָה כְּרַבָּן גַּמְלִיאֵל אַף בָּרִאשׁוֹנָה. מַאי ״אַף בָּרִאשׁוֹנָה״? אַף עַל גַּב דְּאִיכָּא לְמֵימַר אוֹקֵי מָמוֹנָא בְּחֶזְקַת מָרֵיהּ – אָמַר רַבָּן גַּמְלִיאֵל בָּרִי עָדִיף.

And Rav Shmuel bar Yehuda said to Rav Yehuda: Big-toothed one [*shinnana*],[L] **you said to us in the name of Shmuel** that the *halakha* **is in accordance with** the opinion of **Rabban Gamliel even in the first** dispute, the dispute cited in the mishna, which is the first in a series of disputes with regard to conflicting claims. The Gemara asks: **What** is the meaning of **even the first?** What is unique about that dispute relative to the others? The Gemara answers: The novel element in the first dispute is that the claim of the bride is accepted **despite the fact that** although **there is** room **to say: Establish the money in the possession of its owner,** and since the money is in the possession of the husband and the woman is the claimant, **Rabban Gamliel said** that the **certain** claim of the bride **prevails** over the uncertain claim of the groom, who can only speculate about when she was raped.

לֵימָא רַב יְהוּדָה וְרַב הוּנָא דְּאָמְרִי כְּרַבָּן גַּמְלִיאֵל, וְרַב נַחְמָן וְרַבִּי יוֹחָנָן דְּאָמְרִי כְּרַבִּי יְהוֹשֻׁעַ?

The Gemara suggests: **Let us say** that it is **Rav Yehuda and Rav Huna who say** their ruling **in accordance with** the opinion of **Rabban Gamliel,** who says that a certain claim prevails over an uncertain one even to collect money from the possession of the respondent. **And** it is **Rav Naḥman and Rabbi Yoḥanan who say** their ruling **in accordance with** the opinion of **Rabbi Yehoshua,** that one does not collect money based merely on a claim.

אָמַר לָךְ רַב נַחְמָן: אֲנָא דְּאָמְרִי אֲפִילּוּ כְּרַבָּן גַּמְלִיאֵל; עַד כָּאן לָא קָאָמַר רַבָּן גַּמְלִיאֵל הָתָם אֶלָּא דְּאִיכָּא מִגּוֹ, אֲבָל הָכָא – מַאי מִגּוֹ אִיכָּא?

The Gemara rejects that suggestion. **Rav Naḥman** could have **said to you:** That **which I said, is even in accordance with** the opinion of **Rabban Gamliel. Rabban Gamliel says his ruling only there,** with regard to claims of a groom and a bride, **where there is a** ***miggo***,[N] a halakhic argument that the ability to make a more advantageous claim grants credibility to the claim one actually makes, that bolsters the bride's claim. She could have claimed that she wasn't raped at all, but rather that her hymen was ruptured by wood. That is a more advantageous claim because she is not disgraced in the eyes of the groom. Therefore, her claim that she was raped is accorded credibility. **However here,** where one claims that another owes him money, **what** ***miggo*** **is there** bolstering his claim and according it credibility?

אִי נַמִי, עַד כָּאן לָא קָאָמַר רַבָּן גַּמְלִיאֵל הָתָם אֶלָּא דְּאָמְרִינַן אוֹקְמַהּ אַחֶזְקָהּ, אֲבָל הָכָא – מַאי חֶזְקָה אִית לֵיהּ לְהַאי?

Alternatively, Rav Naḥman could have said to you: **Rabban Gamliel says his ruling only there, where we say: Establish her** legal status according to her **presumptive status**[N] as a virgin, and the husband's claim seeks to undermine that presumptive status. **However here, what presumptive status does this** claimant **have** supporting the claim that another owes him money? Therefore, even Rabban Gamliel would concede that his certain claim does not prevail.

הָכִי נַמִי מִסְתַּבְּרָא כִּדְקָא מְשַׁנֵּינַן, דְּרַב נַחְמָן הוּא דַּאֲמַר כְּרַבָּן גַּמְלִיאֵל.

The Gemara notes: **Indeed,** it is **also reasonable** to explain **as we are teaching, that it is Rav Naḥman who said** his ruling **in accordance** with the opinion of **Rabban Gamliel.**

LANGUAGE

Big-toothed one [*shinnana*] – שִׁינָּנָא: A nickname for Rabbi Yehuda, appearing in several places in the Talmud, that was explained by several commentaries to mean sharp or brilliant. However, the *ge'onim* assert that they are certain that this is an expression describing one with large teeth, noting that the expression was still employed in their time.

NOTES

Where there is a *miggo* – דְּאִיכָּא מִגּוֹ: The *miggo* in this case is that the bride could have claimed that her hymen was ruptured by a foreign object. This is a more advantageous claim, as it does not disqualify her from marrying a priest. Moreover, an additional advantage of that claim is that the stigma associated with a claim of rape does not exist (Meiri).

Many reservations were raised with regard to the applicability of the principle of *miggo* in this context. In fact, there are variant readings in which the reason of *miggo* does not appear and only the second reason of presumptive status is cited (see Ritva and Rabbi Aharon HaLevi). The primary difficulty is that, according to most authorities, *miggo* is effective only to exempt from payment, not to collect payment from the possession of its owner, and in this case the bride is receiving payment of her marriage contract from the husband.

Several early commentaries conclude based on this discussion that the principle of *miggo* is effective to collect payment as well (Maharshak; *Haggahot Mordekhai*). Others explain that in this case it is not the *miggo* that is effective in collecting the money. Rather, it is that the certain claim prevails over the uncertain claim (see Ritva and Meiri).

Establish her legal status according to her presumptive status – אוֹקְמַהּ אַחֶזְקָהּ: This is referring to the presumptive status of the bride's body; since she was born as a virgin, she maintains that status until proven otherwise. The Rid and the Rosh add that although the bride does not receive payment of her marriage contract before she enters the wedding canopy, fundamentally, she is entitled to it even after betrothal. They did not want to rely solely on her presumptive status of virginity; that presumption itself was undermined, as she is no longer a virgin when the claim is made. Later commentaries discuss this subject extensively, from various perspectives (see Maharam Schiff and *Shev Shemateta*).

דְּאִם כֵּן קַשְׁיָא הִלְכְתָא אַהִלְכְתָא, דְּקַיְימָא לָן הִלְכְתָא כְּרַב נַחְמָן בְּדִינֵי, וּבְהָא אָמַר רַב יְהוּדָה אָמַר שְׁמוּאֵל הֲלָכָה כְּרַבָּן גַּמְלִיאֵל. אֶלָּא לָאו שְׁמַע מִינָּהּ כִּדְמְשַׁנֵּינַן, שְׁמַע מִינָּהּ.

Because if that were not **so,** it is **difficult,** as there would be a contradiction between one ***halakha*** and another ***halakha.*** **Since,** on the one hand, **we maintain** a principle in halakhic ruling that **the *halakha*** is **in accordance with** the opinion of **Rav Naḥman in civil law; and,** on the other hand, **in that** case involving the claims of the bride and the groom **Rav Yehuda said** that **Shmuel said: The *halakha*** is **in accordance with** the opinion of **Rabban Gamliel. Rather,** can we **not conclude from** this apparent contradiction that the matter must be understood **as we are teaching,** that the opinion of Rav Naḥman can be reconciled with the opinion of Rabban Gamliel? The Gemara affirms: Indeed, **conclude from it** that this is the case.

מתני׳ הִיא אוֹמֶרֶת: ״מוּכַּת עֵץ אֲנִי״, וְהוּא אוֹמֵר: ״לֹא כִּי, אֶלָּא דְּרוּסַת אִישׁ אַתְּ״. רַבָּן גַּמְלִיאֵל וְרַבִּי אֱלִיעֶזֶר אוֹמְרִים: נֶאֱמֶנֶת, וְרַבִּי יְהוֹשֻׁעַ אוֹמֵר: לֹא מִפִּיהָ אָנוּ חַיִּין, אֶלָּא הֲרֵי זוֹ בְּחֶזְקַת דְּרוּסַת אִישׁ עַד שֶׁתָּבִיא רְאָיָה לִדְבָרֶיהָ.

MISHNA In a case where **she says: I am one whose** hymen was **ruptured by wood,** i.e., she admits that her hymen is not intact but claims that it was not ruptured through intercourse, **and the groom says: No; rather, you are** one who was **trampled by a man,**[NH] and your hymen was ruptured through intercourse, **Rabban Gamliel and Rabbi Eliezer say: She is deemed credible** and her claim is accepted because she certainly knows what actually happened. **Rabbi Yehoshua says:** It is **not** based on the statement emerging **from her mouth** that **we conduct our lives; rather, she** retains **the presumptive status of** one who **was trampled by a man, until she brings proof** supporting **her statement** that her hymen was ruptured by wood.

גמ׳ טַעֲנָתַיְיהוּ בְּמַאי? רַבִּי יוֹחָנָן אָמַר: בְּמָאתַיִם וּמָנֶה, רַבִּי אֶלְעָזָר אָמַר: בְּמָנֶה וְלֹא כְלוּם.

GEMARA The Gemara asks: **What are their** respective financial **claims?**[N] **Rabbi Yoḥanan said:** The bride claims that since her hymen was ruptured by wood, her legal status is that of a virgin and she is entitled to a marriage contract of **two hundred** dinars; **and** the groom claims that she engaged in intercourse and is entitled to a marriage contract of **one hundred dinars.**[N] **Rabbi Elazar said:** The bride claims that although her hymen is not intact she did not completely deceive him, as she never engaged in intercourse, and therefore she is entitled to a marriage contract of **one hundred dinars; and** the groom claims that she engaged in intercourse, rendering the betrothal a mistaken transaction, and therefore she is entitled to **nothing at all.**

רַבִּי יוֹחָנָן אָמַר: בְּמָאתַיִם וּמָנֶה, סָבַר לָהּ כְּרַבִּי מֵאִיר, דְּאָמַר: בֵּין הִכִּיר בָּהּ וּבֵין לֹא הִכִּיר בָּהּ – מָאתַיִם. וְרַבִּי אֶלְעָזָר אוֹמֵר: בְּמָנֶה וְלֹא כְלוּם, סָבַר לָהּ כְּרַבָּנַן דְּאָמְרִי: בֵּין הִכִּיר בָּהּ בֵּין לֹא הִכִּיר בָּהּ – מָנֶה.

The Gemara elaborates. **Rabbi Yoḥanan said:** The dispute between the bride and groom is whether the marriage contract **is two hundred** dinars **or one hundred dinars,** because the *tanna* of the mishna **holds in accordance with** the opinion of **Rabbi Meir, who said: Whether** the husband **was aware that her** hymen was ruptured by wood **or whether he was not aware of her** condition, she receives payment of her marriage contract of **two hundred** dinars and it is not a mistaken transaction. **And Rabbi Elazar says: The dispute** between the bride and groom is whether the marriage contract **is one hundred dinars or** whether she is entitled to **nothing at all,** because the *tanna* of the mishna **holds in accordance with** the opinion of **the Rabbis, who said: Whether** the husband **was aware that her** hymen was ruptured by wood or **whether he was not aware of her** condition, she receives payment of her marriage contract of **one hundred dinars.**

NOTES

No, rather you are one who was trampled by a man – **לֹא כִּי אֶלָּא דְּרוּסַת אִישׁ אַתְּ**: In the Jerusalem Talmud the question is raised: How is this exchange possible? The husband has no way of knowing that she her hymen was ruptured through intercourse and not by means of a foreign object. Therefore, the case is explained there that the bride claims she informed the groom before betrothal that her hymen was ruptured by a foreign object, and that he agreed to marry her. The groom claims that he married her based on her presumptive status as a virgin, and he concludes from the fact that she did not tell him that her hymen was ruptured by a foreign object that in fact she lost her virginity through intercourse.

What are their respective financial claims – **טַעֲנָתַיְיהוּ בְּמַאי**: In the *Shita Mekubbetzet* both the question and the basis of the dispute are explained. In the previous mishna (12b), the objective of the claim of each of the parties is articulated. The bride claims that she is entitled to two hundred dinars and the groom claims that she is entitled to nothing, as it is a mistaken transaction. Here, however, the objectives are unarticulated. Therefore, Rabbi Yoḥanan prefers establishing this mishna parallel to the previous mishna, with the bride claiming two hundred dinars despite the fact that this explanation is possible only according to the opinion of Rabbi Meir (11a). Rabbi Elazar prefers establishing this mishna in accordance with the opinion of the Rabbis, although that means that the bride's claim in this mishna is not parallel to the claim in the previous mishna.

Two hundred dinars and one hundred dinars – **בְּמָאתַיִם וּמָנֶה**: Many early commentaries note that ostensibly this is a classic case of partial admission in response to a claim, as the bride claims two hundred dinars and the groom admits that he owes one hundred. In such a case, the Torah imposed an oath upon the respondent. In this case the groom is unable to take the oath, as he does not know what happened, and the principle is that one unable to take an oath is required to pay. Some explain that this principle applies only in a case where there is a reasonable expectation that he knows what happened, but refuses to take an oath. In this case, where there is no such expectation, he is not obligated to pay (Ri, cited in *Tosafot, Bava Kamma* 46a). Many commentaries dispute that explanation. Others explain that the hundred dinars that he acknowledges owing her are not in dispute. They certainly belong to the bride. It is not an admission on his part; rather, the dispute is solely with regard to the additional one hundred dinars, which he completely denies owing (Ritva).

HALAKHA

Ruptured by wood or trampled by a man – **מוּכַּת עֵץ אוֹ דְּרוּסַת אִישׁ**: If a man marries a woman with the presumptive status of a virgin and claims that he discovered that she is not a virgin, and she admits that her hymen was not intact when they consummated the marriage but claims that her hymen was ruptured by a foreign object, her claim is accepted and she is entitled to receive payment of a marriage contract of one hundred dinars. This is in accordance with the opinion of Rabbi Elazar. Even if the husband claims that his wife may have lost her virginity by engaging in intercourse with another man and that the betrothal was a mistaken transaction, his claim is ignored. However, the husband may request that the court excommunicate her if she is lying (Rambam *Sefer Nashim, Hilkhot Ishut* 11:10; *Shulḥan Arukh, Even HaEzer* 68:9).

בִּשְׁלָמָא רַבִּי אֶלְעָזָר לָא קָאָמַר כְּרַבִּי יוֹחָנָן – דְּקָא מוֹקֵי לַהּ כְּרַבָּנַן, אֶלָּא רַבִּי יוֹחָנָן מַאי טַעֲמָא לָא אֲמַר כְּרַבִּי אֶלְעָזָר?

The Gemara asks: **Granted, Rabbi Elazar did not state** his explanation of the mishna **in accordance with** the explanation of **Rabbi Yoḥanan because he** preferred to **establish** the mishna **in accordance with** the opinion of **the Rabbis,** according to which the *halakha* is ruled, and not the opinion of Rabbi Meir. **However, what is the reason that Rabbi Yoḥanan did not state** his explanation of the mishna **in accordance with** the explanation of **Rabbi Elazar?**

קָסָבַר: כְּנָסָהּ בְּחֶזְקַת בְּתוּלָה וְנִמְצֵאת בְּעוּלָה – יֵשׁ לָהּ כְּתוּבָּה מָנֶה. הָכָא, הוּא קָאָמַר מָנֶה וְהִיא קָאָמְרָה מָנֶה, מַאי אִיכָּא בֵּין טַעֲנָה דִּידֵיהּ לְטַעֲנָה דִּידָהּ?

The Gemara answers: The reason that Rabbi Yoḥanan explained the mishna in that manner is that **he holds:** If the groom **married** a woman **with the presumptive status of a virgin, and she is found to be a non-virgin, she** receives payment of her **marriage contract of one hundred** dinars. Therefore, **here,** according to the explanation of Rabbi Elazar, who explains the mishna according to the opinion of the Rabbis, **he is saying** that she engaged in intercourse and is entitled to a marriage contract of **one hundred dinars; and she is saying** that her hymen was ruptured by wood and she is entitled to a marriage contract of **one hundred dinars. What** difference **is there between his claim and her claim?** Therefore, Rabbi Yoḥanan explains the mishna in accordance with the opinion of Rabbi Meir, who holds that the dispute between the bride and the groom is whether she is entitled to a marriage contract of two hundred dinars or a marriage contract of one hundred dinars.

בִּשְׁלָמָא לְרַבִּי אֶלְעָזָר – הַיְינוּ דְּקָתָנֵי תַּרְתֵּי: חֲדָא – לְאַפּוּקֵי מִדְּרָמִי בַּר חָמָא,

Again we question: **Granted, according to Rabbi Elazar,** who explains that the dispute between the bride and the groom is with regard to whether she is entitled to a marriage contract of one hundred dinars because her hymen was ruptured by wood, or whether she is entitled to nothing because she engaged in intercourse, **that is** why the *tanna* **teaches two** similar disputes, in this mishna and in the previous one. **One** dispute, in this mishna, comes **to exclude** the opinion **of Rami bar Ḥama,** who said: If he was not aware that her hymen was ruptured by wood, everyone agrees that she receives no marriage contract at all, as the marriage was a mistaken transaction. From this mishna it is clear that according to her claim that her hymen was ruptured by wood, she is entitled to one hundred dinars.

וַחֲדָא – לְאַפּוּקֵי מִדְּרַב חִיָּיא בַּר אָבִין אָמַר רַב שֵׁשֶׁת. אֶלָּא לְרַבִּי יוֹחָנָן, תַּרְתֵּי לָמָּה לִי?

And one dispute, in the previous mishna, is brought in order **to exclude** that **which Rav Ḥiyya bar Avin** said that **Rav Sheshet said:** If the groom married a woman with the presumptive status of a virgin and she is found to be a non-virgin, she receives payment of her marriage contract of one hundred dinars. In the previous mishna he claims: Before I betrothed you, you were raped and my transaction was a mistaken transaction, indicating that she is entitled to nothing. **However,** according **to Rabbi Yoḥanan, why do I** need the *tanna* to teach **two** similar disputes? In his opinion, the previous mishna could not have been taught to exclude that which Rav Ḥiyya bar Avin said that Rav Sheshet said. It has already been established that Rabbi Yoḥanan agrees with the opinion that if she is found to be a non-virgin, she receives payment of her marriage contract of one hundred dinars.

חֲדָא לְהוֹדִיעֲךָ כֹּחוֹ דְּרַבָּן גַּמְלִיאֵל, וַחֲדָא לְהוֹדִיעֲךָ כֹּחוֹ דְּרַבִּי יְהוֹשֻׁעַ. קַמַּיְיתָא לְהוֹדִיעֲךָ כֹּחוֹ דְּרַבִּי יְהוֹשֻׁעַ, דְּאַף עַל גַּב דְּאִיכָּא לְמֵימַר מִיגּוֹ – לָא מְהֵימְנָא. בַּתְרַיְיתָא לְהוֹדִיעֲךָ כֹּחוֹ דְּרַבָּן גַּמְלִיאֵל, דְּאַף עַל גַּב דְּלֵיכָּא לְמֵימַר מִיגּוֹ – מְהֵימְנָא.

The Gemara answers: The two similar disputes were necessary. **One** is **to convey to you the far-reaching nature** of the opinion **of Rabban Gamliel** and the extent of the credibility that he accords to her claim; **and one** is **to convey to you the far-reaching nature** of the opinion **of Rabbi Yehoshua** and the extent to which he does not accord credibility to her claim. The Gemara elaborates: **The first** mishna, where she admits she was raped but claims that it was after betrothal, **conveys to you the far-reaching nature** of the opinion **of Rabbi Yehoshua: That even though there is** room **to say** that her claim is bolstered by a ***miggo*****, she is not deemed credible. The second** mishna, where she claims that her hymen was ruptured by wood and he claims that she engaged in intercourse, **conveys to you the far-reaching nature** of the opinion **of Rabban Gamliel: That even though there is no** room **to say** that her claim is bolstered by a ***miggo***, in his opinion **she is deemed credible.**

מתני׳ רָאוּהָ מְדַבֶּרֶת עִם אֶחָד, וְאָמְרוּ לָהּ: ״מַה טִּיבוֹ שֶׁל אִישׁ זֶה״? ״אִישׁ פְּלוֹנִי, וְכֹהֵן הוּא״. רַבָּן גַּמְלִיאֵל וְרַבִּי אֱלִיעֶזֶר אוֹמְרִים: נֶאֱמֶנֶת, וְרַבִּי יְהוֹשֻׁעַ אוֹמֵר: לֹא מִפִּיהָ אָנוּ חַיִּין, אֶלָּא הֲרֵי זוֹ בְּחֶזְקַת בְּעוּלָה לְנָתִין וּלְמַמְזֵר, עַד שֶׁתָּבִיא רְאָיָה לִדְבָרֶיהָ.

MISHNA If people **saw** a woman **speaking to one** man, but they did not recognize him, **and they said to her: What is the nature** [*tivo*][L] **of this man?** And she said to them: **He is a man** called **so-and-so and he is a priest;**[N] **Rabban Gamliel and Rabbi Eliezer say: She is deemed credible, and Rabbi Yehoshua says:** It is **not** based on the statement emerging **from her mouth** that **we conduct our lives. Rather, she** assumes **the presumptive status of** one who **engaged in intercourse with a Gibeonite or with a** ***mamzer*****,**[BN] men of flawed lineage who disqualify her from marrying a priest, **until she brings proof** supporting **her statement.**[N]

הָיְתָה מְעוּבֶּרֶת, וְאָמְרוּ לָהּ: ״מַה טִּיבוֹ שֶׁל עוּבָּר זֶה״? ״מֵאִישׁ פְּלוֹנִי, וְכֹהֵן הוּא״. רַבָּן גַּמְלִיאֵל וְרַבִּי אֱלִיעֶזֶר אוֹמְרִים: נֶאֱמֶנֶת, וְרַבִּי יְהוֹשֻׁעַ אוֹמֵר: לֹא מִפִּיהָ אָנוּ חַיִּין, אֶלָּא הֲרֵי זוֹ בְּחֶזְקַת מְעוּבֶּרֶת לְנָתִין וּלְמַמְזֵר, עַד שֶׁתָּבִיא רְאָיָה לִדְבָרֶיהָ.

Similarly, **if** a single woman **was pregnant, and** people **said to her: What is the nature of this fetus?** And she says to them: **It is from a man** called **so-and-so and he is a priest; Rabban Gamliel and Rabbi Eliezer say: She is deemed credible, and Rabbi Yehoshua says:** It is **not** based on the statement emerging **from her mouth** that **we conduct our lives. Rather, she** assumes **the presumptive status of** one who **conceived from a Gibeonite or a** ***mamzer*****, until she brings proof** supporting **her statement.**

גמ׳ מַאי ״מְדַבֶּרֶת״? זְעֵירִי אָמַר: נִסְתְּרָה, רַב אַסִּי אָמַר, נִבְעֲלָה. בִּשְׁלָמָא לִזְעֵירִי – הַיְינוּ דְּקָתָנֵי ״מְדַבֶּרֶת״, אֶלָּא לְרַב אַסִּי מַאי ״מְדַבֶּרֶת״? לִישָּׁנָא מְעַלְּיָא, כִּדְכְתִיב ״אָכְלָה וּמָחֲתָה פִיהָ וְאָמְרָה לֹא פָעַלְתִּי אָוֶן״.

GEMARA The Gemara asks: **What is** the meaning of **speaking**[HN] mentioned in the mishna? **Ze'eiri said:** It means that **she secluded herself** with a man and it is unknown whether she engaged in intercourse. **Rav Asi said:** It means that **she engaged in intercourse. Granted, according to Ze'eiri, that is** why the mishna **teaches** the case employing the term **speaking,** as it is certain only that they were in seclusion. Perhaps all they did was speak. **However, according to Rav Asi, what is** the reason the mishna employed the term **speaking** if the reference is to intercourse? The Gemara answers: The mishna employed **a euphemism, as it is written** with regard to licentious women: **"She eats and wipes her mouth and says: I have done no wickedness"** (Proverbs 30:20). The verse euphemistically ascribes the act of intercourse to the mouth instead of to the appropriate body part.

LANGUAGE

Nature [*tivo*] – **טִיבוֹ:** The meaning of the word *tivo* was discussed by the early commentaries. According to the Rambam it means reason. Others explain that in general it means matter or concern. According to Rabbi Binyamin Musafya it most closely approximates the Hebrew word *teva*, meaning nature. The question then is: What is the nature of this man (see *Melekhet Shlomo*)?

BACKGROUND

Mamzer – **מַמְזֵר:** A *mamzer* is a child born from an incestuous or adulterous relationship, i.e., a child born from relations between a married woman and a man other than her husband, or between relatives for whom relations are proscribed by a prohibition punishable by *karet*. An offspring conceived with a menstruating woman is an exception to this principle, because although the prohibition in that case is punishable by *karet*, the offspring is not a *mamzer*. The offspring born of an unmarried couple is not a *mamzer*. A *mamzer* inherits from his biological father and is considered his son in every respect. A *mamzer* may marry only a female *mamzer* or a convert to Judaism, and the offspring of that union is a *mamzer*. Likewise, a female *mamzer* may marry only a *mamzer* or a convert. The offspring of that union is a *mamzer* as well.

HALAKHA

What is the meaning of speaking – **מַאי מְדַבֶּרֶת:** If an unmarried woman was seen engaging in sexual relations with an unidentified man, and she claims that he is of unflawed lineage, her claim is accepted and she is permitted to marry into the priesthood. Although Rav Asi's opinion is not consistent with the mishna, Ze'eiri does not disagree with his halakhic conclusion (Vilna Gaon; Rambam *Sefer Kedusha, Hilkhot Issurei Bia* 15:11, 18:13; *Shulḥan Arukh, Even HaEzer* 6:17).

NOTES

He is a man called so-and-so and he is a priest – **אִישׁ פְּלוֹנִי וְכֹהֵן הוּא:** Even according to Rabban Gamliel, who says that her claim is accepted, this does not mean that her identification of a man as the one who engaged in intercourse with her or as the father of the child, is similarly accepted. The early commentaries write, and it is likewise cited in the name of the *ge'onim*, that her claim is neither accepted with regard to feeding her child *teruma* if the man she identified as the father was a priest, nor with regard to inheritance, and certainly not with regard to service in the Temple. Others contend that her claim is partially accepted, e.g., to enable her to feed her son produce that is *teruma* by rabbinic law (Meiri). On a similar note, some commentaries maintain that her claim is partially accepted in the sense that if she is the daughter of a priest, she does not forfeit the right to eat *teruma* due to her son. Were he deemed an Israelite and not a priest, she would lose that right.

Engaged in intercourse with a Gibeonite or with a ***mamzer*** – **בְּעוּלָה לְנָתִין וּלְמַמְזֵר:** In the Jerusalem Talmud the dispute is explained in the following manner: Rabbi Yehoshua holds that licentiousness is more common among people of flawed lineage. As the case in question involves licentiousness, there is reason for concern that a man of flawed lineage was involved. The Rabbis, based on the principle: There is no steward for restraining sexual immorality, hold that all men are equally suspect with regard to licentiousness. Later commentaries note that the fact that Rabbi Yehoshua is concerned that perhaps she engaged in intercourse with a *mamzer* or a Gibeonite, and not that she engaged in intercourse with a gentile, although they are more common, proves that the majority is not a factor. Therefore, even in a place where the majority of men are of unflawed lineage, Rabbi Yehoshua does not accept her claim. Furthermore, Rabbi Yehoshua does not accept her claim even in a city where the majority are Jews, where there would be only minor concern that she engaged in intercourse with a *mamzer* (*Ahavat Tziyyon*).

Until she brings proof supporting her statement – **עַד שֶׁתָּבִיא רְאָיָה לִדְבָרֶיהָ:** Rabbi Akiva Eiger asks: Even if she brings proof that the man was of unflawed lineage, since she was immodest with one man there is concern that she was immodest with another, and there is no proof with regard to the anonymous second man. He answers: Once she brings proof for her claim, she restores her presumptive status of unflawed lineage. Even though the possibility exists that she engaged in intercourse with another man, it is a concern by rabbinic law, and everyone agrees that her claim is accepted.

What is the meaning of speaking – **מַאי מְדַבֶּרֶת:** The commentaries explain that since the term speaking is clearly not to be taken literally, as no woman is disqualified from marrying a priest by speaking to a man, the question arises: Is it a euphemism for entering into seclusion or a euphemism for intercourse?

בִּשְׁלָמָא לִזְעֵירִי – הַיְינוּ דְּקָתָנֵי תַּרְתֵּי: ״מְדַבֶּרֶת״ ״וּמְעוּבֶּרֶת״. אֶלָּא לְרַב אַסִי, תַּרְתֵּי לָמָּה לִי?

The Gemara asks: **Granted, according to Ze'eiri,** who said that speaking means that she secluded herself with him, **that is** the reason **that** the *tanna* **teaches two** cases in the mishna: A woman **speaking** to a man **and** a woman who is **pregnant. However, according to Rav Asi,** if speaking means that she engaged in intercourse, **why do I need two** cases addressing the same issue?

חֲדָא לְהַכְשִׁיר בָּהּ, וַחֲדָא לְהַכְשִׁיר בְּבִתָּהּ.

The Gemara answers: The *tanna* teaches **one** case, the case of speaking to a man, **to deem her fit** to marry a priest, because although she engaged in intercourse, Rabbi Eliezer and Rabban Gamliel rule that she is deemed credible and is not considered to have engaged in intercourse with a man of flawed lineage. **And** the *tanna* teaches **one** case, the case of the single woman who is pregnant, in order **to deem her daughter** born from that pregnancy **fit** to marry a priest, as Rabbi Eliezer and Rabban Gamliel rule the mother is deemed credible.

הָנִיחָא לְמַאן דְּאָמַר: לְדִבְרֵי הַמַּכְשִׁיר בָּהּ מַכְשִׁיר בְּבִתָּהּ, אֶלָּא לְמַאן דְּאָמַר: לְדִבְרֵי הַמַּכְשִׁיר בָּהּ פּוֹסֵל בְּבִתָּהּ, מַאי אִיכָּא לְמֵימַר? רַב אַסִי סָבַר כְּמַאן דְּאָמַר לְדִבְרֵי הַמַּכְשִׁיר בָּהּ מַכְשִׁיר בְּבִתָּהּ.

The Gemara asks: **This works out well according to the one who says:** With regard **to the statement of the one who deems her fit** to marry a priest, **he deems her daughter fit**[N] to do so as well. **However, according to the one who says:** With regard **to the statement of the one who deems her fit** to marry a priest, **he** nevertheless **deems her daughter unfit, what is there to say?** Why did the mishna cite two cases addressing the same issue? The Gemara answers: **Rav Asi holds in accordance with** the opinion of **the one who said:** With regard **to the statement of the one who deems her fit** to marry a priest, **he deems her daughter fit** to do so as well.

אָמַר לֵיהּ רַב פַּפָּא לְאַבַּיֵי: לִזְעֵירִי, דְּאָמַר מַאי ״מְדַבֶּרֶת״ נִסְתְּרָה, וְאָמַר רַבִּי יְהוֹשֻׁעַ לָא מְהֵימְנָא – הָאָמַר רַב: מַלְקִין עַל הַיִּחוּד וְאֵין אוֹסְרִין עַל הַיִּחוּד,

Rav Pappa said to Abaye: According **to Ze'eiri, who said: What is** the meaning of the term **speaking?** It means that **she secluded herself, and Rabbi Yehoshua said** that she is **not deemed credible** to say that she engaged in intercourse with a man of proper lineage, but the assumption is that she engaged in intercourse with a man of flawed lineage. **Didn't Rav say: One flogs** a man and a woman **for** entering into **seclusion,**[H] for violating rabbinic law, **but one does not render** a woman **forbidden** to her husband **for** entering into **seclusion?**[N] Only if it is established as a certainty that she engaged in intercourse with a man other than her husband, is she forbidden to her husband.

לֵימָא דְּלָא כְּרַבִּי יְהוֹשֻׁעַ! אֲפִילּוּ תֵּימָא רַבִּי יְהוֹשֻׁעַ, מַעֲלָה עָשׂוּ בְּיוֹחֲסִין.

Let us say that this statement of Rav is **not in accordance with** the opinion of **Rabbi Yehoshua,** as Rabbi Yehoshua rules that she assumes the presumptive status of one who engaged in intercourse with a Gibeonite or with a *mamzer*, and she is forbidden to marry a priest even for entering into seclusion. The Gemara rejects that conclusion. **Even** if you **say** that Rav's statement is **in accordance with** the opinion of **Rabbi Yehoshua,** the Sages **established a higher standard with regard to** matters of **lineage.** Although she is not forbidden to her husband for entering into seclusion, she is deemed unfit to marry a priest.

מֵיתִיבֵי: רָאוּהָ שֶׁנִּכְנְסָה עִם אֶחָד לְסֵתֶר,

The Gemara **raises an objection: If** people **saw that** a woman **entered with one** man **into seclusion,**

HALAKHA

One flogs a man and a woman for entering into seclusion – מַלְקִין עַל הַיִּחוּד: King David's court decreed that a man may not enter into seclusion with an unmarried woman, and if he does so, both he and the woman are flogged with lashes of rebelliousness. However, a married woman is not forbidden to her husband by entering into seclusion with another man, nor is an unmarried woman forbidden to a priest by entering into seclusion with a man of flawed lineage (Rambam *Sefer Kedusha, Hilkhot Issurei Bia* 22:3; *Shulḥan Arukh, Even HaEzer* 22:2).

NOTES

Deems her daughter fit – מַכְשִׁיר בְּבִתָּהּ: The question is not only relevant to a female child but to a male child as well. The Gemara discusses a female child here because she is disqualified by her mother's intercourse with a man of flawed lineage in more ways than male offspring. For example, she may not marry a priest. By contrast, with regard to a male child, the only relevant concerns are whether she engaged in intercourse with a *mamzer* or a Gibeonite, or one with whom relations are forbidden.

One flogs a man and a woman for entering into seclusion but one does not render a woman forbidden to her husband for entering into seclusion – מַלְקִין עַל הַיִּחוּד וְאֵין אוֹסְרִין עַל הַיִּחוּד: The early commentaries discuss whether these two statements refer to the same case or to two different cases, and whether the reference is to a married or an unmarried woman. Most hold that since it is stated in tractate *Kiddushin* that one does not flog a married woman for entering into seclusion with a man, to avoid slandering her children, the Gemara here must be referring to an unmarried woman. *Tosefot Rid*, as well, holds that an unmarried woman is flogged. Others explain that the phrase: One does not render a woman forbidden to her husband for entering into seclusion, is referring specifically to an unmarried woman and her future husband. The Ritva, however, explains that it is referring to a married woman. The Meiri writes that it is referring to both cases, as even an unmarried woman is not rendered forbidden for entering into seclusion with one with whom relations are forbidden, and all the more so a married woman is not rendered forbidden.

אוֹ לְחוּרְבָּה, וְאָמְרוּ לָהּ: ״מַה טִּיבוֹ שֶׁל אִישׁ זֶה״? ״כֹּהֵן הוּא, וּבֶן אֲחִי אַבָּא הוּא״. רַבָּן גַּמְלִיאֵל וְרַבִּי אֱלִיעֶזֶר אוֹמְרִים: נֶאֱמֶנֶת. רַבִּי יְהוֹשֻׁעַ אוֹמֵר: לֹא מִפִּיהָ אָנוּ חַיִּין, אֶלָּא הֲרֵי זוֹ בְּחֶזְקַת בְּעוּלָה לְנָתִין וּלְמַמְזֵר, עַד שֶׁתָּבִיא רְאָיָה לִדְבָרֶיהָ.

or into a ruin, which is typically located outside the city, and if a man and woman meet there it is presumably in order to engage in sexual relations, **and** people **said to her: What is the nature of this man** with whom you secluded? She said to them: **He is a priest, and he is the son of my father's brother,**[N] a respectable person of impeccable lineage. **Rabban Gamliel and Rabbi Eliezer say: She is deemed credible.**[N] **Rabbi Yehoshua says:** It is **not** based on the statement emerging **from her mouth** that **we conduct our lives; rather, she** assumes **the presumptive status of** one who **engaged in intercourse with a Gibeonite or with a** ***mamzer*****,** men of flawed lineage who disqualify her from marrying a priest, **until she brings proof** supporting **her statement.**

בִּשְׁלָמָא לִזְעֵירִי – הַיְינוּ דְּקָתָנֵי תַּרְתֵּי: ״לְסֵתֶר אוֹ לְחוּרְבָּה״. אֶלָּא לְרַב אַסִּי, דְּאָמַר נִבְעֲלָה – תַּרְתֵּי לָמָּה לִי? חֲדָא קָתָנֵי, לְסֵתֶר דְּחוּרְבָּה.

Granted, according to Ze'eiri, who said that speaking means that she secluded herself, **that is** the reason **that** the *tanna* **teaches two** cases where there is merely concern: The case of: **Into seclusion,** where there is lesser concern that she engaged in intercourse, **and** the case of: **Into a ruin,** where there is greater concern. **However, according to Rav Asi, who said** that speaking means that **she had intercourse,** and only in that case is she not deemed credible according to Rabbi Yehoshua, **why do I need two** cases? The Gemara answers: According to Rav Asi, the *tanna* **is teaching one** case: If people saw a woman enter with one man **into the seclusion of a ruin,** where the likelihood is that that they entered to engage in relations.

וְהָא ״לְסֵתֶר אוֹ לְחוּרְבָּה״ קָתָנֵי! חֲדָא לְחוּרְבָּה דְּמָתָא, וַחֲדָא לְחוּרְבָּה דְּדַבְרָא. וּצְרִיכִי, דְּאִי אַשְׁמְעִינַן חוּרְבָּה דְּמָתָא – בְּהָא קָמַכְשַׁר רַבָּן גַּמְלִיאֵל, מִשּׁוּם דְּרוֹב כְּשֵׁרִים אֶצְלָהּ. אֲבָל לְחוּרְבָּה דְּדַבְרָא, דְּרוֹב פְּסוּלִין אֶצְלָהּ – אֵימָא מוֹדֶה לֵיהּ לְרַבִּי יְהוֹשֻׁעַ.

The Gemara asks: **But isn't** the mishna **teaching** two different cases: **Into seclusion or into a ruin?** The Gemara suggests a different explanation. According to Rav Asi, two cases are necessary, **one** with regard **to a ruin in the city and one** with regard **to a ruin in the field,** distant from the city. **And** both cases **are necessary, because if** the *tanna* **taught us** only the case of **a ruin in the city,** one might have concluded that **in that** case **Rabban Gamliel deems her fit** to marry a priest **due to** the fact **that the majority** of the people **in its proximity are honorable** and of impeccable lineage. **However,** with regard **to a ruin in the field, where the majority** of the people **in its proximity are unfit** and of flawed lineage, as people from all over the world pass the ruin in the field and the majority of the people in the world are of flawed lineage, **say** that Rabban Gamliel **concedes to Rabbi Yehoshua** and deems her unfit to marry a priest.

וְאִי אַשְׁמְעִינַן בְּהַהִיא – בְּהַהִיא קָאָמַר רַבִּי יְהוֹשֻׁעַ, אֲבָל בְּהָא – אֵימָא מוֹדֶה לְרַבָּן גַּמְלִיאֵל, צְרִיכָא.

And if the *tanna* **taught us** only **that** case of a ruin in the field, one might have concluded that **in that** case **Rabbi Yehoshua said** she is not deemed credible, because the majority of the people there are of flawed lineage. **However here,** in the case of a ruin in the city, where the majority of the people are of impeccable lineage, **say** that Rabbi Yehoshua **concedes to Rabban Gamliel** that she is deemed credible. Therefore, both cases were **necessary.**

מֵיתִיבֵי: זוֹ עֵדוּת שֶׁהָאִשָּׁה כְּשֵׁרָה לָהּ, וְרַבִּי יְהוֹשֻׁעַ אוֹמֵר: אֵינָהּ נֶאֱמֶנֶת. אָמַר לָהֶם רַבִּי יְהוֹשֻׁעַ: אִי אַתֶּם מוֹדִים בִּשְׁבוּיָה שֶׁנִּשְׁבֵּית וְיֵשׁ לָהּ עֵדִים שֶׁנִּשְׁבֵּית וְהִיא אוֹמֶרֶת ״טְהוֹרָה אֲנִי״, שֶׁאֵינָהּ נֶאֱמֶנֶת?

The Gemara **raises an objection** from the *Tosefta*: **This,** i.e., that she engaged in intercourse with a man of impeccable lineage, **is testimony that a woman is fit** to testify.[N] **And Rabbi Yehoshua says: She is not deemed credible. Rabbi Yehoshua said to the** Sages: **Do you not agree in the case of a woman who was taken captive,**[N] **and she has witnesses** testifying **that she was taken captive,**[H] **and she says: I am pure,** i.e., I was not violated by my captors, **that she is not deemed credible?** The assumption in that case is that most captive women are violated by their captors.

NOTES

And he is the son of my father's brother – וּבֶן אֲחִי אַבָּא הוּא: In the *Shita Mekubbetzet* an explanation is cited asserting that this formulation supports the opinion of Ze'eiri, as it is reasonable to assume that when one asks the woman why she entered into seclusion she would answer that the man was a relative with whom she was speaking. It is also explained there why the Gemara did not cite proof for Ze'eiri's opinion from here.

She is deemed credible – נֶאֱמֶנֶת: The Ramban cites two opinions. The first is that she is deemed credible in a case where the man with whom she engaged in intercourse cannot be located and therefore cannot be questioned. The second, in the name of Ri Migash, is that this is referring to a case where the man confirms that he engaged in intercourse with her but states that he does not know whether she did so with others as well. Later commentaries discuss whether in a case where the man denies having engaged in intercourse with her, Rabban Gamliel would say that her claim is accepted.

This is testimony that a woman is fit to testify – זוֹ עֵדוּת שֶׁהָאִשָּׁה כְּשֵׁרָה לָהּ: The term "this" in the phrase is not to the exclusion of all other testimony, as there are other areas of *halakha* in which a woman is fit to testify. The unique element here is that the woman's testimony is accepted with regard to herself, from which it is inferred that the testimony is accepted with regard to herself and not with regard to her daughter (*Shita Mekubbetzet*).

A woman who was taken captive – שְׁבוּיָה שֶׁנִּשְׁבֵּית: The Ritva explains that in the case of a captive woman there are two factors leading to stringency. First, most men who were in her proximity and potentially violated her while she was in captivity are gentiles, who are sexually immoral and who disqualify her from marrying a priest. Furthermore, she is subject to rape by her captors. Consequently, were she taken captive by Jews, or by gentiles who were unable to rape her, she would not have the legal status of a captive.

HALAKHA

A woman who was taken captive, and she has witnesses that she was taken captive – שְׁבוּיָה שֶׁנִּשְׁבֵּית וְיֵשׁ לָהּ עֵדִים שֶׁנִּשְׁבֵּית: If there are witnesses that the woman was taken into captivity, her claim that she was not violated by her captors is not accepted; rather, she assumes the presumptive status of one who was raped by a gentile and unfit to marry into the priesthood (Rambam *Sefer Kedusha, Hilkhot Issurei Bia* 18:21; *Shulḥan Arukh, Even HaEzer* 7:4).

אָמְרוּ לוֹ: אֲבָל – וּמָה הֶפְרֵשׁ יֵשׁ בֵּין זוֹ לְזוֹ? לָזוֹ – יֵשׁ עֵדִים, וְלָזוֹ – אֵין לָהּ עֵדִים.

The Sages **said to him: But** there is a difference between the cases. **And what difference is there between this** case of a captive, where the woman is not accorded credibility, **and that** case of a woman who secluded herself with a man? **For this** captive, **there are witnesses** that she was taken captive, and due to the prevalent immorality in that situation, she loses the presumptive status of virtue and is considered to have certainly engaged in intercourse. **But for this** woman who secluded herself with a man, **she does not have witnesses** that she engaged in intercourse. Since she could have claimed that she did not engage in intercourse and instead admitted that she engaged in intercourse and claimed that it was with a man of impeccable lineage, she should be accorded credibility.

אָמַר לָהֶם: אַף לָזוֹ יֵשׁ עֵדִים, שֶׁהֲרֵי כְּרֵיסָהּ בֵּין שִׁינֶּיהָ! אָמְרוּ לוֹ: רוֹב גּוֹיִם פְּרוּצִים בַּעֲרָיוֹת הֵם. אָמַר לָהֶן: אֵין אַפּוֹטְרוֹפּוֹס לַעֲרָיוֹת.

Rabbi Yehoshua **said to them: Even for that** woman, the one who secluded herself, **there are witnesses, because her belly is between her teeth,** i.e., her pregnancy is conspicuous and therefore she does not have the option of claiming that she did not engage in intercourse. The Sages **said to him:** There remains a difference between the cases, as **most gentiles are steeped in sexual immorality.** Therefore, presumably, they engaged in intercourse with the captive woman. However, in the case of the woman in seclusion there is no presumption that she engaged in intercourse specifically with a man with flawed lineage. Rabbi Yehoshua **said to them: There is no steward for** restraining **sexual immorality,**[N] and therefore, everyone is suspect in that regard. Therefore, this woman, since she engaged in intercourse, lost her presumptive status of virtue, and there is no basis to trust her that it was with a person of impeccable lineage.

בַּמֶּה דְּבָרִים אֲמוּרִים – בְּעֵדוּת אִשָּׁה בְּגוּפָהּ, אֲבָל עֵדוּת אִשָּׁה בְּבִתָּהּ – דִּבְרֵי הַכֹּל הַוָּלָד שְׁתוּקִי.

The *baraita* continues: **In what** case **are these** divergent **statements** of Rabban Gamliel and Rabbi Yehoshua **said?** It is **in the case of the testimony of a woman with regard to herself,** to render her fit to marry a priest. **However,** in the case of **testimony of a woman with regard to** the fact that the father of **her daughter** is a man of unflawed lineage, **everyone agrees** that her testimony is not deemed credible, and the legal status of **the child** is that of a ***shetuki,***[B] the identity of whose father is unknown and to whom all the stringencies that apply to a *mamzer* apply, due the uncertainty of his lineage.

מַאי קָאָמַר לְהוּ וּמַאי קָמְהַדְרִי לֵיהּ? הָכִי קָאָמְרִי לֵיהּ: הֲשַׁבְתָּנוּ עַל הַמְעוּבֶּרֶת, מַה תְּשִׁיבֵנוּ עַל הַמְדַבֶּרֶת? אָמַר לָהֶם: מְדַבֶּרֶת הַיְינוּ שְׁבוּיָה. אָמְרוּ לוֹ: שָׁאנֵי שְׁבוּיָה דְּרוֹב גּוֹיִם פְּרוּצִים בַּעֲרָיוֹת הֵם. אָמַר לָהֶם: הָא נַמִי, כֵּיוָן דְּאִיסְתַּתַּר – אֵין אַפּוֹטְרוֹפּוֹס לַעֲרָיוֹת.

The Gemara seeks to understand the exchange between Rabbi Yehoshua and the Sages. **What did he say to them and what did they reply to him?** It appears that they were not discussing the same case. **This is what** the Sages **are saying to him: You answered us concerning the pregnant woman,** asserting that there is testimony in the case of the pregnant woman comparable to the testimony in the case of the captive. However, **what will you answer us concerning the** woman who was seen **speaking** to a man? In that case, there is no testimony that she had intercourse. Rabbi Yehoshua **said to them:** The case of **speaking is the same as** the case of the **captive,** as there is reason to believe that she engaged in intercourse. The Sages **said to him:** The case of **a captive is different, as most gentiles are steeped in sexual immorality,** and presumably they engaged in intercourse with the captive woman. Rabbi Yehoshua **said to them:** In **this** case **too, since she secluded herself** with a man, based on the principle: **There is no steward for** restraining **sexual immorality,** presumably she engaged in intercourse with him.

קָתָנֵי מִיהַת תַּרְתֵּי, מְדַבֶּרֶת וּמְעוּבֶּרֶת, תְּיוּבְתָּא דְּרַב אַסִי! תְּיוּבְתָּא.

With regard to the dispute over the meaning of the term: Speaking, the Gemara says: **In any event,** from this discussion it is clear that the *tanna* **is teaching two** different cases, one case of **speaking,** where there is uncertainty whether she engaged in intercourse, **and** one case where she is **pregnant,** and there is no uncertainty in that regard. The Gemara suggests: This is **a conclusive refutation** of the opinion **of Rav Asi,** who explained that speaking in the mishna means that she engaged in intercourse. The Gemara concludes: Indeed, this is **a conclusive refutation** of his opinion.

NOTES

There is no steward for restraining sexual immorality – אֵין אַפּוֹטְרוֹפּוֹס לַעֲרָיוֹת: Rashi explains this to mean that once she entered into seclusion, the Sages cannot guarantee that she did not engage in intercourse. Rabbeinu Ḥananel explains the principle in the way in which it is typically applied: Even the most righteous individual cannot be appointed as a steward for restraining sexual immorality. Therefore, there is no distinction between moral and immoral people in this regard.

BACKGROUND

***Shetuki* – שְׁתוּקִי:** A child whose father's identity is not known is referred to as a *shetuki*, from the Hebrew root *shin, tav, kuf*, meaning silence. The Gemara (*Kiddushin* 70a) explains that he is called *shetuki* because when he calls his father, his mother silences him. His legal status is that of an uncertain *mamzer*.

וְתֵיפּוֹק לֵיהּ דְּהָתָם רוֹב פְּסוּלִין אֶצְלָהּ, וְהָכָא רוֹב כְּשֵׁרִין אֶצְלָהּ! מְסַיַּיע לֵיהּ לְרַבִּי יְהוֹשֻׁעַ בֶּן לֵוִי, דְּאָמַר רַבִּי יְהוֹשֻׁעַ בֶּן לֵוִי: לְדִבְרֵי הַמַּכְשִׁיר – מַכְשִׁיר אֲפִילּוּ בְּרוֹב פְּסוּלִין, לְדִבְרֵי הַפּוֹסֵל – פּוֹסֵל אֲפִילּוּ בְּרוֹב כְּשֵׁרִים.

The Gemara asks with regard to the *baraita*: **And let the** *tanna* **derive** this distinction between a captive woman and a woman who secluded herself with a man from the fact **that there,** in the case of the captive, **the majority** of the men **in her proximity are unfit**[N] and of flawed lineage, **but here,** where she was secluded, **the majority of the men in her proximity are honorable** and of impeccable lineage. Since she is unmarried, most men are not unfit for her. The Gemara notes: The fact that the *tanna* did not derive the distinction from that source **supports** the opinion **of Rabbi Yehoshua ben Levi, as Rabbi Yehoshua ben Levi said:** According **to the statement of** Rabban Gamliel, **the one who deems her fit** to marry a priest, **he deems her fit even in** a case **where the majority of the men** in her proximity **are unfit.**[N] According **to the statement of** Rabbi Yehoshua, **the one who deems her unfit** to marry a priest, **he deems her unfit even in** a case where **the majority** of the men in her proximity **are fit.**

אָמַר רַבִּי יוֹחָנָן: לְדִבְרֵי הַמַּכְשִׁיר בָּהּ – מַכְשִׁיר בְּבִתָּהּ, לְדִבְרֵי הַפּוֹסֵל בָּהּ – פּוֹסֵל בְּבִתָּהּ. וְרַבִּי אֶלְעָזָר אוֹמֵר: לְדִבְרֵי הַמַּכְשִׁיר בָּהּ – פּוֹסֵל בְּבִתָּהּ.

Rabbi Yoḥanan said: According **to the statement of the one who deems her fit** to marry a priest and accepts her claim that she engaged in intercourse with a man of unflawed lineage, **he deems her daughter fit**[HN] as well. According **to the statement of the one who deems her unfit, he deems her daughter unfit** as well. **But Rabbi Elazar says:** According **to the statement of the one who deems her fit, he deems her daughter unfit.**

אָמַר רַבָּה: מַאי טַעְמָא דְּרַבִּי אֶלְעָזָר? בִּשְׁלָמָא אִיהִי – אִית לַהּ חֲזָקָה דְּכַשְׁרוּת, בִּתָּהּ – לֵית לַהּ חֲזָקָה דְּכַשְׁרוּת.

Rabba said: What is the reason for the opinion **of Rabbi Elazar,** who distinguishes between the effectiveness of the woman's claim in determining her own status and its effectiveness in determining the status of her daughter? The reason is that **granted,** her claim is effective with regard to her status because **she has the presumptive status of fitness.** Therefore, until proven otherwise, she retains that status. **Her daughter,** the identity of whose father is unknown, **does not have the presumptive status of fitness.** Therefore, a full-fledged proof is required to establish her fitness.

אֵיתִיבֵיהּ רַבִּי אֶלְעָזָר לְרַבִּי יוֹחָנָן: בַּמֶּה דְּבָרִים אֲמוּרִים – בְּעֵדוּת אִשָּׁה בְּגוּפָהּ. אֲבָל עֵדוּת אִשָּׁה בְּבִתָּהּ – דִּבְרֵי הַכֹּל הַוָּלָד שְׁתוּקִי. מַאי לָאו – שְׁתוּקִי וּפָסוּל? לָא, שְׁתוּקִי וְכָשֵׁר.

Rabbi Elazar raised an objection to the opinion of **Rabbi Yoḥanan** from the *baraita*: **In what** case **are these** disputing **statements** of Rabban Gamliel and Rabbi Yehoshua **said?** It is **in the case of a woman's testimony with regard to herself. However,** in the case of **testimony of a woman with regard to her daughter, everyone agrees** that her testimony is not credible, and the legal status of **the child is** that of **a *shetuki*. What, is it not** that contrary to the opinion of Rabbi Yoḥanan, the *baraita* means that the child is **a *shetuki* and unfit** until proof can be brought that the lineage of the father is unflawed? The Gemara rejects that objection: **No,** the *baraita* means that the child is **a *shetuki*,** as her lineage is unclear, but she is nevertheless **fit.**[N]

HALAKHA

The one who deems her fit…deems her daughter fit – הַמַּכְשִׁיר בָּהּ מַכְשִׁיר בְּבִתָּהּ: If an unmarried woman is pregnant and the identity of the father is unknown, and she claims that the father is a man of unflawed lineage, her claim is accepted, and both she and her daughter born from that pregnancy are fit to marry into the priesthood, in accordance with the opinion of Rabbi Yoḥanan. The ruling is in accordance with his opinion because he was Rabbi Elazar's teacher, and because he holds in accordance with the opinion of Abba Shaul in tractate *Kiddushin*, according to whose opinion the *halakha* was ruled as authoritative (Rosh; Rambam *Sefer Kedusha, Hilkhot Issurei Bia* 15:11; *Shulḥan Arukh, Even HaEzer* 6:17).

NOTES

And let the *tanna* derive from the fact that there the majority of the men in her proximity are unfit – וְתֵיפּוֹק לֵיהּ דְּהָתָם רוֹב פְּסוּלִין אֶצְלָהּ: According to Rashi, this passage is a question on the opinion of Rabbi Yehoshua. According to the Rosh and the Ritva, the difficulty is with regard to the opinion of Rabban Gamliel. In their opinion, the question is: Why did he cite the reason that most gentiles are steeped in sexual immorality? He could have cited a different reason: The majority of the men in her proximity are unfit.

Deems her fit even where the majority of the men in her proximity are unfit – מַכְשִׁיר אֲפִילּוּ בְּרוֹב פְּסוּלִין: Rabbeinu Tam, cited in *Tosafot*, asks: Isn't there a distinction between the case of a captive woman and the case of a woman entering into seclusion? With regard to a captive woman, all the men in her proximity are unfit, not just the majority, as she is subject to coercion and rape by her captors and all intercourse with them renders her unfit. Rabbeinu Tam answers that in this regard there is no halakhic distinction between most and all. Even according to the opinion that the combination of the minority of men who are fit and her presumptive status of fitness neutralizes the majority of unfit men, this situation remains an equally balanced uncertainty in which the ruling is stringent.

Others explain that when Rabbi Yehoshua ben Levi deems her fit even when the majority of men are unfit, he does not distinguish between most and all. Even if all of the men in her proximity are of flawed lineage, perhaps a man of unflawed lineage happened to be there. This is based on the principle: A woman does not engage in intercourse with a man before ascertaining that he is of unflawed lineage.

One who deems her fit…deems her daughter fit – הַמַּכְשִׁיר בָּהּ מַכְשִׁיר בְּבִתָּהּ: The commentaries explain the reason for Rabbi Yoḥanan's opinion in different ways. According to the Rosh, the certain claim of the mother is effective in rendering the daughter fit, as according to the Rabbis when a certain claim clashes with an uncertain claim, one relies on the certain claim unequivocally. According to the *Maggid Mishna*, by Torah law the daughter should be fit, as the Sages said that it is prohibited for a *mamzer* to marry into the congregation of Israel only if he is a definite *mamzer* but not if there is uncertainty with regard to his status.

In cases of uncertainty, the prohibition is by rabbinic law, and in those cases the mother's claim is sufficient to render her daughter fit. Others explain that the mother's presumptive status of fitness, by virtue of which the Rabbis determine that she engaged in intercourse with a man of unflawed lineage, is effective to render the daughter fit as well (*Nimmukei Yosef*; see Ritva; *Shev Shemateta*).

The child is a *shetuki* but she is fit – שְׁתוּקִי וְכָשֵׁר: The *ge'onim* write that based on the conclusion of the Gemara there are two types of *shetuki*. One is a child born to an unmarried woman who does not know the child's father. In that case, due to the possibility that the child is a *mamzer*, he may not marry into the congregation of Israel. The second type of *shetuki* is one born to an unmarried woman who claims that she knows the child's father and he is a man of unflawed lineage. Although, based on her claim, he is neither that man's heir nor fit to perform the Temple service if the man is a priest, he may marry into the congregation of Israel.

וּמִי אִיכָּא שְׁתוּקִי כָּשֵׁר? אִין, כְּדִשְׁמוּאֵל, דְּאָמַר שְׁמוּאֵל: עֲשָׂרָה כֹּהֲנִים עוֹמְדִים, וּפֵירַשׁ אֶחָד מֵהֶם וּבָעַל – הַוָּלָד שְׁתוּקִי.

The Gemara asks: **And is there** a case of **a *shetuki*** who is nevertheless **fit?** The Gemara answers: **Yes, as** in the statement **of Shmuel. As Shmuel said:** If **ten priests** were **standing and one of them left and engaged in intercourse, the child is a *shetuki*,** literally one who is silenced, because the identity of the father is unclear. In that case it is clear that the child is fit, because it is known that the father is a priest of flawless lineage.

מַאי שְׁתוּקִי? אִילֵימָא שֶׁמַּשְׁתִּיקִין אוֹתוֹ מִנִּכְסֵי אָבִיו – פְּשִׁיטָא, וּמִי יָדְעִינַן אֲבוּהּ מַנּוּ? אֶלָּא שֶׁמַּשְׁתִּיקִין אוֹתוֹ מִדִּין כְּהוּנָּה, דִּכְתִיב ״וְהָיְתָה לּוֹ וּלְזַרְעוֹ אַחֲרָיו בְּרִית כְּהֻנַּת עוֹלָם״ – מִי שֶׁזַּרְעוֹ מְיוּחָס אַחֲרָיו, יָצָא זֶה שֶׁאֵין זַרְעוֹ מְיוּחָס אַחֲרָיו.

The Gemara asks: In **what** sense **is this** child **a *shetuki*? If we say** that it means **that one silences him from** a claim to **his father's assets** and he does not inherit his estate, that is **obvious. Do we know who his father is?** It could be any one of the ten. **Rather,** it means **that one silences him from** a claim to **the status of priesthood.**[NH] Although there is no doubt that his father is a priest, the son is not a priest, **as it is written: "And it shall be for him and for his offspring after him an everlasting covenant of priesthood"** (Numbers 25:13). From this it is derived: In the case of a priest **whose offspring are attributed to him,** his offspring are priests; to the **exclusion of this** priest, **whose offspring are not attributed to him,** and whose offspring are not priests. This child, therefore, is a *shetuki* only in the sense that he may not perform the Temple service as a priest. However, he is permitted to marry a Jewish woman.

הַהוּא אָרוּס וַאֲרוּסְתּוֹ דַּאֲתוֹ לְקַמֵּיהּ דְּרַב יוֹסֵף, הִיא אָמְרָה: מִינֵּיהּ, וְהוּא אָמַר:

Apropos paternity, the Gemara relates: There was **a certain betrothed man and his betrothed,** who was pregnant, **who came before Rav Yosef. She said** that she conceived **from** relations with **him, and he said:**

NOTES

One silences him from a claim to the status of priesthood – מַשְׁתִּיקִין אוֹתוֹ מִדִּין כְּהוּנָּה: The Gemara here holds that there is a special *halakha* with regard to the priesthood: Mere knowledge that a child is the son of a priest is not sufficient. Rather, a specific priest must be identified as his father. Early and later commentaries discuss whether his entire lineage must be known or whether it is sufficient if his grandfather can be identified. See *Tosafot*, who explain that this demand is by rabbinic law and the verse cited is merely an allusion. There are early commentaries who disagree and hold that it is a demand by Torah law, although they dispute whether it applies only to Temple service or even to partaking of *teruma* and reciting the Priestly Blessing as well.

HALAKHA

One silences him from a claim to the status of priesthood – מַשְׁתִּיקִין אוֹתוֹ מִדִּין כְּהוּנָּה: If the identity of a child born to an unmarried woman is unknown, he may not function as a priest. For example, if one of a group of ten priests had relations with a woman, but his identity is unknown, the child born of that union is definitely of priestly lineage. If he marries a divorcée or subjects himself to impurity imparted by a corpse, he is flogged, but he may neither perform the Temple service nor partake of *teruma* (Rambam *Sefer Kedusha, Hilkhot Issurei Bia* 20:20; *Shulḥan Arukh, Even HaEzer* 3:9).

אִין, מִינַּאי. אָמַר רַב יוֹסֵף: לְמַאי נֵיחוּשׁ לַהּ? חֲדָא – דְּהָא קָא מוֹדֶה, וְעוֹד: הָא אָמַר רַב יְהוּדָה אָמַר שְׁמוּאֵל: הֲלָכָה כְּרַבָּן גַּמְלִיאֵל.

Yes, she conceived **from** relations with **me.**[NH] **Rav Yosef said:** The ruling here is clear, as **with regard to what** suspicion need we **be concerned? First, he concedes** that he is the father. **And furthermore, didn't Rav Yehuda say**[N] that **Shmuel said: The *halakha* is in accordance with** the opinion of **Rabban Gamliel,**[H] and even if he didn't admit that the child was his, the woman's claim is accorded credibility?

NOTES

Yes, she conceived from relations with me – אִין, מִינַּאי: This entire passage in the Gemara is tied to a passage in tractate *Yevamot* (69b), where a dispute between Rav and Shmuel is cited with regard to the legal status of a child born to a betrothed woman. There, the concern is raised that perhaps she conceived the child of another man. With regard to that concern, two possibilities are raised. Is it a concern only when she has a reputation of promiscuity? Or perhaps it is even a concern when she has no reputation of that sort, and it was apparently her betrothed who impregnated her. Some commentaries explain that the discussion in the Gemara here is based on the first opinion there. Therefore, provided that she does not have a reputation of promiscuity and the man to whom she is betrothed admits that he is the father, the offspring is attributed to him, she may marry into the priesthood, and the lineage of the offspring is unflawed (Ramban; Rashba).

Tosafot hold that the Gemara here is not referring to a case where they engaged in relations once. Rather, it is referring to a case where the betrothed couple lived together as husband and wife. Therefore, the presumptive status of the offspring is that he is the child of her betrothed. This is based on the principle: Most acts of intercourse are attributed to the husband. Others insist that the Gemara here is referring only to a case where the betrothed woman never left the side of her betrothed until she discovered that she was pregnant. Only then can her betrothed state with certainty that the child is his (Rabbi Yosef Migash; Ritva).

And furthermore didn't Rav Yehuda say – וְעוֹד הָא אָמַר רַב יְהוּדָה: The early commentaries disagree with regard to the meaning of the phrase: And furthermore, etc. What was Rav Yosef's opinion? According to *Tosafot*, it means that if her betrothed is not present one relies on the claim of the woman. However, if her betrothed is present, her claim is not accepted at all (Ramban; Rosh; Ran). The Rambam holds that if her claim is contradicted by her betrothed, his statement is not effective to disqualify the woman from marrying into the priesthood, but the offspring is a *mamzer*. Others explain that the claim of the woman is accepted even if it is contradicted by her betrothed, but his statement renders her forbidden to him (*Tosefot Rid*; *Shiltei HaGibborim*). Although the conclusion of the Gemara is that if there is a majority of people of flawed lineage in her proximity she is disqualified from marrying into the priesthood, the offspring is fit to marry into the priesthood because that is a situation after the fact.

HALAKHA

A betrothed woman who becomes pregnant – אֲרוּסָה שֶׁנִּתְעַבְּרָה: If a betrothed woman becomes pregnant before the wedding and claims that the man to whom she is betrothed is the father of her unborn child, and he admits that he is the father or is not present to confirm or deny her claim, the lineage of the child is unflawed and he is considered the groom's child in every sense, even with regard to inheritance (Rema, based on Ran). If the groom denies his paternity the woman remains fit to marry into the priesthood, although his claim renders her forbidden to him. There are additional distinctions with regard to the *halakha* in a case where she has a reputation of promiscuity with others. These are discussed in tractate *Yevamot* (Rambam *Sefer Kedusha, Hilkhot Issurei Bia* 15:17; *Shulḥan Arukh, Even HaEzer* 4:27).

The *halakha* is in accordance with the opinion of Rabban Gamliel – הֲלָכָה כְּרַבָּן גַּמְלִיאֵל: With regard to an unmarried woman who became pregnant and claims that she had relations with a man of unflawed lineage, her claim is accepted and she may marry a priest, even if the majority of men in her proximity are of flawed lineage. The Sages, however, established a higher standard for priestly lineage, and accepted her claim only if there are two majorities of men of unflawed lineage. Otherwise, she is disqualified from marrying a priest (Rambam). Some authorities (*Tur*, citing Ramban and Rashba) maintain that one majority is sufficient (Rambam *Sefer Kedusha, Hilkhot Issurei Bia* 18:13–14; *Shulḥan Arukh, Even HaEzer* 6:17).

אֲמַר לֵיהּ אַבַּיֵי: וּבְהָא, כִּי לָא מוֹדֶה מַכְשַׁר רַבָּן גַּמְלִיאֵל? וְהָאֲמַר לֵיהּ שְׁמוּאֵל לְרַב יְהוּדָה: שִׁינָּנָא! הֲלָכָה כְּרַבָּן גַּמְלִיאֵל, וְאַתְּ לָא תַּעֲבֵיד עוּבְדָא עַד דְּאִיכָּא רוֹב כְּשֵׁרִין אֶצְלָהּ. וְהָכָא – רוֹב פְּסוּלִין אֶצְלָהּ!

Abaye said to him: And in this case, based on the fact that you cited two reasons to deem the child fit, is that to say **when he does not admit** that he is the father **Rabban Gamliel deems** the child **fit?**[N] **But didn't Shmuel say to Rav Yehuda: Big-toothed** one, **the *halakha* is in accordance with** the opinion **of Rabban Gamliel,** i.e., that she is accorded credibility, **but you should not perform an action** based on this ruling **unless the majority of the men in her proximity are honorable** and of impeccable lineage, corroborating her claim. **And here,** since she is betrothed, **the majority of the men in her proximity are unfit,** as a child fathered by any man other than her betrothed is a *mamzer*. Shmuel should not have ruled that the *halakha* was in accordance with the opinion of Rabban Gamliel.

וְלִיטַעֲמִיךְ, תִּקְשֵׁי לָךְ הִיא גּוּפָא: הֲלָכָה – וְאַתְּ לָא תַּעֲבֵיד עוּבְדָא?! אֶלָּא מַאי אִית לָךְ לְמֵימַר: הָא – לְכַתְּחִלָּה, הָא – דִּיעֲבַד, וְהָא נַמִי, כְּדִיעֲבַד דָּמֵי.

Rav Yosef said to Abaye: **And according to your reasoning,** the ***halakha* itself should pose a difficulty for you,** as on the one hand Shmuel rules that it is the ***halakha* and** on the other hand he adds: **But you should not perform an action** based on this ruling. **Rather, what have you to say** to explain this contradiction? **This** statement that one relies on the woman's claim only if a majority of men in her proximity are of unflawed lineage is ***ab initio*. That** statement that one may rely on the woman's claim regardless of the status on the men in her proximity is **after the fact. And this** case of the betrothed woman, **too, is like** a case **after the fact,**[N] as failure to rely on her claim will render her child a *mamzer*. Therefore, in this case, Shmuel would rule that the *halakha* is in accordance with the opinion of Rabban Gamliel.

רָמֵי לֵיהּ אַבַּיֵי לְרָבָא: וּמִי אֲמַר רַבִּי יְהוֹשֻׁעַ אֵינָהּ נֶאֱמֶנֶת? וּרְמִינְהוּ: הֵעִיד רַבִּי יְהוֹשֻׁעַ וְרַבִּי יְהוּדָה בֶּן בְּתֵירָא עַל אַלְמְנַת עִיסָּה שֶׁהִיא כְּשֵׁרָה לִכְהוּנָּה!

§ **Abaye raised a contradiction before Rava** from a mishna (*Eduyyot* 10:3): **Did Rabbi Yehoshua say that** the woman **is not deemed credible** and her claim is not accepted? **And** the Gemara **raises a contradiction: Rabbi Yehoshua and Rabbi Yehuda ben Beteira testified concerning the widow** whose late husband was a member **of a** priestly **family of questionable lineage** [*issa*],[HLN] **that she is fit to** marry into the **priesthood.** Since the matter is uncertain, the woman retains her presumptive status of fitness and her late husband is presumed to be of unflawed lineage.

אָמַר לֵיהּ: הָכִי הָשְׁתָּא! הָתָם – אִשָּׁה נִישֵּׂאת – בּוֹדֶקֶת וְנִישֵּׂאת, הָכָא – אִשָּׁה מְזַנָּה – בּוֹדֶקֶת וּמְזַנָּה?!

Rava **said to him: How can** these cases **be compared? There,** in the case of the widow, one could say: A **woman** who **marries investigates** the lineage of her prospective husband before the wedding **and** only then **marries.**[N] Therefore, one may rely on her presumptive status of fitness and deem her fit to marry a priest. **Here,** can it be said that **a woman** who **engages in licentious intercourse investigates** the lineage of her partner and only then **engages in licentious intercourse?**

HALAKHA

The widow whose late husband was a member of a priestly family of questionable lineage – אַלְמְנַת עִיסָּה: If a woman married a man from a family in which one of the members is an uncertain *ḥalal*, and was then widowed, it is prohibited for her to marry a priest; this is in accordance with the opinion of Rabban Gamliel. However, if she married a priest she may remain married to him, as Rabban Gamliel did not say that it is prohibited for a priest to marry her. Rather, he said that the priests did not accept the leniency (Rambam *Sefer Kedusha, Hilkhot Issurei Bia* 19:23; *Shulḥan Arukh, Even HaEzer* 2:5).

LANGUAGE

A family of questionable lineage [*issa*] – עִיסָּה: Rav Hai Gaon explains that this expression evokes kneaded dough, in which it is difficult to determine exactly what is mixed into the dough. By contrast, the metaphor used to describe a family of impeccable lineage is pure, fine flour. The *Arukh* explains that the reference is to dough from which *ḥalla* was separated, which remains non-sacred. Rashi in tractate *Kiddushin* explains that the reference is to a doughy paste made of grapes from which the juice was squeezed.

NOTES

Rabban Gamliel deems the child fit – מַכְשַׁר רַבָּן גַּמְלִיאֵל: The Ramban cites a variant reading that omits the words: Rabban Gamliel. According to that version, the Gemara is analyzing the opinion of Shmuel and not the opinion of Rabban Gamliel.

And this too is like a case after the fact – וְהָא נַמִי כְּדִיעֲבַד דָּמֵי: The Ra'avad explains that even though with regard to the woman there is an element of after the fact, as she is rendered forbidden to her betrothed, with regard to the offspring the matter is apparently *ab initio*. Nevertheless, he explains that there is an element of a situation after the fact with regard to the offspring. If the question is whether or not her daughter is fit to marry into the priesthood, this would be an *ab initio* situation. However, if the question pertains to classifying the offspring as a *mamzer*, or even worse as an uncertain *mamzer*, who may not marry even another *mamzer*, that is considered after the fact (*Tosafot*; *Tosefot Rid*; Ramban). The Ritva notes that this is the meaning of the phrase: Like a case after the fact, as even though it is not actually after the fact, it is treated as if it were.

The Ra'avad further explains that the use of the term: Like, is due to the fact that they are not yet married and therefore the situation is not actually after the fact. The Ran explains that it is permitted even for the offspring to marry into the priesthood. The reason is that the case is treated as if it were after the fact, because the fate of the woman is tied to the fate of the child. If her betrothed is told that her child is unfit, it is likely that he will divorce the woman.

The widow whose late husband was a member of a priestly family of questionable lineage – אַלְמְנַת עִיסָּה: There are several opinions with regard to the meaning of this concept. Although everyone agrees that there is uncertainty with regard to the *ḥalal* status of the family, there is disagreement with regard to the essence of this uncertainty. Rashi explains that the reference is to a widow whose husband was the son of a priest who married a woman with regard to whom there is uncertainty whether she was a divorcée or whether she was a widow. An example of this would be if her first husband threw a bill of divorce to her and it is unclear whether it landed closer to her or closer to him; and then he died.

Rabbeinu Ḥananel cites two explanations. In one he agrees with Rashi. In the other, he explains that she is the widow of a man whose status as a priest is uncertain, e.g., if two babies were intermingled. See Rashi, who cites an additional explanation in the name of Rabbi Yosef Tuv-Elem.

The *ge'onim*, the Rambam, and *Tosafot* all explain that the reference is to an uncertain *ḥalal* who joined a family or moved to a city, but it is not known who he is. There is a compound uncertainty with regard to the widow of a man from that family. The first uncertainty is whether her late husband is the member of that family with regard to whom the uncertainty exists. Even if it is established that her late husband is indeed the one with regard to whom the uncertainty exists, there remains an uncertainty whether he is in fact a *ḥalal*. The term *issa*, meaning dough, is especially appropriate according to that explanation, as the family is like dough whose ingredients are unknown.

With regard to the legal status of a child born from this union, although the widow enjoys presumptive status of fitness, her offspring does not. Furthermore, as with regard to lineage, the status of the child is determined by the status of the father; since the father is an uncertain *ḥalal*, the same is true of the offspring (*Ayyelet Ahavim*; *Beit Ya'akov*).

A woman who marries, investigates and marries – אִשָּׁה נִישֵּׂאת, בּוֹדֶקֶת וְנִישֵּׂאת: The Rashash explains that since a woman who is getting married plans on spending her entire life with this man, she will investigate his lineage so she does not live her life in sin. However, when it is a one-time, licentious liaison, she is not as careful. Furthermore, before marriage the woman has the time and opportunity to investigate her potential husband. In a licentious liaison, perhaps it is the result of a moment of passion and there is no opportunity to investigate.

אֲמַר רָבָא: דְּרַבִּי יְהוֹשֻׁעַ אַדְּרַבִּי יְהוֹשֻׁעַ קַשְׁיָא, דְּרַבָּן גַּמְלִיאֵל אַדְּרַבָּן גַּמְלִיאֵל לָא קַשְׁיָא? וְהָא קָתָנֵי סֵיפָא, אָמַר לָהֶן רַבָּן גַּמְלִיאֵל: קִבַּלְנוּ עֵדוּתְכֶם, אֲבָל מַה נַּעֲשֶׂה שֶׁהֲרֵי גָּזַר רַבָּן יוֹחָנָן בֶּן זַכַּאי שֶׁלֹּא לְהוֹשִׁיב בֵּית דִּין עַל כָּךְ, שֶׁהַכֹּהֲנִים שׁוֹמְעִין לָכֶם לְרַחֵק אֲבָל לֹא לְקָרֵב!

Rava said with regard to the contradiction that was raised: Is the contradiction between one statement **of Rabbi Yehoshua and** another statement **of Rabbi Yehoshua difficult,** and the contradiction between one statement **of Rabban Gamliel and** another statement **of Rabban Gamliel not difficult? But isn't it taught in the latter clause** of that mishna with regard to the widow whose late husband was from a priestly family of questionable lineage that **Rabban Gamliel said to them: We accept your testimony** that this is the *halakha,* **but what can we do, as Rabban Yoḥanan ben Zakkai decreed not to convene a court for this** purpose of ruling the woman fit, **because the priests obey you** when your ruling calls **to distance** a woman of questionable lineage from marrying them, **but not** when your ruling calls **to bring her near** and deem her fit to marry them. Apparently, Rabban Gamliel did not accept the lenient ruling in the case of the widow, contrary to his statement here that she is accorded credibility.

אֶלָּא אֲמַר רָבָא: דְּרַבָּן גַּמְלִיאֵל אַדְּרַבָּן גַּמְלִיאֵל לָא קַשְׁיָא; הָתָם – בָּרִי, הָכָא – שֶׁמָּא.

Rather, Rava said: The contradiction between one statement **of Rabban Gamliel and** another statement **of Rabban Gamliel is not difficult. There,** in the case of the woman who engaged in intercourse with an unidentified man, her claim that the lineage of the man is unflawed is **a certain** claim. **Here,** in the case of the widow, her claim that his lineage is unflawed is **an uncertain** claim, because there is objective uncertainty with regard to his lineage.

דְּרַבִּי יְהוֹשֻׁעַ אַדְּרַבִּי יְהוֹשֻׁעַ נַמִּי לָא קַשְׁיָא; הָתָם – חַד סְפֵיקָא, הָכָא – תְּרֵי סְפֵיקֵי.

The contradiction between one statement **of Rabbi Yehoshua and** another statement **of Rabbi Yehoshua is** similarly **not difficult. There,** in the case of the woman who engaged in intercourse with an unidentified man, there is only **one uncertainty:**[N] Is the lineage of the man with whom she engaged in intercourse flawed or unflawed? In the case of one uncertainty, the ruling is stringent. **Here,** in the case of the widow, there are **two uncertainties**[N] with regard to the objective situation. It is established that there is uncertainty with regard to one of the members of the family whether or not he is a *ḥalal.* The first uncertainty is whether her late husband is the member of that family with regard to whom the uncertainty exists. Even if it is established that her late husband is indeed the one with regard to whom the uncertainty exists, there remains an uncertainty whether he is in fact a *ḥalal.*

הִלְכָּךְ, לְרַבָּן גַּמְלִיאֵל – אַלִּים לֵיהּ בָּרִי, דַּאֲפִילּוּ בְּחַד סְפֵיקָא נַמִּי מַכְשִׁיר. וְקִיל לֵיהּ שֶׁמָּא, דַּאֲפִילּוּ בִּסְפֵק סְפֵיקָא – נַמִּי פָּסֵיל. לְרַבִּי יְהוֹשֻׁעַ אַלִּים לֵיהּ חַד סְפֵיקָא, דַּאֲפִילּוּ בְּבָרִי נַמִּי פָּסֵיל וְקִיל לֵיהּ סְפֵק סְפֵיקָא, דַּאֲפִילּוּ בְּשֶׁמָּא – נַמִּי מַכְשִׁיר.

Therefore, according **to Rabban Gamliel, a certain** claim is so **powerful for him**[N] **that even in** a case where there is **one uncertainty, he also deems her fit** to marry a priest. **And an uncertain** claim is so **insignificant for him that even in** a case where there is **a compound uncertainty, he also deems her unfit** to marry a priest. According **to Rabbi Yehoshua,** a case where there is **one uncertainty** is so **powerful for him that even in** a case where she makes **a certain** claim, **he also deems her unfit. And** the case of **a compound uncertainty is so insignificant for him that even if she makes an uncertain** claim, **he also deems her fit.**

NOTES

There, there is one uncertainty – הָתָם חַד סְפֵיקָא: Some ask: Isn't there a compound uncertainty in the case of a woman who entered into seclusion as well, the uncertainty whether or not she engaged in intercourse, and even if she did engage in intercourse, perhaps her paramour was of unflawed lineage? The Ramban explains that according to Rabbi Yehoshua, once she enters into seclusion there is no longer uncertainty whether or not she engaged in intercourse, as there is no steward for restraining sexual immorality, i.e., presumably she engaged in intercourse with him.

Here, there are two uncertainties – הָכָא תְּרֵי סְפֵיקֵי: According to the opinion of the Rambam and the *ge'onim* with regard to the widow whose late husband was from a priestly family of questionable lineage, the compound uncertainty is clear: There is uncertainty whether there was a *ḥalal* at all, and even if there was a *ḥalal,* whether her husband was that *ḥalal.* In the *Shita Mekubbetzet* another explanation is cited: Since there is uncertainty with regard to the status of the husband, the resultant uncertainty with regard to his widow is considered a second uncertainty. Since she has the presumptive status of fitness, the flaw in lineage is not dependent on her but originates elsewhere and perhaps there was no flaw at all (see *Beit Shmuel*; *Ayyelet Ahavim*).

A certain claim is so powerful for him – אַלִּים לֵיהּ בָּרִי: The Ritva explains that there is not merely a claim of certainty here. It is bolstered by the presumptive status of her body.

תָּנוּ רַבָּנַן: אֵיזוֹהִי אַלְמְנַת עִיסָּה – כׇּל שֶׁאֵין בָּהּ לֹא מִשּׁוּם מַמְזֵרוּת, וְלֹא מִשּׁוּם נְתִינוּת, וְלֹא מִשּׁוּם עַבְדֵי מְלָכִים. אָמַר רַבִּי מֵאִיר:

§ Apropos the widow, **the Rabbis taught: Who is the widow** whose late husband was a member **of a** priestly **family of questionable lineage** and is fit to marry a priest? It is one who married into **any** family **that does not have** the status of being unfit, **neither due to** uncertain ***mamzer*** **status, nor due to** uncertain **Gibeonite status, nor due to** uncertain status as **slaves of kings,**[N] who would force Jewish women, even daughters of priests, to marry them. **Rabbi Meir said:**

NOTES

Slaves of kings – **עַבְדֵי מְלָכִים**: Most commentaries explain that the concern is due to the prohibition against marrying slaves. The Meiri, however, explains that the reference here is to gentiles, who exercised their power and took Jewish women. Although the *halakha* is that a child born to a Jewish woman and a gentile or slave is permitted to marry into the congregation of Israel, a female child is disqualified from marrying into the priesthood.

Perek **I**
Daf **14** Amud **b**

שָׁמַעְתִּי כׇּל שֶׁאֵין בָּהּ אֶחָד מִכׇּל אֵלּוּ – מַשִּׂיאִין לִכְהוּנָּה.

I heard that with regard to the widow of **any** family **that has none of these** uncertainties associated with it, **one** allows **her to marry** members of **the priesthood.** The only uncertainty where this ruling applies is in the case of uncertain *ḥalal* status.

רַבִּי שִׁמְעוֹן בֶּן אֶלְעָזָר אוֹמֵר מִשּׁוּם רַבִּי מֵאִיר, וְכֵן הָיָה רַבִּי שִׁמְעוֹן בֶּן מְנַסְיָא אוֹמֵר כִּדְבָרָיו: אֵיזוֹהִי אַלְמְנַת עִיסָּה – כׇּל שֶׁנִּטְמַע בָּהּ סְפֵק חָלָל.

Rabbi Shimon ben Elazar says in the name of Rabbi Meir, and likewise Rabbi Shimon ben Menasya would say in accordance with his statement: Who is the widow whose late husband was a member **of a** priestly **family of questionable lineage?** It is a widow who marries into **any** family in **which** a person with regard to whom there is **uncertainty** whether or not he is a ***ḥalal*** **was assimilated** among its members. Therefore, she is referred to as a widow of dough [*issa*]. Just as dough is the result of a mixture of several ingredients, this family too has a person with regard to whom there is uncertainty whether he is a *ḥalal* mixed within it.

מַכִּירִין יִשְׂרָאֵל מַמְזֵרִים שֶׁבֵּינֵיהֶם, וְאֵין מַכִּירִין חֲלָלִין שֶׁבֵּינֵיהֶם.

The reason for the distinction between uncertain *ḥalal* status and uncertain *mamzer* status is that **Jews identify the *mamzerim* that are among them,**[N] and there is no concern lest they assimilate into families of unflawed lineage. **But they do not identify the *ḥalalin* among them.** Therefore, there is concern lest a *ḥalal* assimilate into the family.

אָמַר מָר: אֵיזוֹהִי אַלְמְנַת עִיסָּה – כׇּל שֶׁאֵין בָּהּ לֹא מִשּׁוּם מַמְזֵרוּת, וְלֹא מִשּׁוּם נְתִינוּת, וְלֹא מִשּׁוּם עַבְדֵי מְלָכִים. הָא חָלָל – כָּשֵׁר.

The Gemara analyzes the *baraita*. **The Master said** in the *baraita*: **Who is the widow** whose late husband was a member **of a** priestly **family of questionable lineage?** It is one who married into **any** family **that does not have** the status of being unfit, **neither due to** uncertain ***mamzer*** **status,**[N] **nor due to** uncertain **Gibeonite status, nor due to** uncertain status as **slaves of kings.** The Gemara infers: **However,** if it is due to uncertain ***ḥalal*** status, her marriage to a priest is deemed **fit.**

מַאי שְׁנָא הָנָךְ – דְּאוֹרַיְיתָא, חָלָל נַמִי דְּאוֹרַיְיתָא! וְתוּ, אָמַר רַבִּי מֵאִיר: שָׁמַעְתִּי כׇּל שֶׁאֵין בָּהּ אֶחָד מִכׇּל אֵלּוּ מַשִּׂיאִין לִכְהוּנָּה, הַיְינוּ תַּנָּא קַמָּא!

The Gemara asks: **What is different** about **these** flaws in lineage, uncertain *mamzer* status and Gibeonite status, which render her unfit to marry a priest **by Torah** law?[N] **A *ḥalal*** also renders her unfit **by Torah** law. **And furthermore,** the *baraita* continues: **Rabbi Meir said: I heard** that with regard to the widow of **any** family **that has none of these** uncertainties associated with it, **one marries her to** members of **the priesthood. That is** identical to the opinion of the **first *tanna*.**[N] If there is uncertainty with regard to one in the late husband's family that he is a *mamzer* or a Gibeonite, she is unfit to marry a priest; if the uncertainty is with regard to *ḥalal* status, she is fit to marry a priest. What novel element does Rabbi Meir introduce?

NOTES

Jews identify the *mamzerim* that are among them – **מַכִּירִין יִשְׂרָאֵל מַמְזֵרִים שֶׁבֵּינֵיהֶם**: The same is true of the other men of flawed lineage enumerated there, because people identify all those prohibited from entering the congregation of Israel. However, since the *ḥalal* is prohibited only with regard to the priesthood and the prohibition is irrelevant to all other people, they are likely to forget the prohibition.

That does not have the status of being unfit…due to uncertain *mamzer* status – **שֶׁאֵין בָּהּ לֹא מִשּׁוּם מַמְזֵרוּת**: Most commentaries explain that other examples of flawed lineage by Torah law, e.g., Ammonites, Moabites, Egyptians, and Edomites, were not cited here for various reasons: Ammonites and Moabites because there is a difference between males, who may never enter into the congregation, and females, who may do so immediately; Egyptians and Edomites because they may enter into the congregation three generations after conversion. Rather, only those people of flawed lineage for whom the prohibition is universal and permanent were enumerated here.

These flaws which render her unfit by Torah law – **הָנָךְ דְּאוֹרַיְיתָא**: Rashi explains that all these are derived from the verse: "And if a priest's daughter be married to a common man" (Leviticus 22:12). However, the lack of fitness of a *ḥalal* does not fall into that category because he is a priest, not a common man. The status of a *ḥalal* is derived from a different verse.

That is identical to the opinion of the first *tanna* – **הַיְינוּ תַּנָּא קַמָּא**: Some early commentaries ask: Why didn't the Gemara explain that Rabbi Meir disagrees and holds that the dispute between Rabban Gamliel and Rabbi Yehoshua is limited to a case where there is uncertainty with regard to the fitness of other categories of flawed lineage, but where there is uncertainty with regard to *ḥalal* status Rabban Gamliel would concede? They answer that since all of these categories of flawed lineage are derived from the Torah, there is no reason to distinguish between them (Ramban; Rabbi Aharon HaLevi; Ritva).

וְתוּ, רַבִּי שִׁמְעוֹן בֶּן אֶלְעָזָר אוֹמֵר מִשּׁוּם רַבִּי מֵאִיר, וְכֵן הָיָה רַבִּי שִׁמְעוֹן בֶּן מְנַסְיָא אוֹמֵר כִּדְבָרָיו: אֵיזוֹהִי אַלְמָנַת עִיסָּה – כׇּל שֶׁנִּטְמַע בָּהּ סְפֵק חָלָל, מַכִּירִין יִשְׂרָאֵל מַמְזֵרִים שֶׁבֵּינֵיהֶן וְאֵין מַכִּירִין חֲלָלִין שֶׁבֵּינֵיהֶן, וְהָא אָמְרַתְּ רֵישָׁא חָלָל כָּשֵׁר!

The *baraita* continues: **And furthermore, Rabbi Shimon ben Elazar says in the name of Rabbi Meir, and likewise, Rabbi Shimon ben Menasya would say in accordance with his statement: Who is the widow** whose late husband was a member **of a** priestly **family of questionable lineage?** It is a widow who marries into **any** family in **which** a person with regard to whom there is **uncertainty** whether or not he is a ***ḥalal*** **was assimilated.** Because **Jews identify the *mamzerim* that are among them** there is no concern that they will assimilate into families of unflawed lineage, **but** Jews **do not identify the *ḥalalin* among them.** Due to the concern that a *ḥalal* assimilated into the family, the widow is unfit to marry a priest. The Gemara asks: **But didn't you say in the first clause** of the *baraita* that if there is uncertainty whether or not a ***ḥalal*** was assimilated among its members, her marriage to a priest is deemed **fit?**

אָמַר רַבִּי יוֹחָנָן: "מַמְזֵר" – צוֹוֵחַ, וְ"חָלָל" – שׁוֹתֵק, אִיכָּא בֵּינַיְיהוּ. תַּנָּא קַמָּא סָבַר: כׇּל פְּסוּל דְּקָרוּ לֵיהּ וְשָׁתֵיק – פָּסוּל. וְהָכִי קָאָמַר תַּנָּא קַמָּא: אֵיזוֹהִי אַלְמָנַת עִיסָּה – כׇּל שֶׁאֵין בָּהּ לֹא שִׁתּוּק מַמְזֵרוּת, וְלֹא שִׁתּוּק נְתִינוּת, וְלֹא שִׁתּוּק עַבְדֵי מְלָכִים, וְלֹא שִׁתּוּק חָלָל.

Rabbi Yoḥanan said: The case of one who when called ***mamzer*** **screams** and protests that he is being slandered, **and** when called ***ḥalal*** **is silent,**[N] is the subject of the dispute **between** the *tanna'im* in the *baraita*. **The first *tanna* holds: Anyone who** when others **call him unfit and he is silent, is unfit,**[H] as his silence confirms the allegation. **And this is what the first *tanna* is saying: Who is the widow** whose late husband was a member **of a** priestly **family of questionable lineage,** who is fit to marry a priest? It is one who married into **any** family **that has neither** unfitness due to **silence** in response to allegations of ***mamzer*** **status, nor silence** in response to allegations of **Gibeonite status, nor silence** in response to allegations that they are **slaves of kings, nor silence** in response to allegations of ***ḥalal*** status.[N] Only a woman who was married into a family that protested in response to all these allegations is fit to marry a priest.

וְקָאָמַר לֵיהּ רַבִּי מֵאִיר: הָנָךְ הוּא – דְּקָא פָּסֵיל לֵיהּ בְּקָהָל, אֲבָל שִׁתּוּק חָלָל – כָּשֵׁר, וְהָא דְּשָׁתֵיק – מִשּׁוּם דְּלָא אִיכְפַּת לֵיהּ.

And Rabbi Meir is saying to him: Specifically, each of **those** silent in response to allegations of *mamzer* or Gibeonite status or allegations that they are slaves of kings are rendered unfit **because these** allegations **render him unfit** to marry **into the congregation** of Israel. **However,** despite **silence** in response to allegations of ***ḥalal*** status, her marriage to a priest is deemed **fit. And** the fact **that he is silent is due to his indifference,** as even were he deemed a *ḥalal* the only restriction would be with regard to marriage to priests.

וְקָאָמַר לֵיהּ רַבִּי שִׁמְעוֹן בֶּן אֶלְעָזָר לְתַנָּא קַמָּא דְּרַבִּי מֵאִיר: אִי שְׁמִיעַ לָךְ דְּמַכְשַׁר רַבִּי מֵאִיר בִּשְׁתִיקָה – לָא דְּקָרוּ לֵיהּ חָלָל וְשָׁתֵיק, אֶלָּא דְּקָרוּ לֵיהּ מַמְזֵר וְשָׁתֵיק, וְהַאי דְּשָׁתֵיק – סָבַר: מַמְזֵר קָלָא אִית לֵיהּ. אֲבָל "מַמְזֵר" וְצוֹוֵחַ: "חָלָל" וְשׁוֹתֵק, פָּסוּל, וְהַאי דְּאִשְׁתִּיק – סָבַר: מִיסְתַּיֵּיהּ דְּלָא מַפְּקֵי לֵיהּ מִקָּהָל.

And Rabbi Shimon ben Elazar is saying to the first *tanna* who quoted **Rabbi Meir** as saying: I heard, etc. **If you heard that Rabbi Meir deems** her marriage to a priest **fit, in** a case of **silence** in response to allegations, it is **not** in a case **where they called him *ḥalal* and he is silent; rather,** it is in a case **where they call him *mamzer* and he is silent.** In that case, the reason **he is silent** is **that he holds:** The fact that one is **a *mamzer*** generates **publicity,** and since he is not reputed to be a *mamzer*, he is indifferent to the allegation. **However,** in a case where he is called ***mamzer*** **and he screams** in protest, or where he is called ***ḥalal*** **and he is silent, he is unfit. And** the fact **that he is silent** and does not protest **is** because **he holds:** It is **sufficient for him that they do not expel him from the congregation** of Israel.

NOTES

One who when called *mamzer* screams and protests that he is being slandered, and when called *ḥalal* is silent – מַמְזֵר צוֹוֵחַ וְחָלָל שׁוֹתֵק: The early commentaries discuss the matter of unfitness resulting from the silence of the accused, and there are different explanations with halakhic ramifications. Some explain that according to the first *tanna*, his silence is tantamount to an admission that the allegation of unfitness is accurate (Rambam; Meiri). Some explain that silence is incriminating only if there were rumors of flawed lineage surrounding the accused and his family; otherwise, his silence proves nothing (Ramban; Rashba). The Ra'avad explains that the distinction between screaming and silence was in effect only in those generations when the courts would punish one who slanders another in this manner.

Today, however, the opposite is true. Silence in reaction to an allegation during a quarrel indicates unflawed lineage; it is considered admission of flawed lineage only if the allegation is leveled not in the context of a quarrel. According to these opinions, the matter of one who screams in response to allegations of a *mamzer* is irrelevant. The Ramban cites in the name of Rav Hai Gaon that there is a variant reading that omits the phrase: One who when called *mamzer* screams. However, others hold that confirmation of the allegation is specifically with regard to one who when called *mamzer* screams and protests, and when called *ḥalal* is silent. If one is consistently silent in the face of allegations, perhaps he is one of those people who never scream, even when quarreling with others.

In tractate *Kiddushin*, silence is an indication of impeccable lineage. However, one who screams when called *mamzer* indicates that he reacts to and protests false allegations. If he is then silent when called *ḥalal*, that confirms the allegation (Ritva; Ran).

Silence in response to allegations of *ḥalal* status – שִׁתּוּק חָלָל: The significance of silence in the face of allegations of *ḥalal* is understood according to those who explain that the *ḥalal* is certain that he is a *ḥalal* and it is everyone else who is uncertain. However, according to those opinions who explain that there is an objective uncertainty, how can the silence be considered an admission if the *ḥalal* himself is uncertain of his status? The Ritva explains that his silence is an admission that he is a member of the family with regard to which there is uncertainty.

HALAKHA

Anyone who hears an allegation of unfitness that others call him and is silent, is unfit – כׇּל פְּסוּל דְּקָרוּ לֵיהּ וְשָׁתֵיק פָּסוּל: If one is silent in the face of allegations that he is of flawed lineage, e.g., he is called a *mamzer*, a *ḥalal*, or a Gibeonite, the suspicion is that his silence confirms those allegations, and one may marry him or members of his family only after those allegations are investigated and refuted, in accordance with the opinion of the first *tanna*. Some maintain that this is the case only if it is known that a person of flawed lineage married into the family; otherwise, his silence proves nothing (*Tur*, citing Rabbeinu Yitzḥak; *Beit Yosef*, citing Ramban and Rashba). The Ra'avad explains that the distinction between silence and screaming was in effect only in those generations when the courts would punish one who slanders another in this manner.

Today, however, the opposite is true. Silence in reaction to an allegation during a quarrel indicates unflawed lineage. Yet others hold that his silence confirms the allegations only if he is not silent in response to other allegations (Ran; Rambam *Sefer Kedusha*, *Hilkhot Issurei Bia* 19:22; *Shulḥan Arukh*, *Even HaEzer* 2:4).

תָּנֵי חֲדָא: רַבִּי יוֹסֵי אוֹמֵר שְׁתוּק מַמְזֵר – כָּשֵׁר, שְׁתוּק חָלָל – פָּסוּל. וְתַנְיָא אִידָּךְ: שְׁתוּק חָלָל – כָּשֵׁר, שְׁתוּק מַמְזֵר – פָּסוּל!

The Gemara notes: **It is taught** in **one** *baraita* that **Rabbi Yosei says:** Despite the fact that with **silence** in response to allegations of ***mamzer*** one is **fit; silence** in response to allegations of ***ḥalal*** renders one **unfit. It is taught** in **another** *baraita*: Despite the fact that with **silence** in response to allegations of ***ḥalal*** one is **fit; silence** in response to allegations of ***mamzer*** renders one **unfit.**

לָא קַשְׁיָא; הָא – תַּנָּא קַמָּא אַלִּיבָּא דְּרַבִּי מֵאִיר, הָא – דְּרַבִּי שִׁמְעוֹן בֶּן אֶלְעָזָר אַלִּיבָּא דְּרַבִּי מֵאִיר.

The Gemara explains: The contradiction between the *baraitot* is **not difficult. This** second *baraita* is the opinion of **the first *tanna* in accordance with** the opinion of **Rabbi Meir,** who holds that silence in response to allegations of *ḥalal* does not render one unfit. And **this** first *baraita* is the opinion **of Rabbi Shimon ben Elazar in accordance with** the opinion of **Rabbi Meir,** who holds that silence in response to allegations of *mamzer* is motivated by indifference and does not render him unfit; however, silence in response to allegations of *ḥalal* is an indication that the allegations are true and he is unfit.

מתני׳ אָמַר רַבִּי יוֹסֵי: מַעֲשֶׂה בְּתִינוֹקֶת שֶׁיָּרְדָה לְמַלְּאוֹת מַיִם מִן הָעַיִן וְנֶאֶנְסָה, אָמַר רַבִּי יוֹחָנָן בֶּן נוּרִי: אִם רוֹב אַנְשֵׁי הָעִיר מַשִּׂיאִין לִכְהוּנָּה – הֲרֵי זוֹ תִּינָּשֵׂא לִכְהוּנָּה.

MISHNA **Rabbi Yosei said:** There was **an incident involving a young girl who descended**[N] **to fill** her jug with **water from the spring, and she was raped,** and the identity of the rapist was unknown. **Rabbi Yoḥanan ben Nuri said: If the majority of the people of the city marry** their daughters **to** members of the **priesthood,**[N] **this young girl may be married to** a member of the priesthood.

גמ׳ אֲמַר לֵיהּ רָבָא לְרַב נַחְמָן: רַבִּי יוֹחָנָן בֶּן נוּרִי דַּאֲמַר כְּמַאן? אִי כְּרַבָּן גַּמְלִיאֵל, אֲפִילּוּ בְּרוֹב פְּסוּלִין נַמִי מַכְשַׁר! אִי כְּרַבִּי יְהוֹשֻׁעַ, אֲפִילּוּ בְּרוֹב כְּשֵׁרִים נַמִי פָּסֵיל! אֲמַר לֵיהּ, הָכִי אֲמַר רַב יְהוּדָה אֲמַר רַב:

GEMARA **Rava said to Rav Naḥman: In accordance with whose** opinion is it **that Rabbi Yoḥanan ben Nuri stated** his opinion?[N] **If it is in accordance with** the opinion of **Rabban Gamliel, even in a** case where **the majority** of the people **are of flawed lineage as well, he deems** her **fit** to marry into the priesthood. **If it is in accordance with** the opinion of **Rabbi Yehoshua,**[N] **even in a** case where **the majority** of the people **are of unflawed lineage, he deems** her **unfit** to marry into the priesthood. Rav Naḥman **said to** Rava that **this** is what **Rav Yehuda said** that **Rav said:**

NOTES

A young girl who descended – תִּינוֹקֶת שֶׁיָּרְדָה: One of the questions raised by the early commentaries is whether the girl who was raped claims that she is certain that the man who raped her is of unflawed lineage. The fact is that according to Rabban Gamliel, her certain claim is part of the reason that she is not disqualified. Many prove from the formulation of the mishna, where no claim is mentioned, that the girl made no claim with regard to the identity of the rapist. This is underscored by the fact that the mishna is referring to a young girl and by the fact that the incident transpired among the wagons (see 15a) where there are many strangers whose lineage is unknown (Ramban; Ritva).

If the majority of the people of the city marry their daughters to members of the priesthood – אִם רוֹב אַנְשֵׁי הָעִיר מַשִּׂיאִין לִכְהוּנָּה: Rashi writes that this means simply that most of the people in the city are of unflawed lineage and could marry their daughters to priests. Others explain that it means that most of the residents in fact marry their daughters to priests (*ge'onim*).

In accordance with whose opinion is it that Rabbi Yoḥanan ben Nuri stated his opinion – רַבִּי יוֹחָנָן בֶּן נוּרִי דַּאֲמַר כְּמַאן: The early commentaries ask: Since Rabbi Yoḥanan ben Nuri is a *tanna*, why was it necessary to align his opinion with the opinion of one of the *tanna'im*? Why not say that his is a third opinion? They answer that his opinion was introduced by means of an incident, and the mishna typically cites incidents in support of what was stated previously. Furthermore, were this a third opinion, Rabbi Yosei should have cited it earlier and stated that there is an opinion that the entire matter is dependent on the question whether the majority of the people are of flawed or unflawed lineage (Rabbi Yosef MiGash; Ritva).

If it is in accordance with the opinion of Rabbi Yehoshua – אִי כְּרַבִּי יְהוֹשֻׁעַ: The conclusion of the Jerusalem Talmud differs from the Gemara here. There it is stated that the statement of Rabbi Yoḥanan ben Nuri is in accordance with the opinion of Rabbi Yehoshua. The reason that Rabbi Yoḥanan ben Nuri rules that she is fit to marry into the priesthood is that she was raped. Rabbi Yehoshua deems her unfit because her presumptive status of fitness is compromised by her volitional promiscuity. However, one who is raped does not lose her presumptive status of fitness. That status together with the majority of people of unflawed lineage in her proximity is sufficient to render her fit to marry into the priesthood.

בְּקְרוֹנוֹת שֶׁל צִיפּוֹרִי הָיָה מַעֲשֶׂה, וּכְדְרַבִּי אַמִי, דְּאָמַר רַבִּי אַמִי: וְהוּא שֶׁהָיְתָה סִיעָה שֶׁל בְּנֵי אָדָם כְּשֵׁרִין עוֹבֶרֶת לְשָׁם, וְכִדְרַבִּי יַנַּאי. דְּאָמַר רַבִּי יַנַּאי: נִבְעֲלָה בִּקְרוֹנוֹת – כְּשֵׁרָה לִכְהוּנָּה.

The **incident** transpired **among the wagons** [*keronot*][LN] in the marketplace **of Tzippori**[B] on the market day, and this *halakha* is **in accordance with** the statement of **Rabbi Ami, as Rabbi Ami said: And this is** the ruling only in a case **where there was a contingent of men of unflawed lineage passing there.**[N] Due to the fact that both the lineage of the majority of the people of the city where the girl was raped and the lineage of the majority of the passersby is unflawed, the rape is attributed to a man of unflawed lineage. **And** this ruling is **in accordance with** the statement of **Rabbi Yannai, as Rabbi Yannai said: If she engaged in intercourse in the wagons, she is fit to** marry a member of the **priesthood.**

בִּקְרוֹנוֹת סָלְקָא דַּעְתָּךְ?! אֶלָּא: נִבְעֲלָה בִּשְׁעַת קְרוֹנוֹת – כְּשֵׁרָה לִכְהוּנָּה. אֲבָל פֵּירַשׁ אֶחָד מִצִּיפּוֹרִי וּבָעַל – הַוָּלָד שְׁתוּקִי.

The Gemara asks: Does it **enter your mind** to say that the woman was raped **in the wagons,** in the crowded area of the marketplace where business is conducted? **Rather,** Rabbi Yannai is saying that if **she** was forced to **engage in intercourse at the time of the wagons,** i.e., when the convoys pass, **she is fit to** marry a member of the **priesthood. However,** if **one** individual, whose lineage is unknown, **left Tzippori**[N] **and engaged in intercourse** with a woman, **the child is a *shetuki*** and deemed unfit to marry into the priesthood even though the majority of the inhabitants of city are of unflawed lineage.

כִּי הָא דְּכִי אֲתָא רַב דִּימִי אָמַר זְעֵירִי אָמַר רַבִּי חֲנִינָא, וְאָמְרִי לָהּ אָמַר זְעֵירִי אָמַר רַבִּי חֲנִינָא: הוֹלְכִין אַחַר רוֹב הָעִיר, וְאֵין הוֹלְכִין אַחַר רוֹב סִיעָה.

The Gemara notes: That is **similar** to **this** statement **that when Rav Dimi came** from Eretz Yisrael to Babylonia, **Ze'eiri said** that **Rabbi Ḥanina said, and some say** directly that **Ze'eiri said** that **Rabbi Ḥanina said: One follows the** flawed lineage of the **majority of** the people in **the city and one does not follow** the unflawed lineage of **the majority of the** traveling **contingent,** and the woman who engaged in intercourse with a member of the itinerant contingent is deemed unfit to marry into the priesthood.

כְּלַפֵּי לְיָיא?! הָנֵי נָיְידֵי וְהָנֵי קְבִיעִי וְקַיְימִי!

The Gemara asks: **On the contrary** [***kelapei layya***],[L] the opposite is logical. **These** members of the contingent **are moving,** and in that case the principle is that one follows the majority. **And these** people of the city **are fixed and standing** in one place, and in that case the principle is that even if the lineage of the majority is unflawed, the uncertainty is treated as if it were equally balanced.

LANGUAGE

Wagons [*keronot*] – קְרוֹנוֹת: From the Latin carrum, and perhaps the Greek **κάρρον**, *karron*, meaning carriage or wagon. In the Jerusalem Talmud, the phrase *kerona shel Tzippori* appears, which based on context is from the Greek **κρήνη**, *krēnē*, meaning spring or well. According to that understanding, the reference would be to the spring in Tzippori, corresponding to the mishna that is referring to a young girl who descended to the spring.

On the contrary [*kelapei layya*] – כְּלַפֵּי לְיָיא: This expression is employed in response to a statement that seems contrary to reason. Some say it is a variation of the phrase *kelapei le'an*, meaning: Toward where are you going? Shouldn't you be going in the opposite direction? Some explain it as a contraction of *kelapei alya*, meaning toward the tail, evoking the image of riding a horse facing the tail. That too is contrary to reason.

BACKGROUND

Tzippori – צִיפּוֹרִי: Tzippori was a large town in the Upper Galilee and the perennial rival of Tiberias for recognition as the religious capital of Galilee. During the Second Temple period it enjoyed special status among the towns of the Galilee because of its large and learned Jewish community. Among the *tanna'im* who lived there were Rabbi Yoḥanan ben Nuri, Rabbi Ḥalafta, and his renowned son Rabbi Yosei.

Rabbi Yehuda HaNasi moved to Tzippori toward the end of his life, and it was the seat of the Sanhedrin for approximately one generation. Rabbi Yehuda HaNasi's leading disciples lived in Tzippori: Rabbi Yishmael, son of Rabbi Yosei; Rabban Gamliel, son of Rabbi Yehuda HaNasi, who later succeeded his father as *Nasi*; his brother Rabbi Shimon; Rabbi Ḥanina bar Ḥama, who later headed the Tzippori yeshiva; and Rabbi Yannai. Even after the Sanhedrin moved to Tiberias, Torah scholars continued to live in Tzippori, among them the prominent *amora'im* of Eretz Yisrael, Rabbi Ḥanina of Tzippori and Rabbi Mana.

Ruins at Tzippori

NOTES

Among the wagons – בִּקְרוֹנוֹת: Most commentaries explain that the reference here is to wagons that travel from place to place. Others explain that the reference is to the place where the wagons stop and sell their merchandise, i.e., the marketplace (*Talmidei Rabbeinu Yona*).

And this is where there was a contingent of men of unflawed lineage passing there – וְהוּא שֶׁהָיְתָה סִיעָה שֶׁל בְּנֵי אָדָם כְּשֵׁרִין עוֹבֶרֶת לְשָׁם: There are different opinions regarding the connection of this matter to the dispute between Rabban Gamliel and Rabbi Yehoshua, leading to different halakhic conclusions. According to Rashi, this is in accordance with the opinion of Rabbi Yehoshua; however, he does not explain what Rabban Gamliel would hold in this case. The Ritva explains that according to Rashi, Rabban Gamliel holds that two majorities are no more effective than one, just as he holds that a compound uncertainty is insignificant when the woman's claim is certain. According to most commentaries, there is no dispute between Rabban Gamliel and Rabbi Yehoshua in this case.

Rabbeinu Zeraḥya HaLevi understands Rashi's opinion differently. He explains that this entire discussion is conducted according to the opinion of Rabbi Yehoshua; however, Rabban Gamliel does not require two majorities at all. See the Ramban in *Milḥamot Hashem* with the Ra'avad, both of whom reject that opinion.

However if one left Tzippori – אֲבָל פֵּירַשׁ אֶחָד מִצִּיפּוֹרִי: Most of the early commentaries hold that this ordinance requiring two majorities is universally applied. Therefore, even if it is known that the man with whom she engaged in intercourse was from the city, in the absence of a second majority the child is of flawed lineage. The Meiri disagrees and holds that in this case one majority is sufficient.

אלא: הולכין אחר רוב העיר והוא דאיכא רוב סיעה בהדה. ואין הולכין אחר רוב העיר גרידתא ולא אחר רוב סיעה גרידתא. מאי טעמא – גזרה רוב סיעה אטו רוב העיר.

Rather, this is what Rabbi Yannai is saying: **One follows the** lineage of the **majority of the city,**[N] **and that is** specifically in a case **where there is a majority** of men of unflawed lineage in the passing **contingent**[H] together **with** the city's unflawed majority. In that case, from both perspectives the intercourse can be attributed to a man of unflawed lineage. **However, neither does one follow the** unflawed lineage of the **majority of the city alone, nor** does he **follow the** unflawed lineage of the **majority of the contingent alone. What is the reason** that one does not follow the lineage of the majority of the moving contingent? It is because the Sages issued **a decree** not to follow **the majority of the contingent**[N] **due to the majority of the city,** where one does not follow the majority.

ורוב העיר נמי, אי דקא אזלי אינהו לגבה – כל דפריש מרובא פריש! לא צריכא, דקא אזלא איהי לגבייהו, דהוה ליה קבוע, ואמר רבי זירא: כל קבוע כמחצה על מחצה דמי.

The Gemara asks: **But** aren't there cases where one follows **the majority of the city as well,** as, **if** one of the residents of the city **goes** out of the city **to her** and rapes her, the principle is: The legal status of **any** item **that is separated** from the group is that of one **separated from the majority?**[N] Therefore, there is no reason to issue a decree. The Gemara answers: The decree is **necessary only** due to a case **where she went**[N] into the city **to them,** in which case the rapist **is** an indistinguishable member of a **fixed** set, **and Rabbi Zeira said:** The legal status of uncertainty with regard to **any** item **fixed** in its place is that of an uncertainty that is **equally balanced,** and one does not follow the majority.

ומי בעינן תרי רובי? והתניא: תשע חנויות, כולן מוכרות בשר שחוטה, ואחת מוכרת בשר נבלה, ולקח מאחת מהן ואינו יודע מאי זה מהן לקח – ספיקו אסור. ובנמצא – הלך אחר הרוב!

The Gemara questions the statement of Rabbi Ami: **And do we require two majorities** to overcome the minority? **Isn't it taught** in a *baraita*: With regard to **nine stores**[N] in a city, **all of which sell** kosher **meat** from **a slaughtered** animal,[H] **and one** other store that **sells meat** from unslaughtered **animal carcasses, and** a person **bought** meat **from one of** the stores **and he does not know from which** store **he bought** the meat, in this case of **uncertainty,** the meat **is prohibited.** The legal status of uncertainty with regard to any item fixed in its place is that of an uncertainty that is equally balanced, and one does not follow the majority. This *baraita* continues: **And in** the case of meat **found** in the street, outside the stores, **follow the majority**[H] of stores that sell kosher meat. In other words, the meat is kosher.

NOTES

Rather, one follows the lineage of the majority of the city – אלא הולכין אחר רוב העיר: The Rashba notes that the language used here appears to indicate that the majority of the city is the primary consideration. However, it is clear from the context that this is not the case, as the majority of the city is a fixed majority. Therefore, in order to reconcile the sources, he explains that although the majority of the city is not as significant as the majority of the contingent, it is required in support of the majority of the contingent.

A decree not to follow the majority of the contingent – גזרה רוב סיעה: The Ritva explains that although the fundamental *halakha* in this case is a decree, the second decree is not issued to prevent violation of the first, as both were issued as one decree. In terms of the halakhic ruling, in the *Penei Yehoshua* it is explained based on the *Beit Shmuel* that ultimately, the final conclusion of the Gemara is that this is not a decree. Rather, there is a special ordinance instituted by the Sages to require two majorities in cases relating to lineage. The practical halakhic difference would be in a case where all the people in the city are of unflawed lineage. In that case the decree would not be relevant, even if it is a case where the residents of the city are fixed (see Rashash).

Any item that is separated is separated from the majority – כל דפריש מרובא פריש: The early commentaries explain, and thereby resolve a related contradiction in tractate *Kinnim*, that even though those separated from the majority ultimately returned to their original fixed state, as the man with whom she engaged in intercourse ultimately went home, the determining moment is when the incident took place (Rosh).

The decree is necessary only due to a case where she went – לא צריכא דקא אזלא איהי: There is a variant reading: There are cases where she went. There is a significant difference between the two versions. According to the version in the Gemara, two majorities are required only in a case where it is clear that she went to them. According to the variant reading (Rashi; *Yam shel Shlomo*), the very concern that perhaps she went to them is sufficient for the decree to be issued, and the decree is in effect even in cases where it is unclear whether or not she went to them (see *Beit Yosef*).

Nine stores – תשע חנויות: The distinction here is between fixed items and items that are not fixed. Rabbeinu Ḥananel explains that one does not follow the majority of kosher stores because the price of non-kosher meat is lower and therefore the likelihood that he bought meat in the non-kosher store is greater. Some ask: Even in the case of meat that was found, presumably the meat fell from someone who had purchased it in one of the stores. Why, then, isn't the ruling that it is an equally balanced uncertainty? They answer that the determining moment is the moment that the uncertainty developed. When the question with regard to its status was raised, the item was not fixed (*Shita Mekubbetzet*).

HALAKHA

A majority of the city and a majority of the contingent – רוב העיר ורוב סיעה: With regard to an unmarried woman who engaged in intercourse, even if she became pregnant, and she claims that the man is of unflawed lineage, her claim is accepted and she and her daughter are both fit to marry into the priesthood. That is the *halakha*, provided the majority of the passersby are of unflawed lineage and the majority of the residents of the city from which the passersby came are of unflawed lineage. The Sages established a higher standard with regard to lineage, requiring two majorities.

If there was only one majority, either of the city or of the passersby, she may not marry a priest. However, if she went ahead and married a priest, even if there was a majority of people of flawed lineage, they may remain married (Rambam). If she does not claim that the man was of unflawed lineage, e.g., she did not know his identity, some say that according to the Rambam, unless there are two majorities, she may not marry a priest *ab initio*, and if she does, they may not remain married (*Maggid Mishne*; see Ramban; Rashba; Ran).

Others hold that according to the Rambam, even if there are two majorities, she may not marry a priest *ab initio* (*Beit Yosef*). Others hold that if she claims that she is certain that the man was of unflawed lineage she may marry a priest *ab initio* even if there is only one majority. Furthermore, even if there is a majority of people of unflawed lineage, she may remain married after the fact (Rambam *Sefer Kedusha, Hilkhot Issurei Bia* 18:13–14; *Shulḥan Arukh, Even HaEzer* 6:17).

Nine stores all of which sell meat from a slaughtered animal – תשע חנויות כולן מוכרות בשר שחוטה: If the majority of stores in the city sell kosher meat and a minority of stores sell non-kosher meat, and a person entered one of the stores and purchased meat and does not know which store he entered, since it is a fixed majority, its legal status is that of a balanced uncertainty and the meat is forbidden (Rambam *Sefer Kedusha, Hilkhot Ma'akhalot Assurot* 8:11; *Shulḥan Arukh, Yoreh De'a* 110:3).

And in the case of meat found outside follow the majority – ובנמצא הלך אחר הרוב: With regard to one who finds meat in the marketplace or in the possession of a gentile, one follows the majority; if the majority of stores sell kosher meat, the meat is permitted by Torah law. However, the Sages prohibited all meat that is found and all meat that was out of the sight of Jews even if all those who slaughter and sell meat are Jewish, unless it is clear that it is kosher (Rambam *Sefer Kedusha, Hilkhot Ma'akhalot Assurot* 8:11; *Shulḥan Arukh, Yoreh De'a* 63:1, 110:3).

וְכִי תֵּימָא בְּשֶׁאֵין דַּלְתוֹת מְדִינָה נְעוּלוֹת, דְּקָא אָתֵי לָהּ רוּבָּא מֵעָלְמָא – וְהָא אָמַר רַבִּי זֵירָא: אַף עַל פִּי שֶׁדַּלְתוֹת מְדִינָה נְעוּלוֹת! מַעֲלָה עָשׂוּ בְּיוּחֲסִין.

And if you would say that one follows the majority only in a case **where the gates of the city are unlocked, where** the meat could have **come** to the city **from the majority** of kosher meat **outside** the city and only by combining that majority with the majority of kosher meat stores inside the city, creating two majorities, is the meat ruled kosher; **but didn't Rabbi Zeira say: Even if the city gates are locked,** one follows the majority and the meat is kosher even without a double majority? The Gemara answers: The Sages require two majorities only in cases such as establishing the identity of the child's father, because they **established a higher standard with regard to** matters of **lineage.** However, in other cases, e.g., concerning kosher meat, a single majority is sufficient.

גּוּפָא, אָמַר רַבִּי זֵירָא: כָּל קָבוּעַ כְּמֶחֱצָה עַל מֶחֱצָה דָּמֵי, בֵּין לְקוּלָּא בֵּין לְחוּמְרָא.

§ In terms of the matter **itself, Rabbi Zeira said:** The legal status of uncertainty with regard to **any** item **fixed** in its place is that of an uncertainty that is **equally balanced, both** when it leads to **leniency,** e.g., in a case where, were one to follow the majority, the ruling would be stringent, and when it leads to **stringency,** e.g., in a case where, were one to follow the majority, the ruling would be lenient.

מְנָא לֵיהּ לְרַבִּי זֵירָא הָא? אִילֵימָא מִתֵּשַׁע חֲנוּיוֹת כּוּלָּן מוֹכְרוֹת בְּשַׂר שְׁחוּטָה וְאַחַת בְּשַׂר נְבֵלָה, וְלָקַח מֵאַחַת מֵהֶן, וְאֵינוֹ יוֹדֵעַ מֵאֵיזֶה מֵהֶן לָקַח – סְפֵיקוֹ אָסוּר, וּבַנִּמְצָא – הַלֵּךְ אַחַר הָרוֹב, הָתָם לְחוּמְרָא!

The Gemara asks: **From where does Rabbi Zeira** learn that the legal status of uncertainty with regard to any item fixed in its place is that of an uncertainty that is equally balanced, both when it leads to leniency and when it leads to stringency? **If we say** that it is derived **from** the case of **nine stores** in a city, **all of which sell** kosher **meat** from **a slaughtered** animal, **and one** other store that sells **meat** from unslaughtered **animal carcasses, and** a person **bought** meat **from one of** the stores **and he does not know from which** store **he bought** the meat, in this case of **uncertainty** the meat **is prohibited. And in the** case of meat **found** in the street, outside the stores, **follow the majority** of stores that sell kosher meat, and therefore the meat would be kosher. **There,** in the first case, ruling it an equally balanced uncertainty is **a stringency,** as there is a majority of kosher stores.

אֶלָּא, מִתִּשְׁעָה צְפַרְדְּעִים וְשֶׁרֶץ אֶחָד בֵּינֵיהֶם, וְנָגַע בְּאֶחָד מֵהֶן וְאֵינוֹ יוֹדֵעַ בְּאֵיזֶה מֵהֶן נָגַע, סְפֵיקוֹ טָמֵא. הָתָם נַמִי לְחוּמְרָא!

Rather, Rabbi Zeira learns that *halakha* **from** a different *baraita*. If there were **nine frogs,** which is a creeping animal that does not impart ritual impurity while alive or when dead, **and one** ritually impure **creeping animal,**[HB] whose carcass imparts ritual impurity, **among them, and** a person **touched one of the** ten creatures, **and he does not know which of them he touched,** in this case of **uncertainty** the person is **ritually impure. There too,** ruling it an equally balanced uncertainty is **a stringency,** as the majority of the creeping animals do not impart impurity.

אֶלָּא מִתִּשְׁעָה שְׁרָצִים וּצְפַרְדֵּעַ אֶחָד בֵּינֵיהֶם, וְנָגַע בְּאֶחָד מֵהֶן, וְאֵינוֹ יוֹדֵעַ בְּאֵיזֶה מֵהֶן נָגַע, בִּרְשׁוּת הַיָּחִיד סְפֵיקוֹ טָמֵא, בִּרְשׁוּת הָרַבִּים סְפֵיקוֹ טָהוֹר.

Rather, Rabbi Zeira learns that *halakha* **from** the continuation of that *baraita*. If there are **nine creeping animals,** whose carcasses impart ritual impurity, **and one frog**[H] **among them, and** a person **touched one of them, and he does not know which of them he touched,** if it was **in the private domain,** in this case of **uncertainty** the person is **ritually impure,** as all cases of uncertainty with regard to ritual impurity are ruled impure in the private domain. This is derived from the case of *sota*. However, **in the public domain,** in that case of **uncertainty** the person is **ritually pure.**[N] Although contact with a creeping animal from the majority would render him ritually impure, since the uncertainty is with regard to a fixed group, its legal status is that of an equally balanced uncertainty, and in the public domain he is ritually pure. Rabbi Zeira learns that *halakha* from this case of leniency.

HALAKHA

Nine frogs and one creeping animal – תִּשְׁעָה צְפַרְדְּעִים וְשֶׁרֶץ אֶחָד: If there were nine frogs and one ritually impure creeping animal among them in the private domain, and a person touched one of them but he does not know which, he is ritually impure, as uncertain ritual impurity in the private domain is ritually impure (Rambam *Sefer Tahara*, *Hilkhot Avot HaTumot* 18:2).

Nine creeping animals and one frog – תִּשְׁעָה שְׁרָצִים וּצְפַרְדֵּעַ אֶחָד: If there were nine creeping animals and one frog among them in the private domain, and a person touched one of them and he does not know which, he is ritually impure, as uncertain ritual impurity in the private domain is ritually impure. However, in the public domain he is ritually pure, because the legal status of a fixed majority is that of an equally balanced uncertainty, and uncertain ritual impurity in the public domain is ritually pure (Rambam *Sefer Tahara*, *Hilkhot Avot HaTumot* 18:2).

BACKGROUND

Creeping animal – שֶׁרֶץ: Generally, this term includes rodents, lizards, insects, and any other small creature that crawls. Ritual impurity is imparted by the carcasses of the eight creeping animals enumerated in Leviticus (11:29–37), and the Talmud often refers to these eight creatures with the unmodified term creeping animal. The Sages stated that since the smallest of these eight animals was at least the size of a lentil-bulk at birth, one contracts ritual impurity only through contact with a portion of the carcass of a creeping animal no smaller than a lentil-bulk. Moreover, one is liable to receive lashes for eating a lentil-bulk of a creeping animal.

NOTES

In the public domain, in that case of uncertainty the person is ritually pure – בִּרְשׁוּת הָרַבִּים סְפֵיקוֹ טָהוֹר: The distinction between the private and public domains with regard to uncertain ritual impurity is derived from the case of *sota*, as the *halakha* is that she is forbidden to her husband in a case of uncertainty and her status is expressed in the Torah in terms of ritual impurity. Just as in the case of *sota* the uncertainty developed when the woman entered into seclusion with the man with whom her husband warned her not to seclude herself, which was clearly in the private and not the public domain, so too in a case of uncertain ritual impurity, the person is deemed impure only in the private domain.

Additional details are also derived from *sota*, e.g., the distinction between an item that does not have knowledge to be asked, which is deemed ritually pure in a case of uncertainty, and an item that has knowledge to be asked, which is deemed ritually impure in that case.

HALAKHA

Only in a case where he intends to kill him – עַד שֶׁיִּתְכַּוֵּין לוֹ: One who intended to kill one person but killed another is exempt from court-imposed execution, from payment, and from exile. Therefore, one who throws a stone into a crowd and kills one of those present is exempt, even if the crowd consisted only of Jews.

The Ra'avad wonders why the Rambam ruled in accordance with the opinion of Rabbi Shimon, which is an individual opinion. Some explain that the ruling of the Rambam is not in accordance with the opinion of Rabbi Shimon. Rather, it is in accordance with the opinion of the Sages of the school of Ḥizkiyya (38a), as the discourse in the Gemara is according to his opinion (*Migdal Oz*; *Kesef Mishne*). The second explanation in the *Kesef Mishne* says that the Rambam holds in accordance with the opinion of the Rabbis, and the reason the murderer is exempt is due to the lack of forewarning (Rambam *Sefer Nezikin, Hilkhot Rotze'aḥ UShmirat HaNefesh* 4:1).

וּמִדְּאוֹרַיְיתָא מְנָא לַן? אָמַר קְרָא ״וְאָרַב לוֹ וְקָם עָלָיו״ – עַד שֶׁיִּתְכַּוֵּין לוֹ. וְרַבָּנַן? אָמְרִי דְּבֵי רַבִּי יַנַּאי: פְּרָט לְזוֹרֵק אֶבֶן לְגוֹ.

After citing a tannaitic source for Rabbi Zeira's opinion, the Gemara asks: **And from where in the Torah do we** derive that the legal status of any item fixed in its place is like that of an uncertainty that is equally balanced, both when it leads to leniency and when it leads to stringency? It is derived from **the verse** that **states** with regard to a murderer: **"And lie in wait for him, and rise up against him"** (Deuteronomy 19:11), indicating that one is liable **only** in a case **where he intends to** kill **him.**[HN] One who intended to kill one person and inadvertently killed another is exempt from punishment. **And** how do **the Rabbis,** who hold that one is liable in that case, interpret that verse? The Sages **of the school of Rabbi Yannai say:** It **excludes** the case **of** one who **throws a stone into a crowd** and did not intend to kill a specific person.

הֵיכִי דָמֵי? אִילֵימָא דְּאִיכָּא תִּשְׁעָה גּוֹיִם וְאֶחָד יִשְׂרָאֵל בֵּינֵיהֶם – וְתֵיפּוֹק לֵיהּ דְּרוּבָּא גּוֹיִם נִינְהוּ! אִי נָמֵי פַּלְגָא וּפַלְגָא – סְפֵק נְפָשׁוֹת לְהָקֵל!

The Gemara asks: **What are the circumstances** of the case where he threw the stone and is exempt? **If we say that there are nine gentiles** in the crowd **and one Jew among them,** even without the verse, **let him derive** the exemption from the fact **that they are a majority of gentiles. Alternatively,** even if we say that **half** of the ten people are considered gentiles **and half** are considered Jews, let him derive the exemption from the principle: In a case of **uncertainty** concerning a **life-threatening** situation, the *halakha* **is lenient.**

לָא צְרִיכָא, דְּאִיכָּא תִּשְׁעָה יִשְׂרְאֵלִים וְגוֹי אֶחָד בֵּינֵיהֶם, דַּהֲוָה לֵיהּ גּוֹי קָבוּעַ, וְכׇל קָבוּעַ כְּמֶחֱצָה עַל מֶחֱצָה דָּמֵי.

The Gemara answers: **No,** the verse is **necessary** only in a case where **there are nine Jews and one gentile among them.** Were the ruling to follow the majority the one who threw the stone would be liable. But in that case, **because the gentile is fixed** among them, **and** the legal status of **any** item **fixed** in its place is **like** that of an uncertainty that is **equally balanced,** he is exempt, based on the principle: In a case of uncertainty concerning a life-threatening situation, the *halakha* is lenient. Apparently, even in cases of Torah law in which the result would be a leniency, i.e., exemption from the death penalty for murder, the legal status of any item fixed in its place is like that of an uncertainty that is equally balanced.

אִיתְּמַר רַב חִיָּיא בַּר אָשֵׁי אָמַר רַב: הֲלָכָה כְּרַבִּי יוֹסֵי, וְרַב חָנָן בַּר רָבָא אָמַר רַב: הוֹרָאַת שָׁעָה הָיְתָה.

§ With regard to the matter of following the majority in cases of lineage, it **was stated** that there is an amoraic dispute: **Rav Ḥiyya bar Ashi** said that **Rav said: The** ***halakha*** **is in accordance with** the opinion of **Rabbi Yosei** in the mishna, and it is permitted for the young girl who was raped to marry a priest. **And Rav Ḥanan bar Rava** said that **Rav said:** That **was a provisional edict**[N] issued in exigent circumstances. However, typically, with regard to matters of lineage two majorities are required.

מְתִיב רַבִּי יִרְמְיָה: וּלְיוּחֲסִין לָא בָּעֵינַן תְּרֵי רוּבֵּי? וְהָתְנַן:

Rav Yirmeya raised an objection to the ruling of Rav Ḥiyya bar Ashi, who apparently ruled that even in cases where there is one majority the *halakha* is in accordance with the opinion of Rabbi Yosei: **And in matters of lineage, do we not require two majorities,** a majority of the city's inhabitants and a majority of the passing contingent? **But didn't we learn** in a mishna (*Makhshirin* 2:7):

NOTES

Only in a case where he intends to kill him – עַד שֶׁיִּתְכַּוֵּין לוֹ: According to Rabbi Shimon, one is liable to be executed for murder only if he intended to murder a specific individual. This is consistent with Rabbi Shimon's opinion in many areas of *halakha*; an action is significant only if the result reflects the perpetrator's specific intent. Even according to the opinion of the Rabbis, who hold that one can be liable even if the action does not reflect his specific intent, the question is raised: How can the murderer be executed? Even if he was forewarned, wasn't the forewarning an uncertain forewarning, which is ineffective? The commentaries answer: Since it is possible to forewarn the murderer with regard to both individuals present, it is no longer considered an uncertain forewarning (*Shita Mekubbetzet*).

That was a provisional edict – הוֹרָאַת שָׁעָה הָיְתָה: The simple understanding is that the provisional edict was to be lenient; the Sages issued the edict due to reasons for leniency that existed at that time (see Rashi). However, early commentaries commented that the term provisional edict could be understood in various ways. Some explained that the edict was to be stringent and require two majorities (see *Shita Mekubbetzet*).

מָצָא בָּהּ תִּינוֹק מוּשְׁלָךְ, אִם רוֹב גּוֹיִם – גּוֹי, אִם רוֹב יִשְׂרָאֵל – יִשְׂרָאֵל, מֶחֱצָה עַל מֶחֱצָה – יִשְׂרָאֵל.

If there is a city in which both Jews and gentiles reside, and **one found** an unidentified, **abandoned baby in** the city,[N] **if** there is a **majority of gentiles** in the city the baby is deemed **a gentile; if** there is a **majority of Jews** in the city the baby is deemed **a Jew. If half** the population is gentile and **half** Jewish, the baby is deemed **a Jew.**

וְאָמַר רַב: לֹא שָׁנוּ אֶלָּא לְהַחֲיוֹתוֹ, אֲבָל לְיוּחֲסִין – לֹא, וּשְׁמוּאֵל אָמַר: לְפַקֵּחַ עָלָיו אֶת הַגַּל!

And Rav said with regard to this mishna: The Sages **taught** that if there is a majority of Jews in the city the baby is deemed a Jew **only** with regard **to sustaining him;**[NH] **however,** with regard **to lineage,** e.g., marrying him to a Jewish woman, **no,** he is not deemed a Jew based on the majority and would require conversion. **And Shmuel said:** It was taught that he is deemed a Jew in order **to create an opening** in **a heap** of debris **on his** behalf on Shabbat, i.e., desecrating Shabbat in order to save his life. Apparently, contrary to the ruling of Rav Ḥiyya bar Ashi, Rav holds that a single majority is insufficient to deem him Jewish in matters of lineage.

אִשְׁתְּמִיטְתֵּיהּ הָא דְּאָמַר רַב יְהוּדָה אָמַר רַב: בִּקְרוֹנוֹת שֶׁל צִפּוֹרִי הָוָה מַעֲשֶׂה.

The Gemara answers: Rav Yirmeya **overlooked that which Rav Yehuda said** that **Rav said** with regard to the mishna: The **incident** of the rape of the young girl transpired **among the wagons** in the marketplace **of Tzippori,** and there were two majorities; the majority of the inhabitants of the city and the majority of the passing contingent. Therefore, when Rav Ḥiyya bar Ashi ruled that the *halakha* is in accordance with the opinion of Rabbi Yosei, i.e., that the young girl may marry a priest, it was in a case of two majorities.

וּלְרַב חָנָן בַּר רָבָא דְּאָמַר: הוֹרָאַת שָׁעָה הָיְתָה, קַשְׁיָא. הָא! מַאן דְּמַתְנֵי הָא לָא מַתְנֵי הָא.

The Gemara asks: **And** if the case in the mishna is one of two majorities, according **to Rav Ḥanan bar Rava who said** in the name of Rav: **That was a provisional edict** issued in exigent circumstances, meaning that two majorities were required in that case but typically one majority is sufficient, it is **difficult.** Didn't Rav say that in matters of lineage one majority is insufficient? The Gemara answers: **That** is not difficult. **The one who teaches this,** that the ruling in our mishna was a provisional edict, **does not teach that**[N] statement that Rav Yehuda said that Rav said that the incident took place among the wagons in the marketplace of Tzippori. Rather, he holds that there was a single majority and nevertheless, due to exigent circumstances, the girl was permitted to marry into the priesthood, although generally two majorities are required in cases of lineage.

גּוּפָא, מָצָא בָּהּ תִּינוֹק מוּשְׁלָךְ, אִם רוֹב גּוֹיִם – גּוֹי, אִם רוֹב יִשְׂרָאֵל – יִשְׂרָאֵל, מֶחֱצָה עַל מֶחֱצָה – יִשְׂרָאֵל, אָמַר רַב: לֹא שָׁנוּ אֶלָּא לְהַחֲיוֹתוֹ, אֲבָל לְיוּחֲסִין – לֹא, וּשְׁמוּאֵל אָמַר: לְפַקֵּחַ עָלָיו אֶת הַגַּל.

§ Apropos the case of the abandoned baby, the Gemara analyzes the matter **itself:** If there is a city in which both Jews and gentiles reside, and **one found** an unidentified, **abandoned baby in** the city, **if** there is a **majority of gentiles** in the city the baby is deemed **a gentile. If** there is a **majority of Jews** in the city the baby is deemed **a Jew.** If **half** the population is gentile and **half** Jewish, the baby is deemed **a Jew. Rav said:** The Sages **taught** that the baby is deemed a Jew **only** with regard **to sustaining him; however,** with regard **to lineage, no.**[H] **And Shmuel said:** It was taught that he is deemed a Jew in order **to create an opening** in **a heap** of debris **on his** behalf on Shabbat.

NOTES

One found an unidentified abandoned baby in the city – מָצָא בָּהּ תִּינוֹק מוּשְׁלָךְ: The commentaries ask: Why not resolve the problem by immersing the child for the purpose of conversion? In that way he will grow among the Jews and his legal status will be that of a full-fledged Jew. Several explanations were suggested. According to the opinion that the court converts only a minor who initiates the conversion or who is brought by his parents, in this case conversion is impossible. According to the opinion that the court can initiate conversion, since upon reaching majority the convert can reconsider his conversion, the conversion does not solve the problem (*Shita Mekubbetzet*).

To sustaining him – לְהַחֲיוֹתוֹ: Although it is possible to explain that the term: To sustaining him [*lehaḥayoto*], means saving his life according to Rav, who agrees with Shmuel, the language and context indicate that this was not his intention. Based on this understanding, there is a novel element in Rav's opinion that a Jew is required not merely to save his life but even to tend to his daily needs. There is a novel element in the opinion of Shmuel as well: One may save his life even if it involves desecrating Shabbat.

The one who teaches this does not teach that – מַאן דְּמַתְנֵי הָא לָא מַתְנֵי הָא: Rabbeinu Ḥananel and Rabbi Zeraḥya HaLevi explain: That which Rav Ḥanan does not teach is the segment of Rav's statement: However, with regard to lineage, no. Most of the early commentaries reject that explanation (*Tosafot*; Ramban; Rashba). Most commentaries agree with Rashi, who explains that Rav Ḥanan does not teach the statement cited in the name of Rav that the incident transpired among the wagons of Tzippori. Although that explanation is somewhat problematic as well, as it is difficult to say that their dispute is with regard to the details of an incident that transpired, most early commentaries accept it.

The Ramban in *Milḥamot Hashem* cites a third approach: This *halakha* was not taught in reference to the case of an abandoned baby that was found. Rather, a question was raised from the statement of Rav Yehuda in the name of Rav, who requires two majorities, on the statement of Rav Ḥanan. The Gemara answers that there are two traditions cited in the name of Rav. Early commentaries noted that the expression: The one who teaches this does not teach that, is not typically employed to describe a dispute between two opinions. Rather, it is employed to describe two statements that are redundant or inconsistent in their formulation.

HALAKHA

To sustaining him – לְהַחֲיוֹתוֹ: The legal status of an abandoned baby found in a city with a Jewish majority is that of a Jew in terms of sustaining him. Likewise, if half the population is Jewish and half is gentile, there is a mitzva to sustain the baby (Rambam). The Rema writes that there are those who say that there is a mitzva to sustain him only if there is a Jewish majority (Rashi; *Tosafot*). The dispute is whether Rav's statement in the Gemara addresses the first *halakha* cited in the mishna or the second one (Vilna Gaon; Rambam *Sefer Kedusha, Hilkhot Issurei Bia* 15:26; *Shulḥan Arukh, Even HaEzer* 4:34).

However, with regard to lineage, no – אֲבָל לְיוּחֲסִין לֹא: The legal status of an abandoned baby found in a city with a population of Jews and gentiles, even if there is a Jewish majority, is that of a gentile whose status is uncertain with regard to his lineage. If, after reaching majority, he betrothed a Jewish woman, if he seeks to divorce her he may do so only by giving her a bill of divorce due to that uncertainty, in accordance with the statement of Rav. If he was immersed and converted by the court, or if he himself converted, when he reaches majority his legal status is that of a foundling, and his conversion is effective only in the sense that he is no longer considered a gentile (Rambam *Sefer Kedusha, Hilkhot Issurei Bia* 15:25–26; *Shulḥan Arukh, Even HaEzer* 4:33).

ומי אמר שמואל הכי? והאמר רב יוסף אמר רב יהודה אמר שמואל: אין הולכין בפיקוח נפש אחר הרוב! אלא, כי איתמר דשמואל – ארישא אתמר: אם רוב גוים – גוי, אמר שמואל: ולפקח עליו את הגל – אינו כן.

The Gemara asks: **And did Shmuel say that? But didn't Rav Yosef say** that **Rav Yehuda said** that **Shmuel said: One does not follow the majority in matters** involving **saving a life?**[N] Even if there is the slightest concern that the life of a Jew may be in danger, one takes all steps necessary to save him, even on Shabbat. **Rather, when the statement of Shmuel was stated** with regard to saving a life **it was stated concerning the first clause** of the mishna: **If** there is **a majority of gentiles**[N] in the city the baby is deemed **a gentile. Shmuel said: And** with regard **to creating an opening in a heap** of debris **on his** behalf [*lefake'aḥ alav et hagal*][HN] on Shabbat, **that is not so.** Even if there is a gentile majority in the city, one does not follow the majority in cases involving the saving of a life.

"אם רוב גוים – גוי". למאי הלכתא? אמר רב פפא: להאכילו נבילות.

The mishna continues: **If** there is **a majority of gentiles** the baby is deemed **a gentile.** The Gemara asks: With regard **to what *halakha*** was this stated? **Rav Pappa said:** It was stated in order **to feed** the baby **animal carcasses,**[H] i.e., non-kosher food.

"אם רוב ישראל – ישראל, למאי הלכתא? אמר רב פפא: להחזיר לו אבידה.

And it is taught in the mishna: **If** there is **a majority of Jews** the baby is deemed **a Jew.** The Gemara asks: With regard **to what *halakha*** was this stated?[N] **Rav Pappa said:** It was stated in order **to return lost property to him,**[HN] as one is required to return lost property to a Jew.

HALAKHA

To create an opening in a heap of debris on his behalf – לפקח עליו את הגל: One may create an opening in a heap of debris on Shabbat on behalf of an abandoned baby found in a city in which half the population is Jewish and half is gentile. However, if there is a gentile majority in the city one may not desecrate Shabbat on his behalf. This is the ruling of the Rambam, who holds that Rav and Shmuel disagree about this matter, and the ruling in disputes between Rav and Shmuel is in accordance with the opinion of Rav in ritual matters.

The Rambam, in his responsa to the Sages of Lunel, cites proof from the related discourse in tractate *Yoma* (84b–85a). The Rema cites the opinion of the *Tur* based on the Ramban and the Rashba, which agrees with the opinions of Rashi and *Tosafot*, that even in a city with a gentile majority one may create an opening in a heap of debris on Shabbat on behalf of an abandoned baby that was found. This is because they hold that Rav and Shmuel did not disagree about this matter (Vilna Gaon; Rambam *Sefer Kedusha, Hilkhot Issurei Bia* 15:26 and *Sefer Zemanim, Hilkhot Shabbat* 2:21; *Shulḥan Arukh, Even HaEzer* 4:34).

To feed the baby animal carcasses – להאכילו נבילות: The legal status of an abandoned baby found in a city with a gentile majority is that of a gentile, and one may feed him foods forbidden to Jews, in accordance with the opinion of Rav Pappa (Rambam *Sefer Kedusha, Hilkhot Issurei Bia* 15:26; *Shulḥan Arukh, Even HaEzer* 4:34).

To return lost property to him – להחזיר לו אבידה: The legal status of an abandoned baby found in a city with a Jewish majority is that of a Jew, and one who found lost objects belonging to him returns them to him, in accordance with the opinion of Rav Pappa (Rambam *Sefer Kedusha, Hilkhot Issurei Bia* 15:26; *Shulḥan Arukh, Even HaEzer* 4:34).

NOTES

One does not follow the majority in matters involving saving a life – אין הולכין בפיקוח נפש אחר הרוב: The reason that one does not follow a majority in that case is that once the Gemara interpreted the verse: "And he shall live by them" (Leviticus 18:5) and not that he shall die by them, it means that under no circumstances may he be allowed to die. Therefore, in every case of uncertainty with regard to saving a life, whether due to the situation or due to the identity of the person in danger, one must take the minority into consideration and may not act on the basis of the majority (*Tosafot Yeshanim*; Rosh).

If there is a majority of gentiles – אם רוב גוים: Some explain that this question is posed specifically according to the opinion of Shmuel, as it is possible to say that Rav disagrees with Shmuel and holds that in a case where there is a gentile majority one does not rescue the person from beneath the debris (Ramban). Others disagree, as they maintain that Rav and Shmuel do not disagree with regard to that matter.

To create an opening in a heap of debris on his behalf [*lefake'aḥ alav et hagal*] – לפקח עליו את הגל: The root *peh, kuf, ḥet* in this context is employed in the manner that it is employed throughout the Talmud, in the sense of observation or examination. It refers to opening one's eyes in order to ascertain whether the person under the debris remains alive and to extract him from beneath it. Some explain that it refers not to opening one's eyes but to creating an opening in the heap to release the person who is trapped.

If there is a majority of Jews…with regard to what *halakha* was this stated – אם רוב ישראל...למאי הלכתא: Here too, some explain that this question is posed specifically according to the opinion of Shmuel, who holds that even if there is a gentile majority one rescues the person from beneath the debris (*Shita Mekubbetzet*). Others explain that this question is based on the previous question: If you say that the *halakha* is not in accordance with the opinion of Rav, what is the difference between a situation where the population is half Jewish and half gentile, and a Jewish majority?

To return lost property to him – להחזיר לו אבידה: The commentaries ask: Why is the case of lost property different from the case of damages? The person who found the lost object should say to a person with regard to whom there is uncertainty whether or not he is a Jew who is seeking to recover the lost object: Prove that you are a Jew and take your object. Although there is a Jewish majority, it is not effective in removing property from the hands of the person possessing it.

They answer that there is a distinction between damages and a lost object. In the case of damages, the victim is seeking to receive damages from money that is clearly in the possession of the one who caused the damage. In that case the principle is: The burden of proof is incumbent upon the claimant. However, concerning a lost object, it is not considered completely in the possession of the one who found it, and therefore the majority is effective in facilitating recovery of the object (Ramban; Rashba).

Some later commentaries explain that although in a standard case of one seeking to exact payment from another, possession of the property is the determining factor, in the case of recovery of a lost object, since there is a mitzva to return it, the fact that the object is in one's possession does not supersede the mitzva to return it. See *Tosafot*, where this matter is discussed from a different perspective.

"מחצה על מחצה – ישראל" למאי הלכתא? אמר ריש לקיש: לנזקין. היכי דמי? אי נימא דנגחיה תורא דידן לתורא דידיה – לימא ליה: אייתי ראיה דישראל את ושקול!

And it is taught in the mishna: If **half** the population is gentile and **half** Jewish, the baby is deemed **a Jew.** The Gemara asks: With regard **to what** ***halakha*** was this stated? **Reish Lakish said:** It was stated with regard **to damages.**[H] In terms of payment of damages, the courts judge him as a Jew. The Gemara asks: **What are the circumstances? If we say that our ox,** one belonging to a Jew, **gored his ox,** one belonging to a person of uncertain status, and he claims that he should be compensated for the damages as a Jew, **let the** owner of the ox that gored **say to him: Bring proof that you are a Jew, and take** payment. Due to the uncertainty surrounding his status, he is unable to produce any proof.

לא צריכא, דנגחיה תורא דידיה לתורא דידן. פלגא – משלם, ואידך פלגא – אמר להו: אייתי ראיה דלאו ישראל אנא, ואתן לכון.

Rather, this *halakha* is **necessary only** in a case **where his ox gored our ox,** one belonging to a Jew. In that case, there is no question that **he pays half** the damage, which is the payment when an innocuous ox belonging to a Jew gores an ox belonging to a Jew. **And** with regard to **the other half,** which the owner of the gored ox is claiming, asserting that this person of uncertain status is a gentile and therefore liable to pay full damages, the owner of the ox that gored can **say to** the claimants:[N] **Bring proof that I am not a Jew and I will give you** payment of the other half of the damages. It is with regard to that case that Reish Lakish ruled that in a case of uncertainty, the baby has the presumptive status of a Jew, and it is incumbent upon the claimant to prove otherwise.

הרדן עלך בתולה נשאת

HALAKHA

With regard to damages – לנזקין: In a case where one caused damage to a person who was an abandoned baby found in a city in which half the population is Jewish and half is gentile, or even in a city with a Jewish majority, it is a standard case of uncertainty with regard to monetary matters and the burden of proof is incumbent upon the claimant. If his innocuous ox gored the ox of a full-fledged Jew, he pays half the damage. If the Jew wishes to collect the other half he must bring proof that the owner of the ox is a gentile. If the innocuous ox of a Jew gores his ox, the Jew need not pay him damages, because the owner of the gored ox cannot prove that he is a Jew (Rambam *Sefer Kedusha, Hilkhot Issurei Bia* 15:26; *Tur, Even HaEzer* 4:34).

NOTES

And with regard to the other half, he can say to the claimants – ואידך פלגא אמר להו: The question is raised: Isn't this a case of partial admission in response to a claim, where one is obligated to take an oath on the portion of the claim that he denies? Based on the principle: One who is obligated to take an oath and is unable to take that oath is required to pay, since he is unable to take the oath because there is uncertainty whether he is Jewish, he should be obligated to pay. However, this is not a problem according to the opinion that this principle applies only in a case where there is a reasonable expectation that he could have known what happened but refuses to take an oath; here, therefore, since there is no way to ascertain whether he is a Jew or a gentile he is not required to pay. Even according to those who say that one is required to pay even if he did not take the oath because there is no way for him to know what happened, here he is not required to take an oath at all, as both the claim of the claimant and the claim of the respondent are uncertain (Ritva; *Shita Mekubbetzet*).

Summary of **Perek I**

The Sages designated certain days for marriage because they were assiduous in seeing to the well-being of Jewish women and ensuring that the wedding feast be appropriately elaborate. They also valued the integrity of marriage by scheduling the wedding on a day that would not delay a husband from bringing to court a claim, if he suspected his bride was forbidden to him. Throughout later generations as well, when a wedding could take place any day of the week, including Friday, one must take those two ordinances into account. It is possible to have a wedding on Friday due to the halakhic ruling that it is permitted to engage in intercourse with a virgin on Shabbat. Since there is sanctity and blessing in the wedding celebration, the Sages instituted six special blessings recited whenever and wherever there is a wedding celebration.

With regard to the definition of a virgin in the context of a marriage contract, the Sages determined that a woman who never married and whose hymen is intact is a virgin. The legal status of a woman who married but did not engage in intercourse, or that of a woman whose hymen was ruptured by wood, even though she never engaged in intercourse, is that of a non-virgin. The presumptive status of an unmarried woman with regard to whom there is no information to the contrary is that of a virgin, unless she converted, was liberated from slavery, or was redeemed from captivity after reaching the age of three.

The Gemara concluded that a husband who claims that his bride was not a virgin is deemed credible unless the bride is in possession of proof that his claim is false. However, when there are conflicting claims with regard to the manner in which the bride lost her virginity, with the husband claiming that she engaged in licentious intercourse or that she deceived him and the bride claiming that the circumstances were different, the bride is deemed credible as long as the husband can bring no proof to support his claim.

Just as one relies on the credibility of the bride in this case, so too one relies on her credibility with regard to lineage when she claims that she engaged in intercourse with a man who does not disqualify her from marrying into the priesthood. Likewise, one relies on her credibility to establish the unflawed lineage of an offspring that she conceived while single. The Sages imposed strictures with regard to the *halakhot* of lineage, especially when the woman is unable to identify the father of her unborn child. In order to establish the unflawed lineage of both mother and child, a double majority is required, i.e., a majority of people with unflawed lineage in the place where she engaged in intercourse and a majority of people with unflawed lineage in the place where she originated.

Introduction to **Perek II**

The *halakha* clearly delineates the parameters of valid testimony. For instance, valid testimony requires two valid witnesses, i.e., Jewish males above the age of majority who are related neither to one of the litigants nor to each other. Additionally, one is not allowed to incriminate himself, although he is permitted to obligate himself to pay money by his own admission; and one is not deemed credible to testify about himself.

However, there are various areas that, by Torah law or by rabbinic ordinance, the court deems credible testimony that does not meet all those criteria. The reasons vary. There are cases where the court characterizes the statement of the witnesses as merely revealing a matter, i.e., revealing a fact that by its very nature would have been revealed and publicized. In other cases, the Sages relied on flawed testimony because the problem is rabbinic in nature and they determined that in that case, full-fledged testimony is not required. Furthermore, there are the cases that constitute the bulk of the discussion in this chapter where there is testimony that must either be accepted in its entirety or rejected in its entirety. In those cases, e.g., the mouth that prohibited is the mouth that permitted, one relies on testimony that would not have been accepted in and of itself.

In this chapter, various topics are discussed, such as the *halakhot* relating to both ritual matters, e.g., lineage, priesthood, ritual purity and impurity; and monetary matters, e.g., ratification of documents and repayment of debts, in which one relies on the testimony of witnesses with various flaws, and the parameters of their credibility in each case are delineated. One of the central topics discussed is the testimony of a captive woman. Generally, the assumption is that a woman taken captive is likely to be raped by her captors. Since the wife of a priest who was raped, and any Jewish woman who engages in intercourse with a gentile, are forbidden to a priest, it is prohibited for all women taken captive to marry a priest due to that uncertainty. However, since this prohibition is based upon mere suspicion, the Sages rely on flawed testimony in order to permit a captive woman to marry a priest.

These issues constitute the bulk of this chapter, and related topics will be discussed in the course of the analysis of its central topics.

מתני׳ הָאִשָּׁה שֶׁנִּתְאַרְמְלָה אוֹ שֶׁנִּתְגָּרְשָׁה, הִיא אוֹמֶרֶת: בְּתוּלָה נְשָׂאתַנִי, וְהוּא אוֹמֵר: לֹא כִּי, אֶלָּא אַלְמָנָה נְשָׂאתִיךְ. אִם יֵשׁ עֵדִים שֶׁיָּצָאת בְּהִינוּמָא וְרֹאשָׁהּ פָּרוּעַ – כְּתוּבָּתָהּ מָאתַיִם. רַבִּי יוֹחָנָן בֶּן בְּרוֹקָה אוֹמֵר: אַף חִילּוּק קְלָיוֹת רְאָיָה.

MISHNA With regard to **a woman who was widowed or divorced,** and is now claiming payment of her marriage contract that is not before the court, and **she says: You married me** as **a virgin,** who is entitled to two hundred dinars, **and he says: No; rather, I married you** as **a widow,** who is entitled to one hundred dinars, then, **if there are witnesses that she went out** of her father's house to her wedding **with a** ***hinnuma***[HL] **or** with **her hair uncovered,** in a manner typical of virgins, payment of **her marriage contract is two hundred** dinars. **Rabbi Yoḥanan ben Beroka says: Even** testimony that there was **distribution of roasted grain,** which was customary at weddings of virgins, constitutes **proof** that she is a virgin.

וּמוֹדֶה רַבִּי יְהוֹשֻׁעַ בְּאוֹמֵר לַחֲבֵירוֹ: שָׂדֶה זוֹ שֶׁל אָבִיךָ הָיְתָה, וּלְקַחְתִּיהָ הֵימֶנּוּ – שֶׁהוּא נֶאֱמָן,

Several disputes between Rabban Gamliel and Rabbi Yehoshua were cited previously with regard to the credibility accorded to the respective claims of parties to a dispute. Based on one of those disputes, the *tanna* adds: **And Rabbi Yehoshua concedes in** a case where **one says to another: This field,** which is currently in my possession, **belonged to your father and I purchased it from him, that he is deemed credible,** and his entire claim is accepted. The court accepts not only his admission that it once belonged to the other's father, but also his statement that he purchased it.

HALAKHA

If there are witnesses that she went out with a ***hinnuma*** **– אִם יֵשׁ עֵדִים שֶׁיָּצָאת בְּהִינוּמָא:** A woman claims that she was a virgin when she got married and is consequently entitled to a marriage contract of two hundred dinars, and her husband claims or his heirs claim that she was not a virgin and is entitled to a marriage contract of one hundred dinars, and the marriage contract was lost or, in keeping with local custom, was never written. In such a case, if there are witnesses testifying that actions characteristic of a virgin's wedding were performed at her wedding, she is entitled to a marriage contract of two hundred dinars (Rambam *Sefer Nashim, Hilkhot Ishut* 16:25; *Shulḥan Arukh, Even HaEzer* 96:15).

LANGUAGE

Hinnuma **– הִינוּמָא:** Scholars disagree with regard to the precise source of this word. Many maintain that it is from the Greek **ὑμέναιος**, *hymenaios*, meaning a song sung at a wedding, and it is also used as a general term for a wedding. Rabbeinu Ḥananel suggests that its source is the Greek **ἔννομος**, *ennomos*, a matter performed according to the law (*Arukh*). Others assert that it is related to the Greek **ὑμήν**, *hymen*, meaning thin scarf, or a thin membrane such as the hymen.

Based on the dispute cited in the Gemara (17b) with regard to the precise meaning of this term, and based on the fact that there is a parallel dispute in the Jerusalem Talmud, apparently, the term *hinnuma* does not refer to a specific object but rather to a fixed custom or component of the wedding of a virgin.

שֶׁהַפֶּה שֶׁאָסַר הוּא הַפֶּה שֶׁהִתִּיר. וְאִם יֵשׁ עֵדִים שֶׁהִיא שֶׁל אָבִיו, וְהוּא אוֹמֵר: ״לְקַחְתִּיהָ הֵימֶנּוּ״ אֵינוֹ נֶאֱמָן.

This is so, **as the mouth that prohibited,** i.e., claimed that the field had belonged to the other's father, **is the mouth that permitted,**[N] i.e., claimed that he purchased the field. Even if he had not admitted that it had belonged to the other's father, the field would have remained in his possession. Therefore, his claim is accepted. **However, if there are witnesses that the field belonged to his father, and** the one who has the field in his possession **says: I purchased it from him, he is not deemed credible** and his claim is rejected.

NOTES

The mouth that prohibited is the mouth that permitted – הַפֶּה שֶׁאָסַר הוּא הַפֶּה שֶׁהִתִּיר: Later commentaries sought to clarify whether this principle is an independent legal principle or whether it is based on *miggo*. A *miggo* is a halakhic argument that the ability to make a more advantageous claim grants credibility to the claim one actually makes. That the one who claimed he owned the field could have opted to remain silent but instead admitted that the field was originally not his and that he purchased it indicates that he is telling the truth. The difference between these two understandings is in a case where the two parts of his statement were not stated together. In that case, if his credibility is based on *miggo*, his claim would not be accepted, because a *miggo* cannot be invoked retroactively. The simple understanding of the Gemara is that his credibility is based on *miggo*. However, it is apparent from the early commentaries that they hold that this is an independent principle (see *Kovetz Shiurim*): If one is deemed credible with regard to the statement that is contrary to his interests, there is no reason not to deem him credible with regard to the statement that furthers his interests. This is similar to the reasoning later in the Gemara (26b).

HALAKHA

However if there are no witnesses the husband is deemed credible – הָא לֵיכָּא עֵדִים בַּעַל מְהֵימָן: In a case where the husband claims that he married his wife with the presumptive status of a non-virgin, who is entitled to a marriage contract of one hundred dinars, and she claims that she was a virgin when they married and is consequently entitled to a marriage contract of two hundred dinars, and the marriage contract was lost or, in keeping with local custom, never written, and there are no witnesses, she receives payment of one hundred dinars and the husband must take an oath to exempt himself from paying the additional sum. According to the Rambam it is an oath by Torah law, while according to the Ra'avad it is by rabbinic law. The Rema holds that there is a distinction between a case where no marriage contract was written, when the oath is by rabbinic law, and a case where the marriage contract was lost, where the oath is by Torah law (Rambam *Sefer Nashim, Hilkhot Ishut* 16:25; *Shulḥan Arukh, Even HaEzer* 96:15).

NOTES

And he who asked the question – וּדְקָאָרֵי לַהּ: This expression is a common reaction to an answer so obvious that it calls into question why the question was asked at all. Some suggest that its root is the Hebrew word for teach or instruct [*yara*], and it means: And with regard to the one who taught this matter, what does he hold? The *Arukh* cites the *ge'onim*, who say that its root is the Hebrew word for mixing [*ar*] and that it means: And the one who mixed these matters and taught them, what does he hold?

גמ׳ טַעֲמָא דְּאִיכָּא עֵדִים, הָא לֵיכָּא עֵדִים – בַּעַל מְהֵימָן. לֵימָא תְּנַן סְתָמָא דְּלָא כְּרַבָּן גַּמְלִיאֵל, דְּאִי רַבָּן גַּמְלִיאֵל – הָא אֲמַר אִיהִי מְהֵימְנָא!

GEMARA The Gemara infers: **The reason** that the bride's claim is accepted **is** specifically due to the fact **that there are witnesses** that she went out of her father's house to the wedding with a *hinnuma*. **However, if there are no witnesses,** the **husband is deemed credible.**[H] **Let us say that** the **unattributed** ruling that **we learned** in the mishna **is not in accordance with** the opinion of **Rabban Gamliel, as,** if the ruling was according to **Rabban Gamliel, didn't he say** that **she is deemed credible?**

אֲפִילּוּ תֵּימָא רַבָּן גַּמְלִיאֵל, עַד כָּאן לָא קָאָמַר רַבָּן גַּמְלִיאֵל הָתָם אֶלָּא בְּבָרִי וְשֶׁמָּא, אֲבָל הָכָא, בְּבָרִי וּבָרִי – לָא אֲמַר.

The Gemara answers: **Even** if **you will say** that the ruling in the mishna is in accordance with the opinion of **Rabban Gamliel, Rabban Gamliel stated** his opinion **only there,** in a case where the claim of the bride is **certain and** the claim of the groom is **uncertain,** as the groom does not know what actually happened. **However, here,** in a case where the claim of the bride is **certain and** the claim of the groom is also **certain,** as he is certain that he married her as a widow, Rabban Gamliel **did not say** that her claim is deemed credible.

וּדְקָאָרֵי לַהּ מַאי קָאָרֵי לַהּ? הָא בָּרִי וּבָרִי הוּא! כֵּיוָן דְּרוֹב נָשִׁים בְּתוּלוֹת נִישָּׂאוֹת – כִּי בָּרִי וְשֶׁמָּא דָּמֵי.

The Gemara asks: **And he who asked** the question,[N] **why did he ask it?** The cases are clearly different, as **this is** a case of **a certain** claim **and a certain** claim. The Gemara answers: **Since most women are married** as **virgins,** one might have thought that the legal status in this case **is like** that of a **case of a certain** claim **and an uncertain** claim, as her claim is supported by a majority of cases.

וְהָכִי נַמִי מִסְתַּבְּרָא, מִדְּקָתָנֵי: וּמוֹדֶה רַבִּי יְהוֹשֻׁעַ. אִי אָמְרַתְּ בִּשְׁלָמָא אַיְּירֵי רַבָּן גַּמְלִיאֵל בְּמוֹדֶה – שַׁפִּיר, אֶלָּא אִי אָמְרַתְּ לָא אַיְּירֵי רַבָּן גַּמְלִיאֵל בְּמוֹדֶה – רַבִּי יְהוֹשֻׁעַ לְמַאן מוֹדֶה?

And it also stands to reason that the first clause of the mishna is in accordance with the opinion of Rabban Gamliel, who concedes that without witnesses the woman's claim is not deemed credible, despite the fact that the case is comparable to one of a certain claim and an uncertain claim, as the mishna **teaches: And Rabbi Yehoshua concedes. Granted, if you say that Rabban Gamliel is speaking in** the first clause of the mishna and **he concedes** that even though it is similar to a case of certain and uncertain, her claim is not accepted, it works out **well.** Rabban Gamliel concedes to Rabbi Yehoshua in the first clause of the mishna and the mishna cites a case where Rabbi Yehoshua concedes to Rabban Gamliel. **However, if you say that Rabban Gamliel is not speaking in** the first clause of the mishna and **he** does not **concede, to whom does Rabbi Yehoshua concede** in the latter clause?

מִי סָבְרַתְּ רַבִּי יְהוֹשֻׁעַ אַהַאי פִּירְקִין קָאֵי? אַמִּגּוֹ קָאֵי, וְאַפִּירְקִין קַמָּא קָאֵי.

The Gemara rejects that proof: **Do you think that** the statement of **Rabbi Yehoshua is** in reference **to** a mishna in **this chapter?** Actually, **it is** in reference **to** the principle of *miggo*, **and it is** in reference **to the first chapter.** Rabbi Yehoshua is saying that although he does not accept the claim supported by a *miggo* in the first chapter, here he accepts the claim supported by the principle: The mouth that prohibited is the mouth that permitted, which is based on the same reasoning as *miggo*, i.e., the fact that he could have made a more advantageous claim lends credibility to the less advantageous claim. In this case, he could have remained silent and the field would have remained in his possession. If challenged, he could have claimed that the field was his. Therefore, his less advantageous claim, that the field was not originally his but he purchased it from the father of the claimant, is accepted.

אַהַיָּיא? אִילֵימָא אַהָא: הָיְתָה מְעוּבֶּרֶת, וְאָמְרוּ לָהּ: מַה טִּיבוֹ שֶׁל עוּבָּר זֶה? ״מֵאִישׁ פְּלוֹנִי וְכֹהֵן הוּא״. רַבָּן גַּמְלִיאֵל וְרַבִּי אֱלִיעֶזֶר אוֹמְרִים: נֶאֱמֶנֶת, רַבִּי יְהוֹשֻׁעַ אוֹמֵר: לֹא מִפִּיהָ אָנוּ חַיִּין, הָתָם מַאי מִגּוֹ אִיכָּא? הֲרֵי כְּרֵיסָהּ בֵּין שִׁינֶּיהָ!

The Gemara elaborates: In reference **to which** case in the first chapter did Rabbi Yehoshua make his statement? **If you say** that it is in reference **to this** case (13a): **If** a single woman **was pregnant, and** people **said to her: What is the nature of that fetus, and she says to them: It is from a man** called so-and-so **and he is a priest, Rabban Gamliel and Rabbi Eliezer say: She is deemed credible, and Rabbi Yehoshua says:** It is **not** based on the statement emerging **from her mouth** that **we conduct our lives. There, what** *miggo* **is there** lending credibility to her claim? In that case, **her belly is between her teeth,** i.e., her pregnancy is conspicuous, and consequently she does not have the option of making the more advantageous claim that she did not engage in intercourse.

אֶלָּא אַהָא; רָאוּהָ מְדַבֶּרֶת עִם אֶחָד. וְאָמְרוּ לָהּ: מָה טִיבוֹ שֶׁל אִישׁ זֶה? "אִישׁ פְּלוֹנִי, וְכֹהֵן הוּא". רַבָּן גַּמְלִיאֵל וְרַבִּי אֱלִיעֶזֶר אוֹמְרִים: נֶאֱמֶנֶת, רַבִּי יְהוֹשֻׁעַ אוֹמֵר: לֹא מִפִּיהָ אָנוּ חַיִּין. הָתָם מַאי מִגּוֹ אִיכָּא? הָנִיחָא לִזְעֵירִי דְּאָמַר: מַאי "מְדַבֶּרֶת" נִסְתְּרָה, מִגּוֹ דְּאִי בָּעְיָא אָמְרָה לֹא נִבְעַלְתִּי, וְקָאָמְרָה נִבְעַלְתִּי, מְהֵימְנָא. אֶלָּא לְרַב אַסִי, דְּאָמַר: מַאי "מְדַבֶּרֶת" – נִבְעֶלֶת, מַאי מִגּוֹ אִיכָּא?

Rather, it is in reference **to this** case (13a): **If** people **saw** a woman **speaking to one** man, **and they said to her: What is the nature of this man?** And she said to them: **He is a man** called **so-and-so and he is a priest, Rabban Gamliel and Rabbi Eliezer say: She is deemed credible, and Rabbi Yehoshua says:** It is **not** on based on the statement emerging **from her mouth** that **we conduct our lives.** Again this is challenged: **There, what *miggo* is there? This** works out **well according to Ze'eiri, who said: What** is the meaning of **speaking** mentioned in the mishna? It means that **she secluded herself** with a man. In this case there is a ***miggo*. Since, if she wished** to lie, **she could have said: I did not engage in intercourse** at all, **and** instead **she said: I engaged in intercourse** with a man of unflawed lineage. Therefore, **she is deemed credible** according to Rabban Gamliel. **However, according to Rav Asi, who said: What is** the meaning of **speaking?** It means that **she engaged in intercourse, what *miggo* is there?** There was no better claim available to her.

וְאֶלָּא אַהָא; הִיא אוֹמֶרֶת: מוּכַּת עֵץ אֲנִי, וְהוּא אוֹמֵר: לֹא כִּי, אֶלָּא דְּרוּסַת אִישׁ אַתְּ. רַבָּן גַּמְלִיאֵל וְרַבִּי אֱלִיעֶזֶר אוֹמְרִים: נֶאֱמֶנֶת, וְרַבִּי יְהוֹשֻׁעַ אוֹמֵר: לֹא מִפִּיהָ אָנוּ חַיִּין. הָתָם מַאי מִגּוֹ אִיכָּא?

Rather, it is in reference **to this** case (13a), where **she says:** I am one whose hymen **was ruptured by wood, and** the groom **says: No; rather, you are** one who **was trampled by a man. Rabban Gamliel and Rabbi Eliezer say: She is deemed credible,** and **Rabbi Yehoshua says:** It is **not** on the basis of the statement emerging **from her mouth** that **we conduct our lives. There, what *miggo* is there?**

בִּשְׁלָמָא לְרַבִּי אֶלְעָזָר, דְּאָמַר בְּמָנֶה וְלֹא כְלוּם, מִגּוֹ דְּאִי בָּעְיָא אָמְרָה מוּכַּת עֵץ אֲנִי תַּחְתֶּיךָ, וְאִית לַהּ מָאתַיִם, וְקָאָמְרָה מֵעִיקָּרָא, דְּלֵית לַהּ אֶלָּא מָנֶה – מְהֵימְנָא. אֶלָּא לְרַבִּי יוֹחָנָן, דְּאָמַר בְּמָאתַיִם וּמָנֶה, מַאי מִגּוֹ אִיכָּא?

Granted, according to Rabbi Elazar, who said that the bride claims that she is entitled to a marriage contract of **one hundred dinars, and** the groom claims that she is entitled to **nothing at all,** as in that case, there is a ***miggo*. Since, if she wished** to lie, **she could have said:** I am one whose hymen **was ruptured by wood under your** authority after betrothal, **and she would have** been entitled to **two hundred** dinars, as she was a virgin at betrothal. **And** therefore, when **she says** that her hymen was already ruptured **initially,** prior to betrothal, **when she is** entitled to **only one hundred dinars, she is deemed credible. However, according to Rabbi Yoḥanan, who said:** The bride claims that she is entitled to a marriage contract of **two hundred** dinars; **and** the groom claims that that she is entitled to a marriage contract of **one hundred dinars, what *miggo* is there?** Her claim is the most advantageous claim available to her.

אֶלָּא אַהָא: הַנּוֹשֵׂא אֶת הָאִשָּׁה וְלֹא מָצָא לָהּ בְּתוּלִים, הִיא אוֹמֶרֶת: מִשֶּׁאֵרַסְתַּנִי נֶאֱנַסְתִּי, וְנִסְתַּחֲפָה שָׂדֵהוּ. וְהוּא אוֹמֵר: לֹא כִּי, אֶלָּא עַד שֶׁלֹּא אֵירַסְתִּיךְ.

Rather, it is in reference **to this** case (12b): One **who marries a woman and did not find her hymen** intact, and **she says: After you betrothed me, I was raped and his field was inundated,** i.e., it is attributable to your own misfortune. **And he says: No; rather,** you were raped **before I betrothed you,** and my transaction was a mistaken transaction.

רַבָּן גַּמְלִיאֵל וְרַבִּי אֱלִיעֶזֶר אוֹמְרִים: נֶאֱמֶנֶת, וְרַבִּי יְהוֹשֻׁעַ אוֹמֵר: לֹא מִפִּיהָ אָנוּ חַיִּין. דְּמִגּוֹ דְּאִי בָּעְיָא אָמְרָה מוּכַּת עֵץ אֲנִי תַּחְתֶּיךָ, דְּלָא קָא פָּסְלָה נַפְשָׁהּ מִכְּהוּנָּה, וְקָאָמְרָה נֶאֱנַסְתִּי, דְּקָא פָּסְלָה נַפְשָׁהּ מִכְּהוּנָּה – מִשּׁוּם הָכִי קָאָמַר רַבָּן גַּמְלִיאֵל דִּמְהֵימְנָא. וְקָאָמַר רַבִּי יְהוֹשֻׁעַ לְרַבָּן גַּמְלִיאֵל: בְּהַאי מִגּוֹ דְּהָכָא – מוֹדֵינָא לָךְ, בְּהַהוּא מִגּוֹ דְּהָתָם – פְּלִיגְנָא עִילָּוָךְ.

Rabban Gamliel and Rabbi Eliezer say: She is deemed credible, and **Rabbi Yehoshua says:** It is **not** based on the statement emerging **from her mouth** that **we conduct our lives, as,** in that case there is **a *miggo*. Since, if she wished** to lie, **she could have said:** I am one whose hymen **was ruptured by wood under your** jurisdiction after betrothal, which is a more advantageous claim, **because she does not** thereby **disqualify herself from** marrying into **the priesthood. But she said: I was raped** after betrothal, which is a less advantageous claim, **because she disqualified herself from the priesthood. Therefore, Rabban Gamliel says that she is deemed credible. And Rabbi Yehoshua says to Rabban Gamliel: With regard to this *miggo*** in the mishna **here, I concede to you** that the *miggo* is effective. **With regard to that *miggo* there** in the first chapter, **I disagree with you.**

מִכְּדִי, הַאי מִגּוֹ וְהַאי מִגּוֹ, מַאי שְׁנָא הַאי מִגּוֹ מֵהַאי מִגּוֹ? הָכָא אֵין שׁוֹר שָׁחוּט לְפָנֶיךָ, הָתָם – הֲרֵי שׁוֹר שָׁחוּט לְפָנֶיךָ.

The Gemara asks: But **after all, this is** a case of ***miggo*** **and that is** a case of ***miggo***. In **what** way, in the opinion of Rabbi Yehoshua, **is this *miggo* different from that *miggo*?** The Gemara answers: **Here,** in the case of contested ownership of the field, **there is no slaughtered ox before you,**[N] i.e., there is no reason to question his claim of ownership, as the field is in his possession. However, **there,** in the case of the woman who was found not to be a virgin, **there is a slaughtered ox before you,** i.e., there is reason to question her virginity, and it is only in response to that question that she makes her claim. Therefore, although it is supported by a *miggo*, Rabbi Yehoshua does not accept her claim.

וְכֵיוָן דְּרוֹב נָשִׁים בְּתוּלוֹת נִישָּׂאוֹת, כִּי לָא אָתוּ עֵדִים מַאי הָוֵי? אֲמַר רָבִינָא: מִשּׁוּם דְּאִיכָּא לְמֵימַר רוֹב נָשִׁים בְּתוּלוֹת נִישָּׂאוֹת, וּמִיעוּט אַלְמָנוֹת. וְכָל הַנִּשֵּׂאת בְּתוּלָה – יֵשׁ לָהּ קוֹל,

§ The Gemara resumes discussion of the inference that it drew at the outset with regard to witnesses that the bride was a virgin. **And since** the Gemara established earlier that the woman's claim is supported by the fact **that most women are married** as **virgins, if witnesses did not come, what of it?** That majority should be sufficient to establish that she married as a virgin. **Ravina said:** It is **because there is** room **to say** that although **most women are married** as **virgins and a minority** of women marry as **widows** or non-virgins, there is an additional presumption: The marriage of **anyone who is married** as **a virgin generates publicity,**

NOTES

There is no slaughtered ox before you – אֵין שׁוֹר שָׁחוּט לְפָנֶיךָ: Rashi explains that this means: Just as it would not enter one's mind to ask who slaughtered the ox when there is no slaughtered ox before him, so too, the case of the disputed field is one where it did not enter the mind of the other party to make a claim. However, most early commentaries (*Tosafot*; Ramban; Rashba) reject this explanation, and hold that there it makes no difference whether or not the claimant initiated the litigation. Instead, they explain the expression as a rhetorical flourish meaning that the woman is not deemed credible in a case where the ox is slaughtered before you, i.e., where the facts are indisputable.

Others explain, based on the Gemara in tractate *Ḥullin*, that the presumptive status of a slaughtered ox that is found is that it was properly slaughtered, although while it is alive, proof must be brought that it was properly slaughtered in order to permit its consumption. Similarly, in this case, the facts negate her prior presumptive status of virginity. The *Ba'al HaMaor* cites a variant reading: There, there is no slaughtered ox before you. Just as the presumptive forbidden status of the living animal remains intact until proof is brought that it was properly slaughtered, here too, the money remains in the possession of the husband until the woman brings proof that she was a virgin.

וְזוֹ הוֹאִיל וְאֵין לָהּ קוֹל – אִיתְרַע לָהּ רוּבָּא.

and with regard to **this** woman, **because her** marriage **did not generate publicity, the** effect of the **majority is undermined.**

אִי כָּל הַנִּשֵּׂאת בְּתוּלָה יֵשׁ לָהּ קוֹל, כִּי אָתוּ עֵדִים מַאי הָוֵי? הָנָךְ סָהֲדֵי שַׁקָּרֵי נִינְהוּ! אֶלָּא אֲמַר רָבִינָא: רוֹב הַנִּשֵּׂאת בְּתוּלָה יֵשׁ לָהּ קוֹל, וְזוֹ הוֹאִיל וְאֵין לָהּ קוֹל – אִיתְרַע לָהּ רוּבָּא.

The Gemara asks: **If** in fact, the marriage of **anyone who is married** as **a virgin generates publicity,** and the marriage of this woman did not generate publicity, **when witnesses come, what of it? These are false witnesses,** as their testimony runs counter to the presumption governing all marriages. **Rather, Ravina said** that it is not a universal presumption, but a majority. The marriage of **most** women **who are married** as **virgins generates publicity, but** for **this** woman, **since her** marriage **did not generate publicity, the** effect of the **majority is undermined.** Therefore, the testimony that she went out of her father's house to her wedding with a *hinnuma* overrides the lack of publicity.

״אִם יֵשׁ עֵדִים שֶׁיָּצְתָה בְּהִינּוּמָא״ וכו׳. וְלֵיחוּשׁ דִּלְמָא מַפְּקָא עֵדִים בְּהַאי בֵּי דִינָא וְגָבְיָא, וַהֲדַר מַפְּקָא לָהּ לִכְתוּבָּה בְּהַאי בֵּית דִּין וְגָבְיָא בָּהּ! אָמַר רַבִּי אַבָּהוּ: זֹאת אוֹמֶרֶת: כּוֹתְבִין שׁוֹבֵר. רַב פַּפָּא אֲמַר: בְּמָקוֹם שֶׁאֵין כּוֹתְבִין כְּתוּבָּה עָסְקִינַן.

§ It was stated in the mishna: **If there are witnesses that she went out** of her father's house to her wedding **with a *hinnuma*,** or with her hair uncovered, in a manner typical of virgins, payment of her marriage contract is two hundred dinars. The Gemara asks: **And** since she collects payment without producing her marriage contract, **let us be concerned** that **she might produce witnesses in this court and collect** payment, **and then produce** her **marriage contract in that** other **court and collect with it** payment a second time. **Rabbi Abbahu said: This indicates** that **one writes a receipt**[NHB] indicating that the woman received payment. Were the woman to attempt to collect payment of her marriage contract a second time, her husband would produce the receipt. **Rav Pappa said: We are dealing** in the mishna **with a place where one does not write a marriage contract.**[H] It is only in a case where there is no concern lest she produce her marriage contract that she collects payment based on the testimony of witnesses.

וְאִיכָּא דְּמַתְנֵי לָהּ אַבָּרַיְיתָא: אִיבְּדָה כְּתוּבָּתָהּ, הִטְמִינָה כְּתוּבָּתָהּ, נִשְׂרְפָה כְּתוּבָּתָהּ, רָקְדוּ לְפָנֶיהָ, שִׂחֲקוּ לְפָנֶיהָ, הֶעֱבִירוּ לְפָנֶיהָ כּוֹס שֶׁל בְּשׂוֹרָה, אוֹ מַפָּה שֶׁל בְּתוּלִים, אִם יֵשׁ לָהּ עֵדִים בְּאֶחָד מִכָּל אֵלּוּ – כְּתוּבָּתָהּ מָאתַיִם.

And there are some **who teach** the dispute between Rabbi Abbahu and Rav Pappa with regard **to the *baraita*** that says: In a case where a woman **lost her marriage contract** or **concealed her marriage contract** and she claims that she is unable to find it; or **her marriage contract was burned,** and there is no proof with regard to the sum to which she is entitled; or practices performed exclusively at the weddings of virgins were performed at her wedding, e.g., people **danced before her,** or **played before her,** or **passed before her a cup of** good **tidings**[B] **or a cloth of virginity; if she has witnesses with regard to any one of these** practices, **her marriage contract is two hundred** dinars.

וְלֵיחוּשׁ דִּלְמָא מַפְּקָא עֵדִים בְּהַאי בֵּית דִּין וְגָבְיָא, וַהֲדַר מַפְּקָא לִכְתוּבָּתָהּ בְּהַאי בֵּית דִּין וְגָבְיָא בָּהּ! אָמַר רַבִּי אַבָּהוּ: זֹאת אוֹמֶרֶת: כּוֹתְבִין שׁוֹבֵר. רַב פַּפָּא אָמַר: בְּמָקוֹם שֶׁאֵין כּוֹתְבִין כְּתוּבָּה עָסְקִינַן.

The Gemara asks: **And** since she collects payment without producing her marriage contract, **let us be concerned** that **she might produce witnesses in this court and collect** payment, **and then produce** her **marriage contract in that** other **court and collect** payment **with it** a second time. **Rabbi Abbahu said: This indicates** that **one writes a receipt** indicating that the woman received payment. Were the woman to attempt to collect payment of her marriage contract a second time, her husband would produce the receipt. **Rav Pappa said: We are dealing** in the mishna **with a place where one does not write a marriage contract.**

וְהָא אִיבְּדָה כְּתוּבָּתָהּ קָתָנֵי! דִּכְתַב לָהּ אִיהוּ. סוֹף סוֹף מַפְּקָא לָהּ וְגָבְיָא בָּהּ! מַאי אִיבְּדָה – אִיבְּדָה בָּאוּר.

The Gemara asks: **But** how could Rav Pappa say that the *baraita* is dealing with a place where one does not write a marriage contract? **Isn't it taught** in that *baraita*: If a woman **lost her marriage contract?** The Gemara answers: The *baraita* is referring to a case **where** her husband **wrote her** a marriage contract[N] contrary to the local custom. The Gemara asks: If he wrote her a marriage contract, the concern remains that **ultimately she** will **produce** the marriage contract **and collect** payment **with it** a second time. The Gemara answers: **What** is the meaning of **lost?** The woman **lost** her marriage contract **in the fire.** In that case, there is no longer any concern.

אִי הָכִי הַיְינוּ נִשְׂרְפָה! וְעוֹד: הִטְמִינָה, מַאי אִיכָּא לְמֵימַר? וְתוּ: אִיבְּדָה לָמָּה לִי? אֶלָּא: כָּל אִיבְּדָה – כִּי הִטְמִינָה בְּפָנֵינוּ דָּמֵי, וְלָא יָהֲבִינַן לָהּ עַד דְּאָמְרִי עֵדִים נִשְׂרְפָה כְּתוּבָּתָהּ.

The Gemara asks: **If so, that is** the case of: Her marriage contract **was burned,** listed separately in the *baraita*. **And furthermore, what is there to say** with regard to the case of **concealed,** where the concern that she will collect payment twice remains? **And furthermore,** if burned comes to explain the meaning of lost, **why do I** need the *baraita* to list the case of **lost** at all? It would have been sufficient for the *baraita* to mention the case of a burned marriage contract. **Rather,** the meaning of the *baraita* is: The legal status of **any** case where the woman claims that **she lost** her marriage contract **is like** that of a case **where she concealed** it **before us, and we give her** payment of her marriage contract **only when the witnesses say that her marriage contract was burned.** Otherwise, even if witnesses testify that the practices characteristic of the wedding of a virgin were performed at her wedding, she does not collect payment of her marriage contract.

NOTES

One writes a receipt – כּוֹתְבִין שׁוֹבֵר: There is a dispute among the Sages in a case where the borrower admits his debt and comes to pay it, and the lender says that the promissory note is not accessible and he cannot return it to the borrower. Does the borrower pay his debt and receive a receipt from the lender in lieu of the document itself? Those who maintain that the borrower need not accept a receipt hold that since he would have to keep the receipt indefinitely, as the lender could potentially produce the document and claim the debt at any time, it is unreasonable to require him to do so. Those who maintain that the borrower must pay his debt and accept a receipt hold that the borrower's inconvenience is not a concern, as the verse states: "And the borrower is servant to the lender" (Proverbs 22:7), and the convenience of the lender takes precedence. The early commentaries add that according to the one who maintains that a receipt can serve in lieu of a promissory note, it is not restricted merely to loans, but applies to all financial obligations recorded in documents, including a marriage contract (*Tosafot*; Rashba).

Where her husband wrote her a marriage contract – דִּכְתַב לָהּ אִיהוּ: The Ramban explains, citing the Ra'avad, that the woman admits that although writing a marriage contract was not in keeping with local custom, her husband wrote her a marriage contract. However, she claims that she lost it.

HALAKHA

One writes a receipt – כּוֹתְבִין שׁוֹבֵר: If a debtor comes to pay his debt and the creditor claims that he lost the promissory note, the debtor must pay his debt, and the creditor writes him a receipt. The debtor may not say that he will not pay his debt until the promissory note is returned. However, he may request that the court issue a general ban of excommunication with regard to those who suppress documents and fail to return them. Some say that if the creditor admits that the document is in his possession but is currently unavailable, and he offers to write a receipt, the debtor can refuse to pay until the document is returned (*Tur*). The Rema cites certain cases where a receipt is written for part of the sum (Rambam *Sefer Mishpatim, Hilkhot Malve VeLoveh* 23:16; *Shulḥan Arukh, Ḥoshen Mishpat*, 54:2–3).

With a place where one does not write a marriage contract – בְּמָקוֹם שֶׁאֵין כּוֹתְבִין כְּתוּבָּה: A woman claims that she was a virgin when she was married and the man claims that she was not, and it is a place where the custom is not to write a marriage contract, or the marriage contract was lost. If she can bring witnesses who testify that based on the customs they witnessed at the wedding she was married as a virgin, she receives two hundred dinars (Rambam *Sefer Nashim, Hilkhot Ishut* 16:25; *Shulḥan Arukh, Even HaEzer* 96:15).

BACKGROUND

Writing a receipt – כְּתִיבַת שׁוֹבֵר: It is a matter of dispute whether it is sufficient for the creditor to write a receipt for the debtor when a debt is repaid, or whether the creditor must return the promissory note to the debtor. The reason not to write a receipt is that if the creditor writes one, the debtor must keep the receipt forever. If the debtor loses it, the creditor could then demand payment again. On the other hand, just as when the debtor repays part of the debt, the creditor has no alternative other than to write a receipt, so too, when the debtor repays the entire debt, the creditor may write a receipt.

Cup of good tidings – כּוֹס שֶׁל בְּשׂוֹרָה: Apparently they would pass around this cup after the marriage was consummated and it was confirmed that she was a virgin. Therefore it is called the cup of good tidings, as it apprises everyone that everything is as it should be.

מאן דמתני לה אברייתא – כל שכן אמתניתין, ומאן דמתני לה אמתניתין – אבל אברייתא לא, כי קושיא.

The Gemara notes: **The one who teaches this** dispute between Rabbi Abbahu and Rav Pappa with regard **to the *baraita*, all the more so** would he teach it with regard **to the mishna.** Applying Rav Pappa's opinion to the mishna does not necessitate the emendation and reinterpretation necessitated by its application to the *baraita*. **However, the one who teaches this** dispute with regard **to the mishna** would **not** teach it then with regard **to the *baraita*, in accordance with the difficulty** raised there, as the plain meaning of the *baraita* is that it is a place where one writes a marriage contract.

"אם יש עדים" כו'. וליחוש דלמא מפקא עדי הינומא בהאי בית דין וגביא, והדר מפקא עדי הינומא בבי דינא אחרינא וגביא! במקום דלא אפשר – ודאי כתבינן שובר.

With regard to that same passage in the mishna: **If there are witnesses** that she went out of her father's house to her wedding with a *hinnuma*, or with her hair uncovered, in a manner typical of virgins, payment of her marriage contract is two hundred dinars, the Gemara asks: **But let us be concerned lest she** first **produce witnesses** that she went out with **a *hinnuma*, in this court, and collect** payment, **and then produce witnesses** that she went out with **a *hinnuma*, in that court, and collect** payment a second time. The Gemara answers: **In a place where it is not possible** to guarantee that she will not collect her marriage contract more than once in any other way, **certainly we write a receipt,** even according to the opinion that as a rule, one does not write a receipt.

"העבירו לפניה כוס של בשורה". מאי "כוס של בשורה"? אמר רב אדא בר אהבה: כוס יין של תרומה מעבירין לפניה, כלומר: ראויה היתה זו לאכול בתרומה. מתקיף לה רב פפא: אטו אלמנה מי לא אכלה בתרומה? אלא אמר רב פפא: זו ראשית כתרומה ראשית.

§ It is taught in that *baraita*: Or **passed before her a cup of** good **tidings.** The Gemara asks: **What is a cup of good tidings? Rav Adda bar Ahava says: A cup of *teruma*[B] wine is passed before** the virgin bride, **meaning** that **this** woman **would have been eligible to eat *teruma*** had she married a priest. **Rav Pappa** strongly **objects to** this: **Is that to say** that **a widow does not eat *teruma*** if she marries a priest? Clearly she does. Therefore, what is the proof from *teruma* that she is a virgin? **Rather, Rav Pappa says:** The cup of *teruma* is passed before her to indicate that **this bride is first,** as she has not yet engaged in intercourse, **like *teruma*** that **is** the **first** gift separated from the produce.

תניא, רבי יהודה אומר: חבית של יין מעבירין לפניה. אמר רב אדא בר אהבה: בתולה מעבירין לפניה סתומה, בעולה – מעבירין לפניה פתוחה. אמאי? ניעבר קמי בתולה, וקמי בעולה לא ניעבר כלל! זימנין דתפסה מאתים, ואמרה: אנא בתולה הואי, והאי דלא עברו קמאי – אתנוסי הוא דאתניסו.

It is taught in a *baraita* that **Rabbi Yehuda says:** The custom is that **one passes a barrel of wine before her. Rav Adda bar Ahava said: One passes a sealed** barrel of wine **before a virgin, and one passes an open** barrel of wine **before a non-virgin.** The Gemara asks: **Why** is that necessary? **Let us pass** the sealed barrel **before the virgin, and before the non-virgin let us not pass** a barrel **at all.** Why is it necessary to publicize the fact that she is a non-virgin? The Gemara explains: It is necessary, as, **at times** there could be a case where a non-virgin unilaterally **seized two hundred** dinars as payment for her marriage contract **and said: I was a virgin,** and the fact **that they did not pass** a sealed barrel **before me was due to circumstances beyond their control.** In order to prevent deceit of that kind, an open barrel is passed before the non-virgin, so that people will remember that she is not a virgin.

תנו רבנן: כיצד מרקדין לפני הכלה? בית שמאי אומרים:

§ **The Sages taught: How does one dance before the bride,** i.e., what does one recite while dancing at her wedding? **Beit Shammai say:**

BACKGROUND

Teruma – תרומה: Whenever the term *teruma* appears without qualification, it is referring to *teruma gedola*. The Torah commands that "The first fruit of your grain, of your wine, and of your oil" (Deuteronomy 18:4) are to be given to the priest (see also Numbers 18:12). The Sages extended the scope of this mitzva, which applies only in Eretz Yisrael, to include all produce. After the first fruits have been separated, a certain portion of the produce must be separated for priests.

The Torah does not specify the amount of *teruma* that must be separated; one may theoretically fulfill his obligation by giving even a single kernel of grain from an entire crop. The Sages established a measure: One-fortieth for a generous gift, one-fiftieth for an average gift, and one-sixtieth for a miserly gift. One should not separate the other tithes until he has separated *teruma*.

Teruma is considered sacred and may be eaten only by a priest and his household while they are in a state of ritual purity (see Leviticus 22:9–15). To emphasize that state of ritual purity, the Sages obligated the priests to wash their hands before partaking of *teruma*. This is the source for the practice of washing one's hands before eating. A ritually impure priest or a non-priest who eats *teruma* is subject to the penalty of death at the hand of Heaven. If *teruma* becomes ritually impure, it may no longer be eaten and must be burned. Nevertheless, it remains the property of the priest and he may benefit from its burning.

Nowadays, *teruma* is not given to priests because they have no definite proof of their priestly lineage. Nevertheless, the obligation to separate *teruma* remains. However, only a miniscule portion of the produce is separated.

כַּלָּה כְּמוֹת שֶׁהִיא, וּבֵית הִלֵּל אוֹמְרִים: כַּלָּה נָאָה וַחֲסוּדָה. אָמְרוּ לָהֶן בֵּית שַׁמַּאי לְבֵית הִלֵּל: הֲרֵי שֶׁהָיְתָה חִיגֶּרֶת אוֹ סוּמָא, אוֹמְרִים לָהּ ״כַּלָּה נָאָה וַחֲסוּדָה״? וְהַתּוֹרָה אָמְרָה ״מִדְּבַר שֶׁקֶר תִּרְחָק״! אָמְרוּ לָהֶם בֵּית הִלֵּל לְבֵית שַׁמַּאי: לְדִבְרֵיכֶם, מִי שֶׁלָּקַח מִקָּח רַע מִן הַשּׁוּק – יְשַׁבְּחֶנּוּ בְּעֵינָיו אוֹ יְגַנֶּנּוּ בְּעֵינָיו? הֱוֵי אוֹמֵר – יְשַׁבְּחֶנּוּ בְּעֵינָיו. מִכָּאן אָמְרוּ חֲכָמִים: לְעוֹלָם תְּהֵא דַּעְתּוֹ שֶׁל אָדָם מְעוֹרֶבֶת עִם הַבְּרִיּוֹת.

One recites praise of **the bride as she is,**[N] emphasizing her good qualities. **And Beit Hillel say:** One recites: **A fair and attractive**[N] **bride.**[H] **Beit Shammai said to Beit Hillel:** In a case **where** the bride **was lame or blind,** does one say with regard **to her: A fair and attractive bride? But the Torah states: "Keep you from a false matter"** (Exodus 23:7). **Beit Hillel said to Beit Shammai:** According **to your statement,** with regard to **one who acquired an inferior acquisition from the market,** should another **praise it** and enhance its value **in his eyes or condemn it** and diminish its value **in his eyes? You must say** that **he should praise it** and enhance its value **in his eyes** and refrain from causing him anguish. **From here the Sages said: A person's disposition should always be empathetic with mankind,** and treat everyone courteously. In this case too, once the groom has married his bride, one praises her as being fair and attractive.

כִּי אֲתָא רַב דִּימִי אֲמַר: הָכִי מְשַׁרוּ קַמֵּי כַּלְּתָא בְּמַעַרְבָא: ״לָא כְּחָל וְלָא שְׁרָק וְלָא פִּירְכּוּס, וְיַעֲלַת חֵן״. כִּי סָמְכוּ רַבָּנַן לְרַבִּי זֵירָא שָׁרוּ לֵיהּ הָכִי: ״לָא כְּחָל וְלָא שְׁרָק וְלָא פִּירְכּוּס וְיַעֲלַת חֵן״.

When Rav Dimi came from Eretz Yisrael to Babylonia, **he said: This is what they sing before brides in the West,** in Eretz Yisrael: **No eye shadow, and no rouge, and no braiding** of the hair, **and** yet she is comparable to **a graceful ibex.** The Gemara relates: **When the Sages ordained Rabbi Zeira, this** is what **they** metaphorically **sang** with regard **to him** in his praise: **No eye shadow, and no rouge, and no braiding** of the hair, **and** yet she is comparable to **a graceful ibex.**

כִּי סָמְכוּ רַבָּנַן לְרַבִּי אַמִי וּלְרַבִּי אַסִי שָׁרוּ לְהוּ הָכִי: ״כָּל מִן דֵּין וְכָל מִן דֵּין סְמוֹכוּ לָנָא, לָא תִּסְמְכוּ לָנָא לָא מִן סַרְמִיסִין וְלָא מִן סַרְמִיטִין״. וְאָמְרִי לַהּ: ״לָא מִן חֲמִיסִין וְלָא מִן טוּרְמִיסִין״.

On a related note, the Gemara relates: **When the Sages ordained Rabbi Ami and Rabbi Asi, this** is what **they sang to them: Anyone from** people of **this** kind **and anyone from** people of **that** kind, **ordain** them **for us. Do not ordain for us** others, **neither from** those who **corrupt** [***sarmisin***][N] ***halakhot*****, nor from** those who are **worthless** [***sarmitin***]**. And some say: Not from** those who provide only **one-fifth** [***ḥamisin***] of the reason for a *halakha*, **and not from** those whose knowledge is **incomplete** [***turmisin***].[L]

רַבִּי אַבָּהוּ, כִּי הֲוָה אָתֵי מִמְּתִיבְתָּא לְבֵי קֵיסָר, נָפְקָן אַמְהָתָא דְּבֵי קֵיסָר לְאַפֵּיהּ, וּמְשָׁרִין לֵיהּ הָכִי: ״רַבָּא דְעַמֵּיהּ וּמְדַבְּרָנָא דְאוּמָּתֵיהּ, בּוֹצִינָא דִנְהוֹרָא, בְּרִיךְ מֶתְיָיךְ לִשְׁלָם״.

The Gemara relates another instance of singing the praise of the Sages: **When Rabbi Abbahu would come from the academy to the house of the emperor,**[B] **the maidservants of the emperor's house would go out to greet him, and this** is what **they sang to him: Master of his people and leader of his nation, candle of illumination, blessed is your arrival in peace.**

אָמְרוּ עָלָיו עַל רַבִּי יְהוּדָה בַּר אִילְעַאי שֶׁהָיָה נוֹטֵל בַּד שֶׁל הֲדַס וּמְרַקֵּד לִפְנֵי הַכַּלָּה, וְאוֹמֵר: ״כַּלָּה נָאָה וַחֲסוּדָה״. רַב שְׁמוּאֵל בַּר רַב יִצְחָק מְרַקֵּד אַתְּלָת. אָמַר רַבִּי זֵירָא: קָא מַכְסִיף לַן סָבָא. כִּי נָח נַפְשֵׁיהּ אִיפְסִיק עַמּוּדָא דְנוּרָא בֵּין דִּידֵיהּ לְכוּלֵּי עָלְמָא, וּגְמִירִי דְּלָא אַפְסֵיק עַמּוּדָא דְנוּרָא אֶלָּא אִי לְחַד בְּדָרָא אִי לִתְרֵי בְּדָרָא.

With regard to the mitzva of bringing joy to the bride and groom, the Gemara relates: The Sages **said about Rabbi Yehuda bar Elai that he would take a myrtle branch and dance before the bride, and say: A fair and attractive bride. Rav Shmuel bar Rav Yitzḥak**[P] **would** base his **dance on three** myrtle branches that he would juggle. **Rabbi Zeira said: The old man is humiliating us,** as through his conduct he is demeaning the Torah and the Torah scholars. It is further related: **When** Rav Shmuel bar Rav Yitzḥak **died, a pillar of fire demarcated between him** and **everyone** else, **and we learn** through tradition **that a pillar of fire demarcates only for either one** person **in a generation or for two** people **in a generation.**

PERSONALITIES

Rav Shmuel bar Rav Yitzḥak – רַב שְׁמוּאֵל בַּר רַב יִצְחָק: A member of the second generation of Babylonian *amora'im*, Rav Shmuel bar Rav Yitzḥak was apparently one of the younger disciples of Rav and afterward studied Torah under the tutelage of Rav Huna.

Like many students of Rav Huna, he came to Eretz Yisrael and studied Torah from the preeminent Torah luminary of that generation, Rabbi Yoḥanan. He was already middle-aged when he arrived there. Although no statements in the name of Rabbi Yoḥanan are cited in the Talmud, he engaged in Torah discourse with the students of Rabbi Yoḥanan, some of whom cite statements in his name. His aggadic and halakhic statements are cited in both the Babylonian Talmud and the Jerusalem Talmud. There is no information as to how he earned his livelihood. In terms of his family, it is known that his daughter married Rabbi Hoshaya.

Rav Shmuel bar Rav Yitzḥak conducted himself with great humility, deferring even to those younger than he. A slightly different version of his custom to dance before the bride along with the rest of the incident is related in the Jerusalem Talmud.

NOTES

The bride as she is – כַּלָּה כְּמוֹת שֶׁהִיא: Most commentaries explain as does *Tosafot*, that as she is means according to her good qualities, as every bride has some good quality, e.g., beauty, personality, lineage, or wealth, for which she is praiseworthy. Others explain that the bride as she is means just that, as God created her. It is a neutral statement containing no falsehood.

And attractive – וַחֲסוּדָה: Rashi and others explain that there is a thread of charm drawn over her. This is praise not of her spiritual qualities but of her physical beauty, which attracts onlookers. That is the meaning of the term based on the discussion that follows.

Sarmisin**, etc. – סַרְמִיסִין וכו׳:** The meaning of these words is not clear even though they all have clearly negative connotations. Rashi explains *sarmisin* as meaning those who corrupt *halakhot*. The *ge'onim* explain that *sarmisin* refers to items that are ruined, e.g., a ball of thread that became entangled. Rabbeinu Ḥananel explains that it is an abbreviation for the term: *Sar ḥamishim*, master of fifty, referring to one proficient in only fifty chapters of mishna. Apparently, he interprets the term *ḥamisin* in a similar fashion.

Rashi explains *sarmitin* as a variation of the word *semartutim*, meaning rags. Others cite the interpretation of the *ge'onim* that this refers to untidy penmanship. Rashi interprets *ḥamisin* in tractate *Sanhedrin* as being related to the term *ḥamsanut*, meaning forcibly taking items from another and paying, which in this context refers to people who state matters but do not reveal their reasons, which is also an action that is improperly performed. The *Arukh* explains that it refers to someone who learns only one-fifth [*ḥamishit*] of a tractate, while others have the variant reading of *ḥamitin*, which means wafer and refers to those who snatch items like one snatches a wafer.

In the commentary attributed to Rashi, *turmisin* is linked to the term *tulmisin*, meaning a wicked person. Others cite the *ge'onim*, who explain that dough that is not prepared properly and that remains in the shape of a ball is referred to as *turmisin*. In this context, it refers to people who are incomplete and unrefined. Rabbeinu Ḥananel links it to the term *turmus*, lupine, referring to those whose reasoning is bitter like lupine.

HALAKHA

A fair and attractive bride – כַּלָּה נָאָה וַחֲסוּדָה: It is a mitzva to bring joy to the bride and the groom and to dance before them and recite: A fair and attractive bride, in accordance with the opinion of Beit Hillel (*Shulḥan Arukh, Even HaEzer* 65:1).

LANGUAGE

Those whose knowledge is incomplete [*turmisin*] – טוּרְמִיסִין: Possibly from the Latin tremissis, meaning a Roman coin worth one-third of a dinar. It is used here as a metaphor for people whose knowledge is partial. There is a variant reading, *tolmisin*, from the Greek τόλμησις, *tolmessis*, which is pejorative and means boldness.

BACKGROUND

The house of the emperor – בֵּי קֵיסָר: Rabbi Abbahu lived in Caesarea and was held in high regard by the Roman authorities. Although he had no official position, he was the acting representative of the Jewish people. The emperor's house in this context is apparently the residence of the Roman governor stationed in Caesarea, where Rabbi Abbahu headed his own yeshiva.

אָמַר רַבִּי זֵירָא: אַהֲנְיָיה לֵיהּ שׁוֹטִיתֵיהּ לְסָבָא, וְאָמְרִי לָהּ: שְׁטוּתֵיהּ לְסָבָא, וְאָמְרִי לָהּ: שִׁיטָתֵיהּ לְסָבָא.

Rabbi Zeira said: His branch [*shotitei*] **was effective for the old man,** as it is due to this mitzva that he fulfilled so enthusiastically that he was privileged to receive this great reward. **And some say** that Rabbi Zeira said: **His nonsense** [*shetutei*] was effective **for the old man. And some say** that he said: **His method** [*shittatei*] was effective **for the old man.**

רַב אַחָא מַרְכֵּיב לָהּ אַכַּתְפֵּיהּ וּמְרַקֵּד. אָמְרִי לֵיהּ רַבָּנַן: אֲנַן מַהוּ לְמֶיעֱבַד הָכִי? אֲמַר לְהוּ: אִי דָּמְיָין עֲלַיְיכוּ כְּכָשׁוֹרָא – לְחַיֵּי, וְאִי לָא – לָא.

Rav Aḥa would place the bride **on his shoulders** and dance. **The Sages said to him: What** is the ruling? Is it permitted for **us to do so as well? He said to them: If** brides are **comparable for you to a beam, fine, but if not, no,** you may not.

אָמַר רַבִּי שְׁמוּאֵל בַּר נַחְמָנִי אָמַר רַבִּי יוֹנָתָן: מוּתָּר לְהִסְתַּכֵּל בִּפְנֵי כַּלָּה כָּל שִׁבְעָה, כְּדֵי לְחַבְּבָהּ עַל בַּעְלָהּ. וְלֵית הִלְכְתָא כְּוָותֵיהּ.

Rabbi Shmuel bar Naḥmani said that **Rabbi Yonatan said:** It is **permitted to look at the face of a bride**[H] throughout **all seven** days of the wedding celebration, **in order to endear her to her husband,** whose appreciation of her beauty will be thereby enhanced. The Gemara notes: **And the *halakha* is not in accordance with his** opinion, as it is prohibited to look at any married woman, even a bride.

תָּנוּ רַבָּנַן: מַעֲבִירִין אֶת הַמֵּת מִלִּפְנֵי כַּלָּה, וְזֶה וְזֶה מִלִּפְנֵי מֶלֶךְ יִשְׂרָאֵל. אָמְרוּ עָלָיו עַל אַגְרִיפַּס הַמֶּלֶךְ שֶׁעָבַר מִלִּפְנֵי כַּלָּה, וְשִׁבְּחוּהוּ חֲכָמִים.

§ **The Sages taught: One reroutes** the funeral procession for burial of **a corpse** to yield **before** the wedding procession of **a bride.**[NH] **And both this,** the funeral procession, **and that,** the wedding procession, yield **before a king of Israel.**[H] **They said about King Agrippa** [*Agrippas*][LP] **that** although he was not required to do so, **he rerouted** his entourage **before** the wedding procession of **a bride, and the Sages praised him** for doing so.

שִׁבְּחוּהוּ – מִכְּלָל דְּשַׁפִּיר עֲבַד?! וְהָא אֲמַר רַב אַשִׁי: אֲפִילּוּ לְמַאן דְּאָמַר נָשִׂיא שֶׁמָּחַל עַל כְּבוֹדוֹ – כְּבוֹדוֹ מָחוּל, מֶלֶךְ שֶׁמָּחַל עַל כְּבוֹדוֹ – אֵין כְּבוֹדוֹ מָחוּל; דְּאָמַר מָר: "שׂוֹם תָּשִׂים עָלֶיךָ מֶלֶךְ" – שֶׁתְּהֵא אֵימָתוֹ עָלֶיךָ! פָּרָשַׁת דְּרָכִים הֲוַאי.

The Gemara asks: The Sages **praised him;** is that to say **by inference that he did well** in yielding? **But didn't Rav Ashi say: Even** according **to the one who said** with regard to **a *Nasi*** who **relinquishes the honor** due **him**[H] that **his honor is relinquished,** i.e., he may do so, with regard to **a king who relinquishes** the **honor** due **him,**[H] **his honor is not relinquished. As the Master said** that the meaning of the verse **"You shall place a king over you"** (Deuteronomy 17:15) **is that his awe shall be upon you.** The Torah established that the subjects' awe is an essential component of kingship and it is not the prerogative of the king to waive it. The Gemara answers: **It was at a crossroads** that he encountered the wedding procession, and the fact that he yielded to the bride was not obvious to onlookers. Therefore, the honor due the king was not compromised.

NOTES

One reroutes a corpse to yield before a bride – מַעֲבִירִין אֶת הַמֵּת מִלִּפְנֵי כַּלָּה: The Ramban and the Ra'ah maintain this as a principle: The marriage of a bride takes precedence over burial of a corpse, not only in terms of deference, but also in terms of the allocation of public funds and the like. The reason is that since both of these mitzvot are based on the principle of human dignity, actions designed to enhance the dignity of the living take precedence over those designed to enhance the dignity of the dead. However, others note that the Rambam disagrees.

LANGUAGE

Agrippa [*Agrippas*] – אַגְרִיפַּס: *Agrippas*, Αγρίππας, is the Greek rendition of the Roman name Agrippa.

PERSONALITIES

King Agrippa – אַגְרִיפַּס הַמֶּלֶךְ: This is apparently Agrippa I, the grandson of Herod and Miriam the Hasmonean, who died in 44 CE. Although he spent his youth in Rome involved in the debauchery and machinations of the emperor Tiberius's court, when he ultimately came to Eretz Yisrael and was appointed king over all of the territories that Herod ruled, he underwent a major spiritual transformation that led to the development of a close relationship with the Sages and to scrupulous adherence to the mitzvot. Although the Sages never officially recognized his monarchy, they treated him with deference, and the Talmud recounts several of his good deeds.

Coin with the visage of Agrippa I

HALAKHA

To look at the face of a bride – לְהִסְתַּכֵּל בִּפְנֵי כַּלָּה: It is prohibited to look at the bride, just as it is prohibited to look at any other married woman (*Shulḥan Arukh, Even HaEzer* 65:2).

One reroutes a corpse to yield before a bride – מַעֲבִירִין אֶת הַמֵּת מִלִּפְנֵי כַּלָּה: If a wedding procession and a funeral procession meet, the funeral procession yields to the wedding procession (Rambam *Sefer Shofetim, Hilkhot Evel* 14:8; *Shulḥan Arukh, Even HaEzer* 65:4).

And both this and that before a king of Israel – וְזֶה וְזֶה מִלִּפְנֵי מֶלֶךְ יִשְׂרָאֵל: Both a funeral procession and a wedding procession yield to a king of Israel, in accordance with the *baraita* (Rambam *Sefer Shofetim, Hilkhot Evel* 14:8).

A *Nasi* who relinquishes the honor due him – נָשִׂיא שֶׁמָּחַל עַל כְּבוֹדוֹ: One who sees the *Nasi* of the Sanhedrin stands until the *Nasi* is no longer visible. If a Torah scholar, or even the *Nasi*, relinquishes the honor due him, his honor is relinquished. Nevertheless, it is appropriate to honor him and show him symbolic deference by engaging in a standing-like motion (Rambam *Sefer HaMadda, Hilkhot Talmud Torah* 6:6; *Shulḥan Arukh, Yoreh De'a* 244:14).

A king who relinquishes the honor due him – מֶלֶךְ שֶׁמָּחַל עַל כְּבוֹדוֹ: A king may not relinquish the honor due him, even for the purpose of a mitzva (Rambam *Sefer Shofetim, Hilkhot Melakhim* 2:3).

תָּנוּ רַבָּנַן: מְבַטְּלִין תַּלְמוּד תּוֹרָה לְהוֹצָאַת הַמֵּת וּלְהַכְנָסַת כַּלָּה, אָמְרוּ עָלָיו עַל רַבִּי יְהוּדָה בְּרַבִּי אֶלְעַאי שֶׁהָיָה מְבַטֵּל תַּלְמוּד תּוֹרָה לְהוֹצָאַת הַמֵּת וּלְהַכְנָסַת כַּלָּה. בַּמֶּה דְּבָרִים אֲמוּרִים – כְּשֶׁאֵין עִמּוֹ כׇּל צׇרְכּוֹ, אֲבָל יֵשׁ עִמּוֹ כׇּל צׇרְכּוֹ – אֵין מְבַטְּלִין.

The Sages taught: One suspends the study of Torah to attend **the removal of a corpse**[H] for burial **and to** attend **the entry of a bride into** the wedding canopy. The Sages **said about Rabbi Yehuda, son of Rabbi Elai, that he would suspend the study of Torah to** attend **the removal of a corpse** for burial **and to** attend **the entry of a bride into** the wedding canopy. **In what** case **is this statement said?** In a case **where** there are **not** enough people **with him,** i.e., accompanying the corpse, to satisfy **all his needs,** i.e., to appropriately honor him. **However, if** there are enough people **with him** to satisfy **all his needs, one does not suspend** Torah study.

וְכַמָּה כׇּל צׇרְכּוֹ? אָמַר רַב שְׁמוּאֵל בַּר אִינִי מִשְּׁמֵיהּ דְּרַב: תְּרֵיסַר אַלְפֵי גַּבְרֵי וְשִׁיתָּא אַלְפֵי שִׁיפּוּרֵי. וְאָמְרִי לַהּ: תְּלֵיסַר אַלְפֵי גַּבְרֵי, וּמִינַּיְיהוּ שִׁיתָּא אַלְפֵי שִׁיפּוּרֵי. עוּלָּא אָמַר: כְּגוֹן דְּחָיְיצִי גַּבְרֵי מֵאַבּוּלָא וְעַד סִיכְרָא. רַב שֵׁשֶׁת וְאִיתֵּימָא רַבִּי יוֹחָנָן אָמַר: נְטִילָתָהּ כִּנְתִינָתָהּ, מָה נְתִינָתָהּ בְּשִׁשִּׁים רִבּוֹא – אַף נְטִילָתָהּ בְּשִׁשִּׁים רִבּוֹא. וְהָנֵי מִילֵּי – לְמַאן דְּקָרֵי וְתָנֵי,

The Gemara asks: **And how many** people constitute **all his needs?**[HN] **Rav Shmuel bar Eini said in the name of Rav: Twelve thousand men and six thousand** additional men each sounding **a shofar** to herald the approaching funeral procession. **And some say: Thirteen thousand men and, among them, six thousand** men sounding **a shofar. Ulla said:** All his needs means a crowd large enough **so that the men** in the funeral possession **form a partition** stretching **from the gate of the city** [*abbula*][L] **until the cemetery. Rav Sheshet, and some say Rabbi Yoḥanan, said: The** number of people required for **taking** of the Torah from the Jewish people with the death of a Torah scholar **is equivalent to** the number present at **its giving** to the Jewish people. **Just as its giving** took place **with six hundred thousand** men present at Sinai, **so too,** the **taking** of the Torah at the funeral of a Torah scholar **is with six hundred thousand** men. The Gemara notes: **This applies only to one who read** the Bible **and studied** mishna,[N] i.e., one who is a student of Torah, and consequently worthy of that honor.

LANGUAGE

Gate of the city [*abbula*] – אַבּוּלָא: Most commentaries define *abbula* as the gate of the city, from the Greek ἔμβολος, *embolos*, meaning gatehouse or city gate.

HALAKHA

One suspends the study of Torah to attend the removal of a corpse – מְבַטְּלִין תַּלְמוּד תּוֹרָה לְהוֹצָאַת הַמֵּת: One suspends Torah study for a funeral procession if there are not enough people with the corpse to satisfy all his needs. This is also true for a wedding celebration. However, in both these cases, if there are enough people present one does not suspend Torah study (Rambam *Sefer Shofetim, Hilkhot Evel* 14:9; *Shulḥan Arukh, Yoreh De'a* 361:1).

And how many constitute all his needs – וְכַמָּה כׇּל צׇרְכּוֹ: How many attendees are considered sufficient for a funeral? If the deceased was unlearned in both Bible and mishna, ten men are sufficient. If he was a Torah scholar who studied Bible or mishna himself, which according to the Rema, citing the *Smag*, is the presumptive status of all Jewish people nowadays, six hundred thousand is the requisite number. If he taught Torah to others, everyone must attend his funeral. Nowadays, the prevalent custom is based on the Gemara (*Moed Katan* 27b): In a place where there are different burial societies, each group buries its own dead. Nevertheless, when encountering another funeral procession, one briefly joins the procession in deference to the dead (Rambam *Sefer Shofetim, Hilkhot Evel* 14:11; *Shulḥan Arukh, Yoreh De'a* 361:1).

NOTES

And how many constitute all his needs – וְכַמָּה כׇּל צׇרְכּוֹ: The *ge'onim* write that one may learn from here that although there are prescribed limits to the number of people required to attend a funeral, there is no limit to the number of people required to attend a wedding.

To one who read the Bible and studied mishna – לְמַאן דְּקָרֵי וְתָנֵי: The early commentaries, some of whom cite the *She'iltot*, which is the first source for this opinion, write that for one who has not read any Bible or learned any Mishna, ten men are sufficient to engage in his burial. The commentaries are divided with regard to the burial of a woman. Some say that since she too has presumably neither read the Bible nor learned Mishna, the same applies to her. Others maintain that since the woman has no obligation to study Torah, the legal status of her burial would equal that of a man who read the Bible and learned Mishna, especially if she was a righteous woman (*Talmidei Rabbeinu Yona*).

LANGUAGE

Surḥav – **סוּרְחַב**: This name is related to the Persian suxr, meaning ruddy or red. There are similar names and epithets attached to various Sages, e.g., Yitzḥak the Red [*sumka*].

Veil [*kerita*] – **קְרִיתָא**: There are various opinions with regard to the meaning of this term. Some define it as a diminutive form of the word *kirya*, meaning city. Rabbeinu Ḥananel, cited in the *Arukh*, explains that it is a tiara in the shape of a city that would be placed on the head of the bride. Others say that it was a small structure in which the bride would be seated, or a sedan chair in which the bride was carried. The etymology of the word is unclear.

Roman statue of woman wearing a tiara in the shape of a city

HALAKHA

If there are witnesses that it was the father's field – **אִם יֵשׁ עֵדִים שֶׁהִיא שֶׁלּוֹ**: If one person has witnesses that he is the previous owner of a field currently in the possession of another, and the other person claims that he purchased it from the first, who denies that he sold it and claims that the field is stolen, the first person is deemed credible. He takes an oath of inducement, instituted by the Sages to induce a person to tell the truth, and repossesses his field (Rambam *Sefer Mishpatim*, *Hilkhot To'en VeNitan* 14:3; *Shulḥan Arukh*, *Ḥoshen Mishpat* 140:1).

אֲבָל לְמַאן דְּמַתְנֵי – לֵית לֵיהּ שִׁיעוּרָא.

However, for one who taught others, there is **no measure for** the number of people attending the funeral.

״וְאִם יֵשׁ עֵדִים שֶׁיָּצְתָה בְּהִינּוּמָא״ וכו׳. מַאי הִינּוּמָא? סוּרְחַב בַּר פַּפָּא מִשְּׁמֵיהּ דִּזְעֵירִי אֲמַר: תַּנּוּרָא דְּאָסָא, רַבִּי יוֹחָנָן אָמַר: קְרִיתָא דִּמְנַמְנָה בָּהּ כַּלְּתָא.

The mishna continues: **And if there are witnesses that she went out** of her father's house to her wedding **with a *hinnuma*** her marriage contract is two hundred dinars. The Gemara asks: **What is a *hinnuma*? Surḥav**[L] **bar Pappa said in the name of Ze'eiri:** It is **a canopy of myrtle** over the bride's head. **Rabbi Yoḥanan said:** It is **a veil** [***kerita***][L] covering the bride's face **under which the bride dozes** [***menamna***].

״רַבִּי יוֹחָנָן בֶּן בְּרוֹקָא אוֹמֵר״ וכו׳. תָּנָא: בִּיהוּדָה – רְאָיָה, בְּבָבֶל מַאי? אֲמַר רַב: דַּרְדּוּגֵי דְּמִשְׁחָא אַרֵישָׁא דְּרַבָּנַן. אֲמַר לֵיהּ רַב פַּפָּא לְאַבַּיֵי: מִשְׁחָא דַּחֲפִיפוּתָא קָאֲמַר מָר?! אֲמַר לֵיהּ: יַתְמָא, לָא עָבְדָא לָךְ אִמָּךְ דַּרְדּוּגֵי מִשְׁחָא אַרֵישָׁא דְּרַבָּנַן בִּשְׁעַת מַעֲשֶׂה? כִּי הָא דְּהַהוּא מֵרַבָּנַן דְּאִיעֲסַק לֵיהּ לִבְרֵיהּ בֵּי רַבָּה בַּר עוּלָּא. וְאָמְרִי לַהּ רַבָּה בַּר עוּלָּא אִיעֲסַק לֵיהּ לִבְרֵיהּ בֵּי הַהוּא מֵרַבָּנַן, וְדַרְדֵּיג מִשְׁחָא אַרֵישָׁא דְּרַבָּנַן בִּשְׁעַת מַעֲשֶׂה.

The mishna continues: **Rabbi Yoḥanan ben Beroka says:** Even testimony that there was distribution of roasted grain constitutes **proof** that she is a virgin. It was **taught** with regard to the mishna: **In Judea,** that is **proof**; however, **what are** the customs at the weddings of virgins **in Babylonia? Rav said: Smearing** fragrant oil **on the heads of the Sages** was customary. **Rav Pappa,** who was unfamiliar with that practice, **said to Abaye: Is the Master saying oil for shampooing** the hair? Calling him an orphan because he was ignorant of the custom, **he said to him: Orphan, didn't your mother perform for you smearing of oil on the heads of the Sages at the time of the performance** of your wedding ceremony? **As** this was the case **when one of the Sages who arranged for his son** to marry into **the family of Rabba bar Ulla** attended the wedding, **and some say that** it was **Rabba bar Ulla** who **arranged for his son** to marry into **the family of one of the Sages; and he smeared oil on the heads of the Sages at the time of the performance** of the wedding ceremony.

אַרְמַלְתָּא מַאי? תָּאנֵי רַב יוֹסֵף: אַרְמַלְתָּא לֵית לָהּ כִּיסָּנֵי.

The Gemara asks: **What is the** custom at the wedding of **a widow? Rav Yosef taught: A widow does not have roasted grain** [***kisanei***][N] distributed at her wedding.

״וּמוֹדֶה רַבִּי יְהוֹשֻׁעַ בְּאוֹמֵר לַחֲבֵירוֹ״ כו׳. וְלִיתְנֵי: ״מוֹדֶה רַבִּי יְהוֹשֻׁעַ בְּאוֹמֵר לַחֲבֵירוֹ שָׂדֶה זוֹ שֶׁלְּךָ הָיְתָה וּלְקַחְתִּיהָ מִמְּךָ״!

The mishna continues: **And Rabbi Yehoshua concedes in** a case where **one says to another:** This field belonged to your father, and I purchased it from him, that he is deemed credible. The Gemara asks: **And let** the mishna **teach: Rabbi Yehoshua concedes in** a case where **one says to another: This field belonged to you, and I purchased it from you.**

מִשּׁוּם דְּקָא בָּעֵי לְמִיתְנֵי סֵיפָא: אִם יֵשׁ עֵדִים שֶׁהִיא שֶׁלּוֹ, וְהוּא אוֹמֵר: ״לְקַחְתִּיהָ מִמֶּנּוּ״ – אֵינוֹ נֶאֱמָן. הֵיכִי דָּמֵי?

The Gemara answers: Although Rabbi Yehoshua concedes that his claim is accepted even in that latter case, he addressed the case where the field originally belonged to the father **due to** the fact **that** the *tanna* **wanted to teach in the latter clause that if there are witnesses that it was** the father's field,[H] **and he says: I purchased it from him, he is not deemed credible.** That is the *halakha* only with regard to a field that belonged to the father, and not to the claimant himself. Were it referring to a field that he purchased from the claimant, **what are the circumstances?**

NOTES

A widow does not have roasted grain [*kisanei*] – **אַרְמַלְתָּא לֵית לָהּ כִּיסָּנֵי**: The text of the Gemara is difficult, as the Gemara asks what was the practice characteristic of the wedding of a widow and no answer is provided. *Tosafot* explain that to avoid any potential error, they would take pains to make certain that there was no roasted grain at the wedding of a widow. However, the Ritva cites the opinion of Rabbeinu Tam, who interprets the question as relating to the case of a widow who seized property from her husband's estate and claimed that she had been a virgin. The Gemara answers that if there are witnesses to testify that there was no roasted grain at the wedding ceremony, it serves as proof that she was not a virgin. Since bringing grain does not involve exertion, she cannot claim that there was no grain due to circumstances beyond her control.

Many early commentaries (Rabbeinu Tam in *Sefer HaYashar*; Ramban) cited a variant reading of the text: A widow has *kisanei* at her wedding to distinguish it from the wedding of a virgin, where *kelayot* are brought instead. The *ge'onim* explain that *kisanei* is a dish of wheat, cooked beans, and raisins, and *kelayot* are toasted grain. Rabbeinu Tam explains that *kisanei* is grain toasted in the oven. At the wedding ceremony of a virgin they would bring freshly toasted grain, symbolizing her virginity, and at the wedding of a widow they would bring dried toasted grain.

אִי דַּאֲכָלָהּ שְׁנֵי חֲזָקָה – אַמַּאי לָא מְהֵימַן? וְאִי דְּלָא אֲכָלָהּ שְׁנֵי חֲזָקָה – פְּשִׁיטָא דְּלָא מְהֵימַן!

If it is a case **where** the one in possession of the field **consumed** its produce for the three **years** necessary to establish **presumptive ownership,**[NH] **why is his** claim that he purchased the field **not deemed credible?** After three years of unchallenged possession, the purchaser's claim is sufficient to establish ownership without documentation. **And if he did not consume** its produce for the three **years** necessary to establish **presumptive ownership,** it is **obvious that his** claim **is not deemed credible.** Since the distinction between a case where witnesses are present and a case where there are no witnesses present does not apply when the field in question was the property of the claimant, the *tanna* cited a case where the field belonged to the father.

אִי הָכִי, גַּבֵּי אָבִיו נַמִי, אִי דַּאֲכָלָהּ שְׁנֵי חֲזָקָה – אַמַּאי לָא מְהֵימַן? וְאִי דְּלָא אֲכָלָהּ שְׁנֵי חֲזָקָה – פְּשִׁיטָא דְּלָא מְהֵימַן!

The Gemara asks: **If so,** the same difficulty may be raised **with regard to** a field belonging to the claimant's **father as well: If** the one in possession of the field **consumed** its produce for the three **years** necessary to establish **presumptive ownership, why is his** claim that he purchased the field **not deemed credible? And if he did not consume** its produce for the three **years** necessary to establish **presumptive ownership,** it is **obvious that his** claim **is not deemed credible.** The latter clause is no more applicable to the father's field than it is to the claimant's field. Why did the *tanna* prefer to cite a case where the field belonged to the claimant's father?

בִּשְׁלָמָא גַּבֵּי אָבִיו – מַשְׁכַּחַתְּ לָהּ, כְּגוֹן שֶׁאֲכָלָהּ שְׁתַּיִם בְּחַיֵּי הָאָב וְאַחַת בְּחַיֵּי בְּנוֹ, וְכִדְרַב הוּנָא. דְּאָמַר רַב הוּנָא: אֵין מַחֲזִיקִין בְּנִכְסֵי קָטָן אֲפִילּוּ הִגְדִּיל.

The Gemara answers: **Granted, with regard to** the case where the field belonged to **his father,** a circumstance can **be found** where there is uncertainty with regard to the presumptive ownership of the field, **where** the one in possession of the field **consumed** its produce for **two** of the three years necessary to establish presumptive ownership **during the lifetime of the father**[H] and **one** year **during the lifetime of the son** after the death of his father. **And** this is **in accordance with** the opinion of **Rav Huna, as Rav Huna said: One cannot establish presumptive ownership of the property of a minor, even** after **he reached majority.**[H] This is because the minor is unaware of the property owned by his father, the fact that he did not challenge the claim of the one in possession of the field proves nothing. Therefore, only two of the three years necessary to establish presumptive ownership have passed.

וְרַב הוּנָא מַתְנִיתִין אֲתָא לְאַשְׁמוּעִינַן? אִיבָּעֵית אֵימָא: רַב הוּנָא דִּיּוּקָא דְּמַתְנִיתִין קָאָמַר. וְאִיבָּעֵית אֵימָא: "אֲפִילּוּ הִגְדִּיל" קָא מַשְׁמַע לַן.

The Gemara asks: **And** since the mishna can be explained only in the case delineated by Rav Huna, **did Rav Huna come to teach us a mishna?** There is no need for an *amora* to teach matters that appear in a mishna, as the content of *mishnayot* is known by all. The Gemara answers: **If you wish, say** that **Rav Huna is stating the inference from the mishna,** as the circumstances are not written explicitly in the mishna. **And if you wish, say** instead **that he is teaching us** that even if during the year after the father died his son was no longer a minor, one may not establish presumptive ownership of the property of a minor, **even** after **he reached majority.**[N] From the mishna, one could learn only a case where, during the third year the son was still a minor.

NOTES

Years necessary to establish presumptive ownership – שְׁנֵי חֲזָקָה: The presumptive ownership under discussion here is the ostensible proof that the property legally belongs to the one currently in possession of it. The primary *halakhot* of presumptive ownership are elucidated in tractate *Bava Batra*. Fundamentally, in addition to physical possession of the property, there must also be a claim to legal ownership, i.e., inheritance, purchase, or receipt as a gift. To establish presumptive ownership of land, one must prove that he utilized the land, e.g., that he ate the produce of a field, for three years. Even after three years have elapsed, presumptive ownership does not constitute absolute proof of ownership. Rather, it is effective in that if one claims that he owned the field and brings proof to that effect, and the one in possession of the field claims that ownership was legally transferred to him, he need not document that legal transfer. After three years of uncontested possession of the property, the one in possession of the property is not expected to safeguard the relevant documents any longer.

Even after he reached majority – אֲפִילּוּ הִגְדִּיל: With regard to the practical *halakha*, there are several opinions (see HALAKHA). According to the Rambam the years of possession while the heir was a minor are not included in establishing presumptive ownership; it is established only by means of three years of possession subsequent to his reaching majority. Other early commentaries dispute the Rambam's opinion and contend that since possession of the field began while the heir was a minor and unfamiliar with his father's properties, it is unreasonable to expect him to be familiar with those properties even after he reaches majority. Therefore, they explain, apparently in agreement with the *ge'onim*, that presumptive ownership is established only if possession of the field began after the heir reached majority.

The Rashba explains at length that while the heir is a minor, he lacks the halakhic ability to transfer ownership of the property. A third, and even more extreme, opinion is that of the Rashbam, cited by *Tosafot*, who asserts that in any case where one claims that he assumed possession of the property during the father's lifetime, presumptive ownership cannot be established, as, based on a principle cited in several places in the Talmud, the legal status of an adult heir is equivalent to that of a minor in terms of familiarity with the disposition of his father's properties.

HALAKHA

Consumed its produce for the three years necessary to establish presumptive ownership – אֲכָלָהּ שְׁנֵי חֲזָקָה: If one occupied a field for three years and claims that he acquired it legally, and the previous owner claims that the field was stolen, the first takes an oath of inducement by rabbinic law and maintains possession of the field (Rambam *Sefer Mishpatim, Hilkhot To'en VeNitan* 12:8; *Shulḥan Arukh, Ḥoshen Mishpat* 140:1).

Where one consumed its produce for two years during the lifetime of the father – אֲכָלָהּ שְׁתַּיִם בְּחַיֵּי הָאָב: If one consumed the produce of the field for one year during the lifetime of the previous owner and an additional two years during the lifetime of his son, or if he consumed the produce of the field for two years during the lifetime of the previous owner and an additional year during the lifetime of his son, he thereby established presumptive ownership (Rambam *Sefer Mishpatim, Hilkhot To'en VeNitan* 12:8; *Shulḥan Arukh, Ḥoshen Mishpat* 144:4).

One cannot establish presumptive ownership of the property of a minor, even after he reached majority – אֵין מַחֲזִיקִין בְּנִכְסֵי קָטָן אֲפִילּוּ הִגְדִּיל: The *halakha* of presumptive ownership does not apply to a minor's property, even after he reached majority. For example, if one consumed the produce of the field after the father's death for one year while the son was a minor, and two additional years after he reached majority, presumptive ownership is not established. Only if he maintains possession for three consecutive years after the son reached majority is presumptive ownership established. This is the ruling of the Rambam based on the opinion of the Ri Migash, and the *Shulḥan Arukh*. The Rema, however, rules in accordance with those who disagree with the Rambam, that even if three years passed since the son reached majority, presumptive ownership was not established, as the son may be unaware that the field was stolen from his father (Rashi; Ra'avad; Ramban; Rashba). Some note that both opinions are based on the Gemara here, which is inconclusive (Rambam *Sefer Mishpatim, Hilkhot To'en VeNitan* 14:7 and *Maggid Mishne* there; *Shulḥan Arukh, Ḥoshen Mishpat* 149:19).

וליתנייה בדידיה, ולוקמה כגון שאכלה שתים בפניו ואחת שלא בפניו, וכגון שברח?

The Gemara asks: **And let** the *tanna* **teach** the *halakha* **in** a case where the one in possession of the field says that he purchased the field from the claimant **himself. And let him establish** the mishna in a case **where** the one in possession of the field **consumed** its produce **in the presence** of the claimant, who was the original owner of the field, for **two** of the three years necessary to establish presumptive ownership, **and** consumed its produce not **in his presence** for **one** year. **And** that scenario is in a case **where** the claimant **fled** and therefore, the fact that he did not challenge the claim of the one in possession of the field proves nothing.

ברח מחמת מאי? אי דברח מחמת נפשות – פשיטא דלא מהימן, דלא מצי מחי. ואי דברח מחמת ממון – איבעי ליה למחויי, דקיימא לן: מחאה שלא בפניו – הויא מחאה!

The Gemara asks: That scenario is referring to one who **fled due to what** reason? **If** it is **that he fled due to** the fact that his **life** was in jeopardy, it is **obvious that** the one claiming presumptive ownership **is not deemed credible, since** the owner of the field **is unable to protest,** as he fears for his life. **And if he fled due to money** that he owes,[H] and that is why he does not return to protest the possessor's occupation of the field, **he ought to protest** from afar, **as we maintain that a protest** lodged **not in the presence of** the one using the field[H] **is a legitimate protest.** He could have lodged in a court in his place of exile his protest against the illegal occupation of his field.

דתנן: שלש ארצות לחזקה, יהודה ועבר הירדן והגליל. היה ביהודה והחזיק בגליל, בגליל והחזיק ביהודה – אינה חזקה, עד שיהא עמו במדינה.

This is **as we learned** in a mishna (*Bava Batra* 38a): There are **three** independent **lands** in Eretz Yisrael with regard to establishing **presumptive ownership: Judea, Transjordan, and the Galilee.** If the original owner of the field **was in Judea** and another **occupied** his field **in the Galilee,** or if he was **in the Galilee** and another **occupied** his field **in Judea,** that does **not** establish **presumptive ownership, until** the one occupying the field **will be with** the original owner **in the same country.**

והוינן בה: מאי קסבר: אי קסבר מחאה שלא בפניו הויא מחאה – אפילו ביהודה וגליל נמי, ואי קסבר מחאה שלא בפניו לא הויא מחאה – אפילו יהודה ויהודה נמי לא!

And we discussed that mishna: **What does** this *tanna* **hold? If he holds that a protest** lodged **not in the presence of** the one using the field **is** a legitimate **protest,** then **even in** the case where one is in **Judea and** one is in the **Galilee** the protest should **also** be legitimate. **And if he holds that a protest** lodged **not in the presence of** the one using the field **is not** a legitimate **protest,** then **even** in the case where one is in **Judea and** the other one is in **Judea** as well, the protest should **also not** be legitimate.

אמר רבי אבא בר ממל: לעולם קסבר מחאה שלא בפניו הויא מחאה. ומתניתין בשעת חירום שנו.

Rabbi Abba bar Memel said: Actually the *tanna* **holds that a protest** lodged **not in the presence of** the one using the field **is** a legitimate **protest, and** the Sages **taught this mishna with regard to a crisis period,** when travel is perilous and information cannot be transmitted from Judea to the Galilee. Therefore, although no protest was received from the original owner, the occupier does not establish presumptive ownership of the field, because the lack of protest can be attributed to the perilous situation.

ומאי שנא יהודה וגליל דנקט,

The Gemara asked: **And** if it is due only to the exigent circumstances that the protest is ineffective, **what is different** about **Judea and** the **Galilee** that the *tanna* **cited** specifically these two lands? Ostensibly, even within one of the three lands, if travel and communications are restricted, the same *halakha* would apply.

HALAKHA

Fled due to the fact that his life was in jeopardy…fled due to money he owes – ברח מחמת נפשות...ברח מחמת ממון: If the owner of the field was forced to flee due to the fact that his life was in jeopardy, presumptive ownership of his property cannot be established, because his failure to protest is attributable to the fear that his whereabouts will be discovered. However, based on the Gemara here and in *Bava Batra* (38b), if he fled due to money that he owes, presumptive ownership can be established (Rambam *Sefer Mishpatim, Hilkhot To'en VeNitan* 14:10; *Shulḥan Arukh, Ḥoshen Mishpat* 143:3).

A protest lodged not in the presence of the one using the field – מחאה שלא בפניו: The protest of the previous owner of a field lodged against the occupation of his field by another negates the other's presumptive ownership, even if the protest was not lodged in the other's presence, and even if the protest was lodged in another country, provided lines of communication between the two countries are open (Rambam *Sefer Mishpatim, Hilkhot To'en VeNitan* 11:5; *Shulḥan Arukh, Ḥoshen Mishpat* 146:1).

דִּסְתָם יְהוּדָה וְגָלִיל כִּשְׁעַת חֵירוּם דָּמוּ.

The Gemara answers: The reason that the *tanna* cited specifically a case where each is located in a different land is **that the standard** situation with regard to travel between **Judea and the Galilee is tantamount to a crisis period,** as war was commonplace, and there was a strip of Samaritan territory between Judea and the Galilee.

וְלִיתְנֵי: מוֹדֶה רַבִּי יְהוֹשֻׁעַ בְּאוֹמֵר לַחֲבֵירוֹ: ״מָנֶה לָוִיתִי מִמְּךָ וּפְרַעְתִּיו לְךָ״ – שֶׁהוּא נֶאֱמָן! מִשּׁוּם דְּקָא בָּעֵי לְמִיתְנֵי סֵיפָא: אִם יֵשׁ עֵדִים שֶׁהוּא לָוָה מִמֶּנּוּ, וְהוּא אוֹמֵר ״פְּרַעְתִּיו״ אֵינוֹ נֶאֱמָן, וְהָא קַיְימָא לַן: הַמַּלְוֶה אֶת חֲבֵירוֹ בְּעֵדִים אֵינוֹ צָרִיךְ לְפָרְעוֹ בְּעֵדִים.

The Gemara asks: **And let** the *tanna* **teach** in the mishna: **And Rabbi Yehoshua concedes in** a case where **one says to another: I borrowed one hundred** dinars **from you and repaid** the loan **to you, that he is deemed credible.** The Gemara answers: The *tanna* chose not to teach that case of the mouth that prohibited is the mouth that permitted **due to** the fact **that** the *tanna* **wanted to teach in the latter clause: If there are witnesses that he borrowed** money **from** another, **and he says: I repaid** the loan, **he is not deemed credible.** However, the *tanna* would not be able to distinguish between a case where witnesses testify and a case where there are no witnesses, **as don't we hold** that in the case of **one who lends** money to **another in** the presence of **witnesses,** the borrower **need not repay** the loan **in** the presence of **witnesses?**[H] Therefore, even if witnesses testify that he took the loan, his claim that he repaid the loan is accepted.

וְלִיתְנֵי: מוֹדֶה רַבִּי יְהוֹשֻׁעַ בְּאוֹמֵר לַחֲבֵירוֹ: ״מָנֶה לְאָבִיךָ בְּיָדִי וְהֶאֱכַלְתִּיו פְּרָס״ – שֶׁהוּא נֶאֱמָן!

The Gemara asks: **And let** the *tanna* **teach** in the mishna: **And Rabbi Yehoshua concedes in** a case where **one says to another: Your father has one hundred dinars in my possession**[H] in the form of a loan, **but I provided him** with repayment of **half** that amount, that **his** claim is **deemed credible.**

אַלִּיבָּא דְּמַאן? אִי אַלִּיבָּא דְּרַבָּנַן – הָא אָמְרִי מֵשִׁיב אֲבֵידָה הָוֵי, אִי אַלִּיבָּא דְּרַבִּי אֱלִיעֶזֶר בֶּן יַעֲקֹב – הָא אָמַר שְׁבוּעָה בָּעֵי.

The Gemara answers: There is a tannaitic dispute with regard to that case and the case that the Gemara suggested does not correspond to either opinion. **In accordance with whose** opinion would the mishna be taught? **If** it is **in accordance with** the opinion **of the Rabbis, didn't they say** that in that case **he is** the equivalent of **one returning a lost article?**[N] Since the son is unaware that the borrower owes his father money, and the borrower takes the initiative and admits that he owes part of the sum that he borrowed, it is as if he returned a lost article, and clearly his claim is accepted and no oath is required. **And if** it is **in accordance with** the opinion **of Rabbi Eliezer ben Ya'akov, didn't he say** that in that case the borrower is **required** to take **an oath,** and only then is his claim accepted?

דְּתַנְיָא, רַבִּי אֱלִיעֶזֶר בֶּן יַעֲקֹב אוֹמֵר: פְּעָמִים שֶׁאָדָם נִשְׁבָּע עַל טַעֲנַת עַצְמוֹ. כֵּיצַד? ״מָנֶה לְאָבִיךָ בְּיָדִי וְהֶאֱכַלְתִּיו פְּרָס״ – הֲרֵי זֶה נִשְׁבָּע, וְזֶהוּ שֶׁנִּשְׁבָּע עַל טַעֲנַת עַצְמוֹ, וַחֲכָמִים אוֹמְרִים: אֵינוֹ אֶלָּא כְּמֵשִׁיב אֲבֵידָה, וּפָטוּר.

This dispute is **as it is taught** in a *baraita* that **Rabbi Eliezer ben Ya'akov says:** There are **times when** although no one claimed that another owes him money, **a person takes an oath on** the basis of **his own claim. How** so? If one says to another: **Your father has one hundred dinars in my possession, but I provided him** with repayment of **half** that amount, **he** is required to **take an oath** that he repaid half, **and that is** the case of one **who takes an oath on** the basis of **his own claim. And the Rabbis say:** In that case **he is merely** the **equivalent of one returning a lost article, and is exempt** from taking an oath.

וְרַבִּי אֱלִיעֶזֶר בֶּן יַעֲקֹב לֵית לֵיהּ מֵשִׁיב אֲבֵידָה פָּטוּר? אָמַר רַב: בְּטוֹעֲנוֹ קָטָן. וְהָאָמַר מָר: אֵין נִשְׁבָּעִין עַל טַעֲנַת חֵרֵשׁ שׁוֹטֶה וְקָטָן!

The Gemara asks: **And is Rabbi Eliezer ben Ya'akov not of** the opinion that **one who returns a lost article is exempt from taking an oath** that he did not take part of the sum? He returns what he admitted taking without an oath. **Rav says:** The *baraita* is referring to a case **where a minor makes a claim** against **him.** The lender's minor son claims that the borrower did not repay any part of the loan to his father. The borrower's claim comes in response to that claim. Therefore, his admission is not at all comparable to returning a lost article. The Gemara asks: **But didn't the Master say: One does not take an oath on** the basis of **the claim of a deaf-mute, an imbecile, or a minor?**[HB] Due to their lack of cognition, they are not deemed halakhically competent to require another to take an oath based on their claim.

HALAKHA

In the case of one who lends money…in the presence of witnesses, the borrower need not repay the loan in the presence of witnesses – הַמַּלְוֶה...בְּעֵדִים אֵינוֹ צָרִיךְ לְפָרְעוֹ בְּעֵדִים: If one lends money in the presence of witnesses, without a document or an act of acquisition, the money need not be returned in the presence of witnesses. Therefore, if the borrower claims that he repaid the debt, he is deemed credible without witnesses, although by rabbinic law he must take an oath of inducement (Rambam *Sefer Mishpatim*, *Hilkhot Malve VeLoveh* 11:1; *Shulḥan Arukh*, *Ḥoshen Mishpat* 70:1).

Your father has one hundred dinars in my possession – מָנֶה לְאָבִיךָ בְּיָדִי: If one says to another: My father told me that he lent you one hundred dinars, and the borrower replies: I owe only fifty, the borrower is the equivalent of one who returns a lost object, and he is exempt from paying the other fifty and even exempt from taking an oath of inducement. This is all the more so true if the borrower comes forward of his own volition and says: I borrowed one hundred dinars from your father and repaid fifty.

The Ra'avad, however, rules that the borrower is deemed credible if he takes an oath by Torah law, in accordance with the opinion of Rabbi Eliezer ben Ya'akov, as the *halakha* is always ruled in accordance with his opinion. Others note that Rabbi Eliezer ben Ya'akov requires an oath only when the son made a claim with certainty, i.e., if he witnessed the loan himself. Otherwise the borrower is deemed credible. According to that explanation, the Rambam's ruling is in accordance with all opinions (Rambam *Sefer Mishpatim*, *Hilkhot To'en VeNitan* 4:5; *Shulḥan Arukh*, *Ḥoshen* 75:3).

One does not take an oath on the basis of the claim of a deaf-mute, an imbecile, or a minor – אֵין נִשְׁבָּעִין עַל טַעֲנַת חֵרֵשׁ שׁוֹטֶה וְקָטָן: One does not impose an oath by Torah law based on a partial admission in response to a claim made by a deaf-mute, an imbecile, or a minor, whether the claim is on their own behalf or on behalf of their father. If a minor claims: You borrowed one hundred dinars from my father, and the borrower claims that he owes only fifty dinars, he is exempt by Torah law from taking an oath (Rambam *Sefer Mishpatim*, *Hilkhot To'en VeNitan* 5:9; *Shulḥan Arukh*, *Ḥoshen* 96:1).

NOTES

One returning a lost article – מֵשִׁיב אֲבֵידָה: Rashi and *Tosafot* disagree with regard to the reason behind this *halakha* that one returning a lost object is not obligated to take an oath. According to Rashi, fundamentally, one is required to take an oath. However, the Sages instituted an ordinance for the betterment of the world exempting him from taking that oath, as otherwise people would refrain from returning lost items. According to *Tosafot*, however, the reason is based on the principle of *miggo*, as he could have refrained from returning the article at all.

BACKGROUND

A deaf-mute, an imbecile, or a minor – חֵרֵשׁ שׁוֹטֶה וְקָטָן: Members of these three categories are frequently grouped together because of their actual or presumed limited intellectual capacity or their inability to act responsibly. They are not obligated to perform mitzvot, nor are they held responsible for any damage they may cause. They also lack the legal capacity to act as agents. Although all three are often mentioned together, there are many differences between the *halakhot* governing each of them.

מַאי קָטָן – גָּדוֹל, וְאַמַּאי קָרֵי לֵיהּ קָטָן – דִּלְגַבֵּי מִילֵּי דְּאָבִיו קָטָן הוּא. אִי הָכִי, טַעֲנַת עַצְמוֹ?! טַעֲנַת אֲחֵרִים הִיא! טַעֲנַת אֲחֵרִים וְהוֹדָאַת עַצְמוֹ.

The Gemara answers: In Rav's statement, **what** is the meaning of **minor?** It means one who reached **majority,** and is therefore halakhically competent. **And why does** Rav **call him a minor?** It is due to the fact **that with regard to his father's matters, he is** the equivalent of **a minor,** as he is uncertain about the particulars of his father's dealings. **If so,** i.e., that the son making the claim has already reached majority, the language of the *baraita* is imprecise. Why does the *tanna* refer to this case as one taking an oath on the basis of **his own claim?** This is not his own claim; it **is the claim of others.** The Gemara answers: The *baraita* employed that language for the following reason: It **is the claim of others, but** he is taking an oath on the basis of **his own** partial **admission.**

כּוּלְּהִי טַעֲנָתָא טַעֲנַת אֲחֵרִים וְהוֹדָאַת עַצְמוֹ נִינְהוּ!

The Gemara asks: **All claims** where an oath is required **are** cases of **a claim of others and his own admission.** However, in the *baraita*, Rabbi Eliezer ben Ya'akov introduces his opinion with the phrase: There are times, indicating that the case to which he is referring, that of one taking an oath on the basis of his own claim, is not the standard case of taking an oath.

אֶלָּא הָכָא בִּדְרַבָּה קָמִיפַּלְגִי. דְּאָמַר רַבָּה: מִפְּנֵי מָה אָמְרָה תּוֹרָה מוֹדֶה מִקְצָת הַטַּעֲנָה יִשָּׁבַע – חֲזָקָה, אֵין אָדָם מֵעִיז פָּנָיו בִּפְנֵי בַּעַל חוֹבוֹ. וְהַאי בְּכוּלָּהּ בָּעֵי דְּלִכְפְּרֵיהּ, וְהַאי דְּלָא כָּפַר לֵיהּ – מִשּׁוּם דְּאֵין אָדָם מֵעִיז פָּנָיו הוּא,

Rather, the Gemara suggests an alternative explanation of the tannaitic dispute. **Here,** Rabbi Eliezer ben Ya'akov and the Rabbis **disagree with regard to** the statement of **Rabba,**[N] **as Rabba said: Why did the Torah say**[N] **that** one who **makes a partial admission** in response to **the claim** is required to **take an oath?** It is because there is a **presumption** that **a person** would **not be so insolent**[N] **in the presence of his creditor** as to deny his debt. Presumably, **this** borrower who made a partial admission **would have liked to deny the entire** loan, **and** the fact **that he did not deny** the entire loan **is due to** the fact **that a person** would **not be** so **insolent** in the presence of his creditor.

NOTES

Rather here Rabbi Eliezer ben Ya'akov and the Rabbis disagree with regard to the statement of Rabba – אֶלָּא הָכָא בִּדְרַבָּה קָמִיפַּלְגִי: In this version of the text, which is the version Rashi had, the word rather signifies that the Gemara is retracting the previous explanation that an adult made the claim, and instead explains that the claimant is a minor (see Rashba and *Penei Yehoshua*). Others, however, cite a variant reading in which the word rather does not appear (see Meiri). According to that reading, the claimant remains an adult; however, the Gemara explains the case in a different way (Rashba).

There is an additional opinion, cited in *Shita Mekubbetzet*, based on Rashi's version of the text, but explained differently. The Gemara proceeds to explain the respective opinions of the Rabbis and Rabbi Eliezer ben Ya'akov. The Sages interpret the reasons for mitzvot in accordance with the opinion of Rabbi Shimon, and therefore, they distinguish between the standard case of partial admission and an admission made to a son that one repaid half the amount owed to the father. Rabbi Eliezer ben Ya'akov does not ascribe significance to the reason for the mitzvot. Therefore, the ruling in all cases of partial admission is equal.

Why did the Torah say – מִפְּנֵי מָה אָמְרָה תּוֹרָה: Some say that this is an explanation of why one must take an oath in a case of partial admission and he is not exempt. Based on the principle of *miggo*, he could have denied the entire claim; therefore, his partial admission should be accepted without an oath. The Gemara explains that he could not have totally denied the claim, as a person is not so insolent as to completely deny the debt. Consequently there is no *miggo*. In addition, he is not deemed credible without an oath, even though it is possible that he is just postponing payment until he accrues the requisite funds, since one does not typically repay a debt that he no longer feels the urgency to pay.

The Meiri questions this explanation, as some authorities dispute the basic assumption that a *miggo* exempts one from taking an oath (Ri Migash; Rambam). Furthermore, the Gemara does not appear to be explaining the opinion of the Rabbis; rather, it is providing the reason for the *halakha* in the Torah. Therefore, in his opinion, Rabba's statement comes to explain why the claim of one who totally denies the debt is accepted and no oath is imposed, although one who admits that he owes part of the sum seems more trustworthy, since he is the equivalent of one returning lost property. Rabba explains that since there is a presumption that one would not be so insolent as to deny everything, if he does deny everything, he is deemed credible. However, one who admits that he owes part of the sum is not the equivalent of one returning lost property, as he is clearing his conscience by rationalizing to himself that he is merely postponing repayment of the loan. Therefore, the Torah imposes an oath on him to compel him to admit to the entire sum.

A person would not be so insolent – אֵין אָדָם מֵעִיז פָּנָיו: Rashi explains that a person would not be so insolent to one who did him a favor and lent him money without interest. Others disagree, as an oath in the case of partial admission is imposed in situations where gratitude is not a factor. Therefore other explanations are provided, either similar to that of Rabbeinu Tam, that a person would not be so insolent as to tell a total lie but can rationalize telling a partial truth; or to that of the Riva, that a person would not be so insolent as to lie to one who knows that they are not telling the truth. There are distinct practical halakhic differences between these explanations.

וּבְכוּלָּהּ בָּעֵי דְּלוֹדֵי לֵיהּ, וְהַאי דְּלָא אוֹדֵי לֵיהּ – כִּי הֵיכִי דְּלִישְׁתַּמֵּיט לֵיהּ, וְסָבַר: עַד דַּהֲוָה לִי זוּזֵי וּפָרַעְנָא לֵיהּ. וְרַחֲמָנָא אָמַר: רְמֵי שְׁבוּעָה עֲלֵיהּ כִּי הֵיכִי דְּלוֹדֵי לֵיהּ בְּכוּלֵּיהּ.

And, as a result, **he would have liked to admit to him that** he owes him the **entire** loan. **And** the reason **that he did not admit to him** that he owes him the entire loan is **so that he may** temporarily **avoid** paying **him. And he rationalizes** doing so, saying to himself: I am avoiding him only **until** the time **that I have money, and** then **I will repay him.** Due to the concern that the partial admission is motivated by that rationalization and the claim of the lender is true, **the Merciful One says: Impose an oath upon him so that he will admit that** he owes him the **entire** loan.

רַבִּי אֱלִיעֶזֶר בֶּן יַעֲקֹב סָבַר: לָא שְׁנָא בּוֹ וְלָא שְׁנָא בִּבְנוֹ – אֵינוֹ מֵעִיז, וְהִלְכָּךְ לָאו מֵשִׁיב אֲבֵידָה הָוֵי. וְרַבָּנַן סָבְרִי: בּוֹ הוּא דְּאֵינוֹ מֵעִיז, אֲבָל בִּבְנוֹ מֵעִיז, וּמִדְּלָא הֵעִיז – מֵשִׁיב אֲבֵידָה הָוֵי.

Rabbi Eliezer ben Ya'akov maintains: It is **no different with regard to** the creditor himself, and it is **no different with regard to his son.** The debtor would **not be** so **insolent** as to deny the debt. **And therefore, he is not** considered as **one returning a lost article** on his own initiative. Rather, he is considered as one who partially admits his debt in response to a claim, and is therefore required to take an oath. **However, the Rabbis maintain: In** the presence of the creditor one would **not be insolent, but in** the presence of **his son,** who did not lend him the money, **he** would be **insolent** and deny the claim entirely. Since he had the option of completely denying the loan and opted to admit to part of the claim, **he is** considered as **one returning a lost article** and his claim is accepted without an oath.

מתני׳ הָעֵדִים שֶׁאָמְרוּ: כְּתַב יָדֵינוּ הוּא זֶה, אֲבָל אֲנוּסִים הָיִינוּ, קְטַנִּים הָיִינוּ, פְּסוּלֵי עֵדוּת הָיִינוּ – הֲרֵי אֵלּוּ נֶאֱמָנִים. וְאִם יֵשׁ עֵדִים שֶׁהוּא כְּתַב יָדָם, אוֹ שֶׁהָיָה כְּתַב יָדָם יוֹצֵא מִמָּקוֹם אַחֵר – אֵינָן נֶאֱמָנִין.

MISHNA With regard to **the witnesses who said** in their testimony to ratify their signatures in a document: We signed the document and **this is our handwriting;**[H] **however, we were compelled** to sign,[H] or **we were minors** when we signed, or **we were disqualified witnesses,** e.g., we are relatives of one of the parties, **they are deemed credible.** Since the document is ratified on the basis of their testimony, it is likewise invalidated on the basis of their testimony. **However, if there are** other **witnesses** who testify **that it is their handwriting, or if their handwriting emerges** on a document **from another place,** enabling confirmation of their signatures by comparing the two documents, then the witnesses who signed the document **are not deemed credible.** The document is not invalidated based on their testimony, because ratification of the document is not dependent on their testimony, as their signatures can be authenticated independently.

גמ׳ אָמַר רָמִי בַּר חָמָא: לֹא שָׁנוּ אֶלָּא שֶׁאָמְרוּ ״אֲנוּסִים הָיִינוּ מֵחֲמַת מָמוֹן״, אֲבָל ״אֲנוּסִים הָיִינוּ מֵחֲמַת נְפָשׁוֹת״ – הֲרֵי אֵלּוּ נֶאֱמָנִין.

GEMARA With regard to the latter clause in the mishna, in which it is stated that if there is independent corroboration of the signatures of the witnesses the document is not invalidated based on their testimony, **Rami bar Ḥama says:** The Sages **taught** this *halakha* **only** in a case **where they said: We were compelled** to sign the document **due to a monetary** threat.[N] Their testimony incriminates them, as they testified falsely for money, and the principle is: The testimony of one who incriminates himself is not accepted. **However, if** the witnesses **said: We were compelled** to sign the document **due to** a threat to our **lives, they are deemed credible,** as that testimony is not self-incriminating, since in that case it is permitted to testify falsely.

אֲמַר לֵיהּ רָבָא: כָּל כְּמִינֵּיהּ?! כֵּיוָן שֶׁהִגִּיד – שׁוּב אֵינוֹ חוֹזֵר וּמַגִּיד. וְכִי תֵּימָא: הָנֵי מִילֵּי – עַל פֶּה, אֲבָל בִּשְׁטָר – לָא, וְהָא אָמַר רֵישׁ לָקִישׁ: עֵדִים הַחֲתוּמִים עַל הַשְּׁטָר – נַעֲשָׂה כְּמִי שֶׁנֶּחְקְרָה עֵדוּתָן בְּבֵית דִּין!

Rava said to Rami bar Ḥama: **Is it within their power** to retract their testimony? There is a principle: **Once a** witness **stated** his testimony in court, **he cannot again state** testimony[H] that contradicts his previous testimony. **And if you say** that this principle applies specifically to **oral testimony, but** with regard to **testimony in a document, no,** the principle does not apply and one may retract that testimony, **didn't Reish Lakish say:** The legal status of **witnesses who are signatories on the document**[H] **becomes like those whose testimony was** cross-**examined in court.** Therefore, just as one may not retract oral testimony, neither may he retract written testimony.

HALAKHA

The witnesses who said, this is our handwriting – הָעֵדִים שֶׁאָמְרוּ כְּתַב יָדֵינוּ הוּא זֶה: In a case where witnesses sign a document and later admit that it is their handwriting but add that when they signed the document they were minors or relatives of one of the parties involved and therefore disqualified witnesses, or that they were compelled to sign the document; if they are the only source authenticating their signatures, their testimony is accepted. However, if there is independent authentication of their signatures, e.g., by comparison to other documents or by other witnesses, their statements are not accepted (Rambam *Sefer Shofetim, Hilkhot Edut* 3:6; *Shulḥan Arukh, Ḥoshen Mishpat* 46:37).

We were compelled to sign – אֲנוּסִים הָיִינוּ: In a case where witnesses authenticate their signatures, and there is no independent authentication, and the witnesses claim that they were compelled to sign the document, then, if they were compelled to sign the document due to a threat to their lives, their claim is accepted. However, if they were compelled to sign the document due to a monetary threat, their claim is not accepted, in accordance with the version of the statement of Rami bar Ḥama adopted in the conclusion of the Gemara (Rambam *Sefer Shofetim, Hilkhot Edut* 3:6; *Shulḥan Arukh, Ḥoshen Mishpat* 46:37).

Once a witness stated his testimony in court he cannot again state testimony – כֵּיוָן שֶׁהִגִּיד, שׁוּב אֵינוֹ חוֹזֵר וּמַגִּיד: Once a witness completes his testimony, he may not retract that testimony, unless he does so without pause between the statement and the retraction (*Shulḥan Arukh, Ḥoshen Mishpat* 29:1, and in the comment of Rema).

Witnesses who are signatories on the document – עֵדִים הַחֲתוּמִים עַל הַשְּׁטָר: The legal status of the signatures of witnesses on a document is like that of the oral testimony of witnesses who were cross-examined in court. Therefore, after signing a document, witnesses may not retract their testimony (Rambam *Sefer Shofetim, Hilkhot Edut* 3:6).

NOTES

We were compelled to sign the document due to a monetary threat – אֲנוּסִים הָיִינוּ מֵחֲמַת מָמוֹן: In this first version of Rami bar Ḥama's statement, there are several difficulties, some of which remain after the conclusion of the Gemara. From Rami bar Ḥama's statement it is clear that after signing the document the witnesses can contradict that testimony when they say that they were compelled to sign the document due to a threat to their lives. The Ramban asks: If Rami bar Ḥama holds that once a witness stated his testimony in writing he can again state testimony in court, why are they not able to testify that they were relatives or minors? And if they cannot testify in that case, they should not be allowed to testify that they were compelled by a threat to their lives. The Ramban answers that according to the first version of his statement, Rami bar Ḥama is of the opinion that once a witness stated his testimony in writing, he can again state testimony, in court. The reason they are not deemed credible when they claim to be relatives is that they are incriminating themselves with that claim (see Ritva).

The Rashba explains Rami bar Ḥama's statement in a slightly different manner: The reason that their claim is not accepted according to Rami bar Ḥama is that they are describing an unlikely scenario, because the lender himself initially ascertains that the witnesses are fit to testify and only then has them sign on the document, as the Gemara explains later in the context of analyzing the opinion of Rabbi Meir.

אֶלָּא, כִּי אִתְּמַר – אַרֵישָׁא אִתְּמַר: הֲרֵי אֵלּוּ נֶאֱמָנִין, אָמַר רָמִי בַּר חָמָא: לֹא שָׁנוּ אֶלָּא שֶׁאָמְרוּ: ״אֲנוּסִין הָיִינוּ מֵחֲמַת נְפָשׁוֹת״ אֲבָל אָמְרוּ: ״אֲנוּסִין הָיִינוּ מֵחֲמַת מָמוֹן״ – אֵין נֶאֱמָנִין. מַאי טַעֲמָא – אֵין אָדָם מֵשִׂים עַצְמוֹ רָשָׁע.

Rather, **when** the statement of Rami bar Ḥama **is stated, it is stated with regard to the first clause** of the mishna, that if there is no independent corroboration of their signatures **they are deemed credible. Rami bar Ḥama said:** The Sages **taught** this *halakha* **only** in a case **where** the witnesses **said: We were compelled** to sign the document **due to** a threat to our **lives,** as in that case they do not incriminate themselves. **However,** if the witnesses **said: We were compelled** to sign the document **due to a monetary** threat, **they are not deemed credible. What is the reason** that they are not deemed credible? It is based on the principle: **One does not render himself wicked,** and self-incriminating testimony is not accepted.

תָּנוּ רַבָּנַן: אֵין נֶאֱמָנִים לְפוֹסְלוֹ, דִּבְרֵי רַבִּי מֵאִיר. וַחֲכָמִים אוֹמְרִים: נֶאֱמָנִים. בִּשְׁלָמָא לְרַבָּנַן – כִּי טַעֲמַיְיהוּ, שֶׁהַפֶּה שֶׁאָסַר הוּא הַפֶּה שֶׁהִתִּיר. אֶלָּא לְרַבִּי מֵאִיר – מַאי טַעֲמָא? בִּשְׁלָמָא פְּסוּלֵי עֵדוּת – מַלְוֶה גּוּפֵיהּ מֵעִיקָּרָא מֵידָק דָּיֵיק וּמַחְתָּם, קְטַנִּים נַמִי – כִּדְרַבִּי שִׁמְעוֹן בֶּן לָקִישׁ, דְּאָמַר רֵישׁ לָקִישׁ:

§ **The Sages taught:** Witnesses who testify to invalidate their signatures on a document **are not deemed credible to invalidate** the document; this is **the statement of Rabbi Meir. And the Rabbis say: They are deemed credible.** The Gemara asks: **Granted,** according **to the Rabbis,** their opinion corresponds to **their reasoning** stated previously: **The mouth that prohibited** it, i.e., ratified the document, **is the mouth that permitted** it, i.e., invalidated the promissory note. **However,** according **to Rabbi Meir, what is the reason** that their testimony to invalidate the document is not accepted? **Granted,** their testimony that they were **disqualified witnesses** is not accepted, as **the lender himself initially ascertains** that the witnesses are fit to testify **and** only then **signs** them on the document. **Similarly,** according to Rabbi Meir, their testimony that they were **minors** is **also** not accepted, **in accordance with** the statement of **Rabbi Shimon ben Lakish, as Reish Lakish said:**

Perek **II**
Daf **19** Amud **a**

חֲזָקָה, אֵין הָעֵדִים חוֹתְמִין עַל הַשְּׁטָר אֶלָּא אִם כֵּן נַעֲשָׂה בְּגָדוֹל, אֶלָּא אֲנוּסִין מַאי טַעֲמָא?

There is **a presumption that witnesses sign on the document only**[N] **if** the transaction **was made when** both parties to the transaction are **adults.**[H] A corollary of that presumption is that each party would sign only adult witnesses to the document. **However,** if their testimony was that they were **compelled** to sign the document, **what is the reason** that Rabbi Meir rules that their testimony is not accepted?

אָמַר רַב חִסְדָּא: קָסָבַר רַבִּי מֵאִיר: עֵדִים שֶׁאָמְרוּ לָהֶם ״חִתְמוּ שֶׁקֶר וְאַל תֵּהָרְגוּ״ – יֵהָרְגוּ וְאַל יַחְתְּמוּ שֶׁקֶר,

Rav Ḥisda said that **Rabbi Meir maintains: Witnesses that** others **said to them: Sign** a document containing **a falsehood and** you will **not be killed, should** allow themselves to **be killed and they should not sign** a document containing **a falsehood.**[N] Therefore, even when they testify that they were compelled to sign the document due to a threat to their lives, they are incriminating themselves.

HALAKHA

There is a presumption that witnesses sign on the document only if the transaction was made when both parties are adults – חֲזָקָה, אֵין הָעֵדִים חוֹתְמִין עַל הַשְּׁטָר אֶלָּא אִם כֵּן נַעֲשָׂה בְּגָדוֹל: If the witnesses who signed a document testify that the borrower was a minor when the loan was transacted, they are not deemed credible, as there is a legal presumption that witnesses sign on the document only if the transaction was made when both parties had the status of adults (Rambam *Sefer Mishpatim, Hilkhot Malve VeLoveh* 24:5; *Shulḥan Arukh, Ḥoshen Mishpat* 46:38).

NOTES

Witnesses sign the document only – אֵין הָעֵדִים חוֹתְמִין עַל הַשְּׁטָר אֶלָּא: The question is raised: Why is this additional reason necessary? Ostensibly, the same reason that was cited with regard to disqualified witnesses, i.e., that the lender himself initially ascertains that the witnesses are fit to testify, would have sufficed with regard to minors as well. In *Shita Yeshana*, cited in *Shita Mekubbetzet*, the answer is that although the identity of disqualified witnesses is common knowledge, a minor might appear to have reached majority due to his height, or he might have reached the age of majority without having reached puberty. Therefore, it was necessary to cite the additional reason that witnesses sign the document only when it has been ascertained that the borrower, lender, and witnesses are all adults.

They should be killed and they should not sign a document containing a falsehood – יֵהָרְגוּ וְאַל יַחְתְּמוּ שֶׁקֶר: The early commentaries question this statement, as the widespread consensus is that one is required to give his life and not violate a prohibition only in the case of the three serious offenses of idol worship, forbidden sexual relations, and murder. The Ramban writes that although one is not required to give his life rather than transgress other prohibitions, it is an attribute of piety to do so. Therefore, one could contend that these witnesses incriminate themselves even when they say that they were compelled to sign due to a threat to their lives.

אֲמַר לֵיהּ רָבָא: הָשְׁתָּא, אִילּוּ אָתוּ לְקַמָּן לְאִמְלוּכֵי – אָמְרִינַן לְהוּ: זִילוּ חֲתוּמוּ וְלָא תִּתְקַטְלוּן. דְּאָמַר מָר: אֵין לְךָ דָּבָר שֶׁעוֹמֵד בִּפְנֵי פִּיקּוּחַ נֶפֶשׁ אֶלָּא עֲבוֹדָה זָרָה וְגִלּוּי עֲרָיוֹת וּשְׁפִיכוּת דָּמִים בִּלְבַד. הָשְׁתָּא דַּחֲתַמוּ, אָמְרִינַן לְהוּ אַמַּאי חֲתַמִיתוּ?!

Rava said to him: Now, if the witnesses **came before us to consult** with the Sages, **we say to them: Go sign** the document **and you should not be killed, as the Master said: You have no matter that stands before saving a life,**[H] **other** than **idol worship, forbidden sexual relations, and murder. Now that they signed,** do **we say to them: Why did you sign?** Only in those three cases, when faced with a choice between violating the prohibition and being killed, must one be killed rather than violate the prohibition. Signing a false document does not fall into that category. Why then, according to Rabbi Meir, is their testimony that they were compelled to sign the document not accepted?

אֶלָּא, טַעֲמָא דְּרַבִּי מֵאִיר כִּדְרַב הוּנָא אָמַר רַב. דְּאָמַר רַב הוּנָא אָמַר רַב: מוֹדֶה בִּשְׁטָר שֶׁכְּתָבוֹ אֵין צָרִיךְ לְקַיְּימוֹ.

Rather, the reason for the opinion **of Rabbi Meir is in accordance with** the statement that **Rav Huna said** that **Rav said,**[N] **as Rav Huna said** that **Rav said:** In the case of a borrower who **admits with regard to a document that he wrote it,**[H] the lender **need not ratify** the document in court. Once the borrower admits that he wrote the document, he cannot then claim that it is forged or that the debt was repaid. Similarly, once the witnesses testify that they signed the document, it is a credible document that they cannot then invalidate (*Tosafot*).

גּוּפָא, אָמַר רַב הוּנָא אָמַר רַב: מוֹדֶה בִּשְׁטָר שֶׁכְּתָבוֹ – אֵין צָרִיךְ לְקַיְּימוֹ. אֲמַר לֵיהּ רַב נַחְמָן: גַּנּוּבָא גַּנּוּבֵי לָמָּה לָךְ? אִי סְבִירָא לָךְ כְּרַבִּי מֵאִיר – אֵימָא: הֲלָכָה כְּרַבִּי מֵאִיר!

§ With regard to **the matter itself, Rav Huna said** that **Rav said:** In the case of a borrower who **admits with regard to a document that he wrote it,** the lender **need not ratify** the document in court. **Rav Naḥman said to** Rav Huna: **Why do you** need to **conceal** the reason for your opinion like a **thief? If you hold in accordance with** the opinion of **Rabbi Meir, say: The *halakha* is in accordance with** the opinion of **Rabbi Meir.** Do not state your opinion in a manner that obscures its connection to a tannaitic dispute.

אֲמַר לֵיהּ: וּמָר הֵיכִי סְבִירָא לֵיהּ? אֲמַר לֵיהּ: כִּי אָתוּ לְקַמָּן לְדִינָא אָמְרִינַן לְהוּ: זִילוּ קַיְּימוּ שְׁטָרַיְיכוּ, וְחוּתוּ לְדִינָא.

Rav Huna **said to him: And what does the Master hold** in a case where the borrower admits that he wrote the document? Rav Naḥman **said to him: When** lenders **come before us for judgment, we say to them: Go and ratify your documents and descend** and stand before us **for judgment.** If a lender relies solely on the confession of the borrower, the borrower could claim that although he wrote the document, he then repaid the loan. However, if the document was ratified by the court based on the testimony of the witnesses who signed it, the borrower's claim that he repaid the loan is not accepted.

אָמַר רַב יְהוּדָה אָמַר רַב: הָאוֹמֵר "שְׁטַר אֲמָנָה הוּא זֶה" – אֵינוֹ נֶאֱמָן.

§ **Rav Yehuda said** that **Rav said: One who says** with regard to a document: **This is a document of trust,**[HN] **is not deemed credible.** If one claims that the document is a valid document but that no loan actually took place, and instead the borrower trusted the lender and gave him the document in order to borrow money in the future, or as security, he is not deemed credible.

דְּקָאָמַר מַאן? אִילֵימָא דְּקָאָמַר לֹוֶה – פְּשִׁיטָא, כָּל כְּמִינֵּיהּ?! וְאֶלָּא דְּקָאָמַר מַלְוֶה – תָּבוֹא עָלָיו בְּרָכָה! אֶלָּא, דְּקָאָמְרִי עֵדִים; אִי דִּכְתַב יָדָם יוֹצֵא מִמָּקוֹם אַחֵר – פְּשִׁיטָא דְּלָא מְהֵימְנִי. וְאִי דְּאֵין כְּתַב יָדָם יוֹצֵא מִמָּקוֹם אַחֵר – אַמַּאי לָא מְהֵימְנִי?

The Gemara asks: In the case to **which** Rav's statement is referring, **who is saying** that the document was a document of trust? **If you say** that it is the **borrower who is saying** so, it is **obvious** that he is not deemed credible. **Is it within** the **power** of the borrower to establish that the document is not genuine? **But rather,** say it is the **lender who is saying** that it is a document of trust. In that case, not only is he deemed credible, but **let a blessing come upon him** for admitting that a debt may not be collected with this document. **Rather,** say it is the **witnesses who are saying** that it is a document of trust. If so, the question arises: **If** it is a case **where their handwriting emerges from another place,** it is **obvious** that they are not deemed credible, as the document is ratified. **And if** it is a case **where their handwriting does not emerge from another place,** and the witnesses themselves testify that it is their signatures on the document, but that it was a document of trust, **why are they not deemed credible?** This is a clear case of: The mouth that prohibited is the mouth that permitted.

HALAKHA

You have no matter that stands before saving a life – אֵין לְךָ דָּבָר שֶׁעוֹמֵד בִּפְנֵי פִּיקּוּחַ נֶפֶשׁ: Although there is a mitzva to sanctify the name of God, if someone orders a Jew to violate a Torah prohibition and threatens to kill him if he fails to do so, the Jew should violate the prohibition rather than give his life. This applies to all Torah prohibitions except for idol worship, forbidden sexual relations, and murder. For these he is required to give his life rather than violate the prohibition. In certain circumstances, one is required to give his life rather than violate other prohibitions as well (Rambam *Sefer HaMadda, Hilkhot Yesodei HaTorah* 5:1).

A borrower who admits with regard to a document that he wrote it – מוֹדֶה בִּשְׁטָר שֶׁכְּתָבוֹ: Even if the debtor admits that he wrote a promissory note, the creditor is required to ratify the document. If he fails to ratify the document, the debtor can claim that he repaid the loan, in accordance with the opinion of the Rabbis and the statement of Rav Naḥman (Rambam *Sefer Mishpatim, Hilkhot Malve VeLoveh* 14:5; *Shulḥan Arukh, Ḥoshen Mishpat* 82:1).

One who says, this is a document of trust – הָאוֹמֵר שְׁטַר אֲמָנָה הוּא זֶה: In a case where a creditor admits that a promissory note in his possession is a document of trust, and that there was no loan, then if he owes money to others, and unless he collects the debt he will be unable to repay his debt, and the document was ratified in court or was in the possession of a third party, that admission is not deemed credible, in accordance with Abaye's explanation of Rav Yehuda's statement (Rambam *Sefer Mishpatim, Hilkhot Malve VeLoveh* 2:6; *Shulḥan Arukh, Ḥoshen Mishpat* 47:1).

NOTES

The reason for the opinion of Rabbi Meir is in accordance with the statement that Rav Huna said that Rav said – טַעֲמָא דְּרַבִּי מֵאִיר כִּדְרַב הוּנָא אָמַר רַב: Both in terms of language and in terms of content (see *Tosafot*), Rabbi Meir's statement does not precisely correspond to the opinion of Rav Huna. First, there is a distinction between witnesses and the borrower, as the testimony of witnesses is more authoritative than the statement of the borrower. Second, since the requirement to ratify the documents is by rabbinic law, the signatures on the document constitute a full-fledged proof (Rashba). However, fundamentally, the two opinions are similar.

Rashi has a different opinion and explains the case here as one where the borrower admitted that he wrote the document, obviating the need for the testimony of witnesses. Therefore, the opinions of Rabbi Meir and Rav Huna correspond.

A document of trust – שְׁטַר אֲמָנָה: Rashi explains that this is a document the borrower gives a potential lender before receiving a loan, where the borrower relies on the lender that he will lend him the money at a later date. However, *Tosefot Rid* disputes this and concludes that it is a document drafted to create the impression that the borrower is wealthy, as it enables him to claim that he borrowed money and is in possession of assets, similar to a document of security cited later (19b). The *ge'onim* combine both explanations.

The Meiri explains that a document of trust is one initially drafted with intention to deceive. In a case where one borrows money and does not want to repay, he writes another document creating the impression that he owes money to another, and therefore claims that he does not have funds available to repay the actual loan. According to this explanation, the term injustice used in reference to this document is appropriate.

HALAKHA

A creditor seeks to collect a debt…from another, and the other person seeks to collect a debt from another – נוֹשֶׁה בַּחֲבֵירוֹ...וַחֲבֵירוֹ בַּחֲבֵירוֹ: If a debtor owes money to a creditor, and that creditor owes that amount to another creditor, the money is paid directly from the first debtor to the second creditor, regardless of the order in which the two loans took place, in accordance with the opinion of Rabbi Natan, as, based on the Gemara in tractate *Pesaḥim* (31a), that is Rava's ruling in his dispute with Abaye (*Tosafot*; Rambam *Sefer Mishpatim*, *Hilkhot Malve VeLoveh* 2:6; *Shulḥan Arukh*, *Ḥoshen Mishpat* 86:1).

(סִימָן בא״ש) אֲמַר רָבָא: לְעוֹלָם דְּקָאָמַר לֹוֶה, וְכִדְרַב הוּנָא. דְּאָמַר רַב הוּנָא אָמַר רַב: מוֹדֶה בִּשְׁטָר שֶׁכְּתָבוֹ – אֵין צָרִיךְ לְקַיְּימוֹ.

The Gemara provides **a mnemonic** for the names of the *amora'im* who seek to explain Rav's statement and resolve the problem: ***Beit***, the second letter in the name of Rava; ***alef***, the first letter in Abaye; and ***shin***, the second letter in the name of Rav Ashi. **Rava said: Actually,** it is **the borrower who is saying it, and** it can be explained **in accordance with** the statement of **Rav Huna, as Rav Huna said** that **Rav said:** In the case of a borrower who **admits with regard to a document that he wrote it,** the lender **need not ratify** the document in court. In this case, the borrower admits that he wrote the document and had witnesses sign the document. Rav Yehuda teaches the novel *halakha* that although the borrower later contends that it was a document of trust, once he admits that he wrote the document, that contention is not accepted.

אַבַּיֵּי אֲמַר: לְעוֹלָם דַּאֲמַר מַלְוֶה, וּכְגוֹן שֶׁחָב לַאֲחֵרִים, וּכִדְרַבִּי נָתָן.

Abaye said: Actually, it is **the lender who said** it, **and** it is in a case **where he causes loss to others** by invalidating the document and relinquishing his debt. If the lender owes money to others and lacks funds to repay his debt, then his invalidation of the document creates a situation where his creditor is unable to collect the debt. This is **in accordance with** the opinion of **Rabbi Natan.**

דְּתַנְיָא, רַבִּי נָתָן אוֹמֵר: מִנַּיִן לְנוֹשֶׁה בַּחֲבֵירוֹ מָנֶה, וַחֲבֵירוֹ בַּחֲבֵירוֹ, מִנַּיִן שֶׁמּוֹצִיאִין מִזֶּה וְנוֹתְנִין לָזֶה – תַּלְמוּד לוֹמַר ״וְנָתַן לַאֲשֶׁר אָשַׁם לוֹ״.

As it is taught in a *baraita* that **Rabbi Natan says: From where** is it derived that in a case where **a creditor** seeks to collect a debt **of one hundred dinars from another, and the other** person seeks to collect a debt **from another,**[H] **from where** is it derived **that one takes** money **from this** second debtor **and gives it to the** first creditor without the money passing through the debtor of the first, who is the creditor of the third? It is derived as **the verse states: "And he shall give to the one to whom he is guilty"** (Numbers 5:7). One pays the person to whom the money is owed, even if he did not borrow the money directly from him. When the debtor of the first who is the creditor of the third invalidates the document, he causes a loss to his own creditor.

רַב אַשִׁי אֲמַר: לְעוֹלָם דְּקָאָמְרִי עֵדִים, וּדְאֵין כְּתַב יָדָם יוֹצֵא מִמָּקוֹם אַחֵר. וּדְקָאָמְרַתְּ אַמַּאי לָא מְהֵימְנֵי – כִּדְרַב כָּהֲנָא, דְּאָמַר רַב כָּהֲנָא: אָסוּר לוֹ לְאָדָם שֶׁיַּשְׁהֶה שְׁטַר אֲמָנָה בְּתוֹךְ בֵּיתוֹ, מִשּׁוּם שֶׁנֶּאֱמַר ״אַל תַּשְׁכֵּן בְּאֹהָלֶיךָ עַוְלָה״.

Rav Ashi said: Actually, it is **the witnesses who are saying** it, **and** it is a case **where their handwriting does not emerge from another place. And** with regard to **that which you are saying: Why are they not deemed credible,** it is **in accordance with** the opinion of **Rav Kahana, as Rav Kahana said: It is prohibited for a person to keep a document of trust in his house, as it is stated:** "And **let not injustice dwell in your tents"** (Job 11:14). This false document is likely to engender injustice when the lender seeks to collect payment with it.

Perek **II**
Daf **19** Amud **b**

וַאֲמַר רַב שֵׁשֶׁת בְּרֵיהּ דְּרַב אִידִי: שְׁמַע מִינָּהּ מִדְּרַב כָּהֲנָא, עֵדִים שֶׁאָמְרוּ: ״אֲמָנָה הָיוּ דְּבָרֵינוּ״ אֵין נֶאֱמָנִין. מַאי טַעֲמָא – כֵּיוָן דְּעַוְלָה הוּא, אַעַוְלָה לָא חָתְמֵי.

And Rav Sheshet, son of Rav Idi, says: Conclude from the statement of Rav Kahana that **witnesses who said: Our statement was** a statement of **trust,**[H] and the document we signed was a document of trust, **are not deemed credible. What is the reason? Since** that document **is an injustice, they** would **not sign** a document of **injustice.** Their contention that they signed the document would incriminate them and is therefore not accepted.

HALAKHA

Our statement was a statement of trust – אֲמָנָה הָיוּ דְּבָרֵינוּ: If the witnesses authenticate their signatures on a document but claim that the document is a document of trust, they are not deemed credible, even in a case where there is no independent authentication of the document, in accordance with the opinion of Rav Sheshet, son of Rav Idi; Rav Naḥman; and Mar bar Rav Ashi (Rambam *Sefer Shofetim*, *Hilkhot Edut* 3:7; *Shulḥan Arukh*, *Ḥoshen Mishpat* 46:37).

אמר רבי יהושע בן לוי: אסור לו לאדם שישהה שטר פרוע בתוך ביתו, משום שנאמר "אל תשכן באהליך עולה". במערבא משמיה דרב אמרי: "אם און בידך הרחיקהו" – זה שטר אמנה ושטר פסים: "ואל תשכן באהליך עולה" – זה שטר פרוע.

Rabbi Yehoshua ben Levi said: It is prohibited for a person to keep a repaid document within his house,[H] **due to** the fact **that the verse states:** "And **let not injustice dwell in your tents**" (Job 11:14). Even if he does not use the document to collect payment, the concern is that it might fall into the hands of one who will use it illegally to collect payment. **In the West,** in Eretz Yisrael, **they say in the name of Rav:** With regard to the first half of the verse: **"If iniquity be in your hand, put it far away"** (Job 11:14),[N] **this** is referring to **a document of trust and a document of security** [*passim*].[NL] With regard to the second half of the verse: **"And let not injustice dwell in your tents," this** is referring to **a repaid document.**

מאן דאמר שטר פרוע – כל שכן שטר אמנה, ומאן דאמר שטר אמנה – אבל שטר פרוע לא, דזמנין דמשהי ליה אפשיטי דספרא.

They note: With regard to **the one who said** that **a repaid document** is the injustice referred to in the verse, **all the more so a document of trust** is an injustice and may not be kept, as a document of trust is fundamentally false. **And** with regard to **the one who said** that a **document of trust** is the injustice referred to in the verse, **however,** with regard to **a repaid document,** perhaps it is permitted to keep it, **as, at times** people **keep it** and do not return it to the borrower. This is because in those cases it serves as security **for the coins of the scribe,** whose fee has not yet been paid by the borrower, who is legally responsible to pay the scribe for writing the document.

איתמר, ספר שאינו מוגה, אמר רבי אמי עד שלשים יום מותר לשהותו, מכאן ואילך – אסור לשהותו, משום שנאמר "אל תשכן באהליך עולה".

On a similar note **it is stated,** with regard to keeping items with potential to lead to transgression: With regard to a Torah **scroll that is not proofread**[H] and therefore contains errors, **Rabbi Ami says: It is permitted to keep it** without emending the mistakes for **up to thirty days,** and **from that time onward it is prohibited to keep it, as it is stated:** "And **let not injustice dwell in your tents**" (Job 11:14).

אמר רב נחמן: עדים שאמרו "אמנה היו דברינו" – אין נאמנין: "מודעא היו דברינו" – אין נאמנין. מר בר רב אשי אמר: אמנה היו דברינו" – אין נאמנין, מודעא היו דברינו" – נאמנין. מאי טעמא? האי ניתן ליכתב, והאי לא ניתן ליכתב.

§ **Rav Naḥman said** that **witnesses who say: Our statement was** a statement of **trust** and we signed a document of trust, **are not deemed credible.** Similarly, witnesses who said: **Our statement was** a statement accompanied by **a declaration**[NH] by the person who is rendered a debtor by this document that he was coerced into the agreement, thereby invalidating the document, **are not deemed credible. Mar bar Rav Ashi said** that witnesses who said: **Our statement was** a statement of **trust, are not deemed credible,** but witnesses who said: **Our statement was** a statement accompanied by **a declaration, are deemed credible. What is the reason** for the difference between the cases? **This** document, which was accompanied by a declaration, **may be written,**[N] as it is written under duress. **And this** document of trust **may not be written,** as it is fundamentally unjust.

NOTES

If iniquity be in your hand, put it far away – אם און בידך הרחיקהו: *Tosafot* explain that the distinction between the different documents is deliberate. "If iniquity be in your hand" refers to documents of trust and security, which have no substance and are false from the outset. "And let not injustice dwell in your tents" refers to a paid document, which initially was substantive and now can lead to injustice. Along similar lines, Maharam Schiff adds that the term "put it far away" is appropriate for a document of trust, which should not have been in his house from the outset. Similarly, the phrase "let not injustice dwell in your tents" is appropriate for a repaid document, as, although it was initially legitimate to possess it, it is prohibited to keep it after the debt was repaid.

Document of security – שטר פסים: Some explain that this is a document that one drafts to prevent another from gaining possession of her property, e.g., a woman who writes a document fictitiously transferring her property to another to prevent her husband from gaining possession of it (Rashi on *Ketubot* 99a). Based on the formulation in the Jerusalem Talmud, this is a document given as security for a debt. The Meiri explains that it is a document that one requests to be written to create the impression that he is wealthy, similar to a document of trust. The difference is that the document of trust is given by the borrower to the lender, and the document of security is given by the lender to the borrower.

Our statement was a statement accompanied by a declaration – מודעא היו דברינו: There are two explanations for the problem with testimony stating that there was an accompanying declaration. Some say that oral testimony lacks the authority to nullify a written document (Rashi; *Tosafot*; Rashba). Others explain that because the witnesses knew that this document involved injustice, as the one obligated by the document did not actually want it written, they should not have signed it. Therefore, their claim that it is a document accompanied by a declaration is self-incriminating, and they are not deemed credible to incriminate themselves (Rid; Ran; Rosh). The Meiri writes, citing the early Spanish commentaries, that the discussion here is with regard to a declaration concerning a sale or a gift, where it is possible to contend that one does not perform a transgression by signing the document. However, if they signed a bill of divorce, where the Sages explicitly prohibited issuing a declaration to invalidate a bill of divorce, everyone agrees that they are not deemed credible to say that their statement was accompanied by a declaration.

This may be written – האי ניתן ליכתב: Most commentaries explain that the document may be written despite the declaration, as, if the transaction in the document was made under duress, and the witnesses must be aware of the nature of this duress, the compelled party had no alternative but to do what he did, and therefore writing and signing the document was legitimate (Rashi; Rabbeinu Ḥananel). In the Jerusalem Talmud, it is related that Rav Yirmeya and others signed both the declaration and the document that the declaration undermined. Others explain, citing Rav Nissim Gaon, that the reason that in the case of a declaration the document may be written is that once he informed the witnesses that he was about to write a document under duress, the witnesses could sign the document as a document accompanied by a declaration. In addition, if a separate document of declaration is written and signed before the other document is, everyone agrees that it invalidates the second document. Therefore, they are deemed credible when they testify orally that there was a declaration. The Meiri holds that these two explanations are complementary, while the Ran holds that there is a halakhic difference between them.

LANGUAGE

Document of security [*passim*] – שטר פסים: Some explain that *passim* is related to the term *piyyus*, meaning appeasement, as the document serves to make one amenable to lend another money. However, according to the version in the Jerusalem Talmud, the correct reading is a document of *pastis*, from the Greek πίστις, *pistis*, meaning trust, in which case it is identical to a document of trust.

HALAKHA

It is prohibited for a person to keep a repaid document within his house – אסור לו לאדם שישהה שטר פרוע בתוך ביתו: A lender may not retain a promissory note in his possession after the loan is repaid, in accordance with the opinion of Rabbi Yehoshua ben Levi, even if the borrower did not yet pay the scribe's fee (Ran; *Tur*). However, the *Shakh* cites *Tosafot*, the Rosh, and the Ritva, who rule that it is permitted to retain the document until the scribe's fee is paid (*Shulḥan Arukh, Ḥoshen Mishpat* 57:1).

A scroll that is not proofread – ספר שאינו מוגה: It is prohibited to retain a Torah scroll in one's possession for more than thirty days if it has not been proofread and corrected. Rather, it must be corrected or interred in a repository for unusable sacred objects, in accordance with the opinion of Rabbi Ami. The Rema adds that the same is true for books of the Prophets and Writings, as well as other sacred books, e.g., the Talmud and its commentaries (Rashi; *Haggahot Maimoniyyot*; Rabbeinu Yeruḥam). Others add that the danger is that inadvertent use of corrupted editions of the Talmud and halakhic works could lead to great injustice and mistaken halakhic rulings (Rambam *Sefer Ahava, Hilkhot Sefer Torah* 7:12; *Shulḥan Arukh, Yoreh De'a* 279:1).

Our statement was a statement accompanied by a declaration – מודעא היו דברינו: The Rambam and the *Shulḥan Arukh* rule, in accordance with the opinion of Mar bar Rav Ashi, that if witnesses claim that before they signed a document one of the parties to the transaction declared that he was not acting of his own volition, that they are deemed credible, even if their signatures on the document can be independently authenticated. The *Shakh* and the Gra, however, cite several early commentaries who maintain that the witnesses are deemed credible only when their testimony is the only source authenticating their signatures (*Tosafot*; Rosh; Ran) Yet others (Rav Hai Gaon; Ra'avad) rule that these witnesses are never deemed credible, even when their testimony is the only source authenticating their signatures, in accordance with the opinion of Rav Naḥman, as the *halakha* is ruled in accordance with his opinion in monetary matters (Rambam *Sefer Shofetim, Hilkhot Edut* 3:8; *Shulḥan Arukh, Ḥoshen Mishpat* 46:37).

בעא מיניה רבא מרב נחמן: "תנאי היו דברינו" מהו? מודעא ואמנה היינו טעמא – דקא עקרי ליה לשטרא, והאי נמי – קא עקר לשטרא. או דלמא: תנאי מילתא אחריתי היא? אמר ליה: כי אתו לקמן לדינא אמרינן להו: זילו קיימו תנאייכו, וחותו לדינא.

Rava raised a dilemma before Rav Naḥman: In a case where the witnesses say: **Our statement was a conditional** statement,[NH] i.e., they verify their signatures, but add that the transaction was contingent upon fulfillment of an unwritten condition, **what is** the ruling? Perhaps it is similar to the cases of a statement accompanied by a **declaration**[N] **and** a statement of **trust.** In those latter cases, **this is the reason** that their statement is rejected, **as** in doing so **they undermine the document, and in this case too, he undermines the document. Or perhaps a condition is a different matter,** as it does not necessarily undermine the document. Rav Naḥman **said to him: When** people **come before us for judgment** in this latter case, **we say to them: Go and fulfill your conditions, and** then **descend** before us **for judgment.**

עד אומר: "תנאי" ועד אומר: "אינו תנאי", אמר רב פפא: תרוייהו בשטרא מעליא קא מסהדי, והאי דקאמר "תנאי" – הוה ליה חד, ואין דבריו של אחד במקום שנים.

The Gemara asks: What is the ruling in a case where one **witness says:** There is a **condition** attached to the transaction[NH] **and one witness says: There is no condition? Rav Pappa says: Both are testifying that it is a valid document, and that** witness **who says:** There was a **condition** attached, is only **one** witness whose testimony challenges that validity. **And the statement of one** witness **has no** validity **in a place** where there are **two** witnesses.

מתקיף לה רב הונא בריה דרב יהושע: אי הכי, אפילו תרוייהו נמי! אלא אמרינן: הני למיעקר סהדותייהו קאתו, האי נמי – למיעקר סהדותיה קאתי! והלכתא כרב הונא בריה דרב יהושע.

Rav Huna, son of Rav Yehoshua, strongly **objects to this: If** it is **so** that testifying that there is a condition is considered to undermine the document, then **even if both** of the witnesses testify that there was a condition, their testimony should **also** not be accepted. Once they testified that the document is valid, they cannot give additional testimony that contradicts their original testimony. **Rather, we say: These** two witnesses **are coming to undermine their testimony** that the document is valid. These are not two separate testimonies, one that the document is valid and one with regard to the condition. Rather, the second testimony revokes the first. Similarly, **this** single witness **is coming to undermine his testimony as well.** Therefore, there is only one witness testifying that the document is valid. The Gemara concludes: **The *halakha* is in accordance with** the opinion of **Rav Huna, son of Rav Yehoshua,** and the testimony of even one witness who says that there was a condition attached to the transaction is accepted.

תנו רבנן: שנים חתומין על השטר ומתו, ובאו שנים מן השוק ואמרו: "ידענו שכתב ידם הוא, אבל אנוסים היו, קטנים היו, פסולי עדות היו" – הרי אלו נאמנים. ואם יש עדים שכתב ידם הוא זה, או שהיה כתב ידם יוצא ממקום אחר, משטר שקרא עליו ערער והוחזק בבית דין – אין אלו נאמנין.

§ **The Sages taught:** If **two** witnesses were **signatories on a document and they died,**[H] and **two** strangers **from the marketplace came and said: We know that this is their handwriting, but they were coerced** into signing the document, **or** if they said that **they were minors** when they signed the document, or if they said that **they were disqualified witnesses** when they signed the document, **these** strangers **are deemed credible,** as the mouth that prohibited and ratified the document is the mouth that permitted and undermined the document. **However, if there are** other **witnesses** who testify **that it is their handwriting, or if their handwriting emerges from another place, from a document that one challenged and** that **was deemed valid in court, these** witnesses from the marketplace are **not deemed credible** and their testimony does not undermine the validity of the document.

NOTES

Our statement was a conditional statement – תנאי היו דברינו: Some say that signing a document that has an oral condition attached to it is an injustice, as they are signing a document from which the condition is omitted (Rid). Apparently, if it is explicitly stipulated in the document that there are no conditions the witnesses are not deemed credible if they claim there was a condition, as they are effectively stating that they signed a false document (Ritva).

Declaration and condition – מודעא ותנאי: There are three opinions in the early commentaries with regard to the halakhic ruling in this case, and they explain the Gemara at length according to each. Some maintain that the *halakha* is fundamentally in accordance with the opinion of Mar bar Rav Ashi, who was the latest *amora* whose opinion was cited here, and his ruling that they are deemed credible applies even if their handwriting is authenticated by another document that they signed (Rav Hai Gaon). However, most early commentaries maintain that his ruling applies only to case where their handwriting is not authenticated by another document, as their credibility is based upon the principle: The mouth that prohibited is the mouth that permitted (Rambam). The *ge'onim* themselves disagreed with regard to the ruling here, and some ruled in accordance with the opinion of Rav Naḥman, based on the conclusion of the Gemara in *Bava Batra* (*Sefer HaIttur*; Rid). No proof can be cited from the dilemma raised by Rava, which combines the cases of declaration and trust, as he raised the dilemma before Rav Naḥman, and Mar bar Rav Ashi lived many years after Rava (Meiri).

One witness says there is a condition attached to the transaction – עד אומר תנאי: The early commentaries note that the case cited is one where one witness claims with certainty that there was a condition attached, and the other is uncertain. Were they each to testify with certainty and contradict each other, the document would certainly be rendered invalid, as clearly one of them is lying (Ramban; Rashba; Ran).

HALAKHA

Our statement was a conditional statement – תנאי היו דברינו: If witnesses authenticated their signatures and immediately claimed that there was an unfulfilled oral condition attached to the transaction, they are deemed credible, in accordance with the opinion of Rav Naḥman. However, in a case where their signatures can be independently authenticated, they are not deemed credible (Rashi; Rambam). Others rule that they are deemed credible even in a case where their signatures can be independently authenticated (Rav Hai Gaon; Ra'avad; Rambam *Sefer Shofetim*, *Hilkhot Edut* 3:9). See also the *Shulḥan Arukh*, who rules differently in two separate places (*Ḥoshen Mishpat* 46:37 and 82:12; see *Shakh*).

One witness says there is a condition – עד אומר תנאי: If one of the signatories on a document claims that there was an unfulfilled oral condition attached to the transaction, the defendant is exempt from payment, after taking an oath of inducement by rabbinic law. The authorities disagree about whether this is only in a case where there is no independent authentication of the signatures or if it applies even in a case where there is independent authentication (Rambam *Sefer Shofetim*, *Hilkhot Edut* 3:10; *Shulḥan Arukh*, *Ḥoshen Mishpat* 46:37 and 82:12).

If two witnesses were signatories on a document and they died – שנים חתומין על השטר ומתו: If the witnesses who signed a document have died, and their signatures can be authenticated only by asking other witnesses, but the latter claim that the witnesses were compelled to sign the document or were disqualified from testifying or were minors at the time, their testimony is accepted, and the document is destroyed, in accordance with the *baraita*. If the lender claims that a deadline was set for him to ratify the document, the destruction of the document is delayed. However, if he did not explicitly make that claim, the document is destroyed immediately (Rashba; Rambam *Sefer Shofetim*, *Hilkhot Edut* 7:7; *Shulḥan Arukh*, *Ḥoshen Mishpat* 46:37).

וּמַגְבִּינַן בֵּיהּ כְּבִשְׁטָרָא מַעַלְיָא? וְאַמַּאי? תְּרֵי וּתְרֵי נִינְהוּ!

The Gemara asks: **And** if the testimony of these witnesses is not accepted, is that to say **that we collect** debts with that document as one would collect debts **with a valid document? And why** would that be the case? **Aren't the two** signatories whose signatures were ratified **and the two** witnesses from the marketplace whose testimony invalidates the document contradictory witnesses?[N] Therefore, the document cannot be used to collect payment.

אָמַר רַב שֵׁשֶׁת: זֹאת אוֹמֶרֶת הַכְחָשָׁה תְּחִלַּת הֲזָמָּה הִיא.

Rav Sheshet said: That is to say that **contradiction** of their testimony **is the first** stage in **rendering** them **false, conspiring witnesses,**[H] in the sense that certain restrictions that apply to the latter apply to the former as well.

NOTES

Aren't the two signatories and the two witnesses contradictory witnesses – **תְּרֵי וּתְרֵי נִינְהוּ**: Most commentaries explain that this refers to a case where the second pair of witnesses testifies to invalidate the testimony of the first pair of witnesses, without impugning the witnesses themselves, e.g., the witnesses were minors, relatives, or compelled to sign the document due to a threat to their lives. However, if they testify that the first witnesses are disqualified due to transgressions that they performed, the ruling in that case is like any other case where witnesses testify to disqualify other witnesses, and the testimony of the latter pair of witnesses is accepted (Ri Migash; *Tosafot*; Ramban; Rashba). Others explain that because the first pair of witnesses is dead, even if the second pair of witnesses testifies that the first set is disqualified because they were robbers or the like, the testimony of the second set is considered testimony to contradict their testimony, not to invalidate the witnesses. Therefore, it is a case of contradictory witnesses who negate each other's testimony (*Ba'al HaMaor*; Ritva).

HALAKHA

Contradiction of their testimony is the first stage in rendering them false, conspiring witnesses – **הַכְחָשָׁה תְּחִלַּת הֲזָמָּה הִיא**: Witnesses whose testimony was contradicted and who were later rendered false, conspiring witnesses are subject to the full range of punishments administered to false, conspiring witnesses: Death, lashes, and monetary payment, as contradiction of their testimony is the first stage in rendering them false, conspiring witnesses, in accordance with the statements of Rav Sheshet and Rava (Rambam *Sefer Shofetim, Hilkhot Edut* 18:4; *Tur, Ḥoshen Mishpat* 38).

Perek **II**
Daf **20** Amud **a**

וּכְשֵׁם שֶׁאֵין מְזִימִין אֶת הָעֵדִים אֶלָּא בִּפְנֵיהֶם כָּךְ אֵין מַכְחִישִׁין אֶת הָעֵדִים אֶלָּא בִּפְנֵיהֶם.

And just as witnesses **render** other **witnesses false, conspiring** witnesses **only in their presence,** because with their testimony they render them liable to be punished, **so too,** witnesses **contradict** the testimony of other witnesses **only in their presence.**[N] Since the signatories to the document are dead, their testimony cannot be contradicted.

NOTES

Contradiction of testimony and rendering witnesses false, conspiring witnesses – **הַכְחָשָׁה וַהֲזָמָּה**: There are several differences between these two forms of disallowing the testimony of witnesses. With regard to the testimony of the second pair of witnesses, they render the first pair of witnesses false, conspiring witnesses by testifying that they could not have witnessed what they claim to have witnessed because they were not in the place where they claimed that the incident they witnessed transpired. They contradict the testimony of the first pair of witnesses by partially or completely disputing the content of their testimony.

With regard to the respective consequences, when witnesses are rendered false, conspiring witnesses they receive the punishment that they sought to inflict on the person against whom they testified. The details of these *halakhot* and the exceptions to them are discussed in tractate *Makkot*. In the case of contradiction of testimony, although the first pair of witnesses is suspected of lying, they are not disqualified from testifying in other cases, and they certainly receive no punishment. In addition, with regard to rendering witnesses false, conspiring witnesses, there is a Torah decree that the testimony of the second pair of witnesses is accepted to disqualify the first witnesses. With regard to contradiction of testimony, the testimony of one pair of witnesses is no more accepted than the testimony of the other; they simply neutralize each other (*Talmidei Rabbeinu Yona*).

Rav Sheshet's opinion that contradiction of the witnesses' testimony is the first stage in rendering them false, conspiring witnesses is especially significant with regard to Rava's opinion cited in tractate *Bava Kamma*, which is also the halakhic ruling, that if the testimony of witnesses was contradicted and then those first witnesses were rendered false, conspiring witnesses, they are subject to the full range of punishments administered to false, conspiring witnesses. One does not say that because their testimony was contradicted they are no longer witnesses and cannot be rendered false, conspiring witnesses. The reason is that contradicting witnesses and rendering witnesses false, conspiring witnesses are essentially similar (see Ritva). However, Rabbi Abbahu maintains that since there is so substantive a difference between contradicting witnesses and rendering them false, conspiring witnesses, one cannot derive that restrictions that apply to one apply to the other as well.

אֲמַר לֵיהּ רַב נַחְמָן: אִילּוּ הָווּ קַמָּן וּמַכְחִישִׁין לְהוּ – הֲוָה הַכְחָשָׁה, וְלָא הֲוָה מַשְׁגִּיחִין בְּהוּ, דַּהֲוֵי לָהּ עֵדוּת מוּכְחֶשֶׁת. הָשְׁתָּא דְּלֵיתְנֵהוּ, דְּאִילּוּ הָווּ לְקַמָּן דִּלְמָא הָווּ מוֹדוּ לְהוּ, מְהֵימְנֵי?!

Rav Naḥman said to Rav Sheshet: **If the first pair of witnesses was before us and** the second pair would **contradict** their testimony, **that is contradiction, and we would not consider their** testimony and would not collect money with the document, **as it is contradicted testimony. Now that they are not** before us, and in a case **where if they were before us perhaps they would have admitted to** the second witnesses that the testimony of the second witnesses is correct, **are they deemed credible,** and the document that they signed valid?

אֶלָּא אֲמַר רַב נַחְמָן: אוֹקֵי תְּרֵי לַהֲדֵי תְּרֵי, וְאוֹקֵי מָמוֹנָא בְּחֶזְקַת מָרֵיהּ. מִידֵי דַּהֲוָה אַנִּכְסֵי דְּבַר שַׁטְיָא. דְּבַר שַׁטְיָא זַבֵּין נִכְסֵי. אָתוּ בֵּי תְּרֵי אָמְרִי: כְּשֶׁהוּא שׁוֹטֶה זַבֵּין, וַאֲתוּ בֵּי תְּרֵי וְאָמְרִי: כְּשֶׁהוּא חָלִים זַבֵּין.

Rather, Rav Naḥman said in the case where the testimony of the first witnesses is contradicted not in their presence, the ruling is: **Establish two witnesses against the two** witnesses[NH] who contradict their testimony, thereby neutralizing both testimonies, **and establish the money in the possession of its owner, just as** it was in the case **of the property of bar Shatya.**[L] As when **bar Shatya,** a man who suffered from periodic bouts of insanity, **sold** his **property, two** witnesses **came** and **said: He sold** it **when he was insane; and two** other witnesses **came and said: He sold** it **when he was sane.**[B]

אֲמַר רַב אַשִׁי: אוֹקֵי תְּרֵי לַהֲדֵי תְּרֵי, וְאוֹקֵי מָמוֹנָא בְּחֶזְקַת בַּר שַׁטְיָא. וְלָא אֲמַרַן אֶלָּא דְּאִית לֵיהּ חֲזָקָה דַּאֲבָהָתֵיהּ, אֲבָל לֵית לֵיהּ חֲזָקָה דַּאֲבָהָתֵיהּ – אָמְרִינַן: כְּשֶׁהוּא שׁוֹטֶה זְבַן, וּכְשֶׁהוּא שׁוֹטֶה זַבֵּין.

Rav Ashi said in that case: **Establish two** witnesses **against** the **two** witnesses who contradict the testimony of the first pair, **and establish the money in the possession of bar Shatya.**[NH] The Gemara notes: **We say** that the property remains in the possession of bar Shatya **only when he has** possession of the property based on **the possession of his fathers. However, if he does not have** possession of the property based on **the possession of his fathers,** but he acquired the property himself, **we say: He purchased** his properties **when he was insane, and he sold them when he was insane.** He does not have presumptive ownership of them. Therefore, the property remains in the possession of the person to whom bar Shatya sold it.

אָמַר רַבִּי אַבָּהוּ: אֵין מְזִימִין אֶת הָעֵדִים אֶלָּא בִּפְנֵיהֶן, וּמַכְחִישִׁין אֶת הָעֵדִים שֶׁלֹּא בִּפְנֵיהֶן. וַהֲזָמָה שֶׁלֹּא בִּפְנֵיהֶן, נְהִי דַּהֲזָמָה לָא הָוֵי – הַכְחָשָׁה מִיהָא הָוְיָא.

Rabbi Abbahu disagrees with the opinion of Rav Sheshet and **says:** Witnesses **render** other **witnesses false, conspiring** witnesses **only in their presence,**[H] **but** witnesses **contradict** the testimony of other witnesses **not in their presence. And** with regard to **rendering** other **witnesses false, conspiring** witnesses **not in their presence, although it is not** effective in **rendering them false, conspiring** witnesses in the sense that they are punished for their false testimony, **in any case, it is contradiction** of their testimony.

אָמַר מָר: אִם יֵשׁ עֵדִים שֶׁכְּתַב יָדָם הוּא זֶה, אוֹ שֶׁהָיָה כְּתַב יָדָם יוֹצֵא מִמָּקוֹם אַחֵר, מִשְּׁטָר שֶׁקָּרָא עָלָיו עַרְעָר וְהוּחְזַק בְּבֵית דִּין – אֵין נֶאֱמָנִין. קָרָא עָלָיו עַרְעָר – אִין, לֹא קָרָא עָלָיו עַרְעָר – לָא, מְסַיֵּיעַ לֵיהּ לְרַבִּי אַסִּי, דְּאָמַר רַבִּי אַסִּי: אֵין מְקַיְּימִין אֶת הַשְּׁטָר אֶלָּא מִשְּׁטָר שֶׁקָּרָא עָלָיו עַרְעָר וְהוּחְזַק בְּבֵית דִּין.

§ **The Master said** in the *baraita* cited previously: **If there are** other **witnesses** who testify **that it is their handwriting, or if their handwriting emerges from another place, from a document that one challenged and** that was **deemed valid in court,** these witnesses are **not deemed credible.** The Gemara infers: From a document **that one challenged, yes,** the signatures are authenticated and the testimony of the other witnesses is not accepted; however, **if one did not challenge** the document, **no,** the document cannot be used to authenticate their signatures. This **supports** the statement of **Rabbi Asi, as Rabbi Asi said: One ratifies a document** by authenticating the witnesses' signatures **only from a document that** someone **challenged and** that was **deemed valid in court.**[N]

NOTES

Establish two witnesses against the two witnesses – אוֹקֵי תְּרֵי לַהֲדֵי תְּרֵי: A simple question may be raised: What difference is there whether or not the witnesses are deemed credible? In either case, the money remains with the one in whose possession it is found and the borrower pays nothing. In fact, some commentaries are of the opinion that the only difference is that if the second pair of witnesses is deemed credible, the document is destroyed on the basis of their testimony. If they are not deemed credible, the document is not destroyed, as the borrower could provide another proof. However, most early commentaries agree with Rashi, that the difference between whether or not their testimony is deemed credible is in a case where the lender seizes the property of the borrower. If the witnesses are deemed credible, the lender is not compelled to return the property to the borrower.

Bar Shatya – בַּר שַׁטְיָא: This discussion is based on the principle that the halakhic status of a person who has intermittent periods of sanity and insanity is determined by his condition at the time of his action. During his bouts of insanity, he is not responsible for his actions (Ritva).

One ratifies a document only – אֵין מְקַיְּימִין אֶת הַשְּׁטָר אֶלָּא: There are two fundamental versions of this statement. The version in the Gemara here, which is the version of Rashi and also the Ri Migash, is: One ratifies a document by authenticating the witnesses' signatures only from a document that one challenged. Apparently, one cannot authenticate the signatures by means of a document ratified by the court if that document was not challenged. The reason is that the authentication process is meticulous only when the validity of a document is challenged; therefore one knows that the document is reliable. The Rosh, however, holds that even according to Rashi's version there is no requirement that the proof will be brought from a document that was challenged.

The version of Rif is: One ratifies a document by authenticating the witnesses' signatures from a document that one challenged only if it was deemed valid in court. That is the ruling of several authorities, including the Ramban and the Ritva.

HALAKHA

Establish two witnesses against the two witnesses – אוֹקֵי תְּרֵי לַהֲדֵי תְּרֵי: The witnesses who signed a promissory note died, and other witnesses came to authenticate the signature but claimed that there was some factor disqualifying the signatory witnesses or their signing of the contract. In that case, if there are other witnesses authenticating the signatures, or if their signatures are authenticated by another document that they signed, the document is not destroyed, but the money remains in the possession of the borrower (Rambam *Sefer Shofetim, Hilkhot Edut* 7:7; *Shulḥan Arukh, Ḥoshen Mishpat* 46:37).

And establish the money in the possession of bar Shatya – וְאוֹקֵי מָמוֹנָא בְּחֶזְקַת בַּר שַׁטְיָא: If one who suffers from bouts of insanity sells his property, and one pair of witnesses testifies that he was sane at the time of the sale while another pair of witnesses testifies that he was insane, the status quo is upheld. Therefore, if he sold movable property, it remains in the possession of the buyer. If he sold real estate, it remains in the possession of the seller. Some (*Beit Yosef*; and see the commentary of Rabbi Akiva Eiger to *Shulḥan Arukh*) rule that this is the *halakha* only in the case of inherited real estate, which is in the presumptive possession of the seller (Rambam *Sefer Kinyan, Hilkhot Mekhira* 29:5; *Shulḥan Arukh, Ḥoshen Mishpat* 235:21).

Witnesses render other witnesses false, conspiring witnesses only in their presence – אֵין מְזִימִין אֶת הָעֵדִים אֶלָּא בִּפְנֵיהֶן: A pair of witnesses may contradict the testimony of a pair of witnesses that testified previously, even not in their presence. However, they can render the first pair false, conspiring witnesses only if they are present. Nevertheless, if they testify that the first pair of witnesses was with them elsewhere and could not have witnessed the incident about which they testified, the testimony of the first pair is contradicted, in accordance with the opinion of Rabbi Abbahu (Rambam *Sefer Shofetim, Hilkhot Edut* 18:5).

LANGUAGE

Bar Shatya – בַּר שַׁטְיָא: *Bar* in this context does not mean son of; rather, it is a Hebrew prefix denoting one's attributes, e.g., *ben ḥayil*, referring to a courageous person and *ben beliyya'al*, referring to a wicked person. The term is also used in Aramaic expressions like *bar mitzva*, or *bar pelugta*, referring to an adversary. Here too, bar Shatya refers to one who is known for his insanity.

BACKGROUND

At times sane, at times insane – עִתִּים חָלִים עִתִּים שׁוֹטֶה: Certain types of mental illness, especially bipolar afflictions, are cyclical, where the mentally ill person experiences periods when he is completely sane and periods when his condition deteriorates and his judgment is impaired. The transition from sanity to insanity is gradual. Therefore, there are periods when it is difficult to determine his condition at that point.

אָמְרִי נְהַרְדְּעֵי: אֵין מְקַיְּימִין אֶת הַשְּׁטָר אֶלָּא מִשְּׁתֵּי כְּתוּבּוֹת [אוֹ] מִשְּׁתֵּי שָׂדוֹת, וְהוּא שֶׁאֲכָלוּם בַּעֲלֵיהֶן שָׁלֹשׁ שָׁנִים וּבְשׁוּפִי.

The Sages of Neharde'a[B] say:[N] **One ratifies a document** by authenticating the witnesses' signatures **only from two marriage contracts**[N] **or from** the bills of sale for **two fields** that those witnesses signed. **And** those bills of sale are effective **only** in a case **where their owner ate their** produce for **three years,** the requisite period to establish presumptive ownership of the field, **and in peace,** undisturbed by protest. In that case we can rely on the signatures, and the documents are considered valid.

אָמַר רַב שִׁימִי בַּר אַשִׁי: וּבְיוֹצֵא מִתַּחַת יַד אַחֵר, אֲבָל מִיַּד עַצְמוֹ – לָא. מַאי שְׁנָא תַּחַת יַד עַצְמוֹ דְּלָא – דִּלְמָא זַיּוּפֵי מְזַיֵּיף, מִתַּחַת יְדֵי אַחֵר נַמִי – דִּלְמָא אֲזַל וַחֲזָא, אֲתָא וְזַיֵּיף! כּוּלֵּי הַאי לָא מָצֵי מְכַוֵּין.

Rav Shimi bar Ashi said: Authentication of signatures by comparison to other documents can be accomplished specifically **when** the documents **emerge from the possession of another.**[H] **However,** when the documents emerge **from the possession of** the litigant **himself, no,** they may not be used to authenticate the signatures. The Gemara asks: **What is different** in a case where the documents emerge **from the possession of** the litigant **himself that** they may **not** be used to authenticate the signatures? It is that **perhaps** while the documents were in his possession he learned how to copy the signatures and **forged** them. If so, **also** in a case where the documents emerge **from the possession of another, perhaps he went and saw** the signatures, and **came** back **and forged** them. The Gemara answers: In that case, **he would not be able to accurately** reproduce the signatures **to that extent** based on memory alone.

תָּנוּ רַבָּנַן: כּוֹתֵב אָדָם עֵדוּתוֹ עַל הַשְּׁטָר, וּמֵעִיד עָלֶיהָ אֲפִילּוּ לְאַחַר כַּמָּה שָׁנִים. אָמַר רַב הוּנָא: וְהוּא שֶׁזּוֹכְרָהּ מֵעַצְמוֹ. רַבִּי יוֹחָנָן אָמַר: אַף עַל פִּי שֶׁאֵין זוֹכְרָהּ מֵעַצְמוֹ. אֲמַר רַבָּה: שְׁמַע מִינַּהּ מִדְּרַבִּי יוֹחָנָן: הָנֵי בֵּי תְּרֵי דְּיָדְעִי סַהֲדוּתָא, וּמִנְשֵׁי חַד מִנַּיְיהוּ – מַדְכַּר חַד לְחַבְרֵיהּ.

§ **The Sages taught: A person may write his testimony in a document**[H] **and testify on its** basis **even after several years** have passed. **Rav Huna said: And** that **is** the *halakha* only **if he remembers** the testimony **on his own** and he uses the document merely to refresh his memory with regard to certain details. **Rabbi Yoḥanan said:** One may rely on that written testimony **even if he does not remember** the testimony **by himself** at all. **Rabba said: Conclude from** this statement of **Rabbi Yoḥanan:** With regard to **these two witnesses who know testimony** in a certain case, **and one of them forgot** the testimony, **one** witness **may remind his fellow** witness[H] of the testimony, as according to Rabbi Yoḥanan, even if the witness remembers the testimony only by means of an external stimulus, the testimony is valid.

אִיבַּעְיָא לְהוּ: עַצְמוֹ מַאי? רַב חֲבִיבָא אֲמַר: אֲפִילּוּ עַצְמוֹ. מָר בְּרֵיהּ דְּרַב אַשִׁי אֲמַר: עַצְמוֹ לֹא. וְהִלְכְתָא: עַצְמוֹ לֹא.

A dilemma was raised before the Sages: If the litigant **himself** reminds the witness of the testimony, **what is** the ruling? **Rav Ḥaviva said: Even** if the litigant **himself** reminds the witness, he may testify. **Mar, son of Rav Ashi, said:** If the litigant **himself** reminds the witness, he **may not** testify. **And** the Gemara concludes that **the *halakha* is** that if the litigant **himself** reminds the witness of the testimony, the witness **may not** testify, due to the concern that the litigant influenced the nature of his testimony.

BACKGROUND

The Sages of Neharde'a – נְהַרְדְּעֵי: The Gemara in tractate *Sanhedrin* explains that this is a reference to Rav Ḥama, a fourth-generation Babylonian *amora*. He apparently lived a long life, as his discussions with Sages of the previous generation are recorded in the Talmud. Since he served for over twenty years at the head of the yeshiva in Neharde'a following the death of Rav Naḥman bar Yitzḥak, his *halakhot* are attributed to the Sages of Neharde'a. Apparently, Rav Ḥama was a relative of and served as the scholar of the house of the Exilarch. It is also possible that this is the same Rav Ḥama who met with the king of Persia and discussed matters of Torah with him.

NOTES

The Sages of Neharde'a say – אָמְרִי נְהַרְדְּעֵי: According to most commentaries, there is no dispute here, and the Sages of Neharde'a, supported by the *baraita*, come to complete the statement of Rav Asi. However, there is a dispute with regard to the details. Some explain that to authenticate the witnesses on a document, the Sages of Neharde'a require two ratified documents; one is insufficient (*Halakhot Gedolot*; Ra'avad). Others explain that the Sages of Neharde'a hold that in the absence of one ratified document, one may rely on two unratified documents to authenticate a third, when there are indications that they are indeed authentic signatures (Ritva, citing *Tosafot*).

From two marriage contracts – מִשְּׁתֵּי כְּתוּבּוֹת: The Mordekhai explains that the reason two documents are required is that sometimes signatures are not perfectly consistent, and differences may arise due to the surface on which the witnesses signed their names, or due to the fact that they needed to fit their signatures in limited space. Therefore, two documents present a more complete picture. The Meiri explains that a marriage contract is used for authentication of the signatures because those documents are typically signed in public, and there is no suspicion of forgery. He adds that a document of sale whose accuracy is confirmed by the seller may be used for authentication. In the Jerusalem Talmud there is a discussion with regard to relying on books and letters written by the witnesses, and the Meiri and the Ritva disagree with regard to the interpretation of that discussion. Nevertheless, they both agree that it is problematic to authenticate documents with letters, either because it is unclear who wrote them or because one is not meticulous when writing letters, leading to inconsistencies in the writer's penmanship.

HALAKHA

How his handwriting emerges from another place – כֵּיצַד כְּתַב יָדוֹ יוֹצֵא מִמָּקוֹם אַחֵר: The court authenticates the signatures on a document by comparing them with the signatures on other documents, e.g., two marriage contracts or two deeds of sale of real estate where the purchaser has openly consumed the produce of the field for three years without concern and without protest, in accordance with the opinion of the Sages of Neharde'a. This is the *halakha*, provided that the authenticating document was not produced by the party seeking authentication of the document, due to the suspicion that he forged the signatures, in accordance with the opinion of Rav Shimi bar Ashi. The Rema, citing the *Tur*, rules that this caveat applies even if these documents were ratified, but the Ran, citing the Rambam, disputes this. Similarly, documents whose validity was challenged and that were then ratified by the court may be used to authenticate signatures, in accordance with the *baraita* and the opinion of Rabbi Asi (Rashi; Ra'ah; *Beit Yosef*, citing Rambam). The *Shulḥan Arukh* and the Rema also cite the opinion that ratified documents may be used even if their validity was never challenged (Rosh; *Shakh*, citing Rif and Rambam; Rambam *Sefer Shofetim*, *Hilkhot Edut* 6:3; *Shulḥan Arukh*, *Ḥoshen Mishpat* 46:7).

A person may write his testimony in a document – כּוֹתֵב אָדָם עֵדוּתוֹ עַל הַשְּׁטָר: A witness is permitted to write notes to support his memory and to consult them before testifying, in accordance with the *baraita*. Even if he was unable to remember the incident without consulting the notes, he may testify, in accordance with the opinion of Rabbi Yoḥanan, as the *halakha* is ruled in accordance with his opinion even in disputes with Rav, who was Rav Huna's teacher, and all the more so in disputes with Rav Huna. However, they may testify only if they recall the incident after consulting the notes; they may not testify solely on the basis of what is written (*Tosafot*; Rambam *Sefer Shofetim*, *Hilkhot Edut* 8:1; *Shulḥan Arukh*, *Ḥoshen Mishpat* 28:13).

One witness may remind his fellow witness – מַדְכַּר חַד לְחַבְרֵיהּ: If one is reminded of an incident by another, he may testify, even if the one reminding him is his fellow witness. However, if the one reminding him is a litigant in the case, he may not testify, even if after being reminded he recalls the events himself, in accordance with the opinion of Rabba and Mar bar Rav Ashi (Rambam *Sefer Shofetim*, *Hilkhot Edut* 8:2; *Shulḥan Arukh*, *Ḥoshen Mishpat* 28:14).

ואי צורבא מרבנן הוא – אפילו עצמו. כי הא דרב אשי הוה ידיע ליה בסהדותא לרב כהנא. אמר ליה: מי דכיר מר האי סהדותא? אמר ליה: לא. ולאו הכי והכי הוה? אמר ליה: לא ידענא. לסוף אידכר רב אשי, אסהיד ליה. חזייה לרב כהנא דהוה מחסם. אמר ליה: מי סברת עלך קא סמיכנא? אנא הוא דרמאי אנפשאי ואדכרי.

And if the witness is a Torah scholar,[NH] then **even** if the litigant **himself** jogged the witness's memory, the witness may testify. A Torah scholar would not testify if he did not actually remember the testimony himself, **as in that** case **involving Rav Ashi,**[P] **who knew testimony** relating **to Rav Kahana.** Rav Kahana **said to** Rav Ashi: **Does the Master remember this testimony?** Rav Ashi **said to him: No.** Rav Kahana said to him: **Didn't** the incident transpire in **such and such** a manner? Rav Ashi **said to him: I don't know. Ultimately, Rav Ashi remembered** the testimony and **testified for** Rav Kahana. **He saw that Rav Kahana was hesitant** [*meḥassem*][L] with regard to accepting his testimony, concerned that he had influenced the content of Rav Ashi's testimony. Rav Ashi **said to him: Do you think that I am relying on you? I made an effort, and I remembered** the incident.

תנן התם: התלוליות הקרובות בין לעיר ובין לדרך, אחד חדשות ואחד ישנות – טמאות. הרחוקות, חדשות – טהורות, ישנות – טמאות. איזוהי קרובה? חמשים אמה, ואיזו היא ישנה? ששים שנה. דברי רבי מאיר. רבי יהודה אומר: קרובה – שאין קרובה הימנה, ישנה – שאין אדם זוכרה.

§ Apropos recalling testimony, the Gemara adds that **we learned there** in a mishna (*Oholot* 16:2): **Mounds of dirt**[H] **that are near either to a city or a path, whether** these mounds **are new or whether** they are **old, are ritually impure** due to the concern that a corpse is buried there. With regard to **the** mounds **that are distant** from the city: If they are **new** they are **ritually pure,** as, were there a corpse buried there, someone would remember, and if they are **old** they are **impure.** The mishna elaborates: **What is** a mound that is **near?** It is one at a distance of up to **fifty cubits. And what is** a mound that is **old?** It is one that was there for more than **sixty years;** this is **the statement of Rabbi Meir. Rabbi Yehuda says:** A mound that is **near** is one that there is **no** mound **closer than it. Old** is referring to a mound **that no one remembers.** According to Rabbi Yehuda, the parameters are not quantifiable.

מאי עיר ומאי דרך? אילימא עיר – עיר ממש, דרך – דרך ממש, מספיקא מי מחזקינן טומאה? והאמר ריש לקיש: עילה מצאו וטהרו ארץ ישראל! אמר רבי זירא: עיר – עיר הסמוכה לבית הקברות, ודרך – דרך בית הקברות.

The Gemara asks: **What is a city and what is a path** in this context? **If you say city means an actual city and a path is an actual path** and the mishna is referring to any city or path, the question arises: **Do we presume** the existence of **ritual impurity** in Eretz Yisrael? **But didn't Reish Lakish say** in explaining how the Sages, based on meager proof, deemed an area in Eretz Yisrael ritually pure where uncertainty arose with regard to its purity: **They found a pretext and deemed Eretz Yisrael ritually pure.** Apparently, one does not presume ritual impurity in Eretz Yisrael. Why, then, does the mishna declare that every mound of dirt near a city or a path is impure? **Rabbi Zeira said:** The word **city** in the mishna is referring to **a city adjacent to the cemetery, and** the word **path is** referring to the **path** leading **to the cemetery.** Therefore, the concern that a corpse may be buried in the mound is a reasonable one.

בשלמא דרך בית הקברות – דזמנין דמתרמי בין השמשות, ומקרו קברו בתל. אלא עיר הסמוכה לבית הקברות – כולהי לבית הקברות אזלי!

The Gemara asks: **Granted,** with regard to a mound located adjacent to **the path** leading **to the cemetery,** there is concern that a corpse is buried in the mound, **as sometimes one happens** to go to bury the corpse on Shabbat eve **at twilight,** and to avoid desecrating Shabbat, **it happened that they buried** the corpse **in a mound** on the path. **However,** with regard to **a city adjacent to the cemetery, everyone goes to the cemetery** to bury their dead. Why would anyone bury a corpse in a mound adjacent to the city?

NOTES

And if the witness is a Torah scholar – ואי צורבא מרבנן הוא: Most commentaries follow Rashi, who explains that if the witness is a Torah scholar, even if the litigant reminded him of the facts, he may testify if he ultimately remembers the incident, since a Torah scholar would not testify unless he was certain, and he would not change his testimony due to the influence of the litigant. This can be demonstrated from the incident involving Rav Ashi and Rav Kahana. However, some early commentaries cite an alternative explanation, citing Rav Hai Gaon, that if the litigant is a Torah scholar, it is permitted for him to remind the witness of the incident, since a Torah scholar would certainly relate the circumstances in a manner that will not lead to a perversion of justice and will merely state the facts (Rambam). However, most early commentaries question that explanation, both due to its content, and because it is not supported by the incident involving Rav Ashi.

HALAKHA

And if the witness is a Torah scholar – אי צורבא מרבנן הוא: If the witness is a Torah scholar he may testify, even if the litigant himself reminded him of the incident in question. The Rambam explains that the Gemara is referring to a case where one of the litigants is a Torah scholar. See *Tur* and *Derisha*, who rule according to both interpretations (Rambam *Sefer Shofetim*, *Hilkhot Edut* 8:2; *Shulḥan Arukh*, *Ḥoshen Mishpat* 28:14).

Mounds of dirt – התלוליות: The presumptive status of mounds near a city that is adjacent to a graveyard or to the path leading to a graveyard, whether they are new or old, is that they contain impurity imparted by a corpse, in accordance with the mishna in *Oholot* cited in the Gemara. The word near in this context is referring to the mounds closest to the city, with none closer. However, the presumptive status of a mound that is not near a city is impure only if it is old, which in this context means that no one remembers when it came into being, in accordance with the opinion of Rabbi Yehuda in his dispute with Rabbi Meir, and in accordance with the explanation of Rabbeinu Ḥananel (Rambam *Sefer Tahara*, *Hilkhot Tumat Met* 8:3 and *Kesef Mishne* there).

LANGUAGE

Hesitant [*meḥassem*] – מחסם: There are many variant readings of this term in manuscripts and other sources. There are three principal versions: *Meḥassem*, *mehassem*, and *mehasses*. The last of the three is the one adopted in the Hebrew language, although the other possibilities are also viable. It is unclear whether there is a unique verb form of the root *ḥet*, *samekh*, *mem* in the sense of hesitancy or uncertainty, or whether it is somehow related to other meanings of that verb, e.g., strengthened or withstood.

PERSONALITIES

Rav Ashi – רב אשי: Rav Ashi was a sixth-generation Babylonian Sage whose primary undertaking was the redaction of the Babylonian Talmud together with Ravina. He was born in the year 352 and studied with Rav Kahana. Rav Ashi reestablished the academy in Sura, which had been closed since the time of Rav Ḥisda, and he led the yeshiva for sixty years.

Rav Ashi and Ravina were not the first to edit the Oral Torah, as there are many discussions in the Talmud whose language and style indicate that they were edited long before the time of Rav Ashi. Rav Ashi arranged the material that he received from previous generations, which emanated from different academies and that was written in different styles, to produce an organized and uniform Talmud.

Various factors contributed to Rav Ashi's success in this great project, which ultimately was completed over a period of several hundred years. It is likely that Rav Ashi was assisted by a committee of Sages, who assembled in the academy in Sura. Nevertheless, it was only because of the unique political environment and economic conditions at the time that a project of this scope could be launched. The Persian king Yazdegerd I treated all of his citizens fairly, and expressed particular interest in the Jewish community, whose Sages he respected. Under his regime, the economic situation of the Jews of Babylonia was excellent, and they enjoyed relative freedom. These conditions allowed the Babylonian Sages to commit themselves to this vast enterprise.

אָמַר רַבִּי חֲנִינָא: מִתּוֹךְ שֶׁהַנָּשִׁים קוֹבְרוֹת שָׁם נִפְלֵיהֶן, וּמוּכֵּי שְׁחִין זְרוֹעוֹתֵיהֶם, עַד חֲמִשִּׁים אַמָּה – אָזְלָא אִיהִי לְחוּדָהּ, טְפֵי – דַּבְרָא אִינִישׁ בַּהֲדָהּ, וּלְבֵית הַקְּבָרוֹת אָזְלָא. הִלְכָּךְ, טוּמְאָה בְּאֶרֶץ יִשְׂרָאֵל לָא מַחֲזְקִינַן.

Rabbi Ḥanina said: The mounds could be impure, **since women bury their stillborn** babies adjacent to the city,[N] as there is no funeral in that case, **and** because those **afflicted with boils**[B] bury **their arms**[N] that withered and fell from their bodies. **Until** a distance of **fifty cubits**[N] from the city, the woman **goes alone** and buries the stillborn in a mound. **More** than that distance, **she takes a person with her,** as she fears going alone, **and she goes to the cemetery. Therefore, we are not presuming** the existence of **ritual impurity in Eretz Yisrael.** The case of the mounds is an exception, as there is basis for deeming them impure.

אֲמַר רַב חִסְדָּא: שְׁמַע מִינָּהּ מֵרַבִּי מֵאִיר: הַאי סַהֲדוּתָא, עַד שִׁיתִּין שְׁנִין – מִידְכַּר, טְפֵי – לָא מִידְכַּר. וְלָא הִיא: הָתָם הוּא דְּלָא רָמְיָא עֲלֵיהּ, אֲבָל הָכָא, כֵּיוָן דְּרָמֵי עֲלֵיהּ – אֲפִילּוּ טוּבָא נַמִי.

Rav Ḥisda said: Conclude from the statement of **Rabbi Meir,** who established a time limit beyond which a mound is considered an old mound, that with regard to **testimony, until sixty years** have passed, it is **remembered,** and if **more** than sixty years have passed, it is **not remembered. And** the Gemara rejects that conclusion: **That is not** so. **There,** with regard to the mounds, **it is** a case **where** responsibility to attest to the status of the mound **was not imposed upon him,** and the matter is forgotten after the passage of sixty years. **However, here,** with regard to testimony in general, **since** responsibility to testify **was imposed upon him,**[H] he remembers the testimony **even** after **a greater** period of time than sixty years has passed.

מתני׳ זֶה אוֹמֵר ״כְּתַב יָדִי, וְזֶה כְּתַב יָדוֹ שֶׁל חֲבֵירִי״, וְזֶה אוֹמֵר: ״זֶה כְּתַב יָדִי, וְזֶה כְּתַב יָדוֹ שֶׁל חֲבֵירִי״ – הֲרֵי אֵלּוּ נֶאֱמָנִין. זֶה אוֹמֵר: ״זֶה כְּתַב יָדִי״, – וְזֶה אוֹמֵר זֶה כְּתַב יָדִי צְרִיכִין לְצָרֵף עִמָּהֶם אַחֵר, דִּבְרֵי רַבִּי. וַחֲכָמִים אוֹמְרִים: אֵינָם צְרִיכִין לְצָרֵף עִמָּהֶן אַחֵר, אֶלָּא נֶאֱמָן אָדָם לוֹמַר ״זֶה כְּתַב יָדִי״.

MISHNA If **this** witness whose name is signed on a document **says:** This is **my handwriting**[H] **and this is the handwriting of my fellow** witness, **and that** witness **says: This is my handwriting and that is the handwriting of my fellow** witness, **these** witnesses **are deemed credible** and the document is ratified, as together they provide testimony authenticating both signatures. If **this** witness **says: This is my handwriting, and that** witness **says: This is my handwriting,** and neither testifies with regard to the signature of the other, **they must add another** witness **with them** who will authenticate the signatures of the two witnesses, as otherwise, each of the witnesses would be testifying with regard to half the sum in the document; this is **the statement of Rabbi** Yehuda HaNasi. **And the Rabbis say: They need not add another** witness **with them. Rather, a person is deemed credible to say: This is my handwriting.** The testimony of the two signatories about their own signatures is sufficient.

גמ׳ כְּשֶׁתִּימְצִי לוֹמַר לְדִבְרֵי רַבִּי

GEMARA The Gemara says: **When you analyze** the reasoning for the opinions of the *tanna'im*, **say**[N] that according **to the statement of Rabbi** Yehuda HaNasi,

BACKGROUND

Boils – שְׁחִין: Here the reference is to a variety of the disease that causes limbs to fall off the body. The Gemara describes this affliction in detail later in the tractate (77b).

HALAKHA

Since responsibility to testify was imposed upon him – כֵּיוָן דְּרָמֵי עֲלֵיהּ: Provided a witness recalls an incident that he witnessed, he may testify about that incident forever, and there is no concern that he no longer remembers what transpired (*Shulḥan Arukh, Ḥoshen Mishpat* 28:13).

If this witness says, this is my handwriting – זֶה אוֹמֵר כְּתַב יָדִי: If the two witnesses come to authenticate their signatures, and each one says: This is my handwriting and that is the handwriting of my fellow witness, they are deemed credible. Moreover, the document is ratified even if each authenticates only his own signature, provided that they remember the events recorded in the document, according to the Rambam, who ruled in accordance with the opinion of the Rabbis in their dispute with Rabbi Yehuda HaNasi. Others say that the document is ratified even if the witnesses do not remember the incident and they testify about their signatures alone, provided that an additional witness testifies with regard to both signatures. This ensures that there will be two witnesses for each signature (*Tosafot*, Rosh; *Tur*; Rambam *Sefer Shofetim, Hilkhot Edut* 6:2, 8:4; *Shulḥan Arukh, Ḥoshen Mishpat* 46:7, 10).

NOTES

Since women bury their stillborn babies adjacent to the city – מִתּוֹךְ שֶׁהַנָּשִׁים קוֹבְרוֹת שָׁם נִפְלֵיהֶן: Neither miscarried fetuses nor dismembered limbs require a funeral. They must be buried, however, and it is likely that the public is unaware of the burial and its location. Others suggest that since these women and lepers are ashamed of their situation, the burial is performed as inconspicuously as possible (see *Shita Mekubbetzet*).

And those afflicted with boils bury their arms – וּמוּכֵּי שְׁחִין זְרוֹעוֹתֵיהֶם: Corpses and their body parts impart ritual impurity. The *halakha* is that limbs severed from a living person also impart impurity like the limb of a corpse, where the limb is defined as containing bone, flesh, and sinew.

Until fifty cubits – עַד חֲמִשִּׁים אַמָּה: There are variant readings of the text resulting in different explanations of the Gemara here. The version of the Gemara cited by Rashi is merely: She takes a person with her, and he explains that as the woman would not go a distance greater than fifty cubits by herself but would take another with her, the companion would tell others and the burial would be publicized. Therefore, if there was no publicity, it is possible to conclude that nothing is buried there. According to this interpretation, all old mounds are impure, new mounds close to the city are impure, and new mounds distant from the city are pure.

The version of the Gemara cited by Rabbeinu Ḥananel is as it appears in this edition. If the cemetery is beyond fifty cubits, she takes another with her and performs the burial in the cemetery. Most early commentaries (see *Tosafot*) explain that according to Rabbeinu Ḥananel, there is concern with regard to mounds more than fifty cubits from the city only if they are old, as in the past, there might have been a city or road closer to the mound.

When you analyze the reasoning say – כְּשֶׁתִּימְצִי לוֹמַר: This term used here comes from the Hebrew root meaning exhaust, and in this context means: When one subjects the explicit dispute to exhaustive analysis, one may arrive at a different understanding of the dispute.

על כְּתַב יָדָן הֵם מְעִידִים, לְדִבְרֵי חֲכָמִים עַל מָנֶה שֶׁבַּשְּׁטָר הֵם מְעִידִים.

the witnesses **are testifying about their handwriting** and authenticating their own signatures. Therefore, if each witness testifies only with regard to his own handwriting, there is only one witness authenticating each signature. According **to the Rabbis,** the witnesses **are testifying about** the sum of **one hundred dinars that is in the document**[HN] and are not authenticating the signatures at all. Therefore, the testimony of the two witnesses who signed the document is sufficient to ratify the document.

פְּשִׁיטָא! מַהוּ דְּתֵימָא: לְרַבִּי סְפוּקֵי מְסַפְּקָא לֵיהּ אִי עַל כְּתַב יָדָם הֵם מְעִידִים אוֹ עַל מָנֶה שֶׁבַּשְּׁטָר הֵם מְעִידִים.

The Gemara asks: That is **obvious.** No analysis is necessary to arrive at this explanation of the dispute. The Gemara answers: The analysis is necessary **lest you say** that according to **Rabbi** Yehuda HaNasi there is **uncertainty whether they are testifying about their handwriting or** whether the witnesses **are testifying about** the sum of **one hundred dinars that is in the document,** and due to the possibility that the purpose of the testimony is to authenticate their handwriting, he requires two witnesses for each signature.

וְנַפְקָא מִינַּהּ: הֵיכָא דְּמִית חַד מִינַּיְיהוּ – לִבְעֵי שְׁנַיִם מִן הַשּׁוּק לְהָעִיד עָלָיו,

And the practical difference between whether the opinion of Rabbi Yehuda HaNasi is based on certainty or uncertainty is in a case **where one of** the witnesses who signed the document **died.**[H] If his opinion is based on certainty that they are testifying about the signatures, one other witness testifying to the authenticity of both signatures would suffice, as both that other witness and the surviving signatory would testify to authenticate each signature. However, if his opinion is based on uncertainty, **let them require two** other witnesses **from the street to testify about** the signature of the deceased witness.

דְּאִם כֵּן קָנָפֵיק נְכֵי רִיבְעָא דְּמָמוֹנָא אַפּוּמָא דְּחַד סָהֲדָא.

That is due to the fact that **if** it is **so** that the witnesses are testifying about the sum of one hundred dinars that is in the document and only one other witness joined the surviving witness in testifying with regard to that signature, the result would be that the entire sum **of money, less one-quarter, is collected** based **on the testimony of a single witness.** The surviving signatory authenticates his signature and thereby facilitates collection of half the sum. In addition, his testimony together with the testimony of the witness from the street authenticating the signature of the deceased signatory facilitates collection of the other half. Based on the verse: "At the mouth of two witnesses… shall a matter be established" (Deuteronomy 19:15), each witness is responsible for half the sum.

HALAKHA

They are testifying about the sum of one hundred dinars that is in the document – עַל מָנֶה שֶׁבַּשְּׁטָר הֵם מְעִידִים: When a witness who signed a document comes to court to authenticate his signature and says that he does not recall the actual incident recorded in the document that he signed, his testimony is not accepted. That is because in that case, his testimony is about the sum recorded in the promissory note, in accordance with the opinion of the Rabbis. In any event, if the signatures were already authenticated by other means, e.g., through comparison to another document or through the testimony of other witnesses, whether or not the signatories recall the event is irrelevant (Rambam). Some authorities disagree and rule that the testimony of witnesses authenticating their signatures is valid even if they do not recall the actual event, provided that two witnesses authenticate each signature. This can be accomplished either by each of the witnesses authenticating his own signature and that of his fellow witness, or by each authenticating his own signature and an additional witness testifying to authenticate their signatures (*Tosafot*; Rosh; *Tur*). Others maintain that even the Rambam would agree that an additional witness is effective when the witnesses do not recall the incident (*Beit Yosef*). The *Shakh* proved that Rav Yosef Caro reconsidered and ultimately agreed with most commentaries that the Rambam disagrees in that case as well (Rambam *Sefer Shofetim, Hilkhot Edut* 8:1; *Shulḥan Arukh, Ḥoshen Mishpat* 46:10).

Where one of the witnesses died – הֵיכָא דְּמִית חַד מִינַּיְיהוּ: If one of the signatories to a document dies, the surviving witness may not testify to authenticate both his signature and the signature of the dead witness, as this would lead to most of the money being collected based on the testimony of a single witness. This is in accordance with the Gemara's explanation that the witnesses testify about the sum of one hundred dinars in the document (Rambam *Sefer Shofetim, Hilkhot Edut* 7:5; *Shulḥan Arukh, Ḥoshen Mishpat* 46:13).

NOTES

About the sum of one hundred dinars that is in the document – עַל מָנֶה שֶׁבַּשְּׁטָר: The dispute between the halakhic authorities in this regard (see HALAKHA) is tied to understanding the dispute between the *tanna'im* here. From Rashi's formulation, apparently, the Rabbis, who said that the witnesses are testifying about the sum of one hundred dinars that is in the document, are referring to a case where the witnesses testify: We saw the loan take place. That is the Rid's understanding of Rashi's opinion and is also the opinion of the Rambam, who says that if the witnesses do not remember the actual incident, even if they testify to authenticate their signatures, it is not considered testimony at all. The Rambam even adds that any judge who rules otherwise is lacking in his understanding of civil law. However, many early commentaries object to various aspects of this explanation, as this calls into question the very procedure of ratifying a document by means of authentication of the signatures. Although according to the Rambam there is a distinction between a case where the witnesses say that they do not remember the incident, where their testimony would be disqualified, and a case where the signatures are authenticated and the witnesses say nothing more, where the legal status of their testimony is as though it were cross-examined in court and it is valid.

Some seek to cite proof for the opinion of the Rambam from the parallel discourse on this topic in the Jerusalem Talmud; however, the proof is far from conclusive (see Meiri). Therefore, most other early commentaries agree with *Tosafot*, who explain that the dispute between Rabbi Yehuda HaNasi and the Rabbis is not about the content of the testimony but about its meaning. According to Rabbi Yehuda HaNasi, the testimony of the signatories, of other witnesses, or of the court, who compare the handwriting of the signatories to their signatures in other documents, is authenticating the signatures on the document, and once their signatures are authenticated, the testimony of the signatories becomes like testimony cross-examined in court. The Sages maintain that the authentication of the signatures verifies the original testimony with regard to the hundred dinars recorded in the document. Even if the witnesses do not remember their original testimony, they verify that testimony by authenticating their signatures (see Ritva).

וְהָכָא לְחוּמְרָא וְהָכָא לְחוּמְרָא,

And one would have thought that Rabbi Yehuda HaNasi would rule **stringently here:** When both signatories are alive they must add another witness with them to authenticate the signatures of the two witnesses, as perhaps they are testifying about their handwriting; **and** he would rule **stringently here:** When one of the signatories died they must add two witnesses, as perhaps the witnesses are testifying about the sum of one hundred dinars that is in the document.

קָא מַשְׁמַע לַן: דְּרַבִּי מִיפְשַׁט פְּשִׁיטָא לֵיהּ, בֵּין לְקוּלָּא בֵּין לְחוּמְרָא. דְּאָמַר רַב יְהוּדָה אָמַר רַב: שְׁנַיִם הַחֲתוּמִין עַל הַשְּׁטָר וּמֵת אֶחָד מֵהֶן – צְרִיכִין שְׁנַיִם מִן הַשּׁוּק לְהָעִיד עָלָיו, בְּזוֹ רַבִּי לְקוּלָּא וְרַבָּנַן לְחוּמְרָא.

Therefore, the Gemara **teaches us that** the matter **was clear to Rabbi** Yehuda HaNasi, that they are testifying about their handwriting, and he ruled accordingly **both leniently,** requiring only one additional witness when one of the signatories died, **and stringently,** requiring an additional witness when both signatories are alive. **As Rav Yehuda said** that **Rav said:** With regard to **two** witnesses **who were signatories to a document and one of them died, they require two** others **from the street** to **testify about** the signature of the one who died, and **in this** case, **Rabbi** Yehuda HaNasi rules **leniently** and requires only one additional witness, **and the Rabbis** rule **stringently** and require two additional witnesses.

וְאִי לֵיכָּא תְּרֵי אֶלָּא חַד מַאי? אֲמַר אַבַּיֵי: לִכְתּוֹב חֲתִימַת יְדֵיהּ אַחַסְפָּא, וְשָׁדֵי לֵיהּ בְּבֵי דִינָא, וּמַחְזְקִי לֵיהּ בֵּי דִינָא (וְחָזוּ לֵיהּ), וְלָא צָרִיךְ אִיהוּ לְאַסְהוֹדֵי אַחֲתִימַת יְדֵיהּ, וְאָזֵיל אִיהוּ וְהַאי וּמַסְהֲדֵי אַאִידָךְ.

The Gemara asks: **And if there are not two** witnesses capable of authenticating each signature, **but only one, what** can be done to ratify the document? **Abaye said:** Let the surviving witness **write his signature on an earthenware** shard[NH] **and cast it into the court. And the court** then **ratifies** the document **by seeing** that it is **his** signature. **And** then **he does not need to testify** and authenticate **his signature. But he and this** other witness **go and testify** to authenticate **the other** signature of the deceased witness. In that case, even according to the Rabbis, one additional witness is sufficient.

וְדַוְקָא אַחַסְפָּא, אֲבָל אַמְּגִלְּתָא – לָא. דִּלְמָא מַשְׁכַּח לָהּ אִינִישׁ דְּלָא מַעֲלֵי, וְכָתַב עִילָּוֵיהּ מַאי דְּבָעֵי, וּתְנַן: הוֹצִיא עָלָיו כְּתַב יָדוֹ שֶׁהוּא חַיָּיב לוֹ – גּוֹבֶה מִנְּכָסִים בְּנֵי חוֹרִין.

The Gemara notes: **And** he writes his signature for the purpose of comparison **specifically on an earthenware** shard, **but not on parchment,** due to the concern that **perhaps an unscrupulous person will find it and write on it whatever he wants,** e.g., the undersigned owes him money. **And we learned** in a mishna (*Bava Batra* 175b): If a creditor **produced** a document **about** another written in the other person's **handwriting,**[H] in which it is written **that** the other person **owes him** money, even if there are no witnesses he is obligated to pay, and the claimant **may collect** payment **from unsold property.** One can collect repayment of a loan that is documented on a promissory note signed by two witnesses even from the borrower's land that was sold. With the document signed by the debtor, the creditor may collect payment from unsold property. Due to the potential for deceit with a signature on parchment, one provides a signature sample written on earthenware.

אָמַר רַב יְהוּדָה אָמַר שְׁמוּאֵל: הֲלָכָה כְּדִבְרֵי חֲכָמִים. פְּשִׁיטָא, יָחִיד וְרַבִּים הֲלָכָה כְּרַבִּים! מַהוּ דְּתֵימָא: הֲלָכָה כְּרַבִּי מֵחֲבֵירוֹ, וַאֲפִילּוּ מֵחֲבֵירָיו, קָא מַשְׁמַע לַן.

Rav Yehuda said that **Shmuel said: The *halakha* is in accordance with the statement of the Rabbis** in the mishna that each of the two signatories need testify only about his own signature to ratify the document. The Gemara asks: That is **obvious,** as the principle is: In a dispute between **an individual** Sage **and multiple** Sages, **the *halakha*** is ruled **in accordance with** the opinion of **multiple** Sages. The Gemara answers: **Lest you say** that just as there is a principle: **The *halakha*** is ruled **in accordance with** the opinion of **Rabbi** Yehuda HaNasi in disputes **with his colleague,** there is also a principle that the *halakha* is ruled in accordance with his opinion **even** when he disagrees **with his** multiple **colleagues;** therefore, Rav Yehuda **teaches us** that Shmuel said that the principle applies only to disputes with an individual colleague.

סִימָן נח נד חד. אֲמַר לֵיהּ רַב חִנָּנָא בַּר חִיָּיא לְרַב יְהוּדָה, וְאָמְרִי לָהּ רַב הוּנָא בַּר יְהוּדָה לְרַב יְהוּדָה, וְאָמְרִי לָהּ רַב חִיָּיא בַּר יְהוּדָה לְרַב יְהוּדָה: וּמִי אֲמַר שְׁמוּאֵל הָכִי?

§ The Gemara provides **a mnemonic** for the names and patronyms of the *amora'im* associated with the statement cited below: ***Nun ḥet*** for Rav Ḥinnana bar Ḥiyya, ***nun dalet*** for Rav Huna bar Yehuda, and ***ḥet dalet*** for Rav Ḥiyya bar Yehuda. **Rav Ḥinnana bar Ḥiyya said to Rav Yehuda, and some say** it was **Rav Huna bar Yehuda** who **said** it **to Rav Yehuda, and some say** it was **Rav Ḥiyya bar Yehuda** who **said** it **to Rav Yehuda: And did Shmuel say that** the *halakha* is in accordance with the statement of the Rabbis?

NOTES

Let the surviving witness write his signature on an earthenware shard – לִכְתּוֹב חֲתִימַת יְדֵיהּ אַחַסְפָּא: Ostensibly, this Gemara indicates that one cannot collect payment with a document written on earthenware. The Ramban and others explain that writing on earthenware can easily be forged, and one may not collect a debt with a document that can easily be forged. *Tosafot* question this from the fact that it is stated (*Kiddushin* 9a; 26a) that a document or bill of divorce written on earthenware is a legitimate document. Some answer that the halakhic ruling that earthenware documents are legitimate documents is in accordance with the opinion that it is the witnesses to the transmission of the document who effect the transaction, and therefore the signatures are not significant (*Tosafot*).

Others explain that with regard to a bill of divorce and bills of purchase, whose primary function is to be used at the moment that the document is transferred from the husband to the wife or from the buyer to the seller, there is no insistence that the document be written in a manner where it cannot be forged. The Ritva writes, citing Rabbeinu Tam, that in the case where earthenware documents are legitimate it is referring to text that was chiseled into the earthenware, which cannot be easily forged. Citing Rabbeinu Yeḥiel, others explain that the earthenware then was not smooth and therefore the document could not be easily forged. The reason that the Gemara here suggested writing the signature on earthenware is that people tend not to notice discarded earthenware shards and will therefore not come to use the shard for forgery. Others explain that signing on clay is unusual, and therefore one will take precautions to ensure that his signature on a shard will not be used improperly (Meiri). The simple understanding is that standard procedure was to discard and shatter earthenware with a signature sample that was used in court.

HALAKHA

Let the surviving witness write his signature on an earthenware shard – לִכְתּוֹב חֲתִימַת יְדֵיהּ אַחַסְפָּא: If one of the signatories to a document dies, and the other signatory and one additional witness seek to authenticate the signatures, the surviving witness should not authenticate his own signature. Instead he should write his signature on an earthenware shard in the presence of two independent witnesses, who then authenticate his signature in court. Then, the surviving signatory, together with the additional witness, authenticate the dead witness's signature, in accordance with the opinion of Abaye. The reason that it should be written on a shard or, according to *Tosafot*, at the beginning of a scroll, is to prevent its fraudulent misuse (Rambam *Sefer Shofetim, Hilkhot Edut* 7:5; *Shulḥan Arukh, Ḥoshen Mishpat* 46:13).

If one produced a document about another written in his handwriting – הוֹצִיא עָלָיו כְּתַב יָדוֹ: If a creditor produces a document in which a debtor wrote in his handwriting, or if the debtor signed a document that he owes the creditor money, despite the fact that the document is not signed by witnesses, it may be used to collect from his unsold property. If the alleged debtor authenticates his signature but claims that the loan never took place, the debtor's claim is accepted based on the halakhic principle, known as *miggo*, that the ability to make a more advantageous claim grants credibility to the claim he actually makes, as had he claimed that he repaid the money, the claim would have been accepted. The creditor then takes an oath of inducement instituted by the Sages and is exempt from payment. Others disagree and maintain that one's claim that he repaid a loan that appears in a document written in his handwriting would not be accepted (*Tosafot*; Rambam *Sefer Mishpatim, Hilkhot Malve VeLoveh* 11:3 and see 27:2; *Shulḥan Arukh, Ḥoshen Mishpat* 69:1, 2).

HALAKHA

A witness and a judge join together – **עֵד וְדַיָּין מִצְטָרְפִין**: If there are neither two witnesses to authenticate the signatures of the witnesses nor two witnesses to authenticate the signatures of the judges who ratified the document, and one of the signatory witnesses authenticates his signature and one judge or two independent witnesses authenticate the signature of the judge on the document of ratification, their testimonies do not join together to authenticate the document, because their testimonies are not addressing the same matter, in accordance with the rulings of Rava and Rav Ashi (Rambam *Sefer Shofetim*, *Hilkhot Edut* 4:6; *Shulḥan Arukh*, *Ḥoshen Mishpat* 30:12 and 46:14).

PERSONALITIES

Rami bar Yeḥezkel – **רָמִי בַּר יְחֶזְקֵאל**: Rami, a contraction of Rav Ami bar Yeḥezkel, was the younger brother of Rav Yehuda. Although in his youth he studied Torah under Rav and Shmuel, Rami ascended to Eretz Yisrael where he became familiar with many ancient traditions, principally previously unknown *baraitot*. In the Jerusalem Talmud he appears as Rav Ami or Imi bar Yeḥezkel. Ultimately, he returned to Babylonia, as indicated by the expression: When he came, and he brought with him the Torah of Eretz Yisrael. His traditions were considered precise and significant to the extent that they led to the rejection of statements of Rav Yehuda.

וְהָא הַהוּא שְׁטָרָא דְּנָפֵיק מִבֵּי דִּינָא דְּמָר שְׁמוּאֵל, וַהֲוָה כְּתִיב בֵּיהּ: מִדַּאֲתָא רַב עָנָן בַּר חִיָּיא וְאַסְהֵיד אַחֲתִימוֹת יְדֵיהּ וְאַדְּחַד דְּעִמֵּיהּ, וּמַנּוּ – רַב חָנָן בַּר רַבָּה, וּמִדַּאֲתָא רַב חָנָן בַּר רַבָּה וְאַסְהֵיד אַחֲתִימוֹת יְדֵיהּ וְאַדְּחַד דְּעִמֵּיהּ, וּמַנּוּ – רַב עָנָן בַּר חִיָּיא, אַשְׁרַנוּהִי וְקַיְּימְנוּהִי כִּדְחַזֵּי!

But wasn't there that document that emerged from the court of Master Shmuel, and it was written with regard to that document: **From the fact that Rav Anan bar Ḥiyya came** before the court **and testified about his signature and about** the signature **of the one** who signed the document **with him, and who was that** other signatory, **Rav Ḥanan bar Rabba; and from the fact that Rav Ḥanan bar Rabba came** before the court **and testified about his signature and about** the signature **of the one who** signed the document **with him, and who was that** other signatory, **Rav Anan bar Ḥiyya; we certified and ratified** this document **as appropriate.** If Shmuel ruled in accordance with the opinion of the Rabbis there would have been no need for each to testify about the signature of his fellow witness.

אֲמַר לֵיהּ: הַהוּא שְׁטָרָא דְּיַתְמֵי הֲוָה, וְחָשׁ שְׁמוּאֵל לְבֵית דִּין טוֹעִין. וְסָבַר שְׁמוּאֵל: דִּלְמָא אִיכָּא דִּסְבִירָא לֵיהּ הֲלָכָה כְּרַבִּי מֵחֲבֵירוֹ וְלֹא מֵחֲבֵירָיו, וּבְהָא – אֲפִילּוּ מֵחֲבֵירָיו, סָבַר אַעֲבֵיד רַוְוחָא כִּי הֵיכִי דְּלָא מַפְסְדֵי יַתְמֵי.

Rav Yehuda **said to him: That was a document for** the benefit of **orphans, and Shmuel was concerned** about the potential **for an error of the court. And Shmuel thought: Perhaps there is** a court **that holds** that in general, **the** *halakha* is ruled **in accordance with** the opinion of **Rabbi** Yehuda HaNasi in disputes **with his colleague but not** in disputes **with his** multiple **colleagues, and in this** case, the *halakha* is ruled in accordance with his opinion **even** in disputes **with his** multiple **colleagues,** and the court will not ratify the document if each witness testifies only about his own signature. Therefore **he thought: I will perform** ratification of the document in an **expansive** manner, in accordance with all opinions, to ensure **that the orphans will not lose** money to which they are entitled.

אָמַר רַב יְהוּדָה אָמַר שְׁמוּאֵל: עֵד וְדַיָּין מִצְטָרְפִין.

§ **Rav Yehuda said** that **Shmuel said:** If a document came before a court and the court ratified it, and then the document was produced in order to collect the debt, at which time the borrower contested its validity and claimed that it was forged, one **witness** who was a signatory on the document **and a judge** who ratified the document **join together**[H] to testify that the document is valid.

אֲמַר רָמִי בַּר חָמָא: כַּמָּה מַעַלְיָא הָא שְׁמַעְתָּא. אֲמַר רָבָא: מַאי מַעַלְיוּתָא? מַאי דְּקָא מַסְהֵיד סָהֲדָא לָא קָא מַסְהֵיד דַּיָּינָא, וּמַאי דְּקָא מַסְהֵיד דַּיָּינָא לָא קָא מַסְהֵיד סָהֲדָא!

Rami bar Ḥama said: How excellent is this ***halakha.*** **Rava said:** In **what** way is that **excellence** manifested? **That which the witness testifies,** i.e., authenticating his signature and confirming the incident that he witnessed, **the judge does not testify,** as the judge testifies that the document was ratified. **And that which the judge testifies, the witness does not testify.** There are not two witnesses testifying to either matter.

אֶלָּא, כִּי אֲתָא רָמִי בַּר יְחֶזְקֵאל אָמַר: לָא תְּצִיתִינְהוּ לְהָנֵי כְּלָלֵי דְּכָיֵיל יְהוּדָה אָחִי מִשְּׁמֵיהּ דִּשְׁמוּאֵל.

Rather, when Rami bar Yeḥezkel[P] **came, he said: Do not listen to those principles that my brother** Rav **Yehuda** bar Yeḥezkel **established in the name of Shmuel** with regard to a witness and a judge joining together to testify.

Perek **II**
Daf **21** Amud **b**

אִיקְּלַע רַבְנַאי אֲחוּהּ דְּרַבִּי חִיָּיא בַּר אַבָּא לְמִזְבַּן שׁוּמְשְׁמֵי, וַאֲמַר: הָכִי אֲמַר שְׁמוּאֵל: עֵד וְדַיָּין מִצְטָרְפִין. אֲמַר אֲמֵימָר: כַּמָּה מַעַלְיָא הָא שְׁמַעְתָּא! אֲמַר לֵיהּ רַב אַשִׁי לַאֲמֵימָר: מִשּׁוּם דְּקַלְּסָהּ אֲבוּהּ דְּאִמָּךְ אַתְּ נַמִי מְקַלְּסַתְּ לַהּ? כְּבָר פִּרְכָהּ רָבָא.

The Gemara relates: **Ravnai, brother of Rabbi Ḥiyya bar Abba, happened to** come and **sell sesame, and he said** that **this** is what **Shmuel said: A witness and a judge join** together to testify. **Ameimar said: How excellent is this** ***halakha.*** **Rav Ashi said to Ameimar: Due to the fact that** Rami bar Ḥama, **father of your mother, praised it, you also praise** [***mekallesat***][L] **it? Rava already refuted** that statement and proved it incorrect.

LANGUAGE

Praise [*mekallesat*] – **מְקַלְּסַת**: Apparently from the Greek, this term means praise. Some say that it is from the word καλός, *kalos*, meaning beautiful, or from a similar root. In the Bible the term means the opposite, derision.

אָמַר רַב סָפְרָא אָמַר רַבִּי אַבָּא אָמַר רַב יִצְחָק בַּר שְׁמוּאֵל בַּר מָרְתָא אָמַר רַב הוּנָא, וְאָמְרִי לַהּ אָמַר רַב הוּנָא אָמַר רַב: שְׁלֹשָׁה שֶׁיָּשְׁבוּ לְקַיֵּים אֶת הַשְּׁטָר, שְׁנַיִם מַכִּירִין חֲתִימוֹת יְדֵי עֵדִים וְאֶחָד אֵינוֹ מַכִּיר, עַד שֶׁלֹּא חָתְמוּ – מְעִידִין בְּפָנָיו וְחוֹתֵם, מִשֶּׁחָתְמוּ – אֵין מְעִידִין בְּפָנָיו וְחוֹתֵם.

§ **Rav Safra said** that **Rabbi Abba said** that **Rav Yitzhak bar Shmuel bar Marta said** that **Rav Huna said;** and some say that **Rav Huna said** that **Rav said:** With regard to **three** judges **who convened to ratify a document,**[H] and **two** of them **recognize the signatures of the witnesses** on the document, **and one does not recognize** them; **as long as** the two judges **did not** yet **sign** to ratify the document, they **testify** and authenticate the signatures **before** the third judge, and based on that testimony, the third judge **signs** the document of ratification together with the first two judges. However, **once** the two judges **signed** the ratification, **they may not testify before him and** have him **sign**[N] the ratification. The formula of the ratification is: We verified and ratified this document in a forum of three. Since when the first two judges signed the ratification, they were not a forum of three, the ratification is invalid.

וּמִי כָּתְבִינַן? וְהָאָמַר רַב פַּפִּי מִשְּׁמֵיהּ דְּרָבָא: הַאי אַשְׁרָתָא דְדַיָּינֵי דְּנִיכְתַּב מִקַּמֵּיהּ דְּנִיחְווּ סָהֲדֵי אַחֲתִימַת יְדַיְיהוּ – פְּסוּלָה, דְּמִתְחֲזֵי כְּשִׁקְרָא. הָכָא נַמִי מִתְחֲזֵי כְּשִׁקְרָא!

The Gemara asks: **And do we write** the ratification of a document before all of the judges verify the signatures of the witnesses? **But didn't Rav Pappi say in the name of Rava: This ratification of judges that was written before the witnesses related** testimony **about their signatures is invalid,** even if the witnesses later authenticate their signatures, as **it seems like a lie,** since when they drafted the ratification they were not yet aware that they would be able to ratify the document? **Here too,** when the judges drafted the ratification before the third judge can verify the signatures, **it seems like a lie.**

אֶלָּא אֵימָא: עַד שֶׁלֹּא כָּתְבוּ – מְעִידִין בְּפָנָיו וְחוֹתֵם, מִשֶּׁכָּתְבוּ – אֵין מְעִידִין בְּפָנָיו וְחוֹתֵם.

The Gemara answers: **Rather,** emend the statement and **say: As long as** the two judges **did not** yet **write** the ratification of the document, they **testify** and authenticate the signatures **before** the third judge, and based on that testimony, the third judge **signs** the ratification together with the first two judges. However, **once** the two judges **have written** the ratification, **they may not testify before him and** have him **sign** the ratification.

שְׁמַע מִינַּהּ תְּלָת; שְׁמַע מִינַּהּ: עֵד נַעֲשֶׂה דַּיָּין. וּשְׁמַע מִינַּהּ: דַּיָּינִין הַמַּכִּירִין חֲתִימוֹת יְדֵי עֵדִים אֵינָן צְרִיכִין לְהָעִיד בִּפְנֵיהֶם. וּשְׁמַע מִינַּהּ: דַּיָּינִין שֶׁאֵין מַכִּירִין חֲתִימוֹת יְדֵי עֵדִים – צְרִיכִין לְהָעִיד בִּפְנֵי כׇּל אֶחָד וְאֶחָד.

The Gemara notes: **Conclude from** the statement of Rav Huna **three** *halakhot*: **Conclude from it that a witness** can **become a judge,** as the two judges who testified to authenticate the signatures signed the ratification as judges and were not disqualified due to a conflict of interest. **And conclude from it** that **judges who recognize the signatures of** the **witnesses**[H] **do not require** other witnesses **to testify before them. And conclude from it** that in cases involving **judges who do not recognize the signatures of the witnesses,** witnesses **are required to testify before each and every one of them,** and no judge may issue a ruling based on testimony brought before the other judges.

מַתְקִיף לַהּ רַב אָשֵׁי: בִּשְׁלָמָא, עֵד נַעֲשֶׂה דַּיָּין – שָׁמְעִינַן מִינַּהּ. אֶלָּא דַּיָּינִין הַמַּכִּירִין חֲתִימוֹת יְדֵי עֵדִים אֵין צְרִיכִין לְהָעִיד בִּפְנֵיהֶם, דִּלְמָא לְעוֹלָם אֵימָא לָךְ: צְרִיכִין, וְשָׁאנֵי הָכָא דְּקָא מִקַּיְּימָא הַגָּדָה בְּחַד!

Rav Ashi strongly **objects** to the conclusions drawn by the Gemara. **Granted,** the fact that **a witness** can **become a judge we** can **conclude from** the statement of Rav Huna. **However,** the fact that **judges who recognize the signatures of witnesses do not require** other witnesses **to testify before them** cannot be concluded from the statement of Rav Huna. **Perhaps, I will say to you** that **actually** judges **require** witnesses to testify before them; **and here,** in this case, **it is different,** as the requirement of the **statement** of testimony **is fulfilled with** the testimony of the two judges before the **one** judge[N] who did not recognize the signatures. However, in a case where there is no statement of testimony at all, there could be no ratification of the document.

וְדַיָּינִין שֶׁאֵין מַכִּירִין חֲתִימוֹת יְדֵי עֵדִים צְרִיכִין לְהָעִיד בִּפְנֵי כׇּל אֶחָד וְאֶחָד, דִּלְמָא לְעוֹלָם אֵימָא לָךְ: אֵין צְרִיכִין, וְשָׁאנֵי הָכָא – דְּלָא קָא מִקַּיְּימָא הַגָּדָה כְּלָל!

And furthermore, with regard to the conclusion that in cases of **judges who do not recognize the signatures of the witnesses,** witnesses **are required to testify before each and every one** of them, **perhaps, I will say to you** that **actually,** in general, witnesses **are not required** to testify before each and every judge; **and here,** in this case, **it is different,** as were it not for the testimony of the two judges before the third judge, the requirement of the **statement** of testimony would **not be fulfilled** at all. In a case where there is other testimony, perhaps one may rely on the knowledge of others in order to ratify the document.

HALAKHA

Three judges who convened to ratify a document – שְׁלֹשָׁה שֶׁיָּשְׁבוּ לְקַיֵּים אֶת הַשְּׁטָר: With regard to three judges who convene to ratify a document, two of whom recognize the signatures of the witnesses and one of whom does not, according to several early commentaries (Rif; Rambam; Rashba; *Smag*) they may write the ratification document; the two judges who recognize the signatures then testify before the third, after which all three sign the ratification, in accordance with the opinion of Rav Huna in the name of Rav. Although this is not the Gemara's conclusion, that conclusion is in accordance with the opinion of Rav Pappi that is rejected elsewhere (Radbaz). Others disagree and maintain that writing the ratification to be signed by all three before the two judges testify before the third would create an impression of falsehood. According to this opinion, Rav Pappi's opinion is not rejected with regard to the ratification of documents (Rosh; *Tur*; Rambam *Sefer Shofetim, Hilkhot Edut* 7:6; *Shulḥan Arukh, Ḥoshen Mishpat* 46:24).

Judges who recognize the signatures of the witnesses – דַּיָּינִין הַמַּכִּירִין חֲתִימוֹת יְדֵי עֵדִים: If the judges recognize the signatures of the witnesses they may certify the document without the testimony of witnesses, in accordance with the Gemara's conclusion from that which Rav Huna said that Rav said, which was not rejected due to the difficulty posed by Rav Ashi (*Beit Yosef*; Rambam *Sefer Shofetim, Hilkhot Edut* 6:2; *Shulḥan Arukh, Ḥoshen Mishpat* 46:7).

NOTES

Once they signed they may not testify before him and have him sign – מִשֶּׁחָתְמוּ אֵין מְעִידִין בְּפָנָיו וְחוֹתֵם: Some explain that the reason that the two judges cannot testify before the third once they signed the ratification is because they then become interested parties, as they do not want their signatures invalidated (Rid; *Tosafot*). Others explain that if two judges signed before the third judge heard the testimony, they can no longer testify before the tribunal, as in retrospect it is clear that they signed a false declaration, as they were not permitted to sign the document until all the judges are aware of the matter (Rashi). The Ritva adds that it does not merely seem like a lie, it is actually a lie. Some early and later commentaries (*Talmidei Rabbeinu Yona*; *Korban Netanel*) note that there is a practical difference between these two explanations in a case where it is witnesses and not the other two judges who testify before the third judge. According to the explanation that they signed a false declaration, the document would not be ratified even in this case. Others reject that distinction (Meiri; see Rashi).

As the requirement of the statement of testimony is fulfilled with the testimony of the two judges before the one judge – דְּקָא מִקַּיְּימָא הַגָּדָה בְּחַד: In *Tosafot* and with variations in other early commentaries, the question is raised: Based on the statement of Rav Ashi, it appears that hearing testimony from witnesses is superior to the judge witnessing the incident himself, in direct contradiction of that which is stated in the Gemara with regard to sanctification of the month. Others distinguish between the cases and explain that the concept of a judge witnessing an incident being superior to hearing testimony from witnesses is a principle that applies specifically to the sanctification of the month, with regard to which it is written: "This month shall be for you" (Exodus 12:2), which is interpreted: See this moon and sanctify the month; in other cases, testimony is preferable (Ritva). Others arrive at the same conclusion based on the verse: "And the two men…shall stand before God" (Deuteronomy 19:17), which indicates that in monetary matters testimony is required (Ramban; see *Tosafot*). The Ra'avad distinguishes between different types of testimony. In testimony about the new moon, which is witnessed by all, there is no formal requirement of testimony; however, for testimony about ratification of documents, which involves information that is not universally known, explicit testimony is required.

יָתֵיב רַבִּי אַבָּא וְקָאָמַר לָהּ לְהָא שְׁמַעְתָּא דְּעֵד נַעֲשֶׂה דַּיָּין. אֵיתִיבֵיהּ רַב סָפְרָא לְרַבִּי אַבָּא: רָאוּהוּ שְׁלֹשָׁה וְהֵן בֵּית דִּין – יַעַמְדוּ שְׁנַיִם וְיוֹשִׁיבוּ מֵחַבְרֵיהֶם אֵצֶל הַיָּחִיד, וְיָעִידוּ בִּפְנֵיהֶם, וְיֹאמְרוּ "מְקוּדָּשׁ הַחֹדֶשׁ, מְקוּדָּשׁ", שֶׁאֵין הַיָּחִיד נֶאֱמָן עַל יְדֵי עַצְמוֹ. וְאִי סָלְקָא דַּעְתָּךְ דְּעֵד נַעֲשֶׂה דַּיָּין – לָמָּה לִי כּוּלֵּי הַאי? לֵיתְבוּ בְּדוּכְתַּיְיהוּ וְלִיקַדְּשִׁי!

The Gemara relates: **Rabbi Abba sat and stated this *halakha* that a witness can become a judge.**[H] **Rav Safra raised an objection to** the opinion of **Rabbi Abba** from a mishna (*Rosh HaShana* 25b): If **three** people **saw the new moon**[H] **and they** constitute **a court, two** of them **should stand and seat two of their colleagues** to sit **near** the remaining **individual** judge. **And the** two **should testify before** the three judges, **and they should** then **recite** the standard formula for sanctifying the month: **Sanctified is the month, sanctified.** Two others must join the original judge to form a tribunal of three judges, **as an individual** judge **is not deemed credible** to sanctify the month **by himself. And if it enters your mind** to say **that a witness** can **become a judge, why do I need all this? Let** the three judges remain **seated in their place and sanctify** the month,[B] as they can be both witnesses and judges.

אֲמַר לֵיהּ: אַף לְדִידִי קַשְׁיָא לִי, וּשְׁאֵילְתֵּיהּ לְרַב יִצְחָק בַּר שְׁמוּאֵל בַּר מָרְתָא, וְרַב יִצְחָק לְרַב הוּנָא, וְרַב הוּנָא לְחִיָּיא בַּר רַב, וְחִיָּיא בַּר רַב לְרַב, וַאֲמַר לְהוּ: הַנַּח לְעֵדוּת הַחֹדֶשׁ דְּאוֹרָיְיתָא, וְקִיּוּם שְׁטָרוֹת דְּרַבָּנַן.

Rabbi Abba **said to** Rav Safra: That mishna **was difficult for me** to understand **as well, and I asked Rav Yitzḥak bar Shmuel bar Marta** about **it, and Rav Yitzḥak** asked **Rav Huna, and Rav Huna** asked **Ḥiyya bar Rav, and Ḥiyya bar Rav** asked **Rav, and Rav said to them: Leave** the case of **testimony** to sanctify **the month,** as it is mandated **by Torah** law,[N] and the guidelines are more stringent, **and** the requirement of **ratification of documents is** mandated **by rabbinic** law,[HN] where the guidelines are more lenient. In that case a witness can become a judge.

HALAKHA

A witness can become a judge – עֵד נַעֲשֶׂה דַּיָּין: If a witness testifies in a certain case, he may not also serve as judge in that case, even in monetary cases. If he witnessed the incident but did not testify, he may serve as judge in that case, even if his ruling is influenced by what he saw, in accordance with the opinion of Rabbi Tarfon (*Makkot* 7a; see *Kesef Mishne*). According to *Tosafot* and the Rosh, even if he did not testify he may not serve as a judge in capital cases, in accordance with the opinion of Rabbi Akiva. However, in matters involving rabbinic law, a witness may serve as a judge (Rambam *Sefer Shofetim, Hilkhot Edut* 5:8; *Shulḥan Arukh, Ḥoshen Mishpat* 7:5).

If three people saw the new moon – רָאוּהוּ שְׁלֹשָׁה: If three members of the court saw the new moon after sunset on the twenty-ninth of the month, they seat two other judges with one of them, and the two original judges testify before the three judges, who proceed to sanctify the month (Rambam *Sefer Zemanim, Hilkhot Kiddush HaḤodesh* 2:9).

And the requirement of ratification of documents is by rabbinic law – וְקִיּוּם שְׁטָרוֹת דְּרַבָּנַן: Since the requirement to ratify documents is an ordinance instituted by the Sages, the Rema ruled in several cases that a document may be ratified by a single Torah scholar or expert judge, as, in matters of rabbinic law, he has the authority of a tribunal of three laymen (Rambam *Sefer Shofetim, Hilkhot Edut* 6:1; *Shulḥan Arukh, Ḥoshen Mishpat* 46:4).

BACKGROUND

Sanctification of the month – קִידּוּשׁ הַחוֹדֶשׁ: Sanctification of the month is the process of judicial deliberation and the declaration issued by the ordained court announcing the beginning of a new month. In ancient times, when the new month was determined according to the testimony of witnesses, people who saw the new moon appeared before a central court comprised of members of the Great Sanhedrin to testify. Their testimony was examined, and if it was accepted by the court the new month would be announced and sanctified. Opinions are divided among the *tanna'im* as to whether only a New Moon following a month of twenty-nine days was formally sanctified on the thirtieth day, or whether the New Moon following a month of thirty days was also formally sanctified on the thirty-first day.

The moon's monthly cycle is slightly more than twenty-nine-and-a-half days. In the Talmud, unless stated otherwise, a month consisted of twenty-nine days. Because of this inconsistency, it was frequently necessary to add an additional day to the month. During the long period in antiquity when the Hebrew calendar was established by the court based on the testimony of witnesses who had seen the new moon, the addition of an extra day to a month was determined by their testimony. If the moon was sighted on the night after the twenty-ninth day of the month, the next day was declared the first day of the following month. If, however, the moon was not sighted that night, or if witnesses to the new moon did not appear in Jerusalem to testify the following day, an extra day was added to the previous month, rendering it a month of thirty days. In that case, both the thirtieth and the thirty-first day were celebrated as the New Moon. Since the fourth century CE the Jewish calendar has operated on a fixed astronomical system in which, as a rule, months of twenty-nine days alternate with those of thirty days.

NOTES

Leave the case of testimony to sanctify the month, as it is by Torah law – הַנַּח לְעֵדוּת הַחֹדֶשׁ דְּאוֹרָיְיתָא: Various explanations were provided for the fact that a witness cannot become a judge. Some *ge'onim* write that this is a stringency applicable specifically to the sanctification of the month, as the Festivals are determined based on that sanctification, which therefore could have ramifications involving *karet*, e.g., eating on Yom Kippur, or eating *ḥametz* on Passover. In monetary matters there is no similar requirement. Most commentaries, however, reject that distinction. Some explain that the fact that a witness cannot become a judge is a Torah decree based on the verse: "And the two men…shall stand before God" (Deuteronomy 19:17; see *Tosafot* and Ritva). Others explain that all testimony must be subject to being rendered false, conspiring testimony. If the witnesses were also the judges, they would not allow their testimony to be refuted (see *Tosafot*). Other *ge'onim* explain that the witnesses must testify while standing, and judges are required to sit. Some later authorities ask, based on that understanding, how can a witness ever become a judge? The Gemara answers that it is clear that the requirement for the witnesses to testify while standing does not invalidate testimony given while seated after the fact, as there are cases, e.g., a witness who is a Torah scholar, where it is permitted for the witness to testify while seated (Rashash).

And the requirement of ratification of documents is by rabbinic law – וְקִיּוּם שְׁטָרוֹת דְּרַבָּנַן: Most commentaries understand that by Torah law there is no requirement to ratify a document; the document itself is sufficient unless there was a mistake or a forgery. On that basis, Rav Hai Gaon and others write that if one of the judges who participated in the ratification is disqualified, the ratification is not voided, because it is a requirement only by rabbinic law (see HALAKHA). However, the Rambam apparently explains to the contrary, that the ratification of documents is a leniency. By Torah law, full-fledged testimony is required with regard to the loan itself, and testimony written in a document is ineffective. The Sages instituted that the judges may rely on ratification of the document through authentication of the signatures (see *Shita Mekubbetzet*).

אָמַר רַבִּי אַבָּא אָמַר רַב הוּנָא אָמַר רַב: שְׁלֹשָׁה שֶׁיָּשְׁבוּ לְקַיֵּים אֶת הַשְּׁטָר, וְקָרָא עַרְעָר עַל אֶחָד מֵהֶן, עַד שֶׁלֹּא חָתְמוּ – מְעִידִין עָלָיו וְחוֹתֵם, מִשֶּׁחָתְמוּ אֵין מְעִידִין עָלָיו וְחוֹתֵם.

§ **Rabbi Abba said** that **Rav Huna said** that **Rav said:** In the case of **three** judges **who convened** as a tribunal **to ratify a document, and** a person **raised a challenge** with regard to the fitness **of one of them**[N] to serve as a judge,[H] thereby preventing ratification of the document, **as long as they did not** yet **sign** the ratification, the other two judges **may testify about** the acceptability of the judge whose fitness was challenged, and **he** then **signs** the ratification. However, **once they signed** the ratification, **they may no** longer **testify about his** fitness **and** thereby enable him to **sign** the ratification. Once they sign, their testimony is no longer impartial because there is a conflict of interest as they seek to avoid being associated with a tribunal tainted by an unfit judge.

עַרְעָר דְּמַאי? אִי עַרְעָר דְּגַזְלָנוּתָא

The Gemara elaborates: With regard to **a challenge of what** sort was this *halakha* stated? **If** it was **a challenge** based on an allegation **of theft,**

NOTES

And a person raised a challenge with regard to the fitness of one of them – וְקָרָא עַרְעָר עַל אֶחָד מֵהֶן: Rashi and others explain that after signing the ratification the two judges can no longer testify in support of their colleague due to a conflict of interest, as they do not wish to have their signature on the ratification rendered false. Rabbeinu Ḥananel, however, explains that their conflict of interest is due to the fact that it would become apparent that there was never a legitimate court session, as one of them was not fit to judge. The result is that any rulings that they issued are null and void. According to this opinion, not only is the testimony of the judges ineffective, but even if other witnesses testify after the ratification was signed that the judge is fit, the ruling is similarly null and void.

HALAKHA

And a person raised a challenge with regard to the fitness of one of them to serve as a judge – וְקָרָא עַרְעָר עַל אֶחָד מֵהֶן: If three judges convene to certify a document, and two witnesses testify that one of the judges is guilty of a crime, e.g., robbery, and disqualified from serving as a judge, and two other witnesses testify that the judge has since repented for his crime; if the second pair of witnesses testified before the judges signed the ratification, all three judges may sign the ratification. If the judges signed the ratification before receiving the testimony that the third repented, he is not considered part of the tribunal (Rif; Rambam; based on the explanation of Rabbeinu Ḥananel). Others rule, according to Rashi's interpretation, that the two other judges cannot testify in support of the third after they signed the ratification; however, if witnesses testify that he repented, even after the judges signed the ratification, he is considered a member of the tribunal (Rambam *Sefer Shofetim*, *Hilkhot Edut* 6:7; *Shulḥan Arukh*, *Ḥoshen Mishpat* 46:26).

Perek **II**
Daf **22** Amud **a**

תְּרֵי וּתְרֵי נִינְהוּ, אִי עַרְעָר דִּפְגַם מִשְׁפָּחָה – גִּלּוּי מִלְּתָא בְּעָלְמָא הוּא! לְעוֹלָם אֵימָא לָךְ: עַרְעָר דְּגַזְלָנוּתָא, וְקָאָמְרִי הָנֵי: יָדְעִינַן בֵּיהּ דַּעֲבַד תְּשׁוּבָה.

the witnesses who testified that he is unfit and the judges who testified that he is fit **are two** witnesses **and two** witnesses[NH] who contradict them, and in that case, the allegation of theft is not completely eliminated. **If** it was **a challenge** based on an allegation of **flawed lineage,**[H] e.g., **he is a Canaanite slave and therefore unfit to serve as a judge, that **is a mere revealing of a matter**[N] that will ultimately be revealed in any case and does not require actual testimony. Therefore, there is no conflict of interest preventing the judges from asserting his fitness after they signed. The Gemara concludes: **Actually, I will say to you** that it was **a challenge** based on an allegation **of theft, and these** judges **say: We know about him that he repented** and is now fit to serve as a judge. In that case, their testimony does not contradict the original testimony that he was guilty of theft.

NOTES

They are two witnesses and two witnesses – תְּרֵי וּתְרֵי נִינְהוּ: Rashi explains that since there are two pairs of witnesses that contradict each other, the status of the judge remains uncertain, and the testimony in support of the judge whose fitness was challenged is ineffective. Rabbeinu Ḥananel explains that on the contrary (see *Tosafot*), since this is a case of contradictory testimonies, the judge retains his presumptive status of fitness. In his opinion, the Gemara's question is: If two pairs of witnesses contradict each other, even after they signed the document of ratification, shouldn't the two judges be able to testify with regard to the judge's fitness and retroactively establish that he was fit from the outset? Most commentaries agree with Rashi's opinion, and the Rif adds that in this case of uncertainty there is a confrontation between two presumptions. One, the presumption establishing the money that the lender is seeking to collect in the possession of the borrower, and two, the judge's presumptive status of fitness. Therefore, the judge remains unfit. The early commentaries extensively discuss whether one relies on presumptive status in all cases where it is confronted by the possession of money, or does it take precedence only in specific cases?

That is a mere revealing of a matter – גִּלּוּי מִלְּתָא בְּעָלְמָא הוּא: Since flawed lineage, as opposed to lack of fitness due to transgression such as theft, is a matter of public record, the testimony of the judges and, all the more so, of independent witnesses merely reveal a matter that is already known and is not considered full-fledged testimony. The Ritva adds that the presumptive status of most families, unless proven otherwise, is they are of unflawed lineage; therefore, by testifying that he is of unflawed lineage, they are merely restoring his presumptive status. The Ramban explains that because the witnesses are testifying about the lineage of the entire family, there is no direct testimony with regard to the judge.

HALAKHA

They are two witnesses and two witnesses – תְּרֵי וּתְרֵי נִינְהוּ: If two witnesses testify that a person is disqualified from serving as a witness due to a transgression that he performed, and two witnesses contradict their testimony, he is disqualified from serving as a witness, due to the uncertainty, until witnesses testify that he repented, in accordance with the explanation of Rashi and the ruling of most authorities (Rambam *Sefer Shofetim*, *Hilkhot Edut* 12:3; *Shulḥan Arukh*, *Ḥoshen Mishpat* 34:28).

A challenge based on an allegation of flawed lineage – עַרְעָר דִּפְגַם מִשְׁפָּחָה: If the qualifications of a judge are challenged based on an allegation of flawed lineage, e.g., he is a slave or a gentile, and after the two other judges signed the ratification it is discovered that he is in fact qualified, he may add his signature to the ratification, as the testimony which dismissed the challenge against his qualifications merely revealed the matter of his lineage (Rambam *Sefer Shofetim*, *Hilkhot Edut* 6:7; *Shulḥan Arukh*, *Ḥoshen Mishpat* 46:27).

אָמַר רַבִּי זֵירָא: הָא מִלְּתָא מֵרַבִּי אַבָּא שְׁמִיעַ לִי, וְאִי לָאו רַבִּי אַבָּא דְּמִן עַכּוֹ שְׁכַחְתָּהּ. שְׁלֹשָׁה שֶׁיָּשְׁבוּ לְקַיֵּים אֶת הַשְּׁטָר וּמֵת אֶחָד מֵהֶם – צְרִיכִין לְמִיכְתַּב: ״בְּמוֹתַב תְּלָתָא הֲוֵינָא, וְחַד לֵיתוֹהִי״.

§ **Rabbi Zeira said: This matter, I heard from Rabbi Abba, and if it was not for Rabbi Abba of Akko, I would have forgotten it.** With regard to a case of **three** judges **who convened** as a tribunal **to ratify a document, and one of them died**[H] before signing the ratification, the surviving judges **must** emend the standard formula of the ratification and **write: We were** convened **in a session of three** judges, **and one** of the judges **is no longer** alive. In that way it is clear that although only two judges signed, the document was ratified by three judges.

אֲמַר רַב נַחְמָן בַּר יִצְחָק: וְאִי כָּתַב בֵּיהּ ״שְׁטָרָא דְּנַן נְפַק לְקַדָּמָנָא בֵּי דִינָא״ – תּוּ לָא צְרִיךְ. וְדִלְמָא בֵּית דִּין חָצוּף הוּא? וּכְדִשְׁמוּאֵל, דְּאָמַר שְׁמוּאֵל: שְׁנַיִם שֶׁדָּנוּ – דִּינֵיהֶם דִּין, אֶלָּא שֶׁנִּקְרָא בֵּית דִּין חָצוּף!

Rav Naḥman bar Yitzḥak said: And if the judges **wrote in** the ratification: **This document was produced before us, the court;** they **no longer need** to add that they were three judges, as, when unmodified, the term court connotes a tribunal of three judges. The Gemara asks: **And perhaps it was an impudent court, and** that is **in accordance with** the opinion of **Shmuel,**[N] **as Shmuel said: Two** judges **who** convened a tribunal and **judged, their verdict is a** binding **verdict; however,** because they contravened the rabbinic ordinance mandating that a court be comprised of three judges, **they are called an impudent court.** Therefore, writing: Before us, the court, does not rule out the possibility that the document was ratified by fewer than three judges.

דִּכְתִיב בֵּיהּ: ״בֵּי דִינָא דְּרַבָּנָא אַשִׁי״. וְדִלְמָא רַבָּנַן דְּבֵי רַב אַשִׁי כִּדְשְׁמוּאֵל סְבִירָא לְהוּ? דִּכְתִיב בֵּיהּ: ״וַאֲמַר לָנָא רַבָּנָא אַשִׁי״.

The Gemara answers: It is clear that the document was ratified by the requisite three judges, **as it is written in** the ratification: Before us, **the court of our** teacher **Rav Ashi,** which presumably conforms to rabbinic protocol. The Gemara asks: **And perhaps the Rabbis of the court of Rav Ashi hold in accordance with** the opinion of **Shmuel** and they convened an impudent court, whose ruling is binding. The Gemara answers: It is clear, **as it is written in** the ratification: Before us, the court of our teacher Rav Ashi, **and our** teacher **Rav Ashi said to us**[N] how to ratify the document.

מתני׳ הָאִשָּׁה שֶׁאָמְרָה: ״אֵשֶׁת אִישׁ הָיִיתִי וּגְרוּשָׁה אֲנִי״ – נֶאֱמֶנֶת, שֶׁהַפֶּה שֶׁאָסַר הוּא הַפֶּה שֶׁהִתִּיר. וְאִם יֵשׁ עֵדִים שֶׁהָיְתָה אֵשֶׁת אִישׁ וְהִיא אוֹמֶרֶת: ״גְּרוּשָׁה אֲנִי״ – אֵינָהּ נֶאֱמֶנֶת. אָמְרָה: ״נִשְׁבֵּיתִי וּטְהוֹרָה אֲנִי״ – נֶאֱמֶנֶת, שֶׁהַפֶּה שֶׁאָסַר הוּא הַפֶּה שֶׁהִתִּיר. וְאִם יֵשׁ עֵדִים שֶׁנִּשְׁבֵּית, וְהִיא אוֹמֶרֶת: ״טְהוֹרָה אֲנִי״ – אֵינָהּ נֶאֱמֶנֶת. וְאִם מִשֶּׁנִּשֵּׂאת בָּאוּ עֵדִים – הֲרֵי זוֹ לֹא תֵּצֵא.

MISHNA With regard to **a woman who said: I was a married woman**[H] **and now I am a divorcée, she is deemed credible** and permitted to remarry, **as the mouth that prohibited** and established that she was married **is the mouth that permitted,** and established that she is divorced. **However, if there are witnesses that she was a married woman,**[H] **and she says: I am a divorcée, she is not deemed credible.** Similarly, with regard to a woman who **said: I was taken captive but I am pure,**[HN] as I was not raped in captivity, **she is deemed credible** and permitted to marry a priest, **as the mouth that prohibited** and established that she was taken captive **is the mouth that permitted** and established that she was not defiled. **But if there are witnesses that she was taken captive,**[H] **and she says: I am pure, she is not deemed credible. And if witnesses came after she married,**[H] **this** woman need **not leave** her husband.

HALAKHA

Three judges who convened to ratify a document and one of them died – שְׁלֹשָׁה שֶׁיָּשְׁבוּ לְקַיֵּים אֶת הַשְּׁטָר וּמֵת אֶחָד מֵהֶם: If three judges convene to ratify a document, and one of them dies before signing the ratification, even if they used the term court to describe that tribunal, the document must contain the clause: We were convened in a session of three judges and one of the judges is no longer alive, or a similar formula that makes it clear that there were three judges. This is to prevent those who read the document from concluding that the document was ratified by a court consisting of two judges (Rambam *Sefer Shofetim, Hilkhot Edut* 6:6; *Shulḥan Arukh, Ḥoshen Mishpat* 46:29).

A woman who said, I was a married woman – הָאִשָּׁה שֶׁאָמְרָה אֵשֶׁת אִישׁ הָיִיתִי: If a woman who does not have the presumptive status of a married woman claims that she was a married woman but is now divorced, her claim is accepted. Some add that her claim is accepted only if she states both parts of the claim in the same statement, or only if she provides a rationale for her original statement (Rabbi Moshe HaKohen; Rabbeinu Yona; Rambam *Sefer Nashim, Hilkhot Geirushin* 12:1; *Shulḥan Arukh, Even HaEzer* 152:6).

However if there are witnesses that she was a married woman – וְאִם יֵשׁ עֵדִים שֶׁהָיְתָה אֵשֶׁת אִישׁ: If there are witnesses who testify that the woman was married, her claim that she is now divorced is not accepted, and if she marries, she must leave her husband. That is the ruling even if the witnesses testified after she remarried. However, in terms of marrying a priest and entering into a levirate marriage, she is considered a divorcée based on her claim (Rambam *Sefer Nashim, Hilkhot Geirushin* 12:1; *Shulḥan Arukh, Even HaEzer* 152:7).

I was taken captive but I am pure – נִשְׁבֵּיתִי וּטְהוֹרָה אֲנִי: If a woman comes forward and declares that she was taken captive but that she was not violated, her claim is accepted even if there is one witness who testifies that she was taken captive (Rambam *Sefer Kedusha, Hilkhot Issurei Bia* 18:21; *Shulḥan Arukh, Even HaEzer* 7:4).

But if there are witnesses that she was taken captive – וְאִם יֵשׁ עֵדִים שֶׁנִּשְׁבֵּית: If there are two witnesses who testify that she was taken captive, her claim that she was not violated is accepted only if at least one witness corroborates her claim (Rambam *Sefer Kedusha, Hilkhot Issurei Bia* 18:21; *Shulḥan Arukh, Even HaEzer* 7:4).

Witnesses came after she married – מִשֶּׁנִּשֵּׂאת בָּאוּ עֵדִים: If a woman says: I was taken captive but I am pure, and the court ruled that she may marry a priest *ab initio*, and then witnesses testified that she was taken captive, she remains permitted to marry a priest *ab initio*, in accordance with the mishna and the statement of Rabba bar Avin (Rambam *Sefer Kedusha, Hilkhot Issurei Bia* 18:22; *Shulḥan Arukh, Even HaEzer* 7:6).

NOTES

And perhaps…and that is in accordance with the opinion of Shmuel – וְדִלְמָא...וּכְדִשְׁמוּאֵל: The *ge'onim* disagree whether the *halakha* is ruled in accordance with the opinion of Shmuel or with that of Rabbi Abbahu, who disagrees and says that a tribunal consisting of fewer than three judges is not a court at all. *Tosafot* note that even according to Shmuel, three judges are required to ratify documents. *Tosafot* seek to explain that perhaps the court of Rav Ashi maintains that although the *halakha* is not in accordance with the opinion of Shmuel, since the requirement to ratify documents is mandated by rabbinic law, perhaps a tribunal of two judges is sufficient.

And our teacher Rav Ashi said to us – וַאֲמַר לָנָא רַבָּנָא אַשִׁי: Rashi explains that it is clear that it was a tribunal of three since it was written in the document that Rav Ashi appointed them, and he would not convene a court of two judges. Others explain that Rav Ashi himself was the president of that court, and one can conclude therefore that there were three judges, as they wrote: And Rav Ashi said to us; they were two, and Rav Ashi was the third (*Sefer HaYashar*; see Rashi). Others reject that proof, as were Rav Ashi one of the judges, there would be no uncertainty with regard to whether it was a tribunal of two judges.

I was taken captive, but I am pure – נִשְׁבֵּיתִי וּטְהוֹרָה אֲנִי: The *halakhot* of a woman taken captive are explained in detail later in this chapter. Here, the reference is to a woman who was taken captive by gentiles suspected of sexual immorality; since she was their captive, the concern is that she was raped and therefore disqualified to marry a priest, as a woman who engages in intercourse with a gentile, whether willingly or against her will, is disqualified from marrying into the priesthood. It may be seen later in the Gemara that the Sages were extremely lenient in cases involving captive women, as their disqualification is based on uncertainty.

גמ׳ אָמַר רַב אַסִּי: מִנַּיִן לְהַפֶּה שֶׁאָסַר הוּא הַפֶּה שֶׁהִתִּיר מִן הַתּוֹרָה? שֶׁנֶּאֱמַר ״אֶת בִּתִּי נָתַתִּי לָאִישׁ הַזֶּה לְאִשָּׁה״ ״לָאִישׁ״ – אֲסָרָהּ; ״הַזֶּה״ – הִתִּירָהּ.

GEMARA **Rav Asi said: From where in the Torah** is the principle: **The mouth that prohibited is the mouth that permitted,** derived? It is derived **as it is stated: "I gave my daughter to this man [*la'ish hazeh*] as a wife"** (Deuteronomy 22:16). When the father said that he married her off **"to the man [*la'ish*]"** without revealing his identity, **he rendered her forbidden** to all men. When he then says **"this [*hazeh*],"** thereby identifying the man to whom he married her off, **he renders her permitted** to her husband.

לָמָּה לִי קְרָא? סְבָרָא הִיא: הוּא אֲסָרָהּ וְהוּא שָׁרֵי לַהּ! אֶלָּא, כִּי אִיצְטְרִיךְ קְרָא – לְכִדְרַב הוּנָא אָמַר רַב. דְּאָמַר רַב הוּנָא אָמַר רַב: מִנַּיִן לָאָב שֶׁנֶּאֱמָן לֶאֱסוֹר אֶת בִּתּוֹ מִן הַתּוֹרָה – שֶׁנֶּאֱמַר ״אֶת בִּתִּי נָתַתִּי לָאִישׁ״. ״הַזֶּה״ לָמָּה לִי?

The Gemara asks: **Why do I need** to derive this from **the verse? It is** based on **logic: He rendered her forbidden and he rendered her permitted. Rather, where this verse is necessary, is** in order **to** derive the *halakha* **that Rav Huna said** that **Rav said, as Rav Huna said** that **Rav said: From where in the Torah** is it derived that **a father is deemed credible to render his daughter forbidden?**[H] It is derived **as it is stated: "I gave my daughter to the man [*la'ish*]"** (Deuteronomy 22:16). The Gemara asks: **Why do I** need the subsequent term **"this [*hazeh*]"?**

מִיבְּעֵי לֵיהּ לְכִדְתָנֵי רַבִּי יוֹנָה, דְּתָנֵי רַבִּי יוֹנָה: ״אֶת בִּתִּי נָתַתִּי לָאִישׁ הַזֶּה, ״הַזֶּה״ – וְלֹא לְיָבָם.

The Gemara explains: The verse **is necessary to** derive the *halakha* that **Rabbi Yona taught; as Rabbi Yona taught** in a *baraita* that in the verse: **"I gave my daughter to this man,"** written in the context of a husband slandering his wife, **"this"** is written to infer: The *halakhot* in this passage apply to a man who slanders his wife and **not to the *yavam*,**[H] in the case of levirate marriage.

תָּנוּ רַבָּנַן: הָאִשָּׁה שֶׁאָמְרָה: ״אֵשֶׁת אִישׁ אֲנִי״ וְחָזְרָה וְאָמְרָה: ״פְּנוּיָה אֲנִי״ – נֶאֱמֶנֶת. וְהָא שַׁוְּיַהּ לְנַפְשַׁהּ חֲתִיכָה דְּאִיסּוּרָא! אָמַר רָבָא בַּר רַב הוּנָא: כְּגוֹן שֶׁנָּתְנָה אֲמַתְלָא לִדְבָרֶיהָ. תַּנְיָא נָמֵי הָכִי: אָמְרָה: ״אֵשֶׁת אִישׁ אֲנִי״ וְחָזְרָה וְאָמְרָה: ״פְּנוּיָה אֲנִי״ – אֵינָהּ נֶאֱמֶנֶת, וְאִם נָתְנָה אֲמַתְלָא לִדְבָרֶיהָ – נֶאֱמֶנֶת.

§ **The Sages taught** with regard to **the woman who said: I am a married woman, and then said: I am unmarried,** that **she is deemed credible.** The Gemara asks: **But didn't she render herself an entity of prohibition?** When she said that she was married she rendered herself forbidden to all men. How then can she abrogate the prohibition? The Gemara answers that **Rava bar Rav Huna said:** It is referring to a case **where she provided a rationale [*amatla*]**[L] **for her** initial **statement**[NH] and explained why she said that she was a married woman. **That was also taught** in a *baraita* with regard to **the woman who said: I am a married woman, and then said: I am unmarried,** that **she is not deemed credible. And if she provided a rationale for her** initial **statement, she is deemed credible.**

וּמַעֲשֶׂה נָמֵי בְּאִשָּׁה אַחַת גְּדוֹלָה, שֶׁהָיְתָה גְּדוֹלָה בְּנוֹי, וְקָפְצוּ עָלֶיהָ בְּנֵי אָדָם לְקַדְּשָׁהּ, וְאָמְרָה לָהֶם: ״מְקוּדֶּשֶׁת אֲנִי״. לְיָמִים עָמְדָה וְקִידְּשָׁה אֶת עַצְמָהּ. אָמְרוּ לָהּ חֲכָמִים: מָה רָאִית לַעֲשׂוֹת כֵּן? אָמְרָה לָהֶם: בַּתְּחִלָּה שֶׁבָּאוּ עָלַי אֲנָשִׁים שֶׁאֵינָם מְהוּגָּנִים – אָמַרְתִּי ״מְקוּדֶּשֶׁת אֲנִי״, עַכְשָׁיו שֶׁבָּאוּ עָלַי אֲנָשִׁים מְהוּגָּנִים – עָמַדְתִּי וְקִדַּשְׁתִּי אֶת עַצְמִי. וְזוֹ הֲלָכָה הֶעֱלָה רַב אַחָא שַׂר הַבִּירָה לִפְנֵי חֲכָמִים בְּאוּשָׁא, וְאָמְרוּ: אִם נָתְנָה אֲמַתְלָא לִדְבָרֶיהָ – נֶאֱמֶנֶת.

And there was also an incident involving an important woman who was outstanding in beauty, and many men were clamoring to betroth her. And she said to them: I am already **betrothed. Sometime later she arose and betrothed herself** to a man. **The Sages said to her: What did you see** that led you **to do so? She said to them: Initially, when unscrupulous people approached me** seeking to marry me, **I said: I am betrothed. Now that scrupulous people approached me, I arose and betrothed myself** to one of them. **And** the Gemara notes: **This *halakha* was raised by Rav Aḥa Sar HaBira**[P] **before the Sages in Usha,**[B] the seat of the Sanhedrin, and the Sages **said: If she provided a rationale for her statement, she is deemed credible.**

LANGUAGE

Rationale [*amatla*] – אֲמַתְלָא: From the Aramaic *matla*, meaning parable. The meaning of the term is not limited to fiction, but can refer to any story or incident that is related. In this context, it is a story that one tells to rationalize his actions or his original statement.

NOTES

Where she provided a rationale for her initial statement – כְּגוֹן שֶׁנָּתְנָה אֲמַתְלָא לִדְבָרֶיהָ: The early commentaries write, and it is the *halakha*, that a rationale is effective only if it was examined and deemed plausible. Support for that opinion can be cited from the question of Rav Aḥa Sar HaBira, who asks whether one can rely upon a specific rationale, and from the incident involving the woman who rationalized her statement by saying that she sought to prevent unscrupulous men from seeking to marry her (see *Ḥatam Sofer*).

PERSONALITIES

Rav Aḥa Sar HaBira – רַב אַחָא שַׂר הַבִּירָה: There were apparently two Sages who bore this name. The one mentioned here is a *tanna*, and the other, perhaps one of his descendants (see *Yevamot* 45a), is an *amora*. In both cases, the title *Sar HaBira*, meaning Lord of the Capital, was based on a family legacy. One of their ancestors had been the minister appointed over the capital, i.e., the Temple Mount in Jerusalem, which was also known as the *bira*.

BACKGROUND

Usha – אוּשָׁא: Usha was a town in the Galilee, the seat of the Sanhedrin for a generation (c. 140 CE. After the bar Kokheva revolt (132–135 CE), when the Jewish community in Eretz Yisrael was almost completely destroyed, those scholars who survived the revolt began to congregate in Usha, where the *Nasi* of the Sanhedrin, Rabban Shimon ben Gamliel II, lived. The surviving students of Rabbi Akiva congregated around him. Although they were scattered throughout the Galilee, they recognized Usha as the center of Torah study and as the seat of the Sanhedrin. In Usha, the Sages of that generation instituted many important enactments, known as the rabbinical ordinances instituted in Usha. From there, the Sanhedrin moved to Shefaram.

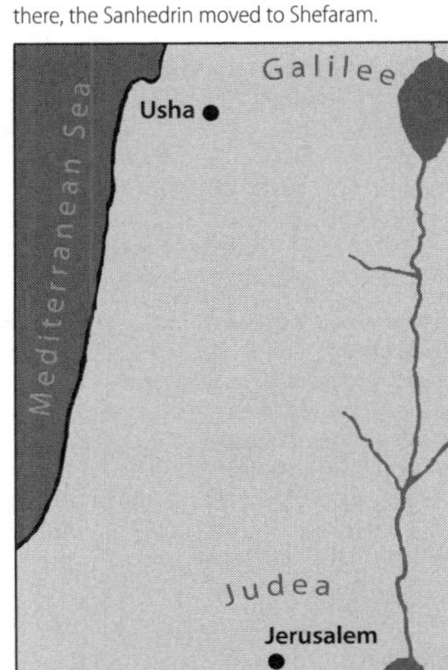

Location of Usha

HALAKHA

A father is deemed credible to render his daughter forbidden – אָב נֶאֱמָן לֶאֱסוֹר אֶת בִּתּוֹ: If a father claims: I betrothed my daughter to a man and received her bill of divorce from him, his claim is accepted. However, if he claims: She was taken captive and I redeemed her, his claim is not accepted, since the Torah deems him credible only with regard to the marital status of his daughter, in accordance with the opinion of Rav Huna (Rambam *Sefer Kedusha, Hilkhot Issurei Bia* 18:24; *Shulḥan Arukh, Even HaEzer* 37:20).

To this man…and not to the *yavam* – לָאִישׁ הַזֶּה...וְלֹא לְיָבָם: A childless widow's brother-in-law who married her through levirate marriage and slandered her and brought false witnesses that she engaged in illicit relations while married to her deceased husband is exempt from receiving lashes and paying the fine, since the Torah category of slander applies exclusively to the husband and not to the *yavam*, in accordance with the opinion of Rabbi Yona (Rambam *Sefer Nashim, Hilkhot Na'ara Betula* 3:9).

Where she provided a rationale for her initial statement – כְּגוֹן שֶׁנָּתְנָה אֲמַתְלָא לִדְבָרֶיהָ: If a woman said that she is married and then claims that she is single, her claim is accepted only if it immediately follows the original statement. However, if she provided a rationale for her original statement, her claim is accepted even if it does not immediately follow the original statement. The Rema, citing the Ra'ah, rules that if she named the man to whom she is married in her original statement, her claim is not accepted even with a rationale (Rambam *Sefer Nashim, Hilkhot Ishut* 9:31; *Shulḥan Arukh, Even HaEzer* 46:4).

בעא מיניה שמואל מרב: אמרה: "טמאה אני" וחזרה ואמרה: "טהורה אני" מהו? אמר ליה: אף בזו, אם נתנה

Shmuel raised a dilemma before Rav: If a woman **said** to her husband: **I am ritually impure** as I am menstruating, **and then said: I am pure,**[H] **what is** the *halakha*? Is she permitted based on her latter statement, or did she render herself an entity of prohibition with her first statement and therefore remains forbidden? Rav **said to him: Even in that case, if she provided a**

HALAKHA

If a woman said, I am ritually impure, and then said, I am pure – אמרה טמאה אני וחזרה ואמרה טהורה אני: If a wife tells her husband that she is ritually impure, and then claims that she is pure, her claim is accepted only if she does so immediately after the original statement. However, if she provided a rationale for her original statement, her claim is accepted even if it does not immediately follow the original statement, in accordance with the opinion of Rav. The Rema adds that although fundamentally her claim is accepted, the pious practice, as adopted by Shmuel, is to be stringent and not accept her claim (Rambam *Sefer Kedusha, Hilkhot Issurei Bia* 4:10; *Shulḥan Arukh, Yoreh De'a* 185:3).

Perek **II**
Daf **22** Amud **b**

אמתלא לדבריה – נאמנת. תנא מיניה ארבעים זימנין, ואפילו הכי לא עבד שמואל עובדא בנפשיה.

rationale for her statement, she is deemed credible. The Gemara relates: Shmuel **learned** this *halakha* **from him forty times** to ensure that he would not forget it, **and even so,** when confronted with a similar situation, **Shmuel did not** rely on that lenient ruling and did not **take action with regard to himself**[N] and his wife.

תנו רבנן: שנים אומרים: "מת", ושנים אומרים: "לא מת", שנים אומרים: "נתגרשה", ושנים אומרים: "לא נתגרשה" – הרי זו לא תנשא, ואם נשאת – לא תצא. רבי מנחם בר יוסי אומר: תצא. אמר רבי מנחם בר יוסי: אימתי אני אומר תצא – בזמן שבאו עדים ואחר כך נשאת, אבל נשאת ואחר כך באו עדים – לא תצא.

§ **The Sages taught** that if **two** witnesses **say:** The husband **died,**[H] **and two** witnesses **say: He did not die;** or if **two** witnesses **say:** This woman **was divorced,**[H] **and two** witnesses **say: She was not divorced, this** woman **may not remarry** as there is no unequivocal testimony that she is unmarried. **And if she remarried,** she need **not leave** her husband. **Rabbi Menaḥem bar Yosei says:** She must **leave** her husband. And **Rabbi Menaḥem bar Yosei said: When do I say** that **she must leave** her husband? It is in a case **where witnesses came** to testify that she is still married **and she remarried thereafter. However, if she remarried and the witnesses came thereafter,** she need **not leave** her husband based on the uncertainty created by contradictory witnesses.

מכדי תרי ותרי נינהו, הבא עליה באשם תלוי קאי! אמר רב ששת: כגון שנשאת לאחד מעדיה. היא גופה באשם תלוי קיימא! באומרת: "ברי לי".

The Gemara asks: **After all, they are two** witnesses testifying that she is married **and two** witnesses testifying that she is not; how then can the ruling be that after remarrying she need not leave her husband? In that case, **one who engages in intercourse with her stands liable** to bring **a guilt-offering for uncertainty.**[N] For any prohibition whose certain violation renders one liable to bring a sin-offering, its uncertain violation renders one liable to bring a guilt-offering for uncertainty. **Rav Sheshet said:** This is a case **where she married one of her witnesses** who testified that she is unmarried. As far as he is concerned, there is no uncertainty. The Gemara asks: **She herself stands liable** to bring **a guilt-offering for uncertainty,** as she has no independent knowledge whether her husband died. The Gemara answers that this is a case **where she says: It is clear to me**[N] that he died.

NOTES

Shmuel did not take action with regard to himself – לא עבד שמואל עובדא בנפשיה: This incident is related in the Jerusalem Talmud and cited by *Tosafot*. Shmuel's wife told him that she was impure and the next day told him that she was pure. On the second day, she explained that on the previous day she had made an excuse not to engage in intercourse because she did not have the energy. Shmuel then asked Rav: What is the *halakha*? In the *Shita Mekubbetzet*, commentaries are cited who questioned this version of the story, and a different version is related in the *She'iltot*. It was customary for the husband to give his wife a drink from the cup of blessing, the cup of wine that accompanies Grace after Meals. If she did not drink from the cup, that would be an indication that her status is that of a menstruating woman. Once, Shmuel hosted Rav, and Shmuel passed the cup of blessing to his wife and she did not accept it. Later, she explained to him that she was pure, but she had refused to accept the cup of blessing because Shmuel's sister was also present, and she did not want to embarrass her sister-in-law by drinking the wine while his sister did not.

A guilt-offering for uncertainty – אשם תלוי: The *halakhot* of a guilt-offering for uncertainty are mentioned briefly in the Torah (see Leviticus 5:17–19) and in detail in tractate *Karetot*. The Sages explained that if one performed an action and does not know whether it involved a prohibition, specifically a prohibition which, when violated unwittingly, requires a sin-offering, he is obligated to bring a guilt-offering for uncertainty. For example, one who consumes the fat of an animal and does not know whether it was forbidden fat, which when consumed intentionally is punishable by *karet* and when consumed unwittingly obligates the bringing of a sin-offering, or whether it was permitted fat, must bring a guilt-offering for uncertainty. If he subsequently discovers that he violated that prohibition, he is obligated to bring a sin-offering.

Where she says, it is clear to me – באומרת ברי לי: Rashi explains that a guilt-offering for uncertainty is brought by one troubled by his conscience. This woman is certain, based on her understanding or feeling, and has no guilty conscience. Some explain that it means that she was actually certain, i.e., she saw him die; however, if that is the case, since the Sages say that the claim of a woman who claims that her husband died is accepted, what is the uncertainty in this case? They answer that the woman's claim is accepted only when it is not contradicted by witnesses (Ra'ah; Ran).

HALAKHA

If two witnesses say the husband died – שנים אומרים מת: If two witnesses say that a woman's husband died and two say that he did not die, she may not remarry. If she remarries, she must leave her husband, as there is uncertainty surrounding her eligibility to marry. If, however, she marries one of the witnesses who testified that her husband died, and she asserts that it is clear to her that her husband is dead, she need not leave her husband, in accordance with the *baraita* and Rav Sheshet's explanation (Rambam *Sefer Nashim, Hilkhot Geirushin* 12:23; *Shulḥan Arukh, Even HaEzer* 17:42).

If two witnesses say this woman was divorced – שנים אומרים נתגרשה: In a case where two witnesses support a woman's claim that she was divorced, and two witnesses testify that she was not divorced, if she remarries she must leave her husband, and the legal status of any child born from the second marriage is that of an uncertain *mamzer*. If she married one of the witnesses who supported her claim, she need not leave her husband. However, if one pair of witnesses testifies that she was just now divorced, even if she confirms that this is the case, and other witnesses testify that she was not just now divorced, if she cannot produce her bill of divorce, her presumptive status is that of a married woman; if she remarries, she must leave her husband, and the legal status of any child born from the second marriage is that of a *mamzer*, in accordance with Rav Asi's explanation of Rabbi Yoḥanan's statement (Rambam *Sefer Nashim, Hilkhot Geirushin* 12:6–7; *Shulḥan Arukh, Even HaEzer* 152:3).

אָמַר רַבִּי יוֹחָנָן: שְׁנַיִם אוֹמְרִים: "מֵת", וּשְׁנַיִם אוֹמְרִים: "לֹא מֵת" – הֲרֵי זוֹ לֹא תִּנָּשֵׂא, וְאִם נִשֵּׂאת לֹא תֵּצֵא. שְׁנַיִם אוֹמְרִים: "נִתְגָּרְשָׁה", וּשְׁנַיִם אוֹמְרִים: "לֹא נִתְגָּרְשָׁה" – הֲרֵי זוֹ לֹא תִּנָּשֵׂא, וְאִם נִשֵּׂאת – תֵּצֵא.

§ **Rabbi Yoḥanan said** that if **two** witnesses **say:** The husband **died, and two** witnesses **say: He did not die, this** woman **may not remarry. And if she remarried** she need **not leave** her husband. If **two** witnesses **say:** This woman **was divorced, and two** witnesses **say: She was not divorced, this** woman **may not remarry. And if she remarried** she must **leave** her husband.

מַאי שְׁנָא רֵישָׁא וּמַאי שְׁנָא סֵיפָא? אָמַר אַבָּיֵי: תַּרְגְּמָה בְּעֵד אֶחָד; עֵד אֶחָד אוֹמֵר: "מֵת" – הֵימְנוּהוּ רַבָּנַן כְּבֵי תְרֵי, וְכִדְעוּלָּא. דְּאָמַר עוּלָּא: כׇּל מָקוֹם שֶׁהֶאֱמִינָה תּוֹרָה עֵד אֶחָד – הֲרֵי כָּאן שְׁנַיִם. וְהַאי דְּקָאָמַר "לֹא מֵת" – הָוֵה לֵיהּ חַד, וְאֵין דְּבָרָיו שֶׁל אֶחָד בִּמְקוֹם שְׁנַיִם.

The Gemara asks: **What is different** in **the first clause** of Rabbi Yoḥanan's statement, where, if she remarried, she need not leave her husband, **and what is the different** in **the second clause,** where, if she remarried, she must leave her husband? **Abaye said: Interpret** Rabbi Yoḥanan's statement **in** a case where each testimony was given by **one witness.**[HN] If **one witness says:** The husband **died, the Sages** instituted an ordinance and **accorded him credibility like** that of **two** witnesses in order to enable his wife to remarry. **And** that is **in accordance with** the opinion of **Ulla, as Ulla said: Wherever the Torah deemed one witness credible,** his legal status **there** is that of **two** witnesses. **And** the legal status of **that** second witness **who says: He did not die, is** that of **one** witness, **and the statement of one** witness has **no** validity **in a place** where there is the testimony of **two** witnesses. Therefore, she need not leave her husband.

אִי הָכִי אֲפִילּוּ לְכַתְּחִלָּה נַמִי! מִשּׁוּם דְּרַב אַסִי: דְּאָמַר רַב אַסִי: "הָסֵר מִמְּךָ עִקְּשׁוּת פֶּה וּלְזוּת שְׂפָתַיִם הַרְחֵק מִמֶּךָּ".

The Gemara asks: **If so,** that this is a case of the testimony of two witnesses against the testimony of one witness, it should be permitted for her to remarry **even *ab initio*.** The Gemara answers that she may not remarry *ab initio* **due to** the opinion of **Rav Asi, as Rav Asi said** that in any case of uncertainty, the verse **"Remove from you a crooked mouth, and perverse lips put far from you"** (Proverbs 4:24) applies. Although it is not a strictly prohibited action, it is, nevertheless, inappropriate.

סֵיפָא, עֵד אֶחָד אוֹמֵר "נִתְגָּרְשָׁה" וְעֵד אֶחָד אוֹמֵר "לֹא נִתְגָּרְשָׁה" – תַּרְוַיְיהוּ בְּאֵשֶׁת אִישׁ קָמַסְהֲדִי, וְהַאי דְּקָאָמַר "נִתְגָּרְשָׁה" – הָוֵה לֵיהּ חַד, וְאֵין דְּבָרָיו שֶׁל אֶחָד בִּמְקוֹם שְׁנַיִם.

In **the latter clause** of Rabbi Yoḥanan's statement, where **one witness says:** This woman **was divorced,**[HN] **and one witness says: She was not divorced, both of them are testifying** that she was **a married woman,**[N] **and that** witness **who says: She was divorced, is one** witness, **and the statement of one** witness has **no** validity **in a place** where there is the testimony of **two** witnesses. Therefore, even if she remarried she must leave her husband.

HALAKHA

In a case where each testimony was given by one witness – בְּעֵד אֶחָד: If one witness testifies that a woman's husband died, and based on that testimony the court permits her to remarry, and then a witness testifies that her husband is alive, she may marry a second husband, in accordance with Abaye's explanation of Rabbi Yoḥanan's statement. The Rema, citing the *Tur*, rules that if she did not yet remarry before the second witness testified, she should not remarry *ab initio*, because it creates the impression of inappropriate behavior, in accordance with the opinion of Rav Asi. Others write that even the Rosh, who is the source for this ruling, agrees that Rav Asi's statement was intended as good advice, not as a prohibition, and that according to the *Kesef Mishne*, Rava completely rejected Rav Asi's opinion (*Ḥelkat Meḥokek*; Rambam *Sefer Nashim, Hilkhot Geirushin* 12:18; *Shulḥan Arukh, Even HaEzer* 17:37).

One witness says this woman was divorced – עֵד אֶחָד אוֹמֵר נִתְגָּרְשָׁה: If one witness testifies that a woman was divorced and one witness testified that she was not, she may not remarry *ab initio*. If her presumptive status is that of a married woman and she remarried, she must leave her husband. If her presumptive status as a married woman was based exclusively on these witnesses, if the one testifying that she was divorced is certain that she was divorced, she may remarry *ab initio* (Rambam *Sefer Nashim, Hilkhot Geirushin* 12:9; *Shulḥan Arukh, Even HaEzer* 152:5).

NOTES

Interpret Rabbi Yoḥanan's statement in a case where each testimony was given by one witness – תַּרְגְּמָה בְּעֵד אֶחָד: The statement of Rabbi Yoḥanan: If two witnesses say, etc., means: One of the two witnesses says. Alternatively, since the Torah deemed the testimony of one witness credible with regard to the death of the woman's husband, his legal status is that of two witnesses (Ritva).

One witness says, this woman was divorced – עֵד אֶחָד אוֹמֵר נִתְגָּרְשָׁה: The early commentaries ask: Even if there is no witness testifying that she was not divorced, because one witness is not deemed credible in matters concerning personal status, it would be prohibited for her to remarry, as the testimony from one witness that she was divorced is not effectual (*Tosefot Yeshanim*; Ramban). They explain that the case here involves a woman whose presumptive status is unmarried, and it is only the testimony of the witnesses that reveal that she was married. The Ramban explains that the case here involves a woman who said: I was a married woman but I am now a divorcée. Others reject that explanation, as it is unlikely that the Gemara would have omitted so significant a detail.

Both of them are testifying that she was a married woman – תַּרְוַיְיהוּ בְּאֵשֶׁת אִישׁ קָמַסְהֲדִי: The commentaries ask: How can one rely on the testimony of these two witnesses? Since they contradict each other, one must be a false witness, and therefore both should be disqualified as witnesses. That is similar to the case of two pairs of contradictory witnesses, where a witness from one pair cannot join a witness from the other pair to testify in another case because one was certainly a false witness. The commentaries explain that the testimony of the witnesses differ with regard to the validity of the bill of divorce. In that case, it could be that neither is lying, but one witness is mistaken in his grasp of the facts (Rashba).

רָבָא אֲמַר: לְעוֹלָם תְּרֵי וּתְרֵי נִינְהוּ, וְרָאָה רַבִּי יוֹחָנָן דְּבָרָיו שֶׁל רַבִּי מְנַחֵם בַּר יוֹסֵי בְּגֵרוּשִׁין, וְלֹא רָאָה בְּמִיתָה. מַאי טַעְמָא? מִיתָה – אֵינָהּ יְכוֹלָה מַכְחַשְׁתּוֹ, גֵּרוּשִׁין – יְכוֹלָה מַכְחַשְׁתּוֹ.

Rava explained the difference between the two cases in Rabbi Yoḥanan's statement and **said: Actually** it is a case where **they are two** witnesses testifying that she is married **and two** testifying that she is not, **and Rabbi Yoḥanan saw the statement of Rabbi Menaḥem bar Yosei** as correct **in** the case of **divorce but did not see** it as correct **in** the case of **death. What is the reason** that he distinguishes between the two cases? In the case of **death,** if ultimately her husband returns alive, **she is unable to deny** that **he** is alive. Therefore, the woman's decision to remarry is credible, as if she were not certain that he was dead, she would not have remarried. However, in the case of **divorce,** if her husband returns and claims that he did not divorce her, **she is able to deny his** claim. Therefore, her decision to remarry is suspect, and the Sages penalized her and established that she must leave her husband.

וּמִי חֲצִיפָה כּוּלֵּי הַאי? וְהָאָמַר רַב הַמְנוּנָא: הָאִשָּׁה שֶׁאָמְרָה לְבַעְלָהּ ״גֵּרַשְׁתַּנִי״ – נֶאֱמֶנֶת, חֲזָקָה, אֵין אִשָּׁה מְעִיזָּה פָּנֶיהָ בִּפְנֵי בַעְלָהּ! הָנֵי מִילֵּי – הֵיכָא דְּלֵיכָּא עֵדִים דְּקָא מְסַיְּיעֵי לָהּ, אֲבָל הֵיכָא דְּאִיכָּא עֵדִים דְּקָא מְסַיְּיעֵי לָהּ – מְעִיזָּה וּמְעִיזָּה.

The Gemara asks: **And is** the woman **impudent** to **that extent,** that she would lie in the presence of her husband and claim that he divorced her? **But didn't Rav Hamnuna say** with regard to a **woman who said to her husband: You divorced me,**[H] **she is deemed credible,** as there is a **presumption that a woman is not insolent in the presence of her husband?** The Gemara answers: **This** statement that she is not insolent **applies only** in a case **where there are no witnesses who are supporting her; however,** in a case **where there are witnesses who are supporting her,**[H] **she would certainly be insolent.**

רַב אַסִי אֲמַר: כְּגוֹן דְּאָמְרִי עֵדִים: ״עַכְשָׁיו מֵת״ ״עַכְשָׁיו גֵּירְשָׁהּ״. מִיתָה – לֵיכָּא לְבֵרוּרָהּ, גֵּירוּשִׁין – אִיכָּא לְבֵרוּרָהּ. דְּאָמְרִינַן לָהּ: אִם אִיתָא דְּהָכִי הֲוָה – אַחֲזֵי לַן גִּיטֵּיךְ.

Rav Asi explained the difference between the two cases in Rabbi Yoḥanan's statement and **said** that it is a case **where the witnesses say: He died now,** or: **He divorced her now.** With regard to the husband's **death, there is no** way to immediately **clarify** whether or not he is dead. With regard to **divorce there is** a way **to** immediately **clarify** whether or not he divorced her, **as we say to** the woman: **If it is so that this** is what happened, **show us your bill of divorce.** Since the testimony was that the divorce was now, it is not feasible that she lost the bill of divorce. If she fails to produce the bill of divorce, the witnesses that testify that she is divorced are apparently false witnesses. Therefore, even if she remarried she must leave her husband.

תָּנוּ רַבָּנַן: שְׁנַיִם אוֹמְרִים: ״נִתְקַדְּשָׁה״ וּשְׁנַיִם אוֹמְרִים: ״לֹא נִתְקַדְּשָׁה״ – הֲרֵי זוֹ לֹא תִּנָּשֵׂא, וְאִם נִשֵּׂאת – לֹא תֵּצֵא. שְׁנַיִם אוֹמְרִים: ״נִתְגָּרְשָׁה״ וּשְׁנַיִם אוֹמְרִים: ״לֹא נִתְגָּרְשָׁה״ – הֲרֵי זוֹ לֹא תִּנָּשֵׂא, וְאִם נִשֵּׂאת – תֵּצֵא.

§ **The Sages taught:** In a case where **two** witnesses **say:** This woman **was betrothed, and two** witnesses **say: She was not betrothed, this** woman **may not marry** another, **and if she remarried,** she need **not leave** her husband. In a case where **two** witnesses **say:** This woman **was divorced, and two** witnesses **say: She was not divorced, this** woman **may not remarry. And if she remarried,** she must **leave** her husband.

HALAKHA

A woman who said to her husband, you divorced me – הָאִשָּׁה שֶׁאָמְרָה לְבַעְלָהּ גֵּרַשְׁתַּנִי: With regard to a woman who was presumed to be married and says to her husband: You divorced me, if she is betrothed by a man other than her presumed husband in the presence of her husband, the betrothal is valid, as her claim that her husband divorced her is accepted. This is because a woman would not be so insolent as to make that claim in the presence of her husband if it were not true.

The Rema writes that some say that her claim is not completely accepted and is not effective as far as enabling her to remarry or to receive payment of her marriage contract (see *Haggahot Maimoniyyot*). Her claim is effective in terms of requiring her to receive a bill of divorce from the one who betrothed her (Ran; Ra'avad). Some authorities add that today, even according to the Rambam, the woman's claim is not accepted because insolence abounds, and the woman would have no problem making a false claim in the presence of her husband. Nevertheless, she requires a bill of divorce from the man who betrothed her in order to remarry (*Beit Yosef*). If another man betrothed her while not in the presence of her husband, the betrothal does not take effect at all, because she would be insolent enough to make a false claim in such a situation. This ruling is in accordance with the opinion of Shmuel, who disagrees with Rav Huna and says that Rav Hamnuna stated his *halakha* only when she made the statement in the presence of her husband. The Ramban says that she requires a bill of divorce even in that case, as he rules stringently based on Rav Huna's opinion (Rambam *Sefer Nashim, Hilkhot Ishut* 4:13 and *Hilkhot Geirushin* 12:4; *Shulḥan Arukh, Even HaEzer* 17:2).

Where there are witnesses who are supporting her – הֵיכָא דְּאִיכָּא עֵדִים דְּקָא מְסַיְּיעֵי לָהּ: There is a presumption that a woman would not be so insolent as to claim in the presence of her husband that he divorced her if it were not true. This applies only when she has no support for her claim. However, if there is support for her claim, she would be so insolent, and therefore her claim is not accepted (*Beit Shmuel*). Some questioned this ruling based on the *Tur*, as the Rosh held that only the support of two witnesses would enable the woman to make a false claim in the presence of her husband (Rambam *Sefer Nashim, Hilkhot Geirushin* 12:6; *Shulḥan Arukh, Even HaEzer* 17:2).

מַאי שְׁנָא רֵישָׁא וּמַאי שְׁנָא סֵיפָא?

The Gemara asks: **What is different** in **the first clause** of the *baraita* with regard to betrothal, where, if she married another, she need not leave her husband; **and what is different** in the **second clause**[N] with regard to divorce, where, if she remarried, she must leave her husband?

אָמַר אַבַּיֵי: תַּרְגְּמַהּ בְּעֵד אֶחָד; עֵד אֶחָד אוֹמֵר "נִתְקַדְּשָׁה" וְעֵד אֶחָד אוֹמֵר "לֹא נִתְקַדְּשָׁה" – תַּרְוַיְיהוּ בִּפְנוּיָה קָמַסְהֲדִי, וְהַאי דְּקָאָמַר "נִתְקַדְּשָׁה" – הָוֵה לֵיהּ חַד וְאֵין דְּבָרָיו שֶׁל אֶחָד בִּמְקוֹם שְׁנַיִם.

Abaye said: Interpret the *baraita* in a case **in** which each testimony was given by **one witness. If one witness says: She was betrothed,**[H] **and one witness says: She was not betrothed, they are both testifying that she was unmarried. And that** witness **who says that she was betrothed is one** witness, **and the statement of one** witness has **no** validity **in a place** where there are **two** witnesses.

סֵיפָא, עֵד אֶחָד אוֹמֵר "נִתְגָּרְשָׁה" וְעֵד אֶחָד אוֹמֵר "לֹא נִתְגָּרְשָׁה" – תַּרְוַיְיהוּ בְּאֵשֶׁת אִישׁ קָמַסְהֲדִי, וְהַאי דְּקָאָמַר "נִתְגָּרְשָׁה" – הָוֵה לֵיהּ חַד, וְאֵין דְּבָרָיו שֶׁל אֶחָד בִּמְקוֹם שְׁנַיִם.

In the latter clause, if **one witness says: She was divorced, and one witness says: She was not divorced, they are both testifying that she was a married woman. And that** witness **who says that she was divorced is one** witness, **and the statement of one** witness has **no** validity **in a place** where there are **two** witnesses. Therefore, even if she remarried she must leave her husband.

רַב אַשִׁי אָמַר: לְעוֹלָם תְּרֵי וּתְרֵי, וְאֵיפוּךְ, שְׁנַיִם אוֹמְרִים "רְאִינוּהָ שֶׁנִּתְקַדְּשָׁה", וּשְׁנַיִם אוֹמְרִים "לֹא רְאִינוּהָ שֶׁנִּתְקַדְּשָׁה" – הֲרֵי זוֹ לֹא תִּנָּשֵׂא, וְאִם נִשֵּׂאת – תֵּצֵא.

Rav Ashi said: Actually it is a case where there are **two** witnesses testifying that she is betrothed and divorced, **and two** testifying that she is not betrothed and divorced. **And** in order to explain the difference between the first and latter clauses, **reverse** the two rulings. In the first clause, if **two** witnesses **say: We saw her that she was betrothed,**[H] **and two** witnesses **say: We did not see her that she was betrothed, this** woman **may not marry, and if she marries** she must **leave** her husband.

פְּשִׁיטָא! "לֹא רְאִינוּהָ" אֵינָהּ רְאָיָה! לָא צְרִיכָא, דְּדָיְירִי בְּחָצֵר אֶחָד. מַהוּ דְּתֵימָא: אִם אִיתָא דְּנִתְקַדְּשָׁה – קָלָא אִית לַהּ לְמִילְּתָא, קָא מַשְׁמַע לָן: דְּעָבְדִי אֱינָשֵׁי דְּמִקַדְּשִׁי בְּצִנְעָא.

The Gemara asks: In that case, it is **obvious** that she must leave her husband, as testimony that **we did not see her is not** effective **proof.** The Gemara answers: **No,** it is **necessary** to teach this *halakha* in a case where the woman and the witnesses **reside in one courtyard. Lest you say: If it is so** that she was **betrothed, the matter generates publicity,** and the fact that the neighbors did not see that she was betrothed indicates that she was not, therefore the *baraita* **teaches us that people are prone to betroth** a woman **in private,** with even their neighbors unaware of the betrothal.

NOTES

What is different in the first clause and what is different in the second clause – מַאי שְׁנָא רֵישָׁא וּמַאי שְׁנָא סֵיפָא: *Tosafot* ask: Ostensibly, the difference is apparent: In the case where the witnesses differ with regard to whether she was betrothed, her presumptive status is that of an unmarried woman; in the case where they differ with regard to whether she was divorced, her presumptive status is that of a married woman. In each case of contradictory testimony, the woman maintains her presumptive status.

Tosefot Rid explains that the *tanna* of this *baraita* holds that the case of two pairs of contradictory witnesses creates uncertainty with regard to Torah law, which negates her presumptive status. The result is that there is uncertainty with regard to her status. The Rashba and others explain in a similar manner: Although the *halakha* is that it is not considered an uncertainty, the Gemara sought to establish this *baraita* according to all opinions, even according to those who maintain that there is uncertainty.

In *Shita Yeshana*, cited in the *Shita Mekubbetzet*, it is explained that if the *baraita* were referring to a woman whose presumptive status is known, there would be nothing novel about this *halakha*. Therefore, one must say that the *baraita* is referring to a woman whose presumptive status is unknown, e.g., where both she and her witnesses came from abroad.

HALAKHA

If one witness says she was betrothed – עֵד אֶחָד אוֹמֵר נִתְקַדְּשָׁה: In a case where one witness testifies that a woman was betrothed and another witness testifies that she was not betrothed, if the second witness testifies that there was no betrothal at all, she may marry *ab initio*. If, however, the witnesses differ about a betrothal with regard to which there is uncertainty, e.g., where the groom threw the money of betrothal to her, and it is unclear whether it landed closer to her, in which case she would be betrothed, or whether it landed closer to him, in which case she would not be betrothed, she may not marry *ab initio*. However, if she married, she need not leave her husband. This ruling is in accordance with Abaye's explanation of the *baraita*, as Rav Ashi does not dispute his ruling, but simply explains the *baraita* in a different manner (*Tosafot*; see *Maggid Mishne*; Rambam *Sefer Nashim, Hilkhot Ishut* 9:31; *Shulḥan Arukh, Even HaEzer* 47:3).

If two witnesses say, we saw her that she was betrothed – שְׁנַיִם אוֹמְרִים רְאִינוּהָ שֶׁנִּתְקַדְּשָׁה: In a case where two witnesses say that they saw a woman betrothed, and two other witnesses say that they did not see her betrothed, even if they were together in the same courtyard at the time of the disputed betrothal, she may not marry *ab initio*. If she does, she must leave her husband. Some authorities rule that if they were all together at the time of the disputed betrothal, and she herself states that it is clear to her that she was not betrothed, if she marries one of the witnesses who supported her claim, she need not leave her husband, in accordance with the opinion of Rav Ashi (*Beit Shmuel*; Rambam *Sefer Nashim, Hilkhot Ishut* 9:30; *Shulḥan Arukh, Even HaEzer* 47:1).

סֵיפָא, שְׁנַיִם אוֹמְרִים ״רְאִינוּהָ שֶׁנִּתְגָּרְשָׁה״, וּשְׁנַיִם אוֹמְרִים ״לֹא רְאִינוּהָ שֶׁנִּתְגָּרְשָׁה״ – הֲרֵי זוֹ לֹא תִּנָּשֵׂא, וְאִם נִשֵּׂאת – לֹא תֵּצֵא. מַאי קָא מַשְׁמַע לַן – אַף עַל גַּב דְּדָיְירֵי בְּחָצֵר אֶחָד. הַיְינוּ הַךְ!

In the **latter clause** of the *baraita*, if two witnesses **say: We saw her that she was divorced,**[H] **and two** witnesses **say: We did not see her that she was divorced, this** woman **may not remarry, and if she remarries,** she need **not leave** her husband. The Gemara asks: **What** is the *baraita* **teaching us?** In this case, too, the fact that the witnesses did not see the divorce proves nothing. The Gemara answers: It teaches that **although** the witnesses and the woman **live in one courtyard** and presumably the witnesses would know if she was divorced, their testimony proves nothing. The Gemara asks: **This is** identical to **that** novel element taught in the first clause, that neighbors are not necessarily aware of what transpires elsewhere in the courtyard.

מַהוּ דְּתֵימָא: גַּבֵּי קִדּוּשִׁין הוּא דַּעֲבִידִי אֱינָשֵׁי דִּמְקַדְּשֵׁי בִּצְנְעָא, אֲבָל גַּבֵּי גֵּירוּשִׁין, אִם אִיתָא דְּאִיגָּרְשָׁא – קָלָא אִית לָהּ לְמִילְּתָא, קָא מַשְׁמַע לַן דַּעֲבִידִי אֱינָשֵׁי דִּמְקַדְּשֵׁי וְדִמְגָרְשֵׁי בִּצְנְעָא.

The Gemara explains that there is a novel element in this *halakha*. **Lest you say** that it is **with regard to betrothal that people are prone to betroth** a woman **in private; however, with regard to divorce, if it is so that she was divorced, it would generate publicity,** as divorce is typically the culmination of a period of incompatibility that is often public. Therefore, the latter clause **teaches us that people are prone to** both **betroth and divorce in private.** Consequently, the fact that the witnesses did not see that she was betrothed and divorced proves nothing.

״וְאִם מִשֶּׁנִּשֵּׂאת בָּאוּ עֵדִים לֹא תֵּצֵא״ כו׳. רַבִּי אוֹשַׁעְיָא מַתְנֵי לָהּ אַרֵישָׁא, רַבָּה בַּר אָבִין מַתְנֵי לָהּ אַסֵּיפָא.

§ We learned in the mishna: **And if the witnesses came after she married,** this woman need **not leave** her husband. Two cases were cited in the mishna, one with regard to a divorcée and one with regard to a woman taken captive, and to which of these cases this *halakha* is referring is a matter of dispute. **Rabbi Oshaya taught** this *halakha* in reference **to the first clause** of the mishna, where the woman claims that she was divorced. **Rabba bar Avin taught** this *halakha* in reference **to the latter clause** of the mishna,[H] where the woman claims that she was taken captive and remained pure.

מַאן דְּמַתְנֵי לָהּ אַרֵישָׁא – כׇּל שֶׁכֵּן אַסֵּיפָא, דְּבִשְׁבוּיָה הֵקִילוּ. וּמַאן דְּמַתְנֵי לָהּ אַסֵּיפָא, אֲבָל אַרֵישָׁא – לָא.

The Gemara notes: **The one who taught** this *halakha* in reference **to the first clause** of the mishna, **all the more so** would he teach it in reference **to the latter clause** of the mishna, **as,** in general, with regard to the status of **a captive woman,** the Sages **were lenient,**[N] because the prohibition is the result of suspicion and uncertainty as far as what transpired during her period of captivity. **And** with regard to **the one who taught** this *halakha* in reference **to the latter clause** of the mishna, **however,** in reference **to the first clause** of the mishna, **no,** he would not necessarily teach this *halakha*.

לֵימָא בִּדְרַב הַמְנוּנָא קָמִיפַּלְגִי, דְּמַאן דְּמַתְנֵי לָהּ אַרֵישָׁא – אִית לֵיהּ דְּרַב הַמְנוּנָא, וּמַאן דְּמַתְנֵי לָהּ אַסֵּיפָא – לֵית לֵיהּ דְּרַב הַמְנוּנָא?

The Gemara explains: **Let us say** it is **with regard to** the presumption of **Rav Hamnuna** that these *amora'im* **disagree. The one who taught** this *halakha* in reference **to the first clause** of the mishna and maintains that if the witnesses came after she married, this woman need not leave her husband, **he holds** in accordance with the presumption of **Rav Hamnuna,** who said that a woman is not insolent in the presence of her husband, and therefore her claim that she was divorced is accepted. **And the one who taught** this *halakha* in reference **to the latter clause** of the mishna and rules that the woman taken captive need not leave her husband the priest, while the woman who claims that she was divorced must leave her husband, **he does not hold** in accordance with the presumption of **Rav Hamnuna.**

לָא, דְּכוּלֵּי עָלְמָא אִית לְהוּ דְּרַב הַמְנוּנָא. וְהָכָא בְּהָא קָמִיפַּלְגִי; דְּמָר סָבַר: כִּי אִיתְּמַר דְּרַב הַמְנוּנָא – בְּפָנָיו, אֲבָל שֶׁלֹּא בְּפָנָיו – מְעִיזָּה, וּמָר סָבַר: שֶׁלֹּא בְּפָנָיו נָמֵי אֵינָהּ מְעִיזָּה.

The Gemara rejects that explanation: **No,** actually **everyone holds** in accordance with the presumption **of Rav Hamnuna, and here** it is **with regard to this that they disagree, as one Sage,** who holds that the woman who claims that she was divorced must leave her husband, **maintains that when** the presumption of **Rav Hamnuna was stated,** it was stated specifically in a case where she was **in his presence;**[H] **however,** when she is **not in his presence, she is insolent. And one Sage,** who holds that the woman who claims that she was divorced need not leave her husband, **maintains that** when **not in his presence she is also not insolent.** Therefore, her claim that she was divorced is accepted.

HALAKHA

If two witnesses say, we saw her that she was divorced – שְׁנַיִם אוֹמְרִים רְאִינוּהָ שֶׁנִּתְגָּרְשָׁה: If two witnesses testify that they saw a woman divorced, and two other witnesses testify that they did not see her divorced, even if they were in the same courtyard, she may not remarry *ab initio*, but if she does, she need not leave her husband, in accordance with Rav Ashi's interpretation of the *baraita*. Some authorities rule that if the witnesses who claim that they did not see her divorced were in a different courtyard, she may remarry *ab initio* (*Beit Shmuel*; Rambam *Sefer Nashim, Hilkhot Geirushin* 12:8; *Shulḥan Arukh, Even HaEzer* 152:4).

Taught this *halakha* in reference to the latter clause of the mishna – מַתְנֵי לָהּ אַסֵּיפָא: If witnesses testify that a woman is married, she is not deemed credible to claim that she is divorced. Therefore, if she remarries, she must leave her husband, even if the witnesses testified after she had already remarried. However, her claim that she was divorced is accepted to prohibit her from marrying a priest or entering into levirate marriage, since her claim rendered her an entity of prohibition (see *Maggid Mishne*; Rambam *Sefer Nashim, Hilkhot Geirushin* 12:1; *Shulḥan Arukh, Even HaEzer* 152:7).

When the presumption of Rav Hamnuna was stated it was stated specifically in a case where she was in his presence – כִּי אִיתְּמַר דְּרַב הַמְנוּנָא בְּפָנָיו: If a woman says in the presence of her husband: You divorced me, her claim is accepted because a woman would not be so insolent as to make that claim in her husband's presence if it were not true. This ruling is in accordance with the opinion of Rav Hamnuna. The Rema writes that some authorities rule that today that presumption is no longer relevant (*Beit Yosef*; Rambam *Sefer Nashim, Hilkhot Ishut* 4:13 and *Hilkhot Geirushin* 12:4; *Shulḥan Arukh, Even HaEzer* 17:2).

NOTES

With regard to the status of a captive woman the Sages were lenient – בִּשְׁבוּיָה הֵקִילוּ: Some explain that the Sages were lenient with regard to a captive woman but displayed no leniency with regard to a married woman. This is because the prohibition against a priest marrying a captive woman, whose legal status is that of a *zona*, is a standard Torah prohibition, while intercourse with a married woman is punishable by death through stoning.

The Ritva rejects that distinction, as the Sages concluded that there is no distinction between more and less severe Torah prohibitions. He explains that the leniency in the case of the captive woman is based on the fact that she attempts to make herself undesirable in the eyes of her captor to avoid being raped, as explained in tractate *Kiddushin* (12b). However, Rashi, both here and elsewhere, explains that the leniency in the case of the captive woman is due to the fact that there is uncertainty whether the captive woman was raped and therefore uncertainty whether she is forbidden. In contrast, in the case of the divorcée, the prohibition is clear as she was a married woman. All three opinions are cited in *Tosafot* on *Kiddushin*.

״וְאִם מִשֶּׁנִּשֵּׂאת בָּאוּ עֵדִים״ וכו׳. אֲמַר אֲבוּהּ דִּשְׁמוּאֵל: לֹא נִשֵּׂאת נִשֵּׂאת מַמָּשׁ, אֶלָּא כֵּיוָן שֶׁהִתִּירוּהָ לִינָּשֵׂא, אַף עַל פִּי שֶׁלֹּא נִשֵּׂאת. וְהָא ״לֹא תֵּצֵא״ קָתָנֵי! לֹא תֵּצֵא מֵהֶתֵּירָהּ הָרִאשׁוֹן.

§ We learned in the mishna: **And if the witnesses came after she married,** this woman need not leave her husband. **The father of Shmuel said: Married** does **not** mean **actually married; rather, once** the court **permitted her to marry, although she has not** yet **married,** she need not leave her husband. The Gemara asks: **But doesn't** the *tanna* **teach: She need not leave,** meaning that she need not leave her husband? The Gemara explains: That phrase in this context means that even if witnesses come, **she does not emerge** from **her initial permitted** status.[H]

תָּנוּ רַבָּנַן: אָמְרָה ״נִשְׁבֵּיתִי וּטְהוֹרָה אֲנִי וְיֵשׁ לִי עֵדִים שֶׁטְּהוֹרָה אֲנִי״. אֵין אוֹמְרִים: נַמְתִּין עַד שֶׁיָּבֹאוּ עֵדִים, אֶלָּא מַתִּירִין אוֹתָהּ מִיָּד. הִתִּירוּהָ לִינָּשֵׂא, וְאַחַר כָּךְ בָּאוּ עֵדִים, וְאָמְרוּ ״לֹא יָדַעְנוּ״ – הֲרֵי זוֹ לֹא תֵּצֵא. וְאִם בָּאוּ עֵדֵי טוּמְאָה, אֲפִילּוּ יֵשׁ לָהּ כַּמָּה בָּנִים – תֵּצֵא.

The Sages taught that if **she said: I was taken captive but I am pure, and I have witnesses** who were with me throughout captivity who can testify **that I am pure,** the court **does not say: We will wait until** those **witnesses come. Rather,** the court **permits her** to marry a priest **immediately.** If the court **permitted her** to marry a priest, **and witnesses came thereafter**[N] **and said: We do not know** whether or not she remained pure, **this** woman **need not leave** her husband, as she was already permitted to marry a priest on the basis of her original statement. **And if witnesses that she was violated came**[H] and testified, **even if she has several children,** she must **leave** the priest to whom she is married.

הָנֵי שְׁבוּיָיתָא דַּאֲתְיָין לִנְהַרְדְּעָא. אוֹתֵיב אֲבוּהּ דִּשְׁמוּאֵל נָטוֹרֵי בַּהֲדַיְיהוּ. אֲמַר לֵיהּ שְׁמוּאֵל: וְעַד הָאִידָּנָא מַאן נַטְרִינְהוּ? אֲמַר לֵיהּ: אִילּוּ בְּנָתָךְ הֲווֹ, מִי הֲוֵית מְזַלְזֵל בְּהוּ כּוּלֵּי הַאי?!

The Gemara relates: There were **these captive women who came to Neharde'a** with their captors so that the local residents would redeem them. **Shmuel's father posted guards with them** to ensure that they would not enter into seclusion with gentiles. **Shmuel said to him: Until now who guarded them?** If there is concern about their status, it should be with regard to the possibility that they engaged in intercourse while in captivity before they were brought to Neharde'a. **He said to** Shmuel: **If they were your daughters, would you treat them with contempt to that extent?** They are no longer captives and deserve to be treated like any Jewish woman of unflawed lineage.

הֲוַאי ״כִּשְׁגָגָה שֶׁיּוֹצָא מִלִּפְנֵי הַשַּׁלִּיט״ וְאִישְׁתַּבְיָין בְּנָתֵיהּ דְּמָר שְׁמוּאֵל, וְאַסְּקִינְהוּ לְאַרְעָא דְּיִשְׂרָאֵל. אוֹקְמָן לְשָׁבוֹיֵינְהוּ מֵאַבְרַאי, וְעַיְילִי לְבֵי מִדְרְשָׁא דְּרַבִּי חֲנִינָא. הָא אָמְרָה: ״נִשְׁבֵּיתִי וּטְהוֹרָה אֲנִי״, וְהָא אָמְרָה: ״נִשְׁבֵּיתִי וּטְהוֹרָה אֲנִי״. שָׁרְינְהוּ.

The statement by the father of Shmuel **was "Like an error that emerges from before the ruler"** (Ecclesiastes 10:5), **and** it was realized. **The daughters of Master Shmuel were taken captive, and** their captors **took them up to Eretz Yisrael** and sought to sell them or ransom them. Shmuel's daughters left **their captors standing outside,** so that they would not come before the court, **and** the women **entered the study hall of Rabbi Ḥanina. This** daughter **said: I was taken captive, and I am pure, and that** daughter **said: I was taken captive, and I am pure, and** the court **permitted them** to marry into the priesthood.

סוֹף עוּל אָתוּ שָׁבוֹיֵינְהוּ. אָמַר רַבִּי חֲנִינָא: בְּנָן דְּמוֹרְיָין אִינּוּן. אִיגְּלַאי מִילְּתָא דִּבְנָתֵיהּ דְּמָר שְׁמוּאֵל הֲווֹ.

Ultimately, their captors came and entered, and it was clear that they were the captors of Shmuel's daughters. However, since the daughters made their claim first and the court permitted them to marry into the priesthood, this remained permitted to them. This is based on the *halakha* that if witnesses subsequently arrive, her initial permitted status need not be revoked. **Rabbi Ḥanina said:** It is clear from their actions that they are the **daughters** of great halakhic **authorities,** as they knew how to conduct themselves in order to retain their presumptive status of purity. The Gemara relates: Ultimately, **the matter became clear, that they were the daughters of Master Shmuel.**[B]

אֲמַר לֵיהּ רַבִּי חֲנִינָא לְרַב שֶׁמֶן בַּר אַבָּא: פּוּק אִיטַּפַּל בִּקְרוֹבוֹתֶיךָ – אֲמַר לֵיהּ לְרַבִּי חֲנִינָא: וְהָאִיכָּא עֵדִים בִּמְדִינַת הַיָּם! הָשְׁתָּא מִיהַת לֵיתְנְהוּ קַמָּן, עֵדִים בְּצַד אַסְתָּן וְתֵאָסֵר?! טַעְמָא – דְּלָא אָתוּ עֵדִים, הָא אָתוּ עֵדִים מִיתַּסְרָא?

Rabbi Ḥanina said to Rav Shemen bar Abba, who was a priest: **Go out and tend to your relatives,** the daughters of Shmuel who were taken captive, and marry one of them. Rav Shemen **said to Rabbi Ḥanina: But aren't there witnesses in a country overseas**[H] who knew before the daughters appeared in court that they were taken captive? Rabbi Ḥanina **said to him: Now, in any event,** those witnesses **are not before us.** He then cited an adage: There are **witnesses in the north** [*astan*][L] **side,** i.e., in a distant place, **and** will the woman **be forbidden?** The Gemara infers from Rabbi Ḥanina's statement: **The reason** that their testimony may be ignored **is** because **the witnesses did not come** to court. **However, were the witnesses** to **come** to court, Shmuel's daughters **would be forbidden** to priests.

HALAKHA

She does not emerge from her initial permitted status – לֹא תֵּצֵא מֵהֶתֵּירָה הָרִאשׁוֹן: In a case where the court rules that it is permitted for a woman to marry a priest on the basis of her claim that she was taken captive but not violated, if witnesses subsequently testify that she was taken captive, her permitted status remains intact. This ruling is in accordance with the opinion of Shmuel's father, according to Rashi's explanation, and the incident involving Shmuel's daughters (Rambam *Sefer Kedusha, Hilkhot Issurei Bia* 18:22; *Shulḥan Arukh, Even HaEzer* 7:6).

And if witnesses that she was violated came – וְאִם בָּאוּ עֵדֵי טוּמְאָה: In a case where a court rules that a woman is permitted to marry a priest on the basis of her claim that she was taken captive but not violated, and two witnesses subsequently testify that she was in fact violated by her captors, if she has already married a priest, she must leave her husband, and children of the priest born to her are disqualified from the priesthood (Rambam *Sefer Kedusha, Hilkhot Issurei Bia* 18:23; *Shulḥan Arukh, Even HaEzer* 7:6).

But aren't there witnesses in a country overseas – וְהָאִיכָּא עֵדִים בִּמְדִינַת הַיָּם: If a woman claims that she was taken captive but not violated, and that she has witnesses supporting her claim that she was not violated, there is no need to wait for the witnesses to testify. Rather, she may marry a priest immediately. Moreover, this is the ruling even if there are rumors that there are witnesses in countries overseas that she was violated (*Tosafot*), as the Sages are lenient with regard to women taken captive, in accordance with the *baraita* and Rav Ashi's conclusion (Rambam *Sefer Kedusha, Hilkhot Issurei Bia* 18:23; *Shulḥan Arukh, Even HaEzer* 7:7).

NOTES

And witnesses came thereafter – וְאַחַר כָּךְ בָּאוּ עֵדִים: Some commentaries explain that there are two reasons that the claim of a woman captive is accepted. First, the principle: The mouth that prohibited is the mouth that permitted, applies because she is the only source for the fact that she was taken captive (see 22a). Second, there is a *miggo*, as she could have claimed that she had never been taken captive. Therefore, even if witnesses come after the court permitted her to marry a priest, rendering the first reason moot, the concept of *miggo*, which accorded her credibility at the time that she made her claim, still applies (*Kovetz Shiurim*).

BACKGROUND

The daughters of Master Shmuel – בְּנָתֵיהּ דְּמָר שְׁמוּאֵל: Neharde'a, where Shmuel's family resided, was adjacent to the border of the Persian and Roman Empires. Therefore, it was attacked and plundered on numerous occasions. Some claim that this incident that befell Shmuel's daughters transpired during the attack of Pappa ben Nazer Odonathus (51b), who destroyed the city in the year 259 CE. Based on data from the Babylonian Talmud and the Jerusalem Talmud, apparently Shmuel had at least three daughters, two of whom were taken captive and brought to Eretz Yisrael. Both later married Rav Shemen bar Abba, one after the death of the other. The third daughter married Issur the convert.

LANGUAGE

North [*astan*] – אַסְתָּן: In Aramaic, this means north, from the Syriac word meaning hidden.

וְהָאָמַר אֲבוּהּ דִּשְׁמוּאֵל: כֵּיוָן שֶׁהִתִּירוּהָ לִינָּשֵׂא – אַף עַל פִּי שֶׁלֹּא נִשֵּׂאת! אָמַר רַב אַשִׁי: עֵדֵי טוּמְאָה אִיתְּמַר.

The Gemara asks: **But didn't Shmuel's father say: Once the** court **permitted** a woman **to marry, even if she has not** yet **married,** she remains permitted? **Rav Ashi said:** The discussion between Rabbi Ḥanina and Rav Shemen **was stated** with regard to **witnesses** who witnessed their **violation.** In that case, were the witnesses to come to court and testify, even if she has several children, she must leave the priest to whom she is married.

Perek **II**
Daf **23** Amud **b**

NOTES

And when this woman testifies about that woman and vice versa – וּבִזְמַן שֶׁהֵן מְעִידוֹת זוֹ אֶת זוֹ: The Gemara explains below (24a) that this is the novel element here: Although there is room for concern lest there is collusion and each woman testify on behalf of the other, the court accepts the testimony.

Yes, the first clause and the last clause – אִין, רֵישָׁא וְסֵיפָא: When the Gemara asks with regard to a mishna or a *baraita*: What are the circumstances, it seeks to ascertain additional factors relevant to the case. In general, the Gemara seeks to establish all the cases in a uniform manner, both in terms of the Sage who stated the *halakha* and in terms of the circumstances of the cases. Different *amora'im* adopted different opinions in *mishnayot* and *baraitot* where interpreting the different clauses uniformly was difficult. Some made every effort to establish the circumstances in a uniform manner even in the face of exegetical or language difficulties, while others, e.g., Rav Yosef and Abaye, preferred explaining the source as it is written even if doing so came at the expense of uniformity.

HALAKHA

And when this woman testifies about that woman and vice versa – וּבִזְמַן שֶׁהֵן מְעִידוֹת זוֹ אֶת זוֹ: The Sages were lenient in cases involving women taken captive. Therefore, they rely on any witness, even a slave or a relative, to permit the woman to marry a priest, and even women who are not deemed credible to testify that a woman's husband died may testify in this case. In addition, the testimony of two women who were in captivity together concerning each other's status is deemed credible (Rambam *Sefer Kedusha, Hilkhot Issurei Bia* 18:17; *Shulḥan Arukh, Even HaEzer* 7:1).

מתני׳ שְׁתֵּי נָשִׁים שֶׁנִּשְׁבּוּ, זֹאת אוֹמֶרֶת: ״נִשְׁבֵּיתִי וּטְהוֹרָה אֲנִי״, וְזֹאת אוֹמֶרֶת: ״נִשְׁבֵּיתִי וּטְהוֹרָה אֲנִי״ – אֵינָן נֶאֱמָנוֹת. וּבִזְמַן שֶׁהֵן מְעִידוֹת זוֹ אֶת זוֹ – הֲרֵי אֵלּוּ נֶאֱמָנוֹת.

MISHNA In a case where witnesses testify that there are **two women who were taken captive,** and **this** woman **says: I was taken captive but I am pure, and that** woman **says: I was taken captive but I am pure, they are not deemed credible. And when this** woman **testifies about that** woman that she is pure and vice versa,[NH] **they are deemed credible.**

גמ׳ תָּנוּ רַבָּנַן: ״אֲנִי טְמֵאָה וַחֲבֶרְתִּי טְהוֹרָה״ – נֶאֱמֶנֶת. ״אֲנִי טְהוֹרָה וַחֲבֶרְתִּי טְמֵאָה״ – אֵינָהּ נֶאֱמֶנֶת. ״אֲנִי וַחֲבֶרְתִּי טְמֵאָה״ נֶאֱמֶנֶת עַל עַצְמָהּ, וְאֵינָהּ נֶאֱמֶנֶת עַל חֲבֶרְתָּהּ. ״אֲנִי וַחֲבֶרְתִּי טְהוֹרָה״ – נֶאֱמֶנֶת עַל חֲבֶרְתָּהּ, וְאֵינָהּ נֶאֱמֶנֶת עַל עַצְמָהּ.

GEMARA **The Sages taught** in the *Tosefta* (2:2): If one of the women says: **I am tainted and my counterpart is pure, she is deemed credible** on both counts. If she says: **I am pure and my counterpart is tainted, she is not deemed credible** with regard to herself nor with regard to her counterpart. If she says: **I and my counterpart are** both **tainted, she is deemed credible with regard to herself but she is not deemed credible with regard to her counterpart.** If she says: **I and my counterpart are** both **pure, she is deemed credible with regard to her counterpart but she is not deemed credible with regard to herself.**

אָמַר מָר: ״אֲנִי טְהוֹרָה וַחֲבֶרְתִּי טְמֵאָה״ – אֵינָהּ נֶאֱמֶנֶת. הֵיכִי דָּמֵי? אִי דְּלֵיכָּא עֵדִים – עַל עַצְמָהּ אַמַּאי לָא מְהֵימְנָא? ״נִשְׁבֵּיתִי וּטְהוֹרָה אֲנִי״ קָאָמְרָה! אֶלָּא פְּשִׁיטָא דְּאִיכָּא עֵדִים.

The Master said in the *baraita* that if she says: **I am pure and my counterpart is tainted, she is not deemed credible.** The Gemara asks: **What are the circumstances? If there are no witnesses** that she was taken captive, **why is she not deemed credible with regard to herself?** If she is saying: **I was taken captive and I am pure,** she is deemed credible based on the principle that the mouth that prohibited is the mouth that permitted. Rather, it is **obvious that there are witnesses** that she was taken captive.

אֵימָא מְצִיעֲתָא: ״אֲנִי וַחֲבֶרְתִּי טְמֵאָה״ – נֶאֱמֶנֶת עַל עַצְמָהּ וְאֵינָהּ נֶאֱמֶנֶת עַל חֲבֶרְתָּהּ. וְאִי דְּאִיכָּא עֵדִים אַמַּאי לָא מְהֵימְנָא? אֶלָּא פְּשִׁיטָא דְּלֵיכָּא עֵדִים.

The Gemara asks: If so, **say the middle clause** of the *baraita*: If she says: **I and my counterpart are** both **tainted, she is deemed credible with regard to herself but she is not deemed credible with regard to her counterpart. And if there are witnesses, why is she not deemed credible** with regard to her counterpart? Once there is testimony that she was taken captive, she no longer has the presumptive status of purity. Rather, it is **obvious that there are no witnesses** that she was taken captive, and therefore her presumptive status of purity is intact.

אֵימָא סֵיפָא: ״אֲנִי וַחֲבֶרְתִּי טְהוֹרָה״ – נֶאֱמֶנֶת עַל חֲבֶרְתָּהּ, וְאֵינָהּ נֶאֱמֶנֶת עַל עַצְמָהּ. וְאִי דְּלֵיכָּא עֵדִים – אַעַצְמָהּ אַמַּאי לָא מְהֵימְנָא? אֶלָּא פְּשִׁיטָא דְּאִיכָּא עֵדִים.

The Gemara asks: If so, **say the last clause** of the *baraita*: If she says: **I and my counterpart are** both **pure, she is deemed credible with regard to her counterpart but she is not deemed credible with regard to herself. And if there are no witnesses** that they were taken captive, **why is she not deemed credible with regard to herself?** Rather, it is **obvious that there are witnesses.**

רֵישָׁא וְסֵיפָא דְּאִיכָּא עֵדִים, מְצִיעֲתָא דְּלֵיכָּא עֵדִים?! אָמַר אַבַּיֵי: אִין, רֵישָׁא וְסֵיפָא – דְּאִיכָּא עֵדִים, מְצִיעֲתָא דְּלֵיכָּא עֵדִים.

The Gemara asks: Is that to say that the *baraita* is formulated in an unusual fashion, with the **first clause and the last clause** pertaining to cases **where there are witnesses, and the middle clause** pertaining to a case **where there are no witnesses? Abaye said: Yes,** the **first clause and the last clause**[N] pertain to cases **where there are witnesses, and the middle clause** pertains to a case **where there are no witnesses.**

רַב פַּפָּא אָמַר: כּוּלָּהּ דְּאִיכָּא עֵדִים, וְאִיכָּא עֵד אֶחָד דְּקָא אַפֵּיךְ. אָמְרָה ״אֲנִי טְמֵאָה וַחֲבֶרְתִּי טְהוֹרָה״ וַאֲמַר לָהּ עֵד אֶחָד ״אַתְּ טְהוֹרָה וַחֲבֶרְתֵּךְ טְמֵאָה״. אִיהִי – שַׁוְּיתָא לְנַפְשָׁהּ חֲתִיכָה דְּאִיסּוּרָא, חֲבֶרְתָּהּ – מִשְׁתַּרְיָא אַפּוּמָּא דִּידָהּ.

Rav Pappa said: The *baraita* in **its entirety** can be explained in a case **where there are witnesses, and there is one witness who is** testifying to the **reverse** of the woman's claim.[NH] If the woman **said: I am tainted and my counterpart is pure, and one witness said to her: You are pure and your counterpart is tainted,** although the witness testified that she was pure, because she admitted that she was tainted **she rendered herself an entity of prohibition. Her counterpart is permitted on the basis of her** claim, which is accepted despite being contradicted by the witness.

״אֲנִי טְהוֹרָה וַחֲבֶרְתִּי טְמֵאָה״ וַאֲמַר לָהּ עֵד אֶחָד: ״אַתְּ טְמֵאָה וַחֲבֶרְתֵּךְ טְהוֹרָה״, אִיהִי כֵּיוָן דְּאִיכָּא עֵדִים – לָאו כָּל כְּמִינָּהּ, חֲבֶרְתָּהּ – מִשְׁתַּרְיָא אַפּוּמָּא דְּעֵד.

If the woman said: **I am pure and my counterpart is tainted, and one witness said to her: You are tainted and your counterpart is pure,** then with regard to **her, since there are witnesses** testifying that she was taken captive, **it is not in her power** to permit herself on the basis of her claim. However, **her counterpart is permitted on the basis of the** testimony of the **witness.**

״אֲנִי וַחֲבֶרְתִּי טְמֵאָה״ וַאֲמַר לָהּ עֵד אֶחָד ״אַתְּ וַחֲבֶרְתֵּךְ טְהוֹרָה״, אִיהִי – שַׁוְּיתָא לְנַפְשָׁהּ חֲתִיכָה דְּאִיסּוּרָא, חֲבֶרְתָּא – מִשְׁתַּרְיָא אַפּוּמָּא דְּעֵד. הָא תּוּ לָמָּה לִי? הַיְינוּ רֵישָׁא!

If the woman said: **I and my counterpart are** both **tainted, and one witness said to her: You and your friend are** both **pure, she rendered herself an entity of prohibition.**[N] However, **her counterpart is permitted on the basis of the** testimony of the **witness.** The Gemara asks: **Why do I** need **this additional** case? **This is** identical **to** that which was taught in the in the **first clause.** The principles governing the first two cases, i.e., she claims that she is tainted and thereby renders herself as an entity of prohibition, and her counterpart is permitted by the testimony of one witness even if that testimony is contradicted, also apply in this case.

מַהוּ דְּתֵימָא: הָנֵי תַּרְוַיְיהוּ טְהוֹרוֹת נִינְהוּ, וְהַאי דְּקָאָמְרָה הָכִי – ״תָּמוֹת נַפְשִׁי עִם פְּלִשְׁתִּים״ הִיא דְּקָא עָבְדָה, קָא מַשְׁמַע לַן.

The Gemara answers: **Lest you say** that in this case, **both of them are** deemed **untainted** in accordance with the testimony of the witness, **and** the fact **that she said that** they are both tainted **was** because **she was acting** with the intention termed: **"Let me die with the Philistines"** (Judges 16:30),[N] i.e., she was willing to implicate herself in order to bolster her credibility so that her testimony against her counterpart would be accepted, the *tanna* therefore **teaches us** that this is not a consideration.

״אֲנִי וַחֲבֶרְתִּי טְהוֹרָה״ וַאֲמַר לָהּ עֵד אֶחָד ״אַתְּ וַחֲבֶרְתֵּךְ טְמֵאָה״, אִיהִי, כֵּיוָן דְּאִיכָּא עֵדִים – לָאו כָּל כְּמִינָּהּ, חֲבֶרְתָּהּ – מִשְׁתַּרְיָא אַפּוּמָּא דִּידָהּ. הָא תּוּ לָמָּה לִי? הַיְינוּ רֵישָׁא דְּרֵישָׁא!

If the woman said: **I and my counterpart are** both **pure, and one witness said to her: You and your counterpart are** both **tainted,** with regard to **her, since there are witnesses** testifying that she was taken captive, **it is not in her power** to permit herself on the basis of her claim. However, **her counterpart is permitted on the basis of her** claim. The Gemara asks: **Why do I** need **this additional** case? **This is** identical **to** that which was taught in the **first part of the first clause.** The principles governing the first two cases, i.e., her claim that she is pure is not accepted when the fact that she was taken captive was established by witnesses, and her counterpart is permitted on the basis of her claim even if that claim is contradicted, also apply in this case.

מַהוּ דְּתֵימָא: כִּי מְהֵימְנָא – בְּמָקוֹם דְּפָסְלָה נַפְשָׁהּ, אֲבָל בְּמָקוֹם דְּמַכְשְׁרָא נַפְשָׁהּ אֵימָא לָא מְהֵימְנָא, קָא מַשְׁמַע לַן.

The Gemara answers: **Lest you say** that **when is she deemed credible** to permit her counterpart, it is only in a case **where she rendered herself unfit** to marry a priest, **but** in a case **where she rendered herself fit, say that she is not deemed credible** with regard to her counterpart; the *tanna* therefore **teaches us** that each segment of the testimony is assessed independently, based on the criteria taught in the first clause.

NOTES

And there is one witness who is testifying to the reverse of the woman's claim – וְאִיכָּא עֵד אֶחָד דְּקָא אַפֵּיךְ: The fundamental explanation of this matter is based on two underlying principles. First, since the status of a captive woman is based on suspicion and the prohibition against her marrying a priest is by rabbinic law, the testimony of one witness is sufficient. The restrictions that apply to cases where the testimony of two witnesses is required are not in effect in cases like these, where the testimony of one witness is accepted. Therefore, the testimony of a woman, a slave, or a maidservant is accepted.

Second, one is deemed credible to disqualify himself or render himself an entity of prohibition. In cases where one witness is deemed credible, his legal status is like that of two witnesses in other cases. Therefore, the testimony of one witness testifying to the contrary is ineffective to contradict that testimony. There is, though, a distinction between a case in which two contradictory single witnesses come together to testify, where each neutralizes the testimony of the other, and a case in which the witness testifying on behalf of the woman comes first, where the testimony of the single witness who comes thereafter cannot neutralize the testimony of the first (see Ramban). Therefore, the early commentaries establish this as a case where the testimony of the woman who testified that her counterpart is pure preceded the contradicting testimony, although that requires changing the order of the statements as they appear in the *baraita* (see Ritva).

She rendered herself an entity of prohibition – אִיהִי שַׁוְּיתָא לְנַפְשָׁהּ חֲתִיכָה דְּאִיסּוּרָא: The Meiri writes that this applies specifically to an unmarried woman. If she claims that she is tainted, her claim is accepted even when there is a witness to the contrary. However, according to the Meiri, with regard to a woman who was married to a priest her claim is not accepted when it is contradicted by a witness, as she does not have the authority to render herself forbidden to her husband. Later authorities disagree with regard to the halakhic ruling in this case.

Let me die with the Philistines – תָּמוֹת נַפְשִׁי עִם פְּלִשְׁתִּים: There is concern that at times a woman hates her counterpart to the extent that she would be willing to harm herself in order to harm that counterpart. Consequently, there are cases where the Sages disqualify the testimony of one woman about another where animosity is common, e.g., the case of the five women related by marriage listed in the mishna in *Yevamot* (117a). In the Gemara here, the woman reasons that were she to claim: I am pure and my counterpart is tainted, her claim would not be accepted. Therefore, she is prepared to claim that she herself is tainted (see *Ḥatam Sofer*).

HALAKHA

And there is one witness who is testifying to the reverse of the woman's claim – וְאִיכָּא עֵד אֶחָד דְּקָא אַפֵּיךְ: If there are two witnesses who testify that a woman was taken captive, and one witness testifies that she was raped, and another testifies that she was not, she is permitted to marry a priest, even if the witness testifying on her behalf is a slave or a woman. This ruling is in accordance with the opinion of Rav Pappa (Rambam *Sefer Kedusha*, *Hilkhot Issurei Bia* 18:21; *Shulḥan Arukh*, *Even HaEzer* 7:5).

מתני׳ וְכֵן שְׁנֵי אֲנָשִׁים, זֶה אוֹמֵר ״כֹּהֵן אֲנִי״ – וְזֶה אוֹמֵר ״כֹּהֵן אֲנִי״ – אֵינָן נֶאֱמָנִין, וּבִזְמַן שֶׁהֵן מְעִידִין זֶה אֶת זֶה – הֲרֵי אֵלּוּ נֶאֱמָנִין. רַבִּי יְהוּדָה אוֹמֵר: אֵין מַעֲלִין לִכְהוּנָּה עַל פִּי עֵד אֶחָד. אָמַר רַבִּי אֶלְעָזָר: אֵימָתַי – בְּמָקוֹם שֶׁיֵּשׁ עוֹרְרִין. אֲבָל בְּמָקוֹם שֶׁאֵין עוֹרְרִין מַעֲלִין לִכְהוּנָּה עַל פִּי עֵד אֶחָד. רַבָּן שִׁמְעוֹן בֶּן גַּמְלִיאֵל אוֹמֵר מִשּׁוּם רַבִּי שִׁמְעוֹן בֶּן הַסְּגָן: מַעֲלִין לִכְהוּנָּה עַל פִּי עֵד אֶחָד.

MISHNA **And likewise,** with regard to **two men** whose lineage is unknown, and **this** man **says: I am a priest,**[H] **and that** man **says: I am a priest,**[N] **they are not deemed credible. And when this** man **testifies about that** man that he is a priest and vice versa,[H] **they are deemed credible. Rabbi Yehuda says: One does not elevate** a man **to priesthood on the basis of one witness.** Two witnesses are required for that purpose. **Rabbi Elazar says: When** is that the ruling? In a case **where there are challengers** to his claim that he is a priest. **However,** in a case **where there are no challengers, one elevates** a man **to priesthood on the basis of one witness. Rabban Shimon ben Gamliel says in the name of Rabbi Shimon, son of the deputy** High Priest:[P] **One elevates** a man **to priesthood on the basis of one witness.**[H]

גמ׳ כָּל הָנֵי לָמָּה לִי? צְרִיכִי; דְּאִי תָּנָא מוֹדֶה רַבִּי יְהוֹשֻׁעַ – מִשּׁוּם דְּאִיכָּא דְּרָרָא דְּמָמוֹנָא, אֲבָל עֵדִים דְּלֵיכָּא דְּרָרָא דְּמָמוֹנָא – אֵימָא לָא.

GEMARA The Gemara asks: **Why do I** need **all these** different cases cited in the *mishnayot* in this chapter? Aren't they all based on the principle: The mouth that prohibited is the mouth that permitted? The Gemara answers: These cases are all **necessary,** as, **if** the *tanna* had **taught** only the case where **Rabbi Yehoshua concedes, in** a case where one says to another: This field, which is currently in my possession, belonged to your father, and I purchased it from him, then one might have thought that his claim is deemed credible **due to** the fact **that there is financial significance** [*derara*][L] in his contention that it belonged to the other's father, and he would not have made that claim if it were not true. **However,** in the case of **witnesses** authenticating their signatures, **where there is no financial significance**[N] for them in their testimony, **say no,** their claim is not accepted.

וְאִי תָּנָא עֵדִים – מִשּׁוּם דִּלְעָלְמָא, אֲבָל אִיהוּ, דִּלְנַפְשֵׁיהּ,

And if the *tanna* **taught** only the case of **witnesses,** one might have thought that their claim is deemed credible **due to** the fact **that** their testimony is relevant **to others. However,** with regard to **him, whose** testimony is relevant **to himself,** as he claims that he purchased the field from the other's father,

NOTES

That man says: I am a priest – **זֶה אוֹמֵר כֹּהֵן אֲנִי**: The Rosh, in tractate *Gittin* (58a), explains that although this seems to be a matter that is likely to be revealed, as one is testifying about a family with whom others are probably familiar and in those cases even one witness is deemed credible, there is still suspicion that he is lying, since there is so much at stake in terms of both social and financial standing for him and his descendants. The *Maggid Mishne* and later authorities rule that today, when there is no special advantage associated with priesthood, but rather it entails several prohibitions, one is deemed credible to testify with regard to his status.

Where there is no financial significance – **דְּלֵיכָּא דְּרָרָא דְּמָמוֹנָא**: The meaning of this phrase in its standard sense is subject to a dispute between the commentaries, and there is disagreement with regard to its meaning in this context as well. According to Rashi here and elsewhere, it means that the witnesses have no financial interest in the case. However, *Tosafot*, citing Rabbeinu Ḥananel, explain that there is no certainty with regard to the identity of the one currently in possession of the money.

LANGUAGE

Significance [*derara*] – **דְּרָרָא**: The commentaries dispute the meaning of this legal term. Some maintain that it is linguistically similar to a term in Syriac that means a disputed matter.

HALAKHA

This man says: I am a priest – **זֶה אוֹמֵר כֹּהֵן אֲנִי**: If a man claims to be a priest, his claim is not accepted. He is not called first to read the Torah, nor does he recite the Priestly Benediction, and all the more so he may not partake of *teruma*, even if it is *teruma* by rabbinic law. However, his claim renders it prohibited for him to marry a divorcée, a widow, or a *zona*, and it is prohibited for him to be exposed to ritual impurity imparted by a corpse. If he violates any of these prohibitions, he is liable to be flogged with lashes of rebelliousness. A woman who engages in intercourse with him assumes the status of an uncertain *ḥalala* and may not marry a priest. The Rema adds, based on the comments of Rabbi Moshe Kohen on the Rambam: Since today no one eats *teruma* at all, one who claims to be a priest is called first to read the Torah and recites the Priestly Benediction based on his claim (Rambam *Sefer Kedusha, Hilkhot Issurei Bia* 20:13; *Shulḥan Arukh, Even HaEzer* 3:1).

And when this man testifies about that man that he is a priest and vice versa – **וּבִזְמַן שֶׁהֵן מְעִידִין זֶה אֶת זֶה**: If each of the two men claiming to be priests testifies on behalf of the other, their testimony is deemed credible (Rambam *Sefer Kedusha, Hilkhot Issurei Bia* 20:11; *Shulḥan Arukh, Even HaEzer* 3:4).

Elevation to the priesthood – **הַעֲלָאָה לִכְהוּנָּה**: A man is elevated to the priesthood on the basis of the testimony of a single witness, in accordance with the opinions of numerous Sages. The Gemara later elaborates on the details of when and in which cases the testimony of a single witness is accepted (Rambam *Sefer Kedusha, Hilkhot Issurei Bia* 20:2 and *Maggid Mishne* there).

PERSONALITIES

Rabbi Shimon, son of the deputy High Priest – **רַבִּי שִׁמְעוֹן בֶּן הַסְּגָן**: According to the Rambam, the reference is to Rabbi Shimon, son of Rabbi Ḥanina the deputy High Priest, who appears throughout the Talmud. Although he is mentioned only a few times in the Mishna, he was one of the most significant Sages in the generation during which the Temple was destroyed. Some hold that Rabbi Shimon, son of the deputy High Priest, is called Rabbi Shimon bar Kahana in the *Tosefta* and other sources. In any event, as the son of the deputy High Priest, his testimony is especially significant with regard to matters of priestly lineage.

אֵימָא לָא.

say no, his claim is not accepted.

וְאִי אַשְׁמְעִינַן הָנֵי תַּרְתֵּי – מִשּׁוּם דְּמָמוֹנָא, אֲבָל אֵשֶׁת אִישׁ דְּאִיסּוּרָא – אֵימָא לָא.

And if the *tanna* **taught us these two** cases, one might have thought that the claim is deemed credible **due to** the fact **that** the cases involve **monetary** matters; **however,** in the case of **a married woman** who claims that she was divorced, **which is a ritual** matter, **say no,** she is **not** deemed credible. Therefore, it was necessary for the *tanna* to teach us all three cases.

״נִשְׁבֵּיתִי וּטְהוֹרָה אֲנִי״ לָמָּה לִי? מִשּׁוּם דְּקָא בָּעֵי לְמִיתְנֵי – ״וְאִם מִשֶּׁנִּשֵּׂאת בָּאוּ עֵדִים הֲרֵי זוֹ לֹא תֵּצֵא״.

The Gemara asks: With regard to the case where one says: **I was taken captive and I am pure, why do I need** the *tanna* to teach that case? There is no novel element in that ruling, as it is merely another application of the same principle. The Gemara answers: The *tanna* taught that case **due to** the fact **that** the *tanna* **sought to teach** based on it: **And if the witnesses came after she married, this** woman need **not leave** her husband.

הָנִיחָא לְמַאן דְּמַתְנֵי לַהּ אַסֵּיפָא, אֶלָּא לְמַאן דְּמַתְנֵי לַהּ אַרֵישָׁא מַאי אִיכָּא לְמֵימַר? מִשּׁוּם דְּקָא בָּעֵי לְמִיתְנֵי ״שְׁתֵּי נָשִׁים שֶׁנִּשְׁבּוּ״.

The Gemara asks: **This** works out **well according to the one who teaches** this *halakha* in reference **to the latter clause** of the mishna with regard to a woman taken captive. **However, according to the one who taught** this *halakha* in reference **to the first clause** of the mishna, with regard to a woman who claimed that she was married and divorced, **what is there to say?** According to that opinion, the ruling with regard to a woman taken captive who claims that she remained pure is superfluous. If a woman is deemed credible in the case where the concern is that she is a married woman, she is all the more so deemed credible when the concern pertains to a less severe prohibition, that of a woman who was violated in captivity marrying a priest. The Gemara answers: The *tanna* taught the superfluous *halakha* that a woman claiming that she was taken captive and remained pure is deemed credible as an introduction, **due to** the fact **that he sought to** subsequently **teach** the case of **two women who were taken captive.**

וּ״שְׁתֵּי נָשִׁים שֶׁנִּשְׁבּוּ״ לָמָּה לִי? מַהוּ דְּתֵימָא: נֵיחוּשׁ לְגוֹמְלִין, קָמַשְׁמַע לַן.

The Gemara asks: **And why do I** need the *tanna* to teach the case of **two women who were taken captive?** What novel element is introduced in that case that did not exist in the case of one woman? The Gemara answers: **Lest you say: Let us be concerned for collusion** between the women, that each would testify for the benefit of the other, the *tanna* therefore **teaches us** that this is not a concern.

״וְכֵן שְׁנֵי אֲנָשִׁים״ לָמָּה לִי? מִשּׁוּם דְּקָא בָּעֵי לְמִיתְנֵי פְּלוּגְתָּא דְּרַבִּי יְהוּדָה וְרַבָּנַן.

The Gemara asks: **And why do I** need the *tanna* to teach the following case: **And likewise two men,** each testifying that the other is a priest? He already taught that if two women each testify that the other is pure, they are deemed credible. The Gemara answers: The *tanna* taught the superfluous *halakha* with regard to two men as an introduction, **due to** the fact **that he sought to** subsequently **teach the dispute between Rabbi Yehuda and the Rabbis,** concerning whether or not the testimony of a single witness is deemed credible to establish another's presumptive status as a priest.

תָּנוּ רַבָּנַן: ״אֲנִי כֹּהֵן וַחֲבֵרִי כֹּהֵן״ – נֶאֱמָן לְהַאֲכִילוֹ בִּתְרוּמָה, וְאֵינוֹ נֶאֱמָן לְהַשִּׂיאוֹ אִשָּׁה, עַד שֶׁיְּהוּ שְׁלֹשָׁה, שְׁנַיִם מְעִידִין עַל זֶה וּשְׁנַיִם מְעִידִין עַל זֶה. רַבִּי יְהוּדָה אוֹמֵר: אַף אֵינוֹ נֶאֱמָן לְהַאֲכִילוֹ בִּתְרוּמָה עַד שֶׁיְּהוּ שְׁלֹשָׁה, שְׁנַיִם מְעִידִין עַל זֶה, וּשְׁנַיִם מְעִידִין עַל זֶה.

§ The Gemara elaborates: **The Rabbis taught** in a *baraita*: In the case of two men, each of whom says: **I am a priest and my counterpart is a priest,** each **is deemed credible** with regard **to enabling his** counterpart **to partake of *teruma*. But he is not deemed credible** with regard to establishing his presumptive status as a priest of unflawed lineage **for** the purpose of **his marrying a woman**[N] **until there are three** people, the two claiming to be priests and an additional witness, so **that** there are **two** witnesses **testifying** with regard **to** the status of **this** person **and two** witnesses **testifying** with regard **to** the status of **that** person. **Rabbi Yehuda says:** Each **is not deemed credible even** with regard **to enabling his** counterpart **to partake of *teruma* until there are three** men, so **that** there are **two** witnesses **testifying** with regard **to this** person **and two** witnesses **testifying** with regard **to that** person.

NOTES

For the purpose of his marrying a woman – לְהַשִּׂיאוֹ אִשָּׁה: Rabbeinu Ḥananel and Rashi both explain that this means: For the purpose of marrying a woman of prestigious descent. However, most early commentaries questioned that explanation, as even if one is not a priest, there is nothing that prevents a non-priest from marrying a woman of unflawed lineage.

Tosafot seek to explain Rashi's opinion and contend that once it is necessary to investigate one's lineage due to the concern that he is a non-priest, they may also investigate other flaws in his lineage that might prohibit him from marrying Jewish women of unflawed lineage, although typically one is not investigated for those flaws. Or, perhaps the mishna is in accordance with the opinion of Rabbi Meir, who holds that there is no presumption of unflawed lineage with regard to each individual. Therefore, his lineage must be investigated.

The Ra'ah adds that this is a case where a rumor spread that his lineage is flawed. Although typically rumors not supported by witnesses are ignored, in this case it is investigated. However, the Rid, Rabbeinu Tam, and most early commentaries explain that it means that even if he marries a woman of unflawed lineage he does not assume the presumptive status of a priest to the extent that it would be permitted for another priest to marry his widow or daughter. The language of the Jerusalem Talmud supports this opinion. It does not state: For the purpose of marrying a woman to him. Rather, it says: For matters of family. This indicates that the *halakha* does not refer specifically to his marriage to a woman.

לְמֵימְרָא דְּרַבִּי יְהוּדָה חָיֵישׁ לְגוּמְלִין וְרַבָּנַן לָא חָיְישִׁי לְגוּמְלִין? וְהָא אִיפְּכָא שְׁמַעִינַן לְהוּ, דִּתְנַן: הַחַמָּרִין שֶׁנִּכְנְסוּ לָעִיר, וְאָמַר אֶחָד מֵהֶן: ״שֶׁלִּי חָדָשׁ וְשֶׁל חֲבֵרִי יָשָׁן״, ״שֶׁלִּי אֵינוֹ מְתוּקָּן וְשֶׁל חֲבֵרִי מְתוּקָּן״ – אֵינוֹ נֶאֱמָן, רַבִּי יְהוּדָה אוֹמֵר: נֶאֱמָן!

The Gemara asks: **Is that to say that Rabbi Yehuda is concerned for collusion** between them, **and the Rabbis are not concerned for collusion? But didn't we learn** that **they** said the **opposite? As we learned** in a mishna: In a case where there were **donkey drivers who entered a city,**[H] **and one of them said: My** produce **is new** from this year's crop, and it is not yet completely dry and therefore of lower quality, **and the** produce **of my counterpart is old** and dry and therefore more durable; or if he said: **My** produce **is not tithed and the** produce **of my counterpart is tithed, he is not deemed credible.** Presumably, there is collusion between the two merchants. In this city, one denigrates the quality of his own produce, enhancing his credibility, while praising the quality of the produce of his counterpart; and his counterpart says the same in the next city that they enter. **And Rabbi Yehuda says: He is deemed credible,** as apparently he is not concerned for collusion between the merchants.

אָמַר רַב אַדָּא בַּר אַהֲבָה אָמַר רַב: מוּחְלֶפֶת הַשִּׁיטָּה. אַבָּיֵי אָמַר: לְעוֹלָם לָא תֵּיפוֹךְ; בִּדְמַאי הֵקִילוּ, רוֹב עַמֵּי הָאָרֶץ מְעַשְּׂרִין הֵן.

Rav Adda bar Ahava said that **Rav said:** The attribution of **the opinions is reversed** in one of the *mishnayot*, so that the opinions of the *tanna'im* are consistent in both the case of the priests and the case of the donkey drivers. **Abaye said: Actually, do not reverse** the attribution, and the fact that Rabbi Yehuda accepts the claim of the donkey driver is because **with regard to doubtfully tithed produce** [*demai*][B] the Sages **were lenient,**[N] because **most** ***amei ha'aretz*** **tithe** their produce. The ordinance of the Sages classifying produce purchased from an *am ha'aretz* as doubtfully tithed produce and requiring its tithing is based on a far-fetched concern. Therefore, testimony of any sort is sufficient to permit its consumption. However, as a rule, Rabbi Yehuda is concerned about collusion.

אֲמַר רָבָא: דְּרַבִּי יְהוּדָה אַדְּרַבִּי יְהוּדָה קַשְׁיָא, דְּרַבָּנַן אַדְּרַבָּנַן לָא קַשְׁיָא?! אֶלָּא, דְּרַבִּי יְהוּדָה אַדְּרַבִּי יְהוּדָה לָא קַשְׁיָא – כִּדְשָׁנֵינַן, דְּרַבָּנַן אַדְּרַבָּנַן לָא קַשְׁיָא, כִּדְאָמַר רַבִּי חָמָא בַּר עוּקְבָא: בִּשֶׁכְּלֵי אוּמָּנוּתוֹ בְּיָדוֹ,

Rava said: Is that to say that the contradiction between one statement **of Rabbi Yehuda** and another statement **of Rabbi Yehuda is difficult,** but the contradiction between one statement **of the Rabbis and** another statement **of the Rabbis is not difficult?** Clearly, the contradiction between the rulings of the Rabbis in the respective *mishnayot* is difficult. **Rather,** the contradiction between one statement **of Rabbi Yehuda** and another statement **of Rabbi Yehuda is not difficult, as we explained** above that Rabbi Yehuda was lenient with regard to doubtfully tithed produce. The contradiction between one statement **of the Rabbis and** another statement **of the Rabbis is** also **not difficult.** Fundamentally, the Rabbis are not concerned for collusion between the two parties. However, in the case of donkey drivers they are concerned, **as Rabbi Ḥama bar Ukva said** in another context that it is referring to a case **where one has the tools of his trade in his hand.**

HALAKHA

Donkey drivers who entered a city – **הַחַמָּרִין שֶׁנִּכְנְסוּ לָעִיר**: If two donkey drivers entered a city and one says: My produce is not tithed and the produce of my counterpart is tithed, he is not deemed credible. This is due to the suspicion of collusion, that in the next city they will reverse roles and his counterpart will make a similar declaration in praise of his produce. This ruling is in accordance with the unattributed mishna. The Rambam omitted the provision with regard to the tools of the trade in his hand, because he ruled in accordance with the second manner of explaining the dispute, according to which that provision is moot (Rambam *Sefer Zera'im*, *Hilkhot Ma'asrot* 12:10).

BACKGROUND

Doubtfully tithed produce [*demai*] – **דְּמַאי**: This is produce, or food prepared from produce, purchased from a person who may not have separated the various tithes as required. The literal meaning of the word is suspicion, as it is produce about which there is suspicion that it was not tithed properly. In the Second Temple period, the Sages decreed that this produce would be accorded uncertain status, even if the owner claims that he tithed the produce. Therefore, the buyer of this produce must tithe it himself. Nevertheless, since the probability is that the produce was in fact tithed, certain leniencies were introduced with regard to partaking and using it.

NOTES

With regard to doubtfully tithed produce the Sages were lenient – **בִּדְמַאי הֵקִילוּ**: Fundamentally, the halakhic status of doubtfully tithed produce (discussed in detail in tractate *Demai*) was established by a rabbinic decree issued with regard to produce purchased from an *am ha'aretz*. The Sages found that a significant number of *amei ha'aretz* would not separate first tithe from their produce. Therefore, all produce of that kind is classified as doubtfully tithed produce, and one who purchases that produce is required to tithe it due to that uncertainty. Since *amei ha'aretz* are suspect with regard to doubtfully tithed produce, they are disqualified from testifying about it. It is clear here and elsewhere that the Sages were lenient with regard to various aspects of doubtfully tithed produce. Although there is a conspicuous minority of *amei ha'aretz* who did not tithe their produce, which led the Sages to issue the decree, the majority do tithe. Since the decree is based on suspicion, not certainty, the Sages were not overly stringent in its regard.

הָכָא נַמִי – בְּשֶׁכְּלֵי אוּמָּנוּתוֹ בְּיָדוֹ.

Here too, it is referring to a case **where** the second donkey driver comes **with the tools of his trade in his hand,** clearly indicating that he too came to sell his produce. Therefore, when the other driver praises his produce, there is room for concern that there was collusion and that in the next city their roles will be reversed. However, when there is no proof of collusion, the Rabbis were not concerned.

וְהֵיכָא אִתְּמַר דְּרַבִּי חָמָא בַּר עוּקְבָא – אַהָא, דִּתְנַן: הַקַּדָּר שֶׁהִנִּיחַ קְדֵירוֹתָיו וְיָרַד לִשְׁתּוֹת (מַיִם מִן הַיְאוֹר) – הַפְּנִימִיּוֹת טְהוֹרוֹת וְהַחִיצוֹנוֹת טְמֵאוֹת.

The Gemara asks: **And where** is the solution **of Rabbi Ḥama bar Ukva stated?** It is stated **concerning that which we learned** in a mishna (*Teharot* 7:1): In the case of **a potter**[N] **who** fashioned his vessels in ritual purity, and **abandoned his pots,**[H] **and descended to drink water from the river,** there is concern that in his absence ritually impure people came into contact with his pots. **The inner** pots **are pure, and the outer** pots **are impure.**

וְהָתַנְיָא: אֵלּוּ וְאֵלּוּ טְמֵאוֹת! אֲמַר רַבִּי חָמָא בַּר עוּקְבָא: בְּשֶׁכְּלֵי אוּמָּנוּתוֹ בְּיָדוֹ, מִפְּנֵי שֶׁיַּד הַכֹּל מְמַשְׁמֶשֶׁת בָּהֶן.

The Gemara asks: **But isn't it taught** in a *baraita*: **Both these** inner pots **and those** outer pots **are ritually impure? Rabbi Ḥama bar Ukva said:** That *baraita* is referring to a case where **the tools of** the potter's **trade are in his hand,** indicating that he intends to sell his pots. **Since all** potential buyers **touch** pots when examining them before purchase, the concern is that among those people there is one who is ritually impure.

וְהָתַנְיָא: אֵלּוּ וְאֵלּוּ טְהוֹרוֹת! אֲמַר רַבִּי חָמָא בַּר עוּקְבָא: בְּשֶׁאֵין כְּלֵי אוּמָּנוּתוֹ בְּיָדוֹ.

The Gemara asks: **But isn't it taught** in another *baraita*: **Both these** inner pots **and those** outer pots **are ritually pure? Rabbi Ḥama bar Ukva said:** That *baraita* is referring to a case where **the tools of** the potter's **trade are not in his hand,** indicating that he does not intend to sell his pots. Therefore, strangers will not touch them at all.

וְאֶלָּא הָא דִּתְנַן: הַפְּנִימִיּוֹת – טְהוֹרוֹת וְהַחִיצוֹנוֹת – טְמֵאוֹת. הֵיכִי מַשְׁכַּחַתְּ לָהּ?

The Gemara asks: **But** if so, the ruling in the mishna: **The inner** pots **are pure and the outer** pots **are impure, under what** circumstances **can** this case **be found?** When the tools of the potter's trade are in his hand, all the vessels are impure, and when the tools of the potter's trade are not in his hand, all the vessels are pure.

דִּסְמִיכָא לִרְשׁוּת הָרַבִּים, וּמִשּׁוּם חִיפּוּפֵי רְשׁוּת הָרַבִּים.

The Gemara answers: The *tanna* of the mishna is referring to a case **where** the tools of the potter's trade are not in his hand. However, he leaves his pots **adjacent to the public domain, and** in an area demarcated from the public domain **due to the stakes** or other objects that are placed on the sides of **the public domain**[B] to distance passersby from the walls of the private domain, and due to crowding, people will be pushed to the sides and inadvertently render the outer pots impure. They do not pass close to the inner pots and will not touch the pots to examine them, because they are not for sale.

וְאִיבָּעֵית אֵימָא: רַבִּי יְהוּדָה וְרַבָּנַן בְּמַעֲלִין מִתְּרוּמָה לְיוּחֲסִין קָמִיפַּלְגִי.

The Gemara proceeds to cite an additional resolution to the contradiction between the opinions of Rabbi Yehuda and the Rabbis, with regard to collusion in terms of the presumptive status of priests and in terms of produce merchants. **And if you wish, say** instead that the dispute between **Rabbi Yehuda and the Rabbis** in the matter of presumptive priestly status is unrelated to collusion. Rather, it is **with regard to** whether **one elevates** one who eats ***teruma*** **to** the presumptive status of priesthood **for** the purpose of **lineage** that **they disagree.**[N] Rabbi Yehuda holds that one elevates from *teruma* to lineage and therefore requires full-fledged testimony by two witnesses to enable the person to partake of *teruma*. The Rabbis maintain that one does not elevate from *teruma* to lineage, and each matter is considered separately. For the purpose of partaking of *teruma*, any testimony is sufficient; for the purpose of lineage, full-fledged testimony by two witnesses is required.

NOTES

Potter – קַדָּר: The Sages decreed that *amei ha'aretz* are always ritually impure because they are not meticulous in distancing themselves from ritual impurity, with the exception of during the Pilgrim Festivals in Jerusalem. Therefore, any object that comes into contact with an *am ha'aretz* assumes the status of an object that became impure with impurity imparted by treading by a *zav*. The potter, in this case, is a *ḥaver* who fashions his pottery in purity. However, his clientele consists of both *ḥaverim* and *amei ha'aretz*, who are ritually impure. The Meiri explains that the potter's tools are the vessels upon which he places the pots in order to sell them.

It is with regard to whether one elevates one who eats *teruma* to the presumptive status of priesthood for the purpose of lineage that they disagree – בְּמַעֲלִין מִתְּרוּמָה לְיוּחֲסִין קָמִיפַּלְגִי: *Tosafot* note that this resolves only the contradiction between the statements of Rabbi Yehuda. However, the contradiction between the statements of the Rabbis with regard to collusion remains difficult. Therefore, this must be taken together with the previous answer, with regard to the tools of the trade. Others claim that this answer reconciles the contradiction between the statements of the Rabbis (*Kesef Mishne*), but the later commentaries question that opinion (see *Tosefot Yom Tov*).

HALAKHA

A potter who abandoned his pots – הַקַּדָּר שֶׁהִנִּיחַ קְדֵירוֹתָיו: If a potter who is scrupulous about ritual purity leaves his pots adjacent to the public domain and goes to drink from the pond, the assumption is that passersby touch the outer pots, nearest the public domain. They are considered ritually impure, and the inner pots are pure. However, in a case where the pots are removed from the public domain, if the potter has the tools of his trade, indicating that the pots are for sale, and passersby touched them, and they are all ritually impure. Otherwise, they are presumed untouched and pure (Rambam *Sefer Tahara, Hilkhot Metamei Mishkav UMoshav* 12:23).

BACKGROUND

Stakes placed on the sides of the public domain – חִיפּוּפֵי רְשׁוּת הָרַבִּים: The term for the stakes, *ḥifufim*, derives from the root *ḥet, peh, peh,* meaning to rub or chafe. This describes the means employed by the homeowners to prevent passersby in the public domain from damaging their walls or fences. They would build protruding stones into the fences or establish a row of stones or stakes at a certain distance from the walls. These stakes created an area that, although technically in the public domain, is not a place through which the multitudes passed. Therefore, in certain respects, its halakhic status was somewhere between a public and a private domain.

Stakes in the public domain

LANGUAGE

Public [*parhesya*] – פַּרְהֶסְיָא: From the Greek παρρησία, *parresia*, meaning freedom of speech, frankness. The Sages expanded it to mean a matter performed openly, in the public view.

אִיבַּעְיָא לְהוּ: מַהוּ לְהַעֲלוֹת מִשְּׁטָרוֹת לְיוּחֲסִין? הֵיכִי דָּמֵי? אִילֵימָא דִּכְתִיב בֵּיהּ ״אֲנִי פְּלוֹנִי כֹּהֵן חָתַמְתִּי עֵד״ – מַאן קָא מַסְהֵיד עִילָּוֵיהּ?

§ **A dilemma was raised before** the Sages: **What is** the *halakha* with regard **to elevating from documents** indicating that one is a priest, to priestly **lineage?**[H] The Gemara asks: **What are the circumstances? If you say that it is written in** the document: **I, so-and-so, a priest, signed as a witness,** in that case **who is testifying about him** that he is a priest? He is the only source asserting his priesthood.

לָא, צְרִיכָא, דִּכְתִיב בֵּיהּ ״אֲנִי פְּלוֹנִי כֹּהֵן לָוִיתִי מָנֶה מִפְּלוֹנִי״ וַחֲתִימוּ סָהֲדֵי, מַאי? אַמָּנֶה שֶׁבַּשְּׁטָר קָא מַסְהֲדֵי אוֹ דִּלְמָא אַכּוּלָּהּ מִילְּתָא קָא מַסְהֲדֵי? רַב הוּנָא וְרַב חִסְדָּא. חַד אֲמַר: מַעֲלִין, וְחַד אֲמַר: אֵין מַעֲלִין.

The Gemara answers: **No,** this *halakha* is **necessary** in a case **where it is written in** the document: **I, so-and-so, a priest, borrowed one hundred dinars from so-and-so, and witnesses signed** the document, **what** is the *halakha*? Do the witnesses **testify** only **concerning the** loan of **one hundred dinars in the document? Or, perhaps they testify concerning the entire matter** and confirm with their signatures that every detail written in the document is true, including the fact that the borrower is a priest. With regard to the halakhic ruling, there is a dispute between **Rav Huna and Rav Ḥisda. One said: One elevates** from documents to priestly lineage, **and one said: One does not elevate.**

אִיבַּעְיָא לְהוּ: מַהוּ לְהַעֲלוֹת מִנְּשִׂיאוּת כַּפַּיִם לְיוּחֲסִין? תִּיבָּעֵי לְמַאן דְּאָמַר מַעֲלִין מִתְּרוּמָה לְיוּחֲסִין, וְתִיבָּעֵי לְמַאן דְּאָמַר אֵין מַעֲלִין;

A dilemma was raised before the Sages: **What is** the *halakha* with regard **to elevating from the lifting of hands** for the Priestly Benediction **to** priestly **lineage?**[H] Is the presumptive status of a person who recites the Priestly Benediction in the synagogue that of a priest in terms of lineage as well? The Gemara notes: **Raise the dilemma** according **to the one who said: One elevates from** ***teruma*** **to lineage; and raise the dilemma** according **to the one who said: One does not elevate** from *teruma* to lineage.

תִּיבָּעֵי לְמַאן דְּאָמַר מַעֲלִין: הָנֵי מִילֵּי – תְּרוּמָה, דַּעֲוֹן מִיתָה הִיא. אֲבָל נְשִׂיאוּת כַּפַּיִם, דְּאִיסּוּר עֲשֵׂה – לָא, אוֹ דִּלְמָא לָא שְׁנָא?

The Gemara notes: **Raise the dilemma** according **to the one who said: One elevates** from *teruma* to lineage. In his opinion, perhaps **this applies** only to ***teruma*****, where** a non-priest who partakes of *teruma* performs **a transgression** whose punishment **is death** at the hand of Heaven. One would not partake of *teruma* and risk that punishment if he were not a priest. **However,** with regard to **the Priestly Benediction,** where a non-priest who recites it violates **a prohibition** stated as **a positive mitzva, no,** one cannot be certain that one would not recite the blessing if he were not a priest. Therefore, one does not elevate from the lifting of hands to priestly lineage. **Or, perhaps** there is **no difference,** and in both cases because there is a transgression involved one can assume that he would not risk performing a transgression were he not a priest.

תִּיבָּעֵי לְמַאן דְּאָמַר אֵין מַעֲלִין: הָנֵי מִילֵּי – תְּרוּמָה דְּמִיתְאַכְלָא בְּצִנְעָא, אֲבָל נְשִׂיאוּת כַּפַּיִם דִּבְפַרְהֶסְיָא, אִי לָאו כֹּהֵן הוּא – כּוּלֵּי הַאי לָא מַחֲצֵיף אֱינָשׁ נַפְשֵׁיהּ, אוֹ דִּלְמָא לָא שְׁנָא?

Raise the dilemma according **to the one who said: One does not elevate** from *teruma* to lineage. In his opinion, perhaps **this applies only** to ***teruma*** **that is eaten in private.** Therefore, a non-priest might partake of *teruma* when he believes that no one is watching. **However,** with regard to **the lifting of hands, which is** recited **in public [*parhesya*],**[L] **if one is not a priest, he would not be insolent to** the **extent that** he would comport himself like a priest in public. Therefore, although partaking of *teruma* is not a clear indicator that he is a priest, reciting the Priestly Benediction is a clear indicator. **Or perhaps,** there is **no difference,** and due to the concern lest a non-priest partake of *teruma* in private and recite the Priestly Benediction in public, neither action can facilitate elevating the person to the presumptive status of a priest in terms of lineage.

HALAKHA

Elevating from documents to priestly lineage – הַעֲלָאָה מִשְּׁטָרוֹת לְיוּחֲסִין: If witnesses signed a document in which it was written that so-and-so the priest borrowed or lent money, the document does not prove priestly descent, since the witnesses signed confirming the loan but not the incidental details. This ruling applies only to matters of lineage. However, with regard to the presumptive status of priesthood in terms of partaking of *teruma* by rabbinic law, it is considered sufficient proof (Rambam *Sefer Kedusha, Hilkhot Issurei Bia* 20:9; *Shulḥan Arukh, Even HaEzer* 3:2).

Elevating from the lifting of hands for the Priestly Benediction to priestly lineage – הַעֲלָאָה מִנְּשִׂיאוּת כַּפַּיִם לְיוּחֲסִין: One does not elevate a person to the presumptive status of priesthood on the basis of his having been seen reciting the Priestly Benediction. The ruling is stringent because the dilemma concerning that case was not resolved in the Gemara and there is a higher standard established for lineage (*Maggid Mishne*; Rambam *Sefer Kedusha, Hilkhot Issurei Bia* 20:4).

רַב חִסְדָּא וְרַבִּי אָבִינָא: חַד אֲמַר: מַעֲלִין, וְחַד אֲמַר: אֵין מַעֲלִין. אֲמַר לֵיהּ רַב נַחְמָן בַּר יִצְחָק לְרָבָא: מַהוּ לְהַעֲלוֹת מִנְּשִׂיאוּת כַּפַּיִם לְיוּחֲסִין? אֲמַר לֵיהּ: פְּלוּגְתָּא דְּרַב חִסְדָּא וְרַבִּי אָבִינָא.

There is a dispute with regard to the halakhic ruling between **Rav Ḥisda and Rabbi Avina. One said: One elevates** from the Priestly Benediction to lineage, **and one said: One does not elevate. Rav Naḥman bar Yitzḥak said to Rava: What is** the *halakha* with regard **to elevating from the lifting of hands to lineage? Rava said to him:** There is **a dispute between Rav Ḥisda and Rabbi Avina.**

הִלְכְתָא מַאי? אֲמַר לֵיהּ: אֲנָא מַתְנִיתָא יָדַעְנָא; דְּתַנְיָא, רַבִּי יוֹסֵי אוֹמֵר: גְּדוֹלָה חֲזָקָה, שֶׁנֶּאֱמַר ״וּמִבְּנֵי הַכֹּהֲנִים בְּנֵי חֲבַיָּה בְּנֵי הַקּוֹץ בְּנֵי בַרְזִלַּי אֲשֶׁר לָקַח מִבְּנוֹת בַּרְזִלַּי הַגִּלְעָדִי אִשָּׁה וַיִּקָּרֵא עַל שְׁמָם. אֵלֶּה בִקְשׁוּ כְתָבָם הַמִּתְיַחְשִׂים וְלֹא נִמְצָאוּ וַיְגֹאֲלוּ מִן הַכְּהוּנָּה. וַיֹּאמֶר הַתִּרְשָׁתָא לָהֶם אֲשֶׁר לֹא יֹאכְלוּ מִקֹּדֶשׁ הַקֳּדָשִׁים עַד עֲמֹד כֹּהֵן לְאוּרִים וְתוּמִּים״.

Rav Naḥman bar Yitzḥak asked Rava: **What is the *halakha*?** Rava **said to him: I know** and base the halakhic ruling on **a *baraita*, as it is taught** in a *baraita* that **Rabbi Yosei says: Great is** the legal authority of **presumptive status,** as one may rely upon it in determining halakhic practice, **as it is stated: "And of the children of the priests: The children of Habaiah, the children of Hakkoz, the children of Barzillai, who took a wife of the daughters of Barzillai the Gileadite, and was called after their name. These sought their register of the genealogy, but it was not found; therefore were they deemed tainted and put from the priesthood. And the Tirshatha said unto them that they should not partake of the most sacred items, until there stood up a priest with Urim VeTummim"** (Ezra 2:61–63).

אָמַר לָהֶם: הֲרֵי אַתֶּם בְּחֶזְקַתְכֶם, בַּמֶּה הֱיִיתֶם אוֹכְלִים בַּגּוֹלָה – בְּקָדְשֵׁי הַגְּבוּל, אַף כָּאן – בְּקָדְשֵׁי הַגְּבוּל. וְאִי סָלְקָא דַּעְתָּךְ מַעֲלִין מִנְּשִׂיאוּת כַּפַּיִם לְיוּחֲסִין, הָנֵי, כֵּיוָן דְּפָרְסֵי יְדַיְיהוּ – אָתֵי לְאַסּוּקִינְהוּ!

Rabbi Yosei explains: Nehemiah **said to** the priests whose status was uncertain: **You maintain your presumptive status. Of what did you partake in the** Babylonian **exile?** It was **the consecrated items** eaten in **the outlying areas,** i.e., *teruma*. **Here too,** you may continue to partake of the **consecrated items** eaten in **the outlying areas,** but you may not partake of offerings, with regard to which you have no presumptive status of priesthood. The Gemara asks: **And if it enters your mind** to say **that one elevates from the lifting of hands to lineage, they will come to elevate those** priests whose status was uncertain to priestly status in terms of lineage, **since they lifted their hands** and recited the Priestly Benediction in exile.

שָׁאנֵי הָכָא, דְּרִיעַ חֶזְקַיְיהוּ. דְּאִי לָא תֵּימָא הָכִי, לְמַאן דַּאֲמַר מַעֲלִין מִתְּרוּמָה לְיוּחֲסִין, כֵּיוָן דְּאָכְלִי בִּתְרוּמָה – אָתֵי לְאַסּוּקִינְהוּ! אֶלָּא לָאו – מִשּׁוּם דְּרִיעַ חֶזְקַיְיהוּ.

The Gemara answers: **Here it is different.** There was no concern lest they elevate them to lineage **because their presumptive status was undermined**[N] by the fact that they did not partake of offerings like the other priests. **As, if you do not say that** one relies on the fact that their status was undermined, **according to the one who said: One elevates from *teruma* to lineage, since they partake of *teruma*,** there should be concern lest **they come to elevate them** to lineage. **Rather,** is the reason that this is not a concern **not due to** the fact **their presumptive status was undermined,** and it is clear to all that there is uncertainty with regard to their status as priests? However, one may not infer from the time of Nehemiah to a time when all priests eat *teruma* and recite the Priestly Benediction, and there is no factor that indicates that they are anything less than full-fledged priests. Perhaps, then, one elevates from *teruma* and from the lifting of hands to lineage.

NOTES

Because their presumptive status was undermined – דְּרִיעַ חֶזְקַיְיהוּ: Rashi explains that their presumptive status as priests is undermined by the fact that everybody knows that they do not partake of consecrated food. Rabbeinu Tam explains that the fact that their presumptive status was undermined explains why they were not elevated to priestly lineage (see *Tosafot*). The reason that their presumptive status was undermined is that there were serious doubts that arose with regard to their lineage. The fact is that they are referred to as the sons of Barzillai, who was not a priest.

Others say that it is clear that they were priests. The concern was that their ancestors married women unfit to marry into the priesthood, rendering each of them a *ḥalal*. However, according to that explanation, it is unclear why an ordinance was necessary to prohibit them from partaking of consecrated food. They explain that the ordinance was not for that particular generation, but for future generations, when the serious doubts with regard to their lineage would be forgotten.

HALAKHA

Now too they partake of *teruma* taken from produce obligated by rabbinic law – הָשְׁתָּא נַמִּי בִּתְרוּמָה דְּרַבָּנַן אֲכוּל: Today, all priests are priests based on their presumptive status and therefore may eat only *teruma* by rabbinic law (Rambam *Sefer Zera'im, Hilkhot Terumot* 6:2, *Sefer Kedusha, Hilkhot Issurei Bia* 20:1).

We elevate from *teruma* to lineage – מַסְּקִינַן מִתְּרוּמָה לְיוּחֲסִין: If two witnesses testify that someone claiming to be a priest eats *teruma* by Torah law, he is deemed a priest of unflawed lineage. The Ran and the *Maggid Mishne* note that, according to the opinion of the Rabbis, who hold that one does not elevate from *teruma* to lineage, the reference is to *teruma* by rabbinic law. However, one does elevate from *teruma* by Torah law, and therefore full-fledged testimony is required to enable one to eat *teruma* by Torah law (Rambam *Sefer Zera'im, Hilkhot Terumot* 6:2 and *Sefer Kedusha, Hilkhot Issurei Bia* 20:4).

From the lifting of hands to *teruma* – מִנְּשִׂיאוּת כַּפַּיִם לִתְרוּמָה: If one was seen reciting the Priestly Benediction or called up first to read the Torah, he is accorded presumptive status of priesthood like all other priests today whose priesthood is presumptive (Rambam *Sefer Kedusha, Hilkhot Issurei Bia* 20:11).

NOTES

And when we elevate from *teruma* to lineage – וְכִי מַסְּקִינַן מִתְּרוּמָה לְיוּחֲסִין: The Ritva explains that this phrase in unrelated to the meaning of Rabbi Yosei's statement: Great is presumptive status. Rather, it is an incidental comment, followed by a return to the main topic.

וְאֶלָּא מַאי גְּדוֹלָה חֲזָקָה? מֵעִיקָּרָא אֲכוּל בִּתְרוּמָה דְּרַבָּנַן, הָשְׁתָּא אֲכוּל בִּתְרוּמָה דְּאוֹרַיְיתָא.

The Gemara asks: **And what, then,** is the meaning of: **Great is** the legal authority of **presumptive status?** This is a standard case of presumptive status, as the practice of the priests remained as it was. There is nothing novel in the application of the principle of presumptive status in this case. The Gemara answers: **Initially,** in the Babylonian exile, they would **partake of *teruma*** taken from produce obligated **by rabbinic** law. **Now,** upon their return to Eretz Yisrael, **they partake of *teruma*** taken from produce obligated **by Torah** law: Grain, wine, and oil, based on their presumptive status.

וְאִי בָּעֵית אֵימָא: הָשְׁתָּא נַמִּי בִּתְרוּמָה דְּרַבָּנַן אֲכוּל, בִּתְרוּמָה דְּאוֹרַיְיתָא לָא אֲכוּל. וְכִי מַסְּקִינַן מִתְּרוּמָה לְיוּחֲסִין – בִּתְרוּמָה דְּאוֹרַיְיתָא, בִּתְרוּמָה דְּרַבָּנַן – לָא מַסְּקִינַן. וְאֶלָּא מַאי גְּדוֹלָה חֲזָקָה? דְּאַף עַל גַּב דְּאִיכָּא לְמִיגְזַר מִשּׁוּם תְּרוּמָה דְּאוֹרַיְיתָא – לָא גָּזְרִינַן.

And if you wish, say instead: **Now too,** upon their return to Eretz Yisrael, **they partake of *teruma*** taken from produce obligated **by rabbinic** law.[H] However, **of *teruma*** taken from produce obligated **by Torah law they may not partake. And when we elevate from *teruma* to lineage,**[HN] this is only **with regard to** one who partakes of ***teruma* by Torah** law. However, in the case of one who partakes of ***teruma* by rabbinic** law, **we do not elevate** him to priestly lineage. The Gemara asks: **And what,** then, is the meaning of: **Great is** the legal authority of **presumptive status?** The Gemara answers: It means that **although there is** reason **to issue a decree** in Eretz Yisrael prohibiting consumption of *teruma* by rabbinic law, **due to *teruma*** that is forbidden **by Torah** law, **we do not issue** that **decree** because: Great is the legal authority of presumptive status.

וּבִתְרוּמָה דְּאוֹרַיְיתָא לָא אֲכוּל? וְהָא כְּתִיב ״אֲשֶׁר לֹא יֹאכְלוּ מִקֹּדֶשׁ הַקֳּדָשִׁים״, מִקֹּדֶשׁ הַקֳּדָשִׁים הוּא דְּלָא אֲכוּל, הָא בִּתְרוּמָה דְּאוֹרַיְיתָא אֲכוּל!

The Gemara asks: **And did** they in fact **not partake of *teruma* by Torah** law? **But isn't it written: "That they should not partake of the most sacred items [*kodesh hakodashim*]"** (Ezra 2:63), from which it may be inferred: It is **of the most sacred items,** i.e., offerings, **that they did not partake; of *teruma* by Torah** law, **they did partake.**

הָכִי קָאָמַר: לָא בְּמִידֵי דְּאִיקְּרִי קֹדֶשׁ, דִּכְתִיב ״וְכָל זָר לֹא יֹאכַל קֹדֶשׁ״, וְלֹא בְּמִידֵי דְּאִיקְּרִי קֳדָשִׁים, דִּכְתִיב ״וּבַת כֹּהֵן כִּי תִהְיֶה לְאִישׁ זָר הִיא בִּתְרוּמַת הַקֳּדָשִׁים לֹא תֹאכֵל״. וְאָמַר מָר: בַּמּוּרָם מִן הַקֳּדָשִׁים לֹא תֹאכַל.

The Gemara answers that **this is** what the verse **is saying: Neither** did they partake **of items called *kodesh*, as it is written: "And no common man may eat of *kodesh*"** (Leviticus 22:10), referring to *teruma*, **nor** did they partake **of items called *kodashim*, as it is written: "And if a priest's daughter be married to a common man, she shall not eat of *terumat hakodashim*"** (Leviticus 22:12). **The Master said** that this means: **Of** that which is **set aside from the offerings [*kodashim*]** to the priests, i.e., the loaves of the thanks-offering and the breast and the shoulder, **they may not partake.** According to neither explanation can any proof be cited from the *baraita* as to whether or not one elevates from *teruma* or from the Priestly Benediction to lineage.

תָּא שְׁמַע: חֲזָקָה לִכְהוּנָּה – נְשִׂיאוּת כַּפַּיִם בְּבָבֶל, וַאֲכִילַת חַלָּה בְּסוּרְיָא, וְחִילּוּק מַתָּנוֹת בִּכְרַכִּין. קָתָנֵי מִיהַת נְשִׂיאוּת כַּפַּיִם, מַאי לָאו לְיוּחֲסִין? לָא, לִתְרוּמָה.

The Gemara suggests: **Come** and **hear** proof from a *baraita*: **Presumptive status for priesthood** is established by **the lifting of hands in Babylonia;** by **partaking of *ḥalla***[B] **in Syria; and** by **distributing** priestly **gifts,**[B] i.e., the foreleg, the jaw, and the maw, **in the cities. In any event,** the *tanna* **teaches** that **the lifting of hands** establishes the presumptive status of priesthood. The Gemara asks: **What, does it not** establish presumptive status **for lineage?** The Gemara answers: **No,** it establishes presumptive status **for *teruma*.**[H]

BACKGROUND

***Ḥalla* – חַלָּה:** The Torah commands the giving of a portion of dough to the priests (Numbers 15:20). This portion is called *ḥalla* and is governed by all the *halakhot* pertaining to *teruma*, the priests' portion of the crop. The Torah does not specify a measure for *ḥalla*. The Sages required a private individual to separate one twenty-fourth of his dough, and a commercial baker one forty-eighth. *Ḥalla* must be taken from dough made from any of the five species of grain, provided that the quantity of flour is at least one-tenth of an ephah in volume. If *ḥalla* is not taken, the dough is considered untithed produce and may not be eaten.

Today, since all Jews are ritually impure, *ḥalla*, like ritually impure *teruma*, must be burned. Accordingly, the measures mentioned above no longer apply. Only a small portion is separated from the dough and burned, and the rest of the dough may be used. A blessing is recited for the separation of *ḥalla*. *Ḥalla* is considered one of the mitzvot practiced particularly by women. The *halakhot* governing this mitzva are discussed comprehensively in tractate *Ḥalla*.

Priestly gifts – מַתָּנוֹת: The Torah commands that one give these portions to a priest when non-sacred animals, e.g., cattle, sheep, and goats, are slaughtered for consumption (Deuteronomy 18:3). No sanctity is attached to these gifts, and once they are given to a priest he may sell or give them to a non-priest.

וְהָא דּוּמְיָא דַּאֲכִילַת חַלָּה קָתָנֵי, מָה אֲכִילַת חַלָּה לְיוֹחֲסִין – אַף נְשִׂיאוּת כַּפַּיִם לְיוֹחֲסִין! לָא, אֲכִילַת חַלָּה גּוּפָהּ לִתְרוּמָה. קָסָבַר: חַלָּה בִּזְמַן הַזֶּה דְּרַבָּנַן, וּתְרוּמָה דְּאוֹרָיְיתָא, וּמַסְּקִינַן מֵחַלָּה דְּרַבָּנַן לִתְרוּמָה דְּאוֹרָיְיתָא. וְכִדְאַפֵּיךְ לְהוּ רַב הוּנָא בְּרֵיהּ דְּרַב יְהוֹשֻׁעַ לְרַבָּנַן.

The Gemara asks: **But isn't** lifting of hands **taught parallel to partaking of *ḥalla*? Just as** with regard to **partaking of *ḥalla*** the *tanna* teaches that it establishes presumptive status **for lineage, so too** with regard to **the lifting of hands** the *tanna* teaches that it establishes presumptive status **for lineage.** The Gemara answers: **No, partaking of *ḥalla* itself** establishes presumptive status only **for *teruma*** and not for lineage. This *tanna* **holds** that **today** the obligation to separate ***ḥalla***[H] from dough **is by rabbinic** law **and** the obligation to separate ***teruma***[HN] **is by Torah** law. The *tanna* teaches that **we elevate from *ḥalla*,** which is an obligation **by rabbinic** law, **to *teruma*,** which is **by Torah** law. **And** this explanation is **in accordance with** the opinion of **Rav Huna, son of Rav Yehoshua,** cited below, **who reversed** the opinion of **the Rabbis** and posited that *ḥalla* today is an obligation by rabbinic law.

תָּא שְׁמַע: חֲזָקָה לִכְהוּנָּה – נְשִׂיאוּת כַּפַּיִם וְחִילּוּק גְּרָנוֹת בְּאֶרֶץ יִשְׂרָאֵל, וּבְסוּרְיָא וּבְכׇל מָקוֹם שֶׁשְּׁלוּחֵי רֹאשׁ חוֹדֶשׁ מַגִּיעִין נְשִׂיאוּת כַּפַּיִם רְאָיָה, אֲבָל לֹא חִילּוּק גְּרָנוֹת.

The Gemara suggests: **Come and hear** proof from a *baraita*: **Presumptive status for priesthood** is established **in Eretz Yisrael** by **the lifting of hands and distribution** of *teruma* at the **threshing floors. And in Syria**[N] **and everyplace** outside Eretz Yisrael **that emissaries** informing residents of the Diaspora of sanctification of **the New Moon arrive, the lifting of hands** constitutes **proof** of presumptive status for priesthood, as the court would investigate the lineage of everyone who recited the Priestly Benediction. **But distribution** of *teruma* at the **threshing floors**[B] **does not**[N] constitute proof of that status, since there is no obligation of *teruma* by Torah law, the courts were not as resolute in examining the lineage of those to whom *teruma* was distributed.

BACKGROUND

Distribution of *teruma* at the threshing floors – חִילּוּק גְּרָנוֹת: In ancient times, stalks of grain would be brought to the threshing floor, a round structure upon which the grain was separated from the stalks by various methods. One common method involved horses or donkeys pulling a threshing sledge that had a rough surface.

Threshing floor

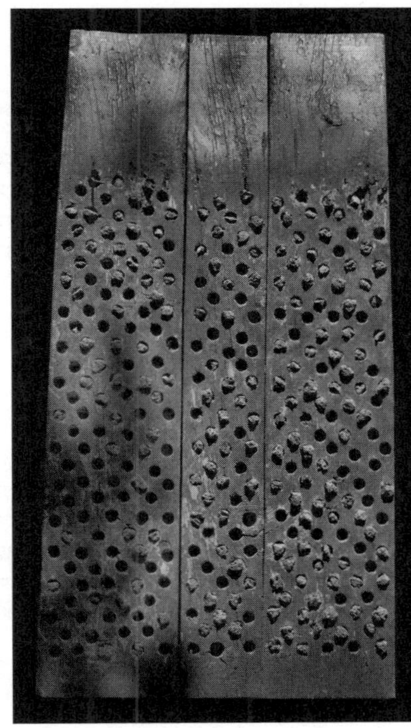

Threshing sledge

HALAKHA

***Ḥalla* today – חַלָּה בִּזְמַן הַזֶּה:** The Torah obligation of *ḥalla* is in effect only in Eretz Israel and only with the presence of the entire Jewish people within its borders. Therefore, even with the return to Zion and the construction of the Second Temple, *ḥalla* was in effect only by rabbinic law, in accordance with the opinion of Rav Huna, son of Rav Yehoshua, as the discussion in the Gemara appears to be conducted according to his opinion (Rambam *Sefer Kedusha, Hilkhot Issurei Bia* 20:3; *Shulḥan Arukh, Yoreh De'a* 322:2).

Today…*teruma* – בִּזְמַן הַזֶּה...תְּרוּמָה: The Rambam writes that since the destruction of the First Temple, the obligation of *teruma* is no longer by Torah law, even in Eretz Israel and even in those places occupied by those returning from Babylonia. The Ra'avad, however, holds that *teruma* in Eretz Israel is an obligation by Torah law even today. The commentaries explain that this question hinges on the dispute between Rabbi Yoḥanan and Reish Lakish in tractate *Yevamot* (81a), where the simple understanding is that Rabbi Yoḥanan holds that the obligation today is by Torah law and Reish Lakish holds that it is by rabbinic law.

The Ra'avad rules in accordance with the opinion of Rabbi Yoḥanan. Apparently, the Rambam rules that only in disputes based on reason between Rabbi Yoḥanan and Reish Lakish is the *halakha* in accordance with the opinion of Rabbi Yoḥanan. However, since there is a tannaitic dispute on the matter, the ruling is in accordance with the opinion of the Rabbis, that the obligation is by rabbinic law (*Maggid Mishne*).

Alternatively, perhaps the dispute between Rabbi Yoḥanan and Reish Lakish is only in accordance with the opinion of Rabbi Yosei, however Rabbi Yoḥanan concedes that the *halakha* is in accordance with the opinion of the Rabbis that *teruma* today is an obligation by rabbinic law (Vilna Gaon). The *Shulḥan Arukh* and the Rashba rule in accordance with the opinion of the Rambam. The Rema writes that others disagree but the normative *halakha* is the ruling of the Rambam (Rambam *Sefer Zera'im*, *Hilkhot Terumot* 1:26; *Shulḥan Arukh, Yoreh De'a* 331:2).

NOTES

Today…*teruma* – בִּזְמַן הַזֶּה...תְּרוּמָה: There are tannaitic and amoraic disputes, as well as a dispute between the early commentaries, whether *teruma* is an obligation by Torah law even nowadays (see HALAKHA). Everyone agrees that the initial consecration of Eretz Yisrael during the conquest of Joshua lapsed with the Babylonian exile. However, they disagree whether the land was entirely reconsecrated with the return to Zion and the construction of the Second Temple. Some say that the reconsecration restored Eretz Yisrael to its previous consecrated status, and the sanctity did not lapse even with the destruction of the Second Temple. Others hold that *teruma* and tithes are tied to the Sabbatical-Year cycle, which in turn is contingent on the Jubilee-Year cycle, which is in effect only when all the Jewish people reside in the land. Once the ten tribes were exiled with the destruction of Samaria, none of those *halakhot* were in effect by Torah law. During the Second Temple, *teruma*, tithes, and the Sabbatical Year were observed voluntarily.

Syria – סוּרְיָא: This is the Greek name for the land of Aram, used in the mishnaic period. These lands were conquered by King David and remained appended to Eretz Yisrael during the reign of his son, Solomon. The question is whether this conquest rendered them part of Eretz Yisrael proper, much like the east bank of the Jordan River, or whether the conquest is considered that of an individual, which does not consecrate the conquered territory. Many Sages hold that since David conquered Syria before completing his conquest of the entire Eretz Yisrael, the conquest was not effective to render the territory as part of Eretz Yisrael. In practice, Syria is accorded intermediate status. In certain respects its status was that of Eretz Yisrael, to the extent that the Sages said that one acquiring land in Syria is considered like one acquiring land on the outskirts of Jerusalem. However, that status was considered a custom by rabbinic law and not a *halakha* by Torah law.

But distribution of *teruma* at the threshing floors does not – אֲבָל לֹא חִילּוּק גְּרָנוֹת: The question arises: Isn't it stated later in the Gemara that one elevates from *teruma* by rabbinic law to *ḥalla* by Torah law? Why then may one not rely on distribution of *teruma* at the threshing floors in Syria, which is by rabbinic law, to establish presumptive status of priesthood, even for matters by Torah law? The Ramban answers that in a place where there is *teruma* by Torah law, greater care is taken, even at a time when it is not in effect by Torah law. However, in Syria, where there never was an obligation of *teruma* by Torah law, distribution of *teruma* at the threshing floor is not proof of priesthood.

BACKGROUND

Alexandria of Egypt – אֲלֶכְּסַנְדְּרִיָּה שֶׁל מִצְרַיִם: There were many cities in Asia and Africa bearing the name Alexandria, e.g., Alexandretta, the largest city in Syria. In order to distinguish between them, the Sages referred to this city as Alexandria of Egypt.

For many generations there was a large and significant Jewish community in Alexandria, with a synagogue renowned for its enormity. Many of the prominent Sages deliberated on various legal problems with the local Jewish population. The cruel suppression of Jewish revolts, in the years 66–115 CE, apparently destroyed the Jewish communal institutions and its central court for an extended period.

וּבָבֶל כְּסוּרְיָא, רַבָּן שִׁמְעוֹן בֶּן גַּמְלִיאֵל אוֹמֵר: אַף אֲלֶכְּסַנְדְּרִיָּא שֶׁל מִצְרַיִם בָּרִאשׁוֹנָה, מִפְּנֵי שֶׁבֵּית דִּין קְבוּעִין שָׁם.

And the status in **Babylonia is like** that in **Syria,** as there, too, there are permanent courts that examine the lineage of those reciting the Priestly Benediction. **Rabban Shimon ben Gamliel says: Even Alexandria of Egypt**[B] **initially** had the same status as Syria, **due to** the fact **that there was a permanent court there** ensuring that the lifting of hands was performed only by a priest.

קָתָנֵי מִיהַת נְשִׂיאוּת כַּפַּיִם, מַאי לָאו לְיוּחֲסִין? לָא, לְחַלָּה. הָא דּוּמְיָא דְּחִילּוּק גְּרָנוֹת קָתָנֵי, מַה חִילּוּק גְּרָנוֹת לְיוּחֲסִין – אַף נְשִׂיאוּת כַּפַּיִם לְיוּחֲסִין! לָא, חִילּוּק גְּרָנוֹת גּוּפָהּ לְחַלָּה. קָסָבַר: תְּרוּמָה בַּזְּמַן הַזֶּה דְּרַבָּנַן, וְחַלָּה דְּאוֹרָיְיתָא, וּמַסְּקִינַן מִתְּרוּמָה דְּרַבָּנַן לְחַלָּה דְּאוֹרָיְיתָא.

In any event, the *tanna* **teaches** that **the lifting of hands** establishes the presumptive status of priesthood. The Gemara asks: **What,** does **it not** establish presumptive status **for lineage?** The Gemara answers: **No,** the lifting of hands establishes presumptive status **for *ḥalla*.** The Gemara asks: **But isn't** the *halakha* of lifting of hands **taught parallel to** the *halakha* of **distribution** of *teruma* at the **threshing floors? Just as distribution** of *teruma* at the **threshing floors** in Eretz Yisrael establishes presumptive status **for lineage, so too, the lifting of hands** establishes presumptive status **for lineage.** The Gemara answers: **No, distribution** of *teruma* at the **threshing floors** establishes presumptive status only **for *ḥalla*** but not for lineage. This *tanna* **holds** that **today** the obligation to separate ***teruma* is by rabbinic law, and *ḥalla* is by Torah** law. The *tanna* teaches that **we elevate from *teruma*,** which is an obligation **by rabbinic** law, to ***ḥalla*,** which is **by Torah** law.

וְכִדְאַשְׁכַּחִינְהוּ רַב הוּנָא בְּרֵיהּ דְּרַב יְהוֹשֻׁעַ לְרַבָּנַן. דַּאֲמַר רַב הוּנָא בְּרֵיהּ דְּרַב יְהוֹשֻׁעַ: אַשְׁכַּחְתִּינְהוּ לְרַבָּנַן בְּבֵי רַב דְּיָתְבִי וְקָאָמְרִי: אֲפִילּוּ לְמַאן דַּאֲמַר תְּרוּמָה בַּזְּמַן הַזֶּה דְּרַבָּנַן – חַלָּה דְּאוֹרָיְיתָא, שֶׁהֲרֵי שֶׁבַע שֶׁכִּיבְּשׁוּ וְשֶׁבַע שֶׁחִילְּקוּ נִתְחַיְּיבוּ בְּחַלָּה וְלֹא נִתְחַיְּיבוּ בִּתְרוּמָה.

And the dispute with regard to the legal status of *teruma* and *ḥalla* today is **as** in the incident **where Rav Huna, son of Rav Yehoshua, found** that this is the opinion of **the Rabbis, as Rav Huna, son of Rav Yehoshua, said: I found the Sages in the study hall of Rav, who were sitting and saying: Even according to the one who said that *teruma* today is** an obligation **by rabbinic** law, the obligation to separate ***ḥalla* is by Torah** law, **as** during the **seven** years **that** the Israelites **conquered** the land of Canaan led by Joshua **and** during the **seven years that they divided** the land,[N] **they were obligated in *ḥalla* but were not obligated in *teruma*.**[N] Today, too, although there is no obligation to take *teruma* in Eretz Yisrael by Torah law, the obligation to separate *ḥalla* is by Torah law.

וְאָמִינָא לְהוּ אֲנָא: אַדְּרַבָּה, אֲפִילּוּ לְמַאן דַּאֲמַר תְּרוּמָה בַּזְּמַן הַזֶּה דְּאוֹרָיְיתָא – חַלָּה דְּרַבָּנַן. דְּתַנְיָא ״בְּבוֹאֲכֶם אֶל הָאָרֶץ״, אִי ״בְּבוֹאֲכֶם״ יָכוֹל מִשֶּׁנִּכְנְסוּ לָהּ שְׁנַיִם וּשְׁלֹשָׁה מְרַגְּלִים – תַּלְמוּד לוֹמַר ״בְּבוֹאֲכֶם״, בְּבִיאַת כּוּלְּכֶם אָמַרְתִּי, וְלֹא בְּבִיאַת מִקְצָתְכֶם. וְכִי אַסְּקִינְהוּ עֶזְרָא,

And I said to them: On the contrary, even according to the one who said that *teruma* today is an obligation **by Torah** law, the obligation to separate ***ḥalla* is by rabbinic** law, **as it is taught** in a *baraita* with regard to the verse concerning *ḥalla*: **"When you come into the land**[N] …from the first of your dough you should separate *teruma*" (Numbers 15:18–19). **If** the obligation is **when you come,** one **might** have thought that it took effect **from** the moment **that two or three spies entered** the land, therefore **the verse states: "When you come,"** from which it is derived that God is saying: **I said** that the obligation takes effect **with the coming of all of you and not with the coming of some of you.** Separating *ḥalla* is an obligation by Torah law only when the entire Jewish people comes to Eretz Yisrael, **and when Ezra took them up** to Eretz Yisrael at the beginning of the Second Temple period,

NOTES

The seven years that they conquered the land and the seven years that they divided the land – שֶׁבַע שֶׁכִּיבְּשׁוּ וְשֶׁבַע שֶׁחִילְּקוּ: Rabbeinu Ḥananel writes that during those years, a large part of Eretz Yisrael remained in the hands of the Canaanites. Proof can be cited from the fact that even when the majority of Eretz Yisrael is not in Jewish hands, the obligation of *ḥalla* is still in effect. This also resolves the problem raised in the *Beit HaLevi*: How can the sanctity of the land be applied selectively? According to Rabbeinu Ḥananel, the status of *ḥalla* is unique, as it is dependent neither upon the sanctity of the land nor upon the presence of the entire Jewish people within its borders.

But were not obligated in *teruma* – וְלֹא נִתְחַיְּיבוּ בִּתְרוּמָה: Some explain that since *teruma* and tithes are associated in the Torah with the Sabbatical-Year cycle, and the *halakhot* of the Sabbatical Year apply only to "your field" (Leviticus 25:4), before the land was divided no individual could be considered as owning inherited property. Therefore, the laws of *teruma* and tithes were not yet in effect. Others explain that the Sabbatical Year is tied to the Jubilee cycle, which is in effect only when the entire Jewish people are within the borders of Eretz Yisrael (see Ritva).

When you come into the land – בְּבוֹאֲכֶם אֶל הָאָרֶץ: Rashi cites the opinion of Rabbi Yishmael from the *Sifrei*, that the term *bevo'akhem*, when you come, is anomalous. Typically, the Torah introduces mitzvot observed exclusively in Eretz Yisrael with the term *ki tavo*, when you will come. Apparently, the dispute in this matter hinges upon the question of whether *bevo'akhem* means any entrance into Eretz Yisrael, even if it is not settlement of the entire land by the entire people, or whether it refers only to the settlement of the entire Jewish people in their land.

לָאו כּוּלְּהוּ סְלוּק.

not all of them ascended. Since the majority of the people did not come to the land, separating *ḥalla* was not restored to the status of an obligation by Torah law.

תָּא שְׁמַע: חֲזָקָה לִכְהוּנָּה – נְשִׂיאוּת כַּפַּיִם, וְחִילּוּק גְּרָנוֹת, וְעֵדוּת. עֵדוּת חֲזָקָה הִיא?! אֶלָּא לָאו הָכִי קָאָמַר: נְשִׂיאוּת כַּפַּיִם כִּי עֵדוּת, מָה עֵדוּת לְיוֹחֲסִין אַף נְשִׂיאוּת כַּפַּיִם לְיוֹחֲסִין. לָא, עֵדוּת הַבָּאָה מִכֹּחַ חֲזָקָה – כַּחֲזָקָה.

The Gemara cites proof from another *baraita* to resolve the dilemma. **Come and hear:** The **presumptive status for priesthood** is established by **Lifting of the Hands** for the Priestly Benediction, **and** by **distribution** of *teruma* at the **threshing floors, and** by **testimony.** The Gemara asks: **Does testimony** merely establish **presumptive status?** Testimony provides absolute proof of his status, not merely a presumption. **Rather is it not** that **this is what** the *tanna* **is saying: Lifting of the Hands** is **like testimony, just as testimony** that one is a priest elevates him to the priesthood **for lineage, so too Lifting of the Hands** establishes presumptive status **for lineage.** The Gemara answers: **No,** when the *tanna* is referring to testimony, he is stating that the legal status of **testimony that is based on presumptive status**[NH] **is like** that of **presumptive status** itself.

כִּי הַהוּא דַּאֲתָא לְקַמֵּיהּ דְּרַבִּי אַמִי, אֲמַר לֵיהּ: מוּחְזְקַנִי בְּזֶה שֶׁהוּא כֹּהֵן. אֲמַר לֵיהּ: מָה רָאִיתָ? אֲמַר לֵיהּ: שֶׁקָּרָא רִאשׁוֹן בְּבֵית הַכְּנֶסֶת. בְּחֶזְקַת שֶׁהוּא כֹּהֵן אוֹ בְּחֶזְקַת שֶׁהוּא גָּדוֹל? שֶׁקָּרָא אַחֲרָיו לֵוִי. וְהֶעֱלָהוּ רַבִּי אַמִי לִכְהוּנָּה עַל פִּיו.

As in the incident involving **a certain** man **who came before Rabbi Ami** and **said to him: That** man established **presumptive status** before **me that he is a priest.** Rabbi Ami **said to him: What did you see** that led you to that conclusion? **He said to** Rabbi Ami: I saw **that he** was called to the Torah and **read first in the synagogue.** Rabbi Ami asked him: Did he read first based **on the presumptive status that he is a priest, or** was it based **on the presumptive status that he is a great** man? The custom was that a priest would be called to the Torah first, unless there was a prominent Torah scholar among the worshippers. He said to Rabbi Ami: He read the Torah as a priest, **as after him a Levite read** the Torah. A Levite is called to the Torah second only when a priest is called first. **And Rabbi Ami elevated him to the priesthood, on the basis of his** statement.

הַהוּא דַּאֲתָא לְקַמֵּיהּ דְּרַבִּי יְהוֹשֻׁעַ בֶּן לֵוִי, אֲמַר לֵיהּ: מוּחְזְקַנִי בְּזֶה שֶׁהוּא לֵוִי. אֲמַר לֵיהּ: מָה רָאִיתָ? אֲמַר לֵיהּ: שֶׁקָּרָא שֵׁנִי בְּבֵית הַכְּנֶסֶת. בְּחֶזְקַת שֶׁהוּא לֵוִי, אוֹ בְּחֶזְקַת שֶׁהוּא גָּדוֹל? שֶׁקָּרָא לְפָנָיו כֹּהֵן. וְהֶעֱלָהוּ רַבִּי יְהוֹשֻׁעַ בֶּן לֵוִי לִלְוִיָּה עַל פִּיו.

The Gemara relates an incident involving **a certain** man **who came before Rabbi Yehoshua ben Levi** and **said to** Rabbi Yehoshua ben Levi: **That** man established the **presumptive status** before **me that he is a Levite.** Rabbi Yehoshua ben Levi **said to him: What did you see** that led you to that conclusion? **He said to** Rabbi Yehoshua ben Levi: I saw **that he** was called to the Torah and that he **read second in the synagogue.** Rabbi Yehoshua ben Levi asked him: Did he read second based **on the presumptive status that he is a Levite, or** was it based **on the presumptive status that he is a great** man? When there is no priest in the synagogue, people in the synagogue are called to the Torah in order of their prominence. Perhaps he was the second most prominent man in the synagogue. He said to Rabbi Yehoshua ben Levi: I am certain that he is a Levite, **as a priest read** the Torah **before him. And Rabbi Yehoshua ben Levi elevated him to Levite status,**[H] **based on his** statement.

הַהוּא דַּאֲתָא לְקַמֵּיהּ דְּרֵישׁ לָקִישׁ, אֲמַר לֵיהּ: מוּחְזְקַנִי בְּזֶה שֶׁהוּא כֹּהֵן. אֲמַר לֵיהּ: מָה רָאִיתָ? [אֲמַר לֵיהּ:] שֶׁקָּרָא רִאשׁוֹן בְּבֵית הַכְּנֶסֶת. אֲמַר לֵיהּ: רְאִיתִיו שֶׁחִילֵּק עַל הַגְּרָנוֹת? אֲמַר לוֹ רַבִּי אֶלְעָזָר: וְאִם אֵין שָׁם גּוֹרֶן בָּטְלָה כְּהוּנָּה?!

The Gemara relates another incident involving **a certain man who came before Reish Lakish** and **said to** Reish Lakish: **That** man established the **presumptive status** before **me that he is a priest.** Reish Lakish **said to him: What did you see** that led you to that conclusion? **He said to** Reish Lakish: I saw **that he** was called to the Torah and **read first in the synagogue.** Reish Lakish, based on his opinion that one's presumptive status as a priest can be established only on the basis of his receiving *teruma*, **said to him: Did you see that he received a share** of *teruma* **at the threshing floor? Rabbi Elazar said to** Reish Lakish: **And if there is no threshing floor**[N] there, does **the priesthood cease** to exist? The testimony that he read from the Torah first is sufficient.

NOTES

Testimony that is based on presumptive status – **עֵדוּת הַבָּאָה מִכֹּחַ חֲזָקָה**: Rashi explains that the witnesses are testifying about presumptive status. The Maharsha writes that the formulation of the Gemara is imprecise, as according to Rashi, the presumption is based on testimony and the testimony is not based on presumptive status. Therefore, *Tosafot* explain that the testimony is based on the presumptive status as a Levite of the one reading the Torah after him.

And if there is no threshing floor – **וְאִם אֵין שָׁם גּוֹרֶן**: Rashi and other commentaries explain this plainly. If this occurs in a place where no crops are grown, e.g., in a big city, there is no proof of priesthood. However, the Ritva explains that even if this transpires in a place where crops are grown, the Sages said that the distribution of *teruma* at the threshing floor does not constitute proof of priesthood (see 25a), there is no proof of priesthood.

HALAKHA

Testimony that is based on presumptive status – **עֵדוּת הַבָּאָה מִכֹּחַ חֲזָקָה**: If one testifies that another is a priest or Levite, the latter assumes that presumptive status based on his testimony. For example, if a witness testified that one was called to read the Torah first and a Levite was called after him, he assumes the presumptive status of a priest (Rambam *Sefer Kedusha*, *Hilkhot Issurei Bia* 20:11).

And…elevated him to Levite status – **וְהֶעֱלָהוּ...לִלְוִיָּה**: If one testifies that he saw another person called to read the Torah second, after a priest, that latter assumes the presumptive status of a Levite (*Maggid Mishne*; Rambam *Sefer Kedusha*, *Hilkhot Issurei Bia* 20:11).

NOTES

If you deem the father credible – אִם אַתָּה מַאֲמִינוֹ: The early commentaries ask: What difficulty did Rabbi Ḥiyya find with the opinion of Rabbi Yehuda HaNasi? Isn't it known that there are many opinions that one elevates to *teruma* on the basis of a single witness, but for lineage two witnesses are required? They answer, in line with *Tosafot*, that Rav Ḥiyya understood from the statement of Rabbi Yehuda HaNasi that one would not be deemed credible in matters of lineage even if he testified together with another witness.

זִימְנִין הֲווּ יָתְבִי קַמֵּיהּ דְּרַבִּי יוֹחָנָן, אֲתָא כִּי הָא מַעֲשֶׂה לְקַמֵּיהּ. אֲמַר לֵיהּ רֵישׁ לָקִישׁ: רְאִיתִיו שֶׁחִילֵּק עַל הַגּוֹרֶן? אֲמַר לֵיהּ רַבִּי יוֹחָנָן: וְאִם אֵין שָׁם גּוֹרֶן בָּטְלָה כְּהוּנָּה?! הֲדַר חַזְיֵיהּ לְרַבִּי אֶלְעָזָר בִּישׁוּת, אֲמַר: שָׁמְעַתְּ מִילֵּי דְּבַר נַפָּחָא וְלָא אָמְרַתְּ לָן מִשְּׁמֵיהּ?!

On another **occasion** Rabbi Elazar and Reish Lakish **sat before Rabbi Yoḥanan.** A matter **similar** to **that incident,** where one testified that another is a priest based on his reading the Torah first, **came before** Rabbi Yoḥanan. **Reish Lakish said to** the person who testified: **Did you see that he received a share** of *teruma* **at the threshing floor? Rabbi Yoḥanan said to** Reish Lakish: **And if there is no threshing floor there,** does **the priesthood cease** to exist? The Gemara relates that Reish Lakish **turned and looked at Rabbi Elazar harshly,** as he understood that on the previous occasion, Rabbi Elazar was citing verbatim a ruling that he heard from Rabbi Yoḥanan. Reish Lakish **said** to Rabbi Elazar: **You heard a statement of bar Nappaḥa,**[P] the son of a blacksmith, an epithet for Rabbi Yoḥanan, **and you did not say it to us in his name?** Had you done so, I would have accepted it from you then.

רַבִּי וְרַבִּי חִיָּיא, חַד הֶעֱלָה בֵּן עַל פִּי אָבִיו לִכְהוּנָּה, וְחַד הֶעֱלָה אָח עַל פִּי אָחִיו לִלְוִיָּה.

The Gemara relates with regard to **Rabbi** Yehuda HaNasi **and Rabbi Ḥiyya** that **one elevated a son to priesthood on the basis of** the statement of **his father, and one elevated a brother to** the **Levite status on the basis of** the statement of **his brother.** It is unclear which of the Sages ruled in which case.

תִּסְתַּיֵּים דְּרַבִּי הֶעֱלָה בֵּן עַל פִּי אָבִיו לִכְהוּנָּה, דְּתַנְיָא: הֲרֵי שֶׁבָּא וְאָמַר ״בְּנִי זֶה, וְכֹהֵן הוּא״ – נֶאֱמָן לְהַאֲכִילוֹ בִּתְרוּמָה, וְאֵינוֹ נֶאֱמָן לְהַשִּׂיאוֹ אִשָּׁה, דִּבְרֵי רַבִּי. אָמַר לוֹ רַבִּי חִיָּיא: אִם אַתָּה מַאֲמִינוֹ לְהַאֲכִילוֹ בִּתְרוּמָה – תַּאֲמִינוֹ לְהַשִּׂיאוֹ אִשָּׁה, וְאִם אִי אַתָּה מַאֲמִינוֹ לְהַשִּׂיאוֹ אִשָּׁה – לֹא תַּאֲמִינוֹ לֶאֱכוֹל בִּתְרוּמָה!

The Gemara notes: **It may be concluded that Rabbi** Yehuda HaNasi is the one who **elevated a son to priesthood on the basis of** the statement of **his father, as it is taught** in a *baraita* that if one **came and said: This is my son and he is a priest,**[H] his statement is **deemed credible to enable** his son **to partake of *teruma*, but** it **is not deemed credible to marry a woman** of superior lineage **to him,** as his testimony is not deemed credible for the purposes of lineage; this is **the statement of Rabbi** Yehuda HaNasi. **Rabbi Ḥiyya said to him: If you deem** the father **credible**[N] **to enable** his son **to partake of *teruma*, deem him credible to marry a woman to** his son. **And if you do not deem him credible to marry a woman to him, do not deem him credible** to enable his son **to partake of *teruma*.**

אָמַר לוֹ: אֲנִי מַאֲמִינוֹ לְהַאֲכִילוֹ בִּתְרוּמָה – שֶׁבְּיָדוֹ לְהַאֲכִילוֹ בִּתְרוּמָה, וְאֵינִי מַאֲמִינוֹ לְהַשִּׂיאוֹ אִשָּׁה – שֶׁאֵין בְּיָדוֹ לְהַשִּׂיאוֹ אִשָּׁה. תִּסְתַּיֵּים. וּמִדְּרַבִּי הֶעֱלָה בֵּן עַל פִּי אָבִיו לִכְהוּנָּה – רַבִּי חִיָּיא הֶעֱלָה אָח עַל פִּי אָחִיו לִלְוִיָּה.

Rabbi Yehuda HaNasi **said to him: I deem him credible to enable** his son **to partake of *teruma*, as it is within his purview to feed** his son ***teruma***, and one is deemed credible with regard to matters that are within his purview. **But I do not deem him credible to marry a woman to** his son, **as it is not within his purview to marry a woman to** his son, and therefore his testimony is not accepted. The Gemara determines: Indeed, it may be **conclude** that it is Rabbi Yehuda HaNasi who elevated a son to priesthood on the basis of the statement of his father. **And from** the fact **that** it is **Rabbi** Yehuda HaNasi who **elevated a son to priesthood on the basis of** the statement of **his father,** clearly it is **Rabbi Ḥiyya** who **elevated a brother to Levite status on the basis of** the statement of **his brother.**

וְרַבִּי חִיָּיא, מַאי שְׁנָא בֵּן דְּלָא, דְּקָרוֹב הוּא אֵצֶל אָבִיו – אָח נַמִּי קָרוֹב הוּא אֵצֶל אָחִיו?

The Gemara asks: **And** according to **Rabbi Ḥiyya, what is different** in the case of a **son, where** a father is **not** deemed credible **because** the son **is a relative of his father,** and therefore the father is disqualified from testifying about his son? **A brother is also a relative of his brother,** and therefore the brother should have been disqualified from testifying about his brother. Rabbi Ḥiyya should accept the testimony in both cases or reject the testimony in both cases.

PERSONALITIES

Bar Nappaḥa – בַּר נַפָּחָא: In several places in the Talmud, primarily in the Jerusalem Talmud, Rabbi Yoḥanan is referred to as bar Nappaḥa, son of the blacksmith. Although there is no information with regard to his family, as he was orphaned at a young age, some say that this was actually his father's profession. Others, among them the second explanation of Rashi in tractate *Sanhedrin* (96a), claim that he was called this due to his extraordinary beauty. The name functioned like a euphemism, but in reverse. Conceivably, his nickname referred to his craftsmanship in Torah (see *Avoda Zara* 50b).

HALAKHA

This is my son and he is a priest – בְּנִי זֶה וְכֹהֵן הוּא: If a priest says: This is my son, and he is a priest, then the son assumes the presumptive status of a priest. He may partake of *teruma* and he has the presumptive status of a priest. However, the father is deemed credible to testify that his son is a priest only if it is established by witnesses that this person is his son, even if the father is of unflawed descent (Rambam *Sefer Kedusha, Hilkhot Issurei Bia* 20:5, 10; *Shulḥan Arukh, Even HaEzer* 3:2).

בְּמֵסִיחַ לְפִי תּוּמוֹ, כִּי הָא דְּאָמַר רַב יְהוּדָה אָמַר שְׁמוּאֵל: מַעֲשֶׂה בְּאָדָם אֶחָד שֶׁהָיָה מֵסִיחַ לְפִי תּוּמוֹ, וְאָמַר: זְכוּרַנִי כְּשֶׁאֲנִי תִּינוֹק וּמוּרְכָּב עַל כְּתֵיפוֹ שֶׁל אַבָּא, וְהוֹצִיאוּנִי מִבֵּית הַסֵּפֶר וְהִפְשִׁיטוּנִי אֶת כּוּתָּנְתִּי, וְהִטְבִּילוּנִי לֶאֱכוֹל בִּתְרוּמָה לָעֶרֶב.

The Gemara answers: Rabbi Ḥiyya is speaking of a case where the brother **speaks offhandedly**[H] in the context of a conversation about a different topic. It was understood from this that his brother is a Levite. This is **similar to that which Rav Yehuda said** that **Shmuel said:** There was **an incident involving a person who was speaking offhandedly and said: I remember when I was a child and** still young enough to be **carried on my father's shoulder, and they took me out of school, and removed my cloak, and immersed me** to purify me from any possible ritual impurity, so that I would be able **to partake of *teruma* that evening.**

וְרַבִּי חִיָּיא מְסַיֵּים בָּהּ: וַחֲבֵירַי בְּדֵילִין מִמֶּנִּי, וְהָיוּ קוֹרִין אוֹתִי "יוֹחָנָן אוֹכֵל חַלּוֹת", וְהֶעֱלָהוּ רַבִּי לִכְהוּנָּה עַל פִּיו.

And Rabbi Ḥiyya, who related that incident, **concluded** the story[N] and related that the man said: **And my friends distanced** themselves **from me, and would call me: Yoḥanan who partakes of *ḥallot*,** as it was prohibited for his friends, who were non-priests, to eat *ḥalla* and *teruma*. **And Rabbi** Yehuda HaNasi **elevated him to priesthood based on his** statement. Just as one's offhanded statement is reliable, so too, is the offhanded statement of one's brother.

תַּנְיָא, רַבִּי שִׁמְעוֹן בֶּן אֶלְעָזָר אוֹמֵר: כְּשֵׁם שֶׁתְּרוּמָה חֲזָקָה לִכְהוּנָּה – כָּךְ מַעֲשֵׂר רִאשׁוֹן חֲזָקָה לִכְהוּנָּה, וְהַחוֹלֵק בְּבֵית דִּין – אֵינָהּ חֲזָקָה.

§ **It is taught** in a *baraita* that **Rabbi Shimon ben Elazar says: Just as *teruma*** establishes the **presumptive status for priesthood, so too the first tithe**[B] establishes the **presumptive status for priesthood. And one who receives a share of *teruma* in court** does **not** establish the **presumptive status** of priesthood.

מַעֲשֵׂר רִאשׁוֹן דִּלְוִי הוּא! כְּרַבִּי אֶלְעָזָר בֶּן עֲזַרְיָה. דְּתַנְיָא: תְּרוּמָה לְכֹהֵן, מַעֲשֵׂר רִאשׁוֹן לְלֵוִי, דִּבְרֵי רַבִּי עֲקִיבָא. רַבִּי אֶלְעָזָר בֶּן עֲזַרְיָה אוֹמֵר: מַעֲשֵׂר רִאשׁוֹן אַף לְכֹהֵן. אֵימוֹר דְּאָמַר רַבִּי אֶלְעָזָר בֶּן עֲזַרְיָה אַף לְכֹהֵן, לְכֹהֵן וְלֹא לְלֵוִי מִי אָמַר?

The Gemara asks: **First tithe is** given **to a Levite.** How does it establish the presumptive status of priesthood? The Gemara answers: This is **in accordance with** the opinion of **Rabbi Elazar ben Azarya, as it is taught** in a *baraita*: ***Teruma* is given to a priest,**[H] **first tithe**[H] **is given to a Levite;** this is **the statement of Rabbi Akiva. Rabbi Elazar ben Azarya says: First tithe** is given **to a priest as well.**[N] The Gemara asks: **Say that Rabbi Elazar ben Azarya said: To a priest as well. Did** actually **he say to a priest and not to a Levite?** Since it is given to both a Levite and a priest, first tithe cannot establish the presumptive status of priesthood.

HALAKHA

The brother speaks offhandedly – מֵסִיחַ לְפִי תּוּמוֹ: If it emerges from one's unconsidered remarks that he is a priest, he assumes the presumptive status of priesthood, which today entitles him to eat *teruma* by rabbinic law. This ruling is based on the incident related in the Gemara about the child who was taken from school and immersed in order to eat *teruma*; and his friends distanced themselves from him and called him: Yoḥanan who partakes of *ḥallot*; and he was elevated to priesthood based on his statement. The *Beit Yosef* and *Beit Shmuel* cite an explanation of *Tosafot* that says that it was necessary to include that this boy was taken from school to establish that he was not a slave. The *Tur* disagrees and holds that all families have the presumptive status of unflawed lineage and no testimony is required to establish that he is not a slave (Rambam *Sefer Kedusha*, *Hilkhot Issurei Bia* 20:14; *Shulḥan Arukh*, *Even HaEzer* 3:1).

***Teruma* is given to a priest – תְּרוּמָה לְכֹהֵן:** Priests, both minor and adult, male and female, are exclusively entitled to partake of *teruma* and the *teruma* of the tithe given by the Levite to the priest from the first tithe. Their wives, their slaves, and their animals are permitted to partake of *teruma* due to their connection to the priest (Rambam *Sefer Zera'im*, *Hilkhot Terumot* 6:1).

First tithe – מַעֲשֵׂר רִאשׁוֹן: If a priest has first tithe or any of the priestly gifts, he is not required to give it to a Levite or a priest. Moreover, Ezra penalized the Levites of his generation, decreeing that first tithe be given to priests instead of Levites. Some note that this penalty was in effect only during Ezra's era; however, in later generations the tithe was given both to Levites and priests. According to that understanding, the ruling of the Rambam could be explained according to all opinions (*Kesef Mishne*; Rambam *Sefer Zera'im*, *Hilkhot Ma'aser Sheni* 1:4).

BACKGROUND

First tithe – מַעֲשֵׂר רִאשׁוֹן: After *teruma* is separated, one-tenth of the remaining produce is given to the Levites. This produce is called first tithe. The owner is permitted to give first tithe to any Levite he chooses. A Levite who received first tithe is required to set aside one-tenth of that produce as *teruma* of the tithe and give it to a priest. The remaining first tithe remains the Levite's property. It has no sanctity and may be eaten by anyone. The legal status of produce from which first tithe was not separated is that of untithed produce and may not be eaten.

NOTES

And Rabbi Ḥiyya concluded the story – וְרַבִּי חִיָּיא מְסַיֵּים בָּהּ: This addition by Rabbi Ḥiyya seems to add nothing of significance. In *Beit Ya'akov*, the explanation is that Rabbi Ḥiyya's statement is consistent with his opinion, as in a previous discussion, Rabbi Ḥiyya maintains that the fact that it is within the father's purview to feed his son *teruma* is not sufficient to deem him credible to testify that his son may partake of *teruma* (25b). Here too, one could say that the fact that his father fed him *teruma* is no proof that he is a priest. Therefore, Rav Ḥiyya added that all of this person's friends referred to him as one who eats *ḥallot*, and this proves that not only his father, but everyone else, knew that he was a priest.

First tithe is given to a priest as well – מַעֲשֵׂר רִאשׁוֹן אַף לְכֹהֵן: Both early and later commentaries discuss this matter at length. From Rashi's and Rashbam's explanations in tractate *Bava Batra* (81b), apparently the dispute arose after the penalty was imposed by Ezra, as, according to Rabbi Akiva, although Ezra penalized the Levites, he established that first tithe would be given to the poor, not to priests. *Tosafot* discuss whether the reference is to the poor in general or only to poor priests. According to Rabbi Elazar ben Azarya, Ezra established that first tithe be given exclusively to priests.

However, according to most commentaries, the dispute is not with regard to the period after the penalty was imposed but with regard to the Torah law itself. According to Rabbi Akiva, first tithe is given exclusively to the Levites, whereas Rabbi Elazar ben Azarya maintains that even by Torah law, the priests are included among the Levites. The Gemara notes in several places that in twenty-four places in the Bible priests are referred to as Levites. However, with regard to the situation after Ezra imposed a penalty, there is a dispute between the early commentaries. Some say that Rabbi Akiva agrees that from then on first tithe was given exclusively to priests, while others contend that even after the decree it was given to Levites, but it could also be given to priests. Most commentaries prefer the latter explanation because it corresponds to the numerous places in the Talmud that refer to a Levite receiving first tithe.

NOTES

But perhaps by happenstance – ודלמא איקרו: The Meiri explains that this is possible in a situation where there are no priests at all. Although Ezra penalized the Levites, he did not want to completely abrogate the mitzva of the first tithe. Therefore, it was occasionally given to the Levites.

אין, בתר דקנסינהו עזרא. ודלמא איקרו ויהבו ליה! אמר רב חסדא: הכא במאי עסקינן – כגון דמוחזק לן באבוה דהאי דכהן הוא, ונפק עליה קלא דבן גרושה ובן חלוצה הוא, וחלקו ליה לדידיה מעשר בבית הגרנות.

The Gemara answers: **Yes,** first tithe can establish the presumptive status of priesthood. **After Ezra penalized** the Levites for failure to return to Eretz Yisrael from Babylonia, he decreed that the people should not give them first tithe. Although by Torah law first tithe may be given to both Levites and priests, after that decree, it was given only to priests. The Gemara asks: How can the presumptive status of priesthood be established? **But perhaps** in this case he was actually a Levite, and **by happenstance**[N] **they gave him** first tithe. **Rav Ḥisda said: With what are we dealing here?** It is a case **where the father of that** man established the **presumptive status of priesthood before us, and a rumor emerged** about the son **that he is the son of a divorced woman or the son of a *ḥalutza*.** As a *ḥalal*, who is disqualified from the priesthood, his legal status is that of an Israelite. **And** it was seen that the son **himself received a share of** first **tithe at the threshing floor.**

לוי – דלאו לוי הוא, מאי איכא למימר – בן גרושה או בן חלוצה הוא, לא מיבעיא למאן דאמר מעשר ראשון אסור לזרים, דלא הוו יהבי ליה, אלא אפילו למאן דאמר מעשר ראשון מותר לזרים, הני מילי – למיספק להו, אבל בתורת חלוקה – לא יהבי ליה.

Therefore, with regard to **Levite** status, it is clear **that he is not a Levite,** as his father is a priest. The Gemara asks: **What** then **is there to say?** Is it that **he is the son of a divorced woman or the son of a *ḥalutza*? It is not necessary to say that** according **to the one who** says that **first tithe is forbidden to non-priests, they would not have given** first tithe to the son of the divorcée, as his legal status is that of a non-priest. **However, even according to the one who says that first tithe is permitted for non-priests,**[H] and therefore the fact that he received first tithe proves nothing, **that** *halakha* **applies only** to the fact that it is permitted for one to whom first tithe produce was distributed **to provide** it to non-priests. **However, in the form of a share** of first tithe **at the threshing floor, one does not give** it **to a** non-priest. Therefore, according to Rabbi Elazar ben Azarya, the fact that one receives a share at the threshing floor proves that he is a priest of unflawed lineage.

"והחולק בבית דין אינה חזקה". אי בבית דין לא הויא חזקה – היכא הויא חזקה?! אמר רב ששת הכי קאמר: החולק תרומה בנכסי אביו עם אחיו בבית דין – אינה חזקה.

It is taught in the same *baraita*: **And one who receives a share** of *teruma* **in court** does **not** establish the **presumptive status** of priesthood. The Gemara asks: **If in court it** does **not** establish the **presumptive status, where does it** establish the **presumptive status?** Isn't court the place where matters are optimally clarified? **Rav Sheshet said** that **this is what** the *tanna* **is saying: One who receives a share of *teruma* from his father's property with his brothers in court**[H] as his portion of the inheritance, in doing so does **not** establish **presumptive status** of priesthood. Even if he is a *ḥalal* and therefore a non-priest, it could be that he owns the *teruma* as part of his inheritance.

פשיטא! מהו דתימא: מדהנך לאכילה האי נמי לאכילה, קא משמע לן: הנך – לאכילה, האי – לזבוני.

The Gemara asks: It **is obvious** that receiving *teruma* in court does not establish the presumptive status. The Gemara answers: **Lest you say** that **from** the fact **that these** brothers receive the *teruma* **to partake** of it, it can be deduced that **that** brother **also** receives the *teruma* **to partake** of it, the *tanna* therefore **teaches us** that **these** brothers receive the *teruma* **to partake** of it and **that** brother receives it **to sell it.** The fact that he may not eat the *teruma* does not prevent him from selling it.

HALAKHA

First tithe is permitted for non-priests – מעשר ראשון מותר לזרים: First tithe may be eaten by non-Levites. Some note that although there is a tannaitic dispute whether or not first tithe may be eaten by non-Levites, the *halakha* is in accordance with the opinion of the Rabbis in their dispute with Rabbi Meir in tractate *Yevamot* (85b) that pertains to the sanctity of first tithe (Rambam *Sefer Zera'im, Hilkhot Ma'aser Sheni* 1:2).

One who receives a share of *teruma*…in court – החולק...בבית דין: If witnesses testify that the son of a priest inherited in court his father's *teruma* in his portion of the inheritance, he does not assume the presumptive status of priesthood. This is because it is conceivable that he is a *ḥalal* who plans to sell his share of the *teruma* (Rambam *Sefer Kedusha, Hilkhot Issurei Bia* 20:12).

״רַבִּי יְהוּדָה אוֹמֵר: אֵין מַעֲלִין לִכְהוּנָּה עַל פִּי עֵד אֶחָד״ וכו׳. רַבָּן שִׁמְעוֹן בֶּן גַּמְלִיאֵל הַיְינוּ רַבִּי אֱלִיעֶזֶר! וְכִי תֵּימָא: עַרְעָר חַד אִיכָּא בֵּינַיְיהוּ: דְּרַבִּי אֱלִיעֶזֶר סָבַר: עַרְעָר חַד, וְרַבָּן שִׁמְעוֹן בֶּן גַּמְלִיאֵל סָבַר עַרְעָר תְּרֵי. הָאָמַר רַבִּי יוֹחָנָן: דִּבְרֵי הַכֹּל אֵין עַרְעָר פָּחוֹת מִשְּׁנַיִם!

§ We learned in the mishna that **Rabbi Yehuda says: One does not elevate** a man **to priesthood on the basis of one witness.** Rabbi Elazar says: In a case where there are no challengers, one elevates a man to priesthood on the basis of one witness. Rabban Shimon ben Gamliel says: One elevates a man to priesthood on the basis of one witness. The Gemara asks: The opinion of **Rabban Shimon ben Gamliel is** identical to the opinion of **Rabbi Eliezer,**[N] as they agree that one elevates a man to priesthood on the basis of one witness when there are no challengers. **And if you would say that there is** a difference **between them** in a case where there is **a challenge** posed by **one** witness, **as Rabbi Eliezer holds: A challenge** posed by **one** witness is sufficient to undermine one's presumptive status of priesthood and two witnesses are required to overcome that challenge, **and Rabban Shimon ben Gamliel holds:** An effective **challenge** requires **two** witnesses, **didn't Rabbi Yoḥanan say: Everyone agrees** that **there is no** effective **challenge** with **fewer than two** witnesses?

אֶלָּא, הָכָא בְּמַאי עָסְקִינַן דְּמוּחְזָק לָן בַּאֲבוּהּ דְּהַאי דְּכֹהֵן הוּא, וּנְפַק עֲלֵיהּ קָלָא דְּבֶן גְּרוּשָׁה אוֹ בֶּן חֲלוּצָה הוּא, וְאַחְתִּינֵיהּ, וַאֲתָא עֵד אֶחָד וְאָמַר: יָדַעְנָא בֵּיהּ דְּכֹהֵן הוּא,

Rather, with what case **are we dealing here?** It is in a case **where the father of that** man established his **presumptive status of priesthood before us, and a rumor emerged about** the son[NH] **that he is the son of a divorced woman or the son of a *ḥalutza*, and** therefore **we downgraded him** from the presumptive status of priesthood. **And one** witness **came and said: I know that he is a priest** of unflawed lineage,

NOTES

The opinion of Rabban Shimon ben Gamliel is identical to the opinion of Rabbi Eliezer – רַבָּן שִׁמְעוֹן בֶּן גַּמְלִיאֵל הַיְינוּ רַבִּי אֱלִיעֶזֶר: This version of the text is Rashi's version, but in manuscripts in the possession of the early commentaries there is a variant reading: The opinion of Rabban Shimon ben Gamliel is identical to the opinion of the first *tanna* (see Rabbeinu Ḥananel). Some explain that there is no difference between the two versions, as the first *tanna* is the first *tanna* whose opinion Rabban Shimon ben Gamliel disputes, i.e., Rabbi Eliezer (Ritva). However, others understand that it is indeed referring to the first *tanna* of the mishna, who says that two men are each deemed credible to testify that their counterpart is a priest. According to this understanding, the difference between the two versions pertains to the matter of collusion. The first *tanna* holds that one witness is deemed credible even when there is suspicion of collusion, and Rabbi Eliezer and Rabban Shimon ben Gamliel disagree (see Ramban).

And a rumor emerged about the son – וּנְפַק עֲלֵיהּ קָלָא: The Ritva explains that the reference here is to a rumor that was confirmed in court. Although there was no clear testimony, the rumor was examined in court and deemed reliable. Therefore, the court decided to downgrade this person from his presumptive status of priesthood. Rashi and *Piskei Riaz* explain that the rumor is unconfirmed, but because of the higher standard set for the priesthood, the rumor is not dismissed, and his status remains uncertain until the matter is clarified.

HALAKHA

And a rumor emerged about the son – וּנְפַק עֲלֵיהּ קָלָא: If one's father has the presumptive status of priesthood and a rumor emerges that he was the son of a divorcée or a *ḥalutza*, the son is downgraded from the presumptive status of priesthood based on the rumor. If one witness then comes and testifies that the son is a legitimate priest, the son is restored to the priesthood. If two witnesses then testify that the son is a *ḥalal*, he is again downgraded. If another single witness then testifies that his lineage is unflawed, his testimony is combined with the testimony of the other witness who testified that he is a legitimate priest, and two witnesses contradict the two who testified against him, so he is restored to his original presumptive status as a legitimate priest, as far as partaking of *teruma* by rabbinic law is concerned (*Beit Shmuel*). This ruling is in accordance with the opinion of Rabban Shimon ben Gamliel and Rav Ashi's explanation, which is the latest amoraic opinion cited, and the principle is that the halakhic ruling is in accordance with the latest opinion (Rambam *Sefer Kedusha*, *Hilkhot Issurei Bia* 20:16; *Shulḥan Arukh*, *Even HaEzer* 3:7).

HALAKHA

Witnesses who did not view the event together – עֵדִים שֶׁלֹּא רָאוּ כְּאַחַת: In monetary cases, the testimony of two witnesses is joined, even if they witnessed an event at different times, in accordance with the opinion of Rabbi Yehoshua ben Korḥa and the ruling in *Sanhedrin* 30a (Rambam *Sefer Shofetim, Hilkhot Edut* 4:1, 3; *Shulḥan Arukh, Ḥoshen Mishpat* 30:6).

וְאַסְּקִינֵיהּ. וַאֲתוֹ בֵּי תְרֵי וְאָמְרִי: בֶּן גְּרוּשָׁה וּבֶן חֲלוּצָה הוּא, וְאַחְתִּינֵיהּ. וַאֲתָא עֵד אֶחָד וְאָמַר: יָדַעְנָא בֵּיהּ דְּכֹהֵן הוּא. וּדְכוּלֵּי עָלְמָא מִצְטָרְפִין לְעֵדוּת,

and therefore we elevated him back to the priesthood, as one witness is sufficient to negate the rumor. **And** then **two** witnesses **came and said: He is the son of a divorced woman or the son of a *ḥalutza*,** and then **we downgraded him**[N] from the priesthood, as two witnesses negated the testimony of one witness. Then **one** witness **came and said: I know that he is a priest** of unflawed lineage. **And everyone agrees** that the two single witnesses **join** together and constitute two witnesses **for** the purpose of **testimony** that he is a priest of unflawed lineage, and fundamentally his presumptive status of priesthood should be restored.

וְהָכָא – בְּמֵיחָשׁ לְזִילוּתָא דְּבֵי דִינָא קָמִיפַּלְגִי. תַּנָּא קַמָּא סָבַר: כֵּיוָן דְּאַחְתִּינֵיהּ – לָא מַסְּקִינַן לֵיהּ, חָיְישִׁינַן לְזִילוּתָא דְּבֵי דִינָא. וְרַבָּן שִׁמְעוֹן בֶּן גַּמְלִיאֵל סָבַר: אֲנַן אַחְתִּינַן לֵיהּ, וַאֲנַן מַסְּקִינַן לֵיהּ, וּלְזִילוּתָא דְּבֵי דִינָא לָא חָיְישִׁינַן.

And here it is **with regard to concern** that it will lead **to contempt for the court** that **they disagree. The first *tanna*,** Rabbi Eliezer, **holds: Once we downgraded him** from the priesthood, **we do not** then **elevate him. We are concerned** that it will lead **to contempt for the court,** as the reversal in the court decisions create the impression that the court does not know what it is doing. **And Rabban Shimon ben Gamliel holds: We downgrade him** from the priesthood **and we** then **elevate him,**[N] **and** as for the possibility that it will lead **to contempt for the court, we are not concerned** about it. The primary concern is that the matter be determined based on the relevant testimonies.

מַתְקִיף לַהּ רַב אַשִׁי: אִי הָכִי אֲפִילּוּ תְּרֵי וּתְרֵי נָמֵי!

Rav Ashi strongly **objects: If so,** if they disagree with regard to contempt for the court, why is it necessary to establish the dispute in a case where the witnesses who testified that he is a priest of unflawed lineage came individually? **If so,** then **even** if **two** witnesses testify together that he is unfit for the priesthood, and the court downgraded him, **and two** witnesses testify together that he is fit for the priesthood, and the court elevated him, the *tanna'im* would **also** disagree, as the same concern for contempt of court applies.

אֶלָּא אָמַר רַב אַשִׁי: בְּמִצְטָרְפִין לְעֵדוּת קָמִיפַּלְגִי, וּבִפְלוּגְתָּא דְּהָנֵי תַּנָּאֵי. דְּתַנְיָא: אֵין עֵדוּתָן מִצְטָרֶפֶת עַד שֶׁיִּרְאוּ שְׁנֵיהֶם כְּאֶחָד, רַבִּי יְהוֹשֻׁעַ בֶּן קָרְחָה אוֹמֵר: אֲפִילּוּ בָּזֶה אַחַר זֶה. וְאֵין עֵדוּתָן מִתְקַיֶּימֶת בְּבֵית דִּין עַד שֶׁיָּעִידוּ שְׁנֵיהֶם כְּאֶחָד,

Rather, Rav Ashi said: It is **with regard to** whether two single witnesses **join** together and constitute two witnesses **for** the purpose of **testimony**[N] that **they disagree, and** it is **in the dispute** between **these *tanna'im*** that they disagree, **as it is taught** in a *baraita*: **The testimony** of individual witnesses **merges** into the testimony of two witnesses **only if the two of them saw** the incident transpire together, **as one. Rabbi Yehoshua ben Korḥa says:** Their testimony merges **even in** a case where **this** witness saw the incident **after that** witness;[H] **however, the testimony** of witnesses **is validated in court only** if **the two of them testify** together **as one.**

NOTES

And we elevated him…and we downgraded him – וְאַסְּקִינֵיהּ...וְאַחְתִּינֵיהּ: The Ramban writes, emphasizing Rashi's comments, that there is a difference between the first time and the second time that the Sages said: We downgraded him. The first time was not a full-fledged downgrade from his presumptive status, as it was merely due to a rumor. In that case, he is temporarily barred from enjoying the benefits of the priesthood until the matter is clarified.

We downgrade him from the priesthood and we then elevate him – אֲנַן אַחְתִּינַן לֵיהּ וַאֲנַן מַסְּקִינַן לֵיהּ: The Rid writes that although this is a case of two witnesses contradicting two others, which, certainly according to the Rid, creates a situation of uncertainty with regard to Torah law, because the discussion here pertains to elevating a person to be eligible to partake of *teruma* by rabbinic law, the uncertainty is with regard to rabbinic law. Rashi asks: Even if there is uncertainty with regard to rabbinic law, why should one be elevated to the priesthood? He explains that this person is restored to the priesthood based on the presumptive status created by the first witness.

Most commentaries reject this explanation and ask: In a case where two witnesses testify that one is a priest, and two others contradict them, clearly one does not assume the presumptive status of priesthood on the basis of the testimony of the first pair of witnesses (see Rashba and Ra'ah). Therefore, most commentaries explain that he is elevated to the priesthood based on the status of his father, who is certainly a priest. That is the formulation of the Rambam as well. The Rosh asks: Wasn't that presumptive status undermined by the rumor that emerged about him, and he was downgraded from the priesthood due to that rumor? On the basis of what presumptive status is he a priest? Although, according to Rashi's opinion, the rumor was not verified in court and it is not sufficiently substantive to undermine his presumptive status, according to others who hold that it was verified in court, the difficulty remains. The Rosh answers that a rumor is dismissed only when its source cannot be determined and refuted. However, here, once witnesses came and rendered him unfit, the source of the rumor is clear. Once those witnesses were contradicted, the rumor no longer has credence.

It is with regard to whether two single witnesses join together and constitute two witnesses for the purpose of testimony – בְּמִצְטָרְפִין לְעֵדוּת: The question arises: If the dispute is with regard to single witnesses joining together, the Gemara could have simply established it in a case where the witnesses did not come to court together. The Ran answers that there is a novel element in the case cited here in the Gemara, as the witnesses join together even in the case cited in the Gemara, where action is taken on the basis of one witness, then rescinded on the basis of two witnesses, and then a second witness testifies. Due to the pair of witnesses that testified in the interim, it appears that the court is relying on one witness.

רַבִּי נָתָן אוֹמֵר: שׁוֹמְעִין דְּבָרָיו שֶׁל זֶה הַיּוֹם, וּכְשֶׁיָּבֹא חֲבֵירוֹ לְמָחָר – שׁוֹמְעִין דְּבָרָיו.

Rabbi Natan says: They need not even testify together, but even if the court **hears the statement of this witness today, and when his fellow** witness **comes tomorrow** the court **hears his statement,**[H] their testimonies merge. Rabbi Eliezer holds in accordance with the opinion of Rabbi Yehoshua ben Korḥa, and therefore the testimony of the second witness cannot be merged with the testimony of the first witness and the person remains a *ḥalal*. Rabban Shimon ben Gamliel holds that the testimony of the two witnesses that he is a priest of unflawed lineage is merged, and his presumptive status of priesthood is restored, as it was already established that his father is a priest.

מתני׳ הָאִשָּׁה שֶׁנֶּחְבְּשָׁה בִּידֵי גוֹיִם, עַל יְדֵי מָמוֹן – מוּתֶּרֶת לְבַעְלָהּ, עַל יְדֵי נְפָשׁוֹת – אֲסוּרָה לְבַעְלָהּ.

MISHNA In the case of **a woman who was imprisoned**[H] **by gentiles due to a monetary** offense committed by her husband, once she is released after he pays his debt, **she is permitted to her husband,** even if he is a priest. There is no concern that they violated her because their objective is to coerce the husband to pay his debt in exchange for her release. Were they to abuse her, it is possible that he would be unwilling to pay. However, if a woman was imprisoned **due to a capital** offense and sentenced to death, once she is released **she is forbidden to her husband**[N] even if he is not a priest due to the concern that perhaps her captors violated her, and she acquiesced to one of them.

גמ׳ אָמַר רַב שְׁמוּאֵל בַּר רַב יִצְחָק אָמַר רַב: לֹא שָׁנוּ אֶלָּא שֶׁיַּד יִשְׂרָאֵל תַּקִּיפָה עַל אוּמּוֹת הָעוֹלָם אֲבָל יַד אוּמּוֹת הָעוֹלָם תַּקִּיפָה עַל עַצְמָן – אֲפִילּוּ עַל יְדֵי מָמוֹן אֲסוּרָה לְבַעְלָהּ.

GEMARA **Rav Shmuel bar Rav Yitzḥak said** that **Rav said: They taught** this mishna **only** in a case **where the authority of the Jewish people is dominant**[H] **over the nations of the world,** and the gentiles are law-abiding citizens. **However, when the authority of the nations of the world is dominant**[N] **over themselves,** a euphemism for dominance over the Jewish people, **even** a woman who was imprisoned **due to a monetary** offense **is forbidden to her husband,** as there is nothing preventing her jailers from violating her.

מְתִיב רָבָא: הֵעִיד רַבִּי יוֹסֵי הַכֹּהֵן וְרַבִּי זְכַרְיָה בֶּן הַקַּצָּב עַל בַּת יִשְׂרָאֵל שֶׁהוּרְהֲנָה בְּאַשְׁקְלוֹן, וְרִיחֲקוּהָ בְּנֵי מִשְׁפַּחְתָּהּ, וְעֵדֶיהָ מְעִידִים אוֹתָהּ שֶׁלֹּא נִסְתְּרָה וְשֶׁלֹּא נִטְמְאָה. וְאָמְרוּ לָהֶם חֲכָמִים: אִם אַתֶּם מַאֲמִינִים שֶׁהוּרְהֲנָה – הַאֲמִינוּ שֶׁלֹּא נִסְתְּרָה וְשֶׁלֹּא נִטְמְאָה, וְאִם אִי אַתֶּם מַאֲמִינִים שֶׁלֹּא נִסְתְּרָה וְשֶׁלֹּא נִטְמְאָה – אַל תַּאֲמִינוּ שֶׁהוּרְהֲנָה.

Rava raised an objection from a mishna (*Eduyyot* 8:2): **Rabbi Yosei the priest and Rabbi Zekharya ben HaKatzav testified about a Jewish woman** about **whom** witnesses testified that **she was taken as collateral** for a debt **in Ashkelon.**[B] **And the members of her family,** who suspected that she engaged in intercourse there, **distanced themselves from her, but her witnesses testified about her that she neither entered into seclusion nor was violated. And the Sages said** to the members of the family: **If you deem** the witnesses **credible**[N] to testify **that she was taken as collateral, deem** the witnesses **credible** to testify **that she neither entered into seclusion nor was violated. And if you do not deem** the witnesses **credible** to testify **that she neither entered into seclusion nor was violated, do not deem** the witnesses **credible** to testify **that she was taken as collateral** at all. In either case, she is permitted to her husband.

וְהָא אַשְׁקְלוֹן, דְּיַד אוּמּוֹת הָעוֹלָם תַּקִּיפָה עַל עַצְמָן, וְקָתָנֵי:

Rava asks: **But** this took place in **Ashkelon, which** is a place **where the authority of the nations of the world is dominant over themselves,** as it was a city of gentiles, **and it is taught:**

NOTES

She is forbidden to her husband – אֲסוּרָה לְבַעְלָהּ: *Tosafot* state explicitly, and it seems that Rashi maintains, that she is forbidden to her husband even if he is not a priest, due to the following concern: Since she is aware that she or her husband was sentenced to execution never to return, she will willingly submit to the prison guards and engage in intercourse with them, in the hope that it will provide her with an opportunity to be rescued.

Furthermore, since the mishna stated without qualification: She is forbidden to her husband, the indication is that she is forbidden even if her husband is a non-priest. However, most early commentaries explain that the reference is specifically to a case where her husband is a priest, and the concern is that she was raped. The Ramban, the Rashba, and the Ritva cite several proofs that there is no concern that she submitted willingly, as the presumption is that Jewish women are not suspected of doing so.

Citing Rabbeinu Ḥananel, some write that in the case of a non-priest, there is a multiple uncertainty: Did she engage in intercourse? If she did, did she do so willingly? In cases of multiple uncertainties, the ruling is lenient. The formulation of the mishna is without qualification because all of the *halakhot* cited in the mishna with regard to women taken captive relate to the wives of priests.

The authority of the nations of the world is dominant – יַד אוּמּוֹת הָעוֹלָם תַּקִּיפָה: The Meiri writes that there is concern when the authority of the nations is dominant, specifically in a place where there is no established regime. However, in a place where there are gentile judges who conduct themselves according to their laws, this is not a concern.

If you deem the witnesses credible – אִם אַתֶּם מַאֲמִינִים: The Rashba and the Ritva explain that these witnesses that testified about the woman must not have been fit witnesses, as the family would have no doubt accepted the testimony of two fit witnesses. Apparently, these witnesses were slaves or maidservants that the family hesitated to deem reliable. The *Penei Yehoshua* cites support from the language of the mishna: Her witnesses, indicating that they were people close to her, e.g., her servants.

BACKGROUND

Ashkelon – אַשְׁקְלוֹן: In the biblical times, Ashkelon was a Philistine city. It became a Hellenist city under the Greeks, although its residents continued to observe aspects of their former religion. Even at the pinnacle of their reign, Ashkelon was never conquered by the Hasmoneans. Under Roman rule it was a free city, where Jews resided; however, it remained a place where the authority of the gentiles was dominant.

HALAKHA

Two witnesses who do not testify at one time – שְׁנֵים הַמְעִידִים שֶׁלֹּא בְּבַת אַחַת: In monetary cases, the witnesses are not required to testify together. Rather, even if they testify on different days, their testimonies are combined into a single testimony and accepted. This ruling is in accordance with the opinion of Rabbi Natan, as he apparently agrees with Rabbi Yehoshua ben Korḥa, in accordance with whose opinion the *halakha* is ruled in the previous note (*Kesef Mishne*; Rambam *Sefer Shofetim*, *Hilkhot Edut* 4:4; *Shulḥan Arukh*, *Ḥoshen Mishpat* 30:9).

A woman who was imprisoned – הָאִשָּׁה שֶׁנֶּחְבְּשָׁה: If a woman was imprisoned by gentiles for a monetary offense, she is permitted to her husband even if he is a priest. However, if she was imprisoned for a capital offense, she is disqualified from marrying a priest; if she is the wife of a priest, she is forbidden to him.

The Rema cites *Tosafot* and the *Tur*, who rule that if she was imprisoned for a capital offense, she is forbidden to her husband, even if he is not a priest, as she is suspected of willingly submitting to her captors. The Rema cites a distinction between a case where the woman is accused of a capital crime, in which she is rendered unfit, and a case where it is her husband who is accused, in which she is not rendered unfit. Others add that even when she is the one accused, if there is a manner in which she could be redeemed, she is not rendered unfit because were they to abuse her, it is possible that she would not be redeemed. During periods of persecution, the ruling of the Rambam, which was more lenient, was adopted (*Terumat HaDeshen*; Rambam *Sefer Kedusha*, *Hilkhot Issurei Bia* 18:30; *Shulḥan Arukh*, *Even HaEzer* 7:11).

In a case where the authority of the Jewish people is dominant – שֶׁיַּד יִשְׂרָאֵל תַּקִּיפָה: The ruling that a woman is permitted to her husband if she is imprisoned for a monetary offense applies only if the authority of the Jewish people is dominant over the gentiles. Otherwise, she is forbidden to her husband even in a monetary case, unless witnesses testify explicitly that she was not violated (Rambam *Sefer Kedusha*, *Hilkhot Issurei Bia* 18:30; *Shulḥan Arukh*, *Even HaEzer* 7:11).

הוּרְהֲנָה – אִין, נֶחְבְּשָׁה – לָא! הוּא הַדִּין אֲפִילּוּ נֶחְבְּשָׁה, וּמַעֲשֶׂה שֶׁהָיָה – כָּךְ הָיָה.

If she was taken as security, in a case where her husband stipulated that if he fails to pay a debt the gentiles may take his wife and do with her as they please, **yes,** she requires witnesses to testify that she was not violated. However, if she was **imprisoned** by the authorities, **no,** she is deemed untainted even without witnesses. Apparently, the distinction is not based on the dominance of the Jewish people. Rather, it is based on the manner in which she was apprehended. The Gemara answers: **The same is true** that she is forbidden to her husband even **if she was imprisoned, and** the reason that the *tanna'im* testified about a case where she was taken as security is because **the incident that transpired, transpired** in **that** manner.

אִיכָּא דְּאָמְרִי, אֲמַר רָבָא: אַף אֲנַן נַמִי תָּנֵינָא: הֵעִיד רַבִּי יוֹסֵי הַכֹּהֵן וְרַבִּי זְכַרְיָה בֶּן הַקַּצָּב עַל בַּת יִשְׂרָאֵל שֶׁהוּרְהֲנָה בְּאַשְׁקְלוֹן וְרִיחֲקוּהָ בְּנֵי מִשְׁפַּחְתָּהּ, וְעֵדֶיהָ מְעִידִים עָלֶיהָ שֶׁלֹּא נִסְתְּרָה וְשֶׁלֹּא נִטְמְאָה. וְאָמְרוּ חֲכָמִים: אִם אַתֶּם מַאֲמִינִים שֶׁהוּרְהֲנָה – הַאֲמִינוּ שֶׁלֹּא נִסְתְּרָה וְשֶׁלֹּא נִטְמְאָה, וְאִם אֵין אַתֶּם מַאֲמִינִים שֶׁלֹּא נִסְתְּרָה וְשֶׁלֹּא נִטְמְאָה – אַל תַּאֲמִינוּ שֶׁהוּרְהֲנָה,

Some say a different version of this tradition. **Rava said** that **we too learn** a proof from a mishna for the statement that Rav Shmuel bar Rav Yitzḥak said that Rav said: **Rabbi Yosei the priest and Rabbi Zekharya ben HaKatzav testified about a Jewish woman** about **whom** witnesses testified that **she was taken as security** for a debt **in Ashkelon. And the members of her family,** who suspected that she engaged in intercourse there, **distanced themselves from her, and her witnesses testified about her that she neither entered into seclusion nor was violated. And the Sages said** to the members of the family: **If you believe** the witnesses **that she was taken as collateral, believe** the witnesses who say **that she neither entered into seclusion nor was violated. And if you do not believe** the witnesses **that she neither entered into seclusion nor was violated, do not believe** the witnesses **that she was taken as collateral** at all.

וְהָא אַשְׁקְלוֹן דְּעַל יְדֵי מָמוֹן הֲוָה, וְטַעֲמָא דְּעֵדִים מְעִידִין אוֹתָהּ, הָא אֵין עֵדִים מְעִידִין אוֹתָהּ – לָא, מַאי לָאו לָא שְׁנָא הוּרְהֲנָה וְלָא שְׁנָא נֶחְבְּשָׁה! לָא, הוּרְהֲנָה שָׁאנֵי.

Rava asks: **But** in the case in **Ashkelon that was due to a monetary** offense, **the reason** that she was permitted is **that witnesses testified about her** that she was untainted. **However, if witnesses did not testify about her, no,** she would not be permitted to her husband, although she was taken due to a monetary offense. What, **is it not** that it **is no different** if she was **taken as collateral and** it **is no different** if she was **imprisoned?** Apparently, if the authority of the gentiles is dominant, even if she was imprisoned for the sake of money there is concern that she was violated. The Gemara rejects the proof: **No,** the case where the woman is **taken as collateral is different,** and only in that case, where her husband stipulated that the gentiles could take her, would the gentiles allow themselves to violate her. However, in a case where she is imprisoned there is no concern of that sort.

אִיכָּא דְּרָמֵי לַהּ מִירְמָא, תְּנַן: עַל יְדֵי מָמוֹן – מוּתֶּרֶת לְבַעְלָהּ. וּרְמִינְהוּ: ״הֵעִיד רַבִּי יוֹסֵי״ כו׳, וְהָא אַשְׁקְלוֹן דְּעַל יְדֵי מָמוֹן, וְקָתָנֵי טַעֲמָא דְּעֵדִים מְעִידִים אוֹתָהּ, הָא אֵין עֵדִים מְעִידִין אוֹתָהּ – לָא!

Some raise it as a contradiction between the sources. **We learned** in the mishna: A woman who was taken hostage **due to a monetary** offense **is permitted to her husband. And they raise a contradiction** from the mishna in *Eduyyot*: **Rabbi Yosei** the priest and Rabbi Zekharya **ben HaKatzav testified** about a Jewish woman about whom witnesses testified that she was taken as collateral for a debt in Ashkelon. **But** this is not the case in **Ashkelon, which was due to a monetary** offense, **and it is taught** that **the reason** that the woman was permitted is **that witnesses testified about her** that she was untainted. **However, if witnesses did not testify about her, no,** she would not be permitted, although she was taken for the sake of money.

וּמְשַׁנֵּי: אֲמַר רַב שְׁמוּאֵל בַּר רַב יִצְחָק: לָא קַשְׁיָא, כָּאן שֶׁיַּד יִשְׂרָאֵל תַּקִּיפָה עַל אוּמּוֹת הָעוֹלָם, כָּאן שֶׁיַּד אוּמּוֹת הָעוֹלָם תַּקִּיפָה עַל עַצְמָן.

And he answers that **Rav Shmuel bar Rav Yitzḥak said:** This is **not difficult. Here,** the mishna is referring to a period **when the authority of the Jewish people is dominant over the nations of the world.** Then, a woman taken hostage for the sake of money is permitted. **There** it is referring to a period **when the authority of the nations of the world is dominant over themselves** and over the Jewish people. Therefore, even a woman taken because of a monetary offense is forbidden unless witnesses testify that she is untainted.

״עַל יְדֵי נְפָשׁוֹת אֲסוּרָה״ וכו׳. אֲמַר רַב: כְּגוֹן נְשֵׁי גַּנָּבֵי. וְלֵוִי אֲמַר: כְּגוֹן אִשְׁתּוֹ שֶׁל בֶּן דּוּנַאי. אָמַר חִזְקִיָּה: וְהוּא שֶׁנִּגְמַר דִּינָן לַהֲרִיגָה. וְרַבִּי יוֹחָנָן אָמַר: אַף עַל פִּי שֶׁלֹּא נִגְמַר דִּינָן לַהֲרִיגָה.

§ We learned in the mishna: A woman who was imprisoned **because of a capital** offense[H] **is forbidden to her husband. Rav said:** The mishna is referring to a case **where the wives of thieves** are involved, as when thieves were apprehended and hanged, their wives were abandoned and made available to all, and they were not protected from potential rapists. **And Levi said:** The mishna is referring to a case **where the wife of ben Donai,**[P] a murderer, is involved, as in that case the government abandons his wife and makes her available to all, which is not the case when one is condemned for theft. **Ḥizkiyya said: And** this abandonment **is** only in a case **where** the husbands **were sentenced to death.**[N] **And Rabbi Yoḥanan said: Although** their husbands **were not sentenced to death,** if the imprisonment is because of a capital offense, the women are abandoned and available to all.

מתני׳ עִיר שֶׁכְּבָשׁוּהָ כַּרְכּוֹם – כָּל כֹּהֲנוֹת שֶׁנִּמְצְאוּ בְּתוֹכָהּ פְּסוּלוֹת. וְאִם יֵשׁ לָהֶן עֵדִים, אֲפִילּוּ עֶבֶד, אֲפִילּוּ שִׁפְחָה – הֲרֵי אֵלּוּ נֶאֱמָנִין. וְאֵין נֶאֱמָן אָדָם עַל יְדֵי עַצְמוֹ.

MISHNA With regard to **a city that was conquered by** an army laying **siege,**[H] **all the women** married to **priests located in** the city **are unfit** and forbidden to their husbands, due to the concern that they were raped. **And if they have witnesses,**[H] **even** if the witness is **a slave, even** if the witness is **a maidservant,** both of whom are generally disqualified as witnesses, **they are deemed credible. And a person is not deemed credible** to establish his status **by his own** testimony. Therefore, a woman is not deemed credible to claim that she was not violated.

גמ׳ וּרְמִינְהוּ: בַּלֶּשֶׁת שֶׁבָּאָה לָעִיר; בִּשְׁעַת שָׁלוֹם, חָבִיּוֹת פְּתוּחוֹת – אֲסוּרוֹת, סְתוּמוֹת – מוּתָּרוֹת. בִּשְׁעַת מִלְחָמָה – אֵלּוּ וָאֵלּוּ מוּתָּרוֹת, לְפִי שֶׁאֵין פְּנַאי לְנַסֵּךְ!

GEMARA The Gemara **raises a contradiction** from a mishna (*Avoda Zara* 70b): If there is a gentile **military unit that entered a city,**[H] if it entered **during peacetime,**[N] after the soldiers leave, the **open barrels** of wine are **forbidden** and the wine in them may not be drunk, due to suspicion that the gentile soldiers may have poured this wine as a libation for idolatry. The **sealed barrels are permitted.** However, if the unit entered **in wartime, both these and those are permitted because** in wartime **there is no respite to pour** wine for idolatry. One can be certain that the soldiers did not do so because the soldiers were preoccupied with preparations for a potential attack by the enemy. Why, then, is the mishna concerned that perhaps the soldiers laying siege to the city rape the women?

PERSONALITIES

Ben Donai – בֶּן דּוּנַאי: Ben Donai is mentioned as a famous murderer in tractate *Sota*, where he is called Elazar ben Dinai, a more common rendition of his name. He was also known as Teḥina ben Perisha.

Ben Dinai is also mentioned in the book of his contemporary Josephus Flavius, where it is related that for a period of approximately twenty years ben Dinai led a gang of robbers and murderers in the Galilee, until he was ultimately deceived and apprehended by the Roman governor and taken to Rome.

Although it is not explicitly stated, apparently ben Dinai was not merely a professional robber. There was a political aspect to his activities, as he was the head of a group of partisans that battled the Romans. Josephus characterizes several leaders of the revolt against Rome as robbers. Perhaps it is due to that political aspect that the Romans opted to try him in Rome rather than trying him in Eretz Yisrael.

According to Roman law at that time, political prisoners who revolted against the government were stripped of all property. In this context, Levi's statement is understandable, as it is only in cases of this kind that the wife of the accused is abandoned and available to all.

NOTES

Where the husbands were sentenced to death – שֶׁנִּגְמַר דִּינָן לַהֲרִיגָה: Although ostensibly the discussion here refers to women apprehended due to the crimes of their husbands, some early commentaries explain that the women are also accused of crimes, as the assumption is that these women were aware of their husbands' actions and possibly even abetted them in their crimes. In the Jerusalem Talmud, it is stated explicitly: Once the court issued her death sentence. This indicates that the woman herself was condemned to death.

A military unit that entered a city during peacetime – בַּלֶּשֶׁת שֶׁבָּאָה לָעִיר בִּשְׁעַת שָׁלוֹם: The Meiri explains that the reference is to soldiers who enter a city, not to wage war, but rather to be temporarily quartered there. During their stay, the authorities empower them to support themselves from the property of the residents of the city. Therefore, the assumption is that they availed themselves of all the open barrels. However, it is clear that they did not touch the sealed barrels, as they would not have expended the effort to reseal barrels that they opened. As mentioned, the concern here is not merely that idolaters came into contact with the wine, but that they actually used it as libation for idolatry, as it was customary to do so before drinking the wine in the barrel.

HALAKHA

Because of a capital offense – עַל יְדֵי נְפָשׁוֹת: If the wife of a priest (Rambam) or the wife of a non-priest (*Tosafot*) was imprisoned by gentiles for a capital offense, she is forbidden to her husband. The language of the Rambam cited in the *Shulḥan Arukh* indicates that he rules in accordance with the opinion of Rav, and the case is one where the women themselves are suspected by the authorities of being aware of their husbands' actions and abetting them. The ruling is in accordance with the opinion of Rav, who, although he was younger than Levi, was the most prominent Sage of his generation and greater then Levi. The fact that the Rambam does not mention that this applies only after the woman was sentenced to death indicates that he rules in accordance with the opinion of Rabbi Yoḥanan in his dispute with his teacher Ḥizkiyya, as that is the Rambam's ruling in virtually all disputes between them (see *Maggid Mishne* and *Beit Yosef*). The Rema writes that women imprisoned due to capital crimes are forbidden to their husbands only if they were accused of the crime. However, if they were imprisoned due to the accusations against their husbands, they would not be victimized until their husbands were actually convicted, in accordance with the opinions of Levi and Ḥizkiyya (Rambam *Sefer Kedusha, Hilkhot Issurei Bia* 18:30; *Shulḥan Arukh, Even HaEzer* 7:11).

A city that was conquered by an army laying siege – עִיר שֶׁכְּבָשׁוּהָ כַּרְכּוֹם: If a city was besieged to the extent that no woman could escape, the legal status of all the women in the city is that of captive women. They are forbidden to priests due to the concern that they were raped (Rambam *Sefer Kedusha, Hilkhot Issurei Bia* 18:26; *Shulḥan Arukh, Even HaEzer* 7:10).

And if they have witnesses – וְאִם יֵשׁ לָהֶן עֵדִים: A woman who was taken captive or was in a city conquered by gentiles and has witnesses that she did not enter into seclusion with a gentile is permitted to a priest. Even a relative, a slave, or a maidservant is deemed credible to testify on her behalf. However, neither her own testimony nor the testimony of her husband, whose legal status is equal to her own for these purposes, is accepted (Rambam *Sefer Kedusha, Hilkhot Issurei Bia* 18:19; *Shulḥan Arukh, Even HaEzer* 7:1).

A military unit that entered a city – בַּלֶּשֶׁת שֶׁבָּאָה לָעִיר: If soldiers entered a city and entered the homes of Jews in peacetime, all the wine in open barrels is forbidden, even if the cover was replaced. However, the wine in the sealed barrels is permitted. If the soldiers pass through a city in wartime, even the wine in the open barrels is permitted (Rambam *Sefer Kedusha, Hilkhot Ma'akhalot Assurot* 12:24; *Shulḥan Arukh, Yoreh De'a* 129:12).

אמר רב מרי: לבעול – יש פנאי, לנסך – אין פנאי. רבי יצחק בר אלעזר משמיה דחזקיה אמר: כאן – בכרכום של אותה מלכות, כאן – בכרכום של מלכות אחרת.

Rav Mari said: To engage in intercourse there is respite;[H] **to pour** wine for idolatry **there is no respite. Rabbi Yitzḥak bar Elazar said in the name of Ḥizkiyya:** There is a different distinction between the cases. **There,** the mishna is referring **to the siege** of a city under the rule **of the same monarchy.**[NH] In that case, the soldiers, acting as the enforcement body of the monarchy, seek to minimize unnecessary damage to the city and will refrain from ruining the wine and raping the women. **Here,** the mishna is referring **to the siege** of a city under the rule **of a different monarchy.** Therefore, there are no restraints with regard to ruining the wine or raping the women.

של אותה מלכות נמי אי אפשר דלא ערק חד מינייהו! אמר רב יהודה אמר שמואל: כשמשמרות רואות זו את זו. אי אפשר דלא נײמא פורתא! אמר רבי לוי: כגון דמהדר לה למתא שושילתא וכלבא וגווזא ואווזא.

The Gemara asks: **Even** in the siege of a city under the rule **of the same monarchy, it is impossible that one of** the soldiers **did not wander off** and rape a woman. **Rav Yehuda said** that **Shmuel said:** This is referring to a case **where** the **sentries see each other** and do not allow the soldiers to plunder the city. The Gemara asks: **It is impossible that** the sentries would **not doze a bit,** enabling some soldiers to enter and plunder the city. **Rabbi Levi said:** It is referring to a case **where they surround the city with chains, and dogs, and branches** [*gavza*],[L] **and geese,**[B] as obstacles preventing unauthorized entry.

אמר רבי אבא בר זבדא: פליגי בה רבי יהודה נשיאה ורבנן, חד אמר: כאן בכרכום של אותה מלכות, כאן בכרכום של מלכות אחרת, ולא קשיא ליה ולא מידי וחד קשיא ליה כל הני, ומשני: כגון דמהדר ליה למתא שושילתא וכלבא וגווזא ואווזא.

Rabbi Abba bar Zavda said: Rabbi Yehuda Nesia, grandson of Rabbi Yehuda HaNasi, redactor of the mishna, **and the Rabbis dispute** this matter. **One said: There,** the mishna is referring **to the siege** of a city under the rule **of the same monarchy. Here,** the mishna is referring **to the siege** of a city under the rule **of a different monarchy, and it was not difficult for him at all,** as in that case there is no concern that perhaps an individual soldier would enter the city. **And for the other one, all these** questions **were difficult, and he answers:** It is referring to a case **where they surround the city**[H] **with chains, and dogs, and branches, and geese.**

אמר רב אידי בר אבין אמר רבי יצחק בר אשיאן: אם יש שם מחבואה אחת – מצלת על הכהנות כולן.

§ With regard to the ruling in the mishna, **Rav Idi bar Avin said** that **Rabbi Yitzḥak bar Ashyan said: If there is a single hideaway there**[H] in the city, where the women could hide from the soldiers, **it saves all the women** married to **priests.** Due to the uncertainty, the presumption is that each of the women found the hideaway, and therefore they are not forbidden to their husbands.

בעי רבי ירמיה: אינה מחזקת אלא אחת, מהו? מי אמרינן: כל חדא וחדא – היינו הא. או דלמא לא אמרינן?

Rabbi Yirmeya raises a dilemma: If the hideaway **holds only one** woman, **what is the ruling? Do we say that** with regard to **each** woman who appears before us, **this is** the one who hid there, and each is permitted to her husband? **Or, perhaps we do not** say that.

NOTES

To the siege of a city under the rule of the same monarchy – בכרכום של אותה מלכות: The Gemara text was emended based on the explanation of Rashi (Rabbeinu Tam in *Sefer HaYashar*). However, almost all of the commentaries and authorities do not accept Rashi's explanation and explain the Gemara differently. The main difference between them is that according to the other commentaries, the siege of a city under the rule of the same monarchy is more dangerous for the women of that city (Rabbeinu Ḥananel; see *Tosafot*; Rambam; Ramban). Since the soldiers need not fear the local army, as they are their comrades in arms, they can ravage the city and its inhabitants at their leisure. The Rashbatz adds that these are troops deployed to suppress a local rebellion, which is typically undertaken ruthlessly. However, when laying siege to a city under the rule of another monarchy, the soldiers fear the local army and cannot proceed at their leisure. According to this opinion, in the Gemara's question: Even in the siege of a city under the rule of the same monarchy, it is impossible that one of them did not wander off, the verb is not masculine, referring to one of the soldiers; rather it is feminine, referring to the women in the city. The siege is typically not so tightly enforced that it would be impossible for one of the besieged people to elude the siege. Indeed, it is related in the Jerusalem Talmud that a blind woman fled the city during a siege. Since the potential of flight exists, the Sages rule leniently with regard to all women in the city. Therefore, Rabbi Levi answered that the reference here is to a particularly harsh siege from which no escape is possible. In the Jerusalem Talmud, the question and the answer correspond to this explanation.

LANGUAGE

Branches [*gavza*] – גווזא: This term comes from the Iranian languages, where it can refer to a mortar, as in Middle Persian gawāz, or a goad or prod, as in the Parthian word gawāz. In Babylonian Jewish Aramaic, it can refer simply to sticks and cut branches.

BACKGROUND

Geese – אווזא: Geese, particularly the ganders, guard their feeding grounds, honking loudly and even attempting to attack any intruder seeking to enter. Therefore, geese were used in lieu of guard dogs to guarantee that trespassers would not pass through certain areas.

HALAKHA

To engage in intercourse there is respite – לבעול יש פנאי: Some authorities say that this is the ruling even if the city was occupied by a foreign army who must be wary of local forces, because the soldiers will find time to engage in intercourse. This ruling is in accordance with the opinion of Rav Mari (Rif; Ramban; Rashba; Rosh; *Shulḥan Arukh, Even HaEzer* 7:10).

To the siege of a city under the rule of the same monarchy – בכרכום של אותה מלכות: The women in the besieged city are forbidden to priests only if the occupying soldiers are from the army of that country, who need not fear local forces, and they have respite to engage in intercourse. However, if the city is occupied by a foreign army whose soldiers are wary of the local army, the women are permitted to priests, in accordance with the statement of Rabbi Yitzḥak bar Elazar in the name of Ḥizkiyya and the explanation of Rabbeinu Ḥananel (Rambam *Sefer Kedusha, Hilkhot Issurei Bia* 18:29; *Shulḥan Arukh, Even HaEzer* 7:10).

Where they surround the city – כגון דמהדר ליה למתא: All the women in the city are forbidden to priests only if the city was surrounded in a manner that renders escape impossible. If it is possible for a woman to flee undetected, the case is parallel to the case of a hideaway with room for one woman, and all the women are permitted. This ruling is in accordance with the opinion of Levi, as explained by Rabbeinu Ḥananel (Rambam *Sefer Kedusha, Hilkhot Issurei Bia* 18:27; *Shulḥan Arukh, Even HaEzer* 7:10).

If there is a single hideaway there – אם יש שם מחבואה אחת: If there is a place to hide in the besieged city, even if there is room for only one woman, none of the women are forbidden to priests; this is in accordance with the opinion of Rabbi Yitzḥak bar Ashyan. Although this question remains unresolved in the Gemara, the ruling is lenient because the prohibition of a captive woman is based on a rabbinic concern that she was violated (Rambam *Sefer Kedusha, Hilkhot Issurei Bia* 18:27; *Shulḥan Arukh, Even HaEzer* 7:10).

וּמַאי שְׁנָא מִשְּׁנֵי שְׁבִילִין, אֶחָד טָמֵא וְאֶחָד טָהוֹר, וְהָלַךְ בְּאֶחָד מֵהֶן וְעָשָׂה טְהָרוֹת, וּבָא חֲבֵירוֹ וְהָלַךְ בַּשֵּׁנִי וְעָשָׂה טְהָרוֹת,

The Gemara asks: **And in what** way is this **different from** the case of **two paths?**[H] As we learned in a mishna: There were two paths, **one** that was **ritually impure** due to a corpse buried there **and one** that was **ritually pure. And** one **walked on one of them,** but he does not remember which, **and** afterward **engaged in** handling items of **ritual purity,** e.g., *teruma* or consecrated items. **And another** person **came and walked on the second** path, and he too does not remember which path it was, **and he** also **engaged in** handling items of **ritual purity.**

רַבִּי יְהוּדָה אוֹמֵר: אִם נִשְׁאַל זֶה בִּפְנֵי עַצְמוֹ וְזֶה בִּפְנֵי עַצְמוֹ – טְהוֹרוֹת, שְׁנֵיהֶם כְּאַחַת – טְמֵאוֹת. רַבִּי יוֹסֵי אוֹמֵר: בֵּין כָּךְ וּבֵין כָּךְ טְמֵאִין.

Rabbi Yehuda says: If this one **asked** a Sage **in and of himself, and that** one **asked** a Sage **in and of himself, they are** both **pure.** When considered separately, each person retains his presumptive status of ritual purity. However, if they **both** came to ask **at the same time, they are** both **ritually impure.** Since one of the two certainly passed on the impure path, although it is uncertain which, both are deemed impure due to that uncertainty. **Rabbi Yosei says: One way or another they are** both **ritually impure.**

וַאֲמַר רָבָא וְאִיתֵּימָא רַבִּי יוֹחָנָן: בְּבַת אַחַת דִּבְרֵי הַכֹּל טְמֵאִין, בָּזֶה אַחַר זֶה דִּבְרֵי הַכֹּל טְהוֹרִים. לֹא נֶחְלְקוּ אֶלָּא בְּבָא לִישָּׁאֵל עָלָיו וְעַל חֲבֵירוֹ, מַר מְדַמֵּי לֵיהּ לְבַת אַחַת, וּמַר מְדַמֵּי לֵיהּ לְבָזֶה אַחַר זֶה. וְהָכָא נַמִּי, כֵּיוָן דְּשָׁרֵי לְהוּ לְכוּלְּהוּ – כְּבַת אַחַת דָּמֵי.

And Rava said, and some say it was **Rabbi Yoḥanan** who elaborates: If they came **at the same time, everyone agrees** that **they are ritually impure,** as even Rabbi Yehuda concedes that this is the *halakha.* If they came independently, **this one after that** one, **everyone agrees** that **they are ritually pure. They disagree only with regard to** a case where one **comes to ask about himself and about the other.**[N] **One Sage,** Rabbi Yosei, **likens it to** a case where they come to ask **at the same time, and Rabbi Yehuda likens it to** a case where **this** one comes **after that** one. The Gemara concludes the analogy: **And here too,** where there was room in the hideout for only one woman, although they came and asked individually, **since they** seek to render **all** the women married to priests **permitted** to their husbands based on that hideout, **it is tantamount to** asking about them all **at the same time,** and they should be deemed forbidden to their husbands.

הָכִי הָשְׁתָּא?! הָתָם – וַדַּאי אִיכָּא טוּמְאָה, הָכָא – מִי יֵימָר דְּאִיטַּמִּי!

The Gemara asks: **How can** these cases **be compared? There,** in the case of the two paths, **there is certainly ritual impurity** in one of the paths, and therefore there is certainly one man who is impure. **Here, who says** any of the women **was violated?** Since there is uncertainty whether any woman was violated at all, one is more likely to rule that each woman was the one who hid than it is to rule that each of the men walked on the ritually pure path.

בָּעֵי רַב אַשִׁי: אָמְרָה ״לֹא נֶחְבֵּאתִי וְלֹא נִטְמֵאתִי״ מַהוּ? מִי אָמְרִינַן:

Rav Ashi raises a dilemma: If there was a hideaway in the city and a woman married to a priest says: **Neither did I hide nor was I violated, what is** the ruling? **Do we say** the principle:

HALAKHA

Two paths – **שְׁנֵי שְׁבִילִין:** If there are two paths, one ritually impure due to a buried corpse and one ritually pure, and one walked on one of them, but he does not remember which, and afterward he engaged in handling items of ritual purity, and another person came and walked on the second path, and he too does not remember which path it was, and he also engaged in handling items of ritual purity, if each comes separately to ask about those items, the ruling is that the items remain ritually pure. If they come together, the ruling is that both items are ritually impure, and they are burned. This ruling is in accordance with the Gemara's conclusion that everyone agrees in a case where these people come together and a case where they come separately. In a case where one of the men asks about his own food and that of another, the ruling is that both items are ritually impure and must be burned, in accordance with the opinion of Rabbi Yosei in his dispute with Rabbi Yehuda (Rambam *Sefer Tahara, Hilkhot She'ar Avot HaTumot* 19:2).

NOTES

Where one comes to ask about himself and about the other – **בְּבָא לִישָּׁאֵל עָלָיו וְעַל חֲבֵירוֹ:** Rashi explains, according to the straightforward meaning of the Gemara, that one comes to ask about himself and about the other person at the same time. However, *Tosafot* state that if one asks about himself and the other person at the same time, even Rabbi Yehuda concedes that he is impure. Therefore, they explain that the case here concerns one who asks first about himself and later he asks about the other person. According to that understanding, the question raised by the Gemara with regard to the hideaway is according to all opinions (see Ritva).

The Ran supports Rashi's explanation that one asks about both of them at the same time: Just as the knowledge that the hideaway is not sufficiently large to house all of the women does not result in a stringent ruling, here too, there is no distinction whether the question is posed at the same time or separately. In both cases, there is awareness of the uncertainty, and nevertheless the ruling is not stringent.

מַה לִּי לְשַׁקֵּר, אוֹ דִּלְמָא לָא אָמְרִינַן?

Why would I lie in so ineffectual a manner, and deem her credible? Had she wanted to lie, she could have claimed that she hid, which is a more effective claim. **Or perhaps we do not say** that principle.

וּמַאי שְׁנָא מֵהַהוּא מַעֲשֶׂה, דְּהַהוּא גַּבְרָא דַּאֲגַר לֵיהּ חֲמָרָא לְחַבְרֵיהּ, אֲמַר לֵיהּ: לָא תֵּיזִיל בְּאוֹרְחָא דִּנְהַר פְּקוֹד, דְּאִיכָּא מַיָּא, זִיל בְּאוֹרְחָא דְּנֶרֶשׁ דְּלֵיכָּא מַיָּא, וַאֲזַל אִיהוּ בְּאוֹרְחָא דִּנְהַר פְּקוֹד, וּמִית חֲמָרָא.

The Gemara asks: **And** in **what** way **is this different from that incident where a certain man who rented a donkey to his colleague said to** the renter: **Do not go on the path of the Pekod River, where there is water,** and the donkey is likely to drown. **Go on the path of Neresh,**[B] **where there is no water. And he went on the path** along **the Pekod River and the donkey died.**

אֲתָא לְקַמֵּיהּ דְּרָבָא. אֲמַר לֵיהּ: אִין, בְּאוֹרְחָא דִּנְהַר פְּקוֹד אֲזַלִי, מִיהוּ לָא הֲווּ מַיָּא. אֲמַר רָבָא: מַה לִּי לְשַׁקֵּר: אִי בָּעֵי אֲמַר לֵיהּ: בְּאוֹרְחָא דְּנֶרֶשׁ אֲזַלִי. וַאֲמַר לֵיהּ אַבָּיֵי: "מַה לִּי לְשַׁקֵּר" בִּמְקוֹם עֵדִים לָא אָמְרִינַן!

The renter **came before Rava** and **said to him: Yes, I went on the path** along **the Pekod River; however, there was no water** there. The donkey's death was caused by other factors. **Rava said:** His claim is accepted based on the principle: **Why would I lie. If he wanted** to lie, he could have **said to him, I went on the path of Neresh. And Abaye said to** Rava: **We do not say** the principle: **Why would I lie, in a situation** where there are **witnesses.**[NH] This principle, which is a form of *miggo*, is effective only when his claim does not contradict established facts. In this case, since it is known to all that there is water on the path along the Pekod River, his claim is not accepted. Similarly, as it is an established fact that the women taken captive were certainly raped, her claim is not accepted even though it is based on a *miggo*.

הָכִי הַשְׁתָּא?! הָתָם – וַדַּאי אִיכָּא עֵדִים דְּאִיכָּא מַיָּא, הָכָא – וַדַּאי אִיטַּמִּי?! חֲשָׁשָׁא הוּא, וּבִמְקוֹם חֲשָׁשָׁא – אָמְרִינַן.

The Gemara asks: **How can** these cases **be compared? There,** in the case of the donkey, **there are certainly witnesses** capable of confirming **that there is water** along that path. **Here,** in the case of the women, is it clearly established that she was **definitely defiled? It is** merely **a concern, and in a situation** where there is merely **a concern** and not an established fact **we say** the principle: Why would I lie,[H] and her claim is accepted.

"אִם יֵשׁ עֵדִים אֲפִילּוּ עֶבֶד וַאֲפִילּוּ שִׁפְחָה נֶאֱמָנִין". וַאֲפִילּוּ שִׁפְחָה דִּידָהּ מְהֵימְנָא? וּרְמִינְהִי: לֹא תִּתְיַיחֵד עִמּוֹ אֶלָּא עַל פִּי עֵדִים,

§ We learned in the mishna: **If** they **have witnesses, even** if the witness is **a slave and even** if the witness is **a maidservant, they are deemed credible.** The Gemara asks: **And** is **even her** personal **maidservant deemed credible?** The Gemara **raises a contradiction** from a mishna (*Gittin* 73a): With regard to one who divorced his wife conditionally, and the condition was not yet fulfilled, the woman **may enter into seclusion with him only on the basis of** the presence of **witnesses,**[H] due to the concern that they will engage in intercourse. If between the drafting of a bill of divorce and its taking effect the husband and wife enter into seclusion together, the bill of divorce must be discarded and a new document drafted in its place.

BACKGROUND

Neresh – נֶרֶשׁ: Neresh is a Babylonian city south of Sura. This was an important agricultural and commercial center that was home to a large number of date palm farmers and alcoholic beverage producers. The city's inhabitants were considered uncultured. Nevertheless, it was home to a Jewish community for many generations, and generated no small number of Sages. At one point, the prominent sage Rav Pappa was the head of the yeshiva in Neresh.

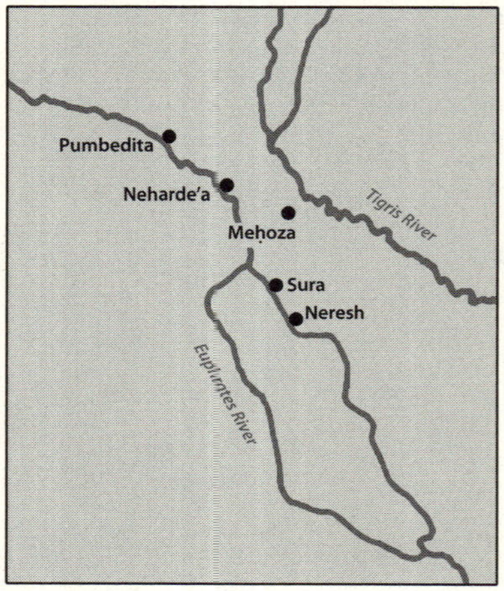

Location of Neresh

NOTES

Why would I lie, in a situation where there are witnesses – מַה לִּי לְשַׁקֵּר בִּמְקוֹם עֵדִים: The authorities unanimously rule in accordance with the opinion of Abaye that the principle of *miggo* does not establish credibility when there are witnesses testifying to the contrary. Clearly, no claim, even one supported by a *miggo*, is effective when it is contradicted by witnesses, as *miggo* establishes that a certain claim is reasonable, while the testimony of witnesses establishes facts. Furthermore, the Ritva writes that in a case where there is explicit testimony contradicting the claim supported by a *miggo*, even Rava would concede that the *miggo* is ineffective. The dispute is only in a case where there is no actual testimony; but instead the *miggo* runs counter to facts that are common knowledge, to which we are all witness, in a sense. Therefore, the principle: Why would I lie, is effective in supporting a claim that cannot otherwise be proven. He is deemed credible due to the assumption that he would not lie unnecessarily, especially when he could have told a more effective lie. However, when there is a reason or witnesses that lead to question the veracity of the claim, the claim is not deemed credible on the basis of *miggo* alone.

HALAKHA

Why would I lie, in a situation where there are witnesses – מַה לִּי לְשַׁקֵּר בִּמְקוֹם עֵדִים: In a case where one rents a donkey to another and tells him to avoid the path along the Pekod River where there is water, and the donkey died, if the renter admits that he took that path but claims that he encountered no water there, he is liable to compensate the owner for the damage to the donkey because of the concept: We are witnesses, i.e., it is common knowledge, that there is water along that route, and we do not say the principle: Why would I lie, in a situation where there are witnesses (Rambam *Sefer Mishpatim*, *Hilkhot Sekhirut* 4:3).

And in a situation where there is merely a concern, we say the principle: Why would I lie – וּבִמְקוֹם חֲשָׁשָׁא אָמְרִינַן: If there was a hideaway in the city, every woman who claims that she was not defiled is deemed credible, as she could have claimed that she hid. When the prohibition is based on uncertainty, the principle of *miggo* is effective, even in a situation where there are witnesses (Rambam *Sefer Kedusha*, *Hilkhot Issurei Bia* 18:28; *Shulḥan Arukh*, *Even HaEzer* 7:10).

The woman may enter into seclusion with him only on the basis of the presence of witnesses – לֹא תִּתְיַיחֵד עִמּוֹ אֶלָּא עַל פִּי עֵדִים: If a husband divorced his wife conditionally and the condition was not yet fulfilled, he may not enter into seclusion with her unless there is a person with them, even if that person is typically disqualified as a witness, e.g., a relative, a slave, or a maidservant. However, he may not enter into seclusion with her if that other person is her own maidservant to whom she is accustomed (Rambam *Sefer Nashim*, *Hilkhot Geirushin* 8:2; *Shulḥan Arukh*, *Even HaEzer* 148:2).

וַאֲפִילּוּ עַל פִּי עֶבֶד. וְעַל פִּי שִׁפְחָה, חוּץ מִשִּׁפְחָתָהּ, מִפְּנֵי שֶׁלִּבָּהּ גַּס בְּשִׁפְחָתָהּ! אֲמַר רַב פַּפִּי: בִּשְׁבוּיָה הֵקִילוּ.

And she may enter into seclusion **even on the basis of** the presence of **a slave and on the basis of** the presence of **a maidservant, except for her** personal **maidservant, due to** the fact **that she is accustomed to her maidservant,** and her presence will not serve as an impediment that would prevent her from engaging in intercourse. Therefore, with regard to the woman taken captive as well, the testimony of the maidservant is not accepted to establish that she was not defiled. **Rav Pappi** resolved the contradiction and **said: With regard to a captive woman,** the Sages **ruled leniently.** Because the prohibition against intercourse with a captive woman is based on the concern that she was violated, the Sages relied on the testimony of her personal maidservant.

רַב פַּפָּא אֲמַר: הָא בְּשִׁפְחָה דִּידָהּ, הָא בְּשִׁפְחָה דִּידֵיהּ.

Rav Pappa resolved the contradiction and **said: This** *halakha* in the case of conditional divorce **is stated with regard to her maidservant,**[H] who is not deemed credible even in the case of a captive woman. **That** *halakha* in the case of the captive woman, where they said even the testimony of the maidservant is accepted, **is stated with regard to his maidservant** to whom the woman is not so accustomed, and therefore her presence serves as an impediment.

וְשִׁפְחָה דִּידָהּ לָא מְהֵימְנָא? הָא קָתָנֵי: אֵין אָדָם מֵעִיד עַל עַצְמוֹ, הָא שִׁפְחָה דִּידָהּ – מְהֵימְנָא! שִׁפְחָתָהּ נַמִי כְּעַצְמָהּ דָּמֵי.

The Gemara asks: **And is her maidservant not deemed credible? But isn't it taught** in the mishna: **A person is not deemed credible** to establish his status **by his own testimony?** From that statement it may be inferred that the woman is not deemed credible to testify about herself, **but her maidservant is deemed credible.** The Gemara answers: The legal status of **her maidservant is like her own** status. Neither is deemed credible.

רַב אַשִׁי אֲמַר: הָא וְהָא בְּשִׁפְחָה דִּידָהּ, וְשִׁפְחָה מִיחֲזָא חַזְיָא וְשָׁתְקָה. הָתָם, דִּשְׁתִיקָתָהּ מַתִּירָתָהּ – לָא מְהֵימְנָא, הָכָא דִּשְׁתִיקָתָהּ אוֹסַרְתָּהּ – מְהֵימְנָא.

Rav Ashi resolved the contradiction and **said: Both** *halakhot* **are** stated **with regard to her maidservant,** but there is a distinction between the cases. **A maidservant sees** what transpires **and is silent,** but does not testify falsely. Therefore, **there,** in the case of conditional divorce, **where** the maidservant's **silence** with regard to whether her mistress engaged in intercourse **renders** the woman **permitted,** as it is sufficient for the maidservant to say merely: I was there, **she is not deemed credible** due to the concern lest she witnessed them engaging in intercourse and remained silent. However, **here,** in the case of the captive woman, **where** the maidservant's **silence would render** her mistress **forbidden,** as a captive woman is presumed to have been violated and the only way to render her permitted is by saying: She was not defiled, **she is deemed credible.**

הָשְׁתָּא נַמִי אָתְיָא וּמְשַׁקְּרָא! תַּרְתֵּי לָא עָבְדָה.

The Gemara asks: **Here too** there should be concern that **she will come and lie** for the benefit of her mistress. The Gemara answers: She would **not perform two** acts of dishonesty. Although there is suspicion that she will refrain from telling the truth, there is no suspicion that she will lie as well. Therefore, if she relates that her mistress was not defiled, she is deemed credible.

כִּי הָא דְּמָרִי בַּר אִיסַק, וְאָמְרִי לָהּ חָנָא בַּר אִיסַק, אֲתָא לֵיהּ אַחָא מִבֵּי חוֹזָאָה. אֲמַר לֵיהּ: פְּלוֹג לִי בְּנִכְסֵי דְּאַבָּא. אֲמַר לֵיהּ: לָא יָדַעְנָא לָךְ. אֲתָא לְקַמֵּיהּ דְּרַב חִסְדָּא, אֲמַר לֵיהּ: שַׁפִּיר קָאָמַר לָךְ, דִּכְתִיב ״וַיַּכֵּר יוֹסֵף אֶת אֶחָיו וְהֵם לֹא הִכִּירֻהוּ״ מְלַמֵּד שֶׁיָּצָא בְּלֹא חֲתִימַת זָקָן וּבָא בַּחֲתִימַת זָקָן.

Proof that one is not suspected of both concealing the truth and lying is cited, **as in that** case **of Mari bar Isak,**[P] **and some say** it was **Ḥana bar Isak,** where someone claiming to be his **brother came to him from Bei Ḥoza'a,**[B] a district located far from the Jewish population centers in Babylonia. This brother **said to him: Apportion me** a share **in my father's property.** Mari **said to him: I do not know you.** The brother **came before Rav Ḥisda** seeking a legal remedy. Rav Ḥisda **said to him:** Your brother **is speaking well** and his response is well founded, **as it is written: "And Joseph recognized his brothers but they recognized him not"** (Genesis 42:8). This **teaches that** Joseph **left** the land of Canaan **without the trace of a beard and came** to meet his brothers **with the trace of a beard.**

HALAKHA

This is with regard to her maidservant – הָא בְּשִׁפְחָה דִּידָהּ: A maidservant is deemed credible to testify that a captive woman was not raped. The woman's own maidservant, however, is not deemed credible, in accordance with the opinion of Rav Pappa. The Ra'avad, however, rules in accordance with the opinion of Rav Ashi, that even her own maidservant is deemed credible (Rambam *Sefer Kedusha, Hilkhot Issurei Bia* 18:19; *Shulḥan Arukh, Even HaEzer* 7:1, 2).

PERSONALITIES

Mari bar Isak – מָרִי בַּר אִיסַק: Mari is mentioned in various places in the Talmud. Some say that there were two people with this name (*Tosafot, Yevamot* 21b), although perhaps the reference is to the same person who lived a long life.

Mari bar Isak was very wealthy, and several of the Sages were visitors to his home. However, as it is stated here, the Sages believed that he used his wealth improperly. That led them to reverse the standard regulations of evidence and place the onus of evidence upon him. His displays of generosity were also treated with suspicion.

BACKGROUND

Bei Ḥoza'a – בֵּי חוֹזָאָה: Bei Ḥoza'a, or Bei Ḥozai, was one of the larger provinces in the Persian Empire. Today it is known by its Persian name, Ḥozistan. This province was far removed from the principal Jewish settlements in Babylonia, which were officially called *Bei Aramai*, and travel between the two was long and arduous. Nevertheless, there were Jewish merchants who traveled there on business, and there was a Jewish community there. Due to the distances and the difficult terrain, ties with Bei Ḥozai were tenuous, and news of events that transpired there did not always reach the major Jewish population centers.

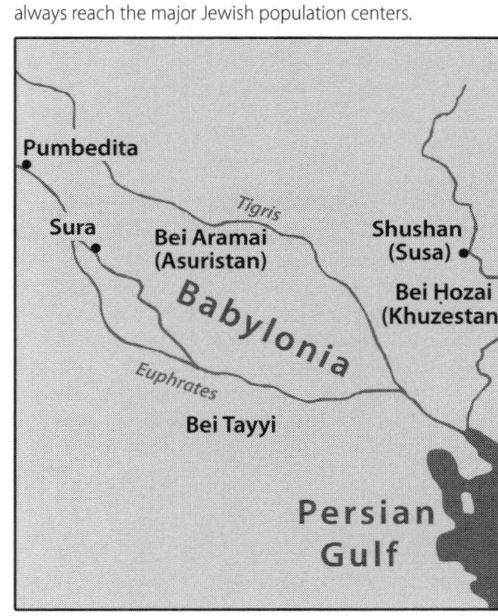

Location of Bei Ḥozai

אֲמַר לֵיהּ: זִיל אַיְיתִי סָהֲדֵי דַּאֲחוּהּ אַתְּ. אֲמַר לֵיהּ: אִית לִי סָהֲדֵי וּמִסְתְּפִינוּ מִינֵּיהּ, דְּגַבְרָא אַלָּמָא הוּא. אֲמַר לֵיהּ לְדִידֵיהּ: זִיל אַיְיתִינְהוּ אַתְּ דְּלָאו אֲחוּךְ הוּא. אֲמַר לֵיהּ: דִּינָא הָכִי?! הַמּוֹצִיא מֵחֲבֵירוֹ עָלָיו הָרְאָיָה! אֲמַר לֵיהּ: הָכִי דָּאֵינְנָא לָךְ וּלְכוּלְּהוּ אַלָּמֵי חַבְרָךְ. – הָשְׁתָּא נַמִּי אָתוּ וּמְשַׁקְּרִי! תַּרְתֵּי לָא עָבְדִי.

Rav Ḥisda **said to him: Go bring witnesses that you are his brother. He said to** Rav Ḥisda: **I have witnesses, but they are afraid of** Mari, **who is a violent man,** and will not testify. Rav Ḥisda **said to** Mari: **Go bring witnesses that he is not your brother.** Mari **said to him: Is that the *halakha*?** Isn't the guiding principle in cases of this sort: **The burden of proof** rests **upon the claimant?** Let the man claiming part of my inheritance bring proof supporting his claim. Rav Ḥisda **said to him: This is how I render judgment for you and for all your fellow violent** men;[H] I place the burden of proof upon them. The Gemara asks: **Now** too, witnesses **will come and lie** in fear of Mari, and what is accomplished by requiring Mari to bring the witnesses? Apparently, one is **not** suspected of **performing two** acts of dishonesty, to both conceal the truth and to lie.

לֵימָא כְּתַנָּאֵי: זוֹ עֵדוּת אִישׁ וְאִשָּׁה, תִּינוֹק וְתִינוֹקֶת, אָבִיהָ וְאִמָּהּ וְאָחִיהָ וַאֲחוֹתָהּ, אֲבָל לֹא בְּנָהּ וּבִתָּהּ, לֹא עַבְדָּהּ וְשִׁפְחָתָהּ. וְתַנְיָא אִידָּךְ: הַכֹּל נֶאֱמָנִין לְהָעִיד, חוּץ מֵהֵימֶנָּה וּבַעְלָהּ.

The Gemara suggests: **Let us say** that the opinions of the *amora'im* with regard to the testimony of her maidservant are **subject to** this dispute between ***tanna'im***. It is taught in one *baraita*: **This testimony** that a captive woman was not defiled with regard to which **a man and a woman, a male child or a female child,** the woman's **father, and her mother, and her brother, and her sister** are deemed credible, **but not her son and her daughter,** and **not her slave or maidservant. And it is taught** in **another** *baraita*: **All are deemed credible to testify** with regard a captive woman, **except for her and her husband.**

דְּרַב פַּפִּי וּדְרַב אַשִׁי – תַּנָּאֵי הִיא. דְּרַב פַּפָּא [מִי] לֵימָא תַּנָּאֵי הִיא?

The Gemara notes: The opinion **of Rav Pappi and** the opinion **of Rav Ashi** are certainly **subject to** the dispute between ***tanna'im***, as they hold that her maidservant is deemed credible contrary to the first *baraita* cited. However, with regard to the opinion **of Rav Pappa,** who distinguishes between her maidservant, who is not deemed credible, and his maidservant, who is, **do we say** that **it is subject to the dispute between *tanna'im*?** Perhaps the *tanna* in each *baraita* holds that her maidservant is not deemed credible, and the *baraita* that deems everyone credible except for the woman and her husband could be explained in another manner, e.g., the legal status of her maidservant is like her own status.

אָמַר לָךְ רַב פַּפָּא: כִּי תַּנְיָא הַהִיא – בִּמְסִיחָה לְפִי תוּמָּהּ.

The Gemara says: There is no proof that Rav Pappa's opinion is contingent upon the tannaitic dispute, as **Rav Pappa** could have **said to you: When that** *baraita* that deems everyone credible except for the woman and her husband **is taught,** it is taught **in** a case where **she is making an unconsidered, incidental remark** in the context of a conversation about an unrelated matter. However, direct testimony of her maidservant is not accepted.

כִּי הָא דְּכִי אֲתָא רַב דִּימִי אֲמַר, רַב חָנָן קַרְטִיגְנָאָה מִשְׁתָּעֵי: מַעֲשֶׂה בָּא לִפְנֵי רַבִּי יְהוֹשֻׁעַ בֶּן לֵוִי, וְאָמְרִי לָהּ רַבִּי יְהוֹשֻׁעַ בֶּן לֵוִי מִישְׁתָּעֵי: מַעֲשֶׂה בָּא לִפְנֵי רַבִּי בְּאָדָם אֶחָד שֶׁהָיָה מֵסִיחַ לְפִי תוּמּוֹ, וְאָמַר: אֲנִי וְאִמִּי נִשְׁבֵּינוּ לְבֵין הַגּוֹיִם, יָצָאתִי לִשְׁאוֹב מַיִם – דַּעְתִּי עַל אִמִּי, לְלַקֵּט עֵצִים – דַּעְתִּי עַל אִמִּי. וְהִשִּׂיאָהּ רַבִּי לִכְהוּנָּה עַל פִּיו.

As in that case **when Rav Dimi came** from Eretz Yisrael to Babylonia; **he said** that **Rav Ḥanan of Carthage relates: An incident came before Rabbi Yehoshua ben Levi** for judgment; **and some say** that **Rabbi Yehoshua ben Levi relates: An incident came before Rabbi** Yehuda HaNasi, **with regard to a person who was making an unconsidered, incidental remark,**[H] **and said: My mother and I were taken captive among the gentiles.** When I **went out to draw water, my thoughts were about my mother; to gather wood, my thoughts were about my mother.** We were never separated. **And Rabbi** Yehuda HaNasi **deemed her** fit **to marry into the priesthood on the basis** of those remarks, even though with regard to testimony about his mother, a son is disqualified as a witness. The same is true of the woman's maidservant.

מתני׳ אָמַר רַבִּי זְכַרְיָה בֶּן הַקַּצָּב: הַמָּעוֹן הַזֶּה! לֹא זָזָה יָדָהּ מִתּוֹךְ יָדִי מִשָּׁעָה שֶׁנִּכְנְסוּ גּוֹיִם לִירוּשָׁלַיִם וְעַד שֶׁיָּצְאוּ. אָמְרוּ לוֹ: אֵין אָדָם מֵעִיד עַל עַצְמוֹ.

MISHNA **Rabbi Zekharya ben HaKatzav**[P] **said:** I swear by **this abode** of the Divine Presence that my wife's **hand did not move from my hand from the time that the gentiles entered Jerusalem until they left,** and I know for a fact that she was not defiled. The Sages **said to him: A person cannot testify about himself.**[H] The legal status of one's wife is like his own status in this regard. Therefore, your testimony is not accepted, and your wife is forbidden to you.

HALAKHA

This is how I render judgment for you and for all your fellow violent men – הָכִי דָּאֵינְנָא לָךְ וּלְכוּלְּהוּ אַלָּמֵי חַבְרָךְ: If the court knows that the defendant is a violent person, and the claimant asserts and brings proof that his witnesses are afraid to testify, the court places the onus of proof upon the defendant and he must bring witnesses to support his claim, in accordance with the opinion of Rav Ḥisda (Rambam *Sefer Shofetim, Hilkhot Edut* 3:12; *Shulḥan Arukh, Ḥoshen Mishpat* 23:5).

A minor who was making an unconsidered, incidental remark – מֵסִיחַ לְפִי תוּמּוֹ: The statement of a minor who makes an unconsidered remark with regard to a captive woman is deemed credible by the court. This is the understanding of Rambam, who explained the incident involving Rabbi Yehuda HaNasi as dealing with a minor and related to the first *baraita*, which listed those deemed credible to testify on behalf of the woman (*Maggid Mishne*). Others rule that a minor's statement is deemed credible even if he intended to testify. That corresponds to the plain understanding of the Gemara that the incident involving Rabbi Yehuda HaNasi relates to the second *baraita* (Ran). According to this understanding, a relative, either minor or adult, is deemed credible only when making incidental remarks, but an unrelated minor is deemed credible to testify directly (Rambam *Sefer Kedusha, Hilkhot Issurei Bia* 18:18; *Shulḥan Arukh, Even HaEzer* 7:1).

A person cannot testify about himself – אֵין אָדָם מֵעִיד עַל עַצְמוֹ: A captive woman's husband is not deemed credible to testify that she was not defiled, because one is not deemed credible to testify about himself, and the status of testimony about his wife is like that of testimony about himself. Others add that this applies only if his testimony was required. However, if the husband was the only one who knew that his wife was taken captive, and he is certain that she was not violated, she is permitted to him (Rambam *Sefer Kedusha, Hilkhot Issurei Bia* 18:19; *Shulḥan Arukh, Even HaEzer* 7:2).

PERSONALITIES

Rabbi Zekharya ben HaKatzav – רַבִּי זְכַרְיָה בֶּן הַקַּצָּב: Rabbi Zekharya ben HaKatzav was a priest and a *tanna* who lived in the generation of the destruction of the second Temple. Apparently, he was one of the older students of Rabbi Yoḥanan ben Zakkai, and that is why he appears both in statements of Rabbi Yoḥanan ben Zakkai's students, where he is cited by name, and in joint statements. Very few of his statements appear in the Mishna, the *Tosefta*, and the Talmud.

גמ׳ תָּנָא: וְאַף עַל פִּי כֵן יִיחֵד לָהּ בַּיִת בַּחֲצֵרוֹ, וּכְשֶׁהִיא יוֹצְאָה – יוֹצְאָה בְּרֹאשׁ בָּנֶיהָ, וּכְשֶׁהִיא נִכְנֶסֶת – נִכְנֶסֶת בְּסוֹף בָּנֶיהָ.

GEMARA The *tanna* **taught** in the *Tosefta*: **And even so,** despite the fact that the Sages ruled his wife forbidden to him because he was a priest, he did not divorce her. **He designated a house in his courtyard for her,**[NH] but did not enter into seclusion with her, **and when she** would **go out** of the courtyard **she** would **go out before her sons** so that she would not be alone in the courtyard with her husband, **and when she** would **enter** the house, **she** would **enter after her sons,** for the same reason.

בָּעֵי אַבָּיֵי: מַהוּ לַעֲשׂוֹת בִּגְרוּשָׁה כֵּן? הָתָם הוּא – דְּבִשְׁבוּיָה הֵקִילוּ, אֲבָל הָכָא – לָא, אוֹ דִּלְמָא לָא שְׁנָא?

Abaye raises a dilemma: What is the *halakha* regarding whether we have **to do likewise with a divorcée?** Can a priest who divorces his wife designate a house for her in the courtyard and rely on the children to ensure that the couple will not enter into seclusion? **Is it** specifically **there,** in the case of Rabbi Zekharya ben HaKatzav **because with regard to a captive woman** the Sages **ruled leniently,** since the prohibition is based on suspicion and not certainty; **however here,** in the case of a divorcée, where there is a certain Torah prohibition, **no,** he may not designate a residence for her in the courtyard? **Or perhaps,** the case of a divorcée **is no different.**

תָּא שְׁמַע, דְּתַנְיָא: הַמְגָרֵשׁ אֶת אִשְׁתּוֹ – לֹא תִּנָּשֵׂא בִּשְׁכוּנָתוֹ,

The Gemara cites proof to resolve the dilemma: **Come** and **hear** proof **as it is taught** in a *baraita*: With regard to **one who divorces his wife, she may not marry** and live **in his** immediate **vicinity,** i.e., his courtyard, due to the concern that because of the intimacy they once shared, her living there will lead to transgression.

NOTES

And even so, he designated a house…for her – וְאַף עַל פִּי כֵן יִיחֵד לָהּ בַּיִת: Rashi explains the phrase: Even so, to mean that although she is forbidden to him, by allowing her to live with him, he treated her in a manner atypical of the manner that a priest treats a woman forbidden to him. However, others explain to the contrary, citing the *ge'onim*; although he knew that she had not been defiled, he took these steps to distance her from him to ensure that he would not enter into seclusion with her.

HALAKHA

He designated a house in his courtyard for her – יִיחֵד לָהּ בַּיִת בַּחֲצֵרוֹ: Since the fact that a captive women is forbidden to a priest is a stringency based on uncertainty, she may continue living in the same courtyard with him, provided that their children are present to ensure that he does not enter into seclusion with her, as was the case in the incident involving Rabbi Zekharya ben HaKatzav (Rambam *Sefer Kedusha, Hilkhot Issurei Bia* 18:25; *Shulḥan Arukh, Even HaEzer* 7:9).

Perek **II**
Daf **28** Amud **a**

וְאִם הָיָה כֹּהֵן – לֹא תָּדוּר עִמּוֹ בְּמָבוֹי. אִם הָיָה כְּפָר קָטָן, זֶה הָיָה מַעֲשֶׂה, וְאָמְרוּ: כְּפָר קָטָן נִידּוֹן כִּשְׁכוּנָה.

And if he was a priest she may not live with him even **in** one **alleyway** that opens into several courtyards, even if she did not remarry, as she is forbidden to him forever. What is the ruling **if it was a small village?** May she live with her ex-husband in the same village? The Gemara relates that **this** case of his divorcée and a small village **was an incident** that transpired **and** the Sages **said: A small village is judged as** his immediate **proximity.**[NH]

מִי נִדְחֶה מִפְּנֵי מִי? תָּא שְׁמַע, דְּתַנְיָא: הִיא נִדְחֵית מִפָּנָיו, וְאֵין הוּא נִדְחֶה מִפָּנֶיהָ. וְאִם הָיְתָה חָצֵר שֶׁלָּהּ – הוּא נִדְחֶה מִפָּנֶיהָ.

The Gemara asks: In cases where they may not reside in the same courtyard or alleyway, **who is ousted in favor of whom?**[H] Which of them must leave? The Gemara suggests: **Come** and **hear** proof **as it is taught** in a *baraita*: **She is ousted in favor of him,** and leaves, **and he is not ousted in favor of her. But if it was her courtyard, he is ousted in favor of her.**

HALAKHA

Distance from his divorcée – הַרְחָקָה מִגְּרוּשָׁתוֹ: A man who divorces his wife may not reside in the same courtyard with her lest they engage in a promiscuous relationship. If the man is a priest, he may not even live with his divorcée in the same alleyway, which includes several courtyards. According to the Rambam, the legal status of a small village is that of an alleyway. The *Maggid Mishne* notes that the Rambam apparently had a variant reading of the Gemara. The Rema adds that if she remarried, even if her former husband was a non-priest, she may not even live in the same alleyway as her former husband (Rambam according to the Ran; Rambam *Sefer Kedusha, Hilkhot Issurei Bia* 21:27; *Shulḥan Arukh, Even HaEzer* 119:7).

Who is ousted in favor of whom – מִי נִדְחֶה מִפְּנֵי מִי: If a man divorced his wife, and it is prohibited for them to reside in the same courtyard: If it is co-owned or co-rented by both of them, the wife must relocate and her ex-husband may remain. However, if it belonged exclusively to her, he must relocate (Rambam *Sefer Kedusha, Hilkhot Issurei Bia* 21:27; *Shulḥan Arukh, Even HaEzer* 119:7).

NOTES

Alleyway and proximity – מָבוֹי וּשְׁכוּנָה: There is a dispute among the commentaries with regard to the definition of these terms. *Tosafot* explain that alleyway refers to a small street, and proximity refers to three adjacent houses. However, the Ran explains that proximity is larger than an alleyway, as the reference is to an entire residential area. This matter depends on the variant readings of the text, as well as on different explanations that led to the development of the variant readings. There are also halakhic ramifications, e.g., whether the legal status of a small village is that of a proximity or an alleyway.

However, the issue is related to a more fundamental dispute with regard to the *halakhot* of distance between the man and the woman. According to the Rambam, the required distance is relative to the severity of the relevant prohibition. Therefore, if the divorcée was married to a non-priest, and not yet remarried, only slight separation would be required, as the prohibition is no more than the prohibition of relations with an unmarried woman. If she was married to a priest, and it is prohibited by Torah law for them to engage in relations, greater separation would be required; and if she remarried, even greater separation would be required, as relations carry the penalty of death. According to *Tosafot* the opposite is true; the more severe the prohibition, the less likely it is that they will violate the prohibition, and less distance is required.

אִיבַּעְיָא לְהוּ: הָיְתָה חָצֵר שֶׁל שְׁנֵיהֶם מַהוּ? תָּא שְׁמַע: הִיא נִדְחֵית מִפָּנָיו. בְּמַאי עָסְקִינַן? אִילֵּימָא בְּחָצֵר שֶׁלּוֹ – פְּשִׁיטָא! וְאֶלָּא בְּחָצֵר שֶׁלָּהּ – וְהָתַנְיָא: אִם הָיְתָה חָצֵר שֶׁלָּהּ – הוּא נִדְחֶה מִפָּנֶיהָ. אֶלָּא לָאו – כִּי הַאי גַּוְונָא. דִּלְמָא דַּאֲגִיר מֵיגָר.

A dilemma was raised before the Sages: If **it was a courtyard** belonging **to both of them, what is the** *halakha*; who is ousted in favor of whom? The Gemara suggests: **Come and hear** proof **as it is taught** in a *baraita*: **She is ousted in favor of him.** The Gemara elaborates: **With what** circumstances **are we dealing? If we say** that the subject of the *baraita* is **with regard to his courtyard,** it is **obvious** that she is ousted. **But rather, is it with regard to her courtyard? Isn't it taught** in a *baraita*: **If it was her courtyard, he is ousted in favor of her? Rather, is it not** that the *baraita* is dealing with **a case like this,** where it was a courtyard belonging to both of them? The Gemara rejects this proof: **Perhaps** the *baraita* is teaching that even in a case **where he rented** the courtyard she is ousted in his favor. Therefore, the dilemma with regard to a courtyard belonging to both of them is unresolved.

מַאי הָוֵי עֲלַהּ? תָּא שְׁמַע: ״הִנֵּה ה׳ מְטַלְטֶלְךָ טַלְטֵלָה גָּבֶר״ וְאָמַר רַב: טַלְטוּלֵי דְּגַבְרָא קְשִׁין מִדְּאִיתְּתָא.

The Gemara asks: **What** halakhic conclusion **was** reached **about** this matter? The Gemara suggests: **Come and hear** proof from the verse: **"The Lord will dislocate you the dislocation of a man"** (Isaiah 22:17), **and Rav said:** This indicates that **the dislocation of a man is more difficult** for him **than** the dislocation of **a woman** is for her.[N] Therefore, the woman is ousted.

תָּנוּ רַבָּנַן: לָוָה הֵימֶנָּה בְּנִכְסֵי אָבִיהָ – אֵינָהּ נִפְרַעַת אֶלָּא עַל יְדֵי אַחֵר. אָמַר רַב שֵׁשֶׁת: וְאִי אָתוּ לְקַמָּן לְדִינָא לָא מִזְדַּקְקִינַן לְהוּ. רַב פָּפָּא אָמַר: שַׁמּוּתֵי מְשַׁמְּתִינַן לְהוּ. רַב הוּנָא בְּרֵיהּ דְּרַב יְהוֹשֻׁעַ אָמַר: נַגּוּדֵי נַמִי מְנַגְּדִינַן לְהוּ. אָמַר רַב נַחְמָן: תָּנָא בְּאֵבֶל רַבָּתִי: בַּמֶּה דְּבָרִים אֲמוּרִים – שֶׁנִּתְגָּרְשָׁה מִן הַנִּשּׂוּאִין, אֲבָל כְּשֶׁנִּתְגָּרְשָׁה מִן הָאֵירוּסִין – נִפְרַעַת עַל יְדֵי עַצְמָהּ, שֶׁאֵין לִבּוֹ גַּס בָּהּ.

The Sages taught: With regard to a priest who **borrowed from** his wife **from** usufruct **property** that she inherited from **her father**[H] and then he divorced her, **she is repaid only by means of another** person and not directly from her husband, to prevent them from engaging in business dealings. **Rav Sheshet said: And if** after engaging in business dealings they **came before us for judgment,**[H] **we do not attend to them** because by engaging in those dealings they were in violation of a transgression. **Rav Pappa said: We excommunicate them** for violating that transgression. **Rav Huna, the son of Rav Yehoshua, said: We also flog them** with lashes.[N] **Rav Naḥman said:** The *tanna* **taught in** ***Evel Rabbati***,[N] one of the minor tractates that deals primarily with the *halakhot* of mourning: **In what case is this statement said?** It is in a case **where she was divorced from marriage. However, when she was divorced from betrothal,**[H] **she is repaid** even directly **by means of** receiving the money **herself, because,** in that case, **he is not** yet **accustomed to her.** Since they never shared intimacy, there is no concern that it will lead to transgression.

הַהוּא אָרוּס וַאֲרוּסָתוֹ דְּאָתוּ לְקַמֵּיהּ דְּרָבָא, יְתֵיב רַב אַדָּא בַּר מַתְּנָא קַמֵּיהּ, אוֹקֵי רָבָא שְׁלוּחָא בֵּינַתַּיְיהוּ. אֲמַר לֵיהּ רַב אַדָּא בַּר מַתְּנָא: וְהָאָמַר רַב נַחְמָן, תָּנָא בְּאֵבֶל רַבָּתִי כו׳! אֲמַר לֵיהּ: קָא חָזֵינַן דְּקָא גַּיְיסֵי בַּהֲדָדֵי.

The Gemara relates: There was an incident concerning **this** divorced, **betrothed man and his betrothed who came before Rava** for judgment, and **Rav Adda bar Mattana was sitting before him** at the time. **Rava placed an intermediary** to separate **between them. Rav Adda bar Mattana said to** Rava: **But didn't Rav Naḥman say:** The *tanna* **taught in** ***Evel Rabbati*** that if she was divorced from betrothal she is paid directly? Rava **said to him:** This applies only in a case where they are not accustomed to each other. However, with regard to these people, **we see that they are accustomed to each other,** and therefore they must be separated.

אִיכָּא דְּאָמְרִי: לָא אוֹקֵי רָבָא שָׁלִיחַ בֵּינַתַּיְיהוּ. אֲמַר לֵיהּ: רַב אַדָּא בַּר מַתְּנָא: נֵיקוּם מָר שְׁלוּחָא בֵּינַתַּיְיהוּ! אֲמַר לֵיהּ: וְהָא [אֲמַר] רַב נַחְמָן: תָּנָא בְּאֵבֶל רַבָּתִי כו׳! אֲמַר לֵיהּ: הָנֵי מִילֵּי – הֵיכָא דְּלָא גָּיְיסֵי בַּהֲדָדֵי, אֲבָל הָנֵי – קָא חָזֵינָא לְהוּ דְּגָיְיסֵי בַּהֲדָדֵי.

Some say that **Rava did not place an intermediary** to separate **between them. Rav Adda bar Mattana said to** Rava: **Let the Master place an intermediary** to separate **between them.** Rava **said to** Rav Adda bar Mattana: **But didn't Rav Naḥman say:** The *tanna* **taught in** ***Evel Rabbati*** that if she was divorced from betrothal she is paid directly? Rav Adda bar Mattana **said to** Rava: **This applies only** in a case **where they are not accustomed to each other. However,** with regard to **these** people, **we see that they are accustomed to each other,** and therefore they must be separated.

מתני׳ וְאֵלּוּ נֶאֱמָנִין לְהָעִיד בְּגוֹדְלָן מַה שֶּׁרָאוּ בְּקוֹטְנָן: נֶאֱמָן אָדָם לוֹמַר ״זֶה כְּתַב יָדוֹ שֶׁל אַבָּא״ וְ״זֶה כְּתַב יָדוֹ שֶׁל רַבִּי״ וְ״זֶה כְּתַב יָדוֹ שֶׁל אָחִי״.

MISHNA **And these are deemed credible to testify in their majority** with regard to **what they saw in their minority. A person is deemed credible to say: This is my father's handwriting,**[H] and to say: **This is my teacher's handwriting;** and to say: **This is my brother's handwriting,** even though he never saw their handwriting after reaching majority.

NOTES

The dislocation of a man is more difficult for him than the dislocation of a woman is for her – טַלְטוּלֵי דְּגַבְרָא קְשִׁין מִדְּאִיתְּתָא: Some commentaries explain that this is because people are more compassionate toward women and even if she is the one required to relocate, she, unlike a man, will have others tend to her needs (Maharsha in tractate *Sanhedrin*). Others explain that this relates to their potential remarriage, as typically the man is responsible for building the house for his wife, and the Sages derived from language in the Torah that it is proper to do so. Therefore, were he required to relocate, he would need to build a new house, unlike a woman, who moves into the house of her new husband (Rashbatz).

We also flog them with lashes – נַגּוּדֵי נַמִי מְנַגְּדִינַן לְהוּ: Although the authenticity of this phrase is uncertain (see *Tosafot*), some explain for various reasons that Rav Huna, son of Rav Yehoshua, seeks to add to the statement of Rav Pappa: Not only are they ostracized, they are also flogged (see *Tosafot*; Ritva). However, the Rambam maintains that Rav Huna, son of Rav Yehoshua, is not suggesting an additional punishment but rather an alternative punishment, the administration of which is left to the discretion of the judges. See *Mo'ed Katan* 17a for a discussion concerning which punishment is considered more severe. Others explain that the punishment according to the Rambam is dependent upon whether she was married to a priest or a non-priest.

***Evel Rabbati* – אֵבֶל רַבָּתִי:** *Evel Rabbati* is one of the minor tractates appended to the Talmud, typically printed at the end of *Seder Nezikin*. These tractates are anthologies of *baraitot* compiled and collected during different periods and they typically address well-defined topics. *Evel Rabbati* addresses the entire range of *halakhot* surrounding death, from the time one is on his deathbed, through burial and mourning. This tractate is euphemistically called tractate *Semaḥot*, celebrations. *Evel Rabbati* literally means greater mourning. A shorter tractate, called *Evel Zutrati*, i.e., lesser mourning, addresses the same subject matter and was published from manuscript relatively recently.

HALAKHA

A priest who borrowed from his wife from usufruct property that she inherited from her father – לָוָה הֵימֶנָּה בְּנִכְסֵי אָבִיהָ: If a man borrowed money from his wife and then divorced her, he must repay her by means of an agent, not directly, in accordance with the *baraita* (Rambam *Sefer Kedusha, Hilkhot Issurei Bia* 21:27; *Shulḥan Arukh, Even HaEzer* 119:8).

If they came before us for judgment – אִי אָתוּ לְקַמָּן לְדִינָא: If a divorced couple come to court together for judgment, they are ostracized or flogged, as no ruling is issued in the dispute about this matter (*Maggid Mishne*). Others note that according to the Rosh, they are ostracized only if the husband is a priest or if the divorcée remarried (*Beit Shmuel*, citing *Beit Yosef*; see *Baḥ*; Rambam *Sefer Kedusha, Hilkhot Issurei Bia* 21:27; *Shulḥan Arukh, Even HaEzer* 119:9).

When she was divorced from betrothal – כְּשֶׁנִּתְגָּרְשָׁה מִן הָאֵירוּסִין: If a man divorces his betrothed bride, they may reside in the same courtyard and come together to court, in accordance with the opinion of Rav Naḥman. However, if that they are accustomed to each other they may not do so, in accordance with the opinion of Rava (Rambam *Sefer Kedusha, Hilkhot Issurei Bia* 21:27; *Shulḥan Arukh, Even HaEzer* 119:10).

This is my father's handwriting – זֶה כְּתַב יָדוֹ שֶׁל אַבָּא: An adult is deemed credible to authenticate the signatures of his father, his teacher, and his brother that he witnessed as a child, provided that he testifies with another witness who witnessed the signature as an adult, in accordance with the opinion of Rav Huna, son of Rav Yehoshua (Rosh, based on the Jerusalem Talmud; *Shakh*; Rambam *Sefer Shofetim, Hilkhot Edut* 7:1, 14:3; *Shulḥan Arukh, Ḥoshen Mishpat* 35:4).

"זָכוּר הָיִיתִי בִּפְלוֹנִית שֶׁיָּצְאָה בְּהִינוּמָא וְרֹאשָׁהּ פָּרוּעַ". וְ"שֶׁהָיָה אִישׁ פְּלוֹנִי יוֹצֵא מִבֵּית הַסֵּפֶר לִטְבּוֹל לֶאֱכוֹל בִּתְרוּמָה". וְ"שֶׁהָיָה חוֹלֵק עִמָּנוּ עַל הַגּוֹרֶן", וְ"הַמָּקוֹם הַזֶּה בֵּית הַפְּרָס". וְ"עַד כָּאן הָיִינוּ בָּאִין בְּשַׁבָּת".

§ Similarly, one is deemed credible to say: **I was reminded of** the wedding of **so-and-so, who went out with a *hinnuma*,**[H] **or** with **her hair uncovered** in a manner typical of virgins, and therefore, her marriage contract is two hundred dinars; **and** to say **that so-and-so would leave school to immerse** in order **to partake of *teruma*,**[H] **and that he would share *teruma* with us at the threshing floor** and therefore he is a priest. Similarly, one is deemed credible to say: **This place is a *beit haperas*,**[L] a field with a grave that was plowed, scattering the bones, and rendering the field a place of uncertain ritual impurity; **and** to say: **Until here we would come on Shabbat**[N] and thereby determine the Shabbat boundary.

אֲבָל אֵין אָדָם נֶאֱמָן לוֹמַר "דֶּרֶךְ הָיָה לִפְלוֹנִי בַּמָּקוֹם הַזֶּה, מַעֲמָד וּמִסְפֵּד הָיָה לִפְלוֹנִי בַּמָּקוֹם הַזֶּה".

However, a person is neither deemed credible to say: So-and-so had a path in this place; nor to say: **So-and-so had** a tract of land where they would perform the ritual of **standing** and sitting **and** deliver **a eulogy in that place,** thereby attesting that the land belongs to that person. The reason he is not deemed credible in those cases is that full-fledged testimony is required to remove property from the possession of its presumptive owner.

גמ׳ אָמַר רַב הוּנָא בְּרֵיהּ דְּרַב יְהוֹשֻׁעַ: וְהוּא שֶׁיֵּשׁ גָּדוֹל עִמּוֹ.

GEMARA Rav Huna, son of Rav Yehoshua, said: And the mishna said that one is deemed credible to testify about handwriting he saw as a minor only **when there is** a witness who saw the handwriting as an **adult** testifying **with him.**[N]

וּצְרִיכָא, דְּאִי אַשְׁמְעִינַן אָבִיו – מִשּׁוּם דִּשְׁכִיחַ גַּבֵּיהּ, אֲבָל רַבּוֹ – לָא. וְאִי אַשְׁמְעִינַן רַבּוֹ – מִשּׁוּם דְּאִית לֵיהּ אֵימְתֵיהּ דְּרַבֵּיהּ, אֲבָל אָבִיו – לָא.

And all of these cases are **necessary,** as one could not have been derived from the other. **As, if** the *tanna* had **taught us** the case of **his father's** handwriting, one might have thought that he is deemed credible **due to** the fact **that he is** often **found with his** father and is familiar with his handwriting; **but** with regard to **his teacher's** handwriting, **no,** he is not deemed credible. **And if** the *tanna* had **taught us** the case of **his teacher's** handwriting, one might have thought that he is deemed credible **due to** the fact **that he has** a sense of **awe of his teacher** and therefore pays attention to his handwriting; **but** with regard to **his father's** handwriting, **no,** he is not deemed credible.

וְאִי אַשְׁמְעִינַן הָנֵי תַּרְתֵּי, אָבִיו – דִּשְׁכִיחַ גַּבֵּיהּ, וְרַבּוֹ – דְּאִית לֵיהּ אֵימְתֵיהּ, אֲבָל אָחִיו דְּלֵית לֵיהּ לָא הָא וְלָא הָא – אֵימָא לָא, קָא מַשְׁמַע לָן: כֵּיוָן דְּקִיּוּם שְׁטָרוֹת מִדְּרַבָּנַן – הֵימְנוּהוּ רַבָּנַן בִּדְרַבָּנַן.

And if the *tanna* had **taught us these two** cases, one might have thought that he is deemed credible with regard to **his father's** handwriting due to the fact **that he is** often **found with him, and his teacher's** handwriting due to the fact **that he has** a sense of **awe of him. But** with regard to **his brother's** handwriting, **which has neither this** factor **nor that** factor, **say no,**[N] he is not deemed credible. Therefore, the *tanna* **teaches us: Since ratification of documents is** required **by rabbinic** law, as by Torah law, the signatories are sufficient proof of a document's validity; **the Sages deemed him credible** to testify in cases that he witnessed as a minor in matters that are **by rabbinic** law, including the case of his brother.

"זָכוּר הָיִיתִי בִּפְלוֹנִית שֶׁיָּצְאָה בְּהִינוּמָא וְרֹאשָׁהּ פָּרוּעַ". מַאי טַעֲמָא? כֵּיוָן דְּרוֹב נָשִׁים בְּתוּלוֹת נִישָּׂאוֹת, גִּלּוּי מִלְּתָא בְּעָלְמָא הוּא.

And the mishna states that one is deemed credible to say: **I was reminded of** the wedding of **so-and-so, who went out with a *hinnuma*, or** with **her hair uncovered. What is the reason** that he is deemed credible? **Since most women are married as virgins,** her presumptive status is that of a virgin even without his testimony. His testimony with regard to what he saw as a minor **is merely revealing of a matter** already presumed true, not actual testimony.

"וְשֶׁהָיָה אִישׁ פְּלוֹנִי יוֹצֵא מִבֵּית הַסֵּפֶר לִטְבּוֹל לֶאֱכוֹל בִּתְרוּמָה". וְדִלְמָא עֶבֶד כֹּהֵן הוּא? מְסַיֵּיעַ לֵיהּ לְרַבִּי יְהוֹשֻׁעַ בֶּן לֵוִי. דְּאָמַר רַבִּי יְהוֹשֻׁעַ בֶּן לֵוִי: אָסוּר לְאָדָם שֶׁיְּלַמֵּד אֶת עַבְדּוֹ תּוֹרָה.

And the mishna states that one is deemed credible to say **that so-and-so would leave school to immerse** in order **to partake of *teruma*,** and therefore he is a priest. The Gemara asks: **And perhaps he is the slave of a priest,**[N] who is also eligible to partake of *teruma*. The Gemara notes: This mishna provides **support for** the opinion of **Rabbi Yehoshua ben Levi, as Rabbi Yehoshua ben Levi said: It is prohibited for a person to teach his slave Torah.**[H] Since the testimony is that he was in school, apparently he is not a slave. Therefore, the fact that he partook of *teruma* indicates that he is a priest.

HALAKHA

Who went out with a *hinnuma* – שֶׁיָּצְאָה בְּהִינוּמָא: An adult is deemed credible to testify that as a child he saw a bride go out with a *hinnuma*, and thereby entitle her to the 200-dinar marriage contract of a virgin, provided that he testifies with another witness who witnessed the event as an adult (Ran; Rosh; and contrary to the *Maggid Mishne*; Rambam *Sefer Nashim, Hilkhot Ishut* 16:25; *Shulḥan Arukh, Even HaEzer* 96:15).

To immerse in order to partake of *teruma* – לִטְבּוֹל לֶאֱכוֹל בִּתְרוּמָה: An adult is deemed credible to testify that as a child he saw someone immerse himself in order to eat *teruma*, and thereby confer the post-Temple presumptive status of priesthood upon that person, and it is permitted for him to eat *teruma* from produce from which one is obligated by rabbinic law to separate *teruma* (Rambam *Sefer Kedusha, Hilkhot Issurei Bia* 20:15; *Shulḥan Arukh, Even HaEzer* 3:5 and *Ḥoshen Mishpat* 35:6).

It is prohibited for a person to teach his slave Torah – אָסוּר לְאָדָם שֶׁיְּלַמֵּד אֶת עַבְדּוֹ תּוֹרָה: A master may not teach his slave Torah, in accordance with the opinion of Rabbi Yehoshua ben Levi (Rambam *Sefer Kinyan, Hilkhot Avadim* 8:18; *Shulḥan Arukh, Yoreh De'a* 267:71).

LANGUAGE

Beit haperas – בֵּית הַפְּרָס: There are differing opinions with regard to the derivation of this term. Rashi and *Tosafot* assert that it is from the term *paras*, meaning break, as a *beit haperas* is impure due to the bones in the grave that are broken by the plow. From the Rambam it appears that this term comes from the word *perisa*, spread, due to the fact that the impurity is spread across the entire field. Others claim that it comes from the Greek πάρος, *paros*, meaning placed before, in the sense that the field is the courtyard of a grave. Yet others attribute it to the Greek ἄπορος, *aporos*, without passage, having no way in or out.

NOTES

Until here we would come on Shabbat – עַד כָּאן הָיִינוּ בָּאִין בְּשַׁבָּת: This testimony is with regard to marking the two-thousand-cubit Shabbat boundary measured from the outskirts of the city, beyond which it is prohibited to walk on Shabbat.

And when there is a witness who saw the handwriting as an adult testifying with him – וְהוּא שֶׁיֵּשׁ גָּדוֹל עִמּוֹ: According to most commentaries, this refers only to testimony about the handwriting of witnesses and the case of the *hinnuma*, which involve a certain monetary element, but not to other matters (see *Tosafot*; *Shita Mekubbetzet*). However, the Ran apparently holds that this *halakha* applies to the case of *teruma* as well, and from Rabbeinu Tam's comments in *Sefer HaYashar*, apparently, it applies to all the matters mentioned in the mishna.

But with regard to his brother's handwriting…say no – אֲבָל אָחִיו...אֵימָא לָא: Some early commentaries say that since the testimony about events that he witnessed in his childhood concerning his brother is deemed credible, the same would be true with regard to others (*Sefer HaIttur*; Razah; Ritva). Others cite proof from the Jerusalem Talmud which states: Provided that it is with regard to matters about which they are familiar. Testimony about what they witnessed as minors is deemed credible exclusively with regard to close relatives with whose signatures they were familiar (Rosh; Meiri).

And perhaps he is the slave of a priest – וְדִלְמָא עֶבֶד כֹּהֵן הוּא: The Ritva explains that this concern was raised specifically here, and not in every case where a witness testifies with regard to one partaking of *teruma*; because it was a minor who witnessed the event, the concern is that he did not pay attention to detail, and consequently became confused between a priest and his slave.

וְלָא? וְהָתַנְיָא: לָוָה הֵימֶנּוּ רַבּוֹ, אוֹ שֶׁעֲשָׂאוֹ רַבּוֹ

The Gemara asks: **And** may one **not** teach his slave Torah? **But isn't it taught** in a *baraita*: A slave **whose master borrowed from him, or whose master made him**

Perek **II**
Daf **28** Amud **b**

HALAKHA

Did not necessarily emerge to freedom – לֹא יָצָא לְחֵירוּת: Even if a master borrows money from his slave, or appoints him steward of his property; or if the slave dons phylacteries or reads from the Torah before his master and the master does not protest, the slave is not thereby liberated, in accordance with the *baraita* (Rambam *Hilkhot Avadim* 8:17; *Shulḥan Arukh*, *Yoreh De'a* 267:70).

One distributes *teruma* to a slave only if his master is with him – אֵין חוֹלְקִין תְּרוּמָה לְעֶבֶד אֶלָּא אִם כֵּן רַבּוֹ עִמּוֹ: One does not distribute *teruma* to a slave at the threshing floor lest people mistakenly conclude that he is a priest (Rambam *Sefer Zera'im*, *Hilkhot Terumot* 12:22).

אַפּוֹטְרוֹפּוֹס, אוֹ שֶׁהִנִּיחַ תְּפִילִּין בִּפְנֵי רַבּוֹ, אוֹ שֶׁקָּרָא שְׁלֹשָׁה פְּסוּקִים בְּבֵית הַכְּנֶסֶת – הֲרֵי זֶה לֹא יָצָא לְחֵירוּת! הָתָם דְּאִיקְרִי עֶבֶד מִדַּעְתּוֹ, כִּי קָאָמְרִינַן – דְּקָא נָהֵיג בֵּיהּ מִנְהַג בָּנִים. "לִטְבּוֹל לֶאֱכוֹל בִּתְרוּמָה". בִּתְרוּמָה דְּרַבָּנַן.

steward over his property, **or** who **donned phylacteries in his master's presence, or** who **read three verses** from the Torah scroll **in the synagogue, did not** necessarily **emerge to freedom.**[H] Apparently, there are slaves who learn Torah to the extent that they are capable of reading the Torah in the synagogue, and conceivably that Torah is learned in school. The Gemara answers that there is no proof from the *baraita*, as **there** it is a case **where the slave read at his own initiative,** and conceivably he taught himself to read the Torah as well. **When we say** in the mishna that it is proof that he is a priest, it is in a case **where he treats him** with **treatment** typical of **children,** not slaves, and sends him to school. When the mishna states that he is deemed credible to testify that as a minor he saw that others went **to immerse** in order **to partake of *teruma*,** the Sages permit them only to partake **of *teruma* by rabbinic** law.

"וְשֶׁהָיָה חוֹלֵק עִמָּנוּ עַל הַגּוֹרֶן". וְדִלְמָא עֶבֶד כֹּהֵן הוּא? תְּנַן כְּמַאן דְּאָמַר: אֵין חוֹלְקִין תְּרוּמָה לְעֶבֶד אֶלָּא אִם כֵּן רַבּוֹ עִמּוֹ. דְּתַנְיָא: אֵין חוֹלְקִין תְּרוּמָה לְעֶבֶד אֶלָּא אִם כֵּן רַבּוֹ עִמּוֹ, דִּבְרֵי רַבִּי יְהוּדָה. רַבִּי יוֹסֵי אוֹמֵר: יָכוֹל הוּא שֶׁיֹּאמַר: אִם כֹּהֵן אֲנִי – תְּנוּ לִי בִּשְׁבִיל עַצְמִי, וְאִם עֶבֶד כֹּהֵן אֲנִי – תְּנוּ לִי בִּשְׁבִיל רַבִּי.

And the mishna states that he is deemed credible to say that they saw **that** so-and-so **would share** *teruma* **with us at the threshing floor,** and therefore he is a priest. The Gemara asks: **And perhaps he is the slave of a priest?** The Gemara answers: **We learned** the mishna **according to the one who says: One distributes *teruma* to a slave only if his master is with him.**[H] Therefore, it is clear that the one sharing *teruma* with them was a priest, not a slave, **as it is taught** in a *baraita*: In the case of the son of a priest's wife and the son of a priest's maidservant who were intermingled at birth, both mothers go to the threshing floor together based on the principle: **One distributes *teruma* to a slave only if his master is with him;** this is **the statement of Rabbi Yehuda. Rabbi Yosei says:** It is **possible that each will say: If I am a priest, give me** *teruma* **for my own sake, and if I am the slave of a priest, give me** *teruma* **for the sake of my master.**

בִּמְקוֹמוֹ שֶׁל רַבִּי יְהוּדָה הָיוּ מַעֲלִין מִתְּרוּמָה לְיוּחֲסִין, בִּמְקוֹמוֹ שֶׁל רַבִּי יוֹסֵי לֹא הָיוּ מַעֲלִין מִתְּרוּמָה לְיוּחֲסִין.

The dispute in the *baraita* is based on the fact that **in the place of Rabbi Yehuda, they would elevate** one who eats ***teruma*** **to the** presumptive status of priesthood **for** the purpose of **lineage.** Therefore, he permitted distributing *teruma* to the slave of a priest only if his master is present, due to the concern that if he were given *teruma* directly, he would be elevated to priesthood. **In the place of Rabbi Yosei, they would not elevate from *teruma* to lineage.** Therefore, he permitted distributing *teruma* directly to the slave of a priest, as there is no concern that the slave would be mistaken for a priest.

תַּנְיָא, אָמַר רַבִּי אֶלְעָזָר בְּרַבִּי יוֹסֵי: מִיָּמַי לֹא הֵעַדְתִּי, פַּעַם אַחַת הֵעַדְתִּי, וְהֶעֱלוּ עֶבֶד לִכְהוּנָּה עַל פִּי. הֶעֱלוּ סָלְקָא דַּעְתָּךְ?! הַשְׁתָּא, וּמָה בְּהֶמְתָּן שֶׁל צַדִּיקִים אֵין הַקָּדוֹשׁ בָּרוּךְ הוּא מֵבִיא תַּקָּלָה עַל יָדָם – צַדִּיקִים עַצְמָם לֹא כׇּל שֶׁכֵּן!

It is taught in a *baraita* that **Rabbi Elazar, son of Rabbi Yosei, said: In all my days, I never** had occasion **to testify** in court. **One time I testified,** and the court **elevated a slave to priesthood on the basis of my** testimony. The Gemara asks: **Does it enter your mind that they** actually **elevated** the slave to priesthood? **Now, just as** with regard to **the animals of the righteous the Holy One, Blessed be He, does not engender a pitfall on their account,** as the Gemara relates with regard to the donkey of Rabbi Pinḥas ben Yair that it would not eat untithed produce (*Ḥullin* 7a), **all the more so** will He not engender a pitfall on account of **the righteous themselves.**

אֶלָּא, בִּקְּשׁוּ לְהַעֲלוֹת עֶבֶד לִכְהוּנָּה עַל פִּי. חֲזָא בְּאַתְרֵיהּ דְּרַבִּי יוֹסֵי, וַאֲזַל וְאַסְהֵיד בְּאַתְרֵיהּ דְּרַבִּי יְהוּדָה.

Rather, the Gemara emends the statement of Rabbi Elazar, son of Rabbi Yosei: **They sought to elevate a slave to priesthood on the basis of my** testimony, but ultimately they did not. Rabbi Elazar **saw** *teruma* distributed directly to the slave of a priest **in the place of Rabbi Yosei,** where one does not elevate from *teruma* to priesthood, **and he went and testified** about what he saw **in the place of Rabbi Yehuda,** where one elevates from *teruma* to priesthood.

״וְשֶׁהַמָּקוֹם הַזֶּה בֵּית הַפְּרָס הוּא״. מַאי טַעְמָא? בֵּית הַפְּרָס דְּרַבָּנַן. דְּאָמַר רַב יְהוּדָה אָמַר שְׁמוּאֵל: מְנַפֵּחַ אָדָם בֵּית הַפְּרָס וְהוֹלֵךְ. וְרַב יְהוּדָה בַּר אַמֵּי מִשְּׁמֵיהּ דְּרַב יְהוּדָה אָמַר: בֵּית הַפְּרָס שֶׁנִּידַּשׁ – טָהוֹר. מַאי טַעְמָא – אִי אֶפְשָׁר לְעֶצֶם כִּשְׂעוֹרָה שֶׁלֹּא נִידַּשׁ בָּרֶגֶל.

And the mishna states that one is deemed credible to testify in his adulthood that as a minor he saw **that this place is a *beit haperas*.**[HN] The Gemara asks: **What is the reason** that he is deemed credible to testify what he witnessed as a minor? The Gemara answers: The ritual impurity of a ***beit haperas*** is **by rabbinic** law,[N] **as Rav Yehuda said** that **Shmuel said: A person** who passes through **a *beit haperas* may blow**[H] on the dust before taking each step, so that if there is a bone beneath the dust he will expose it, avoid it, **and proceed.** One may not rely on that method of examination with regard to impurity by Torah law. **And Rav Yehuda bar Ami, in the name of Rav Yehuda, said: A *beit haperas* that has been trodden** underfoot, creating a path, **is pure. What is the reason?** It is that **it is impossible for a bone** the size **of** a grain of **barley,** whose possible presence led to the decree of impurity, **not to have been trodden underfoot** and rendered smaller. This presumption is possible only in cases of impurity by rabbinic law.

״וְעַד כָּאן הָיִינוּ בָּאִין בְּשַׁבָּת״. קָסָבַר: תְּחוּמִין דְּרַבָּנַן.

And the mishna states that one is deemed credible to testify, in his adulthood, that he saw as a minor: **Until here we would come**[H] **on Shabbat.** The Gemara explains: This *tanna* **maintains** that the Shabbat **boundaries,** beyond which one may not go outside the city on Shabbat, are mandated **by rabbinic** law, and the Sages deemed him credible in matters of rabbinic law.

״וְאֵין נֶאֱמָן לוֹמַר דֶּרֶךְ הָיָה לִפְלוֹנִי בְּמָקוֹם הַזֶּה, מַעֲמָד וּמִסְפֵּד הָיָה לִפְלוֹנִי בְּמָקוֹם הַזֶּה״. מַאי טַעְמָא? אַפּוֹקֵי מָמוֹנָא – לָא מַפְּקִינַן.

And the mishna states that **one is neither deemed credible to say: So-and-so had a path in this place;** nor to say: **So-and-so had** a tract of land where they would perform the ritual of **standing** and sitting **and** deliver **a eulogy in that place.** The Gemara asks: **What is the reason** that he is not deemed credible? It is due to the fact that **we do not remove money** from the possession of its presumptive owner on the basis of testimony about a matter that he witnessed as a minor.

תָּנוּ רַבָּנַן: נֶאֱמָן הַתִּינוֹק לוֹמַר כָּךְ אָמַר לִי אַבָּא: ״מִשְׁפָּחָה זוֹ טְהוֹרָה, מִשְׁפָּחָה זוֹ טְמֵאָה״. טְהוֹרָה וּטְמֵאָה סָלְקָא דַּעְתָּךְ?! אֶלָּא, מִשְׁפָּחָה זוֹ כְּשֵׁרָה, וּמִשְׁפָּחָה זוֹ פְּסוּלָה.

The Sages taught: A child is deemed credible to say when he reaches majority that **this is what my father told me** when I was a minor: **This family is pure, that family is impure.** The Gemara asks: **Does it enter your mind** that his father said **pure and impure?** What do those concepts mean with regard to a family? **Rather,** his father said to him: **This family is of unflawed** lineage,[HN] **and this family is of flawed** lineage.

HALAKHA

That this place is a *beit haperas* – שֶׁהַמָּקוֹם הַזֶּה בֵּית הַפְּרָס הוּא: The mishna states that a man is deemed credible to testify that when he was a child he saw that a certain place was a *beit haperas*, because the impurity of a *beit haperas* is by rabbinic law (Rambam *Sefer Shofetim*, *Hilkhot Edut* 14:3; *Shulḥan Arukh*, *Ḥoshen Mishpat* 35:5).

A person who passes through a *beit haperas* may blow – מְנַפֵּחַ אָדָם בֵּית הַפְּרָס: If one is passing through a *beit haperas*, he may blow on the earth in his path and proceed, and if he does not encounter any bones and thereby does not become ritually impure, he is eligible to sacrifice the Paschal lamb, in accordance with the opinion of Rabbi Yehuda. Likewise, if the *beit haperas* has already been trampled, he may sacrifice the offering (Rambam *Sefer Korbanot*, *Hilkhot Korban Pesaḥ* 6:8).

Until here we would come – עַד כָּאן הָיִינוּ בָּאִין: An adult is deemed credible to testify that he recalls that when he was a child, people would walk only until a certain point on Shabbat (Rambam *Sefer Zemanim*, *Hilkhot Shabbat* 28:19; *Shulḥan Arukh*, *Oraḥ Ḥayyim* 399:11).

This family is of unflawed lineage – מִשְׁפָּחָה זוֹ כְּשֵׁרָה: One is deemed credible to testify that he remembers that when he was a child, people would give priestly gifts and *ḥalla* to a certain priest. Likewise, he is deemed credible to testify that he remembers that as a child his father told him that a certain family was of flawed or unflawed lineage, or that a *ketzatza* ceremony was performed after the wedding of a certain man to a certain woman. Some authorities rule that the testimony of the witness is effective to establish the status of the family's lineage as well as to enable the priest to partake of *teruma*. Others say that only if two witnesses testify in this manner is a definitive determination reached based on their testimony and the family is deemed to be of flawed lineage. If he is one witness, his testimony is sufficient only to cast doubt with regard to the lineage of the family (*Kesef Mishne*, citing Ra'avad; Rambam *Sefer Shofetim*, *Hilkhot Edut* 14:3; *Shulḥan Arukh*, *Ḥoshen Mishpat* 35:6).

NOTES

***Beit haperas* – בֵּית הַפְּרָס:** There are different types of *beit haperas*, but the most common is a field where it is known that there is a grave, and which was consequently plowed. The concern is that bones from the dead body were scattered by the plow, which could render one ritually impure. Therefore, the Sages decreed that an area of one hundred square cubits around the grave would be impure. However, since the decree is based merely on a concern, and one could become impure only by means of impurity imparted by means of a tent (Rashi), and the scattered bones were not sufficiently large to impart impurity in that manner, the Sages relied on the pretext that the bones were trampled, or upon a cursory search, in order to deem anyone who passed through the field ritually pure. The simple understanding of the Gemara is that the testimony given is that the field is impure. However, *Tosafot* suggest that the witness is testifying how far the boundary of the *beit haperas* reaches, beyond which the field is pure. Since the impurity is by rabbinic decree, that testimony is deemed credible.

The impurity of a *beit haperas* is by rabbinic law – בֵּית הַפְּרָס דְּרַבָּנַן: The early commentaries dispute whether this testimony is accepted completely or only partially. The Rid and *Tosafot* maintain that the testimony is deemed credible with regard to what he saw as a child. This is in order to establish that areas previously presumed ritually impure are beyond the boundaries of the *beit haperas* and thereby can be rendered pure. However, the Ritva, among others, maintains that he is not deemed credible to purify an area presumed to be part of a *beit haperas*. Rather, he is deemed credible to establish that a certain area is a *beit haperas* and must be treated as ritually impure.

This family is of unflawed lineage – מִשְׁפָּחָה זוֹ כְּשֵׁרָה: The early commentaries dispute the nature of this testimony and its effect, as ostensibly, even were the father himself to make this claim, it would be considered merely the testimony of one person. The Ra'avad explains that these childhood memories are relied upon only with regard to suspicions about this family's lineage. However, if there were two witnesses, that is full-fledged testimony, which would establish that their lineage was flawed. According to the Ran, this testimony is effective only in a case where it is already known that the lineage of one of two families is flawed, but the identity of that family is unknown, as in that case the testimony can be viewed as merely revealing matters that are already known.

וְ״שֶׁאָכַלְנוּ בִּקְצָצָה שֶׁל בַּת פְּלוֹנִי לִפְלוֹנִי״. וְ״שֶׁהָיִינוּ מוֹלִיכִים חַלָּה וּמַתָּנוֹת לִפְלוֹנִי כֹּהֵן״. עַל יְדֵי עַצְמוֹ, אֲבָל לֹא עַל יְדֵי אַחֵר. וְכוּלָּן, אִם הָיָה גּוֹי וְנִתְגַּיֵּיר, עֶבֶד וְנִשְׁתַּחְרֵר – אֵין נֶאֱמָנִים. וְאֵין נֶאֱמָן לוֹמַר ״דֶּרֶךְ הָיָה לִפְלוֹנִי בַּמָּקוֹם הַזֶּה״, ״מַעֲמָד וּמִסְפֵּד הָיָה לִפְלוֹנִי בַּמָּקוֹם הַזֶּה״. רַבִּי יוֹחָנָן בֶּן בְּרוֹקָא אוֹמֵר: נֶאֱמָנִים.

And he is deemed credible to say **that we ate at the** ***ketzatza***[H] that took place to publicize that the marriage **of the daughter of so-and-so to so-and-so** was unsuitable; **and** to say **that we would bring** ***ḥalla*** **and** priestly **gifts to so-and-so,** who is a **priest.** In that case, he is deemed credible only to testify that he brought the *ḥalla* **by himself, but not by means of another,** as one is certain of matters that he performed himself, even as a minor. However, he is not deemed credible to testify about actions performed by others when he was a minor. **And** with regard to **all these** testimonies, **if he was a gentile**[H] **and he converted,** or **a slave and he was liberated, they are not deemed credible** to testify after their conversion and liberation about matters that transpired beforehand when they were disqualified as witnesses. **And one is neither deemed credible to say** that he remembers that when he was a minor, **so-and-so had a path in this place;** nor that **so-and-so had** a tract of land where they would perform the ritual of **standing** and sitting **and** deliver **a eulogy in that place. Rabbi Yoḥanan ben Beroka says:** They are **deemed credible.**

רַבִּי יוֹחָנָן בֶּן בְּרוֹקָא אַהֵיָּיא? אִילֵימָא אַסֵּיפָא – אַפּוּקֵי מָמוֹנָא הוּא! אֶלָּא אַרֵישָׁא: וְכוּלָּם אִם הָיָה גּוֹי וְנִתְגַּיֵּיר, עֶבֶד וְנִשְׁתַּחְרֵר – אֵין נֶאֱמָנִין, רַבִּי יוֹחָנָן בֶּן בְּרוֹקָא אוֹמֵר: נֶאֱמָנִין.

The Gemara asks: With regard **to which** clause in the *baraita* is **Rabbi Yoḥanan ben Beroka** disputing? **If we say** he is disputing the **last clause** of the *baraita*, which concerns testimony about a path or a place for mourning, **it is** a case of **removing money** from the possession of its presumptive owner. How could his testimony be deemed credible? **Rather,** Rabbi Yoḥanan ben Beroka is certainly disagreeing with the **former clause** of the *baraita*: **And** with regard to **all these** testimonies, **if he was a gentile and he converted,** or **a slave and he was liberated, they are not deemed credible.** It is with regard to that *halakha* that **Rabbi Yoḥanan ben Beroka says:** They are **deemed credible.**

בְּמַאי קָמִיפַּלְגִי? תָּנָא קַמָּא סָבַר: כֵּיוָן דְּגוֹי הוּא – לָא הֲוָה דָּיֵיק, וְרַבִּי יוֹחָנָן בֶּן בְּרוֹקָא סָבַר: כֵּיוָן דְּדַעְתֵּיהּ לְאִיגַּיּוּרֵי – מֵידָק הֲוָה דָּיֵיק.

The Gemara asks: **With regard to what** principle **do they disagree?** The Gemara explains that **the first** ***tanna*** **maintains: Since he was a gentile, he was not exacting** in scrutinizing the matter, as it was irrelevant to him. Therefore, even after he converted he is not deemed credible. **And Rabbi Yoḥanan ben Beroka maintains: Since it was his intention to convert,** he took interest in Judaism and **he was exacting** in scrutinizing the matter, and he is deemed credible.

מַאי קְצָצָה? דְּתָנוּ רַבָּנַן: כֵּיצַד קְצָצָה? אֶחָד מִן הָאַחִין שֶׁנָּשָׂא אִשָּׁה שֶׁאֵינָהּ הוֹגֶנֶת לוֹ, בָּאִין בְּנֵי מִשְׁפָּחָה וּמְבִיאִין חָבִית מְלֵיאָה פֵּירוֹת, וְשׁוֹבְרִין אוֹתָהּ בְּאֶמְצַע רְחָבָה, וְאוֹמְרִים: אַחֵינוּ בֵּית יִשְׂרָאֵל, שִׁמְעוּ! אָחִינוּ פְּלוֹנִי נָשָׂא אִשָּׁה שֶׁאֵינָהּ הוֹגֶנֶת לוֹ, וּמִתְיָירְאִים אָנוּ שֶׁמָּא יִתְעָרֵב זַרְעוֹ בְּזַרְעֵינוּ, בּוֹאוּ וּקְחוּ לָכֶם דּוּגְמָא לְדוֹרוֹת, שֶׁלֹּא יִתְעָרֵב זַרְעוֹ בְּזַרְעֵינוּ. וְזוֹ הִיא קְצָצָה שֶׁהַתִּינוֹק נֶאֱמָן לְהָעִיד עָלֶיהָ.

The Gemara asks about a term employed in the *baraita*: **What is** the meaning of ***ketzatza***? It is **as the Sages taught: How is** ***ketzatza*** performed? If a situation where **one of the brothers who married a woman who is unsuited for him,** due to flawed lineage, occurs, **the family members come and bring** with them **a barrel full of fruits, and break it in the middle of** a public **square** to publicize the matter, **and they say: Our brothers, the house of Israel, listen. Our brother so-and-so married a woman who is unsuited for him, and we fear lest his descendants become intermingled with our descendants.** In order to further underscore the matter, they continue: **Come and take for yourselves a sample** as an indicator for future **generations, so that his descendants will not intermingle with our descendants.** The gathering of the large crowd to take the fruit generates publicity. **And this is the** ***ketzatza*** **that a child** who witnessed it **is deemed credible to testify about it** when he is an adult.

הדרן עלך האשה שנתארמלה

HALAKHA

That we ate at the ***ketzatza*** **– שֶׁאָכַלְנוּ בִּקְצָצָה:** An adult is deemed credible to testify that as a child he ate fruit at a *ketzatza* ceremony held by a certain family to inform the public that one of its sons married a woman unfit for him. The Rema writes that a family has the right to reprimand one of its members who marries an unfit woman, and if he fails to heed their reprimand, they should stage a demonstration to apprise the public of his actions (*Shulḥan Arukh, Even HaEzer* 2:1).

And with regard to all these testimonies, if he was a gentile – וְכוּלָּן אִם הָיָה גּוֹי: Although in all these cases an adult is deemed credible to testify with regard to events that he witnessed as a child, a convert or an emancipated slave is not deemed credible to testify with regard to events that he witnessed as a gentile or a slave respectively, in accordance with the unattributed opinion in the *baraita* (Rambam *Sefer Shofetim, Hilkhot Edut* 14:4; *Shulḥan Arukh, Hoshen Mishpat* 35:7).

Summary of **Perek II**

One of the main topics analyzed in this chapter is the principle: The mouth that prohibited is the mouth that permitted. In other words, in any case where one relies on testimony or the admission of one of the parties, if it is deemed credible it should be accepted in its entirety. Therefore, when one testifies, establishing a fact, whether it relates to him or it relates to another, and he adds certain details that limit or negate the halakhic significance of that testimony, the entire statement of the witness is accepted. This principle applies to ritual matters, e.g., the testimony of a woman regarding with whom she engaged in intercourse, or if she said: I was taken captive but was not violated, or if she said: I was married but now I am divorced; and to monetary matters, e.g., this field belonged to your father and I purchased it from him, or if one said: That is my signature but we were compelled to sign.

There are two restrictions to this form of credibility. First, it is accorded only when there is no independent source of information with regard to that matter. When there is such information, i.e., witnesses or some other source of objective information that is incriminating, the fact that the party admitted it but then negated its significance does not grant him credibility. Second, when a party's claim involves self-incrimination or is suspect of being false for some external reason, it is not granted credibility.

A similar *halakha* exists in cases where one relates a matter that could subject him to a prohibition and he then denies his original statement. In that case, his denial is accepted only if he can provide a rationale explaining why he made his original statement.

Two other significant matters addressed in this chapter were the *halakhot* of ratification of documents and the *halakhot* of a captive woman. With regard to ratification of documents the Gemara concluded that when one seeks to undermine the validity of a document by claiming, for example, that it is a forgery, the document is brought before the court and the court determines, by means of testimony or by comparing the signatures of the witnesses with their signatures on documents previously ratified by the court, whether the witnesses' signatures are legitimate. Since the assumption is that witnesses who sign a document ascertained its validity, their testimony is sufficient to ratify it. It was also concluded that the testimony in the ratification of documents relates to the signatures and not to the content of the document, which led to various conclusions in cases where separate testimony is required for each of the signatures.

With regard to a captive woman, or a woman who was subject to the control of gentiles, e.g., she was in a city under their occupation or she was incarcerated by them, the Sages were concerned that she was raped and therefore forbidden to a priest. However, since it is merely a suspicion, the Sages ruled leniently and relied on testimony that she was not violated from those whose testimony is generally invalid, e.g., one witness, a woman, or a minor. Only the testimony of the woman herself, when there is independent knowledge that she was in captivity, and the testimony of her husband, are invalid.

On a similar note, the Sages relied on flawed testimony from one witness, from a relative, or from a witness who witnessed the incident as a minor in various cases involving rabbinic law, e.g., elevation to priesthood for matters of rabbinic law and for matters of lineage, and for determining the Shabbat boundaries, especially in those matters that entail merely revealing a fact that by its very nature would have been revealed and publicized.

Introduction to **Perek III**

And if a man seduce a virgin who was not betrothed, and lies with her, he shall pay a dowry for her to be a wife to him. If her father refuses to give her to him, he shall weigh money like the dowry of the virgins.

(Exodus 22:15–16)

If a man finds a young woman who is a virgin who was not betrothed, and lay hold on her, and lie with her, and they be found; and the man who lay with her shall give to the father of the young woman fifty shekels of silver, and to him she shall be as a wife, because he tormented her; he may not put her away all his days.

(Deuteronomy 22:28–29)

The *halakhot* of the seducer and the rapist are explicit in the Torah; however, since they are written succinctly, many questions remain that demand practical halakhic resolution.

One of the primary questions relates to the attitude toward the language of the verses: Do the *halakhot* of the seducer and the rapist apply only in the cases delineated in the verse; or does the verse merely cite a specific case in order to illustrate the *halakha*, which applies in other cases as well? This question relates to several details. Does this apply only to a young woman who is a virgin or does it apply to a minor girl and a grown woman as well? Does this apply only to a young woman whose father is alive, or even to an orphan? Is the right of refusal for the marriage of the victim exclusively that of the father and is it applicable only in the case of seduction?

Another related fundamental problem is: What is the *halakha* when there is an additional prohibition associated with this intercourse beyond the seduction and the rape? It could be that the woman is forbidden to the rapist by rabbinic law, due to a positive mitzva, due to a prohibition, or even due to a prohibition punishable by death. Is the perpetrator required to marry his victim in all these cases? Is he obligated to pay the fine? Does he receive only one punishment, or is he is subject to both punishments? These questions require a comprehensive analysis of the general principles of punishment: What is the *halakha* when there is more than one punishment for violating a single prohibition?

Another basic question involves the nature of the payment paid by the seducer and the rapist. Is the sum mentioned in the Torah the total compensation to the victim or is it merely a special fine paid in addition to other payments of compensation like those paid to any other victim of violence? If there are additional payments, how are they assessed and to whom are they paid?

These problems and others that emerge from their resolution constitute the focus of this chapter.

מתני׳ אֵלּוּ נְעָרוֹת שֶׁיֵּשׁ לָהֶן קְנָס: הַבָּא עַל הַמַּמְזֶרֶת, וְעַל הַנְּתִינָה, וְעַל הַכּוּתִית. הַבָּא עַל הַגִּיּוֹרֶת, וְעַל הַשְּׁבוּיָה. וְעַל הַשִּׁפְחָה שֶׁנִּפְדּוּ וְשֶׁנִּתְגַּיְּירוּ וְשֶׁנִּשְׁתַּחְרְרוּ פְּחוּתוֹת מִבְּנוֹת שָׁלֹשׁ שָׁנִים וְיוֹם אֶחָד.

MISHNA These[N] are the cases of **young women**[HB] **for whom there is a fine**[N] paid **to their** fathers by one who rapes them: **One who engages in intercourse with a *mamzeret*,**[N] **or with a Gibeonite woman [*netina*],**[N] who are given [*netunim*] to the service of the people and the altar (see Joshua 9:27), **or with a Samaritan woman [*kutit*].**[N] In addition, the same applies **to one who engages in intercourse with a female convert,**[NH] **or with a captive woman, or with a maidservant,** provided **that** the captives **were ransomed,** or **that** the converts **converted, or that** the maidservants **were liberated** when they were **less than three years and one day old,** as only in that case do they maintain the presumptive status of a virgin.

NOTES

These – **אֵלּוּ**: There was a variant version of the text before the early commentaries that read: And these are the young women. The Rosh justifies the version that appears in the mishna, as the phrase: And these, indicates continuation, and a new topic is addressed in this chapter. However, in the *Shita Mekubbetzet*, the version: And these, is explained. After the women who receive marriage contracts of one hundred or two hundred dinar were enumerated in the earlier chapters, the *tanna* cites an additional list comprised of women for whom there is a fine for rape. In the *Melekhet Shlomo*, support for that contention is cited, as that accounts for the fact that the *tanna* included only young women who are of flawed lineage or otherwise unfit in this list. In addition to the women of unflawed lineage mentioned in the previous chapters, these women, too, are entitled to the fine.

For whom there is a fine – **שֶׁיֵּשׁ לָהֶן קְנָס**: In addition to the fine, the rapist pays compensation for humiliation and degradation as well. However, the *tanna* did not mention those payments here, as he based himself on the verse, which mentions only the fine in the context of a young woman who was raped (*Shita Mekubbetzet*).

One who engages in intercourse with a *mamzeret* – **הַבָּא עַל הַמַּמְזֶרֶת**: In the *Shita Mekubbetzet*, the reason that the mishna is formulated in terms of the rapist: One who engages in intercourse with, instead of simply: These are the young women…a *mamzeret*, a Gibeonite, etc., is addressed. The explanation supports Rabbi Yoḥanan's opinion cited later that the mishna is referring to a case where the rapist was not forewarned. The formulation: One who engages in intercourse with a *mamzeret*, indicates that there was no forewarning.

Gibeonite woman – **נְתִינָה**: The halakhic status of the descendants of the Gibeonites is addressed in several places in the Talmud, primarily in tractates *Yevamot* and *Kiddushin*. Nevertheless, several fundamental questions are not completely resolved and are addressed by the early and later commentaries. From Rashi's commentary here, it appears that the prohibition against the Gibeonites entering the congregation of Israel is not by Torah law but by rabbinic law in the broadest sense of the term, as everyone agrees that it is an early decree dating back to the time of Moses or King David. *Tosafot*, based on the context here and other sources, explain at length that this cannot be the case, and they assert that the prohibition is in fact by Torah law. There are also different opinions with regard to the nature of the prohibition. Some claim that the decree was that the Gibeonites were to be slaves and as such may not marry Jews. That is problematic, because if the legal status of a Gibeonite woman were that of a slave, she would not be entitled to a fine at all. In the Jerusalem Talmud it is explained that the Sages prohibited the Gibeonites from entering the congregation due to concerns about their flawed lineage, although they are still considered Jews. Others explain that the decree accords them the halakhic status of slaves, although fundamentally, they are not actual slaves. Most commentaries contend that Gibeonites are Canaanites, to whom the prohibition "You shall not marry them" (Deuteronomy 7:3) takes effect only after they converted.

Some early commentaries suggest an intermediate opinion. They contend that the first generation of Gibeonites was forbidden by the Torah prohibition: "You shall not marry them"; however, that prohibition did not apply to their children. The extension of the prohibition to their descendants is a decree issued by Joshua or King David (*Talmid HaRa'ah*). *Talmidei Rabbeinu Yona* state, in the name of *Tosefot Rabbi Shimshon of Saens*, that the *tanna* lists a Gibeonite together with a *mamzeret* because they appear together in other contexts, much as a divorcée and a *ḥalutza* are enumerated together as women forbidden to a priest. In both cases, one is prohibited by Torah law, i.e., the *mamzeret* and the divorcée, and one is prohibited by rabbinic law, i.e., the Gibeonite and the *ḥalutza*. The Ritva responds that although there is similarity that would justify listing a divorcée and a *ḥalutza* together, there is no similarity between a *mamzeret* and a Gibeonite. The only justification for listing them together is if they are both prohibited by Torah law.

Samaritan woman – **כּוּתִית**: The status of Samaritans is also subject to a dispute between *tanna'im*. There are two aspects to this matter. First, with regard to their status: Are they considered Jews at all? Second, how does one relate to them in practice? Some *tanna'im* hold that Samaritans are converts coerced by lions (see II Kings, chapter 17), whose conversion never took effect, and they are therefore full-fledged gentiles. The fact that they practice certain mitzvot of the Written Torah does not render them part of the congregation of Israel. Others maintain that they are actual converts. Although they did not initially convert with sincere motives, they later accepted Judaism. According to this opinion, they are full-fledged Jews, despite the fact that their practices deviate from normative *halakha*. Yet even those Sages who deem them Jews disagree with regard to the attitude toward them. Some contend that due to their treatment of the Jewish people, their idolatrous practices, and other reasons, they were penalized to the extent that not only are they kept at a distance, but they are treated as though they are not Jews at all, in the same manner as Jewish apostates. Others assert that it is prohibited to marry them due to concern about their lineage in terms of *mamzerim*, resulting from their lack of observance of *halakha*.

Tosafot, who discuss various aspects of this issue, maintain contrary to the opinion of Rashi that the *tanna* of this mishna holds in accordance with the opinion of Rabbi Meir that the Samaritans were genuine converts. Although Rabbi Meir himself holds that sanctions were imposed upon them with regard to certain monetary matters, he concedes that the fine for rape remains in place, so that the sinner would not profit from his wrongdoing. In the Jerusalem Talmud it is explicitly stated that the mishna is in accordance with the opinion of Rabbi Meir.

One who engages in intercourse with a female convert, etc. – **הַבָּא עַל הַגִּיּוֹרֶת וכו׳**: The Rashash asks why the *tanna* did not list those women forbidden by a standard prohibition, e.g., a *mamzeret*, first, followed by those forbidden by a prohibition punishable by *karet*, e.g., one's sister. Why did he insert the convert between them? The Rashash explains that the *tanna* did so to underscore that although the lineage of a *mamzeret*, a Gibeonite, etc., is flawed, her status is unlike that of a convert or a woman taken captive, whose circumstances rob them of their presumptive status as a virgin.

HALAKHA

These are the cases of young women, etc. – **אֵלּוּ נְעָרוֹת וכו׳**: With regard to one who rapes or seduces a virgin who was forbidden to him by a standard Torah prohibition or by a prohibition punishable by *karet*, if he was forewarned he is flogged and does not pay the fine. If he was not forewarned, he is not flogged, and he pays the fine (Rambam *Sefer Nashim, Hilkhot Na'ara Betula* 1:11; *Tur, Even HaEzer* 177).

One who engages in intercourse with a female convert, etc. – **הַבָּא עַל הַגִּיּוֹרֶת וכו׳**: If a gentile converted, a woman taken captive was redeemed, or a maidservant was freed when they were three years old or less, they are entitled to the fine for rape (Rambam *Sefer Nashim, Hilkhot Na'ara Betula* 1:10; *Tur, Even HaEzer* 177).

BACKGROUND

A young woman – **נַעֲרָה**: The *halakha* recognizes three distinct stages in the development of a woman from childhood to adulthood.

A female minor is a girl who has not yet reached puberty, which takes place at or about age twelve. As a minor, her father has the right to sell her to be a Hebrew maidservant or to betroth her to a man. If he does so, the result is a full-fledged betrothal in every sense. The father also receives his minor daughter's marriage contract and has the exclusive right to accept a bill of divorce on her behalf.

Once she reaches puberty, her legal status is that of a young woman. Although she is no longer a minor, she is not yet a full-fledged adult. Accordingly, her father retains certain authority over her.

Six months later, her legal status is that of a grown woman. From that point on, she is a fully independent adult, and her father no longer has any authority to make decisions on her behalf.

הַבָּא עַל אֲחוֹתוֹ וְעַל אֲחוֹת אָבִיו וְעַל אֲחוֹת אִמּוֹ וְעַל אֲחוֹת אִשְׁתּוֹ וְעַל אֵשֶׁת אָחִיו וְעַל אֵשֶׁת אֲחִי אָבִיו וְעַל הַנִּדָּה – יֵשׁ לָהֶם קְנָס, אַף עַל פִּי שֶׁהֵן בְּהִכָּרֵת – אֵין בָּהֶן מִיתַת בֵּית דִּין.

Similarly, **one who engages in intercourse with his sister,** i.e., he rapes her, **or with his father's sister, or with his mother's sister, or with his wife's sister, or with his brother's wife,**[N] **or with his father's brother's wife** after they divorced, **or with a menstruating woman, there is a fine** paid. **Although there is *karet*** for engaging in relations with any of the women enumerated in this list, one is liable to pay the fine because **there is no court**-imposed **capital punishment.** In cases where there is a court-imposed death penalty, the rapist would be exempt from paying the fine.

גמ׳ הָנֵי נְעָרוֹת פְּסוּלוֹת – אִית לְהוּ קְנָס, כְּשֵׁירוֹת – לָא?! הָכִי קָאָמַר: אֵלּוּ נְעָרוֹת פְּסוּלוֹת שֶׁיֵּשׁ לָהֶם קְנָס: הַבָּא עַל הַמַּמְזֶרֶת וְעַל הַנְּתִינָה וְעַל הַכּוּתִית.

GEMARA The Gemara wonders: Is it **these young women** with **flawed** lineage[N] listed in the mishna, **for whom there is a fine** paid if they are raped, while for young women with **unflawed** lineage, **no,** there is no fine? The Gemara explains that **this** is what the *tanna* **is saying: These are** the **young women** with **flawed** lineage **for whom there is a fine** paid if they are raped. This is not a comprehensive list; rather, the *tanna* enumerates those young women for whom a fine is paid despite their flawed lineage: **One who has relations with a *mamzeret*, or with a Gibeonite woman, or with a Samaritan woman.**

נַעֲרָה – אִין, קְטַנָּה – לָא, מַאן תַּנָּא?

The mishna teaches the *halakha* with regard to a young woman, from which the Gemara infers: With regard to **a young woman, yes,** one is liable to pay the fine if he rapes her, but with regard to **a minor, no,**[N] one is not liable to pay the fine. **Who is the *tanna***[N] who maintains that one is liable for raping a young woman but not a minor?

NOTES

Or with his brother's wife, etc. – **וְעַל אֵשֶׁת אָחִיו וכו׳**: The early commentaries note that the women listed in the mishna as the wife of his brother or of his father's brother are either widowed or divorced, as one who has relations with a married woman is liable to receive the death penalty. Furthermore, they must have been widowed or divorced when they were betrothed, not married, as the fine is imposed only on one who raped or seduced a virgin young woman. A married woman can no longer be considered a virgin young woman even if she did not engage in conjugal relations. That is the understanding that emerges from a careful reading of Rashi. In the Jerusalem Talmud the following question is raised: The wife of one's childless deceased brother is a *yevama*, with regard to whom there is neither prohibition nor fine, as it is a mitzva to have relations with her. They explain that the reference is to the widow of a brother who had children with another woman. Therefore, there is no mitzva of levirate marriage, and the prohibition against relations with one's brother's wife remains intact. Rashi resolves this difficulty by explaining that she is a divorcée, with regard to whom there is no mitzva of levirate marriage.

These young women with flawed lineage, etc. – **הָנֵי נְעָרוֹת פְּסוּלוֹת וכו׳**: The Ritva reinforces this question, as he explains that the term: These, is typically exclusionary, meaning: These and not others. Other early commentaries, however, contend that the term does not always bear that connotation, especially in this case, where there is another list in the next mishna. See also previous note, with regard to the textual variant: And these. A different problem, raised by the Ramban, is that not all of these young women are unfit for marriage; converts, for example, are certainly not barred from entering the congregation of Israel. Therefore, some commentaries explain unfit in this context as referring to women whose lineage is flawed because they were born of a forbidden union or for a different reason. The Ramban himself explains, citing *Tosafot*, that the mishna is referring to a convert, redeemed captive, or liberated slave who was raped by a priest. Since they are forbidden to priests, through intercourse with a priest they are rendered unfit. See the Ritva, who writes contrary to that approach. Several later commentaries question that explanation as well.

A young woman, yes; a minor, no – **נַעֲרָה אִין, קְטַנָּה לָא**: *Tosafot* ask why the Gemara opted for that inference. The Gemara could have inferred: Young women, yes; adult women, no, and then the mishna would be in accordance with the opinions of all the *tanna'im*. *Tosafot* and other early commentaries explain that the inference is based not on the language of the mishna but on the statement later in the Gemara (40b) that the unattributed mishna is in accordance with the opinion of Rabbi Meir. It is therefore reasonable to posit that this mishna follows the same approach. The Ramban explains that had the *tanna* intended merely to exclude grown women, he could have stated: And these are they for whom there is a fine, as it is clear that grown women receive no fine for rape. By specifying young women, he indicates that the *halakha* applies exclusively to young women and not to minors. In the *Shita Mekubbetzet* it is explained that in cases involving a dispute between *tanna'im*, the *tanna* of the mishna usually enters into greater detail. Therefore, the assumption is that he mentioned young women specifically to take a side in the dispute. The *Yam shel Shlomo* explains that had the *tanna* sought to exclude grown women, he could have written: And these are the virgins, as adult women are not considered full-fledged virgins, since in the course of their physical development their hymens do not remain completely intact.

Who is the *tanna* – **מַאן תַּנָּא**: *Tosafot* at the beginning of tractate *Moed Katan* state that typically, the Gemara does not ask: Who is the *tanna*, with regard to a mishna that is in accordance with the opinion of Rabbi Meir, as there is a principle that opinions cited in an unattributed mishna are recognized as those of Rabbi Meir. Still, the question is raised here, and the mishna is attributed to Rabbi Meir. In the *Shita Mekubbetzet* it is explained that since the entire mishna is not in accordance with the opinion of Rabbi Meir, as proven later from the *halakha* of one who rapes his daughter, and according to some commentaries from the *halakha* of a Samaritan woman as well, it was therefore necessary to assert that the primary *halakha* in the mishna is in fact in accordance with the opinion of Rabbi Meir. Other commentaries cite this as proof that the *halakha* is not in accordance with the opinion of Rabbi Meir, as the Gemara's question indicates that this is not an unattributed mishna, in accordance with which the *halakha* is ruled, but the opinion of an individual Sage (see *Mishne LaMelekh*).

אָמַר רַב יְהוּדָה אָמַר רַב: רַבִּי מֵאִיר הִיא. דְּתַנְיָא: קְטַנָּה, מִבַּת יוֹם אֶחָד וְעַד שֶׁתָּבִיא שְׁתֵּי שְׂעָרוֹת – יֵשׁ לָהּ מֶכֶר וְאֵין לָהּ קְנָס. וּמִשֶּׁתָּבִיא שְׁתֵּי שְׂעָרוֹת וְעַד שֶׁתִּיבָּגֵר – יֵשׁ לָהּ קְנָס וְאֵין לָהּ מֶכֶר, דִּבְרֵי רַבִּי מֵאִיר. שֶׁהָיָה רַבִּי מֵאִיר אוֹמֵר: כׇּל מָקוֹם שֶׁיֵּשׁ מֶכֶר – אֵין קְנָס, וְכׇל מָקוֹם שֶׁיֵּשׁ קְנָס – אֵין מֶכֶר.

Rav Yehuda said that **Rav said:** The *tanna* **is Rabbi Meir, as it is taught** in a *baraita*: **With regard to a minor from** the age of **one day old until she grows two** pubic **hairs, there is** the possibility of **sale for her,**[H] as her father may sell her as a Hebrew maidservant, **but there is no fine** paid **for her** if she is raped. **And once she grows two** pubic **hairs,** from that point **until she matures** into a grown woman **there is a fine for her,** as during that period she is a young woman, with regard to whom the Torah law of a rapist and a seducer applies, **but there is no** possibility of **sale for her.** Once she grows two hairs she is no longer under her father's control and can no longer be sold. This is **the statement of Rabbi Meir, as Rabbi Meir would state** a principle: **Any place where there is a sale, there is no fine; and any place where there is a fine, there is no sale.**

וַחֲכָמִים אוֹמְרִים: קְטַנָּה, מִבַּת שָׁלֹשׁ שָׁנִים וְיוֹם אֶחָד וְעַד שֶׁתִּיבָּגֵר – יֵשׁ לָהּ קְנָס. קְנָס אִין, מֶכֶר לָא?! אֵימָא:

And the Rabbis say: With regard to a minor from the age of **three years and one day old until she matures** into a grown woman, **there is a fine for her.**[H] The Gemara asks: Is that to say that a **fine, yes,** there is, but a **sale, no,** there is not? Do the Rabbis maintain that the father has no right to sell his minor daughter? The Gemara emends the text: **Say:**

HALAKHA

There is the possibility of sale for her – יֵשׁ לָהּ מֶכֶר: The father of a minor girl may sell her as a Hebrew maidservant from the day of her birth until she completes her twelfth year and grows two pubic hairs. However, once she has grown two pubic hairs, he may no longer sell her (Rambam *Sefer Kinyan, Hilkhot Avadim* 4:1).

When is there a fine for her – מָתַי יֵשׁ לָהּ קְנָס: A virgin is entitled to a fine for rape from the age of three years and one day old until puberty, in accordance with the opinion of the Rabbis. Although the unattributed mishna is in accordance with the opinion of Rabbi Meir and as a rule the *halakha* is ruled accordingly, the Gemara indicates that the mishna reflects an individual opinion. That is the ruling of Rif, the Rambam, and the Rosh. Rabbeinu Ḥananel and the Ra'avad rule in accordance with the unattributed mishna (Rambam *Sefer Nashim, Hilkhot Na'ara Betula* 1:8; *Shulḥan Arukh, Even HaEzer* 177:1).

אַף קְנָס בִּמְקוֹם מֶכֶר.

There is a **fine even in a place** where there is **sale.** That is, not only can a minor girl from the age of three be sold until she matures, but she also receives payment of the fine.

וְהָנֵי בְּנֵי קְנָסָא נִינְהוּ? וְאַמַּאי? אִיקְּרֵי כָּאן ״וְלוֹ תִהְיֶה לְאִשָּׁה״ – אִשָּׁה הָרְאוּיָה לוֹ! אָמַר רֵישׁ לָקִישׁ: ״נַעֲרָה״, ״נַעֲרָה״, ״הַנַּעֲרָה״; חַד – לְגוּפֵיהּ, וְחַד – לְאַתּוֹיֵי חַיָּיבֵי לָאוִין, וְחַד – לְאַתּוֹיֵי חַיָּיבֵי כָּרֵיתוֹת.

§ The Gemara questions the basic *halakha* that one who rapes young women of flawed lineage is liable to pay the fine: **And are these** young women **entitled** to the **fine?**[N] **But why? I read here** with regard to a rapist: **"And to him she shall be as a wife"** (Deuteronomy 22:29),[N] from which the Sages derived that only **a wife who is suitable for him** is eligible to receive payment of a fine from a rapist. **Reish Lakish said** that one verse states: "If a man finds a young woman" (Deuteronomy 22:28), and another states: "And he shall give to the father of the young woman" (Deuteronomy 22:29). This is tantamount to three mentions: **Young woman, young woman, the young woman,** as the superfluous definite article is interpreted as a third mention of the term. **One** mention is required **to** teach the matter **itself,** that one who rapes a young woman is liable to pay a fine; **and one** is **to include** payment of a fine to those young women for whose rape one is **liable for** violating **prohibitions; and one** is **to include** payment of a fine to those young women for whose rape one is **liable to** receive ***karet.***

רַב פַּפָּא אָמַר: ״בְּתוּלָה״, ״בְּתוּלוֹת״, ״הַבְּתוּלוֹת״ חַד – לְגוּפֵיהּ, וְחַד – לְאַתּוֹיֵי חַיָּיבֵי לָאוִין, וְחַד – לְאַתּוֹיֵי חַיָּיבֵי כָּרֵיתוֹת.

Rav Pappa said: This is derived from the *halakha* of the seducer, as the verses state: "And if a man seduce a virgin … he shall weigh money like the dowry of the virgins" (Exodus 22:15–16). This is tantamount to three mentions: **Virgin, virgins, the virgins. One** mention is required **to** teach the matter **itself; and one** is **to include** those young women for whose rape one is **liable for** violating **prohibitions; and one** is **to include** those young women for whom one who rapes them is **liable to** receive ***karet.***

וְרַב פַּפָּא מַאי טַעְמָא לָא אָמַר כְּרֵישׁ לָקִישׁ? הַהוּא מִיבָּעֵי לֵיהּ לִכְדַאֲבַיֵּי. דְּאָמַר אַבַּיֵּי: בָּא עָלֶיהָ וּמֵתָה – פָּטוּר, שֶׁנֶּאֱמַר ״וְנָתַן לַאֲבִי הַנַּעֲרָה״ – לַאֲבִי נַעֲרָה וְלֹא לַאֲבִי מֵתָה.

The Gemara asks: **And Rav Pappa, what is the reason** that **he did not cite** the source **as Reish Lakish** did? The Gemara answers: **That** derivation from the three instances of the term young woman is **required by him to** teach **in accordance with that** which **Abaye** said, **as Abaye said:** If one **engaged in** forced **intercourse with** a young woman **and she died**[H] before he stood trial, he is **exempt** from paying the fine, **as it is stated: "And he shall give to the father of the young woman"** (Deuteronomy 22:29). From the fact that the verse does not simply say: To her father, it is inferred: **To the father of the young woman and not to the father of a dead** woman. He is liable only if the young woman is still alive.

NOTES

And are these entitled to the fine – וְהָנֵי בְּנֵי קְנָסָא נִינְהוּ: Rashi indicates that this marks the beginning of a new discussion in which the Gemara analyzes the mishna itself. In the *Shita Mekubbetzet* there is an attempt to tie this matter to the previous one. Had the Gemara explained that the mishna is dealing only with the practical *halakha*, the mishna could be explained as teaching that the young women of flawed lineage are not entitled to the fine by Torah law. The Rabbis instituted that the fine should be paid, for the following reason: So that a sinner will not profit. After asserting that the mishna is dealing with Torah law, and that the fine is paid to the father of a young woman and not the father of a minor, this must be reconciled with the verses in the Torah.

I read here: "And to him she shall be a wife" – אִיקְּרֵי כָּאן וְלוֹ תִהְיֶה לְאִשָּׁה: The Ritva contends that this difficulty does not stem from the verse itself, as the verse can be explained in the opposite manner, i.e., that a rapist must marry the woman he raped even if she is unfit to marry him. The *Tosefot Rid* cites the Gemara later (40a), where the question is raised: Why doesn't the positive mitzva to marry the young woman override the prohibition against marrying her? Rather, the difficulty is based primarily on the interpretation of the Sages that "she shall be a wife" refers to a woman suitable for him.

HALAKHA

If one engaged in forced intercourse with a young woman and she died – בָּא עָלֶיהָ וּמֵתָה: If a young woman raped by a man died before he stood trial, he is exempt from paying the fine, as per the opinion of Abaye (Rambam *Sefer Nashim, Hilkhot Na'ara Betula* 1:15; *Tur, Even HaEzer* 177).

וְרֵישׁ לָקִישׁ מַאי טַעְמָא לָא אָמַר כְּרַב פַּפָּא? הַהוּא מִיבָּעֵי לֵיהּ לִגְזֵירָה שָׁוָה. דְּתַנְיָא: ״כֶּסֶף יִשְׁקוֹל כְּמוֹהַר הַבְּתוּלוֹת״ – שֶׁיְּהֵא זֶה כְּמוֹהַר הַבְּתוּלוֹת, וּמוֹהַר הַבְּתוּלוֹת כָּזֶה. וְרֵישׁ לָקִישׁ נַמִי, מִיבָּעֵי לֵיהּ לְכִדְאַבַּיֵי, וְרַב פַּפָּא נַמִי מִיבָּעֵי לֵיהּ לִגְזֵירָה שָׁוָה!

The Gemara asks: **And Reish Lakish, what is the reason that he did not cite** the source **as Rav Pappa** did? The Gemara answers: **That** derivation from the three instances of the term virgin is **required by him to** derive **a verbal analogy,**[B] **as it is taught** in a *baraita* that it is written with regard to a seducer: **"He shall weigh [*yishkol*] money like the dowry of the virgins"** (Exodus 22:16), from which it is derived **that this** fine of a seducer **should be** a sum of fifty *sela* **like the dowry of the virgins**[H] specified in the case of a rapist; **and the dowry of the virgins must be** paid in *sela* **like this** fine of the seducer. Therefore, Reish Lakish holds that no additional matters may be derived from the term virgins. The Gemara asks: **And** for **Reish Lakish too,** isn't it **required by him to** teach **in accordance with that** which **Abaye** said? **And** similarly, for **Rav Pappa,** isn't it **required by him to** derive **a verbal analogy?**

אֶלָּא שִׁיתָּא קְרָאֵי כְּתִיבִי: ״נַעֲרָה״ ״נַעֲרָה״ ״הַנַּעֲרָה״ ״בְּתוּלָה״ ״בְּתוּלוֹת״ ״הַבְּתוּלוֹת״, תְּרֵי – לְגוּפַיְיהוּ, חַד – לְכִדְאַבַּיֵי, וְחַד – לִגְזֵירָה שָׁוָה. אִיַּיתְּרוּ לֵיהּ תְּרֵי, חַד – לְאַתּוֹיֵי חַיָּיבֵי לָאוִין, וְחַד – לְאַתּוֹיֵי חַיָּיבֵי כָּרֵיתוֹת.

Rather, there are **six verses written,**[N] and both Reish Lakish and Rav Pappa derive matters from all of them. In the two passages discussing the rapist and the seducer, it is written: **Young woman, young woman, the young woman; virgin, virgins, the virgins. Two** mentions are required **to** teach the matters **themselves,** the basic *halakhot* of a rapist and a seducer; **one** mention is needed **to** teach **in accordance with that** which **Abaye** said; **and one** mention is necessary **to** derive **a verbal analogy** with regard to the dowry of virgins. **Two** mentions of the term **remain for him; one** is **to include** those young women for whose rape one is **liable for** violating **prohibitions, and one** is **to include** those young women for whom one who rapes them is **liable to** receive ***karet*.** Reish Lakish and Rav Pappa do not disagree; the derivation of each complements that of the other.

וּלְאַפּוֹקֵי מֵהַאי תַּנָּא; דְּתַנְיָא: ״וְלוֹ תִהְיֶה לְאִשָּׁה״, שִׁמְעוֹן הַתִּימְנִי אוֹמֵר: אִשָּׁה שֶׁיֵּשׁ בָּהּ הֲוָיָה. רַבִּי שִׁמְעוֹן בֶּן מְנַסְיָא אוֹמֵר: אִשָּׁה הָרְאוּיָה לְקַיְּימָהּ.

§ The Gemara comments: **And** the mishna comes **to exclude** the opinion **of this *tanna*,**[N] **as it is taught** in a *baraita* that it is written: **"And to him she shall be [*tihye*] as a wife"** (Deuteronomy 22:29). **Shimon HaTimni says:** This is referring to **a woman for whom there is betrothal [*havaya*].**[N] If one betroths a woman with whom relations are punishable by *karet*, the betrothal does not take effect. **Rabbi Shimon ben Menasya says:** This is referring to **a woman who is suitable for** him to **sustain,**[H] whom he need not divorce due to her flawed lineage.

מַאי בֵּינַיְיהוּ? אָמַר רַבִּי זֵירָא: מַמְזֶרֶת וּנְתִינָה אִיכָּא בֵּינַיְיהוּ. לְמַאן דַּאֲמַר יֵשׁ בָּהּ הֲוָיָה – הָא נַמִי יֵשׁ בָּהּ הֲוָיָה, לְמַאן דְּאָמַר רְאוּיָה לְקַיְּימָהּ – הָא אֵינָהּ רְאוּיָה לְקַיְּימָהּ.

The Gemara begins its analysis of the *baraita* with the question: **What is** the practical difference **between** the statements of Shimon HaTimni and Rabbi Shimon ben Menasya? The Gemara explains that **Rabbi Zeira said:** The difference **between their** opinions is with regard to a ***mamzeret* or a Gibeonite woman,** or any other woman who is forbidden but for whom betrothal takes effect. **According to the one who said** that the criterion is whether **there is betrothal,** for **this** woman **there is also betrothal.** If a Jewish man betroths a *mamzeret* or a Gibeonite woman, although it is prohibited to do so, the betrothal takes effect. However, **according to the one who said** that the criterion is whether the woman is **suitable for** him to **sustain, this** woman **is not suitable for** him to **sustain,** since due to the prohibition he is obligated to divorce her.

BACKGROUND

Verbal analogy – גְּזֵירָה שָׁוָה: This is a fundamental talmudic principle of biblical interpretation, appearing in all standard lists of exegetical principles: If the same word or phrase appears in two places in the Torah, and a certain *halakha* is stated explicitly in one of these places, one may infer, on the basis of a verbal analogy, that the same applies in the other case as well. Consequently, inferences drawn on the basis of verbal analogy rely on verbal identity rather than on conceptual similarity. For example, the Torah states concerning those convicted of certain types of sorcery: "Shall be put to death; they shall stone them with stones; their blood shall be upon them" (Leviticus 20:27). Since this verse employs the expression "their blood shall be upon them" when speaking of death by stoning, the Talmud infers by verbal analogy that in all cases where this expression is used, the punishment is capital punishment by stoning.

Generally, inferences are drawn through verbal analogy only if the same word or phrase appears in both of the verses being compared, although verbal analogies are occasionally drawn even if the terms are not identical, if their meanings are similar.

HALAKHA

That this should be like the dowry of the virgins – שֶׁיְּהֵא זֶה כְּמוֹהַר הַבְּתוּלוֹת: One who seduces or rapes a virgin young woman must pay a fine of fifty silver *sela* (Rambam *Sefer Nashim, Hilkhot Na'ara Betula* 1:1).

A woman who is suitable for him to sustain – אִשָּׁה הָרְאוּיָה לְקַיְּימָהּ: Although the Torah states that a rapist is obligated to marry his victim, if she is forbidden to him, even if the prohibition is due to a positive mitzva or by rabbinic law, he may not marry her, in accordance with the opinion of Rabbi Shimon ben Menasya (see *Kesef Mishne* and *Leḥem Mishne*). The *Halakhot Gedolot* states that this *halakha* is based on the later mishna (40a) (Rambam *Sefer Nashim, Hilkhot Na'ara Betula* 1:5; *Shulḥan Arukh, Even HaEzer* 177:4).

NOTES

There are six verses written – שִׁיתָּא קְרָאֵי כְּתִיבִי: In other words, there is no dispute between Reish Lakish and Rav Pappa. Each cited different aspects of the same exposition. One of them specified the terms that include those liable for violating prohibitions, while the other explained the terms that include those liable to receive *karet* (Ritva).

And to exclude the opinion of this *tanna* – וּלְאַפּוֹקֵי מֵהַאי תַּנָּא: The *Tosafot Yeshanim* and the Rosh maintain that the mishna is actually excluding the opinions of two *tanna'im*, Shimon HaTimni and Rabbi Shimon ben Menasya, and the phrase: This *tanna*, is referring to the *tanna* who taught that *baraita* in which their opinions were cited. However, see the alternative versions of the text for readings that do not require this somewhat implausible interpretation.

For whom there is betrothal [*havaya*] – שֶׁיֵּשׁ בָּהּ הֲוָיָה: The term *havaya* is taken from the term used in the Torah: "And if a priest's daughter be married [*tihye*] to a common man" (Leviticus 22:12); "And to him she shall be [*tihye*] as a wife" (Deuteronomy 22:29). *Havaya*, which literally means being, means that the betrothal is effective. Although there is a fundamental dispute between *amora'im* in tractate *Temura* with regard to whether performance of a prohibited action can lead to a halakhically valid result, it is clear from the verses that in certain cases betrothal is effective even though it contravenes Torah law. This is true even according to the extreme opinion of Rabbi Akiva, who says that as a rule, even in cases where one merely violated a prohibition, a child born of that union is a *mamzer*. In this regard, there are many different levels of prohibition and circumstances that affect betrothal differently. Clearly, betrothal of an object or an animal does not take effect. Similarly, since betrothal and marriage are relevant only within the Jewish people, betrothal of a gentile or a slave does not take effect. With regard to other prohibitions there are differences of opinion as to whether the prohibition prevents the betrothal from taking effect, or whether it takes effect only in the sense that it is prohibited for the woman to marry another without first receiving a bill of divorce.

וּלְרַבִּי עֲקִיבָא, דְּאָמַר: אֵין קִידּוּשִׁין תּוֹפְסִין בְּחַיָּיבֵי לָאוִין, מַאי בֵּינַיְיהוּ? אִיכָּא בֵּינַיְיהוּ אַלְמָנָה לְכֹהֵן גָּדוֹל, כְּרַבִּי סִימַאי. דְּתַנְיָא, רַבִּי סִימַאי אוֹמֵר: מִן הַכֹּל עוֹשֶׂה רַבִּי עֲקִיבָא מַמְזֵרִין, חוּץ מֵאַלְמָנָה לְכֹהֵן גָּדוֹל, שֶׁהֲרֵי אָמְרָה תּוֹרָה "לֹא יִקָּח...וְלֹא יְחַלֵּל" – חִילּוּלִין הוּא עוֹשֶׂה, וְאֵין עוֹשֶׂה מַמְזֵרִין.

The Gemara asks: **And according to Rabbi Akiva,**[N] **who said: Betrothal does not take effect for** women for whose rape one is **liable for** violating **prohibitions, what is** the difference **between them?** According to his opinion, betrothal of a *mamzeret* does not take effect either. The Gemara answers: The difference **between their** statements is the case of **a widow** raped **by a High Priest, in accordance with** the opinion of **Rabbi Simai, as it is taught** in a *baraita* that **Rabbi Simai says: Rabbi Akiva deems** children **from all** illicit relations *mamzerim*, **except for** a child born **from a widow to a High Priest, as the Torah said:** "A widow and a divorcée **he shall not take… and he shall not profane** [*yeḥallel*] his seed among his people" (Leviticus 21:14–15), from which it is derived: If he has a child with a widow **he creates *ḥillulin*,**[N] i.e., the male offspring of those relations is a *ḥalal*, disqualified from the priesthood, and the female offspring is a *ḥalala*, unfit to marry a priest, **but he does not create *mamzerim*.** Apparently, in that case, the betrothal does take effect.

וּלְרַבִּי יְשֵׁבָב, דְּאָמַר: בּוֹאוּ וְנִצְוַח עַל עֲקִיבָא בֶּן יוֹסֵף, שֶׁהָיָה אוֹמֵר: כָּל שֶׁאֵין לוֹ בִּיאָה בְּיִשְׂרָאֵל הַוָּלָד מַמְזֵר. מַאי בֵּינַיְיהוּ? אִיכָּא בֵּינַיְיהוּ

The Gemara asks: **And according to Rabbi Yeshevav, who said: Come, let us scream at Akiva ben Yosef,** who is proliferating *mamzerim*, **as he would say:** With regard to **anyone who does not have** the possibility of permitted **relations in the Jewish people,** including a widow with a High Priest, **the offspring is a *mamzer*, what is** the difference **between their** opinions, between the one who said that a fine is paid to women with whom the betrothal takes effect and the one who said that a fine is paid to women suitable for one to sustain? Rabbi Yeshevav maintains that betrothal does not take effect even in the case of a widow to a High Priest. The Gemara answers: **There is** a difference **between them** with regard to

NOTES

And according to Rabbi Akiva – וּלְרַבִּי עֲקִיבָא: *Tosafot* note that this question is irrelevant according to the opinion of Rabbi Shimon HaTimni, as the Gemara in *Yevamot* states explicitly that he disagrees with Rabbi Akiva in this regard and maintains that betrothal takes effect in cases of women for whom one who rapes them is liable for violating a prohibition. Instead, the difficulty is in accordance with the opinion of Rabbi Shimon ben Menasya, whose opinion the Gemara seeks to reconcile with that of Rabbi Akiva. The Ramban cites a similar answer in the name of Rabbi Avraham *Av Bet Din*, and other early commentaries explain likewise. The Ra'ah, however, maintains that the question here is not how to reconcile the opinions of these *tanna'im* with that of Rabbi Akiva. Rather, the Gemara is asking: According to Rabbi Akiva, is there a difference between the two interpretations: A woman for whom there is betrothal, and: A woman who is suitable for him to sustain?

He creates *ḥillulin* – חִילּוּלִין הוּא עוֹשֶׂה: *Tosafot* discuss a different aspect of this dilemma at length: Is *mamzer* status of offspring tied to the question of whether or not there is *havaya*, i.e., whether or not betrothal takes effect, between the man and the woman? They maintain that according to most opinions, *mamzer* status is causally related to the betrothal taking effect. In other words, in any case where betrothal does not take effect, the offspring is a *mamzer*. Admittedly, there are exceptions to this principle, as the child of a Jewish man and a gentile woman or a maidservant is not a *mamzer*. However, that is because no relationship outside the congregation of Israel leads to *mamzer* status, which exists only with regard to Jews. See *Tosafot* for their proof that not everyone agrees that there is necessarily a link between the betrothal not taking effect and *mamzer* status.

Perek **III**
Daf **30** Amud **a**

חַיָּיבֵי עֲשֵׂה – מִצְרִי וַאֲדוֹמִי.

intercourse with women for which one is **liable for** violating a **positive** mitzva,[N] e.g., **an Egyptian** convert **and an Edomite** convert (see Deuteronomy 23:8–9). If he raped a first- or second-generation Egyptian or Edomite convert, even Rabbi Yeshevav agrees that the child is not a *mamzer*, as the betrothal takes effect. On the other hand, it is prohibited for him to sustain her as a wife.

הָנִיחָא לְרַבִּי יְשֵׁבָב, אִי לְאַפּוֹקֵי מִטַּעְמָא דְּרַבִּי סִימַאי קָאָתֵי – שַׁפִּיר. אֶלָּא אִי טַעְמָא דְּנַפְשֵׁיהּ קָאָמַר, כָּל שֶׁאֵין לוֹ בִּיאָה בְּיִשְׂרָאֵל הַוָּלָד מַמְזֵר – וַאֲפִילּוּ חַיָּיבֵי עֲשֵׂה, מַאי בֵּינַיְיהוּ?

The Gemara asks: **This works out well according to Rabbi Yeshevav if he is coming to reject the opinion of Rabbi Simai.** If Rabbi Yeshevav merely takes issue with Rabbi Simai, who said that all offspring of forbidden relations are *mamzerim* according to Rabbi Akiva except for those resulting from relations between a widow and a High Priest, then it may **well** be explained that Rabbi Yeshevav holds that Rabbi Akiva rules that betrothal does not take effect and that there is *mamzerut* when one violates the prohibitions of the priesthood. **However, if he is stating his own opinion,** independent of Rabbi Simai's statement, his ruling is more comprehensive and leads to the conclusion that in the case of relations with **anyone who does not have** the possibility of permitted **relations among the Jewish people, the child is a *mamzer*, and** this is true **even** of women for relations with whom one is **liable for** violating **positive** mitzvot, e.g., Egyptian or Edomite converts. In that case, **what is** the difference **between** the opinions of Shimon HaTimni and Rabbi Shimon ben Menasya?

NOTES

Intercourse with women for which one is liable for violating a positive mitzva – חַיָּיבֵי עֲשֵׂה: The category of positive mitzvot includes all prohibitions that are formulated as a positive mitzva rather than using a negative phrase, e.g.: You may not, lest, do not, take care. One who transgresses and fails to fulfill the command has violated a positive mitzva. In the beginning of tractate *Yevamot* and elsewhere, the Gemara discusses the relative significance of positive mitzvot and prohibitions. There is a fundamental difference between them with regard to punishment: Prohibitions are generally punishable by lashes, whereas positive mitzvot are not. Sexual relations with an Egyptian or Edomite convert are forbidden by a positive mitzva, as explained by Rashi, but there are also other examples of relations forbidden by a positive mitzva. As the Gemara will immediately explain, relations between a non-virgin and a High Priest are also forbidden by a positive mitzva.

אִיכָּא בֵּינַיְיהוּ בְּעוּלָה לְכֹהֵן גָּדוֹל. וּמַאי שְׁנָא? דַּהֲוָה לֵיהּ עֲשֵׂה שֶׁאֵינוֹ שָׁוֶה בַּכֹּל.

The Gemara answers: **There is** a difference **between them** in the case of **a non-virgin** raped **by a High Priest.**[N] **And** the Gemara asks: Here, too, she is a woman for relations with whom one is liable for violating a positive mitzva, as the High Priest fails to fulfill the mitzva "But a virgin of his own people shall he take to wife" (Leviticus 21:14). If Rabbi Akiva rules that betrothal does not take effect when a positive mitzva is violated, **what is different** about this case? The Gemara answers: It is different **because it is a positive** mitzva **whose** application **is not equal for all.**[N] There are two lenient aspects to this mitzva: It is a positive mitzva and not a prohibition, and it applies only to the High Priest and not to all Jews. Even Rabbi Yeshevav would agree that according to Rabbi Akiva, a child born from relations between a High Priest and a non-virgin is not a *mamzer*. However, the High Priest may not sustain the woman as his wife. Therefore, this case is the practical difference between the statements of Shimon HaTimni and Rabbi Shimon ben Menasya.

אָמַר רַב חִסְדָּא: הַכֹּל מוֹדִים בְּבָא עַל הַנִּדָּה שֶׁמְּשַׁלֵּם קְנָס. לְמַאן דְּאָמַר יֵשׁ בָּהּ הֲוָיָה – הָא נַמִי יֵשׁ בָּהּ הֲוָיָה, לְמַאן דְּאָמַר רְאוּיָה לְקַיְּימָהּ – הָא נַמִי רְאוּיָה לְקַיְּימָהּ.

§ **Rav Ḥisda said: Everyone agrees with regard to one who engaged in** forced **intercourse with a menstruating woman**[N] **that he pays** the **fine.** He elaborates: **According to the one who says** that the criterion is whether **there is betrothal,** for **this** woman **too there is betrothal.**[N] **According to the one who says** that the criterion is whether the woman is **suitable for** him to **sustain, this** woman **is suitable for** him to **sustain.**

NOTES

A non-virgin raped by a High Priest – בְּעוּלָה לְכֹהֵן גָּדוֹל: All commentaries grapple with the following fundamental question, which requires explanation of the case of a non-virgin and a High Priest: If the case is that a High Priest raped a non-virgin, he cannot possibly be liable to pay the fine, as the Torah imposes the fine only for rape of a virgin. The case must perforce involve a more intricate situation. Rashi and the Ra'avad explain that the young woman had engaged in anal intercourse, and therefore she is not considered a non-virgin in terms of the prohibition of a High Priest; however, in terms of the fine, she maintains the status of a virgin, even if she engaged in anal intercourse many times. Most commentaries, though, including *Tosafot*, the Ramban, and the Rashba, accept Rabbeinu Ḥananel's interpretation that it refers to a virgin young woman who was raped by the High Priest himself. He thereby rendered her a non-virgin, whose betrothal takes effect, but it is prohibited for him to remain married to her. In the *Shita Mekubbetzet* Rashi's explanation is questioned: If the anal intercourse rendered her a non-virgin in terms of the High Priest, when he rapes her he renders her a *ḥalala*. Consequently, she is forbidden to him by a Torah prohibition and the betrothal does not take effect. The answer in the *Shita Mekubbetzet* is that although he renders her a *ḥalala* by means of the rape, he incurs the obligation to pay the fine when he initiated intercourse, and she is rendered a *ḥalala* at its conclusion.

A positive mitzva whose application is not equal for all – עֲשֵׂה שֶׁאֵינוֹ שָׁוֶה בַּכֹּל: The Gemara explains in several places that a mitzva that is universally applicable, whether it is a positive mitzva or a prohibition, is more severe than one whose applicability is selective. Rabbi Akiva Eiger notes that the prohibition rendering a widow forbidden to a High Priest is also not universally applicable, just like the mitzva that renders a non-virgin forbidden. The essence of his answer, which is rejected by the Rashash, is that the mitzva that renders a non-virgin forbidden to a High Priest has a twofold leniency: It is a positive mitzva, and it is a mitzva that is not universally applicable. The Meiri explains similarly that the reason for leniency with regard to this mitzva is that it applies exclusively to the High Priest and not even to other priests. Furthermore, there are additional lenient aspects to this prohibition, as the Gemara states in tractate *Yevamot*: Ultimately she will be a non-virgin after her marriage to him, and it stands to reason that the fact that the prohibition will eventually be negated on its own renders it a lenient prohibition. In fact, some assert that if a High Priest married a virgin that he raped, he need not divorce her after the fact (see *Tosafot*).

Everyone agrees with regard to one who engaged in forced intercourse with a menstruating woman – הַכֹּל מוֹדִים בְּבָא עַל הַנִּדָּה: The phrase: Everyone agrees, does not include all of the Sages, as from the statement of Rabbi Neḥunya ben HaKana it appears that one who rapes a menstruating woman does not pay the fine. Admittedly, some take issue with this assertion, but the *Tosafot Yeshanim*, citing the Maharam MiRotenburg, bring conclusive proof from the *Tosefta* in which it is explicitly stated that Rabbi Neḥunya ben HaKana exempts one who rapes a menstruating woman from paying the fine. Rather, the phrase: Everyone agrees, refers to the dispute between Shimon HaTimni and Rabbi Shimon ben Menasya, as according to the criteria established by both of them he is obligated to pay the fine, as there, betrothal with a menstruating woman takes effect and she is suitable for him to sustain as his wife (see *Tosafot* and Ritva). This is the understanding in the Babylonian Talmud; however, in the Jerusalem Talmud the understanding is the opposite, and Rabbi Neḥunya ben HaKana agrees that one who has relations with a menstruating woman or with his wife's sister is liable to pay the fine. The reason is that these relationships can become permitted over the course of time, when the menstruating woman immerses in a ritual bath and when one's wife dies, respectively. However, one who rapes a woman that is forbidden to him by a prohibition punishable by *karet* and whom will remain permanently forbidden to him is exempt from payment of the fine. Rabbi Shimon ben Menasya, in contrast, contends that wherever there is liability to receive *karet* he is exempt from payment of the fine.

A menstruating woman has betrothal – נִדָּה יֵשׁ בָּהּ הֲוָיָה: This is derived from the verse "And her menstruation is [*tehi*] upon him" (Leviticus 15:24), which indicates that the *havaya* of betrothal is effective even when she is menstruating. Although the early commentaries disagree as to whether or not marriage to a menstruating woman takes effect, everyone agrees that her betrothal takes effect (see Ritva).

וּלְאַפּוּקֵי מִדְּרַבִּי נְחוּנְיָא בֶּן הַקָּנָה. דְּתַנְיָא: רַבִּי נְחוּנְיָא בֶּן הַקָּנָה הָיָה עוֹשֶׂה אֶת יוֹם הַכִּפּוּרִים כְּשַׁבָּת לְתַשְׁלוּמִין; מַה שַּׁבָּת מִתְחַיֵּיב בְּנַפְשׁוֹ וּפָטוּר מִן הַתַּשְׁלוּמִין – אַף יוֹם הַכִּפּוּרִים מִתְחַיֵּיב בְּנַפְשׁוֹ וּפָטוּר מִן הַתַּשְׁלוּמִין.

§ The Gemara comments: **And** the mishna's ruling that one who has relations with his sister is liable to pay the fine comes **to exclude** the opinion **of Rabbi Neḥunya ben HaKana,**[PN] **as it is taught** in a *baraita*: **Rabbi Neḥunya ben HaKana would render Yom Kippur like Shabbat with regard to payment** for damages.[N] **Just as** one who intentionally desecrates **Shabbat is liable to** receive the **death** penalty **and** is therefore **exempt from** the obligation of **payment** for damages caused while desecrating Shabbat, **so too,** one who intentionally desecrates **Yom Kippur is liable to** receive the **death** penalty **and** is therefore **exempt from** the obligation of **payment** for damages caused while desecrating Yom Kippur.

מַאי טַעֲמָא דְּרַבִּי נְחוּנְיָא בֶּן הַקָּנָה? אֲמַר אַבַּיֵּי: נֶאֱמַר "אָסוֹן" בִּידֵי אָדָם וְנֶאֱמַר "אָסוֹן" בִּידֵי שָׁמַיִם, מָה "אָסוֹן" הָאָמוּר בִּידֵי אָדָם פָּטוּר מִן הַתַּשְׁלוּמִין, אַף "אָסוֹן" הָאָמוּר בִּידֵי שָׁמַיִם פָּטוּר מִן הַתַּשְׁלוּמִין.

The Gemara asks: **What is the rationale** for the opinion **of Rabbi Neḥunya ben HaKana? Abaye said: It states** the word **harm at the hands of man,** in the verse "But if any harm follow, then you shall give a soul for a soul" (Exodus 21:23) **and it states** the word **harm at the hand of Heaven,** in the verse in which Jacob states: "My son shall not descend with you…and harm befalls him on the way" (Genesis 42:38). **Just as** with regard to **harm that is stated at the hands of man,** e.g., one who kills and is liable to be executed, one is **exempt from the** associated **payment,**[H] **so too,** with regard to **harm that is stated at the hand of Heaven,** one is **exempt from the** associated **payment.**

מַתְקִיף לָהּ רַב אַדָּא בַּר אַהֲבָה: מִמַּאי דְּכִי קָא מַזְהַר לְהוּ יַעֲקֹב לִבְנֵיהּ עַל צִינִּים וּפַחִים, דְּבִידֵי שָׁמַיִם נִינְהוּ? דִּלְמָא עַל אַרְיָא וְגַנָּבֵי, דְּבִידֵי אָדָם נִינְהוּ! אַטּוּ יַעֲקֹב אַהָא אַזְהַר, אַהָא לָא אַזְהַר? יַעֲקֹב עַל כָּל מִילֵּי אַזְהַר.

Rav Adda bar Ahava strongly **objects to this: From where** is it derived **that when Jacob is warning his sons** he is warning them **about cold and heat** [*tzinim paḥim*],[LN] **which are at the hand of Heaven? Perhaps** he was warning them **about a lion and thieves, which are** harm **at the hands of man,** meaning that unlike heat and cold, these dangers are not calibrated by God. The Gemara refutes this: **Is that to say** that **Jacob warned** them **about this** harm at the hand of man, but **about that** harm at the hand of Heaven **he did not warn** them? **Jacob warned** them **about all** potentially harmful **matters** that might befall Benjamin, not merely one particular form of catastrophe.

וְצִינִּים פַּחִים בִּידֵי שָׁמַיִם נִינְהוּ? וְהָתַנְיָא: הַכֹּל בִּידֵי שָׁמַיִם חוּץ מִצִּינִּים פַּחִים, שֶׁנֶּאֱמַר "צִנִּים פַּחִים בְּדֶרֶךְ עִקֵּשׁ שׁוֹמֵר נַפְשׁוֹ יִרְחַק מֵהֶם"! וְתוּ: אַרְיָא וְגַנָּבֵי בִּידֵי אָדָם נִינְהוּ? וְהָאָמַר רַב יוֹסֵף, וְכֵן תָּנֵי רַבִּי חִיָּיא: מִיּוֹם שֶׁחָרַב בֵּית הַמִּקְדָּשׁ, אַף עַל פִּי שֶׁבָּטְלוּ סַנְהֶדְרִין – אַרְבַּע מִיתוֹת לֹא בָּטְלוּ? לֹא בָּטְלוּ?! הָא בָּטְלוּ לְהוּ! אֶלָּא:

The Gemara asks: **And are cold** and **heat at the hand of Heaven? Isn't it taught** in a *baraita*: **All** matters are **at the hand of Heaven except for cold** and **heat, as it is stated: "Cold** and **heat are on the path of the crooked, he who guards his soul shall keep far from them"** (Proverbs 22:5)? This indicates that cold and heat are forms of harm caused by man, from which one can protect himself. **And furthermore, are a lion and thieves** forms of harm **at the hands of man? But didn't Rav Yosef say, and similarly,** didn't **Rabbi Ḥiyya teach** a *baraita*: **From the day that the Temple was destroyed,**[N] **although the Sanhedrin was abolished** the **four death** penalties[B] **were not abolished?** The Gemara asks: Were they **not abolished?** It is clear **that they were abolished,** as today there is neither Sanhedrin nor capital punishment. **Rather,** it means that although there are no court-imposed executions,

PERSONALITIES

Rabbi Neḥunya ben HaKana – רַבִּי נְחוּנְיָא בֶּן הַקָּנָה: Rabbi Neḥunya ben HaKana was a *tanna* during the generation when the Second Temple was destroyed. It is possible that he is the same *tanna* occasionally referred to as Rabbi Neḥunya the Great.

Apparently, he had a close relationship with the students of Rabban Yoḥanan ben Zakkai.

Few of Rabbi Neḥunya ben HaKana's halakhic statements were preserved; however, several aggadic statements are cited in his name. The prayer that he recited upon entering the study hall (*Berakhot* 28b) is widely known. Later in this tractate (28a) his positive attributes and his modesty are recounted. Rabbi Neḥunya is credited with development of the hermeneutical method of generalization and detail, and it is generally attributed to Rabbi Yishmael, his most prominent student. Authorship of *Sefer HaBahir*, a kabbalistic midrash, is also attributed to him, as is the prayer: Please, with the might [*ana bekho'aḥ*].

Kana is the name of a city in the tribal territory of Asher (Joshua 19:28). Perhaps his title is attributable to the place where he lived.

HALAKHA

Death at the hands of man, he is exempt from payment – מִיתָה בִּידֵי אָדָם פָּטוּר מִן הַתַּשְׁלוּמִין: If one committed a transgression for which he was liable to be executed, even if he was not forewarned and therefore not actually punished, he is nevertheless exempt from any payment for which he may be liable due to this transgression (Rambam *Sefer Nashim, Hilkhot Na'ara Betula* 1:14 and *Sefer Nezikim, Hilkhot Geneiva* 3:2; *Shulḥan Arukh, Ḥoshen Mishpat* 351).

LANGUAGE

Cold and heat [*tzinim paḥim*] – צִינִּים פַּחִים: Most commentaries on the book of Proverbs agree that *tzinim paḥim* means thorns and traps. However, opinions are divided with regard to its use in the Talmud. *Tosafot* cite several different explanations for these words. Some interpret *tzinim paḥim* as gale-force cold winds (Rabbeinu Gershom on *Bava Batra* 144b). Those commentaries who translate *paḥim* as heat apparently connect it to the term for coals, *peḥamim*, as in the verse "Upon the wicked He shall rain coals [*paḥim*], fire, and brimstone" (Psalms 11:6).

BACKGROUND

The four death penalties – אַרְבַּע מִיתוֹת: There are four forms of court-administered capital punishment in the Torah. They are, in diminishing order of severity: Stoning, burning, decapitation, and strangulation. Capital cases are adjudicated by a court consisting of twenty-three judges.

NOTES

To exclude the opinion of Rabbi Neḥunya ben HaKana – לְאַפּוּקֵי מִדְּרַבִּי נְחוּנְיָא בֶּן הַקָּנָה: Some commentaries maintain that this statement relates to that which Rav Ḥisda said: Everyone agrees with regard to one who engaged in forced intercourse with a menstruating woman that he pays the fine. In that statement, Rav Ḥisda rejects the opinion of Rabbi Neḥunya (*Tosafot*; *Shita Yeshana*, cited in *Shita Mekubbetzet*). However, Rashi and others claim that the Gemara relates to the *halakha* in the mishna with regard to one who rapes his sister. Proof is cited in the *Shita Mekubbetzet* for Rashi's explanation from the fact that the mishna adds the phrase: Although there is *karet* for them, which underscores the fact that despite the prohibition involving *karet* Rabbi Neḥunya's opinion is not taken into account.

The opinion of Rabbi Neḥunya ben HaKana – שִׁיטַת רַבִּי נְחוּנְיָא בֶּן הַקָּנָה: Rabbi Neḥunya's opinion is based on two fundamental reasons that are basically accepted by most *tanna'im*. First, one is not punished twice for the same transgression, as the Gemara later explains at length. Second, there is a principle that one receives the greater of two punishments. Rabbi Neḥunya reasons: Since this transgression entails *karet*, it is sufficient that one receive that severe punishment and not be liable to pay. Another factor taken into consideration by Rabbi Neḥunya, as mentioned in the Gemara briefly, is that wherever the Torah imposes the death penalty it does not render one liable to receive any other punishment, and *karet* is essentially death at the hand of Heaven. The Rabbis respond that these principles apply only to punishments administered by man, but not to penalties administered by Heaven. Furthermore, when one's punishment is at the hand of Heaven he can repent, gain atonement for his sin, and avert his punishment. That is not the case with regard to punishments administered by man (Meiri).

Cold and heat [*tzinim paḥim*] – צִינִּים פַּחִים: Rashi and most commentaries explain these words as meaning cold and heat. The Rashbam maintains that *tzinim* is a form of the word *tzina*, meaning cold, while *paḥim* means trap (see *Tosafot*). Rashi and other commentaries explain the verse in Proverbs in an entirely different manner, unrelated to cold and heat. In any case, the idea is that most suffering cannot be prevented no matter what precautions a person takes, except for those matters caused by negligence (see *Tosafot*; Ramban).

From the day that the Temple was destroyed – מִיּוֹם שֶׁחָרַב בֵּית הַמִּקְדָּשׁ: *Tosafot* question this statement, as it is well known that the courts ceased adjudicating capital cases before the destruction of the Temple. They answer that even so, these judgments were not entirely abrogated at the time. Furthermore, as long as the Temple was standing it afforded atonement for certain types of sins through the priestly vestments and the scapegoat. The *Shita Yeshana*, cited in the *Shita Mekubbetzet*, explains that Rabbi Ḥiyya spoke in general terms and did not insist on precision with regard to the date, as it roughly coincided with the destruction. Likewise, it can be explained that even while the Temple was standing, if the Sanhedrin did not have the authority to impose judgment, violators would be punished at the hand of Heaven.

דִּין אַרְבַּע מִיתוֹת לֹא בָּטְלוּ: מִי שֶׁנִּתְחַיֵּיב סְקִילָה – אוֹ נוֹפֵל מִן הַגַּג, אוֹ חַיָּה דּוֹרַסְתּוֹ. וּמִי שֶׁנִּתְחַיֵּיב שְׂרֵיפָה – אוֹ נוֹפֵל בִּדְלֵיקָה, אוֹ נָחָשׁ מַכִּישׁוֹ. וּמִי שֶׁנִּתְחַיֵּיב הֲרִיגָה – אוֹ נִמְסָר לַמַּלְכוּת, אוֹ לִיסְטִים בָּאִין עָלָיו. וּמִי שֶׁנִּתְחַיֵּיב חֶנֶק – אוֹ טוֹבֵעַ בַּנָּהָר, אוֹ מֵת בִּסְרוּנְכִי? אֶלָּא אֵיפוּךְ: אַרְיָא וְגַנָּבֵי – בִּידֵי שָׁמַיִם, צִינִּים וּפַחִים – בִּידֵי אָדָם.

the **punishment** of the **four death** penalties **was not abolished.**[N] How so? **One who was liable** to be executed by **stoning either falls from the roof or a beast tramples him.** That is similar to stoning, which involves being pushed off an elevated place and then stoned. **And one who was liable** to be executed by **burning either falls into a conflagration or a snake bites him,** which creates a burning sensation. **And one who was liable** to be executed by **decapitation** is **either handed over to the** ruling **monarchy** for execution by sword, **or bandits attack** and kill **him. And one who was liable** to be executed by **strangulation either drowns in a river, or dies of diphtheria** [*serunki*].[L] **Rather, reverse** the order of the previous statement: **A lion and thieves** are cases of harm **at the hand of Heaven,**[N] while **cold and heat** are cases of harm **at the hands of man.**[N]

רָבָא אָמַר: טַעְמָא דְּרַבִּי נְחוּנְיָא בֶּן הַקָּנָה מֵהָכָא: ״וְאִם הַעְלֵם יַעְלִימוּ עַם הָאָרֶץ אֶת עֵינֵיהֶם מִן הָאִישׁ הַהוּא בְּתִתּוֹ מִזַּרְעוֹ לַמֹּלֶךְ וְשַׂמְתִּי אֲנִי אֶת פָּנַי בָּאִישׁ הַהוּא וּבְמִשְׁפַּחְתּוֹ וְהִכְרַתִּי אוֹתוֹ״ אָמְרָה תּוֹרָה: כָּרֵת שֶׁלִּי כְּמִיתָה שֶׁלָּכֶם, מַה מִּיתָה שֶׁלָּכֶם – פָּטוּר מִן הַתַּשְׁלוּמִין, אַף כָּרֵת שֶׁלִּי – פָּטוּר מִן הַתַּשְׁלוּמִין.

Rava said an additional explanation: **The rationale** for the opinion **of Rabbi Neḥunya ben HaKana is from here.** It is written that one who gives his children to Molech is liable to be executed by stoning: **"And if the people of the land do at all hide their eyes**[N] **from that man, when he gives of his seed to Molech,** and do not put him to death; **then I will set My face against that man and against his family, and will cut him off** [*vehikhrati*]" (Leviticus 20:4–5). Through the juxtaposition in this verse **the Torah said: My** *karet* is **like your death** penalty; **just as** one who is liable to receive **your death** penalty **is exempt from the** associated **payments, so too,** one who is liable to receive **My** *karet* **is exempt from the** associated **payments.**

מַאי אִיכָּא בֵּין רָבָא לְאַבַּיֵי? אִיכָּא בֵּינַיְיהוּ זָר שֶׁאָכַל תְּרוּמָה. לְאַבַּיֵי פָּטוּר, וּלְרָבָא חַיָּיב.

The Gemara asks: **What** practical difference **is there between** the opinions of **Rava and Abaye** with regard to the rationale for the opinion of Rabbi Neḥunya ben HaKana? The Gemara answers: **There is** a difference **between them** with regard to **a non-priest who** intentionally **ate** *teruma*.[HN] According **to Abaye** he is **exempt** from paying the priest the value of the *teruma*, as a non-priest who ate *teruma* is liable to receive death at the hand of Heaven. Abaye maintains that the legal status of all forms of death at the hand of Heaven is equivalent to that of death at the hands of man, and therefore, one is exempt from payment. **And** according **to Rava,** who derives the rationale from the juxtaposition between *karet* and death at the hands of man, since a non-priest who ate *teruma* is not liable to receive *karet*, he is **liable** to pay the priest for the *teruma* that he ate.

LANGUAGE

Diphtheria [*serunki*] – **סְרוּנְכִי**: An extension of the Hebrew/Aramaic roots *samekh, nun, kaf* or *shin, nun, kuf*, and the verb, *lesarnek*, meaning strangulation. The reference here is most likely to diphtheria, which causes the blockage of the trachea and death by strangulation.

HALAKHA

A non-priest who ate *teruma* – **זָר שֶׁאָכַל תְּרוּמָה**: A non-priest who intentionally ate *teruma* is liable to receive death at the hand of Heaven. If he was forewarned, he is flogged and need not pay for the *teruma* he ate, as one does not both receive lashes and pay. The *halakha* is not decided based on the Gemara here, which is in accordance with the opinion of Rabbi Neḥunya. Rather, it is in accordance with the conclusion in tractate *Terumot* of the Jerusalem Talmud (Rambam *Sefer Zera'im*, *Hilkhot Terumot* 6:6 and *Kesef Mishne* there).

NOTES

The punishment of the four death penalties was not abolished – **דִּין אַרְבַּע מִיתוֹת לֹא בָּטְלוּ**: *Tosafot* ask: Aren't there many wicked people who die peacefully and are not punished in these manners? They answer that sometimes the punishment is waived if they repented. Similarly, the Rambam writes that their other merits can protect them, as one is not in a position to assess the actions of others and determine the precise punishment that they deserve. In the *Shita Mekubbetzet* and in the commentary of the Ritva, the explanation is that punishment meted out in this world corresponds to the four death penalties. Not all wicked people are punished in this manner, however, as some enjoy peace in this world to facilitate their more severe punishment in the next world. In the *Shita Mekubbetzet* it is explained that only those who were forewarned and sinned in the presence of witnesses are subject to these punishments, and if the courts had the authority they would have administered the four death penalties.

A lion and thieves are at the hand of Heaven – **אַרְיָא וְגַנָּבֵי בִּידֵי שָׁמַיִם**: The early commentaries ask: How can any harm be deemed at the hands of man, if even these are considered to be caused by Heaven? They answer, based on Rashi, that when the verse states: "And yet no harm follow, he shall be punished" (Exodus 21:22), harm refers to court-administered death penalties (Ramban). The Ra'ah likewise explains that since the death penalty is imposed due to the misguided choices of the sinner, it is parallel to cold or heat, as there too one's failure to take precautions leads to harm.

Cold and heat are at the hands of man – **צִינִּים וּפַחִים בִּידֵי אָדָם**: Rabbeinu Ḥananel explains that suffering from cold and heat is sometimes at the hands of man, such as when one carelessly exposes himself to extreme temperatures, and sometimes at the hand of God. Some commentaries maintain that the version of the Gemara before Rabbeinu Ḥananel reflects this explanation.

And if the people of the land do at all hide their eyes – **וְאִם הַעְלֵם יַעְלִימוּ עַם הָאָרֶץ**: In the *Shita Mekubbetzet*, the question is raised: Why does the Gemara cite this verse rather than the preceding one: "And I will set My face against that man, and will cut him off from among his people, because he has given of his seed unto Molech" (Leviticus 20:3)? The answer is that the preceding verse first refers to one who sinned intentionally but without forewarning or without witnesses, and therefore there is no parallel to one who is liable to receive the death penalty. The Gemara therefore cites a verse that deals with one who was liable to receive court-administered execution, in which case the parallel between the death penalties administered by Heaven and by the court is clear.

A non-priest who ate *teruma* – **זָר שֶׁאָכַל תְּרוּמָה**: The punishment for a non-priest who intentionally ate *teruma* is death at the hand of Heaven, as it is written: "And they shall die therein if they profane it" (Leviticus 22:9). In several places the Gemara explains that although *karet* is also a death penalty at the hand of Heaven, there is a difference between the two. *Karet* is a more severe punishment, as one dies younger and sometimes one's family is also eliminated. This is especially true according to the explanation of the Rambam, who maintains that *karet* entails the soul ceasing to exist. Since death at the hand of Heaven is less severe, it is possible that even according to Rabbi Neḥunya the sinner would not be exempt from payment.

וּלְאַבַּיֵי פָּטוּר?! וְהָאָמַר רַב חִסְדָּא: מוֹדֶה רַבִּי נְחוּנְיָא בֶּן הַקָּנָה בְּגוֹנֵב חֶלְבּוֹ שֶׁל חֲבֵירוֹ וַאֲכָלוֹ – שֶׁהוּא חַיָּיב, שֶׁכְּבָר נִתְחַיֵּיב בִּגְנֵיבָה קוֹדֶם שֶׁבָּא לִידֵי אִיסּוּר חֵלֶב. אַלְמָא, דְּמֵעִידָּנָא דְּאַגְבְּהֵיהּ קַנְיֵיהּ, מִתְחַיֵּיב בְּנַפְשׁוֹ לָא הֲוָה עַד דְּאָכֵיל לֵיהּ. הָכָא נַמִי, בְּעִידָּנָא דְּאַגְבְּהֵיהּ קַנְיֵיהּ, מִתְחַיֵּיב בְּנַפְשׁוֹ לָא הָוֵי עַד דְּאָכֵיל לֵיהּ! הָכָא בְּמַאי עָסְקִינַן – כְּגוֹן שֶׁתָּחַב לוֹ חֲבֵירוֹ לְתוֹךְ פִּיו.

The Gemara asks: **And according to Abaye,** is a non-priest actually **exempt** from payment for the *teruma*? **But didn't Rav Ḥisda say that Rabbi Neḥunya ben HaKana concedes**[N] **with regard to** one who **steals another's** forbidden **fat**[B] **and eats it**[H] **that he is obligated** to pay for the fat, even though he is liable to receive *karet*, **as he was already liable for theft before he came** to violate **the prohibition** against eating forbidden **fat? Apparently, from the moment he lifts** the fat to steal **it he acquired it,**[N] and he bears responsibility to repay it, but **he is liable to** receive the **death** penalty **only when he eats it. Here, too,** with regard to a non-priest who ate *teruma*, **at the moment he lifts** the *teruma* **he acquired it** and is responsible to repay it, and **he is liable to** receive the **death** penalty **only when he eats it.** The Gemara answers: **With what are we dealing here?** It is a case **where another inserted** the *teruma* **into his mouth.** In that case, acquisition and liability to receive the death penalty are simultaneous.

סוֹף סוֹף, כֵּיוָן דִּלְעָסֵיהּ – קַנְיֵיהּ, מִתְחַיֵּיב בְּנַפְשׁוֹ לָא הָוֵי עַד דְּבָלְעָהּ! כְּגוֹן שֶׁתָּחַב לוֹ לְתוֹךְ בֵּית הַבְּלִיעָה. הֵיכִי דָּמֵי? אִי דְּמָצֵי לְאַהֲדוּרָהּ – נִיהֲדַר, אִי לָא מָצֵי לְאַהֲדוּרָהּ – אַמַּאי חַיָּיב? לָא צְרִיכָא, דְּמָצֵי לְאַהֲדוּרָהּ עַל יְדֵי הַדְּחָק.

The Gemara asks: **Ultimately, once he chewed** the *teruma* **he acquired it**[N] and is liable to pay, and **he is liable to** receive the **death** penalty **only when he swallows it.**[N] Since the two are not simultaneous, he should be liable to pay. The Gemara answers: It is a case **where** another **inserted it into the pharynx,**[B] so the liability for payment and liability for the death penalty were both achieved through swallowing. The Gemara asks: **What are the circumstances? If** it is **possible to retrieve** the *teruma* by removing it without ruining it, **let him retrieve** it. If one does so, he would not be liable to pay. If he fails to do so, liability or payment precedes liability for the death penalty. **If** it is **not possible to retrieve**[N] the *teruma*, **why** is he **liable?** He did nothing; another person inserted the food in his throat. The Gemara answers: It is **necessary only** in a situation **where** it is **possible to retrieve** the *teruma* **under duress,** with great effort.

רַב פַּפָּא אָמַר: כְּגוֹן שֶׁתָּחַב לוֹ חֲבֵירוֹ מַשְׁקִין שֶׁל תְּרוּמָה לְתוֹךְ פִּיו. רַב אַשִׁי אָמַר: בְּזָר שֶׁאָכַל תְּרוּמָה מִשֶּׁלּוֹ,

Rav Pappa said: It is referring to a case **where another inserted liquids of *teruma* into his mouth.** As soon as the liquid enters his mouth, it is ruined. Therefore, the acquisition and his enjoyment are simultaneous. **Rav Ashi said:** It is referring **to a non-priest who partook of his own *teruma*,**[N] e.g., if the non-priest inherited *teruma* from a priest, or acquired ownership from a priest. In that case, he did not steal the *teruma* and there is no payment for it, but he is liable to receive the death penalty for eating *teruma*,

BACKGROUND

Fat – חֵלֶב: The reference is to forbidden animal fats prohibited by Torah law, in contrast to animal fats that are permitted. One who partakes of forbidden fats of a kosher domesticated animal is liable to receive *karet* (Leviticus 7:22–25). One who partakes of those fats unwittingly is liable to bring a sin-offering. It is permitted to eat the fats of non-domesticated kosher animals and of kosher birds. Among the indicators distinguishing forbidden and permitted fats is that the forbidden fats are concentrated in certain areas in the animal's body, form an independent unit, and are not attached to the muscle. They are surrounded by a thin membrane and can easily be peeled away from the meat. Most forbidden fats of a consecrated animal were offered on the altar.

Pharynx – בֵּית הַבְּלִיעָה: This is located in the back of the mouth. Food reaching the pharynx activates a swallowing reflex. At that point, it is only with great effort that one could prevent the food from being swallowed.

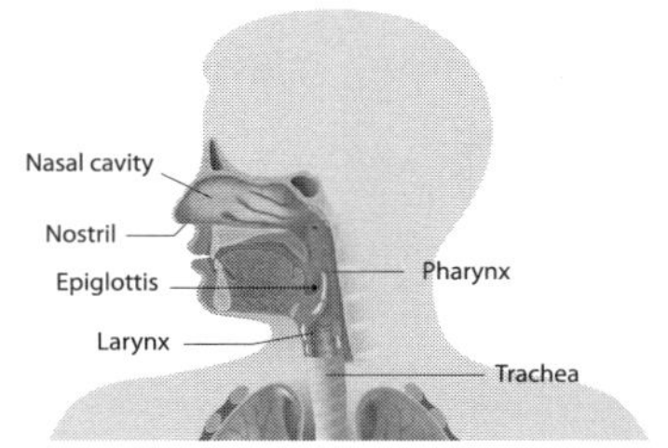

Location of the pharynx

HALAKHA

With regard to one who steals another's forbidden fat and eats it – בְּגוֹנֵב חֶלְבּוֹ שֶׁל חֲבֵירוֹ וַאֲכָלוֹ: One who steals forbidden fat from another and eats it must pay him the value of the fat. The *Sma* and others maintain that this is the *halakha* when one lifted the forbidden fat before consuming it. The *Shakh* notes that this is unnecessary, as the *halakha* is in accordance with the opinion of the Sages that even one who is liable to receive *karet* is obligated to pay for damage that he caused (Rambam *Sefer Nezikim*, *Hilkhot Geneiva* 2:4; *Shulḥan Arukh*, *Ḥoshen Mishpat* 350).

NOTES

Rabbi Neḥunya…concedes, etc. – מוֹדֶה רַבִּי נְחוּנְיָא וכו׳: The Ramban asks: What is novel in Rav Ḥisda's statement, as clearly, with regard to a violation punishable by a court-administered death penalty, Rabbi Neḥunya does not rule more stringently than do the Rabbis, who hold that if one does not incur the liability to be executed and the liability to pay simultaneously he is executed and also pays the damages? The Ramban answers: It is possible that Rav Ḥisda is teaching that the act of lifting the forbidden fat is not considered part of eating but is instead a separate act of acquisition. Furthermore, since Rabbi Neḥunya is lenient with regard to payment, it was necessary to emphasize that even he deems the offender liable in this case.

From from the moment he lifts it he acquired it – מֵעִידָּנָא דְּאַגְבְּהֵיהּ קַנְיֵיהּ: As explained below, it is necessary to precisely define the moment when a particular act is considered theft. Although in the case of misappropriation of a deposit one is liable for merely p anning to do so, that is not the case with regard to theft. Instead, the Sages established lifting as the determining factor in theft. One of the ramifications of this determination is with regard to the liability of the thief for damage to the object from the moment he acquired it through the act of theft, even if he derived no benefit from it. Removing an item from its owner's domain also constitutes an act of theft, even if one did not lift it, as explained later in the Gemara.

Once he chewed it he acquired it – כֵּיוָן דִּלְעָסֵיהּ קַנְיֵיהּ: The Meiri maintains that this phrase is superfluous, as merely holding food in one's mouth acquires the food. He suggests that perhaps the thief must perform an action that demonstrates his consent to the proceedings (see Maharam Schiff).

He is liable to receive the death penalty only when he swallows it – מִתְחַיֵּיב בְּנַפְשׁוֹ לָא הָוֵי עַד דְּבָלְעָהּ: The Rosh asks why he is liable only when he swallows the *teruma* if the *teruma* is already profaned when he chews it. He answers that when the Sages said that one who uses *teruma* profanes it, that is only the case when one uses *teruma* and thereby completes his enjoyment of the food. Here, however, the chewing was not the final stage, as he swallowed it thereafter, and only at that point is the *teruma* profaned (see *Tosafot Yeshanim*).

If it is not possible to retrieve – אִי לָא מָצֵי לְאַהֲדוּרָהּ: The Ritva explains that this can also be referring to a case when another inserted the *teruma* with one's knowledge and consent. *Tosafot* approach this possibility from a different perspective. Some write that although he agreed to have the *teruma* placed in his mouth, he did not intend for it to be shoved in so far that he could not change his mind (see Meiri).

Who partook of his own *teruma* – שֶׁאָכַל תְּרוּמָה מִשֶּׁלּוֹ: The Rashba and others state that this does not mean that it is only in a case where the *teruma* is his; rather, Abaye maintains that he is exempt from punishment for tearing his friend's silk even if the *teruma* was his. An issue addressed by the later commentaries is that if the *teruma* belonged to him he could request that a Sage dissolve the consecration of the *teruma*, as that consecration is like any other vow that can be dissolved in that manner (see *Taz*, *Nekuddot HaKesef*, and *Sefer Hafla'a*).

LANGUAGE

Silk [*shira'in*] – שִׁירָאִין: From the Greek σηρικόν, *sērikon*, a particular variety of silk.

HALAKHA

One who shoots an arrow, etc. – הַזּוֹרֵק חֵץ וכו׳: If one shoots an arrow four cubits in the public domain on Shabbat and it tears silk along its path, he is exempt from payment for the damage as the Shabbat desecration and the damage occur simultaneously. This is in accordance with the statement of Rabbi Avin (Rambam *Sefer Nezikim*, *Hilkhot Geneiva* 3:2).

וְקָרַע שִׁירָאִין שֶׁל חֲבֵירוֹ.

and at the same time **he tore another's silk** [*shira'in*].[LN] The question is whether the liability to receive the death penalty exempts him from the liability for payment incurred at precisely the same moment.

גּוּפָא, אָמַר רַב חִסְדָּא: מוֹדֶה רַבִּי נְחוּנְיָא בֶּן הַקָּנָה בְּגוֹנֵב חֶלְבּוֹ שֶׁל חֲבֵירוֹ וַאֲכָלוֹ – שֶׁהוּא חַיָּיב שֶׁכְּבָר נִתְחַיֵּיב בִּגְנֵבָה קוֹדֶם שֶׁיָּבֹא לִידֵי אִיסּוּר חֵלֶב. לֵימָא פְּלִיגָא דְּרַבִּי אָבִין, דְּאָמַר רַבִּי אָבִין: הַזּוֹרֵק חֵץ מִתְּחִילַּת אַרְבַּע לְסוֹף אַרְבַּע וְקָרַע שִׁירָאִין בַּהֲלִיכָתוֹ – פָּטוּר, שֶׁעֲקִירָה צוֹרֶךְ הַנָּחָה הִיא. הָכָא נַמִי – הַגְבָּהָה צוֹרֶךְ אֲכִילָה הִיא.

§ The Gemara analyzes **the** matter **itself. Rav Ḥisda said: Rabbi Neḥunya ben HaKana concedes in** the case of one who **steals another's** forbidden **fat and eats it that he is obligated** to pay for the fat, **as he is already liable for theft before he comes to** violate **the prohibition** against eating forbidden **fat.** The Gemara comments: **Let us say** that Rav Ḥisda **disagrees** with **Rabbi Avin, as Rabbi Avin said: One who shoots an arrow**[H] **from the beginning of four** cubits **to the end of four** cubits in the public domain on Shabbat, thereby performing a prohibited labor for which he is liable to receive a court-imposed death penalty, **and** the arrow **ripped silk as it proceeds, is exempt** from the obligation to pay for the silk because he is liable for the more severe punishment for desecrating Shabbat. Although the silk was ripped prior to completion of the prohibited labor, as the arrow had not yet come to rest, he is nevertheless exempt, **as lifting is a prerequisite for placement.** The prohibited labor of carrying on Shabbat[N] is comprised of lifting of the object and placement. Once he shot the arrow, its movement through the air is a continuation of his act of Shabbat desecration, for which he is liable to be executed. **Here, too,** say that **lifting** the fat **is a prerequisite for eating,** and therefore he should be exempt from payment.

הָכִי הַשְׁתָּא? הָתָם – אִי אֶפְשָׁר לְהַנָּחָה בְּלֹא עֲקִירָה, הָכָא אֶפְשָׁר לַאֲכִילָה בְּלֹא הַגְבָּהָה, דְּאִי בָּעֵי – גָּחֵין וְאָכֵיל. אִי נַמִי: הָתָם, אִי בָּעֵי לְאַהֲדוּרָה לָא מָצֵי מַהֲדַר לַהּ, הָכָא – מָצֵי מַהֲדַר לַהּ.

The Gemara refutes this argument: **How can** these cases **be compared? There,** in the case of the arrow, **placement is impossible without lifting,** as placement without lifting is not a labor prohibited on Shabbat. Therefore, lifting and placement are a single unit. In contrast, **here, eating is possible without lifting as, if one wishes,** he could **bend down and eat**[N] without lifting the food to his mouth. **Alternatively,** there is another difference between the cases: **There,** in the case of the arrow, even **if he seeks to take back**[N] the arrow after shooting it, **he cannot take it back;** therefore, lifting and placement constitute one action. **Here, he could replace** the fat after lifting it.

NOTES

And he tore another's silk – וְקָרַע שִׁירָאִין שֶׁל חֲבֵירוֹ: Rashi, the Ra'avad, and the Meiri maintain that Rav Ashi's statement is in accordance with the opinion that the principle that a guilty person receives the greater punishment applies in a case where his liability to be executed is due to the effect of his actions on one person and his liability to pay is due to the effect of his actions on another. This applies not only if the two liabilities were incurred by a single act, e.g., killing a slave, which renders him liable to be executed for killing the slave and liable to pay the value of the slave to his master. It applies even if he performed two separate actions, as in this case, when he ate *teruma* and tore silk. Some commentaries explain that this refers to silk wrapped around his neck that he tore in the course of eating the *teruma* (*Shita Mekubbetzet*). However, *Tosafot* and most early commentaries contend that this is not actually a case of death to one person and payment to another, as death at the hand of Heaven is not the result of a sin committed against a particular person. Rather, the novel element is that he is exempt from payment even though he performed two separate actions.

The prohibited labor of carrying out on Shabbat – מְלֶאכֶת הוֹצָאָה בְּשַׁבָּת: One of the thirty-nine categories of labor that are prohibited on Shabbat by Torah law is the labor of carrying out, which is treated in detail in a significant portion of tractate *Shabbat*. The labor of carrying out includes two different situations: First, transfer of an object from the private to the public domain or vice versa, regardless of the distance the item was moved; second, carrying an object four cubits in the public domain. Despite the differences between these scenarios, they share several common elements. In both cases, the object in question is lifted from a significant surface with a minimum requisite area and is then placed on another similar surface. If only one of the stages, lifting or placing, was performed by an individual or if each was performed by a different person, it does not constitute labor prohibited on Shabbat by Torah law.

If one wishes, he could bend down and eat – דְּאִי בָּעֵי גָּחֵין וְאָכֵיל: Consistent with his explanation in parallel discussions, Rashi explains here that one who lifts an object acquires it only if he lifted it more than three handbreadths off the ground. Therefore, if he crouched and stood less than three handbreadths off the ground and ate, he did not acquire the food through lifting. Some early commentaries (*Tosafot*) question Rashi's explanation, as it appears from several sources that one acquires the object even by lifting it by less than three handbreadths off the ground. In fact, the Ran states that according to this opinion one must crouch below one handbreadth, as he maintains that by lifting less than one handbreadth off the ground one does not acquire an object. The Meiri, who agrees with Rashi, resolves the difficulty and explains that those sources according to which an acquisition is accomplished by lifting less than three handbreadths are referring to acquisition by rabbinic law. The early commentaries raise an additional difficulty: Independent of lifting, one should acquire the food when it enters his mouth. Therefore, *Tosafot* and other early commentaries explain that the forbidden fat was on a skewer, and he placed it directly at his pharynx when he crouched. Others explain that this matter of crouching and eating is not the primary answer, which is that lifting and placing are integral to the labor of carrying out, whereas lifting fat is not integral to its consumption (Rashba; Ra'ah).

If he seeks to take back – אִי בָּעֵי לְאַהֲדוּרָה: This appears to mean that the prohibited labor of carrying out begins with the shooting of the arrow, an act that cannot be reversed. The Ramban, however, explains that the shooting of the arrow necessarily entails the tearing of the silk as it moves, which is not the case with the moving knife. Rashi indicates likewise (see Ramban and *Shita Mekubbetzet*).

מַאי אִיכָּא בֵּין הַאי לִישָּׁנָא לְהַאי לִישָּׁנָא? אִיכָּא בֵּינַיְיהוּ הַמַּעֲבִיר סַכִּין בִּרְשׁוּת הָרַבִּים, וְקָרַע שִׁירָאִין בַּהֲלִיכָתוֹ. לְהַךְ לִישָּׁנָא דְּאָמְרַתְּ אִי אֶפְשָׁר לְהַנָּחָה בְּלֹא עֲקִירָה – הָכָא נַמִּי אִי אֶפְשָׁר לְהַנָּחָה בְּלֹא עֲקִירָה. לְהַךְ לִישָּׁנָא דְּאָמְרַתְּ לָא מָצֵי מַהְדַר לַהּ – הָכָא מָצֵי מַהֲדַר לַהּ.

The Gemara asks: **What** practical difference **is there between this formulation,** where the criterion is whether the second stage could be performed independent of the first stage, **and that formulation,** where the criterion is whether the second stage is inevitable after performing the first stage? The Gemara responds: **There is** a practical difference **between them** with regard to **one who carries**[N] **a knife in the public domain and tears silk as he proceeds. According to that formulation, where you said: Lifting is a prerequisite for placement, here too, lifting is a prerequisite for placement.** As these two stages are inexorably connected, they constitute one action, and the one carrying the knife is exempt from paying the damages. Conversely, **according to that formulation where you said: He cannot take back** the arrow and that is why they are considered one action, **here, he can take back** the knife; therefore, lifting and placement are separate actions and he is not exempt from punishment for the damages that he caused.

גּוּפָא, אָמַר רַבִּי אָבִין: הַזּוֹרֵק חֵץ מִתְּחִלַּת אַרְבַּע לְסוֹף אַרְבַּע, וְקָרַע שִׁירָאִין בַּהֲלִיכָתוֹ – פָּטוּר, שֶׁעֲקִירָה צוֹרֶךְ הַנָּחָה הִיא. מְתִיב רַב בֵּיבָי בַּר אַבַּיֵי: הַגּוֹנֵב כִּיס בְּשַׁבָּת – חַיָּיב, שֶׁכְּבָר נִתְחַיֵּיב בִּגְנֵיבָה קוֹדֶם שֶׁיָּבֹא לִידֵי אִיסּוּר סְקִילָה. הָיָה מְגָרֵר וְיוֹצֵא, מְגָרֵר וְיוֹצֵא – פָּטוּר, שֶׁהֲרֵי אִיסּוּר שַׁבָּת וּגְנֵיבָה בָּאִין כְּאֶחָד.

§ The Gemara analyzes **the** matter **itself. Rabbi Avin said:** With regard to **one who shoots an arrow from the beginning of four** cubits **to the end of four** cubits **and** the arrow **rips silk as it proceeds, he is exempt, as lifting is a prerequisite for placement. Rav Beivai bar Abaye raised an objection** from that which is taught in a *baraita*: **One who steals a purse on Shabbat**[H] **is liable** for the theft **because he was already liable for theft** as soon as he lifted the purse. This took place **before he came to** violate **the prohibition** against performing prohibited labor on Shabbat by carrying it into the public domain, a violation punishable by **stoning.** However, if he did not lift the purse but **was dragging** it on the ground **and exiting**[NH] the private domain, **dragging and exiting, he is exempt, as the prohibition** against **theft and the prohibition of Shabbat** are violated **simultaneously** when he drags the purse out of the owner's property and into the public domain.

וְאַמַּאי? הָכָא נַמִּי לֵימָא הַגְבָּהָה צוֹרֶךְ הוֹצָאָה הִיא! הָכָא בְּמַאי עָסְקִינַן – כְּגוֹן שֶׁהִגְבִּיהוֹ עַל מְנָת לְהַצְנִיעוֹ וְנִמְלַךְ עָלָיו וְהוֹצִיאוֹ.

Rav Beivai concludes: **But why** is he liable if he carried the purse? **Here, too, let us say** that **lifting is a prerequisite for carrying out,**[N] and therefore the theft was performed in the course of performance of the prohibited labor and he is exempt. The Gemara answers: **With what are we dealing here?** We are dealing with a case **where he lifted** the pouch **in order to conceal it** in the same domain, not to carry it out into the public domain, **and he reconsidered** his plan with regard to the purse **and carried it out.** In that case the act of lifting was not performed for the purpose of carrying out. Therefore, he is not exempt from the obligation to pay for the theft.

וְכִי הַאי גַּוְונָא מִי חַיָּיב? וְהָאָמַר רַב סִימוֹן אָמַר רַבִּי אַמִי אָמַר רַבִּי יוֹחָנָן: הַמְפַנֶּה חֲפָצִים מִזָּוִית לְזָוִית, וְנִמְלַךְ עֲלֵיהֶם וְהוֹצִיאָן – פָּטוּר, שֶׁלֹּא הָיְתָה עֲקִירָה מִשָּׁעָה רִאשׁוֹנָה לְכָךְ!

The Gemara asks: **And in a case like that,** where he reconsidered, **is** one **liable** for carrying out an object on Shabbat? **But didn't Rav Simon say** that **Rabbi Ami said** that **Rabbi Yoḥanan said: One who moves objects from** one **corner** of his house to another **corner** on Shabbat, **and he reconsidered** his plan in **their** regard after lifting them **and carried them out** into the public domain, he is **exempt, as the** act of **lifting was not initially** performed **for that** purpose of carrying from one domain to another. Here, too, since the thief did not lift the pouch with the intention of carrying it out, he is not liable to be stoned.

NOTES

There is a difference between them with regard to one who carries – אִיכָּא בֵּינַיְיהוּ הַמַּעֲבִיר: The early commentaries point out that the Gemara could also have said that there is a difference between the two opinions with regard to one who ate forbidden fat that was inserted into his throat by another. According to the approach that lifting is a prerequisite for placing, here too, placing food in one's mouth is a prerequisite for eating and the two actions can be regarded as simultaneous. According to the opinion that the decisive factor is one's ability to take back the object, in this case one can extract the food after it was placed in one's mouth and therefore the actions are not regarded as simultaneous. (Ritva).

If he was dragging and exiting – הָיָה מְגָרֵר וְיוֹצֵא: The Ramban asks: If he was dragging the object and never lifted it at all, the prohibited labor of carrying out was never completely performed even when the item reached the public domain. The Ra'avad resolves this difficulty and explains that lifting is required only for carrying four cubits in the public domain. However, for transfer of an object from one domain to another one need not lift it completely off the ground, as the very transfer to a different domain is tantamount to lifting. The Ramban explains that in talmudic times the entrance to the private domain was three handbreadths higher than the private domain, and therefore taking an object out of the private domain would necessarily include lifting. Yet others contend that this is not difficult to explain at all, as lifting is required for the object to be considered to have been moved only with regard to an object that remains in place. However, with regard to an object that one is dragging, where he moves the entire object, that itself is considered full-fledged lifting (*Tosafot* on *Shabbat* 8b; Rashba; Ra'ah).

Lifting is a prerequisite for carrying out – הַגְבָּהָה צוֹרֶךְ הוֹצָאָה הִיא: Here too, it could nevertheless be asserted that lifting is not integral to carrying out, as one could drag the object without lifting it, or, according to the other opinion, one could reverse the process. Some commentaries do state that the Gemara could have raised these questions but opted not to raise all possible difficulties. The Ramban claims that this is not difficult to explain, as the Gemara is saying merely that one cannot be liable for placement without lifting; therefore, from the moment one lifts the object he begins assuming liability (see *Tosafot*).

HALAKHA

One who steals a purse on Shabbat – הַגּוֹנֵב כִּיס בְּשַׁבָּת: One who steals a purse on Shabbat by lifting it in the owner's domain, is obligated to pay damages even if he later carried it out to the public domain, because the theft preceded the desecration of Shabbat. The *Kesef Mishne* notes that the Rambam omits the Gemara's explanation in this regard because he rules in accordance with the formulation that the decisive factor is whether or not one can take back the object. As the discussion in the Gemara is focused on Rabbi Avin's formulation, it is not relevant to the *halakha*. Therefore, the Rambam omits it (Rambam *Sefer Nezikim, Hilkhot Geneiva* 3:2; *Shulḥan Arukh, Ḥoshen Mishpat* 351).

If he was dragging and exiting – הָיָה מְגָרֵר וְיוֹצֵא: If one stole a purse on Shabbat without lifting it, but instead dragged it through the owner's property until he reached the public domain, he is exempt from payment, as the desecration of Shabbat and the theft occur simultaneously (Rambam *Sefer Nezikim, Hilkhot Geneiva* 3:2; *Shulḥan Arukh, Ḥoshen Mishpat* 351).

לָא תֵּימָא עַל מְנָת לְהַצְנִיעוֹ, אֶלָּא אֵימָא עַל מְנָת לְהוֹצִיאוֹ, הָכָא בְּמַאי עָסְקִינַן – כְּשֶׁעָמַד.

The Gemara emends the previous answer: **Do not say** that he lifted it **in order to conceal it;**[N] **rather, say** that he lifted it **in order to carry it out.** Nevertheless, the case of shooting the arrow and the case of stealing the purse are different, as **with what** case **are we dealing here?** It is a case **where he stopped**[H] in the courtyard before taking the pouch out to the public domain. Therefore, the initial lifting is exclusively theft and not the start of a prohibited labor, as by stopping, he separated the lifting from the carrying out.

עָמַד לְמַאי? אִי לְכַתֵּף – אוֹרְחֵיהּ הוּא! אֶלָּא בְּעוֹמֵד לָפוּשׁ, אֲבָל לְכַתֵּף מַאי?

The Gemara asks: This is a case where he **stopped. For what** purpose did he stop? **If** he stopped in order **to** adjust the burden on his **shoulder, that is** the typical **manner** of proceeding and would not be considered an interruption in the process of carrying out the object. **Rather,** it must be **in** a case of one who **stopped to rest,** and when he resumes moving he initiates a separate action. The Gemara infers: **But** if he stopped in order **to** adjust the burden on his **shoulder, what** is the *halakha*?

NOTES

Do not say in order to conceal it, etc. – לָא תֵּימָא עַל מְנָת לְהַצְנִיעוֹ וכו׳: In the *Shita Mekubbetzet* it is explained that many variant versions of the text omit this answer, which may have been inserted under the influence of Rashi's explanation. One can then move to the next explanation in the Gemara with regard to one who stopped, thereby interrupting the transfer of the object.

HALAKHA

Where he stopped – כְּשֶׁעָמַד: One who was carrying an object in the public domain and stopped after walking less than four cubits is exempt. This applies only if he stopped in order to rest; however, if he paused to adjust his burden he is considered to still be in the process of walking, and therefore when he traverses four cubits and stops, he is liable (Rambam *Sefer Zemanim*, *Hilkhot Shabbat* 13:10).

Perek **III**
Daf **31** Amud **b**

פָּטוּר, אַדְּתָנֵי הָיָה מְגָרֵר וְיוֹצֵא מְגָרֵר וְיוֹצֵא פָּטוּר, נִפְלוֹג וְנִיתְנֵי בְּדִידָהּ: בַּמֶּה דְּבָרִים אֲמוּרִים בְּעוֹמֵד לָפוּשׁ, אֲבָל לְכַתֵּף – פָּטוּר!

He would be **exempt.** If that is the case, **rather than teaching:** If **he was dragging and exiting, dragging and exiting, he is exempt, let** the *tanna* **distinguish and teach** the distinction **within** the case of carrying **itself,** as follows: **In what** case **are these matters stated?** It is **in** a case where **he stopped to rest; however,** if **he stopped to** adjust the burden on his **shoulder,** he is **exempt.**

אֶלָּא הָא מַנִּי – בֶּן עַזַּאי הִיא, דְּאָמַר: מְהַלֵּךְ כְּעוֹמֵד דָּמֵי. אֲבָל זוֹרֵק מַאי – פָּטוּר, נִיפְלוֹג [וְנִיתְנֵי] בְּדִידָהּ: בַּמֶּה דְּבָרִים אֲמוּרִים – בִּמְהַלֵּךְ, אֲבָל זוֹרֵק – פָּטוּר!

Rather, the Gemara explains why one is liable in the case where he carries the purse. In accordance with **whose** opinion was **this** *halakha* taught? **It is** in accordance with the opinion of **ben Azzai,** who **said:** The legal status of **one who walks is like** that of **one who stops,**[N] as each step constitutes a pause between the actions of lifting and placement. Therefore, the initial lifting is not part of the prohibited labor of carrying out. The Gemara infers: **But** if **one throws** the object into another domain, **what** is the *halakha*? He would be **exempt** from payment, as the lifting is the start of the prohibited labor of carrying out. If so, **let** the *tanna* **distinguish and teach** the distinction **within** the case **itself,** without resorting to the case of dragging and exiting, as follows: **In what** case **are these matters stated?** It is in the case of **one who walks,** so that there is separation between lifting and carrying out, and therefore the theft and the desecration of Shabbat are not simultaneous. **However, one who throws** is **exempt** from payment, as liability for carrying out and for theft are incurred simultaneously.

מְגָרֵר וְיוֹצֵא אִיצְטְרִיכָא לֵיהּ, סָלְקָא דַּעְתָּךְ אָמִינָא: אֵין דֶּרֶךְ הוֹצָאָה בְּכָךְ, קָא מַשְׁמַע לָן.

The Gemara answers: According to the opinion of ben Azzai, that would in fact be a more appropriate distinction; however, the case of one who was **dragging and exiting was necessary for** the *tanna*[N] to teach because it includes a novel element, as **it might enter your mind to say** that **this is not** a typical **manner of carrying out,** and one is not liable to be executed for performing a prohibited labor in an atypical manner. Therefore, **it teaches us** that this too is a manner of carrying out.

וּבְמַאי? אִי בְּרַבְרְבֵי – אוֹרְחֵיהּ הוּא, אִי בְּזוּטְרֵי – לָאו אוֹרְחֵיהּ הוּא! אֶלָּא, בְּמִיצְעֵי.

And the Gemara asks: **In what** case is this so? **If** it is **in** the case of **large** purses, obviously dragging **is its** typical **manner,** and there is nothing novel in this. **If** it is **in** the case of **small** purses, dragging **is** certainly **not its** typical **manner,** and one would certainly not be liable. **Rather,** it must be referring **to intermediate-sized** purses.[N] Although they are not always carried out in this manner, since they are sometimes dragged, the novelty is that he is liable for desecrating Shabbat and exempt from the payment.

NOTES

The legal status of one who walks is like that of one who stops – מְהַלֵּךְ כְּעוֹמֵד דָּמֵי: Ben Azzai's reasoning is clear: Since the act of walking involves the placement of one foot and the lifting of the other foot, one who walks essentially stops between each step. The problem is that according to that understanding, it is difficult to envision how one could perform the prohibited labor of carrying four cubits on Shabbat at all. *Tosafot* briefly cite three answers to this question, which are discussed in greater detail in other early commentaries. The first explanation is that according to ben Azzai carrying four cubits on Shabbat is a special *halakha*, and although one stops between each step it is considered one continuous action. A second resolution maintains that ben Azzai stated his *halakha* only with regard to one who is walking from a private domain to a public domain or vice versa through an exempt domain, and not with regard to walking in one domain. In the Jerusalem Talmud the explanation is that according to ben Azzai one would be liable for carrying out if he jumped four cubits, and the same would be true for one who threw an object that distance. Yet others suggest that the legal status of carrying four cubits is similar to that of carrying out from domain to domain, as the four cubits are considered one's domain. Ben Azzai's *halakha* is irrelevant in that case.

Dragging and exiting was necessary for the *tanna* – מְגָרֵר וְיוֹצֵא אִיצְטְרִיכָא לֵיהּ: The Ritva had a variant reading of the text: Rather, dragging and exiting was necessary for the *tanna*, etc. The term rather typically signifies a rejection of the previous explanation, and the Ritva explains that the Gemara here is explaining the matter in accordance with the opinion of the Rabbis, and not merely according to ben Azzai. This also resolves the difficulty raised in *Tosafot*. However, the Rashba rejects the variant reading. He claims that the explanation of the Gemara is in accordance with the opinions of both the Rabbis and ben Azzai, although some commentaries maintain that it is only in accordance with the opinion of ben Azzai.

Rather, it must be referring to intermediate-sized purses – אֶלָּא בְּמִיצְעֵי: Some commentaries maintain that the Gemara here disagrees with the Gemara in *Bava Batra* (86a), which states that objects that are typically lifted cannot be acquired with the acquisition of pulling (see Ramban and Rashba).

וּדְאַפְּקֵיהּ לְהֵיכָא? אִי דְּאַפְּקֵיהּ לִרְשׁוּת הָרַבִּים אִיסּוּר שַׁבָּת – אִיכָּא, אִיסּוּר גְּנֵיבָה – לֵיכָּא, אִי דְּאַפְּקֵיהּ לִרְשׁוּת הַיָּחִיד – אִיסּוּר גְּנֵיבָה אִיכָּא, אִיסּוּר שַׁבָּת – לֵיכָּא! לָא צְרִיכָא, דְּאַפְּקֵיהּ לְצִידֵּי רְשׁוּת הָרַבִּים.

The Gemara continues: **And** in this case, **to where** did **he carry out** the pouch? **If he carried it out** from the owner's private domain **to the public domain,**[N] **there is** violation of the **prohibition of Shabbat;** however, **there is no** violation of the **prohibition** against **theft,** as one does not acquire an item by pulling it into the public domain. **If he carried it out** from the owner's private domain **to** his own **private domain, there is** violation of the **prohibition** against **theft;** however, **there is no** violation of the **prohibition of Shabbat.** The Gemara answers: This ruling **is necessary only** in a case **where he carried it out to the sides of the public domain.**[N] This is referring to the area in the public domain adjacent to the houses located on its sides, demarcated from the thoroughfare by small pegs and not by a full-fledged partition.

וּכְמַאן? אִי כְּרַבִּי אֱלִיעֶזֶר, דְּאָמַר: צִידֵּי רְשׁוּת הָרַבִּים כִּרְשׁוּת הָרַבִּים דָּמוּ אִיסּוּר שַׁבָּת אִיכָּא אִיסּוּר גְּנֵיבָה לֵיכָּא. אִי כְּרַבָּנַן, דְּאָמְרִי צִידֵּי רְשׁוּת הָרַבִּים לָאו כִּרְשׁוּת הָרַבִּים דָּמוּ – אִיסּוּר גְּנֵיבָה אִיכָּא, אִיסּוּר שַׁבָּת לֵיכָּא.

The Gemara asks: **And in accordance with whose** opinion is this taught? **If** it is **in accordance with** the opinion of **Rabbi Eliezer, who said:** The legal status of **the sides of the public domain is like** that of **the public domain, there is** violation of the **prohibition of Shabbat;** however, **there is no** violation of the **prohibition** against **theft. If** it is **in accordance with** the opinion of **the Rabbis, who said:** The legal status of **the sides of the public domain is not like** that of **the public domain, there is** violation of the **prohibition** against **theft;** however, **there is no** violation of the **prohibition of Shabbat.**

לְעוֹלָם כְּרַבִּי אֱלִיעֶזֶר, וְכִי אָמַר רַבִּי אֱלִיעֶזֶר צִידֵּי רְשׁוּת הָרַבִּים כִּרְשׁוּת הָרַבִּים דָּמוּ – הָנֵי מִילֵּי לְעִנְיַן חִיּוּבָא דְּשַׁבָּת, דְּזִימְנִין דְּדָחֲקִי רַבִּים וְעַיְילִי לְהָתָם, אֲבָל לְעִנְיַן מִיקְנָא – קָנֵי, מַאי טַעְמָא – דְּהָא לָא שְׁכִיחִי רַבִּים.

The Gemara answers: **Actually,** it is **in accordance with** the opinion **of Rabbi Eliezer, and when Rabbi Eliezer said:** The legal status of **the sides of the public domain is like** that of **the public domain, that applies only with regard to the liability for** performing prohibited labor on **Shabbat, as occasionally the multitudes crowd and enter there. However,** with regard **to the matter of acquiring**[H] an object, one **acquires** it by dragging it there. **What is the reason** for this *halakha*? It is due to the fact **that the public is not** typically **found** there, and acquisition can be effected in a place where the multitudes are not typically found.

רַב אַשִׁי אָמַר: כְּגוֹן שֶׁצֵּירַף יָדוֹ לְמַטָּה מִשְּׁלֹשָׁה וְקִיבְּלוֹ, כְּדְרָבָא. דְּאָמַר רָבָא: יָדוֹ שֶׁל אָדָם חֲשׁוּבָה לוֹ כְּאַרְבָּעָה עַל אַרְבָּעָה. רַב אַחָא מַתְנֵי הָכִי.

Rav Ashi said: Actually, one is exempt when one dragged the object into the public domain in a case **where he joined his hand** to his other hand at a height **below three handbreadths** off the ground **and received** the purse by passing it from one hand into the other as soon as he brought it into the public domain. This is **in accordance with** the opinion of **Rava,**[N] **as Rava said: A person's hand is considered like four by four** handbreadths **for him.**[H] Therefore, an object placed in one's hand is considered placed with regard to Shabbat, and since his hand is his personal domain he has also acquired the stolen item. **Rav Aḥa taught** the entire discussion **this way,** as above.

HALAKHA

Acquisition in the sides of the public domain – קָנִין בְּצִידֵּי רְשׁוּת הָרַבִּים: With regard to an object acquired by pulling in a place that belongs neither to the owner nor to the one acquiring the object, or in the public domain, if the one acquiring the object pulled it into his own domain or into an alleyway, i.e., the sides of the public domain, he acquires it. This is in accordance with the conclusion in the Gemara here that in terms of acquisition, the legal status of the sides of the public domain are not like that of the public domain (Rambam *Sefer Kinyan*, *Hilkhot Mekhira* 4:4; *Shulḥan Arukh*, *Ḥoshen Mishpat* 198:14).

A person's hand is considered like four by four handbreadths for him – יָדוֹ שֶׁל אָדָם חֲשׁוּבָה לוֹ כְּאַרְבָּעָה עַל אַרְבָּעָה: A person's hand is considered for him like a surface with an area of four by four cubits. Consequently, if on Shabbat one carried an object out of one domain and held it in his hand in a different domain, although he did not place it in that domain he is liable for carrying it out, as stated by Rava (Rambam *Sefer Zemanim*, *Hilkhot Shabbat* 13:2).

NOTES

If he carried it out to the public domain, etc. – אִי דְּאַפְּקֵיהּ לִרְשׁוּת הָרַבִּים וכו׳: Some ask: Why not explain that he carried it into another private domain, his own property, via a public domain? The answer is that in that case the prohibition of Shabbat would be violated when the object enters the public domain, and he completes the theft later (*Shita Yeshana*, cited in *Shita Mekubbetzet*).

To the sides of the public domain, etc. – לְצִידֵּי רְשׁוּת הָרַבִּים וכו׳: The definition of public and private domains varies in its application to three different areas of *halakha*: Shabbat, monetary law, and impurity. With regard to monetary law, a private domain is determined by ownership; for Shabbat, a domain is deemed public or private by its area and partitions. With regard to impurity, the decisive factor is the number of people found there. Therefore, it is possible for a place, e.g., the sides of the public domain, to be a private domain with regard to one area of *halakha* and a public domain with regard to another area.

Where he joined his hand below three handbreadths off the ground and received the purse, in accordance with the opinion of Rava – כְּגוֹן שֶׁצֵּירַף יָדוֹ לְמַטָּה מִשְּׁלֹשָׁה וְקִיבְּלוֹ, כְּדְרָבָא: There is a fundamental difficulty with this matter, mentioned in brief by *Tosafot* and discussed at length by the Ramban: Since Rava said in tractate *Shabbat* that the legal status of one's hand is like that of an area of four by four cubits, and therefore an object placed in one's hand is considered as though it were placed in the domain in which he is located, why is it necessary for one to place his hand below three handbreadths? Even if his hand were higher up, the object would still be considered placed in that domain. Apparently, Rashi was aware of this difficulty, as he explains that Rav Ashi's statement that this *halakha* is in accordance with the opinion of Rava is with regard to the *halakhot* of acquisitions, not those of Shabbat. Due to the significance of one's hand, it acquires the object even below three handbreadths. *Tosafot* and others question Rashi's approach, and the early and later commentaries seek to explain Rashi both in terms of different modes of acquisition and in terms of the definition of a person's hand. The *Ḥatam Sofer* writes that according to Rashi, Rava is saying that the legal status of one's hand is that of a larger surface in terms of placement, which explains his opinion with regard to acquisitions. According to *Tosafot*, in contrast, the hand is considered significant but not larger.

The Ramban, consistent with his approach, maintains that the private domain was significantly higher than the public domain, and when the Gemara states that he joined his hand below three handbreadths it means three handbreadths below the private domain, thereby lifting the object above the public domain. The Rid's version, also mentioned by *Tosafot*, reads: Alternatively, it is in accordance with the opinion of Rava. According to this version, the difficulty does not arise at all, as there are two separate answers: First, that he lowered his hand below three handbreadths, and second, that a person's hand is significant, as stated by Rava. The Ramban agrees that this is a worthy reading, but he notes that it does not appear in the manuscripts of Spain (see *Tosafot*).

רָבִינָא מַתְנֵי: לְעוֹלָם דְּאַפְּקֵיהּ לִרְשׁוּת הָרַבִּים וּבִרְשׁוּת הָרַבִּים נַמִי קָנָה. וְתַרְוַיְיהוּ בְּדִיּוּקָא דְּהָא מַתְנִיתִין קָמִיפַּלְגִי, דִּתְנַן: הָיָה מוֹשְׁכוֹ וְיוֹצֵא, וּמֵת בִּרְשׁוּת בְּעָלִים – פָּטוּר, הִגְבִּיהוֹ אוֹ שֶׁהוֹצִיאוֹ מֵרְשׁוּת בְּעָלִים וּמֵת – חַיָּיב.

Ravina taught otherwise: **Actually,** it is a case **where one carried out** the object **to the public domain, and in the public domain he also acquires**[NH] the stolen object by removing it from the owner's domain, even if he does not transfer it to his own domain. The Gemara comments: **And the two of them,** Rav Aḥa and Ravina **disagree with regard to the inference of this mishna, as we learned** in a mishna (*Bava Kamma* 79a) with regard to one who stole an animal: If he **was pulling** the animal **and exiting, and it died in the domain of the owner,** the thief is **exempt** from payment because he did not yet acquire the animal and therefore did not assume liability for its death through circumstances beyond his control. If **he lifted it or took it out of the owner's domain,** thereby acquiring the animal, **and it died,** the thief is **liable** to pay its value because it died in his possession.

רָבִינָא דָּיֵיק מֵרֵישָׁא, רַב אַחָא דָּיֵיק מִסֵּיפָא. רָבִינָא דָּיֵיק מֵרֵישָׁא: הָיָה מוֹשְׁכוֹ וְיוֹצֵא, וּמֵת בִּרְשׁוּת בְּעָלִים – פָּטוּר. טַעֲמָא – דְּמֵת בִּרְשׁוּת בְּעָלִים, הָא הוֹצִיאוֹ מֵרְשׁוּת בְּעָלִים וּמֵת – חַיָּיב. רַב אַחָא דָּיֵיק מִסֵּיפָא: הִגְבִּיהוֹ אוֹ שֶׁהוֹצִיאוֹ, הוֹצָאָה דּוּמְיָא דְּהַגְבָּהָה; מַה הַגְבָּהָה – דְּאָתֵי לִרְשׁוּתֵיהּ, אַף הוֹצָאָה נַמִי – דְּאָתֵי לִרְשׁוּתֵיהּ.

Ravina inferred his conclusion **from the first clause** of the mishna, **and Rav Aḥa inferred** his conclusion **from the latter clause. Ravina inferred** his conclusion **from the first clause:** If he **was pulling** the animal **and exiting, and it died in the domain of the owner,** the thief is **exempt** from payment. **The reason** that the thief is exempt **is that** the animal **died in the owner's domain; by inference,** if **he took it out of the owner's domain**[H] **and it died,** he is **liable** because the thief acquires the item by its very removal from the owner's property, even to the public domain. **Rav Aḥa inferred** his conclusion **from the latter clause** of the mishna: If **he lifted it or took it out of the owner's domain,** he is liable. Based on the juxtaposition of the two, **taking** the animal **out is similar to lifting** it: **Just as lifting** is an act of acquisition through which the animal **comes into his domain, so too, taking** it **out** is referring to a case **where it comes into his domain.**

לְרַב אַחָא קַשְׁיָא רֵישָׁא, לְרָבִינָא קַשְׁיָא סֵיפָא! רֵישָׁא לְרַב אַחָא לָא קַשְׁיָא: כַּמָּה דְּלָא אָתֵי לִרְשׁוּתֵיהּ – רְשׁוּת בְּעָלִים קָרֵינָא בֵּיהּ. סֵיפָא לְרָבִינָא לָא קַשְׁיָא: הוֹצָאָה דּוּמְיָא דְּהַגְבָּהָה – לָא אָמְרִינַן.

The Gemara observes: **For Rav Aḥa the first clause** of the mishna **is difficult,** while **for Ravina the latter clause is difficult.** The Gemara answers: **The first clause is not difficult for Rav Aḥa,** as he could explain it as follows: **As long as** the animal **has not come into one's domain,**[N] even if it has left the owner's property, **we** continue to **call it the owner's domain.** Similarly, **the latter clause is not difficult for Ravina,** as in his opinion **we do not say: Taking** the animal **out is similar to lifting** it. Therefore, the mishna's ruling is that the thief acquires the animal merely through its removal from the owner's property.

״הַבָּא עַל אֲחוֹתוֹ וְעַל אֲחוֹת אָבִיו״ כו׳. וּרְמִינְהוּ: אֵלּוּ הֵן הַלּוֹקִין: הַבָּא עַל אֲחוֹתוֹ, וְעַל אֲחוֹת אָבִיו, וְעַל אֲחוֹת אִמּוֹ, וְעַל אֲחוֹת אִשְׁתּוֹ, וְעַל אֵשֶׁת אָחִיו, וְעַל אֵשֶׁת אֲחִי אָבִיו, וְעַל הַנִּדָּה.

§ The mishna continues: Similarly, **one who has** forced **relations with his sister,** i.e., he rapes her, **or with his father's sister,** or with his mother's sister, or with his wife's sister, or with his brother's wife, or with his father's brother's wife after they divorced, or with a menstruating woman, there is a fine paid. **And** the Gemara **raised a contradiction** from the following mishna (*Makkot* 13a): **And these** people **are flogged:**[NH] **One who has relations with his sister, or with his father's sister, or with his mother's sister, or with his wife's sister, or with his brother's wife, or with his father's brother's wife, or with a menstruating woman.** Anyone who intentionally has relations with any of these women is punished with lashes.

NOTES

In the public domain he also acquires – בִּרְשׁוּת הָרַבִּים נַמִי קָנָה: *Tosafot* point out that this appears to contradict the opinion of Abaye and Rava in *Bava Batra* (84b), who state clearly that pulling, as a mode of acquisition, is not effective in the public domain. In fact, the Rid and other early commentaries maintain that there is a contradiction between the sources in the two tractates, and that is why they do not rule in accordance with the opinion of Ravina (see HALAKHA). Conversely, the Rashba and others accept the explanation of Rabbeinu Yitzḥak in *Tosafot*, who explains that this is not dealing with a standard acquisition; rather, the Gemara is saying that when a thief pulls the object into the public domain he acquires the object to the extent that he is liable for unavoidable accidents that befall the object. However, he does not acquire the object completely. The Ra'ah and the Ritva explain that although pulling does not typically effect acquisition in the public domain, in this case the object was pulled in the public domain after its removal from the owner's domain, and in that case the thief acquires ownership.

As long as it has not come into one's domain, etc. – כַּמָּה דְּלָא אָתֵי לִרְשׁוּתֵיהּ וכו׳: When the mishna refers to the owner's domain, the reference is not to the area currently occupied by the owner but to his domain in terms of legal ownership. Consequently, until the thief acquires the object it remains in the owner's domain (Ritva).

And the Gemara raised a contradiction: These are flogged, etc. – וּרְמִינְהוּ: אֵלּוּ הֵן הַלּוֹקִין וכו׳: Why does the Gemara raise this problem here? The same difficulty could be raised at the beginning of the mishna, as one who rapes a *mamzeret* violates a prohibition and is liable to be flogged. *Tosafot* explain that in fact the Gemara could have raised the question there, but it preferred to cite the question from the mishna in *Makkot*. The Ramban maintains that since the mishna was established earlier in accordance with the opinion of Rabbi Meir, who maintains that one is lashed and pays the fine, as explained later, the difficulty can be raised only with regard to prohibitions punishable by *karet*. In the Jerusalem Talmud there is a different resolution to this problem, as the Gemara there proposes that the mishna is referring to a *mamzer* who raped a *mamzeret*, who is not subject to lashes, as she is permitted to him. According to this interpretation, the novel element in the mishna is that a *mamzeret* is entitled to the fine despite her flawed lineage.

HALAKHA

In the public domain he also acquires – בִּרְשׁוּת הָרַבִּים נַמִי קָנָה: One who stole a purse on Shabbat by dragging it from the owner's domain into the public domain is exempt from payment, as the desecration of Shabbat and the theft occur simultaneously. The *halakha* is in accordance with the opinion of Ravina, as he is a later Sage, and the *halakha* is generally ruled in accordance with his opinion in disputes with Rav Aḥa. The *Tur* rules in accordance with the opinion of Rav Aḥa because according to the Riva in *Tosafot*, this is also the opinion of Abaye and Rava (Vilna Gaon; Rambam *Sefer Nezikim*, *Hilkhot Geneiva* 3:2; *Shulḥan Arukh*, *Ḥoshen Mishpat* 351).

If he took it out of the owner's domain, etc. – הוֹצִיאוֹ מֵרְשׁוּת בְּעָלִים וכו׳: A thief is liable to be punished for theft from the moment he removes an object from its owner's domain, even if it was subsequently destroyed by unavoidable accident. If he did not remove it from the owner's domain he is liable only if he lifted the item, as stated by Ravina (Rambam *Sefer Nezikim*, *Hilkhot Geneiva* 2:16; *Shulḥan Arukh*, *Ḥoshen Mishpat* 348:4).

These are flogged, etc. – אֵלּוּ הֵן הַלּוֹקִין וכו׳: With regard to any prohibition punishable by *karet* and not by court-administered execution, if one violated the prohibition in the presence of witnesses and after forewarning, he is liable to be flogged, as explained in the mishna cited here (Rambam *Sefer Shofetim*, *Hilkhot Sanhedrin* 19:1).

וְקַיְימָא לָן דְּאֵינוֹ לוֹקֶה וּמְשַׁלֵּם! אֲמַר עוּלָּא: לָא קַשְׁיָא; כָּאן – בַּאֲחוֹתוֹ נַעֲרָה, כָּאן – בַּאֲחוֹתוֹ בּוֹגֶרֶת.

And since **we maintain** in general **that one is not** both **flogged and** liable to **pay,** if one receives lashes for having relations with his sister, why must he pay the fine as well? **Ulla said:** This is **not difficult; here,** the *halakha* in the mishna is **with regard to his sister** who is **a young woman,**[N] for whom one pays a fine and is not flogged, whereas **there,** the *halakha* in the mishna is **with regard to his sister** who is a **grown woman,** for whom one does not pay a fine.

אֲחוֹתוֹ בּוֹגֶרֶת נַמִי, הָא אִיכָּא בּוֹשֶׁת וּפְגָם! בְּשׁוֹטָה. וְהָא אִיכָּא צַעֲרָא! בִּמְפוּתָּה.

The Gemara asks: In the case of one who has relations with **his sister** who is a **grown woman, too,** although he does not pay a fine, **isn't there** compensation for **humiliation and degradation?**[H] He should be exempt from lashes in that case as well. The Gemara answers: **There,** the *halakha* in the mishna is **with regard to** his sister who is **an imbecile,**[N] with regard to whom there is no humiliation or degradation beyond her status as an imbecile. The Gemara asks: **But isn't** there payment for **pain**[H] even in the rape of an imbecile? The Gemara responds: The *halakha* is **with regard to a seduced woman,**[H] who is not entitled to payment for pain, as she engaged in relations willingly.

הָשְׁתָּא דְּאָתֵית לְהָכִי, אֲפִילּוּ תֵּימָא אֲחוֹתוֹ נַעֲרָה – בִּיתוֹמָה וּמְפוּתָּה.

The Gemara comments: **Now that you have arrived at this** explanation that the mishna is referring to a seduced woman, the mishna can be understood **even if you say** it is referring **to his sister** who is **a young woman.** The reason that the seducer does not pay the fine is that the *halakha* is **with regard to** one who is **an orphan and a seduced woman.**[N] Were her father alive, he would receive the payment. Because he died, the payment goes to her. Since she willingly participated in the relations, she relinquished her right to the payment, and the seducer is therefore liable to receive lashes.

אַלְמָא קָסָבַר עוּלָּא: כָּל הֵיכָא דְּאִיכָּא מָמוֹן וּמַלְקוֹת – מָמוֹנָא מְשַׁלֵּם, מִילְקָא לָא לָקֵי. מְנָא לֵיהּ לְעוּלָּא הָא? גָּמַר מֵחוֹבֵל בַּחֲבֵירוֹ: מַה חוֹבֵל בַּחֲבֵירוֹ, דְּאִיכָּא מָמוֹן וּמַלְקוֹת, מָמוֹנָא מְשַׁלֵּם, מִילְקָא לָא לָקֵי, אַף כָּל הֵיכָא דְּאִיכָּא מָמוֹן וּמַלְקוֹת, מָמוֹנָא מְשַׁלֵּם, מִילְקָא לָא לָקֵי.

The Gemara observes: **Apparently, Ulla maintains** that in **any** case **where there is** liability to both pay **money and** receive **lashes,** e.g., one who has forced relations with his sister who is a young woman, one **pays money** but **is not flogged.** The Gemara asks: **From where does Ulla** derive **this** principle? The Gemara answers: He **derives** it **from the** *halakha* **of one who injures another. Just as** with regard to **one who injures another where there is** liability to both pay **money** for the injury **and** receive **lashes** for violating the prohibition "Lest he continues to strike him" (Deuteronomy 25:3), the *halakha* there is that one **pays money** but **is not flogged, so too,** in **any** case **where there is** liability to both pay **money and** receive **lashes,** one **pays money** but **is not flogged.**

HALAKHA

In the case of…a grown woman, too, isn't there compensation for humiliation and degradation – בּוֹגֶרֶת נַמִי הָא אִיכָּא בּוֹשֶׁת וּפְגָם: One who rapes a grown woman is not liable to pay the fine, but he pays for her humiliation, degradation, and pain (Rambam *Sefer Nashim, Hilkhot Na'ara Betula* 2:11).

But isn't there payment for pain – וְהָא אִיכָּא צַעֲרָא: One who rapes an imbecile or a deaf-mute is liable to pay only for her suffering (Rambam *Sefer Nashim, Hilkhot Na'ara Betula* 2:11).

With regard to a seduced woman – בִּמְפוּתָּה: One who seduced a grown woman, a deaf-mute, or an imbecile is exempt from payment (Rambam *Sefer Nashim, Hilkhot Na'ara Betula* 2:11).

NOTES

With regard to his sister who is a young woman, etc. – בַּאֲחוֹתוֹ נַעֲרָה וכו׳: Similar answers are provided in the Jerusalem Talmud, with certain differences. The responses attributed here to Ulla are cited there in the name of Rabbi Natan bar Oshaya, while the Sages of Caesarea claim that it refers to a seduced woman or to one who waives her right to the payments.

With regard to an imbecile – בְּשׁוֹטָה: Rashi explains that an imbecile has no value. The Rashash points out that an imbecile does have value with regard to valuations (see *Arakhin* 2a), and he therefore explains that Rashi is referring to her degradation. As explained elsewhere, a woman's degradation is determined by estimating the difference between the amount one would pay to purchase her as a maidservant to marry his Hebrew slave before her rape and the amount one would pay after her rape. That is not relevant with regard to an imbecile.

With regard to one who is an orphan and a seduced woman – בִּיתוֹמָה וּמְפוּתָּה: There is a variant reading cited by some early commentaries: With regard to an orphan who is an imbecile and a seduced woman. Rashi deletes the word imbecile, as it is unnecessary. Even if she is a seduced orphan, she is not entitled to payment. The Ramban agrees with Rashi, adding that the other version resulted from the fact that a minor and an imbecile are typically listed together. Conversely, Rabbi Shmuel HaNagid accepts the variant reading, explaining that orphan is not meant literally; rather, the reference is to a young woman who was betrothed and divorced, whose legal status according to the opinion of Rabbi Yosei HaGelili, cited later (38a), is that of an orphan in her father's lifetime and she is not entitled to a fine. It is necessary to add that she is an imbecile as well, to exempt him from the payments for degradation and humiliation. A different interpretation is suggested by the Ritva. He contends that although an orphan who is not an imbecile waives the payment for her humiliation, she cannot exempt one from the payment for the humiliation suffered by her family. Therefore, the Gemara added that she was an imbecile.

מַה לְּחוֹבֵל בַּחֲבֵירוֹ – שֶׁכֵּן חַיָּיב בַּחֲמִשָּׁה דְּבָרִים, וְאִי מָמוֹנָא לְקוּלָּא, שֶׁכֵּן הוּתַּר מִכְּלָלוֹ בְּבֵית דִּין!

The Gemara asks: **What** is the basis for the comparison between other cases and the case of **one who injures another?** One who injures another cannot serve as a paradigm for cases of liability for both money and lashes because the case of one who injures another is particularly stringent, **as he is liable** to pay **five types** of indemnity:[N] Injury, pain, medical costs, loss of livelihood, and humiliation. **And if** payment of **money** is a more **lenient**[N] form of punishment than lashes, one could infer *a fortiori*: If in the stringent case of injuring another, one receives the more lenient punishment, all the more so would he receive the more lenient punishment in less stringent cases; nevertheless, one who injures another cannot serve as a paradigm for cases of liability for both money and lashes. The reason is that there is also a lenient aspect with regard to injuring another, **as it is permitted,** in departure **from its norm, in court.**[N] The court administers lashes, injuring those convicted. The leniency is that its application is selective.

אֶלָּא גָּמַר מֵעֵדִים זוֹמְמִין, מָה עֵדִים זוֹמְמִין דְּאִיכָּא מָמוֹן וּמַלְקוֹת – מָמוֹנָא מְשַׁלֵּם, מִילְקָא לָא לָקֵי! אַף כָּל הֵיכָא דְּאִיכָּא מָמוֹן וּמַלְקוֹת – מָמוֹנָא מְשַׁלֵּם, מִילְקָא לָא לָקֵי!

Rather, the Gemara states that Ulla **derives** this principle **from** the *halakha* of false, **conspiring witnesses.**[B] **Just as** with regard to **conspiring witnesses, where there is** liability to both pay **money,** if they falsely testified to render one liable for payment, **and** receive **lashes,** for violating the prohibition "You shall not bear false witness against your neighbor" (Exodus 20:12), and the *halakha* is that one **pays money** but **is not flogged, so too,** in **any** case **where there is** liability to both pay **money and** receive **lashes,** one **pays money** but **is not flogged.**

מַה לְּעֵדִים זוֹמְמִין – שֶׁכֵּן אֵינָן צְרִיכִים הַתְרָאָה, וְאִי מָמוֹנָא לְקוּלָּא הוּא – שֶׁכֵּן לֹא עָשׂוּ מַעֲשֶׂה!

The Gemara asks: **What** is the basis for the comparison of other cases to the case of **conspiring witnesses?** Conspiring witnesses cannot serve as a paradigm for cases of liability for both money and lashes because the case of conspiring witnesses is particularly stringent, **as they do not require forewarning.**[H] As a rule, the courts administer punishment only to one who was forewarned not to perform the transgression. The fact that this is not a requirement in the case of conspiring witnesses indicates that it is a particularly stringent prohibition. Therefore, no proof can be cited from the case of conspiring witnesses to other cases with regard to monetary payment instead of lashes. **And if** payment of **money** is a more **lenient** form of punishment than lashes, the case of conspiring witnesses also has a lenient aspect, **as they did not perform an action**[N] but merely spoke.

BACKGROUND

False conspiring witnesses – עֵדִים זוֹמְמִין: These are witnesses who are proven to have perjured themselves in order to cause another to lose a monetary dispute or cause him to be punished by the court. Testimony of witnesses can be invalidated in two manners: (1) Two other witnesses testify that an incident did not transpire as it was described by the first pair of witnesses. In that case, the testimony of neither pair is accepted, and the matter remains unresolved. (2) Two witnesses testify that the first pair of witnesses, whose testimony condemned the defendant, were elsewhere when the incident transpired and could not have witnessed the incident about which they testified. The second pair of witnesses does not contradict the version of events described by the first pair, which may in fact be true. They are merely testifying that the first pair was not present and therefore is not in a position to know what transpired. In that case, the testimony of the second pair of witnesses is accepted, and the testimony of the first pair of witnesses is rejected. Furthermore, the first pair of witnesses, once rendered false conspiring witnesses, are punished with the punishment that they sought to inflict on the defendant through their testimony (see Deuteronomy 19:16–19). Therefore, if their testimony would have resulted in the defendant's execution, they are both executed. If their testimony would have resulted in his receiving lashes, they are both flogged. If their testimony would have resulted in a penalty that cannot be applied to them, e.g., if their evidence would have disqualified the defendant from the priesthood, they are flogged.

HALAKHA

Conspiring witnesses…do not require forewarning – עֵדִים זוֹמְמִין...אֵינָן צְרִיכִים הַתְרָאָה: It is not necessary for conspiring witnesses to be forewarned prior to their testimony; rather, they are punished as soon as they are convicted for giving false testimony, as per the Gemara here and the Gemara in *Makkot* (4b; Rambam *Sefer Shofetim, Hilkhot Edut* 18:4 and *Kesef Mishne* there).

NOTES

What is the comparison to one who injures another, as he is liable to pay five types of indemnity – מַה לְּחוֹבֵל בַּחֲבֵירוֹ שֶׁכֵּן חַיָּיב בַּחֲמִשָּׁה דְּבָרִים: Although not all those who injure others are liable to pay all five indemnities, they all apply potentially: Injury, for permanent damage caused; pain, for the suffering he inflicted; medical costs, for the doctor's treatment and medicine; loss of livelihood, compensation for the period during which the victim was unable to work; and humiliation, for the shame the victim suffered as a result of the attack. Clearly, depending on the circumstances the aggressor might be liable to pay only some of these indemnities, or even only one of them. Apparently, not all of these categories apply to rape, for which one pays the following: The fine; degradation, which is parallel to injury; pain; and humiliation. An earlier version of Rashi's commentary, cited by the *Shita Mekubbetzet*, states that a rapist is not obligated to pay medical expenses. However, the Rid (42a) states that a rapist is sometimes liable to pay medical costs and loss of livelihood as well. However, in that case, the *halakha* of the five types of indemnity is not unique to one who injures another. It is possible that the payments of medical costs and loss of livelihood do not stem from the rape but from injuries one caused. If so, it falls into the category of one who injures another.

And if payment of money is more lenient – וְאִי מָמוֹנָא לְקוּלָּא: The Ritva, elaborating on *Tosafot*, asks: How can it be suggested that payment of money is the more lenient punishment? The Gemara states below that one who inflicts a wound and causes less than a *peruta* worth of damage is liable to be flogged. If he inflicted more serious damage, he pays. If payment of money is a more lenient punishment, he profits from commission of a more egregious transgression. The Ritva suggests that the Torah had compassion on the injured party. Although the aggressor receives a more lenient punishment, the victim receives compensation for his injury. The *Ḥatam Sofer* states that the comparison between the punishments here is not an attempt to determine the overall relationship between payments and lashes. Rather, the Gemara notes that sometimes one is liable to pay a large sum, in which case the payment of money is the more stringent punishment, whereas other times he is liable to pay a small sum, in which case it is a lenient punishment. The punishment of lashes is fixed, while monetary punishment varies.

As this prohibited action is permitted in departure from its norm in court – שֶׁכֵּן הוּתַּר מִכְּלָלוֹ בְּבֵית דִּין: The Ritva asks: How can it be said that the prohibition against injuring another is lenient because injury is permitted in court? Can there be any comparison between one who criminally assaults another to an officer of the court who performs a mitzva by administering lashes to a convicted criminal? He explains that despite this anomaly, the contention of: As this prohibited action is permitted in departure from its norm, is independent of the nature of the leniency. It merely points to the fact that the prohibition is not in effect in all circumstances.

As they did not perform an action – שֶׁכֵּן לֹא עָשׂוּ מַעֲשֶׂה: Although the Gemara in *Bava Metzia* (90b) states: Moving one's lips while speaking is considered an action, there is a difference between a full-fledged action and speech (Rabbeinu Crescas Vidal). The Rashba similarly distinguishes between a significant action and the insignificant action of moving one's lips. The Ritva suggests that the expression: Did not perform an action, is not referring to the fact that they sinned by speaking. Rather, it is a reference to the principle that false conspiring witnesses are executed only if the person they accused was not himself executed. Consequently, they are punished only if their testimony did not cause the performance of an action.

אֶלָּא, גָּמַר מִתַּרְוַיְיהוּ; מָה הַצַּד הַשָּׁוֶה שֶׁבָּהֶן – דְּאִיכָּא מָמוֹן וּמַלְקוּת – מָמוֹנָא מְשַׁלֵּם מִילְקָא לָא לָקֵי, אַף כׇּל הֵיכָא דְּאִיכָּא מָמוֹן וּמַלְקוּת – מָמוֹנָא מְשַׁלֵּם, מִילְקָא לָא לָקֵי. מַה לְּהַצַּד הַשָּׁוֶה שֶׁבָּהֶן – שֶׁכֵּן יֵשׁ בָּהֶן צַד חָמוּר, וְאִי מָמוֹנָא לְקוּלָּא הוּא – שֶׁכֵּן יֵשׁ בָּהֶן צַד הַקַּל!

Rather, Ulla **derives** the principle **from both of them,** the cases of one who injures another and of conspiring witnesses. **The common denominator of** both cases **is that there is** liability to both pay **money and** receive **lashes** and the *halakha* is that one **pays money** but **is not flogged; so too,** in **any** case **where there is** liability to both pay **money and** receive **lashes,** one **pays money** but **is not flogged.** The Gemara asks: **What** is the basis for the comparison of other cases to **the common denominator of** both cases, **as they have an element of stringency**[N] that does not exist in other prohibitions in that one who injures another pays five types of indemnity, and conspiring witnesses are flogged without forewarning? **And if** payment of **money** is a more **lenient** form of punishment than lashes, other cases cannot be derived from it, **as they have an element of leniency** that does not exist in other prohibitions. The prohibition in the case of one who injures another is selectively applied, as it is permitted, in departure from its norm, in court, and the case of conspiring witnesses is lenient because they performed no action.

NOTES

As they have an element of stringency – שֶׁכֵּן יֵשׁ בָּהֶן צַד חָמוּר: This attempt to refute an analogy based on the common denominator appearing elsewhere in the Talmud is questioned by the early commentaries. If an analogy can be refuted due to a common element of stringency, all analogies based on a common denominator can be refuted, as the only reason that the common denominator was necessary is because each of the sources has its own particular stringency or leniency. *Tosafot* explain that this objection is not raised in every case of an analogy based on a common denominator. It is raised only in cases where there is a common extreme stringency or leniency (see *Tosafot*). The Ramban states that the question of whether this explanation fits all the instances in which this refutation is raised requires additional analysis. Rabbeinu Tam in *Tosafot* suggests that the reason this refutation is raised here is because the same stringency and leniency apply in both cases. If conspiring witnesses accused one of injuring another they are liable to pay the five indemnities, and there are certain false testimonies that are permitted in court, with regard to which the prohibition "You shall not bear false witness against your neighbor" (Exodus 20:12) does not apply, e.g., testimony that they saw the new moon. The Ritva and others reject this explanation. A different explanation is suggested by the Ra'ah and his students: The objection of an element of stringency is raised only in cases when the stringent element is the very issue under discussion. In this case, since the relative severity of the various punishments is under discussion, the fact that the two sources both involve especially harsh punishments is in fact a relevant cause for refuting the analogy. By the same token, their particular leniencies are relevant when these *halakhot* are the basis of comparison to other punishments.

Perek **III**
Daf **32** Amud **b**

אֶלָּא, עוּלָּא "תַּחַת" "תַּחַת" גָּמַר, כְּתִיב הָכָא "תַּחַת אֲשֶׁר עִנָּהּ" וּכְתִיב הָתָם "עַיִן תַּחַת עַיִן", מָה הָתָם, מָמוֹנָא מְשַׁלֵּם מִילְקָא לָא לָקֵי – אַף כׇּל הֵיכָא דְּאִיכָּא מָמוֹנָא וּמַלְקוּת – מָמוֹנָא מְשַׁלֵּם, מִילְקָא לָא לָקֵי.

Rather, Ulla derives the fact that one pays and is not flogged by means of a verbal analogy between the terms **for** and **for.** The verse **states** with regard to rape: "And the man who lay with her shall give to the father of the young woman fifty shekels of silver, and to him she shall be as a wife, **because** [*taḥat*] **he tormented her"** (Deuteronomy 22:29), **and it states there,** with regard to injury: **"An eye for** [*taḥat*] **an eye"** (Exodus 21:24). **Just as there,** with regard to injury, one **pays money** and **is not flogged,** so too, in **any** case **where there is** liability to both pay **money and** receive **lashes,** one **pays money** but **is not flogged.**

רַבִּי יוֹחָנָן אָמַר: אֲפִילּוּ תֵּימָא אֲחוֹתוֹ נַעֲרָה. כָּאן – שֶׁהִתְרוּ בּוֹ, כָּאן – שֶׁלֹּא הִתְרוּ בּוֹ.

§ In proposing a different resolution to the apparent contradiction between the mishna here that rules that one pays a fine for raping his sister and the mishna in *Makkot* that rules that one is flogged in that case, **Rabbi Yoḥanan said: Even if you say** that both *mishnayot* are referring to **his sister** who is **a young woman, there** it is referring to a case **where** the witnesses **forewarned him,** and therefore the rapist is flogged; **here,** it is referring to a case **where** the witnesses **did not forewarn him.** Since no lashes are administered without forewarning, the rapist pays the fine.

אַלְמָא קָסָבַר רַבִּי יוֹחָנָן: כׇּל הֵיכָא דְּאִיכָּא מָמוֹן וּמַלְקוּת, וְאַתְרוּ בֵּיהּ, מִילְקָא לָקֵי, מָמוֹנָא לָא מְשַׁלֵּם. מְנָא לֵיהּ לְרַבִּי יוֹחָנָן הָא? אָמַר קְרָא: "כְּדֵי רִשְׁעָתוֹ" – מִשּׁוּם רִשְׁעָה אַחַת אַתָּה מְחַיְּיבוֹ, וְאִי אַתָּה מְחַיְּיבוֹ מִשּׁוּם שְׁתֵּי רִשְׁעָיוֹת, וּסְמִיךְ לֵיהּ "אַרְבָּעִים יַכֶּנּוּ".

The Gemara observes: **Apparently, Rabbi Yoḥanan maintains** that in **any** case **where there is** liability to both pay **money and** receive **lashes, and** the witnesses **forewarned him, he is flogged** but does not **pay money.** The Gemara asks: **From where does Rabbi Yoḥanan** derive **this** principle?[N] The Gemara explains that he derives it from that which **the verse states** with regard to one sentenced to lashes in the court: "The judge shall cause him to lie down, and to be beaten before him, **according to the measure of his wickedness"** (Deuteronomy 25:2), from which it is inferred: **For one** act of **wickedness,** i.e., punishment, **you can render him liable, but you cannot render him liable for two** acts of **wickedness. And juxtaposed to** this it states: **"Forty he shall strike him"** (Deuteronomy 25:3), indicating that the punishment that is administered when one is liable to receive two punishments is lashes and not payment.

NOTES

From where does Rabbi Yoḥanan derive this principle – מְנָא לֵיהּ לְרַבִּי יוֹחָנָן הָא: The Gemara asked earlier: From where did Ulla derive that one pays and is not flogged? This question indicates that without that source, the assumption would have been that one is flogged and does not pay. Here, the Gemara questions Rabbi Yoḥanan's source, indicating that the assumption would have been the opposite. Although the Gemara at times questions a certain opinion based on two conflicting lines of reasoning because neither is clear or obvious, the Gemara here is difficult. *Tosafot Yeshanim* and the Rosh explain that once Ulla cited support for his approach from a verbal analogy, the burden of proof shifts, and the Gemara then seeks the source for Rabbi Yoḥanan's opinion.

וַהֲרֵי חוֹבֵל בַּחֲבֵירוֹ, דְּאִיכָּא מָמוֹן וּמַלְקוֹת – מָמוֹנָא מְשַׁלֵּם, מִילְקָא לָא לָקֵי! וְכִי תֵּימָא: הָנֵי מִילֵּי הֵיכָא דְּלָא אַתְרוּ בֵּיהּ, אֲבָל אַתְרוּ בֵּיהּ – מִילְקָא לָקֵי, מָמוֹנָא לָא מְשַׁלֵּם, וְהָאָמַר רַבִּי אַמִּי אָמַר רַבִּי יוֹחָנָן: הִכָּהוּ הַכָּאָה שֶׁאֵין בָּהּ שָׁוֶה פְּרוּטָה – לוֹקֶה. הֵיכִי דָּמֵי? אִי דְּלָא אַתְרוּ בֵּיהּ – אַמַּאי לוֹקֶה? אֶלָּא פְּשִׁיטָא. דְּאַתְרוּ בֵּיהּ, וְטַעְמָא – דְּלֵית בָּהּ שָׁוֶה פְּרוּטָה, הָא אִית בָּהּ שָׁוֶה פְּרוּטָה – מָמוֹנָא מְשַׁלֵּם, מִילְקָא לָא לָקֵי!

The Gemara asks: **And** what of the case of **one who injures another where there is** liability to both pay **money and** receive **lashes,** in which case one **pays money** but **is not flogged? And lest you say** that **this applies only when** the witnesses **did not forewarn him, but if they forewarned him** before he struck his friend he **is flogged** but **does not pay money, didn't Rabbi Ami** say that **Rabbi Yoḥanan said:** If one **struck** another with **a blow that** does **not** cause damage that amounts to **the value of a** ***peruta***,[H] he is **flogged? The Gemara asks: What are the circumstances** of that case? **If** it is a case **where** the witnesses **did not forewarn him, why is he flogged?** No lashes are administered without forewarning. **Rather, obviously** it is a case **where they forewarned him, and the reason** he is flogged is that **there is not** damage that amounts to **the value of a** ***peruta***. The damages are not quantifiable. The Gemara infers: However, if **there is** damage that amounts to **the value of a** ***peruta***, he **pays money** and **is not flogged,** even though he was forewarned.

כִּדְאָמַר רַבִּי אִילְעָא: בְּפֵירוּשׁ רִיבְּתָה תּוֹרָה עֵדִים זוֹמְמִין לְתַשְׁלוּמִין, הָכָא נָמֵי, בְּפֵירוּשׁ רִיבְּתָה תּוֹרָה חוֹבֵל בַּחֲבֵירוֹ לְתַשְׁלוּמִין. וְהֵיכָא אִיתְּמַר דְּרַבִּי אִילְעָא – אַהָא: מְעִידִין אָנוּ אֶת אִישׁ פְּלוֹנִי שֶׁחַיָּיב לַחֲבֵירוֹ מָאתַיִם זוּז, וְנִמְצְאוּ זוֹמְמִין – לוֹקִין וּמְשַׁלְּמִין, שֶׁלֹּא הַשֵּׁם הַמְבִיאָן לִידֵי מַכּוֹת מְבִיאָן לִידֵי תַשְׁלוּמִין, דִּבְרֵי רַבִּי מֵאִיר, וַחֲכָמִים אוֹמְרִים: כׇּל הַמְשַׁלֵּם אֵינוֹ לוֹקֶה.

The Gemara answers that the fact that conspiring witnesses pay money can be explained **in accordance with that** which **Rabbi Ile'a said** in a different context: **The Torah explicitly amplified** the case of **conspiring witnesses** to include liability **for payment.** The Torah employed language indicating that conspiring witnesses who testified falsely in order to render one liable for payment must pay the sum and are not flogged. **Here, too,** with regard to injury, **the Torah explicitly amplified** the case of **one who injures another** to include liability **for payment.**[H] The Gemara asks: **And where is this** statement **of Rabbi Ile'a stated?** The Gemara answers that it is stated **concerning this** mishna (*Makkot* 4a). If witnesses said: **We testify that so-and-so owes another two hundred dinar, and** these witnesses **were discovered** to be **conspiring** witnesses; **they are flogged and pay, as the source** [*shem*] **that brings them to** liability to receive **lashes does not brings them to** liability for **payment.**[N] Each liability has an independent source; the source for lashes is: "You shall not bear false witness against your neighbor," while the source for payment is: "You shall do unto him as he conspired" (Deuteronomy 19:19). This is **the statement of Rabbi Meir. And the Rabbis say: Anyone who pays is not flogged.**[NH]

וְנֵימָא: כׇּל הַלּוֹקֶה אֵינוֹ מְשַׁלֵּם! אָמַר רַבִּי אִילְעָא: בְּפֵירוּשׁ רִיבְּתָה תּוֹרָה עֵדִים זוֹמְמִין לְתַשְׁלוּמִין. – הֵיכָן רִיבְּתָה תּוֹרָה? מִכְּדֵי כְּתִיב ״וַעֲשִׂיתֶם לוֹ כַּאֲשֶׁר זָמַם לַעֲשׂוֹת לְאָחִיו״. ״יָד בְּיָד״ לָמָּה לִי – דָּבָר הַנִּיתָּן מִיָּד לְיָד. וּמַאי נִיהוּ – מָמוֹן.

And with regard to that mishna, the Gemara asks: **Let us say,** on the contrary, that **anyone who is flogged does not pay. Rabbi Ile'a said: The Torah explicitly amplified** the case of **conspiring witnesses for payment,** not lashes. The Gemara asks: **Where did the Torah amplify** the case of conspiring witnesses? The Gemara explains: **Now, since it states** with regard to conspiring witnesses: **"And you shall do unto him as he conspired to do unto his brother"** (Deuteronomy 19:19); **why do I** require the Torah to state in his punishment: **"A hand for a hand"** (Deuteronomy 19:21)?[N] This indicates that the punishment that takes precedence is one in which there is **an item that is given from hand to hand, and what is that** item? It is **money.**

NOTES

As the source [*shem*] that brings them to liability to receive lashes does not bring them to liability for payment – שֶׁלֹּא הַשֵּׁם הַמְבִיאָן לִידֵי מַכּוֹת מְבִיאָן לִידֵי תַשְׁלוּמִין: According to Rashi, the term: The source [*shem*], is referring to the biblical source for his punishment. Rabbi Meir maintains that conspiring witnesses are liable to payment due to the verse "You shall do unto him as he conspired," and the liability to receive lashes is for their transgression of "You shall not bear false witness." *Tosafot* question this understanding, as they cite proof that Rabbi Meir does not distinguish in that manner, and if the liability for lashes and payment are derived from the same verse, he holds that the sinner is lashed and pays. Some early commentaries claim that Rabbi Meir said his statement only in accordance with the opinion of the Rabbis (see *Tosafot*). Many early commentaries follow the approach of the Ramban in tractate *Makkot* (4b), who asserts that were the liability of conspiring witnesses to receive lashes, in fact, derived from the verse "You shall do unto him as he conspired," the witnesses would not be flogged, as the Torah says that they receive the punishment they plotted to inflict on others, but no more. Since they conspired to obligate the defendant to pay and not to be flogged, they too are liable only to pay and not to be flogged. According to Rabbi Meir, in contrast, it is only the obligation to pay that is derived from the verse "You shall do unto him as he conspired," while their liability to be flogged is derived from a different verse. Since Rabbi Meir maintains in general that one can be flogged and pay for a single transgression, these conspiring witnesses are flogged. According to this approach, the decisive point is not that there are two different verses, but that the source for the witnesses' liability to receive lashes is not their conspiracy but the fact that they gave false testimony. Rabbi Meir contends that their liability in this regard is a general one, unrelated to the particular individual who was the object of their testimony.

Anyone who pays is not flogged – כׇּל הַמְשַׁלֵּם אֵינוֹ לוֹקֶה: Some early commentaries explain that this is as an elaboration on the opinion of the Rabbis: Not only do they reject Rabbi Meir's ruling that conspiring witnesses are flogged due to the verse "You shall not bear false witness," as this is a prohibition that does not entail an action, but in general they maintain that one does not receive two punishments for a single transgression. Others claim that Rabbi Meir made his statement in accordance with the opinion of the Rabbis. He himself is of the opinion that one can both be flogged and pay; however, he contends that in this case even the Rabbis should concede that the witnesses are liable to receive lashes, as their liability stems from a different source. The Rabbis respond that there is no difference whether their liability results from one verse or two (see Ritva).

Why do I require a hand for a hand – יָד בְּיָד לָמָּה לִי: *Tosafot* ask why this exposition is necessary, as the Torah already stated: "As he conspired" indicating that witnesses who sought to render one falsely liable to pay are themselves liable to pay that sum. Why, then, is another exposition necessary to obligate the witnesses to pay for an item that is given from hand to hand? They answer that otherwise the thought would have been that they are liable for payment only if they conspired to obligate him to pay money. In contrast, in a case where they plotted to obligate him to pay and to be flogged, perhaps they receive both punishments. Therefore, the verse teaches that whenever they are obligated to pay, they are not flogged (see Ritva). *Tosafot* suggest that this exposition is in fact unnecessary for conspiring witnesses, but it serves to emphasize the principle that one who injures another is not literally punished with an eye for an eye but with payment. The Ritva asks: Once this derivation is learned, why not say that conspiring witnesses liable to be executed and liable to pay should pay and should not be executed? He answers that with regard to lashes and payment, it is unclear which punishment is more severe, and therefore, the Sages derived that they pay and are not flogged, whether that constitutes a leniency or a stringency. However, the death penalty is clearly a more severe punishment than payment, and the Torah certainly did not intend to be lenient with one liable to be executed.

HALAKHA

If one struck another with a blow that does not cause damage that amounts to the value of a *peruta* – הִכָּהוּ הַכָּאָה שֶׁאֵין בָּהּ שָׁוֶה פְּרוּטָה: If one injured another and the damage amounts to less than the value of a *peruta*, he is flogged and does not pay. The *halakha* is in accordance with the opinion of Rabbi Ami in the name of Rabbi Yoḥanan (Rambam *Sefer Nezikim, Hilkhot Ḥovel UMazik* 5:3; *Shulḥan Arukh, Ḥoshen Mishpat* 420:2).

The Torah explicitly amplified the case of one who injures another to include liability for payment – רִיבְּתָה תּוֹרָה חוֹבֵל בַּחֲבֵירוֹ לְתַשְׁלוּמִין: One who injures another on the Day of Atonement is obligated to pay damages, even though he is liable to receive lashes or *karet* for his action. Although the principle is that one who is liable both to receive lashes and to pay is flogged and does not pay, the Torah explicitly states that one who injures another pays for the injury. The *halakha* is in accordance with the opinion of Rabbi Yoḥanan in his dispute with Ulla (Rambam *Sefer Nezikim, Hilkhot Ḥovel UMazik* 4:9; *Shulḥan Arukh, Ḥoshen Mishpat* 424:2).

Conspiring witnesses for payment – עֵדִים זוֹמְמִין לְתַשְׁלוּמִין: If witnesses who testified that a person owes money were discovered to be false conspiring witnesses, they pay that sum and are not flogged. The *halakha* is in accordance with the opinion of the Rabbis in their dispute with the individual opinion of Rabbi Meir (Rambam *Sefer Shofetim, Hilkhot Edut* 18:1 and *Kesef Mishne* there; *Tur, Ḥoshen Mishpat* 38).

חוֹבֵל בַּחֲבֵירוֹ נַמִי, מִכְּדִי כְּתִיב ״כַּאֲשֶׁר עָשָׂה כֵּן יֵעָשֶׂה לּוֹ״, ״כֵּן יִנָּתֶן בּוֹ״ לָמָּה לִי – דָּבָר שֶׁיֵּשׁ בּוֹ נְתִינָה, וּמַאי נִיהוּ – מָמוֹן.

The same can be said with regard to **one who injures another. Now, since it states:** "And a man who places a blemish upon his counterpart, **as he has done so shall be done to him**" (Leviticus 24:19), **why do I** require the Torah to state: "As one who places a blemish upon a man, **so shall be placed [*yinnaten*] upon him**" (Leviticus 24:20)? This teaches that this is referring to **an item that involves giving [*netina*], and what is that** item? It is **money.**

וְרַבִּי יוֹחָנָן, מַאי טַעְמָא לָא אָמַר כְּעוּלָּא? אִם כֵּן ״בִּטַּלְתָּ עֶרְוַת אֲחוֹתְךָ לֹא תְגַלֶּה״

The Gemara asks: **And Rabbi Yoḥanan, what is the reason** that **he did not say** the same *halakha* **as Ulla,**[N] that where there is liability to both pay money and receive lashes, one pays money but is not flogged? The Gemara answers: **If so,** if that were the case, **you have rendered moot** the prohibition **"The nakedness of your sister…you shall not uncover"** (Leviticus 18:9) in that contrary to the standard prohibitions, no lashes would be administered for its violation.

NOTES

What is the reason that he did not say the same *halakha* as Ulla – מַאי טַעְמָא לָא אָמַר כְּעוּלָּא: The Ramban notes that it is obvious why the Gemara did not ask why Ulla did not say the same *halakha* as Rabbi Yoḥanan, as Ulla derives his *halakha* from a verbal analogy. However, the question of the Gemara is difficult, as it is clear why Rabbi Yoḥanan rejected Ulla's conclusion; it is because he did not accept his verbal analogy. *Tosafot* explain that Ulla's derivation is universally accepted, and therefore it cannot be said that Rabbi Yoḥanan rejects it. Furthermore, as the Ramban himself explains, Ulla's derivation by means of verbal analogy is more authoritative than Rabbi Yoḥanan's derivation by means of juxtaposed verses. According to the Rashba and other early commentaries, that is the basis for the Gemara's question with regard to Rabbi Yoḥanan's approach. The Ramban maintains that the Gemara is not raising a difficulty with regard to the opinion of Rabbi Yoḥanan but merely seeking to clarify the basis for his opinion.

Perek **III**
Daf **33** Amud **a**

חוֹבֵל בַּחֲבֵירוֹ נַמִי, אִם כֵּן, בִּטַּלְתָּ ״לֹא יוֹסִיף פֶּן יוֹסִיף״! עֵדִים זוֹמְמִין נַמִי, אִם כֵּן, בִּטַּלְתָּ ״וְהָיָה אִם בִּן הַכּוֹת הָרָשָׁע״! אֶלָּא עֵדִים זוֹמְמִין אֶפְשָׁר לְקַיּוֹמָהּ בְּבֶן גְּרוּשָׁה וּבֶן חֲלוּצָה. חוֹבֵל בַּחֲבֵירוֹ נַמִי, אִיכָּא לְקַיּוֹמָהּ כְּגוֹן שֶׁהִכָּהוּ הַכָּאָה שֶׁאֵין בָּהּ שְׁוֵה פְּרוּטָה.

The Gemara asks: Based on that reasoning, the same would hold true for **one who injures another as well;**[N] **if so,** if he pays and is not lashed, **you have rendered moot** the prohibition "Forty he shall strike him; **he shall not exceed, lest if he should exceed**" (Deuteronomy 25:3). The same would hold true for **conspiring witnesses as well; if so, you have rendered moot** the verse interpreted as addressing the matter of conspiring witnesses: **"And it shall be if the wicked man deserves to be flogged"** (Deuteronomy 25:2).[N] **Rather,** with regard to **conspiring witnesses,** that verse **can be fulfilled** in the case **of the son of a divorcée or the son of a *ḥalutza*.** If witnesses testified that a priest is the son of a divorcée or a *ḥalutza* and were discovered to be conspiring witnesses, there is no payment and they are flogged. With regard to **one who injures another as well,** the verse **can be fulfilled** in a case **where he struck him** with **a blow that** does **not** cause damage amounting to **the value of a *peruta*.**

אֲחוֹתוֹ נַמִי, אִיכָּא לְקַיּוֹמָהּ בַּאֲחוֹתוֹ בּוֹגֶרֶת! אָמַר לָךְ רַבִּי יוֹחָנָן: הַאי ״תַּחַת אֲשֶׁר עִינָּהּ״ מִיבָּעֵי לֵיהּ לְכִדְאַבַּיֵי, דְּאָמַר אַבַּיֵי: אָמַר קְרָא ״תַּחַת אֲשֶׁר עִינָּהּ״, הַאי – ״תַּחַת אֲשֶׁר עִינָּהּ״, מִכְּלָל דְּאִיכָּא בּוֹשֶׁת וּפְגָם.

The Gemara raises a difficulty: If so, with regard to **one's sister as well,**[N] the lashes **can be fulfilled** in the case of one who had forced relations **with his sister** who is **a grown woman.** Since there is no fine in that case, he is flogged and the verse is not moot. The Gemara answers: **Rabbi Yoḥanan** could have **said to you** that he does not agree with Ulla because **this** verse: **"Because he tormented her"** (Deuteronomy 22:29), is not available for a verbal analogy, as **he requires it to** derive **in accordance with that** which **Abaye** said, **as Abaye said** that **the verse states:** The fine of fifty dinar is payment **"because he tormented her"; by inference** one may conclude **that** beyond the fine, **there is** compensation for **humiliation and degradation.**

וְעוּלָּא נָפְקָא לֵיהּ מִדְּרָבָא. דְּאָמַר רָבָא: אָמַר קְרָא: ״וְנָתַן הָאִישׁ הַשּׁוֹכֵב עִמָּהּ לַאֲבִי הַנַּעֲרָה חֲמִשִּׁים כָּסֶף״, הֲנָאַת שְׁכִיבָה – חֲמִשִּׁים, מִכְּלָל דְּאִיכָּא בּוֹשֶׁת וּפְגָם.

The Gemara asks: **And Ulla,** who uses this verse to derive a verbal analogy, from where does he derive the *halakha* stated by Abaye? The Gemara answers: **He derives it from** the statement of **Rava,** who derives that *halakha* from the same verse, **as Rava said** that **the verse states: "And the man who lay with her shall give to the father of the young woman fifty shekels of silver"** (Deuteronomy 22:29). The superfluous phrase "who lay with her" teaches that it is for **the pleasure of lying** with her that he pays **fifty** shekels, i.e., fifty *sela*; **by inference** one may conclude **that** beyond the fine, **there is** compensation for **humiliation and degradation.**

NOTES

One who injures another as well, etc. – חוֹבֵל בַּחֲבֵירוֹ נַמִי וכו׳: Why was Rabbi Yoḥanan more concerned about rendering the prohibition with regard to one's sister moot than he was with regard to one who injures another or conspiring witnesses? The Ritva explains that there is no independent prohibition with regard to one who injures another. It is derived from the verse written with regard to the officer of the court: "Lest he exceed" (Deuteronomy 25:3). Likewise, the prohibition against conspiring to bear false witness is also derived from a verse written in another context. In contrast, with regard to a sister, the prohibition is explicit: "The nakedness of your sister…you shall not uncover" (Leviticus 18:9).

You have rendered moot: And it shall be if the wicked man deserves to be flogged – בִּטַּלְתָּ וְהָיָה אִם בִּן הַכּוֹת הָרָשָׁע: Why doesn't the Gemara cite the relevant prohibition and say that you have rendered moot the verse "You shall not bear false witness"? One answer is that the prohibition "You shall not bear false witness" is a prohibition that serves as a warning of death at the hands of the court, for which one is not liable to receive lashes (*Shita Yeshana*, cited in *Shita Mekubbetzet*). Alternatively, some Sages maintain that because it is a prohibition that does not involve an action, there are no lashes. Therefore, the Gemara cited the verse from which the punishment of lashes in this case is derived.

One's sister as well, etc. – אֲחוֹתוֹ נַמִי וכו׳: Why didn't the Gemara raise the difficulty that according to Rabbi Yoḥanan this negates the obligation "He shall give to the father of the young woman" in the case of one who rapes his sister? The Rashba explains that this mitzva can be fulfilled in the case of a sister if he received no forewarning, whereas according to Ulla's opinion, there would be no possibility of lashes at all in the case of a virgin sister.

HALAKHA

Conspiring witnesses…are not subject to forewarning – עדים דממין...לאו בני התראה נינהו: Conspiring witnesses do not require forewarning. Although corporal punishment is generally not administered unless the guilty party was forewarned, this does not apply to conspiring witnesses (Rambam *Sefer Shofetim*, *Hilkhot Edut* 18:4).

They could say: We forgot – אמרי אישתלין: One is liable to receive corporal punishment only if he committed the transgression after being forewarned within an interval equivalent to the time of speaking. As explained here, the reason is that otherwise he could claim that he forgot the forewarning (Rambam *Sefer Shofetim*, *Hilkhot Sanhedrin* 12:2).

BACKGROUND

Forewarning – התראה: This is a formal warning to one who is about to violate a prohibition. The forewarning must include the fact that the action that he is about to perform is prohibited, and must also include the punishment that he will receive. Capital and corporal punishment can be administered only with forewarning that is acknowledged by the transgressor. In rare instances, e.g., the cases of false conspiring witnesses or one who incites to idol worship, punishment is administered without forewarning.

רבי אליעזר אומר: עדים זוממין ממונא משלמי ומילקא לא לקי, משום דלאו בני התראה נינהו. אמר רבא: תדע, ניתרי בהו אימת? ניתרי בהו מעיקרא – אמרי אישתלין. ניתרי בהו בשעת מעשה – פרשי ולא מסהדי. ניתרי בהו לבסוף – מאי דהוה הוה.

§ **Rabbi Eliezer says:** The reason that **conspiring witnesses pay money**[N] **but are not flogged** is **due to** the fact **that they are not subject to forewarning,**[HB] and without forewarning there are no lashes. **Rava said: Know** that this is true, since there is no practical manner to forewarn them, as **when** would **we forewarn them?** Perhaps **let us forewarn them initially,** before they come to testify; in that case, the forewarning would be ineffective because they could **say: We forgot**[H] the forewarning. Then **let us forewarn them at the moment of the action,** just before they testify; in that case they will **leave and not testify**[N] at all, as concern for potential repercussions will intimidate them into silence. Or, **let us forewarn them at the end** after their testimony; in that case **that which was, was,**[N] and forewarning at that point is pointless.

מתקיף לה אביי: וניתרי בהו בתוך כדי דבור! מתקיף לה רב אחא בריה דרב איקא: וניתרי בהו מעיקרא, ונרמז בהו רמוזי!

Abaye strongly **objects to this: And let us warn them within** an interval **equivalent** to the time **of speaking,**[N] during the brief period after they completed their statements, at which time the testimony is not yet considered to have concluded. Since they can still retract or amend their testimony during that period, a warning delivered at that point would be timely and effective. **Rav Aha, son of Rav Ika,** also strongly **objects to this: And let us forewarn them initially,** before they testify, **and gesture to them**[N] during the actual testimony, reminding them of the forewarning so they will be unable to claim that they forgot it.

הדר אמר אביי: לאו מילתא היא דאמרי: אי סלקא דעתך עדים זוממין צריכין התראה, כי לא מתרינן בהו לא קטלינן להו – מי איכא מידי דאינהו בעו קטיל בלא התראה, ואינהו בעו התראה? הא בעינן "ועשיתם לו כאשר זמם לעשות לאחיו" וליכא.

Abaye then said: That which I stated is not a significant **matter.** Instead, **if it enters your mind** that **conspiring witnesses require forewarning, when we do not forewarn them we do not kill them.** However, **is there a matter in which they sought to kill** the defendant **without forewarning** him, as their testimony was false, **and** in order to punish them **they require forewarning?**[N] **Don't we require** that their punishment reflect the verse **"And you shall do unto him as he conspired to do unto his brother"** (Deuteronomy 19:19)? **And** if they require forewarning that **is not** the case.

NOTES

Rabbi Eliezer says: Conspiring witnesses pay money – רבי אליעזר אומר: עדים זוממין ממונא משלמי: Most early commentaries continue along lines suggested by Rashi and explain that Rabbi Eliezer contends that since there are two possible punishments, money and lashes, it stands to reason that they would pay and not be flogged because, as a rule, corporal punishment is administered only if there was forewarning, a condition that does not affect payment (Ra'ah; Rashba; Rabbeinu Crescas Vidal). This leads to a question raised by Rashi: If so, why are those who testified that a priest is the son of a divorcée liable to receive lashes? He explains that since fulfillment of the verse "And you shall do unto him as he conspired" is impossible, as explained at length in *Makkot*, the sole option remaining is to administer lashes. Rabbi Eliezer, however, was referring to a situation where the choice is between two available punishments for a single transgression. The Maharsha asks: Why not say that one who is liable to be executed and pay should pay, for the same reason that there is no execution without forewarning? He answers that conspiring witnesses are not liable to be executed because they violated the prohibition "You shall not bear false witness"; rather, they are executed due to the verse "And you shall do unto him as he conspired to do unto his brother."

They will leave and not testify – פרשי ולא מסהדי: Based on Rashi's commentary, apparently they will leave and not testify because they are humiliated by the suspicion that they will testify falsely. The Ritva explains that if they are warned just before they testify they will be concerned that false witnesses might come and render them conspiring witnesses, and they will prefer not to testify at all. The early commentaries inquire into the difference between this *halakha*, where there is concern that they might refrain from testifying, and the *halakha* that in capital cases witnesses are threatened in order to discourage false testimony, where the possibility that they might leave and not testify is not a concern. Several answers were suggested. The most common approach is that in capital cases the witnesses are not actually threatened, as explained in tractate *Sanhedrin*; they are merely informed of the severity of capital cases in general terms, and there is no suspicion voiced that they will testify falsely.

That which was, was – מאי דהוה הוה: Rashi states that they cannot change their testimony once they have delivered it. The *Shita Yeshana*, cited in the *Shita Mekubbetzet*, explains that since they already violated the prohibition with their testimony, warning them is pointless.

Within an interval equivalent to the time of speaking – בתוך כדי דבור: *Tosafot* ask: Doesn't it take longer than that to state the forewarning, and therefore the witnesses would be unable to resume their testimony within that interval? They explain that as long as they remain engaged in the same matter it is considered within an interval equivalent to the time of speaking. A slightly different interpretation is offered by the Ra'avad. He claims that if witnesses require a warning, their testimony would not be complete until after that warning was given. Therefore, the interval is measured only from the conclusion of the warning.

And gesture to them – ונרמז בהו רמוזי: Rashi explains that it is possible to gesture subtly, consistent with his approach that the concern is the embarrassment of the witnesses. The Rashba explains, in keeping with the plain understanding of the Gemara, that the gestures remind them of the earlier warning.

And they require forewarning – ואינהו בעו התראה: Even so, one is not punished for transgressions committed when he was unwitting or unaware. How, then, can it be ascertained that they acted intentionally? One answer is that in general, the assumption is that one is aware that he is violating a prohibition, and therefore the assumption is that a transgressor acted intentionally (*Ketzot HaHoshen* 28:8). However, there is a Torah decree that no punishment may be administered without forewarning adjacent to the act. Here, there is no need for forewarning, as it is clear that they know it is wrong to testify falsely (*Birkat Avraham*).

מַתְקִיף לָהּ רַב סַמָּא בְּרֵיהּ דְּרַב יִרְמְיָה: אֶלָּא מֵעַתָּה, בֶּן גְּרוּשָׁה וּבֶן חֲלוּצָה, דְּלָא מִכִּ״אֲשֶׁר זָמַם״ קָא מִיתְרַבֵּי, לִיבָּעֵי הַתְרָאָה! אָמַר קְרָא: ״מִשְׁפַּט אֶחָד יִהְיֶה לָכֶם״, מִשְׁפָּט הַשָּׁוֶה לְכוּלְּכֶם.

Rav Samma, son of Rav Yirmeya, strongly **objects to this: However, if** what you say is **so,** when witnesses falsely accuse a priest of being **the son of a divorcée or the son of a *ḥalutza*,** as their punishment **is not amplified from** the verse **"As he conspired"** but rather they are punished for violating the prohibition "You shall not bear false witness against your neighbor," **let them require forewarning.** The Gemara answers that **the verse states: "You shall have one manner of law"** (Leviticus 24:22), meaning that there must be **a law equal for all of you.**[N] Since in standard cases of conspiring witnesses no forewarning is required, even in exceptional cases like testimony that a priest is the son of a divorcée or a *ḥalutza*, forewarning is not required.

רַב שֵׁישָׁא בְּרֵיהּ דְּרַב אִידִי אָמַר: חוֹבֵל בַּחֲבֵירוֹ נַמִי, מָמוֹנָא מְשַׁלֵּם וּמִילְקָא לָא לָקֵי – מֵהָכָא: ״וְכִי יִנָּצוּ אֲנָשִׁים וְנָגְפוּ אִשָּׁה הָרָה וְיָצְאוּ יְלָדֶיהָ״, וְאָמַר רַבִּי אֶלְעָזָר: בְּמַצּוּת שֶׁבְּמִיתָה הַכָּתוּב מְדַבֵּר, דִּכְתִיב ״וְאִם אָסוֹן יִהְיֶה וְנָתַתָּה נֶפֶשׁ תַּחַת נָפֶשׁ״.

§ **Rav Sheisha, son of Rav Idi, said:** The fact that in the case of **one who injures another as well**[N] **he pays money and is not flogged** is derived not by means of a verbal analogy but **from here: "If men quarrel and hurt a pregnant woman so that her child departs from her,** and yet no harm follow, he shall be punished as imposed upon him by the woman's husband" (Exodus 21:22). **And Rabbi Elazar said: The verse is speaking of a quarrel that involves death,**[N] i.e., they sought to kill each other, **as it is written: "And if any harm follow, then you shall give a soul for a soul"** (Exodus 21:23).

הֵיכִי דָּמֵי? אִי דְּלָא אַתְרוּ בֵּיהּ – אַמַּאי מִיקְטִיל, אֶלָּא פְּשִׁיטָא דְּאַתְרוּ בֵּיהּ, וּמוּתְרֶה לְדָבָר חָמוּר הָוֵי מוּתְרֶה לְדָבָר הַקַּל, וְאָמַר רַחֲמָנָא ״וְלֹא יִהְיֶה אָסוֹן עָנוֹשׁ יֵעָנֵשׁ״.

The Gemara asks: **What are the circumstances** of this case? **If they did not forewarn one** not to kill the other, **why is he killed** if the death of his opponent ensues? **Rather, obviously** it is a case **where they forewarned him, and** the principle is that **one who is forewarned with regard to a severe matter,** murdering his counterpart, **is forewarned with regard to a lesser matter,**[H] injuring his counterpart. **And** although he is forewarned against injuring another, which violates a prohibition and is punishable by lashes, **the Merciful One states: "And yet no harm follow, he shall be punished"** (Exodus 21:22), indicating that one pays and is not flogged.

מַתְקִיף לָהּ רַב אַשִׁי: מִמַּאי דְּמוּתְרֶה לְדָבָר חָמוּר הָוֵי מוּתְרֶה לְדָבָר הַקַּל, דִּלְמָא לָא הָוֵי? אִם תִּמְצָא לוֹמַר הָוֵי – מִמַּאי דְּמִיתָה חֲמוּרָה,

Rav Ashi strongly **objects to this** proof. First of all, with regard to your initial assumption, **from where** do you ascertain **that one who is forewarned with regard to a severe matter**[N] **is forewarned with regard to a lesser matter? Perhaps he is not** considered forewarned with regard to the lesser matter. Furthermore, even **if you say** that one **is** in fact forewarned with regard to a lesser matter, **from where** do you ascertain **that** the **death** penalty is a more **severe** punishment than lashes?

HALAKHA

Forewarned with regard to a severe matter – מוּתְרֶה לְדָבָר חָמוּר: The question of whether one forewarned with regard to a severe matter is forewarned with regard to a lesser matter remains unresolved. The *Ein Mishpat* claims that the Rambam indicates that one who was forewarned that his action is punishable by death in general is considered forewarned with regard to all forms of executions, regardless of their degree of severity. However, this does not resolve the question with regard to one who was forewarned specifically with regard to a severe death penalty. *Tosafot* suggest that there might be a Torah decree that one must be forewarned specifically with regard to the exact punishment for which he is liable (see Rambam *Sefer Shofetim*, *Hilkhot Sanhedrin* 12:2).

NOTES

A law equal for all of you – מִשְׁפַּט הַשָּׁוֶה לְכוּלְּכֶם: This does not mean that the details of all *halakhot* are the same, as clearly there is a difference between one who injures another, one who pays and is not flogged, and other cases. Rather, the meaning is that when punishment is administered for a particular prohibition, e.g., "You shall not bear false witness," there is no distinction between different cases where the prohibition applies (*Shita Yeshana*, cited in *Shita Mekubbetzet*).

One who injures another as well – חוֹבֵל בַּחֲבֵירוֹ נַמִי: In this context, some commentaries cite the earlier statement of *Tosafot* (32b) that the fact that one who injures another pays and is not flogged is derived from the verse "A hand for a hand" (Deuteronomy 19:21), written with regard to conspiring witnesses. Rabbi Eliezer, at least according to Rava, maintains that this verse is unnecessary in the context of conspiring witnesses, as it can be learned by logical reasoning; therefore, with regard to one who injures another it should be learned by logical reasoning as well (*Shita Mekubbetzet*).

The verse is speaking of a quarrel that involves death – בְּמַצּוּת שֶׁבְּמִיתָה הַכָּתוּב מְדַבֵּר: The verse speaks of two men who were fighting with each other, and in the course of their struggle they hurt a woman. Since "a soul for a soul" is understood literally in this case, although some Sages maintain that here too it is referring to payment of money, the men must have been forewarned not to kill each other. This is according to the opinion that one who intended to kill one person and killed another is liable.

From where do you ascertain that one who is forewarned with regard to a severe matter, etc. – מִמַּאי דְּמוּתְרֶה לְדָבָר חָמוּר וכו׳: The principle that one forewarned with regard to a severe matter is forewarned with regard to a lesser matter seems obvious, since if one is aware that his action is punishable by a severe punishment and decides to perform the action anyway, he certainly accepts a lesser punishment as well. The opposite contention, as explained by *Tosafot*, is that there is a Torah decree that one is punished only if he received forewarning that reflects his precise punishment, whether it is a severe or lesser punishment. Others explain that since it is derived that if a murderer cannot be executed with the death penalty designated for his crime he is executed with another form of death, it can be inferred that those liable to receive other punishments cannot be punished with any other punishment than the one to which they are liable, even if it is a lesser punishment than the designated one (Rabbi David Bonfils on *Sanhedrin* 80b).

דִּלְמָא מַלְקוֹת חָמוּר? דְּאָמַר רַב: אִילְמָלֵי נַגְּדוּהּ לַחֲנַנְיָה מִישָׁאֵל וַעֲזַרְיָה – פָּלְחוּ לְצַלְמָא! אֲמַר לֵיהּ רַב סַמָּא בְּרֵיהּ דְּרַב אַסִי לְרַב אַשִׁי, וְאָמְרִי לָהּ רַב סַמָּא בְּרֵיהּ דְּרַב אַשִׁי לְרַב אַשִׁי: וְלָא שָׁנֵי לָךְ בֵּין הַכָּאָה שֶׁיֵּשׁ לָהּ קִצְבָּה לְהַכָּאָה שֶׁאֵין לָהּ קִצְבָּה?!

Perhaps the punishment of **lashes is** more **severe,**[N] **as Rav said: Had they flogged**[N] **Hananiah, Mishael, and Azariah** (see Daniel, chapter 3) instead of casting them into the fiery furnace, these three **would have** been induced to **worship the** graven **image.** Apparently, the punishment of lashes is more severe than death. **Rav Samma, son of Rav Asi, said to Rav Ashi, and some say Rav Samma, son of Rav Ashi,** said **to Rav Ashi: And is there no difference to you between flogging that has a limit,** e.g., forty lashes by Torah law, which is a less severe punishment, **and flogging that does not have a limit,**[N] i.e., flogging administered to induce compliance, which is more severe?

מַתְקִיף לָהּ רַב יַעֲקֹב מִנְּהַר פְּקוֹד: הָנִיחָא לְרַבָּנַן דְּאָמְרִי נֶפֶשׁ מַמָּשׁ, אֶלָּא לְרַבִּי דְּאָמַר – מָמוֹן מַאי אִיכָּא לְמֵימַר?

With regard to the basic proof from the case of the two men quarreling, **Rav Ya'akov from Nehar Pekod** strongly **objects to this. This** works out **well according to** the opinion of **the Rabbis, who said** that the verse "And you shall give a soul for a soul" (Exodus 21:23) is referring to **an actual life,** and that if he caused the woman's death he is executed. **However, according to Rabbi** Yehuda HaNasi, **who said** that if he did not intend to injure the woman he is not liable to be executed and instead pays **money** as indemnity for causing her death, **what can be said?** According to that opinion, there was no forewarning for lashes at all, and the only liability is payment for injuring another.

אֶלָּא אֲמַר רַב יַעֲקֹב מִנְּהַר פְּקוֹד מִשְּׁמֵיהּ דְּרָבָא: מֵהָכָא, "אִם יָקוּם וְהִתְהַלֵּךְ בַּחוּץ עַל מִשְׁעַנְתּוֹ וְנִקָּה הַמַּכֶּה". וְכִי תַּעֲלֶה עַל דַּעְתְּךָ שֶׁזֶּה מְהַלֵּךְ בַּשּׁוּק וְזֶה נֶהֱרָג? אֶלָּא מְלַמֵּד שֶׁחוֹבְשִׁין אוֹתוֹ, וְאִי מִית – קָטְלִינַן לֵיהּ, וְאִי לָא מִית – "שִׁבְתּוֹ יִתֵּן וְרַפֹּא יְרַפֵּא".

Rather, Rav Ya'akov from Nehar Pekod said in the name of Rava that the *halakha* that one pays and is not flogged is derived **from here.** With regard to one who struck another with a stone or his fist and did not kill him but caused him to be bedridden, it is written: **"If he rises and walks outside with his staff, he who struck him is absolved"** (Exodus 21:19). **And could it enter your mind that this** victim **is walking in the marketplace and that** aggressor **is executed** as a murderer? **Rather,** the verse **teaches that one imprisons** the aggressor[H] while the injured party recuperates, **and if he dies** due to the blow he received, **we kill him. And if he does not die** and recovers, the aggressor's punishment is based on the verse **"His loss of livelihood he shall give, and he shall cause him to be thoroughly healed"** (Exodus 21:19).

הֵיכִי דָּמֵי? אִי דְּלָא אַתְרוּ בֵּיהּ – אַמַּאי מִיקְטִיל? אֶלָּא פְּשִׁיטָא – דְּאַתְרוּ בֵּיהּ, וּמוּתְרֶה לְדָבָר חָמוּר מוּתְרֶה לְדָבָר הַקַּל, וְאָמַר רַחֲמָנָא "שִׁבְתּוֹ יִתֵּן וְרַפֹּא יְרַפֵּא.

The Gemara elaborates: **What are the circumstances? If** the witnesses **did not forewarn him, why is** the offender **killed** if the victim dies? **Rather, obviously** it is a case **where** the witnesses **forewarned him, and one who is forewarned for a severe matter,** such as the potential death penalty, **is** also **forewarned for** the **lesser matter** of injuring another, for which he is liable to be flogged, and nevertheless **the Merciful One states: "His loss of livelihood he shall give, and he shall cause him to be thoroughly healed."** Apparently, despite his liability to be flogged, he pays and is not flogged.

מַתְקִיף לָהּ רַב אַשִׁי: מִמַּאי דְּמוּתְרֶה לְדָבָר חָמוּר הָוֵי מוּתְרֶה לְדָבָר הַקַּל? דִּלְמָא לָא הָוֵי, וְאִם תִּמְצָא לוֹמַר הָוֵי – מִמַּאי דְּמִיתָה חֲמוּרָה, דִּלְמָא מַלְקוֹת חָמוּר? דְּאָמַר רַב: אִילְמָלֵי נַגְּדוּהּ לַחֲנַנְיָה מִישָׁאֵל וַעֲזַרְיָה פָּלְחוּ לְצַלְמָא!

Rav Ashi strongly **objects to this** proof:[N] First of all, with regard to your initial assumption, **from where** do you ascertain **that one who is forewarned with regard to a severe matter is forewarned with regard to a lesser matter? Perhaps he is not** considered forewarned with regard to the lesser matter. Furthermore, even **if you say** that one **is** in fact forewarned with regard to a lesser matter, **from where** do you ascertain **that** the **death** penalty is a more **severe** punishment than lashes? **Perhaps** the punishment of **lashes is** more **severe, as Rav said: Had they flogged Hananiah, Mishael, and Azariah,** instead of casting them into the fiery furnace, **they would have** been induced to **worship the** graven **image.** Apparently, the punishment of lashes is more severe than death.

NOTES

Perhaps the punishment of lashes is more severe – דִּלְמָא מַלְקוֹת חָמוּר: *Tosafot* ask: Why doesn't the Gemara prove that death is the more severe punishment from the fact that it is the punishment administered for the most serious transgressions? The early commentaries suggest various answers, primarily that the issue is not the severity of the punishment itself but its relative harshness from the perspective of the punished. The Ritva states that one sentenced to death might say, as Samson did: "Let me die with the Philistines" (Judges 16:30), and would be prepared to die after murdering his hated enemy. With regard to lashes, in contrast, it is unlikely that one would agree to suffer merely for injuring another. The *Shita Yeshana*, cited in the *Shita Mekubbetzet*, explains that lashes carries with it great suffering and is also very demeaning. Therefore, people consider it a more severe punishment than death.

Had they flogged, etc. – אִילְמָלֵי נַגְּדוּהּ וכו׳: This statement of Rav has raised questions among many early commentaries, as the verse "And you shall love the Lord your God…with all your soul" (Deuteronomy 6:5) indicates that one must be willing to undergo great suffering to sanctify the name of God, as Rabbi Akiva and others did. The Rashba states, citing Rashi, although it does not appear in the standard version of Rashi, that Rav was asking a rhetorical question: Had they been flogged, would they have worshipped the graven image? In any case, Rav's comment proves that lashes are more severe than death. Most early commentaries, however, accept the opinion of *Tosafot* that Nebuchadnezzar's image was not an actual idol, and therefore, by the letter of the law, Hananiah, Mishael, and Azariah were not obligated to give their lives rather than bow to the image. The Ramban agrees with this approach and cites additional proofs that the image was merely an item that could have been mistaken for idolatry and that the three righteous men sought to sanctify the name of God by demonstrating their refusal to accept any authority other than God. He cites a midrash that states that they could have avoided being thrown into the furnace. Others state, citing Rabbi Eliezer, that the *halakha* does not require one to subject himself to suffering greater than death (see *Shita Yeshana*, cited in *Shita Mekubbetzet*).

Flogging that does not have a limit – הַכָּאָה שֶׁאֵין לָהּ קִצְבָּה: In the *Shita Mekubbetzet* it is explained that it is not the number of lashes that determines the sense of the severity of the punishment; rather, it is the very knowledge that the lashes of the court are limited and will eventually end. In contrast, with regard to lashes administered by the monarchy, even if in practice fewer lashes are administered, there is no limit to the lashes that they could inflict.

Rav Ashi strongly objects to this proof – מַתְקִיף לָהּ רַב אַשִׁי: This is difficult, as this statement of Rav Ashi was cited and rejected above. Why is it cited again? In the *Shita Mekubbetzet* it is explained that Rav Ya'akov spoke in accordance with the opinion of Rabbi Yehuda HaNasi that one who sought to kill one person and killed another is exempt. According to that opinion, the questions that Rav Ashi raised are more difficult, as forewarning with regard to one person is ineffective with regard to the other, so forewarning for a severe transgression is ineffective for a lesser transgression.

HALAKHA

The verse teaches that one imprisons the aggressor, etc. – מְלַמֵּד שֶׁחוֹבְשִׁין אוֹתוֹ וכו׳: If one struck another with a stone or his fist, and the court estimated that the blow was capable of killing him, then the aggressor is imprisoned until the fate of the victim is determined. If he dies, the aggressor is executed; if he makes a full recovery, the aggressor pays the five indemnities and is exempt from any other punishment (Rambam *Sefer Nezikim*, *Hilkhot Rotze'aḥ* 4:3).

אֲמַר לֵיהּ רַב סַמָּא בְּרֵיהּ דְּרַב אַסִּי לְרַב אַשִׁי, וְאָמְרִי לָהּ רַב סַמָּא בְּרֵיהּ דְּרַב אַשִׁי לְרַב אַשִׁי: וְלָא שָׁנֵי לָךְ בֵּין הַכָּאָה שֶׁיֵּשׁ לָהּ קִצְבָּה לְהַכָּאָה שֶׁאֵין לָהּ קִצְבָּה?

Rav Samma, son of Rav Asi, said to Rav Ashi, and some say Rav Samma, son of Rav Ashi, said to Rav Ashi: And is there no difference to you between flogging that has a limit, e.g., forty lashes by Torah law, which is a less severe punishment, **and flogging that does not have a limit,** administered to induce compliance, which is more severe?

מַתְקִיף לָהּ רַב מָרִי: מִמַּאי דִּבְמֵזִיד "וְנִקָּה" מִקְּטָלָא, דִּלְמָא בְּשׁוֹגֵג "וְנִקָּה" מִגָּלוּת? קַשְׁיָא.

Rav Mari strongly **objects to this** proof that one pays and is not flogged: **From where** do you ascertain **that** this is referring to one who struck another **intentionally,** and that the verse "He who struck him shall be absolved" means that he **shall be absolved of** the **death** penalty? **Perhaps** the verse is referring to one who struck another **unwittingly, and** the verse means that he **shall be absolved of exile?**[N] In that case, there would be no forewarning. Therefore, no proof may be cited from here that one who injures another pays and is not flogged. The Gemara concludes: This is **difficult,** and no proof may be cited from here.

רֵישׁ לָקִישׁ אֲמַר: הָא מַנִּי – רַבִּי מֵאִיר הִיא, דְּאָמַר: לוֹקֶה וּמְשַׁלֵּם. אִי רַבִּי מֵאִיר – אֲפִילּוּ בִּתּוֹ נַמִּי!

§ The Gemara cites another resolution of the apparent contradiction between the mishna here, which obligates one who rapes his sister to pay a fine, and the mishna in *Makkot*, which rules him liable to be flogged. **Reish Lakish said:** In accordance with **whose** opinion **is this** mishna taught? **It is** in accordance with the opinion of **Rabbi Meir, who said: One is flogged and pays.** The Gemara asks: **If** the mishna is in accordance with the opinion of **Rabbi Meir, even** if one raped **his daughter** he should **also** be obligated to pay the fine. However, the mishna lists only those who raped women for whom one is liable to be punished for violating a prohibition or liable to receive *karet*, not those for whom one is liable to receive court-imposed execution.

וְכִי תֵּימָא רַבִּי מֵאִיר לוֹקֶה וּמְשַׁלֵּם אִית לֵיהּ, מֵת וּמְשַׁלֵּם – לֵית לֵיהּ, וְלָא? וְהָתַנְיָא: גָּנַב וְטָבַח בְּשַׁבָּת, גָּנַב וְטָבַח לַעֲבוֹדָה זָרָה, גָּנַב שׁוֹר הַנִּסְקָל וּטְבָחוֹ – מְשַׁלֵּם תַּשְׁלוּמֵי אַרְבָּעָה וַחֲמִשָּׁה, דִּבְרֵי רַבִּי מֵאִיר, וַחֲכָמִים פּוֹטְרִין.

And lest you say that **Rabbi Meir is of** the opinion that **one is flogged and pays,** but **is not of** the opinion that **one dies** by execution **and pays; and isn't** he of the opinion that one who is executed pays? **But isn't it taught** in a *baraita*: If one **stole** an animal **and slaughtered** it **on Shabbat,**[H] or **stole** it **and slaughtered** it **for idolatry,** or **stole an ox that** was sentenced to be **stoned,**[B] from which one may derive no benefit and is therefore worthless, **and slaughtered it, he pays** the owner **a payment of four or five** times the principal, as he would in any case of stealing and slaughtering an animal? This is **the statement of Rabbi Meir. And the Rabbis exempt him** from payment because he is liable to receive the death penalty for slaughtering on Shabbat or for idolatry. Apparently, Rabbi Meir maintains that one is obligated to pay even when he is liable to receive the death penalty.

הָא אִיתְּמַר עֲלַהּ, אָמַר רַבִּי יַעֲקֹב אָמַר רַבִּי יוֹחָנָן, וְאָמְרִי לָהּ אָמַר רַבִּי יִרְמְיָה אָמַר רַבִּי שִׁמְעוֹן בֶּן לָקִישׁ: רַבִּי אָבִין וְרַבִּי אִילְעָא וְכָל חֲבוּרָתָא מִשְּׁמֵיהּ דְּרַבִּי יוֹחָנָן אָמְרִי: בְּטוֹבֵחַ עַל יְדֵי אַחֵר.

The Gemara refutes this: **Wasn't it stated concerning** this *baraita* that **Rabbi Ya'akov said** that **Rabbi Yoḥanan said, and some say** that **Rabbi Yirmeya said** that **Rabbi Shimon ben Lakish said,** that **Rabbi Avin and Rabbi Ile'a and the entire group said in the name of Rabbi Yoḥanan:** That case is referring **to one who slaughters by means of another?**[H] The thief himself did not slaughter the animal; rather, it was his agent. Consequently, the thief pays because the capital crime was committed by his agent. Therefore, this source is unrelated to Rabbi Meir's opinion with regard to the question of whether one is executed and pays.

וְכִי זֶה חוֹטֵא וְזֶה מִתְחַיֵּיב? אָמַר רָבָא: אָמַר רַחֲמָנָא "וּטְבָחוֹ אוֹ מְכָרוֹ" מָה מְכִירָה עַל יְדֵי אַחֵר – אַף טְבִיחָה עַל יְדֵי אַחֵר.

The Gemara analyzes Rabbi Yoḥanan's explanation: **And does this** agent **sin and that** thief **is liable**[N] to pay four and five times the principal? This violates the principle: There is no agent for matters of transgression. The Gemara explains that this is a *halakha* unique to this case. **Rava said** that **the Merciful One states:** "If a man steal an ox or a sheep **and slaughter it**[N] **or sell it**" (Exodus 21:37). Based on the juxtaposition of slaughter and sale, Rava continues: **Just as sale** is performed **by means of another,** as there is no sale without a buyer, **so too,** one is liable to be punished for **slaughter by means of another.** Although there is no agent for transgression, here there is a Torah decree that one is liable by means of another.

NOTES

Perhaps the verse is referring to one who struck another unwittingly, and the verse means that he shall be absolved of exile – דִּלְמָא בְּשׁוֹגֵג וְנִקָּה מִגָּלוּת: *Tosafot* ask: In light of the principle that one is not exiled if there is the slightest concern that there was an additional complication that contributed to the death of the victim, the fact that the victim did not die immediately should exempt one from exile (see *Tosafot*). The Ritva maintains that the verse is referring to a situation involving exile and not the death penalty. A different objection is raised in the *Shita Mekubbetzet*: As the verse is clearly speaking of one who struck another, how could it be dealing with exile, which only applies to an unintentional murderer? The answer is that exile is conceivable in a case where one intended to strike one person and struck another.

And does this agent sin and that thief is liable – וְכִי זֶה חוֹטֵא וְזֶה מִתְחַיֵּיב: Rashi says that this question is based on the principle: There is no agent for transgression. In *Derush VeḤiddush*, Rabbi Akiva Eiger explains that this is not a case of an agent for transgression, as were he an agent his legal status would be like that of the sender himself, who would not be liable to pay because he would have desecrated Shabbat. Rather, this is a special *halakha* with regard to an action performed by means of another, unrelated to the laws of agency.

Rava said that the Merciful One states: If a man steals an ox or a sheep and slaughter it, etc. – אָמַר רָבָא: אָמַר רַחֲמָנָא וּטְבָחוֹ וכו׳: In the *Sefer Hafla'a* the question is raised: Since there are two expositions cited by earlier Sages for this *halakha*, what did Rava add by citing another source? Furthermore, why does the Gemara cite Rava's proof first? Various answers were suggested. Primary among them is that from Rava's statement it can be derived that this *halakha* applies not only to an agent but to anyone who performs an action of this sort on another's behalf, even if he is ineligible for agency, e.g., a deaf-mute or an imbecile (*Beit Ya'akov*). Alternatively, Rava's statement here is consistent with his opinion elsewhere that the thief is liable even if he slaughtered the animal unwittingly (*Beit Aharon*).

HALAKHA

If one stole and slaughtered on Shabbat, etc. – גָּנַב וְטָבַח בְּשַׁבָּת וכו׳: If one stole an animal and slaughtered it on Shabbat, or stole it and slaughtered it for idolatry, even if he did so unwittingly he is exempt from payment of four or five times the principal, in accordance with the opinion of the Rabbis (Rambam *Sefer Nezikim*, *Hilkhot Geneiva* 3:3).

One who slaughters by means of another – טוֹבֵחַ עַל יְדֵי אַחֵר: If a thief appointed an agent to slaughter the stolen animal on his behalf, and the agent did so on Shabbat, the thief is liable for the payment of four or five times the principal. The Rosh rules that he is exempt, based on the Gemara's statement below that according to the Rabbis, slaughter on Shabbat is considered an unfit act of slaughter (Rambam *Sefer Nezikim*, *Hilkhot Geneiva* 3:6; *Tur*, *Ḥoshen Mishpat* 350).

BACKGROUND

An ox that was sentenced to be stoned – שׁוֹר הַנִּסְקָל: An ox that killed a person is stoned to death, whether or not the ox had previously displayed violent tendencies and whether the victim was an adult, a child, or a Canaanite slave. It is prohibited to derive any benefit from an ox that is stoned, not only after its execution but from the moment the court of twenty-three judges delivered its verdict. The term: Ox that is stoned, is employed to describe any domesticated or non-domesticated animal that killed a person, whether it is a large or small animal, or even a bird.

דבי רבי ישמעאל תנא: "או" – לרבות את השליח. דבי חזקיה תנא: "תחת" – לרבות את השליח.

The Sages **of the school of Rabbi Yishmael taught** a different source for the *halakha* that one is liable for slaughter by means of an agent. It is written: "And slaughter it or sell it"; the term **"or"** comes **to include an agent.**[N] The Sages **of the school of Rabbi Ḥizkiyya taught** a different proof from the same verse: "He shall pay…for an ox…for a sheep"; the term **"for"** comes **to include an agent.**[H]

מתקיף לה מר זוטרא: מי איכא מידי דאילו עבד איהו לא מיחייב, ועביד שליח ומחייב? איהו לאו משום דלא מיחייב, אלא משום דקם ליה בדרבה מיניה.

Mar Zutra strongly **objects to this** *halakha*. **Is there** any **matter** with regard to **which if one performs** it himself, he is not **liable, and** yet if his **agent performs** it he is **liable?** Had he slaughtered the animal himself on Shabbat he would have been exempt from payment. How, then, is he liable if he does so by means of an agent? The Gemara answers: **He** is exempt **not due to** the fact **that he is not liable** for the slaughter; **rather,** he is exempt **due to** the fact **that he receives the greater of** the two punishments, the death penalty, for his desecration of Shabbat. He is liable for both the slaughter and the desecration of Shabbat. In practice, he receives the more severe punishment. However, when he appoints an agent, there is no liability for the desecration of Shabbat, and therefore he must pay for the slaughter.

אי בטובח על ידי אחר, מאי טעמייהו דרבנן דפטרי? מאן חכמים?

The Gemara returns to Rabbi Yoḥanan's explanation of the *baraita*. **If** the *baraita* is referring to the case **of** one **who slaughtered by means of another, what is the** rationale for the opinion **of the Rabbis,**[N] **who exempt** him from payment? As the thief did not perform a transgression for which he is liable to receive the death penalty, why is he exempt from payment for slaughtering the animal? The Gemara answers: **Who are the Rabbis** who disagree with Rabbi Meir in this case?

NOTES

"Or" comes to include an agent – או לרבות את השליח: Ostensibly the term "or" is necessary to rule out the possibility that one would be liable to pay four or five times the principal only if he both slaughtered and stole the animal and did not include an agent. Why, then, is it understood in this manner? One answer is that this derivation is in accordance with the *tanna* who maintains that even when the conjunction "and" [*vav*] is written, it would be understood that either slaughter or sale is sufficient to generate liability. Alternatively, it would have been possible to indicate that one is liable for either one of the actions by reversing the order and writing: And he sold it and slaughtered it, as clearly one could not slaughter the animal after selling it. Therefore, this *halakha* of agency can be derived from the fact that the term "or" is used here (*Shita Mekubbetzet*).

What is the rationale for the opinion of the Rabbis – מאי טעמייהו דרבנן: The question is raised: Couldn't the exemption of the Rabbis be attributed to the fact that they maintain that slaughtering by means of an agent does not render the sender liable? The answer is that the derivation from use of the word "or" is the accepted *halakha*, and the Gemara sought to avoid a difficult response. Furthermore, if there is a dispute with regard to the *halakha* of one who slaughters by means of another, there would have been no point in citing the special cases of one who slaughtered on Shabbat or for idolatry (Ra'ah; Rabbeinu Crescas Vidal).

HALAKHA

Slaughter by means of another – טביחה על ידי אחר: If one stole an ox or sheep and gave it as a gift, or gave it to another to slaughter and the recipient did so, or gave it to another to sell and the recipient sold it, the thief is liable for payment of four or five times the principal, in accordance with the exposition of the Sages here that there is a special *halakha* in the case of one who slaughters a stolen animal (Rambam *Sefer Nezikim*, *Hilkhot Geneiva* 2:10).

Perek **III**
Daf **34** Amud **a**

רבי שמעון היא, דאמר: שחיטה שאינה ראויה – לא שמה שחיטה. התינח עבודה זרה ושור הנסקל, אלא שחיטת שבת – שחיטה ראויה היא, דתנן: השוחט בשבת וביום הכפורים, אף על פי שמתחייב בנפשו – שחיטתו כשרה!

It is Rabbi Shimon, who said: The legal status of **slaughter that is improper,**[HN] in that it does not render the meat fit to be eaten, **is not that of slaughter.** Therefore, one is not liable for slaughter of the animal. The Gemara asks: **This** works out **well** with regard to **idolatry and** the **ox that is stoned,** as their slaughter is ineffective in rendering the meat fit to be eaten; **however, the slaughter on Shabbat is a proper** act of **slaughter, as we learned** in a mishna (*Ḥullin* 14a): In the case of **one who slaughters** an animal **on Shabbat**[N] **or on Yom Kippur,**[H] **although he is liable to** receive the **death** penalty for desecrating Shabbat, **his slaughter is valid** and the meat may be eaten.

HALAKHA

Slaughter that is improper – שחיטה שאינה ראויה: In general the ruling is contrary to the opinion of Rabbi Shimon, and improper slaughter is considered an act of slaughter. Consequently, if a thief slaughtered an ox or lamb that was discovered to be a *tereifa*, he is liable to pay four or five times the principal. Similarly, if an animal was slaughtered in a manner that does not permit its consumption, e.g., it was a *tereifa*, one who slaughters its offspring on the same day is liable for transgressing the prohibition against slaughter of an animal itself and its young on a single day. Nevertheless, one who performs an improper act of slaughter on a bird or undomesticated animal is exempt from covering the blood (see *Ḥullin* 85a), as in that regard it is not considered a bona fide act of slaughter, based on the unattributed mishna in accordance with the opinion of Rabbi Shimon (Rambam *Sefer Kedusha*, *Hilkhot Sheḥita* 12:6, 14:10 and *Sefer Nezikim*, *Hilkhot Geneiva* 2:8; *Shulḥan Arukh*, *Yoreh De'a* 16:9, 28:17; *Tur Ḥoshen Mishpat* 350).

One who slaughters on Shabbat or on Yom Kippur – השוחט בשבת וביום הכפורים: Although one who slaughters an animal on Shabbat is liable to be executed and one who does so on Yom Kippur is liable to receive *karet* or lashes, the slaughter is valid, in accordance with the mishna in *Ḥullin* (Rambam *Sefer Kedusha*, *Hilkhot Sheḥita* 1:29; *Shulḥan Arukh*, *Yoreh De'a* 11:2).

NOTES

Slaughter that is improper – שחיטה שאינה ראויה: Rabbi Shimon defines slaughter as an action that renders the animal fit to be eaten. If the slaughter is ineffective it is not considered slaughter at all; rather, it is as though one killed the animal by some other means. Consequently, wherever a particular *halakha* depends on performance of an act of slaughter, ineffective slaughter does not meet that requirement. Even the Rabbis concede that one who kills an animal in a manner other than slaughter, e.g., by stabbing it, does not meet the requirement of slaughter. *Tosafot* prove that although the term in the Torah in this context is *teviḥa* and not *sheḥita*, which is the standard term for slaughter, the reference is to slaughter.

One who slaughters on Shabbat, etc. – השוחט בשבת וכו׳: The early commentaries ask: Isn't one who desecrates Shabbat an apostate, in which case everyone agrees that his slaughter is invalid? How, then, can one say that slaughter on Shabbat is valid? There are several answers offered. *Tosafot* on *Ḥullin* 14a claim that only one who desecrates Shabbat in public is an apostate. The case here is referring to one who slaughtered the animal in private. Rabbeinu Crescas Vidal agrees. In addition, *Tosafot* explain that the act of slaughter that renders one an apostate is not invalid; rather, all subsequent acts of slaughter are invalid. The Ran in tractate *Ḥullin* explains that it is only the conclusion of the act of slaughter that renders one an apostate, but the slaughter that rendered the animal permitted was already complete. In the Rambam's Commentary on the Mishna, it is explained in *Ḥullin* that this is referring only to one who slaughters unwittingly, and therefore the slaughter is not invalidated as that of an apostate.

סָבַר לַהּ כְּרַבִּי יוֹחָנָן הַסַּנְדְּלָר, דְּתַנְיָא: הַמְבַשֵּׁל בְּשַׁבָּת, בְּשׁוֹגֵג – יֹאכַל, בְּמֵזִיד – לֹא יֹאכַל, דִּבְרֵי רַבִּי מֵאִיר. רַבִּי יְהוּדָה אוֹמֵר: בְּשׁוֹגֵג – יֹאכַל לְמוֹצָאֵי שַׁבָּת, בְּמֵזִיד – לֹא יֹאכַל עוֹלָמִית. רַבִּי יוֹחָנָן הַסַּנְדְּלָר אוֹמֵר: בְּשׁוֹגֵג – יֵאָכֵל לְמוֹצָאֵי שַׁבָּת לַאֲחֵרִים, וְלֹא לוֹ. בְּמֵזִיד – לֹא יֵאָכֵל עוֹלָמִית, לֹא לוֹ וְלֹא לַאֲחֵרִים.

The Gemara answers: The *tanna* of the *baraita* under discussion **holds in accordance with** the opinion of **Rabbi Yoḥanan HaSandlar, as it is taught** in a *baraita*:

With regard to **one who cooks on Shabbat,**[HN] if he did so **unwittingly, he may eat** the food he cooked; if he did so **intentionally, he may not eat** it at all. This is **the statement of Rabbi Meir.**[N]

Rabbi Yehuda says: If he cooked **unwittingly he may eat at the conclusion of Shabbat,**[N] as the Sages penalized even one who sinned unwittingly in that they prohibited him from deriving immediate benefit from the dish that he cooked; if he sinned **intentionally, he may not eat** from it **ever.**

Rabbi Yoḥanan HaSandlar says: If he did so **unwittingly,** the food **may be eaten at the conclusion of Shabbat by others but not by him;** if he did so **intentionally, it may not be eaten ever, neither by him nor by other** Jews. According to Rabbi Yoḥanan HaSandlar, food prepared by means of intentional desecration of Shabbat is unfit to be eaten. That is true with regard to cooking food on Shabbat and with regard to slaughtering an animal on Shabbat.

מַאי טַעְמָא דְּרַבִּי יוֹחָנָן הַסַּנְדְּלָר? כִּדְדָרֵישׁ רַבִּי חִיָּיא אַפִּיתְחָא דְּבֵי נְשִׂיאָה: ״וּשְׁמַרְתֶּם אֶת הַשַּׁבָּת כִּי קֹדֶשׁ הִיא לָכֶם״. מָה קוֹדֶשׁ אָסוּר בַּאֲכִילָה אַף מַעֲשֵׂה שַׁבָּת אֲסוּרִין בַּאֲכִילָה. אִי מָה קוֹדֶשׁ אָסוּר בַּהֲנָאָה אַף מַעֲשֵׂה שַׁבָּת אָסוּר בַּהֲנָאָה – תַּלְמוּד לוֹמַר ״לָכֶם״, שֶׁלָּכֶם יְהֵא.

The Gemara asks: **What is the rationale** for the opinion **of Rabbi Yoḥanan HaSandlar?** The Gemara explains: It is **as Rabbi Ḥiyya taught at the entrance to the house of the** ***Nasi.*** It is written: **"And you shall observe Shabbat, for it is sacred to you;** he who profanes it shall be put to death" (Exodus 31:14); **just as** with regard to **a sacred** item consecrated to the Temple, **eating** it **is prohibited, so too,** with regard to food produced through **action** that desecrates **Shabbat, eating** it **is prohibited.** The Gemara asks: **If** so, perhaps the analogy should be extended to include the following: **Just as** with regard to **a sacred item,** deriving **benefit** from it **is prohibited, so too,** with regard to the product of **an action** that desecrates **Shabbat,** deriving **benefit** from it should be **prohibited.** The Gemara answers: **The verse states:** "It is sacred **to you"** (Exodus 31:14), indicating that **it shall be yours** in the sense that one may derive benefit from it.

יָכוֹל אֲפִילּוּ בְּשׁוֹגֵג. תַּלְמוּד לוֹמַר ״מְחַלְלֶיהָ מוֹת יוּמָת״, בְּמֵזִיד אָמַרְתִּי לָךְ, וְלֹא בְּשׁוֹגֵג.

The Gemara asks: Based on the analogy between actions that desecrate Shabbat and sacred items, one **might** have thought that **even** if the action was performed **unwittingly** it should be prohibited to eat its product, as is the case with regard to sacred items. Therefore, **the verse states: "He who profanes it shall be put to death"** (Exodus 31:14), indicating that it is **with regard to** one who desecrates Shabbat **intentionally** that **I stated to you** this analogy to sacred items,[N] as the verse is clearly referring to one who is liable to receive the death penalty, **and not with regard to** one who desecrates Shabbat **unwittingly,** who is not executed.

HALAKHA

One who cooks on Shabbat – הַמְבַשֵּׁל בְּשַׁבָּת: With regard to a Jew who performed prohibited labor on Shabbat, e.g., cooking, if he did so intentionally, it is permanently prohibited for him to derive benefit from that labor, while others may eat the food immediately at the conclusion of Shabbat. If he did so unwittingly, it is permitted both for him and for others to eat the dish at the conclusion of Shabbat. The *halakha* is ruled in accordance with the opinion of Rabbi Yehuda in his dispute with Rabbi Meir. The Ran adds that the ruling is based on the statement of Rav in *Ḥullin*, where he ruled in accordance with the opinion of Rabbi Meir for Torah scholars but in accordance with the opinion of Rabbi Yehuda for ignorant people, so that they will not come to treat Shabbat prohibitions with contempt (Rambam *Sefer Zemanim*, *Hilkhot Shabbat* 6:23; *Shulḥan Arukh*, *Oraḥ Ḥayyim* 318:1).

NOTES

Benefit from prohibited labor on Shabbat – הֲנָאָה מִמְּלֶאכֶת שַׁבָּת: In the *Shita Mekubbetzet* it is explained that there are three different rationales mentioned here. First, the Sages penalized the sinner so that he would not profit from his transgression. Others explain that the Sages issued a decree penalizing one who acted unwittingly due to an intentional sinner. Second, they did not want people to benefit from prohibited labor performed on Shabbat. Third, due to the verse "It is sacred to you" (Exodus 31:14), the product of labor performed on Shabbat is forbidden.

Intentionally, he may not eat it; this is the statement of Rabbi Meir – בְּמֵזִיד לֹא יֹאכַל דִּבְרֵי רַבִּי מֵאִיר: According to most early commentaries, Rabbi Meir's statement: If he did so intentionally he may not eat it, refers not just to the sinner himself; rather, this dish may not be consumed on Shabbat at all. Rabbi Meir did not formulate his opinion as: It may not be eaten, for stylistic reasons, to use parallel phrasing in both parts of his statement. Similarly, Rabbi Yehuda's statement below must be explained by suggesting that he too employed a uniform mode of expression. The commentaries further state that Rabbi Meir permits even an intentional sinner to partake of the dish after the conclusion of Shabbat. Based on the Gemara in tractate *Ḥullin*, the legal status of an intentional sinner according to Rabbi Meir parallels that of an unwitting transgressor according to Rabbi Yehuda. The legal status of an intentional sinner according to Rabbi Yehuda parallels that of an unwitting sinner according to Rabbi Yoḥanan HaSandlar. However, Rashi here states that according to Rabbi Meir, one who cooks intentionally may never partake of that dish (see *Shita Mekubbetzet*).

He may eat at the conclusion of Shabbat – יֹאכַל לְמוֹצָאֵי שַׁבָּת: Rashi in *Ḥullin* states that this does not mean that the food may be eaten immediately after Shabbat. After the conclusion of Shabbat one must wait until the period of time that would be sufficient for the food to have been prepared from the beginning has elapsed. This is based on the concept that the Sages did not want the sinner to benefit from labor performed on Shabbat.

It is with regard to one who desecrates Shabbat intentionally that I stated to you – בְּמֵזִיד אָמַרְתִּי לָךְ: The Rashash asks why Rabbi Yoḥanan HaSandlar did not explain that the food is prohibited only if one was forewarned, since if he is not forewarned he is not liable to be executed. In fact, in *Gilyon HaShas*, *Sefer HaPardes* is cited, which explains, according to Rashi, that Rabbi Yoḥanan HaSandlar holds that only the product of labor performed on Shabbat by one who was forewarned is permanently forbidden.

פְּלִיגִי בָּהּ רַב אַחָא וְרָבִינָא: חַד אָמַר: מַעֲשֵׂה שַׁבָּת דְּאוֹרַיְיתָא, וְחַד אָמַר: דְּרַבָּנַן, מַאן דְּאָמַר דְּאוֹרַיְיתָא – כִּדְאָמְרַן. מַאן דְּאָמַר דְּרַבָּנַן – אָמַר קְרָא: "קֹדֶשׁ הִיא" – הִיא קוֹדֶשׁ, וְאֵין מַעֲשֶׂיהָ קוֹדֶשׁ.

The Gemara comments: **Rav Aḥa and Ravina disagree with regard to this matter.**[N] **One said:** The product of **an action** that desecrates **Shabbat** is prohibited **by Torah** law, **and one said** that it is prohibited **by rabbinic** law. With regard to the **one who said** that it is prohibited **by Torah** law, it is **as we said,** that it is based on the verse interpreted by Rabbi Ḥiyya. **And** the **one who said** that it is prohibited **by rabbinic** law holds that **the verse states: "It is sacred,"** from which he infers: **It is sacred, but** the product of **its actions is not sacred,** and therefore, by Torah law it may be eaten.

וּלְמַאן דְּאָמַר דְּרַבָּנַן, מַאי טַעֲמַיְיהוּ דְּרַבָּנַן דְּפָטְרִי? כִּי קָא פָּטְרִי רַבָּנַן – אַשְּׁאָרָא.

The Gemara asks: **And** according to the **one who said** it is prohibited **by rabbinic** law, **what is the rationale**[N] for the opinion **of the Rabbis who exempt** the thief from payment for the slaughter performed by his agent on Shabbat? By Torah law, the slaughter is valid. The Gemara answers: **When the Rabbis exempt** the thief from payment, it is with regard **to the rest** of the cases, i.e., one who slaughters for idolatry or an ox sentenced to stoning, not with regard to Shabbat.

טוֹבֵחַ לַעֲבוֹדָה זָרָה, כֵּיוָן דִּשְׁחַט בֵּיהּ פּוּרְתָּא אִיתְּסַר לֵיהּ, אִידָּךְ כִּי קָא טָבַח – לָאו דְּמָרֵיהּ קָא טָבַח! אָמַר רָבָא: בְּאוֹמֵר "בִּגְמַר זְבִיחָה הוּא עוֹבְדָהּ".

The Gemara asks the following question with regard to Rabbi Meir's opinion that **one who slaughters for idolatry** is liable to pay the owner for the animal. **Once he slaughtered** the animal **a bit,**[N] at the very start of the act of slaughter, **it is prohibited for him** to derive benefit from the animal because it is an animal sacrificed to idolatry; **and when he slaughters the rest,** it is **not** the animal that belongs **to its owner** that he **is slaughtering.** Since it is prohibited to derive benefit from the animal, it has no value and there is no ownership. **Rava said:** It is referring **to one who says,** prior to the slaughter, that **he is worshipping** the idol only **at the completion of the slaughter,** and therefore the prohibition takes effect only then.

שׁוֹר הַנִּסְקָל – לָאו דִּידֵיהּ הוּא דְּקָטָבַח! אָמַר רַבָּה: הָכָא בְּמַאי עָסְקִינַן – כְּגוֹן שֶׁמְּסָרוֹ לְשׁוֹמֵר, וְהִזִּיק בְּבֵית שׁוֹמֵר, וְנִגְמַר דִּינֵיהּ בְּבֵית שׁוֹמֵר, וּגְנָבוֹ גַּנָּב מִבֵּית שׁוֹמֵר.

The Gemara asks the following question with regard to Rabbi Meir's opinion that one who slaughters **the ox that is stoned** is liable to pay for the slaughter. Why is he liable? It is **not** the owner's ox that **he is slaughtering,** since once the ox is sentenced to be stoned it is prohibited to derive benefit from it. **Rabba said: With what are we dealing here?** We are dealing with a case **where** the owners **entrusted** the ox **to a bailee and** the ox **injured** another person while **in the bailee's house, and it was sentenced** to be stoned while **in the bailee's house, and** the **thief** then **stole it from the bailee's house** and slaughtered it.

וְרַבִּי מֵאִיר סָבַר לָהּ כְּרַבִּי יַעֲקֹב, וְסָבַר לָהּ כְּרַבִּי שִׁמְעוֹן; סָבַר לָהּ כְּרַבִּי יַעֲקֹב – דְּאָמַר: אַף מִשֶּׁנִּגְמַר דִּינוֹ, הֶחֱזִירוֹ שׁוֹמֵר לִבְעָלָיו – מוּחְזָר. וְסָבַר לָהּ כְּרַבִּי שִׁמְעוֹן, דְּאָמַר: דָּבָר הַגּוֹרֵם לְמָמוֹן כְּמָמוֹן דָּמֵי.

And this solution is based on the fact that **Rabbi Meir holds in accordance with** the opinion of **Rabbi Ya'akov and holds in accordance with** the opinion of **Rabbi Shimon. He holds in accordance with** the opinion of **Rabbi Ya'akov, who said: Even after** the ox **was sentenced** to be stoned, if the **bailee returned it to its owners, it is returned.** Despite the fact that the ox is now worthless, as no benefit may be derived from it, since the bailee returned an ox that is physically intact the owner has no claim against him. **And** Rabbi Meir **holds in accordance with** the opinion of **Rabbi Shimon, who said** that the legal status of **an object that effects monetary** loss[NH] **is like** that of **money.** Even in the case of an object that is worthless, if its elimination causes monetary loss because it must be replaced, it is considered to have value. In this case, although the ox has no value in and of itself, slaughtering the animal prevents the bailee from returning it intact to the owner, requiring him to pay the owner the value of the ox before it was sentenced to be stoned. Consequently, the thief must reimburse the bailee, as the ox has value for the bailee.

רַבָּה אָמַר: לְעוֹלָם בְּטוֹבֵחַ עַל יְדֵי עַצְמוֹ,

Rabba said: Actually, contrary to Rabbi Yoḥanan's explanation of the *baraita*, it is referring **to one who slaughters** the animal **himself,**

NOTES

Rav Aḥa and Ravina disagree with regard to this matter – פְּלִיגִי בָּהּ רַב אַחָא וְרָבִינָא: Most early commentaries, beginning with Rabbeinu Ḥananel, maintain that this is a dispute based only on the opinion of Rabbi Yoḥanan HaSandlar. Even so, most halakhic authorities do not consider this as proof that the *halakha* is in accordance with his opinion, although some *ge'onim* rule based on this Gemara that the *halakha* is in accordance with his opinion. The Ramban cites a different interpretation. He suggests that the *tanna'im* disagree with regard to the correct exposition of the verse "It is sacred to you." Rabbi Meir maintains that the product of prohibited labor is sacred only on the sacred day itself, Rabbi Yehuda claims that it is sacred and prohibited only to one who desecrated Shabbat intentionally, while Rabbi Yoḥanan HaSandlar contends that if Shabbat was willfully desecrated, the resulting product is sacred and prohibited to all.

And according to the one who said it is prohibited by rabbinic law what is the rationale, etc. – וּלְמַאן דְּאָמַר דְּרַבָּנַן מַאי טַעֲמַיְיהוּ וכו׳: The Maharshal asks: Even if the prohibition is by rabbinic law, the meat may not be eaten, and one should therefore be exempt from punishment for the slaughter of the stolen animal. He cites proof from the fact that if one betroths a woman with an object from which it is prohibited to derive benefit by rabbinic law, the betrothal does not take effect even by Torah law. In the *Shita Mekubbetzet* it is explained that the Sages issued the decree that the meat may not be eaten as a stringency, and not as a leniency. The Rashash maintains that there is a difference between the authority of the court to declare one's property ownerless, which influences the legal status of an item even by Torah law, and issuing a decree that slaughter is unfit, which does not influence the legal status by Torah law.

Once he slaughtered the animal a bit – כֵּיוָן דִּשְׁחַט בֵּיהּ פּוּרְתָּא: Even according to the opinion that one cannot render forbidden an object that is not his, that is only with regard to rendering the object forbidden without performing an action. However, if one performs an action that directly affects the object, he renders it forbidden even if it does not belong to him (Ritva; see Rashba).

And Rabbi Meir holds in accordance with the opinion of Rabbi Shimon, who said that the legal status of an object that effects monetary loss – וְסָבַר לָהּ כְּרַבִּי שִׁמְעוֹן דְּאָמַר דָּבָר הַגּוֹרֵם לְמָמוֹן: *Tosafot* ask why this is necessary, as it is well known that Rabbi Meir adjudicates cases of indirect damage. In other words, if one harms another in a manner that is not discernible, or damages an item that is worthless in and of itself, if he causes financial loss he must reimburse his victim. Several answers are offered. Many early commentaries accept the claim of *Tosafot*, who claim that there is a difference between the two cases. Although Rabbi Meir adjudicates cases of indirect damage, that does not mean that he deems the object itself to be worth money. It is merely an obligation by rabbinic law to compensate the victim. Rabbi Shimon, in contrast, maintains that legal status of an object that effects monetary loss is like that of actual money (see Ramban).

HALAKHA

An object that effects monetary loss – דָּבָר הַגּוֹרֵם לְמָמוֹן: If one stole consecrated items from the house of the one who consecrated them, then although the owner is responsible to replace the items the thief is not liable to pay double the principal because, contrary to the ruling of Rabbi Shimon, the legal status of an object that effects monetary loss is not that of money. This is a case of an object that effects monetary loss, as the owner is obligated to bring replacement offerings. The *Shakh* adds that although the *halakha* is that one adjudicates cases of indirect damage and deems one who inflicts that damage liable to pay compensation, most authorities maintain that that is a different issue (Rambam *Sefer Nezikim*, *Hilkhot Geneiva* 2:1; *Shulḥan Arukh*, *Ḥoshen Mishpat* 386:2).

וְרַבִּי מֵאִיר, לוֹקֶה וּמְשַׁלֵּם אִית לֵיהּ, מֵת וּמְשַׁלֵּם לֵית לֵיהּ. וְשָׁאנֵי הָנֵי, דְּחִידּוּשׁ הוּא שֶׁחִידְּשָׁה תּוֹרָה בִּקְנָס, אַף עַל גַּב דְּמִיקְטִיל – מְשַׁלֵּם. וְאָזְדָא רַבָּה לְטַעְמֵיהּ, דְּאָמַר רַבָּה: הָיָה גְּדִי גָּנוּב לוֹ וּטְבָחוֹ בְּשַׁבָּת – חַיָּיב, שֶׁכְּבָר נִתְחַיֵּיב בִּגְנֵיבָה קוֹדֶם שֶׁיָּבֹא לִידֵי אִיסּוּר שַׁבָּת. גָּנַב וְטָבַח בְּשַׁבָּת – פָּטוּר, שֶׁאִם אֵין גְּנֵיבָה – אֵין טְבִיחָה וְאֵין מְכִירָה.

and Rabbi Meir is of the opinion that one **is flogged and pays,** but **is not of** the opinion that one **dies** by execution **and pays. And these** *halakhot* **are different, as it is a novel element that the Torah innovated with regard to** the halakhic category of **fines;**[N] **although he is killed, he pays. And Rabba followed his** line of **reasoning**[N] stated elsewhere, **as Rabba said:** If one **had a stolen kid** in **his** possession that he had stolen previously, **and he slaughtered it on Shabbat,** he is **liable** to pay five times the principal for slaughtering the kid, **as he was already liable for stealing before he came to** violate **the prohibition** against performing labor on **Shabbat.** Although he slaughtered the goat on Shabbat, a capital crime, he is liable for the payment because it is a fine. However, if **he stole** the goat **and slaughtered** it **on Shabbat,**[N] he is **exempt** from the payment of five times the principal **as, if** there is **no** payment for **theft,**[N] due to his liability to receive the death penalty for desecrating Shabbat, and his obligation to repay the theft is not a fine, there is **no** liability for **slaughter and** there is **no** liability for **sale.**

וְאָמַר רַבָּה: הָיָה גְּדִי גָּנוּב לוֹ וּטְבָחוֹ בְּמַחְתֶּרֶת – חַיָּיב, שֶׁכְּבָר נִתְחַיֵּיב בִּגְנֵיבָה קוֹדֶם שֶׁיָּבֹא לִידֵי אִיסּוּר מַחְתֶּרֶת. גָּנַב וְטָבַח בְּמַחְתֶּרֶת – פָּטוּר, שֶׁאִם אֵין גְּנֵיבָה – אֵין טְבִיחָה וְאֵין מְכִירָה.

And Rabba said: If one **had a stolen kid** in **his** possession that he had stolen previously, **and he slaughtered it in** the course of an act of **burglary,**[N] he is **liable** to pay four or five times the principal, **as he was already liable for theft before he came to** violate **the prohibition** against **burglary.** However, if **he stole and slaughtered** an animal **in** the course of an act of **burglary,**[H] he is **exempt.** Because the owner of the house is permitted to kill the burglar, the status of the burglar is tantamount to one liable to receive the death penalty. **As, if** there is **no** payment **for theft,** there is **no** liability for **slaughter and** there is **no** liability for **sale.** Rabba's statements indicate that one pays the fines for slaughter or sale even if he is liable to receive the death penalty.

HALAKHA

If he stole and slaughtered in the course of an act of burglary – גָּנַב וְטָבַח בְּמַחְתֶּרֶת: If a burglar broke into a house and stole an animal and slaughtered it there, he is exempt, as it is permitted to take his life at the time, as per the statement of Rabba (Rambam *Sefer Nezikim, Hilkhot Geneiva* 9:13; *Tur, Ḥoshen Mishpat* 351).

NOTES

As it is a novel element that the Torah innovated with regard to the halakhic category of fines – דְּחִידּוּשׁ הוּא שֶׁחִידְּשָׁה תּוֹרָה בִּקְנָס: In the *Shita Mekubbetzet* it is explained that Rashi is not saying that the novel element in the Torah is that one who is liable to pay a fine is executed and pays. Rather, the novel element is the very imposition of a fine. Therefore, one cannot derive the legal status of fines from other similar payments, and as a result, one is liable to be executed and to pay. Whenever a *halakha* in the Torah is characterized as novel, that means that it is exceptional in certain respects, as the principles in effect in similar cases do not apply. Its *halakhot* are therefore unique; elements of other *halakhot* cannot be derived from it, nor can its elements be derived from other *halakhot*. As for the novel element of fines, the *Ḥatam Sofer* writes that it is not that one pays more than the damage he caused, as that is true about other Torah punishments, e.g., corporal punishment, where there is no necessary connection between the damage caused and the penalty imposed. Instead, the novel element is that the fine is paid to the victim rather than to the public treasury or to the Sanctuary, which is generally the case with regard to sinners.

And Rabba followed his line of reasoning – וְאָזְדָא רַבָּה לְטַעְמֵיהּ: A general question is raised here: When an *amora* repeats a *halakha*, why does the Gemara sometimes react by asking: Didn't he already state that once, while on other occasions the Gemara simply notes: And the Sage followed his line of reasoning stated elsewhere. In *Sefer HaḤokhma*, Rabbeinu Barukh explains that when the statement of the Sage is stated as an elucidation of a mishna or the like, the Gemara says that he followed his standard line of reasoning, as his explanation is consistent with his practical halakhic ruling. However, if both statements are halakhic rulings, the Gemara will question the repetition.

If he stole and slaughtered on Shabbat – גָּנַב וְטָבַח בְּשַׁבָּת: The early and later commentaries discuss the case of one who stole on Shabbat and proceeded to slaughter or sell the animal during the week. The Ritva and others infer from Rashi that in that case he is liable to pay four or five times the principal. The reason is that the theft committed on Shabbat is no longer relevant, and when he takes the animal to slaughter or sells it is as though the theft began at that moment. The Rashba disagrees and maintains that in that case he is exempt, in accordance with the principle that if there is no theft there is no slaughter or sale either. Since one is not liable to pay for theft on Shabbat, there is no liability for slaughter or sale. The *Shita Yeshana*, cited in the *Shita Mekubbetzet* explains likewise. Several later commentaries address the fundamental aspects of this dilemma. It appears that the dispute among the early commentaries is dependent on the precise definition of theft performed in the course of desecrating Shabbat. Is it considered a full-fledged acquisition in every sense but the thief is exempt from payment, or is it viewed as an incomplete acquisition and considered as though there were no theft at all (Rabbi Akiva Eiger; *Or Same'aḥ*; *Kovetz Shiurim*)?

As, if there is no payment for theft, etc. – שֶׁאִם אֵין גְּנֵיבָה וכו׳: Although the fine for slaughter or sale is an independent fine, independent of the mitzva to restore the stolen item to its owner, it is a biblical decree that one is liable to pay four or five times the principal, not merely three or four times. Based on that biblical decree, if one is exempt from the obligation to return the principal, he is exempt from paying the fine as well (Ritva).

The prohibition against burglary – אִיסּוּר מַחְתֶּרֶת: The *halakha* of a burglar who breaks into a private home is stated in the Torah: "If the thief is found breaking in, and is struck and dies, there is no blood for him" (Exodus 22:1). The basic concept, which is elucidated in tractate *Sanhedrin*, is that a thief breaking into a house is considered, with certain exceptions, as one with the intention to commit murder if necessary. Therefore, if the homeowner kills him, he is exempt. Since taking the life of the burglar is permitted, his legal status is like that of one sentenced to death, and therefore he is exempt from payment for any damage that he may have caused at that moment. That status is temporary, as once the burglar leaves the premises it is no longer permitted to kill him and he is liable to pay for any monetary liability that he may incur.

וּצְרִיכָא, דְּאִי אַשְׁמְעִינַן שַׁבָּת – מִשּׁוּם דְּאִיסּוּרָהּ אִיסּוּר עוֹלָם, אֲבָל מַחְתֶּרֶת דְּאִיסּוּר שָׁעָה הוּא – אֵימָא לָא; וְאִי אַשְׁמְעִינַן מַחְתֶּרֶת – מִשּׁוּם דְּמַחְתַּרְתּוֹ זוֹ הִיא הַתְרָאָתוֹ, אֲבָל שַׁבָּת דִּבְעֵיָא הַתְרָאָה – אֵימָא לָא, צְרִיכָא.

The Gemara comments: **And** it was **necessary** for Rabba to state this *halakha* with regard to both Shabbat and burglary; **as, if he** had **taught us**[N] that one is exempt from payment only with regard to **Shabbat,** it is **because** Shabbat is severe since punishment for violation of **its prohibition is an eternal prohibition,** as whenever witnesses testify that one desecrated Shabbat, he can be executed. **However,** in the case of **burglary,** as punishment for violating its **prohibition is transitory,** e.g., it is permitted for the homeowner to kill the burglar only as long as the burglar remains on his property, **say** that he is **not** exempt from payment. **And if he taught us** the exemption only with regard to **burglary,** that would be **because his burglary is his forewarning.** Because he certainly intends to kill the homeowner, it is permitted for the homeowner to kill him without forewarning. In that respect, burglary is a severe prohibition and exempts one from payment. **However, Shabbat, which requires forewarning,** is a less severe prohibition, and in that case, **say** that one **is not** exempt from payment. Therefore, it was **necessary** for Rabba to state the exemption in both cases.

אָמַר רַב פָּפָּא: הָיְתָה פָּרָה גְּנוּבָה לוֹ וּטְבָחָהּ בְּשַׁבָּת – חַיָּיב, שֶׁכְּבָר נִתְחַיֵּיב בִּגְנֵיבָה קוֹדֶם שֶׁיָּבֹא לִידֵי אִיסּוּר שַׁבָּת. הָיְתָה פָּרָה שְׁאוּלָה לוֹ, וּטְבָחָהּ בְּשַׁבָּת – פָּטוּר. אֲמַר לֵיהּ רַב אַחָא בְּרֵיהּ דְּרָבָא לְרַב אָשֵׁי: רַב פָּפָּא פָּרָה אֲתָא לְאַשְׁמוֹעִינַן?!

Rav Pappa said: If one **had a stolen cow** in **his** possession that he had stolen previously **and he slaughtered it on Shabbat,** he is **liable** to pay four or five times the principal **as he was already liable for theft before he came to** violate **the prohibition of Shabbat. If a cow was lent to him and he slaughtered it on Shabbat,**[H] he is **exempt** from paying the fine. **Rav Aḥa, son of Rava, said to Rav Ashi:** Is **Rav Pappa coming to teach us** the case of a **cow?** In other words, what did Rav Pappa add that was not already clear from Rabba's statement? The same principle applies with regard to both a kid and a cow. If one was liable to pay for the theft when he stole the animal, he is liable to pay the fine for slaughter as well, even if he is liable to receive the death penalty.

אֲמַר לֵיהּ: רַב פָּפָּא שְׁאוּלָה אֲתָא לְאַשְׁמוֹעִינַן; סָלְקָא דַּעְתָּךְ אָמֵינָא, הוֹאִיל וְאָמַר רַב פָּפָּא: מִשְּׁעַת מְשִׁיכָה הוּא דְּאִתְחַיַּיב לֵיהּ בִּמְזוֹנוֹתֶיהָ, הָכָא נָמֵי מִשְּׁעַת שְׁאֵלָה אִתְחַיַּיב בְּאוֹנָסֶיהָ. – קָא מַשְׁמַע לַן.

Rav Ashi **said to him: Rav Pappa is coming to teach us** the *halakha* with regard to a **borrowed** cow, as **it could enter your mind to say** that **since Rav Pappa said:** It is **from the moment of pulling** the animal into his domain **that** the borrower **is obligated**[H] **to** provide the animal's **sustenance,** then **here too, from the moment of borrowing**[N] **he is liable** to pay **for its unavoidable accidents.** From that point, the animal is legally in his possession and therefore, even if he slaughtered the animal on Shabbat he should be liable. Therefore, **he teaches us** that one assumes liability for unavoidable accidents only when they actually occur, and if that is on Shabbat, he is exempt.

NOTES

And it was necessary; as, if he had taught us, etc. – וּצְרִיכָא דְּאִי אַשְׁמְעִינַן וכו׳: Rashi and several other commentaries explain that the Gemara here emphasizes that although one might have thought otherwise, in each of these cases one is exempt from punishment. Conversely, *Tosafot* and other early commentaries (Ramban; Rashba) contend that the opposite is true: The point is that one is obligated to pay the fine even though he violated a prohibition that is punishable by death.

Here too, from the moment of borrowing, etc. – הָכָא נָמֵי מִשְּׁעַת שְׁאֵלָה וכו׳: The reason for the difference between these two *halakhot* is that since one who borrows an animal is obligated to guard it from that moment, he is also obligated to see to the animal's sustenance. In contrast, liability to pay for accidental damage does not stem from his obligation to care for the animal; rather, there is an independent obligation to compensate the owner if there is an accident. Therefore, his liability begins only from the moment that the accident transpires.

HALAKHA

If a cow was lent to him and he slaughtered it on Shabbat – הָיְתָה פָּרָה שְׁאוּלָה לוֹ וּטְבָחָהּ בְּשַׁבָּת: One who borrowed a cow from another before Shabbat and stole and slaughtered it on Shabbat is exempt from payment, as the liability to be punished for theft and Shabbat desecration coincide. The *halakha* is in accordance with the opinion of Rav Pappa, as his opinion does not contradict the latter version of Rava's statement. The early commentaries disagree, both in terms of the understanding of the Gemara and in terms of the Rambam's ruling. Some (Meiri; *Netivot HaMishpat, Ḥoshen Mishpat* 341:9) state that he is exempt only from paying four or five times the principal but is liable to pay the principal, while others (Rabbi Meir HaLevi; *Nimmukei Yosef*) state that he is exempt from the principal as well (Rambam *Sefer Nezikim, Hilkhot Geneiva* 3:4; *Tur, Ḥoshen Mishpat* 350).

From the moment of pulling that he is obligated – מִשְּׁעַת מְשִׁיכָה הוּא דְּאִתְחַיַּיב לֵיהּ: One who borrows an animal is obligated to see to its sustenance and is liable for accidents (*Shakh*) from the moment he pulls the animal, as per the opinion of Rav Pappa. The Rema cites the opinion of Rabbeinu Yitzḥak and the Rosh that even without pulling the animal, he is liable from the moment its owners leave (Rambam *Sefer Mishpatim, Hilkhot She'ela* 1:4; *Shulḥan Arukh, Ḥoshen Mishpat* 340:4).

אָמַר רָבָא: הִנִּיחַ לָהֶן אֲבִיהֶן פָּרָה שְׁאוּלָה – מִשְׁתַּמְּשִׁין בָּהּ כׇּל יְמֵי שְׁאֵלָתָהּ, מֵתָה – אֵין חַיָּיבִין בְּאוֹנְסָהּ. כִּסְבוּרִין שֶׁל אֲבִיהֶם הִיא וּטְבָחוּהָ וַאֲכָלוּהָ – מְשַׁלְּמִין דְּמֵי בָשָׂר בְּזוֹל. הִנִּיחַ לָהֶן אֲבִיהֶן אַחֲרָיוּת נְכָסִים – חַיָּיבִין לְשַׁלֵּם.

Rava said: If **their father** died and **left them a borrowed cow,**[H] **they may use it** for **the entire** duration of the **period** for which **it was borrowed.** The right to use a borrowed article continues even after the borrower himself dies. However, if the cow **died, they are not liable** to pay **for its unavoidable accident,**[N] as they did not borrow the animal themselves. Similarly, if **they thought** the cow **was their father's**[H] **and they slaughtered it and ate it, they pay only a reduced** assessment of the **price of the meat.**[N] They are required to pay only for the benefit they received, not the damage they caused the owner. However, if **their father left them**[N] **property** as a **guarantee**[N] for return of the borrowed item, i.e., there was a lien on the father's property during his lifetime, **they are obligated to pay** the entire sum of the damage.

אִיכָּא דְּמַתְנֵי לַהּ אַרֵישָׁא, וְאִיכָּא דְּמַתְנֵי לַהּ אַסֵּיפָא. מַאן דְּמַתְנֵי לַהּ אַרֵישָׁא – כׇּל שֶׁכֵּן אַסֵּיפָא, וּפְלִיגָא דְּרַב פָּפָּא, וּמַאן דְּמַתְנֵי לַהּ אַסֵּיפָא – אֲבָל אַרֵישָׁא לָא, וְהַיְינוּ דְּרַב פָּפָּא.

The Gemara comments: **Some teach this** statement, that if the father left property as a guarantee his heirs are liable to pay the entire damage, **with regard to the first clause** of this *halakha*, **and some teach it with regard to the latter clause.** The Gemara elaborates: According to the **one who teaches it with regard to the first clause,**[N] when the animal died, **all the more so** would he teach this *halakha* **with regard to the latter clause,** as since they slaughtered the animal they must pay full damages. **And** this approach **differs** with the opinion **of Rav Pappa,** who said that a borrower is liable for accidents only when the incident occurs. **And** according to the **one who teaches it with regard to the latter clause,** this *halakha* applies only when they slaughtered and ate it; **however, with regard to the first clause,** when it died, they would **not** be liable, as the *tanna* too maintains that liability for unavoidable accidents begins only when the incident occurs, not from when the cow was borrowed. **And this is** consistent with the ruling **of Rav Pappa.**

HALAKHA

If their father left them a borrowed cow – הִנִּיחַ לָהֶן אֲבִיהֶן פָּרָה שְׁאוּלָה: If one borrowed an animal and died, his heirs may use the animal until the end of the period for which it was borrowed. If the animal dies, they are not liable to pay for the accident, as per the opinion of Rava. However, their liability is like that of paid bailees, as the Gemara states that they are exempt only from accidents, from which it may be inferred that they are liable for theft and loss (*Baḥ*). The Rosh writes that if the lender says to the heirs: Return the article I lent or assume responsibility to pay for accidents, it is binding upon the heirs (Rambam *Sefer Mishpatim, Hilkhot She'ela* 1:5; *Shulḥan Arukh, Ḥoshen Mishpat* 341:3).

If they thought the cow was their father's, etc. – כִּסְבוּרִין שֶׁל אֲבִיהֶם וכו׳: If the heirs inherited no property from their father and slaughtered and ate the borrowed cow under the mistaken impression that it belonged to their father, they are required to pay only for the benefit they received, not the damage they caused the owner. If their father bequeathed property to them and the borrowed cow died or they slaughtered it, they reimburse the owner the full value of his cow from the inherited property. This is the opinion of the Rambam. His view is disputed by the Ramban and the Rashba, who contend that the Rambam's approach corresponds with neither the first version nor the latter version in the Gemara. They rule in accordance with the latter version, and Rava's ruling is parallel to that of Rav Pappa. Therefore, if the cow dies the heirs are exempt from payment even if their father left them property as a guarantee. The Rosh agrees. The *Kesef Mishne* and other commentaries explain that the Rambam had a variant version of the Gemara. The *Shulḥan Arukh*, like most authorities, rules in accordance with the latter version of Rava's statement to exempt the heirs (Rambam *Sefer Mishpatim, Hilkhot She'ela* 1:5; *Shulḥan Arukh, Ḥoshen Mishpat* 341:4).

NOTES

If it died they are not liable for its unavoidable accident – מֵתָה אֵין חַיָּיבִין בְּאוֹנְסָהּ: The Ra'avad states that the heirs are exempt from payments for accidents even if they actually use the animal. He explains that the heirs inherit the rights to use the animal, whereas the obligation to pay for accidents is a personal obligation assumed by the borrower, which lapses upon his death. The heirs never accepted responsibility to pay for accidents. The Rashba questions this approach, in light of the *halakha* that one who borrowed from a hirer is considered to have borrowed from the owner himself. Accordingly, heirs should also be viewed as having borrowed from their father and therefore should be obligated to pay the owner of the animal for accidents. The Ritva answers that even in a case of a second borrower, his liability does not stem from his use of the object but from the fact that he actually borrowed it and thereby incurred the responsibility, as opposed to heirs, who never assumed that. A different explanation is suggested by Rabbi Avraham *Av Beit Din*. He contends that heirs are exempt from financial responsibility for accidents only if they had not made use of the animal, but if they had used it they are considered to have borrowed it themselves. See HALAKHA for further elaboration. The Ra'avad adds that even if they did not use the animal, their responsibility is no less than the responsibility of paid bailees, stemming from their right to use the animal.

Reduced assessment of the price of the meat – דְּמֵי בָשָׂר בְּזוֹל: Based on *Bava Kamma* 146b, Rashi explains that this means that they return the hide to the owner and pay two-thirds of the standard market price of the meat. The Rid agrees. The Ramban maintains that even in *Bava Kamma* that ruling is a later addition by the early *ge'onim*. Therefore, he asserts that there is no connection between the two passages, and the Gemara here simply means the value of meat sold at a reduced price.

If their father left them, etc. – הִנִּיחַ לָהֶן אֲבִיהֶן וכו׳: The rationale for the opinion that this statement relates to the latter clause is subject to dispute among the early commentaries. According to most versions of Rashi's commentary, the heirs are liable due to the fact that they neglected to assess the situation properly, although some (*Shita Mekubbetzet*; Rashash) cite a variant reading that aligns Rashi's opinion with that of most of the other commentaries. The Ramban questions Rashi's interpretation: If that is the reason for their liability, what is the difference whether or not their father left them property? He therefore agrees with *Tosafot* that the heirs' father should have informed them that this cow did not belong to him. Since he neglected to do so, payment is collected from his property, if any of his property remains. Most early commentaries explain in this way, despite the difficulty raised by the Rashba, that it is conceivable that he neglected to inform them due to circumstances beyond his control, e.g., if he died suddenly, a difficulty that does not exist according to Rashi's explanation. Rabbi Meir HaLevi explains that had their father not left them property, there would be no need to consider the possibility that there is some obligation incurred by their father when they come to slaughter the animal, as he left them no property from which it could be collected. Since they did not know the cow was borrowed, they are not liable. If, however, they inherited property from their father, they know that if he was liable, e.g., because he stole the animal, they are obligated to pay due to their own assumption of responsibility for the animal and due to their father's obligation as well.

Property as a guarantee – אַחֲרָיוּת נְכָסִים: According to Rashi this refers specifically to property that can be mortgaged to guarantee a loan, i.e., land. Although there are different versions of the Rambam's ruling, apparently he maintains that after the ordinance instituted by the *ge'onim* that when one takes a loan there is a lien on all of one's property, there is no difference between land and other types of property. The commentaries state that this dispute is related to the issue of whether the ordinance that the debts of the father are bequeathed to an heir is limited to a debt due to a loan or whether it applies to all debts.

The one who teaches it with regard to the first clause, etc. – מַאן דְּמַתְנֵי לַהּ אַרֵישָׁא וכו׳: The Rambam rules that if the heirs thought the cow was their father's and their father left them property, they are obligated to pay even if the cow died. Other early commentaries question this ruling, as it appears to correspond neither with the first nor with the second version of the Gemara. See HALAKHA for further elaboration. The Meiri claims that the duty of the heirs to pay for the dead cow does not result from their liability to pay for accidents, but from their father's obligation to return the article he borrowed. According to his opinion, this *halakha* is unrelated to the Gemara's discussion with regard to the relationship between the statement of Rava and Rav Pappa.

NOTES

What is the reason that he didn't state his opinion in accordance with the opinion of Rabbi Yoḥanan – מַאי טַעְמָא לָא אָמַר כְּרַבִּי יוֹחָנָן: Although ostensibly the Gemara could have said that Reish Lakish bases his opinion on the fact that a careful reading of the mishna leads to the conclusion that it is in accordance with the opinion of Rabbi Meir, it was already proven above that it cannot be said that the entire mishna is in accordance with the opinion of Rabbi Meir. Therefore, that is not sufficient to clarify why he explained it according to Rabbi Meir's opinion (Ritva). In the *Shita Mekubbetzet* it is explained at length that all of the problems of the mishna are resolved by Rabbi Yoḥanan's explanation, including contradictions with other *mishnayot*. That is not the case with the explanation of Reish Lakish.

Those unwittingly liable – חַיָּיבֵי...שׁוֹגְגִין: The word unwittingly is inaccurate here because the same *halakha* applies even if they sinned intentionally, as according to Rabbi Yoḥanan the decisive factor is not their state of mind but whether or not they received a warning and consequently whether or not they are punished. However, it could be explained that Rabbi Yoḥanan deems anyone who acted without forewarning as one who acted unwittingly (Ritva).

בִּשְׁלָמָא רַבִּי יוֹחָנָן לָא אָמַר כְּרֵישׁ לָקִישׁ – דְּקָא מוֹקִים לָהּ כְּרַבָּנַן. אֶלָּא רֵישׁ לָקִישׁ מַאי טַעְמָא לָא אָמַר כְּרַבִּי יוֹחָנָן? אָמַר לָךְ: כֵּיוָן דְּאִילּוּ אַתְרוּ בֵּיהּ – פָּטוּר, כִּי לָא אַתְרוּ בֵּיהּ – נַמִי פָּטוּר.

Several possible solutions were proposed to resolve the apparent contradiction between the mishna here that says that one who rapes his sister pays a fine and the mishna in *Makkot* that says that he is flogged. The Gemara comments: **Granted, Rabbi Yoḥanan,** who explains the mishna as referring to a case where he was not forewarned, **did not state** his opinion **in accordance with** the opinion of **Reish Lakish,** who explains that the mishna is in accordance with the opinion of Rabbi Meir, **as he establishes** the mishna **in accordance with** the opinion of **the Rabbis,** a preferable option, as that aligns the unattributed mishna with the *halakha*. **However, what is the reason** that **Reish Lakish didn't state** his opinion **in accordance with** the opinion of **Rabbi Yoḥanan?**[N] The Gemara answers: Reish Lakish could have **said to you: Since if they forewarned him** he is **exempt** from payment, **when they did not forewarn him,** he is **exempt as well.**

וְאָזְדוּ לְטַעֲמַיְיהוּ: דְּכִי אֲתָא רַב דִּימִי אָמַר: חַיָּיבֵי מִיתוֹת שׁוֹגְגִין וְחַיָּיבֵי מַלְקִיּוֹת שׁוֹגְגִין וְדָבָר אַחֵר, רַבִּי יוֹחָנָן אָמַר: חַיָּיב, וְרֵישׁ לָקִישׁ אָמַר: פָּטוּר. רַבִּי יוֹחָנָן אָמַר: חַיָּיב, דְּהָא לָא אַתְרוּ בֵּיהּ. רֵישׁ לָקִישׁ אָמַר: פָּטוּר, כֵּיוָן דְּאִילּוּ אַתְרוּ בֵּיהּ – פָּטוּר, כִּי לָא אַתְרוּ בֵּיהּ נַמִי פָּטוּר.

And Rabbi Yoḥanan and Reish Lakish each **follow their** standard lines of **reasoning** in this regard, **as when Rav Dimi came** from Eretz Yisrael to Babylonia, **he said:** With regard to **those** who **unwittingly** performed a transgression for which one is **liable**[N] **to** receive the **death** penalty, or **those** who **unwittingly** performed a transgression for which one is **liable** to receive **lashes, and** that transgression also involved **another matter,** monetary payment, **Rabbi Yoḥanan said:** He is **liable** to pay; since he sinned unwittingly he did not receive the severe punishment. **And Reish Lakish said** he is **exempt.** The Gemara clarifies the rationales for their statements. **Rabbi Yoḥanan said** he is **liable; since they did not forewarn him,** he sinned unwittingly. **Reish Lakish said** he is **exempt; since if they forewarned him** he is **exempt** from payment, **when they did not forewarn him,** he is **exempt as well.**

אֵיתִיבֵיהּ רֵישׁ לָקִישׁ לְרַבִּי יוֹחָנָן: ״וְלֹא יִהְיֶה אָסוֹן עָנוֹשׁ יֵעָנֵשׁ״

Reish Lakish raised an objection to the opinion of **Rabbi Yoḥanan** from the following verse, which describes a case where two people fought and during their struggle they hurt a pregnant woman, causing her to miscarry: **"And yet no harm follow, he shall be punished** as imposed upon him by the woman's husband" (Exodus 21:22).

Perek **III**
Daf **35** Amud **a**

מַאי לָאו אָסוֹן מַמָּשׁ? לָא, דִּין אָסוֹן. אִיכָּא דְּאָמְרִי, אֵיתִיבֵיהּ רַבִּי יוֹחָנָן לְרֵישׁ לָקִישׁ: ״וְלֹא יִהְיֶה אָסוֹן עָנוֹשׁ יֵעָנֵשׁ״ מַאי לָאו – דִּין אָסוֹן? לָא, אָסוֹן מַמָּשׁ.

Is this **not** referring to **actual harm,** i.e., the woman's death? And the verse states that he pays only if she did not die, but if she died is he exempt, even if he was not forewarned? The Gemara answers: **No,** the verse can be explained to mean: If there is no **sentence of harm.**[N] If the court does not actually sentence him to death, he pays the damages for the miscarried fetus. He is exempt from payment only if he is actually executed. **Some say** a different version of this exchange: **Rabbi Yoḥanan raised an objection to** the opinion of **Reish Lakish: "And yet no harm follow, he shall be punished"** (Exodus 21:22); **is this not** referring **to a sentence of harm?** The Gemara answers: **No,** the verse can be explained to mean: If there is no **actual harm.**

NOTES

Harm and sentence of harm – אָסוֹן וְדִין אָסוֹן: Rashi explains that the harm referred to in the verse is that of the woman dying. He therefore explains that according to the opinion that the verse refers to actual harm, when it says: "And yet no harm follow, he shall be punished" (Exodus 21:22), it means that whenever the woman dies, the one who caused the miscarriage is not liable. According to the opinion that the verse refers to a sentence of harm, it means that the fact that the woman dies is not sufficient to exempt the aggressor from payment, as there must be a sentence of death for her killer, which can be administered only if there was forewarning.

Rabbeinu Ḥananel's version of the text has the names in the text reversed. Rabbi Yoḥanan asks the first version of the question: Is this not referring to actual harm? Reish Lakish asks the second version: Is this not referring to sentence of harm? Accordingly, he understands the harm mentioned in the verse to be the fate of the killer; Rabbi Yoḥanan asks: Is it not only when the killer experiences actual harm, when he is executed by the court, as there were witnesses and forewarning, that he is exempt from payment? The Gemara's response in defense of Reish Lakish's opinion is that no, the verse is referring to the sentence of harm, i.e. to an action for which one is potentially liable to be executed.

אֲמַר רָבָא: וּמִי אִיכָּא לְמַאן דְּאָמַר חַיָּיבֵי מִיתוֹת שׁוֹגְגִין חַיָּיבִים? וְהָא תָּנָא דְּבֵי חִזְקִיָּה: מַכֵּה אָדָם וּמַכֵּה בְהֵמָה,

Rava said: Is there anyone who said that **those** who **unwittingly** performed a transgression for which one is **liable to** receive the **death** penalty **are obligated** to pay? **But didn't** the Sage **of the school of Ḥizkiyya teach:**[N] The verse speaks of **one who smites a person, and** the verse speaks of **one who smites an animal.**[N] The two cases are juxtaposed in the verse "And one who smites an animal shall pay for it, and one who smites a person shall die" (Leviticus 24:21).

מַה מַּכֵּה בְהֵמָה – לֹא חִילַּקְתָּ בּוֹ בֵּין בְּשׁוֹגֵג בֵּין בְּמֵזִיד, בֵּין מִתְכַּוֵּין לְשֶׁאֵין מִתְכַּוֵּין, בֵּין דֶּרֶךְ יְרִידָה לְדֶרֶךְ עֲלִיָּה, לְפוֹטְרוֹ מָמוֹן אֶלָּא לְחַיְּיבוֹ מָמוֹן – אַף מַכֵּה אָדָם לֹא תַחֲלוֹק בּוֹ בֵּין בְּשׁוֹגֵג בֵּין בְּמֵזִיד, בֵּין מִתְכַּוֵּין לְשֶׁאֵין מִתְכַּוֵּין, בֵּין דֶּרֶךְ יְרִידָה לְדֶרֶךְ עֲלִיָּה – לְחַיְּיבוֹ מָמוֹן, אֶלָּא לְפוֹטְרוֹ מָמוֹן.

Just as in the case of one **who smites an animal, you did not distinguish between** one who did so **unwittingly and** one who did so **intentionally,**[N] **between** one who acted **with intent and one who** acted **with no intent, between** one who smites **in** the course of a **downward motion and** one who smites **in** the course of **an upward motion,** and in all those cases it is not **to exempt** him from paying **money but rather to obligate him to** pay **money; so too, in** the case of one **who smites a person, do not distinguish between** one who did so **unwittingly and** one who did so **intentionally,**[H] **between** one who acted **with intent and one who** acted **with no intent, between** one who smites **in** the course of **a downward motion and** one who smites **in** the course of **an upward motion.** In all those cases as well it is not **to obligate him** to pay **money but rather to exempt him** from paying **money.** The *halakha* in both cases is unconditional; when he smites an animal he is always liable to pay and when he smites a person he is always exempt from payment, regardless of whether or not he is actually executed.

אֶלָּא, כִּי אֲתָא רָבִין אֲמַר: חַיָּיבֵי מִיתוֹת שׁוֹגְגִין כּוּלֵּי עָלְמָא לָא פְּלִיגִי דִּפְטוּרִין. כִּי פְּלִיגִי בְּחַיָּיבֵי מַלְקוֹת שׁוֹגְגִין וְדָבָר אַחֵר. רַבִּי יוֹחָנָן אָמַר: חַיָּיב, חַיָּיבֵי מִיתוֹת אִיתְקוּשׁ, חַיָּיבֵי מַלְקִיּוֹת – לָא אִיתְקוּשׁ. רֵישׁ לָקִישׁ אָמַר: פָּטוּר, בְּפֵירוּשׁ רִיבְּתָה תוֹרָה חַיָּיבֵי מַלְקִיּוֹת כְּחַיָּיבֵי מִיתוֹת.

Rather, when Ravin came from Eretz Yisrael to Babylonia, **he said:** With regard to **those** who **unwittingly** performed a transgression for which one is **liable to** receive the **death penalty, everyone agrees that** they **are exempt,** as per the derivation of the Sages of the school of Ḥizkiyya. **When they disagree** it is **with regard to those** who **unwittingly** performed a transgression for which one is **liable to** receive **lashes, and another matter,**[H] for which he is liable to pay money. **Rabbi Yoḥanan said** that he is **obligated** to pay, as **those liable to** receive the **death penalty are juxtaposed** to cases of monetary payment and are unconditionally exempt from payment. However, **those liable** to receive **lashes are not juxtaposed.** Therefore, in the case of one who is liable to receive lashes, unless one is actually flogged, he is obligated to pay for the damage he inflicted. **Reish Lakish said:** He is **exempt, as the Torah explicitly included those liable to** receive **lashes, like those liable to** receive the **death** penalty, and unconditionally exempted them from payment.

HALAKHA

So too, in the case of one who smites a person, do not distinguish between one who did so unwittingly and one who did so intentionally – אַף מַכֵּה אָדָם לֹא תַחֲלוֹק בּוֹ בֵּין בְּשׁוֹגֵג בֵּין בְּמֵזִיד: If one performed a transgression punishable by death and simultaneously performed an action for which he is liable to pay, he is exempt from that payment even if he sinned unwittingly or with no intent, as per the statement of the Sage of the school of Ḥizkiyya (Rambam *Sefer Nashim, Hilkhot Na'ara Betula* 1:13; *Sefer Nezikim, Hilkhot Ḥovel* 4:7; *Shulḥan Arukh, Ḥoshen Mishpat* 423:4).

When they disagree it is with regard to those who unwittingly performed a transgression for which one is liable to receive lashes, and another matter – כִּי פְּלִיגִי בְּחַיָּיבֵי מַלְקוֹת שׁוֹגְגִין וְדָבָר אַחֵר: One who commits a transgression for which he is liable both to be flogged and to pay is flogged and is exempt from payment. However, if he is not flogged for his transgression, e.g., if he performed it unwittingly or without forewarning, he is obligated to pay. The *halakha* is in accordance with the opinion of Rabbi Yoḥanan in his dispute with Reish Lakish (Rambam *Sefer Nashim, Hilkhot Na'ara Betula* 1:11 and *Sefer Nezikim, Hilkhot Geneiva* 3:1).

NOTES

But didn't the Sage of the school of Ḥizkiyya teach – וְהָא תָּנָא דְּבֵי חִזְקִיָּה: *Tosafot* and other early commentaries discuss whether this statement of the school of Ḥizkiyya is undisputed. In the Jerusalem Talmud there is no dispute in this regard, and both Rabbi Yoḥanan and Reish Lakish accept this exposition completely. The commentaries ask: Couldn't Rabbi Yoḥanan prove from the mishna that one who is liable to receive the death penalty is exempt from paying the fine, as he maintains that the mishna is referring to a sinner who received no forewarning? Why, then, is it necessary for him to cite proof from a different source? The answer is that the difficulty raised from the statement of the school of Ḥizkiyya is also based on this inference from the mishna. The Rashba claims that the Gemara could have cited proof from the mishna, but it preferred to cite an explicit teaching rather than rely on an inference. Furthermore, unlike the statement of the school of Ḥizkiyya, the mishna does not provide the biblical source for the *halakha*.

One who smites a person and one who smites an animal – מַכֵּה אָדָם וּמַכֵּה בְהֵמָה: This exposition is based on the fact that both parts of the verse "And one who smites an animal shall pay for it, and one who smites a person shall die" are superfluous, as the *halakhot* of causing injury to an animal and killing another person are both stated elsewhere. The purpose of this verse, therefore, must be to equate the two *halakhot* (Ramah). It cannot be that the Torah is teaching that one who smites a person is also liable to pay in all cases, as clearly one who commits intentional murder receives the greater of the two punishments and is exempt from payment. He therefore derived that just as one who strikes an animal is liable to pay in every case, so too, one who kills a person is exempt from payment in every case (Ritva).

Between one who did so unwittingly and one who did so intentionally – בֵּין בְּשׁוֹגֵג בֵּין בְּמֵזִיד: *Tosafot* explain that these three categories: Unwitting versus intentional, with intent versus with no intent, and one who smites in the course of a downward motion versus one who smites in the course of an upward motion, refer to three different types of monetary liability. Other early commentaries, and *Tosafot* elsewhere, elaborate on this point. Specifically, they explain that unwitting versus intentional relates to intention to kill, generally determined by forewarning; with intent versus with no intent refers to one who intended to kill one person but killed another; in the course of a downward motion versus in the course of an upward motion is relevant to exile. It is a Torah decree that one is liable to be exiled to a city of refuge only if he killed another in a downward movement, e.g., if one fell on the victim or dropped an object upon him. If one killed another in an upward motion, e.g., one who struck another with an ax while lifting it upward, he is exempt, as explained at length in tractate *Makkot*.

היכן ריבתה תורה? אמר אביי: אתיא "רשע" "רשע". רבא אמר: אתיא "מכה" "מכה". אמר ליה רב פפא לרבא: הי מכה? אילימא "ומכה בהמה ישלמנה ומכה אדם יומת" – האי בקטלא כתיב! אלא האי "מכה": "מכה נפש בהמה ישלמנה נפש תחת נפש" וסמיך ליה "ואיש כי יתן מום בעמיתו [כאשר עשה כן יעשה לו]".

The Gemara asks: **Where did** the **Torah include** those liable to be flogged? **Abaye said:** It is **derived** by means of a verbal analogy between the term **wicked** in the verse "That he is wicked and liable to die" (Numbers 35:31), and the term **wicked**[N] in the verse "That he is wicked and liable to be flogged" (Deuteronomy 25:2). **Rava said:** It is **derived** by means of a verbal analogy between the term **smites** in one verse and the term **smites**[N] in another verse. **Rava Pappa said to Rava:** To **which** term **smites** are you referring? **If we** say that it is the verse **"And one who smites an animal shall pay for it, and one who smites a person shall die"** (Leviticus 24:21), clearly that is not so, as **that is written with regard to death.** Smiting a person in that verse is referring to murder. **Rather,** it is to **this** term **smites** that Rava is referring: **"And he who smites an animal shall pay for it, a life for a life"** (Leviticus 24:18), **and juxtaposed to it,** it is written: **"And a man who places a blemish upon his counterpart, as he has done so shall be done to him"** (Leviticus 24:19). The verses liken those liable to receive lashes to those obligated to pay money, from which it is derived that those liable to receive lashes are exempt from payment.

והאי לאו "מכה" היא! אנן הכאה הכאה קאמרינן. והא כי כתיב – בחובל בחבירו הוא דכתיב, וחובל בחבירו בר תשלומין הוא! אם אינו ענין להכאה שיש בה שוה פרוטה – תנהו ענין להכאה שאין בה שוה פרוטה.

The Gemara raises a difficulty: **But this** term that appears in the latter verse **is** "places a blemish," **not smites.** How, then, can one derive a verbal analogy? The Gemara answers: This is not a verbal analogy based on identical terms; rather, it is based on identical concepts. **We are saying** that it is a verbal analogy between **smiting** an animal in the first verse and **smiting** a person in the latter verse. The Gemara asks: **However, when** the second verse **is written, it is written with regard to one who injures another, and one who injures another is subject to payment** and not to lashes. This undermines the proof, as lashes are not mentioned in either verse. The Gemara answers: **If it is not a matter of smiting that** causes damage equivalent to the **value of a** ***peruta,*** in which case he would pay and would not be flogged, **apply it** to the **matter of smiting that** causes damage that is not equivalent to the **value of a** ***peruta.***[H] Since in that case there is no payment for the injury, one is flogged for striking that blow.

Perek **III**
Daf **35** Amud **b**

סוף סוף לאו בר תשלומין הוא! לא צריכא, דבהדי דמחייה קרע שיראין דיליה.

The Gemara raises a difficulty: **Ultimately,** one who injured another and is flogged **is not subject to payment,** as he inflicted damage worth less than a *peruta*. How then can a principle be derived that one who is liable to receive lashes does not pay even when he is not actually flogged? The Gemara answers: The juxtaposition of the verses is **necessary only** with regard to a situation **where at the same time that he struck**[N] **him he tore his silk.** In that case, where he performed a transgression for which he is liable to be flogged and is also liable to pay damages, it is derived that he would be exempt from paying damages even if he is not actually flogged.

NOTES

It is derived by means of a verbal analogy between the term wicked and the term wicked – אתיא רשע רשע: The Gemara does not specify the verses upon which this verbal analogy is based, as it appears in several places. Although the meaning is not the same in all of those places, the basic comparison between those liable to be executed and those liable to be flogged is an accepted principle, and the Gemara did not find it necessary to elaborate (see *Shita Mekubbetzet*).

It is derived by means of a verbal analogy between the term smites and the term smites – אתיא מכה מכה: The early commentaries discuss the precise nature of this derivation. At first glance, it appears that it is based on juxtaposition of the verses. However, if that is the case, how does the Gemara proceed to reject it based on the term smites when the derivation is not based on a verbal analogy? The Ritva explains that the Gemara was merely questioning the fact that Rava stated that the term smites appears in both verses. *Tosafot* conclude that Rava's derivation is in fact a verbal analogy, which accounts for the question of the Gemara. Accordingly, the phrase: And juxtaposed to it, does not mean that it is a derivation based on juxtaposed verses but is merely noting that the other verse appears adjacent to the first. The notion that a verbal analogy can be based on similar concepts rather than identical terms is well established, as the school of Rabbi Yishmael derives verbal analogies from different words with the same meaning.

HALAKHA

Smiting that causes damage that is not equivalent to the value of a *peruta* – הכאה שאין בה שוה פרוטה: One who struck another with a blow that causes damage that is not the equivalent of a *peruta* is liable to be flogged, as he is exempt from payment. The *halakha* is in accordance with the opinion of Rabbi Yoḥanan (Rambam *Sefer Nezikim, Hilkhot Ḥovel* 4:9, 5:3; *Shulḥan Arukh, Ḥoshen Mishpat* 420:2).

NOTES

Necessary only with regard to a situation where at the same time that he struck, etc. – לא צריכא, דבהדי דמחייה וכו׳: Based on the formulation of the Gemara, this appears to be a continuation of the previous statement, i.e., it is dealing with a blow that caused damage that is not the equivalent of a *peruta*. This is the implied meaning, as the Gemara did not introduce this section with the term: Rather. The Maharshal, however, claims that this solution renders it unnecessary to explain the verse as referring to a blow that caused damage that is not the equivalent of a *peruta* (see *Penei Yehoshua*). The rationale is that the Torah exempted one who injured another from being punished with lashes only if the obligation to pay stems from that very same transgression. If the obligation for payment results from violation of a different prohibition, the injurer is not exempt from being punished with lashes.

אֲמַר לֵיהּ רַב חִיָּיא לְרָבָא: וְלַתַּנָּא דְּבֵי חִזְקִיָּה, דַּאֲמַר: ״מַכֵּה אָדָם וּמַכֵּה בְּהֵמָה״ מִמַּאי דְּבַחוֹל כְּתִיב, וְלֵיכָּא לְאִיפְּלוּגֵי, דִּלְמָא בְּשַׁבָּת כְּתִיב, דְּבִבְהֵמָה גּוּפָהּ אִיכָּא לְאִיפְּלוּגֵי?

§ **Rav Ḥiyya said to Rava: And according to the** derivation **of the** *tanna* **of the school of Ḥizkiyya, who said:** The verse speaks of **one who smites a person, and** the verse speaks of **one who smites an animal. From where** does that *tanna* know **that it is written with regard to a weekday and** therefore **there is no** reason **to distinguish** between an unwitting and a purposeful sinner; **perhaps** this case **is stated with regard to** one who injured an animal on **Shabbat,**[N] **when concerning the animal itself there is** reason **to distinguish** between one who did so unwittingly and one who did so intentionally. In the case of one who acted unwittingly, he is not liable to receive the death penalty and should therefore be obligated to pay, whereas one who acted intentionally is exempt from payment because he receives the death penalty for desecrating Shabbat. If so, there is no source to exempt from payment one who is not actually executed.

לָא סָלְקָא דַּעְתָּךְ, דִּכְתִיב ״וּמַכֵּה בְהֵמָה יְשַׁלְּמֶנָּה וּמַכֵּה אָדָם יוּמָת״. הֵיכִי דָּמֵי? אִי דְּלָא אַתְרוּ בֵּיהּ – מַכֵּה אָדָם אַמַּאי יוּמַת? אֶלָּא פְּשִׁיטָא – דְּאַתְרוּ בֵּיהּ, וְאִי בְּשַׁבָּת – מַכֵּה בְהֵמָה יְשַׁלְּמֶנָּה?! אֶלָּא לָאו – בַּחוֹל.

The Gemara answers: That notion **should not enter your mind, as it is written: "And one who smites an animal shall pay for it, and one who smites a person shall die"** (Leviticus 24:21). **What are the circumstances** discussed in this verse? **If** it is a case **where** the witnesses **did not forewarn him,** i.e., when **one who smites a person** is not forewarned, **why should he be executed?** There is no corporal punishment, neither lashes nor execution, without forewarning. **Rather,** it is **obvious that they forewarned him. And if** the verse is referring to one who sinned **on Shabbat** after forewarning, would **one who smites an animal** be obligated to **pay for it?** He is executed and certainly exempt from payment. **Rather, isn't** the verse clearly referring to a case **during the week?**

אֲמַר לֵיהּ רַב פַּפָּא לְאַבַּיֵי: לְרַבָּה, דְּאָמַר: חִידּוּשׁ הוּא שֶׁחִידְּשָׁה תּוֹרָה בִּקְנָס, וְאַף עַל גַּב דְּמִיקְטִיל מְשַׁלֵּם, מַתְנִיתִין כְּמַאן מוֹקִים לָהּ? אִי כְּרַבִּי מֵאִיר – קַשְׁיָא בִּתּוֹ, אִי כְּרַבִּי נְחוּנְיָא בֶּן הַקָּנָה – קַשְׁיָא אֲחוֹתוֹ, אִי כְּרַבִּי יִצְחָק – קַשְׁיָא מַמְזֶרֶת!

§ **Rav Pappa said to Abaye: According to Rabba,** who **said: It is a novel element that the Torah innovated with regard to** the halakhic category of **fine, and even though he is executed he pays** the fine; **in accordance with whose** opinion **does** Rabba **establish the mishna? If** it is **in accordance with** the opinion of **Rabbi Meir,**[N] it is **difficult;** why is he exempt if he raped **his daughter?** According to Rabba, Rabbi Meir is of the opinion that even one liable to receive the death penalty pays the fine. **If** it is **in accordance with** the opinion of **Rabbi Neḥunya ben HaKana,** it is **difficult,** as why does the mishna rule that he pays the fine for raping **his sister?** Rabbi Neḥunya holds that one liable to receive *karet* is exempt from the fine, like those liable to receive the death penalty. **If** the mishna is **in accordance with** the opinion of **Rabbi Yitzḥak,**[N] who rules that lashes are not administered to those liable to receive *karet* and therefore they are obligated to pay the fine; however, one who is flogged is exempt from payment, it is **difficult,** as why did the mishna rule that he is obligated to pay the fine for raping a ***mamzeret*,**[N] for which he is liable to receive lashes?

NOTES

Perhaps this case is stated with regard to Shabbat – **דִּלְמָא בְּשַׁבָּת כְּתִיב**: Some commentaries explain that the Gemara is not suggesting that the verse refers only to Shabbat, but rather states a principle that applies equally to blows struck on weekdays and those struck on Shabbat. Once it is established that the verse refers to Shabbat as well, an additional distinction can be made between unwitting and intentional actions. If that is the case, this superfluous verse could teach that there is indeed a distinction between unwitting and intentional acts both in the case of one who kills an animal and one who kills a person (Ritva; *Shita Mekubbetzet*).

In accordance with whose opinion…if it is in accordance with Rabbi Meir – **מַתְנִיתִין כְּמַאן...אִי כְּרַבִּי מֵאִיר**: *Tosafot* note that the Gemara did not list all the Sages whose opinions did not correspond with the mishna. Rather, it mentions those opinions cited earlier, and which were suggested as the opinion of the *tanna* of the mishna. Only after listing those *tanna'im* does the Gemara mention Rabbi Yitzḥak, whose opinion was not cited earlier, even though the *mamzeret* appears first in the mishna, (*Shita Mekubbetzet*).

The opinion of Rabbi Yitzḥak – **שִׁיטַת רַבִּי יִצְחָק**: His opinion, which is merely alluded to here, is that even though most of those liable to receive *karet* violate a prohibition, they do not receive lashes. The reason is that just as prohibitions punishable by death at the hands of the court do not render the offender liable to be flogged, the same applies to prohibitions punishable by death at the hand of Heaven, e.g., *karet*.

If the mishna is in accordance with the opinion of Rabbi Yitzḥak, it is difficult…a *mamzeret* – **אִי כְּרַבִּי יִצְחָק קַשְׁיָא מַמְזֶרֶת**: Ostensibly, it could be explained that Rabbi Yitzḥak agrees with Rabbi Meir that one receives lashes and pays, in which case there would be no difficulty from the case of a *mamzeret*. Why then does the Gemara say that it is difficult? Various answers were suggested. The Rashba explains that the Gemara did not want to establish Rabbi Yitzḥak's opinion in accordance with the individual opinion of Rabbi Meir. In the *Shita Mekubbetzet* there is an inference from *Tosafot* that even though the opinion of Rabbi Neḥunya was established in accordance with that of Rabbi Meir, as is indicated in the language of his statement, there is no indication from the statement of Rabbi Yitzḥak that he agrees with Rabbi Meir. Rabbeinu Ḥananel contends that according to Rabbi Yitzḥak lashes are a more severe punishment than *karet*, and those liable to receive *karet* are exempt from lashes only because it is derived from the verses to be lenient in their regard. He therefore maintains that just as those liable to be executed are exempt from payment, the same applies to those who receive lashes. All this is in accordance with the approach of the Gemara.

In the Jerusalem Talmud, it is explained that there is no difficulty, as the mishna can be understood as referring to a *mamzer* who raped a *mamzeret*, in which case there is no liability to receive lashes at all. The Ramban and other commentaries explain that the Gemara does not understand the mishna in this manner because in the case of a *mamzer* who raped a *mamzeret* there is nothing novel, as she is permitted to him, and therefore it is no different from a case of a Jew who rapes a Jewish woman.

הָנִיחָא אִי סָבַר לַהּ כְּרַבִּי יוֹחָנָן – הוּא נַמִּי מְתָרֵיץ לַהּ כְּרַבִּי יוֹחָנָן, אֶלָּא אִי סָבַר כְּרֵישׁ לָקִישׁ – הֵיכִי מְתָרֵיץ לַהּ? עַל כָּרְחָךְ כְּרַבִּי יוֹחָנָן סְבִירָא לֵיהּ.

This works out **well if** Rabba **holds in accordance with** the opinion of **Rabbi Yoḥanan,** who says that one who did not receive forewarning is obligated to pay even if he performed a transgression for which he is liable to be flogged, as **he can explain** the mishna **as well, in accordance with** the opinion of **Rabbi Yoḥanan,** that he is obligated to pay in cases where there was no forewarning. **However, if he holds in accordance with** the opinion of **Reish Lakish,** that one who violated a prohibition for which one is liable to be flogged is exempt from payment even if he was not forewarned, **how does** he **explain** the mishna? The mishna does not correspond to any of the aforementioned opinions. The Gemara answers: **You** must say **perforce** that **he holds in accordance with** the opinion of **Rabbi Yoḥanan**[N] in this regard.

אָמַר לֵיהּ רַב מַתָּנָא לְאַבַּיֵי: לְרֵישׁ לָקִישׁ, דְּאָמַר: בְּפֵירוּשׁ רִיבְּתָה תּוֹרָה חַיָּיבֵי מַלְקִיּוֹת כְּחַיָּיבֵי מִיתוֹת, מַאן תַּנָּא דִּפְלִיג עֲלֵיהּ דְּרַבִּי נְחוּנְיָא בֶּן הַקָּנָה – אִי רַבִּי מֵאִיר, אִי רַבִּי יִצְחָק.

Rav Mattana said to Abaye: According to Reish Lakish, who said that **the Torah explicitly included those** who are **liable to** receive **lashes** and accorded them legal status **like those** who are **liable to** receive the **death** penalty, unconditionally exempting them from payment; **who is the *tanna* who disagrees**[N] **with Rabbi Neḥunya ben HaKana** and obligates one who is liable both to receive *karet* and to be flogged to pay, and the lashes do not exempt him from payment? The Gemara answers: He holds in accordance with **either Rabbi Meir,** who says that one who is liable to receive lashes is liable to pay a fine, **or Rabbi Yitzḥak,** who rules that those liable to receive *karet* are not flogged.

תָּנוּ רַבָּנַן: עֲרָיוֹת וּשְׁנִיּוֹת לָעֲרָיוֹת אֵין לָהֶן לֹא קְנָס וְלֹא פִּיתּוּי. הַמְמָאֶנֶת אֵין לָהּ לֹא קְנָס וְלֹא פִּיתּוּי. אַיְילוֹנִית אֵין לָהּ לֹא קְנָס וְלֹא פִּיתּוּי, וְהַיּוֹצֵאת מִשּׁוּם שֵׁם רַע אֵין לָהּ לֹא קְנָס וְלֹא פִּיתּוּי.

§ The Gemara turns its attention to a related issue. **The Sages taught:** Women who are **forbidden relatives and secondary forbidden relatives**[B] receive **neither** payment **of a fine**[H] for rape **nor** payment of a fine for **seduction.**[N] Similarly, a girl **who refuses**[N] to remain married to her husband receives **neither** payment of **a fine** for rape **nor** payment of a fine for **seduction.**[N] Because she was married, she no longer has the presumptive status of a virgin. **A sexually underdeveloped woman** [*ailonit*] who will never reach puberty and therefore her legal status is not that of a young woman, receives **neither** payment **of a fine** for rape **nor** payment of a fine for **seduction. And one who leaves** her husband **due to a bad reputation** receives **neither** payment of **a fine** for rape **nor** payment of a fine for **seduction.**

BACKGROUND

Secondary forbidden relatives – שְׁנִיּוֹת לָעֲרָיוֹת: These are relatives with whom relations are prohibited as incestuous by rabbinic decree. The Torah (Leviticus, chapters 18 and 20) lists many forbidden incestuous relationships. The Sages expanded this list to include relations with one's maternal and paternal grandmother; the mother of one's maternal and paternal grandfather; the wife of one's maternal and paternal grandfather, even though she is not one's grandmother; the wives of one's father's maternal brothers, while his paternal brother's wives are prohibited by Torah law; the wives of one's maternal uncles; one's son's or daughter's daughter-in-law; one's great-granddaughters; one's wife's great-granddaughters from previous marriages; and one's wife's maternal and paternal great-grandmothers. Relations with these forbidden relatives are also referred to as prohibitions resulting from a mitzva. Violation of these prohibitions is punishable by lashes for rebelliousness administered for transgression of a rabbinic decree.

HALAKHA

These do not have a fine – אֵלּוּ שֶׁאֵין לָהֶן קְנָס: The Rambam writes that one who refuses her husband, a sexually underdeveloped woman [*ailonit*], and a woman with a bad reputation as a minor are not entitled to payment of the fine. The Ra'avad states that the ruling that an *ailonit* does not receive the fine is not the *halakha*, as it is the opinion of Rabbi Meir; while the Rabbis maintain that she is considered a minor until the age of twenty, and she is therefore entitled to the fine. The *Tur* agrees (Rambam *Sefer Nashim*, *Hilkhot Na'ara Betula* 1:9; *Tur*, *Even HaEzer* 177).

NOTES

You must say perforce that he holds in accordance with the opinion of Rabbi Yoḥanan – עַל כָּרְחָךְ כְּרַבִּי יוֹחָנָן: The early commentaries ask: Why not say that Rabba explains the mishna in accordance with the opinion of Ulla that one always pays and is not flogged? Rashi resolves this difficulty and explains that one who does not accept Rabbi Yoḥanan's opinion certainly would not accept Ulla's opinion. Rabbi Aharon HaLevi proves that Ulla's opinion cannot be reconciled with that of Reish Lakish, and the two Sages certainly disagree. The Ramban maintains that it is theoretically possible for Rabba to interpret the mishna in accordance with the opinion of Ulla, but the Gemara does not seek to completely clarify the matter at this juncture. Instead, it merely notes that with regard to the dispute between Reish Lakish and Rabbi Yoḥanan, Rabba's statement is in accordance with the opinion of the latter.

Who is the *tanna* who disagrees, etc. – מַאן תַּנָּא דִּפְלִיג וכו׳: Rashi infers that although Reish Lakish maintains that the mishna disagrees with Rabbi Neḥunya, he cannot establish it in accordance with the opinion of Rabbi Yitzḥak, as explained above with regard to Rabba's statement, but only in accordance with the opinion of Rabbi Meir. Rashi's explanation here is consistent with his opinion that this question does not relate specifically to this mishna in particular, but rather relates to several *mishnayot* that clearly indicate that those liable to receive *karet* must pay as well. Those *mishnayot* correspond to the opinion of Rabbi Yitzḥak. The Ritva agrees. Rabbeinu Ḥananel explains that Reish Lakish maintains that since Rabbi Yitzḥak is of the opinion that no lashes are administered to those liable to receive *karet*, a person can be liable both to receive *karet* and to pay, but not to receive lashes and pay. In the Jerusalem Talmud, it is similarly explained that a person does not receive two punishments for a single transgression if he was convicted by a court, but a liability to be punished at the hand of Heaven does not exempt him from a debt to others.

Neither a fine for rape nor a fine for seduction – לֹא קְנָס וְלֹא פִּיתּוּי: *Tosafot* explain that the term fine is more suitable for a rape, as the perpetrator is also penalized with the obligation to marry his victim. In the *Shita Mekubbetzet* it is explained according to Rashi that the payment is not called a fine in the case of a seduction, as he acted with her consent. Furthermore, a seducer is liable for speaking, whereas a rapist is punished for acting.

A girl who refuses – הַמְמָאֶנֶת: A girl who refuses her husband is a fatherless girl who was married off by her mother or brothers when she was a minor. That marriage is not valid by Torah law, and the Sages ruled that if the minor expresses that she does not wish to remain with her husband, not only does she leave the marriage but the marriage is retroactively negated, and it is as though she was never married. Rashi claims that the reason there is no fine with regard to a girl who refused is that she is no longer considered a virgin because she was married. According to his opinion, this *halakha* contains no novel element, and it is only stated to enable the Gemara to infer that other minors are entitled to the fine.

The Ramban asks: If there are witnesses that she never entered into seclusion with her husband, why shouldn't she be entitled to the fine? And if there are no witnesses to that effect, this *halakha* is obvious. He answers that even if there were witnesses that there was seclusion, one might have thought that since she claims she is a virgin, the rapist should not receive the benefit of the doubt and should be required to pay the fine. The Rashba contends that even if witnesses testified that she was never in seclusion with her husband, she still does not receive the fine, as the witnesses are unable to achieve a degree of certainty that would remove all doubt; the rapist is not required to pay in a case of uncertainty.

Tosafot question Rashi's interpretation, as they point out that according to his approach there is no difference whether he raped or seduced her when she was a minor or whether he did so when she was a young woman, and therefore perhaps the inference should have been that all other young women receive the fine. In the *Shita Mekubbetzet* that assertion is rejected: One who refuses, in present tense, indicates a minor, as she cannot refuse her husband once she reaches puberty. Were the *baraita* referring to a young woman, it should have said: One who refused, in past tense. In any case, *Tosafot* explain otherwise: The Gemara is referring to one who was raped or seduced by her husband while she was still married to him. The novel element is that one does not say that if she refuses him his act is retroactively rendered rape or seduction. Later commentaries explain that the reason that this is not considered rape is that it is deemed rape or seduction only if it is outside the framework of marriage. Otherwise, the categories of rape and seduction are inapplicable.

Nor seduction – וְלֹא פִּיתּוּי: *Tosafot* explain that these words are merely added because the terms are usually listed together, as this *halakha* applies to a young woman as well, and one who seduces a fatherless young woman certainly is not liable to pay the fine, as she consented. The Rashba and the Rosh maintain that even a fatherless minor is not entitled to receive the fine for seduction, as a competent minor can also relinquish her right to the fine, and she does so by agreeing to be seduced. The Ritva disagrees and contends that it can be learned from here that the legal status of the seduction of any minor is like that of rape, as even though she has a certain measure of competency in terms of forgiving a debt, she is not considered to be fully competent in terms of complicity with seduction.

מַאי עֲרָיוֹת וּמַאי שְׁנִיּוֹת לַעֲרָיוֹת? אִילֵימָא עֲרָיוֹת

The Gemara elaborates. **What is** the meaning of **forbidden relatives, and what is** the meaning of **secondary forbidden relatives** in the context of this *baraita*? **If we say** that **forbidden relatives** means

עֲרָיוֹת מַמָּשׁ, שְׁנִיּוֹת – מִדִּבְרֵי סוֹפְרִים, כֵּיוָן דְּמִדְּאוֹרַיְיתָא חֲזָיָא לֵיהּ – אַמַּאי אֵין לָהֶן קְנָס? אֶלָּא: עֲרָיוֹת – חַיָּיבֵי מִיתוֹת בֵּית דִּין, שְׁנִיּוֹת – חַיָּיבֵי כְרֵיתוֹת, אֲבָל חַיָּיבֵי לָאוִין – יֵשׁ לָהֶן קְנָס, וּמַנִּי – שִׁמְעוֹן הַתִּימְנִי הִיא.

actual forbidden relatives[N] prohibited by Torah law, and **secondary relatives** means, as it does in most cases, relatives prohibited **by rabbinic law,**[N] that cannot be, for **since** those secondary relatives **are suitable for him** to marry and are not prohibited **by Torah** law,[N] **why do they not** receive **a fine** if they are raped or seduced? **Rather,** the meaning of these terms in this context is different: **Forbidden relatives** are **those** for which one is **liable** to receive a **court-imposed death** penalty; **secondary relatives** are **those** for which one is **liable** to receive ***karet,*** which are relatively less severe than those for which one is executed. **However, those liable for** violating regular **prohibitions** receive payment of a **fine** if they are raped or seduced. **And** according to **whose** opinion is the *baraita* taught? **It is** the opinion of **Shimon HaTimni,** who exempts from paying a fine only one who rapes a woman with whom betrothal is ineffective.

אִיכָּא דְּאָמְרִי: עֲרָיוֹת – חַיָּיבֵי מִיתוֹת ב״ד וְחַיָּיבֵי כְרֵיתוֹת, שְׁנִיּוֹת – חַיָּיבֵי לָאוִין, מַנִּי – רַבִּי שִׁמְעוֹן בֶּן מְנַסְיָא הִיא.

Some say that we can explain **that forbidden relatives** refers to all relatives with whom relations are forbidden by severe prohibitions, both **those** for which one is **liable to death** by the **court and those** for which he is **liable to *karet,*** and **secondary** relatives refers to **those** relatives with whom one who engages in relations is **liable for** violating regular **prohibitions.** According to this approach, **whose** opinion does this follow? **It is** that of **Rabbi Shimon ben Menasya,** who maintains that even a woman raped by a man forbidden to her by a regular prohibition is not entitled to the fine, despite the fact that betrothal is effective in that case.

״הַמְּמָאֶנֶת אֵין לָהּ לֹא קְנָס וְלֹא פִּיתּוּי״. הָא קְטַנָּה בְּעָלְמָא – אִית לַהּ, מַנִּי – רַבָּנַן הִיא, דְּאָמְרִי: קְטַנָּה יֵשׁ לָהּ קְנָס. אֵימָא סֵיפָא: אַיְילוֹנִית אֵין לָהּ לֹא קְנָס וְלֹא פִּיתּוּי. אֲתָאן לְרַבִּי מֵאִיר, דְּאָמַר: קְטַנָּה אֵין לָהּ קְנָס, וְהָא – מִקַּטְנוּתָהּ יָצְתָה לְבַגֵּר. רֵישָׁא רַבָּנַן וְסֵיפָא רַבִּי מֵאִיר!

§ The *baraita* stated: A girl **who refuses** to remain married to her husband receives **neither** payment of **a fine** for rape **nor** payment of a fine for **seduction,** because she was married and therefore lost her presumptive status as a virgin. The Gemara infers: But **an ordinary minor** girl **has** a fine for rape. If so, in accordance with **whose** opinion is the *baraita* taught? **It is** the opinion of **the Rabbis, who say: A minor** girl **has** a fine for rape. The Gemara asks: **Say the latter clause** of the *baraita*: **A sexually underdeveloped woman [*ailonit*] has neither a fine** for rape **nor** a fine for **seduction,** as she will not develop the signs of puberty and her legal status is that of a minor until she is twenty, at which point she assumes the status of a grown woman. In that *halakha*, the *baraita* **comes to** the opinion of **Rabbi Meir, who said: A minor** girl **does not have** a **fine** for rape, **and** the same is true for **this** *ailonit*, who **emerged from her** status as a **minor** at the age of twenty **to** the status of **a grown woman,** skipping the stage of a young woman. **The first clause** of the *baraita* **is** in accordance with the opinion of **the Rabbis, and the latter clause is** in accordance with the opinion of **Rabbi Meir.**

NOTES

Actual forbidden relatives – עֲרָיוֹת מַמָּשׁ: The phrase: Actual forbidden relatives, refers to those relatives with whom relations are prohibited by Torah law (see Leviticus, chapter 18). An intermediate category of people with whom relations are prohibited by Torah law, even though they do not fall into the category of actual forbidden relatives, is omitted from the *baraita*, which is an additional reason the term: Secondary relatives, should not be interpreted in the standard manner.

Secondary relatives by rabbinic law – שְׁנִיּוֹת מִדִּבְרֵי סוֹפְרִים: As explained by Rashi, there is a list of secondary forbidden relatives, women who are not close relatives by Torah law but are prohibited by rabbinic decree as a safeguard to Torah law. In the second chapter of *Yevamot*, sixteen women are listed as secondary relatives, with whom marriage takes effect but the man is required to divorce her; the Sages penalized these women by stripping them of the right to a marriage contract and other rights to which a married woman is entitled. However, a child born of such a relationship is not rendered unfit, and the woman herself is not disqualified from marrying a priest due to this marriage.

Since they are suitable for him by Torah law – כֵּיוָן דְּמִדְּאוֹרַיְיתָא חֲזָיָא לֵיהּ: The question is raised: With regard to a woman in the category of a secondary forbidden relative, the assertion that since she is suitable for him by Torah law, she is entitled to the fine, is by no means obvious. It could be asserted that since he is required to divorce her and is not allowed to sustain her as his wife, even though it is by rabbinic decree, he does not fulfill the requirement "And to him she shall be as a wife" (Deuteronomy 22:19). The fact is that a Gibeonite woman, who is prohibited by rabbinic law, is listed in the mishna together with a *mamzeret*.

The answer given is that there is a distinction between the *halakha* of a Gibeonite, with regard to whom there is a general rabbinic decree prohibiting her from entering the congregation of Israel, and secondary prohibitions, prohibited as a safeguard, with regard to which the Sages certainly did not deny them their right to the fine (*Shita Mekubbetzet*; *Beit Aharon*).

וְכִי תֵּימָא: כּוּלָּהּ רַבִּי מֵאִיר הִיא, וּבִמְמָאֶנֶת סָבַר לָהּ כְּרַבִּי יְהוּדָה; וּמִי סָבַר לָהּ?! וְהָתַנְיָא: עַד מָתַי הַבַּת מְמָאֶנֶת? עַד שֶׁתָּבִיא שְׁתֵּי שְׂעָרוֹת, דִּבְרֵי רַבִּי מֵאִיר. רַבִּי יְהוּדָה אוֹמֵר: עַד שֶׁיִּרְבֶּה שָׁחוֹר עַל הַלָּבָן!

And if you say that **the entire** *baraita* **is** in accordance with the opinion of **Rabbi Meir, and with regard to** a girl **who refuses** to remain married Rabbi Meir **holds in accordance with** the opinion of **Rabbi Yehuda,** that not only a minor girl but a young woman may also end her marriage through refusal, and the *baraita* is referring to a young woman and not to a minor; **but does he maintain that** opinion? **But isn't it taught** in a *baraita* that he disagrees with Rabbi Yehuda in this matter? It was taught: **Until when can a girl refuse** to remain married?[H] **Until she develops two** pubic **hairs,** signs of puberty rendering her a young woman; this is **the statement of Rabbi Meir. Rabbi Yehuda says:** She can refuse **until** the area covered by the **black** pubic hairs **is greater than the white**[NB] skin of the genital area. That occurs approximately six months later, at which point she becomes a grown woman.

אֶלָּא רַבִּי יְהוּדָה הִיא, וּבִקְטַנָּה סָבַר לָהּ כְּרַבִּי מֵאִיר. וּמִי סָבַר לָהּ? וְהָאָמַר רַב יְהוּדָה אָמַר רַב: זוֹ דִּבְרֵי רַבִּי מֵאִיר. וְאִם אִיתָא, זוֹ דִּבְרֵי רַבִּי מֵאִיר וְרַבִּי יְהוּדָה מִיבָּעֵי לֵיהּ! הַאי תַּנָּא סָבַר לָהּ כְּרַבִּי מֵאִיר בַּחֲדָא, וּפָלֵיג עֲלֵיהּ בַּחֲדָא.

Rather, the Gemara suggests: The *baraita* **is** in accordance with the opinion of **Rabbi Yehuda, and with** regard to **a minor** girl, **he holds in accordance with** the opinion of **Rabbi Meir, who says** that a minor girl does not receive payment of a fine for rape, and therefore, an *ailonit* is not entitled to payment. The Gemara asks: **But does he maintain that** opinion? **But didn't Rav Yehuda say** that **Rav said** with regard to the mishna below (40b), which states: Any case where there is the right of a father to effect the sale of his daughter as a Hebrew maidservant, i.e., when she is a minor, there is no fine if she is raped, **this is the statement of Rabbi Meir? And if it is so** that Rabbi Yehuda maintains that opinion, Rav **should have** said: **This is the statement of Rabbi Meir and Rabbi Yehuda.**[N] Rather, **this** *tanna* of the *baraita* **holds in accordance with** the opinion of **Rabbi Meir with regard to one** *halakha*, that there is no fine for the rape of a minor, **and disagrees with him with regard to one** *halakha*, that a young woman may conclude her marriage through refusal.

רַפְרָם אָמַר: מַאי מְמָאֶנֶת – הָרְאוּיָה לְמָאֵן. וְלִיתְנֵי קְטַנָּה! קַשְׁיָא.

Rafram said: This entire *baraita* is in accordance with the opinion of Rabbi Meir, and **what is** the meaning of the statement: With regard to a girl **who refuses,** there is neither a fine for rape nor a fine for seduction? It is referring to **one who is fit to refuse,** i.e., as long as she is a minor she is not entitled to the fine. The Gemara asks: **And** if that is the case, **let** the *tanna* simply **teach** the *halakha* with regard to **a minor.** Why teach a simple *halakha* in so convoluted a manner? The Gemara concludes: Indeed, this is **difficult.**

״אַיְילוֹנִית אֵין לָהּ לֹא קְנָס וְלֹא פִּיתּוּי״. וּרְמִינְהִי: הַחֵרֶשֶׁת וְהַשּׁוֹטָה וְהָאַיְילוֹנִית יֵשׁ לָהֶן קְנָס וְיֵשׁ לָהֶן טַעֲנַת בְּתוּלִים! וְהָא מַאי רוּמְיָא? הָא – רַבִּי מֵאִיר, הָא – רַבָּנַן. וּדְקָאָרֵי לָהּ מַאי קָאָרֵי לָהּ?

§ The *baraita* stated: **An** *ailonit* **has neither a fine** for rape **nor** a fine for **seduction. And** the Gemara **raises a contradiction** from a *baraita*: **A deaf-mute, an imbecile, and an** *ailonit* **have a fine** for rape **and they have a claim concerning virginity.**[N] If one of these women married with the presumptive status of a virgin and received a corresponding marriage contract, her husband can cause her to lose her marriage contract by claiming that she was not a virgin. The Gemara rejects this argument: **And what is** the **contradiction** in **this?** It can be explained simply: **This** *baraita*, in which it was taught that the *ailonit* receives no fine, is in accordance with the opinion of **Rabbi Meir; that** *baraita*, in which it was taught that the *ailonit* receives a fine, is in accordance with the opinion of **the Rabbis.** The Gemara is puzzled: **And** as the resolution is so obvious, **he who raised** the contradiction, **why did he raise it?** The dispute between Rabbi Meir and the Rabbis in this matter is known.

HALAKHA

Until when can a girl refuse to remain married – עַד מָתַי הַבַּת מְמָאֶנֶת: A girl can refuse to remain married to her husband until two pubic hairs emerge after she reaches the age of twelve years and one day. The *halakha* is in accordance with the opinion of Rabbi Meir in this regard, as the discussion in several places in the Gemara is according to his opinion. If two hairs did not grow and she did not give birth, as that is also a sign of puberty, she remains a minor even after the age of twelve. This applies only if it was definitely determined that the hairs did not grow, as the assumption is that two hairs are present in a girl that age. Even if she was examined and no hairs were discovered, if she engaged in sexual intercourse the assumption is that the hairs were severed as a result. Some authorities maintain that today one should rule stringently and not allow refusal after she reaches the age of twelve under any circumstances (Rambam *Sefer Nashim, Hilkhot Geirushin* 11:4; *Shulḥan Arukh, Even HaEzer* 155:12, and see 19–22).

NOTES

Until the black is greater than the white – עַד שֶׁיִּרְבֶּה שָׁחוֹר עַל הַלָּבָן: Although everyone agrees that the girl becomes a young woman as soon as two pubic hairs emerge, there is a distinction between a young woman and a grown woman, one of whose characteristic signs is the area covered by the black pubic hairs is greater than the white skin of the genital area. A young woman is in certain respects an intermediate stage between a minor and a grown woman, as her father retains certain rights over his daughter while she is still a young woman. Therefore, one might have thought that until she becomes a grown woman, she can refuse to remain married to her husband and dissolve a marriage into which she entered as a minor. According to one opinion in tractate *Yevamot*, even a woman with children can refuse and thereby dissolve a marriage that she entered as a minor.

Rav should have said: This is the statement of Rabbi Meir and Rabbi Yehuda – זוֹ דִּבְרֵי רַבִּי מֵאִיר וְרַבִּי יְהוּדָה מִיבָּעֵי לֵיהּ: This question is unusual, as there is no expectation that all the Sages who share a particular opinion would be listed. Indeed, *Tosafot* prove that other *tanna'im* also agree with Rabbi Meir's opinion. Here, however, the Gemara should have mentioned that this is the opinion of Rabbi Yehuda as well, both because he disagrees with Rabbi Meir with regard to several *halakhot* related to this topic, and because there is an attempt to prove that the *mishnayot* in this chapter are not necessarily all in accordance with the opinion of Rabbi Meir (see *Shita Mekubbetzet*).

They have a claim concerning virginity – יֵשׁ לָהֶן טַעֲנַת בְּתוּלִים: There are two distinct, albeit similar, interpretations of this expression. According to Rashi, it means these women can claim they are virgins, whereas the Rid and Ramban maintain that others can register a claim that contrary to pre-marriage expectations, she was not a virgin. The novel element here is that the Sages did not enact a marriage contract for a deaf-mute, so if there is a claim concerning virginity, the husband must have written a marriage contract for her as a virgin, and he now claims that his was an erroneous transaction.

BACKGROUND

Until the black is greater than the white – עַד שֶׁיִּרְבֶּה שָׁחוֹר עַל הַלָּבָן: One of the first stages is the appearance of pubic hair, which indicates the passage from minority to majority. Only after the passage of time do hairs cover most of the pubic region. The *halakha* does not require that the entire area be covered with hair, but once the area covered by the black pubic hairs is greater than the white skin of the genital area is she considered a grown woman.

מִשּׁוּם דְּאִית לֵיהּ לְמִירְמָא אַחֲרִיתִי עִילָּוֵיהּ: הַחֵרֶשֶׁת וְהַשּׁוֹטָה וְהַבּוֹגֶרֶת וּמוּכַּת עֵץ – אֵין לָהֶן טַעֲנַת בְּתוּלִים, הַסּוּמָא וְאַיְילוֹנִית – יֵשׁ לָהֶן טַעֲנַת בְּתוּלִים. סוּמְכוֹס אוֹמֵר מִשּׁוּם רַבִּי מֵאִיר: סוּמָא אֵין לָהּ טַעֲנַת בְּתוּלִים!

The Gemara answers: He cited this *baraita* **due to the fact that he has another** *baraita* from which **to raise as a contradiction to it: A deaf-mute, and an imbecile, and a grown woman,**[H] **and a woman whose hymen was torn** not in the course of sexual relations,[H] **do not have a claim concerning virginity,** as they do not have the presumptive status of a virgin. However, **a blind** woman **and an** *ailonit*[H] **have a claim concerning virginity. Sumakhos says in the name of Rabbi Meir: A blind** woman **does not have a claim concerning virginity.** The *baraitot* contradict each other with regard to the claim concerning virginity of a deaf-mute and an imbecile.

אָמַר רַב שֵׁשֶׁת: לָא קַשְׁיָא; הָא – רַבָּן גַּמְלִיאֵל, וְהָא – רַבִּי יְהוֹשֻׁעַ. אֵימַר דִּשְׁמַעַתְּ לֵיהּ לְרַבָּן גַּמְלִיאֵל הֵיכָא דְּקָא טָעֲנָה אִיהִי, הֵיכָא דְּלָא קָא טָעֲנָה אִיהִי מִי שָׁמְעַתְּ לֵיהּ? אִין, כֵּיוָן דַּאֲמַר רַבָּן גַּמְלִיאֵל מְהֵימְנָא, כְּגוֹן זוֹ "פְּתַח פִּיךָ לְאִלֵּם" הוּא.

Rav Sheshet said: This is **not difficult,** as **this** *baraita* is in accordance with the opinion of **Rabban Gamliel,**[N] who holds that a woman who, in response to a claim concerning her virginity, is believed if she says that she was raped after her betrothal and therefore does not lose her marriage contract. **And that** *baraita* is in accordance with the opinion of **Rabbi Yehoshua,** who says that a woman is not believed if she makes that claim, and therefore she loses her marriage contract. The Gemara asks: **Say that you heard** that **Rabban Gamliel** accepts her contention in a case **where she claims** that she was raped after the betrothal; however, in a case **where she did not claim** that that was the case, **did you hear** that **he** accepts her contention? The Gemara answers: **Yes, since Rabban Gamliel said** she is **believed** when she states that she was raped after betrothal, the deaf-mute and the imbecile are also believed even though they are unable to make the claim, as in a cases **like that,** it **is** a case of: **"Open your mouth for the mute"** (Proverbs 31:8). When a person lacks the capacity to proffer the claim on his own, the court makes the claim on her behalf.

"וְהַבּוֹגֶרֶת אֵין לָהּ טַעֲנַת בְּתוּלִים". וְהָאָמַר רַב: בּוֹגֶרֶת נוֹתְנִין לָהּ לַיְלָה הָרִאשׁוֹן!

§ The *baraita* stated: **A grown woman does not have a claim concerning virginity**[B] because of changes as her body matures, her hymen is no longer completely intact. The Gemara asks: **But didn't Rav say:** The Sages **give a grown** woman who had relations on her wedding night, **the** entire **first night,**[H] during which she may have relations with her husband several times? Any blood seen during that night is attributed to the blood of her hymen, which is ritually pure, and not menstrual blood. Apparently, even a grown woman has her hymen intact.

HALAKHA

A grown woman – הַבּוֹגֶרֶת: The marriage contract of a grown woman is two hundred dinars, and there is a claim concerning her virginity (Rambam *Sefer Nashim, Hilkhot Ishut* 11:4; *Shulḥan Arukh, Even HaEzer* 68:1).

The claim concerning virginity with regard to a deaf-mute, an imbecile, and a woman whose hymen was torn not in the course of sexual relations – טַעֲנַת בְּתוּלִים בְּחֵרֶשֶׁת וּבְשׁוֹטָה וּבְמוּכַּת עֵץ: Any woman whose marriage contract is one hundred dinars, or for whom the Sages did not institute a marriage contract, is not vulnerable to a claim concerning her virginity. The marriage contract of a woman whose hymen was accidentally torn is one hundred dinars, there is no marriage contract for a deaf-mute, and the marriage of an imbecile does not take effect (Rambam *Sefer Nashim, Hilkhot Ishut* 11:4–5; *Shulḥan Arukh, Even HaEzer* 66:1, and see 67:5 and 67:7–8).

A blind woman and an *ailonit* – הַסּוּמָא וְאַיְילוֹנִית: For a virgin who is blind or an *ailonit* whose status was known at the time of her betrothal, there is a marriage contract of two hundred dinars, and they are vulnerable to a claim concerning their virginity (Rambam *Sefer Nashim, Hilkhot Ishut* 11:4; *Shulḥan Arukh, Even HaEzer* 67:6; 68:1).

Give a grown woman the entire first night – בּוֹגֶרֶת נוֹתְנִין לָהּ לַיְלָה הָרִאשׁוֹן: Fundamentally, as long as a grown woman has not seen the blood of virginity, any blood that she sees after intercourse is attributed to losing her virginity and she is not rendered impure. However, the daughters of Israel imposed a stringency upon themselves, and therefore, even a man who marries a minor virgin must refrain from contact with her after fulfilling the mitzva of consummating the marriage (Rambam *Sefer Kedusha, Hilkhot Issurei Bia* 4:9, 11:8; *Shulḥan Arukh, Yoreh De'a* 193:1).

NOTES

This *baraita* is in accordance with the opinion of Rabban Gamliel – הָא רַבָּן גַּמְלִיאֵל: Rashi explains that this refers to the claim: I was raped after you betrothed me. In the first chapter of this tractate, Rabban Gamliel maintains that a woman is believed when she makes that claim. According to his opinion, although a deaf-mute lacks the halakhic intelligence to make that claim, the court makes the claim on her behalf. The Ramban asks: Isn't a case conceivable where he betrothed her and then consummated the marriage immediately, in which case that claim would not be accepted even from a woman with halakhic intelligence; so how can the court make that claim on behalf of a deaf-mute? Therefore, he explains that the claim made on her behalf is that her hymen was accidentally torn, which is effective even if they had relations immediately after betrothal. Rabbi Meir maintains that a woman in that condition is entitled to a marriage contract of two hundred dinars. This interpretation is especially apt according to Rabbi Shmuel HaNagid's variant reading: This is the opinion of Rabbi Meir in the name of Rabban Gamliel; this is the opinion of Rabbi Meir in the name of Rabbi Yehoshua. Rabbi Zeraḥya HaLevi contends that the reference is to Rabban Gamliel and Rabbi Yehoshua's opinion with regard to the presumptive status of her body. He explains that Rabban Gamliel considers her presumptive status of virginity to be the determining factor, whereas Rabbi Yehoshua rules that the burden of proof is incumbent upon the claimant and the husband's possession of the money is the determining factor (see Ramban and *Tosafot*; Rashba; Rabbi Aharon HaLevi).

BACKGROUND

A grown woman does not have a claim concerning virginity – הַבּוֹגֶרֶת אֵין לָהּ טַעֲנַת בְּתוּלִים: Most women have a natural opening in the hymen, although the ratio between open and blocked areas varies in each woman, just as there are significant differences in the size of the vagina. In any event, while the girl matures and her body develops, the opening in the hymen also grows. In certain cases, the opening can become large enough that a grown woman who is a virgin could have sexual relations with no tearing of the hymen whatsoever. Even in a case where the hymen is torn and bleeds, the hymen might be so small that the husband would not feel its presence at all, and be under the impression that he encountered an open entrance.

אִי דְּקָא טָעֵין טַעֲנַת דָּמִים – הָכִי נַמִי, הָכָא בְּמַאי עָסְקִינַן – דְּקָטָעֵין טַעֲנַת פֶּתַח פָּתוּחַ.

The Gemara answers: If he **proffers a claim** that there was no **blood** after consummating the marriage, **indeed** he can cause her to lose her marriage contract with that claim. However, **with what are we dealing here** in the *baraita*? We are dealing **with** one **who proffers a claim** that he encountered an **open entrance,** i.e., there was no hymen. As the hymen of an adult woman is no longer completely intact, the claim is of no consequence.

״סוּמָכוֹס אוֹמֵר מִשּׁוּם רַבִּי מֵאִיר: סוּמָא אֵין לָהּ טַעֲנַת בְּתוּלִים״. מַאי טַעְמָא דְּסוּמָכוֹס? אָמַר רַבִּי זֵירָא: מִפְּנֵי שֶׁנֶּחְבֶּטֶת עַל גַּבֵּי קַרְקַע. כּוּלְּהוּ נַמִי חַבּוּטֵי מִיחַבְּטִי! כּוּלְּהוּ רוֹאוֹת וּמַרְאוֹת לְאִמָּן, זוֹ אֵינָהּ רוֹאָה, וְאֵינָהּ מַרְאָה לְאִמָּהּ.

The *baraita* continues: **Sumakhos says in the name of Rabbi Meir: A blind** woman **does not have a claim concerning virginity.** The Gemara asks: **What is the rationale** for the statement **of Sumakhos? Rabbi Zeira said: Due to** the fact **that** a blind woman **is struck** by falling **onto the ground,** causing her hymen to break. The Gemara asks: **All** girls tend **to be struck** by falling onto the ground **as well;**[N] what is unique about blind girls? The Gemara answers: When **all of** the other girls fall, they **see** the blood flow **and show** it to **their mother.** The mother would then examine them and discover that her hymen was broken. **This** blind girl **does not see** the flow of blood **and** therefore **does not show** it too **her mother.** Due to that possibility, the man who married the blind woman must have considered the likelihood that her hymen is not intact, and therefore he cannot make a claim concerning virginity.

״וְהַיּוֹצֵאת מִשּׁוּם שֵׁם רַע אֵין לָהּ לֹא קְנָס וְלֹא פִּיתּוּי״. הַיּוֹצֵאת מִשּׁוּם שֵׁם רַע בַּת סְקִילָה הִיא! אָמַר רַב שֵׁשֶׁת: הָכִי קָאָמַר: מִי שֶׁיָּצָא עָלֶיהָ שֵׁם רַע בְּיַלְדוּתָהּ – אֵין לָהּ לֹא קְנָס וְלֹא פִּיתּוּי.

§ The previous *baraita* concluded: **And one who leaves** her husband **due to a bad reputation**[N] **has neither a fine** for rape **nor** a fine for **seduction.** The initial understanding is that the *baraita* is referring to a young betrothed woman who leaves her husband because she committed adultery. The Gemara asks: **One who leaves** her husband **due to a bad reputation is subject to stoning** as an adulteress; clearly she is not entitled to the fine. **Rav Sheshet said: This is what** the *baraita* **is saying: One about whom a bad reputation emerged in her youth** that she engaged in sexual relations **has neither a fine** for rape **nor** a fine for **seduction,** as the assumption is that she is no longer a virgin.

אֲמַר רַב פַּפָּא: שְׁמַע מִינָּהּ, הַאי שְׁטָרָא רִיעָא לָא מַגְבִּינַן בֵּיהּ. הֵיכִי דָּמֵי? אִילֵימָא דְּנָפַק קָלָא עֲלֵיהּ דִּשְׁטָרָא דְּזַיְיפָא הוּא, דִּכְוָותָהּ הָכָא – דְּנָפַק עֲלַהּ קָלָא דִּזְנַאי, וְהָא אֲמַר רָבָא: יָצָא לָהּ שֵׁם מְזַנָּה בָּעִיר – אֵין חוֹשְׁשִׁין לָהּ!

Rav Pappa said: Conclude from it with regard to **this tainted document** whose authenticity was compromised that **we do not collect** a debt **with it.** The Gemara asks: **What are the circumstances? If you say that a rumor emerged about it that it is a forged document,** and in **the corresponding** case **here,** the case of a bad reputation, **that a rumor emerged about her that she engaged in** promiscuous **sexual relations; but didn't Rava say: If a rumor emerged about** a woman **in a town as one who engaged in** promiscuous **sexual relations,**[H] **one** need **not be concerned about it?** The assumption is that it is insubstantial, as a reputation based on rumor is disregarded.

אֶלָּא, דְּאָתוּ בֵּי תְּרֵי וְאָמְרִי: לְדִידְהוּ תַּבְעַתַנְהִי בְּאִיסּוּרָא. דִּכְוָותָהּ הָכָא – דְּאָתוּ בֵּי תְּרֵי וְאָמְרִי: לְדִידְהוּ אֲמַר לְהוּ ״זַיְיפוּ לִי״. בִּשְׁלָמָא הָתָם – שְׁכִיחִי פְּרוּצִין, אֶלָּא הָכָא – אִם הוּא הוּחְזַק – כָּל יִשְׂרָאֵל מִי הוּחְזְקוּ?! הָכָא נַמִי, כֵּיוָן דְּקָא מְהַדַּר אַזִּיוּפָא – אֵימַר זִיּוּפֵי זַיֵּיף וְכָתַב.

Rather, it is **that two witnesses came and said: She propositioned us** to engage **in forbidden** relations,[H] and in **the corresponding** case **here** with regard to a document, it is a case **where two** people **came and said** that **he said to us: Forge** a document **for me.**[N][H] The Gemara asks: **Granted, there,** in the case of the rumor of promiscuity, **immoral men are common,** and even if they refused her, presumably she found someone willing to engage in relations with her. **However, here,** with regard to forgery, even **if he assumed presumptive status** as one seeking a forgery, **do all the Jewish people assume presumptive status** as forgers? Why is the assumption that the document was forged? The Gemara answers: **Here too, since he is** actively **seeking a forgery, say that** he **forged** the document **and wrote** it. Even if others are not suspected of cooperating with him, there is suspicion with regard to the document. Therefore, the case of the tainted document and the woman with a bad reputation are comparable.

NOTES

All girls tend to be struck as well – **כּוּלְּהוּ נַמִי חַבּוּטֵי מִיחַבְּטִי:** Although the Sages stated that the case of a woman's hymen accidentally tearing is rare, there is a difference between one whose genitals tear from direct contact and one whose genitals tear from a fall. Furthermore, only if she was struck with a heavy blow could her hymen be broken (see Rashba). Rabbi Pinehas HaLevi, cited by the Ritva, explains that the statement: When all of the other girls fall they see and show, is for two reasons. First, they can see their surroundings and avoid a heavy blow; and second, if they fall they would show the blood to their mothers.

One who leaves due to a bad reputation – **הַיּוֹצֵאת מִשּׁוּם שֵׁם רַע:** The Gemara's initial assumption is based on the idea that the expression: One who leaves due to a bad reputation, refers to a married woman who was divorced due to rumors of adultery. It cannot be explained that she was divorced due to the rape itself, e.g., if he raped a betrothed maiden, as that is addressed in the next mishna, which enumerates those to whom the fine is not paid based on the principle: One receives the greater of the punishments, in this case, stoning. According to Rashi and most early commentaries, witnesses came and testified that she solicited them to engage in relations with her, and the assumption is that someone accepted her offer and she is no longer a virgin. The Rambam, however, explains that once witnesses testified that she solicited them to engage in relations with her, the claim that she was raped or seduced is rejected, as based on her conduct chances are that she initiated the relations, which exempts him from the fine. The Ran notes that the discussion in the Gemara does not support that interpretation, but several later commentaries explain the Rambam's approach at length, and reconcile it with the Gemara.

He said to us forge a document for me – **לְדִידְהוּ אֲמַר לְהוּ זַיְיפוּ לִי:** The Ritva cites the opinion of certain Sages that if one issued a general request: Forge a document for me, all documents that he produces are suspect. He likewise states in the name of Rabbi Aharon HaLevi that once a person solicits a forgery, any document that he produces is suspected of being forged. The Meiri cites similar opinions (see HALAKHA).

HALAKHA

If a rumor emerged about a woman in a town as one who engaged in promiscuous sexual relations – **יָצָא לָהּ שֵׁם מְזַנָּה בָּעִיר:** If a woman had a reputation of having engaged in promiscuous sexual relations, those rumors are ignored, as per the statement of Rava (Rambam *Sefer Kedusha, Hilkhot Issurei Bia* 17:21; *Shulḥan Arukh, Even HaEzer* 6:16).

She propositioned us to engage in forbidden relations – **לְדִידְהוּ תַּבְעַתַנְהִי בְּאִיסּוּרָא:** If a young woman had a bad reputation, as two men testified that she solicited them to engage in sexual relations, she is not entitled to the fine (Rambam *Sefer Nashim, Hilkhot Na'ara Betula* 1:9; *Shulḥan Arukh, Even HaEzer* 177:4).

He said to us forge a document for me – **לְדִידְהוּ אֲמַר לְהוּ זַיְיפוּ לִי:** If a person produced a promissory note and two witnesses claimed that he had asked them to forge that document, even if the document was ratified by its signatories, it cannot be used to collect the debt. The only way to collect the debt is by producing the witnesses who signed the document to testify that they witnessed the loan, or for others to testify that they saw the pair signing the document and the signatories testify that it is their signature. The Rema states that some authorities disagree and maintain that the testimony validating their signatures is ineffective (*Tur* citing Rabbi Meir HaLevi). However, with regard to other documents that this man produces that affect other people, the debts may be collected, and there is no suspicion that they too were forged (*Shakh*, citing Ran and Rosh; Rambam *Sefer Shofetim, Hilkhot Edut* 11:4; *Shulḥan Arukh, Ḥoshen Mishpat* 63:2).

מתני׳ וְאֵלּוּ שֶׁאֵין לָהֶן קְנָס: הַבָּא עַל הַגִּיּוֹרֶת, וְעַל הַשְּׁבוּיָה, וְעַל הַשִּׁפְחָה, שֶׁנִּפְדּוּ וְשֶׁנִּתְגַּיְּירוּ וְשֶׁנִּשְׁתַּחְרְרוּ יְתֵירוֹת עַל בְּנוֹת שָׁלֹשׁ שָׁנִים וְיוֹם אֶחָד. רַבִּי יְהוּדָה אוֹמֵר שְׁבוּיָה שֶׁנִּפְדֵּית הֲרֵי הִיא בִּקְדוּשָּׁתָהּ, אַף עַל פִּי שֶׁגְּדוֹלָה.

MISHNA And these are the cases of young women **who do not** have **a fine** paid to their fathers when they are raped or seduced: **One who has intercourse with a convert**[H] **or with a captive**[N] woman **or with a gentile maidservant, who were redeemed, converted, or emancipated** when they were **more than three years and one day** old, as presumably they are no longer virgins. **Rabbi Yehuda says: A captive** woman **who was redeemed** remains **in her** state of **sanctity even though** she is **an adult,** as it cannot be stated that she certainly engaged in intercourse.

הַבָּא עַל בִּתּוֹ, עַל בַּת בִּתּוֹ, עַל בַּת בְּנוֹ, עַל בַּת אִשְׁתּוֹ, עַל בַּת בְּנָהּ, עַל בַּת בִּתָּהּ – אֵין לָהֶן קְנָס, מִפְּנֵי שֶׁמִּתְחַיֵּיב בְּנַפְשׁוֹ, שֶׁמִּיתָתָן בִּידֵי בֵּית דִּין, וְכׇל הַמִּתְחַיֵּיב בְּנַפְשׁוֹ אֵין מְשַׁלֵּם מָמוֹן, שֶׁנֶּאֱמַר ״וְאִם לֹא יִהְיֶה אָסוֹן עָנוֹשׁ יֵעָנֵשׁ״.

The mishna resumes its list of the cases of young women who are not entitled to a fine when raped or seduced by the following men: In the case of **one who engages in intercourse with his daughter,**[NH] **with his daughter's daughter,**[N] **with his son's daughter, with his wife's daughter, with her son's daughter,** or **with her daughter's daughter; they do not** receive payment of **a fine.** That is **due to** the fact **that he is liable** to receive the **death** penalty, and **that their death** penalty is administered by **the court, and anyone who is liable** to receive the **death** penalty **does not pay money, as it is stated: "And yet no harm follow, he shall be punished"** (Exodus 21:22). This verse indicates that if a woman dies and the one who struck her is liable to receive the death penalty, he is exempt from payment.

גמ׳ אָמַר רַבִּי יוֹחָנָן: רַבִּי יְהוּדָה וְרַבִּי דּוֹסָא אָמְרוּ דָּבָר אֶחָד; רַבִּי יְהוּדָה – הָא דַּאֲמַרַן, רַבִּי דּוֹסָא – דְּתַנְיָא: שְׁבוּיָה אוֹכֶלֶת בִּתְרוּמָה, דִּבְרֵי רַבִּי דּוֹסָא. אָמַר רַבִּי דּוֹסָא: וְכִי מָה עָשָׂה לָהּ עֲרָבִי הַלָּז? וְכִי מִפְּנֵי שֶׁמִּיעֵךְ לָהּ בֵּין דַּדֶּיהָ פְּסָלָהּ מִן הַכְּהוּנָּה?

GEMARA Rabbi Yoḥanan said: Rabbi Yehuda and Rabbi Dosa[N] **said one** and the same **thing** with regard to a captive woman. The statement of **Rabbi Yehuda** is **that** which **we said** in the mishna. The statement of **Rabbi Dosa** is **as it is taught** in a *baraita*: **A captive** daughter or wife of a priest, who was redeemed, **partakes of *teruma*;**[NH] this is **the statement of Rabbi Dosa.** In explanation, **Rabbi Dosa said: And what did this Arab** who took her captive **do to her? And due to** the fact **that he** lasciviously **squeezed between her breasts,** did he **render her unfit** to marry into **the priesthood?** Although he may have taken liberties with her, there is no concern that he had relations with her.

אֲמַר רַבָּה: דִּלְמָא לָא הִיא; עַד כָּאן לָא קָאָמַר רַבִּי יְהוּדָה הָכָא אֶלָּא שֶׁלֹּא יְהֵא חוֹטֵא נִשְׂכָּר, אֲבָל הָתָם – כְּרַבָּנַן סְבִירָא לֵיהּ. אִי נַמִי: עַד כָּאן לָא קָאָמַר רַבִּי דּוֹסָא הָתָם – אֶלָּא בִּתְרוּמָה דְּרַבָּנַן, אֲבָל קְנָס דְּאוֹרָיְיתָא – כְּרַבָּנַן סְבִירָא לֵיהּ.

Rabba said: Perhaps that is not so, and their opinions differ. Perhaps **Rabbi Yehuda states** his opinion **only here** with regard to payment of a fine, **so that** the **sinner will not profit** through exemption from the fine because this girl was taken captive in her youth. **However, there,** with regard to *teruma*, **he holds in accordance with** the opinion of **the Rabbis,** and she is unfit to marry a priest. **Alternatively,** there is another distinction between their opinions. Perhaps **Rabbi Dosa stated** his opinion **only there, with regard to *teruma*** whose legal status today is **by rabbinic** law, and therefore he rules leniently. **However,** with regard to payment of a **fine,** which is mandated **by Torah law, he holds in accordance with** the opinion of **the Rabbis,** and the rapist is exempt from payment based on the principle: The burden of proof is incumbent upon the claimant, and she cannot prove that her captors did not engage in intercourse with her and that she is a virgin.

NOTES

A captive woman with regard to the matter of a fine – שְׁבוּיָה לְעִנְיַן קְנָס: The early commentaries ask: Doesn't everyone agree that there is merely a suspicion that a captive woman was violated, and it is a rabbinic decree that she does not have the presumptive status of a virgin, so how does the mishna rule unequivocally that she is not entitled to a fine? *Tosafot* explain that if a captive woman was entitled to a fine there is concern lest she marry a priest. In the *Shita Mekubbetzet* it is explained that even though it is based merely on suspicion, her presumptive status as a virgin was undermined, and one does not collect money based on weakened presumptive status.

One who engages in intercourse with his daughter – הַבָּא עַל בִּתּוֹ: In the Jerusalem Talmud the question is raised: If she had relations with another, her father would be entitled to the fine, and therefore it is obvious in this case that she does not receive payment of the fine, as it is her father who would be entitled to the payment. One answer is that this refers to a case where the father died in the meantime, and the fine would therefore have been collected from his estate; his heirs would then have no right to it. The Rashba adds that it could also be referring to a girl who was betrothed and divorced, in accordance with the opinion that in that case the fine is paid to her, as her father is not entitled to the payment after her divorce.

With his daughter's daughter, etc. – עַל בַּת בִּתּוֹ וכו׳: As the mishna includes forbidden relatives by marriage, e.g., relations with his wife's daughter, why doesn't it list his daughter-in-law and other relatives? *Tosafot* maintain that the *tanna* could indeed have enumerated those cases as well, but he taught some cases and omitted others. In the *Shita Mekubbetzet* the suggestion is made that the mishna lists only those cases with regard to which all the Sages agree, even those Sages who maintain that one who was betrothed and divorced is not entitled to the fine.

Rabbi Yehuda and Rabbi Dosa – רַבִּי יְהוּדָה וְרַבִּי דּוֹסָא: In the Jerusalem Talmud, these opinions are also cited, with certain differences. There Rabbi Yoḥanan said that Rabbi Yehuda referred only to the fine, while the Sage of the school of Rabbi Ḥiyya said that Rabbi Yehuda was also referring to the marriage contract, as in the *baraita* quoted below. Reish Lakish alone maintains that the two opinions are equal in all regards, including with regard to the *halakha* of *teruma*.

As it is taught in a *baraita*: A captive partakes of *teruma* – דְּתַנְיָא שְׁבוּיָה אוֹכֶלֶת בִּתְרוּמָה: Although fundamentally, this *halakha* appears in a mishna in tractate *Eduyyot*, since the Gemara adds Rabbi Dosa's rationale for his ruling, which does not appear in the mishna, it introduces the entire passage: As it is taught in a *baraita*.

HALAKHA

A convert, etc. – הַגִּיּוֹרֶת וכו׳: A gentile woman older than the age of three who converted, and likewise a captive older than the age of three who was redeemed, and similarly a maidservant older than the age of three who was freed are not entitled to the fine. The *halakha* is in accordance with the mishna, contrary to the individual opinion of Rabbi Yehuda (Rambam *Sefer Nashim, Hilkhot Na'ara Betula* 1:10).

One who engages in intercourse with his daughter, etc. – הַבָּא עַל בִּתּוֹ וכו׳: One who rapes a woman for whom he is liable to receive a court-administered death penalty, e.g., his daughter or his wife's daughter, whether or not he was forewarned, is exempt from paying the fine (Rambam *Sefer Nashim, Hilkhot Na'ara Betula* 1:13–14).

A captive woman with regard to partaking of *teruma* – שְׁבוּיָה בַּאֲכִילַת תְּרוּמָה: The wife of a priest who was taken captive may not eat *teruma*, due to the concern that she was violated by her gentile captor. However, if she claims that she is pure, or if there were witnesses to that effect, she is permitted to her husband the priest, and she is permitted to eat *teruma*. The *halakha* is in accordance with the opinion of the Rabbis in their dispute with Rabbi Dosa (Rambam *Sefer Zera'im, Hilkhot Terumot* 6:11).

אמר ליה אביי: וטעמיה דרבי יהודה הכא שלא יהא חוטא נשכר הוא? והא תניא, רבי יהודה אומר: שבויה שנשבית הרי היא בקדושתה, אפי׳ בת עשר שנים כתובתה מאתים, והתם – מאי שלא יהא חוטא נשכר איכא? התם נמי, דלמא מימנעי ולא נסבי לה.

Abaye said to Rabba: **And is the rationale** for the opinion of **Rabbi Yehuda here,** in the case of a fine, to ensure **that the sinner will not profit? But isn't it taught** in a *baraita* that **Rabbi Yehuda says: A captive** woman **who was taken captive** remains **in her** state of **sanctity** with the presumptive status of a virgin? **Even** if she was in captivity when she was **ten years old, her marriage contract is two hundred** dinars. **And there,** in that case, **what** relevance **is there** for the rationale: To ensure **that the sinner will not profit?** That *baraita* refers to a marriage contract and no transgression is involved. The Gemara answers: **There too,** Rabbi Yehuda issues the same ruling for a different reason. She receives the marriage contract of a virgin because if she didn't, **perhaps men would refrain and not marry her,** due to their suspicion that her captors violated her.

וסבר רבי יהודה בקדושתה קיימה? והתניא: הפודה את השבויה ישאנה; מעיד בה – לא ישאנה. רבי יהודה אומר: בין כך ובין כך – לא ישאנה! הא גופה קשיא; אמרת: הפודה את השבויה ישאנה, והדר תנא: מעיד בה – לא ישאנה, משום דמעיד בה לא ישאנה?!

The Gemara asks: **And does Rabbi Yehuda maintain** that a captive woman remains **in her** state of **sanctity? But isn't it taught** in a *baraita*: **One who redeems a captive may marry her,** even if he is a priest, but if he **testifies**[H] that **she** did not engage in sexual relations while in captivity, **he may not marry her? Rabbi Yehuda says: Both** in **this** case, where he redeemed her, **and** in **that** case, where he testified, **he may not marry her,** lest she was violated and rendered unfit to marry a priest. The Gemara comments: **This** *baraita* **itself is difficult.** On the one hand **you said: One who redeems a captive may marry her, and then it was taught:** If he **testifies** that **she** did not engage in sexual relations while in captivity, **he may not marry her.** Is that to say that **due to** the fact **that he** also **testifies** that **she** was not violated **he may not marry her?**

הא לא קשיא; הכי קאמר: הפודה את השבויה ומעיד בה – ישאנה, מעיד בה כדי – לא ישאנה.

The Gemara answers: This is **not difficult,** as **this is what** the *baraita* **is saying: One who redeems a captive** woman **and testifies** that **she** was not violated **may marry her.** However, if he **only testifies** that **she** was not violated **he may not marry her.**

מכל מקום קשיא לרבי יהודה! אמר רב פפא: אימא; רבי יהודה אומר בין כך ובין כך – ישאנה. רב הונא בריה דרב יהושע אומר: לעולם כדקתני, רבי יהודה לדבריהם דרבנן קאמר להו: לדידי – בין כך ובין כך ישאנה, אלא לדידכו – בין כך ובין כך לא ישאנה מבעי ליה!

With regard to the apparent contradiction between the two statements of Rabbi Yehuda, the Gemara says: **In any case,** this *baraita* is **difficult** according **to Rabbi Yehuda,** as contrary to his earlier statement, he states that a captive woman does not retain the presumptive status of a virgin. **Rav Pappa said:** Emend the text and **say** that **Rabbi Yehuda says:**[N] **Both** in **this** case and in **that** case **he may marry her. Rav Huna, son of Rav Yehoshua, says: Actually,** do not emend the *baraita* and learn it **as it was taught.** In the *baraita*, **Rabbi Yehuda spoke to them** according **to the statement of the Rabbis.** According **to my** opinion, that the presumptive status of a redeemed captive woman is that of a virgin, **both** in **this** case **and** in **that** case **he may marry her. However,** according **to your** opinion that there is concern lest she was violated, the *halakha* **should be** that **both** in **this** case **and** in **that** case **he may not marry her.**

ורבנן? הפודה את השבויה ומעיד בה ישאנה – לא שדי איניש זוזי בכדי, מעיד בה כדי לא ישאנה – שמא עיניו נתן בה.

The Gemara asks: **And** how do **the Rabbis** explain their ruling? They explain: **One who redeems a captive** woman and **testifies** that **she** was not violated **may marry her,** as **a person does not throw** away **money for nothing.** If he paid the ransom to redeem her, he must be certain that she is a virgin. One who **only testifies** that **she** was not violated **may not marry her, lest he had his eye on her** to marry her and is prepared to lie to facilitate that marriage.

רמי ליה רב פפא בר שמואל לרב יוסף:

Rav Pappa bar Shmuel raised a contradiction before Rav Yosef:

HALAKHA

One who testifies with regard to a captive – המעיד על השבויה: If a priest testifies that a captive woman is pure, he is not permitted to marry her based on his testimony, due to the concern that he lied because he had his eye on marrying her. However, his testimony is accepted to permit her to others (*Beit Shmuel*). If he was not certain that she was not violated, he would not have redeemed her, as he would not have spent his money. If he redeemed her and testified in her regard, he may marry her (Rambam *Sefer Kedusha, Hilkhot Issurei Bia* 18:20; *Shulḥan Arukh, Even HaEzer* 7:3).

NOTES

Say that Rabbi Yehuda says – אימא רבי יהודה אומר וכו׳: The Ritva questions the suggestion that the attribution of the opinion in the *baraita* can be reversed in this manner. He therefore claims that perhaps Rav Pappa is suggesting that Rabbi Yehuda's statement can be read as a question: And may he not marry her? He cites similar instances from elsewhere in the Talmud.

וְסָבַר רַבִּי יְהוּדָה בִּקְדוּשָּׁתָהּ קָיְימָא? וְהָתַנְיָא: הַגִּיּוֹרֶת שֶׁנִּתְגַּיְּירָה וְרָאֲתָה דָּם, רַבִּי יְהוּדָה אוֹמֵר דַּיָּהּ שַׁעְתָּהּ, רַבִּי יוֹסֵי אוֹמֵר: הֲרֵי הִיא כְּכׇל הַנָּשִׁים, וּמְטַמְּאָה מֵעֵת לְעֵת וּמִפְּקִידָה לִפְקִידָה,

And does **Rabbi Yehuda maintain** that a captive woman **remains in her** state of **sanctity? But isn't it taught** in a *baraita*: With regard to a female **convert who converted and saw the** flow of menstrual **blood**[N] on that same day, **Rabbi Yehuda says:** Deeming **her** impure from the **hour** that she saw the menstrual flow **is sufficient for her.** There is no decree of retroactive impurity on objects that she touched earlier, due to the concern that the blood flow might have started earlier. **Rabbi Yosei says: Her** legal status **is like** that of **all** of **the** Jewish **women, and she** therefore **transmits impurity** retroactively **for a twenty-four hour period** following her conversion, or **from examination to examination,** i.e., from the last time she examined herself.

וּצְרִיכָה לְהַמְתִּין שְׁלֹשָׁה חֳדָשִׁים, דִּבְרֵי רַבִּי יְהוּדָה. רַבִּי יוֹסֵי מַתִּיר לֵיאָרֵס וְלִינָּשֵׂא מִיָּד! אֲמַר לֵיהּ: גִּיּוֹרֶת אַשְּׁבוּיָה קָא רָמֵית?! גִּיּוֹרֶת – לָא מְנַטְרָא נַפְשָׁהּ, שְׁבוּיָה – מְנַטְרָא נַפְשָׁהּ.

And a convert **is required to wait**[N] **three months** after her conversion before marrying a Jew, due to the concern that she is pregnant, leading to confusion whether the child was conceived before or after her conversion; this is **the statement of Rabbi Yehuda. Rabbi Yosei permits her to be betrothed and to be married immediately.** Clearly, Rabbi Yehuda is concerned that she engaged in sexual relations prior to her conversion. Rav Yosef **said to** Rav Pappa bar Shmuel: **Are you raising a contradiction** from the *halakha* of **a convert to** that of **a captive** woman? **A convert does not protect herself** from engaging in sexual relations before conversion, whereas **a captive protects herself,** as she is conscious of the sanctity of the Jewish people and does not want to be violated.

וְרָמֵי שְׁבוּיָה אַשְּׁבוּיָה; דְּתַנְיָא: הַגִּיּוֹרֶת וְהַשְּׁבוּיָה וְהַשִּׁפְחָה שֶׁנִּפְדּוּ וְשֶׁנִּתְגַּיְּירוּ, וְשֶׁנִּשְׁתַּחְרְרוּ יְתֵירוֹת עַל בְּנוֹת שָׁלֹשׁ שָׁנִים וְיוֹם אֶחָד – צְרִיכוֹת לְהַמְתִּין שְׁלֹשָׁה חֳדָשִׁים, דִּבְרֵי רַבִּי יְהוּדָה. רַבִּי יוֹסֵי מַתִּיר לֵיאָרֵס וְלִינָּשֵׂא מִיָּד! אִשְׁתִּיק.

And Rav Pappa bar Shmuel **raised a contradiction from** one *halakha* with regard to **a captive to** another *halakha* with regard to **a captive, as it is taught** in a *baraita*: **The convert, or the captive** woman **or the** gentile **maidservant, who were redeemed, converted, or emancipated** when they were **more than three years and one day** old,[N] **are required to wait three months** before marrying; this is **the statement of Rabbi Yehuda. Rabbi Yosei permits** these women **to be betrothed and to be married immediately.** Apparently, Rabbi Yehuda is concerned that she engaged in sexual relations prior to her redemption, contradicting his opinion here. Rav Yosef **was silent,** unable to respond.[H]

HALAKHA

Waiting with regard to a convert and a maidservant – הַמְתָּנָה בְּגִיּוֹרֶת וּבְשִׁפְחָה: An emancipated maidservant and a convert must wait ninety days before they can marry. The *Mishne LaMelekh* claims that this applies only to women who were previously married and therefore took no steps to prevent conception. The same *halakha* applies to a male convert and his wife who converted together; they too must wait so that it can be determined whether conception predated or postdated conversion. That is the ruling in the *Shulḥan Arukh* as well. Although the *Beit Yosef* questions this approach, apparently he reconsidered his ruling (Rambam *Sefer Nashim, Hilkhot Geirushin* 11:21; *Shulḥan Arukh, Even HaEzer* 13:5 and *Beit Shmuel* there).

NOTES

Who converted and saw the flow of menstrual blood – שֶׁנִּתְגַּיְּירָה וְרָאֲתָה דָּם: When a woman sees menstrual blood the concern is whether the blood flowed earlier but was not immediately obvious. Therefore, all pure items with which she came into contact during a previous period of time are rendered ritually impure. The precise length of this period of time is subject to a dispute between Hillel and Shammai at the beginning of tractate *Nidda*. The *halakha* is that this concern extends either for the twenty-four-hour period before she noticed the blood or from her most recent examination, whichever of the two periods is shorter. Consequently, if her last examination was more than twenty-four hours earlier, she renders the items impure retroactively for twenty-four hours, and if she examined herself more recently than that, any pure item with which she came into contact after that examination is impure.

Rashi and most commentaries explain that the convert referred to here saw blood on the day of her conversion. Rabbi Yosei maintains that she is like all Jewish women, and therefore renders items impure retroactively from the time of her conversion, whereas Rabbi Yehuda claims that since it cannot be for the entire twenty-four hour period, as she was a gentile for part of that time, she does not render the items impure retroactively at all, but merely from the moment of her sighting: Deeming her impure from the hour that she saw the menstrual flow is sufficient.

The *Shita Yeshana*, cited in the *Shita Mekubbetzet*, suggests a slightly different interpretation. There it is claimed that the reference is to a convert who saw blood for the first time after her conversion. Accordingly, the dispute is whether a decree is issued in her regard like the decree that applies to all Jewish women, or whether they did not decree impurity in her case, due to her former gentile state.

And a convert is required to wait – וּצְרִיכָה לְהַמְתִּין: The Sages decreed that a woman who was married may not wed another man immediately after the end of her marriage, as she might be unknowingly pregnant from her first husband. In that case, if she gives birth seven months into her second marriage it will be unclear whether the child was born to the first husband after a pregnancy of nine months or to the second husband after a pregnancy of seven months. That would lead to complications with regard to prohibitions, lineage, and inheritance. The Sages therefore required her to wait three months, at which point a pregnancy would be noticeable and it would be clear that the first husband is the father. The *tanna'im* disagreed whether this decree is applied to cases where there is no concern that there might be a previous pregnancy. A similar concern exists in the case of a woman who engaged in forbidden relations, or a convert, where it is necessary to determine whether or not the lineage of the child is flawed. In the case of a convert, there are halakhic ramifications dependent on whether or not the child was conceived and born in sanctity as a member of the Jewish people.

More than three years and one day old – יְתֵירוֹת עַל בְּנוֹת שָׁלֹשׁ שָׁנִים וְיוֹם אֶחָד: *Tosafot* question whether this phrase belongs here. First of all, it does not appear in other places in the Talmud where an identical discussion appears. In addition, it presents a difficulty for the opinion of Rabbi Yehuda, as he does not require a waiting period for a minor who was married. Although some commentaries (Ramban; Rashba) contend that there is no need to be particular in this regard, as adult women are included in this phrase, and the mention of three years and one day is merely the usual expression in this regard, most early commentaries agree that this version is inaccurate.

אֲמַר לֵיהּ: מִידִי שְׁמִיעַ לָךְ בְּהָא? אָמַר לֵיהּ, הָכִי אֲמַר רַב שֵׁשֶׁת: שֶׁרָאוּהָ שֶׁנִּבְעֲלָה. אִי הָכִי מַאי טַעֲמָא דְּרַבִּי יוֹסֵי? אֲמַר רַבָּה: קָסָבַר רַבִּי יוֹסֵי אִשָּׁה מְזַנָּה מְשַׁמֶּשֶׁת בְּמוֹךְ שֶׁלֹּא תִתְעַבֵּר.

Later, Rav Yosef **said to him: Have you heard anything with regard to this** matter? Rav Pappa bar Shmuel **said to him: This** is what **Rav Sheshet said:** Rabbi Yehuda is referring to a captive **whom** witnesses **saw engage in intercourse.** The Gemara asks: **If so, what is the rationale** for the ruling of **Rabbi Yosei** that she may marry immediately? Shouldn't he be concerned lest she is pregnant? **Rabba said: Rabbi Yosei holds** that **a woman who engages in** promiscuous **sexual relations has relations with** a contraceptive **resorbent** at the entrance of her womb, so **that she will not become pregnant.**

בִּשְׁלָמָא גִּיּוֹרֶת, כֵּיוָן דְּדַעְתָּהּ לְאִיגַּיּוּרֵי – מִנַּטְרָא נַפְשָׁהּ; שְׁבוּיָה נַמִי, דְּלָא יָדְעָה הֵיכָא מַמְטוּ לָהּ; שִׁפְחָה נַמִי, דְּשָׁמְעָה מִפִּי מָרָהּ; אֶלָּא יוֹצְאָה בְּשֵׁן וָעַיִן – מַאי אִיכָּא לְמֵימַר?

The Gemara asks: **Granted, a convert** uses the resorbent; **since it is her intention to convert, she protects herself** from pregnancy. **A captive too** uses the resorbent because **she does not know where they are taking her,** and she does not want to become pregnant. **A maidservant** uses the resorbent **too, as she heard from her master** that he intends to free her, and she seeks to avoid confusion with regard to the lineage of her offspring. **However,** with regard a maidservant who **emerges** from slavery **with** the extraction by her master of her **tooth or** her **eye, what is there to say?** She has no advance knowledge that she will be freed and therefore would not take precautions to avoid becoming pregnant, and Rav Sheshet explained that this is a case where she was seen engaging in sexual relations.

וְכִי תֵּימָא כָּל מִמֵּילָא לָא אָמַר רַבִּי יוֹסֵי – הֲרֵי אֲנוּסָה וּמְפוּתָּה, דְּמִמֵּילָא, וְתַנְיָא: אֲנוּסָה וּמְפוּתָּה צְרִיכוֹת לְהַמְתִּין שְׁלֹשָׁה חֳדָשִׁים, דִּבְרֵי רַבִּי יְהוּדָה, רַבִּי יוֹסֵי מַתִּיר לֵיאָרֵס וְלִינָּשֵׂא מִיָּד!

And if you say that with regard to **any** situation that occurs **on its own,** without advance knowledge, **Rabbi Yosei** concedes to Rabbi Yehuda and **did not say** that it is permitted for her to marry immediately, that cannot be so. There is the case of **a raped or seduced** woman, which happens **on its own** without advance knowledge, **and it is taught** in a *baraita*: **A raped woman and a seduced woman must wait three months** before marrying; this is **the statement of Rabbi Yehuda; Rabbi Yosei permits** these women **to be betrothed and to be married immediately.**

אֶלָּא אֲמַר רַבָּה: קָסָבַר רַבִּי יוֹסֵי: אִשָּׁה מְזַנָּה מִתְהַפֶּכֶת כְּדֵי שֶׁלֹּא תִתְעַבֵּר. וְאִידָךְ: חָיְישִׁינַן שֶׁמָּא לֹא נֶהֶפְכָה יָפֶה יָפֶה.

Rather, Rabba said: The rationale for the ruling of Rabbi Yosei is not because the woman uses a contraceptive resorbent that she inserts before engaging in relations. Rather, **Rabbi Yosei holds: A woman** who **engages in** promiscuous **sexual relations**[H] **turns over**[NB] at the conclusion of the sexual act so **that she will not become pregnant.** Therefore, even if she engaged in unplanned sexual relations, she can take steps afterward to prevent unwanted pregnancy. The Gemara asks: **And** how does **the other** *tanna*, Rabbi Yehuda respond to this contention? The Gemara answers: **We are concerned lest** the semen remain in her womb because **she did not turn over properly,** and she will become pregnant.

שֶׁנֶּאֱמַר ״וְלֹא יִהְיֶה אָסוֹן עָנוֹשׁ יֵעָנֵשׁ״ וכו׳. וְהָא מֵהָכָא נָפְקָא? מֵהָתָם נָפְקָא: ״כְּדֵי רִשְׁעָתוֹ״ – מִשּׁוּם רִשְׁעָה אַחַת אַתָּה מְחַיְּיבוֹ, וְאִי אַתָּה מְחַיְּיבוֹ מִשּׁוּם שְׁתֵּי רִשְׁעָיוֹת!

§ The mishna states that one liable to receive the death penalty is exempt from payment, **as it is stated: "And yet no harm follow, he shall be punished, etc."** (Exodus 21:22). The Gemara asks: **And is this** principle **derived from here?** Actually, **it is derived from there:** "And to be beaten before his face **according to the measure of his iniquity**" (Deuteronomy 25:2).[N] From the term: His iniquity, it is inferred: **You can hold** one who performs one action **liable for one iniquity,** i.e., punishment for violating one prohibition, **but you do not hold him liable for two iniquities,** i.e., punishments for violating two prohibitions.

חֲדָא בְּמִיתָה וּמָמוֹן, וַחֲדָא בְּמַלְקוֹת וּמָמוֹן. וּצְרִיכָא: דְּאִי אַשְׁמְעִינַן מִיתָה וּמָמוֹן – מִשּׁוּם דְּאִיכָּא אִיבּוּד נְשָׁמָה, אֲבָל מַלְקוֹת וּמָמוֹן דְּלֵיכָּא אִיבּוּד נְשָׁמָה, אֵימָא לָא.

The Gemara answers: **One** of these derivations, from the verse "And yet no harm follow" is stated **with regard to** one who performed an action for which he is liable to receive the **death** penalty **and** to pay **money,** and the liability to be executed exempts him from payment. **And one** of these derivations, from the verse "According to the measure of his iniquity," is stated **with regard to** one who performed an action for which he is liable to receive **lashes and** to pay **money,** and he receives only one punishment. The Gemara elaborates: **And** both derivations **are necessary, as if** the Torah **taught us** this *halakha* only with regard to **death and money,** one would assert that the exemption from payment is **due to** the fact **that there is loss of life,**[N] the ultimate punishment, leaving no room for additional punishment; **however,** in the case of **lashes and money, where there is no loss of life, say no,** there is no exemption and he is flogged and pays.

HALAKHA

Waiting with regard to a captive, a raped or seduced woman, and one who engaged in promiscuous relations – הַמְתָּנָה בִּשְׁבוּיָה, בַּאֲנוּסָה וּמְפוּתָּה, וּבִמְזַנָּה: A redeemed captive woman need not wait before marrying, even if she was an adult, since she turns over to prevent conception, as stated by Rabbi Yosei. For the same reason a rape victim and seduced woman need not wait three months either, and the same applies to any woman who engaged in promiscuous relations. The Rema states that some authorities, e.g., Rabbi Zeraḥya HaLevi, the Rosh, and the *Tur*, claim that in all cases, if a woman was capable of conception, she must wait, as Shmuel in the latter version of his statement in *Yevamot* (32b) rules in accordance with the opinion of Rabbi Yehuda that there is concern lest she did not turn over properly (Rambam *Sefer Nashim, Hilkhot Geirushin* 11:22; *Shulḥan Arukh, Even HaEzer* 13:6).

NOTES

A woman who engages in promiscuous sexual relations turns over, etc. – אִשָּׁה מְזַנָּה מִתְהַפֶּכֶת וכו׳: Rashi maintains that this reason is accepted; a woman who is freed from enslavement by the loss of a tooth or eye would not have to wait either, as she too would turn over. In his opinion, no woman who engages in acts of promiscuous relations wants to conceive, and therefore she will turn over even if she has no particular reason to protect herself. However, many early commentaries, including *Tosafot* and the Ramban, contend that even Rabbi Yosei agrees that a maidservant is required to wait in that case, as she has no particular reason to prevent conception and therefore would not have turned over. They add that it is possible that she was married to a slave, and as such would certainly have had no reason to avoid conception, as she was engaging in legitimate conjugal relations.

It is derived from there: According to the measure of his iniquity – מֵהָתָם נָפְקָא כְּדֵי רִשְׁעָתוֹ: The Ritva raises the question that although from the verse "According to the measure of his iniquity" it can be derived that one is not punished twice for a single transgression, which of the two punishments he receives cannot be derived. It is only from the verse "And yet no harm follow" that it is derived that he is executed and does not pay. He answers that it is logical that one would not be exempted from the severe punishment of execution, because there is additional liability to pay. The *Beit Aharon* suggests that the question is not why the verse "And yet no harm follow" is necessary; on the contrary, why not suffice with that verse alone, from which both principles can be derived? Although that interpretation resolves the Ritva's question, it does not fit well with the language of the Gemara.

There is loss of life – דְּאִיכָּא אִיבּוּד נְשָׁמָה: Although the *halakha* concludes that he is exempt from any other punishment even if he is not actually executed, the exemption is due to the fact that a transgression that entails the loss of life is so serious that no other punishment would be appropriate. A careful reading of Rashi leads to a similar understanding (*Shita Mekubbetzet*).

BACKGROUND

Turns over – מִתְהַפֶּכֶת: According to modern medicine, turning over after intercourse would be ineffective in preventing conception. Therefore, it stands to reason that the Gemara is not referring merely to turning over; rather, it is referring to additional steps taken to prevent pregnancy. In terms of the language of the Gemara, perhaps it is referring to turning over during the sexual act, leading to an uncommon position that might significantly reduce the odds of conception.

וְאִי אַשְׁמַעִינַן מַלְקוֹת וּמָמוֹן – מִשּׁוּם דְּלָא חֲמִיר אִיסּוּרֵיהּ, אֲבָל מִיתָה וּמָמוֹן דַּחֲמִיר אִיסּוּרֵיהּ אֵימָא לָא, צְרִיכָא.

And if the Torah **taught us** this *halakha* only with regard to **lashes and money,** one would assert that the exemption from payment is **due to** the fact **that** the **prohibition** that he violated **is not severe,** as it is punishable by lashes, and for violating a prohibition that is not severe one does not receive two punishments. **However,** with regard to **death and money, where** the **prohibition** that he violated **is severe, say no,** he is not exempt from receiving two punishments. Therefore, it was **necessary** for the Torah to teach both derivations.

וּלְרַבִּי מֵאִיר, דְּאָמַר לוֹקֶה וּמְשַׁלֵּם, תַּרְתֵּי לָמָּה לִי? חֲדָא בְּמִיתָה וּמָמוֹן

The Gemara asks: **And according to Rabbi Meir, who said** that one **is flogged and pays** in cases where he violated a prohibition punishable by both, **why do I** require **two** derivations teaching that one does not receive the death penalty and pay? The Gemara answers: **One** derivation is **with regard to death and money,** exempting one liable to be executed from payment,

Perek **III**
Daf **37** Amud **b**

וַחֲדָא בְּמִיתָה וּמַלְקוֹת. וּצְרִיכָא; דְּאִי אַשְׁמַעִינַן מִיתָה וּמָמוֹן – מִשּׁוּם דַּחֲדָא בְּגוּפֵיהּ וַחֲדָא בְּמָמוֹנֵיהּ לָא עָבְדִינַן, אֲבָל בְּמִיתָה וּמַלְקוֹת דְּאִידִי וְאִידִי בְּגוּפֵיהּ – אֵימָא מִיתָה אֲרִיכְתָּא הִיא, וְנַעֲבֵיד בֵּיהּ.

and one derivation is **with regard to death and lashes,**[N] exempting one liable to be executed from lashes. The Gemara comments: **And** both verses **are necessary, as if** the Torah **taught us** this *halakha* only with regard to **death and monetary** payment, one would assert that the exemption from payment is **due to** the fact **that we do not administer one** punishment **to his body and one to his money. However, with regard to death and lashes, that both this,** death, **and that,** lashes, are administered **to his body, say it is an extended death** penalty **and let us administer** lashes and then the death penalty **to him** so that his death will ensue from affliction.

וְאִי אַשְׁמַעִינַן מִיתָה וּמַלְקוֹת – דְּתַרְתֵּי בְּגוּפֵיהּ לָא עָבְדִינַן, אֲבָל מִיתָה וּמָמוֹן דַּחֲדָא בְּגוּפֵיהּ וַחֲדָא בְּמָמוֹנֵיהּ – אֵימָא נַעֲבֵיד בֵּיהּ, צְרִיכָא.

And if the Torah **taught us** this *halakha* only with regard to **death and lashes,** one would assert that the exemption from lashes is **due to** the fact **that we do not administer two** punishments **to his body. However,** with regard to **death and money, where one** is administered **to his body and one** is administered **to his money, say: Let us administer** both **to him.** Therefore, both verses are **necessary,** to teach that one receives only one punishment in both cases.

״וְלֹא תִקְחוּ כֹפֶר לְנֶפֶשׁ רֹצֵחַ״ לָמָּה לִי? דְּאָמַר רַחֲמָנָא: לָא תִּשְׁקוֹל מָמוֹנָא מִינֵּיהּ וְתִפְטְרֵיהּ מִקְּטָלָא – ״לֹא תִקְחוּ כֹפֶר לָנוּס אֶל עִיר מִקְלָטוֹ״ לָמָּה לִי? דְּאָמַר רַחֲמָנָא: לָא תִּשְׁקוֹל מָמוֹנָא מִינֵּיהּ וְתִפְטְרֵיהּ מִן גָּלוּת.

The Gemara asks with regard to the verse **"And you shall take no ransom for the life of a murderer,** who is guilty of death" (Numbers 35:31), which means that one does not take payment from a person sentenced to death, **why do I** require this verse, if that principle was already derived from another verse? The Gemara explains **that the Merciful One says: Do not take money from him and exempt him from** the **death** penalty.[H] Similarly, the following verse: **"And you shall take no ransom for him that is fled to his city of refuge"** (Numbers 35:32), **why do I** require this verse? The Gemara explains **that the Merciful One says: Do not take money from him and exempt him from exile.**[H]

וּתְרֵי קְרָאֵי לָמָּה לִי? חַד בְּשׁוֹגֵג וְחַד בְּמֵזִיד, וּצְרִיכִי; דְּאִי אַשְׁמַעִינַן מֵזִיד – מִשּׁוּם דַּחֲמִיר אִיסּוּרֵיהּ, אֲבָל שׁוֹגֵג דְּלָא חֲמִיר אִיסּוּרֵיהּ – אֵימָא לָא. וְאִי אַשְׁמַעִינַן שׁוֹגֵג – מִשּׁוּם דְּלֵיכָּא אִיבּוּד נְשָׁמָה, אֲבָל מֵזִיד דְּאִיכָּא אִיבּוּד נְשָׁמָה – אֵימָא לָא, צְרִיכָא.

The Gemara asks: **And why do I** require **two verses** to teach the same principle? The Gemara explains: **One** verse refers **to** one who killed **unwittingly, and one** verse refers **to** one who killed **intentionally.** The Gemara comments: **And** both verses **are necessary, as if** the Torah **taught us** this *halakha* only with regard to **an intentional** murderer, one would assert that payment is not accepted **due to** the fact **that** the **prohibition** that **he** violated **is severe. However,** with regard to **an unwitting** killer, **where** the **prohibition is not severe, say no,** he may pay in lieu of exile. **And if** the Torah **taught us** this *halakha* only with regard to **an unwitting** killer, one would assert that payment is not accepted **due to** the fact **that there is no loss of life,** as the killer is not executed, and therefore, there is no reason to allow payment in lieu of exile. **However,** with regard to **an intentional** killer, **where there is loss of life,** as he will be executed, **say no,** he may pay in lieu of execution. Therefore, both verses are **necessary.**

NOTES

And one is with regard to death and lashes – וַחֲדָא בְּמִיתָה וּמַלְקוֹת: The Rabbis maintain that no special verse is required for this principle, as it stands to reason that if one is not punished with both lashes and payment, all the more so is he not punished with lashes and execution, as the death penalty is a far more severe punishment than lashes (Rashba; Ritva).

HALAKHA

There is no ransom for a murderer – אֵין כּוֹפֶר לְרוֹצֵחַ: The court may not accept a ransom payment from a murderer in order to exempt him from the death penalty. They may not do so even if he offers all the money in the world, and even if the avenging relative of the victim agrees, as the soul of the murderer does not belong to the avenger but to God (Rambam *Sefer Nezikim, Hilkhot Rotze'aḥ* 1:4).

There is no ransom for exile – אֵין כּוֹפֶר לְגָלוּת: The court may not accept a ransom payment from an unintentional murderer in order to exempt him from exile (Rambam *Sefer Nezikim, Hilkhot Rotze'aḥ* 5:1).

"וְלָאָרֶץ לֹא יְכוּפַּר לַדָּם אֲשֶׁר שׁוּפַּךְ בָּהּ כִּי אִם בְּדַם שׁוֹפְכוֹ" לָמָּה לִי?

The Gemara asks with regard to the following verse: **"And no expiation can be made for the land for the blood that is shed therein, but by the blood of him that shed it"** (Numbers 35:33), which also indicates that he cannot be exempted by money, **why do I** require another verse to teach that one cannot absolve himself from the death penalty by means of payment?

מִבָּעֵי לֵיהּ לִכְדְתַנְיָא: מִנַּיִן שֶׁאִם נִתְעָרְפָה עֶגְלָה וְאַחַר כָּךְ נִמְצָא הַהוֹרֵג, מִנַּיִן שֶׁאֵין פּוֹטְרִין אוֹתוֹ – שֶׁנֶּאֱמַר "וְלָאָרֶץ לֹא יְכוּפַּר לַדָּם אֲשֶׁר שׁוּפַּךְ בָּהּ" וגו׳,

The Gemara explains: **It is necessary** to teach **that which is taught** in a *baraita* with regard to the matter of the calf that is beheaded. If a corpse whose murderer is unknown is found between two towns, the elders of the town nearest to the corpse bring a heifer and behead it in a riverbed, after which they pray for atonement for this murder. The *baraita* states: **From where** is it derived **that if the calf was beheaded and the murderer was found thereafter,**[H] it is derived **that one does not exempt him**[N] from punishment? It is **as it is stated: "And no expiation can be made for the land for the blood that is shed therein,** but by the blood of him that shed it" (Numbers 35:32), from which it is inferred: And not by the blood of the calf.

"וְאַתָּה תְּבַעֵר הַדָּם הַנָּקִי מִקִּרְבֶּךָ" לָמָּה לִי? מִיבָּעֵי לֵיהּ לִכְדְתַנְיָא: מִנַּיִן לַמּוּמָתִים בְּסַיִף שֶׁהוּא מִן הַצַּוָּאר – תַּלְמוּד לוֹמַר "וְאַתָּה תְּבַעֵר הַדָּם הַנָּקִי מִקִּרְבֶּךָ", הוּקְשׁוּ כָּל שׁוֹפְכֵי דָמִים לְעֶגְלָה עֲרוּפָה, מַה לְּהַלָּן מִן הַצַּוָּאר – אַף שׁוֹפְכֵי דָמִים מִן הַצַּוָּאר.

The Gemara asks: What about the following verse, from the conclusion of the chapter of the heifer: The verse **"And so shall you put away the innocent blood from your midst"** (Deuteronomy 21:9) appears to be teaching the very same *halakha*, that a murderer must be executed. **Why do I need it?** The Gemara answers that **it is necessary to teach that which is taught** in a *baraita*: **From where** is it derived **that** with regard to **those executed by sword,** e.g., murderers, their execution **is** administered **from the neck,** and nowhere else? **The verse states: "And so shall you put away the innocent blood from your midst"** (Deuteronomy 21:9), **likening all spillers of blood to the beheaded calf**[B] brought for an unresolved murder. **Just as there,** the calf is beheaded **from the neck, so too, murderers** are beheaded **from the neck.**

אִי מַה לְּהַלָּן בְּקוֹפִיץ, וּמִמּוּל עוֹרֶף, אַף כָּאן בְּקוֹפִיץ וּמִמּוּל עוֹרֶף? אָמַר רַב נַחְמָן אָמַר רַבָּה בַּר אֲבוּהּ: אָמַר קְרָא "וְאָהַבְתָּ לְרֵעֲךָ כָּמוֹךָ" – בְּרוֹר לוֹ מִיתָה יָפָה.

The Gemara asks: **If so, just as there,** in the case of the beheaded calf, it is beheaded **with a cleaver** [*kofitz*][BL] **and at the nape of the neck,**[H] **here too** the court executes murderers **with a cleaver and at the nape of the neck. Rav Naḥman said** that **Rabba bar Avuh said** that **the verse says: "And you shall love your neighbor as yourself"** (Leviticus 19:18),[N] from which it is derived: **Choose for him an agreeable death.**[N] It is prohibited to abuse a guilty person while executing him, and chopping off his head with a cleaver is an unseemly death. The murderer is beheaded from the neck, not with a cleaver, and not by the other methods employed in beheading the calf.

"כָּל חֵרֶם אֲשֶׁר יָחֳרַם מִן הָאָדָם לֹא יִפָּדֶה" לָמָּה לִי? מִיבָּעֵי לֵיהּ לִכְדְתַנְיָא. מִנַּיִן לַיּוֹצֵא לֵיהָרֵג וְאָמַר אֶחָד "עֶרְכּוֹ עָלַי", מִנַּיִן שֶׁלֹּא אָמַר כְּלוּם,

The Gemara asks with regard to the following verse: **"Anything dedicated** [*ḥerem*], **that may be dedicated of men, shall not be redeemed;** he shall surely be put to death" (Leviticus 27:29), which is interpreted here as: Anyone sentenced to be executed shall not be redeemed; this appears to teach the same *halakha* as above, so **why do I need** it? The Gemara explains: **It is necessary** to teach **that which is taught** in a *baraita*: **From where** is it derived **with regard to** one **taken to be executed, and one person said: His valuation**[H] **is upon me** to donate to the Temple, **that he did not say anything** and his vow is not binding?

NOTES

From where is it derived that one does not exempt him – מִנַּיִן שֶׁאֵין פּוֹטְרִין אוֹתוֹ: *Tosafot* note that Rashi on the Torah cites a verse as the source of this *halakha* other than the one cited by the Gemara. They explain that this is related to the dispute concerning whether decapitation or strangulation is the more severe death penalty; *Tosafot* add that the Gemara here does not correspond to the ultimate halakhic ruling. The Ritva and Meiri indicate that the early commentaries had a different version of this passage in *Sanhedrin*, and perhaps Rashi relied on that text. The Rambam, like Rashi on the Torah, cites the verse "And you shall clear away the innocent blood" (Deuteronomy 19:13) as the proof text.

And you shall love your neighbor as yourself – וְאָהַבְתָּ לְרֵעֲךָ כָּמוֹךָ: At first glance, this derivation is difficult, as it applies this significant Torah principle of loving one's neighbor to the choice of an agreeable means of execution. However, the concept is that the mitzva: And you shall love your neighbor applies to all Jews, even to a wicked person facing execution. Therefore every effort must be expended to provide him with an agreeable death. In a homiletic vein, Rabbeinu Meir HaLevi in *Sanhedrin* (52b) reads the term: Your neighbor [*re'akha*], as your wicked [*ra'akha*], meaning that one must love even the wicked members of the Jewish people.

An agreeable death – מִיתָה יָפָה: The use of a cleaver is a less agreeable death as it does not immediately sever all the blood vessels. Furthermore, a cleaver is duller than a sword, and therefore inflicts greater pain (Rabbi Meir HaLevi in *Sanhedrin* 52b).

BACKGROUND

The beheaded calf – עֶגְלָה עֲרוּפָה: When a murder victim's corpse is found outside a town and the identity of the person who caused his death in unknown, the Torah mandates a course of action (Deuteronomy 21:1–9): First, members of the Great Sanhedrin measure the distance between the corpse and the nearest town, to determine which town must perform the rite of the beheaded calf. This measurement is carried out even if it is obvious which town is closest. Afterward, the elders of that town bring a calf that has never been used for any labor, and they behead it in a riverbed that is not tilled. The elders wash their hands and make a statement absolving themselves of guilt. If the murderer is discovered before the calf was killed, the rite is not performed.

Cleaver – קוֹפִיץ:

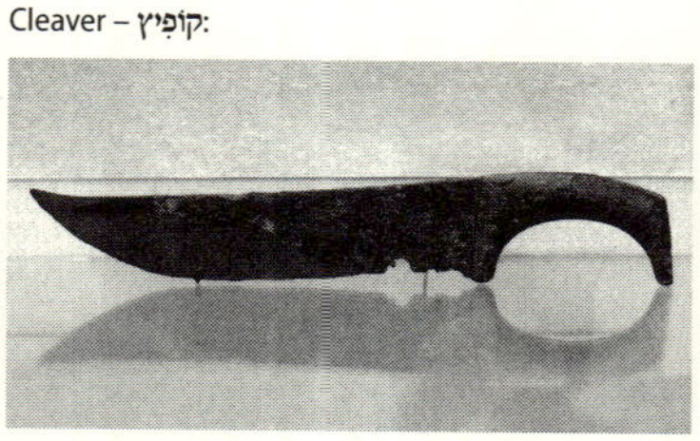

Ancient Roman cleaver

LANGUAGE

Cleaver [*kofitz*] – קוֹפִיץ: From the Greek κοπίς, *kopis*, meaning a thick, large knife.

HALAKHA

The calf was beheaded and the murderer was found thereafter – נִתְעָרְפָה עֶגְלָה וְאַחַר כָּךְ נִמְצָא הַהוֹרֵג: Even if the murderer was discovered only after the calf was beheaded, he is executed (Rambam *Sefer Nezikim, Hilkhot Rotze'aḥ* 10:8).

The manner of beheading the calf – דֶּרֶךְ עֲרִיפַת הָעֶגְלָה: The calf is beheaded by cutting it with a large knife on the back of its neck (Rambam *Sefer Nezikim, Hilkhot Rotze'aḥ* 9:3).

Valuation of one taken to be executed – עֶרְכּוֹ שֶׁל הַיּוֹצֵא לֵיהָרֵג: One condemned to death by a Jewish court has no valuation. In other words, if he or anyone else takes a vow to donate his valuation, the vow does not take effect, in accordance with the opinion of the first *tanna* (Rambam *Sefer Hafla'a, Hilkhot Arakhin* 3:11).

שֶׁנֶּאֱמַר ״כׇּל חֵרֶם אֲשֶׁר יׇחֳרַם מִן הָאָדָם לֹא יִפָּדֶה״. יָכוֹל אַף קוֹדֶם שֶׁנִּגְמַר דִּינוֹ כֵּן – תַּלְמוּד לוֹמַר. ״מִן הָאָדָם״ – וְלֹא כׇּל הָאָדָם.

It is derived **as it is stated: "Anything dedicated [*ḥerem*], that may be dedicated of men [*yoḥoram*], shall not be redeemed"** (Leviticus 27:29). This verse is taken to mean that anything dedicated, through which a man who is condemned [*yoḥoram*] is valuated, shall not be redeemed, as the person in question is already considered dead. One **might** think that **even before his verdict** is issued this should be **so,** and that one who said: The valuation of so-and-so on trial for murder is upon me, said nothing of consequence. Therefore, **the verse states:** "That may be dedicated **of men,**" implying "of men," **but not entire men.** If it is valuation of an entire man, one not yet sentenced to death, it is binding. If it is valuation of a partial man, one sentenced to death, it is not binding.

וּלְרַבִּי חֲנַנְיָא בֶּן עֲקַבְיָא, דְּאָמַר: נֶעֱרָךְ, מִפְּנֵי שֶׁדָּמָיו קְצוּבִין, הַאי ״כׇּל חֵרֶם״ מַאי עָבֵיד לֵיהּ?

The Gemara asks: **And according to Rabbi Ḥananya ben Akavya,** who **said** that even a person taken to his execution **is valuated,**[N] and the vow is binding, **because** the **money** of **his** valuation **is fixed.** The sum of the valuation established in the Torah is not based on the worth of the individual; rather, there is a fixed sum determined by age and gender. Therefore, one may be valuated as long as he is alive. According to that opinion, the question remains with regard to **this** verse: **"Anything dedicated," what does** he derive from **it?**

מִיבָּעֵי לֵיהּ לְכִדְתַנְיָא, רַבִּי יִשְׁמָעֵאל בְּנוֹ שֶׁל רַבִּי יוֹחָנָן בֶּן בְּרוֹקָה אוֹמֵר: לְפִי שֶׁמָּצִינוּ לַמּוּמָתִים בִּידֵי שָׁמַיִם שֶׁנּוֹתְנִין מָמוֹן וּמִתְכַּפֵּר לָהֶן, שֶׁנֶּאֱמַר ״אִם כּוֹפֶר יוּשַׁת עָלָיו״, יָכוֹל אַף בִּידֵי אָדָם כֵּן – תַּלְמוּד לוֹמַר ״חֵרֶם מִן הָאָדָם לֹא יִפָּדֶה״.

The Gemara answers: **He requires it** to teach **that which is taught** in a *baraita*: **Rabbi Yishmael, son of Rabbi Yoḥanan ben Beroka, says: Because we found with regard to those executed at the hand of Heaven,** and not through court-administered execution, **that they give money and their** sins **are atoned, as it is stated:** "The ox shall be stoned, and its owner shall also be put to death. **If there be laid upon him a ransom** then he shall give for the redemption of his life whatsoever is laid upon him" (Exodus 21:29–30). One whose ox kills a person is essentially liable to receive the death penalty at the hand of Heaven, and pays money instead.[H] You **might** think that **even** with regard to those liable to receive the death penalty **at the hands of man** it is **so,** and one can pay in lieu of execution. Therefore, **the verse states: "Dedicated of men shall not be redeemed"** (Leviticus 27:29). One who is executed by man cannot be redeemed with money.

וְאֵין לִי אֶלָּא מִיתוֹת חֲמוּרוֹת, שֶׁלֹּא נִיתְּנָה שִׁגְגָתָן לְכַפָּרָה, מִיתוֹת קַלּוֹת, שֶׁנִּיתְּנָה שִׁגְגָתָן לְכַפָּרָה מִנַּיִן – תַּלְמוּד לוֹמַר ״כׇּל חֵרֶם״.

And I have derived this restriction **only** with regard to prohibitions punishable by **severe** penalties of **death,**[N] e.g., striking one's father, **for which no atonement is designated** in the Torah **for their unwitting** violation. However, with regard to prohibitions punishable by **less severe** penalties of **death,** e.g., performing labor on Shabbat, **for which atonement,** a sin-offering, **is designated** in the Torah **for their unwitting** violation, **from where** is it derived that there is no payment in lieu of execution? **The verse states: "Anything dedicated,"** to include all prohibitions punishable by court-administered execution.

וְלָא מִמֵּילָא, מִ״לֹּא תִקְחוּ כוֹפֶר״ שָׁמְעַתְּ מִינָּהּ: לָא תִּשְׁקוֹל מָמוֹנָא מִינֵּיהּ וְתִיפְטְרֵיהּ, ״כׇּל חֵרֶם״ לָמָּה לִי? אֲמַר רָמִי בַּר חָמָא: אִיצְטְרִיךְ; סָלְקָא דַּעְתָּךְ אָמִינָא:

The Gemara asks: **And didn't you incidentally learn** the following conclusion **from** the verse **"And you shall take no ransom** for the life of a murderer, who is guilty of death" (Numbers 35:31): **Do not take money from him and exempt him** from death? **Why,** then, **do I** require the phrase: **Any *ḥerem*? Rami bar Ḥama said:** It is **necessary,** as **it might enter your mind to say**

HALAKHA

Payment of ransom for death at the hand of Heaven – כּוֹפֶר לַמּוּמָתִים בִּידֵי שָׁמַיִם: The owner of a forewarned ox that killed a person is liable to receive death at the hand of Heaven, in accordance with the verse "And its owner shall also be put to death" (Exodus 21:29). If he pays ransom equivalent to the value of the victim, he thereby gains atonement (Rambam *Sefer Nezikim, Hilkhot Nizkei Mamon* 10:4).

NOTES

Is valuated – נֶעֱרָךְ: The *halakhot* of valuations are detailed in the Torah (Leviticus 27), and an entire tractate, *Arakhin*, is devoted to it. There is a fundamental difference between one who vows to give the monetary worth of a particular person and one who vows to donate his valuation. The former is a vow to donate the monetary value of that person, which is typically determined by his worth in the slave market. In that regard, everyone agrees that one taken to be executed has no monetary value. Valuations, in contrast, are unrelated to one's worth on the slave market, but are fixed sums determined by the age and gender of the subject. The dispute, then, is whether the legal status of one taken to be executed is that of a dead person, who has no valuation, or whether as long as he remains alive he can still be valuated.

Severe penalties of death – מִיתוֹת חֲמוּרוֹת: Rashi and *Tosafot* disagree over whether a murderer is considered one whose punishment is lenient or one whose punishment is severe. They both agree, though, that the determining factor of severity or leniency is whether there is atonement for unwitting transgressors. If that is the case, why doesn't the Gemara explicitly distinguish between capital crimes for unwitting sinners, for which there is atonement, and capital crimes for which there is no atonement; why refer to them cryptically as severe and lenient? Moreover, those transgressions characterized in the Gemara as lenient, e.g., performing prohibited labor on Shabbat, are typically punishable by the more severe penalties of death, stoning, and burning. The *Shita Mekubbetzet* suggests that a prohibition with regard to which the Torah did not specify that it is punishable by *karet* receives a punishment from Heaven as well, rendering his punishment more severe than the punishment of one liable to receive *karet*.

הָנֵי מִילֵּי הֵיכָא דַּהֲרָגוֹ דֶּרֶךְ עֲלִיָּיה, שֶׁלֹּא נִיתְּנָה שִׁגְגָתוֹ לְכַפָּרָה. אֲבָל הֲרָגוֹ דֶּרֶךְ יְרִידָה, דְּנִיתְּנָה שִׁגְגָתוֹ לְכַפָּרָה, אֵימָא נִישְׁקוֹל מָמוֹנָא מִינֵּיהּ וְנִיפַּטְרֵיהּ, קָא מַשְׁמַע לָן.

this principle, that one cannot pay in lieu of execution, **applies only when one** intentionally **killed him in an upward motion,**[NH] **for which no atonement is designated** in the Torah **for its unwitting** performance. **However,** with regard to one who intentionally **killed him in a downward motion, for which atonement,** i.e., exile, **is designated** in the Torah **for its unwitting** performance, **say: Let us take money from him and exempt him.** Therefore, the phrase "any *ḥerem*" **teaches us** that even in that case there is no payment in lieu of execution.

אֲמַר לֵיהּ רָבָא: הָא – מִדְּתָנָא דְּבֵי חִזְקִיָּה נָפְקָא, דְּתָנָא דְּבֵי חִזְקִיָּה: מַכֵּה אָדָם וּמַכֵּה בְהֵמָה,

Rava said to him: That principle **is derived** from that which the Sage **of the school of Ḥizkiyya taught,**[N] **as** the Sage **of the school of Ḥizkiyya taught:** The verse juxtaposes the cases of **one who smites a person, and one who smites an animal** (Leviticus 24:21).

מַה מַּכֵּה בְהֵמָה לֹא חִלַּקְתָּ בּוֹ בֵּין שׁוֹגֵג לְמֵזִיד, בֵּין מִתְכַּוֵּין לְשֶׁאֵין מִתְכַּוֵּין, בֵּין דֶּרֶךְ יְרִידָה לְדֶרֶךְ עֲלִיָּיה, לְפוֹטְרוֹ מָמוֹן אֶלָּא לְחַיְּיבוֹ מָמוֹן, אַף מַכֵּה אָדָם לֹא תַּחֲלוֹק בּוֹ בֵּין שׁוֹגֵג לְמֵזִיד, בֵּין מִתְכַּוֵּין לְשֶׁאֵין מִתְכַּוֵּין, בֵּין דֶּרֶךְ יְרִידָה לְדֶרֶךְ עֲלִיָּיה, לְחַיְּיבוֹ מָמוֹן אֶלָּא לְפוֹטְרוֹ מָמוֹן!

Just as in the case of one **who smites an animal, you did not distinguish between** one who did so **unwittingly and** one who did so **intentionally; between** one who acted **with intent and one who** acted **with no intent; between** one who smites **in** the course of **a downward motion and** one who smites **in** the course of **an upward motion;** and in all those cases it is not **to exempt** him from paying **money but rather to obligate him to** pay **money; so too in** the case of one **who smites a person: Do not distinguish between** one who did so **unwittingly and** one who did so **intentionally; between** one who acted **with intent and one who** acted **with no intent; between** one who smites **in** the course of **a downward motion and** one who smites **in** the course of **an upward motion;** and in all those cases it is not **to obligate him** to pay **money but rather to exempt him** from paying **money.** Apparently, one who kills another in any manner is exempt from payment, and therefore no additional verse is required to derive that principle.

אֶלָּא אֲמַר רָמִי בַּר חָמָא: אִיצְטְרִיךְ; סָלְקָא דַּעְתָּךְ אָמִינָא: הָנֵי מִילֵּי – הֵיכָא דְּסִימֵּא אֶת עֵינוֹ וַהֲרָגוֹ בָּהּ, אֲבָל הֵיכָא דְּסִימֵּא אֶת עֵינוֹ וַהֲרָגוֹ בְּדָבָר אַחֵר – אֵימָא נִישְׁקוֹל מָמוֹנָא מִינֵּיהּ. אֲמַר לֵיהּ רָבָא: הָא נַמִי מֵאִידָּךְ תַּנָּא דְּבֵי חִזְקִיָּה נָפְקָא. דְּתָנָא דְּבֵי חִזְקִיָּה: "עַיִן תַּחַת עַיִן" וְלֹא עַיִן וְנֶפֶשׁ תַּחַת עַיִן!

Rather, Rami bar Ḥama said that the phrase "any *ḥerem*" (Leviticus 27:29) **is necessary, as it might enter your mind to say** that **this** *halakha*, that one who is liable to be executed is exempt from payment, **applies only** in a case **where one blinded** another's **eye and killed him with** that same blow. **However,** in a case **where one blinded** another's **eye and killed him by** means of a **different** blow, **say: Let us take money from him** to pay the damage inflicted to the eye. Therefore, the verse teaches that this is not the case. **Rava said to him: This** case of one who blinded another's eye and killed him **is also derived from** that which **another** ***tanna*** **of the school of Ḥizkiyya** taught, **as the Sage of the school of Ḥizkiyya taught** that the verse states: **"An eye for an eye"** (Exodus 21:24), from which it may be inferred, **but not an eye and a life**[NH] **for an eye.** When he gives his life for killing another while blinding him, he need not pay the worth of the eye as well.

NOTES

When one intentionally killed him in an upward motion – הֵיכָא דַּהֲרָגוֹ דֶּרֶךְ עֲלִיָּיה: *Tosafot* note that killing in an upward motion is considered a less severe crime than killing in a downward motion. The Rambam maintains that this is because an accident of this kind is unusual and it cannot be attributed to negligence. However, *Tosafot* continue, here only one particular aspect of the comparison is under consideration, whether or not atonement is available to one who commits this transgression. Other stringent or lenient elements are not taken into account. The reasoning is that if the Torah provided a remedy for the sin other than the prescribed punishment, it stands to reason that atonement for his transgression could be achieved through monetary payment.

It is derived from that which the Sage of the school of Ḥizkiyya taught – מִדְּתָנָא דְּבֵי חִזְקִיָּה נָפְקָא: Rashi follows his earlier explanation: The main point of the derivation of the Sage of the school of Ḥizkiyya is that there is no monetary payment for violating any prohibition whose violation is punishable by death when it is performed intentionally. According to this, clearly no special derivation is required with regard to one who kills in a downward motion. However, according to the Rambam and others, who maintain that the Sage of the school of Ḥizkiyya is teaching that one does not receive two punishments, the Gemara's statement is difficult, as theoretically, one could be obligated to pay money and at the same time be exempt from any other punishment. The commentaries answer that according to all opinions, the *halakha* is derived from both the statement of the school of Ḥizkiyya and the derivation from the verse "And yet no harm follow" (Exodus 21:22).

An eye for an eye, but not an eye and a life, etc. – עַיִן תַּחַת עַיִן וְלֹא עַיִן וְנֶפֶשׁ וכו׳: This statement of the school of Ḥizkiyya is unrelated to liability for two punishments; rather, as explained by Rashi, it is one of the proofs that the verse "An eye for an eye" is not to be interpreted literally. Were the punishment of one who injured another's eye to have his own eye injured, there is the risk that he might die as a result, meaning that it was an eye and a life for an eye. The early commentaries therefore questioned the relevance of this source to the matter under discussion.

Various explanations of that relevance were proposed. *Tosafot* maintain that the point is from the continuation of the statement of the school of Ḥizkiyya. Just as one does not punished with an eye and a life for an eye, so too, one is not punished with a life and an eye for a life. Others explain that the principle underlying this statement of the school of Ḥizkiyya is that one does not receive two punishments for transgressions committed simultaneously (Rosh; Rabbi Aharon HaLevi; Ritva). An additional interpretation, attributed to one of the Tosafists, is that this is a form of juxtaposition: Just as with regard to the eye of the attacker, he is punished only with payment for one eye, so too, with regard to the eye of the victim, only one punishment is meted out. The Ritva cites Rabbeinu Menaḥem's version of the text: And not an eye for an eye and a life, which is explained like the explanations of the early commentaries.

HALAKHA

Killed him in an upward motion – הֲרָגוֹ דֶּרֶךְ עֲלִיָּיה: One who unintentionally kills another in an upward motion is not liable to be exiled, as detailed in the second chapter of tractate *Makkot* (Rambam *Sefer Nezikim*, *Hilkhot Rotze'aḥ* 6:13).

Not an eye and a life – לֹא עַיִן וְנֶפֶשׁ: One who injures another is not punished by having the same injury inflicted upon him; rather, he pays for the damage he caused. The reason is that inflicting an injury could cause the attacker's death. See *Bava Kama* 84a, where the Gemara derives this principle from this verse (Rambam *Sefer Nezikim*, *Hilkhot Ḥovel* 1:3).

אֶלָּא אֲמַר רַב אַשִׁי: אִיצְטְרִיךְ; סָלְקָא דַּעְתָּךְ אָמִינָא: הוֹאִיל וְחִידּוּשׁ הוּא שֶׁחִידְּשָׁה תּוֹרָה בִּקְנָס, אַף עַל גַּב דְּמִיקְטִיל מְשַׁלֵּם – קָא מַשְׁמַע לָן. וּלְרַבָּה דַּאֲמַר: חִידּוּשׁ הוּא שֶׁחִידְּשָׁה תּוֹרָה בִּקְנָס, אַף עַל גַּב דְּמִיקְטִיל מְשַׁלֵּם, הַאי "כָּל חֵרֶם" מַאי עָבֵיד לֵיהּ? סָבַר לַהּ כְּתַנָּא קַמָּא דְּרַבִּי חֲנַנְיָא בֶּן עֲקַבְיָא.

Rather, after the Gemara rejected the above explanations, **Rav Ashi said:**[N] The phrase "any *ḥerem*" is nonetheless **necessary,** as **it might enter your mind to say: Since it is a novel element that the Torah introduced with regard to** the payment of a **fine,** which is not payment for any damage caused but is a Torah decree, in that case, **even though he is killed he pays** the fine. Therefore, the verse **teaches us** that one who is executed is exempt from payment of the fine. The Gemara asks: **And according to Rabba, who said** that this is indeed the *halakha*: Since **it is a novel element that the Torah introduced with regard to** the payment of **a fine, even though he is killed he pays** the fine, **what does** he **do with this** phrase: **"Any *ḥerem*"?** The Gemara answers: Rabba **holds** with regard **to** this matter **in accordance with** the opinion of **the first *tanna*,** who disagrees with **Rabbi Ḥananya ben Akavya** and explains that the phrase "Any *ḥerem*" teaches that the vow one takes to donate the valuation of one being taken to his execution is not binding.

מתני׳ נַעֲרָה שֶׁנִּתְאָרְסָה וְנִתְגָּרְשָׁה, רַבִּי יוֹסֵי הַגְּלִילִי אוֹמֵר: אֵין לָהּ קְנָס, רַבִּי עֲקִיבָא אוֹמֵר: יֵשׁ לָהּ קְנָס, וּקְנָסָהּ לְעַצְמָהּ.

MISHNA With regard to **a young woman who was betrothed and divorced,**[NH] and then raped, **Rabbi Yosei HaGelili says: She does not** receive payment of a **fine** for her rape. **Rabbi Akiva says: She** receives payment of a **fine** for her rape **and her fine** is paid **to herself,** not her father, as since she was betrothed and divorced she is no longer subject to her father's authority.

גמ׳ מַאי טַעְמָא דְּרַבִּי יוֹסֵי הַגְּלִילִי? אָמַר קְרָא "אֲשֶׁר לֹא אוֹרָשָׂה", הָא אוֹרָסָה – אֵין לָהּ קְנָס. וְרַבִּי עֲקִיבָא: "אֲשֶׁר לֹא אוֹרָשָׂה" – לְאָבִיהָ, הָא אוֹרָסָה – לְעַצְמָהּ,

GEMARA **What is the rationale** for the opinion of **Rabbi Yosei HaGelili?** It is as **the verse states:** "If a man finds a young woman who is a virgin **who was not betrothed"** (Deuteronomy 22:28), from which it may be inferred: If **she was betrothed she does not have** a **fine** for rape. The Gemara asks: **And** how does **Rabbi Akiva** explain this verse? The Gemara answers that the verse states: If it is a young woman **who was not betrothed,** the fine is paid **to her father,** from which it may be inferred: If **she was betrothed,** the fine is paid **to** the betrothed woman **herself.**

אֶלָּא מֵעַתָּה "נַעֲרָה" וְלֹא בּוֹגֶרֶת, הָכִי נַמִי דִּלְעַצְמָהּ? "בְּתוּלָה" וְלֹא בְּעוּלָה, הָכִי נַמִי דִּלְעַצְמָהּ? אֶלָּא, לְגַמְרֵי – הָכָא נַמִי לְגַמְרֵי!

The Gemara asks: **But if** that is **so,** that the inference from the verse is that the fine is levied on one who rapes **a young woman and not** on one who rapes **a grown woman,**[N] **so too,** there is the *halakha* in the latter case that the fine is paid **to** the grown woman **herself.** Similarly, with regard to the inference that the fine is levied on one who rapes **a virgin and not** on one who rapes **a non-virgin, so too,** there is the *halakha* that in the latter case the fine is paid **to** the non-virgin **herself.** A distinction of that kind has never been encountered. **Rather,** with regard to a grown woman and a non-virgin, the rapist is **completely** exempt from paying the fine; **here too,** with regard to a betrothed woman, the rapist is **completely** exempt from paying the fine.

אָמַר לָךְ רַבִּי עֲקִיבָא: הַאי "לֹא אוֹרָשָׂה" מִיבָּעֵי לֵיהּ לְכִדְתַנְיָא: "אֲשֶׁר לֹא אוֹרָשָׂה" – פְּרָט לְנַעֲרָה שֶׁנִּתְאָרְסָה וְנִתְגָּרְשָׁה, שֶׁאֵין לָהּ קְנָס, דִּבְרֵי רַבִּי יוֹסֵי הַגְּלִילִי. רַבִּי עֲקִיבָא אוֹמֵר: יֵשׁ לָהּ קְנָס, וּקְנָסָהּ לְאָבִיהָ. וְהַדִּין נוֹתֵן: הוֹאִיל וְאָבִיהָ זַכַּאי בְּכֶסֶף קִידּוּשֶׁיהָ, וְאָבִיהָ זַכַּאי בְּכֶסֶף קְנָסָהּ, מַה כֶּסֶף קִידּוּשֶׁיהָ, אַף עַל פִּי שֶׁנִּתְאָרְסָה וְנִתְגָּרְשָׁה – לְאָבִיהָ, אַף כֶּסֶף קְנָסָהּ, אַף עַל פִּי שֶׁנִּתְאָרְסָה וְנִתְגָּרְשָׁה – לְאָבִיהָ.

The Gemara answers: **Rabbi Akiva** could have **said to you** that **this** verse: **"Who was not betrothed," is required by him** to teach another *halakha* **that is taught** in a different *baraita*. **"Who was not betrothed"** (Deuteronomy 22:28) comes to **exclude a young woman who was betrothed and divorced** and establish **that she does not** receive payment of a **fine** for her rape; this is **the statement of Rabbi Yosei HaGelili. Rabbi Akiva says: She** receives payment of a **fine** for her rape, **and her fine** goes **to her father,** contrary to the ruling attributed to Rabbi Akiva in the mishna. **And** ostensibly, no verse is required to derive this *halakha*, as **logic dictates** that it is so: **Since her father is entitled to the money of her betrothal**[N] if she is betrothed before she becomes a grown woman, **and** likewise **her father is entitled to the money of her fine; just as the money of her** subsequent **betrothal** as a young woman, **even though she was betrothed and divorced,** is paid **to her father,**[H] **so too, the money of her fine, although she was betrothed and divorced,** is paid **to her father.**

NOTES

Rather, Rav Ashi said, etc. – אֶלָּא אֲמַר רַב אַשִׁי וכו׳: If, as Rav Ashi claims, the phrase "Any *ḥerem*" refers to the case of one who is liable to be executed and to pay a fine, it should have been cited as proof in the mishna, which deals with the fine of a rapist. Why did the mishna cite proof from the verse "And yet no harm follow"? One answer is that the mishna established a principle that one is exempt from payment, even payment of a fine, for a transgression punishable by death, and the *tanna* did not cite all relevant verses. Alternatively, since there is proof for the basic *halakha* from the verse that he cited, the *tanna* did not cite the verse that refers to that particular detail (Rabbi Aharon HaLevi; Ritva).

Who was betrothed and divorced – שֶׁנִּתְאָרְסָה וְנִתְגָּרְשָׁה: The same *halakha* applies if she was betrothed and widowed. Rabbi Yosei HaGelili does not agree with Rabbi Akiva even in that case, but consistently maintains that a young woman who was once betrothed is not entitled to the fine (*Shita Mekubbetzet*).

A young woman and not a grown woman, etc. – נַעֲרָה וְלֹא בּוֹגֶרֶת וכו׳: Rashi notes that since there is no source that requires payment of a fine to a grown woman or a non-virgin, even Rabbi Akiva agrees with this *halakha*. He does not, however, explain why Rabbi Akiva agrees with this *halakha*. One approach is that since ultimately there is a verbal analogy between the seduced and raped woman, the words "young woman" and "virgin" that appear in both passages come to emphasize that only a young woman who is a virgin is entitled to the fine (see *Or Same'aḥ*).

Since her father is entitled to the money of her betrothal – הוֹאִיל וְאָבִיהָ זַכַּאי בְּכֶסֶף קִידּוּשֶׁיהָ: This is problematic, as there is a distinction between a father's right to the money received for his daughter's betrothal and his right to her fine if she is raped. In the case of betrothal, he has the right to betroth her to the man of his choice, but he does not have the right to give her to a man for intercourse outside the context of marriage. Why, then, does he receive the money paid as a fine for her rape? One answer is that Rabbi Akiva maintains that the father's right to the money received for his daughter's betrothal is based on a source other than his discretionary rights with regard to her betrothal, and therefore just as the money of her betrothal goes to her father, so does her fine. As the Meiri stated, betrothal does not release a daughter from her father's authority (see *Shita Mekubbetzet*).

HALAKHA

A young woman who was betrothed and divorced – נַעֲרָה שֶׁנִּתְאָרְסָה וְנִתְגָּרְשָׁה: The fine of one who raped or seduced a girl who was betrothed and divorced is paid to her, as the *halakha* is in accordance with the opinion of Rabbi Akiva in disputes with an individual *tanna* (Rif; Rambam *Sefer Nashim, Hilkhot Na'ara Betula* 2:16).

The money of her betrothal is paid to her father – כֶּסֶף קִידּוּשֶׁיהָ לְאָבִיהָ: With regard to a daughter who was betrothed and divorced or widowed, as long as she remains a young woman, the money of any subsequent betrothal belongs to her father (Rambam *Sefer Nashim, Hilkhot Ishut* 3:11; *Shulḥan Arukh, Even HaEzer* 37:1).

אִם כֵּן, מַה תַּלְמוּד לוֹמַר "אֲשֶׁר לֹא אוֹרָשָׂה" – מוּפְנֶה לְהַקִּישׁ לוֹ, וְלָדוּן הֵימֶנּוּ גְּזֵירָה שָׁוָה: נֶאֱמַר כָּאן "אֲשֶׁר לֹא אוֹרָשָׂה" וְנֶאֱמַר לְהַלָּן "אֲשֶׁר לֹא אוֹרָשָׂה" מַה כָּאן חֲמִשִּׁים – אַף לְהַלָּן חֲמִשִּׁים; וּמַה לְהַלָּן שְׁקָלִים – אַף כָּאן שְׁקָלִים.

If so, and the *halakha* can be logically inferred, **why does the verse state: "Who was not betrothed"?** This verse is **free,** as it is superfluous in its own context, **and** it is written **to liken** another case to it, **and to derive from it a verbal analogy: It is stated here** with regard to a woman who was raped: **"Who was not betrothed," and it is stated below:** "And if a man seduce a virgin **who was not betrothed"** (Exodus 22:15). **Just as here,** with regard to rape, the Torah specifies that the payment is **fifty** silver pieces (Deuteronomy 22:29), **so too below,** with regard to seduction, the payment is **fifty. And just as below,** with regard to seduction, the payment is in **shekels,** as it is written: "He shall weigh [*yishkol*] money" (Exodus 22:16), **so too here,** the payment is in **shekels.**

וְרַבִּי עֲקִיבָא, מַאי חָזֵית דְּ"אֲשֶׁר לֹא אוֹרָשָׂה" לִגְזֵירָה שָׁוָה, וּ"בְתוּלָה" לְמַעוּטֵי בְּעוּלָה,

The Gemara asks: **And Rabbi Akiva, what did you see** that led you to utilize the phrase: **"Who was not betrothed" for a verbal analogy, and** the term **"virgin" to exclude a non-virgin** from the fine?

Perek **III**
Daf **38** Amud **b**

אֵימָא "בְּתוּלָה" – לִגְזֵירָה שָׁוָה וַ"אֲשֶׁר לֹא אוֹרָסָה" – פְּרָט לְנַעֲרָה שֶׁנִּתְאָרְסָה וְנִתְגָּרְשָׁה!

Say to the contrary; the term **"virgin,"** written with regard to both rape and seduction, is **to** derive **a verbal analogy,**[N] and not to exclude a non-virgin, **and** the phrase **"Who was not betrothed"** will be interpreted as Rabbi Yosei HaGelili interpreted it, to **exclude a young woman who was betrothed and divorced.**

מִסְתַּבְּרָא "אֲשֶׁר לֹא אוֹרָסָה" לִגְזֵירָה שָׁוָה, שֶׁהֲרֵי אֲנִי קוֹרֵא בָּהּ "נַעֲרָה בְתוּלָה". אַדְּרַבָּה, "בְּתוּלָה" לִגְזֵירָה שָׁוָה, שֶׁהֲרֵי אֲנִי קוֹרֵא בָּהּ "אֲשֶׁר לֹא אוֹרָסָה"! מִסְתַּבְּרָא, הָא – אִישְׁתַּנֵּי גּוּפָהּ, וְהָא – לָא אִישְׁתַּנֵּי גּוּפָהּ.

The Gemara answers: **It stands to reason** that the phrase **"Who was not betrothed"** is utilized **to** derive **a verbal analogy,** and not to exclude one who was betrothed and divorced, **as** even after the divorce **I can** still **read** the phrase **"A young woman who is a virgin"** as applying **to her.** The Gemara asks: **On the contrary,** utilize the term **virgin to** derive **a verbal analogy, as** even if she is not a virgin, **I can** still **read** the phrase **"Who was not betrothed"** as applying **to her.** The Gemara answers: **It stands to reason** that the term "virgin" excludes a non-virgin, and the phrase "Who was not betrothed" is utilized to derive a verbal analogy, as **this** woman who engaged in relations, **her body changed,**[N] **and that** woman who was betrothed and divorced, **her body did not change,** and therefore her status with regard to the fine should similarly not change.

וְרַבִּי יוֹסֵי הַגְּלִילִי הַאי סְבָרָא מְנָא לֵיהּ? נָפְקָא לֵיהּ מִדְּתַנְיָא: "כֶּסֶף יִשְׁקוֹל כְּמוֹהַר הַבְּתוּלוֹת" – שֶׁיְּהֵא זֶה כְּמוֹהַר הַבְּתוּלוֹת, וּמוֹהַר הַבְּתוּלוֹת כָּזֶה.

The Gemara asks: **And from where** does **Rabbi Yosei HaGelili** derive **this conclusion** with regard to the amount of the payment for seduction and the type of money used in the payment for rape? The Gemara responds: **He derives it from that which was taught** in a *baraita* that it is written with regard to seduction: **"He shall weigh money like the dowry of the virgins"** (Exodus 22:16), from which it is derived **that this** fine for seduction **will be like the dowry** paid **to the virgins** elsewhere for rape, fifty silver coins, **and the dowry** paid **to the virgins** for rape **will be like this** fine for seduction in shekels.

NOTES

Say virgin is to derive a verbal analogy – אֵימָא בְּתוּלָה לִגְזֵירָה שָׁוָה: There is a fundamental difficulty, as this question runs counter to one of the basic principles of verbal analogy, i.e., one may not derive a verbal analogy on his own; only those he has received as a tradition from his teachers are valid. All verbal analogies are based on ancient tradition, like a *halakha* transmitted to Moses from Sinai. Yet here, and in several other places, there appears to be no established tradition. The early commentaries suggest several answers. One approach (Ritva) is that there was a tradition linking two verses by verbal analogy, but it was not clear which particular words served as the basis of the analogy (see *Tosafot*). Others maintain that the terms in the analogy were also part of the tradition, but the meaning of the analogy was not always clear (see *Shita Mekubbetzet*).

This woman, her body changed – הָא אִישְׁתַּנֵּי גּוּפָהּ: This change is obvious in the case of a non-virgin. With regard to a grown woman, some commentaries explain that her body is also considered to have undergone changes over time, affecting her status as a virgin (see *Shita Mekubbetzet*).

קַשְׁיָא דְּרַבִּי עֲקִיבָא אַדְּרַבִּי עֲקִיבָא! תְּרֵי תַּנָּאֵי וְאַלִּיבָּא דְּרַבִּי עֲקִיבָא.

§ The Gemara comments: It is **difficult** as there is a contradiction between one statement **of Rabbi Akiva** and another statement **of Rabbi Akiva.**[N] In the mishna he ruled that the fine for the rape of a young woman who was betrothed and divorced is paid to the woman, and in the *baraita* he ruled that it is paid to her father. The Gemara answers: These are conflicting traditions of **two *tanna'im* in accordance with** the opinion of **Rabbi Akiva.**

בִּשְׁלָמָא רַבִּי עֲקִיבָא דְּמַתְנִיתִין – לָא אָתְיָא גְּזֵירָה שָׁוָה וּמַפְּקָא לֵיהּ לִקְרָא מִפְּשָׁטֵיהּ לְגַמְרֵי, אֶלָּא לְרַבִּי עֲקִיבָא דְּבָרַיְיתָא – אָתְיָא גְּזֵירָה שָׁוָה וּמַפְּקָא מִפְּשָׁטֵיהּ לְגַמְרֵי!

The Gemara observes: **Granted,** the statement of **Rabbi Akiva of the mishna** is reasonable, as **a verbal analogy does not come and divert the verse from its plain meaning entirely.** The plain meaning of the phrase: "Who was not betrothed" is that there is a difference between a young woman who was betrothed, who receives payment of the fine, and one who was not, whose father receives payment of the fine. **However,** according **to Rabbi Akiva of the *baraita*,** does **a verbal analogy come and divert the verse from its plain meaning entirely,**[N] and teach that there is no difference at all between a young woman who was betrothed and one who was not?

אֲמַר רַב נַחְמָן בַּר יִצְחָק: קְרִי בֵּיהּ "אֲשֶׁר לֹא אֲרוּסָה". אֲרוּסָה בַּת סְקִילָה הִיא! סָלְקָא דַּעְתָּךְ אָמִינָא: הוֹאִיל וְחִידּוּשׁ הוּא שֶׁחִידְּשָׁה תּוֹרָה בִּקְנָס, אַף עַל גַּב דְּמִיקְּטִיל – מְשַׁלֵּם.

Rav Naḥman bar Yitzḥak said: Interpret the verse as: **Who is not betrothed.**[N] It does not mean that the young woman was not betrothed in the past, rather, that she is not currently betrothed. The Gemara asks: There is no need for a verse to derive that the rapist is exempt from paying a fine if the young woman is betrothed, as the rape of **a betrothed** young woman **is** punishable **by stoning,** and the rapist is certainly exempt from paying the fine. The Gemara answers: As **it might enter your mind to say: Since it is a novel element that the Torah introduced with regard to** the payment of **a fine, even though he is killed he pays** the fine. Therefore, the verse **teaches us** that one who is executed is exempt from payment of the fine.

וּלְרַבָּה, דַּאֲמַר: חִידּוּשׁ הוּא שֶׁחִידְּשָׁה תּוֹרָה בִּקְנָס, אַף עַל גַּב דְּמִיקְּטִיל מְשַׁלֵּם – מַאי אִיכָּא לְמֵימַר? סָבַר לָהּ כְּרַבִּי עֲקִיבָא דְּמַתְנִיתִין.

The Gemara asks: **And according to Rabba, who said** that this is indeed the *halakha*: Since **it is a novel element that the Torah introduced with regard to** the payment of **a fine, even though he is killed he pays** the fine, **what is there to say?** What is derived from the verse that says that there is no fine if the young woman is betrothed? The Gemara answers: Rabba **holds in accordance with** the opinion of **Rabbi Akiva of the mishna,** who interpreted the verse as it is written, meaning that it is referring to one who was betrothed and divorced.

תָּנוּ רַבָּנַן: קְנָסָהּ לְמִי – לְאָבִיהָ, וְיֵשׁ אוֹמְרִים: לְעַצְמָהּ. לְעַצְמָהּ אַמַּאי? אֲמַר רַב חִסְדָּא: הָכָא בְּנַעֲרָה שֶׁנִּתְאָרְסָה וְנִתְגָּרְשָׁה עָסְקִינַן, וְקָמִיפַּלְגִי בִּפְלוּגְתָּא דְּרַבִּי עֲקִיבָא דְּמַתְנִיתִין וְרַבִּי עֲקִיבָא דְּבָרַיְיתָא.

The Sages taught: With regard to a young woman who was raped, **to whom** is **her fine** paid? It is paid **to her father; and some say:** It is paid **to her.** The Gemara asks: **To her? Why?** The verse explicitly states that the fine is paid to her father. **Rav Ḥisda said: Here we are dealing with a young woman who was betrothed and divorced, and** these *tanna'im* in the *baraita* **disagree in the dispute between Rabbi Akiva of the mishna and Rabbi Akiva of the *baraita*,** with regard to whom the rapist pays the fine in that case.

NOTES

It is difficult as there is a contradiction between one statement of Rabbi Akiva and another statement of Rabbi Akiva – קַשְׁיָא דְּרַבִּי עֲקִיבָא אַדְּרַבִּי עֲקִיבָא: Why did the Gemara postpone raising this contradiction instead of raising it immediately, especially as it provides no novel resolution but merely affirms that these are two opinions? In the *Shita Mekubbetzet* it is explained that since the Gemara elaborates on and provides a source for Rabbi Akiva's opinion, it was necessary to cite the *baraita* in order to explain his reasoning, which appears contrary to the verses. As the *baraita* includes a detailed explanation, the Gemara cannot be dismissed as corrupted and thereby rejected in favor of the mishna (*Shita Mekubbetzet*).

Divert the verse from its plain meaning entirely – מַפְּקָא מִפְּשָׁטֵיהּ לְגַמְרֵי: Even though the ideal verbal analogy is free, i.e., the words that serve as the basis of the analogy are superfluous in their context, the meaning of these words cannot be entirely disregarded just because they were written primarily for the verbal analogy. *Tosafot* note that there are other cases where this is more problematic, as here it is merely the inference of the verse, that a young woman who was betrothed and divorced does not receive the fine, that runs counter to the halakhic conclusion. In other places, the verbal analogy appears to subvert the meaning of the verse entirely (see *Shita Mekubbetzet*).

Interpret the verse as: Who is not betrothed – קְרִי בֵּיהּ אֲשֶׁר לֹא אֲרוּסָה: This does not require adapting the letters or vowels of this word. Rather, the expression "not betrothed" should not be understood in the past tense: Who was not betrothed; rather it is a kind of present participle: One who is not betrothed. This is a common usage in the Bible, particularly in the language of the prophets (Ritva; Rabbeinu Crescas Vidal).

HALAKHA

If one had intercourse with a young woman, and she died – בָּא עָלֶיהָ וּמֵתָה: If the young woman died before the rapist or seducer stood trial, he is exempt from the fine. The *halakha* is in accordance with the opinion of Abaye, as his conclusion is not rejected due to Rava's dilemma (Rambam *Sefer Nashim, Hilkhot Na'ara Betula* 1:15 and the *Kesef Mishna* there; *Tur, Even HaEzer* 177).

אָמַר אַבַּיֵי: בָּא עָלֶיהָ וּמֵתָה – פָּטוּר, שֶׁנֶּאֱמַר "וְנָתַן לַאֲבִי הַנַּעֲרָה" – וְלֹא לַאֲבִי מֵתָה. מִלְּתָא דִּפְשִׁיטָא לֵיהּ לְאַבַּיֵי, מִיבַּעְיָא לֵיהּ לְרָבָא.

§ **Abaye said: If one had intercourse with** a young woman, **and she died**[H] before he was sentenced, he is **exempt** from paying the fine, **as it is stated: "And the man who lay with her shall give to the father of the young woman"** (Deuteronomy 22:29), from which it is inferred, **and not to the father of a dead girl.**[N] The Gemara comments: This **matter that** was **obvious to Abaye** was **raised as a dilemma to Rava.**[N]

דְּבָעֵי רָבָא: יֵשׁ בֶּגֶר בַּקֶּבֶר אוֹ אֵין בֶּגֶר בַּקֶּבֶר? יֵשׁ בֶּגֶר בַּקֶּבֶר – וְדִבְנָהּ הָוֵי, אוֹ דִּלְמָא אֵין בֶּגֶר בַּקֶּבֶר – וְדַאֲבִיהָ הָוֵי?

As Rava raised a dilemma: Is there achievement of **grown-woman status in the grave or is there not** achievement of **grown-woman status in the grave?**[N] The *halakha* is that if a young woman is raped and the rapist did not pay the fine until she became a grown woman, the rapist pays the fine to her and not to her father. Rava's dilemma is in a case where a young woman dies and her rapist was convicted only after the time elapsed that were she alive she would have reached grown-woman status. **Is there** achievement of **grown-woman status in the grave, and** therefore she is entitled to the fine and **it is** the property of **her son**[N] as his mother's heir? **Or perhaps there is no** achievement of **grown-woman status in the grave, and the fine is** the property of **her father,** as she was a young woman when she died.

NOTES

And not to the father of a dead girl – וְלֹא לַאֲבִי מֵתָה: The early commentaries point out that the Gemara does not interpret the term young woman consistently. Sometimes it interprets a young woman as referring to one who was a young woman, even though she is already a grown woman. *Tosafot*, the Rosh, and others explain that it would have been sufficient for it to have been written in the verse: And he gives to her father. The use of the phrase "To the father of the young woman" indicates that she remains a young woman at the time of the rapist's conviction. The *Penei Yehoshua* asks: Wasn't it necessary to write: "To the father of the young woman" to exclude the father of a grown woman? Conceivably, both conclusions may be derived as they emanate from the same principle: The time that determines the father's right to the payment is when the rapist is convicted. If his daughter's status then is no longer what it was at the time of the rape, he forfeits that right.

Raised as a dilemma to Rava – מִיבַּעְיָא לֵיהּ לְרָבָא: Rashi explains later that Rava's dilemma exists neither according to the first version nor according to the second version of Rava's teaching, as in both versions he clearly maintains that death does not release the rapist from the obligation to pay the fine. Rather, the dilemma raised is according to Mar bar Rav Ashi's explanation of Rava's statement.

Is there achievement of grown-woman status in the grave – יֵשׁ בֶּגֶר בַּקֶּבֶר: There are different aspects to the definition of the daughter as a grown woman, both in terms of the changes to her body and in terms of her legal status. The dilemma of whether there is achievement of grown-woman status in the grave is not in terms of her physical state but in terms of her legal status. More specifically, it is with regard to the fact that a grown woman is entirely removed from her father's authority. The problem stems from the fact that a young woman is transformed into a grown woman six months after puberty, which is the time at which she becomes a young woman. The dilemma is as follows: Is the daughter's exit from her father's authority dependent on her development during those six months, which would lead to the conclusion that there is no achievement of grown-woman status in the grave; or is it merely dependent on the passage of time, and once the six months pass she is no longer subject to her father's authority, leading to the conclusion that there is achievement of grown-woman status in the grave (*Birkat Avraham*)?

It is the property of her son – דִּבְנָהּ הָוֵי: The Meiri notes that this son must have been born out of wedlock, as had the daughter been married, her marriage itself would have fully removed her from her father's authority, leaving him with no rights over her.

Many early commentaries question the matter of the son inheriting his mother's fine, as it appears to contradict the principle that one does not bequeath a fine to his heirs, as stated at the start of the next chapter. *Tosafot* discuss this issue at length and provide various resolutions. One approach, attributed to Rabbeinu Yitzḥak, and cited by the Ritva and other early commentaries, is that the principle that one does not bequeath a fine to his heirs refers only to a fine that is not his by right, but which he receives due to actions done to others. Consequently, a father's right to the fine paid by the man who raped his daughter is not inherited by his sons. However, since the rape victim is herself entitled to the fine, she does bequeath it to her heirs. *Tosafot* explain that the discussion here is with regard to payments accompanying the fine, e.g., compensation for humiliation and degradation, and not the fine itself. These are standard monetary payments and therefore are bequeathed to others.

Rabbi Aharon HaLevi states, in the name of Rabbi Zeraḥya HaLevi, that this statement in the Gemara is according to Rabbi Shimon's opinion that if she became a grown woman after the trial she receives the fine herself. Here too, she died after the trial but before she became a grown-woman. The dilemma then is whether she is considered to have achieved grown woman status in the grave, and therefore the money is transferred to her heirs, or perhaps she did not achieve that status, and the money remains her father's. The Rashba rejects this approach. A different interpretation is suggested by the Ramban. He contends that the statement: It is her son's, does not mean literally that it belongs to her son, as a fine cannot be bequeathed. Instead, it means that if there is achievement of grown-woman status in the grave the father no longer has rights to it, as she would have received it, which would have afforded her the theoretical right to give it away or bequeath it. The Ra'avad suggests simply that initially, Rava maintained that a person can bequeath his rights to a fine, and the Gemara could have responded by challenging that assumption. However, the Gemara cited better reasons for rejecting the dilemma. Many early commentaries, including the Ramban and the Rashba, believe that the Ra'avad's answer is the most suitable in the context of the discussion in the Gemara.

וּמִי מִעַבְּרָא? וְהָתָנֵי רַב בֵּיבָי קַמֵּיהּ דְּרַב נַחְמָן: שָׁלֹשׁ נָשִׁים מְשַׁמְּשׁוֹת בְּמוֹךְ, אֵלּוּ הֵן: קְטַנָּה, וּמְעוּבֶּרֶת, וּמֵנִיקָה; קְטַנָּה – שֶׁמָּא תִּתְעַבֵּר וְתָמוּת, מְעוּבֶּרֶת – שֶׁמָּא תַּעֲשֶׂה עוּבָּרָהּ סַנְדָּל, מֵנִיקָה – שֶׁמָּא תִּגְמוֹל אֶת בְּנָהּ.

Rava's dilemma is based on the assumption that a rape victim is able to conceive before she is a grown woman. The Gemara asks: **And can** a minor **conceive? But didn't Rav Beivai teach** a *baraita* **before Rav Naḥman:** It is permitted for **three women** to **engage in relations with** a contraceptive **resorbent.**[N] **These are they: A minor, and a pregnant woman, and a nursing woman.** The *baraita* elaborates: **A minor** may do so **lest she conceive and die;**[NB] **a pregnant** woman, **lest her** existing **fetus** be crushed[B] by another fetus and **assume** the shape of **a sandal** fish[B] if she conceives a second time; and **a nursing** woman, **lest** she conceive, causing her milk to spoil, which will lead **her** to **wean her son** prematurely, endangering his health.

וְאֵיזוֹהִי קְטַנָּה – מִבַּת אַחַת עֶשְׂרֵה שָׁנָה וְיוֹם אֶחָד עַד שְׁתֵּים עֶשְׂרֵה שָׁנָה וְיוֹם אֶחָד. פָּחוֹת מִיכֵּן וְיָתֵר עַל כֵּן – מְשַׁמֶּשֶׁת כְּדַרְכָּהּ וְהוֹלֶכֶת, דִּבְרֵי רַבִּי מֵאִיר. וַחֲכָמִים אוֹמְרִים: אַחַת זוֹ וְאַחַת זוֹ מְשַׁמֶּשֶׁת כְּדַרְכָּהּ וְהוֹלֶכֶת, וּמִן הַשָּׁמַיִם יְרַחֲמוּ, מִשּׁוּם שֶׁנֶּאֱמַר ״שׁוֹמֵר פְּתָאִים ה׳״!

And the *baraita* further states: **What is a minor girl?**[N] A minor girl is a girl **from eleven years and one day old until twelve years and one day old.** If she was **less than that** age or **more than that** age, **she proceeds and engages in relations in her usual manner;** this is **the statement of Rabbi Meir. And the Rabbis say: Both this** woman **and that** woman, i.e., in the cases of all these women, **she proceeds and engages in relations in her usual manner, and from Heaven they will have mercy** and prevent any mishap, **due to the fact that it is stated: "The Lord preserves the simple"** (Psalms 116:6).[N] Apparently, a minor is unable to conceive.

וְכִי תֵּימָא דְּאִיעַבְּרָא כְּשֶׁהִיא נַעֲרָה וְאוֹלִידָה כְּשֶׁהִיא נַעֲרָה, וּבְשִׁיתָּא יַרְחֵי מִי קָא יָלְדָה? וְהָאָמַר שְׁמוּאֵל: אֵין בֵּין נַעֲרוּת לְבַגְרוּת אֶלָּא שִׁשָּׁה חֳדָשִׁים! וְכִי תֵּימָא: בְּצִיר הוּא דְּלֵיכָּא, הָא טְפֵי אִיכָּא – הָא ״אֶלָּא״ קָאָמַר!

And if you say that she conceived when she was a young woman, twelve years old, **and gave birth when she was a young woman,** and died before she reached the status of a grown woman, can a woman **give birth in six months** after conception? **But didn't Shmuel say: There are only six months between** becoming a **young woman and becoming a grown woman?**[H] **And if you say** that Shmuel is saying that it is **less** than six months **that there is not** transition from young woman to grown woman status; however, **more** than six months **there is** transition, as different women develop differently, and therefore she could conceive and give birth while she is a young woman, that is not so, **as Shmuel said: Only,** indicating that the period is neither less nor more than six months.

BACKGROUND

Lest she conceive and die – שֶׁמָּא תִּתְעַבֵּר וְתָמוּת: A minor girl, who has not yet reached puberty, cannot conceive. However, the age of puberty is not uniform but is heavily influenced by genetics and nutrition. There are documented cases of young girls who have indeed conceived and given birth. Regardless, the younger the girl is when she conceives, the greater the danger posed by the pregnancy. Presumably, due to the narrowness of the pelvis of a young girl, she would not survive delivery of her child.

Lest her existing fetus be crushed, etc. – שֶׁמָּא...עוּבָּרָהּ: In the case of twins or simultaneous pregnancies, which are possible albeit infrequent, one of the fetuses occasionally develops more quickly and thereby severely reduces the blood supply to the other fetus. In these situations the undernourished fetus does not develop properly but remains a fleshy mass adjoined to the placenta, similar in shape to the sandal fish.

Sandal fish – סַנְדָּל: This fish is referred to today as the species sole, a group of flatfish, a name derived from the Latin solea, referring to both the fish and the sole of a shoe. The common sole, *Solea solea*, possesses an interesting feature: Both of its eyes are on the right side of its body.

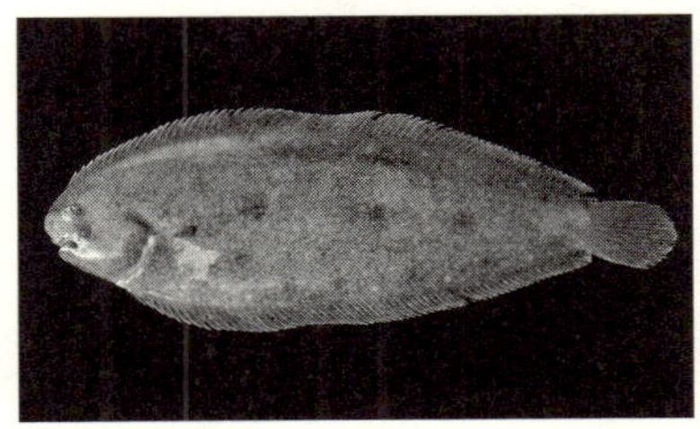

Sandal fish

HALAKHA

There are only six months between becoming a young woman and becoming a grown woman – אֵין בֵּין נַעֲרוּת לְבַגְרוּת אֶלָּא שִׁשָּׁה חֳדָשִׁים: A minor who develops the signs of puberty, two pubic hairs, becomes a young woman. Precisely six months later she becomes a grown woman, as per the statement of Shmuel (Rambam *Sefer Nashim*, *Hilkhot Ishut* 2:2; *Shulḥan Arukh*, *Even HaEzer* 234:1, and in the comment of Rema).

NOTES

It is permitted for three women to engage in relations with a contraceptive resorbent, etc. – שָׁלֹשׁ נָשִׁים מְשַׁמְּשׁוֹת בְּמוֹךְ וכו׳: The early commentaries disagree over the meaning of this statement. Some explain that she inserts the material to cover the entrance of her uterus before engaging in relations, while others maintain that she uses it after intercourse to absorb the semen (see *Tosafot*). The precise nature of this *halakha* is also a matter of dispute among the early commentaries. Rashi maintains that only these three types of women may engage in relations with this resorbent, and it is prohibited for others to do so. However, many other early commentaries, among them Rabbeinu Tam, contend that the Sages were advising or even requiring these three women to use the resorbent due to the danger involved.

Lest she conceive and die – שֶׁמָּא תִּתְעַבֵּר וְתָמוּת: The Gemara's question is clear according to this version of the text, as the indication is that a minor who conceived cannot survive the ordeal of childbirth, and certainly her child will not live. However, according to the variant reading in *Yevamot* (12b): Lest she conceive and lest she die, apparently it is possible for her to conceive and give birth. The Ramban and his students maintain that this version is according to the opinion that children are an indication of grown-woman status, suggesting that she was a grown woman when she conceived, even though both in terms of age and in terms of physical development there was no indication of puberty.

What is a minor girl – אֵיזוֹהִי קְטַנָּה: The meaning is: Whose legal status is that of a minor in terms of this *halakha*? In principle, as long as she has yet to develop the requisite physical indicators, she is still classified as a minor. Here, however, a special definition is necessary, as even Rabbi Meir concedes that under a certain age, there is no concern that a minor might conceive.

The Lord preserves the simple – שׁוֹמֵר פְּתָאִים ה׳: Many commentaries question this attitude: In a life-threatening situation, how can one say that from Heaven they will have mercy, and rely on the notion that the Lord preserves the simple, when the Torah commands that one must avoid all dangers and violate virtually all prohibitions in order to avoid endangering one's life (see *Avoda Zara* 18a)? One opinion is that the Gemara employs this approach only with regard to people conducting themselves in a conventional manner and according to the standard mode of conduct. The assumption is that God protects them, as the fact is that most people are not harmed (*Kovetz Shiurim*). Alternatively, the Gemara employs this approach only in a case where this potential danger affects only a minority of cases, and people need not take special precautions to avoid unlikely occurrences.

אֶלָּא הָכִי קָמִיבַּעְיָא לֵיהּ: יֵשׁ בֶּגֶר בַּקֶּבֶר וּפָקַע אָב, אוֹ דִּלְמָא: אֵין בֶּגֶר בַּקֶּבֶר וְלָא פָּקַע אָב? מָר בַּר רַב אַשִׁי בָּעֵי לָהּ הָכִי: מִיתָה עוֹשָׂה בַּגְרוּת, אוֹ אֵין עוֹשָׂה בַּגְרוּת? תֵּיקוּ.

Rather, Rava's dilemma is unrelated to whether or not her son inherits the fine payment. **This is his dilemma: Is there** achievement of **grown-woman status in the grave and** therefore the right of the **father** to receive payment of the fine **lapsed;** and since there is no one claiming the payment, the rapist need not pay? **Or perhaps there is no** achievement of **grown-woman** status **in the grave, and** the right of the **father did not lapse. Mar bar Rav Ashi raised the dilemma** in **this** manner: Does **death effect grown-woman status**[N] **or does it not effect grown-woman status?** No resolution was found for this dilemma, and the Gemara concludes that the dilemma **stands** unresolved.

בָּעֵי מִינֵּיהּ רָבָא מֵאַבַּיֵּי: בָּא עָלֶיהָ וְנִתְאָרְסָה מַהוּ אֲמַר לֵיהּ: מִי כְּתִיב "וְנָתַן לַאֲבִי הַנַּעֲרָה אֲשֶׁר לֹא אֲרוּסָה"? וּלְטַעֲמִיךְ, הָא דְּתַנְיָא: בָּא עָלֶיהָ וְנִשֵּׂאת – לְעַצְמָהּ, מִי כְּתִיב "וְנָתַן לַאֲבִי הַנַּעֲרָה אֲשֶׁר לֹא נְשׂוּאָה"?

On a similar note, **Rava inquired of Abaye:** If he forcibly **had intercourse with** a young woman **and she was** later **betrothed,**[HN] **what is** the *halakha*? Abaye **said to him: Is it written: And he shall give to the father of the young woman who is not betrothed?** Actually it is written: "If a man finds a young woman…who was not betrothed" (Deuteronomy 22:28), which indicates that the determining factor is whether she was betrothed before the rape and not whether she is engaged at the moment of payment. Rava asked him: **And according to your reasoning, that which was taught** in a *baraita*: If he forcibly **had intercourse** with a young woman **and she** later **married,**[N] the fine is paid **to her,** not to her father. There too, ask: **Is it written: And he shall give to the father of the young woman who is not married?** Even though the verse does not address the moment of payment, if she married the fine is paid to her.

הָכִי הַשְׁתָּא?! הָתָם, הוֹאִיל וּבַגְרוּת מוֹצִיאָה מֵרְשׁוּת אָב, וְנִישּׂוּאִין מוֹצִיאִין מֵרְשׁוּת אָב, מַה בַּגְרוּת, בָּא עָלֶיהָ וּבָגְרָה – לְעַצְמָהּ, אַף נִישּׂוּאִין, בָּא עָלֶיהָ וְנִשֵּׂאת – לְעַצְמָהּ, אֶלָּא אֵירוּסִין – מִי קָא מַפְקֵי מֵרְשׁוּתָא דְּאָב לְגַמְרֵי? הָא תְּנַן: נַעֲרָה הַמְאוֹרָסָה אָבִיהָ וּבַעְלָהּ מְפִירִין לָהּ נְדָרֶיהָ.

Abaye retorted: **How can** these cases be **compared? There,** in the case of marriage, there is reason to diverge from the plain meaning of the verse, **as grown-woman status removes her from** the **authority of the father and marriage removes her from** the **authority of the father. Just as** with regard to **grown-woman status,** if he forcibly **had intercourse with her and she became a grown woman,** the fine is paid **to her,** as it is written: "And he shall give to the father of the young woman" (Deuteronomy 22:29); **so too,** with regard to **marriage,** if he forcibly **had intercourse with her and she** later **married,**[H] the fine is paid **to her. However,** with regard to **betrothal, does it remove**[N] her **from** the **authority of the father entirely? Didn't we learn** in a mishna (*Nedarim* 66b): With regard to **a betrothed young woman, her father and her husband** together **nullify her vows?**[H] Apparently, betrothal does not remove her entirely from her father's authority, and therefore, the *halakha* with regard to betrothal cannot be derived from the *halakha* with regard to grown-woman status. Therefore, Rava's question is not difficult.

HALAKHA

If he forcibly had intercourse with a young woman and she was later betrothed – בָּא עָלֶיהָ וְנִתְאָרְסָה: If a girl who was raped or seduced was later betrothed to another, her fine and the other payments belong to her father, as betrothal does not release her from her father's authority (Rambam *Sefer Nashim, Hilkhot Na'ara Betula* 2:16; *Tur, Even HaEzer* 177).

If he forcibly had intercourse with her and she later married – בָּא עָלֶיהָ וְנִשֵּׂאת: If one who seduced or raped a young woman did not pay the fine and the accompanying payments until she became a grown woman or married, the fine and the other payments are paid to her (Rambam *Sefer Nashim, Hilkhot Na'ara Betula* 2:15).

A betrothed young woman with regard to the nullification of vows – נַעֲרָה הַמְאוֹרָסָה לְהָפֵרַת נְדָרִים: The vows of a betrothed young woman may be nullified only if they are annulled by both the father and the husband. If only one of them annulled her vow, it remains intact, as stated in the mishna in *Nedarim* cited in the Gemara (Rambam *Sefer Hafla'a, Hilkhot Nedarim* 11:9; *Shulḥan Arukh, Yoreh De'a* 374:5).

NOTES

Does death effect grown-woman status – מִיתָה עוֹשָׂה בַּגְרוּת: It is clear from Rashi and other commentaries that the question is not whether death always effects grown-woman status, or even whether she is considered a grown woman in the grave. Rather, this statement should be read in the negative: Does the father forfeit his right to the fine when she dies just as he would if she became a grown woman? The later commentaries add that the difference between these two interpretations is that if she actually were to achieve grown-woman status in the grave, her creditors could collect the debt from the fine.

If he forcibly had intercourse with a young woman and she was later betrothed – בָּא עָלֶיהָ וְנִתְאָרְסָה: The commentaries explain that this is not a question according to the opinions of Rabbi Yosei HaGelili or Rabbi Akiva cited in the *baraita*, but only according to the opinion of Rabbi Akiva of the mishna, who maintains that a betrothed woman is entitled to payment of a fine that is paid directly to her. Others maintain that Rava posed this question according to Abaye's opinion that the decisive time for determining payment of a fine is when the rapist stands trial: Does her change in status mean that she herself receives the payment?

If he forcibly had intercourse with a young woman and she later married – בָּא עָלֶיהָ וְנִשֵּׂאת: In the Jerusalem Talmud, the ruling is that even if she later married, the fine belongs to her father. According to the discussion in the Talmud there, since she was raped while still under her father's authority, the payment is to the father, even if she left his authority entirely in the interim.

Betrothal, does it remove, etc. – אֵירוּסִין מִי קָא מַפְקֵי וכו׳: The Ritva writes that the Gemara sought to cite a proof for this claim from the *halakhot* of vows, as it is clear that with regard to monetary matters, betrothal does not release her from her father's authority. The suggestion is that since payment of the fine is a Torah decree, it should be viewed as a unique *halakha* rather than a standard monetary obligation, and therefore the father could lose the right to this money upon her betrothal.

מתני׳ הַמְפַתֶּה נוֹתֵן שְׁלֹשָׁה דְּבָרִים, וְהָאוֹנֵס אַרְבָּעָה. הַמְפַתֶּה נוֹתֵן בּוֹשֶׁת וּפְגָם וּקְנָס, מוֹסִיף עָלָיו אוֹנֵס שֶׁנּוֹתֵן אֶת הַצַּעַר. מָה בֵּין אוֹנֵס לִמְפַתֶּה? הָאוֹנֵס – נוֹתֵן אֶת הַצַּעַר, וְהַמְפַתֶּה – אֵינוֹ נוֹתֵן אֶת הַצַּעַר. הָאוֹנֵס – נוֹתֵן מִיָּד, וְהַמְפַתֶּה – לִכְשֶׁיּוֹצִיא. הָאוֹנֵס – שׁוֹתֶה בַּעֲצִיצוֹ, וְהַמְפַתֶּה – אִם רָצָה לְהוֹצִיא, מוֹצִיא.

MISHNA **The seducer gives** the father of his victim **three things, and the rapist** gives the father **four.**[H] The mishna specifies: **The seducer gives** the father payments for **humiliation, degradation, and the fine. A rapist adds** an addition to **his** payments, **as he** also **gives** payment for the **pain. What** are the differences **between the** *halakha* of **a rapist and** that of **a seducer? The rapist gives** payment for **the pain, and the seducer does not give** payment for **the pain. The rapist gives** payment **immediately,**[H] **and the seducer** does not pay those payments immediately but only **when he releases** her. **The rapist drinks from his vessel** [*atzitzo*],[BLHN] i.e., marries the woman he raped, perforce, **and the seducer, if he wishes to release** her, **he releases** her.

כֵּיצַד שׁוֹתֶה בַּעֲצִיצוֹ – אֲפִילּוּ הִיא חִיגֶּרֶת, אֲפִילּוּ הִיא סוּמָא, וַאֲפִילּוּ הִיא מוּכַּת שְׁחִין. נִמְצָא בָּהּ דְּבַר עֶרְוָה, אוֹ שֶׁאֵינָהּ רְאוּיָה לָבֹא בְּיִשְׂרָאֵל – אֵינוֹ רַשַּׁאי לְקַיְּימָהּ, שֶׁנֶּאֱמַר ״וְלוֹ תִהְיֶה לְאִשָּׁה״ – אִשָּׁה הָרְאוּיָה לוֹ.

The mishna clarifies: **How does** the rapist **drink from his vessel? Even if** the woman he raped **is lame, even if she is blind, and even if she is afflicted with boils,** he is obligated to marry her and may not divorce her. However, if **a matter of licentiousness is found in her,**[H] e.g., if she committed adultery, **or if she is unfit to enter the Jewish people,** e.g., if she is a *mamzeret*, **he is not permitted to sustain her**[N] as his wife, **as it is stated: "And to him she shall be as a wife"** (Deuteronomy 22:29), from which it is inferred that she must be **a woman who is** legally **suitable for him.**

גמ׳ צַעַר דְּמַאי? אָמַר אֲבוּהּ דִּשְׁמוּאֵל: צַעַר שֶׁחֲבָטָהּ עַל גַּבֵּי קַרְקַע. מַתְקִיף לַהּ רַבִּי זֵירָא: אֶלָּא מֵעַתָּה, חֲבָטָהּ עַל גַּבֵּי שִׁירָאִין הָכִי נָמֵי דְּפָטוּר? וְכִי תֵּימָא הָכִי נָמֵי – וְהָתַנְיָא, רַבִּי שִׁמְעוֹן בֶּן יְהוּדָה אוֹמֵר מִשּׁוּם רַבִּי שִׁמְעוֹן: אוֹנֵס אֵינוֹ מְשַׁלֵּם אֶת הַצַּעַר מִפְּנֵי

GEMARA The mishna taught that a rapist pays for the pain that he caused. The Gemara asks: **For what pain**[N] is he obligated to pay? **Shmuel's father said:** It is for the **pain that** he caused when **he slammed her onto the ground** while raping her. **Rabbi Zeira** strongly **objects to this: But if** what you say is **so,** if **he slammed her onto silk, so too** is the *halakha* **that** he is **exempt** from payment for pain? **And if you say indeed** that it is **so, but isn't it taught** in a *baraita* that **Rabbi Shimon ben Yehuda says in the name of Rabbi Shimon: A rapist does not pay** for **the pain due to** the fact

BACKGROUND

Vessel [*atzitz*] – עָצִיץ: The descriptions of the sources indicate that the reference is to a ceramic or wooden vessel, usually unfinished or not completely fired in the kiln. This type of vessel was used for tasks that required a simple receptacle, but not one with exacting craftsmanship. An *atzitz* was often used for potted plants or as a chamber pot. Sometimes it was crafted from the bottom of a broken jug.

LANGUAGE

Vessel [*atzitz*] – עָצִיץ: Similar to the Arabic اصيص, *'aṣīṣ*, which has the same meaning.

HALAKHA

The seducer gives three things and the rapist four – הַמְפַתֶּה נוֹתֵן שְׁלֹשָׁה דְּבָרִים וְהָאוֹנֵס אַרְבָּעָה: One who seduces a virgin must pay the fine, and the payments for humiliation and degradation. The rapist pays these and must compensate her for her pain as well (Rambam *Sefer Nashim, Hilkhot Na'ara Betula* 2:7; *Shulḥan Arukh, Even HaEzer* 177:1).

The rapist gives payment immediately – הָאוֹנֵס נוֹתֵן מִיָּד: The rapist must pay the four indemnities for which he is liable immediately, and then marry the young woman. In contrast, the seducer pays the fine only if he opts not to take her as a wife (Rambam *Sefer Nashim, Hilkhot Na'ara Betula* 2:7).

Drinks from his vessel – שׁוֹתֶה בַּעֲצִיצוֹ: A man who rapes a virgin is obligated to marry her if she and her father consent. He must do so even if she is lame or blind, and he may never divorce her against her wishes (Rambam *Sefer Nashim, Hilkhot Na'ara Betula* 1:3; *Shulḥan Arukh, Even HaEzer* 177:3).

If a matter of licentiousness is found in her – נִמְצָא בָּהּ דְּבַר עֶרְוָה: If his rape victim was forbidden to him, even if the prohibition is by rabbinic law, he is not permitted to marry. Similarly, if he married her and she acted in a licentious manner, he is required to divorce her (Rambam *Sefer Nashim, Hilkhot Na'ara Betula* 1:5; *Shulḥan Arukh, Even HaEzer* 177:4).

NOTES

Drinks from his vessel – שׁוֹתֶה בַּעֲצִיצוֹ: This refers to a rudimentary earthenware vessel, fit only for potted plants (Rambam's Commentary on the Mishna) or other base uses, such as sewage and the like (*Talmidei Rabbeinu Yona*; see *Shita Mekubbetzet*). In short, this is not a vessel used for drinking and was chosen by the *tanna* for that very reason. Since this man chose to drink from a lowly vessel, he must continue to do so.

The Maharik writes that the *halakha* that a rapist must marry his victim serves to protect the daughters of Israel, so that powerful men will not abuse them. The Radbaz therefore states that this should not be viewed as a penalty but as a positive mitzva. Consequently, even if there were no witnesses and he admits to the rape and is thereby exempted from paying the fine, he is obligated to marry her. As explained above, the reason is that he drinks from his vessel. Once he raped her, he can no longer claim that he does not desire her.

He is not permitted to sustain her – אֵינוֹ רַשַּׁאי לְקַיְּימָהּ: The *tanna* uses this expression in order to include both cases: That of a rapist who married her and later found her behaving in a licentious manner, necessitating their divorce; and one who cannot marry her in the first place because she is prohibited to him. Instead of saying that he divorces her or he may not marry her, the *tanna* states: He may not sustain her (Rashba).

For what pain – צַעַר דְּמַאי: *Tosafot* ask a simple question: Were the Sages unaware that the first time a virgin engages in intercourse it is painful? That seems to be indicated by their question. *Tosafot* and other early commentaries answer that it is clear that this *tanna* does not consider the pain of the tearing of the hymen sufficient to render one liable for payment, as otherwise a seducer would also be deemed liable.

BACKGROUND

Pain – צַעַר: Pain experienced during sexual intercourse might be the result of a lack of lubrication or due to vaginal muscle contractions. Typically, if a woman willingly engages in intercourse, those two problems do not exist, or at least are greatly mitigated. However, a woman who is raped does not want intercourse and does not cooperate in performance of the act, and therefore she could very well experience intense pain that could lead to actual injury. The same applies to a minor girl, as described in *Tosafot*. In contrast, the pain experienced by the breaking of the hymen is not as intense and, as the Gemara describes, is nothing more than a light wound in a sensitive area.

שֶׁסּוֹפָהּ לְהִצְטַעֵר תַּחַת בַּעְלָהּ, אָמְרוּ לוֹ: אֵינוֹ דּוֹמֶה נִבְעֶלֶת בְּאוֹנֶס לְנִבְעֶלֶת בְּרָצוֹן! אֶלָּא אָמַר רַב נַחְמָן אָמַר רַבָּה בַּר אֲבוּהּ: צַעַר שֶׁל פִּיסּוּק הָרַגְלַיִם. וְכֵן הוּא אוֹמֵר: ״וַתְּפַשְּׂקִי אֶת רַגְלַיִךְ לְכׇל עוֹבֵר״.

that she will ultimately suffer[N] the same pain during intercourse when **under** the authority of **her husband? They said to him: One who has intercourse against** her **will is not comparable to one who has intercourse willingly.** Apparently, the pain associated with rape is a direct result of the forced intercourse and not of some associated cause.[B] **Rather, Rav Naḥman said** that **Rabba bar Avuh said:** It refers to the **pain of spreading** her **legs** during intercourse. **And likewise,** the verse **says:**[N] **"And you opened your legs to every passerby"** (Ezekiel 16:25).

אִי הָכִי מְפוּתָּה נָמֵי! אָמַר רַב נַחְמָן אָמַר רַבָּה בַּר אֲבוּהּ: מָשָׁל דִּמְפוּתָּה לְמָה הַדָּבָר דּוֹמֶה – לְאָדָם שֶׁאָמַר לַחֲבֵירוֹ: קְרַע שִׁירָאִין שֶׁלִּי וְהִפָּטֵר. שֶׁלִּי?! דַּאֲבוּהָ נִינְהוּ! אֶלָּא אָמַר רַב נַחְמָן אָמַר רַבָּה בַּר אֲבוּהּ: פִּקְחוֹת שֶׁבָּהֶן אוֹמְרוֹת: מְפוּתָּה אֵין לָהּ צַעַר.

The Gemara asks: **If so, a seduced woman** should **also**[N] be obligated to make that payment as well. **Rav Naḥman said** that **Rabba bar Avuh stated a parable: To what can** this **matter** of a seducer **be compared?** It can be compared **to a person who said to another: Tear my silk**[N] **and be exempt** from payment. Since she engaged in relations of her own volition, she certainly absolved him of payment for the pain. The Gemara asks: Tear **my** silk? It is not her silk, and therefore she may not waive payment for damage to it; **it is** the silk **of her father,** as the fine and the other payments are paid to him. **Rather, Rav Naḥman said**[N] that **Rabba bar Avuh said** that **the clever** women **among them say**[N] that a **seduced woman has no pain** during intercourse, as she is a willing participant.

NOTES

That she will ultimately suffer, etc. – שֶׁסּוֹפָהּ לְהִצְטַעֵר וכו׳: In the Jerusalem Talmud this is deemed comparable to removing the wart from someone who was planning on doing so anyway. She cannot demand compensation as she would have experienced the pain of her loss of virginity at some point. The Rabbis respond that although the act itself would have been performed eventually, her suffering is greater if it is performed against her will. In the Jerusalem Talmud, it is explained that Rabbi Shimon agrees that the rapist must pay for any pain other than the pain of the intercourse itself, e.g., if he pushed her onto thorns, as he disputes the need to pay for pain only with regard to the pain of the sexual act itself. The Ḥatam Sofer asks: Can't the woman claim that she would have never been subject to the pain of intercourse, as since a woman is not obligated to take a husband, she might never have married? He answers that since the fine is compensation for diminishing her prospects of marriage, if she claims she does not want to marry at all, she would no longer be entitled to the fine.

And likewise, the verse says, etc. – וְכֵן הוּא אוֹמֵר וכו׳: Some commentaries explain that this verse is cited in order to explain the spreading of legs to which it refers. The Ritva contends that the meaning of this expression is clear from the context; rather, the verse indicates that this act involves pain, as the prophet is castigating the Jewish people for the fact that it was willing to suffer the pain in order to engage in licentious behavior with others.

If so, a seduced woman should also – אִי הָכִי מְפוּתָּה נָמֵי: The Ramban views the Gemara here as one component of a complex question: If this pain is significant, then a seducer should also have to pay for it, and if it is not significant, the Rabbis should agree that even a rapist should be exempt. The *Shita Mekubbetzet* summarizes the question: The pain of losing her virginity is a one-time occurrence, and therefore she will not experience this pain again. The argument that she will eventually suffer pain during intercourse when under the authority of her husband does not apply to the pain of spreading her legs, as the pain she suffers now will not reduce that of any later cohabitation (see *Tosafot*).

Tear my silk – קְרַע שִׁירָאִין שֶׁלִּי: The logic is that since she suffers the pain to her own body, it is hers and she can waive her right to it (Rabbeinu Crescas Vidal; see Ritva). The *Kovetz Shiurim* explains that her forgiving the debt is insufficient to exempt the rapist for payments of humiliation and degradation, as even though the action that rendered him liable was performed on her body, her father is also affected by the humiliation and degradation. With regard to her pain, in contrast, even when the father is entitled to the payment, the pain affects her exclusively. The Ra'avad rules that the payment for the pain of rape is paid to the victim herself, not to her father.

The *Ḥakham Tzvi* explains that that although a father has the right to give his daughter away in marriage, he cannot give her away to undergo suffering. Apparently, the Torah did not entitle him to the payment for her pain. The Ran, in the next chapter, contends that since he has the right to marry her to a repulsive person, e.g., one who is afflicted with boils, with whom she would only agree to engage in intercourse unwillingly, apparently, he has the right to give her away to undergo suffering, and therefore the payment for her pain also belongs to the father.

Rather, Rav Naḥman said, etc. – אֶלָּא אָמַר רַב נַחְמָן וכו׳: The word rather indicates that Rav Naḥman's statement is not necessarily based on the previous answer with regard to the spreading of legs. Instead, it could be explained that he reverts back to the first opinion, that the pain is the pain of intercourse, and the difference between the two cases is that a seduced woman does not suffer pain. Some commentaries have a variant reading excluding the word rather (see Ritva and *Shita Mekubbetzet*). The later commentaries continue to discuss whether a seduced woman experiences no pain, as any suffering is obscured by the pleasure of the act, or whether she does experience pain but it is not taken into consideration due to her desire.

The clever women among them say, etc. – פִּקְחוֹת שֶׁבָּהֶן אוֹמְרוֹת וכו׳: The significance of clever women is not immediately apparent in this context. The *Shita Mekubbetzet* explains that a significant factor in the pain of intercourse for a woman, even the first time, is the failure to prepare her body properly. Clever women know how to prepare their bodies so that the tearing of their hymens causes merely slight discomfort, as indicated by the various metaphors cited in the Gemara.

וְהָא קָא חָזֵינַן דְּאִית לָהּ! אֲמַר אַבַּיֵי, אָמְרָה לִי אֵם: כְּמַיָּא חֲמִימֵי עַל רֵישֵׁיהּ דְּקָרְחָא. רָבָא אֲמַר: אָמְרָה לִי בַּת רַב חִסְדָּא: כִּי רִיבְדָּא דְּכוּסִילְתָּא. רַב פַּפָּא אֲמַר: אָמְרָה לִי בַּת אַבָּא סוּרָאָה: כִּי נַהֲמָא אַקּוּשָׁא בְּחִינְכֵי.

The Gemara asks: **But don't we see that** even a married woman **has** pain when she engages in sexual relations for the first time? **Abaye said: My** foster **mother told me** that the pain is **like hot water on the head of a bald** man. **Rava said:** My wife, **Rav Ḥisda's daughter, told me** that it is **like the stab of a bloodletting knife. Rav Pappa said:** My wife, **Abba Sura's daughter, told me** that it is **like** the feeling of **hard bread on the gums.** When a woman engages in intercourse willingly, the pain is negligible. Therefore, the seducer is not obligated to pay for pain.

"הָאוֹנֵס נוֹתֵן מִיָּד, הַמְפַתֶּה לִכְשֶׁיּוֹצִיא" וכו׳. לִכְשֶׁיּוֹצִיא, אִשְׁתּוֹ הִיא?! אֲמַר אַבַּיֵי: אֵימָא לִכְשֶׁלֹּא יִכְנוֹס. תַּנְיָא נַמִי הָכִי: אַף עַל פִּי שֶׁאָמְרוּ הַמְפַתֶּה נוֹתֵן לִכְשֶׁלֹּא יִכְנוֹס, בּוֹשֶׁת וּפְגָם – נוֹתֵן מִיָּד. וְאֶחָד הָאוֹנֵס וְאֶחָד הַמְפַתֶּה, בֵּין הִיא וּבֵין אָבִיהָ יְכוֹלִין לְעַכֵּב.

§ The mishna continues: **The rapist gives** payment **immediately, and the seducer when he releases her, etc.** The Gemara asks: **When he releases** her?[N] **Is she his wife?**[N] He did not yet marry her, so how can the mishna use the language of divorce? **Abaye said: Say** that he gives payment **when** he opts **not** to **marry** her.[H] If he marries her he need not pay. **That** opinion **was also taught** in a *baraita*: **Although they said** that **the seducer gives** the fine **when** he opts **not** to **marry** her, the compensation for her **humiliation and degradation he gives immediately.** The *baraita* continues: Although **both the rapist and the seducer** are obligated to marry their victim, **both she and her father**[NH] **are able to prevent** the marriage.

בִּשְׁלָמָא מְפוּתָּה – כְּתִיב "אִם מָאֵן יְמָאֵן אָבִיהָ", אֵין לִי אֶלָּא אָבִיהָ, הִיא עַצְמָהּ מִנַּיִן – תַּלְמוּד לוֹמַר "יְמָאֵן", מִכׇּל מָקוֹם.

The Gemara asks: **Granted,** with regard to **a woman who was seduced, it is written: "If her father refuses** [*maen yemaen*] to give her to him" (Exodus 22:16), and the Sages interpreted: **I have only** derived that **her father** can prevent the marriage; **from where do we** derive that **she herself** can do so? **The verse states:** *Maen yemaen,* a double verb indicating that the marriage can be prevented **in any case,** i.e., she too may do so.

אֶלָּא אוֹנֵס, בִּשְׁלָמָא אִיהִי – כְּתִיב "וְלוֹ תִהְיֶה" – מִדַּעְתָּהּ. אֶלָּא אָבִיהָ מְנָלַן?

However, from where is it derived that they can prevent the marriage in the case of **a rapist? Granted, she** herself can prevent the marriage, as **it is written: "And to him she shall be** as a wife" (Deuteronomy 22:29), and the term "shall be" indicates **with her consent. However, from where do we** derive that **her father** can prevent the marriage?

אָמַר אַבַּיֵי: שֶׁלֹּא יְהֵא חוֹטֵא נִשְׂכָּר. רָבָא אָמַר: קַל וָחוֹמֶר: וּמַה מְפַתֶּה שֶׁלֹּא עָבַר אֶלָּא עַל דַּעַת אָבִיהָ בִּלְבַד, בֵּין הִיא וּבֵין אָבִיהָ יְכוֹלִין לְעַכֵּב, אוֹנֵס שֶׁעָבַר עַל דַּעַת אָבִיהָ וְעַל דַּעַת עַצְמָהּ – לֹא כׇּל שֶׁכֵּן.

Abaye said: No verse is necessary as it stands to reason that the father too can prevent the marriage **so that a sinner will not profit.** If her father could not prevent the marriage, the rapist would acquire the right to marry the young woman despite the father's refusal, a right not accorded to one who seeks to betroth a young woman in a conventional manner. **Rava said** it is derived through **an *a fortiori* inference: Just as** in the case of **a seducer, who contravened only her father's will,** as she acquiesced to his proposition, nevertheless **both she and her father can prevent** the marriage; in the case of **a rapist, who contravened** both **her father's will and her own will, all the more so** is it **not** so that both she and her father can prevent the marriage?

HALAKHA

When does the seducer pay – מָתַי מְשַׁלֵּם הַמְפַתֶּה: A seducer pays compensation for humiliation and degradation immediately, but he pays the fine only if he does not marry his victim (Rambam *Sefer Nashim, Hilkhot Na'ara Betula* 2:7).

Both she and her father, etc. – בֵּין הִיא וּבֵין אָבִיהָ וכו׳: In the cases of both a raped and a seduced young woman, if either she or her father refuses the marriage, the rapist or seducer pays the fine and is not obligated to marry her (Rambam *Sefer Nashim, Hilkhot Na'ara Betula* 1:3).

NOTES

When he releases her – לִכְשֶׁיּוֹצִיא: The Ritva's explanation clarifies the phrase: When he releases her, in this context. He explains that it means that the man releases her in court when he declares that he does not wish to marry her.

Is she his wife – אִשְׁתּוֹ הִיא: Almost all commentaries read this expression in the form of a question: Is she his wife? If he didn't marry her yet, how can he release her? The Ra'avad, however, understands it as a statement: If he married her and she is his wife, upon their divorce he must pay her marriage contract of one hundred dinars, consistent with the Ra'avad's approach with regard to a seduced woman. The Rashba questions this interpretation, for it would mean that the sinner profited, as he paid only one hundred dinars instead of the fifty *sela* fine, which is two hundred dinars, like the dowry of virgins. Furthermore, a seducer can subvert the *halakha* by marrying and immediately divorcing her, thereby saving one hundred dinars.

Both she and her father – בֵּין הִיא וּבֵין אָבִיהָ: *Tosafot* ask: How can the young woman object? After all, her father has the right to marry her to the man of his choice. Some commentaries (Ritva; Rabbeinu Crescas Vidal) maintain that this is referring specifically to an orphan or a grown woman. They explain that the phrase: Both she and her father, refers to different cases. Sometimes she can object, if she is no longer subject to her father's authority, and in other cases, her father has the right of refusal. Others accept Rashi's explanation in tractate *Kiddushin*: Even though her refusal cannot prevent him from marrying her if her father agrees, it obligates the seducer to pay the fine immediately.

Several other interpretations are proposed by the Ran. One suggestion is that if she does not want to be his wife, although her father still retains the power to marry her to him, there is no longer a mitzva for the rapist or seducer to wed her. Alternatively, he suggests that this is a unique *halakha* in that the Torah granted her the right of refusal due to the ordeal she went through, despite the fact that in standard circumstances she cannot refuse her father's choice of a husband for her. The *Yam shel Shlomo* writes that the purpose of the statement that both she and her father can refuse is to emphasize that the mitzva to marry the victim of one's rape and seduction victim applies only to the man, but there is no mitzva incumbent on the woman or her father.

רָבָא לָא אָמַר כְּאַבָּיֵי, כֵּיוָן דְּקָא מְשַׁלֵּם קְנָס – לָאו חוֹטֵא נִשְׂכָּר הוּא. אַבָּיֵי לָא אָמַר כְּרָבָא, מְפַתֶּה דְּאִיהוּ מָצֵי מְעַכֵּב – אָבִיהָ נַמִי מָצֵי מְעַכֵּב, אוֹנֵס דְּאִיהוּ לָא מָצֵי מְעַכֵּב – אָבִיהָ נַמִי לָא מָצֵי מְעַכֵּב.

The Gemara elaborates: **Rava did not say in accordance with** the explanation of **Abaye,** as **since** the rapist **pays the fine he is not a sinner** who **profits,** as he too must pay the dowry of a virgin even if he marries her. Likewise, **Abaye did not say in accordance with** the explanation of **Rava** because in the case of **a seducer, where** the seducer himself **can prevent** the marriage, **her father can also prevent** the marriage. In the case of **a rapist, where** the rapist himself **cannot prevent** the marriage, **her father also cannot prevent** the marriage.

תַּנְיָא אִידָּךְ: אַף עַל פִּי שֶׁאָמְרוּ אוֹנֵס נוֹתֵן מִיָּד, כְּשֶׁיּוֹצִיא הוּא – אֵין לָהּ עָלָיו כְּלוּם. כְּשֶׁיּוֹצִיא? מִי מָצֵי מַפֵּיק לַהּ?! אֵימָא: כְּשֶׁתֵּצֵא הִיא – אֵין לָהּ עָלָיו כְּלוּם. מֵת – יָצָא כֶּסֶף קְנָסָהּ בִּכְתוּבָּתָהּ. רַבִּי יוֹסֵי בְּרַבִּי יְהוּדָה אוֹמֵר: יֵשׁ לָהּ כְּתוּבָּה מָנֶה.

It was taught in **another** *baraita*: **Although** the Sages **said** that **the rapist gives** payment **immediately, when he releases** her **she has no claim upon him.**[N] The Gemara asks: **When he releases** her? **Can he release her?** It is prohibited by Torah law for him to do so. Rather, emend the *baraita* and **say: When she leaves,** if she seeks to divorce him and demands a bill of divorce, **she has no** monetary **claim upon him.** Similarly, if **he died,** the **money of her fine offsets her marriage contract.**[H] The fine, which was the equivalent of the dowry of virgins, replaces her marriage contract. **Rabbi Yosei, son of Rabbi Yehuda, says:** Even a rape victim **has a marriage contract of one hundred dinars,**[N] like the marriage contract of all non-virgin wives.

בְּמַאי קָמִיפַּלְגִי? רַבָּנַן סָבְרִי: טַעְמָא מַאי תַּקִּינוּ רַבָּנַן כְּתוּבָּה – כְּדֵי שֶׁלֹּא תְּהֵא קַלָּה בְּעֵינָיו לְהוֹצִיאָהּ, וְהָא לָא מָצֵי מַפֵּיק לַהּ. וְרַבִּי יוֹסֵי בְּרַבִּי יְהוּדָה סָבַר: הָא נַמִי מְצַעֵר לַהּ עַד דְּאָמְרָה הִיא ״לָא בְּעֵינָא לָךְ״.

The Gemara asks: **With regard to what** principle **do they disagree?** The Gemara explains: **The Rabbis maintain: What is the reason** that **the Sages instituted a marriage contract** for the woman? They instituted it **so that she will not be inconsequential in his eyes,** enabling him **to** easily **divorce her.** Because divorcing her will cost money, he will not do so rashly. **And this** woman whom he raped, **he cannot release her** by Torah law, obviating the need for a marriage contract. **And Rabbi Yosei, son of Rabbi Yehuda, maintains:** With regard to **this** woman **too,** although he cannot divorce her, he can **torment her until she says: I do not want you.** When she initiates the divorce, he can divorce her. Therefore, the Sages instituted that she receives the marriage contract of a non-virgin to prevent him from doing so.

״אוֹנֵס שׁוֹתֶה בַּעֲצִיצוֹ״. אֲמַר לֵיהּ רָבָא מִפַּרְזְקִיָּא לְרַב אַשִׁי: מִכְּדִי, מִגְמַר גָּמְרִי מֵהֲדָדֵי

The mishna continues: **A rapist drinks from his vessel,** and the seducer is not obligated to marry the woman he seduced. **Rava from Parzakya said to Rav Ashi: Since** the *halakhot* of a rapist and a seducer **are derived from each other** with regard to the sum of the fine,

Perek **III**
Daf **40** Amud **a**

לְהָא מִילְּתָא נַמִי לִיגְמְרוּ מֵהֲדָדֵי! אֲמַר קְרָא: ״מָהֹר יִמְהָרֶנָּה לּוֹ לְאִשָּׁה״ לוֹ – מִדַּעְתּוֹ.

for this matter too, marrying the woman against his will, **let them be derived from each other.** Rav Ashi replied that **the verse says** with regard to a seducer: **"He shall pay a dowry for her to be a wife to him"** (Exodus 22:15);[N] **"to him"** means **in accordance with his will.**

NOTES

She has no claim upon him – אֵין לָהּ עָלָיו כְּלוּם: The Gemara provides different explanations for a divorcée and a widow because the reason for the marriage contract varies in each case. With regard to a divorcée the Sages instituted a marriage contract so that her husband would not divorce her lightly, and the Gemara therefore states that there is no need for that ordinance for a rape victim, as he cannot divorce her at all; therefore, she has no claim upon him. In the case of a widow the purpose of her marriage contract is to make her a more attractive marriage prospect, and therefore the Gemara states that she has already received the money in payment of the fine (*Tosafot*; Rosh; Ritva). The Rosh adds that even according to those who maintain that the obligation of the marriage contract of a virgin is by Torah law, since the verse states: "Like the dowry of the virgins" (Exodus 22:16), it is clear that the fine replaces the marriage contract.

The marriage contract of a raped woman – כְּתוּבַּת אֲנוּסָה: The ruling authorities disagree with regard to the basic question of whether or not a rape victim receives a marriage contract. The Rambam maintains that she is not entitled to a marriage contract, whereas the Ra'avad states that she receives a marriage contract of one hundred dinars, like any other non-virgin. The conclusion in the Jerusalem Talmud seems to support the opinion of the Ra'avad. The Gemara there discusses whether a seduced woman or a raped woman is entitled to the other conditions of a marriage contract, such as provision for her male children that predated her marriage, and sustenance for her daughters, among other stipulations.

HALAKHA

The money of her fine offsets her marriage contract – יָצָא כֶּסֶף קְנָסָהּ בִּכְתוּבָּתָהּ: The Sages did not institute a marriage contract for a raped young woman, as it is prohibited for her husband to divorce her. She does not even receive payment of the marriage contract in the event of his death, in accordance with the opinion of the first *tanna* (Rambam *Sefer Nashim, Hilkhot Na'ara Betula* 1:4; *Shulḥan Arukh, Even HaEzer* 177:3).

NOTES

He shall pay a dowry for her to be a wife to him – מָהֹר יִמְהָרֶנָּה לּוֹ לְאִשָּׁה: *Tosafot* ask: If the term "to him" indicates that his consent is required, why not derive a similar *halakha* with regard to a rapist, where it is written: "And to him she shall be as a wife"? The Ritva explains that the derivation is not from the term "to him" but from the phrase "He shall pay a dowry for her," indicating that the seducer's agreement is required. *Talmidei Rabbeinu Yona* maintain that the difference is whether the term "to him" appears at the beginning of a sentence, in which case there is no indication that his agreement is necessary, or whether it appears at the end of the verse, which indicates that his consent is required.

״כֵּיצַד שׁוֹתֶה בַּעֲצִיצוֹ״ כו׳. אֲמַר רַב כָּהֲנָא, אֲמַרִיתָא לִשְׁמַעְתָּא קַמֵּיהּ דְּרַב זְבִיד מִנְּהַרְדְּעָא: נֵיתֵי עֲשֵׂה וְנִדְחֶה לֹא תַעֲשֶׂה!

§ The mishna continues: **How does** the rapist **drink from his vessel?** The mishna proceeds to explain that he is obligated to marry her despite the physical flaws she might have. However, if the marriage is prohibited, either due to the fact that she committed adultery or due to her flawed lineage, he is not obligated to marry her, and therefore he may not marry her. **Rav Kahana said: I stated** this ***halakha*** **before Rav Zevid of Neharde'a,** and I asked him: Let the **positive** mitzva: "And to him she shall be as a wife" (Deuteronomy 22:29), **come and override** the **prohibition**[N] of marriage to a woman who is forbidden to him, according to the principle that positive mitzvot override prohibitions.

אֲמַר לִי: הֵיכָא אָמְרִינַן נֵיתֵי עֲשֵׂה וְנִידְחֵי לֹא תַעֲשֶׂה – כְּגוֹן מִילָה בְּצָרַעַת, דְּלָא אֶפְשָׁר לְקַיּוֹמֵיהּ לַעֲשֵׂה. אֲבָל הָכָא, אִי אָמְרָה דְּלָא בָּעֵינָא מִי אִיתֵיהּ לַעֲשֵׂה כְּלָל?

He said to me: Where do we say the principle that **a positive** mitzva **comes and overrides a prohibition?** It is in a case **where** one performs **circumcision** of a foreskin afflicted **with leprosy.**[H] Although there is a prohibition against removing leprous skin, the positive mitzva of circumcision overrides that prohibition, **as it is not possible to fulfill the positive** mitzva without violating the prohibition. **However, here,** in the case of the rapist, **if** she **says: I do not want him** as a husband, **is there a positive** mitzva **at all?**[N] Since in that case the mitzva need not be performed, as it is negated when the woman refuses to marry him, it does not override the prohibition.

מתני׳ יְתוֹמָה שֶׁנִּתְאָרְסָה וְנִתְגָּרְשָׁה, רַבִּי אֶלְעָזָר אוֹמֵר: הָאוֹנֵס חַיָּיב, וְהַמְפַתֶּה פָּטוּר.

MISHNA With regard to **an orphan who was betrothed**[N] **and divorced, Rabbi Elazar says: One who rapes** her **is obligated** to pay the fine, as she is a virgin young woman, **and one who seduces her is exempt**[H] from payment. Because she is an orphan, or because she was betrothed and divorced, she is independent, and by consenting to the seduction she forgoes her right to the fine.

HALAKHA

Circumcision of a foreskin afflicted with leprosy – מִילָה בְּצָרַעַת: The mitzva of circumcision overrides the prohibition against severing leprosy, whether or not the circumcision is performed at its proper time. Therefore, if there was a leprous spot on the foreskin, one may perform the circumcision and sever it, despite the fact that severing leprosy is prohibited by Torah law (Rambam *Sefer Ahava, Hilkhot Mila Betula* 1:9; *Shulḥan Arukh, Yoreh De'a* 266:1).

One who rapes her is obligated to pay the fine and one who seduces her is exempt – הָאוֹנֵס חַיָּיב וְהַמְפַתֶּה פָּטוּר: If a young woman who was betrothed and divorced was raped, the fine is paid to her. If she was seduced she is not entitled to the fine, as she consented to the act. The *halakha* is in accordance with the opinion of Rabbi Elazar and the ruling of Rav (Rambam *Sefer Nashim, Hilkhot Na'ara Betula* 2:14, 16; *Tur, Even HaEzer* 177).

NOTES

A positive mitzva and a prohibition – עֲשֵׂה וְלֹא תַעֲשֶׂה: The Gemara at the beginning of *Yevamot* explains at length that when there is a conflict between a positive mitzva and a prohibition, and it is impossible to fulfill both, the positive mitzva overrides the prohibition. That is the ruling despite the fact that the punishment for violating a prohibition is generally more severe than the punishment for failure to fulfill a mitzva.

Several questions arise in this regard. One basic issue is the identity of the prohibition in question. Rashi, and most commentaries, explains that it refers to the prohibition of the woman, e.g., a *mamzeret*. *Tosafot* question this approach, as it is derived from the verse "And to him she shall be as a wife" that a rapist is under no obligation to marry a woman prohibited to him. They suggest various answers. Other early commentaries elaborate on *Tosafot*'s answers, and suggest additional answers. The Ramban prefers *Tosafot*'s final answer and explains the Gemara's difficulty as follows: As the Torah establishes here that this positive mitzva does not override a prohibition, why not derive a principle from here that a positive mitzva does not in fact override a prohibition?

Rabbi Aharon HaLevi and his disciples explain that the verse "And to him she shall be as a wife" comes primarily to teach that her consent is required for marriage to the rapist, and it is cited as a mere support for the *halakha*, as the source of that *halakha* is in fact the reason articulated here (see *Tosafot*). The Ritva attributes this approach to the Ramban. The Ramban also maintains that this can be explained in a fundamentally different manner, that the Gemara is not referring to a prohibition of lineage, but to a woman forbidden due to adultery. We can therefore say that even if he found her acting immorally after marriage he is obligated to retain her as a wife, because she was suitable for him when they married. The Ramban is not bothered by *Tosafot*'s rejection of that approach.

Is there a positive mitzva at all – מִי אִיתֵיהּ לַעֲשֵׂה כְּלָל: Rashi explains that because she can neutralize the positive mitzva for the rapist, she is instructed to refuse him. The problem with this interpretation is what happens if the woman does not comply and insists on marrying him? The Ramban answers that according to Rashi it is self-evident that a woman would not want to wed a man with whom marriage is prohibited, and therefore she is induced to refuse him. Most commentaries, however, maintain that the Gemara does not mean that the victim must refuse to marry him. Rather, the very fact that she has the right to do so indicates that it is an insubstantial mitzva and therefore does not override a prohibition (see *Tosafot*, Rid, Ran, and Ramban). The Rid adds that her right of refusal indicates that it is not a full-fledged positive mitzva; rather it is one designed to appease her.

Rabbeinu Crescas Vidal adopts the reading: A positive mitzva overrides a prohibition only when there is no alternative to fulfilling the mitzva and he is completely obligated to perform it. Here, however, the positive mitzva can be bypassed, and therefore it does not negate the prohibition. *Tosafot Yeshanim* suggest that even though the prohibition is overridden by the positive mitzva from the man's perspective, it is also prohibited for her to violate the negative command, and it is certainly not permitted for her to violate a prohibition due to a mitzva incumbent upon him.

An orphan who was betrothed, etc. – יְתוֹמָה שֶׁנִּתְאָרְסָה וכו׳: In the *Shita Mekubbetzet* there are four different interpretations of the term orphan. One possibility is that the mishna is speaking of a single case, an orphan who was betrothed and divorced. Another possibility is that it is referring to a daughter who was betrothed and divorced, and she is called an orphan because her legal status is that of an orphan. A third option is that there are two entirely separate cases; one, an orphan, the other, one who was betrothed and divorced. Finally, the mishna can be explained as dealing with two cases in which the *halakha* is different; an orphan receives no payment, and although a girl who was betrothed and divorced is not entitled to the fine, she receives the payment for degradation. Indeed, the commentaries adopt various interpretations of the mishna. The Ritva explains at length that according to Rashi the word orphan refers literally to a girl without a father and also indicates that the legal status of a girl who was betrothed and divorced is that of an orphan.

גמ׳ אמר רבה בר בר חנה אמר רבי יוחנן: רבי אלעזר בשיטת רבי עקיבא רבו אמרה, דאמר: יש לה קנס, וקנסה לעצמה. ממאי – מדקתני: יתומה, רבי אלעזר אומר: האונס חייב והמפתה פטור.

GEMARA **Rabba bar bar Ḥana said that Rabbi Yoḥanan said: Rabbi Elazar stated** his opinion **in accordance** with the opinion of **Rabbi Akiva, his teacher,**[N] **as** with regard to a young woman who was betrothed and divorced and then raped, Rabbi Akiva **said** in an earlier mishna: **She is entitled to** a fine for rape **and her fine** is paid **to her.** Rabbi Yosei HaGelili says: She is not entitled to a fine for rape. **And from where** do we know that Rabbi Elazar's opinion corresponds to the opinion of his teacher? **From the fact that** the mishna **teaches** with regard to **an orphan** that **Rabbi Elazar says: One who rapes** her **is obligated** to pay the fine **and one who seduces** her **is exempt** from payment.

יתומה פשיטא! אלא הא קא משמע לן: דנערה שנתארסה ונתגרשה כיתומה, מה יתומה לעצמה – אף נערה שנתארסה ונתגרשה לעצמה.

The Gemara asks: **An orphan?** That is **obvious,** as she has no father and is not subject to the authority of anyone else. Clearly the seducer is exempt from payment because she was complicit. **Rather, this** is what the mishna is **teaching us: That** the legal status of **a young woman who was betrothed and divorced,** even if her father is alive, is **like** that of **an orphan: Just as** with regard to **an orphan,** payment of the fine is **to her, so too,** with regard to **a young woman who was betrothed and divorced,**[H] payment of the fine is **to her.**

אמר רבי זירא אמר רבה בר שילא אמר רב המנונא סבא אמר רב אדא בר אהבה אמר רב: הלכה כרבי אלעזר. קרי רב עליה דרבי אלעזר: טובינא דחכימי.

Rabbi Zeira said that **Rabba bar Sheila said** that **Rav Hamnuna the Elder said** that **Rav Adda bar Ahava said** that **Rav said: The** ***halakha*** **is in accordance** with the opinion **of Rabbi Elazar.**[PN] **Rav** would **exclaim about Rabbi Elazar:** He is the **happiest of the Sages,** as he held that the *halakha* was ruled in accordance with his opinion in many instances.

מתני׳ איזהו בושת? הכל לפי המבייש והמתבייש. פגם – רואין אותה כאילו היא שפחה נמכרת בשוק, כמה היתה יפה וכמה היא יפה. קנס שוה בכל אדם. וכל שיש לו קצבה מן התורה – שוה בכל אדם.

MISHNA **What is humiliation?**[N] How is the payment for humiliation during rape or seduction assessed? It is **all based on the one who humiliated and the one who was humiliated.**[HN] The price will vary depending on the lineage of the family of the rape victim and the nature of the attacker. How is her **degradation** assessed? **One considers her as though she were a maidservant sold in the marketplace,** and assesses **how much she was worth** beforehand **and how much she is** currently **worth,** after the rape or seduction. The sum of the **fine is equal for all people,**[H] and the principle is: **Any** payment **that has a fixed sum by Torah law is equal for all people,** regardless of the lineage and the physical state of the attacker or the victim.

HALAKHA

An orphan…one who was betrothed and divorced – יתומה...מי שנתארסה ונתגרשה: The fine for the rape of a girl without a father is paid to her; the same is true for a young woman who was betrothed and divorced (Rambam *Sefer Nashim, Hilkhot Na'ara Betula* 2:14, 16; *Tur, Even HaEzer* 177).

It is all based on the one who humiliated and the one who was humiliated – הכל לפי המבייש והמתבייש: How is the humiliation of a raped woman assessed? It is all based on the one who humiliated and the one who was humiliated. The humiliation of a young woman of significance from a distinguished family is not comparable to the humiliation of a poor girl of lowly lineage. Likewise, the payment to a woman humiliated by a man of significance is lower than the payment to one humiliated by a lowly person (Rambam *Sefer Nashim, Hilkhot Na'ara Betula* 2:4; *Shulḥan Arukh, Even HaEzer* 407:24).

The sum of the fine is equal for all people – קנס שוה בכל אדם: Whether one had relations with the daughter of a High Priest or a *mamzer*, the fine is fifty silver coins (Rambam *Sefer Nashim, Hilkhot Na'ara Betula* 2:3; *Tur, Even HaEzer* 177).

PERSONALITIES

Rabbi Elazar – רבי אלעזר: This is Rabbi Elazar ben Shammua, a *tanna* in the generation prior to the redaction of the Mishna and among the greatest of Rabbi Akiva's students. Rabbi Elazar was a leader of the Jewish people in the years following the persecution in the wake of the failure of the bar Kokheva rebellion. Despite the dire situation, many students studied with him. One of his primary students was Rabbi Yehuda HaNasi, the redactor of the Mishna. Not many of Rabbi Elazar's *halakhot* are cited in the Mishna; however, he was held in high esteem by the Sages of the following generations. Rav, an *amora*, referred to him as the happiest of the Sages, and Rabbi Yoḥanan said of him: The hearts of the early Sages were like the Entrance Hall to the Sanctuary. In the Mishna and in *baraitot*, he is called simply Rabbi Elazar.

Rabbi Elazar ben Shammua lived a long life. According to one tradition he was 105 years old when he was killed. He is listed among the ten martyrs executed by the Romans.

NOTES

Stated it in accordance with the opinion of Rabbi Akiva, his teacher – בשיטת רבי עקיבא רבו אמרה: The Ramban explains that the Gemara is not saying that Rabbi Elazar agrees with Rabbi Akiva as opposed to Rabbi Yosei HaGelili, as that is self-evident. Rather, it is emphasizing that he accepts Rabbi Akiva's opinion cited in the mishna, not the opinion attributed to him in the *baraita*. The Gemara therefore asks: From where is that known; perhaps he agrees with Rabbi Akiva of the *baraita* and that is why he referred specifically to an orphan, as the fine for one who is not an orphan is paid to her father? The Gemara answers that since the mishna mentions an orphan, and there is nothing novel in that *halakha*, as she certainly does not receive payment for willingly performing an act, it is clear that the reference is to a girl who is not an orphan but rather one who was betrothed and divorced. The Ritva adds that by specifying that one who seduces her is exempt, Rabbi Elazar is demonstrating that he is not referring to a literal orphan, as there is no need to state that she receives no payment when she is seduced. Rather, he mentions an orphan in order to explain why she does not receive the fine; a young woman who was betrothed and divorced is considered an orphan in her father's lifetime.

The *halakha* is in accordance with the opinion of Rabbi Elazar – הלכה כרבי אלעזר: The question is raised: Since Rabbi Elazar's opinion is in accordance with the opinion of Rabbi Akiva, why did the Gemara not issue the ruling in accordance with the source of his opinion, Rabbi Akiva? The Ritva explains that had the Gemara issued a ruling in accordance with Rabbi Akiva, there would have been uncertainty whether the reference was to his opinion as cited in the mishna or to the opinion cited in the *baraita*. The Gemara therefore preferred to state that the *halakha* is in accordance with the opinion of Rabbi Elazar, who adopts the opinion of Rabbi Akiva in the mishna, as stated above. The Ritva adds that this is why Rabbi Elazar is called the happiest of the Sages, as he was able to accurately approximate the opinion of his teacher. According to the *Yam shel Shlomo*, Rabbi Elazar indeed adds to Rabbi Akiva's opinion; he teaches that this *halakha* applies to the payments of humiliation and degradation as well as to the fine. This also accounts for the fact that this mishna is placed here, rather than adjacent to Rabbi Akiva's opinion.

What is humiliation – איזהו בושת: The appropriate question would appear to be: How much is the payment of humiliation? After all, that is the topic of the mishna. The *Melekhet Shlomo* explains that since one might have thought that the humiliation and degradation of a rape victim are identical, the mishna underscores that these are two separate *halakhot*.

It is all based on the one who humiliated and the one who was humiliated – הכל לפי המבייש והמתבייש: Rashi here explains that humiliation is greatest when the humiliator is neither particularly prominent nor particularly inconsequential. If he is a person of importance her humiliation is less, and similarly the action of a man of lowly standing is considered insignificant and the humiliation in that case is less. The Rid agrees.

The Ran maintains that this is the case in standard instances of humiliation, but a rape victim is humiliated more when she is violated by a man of lowly standing. He agrees though that a woman raped by a great man suffers less humiliation. See, however, the *Yam shel Shlomo*, who argues to the contrary, and concludes that each case must be considered on its own merits, dependent on time and place. The Meiri agrees with Ran, and cites proof from the Jerusalem Talmud, where it states that the humiliation suffered by a great man is extensive and his humiliation of others is minor, while the humiliation suffered by a lowly man is insignificant while his humiliation of others is major. He explains that the humiliation suffered by a great person corresponds to his significance, and therefore the humiliation payment for a woman of significance will be greater, whereas his humiliation of others is relatively insignificant.

גמ׳ וְאֵימָא חֲמִשִּׁים סְלָעִים אָמַר רַחֲמָנָא, מִכָּל מִילֵּי! אָמַר רַבִּי זֵירָא: יֹאמְרוּ בָּעַל בַּת מְלָכִים – חֲמִשִּׁים, בָּעַל בַּת הֶדְיוֹטוֹת – חֲמִשִּׁים?! אֲמַר לֵיהּ אַבַּיֵי: אִי הָכִי, גַּבֵּי עֶבֶד נַמִי יֹאמְרוּ: עֶבֶד נוֹקֵב מַרְגָּלִיּוֹת – שְׁלֹשִׁים, עֶבֶד עוֹשֶׂה

GEMARA The Gemara asks: **And say that the Merciful One said** that the payment is **fifty** ***sela*** **from all** these **matters,** i.e., the fine, degradation, humiliation, and pain. **Rabbi Zeira said:** That cannot be, as **they will say: If one who engaged in forced intercourse with a daughter of kings** pays a sum of **fifty** *sela*, does **one who engaged in forced intercourse with the daughter of commoners** [*hedyotot*][L] also pay **fifty** *sela*? **Abaye said to him:** This is not a decisive argument, as **if so, with regard to a** Canaanite **slave** killed by an ox, the Torah says that the owner of the ox pays the master of the slave thirty *sela*. There too, **they will say:** For **a slave who pierces** precious **pearls** [*margaliyyot*],[LB] a valuable skill, the fine is **thirty** *sela*, and for **a slave who performs**

LANGUAGE

Commoners [*hedyotot*] – **הֶדְיוֹטוֹת**: From the Greek ἰδιώτης, *idiotēs*, meaning a common man with no official office. The Sages use it to distinguish between a common person, e.g., a common priest, and one with a special position.

Pearls [*margaliyyot*] – **מַרְגָּלִיּוֹת**: From the Greek μαργαρίτης, *margarites*, meaning pearl. Sometimes it is used as a general term for a precious stone, both in Greek and in the language of the Sages.

BACKGROUND

A slave who pierces precious pearls – עֶבֶד נוֹקֵב מַרְגָּלִיּוֹת: Since pearls, especially valuable ones, were usually made into necklaces, they had to be pierced. This was a specialized form of craftsmanship that required expertise. The artisan would choose the ideal place to pierce the jewel, and the resultant hole had to be completely straight so as not to mar the beauty of the pearl. That craftsman was well paid, and a slave who could perform this task would be considered highly valuable.

Perek **III**
Daf **40** Amud **b**

מַעֲשֵׂה מַחַט שְׁלֹשִׁים?!

the **needlecraft** of a tailor, a common, less valuable skill, is the fine also **thirty** *sela*? Rather, just as with regard to the slaves, the sum is not dependent on the standing of the victim, so too with regard to a woman who was raped.

אֶלָּא אָמַר רַבִּי זֵירָא: אִילּוּ בָּאוּ עָלֶיהָ שְׁנַיִם, אֶחָד כְּדַרְכָּהּ וְאֶחָד שֶׁלֹּא כְּדַרְכָּהּ, יֹאמְרוּ: בָּעַל שְׁלֵימָה חֲמִשִּׁים, בָּעַל פְּגוּמָה – חֲמִשִּׁים?! אֲמַר לֵיהּ אַבַּיֵי: אִי הָכִי, גַּבֵּי עֶבֶד נַמִי יֹאמְרוּ, עֶבֶד בָּרִיא – שְׁלֹשִׁים, עֶבֶד מוּכֵּה שְׁחִין – שְׁלֹשִׁים?!

Rather, Rabbi Zeira said a different proof: **Had two** men **engaged in forced intercourse with her, one vaginal intercourse, and one anal intercourse,**[N] **they will say:** If one who **engaged in forced intercourse** with **an untainted** virgin pays **fifty** *sela*, does one who **engaged in forced intercourse** with her when she is **tainted,** i.e., after she has engaged in anal intercourse, also pay **fifty** *sela*? Apparently, the fifty *sela* is the fixed sum of the fine, while the rest of the payment varies on a case-by-case basis. **Abaye said to him:** This too is no proof, as **if so, with regard to a slave as well, they will say** if one whose ox gored **a healthy slave** pays **thirty** *sela*, does one whose ox gored **a slave afflicted with boils** also pay **thirty** *sela*?

אֶלָּא אֲמַר אַבַּיֵי: אָמַר קְרָא ״תַּחַת אֲשֶׁר עִינָּהּ״, הָנֵי – תַּחַת אֲשֶׁר עִינָּהּ, מִכְּלָל דְּאִיכָּא בּוֹשֶׁת וּפְגָם. רָבָא אֲמַר: אָמַר קְרָא ״וְנָתַן הָאִישׁ הַשּׁוֹכֵב עִמָּהּ לַאֲבִי הַנַּעֲרָה חֲמִשִּׁים כָּסֶף״ הֲנָאַת שְׁכִיבָה – חֲמִשִּׁים, מִכְּלָל דְּאִיכָּא בּוֹשֶׁת וּפְגָם.

Rather, Abaye said a different proof. **The verse says:** "Fifty shekels of silver… **because he tormented her**" (Deuteronomy 22:29); **these** fifty *sela* are the fine paid **because he tormented her.** From which it **may be inferred that there are** the additional payments of **humiliation and degradation** beyond that sum mentioned in the verse. **Rava said** an alternative proof. **The verse says: "And the man who lay with her shall give to the father of the young woman fifty shekels of silver"** (Deuteronomy 22:29). For **the pleasure of lying** with her he pays **fifty** *sela*;[H] from which it **may be inferred that there are** the additional payments of **humiliation and degradation,** beyond payment of the fine.

וְאֵימָא לְדִידָהּ? אָמַר קְרָא: ״בִּנְעֻרֶיהָ בֵּית אָבִיהָ״ – כָּל שֶׁבַח נְעוּרֶיהָ לְאָבִיהָ.

The Gemara asks: **And say** that these additional payments are paid **to her?**[N] The Gemara answers that **the verse says:** "Between a father and his daughter, **being in her young womanhood, in her father's house**" (Numbers 30:17), from which it is derived that **all profits** of **her young womanhood** go **to her father.**[H]

NOTES

And one anal intercourse – וְאֶחָד שֶׁלֹּא כְּדַרְכָּהּ: The authorities disagree as to whether a rapist or seducer by means of anal intercourse is liable to pay the fine. According to the Rambam there is no fine for anal intercourse, whereas the Ra'avad deems the rapist liable, as do *Tosafot*. These opinions both depend upon and influence the interpretation of the Gemara. According to those who maintain that there is no fine for anal intercourse, the Gemara is referring to two women, one of whom engaged in anal intercourse before engaging in vaginal intercourse. The Gemara is stating that there is no difference with regard to the sum of the fine for the vaginal intercourse. The other opinion maintains that the Gemara is referring to one woman who receives payment of the fine both from the one who engaged in anal intercourse with her as well as from the one who engaged in vaginal intercourse with her, despite her impaired status. The early commentaries add that it appears that Rashi, at least according to his interpretation here, agrees with the Rambam that the reference is to two women. The Ritva and others note that in the Jerusalem Talmud it is clear that one who performs anal intercourse is also liable to pay the fine.

And say that these additional payments are paid to her – וְאֵימָא לְדִידָהּ: This difficulty hearkens back to the earlier statements of Abaye and Rava. According to Rabbi Zeira's reasoning this is not a question, as he holds that the need to emphasize that fifty *sela* is the sum of the fine is to prevent mistaken impressions and to indicate that the humiliation and degradation are paid to the same person to whom the fine is paid. However, according to Abaye and Rava, who derive this from a verse that indicates that the fine is paid as compensation only for the torment of the intercourse, the question can be raised: Who is entitled to the other payments? (*Shita Mekubbetzet*).

HALAKHA

The pleasure of lying is fifty ***sela*** **– הֲנָאַת שְׁכִיבָה חֲמִשִּׁים:** The fine of fifty *sela* paid by a rapist or a seducer is for the pleasure of the act itself. It does not include other forms of indemnity that he owes her (Rambam *Sefer Nashim*, *Hilkhot Na'ara Betula* 2:1; *Shulḥan Arukh*, *Even HaEzer* 177:1).

All profits of her young womanhood go to her father – כָּל שֶׁבַח נְעוּרֶיהָ לְאָבִיהָ: The four categories of indemnity owed by a rapist and the three owed by a seducer are paid to the girl's father, as all profits of her young womanhood go to her father (Rambam *Sefer Nashim*, *Hilkhot Na'ara Betula* 2:15).

וְאֶלָּא הָא דְּאָמַר רַב הוּנָא אָמַר רַב: מִנַּיִן שֶׁמַּעֲשֵׂה הַבַּת לְאָבִיהָ? שֶׁנֶּאֱמַר ״וְכִי יִמְכּוֹר אִישׁ אֶת בִּתּוֹ לְאָמָה״ מָה אָמָה מַעֲשֵׂה יָדֶיהָ לְרַבָּהּ, אַף בַּת מַעֲשֵׂה יָדֶיהָ לְאָבִיהָ – לָמָּה לִי? תֵּיפוֹק לֵיהּ מִ״בִּנְעוּרֶיהָ בֵּית אָבִיהָ״! אֶלָּא, הַהִיא בַּהֲפָרַת נְדָרִים הוּא דִּכְתִיב.

The Gemara asks: **However,** with regard to **that** which **Rav Huna said** that **Rav said: From where** is it derived **that the handiwork of the daughter** goes **to her father?**[H] It is **as it is stated: "And if a man sells his daughter as a maidservant"** (Exodus 21:7), juxtaposing his daughter to a maidservant: **Just as a maidservant, her handiwork** belongs **to her master,** as she was sold for that purpose; **so too a daughter, her handiwork** goes **to her father. Why do I** need this complicated proof? **Let him derive it** directly from the verse **"Being in her young womanhood, in her father's house." Rather,** this cannot be derived from that verse because **that** verse **is written with regard to the nullification of vows.** A young woman is subject to her father's authority with regard to her vows, which he has the right to nullify. The matter of monetary rights is not addressed in that verse.

וְכִי תֵּימָא: נֵילַף מִינֵּיהּ – מָמוֹנָא מֵאִיסּוּרָא לָא יָלְפִינַן. וְכִי תֵּימָא: נֵילַף מִקְּנָסָא – מָמוֹנָא מִקְּנָסָא לָא יָלְפִינַן. אֶלָּא מִסְתַּבְּרָא דְּאָבִיהָ הָוֵי, דְּאִי בָּעֵי – מָסַר לָהּ לִמְנוּוָּל וּמוּכֵּה שְׁחִין.

And if you say: Let us derive monetary matters **from** vows, i.e., just as she is subject to her father's authority with regard to vows the same is true with regard to monetary matters, **we do not derive monetary** matters **from ritual** matters. **And if you say: Let us derive** that her father receives payment **from** the *halakha* **of a fine,** i.e., just as the fine is paid to her father, as explicitly stated in the Torah, so too, other payments are also paid to her father, **we do not derive monetary** matters **from fines.**[N] The payment of a fine is a novel element decreed by the Torah and cannot serve as a paradigm for standard monetary matters. **Rather,** the Gemara explains that **it is reasonable that** the payments of humiliation and degradation are paid **to her father, as if he wished** to do so he could **give her** hand in marriage **to a repulsive** man[N] **or one afflicted with boils,** thereby humiliating her. Since her humiliation is under his control, payment for her humiliation is similarly his.

״פְּגָם – רוֹאִין אוֹתָהּ כְּאִילּוּ הִיא שִׁפְחָה נִמְכֶּרֶת״. הֵיכִי שָׁיְימִינַן לָהּ? אָמַר אֲבוּהּ דִּשְׁמוּאֵל: אוֹמְדִין כַּמָּה אָדָם רוֹצֶה לִיתֵּן בֵּין שִׁפְחָה בְּתוּלָה לְשִׁפְחָה בְּעוּלָה לְשַׁמְּשׁוֹ,

The mishna continues: How is her **degradation** assessed? **One considers her as though she was a maidservant sold** in the marketplace, and assesses how much she would have been worth beforehand and how much she would be worth currently. The Gemara asks: **How do we assess her** value? **Shmuel's father said: One estimates** the difference **between how much a person is willing to give** to purchase **a virgin maidservant and** how much he is willing to give **to** purchase **a non-virgin maidservant**[N] **to serve him.**

מַאי נָפְקָא לֵיהּ מִינָּהּ? אֶלָּא: בֵּין שִׁפְחָה בְּעוּלָה לְשִׁפְחָה שֶׁאֵינָהּ בְּעוּלָה לְהַשִּׂיאָהּ לְעַבְדּוֹ. וּלְעַבְדּוֹ מַאי נָפְקָא לֵיהּ מִינָּהּ? בְּעֶבֶד שֶׁיֵּשׁ לוֹ לְרַבּוֹ קוֹרַת רוּחַ הֵימֶנּוּ.

The Gemara asks: With regard to **a non-virgin maidservant to serve him;** if he purchases her for service, **what difference is there to him** whether or not she is a virgin? **Rather,** the difference **between a maidservant who engaged in intercourse and a maidservant who did not engage in intercourse** is with regard to how much one is willing **to marry her to his slave.** The Gemara further asks: **And** with regard to marrying her **to his slave, what difference is there to him** whether or not she is a virgin? The Gemara answers: It is **with regard to a slave from whom his master has** a sense of **satisfaction,** and he seeks a virgin for the slave in order to reciprocate. The difference between the price that the master is willing to pay for each of the maidservants is the degradation that the offender pays the victim.[H]

HALAKHA

The handiwork of the daughter goes to her father – מַעֲשֵׂה הַבַּת לְאָבִיהָ: The handiwork of a minor girl, until she becomes a young woman, goes to her father (Rambam *Sefer Nashim, Hilkhot Ishut* 3:11; *Shulḥan Arukh, Even HaEzer* 37:1).

Assessment of degradation – אוֹמְדָן הַפְּגָם: How is the degradation of a rape victim assessed? She is considered as though she was a maidservant for sale in the slave market and the difference between her value as a virgin and her value as a non-virgin is assessed, as a person would pay more for a virgin maidservant in order to marry her to a slave whom he wishes to please (Rambam *Sefer Nashim, Hilkhot Na'ara Betula* 2:6).

NOTES

We do not derive monetary matters from fines – מָמוֹנָא מִקְּנָסָא לָא יָלְפִינַן: The students of the Rashba cite in his name that the reason for this principle is not due to any fundamental difference between payments of money and fines, like the difference between ritual matters and monetary payment. Rather, fines are a novel *halakha* from which a general principle cannot be derived. Consequently, everyone agrees that the *halakhot* of fines can be derived from the *halakhot* of payments of money.

As if he wished to do so he could give her hand in marriage to a repulsive man, etc. – דְּאִי בָּעֵי מָסַר לָהּ לִמְנוּוָּל וכו׳: Rav Hai Gaon explains that he can betroth her to any man he chooses while she is a minor, and the humiliation, degradation, and even the pain resulting from that betrothal would continue into her young womanhood. Therefore, her humiliation and degradation belong to her father. The problem with this explanation is that the same reasoning leads to the conclusion that the humiliation and degradation of a grown woman should also be paid to her father. Rabbi Aharon HaLevi answers that since a grown woman has completely left her father's control, he retains no rights to anything of hers (see Ramban and Rashba).

One estimates…between purchasing a virgin maidservant and purchasing a non-virgin maidservant, etc. – אוֹמְדִין...בֵּין שִׁפְחָה בְּתוּלָה לְשִׁפְחָה בְּעוּלָה וכו׳: *Tosafot* explain that this does not mean every woman is evaluated as though she were a maidservant, as there is certainly no comparison between the degradation of a maidservant to that of an woman of significance from a distinguished family. Rather, the Gemara cited a common case, as only a maidservant can be married to a slave. However, with regard to every woman, the assessment involves that particular woman and how much more a man would be willing to give for her as a virgin. *Tosafot Yeshanim* maintain that degradation is always assessed in terms of a maidservant, as the difference between injury of a woman of significance and injury of a maidservant is covered by the payment for humiliation.

מתני׳ כָּל מָקוֹם שֶׁיֵּשׁ מֶכֶר – אֵין קְנָס, וְכׇל מָקוֹם שֶׁיֵּשׁ קְנָס – אֵין מֶכֶר. קְטַנָּה – יֵשׁ לָהּ מֶכֶר וְאֵין לָהּ קְנָס, נַעֲרָה – יֵשׁ לָהּ קְנָס וְאֵין לָהּ מֶכֶר. הַבּוֹגֶרֶת – אֵין לָהּ לֹא מֶכֶר וְלֹא קְנָס.

MISHNA **Any place where there is sale**[N] by a father of his minor daughter as a Hebrew maidservant, **there is no fine** if she is raped. **And any place where there is a fine,** when a young woman is raped; **there is no sale** by the father. The Gemara specifies: **A minor is subject to sale** by her father, **and she is not entitled to a fine** if she is raped. **A young woman is entitled to a fine** if she is raped **and is not subject to sale. A grown woman is neither subject to sale nor entitled to a fine.**

גמ׳ אָמַר רַב יְהוּדָה אָמַר רַב: זוֹ דִּבְרֵי רַבִּי מֵאִיר, אֲבָל חֲכָמִים אוֹמְרִים: יֵשׁ לָהּ קְנָס בִּמְקוֹם מֶכֶר. דְּתַנְיָא: קְטַנָּה מִבַּת יוֹם אֶחָד וְעַד שֶׁתָּבִיא שְׁתֵּי שְׂעָרוֹת – יֵשׁ לָהּ מֶכֶר וְאֵין לָהּ קְנָס, מִשֶּׁתָּבִיא שְׁתֵּי שְׂעָרוֹת עַד שֶׁתִּיבָּגֵר יֵשׁ לָהּ קְנָס וְאֵין לָהּ מֶכֶר, דִּבְרֵי רַבִּי מֵאִיר, שֶׁהָיָה רַבִּי מֵאִיר אוֹמֵר: כָּל מָקוֹם שֶׁיֵּשׁ מֶכֶר – אֵין קְנָס, וְכׇל מָקוֹם שֶׁיֵּשׁ קְנָס – אֵין מֶכֶר. וַחֲכָמִים אוֹמְרִים: קְטַנָּה מִבַּת שָׁלֹשׁ שָׁנִים וְיוֹם אֶחָד וְעַד שֶׁתִּיבָּגֵר – יֵשׁ לָהּ קְנָס.

GEMARA **Rav Yehuda said** that **Rav said: This** *halakha* in the mishna is **the statement of Rabbi Meir, but the Rabbis say: She is entitled to a fine** even **where** there is **a sale, as it is taught** in a *baraita*: **A minor** girl, **from one day old until she grows two** pubic **hairs, is subject to sale and is not entitled to a fine. From when she grows two** pubic **hairs** and becomes a young woman **until she matures** into a grown woman, **she is entitled to a fine and she is not subject to sale;** this is **the statement of Rabbi Meir, as Rabbi Meir would state** the principle: **Any place where there is a sale there is no fine, and any place where there is a fine there is no sale. And the Rabbis say: A minor** girl **from the age of three years and one day until she matures** into a grown woman **is entitled to a fine.**

קְנָס אִין, מֶכֶר לָא?! אֵימָא: אַף קְנָס בִּמְקוֹם מֶכֶר. אָמַר רַב חִסְדָּא: מַאי טַעְמָא דְּרַבִּי מֵאִיר – אָמַר קְרָא ״וְלוֹ תִהְיֶה לְאִשָּׁה״ – בְּמִהְוָה עַצְמָהּ הַכָּתוּב מְדַבֵּר. וְרַבָּנַן? אָמַר רֵישׁ לָקִישׁ: אָמַר קְרָא ״נַעֲרָ״ – אֲפִילּוּ קְטַנָּה בְּמַשְׁמָע.

The Gemara questions the statement of the Rabbis in the *baraita* with regard to a girl more than three years of age: **A fine, yes, but sale, no?** Do the Rabbis maintain that a father cannot sell his minor daughter as a Hebrew maidservant? Rather, emend the text and **say:** She is **even entitled to a fine**[H] **where** she is subject to **sale. Rav Ḥisda said: What is the rationale** for the opinion **of Rabbi Meir?** It is as **the verse says** with regard to a rapist: "And the man who lay with her shall give to the father of the young woman fifty *sela*, **and to him she shall be as a wife"** (Deuteronomy 22:29). **The verse is speaking with regard to one** halakhically competent to **marry** by **herself,** which means she must be a young woman. The Gemara asks: **And** what is the rationale for the opinion of **the Rabbis? Reish Lakish said** that **the verse says "young woman [*na'ara*]";** however, although the term is pronounced *na'ara*, it is written as *na'ar*,[N] without the letter *heh*, and **even a minor girl is indicated** by that term.

שְׁמָעָהּ רַב פַּפָּא בְּרֵיהּ דְּרַב חָנָן מִבֵּי כְּלוֹחִית, אֲזַל אֲמָרָהּ קַמֵּיהּ דְּרַב שִׁימִי בַּר אַשִׁי. אֲמַר לֵיהּ: אַתּוּן אַהָא מַתְנִיתוּ לַהּ, אֲנַן אַהָא מַתְנִינַן לַהּ: אָמַר רֵישׁ לָקִישׁ: הַמּוֹצִיא שֵׁם רַע עַל הַקְּטַנָּה – פָּטוּר, שֶׁנֶּאֱמַר ״וְנָתְנוּ לַאֲבִי הַנַּעֲרָה״ – נַעֲרָה מָלֵא דִּיבֵּר הַכָּתוּב.

The Gemara relates: **Rav Pappa, son** of **Rav Ḥanan, from** a place called **Bei Keloḥit, heard** this *halakha* and **went and said it before Rav Shimi bar Ashi.** Rav Shimi **said to him: You teach this** statement **concerning that** matter. **We,** based on our traditions, **teach it concerning this** matter, as **Reish Lakish said: One who slanders a minor girl,** falsely claiming that she was not a virgin on the wedding night, **is exempt** from paying the fine, **as it is stated: "And they shall give them to the father of the young woman [*na'ara*]"** (Deuteronomy 22:19). **The verse spoke of *na'ara*,** not only pronounced but written **in full,**[N] indicating that this payment is in effect only with regard to a young woman, not a minor girl.[H] However, in places where the term is written *na'ar*, even a minor girl would be included.

מַתְקִיף לַהּ רַב אַדָּא בַּר אַהֲבָה: טַעְמָא דִּכְתַב רַחֲמָנָא ״נַעֲרָה״, הָא לָאו הָכִי – הֲוָה אָמִינָא אֲפִילּוּ קְטַנָּה? וְהָא כְּתִיב ״וְאִם אֱמֶת הָיָה הַדָּבָר הַזֶּה לֹא נִמְצְאוּ בְתוּלִים לַנַּעֲרָה וְהוֹצִיאוּ אֶת הַנַּעֲרָה אֶל פֶּתַח בֵּית אָבִיהָ וּסְקָלוּהָ״ – וּקְטַנָּה לָאו בַּת עוֹנָשִׁין הִיא! אֶלָּא: כָּאן – נַעֲרָה, הָא כָּל מָקוֹם שֶׁנֶּאֱמַר ״נַעֲרָ״ – אֲפִילּוּ קְטַנָּה בְּמַשְׁמָע.

Rav Adda bar Ahava strongly **objects to this: The reason is that the Merciful One writes "*na'ara*"** with a *heh*. Is that to say that **if that were not the case I would have said that** this *halakha* applies **even to a minor girl?** How is that possible? **But isn't it written: "And if this matter was true, that the hymen of this young woman was not found intact; then they shall remove the young woman to the entrance of her father's house and stone her"** (Deuteronomy 22:20–21). **And** this verse clearly refers to a young woman old enough to be punished, as **a minor is not subject to punishment.**[N] **Rather, here,** with regard to the payment of a slanderer, the verse speaks of **a *na'ara*,** written with a *heh*, and a minor is excluded. This is a paradigm from which **it may be inferred** that in any place **that it is stated "*na'ara*"** without a *heh*, **even a minor girl is indicated.**

NOTES

Any place where there is a sale, etc. – כָּל מָקוֹם שֶׁיֵּשׁ מֶכֶר וכו׳: The *Tosefot Yom Tov* explains that this principle does not teach anything new; it merely serves as a mnemonic for the fact that a minor can be sold but is not entitled to a fine. The *Melekhet Shlomo* contends that there is a new *halakha* that emerges from this principle: Since even a young woman for whom there is no payment of humiliation or degradation, e.g., a deaf-mute or an imbecile, can be sold as a minor, she is entitled to the fine as a young woman.

Na'ara*, with and without the letter *heh – נַעֲרָה מָלֵא וְחָסֵר: Throughout the Torah the word *na'ara* is written without a *heh*, with the lone exception in the case of a slanderer. Admittedly, in certain very ancient Torah scrolls predating Ezra, *na'ara* is consistently written with a *heh*; however, the Masoretic tradition is without the *heh*. As for the derivation itself, one explanation is that when the word is written without a *heh*, it refers to both males and females, and it is only the vocalization that distinguishes between them. Therefore, when it is written without a *heh* it refers even to a minor girl, whose development into a young woman is not yet discernible and is therefore not clearly distinguishable from a male.

The verse spoke of *na'ara* written in full – נַעֲרָה מָלֵא דִּיבֵּר הַכָּתוּב: In the Jerusalem Talmud the question is raised: In the verses concerning the slanderer, other than the single instance where it is written with a *heh*, *na'ara* is written without a *heh* as well. The Gemara there answers that in that context, the fact that it is written without a *heh* indicates that it does not include a minor, but comes to include anal intercourse, which is common to both males and females.

And a minor is not subject to punishment – וּקְטַנָּה לָאו בַּת עוֹנָשִׁין הִיא: *Tosafot* ask: Perhaps the *halakha* of a slanderer applies even if she was a minor, and it is merely the punishment for adultery that is not administered to a minor. They answer that the case of a slanderer is one where a husband is trying to frame his wife and have her executed. As he cannot cause a minor to be executed, he cannot be punished as a slanderer.

HALAKHA

A minor is entitled to a fine – קְטַנָּה יֵשׁ לָהּ קְנָס: With regard to a minor three years and one day old and older, although she can be sold she is nonetheless entitled to the fine if she was raped or seduced, in accordance with the opinion of the Rabbis (Rambam *Sefer Nashim, Hilkhot Na'ara Betula* 1:8; *Shulḥan Arukh, Even HaEzer* 177:1).

One who slanders a minor girl – הַמּוֹצִיא שֵׁם רַע עַל הַקְּטַנָּה: One who slanders a minor girl is exempt from both the fine and lashes, as the term *na'ara* is written with a *heh* in the verse where the punishment is mentioned (Rambam *Sefer Nashim, Hilkhot Na'ara Betula* 3:2).

MISHNA

מתני׳ הָאוֹמֵר: ״פִּתִּיתִי אֶת בִּתּוֹ שֶׁל פְּלוֹנִי״ – מְשַׁלֵּם בּוֹשֶׁת וּפְגָם עַל פִּי עַצְמוֹ, וְאֵין מְשַׁלֵּם קְנָס. הָאוֹמֵר ״גָּנַבְתִּי״ – מְשַׁלֵּם אֶת הַקֶּרֶן עַל פִּי עַצְמוֹ, וְאֵין מְשַׁלֵּם תַּשְׁלוּמֵי כֶפֶל וְתַשְׁלוּמֵי אַרְבָּעָה וַחֲמִשָּׁה. ״הֵמִית שׁוֹרִי אֶת פְּלוֹנִי״ אוֹ ״שׁוֹרוֹ שֶׁל פְּלוֹנִי״ – הֲרֵי זֶה מְשַׁלֵּם עַל פִּי עַצְמוֹ. ״הֵמִית שׁוֹרִי עַבְדּוֹ שֶׁל פְּלוֹנִי״ – אֵין מְשַׁלֵּם עַל פִּי עַצְמוֹ. זֶה הַכְּלָל: כׇּל הַמְשַׁלֵּם יָתֵר עַל מַה שֶּׁהִזִּיק – אֵינוֹ מְשַׁלֵּם עַל פִּי עַצְמוֹ.

MISHNA One who says:[N] **I seduced**[H] **the daughter of so-and-so, pays** compensation for **humiliation and degradation** based **on his own** admission, **but does not pay the fine.** Similarly, **one who says: I stole,**[H] **pays the principal,** the value of the stolen goods, **based on his own** admission, **but does not pay the double payment and** the **payment four and five** times the principal for the slaughter or sale of the sheep or ox that he stole. Likewise if he confessed: **My ox killed so-and-so,**[H] **or:** My ox killed **an ox belonging to so-and-so, this** owner **pays** based **on his own** admission. However, if he said: **My ox killed a slave** belonging **to so-and-so,**[HN] **he does not pay** based **on his own** admission as that payment is a fine. **This is the principle:**[N] **Anyone who pays more than what he damaged,**[N] the payments are fines and therefore **he does not pay** based **on his own** admission. He pays only based on the testimony of others.

GEMARA

גמ׳ וְלִיתְנֵי ״אָנַסְתִּי״! לָא מִבַּעְיָא קָאָמַר; לָא מִבַּעְיָא ״אָנַסְתִּי״ דְּלָא קָא פָּגֵים לַהּ, דִּמְשַׁלֵּם בּוֹשֶׁת וּפְגָם עַל פִּי עַצְמוֹ, אֲבָל ״פִּתִּיתִי״ דְּקָא פָּגֵים לַהּ – אֵימָא לָא מְשַׁלֵּם עַל פִּי עַצְמוֹ – קָא מַשְׁמַע לַן.

GEMARA The Gemara asks: **And let the** *tanna* **teach** this *halakha* with regard to one who said: **I raped**[N] the daughter of so-and-so. Why did the mishna cite the case of seduction? The Gemara answers: The *tanna* **is speaking** employing the style: **It is not necessary. It is not necessary** for the mishna to cite the case of one who says: **I raped** her,[N] **where he does not tarnish her** reputation and merely incriminates himself, as it is obvious that **he pays** compensation for **humiliation and degradation** based **on his own** admission. **However,** in the case of one who says: **I seduced** her, **where he tarnishes her** reputation as he testifies that she willingly engaged in relations with him, and he is not deemed credible to do so, **say** that **he does not pay** based **on his own** admission. Therefore, the mishna **teaches us** that even in the case of seduction he pays compensation for humiliation and degradation based on his own admission.

מַתְנִיתִין דְּלָא כִּי הַאי תַּנָּא; דְּתַנְיָא, רַבִּי שִׁמְעוֹן בֶּן יְהוּדָה אוֹמֵר מִשּׁוּם רַבִּי שִׁמְעוֹן: אַף בּוֹשֶׁת וּפְגָם אֵינוֹ מְשַׁלֵּם עַל פִּי עַצְמוֹ, לֹא כׇּל הֵימֶנּוּ שֶׁיִּפְגּוֹם בִּתּוֹ שֶׁל פְּלוֹנִי.

The Gemara comments: **The mishna is not in accordance with** the opinion of **this** *tanna*, **as it is taught** in a *baraita*: **Rabbi Shimon ben Yehuda says in the name of Rabbi Shimon: Even** the payments of **humiliation and degradation, he does not pay** them based **on his own** admission as **it is not within his power to tarnish** the reputation of **the daughter of so-and-so** based merely on his confession. Consequently, unless his account is corroborated by the testimony of others, his admission that she was complicit in her seduction is rejected.

HALAKHA

One who says: I seduced, etc. – הָאוֹמֵר פִּתִּיתִי וכו׳: One who confesses: I seduced or raped so-and-so's daughter, is exempt from payment of the fine, but is obligated to pay compensation for humiliation and degradation (Rambam *Sefer Nashim*, *Hilkhot Na'ara Betula* 2:12).

One who says, I stole, etc. – הָאוֹמֵר גָּנַבְתִּי וכו׳: One who confesses to stealing and slaughtering or selling is liable to pay only the principal, but is exempt from payment of double or four or five times the principal (Rambam *Sefer Nezikim*, *Hilkhot Geneiva* 3:9; *Tur*, *Hoshen Mishpat* 348).

My ox killed so-and-so, etc. – הֵמִית שׁוֹרִי אֶת פְּלוֹנִי וכו׳: One who confesses that his ox killed so-and-so, or in the case of a forewarned ox, that it killed so-and-so's ox, pays based on his confession (Rambam *Sefer Hafla'a*, *Hilkhot Shevuot* 8:4; *Sefer Shofetim*, *Hilkhot Sanhedrin* 4:14).

My ox killed a slave belonging to so-and-so, etc. – הֵמִית שׁוֹרִי עַבְדּוֹ שֶׁל פְּלוֹנִי וכו׳: One who confesses that his ox killed another person's slave is exempt from paying the thirty *sela*, as it is a fine (Rambam *Sefer Hafla'a*, *Hilkhot Shevuot* 8:2).

NOTES

The order of the mishna – סִדְרָהּ שֶׁל הַמִּשְׁנָה: The commentaries explain that the mishna employs the style: Not only this but also that. In other words, there is a novel element in each succeeding case. The principle here is that one who admits that he is liable to pay a fine is exempt. The mishna teaches that not only is one exempt in a case where he confesses that he raped or seduced a girl, where the exemption could be attributed to the fact that his admission casts aspersions on the girl, but one who confesses that he stole is also exempt from the double payment, although his testimony casts no aspersions. Furthermore, this *halakha* applies not only to a thief, who although he is exempt from the fine, is obligated to pay the principal; it applies even to a case where one confesses that his ox killed a slave, in which case his confession exempts him from any payment. There is a Torah decree that one whose incrimination is based exclusively on his own confession is exempt from the fine (*Melekhet Shlomo*; see *Tosefot Yom Tov*).

My ox killed a slave belonging to so-and-so – הֵמִית שׁוֹרִי עַבְדּוֹ שֶׁל פְּלוֹנִי: In the Jerusalem Talmud, the question is raised with regard to a slave worth less than thirty *sela*: Is part of the sum considered a monetary payment and the rest a fine, or is the entire amount deemed a fine? The *Yam shel Shlomo* explains that the phrase: Anyone who pays more than what he damaged, should not be taken literally, as it is possible that the slave is worth exactly thirty *sela*, in which case he would pay precisely the sum of the damage he caused. Rather, since the sum is fixed and is not always equal to the value of the slave, it is a fine.

This is the principle – זֶה הַכְּלָל: Based on *Tosafot* the commentaries on the mishna explain that the phrase: This is the principle: Anyone who pays more than what he damaged does not pay based on his own admission, comes to include other fines omitted here: The one hundred silver coins that a slanderer pays the father of his wife, and the obligation to free one's slave if he severed one of his extremities, i.e., he is freed with extraction of a tooth or an eye.

Anyone who pays more than what he damaged – כׇּל הַמְשַׁלֵּם יָתֵר עַל מַה שֶּׁהִזִּיק: This principle, which establishes the difference between fines and payments of money, is problematic in the case of the ransom paid by one whose forewarned ox kills a person, as the *tanna'im* disagree about the meaning of the verse "If a ransom is placed upon him, then he shall give the redemption of his soul" (Exodus 21:30). Is this assessment of ransom based on the value of the victim or the value of the owner of the ox? According to the opinion that he pays his own value, in certain cases he pays more than the damage he caused, and therefore the payment should be considered a fine. *Tosafot*, and in greater detail *Tosefot HaRosh* and other commentaries, explain that since he pays the assessment of his own value, it is considered a monetary payment, as he is essentially redeeming himself from death at the hand of Heaven.

And let the ***tanna*** **teach with regard to one who said: I raped** – וְלִיתְנֵי אָנַסְתִּי וכו׳: According to *Tosafot* the question is: Why didn't the *tanna* cite a case of rape rather than one of seduction? The later commentaries add that had the mishna cited the case of rape, there would have been an additional novel element according to the Rambam's opinion that one pays for her pain based on his own admission. However, the Ritva and others claim that the Gemara is merely asking why the *tanna* did not teach both rape and seduction as he did in the other *mishnayot*. See *Tosafot* for a discussion of the novel element in the case of rape.

It is not necessary for the mishna to cite the case of one who says: I raped her, etc. – לָא מִבַּעְיָא אָנַסְתִּי וכו׳: The *ge'onim* had a variant reading of the Gemara, according to which the case of a rapist is unnecessary, as he did not significantly tarnish her reputation, whereas a seducer severely tarnishes her reputation, and therefore one might think that he pays based on his own confession (see also *Shita Mekubbetzet*).

אָמַר לֵיהּ רַב פַּפָּא לְאַבַּיֵי: נִיחָא לָהּ לְדִידָהּ מַאי? דִּלְמָא לָא נִיחָא לֵיהּ לְאָבִיהָ. נִיחָא לֵיהּ לְאָבִיהָ מַאי? דִּלְמָא לָא נִיחָא לְהוּ לִבְנֵי מִשְׁפָּחָה. נִיחָא לְהוּ לִבְנֵי מִשְׁפָּחָה מַאי? אִי אֶפְשָׁר דְּלֵיכָּא חַד בִּמְדִינַת הַיָּם דְּלָא נִיחָא לֵיהּ.

Rav Pappa said to Abaye: According to Rabbi Shimon, if **she herself is amenable** to his claim, and admits that his version of the events is accurate, **what is the** *halakha*? Is he exempt from payments of humiliation and degradation in that case as well? Abaye responded: **Perhaps her father is not amenable** to his daughter's reputation being tarnished. We therefore do not rely on his statement even in this case. Rav Pappa continued: If **her father is** also **amenable** to his claim, **what** is the *halakha*? Abaye responded: **Perhaps her** other **family members are not amenable,** as the reputation of the entire family would be tarnished. Rav Pappa asked: If the **family members** too are **amenable, what** is the *halakha*? Abaye answered: Even if all the local relatives are amenable, **it is impossible that there** will **not** be at least **one** relative **in a country overseas**[N] **who is not amenable** to his claim.

"הָאוֹמֵר גָּנַבְתִּי מְשַׁלֵּם אֶת הַקֶּרֶן" וכו׳. אִיתְּמַר, פַּלְגָּא נִיזְקָא; רַב פַּפָּא אָמַר: פַּלְגָּא נִיזְקָא מָמוֹנָא, רַב הוּנָא בְּרֵיהּ דְּרַב יְהוֹשֻׁעַ אָמַר: פַּלְגָּא נִיזְקָא קְנָסָא.

The mishna continues. **One who says: I stole, pays the principal,** but does not pay the double payment and the payment four and five times the principal. **It is stated** that *amora'im* disagreed with regard to the payment of **half the damage** that the owner of an innocuous ox, which was not yet witnessed goring a person or an ox three times, must pay to the owner of the ox that he gored. **Rav Pappa said: Half the damage** is considered a payment of **money,** compensation for the damage caused. **Rav Huna, son of Rav Yehoshua, said** that **half the damage** is considered payment of a **fine.**

רַב פַּפָּא אָמַר: פַּלְגָּא נִיזְקָא מָמוֹנָא, קָסָבַר: סְתָם שְׁוָורִים לָאו בְּחֶזְקַת שִׁימּוּר קַיְימֵי, וּבְדִין הוּא דִּמְשַׁלֵּם כּוּלֵּיהּ, וְרַחֲמָנָא הוּא דְּחָיֵיס עֲלֵוֵיהּ, דְּאַכַּתִּי לָא אִיַּיעַד תּוֹרָא. רַב הוּנָא בְּרֵיהּ דְּרַב יְהוֹשֻׁעַ אָמַר: פַּלְגָּא נִיזְקָא קְנָסָא. קָסָבַר: סְתָם שְׁוָורִים בְּחֶזְקַת שִׁימּוּר קַיְימֵי, וּבְדִין הוּא דְּלָא לִישַׁלֵּם כְּלָל, וְרַחֲמָנָא הוּא דִּקְנָסֵיהּ, כִּי הֵיכִי דְּנִינְטְרֵיהּ לְתוֹרֵיהּ.

The Gemara elaborates. **Rav Pappa said: Half the damage** is considered a payment of **money,** as **he maintains: Standard oxen do not exist in the presumptive status of safety,**[N] and therefore are likely to cause damage. **And by right,** the owner **should pay the entire** damage caused by his animal, **and it is the Merciful One that has compassion on him, as his ox is not yet forewarned** until it has gored a person or an animal three times. Fundamentally, the payment is for damage that the animal caused. **Rav Huna, son of Rav Yehoshua, said** that **half the damage** is payment of a **fine,** as **he maintains: Standard oxen exist in the presumptive status of safety,** and are not dangerous. **And by right,** the owner **should not pay at all,** as the ox goring could not have been anticipated, and therefore the owner bears no responsibility. **And it is the Merciful One that penalized him so that he would guard his ox.** The sum that he pays is a fine.

סִימָן: היזיק מה והמית כלל. תְּנַן: הַנִּיזָּק וְהַמַּזִּיק בְּתַשְׁלוּמִין. בִּשְׁלָמָא לְמַאן דְּאָמַר פַּלְגָּא נִיזְקָא מָמוֹנָא – הַיְינוּ דְּשַׁיָּיךְ נִיזָּק בְּתַשְׁלוּמִין. אֶלָּא לְמַאן דְּאָמַר פַּלְגָּא נִיזְקָא קְנָסָא – הָשְׁתָּא, דְּלָאו דִּידֵיהּ קָא שָׁקֵיל, בְּתַשְׁלוּמִין אִיתֵיהּ?!

The Gemara provides **a mnemonic**[B] for the proofs cited with regard to this dispute: **Damaged; what; and killed; principle. We learned** in a mishna that if an innocuous ox gored and killed another's ox, both **the damaged and the damager** share **in the payments. Granted, according to the one who said** that **half the damage** is a payment of **money; that** is how the **damaged party shares in the payments.** By right, the owner of the dead ox should be compensated for his entire loss. However, since the ox that gored his ox was innocuous, the owner of the gored ox bears half the costs. The mishna characterizes him as sharing in the payments. **However, according to he who said** that **half the damage** is payment of **a fine,** by right, the injured party himself is entitled to nothing. **Now,** the owner **takes** half the damage **that** by right **is not his;** can **he** be characterized as sharing **in the payments?**

לָא נְצְרְכָא אֶלָּא לְפְחַת נְבֵילָה. פְּחַת נְבֵילָה תְּנֵינָא: תַּשְׁלוּמֵי נֶזֶק מְלַמֵּד שֶׁהַבְּעָלִים מְטַפְּלִין בַּנְּבֵילָה.

The Gemara answers: This *halakha* is **necessary only for the degradation of the carcass.** Initially, half the damage is assessed by calculating the difference between the value of a living ox and the value of its carcass when the owner of the ox that gored the other ox stands trial. The degradation in the value of the carcass from when it was gored until the owner is able to sell it is borne by the owner of the carcass. The owner thereby shares in the payment, as he loses that sum. The Gemara asks: **We** already **learned** the *halakha* with regard to **the degradation of the carcass** in a *baraita* in *Bava Kamma* (10b) in which it is taught that the passage in the mishna: I have become liable to pay **payments of damage,**[N] **teaches that the owners tend to the carcass**[H] and bear the costs of its degradation.

NOTES

Family members in a country overseas – בְּנֵי מִשְׁפָּחָה בִּמְדִינַת הַיָּם: Although her family, certainly those living overseas, have no monetary claim, the issue here is not their monetary or legal rights. Rather, the question is whether the statement that he seduced the daughter constitutes degradation. In this regard, the fact that she has relatives who would be displeased is enough to establish the claim. Consequently, that confession would not be accepted, as it tarnishes the reputation of the family (Rabbi Aharon HaLevi).

Do not exist in the presumptive status of safety – לָאו בְּחֶזְקַת שִׁימּוּר קַיְימֵי: The Ritva and others explain that this does not mean that the assumption is that every ox will gore a person. It means that even those oxen that do not typically gore people must be guarded. Consequently, one who fails to guard them is liable to pay; he cannot be seen as the victim of unavoidable circumstances.

Payments of damage etc. – תַּשְׁלוּמֵי נֶזֶק וכו׳: The inference is as follows: Had it stated simply damage, the understanding would have been that the owner of the ox that gored another ox must pay the victim the entire damage or half the damage in the case of an innocuous ox. In contrast, the phrase: Payments of damage, indicates that he is liable to payment determined when he stands trial, deducting degradation from the sum that he is liable to pay, but not payment to cover all the damage he caused (Rabbeinu Crescas Vidal).

BACKGROUND

A mnemonic – סִימָן: Because the Talmud was studied orally for many generations, mnemonic devices were necessary to facilitate memorizing a series of *halakhot* and the order in which they were taught.

HALAKHA

That the owners tend to the carcass – שֶׁהַבְּעָלִים מְטַפְּלִין בַּנְּבֵילָה: The owner of the ox that was gored bears the cost of the degradation of the carcass. How so? Consider the case of an ox worth two hundred dinars that was gored and killed, and its carcass, which was worth one hundred dinars at the time of its death, was worth only eighty dinars at trial. If the ox that gored a person or animal was forewarned, its owner pays one hundred dinars; if it was innocuous, the owner pays fifty dinars. The owner of the dead ox is not compensated for the twenty dinars of degradation of the carcass. The Rema writes that this *halakha* applies only if the owner of the ox that was gored is immediately apprised of his loss. However, if he was not apprised, and therefore could not have tended to the carcass and sold it immediately, the owner of the ox that gored a person or animal must pay for the degradation in its value. The *Tur* claims that this *halakha* applies also if the market price of the carcass decreased, whereas others contend that the owner of the ox that was gored bears the cost of the decrease in the market price of the carcass (Rambam *Sefer Nezikim, Hilkhot Nizkei Mamon* 7:8; *Shulḥan Arukh, Ḥoshen Mishpat* 403:20).

חֲדָא בְּתָם וַחֲדָא בְּמוּעָד. וּצְרִיכָא, דְּאִי אַשְׁמוּעִינַן תָּם – מִשּׁוּם דְּאַכַּתִּי לָא אִיַּעַד, אֲבָל מוּעָד דְּאִיַּעַד – אֵימָא לָא. וְאִי אַשְׁמוּעִינַן מוּעָד – מִשּׁוּם דְּקָא מְשַׁלֵּם כּוּלֵּיהּ, אֲבָל תָּם – אֵימָא לָא, צְרִיכָא.

The Gemara answers: **One** of these *halakhot* is **with regard to an innocuous** ox **and one** is **with regard to a forewarned** ox. The Gemara adds: **And** it is **necessary** to teach both *halakhot*, **as if** the mishna **had taught us** only with regard to **an innocuous** ox, one would understand that its owner is treated with leniency and the owner of the carcass bears the cost of degradation **due to** the fact **that** the ox **has not yet been forewarned; however,** with regard to **a forewarned** ox, **that was forewarned, say no,** the owner of the carcass does not bear the cost of degradation. **And if** the mishna **had taught us** only with regard to **a forewarned** ox, one would understand that its owner is treated with leniency and the owner of the carcass bears the cost of degradation **due to** the fact **that he pays** for the **entire damage,** and therefore, the relatively insignificant cost of degradation is overlooked. **However,** with regard to **an innocuous** ox, **say no,** since the owner pays only half the damage, he must bear the cost of degradation. Therefore, it was **necessary** to state the *halakha* in both cases. Therefore, there is no proof from this mishna whether half the damage is payment of a money or payment of a fine.

תָּא שְׁמַע: מָה בֵּין תָּם לְמוּעָד? שֶׁהַתָּם מְשַׁלֵּם חֲצִי נֶזֶק מִגּוּפוֹ, וּמוּעָד מְשַׁלֵּם נֶזֶק שָׁלֵם מִן הָעֲלִיָּיה. וְלָא קָתָנֵי שֶׁהַתָּם אֵינוֹ מְשַׁלֵּם עַל פִּי עַצְמוֹ וּמוּעָד מְשַׁלֵּם עַל פִּי עַצְמוֹ!

The Gemara continues. **Come** and **hear** an additional proof from a *baraita*: **What is** the difference **between an innocuous and a forewarned** ox? The difference is **that** the owner of **an innocuous** ox **pays half** of the **damage from its body.** Compensation for the damage may be collected only from the body of the ox that gored another ox. If the ox that gored another ox is worth less than half the damage, e.g., if an inexpensive ox killed an expensive one, the injured party receives less than half the damage. **And** the owner of **a forewarned** ox **pays the entire damage from the** owner's **property,** and the value of the ox that gored another ox has no effect on the payment. The *tanna* **did not teach** an additional difference that the owner of **an innocuous** ox **does not pay** based **on his own** admission **and** the owner of **a forewarned** ox **pays** based **on his own** admission.[H] Apparently, the half damage is a payment of money and not a fine.

תָּנָא וְשִׁיֵּיר. מַאי שִׁיֵּיר דְּהַאי שִׁיֵּיר? שִׁיֵּיר חֲצִי כּוֹפֶר. אִי מִשּׁוּם חֲצִי כּוֹפֶר – לָאו שִׁיּוּרָא הוּא.

The Gemara refutes this claim: This *baraita* is no proof, as the *tanna* **taught** some cases **and omitted** others[N] and did not list all the differences between innocuous and forewarned oxen. The Gemara asks: **What else did he omit that he omitted this?** The failure to include an item in a list can be deemed insignificant only if it is one of at least two omissions. If there is only one omission, apparently it was omitted advisedly. The Gemara replies: **He omitted** the *halakha* of the **half ransom**[H] as well. If a forewarned ox killed a person, its owner pays a ransom, and if an innocuous ox killed a person, the owner does not pay even half the ransom. The Gemara rejects this claim: **If** it is **due to** the **half ransom** that the failure to list the difference with regard to payment based on one's own admission is insignificant, it **is not an omission.**

HALAKHA

Innocuous and forewarned – **תָּם וּמוּעָד**: The owner of a forewarned ox pays full damages from his highest quality property. The same applies to any damage caused by an animal in the course of its typical conduct and which therefore is considered forewarned. If an innocuous ox caused damage its owner pays half of the damage, paid from the body of the ox itself (Rambam *Sefer Nezikim*, *Hilkhot Nizkei Mamon* 1:2–3; *Shulḥan Arukh*, *Ḥoshen Mishpat* 389:2, 9).

Half ransom – **חֲצִי כּוֹפֶר**: The owner of an innocuous ox that killed a person pays nothing, not even half the ransom, as explicitly stated in *Bava Kamma* (Rambam *Sefer Nezikim*, *Hilkhot Nizkei Mamon* 10:2).

NOTES

The *tanna* taught some cases and omitted others – **תָּנָא וְשִׁיֵּיר**: This is a standard response to an attempted inference from an omission in a mishna. The idea is that an omission of a case from a mishna is not significant if the *tanna* did not list all of the possible cases. An alternative manner of expressing the same concept is the phrase: Is that to say that the *tanna* should have continued reckoning cases like a peddler? The immediate rejoinder to this answer, as here, is for the Gemara to inquire: What else did he omit that he omitted this? In other words, in order to assert that the *tanna* did not list all possible cases, it must be proven that the *tanna* omitted additional examples.

הָא מַנִּי – רַבִּי יוֹסֵי הַגְּלִילִי הִיא, דְּאָמַר: תָּם מְשַׁלֵּם חֲצִי כּוֹפֶר.

As it can be explained: According to **whose** opinion **is this** *baraita* taught? **It is** according to the opinion of **Rabbi Yosei**[N] **HaGelili,**[N] **who said:** The owner of **an innocuous** ox **pays half** the **ransom.** According to his opinion, the only differences between innocuous and forewarned oxen are those specified in the mishna.

תָּא שְׁמַע: ״הֵמִית שׁוֹרִי אֶת פְּלוֹנִי״, אוֹ ״שׁוֹרוֹ שֶׁל פְּלוֹנִי״ – הֲרֵי זֶה מְשַׁלֵּם עַל פִּי עַצְמוֹ. מַאי לָאו בְּתָם? לָא, בְּמוּעָד.

The Gemara suggests: **Come** and **hear** an additional proof from the mishna. One who said: **My ox killed so-and-so, or:** My ox killed **an ox** belonging **to so-and-so, this** owner **pays** based **on his own** admission. **What, is** this **not** referring **to an innocuous** ox, for which he pays half the damage, proving that it is a payment of money and not a fine? The Gemara rejects the proof: **No,** the *tanna* is referring **to a forewarned** animal.

אֲבָל בְּתָם מַאי – אֵינוֹ מְשַׁלֵּם עַל פִּי עַצְמוֹ. אַדְּתָנֵי סֵיפָא: ״עַבְדּוֹ שֶׁל פְּלוֹנִי״ אֵינוֹ מְשַׁלֵּם עַל פִּי עַצְמוֹ – נִיפְלוֹג וְנִיתְנֵי בְּדִידַהּ: בַּמֶּה דְּבָרִים אֲמוּרִים – בְּמוּעָד, אֲבָל תָּם אֵינוֹ מְשַׁלֵּם עַל פִּי עַצְמוֹ! כּוּלַּהּ בְּמוּעָד קָמַיְירֵי.

The Gemara asks: **However,** in the case **of an innocuous** ox, **what** is the *halakha*? If it is that **he does not pay** based **on his own** admission, then, **rather than teaching the latter clause** of the mishna: One whose ox **killed a slave** belonging **to so-and-so does not pay** based **on his own** admission, **let him distinguish and teach** the distinction **within the case itself: In what** case **is this statement said?** It is **with regard to a forewarned** ox; **however,** the owner of **an innocuous** ox **does not pay** based **on his own** admission. The Gemara rejects this proof: The **entire** mishna **is speaking of a forewarned** ox, and does not address the *halakha* of an innocuous ox at all. Therefore, no proof can be cited with regard to the nature of half the payment.

תָּא שְׁמַע, זֶה הַכְּלָל: כׇּל הַמְשַׁלֵּם יָתֵר עַל מַה שֶּׁהִזִּיק אֵינוֹ מְשַׁלֵּם עַל פִּי עַצְמוֹ. הָא פָּחוֹת מִמַּה שֶּׁהִזִּיק – מְשַׁלֵּם עַל פִּי עַצְמוֹ! לָא תֵּימָא: הָא פָּחוֹת מִמַּה שֶּׁהִזִּיק, אֶלָּא אֵימָא: הָא כְּמַה שֶּׁהִזִּיק – מְשַׁלֵּם עַל פִּי עַצְמוֹ.

The Gemara suggests: **Come** and **hear** an additional proof from the mishna: **This is the principle: Anyone who pays more than what he damaged,** the payments are fines, and therefore **he does not pay** based **on his own** admission. The Gemara infers: If he pays **less than what he damaged, he pays** based **on his own** admission. Apparently, payment of half the damage is a payment of money, not a fine. The Gemara rejects this proof: **Do not** infer and **say:** If he pays **less than what he damaged,** he pays based on his own admission. Infer and **say:** If he pays precisely **what he damaged, he pays** based **on his own** admission.

אֲבָל פָּחוֹת מַאי – אֵינוֹ מְשַׁלֵּם עַל פִּי עַצְמוֹ. לִיתְנֵי: זֶה הַכְּלָל: כׇּל שֶׁאֵינוֹ מְשַׁלֵּם כְּמַה שֶּׁהִזִּיק – אֵינוֹ מְשַׁלֵּם עַל פִּי עַצְמוֹ, דְּמַשְׁמַע פָּחוֹת וּמַשְׁמַע יָתֵר! תְּיוּבְתָּא.

The Gemara asks: **But** according to that explanation, if he pays **less** than the damage he caused, **what** is the *halakha*? If it is that **he does not pay** based **on his own** admission, **let** the *tanna* **teach** a more general principle: **This is the principle: Anyone who does not pay** the amount **that he damaged does not pay** based **on his own** admission, **as** that formulation both **indicates** one who pays **less and indicates** one who pays **more** than the damage he inflicted. The Gemara concludes: This is **a conclusive refutation** of the opinion of Rav Huna, son of Rav Yehoshua, that payment of half the damage is a fine.

NOTES

According to whose opinion is this *baraita* taught? It is according to Rabbi Yosei, etc. – הָא מַנִּי רַבִּי יוֹסֵי וכו׳: The structure of the Gemara appears to indicate the following: The Gemara attempts to prove that apparently the payment of half the damage is a monetary payment and not a fine, from the fact that the distinction between a forewarned ox, whose owner pays based on his confession, and an innocuous ox, whose owner does not pay based on his confession, was omitted from the mishna. The Gemara answers: The *tanna* taught some cases and omitted others. The Gemara asks: What else did he omit that he omitted this? The Gemara answers: He omitted payment of half the ransom, as there is no payment of ransom at all for an innocuous ox. The Gemara notes: That is not an omission, as the mishna is in accordance with the opinion of Rabbi Yosei HaGelili, who holds that there is a payment of half the ransom in the case of an innocuous ox. Indeed, Rabbeinu Simḥa, cited in *Tosefot HaRosh*, explains the Gemara in this manner. However, that explanation is difficult. The entire difficulty raised by the Gemara is based on establishing that the mishna is according to the individual opinion of Rabbi Yosei HaGelili, which is by no means the most obvious possibility.

The Ra'avad explains in the name of one of his teachers that the contention that the *tanna* included some cases and omitted others is far-fetched, and therefore, the Gemara prefers an explanation of the mishna that does not rely on that contention, even if it requires adoption of a minority opinion. However, some difficulty remains, and therefore, most early commentaries explain the exchange in the Gemara differently. The Gemara is saying that once it was established that the *tanna* omitted the difference between the forewarned and innocuous oxen with regard to ransom, apparently there is another difference that he omitted. It must be that he omitted the difference with regard to liability to pay half the damage based on one's own confession. This proves that the payment of half the damage is a fine and poses a difficulty to the one who holds that it is a monetary payment. The Gemara responds that it is not an absolute proof as it could be established that the mishna is according to the opinion of Rabbi Yosei HaGelili, in which case there is no difference between them with regard to ransom, and therefore there is no need to search for an additional difference with regard to payment based on confession (Ra'avad; Rosh; Ritva).

Rabbi Yosei HaGelili – רַבִּי יוֹסֵי הַגְּלִילִי: *Tosafot* discuss at length why the Gemara attributes this opinion to Rabbi Yosei HaGelili, as there is no source where he is cited expressing this opinion, and it is merely inferred from his statements. Furthermore, if we are willing to ascribe this opinion based on inference, it could be attributed to Rabbi Akiva and to other Sages as well. The Ritva claims that in cases of this kind, the Gemara is not particular about the precise identity of the *tanna*, but is satisfied with the fact that there is a tannaitic opinion to this effect, even if there are other Sages who might also concur with this opinion.

וְהִלְכְתָא: פַּלְגָא נִיזְקָא קְנָסָא. תְּיוּבְתָּא וְהִלְכְתָא?! אִין, טַעְמָא מַאי אִיתּוֹתַב – מִשּׁוּם דְּלָא קָתָנֵי כְּמָה שֶׁהִזִּיק. לָא פְּסִיקָא לֵיהּ, כֵּיוָן דְּאִיכָּא חֲצִי נֶזֶק צְרוֹרוֹת דְּהִלְכְתָא גְּמִירִי לַהּ דְּמָמוֹנָא הוּא – מִשּׁוּם הָכִי לָא קָתָנֵי.

The Gemara further concludes: **And the *halakha* is that** payment of **half the damage**[H] **is a fine.** The Gemara asks: Is there **a conclusive refutation** of the opinion of Rav Huna, son of Rav Yehoshua, **and** the ***halakha***[N] is in accordance with that opinion? The Gemara responds: **Yes,** the *halakha* is in accordance with his opinion, as, **what is the reason** that his opinion **was conclusively refuted?** It is **because** the *tanna* **does not teach:** This is the principle: Anyone who does not pay the amount **that he damaged.** However, the reason the *tanna* did not employ that formulation **is not clear-cut for him, since there is** the payment of **half** the **damage** caused by **pebbles**[H] dispersed by an animal proceeding in its usual manner. **As it is a *halakha* transmitted** to Moses from Sinai **that** the payment for pebbles **is a monetary** payment, not a fine; it is **due to that** fact that the *tanna* **did not teach** the principle: Anyone who does not pay the amount that he damaged does not pay based on his own admission. In the case of pebbles, although he does not pay the amount that he damaged, he pays based on his own admission.

וְהַשְׁתָּא דְּאָמְרַתְּ פַּלְגָא נִיזְקָא קְנָסָא, הַאי כַּלְבָּא דַּאֲכַל אִימְרֵי, וְשׁוּנְרָא דְּאָכֵיל תַּרְנְגוֹלֵי רַבְרְבֵי – מְשׁוּנֶּה הוּא, וְלָא מַגְבִּינַן בְּבָבֶל. אֲבָל זוּטְרֵי – אוֹרְחֵיהּ הוּא, וּמַגְבִּינַן.

Based on that ruling, the Gemara concludes: **And now that you said** that payment of **half the damage is a fine,**[N] **this dog that ate lambs,**[H] **and a cat that ate large roosters,**[N] **is unusual**[N] damage, for which the owner is liable to pay only half the damage if the animal was innocuous, **and** therefore, **we do not collect it in Babylonia.** The payment for unusual damage is a fine, and fines cannot be collected in Babylonia, as there are no ordained judges authorized to adjudicate cases involving fines. **However,** if the cat ate **small** roosters, that **is its usual manner, and we collect** the damages in Babylonia, as it is a payment of money.

HALAKHA

Half the damage – פַּלְגָא נִיזְקָא: The payment of anyone obligated to pay a sum equivalent to the amount of damage caused is considered a monetary payment, whereas the payment of anyone obligated to pay either more or less than the amount of damage caused is a fine. A person is liable to pay a fine based only on the testimony of witnesses (Rambam *Sefer Nezikim, Hilkhot Nizkei Mamon* 2:8).

Half the damage caused by pebbles – חֲצִי נֶזֶק צְרוֹרוֹת: If an animal dispersed pebbles from under its feet in the course of walking, and those pebbles caused damage, it is a sub-category of the primary category of damage of foot, which includes any damage caused by the animal in the course of its standard conduct, and the animal's owner is obligated to remit a monetary payment to the person whose property was damaged, from his highest quality property. However, there is a *halakha* transmitted to Moses from Sinai that he pays only half of the damages (Rambam *Sefer Nezikim, Hilkhot Nizkei Mamon* 2:2; *Shulḥan Arukh, Ḥoshen Mishpat* 390:3).

A dog that ate lambs, etc. – כַּלְבָּא דַּאֲכַל אִימְרֵי וכו׳: If an undomesticated animal killed and ate an animal or ate raw meat, this is typical conduct, and its owner must pay the complete amount of the damage caused. However, in the case of a dog that killed a lamb or in the case of a cat that killed a large rooster and ate it, that is atypical conduct and therefore the owner of the cat or dog is liable to pay only half the damage. A person liable to pay half the damage pays only based on the ruling of judges ordained in Eretz Yisrael (Rambam *Sefer Nezikim, Hilkhot Nizkei Mamon* 3:7; *Sefer Shofetim, Hilkhot Sanhedrin* 5:9; *Shulḥan Arukh, Ḥoshen Mishpat* 391:6; 1:5).

NOTES

A conclusive refutation and *halakha* – תְּיוּבְתָּא וְהִלְכְתָא: There is a difference between the Gemara's use of the expressions conclusive refutation and difficulty. If the opinion of a Sage is characterized as difficult, his opinion was not completely rejected. The Gemara is merely noting that there is a difficulty with that opinion. There is a tradition among the early commentaries that there is an answer to each of those difficulties. Indeed, several books, e.g., Rabbi Yeshaya Berlin's *Kashot Meyushav*, are devoted to providing answers in all of the places where the Gemara concludes that it is difficult. In contrast, when the Gemara concludes that there is a conclusive refutation of an opinion, the difficulty is significant to the extent that the opinion of that Sage is rejected. That explains the astonishment expressed by the Gemara: A conclusive refutation and *halakha*?

And now that you said that payment of half the damage is a fine – וְהַשְׁתָּא דְּאָמְרַתְּ פַּלְגָא נִיזְקָא קְנָסָא: Even though fundamentally, ordained judges are required to adjudicate monetary cases as well as cases of fines, the Sages instituted that in this regard the Sages in each place are the agents of the original ordained Sages. Although they said that this principle is implemented only in common cases, damage caused by animals is deemed a frequent occurrence and is therefore within the jurisdiction of Babylonian judges when the payment for damages is a monetary payment and not a fine (Ritva).

Large roosters – תַּרְנְגוֹלֵי רַבְרְבֵי: The early commentaries state that this distinction between large and small animals applies only to a cat that killed roosters. However, with regard to the case of a dog that ate lambs, it is unusual for a dog to eat even undersized lambs, and therefore those cases may not be adjudicated in Babylonia (Rashi and Meiri on *Bava Kamma*).

It is unusual – מְשׁוּנֶּה הוּא: As explained by Rashi, any damage caused to an object by a domesticated or undomesticated animal eating it falls into the primary category of damage of tooth, which includes any damage caused by the animal by eating an item that it typically eats. However, if the animal ate an item that it does not typically eat, it no longer falls into the category of tooth. Instead, the animal is considered to have acted with the intention to cause damage, which places it in the category of horn, which includes any damage that the animal causes intentionally. Consequently, as long as it was not forewarned, that act has the legal status of goring by an innocuous ox, and the owner only pays half the damage from the animal itself.

וְאִי תָּפַס – לָא מַפְּקִינַן מִינֵּיהּ. וְאִי אֲמַר: אַקְבְּעוּ לִי זִימְנָא לְאֶרֶץ יִשְׂרָאֵל, מַקְבְּעִינַן לֵיהּ, וְאִי לָא אָזֵיל, מְשַׁמְּתִינַן לֵיהּ.

The Gemara comments: **And** in cases of fines, **if** the injured party **seized**[NH] property from the offender in the amount of the fine, even in Babylonia **we do not repossess it from him,** as according to the letter of the law he is entitled to that payment, and the party from whom he seized the property cannot claim that he does not owe that payment. **And if** the injured party **said: Set me a time** to go **to** a court **in Eretz Yisrael,** where cases of fines are adjudicated, **we set** a time **for him, and if** the other disputant **does not go** to Israel as demanded, **we excommunicate him.**

בֵּין כָּךְ וּבֵין כָּךְ מְשַׁמְּתִינַן לֵיהּ. דְּאָמְרִינַן לֵיהּ: סַלֵּיק הֶיזֵּיקָךְ, מִדְּרַבִּי נָתָן. דְּתַנְיָא, רַבִּי נָתָן אוֹמֵר: מִנַּיִן שֶׁלֹּא יְגַדֵּל אָדָם כֶּלֶב רַע בְּתוֹךְ בֵּיתוֹ וְלֹא יַעֲמִיד סוּלָּם רָעוּעַ בְּתוֹךְ בֵּיתוֹ – שֶׁנֶּאֱמַר ״וְלֹא תָשִׂים דָּמִים בְּבֵיתֶךָ״.

The Gemara adds: **Either way,** whether or not he agrees to go to Eretz Yisrael, if he keeps the cause of the damage, **we** in Babylonia **excommunicate him, as we say to him: Remove your** cause of **damage,**[N] in accordance with the opinion of **Rabbi Natan. As it is taught** in a *baraita* that **Rabbi Natan says: From where** is it derived **that a person may not raise a vicious dog**[HB] **in his house, and may not place an unsteady ladder**[H] **in his house?** It is **as it is stated:** "And you shall make a parapet for your roof **that you shall not place blood in your house"** (Deuteronomy 22:8). It is prohibited to leave a potentially dangerous object in one's house, and one who refuses to remove it is excommunicated.

הדרן עלך אלו נערות

NOTES

And if he seized – **וְאִי תָּפַס**: Rabbeinu Tam maintains that seized in this context means that he seized the animal that caused the damage, as, if the legal status of this situation is like that of the damage caused by the horn of an innocuous ox, payment may be collected only from the animal itself, not from the rest of the owner's property. The Meiri agrees. Many early commentaries, however, maintain that since he is not collecting the damages through the legal system but is seizing compensation for the damage he suffered, the above distinction does not apply. As a result, even if the owner of the rooster or the lamb seized other assets of the owner of the dog and the cat, the courts do not repossess them. The Rivan attributes this explanation to Rashi in *Bava Kamma*. This explanation also stands to reason, as it is unlikely that the value of a cat would be sufficient to offset half the damage to a large rooster.

Remove your cause of damage – **סַלֵּיק הֶיזֵּיקָךְ**: The Ritva writes, and the *Nimmukei Yosef* cites in his name, that this principle applies only to a nuisance like a dog, when the owner can be ostracized until he kills it or removes it by some other means. If, however, it was an ox that he utilizes for his work, the court does not compel the owner to remove it from his possession. He is forced to upgrade his supervision over it. In the Jerusalem Talmud, there is an opinion cited by the authorities that even though the party that suffered the damage has the right to seize the possessions of the one whose animal caused the damage, and despite the fact that the latter is required to remove the source of damage from his possession, the owner of the animal that caused the damage is under no obligation, not even by the laws of Heaven, to pay a fine if the court lacks the authority to force him to do so (see *Nimmukei Yosef*).

HALAKHA

And if he seized – **וְאִי תָּפַס**: Even though courts do not collect fines outside Eretz Yisrael, where the judges are not ordained, the person liable to pay the fine is ostracized until he attempts to appease the person who incurred the damage and pays him an appropriate sum. If he does so, the ostracism is repealed, even if the one who incurred the damage refuses to be placated. Similarly, if the victim seizes the property of the person liable to pay the fine equal to the value of the fine, the court does not repossess it from him. The Rema states in the name of the Rosh that although the court does not assess the damage *ab initio* so that if he chooses to do so the victim will know how much to seize, if the victim seized the other's property, the court assesses the damage and informs him whether he is allowed to keep the entire sum that he seized. All these limitations apply to fines fixed by Torah or rabbinic law. However, Sages located in each place have the authority to institute ordinances and collect fines from those who violate their ordinances (Rambam *Sefer Shofetim, Hilkhot Sanhedrin* 5:17; *Shulḥan Arukh, Ḥoshen Mishpat* 1:5).

A vicious dog – **כֶּלֶב רַע**: It is prohibited to raise a vicious dog unless it is tied with iron chains. In a border town one may raise a vicious dog, but he must tie it by day and release it at night. The Rema cites an opinion that if Jews are living among gentiles and require protection they may raise dogs for that purpose; however, if the dog is so vicious that it poses a real danger to people beyond the need for protection, the owner must tie it with chains, as stated here and in *Bava Kamma* 83b (Rambam *Sefer Nezikim, Hilkhot Nizkei Mamon* 5:9; *Shulḥan Arukh, Ḥoshen Mishpat* 409:3).

An unsteady ladder – **סוּלָּם רָעוּעַ**: It is a mitzva to remove any potential danger from one's property. One who keeps a dangerous item in his house has failed to fulfill the positive mitzva of making a parapet and has violated the prohibition: You shall not place blood in your house (Rambam *Sefer Nezikim, Hilkhot Rotze'aḥ UShmirat HaNefesh* 11:4; *Shulḥan Arukh, Ḥoshen Mishpat* 427:8).

BACKGROUND

Damages of cats and dogs – **נִזְקֵי כֶּלֶב וְחָתוּל**: Apparently, based on the Gemara, cats were not completely domesticated and trained in those times. However, some people kept cats in their houses in order to battle snakes, mice, and other small vermin. However, in many cases, the cat would pounce on birds or even on the children of the house.

Most of the dogs in that period were either shepherd dogs or guard dogs. Later in this tractate (61b), it is clear that raising a dog in one's home as a pet was uncommon. Moreover, there were those who kept a vicious dog, a savage guard dog trained to attack and even kill people. It was no wonder that a dog of that kind could pounce on domesticated animals and kill them.

Summary of **Perek III**

In this chapter, the Gemara concluded that one who rapes or seduces a young woman who is forbidden to him, regardless of whether the prohibition is by Torah law or by rabbinic law, need not and may not marry her. However, he is required to pay her father the fine mentioned in the Torah. However, if she was forbidden to him by a prohibition punishable by death, then even if in this particular case the death penalty is not administered, the perpetrator is exempt from paying the fine.

These *halakhot* are based on several principles analyzed in this chapter. One is that a person is not punished with two punishments for one prohibited action; rather he receives the more severe punishment. Another is that in the case of any prohibition whose violation incurs both lashes and monetary payment, one pays and is not flogged. One is obligated to make that payment even if the prohibition was punishable by *karet*.

With regard to the details mentioned in the verse, the Gemara concluded that the rapist is obligated to pay the fine only if the victim is a virgin and not one who lost her presumptive virgin status, e.g., an emancipated maidservant or a woman who participated in a marriage ceremony; however, the rapist is obligated to pay even if he raped a minor girl and not only if the victim is a young woman. Furthermore, even if the victim was a young woman who was betrothed and widowed from betrothal, he is obligated to pay. In addition, although the verse refers to a young woman with a father, even if the victim was an orphan the rapist pays a fine. However, with regard to this detail, there is a difference between the victim of rape and the victim of seduction, as one who seduces an orphaned young woman is exempt, because she was complicit in performing the action. With regard to refusal to marry the perpetrator, the Sages derived that this applies to both the victim of rape and the victim of seduction, and both the father and the daughter have the right of refusal.

The Gemara concluded that the sum written in the Torah is a fine and the perpetrator pays it to every young woman that he victimizes. However, in addition, like any person who injures another, he pays for pain, humiliation, loss of livelihood, medical costs, and degradation. The fine is payment for the act of intercourse alone. Since that sum is a fine and not a monetary obligation, like all fines it is collected only through the testimony of witnesses and not by his own admission and it may be levied and collected only by ordained judges.

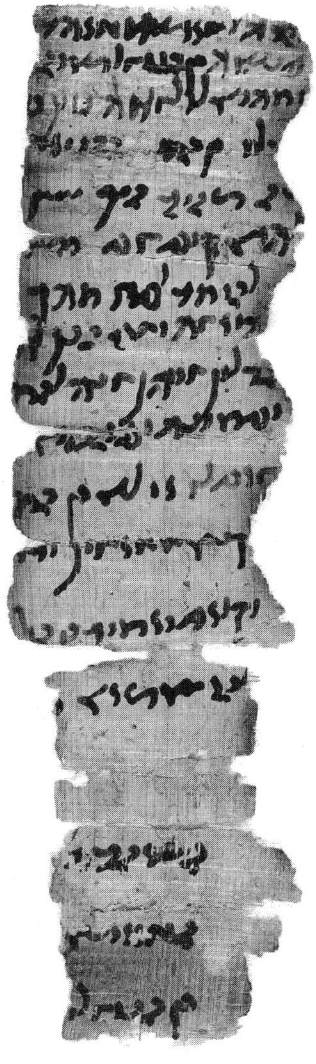

Remnant of an ancient *ketuba*, marriage document, found in a cave in the Judean Desert. Dating back to the second century, it is the oldest *ketuba* ever discovered. It was hidden, along with other objects, by refugees at the end of the bar Kokheva revolt. Although most of the text of the *ketuba* is missing, many significant details can be derived from what remains.

Introduction to **Perek IV**

And if a man sell his daughter to be a maidservant, she shall not go out as the menservants do. If she does not please her master, who has espoused her to himself, then he shall let her be redeemed; he shall have no power to sell her to a foreign people, seeing that he has dealt deceitfully with her. And if he espouse her to his son, he shall deal with her after the manner of daughters. If he takes another wife for himself, her food, her clothing, and her conjugal rights he shall not diminish. And if he does not do these three for her, then she shall go out for nothing, without money.

(Exodus 21:7–11)

If a man take a wife, and go in unto her, and hate her, and place wanton charges against her, and bring up an evil name upon her, and say: I took this woman, and when I came near to her, I did not find in her the tokens of virginity; then the father of the young woman, and her mother, shall take and bring forth the tokens of the young woman's virginity to the Elders of the city in the gate. And the young woman's father shall say to the Elders: I gave my daughter to this man as a wife, and he hates her; and he has placed wanton charges, saying: I did not find in your daughter the tokens of virginity; and these are the tokens of my daughter's virginity. And they shall spread the garment before the Elders of the city. And the Elders of that city shall take the man and chastise him. And they shall fine him a hundred shekels of silver, and give them to the father of the young woman, because he has defamed a virgin of Israel; and she shall be his wife; he may not send her away all his days.

(Deuteronomy 22:13–19)

The Torah states that the fine of the rapist of a young woman must be paid to her father. This chapter analyzes the nature of this rule, which leads to a broader discussion of a father's rights over his daughter. The main sources in the Torah for these rights are the verses that deal with the sale of one's daughter as a maidservant, and there are also several rabbinic ordinances in this regard. The Gemara debates whether these are personal rights, or monetary rights that can be bequeathed to the father's heirs.

Another area of *halakha* in which a father is a party to his daughter's claim is the case of a defamer. Although this situation is described in detail in the Torah, many of its details require clarification. The discussion here focuses on the extent to which the verses must be fulfilled in a literal manner. All agree, for instance, that no punitive measures may be taken as prescribed in the Torah without the testimony of witnesses, which is not mentioned in these verses.

The analysis of the rights of a father over his daughter leads to the central topic of this chapter: The husband's rights with regard to his wife, and his corresponding obligations toward her. The focus of this debate is the marriage contract and its stipulations, which define these rights and obligations. This chapter deals with the obligations of the husband that apply by Torah law, which are derived from the case of the Hebrew maidservant who marries her master. In addition, it discusses those obligations that apply by rabbinic law.

Perek **IV**
Daf **41** Amud **b**

מתני׳ נַעֲרָה שֶׁנִּתְפַּתְּתָה – בּוֹשְׁתָּהּ וּפְגָמָהּ וּקְנָסָהּ שֶׁל אָבִיהָ, וְהַצַּעַר בִּתְפוּסָה. עָמְדָה בַּדִּין עַד שֶׁלֹּא מֵת הָאָב – הֲרֵי הֵן שֶׁל אָב. מֵת הָאָב – הֲרֵי הֵן שֶׁל אַחִין.

MISHNA In the case of **a young woman who was seduced,**[H] the compensation for **her humiliation and her degradation and her fine** belong **to her father. And** the same applies to the compensation for **pain in** the case of a woman who was **raped.** If the young woman **stood trial**[N] against the seducer or rapist **before the father died,**[H] **these** payments belong **to her father,** as stated above. If **the father died** before he collected the money from the offender, the payments belong **to** her **brothers.** As the father's heirs, they inherit the money to which he was entitled before he passed away.

לֹא הִסְפִּיקָה לַעֲמוֹד בַּדִּין עַד שֶׁמֵּת הָאָב – הֲרֵי הֵן שֶׁל עַצְמָהּ, עָמְדָה בַּדִּין עַד שֶׁלֹּא בָּגְרָה – הֲרֵי הֵן שֶׁל אָב. מֵת הָאָב – הֲרֵי הֵן שֶׁל אַחִין. לֹא הִסְפִּיקָה לַעֲמוֹד בַּדִּין עַד שֶׁבָּגְרָה – הֲרֵי הֵן שֶׁל עַצְמָהּ. רַבִּי שִׁמְעוֹן אוֹמֵר: אִם לֹא הִסְפִּיקָה לִגְבּוֹת עַד שֶׁמֵּת הָאָב – הֲרֵי הֵן שֶׁל עַצְמָהּ.

However, if **she did not manage to stand in judgment before the father died,** and she was subsequently awarded the money, the compensation belongs **to her,**[N] as she is now under her own jurisdiction due to the fact that she no longer has a father. If **she stood trial before she reached majority,** the payments belong **to her father,** and if **the father died, they** belong **to** her **brothers,** who inherit the money notwithstanding the fact that she has become a grown woman since the trial. If **she did not manage to stand in judgment before she reached majority,** the money belongs **to her. Rabbi Shimon says:** Even **if** she stood trial in her father's lifetime but **did not manage to collect** the payments **before the father died,** the brothers do not inherit this money, as it belongs **to her.**

NOTES

She stood trial, etc. – עָמְדָה בַּדִּין וכו׳: Some commentaries note that the phrase: She stood trial, does not prove that the father himself cannot sue the offender. Rather, the *tanna* formulates his statement in this manner because the young woman is the sole claimant in the case that follows in the mishna, where the father already died (*Shita Mekubbetzet*). In fact, some early authorities claim the very opposite, that she cannot pursue this claim on her own, as the fact that the money will go to her father indicates that he is the appropriate litigant (Ra'avad; see Rambam).

Belongs to her – הֲרֵי הֵן שֶׁל עַצְמָהּ: Some authorities rule that in this case all of the compensation belongs to her (Rambam; *Tosafot*). Others maintain that with regard to the payments for humiliation and degradation, which are compensation for actual damage caused, the obligation is created automatically at the time of the rape or seduction, which was before the father died. Consequently, the sum belongs to the father even after he has passed away, and the brothers are entitled to this payment as his heirs. It is only the fixed monetary fine that comes into effect due to the court ruling and therefore belongs to the woman (Ramban).

HALAKHA

A young woman who was seduced, etc. – נַעֲרָה שֶׁנִּתְפַּתְּתָה וכו׳: The fine and the compensation for the humiliation and degradation of a seduced young woman and the pain of a raped young woman all belong to her father. If she has no father, she herself is entitled to the money (Rambam *Sefer Nashim, Hilkhot Na'ara Betula* 2:14).

If she stood trial before the father died, etc. – עָמְדָה בַּדִּין עַד שֶׁלֹּא מֵת הָאָב וכו׳: In the case of a seduced or raped young woman who sued only after she reached majority or married, or after her father's death, the fine and the compensation for humiliation, degradation, and, in a case of rape, the pain, all belong to the woman. If she stood trial when she was under her father's authority, the money belongs to her father. If she subsequently reached majority or married, or her father passed away, her brothers collect the money as his heirs, as the father is entitled to them as soon as the court delivers its verdict (Rambam *Sefer Nashim, Hilkhot Na'ara Betula* 2:15).

Perek **IV**
Daf **42** Amud **a**

מַעֲשֵׂה יָדֶיהָ וּמְצִיאָתָהּ, אַף עַל פִּי שֶׁלֹּא גָּבְתָה, מֵת הָאָב – הֲרֵי הֵן שֶׁל אַחִין.

By contrast, with regard to **her earnings and** the lost **items** that **she** has **found, although she has not collected** them,[N] e.g., she had yet to receive her wages, if **the father died they** belong **to** her **brothers.** These payments are considered the property of their father, as he was entitled to them before he passed away.

גמ׳ מַאי קָא מַשְׁמַע לַן? תְּנֵינָא: הַמְפַתֶּה נוֹתֵן שְׁלֹשָׁה דְבָרִים, וְהָאוֹנֵס אַרְבָּעָה, הַמְפַתֶּה נוֹתֵן בּוֹשֶׁת וּפְגָם וּקְנָס, מוֹסִיף עָלָיו אוֹנֵס שֶׁנּוֹתֵן אֶת הַצַּעַר! לְאָבִיהָ אִיצְטְרִיךְ לֵיהּ. לְאָבִיהָ נָמֵי פְּשִׁיטָא, מִדְּקָא יָהֵיב מְפַתֶּה. דְּאִי לְעַצְמָהּ – אַמַּאי יָהֵיב מְפַתֶּה? מִדַּעְתָּהּ עֲבַד!

GEMARA The Gemara asks: **What is** the mishna **teaching us? We** already **learned** this in a mishna (*Ketubot* 39a): **The seducer pays three types of indemnity and the rapist** pays **four. The seducer pays** compensation for his victim's **humiliation and degradation and** for the **fine** the Torah imposes on a seducer. **A rapist adds an additional** payment, **as he pays** compensation for **the pain** she suffered. The Gemara answers: It **is necessary for** the mishna to teach that the money is given **to her father.** The Gemara asks: It **is also obvious** that the money goes **to her father, from** the fact **that a seducer pays** these types of indemnity, **as,** if one claims that the money goes **to her, why does a seducer pay** her at all? After all, **he acted with her consent,**[N] how can she then claim compensation?

NOTES

Although she has not collected them – אַף עַל פִּי שֶׁלֹּא גָבְתָה: The Gemara will inquire into the suitability of the use of the term collected, with regard to a lost object she found. As for the reason why the mishna employs this term, some commentaries write that typically there is no need for a trial in order for someone to collect wages owed to them, whereas in the cases of a rapist and a seducer, the sum due for humiliation and degradation must be determined by the court (*Baḥ* on Rif).

He acted with her consent – מִדַּעְתָּהּ עֲבַד: The commentaries point out that this cannot be speaking of the seduction of a minor. She is not considered to have acted with consent because she is not legally competent to make these decisions.

עָמְדָה בְּדִין אִיצְטְרִיכָא לֵיהּ, פְּלוּגְתָּא דְּרַבִּי שִׁמְעוֹן וְרַבָּנַן.

The Gemara answers: It **was necessary for** the mishna to mention these cases in order to address the case where she **stood for judgment** before her father died, and then he died before collecting payment. In this case, there is **a dispute between Rabbi Shimon and the Rabbis** as to whether the sons inherit these payments from the father or whether the money belongs to the young woman.

תְּנַן הָתָם: ״אָנַסְתָּ וּפִיתִּיתָ אֶת בִּתִּי״, וְהוּא אוֹמֵר: ״לֹא אָנַסְתִּי וְלֹא פִּיתִּיתִי״. ״מַשְׁבִּיעֲךָ אֲנִי״, וְאָמַר: ״אָמֵן״, וְאַחַר כָּךְ הוֹדָה – חַיָּיב.

§ **We learned** in a mishna **there** (*Shevuot* 36b) that if someone said to another: **You raped** my daughter, **or: You seduced my daughter,**[H] **and the other says: I did not rape and I did not seduce,** to which the father replied: **I administer an oath to you,**[N] **and** the defendant **said: Amen, and afterward he admitted** that he had raped or seduced the man's daughter, he is **obligated** both in the payments of a rapist or a seducer as well as an additional one-fifth, and he must bring an offering for swearing falsely that he did not owe the money.

רַבִּי שִׁמְעוֹן פּוֹטֵר, שֶׁאֵינוֹ מְשַׁלֵּם קְנָס עַל פִּי עַצְמוֹ. אָמְרוּ לוֹ: אַף עַל פִּי שֶׁאֵינוֹ מְשַׁלֵּם קְנָס עַל פִּי עַצְמוֹ, אֲבָל מְשַׁלֵּם בּוֹשֶׁת וּפְגָם עַל פִּי עַצְמוֹ.

Rabbi Shimon exempts him, **as he does not pay** the **fine on his own** admission. The accused individual is not considered to have taken a false oath in denial of a monetary charge because he would not have been obligated to pay the fine on the basis of his own admission of guilt. The Rabbis **said to him: Although he does not pay** the **fine on his own** admission, **indeed he does pay** compensation for **the humiliation and degradation on his own** admission. Consequently, he has denied a monetary claim, and therefore his false oath obligates him to add one-fifth and to bring an offering. This concludes the mishna.

בְּעָא מִינֵּיהּ אַבָּיֵי מֵרַבָּה: הָאוֹמֵר לַחֲבֵירוֹ: ״אָנַסְתָּ וּפִיתִּיתָ אֶת בִּתִּי וְהֶעֱמַדְתִּיךָ בַּדִּין וְנִתְחַיַּיבְתָּ לִי מָמוֹן״, וְהוּא אוֹמֵר: ״לֹא אָנַסְתִּי וְלֹא פִּיתִּיתִי וְלֹא הֶעֱמַדְתַּנִי בַּדִּין וְלֹא נִתְחַיַּיבְתִּי לְךָ מָמוֹן״, וְנִשְׁבַּע, וְהוֹדָה, לְרַבִּי שִׁמְעוֹן מַאי?

In light of this mishna, **Abaye raised a dilemma before Rabba:** With regard to **one who says to another: You raped** my daughter, **or: You seduced my daughter, and I made you stand in judgment** for your actions, **and you were found obligated** to pay **me money** but you did not do so, **and** the defendant **says: I did not rape, or: I did not seduce, and you did not make me stand in judgment, and I was not found obligated** to pay **you money,** and the defendant **took an oath** that he was telling the truth **and** subsequently **admitted** his guilt, **according to** the opinion of **Rabbi Shimon, what is** the *halakha*?

כֵּיוָן דַּעֲמַד בַּדִּין – מָמוֹנָא הָוֵאי, וּמִיחַיַּיב עֲלֵיהּ קָרְבַּן שְׁבוּעָה, אוֹ דִּלְמָא: אַף עַל גַּב דַּעֲמַד בַּדִּין – קְנָס הָוֵי? אָמַר לֵיהּ: מָמוֹנָא הָוֵי, וּמִיחַיַּיב עֲלֵיהּ קָרְבַּן שְׁבוּעָה.

Abaye explains the two sides of the dilemma: **Since he stood trial** and was found liable, **is** this considered a regular **monetary** obligation, **and** therefore **he is liable to** bring the **offering** for taking a false **oath** to deny a monetary claim? **Or perhaps** one can argue that **although he stood trial**[N] and the court ordered him to pay, the payment **is** in essence **a fine.** Rabba **said to him:** Since he has already stood trial, **it is** considered a regular **monetary** payment, **and he is liable to** bring the **offering of an oath.**

אֵיתִיבֵיהּ: רַבִּי שִׁמְעוֹן אוֹמֵר: יָכוֹל הָאוֹמֵר לַחֲבֵירוֹ: ״אָנַסְתָּ וּפִיתִּיתָ אֶת בִּתִּי״, וְהוּא אוֹמֵר: ״לֹא אָנַסְתִּי וְלֹא פִּיתִּיתִי״. ״הֵמִית שׁוֹרְךָ אֶת עַבְדִּי״, וְהוּא אוֹמֵר: ״לֹא הֵמִית״. אוֹ שֶׁאָמַר לוֹ עַבְדּוֹ: ״הִפַּלְתָּ אֶת שִׁינִּי וְסִימִּיתָ אֶת עֵינִי״, וְהוּא אוֹמֵר: ״לֹא הִפַּלְתִּי וְלֹא סִימִּיתִי״, וְנִשְׁבַּע, וְהוֹדָה, יָכוֹל יְהֵא חַיָּיב,

Abaye **raised an objection to** Rabba from the following *baraita*. **Rabbi Shimon says:** One **might** have thought that in the case of **one who says to another: You raped** my daughter, **or: You seduced my daughter, and he says: I did not rape** her, **or: I did not seduce** her, or if he claimed: **Your ox killed my slave, and he says:** It **did not kill** him, **or if his slave said to him: You knocked out my tooth, or: You blinded my eye** and you are therefore obligated to emancipate me, **and he says: I did not knock** it **out, or: I did not blind** your eye, **and he takes an oath but** later **admitted** to the truth of the accusation, one **might** have thought that he **should be liable** to bring an offering for a false oath denying a monetary claim.

תַּלְמוּד לוֹמַר ״וְכִחֵשׁ בַּעֲמִיתוֹ בְּפִקָּדוֹן אוֹ בִתְשׂוּמֶת יָד אוֹ בְגָזֵל אוֹ עָשַׁק אֶת עֲמִיתוֹ אוֹ מָצָא אֲבֵידָה וְכִחֶשׁ בָּהּ וְנִשְׁבַּע עַל שָׁקֶר״. מָה אֵלּוּ מְיוּחָדִין – שֶׁהֵן מָמוֹן, אַף כֹּל – שֶׁהֵן מָמוֹן, יָצְאוּ אֵלּוּ שֶׁהֵן קְנָס.

Therefore, with regard to the offering for a false oath in denial of a monetary claim, **the verse states:** "If anyone sin, and commit a trespass against the Lord **and deal falsely with his neighbor in a matter of a deposit or of a pledge or of a robbery or have oppressed his neighbor, or have found that which was lost and deal falsely with it, and swear to a lie**" (Leviticus 5:21–22). **Just as** all these **matters** listed in the verse **are unique** in **that they are monetary** obligations equal in value to the loss one has caused another individual, **so too,** this *halakha* applies to **all** obligations **that are monetary** claims, which **excludes these** payments of a rapist, a seducer, and the like, **as they are fines.**[H]

HALAKHA

You raped or you seduced my daughter, etc. – אָנַסְתָּ וּפִיתִּיתָ אֶת בִּתִּי וכו׳: In a case of one who is accused of perpetrating a crime that would render him liable to pay compensation for the damage he caused, if he falsely swears that he is innocent, he is liable to bring a guilt-offering. However, if he was accused of a crime that would render him liable to pay a fixed monetary fine and he falsely swears that he is innocent, he is not liable to bring a guilt-offering. The reason for this is that his false denial of the claim is not significant, because he would not have been obligated to pay the fine even if he had admitted his guilt. If one was accused of a crime that would render him liable to pay compensation for damage he caused and also a fixed monetary fine, and he swears falsely that he is innocent, he is liable to bring a guilt-offering due to his denial of the regular monetary claim. Consequently, if one accused another of raping his daughter, which includes liability for both a fine as well as compensation for the humiliation and degradation caused to the victim, and the accused swore falsely that he was innocent, he is liable to bring a guilt-offering (Rambam *Sefer Hafla'a*, *Hilkhot Shevuot* 8:3).

Which excludes these, as they are fines – יָצְאוּ אֵלּוּ שֶׁהֵן קְנָס: In a case where one who is sued for a payment he would not have to pay based on his own admission, e.g., a fine, if he denied the claim and swore falsely, he is exempt from bringing a guilt-offering for falsely taking an oath in denial of a monetary claim. However, he is liable for having violated the general prohibition of taking a false oath (Rambam *Sefer Hafla'a*, *Hilkhot Shevuot* 7:2).

NOTES

I administer an oath to you, etc. – מַשְׁבִּיעֲךָ אֲנִי וכו׳: The oath referred to here is the oath on a deposit (see Leviticus 5:20–26). The *halakhot* of this oath are elucidated mainly in tractate *Shevuot*. Although the *halakhot* concerning this oath are numerous and detailed, the basic idea is as follows: When someone has in his possession a deposit belonging to another person or that person's stolen property, and he falsely swears that he does not owe him anything, and he later admits that he lied, he must pay what he owes plus an extra one-fifth of its value. In addition, he must bring an offering, the guilt-offering for robbery. The offender is obligated in the one-fifth and is liable to bring the guilt-offering only if all the conditions of this case are fulfilled. Some commentaries contend that one of these conditions is that the claim must refer to a particular, defined object from which the payment was to be collected (*Tosafot*). In any case, even if the conditions are not precisely fulfilled, he is liable to bring a different offering for his false oath.

Or perhaps, although he stood trial, etc. – אוֹ דִּלְמָא אַף עַל גַּב דַּעֲמַד בַּדִּין וכו׳: The early authorities had other versions of the text that read: Or perhaps, although he stood trial it is a fine, and one who admits to a fine is exempt (see Rabbeinu Ḥananel). However, Rashi does not accept this reading, and the standard text of the Gemara is in accordance with Rashi's version. This difference in the text affects the meaning of both Abaye's question and the rest of the passage.

According to Rashi, the question refers to one issue alone: Do the *halakhot* of a guilt-offering for robbery apply in a case where the source of the monetary obligation was a fine, but the obligation is currently viewed as a regular monetary obligation because the court has already ordered the perpetrator to pay?

Conversely, according to the other reading, Abaye's question refers not only to the *halakhot* of a guilt-offering for robbery, but also to whether the obligation is viewed as a regular monetary obligation with regard to other *halakhot* once the court has ordered him to pay. For instance, if the court that ordered him to pay cannot be contacted to verify its ruling, would the perpetrator be obligated to pay if he admits that he was found guilty in court, or would the *halakha* that one is not liable to a fine by his own admission be relevant in this case as well (see *Tosafot*, Ramban, Rabbeinu Aharon HaLevi, Rashba, and Ritva)?

מַאי לָאו בְּשֶׁעָמַד בַּדִּין! לֹא, בְּשֶׁלֹּא עָמַד בַּדִּין.

What, is it not referring to a case **where he has stood trial,** and yet Rabbi Shimon does not render him liable for the oath as the payment was originally a fine? Rabba refutes this argument: **No,** that *baraita* is referring to a situation **where he has not stood trial.**

וְהָא מִדְּרֵישָׁא בְּשֶׁעָמַד בַּדִּין, סֵיפָא נַמִי בְּשֶׁעָמַד בַּדִּין! דְּקָתָנֵי רֵישָׁא: אֵין לִי אֶלָּא דְּבָרִים שֶׁמְּשַׁלְּמִין עֲלֵיהֶם אֶת הַקֶּרֶן, תַּשְׁלוּמֵי כֵפֶל, תַּשְׁלוּמֵי אַרְבָּעָה וַחֲמִשָּׁה, וְהָאוֹנֵס, וְהַמְפַתֶּה וּמוֹצִיא שֵׁם רַע – מִנַּיִן? תַּלְמוּד לוֹמַר ״וּמָעֲלָה מַעַל״, רִיבָּה.

Abaye persists: **But from** the fact **that** the **first clause** of the *baraita* deals **with** one **who has stood trial,** it follows that the **latter clause also** deals **with one who has stood trial. As** the *baraita* **teaches** in its **first clause: I have** derived the *halakha* **only** for **matters for which one pays the principal.** With regard to **the payments** that are **double** the principal, and **payments** that are **four and five** times the principal, and those of **the rapist, and the seducer, and the defamer, from where** is it derived that all these are included in the liability to bring an offering for falsely taking an oath on a deposit? **The verse states:** "If anyone sin **and commit a trespass** [***ma'ala ma'al***]" (Leviticus 5:21). The doubled usage of the word trespass serves to **amplify** and include any false oath taken in denial of monetary liability.

הֵיכִי דָּמֵי? אִי דְּלָא עָמַד בַּדִּין – כְּפֵילָא מִי אִיכָּא? אֶלָּא פְּשִׁיטָא – בְּשֶׁעָמַד בַּדִּין, וּמִדְּרֵישָׁא בְּשֶׁעָמַד בַּדִּין – סֵיפָא נַמִי בְּשֶׁעָמַד בַּדִּין!

Abaye analyzes this statement: **What are the circumstances? If** this is referring to a situation **when he has not stood trial, is there double** payment in that case? Everyone agrees that one who admits his guilt is exempt from the double payment, and yet this obligation is mentioned in the *baraita*. **Rather,** it **is obvious** that the *baraita* is referring to a case **where** it is claimed that he has already **stood trial** and was declared liable to pay the double payment, and the accused individual denies this claim. Abaye summarizes his question: **And from** the fact **that** the **first clause** of this *baraita* deals **with** one **who has stood trial,** the **latter clause also** deals **with** one **who has stood trial,** and even so Rabbi Shimon does not deem him liable to bring an offering for his oath.

אָמַר לֵיהּ: יָכֵילְנָא לְשַׁנּוּיֵי לָךְ: רֵישָׁא – בְּשֶׁעָמַד בַּדִּין, וְסֵיפָא – בְּשֶׁלֹּא עָמַד בַּדִּין, וְכוּלָּהּ רַבִּי שִׁמְעוֹן הִיא, וְשִׁינּוּיֵי דְּחִיקֵי לָא מְשַׁנֵּינַן לָךְ. דְּאִם כֵּן אָמְרַתְּ לִי: לִיתְנֵי רֵישָׁא ״רַבִּי שִׁמְעוֹן אוֹמֵר״ אוֹ לִיתְנֵי סֵיפָא ״דִּבְרֵי רַבִּי שִׁמְעוֹן״.

Rabba **said to him: I could answer you** that the **first clause** deals **with** one **who** is accused of already having **stood trial** and been deemed liable, **and** the **latter clause** deals **with** one **who has not stood trial, and** this **entire** *baraita* **is** in accordance with the opinion of **Rabbi Shimon.** According to this answer, Rabbi Shimon concedes that after one has been deemed liable in court, the double payment attains the status of a regular monetary obligation rather than a fine, and therefore in the first case in the *baraita* he is liable to bring an offering and a payment for his admission. **But I will not answer you a far-fetched answer, for if** it is **so,** that the entire *baraita* represents the opinion of Rabbi Shimon, **you** could **say to me: Let** the *tanna* of the *baraita* either **teach** explicitly in the **first clause: Rabbi Shimon says, or let him teach** in the **latter clause:** This is **the statement of Rabbi Shimon.**

אֶלָּא, כּוּלָּהּ בְּשֶׁעָמַד בַּדִּין, וְרֵישָׁא רַבָּנַן וְסֵיפָא רַבִּי שִׁמְעוֹן,

Rabba continued: **Rather,** I will say that the **entire** *baraita* is referring **to** one **who has stood trial, and** as for the difference in *halakha,* the **first clause** is in accordance with the opinion of **the Rabbis,** who deem one liable to bring the offering of an oath in a case where the plaintiff says that the defendant stood trial, was found liable, and swore falsely. **And** the **latter clause** represents the opinion of **Rabbi Shimon,** who exempts one who confesses from bringing the offering of an oath.

וּמוֹדֵינָא לָךְ לְעִנְיַן קָרְבַּן שְׁבוּעָה, דְּרַחֲמָנָא פַּטְרֵיהּ מִ״וְּכִחֵשׁ״.

And I concede to you, Abaye, **with regard to** the liability to bring **an offering** for falsely taking **an oath** on a deposit, **that the Merciful One exempts him** from this offering here, **based upon** the verse **"And deal falsely** with his neighbor in a matter of a deposit," (Leviticus 5:21), which indicates that one is liable to bring an offering only if he lied about a claim that was originally a monetary obligation.

BACKGROUND

Until Rav Yosef sat at the head – עַד דְּיָתֵיב רַב יוֹסֵף בְּרֵישָׁא: The Talmud relates how Rav Yosef assumed leadership of the school (see *Berakhot* 64a; *Horayot* 14a). After Rav Yehuda's passing, there were two possible candidates to succeed him as head of the school in Pumbedita, Rabba and Rav Yosef. The younger Rabba was known for his brilliance, whereas Rav Yosef was famed for the breadth of his Torah knowledge. Not knowing who to choose, they asked the Sages of Eretz Yisrael a general question: Who is preferable: Sinai, i.e., a scholar with vast expertise, or one who uproots mountains, i.e., a Sage with a sharp mind? The answer they received was that Sinai is preferable. Nevertheless, Rav Yosef refused the appointment for various reasons, and for the twenty-two years during which Rabba served as head of the school, Rav Yosef did not claim for himself any position of greatness. Rav Yosef agreed to take his place as head of the school only after Rabba passed away.

וְכִי קָאָמִינָא מָמוֹן הָוֵי – לְהוֹרִישׁוֹ לְבָנָיו.

And when I say that Rabbi Shimon maintains that after one is declared liable in court his obligation to pay **is** considered a regular **monetary** payment rather than a fine, that is not to say that he is liable to bring an offering for falsely denying a monetary claim, but rather **to** say that the recipient of the payment **bequeaths it to his sons.** Unlike a fine, which does not pass by inheritance to one's heirs, this is classified as a regular monetary payment. Consequently, if the perpetrator was deemed liable in court and ordered to pay the father of the girl he raped or seduced, and the father died before receiving payment, his sons inherit the right to that payment.

אֵיתִיבֵיהּ: רַבִּי שִׁמְעוֹן אוֹמֵר: אִם לֹא הִסְפִּיקָה לִגְבּוֹת עַד שֶׁמֵּת הָאָב – הֲרֵי הֵן שֶׁל עַצְמָהּ. וְאִי אָמְרַתְּ מָמוֹן הָוֵי לְהוֹרִישׁוֹ לְבָנָיו – לְעַצְמָהּ אַמַּאי? דְּאַחִין בָּעֵי מֵיהֱוֵי!

Abaye **raised an objection to** this last point from the mishna. **Rabbi Shimon says: If** the daughter **did not manage to collect** the payments **before the father died, they** belong **to her. And if you say** that this fine **is a monetary** payment **to** the extent that one can **bequeath it to his sons** after the trial, **why** does the money belongs **to her?** Since the trial has taken place, it **should be** the property **of the brothers** by inheritance from their father, as it is already considered a regular monetary obligation that is owed to the father.

אֲמַר רָבָא, הַאי מִילְּתָא קָשַׁאי בָּהּ רַבָּה וְרַב יוֹסֵף עֶשְׂרִין וְתַרְתֵּין שְׁנִין, וְלָא אִיפְּרַק, עַד דְּיָתֵיב רַב יוֹסֵף בְּרֵישָׁא וּפִירְקָהּ: שָׁאנֵי הָתָם דַּאֲמַר קְרָא "וְנָתַן הָאִישׁ הַשּׁוֹכֵב עִמָּהּ לַאֲבִי הַנַּעֲרָה חֲמִשִּׁים כָּסֶף" – לֹא זִיכְּתָה תּוֹרָה לָאָב אֶלָּא מִשְּׁעַת נְתִינָה.

Rava said: This matter was difficult for Rabba and Rav Yosef for **twenty-two years without resolution, until Rav Yosef sat at the head**[B] of the academy **and resolved it** in the following manner: **There,** in the case of a rape, **it is different, as the verse states: "And the man who laid with her shall give the young woman's father fifty shekels of silver"** (Deuteronomy 22:29), from which it is inferred: **The Torah entitled the father** to this money **only from the time of giving.** Consequently, if the father dies before receiving the money, he does not bequeath his right to the money to his sons. Instead, the daughter is considered to take her father's place as the plaintiff, because she was the victim, and the money is paid to her.

וְכִי קָאָמַר רַבָּה מָמוֹנָא הָוֵי לְהוֹרִישׁוֹ לְבָנָיו – בִּשְׁאָר קְנָסוֹת.

And when Rabba said that the fine imposed by a court **is** considered a regular **monetary obligation** with regard to one's ability **to bequeath it to his sons,** he was not referring to this particular case of a rapist or seducer, but only **to other fines,**[N] which do have the status of regular monetary obligations after the court delivers its verdict.

אֶלָּא מֵעַתָּה, גַּבֵּי עֶבֶד, דִּכְתִיב "כֶּסֶף שְׁלֹשִׁים שְׁקָלִים יִתֵּן לַאדוֹנָיו" הָכִי נַמִי לֹא זִיכְּתָה תּוֹרָה לָאָדוֹן אֶלָּא מִשְּׁעַת נְתִינָה!? "יִתֵּן" לְחוּד "וְנָתַן" לְחוּד.

The Gemara asks: **However, if** that is **so,** that the verb "give" is explained in this manner, **with regard to** an ox that killed **a slave, where it is written: "He shall give to their master thirty shekels of silver"** (Exodus 21:32), **so too** will you say that **the Torah entitled the master only from the time of giving?** The Gemara answers: **"Shall give [*yiten*],"** is distinct, and **"shall give [*venatan*]," is distinct.**[N] The first expression, which is stated with regard to an ox that killed a slave, does not indicate that the recipient acquires the right to the money only from the moment it is given, whereas the formulation employed in the case of rape does indicate that this is the case.

NOTES

And when Rabba said that the fine imposed by the court is considered a regular monetary obligation…only to other fines – וְכִי קָאָמַר רַבָּה מָמוֹנָא הָוֵי...בִּשְׁאָר קְנָסוֹת: The early authorities disagree with regard to Abaye's opinion throughout this discussion. It is unclear whether he even means to express an independent position or whether he raised his question merely for the purpose of clarification. Similarly, it is not entirely clear what Rabba himself holds at the end of the discussion.

Some commentaries maintain that according to Rabba, a father bequeaths all fines to his sons aside from the fine due to be paid by a rapist or seducer, whereas Abaye disagrees. According to this interpretation, this issue is dependent on a dispute in the Jerusalem Talmud over whether the recipient of the payment is considered to be entitled to the money from the time the court issues its verdict or from the time the payment is actually given.

The Ri HaLavan states that everyone agrees that a son inherits all of his father's rights, including fines, with the exception of the fine paid by a rapist or seducer. In his opinion, the discussion does not concern the question of whether the fine is considered a regular monetary obligation for the purposes of inheritance, but only whether it is a monetary payment with regard to an oath imposed by one's sons. In other words, if the sons claim that a certain individual was already pronounced liable to pay their father a fine for having raped his daughter, and the accused man denies the charges and falsely swears to that effect, would he be liable to bring a guilt-offering?

The Ramban argues that although this interpretation fits the logic of the discussion, the phrase: To bequeath it to his sons, indicates that the discussion is about whether the sons inherit the rights to the fine at all. Furthermore, in the Jerusalem Talmud the dispute is understood to pertain to whether or not the sons inherit the rights to the fine.

Shall give [*yiten*] is distinct, and shall give [*venatan*] is distinct – יִתֵּן לְחוּד וְנָתַן לְחוּד: Rashi explains that the difference between these two expressions lies in their grammatical tense. In the word *venatan*, the verb *natan* appears in past tense, and future tense is indicated by the prefix *ve*. This alludes to the fact that the father fully acquires the right to the money only once it has already been given. Conversely, in the word *yiten*, the verb itself is formulated in the future tense.

Alternatively, the Ritva understands the general context of the verses as follows: *Yiten* is referring to the court's order to the aggressor to pay the owner of the slave and indicates that the master has a right to the money from the time of the court's decision. The word *venatan* is referring to the actual payment and indicates that the father of the rape victim is entitled to the money only from the time of the payment.

אִי הָכִי, תַּלְמוּד לוֹמַר ״וְכִחֵשׁ״? תַּלְמוּד לוֹמַר ״וְנָתַן״ מִיבָּעֵי לֵיהּ!

The Gemara raises a difficulty: **If so,** that the main source for this *halakha* is the phrase "shall give [*venatan*]," when it was taught in the *baraita* that a man who rapes or seduces a woman is not liable to bring the offering for a false oath in denial of a monetary claim, rather than saying that this is derived from the fact that **the verse states "and deal falsely,"** he **should have** said that it is derived from the fact that **the verse states "shall give,"** as this is the phrase that teaches that the payment is considered a fine even after he has stood trial.

אֲמַר רָבָא: כִּי אִיצְטְרִיךְ ״וְכִחֵשׁ״ – כְּגוֹן שֶׁעָמְדָה בַּדִּין, וּבָגְרָה וּמֵתָה. דְּהָתָם כִּי קָא יָרֵית אָבִיהָ – מִינָּהּ דִּידָהּ קָא יָרֵית.

In answer to this question, **Rava said: When it was necessary** to cite a proof from **"and deal falsely,"** it was with regard to a situation **where** the young woman's case was **brought to trial,** and the court ruled in her favor, **and she reached majority and** subsequently **died** before the money was paid. The reason that "and deal falsely" is necessary in that case is because **there, when the father inherits,** it is **from her** that **he inherits.**[N]

אִי הָכִי יָצְאוּ אֵלּוּ שֶׁהֵן קְנָס? מָמוֹן הוּא! אָמַר רַב נַחְמָן בַּר יִצְחָק: יָצְאוּ אֵלּוּ שֶׁעִיקָּרָן קְנָס.

The Gemara raises another difficulty: **If so,** the language of the *baraita*: **Excluding these, as they are a fine,** is inaccurate, as **it is** a regular **monetary** payment, not a fine. In answer to this question, **Rav Naḥman bar Yitzḥak said** that this phrase means: **Excluding these, as they are originally a fine,** and it is only once the court orders the man to pay that they are viewed as regular monetary payments.

אֵיתִיבֵיהּ: רַבִּי שִׁמְעוֹן פּוֹטֵר, שֶׁאֵינוֹ מְשַׁלֵּם קְנָס עַל פִּי עַצְמוֹ. טַעֲמָא, דְּלָא עָמַד בַּדִּין. הָא עָמַד בַּדִּין, דִּמְשַׁלֵּם עַל פִּי עַצְמוֹ – קָרְבַּן שְׁבוּעָה נַמִי מִיחַיַּיב!

Abaye **raised an objection to** this explanation of the opinion of Rabbi Shimon, based upon the mishna in *Shevuot* cited above (42a), which states: **Rabbi Shimon exempts** him, **as he does not pay a fine on his own** admission. The Gemara infers: **The reason that** he is not liable to bring a guilt-offering is because **he has not stood trial.** However, if **he has stood trial** and been found guilty, **in which case he pays on his own** admission when he later admits that he was already convicted in court, **he should also be liable to** bring **an offering** if he denies that he was convicted in court and takes **an oath** to that effect. This contradicts the claim that, according to Rabbi Shimon, even after one is convicted in court, the payment is still considered a fine.

רַבִּי שִׁמְעוֹן לְדִבְרֵיהֶם דְּרַבָּנַן קָאָמַר לְהוּ: לְדִידִי, אַף עַל גַּב דְּעָמַד בַּדִּין רַחֲמָנָא פְּטָרֵיהּ מִ״וְּכִחֵשׁ״. אֶלָּא לְדִידְכוּ, אוֹדוּ לִי מִיהַת הֵיכָא דְּלָא עָמַד בַּדִּין, דְּכִי קָא תָּבַע – קְנָסָא קָא תָּבַע.

The Gemara answers: **Rabbi Shimon stated** his opinion **to them in accordance with the statement of the Rabbis** themselves, as follows: **According to my** opinion, **although he has stood trial, the Merciful One exempts him** from the offering, as derived **from** the verse: **"And deal falsely** with his neighbor in a matter of a deposit" (Leviticus 5:21), which indicates that he is liable only for a claim that originally concerned regular a monetary payment. **However, according to your** opinion, you should **at least concede to me** in a case **where he has not stood trial, that when one claims** the money, he **claims a fine** and not a regular monetary payment.

Perek **IV**
Daf **43** Amud **a**

וּמוֹדֶה בִּקְנָס פָּטוּר. וְרַבָּנַן סָבְרִי: כִּי קָא תָּבַע – בּוֹשֶׁת וּפְגָם קָא תָּבַע.

And the principle is that **one who admits** that he is liable to pay **a fine is exempt.** Since the man would not have been liable to pay even if he had admitted his guilt, his denial of guilt is not considered a denial of monetary liability, and even if he swears falsely that he is not liable, he still does not become liable to bring an offering. **And the Rabbis hold** that **when** the father **claims** payment in court, it is the compensation for the **humiliation and degradation** that **he claims.** His main focus is not on the fine, and therefore the denial refers to a regular monetary claim.

NOTES

It is from her that he inherits – מִינָּהּ דִּידָהּ קָא יָרֵית: According to Rabbi Shimon, if the young woman reaches majority before the penalty is paid, she becomes the recipient of the payment. Furthermore, since the phrase "shall give" is stated with regard to money paid to the father, it is limited to that case. If the woman is the recipient, the payment is considered a regular monetary payment rather than a fine, and therefore when she dies, her father inherits the rights to this regular monetary payment. Consequently, the verse states "and deal falsely" to teach that even in this case, where the money has the status of a regular monetary payment rather than a fine, if the rapist denies that he owes the money, he is exempt from bringing an offering because the payment originated as a fine.

בְּמַאי קָא מִיפַּלְגִי? אָמַר רַב פָּפָּא: רַבִּי שִׁמְעוֹן סָבַר: לָא שָׁבֵיק אִינִישׁ מִידֵּי דְּקִיץ וְתָבַע מִידֵּי דְּלָא קִיץ. וְרַבָּנַן סָבְרִי: לָא שָׁבֵיק אִינִישׁ מִידֵּי דְּכִי מוֹדֵי בֵּיהּ לָא מִיפְּטַר, וְתָבַע מִידֵּי דְּכִי מוֹדֶה בֵּיהּ מִיפְּטַר.

The Gemara asks: If this explanation is correct, **with regard to what do the** *tanna'im* **disagree? Rav Pappa said: Rabbi Shimon holds** that **a person does not leave** aside **something that** is **fixed,** e.g., a fine, **and claim something that** is **not fixed,** e.g., the compensation for humiliation and degradation, which need to be assessed by the court. Consequently, a claim of rape is essentially a demand for the fine. **And** conversely, **the Rabbis hold** that **a person does not leave** aside **something that,** if the defendant **admits to it, he is not exempt** from payment, e.g., humiliation and degradation, **and claim something that,** if the defendant **admits to it, he is exempt** from payment. Consequently, they contend that the lawsuit is mainly focused on the compensation for the humiliation and degradation.

בְּעָא מִינֵּיהּ רַבִּי אָבִינָא מֵרַב שֵׁשֶׁת: בַּת הַנִּיזּוֹנֶת מִן הָאַחִין מַעֲשֵׂה יָדֶיהָ לְמִי?

§ **Rabbi Avina raised a dilemma before Rav Sheshet:** With regard to **a daughter who is sustained by** her **brothers,** i.e., an orphan whose brothers provide her with her sustenance from their father's estate, in accordance with the stipulation in the marriage contract between their parents that requires the father to pay for his daughter's sustenance from his property, **to whom do her earnings** belong?

בִּמְקוֹם אָב קַיְימִי: מָה הָתָם – מַעֲשֵׂה יָדֶיהָ לָאָב, הָכָא נַמִי – מַעֲשֵׂה יָדֶיהָ לָאַחִין. אוֹ דִּלְמָא, לָא דָּמֵי לְאָב: הָתָם – מִדִּידֵיהּ מִיתְּזְנָא, הָכָא – לָאו מִדִּידְהוּ מִיתְּזְנָא?

Rabbi Avina explains the sides of the dilemma. One might say that the brothers **stand in place of** the **father: Just as there,** if their father is alive, **her earnings** go **to the father, here too her earnings** go **to the brothers. Or perhaps** this is **not similar** to the case of a living **father.** Why not? Because **there, she is sustained from his** own property, and therefore he is entitled to receive her earnings, whereas **here, she is not sustained from their** possessions but from the estate of their father, and consequently they should not receive her earnings.

אֲמַר לֵיהּ: תְּנֵיתוּהָ: אַלְמָנָה נִיזּוֹנֶת מִנִּכְסֵי יְתוֹמִים, וּמַעֲשֵׂה יָדֶיהָ שֶׁלָּהֶן.

Rav Sheshet **said to him: You** already **learned** the answer to this dilemma from a mishna (*Ketubot* 81a): **A widow is sustained from the property of the orphans,**[H] **and her earnings are theirs.** This indicates that although a widow receives her sustenance from the estate of her deceased husband, in accordance with the stipulations of the marriage contract, the orphans are nevertheless entitled to her earnings. The same reasoning should apply to an orphan sustained by her brothers.

מִי דָּמֵי? אַלְמְנָתוֹ – לָא נִיחָא לֵיהּ בְּהַרְוָוחָה, בִּתּוֹ – נִיחָא לֵיהּ בְּהַרְוָוחָה.

The Gemara refutes this argument: **Are** the two situations **comparable?** In the case of **his widow,** the deceased **is not** necessarily **amenable to her** living **in comfort.**[N] Consequently, she is entitled only to the minimum guaranteed to her in the marriage contract, while her earnings go to his heirs. Conversely, with regard to **his daughter, he is amenable** and is interested **in her** living in **comfort,** and therefore he allows her to retain her earnings so that she can have the extra money.

לְמֵימְרָא דְּבִתּוֹ עֲדִיפָא לֵיהּ מֵאַלְמְנָתוֹ? וְהָאָמַר רַבִּי אַבָּא אָמַר רַבִּי יוֹסֵי: עָשׂוּ אַלְמָנָה אֵצֶל הַבַּת כְּבַת אֵצֶל אַחִין בִּנְכָסִין מוּעָטִין,

The Gemara asks: **Is that to say that** the welfare of **his daughter is** more **preferable to him than** that of **his widow? But didn't Rabbi Abba say that Rabbi Yosei said:** The Sages **established** the *halakha* **of a widow with regard to the daughter,** who is also entitled to sustenance from the estate, **like** the *halakha* of **a daughter with regard to** the **brothers in** a case of **a small estate** that is insufficient for the livelihoods of both the girl and her brothers?

מָה הַבַּת אֵצֶל אַחִין – הַבַּת נִיזּוֹנֶת וְהָאַחִין יִשְׁאֲלוּ עַל הַפְּתָחִים, אַף אַלְמָנָה אֵצֶל הַבַּת – אַלְמָנָה נִיזּוֹנֶת וְהַבַּת תִּשְׁאַל עַל הַפְּתָחִים! לְעִנְיַן זִילוּתָא – אַלְמְנָתוֹ עֲדִיפָא לֵיהּ, לְעִנְיַן הַרְוָוחָה – בִּתּוֹ עֲדִיפָא לֵיהּ.

Rabbi Abba explains: **Just as** in the case of **a daughter with regard to the brothers,** the *halakha* is that **the daughter is sustained** from the father's estate, **and** if **the brothers** have nothing to eat they must go and **beg**[N] for charity **at** people's **doors,**[H] **so too,** in the case of **a widow with regard to the daughter,**[H] **the widow is sustained and the daughters beg** for charity **at** people's **doors.** This indicates that a man is more concerned for his widow than his daughter. The Gemara explains: The two cases are not comparable. **With regard to degradation, one's widow is preferable to him,** i.e., if one of them must be forced to go around requesting handouts, a man would rather it be his daughter than his widow. By contrast, **with regard to comfort,** the comfort of **his daughter is** more **preferable to him** than that of his widow.

HALAKHA

A widow is sustained from the property of the orphans – אַלְמָנָה הַנִּיזּוֹנֶת מִנִּכְסֵי יְתוֹמִים: A widow is entitled to sustenance from the estate of her deceased husband throughout the period of her widowhood, provided that she has not claimed payment of her marriage contract. The right to sustenance applies even if it is not explicitly stated in the document itself. Since the heirs are obligated to sustain the widow, her earnings belong to them (Rambam *Sefer Nashim, Hilkhot Ishut* 18:1; *Shulḥan Arukh, Even HaEzer* 93:3, 95:1).

The daughter is sustained and the brothers must beg for charity at people's doors – הַבַּת נִיזּוֹנֶת וְהָאַחִין יִשְׁאֲלוּ עַל הַפְּתָחִים: If a man died and left sons and daughters, the sons inherit his entire estate. However, their sisters are entitled to sustenance until they mature or are betrothed. This is referring to one who left behind enough property to provide for both his sons and daughters. If his estate suffices only for the daughters, they claim their sustenance from this property, while the sons must go begging if necessary (Rambam *Sefer Nashim, Hilkhot Ishut* 19:17; *Shulḥan Arukh, Even HaEzer* 112:11).

A widow with regard to the daughter – אַלְמָנָה אֵצֶל הַבַּת: If a man left behind a widow and a daughter, and his estate is not large enough to provide for them both, the widow receives her sustenance from the inheritance while the daughter must beg for charity. This is the ruling of the Rambam, in accordance with the opinion of Rabbi Abba here. Others accept the opinion cited in the Jerusalem Talmud (*Bava Batra* 9:1), that each has equal rights to the property, and therefore they may both draw their sustenance from it until nothing is left. It is only in a case of a widow, a son, and a daughter where the children must go and seek charity, while the widow alone receives her sustenance (*Tosafot*; Rosh). The *Shulḥan Arukh* cites the Rambam's opinion as the main ruling, while that of *Tosafot* is mentioned as an alternative opinion (Rambam *Sefer Nashim, Hilkhot Ishut* 19:21; *Shulḥan Arukh Even HaEzer* 93:4).

NOTES

In the case of his widow, the deceased is not necessarily amenable to her living in comfort – אַלְמְנָתוֹ לָא נִיחָא לֵיהּ בְּהַרְוָוחָה: The later authorities explain that a father wants his daughter to get married, which is why he provides her with a dowry in his lifetime, and even after his death he wants her to retain some money that she can add to her dowry. By contrast, he has no particular interest in his widow's marriage to another man. Similarly, with regard to degradation, a man does not want his widow to be degraded and feel the need to marry someone to avoid reliance on others, whereas he prefers that his daughter marry as soon as possible (*Ḥaver ben Ḥayyim*; *Sukkat David*).

The daughter is sustained and the brothers must beg – הַבַּת נִיזּוֹנֶת וְהָאַחִין יִשְׁאֲלוּ: The reason for this difference is that the daughter is entitled to her sustenance due to the stipulation in her mother's marriage contract, which is like any other debt that must be paid from the father's estate. Consequently, although the sons are his heirs, there is a lien upon the father's estate ensuring payment for his daughter's sustenance, and therefore her claim takes precedence over the rights of her brothers. In a case of a widow and a daughter, who are both supported by virtue of the marriage contract, it is necessary to consider other factors to decide between them (see *Tosafot*).

מְתִיב רַב יוֹסֵף: מַעֲשֵׂה יָדֶיהָ וּמְצִיאָתָהּ, אַף עַל פִּי שֶׁלֹּא גָּבְתָה, מֵת הָאָב – הֲרֵי הֵן שֶׁל אַחִין. טַעְמָא – דִּבְחַיֵּי הָאָב, הָא לְאַחַר מִיתַת הָאָב – לְעַצְמָהּ. מַאי לָאו – בְּנִיזּוֹנֶת? לָא בְּשֶׁאֵינָהּ נִיזּוֹנֶת.

Rav Yosef raised an objection to Rav Sheshet's conclusion that the orphan girl's earnings belong to the brothers, from the mishna: With regard to **her earnings and** the lost **items** that **she** has **found, although she has not collected** them, if **the father died, they** belong to **her brothers.** Rav Yosef infers: **The reason** for this *halakha* is that she acquired her earnings **in** her **father's lifetime,** which indicates that the money she earns **after the father's death** belongs **to her. What, is it not** referring even **to** a daughter **who is sustained** from his estate? The Gemara refutes this claim: **No,** it deals **with** a daughter **who is not sustained** from his property but who sustains herself through her own earnings.

אִי בְּשֶׁאֵינָהּ נִיזּוֹנֶת מַאי לְמֵימְרָא? אֲפִילּוּ לְמַאן דְּאָמַר: יָכוֹל הָרַב לוֹמַר לָעֶבֶד ״עֲשֵׂה עִמִּי וְאֵינִי זָנְךָ״, הָנֵי מִילֵּי בְּעֶבֶד כְּנַעֲנִי, דְּלָא כְּתִיב בֵּיהּ ״עִמָּךְ״,

The Gemara asks: **If** the mishna is speaking **of** one **who is not sustained** from his estate, **what** is the purpose **of stating** this? It is obvious that this is the *halakha*, as **even according to the one who said** that **a master can say to** his **slave: Work for me but I will not feed you,**[H] i.e., a master is not legally obligated to provide sustenance to his slave, **this applies only to a Canaanite slave, with regard to whom it is not written** in the Torah: **"With you,"**[N] and therefore his master is not obligated to feed him.

אֲבָל עֶבֶד עִבְרִי דִּכְתִיב בֵּיהּ ״עִמָּךְ״ לָא, כׇּל שֶׁכֵּן בִּתּוֹ!

However, in the case of **a Hebrew slave, as it is written with regard to him: "With you"** (Deuteronomy 15:16), which indicates that he is entitled to live with his master as an equal, the master **may not** compel the slave to serve him unless he feeds him. **All the more so** concerning **his daughter,** it cannot be the case that this young woman has to work and give her wages to the brothers if they are not obligated to sustain her at the same time.

אָמַר רַבָּה בַּר עוּלָּא: לָא נִצְרְכָה אֶלָּא לְהֶעְדֵּפָה. אָמַר רָבָא: גַּבְרָא רַבָּה כְּרַב יוֹסֵף לָא יָדַע דְּאִיכָּא הֶעְדֵּפָה, וְקָמוֹתֵיב תְּיוּבְתָּא?!

Rabba bar Ulla said: It is **necessary only for the surplus.** The mishna is not stating that the brothers take her earnings and do not sustain her, leaving her with nothing. Rather, the question concerns a young woman whose earnings provide her with more than she needs for her sustenance, leaving her with a surplus. It is this surplus that belongs to her brothers. **Rava said** in response to Rabba bar Ulla's explanation: Is it possible that **a man** as **great as Rav Yosef does not know that there is** an explanation according to which the mishna is referring to the **surplus, and** in his ignorance **he raises a refutation** against Rav Sheshet? This certainly cannot be the case.

אֶלָּא אָמַר רָבָא: רַב יוֹסֵף מַתְנִיתִין גּוּפַהּ קַשְׁיָא לֵיהּ, דְּקָתָנֵי: מַעֲשֵׂה יָדֶיהָ וּמְצִיאָתָהּ, אַף עַל פִּי שֶׁלֹּא גָּבְתָה. מְצִיאָתָהּ מִמַּאן גָּבְיָא?

Rather, Rava said: The mishna itself poses **a difficulty to** the opinion of Rav Sheshet, and this difficulty led **Rav Yosef** to his conclusion. This is **as** the mishna **teaches: Her earnings and** the lost **items** that **she** has **found, although she has not collected** them. Rava analyzes this statement: With regard to **items** that **she** has **found, from whom does she collect** them?[N] The concept of collecting is inappropriate in this case.

אֶלָּא לָאו – הָכִי קָאָמַר: מַעֲשֵׂה יָדֶיהָ כִּמְצִיאָתָהּ, מָה מְצִיאָתָהּ – בְּחַיֵּי הָאָב לָאָב, לְאַחַר מִיתַת הָאָב לְעַצְמָהּ, אַף מַעֲשֵׂה יָדֶיהָ נַמִי, בְּחַיֵּי הָאָב לָאָב, לְאַחַר מִיתַת הָאָב לְעַצְמָהּ, שְׁמַע מִינַּהּ.

Rather, is it not the case that **this is what** the mishna **said: Her earnings** are **like items she** has **found: Just as items she** has **found in** her **father's lifetime** belong **to** her **father,** and **after the father's death** they belong **to her, so too,** the same rule applies to **her earnings as well: In the father's lifetime,** they go **to the father,** and **after the father's death** they belong **to her,** even when she is sustained from the inheritance. The Gemara concludes: We can **learn from this** inference that the mishna deals with her earnings themselves, not their surplus, in contrast to the interpretation of Rav Sheshet.

אִיתְּמַר נַמִי, אָמַר רַב יְהוּדָה אָמַר רַב: בַּת הַנִּיזּוֹנֶת מִן הָאַחִין מַעֲשֵׂה יָדֶיהָ לְעַצְמָהּ. אָמַר רַב כָּהֲנָא: מַאי טַעְמָא – דִּכְתִיב ״וְהִתְנַחַלְתֶּם אֹתָם לִבְנֵיכֶם אַחֲרֵיכֶם״, אוֹתָם לִבְנֵיכֶם, וְלֹא בְּנוֹתֵיכֶם לִבְנֵיכֶם, מַגִּיד שֶׁאֵין אָדָם מוֹרִישׁ זְכוּת בִּתּוֹ לִבְנוֹ.

This *halakha* **was also stated** by *amora'im*, as **Rav Yehuda said** that **Rav said:** In the case of **a daughter who is sustained by the brothers,**[H] **her earnings** nevertheless belong **to her. Rav Kahana said: What is the reason** for this? **As it is written** with regard to slaves: **"And you may make them an inheritance for your sons after you"** (Leviticus 25:46), from which it is inferred: It is **them,** slaves alone, that you bequeath **to your sons, and** you do **not** bequeath **your daughters to your sons.** This verse **teaches that a man does not bequeath a right** that he has over his **daughter to his son.** All the rights a man possesses over his daughter are personal rights, which are not transferable by inheritance.

HALAKHA

Work for me but I will not feed you – עֲשֵׂה עִמִּי וְאֵינִי זָנְךָ: A master may say to his Canaanite slave: Work for me but I will not feed you. However, he is obligated to feed a slave who is his wife's usufruct property (Rif; Rambam). The Rema writes that according to some authorities, this *halakha* applies only in normal times. However, during famines, when no one will take pity on the slave and give him charity when he goes begging, the master is required to feed him (*Tosafot*; Rosh; *Tur*; see *Gittin* 12a). Nevertheless, even in this situation, if the slave earns money, the master can tell him to feed himself from his earnings, despite the paucity of the sum (Rambam *Sefer Kinyan*, *Hilkhot Avadim* 8:2; *Shulḥan Arukh*, *Yoreh De'a* 267:20).

A daughter who is sustained by the brothers – בַּת הַנִּיזּוֹנֶת מִן הָאַחִין: When a girl receives her sustenance from her father's estate after his death, her earnings and the items that she has found belong to her. The *halakha* is not in accordance with the opinion of Rav Sheshet. Rather, it follows Rav Ashi's later ruling in accordance with the opinion of Rav, as stated by the Gemara on 43b (Rambam *Sefer Nashim*, *Hilkhot Ishut* 19:10; *Shulḥan Arukh*, *Even HaEzer* 112:2).

NOTES

With regard to whom it is not written in the Torah: With you – דְּלָא כְּתִיב בֵּיהּ עִמָּךְ: Some explain that this is referring to the verse "As a hired worker, and as a settler, he shall be with you" (Leviticus 25:40), which is stated in the form of a command (*Tosafot*). Others maintain that the Gemara is referring to the verse "Because he fares well with you" (Deuteronomy 15:16), which clearly indicates that one must treat a Hebrew slave well, by ensuring that his living conditions are no worse than those of his master (Meiri).

Items she has found, from whom does she collect them – מְצִיאָתָהּ מִמַּאן גָּבְיָא: According to Rav Yosef, it was seemingly unnecessary for the mishna to mention the case of items she has found. Consequently, he understands that it is mentioned in order to indicate that the status of her earnings is like that of items she has found (Ritva).

מַתְקִיף לָהּ רַבָּה: וְאֵימָא בְּפִיתּוּי הַבַּת וּקְנָסוֹת וַחֲבָלוֹת הַכָּתוּב מְדַבֵּר? וְכֵן תָּנָא רַב חֲנִינָא: בְּפִתּוּי הַבַּת וּקְנָסוֹת וַחֲבָלוֹת הַכָּתוּב מְדַבֵּר.

Rabba strongly **objects to this** explanation that the verse is referring to a man's rights to his daughter's earnings: **But** one can **say** that **the verse is speaking of the** fine that a father is paid in the case of the **seduction**[N] **of** his **daughter, and** the **fines** paid to him if she is raped, **and** compensation due to him for **injuries** that she suffered, and the verse indicates that these rights are not bequeathed to his heirs. **And Rav Ḥanina likewise** explicitly **taught** that **the verse is speaking of** payments a father is paid in the case of **the seduction of** his **daughter, and** the **fines** due to him if she is raped, **and** compensation for **injuries** she has suffered.

חֲבָלוֹת – צַעֲרָא דְּגוּפָא נִינְהוּ! אָמַר רַבִּי יוֹסֵי בַּר חֲנִינָא:

The Gemara questions this interpretation: With regard to **injuries, they are** the result of **her bodily pain,** and the guiding principle is that any compensation for a daughter's physical pain does not belong to her father, who merely keeps it in trust for her. If so, the category of injuries should not have been included in this list. **Rabbi Yosei bar Ḥanina said:**

NOTES

But one can say that the verse is speaking of the fine a father is paid in the case of the seduction, etc. – וְאֵימָא בְּפִיתּוּי...הַכָּתוּב מְדַבֵּר וכו׳: On what grounds can one distinguish between the rights to the fine and her earnings? Rashi explains that her earnings are a more common payment, and therefore her retaining of this money is more likely to cause enmity. Others state that according to the opinion of Rav Sheshet, the main concern of the Torah is that the girl's body not be subjugated, and therefore the brothers do not inherit any right that pertains to her body. Since her earnings are merely a monetary right, the daughter does not suffer a loss of dignity if they pass to her brothers (Rabbeinu Crescas Vidal)

Perek **IV**
Daf **43** Amud **b**

שֶׁפְּצָעָהּ בְּפָנֶיהָ. אָמַר רַב זֵירָא אָמַר רַב מַתָּנָה אָמַר רַב, וְאָמְרִי לַהּ אָמַר רַבִּי זֵירָא אָמַר רַב מַתָּנָה אָמַר רַב: בַּת הַנִּיזּוֹנֶת מִן הָאַחִין – מַעֲשֵׂה יָדֶיהָ לְעַצְמָהּ, דִּכְתִיב "וְהִתְנַחַלְתֶּם אוֹתָם לִבְנֵיכֶם אַחֲרֵיכֶם" אוֹתָם לִבְנֵיכֶם וְלֹא בְּנוֹתֵיכֶם לִבְנֵיכֶם, מַגִּיד שֶׁאֵין אָדָם מוֹרִישׁ זְכוּת בִּתּוֹ לִבְנוֹ.

We are dealing with a case **when he injured her in her face,**[HN] and therefore he must also pay for the loss of her value, a sum that belongs to her father. **Rav Zeira said that Rav Mattana said that Rav said, and some say Rabbi Zeira**[B] **said that Rav Mattana said that Rav said:** With regard to **a daughter who is sustained by the brothers, her earnings belong to her, as it is written: "And you may make them an inheritance for your sons after you"** (Leviticus 25:46), which indicates: It is **them,** slaves, that you bequeath **to your sons, and not your daughters to your sons.** This verse **teaches that a man does not bequeath a right** that he has over his **daughter to his son.**

אָמַר לֵיהּ אֲבִימִי בַּר פַּפִּי: שָׁקוּד אֲמָרָהּ. שָׁקוּד מַנּוּ – שְׁמוּאֵל, הָא רַב אֲמָרָהּ! אֵימָא אַף שָׁקוּד אֲמָרָהּ. אֲמַר מָר בַּר אַמֵימַר לְרַב אַשִׁי: הָכִי אָמְרִי נְהַרְדְּעֵי, הִלְכְתָא כְּוָותֵיהּ דְּרַב שֵׁשֶׁת. רַב אַשִׁי אֲמַר: הִלְכְתָא כְּוָותֵיהּ דְּרַב. וְהִלְכְתָא כְּוָותֵיהּ דְּרַב.

Avimi bar Pappi said to Rabbi Zeira: **Shakud**[N] **said** this *halakha*. The Gemara asks: **Who is Shakud?** This is a nickname for **Shmuel.** The Gemara asks: **Didn't Rav say it?** The Gemara answers: One should **say** that Avimi bar Pappi meant that **even Shakud said it,** i.e., Shmuel also agreed with this ruling. **Mar bar Ameimar said to Rav Ashi:** The Sages **of Neharde'a say as follows: The *halakha* is in accordance with** the opinion **of Rav Sheshet,** that brothers who are sustaining their sister are entitled to her earnings. **Rav Ashi said: The *halakha* is in accordance with** the opinion **of Rav,** that her earnings belong to her. The Gemara concludes: **And the *halakha* is in accordance with** the opinion **of Rav.**

HALAKHA

When he injured her in her face – שֶׁפְּצָעָהּ בְּפָנֶיהָ: With regard to one who hurts someone's minor daughter in a manner that reduces her value, whether for work or marriage, e.g., a facial injury, he must pay damages and loss of livelihood to her father. Damages that do not affect her value and the payments for pain, medical costs, and humiliation, belong to the girl herself. Similarly, one who harms his own minor daughter must pay for her pain, medical costs, and humiliation, as stated by Rabbi Yosei bar Ḥanina here and Rabbi Yoḥanan in *Bava Kamma* 88a (Rambam *Sefer Nezikin, Hilkhot Ḥovel* 4:14; *Shulḥan Arukh, Ḥoshen Mishpat* 424:6).

BACKGROUND

The honorifics of Rav and Rabbi – תְּאָרֵי רַב וְרַבִּי: By Torah law, only scholars who received ordination are permitted to serve as judges, as they receive their authority in a chain of transmission reaching back to the court of Moses. Toward the end of the Second Temple period, the custom of addressing ordained Sages with the title of Rabbi was introduced. As explained in *Sanhedrin* 14a, the ordination of Sages may be performed only in Eretz Yisrael. For this reason, even Sages of Babylonia who taught Torah to the masses were entitled Rav rather than Rabbi.

Some Babylonian Sages who ascended to Eretz Yisrael but were not ordained there continued to be called Rav. However, others did receive ordination in Eretz Yisrael (see 17b). Some of these Sages, e.g., Rabbi Abba and Rabbi Elazar, moved to Eretz Yisrael and were ordained when they were young, and therefore they are always referred to in the Gemara as Rabbi. Others, e.g., Rabbi Ami and Rabbi Asi, moved to Eretz Yisrael when they were already prominent Sages. At times they are referred to in the Gemara as Rav, and at times they are referred to by their later title, Rabbi. The case of Rabbi Zeira is similar, as his title serves to distinguish between the *halakhot* he taught in Babylonia, with regard to which he is called Rav Zeira, and his statements in Eretz Yisrael, under the title of Rabbi Zeira.

NOTES

When he injured her in her face – שֶׁפְּצָעָהּ בְּפָנֶיהָ: Rashi here explains that her facial injury reduces her value, which is a loss suffered by her father, as he has the right to sell her as a Hebrew maidservant. Others cite an alternative explanation from a manuscript version of Rashi, that an injury to her face causes humiliation to the rest of her family (*Shita Mekubbetzet*). Yet others explain the Gemara's discussion as follows: If the payment is for her pain, the father has no rights to it at all, and if it is for her loss of livelihood, this certainly belongs to her father, as it is compensation for her inability to work. As for medical costs, these are paid to the doctor. Consequently, there seems to be no reason to state the category of injuries here at all. The Gemara answers that she was injured in the face in a manner which entitles her only to payment for her degradation (Ritva).

Shakud – שָׁקוּד: Rashi explains that Shmuel was diligent [*shakud*] in his studies in order to issue proper halakhic rulings, and in fact, the *halakha* is generally in accordance with his opinion in questions of monetary law. Alternatively, this name reflects in a more general manner Shmuel's great diligence in his studies, unrelated to his preparation when issuing halakhic rulings (see Jerusalem Talmud, *Nedarim* 8:2; *Arukh*). Others interpret *shakud* as speedy. Jeremiah speaks of an almond tree [*makel shaked*], which represents a fast-approaching event (see Jeremiah 1:11–12), because an almond tree bears fruit earlier than other fruit trees. In other words, Shmuel would learn quickly and was able to study large amounts of material (*Ramat Shmuel*). All these interpretations fit the Jerusalem Talmud's version of Shmuel's nickname Shoked. Yet others suggest that Shmuel was called by this name because Rabbi Yehuda HaNasi strove [*shoked*] to ordain him without success.

מתני׳ הַמְאָרֵס אֶת בִּתּוֹ וְגֵירְשָׁהּ, אֵירְסָהּ וְנִתְאַרְמְלָה – כְּתוּבָּתָהּ שֶׁלּוֹ. הִשִּׂיאָהּ וְגֵירְשָׁהּ, הִשִּׂיאָהּ וְנִתְאַרְמְלָה – כְּתוּבָּתָהּ שֶׁלָּהּ. רַבִּי יְהוּדָה אוֹמֵר: הָרִאשׁוֹנָה שֶׁל אָב. אָמְרוּ לוֹ: אִם מִשֶּׁהִשִּׂיאָהּ – אֵין לְאָבִיהָ רְשׁוּת בָּהּ.

MISHNA One who betroths his minor **daughter** to a man,[H] **and** the man subsequently **divorces her,** and her father then **betroths her** to another, **and she is widowed,** the payment specified in **her marriage contract,** even from her second husband, **is his,** i.e., it belongs to the father. However, if her father **married her** off **and** her husband **divorced her,**[H] and her father then **married her** to another man **and she was widowed,** even the payment specified in **her marriage contract** from her first marriage **is hers. Rabbi Yehuda says** that the payment specified in **the first** marriage contract belongs **to the father. They said to him: If** it **was after he married her** off, even the first time, **her father** no longer **has authority over her.**

גמ׳ טַעֲמָא – דְּהִשִּׂיאָהּ וְגֵירְשָׁהּ, הִשִּׂיאָהּ וְנִתְאַרְמְלָה, אֲבָל נִתְאַרְמְלָה תְּרֵי זִמְנֵי – תּוּ לָא חַזְיָא לְאִינְּסוּבֵי. וְאַגַּב אוֹרְחֵיהּ קָא סָתֵים לַן תַּנָּא כְּרַבִּי, דְּאָמַר: בִּתְרֵי זִמְנֵי הָוְיָא חֲזָקָה.

GEMARA The Gemara infers from the language of the mishna: The **reason** is **that** he **married her** off, **and** the husband **divorced her,**[N] and he **married her** off to another man, **and she was widowed. However,** if **she was widowed twice**[H] **she is no longer fit to be married,** due to the concern that she is the cause of her husbands' early demise. The Gemara comments: **And** the ***tanna*** **incidentally** teaches **an unattributed** opinion **in accordance with** the opinion of **Rabbi** Yehuda HaNasi, **who said** that **presumption** is established **by two occasions.** Consequently, she is already considered a danger after two husbands have passed away, as opposed to the opinion that three incidents are required to establish a presumption.

״רַבִּי יְהוּדָה אוֹמֵר: הָרִאשׁוֹנָה שֶׁל אָב״. מַאי טַעֲמָא דְּרַבִּי יְהוּדָה? רַבָּה וְרַב יוֹסֵף דְּאָמְרִי תַּרְוַיְיהוּ: הוֹאִיל וּמִשְּׁעַת אֵירוּסִין זָכָה בָּהֶן הָאָב.

§ The mishna taught that **Rabbi Yehuda says** the payment specified in **the first** marriage contract belongs **to the father.** The Gemara asks: **What is the reason of Rabbi Yehuda?**[N] The Gemara explains that **Rabba and Rav Yosef both say: Since the father is entitled to** the payments of the marriage contract **from the time of** her **betrothal,** when the first husband obligated himself to pay her marriage contract, as the girl was under her father's authority at the time, the father receives the money. Although the money is actually paid only after the girl was married and divorced, at which time she is under her own jurisdiction, her father acquired his right to the marriage contract from the time of her betrothal, when she was under his authority.

HALAKHA

One who betroths his minor daughter to a man, etc. – הַמְאָרֵס אֶת בִּתּוֹ: A father who betrothed his daughter to a man when she was a minor or a young woman is entitled to the payment of her marriage contract if she is widowed or divorced before she reaches majority or before she marries, i.e., while she is still betrothed. This applies even if he then betroths her to another man and she is again widowed or divorced before she reaches majority or before she marries (Rambam *Sefer Nashim, Hilkhot Ishut* 3:11, 10:11; *Shulḥan Arukh, Even HaEzer* 37:3).

If he married her off and her husband divorced her – הִשִּׂיאָהּ וְגֵירְשָׁהּ: Even in the case of a minor daughter, and certainly in the case of a young woman, if she was married off by her father and was subsequently widowed or divorced during his lifetime, she is under her own authority and her father retains no rights over her. Therefore, if she is betrothed again, the marriage contract belongs to her, in accordance with the unattributed opinion in the mishna (Rambam *Sefer Nashim, Hilkhot Ishut* 3:12; *Shulḥan Arukh, Even HaEzer* 37:3, 55:7).

If she was widowed twice – נִתְאַרְמְלָה תְּרֵי זִמְנֵי: If a woman was married or even betrothed to two men who both died, she may not wed a third, as she has a presumption of one whose husbands die, as stated by Rabbi Yehuda HaNasi. If she did marry, or even if she was merely betrothed, her husband does not have to divorce her. Some authorities state that this *halakha* applies only if both husbands became ill and died, but not if one of them died either from a plague that affected a large number of people or from unnatural causes. The Rema notes the practice of many to be lenient with regard to this prohibition (Rambam *Sefer Kedusha, Hilkhot Issurei Bia* 21:31; *Shulḥan Arukh, Even HaEzer* 9:1).

NOTES

The reason is that he married her off and the husband divorced her, etc. – טַעֲמָא דְּהִשִּׂיאָהּ וְגֵירְשָׁהּ וכו׳: If a woman marries multiple men and they die, she is not permitted to remarry, due to the concern that she may be the cause of her husbands' deaths (see *Yevamot* 64b). The *tanna'im* dispute whether this prohibition applies only after the woman's third husband has died or even after her second husband has died. As for the reasoning for this *halakha*, the *amora'im* argue whether it is because her bad fortune causes her husbands to die on her account or whether it is assumed that she has an illness or defect that leads to her husbands' death. There is a practical difference between these two explanations in the case of a woman whose husbands died during their betrothal and in an instance where the husbands passed away as a result of some other clear cause unrelated to their wife, e.g., a war or an accident.

Although the mishna here is not discussing this prohibition, the *tanna* of the mishna did not want to give an example of a tragic case where a woman would not be permitted to remarry (Rashi). According to Rabbi Moshe bar Rabbi Yosef of Narbonne, just as a woman may not remarry after her second husband has died, due to the possibility that she was the cause of his death, she also does not receive payment of her marriage contract from the estate of her second husband. However, the Ramban and Ritva reject this opinion.

The Gemara's inference is based upon the fact that the mishna does not say that she was widowed twice. Rather, it states that she was divorced and widowed. Some commentaries contend, based on Rashi in *Yevamot* (26a), that for this very reason the *tanna* also did not say that she was divorced twice, as a woman who has divorced twice is also prohibited from remarrying. However, others refute this idea, arguing that there is no reason to harbor suspicions against a woman due to a divorce, which must be carried out by her husband (Ritva).

Some commentaries hold that the prohibition against a woman remarrying after two husbands have died applies only if they died after marriage, but not if they died when they were betrothed to her. Nevertheless, the mishna states that the woman was divorced and widowed, instead of widowed twice, even in the first clause, so that the cases would be parallel to the cases mentioned in the mishna's latter clause (Ri HaLavan; Meiri). However, according to the Rambam, even if the husbands died after betrothal and before marriage, the woman is prohibited from remarrying.

What is the reason of Rabbi Yehuda – מַאי טַעֲמָא דְּרַבִּי יְהוּדָה: As opposed to the Gemara here, which relates the dispute to the time of the acquisition of the marriage contract, in the Jerusalem Talmud it is stated that according to the opinion of Rabbi Yehuda, the Sages entitled a father to his daughter's marriage contract in the case under discussion, even if his daughter was married and not merely betrothed, so that he would grant her a generous dowry. Although the *halakha* is in accordance with the opinion of the Sages, in later generations, scholars of several places enacted various decrees obligating the return of all or part of a dowry if the woman dies without children a short while after the marriage.

מְתִיב רָבָא: רַבִּי יְהוּדָה אוֹמֵר: הָרִאשׁוֹנָה שֶׁל אָב, וּמוֹדֶה רַבִּי יְהוּדָה בִּמְאָרֵס אֶת בִּתּוֹ כְּשֶׁהִיא קְטַנָּה, וּבָגְרָה, וְאַחַר כָּךְ נִשֵּׂאת – שֶׁאֵין לְאָבִיהָ רְשׁוּת בָּהּ. אַמַּאי? הָכָא נַמִי לֵימָא: הוֹאִיל וּמִשְּׁעַת אֵירוּסִין זָכָה בָּהֶן הָאָב!

Rava raised an objection from a *baraita*: **Rabbi Yehuda says** that the payment specified in **the first** marriage contract belongs **to** her **father. And Rabbi Yehuda concedes** in the case **of one who betroths his daughter when she is a minor, and she matures and subsequently marries, that her father no** longer **has authority over her** once she becomes an adult, and he does not retain his rights to her marriage contract. According to the above explanation, **why** does Rabbi Yehuda agree in that case? **Here too, let him say: Since the father is entitled to** the payment of her marriage contract **from the time of** her **betrothal,** he receives the payment even if she married after she reached majority.

אֶלָּא, אִי אִתְּמַר הָכִי אִתְּמַר: רַבָּה וְרַב יוֹסֵף דְּאָמְרִי תַּרְוַיְיהוּ: הוֹאִיל וּבִרְשׁוּתוֹ נִכְתָּבִין.

Rather, if this statement **was stated, it was stated as follows: Rabba and Rav Yosef both say: Since** the amounts of the marriage contract **are written under his authority,** as the marriage contract is drafted right before the marriage, at which point the girl was still under her father's jurisdiction, he is therefore entitled to the money. This explains why the ruling is different if she reached majority before her marriage. In this case, the marriage contract was written when she was no longer under her father's jurisdiction, and therefore her father is not entitled to the payment of her marriage contract.

וּמִיגְבָּא מֵאֵימַת גָּבְיָא?

And now that it has been established that even according to the opinion of Rabbi Yehuda, the rights to a marriage contract are determined based upon the time of marriage and not the time of betrothal, despite the fact that its sum is fixed at that time, the Gemara asks: **From when** does the husband's property become liened to ensure **collection** of his wife's marriage contract?[NH] Does the monetary claim take effect at the time of betrothal, so that there is a lien on any property he owned at that time, or is there a lien only on property that the husband owned at the time of marriage?

אָמַר רַב הוּנָא: מָנֶה, מָאתַיִם – מִן הָאֵירוּסִין, וְתוֹסֶפֶת – מִן הַנִּשּׂוּאִין. וְרַב אַסִּי אָמַר: אֶחָד זֶה וְאֶחָד זֶה – מִן הַנִּשּׂוּאִין.

Rav Huna said: With regard to the **one hundred dinars** for a non-virgin and the **two hundred** for a virgin, the basic sums of a marriage contract instituted by the Sages, she has a lien on her husband's property **from the** time of the **betrothal,** as she acquired this amount when she was betrothed, **but** with regard to the **addition,** i.e., additional sums of money stipulated by the husband himself, the wife's lien on his property takes effect only **from the** time of **the marriage. And Rav Asi said:** The lien for **both this and that** take effect only **from the** time of their **marriage.**[N]

וּמִי אֲמַר רַב הוּנָא הָכִי? וְהָאִתְּמַר: הוֹצִיאָה עָלָיו שְׁתֵּי כְתוּבּוֹת, אַחַת שֶׁל מָאתַיִם וְאַחַת שֶׁל שְׁלֹשׁ מֵאוֹת. וְאָמַר רַב הוּנָא: בָּאתָה לִגְבּוֹת מָאתַיִם – גּוֹבָה מִזְּמַן רִאשׁוֹן, שְׁלֹשׁ מֵאוֹת – גּוֹבָה מִזְּמַן שֵׁנִי.

The Gemara asks: **And did Rav Huna** actually **say this,** that a woman has a lien on her husband's property from the time of betrothal with regard to payment of the one hundred or two hundred dinars that constitute the main sum of her marriage contract? **But wasn't it stated** that *amora'im* discussed the case of a woman who **produced against** her husband, upon their divorce, **two marriage contracts,** written at different times, **one of two hundred** dinars **and** the other **one of three hundred? And Rav Huna said:** Since she can claim only one marriage contract, if **she came to collect** the first sum of **two hundred** dinars, **she** can **collect** that amount even **from** property her husband sold after **the first** point in **time,** when this marriage contract was written, and if she wishes to collect the one worth **three hundred** dinars, **she** can **collect from** property her husband sold after **the second** point in **time.**

NOTES

From when does the husband's property become liened to ensure collection of his wife's marriage contract – מִיגְבָּא מֵאֵימַת גָּבְיָא: The commentaries disagree about how to understand the dispute about whether the lien applies from the time of betrothal or from the time of the marriage. According to Rashi, a woman is legally entitled to a marriage contract from the time of betrothal, and if she would be divorced or widowed after betrothal, she would be entitled to payment even if no document had been written. However, it is common custom to write the document right before the marriage. The dispute here is whether the lien on the man's property takes effect from the time when the woman obtains the right to a marriage contract or from the time when the contract is actually written, in accordance with the general policy that only monetary debts for which there is a contract cause a lien on the debtor's property.

Conversely, Rabbeinu Ḥananel holds that a woman is not entitled to a marriage contract until the time of the marriage, but the husband may write one from the time of betrothal if he wishes. The case under discussion is one in which the husband wrote a marriage contract at the time of betrothal for the amount required by the Sages, and then he wrote a new contract at the time of the marriage, which included the obligation to pay an additional sum of money. The question is whether this second contract nullifies the first one, in which case the lien on the husband's property applies only to that which he owned at the time of the marriage, or whether the second contract merely adds an additional sum of money to the previous contract, in which case the lien on his property for the amount specified in the first contract applies to whatever he owned at the time of betrothal, when the first contract was written (see Rosh and Ritva).

Both this and that take effect only from the time of their marriage – אֶחָד זֶה וְאֶחָד זֶה מִן הַנִּשּׂוּאִין: Rav Sherira Gaon's opinion, which provides the basis for the Rambam's ruling, is similar to that of Rabbeinu Ḥananel, only more extreme. He agrees with Rabbeinu Ḥananel that a woman is not entitled to a marriage contract from the time of betrothal. Therefore, even if the husband voluntarily writes a marriage contract, it can be assumed that he does not intend to limit his ability to conduct business by creating a lien on his property before marriage.

HALAKHA

From when does the husband's property become liened to ensure collection of his wife's marriage contract – מִיגְבָּא מֵאֵימַת גָּבְיָא: With regard to one who betrothed a woman and wrote a marriage contract for her but died or divorced her before their marriage, she may collect the basic sum of the marriage contract from property that belonged to her husband at the time of his death. She may not collect her payment from property her husband sold after the betrothal, nor may she collect any additional sum beyond the basic sum of one hundred dinars for a non-virgin or two hundred for a virgin. This is the ruling of the Rambam, in accordance with the opinion of Rav Sherira Gaon. Others rule that she may claim the basic sum of the marriage contract even from property her husband sold after the betrothal (Rambam *Sefer Nashim, Hilkhot Ishut* 10:11; *Shulḥan Arukh, Even HaEzer* 55:6, and *Beit Shmuel* there).

וְאִם אִיתָא – תִּיגְבֵּי מָאתַיִם מִזְּמַן רִאשׁוֹן, וּמֵאָה מִזְּמַן שֵׁנִי!

The Gemara explains the difficulty: **And if it is so,** that Rav Huna maintains that the lien for the basic sum and the addition can be ascribed to different dates, **let her collect two hundred** dinars **from** property sold after **the first** point in **time,** as she was already entitled to the basic sum of her marriage contract from that day, **and** she can collect **the** additional **one hundred** dinars **from** property sold after **the second** point in **time.**

וּלְטַעֲמִיךְ תִּיגְבֵּי חֲמֵשׁ מֵאוֹת כּוּלָּם, מָאתַיִם מִזְּמַן רִאשׁוֹן, תְּלַת מֵאָה מִזְּמַן שֵׁנִי!

The Gemara refutes this argument: **And** even **according to your reasoning, let her collect the entire five hundred** dinars, the sum of both marriage contracts. She should be able to collect **two hundred from** property sold after **the first** point in **time** and **three hundred from** property sold after **the second** stipulated **time.**

אֶלָּא: חֲמֵשׁ מֵאוֹת מַאי טַעֲמָא לָא גָּבְיָא – כֵּיוָן דְּלָא כָּתַב לָהּ ״צָבִיתִי וְאוֹסִיפִית לָךְ תְּלַת מֵאָה אַמָּאתַיִם״ הָכִי קָאָמַר לָהּ: אִי מִזְּמַן רִאשׁוֹן גָּבִיאַת – גָּבְיָא מָאתַיִם, אִי מִזְּמַן שֵׁנִי גָּבִיאַת – גָּבְיָא תְּלַת מֵאָה.

Rather, what is the reason that **she may not collect** the entire sum of **five hundred** dinars? **Since** he did **not write to her** in the second marriage contract: **I chose** to **add to** the payment of **your** marriage contract, and therefore I am writing a contract for **three hundred** dinars in addition **to** the first **two hundred** dinars, it is apparent that **this is what he** meant to **say to her** by writing a second marriage contract: **If you collect from** property sold after **the first** point in **time, you may collect two hundred** dinars; **if you collect from** property sold after **the second** point in **time, you may collect three hundred** dinars.

Perek **IV**
Daf **44** Amud **a**

הָכָא נַמִי הַיְינוּ טַעֲמָא דְּלָא גָּבְיָא, מִדְּלָא כָּתַב לָהּ ״אוֹסִיפִית לָךְ מֵאָה אַמָּאתַיִם״ – אַחוּלֵי אַחִילְתֵּיהּ לְשִׁעְבּוּדָא קַמָּא.

Here too, this is the reasoning for the ruling **that she does not collect** the additional one hundred dinars from the second stipulated time, **as he did not write to her** in the second marriage contract: **I added one hundred** dinars **to your** original marriage contract **of two hundred** dinars. Evidently, he did not add to the existing marriage contract. Rather, **she forgave** her rights **to the first** marriage contract, including the **lien** on his property from the date it was written, in order to accept the second marriage document.

אֲמַר מָר: אִי בָּעֲיָא בְּהַאי – גָּבְיָא, אִי בָּעֲיָא בְּהַאי גָּבְיָא, לֵימָא פְּלִיגָא דְּרַב נַחְמָן, דְּאָמַר רַב נַחְמָן: שְׁנֵי שְׁטָרוֹת הַיּוֹצְאִין בְּזֶה אַחַר זֶה – בִּיטֵּל שֵׁנִי אֶת הָרִאשׁוֹן!

§ After clarifying Rav Huna's opinion, the Gemara turns its attention to a more general issue, connected to his last statement. **The Master,** i.e., Rav Huna, **said,** as indicated in the above discussion, that **if she wishes** she can **collect** the sum specified in **this** marriage contract, and **if she wishes** she can **collect** the sum specified in **that** marriage contract.[H] The Gemara asks: **Shall we say** that this opinion **disagrees** with **that of Rav Naḥman? As Rav Naḥman said:** With regard to **two documents**[N] that pertain to the same issue and **that are produced one after the other,**[H] e.g., a pair of documents that ascribe the transfer of ownership over a particular field to different times, the **second,** later document **nullifies the first.** Here too, the second marriage contract should negate the first one entirely.

NOTES

Two documents – שְׁנֵי שְׁטָרוֹת: Some state that this *halakha* applies only to documents of sale, a gift, or a marriage contract. However, with regard to documents of loans, even if the two amounts were identical but from different dates, they are assumed to refer to different loans (Rif; *ge'onim*). Other early authorities cite support for this opinion from the Jerusalem Talmud in *Ketubot* 9:10 (Ritva). The Gemara there discusses whether one who lends another for a second time, before the first debt is paid off, is required to specify in the second document that he is lending him again. The Gemara concludes that although this is the advisable course of action, as it prevents error, if one does not do so he may nevertheless collect the loans mentioned in both documents.

HALAKHA

She produced two marriage contracts – הוֹצִיאָה שְׁתֵּי כְּתוּבּוֹת: If a woman had two marriage contracts of equal value, the later document cancels the earlier one. She has a lien on her husband's property from the time when the second document was written. If they are not of equal value, she may use whichever one she wishes, and the other is nullified. If the husband wrote in the second document that he was adding an additional sum to that specified in the first document, she has a lien on his property from the time the first document was written vis-à-vis the sum specified in that document, and she has a lien on his property from the time the second document was written vis-à-vis the additional sum specified in that document (Rambam *Sefer Nashim*, *Hilkhot Ishut* 16:29; *Shulḥan Arukh*, *Even HaEzer* 100:14).

Two documents that are produced one after the other – שְׁנֵי שְׁטָרוֹת הַיּוֹצְאִין בְּזֶה אַחַר זֶה: If two identical documents were written about the same transaction, whether a sale or a gift, the second cancels the first. Consequently, if a field is repossessed by creditors of the seller, thereby requiring the seller to compensate the purchaser for his loss, the purchaser may repossess property from the seller only on the basis of the lien created by the second document. If a tax is owed for the field from the period of time between the writing of the two documents, the seller is responsible to pay it. If the purchaser consumed the field's produce during this period of time, he must reimburse the seller. However, some hold that although the purchaser is not entitled to the produce from this period, he does not have to reimburse the owner for anything he took (*Tur*, based on Rosh). The authorities further state that the reputation of the witnesses who signed on the first document is not impaired by this incident, as it is assumed that they acted in good faith (Rambam *Sefer Kinyan*, *Hilkhot Zekhiya* 5:9; *Shulḥan Arukh*, *Ḥoshen Mishpat* 240:2; *Sefer Me'irat Einayim*).

לָאו מִי אִיתְּמַר עֲלַהּ, אָמַר רַב פַּפָּא: וּמוֹדֶה רַב נַחְמָן דְּאִי אוֹסֵיף בֵּיהּ דִּיקְלָא לְתוֹסֶפֶת כְּתָבֵיהּ – הָכָא נַמִי, הָא אוֹסֵיף לַהּ מִידֵּי.

The Gemara refutes this suggestion: **Was it not stated with regard to** this *halakha* of Rav Naḥman that **Rav Pappa said: And Rav Naḥman concedes that if he added** so much as **a palm tree in**[H] the second document,[N] this shows that **he wrote it as an addition**, and therefore the second document does not cancel the first, but adds to its sum? **Here too, he added something for her,** as the sum of money specified in the second marriage contract is larger than that specified in the first.

גּוּפָא, אָמַר רַב נַחְמָן: שְׁנֵי שְׁטָרוֹת הַיּוֹצְאִין בָּזֶה אַחַר זֶה – בִּיטֵּל שֵׁנִי אֶת הָרִאשׁוֹן. אָמַר רַב פַּפָּא: וּמוֹדֶה רַב נַחְמָן דְּאִי אוֹסֵיף בֵּיהּ דִּיקְלָא – לְתוֹסֶפֶת כְּתָבֵיהּ. פְּשִׁיטָא רִאשׁוֹן בְּמֶכֶר וְשֵׁנִי בְּמַתָּנָה – לְיַפּוֹת כֹּחוֹ הוּא דִּכְתַב לֵיהּ, מִשּׁוּם דִּינָא דְּבַר מִצְרָא.

§ Since the Gemara has mentioned the statement of Rav Naḥman, it discusses this matter **itself: Rav Naḥman said:** With regard to **two documents that are produced one after the other,** the **second nullifies the first. Rav Pappa said: And Rav Naḥman concedes that if he added a palm tree to it, he wrote it as an addition.** The Gemara analyzes this *halakha* in detail. It **is obvious** that if the **first** document was a document **of a sale,**[H] **and the second** stated that the same field was given **as a gift,** the second document does not negate the first, as **he wrote** the additional document of a gift **to improve the rights** of the recipient **due to the *halakha*** of one whose field **borders** the field of his neighbor.[N]

וְכׇל שֶׁכֵּן רִאשׁוֹן בְּמַתָּנָה וְשֵׁנִי בְּמֶכֶר, דְּאָמְרִינַן: מִשּׁוּם דִּינָא דְּבַעַל חוֹב הוּא דִּכְתַב כֵּן.

And all the more so, this is the *halakha* if he wrote the **first** document **as a gift and the second** in the form **of a sale, as we say** it was **due to the *halakha*** of **a creditor that he wrote** it in **this way.** Out of concern that his creditor might come and snatch the field from the recipient and leave him without redress, he writes a document of sale for the recipient, so that he can return and collect this sum from him.

HALAKHA

If he added so much as a palm tree – אִי אוֹסֵיף בֵּיהּ דִּיקְלָא: If the second document added to the first, the first document remains valid, as the second one was written only for the additional amount (Rambam *Sefer Kinyan, Hilkhot Zekhiya* 5:9; *Shulḥan Arukh, Ḥoshen Mishpat* 240:2).

If the first document was a document of a sale, etc. – רִאשׁוֹן בְּמֶכֶר וכו׳: If two documents were written for the same transaction, but one was a sale while the other was a gift, the second document does not negate the first, as it is assumed that the second was given to improve the rights of the recipient, as there are advantages to receiving something by sale rather than as a gift, and vice versa (Rambam *Sefer Kinyan, Hilkhot Zekhiya* 5:8; *Shulḥan Arukh, Ḥoshen Mishpat* 240:1).

NOTES

If he added so much as a palm tree in the second document – אִי אוֹסֵיף בֵּיהּ דִּיקְלָא: Rashi and other commentaries maintain that in a case when the second document adds to the first, the recipient has the following choice: He may collect payment with the first document, in which case he receives the smaller sum, but his lien begins from the date when the first document was written. Or, he may collect payment with the second document, in which case he receives the greater sum, but his lien begins from the date when the second document was written. However, many other commentaries hold that he may collect with both documents (Rosh; *Maggid Mishne*). He has a lien on the seller's property from the date when the first document was written vis-à-vis what he received based upon that document, and he has a lien on the seller's property from the date when the second document was written vis-à-vis what was added in the second document.

The *halakha* of one whose field borders the field of his neighbor – דִּינָא דְּבַר מִצְרָא: There is a *halakha* that when someone sells his field, the owner of a bordering field has the first right of purchase. If the seller sells it to someone else, the owner of the bordering field can demand that the purchaser give it to him, although of course he must reimburse him for his purchase. This *halakha* is based on the command: "You shall do that which is right and good" (Deuteronomy 6:18).

The neighbor has a legitimate reason to want this particular field, as it is certainly easier to work and guard two contiguous plots, and since it makes no difference to the seller who gets his field, it would be unfair not to grant ownership to the one who would benefit most.

This *halakha* applies only to a sale, as in the case of a gift the owner might have his reasons for preferring another individual. Consequently, in this case it is possible that the previous owner wrote a document of a gift to help the recipient circumvent the claims of the owner of the adjacent plot.

Most authorities from Rav Hai Gaon onward maintain that the mere act of writing a document of a gift for the field is not enough to remove the complaint of the neighbor, as the neighbor can protest if he knows that the recipient also possesses a document of sale. According to this opinion, the recipient in this case evidently believes that he can show the neighbor the document of gift without it occurring to him that the transaction was actually a sale. Some add that even according to the ruling of the Rambam, that the neighbor has the right to make the recipient swear that he is not cheating him and that it was in fact a gift, it is possible that the document of a gift was written for the purpose of deceiving the neighbor (Ritva). *Tosafot* explain how the rights of the recipient of the field are augmented when he receives the document stating that he received the land as a gift, even if there are no advantages with regard to the *halakha* of one whose field borders on the field of his neighbor.

אֶלָּא, אִי שְׁנֵיהֶם בְּמֶכֶר, שְׁנֵיהֶם בְּמַתָּנָה – בִּיטֵּל שֵׁנִי אֶת הָרִאשׁוֹן. מַאי טַעְמָא? רַפְרָם אֲמַר: אֵימַר אוֹדוּיֵי אוֹדֵי לֵיהּ. רַב אַחָא אֲמַר: אֵימַר אַחוּלֵי אַחְלֵיהּ לְשִׁיעְבּוּדֵיהּ.

Rather, Rav Naḥman meant that **if both of them** were documents **of sale** or **both of them** were documents **of gifts, the second nullifies the first.** The Gemara asks: **What is the reason** for this *halakha*? *Amora'im* argued over this matter. **Rafram said: Say** that the recipient of the field **admitted to him**[N] that the first document was invalid, e.g., it was forged, and he therefore wrote a second, valid document. **Rav Aḥa said: Say** that the recipient **forgave him his lien**[N] from the date of the first document. Consequently, if the seller's creditors collect this field as payment for the debt owed to them, which necessitates the seller reimbursing the buyer for the purchase price of the field, the buyer has a lien only on property owned by the seller from the time of the second document.

מַאי בֵּינַיְיהוּ? אִיכָּא בֵּינַיְיהוּ אוֹרוּעֵי סָהֲדֵי,

The Gemara asks: **What is** the practical difference **between** these two explanations? The Gemara explains: **The** practical difference **between them** involves several cases. First, there is the issue of whether this serves to **impair** the reliability of the **witnesses:**[N] According to Rafram, who assumes that the first document was of questionable validity, the witnesses who signed on that document are likewise under suspicion, and therefore their testimony and signature in other cases are of questionable value.

וּלְשַׁלּוּמֵי פֵּירֵי, וּלְטַסְקָא.

And there is also a difference with regard **to paying** for the **produce** of the property between the dates specified in the two documents. According to Rafram, the transfer of ownership did not take place at the date specified in the first document. Consequently, the recipient of the field must compensate the original owner for the field's produce that he consumed between the two dates. According to Rav Aḥa, the transfer of ownership took place at the time specified in the first document. **And** finally, there is a difference **with regard to** the payment of **the land tax** [***taska***].[L] If the first document was invalid, the previous owner must pay all taxes due during the period between the two documents.

מַאי הֲוֵי עֲלָהּ דִּכְתוּבָּה? תָּא שְׁמַע: דְּאָמַר רַב יְהוּדָה אָמַר שְׁמוּאֵל מִשּׁוּם רַבִּי אֶלְעָזָר בְּרַבִּי שִׁמְעוֹן: מָנֶה מָאתַיִם – מִן הָאֵירוּסִין, וְתוֹסֶפֶת – מִן הַנִּישּׂוּאִין.

§ The above discussion came in the wake of the dispute between Rav Huna and Rav Asi with regard to whether the lien on a husband's property to ensure payment of his wife's marriage contract applies from the time of betrothal or the time of marriage. The Gemara returns to that issue. **What** halakhic conclusion **was** reached **about** this matter of **a marriage contract?** The Gemara responds: **Come** and **hear** the following ruling, **as Rav Yehuda said** that **Shmuel said in the name of Rabbi Elazar, son of Rabbi Shimon:** The lien on his property with regard to the **one hundred dinars** or **two hundred** dinars that comprise the basic sum of a marriage contract applies **from** the time of **the betrothal, and the** lien with regard to the **additional** sum applies **from** the time of **the marriage.**

וַחֲכָמִים אוֹמְרִים: אֶחָד זֶה וְאֶחָד זֶה מִן הַנִּישּׂוּאִין. וְהִלְכְתָא: אֶחָד זֶה וְאֶחָד זֶה מִן הַנִּישּׂוּאִין.

And the Rabbis say: The lien with regard to **both this and that** takes effect only **from** the time of **the marriage.** The Gemara concludes: **And the *halakha*** is that with regard to **both this and that,** the lien takes effect **from** the time of **the marriage,**[H] in accordance with the majority opinion of the Rabbis.

LANGUAGE

Land tax [*taska*] – טַסְקָא: Similar to the Arabic طسق, *ṭasaq*, the *taska* mentioned here is a land tax. This tax was supremely important. According to the Persian law of the time, the payment of the *taska* was considered a sign of ownership of a particular property. Failure to pay the *taska* resulted in expropriation of the land.

HALAKHA

With regard to both this and that, the lien takes effect from the time of the marriage – אֶחָד זֶה וְאֶחָד זֶה מִן הַנִּישּׂוּאִין: If a man wrote two marriage contracts for his wife, one from the time of betrothal and the other from the time of marriage, she may use only the document written at the time of their marriage (*Shulḥan Arukh*, *Even HaEzer* 100:14).

NOTES

Rafram said: Say that the recipient of the field admitted to him, etc. – רַפְרָם אֲמַר אֵימַר אוֹדוּיֵי אוֹדֵי לֵיהּ וכו׳: The Ramban and later commentaries who were influenced by him suggest that this is not an actual dispute between the *amora'im*. Rafram stated his explanation only in cases where the explanation of Rav Aḥa does not apply. Otherwise, it is not assumed that the document is invalid unless there is evidence to this effect.

Forgave him his lien – אַחוּלֵי אַחְלֵיהּ לְשִׁיעְבּוּדֵיהּ: Some infer from this statement that the recipient merely relinquished his lien from the date of the first document, but he did not relinquish his ownership of the field, as one cannot relinquish ownership over land by simply forgoing rights to it without making a formal transaction (Ramban). Others note that *Tosafot* apparently disagree with this conclusion (Ritva; *Nimmukei Yosef*). They suggest that Rav Aḥa's statement actually means that the recipient renounces his ownership rights to the property as guaranteed by the first document. A practical difference between these interpretations would arise in a case where the second document specifies a smaller plot, e.g., half of a field. According to the opinion of the Ramban, the purchaser has not relinquished his right to the entire field, whereas the Ritva and *Nimmukei Yosef* would maintain that the recipient owns only what is specified in the second document.

To impair the reliability of the witnesses – אוֹרוּעֵי סָהֲדֵי: Some explain that the court is suspicious about the veracity of all other testimonies given by the witnesses who signed the first document (Rashi; Meiri). However, most early authorities maintain that people are not invalidated as witnesses because one individual claimed without proof that they signed a forged document. Rather, this *halakha* applies only to documents that are in the possession of the recipient of the field and that were signed by those witnesses. Since the recipient of the field himself argued that the witnesses signed a forged document, he may not collect other claims on the basis of their testimony (Rid; *Tosafot*; Ramban). The Rid adds that the term impair supports this interpretation, as it indicates that the court does not actually invalidate the witnesses but is merely suspicious with regard to them.

מתני׳ הַגִּיּוֹרֶת – שֶׁנִּתְגַּיְּירָה בִּתָּהּ עִמָּהּ וְזִינְּתָה – הֲרֵי זוֹ בְּחֶנֶק. אֵין לָהּ לֹא פֶּתַח בֵּית הָאָב, וְלֹא מֵאָה סֶלַע.

MISHNA In the case of a female **convert**[N] **whose daughter converted**[N] **with her**[H] and later, as a young woman, the daughter **engaged in licentious sexual relations** when she was betrothed, **she is** executed **by strangulation,** not stoning, the method of execution that would be employed had she been born Jewish. **She has neither** the *halakha* of being executed at the **entrance to** her **father's house,**[N] as in the case of a woman who was born Jewish who committed this crime, **nor** does she receive **one hundred *sela*** if her husband defamed her by falsely claiming that she had committed adultery. The reason is that the verses state "Israel" (Deuteronomy 22:19, 21) with regard to these *halakhot*, indicating that these *halakhot* apply only to those born as Jews.

הָיְתָה הוֹרָתָהּ שֶׁלֹּא בִּקְדוּשָּׁה וְלֵידָתָהּ בִּקְדוּשָּׁה – הֲרֵי זוֹ בִּסְקִילָה, וְאֵין לָהּ לֹא פֶּתַח בֵּית הָאָב, וְלֹא מֵאָה סֶלַע. הָיְתָה הוֹרָתָהּ וְלֵידָתָהּ בִּקְדוּשָּׁה – הֲרֵי הִיא כְּבַת יִשְׂרָאֵל לְכׇל דְּבָרֶיהָ.

However, if the daughter's **conception occurred** when her mother **was not** yet **in** a state of **sanctity,**[H] i.e., when she was still a gentile, **but her birth** took place when her mother was **in** a state of **sanctity,** as her mother converted during her pregnancy, **this** daughter is punishable **by stoning** if she committed adultery as a betrothed young woman. However, **she has neither** the *halakha* of being executed at the **entrance to** her **father's house, nor** the right to **one hundred *sela*** if it turns out that her husband defamed her. If **her conception and birth occurred** when her mother **was in** a state of **sanctity,**[H] i.e., after she converted, **she is like a** regular **Jewish woman in all matters.**

יֵשׁ לָהּ אָב וְאֵין לָהּ פֶּתַח בֵּית הָאָב, יֵשׁ לָהּ פֶּתַח בֵּית הָאָב וְאֵין לָהּ אָב – הֲרֵי זוֹ בִּסְקִילָה, לֹא נֶאֱמַר ״פֶּתַח בֵּית אָב״ אֶלָּא לְמִצְוָה.

If a young woman who is betrothed commits adultery and **she has a father but does not have an entrance to** her **father's house,** i.e., if her father does not possess a house of his own, or if **she has an entrance to** her **father's house but does not have a father,**[H] as he has passed away, **she is** nevertheless executed **via stoning,** as the requirement that she is to be executed at the **entrance to her father's house is stated only for a mitzva** but it is not an indispensable requirement.

NOTES

A female convert, etc. – הַגִּיּוֹרֶת וכו׳: With regard to the connection between this *halakha* and the previous *mishnayot*, the commentaries explain that the *mishnayot* clarified the *halakhot* of a rapist and a seducer and then incidentally discussed the rights of a father to his daughter's marriage contract, which is related to his rights to her fine. Subsequently, the mishna addresses the *halakha* of a defamer, whose fine is similar in several regards to that of a rapist (*Melekhet Shlomo*).

A female convert whose daughter converted – הַגִּיּוֹרֶת שֶׁנִּתְגַּיְּירָה בִּתָּהּ: According to most commentaries, this *halakha* applies to all converts, including those who converted at a very young age. Some add that the *tanna* formulated his statement with regard to the daughter of a convert who is also a convert, rather than just referring to a convert, to indicate that the *halakha* applies even to one who converted under the age of three, when she is unable to convert on her own (*Tosafot*). Others state that this *halakha* is referring only to a convert who does not have a presumption of virginity, as stated several times in previous *mishnayot* (Rambam's Commentary on the Mishna). According to this interpretation, the mishna is referring only to a girl who converted when she was older than three.

She has neither the *halakha* of being executed at the entrance to her father's house, etc. – אֵין לָהּ לֹא פֶּתַח בֵּית הָאָב וכו׳: Some commentaries explain that the court does not have to fulfill the requirement to stone her at the entrance of her father's house, as this *halakha* was stated only with regard to a woman who was born Jewish (Rashi; Ritva). Others maintain that once she has converted she is no longer considered halakhically related to her father, and therefore it is impossible to execute her at the entrance of her father's home, similar to the case of a fatherless young woman (*ge'onim*; Rabbeinu Yehonatan; Rid).

HALAKHA

A convert whose daughter converted with her – הַגִּיּוֹרֶת שֶׁנִּתְגַּיְּירָה בִּתָּהּ עִמָּהּ: If a female convert committed adultery as a betrothed young woman, she is executed via strangulation rather than stoning. This applies even if she was younger than three years old when she converted. If her husband defamed her, he is exempt from the fine and from receiving lashes (Rambam *Sefer Kedusha, Hilkhot Issurei Bia* 3:7; *Sefer Nashim, Hilkhot Na'ara Betula* 3:8).

If the daughter's conception occurred when her mother was not yet in a state of sanctity – הָיְתָה הוֹרָתָהּ שֶׁלֹּא בִּקְדוּשָּׁה: If a woman conceived as a gentile and converted before giving birth to her daughter, and the daughter committed adultery as a betrothed young woman, the daughter is executed via stoning. However, she is not stoned at the entrance to her father's house but at the city gates. If her husband defamed her, he is exempt from the fine and from receiving lashes (Rambam *Sefer Kedusha, Hilkhot Issurei Bia* 3:11; *Sefer Nashim, Hilkhot Na'ara Betula* 3:8).

If her conception and birth occurred when her mother was in a state of sanctity – הָיְתָה הוֹרָתָהּ וְלֵידָתָהּ בִּקְדוּשָּׁה: If a girl was conceived after her mother's conversion, she is considered a regular Jewish woman with regard to the *halakhot* of a defamer (Rambam *Sefer Nashim, Hilkhot Na'ara Betula* 3:8).

Does not have a father, etc. – אֵין לָהּ אָב וכו׳: If a betrothed young woman who does not have a father or whose father does not own a house commits adultery, she is stoned in the regular place of stoning (Rambam *Sefer Kedusha, Hilkhot Issurei Bia* 3:11).

גמ׳ מְנָא הָנֵי מִילֵּי? אֲמַר רֵישׁ לָקִישׁ: דְּאָמַר קְרָא ״וָמֵתָה״ – לְרַבּוֹת הוֹרָתָהּ שֶׁלֹּא בִּקְדוּשָּׁה וְלֵידָתָהּ בִּקְדוּשָּׁה.

GEMARA Since the rulings of the mishna are based on the principle that the special *halakhot* of a betrothed young woman who committed adultery apply only to a woman who was born Jewish, the Gemara questions the *halakha* that a woman who was conceived when her mother was a gentile but born when her mother was Jewish is executed via stoning: **From where are these matters** derived? **Reish Lakish said: As the verse states:** "And the men of her city shall stone her with stones **that she die**" (Deuteronomy 22:21). The phrase "that she die" is superfluous and comes **to include** one **whose conception** occurred when her mother **was not** yet **in** a state of **sanctity but her birth** took place when her mother was **in** a state of **sanctity.**

אִי הָכִי, מִילְקָא נַמִי נִילְקֵי, וּמֵאָה סֶלַע נַמִי לְשַׁלֵּם! אָמַר קְרָא: ״וָמֵתָה״ – לְמִיתָה נִתְרַבְּתָה, וְלֹא לִקְנָס. וְאֵימָא: לְרַבּוֹת הוֹרָתָהּ וְלֵידָתָהּ בִּקְדוּשָּׁה! הַהִיא יִשְׂרְאֵלִית מְעַלְּיָיתָא הִיא.

The Gemara asks: **If so,** if the verse equates her to a regular Jewish woman, **let** her husband **also be flogged** if he defames her, **and let him also pay** the **one hundred** *sela.* The Gemara answers that **the verse states: "That she die"** (Deuteronomy 22:21), which indicates that **she was included with regard to** the **death** penalty **but not with regard to** the **fine.** The Gemara asks another question: **Say** that this verse comes **to include** only a girl **whose conception and birth** both occurred when her mother was **in** a state of **sanctity.** The Gemara responds: **That** girl **is a full-fledged Jewish woman,** and there is no difference between her and any other Jewish woman.

וְאֵימָא לְרַבּוֹת הוֹרָתָהּ וְלֵידָתָהּ שֶׁלֹּא בִּקְדוּשָּׁה! אִם כֵּן ״בְּיִשְׂרָאֵל״ מַאי אַהֲנֵי לֵיהּ?

The Gemara asks a question from the opposite perspective: **And say** that the verse comes **to include** even one **whose conception and birth** both occurred when her mother was **not in** a state of **sanctity.** The Gemara answers: **If so,** the phrase **"in Israel"** (Deuteronomy 22:21), **what purpose does it** serve?[N] This expression indicates that this *halakha* applies only to woman who was born Jewish.

אָמַר רַבִּי יוֹסֵי בַּר חֲנִינָא: הַמּוֹצִיא שֵׁם רַע עַל הַיְּתוֹמָה – פָּטוּר, שֶׁנֶּאֱמַר ״וְנָתְנוּ לַאֲבִי הַנַּעֲרָה״ – פְּרָט לָזוֹ שֶׁאֵין לָהּ אָב.

§ **Rabbi Yosei bar Ḥanina said: The defamer of an orphan**[H] girl **is exempt, as it is stated:** "And they shall fine him a hundred shekels of silver, **and give them to the father of the young woman**" (Deuteronomy 22:19), which **excludes this one who does not have a father.**

מְתִיב רַבִּי יוֹסֵי בַּר אָבִין, וְאִיתֵּימָא רַבִּי יוֹסֵי בַּר זְבִידָא: ״וְאִם מָאֵן יְמָאֵן אָבִיהָ״ – לְרַבּוֹת יְתוֹמָה לִקְנָס, דִּבְרֵי רַבִּי יוֹסֵי הַגְּלִילִי.

Rabbi Yosei bar Avin, and some say it was **Rabbi Yosei bar Zevida, raised an objection to this** from the following *baraita*: The verse states with regard to a seduced young woman: **"If her father utterly refuse** [*ma'en yima'en*] to give her to him, he shall pay money according to the dowry of virgins" (Exodus 22:16). The double phrase "utterly refuse [*ma'en yima'en*]" comes **to include an orphan for** the **fine,**[N] i.e., if she does not have a father and she herself refuses to marry her seducer, he must pay her the fine. This is **the statement of Rabbi Yosei HaGelili.** This proves that the fact that the girl does not have a father does not exempt her seducer from paying the fine.

HALAKHA

The defamer of an orphan – הַמּוֹצִיא שֵׁם רַע עַל יְתוֹמָה: If a husband defames his wife and she is an orphan, the one hundred *sela* fine belongs to her, in accordance with the opinion of Rava (Rambam *Sefer Nashim, Hilkhot Na'ara Betula* 3:1, and *Kesef Mishne* there).

NOTES

The phrase "in Israel," what purpose does it serve – בְּיִשְׂרָאֵל, מַאי אַהֲנֵי: The early authorities note that the phrase "in Israel" does not by itself prove that this *halakha* applies only to women born as Jews, as the expression "she has performed a wanton deed in Israel" (Deuteronomy 22:21) can be explained as referring to a convert as well, who has now joined the Jewish people. However, when this verse is combined with the phrase "because he defamed a virgin of Israel" (Deuteronomy 22:19) from the same chapter, in reference to the fine, it is clear that one of the terms is superfluous. It is therefore understood to be teaching that a convert is excluded both from the punishment and the fine.

To include an orphan for the fine – לְרַבּוֹת יְתוֹמָה לִקְנָס: The early authorities question why the seducer would have to pay a fine to the orphan when the *halakha* is that if the fine would be paid to the woman, the seducer is exempt from paying because the woman willingly consented to the act. Some commentaries explain that this verse is referring to a minor who was seduced, as she is considered a victim of a rape due to her age (Ramban in his *Milḥamot Hashem*). One version of the text of the Gemara indicates as much.

The commentaries also question the relevance of the proof from this verse to the discussion at hand. The verse addresses a case of seduction whereas Rabbi Yosei bar Ḥanina's ruling pertains to a case of defamation. Most commentaries accept Rashi's opinion that the *baraita* derives a principle from the verse about seduction. There is a general comparison between the *halakhot* pertaining to a case of seduction and those pertaining to rape. In the case of rape, the Torah says that the fine is paid to the victim's father (Deuteronomy 22:29). The *baraita*, by teaching that if one seduces an orphan he must pay her the fine, indicates that when the Torah says the fine must be paid to the father, that does not mean that no fine is paid in the case of an orphan. Rather, it means simply that if the woman has a father, he has the rights to the fine. The same is true when the Torah states that a defamer must pay a fine to the father of his victim (Deuteronomy 22:19).

HALAKHA

The defamer of a minor – הַמּוֹצִיא שֵׁם רַע עַל הַקְּטַנָּה: If a husband defames his wife and she is a minor, he is exempt from paying the fine and from receiving lashes, as stated by Reish Lakish (Rambam *Sefer Nashim, Hilkhot Na'ara Betula* 3:2).

Witnesses came to testify about her when she was in her father-in-law's house – בָּאוּ לָהּ עֵדִים בְּבֵית חָמִיהָ: If a betrothed young woman committed adultery while living in her father's house, she is stoned at the entrance to her father's house, even if the witnesses testified only after she was married, as taught by Sheila (Rambam *Sefer Kedusha, Hilkhot Issurei Bia* 3:9).

הוּא מוֹתִיב לַהּ וְהוּא מְפָרֵק לַהּ: בְּבָא עָלֶיהָ וְאַחַר כָּךְ נִתְיַתְּמָה.

The Gemara states that Rabbi Yosei bar Avin **raised the objection and he resolved it:** Rabbi Yosei HaGelili refers to **one who had intercourse with her and afterward was orphaned.** Since she had a father when the incident occurred, he is obligated to pay her the fine.

רָבָא אָמַר: חַיָּיב. מִמַּאי – מִדְּתָנֵי אַמֵּי: "בְּתוּלַת יִשְׂרָאֵל" וְלֹא בְּתוּלַת גֵּרִים.

Rava said, in contrast to Rabbi Yosei bar Ḥanina, that one who defames an orphan is **obligated** to pay the fine. **From where** does he learn this? He learns this **from** the fact that **Ami taught** that the fine applies to one who defamed **"a virgin of Israel"** (Deuteronomy 22:19) **and** does **not** apply to one who defamed **a virgin** who is **a convert.**

אִי אָמְרַתְּ בִּשְׁלָמָא כִּי הַאי גַּוְונָא בְּיִשְׂרָאֵל מִיחַיַּיב – הַיְינוּ דְּאִיצְטְרִיךְ קְרָא לְמַעוּטֵי גֵּרִים, אֶלָּא אִי אָמְרַתְּ בְּיִשְׂרָאֵל כְּהַאי גַּוְונָא פָּטוּר, הַשְׁתָּא בְּיִשְׂרָאֵל פָּטוּר – בְּגֵרִים מִיבַּעְיָא?!

Rava elaborates: **Granted, if you say** that **in a case like this,** where a woman has no father, **with regard to** a woman who was born as **a Jew, he is obligated** to pay, **that is** why **it was necessary** for **the verse to exclude converts.** Every convert is considered like an orphan, as the familial connection with her parents is severed upon her conversion, and therefore it is as though she did not have a father. **However, if you say that in a case like this involving** a woman born as **a Jew he is exempt, now** if in a case **involving** a woman born as **a Jew** he is **exempt, is** it **necessary** to derive from a verse **that converts** are not entitled to the fine? The fact that there is such a derivation in the case of converts indicates that in the case of a Jewish-born orphan, the defamer must pay a fine.

אָמַר רֵישׁ לָקִישׁ: הַמּוֹצִיא שֵׁם רַע עַל הַקְּטַנָּה – פָּטוּר, שֶׁנֶּאֱמַר "וְנָתְנוּ לַאֲבִי הַנַּעֲרָה", נַעֲרָה מָלֵא דִּבֵּר הַכָּתוּב.

§ **Reish Lakish said: The defamer** of **a minor**[H] girl **is exempt, as it is stated: "And give them to the father of the young woman** [*na'ara*]" (Deuteronomy 22:19). The word *na'ara* is written in full, with the letter *heh* at the end, whereas elsewhere in the Torah it is written without the *heh*. This indicates that **the verse was speaking** of a female who has **fully** attained the status of **a young woman,** rather than a minor who has not yet reached the state of being a young woman.

מַתְקִיף לַהּ רַב אַחָא בַּר אַבָּא: טַעְמָא דִּכְתִיב בַּהּ "הַנַּעֲרָה" הָא לָאו הָכִי – הֲוָה אָמֵינָא אֲפִילּוּ קְטַנָּה, הָא כְּתִיב "וְאִם אֱמֶת הָיָה הַדָּבָר הַזֶּה לֹא נִמְצְאוּ בְתוּלִים לַנַּעֲרָה וְהוֹצִיאוּ אֶת הַנַּעֲרָה אֶל פֶּתַח בֵּית אָבִיהָ וּסְקָלוּהָ" – וּקְטַנָּה לָאו בַּת עוֹנָשִׁין הִיא!

Rav Aḥa bar Abba strongly **objects to this:** Is it correct that **the reason is that it is written** with regard to **her "*na'ara*"** in full, **but if that were not so, I would say** that **even a minor** is included in this *halakha*? **Isn't it written: "But if this matter is true, that the tokens of virginity were not found in this young woman, then they shall bring out the young woman to the entrance to her father's house and** the men of her city shall **stone her"** (Deuteronomy 22:20–21)? **And** since **a minor is not eligible for punishment,** this verse evidently is referring to a young woman, not a minor, and therefore there is no need for the aforementioned exposition.

אֶלָּא, כָּאן – נַעֲרָה, הָא כׇּל מָקוֹם שֶׁנֶּאֱמַר "נַעַר" – אֲפִילּוּ קְטַנָּה בְּמַשְׁמָע.

Rather, the verse should be understood as follows: **Here,** where it is evident that the Torah is referring to a young woman, it writes *na'ara* with a *heh*, from which it may be inferred that **wherever it is stated *na'ara*** without a *heh* at the end, **it indicates** that the verse is referring **even to a minor** girl. The term *na'ara* without a *heh* is referring to both a minor and a young woman and excludes only an adult woman.

תָּנֵי שֵׁילָא: שָׁלֹשׁ מִדּוֹת בְּנַעֲרָה: בָּאוּ לָהּ עֵדִים בְּבֵית חָמִיהָ שֶׁזִּינְּתָה בְּבֵית אָבִיהָ,

Sheila taught in a *baraita*: There are **three** different **circumstances with regard to a young woman** who has been defamed. If **witnesses came** to testify about **her** when she was **in her father-in-law's house,**[HN] i.e., after she was married, and stated **that she committed adultery in her father's house,** when she was betrothed,

NOTES

Witnesses came to testify about her when she was in her father-in-law's house – בָּאוּ לָהּ עֵדִים בְּבֵית חָמִיהָ: This *halakha* applies to any young woman accused after her marriage of having committed adultery during her betrothal. It makes no difference whether the witnesses came as a result of the fact that her husband defamed her (Ritva).

סוֹקְלִין אוֹתָהּ עַל פֶּתַח בֵּית אָבִיהָ, כְּלוֹמַר: רְאוּ גִּידּוּלִים שֶׁגִּידַּלְתֶּם. בָּאוּ לָהּ עֵדִים בְּבֵית אָבִיהָ שֶׁזִּינְּתָה בְּבֵית אָבִיהָ – סוֹקְלִין אוֹתָהּ עַל פֶּתַח שַׁעַר הָעִיר. סָרְחָה וּלְבַסּוֹף בָּגְרָה – תִּידּוֹן בְּחֶנֶק.

one stones her at the entrance to her father's house, as though to say: See what you have brought up.[N] **If witnesses came** to testify about **her** when she was **in her father's house,**[HN] i.e., when she was betrothed, and testified **that she committed adultery in her father's house, one stones her at the entrance to the gate of the city.** If **she went astray** and sinned when she was a young woman **and subsequently reached majority,**[H] i.e., she became a grown woman, **she is sentenced to strangulation,** which is the punishment for a grown woman who committed adultery.

לְמֵימְרָא דְּכָל הֵיכָא דְּאִישְׁתַּנִּי גּוּפָא אִישְׁתַּנִּי קְטָלָא? וּרְמִינְהִי: נַעֲרָה הַמְאוֹרָסָה שֶׁזִּינְּתָה, וּמִשֶּׁבָּגְרָה הוֹצִיא עָלֶיהָ שֵׁם רַע – הוּא אֵינוֹ לוֹקֶה וְאֵינוֹ נוֹתֵן מֵאָה סֶלַע, הִיא וְזוֹמְמֶיהָ מַקְדִּימִין לְבֵית הַסְּקִילָה.

The Gemara asks with regard to this *halakha*: **Is that to say that** in any case **where her body has changed** after her sin, the manner in which she is put to **death changes** as well? The Gemara **raises a contradiction** from the following *baraita*: If there is **a betrothed young woman who** allegedly **committed adultery, and after she reached majority** she married and her husband **defamed her,** accusing her of having committed adultery during the period of betrothal, **he is not flogged and does not give** the **one hundred** ***sela*** if she is proven innocent, as these punishments are limited to one who defames a young woman (Deuteronomy 22:19). However, if she is guilty, **she and her conspiring witnesses**[N] **are brought early** in the morning **to the place of stoning.**[N] This proves that although her body changed between the time of the sin and the time of her punishment, she is stoned nevertheless.

הִיא וְזוֹמְמֶיהָ סָלְקָא דַעְתָּךְ?! אֶלָּא: אוֹ הִיא אוֹ זוֹמְמֶיהָ מַקְדִּימִין לְבֵית הַסְּקִילָה!

The Gemara digresses to analyze the last clause of this *baraita*: Can it **enter your mind** to say that both **she and her conspiring witnesses,** i.e., witnesses who falsely testified that she committed adultery, are executed? If the witnesses who testified against her were telling the truth and she sinned, only she is liable to be stoned, and if the court discovers that they were false, conspiring witnesses, then they are stoned and she is exempt. **Rather,** the text of the *baraita* should be emended so that it reads: **Either she or her conspiring witnesses are brought early** in the morning **to the place of stoning.**

HALAKHA

Witnesses came to testify about her when she was in her father's house – בָּאוּ לָהּ עֵדִים בְּבֵית אָבִיהָ: The Rambam had a version of the Gemara text that was different than the text printed in the Vilna Talmud. According to his version, Sheila states that if a young woman who was betrothed committed adultery in her father-in-law's house before she entered the wedding canopy, even if witnesses testified about this after she returned to her father's house, she is stoned at the entrance to the city gates (Rambam *Sefer Kedusha, Hilkhot Issurei Bia* 3:9).

If she went astray and subsequently reached majority – סָרְחָה וּלְבַסּוֹף בָּגְרָה: If a betrothed young woman committed adultery in her father's house, even if the witnesses testified after she reached majority or after her husband had intercourse with her, she is liable to be stoned and is executed in the regular place of stoning. This ruling is in accordance with the opinion of Rabbi Yoḥanan (45b), and it is not in accordance with the opinion of Sheila (Rambam *Sefer Kedusha, Hilkhot Issurei Bia* 3:10).

NOTES

See what you have brought up – רְאוּ גִּידּוּלִים שֶׁגִּידַּלְתֶּם: The stoning of a daughter who committed adultery at the entrance to her father's house serves to demonstrate that she did not sin in her father-in-law's house, and he and his family are not responsible for her behavior. Consequently, if the witnesses arrived when she is still in her father's house, it is already evident to all that she sinned there, even if she is not stoned there. Therefore, she is stoned in the most prominent public arena, at the city gates (Ritva, based on Rashi). However, the Rambam rules that even if witnesses came when she was in her father's house, she is stoned at the entrance to his house. Apparently, he maintains that the *tanna* states the clause: Witnesses came when she was in her father-in-law's house, only because it is more likely for matters of this kind to come to light after she has moved out of her father's house (Meiri).

Witnesses came to testify about her when she was in her father's house, etc. – בָּאוּ לָהּ עֵדִים בְּבֵית אָבִיהָ וכו׳: It is clear that some early commentaries had versions of the Gemara text that were different than the version that Rashi had and that is printed in the Vilna Talmud. The Ritva reports that the Ra'avad's text stated: If witnesses came when she was in her father's house to testify that she committed adultery in her father-in-law's house. He explains that this means that she was visiting her father-in-law's house, not that she was married and returned to her father's house. The Ritva adds that the Gemara text of the Rambam read: If witnesses testified when she was in her father-in-law's house that she committed adultery in her father-in-law's house, which means they attested that she sinned after the wedding canopy but before she had intercourse with her husband.

She and her conspiring witnesses – הִיא וְזוֹמְמֶיהָ: The answer of the Gemara is simply that in this context the letter *vav* means: Or, rather than: And.

Brought early in the morning to the place of stoning – מַקְדִּימִין לְבֵית הַסְּקִילָה: Rashi explains that this phrase serves to emphasize that they have no way of escaping this punishment. Others state that the statement that they are brought early means that stoning is the appropriate punishment, notwithstanding the *halakha* that one who cannot be executed in the prescribed manner must be killed by other means (Ritva, citing *Tosafot* on *Makkot* 19b).

אמר רבא: מוציא שם רע קאמרת – שאני מוציא שם רע דחידוש הוא. דהא נכנסה לחופה ולא נבעלה בעלמא, וזינתה – בחנק, ואילו מוציא שם רע – בסקילה.

In answer to the contradiction, **Rava said: A defamer, you said? A defamer is different**[HN] **as it is a novel** *halakha*. Certain aspects of this case do not apply to other *halakhot* **as, generally,** if a woman who **entered the** wedding canopy **and did not** yet **have intercourse** with her husband subsequently **committed adultery,** she is executed **by strangulation,** which is the punishment for a married woman who committed adultery. **However,** in the case of **a defamer,** if the woman is guilty she is executed **by stoning,** despite the fact that if she would commit the sin in her current state, as a married woman, she would be executed via strangulation. This proves that in the case of defamation, the method of execution is determined by the time when the sin was committed, although her status has since changed.

אמר ליה רב הונא בריה דרב יהושע לרבא: דלמא כי חדית רחמנא – היכא דלא אישתני גופא, אבל היכא דאישתני גופא – לא חדית רחמנא!

Rav Huna, son of Rav Yehoshua, said to Rava: Perhaps when the Merciful One introduced the novelty of the *halakha* of a defamer, it was applied only to a case **where her body has not changed** and she is still a young woman. **However,** in a case **where her body has changed** and she has become a grown woman, **the Merciful One did not introduce the novelty** of this *halakha*, and she is liable to strangulation just as she would be liable to strangulation if she had committed the sin as a grown woman.

אלא אמר רב נחמן בר יצחק: אישתני ולא אישתני תנאי היא, דתנן: חטאו עד שלא נתמנו, ונתמנו – הרי הן כהדיוטות.

Rather, Rav Naḥman bar Yitzḥak said: This question of whether the method of her execution **changes or does not change** if her body has changed **is a dispute between** *tanna'im*, **as we learned** in a mishna (*Horayot* 10a), with regard to the special offering of a High Priest or a king who sinned unwittingly (see Leviticus 4:3–12, 22–26): If **they sinned before they were appointed,**[HN] **and they were** subsequently **appointed,** and they became aware of their transgression only after their appointment, **they are like commoners.** They must bring a female sheep or goat, like any ordinary individual who sinned, rather than the bull brought by a High Priest who has sinned or the male goat brought by a king who has sinned.

רבי שמעון אומר: אם נודע להם עד שלא נתמנו – חייבים, משנתמנו – פטורים.

Rabbi Shimon says: If their sin **became known to them before they were appointed,** even if they did not bring their offering before they were appointed, **they are liable** to bring the offering of a commoner. However, if their sin became known to them **after they were appointed, they are** entirely **exempt**[N] from bringing an offering as their change in status necessitates a corresponding change in their offering, and therefore their first obligation is entirely nullified. This shows that according to Rabbi Shimon, a change in status retroactively affects one's liability for a transgression he committed in his previous status. A similar *halakha* should apply in the case of a betrothed young woman who committed adultery and reached majority before her sin became known.

HALAKHA

A defamer is different, etc. – שאני מוציא שם רע וכו׳: If a husband defames his wife by accusing her of having committed adultery before he had engaged in intercourse with her, and witnesses substantiate his claim, the woman is executed via stoning at the entrance to her father's house. This is true if she committed adultery as a young woman who was betrothed. According to the Rambam and the Rashbam, this is true even if she committed adultery after marriage, as long as she had not yet had intercourse with her husband. However, Rabbeinu Ḥananel, the Ra'avad, and many other early authorities rule that if she committed adultery after marriage, she is liable to strangulation (Rambam *Sefer Kedusha*, *Hilkhot Issurei Bia* 3:8, and Ra'avad there).

If they sinned before they were appointed, etc. – חטאו עד שלא נתמנו וכו׳: If an individual committed a transgression for which one is liable to bring a sin-offering and realized that he had done so only after he was appointed to be the High Priest or the king, he nevertheless brings the offering of a commoner (Rambam *Sefer Korbanot*, *Hilkhot Shegagot* 15:10).

NOTES

A defamer is different, etc. – שאני מוציא שם רע וכו׳: Rashi's interpretation of the Gemara's discussion, which is accepted by most early authorities, is as follows: Sheila taught that if a young woman who is betrothed commits adultery and then matures before witnesses testify about her sin, she is executed via strangulation, which is the punishment for a mature woman who has committed adultery. She is not executed via stoning, which is the punishment for a young woman who committed adultery. This is due to the principle that if the individual has changed since the time of the sin, he is punished according to his current status and not according to his status at the time of the sin.

The Gemara raises a question from a *baraita* that indicates that in the case of defamation, even if the woman matures before witnesses testify that she committed adultery, she is stoned. Rava answers that according to Sheila, the entire case of defamation is an exception to the rule, as the woman is stoned when witnesses testify about her crime after she is married, despite the fact that a married woman who commits adultery is executed via strangulation. Consequently, it is not surprising that in the case of defamation, the woman is stoned even if she reached majority between the time of the sin and the time when the witnesses testified about the sin. Rav Huna, son of Rav Yehoshua, questions this logic. He points out that the fact that the method of execution does not change due to the fact that she has married does not mean that it would not change if she had reached majority and thereby underwent a physical change.

The Rashbam, cited in *Tosafot*, suggests an entirely different interpretation of Rava's argument. In his opinion, the novelty of the case of a defamer is that even if the woman committed adultery after marriage, as long as she had not yet had intercourse with her husband, she is liable to be stoned. Conversely, if she committed adultery in a similar circumstance but her husband did not defame her, she is liable to strangulation. The Rambam agrees with this interpretation. Other early authorities disagree. Although this interpretation fits in well with the wording of Rava's statement, it is not reasonable to assume that the woman is liable to be executed more severely, i.e., by stoning, simply because her husband defamed her (see *Tosafot*).

They sinned before they were appointed – חטאו עד שלא נתמנו: Although this case involves a change of status rather than a physical change, it is possible that Rav Naḥman bar Yitzḥak holds in accordance with Rava that there is no difference between a change of status and a physical change. Alternatively, although one cannot prove from the opinion of the Rabbis whether they would agree with the ruling of Sheila, it is clear that Rabbi Shimon would agree with Sheila's ruling. If the offering changes because of a change in status, certainly one's punishment should change due to a physical change in the perpetrator (Ritva).

If their sin became known to them after they were appointed, they are entirely exempt – משנתמנו פטורים: Rabbi Shimon maintains that they cannot bring the offering of a commoner because they are now obligated to bring a different offering. However, they cannot bring an offering according to their current status because they were commoners when they sinned.

אֵימוּר דְּשָׁמְעִינַן לֵיהּ לְרַבִּי שִׁמְעוֹן דְּאָזֵיל אַף בָּתַר יְדִיעָה, דְּאָזֵיל בָּתַר יְדִיעָה וְלָא אָזֵיל בָּתַר חֲטָאָה – מִי שָׁמְעַתְּ לֵיהּ? אִם כֵּן לֵייתֵי קׇרְבָּן כִּי דְּהַשְׁתָּא, מָשׁוּחַ – פָּר, וְנָשִׂיא – שָׂעִיר!

The Gemara questions this comparison: **Say that we heard that Rabbi Shimon follows even** the **awareness,** i.e., Rabbi Shimon takes into consideration the time when the sin became known to the High Priest or king, and maintains that he cannot bring the offering of a commoner. However, **did you hear him** say **that he follows** the time of the **awareness and does not follow** the time of the **sin? If so, let him bring** the **offering that** befits his **current** status: One **anointed** to be the High Priest brings **a bullock, and a prince,** i.e., a king, offers **a goat.** Consequently, there is no proof that, according to Rabbi Shimon, if the sin of a betrothed young woman became known after she reached majority, she is sentenced to strangulation like a grown woman.

הָאָמַר לֵיהּ רַבִּי יוֹחָנָן לְתַנָּא: תְּנֵי "תִּידּוֹן בִּסְקִילָה". וְאַמַּאי? נַעֲרָה הַמְאוֹרָסָה אָמַר רַחֲמָנָא, וְהָא בּוֹגֶרֶת הִיא! אָמַר רַבִּי אֶילְעָא: אָמַר קְרָא "הַנַּעֲרָה" הַנַּעֲרָה שֶׁהָיְתָה כְּבָר.

The Gemara responds: Nevertheless, this issue is subject to a dispute. **Didn't Rabbi Yoḥanan say to** the *tanna*, i.e., the Sage who would recite statements of *tanna'im* before him and who recited Sheila's ruling with regard to a betrothed young woman: **Teach that she is sentenced to stoning**[N] rather than strangulation? The Gemara questions Rabbi Yoḥanan's statement: **But why? The Merciful One says: A betrothed young woman, but this one is a grown woman. Rabbi Ile'a said: The verse states: The young woman, in reference to the young woman that she already was** at the time of her sin, despite the fact that she now has a different status.

אָמַר לֵיהּ רַבִּי חֲנִינָא לְרַבִּי אֶילְעָא: אִי הָכִי – מִילְקָא נַמִּי לִילְקֵי, וּמֵאָה סֶלַע נַמִּי לִישַׁלֵּם! אָמַר לֵיהּ: רַחֲמָנָא נִיצְּלַן מֵהַאי דַּעְתָּא. אַדְּרַבָּה, רַחֲמָנָא נִיצְּלַן מִדַּעְתָּא דִּידָךְ.

Rabbi Ḥanina said to Rabbi Ile'a: If so, if her status is determined according to the time of her transgression, **let** the husband who defames her **also be flogged,**[N] **and let him also pay** the **one hundred** *sela* if his claim turns out to have been unfounded. Rabbi Ile'a **said to him: May the Merciful One save us from** following **this opinion,** as your argument is illogical. Rabbi Ḥanina replied: **On the contrary, may the Merciful One save us from your opinion,** as yours is the baseless opinion.

וְטַעְמָא מַאי? אָמַר רַבִּי יִצְחָק בַּר אָבִין, וְאִיתֵּימָא רַבִּי יִצְחָק בַּר אַבָּא: זוֹ – מַעֲשֶׂיהָ גָּרְמוּ לָהּ, וְזֶה – עֲקִימַת שְׂפָתָיו גָּרְמוּ לוֹ. זוֹ מַעֲשֶׂיהָ גָּרְמוּ לָהּ, כְּשֶׁהִיא זַנַּאי – נַעֲרָה זַנַּאי. וְזֶה עֲקִימַת שְׂפָתָיו גָּרְמוּ לוֹ, אֵימַת קָא מִיחַיַּיב – הַהִיא שַׁעְתָּא, וְהַהִיא שַׁעְתָּא – בּוֹגֶרֶת הֲוַאי.

The Gemara asks: **And what is the reason** that she is considered a young woman with regard to stoning but a grown woman when it comes to the fine? **Rabbi Yitzḥak bar Avin said, and some say** this answer was given by **Rabbi Yitzḥak bar Abba:** With regard to **this one,** i.e., the woman, who sinned, **her act** of adultery **caused her** punishment, **whereas that one,** i.e., the husband who wrongfully defamed his wife, **the twisting of his lips caused his** punishment, i.e., he sinned by speaking. He elaborates: **This one, her action caused her** punishment. **When she committed adultery,** she was **a young woman** who **committed adultery,** and she is sentenced accordingly. **And that one, the twisting of his lips caused his** punishment. **When** does he **become liable?** At **that time** when he defamed her, **and** at **that time** his wife **was a grown woman.**

תָּנוּ רַבָּנַן: נַעֲרָה הַמְאוֹרָסָה שֶׁזִּינְּתָה – סוֹקְלִין אוֹתָהּ עַל פֶּתַח בֵּית אָבִיהָ. אֵין לָהּ פֶּתַח בֵּית הָאָב – סוֹקְלִין אוֹתָהּ עַל פֶּתַח שַׁעַר הָעִיר הַהִיא. וּבְעִיר שֶׁרוּבָּהּ גּוֹיִם – סוֹקְלִין אוֹתָהּ עַל פֶּתַח בֵּית דִּין. כַּיּוֹצֵא בַּדָּבָר אַתָּה אוֹמֵר: הָעוֹבֵד עֲבוֹדָה זָרָה – סוֹקְלִין אוֹתוֹ עַל שַׁעַר שֶׁעָבַד בּוֹ. וּבְעִיר שֶׁרוּבָּהּ גּוֹיִם – סוֹקְלִין אוֹתוֹ עַל פֶּתַח בֵּית דִּין.

§ **The Sages taught** in a *baraita*: In the case of **a betrothed young woman who committed adultery, one stones her at the entrance to her father's house. If she does not have an entrance** to her **father's house, one stones her at the entrance** to the **gate of that city. And in a city that is mostly** populated by **gentiles,**[H] where she cannot be stoned at the city entrance, **one stones her at the entrance** to **the court. In a similar manner, you say:** With regard to **one who engaged in idol worship,**[H] **one stones him at the entrance** to **the gate where he worshipped,**[N] **and in a city that is mostly** inhabited by **gentiles one stones him at the entrance** to **the court.**

HALAKHA

A city that is mostly populated by gentiles – עִיר שֶׁרוּבָּהּ גּוֹיִם: If an individual is supposed to be stoned at the entrance to his city but that city is populated mostly by gentiles, he is stoned at the entrance to the court (Rambam *Sefer Kedusha, Hilkhot Issurei Bia* 3:11).

One who engaged in idol worship – הָעוֹבֵד עֲבוֹדָה זָרָה: One who engaged in idol worship is stoned at the entrance to the city where he committed the sin. If that city is inhabited mostly by gentiles, he is stoned at the entrance to the court (Rambam *Sefer Shofetim, Hilkhot Sanhedrin* 15:2).

NOTES

Teach that she is sentenced to stoning – תְּנֵי תִּידּוֹן בִּסְקִילָה: Some commentaries suggest that it is possible that everyone agrees with this *halakha*, even Rabbi Shimon (Ri HaLavan). Although it can be argued that with regard to an offering, the critical time is when the individual became aware of his sin, with regard to punishments all agree that the critical time is when the sin was committed.

If so, let the husband who defames her also be flogged, etc. – אִי הָכִי מִילְקָא וכו׳: It would seem that this question should not be directed specifically at Rabbi Yoḥanan, as the same question can be raised with regard to the opinion of Sheila. The Ritva explains that according to Sheila, who holds that the case of a defamer is an exception to the general rule, it is possible that the exceptional nature of the case includes the fact that the method through which the woman is executed does not change with her change of status, whereas the husband's punishments do change. By contrast, Rabbi Yoḥanan considers the *halakha* of the defamer to follow the general rules, and therefore it is difficult to understand why some aspects of the case change along with the woman's change of status and others do not.

The gate where he worshipped – שַׁעַר שֶׁעָבַד בּוֹ: The early authorities explain that this does not refer to the actual gate where he worshipped idols; rather, it means the entrance of the city where he committed the transgression. In other words, even if he was sentenced in a different city, the court brings him back to the place where he engaged in idol worship and stones him there (Rabbeinu Aharon HaLevi; Rabbi Crescas Vidal; Meiri).

מְנָא הָנֵי מִילֵּי? דְּתָנוּ רַבָּנַן: "שְׁעָרֶיךָ" – זֶה שַׁעַר שֶׁעָבַד בּוֹ. אַתָּה אוֹמֵר שַׁעַר שֶׁעָבַד בּוֹ, אוֹ אֵינוֹ אֶלָּא שַׁעַר שֶׁנִּידּוֹן בּוֹ?

The Gemara asks: **From where are these matters** derived, that one stones an idol worshipper in the place where he worshipped? **As the Sages taught:** It states with regard to one who worshipped an idol: "Then you shall bring forth that man or that women who have done this evil thing, to your gates … and you shall stone them with stones that they die" (Deuteronomy 17:5). **"Your gates," this is the gate where he worshipped** idolatry. The offender is taken there to be stoned. Do **you say** it is **the gate where he worshipped, or** perhaps **it is only the gate where he was sentenced,** i.e., the gate of the court?

נֶאֱמַר "שְׁעָרֶיךָ" לְמַטָּה, וְנֶאֱמַר "שְׁעָרֶיךָ" לְמַעְלָה, מַה "שְׁעָרֶיךָ" הָאָמוּר לְמַעְלָה – שַׁעַר שֶׁעָבַד בּוֹ, אַף "שְׁעָרֶיךָ" הָאָמוּר לְמַטָּה – שַׁעַר שֶׁעָבַד בּוֹ.

The Gemara answers: **It is stated "your gates" below,** in that verse, **and is stated "your gates" above,** in this verse: "If there is found in the midst of you, within any of your gates … a man or woman who does that which is evil in the sight of the Lord your God, in transgressing His covenant" (Deuteronomy 17:2). **Just as "your gates" stated above** is referring to the **gate where he worshipped, so too** the phrase **"your gates" stated below,** with regard to execution, means the **gate where he worshipped** idols.

דָּבָר אַחֵר: "שְׁעָרֶיךָ" וְלֹא שַׁעֲרֵי גוֹיִם. הַאי "שְׁעָרֶיךָ" הָא אַפִּיקְתֵּיהּ! אִם כֵּן לֵימָא קְרָא "שַׁעַר", מַאי "שְׁעָרֶיךָ"? שְׁמַע מִינָּהּ תַּרְתֵּי.

Alternatively, the idol worshipper is executed at **"your gates," and not** at **the gates of gentiles.** The Gemara asks: **This** term, **"your gates," you have** already **used it** to indicate that he is stoned at the gate of the city where he worshipped idols. How, then, can you derive another *halakha* from this expression? The Gemara answers: **If so,** if it teaches only one *halakha*, **let the verse say** only the word **gate.** For **what** reason does it state **"your gates"?** This indicates that the verse is referring to the gates of cities inhabited by Jews, and therefore one can **conclude two** conclusions **from it.**

אַשְׁכַּחַן עֲבוֹדָה זָרָה, נַעֲרָה הַמְאוֹרָסָה מְנָא לַן?

The Gemara asks: **We found** a source that indicates that in a case of **idolatrous worship,** the perpetrator is stoned at the gate of the city where he committed his sin. **From where do we** derive that **a betrothed young woman** who is not stoned at the entrance to her father's house is stoned at the gate of the city?

אָמַר רַבִּי אַבָּהוּ: גָּמַר "פֶּתַח" מִ"פֶּתַח", וּ"פֶתַח" מִ"שַּׁעַר", וְ"שַׁעַר" מִ"שְּׁעָרֶיךָ".

Rabbi Abbahu said: One **derives** this by verbal analogy, as follows: The meaning of the term **"entrance"** (Deuteronomy 22:21), stated with regard to a betrothed woman who committed adultery, is derived **from** the term **"entrance"** that appears with regard to the Tabernacle, in the verse "The entrance of the gate of the courtyard" (Numbers 4:26); **and** the meaning of this usage of the term **entrance** is derived **from** the term **"gate,"** which appears in the same phrase; **and** the meaning of this usage of the term **"gate"** is derived **from** the term **"your gates"** stated with regard to idolatry. This teaches that a young woman who was betrothed and committed adultery is executed at the gate of the city, similar to one who engaged in idol worship.

תָּנוּ רַבָּנַן: הַמּוֹצִיא שֵׁם רַע – לוֹקֶה וְנוֹתֵן מֵאָה סֶלַע. רַבִּי יְהוּדָה אוֹמֵר: לִלְקוֹת – לוֹקֶה מִכׇּל מָקוֹם. מֵאָה סֶלַע, בָּעַל – נוֹתֵן, לֹא בָּעַל – אֵינוֹ נוֹתֵן.

§ **The Sages taught** in a *baraita*: **One who defames** his wife **is flogged and gives one hundred *sela*. Rabbi Yehuda says:** As for **flogging, he is flogged in any case.** However, with regard to the **one hundred *sela*,** if he defamed her after **he had intercourse** with her, **he gives** the money. If he did **not** yet **have intercourse** with her, **he does not give** her this sum.

קָא מִיפַּלְגִי בִּפְלוּגְתָּא דְּרַבִּי אֱלִיעֶזֶר בֶּן יַעֲקֹב וְרַבָּנַן. וְהָכִי קָאָמַר: הַמּוֹצִיא שֵׁם רַע – לוֹקֶה וְנוֹתֵן מֵאָה סֶלַע, בֵּין בָּעַל בֵּין שֶׁלֹּא בָּעַל, כְּרַבָּנַן. רַבִּי יְהוּדָה אוֹמֵר: לִלְקוֹת – לוֹקֶה מִכׇּל מָקוֹם. מֵאָה סֶלַע, בָּעַל – נוֹתֵן, לֹא בָּעַל – אֵינוֹ נוֹתֵן, כְּרַבִּי אֱלִיעֶזֶר בֶּן יַעֲקֹב.

The Gemara comments: These *tanna'im* **disagree with regard to the dispute between Rabbi Eliezer ben Ya'akov and the Rabbis, and this is what** the first *tanna* **is saying: The defamer is flogged and gives one hundred *sela*, whether he had intercourse** with his wife or **whether he did not have intercourse** with her, **in accordance with** the opinion of **the Rabbis. Rabbi Yehuda says:** As for **flogging, he is flogged in any case,** but with regard to the **one hundred *sela*, if he had intercourse he gives** the money, whereas if **he** did **not have intercourse he does not give** it to her. This is **in accordance with** the opinion of **Rabbi Eliezer ben Ya'akov,** that the *halakha* of a defamer applies only to a husband who had relations with his wife.

אִיכָּא דְּאָמְרִי: כּוּלָּהּ כְּרַבִּי אֱלִיעֶזֶר בֶּן יַעֲקֹב, וְהָכִי קָאָמַר: הַמּוֹצִיא שֵׁם רַע – לוֹקֶה וְנוֹתֵן מֵאָה סֶלַע, וְהוּא שֶׁבָּעַל. רַבִּי יְהוּדָה אוֹמֵר: לִלְקוֹת לוֹקֶה מִכׇּל מָקוֹם.

There are those who say that this entire *baraita* is **in accordance with** the opinion of **Rabbi Eliezer ben Ya'akov, and this is what** the *baraita* **is saying: The defamer is flogged and gives one hundred *sela*, but this** applies only if **he** previously **had intercourse** with his wife. **Rabbi Yehuda says:** As **for flogging, he is flogged in any case,** as only the fine is dependent on the couple having previously had intercourse.

וְסָבַר רַבִּי יְהוּדָה לִלְקוֹת לוֹקֶה מִכׇּל מָקוֹם? וְהָתַנְיָא, רַבִּי יְהוּדָה אוֹמֵר: בָּעַל – לוֹקֶה, לֹא בָּעַל – אֵינוֹ לוֹקֶה! אָמַר רַב נַחְמָן בַּר יִצְחָק: לוֹקֶה מַכַּת מַרְדּוּת, מִדְּרַבָּנַן.

The Gemara asks: **And does Rabbi Yehuda hold** that with regard **to flogging, he is flogged in any case? But isn't it taught** in a *baraita* that **Rabbi Yehuda says:** If **he had intercourse** with his wife before he defamed her, **he is flogged;**[H] but if **he did not have intercourse** with his wife before he defamed her, **he is not flogged?** In answer to this question, **Rav Naḥman bar Yitzḥak said:** When Rabbi Yehuda said that he **is flogged** even if he had not yet had intercourse with his wife, he was referring to **lashes for rebelliousness** [***mardut***],[N] which apply **by rabbinic** law. Since he lied, defamed his wife, and endangered her life by accusing her of a sin that carries the death penalty, the court punishes him, but this punishment does not apply by Torah law.

HALAKHA

If he had intercourse with his wife before he defamed her, he is flogged, etc. – בָּעַל לוֹקֶה וכו׳: A defamer is obligated to pay the fine only if he had typical intercourse with his wife and claimed that he found that she had already engaged in intercourse of this kind. If he did not have typical intercourse with her, even if he had anal intercourse with her, he is exempt. However, he receives lashes for rebelliousness by rabbinic law. The *halakha* is in accordance with the opinion of Rabbi Eliezer ben Ya'akov as explained by Rav Naḥman bar Yitzḥak (Rambam *Sefer Nashim, Hilkhot Na'ara Betula* 3:10; *Tur, Even HaEzer* 177).

NOTES

Lashes for rebelliousness [*mardut*] – מַכַּת מַרְדּוּת: Some explain that *mardut* means rebuke, chastisement (Rav Hai Gaon). Accordingly, Onkelos translates the word chastise in the phrase "to chastise [*leyasra*] you" (Leviticus 26:18) as *lemirdei*, which is a form of the word *mardut*. As for the precise nature of this flogging, some hold that the number of lashes one receives does not have to be divisible by three, one does not have to be beaten with a double strap, and there is no need for a doctor's evaluation as to how many lashes one can withstand, all of which are requirements for flogging by Torah law (*ge'onim*). Others differentiate between various types of lashes for rebelliousness. If the lashes are administered for a one-time sin, the court is more lenient than when it inflicts lashes by Torah law. By contrast, if the beating is inflicted to force someone to fulfill a positive mitzva or to refrain from a persistent transgression, the number of lashes is unlimited (Ritva; Ran).

Perek **IV**
Daf **46** Amud **a**

רַב פַּפָּא אָמַר: מַאי בָּעַל לוֹקֶה דְּקָתָנֵי הָתָם? מָמוֹן. וְקָרֵי לֵיהּ לְמָמוֹן מַלְקוֹת? אִין, וְהָא תְּנַן: הָאוֹמֵר חֲצִי עֶרְכִּי עָלַי – נוֹתֵן חֲצִי עֶרְכּוֹ, רַבִּי יוֹסֵי בְּרַבִּי יְהוּדָה אוֹמֵר: לוֹקֶה וְנוֹתֵן עֵרֶךְ שָׁלֵם. לוֹקֶה אַמַּאי? אָמַר רַב פַּפָּא: לוֹקֶה בְּעֵרֶךְ שָׁלֵם.

Rav Pappa said: What of the statement **that is taught there,** in the *baraita*, that it is only if **he had intercourse** with her that he is **flogged?** It is referring to the **money** of the fine. The Gemara asks: **And** does one **call monetary** payment **flogging?** The Gemara answers: **Yes, and we learned** in a *baraita*: **One who says: Half my valuation**[N] **is upon me,**[H] **he gives half his valuation,** in accordance with the sum fixed by the Torah according to sex and age (see Leviticus 27:2–3). **Rabbi Yosei, son of Rabbi Yehuda, says: He is flogged and gives** his **full valuation.** The Sages inquired: **Why is he flogged?** What transgression did he commit? **Rav Pappa said: He is flogged by** having to pay **a full valuation.** This proves that monetary payment can be referred to as flogging.

מַאי טַעְמָא – גְּזֵירָה חֲצִי עֶרְכּוֹ אַטּוּ עֵרֶךְ חֶצְיוֹ, וְעֵרֶךְ חֶצְיוֹ – הָוֵי לֵיהּ אֵבֶר שֶׁהַנְּשָׁמָה תְּלוּיָה בּוֹ.

The Gemara clarifies: **What is the reason** of Rabbi Yosei, son of Rabbi Yehuda? It is a rabbinic **decree** in the case of one who vows to donate **half of his valuation, due to** a case where one vowed the **valuation of half of himself.**[H] **And** one who vows to donate the **valuation of half of himself has** effectively vowed to donate the valuation of **a limb upon which** his **life depends,** e.g., his head or heart, in which case it is as though he vowed to donate his entire valuation. Consequently, even one who vows to donate half of his valuation must donate his entire valuation.

תָּנוּ רַבָּנַן: ״וְעָנְשׁוּ אוֹתוֹ״ – זֶה מָמוֹן; ״וְיִסְּרוּ״ – זֶה מַלְקוֹת.

§ The Gemara continues to discuss the *halakhot* of the defamer. **The Sages taught** the following *baraita*, based upon the following verses: "And the Elders of that city shall take the man and chastise him. And they shall fine him a hundred shekels of silver, and give them to the father of the young woman" (Deuteronomy 22:18–19). **"And they shall fine** [***ve'anshu***] **him"; this** is referring to **money. "And chastise** him"; **this** is referring to **flogging.**

בִּשְׁלָמָא ״וְעָנְשׁוּ״ זֶה מָמוֹן – דִּכְתִיב ״וְעָנְשׁוּ אוֹתוֹ מֵאָה כֶסֶף וְנָתְנוּ לַאֲבִי הַנַּעֲרָה״ אֶלָּא ״וְיִסְּרוּ״ זֶה מַלְקוֹת מְנָלַן?

The Gemara asks: **Granted,** with regard to the phrase **"and they fine** [***ve'anshu***] **him,"** although the word *ve'anshu* can refer to any punishment, in **this** case it is referring to **money, as it is written: And they shall fine him a hundred shekels of silver, and give them to the father of the young woman. However,** with regard to the statement of the *baraita* that: **"And chastise** him"; **this** is referring to **flogging, from where do we** derive this?

NOTES

Valuations – עֲרָכִין: The *halakhot* of valuations appear in Leviticus (27:1–8) and are clarified in tractate *Arakhin*. A valuation is a vow to donate the value of a particular individual to the Temple treasury. The sum to be paid is not determined by the individual's social stature or by his value as a slave. The Torah provides fixed sums based upon age and sex. If one vows to donate the valuation of a particular limb, his vow is of no consequence, as only a whole person has a valuation. By contrast, one can vow to donate the actual monetary value of a limb to the Temple treasury. Notwithstanding the above distinction, if someone vows to donate the valuation of a critical organ or limb, e.g., if he says: I am obligated in the valuation of my head, it is as though he vowed to donate his full valuation because one cannot live without a head.

HALAKHA

One who says: Half my valuation is upon me – הָאוֹמֵר חֲצִי עֶרְכִּי עָלַי: If one says: Half my valuation is upon me, he must give half the amount of his fixed valuation according to his age and sex, as stated by the unattributed opinion in the mishna (Rambam *Sefer Hafla'a, Hilkhot Arakhin* 2:2).

One vowed the valuation of half of himself – עֵרֶךְ חֶצְיוֹ: If one says: The valuation of half of me is upon me, he must give his entire valuation, as he cannot survive the loss of half of his body (Rambam *Sefer Hafla'a, Hilkhot Arakhin* 2:2).

HALAKHA

The warning for a defamer – אַזְהָרָה לְמוֹצִיא שֵׁם רַע: One who falsely defames a Jewish woman is liable to receive lashes. His warning is in the verse "You shall not go up and down as a talebearer" (Leviticus 19:16; see Rambam *Sefer Nashim, Hilkhot Na'ara Betula* 3:1).

A person should not think impure thoughts – אַל יְהַרְהֵר אָדָם: It is prohibited to think licentious thoughts. One must be wary of any action or sight that will lead him to reflections of this kind (Rambam *Sefer Kedusha, Hilkhot Issurei Bia* 21:5, 21; *Shulḥan Arukh, Even HaEzer* 23:3).

That the court should not be soft to this litigant, etc. – שֶׁלֹּא יְהֵא רַךְ לָזֶה וכו׳: A judge must treat both litigants equally. He must not be pleasant to one party and speak softly to them while displaying a severe countenance and speaking harshly to the other litigant (see Radbaz; Rambam *Sefer Shofetim, Hilkhot Sanhedrin* 21:1; *Shulḥan Arukh, Ḥoshen Mishpat* 17:1).

They testify for him of their own accord – הֵן מְעִידִים אוֹתוֹ מֵאֲלֵיהֶן: If the husband did not bring witnesses to testify that his wife had committed adultery, but they came of their own volition, he is exempt from punishment. This is the case even if they are discovered to have lied (Rambam *Sefer Nashim, Hilkhot Na'ara Betula* 3:11; *Tur, Even HaEzer* 177).

אָמַר רַבִּי אַבָּהוּ: לָמַדְנוּ ״יִסְּרוּ״ מִ״יִּסְּרוּ״ וְ״יִסְּרוּ״ מִ״בֵּן״ וּ״בֵן״ מִ״בִּן״ – ״וְהָיָה אִם בִּן הַכּוֹת הָרָשָׁע״.

Rabbi Abbahu said: We learned the meaning of the word **chastise** in the case of a defamer by verbal analogy **from** the word **chastise** stated in the verse "if a man have a stubborn and rebellious son [*ben*], that will not listen to the voice of his father or the voice of his mother, and though they chastise him, will not listen to them" (Deuteronomy 21:18). **And** the implication of the word **chastise** in that verse is derived **from** the word **son** that appears in the same verse. **And** the implication of the word **son** [*ben*] with regard to a rebellious son is derived **from** the word ***bin*** in the verse **"Then it shall be if the wicked man deserve [*bin*] to be flogged"** (Deuteronomy 25:2).

אַזְהָרָה לְמוֹצִיא שֵׁם רַע מְנָלַן? רַבִּי אֶלְעָזָר אָמַר: מִ״לֹּא תֵלֵךְ רָכִיל״, רַבִּי נָתָן אוֹמֵר: מִ״וְנִשְׁמַרְתָּ מִכֹּל דָּבָר רָע״.

The Gemara asks: **From where do we** derive the **warning,** i.e., the prohibition that serves as the source for the flogging **for a defamer?**[H] **Rabbi Elazar says** that the prohibition is derived **from** the verse **"You shall not go up and down as talebearer"** (Leviticus 19:16). **Rabbi Natan says** that it is derived **from: "Then you shall keep yourself from every evil thing [*davar ra*]"** (Deuteronomy 23:10), which is expounded to mean *dibbur ra*, evil speech.

וְרַבִּי אֶלְעָזָר מַאי טַעְמָא לָא אָמַר מֵהַאי? הַהוּא מִיבְּעֵי לֵיהּ לְכִדְרַבִּי פִּנְחָס בֶּן יָאִיר. ״וְנִשְׁמַרְתָּ מִכֹּל דָּבָר רָע״ מִכָּאן אָמַר רַבִּי פִּנְחָס בֶּן יָאִיר: אַל יְהַרְהֵר אָדָם בַּיּוֹם וְיָבֹא לִידֵי טוּמְאָה בַּלַּיְלָה.

The Gemara asks: **And what is the reason** that **Rabbi Elazar did not state** that it is derived from **this** verse quoted by Rabbi Natan? The Gemara answers: **He requires that** verse **for** the statement of **Rabbi Pineḥas ben Yair,** as it was taught: **"Then you shall keep yourself from every evil thing"; from here Rabbi Pineḥas ben Yair said: A person should not think** impure thoughts[H] **by day and** thereby **come by night to** the **impurity** of an emission.

וְרַבִּי נָתָן, מַאי טַעְמָא לָא אָמַר מֵהַאי? הַהוּא אַזְהָרָה לְבֵית דִּין, שֶׁלֹּא יְהֵא רַךְ לָזֶה וְקָשֶׁה לָזֶה.

The Gemara asks the reverse question: **And what is the reason** that **Rabbi Natan did not state** that it is derived **from that** verse cited by Rabbi Elazar? The Gemara answers: Rabbi Natan explains **that** verse, which includes the term talebearer [*rakhil*], as **a warning to the court that it should not be soft**[N] **to** [*rakh la*] **this** litigant[H] **and harsh to that** one, but it must treat both sides as equals.

לֹא אָמַר לְעֵדִים ״בּוֹאוּ וְהָעִידוּנִי״ וְהֵן מְעִידִים אוֹתוֹ מֵאֲלֵיהֶן – הוּא אֵינוֹ לוֹקֶה וְאֵינוֹ נוֹתֵן מֵאָה סְלָעִים, הִיא וְזוֹמְמֶיהָ מַקְדִּימִין לְבֵית הַסְּקִילָה.

§ The Gemara cites another statement that deals with a defamer: If the husband **did not say to witnesses: Come and testify for me** that my wife committed adultery, **but they testify** for **him of their own accord**[H] and are subsequently discovered to be liars, the husband **is not flogged and does not give the one hundred** ***sela***, as he did not harm her. **She and her conspiring witnesses are brought early to the place of stoning.**

הִיא וְזוֹמְמֶיהָ סָלְקָא דַעְתָּךְ?! אֶלָּא: אוֹ הִיא אוֹ זוֹמְמֶיהָ מַקְדִּימִין לְבֵית הַסְּקִילָה.

The Gemara asks: **Does it enter your mind** to say that **she and her conspiring witnesses** are stoned? If she is liable to be stoned, they are not conspiring witnesses, and conversely, if they are conspiring witnesses, they are stoned and she is exempt. **Rather,** this must mean: **Either she or her conspiring witnesses are brought early to the place of stoning.** If they were telling the truth, she is stoned. If they conspired and offered false testimony, they are liable to be stoned.

טַעְמָא – דְּלָא אֲמַר לְהוּ, הָא אֲמַר לְהוּ – אַף עַל גַּב דְּלָא אַגְרִינְהוּ. לְאַפּוֹקֵי מִדְּרַבִּי יְהוּדָה, דְּתַנְיָא, רַבִּי יְהוּדָה אוֹמֵר: אֵינוֹ חַיָּיב עַד שֶׁיִּשְׂכּוֹר עֵדִים.

The Gemara infers from the *baraita* that the **reason** the husband is not flogged or fined is **that** the husband **did not tell them** to testify, **but if he told them** to testify, **although he did not hire them** but merely persuaded them to testify that his wife had committed adultery as a betrothed woman, he is flogged and must pay the fine. This serves **to exclude** the opinion **of Rabbi Yehuda, as it is taught** in a *baraita* that **Rabbi Yehuda says:** The husband **is liable** to the punishments of a defamer **only if he hired witnesses.**

NOTES

That the court should not be soft, etc. – שֶׁלֹּא יְהֵא רַךְ וכו׳: According to Rabbi Natan, it is not clear that *rakhil* means talebearer, as this word is generally used in the Bible as a reference to commerce. Furthermore, the context indicates that this prohibition is referring to the court, as the previous verse reads: "You shall not respect the person of the poor, nor favor the person of the mighty, but in righteousness you shall judge your neighbor" (Leviticus 19:15). Since the earlier verse deals with judicial matters, this verse is also expounded to refer to the proper behavior of the judiciary.

מַאי טַעְמָא דְּרַבִּי יְהוּדָה? אָמַר רַבִּי אַבָּהוּ: אָתְיָא ״שִׂימָה״ ״שִׂימָה״; כְּתִיב הָכָא ״וְשָׂם לָהּ עֲלִילֹת דְּבָרִים״ וּכְתִיב הָתָם ״לֹא תְשִׂימוּן עָלָיו נֶשֶׁךְ״, מָה לְהַלָּן מָמוֹן – אַף כָּאן מָמוֹן.

The Gemara asks: **What is the reason of Rabbi Yehuda?** Nowhere does the Torah explicitly state that the husband hired false witnesses. The Gemara answers that **Rabbi Abbahu said:** It is **derived** by a verbal analogy between the term **placing,** written with regard to a defamer, and the term **placing,** written with regard to the prohibition against charging interest. **It is written here,** with regard to a defamer: **"And he place wanton charges against her"** (Deuteronomy 22:14), **and it is written there: "Neither shall you place upon him interest"** (Exodus 22:24). **Just as below,** with regard to interest, the verse is referring to **money, so too here,** in the case of a defamer, it is referring to **money,** thereby indicating that the husband paid money in order to substantiate his false accusation.

אָמַר רַב נַחְמָן בַּר יִצְחָק: וְכֵן תָּנֵי רַב יוֹסֵף צִידוֹנִי בֵּי רַבִּי שִׁמְעוֹן בֶּן יוֹחַאי: אָתְיָא ״שִׂימָה״ ״שִׂימָה״.

Rav Naḥman bar Yitzḥak said: Rav Yosef Tzidoni likewise taught in the school of Rabbi Shimon ben Yoḥai: It is **derived** from the verbal analogy between the term **placing,** written with regard to a defamer, and the term **placing,** written with regard to the prohibition against charging interest.

בָּעֵי רַבִּי יִרְמְיָה: שְׂכָרָן בְּקַרְקַע מַהוּ. בְּפָחוֹת מִשָּׁוֶה פְּרוּטָה מַהוּ. שְׁנֵיהֶם בִּפְרוּטָה מַהוּ?

Rabbi Yirmeya raised a dilemma: According to the opinion of Rabbi Yehuda, if the husband **hired** the false witnesses **with land** instead of money, **what is** the *halakha*? If he hired them **with less than the value of a *peruta*, what is** the *halakha*? If he hired **both** witnesses **with a *peruta*, what is** the *halakha*? Since this *halakha* is derived from the case of interest, perhaps, like the prohibition against charging interest, it applies only with regard to money, rather than land, and only with money that is greater than the value of a *peruta*.

בָּעֵי רַב אַשִׁי: הוֹצִיא שֵׁם רַע עַל הַנִּישּׂוּאִין הָרִאשׁוֹנִים מַהוּ, עַל נִשּׂוּאֵי אָחִיו מַהוּ?

Similarly, **Rav Ashi raised a dilemma** concerning a defamer: If **he defamed** his wife **with regard to** their **first marriage,**[H] **what is** the *halakha*? In other words, if a man married a woman, divorced her, remarried her, and subsequently defamed her by claiming that she had committed adultery during the period of betrothal before their first marriage, what is the *halakha*? Similarly, if he performed levirate marriage and then defamed her **with regard to his brother's marriage**[H] to her, **what is** the *halakha*?

פְּשׁוֹט מִיהָא חֲדָא, דְּתָנֵי רַבִּי יוֹנָה: ״אֶת בִּתִּי נָתַתִּי לָאִישׁ הַזֶּה״ לָזֶה – וְלֹא לַיָּבָם.

The Gemara comments: **Resolve at least one** of these dilemmas, **as Rabbi Yona taught** that the verse "And the father of the young woman shall say to the Elders: **I gave my daughter to this man**" (Deuteronomy 22:16) serves to emphasize: I gave him **to this** man **and not to the *yavam*,** i.e., the brother of the original husband. Consequently, if one defames his *yevama* with regard to her original marriage to his brother, the unique *halakhot* of defamation do not apply.

מַאי רַבָּנַן וּמַאי רַבִּי אֱלִיעֶזֶר בֶּן יַעֲקֹב? דְּתַנְיָא: כֵּיצַד הוֹצָאַת שֵׁם רַע? בָּא לְבֵית דִּין, וְאָמַר: ״פְּלוֹנִי, לֹא מָצָאתִי לְבִתְּךָ בְּתוּלִים״. אִם יֵשׁ עֵדִים שֶׁזִּינְּתָה תַּחְתָּיו – יֵשׁ לָהּ כְּתוּבָּה מָנֶה.

§ In the course of the previous discussion, the Gemara mentioned a dispute between the Rabbis and Rabbi Eliezer ben Ya'akov. The Gemara asks: **What** is the opinion of **the Rabbis and what** is the opinion of **Rabbi Eliezer ben Ya'akov,** referred to above (45b)? **As it is taught** in a *baraita*: **How** does the case of **defamation** proceed?[H] It involves a situation where the husband **came to the court and said** to the father: **So-and-so, I have not found** indications of **your daughter's virginity. If there are witnesses** who testify **that she committed adultery under his** authority, i.e., while betrothed to him, **she has a marriage contract of one hundred dinars.**

אִם יֵשׁ עֵדִים שֶׁזִּינְּתָה תַּחְתָּיו יֵשׁ לָהּ כְּתוּבָּה מָנֶה?! בַּת סְקִילָה הִיא! הָכִי קָאָמַר: אִם יֵשׁ עֵדִים שֶׁזִּינְּתָה תַּחְתָּיו – בִּסְקִילָה, זִינְּתָה מֵעִיקָּרָא – יֵשׁ לָהּ כְּתוּבָּה מָנֶה.

The Gemara interrupts its citation of the *baraita*, as this last statement is very surprising: **If there are witnesses** who testify **that she committed adultery under his** authority, does **she have a marriage contract of one hundred dinars? She is** punished **by stoning.** The Gemara explains that **this is what** the *tanna* **said: If there are witnesses** who testify **that she committed adultery under his** authority, she is liable **to** receive the punishment of **stoning.** However, if **she engaged in licentious sexual relations at the outset,** before her betrothal, when she was still a single woman, she is merely guilty of deceiving her husband with regard to her virginity, and therefore **she has a marriage contract of one hundred dinars,** which is the standard marriage contract of a non-virgin.

HALAKHA

If he defamed his wife with regard to their first marriage – הוֹצִיא שֵׁם רַע עַל הַנִּישּׂוּאִין הָרִאשׁוֹנִים: If a man betrothed a woman, divorced her, betrothed her again, and subsequently defamed her and brought witnesses to testify that she had committed adultery during their first betrothal, and the witnesses were later revealed to have testified falsely, the husband is exempt from punishment. Although the Gemara does not resolve this dilemma, the Rambam rules leniently (Rambam *Sefer Nashim, Hilkhot Na'ara Betula* 3:9).

With regard to his brother's marriage – עַל נִשּׂוּאֵי אָחִיו: If a man performed levirate marriage with his *yevama*, and defamed her by bringing witnesses who testified that she had committed adultery when she was betrothed to his brother, and they were found to have testified falsely, the man is exempt from punishment (Rambam *Sefer Nashim, Hilkhot Na'ara Betula* 3:9).

How does the case of defamation proceed – כֵּיצַד הוֹצָאַת שֵׁם רַע: In the case of a defamer, the husband comes to the court with the claim that he had intercourse with his wife for the first time and discovered that she was not a virgin. He then produces witnesses who testify that she committed adultery when she was betrothed to him. If the court examines the matter and finds his claim to be true, she is stoned. If her father brings witnesses who reveal the husband's pair of witnesses to be conspiring witnesses, they are liable to be stoned, and the husband receives lashes and is fined one hundred silver shekels. The Rambam rules in accordance with the opinion of Rabbi Eliezer ben Ya'akov, whose rulings are generally accepted as *halakha*. Additionally, this is the conclusion of the Gemara itself (Rambam *Sefer Nashim, Hilkhot Na'ara Betula* 3:6, and *Kesef Mishne* there).

NOTES

They shall spread that which he placed against her [*sam la*] – פרשו מה ששם לה: Some commentaries maintain that this is not an exposition of the word garment [*simla*] as though it said *sam la*, but rather a reference to the earlier phrase "placed against her [*sam la*] wanton charges" (Deuteronomy 22:17; see *Tosafot* and Ritva). In any case, it is clear that, according to the Rabbis, the term *simla* is not understood to literally refer to a garment. In the Jerusalem Talmud, Rabbi Yishmael is cited as identifying this as one of the three verses in the Torah that cannot be interpreted in a literal manner. Rather, spreading the sheet is to be interpreted allegorically to mean that the case must be investigated thoroughly, as the Rambam says, the witnesses must be interrogated and the case examined in detail. In the Jerusalem Talmud it is indicated that this explanation of the phrase: They shall spread the garment, is accepted by Rabbi Eliezer ben Ya'akov as well the Rabbis.

The matters are as they are written – דברים ככתבן: In the Jerusalem Talmud, where this issue is discussed at length, it is stated that even Rabbi Eliezer ben Ya'akov agrees that this chapter cannot be understood in an entirely literal manner, as neither the lack of a cloth nor the discovery of blood stains on it affords incontrovertible proof of guilt or innocence, as a cloth can get lost or splattered with other types of blood, such as that of a bird. One cannot sentence the young woman to death or penalize the husband on the basis of such flimsy evidence.

Instead, Rabbi Eliezer ben Ya'akov certainly agrees that all claims must be substantiated by witness testimony. Therefore, the dispute between the *tanna'im* is limited to the question of the extent to which the verses are to be understood in a literal manner. The Rabbis maintain that since the basic proof is necessarily provided by witnesses, the entire chapter can be understood in a non-literal fashion, whereas Rabbi Eliezer ben Ya'akov maintains that one must read the verses in as plain a manner as possible.

Consequently, according to many commentaries, Rabbi Eliezer ben Ya'akov holds that the verse is referring to a cloth in order to indicate that the *halakhot* of a defamer apply only if, in addition to bringing witnesses who testify that his wife committed adultery during betrothal, he also had intercourse with his wife and claims that he found her not to be a virgin.

Alternatively, it is possible that the *halakhot* apply as long as the husband and wife engaged in intercourse, even if the husband does not claim to have found at that time that she was not a virgin (see Ramban; Rabbeinu Aharon HaLevi; Ritva; *Nimmukei Yosef*). Others maintain that the husband is punished only if he is impudent enough to claim that his wife was not a virgin despite the fact that the cloth is full of blood (*Tosafot*; Rosh).

נמצא ששם רע אינו שם רע – הוא לוקה ונותן מאה סלע, בין בעל ובין לא בעל. רבי אליעזר בן יעקב אומר: לא נאמרו דברים הללו אלא כשבעל. בשלמא לרבי אליעזר בן יעקב – היינו דכתיב "ובא אליה" "ואקרב אליה".

The Gemara resumes its quotation of the *baraita*: If it was **discovered that the bad name is not a bad name,** i.e., the husband's accusation was false, **he is flogged and gives** her father **one hundred *sela*, whether he had intercourse with her or whether he had not had intercourse with her. Rabbi Eliezer ben Ya'akov says: These matters were stated only** in a case **where he had intercourse** with his wife before defaming her. The Gemara asks: **Granted, according to** the opinion of **Rabbi Eliezer ben Ya'akov, this is as it is written:** "If a man take a wife **and go in unto her"** (Deuteronomy 22:13), and: **"And when I came near to her,** I did not find in her the tokens of virginity" (Deuteronomy 22:14), as both expressions refer to sexual intercourse.

אלא לרבנן – מאי "ובא אליה" "ואקרב אליה"? "ובא אליה" – בעלילות; "ואקרב אליה" – בדברים.

However, according to the opinion of **the Rabbis, what is** the meaning of the phrases **"and go in unto her,"** and **"and when I came near to her,"** if the couple never engaged in intercourse? The Gemara explains that, according to the Rabbis, **"and go in unto her"** is referring **to the wanton charges** the husband leveled against his wife; **"and when I came near to her"** means that he came near **with words,** not intercourse.

בשלמא לרבי אליעזר בן יעקב – היינו דכתיב "לא מצאתי לבתך בתולים". אלא לרבנן – מאי "לא מצאתי לבתך בתולים"? לא מצאתי לבתך כשרי בתולים.

The Gemara asks: **Granted, according to** the opinion of **Rabbi Eliezer ben Ya'akov, this is as it is written: "I did not find in your daughter the tokens of virginity"** (Deuteronomy 22:17), as Rabbi Eliezer ben Ya'akov claims that the husband had relations with her and discovered that she was not a virgin. **However, according to** the opinion of **the Rabbis, what is** the meaning of **"I did not find in your daughter the tokens of virginity,"** if they did not have intercourse? The Gemara answers: The Rabbis explain that he means: **I did not find for your daughter the fitness of virginity,** i.e., I have discovered that she was unfaithful.

בשלמא לרבי אליעזר בן יעקב – היינו דכתיב "ואלה בתולי בתי", אלא לרבנן מאי "ואלה בתולי בתי"? ואלה כשרי בתולי בתי.

The Gemara asks further: **Granted, according to** the opinion of **Rabbi Eliezer ben Ya'akov, this is as it is written** that the father replies: **"And these are the tokens of my daughter's virginity"** (Deuteronomy 22:17). He presents a cloth that proves she was a virgin, in opposition to the husband's claim. **However, according to** the opinion of **the Rabbis, what is** the meaning of **"And these are the tokens of my daughter's virginity"?** The Rabbis answer that the father means: **And these are the** proofs of the **fitness of my daughter's virginity,** i.e., he either brings witnesses to counter the testimony of the husband's witnesses or provides some other proof that his daughter was a virgin at the time of her marriage.

בשלמא לרבי אליעזר בן יעקב – היינו דכתיב "ופרשו השמלה, אלא לרבנן מאי "ופרשו השמלה"?

The Gemara poses yet another question on the same lines: **Granted, according to** the opinion of **Rabbi Eliezer ben Ya'akov, this is as it is written: "And they shall spread the garment"**[H] (Deuteronomy 22:17). The father brings the sheet on which the couple had intercourse and shows that it is stained with blood. **However, according to** the opinion of **the Rabbis,** who claim that a husband can defame his wife even if they have not engaged in intercourse, **what is** the meaning of the phrase **"And they shall spread the garment [*hasimla*]"?**

אמר רבי אבהו: פרשו מה ששם לה. כדתניא: "ופרשו השמלה". מלמד שבאין עדים של זה ועדים של זה, ובוררין את הדבר כשמלה חדשה. רבי אליעזר בן יעקב אומר: דברים ככתבן, שמלה ממש.

Rabbi Abbahu said that the Rabbis interpret this expression as follows: **They shall spread,** i.e., examine, **that which he placed against her [*sam la*].**[N] In other words, they cross-examine the witnesses who testified against her, **as it is taught** in a *baraita*: **"And they shall spread the garment"**; this **teaches that the witnesses of this** husband **come** forward, **and** likewise **the witnesses of that** father come forward, **and** the court **clarifies the matter like a new garment. Rabbi Eliezer ben Ya'akov says: The matters** are **as they are written,**[N] i.e., the verse refers to **an actual cloth.**

HALAKHA

And they shall spread the garment, etc. – ופרשו השמלה וכו': The phrases "they shall spread the garment" and "these are the tokens of my daughter's virginity" are understood to be euphemisms for the court's investigations into private matters. The commentaries wonder why the Rambam interprets these phrases in accordance with the opinion of the Rabbis, while he accepts Rabbi Eliezer ben Ya'akov's ruling as *halakha*. The *Kesef Mishne* states that the Rambam evidently maintains that even Rabbi Eliezer ben Ya'akov agrees that it is not enough merely to spread out a garment or something similar. Rather, he too concedes to the Rabbis that the matter must be clarified by witnesses (Rambam *Sefer Nashim, Hilkhot Na'ara Betula* 3:12).

שָׁלַח רַבִּי יִצְחָק בַּר רַב יַעֲקֹב בַּר גִּיּוֹרֵי מִשְּׁמֵיהּ דְּרַבִּי יוֹחָנָן: אַף עַל גַּב שֶׁלֹּא מָצִינוּ בְּכׇל הַתּוֹרָה כּוּלָּהּ שֶׁחִלֵּק הַכָּתוּב בֵּין בִּיאָה כְּדַרְכָּהּ לְבִיאָה שֶׁלֹּא כְּדַרְכָּהּ לְמַכּוֹת וּלְעוֹנָשִׁין, אֲבָל מוֹצִיא שֵׁם רַע – חִלֵּק: אֵינוֹ חַיָּיב עַד שֶׁיִּבְעוֹל שֶׁלֹּא כְּדַרְכָּהּ, וְיוֹצִיא שֵׁם רַע כְּדַרְכָּהּ.

§ **Rabbi Yitzḥak bar Rav Ya'akov bar Giyyorei sent** a message from Eretz Yisrael to Babylonia **in the name of Rabbi Yoḥanan: Although we have not found in the entire Torah that** any verse **distinguishes between sexual intercourse in a typical manner and sexual intercourse in an atypical manner,**[H] i.e., anal intercourse, **with regard to flogging or** any other **punishment. However,** in the case of the **defamer,** the Torah **does distinguish** in this manner, as the husband **is obligated** to pay the fine **only** if **he had intercourse** with his wife, even it was **in an atypical manner, and** he **defames** her by claiming that she had previously had intercourse **in a typical manner** with someone else.

כְּמַאן? אִי כְּרַבָּנַן – אַף עַל גַּב דְּלָא בָּעַל, אִי כְּרַבִּי אֱלִיעֶזֶר בֶּן יַעֲקֹב,

The Gemara asks: In **accordance with whose** opinion is this ruling of Rabbi Yoḥanan? **If** it is **in accordance with** the opinion of **the Rabbis,** the husband should be liable **even if he did not have intercourse** with his wife. **If** it is **in accordance with** the opinion of **Rabbi Eliezer ben Ya'akov,**

HALAKHA

We have not found…that any verse distinguishes between sexual intercourse in a typical manner and sexual intercourse in an atypical manner, etc. – לֹא מָצִינוּ...שֶׁחִלֵּק הַכָּתוּב בֵּין בִּיאָה כְּדַרְכָּהּ לְבִיאָה שֶׁלֹּא כְּדַרְכָּהּ: One who has intercourse with a woman forbidden to him is liable to his prescribed punishment, either death, *karet*, flogging by Torah law, or lashes for rebelliousness, whether he had relations with her in a typical or atypical manner (Rambam *Sefer Kedusha, Hilkhot Issurei Bia* 1:10; *Shulḥan Arukh, Even HaEzer* 20:1).

אִידִי וְאִידִי כְּדַרְכָּהּ בָּעֵינַן! אֶלָּא שָׁלַח רַב כָּהֲנָא מִשְּׁמֵיהּ דְּרַבִּי יוֹחָנָן: אֵינוֹ חַיָּיב עַד שֶׁיִּבְעוֹל כְּדַרְכָּהּ, וְיוֹצִיא שֵׁם רַע בְּכַדַרְכָּהּ.

we require both this, i.e., the act of intercourse between the husband and wife, **and that,** i.e., the woman's alleged act of intercourse with another man, to be performed in **a typical** manner in order for the laws of a defamer to apply, as Rabbi Eliezer ben Ya'akov interprets the verses literally, meaning that the husband had intercourse with her and discovered she was not a virgin. **Rather, Rav Kahana sent** word **in the name of Rabbi Yoḥanan** that the statement was as follows: **He is obligated** to pay the fine **only**[H] **if he had intercourse** in **a typical** manner **and defamed** her with regard to intercourse performed in **a typical** manner, in accordance with the opinion of Rabbi Eliezer ben Ya'akov.

מתני׳ הָאָב זַכַּאי בְּבִתּוֹ בְּקִידּוּשֶׁיהָ בְּכֶסֶף, בִּשְׁטָר וּבְבִיאָה. זַכַּאי בִּמְצִיאָתָהּ וּבְמַעֲשֵׂה יָדֶיהָ, וּבַהֲפָרַת נְדָרֶיהָ, וּמְקַבֵּל אֶת גִּיטָּהּ, וְאֵינוֹ אוֹכֵל פֵּירוֹת בְּחַיֶּיהָ.

MISHNA **A father has authority** over **his daughter**[N] with regard to **her betrothal**[H] **through money, through** a marriage **document, or through intercourse.**[N] Likewise, a father **is entitled to items she** has **found,**[N] **and to her earnings,**[H] **and to** effect **the nullification of her vows,**[H] i.e., a father may nullify his daughter's vows. **And he accepts her bill of divorce**[H] on her behalf if she is divorced from betrothal before she becomes a grown woman. **And** although he inherits her property when she dies, e.g., property she inherited from her mother's family, **he does not consume the produce** of her property **during her lifetime.**[H]

NOTES

A father has authority over his daughter, etc. – הָאָב זַכַּאי בְּבִתּוֹ וכו׳: The precise meaning of this statement is a matter of dispute. Either it is referring to the father's basic legal right to accept betrothal on behalf of his daughter, or it is referring to his ensuing right to the betrothal money. It appears that the Gemara reads it both ways, depending on whether it is discussing betrothal via money or, alternatively, via a marriage document or intercourse. However, in the Jerusalem Talmud it is stated that it is referring to the monetary rights that accrue to the father. Some commentaries argue that the language of the mishna indicates it is referring to more than just the basic right to accept betrothal (see *Melekhet Shlomo*). It should be noted that this mishna applies specifically when the daughter is a minor or a young woman, but not if she is a grown woman.

Or through intercourse – וּבְבִיאָה: In the Jerusalem Talmud it is asked: In the first two cases, one can explain that a father has rights to his daughter's betrothal money and to use the material on which the marriage document was written as he wishes, but what kind of monetary right does he possess with regard to betrothal via intercourse? The Gemara answers that he has the right to receive pecuniary compensation for allowing the man to betroth her by means of intercourse. The Meiri explains likewise. Apparently the Gemara here does not ask this question because it interprets the mishna as referring to a father's authority to accept betrothal on behalf of his daughter by allowing the man to have intercourse with her, as explained by Rashi.

A father is entitled to items she has found – זַכַּאי בִּמְצִיאָתָהּ: Some commentaries maintain that the father is entitled to lost items that she finds even after her betrothal, provided that she is still a young woman (Meiri). This accounts for the fact that the *tanna* starts a new sentence here and does not state this *halakha* together with the previous ones. Others explain that this is listed as a separate *halakha* because a father's right to items his daughter finds is a rabbinic enactment. Furthermore, this sentence serves as an introduction to the continuation of the mishna, which addresses the rights of a husband, including the rights to items that his wife finds (*Shita Mekubbetzet*).

HALAKHA

He is obligated to pay the fine only, etc. – אֵינוֹ חַיָּיב עַד וכו׳: One who defames his wife is liable only if he had intercourse with her in a typical manner and defames her by claiming that she had committed adultery during betrothal by having intercourse with another man in the typical manner (Rambam *Sefer Nashim, Hilkhot Na'ara Betula* 3:10).

A father has authority over his daughter with regard to her betrothal, etc. – הָאָב זַכַּאי בְּבִתּוֹ בְּקִידּוּשֶׁיהָ וכו׳: A father may betroth his daughter to a man of his choice while she is a minor or a young woman. If the betrothal is performed with money, the money belongs to the father (Rambam *Sefer Nashim, Hilkhot Ishut* 3:11; *Shulḥan Arukh, Even HaEzer* 37:1).

A father is entitled to items she has found and to her earnings – זַכַּאי בִּמְצִיאָתָהּ וּבְמַעֲשֵׂה יָדֶיהָ: A father is entitled to lost items that his daughter has found and to her earnings, until she becomes a grown woman. This applies even if she is not financially dependent upon him (Rambam *Sefer Nashim, Hilkhot Ishut* 3:11; *Sefer Nezikim, Hilkhot Gezeila VaAveda* 17:13; *Shulḥan Arukh, Even HaEzer* 37:1 and *Ḥoshen Mishpat* 270:2).

He is entitled…to effect the nullification of her vows – זַכַּאי...בַּהֲפָרַת נְדָרֶיהָ: A father may nullify his daughter's vows when she is a minor or a young woman (Rambam *Sefer Hafla'a, Hilkhot Nedarim* 11:6; *Shulḥan Arukh, Yoreh De'a* 234:1).

He accepts her bill of divorce – מְקַבֵּל אֶת גִּיטָּהּ: If a father betroths his daughter to a man, and the man then divorces her while she is still a minor, her father accepts her bill of divorce on her behalf, and she is divorced as soon as the document reaches his possession (Rif; Rambam). Others maintain that she, too, can receive her own bill of divorce (*Tosafot*; Razah). Some authorities state that one should be stringent and not allow her to accept her own bill of divorce (Rosh). If he divorces her when she is a young woman, either she or her father can receive the bill of divorce (Rambam *Sefer Nashim, Hilkhot Geirushin* 2:18; *Shulḥan Arukh, Even HaEzer* 141:4).

He does not consume the produce of her property during her lifetime – אֵינוֹ אוֹכֵל פֵּירוֹת בְּחַיֶּיהָ: A father is not entitled to the produce of his daughter's property during her lifetime (see Rambam *Sefer Nezikin, Hilkhot Ḥovel* 4:19; *Shulḥan Arukh, Ḥoshen Mishpat* 424:7).

HALAKHA

The husband consumes the produce of her property during her lifetime – הבעל אוכל פירות בחייה: A husband is entitled to consume the produce of his wife's property (Rambam *Sefer Nashim*, *Hilkhot Ishut* 12:3; 22:7; *Shulḥan Arukh*, *Even HaEzer* 69:3).

He is obligated to provide her sustenance, etc. – חייב במזונותיה וכו׳: A husband is obligated to support his wife, to redeem her if she is captured, and to tend to her burial (Rambam *Sefer Nashim*, *Hilkhot Ishut* 12:2; *Shulḥan Arukh*, *Even HaEzer* 69:2).

May not provide fewer than two flutes, etc. – לא יפחות משני חלילין וכו׳: If a woman dies before her husband, he is obligated to bury her, to pay all the requisite expenses, and to arrange a eulogy for her in accordance with the local practice. If it is the custom to hire people to play the flute and to lament, he must provide at least two flutists, as well as a lamenting woman. As stated by the Gemara (48a), the *halakha* is in accordance with the opinion of Rabbi Yehuda (Rambam *Sefer Nashim*, *Hilkhot Ishut* 14:23; *Shulḥan Arukh*, *Even HaEzer* 89:1).

BACKGROUND

Flutes – חלילין: It was customary during ancient times, including in Eretz Yisrael during the period of the Mishna, to play flutes at funerals in order to stimulate mourning. It seems this custom was widely practiced, since the Mishna (see *Shabbat* 151a) discusses various *halakhot* that concern flutes used at funerals. Later generations discontinued this practice, as they considered it a gentile custom.

Roman relief of a flute player

נשאת – יתר עליו הבעל שאוכל פירות בחייה, וחייב במזונותיה ובפרקונה וקבורתה. רבי יהודה אומר: אפילו עני שבישראל לא יפחות משני חלילין ומקוננת.

If the daughter **married, the husband has more** rights and obligations **than** her father had before the marriage, **as he consumes the produce** of her property **during her lifetime,**[H] **and he is obligated** to provide **her sustenance,**[H] **her redemption** if she is captured, **and her burial** upon her death. **Rabbi Yehuda says: Even the poorest** man **of the Jewish people may not** provide **fewer than two flutes**[HB] **and a lamenting woman,** which it was customary to hire for a funeral, as these too are included in the duties of burial.

גמ׳ בכסף מנלן? אמר רב יהודה: אמר קרא "ויצאה חנם אין כסף" – אין כסף לאדון זה, ויש כסף לאדון אחר, ומנו – אביה.

GEMARA The mishna indicates that a father receives the money of his daughter's betrothal. The Gemara asks: **From where do we** derive that the father is entitled to the **money** of her betrothal? **Rav Yehuda said** that **the verse states,** with regard to an emancipated Hebrew maidservant: **"Then she shall go out for nothing, without money"** (Exodus 21:11), from which it is inferred: **There is no money for this master,** i.e., her master does not receive money when she leaves him, **but there is money for a different master, and who is this? Her father,** who also had authority over her, like her master. When she leaves her father's jurisdiction via betrothal, he is entitled to the betrothal money.

ואימא לדידה? השתא אביה מקבל קידושיה, דכתיב "את בתי נתתי לאיש הזה", איהי שקלא כספא?!

The Gemara asks: **But** one can **say** that the betrothal money should go **to her,** as one can derive from the verse that there is no money for this master but there is money for the woman herself when she leaves her father's domain. The Gemara refutes this suggestion: **Now** consider, **her father accepts her betrothal,**[N] i.e., he can accept the money or document of betrothal from the man of his choice, **as it is written: "I gave my daughter to this man"** (Deuteronomy 22:16). Can one then say that **she takes the money** when her father accepts the betrothal on her behalf?

ואימא: הני מילי – קטנה, דלית לה יד, אבל נערה דאית לה יד – איהי תקדש נפשה, ואיהי תשקול כספא! אמר קרא "בנעוריה בית אביה" – כל שבח נעורים לאביה.

The Gemara raises a difficulty: **But** one can **say** that **this applies** only to **a minor, who does not have a hand,** i.e., she is not legally competent to carry out transactions on her own behalf. **However,** in the case of **a young woman, who does have a hand, she should betroth herself and she should** also **take** her own betrothal **money.** The Gemara answers that there is a different exposition in this regard, as **the verse states: "Being in her youth, in her father's house"** (Numbers 30:17), which teaches that **all gains** that a daughter accrues in her **youth,** i.e., when she is a young woman, belong **to her father.**[N]

ואלא, הא דאמר רב הונא אמר רב: מנין שמעשה הבת לאביה – שנאמר "וכי ימכור איש את בתו לאמה", מה אמה מעשה ידיה לרבה, אף בת מעשה ידיה לאביה – למה לי, תיפוק ליה מ"בנעוריה בית אביה"? אלא, ההוא בהפרת נדרים הוא דכתיב.

The Gemara asks: **But** consider **that which Rav Huna said** that **Rav said: From where** is it derived **that the earnings of a daughter** belong **to her father?** It is **as it is stated: "And if a man sell his daughter to be a maidservant"** (Exodus 21:7); **just as** with regard to **a maidservant, her earnings** belong **to her master, so too** with regard to **a daughter, her earnings** belong **to her father. Why do I need this exposition? Let him derive it from** the phrase **"being in her youth, in her father's house." Rather, that** phrase, "being in her youth, in her father's house," **is written with regard to the nullification of vows,** but it is not referring to monetary matters.

NOTES

Now consider, her father accepts her betrothal, etc. – השתא אביה מקבל קידושיה וכו׳: Rashi explains as follows in tractate *Kiddushin* (3b): Since the Torah would not grant a father the right to betroth his daughter without recompense, he must be entitled to the money she receives. Others commentaries there explain simply that since a father has complete rights over the choice of his daughter's husband, the betrothal is considered a form of transaction in which the father relinquishes his rights to accept betrothal for her in the future, and therefore he is entitled to the money (Ritva on *Kiddushin* 3b).

All gains a daughter accrues in her youth belong to her father – כל שבח נעורים לאביה: Although this teaches that a father is entitled to the money of his daughter's betrothal, it does not directly prove that he has the right to betroth her to the man of his choice. One possibility is that the Gemara's previous argument can now be reversed: If she chooses her husband, why should her father receive the betrothal money? From the fact that he receives the money, it is clear that he has the right to betroth his daughter to the man of his choice (*Ayyelet Ahavim*).

וְכִי תֵּימָא: נֵילַף מִינָּהּ – מָמוֹנָא מֵאִיסּוּרָא לָא יָלְפִינַן. וְכִי תֵּימָא: נֵילַף מִקְּנָסָא – מָמוֹנָא מִקְּנָסָא לָא יָלְפִינַן.

And if you would say: Let us derive from here that just as she is under her father's authority with regard to vows, the same applies to monetary matters, this is not possible, because there is a principle that **we do not derive monetary matters from ritual matters,** as these are two separate areas of *halakha*. **And if you would say: Let us derive** this *halakha* **from** the **fine** paid by the rapist of a young woman, which the Torah explicitly states goes to her father (Deuteronomy 22:29), there is another principle, that **we do not derive monetary matters from fines.** Each fine imposed by the Torah is a novel law, from which nothing can be learned with regard to other monetary liabilities.

וְכִי תֵּימָא: נֵילַף מִבּוֹשֶׁת וּפְגָם – שָׁאנֵי בּוֹשֶׁת וּפְגָם דְּאָבִיהָ נַמִי שַׁיָּיךְ בֵּיהּ.

And if you would say: Let us derive it **from** the compensation paid by a rapist for his victim's **humiliation and degradation,**[N] which is also paid to her father, the compensation for **humiliation and degradation is different, as her father also has a share in it,**[N] because he too is humiliated and harmed by this unfortunate episode, and therefore one cannot learn the *halakhot* of other monetary matters from here.

אֶלָּא, מִסְתַּבְּרָא דְּכִי מְמַעֵט רַחֲמָנָא – יְצִיאָה דִּכְווֹתָהּ קָא מְמַעֵט.

Rather, the Gemara returns to the previous exposition of the verse: "Then she shall go out for nothing, without money" (Exodus 21:11). As for the question of why she does not receive the money herself, the Gemara explains that **it is reasonable** to assume **that when the Merciful One excludes** a case by means of this verse, **He excludes** a case where a girl **leaves** someone's authority **in the corresponding** situation[N] to the case of the Hebrew maidservant.

וְהָא לָא דָּמְיָא הָא יְצִיאָה לְהָא יְצִיאָה, הָתָם גַּבֵּי אָדוֹן – נָפְקָא לָהּ מֵרְשׁוּתֵיהּ לְגַמְרֵי, יְצִיאָה דְּאָב – אַכַּתִּי מְחַסְּרָא מְסִירָה לַחוּפָּה!

The Gemara raises a difficulty: **But this leaving** of her father's authority **is not comparable to that leaving** of her master's authority: **There, with regard to a master,** when he frees her **she leaves his authority entirely,** whereas in the case of a girl who **goes out** from the jurisdiction **of** her **father,** she **still lacks** the process of being **brought to the wedding canopy.** As long as she is not fully married she remains partially under her father's authority, as he is her heir and has rights to her earnings.

מֵהֲפָרַת נְדָרִים מִיהָא נָפְקָא לָהּ מֵרְשׁוּתֵיהּ. דִּתְנַן: נַעֲרָה הַמְאוֹרָסָה אָבִיהָ וּבַעְלָהּ מְפִירִין לָהּ נְדָרֶיהָ.

The Gemara answers: **From** the perspective of her father's right to effect the **nullification of** her **vows, at least,**[N] **she has left his domain** via betrothal, as he no longer maintains exclusive rights to nullify her vows. **As we learned** in a mishna (*Nedarim* 66b): With regard to **a betrothed young woman, her father and her husband nullify her vows** together. Since her father cannot nullify her vows on his own, the two types of leaving are indeed comparable.

"שְׁטָר וּבִיאָה". מְנָא לַן? אָמַר קְרָא: "וְהָיְתָה לְאִישׁ אַחֵר" – אִיתְקוּשׁ הֲוָיוֹת לַהֲדָדֵי.

§ The mishna taught that a father is entitled to accept betrothal of his daughter through a marriage **document or** through **intercourse.** The Gemara asks: **From where do we** derive this? The Gemara answers that **the verse states: "And she becomes another man's wife"** (Deuteronomy 24:2). Since the verse does not specify how she becomes his wife, the different ways of **becoming** a wife **are compared to each other,** i.e., they are considered equal. Accordingly, the various methods of betrothal are the same with regard to the authority of the father.

"זַכַּאי בִּמְצִיאָתָהּ".

The mishna further taught that a father **is entitled to items she** has **found.**

NOTES

Let us derive it from humiliation and degradation – נֵילַף מִבּוֹשֶׁת וּפְגָם: Rashi explains that this refers to the fact that the compensation for a young woman's humiliation and degradation belong to the father, as stated earlier. It has been pointed out that this interpretation is apparently circular, as the very fact that a father is entitled to the compensation for her humiliation and degradation is derived from his ability to accept betrothal on behalf of his daughter, whereas the Gemara here attempt to derive a father's ability to accept betrothal on his daughter's behalf from the fact that he is entitled to the compensation for her humiliation and degradation. Therefore, others explain that this statement refers to the fact that he can hand her over to a man who is repulsive or stricken with boils, which entails causing her humiliation and degradation (Ramban; see 40b).

Her father also has a share in it – אָבִיהָ נַמִי שַׁיָּיךְ בֵּיהּ: According to Rashi, her father has rights to the compensation for her humiliation and degradation because he has the right to betroth her to someone repulsive, which would cause her humiliation and degradation. Conversely, the Ramban explains that the father shares her shame and loss of value because he also suffers as a result of her ordeal. Although not even a husband, whose wife is considered like his own body, has full rights to compensation for her humiliation and degradation, and certainly other relatives do not, it is possible that due to the special closeness between father and daughter her humiliation and degradation are considered his as well. In support of his interpretation, the Ramban cites a version of the parallel passage in *Kiddushin* (3b) which states explicitly that her father also experiences suffering. Some versions of the text of the Gemara here also included that statement. See the Ritva, however, who cites several reasons for accepting Rashi's explanation.

NOTES

He excludes a case where a girl leaves someone's authority in the corresponding situation – יְצִיאָה דִּכְווֹתָהּ קָא מְמַעֵט: The verse indicates that a Hebrew maidservant who reaches majority goes free without payment. If there would be payment, it would be made to the master. This occurs in a case where the maidservant or her family members set her free by offering monetary compensation to the master. A Jewish girl sold as a maidservant remains in that station for a maximum of six years. She can be redeemed by reimbursing the master for a percentage of the purchase price corresponding to the percentage of the six years that she has not yet served. Since the verse indicates that, as opposed to a Hebrew maidservant who goes free because she reached majority, where no money changes hands, in the case of a girl who leaves the jurisdiction of her father via betrothal, money does change hands. The money goes to the father, corresponding to the fact that any money paid in the case of the Hebrew maidservant would have gone to the master.

From the nullification of vows, at least, etc. – מֵהֲפָרַת נְדָרִים מִיהָא וכו׳: This answer is difficult, as the Gemara is seeking to prove that a daughter leaves her father's domain entirely; yet it is clear that with regard to vows he retains a certain right over her, even though he cannot nullify her vows on his own. In fact, Rabbeinu Ḥananel's version of the Gemara did not mention nullification of vows and stated instead: From this matter, at least, she has entirely left his domain. In other words, once the father has accepted betrothal on behalf of his daughter, he no longer has the right to sell her as a Hebrew maidservant. In this sense, she leaves her father's domain in a manner similar to how a Hebrew maidservant leaves her master's domain.

מִשּׁוּם אֵיבָה.

The Gemara explains: The reason is **due to enmity,**[N] so that he should not bear a grudge against her for finding articles and withholding them from him, which might lead him to become reluctant to provide her with sustenance.

״בְּמַעֲשֵׂה יָדֶיהָ״. מְנָלַן? דְּאָמַר רַב הוּנָא אָמַר רַב: מִנַּיִן שֶׁמַּעֲשֵׂה הַבַּת לָאָב? שֶׁנֶּאֱמַר ״וְכִי יִמְכּוֹר אִישׁ אֶת בִּתּוֹ לְאָמָה״ – מָה אָמָה מַעֲשֵׂה יָדֶיהָ לְרַבָּהּ – אַף בַּת מַעֲשֵׂה יָדֶיהָ לְאָבִיהָ. וְאֵימָא: הָנֵי מִילֵּי קְטַנָּה, דְּמָצֵי מְזַבַּן לַהּ, אֲבָל נַעֲרָה, דְּלָא מָצֵי מְזַבַּן לַהּ, מַעֲשֵׂה יָדֶיהָ דִּידָהּ הָווּ!

§ The mishna further taught that a father is entitled **to** his daughter's **earnings.** The Gemara asks: **From where do we** derive this? The Gemara answers: **As Rav Huna said** that **Rav said: From where** is it derived **that the earnings of a daughter** belong **to her father? As it is stated: "And if a man sell his daughter to be a maidservant"** (Exodus 21:7), which indicates that **just as** with regard to **a maidservant, her earnings** belong **to her master,** as she was sold for this purpose, **so too** with regard to **a daughter, her earnings go to her father.** The Gemara asks: **But** one can **say** that **this applies** only to **a minor,** as a father **can sell her** as a maidservant. **However,** with regard to **a young woman, whom he cannot sell,** perhaps **her earnings** should belong **to her.**

מִסְתַּבְּרָא דְּאָבִיהָ הָווּ, דְּאִי סָלְקָא דַּעְתָּךְ מַעֲשֵׂה יָדֶיהָ לָאו דְּאָבִיהָ, אֶלָּא הָא דְּזַכֵּי לֵיהּ רַחֲמָנָא לָאָב לְמִימְסְרָהּ לְחוּפָּה – הֵיכִי מָצֵי מָסַר לַהּ? הָא קָמְבַטֵּל לַהּ מִמַּעֲשֵׂה יָדֶיהָ!

The Gemara responds: It **is reasonable** that her earnings should go **to her father, as, if it should enter your mind** to say that **her earnings** do **not** belong **to her father,** what about the fact **that the Merciful One entitles a father to bring** his daughter, when she is a young woman, **to the wedding canopy?**[N] **How can he bring her** to the wedding canopy? **Doesn't he** thereby **cause her to neglect her earnings** at that time, as she cannot work while getting married? If she has the rights to her own earnings, she can object on these grounds.

פָּרֵיךְ רַב אַחַאי: אֵימָא דְּיָהֵיב לַהּ שְׂכַר פִּקַּעְתָּהּ. אִי נַמִּי: דְּמָסַר לַהּ בְּלֵילְיָא. אִי נַמִּי: דְּמָסַר לַהּ בְּשַׁבָּתוֹת וְיָמִים טוֹבִים!

Rav Aḥai refutes this claim: **Say that** when he brings her to the wedding canopy, **he gives her the wages she neglects** by taking a break from her work, and therefore the above objection does not apply. **Alternatively,** it is referring to a case **where he brought her** to the wedding canopy **at night,** when she does not work. **Alternatively,** it means **that he brought her** to the wedding canopy **on *Shabbatot* or Festivals,** when it is prohibited to work.

אֶלָּא, קְטַנָּה לָא צְרִיכָא קְרָא: הָשְׁתָּא זַבּוּנֵי מְזַבֵּין לַהּ, מַעֲשֵׂה יָדֶיהָ מִיבָּעֵי?! [אֶלָּא] כִּי אִיצְטְרִיךְ קְרָא – לְנַעֲרָה.

Rather, the Gemara reverts to the original exposition based upon the case of a Hebrew maidservant, and argues that with regard to a **minor,** it **is not necessary** to derive from **a verse** that her father is entitled to her earnings, for the following reason: **Now,** if her father has the right to **sell her** as a maidservant, is it **necessary** to state that **her earnings** belong to him? **Rather, when the verse was necessary,** it was **to** teach that the earnings of **a young woman** also belong to her father.

״בַּהֲפָרַת נְדָרֶיהָ״. מְנָלַן? דִּכְתִיב ״בִּנְעוּרֶיהָ בֵּית אָבִיהָ״.

§ The mishna taught that a father is entitled **to** effect **the nullification of** his daughter's **vows.**[N] The Gemara asks: **From where do we** derive this? The Gemara answers **that it is written: "Being in her youth, in her father's house"** (Numbers 30:17), and the Torah proceeds to explain that during this period a father can nullify his daughter's vows.

״וּמְקַבֵּל אֶת גִּיטָּהּ״. מְנָלַן? דִּכְתִיב ״וְיָצְאָה וְהָיְתָה״ – אִיתְקוּשׁ יְצִיאָה לַהֲוָיָה.

The mishna further taught: **And he accepts her bill of divorce** on her behalf. The Gemara asks: **From where do we** derive this? The Gemara answers **that it is written: "And she departs** out of his house and goes **and becomes** another man's wife" (Deuteronomy 24:2). This verse **juxtaposes departing** a marriage **and becoming** a wife, which teaches that the *halakhot* of betrothal apply to her departing her husband's home via a bill of divorce. Consequently, just as a father has the right to accept betrothal on his daughter's behalf, he can also receive a bill of divorce on her behalf.

NOTES

Due to enmity – מִשּׁוּם אֵיבָה: Rashi explains that if the father bears feelings of ill will toward his daughter, he might refuse to provide her with sustenance. *Tosafot* prove that there is no connection between providing her with sustenance and being entitled to her found articles, as even if he does not support her he is still entitled to any lost property she finds. Consequently, they explain that his hostility might lead him to marry her off to an unsuitable man.

Entitles a father to bring his daughter to the wedding canopy – זַכֵּי לֵיהּ...לָאָב לְמִימְסְרָהּ לְחוּפָּה: Rashi cites a proof for this *halakha* from the expression: "I gave my daughter to this man" (Deuteronomy 22:16), which refers to both betrothal and the wedding canopy. Others explain that it is obvious that he can bring her to the wedding canopy, for if he cannot do so, what is the use of betrothing her to someone (Ramban; Rashba; Rabbeinu Crescas Vidal).

The nullification of his daughter's vows – הֲפָרַת נְדָרֶיהָ: Rashi asks why the Gemara cites a verse that merely alludes to this *halakha*, when it could have quoted the explicit phrase: "If her father disallow her on the day that he hears, none of her vows, or her bonds with which she has bound her soul, shall stand" (Numbers 30:6). He explains that the Gemara wanted to cite a proof that this *halakha* applies to a young woman as well as a minor. Other commentaries dismiss this question by stating that it is not unusual for the Gemara to cite one of multiple possible sources for a *halakha*. In these situations, it cites whichever verse is more familiar (Ritva).

״וְאֵינוֹ אוֹכֵל פֵּירוֹת בְּחַיֶּיהָ״. תָּנוּ רַבָּנַן: הָאָב אֵינוֹ אוֹכֵל פֵּירוֹת בְּחַיֵּי בִּתּוֹ. רַבִּי יוֹסֵי בְּרַבִּי יְהוּדָה אוֹמֵר: הָאָב אוֹכֵל פֵּירוֹת בְּחַיֵּי בִּתּוֹ. בְּמַאי קָמִיפַּלְגִי? תַּנָּא קַמָּא סָבַר: בִּשְׁלָמָא בַּעַל תַּקִּינוּ לֵיהּ רַבָּנַן פֵּירֵי, דְּאִם כֵּן מִימְנַע וְלָא פָּרֵיק,

§ The mishna taught that a father **may not consume** the **produce** of his daughter's property **during her lifetime. The Sages taught** in a *baraita*: **A father may not consume the produce** of his daughter's property **during his daughter's lifetime. Rabbi Yosei, son of Rabbi Yehuda, says: A father may consume** this **produce during his daughter's lifetime.** The Gemara asks: **With regard to what** principle **do they disagree?** The Gemara explains that **the first *tanna* holds: Granted,** in the case of **a husband, the Sages decreed for him** that he should consume her **produce, as if** this were not **so, he would refrain from redeeming** her if she were captured. The right of a husband to consume the produce of his wife's property was instituted in order to correspond to his obligation to redeem his wife from captivity.

אֶלָּא אָב מַאי אִיכָּא לְמֵימַר – דְּמִימְנַע וְלָא פָּרֵיק? בְּלָאו הָכִי פָּרֵיק לָהּ! וְרַבִּי יוֹסֵי בְּרַבִּי יְהוּדָה סָבַר: אָב נַמִי מִימְנַע וְלָא פָּרֵיק. סָבַר: כִּיסָא נְקִיטָא עִילָּוָהּ, תֵּיזִיל וְתִפְרוֹק נַפְשָׁהּ.

However, in the case of **a father, what is there to say? That he will refrain from redeeming** her? Even **without this** right to the produce of her property **he will redeem her,** as she is his daughter and he will certainly not turn a blind eye to his own flesh and blood. **And Rabbi Yosei, son of Rabbi Yehuda, holds:** If he is deprived of the right to the produce of his daughter's property, **a father will also refrain from redeeming** her, as he **will reason: A pouch** of money **is held in her** hand for a time of need, so **let her go and redeem herself.**

״נִיסֵּת – יָתֵר עָלָיו הַבַּעַל שֶׁהוּא אוֹכֵל״ כו׳. תָּנוּ רַבָּנַן: כָּתַב לָהּ פֵּירוֹת, כְּסוּת וְכֵלִים שֶׁיָּבוֹאוּ עִמָּהּ מִבֵּית אָבִיהָ לְבֵית בַּעְלָהּ. מֵתָה – לֹא זָכָה הַבַּעַל בִּדְבָרִים הַלָּלוּ. מִשּׁוּם רַבִּי נָתָן אָמְרוּ: זָכָה הַבַּעַל בִּדְבָרִים הַלָּלוּ.

§ The mishna further taught that if the daughter **married, the husband has more** rights **than** her father, **as he consumes** the produce of her property. **The Sages taught** in a *baraita*: If the father **wrote for her** in her marriage contract that he was providing **produce,**[N] **clothing, and vessels that would come with her** as a dowry **from her father's house to her husband's house,** and **she died** during the betrothal period, **the husband does not have the right to these objects. They said in the name of Rabbi Natan: The husband does have the right to these objects.**

לֵימָא בִּפְלוּגְתָּא דְּרַבִּי אֶלְעָזָר בֶּן עֲזַרְיָה וְרַבָּנַן קָמִיפַּלְגִי. דִּתְנַן: נִתְאַרְמְלָה אוֹ נִתְגָּרְשָׁה, בֵּין מִן הַנִּשּׂוּאִין בֵּין מִן הָאֵירוּסִין – גּוֹבָה אֶת הַכֹּל. רַבִּי אֶלְעָזָר בֶּן עֲזַרְיָה אוֹמֵר: מִן הַנִּשּׂוּאִין – גּוֹבָה אֶת הַכֹּל, וּמִן הָאֵירוּסִין – בְּתוּלָה גּוֹבָה מָאתַיִם, וְאַלְמָנָה מָנֶה,

The Gemara suggests: **Let us say that the dispute** of these *tanna'im* **is** parallel to **the dispute** between **Rabbi Elazar ben Azarya and the Rabbis. As we learned** in a mishna (54b): If a woman **was widowed or divorced, whether from marriage or from betrothal, she collects** the **entire** sum specified in her marriage contract, including any extra amount her husband added to the standard sum required by the Sages. **Rabbi Elazar ben Azarya says:** If she was widowed or divorced **from marriage, she collects** the **entire** amount. **But** if she was widowed or divorced **from betrothal,** she is entitled to collect only the standard minimum sum required by the Sages: If she was betrothed as **a virgin she collects two hundred** dinars, **and** if she was **a widow** she is entitled to **one hundred dinars.**

NOTES

He wrote for her in her marriage contract that he was providing produce, etc. – **כָּתַב לָהּ פֵּירוֹת וכו׳**: The early authorities disagree about whether this is referring to a betrothed or a married woman. Some maintain that this is referring to a betrothed woman, which means that even the Rabbis agree in the case of a married woman that the husband receives everything (*ge'onim*; Rabbeinu Ḥananel; Rashi; Rambam). However, others raise several difficulties with this interpretation (Rabbeinu Tam; Razah). First of all, the context is problematic, as this *baraita* is quoted in the context of the Gemara's discussion of married women. Furthermore, the *halakha* is that a husband does not inherit from his wife if they are merely betrothed. Yet another problem is that if this refers to betrothal, the term marriage that appears at the end of the Gemara's discussion of this *baraita* (47b) is unsuitable. Instead, the Gemara should have used a term that refers to betrothal. For these and other reasons, some commentaries explain that this *baraita* is referring to a married woman who has not yet been brought into her husband's house (see *Tosafot* and *Sefer HaYashar*).

Other early authorities offer various resolutions of the difficulties. With regard to the context, some explain that there is a connection between the two discussions according to the opinion of the Rabbis that a husband gains rights to his wife's dowry only from the time of their marriage, not the betrothal (Ramban). As for the difficulty that a husband does not generally inherit his wife's property if she dies while she is betrothed, it is possible that because the father wrote down his obligations, the husband is entitled to whatever was written in the document. Even the problem of the term marriage can be resolved, as from the perspective of the father this relationship is comparable to marriage. Additionally, the opinion of Rabbeinu Tam is not free of difficulties either, and therefore most early authorities accept the interpretation of Rashi and Rabbeinu Ḥananel (see Ritva and *Nimmukei Yosef*).

Perek **IV**
Daf **47** Amud **b**

שֶׁלֹּא כָּתַב לָהּ אֶלָּא עַל מְנָת לְכוֹנְסָהּ. לְמַאן דְּאָמַר לֹא זָכָה – כְּרַבִּי אֶלְעָזָר בֶּן עֲזַרְיָה, וּמַאן דְּאָמַר זָכָה – כְּרַבָּנַן.

The reason is **that he wrote** that she would be entitled to the additional amount **only on the condition** that he would **marry her,** and since he did not marry her, she is not entitled to the extra amount. The Gemara compares the respective opinions: **The one who says** that the husband does **not have the right** to her dowry holds **in accordance with** the opinion of **Rabbi Elazar ben Azarya,** and therefore he rules that just as a husband guarantees his wife an extra sum in her marriage contract only if they actually get married, the wife's father also gives the dowry only the condition that the couple marries. **And the one who said** that the husband does **have the right** to her dowry holds **in accordance with** the opinion of **the Rabbis,** because the document is fully in effect even before marriage.

לָא, דְּכוּלֵּי עָלְמָא כְּרַבִּי אֶלְעָזָר בֶּן עֲזַרְיָה. מַאן דְּאָמַר לֹא זָכָה – כְּרַבִּי אֶלְעָזָר בֶּן עֲזַרְיָה, וּמַאן דְּאָמַר זָכָה – עַד כָּאן לָא קָאָמַר רַבִּי אֶלְעָזָר בֶּן עֲזַרְיָה אֶלָּא מִדִּידֵיהּ לְדִידָהּ, שֶׁלֹּא כָּתַב לָהּ אֶלָּא עַל מְנָת לְכוֹנְסָהּ.

The Gemara refutes this suggestion: **No, everyone agrees** that the *halakha* is **in accordance with** the opinion of **Rabbi Elazar ben Azarya,** and the explanation is as follows: **The one who said** that he does **not have the right** to the dowry clearly holds **in accordance with** the opinion of **Rabbi Elazar ben Azarya,** as stated above; **and the one who says** the husband does **have the right** to her dowry would distinguish between the two cases: **Rabbi Elazar ben Azarya states** that the marriage contract is not fully in effect until marriage **only with regard to** a bestowal **from him to her,** i.e., the extra sum that the husband adds to her marriage contract, **as he wrote** it **for her only on the condition** that he would **marry her,** and he did not intend to give her anything before she became his wife.

אֲבָל מִדִּידָהּ לְדִידֵיהּ – אֲפִילּוּ רַבִּי אֶלְעָזָר בֶּן עֲזַרְיָה מוֹדֵי דְּמִשּׁוּם אִיחַתּוּנֵי הוּא, וְהָא אִיחַתְּנֵי לְהוּ.

However, with regard to that which is given **from her** father **to him,** i.e., the dowry, even **Rabbi Elazar ben Azarya concedes** that the husband is entitled to this money, as the gift of a father **is due to marriage,**[H] i.e., he wants the families to be joined in matrimony, **and they have** already become linked **in marriage.** The dowry given by the father has nothing to do with the transition from betrothal to actual marriage.

״חַיָּיב בִּמְזוֹנוֹתֶיהָ״ וכו׳. תָּנוּ רַבָּנַן: תִּיקְּנוּ מְזוֹנוֹתֶיהָ תַּחַת מַעֲשֵׂה יָדֶיהָ וּקְבוּרָתָהּ תַּחַת כְּתוּבָּתָהּ. לְפִיכָךְ בַּעַל אוֹכֵל פֵּירוֹת.

§ The mishna teaches that a husband **is obligated** to provide his wife with **sustenance,** redemption from captivity, and burial. **The Sages taught** in a *baraita*: The Rabbis **instituted** that a husband must provide his wife with **her sustenance in exchange for** his rights to **her earnings, and** similarly they decreed that a husband must tend to **her burial in exchange for** the fact that he inherits the dowry that she brought into the marriage and which is written in **her marriage contract. Consequently,** the **husband may consume the produce** of her property.

פֵּירוֹת מַאן דְּכַר שְׁמַיְיהוּ?! חַסּוּרֵי מִחַסְּרָא, וְהָכִי קָתָנֵי: תִּיקְּנוּ מְזוֹנוֹתֶיהָ תַּחַת מַעֲשֵׂה יָדֶיהָ, וּפֵירְקוֹנָהּ תַּחַת פֵּירוֹת, וּקְבוּרָתָהּ תַּחַת כְּתוּבָּתָהּ. לְפִיכָךְ בַּעַל אוֹכֵל פֵּירוֹת.

The Gemara expresses surprise at this last statement: **Produce, who mentioned** anything about **that?** The *baraita* did not previously mention produce at all, so how did it arrive at a halakhic conclusion with regard to produce? The Gemara explains that the *baraita* **is incomplete, and this** is what **it is teaching: They instituted** that a husband must provide his wife with **her sustenance in exchange for** his rights to **her earnings; and** it is his duty to provide **her** with **redemption** from captivity **in exchange for** his right to consume the **produce** of her property;[N] **and** it is his obligation to attend to **her burial in exchange for** the fact that he inherits the dowry that she brought into the marriage and which is written in **her marriage contract. Consequently, a husband may consume the produce** of her property.

מַאי לְפִיכָךְ?

Although the Gemara has explained how the *tanna* came to speak about produce, the wording of the *baraita* remains problematic. **What** is the significance of the word **consequently** in this context?

מַהוּ דְּתֵימָא: מֵיכַל לָא נִכְלִינְהוּ, אַנּוּחֵי – נַנְחִינְהוּ, דְּאִם כֵּן מִימְנַע וְלָא פָּרֵיק, קָא מַשְׁמַע לָן דְּהָא עֲדִיפָא, זִימְנִין דְּלָא מָלוּ וּפָרֵיק לָהּ מִדִּידֵיהּ.

The Gemara explains: **Lest you say** that the husband should **not consume the produce** but **leave it**[N] so that if he requires funds to redeem his wife he will have them available, **as, if** he is not compelled to do **so he will refrain from redeeming** her, as he will be unwilling to spend his own money for that purpose; the *tanna* therefore **teaches us that this** arrangement **is preferable,** because **sometimes** the produce **will not amount** to the funds necessary to redeem her from captivity, **and** he would not redeem her if he was expected to use the funds produced by her property. Consequently, the Sages decreed that he consumes the produce immediately and that he must **redeem her from his own** funds if she is taken into captivity.

וְאֵיפוּךְ אֲנָא!

After analyzing the language of the *baraita,* the Gemara turns its attention to the *halakha* itself. **But I can reverse**[N] these connections; why does the *baraita* say that a husband's obligation to provide his wife with sustenance was instituted in exchange for his right to her earnings, as opposed to another of his rights, e.g., his right to consume the produce of her property?

HALAKHA

Due to marriage – מִשּׁוּם אִיחַתּוּנֵי הוּא: If a father assigned money for his daughter's dowry and she died before marriage but after her father had taken leave of her as she went to the wedding canopy, some authorities say that the husband is entitled to the entire amount (Rambam). Others maintain that even after she is actually married, if the husband did not claim the money before her death he receives nothing, as the father intended to give him the sum only for his daughter's benefit (Rabbeinu Tam). Some rule that due to the uncertainty, the father cannot be forced to pay (Maharik).

There are numerous other relevant variables with regard to this *halakha*, e.g., if the money was entrusted to a third party. In practice, different places established protocols that were binding for their communities with regard to the various situations, e.g., the decree of Toledo, and the joint decree of the communities of Speyer, Worms, and Mainz (see Rambam *Sefer Nashim, Hilkhot Ishut* 22:2, 23:15; *Shulḥan Arukh, Even HaEzer* 53:3, and in the comment of Rema).

NOTES

Redemption in exchange for produce of her property – וּפֵירְקוֹנָהּ תַּחַת פֵּירוֹת: Although one might think that the ordinance that the husband has the right to consume the produce of her property is the more basic of the two ordinances, while his obligation to redeem her from captivity was added to correspond to it, most commentaries maintain that the husband's duty to redeem his wife is the main one. The continuation of the Gemara indicates likewise (see *Tosafot* and Ramban). Consequently, a husband cannot relinquish his right to the produce and thereby be released from the obligation to pay for her freedom. This is stated in the Jerusalem Talmud according to some commentaries' version of the text (Meiri). However, some commentaries maintain that the ordinance granting the husband the right to consume his wife's produce is, in fact, the more basic of the two ordinances (Rashbam on *Bava Batra* 49b).

Leave it – אַנּוּחֵי נַנְחִינְהוּ: If the husband is to leave the produce, what benefit does he derive from it? Some commentaries (Ritva, citing *Tosafot*) explain that the husband would use the produce to purchase land in his wife's name, and consume the produce of that land. See *Tosafot* for an alternative explanation.

But I can reverse – וְאֵיפוּךְ אֲנָא: Rashi explains: One can say that his obligation to provide her with sustenance is in exchange for his right to consume the produce of her property. Other commentaries maintain that this cannot be the case. Instead they explain that his right to consume the produce of her property is in exchange for his obligation to attend to her burial (*Tosafot* on 52a; Maharshal).

אָמַר אַבָּיֵי: תִּיקְּנוּ מָצוּי לְמָצוּי, וְשֶׁאֵינוֹ מָצוּי לְשֶׁאֵינוֹ מָצוּי.

Abaye said: The Sages **instituted a common** obligation in exchange **for a common** right, **and** they instituted **an uncommon** obligation in exchange **for an uncommon** right. In other words, the Sages instituted a husband's obligation to provide his wife with sustenance, which is relevant on a regular basis, in exchange for his right to her earnings, which also applies regularly. The other obligations and rights of a husband are relevant less frequently.

אָמַר רָבָא: הַאי תַּנָּא סָבַר מְזוֹנוֹת מִדְּאוֹרַיְיתָא, דְּתַנְיָא: ״שְׁאֵרָהּ״ – אֵלּוּ מְזוֹנוֹת, וְכֵן הוּא אוֹמֵר ״וַאֲשֶׁר אָכְלוּ שְׁאֵר עַמִּי״. ״כְּסוּתָהּ״ – כְּמַשְׁמָעוֹ. ״עוֹנָתָהּ״ – זוֹ עוֹנָה, הָאֲמוּרָה בַּתּוֹרָה, וְכֵן הוּא אוֹמֵר ״אִם תְּעַנֶּה אֶת בְּנוֹתַי״.

§ **Rava said: This *tanna*,** in the *baraita* cited below, **maintains** that the obligation of a husband to provide his wife's **sustenance** applies **by Torah** law, **as it is taught** with regard to the verse pertaining to a husband's obligations toward his wife: "If he takes another wife for himself, her food [*she'era*], her clothing [*kesuta*], and her conjugal rights [*onata*], he shall not diminish" (Exodus 21:10). **"*She'era*"; this is sustenance,**[N] **and it likewise states: "Who also eat the flesh [*she'er*] of my people"** (Micah 3:3). **"*Kesuta*"** is understood **in its literal sense** as referring to clothing. **"*Onata*";**[N] **this is** her **conjugal rights, which is stated in the Torah, and so it says: "If you shall afflict [*te'aneh*] my daughters"** (Genesis 31:50), which indicates that a husband may not deprive his wife of her conjugal rights.[H]

רַבִּי אֶלְעָזָר אוֹמֵר: ״שְׁאֵרָהּ״ – זוֹ עוֹנָה, וְכֵן הוּא אוֹמֵר ״אִישׁ אִישׁ אֶל כׇּל שְׁאֵר בְּשָׂרוֹ לֹא תִקְרְבוּ לְגַלּוֹת עֶרְוָה״. ״כְּסוּתָהּ״ – כְּמַשְׁמָעוֹ. ״עוֹנָתָהּ״ אֵלּוּ מְזוֹנוֹת, וְכֵן הוּא אוֹמֵר ״וַיְעַנְּךָ וַיַּרְעִבֶךָ״.

The *baraita* continues: **Rabbi Elazar says: "*She'era*"; this is** her **conjugal rights, and so it says: "None of you shall approach to any who is near [*she'er*] of kin to him, to uncover their nakedness"** (Leviticus 18:6), which demonstrates that the word *she'er* is used in the context of sexual relations. **"*Kesuta*"** is understood **in its literal sense** as referring to clothing. **"*Onata*"; this is sustenance, and so it says: "And He afflicted you [*vayanekha*], and made you suffer hunger,** and fed you with manna" (Deuteronomy 8:3).

NOTES

She'era, this is sustenance, etc. – שְׁאֵרָה אֵלּוּ מְזוֹנוֹת וכו׳: Apparently, these *tanna'im* maintain that a husband's obligation to provide his wife with sustenance and clothing applies by Torah law. Some suggest that Rava did not explicitly mention this with regard to clothing because all opinions mentioned in the *baraita* agree that it is the plain meaning of the word *kesuta* in the verse, and something that is stated explicitly in the Torah does not have to be mentioned (Ran). However, the Ramban claims that the duties of sustenance and clothing apply by rabbinic law, in accordance with the interpretation of the verse provided by Rav Yosef (see Ramban's Commentary to the Torah, Exodus 21:10).

Onata, etc. – עוֹנָתָהּ וכו׳: The commentaries explain that the term *"onata"* can refer to a period of time [*ona*] as well as suffering [*inui*] (*HaBoneh*). See Rashash, who argues that these *tanna'im* interpret *"onata"* as the prevention of her suffering.

HALAKHA

Food, clothing, and conjugal rights – שְׁאֵר כְּסוּת וְעוֹנָה: By Torah law, there are three obligations of a husband toward his wife: He must provide her with food and with clothing, and he must engage in intercourse with her at regular intervals. This is the ruling of the Rambam, in accordance with the unattributed opinion in the *baraita*. By contrast, the Ramban maintains that only conjugal rights are a Torah obligation, whereas providing her with food and clothing is required by rabbinic law. Some claim (*Maggid Mishne*; see *Beit Shmuel*) that the conjugal rights and clothing apply by Torah law, while providing her with food is by rabbinic law (Rambam *Sefer Nashim*, *Hilkhot Ishut* 12:2; *Shulḥan Arukh*, *Even HaEzer* 69:2).

Perek **IV**
Daf **48** Amud **a**

רַבִּי אֱלִיעֶזֶר בֶּן יַעֲקֹב אוֹמֵר: ״שְׁאֵרָהּ כְּסוּתָהּ״ – לְפוּם שְׁאֵרָהּ תֵּן כְּסוּתָהּ. שֶׁלֹּא יִתֵּן לָהּ לֹא שֶׁל יַלְדָּה לִזְקֵינָה, וְלֹא שֶׁל זְקֵינָה לְיַלְדָּה. ״כְּסוּתָהּ וְעוֹנָתָהּ״ – לְפוּם עוֹנָתָהּ תֵּן כְּסוּתָהּ, שֶׁלֹּא יִתֵּן חֲדָשִׁים בִּימוֹת הַחַמָּה וְלֹא שְׁחָקִים בִּימוֹת הַגְּשָׁמִים.

Rabbi Eliezer ben Ya'akov says that ***she'era*** and ***kesuta***[N] should be interpreted as follows: **In accordance with her flesh [*she'era*],** i.e., her age, **give her clothing [*kesuta*].** This means **that he should not give** the garments **of a young girl to an elderly woman, nor those of an elderly woman to a young girl.** Similarly, ***kesuta*** **and *onata*** are linked: **In accordance with the time** of year **[*onata*], give her clothing [*kesuta*],** meaning **that he should not give new,** heavy clothes[H] **in the summer, nor worn-out** garments **in the rainy season,** i.e., the winter, when she requires heavier, warmer clothes. The entire phrase, therefore, refers only to a husband's obligation to provide clothing for his wife.

תָּנֵי רַב יוֹסֵף: ״שְׁאֵרָהּ״ – זוֹ קֵרוּב בָּשָׂר, שֶׁלֹּא יִנְהַג בָּהּ מִנְהַג פָּרְסִיִּים, שֶׁמְּשַׁמְּשִׁין מִטּוֹתֵיהֶן בִּלְבוּשֵׁיהֶן. מְסַיַּיע לֵיהּ לְרַב הוּנָא, דְּאָמַר רַב הוּנָא: הָאוֹמֵר ״אִי אֶפְשִׁי אֶלָּא אֲנִי בְּבִגְדִי וְהִיא בְּבִגְדָהּ״ – יוֹצִיא וְנוֹתֵן כְּתוּבָּה.

Rav Yosef taught the following *baraita*: **"*She'era*," this** is referring to **closeness of flesh** during intercourse, which teaches **that he should not treat her in the manner of Persians,**[N] **who have conjugal relations in their clothes.** The Gemara comments: This *baraita* **supports** the opinion of **Rav Huna, as Rav Huna said:** With regard to **one who says: I do not want** to have intercourse with my wife **unless I am in my clothes**[H] **and she is in her clothes, he must divorce** his wife **and give** her the payment for her **marriage contract.** This is in keeping with the opinion of the *tanna* of the *baraita* that the Torah mandates the intimacy of flesh during sexual relations.

HALAKHA

He should not give new, heavy clothes, etc. – לֹא יִתֵּן חֲדָשִׁים וכו׳: A husband is obligated to provide his wife with suitable clothing in the winter and the summer, in accordance with the opinion of Rabbi Eliezer ben Ya'akov and the ruling of the mishna in *Ketubot* 64b (Rambam *Sefer Nashim*, *Hilkhot Ishut* 13:1; *Shulḥan Arukh*, *Even HaEzer* 73:1).

I am in my clothes, etc. – אֲנִי בְּבִגְדִי וכו׳: If a husband says he is willing to have relations with his wife only if they both remain clothed, he must divorce her and pay her the marriage contract, as stated by Rav Huna (*Shulḥan Arukh*, *Even HaEzer* 76:13).

NOTES

She'era and *kesuta* – שְׁאֵרָהּ כְּסוּתָהּ: *Tosafot* quote the rest of the *baraita*, which appears in the *Mekhilta* and is also cited in the Jerusalem Talmud (*Ketubot* 5:7). The *baraita* adds that Rabbi Eliezer ben Ya'akov derives the obligations of sustenance and conjugal relations by an *a fortiori* inference. Since a law derived via an *a fortiori* inference has the status of Torah law, *Tosafot* claim that the question of the identity of the *tanna* cited on 47b who maintains that the Sages instituted that a husband must provide food for his wife in exchange for his right to her earnings, indicating that the responsibility to provide her with food is of rabbinic origin, is left unresolved. However, many other early authorities contend that the *baraita* cited by Rav Yosef, which maintains that *she'era* means closeness of flesh, indicates that a husband's obligation to provide food for his wife is of rabbinic origin.

The manner of Persians – מִנְהַג פָּרְסִיִּים: Some commentaries connect this to a statement in *Berakhot* (8a). The problem is that there the Gemara is apparently praising the Persians for their modest conduct during intercourse, whereas here it rejects their conduct. Some commentaries state that even if the husband claims to be acting for reasons of modesty, he must divorce her and pay her the marriage contract (Ritva). Others note the Gemara elsewhere praises those who have relations in their clothes (*Magen Avraham* on *Shulḥan Arukh*, *Oraḥ Ḥayyim* 240:8). The *Magen Avraham* rules that if both partners agree, it is considered a form of modesty (see *Mishna Berura* and *Sha'ar HaTziyyun* on *Shulḥan Arukh*, *Oraḥ Ḥayyim* 240:8).

NOTES

Where it is the common custom for his family, etc. – **כְּגוֹן דְּאוֹרְחֵיהּ דִּידֵיהּ וכו׳**: Some commentaries ask: If the dispute is over whether to follow the custom of his family or hers in a case when his family's custom is to perform a public eulogy for women and her family's custom is not to do so, why does Rabbi Yehuda specify a particular number of flutes that must accompany the eulogy? He should simply state that the eulogy must follow the custom of the husband's family. One answer is that this refers to a situation where his family had the custom to perform a public eulogy, but did not have a clearly defined custom with regard to the number of flutes. Rabbi Yehuda rules that it is not considered a public eulogy, even for the poorest Jew, with fewer than two flutes (*Talmidei Rabbeinu Yona*). Alternatively, even if he is required to arrange a public eulogy, in accordance with the custom of his family, he does not have to provide a eulogy that exactly matches the custom of his family. Rather, it enough if he hires two flutes and a lamenting woman (Ritva).

But not his sons and daughters – **אֲבָל לֹא בָּנָיו וּבְנוֹתָיו**: Later in the Gemara (see 49a–b) there is a detailed discussion of a father's obligation to provide for his children. The duty of a husband to support his wife is either a Torah commandment (see 47b), or an obligation imposed through the marriage contract he gave her. Conversely, with regard to his children there is a difference between children younger than six, minors over the age of six, and grown children.

In addition to the legal obligation, there is also the consideration of whether the court may rely on the fact that the man was supporting his children before he left and can therefore assume that he would want to continue supporting them (see Meiri and Ran).

״רַבִּי יְהוּדָה אוֹמֵר: אֲפִילּוּ עָנִי שֶׁבְּיִשְׂרָאֵל״ וכו׳. מִכְּלָל דְּתַנָּא קַמָּא סָבַר הָנֵי לָא. הֵיכִי דָּמֵי? אִי דְּאוֹרְחָהּ – מַאי טַעְמָא דְּתַנָּא קַמָּא דַּאֲמַר לָא? וְאִי דְּלָאו אוֹרְחָהּ – מַאי טַעְמָא דְּרַבִּי יְהוּדָה?

§ The mishna teaches that **Rabbi Yehuda says: Even the poorest** man **of the Jewish people** may not provide fewer than two flutes and a lamenting woman for his wife's funeral. The Gemara infers: This proves **by inference that the first,** anonymous *tanna* cited in the mishna **holds** that **these are not** part of a husband's obligations. The Gemara asks: **What are the circumstances? If this is** the **common** custom in **her** family at funerals, **what is the reason for** the opinion of **the first** *tanna* **who said** that he does **not** have to do so? If he neglected to provide these items he would be treating her with disrespect. **And if** this **is not** the **common** custom in **her** family, **what is the reason for** the opinion of **Rabbi Yehuda?**

לָא צְרִיכָא, כְּגוֹן דְּאוֹרְחֵיהּ דִּידֵיהּ וְלָאו אוֹרְחָהּ דִּידַהּ. תַּנָּא קַמָּא סָבַר: כִּי אָמְרִינַן עוֹלָה עִמּוֹ וְאֵינָהּ יוֹרֶדֶת עִמּוֹ – הָנֵי מִילֵּי מֵחַיִּים, אֲבָל לְאַחַר מִיתָה – לָא.

The Gemara answers: **No,** it is **necessary** to state their dispute in a case **where** it is the **common** custom for **his** family[N] according to its social status, **but** it is **not common** for **her** family according to its social status. **The first** *tanna* **holds: When we say** that a woman who marries a man **ascends with him,** i.e., she must be treated as equal in status to her husband if his social status is higher than hers, **and does not descend with him** if he is from a lower social status, **this applies only** when they are **alive, but after death** the Sages did **not** enforce this rule.

וְרַבִּי יְהוּדָה סָבַר: אֲפִילּוּ לְאַחַר מִיתָה. אָמַר רַב חִסְדָּא אָמַר מָר עוּקְבָא: הֲלָכָה כְּרַבִּי יְהוּדָה.

And Rabbi Yehuda maintains: Even after death she must be treated in accordance with his status, which means that if those in his family are mourned with flutes and lamenting women, he must provide the same for her funeral. **Rav Ḥisda said** that **Mar Ukva said: The** ***halakha*** **is in accordance with** the opinion of **Rabbi Yehuda.**

וְאָמַר רַב חִסְדָּא אָמַר מָר עוּקְבָא: מִי שֶׁנִּשְׁתַּטָּה – בֵּית דִּין יוֹרְדִין לִנְכָסָיו, וְזָנִין וּמְפַרְנְסִין אֶת אִשְׁתּוֹ וּבָנָיו וּבְנוֹתָיו וְדָבָר אַחֵר. אֲמַר לֵיהּ רָבִינָא לְרַב אָשֵׁי. מַאי שְׁנָא מֵהָא דְּתַנְיָא: מִי שֶׁהָלַךְ לִמְדִינַת הַיָּם וְאִשְׁתּוֹ תּוֹבַעַת מְזוֹנוֹת – בֵּית דִּין יוֹרְדִין לִנְכָסָיו וְזָנִין וּמְפַרְנְסִין אֶת אִשְׁתּוֹ, אֲבָל לֹא בָּנָיו וּבְנוֹתָיו, וְלֹא דָּבָר אַחֵר!

Apropos this ruling, the Gemara cites another statement that **Rav Ḥisda said** that **Mar Ukva said:** With regard to **one who became insane,**[H] the **court enters his property and feeds and provides a livelihood for his wife, his sons, and his daughters, and** it also gives **something else,** as will be explained. **Ravina said to Rav Ashi:** In **what** way **is this** case **different from that which is taught** in a *baraita*: In the case of **one who went overseas**[H] **and his wife claims sustenance,** the **court descends to his property and feeds and provides a livelihood for his wife, but not** for **his sons and daughters**[N] **and** does **not** give **something else.** If a father is not obligated to sustain his children in his absence, what is different about a situation where he is mad?

אֲמַר לֵיהּ: וְלָא שָׁאנֵי לָךְ בֵּין יוֹצֵא לָדַעַת לְיוֹצֵא שֶׁלֹּא לָדַעַת?

Rav Ashi **said to** Ravina: **Is there no difference for you between** a man who **leaves** his responsibilities **knowingly and one who leaves** them **unknowingly?** A father who lost his sanity did not do so by his own choice, and therefore it can be assumed that he would want to provide for his children from his possessions, despite the fact that he is not obligated to do so. By contrast, if he went overseas he freely decided to depart, and one would think that he would leave enough for his sons and daughters. If he failed to do so, he has demonstrated that he does not want to provide for them.

HALAKHA

One who became insane, etc. – **מִי שֶׁנִּשְׁתַּטָּה וכו׳**: If a man lost his sanity, the court uses his property to provide for his wife, as well as for his sons and daughters until their maturity. This is in accordance with the opinion of the *Tur* and the Ran as opposed to that of the Rambam, who rules that if he is not wealthy his property is used to support only his children who are less than six years old (*Ḥelkat Meḥokek*; Rambam *Sefer Nashim, Hilkhot Ishut* 12:17 and *Kesef Mishne* there; *Shulḥan Arukh, Even HaEzer* 71:3).

One who went overseas, etc. – **מִי שֶׁהָלַךְ לִמְדִינַת הַיָּם וכו׳**: If a man left his wife and children and traveled overseas, after three months the court uses his property to support his wife and his children who are younger than six. However, his property is not used to support his children who are age six and older. Some authorities maintain that if the man had been supporting his children before his departure, the court uses his property in order to continue supporting them (Rema, citing Mordekhai). According to the *Tur*, if he is a man of means the court provides sustenance for his older children in all cases. The Rambam disagrees with this ruling (Rambam *Sefer Nashim, Hilkhot Ishut* 12:16; *Shulḥan Arukh, Even HaEzer* 70:5; 71:2).

מַאי דָּבָר אַחֵר? רַב חִסְדָּא אָמַר: זֶה תַּכְשִׁיט – רַב יוֹסֵף אָמַר: צְדָקָה. מַאן דַּאֲמַר תַּכְשִׁיט – כׇּל שֶׁכֵּן צְדָקָה, מַאן דַּאֲמַר צְדָקָה – אֲבָל תַּכְשִׁיט יָהֲבִינַן לָהּ, דְּלָא נִיחָא לֵיהּ דְּתִיתְנַוַּול.

The Gemara asks: **What is** this **something else**[N] mentioned in the *baraita*? **Rav Ḥisda said: This is** a wife's **ornaments,**[H] to which she is entitled in addition to her sustenance. **Rav Yosef said:** It is money for **charity.**[H] The Gemara comments: According to **the one who says** that the court does not pay for a woman's **ornaments** from her husband's property if he has gone overseas, **all the more so** he maintains that the husband's property is not taken for **charity.** Conversely, **the one who says** that the court does not give money for **charity** holds that this applies only to charity, **but it does give her ornaments,** as it is assumed **that it is not satisfactory for him** that his wife **be demeaned** by a lack of jewelry.

אָמַר רַב חִיָּיא בַּר אָבִין אָמַר רַב הוּנָא: מִי שֶׁהָלַךְ לִמְדִינַת הַיָּם וּמֵתָה אִשְׁתּוֹ – בֵּית דִּין יוֹרְדִין לִנְכָסָיו, וְקוֹבְרִין אוֹתָהּ לְפִי כְּבוֹדוֹ. לְפִי כְבוֹדוֹ וְלֹא לְפִי כְבוֹדָהּ?!

Rav Ḥiyya bar Avin said that **Rav Huna said:** In the case of **one who went overseas and his wife died,** the **court enters his property and buries her**[H] **in accordance with his dignity.** The Gemara asks: Does the court act **in accordance with his dignity and not in accordance with her dignity?**[N] What if she came from a more dignified family than her husband?

אֵימָא: אַף לְפִי כְבוֹדוֹ. הָא קָא מַשְׁמַע לַן: עוֹלָה עִמּוֹ וְאֵינָהּ יוֹרֶדֶת עִמּוֹ, וַאֲפִילּוּ לְאַחַר מִיתָה.

The Gemara answers: **Say** that Rav Ḥiyya bar Avin meant: **Even in accordance with his dignity,** i.e., if his family was more distinguished than hers, he must bury her in accordance with the dignity of his family. The Gemara adds: **This** comes to **teach us** that **she ascends with him** to his social status **and does not descend with him, and** this principle applies **even after** her **death,** in accordance with Rabbi Yehuda's opinion in the mishna.

אָמַר רַב מַתָּנָה: הָאוֹמֵר "אִם מֵתָה לֹא תִּקְבְּרוּהָ מִנְּכָסָיו" – שׁוֹמְעִין לוֹ. מַאי שְׁנָא כִּי אָמַר – דְּנָפְלִי נִכְסֵי קַמֵּי יַתְמֵי, כִּי לָא אָמַר נַמִי – נִכְסֵי קַמֵּי יַתְמֵי רְמוּ!

Rav Mattana said: In the case of **one who says** that **if** his wife **dies,** they should **not bury her** using funds **from his property,** the court **listens to him.** The Gemara asks: **What is different** about the case **when** he **says** this command that induces the court to comply with his wishes? It is due to the fact **that the property has come before the orphans** as an inheritance, while the obligation to bury her is not incumbent upon them but is a duty of the inheritors of her marriage contract. However, **even if he did not state** the above preference, **the property is cast before the orphans** and it belongs to them. What does it matter whether or not the husband issued a command to this effect?

אֶלָּא, הָאוֹמֵר "אִם מֵת הוּא לֹא תִּקְבְּרוּהוּ מִנְּכָסָיו" – אֵין שׁוֹמְעִין לוֹ, לָאו כׇּל הֵימֶנּוּ שֶׁיַּעֲשִׁיר אֶת בָּנָיו, וְיַפִּיל עַצְמוֹ עַל הַצִּיבּוּר.

Rather, the Gemara amends Rav Mattana's statement: With regard to **one who says** that **if he** himself **dies,** they should **not bury him** using funds **from his property,**[H] **one does not listen to him,** but the court spends his money without resorting to charity. The reason for this is that it is **not in his power to enrich his sons** by saving them this expense **and to cast himself** as a burden **on the community.**

מתני׳ לְעוֹלָם הִיא בִּרְשׁוּת הָאָב עַד שֶׁתִּכָּנֵס

MISHNA Even after she is betrothed, a daughter **is always under her father's authority until she enters**

NOTES

Something else – **דָּבָר אַחֵר**: Although the Sages established a fixed sum in a marriage contract for the purchase of cosmetics, which is the ornamentation referred to here, since the purpose of these cosmetics is to endear the woman to her husband, one can understand why they are not given to a woman whose husband is overseas (Rivan). This is especially true according to another version of the text, which reads: It is satisfactory for him that his wife be demeaned, i.e., an absent husband has no interest in his wife looking her best, so as not to attract the attentions of other men. Others, who probably had a similar version of the Gemara, maintain that one does not provide ornaments to a wife of a man who lost his sanity, as he does not have the state of mind to desire her (Rid). Yet others explain, in accordance with the standard version of the text, that the court does not force a woman whose husband has become insane to be without cosmetics on a permanent basis, whereas a husband who has gone overseas is expected to return, and therefore she can temporarily do without ornaments (*Beit Shmuel*).

In accordance with his dignity and not in accordance with her dignity – **לְפִי כְבוֹדוֹ וְלֹא לְפִי כְבוֹדָהּ**: Some commentaries note that this question pertains to all opinions, as even those Sages who maintain that she does not ascend with him after death agree that she does not descend from her previous status (Rid).

HALAKHA

Ornaments – **תַּכְשִׁיט**: If a husband traveled overseas and the court ruled that his wife is entitled to receive sustenance, they do not give her money for ornaments. However, a woman whose husband became insane does get an allowance for this purpose. Apparently, the Rambam rules in accordance with the opinion of Rav Ḥisda; however, there are various versions of the text, and therefore it is possible that the Rambam follows Rav Yosef's opinion (Rambam *Sefer Nashim, Hilkhot Ishut* 13:7; *Shulḥan Arukh, Even HaEzer* 70:5–6).

Charity – **צְדָקָה**: If a husband became insane, the court determines the appropriate amount of charity that should be given from his estate (Rambam *Sefer Mishpatim, Hilkhot Naḥalot* 11:11; *Shulḥan Arukh, Ḥoshen Mishpat* 290:15).

Burial – **קְבוּרָה**: In the case of a man who went overseas and his wife died, if necessary the court will sell his property without issuing a public announcement, and bury her in accordance with her husband's status and means, or in accordance with her own status if she came from a more distinguished family. The *halakha* is in accordance with the opinion of Rabbi Yehuda (Rambam *Sefer Nashim, Hilkhot Ishut* 14:24; *Shulḥan Arukh, Even HaEzer* 89:3).

They should not bury him using funds from his property – **לֹא תִּקְבְּרוּהוּ מִנְּכָסָיו**: In the case of one who commands his heirs not to pay for his burial with funds from his estate, the court takes no heed of this directive and forces the heirs to pay for his burial, as well as other items customary for the dead, including a tombstone, in accordance with the opinion of Rav Mattana (Rambam *Sefer Kinyan, Hilkhot Zekhiya* 11:24; *Shulḥan Arukh, Yoreh De'a* 348:2).

לִרְשׁוּת הַבַּעַל לְנִשּׂוּאִין. מָסַר הָאָב לִשְׁלוּחֵי הַבַּעַל – הֲרֵי הִיא בִּרְשׁוּת הַבַּעַל. הָלַךְ הָאָב עִם שְׁלוּחֵי הַבַּעַל, אוֹ שֶׁהָלְכוּ שְׁלוּחֵי הָאָב עִם שְׁלוּחֵי הַבַּעַל – הֲרֵי הִיא בִּרְשׁוּת הָאָב. מָסְרוּ שְׁלוּחֵי הָאָב לִשְׁלוּחֵי הַבַּעַל – הֲרֵי הִיא בִּרְשׁוּת הַבַּעַל.

her **husband's authority in marriage**[N] via the wedding canopy. If the father **delivered** his daughter **to the husband's messengers** to bring her to her husband and the wedding canopy, once she has been handed over **she is under the husband's authority.** However, if **the father went with the husband's messengers, or if the father's messengers went with the husband's messengers, she is** still **under the father's authority,** as he has not fully delivered her to the husband's messengers. If her father sent her with his own messengers **and the father's messengers delivered** the woman **to the husband's messengers,** from that moment onwards **she is under** her **husband's authority.**

גמ׳ מַאי לְעוֹלָם? לְאַפּוּקֵי מִמִּשְׁנָה רִאשׁוֹנָה. דִּתְנַן: הִגִּיעַ זְמַן וְלֹא נִישְּׂאוּ – אוֹכְלוֹת מִשֶּׁלּוֹ וְאוֹכְלוֹת בִּתְרוּמָה. קָא מַשְׁמַע לָן: לְעוֹלָם.

GEMARA The mishna taught that a daughter always remains under her father's authority until she has fully entered her husband's jurisdiction. The Gemara asks: **What is** the significance of the term: **Always,** in the mishna? The Gemara explains: This comes **to exclude** the opinion stated in the **initial** version of the **mishna. As we learned** in a mishna (57a): If **the time** that the groom designated for the wedding **arrived,** and the wedding was postponed, **and they were not married,** the brides are entitled to **eat from his** food **and,** if he is a priest, **eat** ***teruma,*** like married women. The mishna here **teaches us** that the *halakha* is not in accordance with this earlier ruling cited in that mishna. Rather, they are **always** under their father's authority until they actually enter the wedding canopy.

״מָסַר הָאָב לִשְׁלוּחֵי הַבַּעַל הֲרֵי הִיא בִּרְשׁוּת הַבַּעַל״ וכו׳. אָמַר רַב: מְסִירָתָהּ לַכֹּל, חוּץ מִתְּרוּמָה. וְרַב אַסִי אָמַר: אַף לִתְרוּמָה.

§ The mishna taught that if **the father delivered** his daughter **to the husband's messengers, she is under the husband's authority,** unless the father or his messengers accompanied them. **Rav said:** When her father **delivers her** she leaves his jurisdiction **in all** respects, **apart from** the issue of partaking of ***teruma.*** Even if her husband is a priest, if she is not from a family of priests, she may not partake of *teruma* until she is fully married. **And Rav Asi said** that once she has been delivered to the husband's messengers she is under her husband's authority **even** with regard **to** ***teruma.***[N]

אֵיתִיבֵיהּ רַב הוּנָא לְרַב אַסִי, וְאָמְרִי לַהּ חִיָּיא בַּר רַב לְרַב אַסִי: לְעוֹלָם הִיא בִּרְשׁוּת הָאָב, עַד שֶׁתִּכָּנֵס לַחוּפָּה! אֲמַר לְהוּ רַב: לָאו אָמִינָא לְכוּ: לָא תֵּיזְלוּ בָּתַר אִיפְּכָא?! יָכוֹל לְשַׁנּוֹיֵי לְכוּ: מְסִירָתָהּ זוֹ הִיא כְּנִיסָתָהּ לַחוּפָּה.

Rav Huna raised an objection to the opinion of **Rav Asi, and some say** that it was **Ḥiyya, son of Rav,** who raised an objection **to** the opinion of **Rav Asi:** The mishna states that **she is always under her father's authority until she enters the wedding canopy.** According to Rav Asi, however, as soon as her father delivers her to the husband's messengers she is no longer under her father's authority. **Rav said to them: Didn't I tell you not to follow,** i.e., attempt to refute rulings, on the basis of sources that can be explained in **opposing** manners? Rav Asi **can answer you** that the mishna means that **her delivery** to the husband's messengers **is** equivalent to **her entrance to the wedding canopy,** and the same *halakhot* apply in both cases.

וּשְׁמוּאֵל אָמַר: לִירוּשָּׁתָהּ.

And Shmuel said that once a woman's father has delivered her to the messengers of her husband, she is under her husband's authority only with regard **to her inheritance,**[N] i.e., her husband inherits her property upon her death as though she had already entered the wedding canopy.

רֵישׁ לָקִישׁ אָמַר: לִכְתוּבָּתָהּ. כְּתוּבָּתָהּ מַאי הִיא – דְּאִי מֵתָה יָרֵית לָהּ, הַיְינוּ דִּשְׁמוּאֵל! אָמַר רָבִינָא: לוֹמַר כְּתוּבָּתָהּ מֵאַחֵר – מָנֶה.

Reish Lakish said: Her delivery is also effective with regard **to her marriage contract.** The Gemara asks: **What is** Reish Lakish referring to when he says that she is under her husband's authority with regard to **her marriage contract?** If you say it means **that if she dies** he **inherits** all **her** property, including the dowry specified in her marriage contract, **that is** the same as the statement of **Shmuel,** and Reish Lakish has added nothing to his ruling. **Ravina said:** Reish Lakish is coming **to say** that if the man dies before marrying her, and she then marries someone else, **her marriage contract from** the **other** man **is one hundred dinars,** as she is considered a widow from marriage rather than a widow from betrothal.

NOTES

Her husband's authority in marriage – רְשׁוּת הַבַּעַל לְנִשּׂוּאִין: This is the version of the text that Rashi had. However, most early authorities accepted an alternate version of the text that read: A daughter is always under the authority of her father until she enters the wedding canopy. They rejected Rashi's text because of its unusual style and in light of the subsequent Gemara, which appears to quote the mishna in raising a difficulty against the opinion of Rav Asi and cites the alternate version of the text. According to Rashi, it must be explained that the Gemara was citing the meaning of the mishna without quoting it precisely. It appears from the Jerusalem Talmud that the correct version is the text of the authorities who differ with Rashi (see Ritva).

Rav Asi said she is under her husband's authority even with regard to ***teruma*** **– רַב אַסִי אָמַר אַף לִתְרוּמָה:** Rashi explains the dispute between Rav and Rav Asi on the basis of a disagreement (57b) with regard to the reason for the rabbinic decree that a woman whose father is not a priest and who is betrothed to a priest may not partake of *teruma*. Rav Asi follows the opinion that she is prohibited to partake of *teruma* due to a concern that she might give some of it to her brothers and sisters, who are not entitled to eat it. Consequently, as soon as she has been delivered to the husband's messengers, when this concern no longer applies, she may partake of *teruma*. Conversely, Rav accepts the opinion that the concern is that her husband might discover a bodily defect in her which will lead to the retroactive annulment of the marriage, in which case she would have retroactively eaten *teruma* unlawfully. This concern is relevant even after she has been delivered to the husband's messengers, until she actually enters the wedding canopy.

Tosafot question Rashi's explanation, as it apparently does not fit in with the conclusion of the Gemara there, which states that the dispute was only according to the initial version of the mishna; however, according to final *halakha*, which is that a woman betrothed to a priest may not partake of *teruma* until she is married, even if the time designated for the wedding has arrived, all agree that the sole reason is the concern for the discovery of a bodily defect. However, the Rashba claims that this difficulty of *Tosafot* is not irrefutable, as one can explain according to Rashi that Rav Asi offers a third opinion, in addition to the two mentioned in the Gemara there, as he maintains that even according to the final *halakha*, the concern is that she might share *teruma* with her siblings. See the *Shita Mekubbetzet* for a variation of this answer.

Shmuel said she is under her husband's authority only with regard to her inheritance – שְׁמוּאֵל אָמַר לִירוּשָּׁתָהּ: There are differences of opinion among the early commentaries with regard to Shmuel's opinion. Rashi maintains that he is referring only to her inheritance, whereas she is treated as a betrothed woman with regard to all other matters. This explanation widens the gap between the opinion of Shmuel and that of Rav. Conversely, *Tosafot* hold that Shmuel means simply that she is considered married in that her husband inherits from her, but she is not considered married with regard to partaking of *teruma*. According to this opinion, Shmuel agrees with the opinion of Rav cited previously.

רַבִּי יוֹחָנָן וְרַבִּי חֲנִינָא דְּאָמְרִי תַּרְוַיְיהוּ: מְסִירָתָהּ לַכֹּל, אַף לִתְרוּמָה.

Rabbi Yoḥanan and Rabbi Ḥanina both say that a woman's **delivery** to the messengers of her husband causes her to be under his authority **for all** matters, **even** including partaking of ***teruma***.

מֵיתִיבֵי: הָלַךְ הָאָב עִם שְׁלוּחֵי הַבַּעַל, אוֹ שֶׁהָלְכוּ שְׁלוּחֵי הָאָב עִם שְׁלוּחֵי הַבַּעַל, אוֹ שֶׁהָיְתָה לָהּ חָצֵר בַּדֶּרֶךְ וְנִכְנְסָה עִמּוֹ לָלִין, אַף עַל פִּי שֶׁכְּתוּבָּתָהּ בְּבֵית בַּעְלָהּ, מֵתָה – אָבִיהָ יוֹרְשָׁהּ.

The Gemara **raises an objection** from the *Tosefta* (*Ketubot* 4:4): If **the father went with the husband's messengers, or if the father's messengers went with the husband's messengers, or if she owned a courtyard along the way and she entered with** her groom **to lodge,** not for the purpose of marriage but merely to stay overnight until they arrive at his residence, then **even if** the dowry specified in **her marriage contract is** already **in her husband's house,** if **she dies, her father inherits** from **her,** as she is not considered to have entered her husband's domain.

מָסַר הָאָב לִשְׁלוּחֵי הַבַּעַל, אוֹ שֶׁמָּסְרוּ שְׁלוּחֵי הָאָב לִשְׁלוּחֵי הַבַּעַל, אוֹ שֶׁהָיְתָה לוֹ חָצֵר בַּדֶּרֶךְ וְנִכְנְסָה עִמּוֹ לְשׁוּם נִישּׂוּאִין, אַף עַל פִּי שֶׁכְּתוּבָּתָהּ בְּבֵית אָבִיהָ, מֵתָה – בַּעְלָהּ יוֹרְשָׁהּ.

Conversely, if **the father delivered** her **to the husband's messengers, or if the father's messengers delivered** her **to the husband's messengers, or if** the groom **owned a courtyard along the way and she entered with him for the purpose of marriage,** then **even if** the dowry specified in **her marriage contract is** still **in her father's house** and has not yet been given to her husband, if **she dies, her husband inherits** from **her.**[H]

בַּמֶּה דְּבָרִים אֲמוּרִים – לִירוּשָּׁתָהּ. אֲבָל לִתְרוּמָה – אֵין אִשָּׁה אוֹכֶלֶת בִּתְרוּמָה עַד שֶׁתִּכָּנֵס לַחוּפָּה. תְּיוּבְתָּא דְּכוּלְּהוּ! תְּיוּבְתָּא.

The *Tosefta* concludes: **In what case is this statement said?** It is stated with regard to the husband's right **to inherit** from **her. However,** with regard **to *teruma***, the *halakha* is that **a woman** who marries a priest **may not partake of *teruma***[H] **until she** actually **enters the wedding canopy.** This *baraita* is apparently **a refutation of all of them,**[N] i.e., all of the opinions cited previously that hold that once the woman is delivered to the husband's messengers, if the husband is a priest, the woman may partake of *teruma*. The Gemara concludes: Indeed, this is **a conclusive refutation.**

הָא גּוּפָא קַשְׁיָא: אָמְרַתְּ: נִכְנְסָה עִמּוֹ לָלִין. טַעֲמָא דְּלָלִין, הָא סְתָמָא – לְשֵׁם נִישּׂוּאִין; אֵימָא סֵיפָא: נִכְנְסָה עִמּוֹ לְשֵׁם נִישּׂוּאִין, הָא סְתָמָא – לָלִין!

The Gemara asks: **This matter itself is difficult. You said** in the *Tosefta* that if **she entered with him** to her courtyard **to lodge** for one night, and she dies, her father inherits her property. The **reason** is because it specified that they entered only **to lodge** there, from which it may be inferred that if they entered **without specification** it is as though she entered **for the sake of marriage. Say the latter clause** of the *Tosefta*: If **she entered with him** to his courtyard **for the purpose of marriage,** and she dies, her husband inherits her property. This indicates that if she entered **without specification,** i.e., without saying that they were doing so for marriage, it is considered as though they entered merely **to lodge.** The inferences from these two clauses of the *Tosefta* apparently contradict one another.

אֲמַר רַב אַשִׁי: סְתָמֵי סְתָמֵי קָתָנֵי; סְתָם חָצֵר דִּידָהּ – לָלִין, סְתָם חָצֵר דִּידֵיהּ – לְנִשּׂוּאִין.

Rav Ashi said: This is an incorrect interpretation, as the *tanna* **taught** the *halakha* of entering one type of courtyard **without specification** and the *halakha* of entering a different type of courtyard **without specification,** as follows: If they entered **her courtyard without specification** it is assumed that they entered merely **to lodge,** whereas if they entered **his courtyard without specification,** it is assumed that they did so **for** the sake of **marriage,** unless they expressly stated that they had another purpose in mind.[N]

NOTES

A refutation of all of them – תְּיוּבְתָּא דְּכוּלְּהוּ: Rashi and most early authorities maintain that the phrase: All of them, should not be understood literally, as it refers only to those *amora'im* who said that handing her over is effective for everything except inheritance (see *Tosafot*). Apparently, the refutation applies to the opinion of Rav as well, despite the fact that he maintains that the woman cannot partake of *teruma*, as he indicates that it is effective for all other matters, whereas the *baraita* indicates that it affects only the husband's status as her heir (Rabbeinu Crescas Vidal).

Others maintain that the opinion of Reish Lakish is not refuted, as one can say that the *baraita* is speaking only about the relationship between husband and wife, not her relationship with anyone else (Rabbeinu Ḥananel; see Ritva). However, Rabbeinu Ḥananel also had a variant reading of this *baraita*, which states in its first part: He had a different courtyard. He explains that according to the *baraita*, the delivery of a daughter is effective for the husband to inherit from her only if two conditions are fulfilled, namely that she is handed over to the husband or his messengers and that this is performed in a courtyard belonging to him. Accordingly, even Shmuel's opinion that her delivery is effective only for the inheritance is refuted by the *baraita*. Others cite various proofs demonstrating that this version does not fit in well with the continuation of the Gemara, and they stress that the phrase: All of them, does not necessarily mean the refutation of every single opinion (Ramban).

His courtyard and hers – חָצֵר שֶׁלּוֹ וְשֶׁלָּהּ: Since the wedding canopy is not a sacred ritual but merely a symbolic act by which the groom welcomes his bride into his house to commence their married life together, if the groom brings his bride into a courtyard, that may also be considered the equivalent of a wedding canopy. The discussion of the Gemara concerns only the details: When is their lodging together considered a chance event that does not signify his bringing her into his house, and when it is viewed as the equivalent of a wedding canopy (see Meiri and *Shita Mekubbetzet*).

HALAKHA

From when does one inherit from his wife – מֵאֵימָתַי יוֹרֵשׁ אֶת אִשְׁתּוֹ: With regard to a woman who was betrothed, and delivered by her father or his messengers to the husband or his messengers, if she died along the way before the wedding canopy, her husband inherits her property. This is so even if her dowry is still in her father's house. However, the *Tur*, citing the Ran, disagrees in this case, in accordance with the opinion of Rabbeinu Tam. Her husband likewise inherits her property if the father or his messengers accompanied her, and along the way the couple entered a courtyard and was secluded for the purpose of marriage. However, if her father or his messengers went with the husband or his messengers and stayed in a courtyard, in the manner of travelers, then since the husband was not secluded with his wife for the sake of marriage, her father inherits from her if she dies, even if the dowry was in the husband's house. This ruling is as stated in the *baraita* and in accordance with the opinion of Shmuel, consistent with the principle that the *halakha* follows the rulings of Shmuel in monetary law.

Some claim that if the pair entered the husband's courtyard or one that belonged to them both, it is assumed that they were secluded for marriage; whereas if the courtyard belonged to her or if it was not owned by either of them, their seclusion was presumably for the purpose of lodging, as stated by Rav Ashi (Rema; *Maggid Mishne*, citing Ramban and Rashba; Ran). The *Ḥelkat Meḥokek* maintains that this opinion does not dispute the previous ruling of the Rambam (Rambam *Sefer Nashim*, *Hilkhot Ishut* 22:2; *Shulḥan Arukh*, *Even HaEzer* 57:1).

Partaking of *teruma* – אֲכִילַת תְּרוּמָה: An Israelite woman who marries a priest may partake of *teruma*. By Torah law she may partake of *teruma* from the time of her betrothal, but the Sages prohibited her from doing so until she enters the wedding canopy, as stated by Rav (Rambam *Sefer Zera'im*, *Hilkhot Terumot* 6:3).

NOTES

If the father delivered…she is sentenced to strangulation – מָסַר הָאָב...הֲרֵי זוֹ בְּחֶנֶק: Some commentaries write that this *baraita* does not prove that delivering a woman to her husband's messengers changes her status to that of a married woman, and therefore it has no bearing on the earlier dispute (*Shita Mekubbetzet*). This is because the *baraita*, as the Gemara explains, merely proves that a bride who has been transferred to her husband's messenger is no longer classified as a betrothed young woman, as she is not in her father's house. However, this does not necessarily mean that she is considered a married woman (see Rivan).

HALAKHA

The execution of an adulteress – מִיתַת הַנּוֹאֶפֶת: If a betrothed young woman committed adultery, she and the one with whom she committed adultery are sentenced to stoning. If she was a grown woman, or if she had entered the wedding canopy, even if she had not yet engaged in intercourse with her husband, or if her father had delivered her to the husband's messengers, even before the wedding canopy, she is liable to be executed by strangulation, like a regular married woman who committed adultery (Rambam *Sefer Kedusha*, *Hilkhot Issurei Bia* 3:4).

תָּנָא: מָסַר הָאָב לִשְׁלוּחֵי הַבַּעַל וְזִינְּתָה – הֲרֵי זוֹ בְּחֶנֶק. מְנָא הָנֵי מִילֵּי? אָמַר רַבִּי אַמִּי בַּר חָמָא: אָמַר קְרָא ״לִזְנוֹת בֵּית אָבִיהָ״ – פְּרָט לְשֶׁמָּסַר הָאָב לִשְׁלוּחֵי הַבַּעַל.

§ A Sage **taught** in a *baraita*: If **the father delivered** his daughter **to the husband's messengers and she** subsequently **committed adultery, she is** sentenced **to strangulation,**[N] in accordance with the *halakha* of a married woman who committed adultery, rather than stoning, which is the punishment for a betrothed woman who commits adultery.[H] The Gemara asks: **From where are these matters** derived? **Rabbi Ami bar Ḥama said** that **the verse states,** in the context of the command to stone a young woman who commits adultery during betrothal: **"To play the whore in her father's house"** (Deuteronomy 22:21), which **excludes** a case **when the father has delivered** her **to the husband's messengers,** when she is no longer in her father's house.

וְאֵימָא פְּרָט שֶׁנִּכְנְסָה לַחוּפָּה וְלֹא נִבְעֲלָה!

The Gemara raises a difficulty: **But** one can **say** that the verse is **excluding** a case **where she has entered the wedding canopy but she has not** yet **had intercourse,** whereas if her father has merely delivered her to the husband's messengers she is still considered to have sinned in his house and is punishable by stoning like any other betrothed woman.

אָמַר רָבָא, אָמַר לִי אַמִּי: חוּפָּה בְּהֶדְיָא כְּתִיבָא. ״כִּי יִהְיֶה נַעֲרָה בְתוּלָה מְאוֹרָשָׂה לְאִישׁ״, נַעֲרָה – וְלֹא בּוֹגֶרֶת; ״בְּתוּלָה״ – וְלֹא בְּעוּלָה; ״מְאוֹרָשָׂה״ – וְלֹא נְשׂוּאָה.

In answer to this question, **Rava said:** The verse cannot be excluding that case, as **Ami said to me** that the case where she already entered the **wedding canopy is** not derived by inference from that verse; it is **explicitly written** in the following verse: **"If there is a young woman who is a virgin betrothed to a man"** (Deuteronomy 22:23). The terminology of the verse indicates that it applies to a **"young woman" and not to a grown woman;** to a **"virgin" and not** to **a non-virgin;** and to a **"betrothed"** woman **and not** to **a married woman.**

מַאי נְשׂוּאָה? אִילֵימָא נְשׂוּאָה מַמָּשׁ – הַיְינוּ בְּתוּלָה וְלֹא בְּעוּלָה. אֶלָּא לָאו – שֶׁנִּכְנְסָה לַחוּפָּה וְלֹא נִבְעֲלָה.

The Gemara analyzes this statement: **What is** the meaning of the term: **A married woman,** in this context? **If we say** that she is **actually married** and has already engaged in intercourse with her husband, **this** ruling **is** the same as the previous one, that she must be **a virgin and not a non-virgin. Rather, is it not** the case that it is referring to a woman **who has entered the wedding canopy but has not had intercourse,** and yet if she committed adultery at this stage she is sentenced to strangulation, like one who had engaged in relations with her husband? Consequently, the other verse, cited by Rabbi Ami bar Ḥama, cannot be referring to this case.

Perek **IV**
Daf **49** Amud **a**

וְאֵימָא: הֵיכָא דַּהֲדַרָא לְבֵי נָשָׁא – הָדְרָא לְמִילְּתָא קַמַּיְיתָא! אָמַר רָבָא: הַהוּא כְּבָר פַּסְקָהּ תַּנָּא דְּבֵי רַבִּי יִשְׁמָעֵאל.

The Gemara asks another question: **But say** that in a case **where she returns to her father's house,** she **returns** to the **previous matter,** i.e., her former status, as though she had never left her father's authority. **Rava said: That** question **has already been resolved** by **the** *tanna* of the school of **Rabbi Yishmael.**

דְּתָנָא דְּבֵי רַבִּי יִשְׁמָעֵאל: ״וְנֵדֶר אַלְמָנָה וּגְרוּשָׁה כֹּל אֲשֶׁר אָסְרָה עַל נַפְשָׁהּ יָקוּם עָלֶיהָ״, מָה תַּלְמוּד לוֹמַר? וַהֲלֹא מוֹצֵאת מִכְּלַל אָב וּמוֹצֵאת מִכְּלַל בַּעַל!

This is **as** the *tanna* of **the school of Rabbi Yishmael taught: "But the vow of a widow or of a divorcée, everything with which she has bound her soul shall stand against her"** (Numbers 30:10). **What** is the meaning when **the verse states** this? **Is it not** already known that if she is widowed or divorced **she has** already **been removed from the category** of one under the authority of her **father and she has** likewise **been removed from the category** of one under the authority of her **husband?** Who, then, could possibly nullify her vows?

אֶלָּא, הֲרֵי שֶׁמָּסַר הָאָב לִשְׁלוּחֵי הַבַּעַל, אוֹ שֶׁמָּסְרוּ שְׁלוּחֵי הָאָב לִשְׁלוּחֵי הַבַּעַל, וְנִתְאַרְמְלָה בַּדֶּרֶךְ אוֹ נִתְגָּרְשָׁה – הֵיאַךְ אֲנִי קוֹרֵא בָּהּ, בֵּית אָבִיהָ שֶׁל זוֹ אוֹ בֵּית בַּעְלָהּ שֶׁל זוֹ? אֶלָּא לוֹמַר לְךָ: כֵּיוָן שֶׁיָּצְאָה שָׁעָה אַחַת מֵרְשׁוּת הָאָב – שׁוּב אֵינוֹ יָכוֹל לְהָפֵר.

Rather, this is referring to a case **where the father delivered** his daughter **to the husband's messengers or where the father's messengers delivered** her **to the husband's messengers, and she was widowed or divorced on** her **way** to the wedding canopy. **How do I consider her?** Is she a member of **her father's house, or** a member of **her husband's house?** Her status is entirely unclear. **Rather,** this verse comes **to tell you: Since she has left her father's domain** for **a short time** her father **is no longer able to nullify** her vows,[H] as she is considered a widow or a divorcée in all regards. The same applies to the issue at hand: She retains the status of a married woman even if she returns to her father's house.

אֲמַר רַב פַּפָּא: אַף אֲנַן נַמִי תָּנֵינָא: הַבָּא עַל נַעֲרָה הַמְאוֹרָסָה – אֵינוֹ חַיָּיב עַד שֶׁתְּהֵא נַעֲרָה בְּתוּלָה מְאוֹרָסָה, וְהִיא בְּבֵית אָבִיהָ. בִּשְׁלָמָא נַעֲרָה – וְלֹא בּוֹגֶרֶת, בְּתוּלָה – וְלֹא בְּעוּלָה, מְאוֹרָסָה – וְלֹא נְשׂוּאָה: ״בְּבֵית אָבִיהָ״ לְמַעוּטֵי מַאי – לָאו לְמַעוּטֵי מָסַר הָאָב לִשְׁלוּחֵי הַבַּעַל?

Rav Pappa said: We, too, learn this principle in a mishna (*Sanhedrin* 66b): **One who has intercourse with a young woman betrothed** to another **is liable** to stoning **only if she is a virgin, a young woman, betrothed, and she is in her father's house.** The Gemara analyzes this mishna: **Granted,** the term **young woman** indicates that this punishment does **not** apply if she is **a grown woman;** similarly, this punishment applies only if she is **a virgin, but not** if she is **a non-virgin,** and only if she is **betrothed, but not** if she is **a married woman.** However, when the mishna states that she is **in her father's house, what** does that phrase come **to exclude?** Does it **not** serve **to exclude** a case when **the father delivered** her **to the husband's messengers,** indicating that in such a case the punishment of stoning no longer applies?

אֲמַר רַב נַחְמָן בַּר יִצְחָק: אַף אֲנַן נַמִי תָּנֵינָא: הַבָּא עַל אֵשֶׁת אִישׁ, כֵּיוָן שֶׁנִּכְנְסָה לִרְשׁוּת הַבַּעַל לְנִשּׂוּאִין, אַף עַל פִּי שֶׁלֹּא נִבְעֲלָה – הַבָּא עָלֶיהָ הֲרֵי זֶה בְּחֶנֶק. נִכְנְסָה לִרְשׁוּת הַבַּעַל בְּעָלְמָא – שְׁמַע מִינָּהּ.

Rav Naḥman bar Yitzḥak said: We, too, learn this principle in another mishna (*Sanhedrin* 89a): With regard to **one who has intercourse with a married woman, once she has entered her husband's authority for marriage, even though she has not had intercourse** with him, **one who has intercourse with her is** punished **by strangulation,** which is the punishment for adultery with a married woman. It is clear that this *halakha* applies if **she merely entered the husband's authority** for the purpose of marriage, even if they have not yet entered the wedding canopy. The Gemara concludes: Indeed, **learn from here** that this is so.

מתני׳ הָאָב אֵינוֹ חַיָּיב בִּמְזוֹנוֹת בִּתּוֹ. זֶה מִדְרָשׁ דָּרַשׁ רַבִּי אֶלְעָזָר בֶּן עֲזַרְיָה לִפְנֵי חֲכָמִים בְּכֶרֶם בְּיַבְנֶה: הַבָּנִים יִירְשׁוּ, וְהַבָּנוֹת יִזּוֹנוּ. מָה הַבָּנִים אֵינָן יוֹרְשִׁין – אֶלָּא לְאַחַר מִיתַת הָאָב, אַף הַבָּנוֹת אֵין נִיזּוֹנוֹת – אֶלָּא לְאַחַר מִיתַת אֲבִיהֶן.

MISHNA **A father is not obligated to** provide **his daughter's sustenance. This exposition was expounded**[N] **by Rabbi Elazar ben Azarya before the Sages in the vineyard of Yavne:**[N] Since the Sages instituted that after the father's death, **the sons inherit**[N] the sum of money specified in their mother's marriage contract, **and the daughters are sustained** from their father's estate, these the two *halakhot* are equated: **Just as the sons inherit only after the father's death,** not during his lifetime, **so too, the daughters are sustained** from his property **only after their father's death.**

HALAKHA

Since she has left her father's domain for a short time, he is no longer able to nullify her vows – **כֵּיוָן שֶׁיָּצְאָה שָׁעָה אַחַת מֵרְשׁוּת הָאָב שׁוּב אֵינוֹ יָכוֹל לְהָפֵר**: If a betrothed young woman's father, or his messengers, accompanied the husband or his messengers as they brought the woman to the wedding canopy, she does not completely leave her father's authority until she enters the wedding canopy. During this period, her father and her husband together can nullify her vows. However, if her father or his messengers handed her over to the husband or his messengers, the father can no longer nullify her vows. Consequently, even if the groom died before the couple could enter the wedding canopy, and the bride returned to her father's house while she was still a young woman, her father does not regain the right to nullify her vows. However, some hold that the father can nullify vows that she took upon herself after the death of her husband (*Beit Yosef*, citing *Tur*; see *Shakh* and *Taz*; Rambam *Sefer Hafla'a*, *Hilkhot Nedarim* 11:22; *Shulḥan Arukh*, *Yoreh De'a* 234:12).

NOTES

This exposition was expounded – **זֶה מִדְרָשׁ דָּרַשׁ**: In the Jerusalem Talmud this exposition is discussed at length. The basis of this exposition is the fact that these two obligations are juxtaposed in the marriage contract. However, although it is common for the Sages to derive *halakhot* based upon the juxtaposition of laws in the Torah, it is quite unusual for them to derive *halakhot* based upon the juxtaposition of clauses in a legal contract.

In the vineyard of Yavne – **בְּכֶרֶם בְּיַבְנֶה**: As explained by the commentaries, this was the name of the Sanhedrin that presided in Yavne. It was called a vineyard because when it was in session, the Sages themselves, along with their students, would sit in rows, like the rows of a vineyard (Jerusalem Talmud). It is also possible that the Sanhedrin may have been situated near vineyards, lending the name a double meaning. The Rambam in his Commentary on the Mishna (*Eduyyot* 2:4), adds that this name alludes to the entire Jewish people, which is compared by the prophets to a vineyard (see Isaiah 5:1). Although this Sanhedrin did not have the full authority available to a Sanhedrin because it was not located on the Temple Mount, the Sages of this council did meet in order to formally establish *halakhot* for generations to come.

The sons inherit, etc. – **הַבָּנִים יִירְשׁוּ וכו׳**: The commentaries explain that this is not referring to the *halakha* of inheritance according to Torah law. Rather, it is one of the rabbinically instituted stipulations of the marriage contract that the sons born to this wife should inherit their mother's marriage contract, regardless of their share in the inheritance of their father's property. This is known as the marriage document concerning male children (see 52b). Another enactment, also a stipulation of the marriage contract, is that the father is obligated to sustain his daughters. Although the commentaries explain that these two decrees were not enacted at the same time, Rabbi Elazar ben Azarya nevertheless interpreted them as connected (Ritva).

A mitzva to sustain daughters, etc. – מִצְוָה לָזוּן אֶת הַבָּנוֹת וכו׳: The later authorities debate whether there is any practical difference between the opinions of Rabbi Meir and Rabbi Yehuda, both of whom apparently affirm that it is a mitzva to sustain sons and daughters. Some write that the difference concerns a case when there is enough to provide sustenance only for a son or a daughter, as the *tanna'im* dispute which of them takes precedence (Rabbi Akiva Eiger). Others contend that Rabbi Meir's stated reason why it is an *a fortiori* inference that there is a mitzva to sustain the sons, that the sons occupy themselves with Torah study, indicates that the two Sages disagree in a case when the sons are not occupied with studying Torah (*Ḥatam Sofer*).

גמ׳ בִּמְזוֹנוֹת בִּתּוֹ – הוּא דְּאֵינוֹ חַיָּיב, הָא בִּמְזוֹנוֹת בְּנוֹ – חַיָּיב. בִּתּוֹ נַמִּי, חוֹבָה הוּא דְּלֵיכָּא, הָא מִצְוָה – אִיכָּא, מַנִּי מַתְנִיתִין? לָא רַבִּי מֵאִיר, לָא רַבִּי יְהוּדָה, וְלָא רַבִּי יוֹחָנָן בֶּן בְּרוֹקָא.

GEMARA With regard to the mishna's statement that a father is not obligated to provide his daughter's sustenance, the Gemara infers: **It is with regard to** providing **his daughter's sustenance that he is not obligated, but with regard to** providing **his son's sustenance, he is obligated.** Furthermore, with regard to **his daughter, too, there is no obligation,** and therefore the court cannot compel him to provide sustenance for his daughter, **but there is a mitzva,** i.e., it is proper, for him to do so. With this interpretation in mind, **whose** opinion is expressed in **the mishna?** It is **not Rabbi Meir, nor Rabbi Yehuda, nor Rabbi Yoḥanan ben Beroka.**

דְּתַנְיָא: מִצְוָה לָזוּן אֶת הַבָּנוֹת, קַל וָחוֹמֶר לַבָּנִים, דְּעָסְקֵי בַּתּוֹרָה, דִּבְרֵי רַבִּי מֵאִיר. רַבִּי יְהוּדָה אוֹמֵר: מִצְוָה לָזוּן אֶת הַבָּנִים, וְקַל וָחוֹמֶר לַבָּנוֹת, מִשּׁוּם זִילוּתָא. רַבִּי יוֹחָנָן בֶּן בְּרוֹקָא אוֹמֵר: חוֹבָה לָזוּן אֶת הַבָּנוֹת לְאַחַר מִיתַת אֲבִיהֶן, אֲבָל בְּחַיֵּי אֲבִיהֶן – אֵלּוּ וְאֵלּוּ אֵינָן נִיזּוֹנִין.

As it is taught in a *baraita*, it is **a mitzva to sustain daughters,**[N] and the same applies by **an *a fortiori*** inference **to sons, who are engaged in** the study of **Torah.** This is **the statement of Rabbi Meir. Rabbi Yehuda says:** It is **a mitzva to sustain sons,** and the same applies by **an *a fortiori*** inference **with regard to daughters, due to** the **dishonor** they will suffer if they are forced to go around begging. **Rabbi Yoḥanan ben Beroka says:** It is **an obligation to sustain the daughters after their father's death; however, during their father's lifetime** both **these and those,** sons and daughters alike, **are not sustained.**

מַנִּי מַתְנִיתִין? אִי רַבִּי מֵאִיר – הָא אָמַר בָּנִים מִצְוָה, אִי רַבִּי יְהוּדָה – הָא אָמַר בָּנִים נַמִּי מִצְוָה, אִי רַבִּי יוֹחָנָן בֶּן בְּרוֹקָא – אֲפִילּוּ מִצְוָה נַמִּי לֵיכָּא!

The Gemara restates its question: **Whose** opinion is expressed in **the mishna? If** you say it is **Rabbi Meir, didn't he say** that providing sustenance even to one's **sons** is merely **a mitzva,** not an obligation? **If** the mishna expresses the opinion of **Rabbi Yehuda, didn't he say** that providing sustenance to one's **sons** is **also a mitzva,** not an obligation? **If** it is **Rabbi Yoḥanan ben Beroka,** according to his opinion **there is not even a mitzva** to provide sustenance for one's daughters. Consequently, none of opinions of the *tanna'im* of the *baraita* fits the ruling of the mishna.

אִיבָּעֵית אֵימָא רַבִּי מֵאִיר, אִיבָּעֵית אֵימָא רַבִּי יְהוּדָה, אִיבָּעֵית אֵימָא רַבִּי יוֹחָנָן בֶּן בְּרוֹקָא.

The Gemara answers that the mishna can be explained in several different ways. **If you wish, say** that the mishna is in accordance with the opinion of **Rabbi Meir; if you wish, say** that it follows the opinion of **Rabbi Yehuda;** and **if you wish, say** it is the opinion of **Rabbi Yoḥanan ben Beroka.**

אִיבָּעֵית אֵימָא רַבִּי מֵאִיר, וְהָכִי קָאָמַר: הָאָב אֵינוֹ חַיָּיב בִּמְזוֹנוֹת בִּתּוֹ, וְהוּא הַדִּין לִבְנוֹ. הָא מִצְוָה בְּבִתּוֹ – אִיכָּא, קַל וָחוֹמֶר לַבָּנִים. וְהַאי דְּקָתָנֵי בִּתּוֹ – הָא קָא מַשְׁמַע לַן:

The Gemara explains in detail: **If you wish, say** it is **Rabbi Meir, and this is what he said** in the mishna: **A father is not obligated to** provide **his daughter's sustenance, and the same is true with regard to** providing sustenance for **his son.** This indicates that **there is a mitzva,** though not an obligation, to provide for **his daughter,** and by **an *a fortiori*** inference it is a mitzva with regard **to the sons. And** the reason **that** the mishna **teaches** only the case of **his daughter,** and omitted any mention of sons, is not because a father is obligated to feed his sons. Instead, it **teaches us this:**

Perek **IV**
Daf **49** Amud **b**

דַּאֲפִילּוּ בִּתּוֹ, חוֹבָה הוּא – דְּלֵיכָּא, הָא מִצְוָה – אִיכָּא.

That even with regard to **his daughter, there is no obligation** to provide her sustenance, however, **there is a mitzva** to do so.

וְאִיבָּעֵית אֵימָא רַבִּי יְהוּדָה, וְהָכִי קָאָמַר: הָאָב אֵינוֹ חַיָּיב בִּמְזוֹנוֹת בִּתּוֹ, וְכָל שֶׁכֵּן לִבְנוֹ. הָא מִצְוָה בִּבְנוֹ – אִיכָּא, וְקַל וָחוֹמֶר לַבָּנוֹת. וְהָא דְּקָתָנֵי בִּתּוֹ – הָא קָא מַשְׁמַע לַן: דַּאֲפִילּוּ בִּתּוֹ חוֹבָה לֵיכָּא.

And if you wish, say that the mishna is in accordance with the opinion of **Rabbi Yehuda, and this what he said** in the mishna: **A father is not obligated** to provide **sustenance for his daughter, and all the more so** he is not duty-bound to provide **for his son.** It may be inferred from here that **there is** at least **a mitzva with regard to a son, and** the same applies by ***a fortiori*** inference with regard **to the daughters. And** the reason **that** the mishna **teaches** the case of **his daughter** is because it **teaches us this: That even** with regard to **his daughter** there is **no obligation,** despite the mitzva to guard her from dishonor.

וְאִיבָּעֵית אֵימָא רַבִּי יוֹחָנָן בֶּן בְּרוֹקָא, וְהָכִי קָאָמַר: אֵינוֹ חַיָּיב בִּמְזוֹנוֹת בִּתּוֹ, וְהוּא הַדִּין לִבְנוֹ. וְהוּא הַדִּין דַּאֲפִילּוּ מִצְוָה נַמִּי לֵיכָּא, וְאַיְּידֵי דְּבָנוֹת לְאַחַר מִיתַת אֲבִיהֶן חוֹבָה – תָּנָא נַמִּי אֵינוֹ חַיָּיב.

And if you wish, say that the mishna is in accordance with the opinion of **Rabbi Yoḥanan ben Beroka, and this is what he said** in the mishna: A father is **not obligated** to provide **sustenance for his daughter, and the same is true** with regard to providing **for his son. And the same is true** with regard to a mitzva; there is **not even a mitzva** to feed either one's sons or daughters, **but since** the *tanna* wanted to say with regard to **daughters** that **after their father's death** there is **an obligation** to sustain them from his estate, he **also taught** in a parallel manner that the father **is not obligated** to provide sustenance for his daughters during his lifetime. Consequently, it is incorrect to infer from here that there is a mitzva to sustain them despite the lack of obligation; rather, the *tanna* means that there is no obligation and not even a mitzva to do so.

אָמַר רַבִּי אִילְעָא אָמַר רֵישׁ לָקִישׁ מִשּׁוּם רַבִּי יְהוּדָה בַּר חֲנִינָא: בְּאוּשָׁא הִתְקִינוּ שֶׁיְּהֵא אָדָם זָן אֶת בָּנָיו וְאֶת בְּנוֹתָיו כְּשֶׁהֵן קְטַנִּים. אִיבַּעְיָא לְהוּ: הִלְכְתָא כְּוָותֵיהּ אוֹ אֵין הִלְכְתָא כְּוָותֵיהּ? תָּא שְׁמַע: כִּי הֲוָה אָתוּ לְקַמֵּיהּ דְּרַב יְהוּדָה, אָמַר לְהוּ: יָארוֹד יַלְדָה וְאַבְנֵי מָתָא שַׁדְיָא?!

§ **Rabbi Ile'a said** that **Reish Lakish said in the name of Rabbi Yehuda bar Ḥanina: In Usha** the Sages **instituted that a man should sustain his sons and daughters when they are minors. A dilemma was raised before** the Sages: Is **the *halakha* in accordance with his** opinion **or is the *halakha* not in accordance with his** opinion? Must a man feed his young children in practice or not? The Gemara answers: **Come and hear: When they would come before Rav Yehuda** to complain about a father who refused to sustain his children, **he** would **say to them: The jackal** [*yarod*][L] **bears** offspring[N] **and casts** the obligation to feed **them on the residents of the town?** Even a jackal feeds its young, and it is certainly proper for a father to support his children.

כִּי הֲוָה אָתוּ לְקַמֵּיהּ דְּרַב חִסְדָּא, אָמַר לְהוּ: כְּפוּ לֵיהּ אָסִיתָא בְּצִבּוּרָא, וְלֵיקוּם וְלֵימָא: עוּרְבָא בָּעֵי בְּנֵיהּ, וְהַהוּא גַּבְרָא לָא בָּעֵי בְּנֵיהּ. וְעוּרְבָא בָּעֵי בְּנֵיהּ? וְהָכְתִיב "לִבְנֵי עוֹרֵב אֲשֶׁר יִקְרָאוּ"! לָא קַשְׁיָא, הָא – בְּחִיוָּרֵי, הָא – בְּאוּכָּמֵי.

When they would come before Rav Ḥisda to register a similar complaint, **he** would **say to them: Turn over a mortar for him**[N] **in public,** as a raised platform, **and let** that father **stand up and say** about himself: **The raven wants** to care for **its sons, and** yet **this man does not want** to support **his sons.** The Gemara questions this statement: **And does the raven want** to feed **its sons? But isn't it written:** "He gives to the beast its food, **to the young ravens that cry**" (Psalms 147:9)? This verse indicates that the parents of young ravens do not feed them. The Gemara responds: This is **not difficult,** as in **this** case it is referring **to white ones,** and in **that** case it is referring **to black ones.**[N] There are different types of ravens, some of which feed their young while others do not.

כִּי הֲוָה אָתֵי לְקַמֵּיהּ דְּרָבָא, אָמַר לֵיהּ: נִיחָא לָךְ דְּמִיתַּזְנֵי בָּנֶיךָ מִצְּדָקָה?

The Gemara further relates: **When** an incident of this kind **would come before Rava, he** would **say** to the father: Is it **satisfactory to you that your sons are sustained through charity?** All these incidents prove that the *halakha* is not in accordance with the enactment of Usha; although these Sages stated forcefully that it is proper for a father to support his children, they did not force him to do so by the authority of the court.

וְלָא אֲמָרַן אֶלָּא דְּלָא אֲמִיד, אֲבָל אֲמִיד – כָּפֵינַן לֵיהּ עַל כָּרְחֵיהּ. כִּי הָא דְּרָבָא כַּפְיֵיהּ לְרַב נָתָן בַּר אַמִי וְאַפֵּיק מִינֵּיהּ אַרְבַּע מֵאָה זוּזֵי לִצְדָקָה.

The Gemara adds: **And we said** this *halakha* **only when he is not wealthy** and must toil hard to provide food for his children, **but** if he is **wealthy we coerce him against his will**[HN] to sustain them. **Like this** case **of Rava, who coerced Rav Natan bar Ami,** who was a wealthy man, to donate to charity, **and collected from him four hundred dinars for charity.**[H] This shows that even in the absence of a particular obligation, the court will compel a person to give charity if he can afford it. The same reasoning certainly applies to a man's own children.

LANGUAGE

Jackal [*yarod*] – יָארוֹד: The word *yarod*, or *yaror*, according to the version of the *Arukh* and several other sources, is the Aramaic for the Hebrew *tanna* or *tannim*. Several interpretations are offered for this term in the Bible. Some claim it is the name of an animal, the common jackal, whereas others say it is a bird, identified as a nocturnal bird similar to the owl. Rashi occasionally identifies it as a four-legged animal, although elsewhere he says it is a bird. The common denominator between these two creatures is that they both cry out in the night. The *Tosefta* states that *yarodim* are a species of birds. However, it is possible that the term bears both meanings. In any case, the source of the proverb mentioned here with regard to the *yarod* is unclear.

NOTES

The jackal [*yarod*] bears offspring – יָארוֹד יַלְדָה: The commentaries disagree over the meaning of this term. Although the biblical word *tannin*, jackal, is translated as *yarod*, it is possible that *tannin* does not consistently refer to the same animal and can variously refer to a beast or a bird. Some claim that *yarod* is a type of bird that does not feed its young (Rid). However, most commentaries maintain that it refers to the jackal, which is cruel to its young (Rashi). It is noted that according to this interpretation, Rav Yehuda accused the father of being crueler than the *yarod*, which does not neglect to feed its own young despite its cruelty (Ritva; see Rabbi Ovadya Bartenura on the mishna).

Turn over a mortar for him – כְּפוּ לֵיהּ אָסִיתָא: Some commentaries omit the phrase: For him. This reading indicates that someone else would stand on a raised podium and declare this man cruel to his children. Most commentaries, however, maintain that the father himself was compelled to issue this statement and embarrass himself in public. It has even been suggested that one aim of this exercise was to find someone willing to take care of the children in lieu of their father. Some commentaries explain that Rav Yehuda said to overturn a mortar as a curse, i.e., to signify that the father's livelihood should be overturned and diminished (Ritva). Others add that turning over a mortar alludes to the fact that this man has overturned the natural order, as even cruel animals feed their own children (Maharal).

In this case it is referring to white ones and in that case to black ones – הָא בְּחִיוָּרֵי הָא בְּאוּכָּמֵי: Rashi explains that this statement refers to different stages of development of a raven. Initially the young raven is white, and its parents do not have pity on their young, but afterward they turn black, at which point their parents do care for them. Support for his interpretation can be found in *Eikha Rabba* (see also *Arukh*). Others maintain that the Gemara is speaking of two different species of raven, black ones and white ones (*Tosafot*; *Likkutei Ge'onim*).

We coerce him against his will – כָּפֵינַן לֵיהּ עַל כָּרְחֵיהּ: The precise manner in which the father is coerced is not specified by the Gemara. Consequently, many commentaries explain that the court forces him verbally, by reproving and shaming him in public, but it does not actually extract the money from him (Rav Hai Gaon). Others maintain that, if necessary, the court compels him by confiscating his property and using it as needed (see Rambam's Commentary on the Mishna).

HALAKHA

A father's obligation to sustain his children – חוֹבַת הָאָב לָזוּן בָּנָיו: A father is obligated to support his children until they are six years old. The Sages in Usha decreed that a father must support his children even beyond they age of six, until they have matured. If he does not want to support them the court reprimands him and shames him, and publicly declares that he is cruel and does not wish to feed his children, and he is worse than a ritually impure bird, which does feed its young. However, the court cannot compel him to do so, unless he has spare money for charity, in which case the court seizes his property and uses it to feed his children until they mature (Rambam *Sefer Nashim*, *Hilkhot Ishut* 12:14–15; *Shulḥan Arukh*, *Even HaEzer* 71:1).

If he is wealthy the court coerces him…for charity – אֲמִיד כָּפֵינַן לֵיהּ...לִצְדָקָה: All are obligated to give charity to the poor. If someone gives less than the appropriate sum according to his means, the court forces him and administers lashes for rebelliousness until he gives the amount they have deemed appropriate for him (Rambam *Sefer Zera'im*, *Hilkhot Mattenot Aniyyim* 7:10; *Shulḥan Arukh*, *Yoreh De'a* 248:1).

אָמַר רַבִּי אִילְעָא אָמַר רֵישׁ לָקִישׁ: בְּאוּשָׁא הִתְקִינוּ: הַכּוֹתֵב כׇּל נְכָסָיו לְבָנָיו – הוּא וְאִשְׁתּוֹ נִזּוֹנִים מֵהֶם.

§ **Rabbi Ile'a said** that **Reish Lakish said: In Usha** the Sages **instituted** that in a case of **one who writes** a document stating that he is giving **all his property**[N] as a gift **to his sons** in his lifetime, **he and his wife are sustained from** the property until their deaths.

מַתְקִיף לַהּ רַבִּי זֵירָא וְאִיתֵּימָא רַבִּי שְׁמוּאֵל בַּר נַחְמָנִי: גְּדוֹלָה מִזּוֹ אָמְרוּ: אַלְמְנָתוֹ נִזּוֹנֶת מִנְּכָסָיו, הוּא וְאִשְׁתּוֹ מִיבַּעְיָא?!

Rabbi Zeira objects to this, and some say this objection was raised by **Rabbi Shmuel bar Naḥmani:** What is the significance of this ruling? After all, the Sages **said a greater** novelty **than that:** A man's **widow is sustained from his property** even if his estate was inherited by his daughter and therefore belongs to her husband. Although the property is comparable to property from the estate that was sold to a third party, from which a widow is not entitled to claim her sustenance, in this case the Sages decreed that she can claim her livelihood from her late husband's estate to prevent her from losing out entirely. With this in mind, **is it necessary** to state that **he and his wife,** during his lifetime, receive their sustenance from property he gave as a gift to his sons?

דִּשְׁלַח רָבִין בְּאִיגַּרְתֵּיהּ: מִי שֶׁמֵּת וְהִנִּיחַ אַלְמָנָה וּבַת – אַלְמְנָתוֹ נִיזּוֹנֶת מִנְּכָסָיו, נִישֵּׂאת הַבַּת – אַלְמְנָתוֹ נִיזּוֹנֶת מִנְּכָסָיו,

The Gemara provides the background for this ruling: **As Ravin sent in his letter** to Babylonia: With regard to **one who died and left a widow and a daughter,**[H] **his widow is sustained from his property,** as this is a stipulation of the marriage contract. If **the daughter,** who is her father's heir, **married,** the estate is considered usufruct property whose produce belongs to her husband, but even so **his widow is sustained from his property.**

מֵתָה הַבַּת, אָמַר רַבִּי יְהוּדָה בֶּן אֲחוֹתוֹ שֶׁל רַבִּי יוֹסֵי בַּר חֲנִינָא: עַל יָדִי הָיָה מַעֲשֶׂה, וְאָמְרוּ: אַלְמְנָתוֹ נִיזּוֹנֶת מִנְּכָסָיו – הוּא וְאִשְׁתּוֹ מִיבַּעְיָא?!

If **the daughter died** and her husband inherited from her, **Rabbi Yehuda, son of the sister of Rabbi Yosei bar Ḥanina, said: I was involved in an incident** of this kind when this very question came before the Sages for a ruling, **and they said:** Even in this case, **his widow is sustained from his property.** The Gemara reiterates: With all that said, **is it necessary** to state that **he and his wife** are entitled to receive their sustenance from property he gave his son?

מַהוּ דְּתֵימָא: הָתָם הוּא דְּלֵיכָּא דְּטָרַח, אֲבָל הָכָא – נִטְרַח לְדִידֵיהּ וּלְדִידַהּ, קָא מַשְׁמַע לַן.

The Gemara responds: The ordinance is necessary **lest you say** that **it is** in that case **there,** with regard to a widow, that they instituted this *halakha,* **as there is no one to toil** on her behalf, since she is by herself, **but here,** where the husband is alive, **he can toil for himself and for her,** i.e., his wife. The ordinance of Usha therefore **teaches us** that the court does not force him to do so, and they may claim their sustenance from his former property.

אִיבַּעְיָא לְהוּ: הִלְכְתָא כְּווֹתֵיהּ אוֹ לֵית הִלְכְתָא כְּווֹתֵיהּ? תָּא שְׁמַע, דְּרַבִּי חֲנִינָא וְרַבִּי יוֹנָתָן הֲווֹ קָיְימִי, אֲתָא הַהוּא גַּבְרָא, גְּחֵין וּנְשַׁקֵיהּ לְרַבִּי יוֹנָתָן אַכַּרְעֵיהּ. אֲמַר לֵיהּ רַבִּי חֲנִינָא: מַאי הַאי? אֲמַר לֵיהּ: כּוֹתֵב נְכָסָיו לְבָנָיו הוּא,

A dilemma was raised before the scholars: Is **the *halakha* in accordance with** the opinion of Rabbi Ile'a, **or is the *halakha* not in accordance with his** opinion? The Gemara answers: **Come and hear, as Rabbi Ḥanina and Rabbi Yonatan were standing** together, and **a certain man approached, bent over, and kissed Rabbi Yonatan on his foot. Rabbi Ḥanina said to** Rabbi Yonatan: **What is this?** Why does he owe you such a mark of gratitude? **He said to him: He wrote** a document stating that he was giving **his property to his sons,**

NOTES

One who writes that he is giving all his property, etc. – הַכּוֹתֵב כׇּל נְכָסָיו וכו׳: The early authorities state that this ordinance is based on his assumed intention, as it is unlikely that one would give his sons everything and thereby be forced to go begging.

HALAKHA

A widow and a daughter – אַלְמָנָה וּבַת: With regard to a man who died and left a widow and a daughter, whether from that wife or from another woman, if his estate is not large enough to sustain both of them, his widow gets precedence. Even if the daughter married, thereby granting her husband rights to her father's estate, the widow may continue to collect her sustenance from the estate. Furthermore, even if the daughter died and her husband inherited her property, the widow still receives her sustenance from the property, as indicated by the story related in the Gemara (Rambam *Sefer Nashim, Hilkhot Ishut* 19:21; *Shulḥan Arukh, Even HaEzer* 93:4).

ועשיתינהו לזניה. אי אמרת בשלמא לאו דינא – משום הכי עשיינהו, אלא אי אמרת דינא – עשיינהו בעי?!

and I forced them to feed him, for which he is grateful. The Gemara interprets this incident in light of the issue at hand: **Granted, if you say** that this was **not** according to the ***halakha***,[H] i.e., the man's sons had the right to refrain from sustaining him, **due to that** reason Rabbi Yonatan had to **force them** to feed their father; **but if you say** this is the ***halakha***, i.e., the man's sons were required to sustain him, why did he **need to force them**[N] to provide the sustenance of their own accord? The court could have simply requisitioned the necessary amount from the property. This shows that the *halakha* is not in accordance with the opinion of Rabbi Ile'a.

אמר רבי אילעא: באושא התקינו: המבזבז – אל יבזבז יותר מחומש. תניא נמי הכי: המבזבז – אל יבזבז יותר מחומש, שמא יצטרך לבריות. ומעשה באחד שבקש לבזבז [יותר מחומש], ולא הניח לו חבירו, ומנו – רבי ישבב. ואמרי לה: רבי ישבב, ולא הניחו חבירו, ומנו – רבי עקיבא.

§ Apropos the ordinances instituted by the Sages in Usha, the Gemara cites another one. **Rabbi Ile'a said: In Usha** the Sages **instituted** that **one who dispenses** his money to charity **should not dispense more than one-fifth.**[HN] **That** opinion **is also taught** in a *baraita*: **One who scatters should not scatter more than one-fifth, lest he** render himself destitute and **need** the help of other **people. And an incident** occurred **involving a certain** individual **who sought to dispense more than one-fifth** of his property as charity, **and his friend did not let him** act upon his wishes. **And who** was this friend? **Rabbi Yeshevav. And some say** that **Rabbi Yeshevav** was the one who wanted to give too much charity, **and his friend did not let him** do so, **and who was** the **friend? Rabbi Akiva.**

אמר רב נחמן, ואיתימא רב אחא בר יעקב: מאי קרא – "וכל אשר תתן לי עשר אעשרנו לך".

Rav Naḥman said, and some say it was **Rav Aḥa bar Ya'akov** who said: **What is the verse** that alludes to this maximum amount of charity? **"And of all that You shall give me, I will surely give a tenth of it [*aser a'asrenu*] to You"** (Genesis 28:22). The double use of the verb that means to donate one-tenth indicates that Jacob, who issued this statement, was actually referring to two-tenths, i.e., one-fifth.

והא לא דמי עישורא בתרא לעישורא קמא! אמר רב אשי: "אעשרנו" לבתרא כי קמא.

The Gemara asks: **But the latter tenth is not similar to the first tenth,** as it would be one-tenth of what remained after the first tenth had been removed. Consequently, the two-tenths would not equal one-fifth of the original total. The Gemara answers that **Rav Ashi said:** Since the verse could have said: I will surely give one-tenth [*aser a'aser*], and instead stated: **"I will surely give a tenth of it [*aser a'asrenu*],"** it thereby alludes to the fact **that the latter** tenth is **like the first one.**

אמר רב שימי בר אשי: ושמועות הללו מתמעטות והולכות, וסימניך: קטנים כתבו ובזבזו.

With regard to the above statements concerning the Sages' ordinances in Usha, **Rav Shimi bar Ashi said: And these *halakhot* continually decrease.** The first statement was stated by Rabbi Ile'a, quoting a statement by Reish Lakish in the name of Rabbi Yosei bar Ḥanina. The second *halakha* was delivered by Rabbi Ile'a in the name of Reish Lakish, while the third was taught by Rabbi Ile'a without quoting another Sage. **And this is your mnemonic** for the order of these *halakhot*: **Minors wrote and dispensed.** This alludes to the ruling requiring a father to support his children while they are minors, the ruling about one who wrote a document granting all of his property to his sons, and the ruling about one who dispenses large sums to charity.

אמר רב יצחק: באושא התקינו שיהא אדם מתגלגל עם בנו עד שתים עשרה שנה, מכאן ואילך – יורד עמו לחייו. איני?! והא אמר ליה רב לרב שמואל בר שילת: בציר מבר שית – לא תקביל, בר שית – קביל, וספי ליה כתורא!

§ **Rav Yitzḥak said: In Usha** the Sages **enacted that a person should treat his son gently,**[N] even if he does not want to study, **until** his son is **twelve years** old. **From this point forward he harasses him** in all aspects of **his life** in order to force him to study. The Gemara asks: **Is that so? But didn't Rav say to Rav Shmuel bar Sheilat,** who taught children: With regard to a child **less than six years old, do not accept** him; if he is **six years old, accept** him **and stuff him like an ox,** i.e., just as an ox is force-fed, you should force the students to study Torah.

HALAKHA

This was not according to the *halakha* – לאו דינא: If one gives all his property to his sons, leaving nothing for himself, according to the letter of the law neither he nor his wife is entitled to sustenance from the property, as the ordinance of Usha is not accepted as *halakha*. As for the story in which the Sages forced sons to provide for their parents, it is possible that this was in accordance with the *halakha* that the court enforces the bestowal of charity. Consequently, the court can compel any man of means to sustain his father (*Tur, Ḥoshen Mishpat* 257; *Beit Yosef*).

Should not dispense more than one-fifth – אל יבזבז יותר מחומש: The Sages enacted that one should not give away more than one-fifth of his property to charity, so that he not become a burden to the public, in accordance with the ordinance of Usha (Rema, citing *Beit Yosef*). See the Rema and the other commentaries with regard to the application of this principle to different people and times (Rambam *Sefer Hafla'a, Hilkhot Arakhin* 8:13; *Shulḥan Arukh, Yoreh De'a* 249:1, and in the comment of Rema).

NOTES

Why did he need to force them – עשיינהו בעי: The commentaries disagree with regard to the level of force that Rabbi Yonatan applied and to the Gemara's inference on the basis of this incident. Rashi explains that Rabbi Yonatan forced the sons to pay and explains the Gemara's comment as a statement rather than a rhetorical question that asks: Since Rabbi Yonatan was required to force them to pay, why did the father have such an exaggerated level of gratitude? *Tosafot* explain that Rabbi Yonatan merely persuaded the sons to support their father. According to this interpretation, the Gemara's comment means: Why was it necessary to convince the sons if the court could simply have issued a ruling requiring them to support their father and, if necessary, forcibly requisitioned the necessary funds? (see Ritva and *Nimmukei Yosef*).

Should not dispense more than one-fifth – אל יבזבז יותר מחומש: Some commentaries indicate that this prohibition against giving away too much of one's property applies to one who consecrates his possessions to the Sanctuary, whereas one who gives charity may give more than one-fifth as an act of piety (Rivan). It appears that according to the Rambam, it is recommended that one give one-fifth of his money to charity, although this is not obligatory.

Other commentaries, by contrast, accept the opinion of Rashi that the principle stated here, that one should not give away more than one-fifth of his money, includes charity. However, they add that it applies only to one who gives during his lifetime, due to the concern that he might become a burden on others, whereas one who arranges for his property to be distributed after his death may give more (*Halakhot Gedolot*). They further explain that this limitation refers only to the regular bestowal of charity, but in a time of famine, or if the recipient will be in danger if he does not receive more, one may give more. In the Jerusalem Talmud it is explained that giving one-fifth of one's money refers to giving one-fifth of his capital, and then, on an ongoing basis, one-fifth of his earnings.

Treat his son gently – מתגלגל עם בנו: The author of the *Arukh* cites an entirely different interpretation. He maintains that until a son is twelve a father can be easy on him and let him study, but afterward he must teach him a profession from which he can earn a livelihood.

אין, ספי ליה כתורא. מיהו, אינו יורד עמו לחייו עד לאחר שתים עשרה שנה. ואיבעית אימא לא קשיא: הא – למקרא, הא – למשנה.

The Gemara answers: There is no contradiction here, as **yes,** one must **stuff him like an ox** and teach him intensively; **however,** if the student refuses to learn, one **does not harass him** in all aspects of **his life until after** he is **twelve years** old. **And if you wish, say** that this is **not difficult** for a different reason: **This** *halakha*, which prescribes forcing the students to study from the age of six, is referring **to the Bible,** whereas **that** *halakha*, that one should not harass a boy to study until he is twelve, is referring **to the Mishna.**

דאמר אביי: אמרה לי אם: בר שית – למקרא, בר עשר – למשנה, בר תליסר – לתעניתא מעת לעת, ובתינוקת בת תריסר.

This is **as Abaye said:** My foster **mother told me** that **a six-year-old** is ready **for Bible** study and **a ten-year-old** is mature enough **to** study **Mishna.**[H] Additionally, a **thirteen-year-old** is sufficiently developed **to fast for twenty-four hours** like any other adult. **And** as **for a girl,** she must start observing fasts when she is **twelve years old.**

אמר אביי: אמרה לי אם: האי בר שית דטרקא ליה עקרבא ביומא דמישלם שית – לא חיי. מאי אסותיה – מררתא דדיה חיורתא בשיכרא, נשפייה ונשקייה. האי בר שתא דטריק ליה זיבורא ביומא דמישלם שתא – לא חיי. מאי אסותיה – אצותא דדיקלא במיא, נשפייה ונשקייה.

The Gemara cites another statement of Abaye in the name of his foster mother. **Abaye said:** My **mother told me** that **a six-year-old** child **who is stung by a scorpion on the day that** he **completes six** years **will not live** without emergency treatment. **What is his cure? The bile of a white vulture in beer. One should rub him** with this mixture **and make him drink** it. She further said to him: A one-year-old child **who is stung by a hornet**[B] **on the day that** he completes **a year will not live** without emergency treatment. **What is his cure? Palm-tree fiber in water.** Again, **one should rub him** with it **and make him drink** it.

אמר רב קטינא: כל המכניס את בנו פחות מבן שש – רץ אחריו ואינו מגיעו. איכא דאמרי: חביריו רצין אחריו ואין מגיעין אותו. ותרוייהו איתנהו: חליש וגמיר. איבעית אימא: הא – דכחיש, הא – דבריא.

Rav Ketina said: Anyone who brings his son to school when he is **younger than six years old**[B] **will run after him and not catch him.** In other words, he will worry about his welfare for a long time afterward, as the child will be weakened by his studies. **There are those who say that his friends will run after him** in their studies **and not catch him,** i.e., his early start will enable him to be far more successful. The Gemara comments: **And both are** correct; he will **weaken** physically **and learn** well. **If you wish, say** that these two statements can be reconciled differently: **This** case is dealing **with a weak** child, who should not be brought to school at such a young age, whereas **that** statement is referring **to a healthy** boy, who can go to school at a tender age and succeed in his studies.

אמר רבי יוסי בר חנינא: באושא התקינו: האשה שמכרה בנכסי מלוג בחיי בעלה, ומתה – הבעל מוציא מיד הלקוחות. אשכחיה רב יצחק בר יוסף לרבי אבהו דהוה קאי באוכלוסא דאושא. אמר ליה: מאן מרה דשמעתא דאושא? אמר ליה: רבי יוסי בר חנינא. תנא מיניה ארבעין זימנין, ודמי ליה כמאן דמנחא ליה בכיסתיה.

§ **Rabbi Yosei bar Ḥanina said: In Usha** the Sages **instituted** that in the case of **a woman who sold** her **usufruct property,**[H] which is property that belongs to her but whose produce belongs to her husband, **in her husband's lifetime, and** then she **died, the husband** can **repossess** it **from the purchasers.**[N] The Gemara relates: **Rav Yitzḥak bar Yosef found Rabbi Abbahu standing** among the **congregation** [*ukhlusa*][L] **of Usha. He said to him: Who is the Master** who disseminated **the** ***halakha*** that was instituted in **Usha? He said to him: Rabbi Yosei bar Ḥanina. He learned it** from Rabbi Abbahu **forty times,**[N] and from that point onward he remembered it so well that **it seemed to him as though it were placed in his pocket.**

NOTES

The husband can repossess it from the purchasers – הבעל מוציא מידי הלקוחות: This statement implies that the purchaser had already taken possession of the property. However, this is not accurate, because the purchaser cannot actually take possession of the field, due to the right of the husband to the field's produce (see *Shulḥan Arukh, Even HaEzer* 90:9). Rather, the purchaser has the right to take possession of the field if the husband dies before the wife. The statement that the husband can repossess the field should be taken to mean that his rights supersede the purchaser's right to take possession of the field. Alternatively, it might refer to a case when the husband stipulated with his wife that he has no share in the property or its produce during her lifetime, in which case the purchaser may take possession of the land, and upon the woman's death, the husband repossesses it (Rabbeinu Aharon HaLevi; Meiri).

There is a dispute among the *ge'onim* about whether the husband must reimburse the purchaser for the purchase price of the property once he repossesses it. This is a dispute between the Sages of Sura and Pumbedita. Some early authorities rule that he takes the property without having to pay, but if he has the actual money his wife received for the sale, he must return it (Rabbeinu Ḥananel; Rif).

He learned it from Rabbi Abbahu forty times – תנא מיניה ארבעין זימנין: According to Rashi, this means that Rav Yitzḥak bar Yosef learned from Rabbi Abbahu forty times that Rabbi Yosei bar Ḥanina was the Sage who had disseminated the *halakha* instituted in Usha. Some later commentaries explain that this was necessary because he had previously ascribed this to Rabbi Yehuda bar Ḥanina. To rid himself of this entrenched assumption, he had to repeat forty times that it was actually Rabbi Yosei bar Ḥanina who disseminated the *halakha* (*Ḥatam Sofer*). The Maharshal explains that once he heard that it was disseminated by Rabbi Yosei bar Ḥanina, who was a great Sage, he reviewed the *halakha* itself forty times.

HALAKHA

The start of a boy's education – תחילת לימודו של ילד: Once a child starts talking, his father should teach him to say the phrase: Moses instructed us in the Torah, and to say the first verse of *Shema*. He gradually teaches him more and more until he is six years old, or seven, if he is of weak constitution (*Shakh*). At this stage the father should take his son to a teacher. The custom is to take a child to Bible classes when he is five years old, but no earlier. If he is weak, he starts at the age of six. Admittedly, in many places they used to bring boys as young as three to the study halls, but they would say that they were merely seating them alongside their older friends, and that anything they learned was incidental (Rambam *Sefer HaMadda, Hilkhot Talmud Torah* 1:6; *Shulḥan Arukh, Yoreh De'a* 245:5, 8).

A woman who sold her usufruct property – האשה שמכרה בנכסי מלוג: If a married woman sold her usufruct property and subsequently died before her husband, he can repossess the property from the purchasers, in accordance with the ordinance of Usha (Rambam *Sefer Nashim, Hilkhot Ishut* 22:7; *Shulḥan Arukh, Even HaEzer* 90:9).

BACKGROUND

Sting of a scorpion or hornet – עקיצת עקרב וצרעה: The sting of a scorpion, especially certain species, e.g., the yellow scorpion in Eretz Yisrael, causes great pain and in some cases can even be life threatening. The sting of a hornet is usually not as severe, unless the victim suffers an allergic reaction. The level of danger typically corresponds to the ratio between the body weight of the victim and the amount of venom injected by the sting: The smaller the person the more dangerous the sting. It is possible that bile, due to its ability to dilute various substances, could reduce the potential damage of this sting.

Hornet stinger and venom about to enter human skin

Younger than six years old – פחות מבן שש: There are divergent opinions with regard to the most appropriate age to begin regular, concentrated studies. At any event, this is largely dependent on the physical constitution of the child, and more importantly, his emotional maturity. For this reason, there is no clearly established age to commence learning. Nevertheless, it is widely accepted even nowadays that at around the age of six a child achieves the level of maturity necessary for him to begin formal education.

LANGUAGE

Congregation [*ukhlusa*] – אוכלוסא: From the Greek ὄχλος, *okhlos*, meaning a crowd or group of people.

"אַשְׁרֵי שׁוֹמְרֵי מִשְׁפָּט עוֹשֵׂה צְדָקָה בְּכָל עֵת"; וְכִי אֶפְשָׁר לַעֲשׂוֹת צְדָקָה בְּכָל עֵת? דָּרְשׁוּ רַבּוֹתֵינוּ שֶׁבְּיַבְנֶה, וְאָמְרִי לָהּ רַבִּי אֱלִיעֶזֶר: זֶה הַזָּן בָּנָיו וּבְנוֹתָיו כְּשֶׁהֵן קְטַנִּים. רַבִּי שְׁמוּאֵל בַּר נַחְמָנִי אָמַר: זֶה הַמְגַדֵּל יָתוֹם וִיתוֹמָה בְּתוֹךְ בֵּיתוֹ וּמַשִּׂיאָן.

The Gemara discusses a point related to one of the ordinances of Usha. The verse states: **"Happy are they who keep justice, who perform charity at all times"** (Psalms 106:3).[H] **But is it possible to perform charity at all times?** Is one always in the presence of paupers? Therefore, **our Rabbis in Yavne taught, and some say** it was **Rabbi Eliezer: This is** referring to **one who sustains his sons and daughters when they are minors.** As stated above, he is not formally obligated to support them, and therefore when he does so, it is a form of charity that he gives on a constant basis. **Rabbi Shmuel bar Naḥmani said: This is** referring to **one who raises an orphan boy or an orphan girl in his house,** takes care of them, **and marries them off.**

"הוֹן וָעוֹשֶׁר בְּבֵיתוֹ וְצִדְקָתוֹ עוֹמֶדֶת לָעַד", רַב הוּנָא וְרַב חִסְדָּא; חַד אֲמַר: זֶה הַלּוֹמֵד תּוֹרָה וּמְלַמְּדָהּ, וְחַד אֲמַר: זֶה הַכּוֹתֵב תּוֹרָה, נְבִיאִים וּכְתוּבִים, וּמַשְׁאִילָן לַאֲחֵרִים.

The Sages likewise expounded the verse: **"Wealth and riches are in his house, and his charity endures forever"** (Psalms 112:3). How can one's wealth and riches remain in his house while his charity endures forever? **Rav Huna and Rav Ḥisda** disputed this issue. **One said: This** is referring to **one who studies Torah and teaches it.** He loses nothing of his own, while his charity toward others will endure. **And one said: This is one who writes** scrolls of **the Torah, the Prophets, and the Writings, and lends them to others.** The books remain in his possession, but others gain from his charity.

"וּרְאֵה בָנִים לְבָנֶיךָ שָׁלוֹם עַל יִשְׂרָאֵל", אָמַר רַבִּי יְהוֹשֻׁעַ בֶּן לֵוִי: "כֵּיוָן שֶׁבָּנִים לְבָנֶיךָ – שָׁלוֹם עַל יִשְׂרָאֵל, דְּלָא אָתֵי לִידֵי חֲלִיצָה וְיִבּוּם. רַבִּי שְׁמוּאֵל בַּר נַחְמָנִי אָמַר: כֵּיוָן שֶׁבָּנִים לְבָנֶיךָ – שָׁלוֹם עַל דַּיָּינֵי יִשְׂרָאֵל, דְּלָא אָתֵי לְאִינְצוּיֵי.

With regard to the verse: **"And see your son's sons; peace be upon Israel"** (Psalms 128:6), **Rabbi Yehoshua ben Levi said: Once your children** have **children** of their own, there is **peace upon Israel, as they will not come** to require **the ritual through which the** ***yavam*** **frees the** ***yevama*** **of her levirate bonds [*ḥalitza*] or levirate marriage,** which are necessary only if a man dies childless. **Rabbi Shmuel bar Naḥmani said: Once your sons** have **sons** there will be **peace upon the judges of Israel,**[N] as relatives **will not come to quarrel** with the judges over the inheritance.

"זֶה מִדְרָשׁ דָּרַשׁ רַבִּי אֶלְעָזָר לִפְנֵי חֲכָמִים" כו׳.

§ The Gemara returns to the mishna: **This exposition was expounded** by **Rabbi Elazar** ben Azarya **before the Sages** in the vineyard of Yavne: Just as the sons inherit only after the father's death, so too, the daughters are sustained from his property only after their father's death.

HALAKHA

Perform charity at all times – עוֹשֵׂה צְדָקָה בְּכָל עֵת: If one provides for his older children despite the fact that he is not obligated to do so, so that his sons can study Torah and his daughters can follow the proper path, this is counted toward his obligation of charity (Rambam *Sefer Zera'im, Hilkhot Mattenot Aniyyim* 10:16; *Shulḥan Arukh, Yoreh De'a* 251:3).

NOTES

Peace upon the judges of Israel – שָׁלוֹם עַל דַּיָּינֵי יִשְׂרָאֵל: Rashi explains that if there are no sons, other relatives will quarrel over who is the closest heir. Some commentaries ask why this necessitates having sons; if one has daughters and no sons, it is clear that they inherit from their father (Ritva, citing *Tosafot*). The Ritva explains, citing the Ri, that if all his sons have sons of their own he will distribute his property equally among them; but if only one of his sons has sons, he will increase the share of that son, which will cause friction among his children. Others explain that the main point is that the sons are old enough to have their own sons, i.e., they are adults. If his children were minors, the court would have appointed a trustee to oversee the affairs of the orphans and their quarrels with others (*Sefer Hafla'a*). Alternatively, if one has a daughter and a son, and the son dies and leaves a daughter, this would lead to a dispute between the judges of Israel and the Sadducees. The latter maintained that in this case, the property of the deceased is divided equally between the daughter and granddaughter, whereas the Sages held that the son's daughter is the sole heir. This dispute will not arise if his sons have sons of their own (Ritva, citing Rabbeinu Yeḥiel).

Perek **IV**
Daf **50** Amud **b**

יָתֵיב רַב יוֹסֵף קַמֵּיהּ דְּרַב הַמְנוּנָא, וְיָתֵיב רַב הַמְנוּנָא וְקָאָמַר: כְּשֵׁם שֶׁאֵין הַבָּנִים יוֹרְשִׁין אֶלָּא מִן הַקַּרְקַע – כָּךְ אֵין הַבָּנוֹת נִיזּוֹנוֹת אֶלָּא מִן הַקַּרְקַע. אֲוַושׁ עֲלֵיהּ כּוּלֵּי עָלְמָא: דְּשָׁבֵיק אַרְעָא – הוּא דְּיָרְתִי לֵיהּ בְּנֵיהּ, דְּלָא שָׁבֵיק אַרְעָא – לָא יָרְתִי לֵיהּ בְּנֵיהּ?!

The Gemara relates: **Rav Yosef sat before Rav Hamnuna**[B] in the study hall, **and Rav Hamnuna sat and said** the following *halakha*: **Just as sons inherit only from land, so too, daughters are sustained only from land.** When Rav Hamnuna taught this *halakha*, **everyone clamored [*avash*]**[L] **against him,** i.e., all his listeners whispered their surprise to one another: Is it only one **who leaves** behind **land whose sons inherit** from **him,** whereas in the case of one **who does not leave land, his sons do not inherit** from **him?** Rav Hamnuna's statement indicates that sons inherit only land and nothing else.

LANGUAGE

Clamored [*avash*] – אֲוַושׁ: This Aramaic term is related to the Middle Persian awāč, meaning voice. In Aramaic it connotes a murmuring or bustling sound, and can indicate clamor, including the clamor of a shocked audience.

BACKGROUND

Rav Yosef sat before Rav Hamnuna, etc. – יָתֵיב רַב יוֹסֵף קַמֵּיהּ דְּרַב הַמְנוּנָא וכו׳: This story exemplifies some of the conventions in the academies in those days. The leading Sage would sit and expound before his audience. The prominent Sages in attendance would typically sit in the front row, with the other scholars seated behind them. If it was not a lecture open to the wider public, e.g., the public lectures on Festivals, the Sages sitting in front would ask questions and challenge the leading Sage, exchanges that were considered an integral part of the discourse.

אֲמַר לֵיהּ רַב יוֹסֵף: וְדִלְמָא כְּתוּבַּת בְּנִין דִּכְרִין קָאָמַר מָר? אֲמַר לֵיהּ: מָר, דְּגַבְרָא רַבָּא הוּא, יָדַע מַאי קָאָמִינָא.

Rav Yosef said to Rav Hamnuna: **Perhaps the Master was speaking of the marriage document** ensuring the inheritance rights of a woman's **male children,**[H] i.e., her sons' right to inherit the sum stipulated in her marriage contract in addition to their share of the father's estate alongside any other brothers. Rav Hamnuna **said to him: The Master, who is a great man, knows what I said,** i.e., that was indeed my intention, while the others failed to understand me properly.

אֲמַר רַבִּי חִיָּיא בַּר יוֹסֵף: רַב זָן מֵחִיטֵּי דַּעֲלִיָּיה. אִיבַּעְיָא לְהוּ: פַּרְנָסָה הָוְיָא, וּמַאי עֲלִיָּיה – מֵעִילּוּיָא דְאָב, וּכְדִשְׁמוּאֵל. דְּאָמַר שְׁמוּאֵל: לְפַרְנָסָה שָׁמִין בְּאָב.

Rabbi Ḥiyya bar Yosef said: Rav would **sustain** orphan girls **with wheat according to the *aliyya*** if their fathers did not leave land for them. **A dilemma was raised before** the scholars: **Was** this sustenance that Rav provided in the form of **livelihood,** i.e., a dowry so that they could marry, **and what is** the meaning of the term ***aliyya***? It means: In keeping with **the status** [*illuyya*] **of the father,**[N] **and** this is **in accordance with** the opinion **of Shmuel. As Shmuel said: With regard to** the daughters' **livelihood,** i.e., their dowry, the court **assesses** the amount they receive from their father's estate after his death **in accordance with** the temperament and social and financial status of **the father.**[H]

אוֹ דִלְמָא: מְזוֹנֵי מַמָּשׁ הֲוָה, וּמַאי עֲלִיָּיה – מִדְּבָרִים טוֹבִים שֶׁנֶּאֶמְרוּ בַּעֲלִיָּיה. דְּאָמַר רַב יִצְחָק בַּר יוֹסֵף: בַּעֲלִיָּיה הִתְקִינוּ שֶׁיְּהוּ בָּנוֹת נִיזּוֹנוֹת מִן הַמִּטַּלְטְלִין.

Or perhaps it **was actual sustenance,** i.e., provisions so that they would have food, **and what is** the meaning of the term ***aliyya***? It indicates that this *halakha* is one **of the good statements said in the upper chamber** [*aliyya*], **as Rav Yitzḥak bar Yosef said:** When the Sages sat **in the upper chamber** to rule on certain *halakhot*, which they could not do in the study hall at that time due to persecution by gentiles, **they instituted that daughters should be sustained from movable property** in addition to land.

תָּא שְׁמַע: בִּידֵיהּ דְּרַבִּי בְּנַאי, אֲחוּהּ דְּרַבִּי חִיָּיא בַּר אַבָּא, הָווּ מִטַּלְטְלִין דְּיַתְמֵי, אָתוּ לְקַמֵּיהּ דִּשְׁמוּאֵל, אֲמַר לֵיהּ: זִיל זוֹן.

The Gemara suggests: **Come and hear** a resolution to this dilemma: **In the possession of Rabbi Banai, the brother of Rabbi Ḥiyya bar Abba, there was movable property** belonging **to orphans,** deposited with him by their father. The orphan daughters **came before Shmuel,** who **said to** Rabbi Banai: **Go** and **sustain** the daughters from the property.

מַאי לָאו לִמְזוֹנֵי, וּכְדְרַב יִצְחָק בַּר יוֹסֵף סְבִירָא לֵיהּ? לָא, הָתָם לְפַרְנָסָה הֲוַאי. וּשְׁמוּאֵל לְטַעְמֵיהּ, דְּאָמַר שְׁמוּאֵל: לְפַרְנָסָה שָׁמִין בְּאָב.

What, is it not correct to say that this means he should provide them **with sustenance, and** this would indicate that Shmuel **holds in accordance with** the opinion of **Rav Yitzḥak bar Yosef,** that the Sages instituted an ordinance in the upper chamber that daughters are entitled to their sustenance even from movable property? The Gemara refutes this claim: **No, there it is** stated in reference **to** their **livelihood, and Shmuel** conforms **to his** standard line of **reasoning, as Shmuel said: With regard to livelihood,** i.e., the dowry granted to daughters from their father's estate, the court **assesses** the amount they receive **in accordance with** the status of **the father.**

הֲוָה עוּבְדָא בִּנְהַרְדְּעָא, וְדוּן דַּיָּינֵי דִּנְהַרְדְּעָא, בְּפוּמְבְּדִיתָא וְאַגְבֵּי רַב חָנָא בַּר בִּיזְנָא. אֲמַר לְהוּ רַב נַחְמָן: זִילוּ אַהְדְרוּ, וְאִי לָא – מַגְבֵּינָא לְכוּ לְאַפַּדְנַייכוּ מִינַּייכוּ.

The Gemara relates: **There was an incident** of this kind that came before the court **in Neharde'a, and the judges of Neharde'a ruled** that the daughters must be supported from the movable property that their father had left. Likewise, a case occurred **in Pumbedita, and Rav Ḥana bar Bizna collected** the sum from movable property. **Rav Naḥman said to** the judges: **Go reverse** your decisions, **and if not, I will collect your houses** [*appadnaikhu*][L] **from you** in order to compensate those you ruled against.

HALAKHA

The marriage document concerning male children – כְּתוּבַּת בְּנִין דִּכְרִין: If a woman predeceases her husband, her sons inherit the sum stipulated in her marriage contract in addition to their share of the father's estate alongside any other brothers. However, they may inherit this additional sum only from land. The Rambam maintains that even after the *ge'onim* decreed that a woman may collect the payment of her marriage contract from movable property, an ordinance which applies equally to other stipulations of the marriage contract, the stipulation that sons inherit their mother's marriage settlement remains an exception to this principle. Some authorities rule that nowadays even the sons may inherit the sum stipulated in their mother's marriage contract from movable property, like the other stipulations of the marriage contract (Rivash). Others maintain that the institution of the marriage document concerning male children is not practiced at all nowadays (Rema; Rosh; *Maggid Mishne*, citing *ge'onim*). The reason for this is that it is customary to give a far larger dowry to daughters than was customary when the institution was originally established, and the whole point of this institution was to encourage fathers to give their daughters a generous dowry (Rambam *Sefer Nashim*, *Hilkhot Ishut* 16:7; *Shulḥan Arukh*, *Even HaEzer* 111:14, 16).

With regard to the daughters' livelihood the court assesses in accordance with the temperament of the father – לְפַרְנָסָה שָׁמִין בְּאָב: In the case of one who died and left a daughter, the court estimates how much he would have been willing to give her for her dowry, and she takes that sum from his estate. How do they determine his mind-set? They interview his companions and close friends, and examine his manner of conducting business and his social status. If he had married off a different daughter in his lifetime, they give the remaining daughter the same amount he gave his other daughter, as stated by Shmuel (Rambam *Sefer Nashim*, *Hilkhot Ishut* 20:3; *Shulḥan Arukh*, *Even HaEzer* 113:1).

LANGUAGE

House [*appadna*] – **אַפַּדְנָא:** From the Old Persian apadana, meaning palace or audience hall. The term was borrowed from Persian into Aramaic in ancient times and appears in the Bible (Daniel 11:45). It can connote a palace, luxurious home, or fortress.

NOTES

The status of the father – מֵעִילּוּיָא דְאָב: Rabbeinu Ḥananel, cited by *Tosafot*, explains that the maximum amount that would be given to the daughter as a dowry was one-tenth of the estate, and the assessment was conducted in order to determine whether she should receive less than that amount. The ruling authorities discuss whether *Tosafot* accept this opinion, or whether they agree with Rashi, who maintains that one-tenth of the estate was an average amount, and the court would assess whether the father was likely to have given more. Some commentaries contend that a daughter's dowry is basically collected from land alone, and it was collected from movable property only if the court had undertaken to oversee the orphans' assets (see Meiri).

רַבִּי אַמִי וְרַבִּי אַסִי סְבוּר לְמֵיזַן מִמִּטַּלְטְלֵי. אֲמַר לְהוּ רַבִּי יַעֲקֹב בַּר אִידִי: מִילְּתָא דְּרַבִּי יוֹחָנָן וְרֵישׁ לָקִישׁ לָא עָבְדוּ בַּהּ עוּבְדָא, אַתּוּן עָבְדִין בַּהּ עוּבְדָא?!

The Gemara further relates: **Rabbi Ami and Rabbi Asi thought** to issue a ruling requiring a man's heirs **to sustain** his daughters **from** the man's **movable property. Rabbi Ya'akov bar Idi said to them:** This is **a matter** about **which Rabbi Yoḥanan and Reish Lakish did not take action,** i.e., they did not issue a ruling to this effect; will **you take action in** this regard? If those great Sages were not sure enough of the *halakha* to issue a practical ruling, how can you do so?

רַבִּי אֶלְעָזָר סָבַר לְמֵיזַן מִמִּטַּלְטְלִין, אָמַר לְפָנָיו רַבִּי שִׁמְעוֹן בֶּן אֶלְיָקִים: רַבִּי, יוֹדֵעַ אֲנִי בְּךָ שֶׁאֵין מִדַּת הַדִּין אַתָּה עוֹשֶׂה אֶלָּא מִדַּת רַחֲמָנוּת, אֶלָּא, שֶׁמָּא יִרְאוּ הַתַּלְמִידִים וְיִקְבְּעוּ הֲלָכָה לְדוֹרוֹת.

The Gemara relates that **Rabbi Elazar thought** to issue a ruling requiring a man's heirs **to sustain** his daughters **from** his **movable property. Rabbi Shimon ben Elyakim said before him: My teacher, I know about you that you are not acting** according to **the letter of the law,** but **rather** out of **pity** for these daughters, who have no other source of support. **However,** you should still not do this, **lest the students observe and** mistakenly **establish** the ***halakha*** accordingly **for** future **generations.**

הַהוּא דַּאֲתָא לְקַמֵּיהּ דְּרַב יוֹסֵף, אֲמַר לְהוּ: הַבוּ לַהּ מִתַּמְרֵי דְּעַל בּוּדְיָא. אֲמַר לֵיהּ אַבָּיֵי: אִילּוּ בַּעַל חוֹב הֲוָה, כִּי הַאי גַּוְונָא מִי הֲוָה יָהֵיב לֵיהּ מָר?

A certain person **came before Rav Yosef** to inquire about this matter. Rav Yosef **said to** the sons of the deceased man: **Give** the daughter her sustenance **from the dates** that are laid out to dry **on the mats** [***budya***].[BL] These fruits are certainly movable property. **Abaye said to** Rav Yosef: **If it was a creditor** who came to collect a debt, **would the Master give him** the right to collect it **in this** manner? Even a creditor, who may collect his claim by repossessing property that the debtor has sold, cannot take movable property from the possession of orphans. A daughter, who cannot collect her sustenance from property that her father sold, should certainly not have the right to collect her sustenance from movable property that belongs to the male orphans.

אֲמַר לֵיהּ: דְּחַזְיָא לְבוּדְיָא קָאָמִינָא.

Rav Yosef **said to** Abaye: I did not mean actual dates lying on mats; rather, **I spoke** of ripe dates ready for plucking, **which are fit for mats.** Since they are still attached to the ground, they are not considered movable property.

BACKGROUND

Dates laid out to dry on the mats – תַּמְרֵי דְּעַל בּוּדְיָא: Some varieties of dates must be harvested as soon as they ripen, as otherwise they will spoil. Others do not need to be harvested as quickly. It was common to spread mats underneath trees of this latter type, and to allow the dates to fall on their own, after which the dates would be left to dry on the mats. This is what Rav Yosef was referring to.

LANGUAGE

Mats [*budya*] – בּוּדְיָא: An alternative reading is *burya*. This is the Aramaic form, which is derived from the Akkadian burū, meaning reed mat.

Perek **IV**
Daf **51** Amud **a**

סוֹף סוֹף, כָּל הָעוֹמֵד לִגְזוֹז כְּגָזוּז דָּמֵי! דִּצְרִיכָא לְדִיקְלָא קָאָמִינָא.

Abaye asked him: **Ultimately, anything that is about to be sheared is considered sheared,** and therefore these dates should already be classified as movable property, from which her sustenance cannot be collected. Rav Yosef replied: **I spoke** of a case when the fruit is nearly fully ripe, but **is still in need of the palm tree.** Since they are attached to the ground, they may be used for the daughter's sustenance.

הַהוּא יָתוֹם וִיתוֹמָה דַּאֲתוֹ לְקַמֵּיהּ דְּרָבָא, אֲמַר לְהוּ רָבָא: הַעֲלוּ לְיָתוֹם בִּשְׁבִיל יְתוֹמָה. אָמְרִי לֵיהּ רַבָּנַן לְרָבָא: וְהָא מָר הוּא דַּאֲמַר: מִמְּקַרְקְעֵי וְלָא מִמִּטַּלְטְלֵי, בֵּין לִמְזוֹנֵי, בֵּין לִכְתוּבָּה וּבֵין לְפַרְנָסָה!

The Gemara relates: There were **a certain** minor **orphan boy and orphan girl who came before Rava. Rava said to** the trustees of the father's estate: **Increase** the amount you give **to the orphan boy,** so that there should be enough **for the orphan girl** as well. **The Sages said to Rava: But it was the Master who said** that one may collect **from land but not from movable property, whether for sustenance, whether for the marriage contract, or whether for** the daughters' **livelihood.** In this case only movable property was available.

אֲמַר לְהוּ: אִילּוּ רָצָה שִׁפְחָה לְשַׁמְּשׁוֹ – מִי לָא יָהֲבִינַן לֵיהּ? כׇּל שֶׁכֵּן הָכָא, דְּאִיכָּא תַּרְתֵּי.

Rava **said to them: If** this orphan **wanted a maidservant to serve him, would we not give him** one? The court would use his father's property to fund this acquisition. **All the more so here, where there are two** factors, as she is his sister and she will serve him as well. It is therefore appropriate to act in this manner, which is to the benefit of both the boy and the girl.

תָּנוּ רַבָּנַן: אֶחָד נְכָסִים שֶׁיֵּשׁ לָהֶן אַחְרָיוּת וְאֶחָד נְכָסִים שֶׁאֵין לָהֶן אַחְרָיוּת – מוֹצִיאִין לִמְזוֹן אִשָּׁה וְלַבָּנוֹת, דִּבְרֵי רַבִּי. רַבִּי שִׁמְעוֹן בֶּן אֶלְעָזָר אוֹמֵר: נְכָסִים שֶׁיֵּשׁ לָהֶן אַחְרָיוּת – מוֹצִיאִין לַבָּנוֹת מִן הַבָּנִים, וְלַבָּנוֹת מִן הַבָּנוֹת, וְלַבָּנִים מִן הַבָּנִים.

§ The Sages taught: With regard to **both property that has a guarantee,** i.e., real estate, **and property that does not have a guarantee,** i.e., movable objects, the court **removes** them from the orphan heirs **for the sustenance of the wife and for the daughters.** This is **the statement of Rabbi** Yehuda HaNasi. **Rabbi Shimon ben Elazar says:** With regard to **property that has a guarantee,** the court **removes** it **from** the possession of **the sons,** who are the heirs, **for** the sake of the sustenance of **the daughters.**[N] If the deceased had only daughters, and the adult daughters have taken possession of the estate, the court takes some of the property **from the** adult **daughters** in order to give an equal share **to the** young **daughters. And** likewise, one takes some of the property **from the** adult **sons** in order to give an equal share **to the** younger **sons.**

וְלַבָּנִים מִן הַבָּנוֹת בִּנְכָסִים מְרוּבִּין, אֲבָל לֹא לַבָּנִים מִן הַבָּנוֹת בִּנְכָסִים מוּעָטִין.

And in a case where the estate has **a large** amount **of property,** so that there is more than enough to provide sustenance for the daughters, the court takes **from the daughters** the property that is not needed to provide for their sustenance and gives it **to the sons,** who are the true heirs. **However,** in a case where the estate has **a small** amount of **property,** one does not take it **from the daughters** in order to give it **to the sons.**

נְכָסִים שֶׁאֵין לָהֶן אַחְרָיוּת – מוֹצִיאִין לַבָּנִים מִן הַבָּנִים, וְלַבָּנוֹת מִן הַבָּנוֹת, וְלַבָּנִים מִן הַבָּנוֹת, אֲבָל לֹא לַבָּנוֹת מִן הַבָּנִים.

By contrast, with regard to **property that does not have a guarantee,** i.e., movable property, the court **removes** some of it from the possession of **the** adult **sons,** if they have taken it, in order to give a fair share **to the** young **sons, and** similarly, some property is taken **from the** adult **daughters** in order to give a fair share **to the** young **daughters. And** if there are both sons and daughters and the daughters have seized the movable property, it is taken **from the daughters,** who are not entitled to sustenance from movable property, and given **to the sons,** who are the heirs. **However,** they do **not** take any **property from the sons** in order to give it **to the daughters.**

אַף עַל גַּב דְּקַיְימָא לַן הֲלָכָה כְּרַבִּי מֵחֲבֵירוֹ – הָכָא הֲלָכָה כְּרַבִּי שִׁמְעוֹן בֶּן אֶלְעָזָר. דְּאָמַר רָבָא: הִלְכְתָא; מִמְּקַרְקְעֵי וְלָא מִמְּטַלְטְלֵי, בֵּין לִכְתוּבָּה בֵּין לִמְזוֹנֵי בֵּין לְפַרְנָסָה.

The Gemara comments: **Even though we maintain** in general that **the *halakha* is in accordance with** the opinion of **Rabbi** Yehuda HaNasi in disputes with **his colleague,** and therefore the *halakha* should follow his ruling rather than that of Rabbi Shimon ben Elazar, **here the *halakha* is in accordance with** the opinion of **Rabbi Shimon ben Elazar. As Rava said: The *halakha*** is that a woman can collect her claim **from land but not from movable property, whether for the marriage contract,**[H] **for sustenance,**[H] **or for** her **livelihood.**

מתני׳ לֹא כָּתַב לָהּ כְּתוּבָּה – בְּתוּלָה גּוֹבָה מָאתַיִם, וְאַלְמָנָה מָנֶה, מִפְּנֵי שֶׁהוּא תְּנַאי בֵּית דִּין. כָּתַב לָהּ שָׂדֶה שָׁוֶה מָנֶה תַּחַת מָאתַיִם זוּז. וְלֹא כָּתַב לָהּ ״כָּל נְכָסִים דְּאִית לִי אַחֲרָאִין לִכְתוּבָּתֵיךְ״ – חַיָּיב. שֶׁהוּא תְּנַאי בֵּית דִּין.

MISHNA If a husband **did not write a marriage contract for** his wife,[H] **a virgin collects two hundred** dinars **and a widow one hundred dinars** upon divorce or the husband's death, **because it is a stipulation of the court** that a wife is entitled to these amounts. If **he wrote** in **her** marriage contract that she is entitled to **a field worth one hundred dinars**[H] **instead of** the **two hundred dinars** to which she is actually entitled, **and he did not** additionally **write for her: All property I have** shall serve as a **guarantee for** the payment of **your marriage contract,** he is nevertheless **obligated** to pay the full two hundred dinars; and he cannot say that she should take only a mortgaged field for payment of her marriage contract, **as it is a stipulation of the court** that all his property is held as surety for the entire sum.

HALAKHA

From what may a marriage contract be claimed – מִמָּה נִגְבֵּית כְּתוּבָּה: According to the original rabbinic enactment, the sum specified in a marriage contract can be collected only from land. However, the *ge'onim* instituted that it can be claimed even from movable property because in their time, most people did not possess land and relied instead on movable objects. The text of the marriage contract reflects this change. Consequently, a widow may also claim her one hundred dinars from movable property (Rambam *Sefer Nashim, Hilkhot Ishut* 16:7; *Shulḥan Arukh, Even HaEzer* 100:1).

From what may a woman collect sustenance – מִמָּה גּוֹבִים מְזוֹנוֹת: As ruled by the Gemara, the sustenance of a widow and the daughters of the deceased may be collected solely from his land. If he left behind only movable property, the court does not give any of it to his daughters. However, the *ge'onim* instituted that money owed due to the marriage contract and its stipulations may be claimed from movable property as well, with the exception of the marriage document concerning male children. Consequently, daughters receive their sustenance even from movable property. However, even if the estate is small, they cannot collect the entire estate, leaving nothing for the heirs, as they have the right to collect movable property by the enactment of the *ge'onim* and not according to the original letter of the law (*Shulḥan Arukh, Even HaEzer* 112:7).

If a husband did not write a marriage contract for his wife – לֹא כָּתַב לָהּ כְּתוּבָּה: Even if a husband neglected to write a marriage contract for his wife, she is entitled to the basic sum of a marriage contract, i.e., two hundred dinars for a virgin and one hundred dinars for a widow (Rambam *Sefer Nashim, Hilkhot Ishut* 12:5; *Shulḥan Arukh, Even HaEzer* 69:1).

If he wrote in her marriage contract that she is entitled to a field worth one hundred dinars, etc. – כָּתַב לָהּ שָׂדֶה שָׁוֶה מָנֶה וכו׳: If a husband failed to write in the marriage contract: All property I have shall serve as a guarantee for the payment of your marriage contract, even if he set aside land for her that was worth less than the sum specified in the marriage contract, he is responsible to pay the entire amount, as this is a stipulation of the court (Rambam *Sefer Nashim, Hilkhot Ishut* 16:10; *Shulḥan Arukh, Even HaEzer* 100:1).

NOTES

The court removes it…for the sake of the sustenance of the daughters, etc. – מוֹצִיאִין לַבָּנוֹת וכו׳: When a deceased individual has both sons and daughters, only the sons inherit his estate. However, it is a stipulation of the marriage contract that the right of the widow and daughters to receive their sustenance from the estate is considered a preexisting claim, comparable to a lien on the estate due to a debt that the father owed to a third party. Consequently, their sustenance overrides the claims of the heirs to the estate. If the estate is not large, there may be nothing left for the sons once the sustenance is provided to the widow and daughters. However, according to Rabbi Shimon ben Elazar, the stipulations of the marriage contract may be claimed only from real estate and not from movable property.

לֹא כָּתַב לָהּ ״אִם תִּשְׁתַּבַּאי אֶפְרְקִינֵךְ וְאוֹתְבִינֵךְ לִי לְאִינְתּוּ״ וּבְכֹהֶנֶת ״אַהַדְרִינָךְ לִמְדִינָתֵיךְ״ – חַיָּיב, שֶׁהוּא תְּנַאי בֵּית דִּין.

Similarly, if **he did not write for her** in the marriage contract: **If you are taken captive**[H] **I will redeem you and restore you to me as a wife, and in** the case **of a priestess,** i.e., the wife of a priest, who is prohibited to return to her husband if she has intercourse with another man even if she is raped, if he did not write: **I will return you**[H] **to your** native **province,** he is nevertheless **obligated** to do so, **as it is a stipulation of the court.**

נִשְׁבֵּית – חַיָּיב לִפְדוֹתָהּ. וְאִם אָמַר: ״הֲרֵי גִּיטָּהּ וּכְתוּבָּתָהּ, וְתִפְדֶּה אֶת עַצְמָהּ״ – אֵינוֹ רַשַּׁאי. לָקְתָה – חַיָּיב לְרַפְּאוֹתָהּ. אָמַר ״הֲרֵי גִּיטָּהּ וּכְתוּבָּתָהּ, תְּרַפֵּא אֶת עַצְמָהּ״ – רַשַּׁאי.

If a woman **was taken captive,** her husband is **obligated to redeem her.**[H] **And if he said: I hereby** give my wife **her bill of divorce and** the payment of **her marriage contract, and let her redeem herself, he is not permitted** to do so, as he already obligated himself to redeem her when he wrote the marriage contract. If his wife **was struck** with illness, he is **obligated to heal her,**[H] i.e., to pay for her medical expenses. In this case, however, if **he said: I hereby** give my wife **her bill of divorce and** the payment of **her marriage contract, and let her heal herself, he is permitted** to do so.[N]

גמ׳ מַנִּי? רַבִּי מֵאִיר הִיא, דְּאָמַר: כׇּל הַפּוֹחֵת לִבְתוּלָה מִמָּאתַיִם וּלְאַלְמָנָה מִמָּנֶה – הֲרֵי זוֹ בְּעִילַת זְנוּת.

GEMARA The Gemara asks: **Who is** the author of the mishna? **It is Rabbi Meir, who said: Anyone who decreases** the sum guaranteed **to a virgin**[H] in her marriage contract to less **than two hundred** dinars, **or** the sum guaranteed **to a widow** to less **than one hundred dinars,** and proceeds to live with his wife, **this is licentious sexual intercourse.** These sums are fixed by the Sages, and a husband is not permitted to pledge less than the established sum.

דְּאִי רַבִּי יְהוּדָה – הָאָמַר: רָצָה – כּוֹתֵב לִבְתוּלָה שְׁטָר שֶׁל מָאתַיִם, וְהִיא כּוֹתֶבֶת ״הִתְקַבַּלְתִּי מִמְּךָ מָנֶה״, וּלְאַלְמָנָה מָנֶה, וְהִיא כּוֹתֶבֶת ״הִתְקַבַּלְתִּי מִמְּךָ חֲמִשִּׁים זוּז״.

For if you say the mishna is in accordance with the opinion of **Rabbi Yehuda, didn't he say** that if the husband **wants, he may write a document** as a marriage contract **for a virgin** in which he pledges **two hundred** dinars, **and she may** immediately **write: I have received from you one hundred dinars,** thereby waiving her rights to half the sum, so that in practice she gets only one hundred dinars? **And** similarly, **he may pledge one hundred dinars** in the marriage contract **of a widow, and she may write: I have received from you fifty dinars.** This is not in accordance with the mishna, which indicates that he cannot give her less than the minimum amount even with her consent.

אֵימָא סֵיפָא: כָּתַב לָהּ שָׂדֶה שָׁוֶה מָנֶה תַּחַת מָאתַיִם זוּז, וְלֹא כָּתַב לָהּ ״כׇּל נְכָסִים דְּאִית לִי אַחֲרָאִין לִכְתוּבָּתֵיךְ״ – חַיָּיב, שֶׁהוּא תְּנַאי בֵּית דִּין. אֲתָאן לְרַבִּי יְהוּדָה, דְּאָמַר: אַחֲרָיוּת – טָעוּת סוֹפֵר הוּא.

The Gemara raises a difficulty: But now **say the latter clause** of the mishna: If **he wrote in her** marriage contract that she is entitled to **a field worth one hundred dinars instead of** the **two hundred dinars** to which she is actually entitled, **and he did not** additionally **write for her: All property I have** shall serve as a **guarantee for** the payment of **your marriage contract,** he is nevertheless **obligated** to pay the full two hundred dinars, **as it is a stipulation of the court** that all his property is held as surety for the entire sum. In this clause, **we come to** the opinion of **Rabbi Yehuda, who said** that omission of the **guarantee** from a document **is** presumed to be **a scribal error,** unless the document explicitly states that the property of the individual who wrote the document is not liened to guarantee the transaction.

דְּאִי רַבִּי מֵאִיר – הָאָמַר: אַחֲרָיוּת לָאו טָעוּת סוֹפֵר הוּא. דִּתְנַן: מָצָא שִׁטְרֵי חוֹב, אִם

For if this is the opinion of **Rabbi Meir, didn't he say** that omission of the **guarantee** from a document **is not a scribal error,** i.e., a lien can be placed on the property to guarantee the transaction only if the document explicitly states this to be the case. The Gemara cites the source of this dispute. **As we learned** in a mishna (*Bava Metzia* 12b): With regard to one who **found promissory notes, if**

NOTES

Redemption and medical treatment – **פִּדְיוֹן וְרִיפּוּי:** The early authorities addressed the question of why a husband may not absolve himself of the obligation to redeem his wife from captivity by divorcing her, whereas he may absolve himself of the obligation to pay for her medical expenses in this manner. The obligation to redeem one's wife from captivity is treated stringently in general, such that the wife cannot absolve her husband of this obligation (see *Tosafot* on 47b), a factor that may play a role in this discussion. Some commentaries explain that providing medical care is a form of sustenance and, consequently, is limited according to the rules of providing sustenance. Since a man who divorces his wife is no longer obligated to provide her with sustenance, he is also exempt from paying for her medical needs at that time. Conversely, as soon as the woman is taken captive, her husband becomes obligated to redeem her. That preexisting obligation is not canceled by divorce (Rashi; Ramah). Furthermore, the obligation to redeem captives is treated stringently so as to avoid the possibility that the captive will be assimilated among gentiles.

HALAKHA

If he did not write for her: If you are taken captive, etc. – **לֹא כָּתַב לָהּ אִם תִּשְׁתַּבַּאי וכו׳:** If a husband did not write for his wife that if she is taken captive he will redeem her and restore her as his wife, he is nevertheless obligated to do so, as this is a stipulation of the court (Rambam *Sefer Nashim*, *Hilkhot Ishut* 12:5; *Shulḥan Arukh*, *Even HaEzer* 69:1).

And in the case of a priestess, if he did not write: I will return you, etc. – **וּבְכֹהֶנֶת אַהַדְרִינָךְ וכו׳:** A priest must write in his wife's marriage contract: If you are captured I will redeem you and restore you to your native province. Even if he did not include this sentence in the marriage contract, he is obligated to redeem her and return her to her father's house, as it is a stipulation of the court. The reason is that if she is raped by her captors she is prohibited to return to her husband (Rambam *Sefer Nashim*, *Hilkhot Ishut* 14:18; *Shulḥan Arukh*, *Even HaEzer* 78:6).

If a woman was taken captive her husband is obligated to redeem her – **נִשְׁבֵּית חַיָּיב לִפְדוֹתָהּ:** If a man's wife was captured he is obligated to redeem her, and he cannot say: Here is your bill of divorce and the money guaranteed to you in your marriage contract; go and redeem yourself (Rambam *Sefer Nashim*, *Hilkhot Ishut* 14:18; *Shulḥan Arukh*, *Even HaEzer* 78:1).

If his wife was struck with illness he is obligated to heal her – **לָקְתָה חַיָּיב לְרַפְּאוֹתָהּ:** If a woman becomes ill, her husband is obligated to pay her medical expenses. If the husband, seeing that it is a protracted illness, says to her: Either pay for your own expenses with the money of your marriage contract or I will divorce you and give you the marriage contract, he is permitted to do so, but this is not the proper way to behave. Some authorities note that he can remain married to her in this manner only if he allows her to spend the sum of money he included in the marriage contract that is beyond the basic sum required by law, as a couple may not stay together with a marriage contract of less than the minimum amount (*Perisha*). Others add that if she is bedridden he may not divorce her until she recuperates (*Maggid Mishne*, citing Rashba). Nowadays, after Rabbeinu Gershom disallowed divorce that is undertaken without the consent of the wife, it is certainly prohibited to divorce her against her will (see *Ḥelkat Meḥokek* and see *Beit Shmuel*, citing Maharshal; Rambam *Sefer Nashim*, *Hilkhot Ishut* 14:17; *Shulḥan Arukh*, *Even HaEzer* 79:1, 3).

Anyone who decreases the sum guaranteed to a virgin, etc. – **כׇּל הַפּוֹחֵת לִבְתוּלָה, וכו׳:** If a man provides a marriage contract for his wife that specifies a sum that is less than the required amount of two hundred dinars for a virgin or one hundred dinars for a widow, they are not permitted to live together. If they have intercourse, it is considered a licentious act. In this regard, it makes no difference whether he initially wrote a smaller sum or if she wrote that she had received part of her marriage contract. However, the Sages disagreed as to whether this document is of any value. Some maintain that any such document or condition reducing her marriage contract is entirely void and the woman is entitled to the full sum of a marriage contract (Rambam), whereas others rule that if she wrote that she had already received part of the payment, although they may not live together, the document is binding (*Tur*; Rambam *Sefer Nashim*, *Hilkhot Ishut* 12:8; *Shulḥan Arukh*, *Even HaEzer* 66:9).

יֵשׁ בָּהֶן אַחֲרָיוּת נְכָסִים – לֹא יַחֲזִיר, שֶׁבֵּית דִּין נִפְרָעִין מֵהֶן.

they include a property guarantee he may not return them to the lender, as he does not know who lost them. It is possible that the debt has already been paid and the documents were returned to the borrower, and he lost them. He may not give them back to the lender even if the borrower admits that he still owes the money, **as the court collects** the debt **from** purchasers of the borrower's property. There is a concern that the borrower has repaid the loan and he is saying that he did not yet repay it because he has conspired with the lender to convince the court to confiscate liened property that the borrower sold, and the lender and borrower will divide the proceeds.

אֵין בָּהֶן אַחֲרָיוּת נְכָסִים – יַחֲזִיר, שֶׁאֵין בֵּית דִּין נִפְרָעִין מֵהֶן, דִּבְרֵי רַבִּי מֵאִיר. וַחֲכָמִים אוֹמְרִים: אֶחָד זֶה וְאֶחָד זֶה לֹא יַחֲזִיר, שֶׁבֵּית דִּין נִפְרָעִין מֵהֶן.

If, however, the documents were of the kind that **do not include a property guarantee he returns them,** as in this case **the court does not collect from** purchasers of the borrower's property. This is **the statement of Rabbi Meir. And the Rabbis say:** In **both this** case **and that** one, **he may not return** the promissory notes, **as the court collects from** purchasers of the borrower's property[H] regardless, as it is assumed that the omission of the property guarantee from a document is merely a scribal error.

רֵישָׁא רַבִּי מֵאִיר וְסֵיפָא רַבִּי יְהוּדָה! וְכִי תֵּימָא: כּוּלָּהּ רַבִּי מֵאִיר הִיא, וְשָׁאנֵי לֵיהּ לְרַבִּי מֵאִיר בֵּין כְּתוּבָּה לִשְׁטָרֵי – וּמִי שָׁאנֵי לֵיהּ?

If so, **the first clause** of the mishna here **is** in accordance with the opinion of **Rabbi Meir, and the latter clause is** in accordance with the opinion of **Rabbi Yehuda. And if you would say** that the **entire** mishna **is** in accordance with the opinion of **Rabbi Meir, and there is a difference for Rabbi Meir between a marriage contract and** other **documents,** i.e., the guarantee of a marriage contract applies even if it is omitted but the property guarantee in other contracts does not, **is there** really **a difference for him** between the two types of documents?

וְהָתַנְיָא: חֲמִשָּׁה גּוֹבִין מִן הַמְּחוֹרָרִין, וְאֵלּוּ הֵן: פֵּירוֹת, וּשְׁבַח פֵּירוֹת, וְהַמְקַבֵּל עָלָיו לָזוּן אֶת בֶּן אִשְׁתּוֹ וּבַת אִשְׁתּוֹ, וּגְט חוֹב שֶׁאֵין בּוֹ אַחֲרָיוּת, וּכְתוּבַּת אִשָּׁה שֶׁאֵין בָּהּ אַחֲרָיוּת.

Isn't it taught in a *baraita*: **Five** claims **may be collected** only **from free** assets, **and they are as follows: Produce,**[H] **and enhancement** to the **produce.**[HN] **And** likewise, in the case of **one who accepts upon himself** the duty **to sustain his wife's son or his wife's daughter**[H] and then dies, they receive their support only from the estate's free assets. **And** other claims that may be collected only from free assets are **a document of debt that does not include** the clause of property **guarantee, and the marriage contract of a wife that does not include** the clause of property **guarantee.**

מַאן שָׁמְעַתְּ לֵיהּ דְּאָמַר אַחֲרָיוּת לָאו טָעוּת סוֹפֵר הוּא – רַבִּי מֵאִיר, וְקָתָנֵי: כְּתוּבַּת אִשָּׁה!

The Gemara reasons: **Whom have you heard say** that omission of the property **guarantee** from a document **is not a scribal error? Rabbi Meir, and** yet the *baraita* **teaches** that the same applies to the **marriage contract of a wife.** This proves that according to Rabbi Meir, there is no difference between a marriage contract and other documents.

HALAKHA

As the court collects from purchasers of the borrower's property – שֶׁבֵּית דִּין נִפְרָעִין מֵהֶן: With regard to one who finds promissory notes, even if they do not include a clause of guarantee and the borrower admits to owing the money, he may not give them back to the lender. This is the case even if the debt is accredited by others, and even if it is within the time stipulated on the document. The reason is that there is a concern that the pair might have conspired to cheat the purchasers of the borrower's property, as stated by the Rabbis. However, if the document explicitly states that it does not include a guarantee, and the borrower admits he owes the money, it may be returned to the lender. Since property sold by the purchaser cannot be repossessed in this case, there is no concern about a conspiracy, and therefore even the Rabbis concede in this case (*Beit Yosef*; Vilna Gaon; Rambam *Sefer Nezikim, Hilkhot Gezeila VaAveda* 18:1; *Shulḥan Arukh, Ḥoshen Mishpat* 65:6).

Produce – פֵּירוֹת: If someone stole land and ruined it or consumed its produce, when the owner claims reimbursement for the damage or the produce, he may collect it only from the free assets of the robber, but not from property that he sold after he stole the land (Rambam *Sefer Nezikim, Hilkhot Gezeila VaAveda* 9:5; *Shulḥan Arukh, Ḥoshen Mishpat* 372:1).

Enhancement to the produce – שְׁבַח פֵּירוֹת: If someone stole a field and sold it, and the purchaser enhanced it, when the field is later restored to its original owner the following calculation is made: If the added value of the property is greater than the expenses the buyer incurred for this undertaking, the buyer claims his expenses from the owner of the field, while the principal, i.e., the amount he paid for the field, as well as the difference between the expenses he collects from the owner and the amount by which his enhancements raised the value of the field, he collects from the robber. He may claim the principal even by repossessing other property that the robber sold, whereas the added value can be collected only from free assets (Rambam *Sefer Nezikim, Hilkhot Gezeila VaAveda* 9:7; *Shulḥan Arukh, Ḥoshen Mishpat* 373:1).

One who accepts upon himself the duty to sustain his wife's children – הַמְקַבֵּל עָלָיו לָזוּן יַלְדֵי אִשְׁתּוֹ: In the case of a husband who obligated himself to sustain his wife's children from a previous marriage and then died, if this duty was accepted by an act of acquisition or written in a document, the children collect their sustenance even from property that the man sold after accepting this obligation. If he merely gave a verbal promise they may collect their sustenance only from free assets (Rambam *Sefer Nashim, Hilkhot Ishut* 23:18; *Shulḥan Arukh, Even HaEzer* 104:4).

NOTES

Produce and enhancement to the produce – פֵּירוֹת וּשְׁבַח פֵּירוֹת: Rashi explains that this is referring to a case where one inadvertently buys stolen property, e.g., a field, which is then repossessed by its rightful owner, together with the produce growing in the field. The purchaser then has a right to claim reimbursement from the seller for the field, the produce that was growing in the field, and the enhancements that the purchaser made to the field, which are referred to here as enhancement to the produce. The purchaser may collect his claim on the value of the field even from property that the seller sold to others after he sold the stolen property to this purchaser. However, he can collect the value of the produce and the enhancements that he made to the property only from free assets, i.e., assets currently held by the seller. He may not collect these claims from property the seller sold to others because, if he could, there would be no way for the later purchasers to assess the risk that their purchases would be repossessed.

The Ritva comments that the *tanna* specifies these five claims because they may be collected only from free assets even if the individual has a document attesting to his claims. However, all claims that are not documented may be collected only from free assets.

אִיבָּעֵית אֵימָא רַבִּי מֵאִיר, וְאִיבָּעֵית אֵימָא רַבִּי יְהוּדָה; אִיבָּעֵית אֵימָא רַבִּי יְהוּדָה: הָתָם – כָּתְבָה לֵיהּ ״הִתְקַבַּלְתִּי״. הָכָא – לָא כָּתְבָה לֵיהּ ״הִתְקַבַּלְתִּי״.

The Gemara answers: **If you wish, say** that the mishna here is in accordance with the opinion of **Rabbi Meir, and if you wish, say** that it is in accordance with the opinion of **Rabbi Yehuda.** The Gemara elaborates: **If you wish, say** that the mishna is in accordance with the opinion of **Rabbi Yehuda,** and **there,** in the other mishna (54b), the case is where **she wrote to him: I have received** it,[N] thereby waiving her right to part of the marriage contract. In contrast, **here, she did not write to him: I have received** it, and therefore she collects the entire sum from him even if he did not write a marriage contract.

אִיבָּעֵית אֵימָא רַבִּי מֵאִיר: מַאי חַיָּיב דְּקָתָנֵי – מִן הַמְּחוֹרָרִין.

Conversely, **if you wish, say** that the mishna is in accordance with the opinion of **Rabbi Meir.** According to this interpretation, **what is** the meaning of the phrase: He is **obligated, which is taught** in the latter clause of the mishna with regard to the case where the marriage contract did not specify that the husband's property will serve as a guarantee of his obligations toward his wife? It means that the wife's claims may be collected only **from the** husband's **free** assets, i.e., she does not have a lien on his property.

״לֹא כָּתַב לָהּ״ וכו׳. אָמַר אֲבוּהּ דִּשְׁמוּאֵל: אֵשֶׁת יִשְׂרָאֵל שֶׁנֶּאֶנְסָה – אֲסוּרָה לְבַעְלָהּ, חָיְישִׁינַן שֶׁמָּא תְּחִלָּתָהּ בְּאוֹנֶס וְסוֹפָהּ בְּרָצוֹן.

§ The mishna taught that if the husband **did not write for her** that he would redeem her from captivity and restore her to him, he is nevertheless obligated to do so, as this is a stipulation of the court. **Shmuel's father said: The wife of an Israelite who was raped is forbidden to her husband,** as **we are concerned** that **perhaps her** ordeal **started as rape and ended willingly,** i.e., during the act she may have acquiesced, and a married woman who willingly had relations with another man is forbidden to her husband.

אֵיתִיבֵיהּ רַב לַאֲבוּהּ דִּשְׁמוּאֵל: ״אִם תִּשְׁתַּבַּאי אֶפְרְקִינָךְ וְאוֹתְבִינָךְ לִי לְאִינְתּוּ״! אִישְׁתִּיק.

Rav raised an objection to the opinion of **Shmuel's father** from the mishna, which states that one of the stipulations of the marriage contract reads: **If you are taken captive I will redeem you and restore you to me as a wife.** This indicates that despite the possibility that she might have been raped during captivity, she remains permitted to her husband if he is not a priest, and there is no concern that she might have ultimately agreed to the act. Shmuel's father **was silent** and did not respond.

קָרֵי רַב עֲלֵיהּ דַּאֲבוּהּ דִּשְׁמוּאֵל: ״שָׂרִים עָצְרוּ בְמִלִּים וְכַף יָשִׂימוּ לְפִיהֶם״. מַאי אִית לֵיהּ לְמֵימַר – בִּשְׁבוּיָה הֵקִילוּ.

Rav recited the following verse **about Shmuel's father: "The princes refrained from talking and laid a hand upon their mouths"** (Job 29:9). The Gemara comments: The application of this verse to Shmuel's father indicates that he refrained from responding despite the fact that an answer was available. But **what is there for him to say** in reply? The Gemara answers: He could have said that **in** the case of **a captive woman they were lenient.** Since it is uncertain whether she was in fact raped during her captivity, the Sages were lenient. However, it is possible that they were more stringent in the case of a woman who was definitely raped.

וְלַאֲבוּהּ דִּשְׁמוּאֵל, אוֹנֶס דְּשַׁרְיָא רַחֲמָנָא הֵיכִי מַשְׁכַּחַתְּ לַהּ? כְּגוֹן דְּקָאָמְרִי עֵדִים שֶׁצָּוְוחָה מִתְּחִלָּה וְעַד סוֹף.

The Gemara further asks: **According to Shmuel's father, how can you find** a case of **rape where the Merciful One permits** the victim to remain married to her husband? It is always possible that she might have ultimately acquiesced. The Gemara answers: **For example, where witnesses say that she screamed** continuously **from beginning to end.**

וּפְלִיגָא דְּרָבָא, דְּאָמַר רָבָא: כׇּל שֶׁתְּחִלָּתָהּ בְּאוֹנֶס וְסוֹפָהּ בְּרָצוֹן אֲפִילּוּ הִיא אוֹמֶרֶת: הַנִּיחוּ לוֹ, שֶׁאִלְמָלֵא (לֹא) נִזְקַק לָהּ הִיא שׂוֹכַרְתּוֹ – מוּתֶּרֶת, מַאי טַעְמָא – יֵצֶר אַלְבְּשָׁהּ.

The Gemara comments: **And** Shmuel's father **disagrees** with the opinion **of Rava. As Rava said:** With regard to **any** case **that starts as rape and ends willingly,**[H] **even** if **she** ultimately **says: Leave him,** and she further states **that if he had not** forcibly initiated **intercourse with her, she** would **have hired him** for intercourse, **she is** nevertheless **permitted** to her husband. **What is the reason** for this? **The** evil **inclination took hold of her** during the act, and therefore she is still considered to have engaged in intercourse against her will.

NOTES

There the case is where she wrote to him: I have received it – הָתָם כָּתְבָה לֵיהּ הִתְקַבַּלְתִּי: In other words, even Rabbi Yehuda agrees that one cannot violate the enactment of the Sages by writing a marriage contract for less than the minimum amount. His dispute with Rabbi Meir concerns a situation where he accepted the full obligation of the marriage contract, and his wife relinquished her right to part of that sum. In that case it is possible to claim that the marriage was performed appropriately, and she merely forgave him a portion of her monetary claim (Rabbi Aharon HaLevi).

HALAKHA

Starts as rape and ends willingly – תְּחִלָּתָהּ בְּאוֹנֶס וְסוֹף בְּרָצוֹן: If the wife of a regular Israelite, was raped, she is permitted to remain married to her husband. In any situation where the intercourse began against her will she is considered the victim of a rape even if she later consented. The *halakha* is in accordance with the opinion of Rava, as his ruling is supported by a *baraita* (Rambam *Sefer Kedusha*, *Hilkhot Issurei Bia* 1:9; *Shulḥan Arukh*, *Even HaEzer* 6:11).

תניא כוותיה דרבא: "והיא לא נתפשה" – אסורה. הא נתפשה – מותרת. ויש לך אחרת שאף על פי שלא נתפשה – מותרת. ואיזו – זו כל שתחלתה באונס וסופה ברצון.

It **is taught** in a *baraita* **in accordance with** the opinion of **Rava:** The verse states with regard to a *sota*: "And a man lies with her… **and she was not taken**" (Numbers 5:13). This is referring to a woman who had intercourse but was not taken forcefully, i.e., raped, and therefore **she is forbidden** to her husband. It may be inferred from this that if she **was taken** forcefully, she is **permitted** to him. **And** the word "she" teaches **that you have** a case of **another** woman, **where even though she was not taken** forcefully **she is permitted.**[N] **And which** case **is this? This is any** case **that starts as rape and ends willingly.** Although at the conclusion of the act she was not taken forcefully, she is nevertheless permitted to her husband, as stated by Rava.

תניא אידך: "והיא לא נתפשה" – אסורה, הא נתפשה – מותרת. ויש לך אחרת שאף על פי שנתפשה אסורה, ואיזו – זו אשת כהן.

A different inference from the same verse **is taught** in **another** *baraita*: **"And she was not taken"**; in this case, the woman **is forbidden** to her husband. It may be inferred that if **she was taken** forcefully, **she is permitted** to her husband. **And you have another** case **where, even though she was taken** forcefully, **she is forbidden** to her husband. **And which** case **is this? This is** the case of **the wife of a priest,** who is forbidden to her husband even if she is the victim of a rape.[H]

אמר רב יהודה אמר שמואל משום רבי ישמעאל: "והיא לא נתפשה" – אסורה, הא נתפשה – מותרת, ויש לה אחרת שאף על פי שלא נתפשה מותרת, ואיזו – זו שקידושיה קדושי טעות, שאפילו בנה מורכב על כתיפה ממאנת והולכת לה.

Rav Yehuda said another exposition of this same verse that **Shmuel said in the name of Rabbi Yishmael: "And she was not taken"**; in this case **she is forbidden** to her husband. It may be inferred that if she **was taken** forcefully **she is permitted** to her husband. **And there is** a case of **another** woman **where, even though she was not taken** forcefully, she nevertheless remains **permitted. And which** case **is this?** This is referring **to one whose betrothal was a mistaken betrothal,**[H] **as, even if her son** from this marriage **is riding on her shoulders she may refuse** to remain with her husband **and go** off as pleases **her.** Since she was not really married to begin with, an act of intercourse with another man does not render her forbidden to the man with whom she performed a mistaken betrothal.

אמר רב יהודה: הני נשי דגנבו גנבי – שריין לגברייהו. אמרי ליה רבנן לרב יהודה: והא קא ממטיאן להו נהמא! מחמת יראה. והא קא משלחן להו גירי! מחמת יראה. ודאי, שבקינהו ואזלן מנפשייהו – אסירן.

Rav Yehuda said: Those women stolen by kidnappers[H] **are permitted to their husbands,** as, even if they had intercourse with their captors it is considered rape. **The Rabbis said to Rav Yehuda: But** while they are captives **they bring**[N] their kidnappers **bread.** This indicates that they are not acting under duress. He replied: They do so **due to fear.** The Rabbis further inquired: **But they send them arrows.** Rav Yehuda again replied: This too is **due to fear.** However, I **certainly** agree that if the kidnappers **leave them alone, and they go** back to them **of their own accord, they are forbidden** to their husbands, as it is clear that they are no longer acting out of fear.

תנו רבנן: שבויי מלכות – הרי הן כשבויין, גנובי ליסטות – אינן כשבויין. והתניא איפכא!

The Sages taught: With regard to women **captured by the monarchy** for the purpose of having intercourse with the king, **they are** considered to be **like captives,** i.e., they are assumed to have been raped but not to have consented to intercourse. However, **those stolen by bandits are not** considered to be **like captives,**[N] as there is a concern that they might have consented to their captors, thinking that they will marry them. The Gemara raises a difficulty: **But isn't it taught** in a *baraita* that **the reverse** is the case, i.e., women taken by the monarchy are not classified as captives, whereas this status does apply to those abducted by bandits?

NOTES

Where even though she was not taken forcefully she is permitted – שאף על פי שלא נתפשה מותרת: Some commentaries explain this exposition as follows: The term "and she" in the verse is unnecessary, as it is implied by the feminine conjugation of the verb "taken." By adding this extra term, the Torah indicates that as long as there is any compulsion, even if, by the end of the act, the woman was willing, she is not forbidden to her husband (*Talmidei Rabbeinu Yona*). The author of *Shita Mekubbetzet* notes that Rashi explains this differently, that the term "and she" always implies a limitation of the *halakha* stated in the verse.

But while they are captives they bring, etc. – והא קא ממטיאן וכו׳: By behaving in this manner, these women apparently demonstrate that they are not acting under any immediate threat, as they go off and bring bread back to their captors. Similarly, they hand arrows to their captors while they are engaged in combat, despite the fact that they could increase the chances of the bandits being killed if they were to refrain from doing so (*Shita Mekubbetzet*).

Are not considered like captives – אינן כשבויין: Some write that whenever a woman is considered to have engaged in intercourse willingly and was not raped, the obligation to redeem her is no longer in effect, as a penalty for her acquiescence to the act (Rabbi Shmuel HaNagid, citing *ge'onim*).

HALAKHA

The wife of a priest who was raped – אשת כהן שנאנסה: If the wife of a priest had intercourse with another man, even against her will, she is forbidden to her husband (Rambam *Sefer Kedusha*, *Hilkhot Issurei Bia* 18:8; *Shulḥan Arukh*, *Even HaEzer* 6:10).

Whose betrothal was a mistaken betrothal – שקידושיה קדושי טעות: Any woman who is not married or betrothed by Torah law is considered a single woman. Even if she is married by rabbinic law and she has intercourse with another man, she remains permitted to her husband, even if he is a priest (Rambam *Sefer Kedusha*, *Hilkhot Issurei Bia* 3:2, and *Maggid Mishne* there).

Women stolen by kidnappers – נשי דגנבו גנבי: Women who were snatched by bandits are permitted to their husbands if they are non-priests, as it is assumed that the women were raped. However, if they returned to their captors of their own free will after they were released they are forbidden to their husbands, in accordance with the opinion of Rav Yehuda (Rambam *Sefer Nashim*, *Hilkhot Ishut* 24:20).

מַלְכוּת אַמַּלְכוּת לָא קַשְׁיָא; הָא – בְּמַלְכוּת אֲחַשְׁוֵרוֹשׁ, הָא – בְּמַלְכוּת בֶּן נֵצֶר.

The Gemara answers: The apparent contradiction between the ruling of one *baraita* with regard to those captured by the **monarchy** and the ruling of the other *baraita* with regard to those captured by the **monarchy** is **not difficult: This** first *baraita* is referring **to the monarchy of Ahasuerus,** i.e., a powerful king, as the woman is aware that he is merely using her to satisfy his lust and will certainly not marry her, whereas **that** other *baraita* is dealing **with the monarchy of ben Netzer,**[P] a man who established for himself a minor kingdom through robbery and small-scale conquests. It is possible for a woman to suppose that a king like ben Netzer will eventually marry her.

לִיסְטוּת אַלִּיסְטוּת לָא קַשְׁיָא; הָא – בְּבֶן נֵצֶר, הָא – בְּלִיסְטִים דְּעָלְמָא. וּבֶן נֵצֶר, הָתָם קָרֵי לֵיהּ מֶלֶךְ וְהָכָא קָרֵי לֵיהּ לִסְטִים! אִין, גַּבֵּי אֲחַשְׁוֵרוֹשׁ – לִסְטִים הוּא, גַּבֵּי לִסְטִים דְּעָלְמָא – מֶלֶךְ הוּא.

Similarly, the apparent contradiction between the ruling of one *baraita* with regard to those kidnapped by **bandits** and the ruling of the other *baraita* with regard to those kidnapped by **bandits** is **not difficult: This** first *baraita* is referring **to** the banditry of **ben Netzer,**[N] as she might agree to his advances, hoping to become the wife of a king. Conversely, **that** other *baraita* is dealing **with regular bandits** [***listim***],[L] as it can be assumed that the woman did not acquiesce to having intercourse, as, even if he wanted to marry her she would not agree. The Gemara asks: **And** this **ben Netzer,** how can it be that **there he is called a king and here he is called a bandit?** The Gemara answers: **Yes,** when considered **alongside Ahasuerus he is** merely **a bandit,** but when considered **alongside a regular bandit he is** deemed **a king.**

"וּבְכָהֶנֶת אֲהַדְרִינָךְ לִמְדִינָתֵיךְ" וכו׳. אָמַר אַבָּיֵי: אַלְמָנָה לְכֹהֵן גָּדוֹל – חַיָּיב לִפְדוֹתָהּ, שֶׁאֲנִי קוֹרֵא בָּהּ "וּבְכָהֶנֶת אֲהַדְרִינָךְ לִמְדִינָתֵיךְ".

§ The mishna taught: **And in** the case of **a priestess,** i.e., the wife of a priest, even if her husband did not write: If you are taken captive **I will** redeem you and **return you to your** native **province,** he is obligated to do so. **Abaye said:** In the case of **a widow** who was married **to a High Priest,** although the marriage is prohibited by Torah law, if she is taken captive he is **obligated to redeem her, as I apply** to **her** the clause: **And in** the case of **a priestess: I will return you to your** native **province.** Her husband can, and therefore must, fulfill this clause just as he could if he had married a woman who is permitted to him.

LANGUAGE

Bandits [*listim*] – **לִסְטִים**: From the Greek λῃστής, *lēstēs*, meaning robber or bandit.

PERSONALITIES

Ben Netzer – בֶּן נֵצֶר: Ben Netzer is the original family name of a man known as Odenathus, from the city of Tadmor, also known as Palmyra, Syria. Odenathus ruled Palmyra in the middle of the third century, and he succeeded in exploiting the extended conflict between the Romans and the Persians, a war with no clear victor, to increase his power and influence far beyond his city. After he allied himself with the Romans and fought against Shapur I, king of Persia, the Romans appointed him governor of all the adjacent provinces. Nevertheless, he tried to establish his own independent kingdom. Odenathus was murdered in 267 CE, and his grave is found among the ruins of ancient Palmyra. His widow, Queen Zenobia, who ruled in his stead, was able to expand his kingdom as far as the Egyptian border before she was murdered by the Romans. The Sages held this kingdom and its rulers in very low regard, apparently due to their hostile stance toward Jews, as exemplified by their conquest and destruction of the city of Neharde'a, a Jewish center. The Gemara describes ben Netzer's status as somewhere between a king and a bandit.

NOTES

This is referring to ben Netzer – הָא בְּבֶן נֵצֶר: There are differences of opinion as to why women who are captives of the kingdom of ben Netzer differ from captives of other kings or bandits. Some explain that a woman who has relations with a powerful king knows that he has no intention of marrying her, and therefore does not engage in the act willingly. In contrast, ben Netzer was a small-scale king and therefore it is possible that she participated willingly, thinking that he might marry her. In the case of a regular bandit she harbors no desire to marry him, and therefore she is presumed to have been raped (Rashi; Rid; Meiri). Others question this interpretation, claiming that it is unreasonable to suspect a woman of agreeing to intercourse in order to marry her captor (Ramban).

An alternative suggestion is that in the case of a powerful king like Ahasuerus, the woman is aware that there is no escape from him, and she does not bother to scream out in protest. With regard to ben Netzer, however, who was not so powerful, she might have been rescued had she cried out, and therefore if she did not cry out, it is assumed that she participated willingly (Rabbeinu Ḥananel). The Ramban raises various objections to this interpretation as well. One of his difficulties is that according to this reasoning she should be forbidden to her husband in the case of a regular bandit as well. She should certainly have hoped for rescue and cried out, and if she didn't the assumption is that she participated willingly. He further states that Rabbeinu Ḥananel's explanation can be accepted if one adds that in the case of an ordinary bandit she is afraid that he might kill her, whereas it was beneath ben Netzer's dignity to hurt or rape women in his status as king, and therefore he would have let her go had she resisted. A king as powerful as Ahasuerus, however, does not care what others think of him. A different interpretation cited by the Ramban, which he prefers, is that for various reasons they refrained from raping women in the kingdom of ben Netzer, and therefore a woman who had intercourse there must have done so willingly (see also *Nimmukei Yosef*).

NOTES

One who vows that his wife may not derive benefit from him – הַמַּדִּיר אֶת אִשְׁתּוֹ: The details of these *halakhot* are clarified in Chapter Seven. For the purposes of this discussion, it is enough to state that this refers to a vow that prevents the couple from living together and that forces them to divorce.

The wife of a priest – אֵשֶׁת כֹּהֵן: In the case of a non-priest, since he cannot fulfill the clause: I will restore you to me as my wife, he does not have to redeem her. In the case of a priest, the marriage contract stipulates that he will return her to her native province, which he can fulfill even if he pronounced a vow prohibiting her from deriving benefit from him. Although he helps her when he redeems her from captivity, he does not provide her with direct, physical benefit, which is rendered prohibited by his vow.

מַמְזֶרֶת וּנְתִינָה לְיִשְׂרָאֵל – אֵינוֹ חַיָּיב לִפְדּוֹתָהּ, שֶׁאֵין אֲנִי קוֹרֵא בָּהּ ״וְאוֹתְבִינֵךְ לִי לְאִנְתּוּ״. רָבָא אָמַר: כׇּל שֶׁאִיסּוּר שִׁבְיָיה גּוֹרֵם לָהּ – חַיָּיב לִפְדּוֹתָהּ, אִיסּוּר דָּבָר אַחֵר גּוֹרֵם לָהּ – אֵינוֹ חַיָּיב לִפְדּוֹתָהּ.

In the case of a *mamzeret* **or a Gibeonite woman** married **to an Israelite,** who are entitled to a marriage contract despite the fact that the relationship is forbidden and they must get divorced, **he is not obligated to redeem her, as I do not apply to her** the clause: **And I will restore you to me as a wife,** as she is forbidden to him. **Rava said:** In **any** case **where the prohibition of her captivity,** i.e., the fact that she was taken captive, **causes her**[H] to be forbidden to her husband, as in the case of a priest's wife who was taken captive, **he is obligated to redeem her.** However, if **another prohibition causes her** to be forbidden to her husband, e.g., the case of a widow who is married to a High Priest, **he is not obligated to redeem her.**

לֵימָא כְּתַנָּאֵי: הַמַּדִּיר אֶת אִשְׁתּוֹ וְנִשְׁבֵּית, רַבִּי אֱלִיעֶזֶר אוֹמֵר: פּוֹדֶה וְנוֹתֵן לָהּ כְּתוּבָּתָהּ, רַבִּי יְהוֹשֻׁעַ אוֹמֵר: נוֹתֵן לָהּ כְּתוּבָּתָהּ, וְאֵינוֹ פּוֹדֶה.

The Gemara suggests: **Let us say** that this is **parallel to** a dispute between *tanna'im*. As it is taught in a *baraita*: In the case of **one who vows** that **his wife** may not derive benefit from him,[N] in which case he must divorce her, **and she** is then **taken captive,**[H] **Rabbi Eliezer says:** He **redeems** her **and gives her** the payment for **her marriage contract. Rabbi Yehoshua says:** He **gives her** the payment for **her marriage contract but he does not** have to **redeem** her, as he may not take her back as his wife, due to his vow.

אָמַר רַבִּי נָתָן, שָׁאַלְתִּי אֶת סוּמָכוֹס: כְּשֶׁאָמַר רַבִּי יְהוֹשֻׁעַ נוֹתֵן לָהּ כְּתוּבָּתָהּ וְאֵינוֹ פּוֹדֶה – כְּשֶׁהִדִּירָהּ וּלְבַסּוֹף נִשְׁבֵּית, אוֹ בְּנִשְׁבֵּית וּלְבַסּוֹף הִדִּירָהּ?

Rabbi Natan said: I asked Sumakhos: When Rabbi Yehoshua said that he **gives her** the payment for **her marriage contract but he does not** have to **redeem** her, was he referring to a case **where he vowed** that **she** may not derive benefit from him **and she was subsequently taken captive, or** was he speaking **of one who was taken captive and he subsequently vowed** that **she** may not derive benefit from him?

וְאָמַר לִי: לֹא שָׁמַעְתִּי, וְנִרְאִין דְּבָרִים שֶׁהִדִּירָהּ וּלְבַסּוֹף נִשְׁבֵּית. דְּאִי אָמְרַתְּ נִשְׁבֵּית וּלְבַסּוֹף הִדִּירָהּ – אָתֵי לְאִיעֲרוּמֵי.

And he said to me: I have not heard a tradition on this matter, **but it would appear that** Rabbi Yehoshua does not obligate the husband to redeem her in a situation where **he vowed** that **she** may not derive benefit from him **and she was subsequently taken captive. As, if you say** that the same *halakha* applies in a case where **she was taken captive and he subsequently vowed** that **she** may not derive benefit from him, the husband might **come to engage in trickery.** If he wants to release himself from the duty to ransom his wife after she is captured, he can simply vow that she may not derive benefit from him, in which case he would be obligated to pay her only the marriage contract.

מַאי לָאו בְּמַדִּיר אֵשֶׁת כֹּהֵן קָמִיפַּלְגִי, וְאַבַּיֵי דְּאָמַר כְּרַבִּי אֱלִיעֶזֶר, וְרָבָא דְּאָמַר כְּרַבִּי יְהוֹשֻׁעַ?

The Gemara now analyzes the suggested comparison between the opinions cited in this *baraita* and the dispute between Abaye and Rava. **What, is it not** the case that the *tanna'im* **disagree about** a priest **who vows** that his wife, i.e., **the wife of a priest,**[N] may not derive benefit from him? **And Abaye spoke in accordance with** the opinion of **Rabbi Eliezer** when he said that the husband must redeem his wife even if she is forbidden to him due to something other than the fact that she was taken captive, **and Rava spoke in accordance with** the opinion of **Rabbi Yehoshua.**

HALAKHA

Any case where the prohibition of her captivity causes her, etc. – כׇּל שֶׁאִיסּוּר שִׁבְיָיה גּוֹרֵם לָהּ וכו׳: If a woman was forbidden to her husband by a Torah prohibition, and she was taken captive, he is not obligated to redeem her. Rather, he gives her the money of her marriage contract and she must redeem herself. However, in the case of a priest's wife who is forbidden to her husband only due to the fact that she was taken captive, he is obligated to redeem her, as the *halakha* is in accordance with the opinion of Rava (Rambam *Sefer Nashim*, *Hilkhot Ishut* 24:22; *Shulḥan Arukh*, *Even HaEzer* 78:6–7).

One who vows that his wife may not derive benefit from him, and she is then taken captive – הַמַּדִּיר אֶת אִשְׁתּוֹ וְנִשְׁבֵּית: If a man vows that his wife may not derive benefit from him, he is obligated to divorce her and pay her marriage contract. If she is subsequently taken captive, he is not required to redeem her from captivity. However, if she was taken captive before he took this vow, he is required to redeem her. The *halakha* is in accordance with the opinion of Rabbi Yehoshua, not Rabbi Eliezer, and in accordance with the opinion of Sumakhos (Rambam *Sefer Nashim*, *Hilkhot Ishut* 14:21; *Shulḥan Arukh*, *Even HaEzer* 78:5).

לָא, הָכָא בְּמַאי עָסְקִינַן – כְּגוֹן שֶׁנָּדְרָה אִיהִי וְקִיֵּים לָהּ הוּא. רַבִּי אֱלִיעֶזֶר סָבַר: הוּא נוֹתֵן אֶצְבַּע בֵּין שִׁינֶּיהָ, וְרַבִּי יְהוֹשֻׁעַ סָבַר: הִיא נָתְנָה אֶצְבַּע בֵּין שִׁינֶּיהָ.

The Gemara refutes this suggestion: **No; with what are we dealing here?**[N] With a case **where she vowed** not to derive benefit from him, **and** her husband **upheld it for her** by neglecting to nullify her vow when he heard it. The Gemara explains: **Rabbi Eliezer maintains** that **he is putting his finger**[H] **between her teeth,** i.e., he causes the vow to be in effect, and therefore he must redeem her and return her to her native province. **And Rabbi Yehoshua maintains** that **she put her finger between her** own **teeth,** i.e., she is responsible for the vow, because she is the one who initially pronounced it.

אִי הִיא נָתְנָה אֶצְבַּע בֵּין שִׁינֶּיהָ – כְּתוּבָּה מַאי עֲבִידְתָּהּ?

The Gemara asks: **If** Rabbi Yehoshua maintains that **she put her finger between her** own **teeth, what is** the payment of **the marriage contract doing** here? Why must he pay her marriage contract if it is her fault that they cannot remain married?

וְתוּ, אָמַר רַבִּי נָתָן: שָׁאַלְתִּי אֶת סוּמָכוֹס: כְּשֶׁאָמַר רַבִּי יְהוֹשֻׁעַ נוֹתֵן לָהּ כְּתוּבָּתָהּ וְאֵינוֹ פּוֹדֶה – כְּשֶׁהִדִּירָהּ וּלְבַסּוֹף נִשְׁבֵּית, אוֹ בְּשֶׁנִּשְׁבֵּית וּלְבַסּוֹף הִדִּירָהּ? וְאָמַר: לֹא שָׁמַעְתִּי.

And furthermore, it was stated above that **Rabbi Natan said: I asked Sumakhos: When Rabbi Yehoshua said** that he **gives her** the payment for **her marriage contract but he does not** have to **redeem** her, was he referring to a case **where he vowed** that **she** may not derive benefit from him **and she was subsequently taken captive, or** was he speaking **of one who was taken captive and he subsequently vowed** that **she** may not derive benefit from him? **And he said** to me: **I have not heard** a tradition on this matter, but it is reasonable to assume that the case is where he took the vow and she was subsequently taken captive, as otherwise there is a concern that the husband will engage in trickery.

וְאִי דְּנָדְרָה אִיהִי – מַה לִּי הִדִּירָהּ וּלְבַסּוֹף נִשְׁבֵּית, מַה לִּי נִשְׁבֵּית וּלְבַסּוֹף הִדִּירָהּ?

But if this is referring to a case **where she** was the one who **vowed** not to derive benefit from him, **what is** the difference to **me** whether **he** upheld **her vow and she was subsequently taken captive,** and **what is** the difference to **me** whether **she was taken captive and he subsequently** upheld **her vow?** Either way there is no reason to be concerned that he might engage in trickery, since she was the one who took the vow.

אֶלָּא לְעוֹלָם דְּאַדְּרָהּ אִיהוּ, וְאַבַּיֵּי מְתָרֵץ לְטַעֲמֵיהּ, וְרָבָא מְתָרֵץ לְטַעֲמֵיהּ. אַבַּיֵּי מְתָרֵץ לְטַעֲמֵיהּ: אַלְמָנָה לְכֹהֵן גָּדוֹל – כּוּלֵּי עָלְמָא לָא פְּלִיגִי דְּחַיָּיב לְפְדוֹתָהּ, מַמְזֶרֶת וּנְתִינָה לְיִשְׂרָאֵל – כּוּלֵּי עָלְמָא לָא פְּלִיגִי דְּאֵינוֹ חַיָּיב לִפְדוֹתָהּ, מַדִּיר אֵשֶׁת כֹּהֵן נַמִי – כּוּלֵּי עָלְמָא לָא פְּלִיגִי דְּחַיָּיב לִפְדוֹתָהּ, דְּהַיְינוּ אַלְמָנָה [לְכֹהֵן גָּדוֹל].

Rather, this is **actually** referring to a case **where he** was the one who initially **vowed** that **she** may not derive benefit from him. **And Abaye explains** the *baraita* according **to his** line of **reasoning, and Rava explains** the *baraita* according **to his** line of **reasoning. Abaye explains** the *baraita* according **to his** line of **reasoning** as follows: With regard to **a widow** who is married **to a High Priest, everyone agrees** that he is **obligated to redeem her.** If she was **a** *mamzeret* or **a Gibeonite woman** married **to an Israelite, everyone agrees** that he is **not obligated to redeem her.** In the case of a priest **who takes a vow** prohibiting his wife, i.e., **the wife of a priest,** from deriving benefit from him, **likewise everyone agrees** that he is **obligated to redeem her, as this is** the same as the case of **a widow** who is married **to a High Priest,** as he can fulfill the requirement to restore her to her native province.

כִּי פְּלִיגִי – בְּמַדִּיר אֵשֶׁת יִשְׂרָאֵל. רַבִּי אֱלִיעֶזֶר אָזֵיל בָּתַר מֵעִיקָּרָא, וְרַבִּי יְהוֹשֻׁעַ אָזֵיל בָּתַר בַּסּוֹף.

When they disagree it is in the case **of** an Israelite **who vows** that his wife, i.e., **the wife of an Israelite,** may not derive benefit from him. **Rabbi Eliezer follows** the status of the woman **at the outset,** i.e., when the marriage contract was written. Since at that time he could restore her to be his wife, the obligation he took upon himself to redeem her from captivity remains in effect, despite the fact that he can no longer do so due to the vow. **And Rabbi Yehoshua follows** the status of the woman **at the end,** and holds that since, in practice, the husband cannot take her back as a wife because of the vow, he is no longer obligated to ransom her.

רָבָא מְתָרֵץ לְטַעֲמֵיהּ: אַלְמָנָה לְכֹהֵן גָּדוֹל, מַמְזֶרֶת וּנְתִינָה לְיִשְׂרָאֵל – כּוּלֵּי עָלְמָא לָא פְּלִיגִי דְּאֵינוֹ חַיָּיב לִפְדוֹתָהּ, כִּי פְּלִיגִי – בְּמַדִּיר בֵּין אֵשֶׁת כֹּהֵן וּבֵין אֵשֶׁת יִשְׂרָאֵל.

Similarly, **Rava explains** the *baraita* according **to his** line of **reasoning:** In the case of **a widow** married **to a High Priest,** and **a** *mamzeret* **or a Gibeonite woman** married **to an Israelite, everyone agrees** that he is **not obligated to redeem her,** as the prohibition against her remaining married to him results from a cause other than her captivity. **When they disagree** it is with regard to **one who vows** that his wife may not derive benefit from him, **whether** she is **the wife of a priest or the wife of an Israelite.**

NOTES

No, with what are we dealing here, etc. – לָא, הָכָא בְּמַאי עָסְקִינַן וכו׳: The early authorities debate the meaning of the Gemara's refutation here. According to Rashi, the Gemara is saying that the opinions of Rabbi Eliezer and Rabbi Yehoshua cannot be aligned with those of Abaye and Rava, as each of them might agree with either opinion. The *tanna'im* argue only with regard to an Israelite, who is not obligated to redeem a woman forbidden to him: In a case where she is forbidden to him due to a vow that she took and he upheld, is she responsible for the prohibition, in which case the husband is exempt from the obligation to redeem her, or is he responsible for the prohibition, in which case he is obligated to redeem her? Other early authorities raise various difficulties with Rashi's interpretation.

An alternative explanation of the Gemara is presented by the Razah, based upon a slightly different version of the Gemara text. He explains that according to Rava, his dispute with Abaye is the subject of the dispute between the *tanna'im*, and he agrees with the opinion of Rabbi Yehoshua, while Abaye accepts the opinion of Rabbi Eliezer. The Gemara here, which claims that the dispute between the *tanna'im* is not the same as the dispute between Abaye and Rava, is stating this claim only according to Abaye, i.e., Abaye can argue that his opinion accords with both of the *tanna'im* cited in the *baraita*.

Rabbi Aharon HaLevi accepts the standard version of the Gemara text but maintains that the Gemara's answer refers both to Israelites and priests. Rava claims that his opinion accords even with that of Rabbi Eliezer, and since the husband is responsible for the fact that his wife is forbidden to him, even an Israelite husband is obligated to redeem his wife. However, in cases where the husband is not responsible for the prohibition, Rabbi Eliezer concedes that not even a priest is obligated to redeem his wife. Conversely, Abaye explains that even Rabbi Yehoshua exempts the husband from redeeming his wife only because he considers her the cause of her forbidden status, and therefore even a priest is exempt from redeeming his wife. However, if she is not the cause of her forbidden status, even Abaye agrees that the husband is obligated to redeem his wife (see Ramban, Ritva, Meiri, and Rabbi Crescas Vidal).

HALAKHA

He is putting his finger, etc. – הוּא נוֹתֵן אֶצְבַּע וכו׳: If a wife vows to refrain from deriving benefit from her husband, and the husband upholds her vow, or even if he merely fails to nullify it, and he subsequently says that he does not wish to remain with a woman who vows, he may divorce her but he must give her the marriage contract, as he had the opportunity to nullify her vow and chose not to do so. There is a tannaitic dispute with regard to this issue on 71a–b. The opinion accepted as *halakha* is that of Rabbi Yosei (Rambam *Sefer Nashim, Hilkhot Ishut* 12:24; *Shulḥan Arukh, Yoreh De'a* 235:3).

רַבִּי אֱלִיעֶזֶר אָזֵיל בָּתַר מֵעִיקָּרָא, וְרַבִּי יְהוֹשֻׁעַ אָזֵיל בָּתַר בַּסּוֹף.

Rabbi Eliezer follows her status **at the outset** and holds that since he obligated himself to ransom her when he wrote the marriage contract he must act accordingly. **And Rabbi Yehoshua follows** her status **at the end,** and holds that since he cannot fulfill his obligation to restore her as his wife due to a factor other than her captivity, he is entirely exempt from redeeming her.

״נִשְׁבֵּית חַיָּיב לִפְדּוֹתָהּ״ וכו׳. תָּנוּ רַבָּנַן: נִשְׁבֵּית בְּחַיֵּי בַעְלָהּ וְאַחַר כָּךְ מֵת בַּעְלָהּ, הִכִּיר בָּהּ בַּעְלָהּ – יוֹרְשִׁין חַיָּיבִין לִפְדּוֹתָהּ, לֹא הִכִּיר בָּהּ בַּעְלָהּ – אֵין יוֹרְשִׁין חַיָּיבִין לִפְדּוֹתָהּ.

§ The mishna taught that if **she was taken captive,** her husband **is obligated to redeem her. The Sages taught** in a *baraita*: In the case of a wife who was **taken captive in her husband's lifetime and afterward her husband died** before he could redeem her, if **her husband was aware of her** captivity,[N] the **heirs are obligated to redeem her,** but **if her husband was not aware of her** captivity, his **heirs are not obligated**[N] **to redeem her.**

לֵוִי סָבַר לְמֶיעֱבַד עוּבְדָא כִּי הָא מַתְנִיתָא. אָמַר לֵיהּ רַב: הָכִי אֲמַר חֲבִיבִי: לֵית הִלְכְתָא כִּי הָא מַתְנִיתָא, אֶלָּא כִּי הָא דְּתַנְיָא: נִשְׁבֵּית לְאַחַר מִיתַת בַּעְלָהּ – אֵין הַיְּתוֹמִין חַיָּיבִין לִפְדּוֹתָהּ. וְלֹא עוֹד, אֶלָּא אֲפִילּוּ נִשְׁבֵּית בְּחַיֵּי בַעְלָהּ וְאַחַר כָּךְ מֵת בַּעְלָהּ – אֵין הַיְּתוֹמִין חַיָּיבִין לִפְדּוֹתָהּ, שֶׁאֵין אֲנִי קוֹרֵא בָּהּ ״וְאוֹתְבִינַךְ לְאִינְתּוּ״.

The Gemara relates: **Levi thought to act in accordance with this** *baraita*. **Rav said to him: My uncle** [*ḥavivi*],[N] Rabbi Ḥiyya, **said as follows: The** *halakha* **is not in accordance with this** *baraita*. **Rather,** it is **in accordance with that which is taught** in a different *baraita*: If she was **taken captive after the death of her husband, the orphans are not obligated to redeem her. And moreover, even** if she **was taken captive in her husband's lifetime** and he heard about it, **and afterward her husband died, the orphans are not obligated to redeem her,**[H] **as I cannot apply to her** the clause in the marriage contract: **And I will restore you to me as a wife.** Since this stipulation cannot be fulfilled, the obligation to redeem her does not apply.

תָּנוּ רַבָּנַן: נִשְׁבֵּית וְהָיוּ מְבַקְּשִׁין מִמֶּנּוּ עַד עֲשָׂרָה בְּדָמֶיהָ, פַּעַם רִאשׁוֹנָה – פּוֹדֶה, מִכָּאן וְאֵילָךְ, רָצָה – פּוֹדֶה, רָצָה – אֵינוֹ פּוֹדֶה. רַבָּן שִׁמְעוֹן בֶּן גַּמְלִיאֵל אוֹמֵר:

§ **The Sages taught:** If she was **taken captive and they were seeking** ransom **from** her husband of **up to ten times her value,**[H] i.e., far more than the usual ransom for a captive of this kind, on the **first occasion** she is taken captive he must **redeem** her. **From this** point **forward,** i.e., if she was taken captive a second time, if he **wants to, he redeems** her,[N] but if he does not **want** to redeem her, **he does not** have to **redeem** her, as the Sages obligated him to redeem her only once. **Rabban Shimon ben Gamliel says:**

NOTES

If her husband was aware of her captivity – הִכִּיר בָּהּ בַּעְלָהּ: Since he knew what happened to her, his property is mortgaged toward the obligation to redeem her (Rivan).

His heirs are not obligated – אֵין יוֹרְשִׁין חַיָּיבִין: The Rivan and others had a version of the text that states: Brothers-in-law, instead of: Heirs. According to this version, the point is that even the brothers-in-law, with whom the woman has a levirate bond after the death of her husband, are not obligated to redeem her, and certainly other heirs are not obligated (*Talmidei Rabbeinu Yona*).

My uncle [*ḥavivi*] – חֲבִיבִי: This is the meaning in Aramaic. Some understand it as a contraction of the words *aḥi avi*, meaning: My father's brother. Apparently, there is a connection between this use of the term and its other meaning of affection [*ḥibba*].

Rabbi Ḥiyya was Rav's uncle both from his father's and his mother's side. In *Pesaḥim* 4a there is an explanation of this unusual relationship. He was also Rav's primary teacher. It may be for this reason that Rav would refer to Rabbi Ḥiyya with a term that expressed both his familial connection to and his affection for his uncle.

From this point forward if he wants he redeems her – מִכָּאן וְאֵילָךְ רָצָה פּוֹדֶה: Some explain that this means that on the second occasion he does not have to redeem her for more than her value, but he would still be obligated to redeem her for the normal value of a captive similar to her (Rabbeinu Ḥananel, cited by *Tosafot*). Rashi, however, maintains that a husband is obligated to redeem his wife only once. After that, he is not obligated to redeem her at all.

HALAKHA

The orphans are not obligated to redeem her – אֵין הַיְּתוֹמִין חַיָּיבִין לִפְדּוֹתָהּ: The obligation to redeem a wife lapses after her husband's death. There is no duty for the husband's heirs to redeem his widow with the money of his estate, even if she was taken captive during his lifetime and he passed away before he could redeem her (Rambam *Sefer Nashim, Hilkhot Ishut* 18:5; *Shulḥan Arukh, Even HaEzer* 78:8).

They were seeking ransom from her husband of up to ten times her value – הָיוּ מְבַקְּשִׁין מִמֶּנּוּ עַד עֲשָׂרָה בְּדָמֶיהָ: If a woman is taken captive and the captors demand a sum that is larger than the value of her marriage contract, even if it is ten times the value of her marriage contract, her husband is obligated to pay it. However, if she is captured a second time and he wants to divorce her, he may do so and she must redeem herself, as he is obligated to redeem her only once. Some claim that according to the ruling of the Rambam, if the husband does not wish to divorce her he must ransom her even on the second occasion (*Beit Shmuel*, citing *Kesef Mishne*; *Baḥ*; *Derisha*; Rambam *Sefer Nashim, Hilkhot Ishut* 14:19; *Shulḥan Arukh, Even HaEzer* 78:3).

אֵין פּוֹדִין אֶת הַשְּׁבוּיִין יוֹתֵר עַל כְּדֵי דְמֵיהֶם, מִפְּנֵי תִּקּוּן הָעוֹלָם. הָא בִּכְדֵי דְמֵיהֶן – פּוֹדִין, אַף עַל גַּב דְּפִרְקוֹנָהּ יוֹתֵר עַל כְּתוּבָּתָהּ.

One does not redeem captives at more than their value.[H] This policy is **for the betterment of the world,**[N] because if captives are ransomed at exorbitant prices, this will encourage their captors to kidnap more people. The Gemara notes: This implies that if the captors seek a ransom **in** accordance with **their** actual **value one does redeem** captives,[H] **even though** this includes a case where a woman's **redemption** is **more than her marriage contract.**

וּרְמִינְהִי: נִשְׁבֵּית, וְהָיוּ מְבַקְּשִׁין מִמֶּנּוּ עַד עֲשָׂרָה בִּכְתוּבָּתָהּ, פַּעַם רִאשׁוֹנָה – פּוֹדֶה, מִכָּאן וְאֵילָךְ רָצָה – פּוֹדֶה, רָצָה – אֵינוֹ פּוֹדֶה. רַבִּי שִׁמְעוֹן בֶּן גַּמְלִיאֵל אוֹמֵר: אִם הָיָה פִּרְקוֹנָהּ כְּנֶגֶד כְּתוּבָּתָהּ – פּוֹדֶה, אִם לָאו – אֵינוֹ פּוֹדֶה!

And the Gemara **raises a contradiction** from a different *baraita,* which states: If **she was taken captive and** the captors **were seeking from** her husband a ransom of **up to ten times the value of her marriage contract,** on the **first occasion** he must **redeem** her. **From this** point **forward,** if he **wants to he redeems** her, but if he does not **want** to redeem her, **he does not** have to **redeem** her. **Rabban Shimon ben Gamliel says: If** the price of **her ransom was equal to her marriage contract he redeems** her. **If not,** i.e., the price of her ransom was greater than the sum of money guaranteed to her in her marriage contract upon divorce or the death of her husband, **he does not** have to **redeem** her. He can suffice with paying her marriage contract.

רַבָּן שִׁמְעוֹן בֶּן גַּמְלִיאֵל תְּרֵי קוּלֵּי אִית לֵיהּ.

The Gemara answers: **Rabban Shimon ben Gamliel is of** the opinion that there are **two leniencies** with regard to the *halakhot* of redemption. First, he maintains that one does not pay more than the general ransom given for such a captive, and second, a husband does not have to pay more than the sum of his wife's marriage contract.

״לָקְתָה חַיָּיב לְרַפְּאוֹתָהּ״. תָּנוּ רַבָּנַן: אַלְמָנָה נִיזּוֹנֶת מִנִּכְסֵי יְתוֹמִין, וּצְרִיכָה רְפוּאָה – הֲרֵי הִיא כִּמְזוֹנוֹת. רַבָּן שִׁמְעוֹן בֶּן גַּמְלִיאֵל אוֹמֵר: רְפוּאָה שֶׁיֵּשׁ לָהּ קִצְבָּה – נִתְרַפֵּאת מִכְּתוּבָּתָהּ, שֶׁאֵין לָהּ קִצְבָּה – הֲרֵי הִיא כִּמְזוֹנוֹת.

§ The mishna taught (51a) that if a woman **was struck** with illness, her husband is **obligated to heal her,** i.e., to pay for her medical expenses. **The Sages taught** in a *baraita*: In the case of **a widow** who **is sustained from the property of** the **orphans and who requires medical treatment,**[H] her medical needs **are like** her **sustenance,** and the orphans must bear the costs. **Rabban Shimon ben Gamliel** disagrees and **says:** With regard to **treatment that has a fixed** cost, she **is healed from her marriage contract,** i.e., the amount is subtracted from her marriage contract. If it is a treatment **that does not have a fixed** cost, **it is** considered **like sustenance.**

HALAKHA

One does not redeem captives at more than their value – אֵין פּוֹדִין אֶת הַשְּׁבוּיִין יוֹתֵר עַל כְּדֵי דְמֵיהֶם: One may not ransom captives at more than their face value, so as not to encourage enemies to capture more Jews, as stated by Rabban Shimon ben Gamliel. However, it is permitted for one to ransom himself at any price. Similarly, one redeems great Sages, including young scholars who have the potential to become important leaders, even for a hefty sum (see *Tosafot* and Rosh). Some write that it is permitted to ransom one's relatives at a high price, or in fact anyone, if one chooses to do so. The court does not object to this behavior as long as the money does not come from the public purse. This is the accepted practice (Rambam *Sefer Zera'im, Hilkhot Mattenot Aniyyim* 8:12; *Shulḥan Arukh, Yoreh De'a* 252:4).

For their value one does redeem captives – בִּכְדֵי דְמֵיהֶם פּוֹדִים: A husband is obligated to redeem his wife not for more than her value, but only in accordance with the price of similar captives. Some authorities (*Tur* and Rosh, citing Ramah; *Baḥ*) maintain that as his wife is considered like his own body he can spend as much as he wants on her redemption (Rambam *Sefer Nashim, Hilkhot Ishut* 14:19; *Shulḥan Arukh, Even HaEzer* 78:2).

A widow who requires medical treatment – אַלְמָנָה הַצְּרִיכָה לִרְפוּאָה: In the case of a widow sustained from the orphans' property who took ill, if her medical expenses are not fixed, they are categorized as sustenance and the heirs must cover the costs. If her treatment comes at a fixed price, she must pay for it from her marriage contract. There is a general principle that the *halakha* is in accordance with the opinion of Rabban Shimon ben Gamliel in his disputes with other Sages; this is certainly the case here, where the Gemara apparently supports his ruling (Rambam *Sefer Nashim, Hilkhot Ishut* 18:5 and *Maggid Mishne* there; *Shulḥan Arukh, Even HaEzer* 79:1).

NOTES

For the betterment of the world – מִפְּנֵי תִּקּוּן הָעוֹלָם: The Gemara in *Gittin* (45a), which is the source of this *halakha*, inquires as to why exactly it is for the betterment of the world that one does not redeem captives for more than their value. The Gemara there offers two possibilities: It means either that the public will not be able to handle the heavy financial burden of exorbitant ransoms, or that exorbitant ransoms will only encourage criminals to carry out more abductions. The Gemara there does not come to a conclusion as to which reason is correct. Some commentaries suggest that this issue is the subject of dispute in the *baraita* cited here: The first *tanna* maintains that a husband is required to ransom his wife even for a price that is higher than the normal value for such a ransom. Apparently, he holds that the reason captives are generally not ransomed for more than their value is because of the financial burden on the community. Consequently, in this case, where the burden is upon one individual, the captive must be ransomed even for an exorbitant price. Rabban Shimon ben Gamliel, who holds that even a husband does not ransom his wife for an exorbitant fee, must hold that the "betterment of the world" is so as not to encourage criminals from carrying out more kidnappings (Ramban and Rashba on *Gittin* 45a; Rabbi Aharon HaLevi).

Others argue that this discussion provides no proof one way or another. It is possible that even the first *tanna* is generally concerned about giving encouragement to potential kidnappers. However, he holds that there is no limit to the amount one can pay to ransom himself and likewise to ransom his wife, in accordance with the general dictum that one's wife is like oneself (Ritva, citing Rabbeinu Tam; see *Tosafot*). Conversely, it is possible to explain Rabban Shimon ben Gamliel's opinion even according to the reasoning that the concern is for the public purse, as he might be saying that they did not obligate a husband to ransom his wife due to the indirect effect his actions would have on public coffers in future kidnappings, or because the entire community typically shared the costs of the redemption of captives even when the husband was obligated to do so (*Talmidei Rabbeinu Yona*).

אָמַר רַבִּי יוֹחָנָן: עָשׂוּ הַקָּזַת דָּם בְּאֶרֶץ יִשְׂרָאֵל כִּרְפוּאָה שֶׁאֵין לָהּ קִצְבָה. קְרֵיבֵיהּ דְּרַבִּי יוֹחָנָן הֲוָה לְהוּ אִיתַּת אַבָּא דַּהֲוַת צְרִיכָה רְפוּאָה כָּל יוֹמָא. אָתוּ לְקַמֵּיהּ דְּרַבִּי יוֹחָנָן, אֲמַר לְהוּ: אֵיזִילוּ קוֹצוּ לֵיהּ מִידֵי לְרוֹפֵא.

Rabbi Yoḥanan said: The Sages **established** that **in Eretz Yisrael, bloodletting** is considered **like a treatment that does not have a fixed** cost, and therefore the heirs must pay for that treatment. The Gemara relates: **The relatives of Rabbi Yoḥanan had** to take care of the **wife of their father, who required treatment every day,** and therefore her medical expenses were high. **They came before Rabbi Yoḥanan** to ask him what to do. **He said to them: Go** and **fix** a lump **sum with the doctor**[H] for his services. The treatment would then be considered as having a fixed cost, which is deducted from the marriage contract.

אָמַר רַבִּי יוֹחָנָן: עָשִׂינוּ עַצְמֵינוּ כְּעוֹרְכֵי הַדַּיָּינִין. מֵעִיקָּרָא מַאי סָבַר וּלְבַסּוֹף מַאי סָבַר? מֵעִיקָּרָא סָבַר ״וּמִבְּשָׂרְךָ לֹא תִתְעַלָּם״ וּלְבַסּוֹף סָבַר: אָדָם חָשׁוּב שָׁאנֵי.

Later **Rabbi Yoḥanan said** in regret: **We have made ourselves like legal advisors,** who help people with their legal claims. The Gemara asks: **At the outset, what did he hold and ultimately, what did he hold?** The Gemara explains: **At the outset he held** that one should act in accordance with the verse **"and that you do not hide yourself from your own flesh"** (Isaiah 58:7), which indicates that one must help his relatives. **And ultimately he held** that **an important person is different.**[N] If a man of stature offers assistance to his family in a manner that causes a loss to another individual, it appears as though he were unfairly favoring his relatives.

מתני׳ לֹא כָּתַב לָהּ ״בְּנִין דִּכְרִין דְּיֶהֱווּ לִיכִי מִינַּאי אִינּוּן יִרְתוּן כְּסֶף כְּתוּבְּתֵיךְ יָתֵר עַל חוּלַקְהוֹן דְּעִם אֲחוּהוֹן״ – חַיָּיב, שֶׁהוּא תְּנַאי בֵּית דִּין. ״בְּנָן נוּקְבָן דְּיֶהֶוְיָן לִיכִי מִינַּאי יֶהֶוְיָן יָתְבָן בְּבֵיתִי וּמִיתַּזְנָן מִנְּכָסַי עַד דְּתִלָּקְחוּן לְגוּבְרִין״ – חַיָּיב, שֶׁהוּא תְּנַאי בֵּית דִּין.

MISHNA If the husband **did not write for her** in her marriage contract: Any **male children**[H] **you will have from me will inherit the money of your marriage contract in addition to their portion** of the inheritance **that** they receive together **with their brothers,** he is nevertheless **obligated** as though he had written it, **as it is a stipulation of the court** and therefore takes effect even if it is not explicitly stated. Likewise, if he omitted from the marriage contract the sentence: Any **female children**[H] **you will have from me will sit in my house and be sustained from my property until they are taken by men,** i.e., until they are married, he **is** nevertheless **obligated** as though he had written it, **as it too is a stipulation of the court.**

״אַתְּ תְּהֵא יָתְבָא בְּבֵיתִי וּמִיתַּזְנָא מִנְּכָסַי כָּל יְמֵי מֵיגַר אַלְמְנוּתֵיךְ בְּבֵיתִי״ – חַיָּיב, שֶׁהוּא תְּנַאי בֵּית דִּין. כָּךְ הָיוּ אַנְשֵׁי יְרוּשָׁלַיִם כּוֹתְבִין. אַנְשֵׁי גָּלִיל הָיוּ כּוֹתְבִין כְּאַנְשֵׁי יְרוּשָׁלַיִם. אַנְשֵׁי יְהוּדָה הָיוּ כּוֹתְבִין: עַד שֶׁיִּרְצוּ הַיּוֹרְשִׁין לִיתֵּן לָךְ כְּתוּבָּתֵיךְ. לְפִיכָךְ, אִם רָצוּ יוֹרְשִׁין – נוֹתְנִין לָהּ כְּתוּבָּתָהּ, וּפוֹטְרִין אוֹתָהּ.

Similarly, if he omitted from the marriage contract the clause: **You will sit in my house and be sustained from my property**[H] **all the days you live** as **a widow in my house,** he **is** nevertheless **obligated** as though he had written it, **as it is a stipulation of the court.** The mishna comments: **The residents of Jerusalem would write in this manner,** that a widow may remain in her husband's house throughout her widowhood, and **the residents of the Galilee would write** in this manner as well, **like the inhabitants of Jerusalem.** In contrast, **the residents of Judea would write: Until the heirs want to give you your marriage contract. Consequently, if the heirs wish, they may give her marriage contract to her and release her,** and she must find her own living arrangements and provide for herself.

גמ׳ אָמַר רַבִּי יוֹחָנָן מִשּׁוּם רַבִּי שִׁמְעוֹן בֶּן יוֹחַאי: מִפְּנֵי מָה הִתְקִינוּ כְּתוּבַּת בְּנִין דִּכְרִין – כְּדֵי שֶׁיִּקְפּוֹץ אָדָם וְיִכְתּוֹב לְבִתּוֹ כִּבְנוֹ.

GEMARA **Rabbi Yoḥanan said in the name of Rabbi Shimon ben Yoḥai: For what reason did** the Sages **enact the marriage document concerning male children?** It was enacted **so that a man will** be willing to **take the initiative and write** an agreement to give **his daughter** a dowry **as** large as the portion of his possessions that **his son** will receive as an inheritance. The marriage document concerning male children ensures that even if one's daughter dies and her husband inherits her possessions, the dowry will eventually be inherited by her sons when her husband dies. Since the father of the bride knows that his grandchildren will inherit the dowry, he will give a larger dowry.

וּמִי אִיכָּא מִידֵי דְּרַחֲמָנָא אָמַר בְּרָא – לֵירוּת, בְּרַתָּא – לָא תֵּירוּת, וַאֲתוּ רַבָּנַן וּמְתַקְּנֵי דְּתֵירוּת בְּרַתָּא?

The Gemara asks: **And is there anything** that justifies a situation **where the Merciful One says** that **the son inherits** and **the daughter does not inherit, and yet the Sages came and enacted that the daughter should inherit?** The practical effect of their decree is that daughters receive a significant portion of their father's estate, just like sons.

HALAKHA

Go and fix a lump sum with the doctor – אֵיזִילוּ קוֹצוּ לֵיהּ מִידֵי לְרוֹפֵא: If a man's heirs wish to settle with the doctor a fixed price for the widow's medical expenses, so that she should have to pay for it herself out of her marriage contract, they have the right to do so, in accordance with the ruling of Rabbi Yoḥanan (*Shulḥan Arukh, Even HaEzer* 79:2).

If the husband did not write for her: Any male children, etc. – לֹא כָּתַב לָהּ בְּנִין דִּכְרִין וכו׳: One of the stipulations of a marriage contract is that any male children born to this woman will inherit from their father the sum stipulated in their mother's marriage contract in addition to their share of his inheritance. Even if the husband neglected to include this clause in the marriage contract it is in effect, as this is a stipulation of the court (Rambam *Sefer Nashim, Hilkhot Ishut* 12:2; *Shulḥan Arukh, Even HaEzer* 69:2).

Female children, etc. – בְּנָן נוּקְבָן וכו׳: Any female children a man's wife bears to him are entitled to their sustenance from his property until their betrothal, even if this was not stated in the marriage contract, as it is a stipulation of the court (Rambam *Sefer Nashim, Hilkhot Ishut* 12:2; *Shulḥan Arukh, Even HaEzer* 69:2)

A widow is sustained from his property and may live in his house – אַלְמָנָה נִיזּוֹנֶת מִנְּכָסָיו וְגָ־ה בְּבֵיתוֹ: One of the stipulations of a marriage contract, which applies even if it is omitted, is that if the woman is widowed she has the right to receive her sustenance from her late husband's property and to reside in his house throughout her widowhood (Rambam *Sefer Nashim, Hilkhot Ishut* 12:2; *Shulḥan Arukh, Even HaEzer* 69:2).

NOTES

An important person is different – אָדָם חָשׁוּב שָׁאנֵי: This is just one example of several instances where the Gemara states that prominent individuals must be more careful than others in their conduct, because others observe him and learn from him. Certain actions that are usually permitted are considered improper for one of stature. Furthermore, improper conduct on the part of prominent individuals may cause a desecration of God's name.

הָא נַמִּי דְּאוֹרָיְיתָא הוּא, דִּכְתִיב ״קְחוּ נָשִׁים וְהוֹלִידוּ בָּנִים וּבָנוֹת וּקְחוּ לִבְנֵיכֶם נָשִׁים וְאֶת בְּנוֹתֵיכֶם תְּנוּ לַאֲנָשִׁים״. בִּשְׁלָמָא בָּנִים – בִּידֵיהּ קַיְימֵי, אֶלָּא בְּנָתֵיהּ מִי קַיְימָן בִּידֵיהּ?

The Gemara answers: **This also** applies **by Torah** law,[N] **as it is written: "Take wives for yourselves and bear sons and daughters, and take wives for your sons, and give your daughters to husbands"** (Jeremiah 29:6). This verse requires clarification. **Granted, sons are in his hands,** i.e., a father can select wives for them, **but daughters, are they in his power** that he can select husbands for them? It is not the manner of a woman or her family to court a man.

הָא קָא מַשְׁמַע לָן: דְּנַלְבְּשָׁהּ, וְנִיכַסָּהּ, וְנֵיתִיב לָהּ מִידֵי, כִּי הֵיכִי דְּקָפְצִי עֲלָהּ וַאֲתוּ נָסְבִי לָהּ. וְעַד כַּמָּה? אַבַּיֵי וְרָבָא דְּאָמְרִי תַּרְוַיְיהוּ: עַד לְעִישּׂוּר נְכָסֵי.

Rather, the verse **teaches us this, that** the father **should dress her and cover her**[H] **and give her something,** i.e., property, **so that** men **will take the initiative with her and come** to **marry her.** When the verse instructs fathers to marry off their daughters, it means that they must make efforts to ensure this outcome, including bestowing a dowry. The Gemara asks: **And up to how much** must a father give his daughters? **Abaye and Rava both say: Up to one-tenth** of one's **property**[NH] should be handed over to his daughter for her dowry.

וְאֵימָא, דְּאָב – לֵירוּת, דְּבַעַל – לָא לֵירוּת! אִם כֵּן אָב נַמִּי מִימְנָע וְלָא כָּתַב.

The Gemara asks: **But** if this is the reason for the institution of the marriage document concerning male children, **say that** it is only the portion **the** bride's **father** gave as a dowry that her sons **should inherit,** but the money **the husband** guarantees to pay his wife, they **should not inherit.** The Gemara answers: **If so,** the bride's **father will also refrain** from **writing** a large dowry. If his daughter's sons will not inherit the husband's portion of the marriage contract, her father will be reluctant to give generously himself.

וְאֵימָא הֵיכָא דְּכָתַב אָב – לִכְתּוֹב בַּעַל, הֵיכָא דְּלָא כָּתַב אָב – לָא לִכְתּוֹב בַּעַל! לָא פְּלוּג רַבָּנַן.

The Gemara continues to ask: **But** if the concern is that the father will not give, **say** that in a case **where** the **father wrote** a large dowry for his daughter, **let** the **husband** also **write** the stipulation in the marriage document concerning male children, and **when** the **father did not write** a large dowry, **let** the **husband not write** this stipulation. The Gemara replies: **The Sages did not distinguish** between these cases. Although the main purpose of their enactment was to encourage fathers to provide their daughters with generous dowries, the Sages applied their decree equally to all women, even when the father failed to do so.

בַּת בֵּין הַבָּנִים נַמִּי תֵּירוּת! כְּנַחֲלָה שַׁוְיוּהָ רַבָּנַן.

The Gemara poses another question: If the aim is to ensure that the money of the marriage contract will remain with the woman's descendants, in a case when one has **a daughter** from one woman **among** his **sons** from another woman, the daughter should **likewise inherit** her mother's dowry. Why do only male children inherit their mother's dowry? The Gemara responds: **The Sages established** this enactment as **similar to** the *halakha* of **inheritance:** Just as a regular inheritance belongs to sons and not daughters, the same applies to the marriage document concerning male children.

בַּת בֵּין הַבָּנוֹת תֵּירוּת! לָא פְּלוּג רַבָּנַן. וְתִיגְבֵּי מִמְּטַלְטְלֵי! כִּכְתוּבָּה שַׁוְיוּהָ רַבָּנַן.

The Gemara continues to inquire: Why shouldn't one at least say that **a daughter among daughters should inherit?** If he had a daughter from this wife, and his other children are also daughters, in which case all the daughters divide the inheritance, the daughters of each wife should receive the portion her maternal grandfather gave to her mother. The Gemara again answers: **The Sages did not distinguish** between these cases when establishing their decree. The Gemara further asks: **And let** the marriage document concerning male children **be collected** even **from movable property,** if that is all the father possesses. The Gemara replies: **The Sages established** this enactment as **similar to** a regular **marriage contract,** which can be collected only from land.

NOTES

This also applies by Torah law – הָא נַמִּי דְּאוֹרָיְיתָא הוּא: In other words, there is an allusion in the Bible to the idea that a father should do all he can to help his daughters get married, although it is not derived from here that he is duty bound in this regard (Ritva).

Up to one-tenth of one's property – עַד לְעִישּׂוּר נְכָסֵי: Rashi and most commentaries maintain that this is the usual size of a dowry. Some state that one should not give more than this, as it takes away the inheritance from his sons (Rabbeinu Ḥananel). Others add that if one is unable to find a suitable match for his daughter by means of a smaller dowry he should be willing to provide up to this amount (*Talmidei Rabbeinu Yona*).

HALAKHA

The father should dress her and cover her, etc. – נַלְבְּשָׁהּ וְנִיכַסָּהּ וכו׳: The Sages commanded every man to give part of his property to his daughter so as to encourage the attention of suitors. This is known as livelihood [*parnasa*], an obligation derived from the Bible (Rambam *Sefer Nashim*, *Hilkhot Ishut* 20:1, and *Maggid Mishne* there; *Shulḥan Arukh*, *Even HaEzer* 58:1).

Up to one-tenth of one's property – עַד עִישּׂוּר נְכָסֵי: If a man dies and leaves a daughter, the court estimates how much he would have wanted to give her as a dowry. In the *Ba'al HaTurim* it says that if the court has no means of knowing his intention they give her one-tenth of his property, after deducting the costs of his burial (Rambam *Sefer Nashim*, *Hilkhot Ishut* 12:3; *Shulḥan Arukh*, *Even HaEzer* 113:1).

HALAKHA

In a case where their decree would entirely uproot the *halakha* of inheritance, etc. – בְּמָקוֹם דְּקָא מְיעַקְּרָא נַחֲלָה וכו׳: A wife's sons inherit the sum stipulated in her marriage contract only if the estate of the deceased was worth at least a dinar more than the sum stipulated in the marriage contract. If, however, there would be less than a dinar left if they received the sum stipulated in the marriage contract, the entire estate is divided equally, so as not to uproot from the Torah laws of inheritance (Rambam *Sefer Nashim, Hilkhot Ishut* 19:3; *Shulḥan Arukh, Even HaEzer* 111:2).

PERSONALITIES

Abba of Sura – אַבָּא סוּרָאָה: Abba of Sura was Rav Pappa's father-in-law. Later, Abba Mari, Rav Pappa's son from another wife, married a different daughter of Abba of Sura. This double familial connection somewhat explains Abba of Sura's acceptance of the marriage arrangement described here.

Yehuda bar Mareimar – יְהוּדָה בַּר מָרֵימָר: Yehuda bar Mareimar is mentioned in several places in the Talmud as a Torah scholar who studied under Rava. Accordingly, he was approximately the same age and was a colleague of Rav Pappa's. He is sometimes referred to as Yehuda Mar bar Mareimar (see 80b), and some versions of the Gemara text refer to him by that name here. The title Mar generally signifies a member of the Exilarch's family. Due to his status as a Sage and as an Exilarch family member, as well as a colleague of Rav Pappa, it was clear that his very entrance into the house of Abba of Sura would pressure his host into offering Rav Pappa more generous terms.

תִּטְרוֹף מִמְּשַׁעְבְּדֵי! ״יִרְתוּן״ תְּנַן. וְאֵימָא אַף עַל גַּב דְּלֵיכָּא מוֹתַר דִּינָר! בְּמָקוֹם דְּקָא מִיעַקְּרָא נַחֲלָה דְּאוֹרַיְיתָא – לָא תַּקִּינוּ רַבָּנַן.

The Gemara poses yet another question: **Let it be collected** even **from liened** property, i.e., property the father sold after he wrote the marriage contract. The Gemara answers that **we learned** in the mishna: **Will inherit,** and one's heirs do not inherit property that he has sold. The Gemara asks: **But** if this is the reason for this enactment, **say** that it should apply **even though there is no more** than **a dinar** beyond the value of the marriage contract that the father **left over** in his estate. The Sages stated that if no property is left for the inheritance, all the sons share the inheritance equally, in accordance with Torah law. The Gemara answers: **In a case where** their decree **would** entirely **uproot** the *halakha* of **inheritance**[H] **by Torah** law, **the Sages did not enact** the marriage document concerning male children.

רַב פָּפָּא אִיעַסַּק לֵיהּ לִבְרֵיהּ בֵּי אַבָּא סוּרָאָה, אֲזַל לְמִיכְתַּב לַהּ כְּתוּבְּתָהּ. שְׁמַע יְהוּדָה בַּר מָרֵימָר, נְפַק אֲתָא אִיתְחֲזֵי לֵיהּ. כִּי מְטוֹ לְפִיתְחָא הֲוָה קָא מִפְּטַר מִינֵּיהּ. אֲמַר לֵיהּ: נֵיעוּל מָר בַּהֲדַאי!

The Gemara relates: **Rav Pappa,** having **arranged for his son** to marry into **the family of** Abba of **Sura,**[P] **went** to supervise **the writing of** the bride's **marriage contract. Yehuda bar Mareimar**[P] **heard** that Rav Pappa was coming, and **came out** to **present himself before him,** in honor of his arrival. **When they came to the entrance** of Abba of Sura's house, Yehuda bar Mareimar **took his leave of him,** as he did not wish to enter. Rav Pappa **said to him: Let the Master enter** inside **with me.**

Perek **IV**
Daf **53** Amud **a**

BACKGROUND

Shinnana – שִׁינָּנָא: According to Rashi and others, *shinnana* means sharp or witty. Shmuel used this term to show the degree to which he respected his most prominent student, Rav Yehuda. However, the *ge'onim* explain that according to oral tradition, *shinnana* means big toothed, which was a nickname for Rav Yehuda based on his appearance.

HALAKHA

Do not be a partner in the transfer of an inheritance – לָא תֶּיהֱוֵי בְּעַבּוּרֵי אַחְסַנְתָּא: If a man gives his property to people other than his heirs, the recipients acquire full ownership but the Sages are displeased with him, even if his sons were unworthy. It is the custom of pious men not to testify with regard to wills that transfer an estate from the heirs, even from an unfit son to a worthy one, as stated by Shmuel. Some (Rema, citing Mordekhai) add that if a man gave instructions that his property be treated in the best possible manner, it is given to his heirs (Rambam *Sefer Mishpatim, Hilkhot Naḥalot* 6:11; *Shulḥan Arukh, Ḥoshen Mishpat* 282:1).

This applies only if the man gives of his own free will – הָנֵי מִילֵּי מִדַּעְתֵּיהּ: The court does not force a father to marry off his daughters. Even though it is a mitzva for a father to provide a dowry for his daughter, the court does not impose a particular amount. Rather, he gives the sum of his choice (*Shulḥan Arukh, Even HaEzer* 71:1, and in the comment of Rema).

NOTES

This too is an ordinance of the Sages – הַאי נַמִי תַּקַּנְתָּא דְּרַבָּנַן הִיא: Some commentaries are puzzled by this statement, as the Gemara just said (52b) that this is a Torah law (Maharsha). He explains that it is not a full-fledged Torah law, but a rabbinical institution for which they found support in the Torah.

חַזְיֵיהּ דְּלָא הֲוָה נִיחָא לֵיהּ. אֲמַר לֵיהּ: מַאי דַּעְתָּיךְ – מִשּׁוּם דַּאֲמַר לֵיהּ שְׁמוּאֵל לְרַב יְהוּדָה: שִׁינָּנָא, לָא תֶּיהֱוֵי בְּעַבּוּרֵי אַחְסַנְתָּא אֲפִילּוּ מִבְּרָא בִּישָׁא לִבְרָא טָבָא, דְּלָא יְדִיעָא מַאי זַרְעָא נָפֵיק מִינֵּיהּ, וְכׇל שֶׁכֵּן מִבְּרָא לִבְרַתָּא.

Rav Pappa **saw that** Yehuda bar Mareimar **was not amenable** to the idea of entering the house. **He said to him: What is** on **your mind?** Do you not wish to enter **due to that** which **Shmuel said to Rav Yehuda:** *Shinnana*,[B] **do not be** a partner **in the transfer of an inheritance**[H] **even from a bad son to a good son, as it is not known what seed will come from him?** Perhaps the bad son will father worthy children. **And all the more so,** one should not be a partner in the transfer of an inheritance **from a son to a daughter.**

הַאי נַמִי – תַּקַּנְתָּא דְּרַבָּנַן הִיא, דְּאָמַר רַבִּי יוֹחָנָן מִשּׁוּם רַבִּי שִׁמְעוֹן בֶּן יוֹחַי. אֲמַר לֵיהּ: הָנֵי מִילֵּי – מִדַּעְתֵּיהּ, לְעַשּׂוֹיֵיהּ נַמִי? אֲמַר לֵיהּ: אַטּוּ מִי קָאָמֵינָא לָךְ דְּעוּל וְעַשְׂיֵיהּ? עוּל וְלָא תְּעַשְׂיֵיהּ קָאָמֵינָא. אֲמַר לֵיהּ: מֵעַלַּאי דִּידִי הַיְינוּ עַשְׂיֵיהּ.

Rav Pappa continued: Are you worried that your arrival will pressure Abba of Sura to give his daughter a more substantial dowry? But **this too is an ordinance of the Sages,**[N] that a father must provide a dowry for his daughter. This is **as Rabbi Yoḥanan said in the name of Rabbi Shimon ben Yoḥai,** as quoted above, that the Sages enacted this matter so that a man should take the initiative and write an agreement to give his daughter a dowry as large as the portion of his possessions that his son will receive as an inheritance. Yehuda bar Mareimar **said to him: This applies only** if the man gives **of his own** free **will,**[H] but should one **force him as well?** Rav Pappa **said to him: Did I say to you that you should enter and force him?** I merely **said** that you should **enter, but do not force him. He said to him: My** very **entrance is** an act that will effectively **force him,** as he will increase her dowry in my honor.

אַכְפְּיֵיהּ וְעוּל. אִישְׁתִּיק וִיתֵיב. סְבַר הָהוּא – מֵירְתָח רָתַח, כְּתַבִיהּ לְכׇל מַאי דַּהֲוָה לֵיהּ. לְסוֹף אֲמַר לֵיהּ: הַשְׁתָּא נַמִי לָא מִישְׁתָּעֵי מָר? חַיֵּי דְּמָר, לָא שְׁבִיקִי מִידֵּי לְנַפְשַׁאי.

Eventually, Rav Pappa **forced** Yehuda bar Mareimar **and he entered. He was silent, and sat** without uttering a word. Abba of Sura **thought** that Yehuda bar Mareimar **was angry** with him for his failure to grant his daughter a suitable dowry. **He** therefore **wrote** down in the marriage contract **all that he had** as her dowry, to appease him. **Ultimately,** when he observed that Yehuda was still silent, Abba of Sura **said to him: Even now the Master will not talk? By the Master's life, I have left nothing for myself.**

אֲמַר לֵיהּ: אִי מִינַּאי דִּידִי – אֲפִילּוּ הַאי נַמִי דִּכְתַבְתְּ לָא נִיחָא לִי. אֲמַר לֵיהּ: הָשְׁתָּא נַמִי אַהֲדַר בִּי! אֲמַר לֵיהּ: שַׁוְיֵיהּ נַפְשָׁךְ הַדָּרָנָא – לָא קָאָמִינָא.

Yehuda bar Mareimar **said to him: If** you are acting **for my** sake, **that which you wrote is also not amenable to me.** Finally understanding his wishes, Abba of Sura **said to** Yehuda bar Mareimar: **Now too, I will retract,** as I acted in error. Yehuda bar Mareimar **said to him: I did not speak** so that you **should turn yourself into** the kind of person **who retracts** once he gives his word. You should uphold your agreement, but the agreement was not to my liking.

בְּעָא מִינֵּיהּ רַב יֵימָר סָבָא מֵרַב נַחְמָן: מָכְרָה כְּתוּבָּתָהּ לְבַעְלָהּ, יֵשׁ לָהּ כְּתוּבַּת בְּנִין דִּכְרִין אוֹ אֵין לָהּ כְּתוּבַּת בְּנִין דִּכְרִין? אֲמַר לֵיהּ רָבָא: וְתִבָּעֵי לָךְ מוֹחֶלֶת!

§ **Rav Yeimar the Elder raised a dilemma before Rav Naḥman:** If a wife **sold her marriage contract**[N] **to her husband,** i.e., she sold him the right not to have to pay her the marriage contract if they divorce or if she is widowed, does **she have the marriage document concerning male children, or** does **she not have the marriage document concerning male children? Rava said to him: And you can raise** the same **dilemma** with regard to a wife **who forgoes** her right to her marriage contract. Does she retain the marriage document concerning male children in this case?

אֲמַר לֵיהּ הָשְׁתָּא מוֹכֶרֶת קָמִיבַּעְיָא לִי, דְּאַף עַל גַּב דְּאִיכָּא לְמֵימַר זוּזֵי אַנְסוּהָ, דְּאָמִינָא כְּמַאן דְּקָא מָחוּ לָהּ מֵאָה עוּכְלֵי בְּעוּכְלָא, מוֹחֶלֶת מִיבַּעְיָא?!

Rav Yeimar **said to him: Now,** the *halakha* of **one who sells** her marriage contract **is a dilemma for me. As, although there is** room **to say** that **the money forced her,** and **that I say** that she **is like one who is struck** with **a hundred strikes** [*ukelei*][L] **of a hammer** [*ukela*], i.e., she needed liquid assets at the time and therefore she sold her marriage contract unwillingly, even so, I am still willing to entertain the possibility that she has sold the marriage document concerning male children. Then, with regard to **one who forgoes** her marriage contract, **is it necessary** to raise the dilemma?

אֲמַר רָבָא: פְּשִׁיטָא לִי: מוֹכֶרֶת כְּתוּבָּתָהּ לַאֲחֵרִים – יֵשׁ לָהּ כְּתוּבַּת בְּנִין דִּכְרִין, מַאי טַעֲמָא – זוּזֵי אַנְסוּהָ. מוֹחֶלֶת כְּתוּבָּתָהּ לְבַעְלָהּ – אֵין לָהּ כְּתוּבַּת בְּנִין דִּכְרִין, מַאי טַעֲמָא – אַחוּלֵי אַחֵילְתָּא.

Rava said: It **is obvious to me** that if a wife **sells her marriage contract to others,** not to her husband but to someone else who is willing to pay at the present time for the chance to collect the money stated in her marriage contract if she is later divorced or widowed, **she** still **has the marriage document concerning male children. What is the reason? The money forced her** to sell, and she did not mean to renounce all her rights. It is likewise clear to me that **one who forgoes** the right to collect **her marriage contract**[H] from **her husband does not have the marriage document concerning male children. What is the reason? She has forgiven it** all and has no intention of claiming anything from her husband.

בָּעֵי רָבָא: מוֹכֶרֶת כְּתוּבָּתָהּ לְבַעְלָהּ כְּמוֹכֶרֶת לַאֲחֵרִים דָּמֵי, אוֹ כְּמוֹחֶלֶת לְבַעְלָהּ דָּמֵי? בָּתַר דְּבַעְיָא הֲדַר פָּשְׁטָא: מוֹכֶרֶת כְּתוּבָּה לְבַעְלָהּ כְּמוֹכֶרֶת לַאֲחֵרִים דָּמֵי.

However, **Rava raised a dilemma** about the following case: With regard to **one who sells her marriage contract to her husband,** is she **considered like one who sells to others,** i.e., she has not relinquished the marriage document concerning male children, **or is she considered like one who forgoes** her right to collect her marriage contract from **her husband,** i.e., she has forfeited everything? **After he raised the dilemma he subsequently resolved it: One who sells her marriage contract to her husband is considered like one who sells to others,** as she is assumed to have done so due to financial constraints.

מְתִיב רַב אִידִי בַּר אָבִין: מֵתָה – אֵין יוֹרְשִׁין שֶׁל זֶה וְאֵין יוֹרְשִׁין שֶׁל זֶה יוֹרְשִׁין כְּתוּבָּתָהּ. וְהָוֵינַן בָּהּ: כְּתוּבָּתָהּ מַאי עֲבִידְתָּהּ?

Rav Idi bar Avin raised an objection: We learned in a mishna (*Yevamot* 87b) that if a woman's husband went overseas, and after hearing the testimony of one witness that he was dead the woman married again, and then her first husband returned, both husbands must divorce her, and she does not receive payment of her marriage contract from either man. That mishna proceeds to state that if **she died, neither** the **heirs of this** one,[H] the first husband, **nor the heirs of that** one, the second husband, **inherit** the sum stipulated in **her marriage contract. And we discussed** the following question: With regard to **a marriage contract, what is its purpose?** In other words, the mishna just said that she is not entitled to a marriage contract, so how can it even be suggested that the heirs might inherit it?

NOTES

If a wife sold her marriage contract, etc. – **מָכְרָה כְּתוּבָּתָהּ וכו׳**: The early authorities raise a fundamental issue here: What about the third party involved, the sons who stand to gain from the marriage document concerning male children? How can she sell or relinquish their rights? Some maintain that in a case of this kind, when the sons are entitled to the marriage contract not directly but only through their mother, she can forfeit these rights (Rid; see Rashi). Alternatively, when a wife sells or forgoes her marriage contract it is considered as though the document had already been paid, and therefore there is simply nothing left for her to bequeath to her sons (Ritva).

LANGUAGE

Strikes [*ukelei*] – **עוּכְלֵי**: In Aramaic *ukelei* means strikes, while *ukela* means a hammer. Consequently, the expression: One hundred *ukelei be'ukela* means one hundred strikes of a hammer (see Rashi).

HALAKHA

One who sells or forgoes her marriage contract – **מוֹכֶרֶת וּמוֹחֶלֶת כְּתוּבָּתָהּ**: If a wife sells her marriage contract, whether to her husband or to someone else, she has not forfeited the marriage document concerning male children. However, if she forgoes the right to collect her marriage contract, i.e., she cancels the husband's debt rather than transferring rights to collect it, her sons lose the marriage document concerning male children, in accordance with the opinion of Rava (Rambam *Sefer Nashim, Hilkhot Ishut* 17:19; *Shulḥan Arukh, Even HaEzer* 111:15).

Neither the heirs of this one, etc. – **אֵין יוֹרְשִׁין שֶׁל זֶה וכו׳**: If a woman wed someone when she was still married to another man, either because she received a bill of divorce that had actually been canceled or because her husband returned after she had heard that he was dead, she must leave both men, and she requires a divorce from each of them. She is not entitled to a marriage contract, nor to any of the stipulations of a marriage contract from either of them (Rambam *Sefer Nashim, Hilkhot Geirushin* 10:7; *Shulḥan Arukh, Even HaEzer* 17:56).

וַאֲמַר רַב פַּפָּא: כְּתוּבַּת בְּנִין דִּכְרִין. וְאַמַּאי? הָכָא נַמִּי לֵימָא: יֵצֶר אֲנָסָהּ!

And Rav Pappa said: This is referring to **the marriage document concerning male children.** Not only does she forfeit her marriage contract, but she also loses the right to the marriage document concerning male children, as her sons do not inherit from her at all. Rav Idi bar Avin explains his objection. **But** if, according to the above statement, a wife who sells her marriage contract has not relinquished the marriage document concerning male children, **why** does the mishna in *Yevamot* state that none of the woman's heirs inherit the proceeds of her marriage contract? **Here too,** in that mishna, **let us say** that her **desire** to marry another man **forced her** to marry her second husband. Why should she forfeit the marriage document concerning male children?

הָתָם קְנָסָא הוּא דִּקְנָסוּהָ רַבָּנַן.

The Gemara answers: **There it is a penalty** with **which the Sages penalized her.** In other words, the reason is not that she automatically forfeits the marriage document concerning male children, along with the marriage contract itself. Rather, her loss of the marriage document concerning male children is one of several penalties the Sages imposed upon her for remarrying on the basis of the testimony of a single witness without conducting her own thorough investigation into her husband's fate. Therefore, one cannot learn from that *halakha* with regard to the issue at hand.

יְתֵיב רָבִין בַּר חֲנִינָא קַמֵּיהּ דְּרַב חִסְדָּא, וִיתֵיב וְקָאָמַר מִשְּׁמֵיהּ דְּרַבִּי אֶלְעָזָר: מוֹחֶלֶת כְּתוּבָּתָהּ לְבַעְלָהּ – אֵין לָהּ מְזוֹנוֹת. אֲמַר לֵיהּ: אִי לָאו דְּקָאָמְרַתְּ לִי מִשְּׁמֵיהּ דְּגַבְרָא רַבָּא – הֲוָה אָמִינָא לָךְ "מֵשִׁיב רָעָה תַּחַת טוֹבָה לֹא תָמוּשׁ רָעָה מִבֵּיתוֹ".

Ravin bar Ḥanina sat before Rav Ḥisda, and he sat and said the following *halakha* **in the name of Rabbi Elazar: One who forgoes her** right to collect her **marriage contract** from **her husband does not** receive her **sustenance**[N] from him.[H] Rav Ḥisda **said to him: Had you not said** this *halakha* **to me in the name of a great man, I would have said to you** that this is an injustice, in accordance with the verse **"who rewards evil for good, evil shall not depart from his house"** (Proverbs 17:13). After she relinquishes to her husband her right to her marriage contract, which was a favor to her husband, she loses her sustenance as well.

יְתֵיב רַב נַחְמָן וְעוּלָּא וַאֲבִימֵי בַּר רַב פַּפִּי, וִיתֵיב רַב חִיָּיא בַּר אַמִי גַּבַּיְיהוּ. אֲתָא הַהוּא גַּבְרָא דִּשְׁכִיבָא אֲרוּסָתוֹ, אָמְרִי לֵיהּ: זִיל קְבַר, אוֹ הַב לָהּ כְּתוּבָּתָהּ. אֲמַר לְהוּ רַב חִיָּיא, תָּנֵינָא: אִשְׁתּוֹ אֲרוּסָה – לֹא אוֹנֵן וְלֹא מִיטַּמֵּא לָהּ, וְכֵן הִיא – לֹא אוֹנֶנֶת וְלֹא מִיטַּמְּאָה לוֹ, מֵתָה – אֵינוֹ יוֹרְשָׁהּ, מֵת הוּא – גּוֹבָה כְּתוּבָּתָהּ.

The Gemara relates: **Rav Naḥman was sitting, and Ulla and Avimei bar Rav Pappi** were sitting as well, **and Rav Ḥiyya bar Ami was sitting with them,** when **a certain man came** before them **whose betrothed** wife **had died. They said to him:** Go and **bury** her, **or give her** heirs the sum stipulated in **her marriage contract.**[N] **Rav Ḥiyya said to them,** in surprise at their response: But **we learned** that with regard to **one's betrothed wife**[N] he **neither** assumes the status of **an acute mourner nor becomes ritually impure for her**[H] if he is a priest, **and similarly, she neither** assumes the status of **an acute mourner nor becomes ritually impure for him.**[N] If **she died he does not inherit** from **her,**[H] and if **he died she collects** payment of **her marriage contract.**[H]

טַעֲמָא – דְּמֵת הוּא, הָא מֵתָה הִיא – אֵין לָהּ כְּתוּבָּה. מַאי טַעֲמָא? אָמַר רַב הוֹשַׁעְיָא: שֶׁאֵין אֲנִי קוֹרֵא בָּהּ "לִכְשֶׁתִּנָּשְׂאִי לְאַחֵר תִּטְלִי מַה שֶּׁכָּתוּב לֵיכִי".

Rav Ḥiyya infers the following from this statement: The **reason** for this *halakha* is that **he died,** from which it may be inferred that if **she died she does not have a marriage contract,** nor any of the stipulations of a marriage contract. The Gemara asks: **What is the reason** that her marriage contract is canceled upon her death? **Rav Hoshaya said:** The reason is **that I do not read with regard to her** the condition stated in the marriage contract: **When you marry**[N] **another he may take what is written for you,** as she cannot marry another.

NOTES

One who forgoes her marriage contract…does not receive sustenance – מוֹחֶלֶת כְּתוּבָּתָהּ...אֵין לָהּ מְזוֹנוֹת: According to most early authorities, this does not mean that she has waived her right to sustenance from her husband during his lifetime. This is not necessarily due to Rav Ḥisda's claim that the *halakha* is unjust, although some do cite his opinion in support. Rather, it is because a husband is always responsible for his wife's sustenance, either by Torah law or at least by rabbinic ordinance, in exchange for his rights to her earnings. Yet not only does the Rambam rule in accordance with the opinion of Rabbi Elazar, but he maintains that she is not entitled to sustenance even when her husband is alive. Other early authorities discuss the ruling of the Jerusalem Talmud, where it is stated explicitly that even a wife who forgoes her right to collect her marriage contract from her husband is entitled to sustenance from his heirs.

Bury her or give her her marriage contract – קְבַר אוֹ הַב לָהּ כְּתוּבָּתָהּ: The Ramban and the early authorities influenced by him basically accept Rashi's explanation that these Sages, Rav Naḥman, Ulla, and Avimei bar Rav Pappi, initially thought that a husband's obligation to bury his wife is in exchange for the fact that he does not have to pay her marriage contract when she predeceases him. Consequently, if the man had already written his betrothed a marriage contract, he had to either pay it or attend to her burial. Eventually, these Sages conceded that the obligation of burial is in fact in exchange for the husband's right to inherit his wife's dowry. Since a husband inherits his wife's dowry only if they were married and not if they were merely betrothed, then if they were not married he is not required to bury her.

One's betrothed wife – אִשְׁתּוֹ אֲרוּסָה: The main reason for this *halakha* is that with regard to both the ritual impurity of the dead and inheritance the Torah uses the term "his kin" (see Leviticus 21:2 and Numbers 27:11). This term does not apply to a betrothed woman, as there have not been intimate relations between them (*Ba'al Halakhot Gedolot*; see Rashi).

Nor becomes ritually impure for him – וְלֹא מִיטַּמְּאָה לוֹ: Even if she is the daughter of a priest, the prohibition with regard to ritual impurity of the dead does not apply to females. Why, then, may she not defile herself for him? The *ge'onim* and most early authorities explain that this simply means she is not obligated to become ritually impure for him, but she may do so if she wishes. Others state that this refers to the three pilgrimage Festivals, when it is a mitzva for everyone to remain ritually pure. On those days it is prohibited for her to become impure for him (*Tosefot* Rabbi Shimshon of Saens; Rosh; Rashi and *Tosafot* on *Yevamot* 29b).

When you marry, etc. – לִכְשֶׁתִּנָּשְׂאִי וכו׳: It is true that this condition is also not fulfilled if she dies after marriage, but in that case he is obligated to bury her in exchange for the fact that he inherits from her. In the case of a betrothed woman, since he does not inherit from her, one can infer from the language of the marriage contract that he is exempt from paying for her burial (*Shita Mekubbetzet*; see Rashi). The commentaries explain at length that one can infer the parameters of an obligation based upon the standard terminology used in contracts that document the obligation. This is certainly true in the case of a marriage contract, which was instituted by the Sages and whose wording is precise (*Tosafot*).

HALAKHA

Sustenance for one who forgoes the right to collect her marriage contract from her husband – מְזוֹנוֹת בְּמוֹחֶלֶת כְּתוּבָּתָהּ לְבַעְלָהּ: A wife who forgoes her marriage contract has forfeited her rights to sustenance after her husband's death. However, she is entitled to sustenance during his lifetime. The Rambam rules that she is not sustained from his property even while he is alive (see Rambam *Sefer Nashim, Hilkhot Ishut* 12:18; *Shulḥan Arukh, Even HaEzer* 93:9).

He does not become ritually impure for a betrothed woman – אֵין מִיטַּמֵּא לַאֲרוּסָה: If a man's betrothed dies he does not mourn for her or become ritually impure on her account if he is a priest. Likewise, she does not mourn for him and is not obligated to become ritually impure for him (Rambam *Sefer Shofetim, Hilkhot Evel* 2:7; *Shulḥan Arukh, Yoreh De'a* 373:4).

If she died he does not inherit from her – מֵתָה אֵינוֹ יוֹרְשָׁהּ: A man does not inherit from his betrothed upon her death (Rambam *Sefer Nashim, Hilkhot Ishut* 22:2; *Shulḥan Arukh, Even HaEzer* 55:5).

If he died she collects her marriage contract – מֵת הוּא גּוֹבָה כְּתוּבָּתָהּ: A man betrothed a woman and wrote a marriage contract for her, despite the fact that he is not obligated to do so until their marriage. If he subsequently divorced her or died, she may claim the basic amount of her marriage contract, i.e., the sum automatically included in the contract by rabbinic decree, from property that has not been sold. However, she may not collect any additional sum that the husband voluntarily included in the marriage contract (Rambam *Sefer Nashim, Hilkhot Ishut* 10:11; *Shulḥan Arukh, Even HaEzer* 55:6).

כִּי אֲתָא רָבִין אָמַר רֵישׁ לָקִישׁ: אֲרוּסָה שֶׁמֵּתָה – אֵין לָהּ כְּתוּבָּה. אֲמַר לְהוּ אַבָּיֵי: זִילוּ אָמְרוּ לֵיהּ:

The Gemara relates another incident: **When Ravin came** from Eretz Yisrael to Babylonia he said that **Reish Lakish said: A betrothed woman who died does not have a marriage contract. Abaye said to** the scholars who recited this *halakha* in Ravin's name: **Go,** and **say to** Ravin:

Perek **IV**
Daf **53** Amud **b**

שְׁקִילָא טִיבוּתָךְ שַׁדְיָא אַחִיזְרֵי, כְּבָר תַּרְגְּמָא רַב הוֹשַׁעְיָא לִשְׁמַעְתֵּיהּ בְּבָבֶל.

Your good is taken and **cast on thorns,** i.e., we do not owe you a debt of gratitude for informing us of this statement, as **Rav Hoshaya** himself **already interpreted** and ruled this ***halakha*** of yours **in Babylonia.**

״בְּנָן נוּקְבָן דְּיֶהֶוְיָין לִיכִי מִינַּאי״ וכו׳. רַב תָּנֵי: עַד דְּתִלָּקְחָן לְגוּבְרִין, וְלֵוִי תָּנֵי: עַד דְּתִבָּגְרָן. לְרַב – אַף עַל גַּב דְּבָגַר, וְלֵוִי – אַף עַל גַּב דְּאִינְסִיב?

§ The mishna taught that one of the stipulations of the marriage contract is the clause: Any **female children you will have from me** will be sustained from my property. The Gemara notes that **Rav** would **teach** that the daughters are entitled to sustenance **until they are taken** as wives **by men, and Levi** would **teach** that they are entitled to sustenance **until they become grown women.**[H] The Gemara asks: **According to** the opinion of **Rav,** are daughters entitled to sustenance **even though they have become grown women,** if they are still unmarried? Yet how can this be correct? After all, adult daughters are no longer under their father's jurisdiction even in his lifetime. **And** can **Levi** possibly maintain that **even though they are married** they still receive sustenance from their father's estate until they become grown women?

אֶלָּא, בָּגַר וְלָא אִינְסִיב, אִינְסִיב וְלָא בָּגַר – דְּכוּלֵּי עָלְמָא לָא פְּלִיגִי. כִּי פְּלִיגִי – בַּאֲרוּסָה וְלָא בָּגַר. וְכֵן תָּנֵי לֵוִי בְּמַתְנִיתֵיהּ: עַד דְּתִבָּגְרָן וְיִמְטֵי זִמְנֵיהוֹן דְּאִינַּסְבָן. תַּרְתֵּי?! אֶלָּא: אוֹ תִּבָּגְרָן, אוֹ יִמְטֵי זִמְנֵיהוֹן לְאִיתְנַסְבָא.

Rather, in a case where **they became grown women and were not married,**[N] or were **married and had not become grown women, everyone agrees** that they are not entitled to sustenance. **When they disagree** it is **with regard to** a daughter **who was betrothed**[N] **and had not become a grown woman.** Levi maintains that as she is still unmarried she remains under her father's jurisdiction. **And Levi likewise taught** the following version of this stipulation **in his** ***baraita*: Until they become grown women and the time arrives for their marriage.** The Gemara asks: Are these **two** conditions both necessary? She leaves her father's domain when one of these conditions is fulfilled. **Rather,** Levi means that they can continue to receive sustenance **either** until **they become grown women or their time arrives for marriage.**

כְּתַנָּאֵי: עַד מָתַי הַבַּת נִזּוֹנֵית – עַד שֶׁתֵּאָרֵס. מִשּׁוּם רַבִּי אֶלְעָזָר אָמְרוּ: עַד שֶׁתִּבָּגֵר. תָּנֵי רַב יוֹסֵף: עַד דְּיֶהֶוְיָין. אִיבַּעְיָא לְהוּ: הֲוָיָה דְּאֵירוּסִין, אוֹ הֲוָיָה דְּנִישּׂוּאִין? תֵּיקוּ.

The Gemara observes: The dispute between Rav and Levi is **like** a dispute between ***tanna'im*.** As we have learned: **Until when is a daughter sustained** from her father's property? **Until she is betrothed. In the name of Rabbi Elazar they said: Until she becomes a grown woman. Rav Yosef taught** the version: **Until they become** married. The meaning of the expression: Until they become married, is unclear, and therefore **a dilemma was raised before** the scholars: Does this refer to **becoming betrothed or** to **becoming married?** No answer was found, and the Gemara states that the dilemma **shall stand** unresolved.

NOTES

They became grown women and were not married, etc. – בָּגַר וְלָא אִינְסִיב וכו׳: The commentaries explain that there are two opinions with regard to this issue (*Birkat Avraham*). One interpretation is that the key issue is the jurisdiction over the daughter. Once she has left the domain of her father or brothers, whether due to maturity or marriage, they are no longer obligated to give her sustenance (Rashi; *Tosafot*). Alternatively, whether she is entitled to receive sustenance from them depends on whether or not she has another source of sustenance. If she is a grown woman she can support herself by working, and if she is married her husband can provide for her.

When they disagree it is with regard to a daughter who was betrothed, etc. – כִּי פְּלִיגִי בַּאֲרוּסָה וכו׳: Some commentaries explain that this *halakha* applies only to a young woman, but if she was betrothed when she was a minor she does not forfeit her sustenance (Rabbeinu Ḥananel; *Ba'al HaIttur*). According to this opinion, the dispute between Rabbi Yehuda and the Rabbis in the Gemara below with regard to a daughter who refuses her husband is easy to understand. However, those who claim that no betrothed women are entitled to sustenance from their fathers are forced to explain that the ensuing dispute applies only according to one of the opinions here. As for the justification for this difference between a minor and a young woman, the given reason is that the betrothal of a minor is performed with the consent of her brothers or mother, who do not have the power to deprive her of her right to sustenance. Furthermore, as she can refuse this match, it cannot be considered a regular betrothal in all respects.

HALAKHA

Until they are taken…until they become grown women – עַד דְּתִלָּקְחָן...עַד דְּתִבָּגְרָן: One of the stipulations of a marriage contract is that the wife's daughters are entitled to sustenance from their father's property after his death until they are betrothed or reach the age of maturity. If a daughter matured, even if she was not betrothed, or if she was betrothed before she became an adult, she does not receive sustenance from her father's estate, in accordance with the opinion of Rav and the unattributed statement in the *baraita*. Some authorities maintain that a betrothed daughter loses her right to sustenance only if she was betrothed as a young woman; however, while she is a minor she is sustained from her father's property (Rema, citing Rabbeinu Ḥananel and Rashba). Alternatively, this *halakha* applies only if the betrothal was her decision, but if her brothers betrothed her she has not forfeited her sustenance (*Tur*; Ramah; Rambam *Sefer Nashim*, *Hilkhot Ishut* 19:10; *Shulḥan Arukh*, *Even HaEzer* 112:1, 3).

אמר ליה רב חסדא לרב יוסף: מי שמיע לך מיניה דרב יהודה, ארוסה יש לה מזונות או אין לה מזונות? אמר ליה: משמע לא שמיע לי, אלא מסברא לית לה. כיון דאירסה – לא ניחא ליה דתיתזיל.

Rav Ḥisda said to Rav Yosef: Have you heard anything **from Rav Yehuda** with regard to whether **a betrothed** orphan **has sustenance**[NH] from the brothers' inheritance of their father's estate, **or** whether **she does not have sustenance?** Rav Yosef **said to him:** As for **hearing, I have not heard** anything, **but by logical** reasoning I can conclude that **she does not have** sustenance from the inheritance. The reason is that **since** her husband **has betrothed her it is not satisfactory for him that she be demeaned** by having to request her sustenance from the inheritance, when he himself can provide for her.

אמר ליה: אם משמע לא שמיע לך – מסברא אית לה, כיון דלא קים ליה בגוה – לא שדי זוזי בכדי.

Rav Ḥisda **said to** Rav Yosef: **If you have not heard** this *halakha*, **by logical** reasoning **she** should **have** sustenance from the brothers. The reason is that **since** her husband **is not sure** that he will marry **her, he will not throw away money for nothing.**

ואיכא דאמרי, אמר ליה: משמע לא שמיע לי, מסברא אית לה, כיון דלא קים ליה בגוה – לא שדי זוזי בכדי. אמר ליה: אי משמע לא שמיע לך – מסברא לית לה, כיון דאירסה – לא ניחא ליה דתיתזיל.

And some say a different version of this discussion. Rav Yosef **said** to Rav Ḥisda: As for **hearing, I have not heard** anything, but **by logical** reasoning I would say that **she does have** sustenance from the brothers: **Since he is not sure** that he will marry **her, he will not throw away money for nothing.** In response, Rav Ḥisda **said to him: If you have not heard** this *halakha*, **by logical** reasoning **she** should **not have** sustenance from the inheritance: **Since he has betrothed her it is not satisfactory for him that she be demeaned** by having to ask the brothers for food, and he would rather provide for her himself.

סימן דגברי: ש״ק זר״ף, מאנה ויבמה שניה ארוסה ואנסה.

§ The Gemara states **a mnemonic** device **for the men,** i.e., the Sages, who appear in the following discussion: ***Shin, kuf, zayin, reish, peh.*** This refers to Rav Sheshet, Reish Lakish, Rabbi Elazar, Rava, and Rav Pappa. The dilemmas themselves are listed in the following mnemonic: **She refused, and a *yevama*, a secondary** forbidden **relationship, a betrothed woman, and woman who was raped.**

בעו מיניה מרב ששת: ממאנת יש לה מזונות או אין לה מזונות?

The Gemara analyzes these cases one by one: The Sages **raised a dilemma before Rav Sheshet:** With regard to **one who refused,**[N] i.e., a minor orphan girl who was married off by her brothers or mother and then refused her husband, thereby nullifying the marriage, does **she have sustenance** from her father's inheritance **or** does **she not have sustenance?** Is she considered to have been married, and therefore her right to sustenance has lapsed, or does her refusal nullify the marriage to the extent that it is as though she were never married at all, and therefore she is still entitled to sustenance?

אמר להו רב ששת, תניתוה: אלמנה בבית אביה, וגרושה בבית אביה, ושומרת יבם בבית אביה – יש לה מזונות. רבי יהודה אומר: עודה בבית אביה – יש לה מזונות, אינה בבית אביה – אין לה מזונות.

Rav Sheshet said to them: You learned it in the following *baraita*: In the case of **a widow in her father's house,**[N] **or a divorcée in her father's house, or a widow awaiting her *yavam* in her father's house, she has sustenance.**[H] **Rabbi Yehuda says: If she is still in her father's house she has sustenance; if she is not in her father's house she does not have sustenance.**

NOTES

Does a betrothed orphan have sustenance – **ארוסה יש לה מזונות:** There are three interpretations of this dilemma, which depend, among other factors, on variant readings of the Gemara. Rashi maintains that the issue is whether a betrothed orphan is entitled to sustenance from her brothers, i.e., from their late father's estate. If so, this is similar to the previous dispute between Rav and Levi, except that Rav Yosef adds a new consideration, the possibility that her husband might take care of her needs. The other early authorities question Rashi's interpretation for two reasons. First, they say that most versions of the talmudic text do not accord with Rashi's reading. In addition, they explain that on the basis of logical analysis, it is hard to see why a woman should not have the right to sustenance due to the support she receives from her betrothed, when her betrothed is not actually required to support her until they are married or the time for marriage has arrived, i.e., twelve months after the betrothal (see Ramban).

Alternatively, the Gemara is discussing the sustenance of a betrothed woman from her husband's property after his death. The case is where the date for marriage arrived, at which point her husband passed away. Since he is already obligated to sustain her from his property, the question is whether she is considered like a married woman who receives her sustenance from his estate after he has passed away (Rif; see *Talmidei Rabbeinu Yona* and Meiri). Several difficulties have been raised with regard to this interpretation as well. First, the expression: It is not satisfactory for him that she be demeaned, is explained in a far-fetched manner. Second, the context is puzzling, for if this is the dilemma it does not belong here. Rather, it should have been raised in the context of the discussion concerning the obligation of a betrothed man to feed his wife after the time for marriage has arrived.

Yet another interpretation is that the Gemara here in fact refers to the obligation of a betrothed man to provide for his betrothed when she is an orphan receiving her sustenance from her father's property. Admittedly, a man is generally not obligated to feed his betrothed before the prearranged date for marriage, but it is reasonable that he should have to provide for her, as his betrothal caused her to forfeit her sustenance, in accordance with the opinion of Rav (Rabbi Shmuel HaNagid). Many early authorities accept this interpretation, and the Rambam apparently agrees.

One who refused – **ממאנת:** The basic case of refusal concerns a fatherless minor girl. Although her brothers or mother can marry her off, this marriage is not valid by Torah law, but merely by rabbinic decree. Consequently, the Sages ruled that she can annul the marriage entirely by refusing to remain with her husband, which she achieves simply by saying that she does not want to remain with him. In this scenario she is not considered a divorcée. Rather, it is as though the marriage never took place. Apparently, all the commentaries agree that the *halakha* of refusal applies even after marriage, not only after betrothal.

A widow in her father's house, etc. – **אלמנה בבית אביה וכו׳:** There are several explanations of this statement. Rashi and others maintain that it refers only to a widow from the time of betrothal. Others claim that it refers to someone who was widowed or divorced from betrothal and had returned to her father's house during his lifetime (Rabbeinu Ḥananel; Rosh; Ran). Since she was neither a grown woman nor betrothed when her father died, she is entitled to sustenance by virtue of the stipulation in the marriage contract ensuring sustenance for the wife's daughters. Yet others contend that this *halakha* includes a daughter who was widowed or divorced from marriage. If this woman had returned to her father's house by the time he passed away, his heirs are duty bound to provide her sustenance after his death (*Tosafot*, citing Rabbeinu Tam). The Rambam is also of the opinion that the *halakha* refers to a married woman. However, he claims that even if she was widowed after her father's death the heirs are obligated to grant her a livelihood, as she returns to her father's house and is not yet a grown woman.

HALAKHA

The sustenance of a betrothed woman – **מזונות ארוסה:** If a man betroths a girl who is receiving her sustenance from her father's estate, she loses her right to sustenance from that property, and therefore the betrothed man is obligated to support her from the moment of their betrothal. Some say she loses her right to sustenance only if she became betrothed as a young woman, or if she did so without the consent of her brothers (Rambam *Sefer Nashim*, *Hilkhot Ishut* 19:15; *Shulḥan Arukh*, *Even HaEzer* 112:3, and in the comment of Rema).

One who refused, a widow, a divorcée, etc. – **ממאנת, אלמנה, גרושה וכו׳:** If a girl was married off by her mother or brothers and subsequently refused to remain with her husband, or if she was divorced or widowed, even if she was a woman waiting for her *yavam*, then, provided that she returned to her father's house before becoming a grown woman, she is sustained from her father's property until she becomes a grown woman or is betrothed. This is in accordance with the ruling of the *baraita* and the opinion of the first *tanna*, as stated by Rav Sheshet. Some contend that this *halakha* applies only if she was not married but was widowed or divorced from a state of betrothal. The Rema, citing Rashi, *Tosafot*, the Ran, and the *Tur*, says that once she has been married, she is no longer entitled to sustenance. Additionally, the Rema rules that she is entitled to sustenance only if she returned to her father's house while her father was still alive (Rambam *Sefer Nashim*, *Hilkhot Ishut* 19:16; *Shulḥan Arukh*, *Even HaEzer* 112:4).

רַבִּי יְהוּדָה הַיְינוּ תַּנָּא קַמָּא! אֶלָּא לָאו – מְמָאֶנֶת אִיכָּא בֵּינַיְיהוּ, דְּתַנָּא קַמָּא סָבַר: אִית לַהּ, וְרַבִּי יְהוּדָה סָבַר: לֵית לַהּ.

Rav Sheshet analyzes this *baraita*: The opinion of **Rabbi Yehuda is** to all appearances the same as that of **the first *tanna*.** What is their dispute? **Rather, is it not** the case that **there is** a practical difference **between them** concerning a girl **who refused** her husband, **as the first *tanna* maintains** that **she has** sustenance, as her marriage has been annulled and it is as though it never occurred, **and Rabbi Yehuda maintains** that **she does not have** sustenance, as she permanently forfeited this right when she left her father's house in marriage.

בָּעֵי רֵישׁ לָקִישׁ: בַּת יְבָמָה יֵשׁ לָהּ מְזוֹנוֹת אוֹ אֵין לָהּ מְזוֹנוֹת?

Reish Lakish raised a dilemma: With regard to the **daughter** of **a *yevama*,**[NH] i.e., a woman who married her *yavam* in levirate marriage and gave birth to a daughter before he passed away, does **she have sustenance** from the property of the *yavam*, i.e., the girl's father, **or** does **she not have sustenance?**

כֵּיוָן דַּאֲמַר מָר: כְּתוּבָּתָהּ עַל נִכְסֵי בַּעְלָהּ הָרִאשׁוֹן – לֵית לַהּ, אוֹ דִּלְמָא כֵּיוָן דְּאִי לֵית לַהּ מֵרִאשׁוֹן – תַּקִּינוּ לַהּ רַבָּנַן מִשֵּׁנִי, אִית לַהּ? תֵּיקוּ.

The Gemara clarifies the sides of the dilemma: **Since the Master said** that the payment of the **marriage contract** of a *yevama* is taken **from the property of her first husband,** not that of the *yavam*, her daughter should therefore **not have** rights to sustenance from the property of the *yavam*. Her sustenance is a stipulation of the marriage contract, which does not apply to the *yavam*. **Or perhaps, since if she does not have** enough to cover the amount of her marriage contract **from the** property of the **first** husband, **the Sages enacted for her** a marriage contract **from the second** one, i.e., the *yavam*. Therefore, her daughter should **have** sustenance from his property. No answer was found, and the Gemara states that the dilemma **shall stand** unresolved.

בָּעֵי רַבִּי אֶלְעָזָר: בַּת שְׁנִיָּה יֵשׁ לָהּ מְזוֹנוֹת, אוֹ אֵין לָהּ מְזוֹנוֹת?

Rabbi Elazar raised a dilemma: With regard to the **daughter** of **a secondary** forbidden **relationship,** i.e., a girl born to a man and women forbidden to each other by rabbinic law, whose mother is penalized by being deprived of a marriage contract, does her daughter **have sustenance or** does **she not have sustenance?**

NOTES

The daughter of a *yevama* – בַּת יְבָמָה: The question can also be asked with regard to the *yevama* herself: Upon the death of the *yavam*, is the *yevama* entitled to sustenance from his estate, despite the fact that he did not have to write her a marriage contract? If the estate of her first husband can support her, she receives her sustenance from there. If not, most early authorities understood that the *yavam* assumes responsibility to pay her marriage contract, and therefore she would be sustained from his estate (*Tosafot*; Rabbi Aharon HaLevi; Rosh; Ritva). However, some hold that even in this circumstance, she would not have a right to be sustained from the estate of the *yavam* (Rivan; *Shita Mekubbetzet*, citing Rashi).

HALAKHA

The daughter of a *yevama* – בַּת יְבָמָה: In the case of a man who had a daughter with his *yevama* and then passed away, if the woman's first husband left property, the daughter is not entitled to sustenance from either man's estate. The reason for this is that the payment specified in her mother's marriage contract is collected from the estate of the first husband, but the daughter does not receive sustenance by virtue of that marriage contract, as she is not that man's daughter. She is also not entitled to be sustained from her father's property, as the payment specified in her mother's marriage contract is not collected from his estate. However, if the woman's first husband did not leave property, the woman collects the payment specified in her marriage contract from the property of the second husband. Others (*Tur*; Rosh; Ran) explain that this includes all the stipulations of a marriage contract, which means the girl is entitled to sustenance from his estate (Rambam *Sefer Nashim*, *Hilkhot Ishut* 19:14; *Shulḥan Arukh*, *Even HaEzer* 112:5).

Perek **IV**
Daf **54** Amud **a**

כֵּיוָן דְּלֵית לַהּ כְּתוּבָּה – לֵית לַהּ מְזוֹנֵי, אוֹ דִּלְמָא: אִמָּהּ דְּעָבְדָא אִיסּוּרָא – קְנָסוּהָ רַבָּנַן, אִיהִי דְּלָא עָבְדָא אִיסּוּרָא – לָא קְנָסוּהָ רַבָּנַן? תֵּיקוּ.

Once again the Gemara explains the sides of the dilemma: **Since** the Sages penalized the mother and declared that **she does not have a marriage contract,** the daughter **does not have sustenance** either, as her sustenance is guaranteed by her mother's marriage contract. **Or perhaps,** with regard to **her mother, who violated a prohibition, the Sages penalized her** by depriving her of her marriage contract, whereas in the case of the daughter, **who did not violate a prohibition, the Sages did not penalize her.** Once again the Gemara states that the dilemma **shall stand** unresolved.

בָּעֵי רָבָא: בַּת אֲרוּסָה, יֵשׁ לָהּ מְזוֹנוֹת אוֹ אֵין לָהּ מְזוֹנוֹת? כֵּיוָן דְּאִית לָהּ כְּתוּבָּה – אִית לָהּ, אוֹ דִּלְמָא: כֵּיוָן דְּלָא תַּקִּינוּ רַבָּנַן כְּתוּבָּה עַד שְׁעַת נִישּׂוּאִין – לֵית לָהּ? תֵּיקוּ.

Rava raises a dilemma: In the case of the **daughter of a betrothed woman,**[N] i.e., a man betrothed a woman, fathered a daughter with her, and then died, does the daughter **have** the right to receive **sustenance** from his estate, **or** does **she not have** the right to receive **sustenance? Since** the mother **has a marriage contract,** as in this case the man wrote her a marriage contract after betrothing her, it may be argued that the daughter **has** the right to receive sustenance. **Or perhaps, since the Sages did not enact** any requirement for a man to provide his wife with **a marriage contract until the time of marriage,**[N] the stipulations of the marriage contract do not apply until then, and therefore the daughter of this woman **does not have** the right to receive sustenance. Again, the Gemara states that the dilemma **shall stand** unresolved.

בָּעֵי רַב פַּפָּא: בַּת אֲנוּסָה, יֵשׁ לָהּ מְזוֹנוֹת אוֹ אֵין לָהּ מְזוֹנוֹת? אַלִּיבָּא דְּרַבִּי יוֹסֵי בְּרַבִּי יְהוּדָה – לָא תִּיבָּעֵי לָךְ, דְּאָמַר: יֵשׁ לָהּ כְּתוּבָּה מָנֶה.

Rav Pappa raises a dilemma: With regard to **the daughter** of a **raped** woman,[H] i.e., a man raped a young woman, married her, had a child, and died, does **she have** the right to receive **sustenance** from her father's estate **or** does **she not have** the right to receive **sustenance** from his estate? The Gemara comments: **According to** the opinion of **Rabbi Yosei, son of Rabbi Yehuda, do not raise this dilemma, as he said** that a raped woman **has a marriage contract of one hundred dinars,** and therefore she is entitled to the stipulations of a marriage contract, one of which is that if she has a daughter with her husband, the daughter receives sustenance from the husband's estate.

כִּי תִּיבָּעֵי לָךְ – אַלִּיבָּא דְּרַבָּנַן, דְּאָמְרִי: יָצָא כֶּסֶף קְנָסָהּ בִּכְתוּבָּתָהּ – מַאי?

Rather, **let the dilemma be raised according to** the opinion of **the Rabbis, who say** that the **money of her fine fulfilled** his obligation to provide **her** with a **marriage contract,** i.e., since she has already received the fine in compensation for the rape, she is not entitled to further payment in the form of a marriage contract. According to this opinion, **what** is the *halakha*?

כֵּיוָן דְּלֵית לָהּ כְּתוּבָּה – לֵית לָהּ מְזוֹנֵי, אוֹ דִּלְמָא: כְּתוּבָּה טַעֲמָא מַאי? כְּדֵי שֶׁלֹּא תְּהֵא קַלָּה בְּעֵינָיו לְהוֹצִיאָהּ, וְהָא – לָא מָצֵי מַפֵּיק לָהּ? תֵּיקוּ.

The Gemara elaborates: It may be argued that **since** the mother **does not have a marriage contract,** the daughter **does not have** the right to receive **sustenance** from her father's estate. **Or perhaps** one should consider the following: **What is the reason** that **the marriage contract** was enacted? **So that** his wife **will not be demeaned in his eyes such that** he will easily **divorce her. And this one,** his rape victim, **he cannot divorce her** by Torah law, as it is stated: "He may not send her away all his days" (Deuteronomy 22:29). It was therefore unnecessary for the Sages to require that he provide the woman with a marriage contract. However, the reasons for the stipulations included in a marriage contract, e.g., that his daughter receives sustenance from his estate, still apply in this case. Consequently, the Sages stipulated that these provisions still be granted. Yet again the Gemara states that the dilemma **shall stand** unresolved.

"אַתְּ תְּהֵא יָתְבָא בְּבֵיתִי" וכו׳. תָּנֵי רַב יוֹסֵף: בְּבֵיתִי וְלֹא בְּבִיקָתִי. אֲבָל מְזוֹנֵי – אִית לָהּ. מָר בַּר רַב אַשִׁי אֲמַר: אֲפִילּוּ מְזוֹנֵי נַמִי לֵית לָהּ. וְלֵית הִלְכְתָא כְּמָר בַּר רַב אַשִׁי.

§ The mishna taught that one of the stipulations of a marriage contract is: **You will sit in my house** and be sustained from my property all your days as a widow. **Rav Yosef taught: In my house, and not in my hovel** [*bikati*].[L] If there is no room for her in his house, the heirs are not obligated to allow her to stay there. **However,** even in this case, **she has** the right to receive her **sustenance** from the heirs. **Mar bar Rav Ashi said: She does not even have** the right to receive her **sustenance,** as she is entitled to sustenance only when she lives in her husband's house. If she resides elsewhere, for whatever reason, she does not receive this payment. The Gemara concludes: **And the *halakha* is not in accordance with** the opinion **of Mar bar Rav Ashi.**

NOTES

The daughter of a betrothed woman, etc. – בַּת אֲרוּסָה וכו׳: Rashi suggests two interpretations. Either the man wrote a marriage contract for his betrothed by choice, or this discussion is in accordance with the opinion that a betrothed woman is entitled to a marriage contract, in which case she is entitled to it even if he did not actually write the contract. In either case, he did not explicitly write that he is accepting the obligation to support his daughters, and the dilemma is whether the stipulation of the court that imposes this obligation takes effect in this case, even if it is not written in the marriage contract. Others argue that this passage must be in accordance with the opinion that a betrothed woman is entitled to a marriage contract, because if the husband himself decided to give her a marriage contract, it is certain that he is obligated to support his daughters only if he explicitly accepted this obligation upon himself (Rid; see Ritva).

The Sages did not enact a marriage contract until the time of marriage – לָא תַּקִּינוּ רַבָּנַן כְּתוּבָּה עַד שְׁעַת נִישּׂוּאִין: Some commentaries explain that this statement should be understood as follows: Although a betrothed woman is entitled to a marriage contract, the lien on the husband's property in order to guarantee payment of the marriage contract takes effect only upon marriage. Consequently, the provision that a daughter receives her sustenance from her father's estate, which is a stipulation in the marriage contract, takes effect only from the time of the marriage (*Talmidei Rabbeinu Yona*). Yet others explain as follows: The basic idea of a marriage contract applies specifically to a married woman, to prevent the husband from finding it easy to divorce her. Consequently, the marriage contract of a betrothed woman, which lacks this underlying rationale, does not include all the additional stipulations of a marriage contract (Rabbi Crescas Vidal). Some contend that this refers only to a situation where the daughter was born before the marriage, in which case the stipulations of the marriage contract do not apply to her (Ra'avad).

HALAKHA

The daughter of a secondary forbidden relationship, the daughter of a betrothed woman, the daughter of a raped woman – בַּת שְׁנִיָּה, בַּת אֲרוּסָה, בַּת אֲנוּסָה: With regard to the daughter of a woman forbidden to her husband as a secondary forbidden relationship, the daughter of a betrothed woman, and the daughter of a raped woman who married the man who raped her, none of these women are entitled to sustenance after their father's death by virtue of the marriage contract. However, during his lifetime he is obligated to support them, like all other fathers and daughters. The Gemara does not resolve its dilemmas with regard to sustenance after the father's death in these cases, and in uncertain monetary cases the court does not remove money from its owner (Rambam *Sefer Nashim*, *Hilkhot Ishut* 19:14 and *Maggid Mishne* there; *Shulḥan Arukh*, *Even HaEzer* 112:5).

LANGUAGE

My hovel [*bikati*] – בִּיקָתִי: The term *bikta*, which means a very small house, is of unclear origin. The Sages explained that it is a contraction of the two words *bei akta*, meaning a narrow house, or a home so small that one can barely live there.

אָמַר רַב נַחְמָן אָמַר שְׁמוּאֵל: תְּבָעוּהָ לְהִנָּשֵׂא וְנִתְפַּיְּיסָה – אֵין לָהּ מְזוֹנוֹת, הָא לֹא נִתְפַּיְּיסָה – יֵשׁ לָהּ מְזוֹנוֹת? אֲמַר רַב עָנָן: לְדִידִי מְפָרְשָׁא לִי מִינֵּיהּ דְּמָר שְׁמוּאֵל: אָמְרָה ״מֵחֲמַת פְּלוֹנִי בַּעְלִי״ – יֵשׁ לָהּ מְזוֹנוֹת: ״מֵחֲמַת בְּנֵי אָדָם שֶׁאֵינָן מְהוּגָּנִין לָהּ״ – אֵין לָהּ מְזוֹנוֹת.

§ **Rav Naḥman said** that **Shmuel said:** If a man **proposed to marry** a widow **and she agreed,** even if she has not yet married him, **she no** longer **has** the right to receive **sustenance** from the heirs of her previous husband. The Gemara comments: It may be inferred from here that if she had **not agreed,** even if the man had proposed marriage, **she** still **has** the right to receive **sustenance. Rav Anan said: It was explained to me personally by Mar Shmuel** that the *halakha* varies in different cases. If **she said:** I will not marry you **due to so-and-so, my** deceased **husband,** i.e., she still feels connected to him, **she** still **has** the right to receive **sustenance** from his estate. However, if she refused the offer **because** the men who approached her are **people who are unsuitable for her, she does not have** the right to continue to receive **sustenance,** as she has shown that in principle she is willing to remarry.

אָמַר רַב חִסְדָּא: זִינְּתָה – אֵין לָהּ מְזוֹנוֹת. אָמַר רַב יוֹסֵף: כִּיחֲלָה וּפִירְכְּסָה – אֵין לָהּ מְזוֹנוֹת.

Rav Ḥisda said: If **she engaged in licentious sexual relations she does not have** the right to continue receiving **sustenance** from his estate, as she is not acting in a manner befitting a widow. **Rav Yosef said:** If **she painted** her eyes **and dyed** her hair she has clearly done so to attract men for the purposes of marriage, and therefore **she does not have** the right to receive **sustenance** from her husband's estate.

מַאן דְּאָמַר זִינְּתָה – כׇּל שֶׁכֵּן כִּיחֲלָה וּפִירְכְּסָה. מַאן דְּאָמַר כִּיחֲלָה וּפִירְכְּסָה, אֲבָל זִינְּתָה – אִית לָהּ, מַאי טַעְמָא – יֵצֶר אֲנָסָהּ.

The Gemara comments: According to **the one who says** that a widow who **engaged in licentious sexual relations** loses her sustenance, **all the more so** if **she painted** her eyes **and dyed** her hair she loses her sustenance, as her intention to marry is evident. However, according to **the one who says** that if a widow **painted** her eyes **and dyed** her hair she forfeits her right to receive sustenance from her husband's estate, this ruling applies only to that particular situation. **However,** if **she engaged in licentious sexual relations she** still **has** the right to receive sustenance from his estate. **What is the reason?** Her evil **inclination forced her,** i.e., she did not make a decision to remarry but merely succumbed to temptation.

וְלֵית הִלְכְתָא כְּכׇל הָנֵי שְׁמַעְתָּתָא, אֶלָּא כִּי הָא דְּאָמַר רַב יְהוּדָה אָמַר שְׁמוּאֵל: הַתּוֹבַעַת כְּתוּבָּתָהּ בְּבֵית דִּין – אֵין לָהּ מְזוֹנוֹת.

The Gemara concludes: **And the *halakha* is not in accordance with all of these statements.**[N] **Rather,** the *halakha* **is,** in accordance with **that which Rav Yehuda said** that **Shmuel said: One who claims** the payment specified in **her marriage contract in court**[H] **does not have** the right to continue receiving **sustenance,** as she has thereby demonstrated her desire to sever her ties with her late husband.

וְלָא? וְהָתַנְיָא: מָכְרָה כְּתוּבָּתָהּ, וּמִשְׁכְּנָה כְּתוּבָּתָהּ, עָשְׂתָה כְּתוּבָּתָהּ אַפּוֹתֵיקִי לְאַחֵר – אֵין לָהּ מְזוֹנוֹת. הָנֵי – אִין, אֲבָל תּוֹבַעַת – לָא!

The Gemara asks: **And** does she **not** receive sustenance? **But isn't it taught** in a *baraita*: With regard to **one who sold her marriage contract,**[H] **or used her marriage contract as collateral, or established her marriage contract as designated repayment** [*apoteiki*][L] **for** a debt owed to **another** individual, **she does not have** the right to receive **sustenance** from her husband's estate? The Gemara infers from this *baraita*: In **these** cases, **yes,** she forfeits her right to continue to receive sustenance. **However,** in the case of a widow who **claims** her marriage contract, **no,** she does not lose the right to continue to receive sustenance.

הָנֵי – בֵּין בְּבֵית דִּין, בֵּין שֶׁלֹּא בְּבֵית דִּין. תּוֹבַעַת, בְּבֵית דִּין – אִין, שֶׁלֹּא בְּבֵית דִּין – לָא.

The Gemara answers that this argument is incorrect, and one should make the following inference instead: In **these** cases listed in the *baraita,* she forfeits her marriage contract **whether** she took the action **in court** or **whether** she did **not** do so **in court.** However, with regard to **one who claims** her marriage contract, if she issues this claim **in court, yes,** she loses the right to continue to receive her sustenance, but if her claim was **not** issued **in court, no,** she has not forfeited this right.

NOTES

The *halakha* is not in accordance with all of these statements – לֵית הִלְכְתָא כְּכׇל הָנֵי שְׁמַעְתָּתָא: According to *Tosafot*, this should not be read literally; in the case of a woman who agreed to remarry, the *halakha* is that she no longer has the right to receive her sustenance from the estate of her first husband. However, the Rif disagrees and holds that even if the woman agrees to remarry, she maintains the right to receive her sustenance from her first husband's estate until she actually remarries. The Ritva argues that the Gemara would not have used the word all if, as explained by *Tosafot*, it was referring to only two cases.

HALAKHA

One who claims her marriage contract in court – הַתּוֹבַעַת כְּתוּבָּתָהּ בְּבֵית דִּין: A widow who demands payment of her marriage contract in court is no longer entitled to sustenance from her deceased husband's estate. She forfeits her sustenance from the moment she submits this claim, even before she is paid. However, if she demands payment of her marriage contract outside the court, she does not lose her right to sustenance. This follows the Rif's explanation that the Gemara is in accordance with the opinion of Shmuel. Others contend that even when she submits this claim in court, if she was compelled to do so because her husband's heirs were not providing her with proper sustenance, or if they deceived her into issuing this demand, she does not forfeit her sustenance (Rosh, based on the Jerusalem Talmud; Rambam *Sefer Nashim, Hilkhot Ishut* 18:1; *Shulḥan Arukh, Even HaEzer* 93:5).

One who sold her marriage contract, etc. – מָכְרָה כְּתוּבָּתָהּ וכו׳: If, in the presence of three trustworthy men, a woman sold her marriage contract, used it as collateral, or established it as a designated repayment for a debt, whether she did so during her husband's lifetime or after his death, she loses her right to sustenance from her husband's estate, in accordance with the ruling of the *baraita*. Some maintain that she does not lose this right if she performs these transactions when she is not in the presence of at least three trustworthy men. However, the authors of *Beit Shmuel* and *Ḥelkat Meḥokek* hold that she loses her right to sustenance regardless of who was present at the time of the transaction (Rambam *Sefer Nashim, Hilkhot Ishut* 18:1; *Shulḥan Arukh, Even HaEzer* 93:8).

LANGUAGE

Designated repayment [*apoteiki*] – אַפּוֹתֵיקִי: From the Greek ὑποθήκη, *hypothēkē*, meaning mortgage, or a property with a lien. The Sages creatively read it as: *Apo tehei kai*, meaning on this it will stand, i.e., the property is under a mortgage agreement. This was typically a precisely defined property used as a guarantee for the obligation of a certain payment. When a property became an *apoteiki*, the one to whom the money was owed had the right to collect payment from this property before other creditors did so. The property under *apoteiki* was the only guarantee for the payment of this debt, which could not be collected from other properties.

"וכך היו אנשי ירושלים" וכו׳. איתמר, רב אמר: הלכה כאנשי יהודה, ושמואל אמר הלכה כאנשי גליל.

§ The mishna taught: **And the residents of Jerusalem** and of the Galilee **would** write the marriage contract **in this manner,** i.e., that if the woman is widowed, she may remain in her husband's house and receive her sustenance from his property throughout her widowhood. Conversely, the residents of Judea would write that she may live in his house and be sustained from his estate until the heirs decide to give her the marriage contract. **It was stated** that the *amora'im* argued over this issue. **Rav said** that **the *halakha* is in accordance with** the custom of **the residents of Judea, and Shmuel said** that **the *halakha* is in accordance with** the custom of **the residents of the Galilee**[H] and Jerusalem.

בבל וכל פרוודהא נהוג כרב, נהרדעא וכל פרוודהא נהוג כשמואל. ההיא בת מחוזא דהות נסיבא לנהרדעא, אתו לקמיה דרב נחמן, שמעה לקלה דבת מחוזא היא.

The Gemara comments: **Babylonia and all** of its surrounding **towns** [*parvadaha*][L] **act in accordance with** the opinion of **Rav; Neharde'a and all** of its **towns act in accordance with** the opinion of **Shmuel.** The Gemara relates: There was **a certain woman of Meḥoza who was married to** a man from **Neharde'a. They came before Rav Naḥman** to discuss her marriage contract. **He heard from her voice that she was from Meḥoza,** whose residents had a distinctive accent.

אמר להו: בבל וכל פרוודהא נהוג כרב. אמרו ליה: והא לנהרדעא נסיבא! אמר להו: אי הכי – נהרדעא וכל פרוודהא נהוג כשמואל. ועד היכא נהרדעא – עד היכא דסגי קבא דנהרדעא.

Rav Naḥman **said to them: Babylonia and all** of its **towns act in accordance with** the opinion of **Rav. They said to him: But she is marrying** a resident of **Neharde'a. He said to them: If so, Neharde'a and all** of its **towns act in accordance with** the opinion of **Shmuel.** The Gemara asks: **And until where** is the boundary of **Neharde'a? Up to** any place **where the *kav*** measurement **of Neharde'a**[B] **is used.** The entire area that utilizes the system of Neharde'a measurements is considered part of its surroundings for the purposes of this *halakha*.

איתמר: אלמנה, רב אמר: שמין מה שעליה, ושמואל אמר: אין שמין מה שעליה. אמר רב חייא בר אבין: וחילופה בלקיט.

§ **It was stated** that the *amora'im* also argued about the *halakha* **of a widow. Rav said:** When she receives the payment of her marriage contract, the court **appraises** the clothes **that are upon her**[H] and deducts their value from the payment she receives. **And Shmuel said** that the court **does not appraise** the clothes **that are upon her. Rav Ḥiyya bar Avin said: And the reverse** is the case **with regard to a hired worker.** With regard to a hired laborer who lived with his employer and the latter bought clothes for him, Rav and Shmuel disagreed as to whether these garments are appraised and their value deducted from the worker's salary when he leaves his employer's service. However, in this case Rav claims that his clothes are not appraised, whereas Shmuel maintains that they are appraised.

HALAKHA

The *halakha* is in accordance with the residents of the Galilee – **הלכה כאנשי גליל**: A widow is entitled to sustenance from the orphans' property throughout her widowhood, even if this stipulation was omitted from her marriage contract. The heirs cannot pay the one hundred or two hundred dinars specified in her marriage contract and stop providing her with sustenance against her will, before she demands payment of this sum, unless a condition to this effect was explicitly included in the document itself or this was the local custom. Some state that a court can institute this practice as the custom in their area of jurisdiction if they so choose (*Beit Yosef*, based on Rivash). Most early authorities rule in accordance with the custom of the inhabitants of Jerusalem and the Galilee, as the *halakha* is in accordance with the opinion of Shmuel when he disputes Rav in cases involving monetary law (Rambam *Sefer Nashim, Hilkhot Ishut* 18:1; *Shulḥan Arukh, Even HaEzer* 93:3).

The court appraises the clothes that are upon her – **שמין מה שעליה**: If a widow comes to collect payment of her marriage contract, the court evaluates all the clothes she received from her husband, both weekday and Shabbat outfits, and subtracts their value from the sum of the marriage contract. Some add that the same applies to a woman who underwent *ḥalitza* (*Beit Yosef*, citing Rivash). The *halakha* is in accordance with the opinion of Rav, as ruled by Rav Naḥman (Rambam *Sefer Nashim, Hilkhot Ishut* 16:4; *Shulḥan Arukh, Even HaEzer* 99:1).

LANGUAGE

Towns [*parvadaha*] – **פרוודהא**: An alternative reading of this term, *parvaraha*, is provided by the *Arukh*. The phonetically similar word *parvar* appears in the Mishna (*Ḥalla* 4:11) and is Persian in origin, from parwār, suburbs.

BACKGROUND

The *kav* measurement of Neharde'a – **קבא דנהרדעא**: In the past each country had several local measurements that were used only in that particular area. This is still true in certain places nowadays. These local measurements generally existed for volume and weight. Sometimes even two adjacent towns used different measurements. These measurements were perhaps the lingering remnant of an independent authority that once ruled the city or province. Even the Jewish communities of Babylonia were divided into different provinces; in the period of the *ge'onim* the Jewish areas of settlement were even defined by law. Each province had separate customs and accepted the authority of a certain Sage to decide matters of *halakha*. Occasionally they spoke in slightly different dialects and used certain colloquialisms unique to their area. In the case mentioned in the Gemara, Rav Naḥman was able to detect the woman's place of origin from her accent. Ultimately, Rav Naḥman followed the local custom of Neharde'a in his judgment.

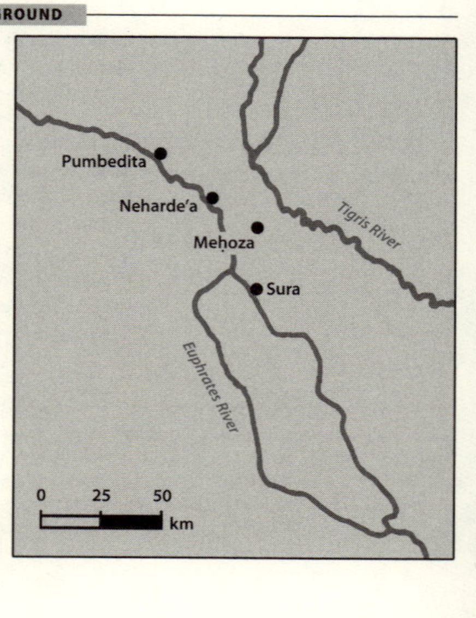

Major cities with large Jewish populations in Babylonia during the time of the Talmud

רַב כָּהֲנָא מַתְנֵי: וְכֵן בְּלָקִיט, וּמַנַּח בָּהּ סִימָנָא: "יַתְמָא וְאַרְמַלְתָּא שְׁלַח וּפוּק".

Conversely, **Rav Kahana** would **teach: And likewise with regard to a hired worker,** their respective opinions are the same in this case as well. Rav rules that one appraises the garments, while Shmuel claims that one does not. **And he would apply a mnemonic** device for Rav's opinion: **An orphan and a widow, disrobe and remove** them. In other words, Rav maintains that both a widow and a hired worker, dubbed an orphan due to his typical poverty, should disrobe, as it were, when the court evaluates the payment to which they are entitled.

אָמַר רַב נַחְמָן: אַף עַל גַּב דִּתְנַן בְּמַתְנִיתִין כְּוָותֵיהּ דִּשְׁמוּאֵל – הִלְכְתָא כְּוָותֵיהּ דְּרַב. דִּתְנַן: אֶחָד הַמַּקְדִּישׁ נְכָסָיו, וְאֶחָד הַמַּעֲרִיךְ אֶת עַצְמוֹ – אֵין לוֹ לֹא בִּכְסוּת אִשְׁתּוֹ, וְלֹא בִּכְסוּת בָּנָיו, וְלֹא בְּצֶבַע שֶׁצְּבָעוֹ לִשְׁמָן, וְלֹא בְּסַנְדָּלִים חֲדָשִׁים שֶׁלְּקָחָן לִשְׁמָן.

Rav Naḥman said: Even though we learned in a mishna in accordance with the opinion of **Shmuel, the** ***halakha*** **is in accordance with** the opinion of **Rav. As we learned** in a mishna (*Arakhin* 24a): With regard to **both one who consecrates his property and one who valuates himself** by donating his fixed value to the Temple, the Temple treasurer has the right to take **neither his wife's clothing,**[H] **nor his children's clothing, nor** new **dyed** clothing **that he dyed** specially **for them,** even if they have yet to wear them, **nor new sandals that he bought for them.** This mishna is apparently in accordance with the opinion of Shmuel that a woman's garments are not considered her husband's property.

אֲמַר לֵיהּ רָבָא לְרַב נַחְמָן: וְכִי מֵאַחַר דִּתְנַן מַתְנִיתִין כְּוָותֵיהּ דִּשְׁמוּאֵל, אַמַּאי הִלְכְתָא כְּוָותֵיהּ דְּרַב? אֲמַר לֵיהּ: לִכְאוֹרָה כִּשְׁמוּאֵל רְהִיטָא, כִּי מְעַיְּינַתְּ בָּהּ – הִלְכְתָא כְּוָותֵיהּ דְּרַב.

Rava said to Rav Naḥman: Once we have learned a mishna in accordance with the opinion of **Shmuel, why is the** ***halakha*** **in accordance with** the opinion of **Rav? He said to him: It would seem** [*likhora*][L] that this mishna agrees **with** the opinion of **Shmuel** when it is **skimmed through** and read superficially. However, **when you examine it** you will see that **the** ***halakha*** is in fact **in accordance with** the opinion of **Rav.**

מַאי טַעְמָא? כִּי אַקְנֵי לַהּ – אַדַּעְתָּא לְמֵיקַם קַמֵּיהּ, אַדַּעְתָּא לְמִשְׁקַל וּלְמֵיפַק – לָא אַקְנֵי לַהּ.

What is the reason for this? **When he bought her** these clothes he did so **with the intention that she should stand before him** and wear them when she is with him. **He did not buy** them for **her with the intention that she should take** them **and leave** him. The reason for the mishna's ruling is in fact that the husband acquires the clothes on behalf of his wife, but this applies only if she is living with him. Consequently, if she is living with him, the treasurer has no right to them. However, if she leaves him, she has no right to them, in accordance with the opinion of Rav.

כַּלְּתָא דְּבֵי בַּר אֶלְיָשִׁיב הֲוָה קָא תָּבְעָה כְּתוּבְּתָהּ מִיַּתְמֵי. הֲוָה קָא מַמְטֵי לְהוּ לְבֵי דִּינָא, אָמְרִי: זִילָא לַן מִילְּתָא דְּתֵיזְלִי הָכִי. אָזְלָא לְבִישְׁתִּינְהוּ וְאִיכַּסְתִּינְהוּ לְכוּלְּהוּ מָנָא. אָתוּ לְקַמֵּיהּ דְּרָבִינָא, אֲמַר לְהוּ: הִלְכְתָא כְּוָותֵיהּ דְּרַב, דְּאָמַר: אַלְמָנָה שָׁמִין מַה שֶּׁעָלֶיהָ.

§ The Gemara relates: The **daughter-in-law of the house of the son of Elyashiv was claiming** payment of **her marriage contract from the orphans,** and **she was** in the process of **bringing them to the court.** The orphans **said** to her: It is **demeaning for us**[N] **that you should go** dressed **in this manner,** in house clothes. We would rather you come in more suitable attire. **She went** and **dressed and covered herself with all of her clothes. They came before Ravina, who said to them: The** ***halakha*** **is in accordance with** the opinion of **Rav,** who **said** that with regard to **a widow,** the court **appraises** the clothes **that are upon her.** Therefore, the court takes everything she is wearing into account in the calculation of her marriage contract payment.

הַהוּא דַּאֲמַר לְהוּ: נְדוּנְיָא לִבְרַת. זַל נְדוּנְיָא. אָמַר רַב אִידִי בַּר אָבִין: פּוּרְנָא לְיַתְמֵי.

The Gemara relates another incident: **A certain** person **said to** his heirs, in his will: Give **a dowry to** my **daughter.**[H] There was an established custom for the amount of money spent on a dowry, including clothing and jewelry. In the meantime, the cost of **a dowry depreciated,** i.e., all these items could be acquired with less money. The question arose concerning the difference between the amount the father wished to give her when he wrote the will and the sum they paid in practice. **Rav Idi bar Avin said:** The **profit** [*purna*],[L] i.e., this difference in price, goes **to the** male **orphans,** not to the daughter.

הַהוּא דַּאֲמַר לְהוּ:

The Gemara cites a related incident: **A certain** person **said to** his heirs, in his will:

HALAKHA

The Temple treasurer has the right to take neither his wife's clothing, etc. – **אֵין לוֹ לֹא בִּכְסוּת אִשְׁתּוֹ וכו׳**: If a man takes a vow or issues a valuation for which he owes money to the Temple Sanctuary, the court takes collateral and claims the debt from his property. However, the court does not take the clothing of his wife or children, nor any new garments that the man dyed for them, nor shoes acquired on their behalf. Similarly, one who states simply that he is consecrating all his possessions has not thereby consecrated his wife's clothing or any of the above items (Rambam *Sefer Hafla'a*, *Hilkhot Arakhin* 3:14).

A dowry to my daughter, etc. – **נְדוּנְיָא לִבְרַת וכו׳**: If a man instructed in his will that his daughter receive a dowry consisting of a certain amount of clothing and other items, and their cost subsequently decreases, she receives these articles in accordance with the cheaper price, with the difference going to her brothers, who are her father's legal heirs, as stated by Rav Idi bar Avin (Rambam *Sefer Kinyan*, *Hilkhot Zekhiya UMattana* 11:22; *Shulḥan Arukh*, *Ḥoshen Mishpat* 253:16).

LANGUAGE

It would seem [*likhora*] – **לִכְאוֹרָה**: The precise source of this common word is unclear. Some claim that it is similar in meaning to *likhura*, i.e., to one who is ugly, where the letter *ayin* replaces the *alef* (Rivan; Rid). If so, it would mean that an ugly man, i.e., one who is not precise in matters, would understand the issue as follows. Others claim that it is an Aramaic term (*ge'onim*). Yet others associate it with *ora*, its light, meaning in the first light, or at first glance.

Profit [*purna*] – **פּוּרְנָא**: From the Greek φερνή, *fernē*, meaning dowry, the money a bride brings to her husband's house upon marriage.

NOTES

It is demeaning for us – **זִילָא לַן מִילְּתָא**: Some explain that the orphans said this because they wanted the court to see how many items of clothing she had (Rivan). The Meiri notes that if the clothes the woman is wearing are considered part of the payment of her marriage contract, certainly the clothes and jewelry she has at home are considered part of the payment. Nevertheless, in this case her husband's heirs were concerned that she would deny having any other clothing or jewelry at home, so they requested that she wear to court whatever she had.

אַרְבַּע מֵאָה זוּזֵי מִן חַמְרָא לִבְרַת. אִייַּקַר חַמְרָא. אֲמַר רַב יוֹסֵף: רַוְוחָא לְיַתְמֵי.

Four hundred dinars of this **wine** you should give **to my daughter,** and **the wine** subsequently **appreciated** in value, so that some money remained. **Rav Yosef said:** The **gain goes to the** male **orphans,** i.e., they are entitled to the leftover sum.

קְרִיבֵיהּ דְּרַבִּי יוֹחָנָן הֲוָה לְהוּ אִיתַּת אַבָּא דַּהֲוָה קָמַפְסְדָה מְזוֹנֵי. אֲתוּ לְקַמֵּיהּ דְּרַבִּי יוֹחָנָן. אֲמַר לְהוּ: אֵיזִילוּ וְאִמְרוּ לֵיהּ לַאֲבוּכוֹן דְּנֵייחֵד לָהּ אַרְעָא לִמְזוֹנָהּ.

The Gemara relates: **The relatives of Rabbi Yoḥanan had a wife of** their **father who would diminish** his resources by spending wastefully on her **sustenance. They came before Rabbi Yoḥanan** to ask his advice. **He said to them: Go and say to your father that he should set aside** a certain portion of **land for her sustenance.** If she agrees to accept this land for her sustenance she has thereby relinquished her claim to the rest of the estate.

אָתוּ לְקַמֵּיהּ דְּרֵישׁ לָקִישׁ, אֲמַר לְהוּ: כׇּל שֶׁכֵּן שֶׁרִיבָּה לָהּ מְזוֹנוֹת! אָמְרוּ לֵיהּ: וְהָא רַבִּי יוֹחָנָן לָא אֲמַר הָכִי! אֲמַר לְהוּ: זִילוּ הֲבוּ לָהּ, וְאִי לָא – מַפֵּיקְנָא לְכוּ רַבִּי יוֹחָנָן מֵאוּנַיְיכוּ. אֲתוּ לְקַמֵּיהּ דְּרַבִּי יוֹחָנָן. אֲמַר לְהוּ: מָה אֶעֱשֶׂה? שֶׁכְּנֶגְדִּי חָלוּק עָלַי.

After their father died, **they came before Reish Lakish**[N] for his ruling, and he **said to them: All the more so, he has increased** the sources of **sustenance** available **to her.** In other words, they are still obligated to support her from their father's estate according to the lifestyle she is accustomed to living, and if they do not, she may use the field to supplement what they give her. **They said to him: But Rabbi Yoḥanan did not say so. He said to them: Go** and **give her** all she requires, **and if not, I will remove for you Rabbi Yoḥanan from your ears,**[N] i.e., I will treat you so harshly that you will forget Rabbi Yoḥanan's ruling. **They approached Rabbi Yoḥanan** to complain, but **he said to them: What can I do?** I cannot impose my opinion, as a man **equal to me disagrees with me.**

אֲמַר רַבִּי אַבָּהוּ, לְדִידִי מְפָרְשָׁא לִי מִינֵּיהּ דְּרַבִּי יוֹחָנָן: אֲמַר ״לִמְזוֹנוֹת״ – רִיבָּה לָהּ מְזוֹנוֹת, אֲמַר ״בִּמְזוֹנוֹת״ – קָצַץ לָהּ מְזוֹנוֹת.

Rabbi Abbahu said: This matter **was explained to me personally by Rabbi Yoḥanan.** All depends on the husband's description of the land. If **he said** that he is giving her land **for her sustenance, he has** thereby **increased** the sources of **sustenance** available **to her.** He will continue to provide her sustenance, but if that amount is insufficient he has also set aside an area of land specifically for that purpose. However, if **he said** to her that he is designating the land **as** her **sustenance, he has** thereby **fixed** this plot of land as the only source of **sustenance** available **to her,** and she can take no more.[H]

הדרן עלך נערה

NOTES

They came before Reish Lakish – אָתוּ לְקַמֵּיהּ דְּרֵישׁ לָקִישׁ: Some explain simply that Rabbi Yoḥanan could not adjudicate their case because he was related to them. Consequently, they had to come before a different judge, whose ruling could not be challenged by Rabbi Yoḥanan (*ge'onim*).

I will remove for you…from your ears [*unaikhu*] – מַפֵּיקְנָא לְכוּ...מֵאוּנַיְיכוּ: In several places Rashi and *Tosafot* explain this expression as a threat of ostracism. Alternatively, the word *unaikhu* is related to *on* meaning power. In other words, I will make sure this Sage will not give you the power to appeal my ruling.

HALAKHA

For sustenance, as sustenance – לִמְזוֹנוֹת, בִּמְזוֹנוֹת: If a man who set aside a portion of land from which his wife can receive her sustenance after his death said: This plot of land shall be for your sustenance, he has increased her sustenance. Therefore, if the produce of the land is insufficient for her needs, she receives the remainder from the rest of his property, whereas if the produce is worth more she takes all the fruit. However, if he said: This plot of land shall be as your sustenance, and she remained silent and did not object, she is entitled to only the produce of that plot of land, in accordance with the opinion of Rabbi Yoḥanan (Rambam *Sefer Nashim*, *Hilkhot Ishut* 18:18; *Shulḥan Arukh*, *Even HaEzer* 93:16).

Summary of
Perek IV

With regard to a father's rights over his daughter, the general principle established by the Sages is that money earned by a daughter in her youth belongs to her father. Until she is a grown woman, a father receives the money of his daughter's betrothal, fines that are paid to her, and any other payment to which she is entitled. Furthermore, her earnings and any articles she finds go to him. However, he may not make use of her personal property, e.g., those items she inherited or received from others. In addition, a father has the right to betroth his minor daughter to the man of his choice, to accept her bill of divorce on her behalf, and to nullify her vows. Most of these rights are personal, and therefore the father cannot bequeath them to his sons. Consequently, his heirs can claim only those payments that were already owed before the father passed away.

These rights of a father are in effect until his daughter becomes a grown woman or marries. Once she has married she has left her father's authority entirely and does not return even if her marriage was annulled. From the perspective of *halakha* she is considered an orphan even though her father is alive.

With regard to a defamer, the verses are fulfilled in accordance with the halakhic midrash, not their literal meaning. In short, the case of the defamer is as follows: A man married a young woman, i.e., neither a minor nor a grown woman, who is not a convert, and he engaged in regular sexual intercourse with her. Subsequently, he claimed in court that she was not a virgin, and he brings witnesses that she committed adultery when she was betrothed to him. If the testimony of these witnesses is accepted, she is stoned at the door of her father's house. Even if she does not have a father, or if her father does not have a house, she is executed regardless. If the father brings witnesses who testify that the first pair were false, conspiring witnesses, the guilty witnesses themselves are stoned, in accordance with the *halakha* of false, conspiring witnesses, while the husband is flogged and must pay the father of the young woman one hundred shekels of silver. Furthermore, he must retain her as his wife and may not divorce her unless she wants to leave him.

The rights of a husband are basically similar to those of a father, as he may nullify his wife's vows, collects her earnings and the articles she finds, and shares the payments for damages that she receives. Unlike a father, a husband is also entitled to the revenue generated by his wife's property, although the wife retains ownership of the property itself. Several obligations are imposed on a husband, corresponding to these rights. By Torah law, he must provide his wife with food, clothing, and fulfill his conjugal duties. In addition, he is obligated by rabbinic law to pay her medical expenses, to redeem her from captivity, and to pay for her burial. There are also several stipulations of the marriage contract that apply after his death. His widow may continue living in his house while receiving her sustenance from his estate, her daughters are also sustained from his property until their marriage or maturity, and her sons inherit their mother's marriage contract in addition to their share of his inheritance. These last two stipulations are known as the marriage document concerning female children and the marriage document concerning male children.

In connection to the marriage document concerning female children, the Gemara discussed the obligation of a father to feed his children during his lifetime. While they are very little, up to the age of six, a father is obligated to provide them with sustenance. Beyond this age, the court will pressure him to feed them until their maturity. If he is wealthy and can afford to do so, he will even be compelled to pay for the sustenance of his children.

Introduction to **Perek V**

This chapter is a continuation of the topics discussed in the previous chapter: The *halakhot* of the marriage contract payment and the stipulations within the contract.

One issue to be determined is the value of the marriage contract payment, both the minimum amount to which the husband must commit and the question of whether this minimum amount is an absolute requirement or can be waived. There is also a discussion concerning an additional sum that the husband may wish to add to his wife's marriage contract and the manner of collecting this additional sum.

Another question that relates to the marriage contract itself is the date at which the stipulations in the marriage contract, particularly the husband's obligation to sustain the wife, take effect. There are three possible points at which this could take place: At the betrothal, at the appointed time designated for the wedding, or when the couple is actually married. In addition to the question of the husband's financial responsibility, there is a non-monetary aspect to this question as well: An Israelite woman married to a priest is entitled to eat *teruma*, and therefore there is a need to clarify when this right begins.

Among the stipulations in the marriage contract is the wife's obligation to perform various tasks for her husband's benefit. This obligation requires definition, in terms of both the nature and the quantity of these tasks. There is also the question of whether this is an absolute obligation for the wife, or whether it is possible to modify it under certain circumstances. This question also has a non-monetary aspect to it: Do the husband or the wife have the power to consecrate the wife's earnings or to prohibit them by means of a vow?

Another fundamental aspect of marriage is the obligation to engage in conjugal relations. Discussing this obligation raises a number of issues, such as the frequency of the set intervals at which the husband is obligated to engage in relations with his wife and the question of how to treat a man or a woman who refuses to fulfill this obligation to his or her spouse.

There is also a need to set a minimum amount to define the husband's obligation to provide his wife with food and clothing. This is particularly necessary during periods when the husband and wife are not together and the husband appoints a third party to provide these necessities for his wife.

The primary topics of this chapter clarify the fundamental and practical aspects of these questions.

מתני׳ אַף עַל פִּי שֶׁאָמְרוּ בְּתוּלָה גּוֹבָה מָאתַיִם וְאַלְמָנָה מָנֶה, אִם רָצָה לְהוֹסִיף, אֲפִילּוּ מֵאָה מָנֶה – יוֹסִיף. נִתְאַרְמְלָה אוֹ נִתְגָּרְשָׁה, בֵּין מִן הָאֵירוּסִין בֵּין מִן הַנִּשּׂוּאִין – גּוֹבָה אֶת הַכֹּל. רַבִּי אֶלְעָזָר בֶּן עֲזַרְיָה אוֹמֵר: מִן הַנִּשּׂוּאִין – גּוֹבָה אֶת הַכֹּל, מִן הָאֵירוּסִין, בְּתוּלָה – גּוֹבָה מָאתַיִם וְאַלְמָנָה מָנֶה, שֶׁלֹּא כָּתַב לָהּ אֶלָּא עַל מְנָת לְכוֹנְסָהּ.

MISHNA Although they said as a principle that **a virgin collects two hundred** dinars as payment for her marriage contract **and** that **a widow** collects **one hundred dinars, if** the husband **wishes to add**[H] **even** an additional **ten thousand** dinars, **he may add** it. If **she is** then **widowed or divorced, whether from betrothal** or **whether from marriage,**[B] **she collects the entire** amount, including the additional sum. **Rabbi Elazar ben Azarya says:** If she is widowed or divorced **from marriage, she collects the total** amount,[H] but if she is widowed or divorced **from betrothal, a virgin collects two hundred** dinars **and a widow one hundred** dinars. This is **because he wrote** the additional amount **for her** in the marriage contract **only in order to marry her.**

רַבִּי יְהוּדָה אוֹמֵר: אִם רָצָה – כּוֹתֵב לִבְתוּלָה שְׁטָר שֶׁל מָאתַיִם, וְהִיא כּוֹתֶבֶת ״הִתְקַבַּלְתִּי מִמְּךָ מָנֶה״, וּלְאַלְמָנָה מָנֶה, וְהִיא כּוֹתֶבֶת ״הִתְקַבַּלְתִּי מִמְּךָ חֲמִשִּׁים זוּז״. רַבִּי מֵאִיר אוֹמֵר: כׇּל הַפּוֹחֵת לִבְתוּלָה מִמָּאתַיִם וּלְאַלְמָנָה מִמָּנֶה – הֲרֵי זוֹ בְּעִילַת זְנוּת.

Rabbi Yehuda says a related *halakha* with regard to the marriage contract: **If he wishes, he may write for a virgin a document for two hundred** dinars as is fitting for her, **and she may** then **write** a receipt stating: **I received one hundred dinars from you.** Even though she has not actually received the money, the receipt serves as a means for her to waive half of the amount due to her for her marriage contract. According to Rabbi Yehuda, the financial commitment in the marriage contract is a right due to the wife, which she may waive if she chooses to do so. **And** similarly, **for a widow** he may write **one hundred dinars** in the contract **and she may write** a receipt stating: **I received from you fifty dinars.** However, **Rabbi Meir says:** It is prohibited to do this, as **anyone who reduces**[N] the amount of the marriage contract to less than **than two hundred** dinars **for a virgin or one hundred dinars for a widow,**[H] **this** marital relationship amounts to **licentious sexual relations** because it is as if he did not write any marriage contract at all.

BACKGROUND

Betrothal and marriage – אֵירוּסִין וְנִשּׂוּאִין: A Jewish wedding is divided into two distinct parts. Betrothal is the first stage of the marriage process. The bond created by betrothal requires that a woman be divorced before she may remarry another man. Starting when a woman is betrothed, sexual relations with another man are considered adulterous and are punishable by death. However, a betrothed couple may not yet live together as husband and wife, and most of the couple's mutual obligations do not yet apply.

Marriage takes effect by means of the wedding ceremony, when the bride and groom come together under the bridal canopy, symbolizing their union. This immediately confers the privileges and the responsibilities associated with marriage upon the newlywed couple. If one spouse dies after marriage, all the *halakhot* of mourning that apply for a close blood relative must also be observed by the surviving spouse. If the wife of a priest dies, he is obligated to make himself ritually impure to bury her. In addition, all the monetary rights and obligations applying to married couples take effect. Nowadays, betrothal and marriage are both performed in a single ceremony, but in talmudic times there was usually a yearlong gap between the two.

HALAKHA

If he wishes to add – אִם רָצָה לְהוֹסִיף: If the husband wishes to add to his wife's marriage contract beyond the set amount specified by the Sages, he may add as much as he wants. The Rema writes that one can derive from the language of the Gemara that there is no need to write the main sum of the marriage contract separately from the additional sum; they may be written as a single sum (Ran, based on Ramban; Rashba). However, some say that the main sum must be written according to the local custom, and consequently the additional sum should be written separately. This is the practice nowadays (Rambam *Sefer Nashim, Hilkhot Ishut* 10:7; *Shulḥan Arukh, Even HaEzer* 66:7).

From marriage, she collects the total amount – מִן הַנִּשּׂוּאִין גּוֹבָה אֶת הַכֹּל: In the case of one who betroths a woman and writes her a marriage contract, if he dies or divorces her, she receives the main sum of the marriage contract from property that is not liened to anyone else, but she does not receive the additional sum. This ruling is in accordance with the opinion of Rabbi Elazar ben Azarya and the conclusion of the Gemara; see 56a (Rambam *Sefer Nashim, Hilkhot Ishut* 10:11; *Shulḥan Arukh, Even HaEzer* 55:6).

Anyone who reduces the amount of his marriage contract to lower than two hundred dinars for a virgin or one hundred dinars for a widow – כׇּל הַפּוֹחֵת לִבְתוּלָה מִמָּאתַיִם וּלְאַלְמָנָה מִמָּנֶה: If someone writes less than the minimum amount set by the Sages in his marriage contract, the sexual relations he has with his wife are considered licentious. This applies whether he wrote a marriage contract with the proper amount and then she wrote a receipt stating that she received part of it although she did not, or whether at the time of the betrothal he included a clause that she would receive less than the required main sum, although this clause is void and she receives the complete amount. This ruling follows the opinion of Rabbi Meir (Rambam *Sefer Nashim, Hilkhot Ishut* 12:8; *Shulḥan Arukh, Even HaEzer* 66:9).

NOTES

Anyone who reduces – כׇּל הַפּוֹחֵת: Rabbi Meir holds that if the husband wrote a marriage contract for less than the minimum amount, this stipulation is entirely void and he is obligated to pay her the full amount, as if he had said nothing. However, the specific formulation of Rabbi Meir's statement emphasizes that despite this fact, intercourse between the couple after the stipulation has been made is tantamount to licentious sexual relations. This is because the woman does not rely on the fact that the stipulation is invalid, but actually believes that the value of her marriage contract is less than the required amount. Consequently, the husband must write her a new marriage contract before they can resume marital relations (Meiri).

גמ׳ פְּשִׁיטָא! מַהוּ דְּתֵימָא: קִיצוּתָא עָבְדוּ רַבָּנַן, שֶׁלֹּא לְבַיֵּישׁ אֶת מִי שֶׁאֵין לוֹ – קָא מַשְׁמַע לַן.

GEMARA The mishna states that if he wishes to add to the obligation in the marriage contract, he may do so. The Gemara asks: **Isn't it obvious** that if he wishes to add he may do so? The Gemara explains: **Lest you say** that **the Sages instituted a fixed** ceiling on the amount one may designate in the marriage contract, in order **not to embarrass one who does not have** sufficient funds, the mishna therefore **teaches us** that the Sages were not specific about this. If he wishes to add to the amount, he may do so.

״אִם רָצָה לְהוֹסִיף״ כו׳. ״רָצָה לִכְתּוֹב לָהּ״ – לָא קָתָנֵי, אֶלָּא ״רָצָה לְהוֹסִיף״. מְסַיַּיע לֵיהּ לְרַבִּי אַיְבוּ אָמַר רַבִּי יַנַּאי. דְּאָמַר רַבִּי אַיְבוּ אָמַר רַבִּי יַנַּאי: תְּנַאי כְּתוּבָּה כִּכְתוּבָּה דָּמֵי.

§ The mishna states that **if he wishes to add** even ten thousand dinars to the marriage contract, he may do so. The Gemara comments: **It does not teach: He wishes to write for her, rather: He wishes to add.** This language indicates that the additional sum he wrote is added to the marriage contract itself, as opposed to being an independent obligation. **This supports** the opinion of **Rabbi Aivu,** who said what **Rabbi Yannai said, as Rabbi Aivu said** that **Rabbi Yannai said: The stipulation in the marriage contract** as well as additional amounts he chooses to add to the contract **are comparable to the marriage contract** itself.[H]

נַפְקָא מִינַּהּ לְמוֹכֶרֶת, וּלְמוֹחֶלֶת, לְמוֹרֶדֶת,

This principle produces **a practical difference** with regard to many issues. It is relevant **to one who sells** her marriage contract, indicating that such a sale includes the additional sum of the marriage contract; **and to one who waives**[H] her marriage contract to her husband or his heirs, teaching that the additional sum is included in this relinquishing of rights to payment of the contract; and **to a rebellious** woman,[H] from whom the court deducts a specific amount from her marriage contract each week until there is nothing left. These deductions come from the additional sum as well.

וּלְפוֹגֶמֶת, לְתוֹבַעַת, וּלְעוֹבֶרֶת עַל דָּת,

And this principle also results in a practical difference **to one who vitiates**[H] her marriage contract, as one who states that she received part of the payment for her marriage contract does not receive the remainder without taking an oath, and the additional sum is included in this *halakha*; **to one who demands**[H] payment for her marriage contract, as the Sages ruled that from the time she begins to demand the payment she waives her right to further sustenance, and this applies with regard to one who demands the additional sum as well; **and to one who violates the precepts**[H] of *halakha* or of Jewish custom, who may be divorced without receiving payment for her marriage contract, including the additional sum.

HALAKHA

The stipulation in the marriage contract as well as additional amounts are comparable to the marriage contract itself – תְּנַאי כְּתוּבָּה כִּכְתוּבָּה דָּמֵי: In most aspects, the main and additional sums of the marriage contract follow the same principles. However, there is a distinction between the two with regard to some details (Rambam *Sefer Nashim, Hilkhot Ishut* 10:7, 18:28; *Shulḥan Arukh, Even HaEzer* 66:7).

One who sells and one who waives – מוֹכֶרֶת וּמוֹחֶלֶת: One who sells or relinquishes her marriage contract without any specifications also sells or relinquishes the additional sum (Rambam *Sefer Nashim, Hilkhot Ishut* 18:28; *Shulḥan Arukh, Even HaEzer* 93:10).

A rebellious woman – מוֹרֶדֶת: The rebellious woman who loses her marriage contract loses both the main and additional sums (Rambam *Sefer Nashim, Hilkhot Ishut* 14:8–9; *Shulḥan Arukh, Even HaEzer* 77:2).

One who vitiates – פּוֹגֶמֶת: A woman who states that she received a portion of the payment for her marriage contract must take an oath in order to receive the remainder, whether her admission was in regard to the main or additional sums (Rambam *Sefer Nashim, Hilkhot Ishut* 16:14; *Shulḥan Arukh, Even HaEzer* 96:7).

One who demands – תּוֹבַעַת: A widow who demands payment for her marriage contract in court without specifying which sum she wants loses her right to sustenance. *Tosafot* conclude that if she demands only the main sum or only the additional sum of the marriage contract, and all the more so if she demands only the dowry, she does not lose her right to sustenance (Rambam *Sefer Nashim, Hilkhot Ishut* 18:1; *Shulḥan Arukh, Even HaEzer* 93:11–12).

One who violates the precepts – עוֹבֶרֶת עַל דָּת: One who violates the precepts of *halakha* or Jewish custom does not receive the main or the additional sums of her marriage contract (Rambam *Sefer Nashim, Hilkhot Ishut* 24:16; *Shulḥan Arukh, Even HaEzer* 115:5).

לָשֶׁבַח, לִשְׁבוּעָה, וְלַשְּׁבִיעִית,

It is also relevant **to an increase in value,**[H] as she does not collect the main or additional sums from the increased value of the property in a case where the husband's estate was not sufficient at the time of his death to pay the entire cost of her marriage contract but the heirs later increased the value of the property; **to an oath,**[H] because if the wife is required to take an oath in order to receive her marriage contract, the additional sum is also included in that oath; **and to the Sabbatical Year,**[BH] as the marriage contract is not annulled with other debts in the Sabbatical Year, and this includes the additional sum as well.

וְלַכּוֹתֵב כׇּל נְכָסָיו לְבָנָיו, לִגְבּוֹת מִן הַקַּרְקַע, וּמִן הַזִּיבּוּרִית, וְכׇל זְמַן שֶׁהִיא בְּבֵית אָבִיהָ, וְלִכְתוּבַּת בְּנִין דִּכְרִין.

And with regard **to one who writes** a document transferring **all of his property to his sons**[H] and leaves his wife a specific plot of land for her marriage contract, this teaches that she receives both the main and the additional sums of her contract only from that land. The aforementioned *halakha* also teaches that she **collects** the payment only **from land,**[H] **and** specifically **from land of inferior quality;**[BH] **and** that a widow loses her ability to collect the main and additional sums **as long as she is in her father's home**[HN] for more than twenty-five years after her husband's death; **and** the principle also applies **to** the stipulation in the **marriage contract** that the **male offspring** inherit their mother's dowry[H] when her husband passes away in addition to the inheritance they receive together with their other brothers. These *halakhot* apply equally to the additional sum of the marriage contract.

BACKGROUND

Sabbatical Year – שְׁבִיעִית: This is the last year of the seven-year Sabbatical cycle. The first such cycle began after the conquest of Canaan by Joshua. The Sabbatical Year is also known as *Shemitta*, which literally means abandonment or release. The *halakhot* of the Sabbatical Year are based on Torah law (see Leviticus 25:1–7 and Deuteronomy 15:1–6), but most authorities maintain that the conditions for the applicability of the Torah mitzva are currently not in effect, and consequently its present-day observance is based on rabbinic decree.

The particular regulations that apply to this year fall into two main categories of *halakhot*: Those pertaining to the imperative that all agricultural land lie fallow, and those pertaining to the cancellation of debts due to loans, as on the last day of the Sabbatical Year all outstanding debts that Jews owe to each other as a result of loans are canceled. This *halakha* does not apply to debts whose payment is not yet due on this day, nor does it apply when collection proceedings have already been initiated in court.

Land of inferior quality – זִיבּוּרִית: When one pays a debt with land rather than with money, differences among gradations of land quality must be taken into consideration. Although the monetary value of the land one receives will be equal whether the debt is paid with a larger portion of inferior-quality land, a smaller quantity of better-quality land, there is nevertheless an established principle that people prefer to receive smaller quantities of high-quality land, as this requires less maintenance. The Torah says explicitly that injured parties receive their damages from highest quality land: "Of the best of his own field, and of the best of his own vineyard, shall he make restitution" (Exodus 22:4). In principle, creditors receive their payment from inferior quality land, but the Sages decreed that a creditor collects from medium-quality land, so as to maintain the incentive to lend money.

HALAKHA

To an increase in value – לָשֶׁבַח: The wife does not receive payment for the main sum or the additional sum of her marriage contract from the increase in value of her husband's property after his death. There are, however, different opinions with regard to a situation where she is the one who caused the property to increase in value (Rambam *Sefer Nashim, Hilkhot Ishut* 16:5; *Shulḥan Arukh, Even HaEzer* 95:7, 100:2).

To an oath – לִשְׁבוּעָה: The woman does not collect the main or additional sums of her marriage contract until after she has sworn to the heirs that her husband did not leave her any other property and that she did not sell or relinquish the contract (Rambam *Sefer Nashim, Hilkhot Ishut* 16:4; *Shulḥan Arukh, Even HaEzer* 96:1).

And to the Sabbatical Year – וְלַשְּׁבִיעִית: A widow in possession of her marriage contract is always entitled to collect payment. The obligation of the husband's heirs to pay is not canceled by the Sabbatical Year, unless she already received a portion of it or solicited payment and converted it into a straightforward loan (Rambam *Sefer Zera'im, Hilkhot Shemitta VeYovel* 9:13; *Shulḥan Arukh, Even HaEzer* 101:1).

To one who writes a document transferring all of his property to his sons – לַכּוֹתֵב כׇּל נְכָסָיו לְבָנָיו: In the case of one who wrote a document transferring all of his property to his sons or daughters, and set aside a specific plot of land to give his wife as payment for her marriage contract, if she was aware of this and did not challenge it, she collects her payment from that piece of land and loses her rights to the remainder of her marriage contract, both the main and additional sums (Rambam *Sefer Kinyan, Hilkhot Zekhiya UMattana* 6:9; *Shulḥan Arukh, Even HaEzer* 106:1).

Collects the payment only from land – לִגְבּוֹת מִן הַקַּרְקַע: Originally, the main and additional sums of the marriage contract were paid only in land. However, the *ge'onim* ordained that a woman can take her marriage contract from movable property as well, and this ordinance spread throughout the Jewish people (Rambam *Sefer Nashim, Hilkhot Ishut* 16:7–10; *Shulḥan Arukh, Even HaEzer* 100:1).

From land of inferior quality – מִן הַזִּיבּוּרִית: Originally, the main and additional sums of the marriage contract were taken from land of the lowest quality in the husband's possession. However, nowadays the accepted custom is to write in the marriage contract: The best and choicest property. The wife thereby collects her marriage contract from the land of the highest quality (Rambam *Sefer Nashim, Hilkhot Ishut* 16:3; *Shulḥan Arukh, Even HaEzer* 100:2; see *Tur, Ḥoshen Mishpat* 108).

As long as she is in her father's home – כׇּל זְמַן שֶׁהִיא בְּבֵית אָבִיהָ: In a case where a widow is not in possession of her marriage document and is living in her father's home, if she does not demand payment within twenty-five years, she cannot collect anything later, as she has presumably relinquished her claim to the marriage contract. This applies equally to the main and additional sums of the marriage contract, as discussed in the Gemara (Rambam *Sefer Nashim, Hilkhot Ishut* 16:23, and *Maggid Mishne* and *Kesef Mishne* there; *Shulḥan Arukh, Even HaEzer* 101:1).

To the stipulation in the marriage contract that the male offspring inherit their mother's dowry – לִכְתוּבַּת בְּנִין דִּכְרִין: One of the conditions of the marriage contract is that if the wife dies before the husband, then when the husband dies, their male children inherit her dowry and the property set aside for their mother's marriage contract, in addition to their portions of the remainder of their father's estate, divided together with their brothers from other wives. The *Shulḥan Arukh* writes that there are some who include the additional sum of the marriage contract in this. The *Beit Shmuel*, *Ḥelkat Meḥokek*, and the Vilna Gaon all express bewilderment at the wording of the *Shulḥan Arukh*, as it implies that there are some who disagree with this ruling. In fact, even the Rambam, who did not explicitly mention the additional sum in this context, seems to agree with this ruling, in accordance with the Gemara here (Rambam *Sefer Nashim, Hilkhot Ishut* 19:1; *Shulḥan Arukh, Even HaEzer* 111:1).

NOTES

And as long as she is in her father's home – וְכׇל זְמַן שֶׁהִיא בְּבֵית אָבִיהָ: This phrase hints to the distinction between a widow who remains in her late husband's home and one who returns to her father's home. This distinction is the subject of a debate among the *tanna'im* (see 104a). According to Rabbi Meir, if she returns to her father's home she can collect payment of the marriage contract whenever she wishes, but if she remains in her husband's home she can collect it for up to only twenty-five years. According to the Rabbis, it is reversed: In her father's home, she can collect for up to twenty-five years and in her husband's home she can collect forever.

Most of the commentaries explain the statement here in accordance with the opinion of the Rabbis: If she returns to her father's home, just as she loses the ability to collect the main sum of the marriage contract after twenty-five years, she also loses the additional sum. However, some explain the statement according to the opinion of Rabbi Meir, meaning that as long as she is in her father's home she can collect her marriage contract, and that this includes the additional sum (Rivan; see *Shita Mekubbetzet*).

אִיתְּמַר כְּתוּבַּת בְּנִין דִּכְרִין, פּוּמְבְּדִיתָא אָמְרִי: לָא טָרְפָא מִמְּשַׁעְבְּדֵי, "יָרְתוּן" תְּנַן,

§ **It was stated** that there was a debate among the Sages with regard to the stipulation in the **marriage contract** that the **male offspring** inherit the sum stipulated in their mother's marriage contract. The Sages of **Pumbedita**[P] **say: It is not seized from liened** property that has been sold[H] by the father. This is because **we learned** in a mishna (52b) that the text of the stipulation is: **They will inherit** the money set aside for their mother's marriage contract. From this phrase it is clear that the stipulation follows the *halakhot* of inheritance, and therefore their inheritance can be taken only from property in the father's possession at the time of his death, but not from property that he had sold.

בְּנֵי מָתָא מְחַסְיָא אָמְרִי: טָרְפָא מִמְּשַׁעְבְּדֵי, "יִסְבוּן" תְּנַן. וְהִלְכְתָא: לָא טָרְפָא מִמְּשַׁעְבְּדֵי, "יָרְתוּן" תְּנַן.

The residents of Mata Meḥasya say: It is seized from liened property that has been sold. Their tradition is that **the mishna states** that the text of the stipulation is: **They will take** the money set aside for their mother's marriage contract. It is as if the husband transferred this property to the sons, and as their acquisition precedes those of the other buyers, they may seize the sold property from the buyers. The Gemara concludes that **the *halakha* is that it is not seized from liened** property that has been sold, as **the mishna states: They will inherit.**

מִטַּלְטְלֵי וְאִיתְנְהוּ בְּעֵינַיְיהוּ – בְּלָא שְׁבוּעָה.

There is another dispute between the Sages of Pumbedita and the residents of Mata Meḥasya, with regard to one who set aside payment for his wife's marriage contract from **movable property, and** these objects **are in their pure,** unadulterated state at the time of the execution of the marriage contract after the husband's death. In this case, all agree that the widow may take them **without an oath** that confirms that her husband did not leave her any other money for the payment of her marriage contract, as it is clear that he set aside these objects for that purpose.

לֵיתְנְהוּ בְּעֵינַיְיהוּ, פּוּמְבְּדִיתָא אָמְרִי: בְּלָא שְׁבוּעָה, בְּנֵי מָתָא מְחַסְיָא אָמְרִי: בִּשְׁבוּעָה. וְהִלְכְתָא: בְּלָא שְׁבוּעָה.

However, if the movable objects **are not in their pure,** unadulterated state,[N] e.g., they were lost, the Sages of **Pumbedita say** that she takes the payment for her marriage contract from other property, as all of the husband's property is liened to the marriage contract **without an oath. The residents of Mata Meḥasya say** she takes her payment only **with an oath,** because of a concern that she may have already received other property as payment for her marriage contract. **And the *halakha*** is that she may take it **without an oath,** in accordance with the opinion of the Sages of Pumbedita.

יִיחֵד לָהּ אַרְעָא, בְּאַרְבָּעָה מִצְרָנָהָא – בְּלָא שְׁבוּעָה. בְּחַד מִצְרָא, פּוּמְבְּדִיתָא אָמְרִי: בְּלָא שְׁבוּעָה, בְּנֵי מָתָא מְחַסְיָא אָמְרִי: בִּשְׁבוּעָה. וְהִלְכְתָא: בְּלָא שְׁבוּעָה.

If **he set aside land for her,**[H] which he demarcated **on all four of its borders,** she seizes the land **without an oath.** If he demarcated it **on** only **one border,**[N] which is not as clear an indication, the Sages of **Pumbedita say** she takes it **without an oath,** and **the residents of Mata Meḥasya say** she takes it **with an oath. And the *halakha*** is that she takes it **without an oath.**

PERSONALITIES

The Sages of Pumbedita – פּוּמְבְּדִיתָא: In tractate *Sanhedrin* (17b), a number of Sages from Pumbedita are identified by name in order to distinguish between the judges of Pumbedita, the sharp-witted scholars of Pumbedita, and the Elders of Pumbedita. The passage here does not clarify to which group it is referring. It appears that this dispute dates to a later period, as Mata Meḥasya did not become an important center of Torah study until the generation of Rav Ashi, near the end of the period of the *amora'im*. From this period onward, there were in fact two great academies: The academy of Pumbedita and the academy of Sura, which is identified with Mata Meḥasya. These academies differed on many matters.

HALAKHA

It is not seized from liened property that has been sold – לָא טָרְפָא מִמְּשַׁעְבְּדֵי: Sons who inherit the property set aside for their mother's marriage contract, based on the stipulation in the marriage contract concerning male children (see previous note), may not collect from liened property, but only from unclaimed property, as with any other inheritance (Rambam *Sefer Nashim*, *Hilkhot Ishut* 19:9; *Shulḥan Arukh*, *Even HaEzer* 111:13).

If he set aside land for her – יִיחֵד לָהּ אַרְעָא: If one set aside land for his wife from which she will collect her marriage contract, whether he marked the land off on all of its borders or only on one side, she may take the land without an oath, in accordance with the opinion of the Sages of Pumbedita (Rambam *Sefer Nashim*, *Hilkhot Ishut* 19:9; *Shulḥan Arukh*, *Even HaEzer* 111:13).

NOTES

Are not in their pure unadulterated state – לֵיתְנְהוּ בְּעֵינַיְיהוּ: Rashi and some other commentaries explain this literally. Even if the objects set aside for her marriage contract are lost forever, she nevertheless collects the payment from other property without an oath. Rashi explains that the reason for a potential oath is due to concern that during the husband's lifetime, he may have given his wife payment for her marriage contract. In the case where the husband gave her objects for her marriage contract while he was alive, if those objects are still available in their original, unadulterated state, there is obviously no concern that he had given her something else as well. However, if those objects were lost, the Sages debated whether there is a concern that he may have reimbursed her with other property, in which case she may be required to take an oath. The conclusion is that one may assume he would not set aside other objects for her, and therefore she may take the payment for her marriage contract without an oath.

However, many of the early authorities explain the statement differently, in accordance with the opinion of Rav Hai Gaon and other *ge'onim*, that this is a case in which the first set of objects are not available, but there are other objects that are known to have been given in place of the original ones. In this case, there is no reason to suspect that he set aside something else for her. Some note that the language of the Gemara supports this explanation, as it does not simply say: They do not exist, but rather: They are not in their pure, unadulterated state, which suggests that there are other objects meant to replace the original ones (Rid). The Ra'avad and the Meiri also discuss whether this applies to an ordinary creditor as well.

On only one border – בְּחַד מִצְרָא: If one demarcates the field on all sides, it is clear that he set the field aside for his wife's marriage contract. However, if he demarcated only one side of the field, it is possible that he meant to leave her only the small strip of land immediately next to the border (Rivan).

אֲמַר לְעֵדִים ״כִּתְבוּ וְחִתְמוּ וַהֲבוּ לֵיהּ״, קָנוּ מִינֵּיהּ – לָא צָרִיךְ אִימְּלוֹכֵי בֵּיהּ, לָא קָנוּ מִינֵּיהּ, פּוּמְבְּדִיתָא אָמְרִי: לָא צָרִיךְ אִימְּלוֹכֵי בֵּיהּ, בְּנֵי מָתָא מְחַסְיָא אָמְרִי: צָרִיךְ אִימְּלוֹכֵי בֵּיהּ. וְהִלְכְתָא: צָרִיךְ אִימְּלוֹכֵי בֵּיהּ.

Furthermore, they had a dispute in a case where someone **told witnesses: Write and sign** a deed of gift **and give it to** the intended recipient[H] of the gift. In such a case, if the witnesses **acquired it from him** on behalf of the recipient by performing a formal act of acquisition, **they do not need to consult with him** again, as there can be no retraction after a formal acquisition. But if **they did not acquire it from him,** the Sages of **Pumbedita say they do not need to consult with him** again, and **the residents of Mata Meḥasya say they must consult with him. And the *halakha* is that they must consult with him** again.

״רַבִּי אֶלְעָזָר בֶּן עֲזַרְיָה״ וכו׳. אִיתְּמַר, רַב וְרַבִּי נָתָן. חַד אֲמַר: הֲלָכָה כְּרַבִּי אֶלְעָזָר בֶּן עֲזַרְיָה, וְחַד אֲמַר: אֵין הֲלָכָה כְּרַבִּי אֶלְעָזָר בֶּן עֲזַרְיָה.

§ The mishna states that **Rabbi Elazar ben Azarya** says that a woman who collects the payment for her marriage contract after marriage receives the main and additional sums, while one who collects it after betrothal receives only the main sum. **It was stated: Rav and Rabbi Natan** differed with regard to this issue. **One said** the ***halakha* is in accordance with** the opinion of **Rabbi Elazar ben Azarya. And one said** the ***halakha* is not in accordance with** the opinion of **Rabbi Elazar ben Azarya.**

תִּסְתַּיֵּים דְּרַבִּי נָתָן הוּא דְּאָמַר הֲלָכָה כְּרַבִּי אֶלְעָזָר בֶּן עֲזַרְיָה, דִּשְׁמָעִינַן לֵיהּ לְרַבִּי נָתָן דְּאָזֵיל בָּתַר אוּמְדָּנָא. דְּאָמַר רַבִּי נָתָן: הֲלָכָה כְּרַבִּי שִׁמְעוֹן שְׁזוּרִי בִּמְסוּכָּן,

It may be concluded that Rabbi Natan is the one who said that the ***halakha* is in accordance with** the opinion of **Rabbi Elazar ben Azarya, as we have heard that Rabbi Natan follows** the principle of **assessing** intention. Even if one did not make an explicit statement, the court assesses what his intention must have been and decides the *halakha* based on that assessment. It is clear that he follows this principle, **as Rabbi Natan said** that the ***halakha* is in accordance with** the opinion of **Rabbi Shimon Shezuri in** the case of an ill person **in danger.**[H] If this person says: Write a bill of divorce for my wife, that is understood as: Write it and give it to her, as his intention is to absolve her from the requirement of levirate marriage by means of the bill of divorce. Although he did not explicitly state this, Rabbi Natan holds that in such a situation the court assesses that this was the husband's intent and follows it.

HALAKHA

Someone told witnesses: Write and sign a deed of gift and give it to the intended recipient – אֲמַר לְעֵדִים כִּתְבוּ וְחִתְמוּ וַהֲבוּ לֵיהּ: If one lends money in the presence of witnesses and performs an act that formalizes the transaction, known as an act of acquisition, the witnesses should record the transaction in a document and give it to the lender, as acquisitions are generally performed in order to be written down. However, if one did not perform an act of acquisition, the witnesses should not write anything unless the borrower requests that they write a document and give it to the lender.

If the borrower requested that the witnesses write it down and deliver the document to the lender, they must return and consult with the borrower before actually giving the document to the lender (Rambam). However, other authorities dispute this ruling and say that it is not necessary to consult with him again. The *Shakh* states that the opinion of most authorities (Rashi; Ra'avad; *Sefer HaIttur*; Ran; *Mishne LaMelekh*) is that the requirement to consult applies only when giving a gift of land or something similar (Rambam *Sefer Mishpatim*, *Hilkhot Malve VeLoveh* 11:1; *Shulḥan Arukh*, *Ḥoshen Mishpat* 39:2–3).

Person in danger – בִּמְסוּכָּן: Usually, if one says: Write a bill of divorce for my wife, the bill of divorce is not delivered to the wife until he explicitly says to do so. However, the *halakha* is different if the husband is departing to travel with a convoy or to sail at sea, or if he is being taken prisoner and led out in chains, or if he has suddenly became severely ill. In all of these cases, if he merely says: Write a bill of divorce for my wife, the bill of divorce is written and delivered to his wife immediately, in accordance with the opinion of Rabbi Shimon Shezuri (Rambam *Sefer Nashim*, *Hilkhot Geirushin* 2:12; *Shulḥan Arukh*, *Even HaEzer* 141:16).

Perek **V**
Daf **55** Amud **b**

וּבִתְרוּמַת מַעֲשֵׂר שֶׁל דְּמַאי.

And the *halakha* is also in accordance with his opinion **with regard to the *teruma* of the tithe**[B] **from doubtfully tithed produce [*demai*].**[H] Produce purchased from a common, uneducated person [*am ha'aretz*] is considered *demai* and by rabbinic law it is regarded as uncertain whether the seller separated tithes and *teruma* of the tithe from it. Rabbi Natan rules in accordance with Rabbi Shimon Shezuri's opinion in a case where, after one bought *demai* and separated *teruma* of the tithe, this *teruma* becomes mingled with the produce from which it was separated. If all of the produce were treated as actual *teruma*, the only solution would be to sell all of the produce to a priest at low cost, as he is the only one who may use it. Rabbi Shimon Shezuri, however, rules that in the case of *demai*, the owner may ask the fruit seller if he properly separated the tithes. If the seller responds that he did, the owner may rely on that, despite the fact that the seller is an *am ha'aretz*, as the Sages do not apply their decree in a case where it would cause significant financial loss.

BACKGROUND

The *teruma* of the tithe – תְּרוּמַת מַעֲשֵׂר: The Levites are commanded to separate one-tenth of the tithe given to them and transfer it to the priests. The Torah calls this "a tithe from the tithe," and the Sages refer to it as the *teruma* of the tithe (see Numbers 18:26–32). All the *halakhot* that apply to *teruma* also apply to *teruma* of the tithe. Even nowadays, *teruma* of the tithe must be separated from produce grown by a Jew in Eretz Yisrael. However, since all Jews today are in a perpetual state of ritual impurity, it cannot be used.

HALAKHA

And with regard to the *teruma* of the tithe from doubtfully tithed produce – וּבִתְרוּמַת מַעֲשֵׂר שֶׁל דְּמַאי: There are differing opinions as to the interpretation of this *halakha*. The Rambam says that it concerns one who is not generally afforded credibility with regard to tithes. In this case, he was seen to separate the *teruma* of the tithe from doubtfully tithed produce and that *teruma* became mixed with other produce. If he says that he subsequently corrected the problem, he is deemed credible, as an *am ha'aretz* is generally cautious with a mixture of *teruma*.

The Ra'avad explains that in a case where the *teruma* fell into the ordinary produce, even if the *teruma* constitutes less than one percent of the mixture, if an *am ha'aretz* reports that he had already separated tithes from the produce and in fact did not need to separate the *teruma* of the tithe, he is deemed credible, as he is presumed to be cautious with a mixture of *teruma* (Rambam *Sefer Zera'im*, *Hilkhot Ma'asrot* 12:4, and *Kesef Mishne* there; see Radbaz).

וְרַב לָא אָזֵיל בָּתַר אוּמְדְּנָא? וְהָא אִיתְּמַר, מַתְּנַת שְׁכִיב מְרַע שֶׁכָּתוּב בָּהּ קִנְיָן, בְּבֵי רַב מִשְּׁמֵיהּ דְּרַב אָמְרִי: אַרְכְּבֵיהּ אַתְּרֵי רִכְשֵׁי, וּשְׁמוּאֵל אֲמַר: לָא יָדַעְנָא מַאי אֵידוּן בָּהּ,

Having established that Rabbi Natan follows the principle of assessment, the Gemara asks: **And does Rav not follow** this principle of **assessing** intention? **But it was stated** that Rav and Shmuel disagreed about a specific case with regard to the **gift** of a person **on his deathbed,**[N] **in which** it was also **written** that the gift was given with an act of **acquisition.**[H] There is a rabbinic ordinance that one on his deathbed can effect the transfer of property without the ordinarily required act of acquisition, but in this case such an act was performed anyway. **In the school of Rav, they say in the name of Rav: He had him ride on two horses,**[N] meaning that he gave him a gift with a document strengthened in two different ways. **And Shmuel said: I do not know what to decide about it.**

בְּבֵי רַב מִשְּׁמֵיהּ דְּרַב אָמְרִי: אַרְכְּבֵיהּ אַתְּרֵי רִכְשֵׁי, הֲרֵי הִיא כְּמַתְּנַת בָּרִיא, וַהֲרֵי הִיא כְּמַתְּנַת שְׁכִיב מְרַע.

The Gemara explains the two opinions: **In the school of Rav, they say in the name of Rav: He had him ride on two horses,** meaning that he performed the transfer in a manner that took advantage of two separate *halakhot* to strengthen its validity. In one aspect, **it is similar to** the **gift of a healthy** person, **and** in a different way **it is similar to** the **gift** of a person **on his deathbed.** Both of these aspects act to strengthen the transfer.

הֲרֵי הִיא כְּמַתְּנַת בָּרִיא – דְּאִם עָמַד אֵינוֹ יָכוֹל לַחֲזוֹר בּוֹ, הֲרֵי הִיא כְּמַתְּנַת שְׁכִיב מְרַע – שֶׁאִם אָמַר ״הִלְוָאָתִי לִפְלוֹנִי״ – הַלְוָאָתוֹ לִפְלוֹנִי.

On the one hand, **it is similar to** the **gift of a healthy** person in **that if he arose** from the bed and recovered **he cannot retract it,** since he performed a proper act of acquisition. On the other hand, **it is like** the **gift** of a person **on his deathbed** in **that if he said: My loan,** i.e., money owed to me, is transferred **to so-and-so**[N] as a gift, **his loan** is in fact transferred **to so-and-so.** Although ordinarily ownership of a debt cannot be transferred without a formal transference of the promissory note, the verbal statement is sufficient to effect the transfer since this is a gift of a person on his deathbed.

וּשְׁמוּאֵל אֲמַר: לָא יָדַעְנָא מַאי אֵידוּן בָּהּ – שֶׁמָּא לֹא גָּמַר לְהַקְנוֹתוֹ אֶלָּא בִּשְׁטָר, וְאֵין שְׁטָר לְאַחַר מִיתָה.

And Shmuel said: I do not know what to decide about it. Perhaps his performance of an act of acquisition indicates that **he resolved to transfer it** to him **only with a bill** of sale. **And** since his intention is that the sale not take effect until he also gives a bill of sale, the transfer does not take effect, as a **bill** of sale is not effective **after the death** of the owner.

HALAKHA

The gift of a person on his deathbed in which it was also written that the gift was given with an act of acquisition – מַתְּנַת שְׁכִיב מְרַע שֶׁכָּתוּב בָּהּ קִנְיָן: If one on his deathbed gives a gift and an act of acquisition is also written in the document, whether the gift involves a portion of his property or all of it, there is a concern that the owner may have meant to give this gift through a document using the ordinary procedures. The gift is therefore annulled, because a deed of transfer of property is not written after the death of the owner. This ruling is in accordance with the opinion of Shmuel, whose opinion is authoritative in monetary matters. However, if the owner explicitly stated that the act of acquisition was performed only in order to give additional force to the transfer, or if this was apparent from his language, the gift is not annulled (Rambam *Sefer Kinyan, Hilkhot Zekhiya UMattana* 8:10; *Shulḥan Arukh, Ḥoshen Mishpat* 250:17–19).

NOTES

The gift of a person on his deathbed – מַתְּנַת שְׁכִיב מְרַע: The Sages established special enactments with regard to gifts given by one on his deathbed. One unique aspect of these gifts is that the Sages exempted them from acts of acquisition, which are ordinarily required. This is because certain items cannot be transferred immediately, and the inability to do so may distress the ill person and cause his condition to worsen. The Sages also established that these special provisions apply only in situations where the ill person gave away all of his property. In that case, all of the gifts are annulled if he becomes healed, as it is apparent that he made these transfers only because he believed he was about to die.

Horses [*rikhshei*] – רִכְשֵׁי: The Hebrew word *rekhesh* appears in the Bible (I Kings 5:8) and seems to indicate an animal used for riding, such as a horse or mule.

If he said: My loan is transferred to so-and-so – אִם אָמַר הִלְוָאָתִי לִפְלוֹנִי: According to Rashi, the novel element in this statement is that he is able to transfer the ownership of money. Money generally cannot be acquired with an exchange transaction, and therefore the act of acquisition is irrelevant with regard to the loan. But in this case, since it is a gift of one on his deathbed, the transaction is effective. However, *Tosafot* and some other early commentaries challenge this explanation. They suggest instead that the novel element is the ability to transfer a loan. Since a loan is not something concrete, under normal circumstances, it cannot be transferred to another using ordinary acts of acquisition.

According to Rabbeinu Ḥananel, this passage is referring to the transference of a promissory note. Although the typical method of transferring a debt is by writing a new document and giving it to the purchaser, in the case of a gift of one on his deathbed, the original document itself can be transferred.

אֶלָּא, תַּרְוַיְיהוּ אָזְלֵי בָּתַר אוּמְדָּנָא.

In any case, it has been established that Rav also follows the principle of assessing one's intention, which calls into question the conclusion that Rabbi Natan is the one who said that the *halakha* is in accordance with the opinion of Rabbi Elazar ben Azarya. **Rather,** the Gemara concludes: **Both** Rav and Rabbi Natan **follow** the principle of **assessing** intention,[H] and the debate can be explained in a different way.

מַאן דְּאָמַר הֲלָכָה – שַׁפִּיר, מַאן דְּאָמַר אֵין הֲלָכָה – הָכָא נַמִי אוּמְדַּן דַּעְתָּא הוּא: מִשּׁוּם אִיקְרוּבֵי דַּעְתָּא הוּא, וְהָא אִיקַּרְבָא לֵיהּ דַּעְתָּא.

According to **the one who says** the ***halakha*** is in accordance with the opinion of Rabbi Elazar ben Azarya, this works out **well.** According to **the one who says** the ***halakha* is not** in accordance with the opinion of Rabbi Elazar ben Azarya, **here too, this is an assessment** of his **intention.** Why did he give her the additional sum of the marriage contract? **It was due to a sense of intimacy** between them, as they were betrothed and were planning to get married. Since **he did** demonstrate **a sense of intimacy** with her, the assessment is that he intended to give her the additional sum.

יְתֵיב רַב חֲנִינָא קַמֵּיהּ דְּרַבִּי יַנַּאי, וְקָאָמַר: הֲלָכָה כְּרַבִּי אֶלְעָזָר בֶּן עֲזַרְיָה. אֲמַר לֵיהּ: פּוּק קְרִי קְרָאָךְ לְבָרָא! אֵין הֲלָכָה כְּרַבִּי אֶלְעָזָר בֶּן עֲזַרְיָה.

Rav Ḥanina,[P] who was known for teaching biblical verses, **sat before Rabbi Yannai and said:** The ***halakha* is in accordance with** the opinion of **Rabbi Elazar ben Azarya.** Rabbi Yannai **said to him: Go out** and **read your verses outside.** Your area of expertise is biblical verses, not *halakha*. What you said is incorrect and should not be said in the study hall, as the ***halakha*** is actually **not in accordance with** the opinion of **Rabbi Elazar ben Azarya.**

אָמַר רַב יִצְחָק בַּר אַבְדִּימִי מִשּׁוּם רַבֵּינוּ: הֲלָכָה כְּרַבִּי אֶלְעָזָר בֶּן עֲזַרְיָה. אָמַר רַב נַחְמָן אָמַר שְׁמוּאֵל: הֲלָכָה כְּרַבִּי אֶלְעָזָר בֶּן עֲזַרְיָה.

Rav Yitzḥak bar Avdimi said in the name of our teacher, Rabbi Yehuda HaNasi: The ***halakha* is in accordance with** the opinion of **Rabbi Elazar ben Azarya. Rav Naḥman said** that **Shmuel said:** The ***halakha* is in accordance with** the opinion of **Rabbi Elazar ben Azarya.**

וְרַב נַחְמָן דִּידֵיהּ אָמַר: אֵין הֲלָכָה כְּרַבִּי אֶלְעָזָר בֶּן עֲזַרְיָה. וּנְהַרְדָּעֵי מִשְּׁמֵיהּ דְּרַב נַחְמָן אָמְרִי: הֲלָכָה כְּרַבִּי אֶלְעָזָר בֶּן עֲזַרְיָה. וְאַף עַל גַּב דְּלָט רַב נַחְמָן, וַאֲמַר: כׇּל דַּיָּינָא דְּדָאֵין כְּרַבִּי אֶלְעָזָר בֶּן עֲזַרְיָה – הָכִי וְהָכִי תֶּיהֱוֵי, אֲפִילּוּ הָכִי הֲלָכָה כְּרַבִּי אֶלְעָזָר בֶּן עֲזַרְיָה. וַהֲלָכָה לְמַעֲשֶׂה – כְּרַבִּי אֶלְעָזָר בֶּן עֲזַרְיָה.

And Rav Naḥman also **said his** own statement: The ***halakha* is not in accordance with** the opinion of **Rabbi Elazar ben Azarya. And** the Sages **of Neharde'a say in the name of Rav Naḥman:** The ***halakha* is in accordance with** the opinion of **Rabbi Elazar ben Azarya.** The Gemara comments: **And although Rav Naḥman cursed** them **and said: Any judge who rules in accordance with** the opinion of **Rabbi Elazar ben Azarya, such and such** unspecified misfortune **will happen to him, even so** the ***halakha* is in accordance with** the opinion of **Rabbi Elazar ben Azarya.** Since the Gemara presented a number of different opinions, it concludes: **And the practical *halakha* is in accordance with** the opinion of **Rabbi Elazar ben Azarya.**[H]

בָּעֵי רָבִין: נִכְנְסָה לַחוּפָּה וְלֹא נִבְעֲלָה מַהוּ? חִיבַּת חוּפָּה קוֹנָה אוֹ חִיבַּת בִּיאָה קוֹנָה?

§ Since the practical *halakha* is that a woman who was divorced or widowed after betrothal receives the main sum of her marriage contract but not the additional sum, **Ravin asks: What is** the *halakha* with regard to a woman who **entered the wedding canopy and** is then widowed or divorced **without having had sexual intercourse?** Does the **affection** manifest in the **wedding effect** the marriage, and therefore she receives the additional sum as a married woman? **Or,** is it the **affection** manifest in the **intercourse** that **effects** the marriage, and consequently this woman is no different than a betrothed woman for the purpose of this *halakha*?

HALAKHA

Follow the principle of assessing intention – אָזְלֵי בָּתַר אוּמְדָּנָא: The court always assesses the intention of one who gives a gift, and if the circumstances indicate what he was thinking, the *halakha* follows this assessment, even if he did not explicitly state his intention (Rambam *Sefer Kinyan, Hilkhot Zekhiya UMattana* 6:1; *Shulḥan Arukh, Ḥoshen Mishpat* 246:1).

The practical *halakha* is in accordance with the opinion of Rabbi Elazar ben Azarya – הֲלָכָה לְמַעֲשֶׂה כְּרַבִּי אֶלְעָזָר בֶּן עֲזַרְיָה: In the case of one who betrothed a woman and wrote main and additional sums in her marriage contract, if he divorces her or he dies without marrying her, she receives only the main sum but not the additional sum (Rambam *Sefer Nashim, Hilkhot Ishut* 10:11; *Shulḥan Arukh, Even HaEzer* 55:6).

PERSONALITIES

Rav Ḥanina – רַב חֲנִינָא: The Rav Ḥanina referred to here is the one generally known as Rav Ḥanina the Bible expert. He was a second-generation *amora* in Eretz Yisrael and a disciple of Rabbi Ḥanina bar Ḥama, known as Rabbi Ḥanina the Great, and of Rabbi Yannai. It appears that he taught Bible to children and also read from the Torah in the synagogue. For this reason, he was sometimes rebuked with the expression: Go out and read your verses outside.

תָּא שְׁמַע, דְּתָנֵי רַב יוֹסֵף: שֶׁלֹּא כָּתַב לָהּ אֶלָּא עַל חִיבַּת לַיְלָה הָרִאשׁוֹן. אִי אָמְרַתְּ בִּשְׁלָמָא חִיבַּת חוּפָּה קוֹנָה – הַיְינוּ דְּאָמַר לַיְלָה הָרִאשׁוֹן, אֶלָּא אִי אָמְרַתְּ חִיבַּת בִּיאָה קוֹנָה – בִּיאָה בַּלַּיְלָה הָרִאשׁוֹן אִיתָא, מִכָּאן וְאֵילָךְ לֵיתָא?!

Come and hear that Rav Yosef taught the following *baraita*: **He wrote** the additional sum in the marriage contract **for her only on account of the affection** characteristic **of the first night** of the marriage. The Gemara asks: **Granted, if you say** that the **affection** manifest in the **wedding effects** the marriage, **this is** why **it says the** affection characteristic of **the first night,** as the wedding ceremony is performed on the first night only. **But if you say** that the **affection** manifest in the **intercourse effects** the marriage, **is there intercourse** only **on the first night** and then **from this** point **forward there is none?** Consequently, the *baraita* implies that the affection manifest in the wedding effects the marriage, and from that point on she is entitled to the additional sum of the marriage contract.

וְאֶלָּא מַאי – חוּפָּה, חוּפָּה בַּלַּיְלָה אִיתָא, בִּימָמָא לֵיתָא? וּלְטַעֲמִיךְ, בִּיאָה בַּלַּיְלָה אִיתָא, בִּימָמָא לֵיתָא? הָא אֲמַר רָבָא: אִם הָיָה בְּבַיִת אָפֵל – מוּתָּר! הָא לָא קַשְׁיָא, אוֹרַח אַרְעָא קָא מַשְׁמַע לָן, דְּבִיאָה בַּלַּיְלָה.

The Gemara rejects this proof: **But rather, what** is the advantage of interpreting the expression: Affection characteristic of the first night, as a reference to the **wedding? Is there a wedding** only **at night** and **not during the day?** The Gemara responds: **And according to your reasoning, is there intercourse** only **at night** and **not during the day?** Didn't **Rava say** that although the Sages generally prohibited engaging in intercourse during the day, **if it was in a dark house**[N] it is **permitted?**[H] The Gemara rejects this question: **This is** not **difficult.** By employing this phrase, **it teaches us the ordinary mode of behavior,** i.e., **that intercourse** generally takes place **at night.**

אֶלָּא חוּפָּה קַשְׁיָא! חוּפָּה נַמִי לָא קַשְׁיָא: כֵּיוָן דִּסְתָם חוּפָּה לְבִיאָה קַיְימָא – אוֹרַח אַרְעָא קָא מַשְׁמַע לָן, דְּבַלַּיְלָה.

Rather, the opinion that the expression is a reference to the **wedding is difficult,** as a wedding does not have to take place at night. The Gemara responds: **The wedding** reference is **also not difficult, since** a reference to **a wedding without specification** means a wedding that **takes place** in order to lead directly **to intercourse.** By using this phrase, **it** similarly **teaches us the ordinary mode of behavior,** i.e., that intercourse generally takes place **at night.** Consequently, this *baraita* cannot be used as a proof for either possibility.

בָּעֵי רַב אַשִׁי: נִכְנְסָה לַחוּפָּה וּפֵירְסָה נִידָּה מַהוּ? אִם תִּימְצֵי לוֹמַר חִיבַּת חוּפָּה קוֹנָה – חוּפָּה דַּחֲזְיָא לְבִיאָה, אֲבָל חוּפָּה דְּלָא חַזְיָא לְבִיאָה – לָא, אוֹ דִּלְמָא לָא שְׁנָא? תֵּיקוּ.

Rav Ashi asks a question similar to Ravin's: If the bride **entered the wedding canopy and began menstruating,** and the husband then died without ever engaging in intercourse with his wife, **what is** the *halakha* with regard to the additional sum of the marriage contract? **If you say** that the **affection** manifest in the **wedding effects** the marriage,[H] does this refer specifically to **a wedding** in which the couple is **fit to** engage in **intercourse,** which involves greater affection, **and a wedding** in which the couple **is not fit to** engage in **intercourse** does **not** effect the marriage? **Or, perhaps it is not different.** The Sages could not answer this, so the question **shall stand** unresolved.

NOTES

If it was in a dark house – אִם הָיָה בְּבַיִת אָפֵל: The Gemara explains that engaging in sexual relations during the daytime is prohibited, because the husband might see something on his wife's body that would cause him to be disgusted with her (*Nidda* 17a). In addition, it says that it is more modest to engage in intercourse in the dark. This demonstrates that relations are not necessarily prohibited during the day; the main point is that it must be dark (see Meiri).

HALAKHA

If it was in a dark house it is permitted – אִם הָיָה בְּבַיִת אָפֵל מוּתָּר: It is prohibited to engage in sexual relations during the daytime, except in a dark house (*Shulḥan Arukh, Oraḥ Ḥayyim* 240:11).

The affection manifest in the wedding effects the marriage – חִיבַּת חוּפָּה קוֹנָה: Once a betrothed woman has entered the wedding canopy, even if she has not yet engaged in sexual intercourse with her husband, she has the status of a married woman for all purposes, e.g., inheritance, her ability to receive the entire sum of her marriage contract, and a priest's obligation to become impure on behalf of his wife if she dies. However, this applies only in a case where she was permitted to engage in sexual relations when she entered the wedding canopy. If she was a menstruating woman at that time, she maintains the status of a betrothed woman for all purposes. The Rosh, however, holds that in the latter case the woman maintains the status of a betrothed woman only with regard to the additional sum of her marriage contract, but for all other matters she has the status of a married woman (Rambam *Sefer Nashim, Hilkhot Ishut* 10:2; *Shulḥan Arukh, Even HaEzer* 61:1).

״רַבִּי יְהוּדָה אוֹמֵר: רָצָה – כּוֹתֵב לִבְתוּלָה״ וכו׳. וְסָבַר רַבִּי יְהוּדָה דְּכוֹתְבִין שׁוֹבֵר? וְהָתְנַן: מִי שֶׁפָּרַע מִקְצָת חוֹבוֹ, רַבִּי יְהוּדָה אוֹמֵר: יַחֲלִיף, רַבִּי יוֹסֵי אוֹמֵר: יִכְתּוֹב לוֹ שׁוֹבֵר!

§ The mishna states: **Rabbi Yehuda says:** If **he wishes, he may write** a marriage contract **for a virgin** for two hundred dinars, and she may then write a receipt as if he had paid part of that sum. They ask: **And did Rabbi Yehuda hold** that one **writes a receipt**[N] for partial payment of a debt? **But didn't we learn** in a mishna (*Bava Batra* 170b): In the case of **one who repaid part of his debt,**[H] **Rabbi Yehuda says: He should exchange** the original promissory note for a new one that states the amount still owed, and **Rabbi Yosei says:** The lender **should write him a receipt** for the money he received? According to Rabbi Yehuda, a new note is preferable to a receipt because if the borrower loses the receipt, the lender is still in possession of a promissory note for the full amount and can collect a second time.

אָמַר רַבִּי יִרְמְיָה: כְּשֶׁשּׁוֹבַרְתָּהּ מִתּוֹכָהּ.

Rabbi Yirmeya said: In the mishna, Rabbi Yehuda is referring to a case **where the receipt is** written **within** the marriage contract itself[N] and not as a separate document. The husband is therefore not required to hold on to a receipt, and consequently Rabbi Yehuda's restriction against writing a receipt is not necessary.

אַבַּיֵי אֲמַר: אֲפִילּוּ תֵּימָא בְּשֶׁאֵין שׁוֹבַרְתָּהּ מִתּוֹכָהּ, בִּשְׁלָמָא הָתָם – וַדַּאי פְּרָעֵיהּ, דִּלְמָא מִירְכַּס תְּבַרְתָּא, וּמַפֵּיק לֵיהּ לִשְׁטָרָא, וַהֲדַר גָּבֵי זִימְנָא אַחֲרִינָא. הָכָא – וַדַּאי יָהֵיב לַהּ? מִילְּתָא בְּעָלְמָא הִיא דְּאָמְרָה לֵיהּ, אִי נָטְרֵיהּ – נָטְרֵיהּ. אִי לָא נָטְרֵיהּ – אִיהוּ הוּא דְּאַפְסִיד אַנַּפְשֵׁיהּ.

Abaye said: Even if **you say** that the mishna is referring to a case **where the receipt is not** written **within it,** it is logical that Rabbi Yehuda would make an exception in this case. **Granted, there,** in an ordinary case of a receipt, **it is certain** that the borrower **repaid** part of the loan, and consequently there is concern that **perhaps** he **will lose the receipt** and the lender will **take out the** promissory **note and return and collect** the entire payment **again.** But **here,** in the mishna, did the husband **definitely give** the wife part of the payment for the marriage contract? The receipt **merely** amounts to **something she said to him** in order to waive part of the payment, although she did not actually receive it. **If he saved** the receipt, **he saved it; if he did not save it, it is he himself who will lose.** Therefore, in this case, Rabbi Yehuda agrees that one writes a receipt.

בִּשְׁלָמָא אַבַּיֵי לָא אֲמַר כְּרַבִּי יִרְמְיָה לָא קָתָנֵי שׁוֹבַרְתָּהּ מִתּוֹכָהּ, אֶלָּא רַבִּי יִרְמְיָה מַאי טַעְמָא לָא אֲמַר כְּאַבַּיֵי? גְּזֵירָה שׁוֹבֵר דְּהָכָא אַטּוּ שׁוֹבֵר דְּעָלְמָא.

They ask: **Granted,** it is understandable why **Abaye did not say** his explanation **in accordance with** the opinion of **Rabbi Yirmeya,** as the mishna **does not teach** explicitly that the **receipt is** written **within** the marriage contract. **However, what is the reason** that **Rabbi Yirmeya did not say** an explanation **in accordance with** the opinion of **Abaye?** Why does Rabbi Yirmeya limit the mishna to a case where the receipt was written within the marriage contract? The Gemara responds: Although this is an unusual case, as there is no concern that the receipt may be lost, there is nevertheless a rabbinic **decree** with regard to **this receipt due to the typical** case of **receipts.** Therefore, Rabbi Yehuda would not allow a receipt unless it was written into the marriage contract itself.

טַעֲמָא – דִּכְתַבָה לֵיהּ, אֲבָל עַל פֶּה – לָא. אַמַּאי? דָּבָר שֶׁבְּמָמוֹן הוּא, וְשָׁמְעִינַן לֵיהּ לְרַבִּי יְהוּדָה דְּאָמַר: דָּבָר שֶׁבְּמָמוֹן – תְּנָאוֹ קַיָּים!

With regard to the crux of the issue, the Gemara notes: **The reason** that Rabbi Yehuda holds that the wife can waive part of the main sum of her marriage contract **is** specifically because **she wrote him** a receipt. **However,** if she said it **verbally, no,** it is not effective, even according to Rabbi Yehuda. The Gemara asks: **Why** not? **This is a monetary matter, and we** have **heard that Rabbi Yehuda said:** With regard to **monetary matters** in which someone makes a verbal stipulation, **his stipulation stands.**

דְּתַנְיָא, הָאוֹמֵר לְאִשָּׁה: הֲרֵי אַתְּ מְקוּדֶּשֶׁת לִי עַל מְנָת שֶׁאֵין לֵיךְ עָלַי שְׁאֵר, כְּסוּת וְעוֹנָה – הֲרֵי זוֹ מְקוּדֶּשֶׁת, וּתְנָאוֹ בָּטֵל, דִּבְרֵי רַבִּי מֵאִיר. רַבִּי יְהוּדָה אוֹמֵר: בְּדָבָר שֶׁבְּמָמוֹן – תְּנָאוֹ קַיָּים.

This is **as it is taught** in the *Tosefta* (*Kiddushin* 3:7): In the case of **one who says to a woman: You are hereby betrothed to me on the condition that you have no** ability to claim **from me food, clothing, or conjugal rights,**[H] **she is betrothed and his stipulation is void;** this is **the statement of Rabbi Meir. Rabbi Yehuda says:** With regard to **monetary matters,** such as food and clothing, **his stipulation stands;** therefore, if she verbally waives part of the marriage contract, and thereby makes a stipulation about a monetary matter, it should be effective.

NOTES

And did Rabbi Yehuda hold that one writes a receipt – וְסָבַר רַבִּי יְהוּדָה דְּכוֹתְבִין שׁוֹבֵר: The Rashba and the Ritva ask: How can this receipt for partial payment of the marriage contract be compared to other receipts? Rabbi Yehuda prohibits use of a receipt only when doing so against the wishes of the borrower, who says that he does not want to be obligated to hold on to the receipt. However, in this case, when it is done with the knowledge and agreement of the husband, why can't she write a receipt? They suggest that since according to Rabbi Yehuda a receipt is not ordinarily used to prove partial payment of a debt, it should not be used in this case either, out of concern that people will see this and demand the use of receipts in other cases. Rather, Rabbi Yehuda should have suggested that the husband write a marriage contract for the full amount and then have the wife return it to him and replace it with a modified contract for the smaller amount.

Where the receipt is written within the marriage contract itself – כְּשֶׁשּׁוֹבַרְתָּהּ מִתּוֹכָהּ: The simplest interpretation of this is that the woman writes the receipt on the marriage contract itself. However, a number of commentaries point out that if this were an acceptable solution, it could also be used in an ordinary case where a borrower paid part of a debt. It must be that this is not allowed, due to concern that the lender cut out or erased the receipt from the document. But if that is so, the question remains: Why does that concern not apply equally to a marriage contract?

A close reading of Rashi's commentary leads to the interpretation that the Gemara means that the receipt must be written into the actual text of the marriage contract itself, before the witnesses sign it. According to this, it is clear that this solution cannot be employed in the case of a promissory note (Ritva; Meiri).

HALAKHA

One who repaid part of his debt – מִי שֶׁפָּרַע מִקְצָת חוֹבוֹ: If one repays part of his debt, then if the lender wishes, the court, but not the witnesses, may write a new document with the remaining amount still owed, and the lender can then collect that amount based on the original date of the loan. Alternatively, the lender may instead write a receipt, even though this will require the borrower to retain the receipt. However, some say that this applies only when the time for payment of the entire loan has come due; if at least part of the money is not yet due, the borrower can demand that the lender have the loan document replaced or record the payment on the document itself (*Shakh*). This ruling is in accordance with the conclusion of the Gemara in tractate *Bava Batra* 170b (Rambam *Sefer Mishpatim, Hilkhot Malve VeLoveh* 23:15; *Shulḥan Arukh, Ḥoshen Mishpat* 54:1).

On the condition that you have no ability to claim from me food, clothing, or conjugal rights – עַל מְנָת שֶׁאֵין לֵיךְ עָלַי שְׁאֵר, כְּסוּת וְעוֹנָה: If the husband made a stipulation with his wife at the time of betrothal that she has no rights to food or clothing, his stipulation stands and he is not obligated to provide food or clothing. However, if he made a stipulation that he will not be required to provide conjugal rights, this stipulation is annulled and he is still obligated to provide them, in accordance with the opinion of Rabbi Yehuda (Rambam *Sefer Nashim, Hilkhot Ishut* 6:9–10, 12:6; *Shulḥan Arukh, Even HaEzer* 38:5, 69:6).

HALAKHA

The marriage contract is a rabbinic law – **כְּתוּבָּה דְּרַבָּנַן**: Most of the halakhic authorities agree that the marriage contract is a rabbinic law (*ge'onim*; Rabbeinu Ḥananel; Rif; Rambam; Maharam of Rothenburg). While some disagree (Rabbeinu Tam; Ri), the *halakha* does not follow this minority (Rambam *Sefer Nashim, Hilkhot Ishut* 10:7, 11:14, 12:2; *Shulḥan Arukh, Even HaEzer* 66:6).

He may actually consume the produce of the produce – **לְעוֹלָם הוּא אוֹכֵל פֵּירֵי פֵּירוֹת**: If one writes or says to his betrothed that he does not have any claim to her property and its produce, then he may not consume the produce, but he may sell it and buy land for his wife with the funds and then consume the produce of the produce. This is the case unless he wrote that he has no claim to her property, its produce, or the produce of its produce forever, in which case only the wife may consume the produce, in accordance with the opinion of Rabbi Yehuda (Rambam *Sefer Nashim, Hilkhot Ishut* 23:4; *Shulḥan Arukh, Even HaEzer* 92:5).

קָסָבַר רַבִּי יְהוּדָה: כְּתוּבָּה דְּרַבָּנַן, וַחֲכָמִים עָשׂוּ חִיזּוּק לְדִבְרֵיהֶם יוֹתֵר מִשֶּׁל תּוֹרָה.

The Gemara answers: **Rabbi Yehuda holds:** The **marriage contract is a rabbinic** law,[H] **and the Sages reinforced their pronouncements with greater** force **than Torah law.** Therefore, if the wife waives part of the main sum of the marriage contract, Rabbi Yehuda holds that her declaration has no force unless it is written down. However, a Torah obligation, such as food and clothing, does not require this reinforcement, and consequently the wife may waive it with a verbal stipulation.

הֲרֵי פֵּירוֹת דְּרַבָּנַן, וְלָא עָבְדוּ לְהוּ רַבָּנַן חִיזּוּק! דִּתְנַן, רַבִּי יְהוּדָה אוֹמֵר: לְעוֹלָם הוּא אוֹכֵל פֵּירֵי פֵּירוֹת, עַד שֶׁיִּכְתּוֹב לָהּ ״דִּין וּדְבָרִים אֵין לִי בִּנְכָסַיִךְ וּבְפֵירוֹתֵיהֶן וּבְפֵירוֹת פֵּירוֹתֵיהֶן עַד עוֹלָם״.

The Gemara challenges this answer: The husband's entitlement to the **produce** of his wife's property **is a rabbinic** decree, **and** nevertheless **the Sages did not reinforce** his rights to **them, as we learned** in a mishna (83a): **Rabbi Yehuda says:** Even if the husband wrote that he waived his rights to the produce of his wife's property, **he may actually consume the produce of the produce**[H] of her property, meaning that he could invest the produce in additional property, which would also belong to his wife, but he would consume its produce. This applies **unless he** explicitly **writes to her: I do not have any claim to your property, its produce, or the produce of its produce, forever.**

Perek **V**
Daf **56** Amud **b**

וְקַיְימָא לַן: מַאי כּוֹתֵב – אוֹמֵר!

And we maintain on this issue: **What is** the meaning of: **Writes?** It means: **Says.** In order to relinquish one's claim to produce of the produce of his wife's property, he does not necessarily need to write this in a document; it is sufficient to say it verbally in front of witnesses. It seems, therefore, that Rabbi Yehuda holds that a verbal stipulation is sufficient for a monetary matter of rabbinic law.

אָמַר אַבָּיֵי: לְכׇל יֵשׁ כְּתוּבָּה, וְלָא לְכׇל יֵשׁ פֵּירוֹת?! מִילְּתָא דִּשְׁכִיחָא עָבְדוּ בָּהּ רַבָּנַן חִיזּוּק, מִילְּתָא דְּלָא שְׁכִיחָא – לָא עָבְדוּ בָּהּ רַבָּנַן חִיזּוּק.

Abaye said: There is a distinction between the two cases. **Every** married woman **has a marriage contract, but not all** husbands **have** the right to **produce,** as not every woman brings property with her into the marriage. Therefore, in relation to **a common matter,** such as a marriage contract, **the Sages reinforced** their pronouncements **about it** by insisting that any stipulations to change the terms must be in writing. However, with regard to **an uncommon matter,** such as the produce of property, **the Sages did not reinforce** their pronouncements **about it,** and a verbal declaration is sufficient.

הֲרֵי חַמָּרִים דִּשְׁכִיחִי, וְלָא עָבְדוּ לָהּ רַבָּנַן חִיזּוּק!

The Gemara challenges this answer: But with regard to the *halakha* of **donkey drivers, which is a common** matter, Rabbi Yehuda does **not** hold that **the Sages reinforced** their pronouncements **about it.**

דִּתְנַן: הַחַמָּרִין שֶׁנִּכְנְסוּ לָעִיר, וְאָמַר אֶחָד מֵהֶן: שֶׁלִּי חָדָשׁ, וְשֶׁל חֲבֵרִי יָשָׁן, שֶׁלִּי אֵינוֹ מְתוּקָּן וְשֶׁל חֲבֵרִי מְתוּקָּן, אֵין נֶאֱמָנִים. רַבִּי יְהוּדָה אוֹמֵר: נֶאֱמָנִים.

This is **as we learned** in a mishna (*Demai* 4:7): In the case of **donkey drivers who entered a city** to sell their wares, **and one of them said: My** produce **is** from the **new** crop and is still moist and not as good, **but my associate's** produce **is** from the **old** crop, or he said: **Mine is not fit** for use, i.e., tithes have not been separated, **but my associate's** produce **is fit** for use, the drivers **are not afforded credibility.** There is a suspicion that they may be lying. They may have an arrangement between them where one will make this statement in one city and in the next city they will alternate, in order to appear credible, so that one will always be able to sell his wares. **Rabbi Yehuda says: They are deemed credible.** This indicates that Rabbi Yehuda holds that a verbal stipulation is sufficient even for a common monetary matter of rabbinic law.

אָמַר אַבַּיֵי: וַדַּאי דְּדִבְרֵיהֶם עָבְדוּ רַבָּנַן חִיזּוּק, סָפֵק דְּדִבְרֵיהֶם – לָא עָבְדוּ רַבָּנַן חִיזּוּק. רָבָא אָמַר: בִּדְמַאי הֵקִילּוּ.

Abaye said: There is a distinction between the cases. With regard to **a certain** matter **involving a rabbinic** decree, such as the main sum of the marriage contract, **the Sages reinforced** their pronouncements, but with regard to **an uncertain** matter **involving a rabbinic** decree, such as the case of the donkey drivers, the **Sages did not reinforce** their pronouncements. **Rava said: The Sages** did not reinforce their pronouncements in the case of the donkey drivers because, in general, **they were lenient about** questions concerning the prohibition of **doubtfully tithed produce [*demai*]**, since the *halakha* of *demai* is itself a stringency, as most *amei ha'aretz* separate tithes from their produce.

״רַבִּי מֵאִיר אוֹמֵר: כׇּל הַפּוֹחֵת״ וכו׳. כׇּל הַפּוֹחֵת – אֲפִילּוּ בִּתְנָאָה. אַלְמָא קָסָבַר: תְּנָאוֹ בָּטֵל, וְאִית לַהּ. וְכֵיוָן דַּאֲמַר לַהּ ״לֵית לִיךְ אֶלָּא מָנֶה״ – לָא סָמְכָא דַּעְתַּהּ, וְהָוְיָא לַהּ בְּעִילָתוֹ בְּעִילַת זְנוּת.

§ The mishna says: **Rabbi Meir says:** In the case of **anyone who reduces** the amount of the marriage contract to less than two hundred dinars for a virgin or one hundred dinars for a widow, this marriage amounts to licentious sexual intercourse. The Gemara makes an inference from the language of the mishna: The phrase: **Anyone who reduces** the amount of the marriage contract, means **even if** he made **a stipulation**[NH] and she agreed. **Apparently,** Rabbi Meir **held** that **his stipulation** in this case **is void and she has** the ability to collect the entire amount set by the Sages, **but** nevertheless **since he said to her: You have only one hundred** dinars, **she does not rely** on the marriage contract and does not see it as a true marriage, **and** therefore the intercourse **becomes licentious sexual intercourse.**

וְהָא שְׁמַעִינַן לֵיהּ לְרַבִּי מֵאִיר, דְּאָמַר: כׇּל הַמַּתְנֶה עַל מַה שֶּׁכָּתוּב בַּתּוֹרָה – תְּנָאוֹ בָּטֵל, הָא בִּדְרַבָּנַן – תְּנָאוֹ קַיָּים! קָסָבַר רַבִּי מֵאִיר כְּתוּבָּה דְּאוֹרָיְיתָא.

But we have **heard** that **Rabbi Meir said** that **anyone who stipulates counter to that which is written in the Torah, his stipulation is void.** This implies that if someone makes a stipulation **on a rabbinic** law **his stipulation** does **stand,** and therefore there is still a question as to why the stipulation about the marriage contract is void, as a marriage contract is a rabbinic ordinance. The Gemara responds: **Rabbi Meir holds** that **a marriage contract is** a requirement of **Torah** law. Consequently, if one made a stipulation to reduce the amount of the marriage contract, this is a stipulation counter to that which is written in the Torah, and it is void.

תַּנְיָא רַבִּי מֵאִיר אוֹמֵר: כׇּל הַפּוֹחֵת לִבְתוּלָה מִמָּאתַיִם, וּלְאַלְמָנָה מִמָּנֶה – הֲרֵי זוֹ בְּעִילַת זְנוּת. רַבִּי יוֹסֵי אוֹמֵר: רַשַּׁאי. רַבִּי יְהוּדָה אוֹמֵר: רָצָה, כּוֹתֵב לִבְתוּלָה שְׁטָר שֶׁל מָאתַיִם, וְהִיא כּוֹתֶבֶת לוֹ ״הִתְקַבַּלְתִּי מִמְּךָ מָנֶה״. וּלְאַלְמָנָה מָנֶה, וְהִיא כּוֹתֶבֶת לוֹ ״הִתְקַבַּלְתִּי מִמְּךָ חֲמִשִּׁים זוּז״.

It **is taught** in a *baraita*: **Rabbi Meir says:** In the case of **anyone who reduces** the amount of the marriage contract to lower **than two hundred** dinars **for a virgin or one hundred** dinars **for a widow, this** marriage amounts to **licentious sexual intercourse. Rabbi Yosei says: One is permitted** to reduce the amount by making a verbal stipulation, provided the wife agrees. **Rabbi Yehuda says: If one wishes, he may write for a virgin a document for two hundred** dinars, **and she may write him** a receipt stating: **I received one hundred** dinars **from you. And** similarly, **for a widow** one may write **one hundred** dinars **and she may write** for **him: I received fifty dinars from you.**

וְסָבַר רַבִּי יוֹסֵי רַשַּׁאי? וּרְמִינְהִי: אֵין עוֹשִׂין כְּתוּבַּת אִשָּׁה מִטַּלְטְלִין מִפְּנֵי תִּיקּוּן הָעוֹלָם. אָמַר רַבִּי יוֹסֵי: וְכִי מָה תִּיקּוּן הָעוֹלָם יֵשׁ בָּזוֹ? וַהֲלֹא אֵין קְצוּבִין, וּפוֹחֲתִין!

The Gemara asks: **And** does **Rabbi Yosei** actually **hold** that **he is permitted** to reduce the amount? The Gemara **raises a contradiction** based on a *baraita*: Collection of **a woman's marriage contract may not be made** dependent upon **movable property.** This is a rabbinic decree enacted **for the betterment of the world. Rabbi Yosei said: What betterment of the world is** accomplished **by this** decree? The Gemara answers: The price of the movable property **is not fixed,** and therefore it might **become devalued.**

תַּנָּא קַמָּא נַמִי ״אֵין עוֹשִׂין״ קָאָמַר! אֶלָּא לָאו – הָכִי קָאָמַר: בַּמֶּה דְּבָרִים אֲמוּרִים – בְּשֶׁלֹּא קִבֵּל עָלָיו אַחְרָיוּת. אֲבָל קִבֵּל עָלָיו אַחְרָיוּת – עוֹשִׂין. וַאֲתָא רַבִּי יוֹסֵי לְמֵימַר: כִּי קִיבֵּל עָלָיו אַחְרָיוּת – אַמַּאי עוֹשִׂין? וַהֲלֹא אֵין קְצוּבִין וּפוֹחֲתִין.

The Gemara analyzes the text of the *baraita*: **The first *tanna* also said:** A marriage contract may **not be made** dependent on movable property. What is Rabbi Yosei's disagreement with him? **Rather, is it not** that **this is what** the first *tanna* **said: In what** case **is this statement said?** In a case where **one did not provide a guarantee** for the movable property. **But if one did provide a guarantee,** the marriage contract **may be made** dependent on it.[H] **And Rabbi Yosei comes to say:** Even **if one provided a guarantee, why can** the marriage contract **be made** dependent on it? The price **is not fixed, and** it may **become devalued.**

NOTES

Anyone who reduces the amount of the marriage contract, even if he made a stipulation – כׇּל הַפּוֹחֵת אֲפִילּוּ בִּתְנָאָה: The early authorities identified two primary difficulties with this statement. The first problem is how this conclusion was derived from Rabbi Meir's statement. Rashi offers one explanation, that it is based on the fact that Rabbi Meir said: Anyone who reduces the amount of the marriage contract, as opposed to: Any woman whose marriage contract does not contain two hundred dinars for a virgin or one hundred dinars for a widow. The language of the statement therefore includes a case where the husband makes a condition that is not effective, so that the wife actually does have the ability to collect the full amount, but since he made a condition reducing the amount, their relationship nevertheless amounts to licentious sexual intercourse.

The Razah and the *Nimmukei Yosef* give a slightly different explanation: Since the language is: Anyone who reduces, and not: One who reduces, this includes one who made a condition to reduce the amount but the condition was not fulfilled. Rabbi Aharon HaLevi suggests another interpretation: This language is meant to include a woman who has a marriage contract but believes she does not have one. This situation can occur only when there is an invalid condition limiting the marriage contract.

HALAKHA

Anyone who reduces the amount of the marriage contract, even if he made a stipulation – כׇּל הַפּוֹחֵת אֲפִילּוּ בִּתְנָאָה: If one makes a condition with his wife that the value of her marriage contract will be less than the amount determined by the Sages, that is to say two hundred dinars for a virgin or one hundred dinars for a widow, this condition is void. This ruling is not due to the reason given by Rabbi Meir, but rather it is in accordance with the opinion of Rabbi Yehuda, that the Sages reinforced their pronouncements with greater severity than they applied to Torah law (Rambam *Sefer Nashim*, *Hilkhot Ishut* 12:8 and *Maggid Mishne* there; *Shulḥan Arukh*, *Even HaEzer* 66:9, 69:6).

But if one did provide a guarantee, the marriage contract may be made dependent upon it – אֲבָל קִבֵּל עָלָיו אַחְרָיוּת, עוֹשִׂין: In a situation where it is not possible for the husband to write a marriage contract, e.g., if it is Shabbat, or if he forgets to write it, he may give her movable property in lieu of her marriage document and provide a guarantee for that property in the event that it is lost or devalued. If he does this, she is permitted to him until he has the opportunity to write her a proper marriage contract, as explained elsewhere by the Gemara (7a) and in accordance with the opinion of the first *tanna* here (*Shulḥan Arukh*, *Even HaEzer* 66:2).

PERSONALITIES

Rami bar Ḥama – רָמִי בַּר חָמָא: Rami, an abbreviation of Rav Ami, bar Ḥama was a prominent fourth-generation Babylonian *amora*. Even in his youth, he was considered the outstanding disciple of Rav Ḥisda and eventually married the latter's daughter. Rami bar Ḥama also studied under Rav Naḥman and Rav Sheshet, and even engaged them in halakhic debate. He was known for his fierce intellect and his masterful memory of the oral tradition. He enjoyed a close relationship with his younger friend and colleague Rava, and after Rami bar Ḥama's death Rava married his widow, the daughter of Rav Ḥisda. The daughter of Rami bar Ḥama's wife was the mother of the *amora* Ameimar.

Rav Avya – רַב אֲוְיָא: A fourth-generation Babylonian *amora*, Rav Avya was a prominent disciple of Rav Huna but he also studied in Eretz Yisrael with Rabbi Ami and Rabbi Yoḥanan. Rav Huna respected him greatly and valued his comments and questions. He married the sister of Rami bar Ḥama and some of his children became *amora'im* themselves, the most famous of whom, Rav Aḥa, son of Rav Avya, is quoted many times in the Talmud as a disciple of Rav Ashi.

הָשְׁתָּא, וּמָה הָתָם דְּדִלְמָא פָּחֲתֵי – חָיֵישׁ רַבִּי יוֹסֵי, הָכָא דְּוַדַּאי קָא פָּחֲתָה – לֹא כׇּל שֶׁכֵּן?! הָכִי הָשְׁתָּא? הָתָם – לָא יָדְעָה דְּתָחֵיל, הָכָא – יָדְעָה וְקָא מָחֲלָה.

Now that the meaning of the *baraita* has been clarified, the Gemara asks: **Just as there,** in the case of movable property, where **perhaps** it will **be devalued, Rabbi Yosei is concerned** that the wife might not receive the full value of her marriage contract, **here,** where it **will definitely be devalued,** is it **not all the more so** clear that he would be concerned? The Gemara responds: **How can** these cases **be compared? There, she does not know** if her marriage contract will be devalued, and there is no reason to suppose **that she will waive** his obligation to her. But **here, she knows and she waived** it.

אַחְתֵּיהּ דְּרָמִי בַּר חָמָא הֲוַת נְסִיבָא לְרַב אֲוְיָא,

The Gemara relates: **The sister of Rami bar Ḥama**[P] **was married to Rav Avya.**[P]

Perek **V**
Daf **57** Amud **a**

אִירְכַס כְּתוּבְּתָהּ. אֲתוֹ לְקַמֵּיהּ דְּרַב יוֹסֵף, אֲמַר לְהוּ: הָכִי אָמַר רַב יְהוּדָה אָמַר שְׁמוּאֵל: זוֹ דִּבְרֵי רַבִּי מֵאִיר,

Her marriage contract was lost, and the woman and her husband **came before Rav Yosef** to ask what they should do. **He said to them: This is** what **Rav Yehuda said** that **Shmuel said: That** ruling, that if someone reduces his wife's marriage contract by even a small amount, their marriage amounts to licentious sexual intercourse, **is the statement of Rabbi Meir.**[N] According to that opinion, the husband and wife were forbidden to each other because she was not in possession of a valid marriage contract.

אֲבָל חֲכָמִים אוֹמְרִים: מְשַׁהֵא אָדָם אֶת אִשְׁתּוֹ שְׁתַּיִם וְשָׁלֹשׁ שָׁנִים בְּלֹא כְּתוּבָּה. אֲמַר לֵיהּ אַבָּיֵי: וְהָא אָמַר רַב נַחְמָן אָמַר שְׁמוּאֵל: הֲלָכָה כְּרַבִּי מֵאִיר בִּגְזֵירוֹתָיו! אִי הָכִי, זִיל כְּתוֹב לַהּ.

But the Rabbis say: Since the woman relies on the fact that she will eventually collect payment for her marriage contract, **a man may maintain his wife for** as long as **two or three years without** a written **marriage contract.** There is no urgent need to write a new one, since the husband's obligation remains intact. **Abaye said to him:** But **didn't Rav Naḥman say** that **Shmuel said** that the ***halakha* is in accordance with** the opinion of **Rabbi Meir** with regard to all of **his decrees?** Since Rabbi Meir's statement about marriage contracts was a form of decree, the *halakha* should be in accordance with his opinion. Rav Yosef responded: **If so, go and write her**[H] a new marriage contract.

NOTES

That ruling is the statement of Rabbi Meir – זוֹ דִּבְרֵי רַבִּי מֵאִיר: The Rivan explains that since Rabbi Meir is of the opinion that if someone reduces the amount of the marriage contract it is as if he engaged in licentious sexual intercourse, he would hold this all the more so with regard to a woman who does not have a marriage contract at all. Rabbi Aharon HaLevi further explains, based on one of Rashi's comments, that when one reduces the amount of the marriage contract, although the stipulation is null and void, Rabbi Meir believes that the woman does not feel confident that she can collect the full sum in case of divorce. Consequently, from her perspective, all sexual intercourse in this marriage is licentious, as she is lacking the financial commitment from her husband which is inherent in a proper marriage. This is even truer when she is not in possession of a marriage contract at all. Although she is entitled to receive payment even without a written marriage contract because there is a stipulation of the court obligating the husband to pay, she does not feel confident that she can collect the money.

HALAKHA

Go and write her – זִיל כְּתוֹב לַהּ: If someone wrote a marriage contract for his wife and it was lost or she waived her right to the payment for the marriage contract by writing a receipt stating that he had paid her, he must write her another document for at least the main sum of the marriage contract, as a man is prohibited from living with his wife for even a short time without a marriage contract. This ruling is in accordance with the opinion of Rabbi Meir, as the *halakha* is in accordance with all of his decrees.

The commentaries add that the ruling that the husband's obligation to write a replacement document does not require him to replace the additional sum of the marriage contract refers only to a situation where the wife waived her rights. But if she lost her marriage contract, he must write her a new document equivalent to the first one, including any additional sum (Rambam *Sefer Nashim, Hilkhot Ishut* 10:10; *Shulḥan Arukh, Even HaEzer* 66:3, and *Ḥelkat Meḥokek* and *Beit Shmuel* there).

כִּי אֲתָא רַב דִּימִי אֲמַר רַבִּי שִׁמְעוֹן בֶּן פָּזִי אֲמַר רַבִּי יְהוֹשֻׁעַ בֶּן לֵוִי מִשּׁוּם בַּר קַפָּרָא: מַחֲלוֹקֶת בַּתְּחִלָּה, אֲבָל בַּסּוֹף – לְדִבְרֵי הַכֹּל אֵינָהּ מוֹחֶלֶת. וְרַבִּי יוֹחָנָן אֲמַר: בֵּין בְּזוֹ וּבֵין בְּזוֹ מַחֲלוֹקֶת. אֲמַר רַבִּי אַבָּהוּ, לְדִידִי מִיפַּרְשָׁא לִי מִינֵּיהּ דְּרַבִּי יוֹחָנָן: דַּאֲנָא וְרַבִּי יְהוֹשֻׁעַ בֶּן לֵוִי לָא פָּלְגִינַן אַהֲדָדֵי.

§ The Gemara relates that **when Rav Dimi came**[B] from Eretz Yisrael to Babylonia, **he said** that **Rabbi Shimon ben Pazi said** that **Rabbi Yehoshua ben Levi** said **in the name of bar Kappara:** This **dispute** between Rabbi Yehuda and Rabbi Yosei concerning whether one may make a verbal stipulation with a woman to reduce her marriage contract is referring only **to the beginning** of the process.[N] **But** with regard **to the end, all agree** that **she cannot waive** her rights[N] by verbal confirmation alone, and she must instead write a receipt. **And Rabbi Yoḥanan said: Both in this** case **and in that** case there is **a dispute. Rabbi Abbahu said:** This **was explained to me** personally **by Rabbi Yoḥanan himself,** who said: **Rabbi Yehoshua ben Levi and I do not** actually **disagree with one another.** We merely used different language to express the same *halakha*.

מַאי בַּתְּחִלָּה דְּקָאֲמַר רַבִּי יְהוֹשֻׁעַ בֶּן לֵוִי – תְּחִלַּת חוּפָּה, וּמַאי סוֹף – סוֹף בִּיאָה. וְכִי קָאָמִינָא אֲנָא בֵּין בְּזוֹ וּבֵין בְּזוֹ מַחֲלוֹקֶת. תְּחִלַּת חוּפָּה וְסוֹף חוּפָּה, דְּהִיא תְּחִילַּת בִּיאָה.

What is the meaning of the term: **To the beginning, which Rabbi Yehoshua ben Levi said?** It is referring to **the beginning of the wedding** ceremony. **And what is** meant by **the end?** It is referring to the **end of intercourse;** Rabbi Yehoshua ben Levi's opinion is that after the marriage has been consummated, Rabbi Yehuda and Rabbi Yosei agree that the wife cannot relinquish her rights verbally. **And when I said** that **both in this** case **and in that** case there is **a dispute,** I was referring to **the beginning** of the **wedding** ceremony **and the end** of the **wedding** ceremony, **which is** also **the beginning of** the time designated for **intercourse.** Consequently, according to Rav Dimi, Rabbi Yehoshua ben Levi and Rabbi Yoḥanan agree that the dispute between Rabbi Yehuda and Rabbi Yosei applies only until the consummation of the marriage. After that point, all agree that she cannot waive her rights verbally.

כִּי אֲתָא רָבִין אֲמַר רַבִּי שִׁמְעוֹן בֶּן פָּזִי אֲמַר רַבִּי יְהוֹשֻׁעַ בֶּן לֵוִי מִשּׁוּם בַּר קַפָּרָא: מַחֲלוֹקֶת לְבַסּוֹף, אֲבָל בַּתְּחִלָּה – דִּבְרֵי הַכֹּל מוֹחֶלֶת. וְרַבִּי יוֹחָנָן אֲמַר: בֵּין בְּזוֹ וּבֵין בְּזוֹ מַחֲלוֹקֶת. אֲמַר רַבִּי אַבָּהוּ: לְדִידִי מִיפַּרְשָׁא לִי מִינֵּיהּ דְּרַבִּי יוֹחָנָן: דַּאֲנָא וְרַבִּי יְהוֹשֻׁעַ בֶּן לֵוִי לָא פָּלְגִינַן אַהֲדָדֵי, מַאי לְבַסּוֹף דַּאֲמַר רַבִּי יְהוֹשֻׁעַ בֶּן לֵוִי – סוֹף חוּפָּה, וּמַאי תְּחִלָּה – תְּחִלַּת חוּפָּה. וְכִי קָאָמִינָא אֲנָא בֵּין בְּזוֹ בֵּין בְּזוֹ מַחֲלוֹקֶת – תְּחִלַּת בִּיאָה וְסוֹף בִּיאָה.

When Ravin came from Eretz Yisrael, he reported this matter differently than Rav Dimi did: **Rabbi Shimon ben Pazi said** that **Rabbi Yehoshua ben Levi said in the name of bar Kappara:** This **dispute** is referring only to **the end** of the process, **but** with regard **to the beginning, all agree** that **she can waive** her rights verbally. **And Rabbi Yoḥanan said: Both in this** case **and in that** case there is **a dispute. Rabbi Abbahu said:** This **was explained to me** personally **by Rabbi Yoḥanan himself,** who said: **I and Rabbi Yehoshua ben Levi do not disagree with one another. What is** the meaning of: **The end, which Rabbi Yehoshua ben Levi said?** The **end of the wedding** ceremony. **And what is** the meaning of the **beginning?** The **beginning of the wedding** ceremony. **And when I said** that **both in this** case **and in that** case there is a **dispute,** I was referring to the **beginning of intercourse and** the **end of intercourse.**

BACKGROUND

When Rav Dimi came – כִּי אֲתָא רַב דִּימִי: Rav Dimi and Ravin were among the Sages who would travel between Eretz Yisrael and Babylonia, primarily to transmit the Torah of Eretz Yisrael to the Torah centers of the Diaspora, although occasionally for business reasons as well. Many questions, particularly those concerning the statements of Sages from Eretz Yisrael, remained unresolved in Babylonia until such travelers arrived and elucidated the *halakha*, the novel expression, or the unique circumstances pertaining to a particular statement that required clarification.

NOTES

This dispute is referring only to the beginning of the process – מַחֲלוֹקֶת בַּתְּחִלָּה: There are two main approaches to understanding the Gemara's discussion. According to Rashi, the debate here revolves around the dispute between Rabbi Yehuda and Rabbi Yosei in the aforementioned *baraita* about a verbal stipulation to reduce the marriage contract (see Ritva and Meiri). However, according to the Rivan, the Rashba, and Rabbi Aharon HaLevi, Rabbi Yehoshua ben Levi and Rabbi Yoḥanan are discussing the dispute between Rabbi Meir and Rabbi Yehuda in the mishna, which pertains to a case where the wife writes a receipt. It appears that according to the Jerusalem Talmud, the discussion is referring to the debate between Rabbi Meir and Rabbi Yehuda.

But with regard to the end, all agree that she cannot waive her rights – אֲבָל בַּסּוֹף לְדִבְרֵי הַכֹּל אֵינָהּ מוֹחֶלֶת: Rashi explains the reason for the distinction between the beginning of the process and the end. At the beginning, before the marriage is finalized, a verbal stipulation is effective. But at the end, when the marriage has already taken effect, the wife can waive her rights only via a written document.

The Rivan gives a different interpretation: If the husband made a stipulation with his wife prior to the marriage, it is possible that she wholeheartedly agreed to the stipulation and waived her right to the rest of the money. However, at the end of the process, since her husband had originally committed to pay her two hundred dinars but then reduced it, this retroactively redefines their marital relationship as licentious sexual intercourse. Alternatively, once she sees that her husband has reduced her marriage contract after the fact, she is no longer confident that she will receive the remaining amount.

אמר רב פפא: אי לאו דאמר רבי אבהו: לדידי מיפרשא לי מיניה דרבי יוחנן דאנא ורבי יהושע בן לוי לא פלגינן אהדדי, הוה אמינא: רבי יוחנן ורבי יהושע בן לוי – פליגי, רב דימי ורבין – לא פליגי,

Consequently, according to Ravin, Rabbi Yehoshua ben Levi and Rabbi Yoḥanan agree that at the time of the of the wedding ceremony the wife can verbally waive her rights, and the dispute of the *tanna'im* is referring to the time after the ceremony, which is also the beginning of the time for consummation of the marriage. **Rav Pappa said: Had Rabbi Abbahu not said: This was explained to me** personally **by Rabbi Yoḥanan himself, that I,** i.e. Rabbi Yoḥanan, **and Rabbi Yehoshua ben Levi do not disagree with one another, I,** i.e., Rav Pappa, **would have said** that the way to understand the various texts is that **Rabbi Yoḥanan and Rabbi Yehoshua ben Levi** do **disagree** with one another, whereas **Rav Dimi** and **Ravin do not disagree** with one another, but rather they both cited the same tradition from Eretz Yisrael.

מאי סוף דקאמר רבין – סוף חופה, ומאי תחלה דקאמר רב דימי – תחלת ביאה.

I would have explained it in the following manner: **What is** the meaning of the word **end, which Ravin said?** It is referring to the **end** of the **wedding** ceremony. **And what is** the meaning of the word **beginning, which Rav Dimi said?** It is referring to the **beginning of** the time designated for **intercourse,** which begins at the end of the wedding ceremony. It would then follow that Rabbi Yehoshua ben Levi and Rabbi Yoḥanan disagreed about the explanation of the dispute between Rabbi Yehuda and Rabbi Yosei, whereas Rav Dimi and Ravin both said the same thing.

מאי קא משמע לן?

What is Rav Pappa **teaching us?** Since he accepts Rabbi Abbahu's statement, he acknowledges that his alternate way of reading the sources is not correct. What, then, is the point of telling us that he would have explained Rabbi Yehoshua ben Levi's and Rabbi Yoḥanan's words differently?

הא קא משמע לן: דפליגי תרי אמוראי אטעמא דנפשייהו, ולא פליגי תרי אמוראי אליבא דחד אמורא.

The Gemara explains: It **teaches us this:** If we were discussing the meaning of an amoraic dispute about which we have different traditions, it is better to explain **that two *amora'im* disagree with regard to their own reasons** and not that **two *amora'im* disagree according to** the opinion of **another *amora*,** as it is more plausible to say that there is a dispute about logical reasoning than that there is a dispute about the correct transmission of a *halakhic* tradition. Consequently, had Rabbi Abbahu not declared that he was told otherwise by Rabbi Yoḥanan, it would have been preferable to explain that there is a logical dispute between Rabbi Yehoshua ben Levi and Rabbi Yoḥanan, rather than saying that the dispute is about the details of the tradition received by Rav Dimi and Ravin.

מתני׳ נותנין לבתולה שנים עשר חודש משתבעה הבעל לפרנס את עצמה וכשם שנותנין לאשה כך נותנין לאיש לפרנס את עצמו ולאלמנה שלשים יום. הגיע זמן ולא נישאו אוכלות משלו ואוכלות בתרומה.

MISHNA One **gives a virgin twelve months**[H] **from** the time **the husband asked** to marry **her** after having betrothed her, in order **to prepare herself** with clothes and jewelry for the marriage. **And just as** one **gives a woman**[H] this amount of time, **so too** does one **give a man** an equivalent period of time **to prepare himself,** as he too needs time to prepare for the marriage. **However, in** the case of **a widow,** who already has items available from her previous marriage, she is given only **thirty days**[H] to prepare. If **the** appointed **time** for the wedding **arrived and they did not get married** due to some delay on the part of the husband, then the woman **may partake of his** food.[H] **And** if her husband is a priest, **she may partake of *teruma*,**[B] even if she is an Israelite woman.

רבי טרפון אומר: נותנין לה הכל תרומה. רבי עקיבא אומר: מחצה חולין ומחצה תרומה.

The *tanna'im* disagree about the permission granted to a priest to sustain his betrothed with *teruma* before she is married to him. **Rabbi Tarfon says: He may give her all** of her required sustenance from ***teruma*.** During her periods of impurity, e.g., menstruation, when she cannot partake of *teruma*, she may sell the *teruma* to a priest and use the proceeds to buy non-sacred food. **Rabbi Akiva says:** He must give her **half** of her needs from **non-sacred** food **and half** may be from ***teruma*,** so that she can eat from the non-sacred food when she is ritually impure.

HALAKHA

One gives a virgin twelve months – נוֹתְנִין לִבְתוּלָה שְׁנֵים עָשָׂר חוֹדֶשׁ: If one betrothed a woman and waited several years before requesting to marry her, if she is still a young woman, she is given twelve months from the date of his request to prepare all her needs and then she must get married (Rambam *Sefer Nashim, Hilkhot Ishut* 10:17; *Shulḥan Arukh, Even HaEzer* 56:1).

Just as one gives a woman – כְּשֵׁם שֶׁנּוֹתְנִין לְאִשָּׁה: Just as a woman is given time to prepare for the marriage after the husband requested to marry her, a man receives time to prepare himself for marriage if the woman requests that he marry her. He is given the same amount of time as she would be. In a case where she would have twelve months to prepare, he also has twelve months; in a case where she would have thirty days, then he too has thirty days.

The later authorities also quote the opinion of the Rosh and the *Tur*, based on the Jerusalem Talmud, that just as there is a distinction between a virgin and a widow there is also a distinction between a bachelor and a widower. A bachelor gets twelve months to prepare from the time his betrothed requests to marry, even if he is marrying a widow. A widower has thirty days to prepare from the time his betrothed requests to marry, even if he marries a virgin. However, according to the *Be'er Heitev*, nowadays, due to changes in the method of preparing for marriage, no one is given so much time to prepare, and the ruling depends on how the judges view the matter (Rambam *Sefer Nashim, Hilkhot Ishut* 10:18; *Shulḥan Arukh, Even HaEzer* 56:2).

In the case of a widow, thirty days – לְאַלְמָנָה שְׁלֹשִׁים יוֹם: One who betroths a woman who has previously been married must give her thirty days from the date that he requests to marry her in order to prepare for the marriage. The widow referred to here is only a widow from marriage, not one who was widowed from her betrothed (Rambam *Sefer Nashim, Hilkhot Ishut* 10:17 and *Maggid Mishne* there; *Shulḥan Arukh, Even HaEzer* 56:1).

May partake of his food – אוֹכְלוֹת מִשֶּׁלּוֹ: If the time that the husband was given has passed and he has not married the woman, he is still obligated to provide for her sustenance (Rambam *Sefer Nashim, Hilkhot Ishut* 10:19; *Shulḥan Arukh, Even HaEzer* 56:3).

BACKGROUND

She may partake of *teruma* – אוֹכְלוֹת בִּתְרוּמָה: Whenever the term *teruma* appears without qualification, it is referring to the great *teruma*. The Torah commands that one must give the priest "the first fruit of your grain, of your wine, and of your oil" (Deuteronomy 18:4, and see Numbers 18:12), and the Sages extended the scope of this mitzva, which applies only in Eretz Yisrael, to include all produce. *Teruma* is sacred and may be eaten only by a priest and his household while they are in a state of ritual purity (see Leviticus 22:9–15). The discussion in the mishna reflects differing opinions with regard to when a woman from a non-priestly family is considered to have become part of her husband's household for the purposes of partaking in *teruma*, as will be explained by the Gemara.

הַיָּבָם אֵינוֹ מַאֲכִיל בִּתְרוּמָה. עָשְׂתָה שִׁשָּׁה חֳדָשִׁים בִּפְנֵי הַבַּעַל, וְשִׁשָּׁה חֳדָשִׁים בִּפְנֵי הַיָּבָם, וַאֲפִילּוּ כּוּלָּן בִּפְנֵי הַבַּעַל חָסֵר יוֹם אֶחָד בִּפְנֵי הַיָּבָם, אוֹ כּוּלָּן בִּפְנֵי הַיָּבָם חָסֵר יוֹם אֶחָד בִּפְנֵי הַבַּעַל – אֵינָהּ אוֹכֶלֶת בִּתְרוּמָה.

The mishna continues: A priest who is a *yavam*, i.e., his brother died childless after betrothing a woman, **does not enable** his *yevama* **to partake**[H] **of *teruma*** by virtue of her relationship with him. **If she** had **completed six months**[N] of the twelve-month wait for marriage **under the aegis of the husband,** and then he died, **and** she waited **six** more **months under the aegis of the *yavam*; or even** if she completed **all of** the necessary time **under the aegis of the husband except for one day** that she was **under the aegis of the *yavam*; or** if she completed **all of** the necessary time **under the aegis of the *yavam* except for one day** that she was **under the aegis of the husband,** she still **may not partake of *teruma*.**

זוֹ מִשְׁנָה רִאשׁוֹנָה. בֵּית דִּין שֶׁל אַחֲרֵיהֶן אָמְרוּ:

This set of rulings, concerning the permission granted a betrothed woman whose wedding date has arrived to partake of *teruma*, is in accordance with **the initial** version of the **mishna.** However, **a court** that convened **after them,** in a later generation, **said:**

NOTES

If she had completed six months – עָשְׂתָה שִׁשָּׁה חֳדָשִׁים: Rashi explains that essentially there is no difference whether she spent six months under the aegis of the husband, or even if she spent twelve months under the aegis of the husband and then began to partake of *teruma* before he died, as the principle is that her relationship with the *yavam* does not enable her to partake of *teruma* at all.

Rabbeinu Tam and the Ramban maintain that when the Sages said that a *yavam* does not enable his *yevama* to partake of *teruma*, they were referring only to a case where, due to Torah law or rabbinic decree, the husband had not enabled the wife to partake of *teruma*. In such a case, even if the *yavam* is a priest, she may not partake of *teruma* until she enters into the actual levirate marriage. But if the situation is such that she would have been able to partake of *teruma* once the appointed time for marriage with the husband arrived, then she may also partake of *teruma* due to the *yavam*. According to this opinion, the sources that maintain that a *yavam* does not enable the *yevama* to partake of *teruma* at all are following the final version of the mishna.

HALAKHA

A *yavam* does not enable his *yevama* to partake – הַיָּבָם אֵינוֹ מַאֲכִיל: An Israelite widow waiting for her *yavam* who is a priest to perform levirate marriage may not partake of *teruma* (Rambam *Sefer Zera'im*, *Hilkhot Terumot* 8:1, 8:5).

Perek **V**
Daf **57** Amud **b**

אֵין הָאִשָּׁה אוֹכֶלֶת בִּתְרוּמָה עַד שֶׁתִּכָּנֵס לַחוּפָּה.

A woman may not partake of *teruma* until she has actually **entered the wedding canopy.**[H]

גמ׳ מְנָא הָנֵי מִילֵּי? אֲמַר רַב חִסְדָּא: דַּאֲמַר קְרָא ״וַיֹּאמֶר אָחִיהָ וְאִמָּהּ תֵּשֵׁב הַנַּעֲרָה אִתָּנוּ יָמִים אוֹ עָשׂוֹר״.

GEMARA The Gemara asks: **From where are these matters** derived,[N] that a virgin is given twelve months to prepare for her wedding? **Rav Ḥisda said** it is based on the fact **that the verse states** with regard to Rebecca: **"And her brother and mother said: Let the damsel abide with us for days, or ten"** (Genesis 24:55).

מַאי ״יָמִים״. אִילֵימָא תְּרֵי יוֹמֵי – מִשְׁתָּעֵי אִינִישׁ הָכִי? אָמְרוּ לֵיהּ: תְּרֵי יוֹמֵי – אֲמַר לְהוּ: לָא. אָמְרוּ לֵיהּ עֲשָׂרָה יוֹמֵי?! אֶלָּא מַאי ״יָמִים״ – שָׁנָה, דִּכְתִיב ״יָמִים תִּהְיֶה גְאוּלָּתוֹ״.

The Gemara first analyzes the language of the verse: **What** is the meaning of **"days"? If we say two days,** the minimum number justifying the use of the plural, does **a person** really **speak like this?** Rebecca's relatives **said to** Abraham's servant that they wanted her to stay for **two days,** after which **he said to them no,** as he did not want to wait even that long. If so, is it possible that after that **they said to him** that they wanted her to stay for **ten days?** Consequently, it is impossible to explain the word "days" as two days and "ten" as ten days. **Rather, what** is the meaning of **"days"?** It means: **A year, as it is written: "For days he shall have redemption"** (Leviticus 25:29), and there it is explained that "days" is referring to a year. Consequently, in the verse **"And her brother and mother said: Let the damsel abide with us for days, or ten"** (Genesis 24:55), "days" refers to a year, and "ten" refers to a shorter period of similar magnitude, i.e. ten months, in order to prepare for her wedding.

NOTES

From where are these matters derived – מְנָא הָנֵי מִילֵּי: The Ritva and *Nimmukei Yosef* state that this is not an actual derivation from a verse, but rather a mere support for the matter. Consequently, the verse provides support only for the case of a virgin, whereas with regard to a widow the source is logical reasoning; it is obvious that she cannot prepare herself adequately in less than a month. The *Nimmukei Yosef* adds that one can perhaps adduce support from the verse for the *halakha* pertaining to a widow as well, since the Gemara originally thought that the word "days" implied a month, which is the amount of time allotted for a widow's preparations.

HALAKHA

A woman may not partake of *teruma* until she has actually entered the wedding canopy – אֵין הָאִשָּׁה אוֹכֶלֶת בִּתְרוּמָה עַד שֶׁתִּכָּנֵס לַחוּפָּה: By Torah law, an Israelite woman who is betrothed to a priest is allowed to partake of *teruma* from the time of her betrothal, but the Sages prohibited her from doing so until she enters the marriage canopy (Rambam *Sefer Zera'im*, *Hilkhot Terumot* 6:3).

וְאֵימָא חוֹדֶשׁ, דִּכְתִיב "עַד חֹדֶשׁ יָמִים"? אָמְרִי: דָּנִין "יָמִים" סְתָם מִ"יָּמִים" סְתָם, וְאֵין דָּנִין "יָמִים" סְתָם מִ"יָּמִים" שֶׁנֶּאֱמַר בָּהֶן "חוֹדֶשׁ".

The Gemara asks: **And** let us **say** that "days" means **a month, as it is written: "But a whole month of days"** (Numbers 11:20), and the verse about Rebecca might then have meant that her family wanted to wait for a month, or at least for ten days. **They say: One derives** the meaning of an **unspecified** use of the term **"days" from** another **unspecified** instance of the term **"days,"** which means a year. **And one does not derive** the meaning of **an unspecified** use of the term **"days" from** an instance of the term **"days," about which** the term **"month" is stated.** Consequently, it can be derived from the verse that the ordinary amount of time required for a virgin to prepare for marriage is twelve months.

אָמַר רַבִּי זֵירָא, תָּנָא: קְטַנָּה, בֵּין הִיא וּבֵין אָבִיהָ יְכוֹלִין לְעַכֵּב. בִּשְׁלָמָא אִיהִי – מָצֵי מְעַכְּבָא, אֶלָּא אָבִיהָ, אִי אִיהִי נִיחָא לָהּ – אָבִיהָ מַאי נָפְקָא לֵיהּ מִינָּהּ? סָבַר: הָשְׁתָּא לָא יָדְעָה, לְמָחָר מִימְרְדָא וְנָפְקָא, וְאָתְיָא וְנָפְלָה עִילָּוַאי.

§ **Rabbi Zeira said:** It was **taught** in the *Tosefta* (*Ketubot* 5:1) with regard to **a minor girl:**[B] **Either she or her father may delay**[H] the wedding until she has reached majority. The Gemara asks: **Granted, she,** the girl herself, **may delay** the wedding if she feels she is not ready, as she is the one who will be directly affected, **but** why should **her father** be allowed to delay her wedding? **If it is suitable for her** to get married, **what difference does it make to her father?** The Gemara answers: **He thinks:** Perhaps she agrees to get married **now** because **she does not** fully **know** what she is doing. But **tomorrow, she will** realize the marriage was a mistake, **rebel, and leave** her husband, **and** then **she will come** back **and become** a burden **to me.** Therefore, her father prefers that she wait until she has reached majority and marry when she is completely aware of what is involved.

אָמַר רַבִּי אַבָּא בַּר לֵוִי: אֵין פּוֹסְקִין עַל הַקְּטַנָּה לְהַשִּׂיאָהּ כְּשֶׁהִיא קְטַנָּה, אֲבָל פּוֹסְקִין עַל הַקְּטַנָּה לְהַשִּׂיאָהּ כְּשֶׁהִיא גְּדוֹלָה. פְּשִׁיטָא! מַהוּ דְּתֵימָא: לֵיחוּשׁ דִּלְמָא מְעַיְּילָא פַּחְדָּא מֵהָשְׁתָּא וְחָלְשָׁה, קָא מַשְׁמַע לָן.

Rabbi Abba bar Levi said: One may not finalize an agreement to marry **a minor girl**[H] in order **to marry her while she is** still **a minor, but one may finalize** an agreement to marry **a minor girl** in order **to marry her when she** becomes **an adult woman.** With regard to the latter *halakha*, the Gemara asks: **Isn't that obvious?** If he will marry her when she becomes an adult woman, there is nothing unusual about this case. The Gemara answers: **Lest you say** that one **should be concerned** that **she might become afraid** of marriage **from** making plans **now, and** this **will** cause her resolve to **weaken,** and then even when she becomes an adult she will maintain reservations about the matter, Rabbi Abba bar Levi therefore **teaches us** that one need not be concerned about this. One may finalize an agreement to marry her as an adult even when she is a minor girl.

אָמַר רַב הוּנָא: בָּגְרָה יוֹם אֶחָד וְנִתְקַדְּשָׁה – נוֹתְנִין לָהּ שְׁלֹשִׁים יוֹם כְּאַלְמָנָה. מֵיתִיבֵי: בָּגְרָה – הֲרֵי הִיא כִּתְבוּעָה, מַאי לָאו – כִּתְבוּעָה דִּבְתוּלָה? לָא, כִּתְבוּעָה דְּאַלְמָנָה.

§ **Rav Huna said:** If **she has reached her majority,** even for just **one day, and** then **she is betrothed,** she is **given her thirty days** to prepare for her wedding, **like a widow,** since prior to reaching adulthood she presumably had already prepared everything needed for her marriage. The Gemara **raises an objection** from a *baraita*: If **she grew up, she is similar to** a betrothed woman **who has been asked** to marry her betrothed. **What, is it not** that she is **similar to a virgin who has been asked** to marry, and she has twelve months to prepare? The Gemara answers: **No,** it means that she is **similar to a widow who has been asked** to marry her betrothed, who gets only thirty days to prepare. Only young women who have not reached majority and who are virgins get a year to prepare; after majority, all women, regardless of whether they are virgins, get thirty days.

תָּא שְׁמַע: בּוֹגֶרֶת שֶׁשָּׁהֲתָה שְׁנֵים עָשָׂר חֹדֶשׁ, רַבִּי אֱלִיעֶזֶר אוֹמֵר: הוֹאִיל וְחַיָּיב בַּעְלָהּ בִּמְזוֹנוֹתֶיהָ – יָפֵר! אֵימָא: בּוֹגֶרֶת וְשֶׁשָּׁהֲתָה שְׁנֵים עָשָׂר חוֹדֶשׁ, רַבִּי אֱלִיעֶזֶר אוֹמֵר: הוֹאִיל וּבַעְלָהּ חַיָּיב בִּמְזוֹנוֹתֶיהָ – יָפֵר.

The Gemara attempts another refutation of Rav Huna's statement: **Come** and **hear** a proof from a mishna (*Nedarim* 73b): **If a grown woman waited twelve months** since betrothal and is still not married, **Rabbi Eliezer says: Since her husband is obligated** to provide **for her sustenance, he may** also **nullify** her vows[N] (see Numbers, chapter 30). It can be inferred from this that the waiting period for a grown woman is also twelve months. The Gemara responds by emending the text of the mishna: **Say** that **if a grown woman** waited thirty days **or** a young woman **waited twelve months, Rabbi Eliezer says: Since her husband is obligated** to provide **for her sustenance, he may nullify** her vows.

BACKGROUND

Minor girl – קְטַנָּה: According to Torah law, a father has the legal authority to marry his daughter off while she is a minor girl. Nevertheless, the Sages decreed that it is prohibited to do so. The father is instructed to wait until his daughter is mature enough to decide on her own whom she would like to marry (*Kiddushin* 41a). If a girl's father is no longer alive, her mother or brothers are given the authority to marry her off with her consent, although this betrothal is valid by rabbinic law, not Torah law, and as a result, a number of halakhic distinctions apply.

It is clear that marriages of minor girls did sometimes take place in Jewish communities, both during the talmudic period and also at later times. However, the extent of such marriages is not known and probably varied greatly in different locales and time periods. Often, these marriages were conducted due to dire circumstances, such as in the case of orphans or other situations of extreme economic distress (*Tosafot*).

HALAKHA

With regard to a minor girl either she or her father may delay – קְטַנָּה בֵּין הִיא וּבֵין אָבִיהָ יְכוֹלִין לְעַכֵּב: If the betrothed of a minor girl requests to marry her, either she or her father may delay the wedding until she grows older and becomes a young woman. If the father wishes her to marry and the daughter consents, the husband may marry her, but it is not proper to do so (Rambam *Sefer Nashim, Hilkhot Ishut* 10:16; *Shulḥan Arukh, Even HaEzer* 56:4).

One may not finalize an agreement to marry a minor girl – אֵין פּוֹסְקִין עַל הַקְּטַנָּה: It is prohibited for one to betroth his minor daughter to a man until she comes of age and expresses her desire to marry a particular person, as explained in tractate *Kiddushin* (41a) and in the Gemara here. The Rema, based on *Tosafot* on tractate *Kiddushin*, writes that despite this people were accustomed to betrothing their minor daughters due to the hardships caused by exile. Parents did not always have the basic requirements of a wedding available, and were not always able to find a suitable match for their daughters, due to the small numbers of Jews in their vicinity. Therefore, if parents found an appropriate match for their daughter and were able to fund the wedding, they would marry her off at that point, due to fear that they would not be able to do so later on. This was the accepted practice, primarily during times of hardship (Rambam *Sefer Nashim, Hilkhot Ishut* 3:19; *Shulḥan Arukh, Even HaEzer* 37:8).

NOTES

Rabbi Eliezer says…he may also nullify her vows – רַבִּי אֱלִיעֶזֶר אוֹמֵר...יָפֵר: The *halakha* is not in accordance with this opinion. Rather, a husband may not nullify his betrothed's vows until she enters the wedding canopy (see Meiri).

תָּא שְׁמַע: הַמְאָרֵס אֶת הַבְּתוּלָה, בֵּין שֶׁתָּבְעָה הַבַּעַל וְהִיא מְעַכֶּבֶת, וּבֵין שֶׁתָּבְעָה הִיא וּבַעַל מְעַכֵּב – נוֹתְנִין לָהּ שְׁנֵים עָשָׂר חֹדֶשׁ מִשְּׁעַת תְּבִיעָה, אֲבָל לֹא מִשְּׁעַת אֵירוּסִין. וּבָגְרָה הֲרֵי הִיא כִּתְבוּעָה. כֵּיצַד? בָּגְרָה יוֹם אֶחָד וְנִתְקַדְּשָׁה – נוֹתְנִין לָהּ שְׁנֵים עָשָׂר חֹדֶשׁ, וְלַאֲרוּסָה שְׁלֹשִׁים יוֹם. תְּיוּבְתָּא דְּרַב הוּנָא! תְּיוּבְתָּא.

The Gemara attempts another refutation of Rav Huna's statement: **Come** and **hear** a *baraita*: **If someone betrothed a virgin, whether the husband asks** to marry **her and she delays** the process because she says that she requires more time **or whether she asks** to marry him **and** the **husband delays** the process because he is not yet ready, **she is given twelve months from the time** the **request** was issued **but not from the time of the betrothal,** even if that was much earlier, and **a grown woman is similar to one who has been asked** to marry.[H] **How is this so? If she has reached her majority** for **one day, and she is** then **betrothed, she** is **given twelve months** from the day of her betrothal, because it is the same as the day of her majority. **One who was** already **a betrothed woman** when she reached majority is given **thirty days.** Therefore, **the refutation** of the opinion **of Rav Huna is a conclusive refutation.**

מַאי וְלַאֲרוּסָה שְׁלֹשִׁים יוֹם? אָמַר רַב פָּפָּא, הָכִי קָאָמַר: בּוֹגֶרֶת שֶׁעָבְרוּ עָלֶיהָ שְׁנֵים עָשָׂר חֹדֶשׁ בְּבַגְרוּת, וְנִתְקַדְּשָׁה – נוֹתְנִין לָהּ שְׁלֹשִׁים יוֹם כְּאַלְמָנָה.

The Gemara asks: **What** is meant by the words: **And one who was** already **a betrothed woman** is given **thirty days? Rav Pappa said: This is what it is saying:** With regard to **a grown woman who has been an adult for twelve months and is** then **betrothed, she** is **given thirty days, like a widow,** and not another twelve months.

״הִגִּיעַ זְמַן וְלֹא נִישְּׂאוּ״. אָמַר עוּלָּא: דְּבַר תּוֹרָה, אֲרוּסָה בַּת יִשְׂרָאֵל אוֹכֶלֶת בִּתְרוּמָה, שֶׁנֶּאֱמַר ״וְכֹהֵן כִּי יִקְנֶה נֶפֶשׁ, קִנְיַן כַּסְפּוֹ״ – וְהַאי נַמִי קִנְיַן כַּסְפּוֹ הוּא. מַה טַּעַם אָמְרוּ אֵינָהּ אוֹכֶלֶת – שֶׁמָּא יִמְזְגוּ לָהּ כּוֹס בְּבֵית אָבִיהָ, וְתַשְׁקֶה לְאָחִיהָ וְלַאֲחוֹתָהּ.

§ The mishna states: **If the** appointed **time** for the wedding **arrived and they did not get married,** she may partake of *teruma*. **Ulla said: By Torah law, the daughter of a non-priest betrothed** to a priest **may partake of *teruma*** immediately, even before the wedding date arrives, **as it is stated: "If a priest buy any soul, the acquisition of his money,** he may eat of it" (Leviticus 22:11), **and this** woman **is also an acquisition of his money** through the betrothal. Therefore, she is entitled to partake of *teruma*. **What,** then, **is the reason** the Sages **said** that **she may not partake?** It is **lest someone pour her a cup** of *teruma* wine while she is **in her father's house.** Although she may drink it as the betrothed of a priest, since she is still living in her father's house there is a concern that **she will give her brother or sister to drink** from the wine, which is prohibited, as they are non-priests.

אִי הָכִי, הִגִּיעַ זְמַן וְלֹא נִישְּׂאוּ נַמִי! הָתָם דּוּכְתָּא מְיַיחֵד לַהּ.

The Gemara asks: **If so,** then **if the time arrived and they did not get married,** there should **also** be concern that she might give it to members of her family, as she is still in her father's house. Why, then, does the mishna say that she is permitted to partake of *teruma* at that time? The Gemara answers: **There,** after the time for the wedding has arrived, **he designates** a specific **place for her.** Since her husband is obligated to provide for her sustenance, he will want to ensure that she receives her food in a particular place so that she not use it to feed her family. This mitigates the concern that she may inadvertently give it to her brother or sister to drink.

אֶלָּא מֵעַתָּה לַקִּיט כֹּהֵן לְיִשְׂרָאֵל לֹא לֵיכוּל בִּתְרוּמָה, דִּלְמָא אָתוּ לְמֵיכַל בַּהֲדֵיהּ! הַשְׁתָּא מִדִּידְהוּ סָפוּ לֵיהּ, מִדִּידֵיהּ אָכְלִי?!

The Gemara asks: **However, if that is so,** then the *halakha* should also be that **a gleaner** who is **a priest** and is employed **by an Israelite may not partake of *teruma*, lest** the other members of the household **come to eat with him** from the *teruma*. The Gemara rejects this: **Now,** even though the members of the Israelite household **feed** the priest **from their** food, as he is their employee, **would they eat from his** food? They would not. Therefore, there is no reason for concern and no reason to prohibit him from eating *teruma*. This is Ulla's opinion.

רַב שְׁמוּאֵל בַּר רַב יְהוּדָה אָמַר: מִשּׁוּם סִימְפּוֹן.

However, **Rav Shmuel bar Rav Yehuda said:** The reason for the rabbinic decree is **due to abrogation** [***simfon***],[L] cancellation of the contract. It may become known after the betrothal that she has blemishes that can retroactively annul the betrothal, and it would then become apparent that she had partaken of *teruma* unlawfully.

HALAKHA

A grown woman is similar to one who has been asked to marry – בָּגְרָה הֲרֵי הִיא כִּתְבוּעָה: If one requests to marry his betrothed after she has reached adulthood, she is given twelve months from the day that she reached majority. Similarly, if she is betrothed during the first twelve months after reaching majority, she has until the end of those twelve months to prepare her wedding, even if he requested an earlier wedding date. If the betrothal or the request occur more than twelve months after her majority, she is given only thirty days, as stated in the *baraita* and in accordance with Rav Pappa, as he is the later *amora* (Rambam *Sefer Nashim*, *Hilkhot Ishut* 10:17; *Shulḥan Arukh*, *Even HaEzer* 56:1).

LANGUAGE

Abrogation [*simfon*] **– סִימְפּוֹן:** Probably from the Greek **σύμφωνον**, *symphonon*, meaning agreement or the conditions of an agreement. The Gemara uses the term to refer to the cancellation of an agreement due to non-fulfillment of the conditions.

HALAKHA

There is no abrogation with regard to slaves – סִימְפּוֹן בַּעֲבָדִים לֵיכָּא: One who buys a slave or maidservant cannot nullify the sale if he discovers a blemish that does not prevent them from performing their labors. This is because he already saw any visible blemishes when he bought and accepted them, and hidden blemishes are irrelevant, since a slave is intended for work. However, if there is a blemish that prevents the slave from performing his work, this is a mistaken acquisition, in accordance with the Gemara (Rambam *Sefer Kinyan*, *Hilkhot Mekhira* 15:12; *Shulḥan Arukh*, *Ḥoshen Mishpat* 232:10).

אִי הָכִי נִכְנְסָה לַחוּפָּה וְלֹא נִבְעֲלָה נַמִי! הָתָם מִיבְדַּק בָּדֵיק לָהּ, וַהֲדַר מְעַיֵּיל.

The Gemara asks: **If so,** if the rabbinic decree that prohibits a woman betrothed to a priest from partaking of *teruma* is due to concern for possible abrogation of the marriage, then a woman who **entered the wedding canopy but has not** yet **engaged in sexual intercourse** should **also** be prohibited from partaking of *teruma*, as the husband does not yet know whether she has blemishes. The Gemara answers: **There,** in that situation, **he investigates her** through the agency of his female relatives **and** only **then enters** the wedding canopy. Consequently, there is no longer any concern about abrogation.

אֶלָּא מֵעַתָּה, עֶבֶד כֹּהֵן שֶׁלְּקָחוֹ מִיִּשְׂרָאֵל לֹא לֵיכוּל בִּתְרוּמָה מִשּׁוּם סִימְפּוֹן! סִימְפּוֹן בַּעֲבָדִים לֵיכָּא; דְּאִי דְּאַבְרָאֵי – הָא קָחָזֵי לֵיהּ, וְאִי דְּגַוָּאֵי – לִמְלָאכָה קָא בָּעֵי, וְשֶׁבַּסֵּתֶר – לָא אִיכְפַּת לֵיהּ. נִמְצָא גַּנָּב אוֹ

The Gemara asks: **However, if that is so,** then according to this rationale, **a priest's slave whom** the priest **purchased from an Israelite should not partake of** *teruma*, **due to** concern of **abrogation.** Perhaps the priest will discover a defect in the slave, resulting in the retroactive cancellation of the acquisition and causing the slave to return to his Israelite master after he had mistakenly eaten *teruma*. The Gemara answers: **There is no abrogation with regard to slaves,**[H] since no type of defect could cause the cancellation of the transaction. The reason for this is **that if** the defect **is external, then he sees it** at the point of sale and accepts it. **And if** the defect **is internal,** since **he needs him for labor, concealed** defects **do not concern him.** With regard to other types of defects, e.g., if **he was discovered** to be **a thief or**

Perek **V**
Daf **58** Amud **a**

LANGUAGE

Gambler [*kuvyustus*] – קוּבְיוּסְטוּס: From the Greek κυβευτής, *kubeutēs*, meaning one who plays with dice, a gambler. The defect is not only the amount of time he wastes by being involved in gambling, but there is also the possibility that he may lose money in the game and steal in order to pay his debts.

קוּבְיוּסְטוּס – הִגִּיעוֹ. מַאי אִיכָּא – לִסְטִים מְזוּיָּין אוֹ מוּכְתָּב לַמַּלְכוּת – הָנְהוּ קָלָא אִית לְהוּ.

a gambler [*kuvyustus*],[LHN] **it has come to him,** meaning that the seller has caught the buyer in a binding transaction, and he cannot annul the sale due to this kind of defect, as these characteristics are common in slaves. **What is** the *halakha* if it was discovered that the slave was **an armed bandit or** that **the king** had **signed** his death warrant, and there is a danger that the government will catch him and execute him? These are serious and uncommon defects that in principle could invalidate a sale. However, **these** defects **generate publicity.**[N] In such unusual and severe circumstances, everyone is aware of them. Therefore, it is assumed that the buyer knew about them as well and nevertheless acquiesced to buy the slave. Consequently, there is no reason to revoke the sale of a slave.

HALAKHA

A thief or a gambler – גַּנָּב אוֹ קוּבְיוּסְטוּס: If one bought a slave and discovered that the slave was an armed robber, this is considered a defect that makes him worthless, since the king will presumably catch the slave and kill him. Similarly, if the slave had been registered as belonging to the king, this is also a defect that voids the transaction. However, if the slave is found to be a thief or a kidnapper, the buyer cannot renege, since it is presumed that slaves act in this way. The Rema writes that discovering the slave to be a kidnapper is akin to finding out that he is an armed robber. But if he turns out to be a gambler, this does not void the transaction (Rambam *Sefer Kinyan*, *Hilkhot Mekhira* 15:13; *Shulḥan Arukh*, *Ḥoshen Mishpat* 232:10).

NOTES

Gambler – קוּבְיוּסְטוּס: This word is from Greek, and there is some dispute among the commentaries about the meaning of the word in the Gemara. Rabbeinu Gershom, Rashi, and the Rivan explain that this is a kidnapper (see Rambam). *Tosafot* express puzzlement at this interpretation and prefer the explanation of Rabbeinu Ḥananel, that it means a gambler.

Generate publicity – קָלָא אִית לְהוּ: Rashi explains that since matters like this generally become public knowledge, if one bought the slave regardless, it appears that he considered this defect and accepted it. Consequently, he may not renege on his transaction. However, Rabbeinu Tam, Rambam, and others explain that if the buyer was unaware of such a major defect or of any hidden blemish that could cause the slave to be idle from work, such as epilepsy or skin boils, the transaction may be annulled. In this case, however, the defect is common knowledge and therefore there is no concern that someone would inadvertently buy such a slave (see Ra'avad).

מִכְּדִי, בֵּין לְמָר וּבֵין לְמָר לָא אָכְלָה. מַאי בֵּינַיְיהוּ? אִיכָּא בֵּינַיְיהוּ: קִבֵּל, מָסַר, וְהָלַךְ.

The Gemara asks: **After all, according to this Sage,** Ulla, **and according to that Sage,** Rav Shmuel bar Rav Yehuda, **she may not partake** of *teruma*, so **what** is the difference **between them?** The Gemara answers: The practical difference **between them is** in cases where **he accepted,** or **he transferred or went.**[N] If the husband explicitly accepted her blemishes, there is no concern with regard to abrogation, but there is still a concern that she will give her family members *teruma* wine. Conversely, if the father transferred his daughter to the agents of the husband and entrusted her to their care, or if the father's own agents went with the girl and the agents of the husband, there is no longer concern that she might give her family members *teruma*, as she is not with them, but there is still a concern about abrogation.

״רַבִּי טַרְפוֹן אוֹמֵר: נוֹתְנִין לָהּ הַכֹּל תְּרוּמָה״ וכו׳. אָמַר אַבָּיֵי: מַחְלוֹקֶת בְּבַת כֹּהֵן לְכֹהֵן, אֲבָל בְּבַת יִשְׂרָאֵל לְכֹהֵן – דִּבְרֵי הַכֹּל מֶחֱצָה חוּלִּין וּמֶחֱצָה תְּרוּמָה.

§ The mishna states that there is a dispute with regard to how a priest must provide for the sustenance of his betrothed once the appointed time for the marriage arrives. **Rabbi Tarfon says: He may give her everything** from **teruma.** Rabbi Akiva says: He must give her half non-sacred food and half may be *teruma*. **Abaye said:** This **dispute** is referring **to a daughter** of **a priest** betrothed **to a priest. But** with regard to **an Israelite woman** who was betrothed **to a priest, all agree** that he must give her **half non-sacred** food **and half** may be ***teruma.*** A priest's daughter is familiar with the *halakhot* of *teruma* and knows how to handle it when she is ritually impure, but when an Israelite woman is not yet familiar with these procedures, there is concern that she might defile the *teruma*. Consequently, she is given some non-sacred food to use as well.

וְאָמַר אַבָּיֵי: מַחְלוֹקֶת בַּאֲרוּסָה, אֲבָל בִּנְשׂוּאָה – דִּבְרֵי הַכֹּל מֶחֱצָה חוּלִּין וּמֶחֱצָה תְּרוּמָה.

And Abaye also **said** that this **dispute** is referring only to **a betrothed woman** whose wedding date has arrived, **but** with regard to **a married woman, all agree** that her husband must give her **half** of her needs from **non-sacred** food **and half** may be ***teruma,*** as it is not appropriate for his wife to have to go to the trouble of selling *teruma* in order to obtain non-sacred food.

תַּנְיָא נָמֵי הָכִי, רַבִּי טַרְפוֹן אוֹמֵר: נוֹתְנִין לָהּ הַכֹּל תְּרוּמָה, רַבִּי עֲקִיבָא אוֹמֵר: מֶחֱצָה חוּלִּין וּמֶחֱצָה תְּרוּמָה. בַּמֶּה דְּבָרִים אֲמוּרִים – בְּבַת כֹּהֵן לְכֹהֵן, אֲבָל בַּת יִשְׂרָאֵל לְכֹהֵן – דִּבְרֵי הַכֹּל מֶחֱצָה חוּלִּין וּמֶחֱצָה תְּרוּמָה. בַּמֶּה דְּבָרִים אֲמוּרִים – בַּאֲרוּסָה, אֲבָל בִּנְשׂוּאָה – דִּבְרֵי הַכֹּל מֶחֱצָה חוּלִּין וּמֶחֱצָה תְּרוּמָה.

This is also taught in a *baraita*: **Rabbi Tarfon says: He may give her everything** from ***teruma,*** and **Rabbi Akiva says: Half** must be **non-sacred** food **and half** may be ***teruma.***[H] **In what** case **is this statement said?** With regard to **a daughter** of **a priest** betrothed **to a priest. But** with regard to **an Israelite woman** betrothed **to a priest, all agree** that she gets **half non-sacred** food **and half** may be ***teruma.* In what case is this statement said? With regard to a betrothed woman, but with regard to a married woman, all agree** that he must give **half non-sacred** food **and half** may be ***teruma.***

רַבִּי יְהוּדָה בֶּן בְּתֵירָא אוֹמֵר: נוֹתְנִין לָהּ שְׁתֵּי יָדוֹת שֶׁל תְּרוּמָה, וְאַחַת שֶׁל חוּלִּין. רַבִּי יְהוּדָה אוֹמֵר: נוֹתֵן לָהּ הַכֹּל תְּרוּמָה, וְהִיא מוֹכֶרֶת וְלוֹקַחַת בִּדְמֵיהֶם חוּלִּין. רַבָּן שִׁמְעוֹן בֶּן גַּמְלִיאֵל אוֹמֵר: כׇּל מָקוֹם שֶׁהוּזְכְּרָה תְּרוּמָה – נוֹתְנִין לָהּ כִּפְלַיִם בְּחוּלִּין.

Rabbi Yehuda ben Beteira says: He need not give half and half, but rather **he may give her two parts *teruma***[N] **and one** part **non-sacred** food. **Rabbi Yehuda says: He may give her all** of it **in *teruma,* but** as the value of *teruma* is lower than that of non-sacred food, the amount must suffice so that when **she sells** *teruma* during the days when she is ritually impure, **she can buy** a sufficient quantity of **non-sacred food with the money. Rabban Shimon ben Gamliel says: Wherever *teruma* is mentioned, he** must **give her double** the amount that she would receive **of non-sacred food,** so that she will not have difficulty locating buyers for her *teruma*. *Teruma* is less popular and its price is significantly lower, since its use is restricted. But if she receives a large amount of *teruma*, she will be able to sell it at an even lower price and locate a buyer more easily.

NOTES

He accepted, or he transferred or went – קִבֵּל מָסַר וְהָלַךְ: Rashi explains here, and in greater detail in a parallel passage in tractate *Kiddushin* (11a), that these three words hint to three different situations. The verb accepted means that the husband declares in advance that he accepts any blemishes that would be found in in his bride. The term transferred is referring to a case where the father had already transferred his daughter into the care of the husband's agents. The word went means that agents of the father accompanied the husband's agents. In the first case, there is no concern about abrogation but there is a concern that the wife might give *teruma* wine to her family members. In the other cases, there is no concern about *teruma* wine but there is concern about abrogation.

Tosafot offer an alternative explanation: In all three cases, there is no concern of abrogation, as the transaction has already been finalized, but there is a concern that the bride may give *teruma* wine to others, as even when she goes with the agents, she might give her father or the agents some *teruma* wine. The Meiri explains that there are really only two situations involved: Accepted, means that the husband accepted the blemishes; transferred and went, means that the father gave his daughter to agents and accompanied them. In the latter case, there is concern about abrogation but not that she may give *teruma* wine to others, as her father is an adult and knows how to take care not to partake of *teruma*. Rabbeinu Crescas Vidal also explains that only two cases are being discussed: The husband accepted the blemishes, or the father transferred and went, meaning he gave his daughter to the agents and went away. Consequently, there is only concern for abrogation.

Rabbi Avraham *Av Beit Din* and the Ra'avad explain differently, that there is only one case here: The father accepted the betrothal money, gave her to the agents, and went away. Consequently, there is concern only for abrogation, but there is no concern that she may give *teruma* wine to those not authorized to drink it.

Two parts *teruma* – שְׁתֵּי יָדוֹת שֶׁל תְּרוּמָה: The explanation for this opinion is fairly simple: If one deducts the period of menstruation and the additional time needed to become ritually pure, the amount of non-sacred food needed comes out to approximately one third of the total allotment (see Maharshal). The *Ḥatam Sofer* says that this calculation is referring to a married woman, who becomes impure periodically due to conjugal relations with her husband as well as during menstruation.

HALAKHA

Half must be non-sacred food and half may be *teruma* – מֶחֱצָה חוּלִּין וּמֶחֱצָה תְּרוּמָה: If the husband is a priest and he supports his wife through a third party, he may give her half *teruma* and half non-sacred food, in accordance with the opinion of Rabbi Akiva. All agree with his opinion with regard to a married woman, and moreover the *halakha* is in accordance with his opinion in his disputes with another *tanna* (Rambam *Sefer Nashim, Hilkhot Ishut* 12:13).

מַאי בֵּינַיְיהוּ? אִיכָּא בֵּינַיְיהוּ טִירְחָא.

The Gemara asks: **What is** the difference **between** the opinions of Rabbi Yehuda and Rabban Shimon ben Gamliel? The Gemara answers: **The** practical difference **between them** is with regard to **effort.** According to Rabbi Yehuda, she must make an effort to find buyers who will provide her with enough non-sacred food for her needs, and consequently, according to him the husband must provide an amount of *teruma* that is equal in value to the amount of non-sacred food to which she is entitled. In contrast, Rabban Shimon ben Gamliel adds additional *teruma* to her allotment beyond this amount, so that she will not be forced to go to as much trouble to sell it.

״הַיָּבָם אֵינוֹ מַאֲכִיל בִּתְרוּמָה״. מַאי טַעְמָא? ״קִנְיַן כַּסְפּוֹ״ אָמַר רַחֲמָנָא, וְהַאי – קִנְיַן דְּאָחִיו הוּא.

§ The mishna states that **a *yavam* does not enable** the *yevama* **to partake of *teruma*.** The Gemara asks: **What is the reason** for this? **The Merciful One states** in the Torah: **"The acquisition of his money"** (Leviticus 22:11) may partake of *teruma*, **but this** woman **is his brother's acquisition** and not his, since a *yavam* does not complete his marriage to the *yevama* until he consummates the marriage.

״עָשְׂתָה שִׁשָּׁה חֳדָשִׁים בִּפְנֵי הַבַּעַל״. הַשְׁתָּא בִּפְנֵי הַבַּעַל אָמְרַתְּ – לָא, בִּפְנֵי הַיָּבָם מִיבַּעְיָא?! זוֹ וְאֵין צָרִיךְ לוֹמַר זוֹ קָתָנֵי.

§ The mishna said that if **she completed six months** from the time of the request for marriage **under the aegis of the husband** and another six months under the aegis of the *yavam*, she may not partake of *teruma*. It then says that this is also true if she completed most of the year under the aegis of the husband, and then it says that this is also true if she completed most of the time under the aegis of the *yavam*. The Gemara asks: **Now** that **you say** that if she completed most of the time **under the aegis of the husband** this does **not** enable her to partake of *teruma*, **is** it **necessary** to say that the same is true if she spent most of the time **under the aegis of the *yavam*?** The Gemara answers: The *tanna* **teaches** the mishna employing the style: **This, and it is unnecessary to say that,** meaning that the cases are organized from the less obvious to the more obvious.

״זוֹ מִשְׁנָה רִאשׁוֹנָה״ כּו׳. מַאי טַעְמָא? אָמַר עוּלָּא וְאִיתֵּימָא רַב שְׁמוּאֵל בַּר יְהוּדָה: מִשּׁוּם סִימְפּוֹן.

§ The mishna states that **this** ruling, that a woman betrothed to a priest may partake of *teruma* while she is still in her father's house if the time for her wedding has arrived, is according to the **initial** version of the **mishna.**[B] But that according to the final version, she may not partake of *teruma* until she has actually entered the wedding canopy. The Gemara asks: **What is the reason** for this later ruling? **Ulla said, and some say** that **Rav Shmuel bar Yehuda** said, that it is **due to** concern about **abrogation,** as the woman may have some blemish that will cause the annulment of the marriage, and it will then be clear that she consumed *teruma* unlawfully.

בִּשְׁלָמָא לְעוּלָּא, קַמַּיְיתָא – שֶׁמָּא יְמַזְגוּ לָהּ כּוֹס בְּבֵית אָבִיהָ, וּבַתְרַיְיתָא – מִשּׁוּם סִימְפּוֹן.

The Gemara comments: **Granted, according to** the opinion of **Ulla, the first** ruling that the Sages taught in the initial version of the mishna, namely that she may not partake of *teruma* in her father's house immediately after betrothal, is because Ulla was concerned **lest** someone **pour her a cup** of *teruma* wine while she would be **in her father's house. And the latter** ruling, that she may not partake of *teruma* until she actually enters the wedding canopy, even after the time for marriage arrives, is **due to** concern about **abrogation.** Consequently, there are two different reasons for the two different rulings.[H]

BACKGROUND

The initial version of the mishna – מִשְׁנָה רִאשׁוֹנָה: This is referring to an ancient Mishna that was in existence long before Rabbi Yehuda HaNasi. Occasionally, statements of *tanna'im* were recorded in written form in early generations. Statements of the initial text of the Mishna are sometimes cited in Rabbi Yehuda HaNasi's version of the Mishna, followed by the version formulated by later Sages. The mention of an initial version of the mishna might be followed by a statement of Rabbi Akiva, as his version of the Mishna and that of his students, e.g., Rabbi Meir, formed the basis of Rabbi Yehuda HaNasi's Mishna. It is often clear from a discussion that a mishna is referring to an earlier version of its ruling, as later Sages dispute the explanation and precise formulation of statements they heard from their teachers. Some *mishnayot* date back to the early days of the Second Temple. Likewise, Beit Shammai and Beit Hillel dispute the meaning of certain initial versions of *mishnayot*.

HALAKHA

The reason for the final version of the mishna – טַעַם מִשְׁנָה אַחֲרוֹנָה: The Rambam writes that the reason for the final ruling of the mishna is the concern that she might serve *teruma* wine to her family members. He does not mention concern for abrogation at all, and it seems that he relies on the Gemara in tractate *Kiddushin* (10b–11a), and a comment of *Tosafot* there (Rambam *Sefer Zera'im*, *Hilkhot Terumot* 6:3).

אֶלָּא לְרַב שְׁמוּאֵל בַּר יְהוּדָה, קַמַּיְיתָא מִשּׁוּם סִימְפּוֹן וּבַתְרַיְיתָא מִשּׁוּם סִימְפּוֹן?! מַאי בֵּינַיְיהוּ?

However, according **to Rav Shmuel bar Yehuda, the first** ruling was **due to abrogation and the latter** ruling was also **due to abrogation.** If so, **what is** the difference **between** the reasoning of the initial version of the mishna and the decision of the court that convened after them?

אִיכָּא בֵּינַיְיהוּ בְּדִיקַת חוּץ. מָר סָבַר: בְּדִיקַת חוּץ – שְׁמָהּ בְּדִיקָה, וּמָר סָבַר: בְּדִיקַת חוּץ לָא שְׁמָהּ בְּדִיקָה.

The Gemara answers: The practical difference **between them is** with regard to **superficial investigation,** i.e., the investigation that could have been conducted on his behalf by his female relatives, which could have been only a superficial investigation. One **Sage holds** that **superficial investigation is considered** a valid **investigation,** and therefore once he requested to marry her and the marriage date arrived, there is no concern of a later abrogation, **and** one **Sage holds** that **superficial investigation is not considered** a valid **investigation,** and consequently there is still concern that when he consummates the marriage he will find some blemish on her and abrogate the marriage.

מתני׳ הַמַּקְדִּישׁ מַעֲשֵׂה יְדֵי אִשְׁתּוֹ – הֲרֵי זוֹ עוֹשָׂה וְאוֹכֶלֶת. הַמּוֹתָר, רַבִּי מֵאִיר אוֹמֵר: הֶקְדֵּשׁ, רַבִּי יוֹחָנָן הַסַּנְדְּלָר אוֹמֵר: חוּלִּין.

MISHNA **If one consecrates his wife's earnings,**[H] meaning anything she produces, such as thread that she spins from wool, which, according to the Sages' ordinance, belongs to her husband, **she may work and sustain** herself from her earnings, as the consecration is ineffective. However, there is a dispute with regard to **the surplus,**[N] meaning any earnings she produces in excess of the amount she is required to produce for her husband. **Rabbi Meir says:** The surplus is **consecrated** property, and **Rabbi Yoḥanan the Cobbler says:** The surplus is also **non-sacred.**

גמ׳ אָמַר רַב הוּנָא אָמַר רַב: יְכוֹלָה אִשָּׁה לוֹמַר לְבַעְלָהּ "אֵינִי נִיזּוֹנֶת וְאֵינִי עוֹשָׂה". קָסָבַר: כִּי תַּקִּינוּ רַבָּנַן מְזוֹנֵי – עִיקָּר, וּמַעֲשֵׂה יָדֶיהָ – מִשּׁוּם אֵיבָה. וְכִי אָמְרָה "אֵינִי נִיזּוֹנֶת וְאֵינִי עוֹשָׂה" – הָרְשׁוּת בְּיָדָהּ.

GEMARA **Rav Huna said** that **Rav said: A woman may say to her husband: I will not be sustained** by you and, in turn, **I will not work,** i.e., you will not keep my earnings. **He holds** that **when the Sages instituted** the various obligations and rights of a husband and wife, the husband's obligation to provide for the wife's **sustenance** was **the primary** one, **and** they then decreed that **her earnings** belong to him in return, **due to** concern about **animosity.** If he would be obligated to provide for her sustenance but she would be allowed to work and keep her earnings, he would resent her. Since her right to sustenance is the primary one, **if she says: I will not be sustained** by you and, in turn, **I will not work,**[H] i.e., you will not keep my earnings, **she has permission to** do so. As the arrangement was established for her benefit, she may cancel it if it is not suitable for her.

מֵיתִיבֵי: תִּקְּנוּ מְזוֹנוֹת תַּחַת מַעֲשֵׂה יָדֶיהָ! אֵימָא: תִּקְּנוּ מַעֲשֵׂה יָדֶיהָ תַּחַת מְזוֹנוֹת.

The Gemara **raises an objection** from a *baraita*: **They instituted** the husband's responsibility for her **sustenance in exchange for** his right to **her earnings.** This indicates that the primary enactment is the husband's right to his wife's earnings, and the ordinance that requires him to provide her with sustenance comes as a result. According to this, the wife would not be allowed to waive the arrangement, contrary to Rav Huna's statement. The Gemara responds: Emend the text of the *baraita* and **say** instead: **They instituted her earnings in exchange for** the husband's responsibility for her **sustenance.**

לֵימָא מְסַיֵּיעַ לֵיהּ: הַמַּקְדִּישׁ מַעֲשֵׂה יְדֵי אִשְׁתּוֹ – הֲרֵי הִיא עוֹשָׂה וְאוֹכֶלֶת. מַאי לָאו – בְּנִיזּוֹנֶת? לָא, בְּשֶׁאֵינָהּ נִיזּוֹנֶת.

The Gemara raises an objection: **Let us say that** the mishna **supports** Rav Huna's opinion, as it is taught: **If one consecrates his wife's earnings, she may work and sustain** herself from her earnings. **What, is it not** discussing a woman **who is sustained** by her husband, meaning that he is willing to sustain her, although she relinquishes her right to sustenance in accordance with Rav Huna's principle? Therefore, her earnings do not belong to him to consecrate. The Gemara answers: **No,** it is discussing a woman **who is not sustained** by her husband, as he does not have sufficient funds to sustain her. Consequently, there is no proof with regard to Rav Huna's statement.

HALAKHA

If one consecrates his wife's earnings – הַמַּקְדִּישׁ מַעֲשֵׂה יְדֵי אִשְׁתּוֹ: If one consecrates his wife's earnings, she can nevertheless sustain herself from her earnings, and the additional amount is also non-sacred, in accordance with the opinion of Rabbi Yoḥanan the Cobbler, as the Gemara (59a) ruled in accordance with his opinion (Rambam *Sefer Hafla'a, Hilkhot Arakhin VaḤaramim* 6:28; *Shulḥan Arukh, Even HaEzer* 81:1).

If she says: I will not be sustained by you and I will not work – אָמְרָה אֵינִי נִיזּוֹנֶת וְאֵינִי עוֹשָׂה: If a woman tells her husband that she will not be sustained from his possessions and will not perform labor for him, her wishes are respected, as the Sages established her earnings in exchange for her sustenance, in accordance with the Gemara's ruling in favor of Rav Huna's opinion (107b). The Rema writes that this stipulation refers only to earnings that a woman produces to provide income, but in all cases she is obligated to see to the needs of her home (Rambam *Sefer Nashim, Hilkhot Ishut* 12:4 and *Maggid Mishne* there; *Shulḥan Arukh, Even HaEzer* 69:4, 80:15).

NOTES

The surplus – הַמּוֹתָר: Rashi, the Rivan, and many other early authorities explain that this clause of the mishna is a separate *halakha* that is not intrinsically connected to the first clause, and that it is referring to one who explicitly stated that he is consecrating the surplus. However, it is suggested in the *Shita Mekubbetzet* that *Tosafot* do not concur with this opinion. Similarly, the Rosh interprets the mishna as referring to one who consecrated all of his wife's earnings without differentiating. However, he says that there is a distinction in the *halakha* between the basic, required amount and the surplus amount she produced. The Meiri explains that the mishna discusses one who consecrated the surplus amount together with the rest of his wife's earnings, in addition to one who explicitly specified the surplus to be consecrated.

There is also a similar dispute with regard to the exact definition of the surplus. Rashi, together with most of the early authorities, explains that the surplus mentioned here has a precise definition, and it refers to whatever a woman produces beyond the quota required of her, as explained in a mishna below (see 64b). Others explain that the surplus is what remains after the wife has sustained herself from her earnings, even if she did not produce more than the required quota (*Talmidei Rabbeinu Yona*). These disparate explanations, which are somewhat connected, form the basis of the different interpretations of this Gemara.

אִי בְּשֶׁאֵינָהּ נִיזּוֹנֶת – מַאי לְמֵימְרָא? אֲפִילּוּ לְמַאן דְּאָמַר יָכוֹל הָרַב לוֹמַר לְעֶבֶד "עֲשֵׂה עִמִּי וְאֵינִי זָנְךָ", הָנֵי מִילֵּי – בְּעֶבֶד כְּנַעֲנִי, דְּלָא כְּתִיב בֵּיהּ "עִמָּךְ". אֲבָל עֶבֶד עִבְרִי דִּכְתִיב בֵּיהּ "עִמָּךְ" – לָא, וְכָל שֶׁכֵּן אִשְׁתּוֹ!

The Gemara asks: If it is discussing a woman **who is not sustained, what** is the purpose **of stating** that he may not consecrate her earnings? **Even according to the one who says** that **a master can say to** his **slave: Work for me but I will not sustain you,**[H] **this applies** only to **a Canaanite slave,**[B] **about whom it is not written: "With you." But** with regard to **a Hebrew slave**[B] **about whom it is written:** "It is good for him **with you"** (Deuteronomy 15:16), this does **not** apply, and the master must sustain him just as he sustains the members of his own household. **And** this is true **all the more so** with regard to **his wife,** as there is a specific obligation of sustenance. Consequently, if he does not do so, he certainly has no right to her earnings.

סֵיפָא אִיצְטְרִיךְ לֵיהּ; מוֹתָר, רַבִּי מֵאִיר אוֹמֵר: הֶקְדֵּשׁ, רַבִּי יוֹחָנָן הַסַּנְדְּלָר אוֹמֵר: חוּלִּין.

The Gemara answers: This *halakha* did not need to be stated, but **the latter clause was necessary,** as it contains a novelty with regard to **the surplus: Rabbi Meir says** that the surplus is **consecrated** property, and **Rabbi Yoḥanan the Cobbler says** it is **non-sacred.**

וּפְלִיגָא דְּרֵישׁ לָקִישׁ. דַּאֲמַר רֵישׁ לָקִישׁ: לָא תֵּימָא טַעֲמָא דְּרַבִּי מֵאִיר מִשּׁוּם דְּקָסָבַר אָדָם מַקְדִּישׁ דָּבָר שֶׁלֹּא בָּא לָעוֹלָם, אֶלָּא טַעֲמָא דְּרַבִּי מֵאִיר: מִתּוֹךְ שֶׁיָּכוֹל לְכוֹפָהּ לְמַעֲשֵׂה יָדֶיהָ – נַעֲשָׂה כְּאוֹמֵר לָהּ "יִקָּדְשׁוּ יָדַיִךְ לְעוֹשֵׂיהֶם".

The Gemara comments: This opinion of Rav Huna **disputes** that **of Reish Lakish, as Reish Lakish said: Do not say** that **the reason for** the opinion of **Rabbi Meir** is that **since he maintains** that **a person may consecrate an object that has not** yet **come into the world,** the consecration can take effect even on her future earnings. **Rather,** say that **the reason for** the opinion of **Rabbi Meir** is that **since he can compel her** to produce **her earnings**[H] for him, it is as if he had a certain legal claim to the products of her hands, i.e., her earnings. Consequently, **he is considered as if he had said to her: Your hands are consecrated to the One Who made them,**[HN] and the consecration can therefore take effect on something that already exists. Since Reish Lakish said that he may compel her to produce earnings for him, the implication is that she may not say: I will not be sustained and I will not work.

וְהָא לָא אֲמַר לָהּ הָכִי! כֵּיוָן דִּשְׁמַעִינַן לֵיהּ לְרַבִּי מֵאִיר דְּאָמַר: אֵין אָדָם מוֹצִיא דְּבָרָיו לְבַטָּלָה – נַעֲשָׂה כְּאוֹמֵר לָהּ "יִקָּדְשׁוּ יָדַיִךְ לְעוֹשֵׂיהֶם".

With regard to Reish Lakish's statement, the Gemara asks: **But he did not say this to her;** rather, he said that he was consecrating her earnings. The Gemara answers: **Since we heard** that **Rabbi Meir said: A person does not say things for naught,** and according to this principle, when one says something that has no halakhic meaning, it is interpreted as if he had said something that does have halakhic relevance, **he is considered as if he had said to her: Your hands are consecrated to the One Who made them.**

HALAKHA

Work for me but I will not sustain you – עֲשֵׂה עִמִּי וְאֵינִי זָנְךָ: A master may tell his Canaanite slave: Work for me but I will not sustain you, and the slave must then go and beg for food and receive his sustenance from charity (Rambam *Sefer Kinyan, Hilkhot Avadim* 9:7).

He can compel her to produce her earnings – יָכוֹל לְכוֹפָהּ לְמַעֲשֵׂה יָדֶיהָ: If a woman refuses to perform labor that she is obligated by marriage to perform, she may be compelled to do so, according to some even by corporal punishment (Rambam *Sefer Nashim, Hilkhot Ishut* 21:10; *Shulḥan Arukh, Even HaEzer* 80:15, and in the comment of Rema).

Your hands are consecrated to the One Who made them – יִקָּדְשׁוּ יָדַיִךְ לְעוֹשֵׂיהֶם: In the case of one who says to his wife: Your hands are consecrated to the One Who made them, all her earnings will be consecrated, since her hands are subjugated to him to perform labor. This is according to the Rambam's understanding that if the husband said this explicitly, the Rabbis concede to Reish Lakish that the consecration takes effect. However, the Ran says that even in this case her earnings are not consecrated, as she has the right to say: I will not be sustained by you, and in turn I will not work (Rambam *Sefer Hafla'a, Hilkhot Arakhin VaḤaramim* 6:28; *Shulḥan Arukh, Even HaEzer* 81:1, and in the comment of Rema).

BACKGROUND

Canaanite slave – עֶבֶד כְּנַעֲנִי: A Canaanite slave is a non-Jewish slave purchased by a Jew (see Leviticus 25:44–46). After he is purchased, such a slave must be immersed in a ritual bath, and, if male, circumcised. These acts signify a change in the slave's status. Although he is not yet a Jew in all respects, a Canaanite slave must observe all of the Torah's prohibitions and must fulfill all positive mitzvot that are not time bound. In many respects, Canaanite slaves are their masters' property and may be sold and purchased like other possessions. His master can free him by giving him a bill of manumission, a document resembling a bill of divorce in its format, but there is a positive mitzva not to free a Canaanite slave without compelling reasons. There is one exception to the above principle: A slave goes free automatically if his master blinds him, knocks out his tooth, or destroys any one of twenty-four other extremities. This applies regardless of whether the master caused the damage intentionally (see Exodus 21:26–27).

A Hebrew slave – עֶבֶד עִבְרִי: A Hebrew slave is an adult male Jew who becomes the slave of another Jew. There are two ways in which a Jew can enter such servitude: (1) The court may sell a thief into slavery if he does not have the means to make restitution for his theft (Exodus 22:2). (2) If a Jew becomes impoverished, he may choose to sell himself to seek relief from his poverty (Leviticus 25:39). A Hebrew slave sold by the court goes free after serving his master for six years (Exodus 21:2), but one who sells himself as a slave may sell himself for six years or for a longer period. In the Jubilee Year, all Hebrew slaves are freed irrespective of how long they have served (Leviticus 25:40). A Hebrew slave may also attain his freedom by paying his master the value of the remainder of the term for which he was sold. If a Hebrew slave has a wife and children, his master is obligated to provide for their sustenance as well.

NOTES

Your hands are consecrated to the One Who made them – יִקָּדְשׁוּ יָדַיִךְ לְעוֹשֵׂיהֶם: The Rashba asks: How can a husband consecrate his wife's hands? Obviously her hands do not belong to him; he cannot sell them or give them away. Even with regard to a slave who is his property, the *halakha* does not allow the owner to consecrate the slave's hands, and therefore he certainly may not do this with his wife. The Rashba therefore explains that it means that he can consecrate her hands vis-à-vis the earnings they produce, just as one can consecrate a tree for its fruit (see *Tosafot* and *Avnei Milluim*).

וְסָבַר רַבִּי מֵאִיר אֵין אָדָם מַקְדִּישׁ דָּבָר שֶׁלֹּא בָּא לָעוֹלָם? וְהָתַנְיָא: הָאוֹמֵר לְאִשָּׁה "הֲרֵי אַתְּ מְקוּדֶּשֶׁת לִי לְאַחַר שֶׁאֶתְגַּיֵּיר" אוֹ "לְאַחַר שֶׁתִּתְגַּיְּירִי", "לְאַחַר שֶׁאֶשְׁתַּחְרֵר", "לְאַחַר שֶׁתִּשְׁתַּחְרְרִי", "לְאַחַר שֶׁיָּמוּת בַּעְלֵיךְ" אוֹ "שֶׁתָּמוּת אֲחוֹתֵיךְ" אוֹ "לְאַחַר שֶׁיַּחֲלוֹץ לֵיךְ יְבָמֵיךְ", רַבִּי מֵאִיר אוֹמֵר: מְקוּדֶּשֶׁת.

The Gemara asks: **Does Rabbi Meir hold** that **a person may not consecrate an object that has not** yet **come into the world?**[H] **Isn't it taught** in a *baraita* that if a gentile **says to a woman: You are hereby betrothed to me after I convert;**[H] **or** if she was a gentile and he said to her: You are hereby betrothed to me **after you convert;** or if he was a slave and said to her: **After I am emancipated;** or if she was a maidservant and he said to her: **After you are emancipated;** or if she was married and he said to her: **After your husband dies; or** if he was married to her sister and he said: **After your sister dies,** as at that point the betrothal could take effect; **or** if she was a widow waiting for her *yavam* and he said to her: **After your** ***yavam*** **performs** ***ḥalitza*** **with you, Rabbi Meir says:** If any of these cases occurred, **she is betrothed.** Apparently Rabbi Meir maintains that betrothal can take effect even on something that has not yet come into being.

מֵהַהִיא – אִין, מֵהָא לֵיכָּא לְמִשְׁמַע מִינַּהּ.

The Gemara answers: Actually, **from that** *baraita,* **one can** learn that this is Rabbi Meir's opinion, but Reish Lakish merely wanted to say that **no** inference is **to be learned from this** mishna, as it is possible to explain Rabbi Meir's words in another way, based on the principle that a person does not say things for naught.

"הַמּוֹתָר, רַבִּי מֵאִיר אוֹמֵר: הֶקְדֵּשׁ". אֵימַת קָדוֹשׁ? רַב וּשְׁמוּאֵל דְּאָמְרִי תַּרְוַיְיהוּ: מוֹתָר לְאַחַר מִיתָה קָדוֹשׁ. רַב אַדָּא בַּר אַהֲבָה אָמַר: מוֹתָר מֵחַיִּים קָדוֹשׁ.

§ The mishna states that with regard to **the surplus, Rabbi Meir says: It is consecrated** property. The Gemara asks: According to this opinion, **when** does the surplus amount become **consecrated? Rav and Shmuel both said: The surplus is consecrated** only **after** the woman's **death. Rav Adda bar Ahava said: The surplus is consecrated while** she is still **alive.**

הֲוֵי בָּהּ רַב פַּפָּא: בְּמַאי? אִילֵימָא בִּמְעַלֶּה לָהּ מְזוֹנוֹת, וּמַעֲלֶה לָהּ מָעָה כֶּסֶף לִצְרָכֶיהָ – מַאי טַעְמָא דְּמַאן דְּאָמַר לְאַחַר מִיתָה קָדוֹשׁ?

Rav Pappa discussed it, as he was perplexed by this dispute: With regard **to what** do they argue? **If we say** that the husband **provides for her sustenance and** additionally **provides her with a silver** ***ma'a*** coin every week **for** the rest of **her needs,** as he is obligated to do (see 64b), then **what is the reason for** the opinion of **the one who said it is consecrated** only **after** her **death?** As the husband has fulfilled all of his obligations and is consequently the owner of his wife's earnings, he should be capable of consecrating them.

וְאֶלָּא כְּשֶׁאֵין מַעֲלֶה לָהּ מְזוֹנוֹת, וְלֹא מַעֲלֶה לָהּ מָעָה כֶּסֶף לִצְרָכֶיהָ – מַאי טַעְמָא דְּמַאן דְּאָמַר מֵחַיִּים קָדוֹשׁ?

And if we **rather** say that **he does not provide for her sustenance and does not provide her with a silver** ***ma'a*** **for her needs,** and she must consequently support herself entirely, then **what is the reason for** the opinion of **the one who said** that **it is consecrated in her lifetime?** It is possible that at some point she will not find sufficient employment, and since her husband does not provide for her sustenance or her other needs, she will need the money for herself and there will not be any surplus at all.

לְעוֹלָם בִּמְעַלֶּה לָהּ מְזוֹנוֹת וְאֵינוֹ מַעֲלֶה לָהּ מָעָה כֶּסֶף לִצְרָכֶיהָ. רַב וּשְׁמוּאֵל סָבְרִי: תִּיקְּנוּ

The Gemara answers: **Actually,** one must explain that they are discussing a situation where **he provides for her sustenance, but does not provide her with a silver** ***ma'a*** **for her needs,** and this is their dispute: **Rav and Shmuel maintain** that the main enactment was that **they established**

HALAKHA

A person may not consecrate an object that has not yet come into the world – אֵין אָדָם מַקְדִּישׁ דָּבָר שֶׁלֹּא בָּא לָעוֹלָם: One may not consecrate objects that have not yet come into the world, in accordance with the opinion of the Rabbis, who disagree with Rabbi Meir (Rambam *Sefer Hafla'a, Hilkhot Arakhin VaḤaramim* 6:26).

You are hereby betrothed to me after I convert, etc. – הֲרֵי אַתְּ מְקוּדֶּשֶׁת לִי לְאַחַר שֶׁאֶתְגַּיֵּיר וכו׳: If a gentile who says to a woman: You are betrothed to me after I convert, or after you convert, she is not betrothed, since he cannot at present betroth her, in accordance with the opinion of the Rabbis, who disagree with Rabbi Meir. However, if one betroths a *yevama,* saying that the betrothal will take effect after the *yavam* performs *ḥalitza,* the woman is of uncertain status with regard to betrothal, as some say that the betrothal can take effect as an uncertain betrothal even before the *ḥalitza* is performed (Rambam *Sefer Nashim, Hilkhot Ishut* 7:14, *Shulḥan Arukh, Even HaEzer* 40:5–6).

מְזוֹנוֹת תַּחַת מַעֲשֵׂה יָדֶיהָ, וּמָעָה כֶסֶף תַּחַת מוֹתָר. וְכֵיוָן דְּלָא קָא יָהֵיב לַהּ מָעָה כֶסֶף – מוֹתָר דִּידַהּ הָוֵי. רַב אַדָּא בַּר אַהֲבָה סָבַר: תִּקְּנוּ מְזוֹנוֹת תַּחַת מוֹתָר, וּמָעָה כֶסֶף תַּחַת מַעֲשֵׂה יָדֶיהָ. וְכֵיוָן דְּקָא יָהֵיב לַהּ מְזוֹנֵי – מוֹתָר דִּידֵיהּ הָוֵי.

sustenance in exchange for her earnings, and the **silver** ***ma'a*** coin that he must give her **in exchange for the surplus** that she continues to make beyond her quota. **And since he does not give her a silver** ***ma'a*** **the surplus is hers,** unless some of it is left after her death, in which case the husband inherits it. **Rav Adda bar Ahava maintains** that **they established sustenance in exchange for the surplus, and a silver** ***ma'a*** **in exchange for her earnings. And since he provides her with sustenance, the surplus is his,** and therefore the sanctity takes effect on it immediately when she produces the surplus.

בְּמַאי קָמִיפַּלְגִי? מָר סָבַר: מִידֵי דִּשְׁכִיחַ מִמִּידֵי דִּשְׁכִיחַ, וּמָר סָבַר: מִידֵי דְּקָיֵיץ מִמִּידֵי דְּקָיֵיץ.

The Gemara asks: **With regard to what do they disagree?** The Gemara explains: One **Sage,** i.e., Rav and Shmuel, **holds that** they established **something common** in exchange **for something common.** Consequently, they established sustenance, which is common, in exchange for earnings, which are also common. **And one Sage,** Rav Adda bar Ahava, **holds that** they established **something** with **a fixed amount** in exchange **for something** with a **fixed amount.** Consequently, since a silver *ma'a* is a fixed amount and the quota of a woman's earnings is also fixed, they established one in exchange for the other.

מֵיתִיבִי: תִּקְּנוּ מְזוֹנוֹת תַּחַת מַעֲשֵׂה יָדֶיהָ! אֵימָא, תַּחַת מוֹתַר מַעֲשֵׂה יָדֶיהָ.

The Gemara **raises an objection** to Rav Adda bar Ahava's opinion from a *baraita*: **They established sustenance in exchange for her earnings.** Apparently, sustenance is not in exchange for the surplus. The Gemara answers by emending the text of the *baraita*: **Say:** They established sustenance **in exchange for the surplus of her earnings.**

תָּא שְׁמַע: אִם אֵינוֹ נוֹתֵן לָהּ מָעָה כֶסֶף לְצוֹרְכֶיהָ – מַעֲשֵׂה יָדֶיהָ שֶׁלָּהּ! אֵימָא, מוֹתַר מַעֲשֵׂה יָדֶיהָ שֶׁלָּהּ. וְהָא עֲלָהּ קָתָנֵי: מָה הִיא עוֹשָׂה לוֹ – מִשְׁקַל חָמֵשׁ סְלָעִים שְׁתִי בִּיהוּדָה!

The Gemara attempts another proof from a mishna (64b): **Come** and **hear: If he does not give her a silver** ***ma'a*** **for her needs, her earnings** belong **to her.** This indicates that the earnings were established in exchange for the silver *ma'a*, as Rav Adda bar Ahava contended. The Gemara rejects this by emending the text of the mishna: **Say: The surplus of her earnings** belongs **to her.** The Gemara challenges the emendation: **But it is taught** in the continuation **of this** mishna: **What** is the fixed amount that **she** must **earn for him?** She must spin the **weight of five** ***sela*** of threads of the **warp in Judea,** which is the equivalent of ten *sela* according to the measurements of the Galilee. This clause implies that the mishna is not discussing the surplus but rather the quota of her required earnings.

הָכִי קָאָמַר: מַעֲשֵׂה יָדֶיהָ כַּמָּה הָוֵי, דְּלֵידַע מוֹתָר דִּידָהּ כַּמָּה – מִשְׁקַל חָמֵשׁ סְלָעִים שְׁתִי בִּיהוּדָה, שֶׁהֵן עֶשֶׂר סְלָעִים בַּגָּלִיל.

The Gemara answers: **This is what it is saying: How much is** the required amount of **her earnings,** so **that** one **can know how much** of what she produces constitutes **the surplus,** and to this the mishna replied: **The weight of five** ***sela*** of threads of the **warp in Judea, which is** the equivalent of **ten** ***sela*** according to the measurements of **the Galilee.**

אָמַר שְׁמוּאֵל: הֲלָכָה כְּרַבִּי יוֹחָנָן הַסַּנְדְּלָר.

§ **Shmuel said:** The ***halakha*** **is in accordance with** the opinion of **Rabbi Yoḥanan the Cobbler.** A husband may not consecrate his wife's earnings at all, as they have not yet come into being.

וּמִי אָמַר שְׁמוּאֵל הָכִי? וְהָתְנַן: ״קוּנָם שֶׁאֲנִי עוֹשָׂה לְפִיךָ״ – אֵינוֹ צָרִיךְ לְהָפֵר. רַבִּי עֲקִיבָא אוֹמֵר: יָפֵר, שֶׁמָּא תַּעֲדִיף עָלָיו יָתֵר מִן הָרָאוּי לוֹ. רַבִּי יוֹחָנָן בֶּן נוּרִי אוֹמֵר: יָפֵר, שֶׁמָּא יְגָרְשֶׁנָּה וּתְהֵא אֲסוּרָה לַחֲזוֹר.

The Gemara asks: **And did Shmuel** actually **say this?** But **didn't we learn** in a mishna (*Nedarim* 85a): If a woman said: **What I make to feed you,** i.e., what I earn for you, is forbidden **like an offering** [***konam***],[NH] the husband **does not need to nullify** this vow. She has a prior obligation to work for him, and therefore the *konam* cannot take effect on something that does not belong to her. **Rabbi Akiva says:** Even so, the husband **should nullify** the vow, **lest she produce more** earnings **than is appropriate for him,** and the *konam* will then take effect on the surplus amount. **Rabbi Yoḥanan ben Nuri said: He should nullify** the vow for a different reason, **lest he divorce her.** Since she rendered her earnings forbidden to him, **she will be prohibited from remarrying** him after her divorce, as it would then be impossible for him to avoid benefiting from his wife's earnings.

NOTES

Konam – קוּנָם: A *konam* is one of various types of vows, and its *halakhot* are explained in tractate *Nedarim*. The word *konam* seems to be an alternate term for an offering, and the basic concept of a *konam* is that one prohibits himself or others from deriving benefit from a particular object by making that object similar to a consecrated item. Despite this, there is a difference between a consecrated item and an object prohibited by a *konam*. Consecration is universal; whatever is consecrated becomes prohibited to everyone. In contrast, a *konam* is an individual prohibition relating either to the one taking the vow or to another specific person. Moreover, consecrated items become the property of the Temple, whereas something prohibited by a *konam* is similar to a consecrated item only with regard to its negative properties. Although it is prohibited to derive benefit from it, the Temple treasury does not have any rights to the item. The continuation of the Gemara discusses the differences between a *konam* and consecration.

HALAKHA

What I make to feed you is like an offering [*konam*] – קוּנָם שֶׁאֲנִי עוֹשָׂה לְפִיךָ: If a married woman said: My hands are consecrated to the One Who made them, or vowed that her husband may not derive benefit from her earnings, it is not prohibited for him to use her earnings, since she is subjugated to him with regard to her earnings. However, he should nullify her vow lest he divorce her, in which case the vow will take effect and it will be prohibited for him to derive benefit from her and to remarry her. According to this, since she made a *konam* vow her earnings are also prohibited, in accordance with the opinion of Rav Ashi (see 59b), who is the later authority. The Rema writes that this vow can take effect only when she says: My hands are consecrated to the One Who made them, and the Rosh, the Ran, and the *Tur*, who maintain that a *konam* vow cannot take effect on an item that does not exist in the world, agree (Rambam *Sefer Hafla'a*, *Hilkhot Nedarim* 12:10 and *Kesef Mishne* there; *Shulḥan Arukh*, *Yoreh De'a* 234:71, *Even HaEzer* 81:2).

וְאָמַר שְׁמוּאֵל: הֲלָכָה כְּרַבִּי יוֹחָנָן בֶּן נוּרִי! כִּי אֲמַר שְׁמוּאֵל הֲלָכָה כְּרַבִּי יוֹחָנָן בֶּן נוּרִי – לְהַעֲדָפָה.

And Shmuel said: The ***halakha*** **is in accordance with** the opinion of **Rabbi Yoḥanan ben Nuri,** who maintains that the wife can render her future earnings prohibited to her husband before these earnings have come into being, with the prohibition to go into effect after she divorces. This would imply that Shmuel holds that it is possible to consecrate an object that has not yet come into the world, contrary to what Rabbi Yoḥanan the Cobbler said. The Gemara answers: **When Shmuel said** that the ***halakha*** **is in accordance with** the opinion of **Rabbi Yoḥanan ben Nuri,** he was referring only to **the surplus.**

וְלֵימָא: הֲלָכָה כְּרַבִּי יוֹחָנָן בֶּן נוּרִי לְהַעֲדָפָה, אִי נַמִי: אֵין הֲלָכָה כְּתַנָּא קַמָּא, אִי נַמִי: הֲלָכָה כְּרַבִּי עֲקִיבָא!

The Gemara asks: If so, **let him say** explicitly that the ***halakha*** **is in accordance with** the opinion of **Rabbi Yoḥanan ben Nuri with regard to the surplus,** or **alternatively,** he should say that the ***halakha*** **is not in accordance with the first** ***tanna,*** or **alternatively,** he should simply say: The ***halakha*** **is in accordance with Rabbi Akiva,** who is concerned about the surplus amount.

אֶלָּא אָמַר רַב יוֹסֵף: קוֹנָמוֹת קָאָמְרַתְּ? שָׁאנֵי קוֹנָמוֹת, מִתּוֹךְ שֶׁאָדָם אוֹסֵר פֵּירוֹת חֲבֵירוֹ עָלָיו – אָדָם מַקְדִּישׁ דָּבָר שֶׁלֹּא בָּא לָעוֹלָם.

Rather, explain it differently, as **Rav Yosef said: Did you speak** about ***konamot*** to prove your contention that one can consecrate objects that have not yet come into the world? ***Konamot*** **are different,** as they have a special status, **since a person can prohibit another's produce to himself.** If one says to another: Your produce is *konam* to me, it is prohibited for him to eat that produce, although it does not belong to him and the prohibition will apply to it only when it reaches his domain. This indicates that a *konam* has unique power that enables **a person** to **consecrate an object that has not** yet **come into the world,** which according to Rabbi Yoḥanan the Cobbler is an exception to the principle. Consequently, Shmuel's ruling in accordance with Rabbi Yoḥanan ben Nuri with regard to *konamot* is not relevant to his opinion on the issue of a wife's earnings.

אֲמַר לֵיהּ אַבָּיֵי: בִּשְׁלָמָא אָדָם אוֹסֵר פֵּירוֹת חֲבֵירוֹ עָלָיו – שֶׁכֵּן אָדָם אוֹסֵר פֵּירוֹתָיו עַל חֲבֵירוֹ, יֶאֱסַר דָּבָר שֶׁלֹּא בָּא לָעוֹלָם עַל חֲבֵירוֹ, שֶׁכֵּן אֵין אָדָם אוֹסֵר פֵּירוֹת חֲבֵירוֹ עַל חֲבֵירוֹ?

Abaye said to him: This analogy cannot serve as a proof. **Granted, a person can prohibit another's produce to himself,** but this is possible **because a person can prohibit his own produce to another.** In both cases there is at least one aspect of the prohibition that is in his domain, either when he forbids another's produce to himself, or when he forbids produce in his own possession to others. However, one cannot **prohibit an object that has not** yet **come into the world to another, since a person cannot prohibit another's produce to another.** Just as he cannot make a *konam* and render prohibited to another person produce that is not in his possession, he also cannot render prohibited to another person produce that has not yet come into the world. If so, how can a woman render her earnings prohibited to her husband by a *konam* if those earnings have not yet come into the world?

אֶלָּא אָמַר רַב הוּנָא בְּרֵיהּ דְּרַב יְהוֹשֻׁעַ: בְּאוֹמֶרֶת "יִקָּדְשׁוּ יָדַי לְעוֹשֵׂיהֶם" דְּיָדַיִם אִיתְנְהוּ בְּעוֹלָם.

Rather, the Gemara rejects that explanation and instead explains as **Rav Huna, son of Rav Yehoshua, said:** The mishna does not refer to a case where she said: My earnings are *konam* to you, but rather to one **when she says: My hands are consecrated to the One Who made them,**[N] and this *konam* can take effect **because the hands** do **exist in the world.**

וְכִי קָאָמְרָה הָכִי מִי מִקַּדְּשָׁן? הָא מְשַׁעְבְּדָא לֵיהּ! דְּאָמְרָה "לִכְשֶׁאֶתְגָּרֵשׁ".

The Gemara asks: **When she says this** in such terms **does it become consecrated? She is subjugated to** her husband with regard to her earnings, so how can she consecrate that which is not hers? The Gemara answers: **She says** that the consecration will take effect **when she will get divorced** from her husband.

וּמִי אִיכָּא מִידֵּי, דְּאִילּוּ הָשְׁתָּא – לָא קָדֵישׁ, וּלְקַמֵּיהּ קָדֵישׁ? אָמַר רַבִּי אֶלְעַאי: אַלְמָה לָא? אִילּוּ הָאוֹמֵר לַחֲבֵירוֹ "שָׂדֶה זוֹ שֶׁאֲנִי מוֹכֵר לָךְ, לִכְשֶׁאֶקָּחֶנָּה מִמְּךָ תִּיקָּדֵשׁ" מִי לָא קָדְשָׁה?

The Gemara asks: **Is there anything** one would do **that if** done **at present,** the **consecration** could **not** take effect **and in the future** the **consecration** could take effect? **Rabbi Elai said: Why not? If one told another: This field that I am selling to you will be consecrated when I buy it** back **from you,**[H] **doesn't** that field **become consecrated** when he buys it back? It appears that one can cause an item to become consecrated in the future although at present he cannot consecrate it.

NOTES

My hands are consecrated to the One Who made them – יִקָּדְשׁוּ יָדַי לְעוֹשֵׂיהֶם: The Rashba writes that the Sages had a tradition that consecrating one's hands for that which they produce is analogous to consecrating a palm tree for its fruit, in which case the sanctity takes effect on the fruit. The fruit is formed inside the tree and within it; similarly, hands craft the handiwork they produce. However, consecrating one's hands is not analogous to setting a trap and consecrating whatever is caught in the trap. The trap itself does not create what it catches, and therefore it cannot consecrate what is in it.

HALAKHA

This field that I am selling you will be consecrated when I buy it back from you – שָׂדֶה זוֹ שֶׁאֲנִי מוֹכֵר לָךְ, לִכְשֶׁאֶקָּחֶנָּה מִמְּךָ תִּיקָּדֵשׁ: If one says to another: This field that I am selling you will be consecrated when I buy it back from you, it becomes consecrated when he repurchases the field. The reason the consecration is effective is that he could have consecrated the field at the time he made the declaration (Rambam *Sefer Hafla'a, Hilkhot Arakhin VaḤaramim* 6:29).

מַתְקִיף לַהּ רַבִּי יִרְמְיָה: מִי דָּמֵי? הָתָם – בְּיָדוֹ לְהַקְדִּישָׁהּ, הָכָא – אֵין בְּיָדָהּ לְגָרֵשׁ אֶת עַצְמָהּ. הָא לָא דָּמְיָא אֶלָּא לָאוֹמֵר לַחֲבֵירוֹ "שָׂדֶה זוֹ שֶׁמָּכַרְתִּי לְךָ לִכְשֶׁאֶקָּחֶנָּה מִמְּךָ תִּיקָּדֵשׁ" – דְּלָא קָדְשָׁה!

Rabbi Yirmeya objects to this: Are these cases **comparable? There,** with regard to a field, since the field that he is selling belongs to him at the time of the sale, **it is in his power to consecrate it** now. Therefore, he can effect sanctity on it at a later point as well. But **here, it is not in her power to divorce herself.** Consequently, the analogy is invalid. Rather, **this is comparable only to** a different case, when **one says to another: This field that I** already **sold to you will be consecrated when I buy it** back **from you.**[H] In that case the field **is not consecrated,** as, when he said this the field was not in his possession, and one cannot consecrate an object that has not yet come into the world.

מַתְקִיף לַהּ רַב פַּפָּא: מִי דָּמֵי? הָתָם – גּוּפָא וּפֵירוֹת בִּיָדָא דְּלוֹקֵחַ, הָכָא – גּוּפָהּ בְּיָדָהּ הוּא! הָא לָא דָּמְיָא אֶלָּא לָאוֹמֵר לַחֲבֵירוֹ

Rav Pappa objects to this: Is Rav Yirmeya's analogy **comparable? There,** the field **itself and** its **produce** are **in the possession of the buyer,** and therefore the seller cannot consecrate them. **Here, her body is in her possession,** as she owns her hands. Rather, **this is comparable only to** a case where **one says to another:**

HALAKHA

This field that I already sold to you will be consecrated when I buy it back from you – שָׂדֶה זוֹ שֶׁמָּכַרְתִּי לְךָ לִכְשֶׁאֶקָּחֶנָּה מִמְּךָ תִּיקָּדֵשׁ: If one said to another: This field that I sold you will be consecrated when I repurchase it from you, then even if he repurchases the field it is not consecrated. Since the field was not in his possession at the time he made the declaration, it was not within his power to consecrate it (Rambam *Sefer Hafla'a*, *Hilkhot Arakhin VaḤaramim* 6:27).

Perek **V**
Daf **59** Amud **b**

"שָׂדֶה זוֹ שֶׁמִּשְׁכַּנְתִּי לְךָ, לִכְשֶׁאֶפְדֶּנָּה מִמְּךָ – תִּיקָּדֵשׁ" – דְּקָדְשָׁה.

This field that I mortgaged to you[H] and from whose produce you are benefiting **will be consecrated when I redeem it from you.** The *halakha* is **that it is consecrated,** since the field itself was not transferred to another's ownership.

מַתְקִיף לַהּ רַב שֵׁישָׁא בְּרֵיהּ דְּרַב אִידִי: מִי דָּמֵי? הָתָם בְּיָדוֹ לִפְדּוֹתָהּ, הָכָא – אֵין בְּיָדָהּ לְגָרֵשׁ עַצְמָהּ. הָא לָא דָּמְיָא אֶלָּא לָאוֹמֵר לַחֲבֵירוֹ "שָׂדֶה זוֹ שֶׁמִּשְׁכַּנְתִּי לְךָ לְעֶשֶׂר שָׁנִים, לִכְשֶׁאֶפְדֶּנָּה מִמְּךָ – תִּיקָּדֵשׁ" דְּקָדְשָׁה.

Rav Sheisha, son of Rav Idi, objects to this: Is it comparable? There, in the case where he mortgaged the field, **it is in his power to redeem it,** whereas **here,** with regard to a woman who renders her earnings prohibited to her husband, **it is not in her power to divorce herself** from her husband. **This is only comparable to one who says to another: This field that I have mortgaged to you for ten years will be consecrated when I redeem it from you.** The *halakha* is **that it is consecrated.** Similarly, in this case, despite the fact that her earnings belong to her husband, when she will be divorced they will revert to her, and since her hands have always belonged to her, she can consecrate her earnings.

מַתְקִיף לַהּ רַב אַשִׁי: מִי דָּמֵי? הָתָם – לְעֶשֶׂר שָׁנִים מִיהָא בְּיָדוֹ לִפְדּוֹתָהּ, הָכָא – אֵין בְּיָדָהּ לְגָרֵשׁ עַצְמָהּ לְעוֹלָם.

Rav Ashi objects to this: Is it comparable? There, after **ten years in any case it will be in his power to redeem it,** whereas **here,** with regard to a woman, **it is never in her power to divorce herself** from her husband. Consequently, there is no way for her to consecrate her future earnings.

HALAKHA

This field that I mortgaged to you – שָׂדֶה זֶה שֶׁמִּשְׁכַּנְתִּי לְךָ: If one said to another: This field that I mortgaged to you will be consecrated when I redeem it from you, then when he redeems the field it becomes consecrated, since it is then in his power to redeem it. Even if the field were mortgaged for a fixed period, it is still consecrated, since it is in his power to redeem the field after that period (Rambam *Sefer Hafla'a*, *Hilkhot Arakhin VaḤaramim* 6:29).

אֶלָּא אָמַר רַב אַשִׁי: קוֹנָמוֹת קָא אָמְרַתְּ? שָׁאנֵי קוֹנָמוֹת דִּקְדוּשַּׁת הַגּוּף נִינְהוּ, וְכִדְרָבָא. דְּאָמַר רָבָא: הֶקְדֵּשׁ, חָמֵץ, וְשִׁחְרוּר – מַפְקִיעִין מִידֵי שִׁיעְבּוּד.

Rather, the contradiction between the two rulings of Shmuel must be resolved in a different manner. **Rav Ashi said: Did you speak** about *konamot*? ***Konamot* are different,**[N] since **they are** a type of **inherent sanctity,**[N] and therefore the *konam* can take effect on an item that is subjugated to another person, **in accordance with** the *halakha* articulated by **Rava. As Rava said: Consecration,**[H] the prohibition of **leavened bread** on Passover,[H] and the **liberation** of a slave[H] can all **abrogate a lien on property.** If property was mortgaged to another person, and then the owner consecrated it, or if leavened bread was mortgaged and Passover arrived and it became prohibited to benefit from it, or if a slave was mortgaged and then liberated by his owner, the lien is abrogated. Since *konam* is a form of consecration, it can take effect on an item even when it is subjugated to another when the owner prohibited it, similar to the case of mortgaged property.

וְנִקְדְּשׁוּ מֵהַשְׁתָּא! אַלִּמוּהָ רַבָּנַן לְשִׁיעְבּוּדֵיהּ דְּבַעַל, כִּי הֵיכִי דְּלָא תִּיקְדַּשׁ מֵהָשְׁתָּא.

The Gemara asks: If it is so, that a *konam* can remove the lien on property, **let her earnings become consecrated from now,** even before her husband divorces her. The Gemara answers: **The Sages reinforced the husband's lien in order that it not become consecrated now.** However, since in general a *konam* can take effect on mortgaged items, it can take effect on her earnings after she leaves her husband's jurisdiction.

מתני׳ וְאֵלּוּ מְלָאכוֹת שֶׁהָאִשָּׁה עוֹשָׂה לְבַעְלָהּ: טוֹחֶנֶת, וְאוֹפָה, וּמְכַבֶּסֶת, מְבַשֶּׁלֶת, וּמֵנִיקָה אֶת בְּנָהּ, מַצַּעַת לוֹ הַמִּטָּה, וְעוֹשָׂה בַּצֶּמֶר. הִכְנִיסָה לוֹ שִׁפְחָה אַחַת – לֹא טוֹחֶנֶת וְלֹא אוֹפָה וְלֹא מְכַבֶּסֶת. שְׁתַּיִם – אֵין מְבַשֶּׁלֶת וְאֵין מֵנִיקָה אֶת בְּנָהּ. שָׁלֹשׁ – אֵין מַצַּעַת לוֹ הַמִּטָּה, וְאֵין עוֹשָׂה בַּצֶּמֶר. אַרְבַּע – יוֹשֶׁבֶת בְּקַתֶּדְרָא.

MISHNA And these are tasks that a wife must **perform**[H] **for her husband: She grinds** wheat into flour, **and bakes, and washes clothes, cooks, and nurses her child, makes** her husband's **bed,**[H] **and makes** thread **from wool**[H] by spinning it. **If she brought him one maidservant,**[H] i.e., brought the maidservant with her into the marriage, the maidservant will perform some of these tasks. Consequently, the wife **does not** need to **grind, and does not** need to **bake, and does not** need to **wash clothes.** If she brought him **two** maidservants,[H] **she does not** need to **cook and does not** need to **nurse her child** if she does not want to, but instead may give the child to a wet nurse. If she brought him **three** maidservants,[H] **she does not** need to **make his bed and does not** need to **make** thread **from wool.** If she brought him **four** maidservants, **she may sit in a chair** [***katedra***][NL] like a queen and not do anything, as her maidservants do all of her work for her.

NOTES

Konamot are different – שָׁאנֵי קוֹנָמוֹת: The Meiri writes that the commentaries dispute whether Rav Ashi's words relate to the *halakha* of *konamot* in general or whether he is discussing only a situation where the woman said: My hands are consecrated to the One Who made them. If the former is true, Shmuel's ruling is to be interpreted as explained by Rav Yosef: Even if the woman consecrated her earnings themselves, the consecration is valid. The latter interpretation is in accordance with the opinion of Rav Huna, son of Rav Yehoshua. This dispute has implications both with regard to Rav Ashi's opinion and the *halakha* itself.

They are a type of inherent sanctity – קְדוּשַּׁת הַגּוּף נִינְהוּ: Rashi explains at length that the term inherent sanctity used in this context does not mean that the item has actual inherent sanctity like consecrated items designated for the altar. Rather, the significance of the term is that if an item was prohibited by a *konam*, it has a similar status to objects that have inherent sanctity, meaning that it cannot be redeemed. If an animal is consecrated for an offering, it has inherent sanctity and its sanctity is irrevocable as long as it is fit to be offered on the altar, which is not the case for items whose sanctity inheres in their value, such as an item consecrated for Temple maintenance, which has no innate sanctity and therefore one can redeem it. An item that was prohibited by a *konam* is similar to an object with inherent sanctity in that it remains prohibited forever, or at least until the vow is revoked. It cannot be redeemed or desacralized.

She may sit in an chair – יוֹשֶׁבֶת בְּקַתֶּדְרָא: *Tosafot* add the following: It would seem from the mishna that, like a woman who brought four maidservants with her into the marriage, a woman who brought three maidservants with her also does not have to perform any tasks. Nevertheless, she is still obligated to do light housework. In contrast, a woman who brought four maidservants does not have to do any work at all.

LANGUAGE

Chair [*katedra*] – קָתֶדְרָא: From the Greek καθέδρα, *kathedra*, meaning chair, specifically a chair of honor used by scholars or rulers.

HALAKHA

Consecration abrogates the lien – הֶקְדֵּשׁ מַפְקִיעַ שִׁעְבּוּד: Consecration removes the lien on property, in accordance with the opinion of Rava, who said that if the borrower consecrates mortgaged property, he abrogates the lien on it, and the creditor cannot collect his debt from that property. According to most ruling authorities, who follow the *ge'onim* and Rashi, this is applicable only if he consecrated the property with inherent sanctity, but if he consecrated it with sanctity that inheres in its value, the consecration cannot abrogate the lien on the property, and the borrower must redeem it with a small sum of money so that people do not say that consecrated items can be desacralized without redemption. However, the Rambam maintains that even sanctity that inheres in an item's value can abrogate the lien until the item is redeemed (Rambam *Sefer Mishpatim*, *Hilkhot Malve VeLoveh* 18:7 and *Sefer Hafla'a*, *Hilkhot Arakhin VaḤaramim* 7:14; *Tur*, *Ḥoshen Mishpat* 117; *Shulḥan Arukh*, *Ḥoshen Mishpat* 117:7, and in the comment of Rema).

The prohibition of leavened bread on Passover abrogates the lien – חָמֵץ מַפְקִיעַ מִשִּׁעְבּוּד: In a case where a Jew borrowed money from a gentile and mortgaged leavened bread as a guarantee against his loan, if Passover elapsed before the loan was repaid, it is permitted to derive benefit from the leavened bread only if he transferred the leavened bread to the gentile's possession as collateral, since the prohibition of leavened bread abrogates the lien (Rambam *Sefer Mishpatim*, *Hilkhot Malve VeLoveh* 18:6; *Shulḥan Arukh*, *Oraḥ Ḥayyim* 441:1).

Liberation of a slave abrogates the lien – שִׁחְרוּר מַפְקִיעַ מִשִּׁעְבּוּד: If a slave was mortgaged as designated repayment for his master's debt and was then liberated by his master, this abrogates the lien, and he is a free man (Rambam *Sefer Kinyan*, *Hilkhot Avadim* 8:16; *Shulḥan Arukh*, *Yoreh De'a* 267:68, *Ḥoshen Mishpat* 117:6).

And these are tasks that a wife must perform – וְאֵלּוּ מְלָאכוֹת שֶׁהָאִשָּׁה עוֹשָׂה: There are some household tasks that a woman must perform for her husband if they are poor: Supervising the grinding of the wheat, baking, cooking, washing clothes, and nursing her child, in accordance with the mishna (Rambam *Sefer Nashim*, *Hilkhot Ishut* 21:5; *Shulḥan Arukh*, *Even HaEzer* 80:6).

Makes her husband's bed – מַצַּעַת לוֹ הַמִּטָּה: A woman is obligated to make her husband's bed. The Rema writes that some say that she is obligated to make all the beds in the house, in accordance with the opinion of the *Maggid Mishne* and the Ran (Rambam *Sefer Nashim*, *Hilkhot Ishut* 21:3; *Shulḥan Arukh*, *Even HaEzer* 80:4).

Makes thread from wool – עוֹשָׂה בַּצֶּמֶר: A woman is obligated to perform tasks that will help sustain her family, in accordance with the custom of her country. If it is the custom for women to weave, she must weave, and if they embroider, she must embroider or spin wool. If it is not the local custom for women to perform these tasks, he can compel her only to spin wool, in accordance with the mishna (Rambam *Sefer Nashim*, *Hilkhot Ishut* 21:1; *Shulḥan Arukh*, *Even HaEzer* 80:1).

If she brought him one maidservant – הִכְנִיסָה לוֹ שִׁפְחָה אַחַת: If a woman brought her husband one maidservant, or property with which to purchase one maidservant, she does not need to supervise the grinding of wheat. She also need not bake, wash clothes or place straw before her husband's animal, in accordance with the mishna (Rambam *Sefer Nashim*, *Hilkhot Ishut* 21:6, *Shulḥan Arukh*, *Even HaEzer* 80:7).

If she brought him two maidservants – הִכְנִיסָה לוֹ שְׁתֵּי שְׁפָחוֹת: If a woman brought him two maidservants, she does not need to cook or to nurse her child, in accordance with the mishna (Rambam *Sefer Nashim*, *Hilkhot Ishut* 21:6; *Shulḥan Arukh*, *Even HaEzer* 80:8).

If she brought him three maidservants – הִכְנִיסָה לוֹ שָׁלֹשׁ שְׁפָחוֹת: If she brought him three maidservants she needs only to make her husband's bed (Ran, citing Rema). Some commentaries say that she needs only to prepare the sheets on his bed, as this is an act of intimacy (*Tur*). The Rambam and the *Shulḥan Arukh* do not cite this *halakha*, as they decided in accordance with Rabbi Eliezer, and do not maintain a distinction between making her husband's bed and making other beds (Rambam *Sefer Nashim*, *Hilkhot Ishut* 21:6 and *Kesef Mishne* there; *Shulḥan Arukh*, *Even HaEzer* 80:8).

NOTES

He can compel her to make thread from wool – כּוֹפָהּ לַעֲשׂוֹת בַּצֶּמֶר: A number of commentaries write that he cannot compel her to make the required amount that other women must make, but only enough so that she will not be totally idle (Rashba; Ritva). There is also a dispute among the early authorities with regard to whether her earnings in this case belong to her or to her husband.

A wife is only for beauty – אֵין אִשָּׁה אֶלָּא לְיוֹפִי: *Tosafot* comment that apparently Rabbi Ḥiyya disagrees with the ruling in the mishna only with respect to tasks that could affect a woman's beauty or refinement, such as grinding or baking, but not tasks like making thread from wool. According to *Melo HaRo'im*, the expression: A wife is only for children, means that a woman should not nurse her baby, since doing so will delay her ability to become pregnant again. According to this interpretation, there is a difference between the statement that a wife is for beauty and the statement that a wife is for children. Others say the opposite: According to the opinion that a wife is for beauty then she does not nurse, whereas according to the opinion that a wife is for children she must also nurse her children (*Ḥever ben Ḥayyim*).

BACKGROUND

Hand mill – רֵיחַיָּא דִּידָא: Hand mills were commonly used in ancient times by women, who would grind grain into flour for household use. The grain was placed in the opening on the top piece and the mill would be turned with the handle while the bottom part stayed still.

When a large amount of flour was needed, it was ground in a large mill that was rotated by water pressure or animals. Although with extreme effort people could also rotate these mills (see Judges 16:21), it is not plausible that such difficult work was done by women.

Hand mill

רַבִּי אֱלִיעֶזֶר אוֹמֵר: אֲפִילּוּ הִכְנִיסָה לוֹ מֵאָה שְׁפָחוֹת – כּוֹפָהּ לַעֲשׂוֹת בַּצֶּמֶר, שֶׁהַבַּטָּלָה מְבִיאָה לִידֵי זִימָּה. רַבָּן שִׁמְעוֹן בֶּן גַּמְלִיאֵל אוֹמֵר: אַף הַמַּדִּיר אֶת אִשְׁתּוֹ מִלַּעֲשׂוֹת מְלָאכָה – יוֹצִיא וְיִתֵּן כְּתוּבָּה, שֶׁהַבַּטָּלָה מְבִיאָה לִידֵי שִׁיעֲמוּם.

Rabbi Eliezer says: Even if she brought him a hundred maidservants, he can compel her to make thread **from wool,**[NH] **since idleness leads to licentiousness.** Consequently, it is better for a woman to be doing some kind of work. **Rabban Shimon ben Gamliel says: Even one who vows that his wife** is prohibited **from doing** any **work**[H] **must divorce** her **and give** her the payment for her **marriage contract, since idleness leads to idiocy.**

גמ׳ טוֹחֶנֶת סָלְקָא דַּעְתָּךְ? אֶלָּא אֵימָא: מַטְחֶנֶת. וְאִיבָּעֵית אֵימָא: בְּרֵיחַיָּא דִּידָא.

GEMARA With regard to the mishna's choice of terminology the Gemara asks: **Could it enter your mind** that she **grinds** the wheat into flour? Ordinarily, grinding is performed in a mill using millstones that are rotated by water or by animals, so the woman herself does not actually grind the wheat. The Gemara answers: **Rather, say** that **she supervises the grinding**[H] by bringing wheat to the mill and ensuring that it is ground properly. Alternatively, **if you wish, say** instead: She can grind the wheat herself **with a hand mill.**[B]

מַתְנִיתִין דְּלָא כְּרַבִּי חִיָּיא. דְּתָנֵי רַבִּי חִיָּיא: אֵין אִשָּׁה אֶלָּא לְיוֹפִי, אֵין אִשָּׁה אֶלָּא לְבָנִים, וְתָנֵי רַבִּי חִיָּיא: אֵין אִשָּׁה אֶלָּא לְתַכְשִׁיטֵי אִשָּׁה. וְתָנֵי רַבִּי חִיָּיא: הָרוֹצֶה שֶׁיְּעַדֵּן אֶת אִשְׁתּוֹ – יַלְבִּישֶׁנָּה כְּלֵי פִשְׁתָּן, הָרוֹצֶה שֶׁיַּלְבִּין אֶת בִּתּוֹ – יַאֲכִילֶנָּה אֶפְרוֹחִים, וְיַשְׁקֶנָּה חָלָב סָמוּךְ לְפִירְקָהּ.

The Gemara comments: **The mishna is not in accordance with** the opinion of **Rabbi Ḥiyya, as Rabbi Ḥiyya teaches: A wife is only for beauty,**[N] and **a wife is only for children,** but not for household tasks. **And Rabbi Ḥiyya teaches: A wife is only for** wearing **a woman's finery. And Rabbi Ḥiyya** similarly **teaches: One who wishes to beautify his wife should clothe her** in **linen garments,** and **one who wishes to whiten his daughter** so that she will have a fair complexion, **should feed her young chickens, and should give her milk to drink toward the time of her maturity.**

״וּמֵנִיקָה אֶת בְּנָהּ״. לֵימָא מַתְנִיתִין דְּלָא כְּבֵית שַׁמַּאי, דְּתַנְיָא: נָדְרָה שֶׁלֹּא לְהָנִיק אֶת בְּנָהּ, בֵּית שַׁמַּאי אוֹמְרִים: שׁוֹמֶטֶת דַּד מִפִּיו, בֵּית הִלֵּל אוֹמְרִים: כּוֹפָהּ וּמְנִיקַתּוֹ. נִתְגָּרְשָׁה – אֵינוֹ כּוֹפָהּ. וְאִם הָיָה מַכִּירָהּ – נוֹתֵן לָהּ שְׂכָרָהּ, וְכוֹפָהּ וּמְנִיקַתּוֹ, מִפְּנֵי הַסַּכָּנָה.

§ The mishna mentions among a wife's obligations that she **nurses her child.** The Gemara suggests: **Let us say that the mishna is not in accordance with** the opinion of **Beit Shammai, as it is taught** in a *baraita*: If a woman **took a vow not to nurse her child,**[H] **Beit Shammai say:** Since she vowed, **she** must **remove** her **nipple from his mouth** and not nurse him. **Beit Hillel say:** Her husband **can compel her, and she** must **nurse** the child even against her will. However, if **she was divorced** and therefore had no further obligations to her husband, **he cannot compel her.**[H] Nevertheless, **if** the baby **recognized her,** then even after the divorce, her husband may **pay her a salary** as a wet nurse **and compel her to nurse due to** the **danger** that the child will starve if he refuses to nurse from another woman. This *baraita* indicates that according to Beit Shammai a woman has no obligation to nurse her child. If she had a prior obligation to her husband to nurse the child, the vow would not take effect.

HALAKHA

He can compel her to make thread from wool – כּוֹפָהּ לַעֲשׂוֹת בַּצֶּמֶר: Even if a woman brought her husband a hundred maidservants, she cannot remain completely idle and not perform any tasks. However, he cannot compel her to work all day, but only enough to prevent her from being idle, which could lead her to licentiousness, in accordance with the opinion of Rabbi Eliezer (Rambam *Sefer Nashim*, *Hilkhot Ishut* 21:2; *Shulḥan Arukh*, *Even HaEzer* 80:2).

One who vows that his wife is prohibited from doing any work – הַמַּדִּיר אֶת אִשְׁתּוֹ מִלַּעֲשׂוֹת מְלָאכָה: One who vows that his wife should not do work must divorce her and give her the payment for her marriage contract, since idleness leads to licentiousness. As explained in the Gemara (61b), this is in accordance with the opinion of Rabbi Eliezer, as opposed to that of Rabbi Shimon ben Gamliel (Rambam *Sefer Nashim*, *Hilkhot Ishut* 21:3; *Shulḥan Arukh*, *Even HaEzer* 80:3).

She supervises the grinding – מַטְחֶנֶת: How does a woman supervise the grinding? She sits in the millhouse and sifts the flour or drives the animal doing the grinding. If it was the custom to grind wheat with a hand mill she must use one, according to both opinions in the Gemara, which are not in dispute with one another (Rambam *Sefer Nashim*, *Hilkhot Ishut* 21:5; *Shulḥan Arukh*, *Even HaEzer* 80:6).

Took a vow not to nurse her child – נָדְרָה שֶׁלֹּא לְהָנִיק אֶת בְּנָהּ: If a woman vows not to nurse her child, she may be compelled to nurse him, in accordance with Beit Hillel's opinion (Rambam *Sefer Nashim*, *Hilkhot Ishut* 21:13; *Shulḥan Arukh*, *Even HaEzer* 82:1).

If she was divorced he cannot compel her – נִתְגָּרְשָׁה אֵינוֹ כּוֹפָהּ: If a woman was divorced she cannot be compelled to nurse her child. If she wishes, her ex-husband can pay her wages as a wet nurse, and if not, she can give the child to him and he must take care of him. If the child knew his mother, and according to some opinions (Rema, citing *Tur*), if he did not want to nurse from others, she can be compelled to nurse him, due to the possible danger involved to the child, and her ex-husband must pay her a salary (Rambam *Sefer Nashim*, *Hilkhot Ishut* 21:16; *Shulḥan Arukh*, *Even HaEzer* 82:5).

אֲפִילּוּ תֵּימָא בֵּית שַׁמַּאי, הָכָא בְּמַאי עָסְקִינַן – כְּגוֹן שֶׁנָּדְרָה הִיא וְקִיֵּים לָהּ הוּא. וְקָסָבְרִי בֵּית שַׁמַּאי: הוּא נוֹתֵן אֶצְבַּע בֵּין שִׁינֶּיהָ. וּבֵית הִלֵּל סָבְרִי: הִיא נָתְנָה אֶצְבַּע בֵּין שִׁינֶּיהָ.

The Gemara rejects this suggestion: **Even if you say** that the mishna is also in accordance with the opinion of **Beit Shammai, here we are dealing with** a case **where she made** this **vow and** her husband **ratified** it **for her** by refraining from nullifying it. **Beit Shammai maintain** that in that case it is considered as if **he had placed his finger between her teeth,** i.e., he caused the vow to be in effect, meaning that in that case the responsibility lies with him. Since he declined the opportunity to nullify the vow, her obligation to nurse is canceled. **Beit Hillel maintain** that in that case **she put her finger between her** own **teeth,** i.e., she caused the vow to remain in effect. Consequently, although he ratified her vow, the responsibility rests on her, and for this reason her obligation is not annulled.

וְנִפְלְגוּ בִּכְתוּבָּה בְּעָלְמָא! וְעוֹד, תַּנְיָא, בֵּית שַׁמַּאי אוֹמְרִים: אֵינָהּ מֵנִיקָה. אֶלָּא מְחַוּוּרְתָּא, מַתְנִיתִין דְּלָא כְּבֵית שַׁמַּאי.

The Gemara asks: If so, that the dispute is about who is responsible when a woman vows and her husband ratifies the vow, and it is not specifically about her obligation to nurse her child, then **let them dispute about a marriage contract in general,** with regard to whether or not a woman is entitled to payment for her marriage contract if she vows to prohibit her husband from deriving benefit from her. **And furthermore, it is taught** in a *baraita* **that Beit Shammai** explicitly **say** with regard to all women, not specifically in the context of vows: **She does not** need to **nurse** if she does not want to. **Rather, it is clear** that **the mishna is not in accordance with** the opinion of **Beit Shammai.**

״אִם הָיָה מַכִּירָהּ״.

The Gemara above quotes a *baraita* where it is taught that **if** the baby **recognized her,** her husband can compel her to continue nursing even after she is divorced, but he must pay her for nursing.

Perek **V**
Daf **60** Amud **a**

עַד כַּמָּה? אָמַר רָבָא אָמַר רַב יִרְמְיָה בַּר אַבָּא אָמַר רַב: שְׁלֹשָׁה חֳדָשִׁים, וּשְׁמוּאֵל אָמַר: שְׁלֹשִׁים יוֹם, וְרַבִּי יִצְחָק אָמַר רַבִּי יוֹחָנָן: חֲמִשִּׁים יוֹם. אָמַר רַב שִׁימִי בַּר אַבָּיֵי: הֲלָכָה כְּרַבִּי יִצְחָק שֶׁאָמַר מִשּׁוּם רַבִּי יוֹחָנָן. בִּשְׁלָמָא רַב וְרַבִּי יוֹחָנָן – כָּל חַד וְחַד כִּי חוּרְפֵיהּ. אֶלָּא לִשְׁמוּאֵל, כִּי הַאי גַּוְונָא מִי מַשְׁכַּחַתְּ לַהּ?

The Gemara asks: **How old** does the child have to be[H] so that one can assume that he already recognizes his mother? **Rava said** that **Rav Yirmeya bar Abba said** that **Rav said: Three months, and Shmuel said: Thirty days, and Rabbi Yitzhak said** that **Rabbi Yoḥanan said: Fifty days. Rav Shimi bar Abaye said:** The *halakha* **is in accordance with** what **Rabbi Yitzḥak said in the name of Rabbi Yoḥanan.** The Gemara asks: **Granted, Rav and Rabbi Yoḥanan** are in dispute with regard to the difference between fifty days and three months, as it is possible that **each** baby varies **according to its intelligence,** as one baby is sufficiently developed at fifty days, while another knows his mother at only three months. **However, according to Shmuel, can you find a case like this,** a one-month-old baby who recognizes his mother?

כִּי אֲתָא רָמֵי בַּר יְחֶזְקֵאל אָמַר: לָא תְּצִיתִינְהוּ לְהָנֵי כְּלָלֵי דְּכַיֵּיל יְהוּדָה אָחִי מִשְּׁמֵיהּ דִּשְׁמוּאֵל. הָכִי אָמַר שְׁמוּאֵל: כָּל זְמַן שֶׁמַּכִּירָהּ.

The Gemara relates: **When Rami bar Yeḥezkel came** from Eretz Yisrael, **he said: Do not listen to,** i.e., do not accept, **those principles that my brother Yehuda said in the name of Shmuel,** as Shmuel did not establish a particular time with regard to this matter. Rather, **this is what Shmuel said: Whenever he recognizes her,**[B] i.e., there is no fixed age at which this occurs. One must check each baby to see whether he recognizes his mother.

HALAKHA

How old does the child have to be – עַד כַּמָּה: If a child has begun to nurse from his mother, one cannot separate him from her due to the possible danger involved. There is no precise stage at which this applies, as it depends on whether the child recognizes his mother, in accordance with the opinion of Shmuel as quoted by Rami bar Yeḥezkel. There are, however, authorities who rule in accordance with Rabbi Yitzḥak, following the ruling of the Gemara (Rif; Rosh). The Rema writes that some authorities maintain that if a child began to nurse from a wet nurse, she can be compelled to continue to nurse him if he recognizes her and resists nursing from another woman (Rambam *Sefer Nashim*, *Hilkhot Ishut* 21:16; *Shulḥan Arukh*, *Even HaEzer* 82:5).

BACKGROUND

Whenever he recognizes her – כָּל זְמַן שֶׁמַּכִּירָהּ: There are several stages of human recognition observed among babies. According to contemporary studies, a newborn can recognize his mother's voice, a capability acquired in the womb, and his mother's scent. At the age of approximately one month an infant begins to demonstrate a certain level of recognition of other people. At about eight weeks a baby may demonstrate signs of interest and affection toward people he recognizes, and his preference for his mother stands out significantly from about six months. These general parameters vary to some extent from child to child; some develop slightly earlier and some later. This type of recognition is present in blind children as well, primarily through the sense of smell.

הַהִיא דַּאֲתַאי לְקַמֵּיהּ דִּשְׁמוּאֵל. אֲמַר לֵיהּ לְרַב דִּימִי בַּר יוֹסֵף: זִיל בְּדַקָהּ. אֲזַל, אוֹתְבָהּ בְּדָרֵי דְּנָשֵׁי, וּשְׁקַלֵיהּ לִבְרָהּ וְקָמְהַדַּר לֵיהּ עֲלַיְיהוּ. כִּי מָטָא לְגַבָּהּ – הֲוַת קָא מַסְוֵי לְאַפָּהּ, כְּבַשְׁתִּנְהִי לְעֵינָהּ מִינֵּיהּ. אֲמַר לָהּ: נְטַף עֵינַיִךְ, קוּם דְּרִי בְּרִיךְ. סוּמָא מְנָא יָדַע? אֲמַר רַב אַשִׁי: בְּרֵיחָא וּבְטַעֲמָא.

The Gemara relates: **A certain** divorcée **came before Shmuel,**[P] as she did not wish to nurse her son. **He said to Rav Dimi bar Yosef: Go and check her,** i.e., verify whether the child recognizes his mother. **He went, placed her in a row of women, and took her son** in his arms **and passed him near them** to see how the child would react. **When** the child **reached her, he looked at her face with joy,** and **she averted her eyes from him,** as she did not want to look at him. **He said to her: Lift up your eyes, get up and take your son,** as it is obvious that he knows you. The Gemara asks: If this is so, then **how does a blind**[H] baby **know** and recognize his mother? **Rav Ashi said: Through smell and through the taste** of her milk.

תָּנוּ רַבָּנַן: יוֹנֵק תִּינוֹק וְהוֹלֵךְ עַד עֶשְׂרִים וְאַרְבָּעָה חֹדֶשׁ, מִכָּאן וְאֵילָךְ – כְּיוֹנֵק שֶׁקֶץ, דִּבְרֵי רַבִּי אֱלִיעֶזֶר. רַבִּי יְהוֹשֻׁעַ אוֹמֵר: אֲפִילּוּ אַרְבַּע וְחָמֵשׁ שָׁנִים, פֵּירַשׁ לְאַחַר עֶשְׂרִים וְאַרְבָּעָה חֹדֶשׁ, וְחָזַר – כְּיוֹנֵק שֶׁקֶץ.

§ Apropos the period of time during which a child nurses, the Gemara continues to debate different aspects of this matter. **The Sages taught** in a *baraita*: **A child may continue to nurse**[H] **until** the age of **twenty-four months, and from this** point **forward,** if he continues to nurse, he is **like one who nurses** from **a non-kosher animal,** as a woman's milk is forbidden to anyone other than a small child; this is **the statement of Rabbi Eliezer. Rabbi Yehoshua says:** A child may continue to nurse **even** for **four or five years,** and this is permitted. However, **if he ceased,**[H] i.e., was weaned, **after twenty-four months and** then **resumed** nursing, he is **like one who nurses** from **a non-kosher animal.**

אָמַר מָר: מִכָּאן וְאֵילָךְ כְּיוֹנֵק שֶׁקֶץ. וּרְמִינְהִי: יָכוֹל יְהֵא חֲלֵב מְהַלְּכֵי שְׁתַּיִם טָמֵא, וְדִין הוּא: וּמַה בְּהֵמָה, שֶׁהֵקַלְתָּ בְּמַגָּעָהּ, הֶחְמַרְתָּ בַּחֲלָבָהּ – אָדָם, שֶׁהֶחְמַרְתָּ בְּמַגָּעוֹ – אֵינוֹ דִּין שֶׁתַּחְמִיר בַּחֲלָבוֹ?

The Master said in the *baraita*: **From this** point **forward** he is **like one who nurses from a non-kosher animal.** The Gemara **raises a contradiction** from a *baraita*: One **might** have thought that the **milk** of **bipeds,** i.e., humans, **would be non-kosher** like that of a non-kosher animal, based on a **logical derivation: Just as** with regard to a non-kosher **animal, where you were lenient with regard to its contact,** meaning that it does not render people or items impure through contact when it is alive, **you were stringent with regard to its milk,** which is prohibited, even more so should this be true with regard to a person. An *a fortiori* inference would indicate that with regard to **a person, where you were stringent about contact,** as people can render other people and objects impure even when they are alive, one should be stricter. So **isn't it logical that you should be stringent with regard to his milk?**

PERSONALITIES

Shmuel – שְׁמוּאֵל: Shmuel was a first-generation *amora* who was born and ultimately passed away in Neharde'a. A child prodigy, he was famous not only for his Torah knowledge, but for his secular learning as well. The Gemara is replete with stories of his expertise in such areas as language, medicine, astronomy, and the natural sciences.

Shmuel traveled to Eretz Yisrael to study with the students of Rabbi Yehuda HaNasi. The Gemara records that he treated Rabbi Yehuda HaNasi's eye ailment there, and that Rabbi Yehuda HaNasi regretted that he was unable to find an opportunity to ordain him. After his return to Babylonia, Shmuel was appointed as one of the judges of the community in the Diaspora.

Together with his colleague Rav, Shmuel raised the standard of Torah study in Babylonia to an advanced level that prompted thousands of students to remain there rather than travel to attend the academy in Eretz Yisrael. Shmuel viewed Babylonia as second in sanctity to Eretz Yisrael and ruled that it is prohibited to leave it to travel to other locations in the Diaspora. He also established a close friendship with King Shapur I of Persia, a benevolent monarch who was tolerant of religious diversity in his kingdom.

Shmuel lived to an advanced age, leaving behind two daughters, both of whom were famous for their wisdom and modesty.

HALAKHA

A blind baby – סוּמָא: Even if a child is blind, one does not separate him from his mother, as he is able to recognize her by taste and smell, according to the statement of Rav Ashi (Rambam *Sefer Nashim, Hilkhot Ishut* 21:16; *Shulḥan Arukh, Even HaEzer* 82:5).

A child may continue to nurse – יוֹנֵק תִּינוֹק וְהוֹלֵךְ: If a child continues to nurse and does not cease at any point during this time, he may nurse until he is four years old if he is healthy, or five years old if he is weak. This ruling is in accordance with the opinion of Rabbi Yehoshua (Rambam *Sefer Kedusha, Hilkhot Ma'akhalot Assurot* 3:5; *Shulḥan Arukh, Yoreh De'a* 81:7).

If he ceased – פֵּירַשׁ: If a child weans before the age of twenty-four months, he may be returned to nursing, even if he had been weaned for a lengthy period. However, after twenty-four months, he cannot be returned to nursing after weaning (Rambam *Sefer Kedusha, Hilkhot Ma'akhalot Assurot* 3:4; *Shulḥan Arukh, Yoreh De'a* 81:7).

תַּלְמוּד לוֹמַר: ״אֶת הַגָּמָל כִּי מַעֲלֵה גֵרָה הוּא״ – הוּא טָמֵא, וְאֵין חֲלֵב מְהַלְּכֵי שְׁתַּיִם טָמֵא, אֶלָּא טָהוֹר. יָכוֹל אוֹצִיא אֶת הֶחָלָב שֶׁאֵינוֹ שָׁוֶה בַּכֹּל, וְלֹא אוֹצִיא אֶת הַדָּם שֶׁהוּא שָׁוֶה בַּכֹּל – תַּלְמוּד לוֹמַר ״הוּא״ הוּא טָמֵא, וְאֵין דַּם מְהַלְּכֵי שְׁתַּיִם טָמֵא, אֶלָּא טָהוֹר.

This is as **the verse states:** "But this you shall not eat, of those that only chew the cud, or of those that only part the hoof; **the camel, because it chews the cud** but does not part the hoof, it is impure for you" (Leviticus 11:4). The somewhat superfluous word "it" teaches that **it** alone **is impure, but the milk** of **bipeds**[H] **is not impure; rather,** it is **kosher.** Furthermore, one **might** have thought that **I should exclude the milk** of humans from the prohibition against consumption, as this issue **does not apply equally to everyone,** since only women produce milk, but **I should not exclude** from the prohibition human **blood,**[H] **which** does **apply equally to everyone.** Consequently, **the verse states "it"** with regard to a camel, to say that **it** alone **is impure,** whereas the **blood** of **bipeds**[N] **is not impure,** but **rather** is **kosher.**

וְאָמַר רַב שֵׁשֶׁת: אֲפִילּוּ מִצְוַת פְּרִישָׁה אֵין בּוֹ!

And Rav Sheshet said about this ruling: **There is not even a** rabbinic **command to refrain**[N] from consuming human milk. Therefore, this presents a contradiction to the statement that a child who nurses beyond a certain age is like one who nurses from a non-kosher animal.

לָא קַשְׁיָא; הָא – דְּפָרֵישׁ, הָא – דְּלָא פָּרֵישׁ.

The Gemara answers: **This is not difficult,** as **this** statement that the milk is permitted is referring to **when it** has been **removed** from the woman's body, and **that** statement, that the milk is forbidden, is referring to **when it** has **not** been **removed.**[N] Fundamentally, human milk is a permitted substance. However, it is prohibited by rabbinic law for anyone other than a very young child to nurse directly from a woman's breasts, and one who does so is considered like one who consumes milk from a non-kosher animal.

וְחַלּוּפָא בְּדָם. כִּדְתַנְיָא: דָּם שֶׁעַל גַּבֵּי כִּכָּר – גּוֹרְרוֹ וְאוֹכְלוֹ, שֶׁבֵּין הַשִּׁינַּיִם – מוֹצְצוֹ וְאֵינוֹ חוֹשֵׁשׁ.

And the opposite applies **to blood:** Human blood that has been removed from the body is forbidden, but if it has not yet been removed, it is permitted. **As it is taught** in a *baraita*: If some human **blood was on a loaf** of bread, one **scrapes off** the blood **and** then he may **eat** the bread. Since the blood was detached from the body, it is forbidden by rabbinic law, but if blood **was between the teeth, he may suck it** and swallow it **without concern,** as the blood is permitted if it has not been removed from the body.

אָמַר מָר, רַבִּי יְהוֹשֻׁעַ אוֹמֵר: אֲפִילּוּ אַרְבַּע וְחָמֵשׁ שָׁנִים. וְהָתַנְיָא, רַבִּי יְהוֹשֻׁעַ אוֹמֵר: אֲפִילּוּ חֲבִילָתוֹ עַל כְּתֵיפָיו! אִידִי וְאִידִי חַד שִׁיעוּרָא הוּא. אָמַר רַב יוֹסֵף: הֲלָכָה כְּרַבִּי יְהוֹשֻׁעַ.

The Master said in the aforementioned *baraita*: **Rabbi Yehoshua says:** A child may continue to nurse **even** for **four or five years. But isn't it taught** in a different *baraita*: **Rabbi Yehoshua says: Even if** he can carry **his package on his shoulder** he can continue to nurse? The Gemara answers: This is not a contradiction, since **both this and that are one,** the same, **measure,** and the difference between them is only semantic. **Rav Yosef said:** The ***halakha* is in accordance with** the opinion of **Rabbi Yehoshua.**

HALAKHA

Milk of bipeds – חֲלֵב מְהַלְּכֵי שְׁתַּיִם: Human milk that has been removed into a vessel is permitted for consumption. According to the Rema, who cites the *Beit Yosef*, it is permitted even if it has been removed into one's hand. However, an adult who nursed directly from a woman's breast is like one who nursed from a non-kosher animal. He receives lashes for rebelliousness, according to the Gemara's conclusion (Rambam *Sefer Kedusha, Hilkhot Ma'akhalot Assurot* 3:4; *Shulḥan Arukh, Yoreh De'a* 81:7).

Human blood – דָּם: If human blood has been removed from the body, it is prohibited to eat it due to the appearance of transgression. Consequently, if one bit into a loaf of bread and blood came out of his mouth onto the bread, he must scrape the blood off the bread and throw it away; the bread can then be eaten. However, if there is blood between one's teeth, since it has not yet been removed from the body, it can be sucked and swallowed (Rambam *Sefer Kedusha, Hilkhot Ma'akhalot Assurot* 6:2; *Shulḥan Arukh, Yoreh De'a* 66:10).

NOTES

Blood of bipeds – דַּם מְהַלְּכֵי שְׁתַּיִם: Most commentaries accept the version of the text that appears in *Torat Kohanim*, which does not mention human blood but rather flesh. According to that version, the *baraita* teaches that human flesh is kosher. The early authorities discussed this matter at length. It seems that one of the principles behind the dispute on this matter is, as described in the *Ḥatam Sofer*, a general question whether man is viewed as a type of animal, as he too is called a "living soul" like the animals (see Genesis 1:24, 2:7); if he is an animal, since he does not have the identifying signs that distinguish kosher animals, he is not kosher. Conversely, it could be argued that the Torah delineated the defining signs of kosher animals with regard to various categories of creatures, e.g., quadrupeds, birds, and fish, and since man is not included in any of these categories, there is no prohibition against consuming human flesh.

The Rambam maintains that there is no prohibition against consuming human flesh, but there is a positive mitzva derived from the verse: "These are the living things that you may eat" (Leviticus 11:2), which excludes human beings. The Ramban questions this opinion, both because this derivation is not in the Talmud and also because if there were a prohibition against eating human flesh, then human milk and blood should also have been included in the prohibition, just as is the case with non-kosher animals. Therefore, he argues that it is permitted to consume flesh from a living person, but he concedes that for other reasons there is a prohibition against eating or deriving any benefit from the flesh of a human corpse and that this prohibition is accepted by all authorities.

Rabbeinu Crescas Vidal writes that there are differences of opinion with regard to human flesh. Some say that it is prohibited to eat it, since a person is not ritually slaughtered (see Ri HaLavan). Others saying it is permitted, since humans do not require ritual slaughter. The Ritva, also quoted in the *Nimmukei Yosef*, accepts the version in the *Torat Kohanim*, according to which human flesh is excluded from the prohibition against consuming non-kosher meat, but he writes that this is prohibited other reasons: There is a prohibition against deriving benefit from a dead person, and flesh from a living person is prohibited due to the prohibition against eating the limb of a living animal. Only in specific cases, such as fish and locusts, which the Torah specifically permitted, does the prohibition against eating the limb of a living animal not apply.

Rabbi Aharon HaLevi writes that the version in our Gemara is the correct version, according to which the exemption derived from the verse is referring only to human blood, whereas with regard to flesh, the fundamental prohibition based on the *a fortiori* inference delineated in the Gemara remains in force. He maintains that there are two exclusions in Leviticus 11:4, based on the words "this" and "it," to exclude the blood and milk of humans, but flesh remains prohibited by the *a fortiori* inference. According to this opinion, there is no principle that the blood, milk, or other objects that come from a non-kosher animal are not kosher. These *halakhot* are learned from specific derivations in each case, and they refer only to animals and not to human beings.

There is not even a rabbinic command to refrain – אֲפִילּוּ מִצְוַת פְּרִישָׁה אֵין בּוֹ: Rashi explains the statement of Rav Sheshet in relation to human milk. The Rivan explains that it indicates that it is permissible to swallow one's own blood that may have come out from in between the teeth, as there is no requirement to refrain from consuming blood that has not been removed from the body.

That statement is referring to when it has not been removed – הָא דְּלָא פָּרֵישׁ: The Sages ruled that it is prohibited for anyone other than a small infant to drink a woman's milk directly from her body. If it were permitted, people might mistakenly conclude that the milk of a non-kosher animal is also permitted. However, once the milk has been removed and it is no longer obvious where it came from, it is permitted (Rivan; *Talmidei Rabbeinu Yona*).

PERSONALITIES

Naḥum of Galia – נַחוּם אִישׁ גַּלְיָא: This sage is mentioned only here and it seems that he was one of the later *tanna'im*. Based on his moniker it appears that he was from Gaul, a region in southern Europe that stretched from the northern part of Italy through France and that included parts of present-day Belgium, Luxembourg, Netherlands, Switzerland and Germany.

LANGUAGE

Weeds [*kashkashin*]– קַשְׁקַשִּׁין: These weeds, which are usually removed by weeding and uprooting, *kishkush* in Hebrew, consist of stubble and plants. Some commentaries explain that they are grass roots.

תַּנְיָא, רַבִּי מָרִינוּס אוֹמֵר: גּוֹנֵחַ יוֹנֵק חָלָב בְּשַׁבָּת. מַאי טַעְמָא – יוֹנֵק מְפָרֵק כִּלְאַחַר יָד, וּבִמְקוֹם צַעֲרָא – לָא גְּזַרוּ רַבָּנַן. אָמַר רַב יוֹסֵף: הֲלָכָה כְּרַבִּי מָרִינוּס.

On the same topic **it is taught** in a *baraita*: **Rabbi Marinos says: One who is coughing** due to an illness that requires milk but did not have milk available **may suck milk** directly from an animal's udders[H] **on Shabbat,** although milking is a prohibited labor on Shabbat. **What is the reason? Sucking** the milk in this way constitutes an act of **extracting[N] in an unusual manner.** Although milking is an example of the labor of extracting, a subcategory of the primary category of threshing, it is prohibited by Torah law only when the labor is performed in its typical manner. One who nurses from an animal is extracting the milk in an unusual manner. Such labor is prohibited by rabbinic law, **but in a situation** involving **pain,** like one who is coughing, **the Sages did not issue a decree. Rabbi Yosef said:** The *halakha* **is in accordance with** the opinion **of Rabbi Marinos.**

תַּנְיָא, נַחוּם אִישׁ גַּלְיָא אוֹמֵר: צִינּוֹר שֶׁעָלוּ בּוֹ קַשְׁקַשִּׁין – מְמַעֲכָן בְּרַגְלוֹ בְּצִנְעָא בְּשַׁבָּת וְאֵינוֹ חוֹשֵׁשׁ. מַאי טַעְמָא – מְתַקֵּן כִּלְאַחַר יָד הוּא, וּבִמְקוֹם פְּסֵידָא לָא גְּזַרוּ בָּהּ רַבָּנַן. אָמַר רַב יוֹסֵף: הֲלָכָה כְּנַחוּם אִישׁ גַּלְיָא.

A ruling similar to the previous *halakha* **is taught** in a *baraita*: **Naḥum of Galia[P] says:** If a drainage **pipe is blocked by weeds** [*kashkashin*][LH] and grass, preventing water from running through the pipe, **one may crush them with his foot in private** on Shabbat **without concern** that he is performing the labor of preparing a vessel. The Gemara explains: **What is the reason** for this leniency? **This is** an example of **repairing** a vessel **in an unusual manner,** since it is uncommon to fix an item without using a tool or one's hands. Performing labor in an unusual manner is ordinarily prohibited by rabbinic decree, **but in a situation** involving financial **loss, the Sages did not issue a decree. Rabbi Yosef said:** The *halakha* **is in accordance with** the opinion of **Naḥum of Galia.**

פֵּירַשׁ לְאַחַר עֶשְׂרִים וְאַרְבָּעָה חֹדֶשׁ, וְחָזַר – כְּיוֹנֵק שֶׁקֶץ. וְכַמָּה? אָמַר רַב יְהוּדָה בַּר חֲבִיבָא אָמַר שְׁמוּאֵל: שְׁלֹשָׁה יָמִים. אִיכָּא דְּאָמְרִי, תָּנֵי רַב יְהוּדָה בַּר חֲבִיבָא קַמֵּיהּ דִּשְׁמוּאֵל: שְׁלֹשָׁה יָמִים.

The Gemara continues discussing the aforementioned *baraita*, which states: If the child **ceased** nursing **after twenty-four months and** then **resumed,** he is **like one who nurses** from **a non-kosher animal.** The Gemara asks: **How long** must he cease nursing to be considered weaned?[H] **Rav Yehuda bar Ḥaviva said** that **Shmuel said: Three days. There are** those **who say** that this was not an amoraic statement, but rather a *baraita* that **is taught** by **Rav Yehuda bar Ḥaviva before Shmuel:** Weaning takes effect after **three days.**

תָּנוּ רַבָּנַן: מֵינֶקֶת שֶׁמֵּת בַּעְלָהּ בְּתוֹךְ עֶשְׂרִים וְאַרְבָּעָה חֹדֶשׁ – הֲרֵי זוֹ לֹא תִתְאָרֵס, וְלֹא תִינָּשֵׂא,

§ The Gemara discusses other *halakhot* relating to nursing. **The Sages taught: A nursing woman whose husband died within twenty-four months** of her child's birth **may not be betrothed and may not get married**

HALAKHA

One who is coughing may suck milk directly from an animal's udders – גּוֹנֵחַ יוֹנֵק חָלָב: One who is coughing and needs to drink milk is permitted to nurse from an animal on Shabbat, as in situations of pain the Sages did not prohibit this. Rabbeinu Tam, the Rosh, and the *Tur* maintain that if one has no ailment other than hunger pangs, it is prohibited to nurse from an animal on Shabbat, in accordance with the opinion of Abba Shaul in tractate *Yevamot* that this is permitted only on a Festival (Rambam *Sefer Zemanim, Hilkhot Shabbat* 21:14; *Shulḥan Arukh, Oraḥ Ḥayyim* 328:33).

If a drainage pipe is blocked by weeds – צִינּוֹר שֶׁעָלוּ בּוֹ קַשְׁקַשִּׁים: If a pipe that conveys water from the roof becomes clogged up with weeds and grass that prevent the water from flowing out, and consequently the water stays on the roof and leaks into the house, one may crush the obstructions with his foot in private. Some say that although it is preferable to crush the weeds in private, if this is not possible it may even be done publicly (*Beur Halakha*). Since this is a rabbinic prohibition and it is being done in an unusual manner, the Sages made an exception in a case where loss is involved, in accordance with Naḥum of Galia and Rav Yosef's ruling (*Shulḥan Arukh, Oraḥ Ḥayyim* 336:9).

How long must he cease nursing to be considered weaned – פֵּירַשׁ...כַּמָּה: A child who is older than twenty-four months and did not nurse for three days may not be returned to nursing, according to the Gemara's conclusion. This *halakha* applies if he stopped nursing while healthy. But if he stopped due to an illness that prevented him from nursing, he may be returned to nursing. If there is some danger involved, he may be returned to nursing, even if he had been weaned for a long time (Rosh, based on Jerusalem Talmud; Rambam *Sefer Kedusha, Hilkhot Ma'akhalot Assurot* 3:5; *Shulḥan Arukh, Yoreh De'a* 81:7).

NOTES

Extracting – מְפָרֵק: The labor of extracting is not enumerated among the thirty-nine labors prohibited on Shabbat. Rashi explains that extracting is a subcategory of threshing, as it involves removing edible contents from an inedible container. *Tosafot* question this interpretation, based on the Gemara elsewhere (*Shabbat* 75a), where it says that the labor of threshing applies only to objects that grew from the ground. Because of this question, Rabbeinu Tam explains that the extracting discussed in the case of milking is actually a subcategory of the labor of smoothing (see *Tosafot* on *Shabbat* 73b), and Rabbi Shimshon of Saens explains that it is a subcategory of shearing.

עַד עֶשְׂרִים וְאַרְבָּעָה חֹדֶשׁ, דִּבְרֵי רַבִּי מֵאִיר. וְרַבִּי יְהוּדָה מַתִּיר בִּשְׁמוֹנָה עָשָׂר חֹדֶשׁ. אָמַר רַבִּי נָתָן בַּר יוֹסֵף: הֵן הֵן דִּבְרֵי בֵּית שַׁמַּאי, הֵן הֵן דִּבְרֵי בֵּית הִלֵּל. שֶׁבֵּית שַׁמַּאי אוֹמְרִים: עֶשְׂרִים וְאַרְבָּעָה חֹדֶשׁ, וּבֵית הִלֵּל אוֹמְרִים: שְׁמוֹנָה עָשָׂר חֹדֶשׁ.

until twenty-four months from the day the child was born. The reason for this decree is to protect the child. If she remarries she may become pregnant and may not be able to continue nursing, but her second husband will not be obligated to support the child who is not his son. This is **the statement of Rabbi Meir. And Rabbi Yehuda permits** getting married **after eighteen months. Rabbi Natan bar Yosef said: These** words **are the same** as **the statement of Beit Shammai, and those** words **are the same** as **the statement of Beit Hillel**, i.e., this is an ancient dispute, **as Beit Shammai say: Twenty-four months, and Beit Hillel say: Eighteen months.**

אָמַר רַבָּן שִׁמְעוֹן בֶּן גַּמְלִיאֵל: אֲנִי אַכְרִיעַ; לְדִבְרֵי הָאוֹמֵר עֶשְׂרִים וְאַרְבָּעָה חֹדֶשׁ – מוּתֶּרֶת לִינָּשֵׂא בְּעֶשְׂרִים וְאֶחָד חֹדֶשׁ, לְדִבְרֵי הָאוֹמֵר בִּשְׁמוֹנָה עָשָׂר חֹדֶשׁ – מוּתֶּרֶת לְהִנָּשֵׂא בַּחֲמִשָּׁה עָשָׂר חֹדֶשׁ, לְפִי שֶׁאֵין הֶחָלָב נֶעְכָּר אֶלָּא לְאַחַר שְׁלֹשָׁה חֳדָשִׁים.

Rabban Shimon ben Gamliel said: I will decide. According to the one who says twenty-four months, she may marry after twenty-one months, since even if she gets pregnant, for the first three months of pregnancy she can still continue to nurse. **According to the one who says eighteen months, she may marry after fifteen months, since the milk becomes spoiled** due to pregnancy[B] **only after three months.**

אָמַר עוּלָּא: הֲלָכָה כְּרַבִּי יְהוּדָה. וְאָמַר מָר עוּקְבָא: לִי הִתִּיר רַבִּי חֲנִינָא לָשֵׂאת לְאַחַר חֲמִשָּׁה עָשָׂר חֹדֶשׁ. אֲרִיסֵיהּ דְּאַבַּיֵּי אֲתָא לְקַמֵּיהּ דְּאַבַּיֵּי, אֲמַר לֵיהּ: מַהוּ לַיָּארֵס בַּחֲמִשָּׁה עָשָׂר חֹדֶשׁ? אֲמַר לֵיהּ: חֲדָא – דְּרַבִּי מֵאִיר וְרַבִּי יְהוּדָה הֲלָכָה כְּרַבִּי יְהוּדָה, וְעוֹד: בֵּית שַׁמַּאי וּבֵית הִלֵּל – הֲלָכָה כְּבֵית הִלֵּל, וַאֲמַר עוּלָּא: הֲלָכָה כְּרַבִּי יְהוּדָה, וַאֲמַר מָר עוּקְבָא: לִי הִתִּיר רַבִּי חֲנִינָא לָשֵׂאת לְאַחַר חֲמִשָּׁה עָשָׂר חֹדֶשׁ, כׇּל שֶׁכֵּן דְּאַתְּ לַיָּארֵס.

Ulla said: The ***halakha*** **is in accordance with** the opinion of **Rabbi Yehuda. And Mar Ukva said: Rabbi Ḥanina allowed me to marry** a nursing woman **after fifteen months.** It is related that **Abaye's tenant farmer came before Abaye**[P] to ask a question. **He said to him: What is** the *halakha* with regard to **betrothing** a nursing woman **after fifteen months?** Abaye **said to him: One** reason it is permitted is that in disputes between **Rabbi Meir and Rabbi Yehuda,** the ***halakha*** **is in accordance with Rabbi Yehuda. And furthermore,** this is actually a dispute between earlier *tanna'im*, and when **Beit Shammai and Beit Hillel** dispute, **the** ***halakha*** **is in accordance with Beit Hillel. And** in addition, **Ulla said:** The ***halakha*** **is in accordance with Rabbi Yehuda. And Mar Ukva said: Rabbi Ḥanina allowed me to marry after fifteen months, and** therefore **all the more so you** are permitted to betroth her, as you are only **betrothing** and not marrying her.

כִּי אֲתָא לְקַמֵּיהּ דְּרַב יוֹסֵף אֲמַר לֵיהּ: רַב וּשְׁמוּאֵל דְּאָמְרִי תַּרְוַיְיהוּ: צְרִיכָה לְהַמְתִּין עֶשְׂרִים וְאַרְבָּעָה חֹדֶשׁ, חוּץ מִיּוֹם שֶׁנּוֹלַד בּוֹ וְחוּץ מִיּוֹם שֶׁנִּתְאָרְסָה בּוֹ. רְהַט בָּתְרֵיהּ תְּלָתָא פַּרְסֵי, וְאָמְרִי לַהּ: פַּרְסָא בְּחָלָא, וְלָא אַדְרְכֵיהּ.

When Abaye **came before Rav Yosef** and told him of the incident, Rav Yosef **said to him** in response: **Rav and Shmuel both say: She must wait twenty-four months**[H] before even becoming betrothed, **excluding the day that** the child **was born and excluding the day she became betrothed.** When Abaye heard this, **he ran three parasangs** after his tenant farmer, **and some say** that he ran **one parasang [*parsa*]**[L] **through sand.** He wanted to inform him that he should not rely on the leniency, but rather he should act in accordance with Rav and Shmuel, who prohibited the betrothal, **but he did not** succeed in **catching up to him.**

BACKGROUND

The milk becomes spoiled due to pregnancy – הֶחָלָב נֶעְכָּר: During pregnancy, different hormones are released in a woman's body. Besides prolactin, which induces milk production, there are also other hormones, progesterone and estrogen, that suppress its production, and were once used to curb milk production in women who did not want to nurse. These hormones generally lead to a reduction or even cessation of milk production in pregnant women, although this does not happen in all cases. Additionally, one must take into account that as long as the fetus is growing, the mother's body gives it precedence in terms of allocating the available resources. Consequently, if a woman is not eating a rich diet, her milk may cease shortly after the onset of pregnancy.

HALAKHA

She must wait twenty-four months – צְרִיכָה לְהַמְתִּין עֶשְׂרִים וְאַרְבָּעָה חֹדֶשׁ: The Sages decreed that one should not marry or betroth a woman who is pregnant with or nursing another man's child, until the child is twenty-four months old, excluding the day of birth and the day of betrothal (*Beit Yosef*). The Rema cites the glosses of the Mordekhai, in which it is stated that these months follow the pattern of the year, whether they are full months or incomplete months. Some say that one must add the extra month in a leap year (*Terumat HaDeshen*; see *Pitḥei Teshuva*; Rambam *Sefer Nashim*, *Hilkhot Geirushin* 11:25–26; *Shulḥan Arukh*, *Even HaEzer* 13:11).

LANGUAGE

Parasang [*parsa*] – פַּרְסָא: In the ancient world, this was the word for a Persian mile, a measurement that was adopted in a number of languages, including Greek, Syriac, and, in this case, the Jewish dialect of Aramaic. Apparently, the word comes from the Middle Iranian frasax. In the talmudic system of measurement, one *parsa* equals four *mil*, approximately 5 km.

PERSONALITIES

Abaye – אַבַּיֵּי: One of the outstanding Sages of the Talmud, Abaye was a fourth-generation Babylonian *amora*. It is possible that his real name was Naḥmani or Kilil and that Abaye was a nickname.

Abaye was orphaned at an early age and raised by his paternal uncle, Rabba. Abaye's foster mother, who was the nursemaid who assisted his uncle in raising him, impressed upon him many life lessons that he quotes in her name. There are several incidents related in the Gemara that illustrate his intelligence even as a child, including some where Rabba tests his knowledge. Although Rabba was a priest and the head of his yeshiva, he lived in poverty, as did Abaye.

Abaye was the primary student of Rabba and also of Rav Yosef. After Rav Yosef's death, Abaye succeeded him as the head of the yeshiva in Pumbedita. He celebrated the study of Torah and would announce a celebration for the scholars whenever one of them completed a tractate. Growing up in his uncle's home, he was aware of the difficulties of scholars who were without financial means. The Gemara in tractate *Berakhot* (35b) relates that he testified that many were successful following the path of Rabbi Yishmael, who instructed his students to plow, plant, and harvest in the appropriate time, and that only very few were successful following the path of Rabbi Shimon bar Yoḥai, who taught that one should devote himself entirely to Torah and ignore worldly concerns. In addition to Abaye's prominence as a Torah scholar, he was known for his righteousness and his acts of kindness.

Abaye's exchanges and halakhic arguments with Rabba and, even more so, with Rav Yosef, can be found throughout the Talmud. However, his disputes with his colleague Rava are especially significant. Their disputes, known as the discussions of Abaye and Rava, are examples of profound and edifying disputes, and they are among the foundations of the Babylonian Talmud. In these disputes, with six exceptions, the *halakha* is ruled in accordance with the opinion of Rava.

NOTES

Even an egg in *kutah* – אֲפִילּוּ בֵּיעֲתָא בְּכוּתְחָא: *Kutah* was a type of popular Babylonian dip made from sour milk and bread crumbs. The Rivan understands that the issue under discussion is simply whether one may eat an egg in *kutah*. However, *Tosafot* and several other early authorities cite and endorse the explanation of the *Arukh* that this does not refer to ordinary eggs, as everyone knows that there is no prohibition against eating eggs with milk, but rather to fully formed eggs found inside a chicken after it was slaughtered. Although these eggs were inside the chicken at the time of slaughter, they are not considered meat and may be eaten with dairy foods. Some question this interpretation: If that is what the Gemara meant, the matter is not simple, and this case should not be cited as a paradigm of a simple question. The Ritva answers that this *halakha* was commonly known at the time, as is apparent from tractate *Beitza*.

BACKGROUND

***Kutah* – כּוּתְחָא:** *Kutah* was a dip made from sour milk and bread crumbs and eaten on bread or as an appetizer. This food was particularly popular in Babylonia and was therefore known as Babylonian *kutah*. It was made with moldy bread, whey, and salt.

Exilarch – רֵישׁ גָּלוּתָא: The Exilarch, who was descended from the kings of the house of David, was recognized by the Jews as the heir to the throne of Judah (see Genesis 49:10) and entrusted with broad official powers. He was the leader of the Jews of the Persian Empire and their representative to the authorities, who regarded him as a member of a royal dynasty. Consequently, the Exilarch was held in high esteem within the Persian court. During various periods, he even ranked third in the royal hierarchy.

אָמַר אַבָּיֵי: הַאי מִילְּתָא דַּאֲמוּר רַבָּנַן: אֲפִילּוּ בֵּיעֲתָא בְּכוּתְחָא לָא לִישְׁרֵי אִינִישׁ בְּמָקוֹם רַבֵּיהּ – לָא מִשּׁוּם דְּמִיחֲזֵי כְּאַפְקִירוּתָא, אֶלָּא מִשּׁוּם דְּלָא מִסְתַּיְּיעָא מִילְּתָא לְמֵימְרָא. דְּהָא אֲנָא הֲוָה גְּמִירְנָא לֵיהּ לְהָא דְּרַב וּשְׁמוּאֵל, אֲפִילּוּ הָכִי – לָא מִסְתַּיְּיעָא לִי מִילְּתָא לְמֵימַר.

Abaye said that he learned from this situation **that which the Sages said: A person should not permit even** eating **an egg in *kutah*,**[NB] a dish made with milk, **in his teacher's vicinity.**[H] This this is a very simple ruling, as an egg is not meat and may unquestionably be eaten with milk. There are no stringencies that apply to this case, but nevertheless one should not rule even on such a *halakha* in his teacher's vicinity. Abaye explained that this is **not because it appears disrespectful** to teach *halakha* in one's teacher's vicinity, as this is a simple matter that does not require great knowledge of *halakha*, **rather because he will not be successful in saying the matter** correctly. An illustration of this principle is what just happened, **since I had learned this** *halakha* **of Rav and Shmuel,** and **even so I was unsuccessful in saying it** correctly, as I ruled in the vicinity of my teacher, Rav Yosef.

תָּנוּ רַבָּנַן: נָתְנָה בְּנָהּ לְמֵינֶקֶת, אוֹ גְּמַלַתּוֹ, אוֹ מֵת – מוּתֶּרֶת לִינָּשֵׂא מִיָּד. רַב פָּפָּא וְרַב הוּנָא בְּרֵיהּ דְּרַב יְהוֹשֻׁעַ סְבוּר לְמֶיעְבַּד עוּבְדָא כִּי הָא מַתְנִיתָא. אֲמַרָה לְהוּ הַהִיא סָבְתָא: בְּדִידִי הֲוָה עוּבְדָא, וַאֲסַר לִי רַב נַחְמָן.

§ **The Sages taught:** If a woman **gave her child to a wet nurse**[H] during the waiting period, **or weaned him,** or the child **died, she is permitted to marry immediately.** It is related that **Rav Pappa and Rav Huna, son of Rav Yehoshua, thought to act in accordance with this *baraita*.** However, **a certain old woman said to them: There was an incident in which I** was involved with regard to this issue **and Rav Naḥman prohibited it for me.**

אִינִי?! וְהָא רַב נַחְמָן שְׁרָא לְהוּ לְבֵי רֵישׁ גָּלוּתָא! שָׁאנֵי בֵּי רֵישׁ גָּלוּתָא, דְּלָא הָדְרִי בְּהוּ.

The Gemara asks: **Is that so? Didn't Rav Naḥman permit this** for the members of **the Exilarch's**[B] **household?** The Gemara answers: **The Exilarch's household is different,** since people employed by them **do not renege** out of fear of the consequences. Consequently, if a woman from that household arranges a wet nurse for her child, it is certain that the wet nurse will keep her commitment, whereas with other people there is a danger that if the mother remarries the child might be left without anyone to feed him.

אֲמַר לְהוּ רַב פָּפֵּי: וְאַתּוּן לָא תִּסְבְּרוּהָ מֵהָא דְּתַנְיָא: הֲרֵי שֶׁהָיְתָה רְדוּפָה לֵילֵךְ לְבֵית אָבִיהָ, אוֹ שֶׁהָיָה לָהּ כַּעַס בְּבֵית בַּעְלָהּ, אוֹ שֶׁהָיָה בַּעְלָהּ חָבוּשׁ בְּבֵית הָאֲסוּרִין, אוֹ שֶׁהָלַךְ בַּעְלָהּ לִמְדִינַת הַיָּם, אוֹ שֶׁהָיָה בַּעְלָהּ זָקֵן אוֹ חוֹלֶה, אוֹ שֶׁהָיְתָה עֲקָרָה, וּזְקֵנָה, אַיְילוֹנִית, וּקְטַנָּה, וְהַמַּפֶּלֶת אַחַר מִיתַת בַּעְלָהּ, וְשֶׁאֵינָהּ רְאוּיָה לֵילֵד – כּוּלָּן צְרִיכוֹת לְהַמְתִּין שְׁלֹשָׁה חֳדָשִׁים, דִּבְרֵי רַבִּי מֵאִיר.

Rav Pappi said to Rav Pappa and Rav Huna, son of Rav Yehoshua: **And do you not maintain** that such a marriage is prohibited **from that which is taught** in a *baraita*: **If** a woman **frequently went to her father's house** and had been there for a long time; **or she had been angry with her husband** and separated from him while still in his **house; or her husband had been incarcerated in prison;** or her husband **had gone overseas; or her husband had been old or ill; or if she was a barren woman, or elderly,** or **a sexually underdeveloped woman, or a minor girl; or if she had miscarried after the death of her husband; or if she was unfit to give birth** for any other reason, although in any of these cases there is no concern that she might be pregnant, **they must all wait** at least **three months.**[H] The Sages said that a woman must wait for three months between marriages, so there would be no doubt as to who is the father of any child she may give birth to, and they did not distinguish between different women with regard to this decree. This is **the statement of Rabbi Meir.**

HALAKHA

In his teacher's vicinity – בְּמָקוֹם רַבֵּיהּ: It is prohibited to rule in the vicinity of one's teacher, within a distance of three parasangs. One who does so is liable to be punished with death at the hand of Heaven, as explained in tractate *Eiruvin* (63a). The Rema writes that this is prohibited in the vicinity of one's preeminent teacher, even if one asked permission from his teacher (Rambam *Sefer HaMadda*, *Hilkhot Talmud Torah* 5:2; *Sefer Shofetim*, *Hilkhot Sanhedrin* 20:9; *Shulḥan Arukh*, *Yoreh De'a* 242:4).

She gave her child to a wet nurse – נָתְנָה בְּנָהּ לְמֵינֶקֶת: Even if a woman gave her child to a wet nurse or weaned him within twenty-four months, and even if the wet nurse vowed publicly not to renege, the mother is prohibited from marrying. This is because the *halakha* is in accordance with Rabbi Meir's opinion with regard to all of his decrees, and there is a concern that people will mistakenly permit a woman's remarriage in a case in which a wet nurse has not taken a vow (Rosh). Some say that in a case where the wet nurse took a vow, if the mother got married she does not need to get divorced (Rema, citing Mordekhai), according to the ruling of Rav Naḥman and the conclusion of the Gemara (Rambam *Sefer Nashim*, *Hilkhot Geirushin* 11:27; *Shulḥan Arukh*, *Even HaEzer* 13:11).

Wait at least three months – לְהַמְתִּין שְׁלֹשָׁה חֳדָשִׁים: Widows and divorcées are prohibited from marrying or betrothing another man within ninety days of their husband's passing. This is in order to determine whether or not the woman is pregnant from her previous husband. According to the rabbinic decree, this applies even where there is no concern that she might be pregnant, e.g., a woman who is incapable of conceiving or one who was widowed or divorced after betrothal (Rambam *Sefer Nashim*, *Hilkhot Geirushin* 11:18–19; *Shulḥan Arukh*, *Even HaEzer* 13:1).

רַבִּי יוֹסֵי מַתִּיר לֵיאָרֵס וְלִינָּשֵׂא מִיָּד. וְאָמַר רַב נַחְמָן אָמַר שְׁמוּאֵל: הֲלָכָה כְּרַבִּי מֵאִיר בִּגְזֵירוֹתָיו!

However, **Rabbi Yosei permits** all the aforementioned women **to be betrothed and to marry immediately,** since there is no concern that they may be pregnant. **And Rav Naḥman said** that **Shmuel said:** The ***halakha* is in accordance with** the opinion of **Rabbi Meir** with regard to all of **his decrees.** In every place where Rabbi Meir was stringent so as to avoid possibility of error, the *halakha* is in accordance with his opinion. Consequently, this ruling should apply also to a nursing mother who wishes to remarry; the restriction should apply equally to a woman who had given her child to a wet nurse, or who had weaned him, or whose child had died.

אָמְרִי לֵיהּ: לָאו אַדַּעְתִּין. וְהִלְכְתָא: מֵת – מוּתֶּר, גְּמָלַתּוּ – אָסוּר. מָר בַּר רַב אָשֵׁי אָמַר: אֲפִילּוּ מֵת נַמִי אָסוּר, דִּלְמָא קָטְלָה לֵיהּ, וְאָזְלָא וּמִינַּסְבָא. הֲוָה עוּבְדָא וַחֲנַקְתֵּיהּ. וְלָא הִיא, הַהִיא שׁוֹטָה הֲוַאי, דְּלָא עָבְדֵי נָשֵׁי דְּחָנְקָן בְּנַיְיהוּ.

They answered him: The matter **was not in our mind,** meaning that we had forgotten this principle. Nevertheless, the Gemara concludes: **The *halakha*** is that if a nursing mother's child **died,** the mother **is permitted** to marry[H] immediately, but if **she had weaned him,** she **is prohibited** from marrying, lest she forcibly wean him prematurely. **Mar bar Rav Ashi said: Even if** the child **died, she is also prohibited** from marrying, because if it were permitted when the child dies, there would be concern that **she might kill him and** then **go and get married.** It is related that **there was an incident** where **a woman strangled** her child for this reason. The Gemara concludes that **that is not so,** i.e., this incident does not affect the *halakha.* **That woman was insane,** and since **women do not** ordinarily **strangle their children,** one need not be concerned about this happening.

תָּנוּ רַבָּנַן: הֲרֵי שֶׁנָּתְנוּ לָהּ בֵּן לְהָנִיק – הֲרֵי זוֹ לֹא תָּנִיק עִמּוֹ לֹא בְּנָהּ וְלֹא בֶּן חֲבֶירְתָּהּ. פָּסְקָה קִימְעָא – אוֹכֶלֶת הַרְבֵּה, לֹא תֹּאכַל עִמּוֹ דְּבָרִים הָרָעִים לֶחָלָב.

§ **The Sages taught:** If **someone gave a child** to a wet nurse, and she agreed **to nurse** him for payment, **she may not nurse her** own **child or another** woman's **child** together **with him,** in order that she not take away milk from the child she is being paid to nurse. Even **if she fixed a small** allowance for food with the payment for nursing, **she must** nevertheless **eat large** quantities[H] so that she will have enough milk. And **she may not eat** together **with him,** i.e., while she is nursing the child, **things** that are **bad for** her **milk.**

הַשְׁתָּא בְּנָהּ אָמְרַתְּ לָא, בֶּן חֲבֶירְתָּהּ מִיבַּעְיָא?! מַהוּ דְּתֵימָא: בְּנָהּ הוּא דְּחָיֵיס עִילָּוֵיהּ – מַמְצִיָא לֵיהּ טְפֵי, אֲבָל בֶּן חֲבֶירְתָּהּ, אִי לָאו דַּהֲוָה לָהּ מוֹתָר – לָא הֲוָה מַמְצְיָא לֵיהּ, קָא מַשְׁמַע לַן.

The Gemara asks about this *baraita*: **Now** that **you said** that she may **not** nurse **her own child** together with her client's child, **is it necessary** to say that she cannot nurse **another woman's child?** The Gemara answers: **Lest you say** that the prohibition is limited to **her child, as** there is a concern that since **she favors him, she will feed him more** milk than the other child, **but** with regard to **another** woman's **child, if she did not have surplus** milk **she would not feed him,** and therefore it should be permitted, the *baraita* therefore **teaches us** not to distinguish between the cases.

פָּסְקָה קִימְעָא אוֹכֶלֶת הַרְבֵּה, מֵהֵיכָא? אָמַר רַב שֵׁשֶׁת: מִשֶּׁלָּהּ.

The *baraita* said that even **if she fixed a small** allowance for food, **she must eat large** quantities. The Gemara asks: **From where** should she get this food if the allowance cannot cover it? **Rav Sheshet said: From her own** funds. Because she accepted an obligation to nurse the child, she must take the necessary steps to fulfill her obligation.

HALAKHA

If the child died, she is permitted to marry – מֵת, מוּתָּר: If a nursing mother's child died, she may get married, and there is no concern that she might kill the child in order to be allowed to remarry. Similarly, if the child weaned in her husband's lifetime, or she could not nurse her child at all, or if she gave her child to a wet nurse three months before her husband's death and did not nurse him at all during this period, she is permitted to marry immediately (Rambam *Sefer Nashim, Hilkhot Geirushin* 11:27; *Shulḥan Arukh, Even HaEzer* 13:11).

Even if she fixed a small allowance for food, she must eat large quantities – פָּסְקָה קִימְעָא, אוֹכֶלֶת הַרְבֵּה: As long as a woman is nursing her child, her husband must provide her with foods that improve her milk output. If she does not receive more food, she must add additional food from her own funds, if she has property of her own. The *Shulḥan Arukh* quotes the Rambam, who writes that if it was agreed to provide her with the appropriate foods and she wishes to eat more food or other foods, her husband cannot deny her these foods because they might be dangerous to her child, since her own personal needs prevail over her child's needs. The Ra'avad disagrees and says that he can deny her these foods (Rambam *Sefer Nashim, Hilkhot Ishut* 21:11; *Shulḥan Arukh, Even HaEzer* 80:11–12).

LANGUAGE

Garden cress [*taḥlei*] – תחלי: This is the Aramaic term for *Lepidium sativum*, the vegetable known in Hebrew as *ḥalim*. It is a garden vegetable used in salads.

Brine [*moninei*] – מוניני: The *Arukh* explains that *moninei* is brine, particularly fish brine, but the term can also be used to refer to locust brine. It appears to be Aramaic, a shortened form of *mei nunei*, meaning fish water.

NOTES

Soil – גרגושתא: The word is of Aramaic origin and it generally refers to the earth used for making seals. It was a type of quality clay used for seals on letters or parcels.

לא תאכל עמו דברים הרעים. מאי נינהו? אמר רב כהנא: כגון כשות, וחזיז, ודגים קטנים, ואדמה. אביי אמר: אפילו קרא וחבושא. רב פפא אמר: אפילו קרא וכופרא. רב אשי אמר: אפילו כמכא והרסנא. מינייהו פסקי חלבא, מינייהו עכרי חלבא.

The *baraita* said: **She may not eat together with him things** that are **bad for her milk.** The Gemara asks: **What are these** foods that are detrimental for milk?[B] **Rav Kahana said: For example, hops; and young, green grain** sprouts; **small fish; and soil. Abaye said: Even pumpkin and quince. Rav Pappa said: Even pumpkin and palm branches** with small, unripe dates. **Rav Ashi said: Even *kutaḥ* [*kamka*] and small fried fish.** All these items are bad, as **some cause milk to dry up** and **some cause milk to spoil.**

דמשמשא בי ריחיא – הוו לה בני נכפי, דמשמשא על ארעא – הוו לה בני שמוטי, דדרכא על רמא דחמרא – הוו לה בני גירדני, דאכלה חרדלא – הוו לה בני זלזלני, דאכלה תחלי – הוו לה בני דולפני, דאכלה מוניני – הוו לה בני מציצי עינא, דאכלה גרגושתא – הוו לה בני מכוערי, דשתיא שיכרא – הוו לה בני אוכמי, דאכלה בישרא ושתיא חמרא – הוו לה בני

The Gemara cites other possible consequences of a mother's behavior that could affect her children: **A woman who engages in intercourse in a mill will have epileptic children;** one who **engages in intercourse on the ground will have long-necked children;** one who **steps on a donkey's dung** when pregnant **will have bald children;** one who **eats mustard** during pregnancy **will have**[B] **gluttonous children;** one who **eats garden cress [*taḥlei*]**[L] **will have tearful children;** one who **eats** fish **brine [*moninei*]**[L] **will have children with blinking eyes;** one who **eats soil**[NB] **will have ugly children;** one who **drinks intoxicating liquor will have black children;** one who **eats meat and drinks wine** during pregnancy **will have children** who are

BACKGROUND

Foods that are detrimental for milk – דברים הרעים לחלב: A woman's diet in general as well as certain specific foods that she eats can affect the quality of her milk and even have an effect on the taste of the milk.

One who eats…will have – דאכלה...הוו לה בני: There is no specific scientific knowledge with regard to this subject, although it seems clear that a woman's diet during pregnancy has an effect on the fetus. Other factors, such as alcohol and drugs, certainly have a significant influence on the development of a fetus, including its color and complexion.

Eating soil – אכילת אדמה: Eating soil during pregnancy is a known phenomenon, as pregnant women sometimes experience cravings for strange foods. At times, they can also suffer from a compulsion to consume non-food items, a psychological disorder known as pica. Cases have been reported of pregnant women eating earth, clay, sand, and other inedible substances. However, certain types of earth may also be eaten for medicinal purposes. The type mentioned in the Gemara may serve to ease heartburn experienced during pregnancy.

Perek **V**
Daf **61** Amud **a**

BACKGROUND

Celery – כרפסא: This is *Apium graveolens*, a garden vegetable used for flavoring and salads.

LANGUAGE

Coriander [*kusbarta*] – כוסברתא: This is a plant used as a spice, with characteristic flavor and aroma. It is known in biblical Hebrew as *gad* and in Modern Hebrew as *kusbar*.

בריי, דאכלה ביעי – הוו לה בני עינני, דאכלה כוורי – הוו לה בני חינני, דאכלה כרפסא – הוו לה בני זיותני, דאכלה כוסברתא – הוו לה בני בישרני, דאכלה אתרוגא – הוו לה בני ריחני. ברתיה דשבור מלכא אכלה בה אמה אתרוגא, והוו מסקי לה לקמיה אבוה בריש ריחני.

healthy; one who **eats eggs will have large-eyed children;** one who **eats fish will have graceful children;** one who **eats celery**[B] **will have beautiful children;** one who **eats coriander [*kusbarta*]**[L] **will have corpulent children;** and one who **eats *etrogim* will have sweet-smelling children.** It is related with regard to **the daughter of King Shapur**[P] of Persia, that **her mother ate *etrogim*** while pregnant with her and **they used to place her in front of her father on top of all the spices,** as she was so fragrant.

PERSONALITIES

King Shapur – שבור מלכא: King Shapur, or Shavor Malka, was the name of several Persian kings. King Shapur I, the second king of the Sassanid dynasty, who lived from 241–272 CE, was tolerant of other faiths. There are many incidents related in the Talmud that reflect his close relationship with the Jewish people, as well as his love and appreciation for Jewish customs. In several places, the Gemara describes his friendship with the *amora* Shmuel.

King Shapur II, who lived from 303–380, was a zealous supporter of Zoroastrianism, a religion he tried to impose on the minorities under his rule, especially Christians. During his reign, the Jewish community suffered from oppressive taxes, levies, and various decrees.

אֲמַר רַב הוּנָא: בָּדַק לָן רַב הוּנָא בַּר חִינָּנָא: הִיא אוֹמֶרֶת לְהָנִיק וְהוּא אוֹמֵר שֶׁלֹּא לְהָנִיק – שׁוֹמְעִין לָהּ, צַעֲרָא דִּידָהּ הוּא. הוּא אוֹמֵר לְהָנִיק וְהִיא אוֹמֶרֶת שֶׁלֹּא לְהָנִיק – מַהוּ? כׇּל הֵיכָא דְּלָאו אוֹרְחָהּ – שׁוֹמְעִין לָהּ, הִיא אוֹרְחָהּ וְהוּא לָאו אוֹרְחֵיהּ – מַאי? בָּתַר דִּידֵיהּ אָזְלִינַן אוֹ בָּתַר דִּידָהּ אָזְלִינַן?

§ **Rav Huna said: Rav Huna bar Ḥinnana tested us,** by asking: **If she says** that she wants **to nurse**[H] **and he says** that he **does not** want her **to nurse** but rather to give the child to a wet nurse, **we accede to her** desires, as **she is the one suffering**[N] from engorgement of her breasts. However, if **he says** that he wants her **to nurse**[H] **and she says** that she does **not** want **to nurse, what is** the *halakha*? He then narrowed the scope of the question: **Anywhere that she is not accustomed,** as the women of her family generally do not nurse their children but give them to wet nurses instead, **we accede to her** desires. However, **if she is accustomed** to nursing **and he is not accustomed,**[N] i.e., the women of her family generally nurse their babies but the women in his family do not, **what** is the *halakha*: Do **we follow his** wishes to follow her family custom **or do we follow her** wishes to follow his family custom?

וּפְשִׁיטְנָא לֵיהּ מֵהָא: עוֹלָה עִמּוֹ וְאֵינָהּ יוֹרֶדֶת עִמּוֹ. אֲמַר רַב הוּנָא: מַאי קְרָאָה – ״וְהִיא בְּעוּלַת בַּעַל״ – בַּעֲלִיָּיתוֹ שֶׁל בַּעַל, וְלֹא בִּירִידָתוֹ שֶׁל בַּעַל. רַבִּי אֶלְעָזָר אֲמַר מֵהָכָא: ״כִּי הִיא הָיְתָה אֵם כׇּל חָי״ – לְחַיִּים נִיתְּנָה, וְלֹא לְצַעַר נִיתְּנָה.

And we answered his question **from this** amoraic statement: When a woman marries a man, **she ascends with him** to his socioeconomic status, if it is higher than hers, **but she does not descend with him** if his status is lower. Consequently, if his family is not accustomed to nurse, she is not obligated to nurse either. **Rav Huna said: What is the verse** from which this is derived? It is derived from: **"She is a man's wife"** (Genesis 20:3). The Gemara explains: The word used here for "wife [*be'ula*]" hints through similar spelling that she ascends in status **with the ascension [*aliya*] of her husband but does not** descend **with the descent of her husband. Rabbi Elazar said:** There is a hint to this principle **from here: "As she was the mother of all living"** (Genesis 3:20), which indicates that **she was given** to her husband **for living** with him, **but was not given to** suffer **pain** with him.

״הִכְנִיסָה לוֹ שִׁפְחָה״ וכו׳. הָא שְׁאָרָא – עָבְדָא. וְתֵימָא לֵיהּ: עַיְילִית לָךְ אִיתְּתָא בַּחֲרִיקַאי! מִשּׁוּם דְּאָמַר לָהּ: הָא טָרְחָא לְדִידִי וּלְדִידָהּ, קַמֵּי דִּידָךְ מַאן טָרַח?

§ The mishna states that **if she brought him one maidservant** into the marriage with her, she does not need to grind wheat, bake, or wash clothes. The Gemara infers from this statement that **she** must nevertheless **perform the other** tasks. The Gemara asks: **Let** the wife **say to him: I brought you a woman in my place [*baḥarikai*]**[L] who can perform all the tasks I am supposed to do, and the wife should be completely exempt. The Gemara answers: This is not a valid argument **because** the husband **can say to her: This** maidservant **toils for me and for herself** like any other woman, but **who will toil for you?** It is necessary for the wife to do some work in order to cover some of her own expenses.

״שְׁתַּיִם אֵינָהּ מְבַשֶּׁלֶת וְאֵינָהּ מֵנִיקָה״ וכו׳. הָא שְׁאָרָא – עָבְדָא. וְתֵימָא לֵיהּ: עַיְילִית לָךְ אִיתְּתָא אַחֲרִיתֵי דְּטָרְחָה לְדִידִי וּלְדִידָהּ, וַחֲדָא לְדִידָךְ וּלְדִידָהּ! מִשּׁוּם דְּאָמַר לָהּ: קַמֵּי אוֹרְחֵי וּפָרְחֵי מַאן טָרַח?

The mishna further said that if she brought him **two** maidservants, **she does not** need to **cook and does not need to nurse** her child. The Gemara infers: **She** must nevertheless **perform the other** tasks. The Gemara asks: **Let** the wife **say to him: I brought you another woman who can toil for me and for herself, and one** who can toil **for you and for herself.** Consequently, I do not need to do any work at all. The Gemara answers: This is also not a valid argument **because he can say to her: Who is going to toil for the guests and wayfarers** who will come because we are a large household? There are still other tasks that need to be performed.

״שָׁלֹשׁ אֵינָהּ מַצַּעַת הַמִּטָּה״. הָא שְׁאָרָא – עָבְדָא. וְתֵימָא לֵיהּ: עַיְילִית לָךְ אַחֲרִיתֵי לְאוֹרְחֵי וּפָרְחֵי! מִשּׁוּם דְּאָמַר לָהּ: נָפֵישׁ בְּנֵי בֵיתָא – נָפֵישׁ אוֹרְחֵי וּפָרְחֵי.

The mishna further said that if she brought him **three** maidservants, **she does not** need to **make his bed** or make thread from wool. The Gemara infers: **She** must nevertheless **perform the other** tasks. The Gemara asks: **Let her say to him: I brought you another** woman to toil **for the guests and wayfarers,** in addition to one to toil for herself and for me, and another to toil for herself and for you. Therefore, I do not need to do any work at all. The Gemara answers: This is also not a valid argument **because he can say to her:** When **the members of the house increase,** the number **of guests and wayfarers** also **increases** and therefore there is still more work to be done.

אִי הָכִי, אֲפִילּוּ אַרְבַּע נַמִי! אַרְבַּע, כֵּיוָן דִּנְפִישֵׁי לְהוּ מְסַיְּיעָן אַהֲדָדֵי.

The Gemara asks: **If so,** then **even** if she brought him **four** maidservants **as well,** she should also have to work, as there will be many more guests. But the mishna says that if she brought four maidservants she does not need to do anything. The Gemara answers: When there are **four, since there are many** of them, **they assist one another** and can complete all the necessary tasks.

HALAKHA

She wants to nurse – הִיא אוֹמֶרֶת לְהָנִיק: If the woman wishes to nurse and her husband does not want her to, the *halakha* rules in her favor (Rambam *Sefer Nashim, Hilkhot Ishut* 21:13; *Shulḥan Arukh, Even HaEzer* 82:2).

He wants her to nurse – הוּא אוֹמֵר לְהָנִיק: Nursing is like any other task that a woman is required to perform if the women in both her family and his are accustomed to it. If she is from a poor family who usually nurse their children, but he is from a wealthy family, then he must hire a wet nurse if she does not want to nurse the baby herself (Rambam *Sefer Nashim, Hilkhot Ishut* 21:14; *Shulḥan Arukh, Even HaEzer* 80:6, 10 and 82:3).

NOTES

She is the one suffering – צַעֲרָא דִּידָהּ הוּא: Rashi understands this to mean that the woman suffers due to engorgement of her breasts, whereas the Rambam explains that she suffers from the baby being taken away from her. The Ri Migash interprets the idea differently: Since the woman alone suffers from nursing, the husband should not have any say in the matter.

She is accustomed to nursing and he is not accustomed – הִיא אוֹרְחָהּ וְהוּא לָאו אוֹרְחֵיהּ: The Rosh writes that this principle applies to all the tasks that a woman is obligated to perform. If it is not the custom of her family or of his family, she is not obligated to perform them. This is also the *halakha* as quoted in the *Shulḥan Arukh*. This case is singled out for discussion because sometimes a woman specifically wants to nurse her child while her husband does not want her to do so.

LANGUAGE

In my place [*baḥarikai*] – בַּחֲרִיקַאי: The *Arukh* and other sources cite a variant text that reads *baharikai*. This term probably derives from the Iranian vihrīq and the Middle Persian guhrīg, which mean equivalent, although in the Babylonian Jewish dialect of Aramaic it means instead of.

NOTES

Once she is able to bring – כֵּיוָן שֶׁרְאוּיָה לְהַכְנִיס: According to Rashi, this means that this *halakha* applies not only when she actually brought him maidservants, but also if there were assets in her dowry that were equal in value to the price of a maidservant. The expression: She reduced her own needs, means that she saved some of the money he gave her, in order to buy a maidservant.

However, the Rif and others have a different version that reads: She found [*matza*] among his possessions, as opposed to: She reduced [*tzimtzema*] her own needs. According to this reading, even if her assets were not sufficient to buy a maidservant, but she determined that he was wealthy and could afford it on his own, she also does not need to perform these tasks. The Ramban and his disciples have a more extreme opinion. They maintain that if the women in the wife's family are not accustomed to doing work themselves but rather to using maidservants, she does not need to perform any task. This interpretation appears to correspond to the idea that she is not obligated to perform tasks to which she is not accustomed.

And make his bed – וּמַצַּעַת לוֹ אֶת הַמִּטָּה: The Rivan does not accept this version, since this is one of the tasks from which the wife is exempt if she brought her husband three maidservants. However, Rashi and *Tosafot* explain that there are two types of bed preparations, one involving heavy work that can be done by a maidservant and another type that is an act of intimacy, and therefore it is not proper for another person to do it.

אָמַר רַב חָנָא וְאִיתֵּימָא רַבִּי שְׁמוּאֵל בַּר נַחְמָנִי: לֹא הִכְנִיסָה לוֹ מַמָּשׁ, אֶלָּא כֵּיוָן שֶׁרְאוּיָה לְהַכְנִיס, אַף עַל פִּי שֶׁלֹּא הִכְנִיסָה. תָּנָא: אֶחָד שֶׁהִכְנִיסָה לוֹ, וְאֶחָד שֶׁצִּמְצְמָה לוֹ מִשֶּׁלָּהּ.

Rav Ḥana, and some say Rav Shmuel bar Naḥmani, said: This does **not** necessarily mean **that she actually brought him** maidservants. **Rather, once she is able to bring**[N] him[H] maidservants, i.e., once her dowry is sufficiently large to buy maidservants, then she is exempt from performing the tasks, **although she did not** actually **bring him** maidservants. The Sages **taught: Whether she brought him** actual maidservants or **whether she reduced her own needs** in order to release enough money to bring a maidservant to work, she is exempt from the tasks.

״אַרְבַּע יוֹשֶׁבֶת בְּקַתֶּדְרָא״. אָמַר רַב יִצְחָק בַּר חֲנַנְיָא אָמַר רַב הוּנָא: אַף עַל פִּי שֶׁאָמְרוּ יוֹשֶׁבֶת בְּקַתֶּדְרָא – אֲבָל מוֹזֶגֶת לוֹ כּוֹס, וּמַצַּעַת לוֹ אֶת הַמִּטָּה, וּמַרְחֶצֶת לוֹ פָּנָיו יָדָיו וְרַגְלָיו.

§ The mishna says that if she brought him **four** maidservants, **she may sit in an chair** and not do anything. **Rav Yitzḥak bar Ḥananya said** that **Rav Huna said: Although they said** that **she may sit in a chair** and does not need to work, **she** should still **pour**[H] **his cup; and make his bed;**[N] **and wash his face, hands, and feet,** as these responsibilities are not household tasks that can be delegated to a maidservant. Rather, they are gestures of affection toward her husband.

אָמַר רַב יִצְחָק בַּר חֲנַנְיָא אָמַר רַב הוּנָא: כׇּל מְלָאכוֹת שֶׁהָאִשָּׁה עוֹשָׂה לְבַעְלָהּ – נִדָּה עוֹשָׂה לְבַעְלָהּ, חוּץ מִמְּזִיגַת הַכּוֹס, וְהַצָּעַת הַמִּטָּה, וְהַרְחָצַת פָּנָיו יָדָיו וְרַגְלָיו.

Rav Yitzḥak bar Ḥananya also **said** that **Rav Huna said** a similar *halakha*: **All tasks that a wife performs for her husband, a menstruating woman may** similarly **perform for her husband,**[H] **except for: Pouring** his **cup;**[H] **and making** his **bed;**[H] **and washing** his **face, hands, and feet.** As explained above, these are acts of affection. If she is menstruating she should not perform them, so as not to lead to forbidden intercourse.

וְהַצָּעַת הַמִּטָּה – אֲמַר רָבָא: לָא אֲמָרַן אֶלָּא בְּפָנָיו, אֲבָל שֶׁלֹּא בְּפָנָיו לֵית לָן בַּהּ. וּמְזִיגַת הַכּוֹס – שְׁמוּאֵל מְחַלְּפָא לֵיהּ דְּבֵיתְהוּ בִּידָא דִּשְׂמָאלָא, אַבַּיֵּי מַנְחָא לֵיהּ אַפּוּמָא דְּכוּבָא. רָבָא אַבֵּי סַדְיָא, רַב פַּפָּא אַשַּׁרְשִׁיפָא.

And With regard to the prohibition against **making** the husband's **bed, Rava said: We said** this **only** if she made the bed **in front of him, but** if it was **not in front of him, we have no problem with it.** With regard to the prohibition against **pouring** his **cup,** the Gemara comments: **Shmuel's wife would change** her practice **toward him** during her menstruation period and pour **with her left hand,** since if she made some change in the manner of pouring, this would serve as a reminder of her status and mitigate the concern that it might lead to intimacy. **Abaye's** wife would **place** his cup **on top of a barrel, Rava's** wife would place it **on his pillow,** and **Rav Pappa's** wife would place it **on the bench** to create a change.

HALAKHA

Once she is able to bring him – כֵּיוָן שֶׁרְאוּיָה לְהַכְנִיס: The *halakha* with regard to a woman who brought maidservants with her into the marriage applies even if she did not actually bring maidservants with her but either her dowry was large enough to purchase maidservants or, in accordance with the version of the text accepted by the Rif and the Rosh, her husband was wealthy enough to purchase maidservants (Rambam *Sefer Nashim, Hilkhot Ishut* 21:6; *Shulḥan Arukh, Even HaEzer* 80:8).

She should still pour his cup – מוֹזֶגֶת לוֹ כּוֹס: Even a woman who is not required to do any work at all must still wash her husband's face, hands, and feet, as well as pour his cup and make his bed, as these are intimate acts that only a wife should perform for her husband (Rambam *Sefer Nashim, Hilkhot Ishut* 21:3; *Shulḥan Arukh, Even HaEzer* 80:4–5).

A menstruating woman may perform for her husband – נִדָּה עוֹשָׂה לְבַעְלָהּ: All the tasks that a woman must perform for her husband can also be done when she is a menstruating woman, apart from pouring his cup; making his bed; and washing his face, hands, and feet. She is not only prohibited from actually washing him, as she may not touch him, but she is also prohibited from pouring the water for him (Rambam *Sefer Nashim, Hilkhot Ishut* 21:8; *Sefer Kedusha, Hilkhot Issurei Bia* 11:19; *Shulḥan Arukh, Yoreh De'a* 195:10).

Pouring his cup – מְזִיגַת הַכּוֹס: A menstruating woman is prohibited from pouring her husband's cup and placing it on the table in the usual matter. She must do so using some sort of conspicuous sign, e.g., pouring with her left hand or placing the cup on the pillow or the blanket, as related in the Gemara (Rambam *Sefer Nashim, Hilkhot Ishut* 21:8; *Shulḥan Arukh, Yoreh De'a* 195:11).

Making his bed – הַצָּעַת הַמִּטָּה: A menstruating woman is prohibited from making her husband's bed in his presence. The commentaries explain that this is referring only to spreading the sheets and other acts of intimacy, but arranging mattresses and other acts that involve exertion are not acts of intimacy and are therefore permitted. If her husband is not present, although he knows that his wife is the one who made the bed, all the actions involved in making the bed are permitted (Rambam *Sefer Nashim, Hilkhot Ishut* 21:8; *Sefer Kedusha, Hilkhot Issurei Bia* 11:19; *Shulḥan Arukh, Yoreh De'a* 195:11).

אָמַר רַב יִצְחָק בַּר חֲנַנְיָא אָמַר רַב הוּנָא: הַכֹּל מַשְׁהִין בִּפְנֵי הַשַּׁמָּשׁ, חוּץ מִבָּשָׂר וְיַיִן. אָמַר רַב חִסְדָּא: בָּשָׂר שָׁמֵן וְיַיִן יָשָׁן. אָמַר רָבָא: בָּשָׂר שָׁמֵן – כָּל הַשָּׁנָה כּוּלָּהּ, יַיִן יָשָׁן – בִּתְקוּפַת תַּמּוּז.

§ Apropos statements by Rav Yitzḥak ben Ḥananya, the Gemara cites other statements in his name. **Rav Yitzḥak bar Ḥananya said** that **Rav Huna said: All** foods may be **withheld from before the waiter,**[H] as one who is a waiter at the meal must wait until the guests have eaten from every food and only then may he eat, **except for meat and wine,** as these foods arouse the appetite more and the waiter would suffer if he could not eat them together with the other participants. **Rav Ḥisda said:** This is referring only to **fatty meat and aged wine. Rava said:** It applies to **fatty meat all year round** but **aged wine** only **during the season of Tammuz,** in the summer. Due to the heat, the aroma of the wine is more pervasive at that time.

אֲמַר רַב עָנָן בַּר תַּחֲלִיפָא: הֲוָה קָאֵימְנָא קַמֵּיהּ דְּמָר שְׁמוּאֵל, וְאַיְיתוּ לֵיהּ תַּבְשִׁילָא דְּאַרְדֵי, וְאִי לָאו דִּיהַב לִי – אִיסְתַּכְּנִי. אֲמַר רַב אַשִׁי: הֲוָה קָאֵימְנָא קַמֵּיהּ דְּרַב כָּהֲנָא, וְאַיְיתוּ לֵיהּ גַּרְגְּלִידֵי דְּלִיפְתָּא בְּחַלָּא, וְאִי לָאו דִּיהַב לִי – אִיסְתַּכְּנִי. רַב פַּפָּא אֲמַר: אֲפִילּוּ תַּמְרְתָּא דְּהִנּוּנִיתָא. כְּלָלָא דְּמִילְּתָא: כָּל דְּאִית לֵיהּ רֵיחָא וְאִית לֵיהּ קִיוְהָא.

Rav Anan bar Taḥalifa said: I was once **standing before Mar Shmuel, and they brought him a cooked dish of mushrooms,**[N] **and if he had not given me** some, **I would have been endangered**[B] due to the craving that I suffered. **Rav Ashi said: I was** once **standing before Rav Kahana, and they brought him slices** [*gargelidei*][L] **of turnip in vinegar, and if he had not given me** some, **I would have been endangered. Rav Pappa said: Even a fragrant date** should be offered to the waiter. The Gemara concludes: **The principle of the matter** is: One should offer some of **everything that** either **has an aroma or** that **has a sharp taste** to whomever is present when it is served, so that no one suffer by being unable to partake of these foods.

אֲבוּהּ בַּר אִיהִי, וּמִנְיָמִין בַּר אִיהִי, חַד סָפֵי מִכָּל מִינָא וּמִינָא, וְחַד סָפֵי מֵחַד מִינָא. מָר – מִשְׁתָּעֵי אֵלִיָּהוּ בַּהֲדֵיהּ, וּמָר – לָא מִשְׁתָּעֵי אֵלִיָּהוּ בַּהֲדֵיהּ.

It is related about two Sages, **Avuh bar Ihi and Minyamin bar Ihi,** that **one of them** was accustomed **to give** his waiter **from every type** of food that he ate, while the other **one would give** him only **one of the types** of food that he ate. The Gemara says: **Elijah spoke with** this **Sage, but Elijah did not speak with that Sage,** since he did not act with piety and caused his waiter to suffer.

הָנְהוּ תַּרְתֵּין חֲסִידֵי, וְאָמְרִי לַהּ רַב מָרִי וְרַב פִּנְחָס בְּנֵי רַב חִסְדָּא, מָר קָדֵים סָפֵי וּמָר מְאַחֵר סָפֵי, דְּקָדֵים סָפֵי – אֵלִיָּהוּ מִשְׁתָּעֵי בַּהֲדֵיהּ, דִּמְאַחֵר סָפֵי – לָא מִשְׁתָּעֵי אֵלִיָּהוּ בַּהֲדֵיהּ.

Similarly, the Gemara relates an incident with regard to **two pious men, and some say** they were **Rav Mari and Rav Pineḥas, the sons of Rav Ḥisda:** One **Sage would give** the waiter something to eat **before** the meal, and the other **Sage would give** the waiter something to eat **after** the guests had eaten. With regard to the one **who gave** it to him **earlier, Elijah spoke with him. But** with regard to the one **who gave** it to him **later, Elijah did not speak with him.**

אֲמֵימָר וּמָר זוּטְרָא וְרַב אַשִׁי הָווּ קָא יָתְבִי אַפִּיתְחָא דְּבֵי אִיזְגּוּר מַלְכָּא, חָלֵיף וְאָזֵיל אַטּוּרְנְגָא דְּמַלְכָּא. חַזְיֵיהּ רַב אַשִׁי לְמָר זוּטְרָא

The Gemara relates another incident with regard to this matter: **Ameimar and Mar Zutra and Rav Ashi were sitting at the entrance to the house of King Izgur.**[P] **The king's chief butler was passing by** with various foods. **Rav Ashi saw Mar Zutra's**[P]

HALAKHA

May be withheld from before the waiter – מַשְׁהִין בִּפְנֵי הַשַּׁמָּשׁ: If a waiter is serving a meal and the foods have a fragrant aroma that causes people to crave them, one must give him some of that food immediately. It is an act of piety to give the waiter some of every food served (Rambam *Sefer Ahava, Hilkhot Berakhot* 7:7; *Sefer Kinyan, Hilkhot Avadim* 9:8; *Shulḥan Arukh, Oraḥ Ḥayyim* 169:1 and *Yoreh De'a* 267:17).

NOTES

Mushrooms – אַרְדֵי: It is known that Shmuel was particularly fond of mushrooms and enjoyed eating them for dessert at the conclusion of his meal.

BACKGROUND

I would have been endangered – אִיסְתַּכְּנִי: The sight of food, and even more so foods with an appealing scent or taste, can have an effect, both physiologically and psychologically, on one who is not eating. Among other things, it can cause secretion of saliva and digestive acids and can cause significant discomfort to the person. It is also possible, under specific conditions, for the experience to cause more serious damage. For example, excessive secretion of digestive acids in a person who has an ulcer can cause extreme pain, a change of complexion, and even fainting.

LANGUAGE

Slices [*gargelidei*] – גַּרְגְּלִידֵי: From the Greek γογγυλίδιον, *goggulidion*, meaning a small turnip.

PERSONALITIES

King Izgur – אִיזְגּוּר מַלְכָּא: This is one of the names of the Persian monarch Yazdegerd I, who ruled from 399–420 CE. He was a peaceable king, and during his reign there were positive relations between Persia and Rome. He also showed great tolerance toward the adherents of other religions among his subjects, for which he was criticized as a sinner by the Persian priests. The favorable conditions extended to the Jews during King Izgur's reign were apparently one of the factors that enabled the beginning of the compilation of the Babylonian Talmud.

Mar Zutra – מָר זוּטְרָא: A colleague of Rav Ashi, Mar Zutra was one of the most prominent Sages of his generation and was a disciple-colleague of his teachers, Rav Pappa and Rav Naḥman bar Yitzḥak. Beyond his greatness in *halakha* and *aggada*, Mar Zutra was noted as a preacher, and his homiletic interpretations are cited throughout the Talmud. He apparently held an official opinion as the scholar and preacher of the House of the Exilarch. Late in his life, he was appointed head of the yeshiva of Pumbedita.

Meetings between Mar Zutra, Ameimar, and Rav Ashi are frequently mentioned in the Talmud, and some of these meetings may well have been at formal conferences of the leaders of Babylonian Jewry of that generation.

דַּחֲוַור אַפֵּיהּ, שָׁקַל בְּאֶצְבְּעָתֵיהּ, אַנַּח לֵיהּ בְּפוּמֵּיהּ. אֲמַר לֵיהּ: אַפְסַדְתְּ לִסְעוּדָתָא דְּמַלְכָּא. אֲמַרוּ לֵיהּ: אַמַּאי תֵּיעֲבֵיד הָכִי? אֲמַר לְהוּ: מַאן דְּעָבֵיד הָכִי – פָּסֵיל לְמַאֲכַל דְּמַלְכָּא. אָמְרוּ לֵיהּ: אַמַּאי? אֲמַר לְהוּ: דָּבָר אַחֵר חֲזַאי בֵּיהּ. בָּדְקוּ וְלָא אַשְׁכְּחוּ. שָׁקַל אֶצְבְּעָתֵיהּ אַנַּח עֲלֵיהּ אֲמַר לְהוּ: הָכָא מִי בְּדַקִיתוּ? בָּדְקוּ אַשְׁכַּחוּ. אָמְרוּ לֵיהּ רַבָּנַן: מַאי טַעֲמָא סָמְכַתְּ אַנִּיסָּא? אֲמַר לְהוּ: חֲזַאי רוּחַ צָרַעַת דְּקָא פָּרְחָה עִילָּוֵיהּ.

face blanch because he craved the food, so he **took** some of the food **with his finger** and **put it in** Mar Zutra's **mouth.** The chief butler **said to him: You have spoiled the king's meal,** as now he will not eat from it. The king's soldiers who were there **said to him: Why did you do this? He said to them: The one who makes such** awful dishes is the one who actually **spoiled the king's food. They said to him: Why** do you say this? **He said to them: I saw something else,** i.e., a leprous infection, **in this** meat. **They checked and didn't find anything. He took his finger and placed it on** the food and **said to them: Did you check here? They** then **checked** that spot and **found** the infection. **The Sages said to** Rav Ashi: **What is the reason** that **you relied on a miracle** and assumed that leprosy would in fact be found there? **He said to them: I saw a leprous spirit**[N] **hovering over** the food and realized that it had this defect.

הַהוּא רוֹמָאָה דַּאֲמַר לָהּ לְהַהִיא אִיתְּתָא: מִינַּסְבַתְּ לִי? אָמְרָה לֵיהּ: לָא. אָזֵיל אַיְיתֵי רִימָּנֵי, פָּלֵי וַאֲכַל קַמַּהּ, כָּל מַיָּא דְּצָעֲרֵי לַהּ – בְּלַעְתֵיהּ, וְלָא הַב לַהּ, עַד דְּזָג לַהּ. לְסוֹף אֲמַר לַהּ: אִי מַסֵּינָא לָךְ מִינַּסְבַתְּ לִי? אָמְרָה לֵיהּ: אִין. אָזֵיל אַיְיתֵי רִימָּנֵי, פָּלֵי וַאֲכַל קַמַּהּ. אֲמַר לַהּ: כָּל מַיָּא דְּצָעֲרֵי לָךְ – תּוּף שְׁדַאי, תּוּף שְׁדַאי. עַד דְּנָפְקָא מִינַּהּ כִּי הוּצָא יָרְקָא, וְאִתַּסִּיאַת.

The Gemara relates another incident with regard to a similar subject: **A certain Roman said to a certain woman: Will you marry me? She said to him: No.** In order to convince her, **he went and brought pomegranates and peeled them and ate** them **in front of her** and did not give her any of them. The aroma of the pomegranates caused her mouth to water, so **she swallowed all** of the **saliva that caused her anguish, but he did not give her** any **until she became ill** and bloated. **Ultimately, he said to her: If I cure you, will you marry me? She said to him: Yes. He went and brought pomegranates, peeled them and ate** them **in front of her. He said to her: All of the saliva that causes you anguish, spit it out, spit it out.** She did this **until** something **like a green leaf came out of her, and** then **she was cured.**

״וְעוֹשָׂה בַּצֶּמֶר״. בַּצֶּמֶר – אִין, בְּפִשְׁתִּים – לָא. מַתְנִיתִין מַנִּי – רַבִּי יְהוּדָה הִיא. דְּתַנְיָא: אֵינוֹ כּוֹפָהּ לֹא לַעֲמוֹד לִפְנֵי אָבִיו, וְלֹא לַעֲמוֹד לִפְנֵי בְּנוֹ, וְלֹא לִיתֵּן תֶּבֶן לִפְנֵי בְּהֶמְתּוֹ. אֲבָל כּוֹפָהּ לִיתֵּן תֶּבֶן לִפְנֵי בְּקָרוֹ. רַבִּי יְהוּדָה אוֹמֵר: אַף אֵינוֹ כּוֹפָהּ לַעֲשׂוֹת בְּפִשְׁתָּן, מִפְּנֵי שֶׁפִּשְׁתָּן מַסְרִיחַ אֶת הַפֶּה וּמְשַׁרְבֵּט אֶת הַשְּׂפָתַיִם. וְהָנֵי מִילֵּי – בְּכִיתָּנָא רוֹמָאָה.

§ The mishna says that a wife must **make** thread **from wool.** The Gemara infers: She **must** make thread **from wool,** but she is **not** obligated to do so **from flax.**[H] The Gemara explains: **Whose** opinion is expressed in the **mishna? It is** in accordance with the opinion of **Rabbi Yehuda, as it is taught** in a *baraita*: A husband **may not compel** his wife **to stand before his father**[H] and serve him, **or to stand before his son** and serve him, **or to place straw before his animals,**[H] i.e., horses and donkeys, **but he can compel her to place straw before his cattle,**[N] i.e., cows and bulls. **Rabbi Yehuda said: He also cannot compel her to make** thread **from flax, because flax,** while it is being spun, **causes the mouth to smell** foul **and the lips to stiffen.**[B] The Gemara comments: **This applies only to Roman flax,** which causes the most damage.

״רַבִּי אֱלִיעֶזֶר אוֹמֵר: אֲפִילּוּ הִכְנִיסָה לוֹ מֵאָה שְׁפָחוֹת״. אֲמַר רַב מַלְכִּיּוּ אֲמַר רַב אַדָּא בַּר אַהֲבָה: הֲלָכָה כְּרַבִּי אֱלִיעֶזֶר.

§ The mishna continues: **Rabbi Eliezer says: Even if she brought him a hundred maidservants,** he may compel her to make thread from wool, since idleness leads to licentiousness. **Rav Malkiyyu said** that **Rav Adda bar Ahava said:** The ***halakha* is in accordance with** the opinion of **Rabbi Eliezer.**

NOTES

I saw a leprous spirit – חֲזַאי רוּחַ צָרַעַת: Rashi and the Rivan explain that Rav Ashi saw a leprous spirit hovering over Mar Zutra. Some commentaries understand this to mean that he therefore understood that Mar Zutra was in an extremely dangerous situation that required him to taste of the food, and this danger outweighed the great risk Rav Ashi took upon himself (Maharsha). However, it is also possible to explain that since he saw a spirit of leprosy over Mar Zutra, he understood that this defect was present in the food as well, and therefore he did not rely on a miracle at all.

His animals and his cattle – בְּהֶמְתּוֹ וּבְקָרוֹ: There are two conflicting versions of the text of this Gemara. The version here is similar to that of French manuscripts, whereas the Spanish manuscripts have an alternative version that is the exact opposite: He cannot compel her to place straw before his cattle but he can compel her to place straw before his animals.

Rashi and the Rivan explain the logic of this *halakha* according to the French version: The term animals is referring to horses and donkeys, which are easily aroused when they are in heat and may injure a woman, whereas this is less common among cattle. Other commentaries offer a different rationale: Since cattle are required for plowing or for milk, their care is part of household maintenance, and it is therefore appropriate to delegate this responsibility to the wife; however the husband's horses or donkeys, which he uses for riding, are not her responsibility (*Talmidei Rabbeinu Yona*; see Ritva). Parallel, opposite logic is used by the commentaries to explain the Spanish version: She is obligated to take care of his horse or donkey, as this is one of the personal tasks she performs for her husband, but she is not obligated to feed the cattle used for plowing, as this is categorized as part of the agricultural work, and it would be difficult and demeaning for her (Rid; *Talmidei Rabbeinu Yona*).

BACKGROUND

Flax causes the mouth to smell foul and the lips to stiffen – פִּשְׁתָּן מַסְרִיחַ אֶת הַפֶּה וּמְשַׁרְבֵּט אֶת הַשְּׂפָתַיִם: People who spin thread typically moisten the fibers with their mouths in order to make the twisting more effective. The fibers of the flax may damage the lips, and excessive spinning of this type of thread causes an enlargement of the lower lip, upon which the spinning thread is usually rested. Additionally, since the method of preparing the tufts of flax for spinning involves causing the stem to begin to rot, a foul odor is caused by the bacteria. Spinning the flax and placing it in one's mouth causes this foul odor to enter the mouth of the spinner as well.

HALAKHA

From wool but not from flax – בַּצֶּמֶר אִין בְּפִשְׁתִּים לָא: If it is the custom of women in a certain country to spin wool or flax, the wife must do this and all other tasks. If it is not their custom to do this kind of work, he may compel her to spin only wool but not flax, since the latter causes damage to the mouth and lips, as the Gemara deduces from the mishna and as explained by Rabbi Yehuda (Rambam *Sefer Nashim*, *Hilkhot Ishut* 21:1; *Shulḥan Arukh*, *Even HaEzer* 80:1).

To stand before his father – לַעֲמוֹד לִפְנֵי אָבִיו: Although a woman must attend to her husband's various needs, she is not obligated to attend to his father or his son. The Rema quotes the Ran, who says that this applies only if the father and son are not being sustained by her husband (Rambam *Sefer Nashim*, *Hilkhot Ishut* 21:3; *Shulḥan Arukh*, *Even HaEzer* 80:4).

To place straw before his animals – לִיתֵּן תֶּבֶן לִפְנֵי בְּהֶמְתּוֹ: One of the tasks that a woman must perform for her husband is placing straw before his animals. Some say that this applies only to the animals he uses for riding purposes (*Ḥelkat Meḥokek*, citing Rosh). She is not, however, obligated to feed his cattle. This follows the version quoted by the Rif, which is the opposite of the version appearing here (Rambam *Sefer Nashim*, *Hilkhot Ishut* 21:5; *Shulḥan Arukh*, *Even HaEzer* 80:6).

אָמַר רַבִּי חֲנִינָא בְּרֵיהּ דְּרַב אִיקָא: שִׁפּוּד, שְׁפָחוֹת וְגוּמּוֹת – רַב מַלְכִּיּוֹ.

Rabbi Ḥanina, son of Rav Ika, said: The *halakha* discussed in tractate *Beitza* (28b) that **a skewer** that had been used for roasting meat but no longer has an olive-bulk of meat on it may be moved to a corner on a Festival; the *halakha* with regard to **maidservants** in the mishna here; **and** the *halakha* discussed in tractate *Nidda* (52a) that if a girl has two hair **follicles** in her pubic region, even if there are no hairs growing from them, she is considered to have reached majority and may perform *ḥalitza*; these three *halakhot* were all stated by **Rav Malkiyyu.**

בְּלוֹרִית, אֵפֶר מִקְלֶה וּגְבִינָה – רַב מַלְכִּיָּא.

However, the *halakha* discussed in tractate *Avoda Zara* (29a) that a Jew who cuts the hair of a pagan must stop at a distance of three fingerbreadths on every side before he reaches his **forelock,** as the pagans would grow their forelocks for idolatry and the Jew must not appear as if he were dressing the forelock for idolatrous purposes; and the *halakha* discussed in tractate *Makkot* (21a) that one may not place **burnt ashes** on a wound, as it looks like a tattoo; **and** the *halakha* discussed in tractate *Avoda Zara* (35b) that **cheese** made by a gentile is forbidden, because gentiles smooth the surface of their cheese with lard; these three *halakhot* were all stated by a different Sage named **Rav Malkiya.**

רַב פַּפָּא אָמַר: מַתְנִיתִין וּמַתְנִיתָא – רַב מַלְכִּיָּא, שְׁמַעְתָּתָא – רַב מַלְכִּיּוֹ. וְסִימָנָךְ: מַתְנִיתָא מַלְכְּתָא. מַאי בֵּינַיְיהוּ? אִיכָּא בֵּינַיְיהוּ שְׁפָחוֹת.

Rav Pappa said: The *halakhot* mentioned above that relate to **a mishna or a *baraita*** were stated by **Rav Malkiya,** whereas amoraic statements of ***halakhot*** that are not related to a mishna or *baraita* were taught by **Rav Malkiyyu. And your mnemonic** to remember this **is: The mishna is a queen [*malketa*],** indicating that the comments that are referring to a mishna were made by Rav Malkiya, whose name is similar to the Aramaic term for queen. The Gemara asks: **What is** the difference **between** Rabbi Ḥanina, son of Rav Ika, and Rav Pappa? The Gemara answers: **There is** a practical difference **between them** with regard to the *halakha* concerning **maidservants.** According to Rabbi Ḥanina, this *halakha* was stated by Rav Malkiyyu, whereas Rav Pappa holds that it was taught by Rav Malkiya, since it is referring to a dispute in a mishna.

״רַבָּן שִׁמְעוֹן בֶּן גַּמְלִיאֵל אוֹמֵר״ וכו׳. הַיְינוּ תַּנָּא קַמָּא! אִיכָּא בֵּינַיְיהוּ דְּמִיטַּלְּלָא בְּגוּרְיָיתָא קִיטַנְיָיתָא וְנַדְרְשִׁיר.

§ The mishna says: **Rabban Shimon ben Gamliel says:** Even one who vows that his wife is prohibited from doing any work[H] must divorce her and give her the payment for her marriage contract, since idleness leads to idiocy. The Gemara asks: **This is** essentially the same as the opinion of **the first *tanna*,** Rabbi Eliezer, who said that idleness leads to licentiousness. The Gemara answers: **The** practical difference **between them is** in a case when **she plays with small dogs [*guriyyata kitanyata*]**[L] **or** with **games [*nadrashir*]**[L] like chess. Since there is something occupying her she is not in danger of idiocy, but occupying oneself with diversions of this type may still lead to licentiousness.

מתני׳ הַמַּדִּיר אֶת אִשְׁתּוֹ מִתַּשְׁמִישׁ הַמִּטָּה, בֵּית שַׁמַּאי אוֹמְרִים: שְׁתֵּי שַׁבָּתוֹת, בֵּית הִלֵּל אוֹמְרִים: שַׁבָּת אַחַת.

MISHNA With regard to **one who vows** that **his wife**[N] may not derive benefit **from marital relations**[H] with him, **Beit Shammai say:** He may maintain this situation for up to **two weeks,** but beyond that he must divorce her and give her the payment for her marriage contract. **Beit Hillel say:** He must divorce her if it continues beyond **one week.**

הַתַּלְמִידִים יוֹצְאִין לְתַלְמוּד תּוֹרָה שֶׁלֹּא בִּרְשׁוּת שְׁלֹשִׁים יוֹם, הַפּוֹעֲלִים שַׁבָּת אַחַת. הָעוֹנָה הָאֲמוּרָה בַּתּוֹרָה: הַטַּיָּילִין – בְּכׇל יוֹם, הַפּוֹעֲלִים – שְׁתַּיִם בְּשַׁבָּת, הַחַמָּרִים – אַחַת בְּשַׁבָּת, הַגַּמָּלִים – אַחַת לִשְׁלֹשִׁים יוֹם, הַסַּפָּנִים – אַחַת לְשִׁשָּׁה חֳדָשִׁים, דִּבְרֵי רַבִּי אֱלִיעֶזֶר.

Apropos the husband's obligation to his wife regarding marital relations, the Gemara mentions other aspects of this issue: **Students may leave** their homes and travel in order **to learn Torah without** their wives' **permission** for up to **thirty days,** and **laborers** may leave their homes without their wives' permission for up to **one week. The set interval** defining the frequency of a husband's conjugal obligation to his wife **stated in the Torah** (see Exodus 21:10),[H] unless the couple stipulated otherwise, varies according to the man's occupation and proximity to his home: **Men of leisure,** who do not work, must engage in marital relations **every day, laborers** must do so **twice a week, donkey drivers once a week, camel drivers once every thirty days,** and **sailors once every six months.** This is **the statement of Rabbi Eliezer.**

HALAKHA

One who vows that his wife is prohibited from doing work – הַמַּדִּיר אִשְׁתּוֹ מִמְּלָאכָה: One who vows to prohibit his wife from doing work must divorce her and give her the payment for her marriage contract, as idleness leads to licentiousness. This ruling is in accordance with Rabbi Eliezer, according to the Gemara's conclusion. For this reason, even if he allows her to occupy herself with other matters so that she not become insane, there is still a concern that she may become licentious (Rambam *Hilkhot Ishut* 21:2; *Shulḥan Arukh, Even HaEzer* 80:2–3).

One who vows that his wife may not benefit from marital relations – הַמַּדִּיר אֶת אִשְׁתּוֹ: One who vows to prohibit his wife from conjugal relations for more than seven days must divorce her and give her the payment for her marriage contract, in accordance with the opinion of Beit Hillel. This is true even if his profession allows for a much longer period of abstinence, as the Gemara (63b) later concludes (Rambam *Sefer Nashim, Hilkhot Ishut* 14:6; *Shulḥan Arukh, Even HaEzer* 76:9).

The set interval defining the husband's conjugal obligation stated in the Torah – הָעוֹנָה הָאֲמוּרָה בַּתּוֹרָה: A husband is obligated to engage in marital relations with his wife according to a frequency dependent upon his virility and occupation. If the couple did not stipulate an agreed-upon frequency between themselves, then a man of leisure must fulfill his conjugal obligation every night, laborers who are employed in the town of their residence must fulfill their obligations twice a week, donkey drivers once a week, camel drivers once every thirty days, and sailors once every six months, in accordance with the opinion of Rabbi Eliezer (Rambam *Sefer Nashim, Hilkhot Ishut* 14:1; *Shulḥan Arukh, Even HaEzer* 76:1–2).

LANGUAGE

Small dogs [*guriyyata kitanyata*] – גּוּרְיָיתָא קִיטַנְיָיתָא: This version of the text, which appears in the *Arukh* as well, is understood to be a term for a specific species of small dogs, which function as pets. However, the exact derivation of the term, and even what language it is from, are unclear.

Games [*nadrashir*] – נַדְרְשִׁיר: The better reading of this term, which appears in some versions, is *nardashir*. It derives from the Middle Persian nēw-ardaxšīr, a term for a backgammon-like game that was named after the first Sasanian king, Ardashir I.

NOTES

One who vows that his wife may not derive benefit – הַמַּדִּיר אֶת אִשְׁתּוֹ: Rashi and a number of other early authorities explain that this cannot mean that he literally prohibited his wife from experiencing the pleasure of relations with him, since such a vow would not take effect. This is because he is obligated to fulfill her conjugal rights, which according to most of the *tanna'im* is an obligation by Torah law. It must therefore be explained that he phrases the vow in such a way that he prohibits himself from deriving benefit from marital relations with her, and such a vow can take effect.

HALAKHA

Even with regard to an unspecified vow – אֲפִילּוּ בִּסְתָם: The time frame established by the Sages for one who vowed to prohibit his wife from marital relations applies whether or not he specified the period of time, in accordance with the opinion of Shmuel. Although generally the *halakha* is in accordance with Rav in matters relating to prohibitions, all of the authorities ruled in accordance with Shmuel in this case in order not to increase the number of divorces (Rambam *Sefer Nashim, Hilkhot Ishut* 14:6; *Shulḥan Arukh, Even HaEzer* 76:9).

גמ׳ מַאי טַעְמָא דְּבֵית שַׁמַּאי? גָּמְרִי מִיּוֹלֶדֶת נְקֵבָה. וּבֵית הִלֵּל? גָּמְרִי מִיּוֹלֶדֶת זָכָר.

GEMARA The Gemara asks: **What is the reason** that **Beit Shammai** say a husband may force abstinence on his wife by a vow for a period of up to two weeks without being compelled to divorce her? **They derive** this from the *halakha* that **a woman who gave birth** to **a female** is ritually impure and prohibited from engaging in conjugal relations with her husband for two weeks after childbirth (see Leviticus 12:5). From this they derive that a period of up to two weeks of abstinence is not deemed undue suffering. **And** from where do **Beit Hillel** derive their opinion? **They derive** it from **a woman who gave birth** to **a male,** as she is ritually impure for one week (see Leviticus 12:1–4).

וּבֵית הִלֵּל נַמִי נִגְמְרוּ מִיּוֹלֶדֶת נְקֵבָה! אִי מִיּוֹלֶדֶת גָּמְרִי לָהּ – הָכִי נַמִי, אֶלָּא בֵּית הִלֵּל מִנִּדָּה גָּמְרֵי לָהּ.

The Gemara asks: **And** if this is so, **Beit Hillel should also derive** the *halakha* **from a woman who gave birth** to **a female,** since it is clear that the Torah does at times mandate a period of abstinence longer than one week. The Gemara answers: **If they derived it from a woman who gave birth,** this is **indeed** how they would have derived it. **Rather, Beit Hillel derived it from** the *halakha* with regard to **a menstruating woman,** who is prohibited from marital relations for seven days according to Torah law.

בְּמַאי קָמִיפַּלְגִי? מָר סָבַר: מִידֵי דִּשְׁכִיחַ מִמִּידֵי דִּשְׁכִיחַ, וּמָר סָבַר: מִידֵי דְּהוּא גָּרֵים לָהּ מִמִּידֵי דְּהוּא גָּרֵים לָהּ.

The Gemara explains: **With regard to what do they disagree?** One **Sage,** Beit Hillel, **holds** that one should derive **a common matter from a common matter.** Consequently, they derive the *halakha* of a permitted abstinence by a husband who vowed not to engage in marital relations with his wife from the *halakha* of a menstruating woman, since both are common cases. **And** one **Sage,** Beit Shammai, **holds** that one should derive **a matter that one caused,** such as a vow, **from a** different **matter that he caused,** i.e., childbirth, and not from menstruation, which was not caused by him at all.

אָמַר רַב: מַחֲלוֹקֶת בִּמְפָרֵשׁ, אֲבָל בִּסְתָם – דִּבְרֵי הַכֹּל יוֹצִיא לְאַלְתַּר, וְיִתֵּן כְּתוּבָּה. וּשְׁמוּאֵל אָמַר: אֲפִילּוּ בִּסְתָם נַמִי יַמְתִּין, שֶׁמָּא יִמְצָא פֶּתַח לְנִדְרוֹ.

Rav said: The **dispute** between Beit Hillel and Beit Shammai **concerns one who specifies** the given period of time in his vow, **but** if he vowed not to engage in marital relations with her for an **unspecified** period of time, **all agree** that **he must divorce** her **immediately and give** her the payment for her **marriage contract.** The reason is that since he did not indicate how long he intended to keep the vow, her suffering begins immediately. **And Shmuel said: Even** with regard to an **unspecified** vow[H] **he should also wait** for the same period of time, as **perhaps he will find an extenuation** enabling the dissolution **of his vow** and then he will not need to divorce her.

הָא פְּלִיגִי בָּהּ חֲדָא זִימְנָא, דִּתְנַן: הַמַּדִּיר אֶת אִשְׁתּוֹ מִלֵּיהָנוֹת לוֹ, עַד שְׁלֹשִׁים יוֹם – יַעֲמִיד פַּרְנָס, יוֹתֵר מִכָּאן – יוֹצִיא וְיִתֵּן כְּתוּבָּה. וְאָמַר רַב: לֹא שָׁנוּ אֶלָּא בִּמְפָרֵשׁ, אֲבָל בִּסְתָם – יוֹצִיא לְאַלְתַּר וְיִתֵּן כְּתוּבָּה. וּשְׁמוּאֵל אָמַר: אֲפִילּוּ בִּסְתָם נַמִי יַמְתִּין, שֶׁמָּא יִמְצָא פֶּתַח לְנִדְרוֹ!

The Gemara asks: **Didn't they disagree about this** issue **once** already? **As we learned** in a mishna (70a): In the case of **one who vows** that **his wife** is prohibited **from benefiting from him** or his property, if his vow will remain in effect for **up to thirty days, he must appoint a trustee** to support her. But if the vow will remain in effect for **more than that** amount of time, **he must divorce** her **and give** her the payment for her **marriage contract. And Rav said** there: **They taught** this **only** with regard to a case **where he specifies** a limited time during which the vow would be in effect, **but** if he vows **without specification, he must divorce** her **immediately and give** her the payment for her **marriage contract. And Shmuel said: Even** when he vowed **without specification, he should also wait,** as **perhaps he will discover an extenuation** enabling the dissolution **of his vow.**

צְרִיכָא, דְּאִי אִיתְּמַר בְּהָא – בְּהָא קָאָמַר רַב, מִשּׁוּם דְּלָא אֶפְשָׁר בְּפַרְנָס. אֲבָל בְּהַהִיא, דְּאֶפְשָׁר בְּפַרְנָס – אֵימָא מוֹדֵי לֵיהּ לִשְׁמוּאֵל. וְאִי אִיתְּמַר בְּהַהִיא – בְּהַךְ קָאָמַר שְׁמוּאֵל, אֲבָל בְּהָא – אֵימָא מוֹדֵי לֵיהּ לְרַב, צְרִיכָא.

The Gemara answers: It is **necessary** to cite the dispute in both cases, as **if it were stated** only **with regard to this** case, of one who vows not to engage in marital relations, one might think that **in this** case **Rav says** he must divorce her **because there is no possibility of** appointing **a trustee, but** that **with regard to that** *halakha*, in the case when he vows not to provide sustenance, **which can be** provided **by a trustee,** one would **say** that Rav **concedes to Shmuel** that he should wait. Conversely, **if** the dispute **was stated with regard to that** case, where a trustee can be appointed, one might think that **in that** case **Shmuel said** to wait, **but in this** case of one who vows not to engage in marital relations, one might **say** that Shmuel **concedes to Rav.** Therefore, **it is necessary** to cite the dispute in both cases.

"הַתַּלְמִידִים יוֹצְאִין לְתַלְמוּד" וכו׳. בִּרְשׁוּת כַּמָּה? כַּמָּה דְּבָעֵי.

§ The mishna said that **students may leave** their homes and travel for up to thirty days in order **to learn Torah,** without their wives' permission. The Gemara asks: If they went **with permission,** for **how long** can they go? The Gemara expresses wonderment at this question: If they went with the permission of their wives, they can go for **as long as they want.** If the husband and wife agree on this, why is there any reason for the court to intervene?

Perek **V**
Daf **62** Amud **a**

אוֹרְחָא דְמִילְּתָא כַּמָּה? אָמַר רַב: חֹדֶשׁ כָּאן וְחֹדֶשׁ בַּבַּיִת, שֶׁנֶּאֱמַר "לְכֹל דְּבַר הַמַּחְלְקוֹת הַבָּאָה וְהַיֹּצֵאת חֹדֶשׁ בְּחֹדֶשׁ לְכֹל חָדְשֵׁי הַשָּׁנָה". וְרַבִּי יוֹחָנָן אָמַר: חֹדֶשׁ כָּאן וּשְׁנַיִם בְּבֵיתוֹ, שֶׁנֶּאֱמַר "חֹדֶשׁ יִהְיוּ בַלְּבָנוֹן שְׁנַיִם חֳדָשִׁים בְּבֵיתוֹ".

The Gemara explains its query: Although a man can legally make any agreement with his wife to limit her conjugal rights, **how much** is an acceptable **manner for this matter?**[N] **Rav said:** The husband may spend **a month here,** in the study hall, **and** then must spend **a month at home.** The allusion to this is **as it is stated** with regard to reserve units serving in King David's army: **"In any matter of the courses, which came in and went out month by month throughout all the months of the year"** (1 Chronicles 27:1). **And Rabbi Yoḥanan said:** He may spend **one month here,** in the study hall, **and** then **two** months **in his home, as it is stated** with regard to workers who worked in the construction of the Temple: **"A month they were in Lebanon, and two months at home"** (1 Kings 5:28).

וְרַב נַמִי: מַאי טַעְמָא לָא אָמַר מֵהַהִיא? שָׁאנֵי בִּנְיַן בֵּית הַמִּקְדָּשׁ, דְּאֶפְשָׁר עַל יְדֵי אֲחֵרִים. וְרַבִּי יוֹחָנָן, מַאי טַעְמָא לָא אָמַר מֵהַהִיא? שָׁאנֵי הָתָם, דְּאִית לֵיהּ הַרְוָוחָה.

The Gemara asks: **And what is the reason** that **Rav did not also say** a proof **from that** source that Rabbi Yoḥanan quoted? The Gemara answers: **The construction of the Temple is different, since it is possible** for this work to be performed **by others,** as there were many people involved in it, but with regard to Torah study, which cannot be performed by others, he is given permission to spend a month here and a month there. The Gemara further questions: **And what is the reason** that **Rabbi Yoḥanan did not say** a proof **from that** source that Rav quoted? The Gemara answers: **There,** with regard to King David, **it is different, since he gains profit** from working for the king; since there is profit involved, his wife might be willing to forgo his staying with her. However, in general a woman wants her husband to spend most of his time at home, so with regard to Torah study, where there is no monetary profit, she will not waive her right for as long.

אָמַר רַב: אֲנָחָה שׁוֹבֶרֶת חֲצִי גּוּפוֹ שֶׁל אָדָם, שֶׁנֶּאֱמַר "וְאַתָּה בֶן אָדָם הֵאָנַח בְּשִׁבְרוֹן מָתְנַיִם וּבִמְרִירוּת תֵּאָנַח". וְרַבִּי יוֹחָנָן אָמַר: אַף כׇּל גּוּפוֹ שֶׁל אָדָם, שֶׁנֶּאֱמַר "וְהָיָה כִּי יֹאמְרוּ אֵלֶיךָ עַל מָה אַתָּה נֶאֱנָח וְאָמַרְתָּ אֶל שְׁמוּעָה כִּי בָאָה וְנָמֵס כׇּל לֵב וְרָפוּ כׇל יָדַיִם וְכִהֲתָה כׇל רוּחַ וְכׇל בִּרְכַּיִם תֵּלַכְנָה מַּיִם".

§ Apropos a dispute between Rav and Rabbi Yoḥanan with regard to the construction of the Temple, the Gemara cites another dispute between them. **Rav said: Groaning breaks half of a person's body, as it is stated: "Groan, therefore, you son of man, with the breaking of your loins, groan so bitterly"** (Ezekiel 21:11), which indicates that groaning breaks half of a one's body, down to his loins. **And Rabbi Yoḥanan said** that groaning breaks **even a person's entire body, as it is stated: "And it shall be, when they say to you: Why are you groaning? That you shall say: Due to the tiding, for it comes, and every heart shall melt, and all hands shall be slack, and every spirit shall be faint, and all knees shall drip with water"** (Ezekiel 21:12).

וְרַבִּי יוֹחָנָן נַמִי, הָכְתִיב "בְּשִׁבְרוֹן מָתְנַיִם"! הַהִיא דְּכִי מַתְחֲלָא – מִמָּתְנַיִם מַתְחֲלָא. וְרַב נַמִי הָכְתִיב "וְנָמֵס כׇּל לֵב וְרָפוּ כׇּל יָדַיִם וְכִהֲתָה כׇּל רוּחַ"! שָׁאנֵי שְׁמוּעָה דְּבֵית הַמִּקְדָּשׁ, דְּתַקִּיפָא טוּבָא.

The Gemara asks: **And** why doesn't **Rabbi Yoḥanan also** say that it breaks half of one's body? **Isn't it written: "With the breaking of your loins,"** implying that it does not break the entire body? The Gemara answers: **This** does not mean that the breakage only reaches the loins, but rather **that when** the sigh **begins** to affect a person, **it begins from his loins.** The Gemara asks: **And** why doesn't **Rav also** say that it breaks the entire body? **Isn't it written: "And every heart shall melt, and all hands shall be slack, and every spirit shall be faint,"** which indicates that groaning causes the entire body to break? The Gemara answers: **The news with regard to** the destruction of **the Temple is different, as it is extremely crushing** and causes great anguish, but in general a sigh causes only half of the body to break.

NOTES

How much is an acceptable manner for this matter – אוֹרְחָא דְמִילְּתָא כַּמָּה: Rashi explains that this question indicates that although one may succeed in persuading his wife to give him permission to leave for an extended period, there is still a concern that she may not have agreed wholeheartedly. Consequently, the Gemara asks about the amount of time for which it can be assumed that a wife would not resent her husband's absence. Rabbi Aharon HaLevi offers an alternative explanation, that the question is referring to a wife who gave her husband permission to leave without specifying a period of time and the Gemara is asking what she meant in doing so.

הַהוּא יִשְׂרָאֵל וְגוֹי דַּהֲווֹ קָאָזְלִי בְּאוֹרְחָא בַּהֲדֵי הֲדָדֵי, לָא אִימְצֵי גּוֹי לְסַגּוּיֵי בַּהֲדֵי יִשְׂרָאֵל. אַדְכְּרֵיהּ חוּרְבַּן בֵּית הַמִּקְדָּשׁ, נְגִיד וְאִיתְנַח, וַאֲפִילּוּ הָכִי לָא אִימְצֵי גּוֹי לְסַגּוּיֵי בַּהֲדֵיהּ. אֲמַר לֵיהּ: לָאו אָמְרִיתוּ אֲנָחָה שׁוֹבֶרֶת חֲצִי גּוּפוֹ שֶׁל אָדָם? אֲמַר לֵיהּ: הָנֵי מִילֵּי מִילְּתָא חַדְתֵּי אֲבָל הָא דִּשְׁנַן בָּהּ – לָא, דְּאָמְרִי אֱינָשֵׁי: דִּמְלַפֵי תִּכְלֵי לָא בָּהֲתָה.

It is related that a **certain Jew and a gentile were walking along the road together. The gentile could not keep up with the Jew,** who was walking faster, and **he** therefore **reminded him of the destruction of the Temple** in order to make the Jew feel sorrowful and slow down. **The Jew sighed and groaned, but even so the gentile could not keep up with him,** as the Jew was still walking faster. The gentile **said to him: Don't you say that groaning breaks half of a person's body?** Why didn't it affect you? **He said to him: This applies only** with regard to **a new** sorrowful **affair, but this,** from **which we have** suffered **repeatedly** and to which we have become accustomed, does **not** affect us as much, **as people say: One who is used to being bereaved** of her children **does not panic** [*bahata*][L] when one of them dies, and similarly, one who is used to a tragedy is not as devastated when being reminded of it.

״הַטַּיָּילִין בְּכָל יוֹם״. מַאי טַיָּילִין? אֲמַר רָבָא: בְּנֵי פִּירְקֵי. אֲמַר לֵיהּ אַבַּיֵי: מַאן דִּכְתִיב בְּהוּ ״שָׁוְא לָכֶם מַשְׁכִּימֵי קוּם מְאַחֲרֵי שֶׁבֶת אוֹכְלֵי לֶחֶם הָעֲצָבִים כֵּן יִתֵּן לִידִידוֹ שֵׁנָא״. וְאָמַר רַב יִצְחָק: אֵלּוּ נְשׁוֹתֵיהֶן שֶׁל תַּלְמִידֵי חֲכָמִים שֶׁמְּנַדְּדוֹת שֵׁינָה מֵעֵינֵיהֶם בָּעוֹלָם הַזֶּה, וּבָאוֹת לְחַיֵּי הָעוֹלָם הַבָּא. וְאַתְּ אָמְרַתְּ בְּנֵי פִּירְקֵי?

§ The mishna said that **men of leisure** must engage in marital relations with their wives **every day.**[H] The Gemara asks: **What** is meant by the term **men of leisure? Rava said:** These are **students** of Torah who go daily to review **their lectures** at a local study hall and return home each evening. **Abaye said to him:** Wives of Torah scholars are **those about whom it is written: "It is vain for you to rise early and sit up late, you that eat the bread of toil, so He gives to His beloved in sleep"** (Psalms 127:2), **and Rabbi Yitzḥak said** in explanation of this verse: **These are the wives of Torah scholars who deprive their eyes of sleep in this world and reach the life of the World-to-Come.** This indicates that Torah scholars exert themselves greatly in their studies and are not home in the evenings, **and you say** that the **students** reviewing **their lectures** are men of leisure, whose wives have conjugal rights for every night?

אֶלָּא, אֲמַר אַבַּיֵי: כִּדְרַב, דַּאֲמַר רַב: כְּגוֹן רַב שְׁמוּאֵל בַּר שֵׁילַת, דְּאָכֵיל מִדִּידֵיהּ וְשָׁתֵי מִדִּידֵיהּ, וְגָנֵי בְּטוּלָּא דְּאַפַּדְנֵיהּ, וְלָא חָלֵיף פְּרִיסְתָּקָא דְּמַלְכָּא אַבָּבֵיהּ. כִּי אֲתָא רָבִין אֲמַר: כְּגוֹן מְפַנְּקֵי דְּמַעַרְבָא.

Rather, Abaye said: The mishna should be explained **in accordance with the opinion of Rav, as Rav said:** This is referring to a man **such as Rabbi Shmuel bar Sheilat,**[N] **who ate his own** food, **drank his own** drinks, **slept in the shade of his own house, and the king's tax collector** [*peristaka*][L] **did not pass by his door,** as they did not know that he was a man of means. A man like this, who has a steady income and no worries, is called a man of leisure. **When Ravin came** from Eretz Yisrael **he said: For example, the** wealthy, **pampered** men **in the West,** Eretz Yisrael, are called men of leisure. Due to the time they have available and the richness of their diet, they have the ability to satisfy their wives every night.

רַבִּי אַבָּהוּ הֲוָה קָאֵי בֵּי בָּאנֵי, הָווּ סָמְכֵי לֵיהּ תְּרֵי עַבְדֵי. אִיפְּחִית בֵּי בָּאנֵי מִתּוּתֵיהּ, אִיתְרְמֵי לֵיהּ עַמּוּדָא, סְלֵיק וְאַסְּקִינְהוּ. רַבִּי יוֹחָנָן הֲוָה קָסָלֵיק בְּדַרְגָּא, הָווּ סָמְכֵי לֵיהּ רַב אַמִּי וְרַב אַסִּי. אִיפְּחִתָא דַּרְגָּא תּוּתֵיהּ, סְלֵיק וְאַסְּקִינְהוּ. אָמְרִי לֵיהּ רַבָּנַן: וְכִי מֵאַחַר דְּהָכִי – לָמָּה לֵיהּ לְמִיסְמְכֵיהּ? אֲמַר לְהוּ: אִם כֵּן מָה אַנִּיחַ לְעֵת זִקְנָה?

To illustrate this point, the Gemara relates two incidents demonstrating the health and strength of the inhabitants of Eretz Yisrael: **Rabbi Abbahu was** once **standing in the bathhouse and two slaves were supporting** his walking. **The bathhouse collapsed under him**[B] and was destroyed. **He found a pillar,** stood on it and **got out, and pulled them** both **up** with him. Similarly, **Rabbi Yoḥanan was** once **going up stairs,** and **Rav Ami and Rav Asi were supporting** him. **The stair collapsed under him, but he went up and pulled them** both **up** with him. **The Sages said to him:** Since it is clear that you are **so** strong, **why do you need** people **to support you? He said to them: If so,** if I were to expend all my strength now, **what will I leave for** myself in my **old age?**

HALAKHA

Men of leisure must engage in marital relations every day – **הַטַּיָּילִין בְּכָל יוֹם**: Men of leisure, meaning men who do not work and have no obligations toward the government, must fulfill their conjugal obligations to their wives every day, in accordance with the mishna and its explanation in the Gemara (Rambam *Sefer Nashim, Hilkhot Ishut* 14:1; *Shulḥan Arukh, Even HaEzer* 76:1).

NOTES

Such as Rav Shmuel bar Sheilat – **כְּגוֹן רַב שְׁמוּאֵל בַּר שֵׁילַת**: Some commentaries write that the Gemara cannot be understood as halakhically defining Rav Shmuel bar Sheilat himself as a man of leisure, as he was a Torah scholar and did not have a set interval of conjugal obligations every day. Rather, his name is cited only to demonstrate an example of a man who does not engage in manual labor.

BACKGROUND

The bathhouse collapsed under him – **אִיפְּחִית בֵּי בָּאנֵי מִתּוּתֵיהּ**: Large bathhouses were built using the Roman method. There was an upper room containing a large pool where the bathers would sit, and underneath was a furnace room containing a fire that would heat the water in the pool. The upper room generally rested on a large number of pillars. At times, due to the heat and weight, the floor of the upper level would collapse.

Roman bath at Masada, with a reconstruction of the floor of the bathhouse resting on pillars

LANGUAGE

Panic [*bahata*] – **בָּהֲתָה**: The *Arukh* defines this word based on the root *beit, heh, tav* according to its ordinary meaning, to be embarrassed. However, it appears that Rashi understood the word according to a meaning it takes in several other sources, in which it is related to the root *beit, ayin, tav*, meaning fear. Consequently, the meaning is that a woman who is accustomed to being bereaved of her children does not panic when tragedy strikes.

Tax collector [*peristaka*] – **פְּרִיסְתָּקָא**: From the Middle Persian frēstak, meaning messenger. In this case it has been understood to refer to a messenger charged with collecting taxes or the like.

"וְהַפּוֹעֲלִים שְׁתַּיִם בְּשַׁבָּת". וְהָתַנְיָא: הַפּוֹעֲלִים אַחַת בְּשַׁבָּת! אָמַר רַבִּי יוֹסֵי בְּרַבִּי חֲנִינָא: לָא קַשְׁיָא: כָּאן – בְּעוֹשִׂין מְלָאכָה בְּעִירָן, כָּאן – בְּעוֹשִׂין מְלָאכָה בְּעִיר אַחֶרֶת. תַּנְיָא נַמִּי הָכִי: "הַפּוֹעֲלִים שְׁתַּיִם בְּשַׁבָּת, בַּמֶּה דְּבָרִים אֲמוּרִים – בְּעוֹשִׂין מְלָאכָה בְּעִירָן, אֲבָל בְּעוֹשִׂין מְלָאכָה בְּעִיר אַחֶרֶת – אַחַת בְּשַׁבָּת.

§ The mishna said: The set interval for **laborers**[H] to fulfill their conjugal obligations to their wives is **twice a week.** The Gemara asks: **Isn't it taught** in a *baraita*: For **laborers, once a week? Rabbi Yosei, son of Rabbi Ḥanina, said:** This is **not difficult: Here,** the case is **where they work in their own city. There,** the case is **where they work in another city. This is also taught** in the *Tosefta* (5:6): For **laborers, twice a week. In what** case **is this statement said?** It is **when they work in their own city, but when they work in another city,** the set interval for their conjugal obligations is **once a week.**

"הַחַמָּרִים אַחַת בְּשַׁבָּת". אֲמַר לֵיהּ רַבָּה בַּר רַב חָנָן לְאַבָּיֵי: אִיכְפַּל תַּנָּא לְאַשְׁמוֹעִינַן טַיָּיל וּפוֹעֵל? אֲמַר לֵיהּ: לָא,

§ The mishna said: The set interval for **donkey drivers** is **once a week,** and for other professions it is even less frequent. **Rabba bar Rav Ḥanan said to Abaye: Did the *tanna* go to all that trouble just to teach us** the *halakha* for **a man of leisure and** for **a laborer?** According to the set intervals given for conjugal obligations, it seems that the *halakha* that one who vowed to prohibit his wife from conjugal relations for longer than a week must divorce her is referring only to a man of leisure or a laborer, whose set interval for conjugal relations is less than that period. However, for other people, whose set interval is once a month or even less frequent, there should be no need to divorce the wife, since the vow does not deprive her of conjugal rights for longer than she would have been deprived anyway. **He said to him: No,**

HALAKHA

The set interval for laborers – הַפּוֹעֲלִים: Laborers who are employed in their own city must fulfill their conjugal obligations to their wives twice a week, and for laborers who are employed in another city, their set interval is once a week. This is in accordance with the Gemara's conclusion, based on the *Tosefta*. The Rema writes in the name of the Maharam of Rothenburg that this applies only to workers who return every night to their homes, but if they sleep in the other city, their set interval for conjugal relations is once every eight days (Rambam *Sefer Nashim, Hilkhot Ishut* 14:1; *Shulḥan Arukh, Even HaEzer* 76:2).

Perek **V**
Daf **62** Amud **b**

אַכּוּלְּהוּ. וְהָא שִׁשָּׁה חֳדָשִׁים קָאָמַר! אֵינוֹ דּוֹמֶה מִי שֶׁיֵּשׁ לוֹ פַּת בְּסַלּוֹ, לְמִי שֶׁאֵין לוֹ פַּת בְּסַלּוֹ.

the *tanna* taught us a *halakha* **with regard to all of them,**[H] not only a man of leisure or a laborer. He asked him: **But** with regard to a sailor **it said** that the set interval for conjugal relations is **six months;** why, then, should he have to divorce her if he vowed to forbid these relations for only a week? He answered him: It is well known that **one who has bread in his basket is not comparable to one who does not have bread in his basket.** On a fast day, one who does not have bread available in his basket suffers more than one who does have bread available and knows that he will be able to eat later. In this case as well, when a woman knows that marital relations are forbidden to her due to a vow, her suffering from waiting for her husband to return is increased.

אֲמַר לֵיהּ רַבָּה בַּר רַב חָנָן לְאַבָּיֵי: חַמָּר וְנַעֲשָׂה גַּמָּל מַאי? אֲמַר לֵיהּ: רוֹצָה אִשָּׁה בְּקַב וְתִיפְלוּת מֵעֲשָׂרָה קַבִּין וּפְרִישׁוּת.

Rabba bar Rav Hanan said to Abaye: If a donkey driver who is already married wants to **become a camel driver,**[H] **what** is the *halakha*? Is he permitted to change his profession in order to earn more money from his work, even though this will mean he reduces the frequency with which he engages in conjugal relations with his wife? **He answered him: A woman prefers a *kav*,** i.e., modest means, **with conjugal relations to ten *kav* with abstinence.** Consequently, he is not allowed to change his profession without her permission.

HALAKHA

With regard to all of them – אַכּוּלְּהוּ: If one vows and prohibits his wife from conjugal relations, whether for an unspecified period of time or for a specified period of more than a week, he must wait for a week and if he has not had his vow dissolved by then, must divorce his wife and give her the payment for her marriage contract. This applies to all men, even to sailors, whose set interval for conjugal obligations is once every six months. This *halakha* is in accordance with the opinion of Abaye (Rambam *Sefer Nashim, Hilkhot Ishut* 14:6; *Shulḥan Arukh, Even HaEzer* 76:9).

A donkey driver wants to become a camel driver – חַמָּר וְנַעֲשָׂה גַּמָּל: A woman may prevent her husband from changing his profession from one where the set interval for his conjugal obligation is more frequent to one where it is less frequent, even if he could make more money from his new profession, in accordance with the opinion of Abaye (Rambam *Sefer Nashim, Hilkhot Ishut* 14:2; *Shulḥan Arukh, Even HaEzer* 76:5).

"הַסַּפָּנִים אַחַת לְשִׁשָּׁה חֳדָשִׁים דִּבְרֵי רַבִּי אֱלִיעֶזֶר". אָמַר רַב בְּרוֹנָא אָמַר רַב: הֲלָכָה כְּרַבִּי אֱלִיעֶזֶר. אֲמַר רַב אַדָּא בַּר אַהֲבָה אָמַר רַב: זוֹ דִּבְרֵי רַבִּי אֱלִיעֶזֶר, אֲבָל חֲכָמִים אוֹמְרִים: הַתַּלְמִידִים יוֹצְאִין לְתַלְמוּד תּוֹרָה שְׁתַּיִם וְשָׁלֹשׁ שָׁנִים שֶׁלֹּא בִּרְשׁוּת. אֲמַר רָבָא: סָמְכוּ רַבָּנַן אַדְּרַב אַדָּא בַּר אַהֲבָה וְעָבְדֵי עוּבְדָא בְּנַפְשַׁיְיהוּ.

§ The mishna stated: For **sailors,** the set interval for conjugal relations is **once every six months. This is the statement of Rabbi Eliezer. Rav Berona said that Rav said:** The ***halakha*** **is in accordance with** the opinion of **Rabbi Eliezer. Rav Adda bar Ahava said that Rav said: This is the statement of Rabbi Eliezer, but the Rabbis say: Students may leave**[H] their homes **to study Torah** for as long as **two or three years without permission** from their wives. **Rava said: The Sages relied on Rabbi Adda bar Ahava's** opinion **and performed an action** like this **themselves,**[N] but the results were sometimes fatal.

כִּי הָא דְּרַב רְחוּמִי הֲוָה שְׁכִיחַ קַמֵּיהּ דְּרָבָא בִּמְחוֹזָא. הֲוָה רְגִיל דַּהֲוָה אָתֵי לְבֵיתֵיהּ כָּל מַעֲלֵי יוֹמָא דְכִיפּוּרֵי. יוֹמָא חַד מְשַׁכְתֵּיהּ שְׁמַעְתָּא, הֲוָה מְסַכְּיָא דְּבֵיתְהוּ: הַשְׁתָּא אָתֵי, הַשְׁתָּא אָתֵי. לָא אֲתָא. חֲלַשׁ דַּעְתָּהּ, אַחֵית דִּמְעֲתָא מֵעֵינָהּ. הֲוָה יְתֵיב בְּאִיגָּרָא – אִפְּחִית אִיגָּרָא מִתּוּתֵיהּ, וְנָח נַפְשֵׁיהּ.

This is as it is related **about Rav Reḥumi, who would commonly** study **before Rava in Meḥoza: He was accustomed to come** back **to his home every** year on the **eve of Yom Kippur. One day he was** particularly **engrossed in** the ***halakha*** he was studying, and so he remained in the study hall and did not go home. **His wife was expecting him** that day and continually said to herself: **Now he is coming, now he is coming.** But in the end, **he did not come. She was distressed** by this and **a tear fell from her eye.** At that exact moment, Rav Reḥumi **was sitting on the roof. The roof collapsed under him and he died.** This teaches how much one must be careful, as he was punished severely for causing anguish to his wife, even inadvertently.

עוֹנָה שֶׁל תַּלְמִידֵי חֲכָמִים אֵימַת? אָמַר רַב יְהוּדָה אָמַר שְׁמוּאֵל: מֵעֶרֶב שַׁבָּת לְעֶרֶב שַׁבָּת. "אֲשֶׁר פִּרְיוֹ יִתֵּן בְּעִתּוֹ" אָמַר רַב יְהוּדָה וְאִיתֵּימָא רַב הוּנָא וְאִיתֵּימָא רַב נַחְמָן: זֶה הַמְשַׁמֵּשׁ מִטָּתוֹ מֵעֶרֶב שַׁבָּת לְעֶרֶב שַׁבָּת.

§ **When** is the ideal **time for Torah scholars** to fulfill their conjugal obligations?[H] **Rav Yehuda said that Shmuel said:** The appropriate time for them is **from Shabbat eve to Shabbat eve,** i.e., on Friday nights. Similarly, it is stated with regard to the verse **"that brings forth its fruit in its season"** (Psalms 1:3): **Rav Yehuda said, and some say** that it was **Rav Huna, and some say** that it was **Rav Naḥman: This** is referring to one **who engages in marital relations,** bringing forth his fruit, **from Shabbat eve to Shabbat eve.**

יְהוּדָה בְּרֵיהּ דְּרַבִּי חִיָּיא חַתְנֵיהּ דְּרַבִּי יַנַּאי הֲוָה אָזֵיל וְיָתֵיב בְּבֵי רַב, וְכָל בֵּי שִׁמְשֵׁי הֲוָה אָתֵי לְבֵיתֵיהּ. וְכִי הֲוָה אָתֵי – הֲוָה קָא חָזֵי קַמֵּיהּ עַמּוּדָא דְנוּרָא. יוֹמָא חַד מְשַׁכְתֵּיהּ שְׁמַעְתָּא. כֵּיוָן דְּלָא חֲזֵי הַהוּא סִימָנָא – אֲמַר לְהוּ רַבִּי יַנַּאי: כְּפוּ מִטָּתוֹ, שֶׁאִילְמָלֵי יְהוּדָה קַיָּים – לֹא בִּיטֵּל עוֹנָתוֹ. הֲוַאי "כִּשְׁגָגָה שֶׁיּוֹצָא מִלִּפְנֵי הַשַּׁלִּיט" וְנָח נַפְשֵׁיהּ.

It is related further that **Yehuda, son of Rabbi Ḥiyya** and **son-in-law of Rabbi Yannai, would go and sit in the study hall, and every** Shabbat eve **at twilight he would come to his house. When he would come,** Rabbi Yannai **would see a pillar of fire preceding him** due to his sanctity. **One day he was engrossed in** the ***halakha*** he was studying, and he stayed in the study hall and did not return home. **When Rabbi Yannai did not see that sign** preceding him, **he said to** the family: **Turn his bed over,** as one does at times of mourning, since he must have died, reasoning that **if Yehuda were alive he would not have missed his set interval** for conjugal relations and would certainly have come home. What he said **became "like an error that proceeds from a ruler"** (Ecclesiastes 10:5), **and** Yehuda, son of Rabbi Ḥiyya, **died.**

HALAKHA

Students may leave – הַתַּלְמִידִים יוֹצְאִין: Torah scholars may leave their homes to study Torah without permission from their wives for up to two or three years, in accordance with Rav Adda bar Ahava. The Rema writes that if the wife gives her husband permission, he may go for as long as she allows, as implied by Rava's words and the continuation of the Gemara (Rambam *Sefer Nashim, Hilkhot Ishut* 14:2; *Shulḥan Arukh, Even HaEzer* 76:5, and see 76:6).

The ideal time for Torah scholars to fulfill their conjugal obligations – עוֹנָה שֶׁל תַּלְמִידֵי חֲכָמִים: Torah scholars must fulfill their conjugal obligations to their wives once a week, and the custom is to do so on Shabbat eve (Rambam *Sefer Nashim, Hilkhot Ishut* 14:1; *Shulḥan Arukh, Even HaEzer* 76:2; see *Ḥelkat Meḥokek* and *Pitḥei Teshuva*).

NOTES

Performed an action like this themselves – וְעָבְדֵי עוּבְדָא בְּנַפְשַׁיְיהוּ: Rashi and the Rivan explain this to mean: They performed an action at the cost of their lives, meaning that they acted according to this ruling and therefore endangered themselves, as is related with regard to Rav Reḥumi. The Rid concludes from this that Rava maintains that those Sages acted incorrectly, and that the *halakha* is not in accordance with the opinion of Rav Adda bar Ahava. However, Rambam and many other authorities rule in accordance with Rav Adda bar Ahava. Apparently they understand Rava's statement to mean that the Sages relied on Rav Adda's opinion because the *halakha* is in accordance with his opinion. Another explanation is that the story of Rav Reḥumi demonstrates that despite this leniency, one must show consideration for his wife, and if he does not do so he is liable to be punished with death at the hand of Heaven (*Talmidei Rabbeinu Yona*).

רַבִּי אִיעֲסַק לֵיהּ לִבְרֵיהּ בֵּי רַבִּי חִיָּיא. כִּי מְטָא לְמִיכְתַּב כְּתוּבָּה נָח נַפְשָׁהּ דְּרָבִיתָא. אֲמַר רַבִּי: חַס וְשָׁלוֹם פְּסוּלָא אִיכָּא? יְתִיבוּ וְעַיְּינוּ בַּמִּשְׁפָּחוֹת: רַבִּי אָתֵי מִשְּׁפַטְיָה בֶּן אֲבִיטַל, וְרַבִּי חִיָּיא אָתֵי מִשִּׁמְעִי אֲחִי דָּוִד.

It is related further that **Rabbi** Yehuda HaNasi **arranged for his son** to marry a daughter of **the household of Rabbi Ḥiyya.**[P] **When he came to write the marriage contract, the girl died. Rabbi** Yehuda HaNasi **said: Is there, Heaven forbid, some disqualification** in these families, as it appears that God prevented this match from taking place? **They sat and looked into the families'** ancestry[N] and found that **Rabbi** Yehuda HaNasi **was descended from Shefatya ben Avital,** the wife of David, whereas **Rabbi Ḥiyya was descended from Shimi, David's brother.**

אָזֵיל אִיעֲסַק לֵיהּ לִבְרֵיהּ בֵּי רַבִּי יוֹסֵי בֶּן זִימְרָא. פָּסְקוּ לֵיהּ תַּרְתֵּי סְרֵי שְׁנִין לְמֵיזַל בְּבֵי רַב. אַחְלְפוּהָ קַמֵּיהּ, אֲמַר לְהוּ: נֶיהֱווֹ שִׁית שְׁנִין. אַחְלְפוּהָ קַמֵּיהּ, אֲמַר לְהוּ: אִיכְנִיס, וַהֲדַר אֵיזִיל. הֲוָה קָא מִכְסִיף מֵאֲבוּהּ. אֲמַר לֵיהּ: בְּנִי, דַּעַת קוֹנְךָ יֵשׁ בְּךָ.

He went and arranged for his son to marry a daughter **of the household of Rabbi Yosei ben Zimra.**[P] **They agreed for him** that they would support him for **twelve years to go to study in the study hall.** It was assumed that he would first go to study and afterward get married. **They passed** the girl **in front of** the groom and when he saw her **he said: Let it be** just **six years. They passed her in front of him** again and **he said to them: I will marry her** now **and then go** to study. **He was** then **ashamed** to see **his father,** as he thought he would reprimand him because when he saw the girl he desired her and could not wait. His father placated him and **said to him: My son, you have your Maker's perception,** meaning you acted the same way that God does.

מֵעִיקָּרָא כְּתִיב "תְּבִיאֵמוֹ וְתִטָּעֵמוֹ" וּלְבַסּוֹף כְּתִיב "וְעָשׂוּ לִי מִקְדָּשׁ וְשָׁכַנְתִּי בְּתוֹכָם".

The proof for this is that **initially it is written: "You bring them and plant them** in the mountain of Your inheritance, the place that You, O Lord, have made for You to dwell in" (Exodus 15:17), which indicates that God's original intention was to build a Temple for the Jewish people after they had entered Eretz Yisrael. **And ultimately it is written: "And let them make Me a Sanctuary, that I may dwell among them"** (Exodus 25:8), i.e., even while they were still in the desert, which indicates that due to their closeness to God, they enjoyed greater affection and He therefore advanced what would originally have come later.

אָזֵיל יְתֵיב תַּרְתֵּי סְרֵי שְׁנֵי בְּבֵי רַב, עַד דַּאֲתָא אִיעַקְּרָא דְּבֵיתְהוּ. אֲמַר רַבִּי: הֵיכִי נַעֲבֵיד? נְגָרְשַׁהּ – יֹאמְרוּ: עֲנִיָּיה זוֹ לַשָּׁוְא שִׁימְּרָה. נִינְסֵיב אִיתְּתָא אַחֲרִיתֵי – יֹאמְרוּ: זוֹ אִשְׁתּוֹ, וְזוֹ זוֹנָתוֹ. בָּעֵי עֲלָהּ רַחֲמֵי וְאִיתַּסִּיאַת.

After his wedding **he went and sat for twelve years in the study hall. By the time he came back his wife had become infertile,** as a consequence of spending many years without her husband. **Rabbi** Yehuda HaNasi **said: What** should **we do? If he will divorce her,** people **will say: This poor woman waited** and hoped **for naught. If he will marry another woman** to beget children, people **will say: This one,** who bears him children, **is his wife and that one,** who lives with him, **is his mistress.** Therefore, her husband **pleaded** with God **to have mercy on her and she was cured.**

NOTES

They sat and looked into the families' ancestry – יְתִיבוּ וְעַיְּינוּ בַּמִּשְׁפָּחוֹת: According to Rashi, they looked into the families and found that the match was not appropriate, as Rabbi Yehuda HaNasi was of royal lineage and Rabbi Ḥiyya, despite being related, was not. However, other commentaries reject this explanation, as there is no indication that even the direct descendants of King David married only women of royal lineage. Therefore, the Maharsha explains the Gemara differently: They looked into the families' ancestry to see whether there was some disqualification, and found that not only was there none, but the families were even related, as both of them descended from Yishai. Therefore, it appeared that the match was particularly appropriate.

PERSONALITIES

Rabbi Ḥiyya – רַבִּי חִיָּיא: Rabbi Ḥiyya ben Abba from the city of Kafri in Babylonia was among the last of the *tanna'im*. He was descended from a family of distinguished lineage that traced its ancestry back to King David and produced many prominent Sages. Even while he was still in Babylonia, Rabbi Ḥiyya was considered a Torah luminary. When he came to Eretz Yisrael, he became a disciple and colleague of Rabbi Yehuda HaNasi, who redacted the Mishna and with whom he had a very close relationship. He was especially close to Rabbi Shimon, son of Rabbi Yehuda HaNasi, who was also his business partner.

In addition to being a prominent Torah scholar, Rabbi Ḥiyya was outstanding in his piety, as reflected in several anecdotes throughout the Talmud. His most significant project was the redaction he did with his disciple-colleague, Rabbi Oshaya, of an anthology of external *mishnayot* to complement the Mishna. Their anthology was considered to be the most authoritative, to the point that it was said that any *baraita* that was not reviewed by them is unfit to enter the study hall. Some believe that he edited the *Tosefta*.

Although apparently Rabbi Ḥiyya initially received financial support from the house of the *Nasi*, he ultimately became a successful merchant in international business ventures, particularly the silk trade.

In addition to the daughter mentioned here who died young, he had twin daughters, Pazi and Tavi, who were the matriarchs of distinguished families of Torah scholars. He also had twin sons: Yehuda, son-in-law of Rabbi Yannai, and Ḥizkiyya. Both were among the leading Torah scholars in the transitional generation between *tanna'im* and *amora'im*, and they apparently replaced him at the head of his private yeshiva in the city of his residence, Tiberias. All of the students of Rabbi Yehuda HaNasi were his colleagues, and he was also close with the *tanna* Rabbi Shimon ben Ḥalafta. The younger students of Rabbi Yehuda HaNasi, namely Rabbi Ḥanina, Rabbi Oshaya, Rabbi Yannai, and others, studied Torah from Rabbi Ḥiyya and were, to a certain degree, his students as well.

His primary disciples were his brothers' sons, Rabba bar bar Ḥana, and above all, the great *amora*, Rav, who, although he was known as the Rabbi of all of Israel, received certain traditions from Rabbi Ḥiyya. He also appears as a central figure in the *Zohar*. Rabbi Ḥiyya was buried in Tiberias, and his two sons were later buried beside him.

Rabbi Yosei ben Zimra – רַבִּי יוֹסֵי בֶּן זִימְרָא: Rabbi Yosei was of the last generation of *tanna'im*. From a source elsewhere in the Talmud it appears that he was a priest and that he was a member of Rabbi Yehuda HaNasi's rabbinical court. He lived a very long life, and therefore many of his statements are relayed by the *amora'im* Rabbi Yoḥanan and Rabbi Elazar. While there are some halakhic statements attributed to him, most of the quotations attributed to him in both Talmuds are of an aggadic nature.

רַבִּי חֲנַנְיָה בֶּן חֲכִינַאי הֲוָה קָאָזֵיל לְבֵי רַב בְּשִׁילְהֵי הִלּוּלֵיהּ דְּרַבִּי שִׁמְעוֹן בֶּן יוֹחַאי. אֲמַר לֵיהּ: אִיעַכַּב לִי עַד דְּאָתֵי בַּהֲדָךְ. לָא אִיעַכְּבָא לֵיהּ. אֲזַל יְתֵיב תְּרֵי סְרֵי שְׁנֵי בְּבֵי רַב. עַד דְּאָתֵי – אִישְׁתַּנּוּ שְׁבִילֵי דְּמָתָא, וְלָא יָדַע לְמֵיזַל לְבֵיתֵיהּ.

Rabbi Ḥananya ben Ḥakhinai[P] **went to the study hall at the end of Rabbi Shimon ben Yoḥai's wedding feast.** Rabbi Shimon **said to him: Wait for me until I can come with you,** after my days of celebration are over. However, since he wanted to learn Torah, **he did not wait** and **went and sat for twelve years in the study hall. By the time he came back, all the paths of his city had changed and he did not know how to go to his home.**

אֲזַל יְתֵיב אַגּוּדָא דְּנַהֲרָא. שְׁמַע לְהַהִיא רְבִיתָא דְּהָווּ קָרוּ לָהּ: בַּת חֲכִינַאי, בַּת חֲכִינַאי, מְלִי קוּלְתֵיךְ וְתָא נֵיזִיל. אֲמַר: שְׁמַע מִינָּהּ, הַאי רְבִיתָא דִּידָן. אֲזַל בַּתְרָהּ, הֲוָה יְתִיבָא דְּבֵיתְהוּ קָא נָהֲלָה קִמְחָא. דָּל עֵינָהּ, חַזְיתֵיהּ, סָוֵי לִבָּהּ, פָּרַח רוּחָהּ. אֲמַר לְפָנָיו: רִבּוֹנוֹ שֶׁל עוֹלָם, עֲנִיָּה זוֹ, זֶה שְׂכָרָהּ?! בְּעָא רַחֲמֵי עֲלָהּ וְחָיְיָה.

He went and **sat on the bank of the river and heard** people **calling to a certain girl: Daughter of Ḥakhinai, daughter of Ḥakhinai, fill your pitcher and come up. He said: I can conclude from this that this is our daughter,** meaning his own daughter, whom he had not recognized after so many years. **He followed her** to his house. **His wife was sitting and sifting flour. She lifted her eyes up, saw him** and recognized him, **and her heart fluttered** with agitation and **she passed away** from the emotional stress. Rabbi Ḥananya **said before** God: **Master of the universe, is this the reward of this poor woman? He pleaded for mercy for her and she lived.**

רַבִּי חָמָא בַּר בִּיסָא אָזֵיל יְתֵיב תְּרֵי סְרֵי שְׁנֵי בְּבֵי מִדְרְשָׁא. כִּי אֲתָא, אֲמַר: לָא אִיעֲבִיד כִּדְעָבֵיד בֶּן חֲכִינַאי. עָיֵיל יְתֵיב בְּמִדְרְשָׁא, שָׁלַח לְבֵיתֵיהּ. אֲתָא רַבִּי אוֹשַׁעְיָא בְּרֵיהּ, יְתֵיב קַמֵּיהּ. הֲוָה קָא מַשְׁאִיל לֵיהּ שְׁמַעְתָּא, חֲזָא דְּקָא מִתְחַדְּדֵי שְׁמַעְתֵּיהּ, חָלַשׁ דַּעְתֵּיהּ, אֲמַר: אִי הֲוַאי הָכָא – הֲוָה לִי זֶרַע כִּי הַאי.

Rabbi Ḥama bar Bisa[P] **went and sat for twelve years in the study hall. When he came** back to his house, **he said: I will not do what the son of Ḥakhinai,** who came home suddenly with tragic consequences for his wife, **did. He went and sat in the study hall** in his hometown, **and sent** a message **to his house** that he had arrived. While he was sitting there **his son Rabbi Oshaya,** whom he did not recognize, **came and sat before him.** Rabbi Oshaya **asked him** questions about ***halakha*****, and** Rabbi Ḥama **saw that the *halakhot*** of Rabbi Oshaya **were incisive,** i.e., he was very sharp. Rabbi Ḥama **was distressed and said: If I had been here** and had taught my son **I would have had a child like this.**

עָל לְבֵיתֵיהּ. עָל בְּרֵיהּ, קָם קַמֵּיהּ. הוּא סָבַר – לְמִשְׁאֲלֵיהּ שְׁמַעְתְּתָא קָא בָּעֵי. אָמְרָה לֵיהּ דְּבֵיתְהוּ: מִי אִיכָּא אַבָּא דְּקָאֵים מִקָּמֵּי בְּרָא? קָרֵי עֲלֵיהּ רָמֵי בַּר חָמָא: "הַחוּט הַמְשׁוּלָּשׁ לֹא בִמְהֵרָה יִנָּתֵק" – זֶה רַבִּי אוֹשַׁעְיָא, בְּנוֹ שֶׁל רַבִּי חָמָא בַּר בִּיסָא.

Rabbi Ḥama **went in to his house** and **his son went in** with him. Rabbi Ḥama then **stood up before him** to honor a Torah scholar, since **he thought** that **he wanted to ask him a matter of *halakha*. His wife said to him: Is there a father who stands up before his son?** The Gemara comments: **Rami bar Ḥama read** the verse **about him: "A threefold cord is not quickly broken"** (Ecclesiastes 4:12). **This** is referring to **Rabbi Oshaya, son of Rabbi Ḥama bar Bisa,** as he represented the third generation of Torah scholars in his family.

PERSONALITIES

Rabbi Ḥananya ben Ḥakhinai – רַבִּי חֲנַנְיָה בֶּן חֲכִינַאי: Rabbi Ḥananya or Ḥannina ben Ḥakhinai, was one of those who deliberated before the Sages in Yavne and was identified as one of the Sages who knew seventy languages. Ben Ḥakhinai was an especially devoted student of Rabbi Akiva. Traditions reported in his name can be found throughout the Mishna, the *Tosefta*, various compilations of halakhic midrash, and the Talmud. In one midrash he is listed among the renowned ten martyrs.

Rabbi Ḥama bar Bisa – רַבִּי חָמָא בַּר בִּיסָא: Rabbi Ḥama was of the last generation of *tanna'im*. He was apparently a member of Rabbi Yehuda HaNasi's rabbinical court, who praised him as a great man. It seems that he lived in the southern part of Eretz Yisrael, perhaps in Lod, and served as a city judge. In most of the places in both the Babylonian and the Jerusalem Talmuds where Rabbi Ḥama's name is mentioned and his statements are quoted, he is referred to by the name of his son: Rabbi Ḥama, father of Rabbi Oshaya. This is because Rabbi Oshaya was one of the leaders of the generation who compiled a collection of important *baraitot*. Very little is known about Rabbi Ḥama's father, Rabbi Bisa, and only one *halakha* is quoted in his name, in a case where he ruled in accordance with the opinion of his grandson Rabbi Oshaya, and contrary to the opinion of his son Rabbi Ḥama.

רַבִּי עֲקִיבָא רָעְיָא דְּבֶן כַּלְבָּא שָׂבוּעַ הֲוָה. חֲזִיתֵיהּ בְּרַתֵּיהּ דַּהֲוָה צְנִיעַ וּמַעֲלֵי, אָמְרָה לֵיהּ: אִי מִקַּדְּשְׁנָא לָךְ אָזְלַתְּ לְבֵי רַב? אֲמַר לַהּ: אִין אִיקַּדְּשָׁא לֵיהּ בְּצִינְעָה, וְשַׁדַּרְתֵּיהּ. שְׁמַע אֲבוּהּ אַפְּקַהּ מִבֵּיתֵיהּ, אַדְּרַהּ הֲנָאָה מִנִּכְסֵיהּ. אֲזַל יְתֵיב תְּרֵי סְרֵי שְׁנִין בְּבֵי רַב, כִּי אֲתָא – אַיְיתֵי בַּהֲדֵיהּ תְּרֵי סְרֵי אַלְפֵי תַּלְמִידֵי. שְׁמַעֵיהּ לְהַהוּא סָבָא דְּקָאָמַר לַהּ: עַד כַּמָּה

The Gemara further relates: **Rabbi Akiva was the shepherd of ben Kalba Savua,**[P] one of the wealthy residents of Jerusalem. The **daughter** of Ben Kalba Savua **saw that he was humble and refined. She said to him: If I betroth myself to you, will you go to the study hall** to learn Torah? **He said to her: Yes. She became betrothed to him privately and sent him** off to study. **Her father heard** this and became angry. **He removed her from his house** and took a **vow** prohibiting her from **benefiting from his property.** Rabbi Akiva **went** and **sat for twelve years in the study hall. When he came** back to his house **he brought twelve thousand students** with him, and as he approached **he heard an old man saying to** his wife: **For how long**

PERSONALITIES

Ben Kalba Savua – בֶּן כַּלְבָּא שָׂבוּעַ: The family of ben Kalba Savua was one of the wealthy and powerful families in Jerusalem at the time of the destruction of the Second Temple. It was said that they were one of the three families who would have had the financial ability to support the entire city for many years of siege. It seems that the family was descended from Caleb, son of Jephunneh, and that this was the source of their name. There is also a poetic extrapolation that he was called that because anyone who entered his home as hungry as a dog [*kalba*] would leave satisfied [*savua*].

In several places, the Talmud describes the difficult life of Rabbi Akiva and his wife during the many years when she was banned from benefitting from her father's property. This Gemara implies that the couple had children; at least one daughter, as mentioned at the end of the discussion in the Gemara, and possibly several sons as well. It seems that Rabbi Akiva also had children from a previous marriage.

Perek **V**
Daf **63** Amud **a**

קָא מְדַבְּרַתְּ אַלְמָנוּת חַיִּים. אָמְרָה לֵיהּ: אִי לְדִידִי צָיֵית – יְתֵיב תְּרֵי סְרֵי שְׁנֵי אַחֲרִינֵי. אֲמַר: בִּרְשׁוּת קָא עָבֵידְנָא. הֲדַר אֲזַל וִיתֵיב תְּרֵי סְרֵי שְׁנֵי אַחֲרִינֵי בְּבֵי רַב. כִּי אֲתָא, אַיְיתֵי בַּהֲדֵיהּ עֶשְׂרִין וְאַרְבְּעָה אַלְפֵי תַּלְמִידֵי. שָׁמְעָה דְּבֵיתְהוּ, הֲוַת קָא נָפְקָא לְאַפֵּיהּ. אָמְרוּ לַהּ שֵׁיבְבָתָא: שְׁאִילִי מָאנֵי לְבוּשׁ וְאִיכַּסַּאי! אָמְרָה לְהוּ: ״יוֹדֵעַ צַדִּיק נֶפֶשׁ בְּהֶמְתּוֹ״. כִּי מְטַיָּא לְגַבֵּיהּ – נָפְלָה עַל אַפָּהּ, קָא מְנַשְּׁקָא לֵיהּ לְכַרְעֵיהּ. הֲווּ קָא מְדַחֲפִי לַהּ שַׁמָּעֵיהּ. אֲמַר לְהוּ: שִׁבְקוּהָ, שֶׁלִּי וְשֶׁלָּכֶם – שֶׁלָּהּ הוּא.

will you lead the life of a **widow of a living man,** living alone while your husband is in another place? **She said to him: If he** would **listen to me, he would sit** and study **for another twelve years.** When Rabbi Akiva heard this **he said: I have permission to do** this. **He went back and sat for another twelve years in the study hall. When he came** back **he brought twenty-four thousand students with him. His wife heard and went out** toward him **to greet him. Her neighbors said: Borrow some clothes and wear them,** as your current apparel is not appropriate to meet an important person. **She said to them: "A righteous man understands the life of his beast"** (Proverbs 12:10). **When she came to him she fell on her face and kissed his feet. His attendants pushed her** away as they did not know who she was, and **he said to them: Leave her** alone, as **my** Torah knowledge **and yours is** actually **hers.**

שְׁמַע אֲבוּהּ דַּאֲתָא גַּבְרָא רַבָּה לְמָתָא, אֲמַר אֵיזִיל לְגַבֵּיהּ אֶפְשָׁר דְּמֵיפֵר נִדְרַאי. אֲתָא לְגַבֵּיהּ אֲמַר לֵיהּ אַדַּעְתָּא דְּגַבְרָא רַבָּה מִי נָדַרְתְּ? אֲמַר לוֹ: אֲפִילּוּ פֶּרֶק אֶחָד וַאֲפִילּוּ הֲלָכָה אַחַת. אֲמַר לֵיהּ: אֲנָא הוּא. נָפַל עַל אַפֵּיהּ, וּנְשַׁקֵיהּ עַל כַּרְעֵיהּ, וְיָהֵיב לֵיהּ פַּלְגָא מָמוֹנֵיהּ. בְּרַתֵּיהּ דְּרַבִּי עֲקִיבָא עָבְדָא לֵיהּ לְבֶן עַזַּאי הָכִי. וְהַיְינוּ דְּאָמְרִי אֱינָשֵׁי: רְחֵילָא בָּתַר רְחֵילָא אָזְלָא, כְּעוֹבָדֵי אִמָּהּ כָּךְ עוֹבָדֵי בְּרַתָּא.

In the meantime **her father heard that a great man came to the town. He said: I will go to him. Maybe he will nullify my vow** and I will be able to support my daughter. **He came to him** to ask about nullifying his vow, and Rabbi Akiva **said to him: Did you vow thinking that** this Akiva **would become a great man? He said to him:** If I had believed he would know **even one chapter or even one *halakha*** I would not have been so harsh. **He said to him: I am he.** Ben Kalba Savua **fell on his face and kissed his feet and gave him half of his money.** The Gemara relates: **Rabbi Akiva's daughter did the same** thing **for ben Azzai,** who was also a simple person, and she caused him to learn Torah in a similar way, by betrothing herself to him and sending him off to study. **This** explains the folk saying **that people say: The ewe follows the ewe; the daughter's actions are the same as her mother's.**

רַב יוֹסֵף בְּרֵיהּ דְּרָבָא שַׁדְּרֵיהּ אֲבוּהִי לְבֵי רַב לְקַמֵּיהּ דְּרַב יוֹסֵף. פָּסְקוּ לֵיהּ שִׁית שְׁנֵי. כִּי הֲוָה תְּלָת שְׁנֵי מְטָא מַעֲלֵי יוֹמָא דְכִפּוּרֵי, אֲמַר: אֵיזִיל וְאִיחֲזִינְהוּ לֶאֱינָשֵׁי בֵּיתִי. שְׁמַע אֲבוּהִי, שְׁקַל מָנָא וּנְפַק לְאַפֵּיהּ. אֲמַר לֵיהּ: זוֹנָתְךָ נִזְכַּרְתָּ? אִיכָּא דְּאָמְרִי, אֲמַר לֵיהּ: יוֹנָתְךָ נִזְכַּרְתָּ? אִיטְרוּד, לָא מָר אִיפְסִיק וְלָא מָר אִיפְסִיק.

On the same subject it is related: **Rav Yosef, son of Rava, was sent by his father to the study hall** to learn **before** the great Sage **Rav Yosef.** They **agreed** that **he** should sit for **six years** in the study hall. **When three years had** passed, **the eve of Yom Kippur arrived** and **he said: I will go and see the members of my household,** meaning his wife. **His father heard and took a weapon,** as if he were going to war, **and went to meet him.** According to one version **he said to him: Did you remember your mistress,** as you are abandoning your studies to see a woman? **There are** those **who say** that he said to him: **Did you remember your dove?** Since both father and son were involved in an argument, **they were preoccupied** and **this Master did not eat the cessation** meal before Yom Kippur **and that Master** also **did not eat the cessation** meal that day.

מתני׳ הַמּוֹרֶדֶת עַל בַּעְלָהּ – פּוֹחֲתִין לָהּ מִכְּתוּבָּתָהּ שִׁבְעָה דִּינָרִין בְּשַׁבָּת, רַבִּי יְהוּדָה אוֹמֵר: שִׁבְעָה טְרַפָּעִיקִין. עַד מָתַי הוּא פּוֹחֵת – עַד כְּנֶגֶד כְּתוּבָּתָהּ. רַבִּי יוֹסֵי אוֹמֵר: לְעוֹלָם הוּא פּוֹחֵת וְהוֹלֵךְ, עַד שֶׁאִם תִּפּוֹל לָהּ יְרוּשָּׁה מִמָּקוֹם אַחֵר גּוֹבֶה הֵימֶנָּה. וְכֵן הַמּוֹרֵד עַל אִשְׁתּוֹ – מוֹסִיפִין עַל כְּתוּבָּתָהּ שְׁלֹשָׁה דִּינָרִין בְּשַׁבָּת, רַבִּי יְהוּדָה אוֹמֵר: שְׁלֹשָׁה טְרַפָּעִיקִין.

MISHNA A woman **who rebels**[H] **against her husband** is fined; **her marriage contract is reduced by seven dinars** each **week. Rabbi Yehuda says: Seven half-dinars** [*terapa'ikin*][L] each week. **Until when does he reduce** her marriage contract? **Until** the reductions are **equivalent to her marriage contract**, i.e., until he no longer owes her any money, at which point he divorces her without any payment. **Rabbi Yosei says: He can always continue to deduct** from the sum, even beyond that which is owed to her due to her marriage contract, **so that if she will receive an inheritance from another source, he can collect** the extra amount **from her. And similarly,** if a man **rebels**[H] **against his wife,** he is fined and an extra **three dinars a week are added to her marriage contract. Rabbi Yehuda says: Three** ***terapa'ikin.***

גמ׳ מוֹרֶדֶת מִמַּאי? רַב הוּנָא אָמַר: מִתַּשְׁמִישׁ הַמִּטָּה, רַבִּי יוֹסֵי בְּרַבִּי חֲנִינָא אָמַר: מִמְּלָאכָה. תְּנַן: וְכֵן הַמּוֹרֵד עַל אִשְׁתּוֹ, בִּשְׁלָמָא לְמַאן דְּאָמַר מִתַּשְׁמִישׁ – לְחַיֵּי, אֶלָּא לְמַאן דְּאָמַר מִמְּלָאכָה – מִי מְשׁוּעְבָּד לָהּ? אִין, בְּאוֹמֵר ״אֵינִי זָן וְאֵינִי מְפַרְנֵס״.

GEMARA The Gemara asks: **Against what** does **she rebel;**[H] what is the nature of the rebellion discussed in the mishna? **Rav Huna said: Against** engaging in **marital relations. Rabbi Yosei, son of Rabbi Ḥanina, said: Against** the **tasks** she is obligated to perform for her husband. The Gemara clarifies this dispute. **The mishna states: Similarly,** if a man **rebels against his wife. Granted, according to the one who says** that the rebellion is **against marital relations, it is well,** as this type of rebellion can apply equally to a husband. **However, according to the one who says** that she rebels **against** performing **tasks, is he subjugated to her** to perform tasks? The Gemara answers: **Yes,** he is, as the mishna is discussing **someone who says: I will not sustain and I will not support** my wife.

וְהָאָמַר רַב: הָאוֹמֵר ״אֵינִי זָן וְאֵינִי מְפַרְנֵס״ – יוֹצִיא וְיִתֵּן כְּתוּבָּה! וְלָאו לְאִמְּלוּכֵי בֵּיהּ בָּעֵי?

The Gemara asks: **But didn't Rav say: One who says: I will not sustain and I will not support** my wife **must** immediately **divorce** her **and give her** the payment for her **marriage contract?** What relevance is there to a discussion of a weekly fine? The Gemara answers: **Shouldn't he be consulted** to investigate whether he will retract his decision? In the interim, while the court discusses the issue with him and explains that he must divorce his wife if he does not retract his decision, he is fined by the addition of three dinars per week to her marriage contract.

מֵיתִיבֵי: אַחַת לִי אֲרוּסָה וּנְשׂוּאָה, וַאֲפִילּוּ נִדָּה, וַאֲפִילּוּ חוֹלָה, וַאֲפִילּוּ שׁוֹמֶרֶת יָבָם.

The Gemara **raises an objection** from a *baraita* with regard to a rebellious woman: **It is the same to me,** i.e., the same *halakha* applies, if the woman who rebelled is **a betrothed woman,**[H] **or a married woman, or even a menstruating woman, or even** if she is **ill,**[H] **or even** if she is **a widow waiting for her** ***yavam***[B] to perform levirate marriage.[H]

בִּשְׁלָמָא לְמַאן דַּאֲמַר מִמְּלָאכָה – שַׁפִּיר. אֶלָּא לְמַאן דַּאֲמַר מִתַּשְׁמִישׁ – נִדָּה בַּת תַּשְׁמִישׁ הִיא? אָמַר לָךְ: אֵינוֹ דּוֹמֶה מִי שֶׁיֵּשׁ לוֹ פַּת בְּסַלּוֹ לְמִי שֶׁאֵין לוֹ.

The Gemara discusses the *baraita*. **Granted, according to the one who says** that her rebelliousness is referring to performing **tasks, it is well. However, according to the one who says** that she rebels **against** engaging in **marital relations,** is **a menstruating woman fit to** engage in **marital relations?** She is not, and therefore there would be no significance to her refusal. The Gemara answers: The one who advocates that opinion could have **said to you: One who has bread in his basket,** i.e., one who has engaged in marital relations with his wife in the past, **is not comparable to one who does not have** bread in his basket. Since she declares her refusal to engage in marital relations, he suffers from this refusal even when she is menstruating or ill.

אִיכָּא דְּאָמְרִי: בִּשְׁלָמָא לְמַאן דַּאֲמַר מִתַּשְׁמִישׁ – הַיְינוּ דְּקָתָנֵי חוֹלָה,

There are those **who say** that the objection was phrased differently. **Granted, according to the one who says** that the rebellion discussed in the mishna is referring to **engaging in marital relations, this** explanation **is** consistent with **that which is taught** with regard to **an ill woman,** that she be fined as a rebellious woman, as even if she is not capable of working, she can still be rebellious with regard to marital relations.

HALAKHA

A woman who rebels – הַמּוֹרֶדֶת: The *halakha* of a rebellious woman does not follow this mishna but rather the later enactment of the Sages, according to which the woman is publicly warned for several weeks and then loses her entire marriage contract if she persists in her rebellion, as explained on 63b (Rambam *Sefer Nashim, Hilkhot Ishut* 14:8; *Shulḥan Arukh, Even HaEzer* 77:2).

A man rebels – מוֹרֵד: If a husband rebels against his wife, meaning that he is willing to support her but is not willing to engage in conjugal relations with her, the court adds the value of thirty-six grains of silver, which is three dinars, to her marriage contract each week, as stated in the mishna. This applies as long as she wants to remain married to him. In addition, each time he deprives her of her conjugal rights he violates the Torah law "He shall not diminish her conjugal rights" (Exodus 21:10). If she does not want to continue to live with him, he is compelled to divorce her immediately and give her the payment for her marriage contract (Rambam *Sefer Nashim, Hilkhot Ishut* 14:15; *Shulḥan Arukh, Even HaEzer* 77:1).

Against what does she rebel – מוֹרֶדֶת מִמַּאי: If a woman withholds conjugal relations from her husband, she is called a rebellious woman. This ruling is in accordance with the opinion of Rav Huna, with which Rabbi Yosei, son of Rabbi Ḥanina, concurs (Rambam *Sefer Nashim, Hilkhot Ishut* 14:8; *Shulḥan Arukh, Even HaEzer* 77:2).

It is the same to me if she is a betrothed woman – אַחַת לִי אֲרוּסָה: If the wedding date of a betrothed woman arrived, and she rebelled against her husband to cause him anguish and does not want to marry him, she is defined as a rebellious woman (Rambam *Sefer Nashim, Hilkhot Ishut* 14:12; *Shulḥan Arukh, Even HaEzer* 77:2).

A menstruating woman or even if she is ill – נִדָּה וַאֲפִילּוּ חוֹלָה: Even if a woman is a menstruating woman or ill and thus not fit to engage in conjugal relations when she rebels, she is nevertheless declared a rebellious woman. The Rema quotes the Rashba, who, based on a statement in the Jerusalem Talmud, distinguishes between a situation where a woman rebels before she begins menstruating, in which case she is a rebellious woman, and one where a woman rebels during her period of menstruation, in which case she is not yet defined as a rebellious woman (Rambam *Sefer Nashim, Hilkhot Ishut* 14:11; *Shulḥan Arukh, Even HaEzer* 77:2).

Or even if she is a widow waiting for her *yavam* to perform levirate marriage – וַאֲפִילּוּ שׁוֹמֶרֶת יָבָם: Some authorities say that not only a woman who agreed to be betrothed to a certain man, but even a *yevama* who refused to enter into levirate marriage in order to cause anguish to her *yavam* is defined as a rebellious woman (Rambam *Sefer Nashim, Hilkhot Ishut* 14:12 and *Hilkhot Yibbum* 2:10; *Shulḥan Arukh, Even HaEzer* 77:2).

LANGUAGE

Half-dinars [*terapa'ikin*] – טְרַפָּעִיקִין: From the Greek τροπαικόν, *tropaikon*, referring to a half-dinar coin. In Latin it was called victoriatus.

BACKGROUND

A widow waiting for her *yavam* – שׁוֹמֶרֶת יָבָם: A woman whose husband dies without children is known by the term: A widow awaiting her *yavam*. If her late husband left behind at least one brother, she is prohibited from marrying anyone else until one of the brothers, preferably the eldest, performs levirate marriage or, alternatively, releases her by performing the *ḥalitza* ceremony. Until one of these procedures is done, the widow is bound to her late husband's brothers by a bond known as a levirate bond. The *amora'im* and *tanna'im* debated the nature and strength of this bond.

אֶלָּא לְמַאן דְּאָמַר מִמְּלָאכָה – חוֹלָה בַּת מְלָאכָה הִיא? אֶלָּא, מִתַּשְׁמִישׁ כּוּלֵּי עָלְמָא לָא פְּלִיגִי דְּהָוְיָא מוֹרֶדֶת. כִּי פְּלִיגִי – מִמְּלָאכָה. מָר סָבַר: מִמְּלָאכָה לָא הָוְיָא מוֹרֶדֶת, וּמָר סָבַר: מִמְּלָאכָה נַמִי הָוְיָא מוֹרֶדֶת.

However, according to the one who says the rebellion is **against** performing **tasks, is an ill woman fit to perform tasks?** Since she is ill, she has no obligation to perform tasks and this is not deemed rebellious behavior. **Rather,** one must explain this as follows: If she rebelled **against** engaging in **marital relations, everyone agrees that she is** defined as **a rebellious** woman. **They disagree** with regard to one who rebels **against** performing **tasks.** One Sage, Rav Huna, **holds** that one who rebels **against performing tasks is not a rebellious woman, and** one Sage, Rabbi Yosei, son of Rabbi Ḥanina, **holds** that one who rebels **against performing tasks is also** considered **a rebellious** woman.

גּוּפָא: הַמּוֹרֶדֶת עַל בַּעְלָהּ פּוֹחֲתִין לָהּ מִכְּתוּבָּתָהּ שִׁבְעָה דִּינָרִים בְּשַׁבָּת, רַבִּי יְהוּדָה אוֹמֵר: שִׁבְעָה טַרְפְּעִיקִין. רַבּוֹתֵינוּ חָזְרוּ וְנִמְנוּ שֶׁיְּהוּ מַכְרִיזִין עָלֶיהָ אַרְבַּע שַׁבָּתוֹת זוֹ אַחַר זוֹ, וְשׁוֹלְחִין לָהּ בֵּית דִּין: הֱוִי יוֹדַעַת שֶׁאֲפִילּוּ כְּתוּבָּתֵיךְ מֵאָה מָנֶה הִפְסַדְתְּ. אַחַת לִי אֲרוּסָה וּנְשׂוּאָה אֲפִילּוּ נִדָּה, אֲפִילּוּ חוֹלָה, וַאֲפִילּוּ שׁוֹמֶרֶת יָבָם.

§ With regard to **the** matter **itself:** A woman who **rebels against her husband** is fined; **we reduce her marriage contract** by **seven dinars** each **week,** and **Rabbi Yehuda says: Seven** ***terapa'ikin***. **Our Sages went back and were counted again,**[H] meaning they voted and decided that instead of deducting a small amount from her marriage contract each week, **they would make** public **announcements**[N] **about her for four consecutive** ***Shabbatot***. **And** they decided **that the court would send** messengers **to her** to inform her: **Be aware that even if your marriage contract is worth ten thousand dinars, you will lose** it all if you continue your rebellion. If she does not retract her rebellion, she forfeits her entire marriage contract. With regard to this enactment, **it is the same to me,** meaning the *halakha* does not change, if she is **a betrothed woman or a married woman,** and **even** if she is **a menstruating woman, and even** if she is **ill, and even** if she is **a widow awaiting her** ***yavam*** to perform levirate marriage.

אֲמַר לֵיהּ רַבִּי חִיָּיא בַּר יוֹסֵף לִשְׁמוּאֵל: נִדָּה בַּת תַּשְׁמִישׁ הִיא? אֲמַר לֵיהּ: אֵינוֹ דּוֹמֶה מִי שֶׁיֵּשׁ לוֹ פַּת בְּסַלּוֹ לְמִי שֶׁאֵין לוֹ פַּת בְּסַלּוֹ.

Rabbi Ḥiyya bar Yosef said to Shmuel: Is a menstruating woman fit to engage in **conjugal relations? He said to him: One who has bread in his basket,** i.e., one who knows that he will be able to engage in relations with his wife after her period of menstrual impurity ends, **is not comparable to one who does not have bread in his basket.**

אָמַר רָמִי בַּר חָמָא: אֵין מַכְרִיזִין עָלֶיהָ אֶלָּא בְּבָתֵּי כְנֵסִיּוֹת וּבְבָתֵּי מִדְרָשׁוֹת. אֲמַר רָבָא: דַּיְקָא נַמִי, דְּקָתָנֵי: אַרְבַּע שַׁבָּתוֹת זוֹ אַחַר זוֹ – שְׁמַע מִינַּהּ. אָמַר רָמִי בַּר חָמָא: פַּעֲמַיִם שׁוֹלְחִין לָהּ מִבֵּית דִּין; אַחַת קוֹדֶם הַכְרָזָה וְאַחַת לְאַחַר הַכְרָזָה.

Rami bar Ḥama said: We make announcements about her only in synagogues[H] **and study halls,** but not in the street. **Rava said: The** language of the *baraita* **is also precise, as it teaches:** They would make announcements on **four consecutive** ***Shabbatot***, which are days when no labor is performed and people are not to be found in the streets, but rather in synagogues and study halls. The Gemara summarizes: **Conclude from** this that this is the case. **Rami bar Ḥama said: The court sends** people to talk **with her twice,**[HN] **once before the announcement and once after the announcement.**

דָּרַשׁ רַב נַחְמָן בַּר רַב חִסְדָּא: הֲלָכָה כְּרַבּוֹתֵינוּ. אֲמַר רָבָא: הַאי בּוּרְכָא. אֲמַר לֵיהּ רַב נַחְמָן בַּר יִצְחָק: מַאי בּוּרְכָתֵיהּ? אֲנָא אֲמַרִיתָהּ נִיהֲלֵיהּ, וּמִשְּׁמֵיהּ דְּגַבְרָא רַבָּה אֲמַרִיתָהּ נִיהֲלֵיהּ, וּמַנּוּ – רַבִּי יוֹסֵי בְּרַבִּי חֲנִינָא.

Rav Naḥman bar Rav Ḥisda taught with regard to this: **The** ***halakha*** **is in accordance with** the decision of **our Sages. Rava said: This is an absurdity** [***burkha***].[L] **Rav Naḥman bar Yitzḥak said to him: What is absurd about this? I said this to him, and I said it to him in the name of a great man. And who is** the great man who ruled this way? **Rabbi Yosei, son of Rabbi Ḥanina.**

וְאִיהוּ כְּמַאן סָבַר? כִּי הָא דְּאִתְּמַר, רָבָא אָמַר רַב שֵׁשֶׁת: הֲלָכָה נִמְלָכִין בָּהּ. רַב הוּנָא בַּר יְהוּדָה אָמַר רַב שֵׁשֶׁת: הֲלָכָה, אֵין נִמְלָכִין בָּהּ.

The Gemara asks: **And in accordance with whose** opinion does Rava **hold?** The Gemara answers: **In accordance with that which was stated: Rava** said that **Rav Sheshet said:** The ***halakha*** **is** that **she is consulted**[H] in an attempt to convince her to retract her decision, and while doing so deductions are made from her marriage contract. But **Rav Huna bar Yehuda** said that **Rav Sheshet said: The** ***halakha*** is that **we do not consult with her.** According to both versions of Rav Sheshet's ruling, she does not lose her marriage contract immediately but rather it is reduced every week. This is the source for Rava's opinion.

HALAKHA

Our Sages went back and were counted again – רַבּוֹתֵינוּ חָזְרוּ וְנִמְנוּ: If a woman rebels against her husband, the court makes daily public announcements about her over a period of four weeks, saying: So-and-so has rebelled against her husband. Some say they do so only on the Shabbat of each of these four weeks (Rema, citing *Tosafot*; Ran). The court informs her that she will forfeit her entire marriage contract if she continues her rebellious behavior. If she does not retract her decision, she forfeits her entire marriage contract, in accordance with the decision of the Sages (Rambam *Sefer Nashim, Hilkhot Ishut* 14:9–10; *Shulḥan Arukh, Even HaEzer* 77:2).

We make announcements…in synagogues – מַכְרִיזִין...בְּבָתֵּי כְנֵסִיּוֹת: The announcements about a rebellious woman are made only in synagogues and study halls, in accordance with Rami bar Ḥama, as no one disputes this (Rambam *Sefer Nashim, Hilkhot Ishut* 14:9; *Shulḥan Arukh, Even HaEzer* 77:2).

Sends people to talk with her twice – פַּעֲמַיִם שׁוֹלְחִין לָהּ: The court sends people to a rebellious woman before it makes an announcement about her, and she is warned that she might forfeit her entire marriage contract. After the announcement, the court sends messengers a second time to warn her again (Rambam *Sefer Nashim, Hilkhot Ishut* 14:10; *Shulḥan Arukh, Even HaEzer* 77:2).

She is consulted – נִמְלָכִין בָּהּ: If she does not retract her rebellious behavior, the court consults with her. If she then does not retract, she forfeits her marriage contract, in accordance with the ruling of Rav Sheshet cited by Rava (Rambam *Sefer Nashim, Hilkhot Ishut* 14:10; *Shulḥan Arukh, Even HaEzer* 77:2).

NOTES

They would make public announcements – שֶׁיְּהוּ מַכְרִיזִין: According to the Rid, the purpose of the announcements is to embarrass her, in the hope that she will retract her decision and change her behavior. Additionally, the announcements will cause her friends and relatives to hear about the issue, and they will try to influence her to end the rebellion.

Sends people to talk with her twice – פַּעֲמַיִם שׁוֹלְחִין לָהּ: Most commentaries understand this to mean that the court sends messengers to her a total of two times: Once before they begin the announcements and once at the end of the four-week period. However, *Talmidei Rabbeinu Yona* cite an alternative explanation in the name of their teacher: The court sends people to her twice for each announcement, for a total of eight times over the course of four weeks of public announcements.

LANGUAGE

Absurdity [*burkha*] – בּוּרְכָא: The *Arukh* explains that this word is a longer form of *bur*, meaning empty or uncultivated. *Burkha* means a hollow or absurd idea with no basis.

הֵיכִי דָּמְיָא מוֹרֶדֶת? אָמַר אֲמֵימַר: דְּאָמְרָה ״בָּעֵינָא לֵיהּ וּמְצַעַרְנָא לֵיהּ״, אֲבָל אָמְרָה ״מָאִיס עֲלַי״ – לָא כָּיְיפִינַן לַהּ. מָר זוּטְרָא אָמַר: כָּיְיפִינַן לַהּ.

§ With regard to this *halakha*, the Gemara asks: **What are the circumstances** in which the *halakha* of **a rebellious** woman applies? **Ameimar said:** The case is where **she says: I want** to be married to **him, but** I am currently refusing him because **I want to cause him anguish**[H] due to a dispute between us. **However,** if **she said: I am disgusted with him,**[HN] **we do not compel her** to remain with him, as one should not be compelled to live with someone who disgusts her. **Mar Zutra said: We do compel her** to stay with him.

הֲוָה עוּבְדָּא, וְאַכְפַּהּ מָר זוּטְרָא, וּנְפַק מִינַּהּ רַבִּי חֲנִינָא מִסּוּרָא. וְלָא הִיא, הָתָם סִיַּיעְתָּא דִשְׁמַיָּא הֲוָה.

It is related: **There was an incident** in which a woman rebelled, claiming that she was disgusted with her husband, **and Mar Zutra compelled her** to stay with him. **And from this** couple **issued Rabbi Ḥanina of Sura.** This demonstrates that even such coercion can cause a blessing. However, the Gemara concludes: **That is not so.** That case should not serve as a precedent, as **there** the positive outcome **was** due to **heavenly assistance.** Ordinarily, nothing good results from conjugal relations that the wife does not desire.

כַּלְּתֵיהּ דְּרַב זְבִיד אִימְרְדָא. הֲוָה תְּפִיסָא חַד שִׁירָא, יָתֵיב אֲמֵימַר וּמָר זוּטְרָא וְרַב אָשֵׁי, וִיתֵיב רַב גַּמְדָּא גַּבַּיְיהוּ. יָתְבִי וְקָאָמְרִי: מָרְדָה – הִפְסִידָה בְּלָאוֹתֶיהָ קַיָּימִין. אֲמַר לְהוּ רַב גַּמְדָּא: מִשּׁוּם דְּרַב זְבִיד גַּבְרָא רַבָּה מַחֲנִיפִיתוּ לֵיהּ? וְהָאָמַר רַב כָּהֲנָא: מִיבַּעְיָא בָּעֵי רָבָא וְלָא פְּשַׁט. אִיכָּא דְּאָמְרִי, יָתְבִי וְקָאָמְרִי: מָרְדָה – לֹא הִפְסִידָה בְּלָאוֹתֶיהָ קַיָּימִין, אֲמַר לְהוּ רַב גַּמְדָּא:

It is related that **the daughter-in-law of Rav Zevid**[P] **rebelled** against her husband. **She was holding a certain garment** in her hands. **Ameimar, Mar Zutra, and Rav Ashi were sitting, and Rav Gamda was sitting with them. They sat and said:** If a woman **rebelled, she lost** her right to **her worn clothes,** meaning she has forfeited the clothes she brought with her for her dowry even if they are still in existence. **Rav Gamda said to them: Because Rav Zevid is a great man,** are **you** willing to **flatter him** with regard to this *halakha*? **Didn't Rav Kahana say: Rava raises a dilemma** about this issue with regard to worn clothes, **and he did not resolve it?** Yet you reached a decision out of respect for Rav Zevid. This is inappropriate. **There are those who say** that this incident happened differently, as these three Sages **sat and said:** If she **rebelled, she did not lose** her right to **her worn clothes. Rav Gamda said to them:**

HALAKHA

I want to be married to him but I want to cause him anguish – בָּעֵינָא לֵיהּ וּמְצַעַרְנָא לֵיהּ: All the *halakhot* of a rebellious woman apply to one who said that she wishes to stay with her husband but wants to cause him anguish due to a quarrel or complaint that she has against him. The Rema writes that the same *halakha* applies if she said that she is disgusted with him but wants to collect her marriage contract from him (Rambam *Sefer Nashim, Hilkhot Ishut* 14:9; *Shulḥan Arukh, Even HaEzer* 77:2).

She said: I am disgusted with him – אָמְרָה מָאִיס עֲלַי: There is a dispute among the authorities with regard to a woman who says: I am disgusted with my husband. The *Shulḥan Arukh* essentially rules in accordance with the Rosh and Rabbeinu Tam, who say that the husband is not compelled to divorce his wife, and contrary to the Rambam, who says that he is compelled. According to this ruling, if she says that her husband disgusts her, the husband is not compelled to divorce her, but if he wishes to do so, she does not receive her marriage contract. According to all authorities, she cannot be compelled to live with him (see Rambam *Sefer Nashim, Hilkhot Ishut* 14:8; *Shulḥan Arukh, Even HaEzer* 77:2).

NOTES

I am disgusted with him – מָאִיס עֲלַי: There is a fundamental dispute among the early authorities with respect to the case of a woman who says: I am disgusted with my husband. The Rambam says that if she says: I am disgusted with him and cannot engage in conjugal relations with him, the court compels him to divorce her. This appears to be Rashi's opinion as well. However, Rabbeinu Tam challenges this opinion on the basis of the fact that the Gemara explicitly mandates compelling a man to divorce his wife only in a few specific cases. He therefore says that if the wife says she is disgusted with her husband, the court does not force him to divorce her. He interprets the Gemara to mean that she is not treated as a rebellious woman with respect to the amount of time allotted to try to appease her or with regard to her rights to her assets. Most authorities rule in accordance with the opinion of Rabbeinu Tam (Ramban; Rashba; Rabbi Aharon HaLevi; Rosh; Ran).

PERSONALITIES

Rav Zevid – רַב זְבִיד: A fifth-generation Babylonian *amora*, Rav Zevid was a close disciple of Abaye and Rava and would often bring up their teachings for discussion among the prominent *amora'im* of his generation. It appears that he also invested considerable time in explaining *baraitot* taught in Rabbi Oshaya's study hall. After Rava's death, his yeshiva split and Rav Zevid took over the Pumbedita branch after Rabbi Ḥama. He headed the yeshiva for about ten years. It is recorded that he was poisoned by servants of the Exilarch, who were upset by his stringent halakhic rulings.

משום דרב זביד גברא רבה הוא אפכיתו ליה לדינא עילויה? האמר רב כהנא: מיבעיא בעי לה רבא ולא פשיט! השתא דלא אתמר לא הכי ולא הכי, תפסה – לא מפקינן מינה, לא תפסה – לא יהבינן לה.

Because Rav Zevid is a great man, and due to his piety and humility he would not challenge the ruling, **you twist the judgment against him? Didn't Rav Kahana say: Rava raises a dilemma** with regard to this issue **and did not resolve** it, so how did you rule that she may retain her worn clothes? The Gemara summarizes: **Now that it was not stated** and concluded **this way or that way, if she seized** an item of her possessions, **we do not take it away from her,**[H] but if she **did not seize** it, **we do not give** it to **her.**

ומשהינן לה תריסר ירחי שתא אגיטא, ובהנך תריסר ירחי שתא לית לה מזוני מבעל.

The Gemara adds another *halakha* with regard to a rebellious woman: **And we delay her bill of divorce** for **twelve months**[N] **of the year**[H] and do not give her a bill of divorce until then. **And during those twelve months of the year she does not** receive **sustenance from** her **husband.**

אמר רב טובי בר קיסנא אמר שמואל: כותבין אגרת מרד על ארוסה, ואין כותבין אגרת מרד על שומרת יבם. מיתיבי: אחת לי ארוסה ונשואה, אפילו נדה, אפילו חולה, ואפילו שומרת יבם!

§ **Rav Tuvi bar Kisna said** that **Shmuel said:** The court **writes a letter of rebellion about a betrothed woman** who is rebelling against her husband. This letter is a court order to deduct value from the marriage contract. **But it does not write a letter of rebellion about a widow awaiting her *yavam*** who does not want to enter into levirate marriage. The Gemara **raises an objection** from a *baraita*: **It is the same to me** if she is **a betrothed woman or a married woman,** and **even** if she is **a menstruating woman,** and **even** if she is **ill, and even** if she is **a widow awaiting her *yavam*.**

לא קשיא; כאן – שתבע הוא, כאן – שתבעה היא. דאמר רב תחליפא בר אבימי אמר שמואל: תבע הוא – נזקקין לו, תבעה היא – אין נזקקין לה.

The Gemara answers: **This is not difficult,** as the contradiction can be resolved in the following way: **Here,** where there is a distinction between a betrothed woman and a widow awaiting her *yavam*, it refers to a case where **he asked** to marry **her** and she is refusing; **there,** where there is no such distinction, the case is where **she asked** to marry **him** and he is refusing. **As Rav Taḥalifa bar Avimi said** that **Shmuel said: If he asked,** the court **responds to his** request and gives her the status of a rebellious woman, **but if she asked, it does not respond to her** request and does not add to her marriage contract.

במאי אוקימתא להא דשמואל – בשתבעה היא, האי כותבין אגרת מרד על ארוסה? לארוסה מיבעי ליה! הא לא קשיא, תני: לארוסה.

The Gemara inquires: **In what** manner **did you establish that which Shmuel** said, that one writes a letter of rebellion about a betrothed woman but not about a widow awaiting her *yavam*? **If** it is a situation where **she asked** to marry him and he did not want, then why phrase **this:** The court **writes a letter of rebellion about a betrothed woman,** which indicates that the bill is written against her. It **should have** said instead: Write a letter of rebellion **for a betrothed woman,** meaning it is written on her behalf against her husband. The Gemara answers: **This is not difficult,** as the text is imprecise. **Teach** the statement instead this way: **For a betrothed woman.**

מאי שנא שומרת יבם דלא – דאמרינן לה: זיל, לא מפקדת. ארוסה נמי – נימא לה: זיל, לא מפקדת! אלא בבאה מחמת טענה, דאמרה: בעינא חוטרא לידא ומרה לקבורה

The Gemara asks: **What is different** about **a widow awaiting her *yavam*,** for whom a letter of rebellion is not written against her husband? **Because we say to her: Go away; you are not commanded** to procreate. Therefore, although she cannot get married, he cannot be compelled to perform an act that the Torah does not specifically command him to perform. The Gemara challenges this answer: If this is the reasoning, then in the case of **a betrothed woman, too, let us say to her: Go away; you are not commanded.**[N] **Rather,** the case where a letter of rebellion is issued must be referring to a woman who **comes with a claim, saying: I want a staff in** my **hand and a hoe for burial,** i.e., I want children who will support me in my old age and attend to my burial after my death. This claim is valid, and therefore the court issues a letter of rebellion against the husband.

HALAKHA

We do not take it away from her – לא מפקינן מינה: In an ordinary case of a rebellious woman, i.e., one who says she wishes to remain married to her husband but rebels in order to cause him anguish, she must return everything she received from her husband if he divorces her. However, guaranteed property that she brought into the marriage and that was recorded in her marriage contract as well as her worn clothes are not taken away from her if she seizes them, but if she did not seize them, they are not given to her. The Rema says that any real estate she brought into the marriage as guaranteed property is returned to her, since this property is viewed as if she had seized it, while her usufruct property always belongs to her. This ruling is in accordance with the interpretation of the Rambam that the Gemara is referring to an ordinary case of a rebellious woman. If she says that she is disgusted with her husband, there are differing opinions among the later authorities concerning the details of the *halakha* (Rambam *Sefer Nashim, Hilkhot Ishut* 14:13; *Shulḥan Arukh, Even HaEzer* 77:3).

We delay her bill of divorce for twelve months of the year – משהינן לה תריסר ירחי שתא: A rebellious woman is not granted a bill of divorce immediately. Rather, she must wait twelve months. During this period she is not entitled to sustenance from her husband. However, her earnings belong to her. Her husband remains obligated to ransom her if she is taken captive and bury her if she dies. In the latter case, her husband inherits her property, in accordance with the ruling of the Rambam.

If, however, she is not rebelling in order to cause her husband anguish, but rather she says that she is disgusted by him, he may divorce her without delay, in accordance with the opinion of the Rambam. This is the accepted ruling, despite the fact that Rambam's ruling with regard to forcing the husband to divorce her in such a case is not accepted (Rambam *Sefer Nashim, Hilkhot Ishut* 14:10; *Shulḥan Arukh, Even HaEzer* 77:2).

NOTES

We delay her bill of divorce for twelve months – ומשהינן לה תריסר ירחי: The commentaries dispute the interpretation of this *halakha*, in accordance with the general dispute concerning the meaning of this entire passage. According to Rashi, who maintains that the Gemara is discussing a wife who says that she is disgusted by her husband, the Sages decreed that she must be given time to change her mind. If she retracts her decision during this twelve-month period, she loses nothing. Accordingly, this enactment is primarily for her benefit.

Others, such as Rabbi Yosef Migash and the Rambam, maintain that this *halakha* is referring only to an ordinary case of a rebellious woman, who says that she wants to remain married to her husband but wants to cause him anguish. But if she says that she is disgusted by him he must divorce her without delay.

The Rosh says that this enactment was established by the later *amora'im*, who observed that women were making rash decisions and were too quick to claim that their husbands disgusted them. Consequently, they decreed that the husband should wait twelve months before granting her a divorce, in order to give her time to reconsider. The Rosh further claims that this enactment annulled the earlier one concerning the four weeks of public announcements.

Let us say to her: Go away, you are not commanded – נימא לה זיל, לא מפקדת: The early commentaries ask: The same could be said to a married woman whose husband rebels against her, as she too is not commanded to procreate. They answer that in the case of a married woman, the claim is not based on the performance of the mitzva, but rather on the fact that by marrying her, her husband obligated himself to fulfill his duty of conjugal relations (Ramban; Rashba; Ritva).

הָכִי נָמֵי שׁוֹמֶרֶת יָבָם – בְּבָאָה מֵחֲמַת טַעֲנָה! אֶלָּא, אִידִי וְאִידִי שֶׁתָּבַע הוּא, וְלָא קַשְׁיָא; כָּאן – לַחֲלוֹץ, וְכָאן – לְיַיבֵּם. דְּאָמַר רַבִּי פְּדָת אָמַר רַבִּי יוֹחָנָן: תָּבַע לַחֲלוֹץ – נִזְקָקִין לוֹ, תָּבַע לְיַיבֵּם – אֵין נִזְקָקִין לוֹ.

The Gemara asks: **So too here,** if she is **a widow awaiting her *yavam* who comes with a claim,** why shouldn't the court listen to her? **Rather,** the Gemara retracts the explanation that she asked him to marry her. Instead, say that both **this and that** are discussing situations **where he asks**[H] her and she rebels, and the question from the *baraita* on Shmuel's statement is **not difficult. Here,** the *baraita* that said that the court writes a letter of rebellion about a widow awaiting her *yavam,* is referring to a case where the *yavam* asked her **to perform *ḥalitza***[B] and she refused. **There,** Shmuel's statement that the court does not write it, is referring to a case where he asked **to consummate the levirate marriage,**[B] **as Rabbi Pedat said** that **Rabbi Yoḥanan said:** If the *yavam* **asked her to perform *ḥalitza***[H] and she refused, the court **responds to him. If he asked to perform levirate marriage,** the court **does not respond to him.**

מַאי שְׁנָא לְיַיבֵּם דְּלָא – דְּאָמְרִינַן לֵיהּ: זִיל וּנְסֵיב אִיתְּתָא אַחֲרִיתִי. לַחֲלוֹץ נָמֵי, נֵימָא לֵיהּ: זִיל וּנְסֵיב אִיתְּתָא אַחֲרִיתִי!

The Gemara asks: **What is different** with regard to the request **to consummate the levirate marriage, that** if a woman refuses the court **does not** write a letter of rebellion against her? **Because we say to him: Go and marry another woman.** He is not required to marry her specifically, if she does not agree to the marriage. Therefore, her refusal is not deemed rebellion. The Gemara challenges that answer: If so, with regard to a request **to perform *ḥalitza* also, let us say to him: Go and marry another woman.** The difference between the two cases is still not clear.

אֶלָּא, דְּאָמַר כֵּיוָן דַּאֲגִידָא בִּי – לָא קָא יָהֲבוּ לִי אַחֲרִיתִי.

Rather, it must be that the reason is because **he says: Since she is attached to me they will not give me another** wife. As long as he has not performed *ḥalitza,* he may have a problem finding another wife, as a potential wife will be concerned that he has a woman attached to him and may eventually enter levirate marriage with him. This is a valid claim, and therefore the court writes a letter of rebellion against her if she refuses *ḥalitza.*

הָכָא נָמֵי כֵּיוָן דַּאֲגִידָא בִּי – לָא קָא יָהֲבוּ לִי אַחֲרִיתִי! אֶלָּא, אִידִי וְאִידִי שֶׁתָּבַע לְיַיבֵּם. וְלָא קַשְׁיָא: כָּאן – כְּמִשְׁנָה רִאשׁוֹנָה, כָּאן – כְּמִשְׁנָה אַחֲרוֹנָה,

The Gemara asks: If so, **here too,** when she refuses a request to consummate the levirate marriage, he may say: **Since she is attached to me they will not give me another.** Why then doesn't the court write a letter of rebellion in this case? **Rather,** one must say that **this and that** are both discussing a case **where he asked to consummate the levirate marriage. And it is not difficult. Here,** in Shmuel's statement, where the court writes a letter of rebellion, it is **in accordance with the first mishna. There,** in the *baraita,* where it doesn't write one, it is **in accordance with the ultimate** version of the **mishna.**

דִּתְנַן: מִצְוַת יִבּוּם קוֹדֶמֶת לְמִצְוַת חֲלִיצָה. בָּרִאשׁוֹנָה, שֶׁהָיוּ מִתְכַּוְּונִין לְשׁוּם מִצְוָה. עַכְשָׁיו שֶׁאֵין מִתְכַּוְּונִין לְשׁוּם מִצְוָה – אָמְרוּ: מִצְוַת חֲלִיצָה קוֹדֶמֶת לְמִצְוַת יִבּוּם.

As we learned in a mishna (*Bekhorot* 13a): **The mitzva of levirate marriage precedes the mitzva of *ḥalitza.***[H] This *halakha* **originally** applied **when** people **would intend** to perform the levirate marriage **for the sake of the mitzva.** At that time, it was customary to compel a woman to enter levirate marriage. If she refused, the court wrote a letter of rebellion about her. However, **now that** people **do not intend** to enter levirate marriage **for the sake of the mitzva,** but may have other intentions, the Sages **said: The mitzva of *ḥalitza* precedes the mitzva of levirate marriage.** Shmuel's statement that the court does not write a letter of rebellion about a widow awaiting her *yavam* is in accordance with the ultimate version of the mishna.

״עַד מָתַי הוּא פּוֹחֵת״ וכו׳. מַאי טְרַפְּעִיקִין? אָמַר רַב שֵׁשֶׁת: אַסְתִּירָא. וְכַמָּה אַסְתִּירָא? פַּלְגָא דְּזוּזָא. תַּנְיָא נָמֵי הָכִי, רַבִּי יְהוּדָה אוֹמֵר: שְׁלֹשָׁה טְרַפְּעִיקִין, שֶׁהֵן תֵּשַׁע מָעִין, מָעָה וָחֵצִי לְכָל יוֹם.

§ The mishna asks: **Until when does he reduce** her marriage contract? And in that context it states that, according to the opinion of Rabbi Yehuda, the sums involved are calculated in *terapa'ikin* and not in dinars. The Gemara asks: **What are *terapa'ikin*? Rav Sheshet said: An *asteira*,**[L] a small coin. **And how much is an *asteira*? A half of a dinar. This is also taught** in a *baraita*: **Rabbi Yehuda says: Three *terapa'ikin*, which are nine *ma'as*, a *ma'a* and a half for each day,** multiplied by six for the six days of the week.

HALAKHA

He asks her to consummate the levirate marriage – תָּבַע הוּא לְיַיבֵּם: This *halakha* is the subject of a dispute among the ruling authorities. If the *yavam* wishes to consummate the levirate marriage and the *yevama* refuses to do so, some claim she is treated as a rebellious woman, in accordance with the first mishna. Others hold that she is not treated as a rebellious woman, in accordance with the ultimate version of the mishna. In any case, the custom in all Ashkenazic communities, as well as in many other communities, is that levirate marriage is not performed at all unless there are special reasons for doing so (Rambam *Sefer Nashim, Hilkhot Yibbum VaḤalitza* 2:10; *Shulḥan Arukh, Even HaEzer* 165:1; see *Pitḥei Teshuva* there).

Asked her to perform *ḥalitza* – תָּבַע לַחֲלוֹץ: If the *yavam* requested to perform *ḥalitza* and the *yevama* refuses both *ḥalitza* and levirate marriage, she has the status of a rebellious woman. If she demands *ḥalitza* and he refuses, he is not forced to comply. Some add that the custom is not to compel him to perform *ḥalitza* at all, even in a situation where he is unable to enter levirate marriage. Rather, the court attempts to work out a compromise between them and persuade him verbally (Rambam *Sefer Nashim, Hilkhot Yibbum VaḤalitza* 2:10; *Shulḥan Arukh, Even HaEzer* 165:1, 3, and in the comment of Rema).

Levirate marriage and *ḥalitza* – יִבּוּם וַחֲלִיצָה: The early commentaries dispute this matter. Some say that the mitzva of levirate marriage takes precedence over the mitzva of *ḥalitza*, in accordance with the ruling of the first mishna (Rif; Rambam). In their opinion, the Gemara here and elsewhere rules in accordance with this opinion. Others maintain that the mitzva of *ḥalitza* takes precedence as stated in the unattributed mishna here (Rashi, and one opinion cited by the Rif). Both opinions are mentioned in the *Shulḥan Arukh* (Rambam *Sefer Nashim, Hilkhot Yibbum VaḤalitza* 1:2, 2:7; *Shulḥan Arukh, Even HaEzer* 165:1, 3).

BACKGROUND

To perform *ḥalitza* – לַחֲלוֹץ: *Ḥalitza* is the ceremony that frees a *yavama*, the widow of a childless man, from the obligation to marry one of her late husband's brothers and allows her to marry someone else (see Deuteronomy 25:7–10). The term *ḥalitza*, meaning removal, is derived from the central element of this ceremony, which involves the widow removing a special sandal from the foot of one of the brothers. *Ḥalitza* must be performed before a rabbinical court. The *halakhot* governing this ceremony are discussed in detail in tractate *Yevamot*.

To consummate the levirate marriage – לְיַיבֵּם: A man whose brother died without children is obliged by Torah law to marry his late brother's widow or to free her by means of a *ḥalitza* ceremony (see Deuteronomy 25:5–10). As long as neither levirate marriage nor *ḥalitza* has taken place, she is prohibited from marrying another man. According to the Torah, levirate marriage is effected by the act of sexual intercourse. The Sages, however, instituted the practice of *ma'amar*, in which the deceased husband's brother betroths the widow, although this betrothal is not effective by Torah law unless the couple engages in intercourse. Sexual relations consummate the marriage between the deceased's brother and the widow, and she is thereafter considered his wife in all respects. Today, in most Jewish communities the brother-in-law is required to free his brother's widow of her obligation through *ḥalitza* and is not permitted to marry her through levirate marriage.

LANGUAGE

***Asteira* – אַסְתִּירָא:** The name of a Greek coin, στατήρ, *statēr*. When made of gold, these coins were worth a *sela*, or four dinars. However, in this case the reference is to the currency of the state, an *asteira* of lesser value, which was worth one-eighth of the larger Tyrian coins, i.e., half a dinar.

אֲמַר לֵיהּ רַבִּי חִיָּיא בַּר יוֹסֵף לִשְׁמוּאֵל: מַאי שְׁנָא אִיהוּ דְּיָהֲבִינַן לֵיהּ דְּשַׁבָּת, וּמַאי שְׁנָא אִיהִי דְּלָא יָהֲבִינַן לָהּ דְּשַׁבָּת? אִיהִי דְּמִיפַּחֲתָא קָא פָּחֵית – לָא מֶיחֱזֵי כִּשְׂכַר שַׁבָּת, אִיהוּ דְּאוֹסוּפֵי קָא מוֹסְפָא,

Rabbi Ḥiyya bar Yosef said to Shmuel: What is different when she is the one rebelling against **him, that we give him** compensation **for Shabbat,** as her marriage contract is reduced by seven dinars a week, which is one dinar per day including Shabbat, and **what is different** for **her that we do not give her** compensation **for Shabbat** but rather only for six days? The Gemara explains: When it is **she who** is fined and her marriage contract **is reduced,** it **does not appear to be Shabbat wages,**[N] money paid for services rendered on Shabbat, which is prohibited. Whereas when it is **he who** is fined and compelled to **add** additional money every day to her marriage contract,

NOTES

It is reduced and it does not appear to be Shabbat wages – דְּמִיפַּחֲתָא קָא פָּחֵית לָא מֶיחֱזֵי כִּשְׂכַר שַׁבָּת: The Sages prohibited receiving wages for work performed on Shabbat, even if no prohibited labors are involved in the work. This is a rabbinic law designed to prevent people from engaging in prohibited commerce on Shabbat (Rashi).

Perek **V**
Daf **64** Amud **b**

מֶיחֱזֵי כִּשְׂכַר שַׁבָּת.

it does **appear to be Shabbat wages.** Consequently, the Sages decreed that he should not give her money for Shabbat.

אֲמַר לֵיהּ רַבִּי חִיָּיא בַּר יוֹסֵף לִשְׁמוּאֵל: מַה בֵּין מוֹרֵד לְמוֹרֶדֶת? אֲמַר לֵיהּ: צֵא וּלְמַד מִשּׁוּק שֶׁל זוֹנוֹת. מִי שׂוֹכֵר אֶת מִי? דָּבָר אַחֵר: זֶה – יִצְרוֹ מִבַּחוּץ, וְזוֹ – יִצְרָהּ מִבִּפְנִים.

On the same issue, **Rabbi Ḥiyya bar Yosef said to Shmuel: What is** the reason for the difference in *halakha* **between a rebellious** man **and a rebellious** woman?[N] According to all opinions, a rebellious wife's fine is greater than that of a rebellious husband. **He said to him: Go and learn from the market of prostitutes. Who hires whose** services? Clearly, a man suffers more from lack of sexual intercourse, and therefore the penalty for a rebellious wife is greater. **Alternatively,** when **he** desires sexual relations, **his inclination** is noticeable **on the outside,** and therefore he feels shame as well as pain. **But** for **her, her inclination is on the inside,** and is not obvious.

מתני׳ הַמַּשְׁרֶה אֶת אִשְׁתּוֹ עַל יְדֵי שָׁלִישׁ – לֹא יִפְחוֹת לָהּ מִשְּׁנֵי קַבִּין חִטִּין, אוֹ מֵאַרְבָּעָה קַבִּין שְׂעוֹרִין. אָמַר רַבִּי יוֹסֵי: לֹא פָּסַק לָהּ שְׂעוֹרִין אֶלָּא רַבִּי יִשְׁמָעֵאל, שֶׁהָיָה סָמוּךְ לֶאֱדוֹם. וְנוֹתֵן לָהּ חֲצִי קַב קִיטְנִית, וַחֲצִי לוֹג שֶׁמֶן, וְקַב גְּרוֹגָרוֹת, אוֹ מָנֶה דְּבֵילָה. וְאִם אֵין לוֹ – פּוֹסֵק לְעוּמָּתָן פֵּירוֹת מִמָּקוֹם אַחֵר.

MISHNA If someone **feeds his wife by means of a third party** serving as a trustee, while the husband himself is not living with her for some reason, he may **not** give **her less than two *kav***[H] of **wheat or four *kav*** of **barley** a week for her sustenance. **Rabbi Yosei said: Only Rabbi Yishmael, who was near Edom, allotted her barley. And he** must **give her half a *kav*** of **legumes, and half a *log*** of **oil, and a *kav*** of **dried figs or** the weight of **a *maneh***[B] of **fig cakes. And if he does not have** these fruits, **he** must **apportion** for her **a corresponding** amount of **fruit from elsewhere.**

וְנוֹתֵן לָהּ מִטָּה, מַפָּץ וּמַחֲצֶלֶת, וְנוֹתֵן לָהּ כִּפָּה לְרֹאשָׁהּ וַחֲגוֹר לְמָתְנֶיהָ, וּמִנְעָלִים מִמּוֹעֵד לְמוֹעֵד, וְכֵלִים שֶׁל חֲמִשִּׁים זוּז מִשָּׁנָה לְשָׁנָה. וְאֵין נוֹתְנִין לָהּ לֹא חֲדָשִׁים בִּימוֹת הַחַמָּה, וְלֹא שְׁחָקִים בִּימוֹת הַגְּשָׁמִים. אֶלָּא נוֹתֵן לָהּ כֵּלִים שֶׁל חֲמִשִּׁים זוּז בִּימוֹת הַגְּשָׁמִים, וְהִיא מִתְכַּסָּה בִּבְלָאוֹתֵיהֶן בִּימוֹת הַחַמָּה, וְהַשְּׁחָקִים שֶׁלָּהּ.

And he must **give her a bed,**[N] **a soft mat,**[B] **and** a hard **mat. And he** must **give her a cap**[B] **for her head, and a belt for her waist, and** new **shoes from Festival to Festival,** i.e., he must buy her new shoes each Festival. **And** he must purchase **garments**[H] for her with a value **of fifty dinars from year to year.** The mishna comments: **And he may not give her new** clothes, which tend to be thick and warm, **in the summer, nor worn** garments **in the rainy season,** as these are too thin and she will be cold. **Rather, he should give her clothes** at a value **of fifty dinars in the rainy season, and she covers herself with** these same **worn** garments **in the summer** as well. **And** the leftover, **worn** clothes belong **to her.**

NOTES

What is the difference between a rebellious man and a rebellious woman – מַה בֵּין מוֹרֵד לְמוֹרֶדֶת: The commentaries infer from this passage that the *halakha* pertaining to a rebellious woman is in accordance with the opinion of Rav Huna, who maintains that the rebellion refers to the denial of sexual relations. According to the opinion of Rabbi Yosei bar Rabbi Ḥanina, that the rebellion concerns the tasks she is obligated to perform, this discussion does not make sense at all.

And he must give her a bed – וְנוֹתֵן לָהּ מִטָּה: The early commentaries note that the mishna lists only those items of food and clothing required for her physical needs. However, it does not mention other articles needed for the preparation of her food. These additional objects, which include a lamp and a wick, are listed in the *Tosefta*.

BACKGROUND

***Maneh* – מָנֶה:** In this context, *maneh* is referring to a weight that is not identical to the coin of the same name, although they were likely of the same weight. There is a difference in weight between the Greek and the Italian *maneh*, and the Gemara is probably referring to the Italian *maneh*, which weighed roughly 327 g.

Soft mat – מַפָּץ: This refers to a type of mat woven out of reeds. The difference between a soft and a hard mat is probably that a hard mat was woven out of whole reeds, whereas a soft mat was comprised of parts of reeds, perhaps their soft inner sections.

Cap – כִּפָּה: Women would cover their hair with a large cap made from wool or some other material. This cap would cover most of their hair. Usually, a woman would not venture into the street wearing only a cap. Rather, she would add a scarf, a kerchief, or some other kind of head covering or ornamentation.

Bust of a Roman woman, with head covering of several layers

HALAKHA

Two *kav* – שְׁנֵי קַבִּין: How much food must a husband provide for his wife? He must give her bread for two meals a day and a minor dish to go with it. For Shabbat, he must give her food for three meals. The Rambam writes that he must provide her with the type of food eaten by the residents of their place, either wheat or barley, or even rice or millet, if these are the staple grains (Rambam *Sefer Nashim*, *Hilkhot Ishut* 12:10; *Shulḥan Arukh*, *Even HaEzer* 70:3).

And garments – וְכֵלִים: A husband must provide his wife with clothes worth fifty dinars every year. He buys her new clothes in the rainy season, which she wears through the summer. The worn clothes belong to her. Furthermore, he must provide her with a garment for her waist, a cap for her head, and new shoes every Festival. His obligation to clothe her includes also the provision of household vessels, i.e., a ready bed and a soft or hard mat. The Rambam writes that this list is referring to Eretz Yisrael at that time. In other locations, the details vary. The principle is that he must give her suitable attire for the summer and the rainy season, which consists of the simplest of garments customarily worn in that time and place (Rambam *Sefer Nashim*, *Hilkhot Ishut* 13:1–3; *Shulḥan Arukh*, *Even HaEzer* 73:1).

BACKGROUND

The warp and the woof – שְׁתִי וָעֵרֶב: The act of weaving was performed using the threads of the warp, which were mainly fixed in the loom. In certain cases, these threads could be lifted up, but generally they were firmly attached. The threads of the warp form the basis of the woven material, while the threads of the woof are passed through those of the warp by various means. Since the threads of the warp hold the woven material together, they must be far stronger than those of the woof, despite the fact that they are often significantly thinner. Consequently, the spinning of the warp must be very precise and much stronger than that of the woof. Therefore, the Sages determined that twice as much work is required to manufacture an equal weight of threads suitable for warp as for threads to be used for woof.

***Pundeyon* – פּוּנְדְּיוֹן:** A *pundeyon* is a coin worth two *issar*. There are twelve *pundeyon* in a dinar and forty-eight *pundeyon* in a *sela*. The source of the word is the Latin dupondius, meaning two *assarii*, which were Roman coins.

Dupondius coin struck in Rome for the emperor Augustus

The *se'a* and the *kav* – סְאָה וְקַב: The *se'a* is a basic measure of volume in the Bible and the Talmud. A *se'a* is six *kav*. Accordingly, four *se'a* equal twenty-four *kav*. The loaf referred to here, which is one forty-eighth of this amount, is therefore half a *kav* in volume.

נוֹתֵן לָהּ מָעָה כֶּסֶף לְצוֹרְכָּהּ, וְאוֹכֶלֶת עִמּוֹ מִלֵּילֵי שַׁבָּת לְלֵילֵי שַׁבָּת. וְאִם אֵין נוֹתֵן לָהּ מָעָה כֶּסֶף לְצוֹרְכָּהּ – מַעֲשֵׂה יָדֶיהָ שֶׁלָּהּ.

In addition to the above, **he** must **give her** another **silver *ma'a***[H] coin **for** the rest of **her needs. And she eats with him**[H] **from Shabbat evening to Shabbat evening.** Although he may provide for her sustenance via a third party throughout the week, on Shabbat evening she has the right to eat together with him. **And if he does not give her a silver *ma'a* coin for her needs, her earnings** belong **to her.**

וּמַה הִיא עוֹשָׂה לוֹ – מִשְׁקַל חָמֵשׁ סְלָעִים שְׁתִי בִּיהוּדָה, שֶׁהֵן עֶשֶׂר סְלָעִים בַּגָּלִיל. אוֹ מִשְׁקַל עֶשֶׂר סְלָעִים עֵרֶב בִּיהוּדָה, שֶׁהֵן עֶשְׂרִים סְלָעִים בַּגָּלִיל. וְאִם הָיְתָה מֵנִיקָה – פּוֹחֲתִין לָהּ מִמַּעֲשֵׂה יָדֶיהָ, וּמוֹסִיפִין לָהּ עַל מְזוֹנוֹתֶיהָ. בַּמֶּה דְּבָרִים אֲמוּרִים – בְּעָנִי שֶׁבְּיִשְׂרָאֵל, אֲבָל בִּמְכוּבָּד – הַכֹּל לְפִי כְּבוֹדוֹ.

And what is the fixed amount **that she** must **earn for him?** She must spin wool in the **weight of five *sela*** of threads of the **warp in Judea, which are** equivalent to **ten *sela*** according **to** the measurements of the **Galilee, or the weight of ten *sela*** of the threads of the **woof,**[B] which are easier to prepare, **in Judea, which are** equivalent to **twenty *sela*** according **to** the measurements used in the **Galilee. And if she is nursing**[H] at the time, the required amount **is reduced from her earnings and is added** to the sum she receives **for her sustenance. In what** case **is this statement**, i.e., all these amounts and measurements, **said? With** regard to **the poorest**[H] **of Jews**, i.e., these are the minimum requirements. **However, in the case of** a financially **prominent man, all** the amounts are increased **according to his prominence.**

גמ׳ מַנִּי מַתְנִיתִין? לָא רַבִּי יוֹחָנָן בֶּן בְּרוֹקָא, וְלָא רַבִּי שִׁמְעוֹן. דִּתְנַן: וְכַמָּה שִׁיעוּרוֹ – מְזוֹן שְׁתֵּי סְעוּדוֹת לְכָל אֶחָד וְאֶחָד, מְזוֹנוֹ לַחוֹל וְלֹא לַשַּׁבָּת, דִּבְרֵי רַבִּי מֵאִיר. רַבִּי יְהוּדָה אוֹמֵר: לַשַּׁבָּת וְלֹא לַחוֹל, וְזֶה וְזֶה מִתְכַּוְּונִין לְהָקֵל.

GEMARA **Whose** opinion is expressed in **the mishna?** It is **not Rabbi Yoḥanan ben Beroka and** it is **not Rabbi Shimon, as we learned** in a mishna (*Eiruvin* 82b): **What is the measure** for a joining of Shabbat boundaries [*eiruv*]? It consists of a quantity of **food** sufficient for **two meals for each and every one** of those included in the *eiruv*. The *tanna'im* disagree with regard to the definition of these two meals: It is referring to **one's food** that he eats **on a weekday and not on Shabbat;** this is **the statement of Rabbi Meir. Rabbi Yehuda says:** It is referring to the amount he eats **on Shabbat and not on a weekday. And** both **this** Sage, Rabbi Meir, **and that** Sage, Rabbi Yehuda, **intend to be lenient,** as Rabbi Meir maintains that people eat more food on Shabbat, whereas Rabbi Yehuda believes that they consume more on a weekday.

רַבִּי יוֹחָנָן בֶּן בְּרוֹקָא אוֹמֵר: כִּכָּר הַלָּקוּחַ בְּפוּנְדְּיוֹן. מֵאַרְבַּע סְאִין לְסֶלַע. רַבִּי שִׁמְעוֹן אוֹמֵר: שְׁתֵּי יָדוֹת לְכִכָּר, מִשָּׁלֹשׁ כִּכָּרוֹת לְקַב.

Rabbi Yoḥanan ben Beroka says:[H] Food for two meals is the size of **a loaf bought with a *pundeyon*,**[B] which is one forty-eighth of a *sela*, **when four *se'a*** of wheat are sold **for a *sela*.** According to this calculation, a *pundeyon* can purchase one-twelfth of a *se'a* of wheat, which is equivalent to half of a *kav*, as there are six *kav* in a *se'a*. Therefore, according to Rabbi Yoḥanan ben Beroka, one quarter of a *kav* is sufficient for a single meal. **Rabbi Shimon says:** Food for two meals is **two** of three **parts of a loaf, when three loaves** are prepared **from a *kav***[B] of wheat. According to Rabbi Shimon, therefore, one-ninth of a *kav* of wheat is sufficient for a meal.

HALAKHA

A silver *ma'a* – מָעָה כֶּסֶף: The husband must give his wife a silver *ma'a* every week for the rest of her requirements (Rambam *Sefer Nashim*, *Hilkhot Ishut* 12:10; *Shulḥan Arukh*, *Even HaEzer* 70:3).

And she eats with him – וְאוֹכֶלֶת עִמּוֹ: If a husband wants to give his wife the food she requires while she eats her meals by herself, he is permitted to do so. However, he must dine with her on Shabbat evening, in accordance with the explanation of Rav Naḥman. Some claim that he may not require his wife to eat alone without her acquiescence (Rambam *Sefer Nashim*, *Hilkhot Ishut* 12:12; *Shulḥan Arukh*, *Even HaEzer* 70:2, and in the comment of Rema).

If she is nursing – אִם הָיְתָה מֵנִיקָה: During the period when a wife is nursing her child, the amount of the earnings she must provide for her husband is reduced while her sustenance is increased (Rambam *Sefer Nashim*, *Hilkhot Ishut* 21:11; *Shulḥan Arukh*, *Even HaEzer* 80:11).

In what case is this statement said, with regard to the poorest – בַּמֶּה דְּבָרִים אֲמוּרִים, בְּעָנִי: All these amounts of food and clothing that a husband must give his wife were stated with regard to the poorest of Jews. However, a wealthy man must provide for his wife in accordance with his means (Rambam *Sefer Nashim*, *Hilkhot Ishut* 12:11, 13:5; *Shulḥan Arukh*, *Even HaEzer* 70:3, 73:4).

Rabbi Yoḥanan ben Beroka says – רַבִּי יוֹחָנָן בֶּן בְּרוֹקָא אוֹמֵר: The size of a joining of boundaries on Shabbat [*eiruv*] must be two meals for each member of the *eiruv*, which is roughly the volume of six medium eggs. The *halakha* is in accordance with the opinion of Rabbi Yoḥanan ben Beroka, as in tractate *Eiruvin* his ruling is attributed to the Rabbis (Rambam *Sefer Zemanim*, *Hilkhot Eiruvin* 1:9, 6:7, and *Maggid Mishne* there; *Shulḥan Arukh*, *Oraḥ Ḥayyim* 386:6, 409:7).

חֶצְיָהּ – לְבֵית הַמְנוּגָּע, וַחֲצִי חֶצְיָהּ – לִפְסוֹל אֶת הַגְּוִיָּה, וַחֲצִי חֲצִי חֶצְיָהּ – לְקַבֵּל טוּמְאַת אוֹכָלִין.

Having discussed the various opinions with regard to the size of a loaf of bread sufficient for a meal, the mishna states that **half** of this loaf is the amount called a half [*peras*], a measure relevant **for** the *halakhot* of **a leprous house.**[HB] If one enters a house afflicted with leprosy and remains there long enough to eat this amount of food, the clothes he is wearing become ritually impure. **And half of its half,** one quarter of a loaf this size, is the amount of ritually impure food that **renders the body unfit.**[H] In other words, impure food of this amount imparts ritual impurity to the body of the eater and disqualifies him by rabbinic law from eating *teruma*. **And half of one half of its half,** one-eighth of this loaf, is the minimum measure of food that is **susceptible to ritual impurity as food.**[H]

מַנִּי? אִי רַבִּי יוֹחָנָן בֶּן בְּרוֹקָא – תְּמָנֵי הָוְיָין, וְאִי רַבִּי שִׁמְעוֹן – תְּמָנֵי סְרֵי הָוְיָין!

After the citing the mishna, the Gemara returns to its question: **Who is** the author of **the mishna** here, which says a husband must provide two *kav* of wheat per week for his wife's sustenance? **If** it is **Rabbi Yoḥanan ben Beroka,** who maintains that one quarter of a *kav* is sufficient for a single meal, there **are** only **eight** meals in two *kav*, and the wife requires at least fourteen meals for a week, as it was customary to eat two meals each day. **And if** it is **Rabbi Shimon,** who holds that one-ninth of a *kav* is sufficient for a meal, two *kav* **are** enough for **eighteen** meals, and therefore the mishna requires more than she actually needs.

לְעוֹלָם רַבִּי יוֹחָנָן בֶּן בְּרוֹקָא, וּכְדַאֲמַר רַב חִסְדָּא: צֵא מֵהֶן שְׁלִישׁ לַחֶנְווֹנִי. הָכָא נַמִי – אַיְיתִי תִּילְתָּא שְׁדֵי עֲלַיְיהוּ. אַכַּתִּי תַּרְתֵּי סְרֵי הָוְיָין! אוֹכֶלֶת עִמּוֹ לֵילֵי שַׁבָּת.

The Gemara answers: **Actually,** the mishna is in accordance with the opinion of **Rabbi Yoḥanan ben Beroka, and** this is **as Rav Ḥisda said** in explanation of Rabbi Yoḥanan ben Beroka's opinion: **Deduct one-third for the grocer's** markup, as he takes one-third as profit. This adds one half to the total cost. **Here, too, bring one-third** and **add** it **to** the total amount of meals that can be provided by two *kav* of wheat. The Gemara raises a difficulty: **Still,** after adjusting the calculation by adding an additional half, a measurement known by the term: Outside third, to the amount of meals that can be eaten from two *kav* of wheat, **they are** equal to **twelve meals.** This is still not sufficient, as the wife requires fourteen. The Gemara answers: **She eats with him on Shabbat evening.** Consequently, this meal is not included in the amount that must be provided through the third party.

הָנִיחָא לְמַאן דַּאֲמַר אֲכִילָה מַמָּשׁ, אֶלָּא לְמַאן דַּאֲמַר אֲכִילָה תַּשְׁמִישׁ – מַאי אִיכָּא לְמֵימַר? וְעוֹד: תְּלֵיסַר הָוְיָין! אֶלָּא, כִּדְאָמַר רַב חִסְדָּא: צֵא מֵהֶן מֶחֱצָה לַחֶנְווֹנִי, הָכִי נַמִי אָתְיָא פַּלְגָּא וּשְׁדֵי עֲלַיְיהוּ.

The Gemara asks: **This works out well according to the one who says** that when the mishna is referring to eating, it means **literal eating. However, according to the one who says** that this **eating** on Shabbat evening is a euphemism, and it is actually referring to **conjugal relations, what can be said? And furthermore,** even if the meal on Shabbat evening is omitted, **they are** still **thirteen** meals that she requires but she has enough for only twelve. **Rather,** this is **as Rav Ḥisda said,** with regard to Rabbi Yoḥanan ben Beroka's opinion: **Deduct one-half for the grocer's** markup. **So too** here, **bring a half and add** it **to** the total amount, which means she has enough for sixteen meals, not eight.

קַשְׁיָא דְּרַב חִסְדָּא אַדְּרַב חִסְדָּא! לָא קַשְׁיָא; הָא – בְּאַתְרָא דְּיָהֲבֵי צִיבֵי, הָא – בְּאַתְרָא דְּלָא יָהֲבֵי צִיבֵי.

The Gemara asks: This is **difficult** with regard to one statement **of Rav Ḥisda,** which seemingly contradicts the other statement **of Rav Ḥisda.** The Gemara answers: This is **not difficult. This** statement, that the grocer's markup adds one-third to the price, is referring **to a place where they** also **give** money as a separate payment for the **wood** required to bake bread. **That** statement, that the grocer's markup adds half, is referring **to a place where they do not give** money for **wood,** and therefore the markup must be higher to cover those costs.

אִי הָכִי שִׁיתְּסְרֵי הָוְיָין? כְּמַאן – כְּרַבִּי חִידְקָא, דְּאָמַר: אַרְבַּע סְעוּדוֹת חַיָּיב אָדָם לֶאֱכוֹל בְּשַׁבָּת?

After reconciling the apparent contradiction between the two statements of Rav Ḥisda, the Gemara returns to the opinion of Rabbi Yoḥanan ben Beroka. **If so,** according to the above calculation, there **are sixteen** meals, which is more than a woman requires in a week. The Gemara suggests: In that case, **who is** the author of **the mishna?** Is it **in accordance with** the opinion of **Rabbi Ḥidka, who said** that **a person is obligated to eat four meals on Shabbat?** Since two meals are eaten on an ordinary weekday, this results in a total of sixteen meals a week.

HALAKHA

Half for a leprous house – חֶצְיָהּ לְבֵית הַמְנוּגָּע: If someone enters a leprous house, his body is immediately rendered ritually impure. However, his clothes and shoes remain pure until he has stays there long enough for one to recline and eat a half-loaf of wheat bread together with condiments. This amount is roughly the volume of six eggs, in accordance with the opinion of Rabbi Yoḥanan ben Beroka (Rambam *Sefer Tahara, Hilkhot Tumat Tzara'at* 16:6).

And half of its half renders the body unfit – וַחֲצִי חֶצְיָהּ לִפְסוֹל הַגְּוִיָּה: One who eats ritually impure food is disqualified from partaking of *teruma* if he eats an amount equivalent to the volume of an egg and a half, which is equivalent to half of a half-loaf of bread, in accordance with the opinion of Rabbi Yoḥanan ben Beroka (Rambam *Sefer Tahara, Hilkhot Tumat Okhalin* 4:1).

And half of one half of its half is susceptible to ritual impurity as food – וַחֲצִי חֲצִי חֶצְיָהּ לְטוּמְאַת אוֹכָלִין: Food imparts ritual impurity to other food or drink or to the hands, only if it contains the volume of an egg without its shell (Rambam *Sefer Tahara, Hilkhot Tumat Okhalin* 4:1, and *Kesef Mishne* there).

BACKGROUND

A leprous house – בֵּית הַמְנוּגָּע: By Torah law (see Leviticus 14:33–57), if leprous spots appear in a house, all the objects in the house must be removed in order to prevent them from becoming ritually impure, after which a priest is brought to examine the house. If the priest confirms that there is evidence of leprosy, the house is quarantined for a week, after which it is reexamined by the priest. If the leprous spots darkened or disappeared, the house is declared ritually pure. If the spots remained unchanged, the house is quarantined for a second week. If, after the second week, the spots have then darkened, the house is declared ritually pure after it undergoes the purification process described below. However, if the spots remain unchanged or have spread, the affected parts of the house are removed and replaced with new materials, after which the house is quarantined for a third week. If the spots reappear, the entire house must be destroyed, and its stones are disposed of in a ritually impure place.

A leprous house renders people and objects inside it ritually impure, with the exception of objects in hermetically sealed earthenware containers. If the house is declared free of leprosy, it is purified by a process involving birds, cedar wood, and red thread, parallel to the purification process of a leper. There are many halakhic restrictions with regard to the applicability of the *halakhot* pertaining to leprous houses, including the restriction that they apply only to structures at least four by four cubits in size.

HALAKHA

You can even say the Rabbis – אֲפִילּוּ תֵּימָא רַבָּנַן: One must eat three meals on Shabbat, in the evening, morning, and afternoon. The *halakha* is in accordance with the opinion of the Rabbis, not the minority opinion of Rabbi Ḥidka (Rambam *Sefer Zemanim, Hilkhot Shabbat* 30:9; *Shulḥan Arukh, Oraḥ Ḥayyim* 291:1).

BACKGROUND

Edomite barley – שְׂעוֹרִין אֲדוֹמִיּוֹת: Since barley can withstand extreme weather conditions better than wheat, it can be cultivated in hot regions. Generally speaking, in a place where there is less water, the barley harvest will yield less grain and the kernels will be smaller. This is probably why barley in the south of Judea, near Edom, was worse than that of other areas. It is also possible that farmers in that region used a particular species of barley, one that was suitable for the arid climate but was inferior in taste and nutritional value.

אֲפִילּוּ תֵּימָא רַבָּנַן, דַּל חֲדָא לְאָרְחֵי וּפָרְחֵי.

The Gemara rejects this suggestion: **You** can **even say** that the mishna is in accordance with the opinion of **the Rabbis,**[H] who maintain that one is obligated to eat only three meals on Shabbat, as you should **remove one meal for guests and wayfarers.** In other words, the husband cannot give his wife the absolute minimum amount she requires for herself and no more. He must give her enough to provide for the occasional visitor. Consequently, the total sum is somewhat more than was originally assumed.

הַשְׁתָּא דְּאָתֵית לְהָכִי – אֲפִילּוּ תֵּימָא רַבִּי שִׁמְעוֹן. לְרַבָּנַן – דַּל תְּלָת לְאָרְחֵי וּפָרְחֵי, לְרַבִּי חִידְקָא – דַּל תַּרְתֵּי לְאָרְחֵי וּפָרְחֵי.

The Gemara adds: **Now that you have arrived at this** answer, **you** can **even say** that the mishna is in accordance with the opinion of **Rabbi Shimon,** who maintains that two *kav* is sufficient for eighteen meals. This can be explained either by saying that Rabbi Shimon agrees with the opinion **of the Rabbis,** that one eats three meals on Shabbat, if you **remove three** meals **for guests and wayfarers,** or that Rabbi Shimon agrees with the opinion **of Rabbi Ḥidka,** that four meals are eaten on Shabbat, in which case you must **remove two** meals **for guests and wayfarers.** In this manner, the mishna can be reconciled with all opinions.

״אָמַר רַבִּי יוֹסֵי לֹא פָּסַק שְׂעוֹרִין״ וכו׳. אֶלָּא בֶּאֱדוֹם הוּא דְּאָכְלִין שְׂעוֹרִים, בְּכוּלֵּי עָלְמָא לָא אָכְלִי?! הָכִי קָאָמַר: לֹא פָּסַק שְׂעוֹרִים כִּפְלַיִם בְּחִטִּין אֶלָּא רַבִּי יִשְׁמָעֵאל, שֶׁהָיָה סָמוּךְ לֶאֱדוֹם, מִפְּנֵי שֶׁשְּׂעוֹרִין אֲדוֹמִיּוֹת רָעוֹת הֵן.

§ The mishna teaches that **Rabbi Yosei said: Only** Rabbi Yishmael, who was near Edom, **allotted her barley.** The Gemara asks: **But** does this indicate that **it is only in Edom that they eat barley,** whereas **in the rest of the world they do not eat** barley? This cannot be the case, as barley was eaten by the poor everywhere. The Gemara explains: **This is what** Rabbi Yosei **is saying: Only Rabbi Yishmael, who was near Edom, allotted her a double** amount **of barley** to that **of wheat, since Edomite barley**[B] **is bad,** whereas elsewhere the barley is of a higher quality, and therefore the difference between barley and wheat is less marked.

״וְנוֹתֵן לָהּ חֲצִי קַב קִיטְנִית״. וְאִילּוּ יַיִן – לָא קָתָנֵי. מְסַיֵּיע לֵיהּ לְרַבִּי אֶלְעָזָר, דְּאָמַר רַבִּי אֶלְעָזָר:

§ The mishna further taught: **And he** must **give her half a** *kav* of **legumes** as well as oil and fruit. The Gemara comments: **And yet wine is not taught** in the mishna. **This supports** the opinion **of Rabbi Elazar, as Rabbi Elazar said:**

Perek **V**
Daf **65** Amud **a**

BACKGROUND

Neviraya – נְבִירָיָא: Apparently, this village of Neviraya, or Nevuraya, was also called Nevor Ḥayil, Nefor Ḥayil, or, according to some versions of the text, Gevuraya or Gevor Ḥayil. This village was probably located north of Safed, but only its ruins remain nowadays, including the ruins of its ancient synagogue.

אֵין פּוֹסְקִין יֵינוֹת לְאִשָּׁה. וְאִם תֹּאמַר ״אֵלְכָה אַחֲרֵי מְאַהֲבַי נוֹתְנֵי לַחְמִי וּמֵימַי צַמְרִי וּפִשְׁתִּי שַׁמְנִי וְשִׁקּוּיָי״ – דְּבָרִים שֶׁהָאִשָּׁה מִשְׁתּוֹקֶקֶת עֲלֵיהֶן, וּמַאי נִינְהוּ – תַּכְשִׁיטִין.

Wines are not allotted to a wife. And if you say that in the verse: **"I will go after my lovers who give me my bread and my water, my wool and my flax, my oil and my drink"** (Hosea 2:7), "drink [*shikkuyai*]" is apparently a reference to wine, which indicates that it is usual for a woman to receive wine, this is invalid, since actually *shikkuyai* is not referring to wine but rather to **items that a woman desires [*mishtokeket*]. And what are these? Jewelry** or other ornaments, not wine.

דָּרַשׁ רַבִּי יְהוּדָה אִישׁ כְּפַר נְבִירָיָא, וְאָמְרִי לַהּ אִישׁ כְּפַר נְפוֹר חַיִל: מִנַּיִן שֶׁאֵין פּוֹסְקִין יֵינוֹת לְאִשָּׁה – שֶׁנֶּאֱמַר ״וַתָּקָם חַנָּה אַחֲרֵי אָכְלָה בְשִׁלֹה וְאַחֲרֵי שָׁתֹה״. ״שָׁתֹה״ וְלֹא שָׁתַת.

Rabbi Yehuda of the village of Neviraya,[B] **and some say of the village of Nefor Ḥayil, interpreted** a verse: **From where** is it derived **that one does not allot wines for a woman? As it is stated: "So Hannah rose up after she had eaten in Shiloh and after he had drunk"** (I Samuel 1:9). It states: **"He had drunk," and not: She had drunk.** This teaches that although she ate, she did not drink wine.

אֶלָּא מֵעַתָּה ״אָכְלָה״ וְלֹא אָכַל הָכִי נָמֵי?! אֲנַן מִדְּשַׁנֵּי קְרָא בְּדִבּוּרֵיהּ קָאָמְרִינַן, מִכְּדֵי בְּגַוַּהּ קָא עָסֵיק וְאָתֵי, מַאי טַעְמָא שַׁנֵּי? שְׁמַע מִינַּהּ: ״שָׁתֹה״ – וְלֹא שָׁתַת.

The Gemara asks: **However, if that is so,** by the same reasoning, should the phrase **"she had eaten,"** which is in the feminine, **indeed** be interpreted to mean that only she ate, **and that he did not eat? The Gemara answers: We say** this interpretation **from** the fact **that the verse changed its language. Since the verse was already dealing with her, what is the reason** that it **changed** the terminology and did not state: And had drunk, in the feminine? One can **learn from this** that **"he had drunk"** means that he drank, **but she did not drink.**

מֵיתִיבֵי: רְגִילָה נוֹתְנִין לָהּ! רְגִילָה שָׁאנֵי. דְּאָמַר רַב חִינָּנָא בַּר כָּהֲנָא אָמַר שְׁמוּאֵל: רְגִילָה – נוֹתְנִין לָהּ כּוֹס אֶחָד, שֶׁאֵינָהּ רְגִילָה – נוֹתְנִין לָהּ שְׁנֵי כּוֹסוֹת.

The Gemara **raises an objection** from a *baraita*: If a woman is **accustomed** to wine, **she is given** wine. The Gemara explains: If the woman is **accustomed** to wine it **is different, as Rav Ḥinnana bar Kahana said** that **Shmuel said:** If a woman is **accustomed** to drinking wine, **she is given one cup,** and if she **is not accustomed** to wine, **she is given two cups.**

מַאי קָאָמַר? אָמַר אַבַּיֵי, הָכִי קָאָמַר: רְגִילָה – בִּפְנֵי בַעְלָהּ שְׁנֵי כוֹסוֹת, שֶׁלֹּא בִּפְנֵי בַעְלָהּ – נוֹתְנִין לָהּ כּוֹס אֶחָד. אֵינָהּ רְגִילָה – בִּפְנֵי בַעְלָהּ אֶלָּא כּוֹס אֶחָד, שֶׁלֹּא בִּפְנֵי בַעְלָהּ – אֵין נוֹתְנִין לָהּ כָּל עִיקָּר.

The Gemara asks: **What is** Shmuel **saying?** His statement is the opposite of what one would logically expect. **Abaye said: This is what** he **is saying:** If **she is accustomed** to wine, then **in the presence of her husband** she is given **two cups,** and if she **is not in the presence of her husband she is given one cup.** If she **is not accustomed** to drinking wine, then **in the presence of her husband** she is given **only one cup,** and if she **is not in the presence of her husband she is not given** wine **at all.**

וְאִי בָּעֵית אֵימָא: רְגִילָה – נוֹתְנִין לָהּ לְצִיקֵי קְדֵירָה. דְּאָמַר רַבִּי אַבָּהוּ אָמַר רַבִּי יוֹחָנָן: מַעֲשֶׂה בְּכַלָּתוֹ שֶׁל נַקְדִּימוֹן בֶּן גּוּרְיוֹן שֶׁפָּסְקוּ לָהּ חֲכָמִים סָאתַיִם יַיִן לְצִיקֵי קְדֵירָה מֵעֶרֶב שַׁבָּת לְעֶרֶב שַׁבָּת. אָמְרָה לָהֶן: כָּךְ תִּפְסְקוּ לִבְנוֹתֵיכֶם. תָּנָא: שׁוֹמֶרֶת יָבָם הָיְתָה, וְלֹא עָנוּ אַחֲרֶיהָ אָמֵן.

And if you wish, say instead: If **she is accustomed** to wine, **she is given** wine, but not for drinking, rather **for** meat **pudding** [*tzikei*],[B] made with wine, flour, and leftover meat **in a pot. As Rabbi Abbahu said** that **Rabbi Yoḥanan said: An incident** occurred **involving the daughter-in-law of Nakdimon ben Guryon,**[P] whose husband had died. **The Sages apportioned for her** from his estate **two** ***se'a*** **of wine for pudding, from one Shabbat eve to another. She said to them,** as a blessing out of gratitude: **So may you apportion for your** own **daughters** an amount as large as this. It was **taught: She was a widow waiting for her** ***yavam*****, and** consequently, **the Sages did not answer amen after her** blessing, as they did not want their daughters to reach her unfortunate state.

תָּנָא: כּוֹס אֶחָד – יָפֶה לְאִשָּׁה, שְׁנַיִם – נִיוּוּל הוּא, שְׁלֹשָׁה – תּוֹבַעַת בַּפֶּה, אַרְבָּעָה – אֲפִילּוּ חֲמוֹר תּוֹבַעַת בַּשּׁוּק, וְאֵינָהּ מַקְפֶּדֶת. אָמַר רָבָא: לֹא שָׁנוּ אֶלָּא שֶׁאֵין בַּעְלָהּ עִמָּהּ, אֲבָל בַּעְלָהּ עִמָּהּ – לֵית לָן בָּהּ.

It was **taught** in a *baraita*: **One cup** of wine is **good for a woman; two cups is a disgrace,**[B] as she will start to become drunk; after **three** cups, she will become lustful and **verbally request** sexual intercourse, which is unseemly; after **four** cups of wine, she will **even request** intercourse from **a donkey in the marketplace, as** at this stage she is so drunk that **she is not particular** about with whom she has relations. **Rava said: They taught** that a woman should not drink much wine **only if her husband is not with her. However,** if **her husband is with her, we have no** problem **with it.** If she feels an urge for intercourse her husband is available.

וְהָא חַנָּה דְּבַעְלָהּ עִמָּהּ הֲוַאי! אַכְסְנַאי שָׁאנֵי. דְּאָמַר רַב הוּנָא: מִנַּיִן לְאַכְסְנַאי שֶׁאָסוּר בְּתַשְׁמִישׁ הַמִּטָּה – שֶׁנֶּאֱמַר "וַיַּשְׁכִּמוּ בַבֹּקֶר וַיִּשְׁתַּחֲווּ לִפְנֵי ה׳ וַיָּשׁוּבוּ וַיָּבֹאוּ אֶל בֵּיתָם הָרָמָתָה וַיֵּדַע אֶלְקָנָה אֶת חַנָּה אִשְׁתּוֹ וַיִּזְכְּרֶהָ ה׳". הַשְׁתָּא – אִין, מֵעִיקָּרָא – לָא.

The Gemara raises a difficulty: **But** the case of **Hannah was** one **in which her husband was with her,** and yet this episode is cited as a source for the *halakha* that a woman should not drink wine. The Gemara answers: The case of **a guest is different, as Rav Huna said: From where** is it derived **that a guest is prohibited from** engaging in **conjugal relations?**[H] **As it is stated: "And they rose up in the morning early, and worshipped before the Lord, and returned, and came to their house to Ramah; and Elkanah knew Hannah his wife; and the Lord remembered her"** (I Samuel 1:19). This verse indicates that **now,** after they returned home, **yes,** they engaged in relations; **at the outset,** when they were still in Shiloh, **no,** they did not. Therefore, Hannah did not drink wine in Shiloh.

BACKGROUND

Pudding [*tzikei*] – צִיקֵי: This meat pudding is probably called by this name because it contains liquids that one pours [*yotzek*] into the pot. The ingredients of this pudding included the leftover juices of various types of meat that were cooked, to which wine and spices were added.

Two cups is a disgrace – שְׁנַיִם נִיוּוּל הוּא: Consumption of alcohol may have an effect on one's sexual behavior, primarily for psychological reasons. Alcohol may remove one's normal inhibitions and scruples, and consumption of a relatively large amount of wine, especially when the drinker is not used to alcohol, can arouse lust and irregular sexual behavior. A particularly large consumption of wine is likely to impair sexual performance in men, but this is not the case for women.

PERSONALITIES

Nakdimon ben Guryon – נַקְדִּימוֹן בֶּן גּוּרְיוֹן: Nakdimon ben Guryon, whose Hebrew name was Boni, was one of the wealthiest residents of Jerusalem in the generation that lived during the destruction of the Second Temple. The Gemara in tractate *Ta'anit* (19b) recounts that he gave large sums for communal causes, and a great miracle happened to him in the merit of his efforts. There had been a drought and there was not enough water for the pilgrims who has ascended to Jerusalem for the Festival. Nakdimon borrowed twelve wells of water from a gentile officer and promised him a large sum of money if it did not rain by a certain date. At the last moment, Nakdimon prayed to God and a large amount of rain suddenly fell.

HALAKHA

A guest is prohibited from engaging in conjugal relations – אַכְסְנַאי אָסוּר בְּתַשְׁמִישׁ הַמִּטָּה: One who is a guest should not engage in conjugal relations, due to the lack of privacy, but should wait until he returns to his home. However, if the couple is provided with a room to themselves, they are permitted to engage in relations, provided that they do not use their host's bedding, as it may become soiled (Rambam *Sefer Kedusha, Hilkhot Issurei Bia* 21:15; *Shulḥan Arukh, Oraḥ Ḥayyim* 240:13 and *Even HaEzer* 25:7).

חוּמָא דְּבֵיתְהוּ דְּאַבָּיֵי אֲתַאי לְקַמֵּיהּ דְּרָבָא. אָמְרָה לֵיהּ: פְּסוֹק לִי מְזוֹנֵי! פָּסַק לָהּ. פְּסוֹק לִי חַמְרָא! אֲמַר לֵיהּ: יָדַעְנָא בֵּיהּ בְּנַחְמָנִי, דְּלָא הֲוָה שָׁתֵי חַמְרָא. אָמְרָה לֵיהּ: חַיֵּי דְּמָר, דַּהֲוֵי מַשְׁקֵי לֵיהּ בְּשׁוּפְרָזֵי כִּי הַאי. בַּהֲדֵי דְּקָא מַחְוְיָא לֵיהּ אִיגַּלִּי דַּרְעָא, נְפַל נְהוֹרָא בְּבֵי דִּינָא.

The Gemara relates: **Abaye's wife, Ḥoma,**[P] **came before Rava**[P] after Abaye died, as Rava was the local judge. **She said to him: Apportion sustenance for me,** as I am entitled to be sustained by Abaye's heirs. Rava **apportioned** sustenance **for her.** She subsequently said to him: **Apportion wine for me** as well. Rava **said to her: I know that Naḥmani,** i.e., Abaye, **did not drink wine.** Since you were not accustomed to drinking wine during your husband's lifetime, you are not entitled to it after his death. **She said to him: By the Master's life,** this is not correct. In fact, **he would give** me wine **to drink in cups** [***shufrazei***][L] **as large as this.** She gestured with her hands to show how large the cups were. **While she was showing him** the size of the cups, **her arm became uncovered,** and she was so beautiful that it was as though **a light had shined in the courtroom.**

קָם רָבָא, עָל לְבֵיתֵיהּ, תַּבְעָהּ לְבַת רַב חִסְדָּא. אָמְרָה לֵיהּ בַּת רַב חִסְדָּא: מַאן הֲוֵי הָאִידָּנָא בְּבֵי דִינָא? אֲמַר לָהּ: חוּמָא דְּבֵיתְהוּ דְּאַבָּיֵי. נָפְקָא אַבָּתְרָהּ, מַחְתָא לָהּ בְּקוּלְפֵי דְּשִׁידָּא עַד דְּאַפְּקָהּ לָהּ מִכּוּלֵּי מְחוֹזָא. אָמְרָה לָהּ: קְטַלְתְּ לֵיךְ תְּלָתָא, וַאֲתַת לְמִיקְטַל אַחֲרִינָא?!

Rava arose, went home, and **requested** intercourse **from** his wife, the **daughter of Rav Ḥisda. The daughter of Rav Ḥisda said to him: Who was just now in the courtroom?** Noticing his unusual behavior, she suspected that there must have been a woman in the court. **He said to her: Ḥoma, Abaye's wife,** was there. Upon hearing this, Rava's wife **went after** Ḥoma and **struck her with the lock of a chest** [***kulpei deshida***][L] **until she drove her out of the entire** city **of Meḥoza, saying to her: You have** already **killed three** men, as Abaye was your third husband, **and now you come to kill another** one, my husband Rava? Since you showed him your beauty, he will want to marry you.

דְּבֵיתְהוּ דְּרַב יוֹסֵף בְּרֵיהּ דְּרָבָא אֲתַאי לְקַמֵּיהּ דְּרַב נְחֶמְיָה בְּרֵיהּ דְּרַב יוֹסֵף. אָמְרָה לֵיהּ: פְּסוֹק לִי מְזוֹנֵי! פָּסַק לָהּ. פְּסוֹק לִי חַמְרָא! פָּסַק לָהּ. אֲמַר לָהּ: יָדַעְנָא בְּהוּ בִּבְנֵי מְחוֹזָא דְּשָׁתוּ חַמְרָא.

The Gemara relates a similar incident: **The wife of Rav Yosef, son of Rava, came before Rav Neḥemya, son of Rav Yosef,** for judgment. **She said to him: Apportion sustenance for me.** Rav Neḥemya **apportioned** a certain amount of sustenance **for her. She said to him: Apportion wine for me** as well. **He apportioned** wine **for her. He said to her: I know that the residents of Meḥoza** are accustomed to **drinking wine,**[H] and therefore you, too, are entitled to wine, in accordance with the local custom.

דְּבֵיתְהוּ דְּרַב יוֹסֵף בְּרֵיהּ דְּרַב מְנַשְּׁיָא מִדְּוִיל אֲתַאי לְקַמֵּיהּ דְּרַב יוֹסֵף, אָמְרָה לֵיהּ: פְּסוֹק לִי מְזוֹנֵי! פָּסַק לָהּ. פְּסוֹק לִי חַמְרָא! פָּסַק לָהּ. פְּסוֹק לִי שִׁירָאֵי! אֲמַר לָהּ: שִׁירָאֵי לָמָּה? אָמְרָה לֵיהּ: לָךְ, וּלְחַבְרָךְ, וּלְחַבְרוּוָךְ.

Similarly, **the wife of Rav Yosef, son of Rav Menashya of D'vil, came before Rav Yosef. She said to him: Apportion sustenance for me. He apportioned** sustenance **for her.** She added: **Apportion wine for me. He apportioned** wine **for her.** She continued: **Apportion silk** garments **for me.** Rav Yosef **said to her: Why do** you need **silk** garments? **She said to him: For you, for your friends, and for your friends' friends.** Even as a widow, I should not have to be ashamed in front of you and your colleagues.

״וְנוֹתֵן לָהּ מִטָּה וּמַפָּץ״ וכו׳. מַפָּץ וּמַחֲצֶלֶת לָמָּה לָהּ דְּיָהֵיב לָהּ? אֲמַר רַב פַּפָּא: בְּאַתְרָא דִּנְהִיגִי דְּמָלוּ פּוּרְיָא בְּחַבְלֵי, דִּמְבַגֵּר לָהּ.

§ The mishna taught: **And he** must **give her a bed, a soft mat,** and a hard mat. The Gemara asks: **Why does he** need **to give her a soft mat and** a hard **mat** if she already has a bed? **Rav Pappa said:** The mishna is speaking **of a place where it is the custom to fill a bed with ropes.**[B] **Because** these ropes cause her suffering and **age** [***mevager***][L] **her,** she covers them with a mat, which serves as a kind of mattress upon which she can lie in comfort.

PERSONALITIES

Ḥoma – חוּמָא: Ḥoma was the daughter of Isi ben Rav Yitzḥak ben Rav Yehuda. She was originally married to Raḥava from Pumbedita, and after his death she married Rav Yitzḥak, son of Rabba bar bar Ḥana. When her second husband also passed away, Abaye took her as his wife, despite the prohibition against marrying a woman whose previous husbands have died, as he relied on the opinion that a woman is considered a danger to her husband only if three previous husbands have died. Apparently, Rava's wife was worried that due to Ḥoma's beauty and lineage, other men would also want to marry her.

Rava – רָבָא: Rava, one of the most prominent fourth-generation *amora'im* in Babylonia, was the son of the *amora* Rav Yosef bar Ḥama and the colleague of Abaye. Rava was born in the town of Meḥoza, where he studied Torah under Rav Naḥman bar Ya'akov and Rav Ḥisda. The Gemara relates that Rava and his study partner, Rami bar Ḥama, were visiting their teacher, Rav Ḥisda, while the latter's young daughter sat on his lap. Rav Ḥisda playfully asked her which of the scholars she would fancy marrying. The girl diplomatically answered that she would like to marry both of them, whereupon Rava responded that he would be last. The daughter ended up marrying Rami bar Ḥama. After he passed away, she married Rava (*Bava Batra* 12b).

Rava considered Rav Yosef to be his primary teacher and would depart his company by walking backward, causing himself multiple injuries to his heels. Upon Rav Yosef's death, Abaye was chosen to succeed him as head of the yeshiva of Pumbedita and Rava subsequently opened a new yeshiva at Meḥoza.

The Talmud records innumerable debates between Rava and Abaye, which were ruled in accordance with Rava in all but six instances. Rava did become head of the Pumbedita yeshiva when Abaye died, but he transferred his teacher's academy to his adopted locale of Meḥoza. This resulted in Rava's yeshiva standing as the single Babylonian house of study during this period.

HALAKHA

I know that the residents of Meḥoza are accustomed to drinking wine – יָדַעְנָא בְּהוּ בִּבְנֵי מְחוֹזָא דְּשָׁתוּ חַמְרָא: In a place where the custom is that women drink wine, the husband must give his wife a small amount of wine, as indicated by the stories related in the Gemara (Rambam *Sefer Nashim, Hilkhot Ishut* 12:10; *Shulḥan Arukh, Even HaEzer* 70:3).

BACKGROUND

To fill a bed with ropes – דְּמָלוּ פּוּרְיָא בְּחַבְלֵי: The ordinary method of constructing a bed was to stretch out ropes between the poles that formed the frame of the bed. These ropes created a kind of netting that served as a base on which a mat would be placed. By contrast, in certain places, as described here, the bed was filled with ropes, i.e., they wove many ropes in a tight formation, so that there was no need for a mat. Although it was possible to lie on these beds, they were uncomfortable due to the hardness and coarseness of the ropes.

LANGUAGE

Cups [*shufrazei*] – שׁוּפְרָזֵי: The *Arukh* suggests that *shufrazei* refers to long glass receptacles, similar to the *barzina* mentioned elsewhere (*Shabbat* 109b). It is also possible that the word *shufrazei* is related to *shofar*, horn.

The lock of a chest [*kulpei deshida*] – קוּלְפֵי דְשִׁידָּא: Some associate *kulpei* with the Greek κόλαφος, *kolafos*, a blow. Others state, in accordance with the version of the *Arukh* in several places in the Gemara, that it should be read as *kupla desherai*, from the Persian kopel, meaning a thick stick or a club, and the Aramaic *desherai*, meaning silk weavers. According to this interpretation, Rava's wife fashioned a kind of silk stick that she used to strike Ḥoma.

Age [*mevager*] – מְבַגֵּר: Rashi and several later linguistic scholars maintain that this term is similar in meaning to the usual form, *bagar*, aged. That is, the ropes cause her pain and make her body age. Alternatively, *bagar* may be derived from the Syriac *pagar*, meaning a cut or slice, i.e., the ropes cut her body.

תָּנוּ רַבָּנַן: אֵין נוֹתְנִין לָהּ כַּר וְכֶסֶת. מִשּׁוּם רַבִּי נָתָן אָמְרוּ: נוֹתְנִין לָהּ כַּר וְכֶסֶת. הֵיכִי דָּמֵי? אִי דְּאוֹרְחָהּ – מַאי טַעֲמָא דְּתַנָּא קַמָּא? וְאִי דְּלָאו אוֹרְחָהּ – מַאי טַעֲמָא דְּרַבִּי נָתָן?

The Sages taught: One does not give a poor woman **a pillow and a cushion. In the name of Rabbi Natan, they said: One** does **give her a pillow and a cushion.** The Gemara asks: **What are the circumstances? If it is her** usual **manner** to use a pillow and cushion, **what is the reason for** the opinion of **the first** ***tanna*** that she is not given these items? **And if it is not her** usual **manner, what is the reason for** the opinion of **Rabbi Natan?**

לָא צְרִיכָא, כְּגוֹן דְּאוֹרְחֵיהּ דִּידֵיהּ וְלָאו אוֹרְחָהּ דִּידָהּ. תַּנָּא קַמָּא סָבַר: אֲמַר לָהּ: כִּי אָזֵילְנָא – שָׁקֵילְנָא לְהוּ, וְכִי אָתֵינָא – מַיְיתֵינָא לְהוּ בַּהֲדַאי. וְרַבִּי נָתָן סָבַר: אָמְרָה לֵיהּ: זִימְנִין דְּמִיתְרְמֵי בֵּין הַשְּׁמָשׁוֹת וְלָא מָצֵית מַיְיתֵי לְהוּ, וּשְׁקַלְתְּ לְהוּ לְדִידִי, וּמַגְנֵית לִי עַל אַרְעָא.

The Gemara answers: **No,** it is **necessary** in a case **where** it is **his manner** to use a pillow and cushion, **but** it is **not her manner. The first** ***tanna*** **holds** that the husband **says to her: When I go away** from you, **I will take** my bedding with me, **and when I come** back **I will bring it with me. And Rabbi Natan holds** that **she** can **say to him: Sometimes it happens** that you arrive **at twilight and you are unable to bring it** with you, **and you** will **take my** bedding **and you** will **make me lie on the ground.** Therefore, I require extra pillows and cushions.

״וְנוֹתֵן לָהּ כִּפָּה״. אֲמַר לֵיהּ רַב פַּפָּא לְאַבָּיֵי:

§ The mishna further taught: **And he** must **give her a cap,** and shoes every Festival, and clothes once a year. **Rav Pappa said to Abaye:**

הַאי תַּנָּא – שְׁלִיחַ עַרְטְלַאי וְרָמֵי מְסָאנֵי! אֲמַר לֵיהּ: תַּנָּא בִּמְקוֹם הָרִים קָאֵי, דְּלָא סַגְיָא בְּלָא תְּלָתָא זוּגֵי מְסָאנֵי. וְאַגַּב אוֹרְחֵיהּ קָא מַשְׁמַע לָן דְּנִיתְבִינְהוּ נִיהֲלָהּ בַּמּוֹעֵד, כִּי הֵיכִי דְּנֶיהֱוֵי לָהּ שִׂמְחָה בְּגַוַּיְיהוּ.

This ***tanna*** creates a bizarre situation in which the woman is **left naked but wearing shoes,** as the husband must give his wife shoes three times a year but new clothing only once a year. Abaye **said to him: The** ***tanna*** **is standing,** i.e., speaking of, **a mountainous region,**[N] **in which she cannot do without three pairs of shoes,** as shoes wear out quickly in hilly areas. **And in passing,** the ***tanna*** **teaches us that he should give them to her on a Festival, so that she will rejoice in them** during the Festival.

״וְכֵלִים שֶׁל חֲמִשִּׁים זוּז״. אֲמַר אַבָּיֵי: חֲמִשִּׁים זוּזֵי פְּשִׁיטֵי. מִמַּאי? מִדְּקָתָנֵי: בַּמֶּה דְּבָרִים אֲמוּרִים – בְּעָנִי שֶׁבְּיִשְׂרָאֵל, אֲבָל בִּמְכוּבָּד – הַכֹּל לְפִי כְּבוֹדוֹ. וְאִי סָלְקָא דַּעְתָּךְ חֲמִשִּׁים זוּז מַמָּשׁ, עָנִי חֲמִשִּׁים זוּז מְנָא לֵיהּ? אֶלָּא שְׁמַע מִינָּהּ – חֲמִשִּׁים זוּזֵי פְּשִׁיטֵי.

§ The mishna teaches: **And he** must **give her clothes** with a value **of fifty dinars. Abaye said:** This is referring to **fifty simple** [***peshitei***][L] **dinars,**[B] used as the money of the state, which are worth only one-eighth of Tyrian dinars. **From where** did Abaye derive this? **From the fact that it teaches: In what** case **is this statement said?** It is **with** regard to **the poorest of Jews. However,** in the case **of a prominent man, all** the amounts are increased **in accordance with his prominence. And if it enters your mind** that the mishna means **literally fifty dinars, from where** would such **a poor man** get **fifty dinars?** How could a pauper afford to give such a large sum to his wife for her clothing? **Rather, learn from this** that the mishna is referring to **fifty simple dinars.**

NOTES

The ***tanna*** **is standing, speaking of, a mountainous region –** **תַּנָּא בִּמְקוֹם הָרִים קָאֵי:** The *Maggid Mishne* cites this as proof for the Rambam's opinion that all the details in this chapter describing the exact items and quantities a husband must provide for his wife are limited to particular times and places. In practice, a husband must provide her with the ability to live in a manner considered acceptable in their community, in accordance with the principles delineated here.

LANGUAGE

Simple [*peshitei*] – פְּשִׁיטֵי: Some explain this term literally as referring to simple copper coins. Others relate this word to the Middle Persian pišīz, meaning a small coin.

BACKGROUND

Simple dinars – זוּזֵי פְּשִׁיטֵי: Generally speaking, two monetary systems were in use during the talmudic period. One of these was based on a silver standard. This system, which was used in the Bible, is called Tyrian money by the Sages. The other system, known as money of the state, used the same names for its coins, but the value of each coin was one-eighth of the value of the coin with the same name in the Tyrian system. Using the same name for coins of different value was common and still exists in some places today. Consequently, it is necessary to clarify in each case whether the sum in question refers to silver dinars or simple dinars.

״וְאֵין נוֹתְנִין לָהּ לֹא חֲדָשִׁים״ וכו׳. תָּנוּ רַבָּנַן: מוֹתַר מְזוֹנוֹת – לַבַּעַל, מוֹתַר בְּלָאוֹת – לָאִשָּׁה. מוֹתַר בְּלָאוֹת לָאִשָּׁה לָמָּה לָהּ? אָמַר רַחֲבָה: שֶׁמִּתְכַּסָּה בָּהֶן בִּימֵי נִדָּתָהּ, כְּדֵי שֶׁלֹּא תִּתְגַּנֶּה עַל בַּעְלָהּ.

§ The mishna further states: **And he may not give her new** clothes in the summer, nor worn garments in the rainy season, and the leftover, worn clothes belong to her. **The Sages taught: Leftover sustenance** belongs **to the husband,**[H] whereas **leftover, worn clothes** belong **to the wife.**[H] The Gemara asks: With regard to the statement that **worn clothes** belong **to the wife, why** does **she** need these old clothes? **Raḥava said:** She requires them, **as she covers herself with them during her days of menstruation, so that she does not become repulsive to her husband.** If she wears her normal clothes when she is menstruating, he will later be disgusted by her.

אָמַר אַבַּיֵי, נְקִיטִינַן: מוֹתַר בְּלָאוֹת אַלְמָנָה – לְיוֹרְשָׁיו. הָתָם הוּא דְּלָא תִּתְגַּנֵּי בְּאַפֵּיהּ, הָכָא – תִּתְגַּנֵּי וְתִתְגַּנֵּי.

Abaye said: We have a tradition that the **leftover, worn clothes of a widow**[H] belong **to** the husband's **heirs.** The reason is that **it is** only in that case **there,** concerning a woman whose husband is alive, that the reasoning **so that she does not become repulsive to her husband** can be applied. Whereas **here,** when he is dead, **let her become repulsive.** There is no need to ensure that she find favor in the eyes of his heirs.

״נוֹתֵן לָהּ מָעָה כֶּסֶף״ וכו׳. מַאי אוֹכֶלֶת? רַב נַחְמָן אָמַר: אוֹכֶלֶת מַמָּשׁ. רַב אַשִׁי אָמַר: תַּשְׁמִישׁ.

§ The mishna teaches that **he gives her a silver *ma'a*,** and she eats with him from one Shabbat evening to the next. The Gemara asks: **What is** the meaning of the phrase: **She eats,** in this context? **Rav Naḥman said:** It means **literally** that **she eats** with him[H] once a week. **Rav Ashi said:** This is referring to **sexual relations.**

תְּנַן: אוֹכֶלֶת עִמּוֹ לֵילֵי שַׁבָּת. בִּשְׁלָמָא לְמַאן דְּאָמַר אֲכִילָה – הַיְינוּ דְּקָתָנֵי ״אוֹכֶלֶת״, אֶלָּא לְמַאן דַּאֲמַר תַּשְׁמִישׁ – מַאי ״אוֹכֶלֶת״? לִישָּׁנָא מְעַלְּיָא, כְּדִכְתִיב ״אָכְלָה וּמָחֲתָה פִיהָ וְאָמְרָה לֹא פָעַלְתִּי אָוֶן״.

The mishna states: And she eats with him from **Shabbat evening** to Shabbat evening. **Granted, according to the one who says** that it means actual **eating, this** explanation **is** consistent with **that which is taught: She eats. However, according to the one who says** that it is referring to **sexual relations, what is** the meaning of: **She eats?** The Gemara explains: It is **a euphemism, as it is written:** "So is the way of an adulterous woman; **she eats, and wipes her mouth, and says: I have done no wickedness"** (Proverbs 30:20).

מֵיתִיבֵי, רַבָּן שִׁמְעוֹן בֶּן גַּמְלִיאֵל אוֹמֵר: אוֹכֶלֶת בְּלֵילֵי שַׁבָּת וְשַׁבָּת. בִּשְׁלָמָא לְמַאן דְּאָמַר אֲכִילָה – הַיְינוּ דְּקָתָנֵי ״וְשַׁבָּת״. אֶלָּא לְמַאן דְּאָמַר תַּשְׁמִישׁ – תַּשְׁמִישׁ בְּשַׁבָּת מִי אִיכָּא? וְהָאָמַר רַב הוּנָא: יִשְׂרָאֵל קְדוֹשִׁים הֵן, וְאֵין מְשַׁמְּשִׁין מִטּוֹתֵיהֶן בַּיּוֹם! הָאֲמַר רָבָא: בְּבַיִת אָפֵל – מוּתָּר.

The Gemara **raises an objection: Rabban Shimon ben Gamliel says,** disagreeing with the *tanna* of the mishna: **She eats on Shabbat evening and** on **Shabbat. Granted, according to the one who says** that it means actual **eating, this** explanation **is** consistent with **that which is taught: And Shabbat,** i.e., she dines with him also on the day of Shabbat. **However, according to the one who says** that it is referring to **sexual relations, are there sexual relations on** the day of **Shabbat? But didn't Rav Huna say: The Jewish people are holy** and therefore **do not engage in sexual relations during the day?** The Gemara answers that **Rava said:** If they are **in a dark house, it is permitted** to engage in relations even during the day.

״וְאִם הָיְתָה מֵנִיקָה״. דָּרַשׁ רַבִּי עוּלָּא רַבָּה אַפִּיתְחָא דְּבֵי נְשִׂיאָה: אַף עַל פִּי שֶׁאָמְרוּ אֵין אָדָם זָן אֶת בָּנָיו וּבְנוֹתָיו כְּשֶׁהֵן קְטַנִּים, אֲבָל זָן קְטַנֵּי קְטַנִּים.

§ The mishna teaches: **And if she is nursing,** the required amount is reduced from her earnings and is added to the sum she receives for her sustenance. **Rabbi Ulla the Great taught at the entrance to the house of the *Nasi*: Although** the Sages **said** that **a person is not** obligated **to sustain his sons and daughters when they are young, still, he** must **sustain the very young ones.**[H]

HALAKHA

Leftover sustenance belongs to the husband – מוֹתַר מְזוֹנוֹת לַבַּעַל: If sustenance was apportioned for a wife and some is left over, it belongs to her husband. Many authorities maintain that this *halakha* applies only if there are leftovers due to a reduction in the price of food, but if she ate less than usual, the leftovers belong to her (Rambam *Sefer Nashim, Hilkhot Ishut* 12:13; *Shulḥan Arukh, Even HaEzer* 70:3, and in the comment of Rema).

Leftover, worn clothes belong to the wife – מוֹתַר בְּלָאוֹת לָאִשָּׁה: If a husband gave his wife clothes and they wore out, they belong to her (Rambam *Sefer Nashim, Hilkhot Ishut* 13:1; *Tur, Even HaEzer* 73).

Leftover, worn clothes of a widow – מוֹתַר בְּלָאוֹת אַלְמָנָה: The leftover, worn clothes of a widow belong to her husband's heirs (Rambam *Sefer Nashim, Hilkhot Ishut* 18:4; *Shulḥan Arukh, Even HaEzer* 95:5).

It means literally that she eats with him – אוֹכֶלֶת מַמָּשׁ: Even if a husband provides his wife with food by means of a third party, he must eat with her every Shabbat evening. The *halakha* is in accordance with the opinion of Rav Naḥman, as is usual for cases involving monetary judgment (Rambam *Sefer Nashim, Hilkhot Ishut* 12:12; *Shulḥan Arukh, Even HaEzer* 70:2).

Sustain the very young ones – זָן קְטַנֵּי קְטַנִּים: Just as a husband is obligated by Torah law to sustain his wife, he is likewise obligated by Torah law to provide sustenance for his young sons and daughters until they reach the age of six. From this age onward, the obligation to sustain them is by rabbinic law. The *halakha* is in accordance with the opinion of Rabbi Ulla the Great (Rambam *Sefer Nashim, Hilkhot Ishut* 12:14; *Shulḥan Arukh, Even HaEzer* 71:1).

עַד כַּמָּה – עַד בֶּן שֵׁשׁ. כִּדְרַב אַסִי, דְּאָמַר רַב אַסִי: קָטָן בֶּן שֵׁשׁ יוֹצֵא בְּעֵירוּב אִמּוֹ.

The Gemara asks: **Until when** are they considered very young? **Until the age of six, in accordance with** the opinion of **Rav Asi, as Rav Asi said: A six-year-old minor may go out by** means of **his mother's *eiruv*,**[H] if she prepared an *eiruv* on one side of the city. He is included in his mother's *eiruv* rather than that of his father, as he is considered subordinate to his mother.

מִמַּאי – מִדְּקָתָנֵי: הָיְתָה מֵנִיקָה – פּוֹחֲתִין לָהּ מִמַּעֲשֵׂה יָדֶיהָ, וּמוֹסִיפִין לָהּ עַל מְזוֹנוֹתֶיהָ. מַאי טַעְמָא? לָאו מִשּׁוּם דְּבָעֵי לְמֵיכַל בַּהֲדָהּ? וְדִלְמָא מִשּׁוּם דְּחוֹלָה הִיא.

The Gemara asks: **From where** is this *halakha* that Rabbi Ulla taught derived? The Gemara explains that it is derived **from** the fact **that it teaches: If she is nursing,** the required amount **is reduced from her earnings and is added** to the sum she receives **for her sustenance. What is the reason** for this? Is it **not because** the baby **needs to eat** together **with her?** This shows that a father is responsible to provide for his young child. The Gemara rejects this proof: **But perhaps** he increases her sustenance not due to the baby but **because she is** considered **ill** due to her weakness while nursing, in which case the obligation stems from his obligation to his wife, not to his child.

אִם כֵּן לִיתְנֵי "אִם הָיְתָה חוֹלָה", מַאי "אִם הָיְתָה מֵנִיקָה"? וְדִלְמָא הָא קָא מַשְׁמַע לַן: דִּסְתָם מֵנִיקוֹת חוֹלוֹת נִינְהוּ. אִיתְּמַר, אָמַר רַבִּי יְהוֹשֻׁעַ בֶּן לֵוִי: מוֹסִיפִין לָהּ יַיִן, שֶׁהַיַּיִן יָפֶה לֶחָלָב.

The Gemara retorts: **If so, let** the mishna **teach: If she was ill. What** is the reason that it specifies: **If she was nursing?** The reason for this *halakha* must certainly be due to the child. The Gemara again rejects this answer: **But perhaps** the mishna **teaches us this,** that in an **ordinary** situation, **nursing women are** considered **ill,** and that a husband must increase the sustenance all the more so if his wife is actually ill. Consequently, this does not prove that a father is obligated to sustain his very young child. **It was stated** that **Rabbi Yehoshua ben Levi said: Wine is added for** a nursing woman,[H] **as wine is good for milk.**[N]

הדרן עלך אף על פי

HALAKHA

A six-year-old minor may go out by means of his mother's *eiruv* – קָטָן בֶּן שֵׁשׁ יוֹצֵא בְּעֵירוּב אִמּוֹ: Up to and including the age of six, a child may use his mother's *eiruv*, without contributing the standard two meals toward the *eiruv*. The *halakha* is in accordance with the opinion of Rav Asi (Rif; Rambam; *Smag*; *Smak*). However, other sources (Rosh; *Tur*; *Mishna Berura*, based on *Eliyya Rabba*) indicate that a four- or five-year-old child who is not dependent upon his mother may not rely on her *eiruv* (Rambam *Sefer Zemanim*, *Hilkhot Eiruvin* 6:21; *Shulḥan Arukh*, *Oraḥ Ḥayyim* 414:2).

Wine is added for a nursing woman – מוֹסִיפִין לָהּ יַיִן: During the period that a woman is nursing, a husband must provide her with foods that are beneficial for her milk in addition to her regular sustenance, e.g., wine (Rambam *Sefer Nashim*, *Hilkhot Ishut* 21:11; *Shulḥan Arukh*, *Even HaEzer* 80:11).

NOTES

Wine is good for milk – הַיַּיִן יָפֶה לֶחָלָב: Most commentaries consider this statement conclusive proof that the increase in sustenance is for the benefit of the child rather than the mother, as Rabbi Yehoshua ben Levi says that wine is good for milk, not for the nursing mother (see Rivan and Ri Migash).

Summary of **Perek V**

With regard to the sums in the marriage contract, the conclusion is that a man can add as large an additional sum as he likes. However, the additional sum can be collected only by a woman who was widowed or divorced after marriage. If the relationship ends during the betrothal stage, the woman receives only the main sum of her marriage contract, but not the additional sum.

By rabbinic law, the husband is prohibited from reducing the sum below the minimum amount, even if his wife agrees. If a man does not write a marriage contract at all, or writes one for less than the minimum amount, their relationship amounts to licentious sexual intercourse.

After betrothal, unless the couple agrees otherwise, there is generally an appointed date set for the marriage. Once this date arrives, the woman is entitled to be sustained from the husband's assets. Nevertheless, due to various considerations, the Sages ruled that a woman who is betrothed to a priest may not partake of *teruma* until they are actually married.

With regard to the wife's obligation to perform tasks, the conclusion is that she is responsible for the primary maintenance of the household: Preparing food and caring for the young children, and other household duties. Additionally, she must do some work to aid in producing income for the family. Nevertheless, these are not absolute obligations, as a woman has the prerogative to declare that she will forfeit the right to sustenance from her husband in return for being able to keep her earnings. Additionally, if the wife brings property into the marriage from her dowry, or if the husband or wife is from a family that is not accustomed to performing household tasks, she is exempt from those tasks, due to the *halakha* that a woman ascends with her husband to his social status but does not descend from her status if his is lower.

Despite this, even a wealthy woman must perform certain acts of affection for her husband. These are tasks that do not require great effort but create feelings of closeness between them. Also, a woman may not be completely idle, as this leads to sin. For these and other reasons, the conclusion is that the husband cannot consecrate his wife's earnings.

The Sages delineated specific intervals at which the husband must engage in sexual relations with his wife, depending on his occupation, and he is not permitted to reduce the frequency of his conjugal obligations below this minimum without the wife's agreement. Nevertheless, he is permitted to leave her for a time in order to study Torah, despite the resultant neglect of his conjugal obligations during his absence.

The conjugal obligations are so significant that if one of the parties becomes completely unable to fulfill them, the couple is required to get divorced. If the husband is the one who deprives his wife of sexual intercourse, he must divorce her and give her the payment of her marriage contract. If the wife deprives the husband, she may be divorced without payment of her marriage contract. Furthermore, if one spouse refuses to engage in conjugal relations with the other due to a disagreement between them, this spouse is declared rebellious and is subject to monetary fines. And the Sages decreed that if the disagreement is not resolved within a short time, the couple should get divorced.

The Sages also set minimum amounts of food, clothing, and household necessities that the poorest of Jewish husbands must provide for their wives. These amounts, like other details of the stipulations in the marriage contract, fluctuate with the accepted practice in each community. Additionally, the couple has the right to stipulate different terms between them.

Index of **Background**

Index of **Background**

Index of **Language**

Index of **Personalities**

Image **Credits**

p21 1st image © Magnus Manske; **p21** 2nd image © acquired by Henry Walters, 1914; **p22** © Galyn Wiemers; **p32** top left image © andrewgabrielrose; **p32** bottom left image © Chmee2; **p79** © Ori~; **p100** © Dave and Margie Hill/Kleerup; **p208** © Wolfgang Sauber; **p215** © Hans Hillewaert; **p262** © Jastrow; **p278** © Biehler Michael, www.shutterstock.com; **p336** © Matthias Kabel; **p363** © Giovanni Dall'Orto; **p364** © Guy de la Bedoyere; **p233** © Shai Halevi, Clara Amit, Yoram Lehman, Yael Yolovitch, Miki Koren, and Mariana Salzberger, courtesy of the Israel Antiquities Authority

תלמוד בבלי

— מהדורת נאה —

כתובות א

Shefa

ירושלים

KOREN

תלמוד בבלי

הוצאת קורן ירושלים

— מהדורת נאה —

כתובות א

COMMENTARY BY

Rabbi Adin Even-Israel Steinsaltz

EDITOR-IN-CHIEF

Rabbi Dr Tzvi Hersh Weinreb

EXECUTIVE EDITOR

Rabbi Joshua Schreier

•

SHEFA FOUNDATION

KOREN PUBLISHERS JERUSALEM

בְּתוּלָה

*א נִשֵּׂאת לְיוֹם הָרְבִיעִי, וְאַלְמָנָה לְיוֹם הַחֲמִישִׁי. שֶׁפַּעֲמַיִם בְּשַׁבָּת בָּתֵּי דִינִין יוֹשְׁבִין בָּעֲיָירוֹת: בַּיּוֹם הַשֵּׁנִי וּבַיּוֹם הַחֲמִישִׁי, שֶׁאִם הָיָה לוֹ טַעֲנַת בְּתוּלִים הָיָה מַשְׁכִּים לְבֵית דִּין.§ **גמ'** אָמַר רַב יוֹסֵף אָמַר רַב יְהוּדָה אָמַר שְׁמוּאֵל: מִפְּנֵי מָה אָמְרוּ בְּתוּלָה נִשֵּׂאת לְיוֹם הָרְבִיעִי — לְפִי שֶׁשָּׁנִינוּ: *הִגִּיעַ זְמַן וְלֹא נִישְּׂאוּ — אוֹכְלוֹת מִשֶּׁלּוֹ, וְאוֹכְלוֹת בִּתְרוּמָה. יָכוֹל הִגִּיעַ זְמַן בְּאֶחָד בְּשַׁבָּת יְהֵא מַעֲלֶה לָהּ מְזוֹנוֹת — לְכָךְ שָׁנִינוּ: בְּתוּלָה נִשֵּׂאת לְיוֹם הָרְבִיעִי. אָמַר רַב יוֹסֵף: *מָרֵיהּ דְּאַבְרָהָם! תָּלֵי תַּנְיָא בִּדְלָא תַּנְיָא. הֵי תַּנְיָא וְהֵי לָא תַּנְיָא? הָא תַּנְיָא וְהָא תַּנְיָא! אֶלָּא: תָּלֵי תַּנְיָא דִּמְפָרֵשׁ טַעֲמָא, בִּדְתַנְיָא דְּלָא מְפָרֵשׁ טַעֲמָא! אֶלָּא, אִי אִיתְּמַר הָכִי אִיתְּמַר, אָמַר רַב יְהוּדָה אָמַר שְׁמוּאֵל: מִפְּנֵי מָה אָמְרוּ בְּתוּלָה נִשֵּׂאת לְיוֹם הָרְבִיעִי — שֶׁאִם הָיָה לוֹ טַעֲנַת בְּתוּלִים הָיָה מַשְׁכִּים לְבֵ"ד. וְתִינָּשֵׂא בְּאֶחָד בְּשַׁבָּת, שֶׁאִם הָיָה לוֹ טַעֲנַת בְּתוּלִים הָיָה מַשְׁכִּים לְבֵית דִּין? *ב שָׁקְדוּ חֲכָמִים עַל תַּקָּנַת בְּנוֹת יִשְׂרָאֵל, שֶׁיְּהֵא טוֹרֵחַ בִּסְעוּדָה שְׁלֹשָׁה יָמִים: אֶחָד בְּשַׁבָּת וְשֵׁנִי בְּשַׁבָּת וּשְׁלִישִׁי בְּשַׁבָּת, וּבָרְבִיעִי כּוֹנְסָהּ. וְעַכְשָׁו שֶׁשָּׁנִינוּ "שָׁקְדוּ", אוֹתָהּ שֶׁשָּׁנִינוּ הִגִּיעַ זְמַן וְלֹא נִישְּׂאוּ אוֹכְלוֹת מִשֶּׁלּוֹ וְאוֹכְלוֹת בִּתְרוּמָה, ג הִגִּיעַ זְמַן בְּאֶחָד בְּשַׁבָּת, מִתּוֹךְ שֶׁאֵינוֹ יָכוֹל לְכוֹנְסָהּ — אֵינוֹ מַעֲלֶה לָהּ מְזוֹנוֹת. לְפִיכָךְ, ד חָלָה הוּא, אוֹ שֶׁחָלְתָה הִיא, אוֹ שֶׁפֵּירְסָה נִדָּה — אֵינוֹ מַעֲלֶה לָהּ מְזוֹנוֹת. וְאִיכָּא דְּבָעֵי לָהּ מִיבְּעָיָא: חָלָה הוּא מַהוּ? הָתָם טַעֲמָא מַאי — מִשּׁוּם דַּאֲנִיס, וְהָכָא נַמִי — הָא אֲנִיס. אוֹ דִּלְמָא: הָתָם אֲנִיס בְּתַקַּנְתָּא דְּתַקִּינוּ לֵיהּ רַבָּנַן, הָכָא — לָא. וְאִם תִּמְצֵי לוֹמַר חָלָה הוּא מַעֲלֶה לָהּ מְזוֹנוֹת, חָלְתָה הִיא מַהוּ? מָצֵי אָמַר לָהּ: אֲנָא הָא קָאֵימְנָא, אוֹ דִּלְמָא, מָצְיָא אָמְרָה לֵיהּ "נִסְתַּחֲפָה שָׂדֵהוּ"? וְאִם תִּמְצֵי לוֹמַר אָמְרָה לֵיהּ "נִסְתַּחֲפָה שָׂדֵהוּ", פֵּירְסָה נִדָּה מַהוּ? בִּשְׁעַת וְסְתָּהּ — לָא תִּיבָּעֵי לָךְ, דְּלָא

רש"י

בְּתוּלָה נִשֵּׂאת לְיוֹם הָרְבִיעִי. תַּקָּנַת חֲכָמִים הִיא שֶׁתִּנָּשֵׂא בָּרְבִיעִי בְּשַׁבָּת, כִּדְמְפָרֵשׁ טַעְמָא. שֶׁפַּעֲמַיִם בְּשַׁבָּת. אַבְּתוּלָה קָאֵי. בְּשֵׁנִי וּבַחֲמִישִׁי. אַחַת מֵעֶשֶׂר תַּקָּנוֹת שֶׁתִּיקֵּן עֶזְרָא. בְּבָבָא קַמָּא בְּפֶרֶק "מְרוּבֶּה" (דף פב.) מְפָרֵשׁ לְכוּלְּהוּ. וּלְכָךְ תִּקְּנוּ שֶׁתִּנָּשֵׂא בָּרְבִיעִי, שֶׁאִם הָיָה לוֹ טַעֲנַת בְּתוּלִים — יַשְׁכִּים לְבֵ"ד בְּעוֹד כַּעֲסוֹ עָלָיו. [וְאִם יֵשׁ שָׁהוּת בֵּינְתַיִם — יֵשׁ לָחוּשׁ] שֶׁמָּא יִתְפַּיֵּיס וְתִתְקָרֵר דַּעְתּוֹ, וִיקַיְּימֶנָּה. וְשֶׁמָּא הִיא זִינְּתָה תַּחְתָּיו, וְנֶאֶסְרָה עָלָיו, כִּדְיָלְפִינַן (סוטה דף כח.) מִ"וְנִסְתְּרָה וְהִיא נִטְמָאָה", וּמִתּוֹךְ שֶׁיָּבֹא לְבֵית דִּין — יִתְבָּרֵר הַדָּבָר כְּשֶׁיֵּצֵא הַקּוֹל, שֶׁמָּא יָבוֹאוּ עֵדִים. וּבַגְּמָרָא פָּרֵיךְ: וְתִינָּשֵׂא בְּאֶחָד בְּשַׁבָּת! **גמ'** לְפִי שֶׁשָּׁנִינוּ כו'. לְקַמָּן מַקְשֵׁי עֲלַהּ. הִגִּיעַ זְמַן וְלֹא נִישְּׂאוּ. לְקַמָּן בְּפֶרֶק "אַף עַל פִּי" תְּנַן: נוֹתְנִין לִבְתוּלָה שְׁנֵים עָשָׂר חֹדֶשׁ מִשֶּׁתְּבָעָהּ הַבַּעַל וְהִזְהִיר עַל הַנִּישּׂוּאִין, לְפַרְנֵס עַצְמָהּ בְּתַכְשִׁיטִין. לְפַרְנֵס = קנדיר"ר בְּלַעַ"ז. וּלְאַלְמָנָה שְׁלֹשִׁים יוֹם. הִגִּיעַ זְמַן. זֶה וְלֹא נִישְּׂאוּ לַחוּפָּה, לְקַמָּן מְפָרֵשׁ שֶׁעִכֵּב הַבַּעַל. אוֹכְלוֹת מִשֶּׁלּוֹ. שֶׁהַבַּעַל חַיָּיב בִּמְזוֹנוֹת אִשְׁתּוֹ מִתַּקָּנַת ב"ד, כִּדְלְקַמָּן בְּפֶרֶק "נַעֲרָה" (דף מו:). וְאוֹכְלוֹת בִּתְרוּמָה. אִם כֹּהֵן הוּא וְהִיא בַּת יִשְׂרָאֵל. שֶׁהַכֹּהֵן מַאֲכִיל אֶת אִשְׁתּוֹ תְּרוּמָה, כִּדְיָלֵיף (לקמן דף נז:) מִ"וְכֹהֵן כִּי יִקְנֶה נֶפֶשׁ". לְכָךְ שָׁנִינוּ בְּתוּלָה נִשֵּׂאת כו'. לְהוֹדִיעַ שֶׁתַּקָּנַת חֲכָמִים מְעַכַּבְתּוֹ מִלִּכְנוֹס, וְאֵין עַכָּבָה זוֹ שֶׁלּוֹ. מָרֵיהּ דְּאַבְרָהָם כו'. תָּמַהּ עַל דִּבְרֵי רַבּוֹ, וְאָמַר: מָרֵיהּ דְּאַבְרָהָם! מַה זֶּה הָיָה לִשְׁמוּאֵל לוֹמַר כֵּן? וְעוֹד, שֶׁחָלָה רַב יוֹסֵף וְשָׁכַח תַּלְמוּדוֹ, וְתוֹהֶה עַל דְּבָרָיו הָרִאשׁוֹנִים. תָּלֵי תַּנְיָא בִּדְלָא תַּנְיָא. תּוֹלֶה טַעַם מִשְׁנָה שְׁנוּיָה בְּמִשְׁנָה שֶׁאֵינָהּ שְׁנוּיָה: וּמַקְשִׁינַן לְרַב יוֹסֵף. הֵי תַּנְיָא וְהֵי לָא תַּנְיָא? הָא תַּנְיָא וְהָא תַּנְיָא. זוֹ שְׁנוּיָה וְזוֹ שְׁנוּיָה. אֶלָּא תָּלֵי תַּנְיָא דִּמְפָרֵשׁ טַעְמָא בִּדְתַנְיָא דְּלָא מְפָרֵשׁ טַעְמָא. מִשְׁנָתֵינוּ טַעְמָהּ מְפוֹרָשׁ בְּתוֹכָהּ — כְּדֵי שֶׁיַּשְׁכִּים לְבֵית דִּין. וְהִגִּיעַ זְמַן אֵין שׁוּם טַעַם מְפוֹרָשׁ בָּהּ, לוֹמַר מִפְּנֵי מָה אִם הִגִּיעַ זְמַן בְּאֶחָד בְּשַׁבָּת אֵינוֹ מַעֲלֶה לָהּ מְזוֹנוֹת. וְתִינָּשֵׂא בְּאֶחָד בְּשַׁבָּת. כּוּלָּהּ רַב יוֹסֵף קָאָמַר לָהּ. וְעַכְשָׁיו שֶׁשָּׁנִינוּ שָׁקְדוּ. וּבִשְׁבִיל תַּקָּנָה זוֹ הוּא מְעוּכָּב מִלִּכְנוֹס בְּאֶחָד בְּשַׁבָּת, מֵעַתָּה אוֹתָהּ שֶׁשָּׁנִינוּ כו'. לְפִיכָךְ. רַב יוֹסֵף מְסַיֵּים לָהּ מִשְּׁמֵיהּ דְּנַפְשֵׁיהּ וּמִסְּבָרֵיהּ, וְאָמַר: לְפִיכָךְ, הוֹאִיל וְלָמַדְנוּ שֶׁהַמְעוּכָּב מֵחֲמַת אוֹנֶס אֵינוֹ חַיָּיב לְזוּנָהּ — חָלָה הוּא כו'. הָא קָאֵימְנָא. הִנְנִי מְזוּמָּן. נִסְתַּחֲפָה שָׂדֵהוּ. לְשׁוֹן "מָטָר סוֹחֵף" (משלי כח) נִשְׁטְפָה שָׂדְךָ, כְּלוֹמַר: מַזָּלְךָ גָּרַם, כִּי מֵהַיּוֹם אֲנִי מוּטֶּלֶת עָלֶיךָ לָזוּן. פָּשִׁיט

תוספות

בתולה · הא דלא קתני "הבתולה" כדתני "האשה נקנית", "היבמה ניקנית" (קדושין דף ב.) – משום דהתם אקרא קאי "כי יקח איש אשה" (דברים כב) – האשה הכתובה, וכן היבמה, אבל הכא – לא קאי אקרא. והא דלא תנן בפ"ק דקידושין (דף יד:) "העבד עברי" אף על פי דכתיב בקרא (שמות כא) "כי תקנה עבד עברי" – משום דא"כ ה"ל למתני "העבד העברי", שאינו דנוק, ואין דרך התלמוד לדבר כן. ומיהו, גבי איש ואשה רגילים בכל מקום לשנות בה' אע"ג דלא קאי אקרא כמו "האשה שהלכה" (יבמות דף קיד:) "האשה שנתארמלה" (לקמן דף טו:) "האיש מדיר את בנו בנזיר" (נזיר ד' כח:).

נשאת · הא דלא קתני "נושאין את הבתולה" כמו "האיש מקדש" (קדושין דף מא.) – לפי שעתה מקלר יותר. ועוד: דאי תנא הכי ה"א אפי' בעל כרחה, כדמשני (שם דף ג:) גבי הא דפריך וליתני "האיש קונה". ועוד, דהתם אקרא קאי כי יקח איש אשה".

ליום הרביעי. ולא בליל חמישי, כדאמר בפרק בתרא דנדה (דף סה:) *דליכא כתובה דלא רמו בה תיגרא. כ"ש אם יעשה נשואין בליל ה', דאיכא למיחש שיטרד בנשואין וכתובה ולא יבעול.

שאם היה לו טענת וכו'. ואם תאמר: הא תינח אשת כהן או פחותה מבת שלש דליכא אלא חד ספיקא, כדאמרינן בגמרא (לקמן ט.) אבל בשאר נשים, דאיכא ספק ספיקא – אמאי תנשא ליום ד'? ואומר ר"ת: דלא פלוג רבנן בתקנתא, ומשום אשת כהן ופחותה מג' תקנו בכל הנשים שינשאו ביום ד'. ובקונטרס פי': שמתוך כך יתברר הדבר ויבואו עדים שזינתה ברלון. וקשה לפירושו, דאמרינן בגמרא (שם:) אמר אביי אף אנן נמי תנינא, דהאומר פתח פתוח מלאתי נאמן לאוסרה עליו: בתולה נשאת כו', מאי לאו דקטעין פתח פתוח? והשתא היכי מייתי ראיה לפ"ה? הא אע"ג דאינו נאמן – מכל מקום ישכים לבית דין, שמתוך כך יצא הקול ויבואו עדים ויתברר הדבר? וי"ל: דלא מייתי אביי ראיה לרבי אלעזר אלא שהוא בקי ומכיר אם הוא פתח פתוח, דאם אינו בקי – לא יצא הקול, ולא יבא לידי בירור, כי יאמרו שהוא טעה וסבור שמלא פתח פתוח ואינו כן, ולא יחושו לדבריו. ועי"ל: דגם לפ"ה לא היו מתקנים שתהא ניסת ליום ד' משום שמא יתברר על ידי עדים, אבל כיון דבאשת כהן ובפחותה מבת שלש, דנאמן לאוסרה עליו, תקנו שתהא ניסת ברביעי – גם בשאר נשים תקנו, משום שמתוך כך יצא הקול ויתברר הדבר על ידי עדים. והשתא מייתי אביי שפיר ממתניתין דבאשת כהן ובפחותה מבת שלש נאמן לאוסרה עליו. ותימה: דהכא משמע דמשום חששא דזנות תקנו שתהא ניסת ברביעי, ובפ"ב דגטין (דף יז. ושם) איכא מ"ד דתקנו זמן בגטין משום פירי, אבל משום שמא יחפה על בת אחותו לא חיישינן, משום דזנות לא שכיח? וי"ל: דהתם קאמר זנות דאתי לידי מיתה, דהיינו בהתראה ובעדים, לא שכיח. אי נמי: הכא שלא תשב עמו באיסור כל ימיו – חשו אפילו לזנות, אע"ג דלא שכיח.

מפני מה אמרו בתולה נשאת ליום הרביעי לפי ששנינו כו'. אין שואל הטעם למה נשאת ברביעי, דאם כן לא הוה משני מידי. אלא הכי פירושו: "מפני מה אמרו" כלומר, מאי נפקא מינה שתיקנו שנשאת ברביעי? ומשני: נפקא מינה לענין מזונות ותרומה. ורב יוסף קא מתמה "מריה דאברהם", דהא נפקותא מפרשה בהדיא "שאם היה לו טענת בתולים", והוא מניח נפקותא זו המפורשת ותופס נפקותא אחרינא.

אלא אי אתמר הכי אתמר א"ר יהודה אמר שמואל. ולא גרסינן רב יוסף, דהא רב יוסף גופיה קאמר: אלא אי איתמר.

מפני מה אמרו כו'. בניחותא גרסינן לה, ולא בא להקשות אלא "ותנשא באחד בשבת".

ותנשא באחד בשבת. לא בעי לשנויי דנשאת ברביעי כדי שתבעל בחמישי משום ברכה שנאמרה בו לדגים, כדאמרינן לקמן (דף ה.)! ועוד: למה לי טעם דשקדו? תיפוק ליה משום ברכה! ואומר ר"י: דטעם דברכה אינה אלא עלה טובה, ולא מקרי עבריינא. אבל משום שקדו – מקרי עבריינא. וכן משמע לקמן דאמר טעמא משום ברכה. אבל משום איקרורי דעתא – לא חיישינן, ומאי נפקא מינה? אלא ודאי דמשום ברכה לא מקרי עבריינא.

מליא

עין משפט נר מצוה

א א ב מיי' פ"י מהל' אישות הל' טו סמג עשין מח טוש"ע אה"ע סימן סד סעי' ג:

ב ג ד מיי' שם הלכה יט וסמג שם טוש"ע שם סי' נו סעי' ג:

[הך דליכא כתובה וכו' ליתא בנדה אך בשבת קל. ונראה כוונת התוס' כמ"ש כדאמר בפ' בתרא דנדה סה: ר"ל שאמרו שם שאני כתובה דמגהי בה טפי ע' רש"י וערוך שם והא דכתבו דליכא כתובה הוא טעס בפ"ע]

תוספות רי"ד

בתולה נשאת ביום ד' ואלמנה ביום ה' שפעמים בשבת ב"ד יושבין בעיירות ביום ב' וביום ה' ואם היה לו טענת בתולים היה משכים לב"ד. פי' חכמים תקנו שתנשא הבתולה בד' כדי שיבעול בליל ה' ואם לא ימצא לה בתולים ילך בבוקר לב"ד טרם שיתקרר דעתו שיפיים עמה ויחקרו ב"ד מתי זינתה שמא תחתיו זינתה והיא אסורה לו. שפעמים בשבת וכו'. פי' אבתולה יהיב טעמא וטעמא דאלמנה מפרש לקמן. ותקנות עזרא הוא שישבו ב"ד בעיירות בב' ובה'. כדאמרינן בפ' מרובה מי' תקנות שתיקן עזרא. ואע"פ שבכל עיר ועיר היתה סנהדרין קבוע. בכל ימות השבוע היו עוסקים בתורה ובב' ובה' עוסקים בדינים. ולקמן פריך ותנשא באחד בשבת: אמר ר"י מפני מה אמרו בתולה נשאת בד' שאם היה לו טענת בתולים היה משכים לב"ד. ותנשא בא' בשבת ואם היה לו טענת בתולים היה משכים לב"ד שקדו חכמים על תקנות בנות ישראל שיהא טורח ג' ימים בסעודה א' בשבת שני ושלישי וברביעי כונסה. ועכשיו ששנינו שקדו. אותה ששנינו לקמן בפ' אע"פ נותנים לבתולה י"ב חודש משתבעה הבעל לפרנס א"ע. כשם שנותנים לאשה כך נותנים לאיש לפרנס א"ע ולאלמנה ל' יום הגיע זמן ולא נשאו אוכלות משלו. פי' וכגון שהבעל מעכב הגיע זמן בא' בשבת מתוך שאינו יכול לכונסה אינו מעלה לה מזונות לפיכך חלה הוא או שחלתה היא או שפירסה נדה אינו מעלה לה מזונות. א"ר שמואל בר רב יצחק ל"ש אלא מתקנות עזרא ואילך שאין ב"ד יושבין אלא בב' ובה'. אבל אי איכא ב"ד קבועים בכל יום כקודם תקנות עזרא אשה נשאת בכל יום והא בעינן שקדו דטריח לה. והכי אסיק רב אחא דכל אונסא לא אכלה בין חלתה היא ובין חלה הוא. והכי הילכתא:

מסורת הש"ס

נ"י כ"י

לקמן ט:

לקמן מח. נז. ע: [נדרים עג:]

ב"ב קלב: שבת כב. [עירובין עה:]

לקמן ג. ה.

ג א מיי' פ"ט מהל' גירושין הל' ח סמג עשין נ טוש"ע אה"ע סי' קמד סעי' א:
ד ב מיי' שם הל' ב (טוש"ע שם סעי' ב):
ה ג מיי' שם הל' יב סמג שם טוש"ע שם סי' קמה סעי' א:
ו ד מיי' שם הל' יא וסמג שם טוש"ע שם סי' קמד סעי' ג:
ז ה מיי' שם הל' ח טוש"ע שם סעי' א:

דְּלָא מָצְיָא אָמְרָה לֵיהּ "נִסְתַּחֲפָה שָׂדֵהוּ". כִּי תִּיבָּעֵי לָךְ — שֶׁלֹּא בְּשַׁעַת וִוסְתָּהּ מַאי? כֵּיוָן דְּלָאו בְּשַׁעַת וִוסְתָּהּ הֲוַיָא — מָצְיָא אָמְרָה לֵיהּ "נִסְתַּחֲפָה שָׂדֵהוּ", אוֹ דִלְמָא, כֵּיוָן דְּאִיכָּא נָשֵׁי דְּקָא מְשַׁנְּיָא וִוסְתַּיְיהוּ, כְּשַׁעַת וִוסְתָּהּ דָּמֵי? פָּשֵׁיט רַב אַחַאי: הִגִּיעַ זְמַן וְלֹא נִישְּׂאוּ אוֹכְלוֹת מִשֶּׁלּוֹ וְאוֹכְלוֹת בִּתְרוּמָה. "לֹא נָשְׂאוּ" לָא קָתָנֵי, אֶלָּא "לֹא נִישְּׂאוּ", הֵיכִי דָּמֵי, אִי דְּקָא מְעַכְּבָן אִינְהִי — אַמַּאי אוֹכְלוֹת מִשֶּׁלּוֹ וְאוֹכְלוֹת בִּתְרוּמָה? אֶלָּא לָאו דְּאִיתְּנִיס כִּי הַאי גַּוְונָא, וְקָתָנֵי: אוֹכְלוֹת מִשֶּׁלּוֹ וְאוֹכְלוֹת בִּתְרוּמָה! אָמַר רַב אָשֵׁי: לְעוֹלָם אֵימָא לָךְ: כָּל אוּנְסָא לָא אָכְלָה, וּדְקָא מְעַכְּבִי אִינְהוּ, וּבְדִין הוּא דְּאִיבָּעֵי לֵיהּ לְמִיתְנֵי "לֹא נָשְׂאוּ", וְאַיְּידֵי דְּתָנָא רֵישָׁא בְּדִידְהִי תָּנָא נַמִי סֵיפָא בְּדִידְהִי.§ אָמַר רָבָא: וּלְעִנְיַן גִּיטִּין אֵינוֹ כֵּן. [א]אַלְמָא קָסָבַר רָבָא: *אֵין אוֹנֶס בְּגִיטִּין. מְנָא לֵיהּ לְרָבָא הָא? אִילֵימָא מֵהָא דִּתְנַן: *[ב]"הֲרֵי זֶה גִּיטֵּיךְ אִם לֹא בָּאתִי מִכָּאן וְעַד שְׁנֵים עָשָׂר חֹדֶשׁ", וּמֵת בְּתוֹךְ שְׁנֵים עָשָׂר חֹדֶשׁ, אֵינוֹ גֵּט. מֵת — הוּא דְּאֵינוֹ גֵּט, הָא חָלָה — הֲרֵי זֶה גֵּט. וְדִלְמָא לְעוֹלָם אֵימָא לָךְ: חָלָה נַמִי אֵינוֹ גֵּט, וְהִיא גּוּפָא קמ"ל: דְּאֵין גֵּט לְאַחַר מִיתָה? אֵין גֵּט לְאַחַר מִיתָה — הָא תָּנָא לֵיהּ רֵישָׁא: [ג]"הֲרֵי זֶה גִּיטֵּיךְ אִם *מַתִּי" "הֲרֵי זֶה גִּיטֵּיךְ מֵחוֹלִי זֶה" "הֲרֵי זֶה גִּיטֵּיךְ לְאַחַר מִיתָה" — לֹא אָמַר כְּלוּם. דִּלְמָא לְאַפּוּקֵי מִדְּרַבּוֹתֵינוּ? דְּתַנְיָא: וְרַבּוֹתֵינוּ הִתִּירוּהָ לְהִנָּשֵׂא, וְאָמְרִינַן: מַאן רַבּוֹתֵינוּ? אָמַר רַב יְהוּדָה אָמַר שְׁמוּאֵל: בֵּי דִינָא דְּשָׁרוּ מִשְׁחָא. סָבְרִי לָהּ כְּרַבִּי יוֹסֵי, דְּאָמַר: זְמַנּוֹ שֶׁל שְׁטָר מוֹכִיחַ עָלָיו. וְאֶלָּא מִסֵּיפָא: *[ד]"מֵעַכְשָׁיו אִם לֹא בָּאתִי מִכָּאן וְעַד י"ב חֹדֶשׁ" וּמֵת בְּתוֹךְ שְׁנֵים עָשָׂר חֹדֶשׁ — הֲרֵי זֶה גֵּט. מֵת — וְהוּא הַדִּין לְחָלָה. דִּלְמָא מֵת דַּוְקָא, דְּלָא נִיחָא לֵיהּ דְּתִפּוֹל קַמֵּי יָבָם! אֶלָּא מֵהָא: *דְּהַהוּא דַּאֲמַר לְהוּ "אִי לָא אָתֵינָא מִיכָּן וְעַד תְּלָתִין יוֹמִין לֶיהֱוֵי גִּיטָּא", אֲתָא בְּסוֹף תְּלָתִין יוֹמִין [ה]וּפְסַקֵיהּ מַבְרָא, אֲמַר לְהוּ: "חֲזוּ דַּאֲתַאי, חֲזוּ דַּאֲתַאי!" אָמַר שְׁמוּאֵל: לָאו שְׁמֵיהּ מָתְיָא. וְדִלְמָא אוּנְסָא דִּשְׁכִיחַ שָׁאנֵי, דְּכֵיוָן דְּאִיבָּעֵי לֵיהּ לְאַתְנוּיֵי וְלָא אַתְנֵי — אִיהוּ דְּאַפְסֵיד אַנַּפְשֵׁיהּ! אֶלָּא רָבָא סְבָרָא דְּנַפְשֵׁיהּ קָאָמַר, מִשּׁוּם צְנוּעוֹת וּמִשּׁוּם פְּרוּצוֹת; מִשּׁוּם צְנוּעוֹת, דְּאִי אָמְרַתְּ לָא לֶהֱוֵי גֵּט — זִימְנִין

מציא אמרה ליה נסתחפה שדהו. ואינו יכול לטעון: דאדרבה מזלה גרס. דכיון דלא מיפקדא אפריה ורביה לא מיענשא, כדאמרינן ב"הבא על יבמתו" (יבמות דף סד:) ועוד: דהאשה היא שדה של הבעל, ואין הבעל שדה שלה. לפיכך חלה הוא אינו מעלה לה מזונות. קשה לר"י: דאמר ב"החולץ" (שם דף מא: ושם) עמד בדין וברח — נזונת משל יבם, ומפרש בירושלמי: ברח — ה"ה חלה, והכא אמרי' דחלה אין מעלה לה מזונות! ואור"י: דהתם חלה או ברח לאחר שעמד בדין, שכבר נתחייב לה במזונות. אבל הכא בחלה קודם הגעת הזמן. ובקונט' פי' שם: דוקא ברח, אבל חלה — לא, ואין נראה, כדמשמע בירושלמי. ולפירושו אין להקשות מאיכא דבעו לה מיבעיא, אמאי לא פשיט לה מהתם? דיש לומר: דארוסתו אגידא ביה טפי מיבמתו, כדאמרינן ביבמות בכמה דוכתי. פשיט רב אחאי. לא כמו שפירש רשב"ס דהיינו רב אחאי גאון שעשה שאלתות, והיה בסוף כל האמוראים, ולכך משנה לשונו בכל התלמוד: פריך רב אחאי: פשיט רב אחאי. שהרי כאן רב אשי *עונה על דבריו. אלא אומר רבינו תם שהוא אמורא, וכל אמורא היה תופס לשונו, כמו: מגדף בה ר' אבהו (סנהדרין ג:) תהי בה ר' יוחנן (ב"ק קיב:), לייט עלה אביי (ברכות כט.).

לא נשאו לא קתני אלא לא נישאו. מקובלין היו כך לקרות "לא נישאו". ועוד: דאי "לא נשאו" האנשים קאי — ה"ל למימר נמי בלשון רבים: ואוכלות משלהם. אלא לא נישאו. פירוש: דמשמע נמי דמעכבי אינהי. אבל אין לומר דמשמע דוקא דמעכבי אינהי אבל לא אינהו, מדקאמר: לעולם דמעכבי אינהו, ואיידי דתנא רישא בדידהי כו', דמשום איידי אין לשנות טעות בסיפא. מת הוא דאינו גט. דאין גט לאחר מיתה, הא חלה — הרי זה גט. דאי חלה נמי אינו גט, וטעמא דהכא דאינו גט משום אונס — אם כן לישמעינן חלה, דהוי אונס מועט, וכ"ש מת! דהשתא אכתי לא אסיק אדעתיה דמת איכא למימר ניחא ליה דלא תפול קמי יבם. ודלמא לעולם אימא לך חלה נמי אינו גט. ויש טענת אונס. ודקאמר ליתני חלה וכ"ש מת, הא דקתני מת — הא קמ"ל דאין גט לאחר מיתה. ואתא לאשמועינן תרוייהו: דיש אונס, ואין גט לאחר מיתה. דאי יש אונס גרידא אתא לאשמועינן, אבל יש גט לאחר מיתה — הוה ליה למינקט חלה, ואי אין גט לאחר מיתה גרידא הוה בעי לאשמועינן — לא הוה ליה למינקט הרי זה גיטך אם לא באתי, שעושה תנאי, אלא הרי זה גיטך לאחר מיתה. הרי זה גיטך אם מתי מחולי זה לאחר מיתה. לאחר מיתה הוי טעמא דכולהו כמו "אתם" — ולא אפוטרופסין ולא שותפין ולא אריסין. ולא כל התורס את שאינו שלו (גיטין דף נב.) דכולהו הוו משום תורס את שאינו שלו. וא"ת: ההיא משנה גופה אמאי איצטריך? הא תנן בהדיא בפ"ק דגיטין (דף יג. שם): דאין גט לאחר מיתה, דתנן: האומר תנו גט זה לאשתי — לא יתנו לאחר מיתה. ובפרק קמא דגיטין (שם ד"ה "לא") פירשנו. דלמא לאפוקי מדרבותינו. אבל מההיא דרישא לא שמעינן לאפוקי מדרבותינו, דאיכא לאוקמה בשאין כתוב זמן בשטר. והא דאמרינן (בגיטין דף פו.) שלשה גיטין פסולין וחד מינייהו שאין בו זמן — הא אמרינן אם נשאת הולד כשר, ומשום דאין גט לאחר מיתה קתני הכא לא אמר כלום, אפילו נשאת. אי נמי בשכתוב בו *שבוע או שנה או חדש, דאמר בפרק שני דגיטין (דף יז:) דכשר ואין זמנו מוכיח עליו. אי נמי במאוחר. דלמא מת דוקא דלא ניחא ליה דתפול קמי יבם. וא"ת: בפרק "מי שאחזו" (גיטין דף עג. ושם) דאמרי': אכלו ארי אין לנו. פירוש: אין לנו שיהא גט. ואמאי לא הוי גט? הא לא ניחא ליה דתפול קמי יבם? וי"ל: דבאונס דלא שכיח כלל לא אסיק אדעתיה שירלה שיהא גט. וסברה

פְּשִׁיט רַב אַחַאי. הָךְ בְּעָיָא מִמַּתְנִיתִין, דְּקָתָנֵי: לֹא נִישְּׂאוּ, וְלָא קָתָנֵי לֹא נָשְׂאוּ, דְּלִישְׁתַּמַּע שֶׁהַבְּעָלִים מְעַכְּבִים. אֶלָּא לֹא נִישְּׂאוּ. הֵן לַבְּעָלִים, תָּלָה הָעַכָּבָה בַּנָּשִׁים. וְאַיְּידֵי דְּתָנָא רֵישָׁא בְּדִידְהִי. נוֹתְנִין לִבְתוּלָה שְׁנֵים עָשָׂר חֹדֶשׁ, וּלְאַלְמָנָה שְׁלֹשִׁים יוֹם. וּלְעִנְיַן גִּיטִּין אֵינוֹ כֵּן. אַלְּפִיכָךְ קָאֵי, דְּאַשְׁמְעִינַן שֶׁעַכָּבַת הָאוֹנֶס פּוֹטַרְתּוֹ מִן הַמְּזוֹנוֹת — לְעִנְיַן גִּיטִּין אֵין טַעֲנַת אוֹנֶס מוֹעֶלֶת; אִם נָתַן גֵּט לְאִשְׁתּוֹ ע"מ אִם לֹא אָבֹא עַד זְמַן פְּלוֹנִי יְהֵא גֵּט, [וְנֶאֱנַס] וְלֹא בָּא — הֲרֵי זֶה גֵּט, וְאֵינוֹ יָכוֹל לוֹמַר אָנוּס הָיִיתִי. אַלְמָא קָסָבַר אֵין אוֹנֶס בְּגִטִּין. אֵין טַעֲנַת אוֹנֶס בְּגִיטִּין. וּלְקַמֵּיהּ מְפָרֵשׁ טַעְמָא. אֵינוֹ גֵּט. וְאִם אֵין לָהּ בָּנִים זְקוּקָה לְיָבָם. מֵת הוּא דְּאֵינוֹ גֵּט. דְּהָא לָא שַׁוְיָא גִּיטָּא עַד י"ב חֹדֶשׁ, וְהוּא מֵת בְּתוֹךְ הַזְּמַן, וּמַאן קָא מְגָרֵשׁ לָהּ מֵהָשְׁתָּא? אֵין הַמֵּתִים מְגָרְשִׁים. מֵת הוּא דְּאֵינוֹ גֵּט. מִשּׁוּם דְּאֵין גֵּט לְאַחַר מִיתָה. אֲבָל מִשּׁוּם אוֹנֶס אַחֲרִינָא — לָא מַפְקַע גִּיטָּא. אַלְמָא: אֵין אוֹנֶס בְּגִטִּין. דְּאִי סָלְקָא דַּעְתָּךְ חָלָה נַמִי אֵינוֹ גֵּט — נִיתְנֵי חָלָה וְכָל שֶׁכֵּן מֵת, שֶׁאֵין אוֹנֶס גָּדוֹל מִזֶּה. הִיא גּוּפָא קמ"ל. כְּלוֹמַר: הַאי דְּתָנָא מֵת לָאו לְדִיוּקָא דִּילָהּ תַּנְיָהּ, לְמֵידַק: הָא חָלָה — הֲרֵי זֶה גֵּט; אֶלָּא לְאַשְׁמְעִינַן הִיא גּוּפָא, דְּאֵין גֵּט לְאַחַר מִיתָה, וַאֲפִי' בְּלֹא תְּנַאי. כְּגוֹן, הָאוֹמֵר לְאִשְׁתּוֹ: הֲרֵי זֶה גִּיטֵּיךְ לְאַחַר מוֹתִי — אֵינוֹ גֵּט לְפוֹטְרָהּ מִן הַיָּבָם. זֶה גִּיטֵּךְ אִם מַתִּי. שֶׁכִּיב מְרַע שֶׁכָּתַב גֵּט לְאִשְׁתּוֹ בְּאֶחָד מִן הַלְּשׁוֹנוֹת הַלָּלוּ: זֶה גִּיטֵּךְ אִם מַתִּי, אוֹ זֶה גִּיטֵּךְ מֵחוֹלִי זֶה — מִשֶּׁיִּפְסוֹק חוֹלִי זֶה (מֵעָלַי) מַשְׁמַע, וְהוּא מֵת מֵאוֹתוֹ חוֹלִי — לֹא אָמַר כְּלוּם, שֶׁהֲרֵי מִשֶּׁפָּסַק אֵינוֹ בַּחַיִּים וְאֵינוֹ יָכוֹל לְגָרֵשׁ. דִּלְמָא. הָא דְּאִיצְטְרִיךְ סֵיפָא אִם לֹא בָּאתִי וכו' — לְאַפּוּקֵי מִדְּרַבּוֹתֵינוּ אִיצְטְרִיךְ, דִּפְלִיגִי עֲלַהּ, וְאָמְרִי דְּאֵין גֵּט לְאַחַר מִיתָה הוּא, דְּכֵיוָן דִּכְתוּב בַּגֵּט זְמַן כְּתִיבָתוֹ — הוּא מוֹכִיחַ שֶׁכָּךְ אָמַר לָהּ: אִם לֹא בָּאתִי לְאוֹתוֹ זְמַן — יְהֵא גֵּט לְמַפְרֵעַ מֵהַיּוֹם. דְּאִי לָא מְשַׁוֵּי גִּיטָּא עַד שְׁנֵים עָשָׂר חֹדֶשׁ, לָמָּה כָּתַב יוֹם כְּתִיבַת הַגֵּט בְּתוֹכוֹ? לִכְתּוֹב: אִם לֹא בָּאתִי לר"ח פְּלוֹנִי יְהֵא גֵּט. הִתִּירוּהָ לִינָּשֵׂא. בְּלֹא חֲלִיצָה, לְהָהִיא דְּ"אִם לֹא בָּאתִי". זְמַנּוֹ שֶׁל שְׁטָר מוֹכִיחַ עָלָיו. לֹא לְחִנָּם נִכְתַּב זְמַנּוֹ לְתוֹכוֹ, אִם לֹא לְהוֹדִיעַ שֶׁמִּיּוֹם הַכְּתִיבָה וְהַמְּסִירָה הוּא מְגָרְשָׁהּ אִם לֹא יָבֹא לְאוֹתוֹ זְמַן. הִלְכָּךְ, אַע"ג דְּלֹא כָּתַב: זֶה גִּיטֵּךְ מֵהַיּוֹם אִם לֹא בָּאתִי כו' — כְּמַאן דִּכְתַב "מֵהַיּוֹם" דָּמֵי. וּבְבָבָא בַּתְרָא (דף קלו.) אֲמָרָהּ רַבִּי יוֹסֵי, דִּתְנַן: הַכּוֹתֵב נְכָסָיו לִבְנוֹ צָרִיךְ שֶׁיִּכְתּוֹב "מֵהַיּוֹם וּלְאַחַר מִיתָה", וְאִם לֹא כָּתַב "מֵהַיּוֹם" — אֵינָהּ מַתָּנָה. רַבִּי יוֹסֵי אוֹמֵר: אֵינוֹ צָרִיךְ. וְאֶלָּא מִסֵּיפָא. גָּמַר רָבָא דְּאֵין אוֹנֶס בְּגִיטִּין. הֲרֵי זֶה גֵּט. וְאַע"ג דְּאֵין אוֹנֶס גָּדוֹל מִמִּיתָה. אַלְמָא: אֵין אוֹנֶס בְּגִיטִּין, וְהוּא הַדִּין לְחָלָה. דִּלְמָא מֵת דַּוְקָא. דְּכָל עַצְמוֹ שֶׁכָּתַב לָהּ גֵּט מֵחֲמַת כֵּן כָּתַב לָהּ, שֶׁאִם יָמוּת יִהְיֶה גֵּט לְמַפְרֵעַ, שֶׁלֹּא תִּזָּקֵק לְיָבָם. וּבְהַאי אוּנְסָא לָא נִיחָא לֵיהּ לְמִיבְטַל גִּיטָּא. אֲבָל בְּאוּנְסָא אַחֲרִינָא, דְּנִיחָא לֵיהּ לְבַטּוּלֵי גִּיטָּא בֵּיהּ — אֵימָא לָךְ: יֵשׁ אוֹנֶס בְּגִיטִּין. וּפְסַקֵיהּ מַבְרָא. הַנָּהָר הִפְסִיקוֹ. שֶׁהָיְתָה הַמַּעְבּוֹרֶת מִצַּד הָעִיר, וְלֹא יָכוֹל לַעֲבוֹר. חֲזוּ דַּאֲתַאי. שֶׁבָּאתִי. לָא שְׁמֵיהּ מָתְיָא. וְהָוֵי גִּיטָּא. וְאִם רָצְתָה — תִּינָּשֵׂא לְאַחֵר, וְגַם לִכְהוּנָּה נִפְסֶלֶת מֵהַיּוֹם.

תוספות רי"ד

אמר רבא ולענין גיטין אינו כן. פי' לענין גיטין אין טענת אונס מועלת שאם נתן גט לאשתו שאם לא אבוא עד זמן פלוני יהא גט. ונאנס ולא בא ה"ז גט ואין יכול לומר אנוס הייתי. אלמא קסבר אין אונס בגיטין. א"ד אמר רבא וכן לענין גיטין. אלמא קסבר יש אונס בגיטין. ואע"ג דקי"ל הלכה כלישנא בתרא. הכא הלכה כלישנא קמא דהכי אמרי' בגיטין בשמעתא קמייתא בפ' השולח. ההוא דא"ל אי לא נסיבנא מכאן ועד תלתין יומין להוי גיטא כי מטא יום תלתין א"ל הא טרחנא למאי נחוש לה. אי משום אונסא אין אונס בגיטין. אלמא קסבר לה לתלמודא דאין אונס בגיטין:

מסורת הש"ס

[וע' תוס' זבחים קב: ד"ה פליך]
[גיטין ל. לד.]
גיטין עו: ע"ז לז.
גיטין עב. ב"ב קלז.
גיטין עו:
שם ל. לד. נדרים כז:
[שבוע שנה חודש כצ"ל]

גליון הש"ס

תוס' ד"ה לא נשאו וכו' מקובלין היו כך. וכן בנדרים דף לה ע"א בר"ן ד"ה דיקא נמי:

זימנין דלא אניס, וסברה דאניס, ומיעגנא ויתבה. ומשום פרוצות, דאי אמרת לא ליהוי גיטא, זימנין דאניס ואמרה לא אניס, ואזלא ומינסבא, ונמצא גט בטל ובניה ממזרים. ומי איכא מידי דמדאורייתא לא להוי גט ומשום צנועות ומשום פרוצות שרינן אשת איש לעלמא?! אין, *כל דמקדש – אדעתא דרבנן מקדש, °ואפקעינהו רבנן לקידושי מיניה. אמר ליה רבינא לרב אשי: תינח קדיש בכספא, קדיש בביאה מאי איכא למימר? שויוה רבנן לבעילתו בעילת זנות. איכא דאמרי, אמר רבא: וכן לענין גיטין. אלמא קסבר רבא: יש אונס בגיטין, מיתיבי: "הרי זה גיטיך אם לא באתי מכאן ועד שנים עשר חדש" ומת בתוך שנים עשר חדש – אינו גט. מת – הוא דאינו גט, הא חלה – הרי זה גט! לעולם אימא לך חלה נמי אינו גט, והיא גופה קמ"ל, דאין גט לאחר מיתה. אין גט לאחר מיתה – הא תנא ליה רישא! דלמא לאפוקי מדרבותינו. ת"ש: "מעכשיו אם לא באתי מכאן ועד שנים עשר חדש" ומת בתוך שנים עשר חדש – הרי זה גט. מאי לאו – הוא הדין לחלה? לא, מת דוקא, דלא ניחא ליה דתפול קמי יבם. ת"ש: מההוא דאמר להו: "אי לא אתינא מכאן ועד שלשים יום ליהוי גיטא", אתא בסוף תלתין יומין ופסקיה מברא, ואמר להו: "חזו דאתאי, חזו דאתאי!" ואמר שמואל: לא שמיה מתיא. אונסא דשכיח שאני, דכיון דאיבעי ליה לאתנויי ולא אתני – איהו הוא דאפסיד אנפשיה. אמר רב שמואל בר יצחק: לא שנו אלא מתקנת עזרא ואילך, שאין בתי דינין קבועין אלא בשני ובחמישי. אבל קודם תקנת עזרא, שבתי דינין קבועין בכל יום – אשה נשאת בכל יום. קודם תקנת עזרא? מאי דהוה הוה! הכי קאמר: [א]אי איכא בתי דינין דקבועין האידנא כקודם תקנת עזרא – אשה נשאת בכל יום. הא בעינן *שקדו! דטריח ליה. מאי

זימנין דלא אניס. והוי גיטא. **וסברה.** דלמא אניס, ואינו גט, ותדאג להינשא. **ומינסבא.** וכשיבא ויאמר "נאנסתי" – נמלא גט בטל, ובניה מן האחרון ממזרים. לפיכך אמרו יהא גט. **דמדאורייתא לא הוי גיטא.** שמלינו טענת אונס מן התורה, שנאמר (דברים כב) "ולנערה לא תעשה דבר". **כל המקדש.** כל המקדש אשה – על דעת שהנהיגו חכמי ישראל בישראל הוא מקדשה, שיהיו קיימין קידושין לפי דברי חכמים, ויהיו בטילים לפי דברי חכמים, על ידי גיטין שהכשירו חכמים. **ואפקעוה רבנן לקידושין.** כשיבא גט כזה אחריהם. **תינח.** למימר אפקעתא כדקדיש בכספא, דנימא: גט זה עוקר הקידושין, ועושה מעות מתנה מעיקרן. **קדיש בביאה מאי.** אפקעתא מעיקרא איכא? בשלמא על ידי גט כשר, אע"פ שהקידושין קיימים עד עכשיו – גזירת הכתוב היא שהגט כורתו ומתיר איסורו מכאן ולהבא. אבל זה, שאינו גט מן התורה, ואתה מכשירו מפני דעתו של זה שקידשה על דעת חכמים, ושביטלו על פי חכמים – צריך אתה לומר שמעיקרן לא יהו קידושין, ואי קדיש בביאה, ואתה עוקר קידושין למפרע, מה תהא על ביאתו? **שויוה רבנן לבעילתו.** למפרע, על ידי גט שהוא מדבריהם, בעילת זנות. ויש בהן כח לעשות כן, שהרי הוא תלה בהן. שמעתי כל רבותי מפרשים "דקדיש בכספא" – דקידושי דרבנן נינהו. ואי אפשר לומר כן. חדא: דגזירה שוה היא "קיחה" "קיחה" משדה עפרון (קידושין דף ב.), וכל הלמד מגזירה שוה כמו שכתוב מפורש הוא לכל דבר. ועוד: אי דרבנן נינהו – היאך סוקלין על ידו, ומביאין חולין לעזרה על שגגתן? וסוף סוף כי קא משנינן שויוה רבנן לבעילתו בעילת זנות – על כרחך צריך אתה לפרש כמו שפירשתי, שהקידושין נעקרין מעיקרן ולא מכאן ולהבא. והמפרש לומר שויוה רבנן לכל מקדשי בביאה בעילת זנות – טעות גמור הוא, ובא להתיר אשת איש המתקדשת בביאה בלא גט מן הטעם הזה, ולא מלינו זאת בהתלמוד. **וכן לענין גיטין.** אלפיכך קאי, דטענינן טענת אונס בתנאי הגט להפקיעו. **שבתי דינין קבועין בכל יום.** כלומר, שקביעות כל הימים שוה. **והא בעינן שקדו.** שיהא טורח בסעודה שלשה ימים. **דטריח ליה.** אם טרח לפני השבת ותיקן צרכי סעודה – כונסה באחד בשבת או בשני בשבת. מאי

וסברה דאנים. ומן הדין לית לן למיחש דלמא אנים הוא, דרובן לא אניסי. ולהכי קרי להו צנועות, שמחמירים על עצמן אע"ג דמצי לאינסובי. [א] וגבי פרוצות לא גרסינן וסברה דלא אנים, אלא: ואמרה דלא אנים. פי': אפילו כשיצא הקול דאנים, אמרה דלא אנים. או אפילו כשתדע היא עצמה דאנים, ואחרים לא ידעו. ואם תאמר: מת תוך י"ב חודש נמי יהא גט מהאי טעמא? דזימנין דלא מת וסברה דמת, ומיעגנא ויתבה! ויש לומר: דמיתה קלא אית לה.

אדעתא דרבנן מקדש. לכן אומרים בשעת קידושין "כדת משה וישראל".

ואפקעינהו רבנן לקידושין מינה. בריש "השולח" (גיטין לג.) פירשתי.

תינח דקדיש בכספא. דהפקר ב"ד היה הפקר, והוו מעות מתנה, וממילא יהו כל בעילותיו זנות. קדיש בביאה מאי איכא למימר, איך יפקיעו ביאה של קידושין? ואפי' למ"ד ב"האשה רבה" (יבמות פט: ושם) דיש כח לחכמים לעקור דבר מן התורה – היינו כגון דליכא עבירה, כההיא ד"האשה רבה" דהדר לטיבלא. אבל היכא דאיכא עבירה, דמקודשת היא בביאה – מאי איכא למימר? ומשני: שויוה רבנן בעילותיו בעילת זנות, ואין כאן קדושין*.

איכא דאמרי אמר רבא וכן לענין גיטין. פסק ר"ח כלישנא קמא, דאין אונס בגיטין. והביא ראיה מדקאמר סתמא התלמוד בריש "השולח" (גיטין לד. ושם) גבי ההוא דאמר אי לא נסיבנא עד תלתין יומין ליהוי גיטא כו', ואי משום אונס – אין אונס בגיטין. וכן נראה, דאליבא דאיכא דאמרי הוו פירכי מכל הני דמייתי סייעתא ללישנא קמא, ולא סמכינן אשינויי דחיקי. וקשה לר"י: דמסיק בפרק "מי שאחזו" (שם עג. ושם) דבין דאמר הרי זה גיטיך אם מתי מחולי זה, בין אם אמר אם לא אעמוד מחולי זה, ונפל עליו הבית או נשכו נחש או אכלו ארי – דלא הוי גט. אלמא דיש אונס בגיטין! וליכא למימר דהתם לא מטעם דיש אונס קאמר דלא הוי גט, אלא משום דבין אם מתי מחולי זה בין אם לא אעמוד – משמע שימות מחמת זה החולי, וכשנפל עליו הבית או נשכו נחש – אינו גט דאין זה מחולי זה. דהא מוכח בהדיא התם דמטעם דיש אונס הוא, גבי ההוא גברא דזבין ארעא לחבריה וקביל עליה כל אונסא דאיתיליד בה כו', אמר רבא: אונס דלא שכיח הוא. ומייתי רבא סייעתא מהא דאכלו ארי אינו גט, אלמא אונס דלא שכיח יש טענת אונס לרבא, והכא קאמר רבא גופיה בלישנא קמא, שהוא עיקר, דאין אונס אפילו באונס דלא שכיח, כדמוכח הסוגיא! ואור"י: דג' ענייני אונס הן; דאונס דלא שכיח כלל כההיא ד"מי שאחזו", אפי' ללישנא קמא דרבא דהכא – יש אונס, דלא שייך התם לתקן משום צנועות ומשום פרוצות, דלעולם לא סברי צנועות דנפל עליו הבית או שהכישו נחש, כיון דלא שכיח כלל. ומשום פרוצות נמי ליכא למיחש, כיון דלא שכיח שיעשה כן. ואונס דשכיח, כגון ההיא דפסקיה מברא – אפילו לאיכא דאמרי אין אונס, דאיבעי ליה לאתנויי. אבל אונס דשכיח ולא שכיח – פליגי תרי לישני דרבא. והלכתא כלישנא קמא דרבא כדפירשנו. **שבתי** דינין קבועים בכל יום. וא"ת: וכי תיקן עזרא שלא יהו בתי דינין קבועים בכל יום אלא בב' ובה' בלבד? ועוד קשה: דאמרינן בשבת (ד' קכט: ושם) מי שיש לו זכות אבות יקיז בב' ובה'. וכי קודם עזרא לא היו מקיזין כל עיקר? ואומר ר"ת: דקודם תקנת עזרא לא היו קבועים בכל יום, אלא כשהיו צריכין לשום דין היו יושבין בכל יום, ועזרא תיקן שיהיו קבועין בב' ובה', וכל הרוצה לדון יבא וידון. והיו יכולין להקיז בכל יום קודם תקנת עזרא, כיון שלא היו קבועים. ור"י מירץ: שלא היו קבועים תחלה אלא בעיר אחת, ועזרא תיקן בכל עיר ועיר בב' ובה'. **אשה** נשאת בכל יום. קשה לרשב"א: אמאי נשאת בכל יום? תהא כאלמנה ותינשא בה' ותיבעל בששי, לפי שנאמר בו ברכה לאדם! וי"ל: דמשום ברכה לא היו קובעים יום, כדפרישית לעיל. ובאלמנה נמי לא קבעו שתיבעל בששי משום ברכה גרידא, אלא משום שקדו, שיהא שמח עמה ג' ימים, כדאמר לקמן (דף ה.). ובתולה דלא שייך ההוא טעמא, דליכא למימר משכים לאומנתו והולך לו, לפי שיש בה שבעת ימי המשתה – הלכך משום ברכה גרידא לא היו קובעים יום. **אי** איכא בתי דינין כו'. נראה לר"י: דמכל מקום אין נשאת בששי, דהא אין דנין בשבת, ועתה נוהגין לישא אף בששי, משום דאין ב"ד קבועין. ואם יש לו טענת בתולין – יכול לקבול בשבת בפני שלשה כמו בשאר ימות השבוע. ועוד: לפירוש הקונטרס, דוקא בימיהם קבעו יום הנישואין משום שעל ידי כך יתברר הדבר ויבואו עדים, מתוך שמתאספים העם לב"ד, ואין שייך לומר עכשיו כן.

ובשני

יבמות ל: קי. גיטין לג. עג. בבא בתרא מח:

[לעיל ב. לקמן ה.]

ח א מיי' פ"י מהל' אישות הל' טו סמג עשין מח טוש"ע אה"ע סי' סד סעי' ג:

[ועי' תוס' ב"ב מח:]

גליון הש"ס

גמ' ואפקעינהו רבנן. עי' תשובת רשב"א סי' אלף קסב:

הגהות מהר"ב רנשבורג

א] תד"ה וסברה דאניס וכו' וגבי פרוצות ל"ג וכו'. עי' נדה יב ע"א תד"ה צנוע וכו':

מַאי שָׁקְדוּ? דְּתַנְיָא: מִפְּנֵי מָה אָמְרוּ בְּתוּלָה נִשֵּׂאת לְיוֹם הָרְבִיעִי — שֶׁאִם הָיָה לוֹ טַעֲנַת בְּתוּלִים הָיָה מַשְׁכִּים לְב"ד. וְתִנָּשֵׂא בְּאֶחָד בְּשַׁבָּת, וְאִם הָיָה לוֹ טַעֲנַת בְּתוּלִים — הָיָה מַשְׁכִּים לְב"ד! שָׁקְדוּ חֲכָמִים עַל תַּקָּנַת בְּנוֹת יִשְׂרָאֵל, שֶׁיְּהֵא אָדָם טוֹרֵחַ בִּסְעוּדָה שְׁלֹשָׁה יָמִים: אֶחָד בְּשַׁבָּת, וְשֵׁנִי בְּשַׁבָּת, וּשְׁלִישִׁי בְּשַׁבָּת, וּבָרְבִיעִי כּוֹנְסָהּ. וּמִסַּכָּנָה וָאֵילָךְ נָהֲגוּ הָעָם לִכְנוֹס בִּשְׁלִישִׁי, וְלֹא מִיחוּ בְּיָדָם חֲכָמִים. וּבְשֵׁנִי לֹא יִכְנוֹס, וְאִם מֵחֲמַת הָאוֹנֶס — מוּתָּר. וּמַפְרִישִׁין אֶת הֶחָתָן מִן הַכַּלָּה לֵילֵי שַׁבָּת תְּחִלָּה, מִפְּנֵי שֶׁהוּא עוֹשֶׂה חַבּוּרָה. מַאי סַכָּנָה? אִילֵימָא דְּאָמְרִי: בְּתוּלָה הַנִּשֵּׂאת לְיוֹם הָרְבִיעִי תֵּיהָרֵג — נָהֲגוּ?! לְגַמְרֵי נִיעַקְרֵיהּ! אָמַר רַבָּה, דְּאָמְרִי: בְּתוּלָה הַנִּשֵּׂאת בְּיוֹם הָרְבִיעִי — תִּיבָּעֵל לַהֶגְמוֹן תְּחִלָּה. הַאי סַכָּנָה?! אוֹנֶס הוּא! מִשּׁוּם דְּאִיכָּא צְנוּעוֹת דְּמָסְרָן נַפְשַׁיְיהוּ לִקְטָלָא, וְאָתְיָין לִידֵי סַכָּנָה. וְלִידְרוֹשׁ לְהוּ דְּאוֹנֶס שָׁרֵי! אִיכָּא פְּרוּצוֹת, וְאִיכָּא נַמִי כֹּהֲנוֹת. וְלִיעַקְרֵיהּ! גְּזֵירָה עֲבִידָא דְּבָטְלָא, וְתַקַּנְתָּא דְּרַבָּנַן מִקַּמֵּי גְּזֵירָה לָא עָקְרִינַן. אִי הָכִי בִּשְׁלִישִׁי נַמִי אָתֵי וּבָעֵיל! מִסְּפֵיקָא לָא עָקַר נַפְשֵׁיהּ. וּבְשֵׁנִי לֹא יִכְנוֹס, וְאִם מֵחֲמַת הָאוֹנֶס — מוּתָּר. מַאי אוֹנֶס? אִילֵימָא הָא דַּאֲמַרַן — הָתָם קָרֵי לֵיהּ סַכָּנָה וְהָכָא קָא קָרֵי לֵיהּ אוֹנֶס? וְתוּ, הָתָם נָהֲגוּ, הָכָא — מוּתָּר! אָמַר רָבָא: דְּאָמְרִי שַׂר צָבָא בָּא לָעִיר. ה"ד? אִי דְּאָתֵי וְחָלֵיף — לִיעַכַּב! לָא צְרִיכָא, דְּאָתֵי וְקָבַע. בְּג' מִיהָא לִכְנוֹס! אַסְפַּרְוָוא דִּידֵיהּ בְּג' קָאָתוּ. וְאִיבָּעֵית אֵימָא: מַאי מֵחֲמַת הָאוֹנֶס — כִּדְתַנְיָ': הֲרֵי שֶׁהָיָה פִּתּוֹ אָפוּי, וְטִבְחוֹ טָבוּחַ, וְיֵינוֹ מָזוּג, וּמֵת אָבִיו שֶׁל חָתָן אוֹ אִמָּהּ שֶׁל כַּלָּה — מַכְנִיסִין אֶת הַמֵּת לְחֶדֶר, וְאֶת הֶחָתָן וְאֶת הַכַּלָּה לַחוּפָּה

וּבוֹעֵל

מַאי שֶׁקָּדוּ. הֵיכָן שָׁנִינוּ שֶׁקָּדוּ דְּמַקְשִׁינַן לָהּ הָכָא? אִי מִשּׁוּם דַּאֲמַר שְׁמוּאֵל לְעֵיל – לֵית לָן לְאוֹתְבֵיהּ מִינָּהּ לַאֲמוֹרָאָה אַחֲרִינָא. וּמִן הַסַּכָּנָה וְאֵילָךְ. לְקַמָּן מְפָרֵשׁ לָהּ. וּבְשֵׁנִי לֹא יִכְנוֹס. בִּשְׁבִיל אוֹתָהּ סַכָּנָה, וְאֵין צָרִיךְ לַעֲקוֹר בִּשְׁבִילָהּ תַּקָּנַת חֲכָמִים אֶלָּא יוֹם אֶחָד, וְיִהְיֶה טוֹרֵחַ מִיהַת שְׁנֵי יָמִים בְּצׇרְכֵי סְעוּדָה. וְאִם מֵחֲמַת הָאוֹנֶס. לְקַמָּן מְפָרֵשׁ. תְּחִלָּה. אִם בִּיאָה רִאשׁוֹנָה הִיא, מַפְרִישִׁין אוֹתָהּ מִמֶּנּוּ לֵילֵי שַׁבָּת. נָהֲגוּ. בִּתְמִיָּה. סַכָּנַת נְפָשׁוֹת הִיא, וְאַתְּ אָמְרַתְּ נָהֲגוּ לִכְנוֹס בְּיוֹם שְׁלִישִׁי, אֲבָל מִיעֲקַר רְבִיעִי לְגַמְרֵי לֹא עָקְרוּ? נִיעַקְרֵיהּ. וְיַתְקְנוּ לָהֶם יָמִים אֲחֵרִים. וְלִדְרוֹשׁ לְהוּ דְּאוֹנֶס שָׁרֵי. דְּנִבְעֶלֶת בְּאוֹנֶס אֵינָהּ נֶאֱסֶרֶת עַל בַּעְלָהּ, דְּיָלְפִינַן לְקַמָּן בְּפֶרֶק ד' (דף נא:) מִ"וְהִיא לֹא נִתְפָּשָׂה", וְלָא לִימְסְרוּ נַפְשַׁיְיהוּ לְמִיתָה. אִיכָּא פְּרוּצוֹת. דְּאִי מְקִילִינַן לְהוּ עָבְדִי בְּרָצוֹן, וְנֶאֱסָרוֹת עַל בַּעֲלֵיהֶן. וְאִיכָּא נַמִי כֹּהֲנוֹת. שֶׁנֶּאֱסָרוֹת עַל בַּעֲלֵיהֶן אַף בְּאוֹנֶס. וְאִינְהוּ מָסְרָן נַפְשַׁיְיהוּ לְמִיתָה, דְּאֵשֶׁת כֹּהֵן שֶׁנֶּאֶנְסָה אֲסוּרָה לְבַעְלָהּ, וּלְקַמָּן בְּפֶרֶק ד' (שם) יָלְפִינַן לָהּ. וְלִיעַקְרֵיהּ. הוֹאִיל וְזִמְנִין דְּאִיכָּא סַכָּנָה. בִּשְׁלִישִׁי נַמִי אָתֵי וּבָעֵיל. כֵּיוָן דְּיָדַע שֶׁהִתְחִילוּ לִנְהוֹג בִּשְׁלִישִׁי. מִסְּפֵיקָא לָא עָקַר נַפְשֵׁיהּ. כֵּיוָן דְּלָאו קְבִיעוּת גָּמוּר הוּא עַל יְדֵי תַּקָּנַת ב"ד, סְפֵיקָא הִיא לוֹ אִם יֵשׁ נִישּׂוּאִין הַיּוֹם בָּעִיר, וְלָא עָקַר נַפְשֵׁיהּ לָבֹא בָּעִיר. הָתָם נָהֲגוּ. מַשְׁמַע רוּבָּם נָהֲגוּ. הָכָא מוּתָּר. לָא גָּרְסִינַן לְכַתְּחִילָּה. וְהָכִי קָא מַתְמַהּ: הָכָא מוּתָּר קָתָנֵי, דְּמַשְׁמַע: אִם יִמָּלֵךְ אִישׁ יְחִידִי בְּבֵית דִּין – יַתִּירוּ לוֹ, אֲבָל נָהֲגוּ – לָא קָתָנֵי. שַׂר צָבָא בָּא לָעִיר. וְיַחְטְפוּ צׇרְכֵי סְעוּדָה מֵאֲשֶׁר יִמְלְאוּ. וְחָלֵיף. לְאַחַר רְבִיעִי. לִיעַכַּב. עַד יוֹם רְבִיעִי שֶׁל שַׁבָּת הַבָּא. בִּשְׁלִישִׁי לִכְנוֹס. לָמָּה נַתִּיר לוֹ לִקְדּוֹם כׇּל כָּךְ, שֶׁלֹּא יַטְרִיחַ בִּסְעוּדָה אֶלָּא יוֹם אֶחָד, וּמִיעַקְרָא תַּקַּנְתָּא דְּשָׁקְדוּ? אִיסְפְּרָווֹא דִּידֵיהּ. חֵיל מְשָׁרְתָיו הַמְּכִינִים לוֹ צׇרְכֵי סְעוּדָה, בִּלְשׁוֹן לַעַז הירניי"ש. כִּדְתַנְיָא. חָתָן שֶׁמֵּת אָבִיו בְּשֵׁנִי וְאֵין יָכוֹל לְהַמְתִּין עַד לְמָחָר, שֶׁצָּרִיךְ לְהַשְׁהוֹת אֶת הַמֵּת עַד שֶׁיִּכָּנְסוּ לַחוּפָּה. וְיֵינוֹ מָזוּג. בְּמַיִם, שֶׁיְּהֵא רָאוּי לִשְׁתִיָּה, וְשׁוּב אֵינוֹ מִתְקַיֵּים. אָבִיו שֶׁל חָתָן אוֹ אִמָּהּ שֶׁל כַּלָּה. דַּוְקָא נָקַט אָבִיו שֶׁל חָתָן, שֶׁהוּא הַטּוֹרֵחַ בְּצׇרְכֵי סְעוּדָה, וְאִמָּהּ שֶׁל כַּלָּה הִיא הַמְּכִינָה לָהּ תַּכְשִׁיטִין. לְפִיכָךְ, אִם יַעֲבוֹר הַמּוֹעֵד שׁוּב אֵין מֵכִין לָהֶם, וְהִתִּירוּ לָהֶם לְהַכְנִיס אֶת הַמֵּת לְחֶדֶר שֶׁלֹּא יִקְבְּרוּהוּ, דְּאִם כֵּן חָלָה אֲבֵילוּת עַל הָאָבֵל בִּסְתִימַת הַגּוֹלֵל, כִּדְלְקַמָּן, וְשׁוּב לֹא יוּכַל לִכְנוֹס עַד שֶׁיַּעֲבוֹר הָאֲבֵילוּת.

וּפוֹרֵשׁ

ובשני לא יכנום. פ"ה: אפילו בשעת הסכנה, דאין לעקור בשבילה תקנת חכמים אלא יום אחד. וקשה לר"י, דאמר לקמן: מאי אונס? אילימא הא דאמרן התם קרי ליה כו', הוה ליה למיפרך טפי רישא לסיפא, דקתני רישא ובשני לא יכנוס אפי' בשעת הסכנה! ואומר ריצב"א: דמשום הכי לא פריך ליה משום דאיכא לפרושי ואם מחמת האונס, פירוש: שיש סכנה אף ביום שלישי – מותר לכנוס בשני. ונראה לר"י: דמילתא באנפי נפשה היא, ולא איירי בסכנה. ובשני לא יכנוס – הוא הדין בג', אלא נקט בב' משום דבעי למיתני: ואם מחמת האונס מותר. **ולדרוש** להו דאונס שרי. וא"ת: והא אמרינן בפ' "בן סורר ומורה" (סנהדרין עד. ושם) על כל עבירות יעבור ואל יהרג, חוץ מעבודה זרה וג"ע וש"ד! ותירץ ר"ת: דאין חייבין מיתה על בעילת נכרי, דרחמנא אפקריה לזרעיה דנכרי, דכתיב (יחזקאל כג) "וזרמת סוסים זרמתם". ומייתי ראיה, דפריך בפ' "בן סורר ומורה" (שם:): הא אסתר פרהסיא הואי! ולא פריך והא אסתר גילוי עריות הויא, משמע דמשום עריות לא הוה מיחייבא. ומתוך כך התיר ר"ת לבת ישראל שהמירה ובא עליה גוי לקיימה לאותו גוי כשנתגייר, דלא שייך למימר אחד לבעל ואחד לבועל בביאת נכרי דהויא כביאת בהמה. ואין נראה לריב"ם, דהא ע"י ביאת גוי נאסרה לבעלה, כדאמר הכא דאיכא פרוצות. ובפ' "האשה שנתארמלה" (לקמן כו: ושם) גבי האשה שנחבשה בין הגוים אמרי' דברצון אסורה לבעלה. ואמר נמי במגילה (דף טו.): "כאשר אבדתי אבדתי" כאשר אבדתי מבית אבא אבדתי ממך, אלמא לגבי בעלה לא חשיבא בעילת נכרי כביאת בהמה, והוא הדין לבועל. אע"ג דאין זנות לבהמה ואין ביאת בהמה פוסלת ואוסרת, כדאמרי' בפ' "הבא על יבמתו" (יבמות נט:), ביאת נכרי הויא ביאה, וכי אפקריה רחמנא לזרעיה – הני מילי לענין דאין לו יחס, וזרעו חשוב כזרע בהמה! ויש לומר, דהכי פריך: ולדרוש להו דאונס שרי, לפי שהאשה היא קרקע עולם ולא עבדה מעשה, כדמשני בפרק "בן סורר ומורה": אסתר קרקע עולם היתה. והא דלא פריך התם גילוי עריות הויא – דפשיטא ליה דאיכא לשנויי קרקע עולם היא ואין לה למסור עצמה, אבל לענין חילול השם לא היה נראה לו שיועיל טעם דקרקע עולם, ומשני: קרקע עולם היתה, ואפילו חילול השם ליכא. ובפרק "מצות חליצה" (שם קג. ושם) דפריך גבי יעל: והא קמתהניא מעבירה! ומשני: טובתן של רשעים רעה היא אצל צדיקים, שהטיל בה זוהמא. ולא משני קרקע עולם היתה – משום דהתם לא פריך אמאי לא מסרה עצמה, דהא לא היה רוצה להמיתה, דאדרבה היה צריך שתשמרהו, אלא הכי פירושו: והא מתהניא מעבירה, למה משבחה הכתוב "מנשים באהל תבורך" ודרשינן בנזיר (דף כג: שם): גדולה עבירה לשמה ממצוה שלא לשמה, ופריך דיעל נמי הוה עבירה שלא לשמה, דהא מתהניא מעבירה! ומשני: דלא מתהניא, ועשתה עבירה לשמה כדי להציל את ישראל. **בתולה** הנשאת ברביעי תיבעל. לאו דוקא ברביעי, מדפריך לקמן: בשלישי נמי אתי ובעיל, שאינו מתכוין אלא להנאתו, אלא אגב דנקט לעיל שנשאת ברביעי תיהרג, דהתם מקפידים על קביעות יום כדי להעבירם על דתם, נקט ליה נמי הכא ברביעי. **ולדרוש** להו דאונס שרי. אין לפרש דפריך הכי: לדרוש כו' דשוב לא יהא סכנה אלא אונס, ואמאי קאמר ומסכנה ואילך, הוה ליה למימר ומן האונס ואילך! דא"כ – מאי משני משום פרוצות? דהא אפילו לא דרשינן להו דאונס שרי לא מסרי נפשייהו. דדוקא לצנועות אמרינן דמסרי נפשייהו. ועוד: וכי משום פרוצות יניחו להרוג הצנועות? אלא הכי פירושו: ולדרוש להו דאונס שרי, וכיון דליכא סכנה – אמאי לא מיחו בידם חכמים? ומשני: משום פרוצות לא מיחו בידם, אי נמי משום כהנות. **ותו** התם. בשלישי נהגו. ואמרינן בפ' בתרא דתענית (דף כו:): מאן דאמר נהגו – אורויי לא מורינן, והכא בשני – מותר לכתחלה. ופי' הקונטרס דפירש נהגו – רובא דעלמא, והכא מותר – יחידי, ולא גרסינן 'לכתחלה', אינו מיושב. **אי** דאתי וחליף ליעכב. פ"ה: חליף לאחר ד', וליעכב עד יום ד' של שבת הבא: וקשה לר"י: דאם כן מאי משני לא צריכא דאתי וקבע? אכתי ליעכב חדש או חדשים עד שילך! על כן נראה לר"י: שאם יתעכב כל יום ד' – אין לו לעכב עד יום ד' אחר, אלא יכנוס בג'. והכי פריך: אי אתי וחליף בד' גופיה – ליעכב עד דחליף! ומשני: דאתי וקבע כל יום ד'. **בשלישי** מיהא לכנום. ולא בעי למימר דאתי שר הצבא בג' – דא"כ יכנוס בד'. **איספרווא** דידיה בג' אתא. אין לתמוה: משום סעודה עקרינן תקנתא דרבנן ב' ימים, ומשום סכנה לא עקרינן אלא יום אחד?! דבעילת הגמון שכיח, שרגיל לבא ולבעול. ואי עקרינן שני ימים – אתא להשתכח. אבל אונס שר צבא – אינו אלא אקראי בעלמא: (לעיל) **תקנה** דרבנן מקמי גזרה לא עקרינן. כי פריך לעיל ליעקרוה לא משני תקנה דרבנן מקמי גזרה כו' כדמשני הכא משום דלעיל פריך וליעקרוה ויקבעו יום אחר כיון דאינו מתכוין אלא להעבירם על דת כשיקבעו יום אחר לא יחושו ולא מיעקרא תקנתא דרבנן הואיל ויהא יום אחד קבוע אבל הכא פריך וליעקרוה ולא יהא שום יום קבוע שאם יקבעו יום אתי ובעיל באותו יום ולהכי משני מקמי גזרה לא עקרינן תקנה דרבנן שלא יהא שום יום קבוע. (לעיל) **אי** הכי בשלישי נמי אתי ובעיל. פי' *אי אמרת בשלמא כדמעיקרא דאמרי בתולה שנשאת בד' תיהרג ואינן מתכוונין אלא להעבירם לא יחושו אם יעשו ביום ג' אלא אי אמרת משום בעילת ההגמון כיון שמתכוין להנאתו בשלישי נמי אתי ובעיל. [וע' תוס' שבת קכ:]

בועל

תניא הרי שהיה פתו אפויה וטבחו טבוח ויינו מזוג ונתן מים ע"ג בשר ומת אביו של חתן או אמו של כלה מכניסין את המת לחדר ואת החתן ואת הכלה לחופה ובועל בעילת מצוה ופורש ונוהג ז' ימי משתה ואח"כ נוהג ז' ימי אבילות וכל אותן הימים הוא ישן בין האנשים והיא ישנה בין הנשים. וכן מי שפירסה אשתו נדה ואין מונעים תכשיטין מן הכלה כל ל'. פי' מכניסים את וכו'. שלא יקברוהו ותחול עליו האבילות בסתימות הגולל ושוב לא יוכל לכונסה עד שיעבור ז' ימי האבל. אלא כונס תחלה ואח"כ יקברו המת וכיון דחלה עליו חתונה הויא גביה כרגל שלא אתיא אבילות וחיילא עליה. ונוהג ז' ימי המשתה תחלה ואח"כ ז' ימי האבילות וכל אותן הימים אינו מתיחד עמה שמא יבעול. ואבל אסור בתשמיש המטה ואף בז' ימי המשתה שהן אצלו כרגל דברים של צנעה נוהג ואין מונעים וכו' ואע"פ שהיא אבילה שלא תתגנה על בעלה. ודוקא אביו של חתן הטורח בצרכי סעודה. ואמה של כלה המכינה לה לתכשיטין דליכא איניש דטרח להו. אבל איפכא לא:

וּבוֹעֵל בְּעִילַת מִצְוָה וּפוֹרֵשׁ, וְנוֹהֵג שִׁבְעַת יְמֵי הַמִּשְׁתֶּה, וְאַחַר כָּךְ נוֹהֵג שִׁבְעַת יְמֵי אֲבֵילוּת. וְכָל אוֹתָן הַיָּמִים הוּא יָשֵׁן בֵּין הָאֲנָשִׁים וְהִיא יְשֵׁנָה בֵּין הַנָּשִׁים. *וְאֵין מוֹנְעִין תַּכְשִׁיטִין מִן הַכַּלָּה כָּל שְׁלֹשִׁים יוֹם. [א]וְדַוְקָא אָבִיו שֶׁל חָתָן אוֹ אִמָּהּ שֶׁל כַּלָּה, דְּלֵיכָּא אִינִישׁ דְּטָרַח לְהוּ, אֲבָל אִיפְּכָא — לָא. אָמַר רַפְרָם בַּר פַּפָּא אָמַר רַב חִסְדָּא: לֹא שָׁנוּ אֶלָּא שֶׁנָּתַן מַיִם עַל גַּבֵּי בָשָׂר. אֲבָל לֹא נָתַן מַיִם עַל גַּבֵּי בָשָׂר — מִזְדַּבַּן. אָמַר רָבָא: וּבִכְרַךְ, אע"פ שֶׁנָּתַן מַיִם עַל גַּבֵּי בָשָׂר — מִזְדַּבַּן. אָמַר רַב פָּפָּא: וּבִכְפָר, אע"פ שֶׁלֹּא נָתַן מַיִם עַל גַּבֵּי בָשָׂר — לָא מִזְדַּבַּן. וְאֶלָּא, דְּרַב חִסְדָּא הֵיכִי מַשְׁכַּחַתְּ לָהּ? אָמַר רַב אַשִׁי: כְּגוֹן מָתָא מְחַסְיָא, דְּמַפְקָא מִכְּרַךְ וּמַפְקָא מִכְּפָר. תַּנְיָא כְּוָותֵיהּ דְּרַב חִסְדָּא: [ב]הֲרֵי שֶׁהָיָה פִּתּוֹ אֲפוּיָה וְטִבְחוֹ טָבוּחַ וְיֵינוֹ מָזוּג, וְנָתַן מַיִם עַל גַּבֵּי בָשָׂר, וּמֵת אָבִיו שֶׁל חָתָן אוֹ אִמָּהּ שֶׁל כַּלָּה — מַכְנִיסִין אֶת הַמֵּת לְחֶדֶר וְאֶת הֶחָתָן וְאֶת הַכַּלָּה לַחוּפָּה, וּבוֹעֵל בְּעִילַת מִצְוָה וּפוֹרֵשׁ, וְנוֹהֵג שִׁבְעַת יְמֵי הַמִּשְׁתֶּה, וְאח"כ נוֹהֵג שִׁבְעַת יְמֵי אֲבֵילוּת. וְכָל אוֹתָן הַיָּמִים הוּא יָשֵׁן בֵּין הָאֲנָשִׁים וְאִשְׁתּוֹ יְשֵׁנָה בֵּין הַנָּשִׁים. וְכֵן *מִי שֶׁפֵּירְסָה אִשְׁתּוֹ נִדָּה — הוּא יָשֵׁן בֵּין הָאֲנָשִׁים וְהִיא יְשֵׁנָה בֵּין הַנָּשִׁים. *[ג]וְאֵין מוֹנְעִין תַּכְשִׁיטִין מִן הַכַּלָּה כָּל ל' יוֹם. בֵּין כָּךְ וּבֵין כָּךְ לֹא יִבְעוֹל לֹא בְּעֶרֶב שַׁבָּת וְלֹא בְּמוֹצ"שׁ. אָמַר מָר: הוּא יָשֵׁן בֵּין הָאֲנָשִׁים וְהִיא יְשֵׁנָה בֵּין הַנָּשִׁים. מְסַיֵּיעַ לֵיהּ לְרַבִּי יוֹחָנָן. דְּאָמַר רַבִּי יוֹחָנָן: [ד]אע"פ שֶׁאָמְרוּ אֵין אֲבֵילוּת בַּמּוֹעֵד — אֲבָל דְּבָרִים שֶׁל צִינְעָא נוֹהֵג. דָּרַשׁ רַב יוֹסֵף בְּרֵיהּ דְּרָבָא מִשְּׁמֵיהּ דְּרָבָא: [ה]ל"שׁ אֶלָּא שֶׁלֹּא בָּעַל, אֲבָל בָּעַל — אִשְׁתּוֹ יְשֵׁנָה עִמּוֹ. וְהָא הָכָא, דְּבְבָעַל עָסְקִינַן, וְקָתָנֵי: הוּא יָשֵׁן בֵּין הָאֲנָשִׁים וְהִיא יְשֵׁנָה בֵּין הַנָּשִׁים! כִּי קָאָמַר — [ו]אַפֵּירְסָה אִשְׁתּוֹ נִדָּה. הָא "וְכֵן" קָתָנֵי! הָכִי

ופורש. וְיִקָּבְרוּ אֶת הַמֵּת מִיָּד. דְּכֵיוָן דְּחָלָה עָלָיו אֲנִינוּת – הָוְיָא לְגַבֵּיהּ כְּרֶגֶל, וְלָא אָתְיָא אֲבֵילוּת וְחָיְילָא, וְנוֹהֵג שִׁבְעַת יְמֵי הַמִּשְׁתֶּה כו'. וְכָל אוֹתָן הַיָּמִים. שֶׁל יְמֵי הַמִּשְׁתֶּה וְשֶׁל אֲבֵילוּת. הוּא יָשֵׁן כו'. וְאֵין מִתְיַחֲדִין זֶה עִם זֶה, שֶׁמָּא יִבְעוֹל, וְאָבֵל אָסוּר בְּתַשְׁמִישׁ הַמִּטָּה, כִּדְיָלְפִינַן בְּ"אֵלּוּ מְגַלְּחִין" (מו"ק דף טו:). וְאַף בְּשִׁבְעַת יְמֵי הַמִּשְׁתֶּה שֶׁהֵן כְּרֶגֶל נוֹהֵג הוּא אֲבֵילוּת שֶׁל דִּבְרֵי צִינְעָא, דְּהַיְינוּ אִיסּוּר תַּשְׁמִישׁ, כִּדְלְקַמָּן. וְאֵין מוֹנְעִין. בִּשְׁבִיל הָאֲבֵילוּת אֵין אוֹסְרִין עָלֶיהָ תַּכְשִׁיטֶיהָ, שֶׁלֹּא תִּתְגַּנֶּה עַל בַּעְלָהּ. כָּל שְׁלֹשִׁים יוֹם. וְאע"פ שֶׁהֵן יְמֵי אֲבֵילוּת לִשְׁאָר בְּנֵי אָדָם, וְכָל שֶׁכֵּן מִשְּׁלֹשִׁים וְאֵילָךְ. דְּלֵיכָּא אִינִישׁ דְּטָרַח. אִם יַפְסִידוּ מַה שֶּׁהֵכִינוּ. שֶׁנָּתַן מַיִם עַל גַּבֵּי בָשָׂר. שׁוּב אֵינוֹ רָאוּי לְמוֹכְרוֹ בַּמַּקּוּלִין. בִּכְרַךְ. שְׁכִיחִי אֱינָשֵׁי טוּבָא, וְיֵשׁ קוֹפָּלִים הַרְבֵּה. אֶלָּא דְּרַב חִסְדָּא. דְּמַפְלִיג בֵּין נָתַן לְלֹא נָתַן. הֵיכִי מַשְׁכַּחַתְּ לָהּ. לֹא בִּכְרַךְ וְלֹא בִּכְפָר. דְּמַפְקָא מִכְּרַךְ וּמַפְקָא מִכְּפָר. מוּפְלָאָה מִכְּלַל כְּרַךְ, וּמוּפְלָאָה מִכְּלַל כְּפָר. גְּדוֹלָה מִכְּפָר וּקְטַנָּה מִכְּרַךְ. תַּנְיָא כְּרַב חִסְדָּא. דְּמוֹקֵי לָהּ בְּנָתַן מַיִם עַל גַּבֵּי בָשָׂר. וְכֵן מִי שֶׁפֵּירְסָה אִשְׁתּוֹ נִדָּה. בִּכְנִיסָתָהּ לַחוּפָּה. הוּא יָשֵׁן כו'. וְאֵין נֶאֱמָנִין זֶה עִם זֶה. בֵּין כָּךְ וּבֵין כָּךְ. בֵּין יֵשׁ אוֹנֶס בֵּין אֵין אוֹנֶס. לֹא יִבְעוֹל. בְּעִילָה רִאשׁוֹנָה. לֹא בְּעֶרֶב שַׁבָּת כו'. בְּלֵיל שַׁבָּת, מִפְּנֵי שֶׁעוֹשֶׂה חַבּוּרָה. וְלֹא בְּמוֹצ"שׁ. לְקַמָּן מְפָרֵשׁ. מְסַיֵּיעַ לֵיהּ. הָא דְּקָתָנֵי דְּאָסוּר בְּתַשְׁמִישׁ בְּשִׁבְעַת יְמֵי הַמִּשְׁתֶּה, שֶׁהֵן לוֹ כְּרֶגֶל. שֶׁל צִינְעָא. שֶׁאֵינוֹ נִיכָּר לַבְּרִיּוֹת שֶׁהוּא אָבֵל בְּכָךְ. לֹא שָׁנוּ. דְּאֵין נֶאֱמָנִין לְהִתְיַיחֵד. אֶלָּא שֶׁלֹּא בָּעַל. דְּתַקִּיף לֵיהּ יִצְרֵיהּ. דִּבְבָעַל עָסְקִינַן. דְּקָתָנֵי בּוֹעֵל בְּעִילַת מִצְוָה לִפְנֵי קְבוּרַת הַמֵּת. כִּי קָאָמַר. רָבָא לֹא שָׁנוּ, אַפֵּירְסָה אִשְׁתּוֹ נִדָּה קָאָמַר. דְּכֵיוָן דְּנִדָּה חֲמוּרָה, בַּעַל מְהֵימַן עֲלָהּ, דְּלָא אָתֵי לְזַלְזוּלֵי בְּאִיסּוּר כָּרֵת. הָא וְכֵן קָתָנֵי. קס"ד אַכּוּלָּהּ מִילְּתָא דַּאֲבֵילוּת מְדַמֵּינַן לֵיהּ, וּבַאֲבֵילוּת דְּבַעַל עָסְקִינַן. ה"ק

בועל בעילת מצוה ופורש. קודם שיקבר המת. אבל לאחר שנקבר – לא. כדאמרינן בסמוך: דברים של צינעא נוהג. ודייק לה מדקתני כל אותן הימים הוא ישן בין האנשים כו'. מיהו, מרישא דהכא לא ה"מ למידק דדוקא כשהמת בחדר הוא דשרי בעילת מצוה. דמצי לדחויי: דבועל בעילת מצוה – היינו אפי' לאחר שחל עליו אבילות. אבל קשה לרשב"א: אמאי לא דייק מדקתני "ופורש", מכלל דנוהג דברים של צינעא, מדלא התיר אלא בעילת מצוה דוקא! ואור"י: דהמ"ל פורש משום דם בתולים, כדאמרינן בפ' "תינוקת" (נדה דף סה:). אבל מ"הוא ישן בין האנשים" דייק שפיר דהוי משום אבילות, דאי משום נדות, כיון דבעיל – אשתו ישנה עמו, כדאמר רב יוסף בסמוך. ועוד: דכל אותן הימים משמע דבכולהו הוי חד טעמא, דהיינו משום אבילות. והשתא מקילינן טפי באנינות דאורייתא מבאבילות דרבנן, מידי דהוה אנעילת סנדל ועטיפת הראש וכפיית המטה. **בעילת** מצוה. קרי לה בעילת מצוה משום דכתיב "כי בועליך עושיך" ואמרי' (סנהדרין דף כב:): אין אשה כורתת ברית אלא למי שעושה אותה כלי. וע"י כך מידבק בה, ובאין לידי פריה ורביה. ולהכי קרי לה לבעילה ראשונה בעילת מצוה. **אבל** איפכא לא. וה"ה אם אבלים מחמת שאר קרובים. תימה: דאמר בפ"ג דמועד קטן (דף כג. ושם): מתה אשתו – אסור לישא עד שיעברו ג' רגלים, ואם אין לו בנים – מותר לישא לאלתר משום פריה ורביה. הניחה לו בנים קטנים – מותר לישא לאלתר, משום פרנסתם. והכא אמר אבל איפכא לא, ומשמע דבאין לו בנים עסקינן, מדקאמר דליכא דטרח להו, משמע דבבחור איירי! וי"ל: דלאלתר לאו דוקא, אלא כלומר מותר לאחר ז'. ומיהו, לבעול אסור עד לאחר ל', כדמוכח בתר הכי במעשה שמתה אשתו של יוסף הכהן, ואמר לאחותה בבית הקברות: לאי ופרנסי בני אחותיך, ואעפ"כ לא בא עליה עד זמן מרובה, מאי זמן מרובה – שלשים יום, מכלל דכנסה תוך ל'. ותוך שבעה ודאי אסור, כדמוכח הכא. ומה שאמר לה בבה"ק לא היה זה כניסה אלא שידוכין בעלמא. ונראה לר"י: דודאי אותו שיש לו בנים קטנים מותר לישא תוך ל', כדמשמע בעובדא דיוסף הכהן. אבל אותו שאין לו בנים כלל – אסור לישא עד לאחר שלשים, כיון שאין יכול לבעול תוך שלשים. וכן משמע במס' שמחות (פ"ז), דתניא: בד"א – כשיש לו בנים גדולים, אבל אין לו בנים או שיש לו בנים קטנים – מותר לישא אחרת לאחר ל'. משמע דאסור אפי' לישא תוך שלשים. ואע"ג דיש לו בנים קטנים מותר לישא תוך שלשים – מ"מ נקט אחר שלשים משום אין לו בנים. ור"ת ר"ל: דבאין לו בנים – אפי' לבעול שרי תוך שלשים אחר ז', משום פריה ורביה. וההיא דשמחות אינה מתיישבת כפי'. ונראה דבים לו בנים קטנים שרי לישא, ואפי' אם היא נמי אבילה – מפני שמפרנסת בניו. ואע"פ שאפשר באחרת, כדמוכח בעובדא דיוסף הכהן שהיתה אבילה מאחותה. ומיהו, אין כל כך ראיה, דשמא שאני התם לפי שהיא תרחם על בני אחותה יותר מאחרת. ואע"ג דתנן בפרק "החולץ" (יבמות דף מא. ושם): כל הנשים יתארסו חוץ מאלמנה, מפני האיבול, ולא מפליג מידי, משמע שאסורה אפי' למי שיש לו בנים קטנים כשהיא אבילה – התם משום דבלאו הכי אסורה, דצריכה להמתין ג' חדשים משום הבחנה. ואור"ת: דאפי' מתו אביו ואמו יכול לכנוס אחר ל'. והא דאמרי' במועד קטן (דף כב:): על כל המתים נכנס לבית המשתה אחר ל', על אביו ועל אמו אחר י"ב חדשים – ה"מ בשאר שמחות, אבל לישא אשה, שהיא מצוה יתירה – מותר, ואפי' יש לו בנים, משום שנאמר (קהלת יא) "בבקר זרע [את] זרעך ולערב אל תנח ידך". והביא ראיה מדתניא סתם כל ל' יום לנישואין, ולא מפליג בין אביו ואמו לשאר קרובים – משמע דבכולהו לאחר ל' מותר. וה"ר יוסף הביא ראיה לדבריו, דתנן במסכת שמחות (פ"ט) בהדיא: על כל המתים אסור לילך לבית המשתה עד שישלימו ל' יום, ועל אביו ועל אמו אסור כל שנים עשר חדש, אא"כ היה של מצוה. אלמא שרי בכל משתה של מצוה. ול"ע אי קאי נמי ארישא, ושרי אפי' תוך ל' יום. **כגון** מתא מחסיא. תימה: רב חסדא מאי דוחקיה לאוקומי בנתן מים על גבי בשר? נוקמה בכפר, אע"פ שלא נתן מים על גבי בשר! ויש לומר: משום דניחא ליה לרב חסדא לאוקמה ברוב עיירות שהן בינוניות. וה"ק: כגון מתא מחסיא ורוב עיירות. ומש"ה נקט נמי בברייתא דמייתי "ונתן מים על גבי בשר", משום דאיירי ברוב עיירות. **מסייע** ליה לר' יוחנן כו'. מועד וחתן משוה אותן בכ"מ, כההיא דתניא בפ"ק דמועד קטן (דף ז: ושם): חתן שנולד בו נגע – נותנין לו ז' ימי המשתה לו ולאיצטליתו ולכסותו, וכן ברגל נותנין לו כל ימות הרגל. **אבל** דברים של צינעא נוהג. פי': חובה לעשות כן, ולא רשות. מדמייתי סייעתא מן הברייתא. וא"ת: רב ושמואל, דאמרי בפרק בתרא דמועד קטן (דף כד.): דתשמיש המטה בשבת של ז' ימי אבילות רשות, תיקשי להו ברייתא דהכא! ואין סברא לחלק בין מועד לשבת, ומקילין בשבת טפי. אלא נראה לר"י: דרב ושמואל מפלגי בין חתן למועד ושבת. אבל קשה: דכל איתן הימים הוא ישן בין האנשים – משמע אפי' בשבת! ופסקו ה"ג כר' יוחנן, ופירשו: אע"ג דקיימא לן כדברי המיקל באבל – ה"מ בתנאי, אבל באמוראי לא. ואור"י: דודאי נראה דהלכה כר' יוחנן, מדאמר התלמוד הכא מסייע ליה לר' יוחנן.

והלעת

ט א ב מיי' פי"א מהל' אבל הל' ח סמג עשין ב טוש"ע יו"ד סי' שמב וסי' שפג סעי' ב [רב אלפס כאן ובמ"ק פ"ג דף רלא.]

י ג מיי' וסמג שם טוש"ע שם סי' שפא סעי' ו:

יא ד מיי' פ"י שם הל' ג סמג שם טוש"ע שם סי' שלט סעי' ב [עי' כ"מ]:

יב ה ו מיי' פכ"ב מהל' איסורי ביאה הל"א סמג לאוין קכו טוש"ע אה"ע סי' כב סעי' א וטוש"ע יו"ד סי' שפג סעי' ב:

תוספות רי"ד

אמר רפרם בר פפא א"ר חסדא לא שנו אלא שניתן מים ע"ג בשר אבל לא ניתן מים ע"ג בשר מיזדבן. אמר רבא ובכרך אע"פ שניתן מים על גבי בשר מיזדבן. א"ר פפא ובכפר אע"פ שלא ניתן מים ע"ג בשר לא מיזדבן. ואלא דרב חסדא היכי משכחת לה כגון מתא מחסיא דמפקא מכפר ומפקא מכרך: אמר מר הוא ישן בין האנשים וכו'. מסייע ליה לר' יוחנן דאמר ר"י אע"פ שאמרו אין אבילות במועד אבל דברים שבצנעה נוהג. פי' ז' ימי חתונות כשבעת ימי הרגל הן לו. ומפני שתשמיש המטה הוי דבר של צנעה שאין בני העולם מרגישים אסור: דרש ר"י ברי' דרבא משמיה דרבא לא שנו אלא שלא בעל שיצרו תוקפו אבל בעל אשתו ישנה עמו בבית. והא הכא בבעל עסקינן וקתני הוא ישן בין האנשים וכו'. כי קאמר ר"י אפירסה נדה. והא וכן קתני ה"ק וכן מי שפירסה אשתו נדה ולא בעל הוא ישן בין האנשים ואשתו ישנה בין הנשים פי' אבל [בעל] כל נדה דעלמא מתקיים בעלה בבית וכשמת אביו של חתן או אמה של כלה צריכי שימור:

[יומא עח:]

[עי' תוס' יומא יח: ד"ה יחודי וכו' אריכות בסוגיא דהכא]

יומא דף עח:

גליון הש"ס

רש"י ד"ה כל ל' יום. ע' מג"א סי' תרי"ג ס"ק י"ב:

הָכִי קָאָמַר: וְכֵן מִי שֶׁפֵּירְסָה אִשְׁתּוֹ נִדָּה וְלֹא בָּעַל — הוּא יָשֵׁן בֵּין הָאֲנָשִׁים, וְאִשְׁתּוֹ יְשֵׁנָה בֵּין הַנָּשִׁים. לְמֵימְרָא דַּאֲבֵילוּת קִילָּא לֵיהּ מִנִּדָּה? וְהָאָמַר רַבִּי יִצְחָק בַּר חֲנִינָא אָמַר רַב הוּנָא: *[א] כָּל מְלָאכוֹת שֶׁאִשָּׁה עוֹשָׂה לְבַעְלָהּ, נִדָּה עוֹשָׂה לְבַעְלָהּ, חוּץ מִמְּזִיגַת הַכּוֹס וְהַצָּעַת הַמִּטָּה וְהַרְחָצַת פָּנָיו יָדָיו וְרַגְלָיו. וְאִלּוּ גַּבֵּי אֲבֵילוּת תַּנְיָא: אע"פ שֶׁאָמְרוּ: אֵין אָדָם רַשַּׁאי לָכוֹף אֶת אִשְׁתּוֹ לִהְיוֹת כּוֹחֶלֶת וְלִהְיוֹת פּוֹקֶסֶת, [ב] בֶּאֱמֶת אָמְרוּ: מוֹזֶגֶת לוֹ הַכּוֹס, וּמַצַּעַת לוֹ הַמִּטָּה, וּמַרְחֶצֶת לוֹ פָּנָיו יָדָיו וְרַגְלָיו! לָא קַשְׁיָא, כָּאן — בַּאֲבֵילוּת דִּידֵיהּ, כָּאן — בַּאֲבֵילוּת דִּידָהּ. וְהָא אָבִיו שֶׁל חָתָן אוֹ אִמָּהּ שֶׁל כַּלָּה קָתָנֵי! כִּי קָתָנֵי — אַשְּׁאָרָא. וּמִי שָׁאנֵי בֵּין אֲבֵילוּת דִּידֵיהּ לַאֲבֵילוּת דִּידָהּ? וְהָתַנְיָא: *מִי שֶׁמֵּת חָמִיו אוֹ חֲמוֹתוֹ [ג] אֵינוֹ יָכוֹל לָכוֹף אֶת אִשְׁתּוֹ לִהְיוֹת כּוֹחֶלֶת וְלִהְיוֹת פּוֹקֶסֶת, אֶלָּא כּוֹפֶה מִטָּתוֹ וְנוֹהֵג עִמָּהּ אֲבֵילוּת. וְכֵן הִיא שֶׁמֵּת חָמִיהָ אוֹ חֲמוֹתָהּ אֵינָהּ רַשָּׁאָה לִהְיוֹת כּוֹחֶלֶת וְלִהְיוֹת פּוֹקֶסֶת, אֶלָּא כּוֹפָה מִטָּתָהּ וְנוֹהֶגֶת עִמּוֹ אֲבֵילוּת! תְּנֵי בַּאֲבֵילוּת דִּידֵיהּ: הוּא יָשֵׁן בֵּין הָאֲנָשִׁים וְאִשְׁתּוֹ יְשֵׁנָה בֵּין הַנָּשִׁים. הָא "וְכֵן" קָתָנֵי! כִּי קָתָנֵי — אַכִּיחוּל וְאַפִּירְכּוּס. וְהָא "עִמּוֹ" קָתָנֵי, מַאי לָאו עִמּוֹ בַּמִּטָּה? לֹא, עִמּוֹ בַּבַּיִת. *וּכְדַאֲמַר לֵיהּ רַב לְחִיָּיא בְּרֵיהּ: [ד] בְּאַפַּהּ — נְהוֹג אֲבֵילוּתָא, דְּלָא בְּאַפַּהּ — לָא תִּנְהוֹג אֲבֵילוּתָא. רַב אַשִׁי אָמַר: מִי קָמְדַמֵּית אֲבֵילוּתָא דְּהָכָא לַאֲבֵילוּתָא דְּעָלְמָא? ●אֲבֵילוּתָא דְּעָלְמָא — חֲמִיר, וְלָא אָתֵי לְזַלְזוּלֵי בֵּיהּ. אֲבֵילוּת דְּהָכָא, כֵּיוָן דְּאַקִילוּ רַבָּנַן — אָתֵי לְזַלְזוּלֵי בֵּיהּ. מַאי קוּלָּא? אִילֵימָא דְּקָתָנֵי בּוֹעֵל בְּעִילַת מִצְוָה וּפוֹרֵשׁ — הָתָם מִשּׁוּם דְּלָא חָל עָלָיו אֲבֵילוּתָא; אִי לְרַבִּי אֱלִיעֶזֶר — *עַד שֶׁיֵּצֵא מִפֶּתַח הַבַּיִת, אִי לְרַבִּי יְהוֹשֻׁעַ — עַד שֶׁיִּסָּתֵם הַגּוֹלֵל! אֶלָּא דְּקָתָנֵי: נוֹהֵג שִׁבְעַת יְמֵי הַמִּשְׁתֶּה, וְאח"כ נוֹהֵג שִׁבְעַת יְמֵי אֲבֵילוּת. אָמַר מָר: [ה] בֵּין כָּךְ וּבֵין כָּךְ לֹא יִבְעוֹל לֹא בְּעֶרֶב שַׁבָּת וְלֹא בְּמוֹצ"שׁ. בִּשְׁלָמָא בְּעֶרֶב שַׁבָּת — מִשּׁוּם חַבּוּרָה, אֶלָּא בְּמוֹצָאֵי שַׁבָּת אַמַּאי לֹא? אָמַר רַבִּי זֵירָא: מִשּׁוּם

רש"י

ה"ק כו'. כְּלוֹמַר, כִּי קָאָמַר 'וְכֵן' — אַהוּא יָשֵׁן בֵּין הָאֲנָשִׁים וְהִיא יְשֵׁנָה בֵּין הַנָּשִׁים קָאָמַר, וּלְעוֹלָם הָךְ דְּשֶׁלֹּא בָּעַל קָאֵי. קִילָּא לֵיהּ. לַעֲבוֹר עָלֶיהָ מִנִּדָּה, דַּאֲבֵילוּת לָא מְהֵימְנַתְּ לֵיהּ וְאַנִּדָּה מְהֵימְנַתְּ לֵיהּ. מְלָאכוֹת שֶׁהָאִשָּׁה עוֹשָׂה לְבַעְלָהּ. לְקַמָּן תָּנֵי לְהוּ בְּפֶרֶק "אַף עַל פִּי". חוּץ מִמְּזִיגַת הַכּוֹס. לְהוֹשִׁיט לוֹ. וְהַצָּעַת הַמִּטָּה וְהַרְחָצַת פָּנָיו כו'. שֶׁדֶּרֶךְ קֵירוּב וְחִיבָּה הֵן, וּבָאִין לִידֵי הֶרְגֵּל דָּבָר. אֵין אָדָם רַשַּׁאי לָכוֹף אֶת אִשְׁתּוֹ. בִּימֵי אֶבְלָהּ, כְּשֶׁמֵּת אָבִיהָ אוֹ אִמָּהּ. פּוֹקֶסֶת. מַעֲבֶּרֶת שְׂרָק עַל פָּנֶיהָ. מוֹזֶגֶת לוֹ. וְלָא חָיְישִׁינַן לְהֶרְגֵּל דָּבָר. אַלְמָא: אֲבֵילוּת חֲמִירָא לֵיהּ. כָּאן בַּאֲבֵילוּת דִּידֵיהּ. לְעוֹלָם אֲבֵילוּת קִילָּא לֵיהּ מִנִּדָּה, וְהָנֵי מַתְנִיָתָא הָכִי מְתָרְצָן: הָא דְּקָתָנֵי לְעֵיל הוּא יָשֵׁן בֵּין הָאֲנָשִׁים כו' — בַּאֲבֵילוּת דִּידֵיהּ, וְהָךְ דְּקָתָנֵי מוֹזֶגֶת לוֹ כו' — בַּאֲבֵילוּת דִּידָהּ קָאֵי. דְּקָתָנֵי: אֵין אָדָם רַשַּׁאי לָכוֹף כו'. אַלְמָא בַּאֲבֵילוּת דִּידָהּ קָיְימִינַן, שֶׁאֵינָהּ רוֹצָה לִכְחוֹל וְלִפְקוֹס. וְהַיְינוּ טַעְמָא דְּמוֹזֶגֶת, דְּאִם יִתְגַּבֵּר יִצְרוֹ עָלָיו, כֵּיוָן דַּאֲבֵילוּת דִּידָהּ הוּא — אֵינָהּ שׁוֹמַעַת לוֹ. וְהָא אָבִיו שֶׁל חָתָן כו'. אַלְמָא בַּאֲבֵילוּת דִּידָהּ נַמִּי אַחְמִיר תַּנָּא דִּלְעֵיל. כִּי קָתָנֵי. אִמָּהּ שֶׁל כַּלָּה — אַשְּׁאָרָא, אַ"מַכְנִיסִים הַמֵּת לְחֶדֶר". אֲבָל "הוּא יָשֵׁן בֵּין הָאֲנָשִׁים" — אַאֲבֵילוּת דְּחָתָן קָאֵי. וְנוֹהֶגֶת עִמּוֹ אֲבֵילוּת. אַלְמָא מִדְּלָא קָתָנֵי בַּאֲבֵילוּת דִּידֵיהּ הוּא יָשֵׁן בֵּין הָאֲנָשִׁים — שְׁמַע מִינָּהּ חֲמִיר לֵיהּ, וְלָא שָׁנֵי לָן. ה"ג: תְּנֵי בַּאֲבֵילוּת דִּידֵיהּ הוּא יָשֵׁן כו'. הָכִי גָּרְסִינַן. וְהָא עִמּוֹ קָתָנֵי מַאי לָאו עִמּוֹ בַּמִּטָּה. אַלְמָא אֲבֵילוּת דִּידֵיהּ נַמִּי מְהֵימָן. לֹא עִמּוֹ בַּבַּיִת. וְטַעְמָא לָאו מִשּׁוּם דִּמְהֵימָן נָקַט לָהּ, אֶלָּא לְאַשְׁמוֹעִינַן דְּאֵין אֲבֵילוּתוֹ מוּטָּל עָלֶיהָ אֶלָּא בְּפָנָיו מִשּׁוּם כְּבוֹדוֹ. וְכֵן הוּא אֵין אֲבֵילוּתָהּ מוּטָּל עָלָיו אֶלָּא לְפָנֶיהָ וְלִכְבוֹדָהּ. כְּדַאֲמַר לֵיהּ רַב לְחִיָּיא בְּרֵיהּ. כְּשֶׁמֵּת חָמִיו: בְּאַפַּהּ נְהוֹג אֲבֵילוּתָא כו'. פְּלוּגְתָּא דְּרַבִּי אֱלִיעֶזֶר וְרַבִּי יְהוֹשֻׁעַ בְּמוֹעֵד קָטָן. גּוֹלֵל. זֶהוּ כִּסּוּי שֶׁל אֲרוֹן הַמֵּת. מִשּׁוּם

תוספות

והצעת המטה. נראה לר"י דהצעת המטה דהכא היינו פריסת סדינין, שהוא דבר של חיבה. אבל הצעת כרים וכסתות, שאינן דברים של חיבה — שרי לנדה. והביא ראיה מדתנן בפ' "אע"פ" (לקמן נט:): הכניסה לו ג' שפחות — אינה מצעת לו המטה ואינה עושה בצמר. ארבע — יושבת בקתדרא. ואמרינן בגמרא: אע"פ שאמרו ד' יושבת בקתדרא — אבל מוזגת לו כוס, ומצעת לו המטה, ומרחצת לו פניו ידיו ורגליו. ופי' בקונטרס: דהא דתנא ג' אינה מצעת לו המטה — היינו הצעת כרים וכסתות, דהוי דבר שיש טורח. אבל מצעת לו המטה — היינו פריסת סדין ולבדין, דמילי דחיבה נינהו שתחבב עליו, ואין בו טורח. וההיא הצעה של חיבה נראה דדוקא אסור. וכן משמע, דמזכירה בהדי מזיגת כוס והרחצת פניו ידיו ורגליו כי התם. מיהו, לספרים דל"ג במשנה אלא: ואינה מצעת המטה, ול"ג 'לו' ובגמרא גרסינן 'לו' — אין ראיה משם שיהו תרי גווני הצעה, דמתני' איירי בהצעת שאר מטות, ובגמרא איירי בהצעת מטה לבעלה לבדו.

פוקסת. פ"ה: מעברת שרק על פניה. ואין נראה, דאמר בפ"ב לקמן (דף יז.): לא שרק ולא פירכוס. משמע דתרי מילי נינהו. דפוקסת דהכא — היינו פירכוס, כדאמרי' בסמוך: כי קתני — אכיחול ואפירכוס. ובשילהי "המצניע" (שבת צה.) קתני: פוקסת ומעברת שרק על פניה. ולקמן בפ"ב פ"ה: פירכוס — קליעת שער. וקשה לר"י: דבשילהי "המצניע" (שם צד: ושם) קתני גודלת ופוקסת? אלא נראה דאחד מתיקוני נשים הוא.

ומי שאני בין אבילות דידיה לאבילות דידה. תימה: דבלאו מילתא דרב יוסף הוי מצי למיפרך ברייתות אהדדי! וי"ל: דאי לאו הוה מילתא דרב יוסף הוה מפלגינן בין שעת חופה לשלא בשעת חופה. דבשעת חופה — יצרו תוקפו אע"ג דבעל. אבל לרב יוסף לא מצי לפלוגי בהכי, דהא בבעל חשיב ליה כאשתו ישנה, דאפי' בשעת חופה אשתו ישנה עמו בנדה ובאבילות דידה, ואפילו הכי באבילות דידיה קתני: הוא ישן בין האנשים, ולהכי פריך שפיר. ולרשב"א נראה דאי לאו דרב יוסף — לא הוה קשה מידי. דעמו ועמה קתני בברייתא — לאו עמו במטה אלא עמה בבית, אבל לרב יוסף דבאבילות דידה אשתו ישנה עמו — א"כ הא דקתני נוהג עמה אבילות היינו עמה במטה, דומיא דהכא באבילות דידיה הוי עמו במטה. והא דמשני תני באבילות דידיה הוא ישן — אינו מגיה הברייתא, אלא מפרש ד'עמו' דקתני בברייתא דהכי הוא. ופריך: והא 'עמו' קתני, מאי לאו עמו במטה? פי': דומיא ד'עמה', ומשני: לא, עמו בבית, כדא"ל רב כו'.

עד שיסתם הגולל. בכמה מקומות פי' רש"י דגולל הוי כיסוי ארון, ודופק היינו קרשים שבצידי הארון. ונקרא דופק על שם שהגולל דופק עליו.

וכעין זה פי' בערוך. וקשה לר"ת: דאמר בפרק "מי שמתו" (ברכות יט: ושם): מדלגין היינו על גבי ארונות. ואיך היו מדלגין? והלא הגולל והדופק מטמא באהל, כדאמרינן ב"העור והרוטב" (חולין קכו: ושם)! ועוד, דבפרק "בהמה המקשה" (שם עב:) דריש: "על פני השדה" — לרבות גולל ודופק. ולפ"ה הלא ארון אינו על פני השדה! ואומר ה"ר דוד מנלינבורק כי לפרש"י [דריש] לרבות גולל ודופק שפירש דלא מרבינן מעל פני השדה דמטמא אלא כשפירש, אבל בעוד שהוא טמון — בטל אגב קרקע, ולא מטמא באוהל. והשתא אתי נמי שפיר ההיא דמדלגים היינו על גבי ארונות. ועוד י"מ: אע"ג דגולל מטמא באהל — מ"מ יכולין לדלג ולטמאות עצמם בגולל, דתניא במס' שמחות (פ"ד): כל טומאה שאין נזיר מגלח עליה — אין כהן מוזהר עליה. ואר"ת: דמשובשת היא, דהא רביעית דם אין נזיר מגלח עליה, כדתנן בנזיר (דף נד. ושם) וכהן מוזהר עליה. ועוד הקשה: דתניא בעירובין (דף טו:): כל דבר שיש בו רוח חיים אין עושין ממנו לא גולל לקבר כו', ולפ"ה וכי דרך לעשות כסוי ארון מבעלי חיים? ויש לומר אע"ג דאין דרך לעשות כסוי ארון מבעלי חיים — מכל מקום כמה דברים אשכחן דלא שכיח, ומיירי בהן התלמוד לדרוש ולקבל שכר, כדאמרינן בפרק "המקשה" (חולין ע.): בלעתו חולדה והוציאתו והכניסתו והקיאתו ויצא מאליו מהו? הדביק שני רחמים ויצא מזה לזה מהו? אף על פי שלא יבא לעולם. ור"ת מפרש: דגולל היינו מצבה, שהיא אבן גדולה. ולשון גולל שייך על האבן, כדכתיב "וגללו את האבן" (בראשית כט). ודופק הן שתי אבנים, אחת לראשה ואחת לרגלה של מצבה. ופעמים כשאין המצבה מזומנת מעמידין שם בהמה או דבר אחר לסימן; ובההיא דמדלגין לא היה שם מצבה. ומחמת המת לא היו מיטמאין, דרוב ארונות יש בהן פותח טפח. ולא תקשה לר' יהושע מאימת חל אבילות כשאין שם מצבה, די"ל: דכי מהדרי אפייהו דקוברין, כדאמרינן במועד קטן (דף כב.) דהנהו דלא אזלי בתר שכבא מכי מהדרי אפייהו. וקשה לר"י על פירוש רבינו תם: דתניא בתוספתא דאהלות בפרק ד': אמר רבי יהודה שתי אבנים גדולות של

עין משפט נר מצוה

יג א מיי' פי"א מהל' איסורי ביאה הל' יט סמג לאוין קיא טוש"ע יו"ד סי' קצה סעי' י:

יד ב (מיי' פ"ב מהל' אבל) סמג עשין ב טוש"ע שם סי' שפג סעי' א:

טו ג [מיי' פ"ב מהל' אבל הל' ה] טוש"ע שם סי' שעד סעי' ו וסי' שפא סעי' ו:

טז ד מיי' פ"ב שם הל' ה סמג שם (טוש"ע יו"ד סי' שעד סעי' ו):

יז ה מיי' פ"י מהל' אישות הל' יד טוש"ע אה"ע סי' סד סעי' ג:

תוספות רי"ד

למימרא דאבילות קילא [ליה] מנדה דהא בנדה [אינה] צריכה שימור אם בעל ואבילות (לא) מצרכינן שימור אע"פ שבעל. והא אר"י ב"ח א"ר פפא כל מלאכות שהאשה עושה לבעלה נדה עושה לבעלה חוץ ממזיגת הכוס והצעת המטה והרחצת פניו ידיו ורגליו ואילו גבי אבילות תניא אע"פ שאמרו אין אדם רשאי לכוף את אשתו לא להיות כוחלת ולא להיות פוקסת באמת אמרו מוזגת לו הכוס ומצעת לו המטה ורוחצת פניו ידיו ורגליו ומסיק ר"א מי קא מדמית אבילות דהכא לאבילות דעלמא. אבילות דעלמא חמירא ליה ולא אתי לזלזולי בה. אבל אבילות דהכא כיון דאקילי בה רבנן אתי לזלזולי בה ומאי קילותא דקתני נוהג ז' ימי המשתה ואח"כ נוהג ז' ימי אבילות: תניא מי שמת חמיו או חמותו אינו רשאי לכוף את אשתו להיות פוקסת אבל כופה מטתו ונוהג עמה אבילות ודוקא בפניה אבל שלא בפניה לא. כדא"ל רב לחייא בריה באפה נהוג אבילות שלא באפה לא תנהוג אבילות:

מסורת הש"ס

לקמן סח.

מ"ק כ: שמחות פי"א

ג"ז שם

מ"ק כז. סנהדרין מז: [שבת קנב:]

גליון הש"ס

גמ' אבילותא דעלמא חמיר. ע' סוטה ז ע"א תוס' ד"ה אמר:

משום חשבונות. אמר ליה אביי: וחשבונות של מצוה מי אסירי? והא רב חסדא ורב המנונא דאמרי תרוייהו: *[א]חשבונות של מצוה מותר לחשבן בשבת! וא"ר אלעזר: [ב]פוסקין צדקה לעניים בשבת! ואמר ר' יעקב אמר ר' יוחנן: [ג]הולכין לבתי כנסיות ולבתי מדרשות לפקח על עסקי רבים בשבת. ואמר רבי יעקב בר אידי אמר רבי יוחנן: מפקחין פיקוח נפש בשבת. ואמר רב שמואל בר נחמני אמר רבי יונתן: הולכין לטרטייאות ולקרקייאות לפקח על עסקי רבים בשבת. ותנא דבי מנשיא: [ד]משדכין על התינוקת ליארס בשבת, ועל התינוק ללמדו ספר וללמדו אומנות! אלא אמר רבי זירא: גזירה שמא ישחוט בן עוף. א"ל אביי: אלא מעתה, יום הכפורים שחל להיות בשני בשבת ידחה, גזירה שמא ישחוט בן עוף! התם, דלנפשיה, לא טריד, הכא דלאחרים – טריד. אי נמי: התם – אית ליה רווחא, הכא – לית ליה רווחא. השתא דאתית להכי – ערב שבת נמי, גזירה שמא ישחוט בן עוף. איבעיא להו: בתולה נשאת ברביעי ונבעלת ברביעי, ולא חיישינן לאיקרורי דעתא, או דלמא: בתולה נשאת ברביעי ונבעלת בחמישי, דחיישינן לאיקרורי דעתא? ת"ש, דתני בר קפרא: בתולה נשאת ברביעי [ה]ונבעלת בחמישי, הואיל ונאמרה בו ברכה לדגים. אלמנה נשאת בחמישי ונבעלת בששי, הואיל ונאמרה בו ברכה לאדם. טעמא – משום ברכה, אבל משום איקרורי דעתא – לא חיישינן. אי הכי, אלמנה נמי תיבעל בחמישי, הואיל ונאמרה בו ברכה לדגים! ברכה דאדם עדיפא ליה. ואי נמי – משום שקדו. דתניא: מפני מה אמרו אלמנה נשאת בחמישי ונבעלת בששי? שאם אתה אומר תיבעל בחמישי – למחר משכים לאומנתו והולך לו, *שקדו חכמים על תקנת בנות ישראל, [ו]שיהא שמח עמה שלשה ימים: חמישי בשבת, וערב שבת, ושבת. מאי איכא בין "ברכה" ל"שקדו"? איכא בינייהו אדם בטל, אי נמי יום טוב שחל להיות בערב שבת. דרש בר קפרא: גדולים מעשה צדיקים יותר ממעשה שמים וארץ, דאילו במעשה שמים וארץ כתיב: °"אף ידי יסדה ארץ וימיני טפחה שמים" ואילו במעשה ידיהם של צדיקים כתיב: °"מכון לשבתך פעלת ה' מקדש אדני כוננו ידיך". השיב בבלי אחד, ור' חייא שמו: °"ויבשת ידיו יצרו"! "ידו" כתיב. והכתיב "יצרו"! א"ר נחמן בר יצחק: יצרו אצבעותיו, כדכתיב: °"כי אראה שמיך מעשה אצבעותיך ירח וכוכבים אשר כוננתה". מיתיבי: °"השמים מספרים כבוד אל ומעשה ידיו מגיד הרקיע"! הכי קאמר: מעשה ידיהם של צדיקים מי מגיד – הרקיע, ומאי ניהו – מטר. דרש בר קפרא: מאי דכתיב °"ויתד תהיה לך על אזנך" – אל תקרי "אזנך" אלא "על אזנך", שאם ישמע אדם דבר שאינו הגון,

יניח

ישעיה מח | שמות טו | תהלים צה | שם ח | שם יט | דברים כג

רש"י

משום חשבונות. שאם יכנוס למוצאי שבת יעשה סעודה בלילה, ויחשוב בשבת מהו צריך להוציא, וכתיב "ודבר דבר" (ישעיה נח). מפקחים. מוציאין לאור. פיקוח. פוסקונברמ"ש בלע"ז. טרטיאות. פלטי מלכים ושלטונים. ללמדו אומנות. מצוה הוא, דכתיב (קהלת ט) "ראה חיים עם אשה אשר אהבת" – תורה אור למוד אומנות שתחיה הימנו עם התורה. ואמרינן בקידושין (דף כט.) שאביו חייב ללמדו אומנות. שמא ישחוט בן עוף. בשבת, לצורך מוצאי שבת. שיהא טרוד וישכח שהוא שבת. שחל להיות בשני בשבת. שצריכין להרבות בסעודה אחר השבת, שהוא ערב יום כפורים. ידחה. לשלישי בשבת, שמא ישחוט בן עוף לצורך סעודת מחר. אית ליה רווחא. לשחוט בלילה, שהסעודה אינה עד למחר. הכא לית ליה רווחא. שהסעודה בלילה אחר השבת משחשיכה מיד. ולא חיישינן לאיקרורי דעתא. אם לא ימצא לה בתולים – לא חיישינן שיתקרר כעסו בהאי פורתא. ונבעלת בחמישי. משתחשך ברביעי ותיכנס ליל חמישי. ברכה לדגים. "פרו ורבו ומלאו את המים" כו' (בראשית א). הואיל ונאמרה בו ברכה לאדם. "פרו ורבו ומלאו את הארץ" (שם). טעמא משום ברכה. אבל מאן דלא קפיד אברכה, משום איקרורי דעתא – לא חיישינן משום האי פורתא. ברכה דאדם עדיפא ליה. ומיהו, בששי לא תנשא בתולה, דבזמן ארוך עד שני בשבת דאתו דייני חיישינן לאיקרורי. אבל מרביעי עד חמישי – לא חיישינן. למחר משכים לאומנתו והולך. שאין משתה אלמון באלמנה אלא יום אחד, כדלקמן בפירקין (דף ז.). חמישי בשבת. יום חופה. וששי בשבת. ביאה. אדם בטל. למ"ד ברכה דאדם עדיפא – אף זו תיבעל בששי, למ"ד משום שקדו – נבעלת בחמישי, דהא לא ישכים לאומנתו. גדולים מעשה צדיקים ממעשה יצירת שמים וארץ. ומשום בר קפרא נקט לה, דאיירי לעיל באגדה. אף ידי. חדא יד. מקדש מעשה ידי לצדיקים הוא. הכי קאמר. האי "ומעשה ידיו" במעשה הצדיקים כתיב, שקרוין מעשה שלהם מעשה ידיו של הקב"ה. וה"ק: ומעשה ידיו, דהוא מעשה הצדיקים – מגיד הרקיע. שהרקיע מעיד עליהם לבריות שהם צדיקים, שמתפללין על הגשמים ומטר יורד. יתד. קביל"י בלע"ז.

שבת קנ. | [לעיל ב. ג. לקמן ז.]

תוספות

של ארבעה ארבעה טפחים, שעשאן גולל לקבר המאהיל על גבי שתיהם – טמא. ניטלה אחת מהן – המאהיל על גבי השניה טהור, מפני שיש לטומאה דרך שילא. מה שייך דרך שילא לפר"ת? ובתוספתא דאהלות ספ"ג תניא: מעשה באחד שמת בערב הפסח ולא רצו לקוברו, ונכנסו הנשים וקשרו החבל בגולל, משכו האנשים מבחוץ וקברוהו הנשים והלכו האנשים ועשו פסחיהן לערב. משמע שלא היו יכולין הנשים לקוברו עד שמשכו האנשים מבחוץ את הגולל. ואם גולל הויא מצבה – למה לא קברוהו בלא מצבה עד אחר הפסח? אלא ודאי הוא כסוי ארון, כפירוש הקונטרס. ולפי שהיה של אבן היה כבד כל כך*.

שמא ישחוט בן עוף. יש גורסים: בו עוף. אע"ג דשבת לשון נקבה היא, דכתיב (שמות לא) "מחלליה מות יומת" – ה"נ הוי לשון זכר "כל העושה בו מלאכה" (שם לה), "שומר שבת מחללו" (ישעיה נו). ושפיר גרסינן נמי בן עוף, דדרך בני אדם לשחוט הרכין והקטנים, כדכתיב (ויקרא ה) "שני בני יונה". ובפרק קמא דקידושין (דף לו: ושם) אתיא מבן עוף, מה לבן לאן שכן קבע לו כו'.

אלא מעתה יום הכפורים שחל להיות בשני כו'. תימה: אמאי נקט יום כפורים דלא הוי אלא לרבי יוסי הגלילי? כדתנן (חולין דף פג.): בד' פרקים בשנה המוכר בהמה לחבירו צריך להודיעו: אמה מכרתי לשחוט כו', וכדברי רבי יוסי הגלילי אף ערב יום הכפורים בגליל. אמאי לא נקט חד מד' פרקים דהוי לכ"ע? וי"ל: דבערב יום הכפורים היו רגילין להרבות בעופות ובדגים, כדמשמע בבראשית רבה (פי"א) גבי ההוא חייטא דזבן נונא כו' משום דהוי יום סליחה וכפרה. ובהנהו ד' פרקים היו מרבים בבהמות, דליכא למגזר שמא ישחוט.

אי הכי אלמנה נמי תיבעל בחמישי. פי': בשלמא אי הוה תני בברייתא דבתולה נבעלת בחמישי משום איקרורי דעתא, כדקמיבעיא לן, ולא משום ברכה לדגים דלא חשיבא – הוי ניחא לן באלמנה דנבעלת בששי משום ברכה. אבל השתא דטעמא דבתולה משום ברכה – אלמנה נמי תיבעל בחמישי!

אי נמי משום שקדו. וא"ת: והיכי מצי למימר משום שקדו, הא בברייתא קתני בהדיא משום ברכה! וי"ל: דלהאי שינויא הוי פירוש הברייתא הכי: אלמנה נשאת בחמישי ונבעלת בששי. פי': משום שקדו, כמו שמפורש בברייתא אחרת, וא"ת: משום ברכה דדגים היה להם להניח תקנת שקדו – לא חשו לכך, הואיל ובששי נמי נאמרה ברכה לאדם.

מאי איכא בין ברכה לשקדו. אע"ג דמשום ברכה לא מיקרי עבריינא, מכל מקום בעי למה לי טעמא דברכה. אי נמי, בעי: מאי איכא בין לישנא דמשני ברכה דאדם עדיפא ליה, ובין לישנא דאי נמי משום שקדו? ומשני: דאיכא בינייהו אדם בטל, אי נמי י"ט שחל להיות כו'. דללישנא דטעמא דברייתא משום שקדו ולא משום ברכה, הכא דליכא שקדו – נבעלת אם ירצה בחמישי. אבל ללישנא קמא, דטעמא דברייתא משום ברכה, כדמשמע פשטא דברייתא – אפילו באדם בטל או בי"ט שחל להיות בערב שבת, דליכא משום שקדו, מכל מקום משום ברכה תבעל בששי. ואפילו להאי לישנא, אי לאו שתקנו משום שקדו –משום ברכה לחודה לא היו קובעים יום, כדפרישית לעיל גבי ותנשא באחד בשבת.

דאילו בשמים ובארץ כתיב אף ידי וגו'. דמשמע חדא, אע"ג דמסיים קרא "וימיני טפחה שמים", ואמר בשילהי "הקומץ רבה" (מנחות לו: ושם) דיד היינו שמאל, א"כ תרתי כתיב – מ"מ בחד מעשה ליכא אלא חד. אבל במעשה צדיקים בחד מעשה, כמו בית המקדש, כתיב תרתי ידים.

זה

עין משפט נר מצוה

יח א ב ג ד מיי' פכ"ד הל' שבת הל"ה סמג לאוין סה טוש"ע או"ח סי' שו סעי' ו:

יט ה טוש"ע אה"ע סי' סד:

כ ו מיי' פ"י מהל' אישות הל' יב סמג עשין מח טוש"ע אה"ע סי' (סג) [סד] סעי' ג:

[וע' בתוס' שבת קנב: וסוכה כג. ד"ה ולא ותוס' סנהדרין מז:]

תוספות רי"ד

ר"ח ורב המנונא דאמרי תרוייהו חשבונות של מצוה מותר לחשבן בשבת וא"ר אלעזר פוסקין צדקה לעניים בשבת. וא"ר יעקב ב"א אר"י מפקחין פקוח נפש בשבת והולכים לב"כ ולבתי מדרשות לפקח על עסקי רבים בשבת. ותנא דבי מנשה משדכין על התינוקת לארס בשבת ועל התינוק ללמדו ספר וללמדו אומניות בשבת. וא"ר שמואל בר נחמני אר"י הולכין לטרטראיות ולקרקסאות לפקח על עסקי רבים בשבת: תני בר קפרא בתולה נשאת בד' ונבעלת בה' הואיל ונאמרה בו ברכה לדגים ואלמנה נשאת בה' ונבעלת בששי הואיל ונאמרה בו ברכה לאדם ותניא מפני מה אמרו אלמנה נשאת בחמישי ונבעלת בו' שאם אתה אומר תבעל בחמישי למחר משכים הוא לאומנותו והולך. שקדו חכמים על תקנות בנות ישראל שיהא שמח עמה ג' ימים ה' בשבת ו' בשבת ושבת:

איבעיא להו מהו לבעול בתולה בשבת. ומסיק תלמודא והלכתא מותר לבעול בשבת:

יַנִּיחַ אֶצְבָּעוֹ בְּאָזְנָיו. וְהַיְינוּ דְּאָמַר ר' אֶלְעָזָר: מִפְּנֵי מָה אֶצְבְּעוֹתָיו שֶׁל אָדָם דּוֹמוֹת לִיתֵידוֹת? מַאי טַעֲמָא? אִילֵימָא מִשּׁוּם דִּמְחַלְּקָן — כָּל חֲדָא וַחֲדָא לְמִילְּתֵיהּ עֲבִידָא, דְּאָמַר מָר: *זוֹ זֶרֶת, זוֹ קְמִיצָה, זוֹ אַמָּה, זוֹ אֶצְבַּע, זֶה גּוּדָל! אֶלָּא: מַה טַּעַם מְשׁוּפּוֹת כִּיתֵידוֹת? שֶׁאִם יִשְׁמַע אָדָם דָּבָר שֶׁאֵינוֹ הָגוּן יַנִּיחַ אֶצְבְּעוֹתָיו בְּאָזְנָיו. תָּנָא דְּבֵי רַבִּי יִשְׁמָעֵאל: מִפְּנֵי מָה אוֹזֶן כּוּלָּהּ קָשָׁה וְהָאַלְיָה רַכָּה? שֶׁאִם יִשְׁמַע אָדָם דָּבָר שֶׁאֵינוֹ הָגוּן — יָכוֹף אַלְיָה לְתוֹכָהּ. ת"ר: *אַל יַשְׁמִיעַ אָדָם לְאָזְנָיו דְּבָרִים בְּטֵלִים מִפְּנֵי שֶׁהֵן נִכְווֹת תְּחִלָּה לְאֵיבָרִים. אִיבַּעְיָא לְהוּ: מַהוּ לִבְעוֹל בַּתְּחִלָּה בְּשַׁבָּת, דָּם מִיפְקַד פְּקִיד אוֹ חַבּוּרֵי מִיחַבַּר? וְאִם תִּימְצֵי לוֹמַר דָּם מִיפְקַד פְּקִיד, לְדָם הוּא צָרִיךְ — וְשָׁרֵי, אוֹ דִּלְמָא לְפֶתַח הוּא צָרִיךְ — וַאֲסִיר? וְאִם תִּימְצֵי לוֹמַר לְדָם הוּא צָרִיךְ, וּפֶתַח מִמֵּילָא קָאָתֵי, הֲלָכָה כְּר"ש *דְּאָמַר: דָּבָר שֶׁאֵין מִתְכַּוֵּין מוּתָּר, °אוֹ הֲלָכָה כְּרַבִּי יְהוּדָה דְּאָמַר: דָּבָר שֶׁאֵין מִתְכַּוֵּין אָסוּר? וְאִם תִּימְצֵי לוֹמַר הֲלָכָה כְּר' יְהוּדָה — מְקַלְקֵל הוּא אֵצֶל הַפֶּתַח אוֹ מְתַקֵּן הוּא אֵצֶל הַפֶּתַח? אִיכָּא דְּאָמְרִי: וְאִם תִּימְצֵי לוֹמַר דָּם חַבּוּרֵי מִיחַבַּר — לְדָם הוּא צָרִיךְ וְאָסוּר, אוֹ דִּלְמָא לַהֲנָאַת עַצְמוֹ הוּא צָרִיךְ וְשָׁרֵי? וְאִם תִּימְצֵי לוֹמַר לַהֲנָאַת עַצְמוֹ הוּא צָרִיךְ, וְדָם מִמֵּילָא קָאָתֵי — הֲלָכָה כְּרַבִּי יְהוּדָה אוֹ הֲלָכָה כְּר"ש? וְאִם תִּימְצֵי לוֹמַר הֲלָכָה כְּר' יְהוּדָה — מְקַלְקֵל בְּחַבּוּרָה אוֹ מְתַקֵּן בְּחַבּוּרָה הוּא? וְאִם תִּימְצֵי לוֹמַר מְקַלְקֵל בְּחַבּוּרָה הוּא — בִּמְקַלְקֵל הֲלָכָה כְּרַבִּי יְהוּדָה אוֹ

זה גודל. פי' בקונטרס לענין בהן יד דמלורע. ואין נראה, דאם כן הוה ליה למימר זה בהן! ועוד, דאפילו לא מחלק מלי מסוי על בהן שהוא קלר מכולם. ונראה דלענין קמילה קאמר, כדתנן (מנחות דף יא.): מוחק בגודל מלמעלה. אבל בידו אחרת לא יוכל לעשות, דבעינן עבודה בימין.

מהו לבעול בתחלה בשבת. אף על גב דתקנו שתהא בתולה נשאת ברביעי, בכל מקום אם אירע לו שלא בעל בליל חמישי — לא חייבוהו חכמים להמתין עד יום חמישי אחר, או עד יום ב', להכי בעי אם מותר לבעול בשבת אם לאו. אע"ג דתניא לעיל ומפריסין חתן מן הכלה לילי שבת תחלה מפני שהוא עושה חבורה, ותניא נמי באידך ברייתא: בין כך ובין כך לא יבעול לא בערב שבת ולא כו'. פי' בקונטרס דלא הוה ידע לה. א"נ ידע לה, ובעי היכי הלכתא. דאיכא למימר דפליגי בה ר' יהודה ור"ש. ומיהו, על כרחך נראה דלא ידע הברייתא דחיישינן שמא ישחוט בן עוף. דאי הוה ידע לה – מאי קמיבעיא ליה? הא בהא לא פליגי ר' יהודה ור"ש. והא דלא פשיט מינה לבסוף – משום דמשכח תנאי דפליגי עלה.

דם מיפקד פקיד או חבורי מיחבר. טעמא דחבורה לא כפרש"י דפירש בפרק "שמונה שרצים" (שבת קז:) דחייב משום לובע גבי ח' שרצים, דתנא התם: נצרר הדם אע"פ שלא יצא. וקשה לר"י: דב"אלו טריפות" (חולין מו:) בשמעתא דריאה תניא: ושאר שקצים ורמשים – עד שיצא מהם דם. והשתא התם מאי לובע איכא? הא לית להו עור! וה"נ, מאי לביעה איכא בהך חבורה? וכן גבי חבורה דמילה לא שייך לביעה! ועוד: דעל כרחך לשמואל איכא טעמא אחרינא, דבפרק "כלל גדול" (שבת עה. וש"נ) קאמר דשוחט לא מחייב משום לובע אלא משום נטילת נשמה. אלמא טעמא דחבורה הוי משום נטילת נשמה, כדקאמר שמואל התם. ורב דאמר התם משום לובע – אף משום לובע קאמר. ונטילת נשמה אין לפרש דטעמא משום הכחשה, שמחלישו ונוטל קלת נשמתו, דהכא אין לריך לחלישות האשה, ומיהו איסורא דקאמר הכא – איכא למימר דהויא דרבנן. אבל גבי מילה משמע דאיכא איסורא דאורייתא בהוצאת דם, דאמרינן בפרק "ר' אליעזר" (שם קלג:): האי אומנא דלא מייץ – סכנתא הוא, ומעברינן ליה. פשיטא מדקא מחללין שבת עליה! מהו דתימא: דם מיפקד פקיד, קמ"ל דחבורי מיחבר. ואי הוה משום החלשה – ליכא חילול שבת, דהויא מלאכה שאין לריכה לגופה, דאין לורך להחליש התינוק! ונראה לר"ת לפרש דהוצאת דם חשיבה נטילת נשמה, כי הדם הוא הנפש, וכשנוטל מקלתו נוטל מקלת נשמה. וקשה לר"י, דאמרי' בפרק "כלל גדול" (שם עה. ושם) גבי הלד חלזון והפולעו: וליחייב נמי משום נטילת נשמה! ומשני: מתעסק הוא אלל נטילת נשמה, דכל כמה דאית ביה נשמה טפי ניחא ליה כו'. ולפי זה, אפילו הוא חי גמור – הרי יש כאן נטילת נשמה! ואומר ר"ת: כי דם חלזון שלובעין בו הוא מיפקד פקיד, ועל אותו אינו חייב משום נטילת נשמה, ועל שאר הדם שמחובר – חשיב ליה מתעסק.

לדם הוא צריך ושרי. וא"ת: והא פסיק רישיה הוא לענין הפתח! וי"ל: שיכול להוציא הדם בלא עשיית הפתח. פי' ר"ת: שלריך להוציא הדם שלא יתלכלך פעם אחרת כשיבעול. ולפירושו לקמן דקאמר: דם חבורי מיחבר, אי לדם הוא לריך ואסור. אף על גב דהויא מלאכה שאינה לריכה לגופה דשריא במקום לערא גבי מורסא, הכא גבי מלוה – אסור. ולקמן נפרש הא דפריך ממפיס מורסא לפירושו. ור"י מפרש: לדם הוא לריך – שלריך לראות אם היא בתולה.

אם תימצי לומר הלכה כרבי יהודה מקלקל **הוא אצל הפתח** ושרי. פי': דרבי יהודה אית ליה דמקלקל בחבורה פטור. אף על גב דפטור אבל אסור – מיהו הכא מותר לכתחלה, משום דאיכא תרתי: מקלקל בחבורה, ודבר שאינו מתכוין. וקשה, דבגרירה אסר ר' יהודה אע"ג דאיכא תרתי, דאין מתכוין ומקלקל נמי הוי, כדאמרינן בשילהי פ"ק דחגיגה (דף י.) דמוקי הך דחופר גומא ואין לריך אלא לעפרה דפטור אפי' כר' יהודה דמחייב מלאכה שאינה לריכה לגופה, וטעמא דפטור – משום דמקלקל הוי. ובפרק "י"ט" (ביצה כג. ושם) אסר רבי יהודה קירוד אף על גב דאין מתכוין ומקלקל! ויש לומר: דהכא שרי טפי משום דאיכא נמי מלוה. א"נ, שלא במקום מלוה נמי היכא דאיכא תרתי – שרי. וגבי חריץ יש להעמיד כגון שאינו מקלקל לגמרי אלא מתקן קלת, דמשוי גומות מלד אחד. וגבי קירוד נמי, במה שמוליא דם – מיקל לבהמה קלת, כמו דם הקזה*.

את"ל הלכה כרבי יהודה מקלקל בחבורה **הוא** כו'. משמע דאי הלכה כרבי שמעון שרי אפילו הוא מתקן, כיון דאין מתכוין. וקשה: דבשילהי פרק "ספק אכל" (כריתות יט: ושם) *אמר: לרבי שמעון, הואיל ומקלקל בחבורה חייב – מתעסק נמי חייב. ומאי שנא דאין מתכוין פוטר רבי שמעון בחבורה טפי ממתעסק? וי"ל: דמתעסק שמתכוין למלאכה – לא מיפטר בשבת אלא משום דאין זה מלאכת מחשבת, ומשום הכי חייב לרבי שמעון מתעסק בחבורה כמו מקלקל בחבורה, דמחייב רבי שמעון אע"ג דאין זה מלאכת מחשבת. ולהכי תלינן ליה במקלקל

יַנִּיחַ אֶצְבָּעוֹ. שֶׁהִיא שְׁפוּיָה כְּיָתֵד. מ"ט. כְּלוֹמַר, בְּמַאי דּוֹמוֹת כִּיתֵידוֹת? **אִי נֵימָא דִּמְחַלְּקָן.** שֶׁמְּחוּלָּקוֹת זוֹ מִזּוֹ, וְאֵינָן מְחוּבָּרוֹת יַחַד. **חֲדָא חֲדָא לְמִילְּתֵיהּ.** קוּשְׁיָא הִיא: כָּל אַחַת יֵשׁ בָּהּ צוֹרֶךְ, וְאַף בְּצוֹרְכֵי גָבוֹהַּ. זוֹ זֶרֶת. מִן הַקְּטַנָּה מוֹדְדִין זֶרֶת שֶׁל חוֹשֶׁן. זוֹ קְמִיצָה. מֵאֶצְבַּע שֶׁאֵצֶל הַקְּטַנָּה מַתְחִילִין לִקְמוֹץ. חוֹפֶה שָׁלֹשׁ אֶצְבָּעוֹת עַל פַּס יָדוֹ, הַקְּמִיצָה וְהָאַמָּה וְהָאֶצְבַּע, וְקוֹמֵץ. **זוֹ אַמָּה.** מֵהַגְּדוֹלָה מוֹדְדִין אַמַּת בִּנְיָן וְאַמַּת כֵּלִים. **זוֹ אֶצְבַּע.** לְמַתַּן דָּמִים שֶׁל חַטָּאת, דִּכְתִיב בֵּיהּ "בְּאֶצְבָּעוֹ" (ויקרא ד). **זֶה גּוּדָל.** לְבֹהֶן יָד דְּאַהֲרֹן (שם ח) וְדִמְצוֹרָע (שם יד). **מְשׁוּפּוֹת.** אגויישיד"ש בְּלַעַז. **אַלְיָה.** בָּשָׂר שֶׁבְּסוֹף הָאוֹזֶן. **נִכְוֵית תְּחִילָּה לְאֵבָרִים.** רַכּוֹת וְדַקּוֹת לִיכָּווֹת מִכּוּלָּם. וְהָכִי נַמִי אָמְרִינַן בְּמַסֶּכֶת ע"ז (דף לח.): הַאי גּוֹי דַּחֲרֵיךְ רֵישָׁא – שָׁרֵי לְמֵיכַל אֲפִילּוּ מֵרֵישׁ אוּדְנֵיהּ, וְאע"פ שֶׁמְּמַהֵר לִיבָּשֵׁל. **מַהוּ לִבְעוֹל בַּתְּחִלָּה.** לָא שְׁמִיעַ לְהוּ הָךְ מַתְנִיתָא דִּלְעֵיל*. א"נ, שְׁמִיעַ לְהוּ, וּמִיבַּעְיָא לְהוּ: הֲלָכָה אוֹ אֵין הֲלָכָה. **מִיפְקַד פְּקִיד.** כְּמוֹ פִּקָּדוֹן, כָּנוּס וְעוֹמֵד וְאֵינוֹ נִבְלָע בְּדוֹפְנֵי הָרֶחֶם, לִהְיוֹת יְלִיאָתוֹ עַל יְדֵי חַבּוּרָה. אֶלָּא שֶׁהַפֶּתַח נָעוּל בְּפָנָיו, וּפוֹתְחִין לוֹ וְיוֹצֵא. **אוֹ חַבּוּרֵי מִיחַבַּר.** דַּם בְּתוּלִים הַיּוֹצֵא, עַל יְדֵי חַבּוּרָה הוּא בָּא, שֶׁהַדּוֹפֶן מִתְפָּרֵק מֵחֲבֵרוֹ. **אִם תִּימְצֵי לוֹמַר מִיפְקַד פְּקִיד.** וְאֵין בּוֹ מִשּׁוּם חַבּוּרָה, כַּוָּונַת הַמּוֹצִיאוֹ לְמַאי? לְדָם הוּא צָרִיךְ וּמִתְכַּוֵּין לְהוֹצִיאוֹ. **וְשָׁרֵי.** דְּהָא מִיפְקַד פְּקִיד. **אוֹ דִּלְמָא לְפֶתַח מִתְכַּוֵּין.** וַהֲרֵי הוּא כְּבוֹנֶה, וְאָסוּר. **וְאִם תִּימְצֵי לוֹמַר לְדָם הוּא מִתְכַּוֵּין.** וְלֹא לְפֶתַח, וּמִיהוּ עַל כָּרְחָךְ פִּיתְחָא מִמֵּילָא הָוֵי. **הֲלָכָה כְּרַבִּי יְהוּדָה.** בְּדָבָר שֶׁאֵין מִתְכַּוֵּין, וְאָסוּר. **אוֹ כְּר"ש.** וּמוּתָּר. וְא"ת: פְּסִיק רֵישֵׁיהּ וְלֹא יָמוּת הוּא! הָא פָּרְכִינַן לָהּ לְקַמָּן, וּמְשַׁנֵּינַן: יֵשׁ שֶׁבְּקִיאִין בְּהַטָּיָה, וְאֵין דָּם יוֹצֵא, וְאַף אֵין פֶּתַח נִפְתָּח. הִלְכָּךְ, לָאו פְּסִיק רֵישֵׁיהּ וְלֹא יָמוּת הוּא. **וְאת"ל הֲלָכָה כְּרַבִּי יְהוּדָה.** אַכַּתִּי אִיכָּא לְמִיבְּעֵי, דְּקַיְימָא לָן (שבת ד' קו.) כִּי אָמַר רַבִּי יְהוּדָה – בִּמְתַקֵּן, אֲבָל בִּמְקַלְקֵל – אֵינָהּ מְלָאכָה. וְיֵשׁ לִשְׁאוֹל עַל פֶּתַח זֶה, אִם תִּקּוּן הוּא אֶצְלָהּ אוֹ קִלְקוּל הוּא אֶצְלָהּ, שֶׁהַבְּתוּלָה חֲשׁוּבָה מִן הַבְּעוּלָה. **וְאת"ל מְקַלְקֵל הוּא** ל"ג, דְּאִי מְקַלְקֵל – לְדִבְרֵי הַכֹּל מוּתָּר, שֶׁאֵין לָךְ מְקַלְקֵל חַיָּיב אֶלָּא חוֹבֵל וּמַבְעִיר אַלִּיבָּא דְּרַבִּי שִׁמְעוֹן, וְהָכָא לָאו חוֹבֵל הוּא, דְּהָא בְּאת"ל דָּם מִיפְקַד פְּקִיד בָּעֵי לָהּ וְאָזֵיל. וְדָם מִמֵּילָא קָא הָוֵי. הוּא אֵינוֹ מִתְכַּוֵּין לְהוֹצִיאוֹ, אֲבָל הוּא יוֹצֵא, וְנִמְצֵאת חַבּוּרָה נַעֲשֵׂית שֶׁלֹּא בְּכַוָּונָה. **הֲלָכָה כְּרַבִּי יְהוּדָה.** בְּדָבָר שֶׁאֵינוֹ מִתְכַּוֵּין, וְשֶׁמָּא מְתַקֵּן הוּא וְאָסוּר. **אוֹ הֲלָכָה כְּר"ש.** דְּדָבָר שֶׁאֵין מִתְכַּוֵּין מוּתָּר. **וְאִם תִּימְצֵי לוֹמַר הֲלָכָה כְּרַבִּי יְהוּדָה.** קִלְקוּל הוּא וּמוּתָּר, אוֹ תִּקּוּן הוּא וְאָסוּר? וַאֲפִי' אִם קִלְקוּל הוּא יֵשׁ לְמִצְוָה צַד אִיסּוּר, אִם בְּדָבָר שֶׁאֵין מִתְכַּוֵּין סְבִירָא לָן כְּרַבִּי יְהוּדָה, וּבִמְקַלְקֵל בְּחַבּוּרָה סְבִירָא לָן כְּר"ש דִּמְחַיֵּיב. דְּאָמְרִינַן: כָּל הַמְקַלְקְלִין פְּטוּרִין חוּץ מֵחוֹבֵל וּמַבְעִיר, וְאוֹקִימְנָא כְּר"ש בְּפֶרֶק "הָאוֹרֵג" (שבת קו.). **הֲלָכָה כְּרַבִּי יְהוּדָה בִּמְקַלְקֵל.** וּמוּתָּר, דְּכִי אָמַר רַבִּי יְהוּדָה דָּבָר שֶׁאֵין מִתְכַּוֵּין אָסוּר – בִּמְתַקֵּן, אֲבָל בִּמְקַלְקֵל לָא אָמַר. אוֹ

מנחות יא. | [מס' ד"א זוטא פ"ד] | [דף ג:] | ביצה כג. [שבת מא: וש"נ] | [ועי' תוס' בכורות כד: ד"ה והיינו] | ליתא שם האי לישנא

גליון הש"ס
גמ' או הלכה כר"י דאמר דשא"מ אסור. ע' פסחים כה ע"ב תד"ה לא אפשר:

או הֲלָכָה כְּר"ש? (אִיתְּמַר), בְּבֵי רַב אָמְרִי: רַב שָׁרֵי וּשְׁמוּאֵל אָסַר. בִּנְהַרְדְּעָא אָמְרִי: רַב אָסַר וּשְׁמוּאֵל שָׁרֵי. אָמַר רַב נַחְמָן בַּר יִצְחָק, וְסִימָנֵיךְ: אֵלּוּ מְקִילִין לְעַצְמָן וְאֵלּוּ מְקִילִין לְעַצְמָן. וְרַב שָׁרֵי?! *וְהָאָמַר רַב שִׁימִי בַּר חִזְקִיָּה מִשְּׁמֵיהּ דְּרַב: [א]הַאי מְסוֹכְרִיָּא דְּנַזְיָיתָא אָסוּר לַהֲדוּקָהּ בְּיוֹמָא טָבָא! בְּהַהוּא אֲפִילּוּ ר"ש מוֹדֶה. דְּאַבַּיֵּי וְרָבָא דְּאָמְרִי תַּרְוַיְיהוּ: מוֹדֶה ר"ש *בִּפְסִיק רֵישֵׁיהּ וְלֹא יָמוּת. וְהָא אָמַר רַב חִיָּיא בַּר אַשִׁי אָמַר רַב: הֲלָכָה כְּרַבִּי יְהוּדָה, וְרַב חָנָן בַּר אַמִי אָמַר שְׁמוּאֵל: הֲלָכָה כְּרַבִּי שִׁמְעוֹן. וְרַב חִיָּיא בַּר אָבִין מַתְנֵי לָהּ בְּלָא גַּבְרֵי, רַב אָמַר: הֲלָכָה כְּר' יְהוּדָה, וּשְׁמוּאֵל אָמַר: הֲלָכָה כְּרַבִּי שִׁמְעוֹן! לְעוֹלָם רַב כְּרַבִּי יְהוּדָה סְבִירָא לֵיהּ לְהָךְ לִישָּׁנָא דְּאָמַר דָּם מִיפְקַד פְּקִיד — מְקַלְקֵל הוּא אֵצֶל הַפֶּתַח. לְהָךְ לִישָּׁנָא דְּאָמַר דָּם חַבּוּרֵי מִיחַבַּר — מְקַלְקֵל בְּחַבּוּרָה הוּא. מְתִיב רַב חִסְדָּא: *תִּינוֹקֶת שֶׁלֹּא הִגִּיעַ זְמַנָּהּ לִרְאוֹת וְנִשֵּׂאת, ב"ש אוֹמְרִים: נוֹתְנִין לָהּ אַרְבָּעָה לֵילוֹת, וּב"ה אוֹמְרִים: [ב]עַד שֶׁתַּחְיֶה הַמַּכָּה. הִגִּיעַ זְמַנָּהּ לִרְאוֹת וְנִשֵּׂאת. בש"א: נוֹתְנִין לָהּ לַיְלָה הָרִאשׁוֹן. וּבֵית הִלֵּל אוֹמְרִים: עַד מוֹצָאֵי שַׁבָּת, [ג]אַרְבָּעָה לֵילוֹת. מַאי

רש"י

או הֲלָכָה כְּר"ש. דִּמְקַלְקֵל בְּחַבּוּרָה חַיָּיב, כֵּיוָן דְּתִימְלֵי לוֹמַר הֲלָכָה כְּר' יְהוּדָה בְּדָבָר שֶׁאֵין מִתְכַּוֵּין דְּאָסוּר. **בִּנְהַרְדְּעָא.** מְקוֹמוֹ שֶׁל שְׁמוּאֵל. **וְסִימָנֵיךְ.** שֶׁלֹּא תִּטְעֶה לְהַחֲלִיף שְׁמַעְתָּא דְּבֵי רַב לִנְהַרְדְּעָא, וּדִנְהַרְדְּעָא לְדְבֵי רַב. **אֵלּוּ מְקִילִין לְעַצְמָן.** דְּבֵי רַב שֶׁצְּרִיכִים לַעֲשׂוֹת כְּדִבְרֵי רַבָּן, אוֹמְרִים שֶׁרַבָּן הִתִּיר. וּנְהַרְדְּעָא, הָעוֹשִׂים כִּשְׁמוּאֵל רַבָּן, אוֹמְרִים שְׁמוּאֵל הִתִּיר. **וְרַב שָׁרֵי.** בִּתְמִיָּה, אַלְמָא דָּבָר שֶׁאֵין מִתְכַּוֵּין מוּתָּר סְבִירָא לֵיהּ. **מְסוֹכְרִיָּא דְּנַזְיָיתָא.** סְתִימַת נֶקֶב גִּיגִית שֶׁמּוֹצִיאִין הַשֵּׁכָר דֶּרֶךְ הַנֶּקֶב וְסוֹתְמִין אוֹתוֹ בִּבְלָאֵי בְּגָדִים. **אָסוּר לַהֲדוּקָהּ.** מִשּׁוּם סְחִיטָה. **מוֹדֶה ר"ש כו'.** אֲבָל כָּאן יֵשׁ שֶׁבְּקִיאִים בַּהֲטָיָיה, כִּדְלְקַמָּן. **הֲלָכָה כְּרַבִּי יְהוּדָה.** בְּאֵין מִתְכַּוֵּין. **בְּלָא גַּבְרֵי.** בְּלֹא אֲמוֹרָאֵי אַלִּיבָּא דְּרַב וְאַלִּיבָּא דִּשְׁמוּאֵל, אֶלָּא רַב וּשְׁמוּאֵל גּוּפַיְיהוּ. **לְהָךְ לִישָּׁנָא** דְּאָמְרַתְּ דָּם מִיפְקַד פְּקִיד. וְהָאִיסּוּר מִשּׁוּם פֶּתַח הוּא. **מְקַלְקֵל הוּא אֵצֶל הַפֶּתַח.** וּבִמְקַלְקֵל מוֹדֶה רַבִּי יְהוּדָה. **מְקַלְקֵל בְּחַבּוּרָה הוּא.** וְרַב סָבַר לָהּ כְּרַבִּי יְהוּדָה אַף בִּמְקַלְקֵל בְּחַבּוּרָה לְקוּלָּא, דְּקָא פָּטַר בָּהּ רַבִּי יְהוּדָה. **שֶׁלֹּא הִגִּיעַ זְמַנָּהּ לִרְאוֹת.** בְּמַסֶּכֶת נִדָּה אָמַר: אֵימָתַי הִגִּיעַ זְמַנָּהּ לִרְאוֹת — מִשֶּׁיַּגִּיעוּ יְמֵי הַנְּעוּרִים. **נוֹתְנִין לָהּ אַרְבָּעָה לֵילוֹת.** שֶׁכָּל דָּמִים שֶׁתִּרְאֶה בָּהֶן מֵחֲמַת תַּשְׁמִישׁ מַחְזְקִינַן לְהוּ בְּדַם בְּתוּלִים. **עַד שֶׁתִּחְיֶה הַמַּכָּה.** כָּל זְמַן שֶׁאֵינָהּ מְשַׁמֶּשֶׁת בְּלֹא דָּם לֹא חָיְתָה הַמַּכָּה. **הִגִּיעַ זְמַנָּהּ לִרְאוֹת.** וְלֹא רָאֲתָה. **לַיְלָה הָרִאשׁוֹן.** אֲפִילּוּ לִבְעִילוֹת הַרְבֵּה. מַאי

תוספות

במקלקל משום דטעם שניהם דפטורין בשאר מלאכות שבת הוי משום דבעינן מלאכת מחשבת, אבל שאינו מתכוין כלל למלאכה לא משום דבעינן מלאכת מחשבת מיפטר, דהא בשאר מקומות נמי מיפטר אין מתכוין, כגון גבי כלאים, דמוכרי כסות מוכרין כדרכן ובלבד שלא יתכוין כו' (כלאים פ"ט מ"ה), ותנן נמי: נזיר חופף ומפספס כו' (נזיר דף מב.), הילכך בחבורה נמי שרי.

האי מסוכרייתא **דנזייתא אסור** להדוקה כו'. פירש בקונטרס, וכן ר"ח ובערוך* בחד לישנא, וכן בסדר תנאים ואמוראים, דאסור משום סחיטה. וקשה לר"ת: דהא סחיטה משום ליבון, ולא שייכא בשאר משקים. דכל דבר המלכלך את בולעו, כגון יין ושכר ושמן — לא שייך ליבון בסחיטתו, אלא דוקא במים. וראיה לדבר — מדלא גזרינן בהו שמא יסחוט כמו גבי מים, כדאמרינן ב"אלו קשרים" (שבת דף קיג.): היה מהלך בשבת ופגע באמת המים כו' היכי ליעביד? ליזיל במיא — אתי לידי סחיטה. ותניא נמי בפרק "חבית" (שם דף קמז: ושם): ומסתפג באלונטית ולא יביאה בידו, ומפרש בגמ' דאתי לידי סחיטה. ובפ"ב דביצה (דף יח. ושם) אומר דלכ"ע אין מטבילין את הכלים, ומפרש בגמרא גזירה משום סחיטה. ואילו בפרק "תולין" (שבת דף קלט:) תנן: מסננין את היין בסודרין. אלמא לגבי יין לא גזרינן משום סחיטה! ובריש "המביא" (ביצה דף ל.) נמי קאמר: ליפרוס סודרא עליה, ולא קאמר אתי לידי סחיטה, והיינו משום דלא שייך ליבון אלא גבי מים. והא דאמרינן בפרק "מפנין" (שבת דף קכח:): אם היתה צריכה שמן חבירתה מביאה לה בשערה. ופריך: והא אתי לידי סחיטה? ומשני: אין סחיטה בשער. משמע דשייך סחיטה בשמן. וכן בפ' "נוטל" (שם דף קמג.): ספוג, אם יש לו בית אחיזה — מקנחין בו, ואם לאו — אין מקנחין בו, משום דאתי לידי סחיטת שמן הנבלע בו! ההיא סחיטה אור"ת דהויא משום מפרק, ואסורה כמו סחיטת זיתים וענבים. והכא אומר ר"ת דליכא למימר דאסור משום מפרק, כיון שהנסחט הולך לאיבוד, *אע"ג דהוי פסיק רישיה. וכן פירש בערוך דכל פסיק רישיה דלא ניחא ליה שרי. ועיקר ראייתו מפרק "כל התדיר" (זבחים דף צא: ושם) אליבא דר"ש מזלפין יין על גבי האישים אע"ג דפסיק רישיה הוא, דודאי מכבה הוא, כיון דלא ניחא ליה בהאי כיבוי — שרי. ועוד מייתי ראיה מ"לולב הגזול" (סוכה דף לג: ושם) דקאמר ר"א בר"ש: ממעטים ענבים בי"ט, פי' ענבי הדס. ופריך: והא מתקן מנא! ומוקים לה במתכוון לאכילה, סבר לה כאבוה. ופריך: והא מודה ר"ש בפסיק רישיה כו'! ומשני: לא צריכא דאית ליה הושענא אחריתי. אלמא כיון דלא ניחא ליה, ולא חייש בהאי תיקון — שרי, אע"ג דפסיק רישיה הוא. ונראה לר"י דלא קשה מידי; דאיכא למימר דאסור לסחוט בשאר משקה משום ליבון כמו במים, ומ"מ לא חיישינן בהו שמא יסחוט, כיון שהטעם והריח נשארים בבגדים ומעט היה נהנה בסחיטתו. ומצינן למימר נמי דאסור משום מפרק. ואף ע"ג דהוי פסיק רישיה דלא ניחא ליה — אסור לכתחילה לר"ש, כמו במלאכה שאינה צריכה לגופה. וראיות הערוך אינן ראיות; דההיא דמתיר ר"ש לזלף יין על גבי האישים — איכא למימר דמצוה שאני. וכן ההיא דאית ליה הושענא אחריתי, איכא למימר דשרי משום מצוה. א"נ הכי פי': והא פסיק רישיה הוא! דאית ליה הושענא אחריתי, והואיל וכן — שרי לר"ש, דשמא לא יצטרך לה ונמצא שלא תיקן כלי, והלכך לאו פסיק רישיה הוא. אבל לר"י אסור, דשמא יצטרך לה ואגלאי מילתא דכלי עבד. ועל פי' הערוך קשה: דתנן בפרק "שמונה שרצים" (שבת דף קז.): המפיס מורסא בשבת, אם לעשות לה פה — חייב, ואם להוציא ממנה ליחה — פטור, ודוקא משום צערא פטור ומותר, אבל אי לאו משום צערא היה אסור, אע"ג דלא ניחא ליה בפה כלל, דאי ניחא ליה מן הפה — כי לא מתכוין נמי חייב! וכן מחט של יד ליטול בה את הקוץ דשרי — משום צערא, אבל אי לאו הכי — אסור, אע"ג דלא ניחא ליה כלל! אבל קצת קשה: אי פסיק רישיה דלא ניחא ליה אסור, אמאי קאמר רב בפרק "חבית" (שם קמה.) כבשים שסחטן לגופן פטור ומותר, הואיל וא"ל למים היוצאין, והשתא אע"ג דא"ל — היה להיות אסור! ואור"י: דמצינן למימר דדוקא כבשים שרי, דהוי הנסחט מהם כמו אוכלא דאיפרת, ואין שם משקה עליו, כדאמרינן דאפי' למימיהם פטור אבל אסור. ועוד י"ל: דכל דבר שאדם עושה במזיד, לא שייך למימר שמא יסחוט. דסברא הוא, כיון דלדעת כן הוא עושה. ולהכי, גבי מסננין את היין לא חיישינן שמא יסחוט. ואתיא שפיר האי דנדה מערמת וטובלת בבגדיה (ביצה דף יח.). וכן בפ"ח דיומא (דף עז:): ההולך להקביל פני רבו עובר עד צוארו במים, ולא גזרינן שמא יסחוט, לפי שלדעת כן הוא עושה. *ועוד איכא למימר התם דמצוה שאני. ובערוך פירש לשון אחר: מסוכרייא דנזייתא, סתימת גיגית של שכר אסור להדוקה, דשמא תבטל הסתימה אצל הגיגית ויעשה כלי בשבת. ואין נראה לר"י, דהיכי דמי, דאם בדעתו לבטל שם בשעת הנחה — מאי פסיק רישיה שייך כאן? מיד הוא עושה כלי, דמתכוין לעשותו! ואם אין בדעתו לבטלה שם — א"כ לא הוי פסיק רישיה שיעשנה כלי! וי"ל בדוחק: שהוא מתכוין לבטלה ואינו מתכוין לעשות כלי, ושייך ביה פסיק רישיה הואיל ואינו מתכוין לגמרי לעשות כלי*. **לעולם** רב כר"י ס"ל כו'. לשמואל נמי איכא לשנויי לעולם כר"ש ס"ל, להך לישנא דאמר דם מיפקד פקיד — לפתח הוא צריך, ולהך לישנא דאמר חבורי מחבר — לדם הוא צריך: *מאי **לאו דאי לא בעיל מצי בעיל.** דלמאי נקט עד מוצאי שבת, אי לאו דאתא לאשמועינן דמצי בעיל בשבת, אע"ג דמשיר בתולים. דליכא למימר דנקט עד מוצ"ש לאשמועי' דבעינן רצופין — דהא לא בעינן שיהו רצופין, כדתניא בפרק בתרא דנדה (דף סד: ושם): מעשה ונתן לה ד' לילות מתוך י"ב חדש. והכי פי': נותנין לה ד' לילות עד מוצ"ש, שיבעול בכל לילה ויסיר מקצת בתולים עד מוצ"ש. ואשמועינן דשרי להסיר בתולים בשבת! ומשני: לא, לבר משבת. ומוצאי שבת נקט לאשמועינן דבעינן רצופים. והוה מצי למיפרך מברייתא דפרק בתרא דנדה, דמוכח דאפי' מפוזרין, אלא דפריך ליה מגופה דברייתא: והא עד מוצאי שבת ארבעה לילות קתני! וא"ת: מעיקרא דמשני לבר משבת — מה עלה בדעתו? והא קתני בהדיא ד' לילות! וי"ל: דהוה ס"ד דהכי פירושו: נותנין לה עד מוצאי שבת לבר משבת, שהן בין הכל ד' לילות. ואיהו פריך: דמשמע דבעיל ד' לילות! ומשני: כשבעל. וקמ"ל כמו שמפרש בתר הכי: אע"ג דהוי פירצה דחוקה, דהא אי חזיא תלינן בדם בתולין, אפ"ה שרי. מאי

מסורת הש"ס

ס"א ל"ג

שבת קיא. בכורות כה. [ע"ש]

שבת עה. קג. קיא: קיז. קכ: קלג. קמג. בכורות כה. סוכה לג: [ביצה לו.]

נדה יח: סד:

[אע"ג דמלאכה שא"צ לגופה אסור לר"ש היכא דלא ניחא ליה כלל שרי טפי כ"ה הנוסחא בתשובת רא"מ סי' לד]

רש"ל גורס ומיהו

[ועי' תוס' שבת מא: ד"ה מיחם]

עין משפט נר מצוה

כא א טוש"ע א"ח סימן שכ סעיף יח:

כב ב ג מיי' פ"ה מהל' איסורי ביאה הל' יח יט סמג לאוין קיא (טוש"ע אה"ע סימן סב סעיף א וטוש"ע י"ד סימן קצג סעיף א):

[ערך סחר]

תוספות רי"ד

האי מסוכרייתא דנזייתא אסור להדוקה ביומא טבא ואפילו ר"ש מודה בהא דאביי ורבא דאמרי תרוייהו מודה ר"ש בפסיק רישי' ולא ימות. פי' המורה סתימת נקב גיגית שמוציאים ממנו השכר וסותמים אותו בבלאי בגדים אסור להדוקה משום סחיטה. ואינו נראה כלל שמה שמשימים בנקב שמוציא ממנו מים או יין בלאי בגדים אין בו משום סחיטה שאינו מוכנין לא ללבנם ולא לקבל ממנו משקה ולאיבוד אזיל א"כ אמאי ליתסר. ור' נתן בעל הערוך פי' משום ר"ח ז"ל מטלית שמשימים על הגיגית לסתום פי' (ומפרקת) [ומהדקה] המטלית שם וזהו פתרון יפה. דודאי באותו המטלית קפיד אם תשרה. א) ומה שסוחט ממנו אסור משום מלבן שדומה לסוחט בגדים שרויים. וזה שאנו משימין בברזא של חביות מתיר ר' נתן בפירוש מפני שהולך לאיבוד:

א) עי' בערוך ערך סחר ה' דפירש שם לאסור משום סחיטה דניחא ליה שיזוב היין בתוך הכלי ע"ש ומשמע לאסור משום מפרק וצ"ע.

שייך לע"ב

מאי לאו דאי לא בעל מצי בעיל אפילו בשבת! אמר רבא: לא, לבר משבת. אמר ליה אביי: והא עד מוצאי שבת ארבעה לילות קתני! אלא אמר רבא: כשבעל. אי כשבעל — מאי קמ"ל? קמ"ל דשרי למיבעל בשבת, כדשמואל. דאמר שמואל: *פירצה דחוקה מותר ליכנס בה בשבת, ואע"פ שמשיר צרורות. מתיב רב יוסף: *[א]חתן פטור מקרית שמע לילה הראשון עד מוצאי שבת אם לא עשה מעשה. מאי לאו — דטריד, דבעי למיבעל? אמר ליה אביי: לא, דטריד דלא בעיל. אמר ליה רבא: ומשום טירדא פטור?! אלא מעתה טבעה ספינתו בים הכי נמי דפטור?! וכי תימא ה"נ — והאמר רבי אבא בר זבדא אמר רב: *אבל חייב בכל המצות האמורות בתורה חוץ מן [ב]התפילין, שנא' בהן "פאר" (יחזקאל כד)! אלא אמר רבא: תנאי היא. דתנא חדא: אם לא עשה מעשה בראשון — פטור אף בשני, בשני — פטור אף בשלישי. ותניא אידך: ראשון ושני — פטור, שלישי — חייב. ואביי: התם נמי בטירדא פליגי. והני תנאי כי הני תנאי; דתניא: הכונס את הבתולה לא יבעול בתחלה בשבת, וחכמים מתירין. *מאן חכמים? אמר רבה: רבי שמעון היא, *דאמר: דבר שאין מתכוין מותר. אמר ליה אביי: והא מודה ר' שמעון בפסיק רישיה ולא ימות! אמר ליה: לא כהללו בבליים שאין בקיאין בהטייה, אלא יש בקיאין בהטייה. א"כ טורד למה? לשאינו בקי. יאמרו: בקי — מותר, שאינו בקי — אסור! רוב בקיאין הן. אמר ליה רבא בר רב חנן לאביי: אלא מעתה שושבינין למה? מפה למה? א"ל: התם שמא יראה ויאבד. מתיב רבי אמי: *[ג]המפים מורסא בשבת, אם לעשות לה פה — חייב. ואם להוציא ממנה ליחה — פטור

מאי לאו. הנך ארבעה לילות עד מוצאי שבת דקתני, להכי תני להו: דאי לא בעל בעילה גמורה — מצי למיבעל, וכל דם שהוא מוציא תמיד *בהערותיו הוו דם בתולים. ושמעינן מינה נמי, דמותר לבעול בתחבורה בשבת. והא ארבעה לילות עד מוצאי שבת קתני. ולא משכחת ליה לבר משבת, דהא ברביעי ניסת, ויש כאן לילי חמישי ושישי ושבת ומוצאי שבת. אי כשבעל. ולא אתא לאורויי לן אלא היתר דם בתולים, האי דנקט עד מוצאי שבת מאי קמ"ל? ליתני: נותנין לה ארבעה לילות. על כרחך משום בעילת שבת נקט לה. שמשיר צרורות. והאי נמי דלא מחבל פורתא, ומספיקא לא אסרינן ליה. מאי לאו. האי דפטר ליה מק"ש בלילי שבת משום דטריד במצוה, דבעי למיבעל, והעוסק במצוה פטור מן המצוה. דטריד דלא בעל. מצטער שלא בעל. משום דטריד פטור. בתמיה. ומשום צער פטור?! מאחר שאינו מחשב לעסוק במצוה. שנאמר בהן פאר. "פארך חבוש עליך" (יחזקאל כד), ואבל מעולל בעפר קרנו וראשו, ואין זה פאר לתפילין. [אלא אמר רבא ודאי לא מצית לתרוצי הא דחתן פטור מק"ש משום דלא מצי בעיל, דא"כ לא הוה פטור, דהא לא טריד בדבר מצוה. תנאי היא. בעילת חבורה בשבת, ומאן דאסר לבעול בשבת — כתנאי אמרה לשמעתיה, דאיכא תנא אחרינא דאסר למיבעל. דתנא חדא כו']. פטור. מקריאת שמע. שלישי חייב. דשבת הוא, ואסור לבעול. ואביי. אמר לך: הנך תנאי נמי בטירדא פליגי, והאי דפטר ליה מק"ש — לאו משום דשרי למיבעל, אלא קסבר המצטער לצער של מצוה פטור מקריאת שמע. ולא דמי לאבל דטריד טירדא דרשות, שאין צערו מצוה, אע"פ שאבילותו מצוה. ומאן דמחייב סבר: טירדא לא פטר. [ורבא אמר דבמותר לבעול פליגי, והני תנאי כהני תנאי]. בהטייה. שמטין לצדדין, ואין מוציאים דם. אם כן. דבקיאים. טורד למה. מהו טרדו להפטר מק"ש. בקי מותר. לבעול בשבת, דלא פסיק רישיה ולא ימות הוא. רוב בקיאין הן. הילכך סתמא לאו פסיק רישיה ולא ימות הוא. שושבינין למה. מאחר שיש בקיאין לבעול בלא דם — הא דתניא לקמן (דף יב.): היו מעמידין להן שני שושבינין אחד לו ואחד לה, כדי לשמש את החתן ואת הכלה. כלומר, לבקר אחריהם שלא יהגו בה רמאות בטענת בתולים. ואי בקיאין בהטייה — מה שושבינין מועילין? מפה למה. לברר את הבתולים. וליטעמיך ל"ג, אלא ה"ג: שושבינין למה? מפה למה? אמר ליה שמא יראה ויאבד. שמא לא יטה, ויוציא דם ויאבדנו, ויאמר לא מצאתי דם, דאילו בהטייה, אם בא לטעון — תאמר לו: עדיין בתולה אני. המפים מורסא. הפותח פה נפש, שקורין קלו"ג. אם לעשות לה פה. שמתכוין ליפותה ולהיות לה פתח זה ליום מחר. חייב. שהוא מתקן פתח, וחייב משום בונה, °דאשכחן בנין בבעלי חיים, דכתיב "ויבן את הצלע" (בראשית ב).

פטור

מאי קמ"ל. במאי דנקט עד מוצאי שבת, דלענין רצופים ליכא למימר, כדפרישית. מאי לאו דטריד דבעי למיבעל. הכא ליכא לשנויי לבר משבת כדלעיל — דא"כ אינו פטור עד מוצאי שבת, וקא משוית ליה לתנא טועה, דפטר ליה עד מוצאי שבת. אבל לעיל, אפילו כי אמרינן לבר משבת, ולא מצי למיבעל בשבת, מכל מקום דוקא נקט עד מוצאי שבת, משום דעד למוצאי שבת תולין בדם בתולים היכא דעבר ובעל. והא אמר ר' אבא אבל חייב בכל המצות כו'. ואביי סבר דטירדא דליכא מצוה כלל — מחייב, אבל טירדא דלא מצי בעיל — חשיב טירדא דמצוה, כיון שטרוד במה שאינו יכול לעשות מצוה. חוץ מן התפילין שנאמר בהן פאר. ואמרינן בפרק בתרא דמועד קטן (דף טו.): מדאמר ליה רחמנא ליחזקאל "פארך חבוש עליך" מכלל דלעלמא אסור. ובקונטרס דפי' שנאמר בהן 'פאר', ואבל מעולל בעפר קרנו וראשו, היינו ליתן טעם דלא נילף שאר מצות מתפילין. וא"ת: ומאי שנא לגבי תפילין אמרינן דדוקא ליחזקאל נאמר, ולא לשאר אבלים, וגבי תלמוד תורה ילפינן שאר אבלים מיחזקאל, דאמרינן (שם): אבל אסור בתלמוד תורה, מדאמר ליה רחמנא ליחזקאל "האנק דום"! ויש לומר: דלאסור גמרינן, דמדאסר רחמנא ליחזקאל — לכ"ע נמי אסור. אבל להתיר — לא גמרינן, דליה לחודיה למשרי אתא. והני תנאי כי הני תנאי. אע"ג דפליגי תנאי בהדיא בהכי — מכל מקום דחיק אביי לעיל, דחשיב טירדא דמצוה הא דלא מצי בעיל, דניחא ליה לאוקומי מתני' כשמואל דאסר לבעול. ומוקי נמי פלוגתא דברייתא אי חשיב טירדא הא דלא מצי בעיל, כדי לאוקמי כשמואל כל מה שיכול. לא כהללו בבליים שאין בקיאין בהטייה. פירוש: אינו פסיק רישיה, דכל העולם אינן כמו בבליים, אלא בקיאין הן. הילכך שרי להו למיבעל, ובלבד שלא יתכונו לבעול בעילה גמורה. ופריך: אם כן טורד למה? פירוש: בשבת אמאי פטר ליה לעיל מק"ש, כיון דבקיאין הן? בשלמא בחול איכא טירדא — לפי שמתכוין לבעול בעילה גמורה, ואף לבקיאין יש טירדא לבעול בעילה גמורה, כדאמר בפרק שני דברכות (דף טז. ושם) דר"ג היה פטור ומחמיר על עצמו, אע"ג דבקי היה, שלא היה בבלי. אבל בשבת שאינו מתכוין לבעול בעילה גמורה — טורד למה? ומשני: לשאינו בקי. פי': לפי שאינו בקי בשעת ק"ש, דאפי' הבקיאין בשעת מעשה — קודם מעשה יראים שלא יהיו בקיאין, הילכך טרודים כולם. רוב בקיאין הן. וכל חד וחד מספקינן ליה ברוב, וכולם מותרים. משמע הכא דרובן בקיאין בהטייה. וא"ת: דאמרינן בפ"ב דחגיגה (דף יד: ושם): בתולה שעיברה מהו לכהונה? כגון שבדקוה על פי חבית ולא היה ריחה נודף, מי חיישינן לדשמואל דאמר יכולני לבעול כמה בעילות בלא דם או דלמא באמבטי עיברה? ומסיק: דשמואל לא שכיח! ובפרק בתרא דנדה (דף סד: ושם) נמי קאמר: שאני שמואל דרב גובריה הוא. והא אמרינן הכא דרוב בקיאין הן! וי"ל: דשמואל היה יכול לבעול בעילה גמורה שאשה מתעברת בו, בלא דם. אבל בהטייה אין אשה מתעברת. ולהכי בההיא דחגיגה ליכא למיחש בהטייה אלא לדשמואל. אלא מעתה שושבינין למה מפה למה. פי' בקונטרס: כיון שהן בקיאין לבעול בלא דם — שמא יטה והיא לא תפיק אדעתה שהטה? ומשני: דשושבינין ומפה הם שאם לא יטה ויבעול בעילה גמורה, ויאבד המפה. ואם יטה ויאמר שלא מצא לה בתולים יכולה לומר עדיין בתולה אני. וקשה לר"י: דאינו מתרץ ממה שהקשה לו, דהוי ליה לשנויי דמסקא אדעתה לומר עדיין בתולה אני, ועיקר התירוץ חסר מן הספר! ונראה לר"י כפירוש ר"ת: דדוקא משבת קא פריך דמפה ושושבינין למה, דצריך לבעול בהטייה, דמעשה בכל יום שעושין שושבינין אפילו בשבת! ומשניך שמא יארע שלא יטה ויבעול בעילה גמורה ויאבד דם בתולים. והויא דומיא דטורד למה, דפריך נמי משבת. אם לעשות לה פה חייב. דפתח זה עשויה להכניס ולהוציא, להכנים אויר ולהוציא ליחה. ואם להוציא ממנה ליחה פטור. בפרק "שמונה שרצים" (שבת דף קז: ושם) מוקמינן לה כרבי שמעון. וסלקא דעתיה דרבי אמי דמותיב דדם מיפקד פקיד, ולדם הוא צריך ולא לפתח, ואפ"ה אסר שמואל כרבי שמעון, דהוי מלאכה שאינה צריכה לגופה. ולהכי פריך ממפים מורסא, דכי היכי דלהוציא ממנה ליחה פטור, וקיימא לן דפטור ומותר כיון דאינו צריך לפתח, אף על גב דשאר מלאכה שאינה צריכה לגופה פטור אבל אסור — במורסא שרי משום צער. הכא נמי, משום מצוה הוי לן למשרי. ועוד: אפילו שרינן משום צערא טפי ממשום מצוה, כדפירש ר"ת לעיל, פריך שפיר; דהכא ודאי דהוי פסיק רישיה לענין פתח, אי לאו משום צערא היה אסור. אבל

גבי

עין משפט נר מצוה

כג א מיי' פ"ד מהל' ק"ש הל' א סמג עשין יח טוש"ע א"ח סי' ע סעי' ג:

כד ב מיי' פ"ד מהל' תפילין הל' יג ופ"ד מהל' אבילות הל' ט סמג עשין דרבנן ב טוש"ע א"ח סימן לח סעי' ה וטוש"ע יו"ד סי' שפח סעי' א:

כה ג מיי' פ"י מהל' שבת הל' יז סמג לאוין סה טוש"ע או"ח סי' שכח סעי' כח:

מסורת הש"ס

נ"ל בהערותיו. יעב"ץ

נדה סד:

ברכות טז.

סוכה כה. ברכות יא. טז: מו"ק טו. ע"ש [שמחות פ"ו]

[עירובין פג. וש"נ]

[לעיל ה. וש"נ]

נ"י כ"י

שבת קז. ושם: עדיות פ"ב מ"ה

גליון הש"ס

רש"י ד"ה חייב וכו' דאשכחן בנין בבע"ח. שבת לה ע"א.

כו א מיי' פ"י מהל' אישות הל' ט סמג עשין מח טוש"ע אה"ע סי' סו סעי' ב:
כז ב מיי' פ"ב מהל' נזירות הל' כא:
כח ג מיי' פ"ט מהל' שחיטה הל' א סמג עשין סג טוש"ע יו"ד סי' לב סעי' א:
[נ"ל בפ' כירה שבת מב.]
כט ד מיי' פ"ל מהל' שבת הל' יד סמג לאוין סה ועשין מח טוש"ע אה"ע סימן סב סעיף א וטוש"ע א"ח סי' רפ סעי' ב:
ל ה מיי' פ"ב מהל' ברכות הל' ט ומיי' פ"י מהל' אישות הל' ה סמג עשין מח טוש"ע אה"ע סי' סא סעי' ד:
לא ו ז מיי' פ"ב מהלכות ברכות הל' ט סמג שם טוש"ע שם סעי' ו:
לב ח מיי' פ"י מהלכ' אישות הל' י"ב סמג שם טוש"ע שם סי' סא סעי' ב [ועי' מ"מ]:
לג ט מיי' פ"ב מהל' ברכות ה"ט סמג שם טוש"ע שם סעי' ו:

פטור! התם פקיד ועקיר, הכא – פקיד ולא עקיר. רבי אמי שרא למיבעל בתחלה בשבת. אמרי ליה רבנן: והא לא כתיבא כתובתה! אמר להו: *[א]אתפסוה מטלטלין. רב זביד שרא למיבעל בתחלה בשבת. איכא דאמרי: רב זביד גופיה בעל בתחלה בשבת. רב יהודה שרא למיבעל בתחלה ביו"ט. אמר רב פפי משמיה דרבא: לא תימא ביו"ט דשרי, הא בשבת אסור – דהוא הדין דאפילו בשבת נמי שרי, *ומעשה שהיה כך היה. רב פפא משמיה דרבא אמר: ביו"ט – שרי, בשבת – אסור. א"ל רב פפי לרב פפא: מאי דעתיך, מתוך שהותרה חבורה לצורך הותרה נמי שלא לצורך? אלא מעתה מותר לעשות מוגמר ביו"ט, *דמתוך שהותרה הבערה לצורך – הותרה נמי שלא לצורך! אמר ליה: עליך אמר קרא °"אך אשר יאכל לכל נפש" דבר השוה לכל נפש. אמר ליה רב אחא בריה דרבא לרב אשי: אלא מעתה, נזדמן לו צבי ביו"ט, הואיל ואינו שוה לכל נפש – ה"נ דאסור למשחטיה?! אמר ליה: אנא דבר הצורך לכל נפש קאמינא, צבי צריך לכל נפש הוא. אמר רבי יעקב בר אידי: הורה רבי יוחנן בצידן: אסור לבעול בתחלה בשבת. ומי איכא הוראה לאיסור? אין. והתנן: *הורוה בית הלל [ב]שתהא נזירה עוד שבע שנים אחרות, ואי נמי כי הא, דתניא: *[ג]חוט השדרה שנפסק – ברובו, דברי רבי. ר' יעקב אומר: אפי' ניקב. הורה רבי כר' יעקב. אמר רב הונא: אין הלכה כר' יעקב. רב נחמן בר יצחק מתני הכי: אמר ר' אבהו שאל ר' ישמעאל בן יעקב דמן צור את רבי יוחנן בצידן, ואנא שמעי: מהו לבעול בתחלה בשבת? ואמר ליה: אסור. והלכתא: [ד]מותר לבעול בתחלה בשבת.§ אמר רבי חלבו אמר רב הונא א"ר אבא בר זבדא אמר רב: אחת בתולה ואחת אלמנה טעונה ברכה. ומי אמר רב הונא הכי? והאמר רב הונא: אלמנה אינה טעונה ברכה! לא קשיא; כאן – בבחור שנשא אלמנה, כאן – באלמון שנשא אלמנה. ואלמון שנשא אלמנה לא? והאמר רב נחמן, אמר לי הונא בר נתן, תנא: מנין [ה]לברכת חתנים בעשרה? שנאמר: °"ויקח עשרה אנשים מזקני העיר ויאמר שבו פה וישבו", ובועז אלמון שנשא אלמנה הוה! מאי אינה טעונה ברכה דאמר רב הונא – אינה טעונה ברכה כל ז' – [ו]אבל יום אחד טעונה ברכה. אלא הא דתניא: *שקדו חכמים על תקנת בנות ישראל שיהא שמח עמה ג' ימים, במאי? אי בבחור – האמרת שבעה, אי באלמון – האמרת יום אחד! איבעית אימא: [ז]באלמון – יום אחד לברכה [ח]ושלשה לשמחה, ואיבעית אימא: [ט]בבחור – שבעה לברכה ושלשה לשמחה.

מיתיבי

שמות יב

רות ד

[לעיל ה.]

פטור. וקיימא לן: פטור ומותר לכתחלה, ב"יציאות השבת" (דף ג.). קשיא למאן דאסר, דהאי נמי להוציא דם הוא. התם. גבי ליחה. פקיד. כנוס ביחד. ועקיר. כולו מן הבשר, ועומד לצאת. הכא. דם בתולים. פקיד הוא ולא עקיר. לגמרי, אלא נבלע קצת בכתלים, אע"פ שאינו מחובר כבשר דם תורה אור האברים אלא כנוס. מיהו, דומה למחובר הוא, שאינו מוכן לצאת כליחה. אתפסוה מטלטלי. תנו לה מטלטלין תחת ידה במשכון לשיעבוד כתובתה, עד שיכתבו שטר כתובתה בשעבוד קרקעות. מאי דעתיך. למישרי יו"ט יותר מבשבת. לצורך. אוכל נפש, כגון שחיטה. מוגמר. בשמים על האש, לגמר את הכלים ואת הבגדים. עליך אמר קרא לכל נפש דבר השוה לכל נפש. מותר, ובעילה שוה לכל, אבל מוגמר אינו אלא למפונקים. ומי איכא הוראה לאיסור. ומי קרי איסור "הוראה"? משום דכל אדם רשאי להחמיר, והאוסר אין זה סמיכת דברים, שאפי' מן הספק, שאין ההלכה ברורה לו, הוא בא ואוסר. אבל המתיר סומך על שמועתו, או על סברת חכמתו, והיא "הוראה". הורוה ב"ה. משנה היא במסכת נזיר, בהילני המלכה שיצא בנה למלחמה, ונדרה שבע שנים בנזיר *בחוצה לארץ, ועלתה לארץ, הורוה ב"ה שתהא נזירה עוד ז' שנים אחרות. חוט השדרה שנפסק ברובו. טריפה. טעונה ברכה. ברכת חתנים. בועז אלמון הוה. דאמר מר: אבצן זה בועז, וכבר היו לו ל' בנים ושלשים בנות, כדאמרינן בבבא בתרא (דף קכ.). האמרת שבעה. דמדאינה טעונה דקאמר רב הונא אוקימנא דאינה טעונה שבעה, מכלל דטעונה דקאמר רבי אבא – שבעה.

מברכין

[עי' תוס' לקמן נו: ד"ה אין]

[עירובין סח. וש"נ]

[פסחים ה: ביצה יב:]

ומנחה בה"ל ועלתה לארץ כצ"ל. רש"ל

נזיר יט:

חולין מה.

גבי בעילה אית לן למשרי אע"ג דליכא לערל, כיון דלא הוי פסיק רישיה לענין פתח, כיון דאפשר להוציא דם בלא עשיית פתח כדמוכח לעיל (דף ה:). ומשני, הכא פקיד ולא עקיר, דקסבר דם חבורי מיחבר. והוא הדין דהוי מצי לשנויי דלפתח הוא צריך, אלא לפי מאי דקים ליה דלדם הוא צריך משני ליה. ותימה: דהא שמואל במלאכה שאינה צריכה לגופה סבר לה כר' יהודה, כדאמרי' בפ' *"המצניע" (ד' פא. ושם) ובפ' "כל התדיר" (זבחים ד' צא.)! ועוד, דמדבר שאין מתכוין דשרי ר"ש ה"ל לאקשויי, ולא ממלאכה שאינה צריכה לגופה, כיון דרוב בקיאין ולא הוי פסיק רישיה.

מתוך שהותרה לצורך. פירוש: לצורך אוכל נפש, הותרה נמי שלא לצורך אוכל נפש, ובלבד שיהא צורך הנאת היום, או צורך קיום מצוה ביו"ט. כההיא דהוצאת קטן למולו, וספר תורה לקרות בו, ולולב לצאת בו (ביצה דף יב.). אבל שלא לצורך היום כלל – לא, כמו הוצאת אבנים דמיחייב, והאופה מיו"ט לחול לרב חסדא דאמר לוקה (שם דף כא.), משום דלית ליה "הואיל". ושחיטת עולת נדבה דשרי לב"ה (שם דף כ:) היינו משום שלא יהא שלחנך מלא ושלחן רבך חסר. ומוצא חמץ בתוך ביתו דאמרינן בפ"ק דפסחים (דף ו. ושם) דכופה עליו כלי ולא שרינן לשורפו – משום "מתוך", היינו: משום דאסור לשורפו מדרבנן משום מוקצה, דאסור לטלטלו. אבל אין לומר דאיירי כשביטלו, דמכל מקום מדרבנן מצוה לשורפו, והוי צורך היום, דבמצוה דרבנן נמי שרינן היכא דאיכא למימר "מתוך". והא דפליגי ב"ש וב"ה (ביצה דף יב:) במבשל גיד הנשה ביו"ט ואכלו, דלב"ש דלית להו "מתוך" לוקה, ולב"ה דאית להו "מתוך" – אינו לוקה, צריך לומר: אע"ג דלא חשיב אוכל נפש, משום איסור דרכיב עליה, מכל מקום צורך היום הוא, כיון דאכיל ליה. ונראה לר"י: דהוצאת תינוק לטייל – הוי צורך היום. ומיהו, הוצאה לצורך גוי נראה דאסור. ומה שנהגו עתה להוציא לצורך גוי היה נראה לרשב"א משום דרשות הרבים דידן לא הוי אלא כרמלית, דאין רחבין ט"ז אמה, וגבי יו"ט לא גזור רבנן, כי היכי דלא תקון רבנן עירובי חצירות ביו"ט, כדמשמע בריש פרק שני דביצה (דף טז:) דאמר: יו"ט שחל להיות ערב שבת כו' רבי אומר מערבין עירובי חצירות אבל לא עירובי תחומין, לפי שאתה אוסרו בדבר האסור לו ואי אתה אוסרו בדבר המותר לו. אלמא לא תקון עירובי חצירות ביו"ט. והוא הדין דלא גזרו בכרמלית. והא דקיימא לן בפרק "אמרו לו" (כריתות דף יד. ושם) ובפרק קמא דביצה (דף יב. ושם) דיש עירוב והוצאה ליו"ט – נראה דאיירי בעירובי תחומין. ושוב חזר בו, דמהלך שאינה מעורבת אין ללמוד ממנה לכרמלית, דחמיר טפי, כמו שפירשתי במסכת שבת (דף קיז.). ועוד נראה: דהא דקיימא לן דיש עירוב והוצאה ליו"ט – בעירובי חצירות איירי, מדבעי למימר בפרק "אמרו לו" (כריתות דף יד. ושם) דאין עירוב והוצאה ליוה"כ, מדתנן התם: אם היתה שבת והוציאו בפיו – חייב, וכן בביצה (דף יב. ושם) בעי למידק דאין עירוב והוצאה ליו"ט מדשרו בית הלל להוציא קטן ולולב –והיינו עירובי חצרות, דהשתא מוכח לה שפיר מדשרו הוצאה, דלא גזרו רבנן אעירובי חצירות אלא משום הוצאה, אבל עירובי תחומין אין ענייניה להוצאה. והא דקאמר ואי אתה אוסרו בדבר המותר לו – היינו משום דמותר להוציא לצורך. **אלא** מעתה יהא מותר לעשות מוגמר ביו"ט. ואם תאמר: לדידיה נמי תקשי, וכי לא סבר דאמרינן "מתוך"? הא טעמא דב"ה הכי הוא! ויש לומר: שהיה סובר דטעמא דבית הלל משום דאין עירוב והוצאה, כדקא ס"ד מעיקרא בביצה. אע"ג דהתם פריך עלה – דלמא לרב פפי לא שמיע לה. ועוי"ל: שהיה סובר הותרה שלא לצורך ובלבד שיהא דבר הרגיל. ולהכי פריך, דזה אינו רגיל טפי מוגמר. **אמר** ליה אנא דבר הצריך לכל נפש קאמינא וצבי צריך לכל נפש. וכן ביצה. וקשה לר"י: דאמר בסוף פ"ב דביצה (דף כב.) מהו לכבות הנר מפני דבר אחר – ומסיק דאסור. הא הכא שרי, משום דצריך לכל נפש! וי"ל: דהכא דוקא בבעילה ראשונה, דמצוה היא, דהוי צורך מצות היום. אבל שאר בעילות – אין כל כך צורך היום. ועי"ל, דכיבוי הנר מפני דבר אחר הוי כמו מכשירין, דאפילו באוכל נפש אסור. וכן מוכח התם, דפריך עלה מהא דתניא דמכבין את הבקעת כדי שלא יתעשן הבית, ומשני: ההיא רבי יהודה היא דשרי מכשירי אוכל נפש, כי קאמינא לרבנן. **והלכתא** מותר לבעול בתחלה בשבת. ולא חיישינן שמא ישחוט בן עוף. והאי סמכינן למיעבד סעודה בשבת.

במקהלות

תוספות רי"ד

א"ל והא לא כתיבא כתובה ואסרו חכמים לשהות אדם את אשתו שעה אחת בלא כתובה א"ל אתפסוה מטלטלי שיעור כתובתה. פי' שיהיה משכון בידה עד שיכתבו לה שטר כתובתה: א"ר חלבו א"ר אדא בר זבדא אמר רב א' בתולה וא' אלמנה טעונה ברכה [כל] שבעה. פי' טעונה ברכות כל ז' ימים ולקמן מוקי לה בדאיכא פנים חדשות: ומי אמר רב הכי והא"ר הונא אלמנה אינה טעונה ברכה כל ז' אלא יום א'. ל"ק כאן בבחור שנשא אלמנה כאן באלמון שנשא אלמנה. מיתיבי מברכים לבתולה ז' ולאלמנה יום א' מאי לאו לאלמנה שנשאת לבחור. לא לאלמון. אבל לבחור מאי ז'. א"ה ליתני מברכין לבתולה ז' ולאלמנה שנשאת לבחור ז' ולאלמנה שנשאת לאלמון יום א'. מילתא פסיקא קתני ליכא בתולה דבצירא מז' פי' ואפילו נשאת לאלמון. וליכא אלמנה דבצירא מיום א': אלא הא דתניא שקדו חכמים על תקנת בנות ישראל שיהא שמח עמה ג' ימים במאי אי בבחור הא אמרת ז' אם באלמון הא אמרת יום א'. איבעית אימא בבחור ז' לברכה וג' לשמחה איבע"א באלמון יום א' לברכה וג' לשמחה:

לד א מיי' פ"ח מהל' זכיה הל' ה סמג עשין פג טוש"ע חו"מ סי' רי סעי' א:

[בספר תהלים שלפנינו נדפס מלא]

לה ב מיי' פ"ב מהל' ברכות הל' ט ופ"י מהל' אישות הל' ג סמג עשין מח טוש"ע אה"ע סימן סא סעי' א:

לו ג מיי' פ"י מהל' אישות הל"ו טוש"ע שם סי' נה סעי' א:

לז ד ה מיי' פ"ג שם הל' כד סמג שם טוש"ע שם סי' לד סעי' א:

לח ו מיי' פ"ב מהל' ברכות הל' י סמג שם טוש"ע שם סימן סב סעי' ז ח [עי' כ"מ]:

במקהלות ברכו אלהים. אע"ג ד"מקהלות" – תרי קהלות משמע – אין סברא לחלק בין עשרה לעשרים לענין שום מילתא, ומקהלות דעלמא בעי למימר. ומיהו, בירושלמי דריש: "במקהלת" כתיב *חסר וי"ו. **המזכה** לעובר קנה. אע"ג דשמואל גופיה פסיק כרבי יוחנן הסנדלר (לקמן דף נח:) דמקדיש מעשה ידי אשתו – המותר חולין, דאין אדם מקדיש דבר שלא בא לעולם, וכל שכן לדבר שלא בא לעולם, דגרע טפי; כדאמרינן בסוף פרק קמא דגיטין (דף יג: ושם) דקאמר: אפילו לרבי מאיר דאמר: אדם מקנה דבר שלא בא לעולם – הני מילי לדבר שבא לעולם, אבל לדבר שלא בא לעולם – לא אמר! מ"מ, שמואל חשיב עובר בא לעולם. אי נמי: שמואל אית ליה טפי אדם מקנה לדבר שלא בא לעולם. ממה שמקנה דבר שלא בא לעולם והיא סוגיא דפרק קמא דגיטין (ג"ז שם) אתיא אליבא דרב הונא. וכן מצינו רב נחמן דבהדיא סברתו הפוכה מדרב הונא, [יבמות לג.] דרב הונא אית ליה* בפירות דקל משבאו לעולם אין יכול לחזור בו, [ב"ב קמב.] וגבי עובר קאמר* אף לכשתלד – לא קנה. ורב נחמן סבר לכשתלד קנה, ובפירות דקל קאמר אף משבאו לעולם יכול לחזור בו. (שייך לע"א) **הורוה** בית הלל. גבי הילני המלכה. אע"ג דמבית חשמונאי היתה, שהרי אם מונבז המלך היתה, כדאמר ביומא (דף לז. ושם), ומלכות הורדוס מאה ושלש שנה בפני הבית, והלל לא נהג נשיאותו עד שלש שנים לאחר מלכות הורדוס, כדאמרינן (שבת טו.): הלל ושמעון, גמליאל ושמעון נהגו נשיאותן בפני הבית מאה שנה – מכל מקום כבר היו לו אז תלמידים שהורו. (שייך לע"א) **והא** בועז אלמון שנשא אלמנה הוה. לאו דוקא אלמנה, דכשנשאת למחלון (וכליון) היתה גויה, אלא כיון דבעולה – היא כאלמנה חשיב לה. (שייך לע"א) **באלמנה** שנשאת לבחור. דכיון שאין שניהם אלמונים – יש לברך כל שבעה. **שנאמר** ויקח בועז עשרה אנשים. ובמסכת כלה דמייתי קרא ד"ויברכו את רבקה" (בראשית כד) איכא למימר דהתם ברכת אירוסין, והכא ברכת נישואין. ויש ללמוד מכאן שיש לברך ברכת אירוסין לאשה המתקדשת על ידי שליח, שהרי אליעזר שליח היה. ונראה דאסמכתא בעלמא היא, דעשרה לא מישתמע מהתם, ולא איירי פשטיה דקרא בברכת אירוסין. **רבי** יהודה אומר אף בבית האירוסין מברכין אותה מפני שמתייחד עמה. ואמרי': כלה בלא ברכה אסורה לבעלה כנדה. ולפי שפעמים בא עליה שלא לשם חופה – עושין ברכה מתחלה, כדי שתבא כלה בברכה. **מאן** דלא חתים מידי דהוה אברכת פירות. שאין בה אריכות. והאי נמי אינה ארוכה, ולא דמי לקידושא דאריך טפי. ומאן דחתים – מידי דהוה אקידושא דחתים ביה משום דאריך, והאי נמי חשיבא ארוכה. ומה שפירש בקונטרס דמשום דבלשון קדושה היא חתמי בה כמו בקידושא – אינו נראה. ק"ק: מאן דלא חתים בה, מאי שנא מברכת התורה דחתמינן בה ב"אשר בחר בנו" אע"ג דברכת אירוסין אריכא טפי מינה? ושמא לא היה חותם בה. **והוא** שבאו פנים חדשות. אור"י: דפנים חדשות אין קורא אלא בני אדם שמרבים בשבילם השמחה יותר. ושבת דחשבינן פנים חדשות, דאמרינן באגדה: מזמור שיר ליום השבת, אמר הקב"ה: פנים חדשות באו לכאן, נאמר שירה – התם נמי מרבין לכבוד השבת בשמחה ובסעודה.
שהכל

מיתיבי: מברכין לבתולה שבעה ולאלמנה יום אחד. מאי לאו – אפילו אלמנה שנשאת לבחור! לא, לאלמון. אבל לבחור מאי – שבעה, אי הכי ליתני: מברכין לבתולה שבעה, ולאלמנה שנשאת לבחור שבעה, ולאלמנה יום אחד! מילתא פסיקתא קתני, דליכא בתולה דבצרה משבעה, וליכא אלמנה דבצרה מיום אחד. § גופא, אמר רב נחמן: אמר לי הונא בר נתן, תנא: מנין לברכת חתנים בעשרה – שנאמר: °"ויקח עשרה אנשים מזקני העיר ויאמר שבו פה". (רות ד) ורבי אבהו אמר מהכא: °"במקהלות ברכו אלהים ה' ממקור ישראל" (תהלים סח) ורב נחמן בהאי קרא דרבי אבהו מאי דריש ביה? מיבעי ליה לכדתניא, היה ר"מ אומר: *מנין שאפילו עוברים שבמעי אמן אמרו שירה על הים? שנאמר: "במקהלות ברכו אלהים ה' ממקור ישראל". ואידך – אם כן לימא קרא "מבטן", מאי "ממקור" – על עסקי מקור. ורבי אבהו בהאי קרא דרב נחמן מאי דריש ביה? ההוא מיבעי ליה למידרש: *עמוני ולא עמונית, מואבי ולא מואבית. דאי סלקא דעתך לברכה – לא סגיא דלאו זקנים? ואידך: אי סלקא דעתך למידרש – לא סגיא דלאו עשרה? אין, לפרסומי מילתא. *וכדאמר ליה שמואל לרב חנא בגדתאה: פוק ואייתי לי בי עשרה, ואימא לך באנפייהו: המזכה לעובר – קנה. והלכתא: [א]המזכה לעובר – לא קנה. § תנו רבנן: מברכין •ברכת חתנים [ב]בבית חתנים. ר' יהודה אומר: אף בבית האירוסין מברכין אותה. אמר אביי: וביהודה שנו, [ג]מפני שמתייחד עמה. תניא אידך: מברכין ברכת חתנים בבית חתנים, וברכת ארוסין בבית האירוסין, ברכת האירוסין מאי מברך? רבין בר רב אדא ורבה בר רב אדא, תרוייהו משמיה דרב יהודה אמרי: [ד]בא"י אמ"ה אשר קדשנו במצותיו וצונו על העריות ואסר לנו את הארוסות והתיר לנו את הנשואות על ידי חופה וקידושין. רב אחא בריה דרבא מסיים בה משמיה דרב יהודה: [ה]בא"י מקדש ישראל על ידי חופה וקידושין. מאן דלא חתים – מידי דהוה אברכת פרות ואברכת מצות, ומאן דחתים – מידי דהוה אקידושא. § ת"ר: מברכין ברכת חתנים בעשרה כל שבעה. אמר רב יהודה: [ו]והוא שבאו פנים חדשות. מאי מברך? אמר רב יהודה: בא"י אמ"ה שהכל

מברכין לבתולה שבעה. לקמן מפרש כשבאו פנים חדשות מברך כולן כל ימי המשתה, ואי לא – מברך חדא. במקהלות ברכו אלהים ה' ממקור ישראל. על ברכת מקור צריך קהל, והיינו עשרה כמו "הקהל את העדה" (במדבר כ), ואין הקהל פחות מעדה, ועדה עשרה, כדילפינן (ברכות דף כא:) מעדת מרגלים "עד מתי לעדה הרעה" – יצאו יהושע וכלב. בגדתאה. עיר שבבבל ושמה בגדת. בפסק סדרו של רב שרירא גאון היא נזכרת. המזכה. מתנה על ידי אחר. לעובר. שבמעי אמו, קנה. בבית חתנים. כשנכנסה לחופת נישואין. אף בבית האירוסין. כשמקדשה, מברכין כל ברכת חתנים, כדמפרש. אמר אביי וביהודה שנו. [הא דר"י ביהודה שנו]. שמתייחד עמה. באירוסין, כדי שיהא לבו גס בה, כדלקמן (דף יב.). לפיכך מברכין ברכת חתנים מתחלה, דתניא במסכת כלה: כלה בלא ברכה אסורה לבעלה כנדה. ואסר לנו את הארוסות. מדרבנן, שגזרו על הייחוד של פנויה, ואף ארוסה לא התירו עד שתיכנס לחופה, ובברכה, כדפרישית: כלה בלא ברכה אסורה לבעלה כנדה. ואדרבנן נמי מברכין "וצונו", "ואסר לנו", כדאשכחן בנר חנוכה (שבת דף כג.). והתיר לנו. את נשותינו הנשואות לנו על ידי חופה וקידושין. אברכת פירות. בורא פרי העץ. ברכת מצות. על השחיטה, ועל המילה. דכיון דכולה חדא הודאה היא, ואין הפסק בקשה בינתיים – לא בעיא חתימה. כדאמר ב"ערבי פסחים" (פסחים דף קה.): ברכת המצות טעמא מאי – משום דהודאה היא, הא נמי – כולה הודאה היא. מידי דהוה אקידושא. כיון דבלשון קדושה היא כקידוש היום, חתמינן בה כי התם, דבההיא חתמינן משום דיש בה הפסק, כגון "כי הוא יום תחלה למקראי קודש". והוא שבאו. אל המשתה. פנים חדשות. בכל יום, שלא היו שם אתמול. מאי מברך אמר רב יהודה כו'. נראה בעיני: סדר ברכות שנסדרו על עסקי הזווג אינו אלא מ"אשר יצר" ואילך, שאותה ברכה מתחלת לדבר בשניהם; "אשר יצר את האדם" מדבר בזכר, והתקין

ברכות נ.
[יבמות סט. וש"נ]
יבמות מז. ב"ב קמב: [זבחים לג.]

גליון הש"ס
גמ' ברכת חתנים בבית חתנים. ע' סוכה כה ע"ב תד"ה אין שמחה.

תוספות רי"ד

א"ר נחמן א"ר הונא תנא מנין לברכת חתנים שהוא בעשרה שנאמר ויקח בועז עשרה אנשים וכו'. ור' אבהו אמר במקהלות ברכו אלהים ה' ממקור ישראל. פי' בה"ג בשעה שאתה מברך על המקור משום פריה ורביה עשה קהילה. א"ר יוסף הלוי הני ז' ברכות דמברכים בבית חתנים בין בשעת הכניסה בין בשעת המשתה בדאיכא פנים חדשות בין אשר ברא. בדליכא פנים חדשות לא מברכינן לה אלא בעשרה. דאר"י אר"י מברכין ברכת חתנים בעשרה כל ז' וחתנים מן המנין. ואשר ברא כיון דמברכת חתנים הוא לא מברכין לה בדליכא פנים חדשות אלא בעשרה. ואינו נ"ל דכל היכא דאמרי ברכת חתנים לא משמע אלא ז' ברכות ולא אשר ברא בלחוד דהכי אמרינן ברכת חתנים כל ז'. ואמר רב יהודה והוא שבאו פנים חדשות. אלמא לא מיקרייא ברכת חתנים אלא ז' ברכות. דהא אשר ברא בלחוד לא בעיא פנים חדשות. והלכך כי אר"י מברכין ברכת חתנים בעשרה כל ז' על ז' ברכות קאמר ובדאיכא פנים חדשות. אבל אשר ברא נ"ל כיון שהוא עיקר ברכת חתנות שחייב לברכה בכל יום אפילו אם אכל החתן יחיד חייב לאומרה. הגה"ה (והרב פוסק (כר') [בשם רבינו] יצחק הלוי ואפי' ברכת אשר ברא לבדו צריכה עשרה.) ת"ר מברכין ברכת חתנים בבית חתנים ר"י אומר אף בבית האירוסין מברכין אותן. אמר אביי ביהודה שנו מפני שמתיחד עמה. פי' ביהודה הי' מיחדים אותם משעת אירוסין כדי שיהא לבו גס בה. ולפיכך מברכים אותם ברכת חתנים תחלה ותניא במס' כלה כלה בלא ברכה אסורה לבעלה כנדה. ואע"ג דהוו מברכי להו משעת אירוסין דין ארוסה יש לה ולא דין נשואה ואינו זכאי לא במציאותי' ולא במעשה ידיה ולא בהפרת נדריה. ואם מתה אינה יורשה וכן הוא אינו חייב לה בשאר כסות ועונה ולא נקראת אשתו נשואה אלא כשמוסרים אותה לו לשם נשואין. דמסירה קונה שתהיה אשתו לכל דבר ולא ז' ברכות דז' ברכות לא עבדי אלא שיהא מותר להתיחד עמה. וכן דרך קהילות ממגיאה שמברכים ז' ברכות משעת אירוסין ועומדים זמן הרבה. ואח"כ מוסרים אותה לו לחופה לשם נשואין. ומ"ה תנן בפירקין לקמן. חוץ מן הארוסה שביהודה. שאע"פ שהיו מברכים ברכות אירוסין אכתי ארוסה קרי לה עד שימסרנה לו לשם נשואין ונ"ל שכיון שבירך ז' ברכות משעת אירוסין אסור עוד לברכה בשעת נשואין דהוה להו ברכה לבטלה. א"נ י"ל משום אפושי שמחה. וכל מה שמברכין בתוך ז' ימי החתונה אין בם משום ברכה לבטלה והכי נמי עיקר חיתונים הנשואים הם שמה שבירך בשעת האירוסין לא בירך אלא להתיר היחוד ועיקר חתנותיה זו היא. הלכך מברכין אותם בשעת הנשואים: תניא אידך מברכין ברכות חתנים בבית חתנים וברכת האירוסין בבית האירוסין. ברכת האירוסין מאי מברך רבין בר אדא ורב' בר רב אדא תרווייהו משמיה דר"י אמרי. בא"י אמ"ה אקב"ו על העריות ואסר לנו את הארוסות והתיר לנו את הנשואות ע"י חופה וקידושין. רב אחא משמיה דרבא מסיים בא"י מקדש ישראל ע"י חופה וקידושין מאן דלא מסיים סבר מידי דהוי אברכת פירות ואברכת מצות. ומאן דמסיים סבר מידי דהוי אקדושא דעלמא. פי' שמאריך בה דבריו צריך חתימה וכך הלכה. והאי ואסר לנו את הארוסות היא מדרבנן שאמרו כלה בלא ברכה אסורה לבעלה כנדה ואפ"ה מברך עליה מידי דהוה אנר חנוכה. ונ"ל דאע"ג שכל המצות מברך עליהן עובר לעשייתן הכא ברישא מקדש והדר מברך. מפני שהוא תלוי בדעת אחרים ושמא יחזרו בהן והוו לבטלה: ת"ר מברכין ברכת חתנים כל ז'. אמר ר"י והיא שבאו פנים חדשות. פי' ברכות חתנים הוא ז' ברכות. ומ"ה צריך פנים חדשות אדם
שעדיין

תורה אור

א"שֶׁהַכֹּל בָּרָא לִכְבוֹדוֹ", וְ"יוֹצֵר הָאָדָם", וַ"אֲשֶׁר יָצַר אֶת הָאָדָם בְּצַלְמוֹ בְּצֶלֶם דְּמוּת תַּבְנִיתוֹ וְהִתְקִין לוֹ מִמֶּנּוּ בִּנְיַן עֲדֵי עַד בָּרוּךְ אַתָּה ה' יוֹצֵר הָאָדָם", "שׂוֹשׂ תָּשִׂישׂ וְתָגֵל הָעֲקָרָה בְּקִבּוּץ בָּנֶיהָ לְתוֹכָהּ בְּשִׂמְחָה בָּרוּךְ אַתָּה ה' מְשַׂמֵּחַ צִיּוֹן בְּבָנֶיהָ", "שַׂמֵּחַ תְּשַׂמַּח רֵיעִים הָאֲהוּבִים כְּשַׂמֵּחֲךָ יְצִירְךָ בְּגַן עֵדֶן מִקֶּדֶם בָּרוּךְ אַתָּה ה' מְשַׂמֵּחַ חָתָן וְכַלָּה", "בָּרוּךְ אַתָּה ה' אמ"ה אֲשֶׁר בָּרָא שָׂשׂוֹן וְשִׂמְחָה חָתָן וְכַלָּה גִּילָה רִינָּה דִּיצָה חֶדְוָה אַהֲבָה וְאַחֲוָה וְשָׁלוֹם וְרֵיעוּת, מְהֵרָה ה' אֱלֹהֵינוּ יִשָּׁמַע בְּעָרֵי יְהוּדָה וּבְחוּצוֹת יְרוּשָׁלַיִם קוֹל שָׂשׂוֹן וְקוֹל שִׂמְחָה קוֹל חָתָן וְקוֹל כַּלָּה קוֹל מִצְהֲלוֹת חֲתָנִים מֵחוּפָּתָם וּנְעָרִים מִמִּשְׁתֵּה נְגִינָתָם בא"י מְשַׂמֵּחַ חָתָן עִם הַכַּלָּה". לֵוִי אִיקְלַע לְבֵי רַבִּי בְּהִלּוּלֵיהּ דְּר"ש בְּרֵיהּ, בְּרִיךְ חָמֵשׁ. רַב אַסִּי אִיקְלַע לְבֵי רַב אַשִׁי בְּהִלּוּלֵיהּ דְּמָר בְּרֵיהּ, בְּרִיךְ שִׁית. לֵימָא בְּהָא קָמִיפַּלְגִי, דְּמ"ס חֲדָא יְצִירָה הֲוַאי, וּמ"ס: שְׁתֵּי יְצִירוֹת הֲוַאי? לָא, דְּכ"ע חֲדָא יְצִירָה הֲוַאי, מ"ס: בָּתַר מַחֲשָׁבָה אָזְלִינַן, וּמ"ס: בָּתַר מַעֲשֶׂה אָזְלִינַן. כִּי הָא *דְּרַב יְהוּדָה רָמֵי, כְּתִיב: °"וַיִּבְרָא אֱלֹהִים אֶת הָאָדָם בְּצַלְמוֹ", וּכְתִיב: °"זָכָר וּנְקֵבָה בְּרָאָם", הָא כֵּיצַד? בַּתְּחִלָּה עָלָה בְּמַחֲשָׁבָה לְבָּרְאוֹת שְׁנַיִם, וּלְבַסּוֹף נִבְרָא אֶחָד. רַב אַשִׁי אִיקְלַע לְבֵי רַב כָּהֲנָא, יוֹמָא קַמָּא בְּרִיךְ כּוּלְּהוּ, מִכָּאן וְאֵילָךְ, באִי אִיכָּא פָּנִים חֲדָשׁוֹת – בְּרִיךְ כּוּלְּהוּ, וְאִי לָא – אַפּוּשֵׁי שִׂמְחָה בְּעָלְמָא הוּא, מְבָרֵךְ "שֶׁהַשִּׂמְחָה בִּמְעוֹנוֹ" וַ"אֲשֶׁר בָּרָא". מִשִּׁבְעָה וְעַד שְׁלֹשִׁים, בֵּין אֲמַר לְהוּ מֵחֲמַת הִלּוּלָא וּבֵין לָא אֲמַר לְהוּ מֵחֲמַת הִלּוּלָא – מְבָרֵךְ "שֶׁהַשִּׂמְחָה בִּמְעוֹנוֹ". מִכָּאן וְאֵילָךְ, אִי אֲמַר לְהוּ מֵחֲמַת הִלּוּלָא – מְבָרֵךְ "שֶׁהַשִּׂמְחָה בִּמְעוֹנוֹ", וְאִי לָא – לָא. וְכִי א"ל מֵחֲמַת הִלּוּלָא עַד אֵימַת? אָמַר רַב פַּפִּי מִשְּׁמֵיהּ דְּרָבָא: געַד תְּרֵיסַר יַרְחֵי שַׁתָּא. וּמֵעִיקָּרָא מֵאֵימַת? *אָמַר רַב פַּפָּא: מִכִּי רָמוּ שַׂעֲרֵי בְּאַסִּינְתָּא. אִינִי? וְהָא רַב פַּפָּא אִיעֲסַק לְאַבָּא מָר בְּרֵיהּ, וּבְרִיךְ מִשְּׁעַת אֵירוּסִין! שָׁאנֵי רַב פַּפָּא דַּהֲוָה טְרִיחַ לֵיהּ. רָבִינָא אִיעֲסַק לֵיהּ לִבְרֵיהּ בֵּי רַב חֲבִיבָא, וּבְרִיךְ מִשְּׁעַת אֵירוּסִין. אֲמַר: קִים לִי בְּגַוַּיְיהוּ דְּלָא הָדְרֵי בְּהוּ. לָא אִסְתַּיַּיע מִילְּתָא, וְהָדְרִי בְּהוּ. רַב תַּחְלִיפָא בַּר מַעַרְבָא אִיקְלַע לְבָבֶל, בְּרִיךְ שִׁית אֲרִיכָתָא. וְלֵית הִלְכְתָא כְּוָותֵיהּ. רַב חֲבִיבָא אִיקְלַע לְבֵי מְהוּלָא, בְּרִיךְ "שֶׁהַשִּׂמְחָה בִּמְעוֹנוֹ", וְלֵית הִלְכְתָא כְּוָותֵיהּ, מִשּׁוּם דִּטְרִידִי, דְּאִית לֵיהּ צַעֲרָא לְיָנוֹקָא. א"ר נַחְמָן אָמַר רַב: דחֲתָנִים מִן הַמִּנְיָן, *וְאֵין אֲבֵלִים מִן הַמִּנְיָן. מֵיתִיבֵי: חֲתָנִים וַאֲבֵלִים מִן הַמִּנְיָן! מַתְנִיתָא קָא רָמֵית עֲלֵיהּ דְּרַב?! *רַב תַּנָּא הוּא, וּפָלֵיג. אִיתְּמַר, *אָמַר ר' יִצְחָק א"ר יוֹחָנָן: חֲתָנִים מִן הַמִּנְיָן, וְאֵין אֲבֵלִים מִן הַמִּנְיָן. מֵיתִיבֵי: חֲתָנִים וַאֲבֵלִים מִן הַמִּנְיָן!

כִּי

רש"י

וְהִתְקִין לוֹ מִמֶּנּוּ בִּנְיַן עֲדֵי עַד. הִיא הַנְּקֵבָה. שׂוֹשׂ תָּשִׂישׂ. לְפִי שֶׁאָנוּ צְרִיכִין לְהַעֲלוֹת זִכְרוֹן יְרוּשָׁלַיִם עַל רֹאשׁ שִׂמְחָתֵנוּ, שֶׁנֶּאֱמַר (תהלים קלז) "תִּדְבַּק לְשׁוֹנִי לְחִכִּי" וגו'. שַׂמֵּחַ תְּשַׂמַּח. בְּרָכָה לְחָתָן וְכַלָּה שֶׁיַּגִּילוּ בְּשִׂמְחָה וְטוּב לֵב. וַ"אֲשֶׁר בָּרָא" – לְשֵׁם כָּל יִשְׂרָאֵל. וּלְפִי שֶׁהַסֵּדֶר מַתְחִיל מֵ"אֲשֶׁר יָצַר", לְפִיכָךְ פָּתַח בָּהּ בְּבָרוּךְ וְחָתַם בָּהּ בְּבָרוּךְ, כְּדֶרֶךְ כָּל רָאשֵׁי סִדְרֵי בְּרָכוֹת. וְ"שׂוֹשׂ תָּשִׂישׂ" וְ"שַׂמֵּחַ תְּשַׂמַּח" – מִפְּנֵי שֶׁהֵן בְּרָכָה הַסְּמוּכָה לַחֲבֶרְתָּהּ לֹא פָּתַח בָּהּ בְּבָרוּךְ, שֶׁכֵּן תִּיקְּנוּ לְכָל הַבְּרָכוֹת שֶׁסְּמוּכוֹת אַחַר הָרִאשׁוֹנָה עַל הַסֵּדֶר. וַ"אֲשֶׁר בָּרָא" מִפְּנֵי שֶׁהִיא נֶאֱמֶרֶת יְחִידִית בְּרוֹב יְמֵי הַמִּשְׁתֶּה, כְּשֶׁאֵין שָׁם פָּנִים חֲדָשׁוֹת – לְפִיכָךְ אֵינָהּ מִן הַסְּמוּכוֹת, וְהוּצְרַךְ לִפְתּוֹחַ בָּהּ בְּבָרוּךְ וּלְסַיֵּים בָּהּ בְּבָרוּךְ. אֲבָל "שֶׁהַכֹּל בָּרָא לִכְבוֹדוֹ" אֵינָהּ מִן הַסֵּדֶר, אֶלָּא לַאֲסִיפַת הָעָם הַנֶּאֱסָפִים שָׁם לִגְמוֹל חֶסֶד, זֵכֶר לְחַסְדֵי הַמָּקוֹם שֶׁנָּהַג עִם אָדָם הָרִאשׁוֹן, שֶׁנַּעֲשָׂה לוֹ שׁוֹשְׁבִין וְנִתְעַסֵּק בּוֹ. וַאֲסִיפָה זוֹ כְּבוֹד הַמָּקוֹם הִיא, וּבְרָכָה זוֹ לְכָךְ נִתְקְנָה. וּמַשְׁמָעוּת אֲסִיפָה הִיא רְאוּיָה לְבָרֵךְ, אֶלָּא מִפְּנֵי שֶׁיֵּשׁ בְּרָכָה עַל הַכּוֹס הִזְקִיקוּהָ לְסַדְּרָהּ עָלָיו, מִידֵי דַּהֲוָה אַבִּרְכַּת בְּשָׂמִים וּבִרְכַּת עַל הָאוֹר בְּמוֹצָאֵי שַׁבָּת, דְּאָמְרִי' *(ירושלמי *דפסחים פ"י): רַבִּי מְפַזְּרָן וְחוֹזֵר וְסוֹדְרָן עַל הַכּוֹס, וְרַבִּי חִיָּיא מְכַנְּסָן, הוֹאִיל וְיֵשׁ שָׁם כּוֹס. וּלְפִי שֶׁאֵינָהּ מִשְּׁאָר סֵדֶר הַבְּרָכוֹת, וּבְרָכָה הוֹדָאָה אַחַת – לֹא חָתְמוּ בָּהּ בְּבָרוּךְ, מִידֵי דַּהֲוָה אַבִּרְכַּת פֵּירוֹת וּמִצְוֹת. וְכֵן בִּרְכַּת "יוֹצֵר הָאָדָם" שֶׁתִּיקְּנוּהָ לִיצִירָה רִאשׁוֹנָה שֶׁל אָדָם הָרִאשׁוֹן כִּדְלְקַמָּן, אִי לְמ"ד ב' יְצִירוֹת הֲווּ, אִי לְמ"ד ב' יְצִירוֹת עָלוּ בְּמַחֲשָׁבָה וּבָתַר מַחֲשָׁבָה אָזְלִינַן – מ"מ אֵינָהּ מִסֵּדֶר בִּרְכוֹת הַזִּוּוּג. דְּהָא בִּיצִירָה רִאשׁוֹנָה אַכַּתִּי נְקֵבָה לָא הֲוַאי. וְא"ת: לָמָּה הִיא בָּאָה? מִתּוֹךְ שֶׁאָנוּ מְבָרְכִין עַל יְצִירָה הַשְּׁנִיָּה, תִּקְּנוּ אַף עַל הָרִאשׁוֹנָה שֶׁהִיא עִיקָּר וּתְחִילָּתוֹ. וְהִתְקִין לוֹ מִמֶּנּוּ. מִגּוּפוֹ, מִצַּלְעוֹתָיו. בִּנְיַן עֲדֵי עַד. בִּנְיָן נוֹהֵג לְדוֹרוֹת. וְחַוָּה קָרֵי לָהּ בִּנְיָן עַל שֵׁם "וַיִּבֶן אֶת הַצֵּלָע" (בראשית ב). עֲקָרָה. יְרוּשָׁלַיִם. רֵיעִים הָאֲהוּבִים. הֶחָתָן וְהַכַּלָּה, שֶׁהֵן רֵיעִים הָאוֹהֲבִים זֶה אֶת זֶה. כְּשַׂמֵּחֲךָ יְצִירְךָ. כְּמוֹ שֶׁשִּׂמַּחְתָּ אֶת אָדָם הָרִאשׁוֹן. בְּגַן עֵדֶן מִקֶּדֶם. דִּכְתִיב "וַיִּטַּע גַּן בְּעֵדֶן מִקֶּדֶם, וַיָּשֶׂם שָׁם" וגו' (שם). מְשַׂמֵּחַ חָתָן וְכַלָּה. וּבָאַחֲרוֹנָה "מְשַׂמֵּחַ חָתָן עִם הַכַּלָּה". לְפִי שֶׁשִּׂמְחַת בְּרָכָה הָרִאשׁוֹנָה לֹא בְּשִׂמְחַת חֲתוּנָּה אָנוּ אוֹמְרִים, שֶׁהֲרֵי תְּפִלָּה הִיא שֶׁמִּתְפַּלְּלִים וּמְבָרְכִין שֶׁיִּהְיוּ שְׂמֵחִים בְּהַצְלָחָה כָּל יְמֵיהֶם, לְפִיכָךְ אֵין לַחְתּוֹם "מְשַׂמֵּחַ חָתָן עִם הַכַּלָּה", דְּמַשְׁמַע אִישׁ בְּאִשְׁתּוֹ, אֶלָּא בָּרוּךְ ה' מְשַׂמֵּחַ אֶת שְׁנֵיהֶם לְעוֹלָם, בְּסִיפּוּק מְזוֹנוֹת וְכָל טוּב. וּבָאַחֲרוֹנָה שֶׁבַח שֶׁמְּשַׁבֵּחַ לְהקב"ה שֶׁבָּרָא חֲתוּנַּת דִּיבּוּק אִישׁ בְּאִשָּׁה עַל יְדֵי שִׂמְחָה וְחֶדְוָה, לְפִיכָךְ יֵשׁ לַחְתּוֹם "מְשַׂמֵּחַ חָתָן עִם הַכַּלָּה", שֶׁהוּא לְשׁוֹן שִׂמְחַת אִישׁ בְּאִשָּׁה. בְּרִיךְ חָמֵשׁ. "שֶׁהַכֹּל" וַ"אֲשֶׁר יָצַר" וְ"שׂוֹשׂ תָּשִׂישׂ", "שַׂמֵּחַ תְּשַׂמַּח", "אֲשֶׁר בָּרָא". בְּרִיךְ שִׁית. "יוֹצֵר הָאָדָם" הוֹסִיף. חֲדָא יְצִירָה הֲוַאי. כְּמַאן דְּאָמַר בְּעֵירוּבִין (דף יח.) "וַיִּבֶן אֶת הַצֵּלָע" – פַּרְצוּף. שֶׁמִּתְּחִילַּת בְּרִיָּיתוֹ נִבְרָא שְׁנֵי פַּרְצוּפִין, זָכָר מִלְּפָנָיו וּנְקֵבָה מֵאָחוֹר. שְׁתֵּי יְצִירוֹת. כְּמַאן דְּאָמַר זָנָב הָיָה, וּמִמֶּנּוּ נִבְרֵאת הָאִשָּׁה, וַהֲרֵי כָּאן שְׁתֵּי יְצִירוֹת. בָּתַר מַחֲשָׁבָה אָזְלִינַן. שֶׁשְּׁנַיִם עָלוּ בְּמַחֲשָׁבָה לְהִבָּרְאוֹת, וְנִבְרָא אֶחָד. בְּעֵירוּבִין בְּפֶ' "עוֹשִׂין פַּסִּין". מְבָרֵךְ שֶׁהַשִּׂמְחָה בִּמְעוֹנוֹ. בִּתְחִילַּת הַזִּימּוּן. בֵּין אָמַר לְהֶן. לַקְּרוּאִין. מֵחֲמַת הִילּוּלָא. קְרָאתִי לָכֶם הֲלוֹם לִסְעוּדָה. מֵעִיקָּרָא. קוֹדֶם הַחוּפָּה, אִם הִזְמִין קְרוּאִים, וְאָמַר לָהֶם: מֵחֲמַת שֶׁאֲנִי רוֹצֶה לְהַכְנִיס בְּנִי לַחוּפָּה. מֵאֵימָתַי. הָוְיָא הַתְחָלַת שִׂמְחַת חוּפָּה, לְבָרֵךְ "שֶׁהַשִּׂמְחָה בִּמְעוֹנוֹ". מִכִּי רָמֵי שַׂעֲרֵי בְּאַסִּינְתָּא. יֵשׁ שׁוֹרִין שְׂעוֹרִים בַּעֲרֵיבַת מַיִם *לְהָטִיל שֵׁכָר לְצוֹרֶךְ חוּפָּה. וי"א: לְשֵׁם הֶחָתָן וְהַכַּלָּה זוֹרְעִין שְׂעוֹרִין בְּעָצִיץ, לוֹמַר: פְּרוּ וּרְבוּ וְצִמְחוּ כַּשְּׂעוֹרִים הַלָּלוּ. דַּהֲוָה טָרַח לֵיהּ. מְתוּקָּנִים הָיוּ לוֹ כָּל צָרְכֵי חוּפָּה וּסְעוּדָה. אִיעֲסַק לִבְרֵיהּ. שִׁידֵּךְ לוֹ אִשָּׁה. וּבְרִיךְ מִשְּׁעַת אֵירוּסִין. שֶׁהַשִּׂמְחָה בִּמְעוֹנוֹ. וְהָדְרִי בְּהוּ. לֹא נָתְנוּ לוֹ הָאִשָּׁה. שִׁית אֲרִיכָתָא. הוֹסִיף דְּבָרִים עַל "שֶׁהַכֹּל" וְעַל בִּרְכַּת יְצִירָה רִאשׁוֹנָה, וְחָתַם בָּהֶם בְּבָרוּךְ. וְלֵית הִלְכְתָא כְּוָותֵיהּ. כִּדְפֵי' לְעֵיל. לְבֵי מְהוּלָא. לִסְעוּדַּת מִילָה. חֲתָנִים מִן הַמִּנְיָן. לְקַמָּן מְפָרֵשׁ לְמַאי הִלְכְתָא.

בְּבִרְכַּת

תוספות

שהכל ברא לכבודו ויוצר האדם. פותחת בברוך אע"פ שכל אחת סמוכה לחבירתה, כיון דקצרות הן, אם לא היה פותח בברוך היה נראה הכל ברכה אחת. וכן "אשר יצר" אם לא היה פותח בברוך היה נראה שהיתה מתחלת מ"ברוך יוצר האדם אשר יצר". אבל "שוש תשיש" שהיא אחר ברכה ארוכה אין צריך לפתוח בברוך. ו"אשר ברא" פותחת בברוך, לפי שמברכים אותה בפני עצמה כשאין פנים חדשות, כדפירש בקונטרס. ועל "שהכל ברא לכבודו" ו"יוצר האדם" פי' בקונטרס טעם אחר. ור"ת פירש: ד"יוצר האדם" פותחת בברוך, לפי שיש שלא היו אומרים אותה, כדאמר בסמוך. ואור"ת דבפרק קמא דברכות (דף יא:), גבי ברכת התורה גרסי': ר' יוחנן מסיים בה הכי "והערב נא" דברכה אחת היא, דאי הוו שתי ברכות – היה צריך לפתוח בברוך, אע"ג דסמוכה לחברתה, כיון שאותה שלפניה היא קצרה. ובתר הכי גרסינן: הלכך נימרינהו לתרוייהו, ולא גרסינן "לכולהו" – דאם כן הוה משמע דשלש ברכות הן. חדא יצירה הואי. צריך לומר דהיינו כמאן דאמר פרצוף אחד, מדקאמר בתר הכי: דכולי עלמא חדא יצירה הואי, מר סבר בתר מחשבה אזלינן. וכריש פרק שני דעירובין (דף יח. ושם) משמע בהדיא דלמאן דאמר פרצוף אחד – הוה עלה במחשבה להבראות שנים. אבל למאן דאמר התם שני פרצופים – לא סבירא ליה הכי. כך פירש רשב"ם.

רב תנא הוא ופליג. לא בעי לשנויי כי תניא ההיא בברכת המזון כדמשני רבי יוחנן, דנראה לו דוחק להעמיד כן, ונוח לו טפי לומר דפליג. ומדלא קאמר ר' יוחנן *תנא ופליג – יש להוכיח דר"י אמורא היה, דאי הוה תנא – הוה משני כדמשני לרב. ואין להקשות: דאמאי לא משני רבי יוחנן אנא דאמרי כרב דתנא הוא? דרבי יוחנן לא היה מחזיק רב כתנא, דפליג עליו בכל דוכתא. ומיהו, איכא נמי רבי יוחנן שהיה תנא, דתניא בשילהי דנזיר (דף סה. ושם): וכמה שיעור תפיסה פירש רבי יוחנן כו'.

כי

עין משפט נר מצוה

לט א מיי' פ"ב מהל' ברכות הל' יא ופ"י מהל' אישות הל' ג סמג עשין מח טוש"ע אה"ע סי' (סא) [סב] סעי' א:
מ ב מיי' שם הל' י טוש"ע שם סעיף ז:
מא ג מיי' פ"י מהל' אישות ה"ו טוש"ע שם סעיף יג:
מב ד מיי' שם הל' ה ופ"ב מהל' ברכות ה"י טוש"ע שם סעיף ז:

מסורת הש"ס

פסחים נג.
ל"ל דברכות פ"ח ה"א
בראשית א | שם ה
[עירובין יח. ע"ש היטב וע' גם ברכות סא. ומגלה לייכב. ושם תוספות ר' אבהו וכ"ה בשאילתות.]
[ע"ז ח:]
[סנהדרין יט.]
[עירובין נ: וש"נ]
[מגילה כג:]
[עיין תוס' ע"ז ח: ד"ה מכי וכו' הכינו על פירוש זה]

תוספות רי"ד

שעדיין לא שמען: מאי מברך אר"י שהכל ברא לכבודו. יוצר האדם. אשר יצר. שוש תשיש. שמח תשמח. אשר ברא. פי' תחלה מברך שהכל ברא לכבודו משום דברכת חתנים צריכה עשרה כדכתיב במקהלות ברכו ה' וכתיב ברוב עם הדרת מלך. וזו האסיפה היא על כבודו לברכו ברבים מ"ה מתחיל ומברך שהכל. אח"כ מברך יוצר האדם כנגד יצירה ראשונה שנברא לבדו. אח"כ מברך על יצירת שניהם האיך הפריד לו אשה מצלעותיו ומפני שמאריך דבריו חותם בה. אבל השתים הראשונות שהן קצרות אינו חותם בהן ואע"פ שהיא סמוכה לשלש ראשונות שבירך כבר פותח בה בברוך מפני שהשלש ראשונות פתיחה בברוך יש בהן. אבל חתימה אין בהם ואיזו נקרא ברכה הסמוכה לחברתה שאין פותחים בה בברוך כשמתחיל לאחרי' כגון ברכות י"ח וברכות ק"ש. אבל הסמוכה לברכה קטנה פותחים בה בברוך כמו שאנו עושים בק' ברכות שאותן שהם קצרות מברכין על כ"א וא' בפתיחה ולא יותר וכשמתחיל לברך ברכות הארוכות פותח בה בברוך. ואין סמיכות ברכות הקצרות פוטרת מלפתוח בה בברוך. ונ"ל שטועים הם בני אדם שמתחילים מאה ברכות מאלהי נשמה מפני שלא מצינו בשום מקום שיתחיל בברכות בלא פתיחת ברוך. וכך ראוי להתחיל ברוך אשר יצר את האדם בחכמה. ויש בה פתיחה לפניה וחתימה לאחריה. ואח"כ אומר אלהי נשמה וחותם בה בברוך ואינו פותח בה בברוך מפני שהיא סמוכה להו. אח"כ אומר כל הקצרות. ואח"כ אומר המעביר שינה. ופותח בברוך. מפני שסמיכות ברכות הקטנות אינה פוטרתה. ובברכת התורה פותח בה בברוך מפני שלא נתקנה עם סדר ק' ברכות אלא כשצריך ללמוד הילכך יש בה פתיחה. אח"כ מברך שוש תשיש קודם שיברך על שמחת החתן דכתיב אם לא אעלה את ירושלים על ראש שמחתי. ומפני שהיא סמוכה לחתימת אשר יצר אינו פותח בה בברוך. אח"כ אומר שמח תשמח שישמח החתן והכלה כל ימיהם ואין זו שמחת הזיווג ומסיים בה משמח חתן וכלה ואינו פותח בה בברוך מפני שסמוכה היא לחתימת שוש תשיש. אח"כ אומר אשר ברא שהוא שמחת הזיווג וחותם בה משמח חתן עם הכלה ששמחים כשמזדווגים זה עם זה ואע"פ שהיא סמוכה לחתימה הראשונה שלפניה ודין הוא שלא נפתח בה בברוך. אפ"ה מפני שמברכים אותה לבדה בדליכא פנים חדשות הוא פותח בה בברוך: רב אשי איקלע לבי רב כהנא יומא קמא בריך כולהו מכאן ואילך אמר אי איכא פנים חדשות נבריך כולהו. ואי לא אפושי שמחה בעלמא הוא. מברך שהשמחה במעונו ואשר ברא. פי' יומא קמא בין בשעת כניסתן לחופה בין בסעודה מברך כולהו ואין צריך פנים חדשות דהא מכאן ואילך לא הוי אלא בסעודה. א"כ יומא קמא אפילו בסעודה מברך ז' ברכות בלא פנים חדשות. ומכאן ואילך בלא פנים חדשות מברך שהשמחה במעונו בברהמ"ז ואשר ברא שהוא עיקר ברכת החתונות בסוף ברהמ"ז. מז' ועד ל' בין אמר מחמת הלולא בין לא אמר מחמת הילולא מברך שהשמחה במעונו. פי' אבל לא אשר ברא שהוא ברכת החתונות. וכיון שעברו ז' ימי חתונות אינו ראו לברכם. מכאן ואילך אי אמר מחמת הלולא מברך שהשמחה במעונו ואי לא לא. וכי אמר מחמת הלולא עד אימת. א"ר פפי משמיה דרבא עד תריסר ירחי שתא. מעיקרא מאימת א"ר פפא מכי רמו שערי באסותא פי' כיון שמשליך השעורים בגיגית לעשות מהן שכר לצורך הסעודה מברך הסעודה אבל לא משעת אירוסין: רבינא איעסיק ליה לבריה בי רב חביבא בריך משעת אירוסין. אמר קים לי בגווייהו דלא הדרי ביה ולא אסתעייא מילתא והדרי ביה: רב תחליפא איקלע לבבל בריך שית אריכתא. פי' הוסיף דברים על שהכל ועל יוצר האדם. והאריך בהן וחתם בהם ופסיק תלמודא ולית הלכתא [כוותיה]: רב חביבא איקלע לסעודת המילה בריך שהשמחה במעונו ופסיק תלמודא ולית הלכתא [כוותיה] משום דאית ליה צערא לינוקא. אר"י אמר ר"י מברכין ברכת חתנים בעשרה כל ז'. וחתנים מן המנין ואין אבלים מן המנין. מאי ברכת אבלים ברכת רחבה פי' היו מברין את האבל ברחובה של עיר ומברכין שם כנגד השם וכנגד אבלים וכנגד המנחמים וכנגד כל ישראל כדמפרש בגמרא וצריכה עשרה ובאותן יו"ד אין אבלים מן המנין כברכת המזון כגון ג' לזימון ויו"ד לאלהינו:

מג א מיי' פ"ד מהלכות אבל הלכה ו טוש"ע יו"ד סי' שעט סעיף ה:
מד ב מיי' פי"ג שם הלכה א סמג עשין דרבנן ב:
מה ג מיי' שם הל"ח סמג שם:
מו ד מיי' פ"ד שם הל"א סמג שם טוש"ע יו"ד סי' שנב סעי' ב:

כי תניא ההיא בברכת המזון. פי' בקונטרס: להצטרף עם ג' לזימון, שהרי הוא חייב בכל המצות. ואין נראה לר"י, דא"כ לא אתא לאשמועינן אלא דחייב במצות – והוה ליה למימר בהדיא דחייב במצות! ועוד: דא"כ מאי פריך ליה מברכת אבלים בעשרה ואין אבלים מן המנין, דקאמר ברכה בשורה מי איכא? אלא ע"כ היינו ברכת המזון, והדרן קושיא לדוכתין, דקתני ואבלים מן המנין, ואוקמינן בברכת המזון. ולפירש הקונטרס לא קשיא מידי, דכי קתני ואבלים מן המנין – היינו להצטרף לזימון, לומר "נברך שאכלנו משלו", אבל ברכת אבלים שמברכים בברכת המזון – קאמר רבי יוחנן דאינו מן המנין. לכך צריך לפרש: כי תניא ההיא בברכת המזון – היינו ברכת אבלים שבברכת המזון. מכאן משמע שברכת אבלים שבברכת המזון לא הוי אלא בעשרה, מדסליק אדעתיה דמקשן דאיירי בברכת אבלים שבברכת המזון, וקאמר בעשרה, והוה ניחא ליה בהכי אי לאו משום דקתני לעיל בברייתא ואבלים מן המנין, אם כן צריך עשרה.

אלא כי קאמר ר' יוחנן ברחבה. אי גרסינן "אלא" משמע דההיא דלעיל נמי מעמיד ברחבה. ותימה: למה הוצרכו תרי מילי דר' יוחנן, ההיא דלעיל והך? וצריך לומר דחדא מכלל חברתה אתמר, ההיא דלעיל מכללא דהך. אבל אי ל"ג "אלא" – ניחא, דלעיל איירי בשורה והכא ברחבה בלא פנים חדשות. ומימרא שלישית של רבי יוחנן הוצרך להשמיענו דבפנים חדשות אין אבלים מן המנין. ואי נקט ההיא – ה"א איפכא דוקא מיום ראשון ואילך, אבל ביום ראשון שייכי טפי ומברכים לה בלא י'.

תורה אור

כִּי תַּנְיָא הַהִיא — א בְּבִרְכַּת הַמָּזוֹן, כִּי קָאָמַר רַבִּי יוֹחָנָן — ב בְּשׁוּרָה. וְאֶלָּא הָא *דְּאָמַר רַבִּי יִצְחָק אָמַר רַבִּי יוֹחָנָן: *מְבָרְכִים בִּרְכַּת חֲתָנִים בַּעֲשָׂרָה — וַחֲתָנִים מִן הַמִּנְיָן, וּבִרְכַּת אֲבֵלִים בַּעֲשָׂרָה — וְאֵין אֲבֵלִים מִן הַמִּנְיָן. בְּרָכָה בְּשׁוּרָה מִי אִיכָּא? אֶלָּא, כִּי קָאָמַר רַבִּי יוֹחָנָן — בִּרְחָבָה. וְאֶלָּא הָא דְּאָמַר רַבִּי יִצְחָק אָמַר רַבִּי יוֹחָנָן: מְבָרְכִין בִּרְכַּת חֲתָנִים בַּעֲשָׂרָה כָּל שִׁבְעָה — וַחֲתָנִים מִן הַמִּנְיָן, וּבִרְכַּת אֲבֵלִים בַּעֲשָׂרָה כָּל שִׁבְעָה — וְאֵין אֲבֵלִים מִן הַמִּנְיָן, בִּרְכַּת רְחָבָה כָּל שִׁבְעָה מִי אִיכָּא? מַשְׁכַּחַתְּ לָהּ בְּפָנִים חֲדָשׁוֹת. כִּי הָא דְּרַב חִיָּיא בַּר אַבָּא מַקְרֵי בְּנֵיהּ דְּרֵישׁ לָקִישׁ הֲוָה, וְאָמְרִי לָהּ מַתְנֵי בְּרֵיהּ דְּרֵישׁ לָקִישׁ הֲוָה. שְׁכֵיב לֵיהּ יָנוּקָא. יוֹמָא קַמָּא לָא אֲזַל לְגַבֵּיהּ, לְמָחָר דַּבְרֵיהּ לִיהוּדָה בַּר נַחְמָנִי מְתוּרְגְּמָנֵיהּ, אֲמַר לֵיהּ: קוּם אֵימָא מִלְּתָא כָּל קְבֵיל יָנוּקָא. פְּתַח וַאֲמַר: °"וַיַּרְא ה' (דברים לב) וַיִּנְאָץ מִכַּעַס בָּנָיו וּבְנוֹתָיו", דּוֹר שֶׁאָבוֹת מְנָאֲצִים לְהקב"ה — כּוֹעֵס עַל בְּנֵיהֶם וְעַל בְּנוֹתֵיהֶם, וּמֵתִים כְּשֶׁהֵם קְטַנִּים. וְאִיכָּא דְּאָמְרִי: בָּחוּר הֲוָה, וְהָכִי קָאָמַר לֵיהּ: °"עַל כֵּן (ישעיה ט) עַל בַּחוּרָיו לֹא יִשְׂמַח ה' וְאֶת יְתוֹמָיו וְאֶת אַלְמְנוֹתָיו לֹא יְרַחֵם כִּי כֻלּוֹ חָנֵף וּמֵרַע וְכָל פֶּה דֹּבֵר נְבָלָה בְּכָל זֹאת לֹא שָׁב אַפּוֹ וְעוֹד יָדוֹ נְטוּיָה", *מַאי "וְעוֹד יָדוֹ נְטוּיָה"? אָמַר רַב חָנָן בַּר רַב: הַכֹּל יוֹדְעִין כַּלָּה לָמָּה נִכְנְסָה לַחוּפָּה, אֶלָּא ה כָּל הַמְנַבֵּל פִּיו וּמוֹצִיא דְּבַר נְבָלָה מִפִּיו, אֲפִילּוּ נֶחְתַּם לוֹ גְּזַר דִּינוֹ שֶׁל שִׁבְעִים שָׁנָה לְטוֹבָה — נֶהְפָּךְ עָלָיו לְרָעָה. אֲתָא לְנַחוּמֵי, צַעוּרֵי קָמְצַעֵר לֵיהּ?! הָכִי קָאָמַר לֵיהּ: חָשֵׁיב אַתְּ לְאִתְפּוּסֵי אַדְּרָא. אֲמַר לֵיהּ: קוּם אֵימָא מִלְּתָא כְּנֶגֶד שִׁבְחוֹ שֶׁל הקב"ה. פְּתַח וַאֲמַר: הָאֵל הַגָּדוֹל בְּרוֹב גָּדְלוֹ, אַדִּיר וְחָזָק בְּרוֹב נוֹרָאוֹת, מְחַיֵּה מֵתִים בְּמַאֲמָרוֹ, עוֹשֶׂה גְדוֹלוֹת עַד אֵין חֵקֶר וְנִפְלָאוֹת עַד אֵין מִסְפָּר, בא"י מְחַיֵּה הַמֵּתִים. א"ל: קוּם אֵימָא מִלְּתָא כְּנֶגֶד אֲבֵלִים. פְּתַח וַאֲמַר: אַחֵינוּ הַמְיוּגָּעִים הַמְדוּכָּאִין בָּאֵבֶל הַזֶּה, תְּנוּ לְבַבְכֶם לַחֲקוֹר אֶת זֹאת. זֹאת הִיא עוֹמֶדֶת לָעַד, נָתִיב הוּא מִשֵּׁשֶׁת יְמֵי בְרֵאשִׁית, רַבִּים שָׁתוּ רַבִּים יִשְׁתּוּ, כְּמִשְׁתֵּה רִאשׁוֹנִים כָּךְ מִשְׁתֵּה אַחֲרוֹנִים. אַחֵינוּ, בַּעַל נֶחָמוֹת יְנַחֵם אֶתְכֶם, בָּרוּךְ מְנַחֵם אֲבֵלִים. אָמַר אַבָּיֵי: "רַבִּים שָׁתוּ" — לֵימָא, "רַבִּים יִשְׁתּוּ" — לָא לֵימָא. "מִשְׁתֵּה רִאשׁוֹנִים" — לֵימָא, "מִשְׁתֵּה אַחֲרוֹנִים" — לָא לֵימָא. דְּאָר"ש בֶּן לָקִישׁ, וְכֵן תָּנָא מִשְּׁמֵיהּ דְּר' יוֹסֵי: *לְעוֹלָם אַל יִפְתַּח אָדָם פִּיו לַשָּׂטָן. אָמַר רַב יוֹסֵף: מַאי קְרָא — °"כִּסְדוֹם הָיִינוּ לַעֲמוֹרָה דָּמִינוּ", מַאי אַהֲדַר לֵיהּ — (שם א) "שִׁמְעוּ דְבַר ה' קְצִינֵי סְדוֹם וגו'". א"ל: קוּם אֵימָא מִלְּתָא כְּנֶגֶד מְנַחֲמֵי אֲבֵלִים. פְּתַח וַאֲמַר: אַחֵינוּ גּוֹמְלֵי חֲסָדִים בְּנֵי גּוֹמְלֵי חֲסָדִים, הַמַּחֲזִיקִים בִּבְרִיתוֹ שֶׁל אַבְרָהָם אָבִינוּ, (שֶׁנֶּאֱמַר: °"כִּי יְדַעְתִּיו (בראשית יח) לְמַעַן אֲשֶׁר יְצַוֶּה אֶת בָּנָיו וגו'"). אַחֵינוּ, בַּעַל הַגְּמוּל יְשַׁלֵּם לָכֶם גְּמוּלְכֶם, בָּרוּךְ אַתָּה מְשַׁלֵּם הַגְּמוּל. א"ל: קוּם אֵימָא מִלְּתָא כְּנֶגֶד כָּל יִשְׂרָאֵל. פְּתַח וַאֲמַר: רִבּוֹן הָעוֹלָמִים, פְּדֵה וְהַצֵּל מַלֵּט הוֹשַׁע עַמְּךָ יִשְׂרָאֵל מִן הַדֶּבֶר, וּמִן הַחֶרֶב, וּמִן הַבִּיזָּה, וּמִן הַשִּׁדָּפוֹן, וּמִן הַיֵּרָקוֹן, וּמִכָּל מִינֵי פוּרְעָנִיּוֹת הַמִּתְרַגְּשׁוֹת וּבָאוֹת לָעוֹלָם. טֶרֶם נִקְרָא וְאַתָּה תַעֲנֶה, בָּרוּךְ אַתָּה עוֹצֵר הַמַּגֵּפָה. אָמַר עוּלָּא, וְאָמְרִי לָהּ בְּמַתְנִיתָא תָּנָא: *ג עֲשָׂרָה כּוֹסוֹת תִּקְּנוּ חֲכָמִים בְּבֵית הָאֵבֶל; שְׁלֹשָׁה קוֹדֶם אֲכִילָה — כְּדֵי לִפְתּוֹחַ אֶת בְּנֵי מֵעָיו, שְׁלֹשָׁה בְּתוֹךְ אֲכִילָה — כְּדֵי לִשְׁרוֹת אֲכִילָה שֶׁבְּמֵעָיו, וְאַרְבָּעָה לְאַחַר אֲכִילָה — [א] אֶחָד כְּנֶגֶד "הַזָּן", וְאֶחָד כְּנֶגֶד בִּרְכַּת הָאָרֶץ, וְאֶחָד כְּנֶגֶד "בּוֹנֵה יְרוּשָׁלַיִם", וְאֶחָד כְּנֶגֶד "הַטּוֹב וְהַמֵּטִיב". הוֹסִיפוּ עֲלֵיהֶם אַרְבָּעָה: אֶחָד כְּנֶגֶד חַזָּנֵי הָעִיר, וְאֶחָד כְּנֶגֶד פַּרְנָסֵי הָעִיר, וְאֶחָד כְּנֶגֶד בֵּית הַמִּקְדָּשׁ, וְאֶחָד כְּנֶגֶד רַבָּן גַּמְלִיאֵל. הִתְחִילוּ, הָיוּ שׁוֹתִין וּמִשְׁתַּכְּרִין. הֶחֱזִירוּ הַדָּבָר לְיוֹשְׁנָהּ. מַאי רַבָּן גַּמְלִיאֵל? דְּתַנְיָא: *בָּרִאשׁוֹנָה הָיְתָה הוֹצָאַת הַמֵּת קָשָׁה לִקְרוֹבָיו יוֹתֵר מִמִּיתָתוֹ, עַד שֶׁהָיוּ מַנִּיחִים אוֹתוֹ וּבוֹרְחִין. עַד שֶׁבָּא רַבָּן גַּמְלִיאֵל וְנָהַג קַלּוּת בְּעַצְמוֹ, וְהוֹצִיאוּהוּ בִּכְלֵי פִשְׁתָּן. וְנָהֲגוּ ד כָּל הָעָם אַחֲרָיו לְהוֹצִיא בִּכְלֵי פִשְׁתָּן, אָמַר רַב פַּפָּא: וְהָאִידָּנָא נָהוּג עָלְמָא אֲפִילּוּ *בְּצַרְדָּא בַּר זוּזָא. § אָמַר רַבִּי אֶלְעָזָר הָאוֹמֵר

בְּבִרְכַּת הַמָּזוֹן. לְהִצְטָרֵף לְג' לְזַמֵּן עָלָיו, שֶׁהֲרֵי הוּא חַיָּיב בְּכָל הַמִּצְוֹת. **בְּשׁוּרָה.** כְּשֶׁהָיוּ חוֹזְרִין מִן הַקֶּבֶר הָיוּ עוֹשִׂין שׁוּרָה סָבִיב הָאָבֵל לְנַחֲמוֹ, וּמוֹשִׁיבִין אוֹתוֹ, וְהֵן עוֹמְדִים סָבִיב. וְאָמְרִי' בְּסַנְהֶדְרִין (דף יט.): אֵין שׁוּרָה פָּחוּת מִי'. **בִּרְחָבָה.** כְּשֶׁמַּבְרִין אֶת הָאָבֵל סְעוּדָה רִאשׁוֹנָה מִשֶּׁל אֲחֵרִים, כִּדְאָמְרִינַן בְּמוֹעֵד קָטָן (דף כז:), הָיוּ מַבְרִין אוֹתוֹ בָּרְחָבָה וּמְבָרְכִין שָׁם בִּרְכַּת אֲבֵלִים, כִּדְמְפָרֵשׁ לְקַמֵּיהּ, "בָּרוּךְ מְנַחֵם אֲבֵלִים". **אֲמַר לֵיהּ.** לִמְתוּרְגְּמָנֵיהּ. **כָּל קְבֵיל יָנוּקָא.** לְנֶגֶד הַמְּאוֹרָע, דְּבָרִים נִיחוּמִים עַל מִיתַת הַיֶּלֶד. **וַיַּרְא ה'.** מֶה עָשׂוּ אָבוֹת. **וַיִּנְאָץ מִכַּעַס.** שֶׁהִכְעִיסוּהוּ, וְגָרְמוּ לוֹ לִפְקוֹד עַל בְּנֵיהֶם וּבְנוֹתֵיהֶם. **וְאִית דְּאָמְרִי.** לֹא תִּינוֹק הָיָה הַמֵּת אֶלָּא בָּחוּר הָיָה, וְהָכִי קְרָא אֲמַר: "עַל בַּחוּרָיו" וגו'. **שֶׁל ע' שָׁנָה.** "וְעוֹד" דָּרֵישׁ כְּמוֹ "וָעֶד", עוֹלָמוֹ שֶׁל אָדָם, נְטוּיָה — נֶהְפֶּכֶת מִטּוֹב לְרָע. **אֲתָא לְנַחוּמֵי צַעוּרֵי מְצַעֵר לֵיהּ.** בִּתְמִיָּה: מוֹכִיחַ עַל פָּנָיו שֶׁבִּשְׁבִיל עֲוֹנוֹ מֵת בְּנוֹ?! **חָשֵׁיב אַתְּ לְאִתְפּוּסֵי אַדְּרָא.** חָשׁוּב אַתָּה לְמַעְלָה לְתוֹפְסְךָ וְאֶת בָּנֶיךָ בַּעֲוֹן הַדּוֹר, דְּקַיְ"ל: *בִּזְמַן שֶׁצַּדִּיקִים בַּדּוֹר — צַדִּיקִים נִתְפָּסִים עַל הַדּוֹר, שֶׁנֶּאֱמַר "וּמִמִּקְדָּשִׁי תָּחֵלּוּ" (יחזקאל ט). **הָאֵל הַגָּדוֹל בְּרוֹב גּוֹדְלוֹ.** בְּבָרוּךְ פָּתַח בָּהּ, "בָּרוּךְ אַתָּה ה' אֱלֹהֵינוּ מֶלֶךְ הָעוֹלָם הָאֵל הַגָּדוֹל" וכו'. **אַחֵינוּ הַמְיוּגָּעִים כו'.** בְּרָכָה הַסְּמוּכָה לַחֲבֶרְתָּהּ הִיא, וְכֵן סְדוּרוֹת עַל הַסֵּדֶר. **בָּאֵבֶל הַזֶּה** תְּנוּ לְבַבְכֶם לַחֲקוֹר זֹאת שֶׁזֹּאת עוֹמֶדֶת לָעַד. שֶׁהַכֹּל מֵתִים, וְלֹא תִּבְכּוּ יוֹתֵר מִדַּאי. **מִשְׁתֵּה הָרִאשׁוֹנִים לֵימָא.** מִשְׁתֵּה רִאשׁוֹנִים הוּא. **בִּבְרִיתוֹ שֶׁל אַבְרָהָם.** שֶׁגָּמַל חֲסָדִים, דִּכְתִיב (בראשית כא) "וַיִּטַּע אֶשֶׁל", ר"ת: אֲכִילָה שְׁתִיָּה לְוָיָה*. **עֲשָׂרָה כּוֹסוֹת.** לְהַרְבּוֹת לוֹ בִּשְׁתִיָּה, כִּדְכְתִיב (משלי לא) "תְּנוּ שֵׁכָר לְאוֹבֵד, וְיַיִן לְמָרֵי נָפֶשׁ". **קוֹדֶם אֲכִילָה.** שֶׁהָיוּ רְגִילִין לְהַמְשִׁיךְ פַּרְפְּרָאוֹת לִפְנֵי סְעוּדָה, כְּגוֹן כִּיסָנִין וְסוּפְגָּנִין וְאִיסְקְרִיטִין, וּבְאוֹתָם פַּרְפְּרָאוֹת מַשְׁקִין לָאָבֵל ג' כּוֹסוֹת. **אֶחָד כְּנֶגֶד הַזָּן.** עַל כָּל בְּרָכָה שׁוֹתֶה הַכּוֹס, וּמוֹזְגִין לוֹ אַחֵר. **כְּנֶגֶד חַזָּנֵי הָעִיר.** תִּקְּנוּ לָהֶם בְּרָכָה עָלָיו, לְפִי שֶׁהָיוּ שַׁמָּשֵׁי הָעִיר לְהִתְעַסֵּק בַּמֵּתִים וּבִשְׁאָר צָרְכֵי צִיבּוּר. **פַּרְנָסֵי הָעִיר.** שֶׁהָיוּ עֲשִׁירִים מְבַזְבְּזִים מָמוֹנָם לִקְבוּרַת עֲנִיִּים. **כְּנֶגֶד בהמ"ק.** תִּקְּנוּ עָלָיו בִּרְכַּת נִיחוּמִים, שֶׁיְּנַחֲמֵנוּ הַמָּקוֹם בְּבִנְיָינוֹ מֵאֶבְלֵנוּ, שֶׁאָנוּ מִתְאַבְּלִים עָלָיו כְּעַל מֵת. **כְּנֶגֶד ר"ג.** לְקַמָּן מְפָרֵשׁ. **לְיוֹשְׁנָהּ.** עֲשָׂרָה כּוֹסוֹת. **הוֹצָאַת הַמֵּת.** שֶׁהָיוּ קוֹבְרִים אוֹתוֹ בְּכֵלִים יְקָרִים כְּגוֹן שִׁירָאִין וּסְרָקוֹת. **בְּצַרְדָּא בַּר זוּזָא.** בֶּגֶד קַנְבּוֹס שֶׁאֵינוֹ שָׁוֶה אֶלָּא דִּינָר. הָאוֹמֵר

מגילה כג: [תוספתא מגילה פ"ג]
[שבת לג:]
שבת דף לג.
[וע"ע רש"י סוטה י. ד"ה פונדק]
ברכות יט. ס. ע"ש
שמחות פי"ד [פסחים קי.]
מ"ק כז: [תוספתא נדה פ"ט]
ס"א איתו

הגהות הגר"א

[א] גמ' (אחד כנגד הזן כו' על הטוב והמטיב) תא"מ (ואפשר דהם כנגד ד' ברכות האמורים למעלה פתח ואמר כו' ואולי על כל כוס אומר ברכה א'):

גליון הש"ס

גמ' כל המנבל פיו. עיין ט"ז יו"ד רסי' קכד:

[גי' הערוך צדרא ועיין ב"מ נא. לאיתא צדרייתא ופרש"י בגדי קנבוס אבל בשאלתות איתא בצרדא כדאיתא לפנינו]

הָאוֹמֵר "פֶּתַח פָּתוּחַ מָצָאתִי" — נֶאֱמָן לְאוֹסְרָהּ עָלָיו — וְאַמַּאי? אסָפֵק סְפֵיקָא הוּא: סָפֵק תַּחְתָּיו סָפֵק אֵין תַּחְתָּיו, וְאִם תִּמְצָא לוֹמַר תַּחְתָּיו — סָפֵק בְּאוֹנֶס סָפֵק בְּרָצוֹן! לָא צְרִיכָא בבְּאֵשֶׁת כֹּהֵן. וְאִיבָּעֵית אֵימָא גבְּאֵשֶׁת יִשְׂרָאֵל, וּכְגוֹן דְּקַבֵּיל בָּהּ אֲבוּהּ קִידּוּשִׁין פְּחוּתָה מִבַּת ג' שָׁנִים וְיוֹם אֶחָד. מַאי קמ"ל? תָּנֵינָא. *דהָאוֹמֵר לְאִשָּׁה "קִדַּשְׁתִּיךְ". וְהִיא אוֹמֶרֶת "לֹא קִדַּשְׁתַּנִי" — הִיא מוּתֶּרֶת בִּקְרוֹבָיו, וְהוּא אָסוּר בִּקְרוֹבוֹתֶיהָ! מַהוּ דְּתֵימָא: הָתָם דְּוַדַּאי קִים לֵיהּ, אֲבָל הָכָא — מֵיקָם הוּא דְּלָא קִים לֵיהּ, קמ"ל. וּמִי אָמַר רַבִּי אֶלְעָזָר הָכִי? וְהָאָמַר רַבִּי אֶלְעָזָר: אֵין הָאִשָּׁה נֶאֱסֶרֶת עַל בַּעְלָהּ, אֶלָּא עַל עִסְקֵי קִינּוּי וּסְתִירָה, וּכְמַעֲשֶׂה שֶׁהָיָה! וְתִסְבְּרָא, מַעֲשֶׂה שֶׁהָיָה בְּקִינּוּי וּסְתִירָה הֲוָה?! וְעוֹד: מִי אֲסָרוּהָ? הָא לָא קַשְׁיָא; הָכִי קָאָמַר: אֵין הָאִשָּׁה נֶאֱסֶרֶת עַל בַּעְלָהּ אֶלָּא עַל עִסְקֵי קִינּוּי וּסְתִירָה, מִמַּעֲשֶׂה שֶׁהָיָה דְּלָא הֲוָה קִינּוּי וּסְתִירָה, וְלָא אִיתַּסְרָא. מִכָּל מָקוֹם קַשְׁיָא: קִינּוּי וּסְתִירָה — אִין, פֶּתַח פָּתוּחַ — לָא! וּלְטַעְמִיךְ, קִינּוּי וּסְתִירָה — אִין, עֵדִים — לָא?! אֶלָּא הָכִי קָאָמַר: האֵין הָאִשָּׁה נֶאֱסֶרֶת עַל בַּעְלָהּ בְּעֵד אֶחָד אֶלָּא בִּשְׁנֵי עֵדִים, וְקִינּוּי וּסְתִירָה — אֲפִילּוּ בְּעֵד אֶחָד נַמִי, וּפֶתַח פָּתוּחַ — כִּשְׁנֵי עֵדִים דָּמֵי. וְכִי תֵּימָא: מַעֲשֶׂה שֶׁהָיָה מִפְּנֵי מָה לֹא אֲסָרוּהָ — והָתָם אוֹנֶס הֲוָה. וְאִיבָּעֵית אֵימָא, כִּי הָא דְּאָמַר רַבִּי שְׁמוּאֵל בַּר נַחְמָנִי אָמַר רַבִּי יוֹנָתָן:
כָּל

רש"י

הָאוֹמֵר פֶּתַח פָּתוּחַ מָצָאתִי. וְטַעֲנַת דָּמִים אֵין לוֹ, כְּגוֹן שֶׁהִיא מִמִּשְׁפַּחַת דּוֹרְקְטִי שֶׁאֵין לָהֶם דַּם בְּתוּלִים, כִּדְלְקַמָּן (דף י), אוֹ שֶׁנֶּאֶבְדָה מִמֶּנּוּ מַפָּה, וְלֹא יָדַע אִם הָיָה דָּם אִם לָאו. אֲבָל זֹאת בְּרוּרָה לוֹ, שֶׁפֶּתַח פָּתוּחַ מָצָא. נֶאֱמָן לְאוֹסְרָהּ עָלָיו. וְאַעַ"פ שֶׁאֵין הַדָּבָר הַזֶּה יָכוֹל לְהִתְבָּרֵר אֶלָּא עַל פִּיו, לְגַבֵּי נַפְשֵׁיהּ הָוֵי מְהֵימָן לְשַׁוְּיֵהּ עֲלֵיהּ חֲתִיכָה דְּאִיסּוּרָא, אֲבָל לְהַפְסִידָהּ כְּתוּבָּתָהּ — לֹא מְהֵימָן. וְאַמַּאי. מִיתַּסְרָא עֲלֵיהּ, אֲפִי' אִי מְהֵימְנַתְּ לֵיהּ דְּנִבְעֲלָה. סָפֵק תַּחְתָּיו. מִשֶּׁנִּתְאָרְסָה זִינְּתָה. סָפֵק אֵין תַּחְתָּיו. אֶלָּא קוֹדֶם שֶׁנִּתְאָרְסָה זִינְּתָה. סָפֵק בְּאוֹנֶס. וַאֲנוּסָה שַׁרְיָא בְּאֵשֶׁת יִשְׂרָאֵל, כִּדְלְקַמָּן (דף נא:) מִ"וְהִיא לֹא נִתְפָּשָׂה". בְּאֵשֶׁת כֹּהֵן. שֶׁהָאוֹנֶס אָסוּר בָּהּ. הִלְכָּךְ, חַד סָפֵק הוּא. פְּחוּתָה מִבַּת ג' שָׁנִים. וְעַכְשָׁיו הִיא גְּדוֹלָה, וּפִיתּוּיָהּ פִּיתּוּי וְאֵינוֹ אוֹנֶס. הִלְכָּךְ, חַד סָפֵק אִיכָּא — סָפֵק אוֹנֶס סָפֵק רָצוֹן. אֲבָל סָפֵק תַּחְתָּיו סָפֵק אֵין תַּחְתָּיו — לֵיכָּא, שֶׁאִילּוּ נִבְעֲלָה קוֹדֶם לָכֵן — הָיוּ בְּתוּלֶיהָ חוֹזְרִים, כִּדְתְנַן בְּמַסֶּכֶת נִדָּה (דף מד:): פָּחוֹת מִכָּאן — כְּנוֹתֵן אֶצְבַּע בָּעַיִן, שֶׁהַדִּמְעָה יוֹצֵאת וְחוֹזֶרֶת. מַאי קמ"ל תָּנֵינָא. שֶׁאָדָם נֶאֱמָן עַל עַצְמוֹ לֶאֱסוֹר לוֹ אֶת הַמּוּתָּר עַל פִּיו. הוּא אָסוּר בִּקְרוֹבוֹתֶיהָ. בְּאִמָּהּ וּבִתָּהּ וַאֲחוֹתָהּ, דְּשַׁוִּינְהוּ אַנַּפְשֵׁיהּ חֲתִיכָה דְּאִיסּוּרָא. וְהִיא מוּתֶּרֶת בִּקְרוֹבָיו. שֶׁהֲרֵי אֵינָהּ מוֹדָה בַּקִּידּוּשִׁין. וּבְמַסֶּכֶת קִידּוּשִׁין מוֹקְמִינַן לָהּ בְּאוֹמֵר: קִידַּשְׁתִּיהָ בִּפְנֵי עֵדִים, וְהָלְכוּ לָהֶם לִמְדִינַת הַיָּם. דְּוַדַּאי קִים לֵיהּ. שֶׁקִּידְּשָׁהּ. אֲבָל הָכָא. אֵימָא: מִתּוֹךְ שֶׁפָּנוּי הָיָה, וְאֵינוֹ בָּקִי — מֵיקָם הוּא דְּלָא קִים לֵיהּ. כְּסָבוּר שֶׁמָּצָא פֶּתַח פָּתוּחַ, וְאֵינוֹ כֵּן, וְלֹא תֵּיאָסֵר, קָמַשְׁמַע לָן. וּמִי אָמַר רַבִּי אֶלְעָזָר הָכִי. דְּאִשָּׁה מְזַנָּה נֶאֱסֶרֶת עַל פִּי בַּעְלָהּ. קִינּוּי. שֶׁאָמַר לָהּ: אַל תִּסָּתְרִי עִם פְּלוֹנִי. וּסְתִירָה. שֶׁבָּאוּ עֵדִים שֶׁנִּסְתְּרָה עִמּוֹ אַחַר קִינּוּי. וּכְמַעֲשֶׂה שֶׁהָיָה. דְּבַת שֶׁבַע. וְתִסְבְּרָא. דְּהָכִי א"ר אֶלְעָזָר? מַעֲשֶׂה שֶׁהָיָה מִי הֲוָה בֵּיהּ קִינּוּי? וְעוֹד מִי אֲסָרוּהָ. עַל אוּרִיָּה? דְּאִילּוּ נֶאֶסְרָה עַל אוּרִיָּה — נֶאֶסְרָה אַף עַל דָּוִד, דְּקַיְימָא לָן (סוטה דף כז:): כְּשֵׁם שֶׁאֲסוּרָה לַבַּעַל, כָּךְ אֲסוּרָה לַבּוֹעֵל. הָא לָא קַשְׁיָא. כְּלוֹמַר, מִשּׁוּם הָא קוּשְׁיָא לָא תִּדְחֲיֵיהּ לְרַבִּי אֶלְעָזָר. הָכִי קָאָמַר אֵין הָאִשָּׁה נֶאֱסֶרֶת עַל בַּעְלָהּ אֶלָּא עַל עִסְקֵי קִינּוּי וּסְתִירָה מִמַּעֲשֶׂה שֶׁהָיָה. מִמַּעֲשֶׂה דְּבַת שֶׁבַע לָמְדוּ לְמִדִּין כֵּן, שֶׁלֹּא הָיָה שָׁם קִינּוּי וּסְתִירָה, וְלֹא אֲסָרוּהָ. עֵדִים לָא. בִּתְמִיָּה: אֲפִי' יֵשׁ עֵדִים שֶׁזִּינְּתָה, שֶׁמָּא אֵינָהּ נֶאֱסֶרֶת בְּלֹא קִינּוּי?! וְהָא כְּתִיב (דברים כד) "כִּי מָצָא בָהּ עֶרְוַת דָּבָר". וְעוֹד, הָא לֹא נִתְפְּשָׂה אֲסוּרָה? אֵין הָאִשָּׁה נֶאֱסֶרֶת עַל בַּעְלָהּ בְּעֵד אֶחָד. דְּיָלֵיף (סוטה דף ג:) "דָּבָר" "דָּבָר" מִמָּמוֹן. וְקִינּוּי וּסְתִירָה. אִם יֵשׁ עֵדִים שֶׁקִּינֵּא לָהּ, וְיֵשׁ עֵדִים שֶׁנִּסְתְּרָה אַחַר קִינּוּי. אֲפִי' בְּעֵד אֶחָד. אֲפִי' אֵין בַּטּוּמְאָה אֶלָּא עֵד אֶחָד — נֶאֱמָן, דִּכְתִיב (במדבר ה) "וְעֵד אֵין בָּהּ", וְאָמַר מַר (סוטה ב:): כָּל מָקוֹם שֶׁנֶּאֱמַר "עֵד" — הֲרֵי כָּאן שְׁנַיִם, וְקָאָמַר רַחֲמָנָא "עֵד אֵין בָּהּ" תְּרֵי, אֶלָּא חַד. "וְהִיא לֹא נִתְפָּשָׂה" — אֲסוּרָה, שֶׁרַגְלַיִם לַדָּבָר שֶׁזִּינְּתָה, שֶׁהֲרֵי קִינֵּא לָהּ וְנִסְתְּרָה, וְעֵד אֶחָד מְעִידָהּ שֶׁהִיא טְמֵאָה. וּמֵהַשְׁתָּא לָא תִּקְשֵׁי לָךְ דְּרַבִּי אֶלְעָזָר, דְּפֶתַח פָּתוּחַ לְאוֹסְרָהּ עַל עַצְמוֹ כִּשְׁנֵי עֵדִים דָּמֵי, שֶׁהֲרֵי דָּבָר בָּרוּר הוּא לוֹ שֶׁנִּבְעֲלָה. מִפְּנֵי מָה לֹא אֲסָרוּהָ. עַל דָּוִד, שֶׁהֲרֵי עֵדִים הַרְבֵּה יָדְעוּ.
גֵּט

קדושין סה.

תוספות

האומר פתח פתוח מצאתי כו'. פירש בקונטרס דטענת דמים לא קאמר, כגון שנאבדה המפה או שהיא ממשפחת דורקטי שאין להם דמים. ור"ת מפרש: דבוגרת ומוכת עץ אין להם דמים, אבל אין פתחן פתוח ויכול לטעון טענת פתח פתוח. וקשה לפר"ת, דאמרי' ב"אלו נערות" (לקמן לו. ושם:): ובוגרת אין לה טענת בתולים? והאמר רב בוגרת נותנים לה לילה ראשונה. ומשני: אי דקא טעין טענת דמים — ה"נ, הב"ע — דקטעין טענת פתח פתוח. משמע דפתחה פתוח, ויש לה דמים! וי"ל: דר"ת גרים כגירסא ראשונה שהיתה בספרים; *אי דקא טעין טענת פתח פתוח — הכי נמי, הב"ע — דקא טעין טענת דמים. וה"פ: והאמר רב בוגרת נותנין לה לילה הראשונה, ומדתלינן כל הלילה בדם בתולים — משמע דאיכא בוגרת דאית לה דם בתולים טובא, אם כן אי אפשר לשום בוגרת שלא יהא פתחה סתום, אפילו אין לה דמים, וא"כ יש לה טענת בתולים בפתח פתוח! ומשני: אי דקטעין פתח פתוח — ה"נ דיש לה טענת בתולים. הב"ע דלית לה טענת בתולים — בטענת דמים, משום דאיכא בוגרת דדמיה כלין. ומיהו, בירושלמי משמע לא כפר"ת, דקאמר התם ר' יונה בשם ר' קריספא: בוגרת כחבית פתוחה של יין! ויש ליישב: דלענין דמים קאמר, משום דסתם חבית סתומה לעולם יש בה יין, שאין דרך לסתום חבית ריקנית. אבל חבית פתוחה — פעמים יש בה יין, פעמים אין בה יין. כך בוגרת, פעמים אין לה דמים פעמים יש לה. ומשום הכי אין לה טענת דמים כדפר"ת. וכדאמר בפרק "הבא על יבמתו" (יבמות נט. ושם): פרט לבוגרת שכלו בתוליה. **לא** צריכא באשת כהן. וא"ת: ונוקמה אחזקתה שהיא כשרה לכהונה, ונימא דלאו תחתיו זינתה! וי"ל: דאדרבה, אית לן למימר דהשתא נבעלה, דאוקמה אחזקת הגוף שהיתה בתולה. **ואי** בעית אימא באשת ישראל דקביל בה אביה קידושין פחותה מבת ג' שנים. וא"ת: אכתי איכא ספק ספיקא; ספק באונס ספק ברצון, ואת"ל ברצון — ספק כשהיא קטנה, ופתוי קטנה אונס הוא, כדאמרינן ב"הבא על יבמתו" (שם סא:)! וי"ל: דשם אונס חד הוא. וא"ת: ונוקמה בחזקת היתר לבעלה! וי"ל: דאונסא קלא אית לה, כדאמרינן בירושלמי [אונסא יש לו קול], והשתא דליכא קלא — הוי ליה רצון רובא ומיעוט אונס, ורובא וחזקה רובא עדיף. וא"ת: א"כ בספק ספיקא נמי תיאסר, דספק אונס כמאן דליתיה דמי, ולא נשאר אלא חד ספק; ספק תחתיו, ובהא לא שייך לאוקמה בחזקת היתר, כדפי'! א] ואומר ר"י: דהאי רובא דברצון אינו רוב גמור, אלא הוי מדרבנן, והלכך במקום ספק ספיקא — שרי, ובמקום חד ספיקא — חשבי רבנן רצון לגבי אונס רובא. ואשכחן כי האי גוונא גבי תינוק שנמצא בצד העיסה (קדושין דף פ.), דלא הוי רובא אלא מדרבנן, ולהכי קאמר ר' יוחנן התם דאין שורפין עליו את התרומה. וא"ת: אכתי באשת כהן ובקיבל אביה קדושין פחותה מבת שלש לישראל איכא ספק ספיקא, דספק מוכת עץ ספק דרוסת איש, [באשת כהן אית לן למימר: את"ל דאינה מוכת עץ — מ"מ ספק תחתיו ספק אין תחתיו. אשת ישראל, את"ל דאינה מוכת עץ — ספק באונס ספק ברצון]. ואין לומר דמוכת עץ לא שכיח, דהא אמרינן ב"אלו נערות" (לקמן לו:) גבי סומא שאין לה טענת בתולין מפני שנחבטה על גבי קרקע. ופריך: כולהו נמי חבוטי מיחבטן! א"כ שכיח! ולפירוש ר"ת דמוכת עץ פתחה סתום — אתי שפיר. וי"ל: דאם איתא דמוכת עץ היא — הויא טוענת, דאין גנאי בכך כמו בביאת אונס, ומדלא טענה — אין להסתפק בכך. **ומי** אמר ר' אלעזר הכי והאמר ר"א כו'. תימה: השתא דבעי למימר דלא מהימן אפי' לשוייה עליה חתיכה דאיסורא — תיקשי ליה מתני' דהאומר לאשה קידשתיך אסור בקרובותיה! וי"ל: דסבירא ליה למקשן דאין דבר שבערוה פחות משנים, ואפי' ראה אדם שזינתה אשתו, רק שלא היה שם עדים — לא היתה נאסרת עליו. והלכך, ממתני' לא קשיא ליה מידי, דקדשתיך בעדים קאמר, דמקדש אפי' בעד אחד — אין חוששין לקדושיו*. אבל אהא דאמר ר' אלעזר דנאמן בלא עדים לומר דמצא פתח פתוח — פריך שפיר. **קינוי** וסתירה אין עדים לא. הכי נמי דלא אתא למעוטי על פי עצמו, דכעדים דמי, כיון דקים ליה. **מפני** מה לא אסרוה. פירש הקונטרס: והלא אותו מעשה בעדים הוה. ואין נראה, דנהי דידוע לרבים הוה שהביאה לביתו — מ"מ לא ראו כמכחול בשפופרת, שבפני בני אדם לא שמש! ונראה לר"י לפרש: וא"ת דפתח פתוח כשני עדים דמי — אמאי לא אסרוה לדוד? דדוד היה יודע בודאי שנבעלה, ואע"פ שעשה תשובה מכל מקום עיכבה. ואם היתה אסורה לו — לא היה אותו צדיק לוקחה לו לאשה.
כל

[כלאיתא קדושין סה.]

עין משפט נר מצוה

מז א ב ג מיי' פי"ח מהל' איסורי ביאה הל' י יא סמג לאוין קנא טוש"ע אה"ע סי' ו סעי' יד וסימן סח סעי' ז:

מח ד מיי' פ"ט מהל' אישות הל' טו טוש"ע שם סי' מח סעי' א.

מט ה מיי' פכ"ד מהל' אישות הל' יח סמג עשין מח טואה"ע סי' קטו וטוש"ע שם סי' יא סעי' א [וברב אלפס קידושין פ"ג ד' רלח:]

[ועיין היטב ערוך ערך פתח א']

נ ו מיי' פ"א מהל' סוטה הל' טו סמג עשין נו טוש"ע אה"ע סי' קעח סעי' יד [וברב אלפס שם]:

תוספות רי"ד

אמר ר"א האומר פתח פתוח מצאתי נאמן לאוסרה עליו. פי' שלא טען טענות דמים לומר בעלתי ולא מצאתי דמים כגון שהיתה בוגרת או שהיתה ממשפחת דורקטי נאמן לאוסרה עליו. פי' המורה ואע"פ שאין הדבר הזה יכול להתברר אלא על פיו לגבי נפשיה הוי מהימן לשוויה עליה חתיכה דאיסורא אבל להפסיד כתובה לא מהימן. ואמאי ספק ספיקא הוא ספק תחתיו זינתה וספק לא זינתה תחתיו ואת"ל תחתיו זינתה ספק באונס ספק ברצון. ל"צ באשת כהן פי' דאפילו באונס אסורה לו הלכך חד ספק הוא ואבע"א באשת ישראל וכגון דקיבל [בה] אבוה קידושין פחות מבת ג' שנים פי' שאין לומר קודם שאירסה זינתה שהרי בתוליה חוזרים ולא נשאר שם אלא חד ספק ומספיקא היא נאסרה לו: מאי קמ"ל תנינא פי' שאדם נאמן על עצמו לאסור לו את המותר עליו. האומר לאשה קדשתיך והיא אומרת לא קדשתני הוא אסור בקרובותיה פי' באמה ובתה ואחותה דשווינהו אנפשיה חתיכה דאיסורא והיא מותרת בקרוביו פי' שהרי אינה מודה בקידושיו ובמס' קידושין מוקי לה באומר לה קדשתיך בפני עדים והלכו להם למדינות הים. מהו דתימא התם הוא דודאי קים ליה פי' שקדשה אבל הכא מיקם הוא דלא קים ליה פי' מפני שהוא פנוי ויש לומר בחוצפא בעל וג"ל כי פתוח היה ואינו כן א"כ לא תיתסר קמ"ל וכ"ש אם טען בעלתי ולא מצאתי דם בנערה שלא בגרה ואינה ממשפחת דורקטי שהוא נאמן לאוסרה עליו שהוא טענה ודאית יותר מפתח פתוח: ומי א"ר אלעזר הכי פי' דאשה מזנה נאסרת ע"פ עצמו והא א"ר אלעזר אין האשה נאסרת על בעלה אלא על ידי קינוי וסתירה.

גליון הש"ס

גמ' התם אונס הוה. ע' יבמות לה ע"א תד"ה אע"פ:

הגהות מהר"ב רנשבורג

א] תד"ה וא"א וכו' ואור"י דהאי רובא דברצון אינו רוב גמור. עי' פ"י ושו"ת הריב"ש סי' שע"ב וסדרי טהרה בנדה יח ע"א בתוס' ד"ה שליא וכו' ודו"ק:

ולטעמיך קינוי וסתירה אין עדים לא פי' אם יש עדים שזינתה שמא אינה נאסרת בלא קינוי והכתיב כי מצא בה ערות דבר. אלא הכי קאמר אין האשה נאסרת על בעלה בעד א' אלא בשני עדים. וקינוי וסתירה אפילו בע"א. ופתח פתוח מצאתי כב' עדים דמי. פי' אע"פ שעד אחד נאמן באיסורין. היכא דאמר ליה ע"א אשתך זינתה אינו נאמן שאין דבר שבערוה פחות משנים ואם קינא ונסתרה ובא ע"א (יאמר) [ואמר] נטמאת נאמן וקורעת כתובתה ויוצאה ואם רוצה לשתות אין משקין אותה. גם אם אמר פתח פתוח מצאתי נאמן על עצמו כשני עדים ושוי אנפשיה חתיכה דאיסורא:

*כָּל הַיּוֹצֵא לְמִלְחֶמֶת בֵּית דָּוִד גֵּט כְּרִיתוּת כּוֹתֵב לְאִשְׁתּוֹ, דִּכְתִיב: °"וְאֶת אַחֶיךָ תִּפְקֹד לְשָׁלוֹם וְאֶת עֲרֻבָּתָם תִּקָּח". מַאי "וְאֶת עֲרֻבָּתָם תִּקָּח" – תָּנֵי רַב יוֹסֵף: דְּבָרִים הַמְעוֹרָבִין בֵּינוֹ לְבֵינָהּ. אָמַר אַבַּיֵי: אַף אֲנַן נַמִי תְּנֵינָא, *בְּתוּלָה נִשֵּׂאת לְיוֹם הָרְבִיעִי. לְיוֹם רְבִיעִי – אִין, לְיוֹם חֲמִישִׁי – לָא, מַאי טַעֲמָא – מִשּׁוּם אִיקְרוּרֵי דַּעְתָּא. וּלְמַאי? אִי לְמֵיתַב לָהּ כְּתוּבָּה – נֵיתִיב לָהּ, אֶלָּא לְאוֹסְרָהּ עָלָיו, וּדְקָא טָעֵין טַעֲנָה. מַאי לָאו דְּקָטָעֵין טַעֲנַת "פֶּתַח פָּתוּחַ"! אלָא, דְּקָטָעֵין טַעֲנַת דָּמִים. אָמַר רַב יְהוּדָה אָמַר שְׁמוּאֵל: הָאוֹמֵר "פֶּתַח פָּתוּחַ מָצָאתִי" נֶאֱמָן לְהַפְסִידָהּ כְּתוּבָּתָהּ. אָמַר רַב יוֹסֵף: מַאי קמ"ל? תְּנֵינָא: *הָאוֹכֵל אֵצֶל חָמִיו בִּיהוּדָה שֶׁלֹּא בְּעֵדִים – אֵינוֹ יָכוֹל לִטְעוֹן טַעֲנַת בְּתוּלִים, מִפְּנֵי שֶׁמִּתְיַיחֵד עִמָּהּ. בִּיהוּדָה הוּא דְּלָא מָצֵי טָעֵין, הָא בַּגָּלִיל – מָצֵי טָעֵין. וּלְמַאי? אִי לְאוֹסְרָהּ עָלָיו – בִּיהוּדָה אַמַּאי לָא? אֶלָּא לָאו – לְהַפְסִידָהּ כְּתוּבָּתָהּ, וּדְקָא טָעֵין טַעֲנָה, *מַאי לָאו דְּקָא טָעֵין טַעֲנַת "פֶּתַח פָּתוּחַ"! לָא, דְּקָא טָעֵין טַעֲנַת דָּמִים. אִיתְּמַר

תורה אור
ש"א יז

רש"י

גֵּט כְּרִיתוּת כּוֹתֵב לְאִשְׁתּוֹ. שֶׁאִם יָמוּת בַּמִּלְחָמָה יְהֵא גֵּט מִיּוֹם כְּתִיבָתוֹ. וַהֲרֵי מֵת אוּרִיָּה בַּמִּלְחָמָה. דִּכְתִיב. בְּמִלְחֶמֶת שָׁאוּל "וְאֶת אַחֶיךָ" כו', וְדָוִד לָמַד מִיִּשַׁי אָבִיו לְהַנְהִיג שֶׁאַף הַיּוֹצְאִין לְמִלְחֲמוֹתָיו עוֹשִׂין כֵּן. דְּבָרִים הַמְעוֹרָבִים בֵּינוֹ לְבֵינָהּ. אֵלּוּ קִדּוּשִׁין. תִּקָּח. תְּטוֹל מִבֵּינֵיהֶם עַל יְדֵי גֵּט. אַף אֲנַן נַמִי תְּנֵינָא. דְּטוֹעֵן "פֶּתַח פָּתוּחַ מָצָאתִי" אֲסוּרָה עָלָיו, וְלָא אָמְרִינַן לָא קִים לֵיהּ. אִיקְרוּרֵי דַּעְתָּא. עַד שֵׁנִי בְּשַׁבָּת הַבָּאָה. וּלְמַאי. קָפְדִי רַבָּנַן אִי מִקַּרְרָא דַּעְתֵּיהּ. נֵיתִיב לָהּ. מַה לָּנוּ לְהַפְסִידָהּ? וַהֲרֵי הוּא נוֹתֵן מִדַּעַת. אֶלָּא לָאו לְאוֹסְרָהּ. הוּא דְּקָפְדִינַן, שֶׁלֹּא יְקָרֵר דַּעְתּוֹ וִיקַיֵּים אֶת הָאֲסוּרָה לוֹ. אַלְמָא, כִּי אָתֵי וְטָעֵין – אָסְרִינַן לָהּ עֲלֵיהּ. טַעֲנַת דָּמִים. דְּטַעֲנָה מְבוֹרֶרֶת הִיא, וְלֵיכָּא לְמֵימַר לָא קִים לֵיהּ. אֲבָל בְּפֶתַח פָּתוּחַ – אֵימָא לָךְ לָא קִים לֵיהּ. לְהַפְסִידָהּ כְּתוּבָּתָהּ. עַל פִּי עַצְמוֹ, וְטַעְמָא לְקַמָּן מְפָרֵשׁ: חֲזָקָה אֵין אָדָם טוֹרֵחַ בִּסְעוּדָה וּמַפְסִידָהּ. הָאוֹכֵל אֵצֶל חָמִיו. בַּיָּמִים שֶׁבֵּין אֵירוּסִין לְנִשּׂוּאִין. אֵין יָכוֹל לִטְעוֹן טַעֲנַת בְּתוּלִים. כְּשֶׁתִּכָּנֵס לַחוּפָּה. מִפְּנֵי שֶׁמִּתְיַיחֵד עִמָּהּ. בִּיהוּדָה הָיוּ מְיַיחֲדִין אוֹתָם כְּדֵי שֶׁיְּהֵא לִבּוֹ גַּס בָּהּ. בִּיהוּדָה אַמַּאי לָא. הָאוֹמֵר פְּשִׁיטָא לִי שֶׁלֹּא בָּאתִי אֵלֶיהָ, וְהָא וַדַּאי מֵאַחֵר זִינְּתָה – שַׁוְיַהּ עֲלֵיהּ חֲתִיכָה דְּאִיסּוּרָא, מַה לִּי גָּלִיל מַה לִּי יְהוּדָה. אֶלָּא לָאו לְהַפְסִידָהּ כְּתוּבָּתָהּ. וּבִיהוּדָה לָא מַפְסִידָהּ עַל פִּיו, דְּאָמְרִינַן הוּא בָּא עָלֶיהָ בָּאֵרוּסִין, וּבַגָּלִיל מָצֵי טָעֵין, דְּהָא לָא נִתְיַיחֵד. מַאי לָאו דְּקָטָעֵין טַעֲנַת פֶּתַח פָּתוּחַ מָצָאתִי. דְּאַע"ג דְּאֵין עֵדִים בְּדָבָר זֶה וְלָא טַעֲנָה מוּכַחַת, אֶלָּא עֲלֵיהּ סָמְכִינַן. דְּאָמְרִינַן: אִי לָאו דְּקוּשְׁטָא הוּא – לָא הָיָה מַפְסִיד סְעוּדָתוֹ. וְאִם הָיָה שׂוֹנְאָהּ – מִתְּחִלָּה הָיָה מְגָרְשָׁהּ, וְלָא טָרַח בִּסְעוּדַת נִשּׂוּאִין. וּמִיהוּ, בִּיהוּדָה לָא מְהֵימַן, שֶׁמָּא בָּעַל בִּימֵי אֵירוּסִין וְשָׁכַח, אוֹ הֶעֱרָה בָּהּ מִתּוֹךְ חִבָּתָהּ, וְלָא יָדַע שֶׁשִּׁיבֵּר בְּתוּלֶיהָ. לָא דְּקָא טָעֵין טַעֲנַת דָּמִים. לְעוֹלָם אֵימָא לָךְ: בְּדָבָר שֶׁאֵינוֹ יָכוֹל לְבָרְרוֹ – אֵינוֹ נֶאֱמָן לְהַפְסִיד כְּתוּבָּתָהּ. וְדִיוּקָא דְּמַתְנִי', דְּדָיְיקִינַן הָא בַּגָּלִיל מָצֵי טָעֵין – דְּטָעֵין טַעֲנַת דָּמִים. וּכְגוֹן שֶׁהָיוּ לָהֶם שׁוֹשְׁבִינִים שֶׁמְּמַשְׁמְשׁוּ אוֹתָן, וְלֹא נַעֲשֵׂית אוֹנָאָה בַּדָּבָר, וְלֹא רָאָה וְאִיבֵּד, וְטַעֲנָה בְּרוּרָה הִיא. חֲכָמִים

תוספות

כל היוצא למלחמת בית דוד גט כריתות כותב לאשתו. פי' בקונטרס: שאם ימות במלחמה – יהא גט משעת כתיבתו. וקשה לר"ת: דא"כ מאי כל היוצא, אם לא מהני אלא למי שאין לו בניס ויש לו יבם? ועוד: דתנן ב"מי שאחזו" (גיטין עג. ושם) מה היא באותן הימים? רבי יהודה אומר: הרי היא כאשת איש לכל דבריה, וקאי אמאי דקתני לעיל מינה: "הרי זה גיטך מהיום אם מתי". וכן משמע בתוספתא. אלמא, אע"ג דאמר "מהיום" – הויא אשת איש גמורה, כדמפרש בגמרא באומר "מעת שאני בעולם". פירוש: דהאי דאמר "מהיום" לא שיחול מיד, אלא דעתו שיחול שעה אחת קודם מיתתו, דהיינו מעת שהוא בעולם. ולא אמר "מהיום" אלא למעוטי לאחר מיתה, כלומר: מאותו יום שאני בעולם יהא גט. ומיהו, יש לחלק בין "מהיום" לפירש בהדיא שיחול משעת כתיבה – דע"כ משעת כתיבה קאמר שיהא גט. ועוד נראה: דאפי' אמר "מהיום" יש ליישב פי' הקונטרס, דלאו דוקא פירש שאם ימות במלחמה, אלא היו מתנים אם לא יחזור מן המלחמה. ואגב ריהטיה נקט בקונטרס אם ימות, דסתם מי שאינו חוזר מן המלחמה אינו חוזר לפי שמת. אלא ה"ה אם נשבה. והשתא "מהיום" דהכא אין שייך לומר "מעת שאני בעולם" כההוא ד"מי שאחזו", אלא "מהיום" – מיום כתיבה קאמר.

ואם תאמר: והרי חזר אוריה ונתבטל הגט! ויש לומר: שהיה מתנה אם לא יחזור בסוף המלחמה, והרי לא חזר לבסוף. וניחא לפירוש זה הא דאמרינן בפרק "הזהב" (ב"מ נט. ושם): נוח לו לאדם שיבעול ספק אשת איש ואל ילבין פני חבירו ברבים. ומפיק ליה מהאי מעשה דבת שבע, דספק אשת איש הואי, דדלמא יחזור מן המלחמה. ור"ת מפרש: כותב גט כריתות לגמרי, בלא שום תנאי. ולפי' קשה: אמאי קרי לה ספק אשת איש? הא הואי גרושה גמורה! ואר"ת: דקרי לה ספק אשת איש לפי שהיו מגרשין בצינעא, שלא יהא נודע ויקפצו עליהם בני אדם לקדשם. ולפי' הקונטרס קשה קצת איך בא עליה? למה לא היה ירא שמא יחזור! **אי** למיתב לה כתובה כו'. משמע, אם היה בא לב"ד – היה נאמן להפסידה כתובתה, אע"פ שלאוסרה עליו לא היה נאמן, משום דאית לן למימר דשמא אינו בקי בפתח פתוח, ואוקמה בחזקת היתר. אבל מ"מ כתובתה הפסידה, אע"פ שיש לנו לומר שהוא טועה בפתח פתוח, דאית לן למימר אוקי ממונא בחזקת מריה. וקשה: דאמאי מפסידה כתובתה? והא הוה א] ספק ספיקא; ספק אי הוא בקי בפתח פתוח אם לאו, ואם תמצא לומר פתח פתוח הוה – ספק באונס ספק ברצון, דאפי' אשת כהן באונס לא מפסדה כתובתה! ואין לומר דאפי' בספק ספיקא מפסדה כתובתה משום דמוקמינן ממונא בחזקתיה – דהא לקמן (דף יב:) גבי "משארסתני נאנסתי", והוא אומר "לא כי אלא עד שלא ארסתיך נאנסת והיה מקחי מקח טעות", ואיכא מאן דמפרש לקמן (דף יא:): מקח טעות ממאתים, אבל מנה אית לה. אלמא משום דאותו מנה הוי ספק ספיקא – לא מפסדה; דספק קודם שנתארסה ספק אחר שנתארסה, ואם תמצא לומר אחר שנתארסה – אימור באונס הוה. דאי אמרת דאפי' בספק ספיקא מפסדה – אמאי אית לה אפי' מנה? וי"ל: דלא חשיב ספק ספיקא כהאי גוונא, משום דהאי ספיקא שמא באונס היה – לא חשיב ספיקא גמורה למיתב לה כתובה, דאימור קודם שנתארסה נאנסה. והשתא אתי שפיר הא דתנן במתני' (לקמן דף יג.): היא אומרת "מוכת עץ אני", והוא אומר "לא כי אלא דרוסת איש את" וקאמר ר' יהושע שאינה נאמנת ומפסדת כתובתה, אי לר' יוחנן – מנה, אי לר' אלעזר – ולא כלום. ואע"ג דהוי ספק ספיקא; ספק מוכת עץ ויש לה כתובה, ואפי' אם תמצא לומר דרוסת איש – אימור תחתיו נאנסה ונסתחפה שדהו ויש לה כתובה. אלא ודאי ספק באונס לא חשיב ספק, ב] דאימור קודם שנתארסה נאנסה. ועוד אומר רבינו יצחק: דמוכת עץ לא שכיח, דהא דאמרינן (לקמן לו:): כולהו נמי חבוטי מיחבטן – היינו אליבא דר"ג, אבל רבי יהושע שמעינן דלית ליה טעמא דמיחבטן, דקאמר התם (לקמן לו.): חרשת ושוטה יש להן טענת בתולין, והיינו משום דס"ל דחבטא לא שכיחא. **מאי** לאו דקא טעין טענת פתח פתוח. נראה לפרש דקס"ד דבטענת דמים *ליכא למיחש לאיקרורי דעתא, דכיון דליכא דם לבו נוקפו ואין מתקרר. אבל בפתח פתוח – איכא למיחש שמא יתקרר. **נאמן** להפסידה כתובתה. אור"י: דשמואל מודה שפיר דנאמן לאוסרה עליו. ולהפסידה כתובתה איצטריך ליה לאשמעינן, דלא תימא דלא יהא נאמן, אע"ג דקים ליה בפתח פתוח דנימא במזיד משקר להפסידה כתובתה. ור"א נמי מאי סבר דנאמן להפסידה, ונקט לאוסרה לרבותא, וכ"ש דנאמן להפסיד כתובתה, כדמוכח הסוגיא דלעיל. [ומיהו, בירושלמי משמע דלר"א אינו נאמן להפסיד כתובתה]. **אבל** בגליל מצי טעין. וא"ת: מנא ליה? דלמא ביהודה נאמנת לומר שבא עליה באירוסין ולא בגליל, אבל כשטוענת בתולה הייתי – בגליל נמי מהימנא? וי"ל: דמשמע ליה אינו יכול לטעון טענת בתולים בכל ענין, בין שאומרת שבא עליה מן האירוסין בין שאומרת פתח נעול מלא. דביהודה נאמנת במגו דאי בעיא אמרה באירוסין בא עליה. ולא בגליל, דליכא מגו. אבל קשה: דמייתי מדיוקא, והוה ליה לאתויי מרישא. דקתני (לקמן דף י:): בתולה אלמנה מן האירוסין כו' ויש להן טענת בתולין. וע"כ לענין כתובה איירי, דלאוסרה עליו – אפילו מן הנשואין נמי יש לה טענת בתולין, כיון דכנסה בחזקת בתולה, כדמוכח לקמן (דף יב.), דפריך: וניחוש שמא תחתיו זינתה! **מאי** לאו דקא טעין טענת פתח פתוח. וביהודה אע"ג דאיכא חזקה לא מהימן, כדפי' בקונטרס. א"נ: כיון דמתייחד עמה – ודאי בא עליה, דלא מוקי איניש אנפשיה. ואע"ג דגבי יבמה אמרינן (יבמות דף קיא:) דעד ל' יום מוקי אנפשיה – רוב פעמים לא מוקי אנפשיה אפי' שעה אחת, דעל דעת כן מתייחד *[עמה], ואיתרע חזקה.

לא דקא טעין טענת דמים. דהויא טענה ברורה, מדאין סדינין מלוכלכים בדם. ונראה דבטענת פתח פתוח וטענת דמים דשמעתין, איירי שהיא טוענת שהוא בא עליה באירוסין, או אומרת בתולה הייתי. וא"ת: ונהימנא לדידה במגו דאי בעיא אמרה משארסתני נאנסתי דנאמנת לר"ג, דפסקינן לקמן (דף יג.) כוותיה! וי"ל: דאינה מודה ברצון שנבעלה מאחר. ועוד: דאין זה מגו, דמיפסלא נפשה מכהונה. אבל קשה: דליהמנה במגו דאי בעיא אמרה מוכת עץ אני, אפי' לרבנן דלקמן (דף יא:) דאמרי מוכת עץ כתובתה מנה, דאין זה מגו דאינה רוצה להפסיד כלום מכתובתה – מ"מ נאמנת במגו, דאי בעיא אמרה מוכת עץ אני תחתיך, ונסתחפה שדהו! לכך נראה דהוי מגו במקום חזקה, דאין אדם טורח בסעודה ומפסידה. אע"ג דבעי' היא בפ"ק דבבא בתרא (דף ה: ושם) אי אמרינן מגו במקום חזקה או לא, שמא חזקה דהכא עדיפא. ואי לא אמרינן מגו להוציא – אתי נמי שפיר:

אמר

עין משפט נר מצוה

נא א מיי' פי"א מהל' אישות הלכה יב יג טוש"ע אה"ע סימן סח סעיף ג וסעיף ו

מסורת הש"ס

שבת נו.

[לעיל ב.]

לקמן יב.

כ"ה בדפו"י

הגהות

א] בת"י עה"ג וי"מ דהכא לא חשיב ספק ספיקא דאין יכולין להתהפך ולומר בריש' ספק באונס ספק ברצון ואת"ל ברצון ספק וכו' ולהכי לא חשיב אלא חדא ספיקא וה"נ י"ל בע"א דרוב בקיאין בפתח פתוח והוה ליה לענין כתובה רובא וחזקת ממונא ותו ליכא אלא חדא ספיקא אבל לענין לאוסרה איכא למימר סמוך מיעוטא דאין בקיאין לחזקה ואיתרע רובא והוי ליה פלגא ופלגא והוי ספק ספיקא ול"נ דה"פ אי למיתב לה כתובה ואיירי בטענת דמים לענין כתובה איכא למיחש לאיקרורי דעתיה בטענת דמים

[דטענת דמים מסתבר כשנתייחד עמה אם היו אז דמים בשעת תשמיש היתה מראה לאביה ולאמה או לבעלה כדי שלא יהא לו לב עליה כשישאנה וס"ד דטענת דמים אף ביהודה יכול לטעון אבל בפתח אינה מכרת אם פתחה נעול או לאו ואינה מגדת והשתא אתי שפיר דלא פריך מרישא דבפשיטות איכא לאוקמי בטענת דמים. ת"י עה"ג. ובתוס' הרשב"א מצאתי דפי' דבטענת דמים ביהודה נמי ס"ד דמהימן דליכא למימר שכח דאם איתא דהוה דם כשנתייחד עמה לא היה שוכח אבל בפתח פתוח איכא למימר דלא אסיק אדעתיה וא"ת מ"מ אם איתא דפתח לה פתח הוי דם וי"ל דאפשר למיפתח פתח בלא דם ולפי' ר"ח איכא לאוקמי בבוגרת שכלו דמיה שפתח פתחא ולאו אדעתיה כיון דליכא דם ובכל בתולה אפשר לפותחה בלא דם כדשמואל מיהו הסיא דשמואל נמי משמע דפתחה נעול מדאין ריחה נודף ושמא יש לומר דמחמת דם נמי אין ריחה נודף. ע"כ]:

ב] [ולהאי שינויא לא מיתוקמא מתני' בפחות מג' שנים. ת"י עה"ג]

[*ולפי פי' ר"ח אתי שפיר דמיסתבר ליה לאוקמי מתני' בכל הנשים אפי' בבוגרת ומוכת עץ דלאין להם דמים ועי"ל מאי לאו דקטעין אף פתח פתוח דאיירי מתני' בכל ענין שיטעון]

עין משפט נר מצוה

נב א מיי' פי"א מהל' אישות הל' א סמג עשין מח טוש"ע אה"ע סי' סה סעי' א וסעי' ח:

נג ב מיי' פט"ז שם הל' ג סמג שם טוש"ע שם סי' ק סעי' ב:

נד ג מיי' פי"י שם הל' ז טוש"ע שם סימן סו סעיף ו:

נה ד טוש"ע שם סי' סח סעי' ו בהגהה:

[ועי' תוס' סוטה כז. ד"ה אינן]

נו ה ו מיי' פי"א שם הל' יב טוש"ע שם:

מסורת הש"ס

קדושין מה: [יבמות קז.] | נ"י כ"י | [לקמן נו:] | לקמן לח: [כתו:] | [ועי' תוס' סוטה כז. ד"ה אינן] | לקמן קי: | שמות כב

גמרא

איתמר, אמר רב נחמן אמר שמואל משום רבי שמעון בן אלעזר: א חכמים תקנו להם לבנות ישראל, לבתולה מאתים, ולאלמנה מנה. והם האמינוהו, שאם אמר "פתח פתוח מצאתי" נאמן. א"כ מה הועילו חכמים בתקנתם? אמר רבא: *חזקה, אין אדם טורח בסעודה ומפסידה. תנא: הואיל וקנס חכמים הוא — לא תגבה אלא מן הזיבורית. קנסא?! מאי קנסא? אלא אימא: ב הואיל ותקנת חכמים הוא — לא תגבה אלא מן הזיבורית. רבן שמעון בן גמליאל אומר: *כתובת אשה מן התורה — ומי אמר רבן שמעון בן גמליאל הכי? *והתניא: °"כסף ישקל כמהר הבתולות" שיהא זה כמוהר הבתולות, ומוהר הבתולות כזה. ג מכאן *סמכו חכמים לכתובת אשה מן התורה. רבן שמעון בן גמליאל אומר: כתובת אשה אינה מדברי תורה, אלא מדברי סופרים! איפוך. ומאי חזית דאפכת בתרייתא? איפוך קמייתא! הא שמעינא ליה לרבן שמעון בן גמליאל דאמר כתובת אשה מדאורייתא, דתנן: *רבן שמעון בן גמליאל אומר: נותן לה ממעות קפוטקיא. ואי בעית אימא: כולה רבן שמעון בן גמליאל היא, וחסורי מיחסרא והכי קתני: מכאן סמכו חכמים לכתובת אשה מן התורה. כתובת אלמנה אינה מדברי תורה אלא מדברי סופרים, שרבן שמעון בן גמליאל אומר: כתובת אלמנה אינה מדברי תורה אלא מדברי סופרים. ההוא דאתא לקמיה דרב נחמן, אמר ליה: פתח פתוח מצאתי. אמר ליה רב נחמן: אסבוהו כופרי, מברכתא חביטא ליה. והא רב נחמן הוא דאמר מהימן! מהימן, ומסבינן ליה כופרי. רב אחאי משני: ד כאן — בבחור, כאן — בנשוי. ההוא דאתא לקמיה דרבן גמליאל, אמר ליה: פתח פתוח מצאתי. אמר ליה: ה שמא הטיתה? אמשול לך משל, למה הדבר דומה — לאדם שהיה מהלך באישון לילה ואפילה, היטה — מצאו פתוח, לא היטה — מצאו נעול. איכא דאמרי, הכי אמר ליה: ו שמא במזיד הטיתה ועקרת לדשא ועברא? אמשול לך משל למה הדבר דומה — לאדם שהוא מהלך באישון לילה ואפילה; היטה במזיד — מצאו פתוח. לא היטה במזיד — מצאו נעול. ההוא דאתא לקמיה דרבן גמליאל בר רבי, אמר ליה: רבי, בעלתי ולא מצאתי דם. אמרה לו: רבי, בתולה הייתי. אמר להם: הביאו לי אותו סודר. הביאו לו הסודר ושראו במים, וכבסו, ומצא עליו כמה טיפי דמים. אמר לו: לך זכה במקחך. אמר ליה הונא מר בריה דרבא מפרזקיא לרב אשי: אנן נמי נעביד הכי! אמר ליה:

גיהוץ

רש"י

חכמים תקנו לאשה כו'. כלומר: אי הואי כתובתה דאורייתא, לא הוי נאמן להפקיעה אלא בעדות ידועה. אבל כתובתה — חכמים תיקנוה, הם אמרו והם אמרו. הם שתיקנוה אמרו שהוא נאמן להפסידה אף בטענת פתח פתוח. א"כ. שבידו להפקיעה. מה הועילו חכמים בתקנתן. שתקנו לה כתובה. חזקה אין אדם טורח בסעודה כו'. אין לחוש שיטעון אדם כך אלא באמת. שאם היה שונא אותה מתחילה — לא היה טורח בסעודה וכונסה ומפסיד סעודתו חנם, אלא היה מגרשה מתחילה. אלא מן הזיבורית. אם באת לגבות כתובתה, ויש לו עידית וזיבורית ובינונית — אינה יכולה לומר תן לי עידית או בינונית בשוויה; אלא אם בא ליתן לה זיבורית בשוויה — יתן. [מאי קנסא. כלומר מאי פשע דקא קנסינן ליה]. מן התורה. מ"כסף ישקול" כדלקמן. כסף ישקול. במפתה נאמר. כמוהר הבתולות. האמור במאנס את הבתולה (דברים כב), קנסו הכתוב נ' כסף בשביל מוהר בתוליה. שיהא זה כמוהר הבתולות. הקיש הכתוב קנס המפתה לקנס האונס: מה להלן נ' — אף כאן נ'. ומה כסף האמור כאן שקלים, דכתיב "ישקול" — אף להלן שקלים, דלא תימא מעות. מכאן סמכו. מדקרי לה מוהר. נותן לה ממעות קפוטקיא. בפרק בתרא תנן: נשא אשה בא"י וגירשה בקפוטקיא — נותן לה ממעות א"י, שהן קלות. נשא אשה בקפוטקיא וגירשה בא"י — נותן לה ממעות א"י מנין הכתוב בכתובה, דאזלינן לקולא. רשב"ג אומר: נותן לה ממעות קפוטקיא, שנשתעבד בהן, כשאר מלוה, דקסבר: כתובה דאורייתא. אסבוהו כופרי. הלקוהו מלקיות במקלות חריות של דקל, שיש בהן עוקצין כמין קוצין, כדאמרינן בסוכה (דף לג.): ואימא כופרא — "דרכיה דרכי נועם" כתיב. מברכתא חביטא ליה. זונות העיר הזאת, ששמה מברכתא, חבוטות ושוכבות תמיד לפניו לזנות, מאחר שהוא בקי בפתח פתוח. בחור — לא מהימן, ומסבינן ליה כופרי על שמעיז פניו. נשוי — מהימן, ולא מסבינן ליה כופרי. הטה. כשהגיע לפתח ביתו הסגור ויש בו דבר מעכבו מלפתוח, וכשמטין אותו לצדדין — נפתח. איכא דאמרי. בלא מתכוין לא שכיח הטייה, ולא אמרי' שמא הטה. אלא כך בדקו: שמא במזיד הטית ועקרת לדשא ועברא = עקרת הדלת והבריח. הטה במזיד. במתכוין ובכח. וכבסו. שהיו טיפי הדמים מכוסים בשכבת זרע.

גיהוץ

תוספות

אמר רב נחמן אמר שמואל חכמים תיקנו כו'. משמע דכתובה דרבנן. וכן ב"האשה רבה" (יבמות פט. ושם) גבי אין לה כתובה קאמר: מאי טעמא תקינו לה רבנן כתובה — שלא תהא קלה בעיניו להוציאה כו'. אלמא סתמא דהתלמוד סבר דכתובה דרבנן, וקשה: דנהגו לכתוב בכתובה "כסף זוזי מאתן דחזו ליכי מדאורייתא"! ואור"ת: דסמכינן ארשב"ג דמתני' דפרק בתרא (דף קי:) דמייתי לה נמי בסמוך, דאמר: נותן לה ממעות קפוטקיא, דקסבר כתובה דאורייתא. *וקי"ל כרשב"ג במשנתנו. ועוד אור"י: דלא קיימא לן כר"נ, דאשכחנא רב אשי דהוא בתראה דפליג עליה, כדמתרץ לקמן ברייתא (דף יב.) תני: כל שלא מושמש אינו יכול לטעון טענת בתולים. אלמא דחייש לשמא משקר, ולא אמרינן חזקה אין אדם טורח בסעודה ומפסידה. וכן פי' רבינו יצחק בן רבינו מאיר דרב אשי פליג אדרב נחמן. והא דאמרינן ב"האשה רבה" (יבמות פט. ושם): מ"ט תקינו רבנן כתובה — ה"פ: מ"ט תקינו רבנן כתובה היכא דתקינו, כגון באלמנה — שלא תהא קלה בעיניו להוציאה. ה"נ תקינו שלא יהא לה, כדי שתהא קלה בעיניו להוציאה.

חזקה אין אדם טורח כו'. תימה: תינח באשת כהן או בפחותה מג' דמיתסרא עליה, הילכך כיון דמפסידה — נאמן. ולמ"ד נמי לקמן כנסה בחזקת בתולה ונמצאת בעולה אין לה כתובה כלל — ניחא, דהשתא נמי מפסידה, שהרי מקח טעות הוא. אבל למ"ד יש לה כתובה מנה — לא מפסיד מידי, אלא שבא להפסידה מכתובתה מנה. אבל הסעודה לא מפסיד, ואמאי מהימן? ונראה דלא מהימן.

הואיל ותקנת חכמים היא לא תגבה כו'. תימה: דר"מ אית ליה לקמן בפרק "אע"פ" (נו: ושם) דכתובה דאורייתא, ובפ' "הניזקין" (גיטין מח: ושם) אמרי' דקסבר ר"מ דכתובת אשה בבינונית, משום חינא. וכיון דהויא דאורייתא — דינה בעידית, כדנפקא לן בריש ב"ק (דף ה.): וכולן כאבות לשלם ממיטב, דאתיא "תחת" "נתינה" "ישלם" "כסף", ואמאי הפקיעו דינה? ועוד, דלא מישתמיט תנא בשום מקום דאית ליה כתובת אשה ממטלטלי אלא לר"מ, כדאמרינן בכל דוכתין (יבמות לט.): הא מני — ר"מ היא, דאמר מטלטלי משתעבדי לכתובה. ולמ"ד דאורייתא — אמאי לא גבי ממטלטלי כמו ניזקין, כיון דמהתם ילפינן? וי"ל: דטעמא, שלא יפרשו מהן בני אדם אם יצטרכו למכור עידית או מטלטלים, וחשו כדי שיקפצו עליהן בני אדם.

נותן לה ממעות קפוטקיא. תימה לר"י: מה ריוח הוא לה שנותן לה מאותם המעות? מ"מ אינו נותן לה אלא שוה נ' שקלים! ואם היינו אומרים דלעולם צריך ליתן לה שקלים שעומדין שם בקפוטקיא נ' שקלי קפוטקיא, ובארץ ישראל נ' שקלים של ארץ ישראל — הוה ניחא. כדאמרינן גבי ה' סלעים דפדיון בכור בפ' "יש בכור" (בכורות נ. ושם): לישדר מר תילתא אחרינא דאוסיפו עלייהו, ושדר להו. מיהו אין נראה, דהתם כשהוסיפו — בכל מקום הוסיפו, אבל כשמוסיפין במקום אחד — אין נראה שבכך תשתנה מדה דאורייתא. ומיהו, בירושלמי דפירקין גרסינן אמתניתין דכתובה מאתים: רבי מונא בשם שמואל אמר: בשקל הקדש, רבי אבא בר זונא אמר: מטבע יוצא, וכן מסקי התם כמה אמוראי.

מברכתא חביטא ליה. פירוש: הלקוהו שמוליא ש"ר על בת ישראל, שהרי משקר. וכי זונות חבוטות לפניו שיהיה בקי? הלכך לא מהימן. והא אמר רב נחמן מהימן? ומשני: מהימן, ומסבינן ליה כופרי. ורב נחמן דאמר אסבוהו — לא משום שלא היה מאמינו, אלא היה מאמינו, ואמר להלקותו לפי שחשוד על הזנות. ורב אחא משני כדסבירא לן מעיקרא דלא מהימן, ואיירי בבחור. ועי"ל בניחותא: מברכתא חביטא ליה, אף על פי שהוא נאמן — הלקוהו, לפי שחשוד על הזנות. והאמר רב נחמן נאמן, ולא פירש להלקותו! ומשני: מהימן ומסבינן ליה, ורב נחמן לא איירי במלקות. רב אחא אמר: לעולם נאמן דאמר רב נחמן — היינו בלא מלקות, ובנשוי.

בתולה

תוספות רי"ד

אמר ר"נ אמר שמואל משום ר"ש ב"א חכמים תקנו להם לבנות ישראל לבתולה מאתים ולאלמנה מנה. והם הימנוהו שאם אמר פתח פתוח מצאתי נאמן א"כ מה הועילו חכמים בתקנתם. א"ר חזקה אין אדם טורח בסעודה ומפסידה. פי' המורה אין לחוש שיטעון כך אלא באמת שאם היה שונאה מתחילה לא היה טורח בסעודה לכונסה ומפסיד סעודתו חנם אלא מתחלה [היה] מגרשה והגאון פי' אימתי הבעל מהימן כששניהם טוענים ברי על הפתח הבעל אומר פתח פתוח מצאתי והיא טוענת לא כי אלא פתח נעול מצאת ותרווייהו טענו טענות ברי אז הבעל מהימן אבל אם היא מודה ליה אין פתח פתוח מצאת אבל תחתיך נאנסתי ונסתפחה שדך או מוכת עץ אני ואית לי כתובה ואיהו אמר שמא עד שלא ארסתיך והיה מקחי מקח טעות כיון דאיהי טוענת ודאי ואיהו ספק אינו נאמן כדאמר לקמן דפסק שמואל הלכתא כרבן גמליאל דאמר דאשה נאמנת ולא קשיא דשמואל אדשמואל דלא דמי תרתי טעניתא להדדי דהכא טענו ברי וברי והתם טענו ברי ושמא ואית לה מיגו וחזקה. פי' מיגו דאי בעי אמרה מוכת עץ אני תחתיך ולא פסלה נפשה מכהונה וכו' וחזקה דגופה דבתולה נולדה: וראיתי כתוב בה"ג דאי עביד בעל סעודה רבתי דינא הוא דשקיל אודינא מן האשה מטעם רבה ואינו נ"ל דעד כאן לא האמינוהו אלא להפסידה כתובתה שהוא מוחזק בה אבל להוציא ממון ממנה אינו נאמן בטענתו. וכתב רבינו יצחק ז"ל חזינן לגאון דקאמר ה"מ לענין מנה מאתים אבל לתוספת לא מהימן וטעמא דמסתבר הוא דלא תקינו רבנן אלא מנה מאתים אבל תוספת איהו כתב לה מנפשיה הלכך לא מהימן: תנא הואיל וכן דכתובתה תיקון חכמים היא לא תגבה אלא מן הזיבורית. פי' אם באת לגבות כתובתה ויש לו עידית בינונית וזיבורית אין יכולה לומר תן לי עידית או בינונית ובשוויה אלא זיבורית נותן לה ובשוויה: רשב"ג אומר כתובת אשה מן התורה. ומי ארשב"ג הכי והא תניא כסף ישקול כמוהר הבתולות מכאן סמכו חכמים לכתובת אשה מן התורה. רשב"ג אומר כתובת אשה אינה מה"ת אלא מדברי סופרים. איפוך ומאי חזית דאפכית בתרייתא איפוך קמייתא. דהא שמעינן ליה לרשב"ג דאמר כתובת אשה דאורייתא פי' דתנן בפ' בתרא דמכילתין נשא אשה בא"י וכו' רשב"ג אומר נותן לה ממעות קפוטקיא פי' נשתעבד בהן כשאר מלוה דקסבר כתובה דאורייתא. ע' בסו"פ: ההוא דאתא לקמיה דרב נחמן אמר פתח פתוח מצאתי אמר להו ר"נ אסבוהו כופרא. פי' חריות של דקל שיש בהן עוקצין כמין קוצין: מברכתא חביטא ליה. פי' זונות מופקרות היו חבוטות לו שמכיר בפתח פתוח. והאר"נ האומר וכו' נאמן. נאמן ומספינן ליה כופרא. רב אחא משני כאן בבחור כאן בנשוי. פי' בחור לא מהימן ומספינן ליה כופרי נשוי מהימן ולא מספינן ליה כופרי: ההוא דאתא לקמיה דר"ג א"ל פ"פ מצאתי. א"ל שמא הטית אמשול לך משל למה הדבר דומה לאדם שמהלך באישון לילה ואפילה הטה מצאו פתוח לא הטה מצאו נעול. פי' בהגיעו לפתח ביתו הסגור ויש בו המעכבו מלפתוח. וכשמטין אותו לצדדין נפתח. ואי קשיא היכא שריא ליה. והא אמרן לעיל האומר פ"פ מצאתי מהימן לאוסרה עליו. תשובה אי הוה מהדר ליה ברי לי שלא הטיתי הוה אסורה עליו. אבל כיון דשתיק הרגיש ר"ג מתוך דבריו כמספקא ליה ואין טענתו טענה ברורה ולפיכך שריא עליה:

גליון הש"ס

גמ' חכמים תקנו להם. עיין סנהדרין ח ע"א תד"ה מוציא שם רע:

נז א מיי׳ פי״א מהל׳ אישות הל׳ יב טוש״ע אה״ע סי׳ סא סעי׳ ד [עי׳ מ״מ]:

נח ב ג מיי׳ שם טור שו״ע שם סעיף ה:

נט ד מיי׳ פ״י שם הל׳ ט סמג עשין מח טוש״ע שם סי׳ סו סעי׳ ו:

ס ה מיי׳ פי״א שם הל׳ א והלכה ח סמג שם טוש״ע שם סימן סז סעיף א:

סא ו מיי׳ פ״א מהל׳ ביאת מקדש הל״ג (סמג לאוין ס) טוש״ע יו״ד סימן רמב סעיף יג בהגהה:

בתולה אלמנה גרושה וחלוצה. נראה לפרש דלרבותא נקט חלוצה. דסלקא דעתך אמינא: כיון דשומרת יבם לא מיתסרא כניסה לחופה, שהרי יבמה יבא עליה בעל כרחה, וה״א דכנשואה דמיא, קמ״ל. **אלמנה** דכתיבא באורייתא מאי איכא למימר. והא ליכא למימר דתפשוט מהכא דכתובת אלמנה מנה מדאורייתא — דהא מנה לא היה בימי משה, דלא הזכירה תורה אלא ככר. והא דאמרינן בבכורות (דף ה. ושם): משה רבינו נאמן היה ובקי בחשבונות, אלא שמנה של קודש כפול היה — לא שהיה מנה בימי משה, אלא כלומר: כמו שמנה של קודש בימי יחזקאל כפול היה — כך היה ככר של קודש כפול בימי משה. **ותנא** רב יוסף אשור זו סליקא ומי הואי. פי׳ בקונטרס: ומי הואי בבריאת עולם? ובלא רב יוסף מ״אשור״ וכן מ״כוש״ לא מצי למיפרך, דמצינן למימר דאשור וכוש שם המחוז ולא שם העיר, ומימות עולם היה שמם כך. אבל קשה: דמאי מייתי מאשור? דאשור, אע״ג דלא הוה בבריאת עולם, כיון דהוה בימי משה — שפיר הוה ליה למכתב, אבל מנה לא היה לו לכתוב, כיון שעדיין לא היה בדורו! ונראה לר״י לפרש: דסליקא בימי משה מי הואי? דקים ליה דסליקא לא היה בימי משה, וסביב סליקא הולך חדקל, ולא אבל אשור שהיה בימי משה.

אמר רב אכל תמרים אל יורה. ואם תאמר: דבפ״ג דכריתות (דף יג: ושם) (אמר רב הונא) אמר רב: הלכה כר׳ אלעזר, דאינו מחייב על שאר משכרין אלא על היין בלבד! וי״ל: אע״ג דלא מחייב על ביאת מקדש — אסור להורות. *) וה״נ משמע בס״פ ״אלו מומין״ (בכורות מה:) דפסול לעבודה למאן דלא מחייב אשאר משכרין, אף על גב דעבודה לא אחיל — הוא הדין נמי דאל יורה.

מטבילין

*) [בכריתות תירצו דהתם מדאורייתא והכא מדרבנן הוא דאסור]

תורה אור

*גיהוץ שלנו כבבוס שלהם. ואי אמרת ניעבד גיהוץ — מעברא ליה חומרתא. ההוא דאתא לקמיה דרבן גמליאל ב״ר, אמר ליה: רבי, בעלתי ולא מצאתי דם. אמרה ליה: רבי, עדיין בתולה אני. א אמר להן: הביאו לי שתי שפחות, אחת בתולה ואחת בעולה. הביאו לו, והושיבן *על פי חבית של יין. בעולה — ריחה נודף, בתולה — אין ריחה נודף, אף זו הושיבה, ולא היה ריחה נודף, אמר לו: לך זכה במקחך. ונבדוק מעיקרא בגווה? גמרא הוה שמיע ליה, מעשה לא הוה חזי, וסבר דלמא לא קים ליה בגווה דמלתא שפיר, ולאו אורח ארעא לזלזולי בבנות ישראל. ההוא דאתא לקמיה דרבן גמליאל הזקן, אמר לו: רבי, בעלתי ולא מצאתי דם. ב אמרה לו: רבי, ממשפחת דורקטי אני, שאין להן לא דם נדה ולא דם בתולים. בדק רבן גמליאל בקרובותיה ומצא כדבריה. אמר לו: לך זכה במקחך, אשריך שזכית למשפחת דורקטי. *מאי דורקטי — דור קטוע.* אמר רבי חנינא: תנחומים של הבל ניחמו רבן גמליאל לאותו האיש. דתני רבי חייא: כשם *שהשאור יפה לעיסה כך דמים יפים לאשה. ותנא משום רבי מאיר: כל אשה שדמיה מרובין — בניה מרובים. איתמר, רבי ירמיה בר אבא אמר: ״זכה במקחך״ אמר ליה. ורבי יוסי בר אבין אמר: ״נתחייב במקחך״ אמר ליה. בשלמא למאן דאמר ״נתחייב״ — היינו דרבי חנינא, אלא למאן דאמר ״זכה״ — מאי זכותא? דלא אתי לידי ספק נדה. ההוא דאתא לקמיה דרבי, אמר ליה: רבי, בעלתי ולא מצאתי דם. ג אמרה לו: רבי, עדיין בתולה הייתי, ושני בצורת הוה. ראה רבי שפניהם שחורים, צוה עליהן והכניסום למרחץ, והאכילום והשקום, והכניסום לחדר, בעל ומצא דם. אמר לו: לך זכה במקחך. קרי רבי עליהם: ״°צפד עורם על עצמם יבש היה כעץ״. (איכה ד) § **מתני׳** ד בתולה כתובתה מאתים ואלמנה מנה. ה בתולה, אלמנה, גרושה, וחלוצה מן האירוסין — כתובתן מאתים, ויש להן טענת בתולים. § **גמ׳** מאי אלמנה? אמר רב חנא בגדתאה: אלמנה — על שם מנה. אלמנה מן האירוסין מאי איכא למימר? איידי דהא קרי לה אלמנה — הא נמי קרי לה אלמנה. אלמנה דכתיבא באורייתא מאי איכא למימר? דעתידין רבנן דמתקני לה מנה. ומי כתב קרא לעתיד? אין, דכתיב: °״ושם הנהר (בראשית ב) השלישי חדקל הוא ההולך קדמת אשור״, ותנא רב יוסף: *אשור זו סליקא. ומי הואי? אלא דעתידה, הכא נמי — דעתידה. ואמר רב חנא בגדתאה: מטר משקה, מרוה, ומזבל, ומעדן, וממשיך. אמר רבא בר רבי ישמעאל ואיתימא רב ייmar בר שלמיא: מאי קרא — °״תלמיה רוה נחת גדודיה ברביבים תמוגגנה (תהלים סה) צמחה תברך״. אמר רבי אלעזר: מזבח — מזיח, ומזין, מחבב, מכפר. היינו מכפר היינו מזיח! מזיח גזירות ומכפר עונות. ואמר רב חנא בגדתאה: *תמרי משחנן, משבען, משלשלן, מאשרן ולא מפנקן. אמר רב: אכל תמרים ו אל יורה. מיתיבי: תמרים, שחרית וערבית — יפות, במנחה — רעות, בצהרים — אין כמותן. ומבטלות שלשה דברים: מחשבה רעה, וחולי מעים, ותחתוניות! מי אמרינן דלא מעלו? עלויי מעלו, ולפי שעתא טרדא. מידי דהוה אחמרא, *דאמר מר *השותה רביעית יין אל יורה. ואיבעית אימא: לא קשיא; הא — מקמי נהמא, הא — לבתר נהמא. דאמר אביי, *אמרה לי אם: תמרי מקמי נהמא — כי נרגא לדיקולא, בתר נהמא — כי עברא לדשא. *דשא, אמר רבא: דרך שם. דרגא, אמר רבא: דרך גג. פוריא, א״ר פפא: שפרין ורבין עליה. אמר רב נחמן בר יצחק:

אף

גיהוץ. לשיקיי״ר, באבן הזכוכית. כבבוס שלהן. שהיו מימיהם יפים לכבס, או סממנין יפים היו להן לכבס. ובכיבוס שלנו אין הבגד מלובן עד שיהיה מגוהץ. מעברא ליה חומרתא. שפשוף האבן מעביר את הדם. חומרתא. אבן, כדאמרינן בגיטין (דף סט:): ונזדהר בחומרתא דנפק מיניה, אבן המגלאת בחמה מחמת חולי. ריחה נודף. מפיה מריחין ריח היין שנכנס לה דרך פתח הפתוח. גמרא הוה שמיע ליה. שעשו כן לבנות יבש גלעד, במסכת יבמות (דף ס:). דור קטוע. שאין להם לא דם נדה ולא דם בתולים. יפין לאשה. למהר לה הריון. נתחייב במקחך. על כרחך תקבל חובה הבאה לך במקחך, לשון: אין חבין לאדם (לקמן דף יא.) — דבר שהוא לרעתו קרוי חובה. שפניהם שחורים. מחמת רעבון. צפד עורם. דונש פירש: כמו דבק עורם על עצמם, ומנחם פירש: שחר עורם. **מתני׳** בתולה אלמנה וגרושה. בין בתולה שהיא אלמנה, או גרושה או חלוצה מן האירוסין, וחזרה ונשאת. כתובתה. מן השני. מאתים. שהרי בחזקת בתולה היא נשאת לו. ויש להם טענת בתולים. אם לא מצאה הב׳ בתולה — אבדה כל כתובתה, דמקח טעות היא לו. **גמ׳** בגדתאה. דמן בגדת. על שם מנה. שאם נשאת משנתאלמנה — אין לה כתובה אלא מנה. דכתיבא באורייתא. ועדיין לא נתקנו כתובות. ומי כתיב קרא. לקרות על שם דבר העתיד. זו סליקא. שם עיר. ומי הואי. העיר בנויה בבריאת עולם, דכתיב ״ההולך קדמת אשור״. [מטר. ולא מאותיות דריש הכי, אלא לפום סברא]. מזבל. את הארץ. מעדן. נותן עדנה וזיו בפירות. תלמיה. של א״י. רוה נחת גדודיה כאשר ברביבים תמוגגנה. ״רוה״ — הרי משקה ומרוה. ״תמוגגנה״ — הרי מזבל, מעדן. וממשיך את הפירות — נפקא מ״צמחה תברך״. תמוגגנה = דישטנפי״ר. מזיח. קס״ד: מזיח עונות. מזין. בזכות הקרבנות העולם נזון, שהקרבנו׳ באין מן המזון וגורמין לו ברכה. מחבב. את ישראל אל אביהם. היינו מזיח היינו מכפר. הי ניהו מזיח, הי ניהו מכפר? מזיח גזירות. רעות מעל ישראל. משחנן. מחממות. משלשלן. שלשול. מאשרן. מחזיקות כח, כמו ״אשרו חמוץ״ (ישעיהו א). ולא מפנקן. אינן מרבות אסטניסא על הלב, וכלן לשבח. אל יורה. שום הוראה, לפי שטורדות דעתו כשיכור. שחרית וערבית יפות. כללא דמילתא, לאחר אכילה — יפות. שחרית, דרכן של בני אדם בפת שחרית, כדאמר ב״המקבל״ (ב״מ קז:) ערבית — לאחר אכילה. במנחה רעות. שהן קודם אכילה, לאחר שינת הצהרים. בצהרים. לאחר הסעודה, שאכל ושבע. אין כמותם. וטובות יותר מערבית. לפי שאינו מעוכב ביום מילך לשדות לבית הכסא בכל עת שירצה, אבל בלילה טורח הוא לו. מבטלות מחשבה רעה. דאגה, לפי שמשמחות את הלב, והרהורים שעת אורה וגילה היא. כי עברא לדשא. מחזיקות את הגוף כבריח את הדלת.

אף

תוספות רי״ד

ההוא דאתא לקמיה דר״ג. א״ל בעלתי ולא מצאתי דם. אמרה לו רבי עדיין בתולה אני. אמר להן הביאו לי שתי שפחות א׳ בעולה וא׳ בתולה הביאו לו הושיבם על פי חבית של יין. בתולה אין ריחה נודף. בעולה ריחה נודף מפיה (כרימון) [כריח] בית היין. שנכנס לה דרך (הפגם הפגום) [פתח הפתוח] הושיבוה ולא היה ריחה נודף. אמר ליה לך זכי במקחך. ההוא דאתא לקמיה דר״ג הזקן א״ל רבי בעלתי ולא מצאתי דם. אמרה לו רבי בתולה שלימה נבעלתי אלא ממשפחת דורקטי אני שאין להם לא דם בתולות ולא דם נדה בדק ר״ג בקרובותי׳ ומצא כדבריה א״ל לך זכי במקחך: ההוא דאתא לקמיה דרבי. א״ל רבי בעלתי ולא מצאתי דם אמרה לו בתולה שלימה אני. אלא שני בצורת הם. ראה פניה מוריקות. פי׳ מושחרים מחמת רעבון. צוה עליהם והכניסם למרחץ והאכילם והשקם והכניסם לחופה ובעל ומצא דם. א״ל לך זכי במקחך. קרא עליהם צפד עורם על עצמם יבש היה כעץ. צפד פי׳ לשון דבק: **מתני׳** בתולה כתובתה מאתים. ואלמנה מנה. בתולה אלמנה גרושה וחלוצה מן האירוסין כתובתן מאתים מן הנשואין כתובתן מנה. פי׳ בתולה שהיא אלמנה או גרושה וחלוצה מן האירוסין ונשאת. כתובתה מן השני מאתים שהרי בחזקת בתולה נשאת לו ויש לה טענות בתולים:

[תענית כט:]

[יבמות ס:]

[בערוך איתא מאי דורקטי תנא דור קטוע]

נדה ח: סד:

נ״י כ״י

יומא י

גיטין ע.

[וע׳ תוס׳ סנהדרין מב. ד״ה הטעוסקים]

[קדושין לח. וש״נ]

עירובין סד. [נזיר לח.]

[שבת עז:]

אַף אָנוּ נֹאמַר: אַיְילוֹנִית – דּוּכְרָנִית דְּלָא יָלְדָה.§ **מתני'** [א]הַגִּיּוֹרֶת וְהַשְּׁבוּיָה וְהַשִּׁפְחָה, שֶׁנִּפְדּוּ וְשֶׁנִּתְגַּיְּירוּ וְשֶׁנִּשְׁתַּחְרְרוּ פְּחוּתוֹת מִבְּנוֹת שָׁלֹשׁ שָׁנִים וְיוֹם אֶחָד – כְּתוּבָּתָן מָאתַיִם, וְיֵשׁ לָהֶן טַעֲנַת בְּתוּלִין.§ **גמ'** אָמַר רַב הוּנָא: [ב]גֵּר קָטָן מַטְבִּילִין אוֹתוֹ עַל דַּעַת בֵּית דִּין. מַאי קמ"ל – *דִּזְכוּת הוּא לוֹ, וְזָכִין לְאָדָם שֶׁלֹּא בְּפָנָיו – תְּנֵינָא: *[ג]זָכִין לְאָדָם שֶׁלֹּא בְּפָנָיו, וְאֵין חָבִין לְאָדָם שֶׁלֹּא בְּפָנָיו! מַהוּ דְּתֵימָא: גּוֹי בְּהֶפְקֵירָא נִיחָא לֵיהּ, דְּהָא קַיְימָא לָן *דְּעֶבֶד וַדַּאי בְּהֶפְקֵירָא נִיחָא לֵיהּ, קמ"ל: דְּהָנֵי מִילֵּי – גָּדוֹל, דְּטָעַם טַעַם דְּאִיסּוּרָא. אֲבָל קָטָן – זְכוּת הוּא לוֹ. לֵימָא מְסַיַּיע לֵיהּ: הַגִּיּוֹרֶת וְהַשְּׁבוּיָה וְהַשִּׁפְחָה שֶׁנִּפְדּוּ וְשֶׁנִּתְגַּיְּירוּ וְשֶׁנִּשְׁתַּחְרְרוּ פְּחוּתוֹת מִבְּנוֹת שָׁלֹשׁ שָׁנִים וְיוֹם אֶחָד. מַאי לָאו – דְּאַטְבְּלִינְהוּ עַל דַּעַת בֵּית דִּין? לָא, הָכָא בְּמַאי עָסְקִינַן, בְּגֵר שֶׁנִּתְגַּיְּירוּ בָּנָיו וּבְנוֹתָיו עִמּוֹ, [ד]דְּנִיחָא לְהוּ בְּמַאי דְּעָבֵיד אֲבוּהוֹן. אָמַר רַב יוֹסֵף: [ה]הִגְדִּילוּ יְכוֹלִין לִמְחוֹת. אִיתִיבֵיהּ אַבַּיֵי: הַגִּיּוֹרֶת וְהַשְּׁבוּיָה וְהַשִּׁפְחָה שֶׁנִּפְדּוּ וְשֶׁנִּתְגַּיְּירוּ וְשֶׁנִּשְׁתַּחְרְרוּ פְּחוּתוֹת מִבְּנוֹת שָׁלֹשׁ שָׁנִים וְיוֹם אֶחָד – כְּתוּבָּתָן מָאתַיִם. וְאִי ס"ד הִגְדִּילוּ יְכוֹלִין לִמְחוֹת – יָהֲבִינַן לָהּ כְּתוּבָּה דְּאָזְלָה וְאָכְלָה בְּגֵיוּתָהּ?! [ו]לְכִי גָּדְלָה. לְכִי גָּדְלָה נַמִי, מְמַחְיָיא וְנָפְקָא! [ז]כֵּיוָן שֶׁהִגְדִּילָה *שָׁעָה אַחַת וְלֹא מִיחֲתָה – שׁוּב אֵינָהּ יְכוֹלָה לִמְחוֹת. מְתִיב רָבָא: *אֵלּוּ נְעָרוֹת שֶׁיֵּשׁ לָהֶן קְנָס: הַבָּא עַל הַמַּמְזֶרֶת, וְעַל הַנְּתִינָה, וְעַל הַכּוּתִית, וְעַל הַגִּיּוֹרֶת, וְעַל הַשְּׁבוּיָה, וְעַל הַשִּׁפְחָה שֶׁנִּפְדּוּ וְשֶׁנִּתְגַּיְּירוּ וְשֶׁנִּשְׁתַּחְרְרוּ פְּחוּתוֹת מִבְּנוֹת שָׁלֹשׁ שָׁנִים וְיוֹם אֶחָד – יֵשׁ לָהֶן קְנָס. וְאִי אָמְרַתְּ הִגְדִּילוּ יְכוֹלִין לִמְחוֹת – יָהֲבִינַן לָהּ קְנָס דְּאָזְלָה וְאָכְלָה בְּגֵיוּתָהּ?! לְכִי גָּדְלָה. לְכִי גָּדְלָה נַמִי, מְמַחְיָיא וְנָפְקָא! כֵּיוָן שֶׁהִגְדִּילָה שָׁעָה אַחַת וְלֹא מִיחֲתָה, שׁוּב אֵינָהּ יְכוֹלָה לִמְחוֹת. אַבַּיֵי לֹא אָמַר כְּרָבָא – הָתָם קְנָסָא, הַיְינוּ טַעֲמָא *שֶׁלֹּא יְהֵא חוֹטֵא נִשְׂכָּר. רָבָא לֹא אָמַר כְּאַבַּיֵי – *[ח]כְּתוּבָּה הַיְינוּ טַעֲמָא – שֶׁלֹּא תְּהֵא קַלָּה בְּעֵינָיו לְהוֹצִיאָהּ.§ **מתני'** [ט]הַגָּדוֹל שֶׁבָּא עַל הַקְּטַנָּה, וְקָטָן שֶׁבָּא עַל הַגְּדוֹלָה, וּמוּכַּת עֵץ – כְּתוּבָּתָן מָאתַיִם, דִּבְרֵי רַבִּי מֵאִיר. *וַחֲכָ"א: [י]מוּכַּת עֵץ – כְּתוּבָּתָהּ מָנֶה. [כ]בְּתוּלָה, אַלְמָנָה, גְּרוּשָׁה וַחֲלוּצָה מִן הַנִּישּׂוּאִין – כְּתוּבָּתָן מָנֶה, וְאֵין

[לקמן כט. ב"ק לח:]

רש"י

אף אנו נאמר. אף אנו נדרוש את השמות, מה לשון איילונית שקראו חכמים לאשה שאינה ראויה לילד. דוכרנית. לשון "איל תמים" דמתרגמינן דכר שלים (ויקרא ה) – הרי היא כאיל שאינו יולד. **גמ'** (*על דעת ב"ד). אם אין לו אב, ואמו הביאתו להתגייר. מטבילין. דאין לך גר בלא מילה וטבילה. על דעת בית דין. שלשה יהו בטבילתו, כדין כל טבילת גר שצריכים ג'. והן נעשין לו אב, והרי הוא גר על ידיהן, ומגעו ביין כשר. מהו דתימא גוי בהפקירא ניחא ליה. וחוב הוא לו, ואין אדם נעשה שליח לאדם לחובתו שלא בפניו, כלומר שלא מדעתו. וקטן לאו בר דיעה הוא. דהא גבי עבד קי"ל. בפ"ק דגיטין (דף יג.) דודאי בהפקירא ניחא ליה, נוח לו להיות עבד ויהא מותר בהפקר זימת השפחות, מהיות בן חורין להיות מותר בבת ישראל, דלא זילא ליה ולא שכיחא ליה להפקירא. קמ"ל. הכא, דגבי גוי קטן לא אמרינן הכי. דהני מילי. דניחא ליה בהפקירא. גדול. שגדל [במדות] הפקירות, וטעים ליה טעמא דאיסורא. הגדילו. קטנים שנתגיירו, ואפי' עם אביהן. יכולין למחות. ולומר: אי אפשינו להיות גרים. וחוזרין לסורן, ואין לנו לענשן בב"ד, ואפי' ידינו תקיפה. ואם קידש אשה משמיחה – אינה צריכה גט להיות כישראל מומר. לכי גדלה. לא יהבינן לה עד שתגדיל. שוב אינה יכולה למחות. ואם מיחתה – הרי היא כישראל מומרת, ליענש בכל עונשי ב"ד. שיש להן קנס. נ' כסף אם יאנסו. הבא על הממזרת. ואע"ג דלא קרינן ביה "ולו תהיה לאשה", שהרי אינה ראויה לקיימה – אפילו הכי יש לה קנס, כדלקמן. אביי לא אמר כרבא. דמותיב מקנסא, דקסבר לאו תיובתא היא, דטעמא דקנסא – שלא יהא חוטא נשכר להפטר. רבא לא אמר כאביי. דמותיב מכתובה, דהתם טעמא מאי תקינו לה רבנן כתובה – שלא תהא קלה בעיניו להוציאה, וכל זמן שלא מיחתה – גיורת היא, ועבדינן לה תקנתא. **מתני'** הבא על הקטנה. פחותה מבת שלש, שאין ביאתה ביאה, שהרי בתוליה חוזרין. וקטן. פחות מבן תשע, שאמרו חכמים: אין ביאתו ביאה, ובא על הגדולה. ומוכת עץ. שנתקע לה עץ באותו מקום. כתובתן מאתים. אם נשאו לאיש אחרי כן – לא איבדו בכך את כתובתן, אם נשאה סתם ולא פירש לה כלום. בתולה. שהיא אלמנה או גרושה או חלוצה. מן הנישואין. כגון שנכנסה לחופה, ומת בעלה בחזקת שלא נבעלה. כתובתה מנה. אם ניסת לאחר סתם, כתובתה מנה, דבחזקת בעולה קיימא משנכנסה לחופה. ואין

תוספות

מטבילין אותו על דעת ב"ד משום דזכות הוא. ותימה: דהא זכייה הוי מטעם שליחות, דכיון דזכות הוא לו – אנן סהדי דעביד ליה שליח, כדמוכח בפ"ק דב"מ (דף יב.) גבי חצר משום יד איתרבאי, ולא גרע משליחות. וא"כ היאך זכין לקטן? והלא אין שליחות לקטן, כדאמרינן ב"איזהו נשך" (שם עא:)! ועוד, דאכתי גוי הוא, ואמרי' התם: דקטן דאתי לכלל שליחות – אית ליה זכייה מדרבנן, גוי דלא אתי לכלל שליחות – אפילו זכייה מדרבנן לית ליה! ונראה לר"י: דהכא נמי דזכין לו – מדרבנן, כדאמרינן התם דקטן אית ליה זכייה מדרבנן. ואע"ג דאכתי גוי הוא – הא אתי לכלל שליחות. א"נ, כיון דבהך זכייה נעשה ישראל – הוה ליה כישראל גמור לעניין זכייה. וא"ת: היכי הוי גר מדרבנן, ושרינן ליה בבת ישראל, וקידושיו קידושין, הא מן התורה גוי הוא! וי"ל: דקסבר כמ"ד ב"האשה רבה" (יבמות דף פט:) דיש כח ביד חכמים לעקור דבר מן התורה בקום ועשה. וכי פריך מאי קמ"ל – הוה מצי לשנויי קמ"ל דיש כח ביד חכמים לעקור דבר מן התורה בקום ועשה, וחד מתרי טעמי נקט. והא דאמרי' בריש "בן סורר" (סנהדרין דף סח: ושם) גבי גזל הגר "אם אין לאיש גואל", איש – אתה צריך לחזר אחריו אם יש לו גואל, אבל קטן – אי אתה צריך לחזר אחריו כו' – משכחת לה גר קטן מן התורה במעוברת שנתגיירה, *כדאמרי' בפרק "הערל" (יבמות דף עח. ושם): גויה מעוברת שנתגיירה – בנה אין צריך טבילה, והוי גר מן התורה, דישראל גמור הוא. ואית ליה ממון מן התורה – כגון שירש את אמו. ואי אתה צריך לחזר עליו – שאין לו יורשין, שאינו מוליד, ואחיו מן האם אין יורשין אותו. ולפי ספרים דגרסינן בב"מ (דף עא:): זכייה מיהא אית ליה, ולא גרס מדרבנן – ניחא, דמצי למימר דאית ליה זכייה מן התורה. וגוי קטן, כיון דבא להתגייר – חשבינן ליה כישראל קטן. ואע"ג דזכייה הוי מטעם שליחות, ואין לו שליחות מן התורה – ה"מ בדבר שיש בו קצת חובה, כגון להפריש תרומתו, דשמא היה רוצה לפוטרה בחטה אחת, או שמא היה רוצה להעדיף. אבל הכא, שזכות גמור הוא לו – יש לו שליחות. **מהו** דתימא גוי בהפקירא ניחא ליה. ואע"ג דרבנן פליגי אר' מאיר בפ' קמא דגיטין (דף יג. ושם), ולית להו טעמא דבהפקירא ניחא ליה – ה"מ גבי עבד שאינו חושש בהפקירא, שמפקיע עצמו מן השעבוד. אבל גבי גוי, שאינו משועבד – ניחא ליה בהפקירא. וכן נראה, דאי לא תימא הכי – היכי מייתי סייעתא מההוא דגיורת? דלמא רבנן היא, דאפילו בגדול לית להו בהפקירא ניחא ליה. **אבל** קטן זכות הוא לו. והא דתנן בפרק קמא דגיטין (ג"ז שם) האומר: תנו גט זה לאשתי ושיחרור זה לעבדי, רצה לחזור בשניהם – יחזור, דברי רבי מאיר. היינו בעבד גדול, דבקטן מודה רבי מאיר דזכות הוא לו, דלא ניחא ליה בהפקירא, כדאמרינן הכא, משום דלא טעים טעמא דאיסורא. א"נ, איירי אף בעבד קטן, וכגון שהוא של כהן, דחוב הוא לו שיצא לחירות, לפי שמפסידו מלאכול בתרומה. **לכי** גדלה. וא"ת: והלא כבר גדולה היא; שהיא נערה כיון שהיא בת קנס! ומפרש ר"י: לכי גדלה ונהגה מנהג יהודית. **אביי** לא אמר כרבא שלא יהא חוטא נשכר. משמע דרבא לית ליה טעמא דשלא יהא חוטא נשכר. וקשה: דאמרי' בפ' "שור שנגח ד' וה'" (ב"ק דף לח: ושם): קסבר רבי מאיר כותים גירי אמת הן, וקנס הוא דקניס ר"מ בממונם לענין שור שנגח, שלא יטמעו בהן. ופריך: אלו נערות שיש להן קנס – הבא על הכותית. ואי קניס ר"מ בממונם – ה"נ ניקנוס! ומשני: דהכא לא בעי למקנס, שלא יהא חוטא נשכר. והשתא לרבא, דלית ליה הכא טעם דחוטא נשכר, היכי מצי משני התם? וי"ל: דהתם אית ליה שפיר האי טעמא, כיון דבדין יש להן קנס, דגרי אמת הן, אלא דבעי' למקנס להו. סברא הוא, דמשום טעמא שלא יהא חוטא נשכר מוקמינן לה אדינא. אבל הכא סבירא ליה לרבא, דמשום טעמא שלא יהא חוטא נשכר אין ליתן לה, כיון דמן הדין לית לה, שהרי גויה גמורה היא אם תמחה. ובפ' "אלו נערות" (לקמן דף לו:) דאית ליה לרבא שלא יהא חוטא נשכר גבי שבויה – משום דמוקמינן לה בקדושתה. ושמואל

תוספות רי"ד

הגיורת והשבויה והשפחה שנפדו ושנתגיירו ושנשתחררו פחותות מבנות ג' שנים ויום אחד כתובתן מאתים ויש להן טענת בתולים. פי' בחזקת בתולות הן. ואם נמצאת בעולה אומר לה מקחי מקח טעות ואבדה כל כתובתה. אמר ר"ה גר קטן מטבילין אותו ע"ד ב"ד. פי' אע"פ שאין לו אב ואם כגון תינוק שנמצא מושלך או ששבו ישראל קטני פלשתים ב"ד מלין אותם והם כישראל לכל דבר. והמורה פי' מטבילין אותו. דאינו גר עד שימול ויטבול. עיין פרק החולץ [דף מו] ובפ"ח דיבמות [דף ע"א]. מאי קמ"ל דזכין לאדם שלא בפניו תנינא זכין לאדם שלא בפניו ואין חבין לו לאדם אלא בפניו. מ"ד בהפקירא ניחא ליה וחוב הוא לו. פי' שאין אדם נעשה שליח לחובתו שלא בפניו כלומר שלא מדעת. קמ"ל דה"מ גדול דטעים טעמא דאיסורא אבל קטן זכות הוא [לו]. אמר ר"י ואם הגדילו. פי' הקטנים שנתגיירו ואפי' עם אביהן יכולין למחות. פי' יכולין לומר אי אפשינו להיות גרים ואין לנו לעונשם בב"ד. ואפילו ידינו תקיפה. ואם קידש אשה משמיחה אינה צריכה גט להיות כישראל מומר. ודוקא שלא הגיעו לכלל שתי שערות אבל אם הגדילו ולא מיחו אין יכולין למחות ואם מיחו הרי הן כישראל מומר וקדושי' קדושין. א) והגדילו דר"י לאו דוקא שבאו לכלל עונשין אלא שבאו לכלל דעת ועדיין לא באו לכלל עונשין: **מתני'** הגדול שבא על הקטנה וקטן שבא על הגדולה ומוכת עץ כתובתן מאתים. דברי ר"מ וחכ"א מוכת עץ כתובתן מנה. פי' קטנה פחותה מבת ג' שנים ויום אחד שאין ביאתה ביאה שהרי בתוליה חוזרין. וקטן פחות מבן ט' שאמרו חכמים אין ביאתו ביאה לקנות קנין גמור. כגון אם בא על יבמתו דהתם אמרי' אין ביאתו ביאה ב) חשובה לקנות לגמרי. פי' לא גרעה אותה ביאה ממאמר בגדול. שכמו שמאמר בגדול פוסלה על שאר האחין. כך ביאת [פחות] בן ט' פסלה על האחין. עיין בפ' האשה רבה: מוכת עץ שנתקע לה עץ באותו מקום ויצאו בתוליה כתובתה מאתים. פי' לא הפסידו כתובתן אם נישאו סתם וחכ"א מוכת עץ כיון שאיבדה בתוליה כתובתה מנה: איתמר

א) ובזה מיושב קושיית התוס' כאן בד"ה קסה ועי"ש. ב) ע"ש ביבמות דף נו דמיירי שם בביאת בן תשע דעשו כמאמר בגדול אבל בפחות מבן תשע לא מיירי התם כלל וצ"ע.

עין משפט נר מצוה

סב א מיי' פי"א מהל' איסות הל' א' סמג עשין מח טוש"ע אה"ע סי' סז סעי' ג:
סג ב מיי' פי"ג מהל' איסורי ביאה הל' ז סמג לאוין קיז טוש"ע יו"ד סי' רסח סעי' ז:
סד ג מיי' פ"ד מהל' זכיה הל"ב סמג עשין פ"ב טוש"ע חו"מ סי' רמג סעי' א וטוש"ע יו"ד סי' רסח סעי' ז':
סה ד ה ו ז מיי' פ"י מהל' מלכים הל"ג טוש"ע יו"ד סי' רסח סעי' ז':
סו ח מיי' פ"י מהל' איסות הל"ז טור אה"ע סי' סו:
סז ט מיי' פי"א מהל' איסות הל"ג סמג עשין מח טוש"ע שם סי' סז סעיף ד:
סח י מיי' שם טוש"ע שם סעיף ה:
סט כ מיי' שם הל' א טוש"ע שם סעי' ב:

מסורת הש"ס

[ג"ל גר קטן]

[ע' תוס' גיטין ה: ד"ה והא קי"ל] [עירובין פא: יבמות קיח: וש"נ]

[גיטין יג. ע' תוס' שם]

[קשה א"כ מתי תדע שעת המחאה דהא בקטנות אינה יכולה למחות כרי"ל כגון שבתחילה מנהג גיות יום לפני גדלותה וכן נהגה יום או יומים לאחר גדלותה. תפ"י עה"ג]

[יבמות נב: וש"נ]

[יבמות פט. לקמן לט: כז.]

[לקמן יג.]

[וע' תוס' ב"ק קט: ד"ה קטן ותוס' סנהדרין סח:]

גליון הש"ס

גמ' שלא יהא חוטא נשכר. פ"ב דחלה מ"ז נדה דף ד ע"ב: תום' ד"ה לכי גדלה. וא"ת והלא כבר גדולה. עיין נדה מד ע"ב תוס' ד"ה שלשים יום:

עין משפט נר מצוה

ע א מיי' פי"א מהל' אישות הל"א טוש"ע אה"ע סי' סז סעי' ג:

עא ב מיי' שם הל"ג טוש"ע שם סעי' ד:

עב ג ד מיי' שם טוש"ע שם סעי' ה:

עג ה טוש"ע שם סעי' ב:

וְאֵין לָהֶן טַעֲנַת בְּתוּלִים. [א]הַגִּיּוֹרֶת וְהַשְּׁבוּיָה וְהַשִּׁפְחָה שֶׁנִּפְדּוּ וְשֶׁנִּתְגַּיְּירוּ וְשֶׁנִּשְׁתַּחְרְרוּ יְתֵירוֹת עַל בְּנוֹת שָׁלֹשׁ שָׁנִים וְיוֹם אֶחָד — כְּתוּבָּתָן מָנֶה, וְאֵין לָהֶן טַעֲנַת בְּתוּלִין.§ **גמ'** אָמַר רַב יְהוּדָה אָמַר רַב: קָטָן הַבָּא עַל הַגְּדוֹלָה עֲשָׂאָהּ מוּכַּת עֵץ. כִּי אָמְרִיתָהּ קַמֵּיהּ דִּשְׁמוּאֵל, אָמַר: [ב]אֵין מוּכַּת עֵץ בְּבָשָׂר. אִיכָּא דְּמַתְנֵי לָהּ לְהָא שְׁמַעְתָּא בְּאַפֵּי נַפְשָׁהּ: קָטָן הַבָּא עַל הַגְּדוֹלָה, רַב אָמַר: עֲשָׂאָהּ מוּכַּת עֵץ, וּשְׁמוּאֵל אָמַר: אֵין מוּכַּת עֵץ בְּבָשָׂר. מְתִיב רַב אוֹשַׁעְיָא: גָּדוֹל שֶׁבָּא עַל הַקְּטַנָּה, וְקָטָן הַבָּא עַל הַגְּדוֹלָה, וּמוּכַּת עֵץ — כְּתוּבָּתָן מָאתַיִם, דִּבְרֵי ר"מ. וַחֲכָמִים אוֹמְרִים: מוּכַּת עֵץ כְּתוּבָּתָהּ מָנֶה! אָמַר רָבָא: הָכִי קָאָמַר גָּדוֹל הַבָּא עַל הַקְּטַנָּה — וְלֹא כְלוּם, *דְּפָחוֹת מִכָּאן כְּנוֹתֵן אֶצְבַּע בָּעַיִן דָּמֵי. וְקָטָן הַבָּא עַל הַגְּדוֹלָה — עֲשָׂאָהּ מוּכַּת עֵץ, וּמוּכַּת עֵץ גּוּפָא — פְּלוּגְתָּא דְּר"מ וְרַבָּנַן. אָמַר רָמִי בַּר חָמָא: *מַחֲלוֹקֶת כְּשֶׁהִכִּיר בָּהּ; דְּר"מ מְדַמֵּי לָהּ לְבוֹגֶרֶת, וְרַבָּנַן מְדַמּוּ לָהּ לִבְעוּלָה. אֲבָל לֹא הִכִּיר בָּהּ — דִּבְרֵי הַכֹּל וְלֹא כְלוּם. וְר"מ אַמַּאי מְדַמֵּי לָהּ לְבוֹגֶרֶת? נְדַמְּיָיהּ לִבְעוּלָה! בְּעוּלָה אִיתְעֲבֵיד בָּהּ מַעֲשֶׂה בִּידֵי אָדָם. הָא — לָא אִיתְעֲבֵיד בָּהּ מַעֲשֶׂה בִּידֵי אָדָם. וְרַבָּנַן, אַדִּמְדַמּוּ לָהּ לִבְעוּלָה נְדַמְּיָיהּ לְבוֹגֶרֶת! בּוֹגֶרֶת לָא אִיתְעֲבֵיד בָּהּ מַעֲשֶׂה כְּלָל, הָא — אִיתְעֲבֵיד בָּהּ מַעֲשֶׂה, אֲבָל לֹא הִכִּיר בָּהּ — לְדִבְרֵי הַכֹּל וְלֹא כְלוּם. מְתִיב רַב נַחְמָן: *הִיא אוֹמֶרֶת "מוּכַּת עֵץ אֲנִי" וְהוּא אוֹמֵר "לֹא כִּי, אֶלָּא דְּרוּסַת אִישׁ אַתְּ". ר"ג וְר' אֱלִיעֶזֶר אוֹמְרִים: נֶאֱמֶנֶת! אֶלָּא אָמַר רָבָא: בֵּין הִכִּיר בָּהּ וּבֵין לֹא הִכִּיר בָּהּ, לְר"מ — מָאתַיִם, לְרַבָּנַן; הִכִּיר בָּהּ — מָנֶה, לֹא הִכִּיר בָּהּ — וְלֹא כְלוּם. וַהֲדַר בֵּיהּ רָבָא, דְּתַנְיָא: כֵּיצַד *הוֹצָאַת שֵׁם רַע? בָּא לְבֵית דִּין וְאָמַר: פְּלוֹנִי, לֹא מָצָאתִי לְבִתְּךָ בְּתוּלִים. אִם יֵשׁ עֵדִים שֶׁזִּינְּתָה תַּחְתָּיו — יֵשׁ לָהּ כְּתוּבָּה מָנֶה. אִם יֵשׁ עֵדִים שֶׁזִּינְּתָה תַּחְתָּיו?! בַּת סְקִילָה הִיא! הָכִי קָאָמַר: אִם יֵשׁ עֵדִים שֶׁזִּינְּתָה תַּחְתָּיו — בִּסְקִילָה, זִינְּתָה מֵעִיקָּרָא — יֵשׁ לָהּ כְּתוּבָּה מָנֶה. *וְאָמַר רַב חִיָּיא בַּר אָבִין אָמַר רַב שֵׁשֶׁת: זֹאת אוֹמֶרֶת כְּנָסָהּ בְּחֶזְקַת בְּתוּלָה וְנִמְצֵאת בְּעוּלָה — יֵשׁ לָהּ כְּתוּבָּה מָנֶה. וּמְתִיב רַב נַחְמָן: *הַנּוֹשֵׂא אֶת הָאִשָּׁה וְלֹא מָצָא לָהּ בְּתוּלִים, הִיא אוֹמֶרֶת "מִשֶּׁאֵרַסְתַּנִי נֶאֱנַסְתִּי וְנִסְתַּחֲפָה שָׂדֵהוּ" וְהוּא אוֹמֵר "לֹא כִּי, אֶלָּא עַד שֶׁלֹּא אֵירַסְתִּיךְ, וְהָיָה מִקָּחִי מִקַּח טָעוּת", וְלֵית לָהּ כְּלָל? וַאֲמַר לְהוּ רַב חִיָּיא בַּר אָבִין: אֶפְשָׁר רַב עַמְרָם וְכָל גְּדוֹלֵי הַדּוֹר יָתְבִי כִּי אֲמַר רַב שֵׁשֶׁת לְהָא שְׁמַעְתָּא, וְקַשְׁיָא לְהוּ, וְשַׁנֵּי: מַאי מִקַּח טָעוּת — נַמִי מִמָּאתַיִם, אֲבָל מָנֶה — אִית לָהּ. וְאַתְּ אָמְרַתְּ לֵית לָהּ כְּלָל?! °וְאָמַר רָבָא: מַאן דְּקָא מוֹתִיב — שַׁפִּיר קָא מוֹתִיב, [ג]מִקַּח טָעוּת — לְגַמְרֵי מַשְׁמַע. וְאֶלָּא קַשְׁיָא הַךְ! תְּרֵיץ וְאֵימָא הָכִי: אִם יֵשׁ עֵדִים שֶׁזִּינְּתָה תַּחְתָּיו — בִּסְקִילָה, זִינְּתָה מֵעִיקָּרָא — וְלֹא כְלוּם, [ד]נִמְצֵאת מוּכַּת עֵץ — יֵשׁ לָהּ כְּתוּבָּה מָנֶה. וְהָא רָבָא הוּא דַּאֲמַר לְרַבָּנַן לֹא הִכִּיר בָּהּ וְלֹא כְלוּם! אֶלָּא ש"מ: הֲדַר בֵּיהּ רָבָא מֵהַהִיא. ת"ר: כְּנָסָהּ רִאשׁוֹן לְשׁוּם נִישּׂוּאִין, [ה]וְיֵשׁ לָהּ עֵדִים שֶׁלֹּא נִסְתְּרָה. אִי נַמִי, נִסְתְּרָה וְלֹא שָׁהֲתָה כְּדֵי בִיאָה — אֵין הַשֵּׁנִי יָכוֹל לִטְעוֹן טַעֲנַת בְּתוּלִים, שֶׁהֲרֵי כְּנָסָהּ רִאשׁוֹן.

אמר

*) ועוד נ"ל דניחא ליה טפי דלרבנן לא הכיר בה מנה להשתא מיתוקמא מתני' וברייתא נמי כרבנן. ת"י עה"ג

רש"י

וְאֵין לָהֶן טַעֲנַת בְּתוּלִין. אֵין יָכוֹל לְהַפְסִידָהּ אוֹתָהּ מָנֶה, וְלוֹמַר: בְּחֶזְקַת בְּתוּלָה נְשָׂאתִיךְ, וַהֲרֵי מִקָּחִי מִקַּח טָעוּת. **גמ'** עֲשָׂאָהּ מוּכַּת עֵץ. נְהִי דְּאֵין בִּיאָתוֹ בִּיאָה, מִיהוּ לָא גָּרַע מֵעֵץ הַנִּתְקָע. וּלְרַבָּנַן דִּפְלִיגִי אַמּוּכַּת עֵץ כְּתוּבָּתָהּ מָנֶה, וְכֵן לְעִנְיַן כֹּהֵן גָּדוֹל, דִּתְנַן (יבמות דף נט.): לֹא יִשָּׂא אֶת מוּכַּת עֵץ — הָא נַמִי אֲסִירָא לֵיהּ. אֵין מוּכַּת עֵץ בְּבָשָׂר אָדָם. וְאִי בְּעוּלָה לָא הָוְיָא — מוּכַּת עֵץ נַמִי לֵיתָא. בְּאַפֵּי נַפְשָׁהּ. בְּלָא גַּבְרֵי. דְּלָא אֲמַר רַב יְהוּדָה מִשְּׁמֵיהּ דְּרַב וּמִשְּׁמֵיהּ דִּשְׁמוּאֵל, אֶלָּא אִינְהוּ גּוּפַיְיהוּ אִיפְלוּג בָּהּ. וְקָטָן שֶׁבָּא עַל הַגְּדוֹלָה וּמוּכַּת עֵץ. וּמִדְּפַלְגִינְהוּ תַּנָּא לְתַרְתֵּי, וְלָא אִיפְלוּג רַבָּנַן אֶלָּא בְּמוּכַּת עֵץ — שָׁמְעַתְּ מִינָּהּ: אֵין מוּכַּת עֵץ בְּבָשָׂר. הָכִי קָאָמַר גָּדוֹל הַבָּא עַל הַקְּטַנָּה וְלֹא כְלוּם. אֵינָהּ בִּיאָה לְדִבְרֵי הַכֹּל. הִלְכָּךְ, כְּתוּבָּתָהּ מָאתַיִם. וְלָא אִיפְלוּג רַבָּנַן עֲלָהּ, דְּפָחוֹת מִכָּאן כְּנוֹתֵן אֶצְבַּע בָּעַיִן. דִּתְנַן בְּמַסֶּכֶת נִדָּה (דף מד) גַּבֵּי בַּת פְּחוּתָה מִג' שָׁנִים וְיוֹם אֶחָד: מַה הַדִּמְעָה הַיּוֹצֵאת ע"י אֶצְבַּע בָּאָה אַחֶרֶת תַּחְתֶּיהָ, אַף בְּתוּלִים שֶׁל פָּחוֹת מִכֵּן — חוֹזְרִין אֲחֵרִים תַּחְתֵּיהֶם. וְקָטָן שֶׁבָּא עַל הַגְּדוֹלָה. מוּכַּת עֵץ הִיא זוֹ, וּכְתוּבָּתָהּ מָאתַיִם, דִּבְרֵי רַבִּי מֵאִיר. וַחֲכָמִים אוֹמְרִים: כָּל מוּכַּת עֵץ כְּתוּבָּתָהּ מָנֶה. וְהָא נַמִי, דְּקָא מְשַׁוֵּית לָהּ מוּכַּת עֵץ — כְּתוּבָּתָהּ מָנֶה. כְּשֶׁהִכִּיר בָּהּ. כְּשֶׁכְּנָסָהּ וְכָתַב לָהּ כְּתוּבָּה, הָיָה יוֹדֵעַ שֶׁהִיא מוּכַּת עֵץ. מְדַמֵּי לָהּ לְבוֹגֶרֶת. דְּקַיְימָא לָן שֶׁכָּלוּ בְּתוּלֶיהָ, בְּמַסֶּ' יְבָמוֹת (דף נט.), דְּקָתָנֵי: "בִּבְתוּלֶיהָ" — פְּרָט לְבוֹגֶרֶת שֶׁכָּלוּ בְּתוּלֶיהָ, וַאֲפִי' הָכִי — כְּתוּבָּתָהּ מָאתַיִם. וְלֹא כְלוּם. דְּמִקַּח טָעוּת הוּא, וַאֲפִי' מָנֶה אֵין לָהּ. הִיא אוֹמֶרֶת מוּכַּת עֵץ אֲנִי. מִשְׁנָתֵנוּ הִיא. וְהוּא אוֹמֵר לֹא כִּי אֶלָּא דְּרוּסַת אִישׁ אַתְּ. הַנּוֹשֵׂא אֶת הָאִשָּׁה בְּחֶזְקַת בְּתוּלָה וְלֹא מָצָא לָהּ בְּתוּלִים, הִיא אוֹמֶרֶת מוּכַּת עֵץ אֲנִי כו'. ש"מ אִית לָהּ כְּתוּבָּה, אוֹ מָנֶה אוֹ מָאתַיִם, דְּאִי לֵית לָהּ — מַאי נֶאֱמֶנֶת דְּקָאָמַר רַבָּן גַּמְלִיאֵל? אַלְמָא: מוּכַּת עֵץ שֶׁלֹּא הִכִּיר בָּהּ — יֵשׁ לָהּ כְּתוּבָּה, תְּיוּבְתָּא דְּרָמִי בַּר חָמָא דְּאָמַר לֹא הִכִּיר בָּהּ דִּבְרֵי הַכֹּל וְלֹא כְלוּם. אֶלָּא אָמַר רָבָא לְר"מ בֵּין הִכִּיר בָּהּ בֵּין לֹא הִכִּיר בָּהּ מָאתַיִם. וּמַתְנִי' דְּקָתָנֵי הִיא אוֹמֶרֶת מוּכַּת עֵץ אֲנִי, וְקָא תָּבְעָה מָאתַיִם — רַבִּי מֵאִיר הִיא. לְרַבָּנַן הִכִּיר בָּהּ מָנֶה. וּמַתְנִי' דְּהָכָא דְּקָתָנֵי: וַחֲכָמִים אוֹמְרִים מוּכַּת עֵץ מָנֶה — כְּשֶׁהִכִּיר בָּהּ. לֹא הִכִּיר בָּהּ וְלֹא כְלוּם. וְהָא לָא מָצֵינוּ לְמֵימַר: לְר' מֵאִיר הִכִּיר בָּהּ מָאתַיִם, לֹא הִכִּיר בָּהּ — מָנֶה. דְּאִי בְּמִקַּח טָעוּת מַחְזְקִינַן לֵיהּ מִשּׁוּם דְּלֹא הִכִּיר בָּהּ — לֵית לָהּ מִידֵי. וְאִי לָאו מִקַּח טָעוּת הוּא – אֵין חִילּוּק בֵּין הִכִּיר לְלֹא הִכִּיר. וְהָדַר בֵּיהּ רָבָא גַּרְ'. וְל"ג מֵהַהִיא. וְהָדַר בֵּיהּ רָבָא מִמַּאי דְּאָמַר לְרַבָּנַן לֹא הִכִּיר בָּהּ וְלֹא כְלוּם, אֶלָּא: בֵּין הִכִּיר בֵּין לֹא הִכִּיר – יֵשׁ לָהּ מָנֶה לְרַבָּנַן, וּמָאתַיִם לְר"מ. וּמַתְנִי' דְּהָכָא – דִּבְרֵי הַכֹּל. הוֹצָאַת שֵׁם רַע. לֵיעָנֵשׁ מֵאָה כֶּסֶף אִם שֶׁקֶר, וְלִיסָּקֵל אִם אֱמֶת הָיָה. בָּא לְב"ד. זָקוּק לָבֹא לְב"ד וְאוֹמֵר כו'. וְאָמַר רַב חִיָּיא גַּרְסִי'. וּמוֹתִיב רַב נַחְמָן גַּרְ'. נִסְתַּחֲפָה שָׂדֵהוּ. מַזָּלֵךְ גָּרַם, כְּאָדָם שֶׁנִּסְתַּחֵף לוֹ שָׂדֵהוּ וְסוֹחֵף אֶת זַרְעוֹ וְעוֹקְרָהּ. מִקַּח טָעוּת לְגַמְרֵי מַשְׁמַע. וְאֵין לָהּ כְּלוּם. כִּי אָמְרָה רַב שֵׁשֶׁת לְהָא שְׁמַעְתָּא. לְהָכִי זֹאת אוֹמֶרֶת דִּלְעֵיל, דְּיֵשׁ לָהּ כְּתוּבָּה מָנֶה. וְקַשְׁיָא לְהוּ. הָא דְּאוֹתְבִינַן. וְאָמַר רָבָא גַּרְסִי'. וְאֶלָּא קַשְׁיָא הַךְ. וְקַשְׁיָא לְרָבָא, אֶלָּא קַשְׁיָא הַךְ דִּלְעֵיל דְּקָתָנֵי זִינְּתָה מֵעִיקָּרָא יֵשׁ לָהּ כְּתוּבָּה מָנֶה. תְּרֵיץ. לְהָהִיא דִּלְעֵיל דְּקָא הוֹצָאַת ש"ר, תִּירוּצָא דְּקַלָּלָא לָהּ לָא תְּקַלְּהָ הָכִי, אֶלָּא הָכִי: אִם יֵשׁ עֵדִים כו'. נִמְצֵאת. לֹא הִכִּיר בָּהּ קָאָמַר. וְקָא מוֹתֵיב: יֵשׁ לָהּ כְּתוּבָּה מָנֶה, אַלְמָא הָדַר בֵּיהּ מֵהַהִיא דִּלְעֵיל, דְּהָא אִיהוּ אָמַר: לְרַבָּנַן וְלֹא כְלוּם. וְכִרְבִּי מֵאִיר נָמֵי לָא אוֹקְמָהּ, דְּהָא רַבִּי מֵאִיר מָאתַיִם קָאָמַר. וְיֵשׁ לָהּ עֵדִים שֶׁלֹּא נִסְתְּרָה. רְבוּתָא אַשְׁמְעִינַן, דְּאַף עַל פִּי שֶׁהָיָה לָהּ אֵין הַשֵּׁנִי יָכוֹל לִטְעוֹן טַעֲנַת בְּתוּלִים לְהַפְסִידָהּ כְּתוּבָּתָהּ, וְלֵימָא מִקַּח טָעוּת הוּא. שֶׁהֲרֵי כְּנָסָהּ רִאשׁוֹן. וְעָלָיו לָדַעַת שֶׁנִּבְעֲלָה.

זאת

תוספות

ושמואל אמר אין מוכת עץ בבשר. בלא הסיר בתולין איירי, דאי בהסיר – למה יש לה להיות פחותה ממוכת עץ.

לרבנן הכיר בה מנה לא הכיר בה ולא כלום. ומתני' ר"מ היא ולא רבנן. ואם תאמר: אמאי לא קאמר לרבנן בין הכיר בה בין לא הכיר בה מנה, כדקאמר במסקנא, ותיתי מתניתין לדברי הכל! וי"ל: דלא ניחא ליה למימר הכי, דכיון דרבנן מדמו לה לבעולה – הויא בלא הכיר בה כמו כנסה בחזקת בתולה ונמצאת בעולה, וסבירא ליה דלית לה ולא כלום. ובמסקנא סבר הא דמדמו לה לבעולה – היינו לענין מנה, אבל מקח טעות – לא הויא כמו בעולה, דאינו מקפיד כ"כ במוכת עץ שיהא מקח טעות.

הדר ביה רבא מההיא. אבל מהא לא בעי למימר דהדר ביה, משום דמקח טעות – לגמרי משמע. וא"ת: מנא לן דהדר ביה ממה שאמר לרבנן לא הכיר בה ולא כלום? נאמר שחזר בו ממה שאמר לא הכיר בה לר"מ מאתים, אלא נפרש לא הכיר בה – מנה, ונוקי ברייתא כרבי מאיר! וי"ל כדפי' לעיל בקונטרס: דאין זה סברא, דאי חשיב מקח טעות לא יהא לה כלום, ואי לא חשיב מקח טעות – למה לא יהא לה מאתים? כיון דמדמה לה לבוגרת, דאטו לבוגרת פוחתין לה מכתובתה*)!

אמר

תוספות רי"ד

איתמר קטן שבא על הגדולה רב אמר עשאה מוכת עץ. פי' דכיון שהוציא בתוליה אע"ג שאין ביאתו ביאה לא גרע מעץ הנתקע וכתובתה מנה לרבנן ושמואל אמר אין מוכת עץ בבשר פי' בבשר אדם. ואי בעולה לא הויא מוכת עץ נמי לא הויא והרי היא כאילו מיעכה היא באצבעה שהממעכת בתוליה באצבעה לא הפסידה מאתים דדוקא דרוסת איש ומוכת עץ לרבנן הפסידה המאתים אבל במיעוך לא הפסידה המאתים כיון שאין כוונתה אלא שלא להצטער תחת בעלה ובמוכת עץ דפליגי רבנן משום דהוי שלא לדעתה ומיסניא בהכי. אמרי' בפ' ד' אחין כל הני מיעכות של בית ר' תמר שמן וקי"ל כשמואל בדיני: אמר רמב"ח מחלוקת כשהכיר בה. פי' כשכונסה וכתב לה כתובה היה יודע שהיא מוכת עץ דר"מ מדמי לה לבוגרת פי' דקי"ל דכלו בתוליה ואפ"ה כתובתן מאתים ורבנן מדמו לה לבעולה ור"מ אדמדמי לה לבוגרת לדמו לה לבעולה בעולה איתעביד בה מעשה (בוגרת) [בידי אדם הא] לא איתעביד בה מעשה ורבנן אדמדמו לה לבעולה לדמו לה לבוגרת בוגרת לא איתעביד בה מעשה כלל הא איתעביד בה מעשה. אבל לא הכיר בה ד"ה ולא כלום פי' שמקח טעות הוא. ורבא אסיק דבין הכיר בה ובין לא הכיר בה לר"מ כתובתה מאתים לרבנן כתובתה מנה. וקי"ל כרבנן ולא כר"מ דיחיד ורבים הלכה כרבים: **מתני'** בתולה אלמנה גרושה וחלוצה מן הנשואין כתובתן מנה ואין להן טענת בתולים. הגיורת והשבויה והשפחה שנפדו ושנתגיירו ושנשתחררו יתירות על ג' שנים ויום א' כתובתן מנה ואין להן טענת בתולים. פי' בתולה מן הנשואין וכגון שנכנסה לחופה ומת בעלה בחזקת בעולה קיימא משעה שנכנסה תחתיו וכתובתה מנה אם נשאת לאחר מכאן אין להם טענת בתולים להפסידה אותה מנה ולומר בחזקת בתולה נשאתיך והרי מקחי מקח טעות: תנו רבנן כנסה הראשון לשם נשואין ויש לה עדים שלא נסתרה או שנסתרה אלא שלא שהתה עמו כדי ביאה אין השני יכול לטעון טענת בתולים פי' להפסידה מנה הראוי לאלמנה מן הנשואין שהרי כנסה הראשון. ואע"פ שהעדים מעידין אינו יכול לטעון. אמר

מסורת הש"ס

(יבמות דף נט.) [נדה מד:] [לקמן יג.] לקמן יג. [טז.] לקמן מו. [לקמן יג.] [לקמן יב: טז.]

גליון הש"ס

גמ' ואמר רבא מאן דקא מותיב שפיר. שבת קכג ע"א ר"ה ו ע"ב:

נ"ל אברייתא

אמר רבה: זאת אומרת; כנסה בחזקת בתולה ונמצאת בעולה יש לה כתובה מנה. רב אשי אמר: בעלמא לעולם אימא לך — לית לה כלל, ושאני הכא — שהרי כנסה ראשון. וניחוש שמא תחתיו זינתה! אמר רב שרביא: כגון שקידש ובעל לאלתר. ואיכא דמתני לה אמתניתין: בתולה אלמנה, גרושה, חלוצה, מן הנישואין — כתובתן מנה, ואין להן טענת בתולין. בתולה מן הנישואין היכי משכחת לה? כגון שנכנסה לחופה ולא נבעלה. אמר רבה: זאת אומרת, כנסה בחזקת בתולה ונמצאת בעולה — כתובתה מנה. רב אשי אמר: לעולם אימא לך בעלמא לית לה כלל, ושאני הכא שהרי נכנסה לחופה. וליחוש שמא תחתיו זינתה! אמר רב שרביא: כגון שקידש ובעל לאלתר. מאן דמתני לה אברייתא — כל שכן אמתניתין, ומאן דמתני לה אמתני' — אבל אברייתא לא, משום דמצי אמר לה: אנא אעדים סמכי.§

מתני' *א האוכל אצל חמיו ביהודה שלא בעדים — אינו יכול לטעון טענת בתולים, מפני שמתייחד עמה.§ גמ' מדקתני "האוכל" מכלל דאיכא דוכתא ביהודה נמי דלא אכיל! אמר אביי: ש"מ ביהודה נמי מקומות מקומות יש. כדתניא, א"ר יהודה: *ביהודה, בראשונה היו מייחדין את החתן ואת הכלה שעה אחת קודם כניסתן לחופה, כדי שיהא לבו גס בה. ובגליל לא היו עושין כן. ביהודה, בראשונה היו מעמידין להם שני שושבינין, אחד לו ואחד לה, כדי למשמש את החתן ואת הכלה בשעת כניסתן לחופה, ובגליל לא היו עושין כן. ביהודה, בראשונה היו שושבינין ישנים בבית שחתן וכלה ישנים בה, ובגליל לא היו עושין כן. וכל שלא נהג כמנהג הזה אינו יכול לטעון טענת בתולים. אהייא? אילימא ארישא — "כל שנהג" מיבעי ליה! אלא אסיפא — "כל שלא מושמש" מיבעי ליה! אמר אביי: לעולם ארישא, ותני: "כל שנהג". אמר ליה רבא: והא "כל שלא נהג" קתני! אלא אמר רבא, הכי קאמר: כל שלא נהג מנהג גליל בגליל אלא מנהג יהודה בגליל אינו יכול לטעון טענת בתולים. רב אשי אמר: לעולם ב אסיפא, ותני: "כל שלא מושמש".§ מתני' אחת אלמנת ישראל ואחת אלמנת *כהנים כתובתה מנה. בית דין של כהנים היו גובין לבתולה ארבע מאות זוז, ולא מיחו בידם חכמים.§ גמ' תנא: ואלמנת כהנים כתובתה מאתים. והאנן תנן: אחת אלמנת ישראל ואחת אלמנת כהנים כתובתן מנה! אמר רב אשי: שתי תקנות הוו; מעיקרא תקינו לבתולה ארבע מאות זוז, ולאלמנה מנה. כיון

רש"י

זאת אומרת כו'. דהא ודאי בחזקת בתולה כנסה, דסמך אעדים, וקאמר אין יכול להפסידה מנה הראוי לאלמנה מן הנישואין. וניחוש שמא תחתיו זינתה. *אמתניתין פריך, דקתני אין השני יכול לטעון טענת בתולים, ולא מזקיקינן ליה לבא לבית דין, ולא יתברר הדבר אם תחתיו זינתה אם לא, ושמא אסורה היא לו? בשלמא אהך דלעיל, דאמרן כנסה בחזקת בתולה ונמצאת בעולה יש לה כתובה — לא מקשינן, דאיכא למימר כשבא לבית דין ובאו עדים שזינתה קודם לכן. אבל הכא קתני: אין יכול לטעון — מתוך כך לא יבא לב"ד. כשקידש ובעל לאלתר גרסינן, ולא גרסינן כשקידש לאלתר ובעל לאלתר — שלא פירש ממנה בין קידושין לבעילה, דודאי לא תחתיו זינתה. ואיכא דמתני לה. להא דרבה ורב אשי ורב שרביא אמתני'. זאת אומרת. מדקתני מתני' אין להן טענת בתולים. וליחוש שמא תחתיו זינתה. ואמאי תני אין להן טענת בתולים. מאן דמתני לה. להא דרבה ורב אשי אברייתא. כ"ש אמתני'. דכיון דאברייתא, אע"ג דאמרו עדים לא נסתרה לראשון, ושני זה בחזקת בתולה כנסה, ואפילו הכי אהדר ליה רב אשי לרבה: לעולם לא תשמע כנסה בחזקת בתולה ונמצאת בעולה יש לה כתובה, דשאני הכא שהרי כנסה ראשון. כל שכן אמתניתין, דלא הבטיחוהו עדים על כך, איכא למתנייה לדרבה, ומאי דאהדר ליה רב אשי. ומאן דתני לה. דרבה ורב אשי אמתניתין. אבל אברייתא לא. מתני להו, דמברייתא ודאי שפיר ש"מ זאת אומרת דרבה, ועלה לא הוה לרב אשי לאהדורי שאני הכא שהרי כנסה ראשון — דמצי אמר: אנא אעדים סמכי, וכיון דקתני אין השני יכול לטעון טענת בתולים — שמעינן ודאי דזאת אומרת: כנסה בחזקת בתולה ונמצאת בעולה — יש לה כתובה. מקומות מקומות יש. שחלוקין במנהגם. ונפקא מינה, דהיכא דלא נהיגי לייחד — יכול לטעון. כדתניא. דמקומות מקומות יש. למשמש. לפשפש ולמשמש במעשיהן באותו הלילה, שלא יקלקלו זה את זה במעשיהם בתרמית. שלא יראה זה דם בתולים ויאבד, וזו לא תביא מפה שיש עליה טיפי דמים. ובמקום שנהגו למשמש לא נהגו לייחד. דאילו במקום שנהגו לייחד, מאי מישמוש בעי? הרי אין שם טענת בתולים. אלמא ביהודה מקומות מקומות יש. אילימא ארישא. אמנהג דמייחדין. כל שנהג להתייחד מיבעי ליה. דאין יכול לטעון. אלא אסיפא. אמנהג דמשמוש שושבינין. כל שלא מושמש מיבעי ליה. דהטוען טענת בתולים הוא הבעל, והוא אינו נוהג מישמוש שבו [שאינו תלוי בבעל], אלא על ידי הכלה למשמשו שלא יאבד את בתוליה. ומשמוש בכלה, שלא תביא דם מן החוץ — תלוי בבעל. והיכי תני כל בעל שלא נהג מישמוש אינו יכול לטעון טענת בתולים? כ"ש דאם לא נהג למשמש והם מישמשו אותו, דיכול לטעון! הכי איבעי ליה למתני: כל שלא מושמש אינו יכול לטעון, דשמא ראה ואבד. אלא אמר רבא. האי כל שלא נהג — אמנהג דגליל קאי, דתנא בברייתא: ובגליל לא היו עושין כן, ועלה קאי: כל שלא נהג כמנהג הזה בגליל, אלא נתייחד כמנהג שביהודה — אינו יכול לטעון. מתני' אלמנת כהנים. אלמנה בת כהן. היו גובין לבתולה. בת כהן כשנישאת לכהן, וכ"ש כשנישאת לישראל. גמ' שתי תקנות הוו. לאלמנה בת כהן. דמזלזלי

[לעיל ט:]

[תוספתא פ"א]

[במשנה שבמשניות ליתא כהן]

תוספות

אמר רבה זאת אומרת. נראה דהכא גרסינן רבה, דהא רבא קאמר לעיל דמקח טעות לגמרי משמע. ואי גרסינן הכא רבא — א"כ תיקשי מתניתין רישא לסיפא, דהא זאת אומרת איכא למידק נמי ממתניתין, כדאמרינן בסמוך. אלא ודאי נראה דהכא גרס רבה. דרבא דאמר לעיל מקח טעות לגמרי משמע, יפרש כמו רב אשי.

כנסה בחזקת בתולה ונמצאת בעולה יש לה מנה. והא דקתני שהרי כנסה ראשון — פירש ריב"ם דהכי משמע ליה: אין לשני טענת בתולין לחסרה מכתובתה כלום, שהרי כנסה ראשון וגרם להיות כתובתה מנה, ואינו יכול לחסרה כלום מאותה מנה, דלא מהניא טענת בתולין אלא ממנה דבתולין. שאני הכא שהרי כנסה ראשון. ואדעתא דבעולה נישאת. ואע"ג דעדים מעידים שלא נבעלה — אינו סומך על זה, מאחר שהיו נישואין, וסבר דלשבחה אומרים כן.

וניחוש שמא תחתיו זינתה. אין לומר דפריך אמאי אינו יכול לטעון טענת בתולים לאוסרה עליו, ניחוש באשת כהן שמא תחתיו זינתה, דליכא אלא חדא ספיקא; ספק תחתיו ספק אין תחתיו. דהא מצי לשנויי דהא דאינו יכול לטעון — היינו להפסידה מכתובתה, דאיכא ספק ספיקא: דאפי' תחתיו — אימור באונס הוה. ואין זה דוחק, דלעיל נמי מפרש אינו יכול לטעון טענת בתולים הכי. דקאמר: למאי? אי לאוסרה עליו — ביהודה אמאי לא כו', אלא אכתובה פריך, אמאי אינו מפסיד לה. ונראה לר"י דלרב אשי פריך: כיון דבעלמא אית ליה דאין לה כלום, והכא יש לה לפי שכנסה ראשון — א"כ יבא לידי איסור, שזה האיש סבור כיון שזו יש לה, אע"ג דבעלמא לית לה — אם כן מחזיקין אותה ודאי בעולה מבעל ראשון, ואדעת כן רוצים לומר שנשאתי, ובחנם אטרח לבית דין, שודאי לא יאסרוה עלי. ולכך היה לנו להפסיד כתובתה, שיבא לב"ד ולא יטעה לומר שמותרת לו. ואפי' באשת ישראל יש לנו להפסידה, גזירה שיראה כהן שזו לא תאבד כתובתה, ויסבור אף בשלו כן, ולא יבא לב"ד. אבל לרבה לא פריך מידי, כיון דבעלמא נמי יש לה — ליכא למיטעי.

כגון שקידש ובעל לאלתר. וכן צריך נמי להעמיד שהראשון אחר שקידש כנסה לאלתר ומת מיד, ועדים מעידים שלא זינתה תחתיו. דאם נבעלה תחת הראשון — הרי נבעלה לפסול לה, ואסורה לכהונה.*)

שתי תקנות הוו. וליכא למימר דחדא תקנה הואי, ומתני' קודם תקנה וברייתא לאחר תקנה שתיקנו לאלמנה מאתים — דהא חזינן השתא דלית להו מאתים. וליכא למימר נמי דמעיקרא כי תקינו לבתולה ארבע מאות תקינו גם כן לאלמנה מאתים — דאין סברא לתקן לאלמנה מאתים אם לא אחר שראו צורך, דמזלזלי בהו. [הילכך, מעיקרא לא רצו לשנותה משאר אלמנה, וכיון דחזו דקא מזלזלי בהו — ראו שהיה צורך, תקנו להם מאתן. וכיון דחזו דפרשי מינייהו — אהדרינהו למילתייהו]. ולכך הוצרך לומר שתי תקנות הוו. כיון

עין משפט נר מצוה

עד א מיי' פי"א מהל' אישות הלכה ח סמג עשין מח טוש"ע אה"ע סימן סח סעיף א:
עה ב טוש"ע שם ס"ב:

תוספות רי"ד

אמר רבא זאת אומרת כנסה בחזקת בתולה ונמצאת בעולה יש לה כתובה מנה. פי' כיון שהעדים מבררים ומעידים שלא בא עליה כשכנסה [ראשון] א"כ בחזקת בתולה כונסה וש"מ כנסה בחזקת בתולה ונמצאת בעולה כתובתה מנה. ר"א אמר בעלמא לעולם אימא לך דלית לה מידי ושאני הכא שכבר כנסה הראשון. פי' ואע"פ שמעידים העדים שלאחר שכנסה לא בא עליה יש לומר כיון שנתרצית לו לכונסה מאותה שעה היא נשאת לו. והל' כרב אשי דכנסה בחזקת בתולה ונמצאת בעולה אין לה כלום ורבא נמי הכי אמר לעיל במאי דתנן הנושא את האשה ולא מצא לה בתולים וכו' ואמר רבא מקח טעות לגמרי משמע ולית לה כלל. והכא דקאמר זאת אומרת דיוקא בעלמא סבר לדייק מינה ולמימר דתנא דהאי מתניתא ס"ל הכי וליתא אלא כדתרצה רב אשי. ומקשה וליחוש שמא תחתיו זינתה וא"ר שרביא כגון שקידש ובעל לאלתר. פי' כל היכא דהיא טענה טענת ברי ובעל טעין טענת שמא כגון תחתיך נאנסתי או מוכת עץ אני נאמנת ושקלא כתובה ושריא לבעלה כדלקמן ואפילו ר' יהושע דאמר לקמן בראוה מדברת חיישינן שמא נבעלה לנתין ולממזר דוקא להנשא לכהונה אבל לאוסרה על בעלה בייחוד בעלמא הא אמרי' לקמן דמודה ר"י דלא אסרה לה אפי' אם הוא כהן וה"נ אילו טענה האשה ואמרה שבעלי בא עלי קודם נשואין לא הוה מקשי' וליחוש שמא תחתיו זינתה דהיא נאמנת אלא התנא לא שנה טענת האשה אלמא לא טענה הכי ואפ"ה אומר' לו ב"ד שאינך יכול לטעון טענת בתולים שמא בא עליה קודם נשואין משעה ששניהם נאותו לכנוס ואע"פ שהאשה אינה יודעת לטעון. י"ל שלמפרע היה מערה בה והוציא בתוליה ולא הרגישה שלא עלו במטה כדרך חתן וכלה אלא עד אז היה מערה בה ולא שתה לבה ולא ידעה ומ"ה פריך וליחוש שמא תחתיו זינתה דהניחא שלא להפסידה כתובתה אמרי' שמא בעלה בא עליה ולא תפסיד כתובה מספק אבל מספקא תאסר עליו כיון שעדים מעידים שלאחר שכנסה לא בא עליה והיא נמי לא טענה טענה ודאית תאסר עליו מספק שמא תחתיו זינתה ולהכי איצטריך רב שרביא לומר שקידש ובעל לאלתר שיצאנו מזה הספק ויש כאן ספק שמא בעולה היתה מקודם לכן והרי מקחו מקח טעות

בזה הספק אנו תולין כי בעלה בא עליה ואין כאן מקח טעות א) פי' המורה וניחוש שמא תחתיו זינתה אמתניתין פריך דקתני אין השני יכול לטעון טענת בתולים ולא מזקיקנן ליה לבוא לב"ד ולא מתברר אם זינתה תחתיו אם לאו ושמא אסורה לו דבשלמא אהך דלעיל דאמרת כנסה בחזקת בתולה ונמצאת בעולה יש לה כתובה מנה לא מקשי' דא"ל כשבא לב"ד באו עדים שזינתה קודם לכן אבל הכא קתני אין יכול לטעון מתוך כך לא יבא לב"ד אמר רב שרביא כשקידש ובעל לאלתר. פי' שלא פירשה ממנו בין קידושין לבעילה דודאי לא ניחוש לזינתה: מתני' האוכל אצל חמיו ביהודה שלא בעדים אינו יכול לטעון טענת בתולים מפני שמתיחד עמה. אחד אלמנת ישראל ואחד אלמנת כהנים כתובתן מנה ב"ד של כהנים היה גובין לבתולה ד' מאות זוז ולא מיחו בידם חכמים: תניא א"ר יהודה בראשונה ביהודה (היה) [היו] מיחדים את החתן ואת הכלה שעה אחת קודם כניסתן לחופה כדי שיהיה לבו גס בה ובגליל לא היו עושים כן. ביהודה בראשונה (היה) [היו] מעמידים להם שני שושבינים אחד לו ואחד לה כדי למשמש את החתן ואת הכלה בשעת כניסתן לחופה פי' למשמש ולפשפש באותו הלילה במעשיהן שלא יקלקלו זה על זה שלא יראה זה דם בתולים ויאבד וזו תביא מפה שיש עלי' טפת דם ובגליל לא היו עושין כן. פי' גם ביהודה הי' מקומות שלא היו מעמידים שושבינין דאי במקום שהיו מייחדים לא יועילו שושבינין שהרי אין שם טענת בתולים. ביהודה בראשונה היו שושבינים ישינים בבית שחתן וכלה ישינים בו ובגליל לא היו עושים כן. וכל שלא נהג במנהג זה אינו יכול לטעון טענות בתולים. שהרי נתיחד עמה. אבל נהג מנהג גליל ולא נתייחד יכול לטעון ומהימן ורב אשי פי' כל שלא משמש ביהודה אינו יכול לטעון פי' כיון שביהודה ממשמשים והוא לא משמש אמרי' לכתחלה עשה כדי להעליל עלילה עלי' אבל בגליל שלא נהגו מצי טעין אע"פ שלא משמש. ושמואל דאמר נאמן להפסידה כתובתה בטענת פתח פתוח דליכא למיקם עלה דמלתא להתברר ע"י שושבינים. וכגון שהיתה בוגרת שכלו בתוליה או אם היתה ממשפחת דורקטי אבל בטענות דמים אם נהגו למשמש ולא משמש אינו נאמן ובמקום שלא נהגו למשמש נאמן: ב"ד

א) נ"ל והמורה פירש. ור"ל דרשי ז"ל פירש.

*) [רב אשי אומר תני כל שלא מושמש. אומר רבינו יצחק בן רבינו מאיר דרב אשי פליג אדרב נחמן דלית לי' חזקה דאין אדם טורח כו' כדפי' לעיל. ור"ת אומר דלא פליג דדוקא ביהודה שנהגו למשמש ואירע שלא משמש אינו יכול לטעון דדומה לדבר שבא בכרמאות גילגל שלא מישמשוהו וכן משמע קצת דהא קתני ביהודה אינו יכול לטעון הא בגליל מצי טוען כדדייק לעיל אע"ג דבגליל לא היו ממשמשין כדקתני בברייתא ומיהו יש לפרש הא בגליל מצי טוען היינו אם אירע שמישמשוהו וע"כ צריך לפרש כן למאי דדחי לעיל לא דקא טעין טענת דמים ולא אמרי' חזקה דאין אדם טורח כו']:

עו א טוש"ע אה"ע סי' סו סעיף ז:
עז ב מיי' פ"א מהל' אישות הל' יא סמג עשין מח טוש"ע שם סי' סח סעיף ב:
עח ג מיי' פ"ה מהל' טוען ונטען הל' ט סמג עשין צה טוש"ע ח"מ סימן עה סעיף ט:

כיון דחזו דמזלזלי בהו – תקינו להו מאתן. כיון דחזו דקא פרשין מינייהו, דאמרי: עד דנסבינן אלמנת כהנים – ניזיל ניסיב בתולה בת ישראל, אהדרינהו למלתייהו.§ בית דין של כהנים כו'.§ אמר רב יהודה אמר שמואל: לא ב"ד של כהנים בלבד אמרו, אלא אפי' משפחות המיוחסות בישראל, אם רצו לעשות כדרך שהכהנים עושין – עושין. מיתיבי: הרוצה לעשות כדרך שהכהנים עושין, כגון בת ישראל לכהן ובת כהן לישראל – עושין. בת ישראל לכהן, ובת כהן לישראל הוא דאיכא צד כהונה, אבל בת ישראל לישראל – לא! לא מבעיא קאמר; לא מבעיא בת ישראל לישראל, דלא מצי אמר לה עלויי קא מעלינן ליך, אבל בת ישראל לכהן, דמצי אמר לה עלויי קא מעלינן ליך, אימא לא, קמ"ל.§ **מתני'** הנושא את האשה ולא מצא לה בתולים, היא אומרת: משארסתני נאנסתי, ונסתחפה שדהו. והוא אומר: לא כי, אלא עד שלא ארסתיך, והיה מקחי מקח טעות. רבן גמליאל ורבי אליעזר אומרים: נאמנת. רבי יהושע אומר: לא מפיה אנו חיין, אלא הרי זו בחזקת בעולה עד שלא תתארס והטעתו, עד שתביא ראיה לדבריה.§ **גמ'** אתמר, "מנה לי בידך" והלה אומר "איני יודע". רב יהודה ורב הונא אמרי: חייב, ורב נחמן ורבי יוחנן אמרי: פטור. רב הונא ורב יהודה אמרי: חייב, ברי ושמא – ברי עדיף. רב נחמן ורבי יוחנן אמרי: פטור, אוקי ממונא בחזקת מריה. א"ל אביי לרב יוסף: הא דרב הונא ורב יהודה – דשמואל היא. דתנן: היתה מעוברת, ואמרו לה: מה טיבו של עובר זה? מאיש פלוני, וכהן הוא. רבן גמליאל ורבי אליעזר אומרים: נאמנת. ואמר רב יהודה אמר שמואל: הלכה כרבן גמליאל. ואמר ליה רב שמואל בר יהודה לרב יהודה: שיננא, אמרת לן משמיה דשמואל הלכה כרבן גמליאל אף בראשונה. מאי "אף בראשונה"? אע"ג דאיכא למימר אוקי ממונא בחזקת מריה – אמר רבן גמליאל ברי עדיף. לימא רב יהודה ורב הונא דאמרי כר"ג, ורב נחמן ורבי יוחנן דאמרי כרבי יהושע? אמר לך רב נחמן: אנא דאמרי אפילו כרבן גמליאל; עד כאן לא קאמר ר"ג התם אלא דאיכא מגו, אבל הכא – מאי מגו איכא? אי נמי, עד כאן לא קאמר רבן גמליאל התם אלא דאמרינן אוקמה אחזקה, אבל הכא – מאי חזקה אית ליה להאי? הכי נמי מסתברא כדקא משנינן, דרב נחמן הוא דאמר כר"ג. דאם

רש"י

דמזלזלי בהו. באלמנות, קלות בעיניהם להוציאן מפני שכתובתן מועטת, תקינו להו מאתן, דגנאי היה להן. ואע"פ שאלמנות ישראל נמי כתובתן מנה, מיהו כהנים חשידי טפי, וגנאי להם גירושי בנותיהן יותר מישראל. **מתני'** נאמנת. קא סלקא דעתך משום דברי ושמא ברי עדיף. הרי זו בחזקת. שנבעלה עד שלא תתארס, והטעתו. **גמ'** חייב. לשלם. פטור. מלשלם. ומכל מקום משביעינן ליה שבועת היסת שכן הוא כדבריו, שאינו יודע שהוא חייב לו. וכהן הוא. כלומר מיוחס הוא. אף בראשונה. גבי תביעת כתובה. [אוקי כתובה אחזקתה. אחזקת הבעל. ה"נ גבי מנה לי בידך, איכא למימר נמי: אוקי ממונא בחזקת מריה, ופטור. אלא דאיכא מגו]. כגון "משארסתני נאנסתי", וכגון היא אומרת "מוכת עץ אני", דאמרינן מגו דאי בעיא טענה טענה מעלייתא מהך, כגון גבי "משארסתני נאנסתי" הוה טענה "מוכת עץ אני" [טענה מעלייתא], דלא פסלה נפשה מכהונה. וקאמרה "נאנסתי [משארסתני]", וקא מיפסלה נפשה, דאשת ישראל שנאנסה אסורה לכהן – ש"מ קושטא קאמרה. וגבי היא אומרת "מוכת עץ אני", אי בעיא אמרה "מוכת עץ אני תחתיך" ואית לה מאתן, וקא אמרה "מוכת עץ אני קודם לכן, ואין לי אלא מנה". אבל הכא. גבי האי תובע, מאי מגו איכא דלהמניה? הלכך אוקי ממונא בחזקת מריה. אוקמה אחזקה. מספקא לן אשעת ארוסין, אי בתולה הואי ונשתעבד לה למאתים, אי בעולה הואי – העמד אשה על חזקתה ובתולה נולדה, והך השתא הוא דאיתניסה אחר אירוסין. מאי חזקה אית ליה להאי. תובע, דנוקמיה אחזקיה לגבות? הלכך זיל בתר חזקה דממונא. דא"כ

תוספות

כיון דחזו דמזלזלי בהו. פירש בקונטרס: שהיו קלות בעיניהן להוציאן, לפי שהיתה כתובתן מועטת. וקשה: דמעיקרא נמי הוו ידעי שקלות בעיניהן להוציאן כיון דמנה חשיב דבר מועט! ונראה לר"י לפרש: דמזלזלי בהו – שמקלת בני אדם היו נמנעים מלנושאם, לפי שהיו קלות בעיניהן, שאין לה כתובה אלא רביע ממה שיש לה לבתולה, ותקינו לה מאתן. כיון דחזו דפרשי מינייהו לגמרי, והיו קופצים קודם על בתולות ישראל, ולא היה שום אדם קופץ עליהם – אהדרינהו למילתייהו. היינו דנקט מעיקרא מזלזלי, שהיו נמנעים ולא לגמרי פורשים, ובתר הכי נקט "ופרשי". **בית** דין של כהנים היו גובין כו' ולא מיחו בידם חכמים. אע"פ שלא כתב בלשון תוספת, אלא ארבע מאות דחזו ליכי. וקא ס"ד דלא תגבה, דלא חזו, ובלשון תוספת לא כתב – קא משמע לן דמנהג טוב מאד הוא, וראוי להיות בכהונה ובמשפחות המיוחסות. ושייך בהו למימר דחזו ליכי, ואפי' לא כתב לה כתובה – גובה ארבע מאות בתנאי ב"ד, כמו בבנות ישראל מאתים, דתקנה גמורה היא. **והוא** אומר לא כי כו'. אע"ג דבסוף "המניח" (ב"ק דף לה: ושם) דייק מדקתני "לא כי" דמיירי בברי, הכא דליכא למיטעי – קתני "לא כי" אע"ג דאיירי בשמא. **מנה** לי בידך והלה אומר איני יודע. פי': איני יודע אם הלויתני מעולם. אבל הלויתני ואיני יודע אם פרעתיך – תנן בהדיא ב"הגוזל בתרא" (שם קיח.) דחייב. **רב** הונא ורב יהודה אמרי חייב. לכאורה נראה דלית להו דרבי אבא דאמר: מתוך שאינו יכול לישבע משלם. דטעמיה דר' אבא משום דדריש (שבועות ד' מז.) "שבועת ה' תהיה בין שניהם" – ולא בין שני היורשין. כגון, אמר מנה לאבא ביד אביך, ואמר: חמשין ידענא, וחמשין לא ידענא. ואבוה כה"ג, מתוך שאין יכול לישבע – משלם. ואי מנה לי בידך והלה אומר איני יודע חייב – אין כאן שבועה, דאפי' הוא אומר אין יודע בכל – חייב. ותימה: דבפרק "יש נוחלין" (ב"ב דף קלה. ושם) גבי האומר זה אחי, משמע דאביי אית ליה מנה לי בידך והלה אומר איני יודע חייב. ובפ' "חזקת הבתים" (שם לד. ושם) משמע דאית ליה לדר' אבא! וי"ל: דאפי' למ"ד חייב, איכא למידרש "שבועת ה' תהיה בין שניהם" – ולא בין היורשין, דשניהם לא ידעי, אלא שעד אחד מעיד שאחד חייב לחבירו מנה. דאבוה, מתוך שאינו יכול לישבע – משלם. תימה: דרב יהודה גופיה אית ליה בריש "הפרה" (ב"ק מו. ושם) אפילו ניזק אומר ברי ומזיק אומר שמא – המע"ה! ואין לומר דרב יהודה כסומכוס דאמר: ממון המוטל בספק חולקין, ולא אזיל בתר חזקת ממון, ולהכי כי איכא ברי ושמא – נוטל הכל, והתם דקאמר אמר רב יהודה אמר שמואל: זו דברי סומכוס, אבל חכמים אומרים: זה כלל גדול בדין כו' – אליבא דרבנן קאמר, וליה לא סבירא ליה. דהתם (בב"ב דף לג:) משמע דסבר כרבנן, גבי מוכר שור לחבירו ונמצא נגחן. ועוד, דתנן בפרק "השואל" (ב"מ לז. ושם): המשאיל אומר שאולה מתה והלה אומר איני יודע – חייב. וקאמר בגמרא: לימא תיהוי תיובתא דרב נחמן ור' יוחנן. ומאי קושיא? הא ע"כ מתני' כסומכוס אפי' לרב יהודה, דלרבנן מודה רב יהודה דפטור, ורב נחמן ורבי יוחנן ע"כ כרבנן, דלסומכוס לכל הפחות חולקין! אבל אי פליגי אליבא דרבנן, ולסומכוס לעולם חולקין, אפי' בברי ושמא – פריך שפיר ממתני', דכרבנן אתיא, דלסומכוס חולקין! וי"ל: דהתם ברי גרוע ושמא טוב, דלפי שהמזיק לא היה שם טוען זה ברי, ושמא דמזיק טוב – דלא הוה ליה למידע. אבל מנה לי בידך – הברי טוב והשמא גרוע, דהוה ליה לידע אם חייב אם לאו. אבל קשה: דבעי למימר הכא הא דרב יהודה דשמואל היא, דפסק כרבן גמליאל, והתם ברי גרוע ושמא טוב, שהבעל אינו יודע מתי נבעלה, ואם כן תיקשי דשמואל אדשמואל דפ' "הפרה" (ב"ק מו. ושם)! ויש לומר: דה"מ למימר וליטעמיך. ועוד יש לומר: דסוגיא דהכא סברה דזה כלל גדול בדין – לא לניזק אומר ברי ומזיק אומר שמא, אלא כדקאמר התם: אי נמי לכי הא. וקשה על זה דאפילו לפי אי נמי דהתם לא אתי שפיר, דהא בסוף "המניח" (שם דף לה: ושם) אית להו לרבנן בהדיא, דאפי' ניזק אומר ברי כו', ושמואל סובר כרבנן כדמוכח ב"המוכר שור לחברו"! **אלא** דאיכא מגו. הא' שנויא לא אתיא אלא לרב נחמן, דלר' יוחנן בהדיא דמוכת עץ ליכא מגו, כדמוכח לקמן. הקשה ה"ר יעקב מקורבי"ל: אכתי, ע"כ הא דרב יהודה דשמואל היא, דאי לשמואל פטור – תקשי ליה ממתניתין ד"השואל" (ב"מ ד' לז. ושם): המשאיל אומר שאולה מתה, והלה אומר איני יודע – חייב, דלשמואל ליכא לשנויי כדמשני לרב נחמן ולרבי יוחנן כגון שיש עסק שבועה ביניהן, ומתוך שאינו יכול לישבע משלם, דשמואל אית ליה בהדיא בפ' "כל הנשבעין" (שבועות ד' מז. ושם) דחזרה שבועה לסיני, ולא משלם! וי"ל: דאיכא למימר דלעולם מנה לי בידך והלה אומר איני יודע – לשמואל פטור, ומוקי שמואל מתני' ד"השואל" כשיש עסק שבועה, וכההוא תנא דאית ליה מתוך שאינו יכול לישבע משלם, והוא סבר כאידך תנא, דפלוגתא דתנאי היא בפרק "כל הנשבעין" (שם). [ועי' ביתר ביאור תוס' ב"מ לז: סד"ה רב הונא].

גליון הש"ס

גמ' הא דרב הונא ורב יהודה דשמואל היא. עיין יבמות יח ע"ב תד"ה לאו דרבי.

תוספות רי"ד

תוספות רי"ד

עט א מיי' פי"א מהל' אישות הלכה ב סמג עשין מח טוש"ע אה"ע סימן סח סעיף ט: פ ב ג ד ה מיי' פי"ח מהלכות איסורי ביאה הלכה יג ופי"ח הלכה יג סמג לאוין קכא טוש"ע שם סי' ו סעיף יז: פא ו מיי' פכ"ב שם הל' ג סמג לאוין קכו טוש"ע שם סימן כב סעיף ב:

דְּאִם כֵּן קַשְׁיָא הִלְכְתָא אַהִלְכְתָא, דְּקַיְימָא לָן *הִלְכְתָא כְּרַב נַחְמָן בְּדִינֵי, וּבְהָא אָמַר רַב יְהוּדָה אָמַר שְׁמוּאֵל הֲלָכָה כְּרַבָּן גַּמְלִיאֵל. אֶלָּא לָאו ש"מ כִּדְמְשַׁנֵּינַן, ש"מ.§ **מתני'** *הִיא אוֹמֶרֶת: "מוּכַּת עֵץ אֲנִי", וְהוּא אוֹמֵר: "לֹא כִּי, אֶלָּא דְּרוּסַת אִישׁ אַתְּ". ארַבָּן גַּמְלִיאֵל וְרַבִּי אֱלִיעֶזֶר אוֹמְרִים: נֶאֱמֶנֶת, וְרַבִּי יְהוֹשֻׁעַ אוֹמֵר: לֹא מִפִּיהָ אָנוּ חַיִּין, אֶלָּא הֲרֵי זוֹ בְּחֶזְקַת דְּרוּסַת אִישׁ עַד שֶׁתָּבִיא רְאָיָה לִדְבָרֶיהָ.§ **גמ'** טַעֲנָתַיְיהוּ בְּמַאי? *רַבִּי יוֹחָנָן אָמַר: בְּמָאתַיִם וּמָנֶה, רַבִּי אֶלְעָזָר אָמַר: בְּמָנֶה וְלֹא כְלוּם. רַבִּי יוֹחָנָן אָמַר: בְּמָאתַיִם וּמָנֶה, סָבַר לָהּ *כְּר"מ, דְּאָמַר: בֵּין הִכִּיר בָּהּ וּבֵין לֹא הִכִּיר בָּהּ — מָאתַיִם. וְרַבִּי אֶלְעָזָר אוֹמֵר: בְּמָנֶה וְלֹא כְלוּם, סָבַר לָהּ כְּרַבָּנַן דְּאָמְרִי: בֵּין הִכִּיר בָּהּ בֵּין לֹא הִכִּיר בָּהּ — מָנֶה. בִּשְׁלָמָא ר' אֶלְעָזָר לָא קָאָמַר כְּר' יוֹחָנָן — דְּקָא מוֹקֵי לָהּ כְּרַבָּנַן, אֶלָּא רַבִּי יוֹחָנָן מ"ט לֹא אָמַר כְּר' אֶלְעָזָר? קָסָבַר: כְּנָסָהּ בְּחֶזְקַת בְּתוּלָה וְנִמְצֵאת בְּעוּלָה — יֵשׁ לָהּ כְּתוּבָּה מָנֶה. הָכָא, הוּא קָאָמַר מָנֶה וְהִיא קָאָמְרָה מָנֶה, מַאי אִיכָּא בֵּין טַעֲנָה דִּידֵיהּ לְטַעֲנָה דִּידָהּ? בִּשְׁלָמָא לְר' אֶלְעָזָר — הַיְינוּ דְּקָתָנֵי תַּרְתֵּי: חֲדָא — לְאַפּוֹקֵי מִדְּרָמֵי בַּר חָמָא, וַחֲדָא — לְאַפּוֹקֵי מִדְּרַב חִיָּיא בַּר אָבִין א"ר שֵׁשֶׁת. אֶלָּא לְר' יוֹחָנָן, תַּרְתֵּי לָמָּה לִי? חֲדָא לְהוֹדִיעֲךָ כֹּחוֹ דְּרַבָּן גַּמְלִיאֵל, וַחֲדָא לְהוֹדִיעֲךָ כֹּחוֹ דְּרַבִּי יְהוֹשֻׁעַ. קַמַּיְיתָא לְהוֹדִיעֲךָ כֹּחוֹ דְּרַבִּי יְהוֹשֻׁעַ, דְּאַף עַל גַּב דְּאִיכָּא לְמֵימַר מִיגּוֹ — לָא מְהֵימְנָא, בַּתְרַיְיתָא לְהוֹדִיעֲךָ כֹּחוֹ דְּרַבָּן גַּמְלִיאֵל, דְּאע"ג דְּלֵיכָּא לְמֵימַר מִיגּוֹ — מְהֵימְנָא.§ **מתני'** *רָאוּהָ מְדַבֶּרֶת עִם אֶחָד, וְאָמְרוּ לָהּ: "מַה טִּיבוֹ שֶׁל אִישׁ זֶה?" — "אִישׁ פְּלוֹנִי, וְכֹהֵן הוּא". ברַבָּן גַּמְלִיאֵל וְרַבִּי אֱלִיעֶזֶר אוֹמְרִים: נֶאֱמֶנֶת, וְר' יְהוֹשֻׁעַ אוֹמֵר: לֹא מִפִּיהָ אָנוּ חַיִּין, אֶלָּא הֲרֵי זוֹ בְּחֶזְקַת בְּעוּלָה •לְנָתִין וּלְמַמְזֵר, עַד שֶׁתָּבִיא רְאָיָה לִדְבָרֶיהָ. *הָיְתָה מְעוּבֶּרֶת, וְאָמְרוּ לָהּ: "מַה טִּיבוֹ שֶׁל עוּבָּר זֶה"? "מֵאִישׁ פְּלוֹנִי, וְכֹהֵן הוּא". גרַבָּן גַּמְלִיאֵל וְרַבִּי אֱלִיעֶזֶר אוֹמְרִים: נֶאֱמֶנֶת, וְר' יְהוֹשֻׁעַ אוֹמֵר: לֹא מִפִּיהָ אָנוּ חַיִּין, אֶלָּא הֲרֵי זוֹ בְּחֶזְקַת מְעוּבֶּרֶת לְנָתִין וּלְמַמְזֵר, עַד שֶׁתָּבִיא רְאָיָה לִדְבָרֶיהָ.§ **גמ'** מַאי "מְדַבֶּרֶת"? *זְעֵירִי אָמַר: נִסְתְּרָה, רַב אַסִי אָמַר, דנִבְעֲלָה. בִּשְׁלָמָא לִזְעֵירִי — הַיְינוּ דְּקָתָנֵי "מְדַבֶּרֶת", אֶלָּא לְרַב אַסִי מַאי "מְדַבֶּרֶת"? *לִישָּׁנָא מַעַלְיָא, כְּדִכְתִיב: °"אָכְלָה וּמָחֲתָה פִיהָ וְאָמְרָה לֹא פָעַלְתִּי אָוֶן". בִּשְׁלָמָא לִזְעֵירִי — הַיְינוּ דְּקָתָנֵי תַּרְתֵּי, "מְדַבֶּרֶת" וּ"מְעוּבֶּרֶת". אֶלָּא לְרַב אַסִי, תַּרְתֵּי לָמָּה לִי? החֲדָא לְהַכְשִׁיר בָּהּ, וַחֲדָא לְהַכְשִׁיר בְּבִתָּהּ. *הָנִיחָא לְמַאן דְּאָמַר: לְדִבְרֵי הַמַּכְשִׁיר בָּהּ מַכְשִׁיר בְּבִתָּהּ, אֶלָּא לְמ"ד: לְדִבְרֵי הַמַּכְשִׁיר בָּהּ פּוֹסֵל בְּבִתָּהּ, מַאי אִיכָּא לְמֵימַר? רַב אַסִי סָבַר כְּמ"ד לְדִבְרֵי הַמַּכְשִׁיר בָּהּ מַכְשִׁיר בְּבִתָּהּ. א"ל רַב פָּפָּא לְאַבַּיֵי: לִזְעֵירִי, דְּאָמַר מַאי "מְדַבֶּרֶת" נִסְתְּרָה, וְא"ר יְהוֹשֻׁעַ לָא מְהֵימְנָא — הָאָמַר רַב: *ומַלְקִין עַל הַיִּחוּד וְאֵין אוֹסְרִין עַל הַיִּחוּד, לֵימָא דְּלָא כְּר"י! אֲפִי' תֵּימָא ר' יְהוֹשֻׁעַ, *מַעֲלָה עָשׂוּ בְּיוּחֲסִין. מֵיתִיבֵי: רָאוּהָ שֶׁנִּכְנְסָה עִם אֶחָד לְסֵתֶר, אוֹ

מִשלי ל

דא"כ. דרב נחמן לא מיתוקם כרבן גמליאל אלא כרבי יהושע, קשיא הלכתא אהלכתא. **מתני'** דרוסת איש את. קודם שארסתיך. **גמ'** טענתייהו במאי. מה היא תובעתו, ומה הוא רוצה ליתן? במאתים ומנה. היא אומרת: "מוכת עץ אני, ויש לי מאתים, ואע"פ שלא הכרת בי", והוא אומר: "דרוסת איש את, ואין לך אלא מנה". וקסבר: כנסה בחזקת בתולה ונמצאת בעולה – יש לה כתובה מנה. במנה ולא כלום. היא תובעת מנה, והוא אומר: "אין ליך כלום". סבר לה. תנא דמתני'. דאילו רבי יוחנן לא שביק רבנן ועביד כר"מ. קסבר. ר' יוחנן, כנסה בחזקת בתולה ונמצאת בעולה – יש לה מנה. הלכך, על כרחך מוכת עץ דמתני' ר"מ היא, דאמר מאתים. והוא אומר: "דרוסת איש את, ויש ליך מנה". דאי רבנן היא – לא תבעה אלא מנה, והוא אומר: "דרוסת איש את ויש לך מנה" – מאי איכא בין טענתא דידיה לטענתא דידה? בשלמא לרבי אלעזר. דאמר דרוסת איש אין לה כלום. היינו דקתני תרתי. בבי במתני', גבי פלוגתא דממונא: "היא אומרת משארסתני נאנסתי" ו"היא אומרת מוכת עץ אני". חדא לאפוקי מדרמי בר חמא וחדא לאפוקי כו'. "היא אומרת משארסתני נאנסתי" תנא למיתני בה "והיה מקחי מקח טעות" – לגמרי משמע, ואין לה כלום, לאפוקי מדרב חייא בר אבין דאמר לעיל (דף יא:): כנסה בחזקת בתולה ונמצאת בעולה – יש לה כתובה מנה. ותנא היא אומרת "מוכת עץ אני" – לאפוקי מדרמי בר חמא, דאמר לעיל גבי מוכת עץ: אבל לא הכיר בה – דברי הכל ולא כלום. **אלא** לרבי יוחנן. דאמר כנסה בחזקת בתולה ונמצאת בעולה – יש לה כתובה מנה. אם כן, מאי מקח טעות דקתני – אמאתים, אבל מנה – יש לה. למה לי למיתני כלל להאי? אי לאשמועינן פלוגתא דרבן גמליאל ור' יהושע בברי ושמא, ואוקי ממונא בחזקת מריה, ליתני חדא לאפוקי מדרמי בר חמא, ולאשמעינן פלוגתייהו. **דאיכא** למימר מגו. מגו דאי בעיא אמרה "מוכת עץ אני". בתרייתא. ליכא למימר מגו לר' יוחנן, דמוקי מתני' כרבי מאיר, דאמר: מוכת עץ שלא הכיר בה – כתובתה מאתים, ליכא שום מגו, דמה לי אומרת "מוכת עץ אני תחתיך", מה לי אמרה "מעיקרא". **מתני'** *[ראוה מדברת. בפנויה, ומשום חששא דפסולין לנתין ולממזר, וכיון שנבעלה לפסול – פסלה מן הכהונה]. נאמנת. וכשרה לכהונה, ולא מספקינן לה בנבעלה לפסול לה. היתה מעוברת כו'. בגמ' מפרש תרתי למה לי. **גמ'** נסתרה. ואע"פ שלא ראוה שנבעלה – נפסלה לכהונה לרבי יהושע, כדלקמן, דמעלה עשו ביוחסין. אכלה ומחתה פיה. אלמא נקט תשמיש בלשון אכילה. **בשלמא** לזעירי היינו דקתני תרתי. מדברת, להודיעך כחו דר' יהושע, דאע"ג דלא ראוה שנבעלה – פסולה. ומעוברת – להודיעך כחו דרבן גמליאל. בבתה. אם העובר הזה נקבה תנשא לכהונה לר"ג. דאי אשמועינן בדידה – הוה אמינא: איהי, הואיל דהוה לה חזקה דכשרות מעיקרא – אמרי' אוקמה אחזקה ואל תפסילנה מספק. אבל עובר, דלא הוה ליה חזקה דכשרות – אימא לא. **הניחא** למ"ד כו'. לקמן בשמעתין. **מאי איכא** למימר. תרתי להכשיר בה למה לי? כיון דמדברת ברואה שנבעלה. מלקין על היחוד. מכת מרדות. **ואין אוסרין.** אשה על בעלה בשביל יחוד בעלמא. **לימא** דלא כרבי יהושע. דמשום יחוד מחזיק לה בנבעלת. ביוחסין. בכהונה. לסתר. משמע יחוד בעלמא. לחורבה

[קדושין נט: ב"מ קי.] [לעיל יא: לקמן טז.] [לקמן טז.] [לעיל יא.] [לקמן טז.] [קדושין עד. [עה.] נ"י כ"י [לקמן טז. יבמות יח:] [פסחים ג. וש"נ] [קדושין עד.] שם פא. [קדושין עג. לקמן טו.]

רב אסי אמר נבעלה. אבל נסתרה, מודה ר' יהושע דנאמנת לומר לכשר נבעלתי, במגו דאי בעיא אמרה לא נבעלתי. וא"ת: והא רבי יהושע לית ליה מגו גבי משארסתני נאנסתי! ויש לומר: דהתם לא הוי מגו גמור, דהא אפילו אמרה מוכת עץ אני – אינה נאמנת לרבי יהושע. כדתנן במתני'. ולא קרי ליה מגו אלא לפי שהיא •טענה מעולה ביותר.

חדא להכשיר בה וחדא להכשיר בבתה. וצריכי תרווייהו: חדא להודיעך כחו דרבן גמליאל, וחדא להודיעך כחו דרבי יהושע.

לדברי המכשיר בה פוסל בבתה. ומעוברת דנקט – משום לישנא מעליא. **ואין** אוסרין על היחוד לימא דלא כרבי יהושע. תימה לרשב"א: דלזעירי (נמי) דאמר נסתרה, איירי כגון דמודה היא שנבעלה. דאי אמרה לא נבעלתי – אם כן הוי ספק ספיקא, דמכשיר רבי יהושע, כדאמר לקמן: התם – ספק ספיקא! ויש לומר: דלעולם איירי דקאמרה לא נבעלה, וחשיב ליה חדא ספיקא, משום דאין אפוטרופוס לעריות. אבל קשה! דבהדי' משמע בריש פרק שני (לקמן טז.) דאיירי בנבעלת, דקאמר: הניחא לזעירי דאמר מאי מדברת נסתרה, דמגו דאי בעיא אמרה לא נבעלתי – מהימנא כו'! לכך נראה דפריך לזעירי, דבספיקא חדא אסרינן לה, והא יחוד דאשת איש דספיקא חדא היא, ואין אוסרים על היחוד! וק"ק: דלכאורה נראה דיחוד איסור פריך, מדפריך לזעירי ולא לרב אסי! **מעלה** עשו ביוחסין. תימה: דמשמע דאין אוסרין על היחוד איירי באשת איש, ולא בפנויה. ובסוף קדושין (דף פא. ושם) מוקי מלקין על היחוד – דוקא בפנויה, אבל באשת איש – לא, דאתה מוציא לעז על בניה. ואפי' למר זוטרא דמלקין ומכריז באשת איש, מודה דבפנויה נמי איירי! ואור"ת: דאף על גב דמלקין על היחוד איירי בפנויה, אין אוסרין על היחוד – לא איירי אלא באשת איש. *וא"ת: והא אמרינן בפ' בתרא דנדרים (דף צא:) גבי ההוא נואף דעייל לגבה דההיא איתתא, אמר ליה נואף: לא תיכול מינהון, דטעמינהו חויא. אמר רבא: איתתא שריא, אם איתא דעבד איסורא – ניחא ליה דלימות. משמע דאי לאו האי טעמא – היתה נאסרת על ידי יחוד! ויש לומר דנואף שאני. וה"ר יוסף דשליטן תירץ: דאין אוסרים על היחוד – איירי בפנויה, כמו מלקין על היחוד. ולא איירי לכהונה, אלא אין אוסרין אותה לבנו כשמתייחד עם אביו, לרבי יהודה דאסר באנוסת אביו (יבמות דף צז.).

הסכמתו

[מיהו קשה לאפריך מרב דאמר אין אוסרין על היחוד הוה ליה למיפרך מהא דקי"ל בכולי תלמודא וסתם משניות דאין אשה נאסרת על בעלה אלא על ידי קינוי וסתירה לכך נ"ל דרב איירי בפנויה דוקא וה"פ דמעלה עשו ביוחסין לאסור היכא דאמרה לכשר נבעלתי דמודה מיהא ולא מהימנינן לה במגו אבל אי אמרה לא נבעלתי בהא לא עשו מעלה ובהא איירי רב. ת"י]

גליון הש"ס

מתני' לנתין ולממזר עי' גיטין פט ע"א תוס' ד"ה כשולה ובמהרש"א שם: **תוס'** ד"ה רב אסי וכו' טענה מעולה ביותר. וכ"כ הרשב"א קדושין דף כ ע"א ד"ה הא:

תוספות רי"ד

דא"כ קשה הלכתא אהלכתא דקי"ל הלכה כר"נ בדיני. ובהא אמר ר"י אמר שמואל הלכה כר"ג ש"מ: **מתני'** היא אומרת מוכת עץ אני והוא אומר לא כי אלא דרוסת איש את ר"ג ור"א אומרים נאמנת ור"י אומר לא מפיה אנו חיין אלא ה"ז בחזקת דרוסת איש עד שתביא ראיה לדבריה: טענתייהו במאי. פי' מה היא תובעתו ומה הוא רוצה ליתן ר' יוחנן אמר במאתים ומנה פי' היא אומרת מוכת עץ אני ויש לי מאתים ואע"פ שלא הכרת בי והוא אומר דרוסת איש את ואין לך אלא מנה וכנסה בחזקת בתולה ונמצאת בעולה יש לה כתובה מנה וסבר לה כר"מ דאמר מוכת עץ בין הכיר בה בין לא הכיר בה כתובתה מאתים וכנסה בחזקת בתולה ונמצאת בעולה כתובתה מנה הלכך ע"כ מוכת עץ דמתני' ר"מ היא דאמר מאתים והוא אומר דרוסת איש את ואין לך אלא מנה דאי רבנן היא לא טענה אלא מנה מאי איכא בין טענה דידיה לטענה דידה במנה טענה לו ומנה מודה לה ופי' [המורה] סבר לה דלעיל סבר לה תנא דמתני' דאילו ר' יוחנן לא שביק רבנן ועביד כר"מ ור"א סבר במנה ולא כלום סבר לה כרבנן דאמרי בין הכיר בה בין לא הכיר בה כתובתה מנה וכנסה בחזקת בתולה ונמצאת בעולה אין לה כלום בשלמא ר"א לא אמר כר"י דקא מוקי לה כרבנן פי' במנה ולא כלום: היינו דקתני תרי בבא במתני' גבי פלוגתא דממונא היא אומרת משארסתני נאנסתי וכו' והוא אומר לא כי והיה מקחי מקח טעות ומקח טעות לגמרי משמע ואין לה כלום אלא ר"י מ"ט לא אמר כר"א קסבר כנסה בחזקת בתולה ונמצאת בעולה יש לה כתובה מנה הכא הוא אומר מנה והיא אומרת מנה מאי איכא בין טענתיה לטענתה והלכתא כר"א דקיימי רבא ורב אשי כוותיה דכנסה בחזקת בתולה ונמצאת בעולה אין לה כלום כדכתיבנא לעיל ובמוכת עץ נמי הלכתא כרבנן דאמרי מנה: **מתני'** ראוה מדברת עם א' מה טיבו של זה איש פלוני וכהן הוא ר"ג ור"א אומרים נאמנת ור"י אומר לא מפיה אנו חיין אלא ה"ז בחזקת בעולה לנתין ולממזר עד שתביא ראיה לדבריה היתה מעוברת מה טיבו של עובר זה מאיש פלוני וכהן הוא ר"ג ור"א אומרים נאמנת ור"י אומר לא מפיה אנו חיין אלא ה"ז בחזקת מעוברת מנתין וממזר עד שתביא ראיה לדבריה: וכהן הוא פי' מיוחס ולא כהן ממש שאינה נאמנת להחזיק העובר בחזקת כהן אלא בחזקת כשר שאם הוא בת תנשא לכהונה: מאי מדברת זעירא אמר נסתרה ואע"פ שלא ראוה שנבעלה פסולה לכהונה לר"י כדלקמן שמעלה עשו ביוחסין ור"א אמר נבעלה בשלמא לזעירא היינו דקתני מדברת אלא לר"א מאי מדברת לישנא מעליא כדכתיב אכלה ומחתה פיה וגו' פי' נקט תשמיש בלשון אכילה בשלמא לזעירי היינו דקתני תרתי מדברת ומעוברת פי' מדברת להודיע כחו דר"י דאפילו בעדי יחוד בלבד אסורה היא לכהן משום דמעלה עשו ביוחסין ומעוברת להודיע כחו דר"ג אלא לר"א תרתי למה לי פי' לתני מדברת וכ"ש מעוברת. חדא להכשיר בה וחדא להכשיר בבתה דאתמר ר"י אמר לדברי המכשיר בה מכשיר בבתה לדברי הפוסל בה פוסל בבתה ור"א אומר אף לדברי המכשיר בה פוסל בבתה דבשלמא איהי אית לה חזקה דכשרות פי' מעיקרא ואוקמה אחזקה ולא תפסלנה מספק אבל בתה לית לה חזקה דכשרות והלכתא כר' יוחנן דהוא רביה דר"א שאין הלכה כתלמיד במקום הרב ותו דקאי כאבא שאול דתנן בעשרה יוחסין אבא שאול היה קורא לשתוקי בדוקי ואמרי' בגמ' מאי בדוקי שבודקין את אמו ואי אמרה לכשר נבעלתי נאמנת ואע"ג דאיכא רוב פסולים אצלה וא"ר הל' כאבא שאול: א"ל ר"פ לאביי לזעירי דאמר נסתרה ואר"י דלא מהימנא הא דאמר רב מלקין על היחוד

תורה אור

אוֹ לְחוּרְבָּה, וְאָמְרוּ לָהּ: "מַה טִּיבוֹ שֶׁל אִישׁ זֶה?" "כֹּהֵן הוּא, וּבֶן אֲחִי אַבָּא הוּא". רַבָּן גַּמְלִיאֵל וְר"א אוֹמְרִים: נֶאֱמֶנֶת. רַבִּי יְהוֹשֻׁעַ אוֹמֵר: לֹא מִפִּיהָ אָנוּ חַיִּין, אֶלָּא הֲרֵי זוֹ בְּחֶזְקַת בְּעוּלָה לְנָתִין וּלְמַמְזֵר, עַד שֶׁתָּבִיא רְאָיָה לִדְבָרֶיהָ. בִּשְׁלָמָא לִזְעֵירִי — הַיְינוּ דְּקָתָנֵי תַּרְתֵּי, "לְסֵתֶר אוֹ לְחוּרְבָּה". אֶלָּא לְרַב אַסִּי, דְּאָמַר נִבְעֲלָה — תַּרְתֵּי לָמָּה לִי? חֲדָא קָתָנֵי, לְסֵתֶר דְּחוּרְבָּה. וְהָא "לְסֵתֶר אוֹ לְחוּרְבָּה" קָתָנֵי! חֲדָא לְחוּרְבָּה דְּמָתָא, וַחֲדָא לְחוּרְבָּה דְּדַבְרָא. וּצְרִיכִי, דְּאִי אַשְׁמְעִינַן חוּרְבָּה דְּמָתָא — בְּהָא קָמַכְשַׁר רַבָּן גַּמְלִיאֵל, מִשּׁוּם דְּרוֹב כְּשֵׁרִים אֶצְלָהּ. אֲבָל לְחוּרְבָּה דְּדַבְרָא, דְּרוֹב פְּסוּלִין אֶצְלָהּ — אֵימָא מוֹדֶה לֵיהּ לְרַבִּי יְהוֹשֻׁעַ. וְאִי אַשְׁמְעִינַן בְּהַהִיא — בְּהַהִיא קָאָמַר רַבִּי יְהוֹשֻׁעַ, אֲבָל בְּהָא — אֵימָא מוֹדֶה לְר"ג, צְרִיכָא. מֵיתִיבֵי: *זוֹ עֵדוּת שֶׁהָאִשָּׁה כְּשֵׁרָה לָהּ, וְרַבִּי יְהוֹשֻׁעַ אוֹמֵר: אֵינָהּ נֶאֱמֶנֶת. אָמַר לָהֶם ר"י: אִי אַתֶּם מוֹדִים [א]בִּשְׁבוּיָה שֶׁנִּשְׁבֵּית וְיֵשׁ לָהּ עֵדִים שֶׁנִּשְׁבֵּית וְהִיא אוֹמֶרֶת "טְהוֹרָה אֲנִי", שֶׁאֵינָהּ נֶאֱמֶנֶת? אָמְרוּ לוֹ: אֲבָל. וּמָה הֶפְרֵשׁ יֵשׁ בֵּין זוֹ לָזוֹ? לָזוֹ — יֵשׁ עֵדִים, וְלָזוֹ — אֵין לָהּ עֵדִים. אָמַר לָהֶם: אַף לָזוֹ יֵשׁ עֵדִים, שֶׁהֲרֵי כְּרֵיסָהּ בֵּין שִׁנֶּיהָ! אָמְרוּ לוֹ: רוֹב גּוֹיִם פְּרוּצִים בַּעֲרָיוֹת הֵם. אָמַר לָהֶן: *אֵין אַפּוֹטְרוֹפּוֹס לַעֲרָיוֹת. בד"א — בְּעֵדוּת אִשָּׁה בְּגוּפָהּ, אֲבָל עֵדוּת אִשָּׁה בְּבִתָּהּ — דִּבְרֵי הַכֹּל הַוָּלָד שְׁתוּקִי. מַאי קָאָמַר לְהוּ וּמַאי קָמַהְדְּרִי לֵיהּ? הָכִי קָאָמְרִי לֵיהּ: הֲשֵׁבוֹתָנוּ עַל הַמְעוּבֶּרֶת, מַה תְּשִׁיבֵנוּ עַל הַמְדַבֶּרֶת? אָמַר לָהֶם: מְדַבֶּרֶת הַיְינוּ שְׁבוּיָה. אָמְרוּ לוֹ: שָׁאנֵי שְׁבוּיָה דְּרוֹב גּוֹיִם פְּרוּצִים בַּעֲרָיוֹת הֵם. אָמַר לָהֶם: הָא נַמִי, כֵּיוָן דְּאִיסְתַּתַּר — אֵין אַפּוֹטְרוֹפּוֹס לַעֲרָיוֹת. קָתָנֵי מִיהַת תַּרְתֵּי, מְדַבֶּרֶת וּמְעוּבֶּרֶת, תְּיוּבְתָּא דְּרַב אַסִּי! תְּיוּבְתָּא. וְתִיפּוֹק לֵיהּ דְּהָתָם רוֹב פְּסוּלִין אֶצְלָהּ, וְהָכָא רוֹב כְּשֵׁרִין אֶצְלָהּ! מְסַיֵּיעַ לֵיהּ לְרַבִּי יְהוֹשֻׁעַ בֶּן לֵוִי, דְּאָמַר רַבִּי יְהוֹשֻׁעַ בֶּן לֵוִי: לְדִבְרֵי הַמַּכְשִׁיר — מַכְשִׁיר אֲפִילּוּ בְּרוֹב פְּסוּלִין, לְדִבְרֵי הַפּוֹסֵל — פּוֹסֵל אֲפִילּוּ בְּרוֹב כְּשֵׁרִים. א"ר יוֹחָנָן: *[ב]לְדִבְרֵי הַמַּכְשִׁיר בָּהּ — מַכְשִׁיר בְּבִתָּהּ, לְדִבְרֵי הַפּוֹסֵל בָּהּ — פּוֹסֵל בְּבִתָּהּ. וְרַבִּי אֶלְעָזָר אוֹמֵר: לְדִבְרֵי הַמַּכְשִׁיר בָּהּ — פּוֹסֵל בְּבִתָּהּ. אָמַר רַבָּה: מ"ט דר"א? בִּשְׁלָמָא אִיהִי — אִית לָהּ חֲזָקָה דְּכַשְׁרוּת, בִּתָּהּ — לֵית לָהּ חֲזָקָה דְּכַשְׁרוּת. אֵיתִיבֵיהּ ר"א לְרַבִּי יוֹחָנָן: בד"א — בְּעֵדוּת אִשָּׁה בְּגוּפָהּ. אֲבָל עֵדוּת אִשָּׁה בְּבִתָּהּ — דִּבְרֵי הַכֹּל הַוָּלָד שְׁתוּקִי. מַאי לָאו — שְׁתוּקִי וּפָסוּל? לָא, שְׁתוּקִי וְכָשֵׁר. וּמִי אִיכָּא שְׁתוּקִי כָּשֵׁר? אִין, כִּדִשְׁמוּאֵל, דְּאָמַר שְׁמוּאֵל: *עֲשָׂרָה כֹּהֲנִים עוֹמְדִים, וּפֵירַשׁ אֶחָד מֵהֶם וּבָעַל — הַוָּלָד שְׁתוּקִי. מַאי שְׁתוּקִי? אִילֵימָא שֶׁמְּשַׁתְּקִין אוֹתוֹ מִנִּכְסֵי אָבִיו — פְּשִׁיטָא, וּמִי יָדְעִינַן אֲבוּהּ מַנּוּ? [ג]אֶלָּא שֶׁמְּשַׁתְּקִין אוֹתוֹ מִדִּין כְּהוּנָּה, דִּכְתִיב: "°וְהָיְתָה לוֹ וּלְזַרְעוֹ אַחֲרָיו בְּרִית (במדבר כה) כְּהֻנַּת עוֹלָם" — מִי שֶׁזַּרְעוֹ מְיוּחָס אַחֲרָיו, יָצָא זֶה שֶׁאֵין זַרְעוֹ מְיוּחָס אַחֲרָיו. [ד]הַהוּא אָרוּס וַאֲרוּסָתוֹ דַּאֲתוֹ לְקַמֵּיהּ דְּרַב יוֹסֵף, הִיא אָמְרָה: מִינֵּיהּ, וְהוּא אָמַר: אִין

רש"י

לְחוּרְבָּה. סְתָמָא לִבְעִילָה, שֶׁהוּא מָקוֹם לִזְנוּת. חוּרְבָּה דְּמָתָא. סְתָם בְּעִילָתָהּ מֵאֶחָד מִבְּנֵי הָעִיר. וְאִיכָּא לְמֵימַר בְּעִיר שֶׁרוּבָּהּ יִשְׂרָאֵל כְּשֵׁרִים קָאָמַר. דְּדַבְרָא. סָפֵק אֶחָד מִסּוֹף הָעוֹלָם בָּא לְכָאן. וְרוֹב הָעוֹלָם גּוֹיִם הֵם, וּפוֹסְלִים אִשָּׁה בְּבִיאָתָם לִכְהוּנָּה, כִּדְאָמַר בִּיבָמוֹת (דף מה.) וּבְקִדּוּשִׁין (דף עה:): יָלְאוּ גּוֹי וְעֶבֶד שֶׁאֵין לוֹ אַלְמָנוּת וְגֵירוּשִׁין בָּהּ. זוֹ עֵדוּת שֶׁהָאִשָּׁה. עַצְמָהּ כְּשֵׁרָה לוֹמַר: לְכָשֵׁר נִבְעַלְתִּי. אֵינָהּ נֶאֱמֶנֶת. לִינָּשֵׂא לְכֹהֵן. אָמְרוּ לוֹ אֲבָל. הֵן, כְּמוֹ "אֲבָל שָׂרָה אִשְׁתְּךָ" (בראשית יז) דִּמְתַרְגְּמִינַן: בְּקוּשְׁטָא. וּמַה הֶפְרֵשׁ בֵּין זוֹ לָזוֹ. ר' יְהוֹשֻׁעַ קָאָמַר לָהּ. לָזוֹ יֵשׁ עֵדִים. שֶׁנִּבְעֲלָה, דְּכֵיוָן דְּנִשְׁבֵּית לְבֵין הַגּוֹיִם, וְהֵם פְּרוּצִים בַּעֲרָיוֹת, כּוּלָּנוּ עֵדִים שֶׁנִּבְעֲלָה. וְלָזוֹ אֵין עֵדִים. שֶׁנִּבְעֲלָה, שֶׁלֹּא רָאוּהָ אֶלָּא מְדַבֶּרֶת, וּמִיגּוֹ דְּאִי בָּעֲיָא אָמְרָה לֹא נִבְעַלְתִּי, כִּי אָמְרָה נַמִי לְכָשֵׁר נִבְעַלְתִּי — מְהֵימְנָא. אַף לָזוֹ. כְּלוֹמַר, אַף כָּאן יֵשׁ אַחַת שֶׁיֵּשׁ לָהּ עֵדִים, וְאַתֶּם חוֹלְקִים עָלַי, בִּהְיוֹתָהּ מְעוּבֶּרֶת. אָמְרוּ לֵיהּ כו'. לְקַמֵּיהּ מְפָרֵשׁ מַאי קָא מְהַדְּרֵי לֵיהּ עַל מַאי דְּקָאָמַר לְהוּ. אֵין אַפּוֹטְרוֹפּוֹס כו'. [תוספתא סוף פרק א] לְקַמָּן מְפָרֵשׁ. בד"א. דְּנֶאֱמֶנֶת לְר"ג. בְּעֵדוּת אִשָּׁה בְּגוּפָהּ. כְּלוֹמַר, לְהַכְשִׁיר אֶת עַצְמָהּ לִכְהוּנָּה, דְּלָא מַחְזְקִינַן לָהּ בְּנִבְעֲלָה לְפָסוּל. מַאי קָאָמַר לְהוּ כו'. כְּלוֹמַר, מַאי קָאָמַר לְהוּ אִיהוּ, דְּקָא מְהַדְּרִי לֵיהּ אִינְהוּ רוֹב גּוֹיִם פְּרוּצִים בַּעֲרָיוֹת. כְּלוּם תְּשׁוּבָה הִיא זוֹ עַל מַה שֶּׁאָמַר לָהֶם אַף לָזוֹ יֵשׁ לָהּ עֵדִים? [חולין יא: נדה לג.] אֵין לְךָ פָּרוּץ גָּדוֹל מִזֶּה, דְּקָחָזֵינַן דְּנִתְעַבְּרָה מִמֶּנּוּ. הֲשֵׁבוֹתָנוּ עַל הַמְעוּבֶּרֶת. תְּשׁוּבָה גְּמוּרָה וְנָכוֹנָה. מְדַבֶּרֶת הַיְינוּ שְׁבוּיָה. מַה מְּדַבֶּרֶת אֵין לָהּ עֵדִים — אַף שְׁבוּיָה אֵין לָהּ עֵדִים בִּבְעִילָה, וְאַתֶּם מַחֲזִיקִים אוֹתָהּ כְּנִבְעֲלָה. פְּרוּצִים בַּעֲרָיוֹת. וְהָא וַדַּאי נִבְעֲלָה. אֵין אַפּוֹטְרוֹפּוֹס לַעֲרָיוֹת. אֵין אַתֶּם יְכוֹלִים לִהְיוֹת לָהּ אַפּוֹטְרוֹפּוֹס, לוֹמַר: לֹא נִבְעֲלָה. וְתִיפּוֹק לֵיהּ וכו'. לְרַבִּי יְהוֹשֻׁעַ פָּרֵיךְ: נְהִי נַמִי דְּאֵין אַפּוֹטְרוֹפּוֹס לַעֲרָיוֹת, תֵּיפּוֹק לֵיהּ דְּלָא דָּמֵי לִשְׁבוּיָה, דְּהָתָם רוֹב פְּסוּלִין כו'. מַכְשִׁיר אֲפִי' בְּרוֹב פְּסוּלִים. דְּאָמְרִינַן: אוֹקְמָהּ אַחֲזָקָהּ. וְעַל רוֹב פְּסוּלִים, שֶׁהָיוּ מַכְשִׁירִים אוֹתָהּ, הֵבִיא הוּא לָהֶם רְאָיָה מִן הַשְּׁבוּיָה. אִית לָהּ [קדושין עד.] חֲזָקָה דְּכַשְׁרוּת. וְי"ל: אִשָּׁה זוֹ בְּחֶזְקַת כַּשְׁרוּת עוֹמֶדֶת, וּמִסָּפֵק אַתָּה בָּא לְפוֹסְלָהּ — אַל תְּפַסְּלֶנָּה מִסָּפֵק. לָא שְׁתוּקִי וְכָשֵׁר. כְּלוֹמַר, שְׁתוּקִי הוּא בְּמִקְצָת, שֶׁאִם כֹּהֵן הָיָה הַבּוֹעֵל וְהָעוּבָּר יִהְיֶה זָכָר — מְשַׁתְּקִין אוֹתוֹ מִדִּין כְּהוּנָּה, כִּדְלְקַמָּן. אֲבָל כָּשֵׁר הוּא לְיוֹחֲסִין, שֶׁאִם נְקֵבָה הִיא — תִּינָּשֵׂא לִכְהוּנָּה, וְאִם זָכָר הוּא — בִּתּוֹ וְאַלְמְנָתוֹ כְּשֵׁרוֹת לִכְהוּנָּה. וּפֵירַשׁ אֶחָד מֵהֶן. וְאֵין יָדוּעַ אֵיזֶה הוּא. הַוָּלָד שְׁתוּקִי. וְאַע"פ שֶׁבָּרוּר לָנוּ שֶׁמִּכֹּהֵן (יבמות ק.) כָּשֵׁר בָּא. וְהַאי שְׁתוּקִי עַל כָּרְחָךְ כָּשֵׁר לְיוֹחֲסִין, וְאִם נְקֵבָה הִיא — רְאוּיָה לְכֹהֵן, וְקָרֵי לֵיהּ שְׁתוּקִי. מִדִּין כְּהוּנָּה. שֶׁלֹּא יַעֲבוֹד עֲבוֹדָה, וְלֹא יֹאכַל תְּרוּמָה. מְיוּחָס אַחֲרָיו. שֶׁאָנוּ יוֹדְעִין מִי אָבִיו.

תוספות

השבתנו על המעוברת. פי': לדידן ניחא, דאשה מזנה בודקת ומזנה, ולא דמיא לשבויה. אלא לדידך, דלית לך הך סברא — תינח מעוברת, אבל מדברת אפילו לפי דבריך יש הפרש, דלזו יש עדים ולזו אין עדים, ואיכא מיגו! אמר להם: מדברת היינו שבויה, וכמו ששבויה אין נאמנת לומר לא נבעלתי — ה"נ מדברת, כדמסיק: לפי שאין אפוטרופוס לעריות. ומיהו, פי' זה לא יתכן למאי דפרישית לעיל, דלר' יהושע נאמנת לומר לא נבעלתי. ופר"י בדוחק: מדברת היינו שבויה, דכמו *ששבויה בחזקת בעולה — כך מדברת בחזקת בעולה, לענין שאם אמרה לכשר נבעלתי שאינה נאמנת במיגו, לפי שיראה לומר לא נבעלתי. ולהכי אהני דאין אפוטרופוס לעריות דלא חשבינן ליה מיגו. **מסייע** ליה לר' יהושע בן לוי. הקשה ר"ת: אכתי תיפוק ליה, דהתם בשבויה — כל פסולים, והכא בחורבה דדברא — רובא! ותירץ: דרוב ככל. וליכא למימר, במדברת דליכא אלא רוב איכא למימר סמוך מיעוטא לחזקה, ואיתרע לה רובא, דאפילו אית להו סמוך מיעוטא לחזקה לר"ג ור' יהושע — מ"מ לא הוי אלא פלגא ופלגא, ודין הוא שתאסר מספק, דספק איסורא לחומרא. ולא דמי לתינוק שנמצא בצד העיסה בפרק "עשרה יוחסין" (קדושין דף פ. ושם) דמטהרין מטעם סמוך מיעוטא לחזקה, דאם אמרו ספק טומאה לטהר יאמרו ספק איסור להתיר?! כדאמרינן פרק "כיסוי הדם" (חולין דף פו:). **מכשיר** אפילו ברוב פסולים. והא דקאמרינן בפ' "עשרה יוחסין" (קידושין עד. ושם) גבי אבא שאול היה קורא לשתוקי בדוקי, ומפרש בגמרא שבודקין אמו, ואומרת: לכשר נבעלתי. ופריך: כמאן – כר"ג, תנינא חדא זימנא: היתה מעוברת כו', פי': והוה ליה למתני וכן אמר אבא שאול? וכן פי' שם בקונטרס. ומשני: דאבא שאול עדיפא מר"ג, דאי מהתם — הוה אמינא ברוב כשרים אבל כו', אע"ג דאמרי' הכא דר"ג מכשיר אפילו ברוב פסולין — אבא שאול קאי אמתני', וממתני' לא משמע מידי דאיירי ברוב פסולין. והא דפריך התם לעיל, למאי דהוה בעי למימר דאבא שאול אתא להכשיר בבתה: ניחא למ"ד לדברי המכשיר בה פוסל בבתה, אבל למ"ד מכשיר בבתה — מאי איכא למימר? התם פריך שפיר, דאפי' לזעירי לשון המשנה דקתני: מה טיבו של עובר זה, משמע דאתא להכשיר בבתה. **פשיטא** מי ידעינן אבוה מנו. הכא לא בעי לשנויי לא צריכא דאי תפס, כדמשני בפרק "עשרה יוחסין" (שם דף עה. ושם) גבי ארוסה שעיברה. דהתם רגלים לדבר דמארוס נתעברה, ואיכא למיתלי ביה טפי מבאינש דעלמא. **בעינן** זרעו מיוחס אחריו. והא דאמר ב"החולץ" (יבמות דף לז.): ראשון ראוי להיות כ"ג, גבי ספק בן תשע לראשון – בפרק "נושאין על האנוסה" (שם דף ק:) פריך לה, ומשני: זרעו מיוחס אחריו – דרבנן, וקרא אסמכתא בעלמא הוא, וכי גזור רבנן – בזנות. בנישואין לא גזור.

[**ההוא** ארוס וארוסתו. והא דאמר ב"עשרה יוחסין" (קדושין דף עה.), איתמר: הבא על ארוסתו בבית חמיו, רב אמר: הולד ממזר, ושמואל אמר: הולד שתוקי – כשלא בדקו את אמו. דאי כשבדקו – קשיא דשמואל אדשמואל. דהכא אמר שמואל דנאמנת, דהלכה כרבן גמליאל דנאמנת, והתם קאמר איפוך, שמואל אמר: הולד ממזר. וכן משמע, דבמסקנא משני התם: לעולם לא תיפוך כו'. ומפרש: מאי שתוקי – שבודקין את אמו, ואומרת לכשר נבעלתי. ואם תאמר: אכתי לשמואל, דהתם משמע דוקא בבא על ארוסתו בבית חמיו מהני בדיקה, והכא משמע אפילו כי לא מודה – אמר שמואל דנאמנת, כרבן גמליאל! ויש לומר: דהא דנקט בא – היינו משום רבותא דרב נקטיה, דאפילו הכי אמר הולד ממזר. אי נמי, התם הוא דבעינן בא – משום דאיירי בדליכא מעלמא, כדאמר רבא ביבמות בשלהי "אלמנה לכהן גדול": מסתברא מילתא דרב בדליכא מעלמא, והכא בדלא דיימא מעלמא מיירי. ועוד: דבכל הספרים גרס בקדושין: ארוסה שעיברה, והשתא דוקא קאמר שבודקין. אבל – א"נ בדיקה. ומיהו, קשה ללישנא קמא ביבמות בסוף פ' "אלמנה", דפליגי רב ושמואל בבא, ומסיק התם אביי דאע"ג דלא דיימא מעלמא פליגי, דדלמא מדאפקרה נפשה לגבי ארוס מפקרה נפשה לגבי עלמא, הא אמר הכא חדא דקא מודה, ומשמע דכשר אפילו לר' יהושע, ובא כמודה דמי

עין משפט נר מצוה

פב א מיי' פי"ח מהל' איסורי ביאה הלכה כא סמג לאוין קכא טור ש"ע אה"ע סימן ז ס"ד:

פג ב מיי' פט"ו שם הלכה יא סמג שם טוש"ע שם סי' ו סעיף יז:

ואע"ג דמיעוט עובדי כוכבים אין פרוצים מ"מ חשבינן לה ודאי בעולה מן הרוב הפרוצים. ת"י:

פד ג מיי' פ"כ שם הל' כ סמג לאוין קכב טוש"ע שם סימן ג סעיף ט:

פה ד מיי' פט"ו שם הלכה יז טוש"ע שם סימן ד סעיף כז [וברב אלפס עוד ביבמות פ"ז דף כז ע"א]:

תוספות רי"ד

היחוד ואין אוסרים על היחוד לימא דלא כר"י פי' דמשום יחוד מחזיק לה כנבעלה פי' מלקין מכות מרדות לאשת איש שנתייחדה עם א' אבל אין אוסרין אותה על בעלה בעידי יחוד אלא היכא דקינא לה מעיקרא בפני שנים ואמר לה אל תסתרי עם איש פלוני אם נסתרה עמו היא סוטה האמורה בתורה והיא אסורה לו עד שתובדר במים המאררים אבל בלא קינוי מעיקרא אינה נאסרת לו בסתירה בלחוד. ומהדר מעלה עשו ביוחסין פי' דלא אסרה ר"י אלא אם היתה פנויה שלא תנשא לכהן דאמרינן דלמא נבעלה לפסול לה אבל לבעלה לא אסרה ואפי' אם היה בעלה כהן. אר"י א"ש הלכה כר"ג אריב"ל לדברי המכשיר מכשיר אפילו ברוב פסולים לדברי הפוסל פוסל אפי' ברוב כשרים: ההוא ארוס וארוסתו דאתו לקמיה דר"י היא אומרת מיני' והוא אומר

פו א ב מיי' פט"ו מהל' איסורי ביאה הלכה יח ופי"ח הלכה יג, יד סמג לאוין קכא טוש"ע אה"ע סימן ו סעיף יז [וברב אלפס עוד ביבמות פ"ז דף כ"ז]:

פז ג ד ה מיי' פי"ט שם הלכה יב טור אה"ע סימן ו וש"ע אה"ע סימן ג סעיף ה.

אין, מינאי. אמר רב יוסף: למאי ניחוש לה? חדא – דהא קא מודה, ועוד: הא *אמר רב יהודה אמר שמואל: הלכה כרבן גמליאל. א]אמר ליה אביי: *ובהא, כי לא מודה מכשר רבן גמליאל? והאמר ליה שמואל לרב יהודה: שיננא! אהלכה כר"ג, ואת לא תעביד עובדא עד דאיכא רוב כשרין אצלה. והכא – רוב פסולין אצלה! וליטעמיך, תקשי לך היא גופא: הלכה – ואת לא תעביד עובדא?! אלא מאי אית לך למימר: בהא – לכתחלה, הא – דיעבד, והא נמי, כדיעבד דמי. רמי ליה אביי *לרבא: ומי אמר רבי יהושע אינה נאמנת? ורמינהו: *העיד ר' יהושע ורבי יהודה בן בתירא געל אלמנת עיסה שהיא כשרה לכהונה! א"ל: הכי השתא! התם – אשה נישאת – בודקת ונישאת, הכא – אשה מזנה – בודקת ומזנה?! אמר רבא: דרבי יהושע אדרבי יהושע קשיא, דרבן גמליאל אדרבן גמליאל לא קשיא? והא קתני סיפא, אמר להן רבן גמליאל: קבלנו עדותכם, דאבל מה נעשה שהרי גזר רבן יוחנן בן זכאי שלא להושיב בית דין על כך, שהכהנים שומעין לכם לרחק אבל לא לקרב! אלא אמר רבא: דרבן גמליאל אדרבן גמליאל לא קשיא; התם – ברי, הכא – שמא. דר' יהושע אדר' יהושע נמי לא קשיא; התם – חד ספיקא, הכא – תרי ספיקי. הלכך, לרבן גמליאל – אלים ליה ברי, דאפילו בחד ספיקא נמי מכשיר. וקיל ליה שמא, דאפילו בספק ספיקא – נמי פסיל. לרבי יהושע אלים ליה חד ספיקא, דאפילו בברי נמי פסיל וקיל ליה ספק ספיקא, דאפילו בשמא – נמי מכשיר. תנו רבנן: *איזוהי אלמנת עיסה – הכל שאין בה לא משום ממזרות, ולא משום נתינות, ולא משום עבדי מלכים. אמר רבי מאיר: שמעתי

רש"י

אין מינאי. אמת, ממני הוא. ובהא כי לא מודי כו'. דקא אמרת ועוד. ארוסה הכל פסולין אצלה חוץ מן הארוס. הא לכתחלה. אם בא כהן לימלך לבית דין, לא שרינן ליה לכונסה אא"כ היו רוב כשרים אצלה. דיעבד. אם נשאה כהן ולא נמלך, לא מפקינן לה מיניה. והא נמי כדיעבד דמי. שנתעברה ואתה בא לפסול העובר ולאוסרה על הארוס, דאם אין אתה מאמינה הרי אתה מוציאה מבעלה. מי אמר רבי יהושע אינה נאמנת. אלמא לא מוקמינן לה אחזקה. עיסה. לשון ספק. על אלמנת עיסה. שהיא באה מכח ספק חלל, כדלקמן, שנטמע בה ספק חלל, כגון שנזרק בעל אמו הראשון לה גט, ספק קרוב לו ספק קרוב לה, ומת. ונמצאת זו ספק גרושה ספק אלמנה, ונשאה כהן והוליד ממנה בן – זהו ספק חלל. והעיד ר"י על אלמנתו של זה שהיא כשרה. אלמא מוקמינן לה אחזקה, ואמרינן: אל תפסילנה לזו מספק, כלומר שמא בעלה חלל היה. בודקת וניסת. ו"י שבדקה אחר אותן גירושין, והוגד לה שקרוב לו היו, ולא נתגרשה כלל, ואלמנה היתה, וכשרה לכהן. בודקת ומזנה. בתמיה. דרבן גמליאל אדרבן גמליאל לא קשיא. בתמיה, דלא חיישת לתרוציהו. הא קתני סיפא. דההיא אמר להן כו'. קבלנו עדותכם. נאמנים אתם לנו שכך שמעתם. על כך. להתירה לכהונה, דודאי אסורה. שהכהנים שומעין לכם. אם תאמרו אסורה. אבל לא לקרב. אם תאמרו מותרת. התם ברי. מתניתין, היא אומרת: ברי לי שלכשר נבעלתי. הכא. גבי אלמנת עיסה, כי היכי דלדידן מספקא לן, לדידה נמי מספקא לה, וליכא למימר בה: ברי ושמא – ברי עדיף. חד ספיקא. מתניתין חד ספיקא היא – ספק נבעלה לכשר, ספק נבעלה לפסול; שהרי לא בא זה לפנינו, ואילו בא – שמא היינו מכירים בו שהוא פסול. הכא. גבי אלמנת עיסה. תרי ספיקי. אמו של ספק חלל זה – בה נולד הספק, והיא עצמה לא נאסרה אלא מספק. וזו שבאה מחמת בנה קרי לה ספק ספיקא. ומדברי רבי יוסף טוב עלם מצאתי: [אלמנת עיסה] – אשה שיש בבעלה ספק ספיקא, כגון שנתגרשה אמו מבעלה הראשון, ספק קרוב לו ספק קרוב לה, ומת בתוך שלשה חדשים, ונשאת לכהן תוך שלשה חדשים, וילדה את זה; ספק שהוא בן תשעה לראשון וכשר, ואפילו היתה מגורשת, שהרי קודם לגט נתעברה, והוא ישראל ולא כהן. וספק בן שבעה לאחרון, ואם תמצא לומר של כהן הוא, והרי הוא ספק חלל. הרי ספק ספיקא: שמא אינו בנו של כהן, ואת"ל בנו הוא – שמא לא היתה אמו גרושה אלא אלמנה. ולהכי קרי לה עיסה, שיש בה עירובי ספיקות הרבה, כעיסה זו שהיא בלוסה. והא דאמרינן לקמן "כל שנטמע בה ספק חלל" – היינו פירושה: כל שנטמעו בה ספק עירובי חלל. נטמע. נתערב. איזוהי אלמנת עיסה. שהעידו עליה שהיא כשרה. כל שאין. בעירובי ספיקותיה לא ספק ממזרות ולא ספק נתינות ולא ספק עבדי מלכים, אלא ספק חלל לבדו. מש"ה נקט עבדי מלכים, משום עבדי שלמה *שהיו עשירים ובעלי זרוע ונשאו להם בנות ישראל. וכגון זרעו של הורדוס שהיה' עבד לבית חשמונאי, וגברה ידו ומלך. שמעתי

תוספות

דמי, דהא מודה דהכא אינו אלא שהיה אומר שבא עליה, דפשיטא שלא היה מזנב אחריה לאורבה שלא תזנה, ובין לרב ובין לשמואל אסור הוא בבת ישראל, דשתוקי דקאמר לשמואל היינו – דאסור בבת ישראל לכולהו לישני דבפרק בתרא דקדושין! וללישנא דבדוקי נמי קשה טפי, דמשמע דאפילו ע"י בדיקת האם לא מיתכשר אלא לר"ג, אבל לרבי יהושע לא, והכא אמר דהא קא מודה, וכשר לכ"ע! ושמא יש לחלק: דבא דהתם – היינו שפעם אחת בא עליה, אבל מודה דהכא דקאמר מיניה – היינו שבא עליה ביאות הרבה, והיה רגיל אצלה תמיד, וכדאמרינן: רוב בעילות הלך אחר הבעל. **חדא** דקא מודה. וללישנא קמא דיבמות – דלא דיימא מעלמא, ולאיכא דאמרי – דאפילו דיימא מעלמא, כיון דקא מודה – בתריה דידיה שדינן ליה. **חדא** דקא מודה. מלינן לפרש דאיירי לענין לאוסרה על הארוס, וה"פ: חדא דקא מודה – הלכך אינה נאסרת עליו, ועוד הא רב יהודה כו', לא קאמר ועוד אפילו לא מודה, דאם אינו מודה – פשיטא דנאסרת עליו. אלא כלומר, אפילו כי ליכא טעמא דמודה, כגון לאביי דס"פ "אלמנה": מדאפקרה נפשה לגבי ארוס מפקרה נפשה נמי לגבי עלמא – אפ"ה אינה נאסרת עליו משום דנאמנת כר"ג, כן פי' לנו ר"י. ואי אפשר להעמידה. דלפי דבריו, אם כן הא דאמר אביי "מדאפקרה נפשה" – היינו בשלא בדקו את אמו. וזה אינו, דהא אפלוגתא דרב ושמואל קאי, דמוקמי בקדושין מאי שתוקי – בדוקי! ולמאי דגרסינן בקדושין: ארוסה שעיברה – לא קשה מידי. על כן צריך לפרש דהכא לא איירי לאוסרה עליו, אלא לענין להכשיר את הולד. והשתא הוי "ועוד" כפשוטו: ועוד, דאפילו לא יודה. ולאו דקאמר דלאו מיניה – דבהא לא מכשיר ר"ג כיון דהוי ברי וברי, כדאמר ברפ"ב, אלא כגון שמת או דליתיה קמן דלישיילוה. והא דחשיב ליה בסמוך דיעבד – לפי שלא היה יכול הולד להינשא לבת ישראל, ואפילו לממזרת אסור, דמדאורייתא כשר הוא, דהאי הוי כדיעבד, הלכה כר"ג]: (מן ד"ה ההוא ארוס עד"כ היה חסר מהתוספות).

אלמנת עיסה. פירש בקונטרס שני פירושין, ושניהם דחוקים. דהא אמרינן לקמן: איזו היא אלמנת עיסה – כל שנטמע בה ספק חלל. *) ומה טימוע שייך במה שנישאת לספק חלל? ועוד: דאין לשון עיסה נופל על אדם אחד, אלא על משפחה שייך לשון עיסה, כדאמרינן (קידושין דף סט:): כל הארצות עיסה לארץ ישראל, וא"י עיסה לבבל. ובתוספתא תניא: מפני מה אמרו עיסה פסולה – מפני ספיקי חללין. ומה ספיקי חללין שייך לאלו הפירושין?! ונראה לר"י ולריב"א: דעיסה קורא המשפחה שנטמע בהם ספק חלל אחד, או הרבה ספיקי חללים. ולהכי חשיב ליה לקמן ספק ספיקא, דכל אחד מבני המשפחה ספק אם הוא אותו ספק שנתערב בהן, אם לאו. ולקמן גרסינן: איזהו עיסה – כל שנטמע בה כו', ולא גרסינן אלמנת. והכי איתא בירושלמי. ואפילו גרסינן אלמנת, כל שנטמע בה – קאי אעיסה. ואם תאמר: דבפרק "עשרה יוחסין" (שם דף עה.) משמע דאפילו מאן דמכשר אלמנת עיסה מודה בבת דפסולה, גבי הא דאמר רב חסדא: הכל מודים באלמנת עיסה שפסולה לכהונה כו', ולאפוקי מהני תנאי, דתנן: העיד רבי יהושע כו', ומה לי אלמנה מה לי בת, דבת נמי הוי ספק ספיקא כמו באלמנה! וי"ל: דבת העיסה אין לה חזקה דכשרות, ואע"ג דבעלמא מקילין בספק ספיקא – הכא מעלה עשו ביוחסין, כי היכי דמצריך לקמן תרי רובי להכשיר אף על גב דבעלמא סגי בחד רובא. **דרבי** יהושע אדר"י לא קשיא. והשתא לא מצי לשנויי דבודקת ונישאת כדמשני לעיל, כיון דהשתא אוקימנא באומרת שמא. **תנו** רבנן איזו היא אלמנת עיסה. קשה לרבינו תם על גרסת הספרים דגרסי אלמנת עיסה, דאם כן אית ליה לרבי יוסי דאלמנת עיסה כשרה, דהא מכשר לקמן שתוק ממזר, וכל שכן דמכשר באלמנת עיסה, כדמוכח הסוגיא. ובפרק "עשרה יוחסין" (ג"ז שם) אמר בהדיא דלרבי יוסי אלמנת עיסה פסולה! לכך מוחק רבינו תם "אלמנת", וגרים: איזוהי עיסה. ולענין בת קתני, וקאי אהאי דתנא בשילהי עדיות: העיסה נאמנת לטהר ולטמא, לרחק ולקרב, לאסור ולהתיר. וה"פ: נאמנת לטהר עצמה בלויה או בשתיקה, למר כדאית ליה ולמר כדאית ליה. לטמא ולטהר – שייך לענין ממזרות ונתינות, כדתנן (קדושין דף עב:) ממזרים ונתינים עתידין ליטהר. לרחק ולקרב – שייך אחללות, כדתנן: הכהנים שומעים לכם לרחק ולא לקרב, וכן לקמן (דף כ.) "וריחקום בני משפחה". ולאסור ולהתיר – שייך אעבדים. והא דפריך בפ"ב (לקמן דף כח:) טמאה וטהורה ס"ד – התם דכייל כל פסולי בחד לישנא, הוה ליה למיתני: משפחה זו כשרה וזו פסולה, אבל אממזרות ונתינות לחודא – שייך שפיר לשון טומאה וטהרה. ונאמנת נקט – משום לטהר לקרב ולהתיר, אע"ג דלטמא ולרחק ולאסור בלויה או בשתיקה לא שייך נאמנות, ועלה קתני בברייתא דהכא: איזו היא עיסה שנאמנת בלויה או בשתיקה ולטהר את הבת – כל שאין בה כו', והכי משמע בתוספתא, דקתני: נאמנת עיסה לטהר ולטמא, לרחק ולקרב, לאסור ולהתיר, ובאלמנת עיסה לא נגעו. והשתא לא קשה דרבי יוסי אדרבי יוסי, דהא דלמכשר רבי יוסי בשתוק ממזר – אגוף העיסה קאי, להכשיר את הבת, אבל במקום שמוזיר אלמנת עיסה להכשיר – דוקא אלמנה, ולא הבת, כדמוכח בקדושין (דף עה.) ושם ולא פוסל רבי יוסי אפילו את האלמנה, כדמוכח נמי בקדושין. ולדברי ר"ת משמע בירושלמי, דקתני: איזוהו עיסה – כל שאין בה לא ממזר ולא נתין ולא עבדי מלכים. רבי מאיר אומר: כל שאין בה אחד מכל אלו בתה כשרה, אלמא דבכשרות דבת מיירי, ולא באלמנה. ומיהו קשה לרשב"א: כיון דהך ברייתא קיימא לפרושי ההיא דסוף עדיות, אם כן רבי מאיר דסבר דחלל בין נווח בין שתק כשר, היכי מפרש הא דקתני לרחק? ואור"י: הא דמכשר ר"מ חלל שותק – הני מילי כשאמרי כן שואלין ממנו אם הוא חלל אם לאו, ולוו, אבל אם לעולם שותק – פשיטא דפסול. והא דקתני דנאמנת לרחק – אם לעולם שותק.

לא

*) [וגם על חלל עצמו אין שייך לשון טימוע]

תוספות רי"ד

אין מינאי הוא אר"י למאי ניחוש לה חדא דהא קא מודי ותו האר"י אמר שמואל הל' כר"ג פי' דכי אומרת מאיש פלוני וכהן הוא נאמנת ואע"ג דאתי ההוא פלוני ומכחיש לה ואמר לא באתי עלי' מעולם היא נאמנת דאי איתא דהיכא דקא מכחיש לה לא מהימנא א"כ אמאי מהימן לה ר"ג מסתמא יבוא אותו פלוני ויאמר אם בא עליה אם לאו אלא ודאי דאע"ג דהוה אתי ומכחיש לה היא נאמנת בין להכשיר בה בין להכשיר בתה והכא נמי אע"ג דאתי ארוס ואמר מעולם לא באתי עליה היא נאמנת להכשיר העובר ולהכשיר עצמה אם תתאלמן אבל לארום ודאי אסורה דשויא אנפשיה חתיכה דאיסו' א"ל אביי ובהא כי לא מודה מי מכשיר ר"ג והא"ל שמואל לר"י שיננא הלכתא כר"ג ואת לא תעביד עובדא [עד] דאיכא רוב כשרים אצלה והכא רוב פסולים אצלה פי' ארוסה הכל פסולין אצלה חוץ מן הארום וליטעמך תיקשי לך היא גופא הלכה ואת לא תעביד עובדא. אלא הא לכתחלה הא דיעבד והכא נמי כדיעבד דמי פי' אם בא כהן לימלך לב"ד לא שרינן ליה לכתחלה אלא א"כ הוי רוב כשרים אצלה והא דיעבד פי' המורה אם נשאה כהן ולא נמלך לא מפקינן לה מיניה והא נמי כדיעבד דמי שנתעברה ואתה בא לפסול העובר ולאסרה על הארום אם אין אתה מאמינה הרי אתה מוציאה מבעלה. ואינו נ"ל דאפי' אם מהימנינן לה ה"מ להכשיר גופה ובתה לכהונה אבל על בעלה לא ומשום דשויתה אנפשיה חתיכה דאיסורא אלא נ"ל כך [פירושו] אי לא מהימנינן לה משוינן לבתה ממזרת ואסורה לבא בקהל ולא דמיא לפנויה שנתעברה דאע"ג דפסיל לה לכהונה לא פסיל לה לקהל דאימר לחלל נבעלה ואסורה לכהן ומותרת לישראל אבל הכא אי מספקת לה דנתעברה מאחר הויא לה ממזרת ומה לי לאפוקי מקהל ומה לי לאפקה מבעלה וכי היכי דדיעבד דהתם אמרת נאמנת הכא נמי נאמנת ומותרת בתה לכהן כדי שלא תוציאנה מקהל והא דר"י אתיא כשמואל דבפרק אלמנה לכ"ג פליגי רב ושמואל בארוסה שעיברה דרב אמר הולד ממזר ושמואל אמר הולד שתוקי ובפרק עשרה יוחסין מפרש' אמילתא דשמואל מאי שתוקי בדוקי' כאבא שאול דבדיק' לאימ' ואי אמרה מארוסה נתעברה

[לעיל יג:]

[עי' תוס' יבמות קטו: ד"ה וכן תוס' וע"ש תוס' ב"מ ע. ד"ה אתא ותוס' לקמן פה: ד"ה ועוד]

[ג"ל לרבה]

קדושין עה. עדיות פ"ח מ"ג

[תוספתא קדושין פ"ה]

[יבמות עז.]

הגהות מהר"ב רנשבורג

א] גמ' א"ל אביי ובהא כי לא מודה מי מכשיר כו'. עיין ב"מ ע ע"א תד"ה אתא מריה וכו'.

עין משפט נר מצוה

פח א מיי' פי"ט מהל' איסורי ביאה הלכה כב טוש"ע אה"ע סימן ג סעיף ד:

[ושמא לא נקיט אלא מאי דאכשר ר"מ ור"ש בן אלעזר פוסל. ת"י.]

שָׁמַעְתִּי כָּל שֶׁאֵין בָּהּ אֶחָד מִכָּל אֵלּוּ — מַשִּׂיאִין לִכְהוּנָּה. ר"ש בֶּן אֶלְעָזָר אוֹמֵר מִשּׁוּם ר"מ, וְכֵן הָיָה ר"ש בֶּן מְנַסְיָא אוֹמֵר כִּדְבָרָיו: אֵיזוֹהִי אַלְמָנַת עִיסָּה — כָּל שֶׁנִּטְמַע בָּהּ סְפֵק חָלָל. מַכִּירִין יִשְׂרָאֵל מַמְזֵרִים שֶׁבֵּינֵיהֶם, וְאֵין מַכִּירִין חֲלָלִין שֶׁבֵּינֵיהֶם. אָמַר מָר: אֵיזוֹהִי אַלְמָנַת עִיסָּה — כָּל שֶׁאֵין בָּהּ לֹא מִשּׁוּם מַמְזֵרוּת, וְלֹא מִשּׁוּם נְתִינוּת, וְלֹא מִשּׁוּם עַבְדֵי מְלָכִים. הָא חָלָל — כָּשֵׁר. מַאי שְׁנָא הָנָךְ — דְּאוֹרַיְיתָא, חָלָל נַמִי דְּאוֹרַיְיתָא! וְתוּ, אָמַר רַבִּי מֵאִיר: שָׁמַעְתִּי כָּל שֶׁאֵין בָּהּ אֶחָד מִכָּל אֵלּוּ מַשִּׂיאִין לִכְהוּנָּה, הַיְינוּ תַּנָּא קַמָּא! וְתוּ, ר"ש בֶּן אֶלְעָזָר אוֹמֵר מִשּׁוּם ר' מֵאִיר, וְכֵן הָיָה ר"ש בֶּן מְנַסְיָא אוֹמֵר כִּדְבָרָיו: אֵיזוֹהִי אַלְמָנַת עִיסָּה — כָּל שֶׁנִּטְמַע בָּהּ סְפֵק חָלָל, מַכִּירִין יִשְׂרָאֵל מַמְזֵרִים שֶׁבֵּינֵיהֶן וְאֵין מַכִּירִין חֲלָלִין שֶׁבֵּינֵיהֶן, וְהָא אָמְרַתְּ רֵישָׁא חָלָל כָּשֵׁר! א"ר יוֹחָנָן: "מַמְזֵר" — צוֹוֵחַ, וְ"חָלָל" — שׁוֹתֵק, אִיכָּא בֵּינַיְיהוּ. תַּנָּא קַמָּא סָבַר: [א]כָּל פָּסוּל דְּקָרוּ לֵיהּ וְשָׁתֵיק — פָּסוּל. וְהָכִי קָאָמַר ת"ק: אֵיזוֹהִי אַלְמָנַת עִיסָּה — כָּל שֶׁאֵין בָּהּ לֹא שְׁתוּק מַמְזֵרוּת, וְלֹא שְׁתוּק נְתִינוּת, וְלֹא שְׁתוּק עַבְדֵי מְלָכִים, וְלֹא שְׁתוּק חָלָל. וְקָאָמַר לֵיהּ ר"מ: הָנָךְ הוּא — דְּקָא פָּסֵיל לֵיהּ בְּקָהָל, אֲבָל שְׁתוּק חָלָל — כָּשֵׁר, וְהָא דְּשָׁתֵיק — מִשּׁוּם דְּלָא אִיכְפַּת לֵיהּ. וְקָאָמַר לֵיהּ ר"ש בֶּן אֶלְעָזָר לְתַנָּא קַמָּא דְּר' מֵאִיר: אִי שְׁמִיעַ לָךְ דְּמַכְשַׁר ר"מ בִּשְׁתִיקָה — לָא דְּקָרוּ לֵיהּ חָלָל וְשָׁתֵיק, אֶלָּא דְּקָרוּ לֵיהּ מַמְזֵר וְשָׁתֵיק, וְהַאי דְּשָׁתֵיק — סָבַר: מַמְזֵר קָלָא אִית לֵיהּ. אֲבָל "מַמְזֵר" וְצוֹוֵחַ, "חָלָל" וְשׁוֹתֵק, פָּסוּל, וְהַאי דְּאִשְׁתִּיק — סָבַר: מִיסְתַּיֵּיהּ דְּלָא מַפְּקֵי לֵיהּ מִקָּהָל. תָּנֵי חֲדָא: ר' יוֹסֵי אוֹמֵר שְׁתוּק מַמְזֵר — כָּשֵׁר, שְׁתוּק חָלָל — פָּסוּל. וְתַנְיָא אִידָךְ: שְׁתוּק חָלָל — כָּשֵׁר, שְׁתוּק מַמְזֵר — פָּסוּל! לָא קַשְׁיָא; הָא — ת"ק אַלִּיבָּא דְּר"מ, הָא — דְּר"ש בֶּן אֶלְעָזָר אַלִּיבָּא דְּר"מ.§

מתני' א"ר יוֹסֵי: מַעֲשֶׂה בְּתִינוֹקֶת שֶׁיָּרְדָה לְמַלְּאוֹת מַיִם מִן הָעַיִן, וְנֶאֶנְסָה, אָמַר רַבִּי יוֹחָנָן בֶּן נוּרִי: אִם רוֹב אַנְשֵׁי הָעִיר מַשִּׂיאִין לִכְהוּנָּה — הֲרֵי זוֹ תִּינָּשֵׂא לִכְהוּנָּה.§

גמ' אֲמַר לֵיהּ רָבָא לְרַב נַחְמָן: ר' יוֹחָנָן בֶּן נוּרִי דְּאָמַר כְּמַאן? אִי כְּרַבָּן גַּמְלִיאֵל — אֲפִילּוּ בְּרוֹב פְּסוּלִין נַמִי מַכְשַׁר, אִי כְּרַבִּי יְהוֹשֻׁעַ — אֲפִילּוּ בְּרוֹב כְּשֵׁרִים נַמִי פָּסֵיל! אֲמַר לֵיהּ: הָכִי אָמַר רַב יְהוּדָה אָמַר רַב:

בְּקְרוֹנוֹת

רש"י

שָׁמַעְתִּי כו'. לְקַמֵּיהּ פָּרֵיךְ: הַיְינוּ תַּנָּא קַמָּא, דְּתַנָּא קַמָּא נַמִי הָכִי אָמַר, דְּמִשּׁוּם דְּאֵין בָּהּ אֶחָד מִכָּל אֵלּוּ הֵעִידוּ עָלֶיהָ לְהַכְשִׁיר. מַכִּירִין יִשְׂרָאֵל מַמְזֵרִין שֶׁבֵּינֵיהֶן. וּסְפֵק מַמְזֵר יֵשׁ לְךָ לְהַכְשִׁיר, דְּאִי מַמְזֵר הֲוָה — מֵידַע הֲווּ יָדְעִי בֵּיהּ. וְאֵין מַכִּירִין חֲלָלִין שֶׁבֵּינֵיהֶן. וּסְפֵק חָלָל יֵשׁ לְךָ לִפְסוֹל. וּלְקַמֵּיהּ פָּרֵיךְ: הָא אָמְרַתְּ רֵישָׁא: אֵיזוֹהִי אַלְמָנַת עִיסָּה — כָּל שֶׁנִּטְמַע בָּהּ סְפֵק חָלָל, אַלְמָא סְפֵק חָלָל כָּשֵׁר. הָא חָלָל כָּשֵׁר. מִשּׁוּם סְפֵק חָלָל לָא פָּסֵיל לָהּ. מַאי שְׁנָא הָנָךְ. דְּפָסֵיל לָהּ סָפֵק דִּידְהוּ. דְּאוֹרַיְיתָא. מִשּׁוּם דְּוַדַּאי פּוֹסְלִין מִן הַתּוֹרָה בְּבִיאָה, דְּנָפְקָא לָן בִּיבָמוֹת (דף סח.) מִ"כִּי תִהְיֶה לְאִישׁ זָר", כֵּיוָן שֶׁנִּבְעֲלָה לְפָסוּל לָהּ — פְּסָלָהּ. חָלָל נַמִי. וַדַּאי פָּסוּל מִדְּאוֹרַיְיתָא, דְּיָלְפִינַן לָהּ הָתָם מִ"לֹא יְחַלֵּל זַרְעוֹ", מַקִּישׁ זַרְעוֹ לוֹ, מָה הוּא פּוֹסֵל בְּבִיאָתוֹ — אַף זַרְעוֹ פּוֹסֵל. וְהוּא גּוּפֵיהּ נָפְקָא לָן מִ"לֹא יְחַלֵּל", שְׁנֵי חִילּוּלִין מַשְׁמַע, אֶחָד לְזַרְעוֹ וְאֶחָד לְאִשְׁתּוֹ. ר"ש בֶּן אֶלְעָזָר כו'. סֵיפָא דְּמִילְּתֵיהּ אַרֵישָׁא דְּמִילְּתֵיהּ פָּרֵיךְ, דְּקָתָנֵי סֵיפָא: אֵין מַכִּירִין חֲלָלִין שֶׁבֵּינֵיהֶן, מַשְׁמַע אֶפְשָׁר שֶׁהָיָה חָלָל אֲבָל לֹא הָיוּ מַכִּירִין בּוֹ, אַלְמָא אִית לֵיהּ דְּפָסֵיל. וְרֵישָׁא אָמַר: אֵיזוֹהִי אַלְמָנַת עִיסָּה, וְהִכְשִׁיר כָּל שֶׁנִּטְמַע בָּהּ סְפֵק חָלָל. אָמַר ר' יוֹחָנָן מַמְזֵר צוֹוֵחַ וְחָלָל שׁוֹתֵק **איכא** בֵּינַיְיהוּ. אָדָם שֶׁכְּשֶׁקּוֹרִין אוֹתוֹ מַמְזֵר הוּא צוֹוֵחַ, וּכְשֶׁקּוֹרִין אוֹתוֹ חָלָל — שׁוֹתֵק, אִיכָּא בֵּין ר"מ לְת"ק וּבֵין תַּנָּא קַמָּא, דִּבְרַיְיתָא אַלִּיבָּא דְּר"מ וְר"ש בֶּן אֶלְעָזָר אַלִּיבָּא דְּר"מ. תַּנָּא קַמָּא סָבַר כָּל פָּסוּל דְּקָרוּ לֵיהּ וְשָׁתֵיק פָּסוּל. דְּהוֹדָאָה הִיא. וְכָל שֶׁאֵין בָּהּ לֹא מִשּׁוּם מַמְזֵרוּת כו' דְּקָאָמַר — אַשְּׁתִיקוֹת קָאֵי. וְהָכִי קָאָמַר אֵיזוֹהִי אַלְמָנָה עִיסָּה. לְהַכְשִׁיר. כָּל שֶׁאֵין בָּהּ לֹא שְׁתוּק מַמְזֵרוּת וְלֹא שְׁתוּק נְתִינוּת. וְכֵיוָן דְּתָלָה טַעְמָא בִּשְׁתִיקָה, הוּא הַדִּין לְכָל שְׁתוּקֵי פְּסוּל, וְלֹא הוּצְרַךְ לִמְנוֹת אֶת כּוּלָּם. וּבְאֵיזוֹ הִכְשִׁירוּ — בְּאֵשֶׁת סְפֵק חָלָל שֶׁאָנוּ מַכִּירִין אֶת סְפֵיקוֹ, שֶׁנִּתְגָּרְשָׁה אִמּוֹ סָפֵק. אֲבָל מִי שֶׁאֵין מַכִּירִין בּוֹ, וְשָׁמַעְנוּ שֶׁפּוֹסְלִין אוֹתוֹ וְשׁוֹתֵק — פָּסוּל. וְקָאָמַר לֵיהּ ר"מ. דַּוְקָא הָנֵי, אֲבָל שְׁתוּק חָלָל לָא פָּסוּל. וְהָא דְּשָׁתֵיק. לָאו מִשּׁוּם דְּאוֹדֵי, אֶלָּא מִשּׁוּם דְּלָא אִיכְפַּת לֵיהּ, הוֹאִיל וְלָאו פְּסוּל קָהָל הוּא. וְהַיְינוּ דְּקָאָמַר כָּל שֶׁאֵין בָּהּ אֶחָד מִכָּל אֵלּוּ שְׁתִיקוֹת — מַשִּׂיאִין בְּנוֹתֵיהֶן לִכְהוּנָּה, וַאֲפִי' יֵשׁ בּוֹ שְׁתוּק חָלָל. וְקָאָמַר לֵיהּ ר"ש לְתַנָּא קַמָּא. לָאו לְתַנָּא קַמָּא דִּבְרַיְיתָא קָאָמַר, דְּהַהִיא רַבָּנַן הִיא. אֶלָּא לְתַנָּא שֶׁשָּׁנָה דִּבְרֵי ר"מ בְּבֵית הַמִּדְרָשׁ, וְאָמַר בְּשֵׁם ר"מ שָׁמַעְתִּי כָּל שֶׁאֵין בָּהּ כו'. אִי שְׁמִיעַ לָךְ כו'. וְהָכִי קָאָמַר: אֵיזוֹ הִיא אַלְמָנַת עִיסָּה — כָּל שֶׁנִּטְמַע בָּהּ סְפֵק חָלָל שֶׁאָנוּ מַכִּירִין אֶת פְּסוּלוֹ, שֶׁהָיְתָה אִמּוֹ סָפֵק גְּרוּשָׁה. אֲבָל שְׁתוּק חָלָל וְאֵין אָנוּ מַכִּירִין בּוֹ — פָּסוּל, כְּתַנָּא קַמָּא. וּמִיהוּ, בְּהָא פָּלֵיג רַבִּי מֵאִיר אַתַּנָּא קַמָּא: דְּאִיהוּ כָּל פְּסוּל דְּשָׁתֵיק בֵּיהּ פָּסֵיל, וּלְרַבִּי מֵאִיר חָלָל שְׁתוּק הוּא דְּפָסוּל, דְּסָבַר מִסְתַּיֵּיהּ דְּלָא מַפְּקֵי לֵיהּ מִקָּהָל, וְאִם אֲנִי צוֹוֵחַ — יַכְרִיזוּ עָלַי, וְיִוָּדַע פְּסוּלִי בְּבֵרוּר. וְעַכְשָׁיו אֵין מַכִּירִין יִשְׂרָאֵל חֲלָלִין שֶׁבֵּינֵיהֶם. אֲבָל שְׁתוּק מַמְזֵר — כָּשֵׁר, דְּהַאי דְּשָׁתֵיק, סָבַר: הַכֹּל יוֹדְעִין שֶׁאֵינִי מַמְזֵר, דְּמַכִּירִין יִשְׂרָאֵל מַמְזֵרִין שֶׁבֵּינֵיהֶן. **מתני'** מִן הָעַיִן. מִן הַמַּעְיָין. אִם רוֹב הָעִיר. כְּשֵׁרִין לְהַשִּׂיא בְּנוֹתֵיהֶן וְאַלְמְנוֹתֵיהֶן לִכְהוּנָּה, שֶׁאֵין רוֹב בְּנֵי הָעִיר מִן הַפּוֹסְלִין אִשָּׁה לִכְהוּנָּה בְּבִיאָתָן — אַף זוֹ תִּינָּשֵׂא לִכְהוּנָּה. **גמ'** דְּאָמַר כְּמַאן. דְּבָעֵי רוֹב כְּשֵׁרִין. אֲפִילּוּ בְּרוֹב פְּסוּלִין נַמִי מַכְשַׁר. דְּאִית לֵיהּ: הַעֲמֵד אִשָּׁה עַל חֶזְקָתָהּ. אָמַר לֵיהּ הָכִי אָמַר כו'. לְעוֹלָם כְּרַבִּי יְהוֹשֻׁעַ, וְהָכָא מִשּׁוּם דְּאִיכָּא תְּרֵי רוּבֵּי לְכַשְׁרוּת — אַכְשְׁרָהּ, וּכְדְרַב יְהוּדָה. וּלְקַמָּן מְפָרֵשׁ טַעְמָא וְאָזֵיל מַאי שְׁנָא תְּרֵי רוּבֵּי מֵחַד רוּבָּא.

בְּקְרוֹנוֹת

תוספות

לא משום ממזרות כו'. הא דלא חשיב עמוני ומואבי — משום דלא פסיקא, דזכרים אסורין ונקבות מותרות. ומצרי ואדומי לא חשיב, דאינן אסורין אלא עד דור שלישי. **ותו** ר"ש בן אלעזר אומר איזוהי עיסה כל שנטמע בה ספק חלל והאמרת רישא חלל כשר. ה"ג בכל הספרים, ובפירוש ר"ת. ומפרש: כל שנטמע בה ספק חלל, הא ודאי חלל — פסול. והא אמרת רישא חלל כשר, והיינו ודאי חלל! ואין נראה, דמאי פריך מתנא קמא? דלמא ת"ק פליג עליה! ופירוש הקונטרס וגרסתו עיקר. **ממזר** צווח וחלל שותק **איכא** בינייהו. תימה: דהוה ליה למימר ממזר צווח ושותק וחלל שותק איכא בינייהו! דבממזר שותק נמי פליגי, דהא מכשר ליה ר"ש בן אלעזר*! **אבל** ממזר צווח וחלל שותק פסול. וא"ת: ממזר צווח מנא ליה דפסל ר"ש בן אלעזר? ואומר ר"י: מדקתני במילתיה איזוהי עיסה — כל שנטמע בה ספק חלל. דלא הוה ליה למימר אלא מכירין ישראל ממזרים שביניהם, ואין מכירין חללין שביניהם, דמינה שמעינן בחלל צווח דכשר, כי היכי דלא הוצרך להשמיענו כל שנטמע בה ספק ממזר. אלא ודאי אתא למידק דחלל צווח דוקא כשר, הא ממזר צווח — פסול. **מסתייה** דלא מפקינן ליה מקהל. וא"ת: מה צריך להאי טעמא? לימא: הא דשתיק — משום דאודויי קא מודי, דהא ממזר שותק פסול לת"ק משום דשתיקה כהודאה, וה"ה דחלל שותק לר"ש, דפסול מהאי טעמא! ואע"ג דגבי ממזר שותק לדידיה לא הוי שתיקה כהודאה — היינו משום דסבר דממזר קלא אית ליה. וי"ל: דהכי פירושא: סבר מסתייה דלא מפקינן ליה מקהל (כהונה). פי': אפי' מקהל כהונה, אע"פ שזה מחרפו וקורהו חלל — סבור דאין מוציאין אותו מקהל כהונה, וסבור אם יצווח יחזרו לברר הדבר ויפסלוהו, וטעם זה שייך גם בממזר שותק לת"ק, ולא נאמר דשתיקה כהודאה. וכן פירש בקונטרס. **כמאן** אי כר"ג אפילו ברוב פסולין נמי מכשר. וא"ת: והא לא מכשר ברוב פסולין אלא כשטוענת ברי, ואית לה מיגו דאי בעיא אמרה לא נבעלתי, או בלא מגו היכא דאיכא למימר בודקת ומזנה. אבל הכא, אפילו טוענת ברי — הא לית לה מגו. וליכא למימר בודקת ומזנה, דהא נאנסה! ואפי' אם נאמר דהכא לא ראוה שנאנסה, אלא היא אמרה כן, דאית לה מגו — א"כ תקשי הלכתא אהלכתא, דלקמן פסיק רב הלכה כר' יוסי, ולעיל פסיק רב יהודה אמר שמואל הלכה כר"ג! ואין נראה לומר דפליגי, דא"כ מאי מייתי אעובדא דארום וארוסתו מרב יהודה אמר שמואל, וכן לעיל (דף יג.) פריך הלכתא אהלכתא, קי"ל כרב נחמן בדיני כו' ואדרבה הא רב פסיק כר' יהושע וקי"ל כרב באיסורי! ויש לומר, דהכי פירושו: כמאן, אי כר"ג ובטוענת ברי, ובלא ראוה שנאנסה, דאיכא מגו — אפילו ברוב פסולים נמי מכשר, ואיירי נמי כשראוה מדברת, דאי לא ראוה מדברת — מאי פריך אי כרבי יהושע אפילו ברוב כשרים נמי פסול? ומשני

אמר

תוספות רי"ד

נאמנת: **מתני'** א"ר יוסי מעשה בתינוקת שירדה למלאות מים מן המעיין ונאנסה ואר"י בן נורי אם רוב העיר משיאים לכהונה ה"ז תנשא [לכהונה] אר"י אמר רב

גליון הש"ס

מתני' א"ר יוסי מעשה בתינוקת. עיין יבמות דף סז ע"ב תוס' ד"ה אין חוששין:

בְּקְרוֹנוֹת שֶׁל צִיפּוֹרִי הָיָה מַעֲשֶׂה, וּכְדְרַבִּי אַמִי, דְּאָמַר רַבִּי אַמִי: וְהוּא שֶׁהָיְתָה סִיעָה שֶׁל בְּנֵי אָדָם כְּשֵׁרִין עוֹבֶרֶת לְשָׁם, וּכְדר' יַנַּאי. דְּאָמַר ר' יַנַּאי: נִבְעֶלֶת בִּקְרוֹנוֹת — כְּשֵׁרָה לִכְהוּנָּה. בִּקְרוֹנוֹת סָלְקָא דַעְתָּךְ?! אֶלָּא: נִבְעֶלֶת בִּשְׁעַת קְרוֹנוֹת — כְּשֵׁרָה לִכְהוּנָּה. אֲבָל פֵּירַשׁ אֶחָד מִצִּיפּוֹרִי וּבָעַל — הַוָּלָד שְׁתוּקִי. כִּי הָא דְּכִי אֲתָא רַב דִּימִי אָמַר זְעֵירִי א"ר חֲנִינָא, וְאָמְרִי לָהּ אָמַר זְעֵירִי אָמַר ר' חֲנִינָא: הוֹלְכִין אַחַר רוֹב הָעִיר, וְאֵין הוֹלְכִין אַחַר רוֹב סִיעָה. כְּלַפֵּי לַיָּיא?! הָנֵי נָיְידִי וְהָנֵי קְבִיעִי וְקַיְימִי! אֶלָּא: [א]הוֹלְכִין אַחַר רוֹב הָעִיר וְהוּא דְּאִיכָּא רוֹב סִיעָה בַּהֲדָהּ. וְאֵין הוֹלְכִין אַחַר רוֹב הָעִיר גְּרֵידְתָא וְלֹא אַחַר רוֹב סִיעָה גְּרֵידְתָא. מ"ט — גְּזֵרָה רוֹב סִיעָה אַטּוּ רוֹב הָעִיר. וְרוֹב הָעִיר נַמִי, *אִי דְּקָא אָזְלֵי אִינְהוּ לְגַבָּהּ — כָּל דְּפָרֵישׁ *מֵרוּבָּא פָּרֵישׁ! [ב]*לָא צְרִיכָא, דְּקָא אָזְלָא אִיהִי לְגַבַּיְיהוּ, דַּהֲוָה לֵיהּ קָבוּעַ, וְא"ר זֵירָא: כָּל קָבוּעַ כְּמֶחֱצָה עַל מֶחֱצָה דָּמֵי. וּמִי בָּעֵינַן תְּרֵי רוּבֵּי? וְהָתַנְיָא: *[ג]תֵּשַׁע חֲנוּיוֹת, כּוּלָּן מוֹכְרוֹת בְּשַׂר שְׁחוּטָה, וְאַחַת מוֹכֶרֶת בְּשַׂר נְבֵלָה, וְלָקַח מֵאַחַת מֵהֶן וְאֵינוֹ יוֹדֵעַ מֵאֵי זֶה מֵהֶן לָקַח — סְפֵיקוֹ אָסוּר. [ד]וּבַנִּמְצָא — הַלֵּךְ אַחַר הָרוֹב! וְכִי תֵּימָא כְּשֶׁאֵין דַּלְתוֹת מְדִינָה נְעוּלוֹת, דְּקָא אָתֵי לָהּ רוּבָּא מֵעָלְמָא — וְהָא א"ר זֵירָא: *אע"פ שֶׁדַּלְתוֹת מְדִינָה נְעוּלוֹת! *מַעֲלָה עָשׂוּ בְּיוּחֲסִין. גּוּפָא, א"ר זֵירָא: כָּל קָבוּעַ כְּמֶחֱצָה עַל מֶחֱצָה דָּמֵי, בֵּין לְקוּלָּא בֵּין לְחוּמְרָא. מְנָא לֵיהּ לְר' זֵירָא הָא? אִילֵימָא מִתֵּשַׁע חֲנוּיוֹת כּוּלָּן מוֹכְרוֹת בְּשַׂר שְׁחוּטָה וְאַחַת בְּשַׂר נְבֵלָה, וְלָקַח מֵאַחַת מֵהֶן, וְאֵינוֹ יוֹדֵעַ מֵאֵיזֶה מֵהֶן לָקַח — סְפֵיקוֹ אָסוּר, וּבַנִּמְצָא — הַלֵּךְ אַחַר הָרוֹב, הָתָם לְחוּמְרָא! אֶלָּא, *[ה]מִתִּשְׁעָה צְפַרְדְּעִים וְשֶׁרֶץ אֶחָד בֵּינֵיהֶם, וְנָגַע בְּאֶחָד מֵהֶן וְאֵינוֹ יוֹדֵעַ בְּאֵיזֶה מֵהֶן נָגַע, סְפֵיקוֹ טָמֵא. הָתָם נַמִי לְחוּמְרָא! אֶלָּא [ו]מִתִּשְׁעָה שְׁרָצִים וּצְפַרְדֵּעַ אֶחָד בֵּינֵיהֶם, וְנָגַע בְּאֶחָד מֵהֶן, וְאֵינוֹ יוֹדֵעַ בְּאֵיזֶה מֵהֶן נָגַע, ברה"י סְפֵיקוֹ טָמֵא, בִּרְשׁוּת הָרַבִּי' סְפֵיקוֹ טָהוֹר. וּמִדְּאוֹרַיְיתָא מְנָא לָן? *אָמַר קְרָא: °"וְאָרַב לוֹ וְקָם עָלָיו" — [ז]עַד שֶׁיִּתְכַּוֵּין לוֹ. וְרַבָּנַן? אָמְרִי דְּבֵי ר' יַנַּאי: פְּרָט לַזּוֹרֵק אֶבֶן לְגוֹ. *הֵיכִי דָּמֵי? אִילֵימָא דְּאִיכָּא תִּשְׁעָה גּוֹיִם וְאֶחָד יִשְׂרָאֵל בֵּינֵיהֶם — וְתֵיפּוֹק לֵיהּ דְּרוּבָּא גּוֹיִם נִינְהוּ! אִי נַמִי פַּלְגָא וּפַלְגָא — *סְפֵק נְפָשׁוֹת לְהָקֵל! לָא צְרִיכָא, דְּאִיכָּא תִּשְׁעָה יִשְׂרְאֵלִים וְגוֹי אֶחָד בֵּינֵיהֶם, דַּהֲוָה לֵיהּ גּוֹי קָבוּעַ, וְכָל קָבוּעַ כְּמֶחֱצָה עַל מֶחֱצָה דָּמֵי. אִיתְּמַר רַב חִיָּיא בַּר אַשִׁי אָמַר רַב: הֲלָכָה כְּרַבִּי יוֹסֵי, וְרַב חָנָן בַּר רָבָא אָמַר רַב: הוֹרָאַת שָׁעָה הָיְתָה. מְתִיב רַבִּי יִרְמְיָה: וּלְיוּחֲסִין לָא בָּעֵינַן תְּרֵי רוּבֵּי? וְהָתְנַן: מָצָא

רש"י

בִּקְרוֹנוֹת שֶׁל צִיפּוֹרִי. בְּיוֹם הַשּׁוּק, שֶׁסִּיעוֹת וְשַׁיָּירוֹת מִמָּקוֹם אַחֵר בָּאוֹת שָׁם. וּכְדְרַבִּי אַמִי. דְּהַשְׁתָּא אִיכָּא רוֹב סִיעָה וְרוֹב הָעִיר. נִבְעֶלֶת בִּקְרוֹנוֹת. מַשְׁמַע עַל הַקָּרוֹן. בִּשְׁעַת קְרוֹנוֹת. שֶׁהַשַּׁיָּירוֹת בָּאוֹת לָעִיר. כְּשֵׁרָה לִכְהוּנָּה. כִּדְקָאָמַר: וְהוּא שֶׁהָיְתָה סִיעָה שֶׁל בְּנֵי אָדָם כְּשֵׁרִים עוֹבֶרֶת שָׁם, דְּאִיכָּא לְמֵימַר שֶׁמֵּהֶם הָיָה. אֲבָל פֵּירַשׁ אֶחָד מִצִּיפּוֹרִי. דְּיָדְעִינַן וַדַּאי דְּמִן הָעִיר הָיָה, אע"פ שֶׁצִּיפּוֹרִי עִיר שֶׁרוּבָּהּ מַשִּׂיאִין לִכְהוּנָּה. הַוָּלָד שְׁתוּקִי. דִּבְחַד רוּבָּא לָא מַכְשַׁר. וְכִי הָא דְּכִי אֲתָא רַב דִּימִי אָמַר זְעֵירִי אָמַר רַבִּי חֲנִינָא וְאָמְרִי לָהּ. שֶׁלֹּא הוּזְכַּר רַב דִּימִי כָּאן, אֶלָּא זְעֵירִי אָמַר רַבִּי חֲנִינָא, דְּבָעֵינַן תְּרֵי רוּבֵּי. וּכְדִמְפָרֵשׁ טַעְמָא. הוֹלְכִין אַחַר רוֹב הָעִיר. לְהַכְשִׁיר. וְאֵין הוֹלְכִין אַחַר רוֹב סִיעָה. כְּגוֹן בְּמָקוֹם רָחוֹק מִן הָעִיר, דְּבְוַדַּאי מֵאַנְשֵׁי הַסִּיעָה הֲוָה — אֵין מַכְשִׁירִין אוֹתָהּ, וַאֲפִילּוּ רוּבָּן כְּשֵׁרִין. וְקַשְׁיָא לָן כְּלַפֵּי לַיָּיא. כְּנֶגֶד אֵיפוֹא הַדָּבָר הַזֶּה סוֹבֵב?! הָנֵי נָיְידִי. רוֹב סִיעָה נָיְידִי, וְיֵשׁ לְהַלֵּךְ בָּהֶן אַחַר הָרוֹב. וְהָנֵי. שֶׁל עִיר. קְבִיעִי. וְאָמְרִינַן לְקַמָּן: כָּל קָבוּעַ כְּמֶחֱצָה עַל מֶחֱצָה דָּמֵי, וַאֲפִילּוּ אֵין שָׁם אֶלָּא אֶחָד — פְּסוּלָה. וְלֹא אַחַר רוֹב סִיעָה גְּרֵידְתָא. וְהָכִי קָאָמַר: אֵין הוֹלְכִין אַחַר רוֹב סִיעָה לְבַדָּהּ, וְכָל שֶׁכֵּן אַחַר רוֹב הָעִיר לְבַדָּהּ. מ"ט. אַחַר רוֹב סִיעָה לֹא. גְּזֵרָה אַטּוּ רוֹב הָעִיר. דִּקְבִיעִי. וּפָרְכִינַן. רוֹב הָעִיר נַמִי. אִי עָקַר הַבּוֹעֵל מִבֵּיתוֹ וְאָזַל לְגַבָּהּ — הֲוָה נָיֵיד, וְקי"ל: כָּל דְּפָרֵישׁ מֵרוּבָּא פָּרֵישׁ! וּמְשַׁנֵּי. אִיכָּא דְּקָאָזְלָא לְגַבַּיְיהוּ כו', וְלָא גָּרְסִינַן *מַאי אִיכָּא, יֵשׁ שֶׁהוֹלֶכֶת הִיא אֶצְלוֹ וְהָוֵה לֵיהּ קָבוּעַ. הִלְכָּךְ, אֲפִילּוּ בְּרוֹב כְּשֵׁרִים, אוֹ רוֹב הָעִיר אוֹ רוֹב סִיעָה — פָּסוּל, כְּרַבִּי יְהוֹשֻׁעַ. וּמִשּׁוּם תְּרֵי רוּבֵּי אַכְשְׁרָהּ, דְּלֵיכָּא לְמִיגְזַר מִידֵי. וְלָקַח בָּשָׂר מֵאַחַת מֵהֶן. בִּמְקוֹם קְבִיעוּת. סְפֵיקוֹ אָסוּר. דְּכָל קָבוּעַ כְּמֶחֱצָה עַל מֶחֱצָה דָּמֵי. וּבַנִּמְצָא. בָּשָׂר הַנִּמְצָא בַּשּׁוּק, וְלָא יָדְעִינַן מֵאֵיזֶה פֵּירַשׁ. הַלֵּךְ אַחַר הָרוֹב. הוֹאִיל וְהַבָּא לְפָנֵינוּ לֹא בִּמְקוֹם קְבִיעוּת לְקָחָהּ, וּכְבָר פֵּירְשָׁה עַל יְדֵי אַחֵר, וְכָל דְּפָרֵישׁ מֵרוּבָּא פָּרֵישׁ. דְּקָאָתֵי לָהּ רוּבָּא מֵעָלְמָא. וּכְגוֹן שֶׁרוֹב סִיעַת טַבָּחֵי יִשְׂרָאֵל כְּשֵׁרִים בָּאוּ לְכָאן, דְּאִיכָּא תְּרֵי רוּבֵּי. אוֹ שֶׁרוֹב טַבָּחֵי כָּל הַמְּדִינָה יִשְׂרָאֵל, דְּאִיכָּא תְּרֵי רוּבֵּי: רוֹב הָעִיר, וְרוֹב הַמְּדִינָה דְּנָיְידִי. אֶלָּא מִתִּשְׁעָה צְפַרְדְּעִים כו'. תּוֹסֶפְתָּא הִיא בְּמַסֶּ' טְהָרוֹת: תִּשְׁעָה צְפַרְדְּעִים מֵתִים בִּרְשׁוּת הַיָּחִיד, וְשֶׁרֶץ אֶחָד כְּגוֹן לְטָאָה שֶׁהוּא דּוֹמֶה לִצְפַרְדֵּעַ, בֵּינֵיהֶם, וְנָגַע בְּאֶחָד מֵהֶן — סְפֵיקוֹ טָמֵא. אֶלָּא מִתִּשְׁעָה שְׁרָצִים כו'. אַף הִיא תּוֹסֶפְתָּא בְּמַסֶּ' טְהָרוֹת, וְקָתָנֵי: בִּרה"י סְפֵיקוֹ טָמֵא, בִּרה"ר סְפֵיקוֹ טָהוֹר, אַלְמָא כְּמֶחֱצָה דָּמֵי וּלְקוּלָּא. דְּאִי לָאו כְּמֶחֱצָה דָּמֵי — אֵין כָּאן סְפֵק טוּמְאָה אֶלָּא וַדַּאי טוּמְאָה, דְּהָא רוּבָּא שְׁרָצִים. אָמַר קְרָא וְאָרַב לוֹ עַד שֶׁיְּהֵא מִתְכַּוֵּין לוֹ. פְּרָט לְמִתְכַּוֵּין לַהֲרוֹג אֶת זֶה וְהָרַג אֶת זֶה. הָכִי דָּרֵישׁ לֵיהּ ר"ש בְּסַנְהֶדְרִין. וְאָמְרִינַן הָתָם: וְרַבָּנַן הֵיכִי דָּרְשֵׁי לֵיהּ? אָמְרֵי דְּבֵי ר' יַנַּאי פְּרָט לַזּוֹרֵק אֶבֶן לְגוֹ. לְתוֹךְ חֲבוּרַת בְּנֵי אָדָם גּוֹיִם וְיִשְׂרְאֵלִים. אֲבָל שְׁנֵי יִשְׂרְאֵלִים עוֹמְדִין, וְנִתְכַּוֵּין לַהֲרוֹג (א) זֶה (וְהָרַג זֶה) וְהִתְרוּ בּוֹ וְקִבֵּל הַתְרָאָה, וְנָפְלָה הַמַּכָּה עַל חֲבֵירוֹ — חַיָּיב. וְהַיְינוּ טַעְמָא דְּקָאָמַר הָכָא וְרַבָּנַן, מִשּׁוּם דִּבְסַנְהֶדְרִין הָכִי אִיתָא. תֵּיפּוֹק לֵיהּ דְּרוּבָּא גּוֹיִם נִינְהוּ. וְלָמָּה לִי קְרָא? וְאִי נַמִי פַּלְגָא וּפַלְגָא, אַכַּתִּי לָא אִיצְטְרִיךְ קְרָא, דְּמֵהֵיכָא תֵּיתֵי דְּנִיקְטְלֵיהּ? סְפֵק נְפָשׁוֹת. דִּינֵי נְפָשׁוֹת לְהָקֵל, דְּהָא "וְהִצִּילוּ הָעֵדָה" כְּתִיב (במדבר לה). דַּהֲוָה לֵיהּ גּוֹי קָבוּעַ בֵּינֵיהֶם. וְאַשְׁמוּעִינַן הַאי קְרָא דְּכָל קָבוּעַ כְּמֶחֱצָה עַל מֶחֱצָה דָּמֵי. הוֹרָאַת שָׁעָה הָיְתָה. סָךְ דְּרִיבָ"ן לוֹרֶךְ שָׁעָה הָיְתָה, אוֹ רָאוּ שָׁם שֶׁאָר לְיָדֵי הֶיכֵּר דְּבָרִים לְהַתִּיר, אֲבָל לְדוֹרוֹת — תְּרֵי רוּבֵּי בָּעֵינַן. מֵתִיב רַבִּי יִרְמְיָה כו'. קס"ד דְּמִשּׁוּם רוֹב הָעִיר גְּרֵידְתָא אַכְשְׁרוּהָ, וַאֲמַר רַב הֲלָכָה כְּרַבִּי יוֹסֵי. מָצָא

תוספות

אמר רב בקרונות של צפורי היה מעשה כו' – פי': לעולם דלא טוענה ברי. ור' יוחנן בן נורי בתרוייהו היכא דלא טוענה ברי – לכ"ע בעינן תרי רובי. והא דלא קאמר בשניה לעולם דלא טוענה ברי, משום דנאתקפתא לא קאמר אי בטוענת ברי כו'. אי נמי נוכל לפרש, דבשניה נמי איירי בברי, ודאיכא מגו. ולא תקשי הלכתא אהלכתא, דדוקא דיעבד פסיק שמואל כר"ג כדאמר לעיל: ואת לא תעביד עובדא עד דאיכא רוב כשרין. אף על גב דלעיל משמע דברוב אחד שרי לכתחלה, רב חייא בר אשי סבר דלכתחלה בעינן תרי, רובי ומתני' קתני הרי זו תנשא – דמשמע לכתחלה.

דלמא אזלא איהי לגבייהו. פי' לתוך ביתם, דאפילו בתוך העיר לא חשיב קבוע, דדמי לנמצא בין החנויות, דלא חשיב קבוע. וכן גבי תינוק מושלך בעיר לא חשיב קבוע, הואיל ולא נמצא בבית. ולכך פירש בקונטרס שפירש בועל מביתו. וא"ת: דבנזיר פ"ב (דף יב. ושם) פריך אהא דאמר: האומר לשלוחו "צא וקדש לי אשה סתם" – אסור בכל הנשים, שבעולם מקן סתומה, ומסיק: אמינא לך אנא אשה דלא ניידא, ואת אמרת לי איסורא דנייד? וכי תימא ה"נ בשוקא אשכחה וקדיש – התם הדרא לניחותא. משמע לגבי אדם לא שייך כל דפריש מרובא פריש משום דהדר לניחותיה! ולאו פירכא היא, דהתם בשעת האיסור כשזה בא על שום אשה הדרא לניחותא האשה שקידש השליח. אבל הכא, כי אזלי אינהו לגבה בשעה שאוסרה הרי הוא נייד.

פרט לזורק אבן לגו. תימה: דלר' שמעון קבוע מנא ליה? ואין לומר דמסקינן בפ' "הנשרפין" (סנהדרין דף עט. ושם) דר"ש סבר כרבי דיליף "נתינה" "נתינה" ואייתר ליה "וארב לו" לקבוע – דאכתי לתנא דבי חזקיה מנא ליה קבוע? דלית ליה דרבי, דהא באין מתכוין פטור ממנון*.

וספק נפשות להקל. תימה: למ"ד: התראת ספק לא שמה התראה, אפילו ספק נפשות להחמיר – פטור, משום דהתראת ספק היא! ואי למ"ד שמה התראה – היכי פטרינן ליה כשנמצא שישראל הרג? הא מיחייב בהכה את זה וחזר והכה את זה*, ובנותר כשאמרו לו אל תותיר, אע"ג דספק הוא! וי"ל: דשאני התם שיודע בודאי שיבא לידי איסור אם יותיר או יכה שניהם – מש"ה שמה התראה, אבל הכא – אינו יודע שודאי יבוא לידי איסור, שאינו יודע את מי יכה.

וליוחסין לא בעינן תרי רובי ורמינהי כו'. הוה מצי לשנויי: שאני תינוק דלית לי' חזק' דכשרו'.

ולרב

עין משפט נר מצוה

פט א ב מיי' פי"ח מהלכות איסורי ביאה הל' יד סמג לאוין קכא טוש"ע אה"ע סימן ו סעיף יז יח:

צ ג מיי' פ"ח מהלכות מאכלות אסורות הל' יא סמג לאוין קמא טור ש"ע י"ד סימן קי סע"ג:

צא ד מיי' שם וטוש"ע שם ובסי' סג ס"א:

צב ה ו מיי' פי"ח מהלכות אבות הטומאות הלכה ב:

צג ז מיי' פ"ד מהל' רוצח הלכה א סמג לאוין קמג.

מסורת הש"ס

[קדושין עג.] [ברכות כח. וש"נ] פסחים ט: חולין לה. נדה יח. נ"ל מאי רוב העיר איכא כו' רש"ל. נדה יח. ע"ש תוספתא טהרות פ"ו. ב"ק מד: סנהדרין עט. [יומא פד.] [שבת קכט. וש"נ] דברים יט.

[רש"ל מוחק וכ"ב גירסת רש"י איכא דקאזלה לגבייהו ועי' ב' גירסות בב"י אה"ע סימן ו] [לעיל יג. וש"נ] [ובסנהדרין עט. ד"ה וכל כתבו תוס' תירוץ לזה וכ"כ בב"ק מד: ד"ה כל ועי' תוספות נדה יח. ד"ה ספיקא] יבמות קא.

הגהות הב"ח

(א) רש"י ד"ה אמרי וכו' להרוג את זה והרג את זה:

תוספות רי"ד

בקרונות של צפורי היה מעשה וכדר' ינאי דאמר נבעלה בשעת קרונות כשירה לכהונה פי' קרוניות הבאים ממקום אחר ומתקבצים שם ליום השוק והוא שהיתה סיעה של בני אדם כשרים עוברים שם דהוה תרי רובא לכשרות רוב העיר ורוב סיעה. פי' כל זה מפני שלא ידעה למי נבעלה אבל אי ידעה ואמרה לכשר נבעלתי הלכה כר"ג ונאמנת אפילו ברוב פסולים: ומקשי' ומי בעי תרי רובי והתניא ט' חנויות כולן מוכרות בשר שחוטה ואחת מוכרת בשר נבילה ולקח מאחת מהן ואינו יודע מאיזה מהן לקח ספיקו אסור שכל קבוע כמחצה על מחצה דמי ובנמצא הלך אחר הרוב דכל דפריש מרובא פריש. ומהדר מעלה עשו ביוחסין: איתמר אר"ח אמר רב הלכה כר' יוסי פי' דבעי' תרי רובי: א"ר זירא כל קבוע כמחצה על מחצה דמי בין לקולא בין לחומרא כגון ט' חנויות דאמרן. א"נ ט' צפרדעים ושרץ א' ביניהם ברה"י ונגע באח' מהן ואינו יודע באיזה מהן נגע ספיקו טמא. לקולא כגון ט' שרצים וצפרדע א' ביניהן ברה"ר ונגע באח' מהן וא"י באיזה מהן נגע ספיקו טהור אלא כמחצה על מחצה דמי ולקולא. דאי לאו כמחצה על מחצה דמי אין כאן ספק טומאה אלא ודאי טומאה דהא רובא שרצים: האשה

צד א מיי' פט"ו מהל' איסורי ביאה הלכה כה טוש"ע אה"ע סימן ד סעיף לג:

צה ב ג ד ה מיי' שם הל' כו וטור שו"ע שם סעיף לד:

א ו מיי' פט"ז מהלכות אישות הלכה כה טור ש"ע שם סי' נו סעיף ט:

*מצא בה תינוק מושלך, אם רוב גוים — גוי, אם רוב ישראל — ישראל, מחצה על מחצה — ישראל. ואמר רב: לא שנו אלא להחיותו, [א]אבל ליוחסין — לא, ושמואל אמר: לפקח עליו את הגל! אשתמיטתיה הא דא"ר יהודה אמר רב: בקרונות של צפורי הוה מעשה. ולרב חנן בר רבא דאמר: הוראת שעה היתה, קשיא הא! מאן דמתני הא לא מתני הא. גופא, מצא בה תינוק מושלך, אם רוב גוים — גוי, אם רוב ישראל — ישראל, מחצה על מחצה — ישראל, אמר רב: לא שנו אלא להחיותו, אבל ליוחסין — לא, ושמואל אמר: לפקח עליו את הגל. ומי אמר שמואל הכי? והאמר רב יוסף אמר רב יהודה אמר שמואל: אין הולכין בפיקוח נפש אחר הרוב! אלא, כי איתמר דשמואל — ארישא איתמר: אם רוב גוים — גוי, אמר שמואל: *[ב]ולפקח עליו את הגל — אינו כן. "אם רוב גוים — גוי". למאי הלכתא? אמר רב פפא: [ג]להאכילו נבילות. "אם רוב ישראל — ישראל", למאי הלכתא? אמר רב פפא: [ד]להחזיר לו אבידה. "מחצה על מחצה — ישראל" למאי הלכתא? אמר ריש לקיש: [ה]לנזקין. ה"ד? אי נימא דנגחיה תורא דידן לתורא דידיה — לימא ליה: אייתי ראיה דישראל את ושקול! לא צריכא, דנגחיה תורא דידיה לתורא דידן. פלגא — משלם, ואידך פלגא — אמר להו: אייתי ראיה דלאו ישראל אנא, ואתן לכון.§

הדרן עלך בתולה נשאת

האשה *שנתארמלה או שנתגרשה, היא אומרת: בתולה נשאתני, והוא אומר: לא כי, אלא אלמנה נשאתיך. [ו]אם יש עדים שיצאת בהינומא וראשה פרוע — כתובתה מאתים. רבי יוחנן בן ברוקה אומר: אף חילוק קליות ראיה. ומודה רבי יהושע באומר לחבירו: שדה זו של אביך היתה, ולקחתיה הימנו — שהוא נאמן, שהפה

מצא בה תינוק מושלך. משנה היא בסדר טהרות גבי עיר שישראלים וגוים דרים בה. מחצה על מחצה ישראל. לקמיה מפרש מאי איכא בין רוב ישראל למחצה על מחצה, דפליג להו בתרי. לא שנו. דאם רוב ישראל ישראל. אלא להחיותו. ב"ד מצווין לפרנסו, משום "וחי אחיך עמך" (ויקרא כה). אבל ליוחסין לא. דאם בת היא — אסורה לכהן, ואפי' ליכא למיחש משום אסופי, כגון הנך דאמרינן בעשרה יוחסין (קדושין עג:): *משלטי הדמיה, תלי פיתקא, תלי קמיעא — מיהו חיישינן שמא בת גוי היא. (א) ולמ"ד גיורת פסולה לכהונה — אפילו קטנה זו אסורה לכהן, דתרי רובי בעינן ליוחסין. ושמואל אמר אף לפקח עליו את הגל. בשבת, חשבינן ליה לישראל. אשתמיטתיה. לרבי ירמיה. הא דאמר רב יהודה. דהכא נמי תרי רובי הוו. ולרב חנן בר רבא דאמר. משמיה דרב. הוראת שעה היתה. והתם תרי רובי הוו, וקאמר: הוראת שעה היתה, אבל לדורות — לא בעינן תרי רובי. קשיא הא. דרב, דאמר: אבל ליוחסין לא. אלמא רב תרי רובי בעי. לא מתני הא. דאמר רב יהודה אמר רב בקרונות של צפורי הוה מעשה, וחד רובא הוה. הלכך, הוראת שעה היתה. מי אמר שמואל הכי. דלענין פיקוח נפש בעינן רובא. אין הולכין כו'. דאפילו בספק גוי ספק ישראל, ברוב גוים — מפקחין. ולענין פיקוח נפש אינו כן. דאפילו ברוב גוים מפקחין, דאין הולכין בו אחר הרוב. למאי הלכתא. כיון דאמר שמואל מפקחין עליו את הגל — אלמא לאו גוי הוא לכל מילי, ולמאי הלכתא חשיב ליה גוי? להאכילו נבלות. בידים, וכ"ש שלא יחזירו לו אבידה ולנזקין. להחזיר לו אבידה. רבותא היא, דמוליאין מיד ישראל הזוכה בה. ועוד, דאמור רבנן (סנהדרין דף עו:): המחזיר אבידה לגוי, עליו הכתוב אומר "למען ספות הרוה את הצמאה", שהשוה מגרים לחשיבתן של ישראל, ונאמר "לא יאבה ה' סלוח לו". מחצה על מחצה ישראל למאי הלכתא. להחזיר לו אבידה לא מצית אמרת דא"כ למאי הלכתא פלגינהו מהדדי. לנזקין. דתנן ב"ק (דף לז:): שור של ישראל שנגח לשור של גוי פטור ושור של גוי שנגח לשור של ישראל בין תם בין מועד משלם נזק שלם וישראל לישראל תם משלם חצי נזק ומועד משלם נזק שלם. אילימא כו'. וקאמרת דדיינינן ליה כישראל ומחייבת ליה לשלם לו חצי נזקו. לימא ליה. ישראל אייתי ראיה דהא מחצה על מחצה הוא וספיקא הוא. לא צריכא כו'. וקא תבע ליה ישראל נזק שלם לתם כדין גוי ואשמעינן תנא דכישראל דיינינן ליה ולא משלם אלא חצי נזק דא"ל אייתי ראיה.

הדרן עלך בתולה נשאת

האשה שנתארמלה או נתגרשה. ותובעת כתובתה. והוא אומר. אנתגרשה קאי. ולאלמנה היורשין אומרים לה: אלמנה נשאך אבינו, ואין לך אלא מנה. ושטר הכתובה אבד. אם יש עדים. על נשואיה שיצאת מבית אביה לבית בעלה. בהינומא. בגמ' מפרש. וראשה פרוע. אילטייבליד"ה = שערה על כתפיה. כך היו נוהגין להוציא את הבתולות מבית אביהן לבית החתונה. אף חילוק קליות. רגילים היו לחלק קליות להתינוקות בנישואי הבתולות. קליות. כשהשבולין לחין מייבשין אותן בתנור והן קליות ומתוקין לעולם. ומודה ר' יהושע. מפרש בגמ' היכא קאי ומאי מודה. שהפה

ולרב חנן דאמר הוראת שעה היתה. ולדורות סגי בחד רובא — קשיא הך. ולא מיסתברא ליה למימר דהוראת שעה היתה שהתיר בתרי רובי. אבל לדורות לא סגי אפילו בתרי רובי. **מאן** דמתני הא לא מתני הא. פי' בקונטרס: דרב חנן לא מתני דבקרונות של צפורי היה מעשה, ולא הוה אלא חד רובא. ולפירושו לא פליגי דלדורות לכ"ע בעינן תרי רובי, ולא פליגי אלא במעשה היכי הוה. ור"ת פי': דרב חנן לא מתני אבל ליוחסין לא, וסגי לדידיה לדורות בחד רובא. אבל קשה לפירושו: לרב חנן תקשי ר' יוחנן בן נורי דאמר כמאן דסגי בחד רובא, כדפריך לעיל! ועוד: דלא מיסתבר דשום אמורא יחלוק אההיא דאבל ליוחסין לא, דרב גופיה קאמר לה בלא אמורא. ולהכי אפירכא דרבי ירמיה לא משני מאן דמתני הא לא מתני הא. **אם** רוב גוים גוי למאי הלכתא. לא מצי למימר לענין שלא להחיותו, דמאי איריא רוב גוים — אפילו מחצה נמי, דדוקא ברוב ישראל קאמר רב דהוי ישראל להחיותו. **להחזיר** לו אבדה. הוה מצי למימר להחיותו, כדאמר רב. אלא נקט להחזיר לו אבדה דהוי רבותא טפי, דאיסור גדול הוא *משום "למען ספות הרוה וגו'". אבל להחיותו לא הוי רבותא כל כך, דהא *מפרנסין עניי גוים עם עניי ישראל. ואפי' לשמואל דאמר *אין הולכין בממון אחר הרוב, היינו, *במוכר שור לחבירו ונמצא נגחן, שבהיתר בא המעות לידו, ומדעתו נתנם לו הלוקח, אבל הכא מודי דאזלינן בתר רובא. **לא** צריכא דנגחיה תורא דידיה כו'. תימה: דהכי נמי הוה מצי למימר מחצה על מחצה גוי, ומנגח תורא דידן לתורא דידיה, [כולה מילתא הוי מצי למימר לענין נגיחה. אלא ניחא בכל חד למצוא דבר חדש. מהר"ס].

הדרן עלך בתולה נשאת

האשה. אם יש עדים שיצאת בהינומא כו'. בדלא נקיטא כתובה איירי, דאי איכא כתובה — ניחזי כתובתה, אם היא בתולה או אלמנה. ואפילו למ"ד: *הטוען אחר מעשה ב"ד ואמר פרעתי נאמן — מ"מ אין נאמן לומר כאן "אלמנה נשאתיך" מגו דאי בעי אמר "פרעתי" — דמגו במקום עדים הוא.

ומודה רבי יהושע באומר שדה כו' דנאמן. מתוך פירוש הקונט' משמע דדוקא כשאין הלה תובעו, ונאמן במגו דאי בעי שתיק. אבל אם תובעו — אינו נאמן. ואינו נראה, דהא קתני סיפא: ואם יש עדים כו'! משמע דדוקא אם יש עדים שהיתה של אביו אינו נאמן. אבל אם אין עדים, אע"ג דהלה תובעו — נאמן, מגו דאי בעי אמר לא היתה של אביך מעולם, מדלא נקט אם תובעו אינו נאמן. ובגמרא נמי פריך: וליתני שדה זו שלך היתה! משמע דבהלה תובעו איירי, ולכך משיב: ודאי שלך היתה ולקחתיה ממך. אבל אם לא תובעו, אין שייך לומר שלך היתה, כי מסתמא הוא יודע בעצמו דבר זה. דאי

תוספות רי"ד

האשה שנתאלמנה או שנתגרשה היא אומרת בתולה נשאתני והוא אומר לא כי אלא אלמנה נשאתיך אם יש עדים שיצאת בהינומא וראשה פרוע כתובתה מאתים ר"י אומר אף חילוק קליות ראיה. פי' הוא אומר אנתגרשה קאי ולאלמנה אומרים לה היורשים אבינו אלמנה נשאך ואין לך אלא מנה ושטר כתובה אבד אם יש עדים על נשואיה שיצאת מבית אביה לבית בעלה בהינומא שהיא סימן הבתולות כדמפרש לקמן וראשה פרוע שערה על כתפה וכך היה מוציאים הבתולות מבית אביהן לבית החתונה. אף חילוק וכו' רגילין היו לחלק מיני פירות וקליות שהיו מיבשין השבלים כשהם לחים בתנור והם מתוקין ובנשואי הבתולות נותנים ומחלקין מהם לתינוקות ואי איכא עדי הינומא אע"ג שהיא אלמנה גביא בעדי הינומא ואע"ג דאיכא למיחש לפרעון וכל טענה דהוה מצי למיטען איהו ב"ד טוענין בעבור היתומים גביא כתובתה דהכי אמרינן בשנים אוחזין הטוען אחר מעשה ב"ד לא אמר כלום דכל מעשה ב"ד כמאן דנקט שטרא בידיה דמי ותנן נמי בפרק הכותב הוציאה גט ואין עמה כתובה גובה כתובתה ולא מצי למטען פרעתי עד שיראה שטר כתובתה קרוע או שובר והתם מוכח דלא מבעי' במנה מאתים שהיא תנאי ב"ד דגביא אלא אפילו תוספת בלא כתובה נמי גביא ולא מהימן לומר פרעתיך הלכך ה"נ מיתמי

כדאיתא סנהדרין עו:

כדאיתא גיטין סא.

[ב"ק מו: וב"ב לב:]

[עי' תוס' ב"ק מו: ותוס' ב"מ כ: ד"ה אוכלא ותוס' סנהדרין ג: ד"ה דיני ותוס' יומא פה.]

[עי' תוס' לקמן פח: ופט. בד"ה הלכתא וכו' וא"ל אי שמואל לית ליה דר' יוחנן וכו']

מכשירין פ"ב מ"ז יומא פד:

הגה"ה פי' משלטי הדמיה. מתוקנין אבריו. פיתקא. קמיע של כתב. קמיעא. קמיע של עיקרין דהא חסה על חייו והוכיח תחלתו שאוהבת אותו ולא השליכתו למות:

[נראה לר"י דמשום דדרשינן וחי בהם ולא שימות בהם ומשמע שלא יבוא לידי מיתה בשום ענין לכך יש לחוש למיעוט ישראל. ת"י]

ב"ב לב: [ושם איתא שנתלאמנה]

הגהות הב"ח

(א) רש"י ד"ה אבל כו' ולמ"ד גיורת. נ"ב בפרק הבא על יבמתו דף ס ע"ב:

שֶׁהַפֶּה שֶׁאָסַר הוּא הַפֶּה שֶׁהִתִּיר. וְאִם יֵשׁ עֵדִים שֶׁהִיא שֶׁל אָבִיו, וְהוּא אוֹמֵר: "לְקַחְתִּיהָ הֵימֶנּוּ" אֵינוֹ נֶאֱמָן.§ **גמ'** טַעֲמָא [א]דְּאִיכָּא עֵדִים, הָא לֵיכָּא עֵדִים — בַּעַל מְהֵימָן. לֵימָא תְּנַן סְתָמָא דְּלָא כְּרַבָּן גַּמְלִיאֵל, דְּאִי ר"ג — הָא אָמַר אִיהִי מְהֵימְנָא! אֲפִילּוּ תֵּימָא רַבָּן גַּמְלִיאֵל, עַד כָּאן לָא קָאָמַר ר"ג הָתָם אֶלָּא בְּבָרִי וְשֶׁמָּא, אֲבָל הָכָא, בְּבָרִי וּבָרִי — לֹא אָמַר. *וּדְקָאָרֵי לָהּ מַאי קָאָרֵי לָהּ? הָא בָּרִי וּבָרִי הוּא! *כֵּיוָן דְּרוֹב נָשִׁים בְּתוּלוֹת נִישָּׂאוֹת — כִּי בָּרִי וְשֶׁמָּא דָּמֵי. וְהָכִי נַמִי מִסְתַּבְּרָא, מִדְּקָתָנֵי: וּמוֹדֶה רַבִּי יְהוֹשֻׁעַ. אִי אָמְרַתְּ בִּשְׁלָמָא אַיְירִי ר"ג בְּמוֹדֶה — שַׁפִּיר, אֶלָּא אִי אָמְרַתְּ לָא אַיְירִי ר"ג בְּמוֹדֶה — רַבִּי יְהוֹשֻׁעַ לְמַאן מוֹדֶה? מִי סָבְרַתְּ ר' יְהוֹשֻׁעַ אַהַאי פִּירְקִין קָאֵי? אַמִּגּוֹ קָאֵי, וְאַפִּירְקִין קַמָּא קָאֵי. אַהַיָּיא? אִילֵימָא אַהָא: *הָיְתָה מְעוּבֶּרֶת, וְאָמְרוּ לָהּ: מַה טִּיבוֹ שֶׁל עוּבָּר זֶה? "מֵאִישׁ פְּלוֹנִי וְכֹהֵן הוּא". ר"ג וְר"א אוֹמְרִים: נֶאֱמֶנֶת, רַבִּי יְהוֹשֻׁעַ אוֹמֵר: לֹא מִפִּיהָ אָנוּ חַיִּין, הָתָם מַאי מִגּוֹ אִיכָּא? הֲרֵי כְּרֵיסָהּ בֵּין שִׁינֶּיהָ! אֶלָּא אַהָא; *רָאוּהָ מְדַבֶּרֶת עִם אֶחָד. וְאָמְרוּ לָהּ: מַה טִּיבוֹ שֶׁל אִישׁ זֶה? "אִישׁ פְּלוֹנִי, וְכֹהֵן הוּא". ר"ג וְר"א אוֹמְרִים: נֶאֱמֶנֶת, רַבִּי יְהוֹשֻׁעַ אוֹמֵר: לֹא מִפִּיהָ אָנוּ חַיִּין. הָתָם מַאי מִגּוֹ אִיכָּא? הָנִיחָא *לִזְעֵירִי דְּאָמַר: מַאי "מְדַבֶּרֶת" נִסְתְּרָה, מִגּוֹ דְּאִי בָּעֲיָא אָמְרָה לֹא נִבְעַלְתִּי, וְקָאָמְרָה נִבְעַלְתִּי, מְהֵימְנָא. אֶלָּא לְרַב אַסִּי, דְּאָמַר: מַאי "מְדַבֶּרֶת" — *נִבְעֶלֶת, מַאי מִגּוֹ אִיכָּא? וְאֶלָּא אַהָא; *הִיא אוֹמֶרֶת: מוּכַּת עֵץ אֲנִי, וְהוּא אוֹמֵר: לֹא כִּי, אֶלָּא דְּרוּסַת אִישׁ אַתְּ. ר"ג וְר"א אוֹמְרִים: נֶאֱמֶנֶת, וְרַבִּי יְהוֹשֻׁעַ אוֹמֵר: לֹא מִפִּיהָ אָנוּ חַיִּין. הָתָם מַאי מִגּוֹ אִיכָּא? בִּשְׁלָמָא לְרַבִּי אֶלְעָזָר, דְּאָמַר בְּמָנֶה וְלֹא כְּלוּם, מִגּוֹ דְּאִי בָּעֲיָא אָמְרָה מוּכַּת עֵץ אֲנִי תַּחְתֶּיךָ, וְאִית לָהּ מָאתַיִם, וְקָאָמְרָה מֵעִיקָּרָא, דְּלֵית לָהּ אֶלָּא מָנֶה — מְהֵימְנָא. אֶלָּא לְר' יוֹחָנָן. דְּאָמַר בְּמָאתַיִם וּמָנֶה, מַאי מִגּוֹ אִיכָּא? אֶלָּא אַהָא: *הַנּוֹשֵׂא אֶת הָאִשָּׁה וְלֹא מָצָא לָהּ בְּתוּלִים, הִיא אוֹמֶרֶת: מִשֶּׁאֵרַסְתַּנִי נֶאֱנַסְתִּי, וְנִסְתַּחֲפָה שָׂדֵהוּ. וְהוּא אוֹמֵר: לֹא כִּי, אֶלָּא עַד שֶׁלֹּא אֵירַסְתִּיךְ. ר"ג וְר"א אוֹמְרִים: נֶאֱמֶנֶת, וְר' יְהוֹשֻׁעַ אוֹמֵר: לֹא מִפִּיהָ אָנוּ חַיִּין. דְּמִגּוֹ דְּאִי בָּעֲיָא אָמְרָה מוּכַּת עֵץ אֲנִי תַּחְתֶּיךָ, דְּלָא קָא פָּסְלָה נַפְשָׁהּ מִכְּהוּנָּה, וְקָאָמְרָה נֶאֱנַסְתִּי, דְּקָא פָּסְלָה נַפְשָׁהּ מִכְּהוּנָּה — מִשּׁוּם הָכִי קָאָמַר ר"ג דִּמְהֵימְנָא. וְקָאָמַר רַבִּי יְהוֹשֻׁעַ לְר"ג: בְּהַאי מִגּוֹ דְּהָכָא — מוֹדֵינָא לָךְ, בְּהַהוּא מִגּוֹ דְּהָתָם — פְּלִיגְנָא עִילָּוָךְ. מִכְּדִי, הַאי מִגּוֹ וְהַאי מִגּוֹ, מַאי שְׁנָא הַאי מִגּוֹ מֵהַאי מִגּוֹ? הָכָא אֵין שׁוֹר שָׁחוּט לְפָנֶיךָ, הָתָם — הֲרֵי שׁוֹר שָׁחוּט לְפָנֶיךָ. וְכֵיוָן דְּרוֹב נָשִׁים בְּתוּלוֹת נִישָּׂאוֹת, כִּי לָא אָתוּ עֵדִים מַאי הָוֵי? *אָמַר רָבִינָא: מִשּׁוּם דְּאִיכָּא לְמֵימַר רוֹב נָשִׁים בְּתוּלוֹת נִישָּׂאוֹת, וּמִיעוּט אַלְמָנוֹת. וְכָל הַנִּשֵּׂאת בְּתוּלָה — יֵשׁ לָהּ קוֹל, וְזוֹ

רש"י

שֶׁהַפֶּה שֶׁאָסַר. זֶה אֵינוֹ יוֹדֵעַ שֶׁהָיְתָה שֶׁל אָבִיו, אֶלָּא עַל פִּיו שֶׁל זֶה, וּמַה שֶּׁאָסַר – הֲרֵי הִתִּיר. **גמ'** טַעֲמָא דְּאִיכָּא עֵדִים. דְּיָצְאָה בְּהִינּוּמָא. הַבַּעַל מְהֵימָן. וְלָא אָמְרִינַן: הוֹאִיל וּמִסְתַּפְּקָא לָן עַל יוֹם נִישּׂוּאֶיהָ אִם בְּתוּלָה הָיְתָה אִם בְּעוּלָה – הַעֲמֵד אוֹתָהּ עַל חֶזְקָתָהּ שֶׁל קוֹדֶם לָכֵן, וּמִתְּחִלָּה בְּתוּלָה הָיְתָה. הִיא נֶאֱמֶנֶת. דְּאָזֵיל בָּתַר חֲזָקָה דְּגוּפָא. בְּבָרִי וְשֶׁמָּא. גַּבֵּי מִשֶּׁאֵרַסְתַּנִי נֶאֱנַסְתִּי, הִיא טוֹעֶנֶת בָּרִי לִי הוּא, וְהוּא אֵינוֹ טוֹעֵן אֶלָּא שֶׁמָּא עַד שֶׁלֹּא אֵרַסְתִּיךְ. דְּהָא אֵינוֹ יוֹדֵעַ מָתַי נֶאֶנְסָה. וּדְקָאָרֵי לָהּ. לְמֵימַר סְתָמָא דְּלָא כְּרַבָּן גַּמְלִיאֵל. מַאי קָאָרֵי לָהּ. וּמַאי עָלְתָה בְּדַעְתּוֹ לְאַפּוֹקֵי מִדְּר"ג, הָא לָא דָּמְיָא לָהּ! כֵּיוָן דְּרוֹב נָשִׁים בְּתוּלוֹת נִישָּׂאוֹת. קְרוֹבָה טַעֲנָתָהּ לִהְיוֹת אֱמֶת יוֹתֵר מִשֶּׁלּוֹ, וּכְבָרִי וְשֶׁמָּא דָּמְיָא. וְהָכִי נַמִי מִסְתַּבְּרָא. דְּר"ג מוֹדֶה בָּהּ דְּבַעַל מְהֵימָן. אִי אָמְרַתְּ בִּשְׁלָמָא אַיְירִי ר"ג בְּמוֹדֶה. דְּהָךְ רֵישָׁא הוֹדָאָה הוּא דְּקָא מוֹדֶה ר"ג לְרַבִּי יְהוֹשֻׁעַ, וְאָמַר: אע"ג דִּפְלִיגְנָא עֲלָךְ בְּבָרִי וְשֶׁמָּא – מוֹדֵינָא לָךְ בְּבָרִי וּבָרִי – הַיְינוּ דְּשַׁיָּיךְ לְמִיתְנֵי בַּתְרֵיהּ וְר' יְהוֹשֻׁעַ מוֹדֶה לְר"ג בְּהָאוֹמֵר לַחֲבֵרוֹ שָׂדֶה זוֹ כו'. דְּאע"ג דִּפְלִיגְנָא בְּפ"ק בְּמִשֶּׁאֵרַסְתַּנִי נֶאֱנַסְתִּי, דְּאע"ג דְּאִיכָּא לְמֵימַר מִגּוֹ לָא מְהֵימְנָא, מוֹדֵינָא בְּהַאי מִגּוֹ דְּאִי בָּעֵי שָׁתֵיק וְלָא א"ל שֶׁל אָבִיךָ הָיְתָה, כִּי אָמַר לֵיהּ נַמִי לְקַחְתִּיהָ הֵימֶנּוּ – מְהֵימָן, כִּדִלְקַמָּן. אֶלָּא אִי אָמְרַתְּ לָא אַיְירִי. רֵישָׁא בְּמוֹדֶה ר"ג, מַאי "מוֹדֶה רַבִּי יְהוֹשֻׁעַ"? מַאי שַׁיָּיךְ לְמִיתְנְיֵיהּ הָכָא, וְאַהֵיכָא קָאֵי? אַמִּגּוֹ קָאֵי. אַפְּלוּגְתָּא דְּאִיכָּא לְמֵימַר בָּהּ מִגּוֹ בְּפֶ' קַמָּא קָאֵי, וְקָאָמַר: אע"ג דִּפְלִיגְנָא בְּמִגּוֹ דְּהָתָם – בְּמִגּוֹ דְּהָכָא מוֹדֵינָא, כִּדִלְקַמָּן. אַהַיָּיא. אִיכָּא מִגּוֹ. הֲרֵי כְּרֵיסָהּ בֵּין שִׁינֶּיהָ. וְאֵינָהּ יְכוֹלָה לוֹמַר לֹא נִבְעַלְתִּי. וְקָאָמְרָה נִבְעַלְתִּי. וּלְכָשֵׁר נִבְעַלְתִּי, מְהֵימְנָא. בִּשְׁלָמָא לְר' אֶלְעָזָר דְּאָמַר. בְּפֶרֶק קַמָּא טַעֲנָתַיְיהוּ בְּמָנֶה וְלֹא כְלוּם. מוּכַּת עֵץ שֶׁלֹּא הִכִּיר בָּהּ – אֵינָהּ יְכוֹלָה לְתוֹבְעוֹ אֶלָּא מָנֶה, וְהוּא אוֹמֵר: דְּרוּסַת אִישׁ אַתְּ, וְאֵין לִיךְ כְּלוּם. אִיכָּא מִגּוֹ, דְּאִי בָּעֲיָא אָמְרָה מוּכַּת עֵץ אֲנִי תַּחְתֶּיךָ. *מִשֶּׁאֵרַסְתַּנִי. אֵירַע לִי וְנִסְתַּחֲפָה שָׂדֵהוּ, וְאִית לִי מָאתַיִם. וְקָאָמְרָה. מוּכַּת עֵץ אֲנִי מֵעִיקָּרָא, וְלֹא תָּבְעָה אֶלָּא מָנֶה – מְהֵימְנָא. אֶלָּא לְר' יוֹחָנָן. דְּאָמַר: טַעֲנָתַיְיהוּ בְּמָאתַ' וּמָנֶה, שֶׁהִיא תּוֹבַעְתּוֹ מָאתַיִם – לֵיכָּא מִידֵּי בֵּין תַּחְתָּיו לְמֵעִיקָּרָא, מַאי מִגּוֹ אִיכָּא? הָכָא. גַּבֵּי שָׂדֶה אֵין שׁוֹר שָׁחוּט לְפָנֶיךָ, שֶׁיַּעֲלֶה עַל לֵב בְּעָלָיו לִתְבּוֹעַ מִי שְׁחָטוֹ. כְּלוֹמַר, אִם שָׁתַק זֶה – לֹא הָיוּ לוֹ עוֹרְרִים. הִלְכָּךְ, אִי לָאו דְּדָבָר פָּשׁוּט הוּא שֶׁלְּקָחָהּ הֵימֶנּוּ – לֹא הָיָה אוֹמֵר לוֹ שֶׁל אָבִיךָ הָיְתָה. הִלְכָּךְ אָמְרִי' מִגּוֹ. אֲבָל גַּבֵּי לֹא מָצָא לָהּ בְּתוּלִים – שׁוֹר שָׁחוּט לְפָנֶיךָ, בְּתוּלִים שֶׁלֹּא מָצָא לָהּ הֵם הֱסִיתוּהוּ לָבֹא לְבֵ"ד, וְאע"פ שֶׁיֵּשׁ לָהּ לְהָשִׁיב טַעֲנָה טוֹבָה מִזּוֹ – לָא אָמְרִינַן מִגּוֹ, דִּלְמָא לָא אַסְּקָהּ אַדַּעְתָּהּ. א"נ, אִיעֲרוּמֵי קָא מְעָרְמָא. וְכֵיוָן שֶׁרוֹב נָשִׁים. קוּשְׁיָא הִיא. יֵשׁ לָהּ קוֹל. וְהַרְבֵּה יוֹדְעִים שֶׁיָּצְאָה בְּהִינּוּמָא.
וְזוֹ

תוספות

דאי רבן גמליאל הא אמר איהי מהימנא. נראה דלמ"ד *הטוען אחר מעשה ב"ד לא אמר כלום פריך, דלמ"ד דמלי טעין פרעתי – הכא נאמן הבעל, אפילו לר"ג לומר: אלמנה נשאתיך, במגו דאי בעי אמר פרעתי. **הכי** נמי מסתברא. פי' בקונטרס: הכי נמי מסתברא דמתני' אתיא כרבן גמליאל, כדמשנינן דבברי וברי מודה, מדקתני ומודה ר' יהושע כו'. וקשה לפי': דכי לא איירי נמי ר"ג במודה אתי שפיר ומודה רבי יהושע, כלומר, אע"ג דברישא פליגנא עלך – בסיפא מודינא לך, אע"ג דרישא וסיפא אינן מענין אחד. כי היכי דאתיא ליה שפיר ומודה רבי יהושע, אי איירי ר"ג במודה, אע"ג דמודה דר' גמליאל אינו מענין ומודה דרבי יהושע! ויש ליישב, דודאי כי איירי ר"ג במודה שייך למיתני שפיר ומודה רבי יהושע, אע"ג דלא הוי מענין אחד. כלומר: דאגב דתנא מילתא דמודה ר"ג – תני נמי מילתא דמודה בה רבי יהושע, אבל אי לא איירי רבן גמליאל במודה – לא שייך למיתני ומודה רבי יהושע לאשמועינן אע"ג דפליג ברישא מודה בסיפא, כיון דרישא וסיפא אינם מענין אחד. אבל קשה: דלא הוה ליה למימר אמגו קאי, דעד השתא נמי לפ"ה אמגו הוי קאי! ונראה לר"י דה"פ: הכי נמי מסתברא דכברי ושמא דמי, ולא בא לומר דפליג רבן גמליאל ברישא, אלא אע"ג דכברי ושמא דמי – מודה ר"ג, משום דלאו שמא ממש הוא. מדקאמר ומודה רבי יהושע, אי אמרת בשלמא איירי ר"ג במודה, כלומר, אע"ג דכברי ושמא דמי – מודה ר"ג דבעל נאמן – היינו דקתני ומודה רבי יהושע דבהאי ברי נאמן. דס"ד דטעמא דרבי יהושע משום ברי ושמא, דזה אינו תובעו, כדפי' בקונט'. והשתא הוה מודה דר"ג ומודה דר"י מענין אחד. אלא אי אמרת דרישא בברי וברי גמור הוא, ולא איירי רבן גמליאל במודה, דפשיטא דכיון דברי וברי הוא דלא פליג ר"ג – מאי ומודה? וקאמר: מי סברת דארישא קאי, וטעמא דר"י משום ברי ושמא – אמגו קאי. דטעמא דר' יהושע משום מגו, ונאמן אפי' הלה תובעו, ואפירקין קמא קאי.
התם שור שחוט לפניך. פירש בקונטרס: שהוא טוען עד שלא אירסתיך נאנסת. והכא אין שור שחוט לפניך, דאין הלה תובעו. ור"י מפרש: דהכא נמי איירי בהלה תובעו, כדפי', וה"פ: התם שור שחוט לפניך, דהרי אין לה בתולים, ואינה יכולה לומר בתולה אני, כמו בשור שחוט שאין יכול לומר חי הוא. ולהכי, בין אומרת משארסתני נאנסתי, בין אומרת מוכת עץ אני תחתיך – לא מהימנא. הכא, אין שור שחוט לפניך ונאמן במגו, דאי בעי אמר: לא היתה של אביך מעולם.
כיון דרוב נשים בתולות נישאות כי ליכא עדים מאי הוי. לרב פריך, דאית ליה *הולכין בממון אחר הרוב*.
וזו

[ב"מ יז.]
ב א מיי' פט"ז מהלכות אישות הלכה כה סמג עשין מח טוש"ע אה"ע סימן נו סעיף טו:

תוספות רי"ד

מיתמי גובה בלא כתובה ודייקינן טעמא דאיכא עדים פי' שיצאת בהינומא ורא{ש}ה פרוע הא ליכא עדים בעל מהימן פי' ולא אמרינן הואיל ומספקא לן על יום נשואיה אם היתה בעולה או בתולה העמד אותה על חזקתה של קודם לכן ובתולה היתה לימא תנן סתמא דלא כר"ג דאי ר"ג האמר איהי מהימנא פי' דאזיל בתר חזקה דגופה וה"נ נימא העמד אשה על חזקתה ובתולה היתה ומהדר אפילו תימא ר"ג ע"כ לא קאמר ר"ג אלא ברי ושמא אבל ברי וברי לא אמר עיין בפ"ק. ודקארי לה מאי קארי לה. כיון דרוב נשים בתולות נשאות כברי ושמא דמי. וכיון דרוב נשים בתולות נשאות כי לא אתי עדי הינומא מאי הוה ניזיל בתר רובא. פי' ואע"ג דיש פלוגתא בהא מילתא רב ושמואל בפרק המוכר פירות דרב אמר הולכין בממון אחר הרוב ושמואל אמר אין הולכין בממון אחר הרוב וקי"ל הלכה כשמואל הכא משום דאיכא תרתי רובא וחזקה העמד אשה על חזקתה ובתולה היתה אפי' שמואל מודה. אמר רבינא משום דא"ל דרוב נשים בתולות נשאות ומיעוט אלמנות ורוב הנשאת בתולה יש לה קול וזו הואיל ואין לה קול איתרע לה רובא:

לעיל יב:

גליון הש"ס

גמ' ודקארי לה מאי קארי לה. לקמן לו ע"א [יומא ל ע"ב] יבמות יא ע"א יד ע"א [עב ע"א. גיטין סא ע"ב ב"ק מז ע"ב] ב"ב ב ע"ב [יז ע"ב] קמז ע"א [בכורות ד ע"ב] נדה סד ע"א:

[ב"ק מו: ב"ב לב:]
*אפשר דאפילו לשמואל הוה לן למיזל בתר רובא ולא אחר חזקת ממון כיון דחזקת הגוף מסייע לרוב ופריך שפיר אפילו אליביה דשמואל קאי אמאי דאמרינן

ב"ב לב: [עי' פרש"י לקמן לו. ד"ה ודקארי] לקמן כח.
לעיל יג.
שם
[שם]
...ע"ג דאיתותב כו' מ"מ ...עי נמי לשנויי מתני' אליביה. ת"י
...ד"ז שייך לקמן אחר ד"ה ...לא לר' יוחנן ויותר טפי ...ם לדיבור זה שייכות לעיל יב: במשנה הנושא וכו']
[ב"ב לב:]

לעיל כיון דרוב נשים בתולות נישאות הוי ליה ברי דידיה כי שמא ובברי ושמא פסק שמואל כר"ג הכא דמהני לה חזקת הגוף לחד לישנא דפ"ק להכי פריך וניזיל בתר רובא דס"ד דהוי רוב גמור. ת"י.

וְזוֹ הוֹאִיל וְאֵין לָהּ קוֹל — אִיתְרַע לָהּ רוּבָּא. אִי כָּל הַנִּשֵּׂאת בְּתוּלָה יֵשׁ לָהּ קוֹל, כִּי אָתוּ עֵדִים מַאי הָוֵי? הָנָךְ סָהֲדֵי שַׁקָּרֵי נִינְהוּ! אֶלָּא אָמַר רָבִינָא: רוֹב הַנִּשֵּׂאת בְּתוּלָה יֵשׁ לָהּ קוֹל, וְזוֹ הוֹאִיל וְאֵין לָהּ קוֹל — אִיתְרַע לָהּ רוּבָּא.§ אִם יֵשׁ עֵדִים שֶׁיָּצְתָה בְּהִינּוּמָא וכו'.§ וְלֵיחוּשׁ דִּלְמָא מַפְּקָא עֵדִים בְּהַאי בֵּי דִינָא וְגָבְיָא, וַהֲדַר מַפְּקָא לָהּ לִכְתוּבָּה בְּהַאי ב"ד וְגָבְיָא בָּהּ! א"ר אַבָּהוּ: זֹאת אוֹמֶרֶת: *כּוֹתְבִין שׁוֹבֵר. רַב פַּפָּא אָמַר: [א]בְּמָקוֹם שֶׁאֵין כּוֹתְבִין כְּתוּבָּה עָסְקִינַן. וְאִיכָּא דְּמַתְנֵי לָהּ אַבָּרַיְיתָא: אִיבְּדָה כְּתוּבָּתָהּ, הִטְמִינָה כְּתוּבָּתָהּ, נִשְׂרְפָה כְּתוּבָּתָהּ, רָקְדוּ לְפָנֶיהָ, שִׂחֲקוּ לְפָנֶיהָ, הֶעֱבִירוּ לְפָנֶיהָ כּוֹס שֶׁל בְּשׂוֹרָה, אוֹ מַפָּה שֶׁל בְּתוּלִים, אִם יֵשׁ לָהּ עֵדִים בְּאֶחָד מִכָּל אֵלּוּ — כְּתוּבָּתָהּ מָאתַיִם. וְלֵיחוּשׁ דִּלְמָא מַפְּקָא עֵדִים בְּהַאי ב"ד וְגָבְיָא, וַהֲדַר מַפְּקָא לִכְתוּבָּתָהּ בְּהַאי ב"ד וְגָבְיָא בָּהּ! א"ר אַבָּהוּ: זֹאת אוֹמֶרֶת: *[ב]כּוֹתְבִין שׁוֹבֵר. רַב פַּפָּא אָמַר: בְּמָקוֹם שֶׁאֵין כּוֹתְבִין כְּתוּבָּה עָסְקִינַן. וְהָא אִיבְּדָה כְּתוּבָּתָהּ קָתָנֵי! דְּכָתַב לָהּ אִיהוּ. סוֹף סוֹף מַפְּקָא לָהּ וְגָבְיָא בָּהּ! מַאי אִיבְּדָה — אִיבְּדָה בָּאוּר. א"ה הַיְינוּ נִשְׂרְפָה! וְעוֹד: הִטְמִינָה, מַאי אִיכָּא לְמֵימַר? וְתוּ: אִיבְּדָה לָמָּה לִי? אֶלָּא: כָּל אִיבְּדָה — כִּי הִטְמִינָה בְּפָנֵינוּ דָּמֵי, וְלָא יָהֲבִינַן לָהּ עַד דְּאָמְרִי עֵדִים נִשְׂרְפָה כְּתוּבָּתָהּ. מַאן דְּמַתְנֵי לָהּ אַבָּרַיְיתָא — כָּל שֶׁכֵּן אַמַּתְנִי', וּמַאן דְּמַתְנֵי לָהּ אַמַּתְנִי' — אֲבָל אַבָּרַיְיתָא לָא, כִּי קוּשְׁיָא.§ אִם יֵשׁ עֵדִים כו'.§ וְלֵיחוּשׁ דִּלְמָא מַפְּקָא עֵדֵי הִינּוּמָא בְּהַאי ב"ד וְגָבְיָא, וַהֲדַר מַפְּקָא עֵדֵי הִינּוּמָא בְּבֵי דִינָא אַחֲרִינָא וְגָבְיָא! בְּמָקוֹם דְּלָא אֶפְשָׁר — וַדַּאי כָּתְבִינַן שׁוֹבֵר.§ הֶעֱבִירוּ לְפָנֶיהָ כּוֹס שֶׁל בְּשׂוֹרָה.§ מַאי "כּוֹס שֶׁל בְּשׂוֹרָה"? אָמַר רַב אַדָּא בַּר אַהֲבָה: כּוֹס יַיִן שֶׁל תְּרוּמָה מַעֲבִירִין לְפָנֶיהָ, כְּלוֹמַר: רְאוּיָה הָיְתָה זוֹ לֶאֱכוֹל בִּתְרוּמָה. מַתְקִיף לָהּ רַב פַּפָּא: אַטּוּ אַלְמָנָה מִי לָא אָכְלָה בִּתְרוּמָה? אֶלָּא אָמַר רַב פַּפָּא: זוֹ רֵאשִׁית כִּתְרוּמָה רֵאשִׁית. תַּנְיָא, רַבִּי יְהוּדָה אוֹמֵר: חָבִית שֶׁל יַיִן מַעֲבִירִין לְפָנֶיהָ. אָמַר רַב אַדָּא בַּר אַהֲבָה: בְּתוּלָה מַעֲבִירִין לְפָנֶיהָ סְתוּמָה, בְּעוּלָה — מַעֲבִירִין לְפָנֶיהָ פְּתוּחָה. אַמַּאי? נִיעֲבַר קַמֵּי בְּתוּלָה, וְקַמֵּי בְּעוּלָה לָא נִיעֲבַר כְּלָל! זִימְנִין דְּתָפְסָה מָאתַיִם, וְאָמְרָה: אֲנָא בְּתוּלָה הֲוַאי, וְהַאי דְּלָא עֲבָרוּ קַמָּאי — אִתְנוּסֵי הוּא דְּאִתְנִיסוּ. *תָּנוּ רַבָּנַן: כֵּיצַד מְרַקְּדִין לִפְנֵי הַכַּלָּה? בֵּית שַׁמַּאי אוֹמְרִים:

כַּלָּה

רש"י

וְזוֹ הוֹאִיל וְאֵין לָהּ קוֹל. שֶׁאֵין מֵעִיד עָלֶיהָ שֶׁיָּצְאָה בְּהִינּוּמָא. **כִּי אָתוּ** עֵדִים מַאי הָוֵי. כֵּיוָן דַּחֲזָקָה דְּיֵשׁ לָהּ קוֹל, הַרְבֵּה הָיוּ יוֹדְעִין. **דִּלְמָא** **מַפְּקָא** עֵדִים. עֵדֵי הִינּוּמָא. כּוֹתְבִין שׁוֹבֵר. שֶׁכְּשֶׁיִּפָּרַע לָהּ כְּתוּבָּתָהּ תִּכְתּוֹב לוֹ שֶׁקִּבְּלָה כְּתוּבָּתָהּ, וְיִהְיֶה בְּיָדוֹ לִזְכוּת. **זֹאת אוֹמֶרֶת.** וּדְלָא כְּמַאן דְּאָמַר אֵין כּוֹתְבִין, בְּבָבָא בַּתְרָא. רַב **פַּפָּא אָמַר.** לְעוֹלָם אֵין כּוֹתְבִין, דְּנִמְצָא זֶה צָרִיךְ לִשְׁמוֹר שׁוֹבְרוֹ מִן הָעַכְבָּרִים. וּמִי שֶׁיֵּשׁ לוֹ שְׁטָר עַל חֲבֵרוֹ – אוֹ יָבִיא הַשְּׁטָר וְיַחֲזִירֶנּוּ, אוֹ לֹא יִטּוֹל כְּלוּם. וּמַתְנִי' בְּמָקוֹם שֶׁאֵין כּוֹתְבִין כְּתוּבָּה, אֶלָּא סוֹמְכִין עַל תְּנַאי בֵּית דִּין שֶׁתִּקְּנוּ לִבְתוּלָה מָאתַיִם וּלְאַלְמָנָה מָנֶה, דְּלֵיכָּא לְמֵיחַשׁ לְדִלְמָא הָדְרָה וּמַפְּקָא לָהּ. דְּמַתְנֵי לָהּ. לְדְרַבִּי אַבָּהוּ וּלְדְרַב פַּפָּא. הִטְמִינָה כְּתוּבָּתָהּ. וְהִיא תּוֹבַעַת מָאתַיִם, וְהוּא אוֹמֵר אַלְמָנָה נְשָׂאתִיךְ. רָקְדוּ לְפָנֶיהָ. אִם יֵשׁ עֵדִים שֶׁרָקְדוּ לְפָנֶיהָ בְּיוֹם נִשּׂוּאֶיהָ. כּוֹס שֶׁל בְּשׂוֹרָה. הַמְבַשֵּׂר עָלֶיהָ סִימָנֵי בְּתוּלוֹת. וּלְקַמָּן מְפָרֵשׁ מַאי הִיא. **אֶלָּא.** הָכִי קָאָמַר: כָּל אִיבְּדָה כְּמִי שֶׁהִטְמִינָה בְּפָנֵינוּ דָּמֵי, וְלָא גָּבְיָא. וְהָכִי קָתָנֵי: אִיבְּדָה כְּתוּבָּתָהּ, הִטְמִינָה כְּתוּבָּתָהּ, נִשְׂרְפָה כְּתוּבָּתָהּ, אִם רָקְדוּ לְפָנֶיהָ וכו'. וְהָכִי פֵּירוּשָׁהּ: אָמְרָה אָבַד שְׁטַר כְּתוּבָּתָהּ – הֲרֵי הִיא כְּמוֹ שֶׁהִטְמִינָה כְּתוּבָּתָהּ בְּפָנֵינוּ כְּדֵי לְהוֹצִיא וְלִגְבּוֹת פַּעַם שְׁנִיָּה, וְאֵינָהּ גּוֹבָה כְּלוּם, אא"כ תָּבִיא הַשְּׁטָר. וְאִם אָמְרָה נִשְׂרְפָה, וְיֵשׁ עֵדִים שֶׁנִּשְׂרְפָה, דְּהַשְׁתָּא לֵיכָּא לְמֵיחַשׁ לְמִידֵי – תָּבִיא עֵדִים שֶׁרָקְדוּ לְפָנֶיהָ, שֶׁזֶּהוּ סִימָן לִבְתוּלָה, וְתִגְבֶּה מָאתַיִם. מַאן דְּמַתְנֵי לָהּ. לְדְרַבִּי אַבָּהוּ וְרַב פַּפָּא אַבָּרַיְיתָא. כָּל שֶׁכֵּן **אַמַּתְנִיתִין.** דְּכֵיוָן דְּאַבָּרַיְיתָא דְּקָתָנֵי בְּהֶדְיָא אִיבְּדָה כְּתוּבָּתָהּ גָּבְיָא, וַעֲלָהּ קָאָמַר רַב פַּפָּא דְּלָא גָּבְיָא. וּמְתָרֵץ לָהּ דַּחֲדָא קָתָנֵי: אִיבְּדָה כְּתוּבָּתָ' הֲרֵי הִיא כְּמוֹ שֶׁהִטְמִינָה, וּכְשֶׁנִּשְׂרְפָה הוּא דְּקָא גָּבְיָא, וּלְעוֹלָם אֵין כּוֹתְבִין שׁוֹבֵר, כָּל שֶׁכֵּן דְּאַמַּתְנִי' אִיכָּא לְמִיתְנֵי פְּלוּגְתָּא דְּרַב פַּפָּא אַדְּר' אַבָּהוּ, לְמֵימַר דִּבְמָקוֹם שֶׁאֵין כּוֹתְבִין כְּתוּבָּה עָסְקִי'. וּמַאן דְּמַתְנֵי. פְּלוּגְתָּא דְּרַב פַּפָּא וּדְר' אַבָּהוּ אַמַּתְנִי'. **אֲבָל אַבָּרַיְיתָא לָא.** מַתְנֵי לֵיהּ, דְּוַדַּאי שָׁמְעִינַן מִינָּהּ דְּכוֹתְבִין שׁוֹבֵר, דְּהָא בְּמָקוֹם שֶׁכּוֹתְבִין כְּתוּבָּה עָסְקִינַן. כִּי קוּשְׁיַין. דְּקָתָנֵי אִיבְּדָה כְּתוּבָּתָהּ. וְלָא נִיחָא לְשַׁנּוּיֵי שִׁינּוּיָא דְּחִיקָא, לְמֵימַר אִיבְּדָה כְּתוּבָּתָ' כְּהִטְמִינָה כְּתוּבָּתָהּ קָאָמַר. כֵּיוָן דְּלָא **אֶפְשָׁר.** כְּגוֹן בְּמָקוֹם שֶׁאֵין כּוֹתְבִין כְּתוּבָּה, וְגוֹבוֹת עַל פִּי עֵדִים, וְיֵשׁ לָחוּשׁ שֶׁמָּא תֵּלֵךְ לְב"ד אַחֵר וְתָבִיא עֵדִים אֲחֵרִים וְתִגְבֶּה פַּעַם שְׁנִיָּה – וַדַּאי כָּתְבִינַן שׁוֹבֵר. רְאוּיָה הָיְתָה זוֹ לֶאֱכוֹל בִּתְרוּמָה. אִי נִישֵּׂאת לְכֹהֵן, דִּבְתוּלָה שְׁלֵמָה נִמְצֵאת וְלֹא בְּעוּלָה, שֶׁתִּפָּסֵל לְכֹהֵן מֵחֲמַת זְנוּת. מַתְקִיף לָהּ רַב **פַּפָּא.** וּמַה זּוֹ עֵדוּת לְלֹא נִישֵּׂאת אַלְמָנָה? **אַטּוּ.** אִי נִישֵּׂאת כְּשֶׁהִיא אַלְמָנָה לְכֹהֵן הֶדְיוֹט, מִי לָא אָכְלָה בִּתְרוּמָה? זוֹ **רֵאשִׁית.** בְּעִילָתָהּ רֵאשִׁית. זִימְנִין דְּתָפְסָה **מָאתַיִם.** בְּלֹא בֵּית דִּין. וְכִי בָּעֵינַן לְאַפּוּקֵי מִינָּהּ, מִשּׁוּם דְּאֵין עֵדִים שֶׁהֶעֱבִירוּ לְפָנֶיהָ, אָמְרָה: אִיתְנוּסֵי הוּא דְּאִיתְנִיסוּ. שִׁיכּוֹרִים הָיוּ מֵאוֹנֶס יֵין הַמִּשְׁתֶּה. הִלְכָּךְ, הַשְׁתָּא אָתוּ עֵדִים שֶׁהֶעֱבִירוּ לְפָנֶיהָ פְּתוּחָה – וְתוּ לֵיכָּא מִידֵי. **כֵּיצַד** מְרַקְּדִים. מָה אוֹמְרִים לְפָנֶיהָ.

כְּמוֹת

תוספות

וזו הואיל ואין לה קול **איתרע** לה רובא. תימה: דתנן בפירקין (לקמן כח.): אלו נאמנים להעיד בגודלן מה שראו בקטנותן: זכורני בפלונית שיצאה בהינומא וראשה פרוע. וקאמר בגמ': מ"ט – כיון דרוב נשים בתולות נישאות, גילוי מילתא בעלמא הוא. והשתא היכי מיירי? אם יש לה קול – למה צריך שום עדות לרב ניזיל בתר רובא, כדפריך הכא. ואי אין לה קול – א"כ איתרע לה רובא, ויצטרך שני עדים כשרים! וכי תימא דכשמעיד הוא שראה בקוטנו ואחר עמו חשבינן קול – הא פריך הכא: סהדי שקרי נינהו! ויש לומר: דרוב נשים בתולות נישאות עדיף מרוב נשים הנישאות בתולות יש לה קול, וכי אין לה קול – לא יתרע כל כך רוב דבתולות נישאות, שלא יועיל עדות דראה בקוטנו ואחר עמו.

וליחוש דלמא מפקא כו'. ואפי' ע"י עדי הינומא לא היה לה לגבות עד שתחזיר לו הכתובה, כיון שיכול לבא לידי הפסד במה שנשארה כתובה תחת ידה. דלא מיבעיא למ"ד דיכול לטעון אחר מעשה ב"ד דמפסיד, דאם לא יהיה לה כתובה יהי' נאמן לומר פרעתי. אלא אפילו למ"ד דלא מצי טעין אחר מעשה בית דין מפסיד במה שהכתובה תחת ידה, שאם תתבענו פעם אחרת ולא יהיו לה עדי הינומא – יהא נאמן לומר פרעתי מנה, במגו דאי בעי אמר אלמנה נשאתיך. או אם יהא במקום שאין מכירין אם היא אשתו – יהיה נאמן לומר פרעתי הכל, במגו דאי בעי אמר אין את אשתי. והשתא שהכתובה בידה – תוציא מאתים, וכיון שיכול לבא לידי הפסד – אין לו לפרוע. **זאת** אומרת כותבין שובר. אע"ג דהכא לא אפשר, דאיכא למיחש דלמא תשרוף כתובתה בעדים והדרא וגביא בעדי הינומא, כדאמרינן בסמוך: ודלמא הדרא ומפקא בעדי הינומא וגביא, למ"ד הטוען אחר מעשה בית דין לא אמר כלום, וע"כ זקוק הוא לשובר – מ"מ דייק שפיר דבעלמא נמי כותבין שובר, דאי אין כותבין בעלמא – למה יפרע כאן, כיון שיכול לבא לידי הפסד במה שהכתובה בידה, כדפירשנו.

כותבין שובר. אע"ג דבפרק "גט פשוט" (ב"ב קע"א: ושם) מפרש טעמא דמאן דאמר כותבין שובר משום ד"עבד לוה לאיש מלוה" – לאו דוקא לוה, אלא הוא הדין בכל חוב כמו כתובה דהכא, ושטרי מקח, דאמר התם דכותבין שובר. **מאי** איבדה איבדה באור. וא"ת: א"כ אפי' במקום שכותבין הוה ליה לאוקמי, ומאי דוחקא לאוקמי במקום שאין כותבין וכתב לה איהו? ואור"ת: דבמקום שכותבין ונשרפה – איכא למיחש שכתב לה כתובה אחרת, דאסור להשהותה בלא כתובה. מיהו, הוה מצי לאוקומה במקום שכותבין ונשרפה אחר הגירושין, דליכא למיחש שמא כתב לה אחרת, אלא שנראה לו דוחק. **ותו** איבדה למה לי. אף על גב דלכאורה היינו פירכא קמייתא דפריך: היינו נשרפה – יש ליישב דהכי קאמר: ותו, אפילו אם נאמר דנשרפה הוי פירושא דנאבדה – מכל מקום תקשי: איבדה למה לי? **איתנוסי** הוא דאיתניסו. נראה דמיירי כגון דאיכא מגו, דאי בעיא אמרה אין בידי כלום. דאי לאו הכי – אמאי מהימנא? ואם תאמר: בחילוק קליות דאמר לקמן ארמלתא לית לה כסני, אמאי לא חיישינן דלמא תפסה כו' כדאמר הכא? ואומר רבינו תם: דדוקא בדבר שיש טורח, כגון חבית דהכא, יכולה לומר דאיתניסו, אבל קליות ושאר דברים שהן קלים לעשות – לא.

כלה

עין משפט נר מצוה

ג א מיי' פט"ז מהלכות אישות הלכה כ סמג עשין מח טוש"ע אה"ע סימן צו סעיף טו:
ד ב מיי' פכ"ג מהלכות מלוה הלכה טו טז סמג עשין צד טוש"ע ח"מ סימן נד סעיף ב:

תוספות רי"ד

וליחוש דלמא מפקא עדי הינומא בהאי בי דינא וגביא ומפקא כתובתה או עדי הינומא בב"ד אחרינא וגביא א"ר אבהו זאת אומרת כותבין שובר פי' ולא מצי אידך למימר א"א לשמור שוברי מפני העכברים אלא או תקרע לי שטרא או לא אית לך כלום אלא פורעו בע"כ והוא כותב לו שובר ודלא כמ"ד בב"ב דאין כותבין שובר והכי אסיקנא שם בג"פ [דף קעא ע"ב] דכותבין שובר: ת"ר כיצד מרקדין לפני הכלה. ב"ש אומרים

גליון הש"ס

גמ' אי כל הנישאת. כעין זה נדה דף כט ע"א:

מסורת הש"ס

[שבת עט. לקמן נו. פט. סוטה ז: ב"ב קע: קעא:]

שבת עט. ב"ב קעא:

מסכת דרך ארץ פ"ה

ה א טוש"ע אה"ע סימן סה סעיף א:
ו ב מיי' פ"ו מהלכות דעות הלכה א:
ז ג טוש"ע שם סימן סה סעיף ב:
ח ד מיי' פי"ד מהל' אבל הלכה ח סמג עשין דרבנן ב טוש"ע י"ד סימן שם וטוש"ע אה"ע סי' סה סעיף ד:
ט ה מיי' שם הלכה ח:
י ו מיי' פ"ז מהלכות ת"ת הלכה יג סמג עשין יג טוש"ע י"ד סי' רמד סעיף יד:
[סנהדרין יד.]
יא ז מיי' פ"ב מהלכות מלכים הלכה ג סמג עשין ה:
יב ח ט י כ מיי' פי"ד מהלכות אבל הלכה ט והלכה יא טוש"ע י"ד סימן שסא סעיף א:
[בערוך ערך חמס האריך לפרש כל המלות אלו בכמה אופנים קח נא משם]

תורה אור

כלה כמות שהיא, ובית הלל אומרים: [א]כלה נאה וחסודה. אמרו להן ב"ש לב"ה: הרי שהיתה חיגרת או סומא, אומרי' לה "כלה נאה וחסודה"? והתורה אמרה: "°מדבר שקר תרחק"! (שמות כג) אמרו להם ב"ה לב"ש: לדבריכם, מי שלקח מקח רע מן השוק – ישבחנו בעיניו או יגננו בעיניו? הוי אומר – ישבחנו בעיניו. מכאן אמרו חכמים: [ב]לעולם תהא דעתו של אדם מעורבת עם הבריות. כי אתא רב דימי אמר: הכי משרו קמי כלתא במערבא: "לא כחל ולא שרק ולא פירכוס, ויעלת חן". *כי סמכו רבנן לרבי זירא שרו ליה הכי: "לא כחל ולא שרק ולא פירכוס ויעלת חן". כי סמכו רבנן לרבי אמי ולרבי אסי שרו להו הכי: "כל מן דין וכל מן דין סמוכו לנא, לא תסמכו לנא לא מן סרמיסין ולא מן סרמיטין". ואמרי לה: "לא מן חמיסין ולא מן *טורמיסין". ר' אבהו, כי הוה אתי ממתיבתא לבי קיסר, נפקן אמהתא דבי קיסר לאפיה, ומשרין ליה הכי: "רבא דעמיה ומדברנא דאומתיה, בוצינא דנהורא, בריך מתייך לשלם". אמרו עליו על רבי יהודה בר אילעאי שהיה נוטל בד של הדס ומרקד לפני הכלה, ואומר: "כלה נאה וחסודה". רב שמואל בר רב יצחק מרקד אתלת. א"ר זירא: קא מכסיף לן סבא. כי נח נפשיה *איפסיק עמודא דנורא בין דידיה לכולי עלמא, וגמירי דלא אפסיק עמודא דנורא אלא אי לחד בדרא אי לתרי בדרא. א"ר זירא: אהנייה ליה שוטיתיה לסבא, ואמרי לה: שטותיה לסבא, ואמרי לה: שיטתיה לסבא. רב אחא מרכיב לה אכתפיה ומרקד. אמרי ליה רבנן: אנן מהו למיעבד הכי? אמר להו: אי דמיין עלייכו ככשורא – לחיי, ואי לא – לא. א"ר שמואל בר נחמני א"ר יונתן: מותר להסתכל בפני כלה כל שבעה, כדי לחבבה על בעלה. [ג]ולית הלכתא כוותיה. ת"ר: *[ד]מעבירין את המת מלפני כלה, [ה]וזה וזה מלפני מלך ישראל. אמרו עליו על אגריפס המלך שעבר מלפני כלה, ושבחוהו חכמים. שבחוהו – מכלל דשפיר עבד?! *והא א"ר אשי: אפילו למ"ד [ו]נשיא שמחל על כבודו – כבודו מחול, [ז]מלך שמחל על כבודו – אין כבודו מחול; דאמר מר: *"°שום תשים עליך מלך" (דברים יז) – שתהא אימתו עליך! פרשת דרכים הואי. תנו רבנן: *[ח]מבטלין תלמוד תורה להוצאת המת ולהכנסת כלה, אמרו עליו על רבי יהודה ברבי אלעאי שהיה מבטל תלמוד תורה להוצאת המת ולהכנסת כלה. במה דברים אמורים – [ט]כשאין עמו כל צרכו, אבל יש עמו כל צרכו – אין מבטלין. וכמה כל צרכו? אמר רב שמואל בר איני משמיה דרב: תריסר אלפי גברי ושיתא אלפי שיפורי. ואמרי לה: *תליסר אלפי גברי, ומינייהו שיתא אלפי שיפורי. עולא אמר: כגון דחייצי גברי מאבולא ועד סיכרא. רב ששת ואיתימא רבי יוחנן אמר: [י]נטילתה כנתינתה, מה נתינתה בששים רבוא – אף נטילתה בששים רבוא. [כ]וה"מ – למאן דקרי ותני, אבל

רש"י

כמות שהיא. לפי יופיה וחשיבותה מקלסין אותה. חסודה. חוט של חסד משוך עליה. מכאן אמרו. מדברי ב"ה שאמרו ישבחנה. תהא דעתו של אדם מעורבת עם הבריות. לעשות לאיש ואיש כרצונו. משרו. משוררים. לא כחל. אינה צריכה כחל. ולא שרק. צבע המאדים את הפנים. פירכוס. קליעת שיער. זו לא כחלה ולא שרקה ולא פירכסה, והרי היא יעלת חן. כל מן דין. כל כמות אלו הוו סומכין לנו, לקרותן רבי ולמנותם דיינין. סרמיסין. מסרסין הלכות דהיפך טעמיהן. סרמיטין. לשון סמרטוטין. חמיסין. אומרים חמישית הטעם*. טורמיסין. לא איתפרש. (*טורמיסין כי הא דאמר בב"ר (פ' מ"א) על טורמיסין למיקרב למסאנא דמטרוניתא – אנשים ריקנים*). ממתיבתא. מבית המדרש. רבא דעמיה. נשיא בעמו. מדברנא. מנהיג. בריך מתייך לשלם. ברוך בואך לשלום. בוצינא דנהורא. על שהיה קלסתר פניו מבהיק, כדאמרינן בב"ב (דף נח): שופריה דרבי אבהו מעין שופריה *דרבי יוחנן, דנפקי זיהרורית מיניה, כדמפרש התם. אתלת. שלש בדין, זורק אחת ומקבל אחת. מכסיף לן סבא. שמזלזל בכבוד תלמידי חכמים, ונוהג קלות ראש בעצמו. שוטיתיה. שוט של הדס שהיה מרקד בו. שיטתיה. שיטתו ומנהגו. שטותיה. שהיה מתנהג כשוטה. מרכיב לה אכתפיה. את הכלה. כי כשורא. כקורה בעלמא, שאין אתם מהרהרין עליה. לחבבה. כשרואה הכל מסתכלים בה – נכנס יופיה בלבו. מעבירין. כשכלה יוצאה מבית אביה לבית חתונתה, ונושאי מת יוצאים, ובזו ובזו אוכלוסים הרבה ואין רוצין להתערב – מעבירין את המת (אפילו) דרך אחרת. אפילו למ"ד. פלוגתא בפרק קמא דקידושין. שום תשים עליך מלך. ישראל הוזהרו שישימו עליהם שימות הרבה, כלומר: שתהא אימתו עליהם. הלכך אין כבודו מחול, שלפיכך ריבה הכתוב שימות הרבה. פרשת דרכים הוה. ולא ניכר שעבר מלפניה, אלא כאילו הוא צריך לפנות לאותו הדרך. שיפורי. מכריזין עליו, שיבואו לכבדו. דחייצי גברי מאבולא לסיכרא. משער העיר ההיא, עד הקבר. נטילתה. של תורה ממנו כנתינתה בסיני. נטילתה – היינו כשמת, ותלמודו בטל. למאן דקרי. מקרא. ותני. משנה, אבל עדיין לא שנה לתלמידים.

תוספות

כלה כמות שהיא. ואם יש בה מום – ישתקו, ולא ישבחוה. אי נמי – ישבחוה בדבר נאה שיש בה, כגון בעיניה או בידיה, אם הם יפות. וב"ה אומרים: ישבחוה לגמרי, דכשמזכירין מה שיש בה לשבח – מכלל דשאר לגנאי. ישבחנו בעיניו או יגננו בעיניו. וב"ש סברי: אע"ג דישבחנו בעיניו – אין להם לחכמים לתקן להזקיק לומר שקר, דהתורה אמרה "מדבר שקר תרחק". שיטתיה לסבא. פר"ח: לשון "שיטה והדס" (ישעיה מ"א). אע"ג דלא הוי ממש מין אחד – מ"מ שניהם מין ארז. וא"ת: ומנא ליה דבשביל כן זכה? וי"ל: דעמוד דנורא היה כעין שיבשא דהדס, כדאמרינן בבראשית רבה (פ' סא): נחת שיבשא דנורא ואיתעבידא כעין שיבשא דהדס, ואפסקת בין דידיה לחברוהי. אמרי: חמית הדין סבא דקאי שיבשא דנורא קומיה משום דעביד קמוהי דכלתא. מלך שמחל על כבודו אין כבודו מחול. אע"ג דלא היה מלך גמור, כדמשמע ב"אלו נאמרין" (סוטה דף מא.), מ"מ היו נוהגין בו כבוד כמלך גמור. פרשת דרכים הואי. הכא לא מצי לשנויי מצוה שאני, כדמשני ב"אלו נאמרין" (ג"ז שם) גבי שקרא מעומד. דהתם מצוה הוא, שיש למלך לחלוק כבוד לתורה החשובה ממנו, אבל הכא ליכא מצוה, דכבודו עדיף מכבוד הכלה.

[ת"ר מעבירין את המת מלפני הכלה. מכאן משמע כשיש אבל וחתן בבית הכנסת – החתן יוצא תחלה ושושביניו, ושוב יוצא האבל ומנחמיו. וגם הקרובים לחתן ולאבל יאכלו בבית החתן אם ירצו, דהא כבודו קודם. וכן בבקר, כשמוליכים הכלה לבית החתן – מוליכין הכלה תחלה אם יש מת בעיר, או יקברוהו קודם שיגיע הזמן דהכנסת כלה. להראב"ה].

מבטלין תלמוד תורה להוצאת המת. וקשה, *דבהלכות דרך ארץ אמר ר"ע: תחלת תשמישי לפני חכמים, פעם אחת הייתי מהלך בדרך ומצאתי מת מצוה ונטפלתי בו ד' מילין עד שהבאתיו לבית הקברות, וקברתיו. וכשבאתי והרציתי דברי לפני ר"א ור' יהושע, אמרו לי: על כל פסיעה ופסיעה כאילו שפכת דם נקי? וי"ל: דהתם לאו משום ביטול תורה, אלא משום דמת מצוה קנה מקומו, והיה לו לקוברו במקום שמצאו. וכן משמע במס' שמחות (פ"ד) דקאמר: מת מצוה קנה מקומו, *והעובר על דברי חכמים חייב מיתה. *) וכן אמר ר' עקיבא: תחלת תשמישי כו'. והר"ר יהודה מקורביי"ל תירץ: דהתם משום דביטל עצמו משימוש ת"ח קאמר, דגדול שימושה יותר מלימודה. להוצאת המת. לא במת מצוה איירי, אלא בכל המתים. ואע"ג דבפ"ק דמגילה (דף ג: ושם) אומר: פשיטא דמת מצוה ותלמוד תורה – מת מצוה עדיף, דתניא: מבטלין ת"ת להוצאת המת. נקט מת מצוה אגב מילי אחריני דהתם, דהוו דווקא מת מצוה. והא דאמר ב"אלו מגלחין" (מו"ק דף כז:): מת בעיר – כל בני העיר אסורים בעשיית מלאכה. ומוקי לה בדליכא חברותא, אבל אי איכא חברותא – מותרין השאר. פירוש חברותא – שנחלקו בני העיר לחבורות, שתעסוק כל אחת במת שלה בפני עצמה – היינו שלא בשעת הוצאה, אבל בשעת הוצאה – כולם צריכין לצאת. אבל

*) [ברכות ז: עירובין כא:]

תוספות רי"ד

כלה כמות שהיא פי' לפי יפיה וחשיבותה מקלסין אותה ולא במה שאין בה ובה"א כלה נאה וחסודה חוט של חסד משוך עליה ומראיתה נאה פי' נאה בעיני הבריות אמרי ב"ש לב"ה לדבריך הרי שהיתה חגרת או סומא אומרים לה כלה נאה וחסודה והתורה אמרה מדבר שקר תרחק א"ל ב"ה לדבריכם מי שלקח מקח רע מן השוק ישבחנו בעיניו או יגננו בעיניו הוי אומר ישבחנו בעיניו מכאן אמרו חכמים תהא דעתו של אדם מעורבת עם הבריות פי' לומר דבר המתקבל ואע"פ שאומר שקר: ת"ר מעבירין את המת מלפני הכלה וזה וזה מלפני מלך ישראל. ת"ר מבטלין ת"ת להוצאת המת ולהכנסת כלה אמרו עליו על ר"י בר אלעאי שהיה מבטל ת"ת להוצאת המת ולהכנסת כלה בד"א כשאין עמו כל צרכו אבל יש עמו כל צרכו אין מבטלין וכמה כל צרכו אמר ר"ש בר (איקא) [איני] משמיה דרב תליסר אלפי גברי ושיתא אלפי שיפורי ואמרי לה תריסר אלפי גברא ומינייהו שיתא אלפי שיפורי פי' מכריזין עליו שיבואו לכבדו וגם מקוננים ומספידים אותו בחלילים עולא אמר כגון דחייצי גברא מאבולא ועד סכרא פי' מפתח העיר עד הקבר ר"ש ואיתימא ר' אמי ואיתימא רבי יוחנן נטילתה כנתינתה מה נתינתה בס' רבוא אף נטילתה בס' רבוא וה"מ למאן דקרי ותני אבל למאן דמתני לית ליה שיעורא פי' דקרי מקרא ותני משנה אבל עדיין לא שנה לתלמידים אבל למתני לתלמידים לית ליה שיעורא וכתב המורה וממילא שמעינן דלמאן דלא

[וז"ל הערוך בערך חמס חמיסין שבונין חומשה של מסכת ועיין רש"י בסנהדרין מפרק מלמון חמסנין שמונגנין מלומר טעמי תורה]

*שם בכ"י הגירסא טולמוסין ופרש"י בפירושו שם טולמוסין אנשי חמס מתרגום אדם בליעל (משלי ו יב) בר נש טולמוס וכו' כמ"ש ערך טרמס.

[ליתא הכי לא בכ"ב גם בכ"מ פ"ד. קאמר להדיא טעם דלא חשיב שופריה דר' יוחנן והנה בר"ש בסנהדרין יז. ד"ה בוצינא וכו' אפשר לתקן ולומר דל"ל מעין שופריה דיעקב דנפקי זיהרורית מיניה כדמפרש התם מצוה לעשות ולתקן באופן אחר]

גליון הש"ס

גמ' מרקד אתלת. ירושלמי פ"א דפאה על מתני' א' ובשינוי קצת ועוד במ"ר בראשית פ' נט: תום' ד"ה מבטלין וכו' דגדול שימושה. ברכות דף ז ע"ב:

[שמחות פ"א ע"ש]

קדושין לב: סוטה מח: סנהדרין יט:

[שם ובסנהדרין כב.]

[מגילה ג: כט.]

[נ"ל תריסר וכן איתא במגילה]

לקמן עז.

[נ"ל דבמסכת דרך ארץ זוטא פ"ח]

יג א מיי' פי"ד מהלכות טוען ונטען הלכה ג סמג עשין לה טוש"ע ח"מ סימן קמ סעיף א:
יד ב מיי' פי"ב שם הל' ח סמג שם טוש"ע שם סימן קמט סעיף ד:
טו ג מיי' פי"ד שם הל' ז טוש"ע שם סימן קמט סעיף יט:
טז ד מיי' פי"ב שם הלכה י סמג שם טוש"ע שם סימן קמג סעיף ג:
יז ה מיי' שם פי"ח הלכה ה טוש"ע שם סימן קמו סעיף א:

אבל למאן דמתני – לית ליה שיעורא.§ ואם יש עדים שיצתה בהינומא וכו'.§ מאי הינומא? סורחב בר פפא משמיה דזעירי אמר: תנורא דאסא, רבי יוחנן אמר: קריתא דמנמנה בה כלתא.§ רבי יוחנן בן ברוקא אומר וכו'.§ תנא: ביהודה – ראיה, בבבל מאי? אמר רב: דרדוגי דמשחא ארישא דרבנן. אמר ליה רב פפא לאביי: משחא דחפיפותא קאמר מר?! אמר ליה: יתמא, לא עבדא לך אמך דרדוגי משחא ארישא דרבנן בשעת מעשה? כי הא דההוא מרבנן דאיעסק ליה לבריה בי רבה בר עולא. ואמרי לה רבה בר עולא איעסק ליה לבריה בי ההוא מרבנן, ודרדיג משחא ארישא דרבנן בשעת מעשה. ארמלתא מאי? תאני רב יוסף: ארמלתא לית לה כיסני.§ ומודה רבי יהושע באומר לחבירו כו'.§ וליתני: "מודה ר' יהושע באומר לחבירו שדה זו שלך היתה ולקחתיה ממך"! משום דקא בעי למיתני סיפא: אאם יש עדים שהיא שלו, והוא אומר: "לקחתיה ממנו" – אינו נאמן. היכי דמי? אי דאכלה שני חזקה – אמאי לא מהימן? ואי דלא אכלה שני חזקה – פשיטא דלא מהימן! אי הכי, גבי אביו נמי, אי דאכלה שני חזקה – אמאי לא מהימן? ואי דלא אכלה שני חזקה – פשיטא דלא מהימן! בשלמא גבי אביו – משכחת לה, *כגון בשאכלה שתים בחיי האב ואחת בחיי בנו, וכדרב הונא. *דאמר רב הונא: גאין מחזיקין בנכסי קטן אפילו הגדיל. ורב הונא *מתניתין אתא לאשמועינן? איבעית אימא: רב הונא •דיוקא דמתני' קאמר. ואיבעית אימא: "אפילו הגדיל" קמ"ל. וליתנייה בדידיה, ולוקמה כגון שאכלה שתים בפניו ואחת שלא בפניו, וכגון שברח? ברח מחמת מאי? אי דדברח מחמת נפשות – פשיטא דלא מהימן, דלא מצי מחי. ואי דברח מחמת ממון – איבעי ליה למחויי, הדקי"ל: מחאה שלא בפניו – הויא מחאה! דתנן: *שלש ארצות לחזקה, יהודה ועבר הירדן והגליל. היה ביהודה והחזיק בגליל, בגליל והחזיק ביהודה – אינה חזקה, עד שיהא עמו במדינה. והוינן בה: *מאי קסבר: אי קסבר מחאה שלא בפניו הויא מחאה – אפילו ביהודה וגליל נמי, ואי קסבר מחאה שלא בפניו לא הויא מחאה – אפילו יהודה ויהודה נמי לא! אמר רבי אבא בר ממל: לעולם קסבר מחאה שלא בפניו הויא מחאה. ומתניתין בשעת *חירום שנו. ומאי שנא יהודה וגליל דנקט – דסתם

רש"י

אבל למאן דמתני. לאחרים. לית ליה שיעורא. וממילא שמעינן דלמאן דלא קרי ולא תני אין מבטלין אם יש לו מתעסקין כדי קבורה בעלמא – בשאלתות דרב אחאי *מצאתי כן. תנורא דאסא. כמין חופה של הדס עגולה. קריתא. צעיף על ראשה משורבב על עיניה, כמו שעושין במקומינו. ופעמים שמנמנמת בתוכו, מתוך שאין עיניה מגולין, ולכך נקרא הינומא, על שם תנומה. ביהודה ראיה. כל הני דמתני', ששם היו רגילין בסימנין הללו לבתולה. דרדוגי מישחא. הנשים נותנים שמן בראש התלמידים, ושפות. מישחא דחפיפותא. [שמן של בשמים שמתוקן *לחופת] קאמר מר – וכי בעלי חפיפות הן, לסוכן שמן? יתמא. יתום ממנהג הנוהג. איעסק לבריה. לישא לו אשה. ודרדיג מישחא. שף שמן בראש התלמידים. ארמלתא מאי. מה סימנין עושים לאלמנה להודיע שאלמנה נישאת. לית לה כיסני. אין לה קליות, וזה סימנה. וליתני מודה ר' יהושע כו' שדה זו שלך היתה. כיון דטעמא משום דאין שור שחוט לפניו הוא, שלא היה אדם תובעו – מה לי של אביו ומה לי שלו, ומאי שנא של אביך דנקט? שני חזקה. שלש שנים שתיקנו חכמים לכל מחזיקים בקרקע, דמשאכלה שלש שנים בלא עירעור – נאמן לומר לקחתיה ואבד שטרי, דכולי האי לא מזדהר איניש בשטרא. בשלמא גבי אביו משכחת לה. דאיצטריך למיתנייה, כגון דאכלה שני חזקה ואפילו הכי לא מהימן. וכגון שאכלה שתי שנים ראשונות בחיי אביו, ומת. ואכלה השלישית לפני הבן הזה, והוא היה קטן ולא עירער. ואיצטריך לאשמועינן, דכיון דקטן היה – אין השנה הזאת עולה מן המנין. וכדרב הונא דאמר אין מחזיקין בנכסי קטן. המחזיק בנכסי קטן שלש שנים אינה חזקה. דהאי דלא מיחה – משום דקטן הוא, ואפילו הגדיל לאחר מיכן והחזיק זה בפניו כמה שנים – אינה חזקה, הואיל ותחלתו כשהוא קטן דאהו מוחזק בה – לא ידע כשהגדיל שהיתה של אביו, עד ששומע מפי אחרים. ורב הונא מתניתין אתא לאשמועינן. בתמיה. כיון דמתניתין בהכי עסקינן, ולא מיתוקמא אלא בהכי – מאי אתא רב הונא לאשמועינן? הרי כבר שנויה ועומדת, ודבר השנוי במשנתינו שגור בפי הכל. דיוקא דמתניתין אתא לאשמועינן. משום דמתני' לא מיפרשא בהדיא דבהכי עסקינן, ואתא רב הונא לאשמועינן בהדיא, ומדיוקא דמתני' קא יליף לה. וליתנייה בדידיה. שדה זו שלך היתה אם יש עדים כו' אינו נאמן, ואע"ג שאכלה שני חזקה, וכגון שהיו שתים בפניו ואחת שלא בפניו. כגון שברח. ואשמעינן דההיא שתא לא סלקא ליה. אי ברח מחמת ממון. שאינו ירא מן המלכות, אלא מנעקת הנועקים בעיר. איבעי ליה למחויי. במקום שהוא שם, וכיון דלא מיחה – חזקה מעלייתא היא. שלש ארצות לחזקה. שלש ארצות של א"י חשובות חלוקות זו מזו לענין חזקה, כאילו הן ארצות נכריות. ואם היה בזו והחזיק אחר בקרקע שיש לו בחברתה – אינה חזקה. במדינה. או שניהם בגליל, או שניהם ביהודה, ואפי' הן בשתי עיירות. אפי' יהודה וגליל נמי. הוה ליה למחויי היכא דהוי, ומדלא מחי – תיהוי חזקה. ואי קסבר מחאה שלא בפניו לא הויא מחאה. כגון אם היה בעיר אחת, ומיחה שלא בפניו בפני שנים בעיר אחרת. אפילו יהודה ויהודה. בשתי עיירות נמי לא תיהוי חזקה, דלא הוה ליה למחויי שלא בפניו. הויא מחאה. דחברך חברא אית ליה, דהני דמחי באנפייהו מגלו לאחריני, ובא הדבר לאזני המחזיק, וה"ל לאזדהורי בשטריה. ומתני'. דקתני יהודה וגליל לא. בשעת חירום שנו. דיכול לומר: לא נגלית לי מחאתו שאשמור את שטרי. ומאי שנא יהודה וגליל דנקט. אם יש חירום נמי מעיר לעיר, אפי' שתי עיירות באותה מדינה נמי לא.

וליתני

תוספות

אבל מאן דמתני לית ליה שיעורא. בשאלתות דרב אחאי כתוב: וממילא שמעינן למאן דלא קרי ולא תני – אין מבטלין, אם יש לו מתעסקין כדי קבורה. ונראה לר"י דלענין מלאכה מבטלין כל בני העיר, ואסור אפילו למאן דלא קרי ולא תני, דלא מפליג מידי ב"אלו מגלחין" (מו"ק דף כז:) בהכי. אלמנה מאי. ביהודה בעי, שלא היה אלא חילוק קליות – לכך בעי אלמנה מאי, והלא פעמים אפילו בלא חופה היו רגילין לחלק, ויש לחוש שמא חילקו בחופת אלמנה! ומשני: לית לה כיסני, פירוש: היו נזהרין הרבה שלא יחלקו קליות בחופת אלמנה. וליתני מודה רבי יהושע שדה זו שלך היתה. דהוי רבותא טפי, דהוי ברי וברי. ואחת בחיי הבן. ודווקא שהוא קטן, כפי' הקונט'. אבל אם הוא גדול – הוי חזקה, כדאמרי' ב"חזקת הבתים" (ב"ב דף מב. ושם): אכלה בפני האב שנה ובפני הבן שנה ובפני לוקח שנה – הרי זו חזקה. ורבינו שמואל פי' אהא דאמר בסמוך ואפילו הגדיל – אפילו הגדיל בחיי האב, דגדול לגבי מילי דאבוה קטן הוא. ואור"ת: דלפירושו הא דאמר ב"חזקת הבתים" (ג"ז שם) דהויא חזקה בפני הבן – היינו כשהיה גדול בתחילת חזקה. ורב הונא מתני' אתא לאשמועינן. לאו דווקא נקט רב הונא, דהא לא איירי רב הונא התם *אלא במורידין קרוב לנכסי קטן, והא לא שמעינן ממתני'. אלא כלומר, רבא דדייק התם: *ש"מ מדרב הונא דאין מחזיקין בנכסי קטן – מאי אתא לאשמועינן! מחאה שלא בפניו כו'. תימה: אמאי נקט בכל דוכתא מחאה שלא בפניו? הוה ליה למינקט: חזקה שלא בפניו כו'! וי"ל דעיקר הטע' תלוי במחאה, דחזקה ודאי יש לה קול אפי' שלא בפניו, ואפ"ה אי מחאה אין לה קול – לא הוי חזקה, ולהכי נקט מחא'.

דסתם

תוספות רי"ד

דלא קרי ולא תני אין מבטלין ת"ת אם יש לו מתעסקים כדי קבורה בעלמא בשאלתות דרב אחא מצאתי כן: אם יש עדים שיצאת בהינומא מאי הינומא סורחב בר פפא אמר משמיה דזעירי תנורא דאסא פי' כמין כיפה של הדס עגולה ר"י אמר קריתא ומנמנמא בה כלה פי' צניף על ראשה משורבב על עיניה כמו שעושים בהרבה מקומות ופעמים שמנמנמת בתוכו מתוך שאין עיניה מגולות ולכך נקרא הינומא ע"ש תנומה: מתני' ומודה ר"י באומר לחבירו שדה זו של אביך היתה ולקחתיה ממנו נאמן שהפה שאסר הוא הפה שהתיר ואם יש עדים שהוא של אביו והוא אומר לקחתיה הימנו אינו נאמן ואסיקנא ר' יהושע אפרק קמא קאי ואהא קאי דתנן הנושא את האשה ולא מצא לה בתולים היא אומרת משארסתני נאנסתי ונסתחפה שדך והוא אומר לא כי אלא עד שלא ארסתיך והיה מקחי מקח טעות ר"ג ור"א [אומרים] נאמנת ור"י אומר לא מפיה אנו חיין והתם מאי מיגו איכא מיגו דאי בעי אמרה מוכת עץ אני ולא פסלה נפשה מכהונה וקאמרה נאנסתי דפסלה נפשה מכהונה מהימנא וא"ל ר"י לר"ג בההיא מיגו דהכא מודינא לך בההיא מיגו דהתם פליגנא עלך. מ"ש הכא ומ"ש התם הכא אין שור שחוט לפניך. פי' ואם רוצה לומר אינו של אביך ולהכחישו יכול גם עתה כשהודה שהיתה של אביו ולקחה ממנו נאמן אבל התם גבי אשה אם תרצה להכחישו ולומר בתולה הייתי אינה יכולה שהרי [שור] שחוט לפניך השושבינים המעידים שלא נמצאו לה בתולים הלכך כל טענה דאמרה בין מוכת עץ אני בין נאנסתי תחתיך לא מהימנא:

מתני'

מסורת הש"ס

[פרשת ויחי סימן לב]

נ"ל לחפיפות. יעב"ץ

[ב"מ לט.]

[שם]

ב"ב מב.

ב"מ לט.

[פסחים קח: ר"ה ח.]

ב"ב לח.

[שם ע"ש]

[פי' בערוך ערך חרס א סיכסוך איש באחיו ובעיר בעיר]

גליון הש"ס

גמ' דיוקא דמתניתין קאמר. שבת דף לו ע"ב שבועות דף כט ע"ב:

ולתני מנה לויתי ממך. מלתיה דר' יהושע דאשמועינן דמודה היכא דאין שור שחוט לפניך, מאי שנא דאשמעינן בקרקע, ואיצטריך למתנייה באביו משום סיפא? לנקוט מלתיה במטלטלין, ולישמעינן בדידיה גופיה! נאמן. מדאורייתא, בלא שבועה. וניתני מודה ר' יהושע כו' והאכלתיו פרס. פרעתיו חציו, שהוא נאמן בלא שבועה, הואיל ואין שור שחוט לפניו. דאשמועינן רבותא, דאע"ג דמודה במקצת – פטור, הואיל ואינו תובעו. אליבא דמאן. תנאי פליגי בהא מילתא בשבועות (דף מב.), ואי אמר רבי יהושע הכי – לא כחד מנייהו הוא. דאי כרבנן הא אמרי אפי' תובעו וזה מודה במקצת – משיב אבידה הוא, דתנן בשבועות: "מנה לאבא בידך" – "אין לך בידי אלא חמשים דינר" – פטור, משום שהוא כמשיב אבידה. ומאי אשמעינן רבי יהושע באין שור שחוט? אפי' שור שחוט לפניו נמי נאמן! ואי אליבא דר' אליעזר בן יעקב, כי לא תבע ליה נמי – הא אמר שבועה בעי! ורבי אליעזר לית ליה משיב אבידה פטור. מן השבועה?! בתמיה. הא תקנתא דרבנן היא, במס' גיטין (דף מח:): המוצא מציאה לא ישבע, מפני תיקון העולם. וכיון דכי אינו תובעו נמי מחייב ליה שבועה – הרי אין לך משיב אבידה גדולה מזה, וחייב. אין נשבעין על טענת חרש שוטה וקטן. משנה היא בשבועות. טענת אחרים הוא. ומאי "פעמים" דקאמר? ומאי "טענת עצמו"? אלא הכא בדרבה קא מיפלגי. לעולם בטוענו קטן. ודקשיא לך, אין נשבעין על טענת קטן – הני מילי בשטוענו קטן "אני נתתיו לך", וקרא כתיב "כי יתן איש אל רעהו" – ולא קטן, ומהכא יליף לה בשבועות. אבל הכא שבא בטענת אביו – אית ליה לרבי אליעזר בן יעקב נשבעין. ורבנן פליגי עליה אפילו בטוענו גדול, וקרו ליה משיב אבידה, ובדרבה קא מיפלגי.

לא

דסתם יהודה וגליל כשעת חירום דמו. *וליתני: מודה רבי יהושע באומר לחבירו: "מנה לויתי ממך ופרעתיו לך" – שהוא נאמן! משום דקא בעי למיתני סיפא: אם יש עדים שהוא לוה ממנו, והוא אומר "פרעתיו" אינו נאמן, והא *קיימא לן: אהמלוה את חבירו בעדים אינו צריך לפרעו בעדים. וליתני: מודה ר' יהושע באומר לחבירו: "מנה לאביך בידי והאכלתיו פרס" – שהוא נאמן! אליבא דמאן? אי אליבא דרבנן – הא אמרי משיב אבידה הוי, אי אליבא דרבי אליעזר בן יעקב – הא אמר שבועה בעי. דתניא, *רבי אליעזר בן יעקב אומר: פעמים שאדם נשבע על טענת עצמו. כיצד? "מנה לאביך בידי והאכלתיו פרס" – הרי זה נשבע, וזהו שנשבע על טענת עצמו, וחכמים אומרים: באינו אלא כמשיב אבידה, ופטור. ור' אליעזר בן יעקב לית ליה משיב אבידה פטור? אמר רב: בטוענו קטן. *והאמר מר: גאין נשבעין על טענת חרש שוטה וקטן! מאי קטן – גדול, ואמאי קרי ליה קטן – דלגבי מילי דאביו קטן הוא. אי הכי, טענת עצמו?! טענת אחרים היא! טענת אחרים והודאת עצמו. כולהי טענתא טענת אחרים והודאת עצמו נינהו! אלא הכא בדרבה קמיפלגי. דאמר רבה:* מפני מה אמרה תורה מודה מקצת הטענה ישבע – חזקה, אין אדם מעיז פניו בפני בעל חובו. והאי בכולה בעי דלכפריה, והאי דלא כפר ליה – משום דאין אדם מעיז פניו הוא,

ובכולה

דסתם יהודה וגליל בשעת חירום דמי. תימה: דבריש גיטין (דף ד: ושם) תנן: דבארץ ישראל א"צ לומר בפני נכתב ובפני נחתם, אפי' מיהודה לגליל, משום דאיכא עולי רגלים, ובתי דינין, ועדים מצויין לקיימו! ויש לומר: דהתם האשה מחזרת אחר עדי קיום, אע"ג דיהודה וגליל כשעת חירום דמי – תמצא עדי קיום, כיון דאיכא עולי רגלים. אבל המחזיק – אין רגיל לחזור אחר עדי מחאה. ואם תאמר: התם *דאמר: שאני בני מחוזא דניידי, וצריך לומר אפי' באותה שכונה "בפני נכתב" (א), דאין עדים מצויין לקיימו, אטו במחוזא לא תועיל מחאה שלא בפניו? וי"ל: דהתם דרך הליכתן מן העיר, כששמעו מחאה – רגילות הוא לומר פלוני מיחה. ושומעין אחרים עד שנשמע הקול למחזיק. אבל גבי גט – אין רגיל שיאמרו בהליכתן: אנו חתמנו על הגט [או מכירין אנו חתימת עדים החתומים]. **אין** צריך לפרעו בעדים. ואם תאמר: למאן דאמר צריך לפרעו בעדים – תקשי ליה מתניתין דהכא, דליתני "מנה לך בידי"! ויש לומר: דפלוגתא דתנאי היא בפרק "שבועת הדיינין" (שבועות דף מא:) אי נמי: דלא חשיב לה פירכא, דניחא ליה לאשמועינן דאין מחזיקין בנכסי קטן. ואם תאמר: מאי משני? אכתי ליתני: ואם יש עדים ואמר לו: "אל תפרעני אלא בפני פלוני ופלוני" – אינו נאמן! וי"ל דלא היה רוצה להאריך בלשונו, או שמא מילתא דפשיטא הוא. **אי** אליבא דרבנן הא אמרי משיב אבידה הוי. כדמסיק דבכנו מעיז, וא"כ לא מצי למיתני ואם יש עדים אינו נאמן – דלעולם נאמן במגו, דאי בעי אמר פרעתי הכל, דבכנו מעיז ומעיז. **ורבי** אליעזר בן יעקב לית ליה משיב אבידה פטור. פי' בקונטרס: התנן המוצא מציאה לא ישבע מפני תיקון העולם, ואית ספרים דגרסי הכי בהדיא. ואין נראה לרבינו יצחק, דמשיב אבידה פטור מדאורייתא מטעם מגו. ולא מכח ההיא משנה פריך, אלא פריך: וכי לית ליה מגו? וכן משמע ב"הניזקין" (גיטין דף נא. ושם) דפריך: ולית ליה לרבי יצחק המוצא מציאה כו'? ומשני: הוא דאמר כר"א בן יעקב דאמר: פעמים שאדם נשבע וכו'. ופריך: ור"א בן יעקב לית ליה משיב אבידה פטור! והשתא, אי מכח מתני' פריך – הוה ליה למימר: ולית ליה לר"א בן יעקב המוצא מציאה? כדקאמר ארבי יצחק! ועוד, כיון דמשני הוא דאמר כר"א בן יעקב – א"כ רוצה לומר דר"א פליג אמתניתין, א"כ מאי פריך ור"א בן יעקב לית ליה משיב אבידה פטור? אין הכי נמי דלית ליה! אלא מכח מגו פריך, כדפרישית. **אלא** הכא בדרבה קא מיפלגי. פירש בקונטרס: לעולם בטוענו קטן, ודקא קשיא לך הא אין נשבעין על טענת קטן – ה"מ בבא בטענת עצמו, אבל בבא בטענת אביו – טענה חשובה היא. וכי תימא מ"ט דרבנן? דאין סברא לומר דסברי דאף בבא בטענת אביו לית ביה ממשא, אלא בדרבה קמיפלגי. ונראה דמשום דקרי ליה טענת עצמו דחקו להעמיד בטוענו קטן. אבל קשה: דעיקר התירוץ חסר מן הספר! ועוד: דב"הגוזל קמא" (ב"ק דף קו: ושם) ממעטינן נתנו כשהוא קטן ותבעו כשהוא גדול עד שתהא תביעה ונתינה שוין בגדלות, וה"ה דמהאי קרא ממעט נתנו כשהוא גדול ותבעו כשהוא קטן, דהיינו כגון שנתן לו אביו ותבעו בקטנות! ונראה דה"פ: לעולם בגדול מיירי, אלא לא תימא דקרי ליה טענת עצמו משום דהודאת עצמו היא, אלא בדרבה קמיפלגי. ולרבנן דסברי דבכנו מעיז – טענת עצמו היא, וה"ק ראב"י: פעמים שאדם נשבע על מה שאתם מחשיבים טענת עצמו, אבל לדידי דאינו מעיז – טענת אחרים היא. ובסוף "שבועת הדיינין" (שבועות דף מב. ושם) דתנן: אבל נשבעין לקטן, ומפרש בבא בטענת אביו, וראב"י היא – ההוא קטן נמי לאו דווקא, אלא גדול, וקרי ליה קטן – משום דלגבי מילי דאבוה קטן הוא, כדמפרש הכא. וקשה קצת: דהוה ליה לאקשויי ולשנויי אמתניתין דהתם כמו שמקשה על רב, דבההיא שמעתא גופה לא מקשה על המשנה אלא על רב. **מפני** מה אמרה תורה מודה מקצת הטענה ישבע. אפילו לרבנן דר"ש, דלא דרשי טעמא דקרא, קא בעי רבה שפיר: מפני מה אמרה תורה כו'. דאמאי לא מהימן בלא שבועה במגו דאי בעי כפר הכל, או נילף מהכא דלא אמרינן מגו! ומשני: דאין זה מגו, דאין אדם מעיז לכפור. ואף על גב דבפרק "שבועת הדיינין" (שם דף מ:) אמרינן: בכופר הכל, משביעין אותו שבועת היסת, משום דחזקה אין אדם תובע אלא אם כן יש לו. ופריך: אדרבה, חזקה דאין אדם מעיז פניו בפני בעל חובו! ומשני: דאשתמוטי קמשתמיט, אלמא בכופר בכל נמי אדם מעיז לכפור, דאשתמוטי קא משתמיט, כמו במודה מקצת! מ"מ קאמר הכא שפיר, חזקה דאין אדם מעיז לכפור הכל כל כך, ולא הוי מגו. דיותר ברצון הוא מודה במקצת הטענה, דאינו מעיז כל כך. אבל אין לפרש דרבה אתא לפרושי מפני מה אמרה תורה מודה מקצת ולא כופר הכל, וקאמר: חזקה דאין אדם מעיז, לכך נאמן כשכופר הכל – דאם כן במקום שיכול להעיז – אפילו כופר הכל חייב, ובסמוך אמרינן איפכא, לרבנן, דבכנו מעיז ופטור אף מודה מקצת הטענה, משום דמשיב אבידה הוא, מגו דאי בעי כפר הכל. ואם תאמר: ומנלן דכופר הכל פטור? וליכא למימר מדאצטריך קרא לחייב שבועה בעד אחד, מכלל דכופר הכל פטור – דהא איצטריך להיכא שמעידים שגנב לו והוא אינו יודע. אלא י"ל: דגזירת הכתוב היא ד"כי הוא זה" משמע דבעינן כפירה והודאה, ועוד: מודה מקצת יש להשביעו שחייב לו ממון שהודה, ועל ידי כך מגלגל עליו שבועה כעין גלגול, אבל כופר הכל – נסתלק לגמרי ממנו. **חזקה** אין אדם מעיז פניו. לא כמו שפי' בקונטרס ב"הגוזל" (ב"ק דף קז.) דאין אדם מעיז לפי שעשה לו טובה שהלוהו, דאם כן – בפקדון מודה מקצת נמי יהא פטור, במגו דאי בעי כופר הכל. ובכל דוכתא משמע דמודה מקצת חייב בפקדון, גבי עשר גפנים טעונות מסרתי לך כו' (שבועות דף מג:) דמשמע דאיירי בפקדון, וגבי סלע הלויתני עליו ושתים היה שוה (שם מג.), וגבי מציאה נמי אמרי' ב"הניזקין" (גיטין נא. ושם) דמודה מקצת חייב, ולא מהימן במגו! אלא אור"ת: דהיינו כגון חזקה שאין האשה מעיזה פניה בפני בעלה, שאין לאדם פנים לכפור הכל. וריב"א פי': אין אדם מעיז היכא שחבירו מכיר בשקרו, ואין להאריך*.

ובכולי

מסורת הש"ס:
[השמטת קס"ד דהמלוה את חבירו בעדים צריך לפרעו בעדים ואין נאמן לומר פרעתי כיון דלית ליה מגו ומסיק דקי"ל דא"צ לפרעו בעדים ונאמן לומר פרעתי אפילו בלא מגו ה"י]
גיטין נא: שבועות מב.
שם
גיטין נא: ב"ק קו. שבועות מב: ב"מ ג.

עין משפט נר מצוה:
יח א מיי' פי"א מהל' מלוה ולוה הלכה א סמג עשין צד טוש"ע ח"מ סימן ע סעיף א:
יט ב מיי' פ"ד מהלכות טוען ונטען הלכה ה סמג שם טוש"ע שם סי' עה סעיף ג:
[ושם דף ו.]
כ ג מיי' פ"ה שם הל' ט סמג שם טוש"ע שם סימן צו סעיף א:
שם
ב"ב קנ. שבועות מא: [ועיין קדושין מג:]
נ"י כ"י
[ובתוס' ב"ק קז. ד"ה עירוב וכו' האריכו טובא]

הגהות הב"ח
(א) תוס' ד"ה דהתם וכו' בפני נכתב ובפני נחתם דאין עדים:

ובכולה בעי דלודי ליה, והאי דלא אודי ליה — כי היכי דלישתמיט ליה, וסבר: עד דהוה לי זוזי ופרענא ליה. ורחמנא אמר: רמי שבועה עליה כי היכי דלודי ליה בכוליה. רבי אליעזר בן יעקב סבר: לא שנא בו ולא שנא בבנו — אינו מעיז, והלכך לאו משיב אבידה הוי. ורבנן סברי: בו הוא דאינו מעיז, אבל בבנו מעיז, ומדלא העיז — משיב אבידה הוי.§ **מתני'** [א]העדים שאמרו: כתב ידינו הוא זה, אבל אנוסים היינו, קטנים היינו, פסולי עדות היינו — הרי אלו נאמנים. ואם יש עדים שהוא כתב ידם, או שהיה כתב ידם יוצא ממקום אחר — אינן נאמנין.§ **גמ'** אמר רמי בר חמא: לא שנו אלא שאמרו "אנוסים היינו מחמת ממון", אבל "אנוסים היינו מחמת נפשות" — הרי אלו נאמנין. אמר ליה רבא: כל כמיניה?! *כיון שהגיד — שוב אינו חוזר ומגיד. וכי תימא: הני מילי — על פה, אבל בשטר — לא, והא אמר ריש לקיש: *עדים החתומים על השטר — *נעשה כמי שנחקרה עדותן בב"ד! אלא, כי אתמר — ארישא אתמר: הרי אלו נאמנין, אמר רמי בר חמא: לא שנו אלא שאמרו: "אנוסין היינו מחמת נפשות" אבל אמרו: "אנוסין היינו מחמת ממון" — אין נאמנין. *מאי טעמא — אין אדם משים עצמו רשע. תנו רבנן: *אין נאמנים לפוסלו, דברי רבי מאיר. וחכמים אומרים: נאמנים. בשלמא לרבנן — כי טעמייהו, שהפה שאסר הוא הפה שהתיר. אלא לר' מאיר — מ"ט? בשלמא פסולי עדות — מלוה גופיה מעיקרא מידק דייק ומחתם, קטנים נמי — כדרשב"ל, דאמר ריש לקיש:

חזקה

לא שנא בו ולא שנא בבנו. ואפילו הוא קטן. אינו מעיז. ולהכי קרי ליה טוענת עצמו, משום דטענת קטן בעלמא לית בה ממשא. אבל בבנו מעיז. ואפילו הוא גדול. **מתני'** העדים שאמרו כו'. שהיו מעידים על חתימתם לקיים את השטר. פסולי עדות היינו. קרובים, או משחקים בקוביא. הרי אלו נאמנים. כיון דאין כתב ידם ניכר אלא על פיהם — הפה שאסר הוא הפה שהתיר. כי היכי דמהימנת להו אהא — הימנינהו אהא. יוצא ממקום אחר. חתומים בשטר אחר שהוחזק בב"ד, וכתוב בו הנפק. ובא אותו שטר לפנינו עם זה, וכתב חותמין דומין של זה לשל זה — אין כאן הפה שאסר, ואין נאמנים לומר פסולים היינו. **גמ'** לא שנו. דאם כתב ידן יוצא ממקום אחר — אין נאמנין. אלא שאמרו אנוסים היינו מחמת ממון. דלאו כל כמינייהו לשוויי נפשייהו רשעים בעדות פיהם, ולפסול את השטר. דאדם קרוב אצל עצמו, ואינו נאמן על עצמו לא לזכות ולא לחובה בדיני נפשות, ובפסולי עדות להעשות רשע ופסול על פיו, ואלו פוסלים עצמן באומרם "חתמנו שקר בשביל אונס ממון". ורישא טעמא משום הפה שאסר הוא הפה שהתיר. מחמת נפשות. שאמר בעל השטר הזה להרגנו, ואדם חזק הוא. כיון שהגיד שוב אינו חוזר ומגיד. דגבי עדות חדא הגדה כתיבא, "אם לא יגיד" וגו' (ויקרא ה). והכא נמי, כיון דחתימי בשטרא — היינו הגדה דידהו, והיכי מהימני תו למיעקר, הואיל וכתב ידן יוצא ממקום אחר? בהא רישא, כשאין כתב ידן יוצא ממקום אחר, ועלייהו סמכינן — הואלה חדא הגדה היא, דהא באותו דבור [בכדי] שאילת שלום קאמרי "אבל אנוסים היינו". אבל הכא לאו אפומייהו סמכינן. הני מילי על פה. כגון המעיד בב"ד, ולאחר כדי דבור בא לשנות בו. אבל בשטר לא. דהגדה כתיב. לא שנו. דקאמרינן הפה שאסר כו'. אלא דאמרי מחמת נפשות. נאנסנו, דלא משוו נפשייהו רשעים. וכיון דעלייהו סמכינן — הא בתוך כדי דבור עקרוה לסהדותייהו, והפה שאסר התיר. אין אדם משים עצמו רשע. אינו נאמן לפסול את עצמו מחזקתו. דקרוב הוא אצל עצמו, וקרוב פסול לעדות. אין נאמנין לפוסלו. ארישא דמתניתין פליג: העדים שאמרו כתב ידינו הוא אבל אנוסים היינו כו'. הפה שהתיר. וכיון דמחמת נפשות קאמרי נאנסנו — לא משוו נפשייהו רשעים. ופסולי עדות דקאמרי — היינו טעמא: דלאו בעדותן משוו נפשייהו רשעים, אלא דאמרי קרובים או עבדים היינו, ועכשיו אנו משוחררים. בשלמא פסולי עדות. או קטנים, כיון דמודים הם שהשטר כדין נכתב, שהמלוה או המקח אמת, אבל אנחנו לא היינו ראוים, והויא לה כמלוה על פה, או אי מכירה היא לא נקנה הקרקע בשטר זה — אמר ר"מ דלא מהימני, דא"כ מלוה לא שדי זוזי בכדי, וכי מחתים עדים על שטרו — מידק דייק שיהו כשרים.

אלא

ובכולי בעי דלודי. פירש בקונטרס בב"מ (דף ג: ושם) דאתא לפרש דלא תימא אמאי נשבע? נימא: מגו דחשיד אממונא — חשיד נמי אשבועתא, ולהכי קאמר: ובכולי בעי דלודי ליה, ולא חשיד אממונא. וקשה לר"י: דהא אמר בפ"ק דב"מ (דף ה:) דלא אמרינן מגו דחשיד אממונא חשיד נמי אשבועתא. ואין לומר דמן התורה חשיד נמי אשבועתא, ומדרבנן הוא דאמרינן דלא חשיד, לפי שראו שהיו מקילין בממון יותר מבשבועה, ותקנו שבועה על החשודים כל זמן שלא נודע שהוא גזלן, שכשר מן התורה עדיין. אבל גזלן ידוע, שפסול מן התורה — לא תקנו. ולפי זה שבועה שלא שלחתי בו יד היא מדרבנן, [ולא הויא דאורייתא אלא שבועה שלא פשעתי בה]. והא דכתיב "אם לא שלח" — לא שנשבע שלא שלח, אלא ה"ק קרא: נשבע שלא פשע, אימתי — בזמן שלא שלח בו יד, דאם שלח בו יד חייב אפילו שלא פשע, דנתחייב באונסים. דהא גבי נסכא דרבי אבא (שבועות דף לב:) משמע דאי אמר לא חטפי — היה נשבע להכחיש את העד, אע"ג דחשיד אממונא. והתם הויא שבועה דאוריית', דבשבועה דרבנן לא אמרינן מתוך שאינו יכול לישבע משלם, כדמשמע בפ"ק דב"מ (שם) גבי ההוא רעיא. ונראה דאתא לפרש דלא תקשי, כיון דאין אדם מעיז — יהא נאמן במה שכפר מקצת, וכיון דמחייבינן שבועה — אם כן מחשבו עזות פנים, א"כ יהא נאמן במגו, דאי בעי כפר הכל. וקאמר דאין זה עזות מה שכופר קצת. וא"ת: כיון דלא חשיד אשבועתא — למה גזלן פסול לשבועה? ותירץ הר' יהודה חסיד: דדוקא כשהוא חשוד על אותו ממון שבא לישבע אמרינן דלא חשיד אשבועתא, דעל ידי השבועה יפרוש. אבל אותו ממון שכבר גזל — לא יפרוש ע"י השבועה. וגבי ההוא רעיא דחשיב ליה גזלן משום דאכל תרי מינייהו, אע"פ שצריך לפרוע הני תרי דאכל — מ"מ לא יפרוש מן השאר משום שבועה, דמה שמשלם בע"כ אין זה השבה מעליא. וי"מ: דגזלן כשר לשבועה מן התורה, דלא חשיד אשבועתא, אלא דמדרבנן פסלוהו כשהוא גזלן. ואם תאמר: ומאי שנא דלעדות פסול — כדכתיב "אל תשת ידך עם רשע וגו'" ולשבועה כשר? וי"ל: דבשבועת שקר יש בה עונש גדול דכתיב בה "לא ינקה", וכדאמר ב"שבועת הדיינין" (שבועות דף לט.), שכל העולם כולו נזדעזע כשאמר הקב"ה (לא תשבעו ו) "לא תשא". ועוד: דבעדות שקר ליכא אלא "לא תענה", ובשבועת שקר איכא "לא תגזול" ו"לא תשבעו* לשקר". **הרי אלו** נאמנים. וא"ת: ולמה נאמנים? והא מגו במקום עדים הוא, דאנן סהדי שלא היו אנוסים ולא פסולי עדות, דהא לקמן אמרינן תרי ותרי נינהו! וי"ל: כיון דהצריכו חכמים קיום — הכא לא חשיב כלל קיום מה שאומרים "כתב ידינו הוא זה", כיון דאינהו גופייהו אמרי תוך כדי דבור "קטנים או אנוסים היינו". אבל לקמן חשבינן להו כשני עדים, כיון דכבר מקויים הוא, שכתב ידן יוצא ממקום אחר: **אין** נאמנים — הכא ליכא לאקשויי להימנו במגו, דאי בעו אמרי פרוע הוא! דכיון דמקויים הוא — הוי מגו במקום עדים, כדפירשנו. ועוד: דחוזרים ומגידים הם, וכיון שהגיד — שוב אינו חוזר ומגיד, כדאמרי' בגמרא. ועוד: דבשני עדים לא אמרינן מגו. וברישא נאמנים — משום דאי בעו שתקי. **לא** שנו אלא שאמרו אנוסים היינו מחמת ממון. דלא מהימני משום דלא משוו נפשייהו רשעים. וקטנים — כדרשב"ל. ופסולי עדות — משום דמלוה גופיה מידק דייק, כדאמרינן בסמוך. **מחמת** נפשות הרי אלו נאמנים. וא"ת: וכי אמרו קטנים היינו או אנוסים מחמת ממון היינו — להימנו במגו דאמרי אנוסים היינו מחמת נפשות! דהא ברישא דאיכא מגו, נאמנים לומר אנוסים היינו מחמת ממון! וי"ל: דאונס מחמת נפשות לא שכיח.[א] ועוד, דבשני עדים לא אמרינן מגו, כדפרישית. **ואין** אדם משים עצמו רשע. וא"ת: והא קסבר רבא דפלגינן דיבורא בפ"ק דסנהדרין (דף ט: ושם) גבי פלוני רבעני לרצוני, ופלוני בא על אשתי — אם כן הכא נהימנו דאנוסים היו, אבל לא מחמת ממון אלא מחמת נפשות, דאליבא דרבא קיימא! וי"ל: כיון דקיום שטרות דרבנן — לא פלגינן דיבורא כדי לפסול השטר. ועוד: דאין לנו לומר מעצמינו דאנוסים היו מחמת נפשות, דאונס מחמת נפשות לא שכיח, כדפרישית. אבל התם שכיח שבא על אשת איש אחרת כמו על אשתו, או שרבעו אדם אחר. וכן בהרגתיו בספ"ב דיבמות (דף כה: ושם) יכול להיות דאדם אחר הרגו. אי נמי: שאני הכא דמחמת ממון או מחמת נפשות הוי פירושא דאנוסים היינו, הלכך לא פלגינן דיבורא. אבל לרצונו ובא על אשתו הוי דיבור בפ"ע. א"נ: הכא עיקר עדות הוא במה שאומרים אנוסים היינו, שבאו לומר שלא ראו המלוה — א"כ מיד עושין עצמן רשעים כיון שחתמו אם לא יעשו פירוש לדבריהם, הלכך לא שייך הכא פלגינן דיבורא. אבל ההיא דהרגתיו — עיקר עדות הוא לומר שנהרג, להשיא את אשתו. וכן פלוני רבעו, או בא על אשתו — עיקר עדות להרוג פלוני. הלכך פלגינן דיבורא. ולגבי להשים עצמו רשע או לגבי אשתו — לא יהא נאמן. **מלוה** גופיה מידק דייק. ולרבנן אפי' מלוה על פה לא הויא, דבעינן שיהא תחלתו וסופו בכשרות, כדאמרי' ב"יש נוחלין" (ב"ב דף קכח. ושם). **קטנים** נמי כדרשב"ל. ה"מ למימר: וקטנים נמי משום דמלוה גופיה מידק דייק, אלא דניחא ליה למינקט בכל חד טעמא אחרינא. א"נ: טעמא דריש לקיש גופיה נמי משום דמלוה מידק דייק. והא דלא מייתי דרשב"ל אפסולי עדות — משום דר"ל לא הזכיר אלא קטנים בדבריו.

חזקה

כא א ב ג מיי' פ"ג מהלכות עדות הל' ו ז סמג עשין קט טוש"ע ח"מ סימן מו סעיף לו [וברב אלפס כאן ובסנהדרין פ"ק דף רסג]

נ"י כ"י

תוספות רי"ד

מתני' העדים שאמרו כתב ידינו הוא זה אבל אנוסים היינו קטנים היינו פסולי עדות היינו הרי אלו נאמנים ואם יש עדים שהוא כתב ידן או שכתב ידן יוצא ממקום אחר אין נאמנים. פי' ראובן הוציא שט"ח על שמעון ושמעון טען איני מכיר חתימת העדים ושמא מזויף הוא אינו יכול ראובן לגבות בו עד שלא יקיים שטרו ואם באו העדים החתומים בו לפני ב"ד ואמרו כתב ידינו הוא זה וקיימוהו וחזרו ואמרו אנוסים היינו מחמת נפשות כדאמר לקמן ובשקר חתמנו אלא כדי להציל את נפשינו עשינו וחתמנו שאין לך דבר שעומד בפני פקוח נפש או שאמרו קטנים היינו בשעה שחתמנו או בעת שראינו ההלואה בעינינו וראיית הקטן אינה ראייה ואע"פ שבשעת הגדה הוא גדול דכתיב או ראה או ידע אם לא יגיד ונשא עונו בעינן שתהא הראייה והגדה בכשרות או שאמרו פסולים היינו מחמת קורבה שהיינו בשעת הכתיבה או בעת המלוה קרובים למלוה או ללוה או העדים זה לזה ונתרחקנו עכשיו ועדותנו הוא בטלה הרי אלו נאמנים משום מגו. מגו הוי בעי אמרי אין זה כתב ידינו ועכשיו אומרים כתב ידינו הוא אבל אנוסים היינו מחמת הטענות האלו הם נאמנים אבל אם יש עדים אחרים שמכירים חתימתן ואומרים לב"ד שזו היא חתימתן ומקיימים השטר על פיהם או שכתב ידן יוצא ממקום אחר שבשטר אחר חתמו בשטר שהוחזק ונתקיים בב"ד וב"ד רואים זה וזה ומשוין אותן ומתברר שזו היא חתימתן ואומרים אלו הטענות לבטל השטר אין נאמנים שכיון שחתמו השטר בחזקת כשרות הוא דסתמא דמילתא החותם השטר בכשרות חותם וכיון שהגידו שוב אינן חוזרין ומגידים דברישא דאית להו מגו מהימנו אבל השתא דליכא להו מגו לא מהימנו אלא השטר מקוים ע"פ אחרים ופי' המורה פסולים היינו קרובים או משחקים בקוביא ואינו נ"ל שיהיו נאמנין לומר משחקי בקוביא דאמרינן לקמן שאין אדם נאמן לשום עצמו רשע ואפילו ע"י מגו הלכך אין לפרש פסולים היינו אלא מחמת קורבה: א"ר ב"ח לא שנו פי' שאם כתב ידם יוצא ממקום אחר אינן נאמנים אלא שאמרו אנוסים היינו מחמת ממון פי' שהיה אונס את ממוננו אם לא היינו חותמנו לו שקר בזה ודאי אין נאמנים כשהשטר מתקיים ע"פ אחרים שאין אדם רשאי לחתום שקר כדי להציל ממונו והמורה פי' דלאו כל כמינייהו לשווי נפשייהו רשיעי בעדות פיהם ולפסול השטר דאדם קרוב אצל עצמו ואין נאמן על עצמו לא לזכות ולא לחובה אבל אנוסים היינו מחמת נפשות נאמנים פי' שאין לך דבר שעומד בפני פיקוח נפש. א"ל רבא כיון שהגיד שוב אינו חוזר ומגיד וכ"ת ה"מ ע"פ פי' כגון המעיד בב"ד ולאחר כדי דיבור בא לשנות בו אבל בשטר לא והאמר ר"ל עדים החתומים בשטר נעשה כמי שנחקרה עדותן בב"ד פי' מ"ה אמר כמו שנחקרה עדותן ולא אמר כמו שהגידו עדותן בב"ד שאם הגידו ועדיין לא נחקרה עדותן יכולין לחזור בהם ולומר שקר העדנו דתניא בתוספתא דפ"ב דכתובות העדים שאמרו מעידים אנו בפלוני שהוא בן גרושה בן חלוצה נתין וממזר עד שלא נחקרה עדותן אמרו בדאים אנו נאמנים ואם משנחקרה עדותן אמרו בדאים אנו אין נאמנים כללו של דבר העדים שהעידו לטמא ולטהר לקרב ולרחק עד שלא נחקרה עדותן אמרו בדאים אנו נאמנים ואם משנחקרה עדותן אין נאמנים. אלא אי אתמר ארישא אתמר הרי אלו נאמנים ארמב"ח לא שנו פירוש דאמרינן הפה שאסר הוא הפה שהתיר אלא שאמרו אנוסים היינו מחמת נפשות אבל אמרו אנוסים היינו מחמת ממון אין נאמנים שאין אדם משים עצמו רשע ואפילו ע"י מגו פי' אינו נאמן לפסול עצמו מחזקתו דקרוב הוא אצל עצמו וקרוב פסול לעדות:

אמר

[ב"ב קסח. סנהדרין מד. מכות ג:]

גיטין ג.

[עי' תוספות לקמן כח. ד"ה קיום]

סנהדרין ט: כה. יבמות כה: ב"ב קנד.

הגהות מהר"ב רנשבורג

א] תד"ה מחמת כו' ועוד דבשני עדים לא אמרינן כו'. עי' קונטרס מג ע"ב תד"ה והשתא וכו'.

גמרא

ᵃחֲזָקָה, אֵין הָעֵדִים *חוֹתְמִין עַל הַשְּׁטָר אא"כ נַעֲשָׂה בְּגָדוֹל, אֶלָּא אֲנוּסִין מ"ט? אֲמַר רַב חִסְדָּא: קָסָבַר ר"מ: עֵדִים שֶׁאָמְרוּ לָהֶם "חִתְמוּ שֶׁקֶר וְאַל תֵּהָרְגוּ" – יֵהָרְגוּ וְאַל יַחְתְּמוּ שֶׁקֶר, אֲמַר לֵיהּ רָבָא: הַשְׁתָּא, אִילּוּ אָתוּ לְקַמָּן לְאִימְּלוּכֵי – אָמְרִינַן לְהוּ: זִילוּ חֲתוּמוּ וְלָא תִּתְקַטְלוּן. *דְּאָמַר מָר: ᵇאֵין לְךָ דָּבָר שֶׁעוֹמֵד בִּפְנֵי פִּיקּוּחַ נֶפֶשׁ אֶלָּא עֲבוֹדָה זָרָה וְגִלּוּי עֲרָיוֹת וּשְׁפִיכוּת דָּמִים בִּלְבָד. הַשְׁתָּא דְּחָתְמוּ, אָמְרִינַן לְהוּ אַמַּאי חֲתַמִיתוּ?! אֶלָּא, טַעֲמָא דְּר"מ כִּדְרַב הוּנָא אָמַר רַב. דְּא"ר הוּנָא אָמַר רַב: *מוֹדֶה בִּשְׁטָר שֶׁכְּתָבוֹ אֵין צָרִיךְ לְקַיְּימוֹ. גּוּפָא, אָמַר רַב הוּנָא אָמַר רַב: מוֹדֶה בִּשְׁטָר שֶׁכְּתָבוֹ – אֵין צָרִיךְ לְקַיְּימוֹ. א"ל רַב נַחְמָן: *גְּנוּבָא גְּנוּבֵי לָמָּה לָךְ? אִי סְבִירָא לָךְ כְּר"מ – אֵימָא: הֲלָכָה כְּר"מ! אֲמַר לֵיהּ: וּמָר הֵיכִי סְבִירָא לֵיהּ? אֲמַר לֵיהּ: כִּי אָתוּ לְקַמָּן לְדִינָא אָמְרִינַן לְהוּ: ᵍזִילוּ קַיְּימוּ שְׁטָרַיְיכוּ, וְחוּתוּ לְדִינָא. א"ר יְהוּדָה אָמַר רַב: הָאוֹמֵר "שְׁטַר אֲמָנָה הוּא זֶה" – אֵינוֹ נֶאֱמָן. דְּקָאָמַר מַאן? אִילֵימָא דְּקָאָמַר לֹוֶה – פְּשִׁיטָא, כָּל כְּמִינֵּיהּ?! וְאֶלָּא דְּקָאָמַר מַלְוֶה – תָּבוֹא עָלָיו בְּרָכָה! אֶלָּא, דְּקָאָמְרִי עֵדִים; אִי דִּכְתַב יָדָם יוֹצֵא מִמָּקוֹם אַחֵר – פְּשִׁיטָא דְּלָא מְהֵימְנֵי. וְאִי דְּאֵין כְּתַב יָדָם יוֹצֵא מִמָּקוֹם אַחֵר – אַמַּאי לָא מְהֵימְנֵי? (סִימָן בא"ש) אָמַר רָבָא: לְעוֹלָם דְּקָאָמַר לֹוֶה, וְכִדְרַב הוּנָא. דְּא"ר הוּנָא אָמַר רַב: מוֹדֶה בִּשְׁטָר שֶׁכְּתָבוֹ – אֵין צָרִיךְ לְקַיְּימוֹ. אַבַּיֵי אָמַר: לְעוֹלָם דְּאָמַר מַלְוֶה, ᵈוּכְגוֹן שֶׁחָב לַאֲחֵרִים, וְכִדְרַבִּי נָתָן. *דְּתַנְיָא, רַבִּי נָתָן אוֹמֵר: ᵉמִנַּיִן לְנוֹשֶׁה בַּחֲבֵירוֹ מָנֶה, וַחֲבֵירוֹ בַּחֲבֵירוֹ, מִנַּיִן שֶׁמּוֹצִיאִין מִזֶּה וְנוֹתְנִין לָזֶה – תַּלְמוּד לוֹמַר: °"וְנָתַן לַאֲשֶׁר אָשַׁם לוֹ". רַב אַשִׁי אָמַר: לְעוֹלָם דְּקָאָמְרִי עֵדִים, וּדְאֵין כְּתַב יָדָם יוֹצֵא מִמָּקוֹם אַחֵר. וּדְקָאָמְרַתְּ אַמַּאי לָא מְהֵימְנֵי – כִּדְרַב כָּהֲנָא, דְּא"ר כָּהֲנָא: אָסוּר לוֹ לָאָדָם שֶׁיַּשְׁהֶה שְׁטַר אֲמָנָה בְּתוֹךְ בֵּיתוֹ, מִשּׁוּם שֶׁנֶּאֱמַר: °"אַל תַּשְׁכֵּן בְּאֹהָלֶיךָ עַוְלָה".

וְאָמַר

(במדבר ה; איוב יא)

רש"י

אֶלָּא אֲנוּסִים מ"ט לָא. גֵּימָא: הַפֶּה שֶׁאָסַר הוּא שֶׁהִתִּיר. *אא"כ נַעֲשָׂה בְּגָדוֹל. כָּל מַעֲשֵׂה הַשְּׁטָר בִּגְדוֹלִים, הַלּוֹקֵחַ וְהַמּוֹכֵר. וְגַבֵּי עֵדִים נַמִי אָמְרִי': חֲזָקָה אֵין הַלּוֹקֵחַ מַחְתִּים בּוֹ קְטַנִּים. יֵהָרְגוּ וְאַל יַחְתְּמוּ שֶׁקֶר. הִלְכָּךְ כִּי אָמְרִי נַמִי "אֲנוּסִים הָיִינוּ מֵחֲמַת נְפָשׁוֹת" – מְשַׁוּוּ נַפְשַׁיְיהוּ רְשָׁעִים. מוֹדֶה בִּשְׁטָר שֶׁכְּתָבוֹ. לֹוֶה שֶׁהוֹדָה בִּשְׁטָר שֶׁכְּתָבוֹ, וְעַל פִּיו נֶחְתְּמוּ הָעֵדִים. אֵין הַמַּלְוֶה צָרִיךְ לְקַיְּימוֹ. בְּעֵדִים הַחֲתוּמִים בּוֹ, שֶׁאֵין הַלֹּוֶה שׁוּב נֶאֱמָן לוֹמַר פְּרַעְתִּיו. וְלָא אָמְרִינַן בְּהַאי הַפֶּה שֶׁאָסַר הוּא שֶׁהִתִּיר, דְּמִכֵּיוָן שֶׁאָמַר כָּשֵׁר הָיָה – הֲרֵי הוּחְזַק הַשְּׁטָר. וְכִי אָמַר "פְּרַעְתִּיו" – לָא מְהֵימַן, שֶׁהֲרֵי בְּיַד הַמַּלְוֶה הוּא. וְר"מ נַמִי, דְּאָמַר אֵין נֶאֱמָנִים לְפוֹסְלוֹ – בְּמוֹדֶה לֹוֶה שֶׁכְּתָבוֹ קָאָמַר. וְקָסָבַר לָא צְרִיכִינַן תּוּ לְעֵדִים, וְלָאו אַפּוּמַּיְיהוּ מִיקַּיֵּים שְׁטָרָא. גְּנוּבָא. מִתְגַּנֵּב אַתָּה לוֹמַר דְּבָרֶיךָ בְּלָשׁוֹן שֶׁלֹּא נֶחְלְקוּ בּוֹ הַיָּחִיד וְהַמְרוּבִּים, כְּדֵי שֶׁלֹּא יְבַטְּלוּ אֶת דְּבָרֶיךָ, דְּאָמְרַתְּ כְּיחִידָאָה. אִי סְבִירָא לָךְ כְּר"מ אֵימָא הֲלָכָה כְּר"מ. וְלָא תִּנְקוֹט לָהּ כְּמִילְּתָא בְּאַנְפֵּי נַפְשָׁהּ. וּמַר הֵיכִי סְבִירָא לֵיהּ. בְּמוֹדֶה בִּשְׁטָר שֶׁכְּתָבוֹ. כִּי אָתוּ לְקַמָּן. מַלְוִין מְבִיאִין שְׁטָרוֹת. קַיְּימוּ שְׁטָרַיְיכוּ. כָּךְ אֲנִי רָגִיל לוֹמַר לְמַלְוִים הַמְּבִיאִים שְׁטָרוֹתֵיהֶם לְפָנַי וְאֵין עֵדֵיהֶם עִמָּהֶם, אֲנִי אוֹמֵר לָהֶם: לְכוּ וּבַקְּשׁוּ עֵדֵיכֶם וְקַיְּימוּהוּ. דְּאִי לָאו הָכִי, אע"ג דְּמוֹדֶה לֹוֶה שֶׁכְּתָבוֹ – מָצֵי לְמֵימַר פְּרַעְתִּיו. שְׁטַר אֲמָנָה. לֹא לָוָה כְּלוּם, אֶלָּא כְּתָבוֹ וּמְסָרוֹ לַמַּלְוֶה, שֶׁאִם יִצְטָרֵךְ לִלְוֹת – יַלְוֶה. וְהֶאֱמִינוֹ שֶׁלֹּא יִתְבָּעֶנּוּ אא"כ מַלְוֵהוּ. כָּל כְּמִינֵּיהּ. וַהֲלֹא עֵדִים חֲתוּמִים בּוֹ, פְּשִׁיטָא דְּיִתְקַיֵּים בְּחוֹתְמָיו! כִּדְרַב הוּנָא. וְאַשְׁמְעִינַן רַב יְהוּדָה נַמִי הָכִי: דְּלֹוֶה שֶׁאָמַר כְּתַבְתִּיו וּמְסַרְתִּיו לוֹ, אֲבָל שְׁטַר אֲמָנָה הוּא – אֵין צָרִיךְ הַמַּלְוֶה לַחֲזוֹר וּלְהָבִיא לְהָעִיד עַל הַחֲתִימָה, דְּאֵין נֶאֱמָן לֹוֶה לְפוֹסְלוֹ, דְּלָא עָבֵיד אִינִישׁ דְּכָתַב וּמָסַר בְּלֹא הַלְוָאָה. שֶׁחָב לַאֲחֵרִים. בְּהוֹדָאָה זוֹ, שֶׁהוּא מוֹדֶה שֶׁהוּא שְׁטַר אֲמָנָה – חָב וּמַפְסִיד אֶת אֲחֵרִים הַנּוֹשִׁים בּוֹ, וְאֵין לוֹ מַה לְהַגְבּוֹתָם, וְהָיוּ רוֹצִים לִגְבּוֹת חוֹב זֶה. וְנָתַן לַאֲשֶׁר אָשֵׁם לוֹ. וְלֹא כָּתַב "לַאֲשֶׁר הִלְוָהוּ", אֶלָּא לַאֲשֶׁר הָאָשָׁם שֶׁלּוֹ. וְאָשָׁם הוּא קֶרֶן, כִּדְאָמְרִי' בְּ"הַגּוֹזֵל" (ב"ק דף קי.) – לְמִי שֶׁהַקֶּרֶן שֶׁלּוֹ.

תוספות

חזקה אין כו'. הכא משמע דלא אמרינן מגו במקום חזקה, ולרבנן אמרינן. וצ"ע: דבעיא היא בפרק קמא דב"ב (דף ה: ושם) ולא אפשיטא, גבי תבע אחר זמנו, ואמר ליה פרעתיך תוך זמני.

דאמר מר אין לך דבר כו'. פירוש: אפי' מאן דמחמיר – לא מחמיר אלא בהנך, דרבא גופיה קסבר דאפילו בהני אינו חייב למסור עצמו בלינעא, במס' ע"ז בפרק "ר' ישמעאל" (דף נד. ושם), ואין חילוק בין הנך לשאר, ובפרהסיא – בכולהו יהרג ולא יעבור*.

טעמא דר"מ כדרב הונא כו'. פירש בקונטרס: דמיירי פלוגתייהו במודה לוה שכתבו. והיינו טעמא דר"מ דאין נאמנין – דהואיל ולוה קיימו – לא צריכי תו לעדים, ולאו אפומייהו מקיים שטרא. ורבנן סברי צריך לקיימו. וקשה לר"י: דא"כ ליפלגו בלא עדים בלוה גופי', הואיל וטעמייהו תלי בלוה! ועוד: דבפרק "מי שמת" (ב"ב דף קנד: ושם) משמע דלא פליגי בלוה, דקאמר רבי יוחנן: שאני אומר מודה בשטר שכתבו א"צ לקיימו דברי הכל היא. ופריך: והא מפלג פליגי אין נאמנים לפוסלו כו' אמר ליה: אי אלימי עדים לאורועי שטרא – איהו כל כמיניה?! ועוד: דהוה ליה למימר בדרב הונא קמיפלגי! ונראה לר"ת ולר"י דה"פ: טעמא דר"מ כדרב הונא, דכמו שאומר רב הונא דלא אמרינן מגו לפסול השטר בלוה – ה"נ אמר ר"מ בעדים, דאע"ג דאלימי לא פסלי שטרא במגו.

מודה בשטר שכתבו א"צ לקיימו. וא"ת: ומ"ט לא מהימן במגו דאי בעי אמר מזויף? וי"ל: דשמא ירא לוה לומר מזויף, פן יכחישוהו, וליכא מגו. ופירש הקונט' במקום אחר: דטעמא משום דדבר תורה א"צ קיום, דעדים החתומים על השטר נעשה כמי שנחקרה עדותן בב"ד, ורבנן הוא דאצרכוהו קיום – כי טעין מזויף הוא, אבל בשאר טענות, כגון פרוע הוא – לא הצריכוהו קיום. וכן נראה לר"י. *)אבל אין לפרש דלא מהימן במגו לומר פרוע הוא, משום דאי פרעיה – שטרא בידיה מאי בעי, דהא כי טעין נמי אמנה הוא מסקינן בסמוך אמילתיה דרב דלא מהימן, והתם לא שייך האי טעמא. **אי** סבירא לך כר"מ כו'. וא"ת: ודלמא משום הכי לא קאמר הלכה כר"מ, משום דאיכא בפ' "מי שמת" (ב"ב קנד: ושם) דמפיך דר"מ לרבנן! ויש לומר: דהוה מצי למימר דהלכה כרשב"ג, דאית ליה בהדיא בפ"ק דב"מ (דף ז.) דמודה בשטר שכתבו אין צריך לקיימו.

אימא הלכה כרבי מאיר. תימה: דאפילו כרבנן נמי מצי סבר, ושאני עדים דאלימי לאורועי שטרא, דהכי אית ליה לרבי יוחנן! ויש לומר: דרב נחמן אין נראה לו לחלק. ואם תאמר: ודלמא רב הונא מיירי במודעא ואמנה, דאפילו רב נחמן מודה לקמן! ויש לומר: דרב הונא סתם קאמר, ולא מפליג. **לעולם** דקאמר לוה וכדרב הונא כו'. ואם תאמר: ואמאי לא קאמר נמי לעולם דקאמרי עדים, וכדרב הונא? ויש לומר: דלא ניחא ליה לאוקמי דלא כרבנן, דאמרי אלימי עדים לאורועי שטרא. **וכדרב** הונא אמר רב. וא"ת: תרתי מילי דרב למה ליה? וי"ל: דחדא מכלל חבירתה אתמר. **וכגון** שחב לאחרים. וא"ת: ולהימניה במגו, דאי בעי מחיל ליה, דהא המוכר שטר חוב לחבירו וחזר ומחלו – מחול (לקמן דף פה:)! ויש לומר: דלאו מגו הוא, דשמא אין דעתו למחול ולהפסיד חובו, דעכשיו שאומר אמנה הוא – לא מפסיד מידי, כיון שאין הלוה גזלן. אע"ג דבספ"ק דב"מ (דף כ: ושם) אמרינן מגו כה"ג, גבי מצא שובר בזמן שהאשה מודה יחזיר לבעל, דקאמר: ש"מ איתא לדשמואל – שמא התם סמכינן אמגו כל דהו, משום דאיכא שובר דמוכח. ואם נאמר דמכירת שטר חוב אינו אלא מדרבנן – הוה אתי שפיר, דמצינן למימר: דווקא מוכר שטר חוב דהוי מדרבנן יכול למחול, אבל בנושה בחבירו כו', דחייב לו מן התורה, אינו יכול למחול. וכן משמע בפרק "מי שמת" (ב"ב דף קמז: ושם): דקאמר: ומודה שמואל דאם נתנו במתנת ש"מ שאינו יכול למחול. ומסיק: מתנת ש"מ דאורייתא, ואינו יכול למחול. דאי ס"ד מדרבנן – אמאי אינו יכול למחול? משמע דבמידי דאורייתא אינו יכול למחול! ויש לדחות: דהתם ודאי אי מתנת שכיב מרע דאורייתא – אין היורש יכול למחול, דמאי אולמיה האי יורש מהאי יורש? ועוד יש להביא ראיה דנושה בחבירו וחבירו בחבירו אינו יכול למחול, דאמרי' בסוף "האשה שנפלו" (לקמן פא:): הרי שהיה נושה באחיו מנה, ומת, והניח שומרת יבם, לא יאמר הואיל ואני יורש החזקתי, אלא מוציאין מידו ולוקח בהן קרקעות, והוא אוכל פירות. ומוקמי' לה כר' נתן. דהא הוי כמו נושה בחבירו מנה וחבירו בחבירו, דכל אשר לבעלה משועבד לה לכתובתה. ואי יכול למחול – אמאי ילקח בהן קרקע? ימחול לעצמו, שהוא יורש ויכול למחול. ויש לדחות: דשאני התם, דאין יורש אלא מכחה, ואינו יכול להפקיע זכותה. [וי"מ דדוקא במוכר שט"ח יכול למחול, שקדם חובו לחוב של מוכר. אבל הנושה בחבירו, שקדם חובו לחוב של חבירו – אינו יכול למחול. ושומרת יבם נמי, קדם שטר חובה לחוב בעלה]. וא"ת: אכתי נהימניה במגו דאי בעי קלתיה, כדאמרינן בסוף "זה בורר" (סנהדרין דף לא:)! ויש לומר: דהכא אתחזק בבי דינא, דאמרינן התם כיון דאתחזק בבי דינא – אי בעי קלתיה לא אמרינן. אי נמי: הכא מיירי כשהשטר הוא ביד שליש. **מנין** לנושה בחבירו כו'. משמע דהלכה כר' נתן, ובגיטין (דף לז.) פירשנוה. **)אעולה** לא חתמי. והא דכותבין שטר ללוה אע"פ שאין מלוה עמו – היינו למוסרו ללוה, ולא למלוה.

אס

*) [ועיין תוס' לקמן כח. ד"ה קיום]

**) שייך לע"ב

תוספות רי"ד

אמר ר"ה א"ר מודה בשטר שכתבו א"צ לקיימו. פי' לוה שהודה שכתבו ועל פיו נחתמו העדים אין המלוה צריך לקיימו בעדים החתומים בו שכבר קיימו הלוה שהודה לו כי הוא כתבו והחתימו ואם טוען הלוה פרעתיך אינו נאמן שכבר השטר מקוים דכל שטר מקוים אין הלוה יכול לומר פרעתי דא"ל מלוה שטרך בידי מאי בעי ול"א בזה הפה שאסר הוא הפה שהתיר: א"ל ר"נ גנובא גנובא למה לך פי' המורה מתגנב אתה לומר דבריך בלשון שלא נחלקו היחיד והרבים כדי שלא יבטלו את דבריך דאמרת כיחידאה אי ס"ל כרבי מאיר אימא הלכה כר"מ פי' דפלוגתא דר"מ ורבנן הוא דר"מ אומר אצ"ל ורבנן אמרו צריך לקיימו ולא תנקוט לה למילתא באנפי נפשי' א"ל ומר היכי ס"ל פי' במודה בשטר שכתבו א"ל כי אתו לקמן פי' מלוים [המביאין] שטרות אמרינן להו זילו קיימו שטרייכו וחותו לדינא פי' כך אני רגיל לומר למלוים המביאים שטרותיהם לפני ואין עדיהם עמהן לכו ובקשו עדיכם וקיימוהו שאם לא תקיימוהו קומו של לוה שמודה שכתבו אינו מועיל לך שהרי חוזר ואומר פרעתיך ויש להאמינו ע"י מיגו ומש"ה טרח לקיים שטרך ושוב לא יהא נאמן לומר פרעתי והל' כר"נ בדיני שאינו נאמן עיין בפסקי בפ' מי שמת עיין לקמן: **אמר** ר"י א"ר האומר שטר אמנה הוא זה אינו נאמן. פי' המורה שטר אמנה שלא לוה כלום אלא כתבו ומסרו למלוה שאם יצטרך ללוות ילוהו והאמינו שלא יתבענו אא"כ מלוהו ואינו נ"ל דמשמע מפירושו שהעדים נתנוהו ללוה והוא נתנו למלוה וא"כ אמאי קרי לי' לקמן עולה ולא מהימני עדים בזה והתנן כותבין שטר ללוה אע"פ שאין מלוה עמו וכ"ת הא אוקימנא לההוא בשטרא אקנייתא פי' שמקנהו לו נכסיו מהיום בין ילוה בין לא ילוה יגבה מהן לאותו זמן מהיום הרי אביי מעמידה בשטרי דלאו אקנייתא דאמר אביי הא דתנן כותבין שטר ללוה בלא מלוה אפילו בשטרא דלאו אקנייתא נמי וא"נ אתי למיטרף לקוחות מהיא זמנא והוא לא לוה עד תשרי לאו שלא כדין טריף דעדיו בחתומין זכין לו פי' מיום שחתמוהו יחול השעבוד ואפילו לא לוה המעות עד תשרי וכל ההיא חששא אינה שמא כתב ללוות בניסן ולא לוה עד תשרי ואתי למטרף לקוחות שלא כדין אבל לשמא לא הלוהו כלל לא חיישינן דאיהו דאפסיד אנפשי' דהימני' ומאי עולה איכא גביה סהדי אי איהו מהימן ליה וגם שטר אמנה מנין שלא יהיה אפילו בשטרא אקנייתא ואם העדים נתנוהו למלוה ברצון הלוה שצוה להם ליתנו לו אע"פ שלא ראו ההלואה בעיני' כשר וכשר הוא שאם הלוה רוצה להאמין למלוה שילוהו מה יש לעדים לומר לא ניתן לו השטר עד שנראה ההלואה בעינינו (דשמא לא ילוך הוא בושת עלי ומאמין בו ואומר להם תנו לו השטר והעדים יעברו ע"י שלא ליתן) ובמתני' הכי תנן

ואין

תוספות רי"ד

אין כותבין למלוה עד שיהא לוה עמו ולא קתני עד שיראו מתן מעות אלא עד שיהא הלוה עמו דכיון דלוה עמו אם רוצה שיתנוהו למלוה יתנו ואם לאו לא יתנו האיך קרי לה עולה דלמא יהיב ליה בינו לבינו ואי לא יהיב לה לעולם איהו הוא דאפסיד אנפשיה ושטר כשר הוא וגובה בו ממשעבדי אלא ודאי שטר אמנה הוא שלא עשה מתחלה ללוות בו אלא הלוה עשאו כדי להראות עצמו לעולם שאינו עשיר שהרי לוה מאחרים ומוסרו למלוה מאמין בו שלא יתבענו כלום אלא שיראה לעולם כי הוא חייב לו מחפה עליו שלא יראה עשיר מפני שהוא אוהבו דומה הוא לשטר פסים שלא נעשה בתחלה בעבור הלואה אלא המלוה פיים את הלוה עשה לי שטר שאתה חייב לי כך וכך כדי שיראה עשיר ויתנו לי אשה והאמן באהבתי שלעולם לא אתבעך בו ולשניהם פתרון א' אלא זה שעושה המלוה כדי שיראה עשיר קורא שטר פסים שצריך לפיים את הלוה שיעשה עליו שט"ח כי הוא חייב לו ויאמין בו שלא יתבענו ומה שהלוה כותב על עצמו כדי שיראה עני קורא אמנה שא"צ לפיים את המלוה בזה ושטר אמנה כזה ודאי הוא עולה שלא נעשה בשביל הלואה ואין העדים רשאים לחתום בו אבל שטר הלואה שנעשה כדי ללוות אין בו שום עולה כדפרי': ואמרינן דקאמר מאן אי לימא דקאמר לוה פשיטא פי' והלא עדים חתומים בו ופשיטא דיתקיים בחותמיו כל כמיניה ואלא דקאמר מלוה תבא עליו ברכה ואלא דקאמרו עדים אי כת"י יוצא ממקום אחר פשיטא דלא מהימני ואי אין כת"י יוצא ממ"א אמאי לא מהימני פי' והאיכא הפה שאסר הוא הפה שהתיר ומיגו דאי בעי אמרי לא חתמנו והשתא דאמרו חתמנו וכך היה ליהמנו א"ר לעולם דקאמר לוה וכדר"ה א"ר פי' כלומר ור"י נמי אשמעינן הכי דלוה שאומר כתבתיו ומסרתיו לו אבל שטר אמנה הוא א"צ המלוה לחזור ולהביא עדים להעיד על החתימה שאין נאמן לוה לפוסלו דלא עביד איניש דכתב ומסר בלא הלואה דאר"ה א"ר מודה בשטר שכתבו אצ"ל פי' וליתא לדרבא דאיהו מתרץ מילתא דרב אליבא דידיה דר"ה משמיה דרב קאמר ליה וכבר ר"נ פליג עלויה ואוקי מילתא כר"מ ולא כרבנן למימר דלית הל' כוותיה: אביי אמר לעולם דקאמר מלוה וכגון שחב לאחרים וכדר"נ דתניא ר"נ אומר מנין לנושה בחבירו מנה וחבירו לחבירו מנין שמוציאים מזה ונותנים לזה שנאמר ונתן לאשר אשם לו וקי"ל כיון דאמרי' המוכר שט"ח לחבירו וחזר ומחלו מחול יהיה נאמן לומר שטר אמנה ע"י מיגו דמה לו לשקר איבעי למיפטרי הלוה מיד הנושים בו הוה מחיל ליה השתא דאמר שטר אמנה הוא יהיה נאמן דהכי אמרי' בשנים אוחזין ת"ר מצא שובר פי' שכתבה אשה לבעלה התקבלתי כתובתי ועודה תחתיו בזמן שהאשה מודה יחזיר לבעל אין האשה מודה לא יחזיר לא לזה ולא לזה ודיקינן עלה בזמן שהאשה מודה מיהת יחזיר לבעלה ואמאי ניחוש דלמא כתבה ליה בניסן ולא נתנה עד תשרי הוא לא פרע עד תשרי ואזלא היא בעודה תחתיו בין ניסן לתשרי וזבנה לכתובתה לאחר בטובת הנאה מניסן ועד תשרי פי' בזול לפי שנותן מעותיו בספק שאם תמות היא ירשנה בעלה ומפסיד לוקח שלקחה ואם ימות הבעל או יגרשנה יהיה הלוקח במקומה לגבות כתובתה ושוב אין לבעלה לפרוע כתובתה אלא ללוקח ושובר שנכתב בשמה אינה כלום ומפיק ליה לשובר דכתב בניסן ואתי למיטרף לקוחות שלא כדין פי' שהשובר קודם לשטרו של לוקח ויחזיק הבעל בקרקע המיוחד לכתובתה ומהדרי' א"ר ש"מ איתא לדשמואל דאמר המוכר שט"ח לחבירו וחזר ומחלו מחול פי' ש"מ מדלא חיישינן להכי דא"נ הוה הכי שפיר זכה בעל השובר שנכתב בשמה הלכך אם

מכרה

עין משפט נר מצוה

כב א מיי' פכ"ד מהל' מלוה ולוה הלכה ה טוש"ע ח"מ סימן מו סעיף ח:

כג ב מיי' פ"ה מהלכות יסודי התורה הלכה א ב טוש"ע י"ד סימן קנז סעיף א:

[וע"ע תוס' ע"ז כז: ד"ה יכול]

כד ג מיי' פי"ד מהלכות מלוה ולוה הל' ה ע... סמג עשין צד טוש"ע ח"מ סימן מו סעיף ... וסימן פב סעיף א:

כה ד מיי' שם פ"ב שם הל' ה סמג שם טוש"ע ח"מ סימן מז סעיף א:

כו ה מיי' שם הלכה ו וסמג שם טוש"ע ח"מ סימן מו סעיף לח:

מסורת הש"ס

[לדבור זה שייך לעיל קודם לדבור אלא אנוסים וכו']

ב"ב קנה. סנהדרין כט:

סנהדרין עד.

שבת קלב. עב: ב"ב קנד. קעו.

[יבמות לג. ב"ב קלג.]

פסחים לא. לקמן פב. גיטין לז. ב"ק מ: [קדושין טו.]

גליון הש"ס

גמ' אין לך דבר שעומד בפני פיקוח נפש. עיין סוטה דף ז ע"ב תוס' ד"ה ... תוס' ד"ה וכדרב הונא ... באד"ה לחלק מכלל חבירתה ...

עין משפט נר מצוה

כז א מיי' פ"ג מהלכות עדות הלכה ז סמג עשין קט טוש"ע ח"מ סי' מו סעיף לז:

כח ב טוש"ע ח"מ סימן נז סעיף א:

כט ג מיי' פ"ז מהלכות ס"ת הלכה יב סמג עשין כה טוש"ע י"ד סי' רעט סעיף א [וברב אלפס עוד בריש הלכות ספר תורה דף סה:]:

ל ד ה ו ז ח מיי' פ"ג מהל' עדות הל' ז ח ט ופ"ז הל' ז סמג עשין קט טוש"ע ח"מ סי' מו סעי' לז [וסי' כט סעיף א]:

פי' שפייסו להלוות לו שטר

לא ט מיי' פי"ח מהל' עדות הלכה ד סמג עשין קי טור ח"מ סי' לח:

וְאָמַר רַב שֵׁשֶׁת בְּרֵיהּ דְּרַב אִידִי: ש"מ מִדְּרַב כָּהֲנָא, עֵדִים שֶׁאָמְרוּ: א"אֲמָנָה הָיוּ דְּבָרֵינוּ" אֵין נֶאֱמָנִין. מַאי טַעְמָא — כֵּיוָן דְּעַוְלָה הוּא, אַעַוְלָה לָא חָתְמֵי. *אָמַר רַבִּי יְהוֹשֻׁעַ בֶּן לֵוִי: באָסוּר לוֹ לְאָדָם שֶׁיַּשְׁהֶה שְׁטָר פָּרוּעַ בְּתוֹךְ בֵּיתוֹ, מִשּׁוּם שֶׁנֶּאֱמַר: °"אַל תַּשְׁכֵּן בְּאֹהָלֶיךָ עַוְלָה". בְּמַעֲרָבָא מִשְּׁמֵיהּ דְּרַב אָמְרִי: °"אִם אָוֶן בְּיָדְךָ הַרְחִיקֵהוּ" — זֶה שְׁטַר אֲמָנָה וּשְׁטַר *פַּסִּים, "וְאַל תַּשְׁכֵּן בְּאֹהָלֶיךָ עַוְלָה" — זֶה שְׁטָר פָּרוּעַ. מַאן דְּאָמַר שְׁטָר פָּרוּעַ — כׇּל שֶׁכֵּן שְׁטַר אֲמָנָה, וּמַאן דְּאָמַר שְׁטַר אֲמָנָה — אֲבָל שְׁטָר פָּרוּעַ לָא, דְּזִמְנִין דְּמַשְׁהֵי לֵיהּ אַפְּשִׁיטֵי דְּסַפְרָא. אִתְּמַר, גסֵפֶר שֶׁאֵינוֹ מוּגָּה, אָמַר רַבִּי אַמִּי עַד ל' יוֹם מוּתָּר לְשַׁהוֹתוֹ, מִכָּאן וְאֵילָךְ — אָסוּר לְשַׁהוֹתוֹ, מִשּׁוּם שֶׁנֶּא': "אַל תַּשְׁכֵּן בְּאֹהָלֶיךָ עַוְלָה". *אר"נ: עֵדִים שֶׁאָמְרוּ "אֲמָנָה הָיוּ דְּבָרֵינוּ" — אֵין נֶאֱמָנִין, "מוֹדָעָא הָיוּ דְּבָרֵינוּ" — אֵין נֶאֱמָנִין. מָר בַּר רַב אַשִׁי אָמַר: ד"אֲמָנָה הָיוּ דְּבָרֵינוּ" — אֵין נֶאֱמָנִין, ה"מוֹדָעָא הָיוּ דְּבָרֵינוּ" — נֶאֱמָנִין. מ"ט? הַאי נִיתָּן לִיכָּתֵב, וְהַאי לֹא נִיתָּן לִיכָּתֵב. בְּעָא מִינֵּיהּ רָבָא מֵרַב נַחְמָן: "תְּנַאי הָיוּ דְּבָרֵינוּ" מַהוּ? מוֹדָעָא וַאֲמָנָה הַיְינוּ טַעְמָא — דְּקָא עָקְרִי לֵיהּ לִשְׁטָרָא, וְהַאי נַמִי — קָא עָקַר לִשְׁטָרָא. אוֹ דִּלְמָא: תְּנַאי מִילְּתָא אַחֲרִיתִי הִיא? א"ל: כִּי אָתוּ לְקַמָּן לְדִינָא אָמְרִינַן לְהוּ: וזִילוּ קַיִּימוּ תְּנָאַיְיכוּ, וְחוּתוּ לְדִינָא. עֵד אוֹמֵר: "תְּנַאי" וְעֵד אוֹמֵר: "אֵינוֹ תְּנַאי", א"ר פַּפָּא: תַּרְוַיְיהוּ בִּשְׁטָרָא מַעַלְיָא קָא מַסְהֲדִי, וְהַאי דְּקָאָמַר "תְּנַאי" — הָוֵה לֵיהּ חַד, וְאֵין דְּבָרָיו שֶׁל אֶחָד בִּמְקוֹם שְׁנַיִם. מַתְקִיף לָהּ רַב הוּנָא בְּרֵיהּ דְּרַב יְהוֹשֻׁעַ: אִי הָכִי, אֲפִי' תַּרְוַיְיהוּ נַמִי! אֶלָּא אָמְרִינַן: הָנֵי לְמֵיעֲקַר סַהֲדוּתַיְיהוּ קָאָתוּ, הַאי נַמִי — לְמֵיעֲקַר סַהֲדוּתֵיהּ קָאָתֵי! זוְהִלְכְתָא כְּרַב הוּנָא בְּרֵיהּ דְּרַב יְהוֹשֻׁעַ. ת"ר: ח"שְׁנַיִם חֲתוּמִין עַל הַשְּׁטָר וּמֵתוּ, וּבָאוּ שְׁנַיִם מִן הַשּׁוּק וְאָמְרוּ: "יָדַעְנוּ שֶׁכְּתַב יָדָם הוּא, אֲבָל אֲנוּסִים הָיוּ, קְטַנִּים הָיוּ, פְּסוּלֵי עֵדוּת הָיוּ" — הֲרֵי אֵלּוּ נֶאֱמָנִים. וְאִם יֵשׁ עֵדִים שֶׁכְּתַב יָדָם הוּא זֶה, אוֹ שֶׁהָיָה כְּתַב יָדָם יוֹצֵא מִמָּקוֹם אַחֵר, מִשְּׁטָר שֶׁקָּרָא עָלָיו עַרְעָר וְהוּחְזַק בְּבֵ"ד — אֵין אֵלּוּ נֶאֱמָנִין. וּמַגְבִּינַן בֵּיהּ כְּבִשְׁטָרָא מַעַלְיָא? וְאַמַּאי? תְּרֵי וּתְרֵי נִינְהוּ! אֲמַר רַב שֵׁשֶׁת: טזֹאת אוֹמֶרֶת: *)טהַהַכְחָשָׁה תְּחִלַּת הֲזָמָּה הִיא,

*) [ב"ק עג:]

רש"י

וְאָמַר רַב שֵׁשֶׁת גָּרְסִי'. אַעַוְלָה לָא חָתְמֵי. וְכִי אָמְרִי "חָתַמְנוּ" — אֵין נֶאֱמָנִים לְהַרְשִׁיעַ אֶת עַצְמָן. עַל פְּשִׁיטֵי דְּסַפְרָא. שֶׁעַל הַלֹּוֶה לִיתֵּן שְׂכַר הַסּוֹפֵר, וּפְעָמִים שֶׁאֵין לוֹ, וְנוֹתְנוֹ הַמַּלְוֶה, וְחוֹזֵר וְגוֹבֵהוּ מִמֶּנּוּ בִּשְׁעַת פֵּרָעוֹן, וּמְעַכֵּב הַשְּׁטָר עָלָיו. סֵפֶר שֶׁאֵינוֹ מוּגָּה. תּוֹרָה נְבִיאִים וּכְתוּבִים. מוּגָּה. מִן טָעֻיּוֹת שֶׁבּוֹ. עֵדִים. הַחֲתוּמִים בַּשְּׁטָר, וְאָמְרוּ: אֲמָנָה הָיוּ דְּבָרֵינוּ. לֹא הִלְוָהוּ כְּלוּם, אֶלָּא כָּתַבְנוּ לוֹ — לִכְשֶׁיִּצְטָרֵךְ יַלְוֶה לוֹ. וְזֶה שֶׁיִּעֵבֵּד לוֹ נְכָסָיו מֵעַכְשָׁיו אִם יַלְוֶה אֲפִילּוּ לְאַחַר זְמַן, דְּלָאו מוּקְדָּם לֶיהֱוֵי לִטְרוֹף שֶׁלֹּא כַּדִּין. מוֹדָעָא הָיוּ דְּבָרֵינוּ. אִם שְׁטַר מֶכֶר הוּא, וְאָמְרוּ עֵדִים הַחֲתוּמִים בּוֹ: הַמּוֹכֵר מָסַר מוֹדָעָא בְּפָנֵינוּ וְהֶרְאָנוּ אוֹנְסוֹ, וְהִכַּרְנוּ בּוֹ. אֵין נֶאֱמָנִין. דְּלָא אָתֵי עַל פֶּה וּמֵרַע לֵיהּ לִשְׁטָרָא. מוֹדָעָא נִיתָּן לָעֵדִים לִכְתּוֹב אֶת הַשְּׁטָר כְּדֵי לְהַצִּיל הָאָנוּס מֵאוֹנְסוֹ, אֲמָנָה לֹא נִיתָּן לְהִכָּתֵב, דְּעַוְלָה הֲוַאי, וְכִי אָמְרוּ חָתַמְנוּ — מְשַׁוּוּ לְנַפְשַׁיְיהוּ רְשָׁעִים, וְאֵין אָדָם נֶאֱמָן לָשׂוּם עַצְמוֹ רָשָׁע. תְּנַאי הָיוּ דְּבָרֵינוּ. עַל תְּנַאי מְכָרָהּ לוֹ, שֶׁיַּעֲשֶׂה לוֹ כָּךְ וְכָךְ, וְלֹא רָאִינוּ שֶׁקִּיֵּים לוֹ תְּנָאוֹ. וְזֶה אוֹמֵר: לֹא קִיֵּים לִי, וְאֵינוֹ מֶכֶר. מוֹדָעָא וַאֲמָנָה. טַעְמָא מַאי קָאָמַר מַר אֵין נֶאֱמָנִין. דְּקָא עָקְרִי לֵיהּ לִשְׁטָרָא. בְּעֵדוּתָן זֶה, וְלָא אָתֵי עַל פֶּה וּמֵרַע לִשְׁטָרָא. הָכָא נַמִי כו'. אוֹ דִלְמָא. הָא לָא עֲקִרְתָּא דִּשְׁטָרָא הוּא, דְּמוֹדִים הֵם שֶׁהַשְּׁטָר אֱמֶת, אֶלָּא שֶׁתְּנַאי הָיָה בֵּינֵיהֶם, וְזוֹ עֵדוּת אַחֶרֶת הִיא, וּשְׁטָרָא מִמֵּילָא מִיעֲקַר לְאַחַר זְמַן, בַּיּוֹם שֶׁלֹּא קִיֵּים תְּנָאוֹ בִּזְמַנּוֹ. כִּי אָתוּ לְקַמָּן. לָקוֹחוֹת שֶׁעֵדֵיהֶם מְעִידִים שֶׁתְּנַאי הָיוּ דִּבְרֵיהֶם. אָמְרִי' לְהוּ זִילוּ קַיִּימוּ תְּנָאַיְיכוּ. לַבְּעָלִים. וְחוּתוּ לְדִינָא. אִם יְעַכֵּב שׁוּב הַקַּרְקַע. תַּרְוַיְיהוּ בִּשְׁטָרָא מַעַלְיָא קָא מַסְהֲדִי. שְׁנֵיהֶם מְעִידִים שֶׁהַשְּׁטָר אֱמֶת, וּכְמוֹת שֶׁהוּא כָּתוּב בְּלֹא תְּנַאי, חֲתָמוּהוּ. וְהַאי דְּקָאָמַר תְּנַאי חַד הוּא. וְאֵינוֹ נֶאֱמָן לַעֲקוֹר שְׁטָר שֶׁשְּׁנֵיהֶם חֲתוּמִים בּוֹ. אִי הָכִי אֲפִילּוּ תַּרְוַיְיהוּ נַמִי אֶלָּא אָמְרִינַן כו'. אִי הָכִי דְּכֵיוָן שֶׁהֵעִיד עַל כְּתַב יָדוֹ עָשִׂיתָ לָזֶה אֶחָד מִמְּקַיְּימֵי הַשְּׁטָר כְּמוֹת שֶׁהוּא כָּתוּב בְּלֹא תְּנַאי, וַהֲוֵי לְהוּ עֵדָיו שְׁנַיִם, וְעֵדוּת אַחֲרוֹנָה דִּבְרֵי אֶחָד בִּמְקוֹם שְׁנַיִם. אֲפִי' תַּרְוַיְיהוּ נַמִי. אָמְרֵי: תְּנַאי הָיוּ דְּבָרֵינוּ — לָא לֵיתְהֵימְנוּ. דְּכֵיוָן שֶׁהֵעִידוּ עַל כְּתַב יָדָן — קִיְּימוּ הַשְּׁטָר כְּמוֹת שֶׁהוּא כָּתוּב, וְכִי אָמְרֵי תְּנַאי הָיוּ דְּבָרֵינוּ — הָווּ לְהוּ מַגִּידִים וְחוֹזְרִים וּמַגִּידִים, וְאַמַּאי אֲמַר רַב נַחְמָן קַיְּימוּ תְּנָאַיְיכוּ כו'? אֶלָּא. עַל כָּרְחָךְ לָאו חֲתִימָה מְקוּיֶּימֶת הוּא, דְּכֵיוָן דְּתוֹךְ כְּדֵי דִבּוּר מַסְּקֵי דִּבּוּרַיְיהוּ וְאָמְרֵי: אֲבָל תְּנַאי הָיָה בֵּינֵיהֶן, אָמְרִינַן: הָנֵי לְמֵיעֲקַר סַהֲדוּתַיְיהוּ שֶׁאָמְרוּ "כְּתַב יָדֵינוּ הוּא" קָאָתוּ, וְלוֹמַר: לֹא חָתַמְנוּ אֶלָּא ע"מ שֶׁיִּתְקַיֵּים אֶת הַתְּנַאי, וְכֵיוָן דִּתְנַאי מִלְּתָא אַחֲרִיתִי הִיא, שֶׁאֵינָהּ עוֹקַרְתּוֹ אֶלָּא לְאַחַר זְמַן — לָא דָּמְיָא לְמוֹדָעָא וַאֲמָנָה, וּמְהֵימְנֵי, דְּעֵדוּת בִּפְנֵי עַצְמָהּ הִיא. הַאי נַמִי. כִּי סַיֵּים וְאָמַר תְּנַאי הֲוָה — עָקַר לַחֲתִימַת יָדֵיהּ, לוֹמַר: לֹא חָתַמְתִּי אֶלָּא עַל מְנָת כֵּן. וְכֵיוָן דְּאִית לָן דְּמִלְּתָא אַחֲרִיתִי הִיא, וּשְׁטָרָא מִמֵּילָא מִיעֲקַר — אִשְׁתַּכַּח דְּאֵין בַּשְּׁטָר חָתוּם אֶלָּא ע"א. שֶׁקָּרָא עָלָיו עַרְעָר. שֶׁרְנָנָה הַנִּתְבָּע לְפוֹסְלוֹ. וּמַגְבִּינַן בֵּיהּ. בִּתְמִיָּה. תְּרֵי וּתְרֵי נִינְהוּ. עֵדֵי הַשְּׁטָר ב', וְאֵלּוּ ב' מְעִידִים עֲלֵיהֶם שֶׁפְּסוּלִים הָיוּ בְּאוֹתָהּ שָׁעָה.

וּכְשֵׁם

תוספות

אם און בידך הרחיקהו זה שטר פסים ושטר אמנה. דהכי משמע לשון "און" – דמעיקרא הוי שקר. "ואל תשכן באהליך עולה" זה שטר פרוע, שעתה הוא עולה, אבל מעיקרא הוא אמת. **זמנין** דמשהי ליה אפשיטי דספרא. וע"י אותה שהייה אישתלי ליה שהותא פעם אחרת, הלכך לא קרי ליה "עולה". ומ"ד שטר פרוע – היה לו ליזהר. אבל אין לפרש דמשום שהייתו אפשיטי דספרא קרי ליה "עולה", דמה פשע? **אמר** רב נחמן עדים שאמרו אמנה היו דברינו אין נאמנים. ע"כ באין כתב ידן יוצא ממקום אחר איירי, דאי כתב ידן יוצא ממקום אחר – פשיטא. דהכי פריך לעיל. ועוד: דמר בר רב אשי קאמר דאין נאמנים משום דלא ניתן לכתב, ואי בכתב ידן יוצא ממקום אחר – אפילו ניתן לכתב פשיטא דאין נאמנים. וקשה: דאמאי לא מהימני במיגו? דהא רב נחמן גופיה אית ליה לעיל מגו לפסול השטר, דקאמר: כי אתו לקמן לדינא אמרינן להו זילו קיימו שטרייכו וחותו לדינא, דמהימן לומר פרוע במגו דמזויף. וכ"ש עדים, דאלימי לאורועי שטרא, כדאמר ב"מי שמת" (ב"ב דף קנד.)! ותירץ ר"י: דהיינו טעמא דמודעא, הואיל ומודים שהשטר נכתב ונמסר כהלכתו – שוב לא אתי על פה ומרע לשטרא אפילו במגו. ולא דמי לאנוסים וקטנים דמתניתין, שאין מודים שהיה שטר כשר כלל, אלא סותרין אותו – הלכך מהימני במגו, דלא שייך כאן לומר דלא אתי על פה ומרע לשטרא, שהרי אינם מודים שהיה שטר. ואמנה נמי נראה דהיינו טעמא דלא מהימני לרב נחמן, דלא מרעי לשטרא, הואיל ומודים שהשטר נכתב כדין מדעת הלוה. דלא מפרש טעמא דאמנה משום דלא ניתן לכתב אלא מר בר רב אשי, אבל לרב נחמן – טעם אמנה ומודעא שניהם שוה. והא דאית ליה לרב נחמן דנאמן לומר פרוע הוא במגו דמזויף – התם נמי לא מרע לשטרא כלל, הלכך מהימן במגו. ואתי שפיר רב נחמן כרבנן דר"מ. והיא ברייתא ד"מי שמת" (ג"ז שם:) דשטר אמנה הוא זה דאינו נאמן, דבעי לאוקמי כר"מ – רב נחמן מוקי לה לדברי הכל. **או** דלמא תנאי מילתא אחריתי היא. פי': לדבר אחר הן באין, ולא לעקירת השטר, אלא תוספת בעלמא, שמפרשים עדותן היאך. ועד השתא קיים השטר, ואינו נעקר אם יתקיים התנאי, הלכך אין כאן הורעת השטר. אבל אין לפרש: מילתא אחריתי היא לגמרי, ולא שייך לעדותן ראשונה, כמו שאם היו מעידין שהוא פרוע שהן נאמנים – דא"כ מאי פריך בסמוך: א"ה אפי' תרי נמי! דכיון דתנאי מילתא אחריתי הוא לגמרי – תרי נאמנים אפילו בכתב ידן יוצא ממקום אחר. אבל חד לעולם אימא לך דלא מהימן, כי היכי דלא מהימן לומר פרוע הוא. לכך נראה כדפירשנו. **ואם** כתב ידן יוצא ממקום אחר אין נאמנים. ופסולי עדות דקתני, לא שאומרים שעדיין פסולים – דאם כן אמאי אין נאמנים? אלא פסולי עדות הוו אז, ועתה מודים שהם כשרים. וא"ת: ומכל מקום, אמאי אין נאמנים? להימנו במגו, דאי בעו אומרים עדיין הם פסולים! [וכן בכל] שתי כתי עדים המכחישות זו את זו, אמאי לא מהימני בתראי במגו דאי בעו פסלי לקמאי בגזלנותא? ואור"י דבשני עדים לא שייך מגו, דאין אחד יודע מה בלב חבירו*). **אמר** רב ששת זאת אומרת הכחשה תחלת הזמה היא. וא"ת: תקשי לרב ששת ברייתא ד"מי שמת" (ג"ז שם) דקתני: אם אמר שטר אמנה הוא, אם יש עדים, פירוש: דשטר אמנה הוא – הלך אחר עדים, ואם לאו – הלך אחר השטר. אלמא אע"ג דאין השטר צריך, קיום כדאמר הלך אחר השטר, שמודה הלוה שכתבו כדאיתא התם, [ואפילו הכי], אם יש עדים – הלך אחר עדים, ולא אמרינן הכחשה תחלת הזמה! וי"ל: דזאת אומרת קאמר, אבל ההיא פליג.

*) ובאין כתב ידן יוצא ממקום אחר נאמנין שפיר במגו דאי בעי שתקי אי נמי מגו במקום עדים הוא אי נמי הא דבתראי מהימני חידוש הוא דמאי חזית דסמכת אהני כו' הלכך אין נאמנין במגו שיכולים לפוסלן בגזלנותא אלא כשאומרים כן בפירוש:

ואוקי

תוספות רי"ד

מכרה היא כתובתה באייר דהיינו שטר חוב וחזרתה ומחלתה לבעלה בתשרי שפיר טרף בעלה וכיון א) שיכולה למחול אותה לבעלה אי לקנוניא בע"י להפסיד הלקוחות כלל למחול לבעלה ומדלא מחלה ש"מ קושטא קאמרה וה"נ הכא נהימניה על ידי ההיא מיגו ונ"ל לתרץ דדוקא גבי מוכר לחבירו יכול למחול מפני שאינו יכול להקנות לחבירו גוף המנה שאינו בעין אבל ב) מלוה שלא יכול לומר הלוה ללוקח לאו בע"ד דידי את דלא יהא אלא שהרשהו לגבות ממנו ומפני כך יכול המלוה למחול אבל כשחב לאחרים שהוא ד"ת אינו יכול למחול שמשעה שחב לאחרים נשתעבד המנה הזה לאותו ושוב אינו המלוה יכול למוחלו ומ"ה אוקימנא כשחב לאחרים ולא כשמכרו לאחרים דהתם ודאי דמצי מחיל הנה נאמן ע"י מיגו אבל הכא לא מצי מחיל ומ"ה לא מהימן: ר"א אמר לעולם דקאמרו עדים ודאין כת"י יוצא ממקום אחר ודקאמרת אמאי לא מהימנו כדר"כ דאר"כ אסור לאדם שישהה שטר אמנה בתוך ביתו שנאמר אל תשכן באהליך עולה: **א"ר** [ששת] (אשישא) בריה דר"א ש"מ מדר"כ העדים שאמרו אמנה היה דברינו אין נאמנים מ"ט כיון דעולה היא אעולה לא חתמו ואע"פ שיש להן מיגו אין נאמנים: אריב"ל אסור לאדם שישהא שטר [illegible] לו לפרוע ללוה כדתנן והלוה נותן שכר הסופר ויפרעם המלוה ודוקא אפשיטי דספרא פליגי אבל אם חייב לו קצת מן החוב ליכא מאן דפליג שיכול להשהותו אצלו עד שיפרענו וא"צ לכתוב לו שובר כדי שיהא לו כפוף שיפרענו: במערבא אמרי משמיה דר"א אם אין בידך הרחיקהו זה שטר פסים ושטר אמנה ואל תשכן באהליך עולה זו שטר פרוע: איתמר ס"ת שאינו מוגה א"ר אמי עד ל' יום מותר להשהותו מכאן ואילך אסור להשהותו משום אל תשכן באהליך עולה: א"ר נחמן עדים שאמרו אמנה היה דברינו מודעא היה דברינו אין נאמנים פי' עדים החתומים בשטר ואמרו אמנה היה לא הלוה לו פלוני אלא כתבנוהו לו ולכשיצטרך ילוה בו וזה שיעבד לו נכסיו מעכשיו אם ילוה לו לאחר זמן דלא להוי יכול לטרוף שלא כדין ולא מיבעיא אם כת"י יוצא ממ"א דלא מהימנו לעוקרו דלא הפה שאסר הפה שהתיר איכא אלא אפילו אם הן עצמם מקיימים אותו ואומרים כת"י הוא אבל אמנה היה דברינו אין נאמנים שמאחר שמודים שנכתב בכשרות הרי חתימתן שבשטר כאילו העידו בב"ד שכל מה [שכתוב] בשטר הלוהו מלוה ללוה וכיון שהגיד שוב אין חוזר ומגיד ותו דלא אתי ע"פ ומרע לשטרא אבל שטרא מרע לשטרא מודעא היה דברינו אין נאמנים פי' אם שטר מכר הוא ואמרו עדים החתומים בו המוכר מסר מודעא והראה אונסו והכרנו בו אין נאמנים דלא אתי ע"פ ומרע לשטרא: מר בר ר"א אמר אמנה היה דברינו אין נאמנים אבל מודעא היה דברינו נאמנים מ"ט האי ניתן לכתב והאי לא ניתן לכתב פירוש מודעא היה דברינו שאומר אם היה שטר מכר לא ברצונו מכר לו אלא אנוס היה ומסר מודעא לפנינו וקסבר ר"נ כיון שהיה אנוס ודאי ג) אונסו א"כ לא היה להם לחתום השטר מכירה וא"ת בשביל זה חתמו בו כדי להציל את המוכר מיד הלוקח שהיה אונס אותו והוא פייסם שיכתבו לו ויחתמוהו היה להם לכתוב שטר מודעא ברישא דמודעי ניתן לכתב והדר ליכתבו ליה להאי שטרא מכר והוי אתיא מודעא ומבטלא לשטרא והשתא דלא כתבו מודעא ברישא לא הוה להו לחתום בו וחתמו עולה מכירה ואאשקלתא פי' גם על שטר מכירה חתם מאן דחתם אמודעי וכו' דאע"ג דתלויה וזבין זביניה היכא דלא מסר מודעא אבל המודעא שנכתב תבטל שטר המכירה ומאן דחתם אאשקלתא וזבין זביניה זביני כדאסיקנא ר"ה לטעמיה וכו' ור' יצחק אלפסי פסיק הל' כמר בר רב אשי רבא מר"נ תנאי היה דברינו מהו מודעא ואמנה טעמא מאי דעקר לי' לשטרא והאי נמי עקר לה דלמא תנאי מילתא אחריתי (והרב מוליך השיטה בשכת"י יוצא ממקום אחר ובעי' דרבא כשת"י מודעא ואמנה מ"ט אמרת דאין נאמנים אע"פ שאין כת"י יוצא ממקום אחר משום דעקרי לה בעדותן והלכך אמרינן להו א"כ דאמנה היה ולא הלוה לו או מודעא היה ולא מכר לו מרצונו למה ורשע עשיתם לפי דבריכם וכיון דמשוי נפשייהו רשיעי אין נאמנים וה"נ קעקרי לה לשטרא היה דברינו באמרו להו כיון שעל תנאי היה המכר כגון אם יבא פלוני ממקום פלוני ויסכים בדבר ואם לא לא יהא מכר למה חתמתם בשטר המכר שבלא שום תנאי מכר לו לא היה לכם לעשות גם זה עולה הוא דומיא דשטר אמנה אע"פ שהאמינו המוכר שאם לא יקיים תנאו שיהא המכר להם לחתום כדאמרינן בשטר אמנה שאע"פ שהאמינו שילוהו ויקרא עולה ואין לחתום בו או דלמא אחריתי הוא פי' שכיון שמכר לו מכר מקוים אע"פ שהתלה המכר על תנאי שאמר אם יבא ויסכים יהא קיים ואם לאו יהא בטל רשאים העדים לחתום בו כיון שהמוכר מאמינו ולא רצה בתוך השטר א"ל כי אתי לקמן פי' לקוחות שעדיהם מעידים שתנאי היה דבריהם אמרינן ל תנאייכו פי' לבעל וחותו לדינא פי' אם יעכב שוב הקרקע שנאמנים לומר תנאי היה דברינו וכי

הוא כמו שטר אמנה ואע"פ שאין כת"י ימ"א דמהימני ע"י מיגו דאמרו לא חתמנו כדלעיל ואתי ע"פ דידהו ומרע לשטרא ה"מ בקטנים היינו קרובים היינו אנוסים היינו מחמת נפשות דלא הוי עולה ולא משוי נפשייהו רשיעא אבל במודעא היה דברינו שהוא עולה כמו אמנה היה דברינו אפילו על ידי מיגו אין נאמנים שאין אדם משים עצמו רשע פירוש תרוייהו מודי דשטרא מעליא הוא ועכשיו באים לבטלו ע"י עדות מודעא וזה נקרא חוזר ומגיד וכיון שהגיד עדותו בשטר שוב אינו חוזר ומגיד ע"פ פעם שני. ומר בר ר"א סבר אמנה לא ניתן לכתב מש"ה אין נאמנים אפילו ע"י מיגו משום דעולה היא וכי אמרו חתמנו משוי נפשייהו רשיעא ואין אדם משים עצמו רשע אבל מודעא ניתן לכתב כדי לפצות המוכר מאונסו מאי אמרת הוו להו למיכתב מודעא ברישא מירתת מוכר דלמא מרגיש לוקח ואנים ליה טפי ואי אמרת ומשום אונסיה היכי חתמו שקרא מימר אמר להו סוף סוף על פומייכו בעי לאיתקיימא שטרא אתון דמיתקיימתון ליה אתון אמריתו דאנוס הייתי ותהימנו ע"י מיגו מש"ה סבר מר בר"א דניתן לכתוב ונאמנים ור"נ סבר דלמא לא מקיים שטרא מפומייהו אלא אפומי דסהדי אחרינא או מכת"י יוצא ממקום אחר דתו ל"ל מיגו נמצא שחתמו' על שקר הלכך לא ניתן לכתב והל' כר"נ דמסתבר טעמי' ותו דבחזקת הבתים מקשי [illegible]

א) אולי צ"ל וכיון שיכולה למחול אותה לבעלה יכולה נמי לעשות קנוניא כדי להפסיד הלקוחות ואף שאין כוונתה כלל למחול לבעלה וכו'. ב) נראה דצ"ל ולא מהני המכירה רק שלא יכול לומר וכו'. ג) נראה דצ"ל וודאי אינה מכירה וא"כ.

גליון הש"ס גמ' זאת אומרת הכחשה. עיין שיטה מקובצת בב"מ דף קב ע"א ד"ה אר"א זאת אומרת בשם רבי סעדי' גאון:

וְכִשֵׁם שֶׁאֵין מְזִימִין אֶת הָעֵדִים אֶלָּא בִּפְנֵיהֶם כָּךְ אֵין מַכְחִישִׁין אֶת הָעֵדִים אֶלָּא בִּפְנֵיהֶם. אֲמַר לֵיהּ רַב נַחְמָן: אִילּוּ הָווּ קַמָּן וּמַכְחִישִׁין לְהוּ – הֲוָה הַכְחָשָׁה, וְלָא הֲוָה מַשְׁגִּיחִין בְּהוּ, דְּהָוֵי לָהּ עֵדוּת מוּכְחֶשֶׁת. הַשְׁתָּא דְּלֵיתְנְהוּ, דְּאִילּוּ הָווּ לְקַמָּן דִּלְמָא הָווּ מוֹדוּ לְהוּ, מְהֵימְנֵי?! אֶלָּא אָמַר רַב נַחְמָן: [א]אוֹקֵי תְּרֵי לַהֲדֵי תְּרֵי, וְאוֹקֵי מָמוֹנָא בְּחֶזְקַת מָרֵיהּ. *מִידֵי דַּהֲוָה אַנִּכְסֵי דְּבַר שָׁטְיָא. דְּבַר שָׁטְיָא זַבֵּין נִכְסֵי. אֲתוּ בֵּי תְּרֵי אָמְרִי: כְּשֶׁהוּא שׁוֹטֶה זַבֵּין, וַאֲתוּ בֵּי תְּרֵי וְאָמְרִי: כְּשֶׁהוּא חָלִים זַבֵּין. אָמַר רַב אַשִׁי: [ב]אוֹקֵי תְּרֵי לַהֲדֵי תְּרֵי, וְאוֹקֵי *מָמוֹנָא בְּחֶזְקַת בַּר שָׁטְיָא. וְלָא אֲמָרַן [ג]אֶלָּא דְּאִית לֵיהּ חֲזָקָה דַּאֲבָהָתֵיהּ, אֲבָל לֵית לֵיהּ חֲזָקָה דַּאֲבָהָתֵיהּ – אָמְרִינַן: כְּשֶׁהוּא שׁוֹטֶה זָבַן, *וּכְשֶׁהוּא שׁוֹטֶה זַבֵּין. א"ר אַבָּהוּ: [ד]אֵין מְזִימִין אֶת הָעֵדִים אֶלָּא בִּפְנֵיהֶן, וּמַכְחִישִׁין אֶת הָעֵדִים שֶׁלֹּא בִּפְנֵיהֶן. וַהֲזָמָה שֶׁלֹּא בִּפְנֵיהֶן, נְהִי דַּהֲזָמָה לָא הָוֵי – הַכְחָשָׁה מִיהָא הָוְיָא. אָמַר מָר: אִם יֵשׁ עֵדִים שֶׁכָּתַב יָדָם הוּא זֶה, אוֹ שֶׁהָיָה כְּתַב יָדָם יוֹצֵא מִמָּקוֹם אַחֵר, מִשְּׁטָר שֶׁקָּרָא עָלָיו עַרְעָר וְהוּחְזַק בְּב"ד – אֵין נֶאֱמָנִין. (א) קָרָא עָלָיו עַרְעָר – אִין, לֹא קָרָא עָלָיו עַרְעָר – לָא, מְסַיַּיע לֵיהּ לְרַבִּי אַסִי, דְּאָמַר רַבִּי אַסִי: [ה]אֵין מְקַיְּימִין אֶת הַשְּׁטָר אֶלָּא מִשְּׁטָר שֶׁקָּרָא עָלָיו עַרְעָר וְהוּחְזַק בְּב"ד. אָמְרִי נְהַרְדְּעֵי: [ו]אֵין מְקַיְּימִין אֶת הַשְּׁטָר אֶלָּא מִשְּׁתֵּי כְּתוּבּוֹת [אוֹ] מִשְּׁתֵּי שָׂדוֹת, וְהוּא שֶׁאֲכָלוּם בַּעֲלֵיהֶן ג' שָׁנִים וּבְשׁוּפִי. א"ר שִׁימִי בַּר אַשִׁי: [ז]וּבְיוֹצֵא מִתַּחַת יַד אַחֵר, אֲבָל מִיַּד עַצְמוֹ – לֹא. מַאי שְׁנָא תַּחַת יַד עַצְמוֹ דְּלָא – דִּלְמָא זִיּוּפֵי מְזַיֵּיף, מִתַּחַת יְדֵי אַחֵר נַמִי – דִּלְמָא אֲזַל וַחֲזָא, אֲתָא וְזַיֵּיף! כּוּלֵּי הַאי לָא מָצֵי מְכַוֵּין. ת"ר: *[ח]כּוֹתֵב אָדָם עֵדוּתוֹ עַל הַשְּׁטָר, וּמֵעִיד עָלֶיהָ אֲפִילּוּ לְאַחַר כַּמָּה שָׁנִים. אָמַר רַב הוּנָא: וְהוּא שֶׁזּוֹכְרָהּ מֵעַצְמוֹ. רַבִּי יוֹחָנָן אָמַר: [ט]אע"פ שֶׁאֵין זוֹכְרָהּ מֵעַצְמוֹ. אָמַר (א) רַבָּה: ש"מ מִדְּרַבִּי יוֹחָנָן: [י]הָנֵי בֵּי תְּרֵי דְּיָדְעִי סַהֲדוּתָא, וּמִנְשֵׁי חַד מִנַּיְיהוּ – מַדְכַּר חַד לְחַבְרֵיהּ. אִיבַּעְיָא לְהוּ: עַצְמוֹ מַאי? רַב חֲבִיבָא אָמַר: אֲפִילּוּ עַצְמוֹ. מָר בְּרֵיהּ דְּרַב אַשִׁי אָמַר: עַצְמוֹ לֹא. וְהִלְכְתָא: [כ]עַצְמוֹ לֹא.
וְאִי

[יבמות לא:]

רש"י

וכשם שאין מזימין העדים אלא בפניהם. שהרי הם באין לחייבן כדי לעונשן או נפש או ממון, והתורה אמרה "והועד בבעליו" – יבא בעל השור ויעמוד על שורו (ב"ק דף קיב:). כך אין מכחישין. אפילו לבטל עדותן. לא הוו משגיחין בהו. בעדי השטר לגבות על פיהם. השתא. דאיכא למימר אילו הוו קמן הוו מודו להני, אמרת מהימני?! ואוקי ממונא בחזקת מריה. בחזקת הלוה. ואם קרקע היא – תעמוד בחזקת המוכר. ודקתני 'בדברי' אין נאמנים – לא דליהוי שטרא מעליא למיגבי ביה, אלא דלא קרעינן ליה. ואי תפיס מידי והדר אתי האי ותבע מיניה – לא מפקינן מיניה, דאמרינן: אוקי תרי בהדי תרי, וממונא בחזקת היכא דקאי. זבין נכסיה. מכר קרקעותיו. חלים. בריא. ולא אמרן. דאוקי נכסי בחזקת בר שטיא. אלא דאית ליה. בנכסים הללו חזקה דאבהתא, שהיו של אבותיו, דחזקה מעלייתא היא. אבל לית ליה בהו חזקה דאבהתא. אלא חזקה דנפשיה, שקנאן הוא והוחזקו בידו – כקנייתו כך מכירתו, ואין חזקתו חזקה לבטל מכירתו. נהי דהזמה לא הויא. לעונשם לא נפש ולא ממון, הכחשה הויא לבטל עדותן. אין מקיימין את השטר. מתוך שטר אחר. אא"כ קרא ערער. על אותו שטר האחר, והוחזק בב"ד על ידי עדיו. דאי לא קרא עליו ערער – חיישינן דלמא ההוא גופיה מזוייף הוא. משתי שדות. מעדים הללו, אם חתומים על שני שטרות אחרים, שהן מכר שתי שדות, ואכלום הלקוחות ע"י שטרות הללו שלש שנים – מקיימין שטר שלישי מהן, אם החתימות דומות. בשופי. בלא ערעור. וביוצא מתחת ידי אחר. שהשטרות הללו שמקיימין את השלישי מהם יוצא מתחת ידי אחר, ולא מתחת ידיו של זה המוציא את השלישי. זיופי זייף. הסתכל בכתב של אותן שטרות, וכיון וחתם הוא עצמו את השלישי דוגמת אותה חתימה. מכוין. מלמד כתב בכתב, הואיל ואינו לפניו. כותב אדם. אם עשאוהו עד בדבר, וירא לשוכחו – כותבו על חתיכת קלף ומצניעה. ומעיד. ע"פ אותו כתב, אפי' לאחר כמה שנים. שזוכרה מעצמו. בלא ראיית השטר נזכר קצת מעדותו מאליו. אע"פ שאין זוכרה מעצמו. אלא לאחר שרואה בשטר נתן בלבו ונזכר, שלא נשתכח ממנו כל כך, שכשמזכירים לו נזכר. אבל אינו נזכר לגמרי – לא, דרחמנא אמר: מפיהם, ולא מפי כתבם. עצמו מאי. אם בעל דין עצמו מזכירו עד שנזכר, מאי.
ואי

תוספות

ואוקי ממונא בחזקת מריה. פירש בקונט': ואין נאמנין דקתני – לאו דמגבינא בשטרא, אלא דלא קרעינן ליה. ונפקא מינה, דאי תפס לא מפקינן מיניה. וקשה: דאמר בפ"ק דב"מ (דף ו: ושם) גבי ספק בכור, תקפו כהן – מוציאין אותו מידו. אלמא תפיסה דלאחר ספיקא – לאו כלום היא! ומיהו ההוא דסוף "השואל" (שם דף קב: ושם) לא קשה מידי, דאמרי' גבי משכיר בית לחבירו בי"ב זהובים לשנה מדינר זהב לחדש; בא בתחלת החדש – כולו למשכיר. אלמא דבחזקת משכיר הוא, ואפ"ה קאמר: בא בסוף החדש – כולו לשוכר. דשאני התם, דכיון דלא בא בתחלת החדש – איכא למימר דאודויי אודי ליה. ויש לומר: דשאני גבי בכור, שכהן תופס מספק, דאין יודע אם בכור הוא, אבל הכא שטוען ברי – מהניא תפיסה. וא"ת: ב"חזקת הבתים" (ב"ב דף לד:) גבי זה אומר של אבותי כו' אמר ר"נ: כל דאלים גבר, ופריך מהמחליף פרה בחמור, זה אומר ברשותו ילדה וזה אומר כו' – יחלוקו, ומאי קושיא? הא ההיא אתיא כסומכוס, ורב נחמן כרבנן. דלרבנן דאמרי המע"ה, היינו דינא דכל דאלים גבר, כיון דמהניא תפיסה כשטוען ברי! ויש לומר דהכי פריך: דאפי' רבנן לא פליגי אסומכוס אלא משום דחד מינייהו מוחזק, ואיכא למימר, המע"ה, אבל הכא דאין אחד מוחזק יותר מחבירו, מודו לסומכוס דיחלוקו. ועי"ל: דהכא מיירי כשתפס קודם שנולד הספק. ורשב"א נראה לו להעמיד הברייתא בשוכר, ולהכי אין נאמנין, דאוקי ממונא בחזקת מריה, ומחזקינן עדי שוכר בכשרים, ולא יפרעו. **אלא** אמר ר"נ אוקי תרי להדי כו'. וא"ת: ולר"נ אמאי לא מגבינן ביה בשטרא? הא סבר ר"נ כרב הונא (שבועות מז) [ב"ב דף לא:] בשני כתי עדים המכחישות זו את זו, דכל אחת באה בפ"ע ומעידה, אע"ג דלפי עדות כל אחת חבירתה פסולה לכל עדיות. הכא נמי, כיון דאין מכחישין אותן לומר שלא לוה כלום, אלא אומרים אינכם נאמנים בדבר זה, דפסולין הייתם, ליתכשרו. ואמאי לא מגבינן ביה בשטר? ויש לומר: דהתם באה כל אחת בפ"ע ומעידה, משום דמוקמינן כל אחת בחזקת כשרות, אבל הכא שאומרים קטנים היו או קרובים משנולדו עד עתה שנתרחקו – ליכא למימר אוקמינהו אחזקייהו, דפסלינן אותן משנולדו. ואנוסים היו נמי מחמת נפשות, לא שייך לאוקמי אחזקה, דהא לא פסלי להו כלל. ורשב"א אומר: דהכא לא מוקמינן להו אחזקה כדאמר לעיל, משום דאילו הוו קמן דלמא הוו מודו.

ואוקי ארעא בחזקת בר שטיא. דוקא בקרקע הוא דאמרינן הכי, אבל במטלטלים אמרינן דהוו בחזקת המוחזק, כדאמר בפרק "השואל" (ב"מ דף ק.) גבי המחליף פרה בחמור, דפריך: וליחזי פרה ברשותא דמאן קיימא, ולהוי אידך המע"ה? ומשני: דקיימא באגם. אומר ר"י: דהכא לא שייך למימר כדאמרי' בסוף קדושין (דף עט:) וב"מי שמת" (ב"ב דף קנג: ושם): אם שכיב מרע הוא – עליהם להביא ראיה שבריא היה, ואם בריא הוא כו', דבר שטיא דהכא כיון דעתים חלים ועתים שוטה, אין ראיה ממה שהוא עכשיו. **דלמא** זיופי זייף. אור"ת: *דדוקא היכא שאין אנו מכירין החתימה אלא ע"י דמיון החתימה להחתימה, אבל היכא דמכירין חתימת העדים בטביעת עין, אע"פ שיש לו חתימה אחרת תחת ידו – ליכא למיחש דלמא זייף, דכיון דמכירין החתימה – אם זייף היה ניכר היטב. **ורבי** יוחנן אומר אע"פ שאין זוכרה מעצמו. פי': אבל ע"י השטר זוכרה. אבל אם אין זוכרה כלל – לא, דמפיהם ולא מפי כתבם, כדאמרינן פ' "ד' אחין" (יבמות דף לא: ושם) גבי מפני מה לא תקנו זמן בקדושין, דקאמר: לינהו גבי עדים, אי דכירי – ליתו ולסהדו, ואי לא – זימנין דחזו בכתבא, ואתו ומסהדי, ואמר רחמנא "מפיהם" – ולא מפי כתבם. וא"ת: הכא נמי, אמאי לא אסריך לכתוב עדות על השטר, שמא ישכח לגמרי ואתו ומסהדי מכתבא, כדחיישינן התם? ויש לומר: דודאי התם חשו חכמים, לפי שב"ד מוסרין לו השטר, ויסבור שלכך מסרוהו לו שיעיד אפי' לא יזכור. אבל הכא, שמעצמו כותב עדותו על השטר – לא חשו חכמים לכך. וא"ת: ואמאי לא מלו חזו בכתבא ולאסהודי? הא תנן ב"גט פשוט" (ב"ב דף קסח.): מי שנמחק שטר חובו – מעמיד עליו עדים, ובא לב"ד ועושין לו קיומו. ומפרש בגמ' מהו קיומו. וכן ב"הגוזל קמא" (ב"ק דף לח.) דאמרינן גבי שורף שטרותיו של חבירו: פטור מדיני אדם כו', ה"ד? אי דאיכא סהדי דידעי מה הוה כתוב ביה בשטרא – נכתוב ליה שטרא אחרינא, אלמא לא חשבינן ליה מפיהם ולא מפי כתבם! וי"ל: דבפ' "ד' אחין" (יבמות לא: ושם) חיישינן דלמא אתו ומסהדי בסתם כאילו זוכרין העדות, אבל ודאי, אם היו מעידין שכך ראו בחתימתן – הא לא חשיב מפיהם ולא מפי כתבם, דעדים החתומין על השטר נעשה כמי שנחקרה עדותן בבית דין, והוי כאילו מעידין ראינו עדות שנחקרה בבית דין. ואם תאמר: והכא אפילו אין זה זוכרה כלל מה בכך? יעיד
שטרו

א) [נ"ל רבא וכן איתא בשאלתות פ' יתרו סימן נה וכ"א ברי"ף והרא"ש] ב) [וע"ע תוס' ב"ב קה. ד"ה אבל]

עין משפט נר מצוה

לב א מיי' פ"ז מהלכות עדות הלכה ז סמג עשין קט טוש"ע ח"מ סימן מו סעיף ח:
לג ב מיי' פכ"ב מהל' מכירה הלכה ז סמג עשין פב טוש"ע ח"מ סי' רלה סעיף כא בהגה"ה:
לד ג ב"י
לה ד מיי' פ"ח מהל' עדות הלכה ב סמג עשין קו טור ח"מ סימן מו:
לו ה ו ז מיי' פ"ו שם הלכה ג סמג שם טוש"ע ח"מ סימן מו סעיף ז:
לז ח ט מיי' פ"ח מהל' עדות הלכה א סמג עשין קט טוש"ע ח"מ סימן כח סעיף יג:

[נ"ל ארעא וכן איתא ביבמות לא: וכן העתיק הרשב"א בב"צ מג: ד"ה ואי בעית אימא]

לח י כ מיי' שם הלכה ב טוש"ע ח"מ סימן מו סעיף יז:

תוספות רי"ד

יוצא ממקום אחר ולא דמי לא למודעא ולא לאמנה דמודעא הא קא חזי דאנוס הוה ולא היה להם לחתום עד שלא יכתבו לו שטר מודעא אאמנה נמי לא אע"ג דאמרינן שאע"פ שהלוה מאמינו למלוה שילוהו אפ"ה אין לחתום בו דהתם לאו משום פסידא דלוה שכיון שהוא מתרצה בכך אין אנו חוששים בדבר אלא משום פסידא דלקוחות הוא כדאמרינן הכי שכיון שכתב ללוות ולא לוה אתי לאטעויי לקוחות שלא ידעו דהכי הוא דהא בשטרא דלאו אקניתא אין כותבין שטר ללוה אין שיהא מלוה עמו משום פסידא דלקוחות אבל בשטרא אקניתא כותבין דאי טריף בעל כרחו טריף ואע"ג דאיכא למיחש דלמא ממטי ליה לוה למלוה ומאמנו עד שילוהו ולבסוף לא ילוהו אפ"ה לא חיישינן כיון שהוא מאמינו דהוא מאמינו היה לו לכתוב שאם לא יתקיים התנאי יבטל המכר אין לנו לחוש להפסדו והלכך רשאים לחתום בו ולא היו עדיו כיון דלא מפסיד לאחריני אבל אם הוא כת"י יוצא ממקום אחר אין נאמנים שכיון שהגיד שוב אין חוזר ומגיד (א"כ) [א"נ] י"ל כיון דפשיט ליה דהוא מילתא אחריתי הוא ואינה עולה מהימני הוא על פי שכת"י יוצא ממקום אחר אין נאמנים דמה לי אחרים מעידים הם כמו שאם מעידים אחרים עליהם שאינם נאמנים כמו כן משעידו הן בעצמן אינן נאמנים והרבה בני אדם עושים דבר זה שטוב עשאו להזכיר שום דבר שהוא עתיד להתקיים ימים רבים ואומר להם לפני עדי השטר שלא יכפור איש לחבירו הלכך אע"ג דליכא מיגו מהימן: עד אומר אני ועד אומר אנו תנאי א"ר פפא תרוויהו בשטר מעליא קמסהדי והאי דאמר תנאי הו"ל חד ואין דבריו של אחד במקום שנים מתקיף ליה ר"ה בריה דר"י א"ה אפילו תרוויהו נמי אלא אמרי' הני למיעקר סהדותייהו קאתי חד נמי למיעקר סהדותיה קאתי פי' א"ה כיון שהעיד על כת"י עשיתם לזה א' ממקיימי השטר שהוא כתוב בלא תנאי והוי ליה עידיו שנים ועדות אחרונה דברי אחד במקום שנים אפי' תרוייהו נמי אמרו תנאי היה דברינו לא להימנו כיון שהעידו על כת"י קימו השטר שהוא כמו שהוא כתוב וכי אמרו תנאי היה דברינו הו"ל מגידים וחוזרים ומגידים ואמאי הם נאמנים אלא ע"כ לא חתימה מקויימת הוא דכיון דבתוך כ"ד מסקי דבורייהו ואמרו אבל תנאי היה ביניהן אמרי' הני למיעקר סהדותייהו קאתי שאמרו כת"י הוא ועכשיו אומרים לא חתמנו אלא על מנת שיתקיים התנאי וכיון דתנאי מילתא אחריתא היא שאינה עוקרתו אלא לאחר זמן לא דמיא למודעא ואמנה ומהימני

דלאו עולה היא שהרי עדות היא בפ"ע האי חד נמי כי סיים ואמר תנאי הוה עקר לחתימת ידיה לומר לא חתמתי אלא על מנת כן וכיון דלאו עולה הוא מהימן ואשתכח דאין בשטר חתום אלא ע"א ומסיק תלמודא והל' כר"ה [בריה] דר"י: ת"ר שנים החתומים על השטר ומתו ובאו שנים ואמרו ידענו שכת"י הוא זה אבל אנוסים היו קטנים היו פסולי עדות היו הרי אלו נאמנים ואם יש עדים שהוא כת"י או שכת"י יוצא ממקום אחר משטר שקרא עליו ערעור פי' שרצה הנתבע לפוסלו והוחזק בב"ד אין נאמנים פי' היכא דאיכא מיגו נאמנים ולא מגבינן ביה והיכא דליכא מיגו אין נאמנים ומגבינן ביה ומקשה אין נאמנים ומגבינן ביה תרי ותרי נינהו פי' אלו אומרים שהיו קטנים או אנוסים או פסולי עדות והשטר חתום מסתמא בכשרות וכאילו קיימו סהדי דשטרא קדמנא ואמרו גדולים היינו ורחוקין ולא היינו אנוסים דמי והוי להו תרי ותרי ולמה אתה מאמין אלה החתומים בשטר יותר מאלה האחרונים ואתה מגבה בו כתב רבינו יוסף הלוי ז"ל נראין הדברים שזו הקושיא לא אכולהו היא אלא אאנוסים בלחוד היא שנמצאו מעידים שהעדות לא היתה אמת ולפיכך הקשינו והא תרי ותרי נינהו אבל קטנים [illegible]

תוספות רי"ד

על קטנים ופסולים הוו שיהיה אלו האחרונים נאמנים ולא נימא תרי ותרי נינהו אלא נקרע' להאי שטרא לגמרי כיון שהאלו האחרונים' מעידין על גופן של הראשונים שהיו פסולים א"ו בין כשאומרי' אלו האחרונים על הראשונים' קטנים היו פסולי עדות היו בין כשאומרים אנוסים היו אומר הברייתא שאין נאמנים ועל כלם אנו מקשים תרי ותרי נינהו ואע"פ שהן מעידין על גופן של ראשונים לפוסלן אין אנו דוחין את הראשונים לגמרי שאם יבואו שנים אחרים ויאמרו לראשונ' פסולי' הייתם או קטנים והן אומרים לא אלא גדולים וכשרים היינו אמרינן תרי ותרי נינהו חוץ מעדים זוממים שהאחרונים באים ומעידים על הראשונים ואומרים ביום פלוני עמנו הייתם במקום פ' שהאמינה התורה את האחרונים ואמרינן דחידוש הוא ולא משום תרי ותרי נינהו אבל בכ"מ אין אנו מאמנים את האחרונים יותר מן הראשונים אלא אמרינן תרי ותרי נינהו אבל ודאי יש לברר דבר זה שאילו באו שנים והעידו על שנים אחרים שהם גולנים או משחקי בקוביא או שהן קרובים למלוה או ללוה נאמנים הם ולא אמרינן תרי ותרי נינהו שאלו אומרים גולנים הן ואלו אומרים אין אנו גולנים ובדאים אתם אלא נאמנים הם לפוסלן כדאמרינן בפרק דיני ממונות בתרא גבי עד זומם דאמר רבא מכאן ולהבא הוא נפסל משום תרי טעמא חדא דחידוש הוא ואין לך בו אלא חדושו וחדא משום הפסד לקוחות ואמרינן מאי איכא בין הני תרי טעמא א"ב דאמדהדו תרי בחד א"נ דפסלינהו בגזלנותא אלמא כל היכא

דפסלינהו בגזלנותא לא אמרינן תרי ותרי נינהו אלא נאמנים ומחזיקים להו בגזלנותא על פיהם [illegible] משוי גופייהו גזלנים אלא מכחישים אותם ואמרו דההוא סהדותא לא הות בן אמרינן תרי ותרי [illegible] אמאן נסמוך אי אהני אי אהני אך אם יכחישו בדרך הזמה שאמרו עמנו הייתם במקום פלוני [illegible] וגזירת מלך אבל אם אמרו עמנו הי' המלוה או הלוה במקום פלוני לא ידעינן אמאן נסמוך [illegible] ותרי נינהו ואי פסלו להו לגופייהו בגזלנותא או ע"י קורבה מהימנינן בתראי ומבטלין לסהדותא משום דכי מסהדי על גופייהו דגזלנין נינהו פסלו להו לכל עדות דעלמא וכן כי מסהדי שהן [illegible] או ללוה פסלו להו לכל עדיות דעלמא הלכך מהימני' לבתראי ולא אמרינן תרי ותרי נינהו דהא [illegible] עדים שלא יהיו עדים גם בשאר עדיות אבל כשמכחישין אותן שאומרים עמנו היה המלוה או הל[illegible] אותן לשאר עדיות כי אם בעדות זה בלבד אומרים ששקר העידו ואע"פ שלפי דבריהם ממיל[illegible] שהן אינן מעידים עליהם אלא בעדות זה ולא החזיקו את גופן פסולין אפי' בעדות זו תרי ות[illegible] [illegible]

הגהות הב"ח (א) גמ' מיהת קרא עליו וכו' עד ערער לא. נ"ב [illegible]

גליון הש"ס גמ' וכשהוא שוטה זבין. [illegible] תוס' ד"ה דלמא וכו' אור"ת דדוקא וכו'. [illegible]

עין משפט נר מצוה

לט א מיי' פ"ח מהל' עדות הלכה ג סמג עשין קט טוש"ע ח"מ סימן כח סעיף יז.

מ ב ג ד ה מיי' פ"ח מהלכות טומאת מת הלכה ג:

מא ו טוש"ע ח"מ סימן כח סעיף (ג) [יג]:

מב ז ח טוש"ע ח"מ סימן מו סעיף י:

וְאִי צוּרְבָא מֵרַבָּנַן הוּא — אֲפִילּוּ עַצְמוֹ. כִּי הָא דְּרַב אַשִׁי הֲוָה יְדִיעַ לֵיהּ בְּסַהֲדוּתָא לְרַב כָּהֲנָא. אֲמַר לֵיהּ: מִי דְּכִיר מָר הַאי סַהֲדוּתָא? אֲמַר לֵיהּ: לָא. וְלָאו הָכִי וְהָכִי הֲוָה? א"ל: לָא יָדַעְנָא. לְסוֹף אִידְכַּר רַב אַשִׁי, אַסְהֵיד לֵיהּ. חַזְיֵיהּ לְרַב כָּהֲנָא דַּהֲוָה מְחַסֵּם. א"ל: מִי סָבְרַתְּ עֲלָךְ קָא סָמֵיכְנָא? אֲנָא הוּא דִּרְמַאי אַנַּפְשַׁאי וְאַדְּכְרִי. *תְּנַן הָתָם: הַתְּלוּלִיּוֹת הַקְּרוֹבוֹת בֵּין לָעִיר וּבֵין לַדֶּרֶךְ, אֶחָד חֲדָשׁוֹת וְאֶחָד יְשָׁנוֹת — טְמֵאוֹת. הָרְחוֹקוֹת, חֲדָשׁוֹת — טְהוֹרוֹת, יְשָׁנוֹת — טְמֵאוֹת. אֵיזוֹהִי קְרוֹבָה? חֲמִשִּׁים אַמָּה, וְאֵיזוֹ הִיא יְשָׁנָה? שִׁשִּׁים שָׁנָה. דִּבְרֵי ר"מ. רַבִּי יְהוּדָה אוֹמֵר: קְרוֹבָה — שֶׁאֵין קְרוֹבָה הֵימֶנָּה, יְשָׁנָה — שֶׁאֵין אָדָם זוֹכְרָהּ. מַאי עִיר וּמַאי דֶּרֶךְ? אִילֵימָא עִיר — עִיר מַמָּשׁ, דֶּרֶךְ — דֶּרֶךְ מַמָּשׁ, מִסְפֵּיקָא מִי מַחְזְקִינַן טוּמְאָה? וְהָאָמַר רֵישׁ לָקִישׁ: *עִילָּה מָצְאוּ וְטִהֲרוּ אֶרֶץ יִשְׂרָאֵל! א"ר זֵירָא: עִיר — עִיר הַסְּמוּכָה לְבֵית הַקְּבָרוֹת, וְדֶרֶךְ — דֶּרֶךְ בֵּית הַקְּבָרוֹת. בִּשְׁלָמָא דֶּרֶךְ בֵּית הַקְּבָרוֹת — דִּזְמְנִין דְּמִתְרַמֵּי בֵּין הַשְּׁמָשׁוֹת, וּמַקְרוּ קָבְרוּ בְּתֵל. אֶלָּא עִיר הַסְּמוּכָה לְבֵית הַקְּבָרוֹת — כּוּלְּהִי לְבֵית הַקְּבָרוֹת אָזְלֵי! אָמַר רַבִּי חֲנִינָא: מִתּוֹךְ שֶׁהַנָּשִׁים קוֹבְרוֹת שָׁם נִפְלֵיהֶן, וּמוּכֵּי שְׁחִין זְרוֹעוֹתֵיהֶם, עַד חֲמִשִּׁים אַמָּה — אָזְלָא אִיהִי לְחוּדָהּ, טְפֵי — דְּבָרָא אִינִישׁ בַּהֲדָהּ, וּלְבֵית הַקְּבָרוֹת אָזְלָא. הִלְכָּךְ, טוּמְאָה בְּאֶרֶץ יִשְׂרָאֵל לָא מַחְזְקִינַן. אָמַר רַב חִסְדָּא, ש"מ מֵרַבִּי מֵאִיר: הַאי סַהֲדוּתָא, עַד שִׁיתִּין שְׁנִין — מִידְכַּר, טְפֵי — לָא מִידְכַּר. וְלָא הִיא: הָתָם הוּא דְּלָא רָמְיָא עֲלֵיהּ, אֲבָל הָכָא, כֵּיוָן דְּרָמֵי עֲלֵיהּ — אֲפִילּוּ טוּבָא נַמִי.§

מתני' זֶה אוֹמֵר "כְּתַב יָדִי, וְזֶה כְּתַב יָדוֹ שֶׁל חֲבֵירִי", וְזֶה אוֹמֵר: "זֶה כְּתַב יָדִי, וְזֶה כְּתַב יָדוֹ שֶׁל חֲבֵירִי" — הֲרֵי אֵלּוּ נֶאֱמָנִין. זֶה אוֹמֵר: "זֶה כְּתַב יָדִי", — וְזֶה אוֹמֵר זֶה כְּתַב יָדִי צְרִיכִין לְצָרֵף עִמָּהֶם אַחֵר, דִּבְרֵי רַבִּי. וַחֲכָמִים אוֹמְרִים: אֵינָם צְרִיכִין לְצָרֵף עִמָּהֶן אַחֵר, אֶלָּא נֶאֱמָן אָדָם לוֹמַר "זֶה כְּתַב יָדִי".§ **גמ'** כְּשֶׁתִּימְצֵי לוֹמַר לְדִבְרֵי רַבִּי עַל

רש"י

וְאִי צוּרְבָא מֵרַבָּנַן הוּא. חָעֵד. אֲפִי' לְעַצְמוֹ. שֶׁל בַּעַל דִּין. דְּלוּרְבָא דְּרַבָּנַן, אִי לָאו דְּכִי רָמֵי אַנַּפְשֵׁיהּ מִדְּכַר שַׁפִּיר — לָא הֲוָה סָמֵיךְ אַסְפֵּיקָא לְמֵיקַם וְאַסְהוֹדֵי. מְחַסֵּם. מְגַמְגֵּם, תָּמֵהַּ עַל רַב אַשִׁי שֶׁהֵעִיד בַּדָּבָר. הַתְּלוּלִיּוֹת. תִּילֵּי קַרְקַע. וְדֶרֶךְ בְּנֵי אָדָם לִקְבּוֹר בְּתֵל, מִשּׁוּם דְּאֵין בְּנֵי אָדָם מַטִּין מִן הַדֶּרֶךְ לַעֲבוֹר עָלָיו. וְעִיר וְדֶרֶךְ לְקַמָּן מְפָרֵשׁ לְהוּ. אֶחָד חֲדָשׁוֹת. שֶׁאֵין זְמַן רָחוֹק שֶׁלֹּא הָיָה כָּאן תֵּל, דְּאִיכָּא לְמֵימַר: כֵּיוָן דַּחֲדָשָׁה הִיא, אִם אִיתָא שֶׁנִּקְבַּר שָׁם מֵת — מִדְּכַר דְּכִיר לֵיהּ, אַפ"ה טְמֵאוֹת מִסָּפֵק; דְּכֵיוָן דִּסְמוּכָה לָעִיר, אִיכָּא לְמֵימַר: אִשָּׁה יְחִידָה הָלְכָה וְקָבְרָה שָׁם נֵפֶל שֶׁלָּהּ. הָרְחוֹקוֹת. דְּאֵין אִשָּׁה יְחִידָה הוֹלֶכֶת שָׁם. חֲדָשׁוֹת טְהוֹרוֹת. דְּאִם אִיתָא דְּנִקְבַּר בֵּיהּ — הֲווּ יָדְעֵי לֵיהּ. יְשָׁנוֹת טְמֵאוֹת. שֶׁכְּבָר נִשְׁתַּכַּח הַדָּבָר מִן הַיּוֹדְעִים. וְאֵיזוֹ הִיא קְרוֹבָה. לָעִיר, שֶׁאָנוּ אוֹמְרִים עָלֶיהָ שֶׁאַף הַחֲדָשָׁה טְמֵאָה — חֲמִשִּׁים אַמָּה. וְאֵיזוֹ הִיא יְשָׁנָה. שֶׁאָנוּ אוֹמְרִים עָלֶיהָ שֶׁאֲפִי' הִיא רְחוֹקָה טְמֵאָה — שִׁשִּׁים שָׁנָה. שֶׁאֵין קְרוֹבָה הֵימֶנָּה. אֲבָל אִם יֵשׁ קְרוֹבָה הֵימֶנָּה, אֲפִי' הִיא בְּתוֹךְ חֲמִשִּׁים אַמָּה — הָוְיָא כִּרְחוֹקָה. וַחֲדָשָׁה טְהוֹרָה, דְּאִם אִיתָא דְּהָלְכָה אִשָּׁה יְחִידָה לִקְבּוֹר — לָא שָׁבְקָה קְרוֹבָה הֵימֶנָּה וְאָזְלָא לְגַבֵּי דִּידָךְ. שֶׁאֵין אָדָם זוֹכְרָהּ. שֶׁאֵין אָדָם אוֹמֵר: זָכוּר אֲנִי שֶׁלֹּא הָיָה כָּאן תֵּל וּבְיָמַי נַעֲשָׂה תֵּל זֶה כָּאן. עִילָּה מָצְאוּ. עֲלִילָה בְּעָלְמָא מָצְאוּ חֲכָמִים, וְהֶחְזִיקוּ בָּהּ לִתְלוֹת עָלֶיהָ וּלְטַהֵר אֶת אֶרֶץ יִשְׂרָאֵל, בְּמַסֶּכֶת נָזִיר בְּפֶרֶק בַּתְרָא. אַלְמָא מִסְּפֵיקָא לָא מַחְזְקִינַן טוּמְאָה בְּקַרְקָעָהּ שֶׁל אֶרֶץ יִשְׂרָאֵל. וְטִיהֲרוּ אֶת א"י גָּרְסִי', וְלָא גָּרְסִינַן כָּל. דְּמִתְרַמֵּי בֵּין הַשְּׁמָשׁוֹת. שֶׁל עֶרֶב הַשַּׁבָּת, וְאֵין שָׁהוּת לֵילֵךְ עַד בֵּית הַקְּבָרוֹת. וּמוּכֵּי שְׁחִין. שֶׁאֵבְרֵיהֶן נוֹפְלִין, אוֹ שֶׁחוֹתְכִין אוֹתָן. וְאֵבֶר מִן הַחַי מְטַמֵּא כְּאֵבֶר מִן הַמֵּת, כִּדְאָמְרִינַן בְּ"הָעוֹר וְהָרוֹטֶב" (חולין קכט:). ש"מ. מִדְּקָתָנֵי לְעֵיל: אֵיזוֹ הִיא יְשָׁנָה שִׁשִּׁים שָׁנָה, וְטַעְמָא מִשּׁוּם דְּלָא דְּכִירֵי לָהּ הוּא — הַאי סַהֲדוּתָ' כו'. אֲבָל הָכָא. שֶׁעֲשָׂאוּהוּ עֵד בַּדָּבָר, אֲפִילּוּ טוּבָא נַמִי סָמְכִינַן אַסַּהֲדוּתֵיהּ, אִי מַסְהֵיד. **מתני'** הֲרֵי אֵלּוּ נֶאֱמָנִין. דְּאִיכָּא תְּרֵי סָהֲדֵי דִּמְסַהֲדֵי אַכָּל כְּתָב וּכְתָב. צְרִיכִים לְצָרֵף עִמָּהֶן אַחֵר. שֶׁיַּכִּיר כְּתַב יְדֵי שְׁנֵיהֶם, דִּתְרֵי סָהֲדֵי בָּעֵינַן אַכָּל כְּתָב וּכְתָב, וְטַעְמָא מְפָרֵשׁ בַּגְּמָרָא. **גמ'** כְּשֶׁתִּימְצֵי לוֹמַר לְדִבְרֵי רַבִּי. כְּשֶׁתַּעֲמוֹד לְסוֹף דְּבָרָיו, קָסָבַר עַל

תוספות

שטרו בב"ד! ויש לומר: דע"א בשטר לא חשיב שטר אלא אותו שיש בו שני עדים, דומיא דספר מקנה. והא דאמר ב"גט פשוט" (ב"ב דף קסה.): עד אחד בכתב ועד אחד בעל פה — אין מצטרפין, דמשמע: הא שניהם בשטר, אפילו בשתי אגרות — מצטרפין, התם מיירי כגון שהאחד בשטר והאחד בעל פה, לא שאומר שראה הוא המלוה, אלא שראה מסירת השטר מלוה למלוה, דהוי כשנים החתומים בשטר, לר"א דאמר עדי מסירה כרתי. ועוד: דבירושלמי מפרש עד א' בשטר — היינו שנים חתומים בשטר, וקיימו כתב ידו של אחד, ולא מצאו לקיים כתב ידו של שני. ומ"מ, נהי דעד אחד לא חשיב שטר לענין שאם יבואו עדים ויאמרו "כך ראינו בשטר" דחשבינן להו כעד מפי עד — עדות מיהא הוי, ויכול לשלוח כתב ידו לב"ד, ולא חשיב מפיהם ולא מפי כתבם כיון שהוא זוכר העדות. ורש"י פי' בפירוש החומש: *מפיהם ולא מפי כתבם — שלא ישלח בכתב עדותו לב"ד. א"נ אומר ר"י: דע"א מועיל בשטר, אם יש שני שטרות בכל אחד חתום עד א' — חשוב כשטר שלם. וכ"ת: א"כ בשמעתין יביא כתבו לב"ד אפילו אינו זוכר כלל! ויש לומר: דלא חשיב שטר אלא כשעשוי מדעת שניהם, מדעת הלוה שהוא חייב — אז חשיב שטר. אבל הכא, שכותב עדותו שלא מדעת הלוה — לא חשיב שטרא. והקשה ה"ר שמואל מוורדו"ן: דאמר ב"חזקת הבתים" (ב"ב דף מ. ושם): מחאה בפני שנים וא"צ לומר "כתובו". ומה מועיל "כתובו" כיון דאין עשוי מדעת המחזיק? ולפי מה שפירשנו דעדות מיהא הוי כל זמן שזוכר — אתי שפיר. מיהו, בלאו הכי מתרץ ר"י דגבי מחאה הקילו, שאינה אלא מדרבנן. דהכי נמי הקילו לומר דמחאה שלא בפניו הויא מחאה, אע"פ שלפעמים לא ישמע, וסמכו על זה דחברך חברא אית ליה. וכן במודעא בפני שנים הקילו לכתוב, להציל אנוס מאונסו. ועוד אומר ר"י: דלא בעינן דעת שניהם. והכא היה יכול להביא שטרו אם היה כתוב כתיקון שטרות, אבל הכא מיירי שאינו כתוב כסדר השטר, אלא זכרון דברים בעלמא. ומתוך הירושלמי נראה לפ' בענין אחר סוגיא זו, דקאמר התם: רב הונא כרבי, ור' יוחנן כרבנן. פירוש: כשהעדים באים לקיים חתימתן, אם זוכרין המלוה בלא שטר — אפי' לרבי א"צ לצרף עמהן אחר מן השוק, דעל מנה שבשטר הן מעידין. וכשאין זוכרים המלוה אפילו ע"י השטר — אפי' רבנן מודו דצריכין לצרף עמהן, דעל כרחין אין מעידין אלא על כתב ידן. וכי פליגי — היינו כשזוכרין המלוה ע"י השטר, דלרבנן חשיב זכירה ועל מנה הן מעידין, ולרבי לא חשיב זכירה. ולשון "כותב אדם" לא משמע הכי.

אחד חדשות ואחד ישנות. תימה: דהכא מזכיר שאינו פשוט קודם. וכן ב"החולץ" (יבמות דף מא.): לא יתארסו ולא ינשאו עד שיהו להן ג' חדשים, אחד בתולות ואחד בעולות — מזכיר אירוסין קודם נישואין ובתולות קודם בעולות, דהיינו: שאינו פשוט קודם. ובר"ה (דף כט:) תנן: אחד יבנה ואחד כל מקום שיש בו ב"ד — התם נקט דבר פשוט ברישא. וכן בב"ק (דף נ:): אחד החופר בור שיח ומערה. ובמס' סוטה (דף מג.): אחד הבונה ואחד הלוקח כו' גבי מערכי מלחמה. ורש"י נמי גריס בפ"ק דסוכה (דף כ. ושם) גבי מחצלת גדולה שעשאה לשכיבה טמאה ואין מסככין בה, רבי אליעזר אומר: אחת קטנה ואחת גדולה. ופריך: א' גדולה וא' קטנה מבעי ליה? והיה כתוב בספרים להפך, ורש"י מהפך הגירסא משום דדרך התנאים להזכיר הפשוט קודם. ואומר ר"י: א) דהיכא דקאי אפלוגתא או אקרא — מזכיר הפשוט קודם, כי ההיא דפליג ר' אליעזר את"ק בסוכה, והוה ליה למימר אחת גדולה שאתה מודה לי — כך תודה בקטנה. וכן "אחד יבנה" פליג אדר' אליעזר דאמר לא התקין רבן יוחנן בן זכאי שיהו תוקעין אלא ביבנה בלבד. ובב"ק (דף נ:) ובסוטה (דף מג.) קאי קרא. אבל הכא וב"החולץ" לא קאי אמידי, אין להקפיד איזה נשנה תחלה: [וע' תוס' שבת כ: ד"ה "אחד מבושל" פסחים פה. קח: סוכה כ. זבחים לג: ד"ה "אי הכי", ומנחות סג: ד"ה "אחד שבת". וע' תוס' קדושין יג. ד"ה "כסס"].

טמאות • פירש בקונטרס דבקרובות אפילו חדשות טמאות, משום דאזלא איהי לחודה, ואין ידוע אם קברה שם. אבל רחוקה, דדברא איניש בהדה, ואלמלי קברה איניש דאזיל בהדה היה מגלה. ולפיכך ישנות טמאות דאע"פ דדברא איניש בהדה נשתכח הדבר. וקשה [לר"י]: דאם כן, אמאי ב) נ"ל נסמוך דדברא איניש בהדה ולבית הקברות אזלא, לא הוה ליה למימר אלא: דברא איניש בהדה, ותו לא. ולכך טפי חדשות טהורות, דאם איתא דקברה שם — היה הדבר ידוע! ועוד: אי לבית הקברות אזלא — ישנות אמאי טמאות? ונראה לר"י כר"ח דפירש: דישנות טמאות אפילו רחוקות, דחיישינן שמא קרובות היו, שהיה העיר אצלה וחרב. ולפי זה לא נאמר משום דדברא איניש בהדה היה ידוע יותר, ולהכי איצטריך לומר: ולבית הקברות אזלא. **עילה** מצאו. פירש רבינו חננאל: גלע, ותלו הטומאה באותה גלע והשאר טהרו.

א) [וי"מ הכא דנקט אחד חדשות לפי שכל דבר חדש הוא תחלה ואח"כ ישן וכמו כן באירוסין קודם נישואין ובתולות שהם קודם בעולות. ומ"מ קשה דבפרק כילד צולין (דף פה.) קאמר אחד עצם שיש בו מוח ואחד עצם שאין בו מוח אע"ג שאין בו מוח פשוט יותר שיש בו משום ועצם לא תשברו בו והתם לא שייך האי טעמא וצריך לפרש כדפר"י. ת"י עה"ג]:
ב) ומאי למימר דתרי טעמי לטיבותא נקט. [ת"י]:

תוספות רי"ד

מעידים ולמה אומר הברייתא שאין נאמנים ור"נ אמר תרי ותרי נינהו תשובה בודאי כי אמרי להו גזלנים אתם או קרובים אתם נאמנים משום דמסלקי להו מתורת עדות לגמרי אבל כשאומרים קטנים הייתם או קרובים הייתם כיון דמודו דהשתא בני עדות נינהו ומסהדי על ההיא זימנא בלחוד הוו להו תרי ותרי דהא השתא הם כשרי' לעדות ואמרי לא היינו קטנים לא היינו קרובים ומש"ה לא מהימנינן לבתראי. ומקשינן אמאי קאמר ת"ק שאין נאמנים ומגבינן ביה תרי ותרי נינהו ועל כולן מקשינן בין על אנוסים היו בין על קטנים היו בין על קרובים היו אלא א"ר נחמן אוקי תרי לבהדי תרי ואוקי ממונא בחזקת מריה מידי דהוה אנכסי דבר שטיא דבר שטיא זבין נכסיה פירוש מכר קרקעותיו אתו בי תרי ואמרי כשהוא חלים זבן פי' בריא ואתו בי תרי ואמרו כשהוא שוטה זבן ואר"א אוקי תרי לבהדי תרי ואוקי נכסים בחזקת בר שטיא פי' ואע"פ שתפס המלוה מוציאים מידו דשלא כדין תפס דומיא דבר שטיא שהיה הנכסים ביד הלוקח ואר"נ דאוקי נכסים בחזקת בר שטיא ולא אמרן פי' אוקי נכסים בחזקת בר שטיא אלא דאית ליה חזקה דאבהתיה פירוש חזקה שנכסים הללו היו של אבותיו אבל לית ליה חזקה דאבהתיה אלא חזקה דנפשיה פירוש שקנאם הוא והוחזקו בידו אמרינן כשהוא שוטה זבן וכשהוא שוטה זבין פי' בקנייתו כך מכירתו ואין חזקתו חזקה לבטל מכירתו ע' בפ"ג דיבמות: א"ר אבהו אין מזימין את העדים אלא בפניהם ומכחישין את העדים שלא בפניהם והזמה שלא בפניהם נהי דהזמה לא הוי הכחשה מיהא הוי פירוש בהזמה דמענש בכאשר זמם בעי' בפניהם אבל בהכחשה דלא מיענש לא בעי' בפניהם א) פי' המורה נהי דהזמה לא הוי לעונשן לא נפשות ולא ממון הכחשה הוי לבטל עדותן: אמר מר או שכת"י יוצא ממקום אחר משטר שקרא עליו ערעור והוחזק בב"ד אין נאמנים קרא עליו ערעור אין לא קרא עליו ערעור והוחזק בב"ד לא מסייע ליה לרבי אסי דאמר ר"א אין מקיימין את השטר אלא משטר שקרא עליו ערעור והוחזק בב"ד פי' אין מקיימין את השטר מתוך שטר אחר אלא אם כן קרא ערעור על אותו שטר האחר והוחזק בב"ד ע"י עדיו דאי לא קרא עליו ערעור חיישינן דלמא ההוא גופיה מזויף הוא: אמרי נהרדעא אין מקיימין את השטר אלא משתי שדות והלקוחות אכלו ג' שנים ע"י שטרות הללו מקיימין שטר שלישי מהם אם דומין החתימות ובשופי פי' כשהן בלא ערעור ולא פליגי נהרדעאי אברייתא דהאי דבעי שתי שטרות של שתי שדות כגון דלא מקיימי מש"ה בעי' שאכלום בעליהם בשופי ג' שנים אבל אם [הם] מקיימין אפי' מחד מקיימין אמר ר"ש בר אשי וביוצא מת"י אחר פי' ששני שטרות הללו שמקיימין השלישי מהן יוצאים מת"י איש אחר אבל מתחת ידו לא פי' של זה המוציא את השלישי מ"ש מתחת ידו דלא דלמא זיופי זייף פי' הסתכל בכתב של אותן שני שטרות וכוון וחתם הוא בעצמו את השלישי דומנת אותן חתימות מתחת יד אחר נמי דלמא אזיל והוא ואתא וזייף כולי האי לא מצי מכוין אי שהמזייף צריך שיהא הכתב לפניו ויראה אות באות והלואי שיוכל לכוין ולצמצם ולעשות כמוהו: ת"ר כותב אדם עדותו על השטר ומעיד עליה אפילו לאחר כמה שנים פי' אם עשאו עד בדבר ויראו לשכחו כותבו על חתיכת קלף ומצניעה ומעיד ע"פ אותו כתב אפילו לאחר כמה שנים א"ר הונא והוא שזוכרה מעצמו פי' בלא ראיית השטר זוכר קצת מעדותו מאליו ואין זה מדבר משטר שיצא מת"י ומסרו למלוה או ללוקח דהתם אע"ג דלא דכירי לסהדותייהו כלל כיון שמעיד שזה כת"י ומקיים חתימותו אם יש אחרים מעידין על חתימתו השטר קיים ואף על פי שאינו זוכר עדות ואעפ"כ שמת חתימתו קיימת שעדים המעידים על השטר נעשה כמי שנחקרה עדותן בב"ד ולא מיירי הכא אלא בעדותו תחת ידו כגון ספר זכרונות שאדם כותב בו עסקיו שלא ישכחם הן העדות זו שנאמרה לו בפה כתבה שם שלא ישכחנה ומ"ה א"ר הונא והוא שזוכרה מעצמו אבל אם שכחה בטל כתבו ואל יראה ויעיד מתוך כתבו ואהני ליה כתבא שיעיין שם לפרקים ולא (יטרדנה) [ישכחנה] ור"י אמר אף על פי שאינו זוכרה מעצמו פי' אלא לאחר שראה השטר נותן בלבו ויזכיר שלא נשתכחה ממנו כל כך רק כשמזכירים אותו נזכר אבל אם אינו נזכר כלל לא דהכי אמרינן בפרק ד' אחין לינהוו גבי עדים אם מדכירי ליתי ולסהדו ואי לא זמנין דחזו מכתבא ומסהדי ורחמנא אמר מפיהם ולא מפי כתבם: (ארב"א) [אמר רבא] שמע מיניה מר' יוחנן הני תרי דידעי בסהדותא ומינשי חד מינייהו מדכיר ליה חבר' ומדכר איבעיא להו מלוה בעצמו מאי פי' אם בעל דין מזכירו עד שנזכר מאי ר"ח אמר אפילו מלוה בעצמו מר בר אשי אמר (אפי') מלוה בעצמו לא ולהלכתא מלוה בעצמו לא ואי צורבא מרבנן אפילו מלוה בעצמו פי' דאי לאו רמי אנפשי' ומדכר שפיר לא הוי סמיך אספיקא למיקם לאסהודי כי הא דרב אשי הוה ידע סהדותא לרב כהנא א"ל מי מדכיר מר ההוא סהדותא א"ל לא א"ל ולאו הכי והכי הוה א"ל לא ידענא לסוף אדכר ר"א ואזיל אסהיד ליה חזי' לרב כהנא דהוה קא מהסם פי' מגמגם פי' לתמוה על ר"א שהעיד בדבר א"ל מי סברת עלך קסמכנא אנא רמאי אנפשאי ואידכרי עיין בפסקי בפרק ד' אחין: **מתני'** זה אומר זה כתב ידי וזה כתב ידו של חבירו וזה אומר זה כת"י וזה כת"י של חבירי הרי אלו נאמנים זה אומר זה כתב ידי וזה אומר זה כת"י צריכים שיצטרף אחר עמהן דברי רבי וחכ"א אין צריכין לצרף עמהן אחר אלא נאמן אדם לומר זה כתב ידי. רבי סבר תרי סהדי בעי' אכל חתימה וחתימה וחתימה הלכך אם כל אחד העיד על שלו ועל של חבירו יש שני עדים אבל חתימה וחתימה ואם כל אחד ואחד מעיד על שלו ולא על של חבירו צריכים לצרף עמהן אחר שיכיר שתי החתימות שיבואו על כל חתימה שני עדים. וחכמים סברי כל אחד נאמן על חתימתו שבוודאי כשבאו העדים לקיים חתימת עדים אחרים צריכים להיות שנים על כל חתימה וחתימה אבל כשעדי השטר הן בעצמן מקיימין חתימתן אין צריכין צירוף אלא כל אחד נאמן לומר זה כתב ידי ופריש תלמודא טעמייהו כשתמצא

א) נ"ל והזמה שלא בפניהם הכחשה מיהו הוי פי' המורה וכו'.

גליון הש"ס גמ' שאין אדם זוכרה. עיין תוס' יו"ט פ"ב מ"ג דב"ב ד"ה לא יסמוך:

על כתב ידן הם מעידים, לדברי חכמים [א]על מנה שבשטר הם מעידים. פשיטא! מהו דתימא: לרבי ספוקי מספקא ליה אי על כתב ידם הם מעידים או על מנה שבשטר הם מעידים. ונפקא מינה: [ב]היכא דמית חד מינייהו – לבעי שנים מן השוק להעיד עליו, דאם כן קנפיק נכי ריבעא דממונא אפומא דחד סהדא. והכא לחומרא והכא לחומרא, קמ"ל: דרבי מיפשט פשיטא ליה, בין לקולא בין לחומרא. דאמר רב יהודה אמר רב: [ג]שנים החתומין על השטר ומת אחד מהן – צריכין שנים מן השוק להעיד עליו, בזו רבי לקולא ורבנן לחומרא. ואי ליכא תרי אלא חד מאי? אמר אביי: [ד]לכתוב חתימת ידיה אחספא, ושדי ליה בבי דינא, (א) ומחזקי ליה בי דינא (וחזו ליה), ולא צריך איהו לאסהודי אחתימת ידיה, ואזיל איהו והאי ומסהדי אאידך. ודוקא אחספא, *אבל [ה]אמגלתא – לא. דלמא משכח לה איניש דלא מעלי, וכתב עילויה מאי דבעי, ותנן: *[ו]הוציא עליו כתב ידו שהוא חייב לו – גובה מנכסים בני חורין. א"ר יהודה אמר שמואל: הלכה כדברי חכמים. *פשיטא, יחיד ורבים הלכה כרבים! מהו דתימא: *הלכה כרבי מחבירו, ואפילו מחביריו, קא משמע לן.§ סימן נח נד חד.§ אמר ליה רב חננא בר חייא לרב יהודה, ואמרי לה רב הונא בר יהודה לרב יהודה, ואמרי לה רב חייא בר יהודה לרב יהודה: ומי אמר שמואל הכי? והא ההוא שטרא דנפיק מבי דינא דמר שמואל, והוה כתיב ביה: מדאתא רב ענן בר חייא ואסהיד אחתימות ידיה ואדחד דעמיה, ומנו – רב חנן בר רבה, ומדאתא רב חנן בר רבה ואסהיד אחתימות ידיה ואדחד דעמיה, ומנו – רב ענן בר חייא, אשרנוהי וקיימנוהי כדחזי! א"ל: ההוא שטרא דיתמי הוה, וחש שמואל *לב"ד טועין. וסבר שמואל: דלמא איכא דסבירא ליה הלכה כרבי מחבירו ולא מחביריו, ובהא – אפילו מחביריו, סבר אעביד רווחא כי היכי דלא מפסדי יתמי. אמר רב יהודה אמר שמואל: עד ודיין מצטרפין. אמר רמי בר חמא: כמה מעליא הא שמעתא. *אמר רבא: מאי מעליותא? מאי דקא מסהיד סהדא לא קא מסהיד דיינא, ומאי דקא מסהיד דיינא לא קא מסהיד סהדא! אלא, כי אתא רמי בר יחזקאל אמר: [ז]לא תציתינהו להני כללי דבייל יהודה אחי משמיה דשמואל.

איקלע

רש"י

על כתב ידן הן באין להעיד, כשמקיימין השטר בב"ד. לפיכך צריך שנים על כל כתב וכתב. לדברי חכמים על מנה שבשטר הם מעידים. אנחנו ראינו המלוה וחתמנו. הלכך בתרי סגי, ולא צריך חד מינייהו לאסהודי אחבריה. מהו דתימא לרבי ספוקי מספקא ליה אי על כתב ידן. אנו זקוקין שיעידו. או על מנה שבשטר. ומשום שמא על כתב ידן הן מעידין – מצריך תרי לכל כתב וכתב. ומיפשט מיהא לא פשיטא ליה. ונפקא מינה. בין ספק לודאי, לשנים החתומים על השטר ומת אחד מהן – צריך שנים מן השוק להעיד עליו, ואין זה כשר להעיד על כתב ידו ועל של חבירו ולצרף אחד עמו שיעיד על שתיהן. דדלמא על מנה שבשטר הן מעידין, וכי אומר זה כתב ידי – נפיק פלגא דממונא אפומיה, וזה שמעיד עמו על חתימתו – לא מעלה ולא מוריד, דאינו צריך לו. וכי הדר מצטרף עם ההוא מן השוק להעיד על חתימת המת – הדר נפיק ריבעא דממונא אפומיה, אשתכח דכולא ממונא נכי ריבעא נפיק אפומיה, ואנן "על פי שנים עדים" בעינן, חצי דבר על פיו של זה וחצי דבר על פיו של זה, הלכך ניבעי תרי. דכיון דספיקא היא – ניזיל הכא לחומרא והכא לחומרא: היכא דשניהם קיימים אזלינן לחומרא, ואמרינן: על כתב ידן הן מעידין, ובעינן תרין על כל כתב וכתב. והיכא דמית חד מינייהו – בעינן תרין מן השוק, שיעיד האחד על כתב יד המת, ואחד מהן יעיד על כתב יד המת והחי. דאי הוה פשיטא לן דעל כתב ידן מעידין – הוי סגי בחד מן השוק שיעיד על שתי החתימות, והחי יעיד גם הוא על שתיהם, ולא נפיק כולא ממונא נכי ריבעא אפומא דחד – דאיהו נמי צריך לאותו מן השוק שיעיד על חתימתו. אבל השתא דמספקא לן דלמא על מנה שבשטר הן מעידין, ועל כתב ידו הוא נאמן ואין צריך לצירוף, ועוד אנו צריכים לו שיעיד על חותם המת – נפקי תלתא ריבעי אפומיה, אי ליכא תרין מן השוק שלא יהא זה צריך להעיד על המת. קמ"ל דפשיטא ליה, וסגי בחד מן השוק, ושניהם יעידו על שתיהן. בין לקולא. כי הכא, דאילו לרבנן בעי שנים מן השוק שיעידו על של מת, וזה לבדו יעיד על חתימתו. נכי ריבעא. חסר ריבעא. צריך שנים. לדברי חכמים. ואי ליכא שנים. שיכירו כתב המת. אלא חד. וזה החי נמי מכירה, מאי ניעביד? לכתוב. זה שנשאר בחיים. חתימת ידיה אחספא ונשדייה בבי דינא. ויטלוה הדיינים, ויקיפוה אצל חתימתו שבשטר. ומחזקי. ההיא דשטרא מהך דאחספא, דלא צריך לאסהודי אחתימת ידיה. וכתב עליה מאי דבעי. למעלה מן החתימה יכתוב שזה החתום לוה ממנו מנה, וכותב כך: אני פלוני החתום למטה לויתי מנה מפלוני. מנכסים בני חורין. ומשעבדי לא, דלית ליה קלא לדבר שאינו עשוי בעדים. מהו דתימא. כי היכי דהלכה כרבי מחבירו – ה"נ אפילו מחביריו. דנפיק מבי דינא דמר שמואל. שקיימוהו בבית דינו, וכך נמצא כתוב בהנפק שכתבו הדיינים בו. מדאתא רב ענן כו'. אלמא כרבי ס"ל, שצריך לומר: זה כתב ידי וזה כתב ידו של חבירי. שטרא דיתמי הוה. שהולך לעיין בתקנתם. וחש שמואל. שאם לא כתב בו אלא: פלוני העיד על כתב ידו ופלוני על כתב ידו, שמא כשיוציאו היתומים שטר זה בב"ד לגבות יהא אותו ב"ד טועה לומר שהלכה כרבי, ויאמרו שאין זה קיום. איכא דס"ל. בעלמא ולא מחביריו, ובהא אפי' מחביריו. עד ודיין. שטר שכתוב בו הנפק, וחתמו הדיינין על הנפק שלו, ולאחר זמן, כשהוציאו המלוה לגבות, ערער הלוה לומר מזוייף הוא, ובא אחד מעדי השטר והעיד על כתב ידו, ואחד מן הדיינים העיד על כתב ידו – מצטרפין להכשירו. מאי דקא מסהיד סהדא כו'. עדי השטר מעידין על מנה שבשטר כרבנן, והדיינין מעידין: בפנינו נתקיים. רב יהודה אחוה דרמי בר יחזקאל הוה.

איקלע

תוספות

על כתב ידן הן מעידין. נראה, דלרבי אפילו אומרים בפירוש דמעידין על מנה שבשטר – חשיב כאילו מעידין על כתב ידן. וכן לרבנן אפי' אומרי' בהדיא דעל כתב ידן הן מעידין. מדאמרי' בסמוך ואי ליכא תרי אלא חד היכי נעביד, משמע דלא יועיל לרבנן אם יעידו בהדיא על כתב ידן. ודוקא אחספא. וה"ה אריסא דמגלתא, כדאמר ב"גט פשוט" (ב"ב דף קס: ושם) דליכא למיחש למידי, והא דתניא בפ"ק דקדושין (דף ט. ושם): כתב על הנייר או על החרס "בתך מקודשת לי כו'", וכן גבי שדה (שם כו.): כתב על הנייר או על החרס כו' – הרי זה מכורה, נראה דאתיא כר"א, דאמר: *עדי מסירה כרתי. דלר"מ כיון דעדי חתימה כרתי – לא מהני על דבר שיכול לזייף. כדאמר בפרק ב' דגיטין (דף כא: ושם): אין כותבין לא על הנייר כו', וחכמים מכשירין. ומפרש בגמרא *מאן חכמים – ר"א. ואע"ג דאמר התם: לא הכשיר ר"א אלא בגיטין, אבל בשאר שטרות לא – ה"פ: אלא בגיטין ודכוותייהו, דהיינו בשטרות שאין עומדין לראיה, כגון אותו שאינו עשוי אלא לקנות בו אשה ושדה. כעין גיטין שעשוין לפי שעה לגרש בו, ואע"פ שיכול השטר של קנין להועיל לראיה – גם הגט יכול להועיל, כדאמר ב"הכותב" (לקמן דף פט:) ובפ"ק דב"מ (דף יח. ושם): וכ"ת נקרעיה – בעינא לאנסובי ביה. אלא שעיקרן לא לכך נעשו, ולא ממעט אלא שטרות שעיקרן לראיה, ועשוין לעמוד ימים רבים, כדמייתי התם קרא ונתתם בכלי חרש וגו'.

הוציא עליו כתב ידו שהוא חייב לו גובה מנכסים בני חורין. פסק רב אלפס: דווקא כשאומר לא היו דברים מעולם, אבל נאמן הוא לומר פרעתי, ולא מצי א"ל "שטרך בידי מאי בעי" אלא בשטר שיש בו עדים, דגובה בו מנכסים משועבדים. ואין נראה לרבינו יצחק, כי מנין לו זה החילוק? כי סבר דבכל שטר איני רגיל לפרוע עד שיחזיר לו שטרו.

עד ודיין מצטרפין. משמע דאפילו בשטר מקויים חיישינן שמא זייף לחתימת הדיינין. וכן משמע בירושלמי דגיטין, ובפרק "בן סורר". והא דתניא בתוספתא דשביעית: פרוזבול המקושר, ר' יהודה אומר: עדים חותמין מבחוץ והדיינים מבפנים. אמרו לו: אין מעשה בית דין צריך קיום – היינו דווקא בפרוזבול, משום דנאמן אדם לומר פרוזבול היה לי ואבד, ואפי' למ"ד אינו נאמן – מודה הוא דלא בעי קיום.

האמר

עין משפט נר מצוה

מג א ב מיי' פ"ז מהל' עדות הלכה ג סמג עשין קט טוש"ע ח"מ סימן (כח) [מו] סעיף י יא:

מד ג ד מיי' שם הל' ה טוש"ע שם סעיף יג:

מה ה טוש"ע שם סי' סט סעיף ב:

מו ו מיי' פי"א מהל' מלוה ולוה הלכה ג ופכ"ז הלכה ב סמג עשין צד טוש"ע שם סימן לט סעיף א וסימן סט סעיף א:

[בגיטין פו.]

[שם כב.]

מסורת הש"ס

רש"ל מ"ז

ב"ב קעה:

[ברכות ע. וש"נ]

[לקמן נא. עירובין מו: פסחים כז. ב"ב קכד:]

[יבמות קו. ב"ב קלח: קסז. סנהדרין ל.]

גי' רש"ל אמר ליה רבא

הגהות הב"ח

(א) גמ' ושדי ליה בבי דינא וחזו ליה ומחזקי ליה בי דינא ולא צריך כצ"ל:

גליון הש"ס

גמ' אבל אמגלתא לא. עיין ב"ב דף קס ע"א תוס' ד"ה מקושר עדיו מאחוריו: שם כמה מעליא. כעין זה שבועות דף מז ע"ב: שם לא תציתינהו. לקמן דף ס ע"א ודף עו ע"ב חולין דף מד ע"א:

תוספות רי"ד

כשתמצא לומר לדברי רבי על כת"י הן מעידין ולפיכך צריך שיצטרף עמהן אחר ולדברי חכמים על מנה שבשטר הן מעידין והרי הם שנים ופי' המורה שהם זקוקין לומר אנחנו ראינו המלוה וחתמנו ואינו נ"ל שבין שזוכרין אותה ומעידין עליה בין אין זוכרין אותה שכבר שכחו העדות אלא שמכירין חתימתן ומעידין עליה. פליגי רבי ורבנן רבי סבר אע"פ שזוכרים ההלואה ומעידים עליה אפ"ה על כת"י מעידין שאם לא יקיימו החתימה הוה לה מלוה ע"פ ולא טרפא ממשעבדי א"נ מצי אידך למיטען פרעתי הלכך זקוקים אנו לעדותן לומר מכירים אנו חתימתינו ולשויי שטרא מעליא למיטרף מן הלקוחות ושלא לטעון פרעתי ורבנן סברי לא מיבעי אם זוכרים המלוה ומעידים עליה אלא אע"פ שאין זוכרים אותה כי אם מכירין חתימתן על מנה שבשטר מעידין שמתחלה כשחתמו העידו כל אחד על המנה גם עתה שבאים לקיים חתימתן כל עדותן אינה באה אלא על המנה א) ואע"פ שעכשיו אינן זוכרין אותו שכיון שבאים לקיים החתימה שנעשית על המנה נמצא שכל עדותן על זו הוא: אר"י אמר שמואל הל' כחכמים פשיטא יחיד ורבים הלכה כרבים מ"ד הל' כרבי מחבירו ב) ובהא אפי' מחביריו קמ"ל: אר"י א"ר שנים החתומים על השטר ומת אחד מהן צריכים שנים מן השוק להעיד עליו ואל יצטרף הוא עם א' כי היכי דלא ליפוק נבי רבעא דממונא אפומא דחד סהדא פי' הוא שהעיד על חתימתו נאמן וא"צ לצירוף מן השוק אבל חבירו שמת צריכים שנים מן השוק להעיד על חתימתו עכשיו ואם יצטרף הוא עם אחר נמצא שיצאו שלשת חלקי המנה שבשטר ע"פ זה והתורה אמרה על פי שנים עדים יקום דבר חצי דבר ע"פ זה וחצי דבר ע"פ זה ופי' נבי חסר: ואי ליכא אלא חד מהו פי' שמכירה מאי ליעבד אמר אביי כותב האיך פי' שנשאר בחיים חתימות ידו אחספא ושדי ליה בב"ד וחזי ליה ב"ד פי' ויטלוה הדיינים ויקיפוה אצל חתימות שבשטר ומחזקי ליה פי' ההיא דשטרא מהך דחספא ולא יצטריך איהו לאסהודי אחתימות ידיה ואזיל איהו והאי ומסהיד אאידך ודוקא אחספא אבל אמגילתא לא דלמא משכח ליה איניש דלא מעלי וכתב עלויה מה דבעי ותנן הוציא עליו כת"י שהוא חייב לו גובה מנכסים בנ"ח פי' ממשעבדי לא דל"ל קלא שאינו עשוי בעדים וכן נמי יכול לכתוב אריש מגילתא כדאמרי' בפ' ג"פ האי מאן דמחוי חתימות ידיה בב"ד לא לחוי בסוף מגילתא אלא ברישא דלמא משכח ליה אחר וכתב אגבי' דמסיק בי' פי' יכתוב מלמעלה אני החתום לויתי מפלוני מנה עיין בפ"ק דקדושין בהלכה ובשטר (דף כ"ו): אר"י א"ש עד ודיין מצטרפים פי' ראובן שהוציא על שמעון שטר חתום ואשרתא דדייני מלמטה שחתמו הדיינים שם שקיימו החתימה וטען שמעון איני מכיר לא חתימת העדים ולא חתימת הדיינים ושמא הוא זייף הכל ובא ע"א מעדי השטר והעיד על חתימתו ואחד מן הדיינים בא והעיד על חתימתו מצטרפים זה עם זה דכולהו לקיומא שטרא אתו. אמר רמב"ח כמה מעליא האי שמעתא א"ל מאי מעליותא מאי דמסהיד סהדא לא מסהיד דיינא ומאי דמסהיד דיינא לא מסהיד סהדא. אלא כי אתא רמי בר יחזקאל אמר לא תציתו להו להני כללי דבייל יהודה אחי משמי' דשמואל

דאיקלע

א) והיינו כדעת הראב"ד בהשגות פ"ח מהלכות עדות הלכה ד' ע"ש. ב) נראה דרבינו היה גורס כאן ובהא אפילו מחביריו וכ"ה הגירסא באמת בפסחים כז.

עין משפט נר מצוה

מח א מיי' פ"ז מהל' עדות הלכה ו סמג עשין קט טוש"ע ח"מ סימן מו סעיף כד:

מט ב מיי' פ"ו שם הל' ב סמג שם טוש"ע שם סעיף ז:

נ ג מיי' פ"ב מהלכות קידוש החדש הלכה ט:

נא ד מיי' פ"ה מהלכות עדות הלכה ט סמג עשין קט טוש"ע ח"מ סי' ז סעיף ה:

נב ה מיי' פ"ו שם הל' א ופ"ז הלכה ו סמג עשין פב טוש"ע שם סימן מו סעיף ד בהג"ה:

נג ו מיי' שם טוש"ע שם סעיף כו:

תוספות

האמר רב פפי **האי אשרתא.** תימה: דפריך מדרב פפי, ובפרק "הכותב" (לקמן דף פה. ושם) מסיק דליתא לדרב פפי מדרב נחמן כו'! ועוד דבפ' "כל הגט" (גיטין כו: ושם) מסיק דרב לית ליה דרב פפי. והיכי פריך הכא מדרב פפי אמילתיה דרב? מיהו, הא איכא לתרץ: דאלישנא דאמרי לה משמיה דרב הונא פריך. ואין לומר דהכי פריך: כיון דאמר משחתמו אין מעידין לפניו וחותם – אלמא חיישינן למיחזי כשקרא, אם כן משכתבו עד שלא חתמו נמי, דכתיבה נמי מיחזי כשקרא. דא"כ הוה קשיא דרב אדרב, דהכא חייש למיחזי כשקרא, ובפרק "כל הגט" (שם) לא חייש. אלא טעמא, דמשחתמו דמי לנוגעים בעדות, כעין שפירש בקונט' גבי ההוא שקרא ערער על אחד מהן. ותירץ ר"ת: *דדרך התלמוד להקשות אפילו מדבר דלא הוי הלכתא הכי. ופוסק ר"ת דכתבינן *אורכתא אפילו אמטלטלי דכפריה, דלא קיי"ל כרב פפי דחייש למיחזי כשקרא. אע"ג דפריך מינה, ופריך נמי מנהרדעי בכמה מקומות בפרק "שבועת העדות" (שבועות דף לג: ושם) ובפרק "יש בכור" (בכורות דף מט.): והאמרי נהרדעי לא כתבינן אורכתא כו'. וי"מ: וליתא דקאמר ב"הכותב" ובפ' "כל הגט" (גיטין דף כו: ושם) דלא בעי למימר דליתא לדרב פפי, אלא דליתא לקושיא, שאין לדמות אשרתא שהוא מעשה ב"ד לשאר שטרות, דבמעשה ב"ד לכ"ע חיישינן למיחזי *כשקרא. ור"י מדנפי"ר תירץ: דלכתחלה ודאי חיישינן למיחזי כשקרא, כדאמר להו רב לספרי: כי יתביתו בהיני כו' (ב"ב דף קעב.) אבל בדיעבד – לא חיישינן. ולהכי פריך הכא, דהוי לכתחלה. והא דקאמר דליתא לדרב פפי – היינו דיעבד. דההיא איתתא ד"הכותב" (לקמן דף פה. ושם) כיון שהיתה צריכה לחזור לב"ד כדיעבד דמי. והרשאה נמי דכתבינן אמטלטלי דכפריה – היינו משום כיון דאינו יכול לילך שם – כדיעבד דמי*.

[וע"ע בתוס' ב"מ קיג. ד"ה מחזיר] [פי' הרשאה] [והכותב להכותב לא חשיב מעשה ב"ד דכעדים סגי שיעידו שנכתבה. ת"י] [וע"ע תוס' גיטין כו. ד"ה ליתא וכ"מ יב: ד"ה כותבין]

וש"מ דיינין המכירין חתימת עדים **א"צ להעיד בפניהם.** דקס"ד דצריך להעיד בפניהם, אע"ג דלא תהא שמיעה גדולה מראייה, לפי שהיו נראין יותר בית דין. דכשאין מעידין בפניהם – אין נראה אלא כעד מפי עד. ומטעם זה הצריכו ג' בקיום שטרות, דהוה סגי בב', אלא משום דבעינן שיהא ב"ד כדפרישית. ועוד אומר ר"י: דס"ד דצרי' להעיד בפניהם משום דפעמים אין מכירין אלא על ידי שראו בלילה, דליכא למימר לא תהא שמיעה גדולה מראייה, דשמיעה אינה יכולה להיות בלילה כדאמר בר"ה (דף כה: ושם) דחקירת עדים כתחלת דין דמי, ותחלת דין אינו אלא ביום, כדאמרינן בסנהדרין (דף לב.). **בפני** כל אחד ואחד. דס"ד כיון שהעידו בפני שנים – יכול השלישי לכתוב על סמך השנים, אע"פ שלא העידו בפניו. **הנח** לעדות החדש דאורייתא. ובדאורייתא אין עד נעשה דיין. וטעמא דאין עד נעשה דיין – משום דבעינן שיעידו לפני הדיינין, כמו שמפרש רשב"ם, דכתיב "ועמדו שני האנשים" – אלו העדים, "לפני ה'" אלו הדיינין. וי"מ: משום דבעינן עדות שאתה יכול להזימה, ואם העדים נעשו דיינין – עדות שאין אתה יכול להזימה היא, שלא יקבלו הזמה על עצמן. ומיהו, לפי טעם זה, אם העדים קרובים לדיינין – אינם יכולים להעיד, דלא יקבלו הזמה עליהם. אלא כיון דבני הזמה נינהו בב"ד אחר – עדות שאתה יכול להזימה קרינא בהו, ה"נ יהיה הדיין נעשה עד. *)ודוקא בעד המעיד אמרינן דאין עד נעשה דיין, דשייכי הני טעמי. אבל עד שאינו צריך להעיד, כגון שיש אחרים שיעידו, או כגון שראוהו ביום שאינו צריך להעיד, דלא תהא שמיעה גדולה מראייה – נעשה דיין. ודווקא בדיני ממונות, אבל בדיני נפשות – אפילו עד שאין צריך להעיד אין נעשה דיין לר"ע דאמר במסכת מכות (דף ו. ושם): אפילו הן מאה – כולן עדים. וטעמא מפרש בפרק "ראוהו ב"ד" (ר"ה דף כו. ושם) משום דכתיב "והצילו העדה", והנך כיון דחזו דקטל – תו לא חזי ליה זכותא. ודווקא בדאורייתא, אבל בדרבנן – אפילו עד המעיד נעשה דיין.

*) [וע"ע מ"ש תוס' ב"ק ל: ד"ה כגון שראוהו בלילה כו' טעם אחר בשם ר"י דנפקא לן מביום הנחילו כו']

גמרא

איקלע רבנאי אחוה דר' חייא בר אבא למזבן שומשמי, ואמר: הכי אמר שמואל: עד ודיין מצטרפין. אמר אמימר: כמה מעליא הא שמעתא! אמר ליה רב אשי לאמימר: משום דקלסה אבוה דאמך את נמי מקלסת לה? כבר פרכה רבא.§ אמר רב ספרא אמר רבי אבא אמר רב יצחק בר שמואל בר מרתא אמר רב הונא, ואמרי ליה אמר רב הונא אמר רב: אשלשה שישבו לקיים את השטר, שנים מכירין חתימות ידי עדים ואחד אינו מכיר, עד שלא חתמו – מעידין בפניו וחותם, משחתמו – אין מעידין בפניו וחותם. ומי כתבינן? והאמר רב פפי משמיה דרבא: *האי אשרתא דדייני דניכתב מקמיה דניחוו סהדי אחתימת ידייהו – פסולה, דמתחזי כשקרא. הכא נמי מתחזי כשקרא! אלא אימא: עד שלא כתבו – מעידין בפניו וחותם, משכתבו – אין מעידין בפניו וחותם. ש"מ תלת; ש"מ: *עד נעשה דיין. וש"מ: בדיינין המכירין חתימות ידי עדים אינן צריכין להעיד בפניהם. וש"מ: דיינין שאין מכירין חתימות ידי עדים – צריכין להעיד בפני כל אחד ואחד. מתקיף לה רב אשי: בשלמא, עד נעשה דיין – שמעינן מינה. אלא דיינין המכירין חתימות ידי עדים אין צריכין להעיד בפניהם, דלמא לעולם אימא לך: צריכין, ושאני הכא דקא מקיימא הגדה בחד! ודיינין שאין מכירין חתימות ידי עדים צריכין להעיד בפני כל אחד ואחד, דלמא לעולם אימא לך: אין צריכין, ושאני הכא – דלא קא מקיימא הגדה כלל! יתיב ר' אבא וקאמר לה להא שמעתא דעד נעשה דיין. איתיביה רב ספרא לרבי אבא: *גראוהו שלשה והן בית דין – יעמדו שנים ויושיבו מחבריהם אצל היחיד, ויעידו בפניהם, ויאמרו "מקודש החדש, מקודש", שאין היחיד נאמן על ידי עצמו. ואי סלקא דעתך דעד נעשה דיין – למה לי כולי האי? ליתבו בדוכתייהו וליקדשי! אמר ליה: אף לדידי קשיא לי, ושאילתיה לרב יצחק בר שמואל בר מרתא, ורב יצחק לרב הונא, ורב הונא לחייא בר רב, וחייא בר רב לרב, ואמר להו: הנח דלעדות החדש דאורייתא, *הוקיום שטרות דרבנן. אמר רבי אבא אמר רב הונא אמר רב: ושלשה שישבו לקיים את השטר, וקרא ערער על אחד מהן, עד שלא חתמו – מעידין עליו וחותם, משחתמו אין מעידין עליו וחותם. ערער דמאי? אי ערער דגזלנותא

תרי

רש"י

איקלע רבנאי למיזבן שומשמי גרסי', ולא גרסי' דאיקלע, ולא גרסינן לגבן. ולאו רמי אמרה, דא"א לומר כן שאמר רמי עדות זו על אמימר ורב אשי, שהרי רב אשי כמה דורות היה אחריו, דאמרינן בקדושין (דף עב:): יום שמת רב יהודה נולד רבא, יום שמת רבא נולד רב אשי. **אבוה דאמך.** רמי בר חמא. **שלשה שישבו.** בב"ד. **לקיים השטר.** ובלא העדאת עדים שיעידו על כתב ידן, לפי שהדיינין עצמן מכירין אותה. **השנים מכירין** אותה ואחד אינו מכיר. **עד שלא חתמו.** השנים על ההנפק. **מעידין.** לפני השלישי שזהו כתב ידן של חתומים. **וחותם.** עמהם על מה שכותבין "אשרנוהי וקיימנוהי לשטרא דנן כמותב תלתא דאשתמודענא דחתימת ידא דסהדי היא". **משחתמו אין מעידין.** דחתימה קמייתא בשקרא הואי, דלאו תלתא הוו דידעי. **ומי כתבינן.** לאשרתא דידיה? בתמיה. וכי קודם שנתקיים לפני שלשתן יכתבו "במותב תלתא הוינא ואשתמודענא" כו'. **אשרתא.** לשון חוזק, שמחזיקים [את השטר] וכותבין אשרנוהי. **דנכתבא מקמי דניחוו סהדי כו'.** עד שלא העידו העדים על כתב ידם כתבו הדיינין "במותב תלתא הוינא ונפיק שטרא דנן קדמנא ואסהידו פלוני ופלוני אחתימת ידייהו ואשרנוהי וקיימנוהי". **עד נעשה דיין.** שהרי השנים העידו על החתימות. **צריכין להעיד בפני כל אחד ואחד.** שאם העידו בפני השנים – אין הג' יכול לחתום, דהא הכא הוצרכו השנים להעיד בפני הג'. **דלמא לעולם צריכין.** להעיד, שאין עדות אלא ע"י הגדת עדות. **ושאני הכא דקא מקיימא הגדה.** בפני היחיד שאינו מכיר. **דלא מקיימא הגדה כלל.** אי לא הוו מסהדי באפיה. **ראוהו ג'.** בעדות החדש קאי. **והן בית דין.** מסנהדרין המקדשין את החדש. **יעמדו השנים.** להיות עדים. **והתם פרכינן:** לא תהא שמיעה גדולה מראיה! ומוקמינן לה כשראוהו בלילה. לפיכך אם לא יעידו לבקר – על מה יאמרו מקודש. **שאין היחיד נאמן.** לקדש החדש ביחידי. **ליתבו בדוכתייהו.** אחר שהעידו בפניו. **וקרא ערער על הא'.** שהוא פסול. **עד שלא חתמו.** השני דיינים על האשרתא. **מעידין.** על זה שהוא כשר. **משחתמו.** הוו להו נוגעין בעדות, שגנאי להם שישבו עם פסול בדין.

מסורת הש"ס

גיטין כו: לקמן פה. [וע' בטוש"ע ח"מ סימן מו סעיף כד ובש"ך ובסמ"ע שם]

סנהדרין לד: ר"ה כו. גיטין ה: ב"ק ל: ב"ב קיד.

ר"ה כה:

[לקמן כח. ע"ש בתוס']

תוספות רי"ד

דאיקלע רבנאי אחוה דר' חייא בר אבין לקמן למיזבן שומשמי ואמר הכי אמר שמואל עד ודיין אין מצטרפים וכך הלכה: אר"ה א"ר ג' שישבו לקיים את השטר פי' בלא העדאת עדים שיעידו על כת"י לפי שהדיינים עצמם מכירין אותה ב' מהן מכירין חתימת ידי העדים וא' אינו מכיר עד שלא חתמו פי' בהנפק מעידים בפניו וחותם פי' לפני השלישי שזה כת"י החתומים משחתמו אין מעידין בפניו וחותם פירוש (אחר) עד שלא חתמו הן בההיא אשרתא מעידים בפני זה וחותם עמהן וכותבין כך נפק שטרא דנן קדמנא ונתבררנו שהוא חתימות העדים ואשרנוהו וקיימנוהו כדחזי אבל אחר שחתמו אין מעידין בפניו מפני שהן נוגעים בעדותן שנראה שמה שמעידים כך כדי לקיים חתימתן שלא תבטל: ש"מ תלת ש"מ עד נעשה דיין פי' אחר שהעיד ונעשה עד חוזר עוד ונעשה דיין וש"מ דדיינים המכירים חתימת ידי העדים א"צ להעיד בפניהם וש"מ דיינים שאין מכירין חתימות העדים צריכים להעיד בפני כאו"א פי' שאם העידו בפני הב' אין הג' יכול לחתום שהרי כאן הצריכו להעיד בפני הג' ולא יועיל הנה שיעידו בפני ב' והב' יעידו לג' כדאמרינן בשנים מכירין משום דהוי להו עד מפי עד אבל כשמכירין מעצמן אינו עד מפ"ע: איתבי' רב ספרא לר"א ועד מי נעשה דיין והתנן ראוהו ג' והם ב"ד פי' מסנהדרין שמקדשים את החדש יעמדו ב' ויושיבו מחבריהם אצל היחיד ויעידו בפניהם ויאמרו מקודש מקודש שאין היחיד נאמן ע"י עצמו והתם פרכינן ולא תהא שמיעה גדולה מראייה ומתוקמ' לה כשראוהו בלילה לפיכך אם לא יעידו בבקר על מה יאמרו מקודש אין היחיד ראוי לקדש את החדש דקידוש החדש צריך שלשה והלכך יושיבו ב' דיינים אחרים מחבריהם מיושבי סנהדרין ואלה הב' שראו יעמדו בפניהם והם יקדשוהו ואי איתא ליתבו בדוכתייהו ולקדשו פי' אי איתא דעד שהעיד נעשה דיין מה צריך להושיב מחבריהם אצל היחיד הם שהעידו יצטרפו עמו לקדש אלא לאו ש"מ אין עד שהגיד עדותו כשר להיות דיין והכא היכי אמרינן דמעידים ומסיק הנח לעדות החודש דאורייתא ובדאורייתא אין עד נעשה דיין אבל קיום שטרות דרבנן ובדרבנן עד נעשה דיין פי' מה"ת ליכא למיחש לזויפא אלא בלי קיום יגבה ולכי מתברר דזייף מהדר ליה ורבנן הוא דאצרכו' לקיומי' ועד דלא מקיים לא גבי. ע' דיני עד נעשה דיין בס"פ ששם ביארתי שאם יש עדים רבים שיגמר הדין ע"פ שנים עדים ושלשה דיינים עד שהגיד עדותו נעשה דיין: אמר ר"פ משמיה דרבא האי אשרתא דדיינא דכתיבא מקמי דנחזו סהדי אחתימות ידיהו פסולה משום דמיחזי כשיקרא וליתא הל' הכי דלקמן בפ' הכותב ובגיטין בפ' כל הגט מתיב' ליה ואמרינן וליתא לדר"פ: אמר ר' אבא אר"ה א"ר ג' שישבו לקיים את השטר וקרא ערעור על א' מהן עד שלא חתמו פי' השנים על אשרתא מעידים עליו על זה שהוא כשר וחותם משחתמו אין מעידין עליו וחותם פי' כיון שחתמו הן נוגעים בעדות שהם מתכוונים שלא תבטל חתימתן וגם גנאי הוא להם שיאמרו עם הפסול חתמו. וערעור דמאי אי ערעור דגזלנותא

תרי

תְּרֵי וּתְרֵי נִינְהוּ, א אִי עַרְעָר דִּפְגַם מִשְׁפָּחָה – גִּלּוּי מִלְּתָא בְּעָלְמָא הוּא! לְעוֹלָם אֵימָא לָךְ: עַרְעָר דְּגַזְלָנוּתָא, וְקָאָמְרִי ב הָנֵי: יָדְעִינַן בֵּיהּ דַּעֲבַד תְּשׁוּבָה. א"ר זֵירָא: הָא מִלְּתָא מֵרַבִּי אַבָּא שְׁמִיעַ לִי, וְאִי לָאו רַבִּי אַבָּא דְּמִן עַכּוֹ שְׁכַחְתָּהּ. ג ג' שֶׁיָּשְׁבוּ לְקַיֵּים אֶת הַשְּׁטָר וּמֵת אֶחָד מֵהֶם – צְרִיכִין לְמִיכְתַּב: "בְּמוֹתַב תְּלָתָא הֲוֵינָא, וְחַד לֵיתוֹהִי". אָמַר רַב נַחְמָן בַּר יִצְחָק: וְאִי כָּתַב בֵּיהּ "שְׁטָרָא דְּנַן נְפַק לְקַדָּמָנָא בֵּי דִינָא" – תּוּ לָא צְרִיךְ. וְדִלְמָא בֵּית דִּין חָצוּף הוּא? וּכְדִשְׁמוּאֵל, דְּאָמַר שְׁמוּאֵל: *שְׁנַיִם שֶׁדָּנוּ – דִּינֵיהֶם דִּין, אֶלָּא שֶׁנִּקְרָא ב"ד חָצוּף! דִּכְתִיב בֵּיהּ: "בֵּי דִינָא דְּרַבָּנָא אַשִׁי". וְדִלְמָא רַבָּנַן דְּבֵי רַב אַשִׁי כִּדְשְׁמוּאֵל סְבִירָא לְהוּ? ד דִּכְתִיב בֵּיהּ: "וַאֲמַר לָנָא רַבָּנָא אַשִׁי".§

מתני' *ה הָאִשָּׁה שֶׁאָמְרָה: "אֵשֶׁת אִישׁ הָיִיתִי וּגְרוּשָׁה אֲנִי" – נֶאֱמֶנֶת, שֶׁהַפֶּה שֶׁאָסַר הוּא הַפֶּה שֶׁהִתִּיר. ו וְאִם יֵשׁ עֵדִים שֶׁהָיְתָה אֵשֶׁת אִישׁ וְהִיא אוֹמֶרֶת: "גְּרוּשָׁה אֲנִי" – אֵינָהּ נֶאֱמֶנֶת. ז אָמְרָה: "נִשְׁבֵּיתִי וּטְהוֹרָה אֲנִי" – נֶאֱמֶנֶת, שֶׁהַפֶּה שֶׁאָסַר הוּא הַפֶּה שֶׁהִתִּיר. ח וְאִם יֵשׁ עֵדִים שֶׁנִּשְׁבֵּית, וְהִיא אוֹמֶרֶת: "טְהוֹרָה אֲנִי" – אֵינָהּ נֶאֱמֶנֶת. ט וְאִם מִשֶּׁנִּשֵּׂאת בָּאוּ עֵדִים – הֲרֵי זוֹ לֹא תֵּצֵא.§

גמ' א"ר אַסִי: מִנַּיִן לַהַפֶּה שֶׁאָסַר הוּא הַפֶּה שֶׁהִתִּיר מִן הַתּוֹרָה? שֶׁנֶּאֱמַר: °"אֶת בִּתִּי נָתַתִּי לָאִישׁ הַזֶּה לְאִשָּׁה" "לָאִישׁ" – אֲסָרָהּ, "הַזֶּה" – הִתִּירָהּ. °ל"ל קְרָא? סְבָרָא הִיא: הוּא אֲסָרָהּ וְהוּא שָׁרֵי לָהּ! אֶלָּא, כִּי אִיצְטְרִיךְ קְרָא – לְכִדְרַב הוּנָא אָמַר רַב. דְּא"ר הוּנָא אָמַר רַב: *מִנַּיִן לָאָב שֶׁנֶּאֱמָן לֶאֱסוֹר אֶת בִּתּוֹ מִן הַתּוֹרָה – שֶׁנֶּאֱמַר: "אֶת בִּתִּי נָתַתִּי לָאִישׁ". "הַזֶּה" לָמָּה לִי – מִיבָּעֵי לֵיהּ לְכִדְתָנֵי ר' יוֹנָה, דְּתָנֵי ר' יוֹנָה: "אֶת בִּתִּי נָתַתִּי לָאִישׁ הַזֶּה", *"הַזֶּה" – כ וְלֹא לַיָּבָם. ת"ר: ל הָאִשָּׁה שֶׁאָמְרָה: "אֵשֶׁת אִישׁ אֲנִי" וְחָזְרָה וְאָמְרָה: "פְּנוּיָה אֲנִי" – נֶאֱמֶנֶת. וְהָא שַׁוְּיַהּ לְנַפְשַׁהּ חֲתִיכָה דְּאִיסּוּרָא! אָמַר רָבָא בַּר רַב הוּנָא: כְּגוֹן מ שֶׁנָּתְנָה אֲמַתְלָא לִדְבָרֶיהָ. תַּנְיָא נַמִי הָכִי: אָמְרָה: "אֵשֶׁת אִישׁ אֲנִי" וְחָזְרָה וְאָמְרָה: "פְּנוּיָה אֲנִי" – אֵינָהּ נֶאֱמֶנֶת, וְאִם נָתְנָה אֲמַתְלָא לִדְבָרֶיהָ – נֶאֱמֶנֶת. וּמַעֲשֶׂה נַמִי בְּאִשָּׁה אַחַת גְּדוֹלָה, שֶׁהָיְתָה גְּדוֹלָה בְּנוֹי, וְקָפְצוּ עָלֶיהָ בְּנֵי אָדָם לְקַדְּשָׁהּ, וְאָמְרָה לָהֶם: "מְקוּדֶּשֶׁת אֲנִי". לְיָמִים עָמְדָה וְקִידְּשָׁה אֶת עַצְמָהּ. אָמְרוּ לָהּ חֲכָמִים: מָה רָאִית לַעֲשׂוֹת כֵּן? אָמְרָה לָהֶם: בַּתְּחִלָּה שֶׁבָּאוּ עָלַי אֲנָשִׁים שֶׁאֵינָם מְהוּגָּנִים – אָמַרְתִּי "מְקוּדֶּשֶׁת אֲנִי", עַכְשָׁיו שֶׁבָּאוּ עָלַי אֲנָשִׁים מְהוּגָּנִים – עָמַדְתִּי וְקִדַּשְׁתִּי אֶת עַצְמִי. וְזוֹ הֲלָכָה הֶעֱלָה רַב אַחָא שַׂר הַבִּירָה לִפְנֵי חֲכָמִ' בְּאוּשָׁא, וְאָמְרוּ: אִם נָתְנָה אֲמַתְלָ' לִדְבָרֶיהָ – נֶאֱמֶנֶת. בְּעָא מִינֵּיהּ שְׁמוּאֵל מֵרַב: אָמְרָה: "טְמֵאָה אֲנִי" וְחָזְרָה וְאָמְרָה: "טְהוֹרָה אֲנִי" מַהוּ? אָמַר לֵיהּ: נ אַף בְּזוֹ, אִם נָתְנָה אֲמַתְלָא

תורה אור: דברים כב

תְּרֵי וּתְרֵי נִינְהוּ. כִּי אָמְרִי לֹא גָזַל – הָווּ לְהוּ תְּרֵי וּתְרֵי, וְלֹא מִתְכַּשַּׁר בְּהָכִי. דְּקַיְ"ל לְקַמָּן בְּפִרְקִין (דף כו.): אֵין עַרְעָר פָּחוֹת מִשְּׁנַיִם. דִּפְגַם מִשְׁפָּחָה. שֶׁהֵעִידוּ עָלָיו שֶׁהוּא עֶבֶד, וְעֶבֶד פָּסוּל לְדִין וּלְעֵדוּת ק"ו מֵאִשָּׁה, כִּדְאָמַר בְּפֶ' "הַחוֹבֵל" (ב"ק פח.). גִּלּוּי מִילְּתָא בְּעָלְמָא הוּא. מִשֶּׁחָתְמוּ אַמַּאי אֵין מְעִידִין עָלָיו? מַאי חֲשַׁד נוֹגֵעַ בְּעֵדוּת אִיכָּא הָכָא? דָּבָר זֶה צְרִיכִין הֵן לְבָרֵר, וְדָבָר הֶעָשׂוּי לְגַלּוֹת הוּא, שֶׁיִּבְדְּקוּ אַחֲרָיו עַד שֶׁיִּתְבָּרֵר הַדָּבָר. וְאֵין עֵדוּתָן שֶׁל אֵלּוּ תָּלוּי בְּהַגָּדָתָן, וְאֵינָן אֶלָּא מְגַלֵּי דָבָר בְּעָלְמָא. דַּעֲבַד תְּשׁוּבָה. וְהֵשִׁיב אֶת הַגְּזֵלָה. וְאִי לָאו רַבִּי אַבָּא דְּמִן עַכּוֹ. שֶׁהִזְכִּירָהּ לִי לְאַחַר זְמַן. שְׁכַחְתָּהּ. שְׁכַחְתִּיהָ. וּמֵת אֶחָד מֵהֶן. עַד שֶׁלֹּא חָתְמוּ. צְרִיכִין לְמִיכְתַּב כו'. דְּקִיּוּם הַשְּׁטָר בִּשְׁלֹשָׁה, וְהָרוֹאֶה שְׁנַיִם חֲתוּמִין בּוֹ – יֹאמַר שֶׁבִּשְׁנַיִם קִיְּימוּהוּ. וְאִי כָּתַב בֵּיהּ שְׁטָרָא דְּנַן נְפַק קֳדָמָנָא בֵּי דִינָא תּוּ לָא צְרִיךְ. דְּלָא מִקְרֵי בֵּי דִינָא בְּצִיר מִתְּלָתָא. בֵּי דִינָא דְּרַבָּנָא אַשִׁי. אוֹרְחָא דְּמִילְּתָא נָקַט, שֶׁהוּא הָיָה רֹאשׁ יְשִׁיבָה בְּמָתָא מַחְסְיָא בִּימֵי רַב נַחְמָן בַּר יִצְחָק דְּהוּא מָרָא דִּשְׁמַעְתָּא, וַדַּאי בֵּי דִינָא דְּרַב אַשִׁי לָא עָבְדִין בִּתְרֵין. וַאֲמַר לָנָא רַבָּנָא אַשִׁי. לְאִזְדַּקּוֹקֵי לֵיהּ וּלְקַיּוּמֵי. דְּכֵיוָן דְּרַב אַשִׁי גּוּפֵיהּ הִזְקִיקָן – אִיהוּ וַדַּאי לִתְלָתָא אָמַר. וְיֵשׁ מְפָרְשִׁין: וַאֲמַר לָנָא רַבָּנָא אַשִׁי – תְּלָתָא נִינְהוּ. וְלָא נְהִירָא לִי; דְּאִי רַב אַשִׁי חַד מִנַּיְהוּ, מַאי וַאֲמַר לָנָא דִּכְתָבֵי בֵּיהּ?

מתני' נִשְׁבֵּיתִי. לְבֵין הַגּוֹיִם. וּטְהוֹרָה אֲנִי. שֶׁלֹּא נִבְעַלְתִּי לְגוֹי. נֶאֱמֶנֶת. וּמוּתֶּרֶת לְכֹהֵן. וְאִם מִשֶּׁנִּיסֵּת בָּאוּ עֵדִים. בַּגְּמָרָא מְפָרֵשׁ הֵיכִי קָאֵי. גמ' נָתַתִּי לָאִישׁ אֲסָרָהּ. לְכָל הָעוֹלָם, דְּלָא יָדְעִינַן לְמַאן. וְכִי אָמַר "הַזֶּה" – הִתִּירָהּ לוֹ. שֶׁנֶּאֱמָן לֶאֱסוֹר אֶת בִּתּוֹ. כְּשֶׁהִיא קְטַנָּה אוֹ נַעֲרָה, שֶׁבְּיָדוֹ לְקַדְּשָׁהּ. כִּדְאָמְרִי' בְּפֶ' "נַעֲרָה שֶׁנִּתְפַּתְּתָה": מִנַּיִן שֶׁאִם אָמַר קִדַּשְׁתִּיהָ לִפְלוֹנִי שֶׁהוּא נֶאֱמָן לְאוֹסְרָהּ עַל הַכֹּל? אֶת בִּתִּי נָתַתִּי. אַלְמָא בְּדִידֵיהּ תַּלְיָא נְתִינָה, וְהֵימְנֵיהּ קְרָא לְמֵימַר הָכִי. הַזֶּה לָמָּה לִי. כֵּיוָן דְּלָאו לְהַפֶּה שֶׁאָסַר מִיבָּעֵי לֵיהּ. וְלֹא לַיָּבָם. אִם הוֹצִיא שֵׁם רַע עַל נִישּׂוּאֵי אָחִיו. שֶׁאֵין הַיָּבָם נִידּוֹן כְּמוֹצִיא שֵׁם רַע לֵיעָנֵשׁ בְּמֵאָה כֶּסֶף. וְהָכִי מוּכָח לְקַמָּן בְּפֶרֶק "נַעֲרָה".

אֲמַתְלָא

תרי ותרי נינהו. פירש בקונטרס: וכי אמרי לא גזל – הוו להו תרי ותרי, ולא מתכשר בהכי. וקשה דהכא אליבא דרב הונא קיימינן. דאית ליה (שבועות דף מז:) דזו באה בפני עצמה ומעידה, דאית לן למימר אוקי גברא אחזקתיה. ועוד דלרב חסדא דאמר (שם): בהדי סהדי שקרי למה לי – מודה הכא דהאי גברא ממילא מתכשר, שהרי אם כת אחת מאלו מעידה על אדם אחד שהוא פסול, לרב חסדא דחשיב להו סהדי שקרי – לא היתה נאמנת, אע"ג דאין אדם מכחישה, וכ"ש היכא דאיכא סהדי דמכחשי. דלא מהימני. וע"ק לר"י דקאמר אי ערער דפגם משפחה – גלוי מילתא בעלמא הוא. ופי' הקונט': דדבר העשוי ליגלות הוא, שיבדקו עד שיתברר הדבר. וזהו תימה: איך יתברר הדבר לעולם? כיון שאלו ב' אומרים שהוא עבד – אין כל העולם יכולים להכחישן, דתרי כמאה! על כן נראה כפר"ת: דלא איירי בעדות דיינין אלא בעדות אחרים. וה"פ: אם עד שלא חתמו קרא ערער על אחד מהם – מעידים שנים מן השוק עליו וחותם, דהוי כאילו ישבו בית דין אחר שהכשירוהו, ולא בטל וועד המושב, וחותמין. משחתמו השנים ולא הספיק השלישי לחתום עד שקרא עליו ערער, בא ערער וביטל וועד המושב של אותו ב"ד. אע"פ שאחרי כן העידו אחרים שהוא כשר, כיון שביטל ההוא מושב – בטל. וצריך לחזור ולהושיב ב"ד על כך. ערער דמאי? אי ערער דגזלנותא – תרי ותרי נינהו, ולא מיפסיל. דאוקי תרי בהדי תרי, ואוקי גברא אחזקתיה. וכיון דאיגלאי מלתא דמעולם לא היה פסול – הרי לא היה בטל וועד המושב של אותו ב"ד. אי ערער דפגם משפחה, שאמרו עליו שהוא עבד, ואלו מזימים אותם. דאי אומרים שאינו עבד – א"כ היה נפסל! דליכא למימר אוקי גברא אחזקה, דאם הוא עבד לא היה לו חזקת כשרות מעולם – *א"כ גלוי מילתא בעלמא הוא, דכיון דאיגלאי מלתא דכשר היה – מה איכפת לן בההוא ערעור, ולא בטל וועד המושב לעולם. ערער דגזלנותא, ודקאמרי הנך סהדי ידעינן ביה דעבד תשובה. וכיון דמודו לקמאי דגזלן הוא – הוה ערער דידהו ערער, ובטל וועד המושב. דהואיל ואמת הוא שנפסל – הוי בחזקת פסלות עד שנודע לנו כשרותו.

במותב תלתא כחדא הוינא וחד ליתוהי. פירוש: צריך לכתוב "וחד ליתוהי", כיון דכתב בהדיא "במותב תלתא הוינא", ואין חותמין בו כי אם שנים. אבל ודאי, אם לא כתב "וחד ליתוהי" – כשר. תדע, מדקאמר ואי כתב ביה "בי דינא" – תו לא צריך. ומיירי דלא כתב "וחד ליתוהי", מדפריך: ודלמא ב"ד חצוף הוה.

ודלמא רבנן דבי רב אשי כשמואל סבירא להו. פי': כמו שסובר שמואל בעלמא כן סבירא להו בקיום שטרות. אבל שמואל מצי סבר שפיר דקיום שטרות בעי ג'. דהא רב נחמן סבר לה כשמואל בפ"ק דסנהדרין *)(דף ג. ושם) דשנים שדנו דיניהם דין. ורב נחמן גופיה סבר דקיום שטרות בשלשה בפ' "חזקת הבתים" (ב"ב מ.) גבי ג' ארכות לחזקה.

מנין להפה שאסר הוא הפה שהתיר מן התורה שנאמר "את בתי נתתי לאיש וגו'". משמע דאין האב נאמן להתיר את בתו כשאסרה אלא מטעם מגו. ותימה: דאם בא אחד ואמר "קדשתי את בתי", ולאחר שעה או למחר אמר: "לפלוני קדשתיה" לא יהא נאמן, כיון דהשתא ליכא מגו? ואומר ר"י: דבענין זה, שאינו סותר דבריו הראשונים ולא בא אלא לפרש דבריו הראשונים – מהימן, אע"ג דליכא מגו. והכא דריש מ"את בתי" הפה שאסר הוא הפה שהתיר, כגון דקאי האיש שקידש לו קמיה, וקאמר "את בתי נתתי לאיש" ושתיק, דמשמע ודאי שאינו מכיר שזה חתנו, מדלא אמר "את בתי נתתי לזה", או "לאיש הזה" ביחד, בלא הפסק מרובה, הלכך לא יהא נאמן אחר כך. אלא תוך כדי דבור, דאיכא מגו. ועוד אומר ר"י: דאיכא למימר אפילו בכה"ג מהימן בלא מגו, וקרא יתירא קדריש, ואם אינו ענין כאן, דאפילו לאחר זמן נאמן, דסברא הוא שיהא נאמן לפרש למי נתנה, אע"פ שלא פירש מתחלה, שלא היה חושש לפרש – תנהו ענין להיכא דאינו נאמן לאחר זמן, שיהא נאמן בתוך כדי דבור במגו.

[מנין לאב שנאמן לאסור וכו'. תימה: מה צריך קרא? תיפוק ליה דנאמן, הואיל ובידו לקדשה, כדאמר ב"ש נוטלין" (ב"ב קלד:): בעל שאמר "גרשתי את אשתי" – נאמן, הואיל ובידו לגרשה! וי"ל: דהכא אין בידו כל כך, דשמא לא ימצא אדם שיקדשנה (כדאיתא קידושין סד.) להכי איצטריך קרא. ומיהו, אם אמר על בתו בוגרת "קדשתיה כשהיתה נערה" – או קטנה נראה דאינו נאמן, דהשתא אין בידו כלל. דאף על גב דלקמן בפרק "נערה שנתפתתה" (דף מו:) פריך: ואימא הנ"מ קטנה, אבל נערה – איהי תיקדש נפשה! לפי זה היה נ"ל דנאמן לאסור אפילו בשעה שאין בידו לקדשה, דקרא בנערה כתיב, ובעי למימר דאין בידו לקדשה, ו"את בתי נתתי" כשהיתה קטנה, וגזרת הכתוב הוא דנאמן אע"פ שאין בידו. אבל לפי המסקנא לא נאמר כן].

*) [ה: ועי' תוס' שם ג. ד"ה לרבא]

חזרה

נד א מיי' פ"ו מהלכות עדות הלכה ז טוש"ע ח"מ סי' מו סעיף כז:

נה ב מיי' שם טוש"ע שם סעיף כו:

נו ג ד מיי' שם הלכה ו טוש"ע שם סעיף כט:

נז ה מיי' י"ב מהלכות גירושין הלכה א סמג עשין מח טוש"ע אה"ע סימן קנב סעיף ו:

נח ו מיי' שם טוש"ע שם סעיף ז:

נט ז ח מיי' פי"ח מהל' איסורי ביאה הלכה כא סמג לאוין קכא טוש"ע אה"ע סימן ז סעיף ד:

ס ט מיי' שם הלכה כב טוש"ע שם סעיף ו:

סנהדרין ג. ה: ל. פז:

[בכורות לו.]

סא י מיי' פ"ט מהלכות אישות הל' ג ופי"ח מהלכות איסורי ביאה הלכה כד סמג עשין מ טוש"ע אה"ע סימן לז סעיף כח:

סב כ מיי' פ"ג מהל' נערה בתולה הלכה ט סמג עשין כה:

סג ל מיי' פ"ט מהל' אישות הלכה לא סמג עשין מח טוש"ע אה"ע סימן מו סעיף ד:

סד נ מיי' פ"ד מהלכות איסורי ביאה הל' י סמג לאוין קיא טוש"ע י"ד סימן קפה סעיף ג:

קדושין סד. [ע"ש]

[וה"ה דהוה מצי למימר בערער דפגם משפחה וכגון דקאמרי ידעינו שנשתחרר. ת"י עה"ג]

תוספות רי"ד

תרי ותרי נינהו פי' ועד שלא חתמו אמאי מעידין והא אין ערער פחות מב' שאין משגיחים בדברי היחיד וכיון שב' אומרים גזלן הוא ואלו אומרים שלא גזל הו"ל תרי ותרי וכל תו"ת הו"ל ספיקא דאורייתא ובספיקא דאורייתא לא אמרינן אוקי גברא אחזקתיה כדאמרינן לקמן בפירקין וכיון דהאידנא איתוקם בספק גזלן היכי מחתמינן ליה ומפקינן ממונא אפומיה הלכך אע"פ שלא חתמו לא יכלו להכשירו ואי ערעור דפגם משפחה גלוי מילתא בעלמא הוא ואפי' משחתמו מעידים פי' ערעור דפגם משפחה שאלו השנים שבאו לפוסלו לא העידו עליו עדות ברורה אלא העידו שבמשפחתו נטמע שם עבד שהוא פסול לעדות וכל המשפחה הן בחזקת שהוא ספק פסול שמא מזרע אותו עבד נולד ואלה מעידים שזה אינו מן המסופקין דברי לן שמייחום כשרות הוא בא ואינן מכחישין את העדים אלא מוציאים את זה מספק פסול שלא יהיה מסופק כשאר כל בני המשפחה וזהו גילוי מילתא שיכול להתברר ע"פ אחרים שנבדוק אחריו ויתברר אם נולד מן הכשרים או מן הפסולין ובמילתא דעביד לגלויי לא משקרי אינשי והלכך אע"פ שחתמו והן נוגעים בעדות נאמנים דבאיזה עדות אינן נאמנין בדבר שלא נוכל להתברר על ידי אחרים כ"א על פיהם כדלקמן שמעידין שעשה תשובה שאין מכירין תשובתו אלא הם אבל ייחום האדם דהוא מילתא דעביד לגלויי ע"פ אחרים אע"פ שהן נוגעים בעדותן נאמנים הם. לעולם ערער דגזלנותא ודקאמרי הני ידעי' ביה דעשה תשובה שהחזיר את הגזילה ואין כאן משום הכחשה הלכך עד שלא חתמו מעידין עליו וחותם ומשחתמו שהן נוגעים בעדות אין מעידין עליו וחותם עי' בס"ה בערך מ"ר: א"ר זירא האי מילתא מר' אבא שמיעא לי שלשה שישבו לקיים את השטר ומת אחד מהן צריכים למיכתב במותב תלתא כחדא הוינא וחד ליתוהי פי' צריכים להודיע למה לא חתם הג' שיש לך לומר הא' היה קרובו או פסול ומפני זה לא חתם ובעבור זה האשרתא היא פסולה והמורה פי' צריכים לכתוב קודם שיחתמוהו דקיום שטרות בשלשה והרואה ב' חתומים יאמר שבשנים קיימוהו ואי כתיב [ביה] הא שטרא דנן נפק קדמנא בב"ד תו לא צריך דלא מקרי ב"ד בציר מתלתא. והגאון פי' אם כתבו בפנינו בב"ד הנפק שטרא דנן ואע"ג דלא כתבו במותב תלתא תו לא צריך למכתב וחד ליתוהי דסתם ב"ד כשרי' משמע ולא פסולים ולא קרובים ומקשינן דלמא ב"ד חצוף הוא דאמר שמואל שנים שדנו דיניהם דין אלא שנקרא ב"ד חצוף פי' והאשרתא בטילה דלית הלכתא כשמואל אלא כר' אבהו דאמר אין דיניהם דין ומהדר דכתיב ביה בי דינא דרבנא אשי פי' ב"ד מומחה שבדור והמורה פי' אורחא דמילתא נקט שהוא היה ראש ישיבה במתא מחסי' בימי רנב"י דהוא מרה שמעתתא ובודאי בי דינא דר' אשי לא עביד בתרין ומקשי' ודלמא ב"ד דר' אשי כשמואל ס"ל ואין הלכה כמותן ומהדר דכתיב ביה אמר לנא רבנא אשי פי' רב אשי צוה לנו להזקק לו וכיון שע"פ ר"א עשו בוודאי בי ג' היו דר"א לא טעה בדשמואל דלית הל' כוותיה וכ"ש אם כתבו בבי ב"ד במותב תלתא כחדא הוינא דתו ליכא למיחש לא לדשמואל ולא לקרוב ופסול שחותמים בו שנים ואין צריכין לומר וחד ליתוהי ודוקא אם מת אבל אם חי צריך לחתום שלא יאמרו השנים שהעידו בפניהם חתמו והשלישי לא העידו בפניו ומש"ה לא חתם והאשרתא בטלה: **מתני'** האשה שאמרה אשת איש הייתי וגרושה אני נאמנת שהפה שאסר הוא הפה שהתיר ואם יש עדים שהיא אשת איש והיא אומרת גרושה אני אינה נאמנת. ת"ר אמרה אשת איש אני וחזרה ואמרה פנויה אני אינה נאמנת ואם נתנה אמתלא לדבריה נאמנת ומעשה באשה אחת שהיתה גדולה בנוי וקפצו עליה בני אדם לקדשה וא"ל מקודשת אני לימים עמדה וקדשה א"ע א"ל חכמים מה ראית א"ל בתחלה שבאו עלי בני אדם שאינם מהוגנים אמרתי מקודשת אני עכשיו שבאו עלי בני אדם שהן הגונים לי עמדתי וקדשתי את עצמי וזו הלכה העלה ר"א שר הבירה לפני חכמים ואמרו אם נתנה אמתלא לדבריה נאמנת בעא מיניה שמואל מרב אמרה טמאה אני פי' נדה וחזרה ואמרה טהורה אני מהו א"ל אף בזו אם נתנה אמתלא לדבריה נאמנת: *)תנא מיניה מ' זמנין ואפ"ה לא עביד שמואל עובדא בנפשיה פי' פעם אחת אמרה לו אשתו כן ונתנה אמתלא לדבריה ופירש ממנ' עד שטבלה: ת"ר שנים אומרים מת ושנים אומרים לא מת שנים אומרים נתגרשה ושנים אומרים לא נתגרשה ה"ז ל"ת ואם נשאת לא תצא מכדי תרי ותרי נינהו הבא עליה באשם תלוי קאי פי' בא על ספק כרת אר"ש כגון שנשאת לאחד מעדיה פי' שאמרו מת שאין אשם תלוי אלא למי שלבו נוקפו אבל זה אומר ברי לו אבל לאיניש דעלמא תצא ואע"ג דתנן בפ"ב דיבמות מת לא ישא את אשתו דוקא בחד אבל בתרי ליכא למיחש כדאוקימנא התם דתרי לא חשידי. היא גופה באשם תלוי קימא באומרת ברי לי פי' שבאתה גם היא משם ואומרת מת בעלי ואם על העדים סמכה תצא ור"מ ב"י פליג ואמר שאם באו עדי האוסרים תחלה ואח"כ נשאת ואפילו לאחד מעדיה ואע"ג דאמרה ברי לי תצא עיין בהאשה רבה. אר"י ב' אומרים מת וב' אומרים לא מת ה"ז לא תנשא ואם נשאת ל"ת ב' אומרים נתגרשה וב' אומרים לא נתגרשה ה"ז לא תנשא ואם נשאת תצא מ"ש רישא ומ"ש סיפא ואוקמי' רבא דראה ר"י דברי ר' מנחם בר"י בגירושין ולא ראה דבריו במיתה מ"ש מיתה אינה יכולה להכחישתו פי' אם יבא בעלה א"י לומר לו מת אתה הלכך אי לא דברי לה שמת מירתתא ולא מינסבא עד דדייקא שפיר דחיישי לקלקולא גירושין יכולה להכחישתו פי' אם יבא ויאמר לא גרשתיך היא תאמר גרשתני הלכך אי שרית לה סמכא אדעתא ומינסבא ע"פ עדות הללו מספק

*) שייך לע"ב

גליון הש"ס גמ' למה לי קרא סברא. ב"ק מו ע"ב נדה כה ע"א:

אֲמַתְלָא לִדְבָרֶיהָ — נֶאֱמֶנֶת. תָּנָא *מִינֵּיהּ אַרְבָּעִים זִימְנִין, וַאפ"ה לָא עֲבַד שְׁמוּאֵל עוּבְדָא בְּנַפְשֵׁיהּ. *ת"ר: שְׁנַיִם אוֹמְרִים: "מֵת", וּשְׁנַיִם אוֹמְרִים: "לֹא מֵת", שְׁנַיִם אוֹמְרִים: "נִתְגָּרְשָׁה", וּשְׁנַיִם אוֹמְרִים: "לֹא נִתְגָּרְשָׁה" — הֲרֵי זוֹ לֹא תִּנָּשֵׂא, וְאִם נִשֵּׂאת — לֹא תֵּצֵא. רַבִּי מְנַחֵם בַּר יוֹסֵי אוֹמֵר: תֵּצֵא. אָמַר רַבִּי מְנַחֵם בַּר יוֹסֵי: אֵימָתַי אֲנִי אוֹמֵר תֵּצֵא — בִּזְמַן שֶׁבָּאוּ עֵדִים וְאח"כ נִשֵּׂאת, אֲבָל נִשֵּׂאת וְאח"כ בָּאוּ עֵדִים — לֹא תֵּצֵא. *מִכְּדִי תְּרֵי וּתְרֵי נִינְהוּ, הַבָּא עָלֶיהָ בְּאָשָׁם תָּלוּי קָאֵי! א"ר שֵׁשֶׁת: כְּגוֹן [א]שֶׁנִּשֵּׂאת לְאֶחָד מֵעֵדֶיהָ. הִיא גּוּפָהּ בְּאָשָׁם תָּלוּי קַיְימָא! [ב]בְּאוֹמֶרֶת: "בָּרִי לִי". אָמַר רַבִּי יוֹחָנָן: [ג]שְׁנַיִם אוֹמְרִים: "מֵת", וּשְׁנַיִם אוֹמְרִים: "לֹא מֵת" — הֲרֵי זוֹ לֹא תִּנָּשֵׂא, וְאִם נִשֵּׂאת לֹא תֵּצֵא. [ד]שְׁנַיִם אוֹמְרִים: "נִתְגָּרְשָׁה", וּשְׁנַיִם אוֹמְרִים: "לֹא נִתְגָּרְשָׁה" — הֲרֵי זוֹ לֹא תִּנָּשֵׂא, וְאִם נִשֵּׂאת — תֵּצֵא. מַאי שְׁנָא רֵישָׁא וּמַאי שְׁנָא סֵיפָא? אָמַר אַבַּיֵי: תַּרְגְּמָהּ בְּעֵד אֶחָד; [ה]עֵד אֶחָד אוֹמֵר: "מֵת" — הֵימְנוּהוּ רַבָּנַן כְּבֵי תְרֵי, וְכִדְעוּלָּא. דְּאָמַר עוּלָּא: כָּל מָקוֹם *שֶׁהֶאֱמִינָה תּוֹרָה עֵד אֶחָד — הֲרֵי כָּאן שְׁנַיִם. וְהַאי דְּקָאָמַר "לֹא מֵת" — הֲוָה לֵיהּ חַד, וְאֵין דְּבָרָיו שֶׁל אֶחָד בִּמְקוֹם שְׁנַיִם. אִי הָכִי אֲפִי' לְכַתְּחִלָּה נָמֵי! מִשּׁוּם דְּרַב אַסִי, דְּא"ר אַסִי: *°"הָסֵר מִמְּךָ עִקְּשׁוּת פֶּה וּלְזוּת שְׂפָתַיִם הַרְחֵק מִמֶּךָּ". סֵיפָא, [ו]עֵד אֶחָד אוֹמֵר "נִתְגָּרְשָׁה" וְעֵד אֶחָד אוֹמֵר "לֹא נִתְגָּרְשָׁה" — תַּרְוַיְיהוּ בְּאֵשֶׁת אִישׁ קָמַסְהֲדֵי, וְהַאי דְּקָאָמַר "נִתְגָּרְשָׁה" — הֲוָה לֵיהּ חַד, וְאֵין דְּבָרָיו שֶׁל אֶחָד בִּמְקוֹם שְׁנַיִם. רָבָא אָמַר: לְעוֹלָם תְּרֵי וּתְרֵי נִינְהוּ, וְרָאָה ר' יוֹחָנָן דְּבָרָיו שֶׁל ר' מְנַחֵם בַּר יוֹסֵי בְּגֵרוּשִׁין, וְלֹא רָאָה בְּמִיתָה. מ"ט? מִיתָה — אֵינָהּ יְכוֹלָה מַכְחַשְׁתּוֹ, גֵּרוּשִׁין — יְכוֹלָה מַכְחַשְׁתּוֹ. וּמִי חֲצִיפָה כּוּלֵּי הַאי? וְהָאָמַר רַב הַמְנוּנָא: *[ז]הָאִשָּׁה שֶׁאָמְרָה לְבַעְלָהּ "גֵּרַשְׁתַּנִי" — נֶאֱמֶנֶת, חֲזָקָה, אֵין אִשָּׁה מְעִיזָּה פָּנֶיהָ בִּפְנֵי בַּעְלָהּ! הָנֵי מִילֵּי — הֵיכָא דְּלֵיכָּא עֵדִים דְּקָא מְסַיְּיעֵי לָהּ, [ח]אֲבָל הֵיכָא דְּאִיכָּא עֵדִים דְּקָא מְסַיְּיעֵי לָהּ — מְעִיזָּה וּמְעִיזָּה. רַב אַסִי אָמַר, כְּגוֹן דְּאָמְרִי עֵדִים: "עַכְשָׁיו מֵת" "עַכְשָׁיו גֵּירְשָׁהּ". מִיתָה — לֵיכָּא לְבֵרוּרָה, [ט]גֵּירוּשִׁין — אִיכָּא לְבֵרוּרָה. דְּאָמְרִינַן לָהּ: אִם אִיתָא דְּהָכִי הֲוָה — אַחְזִי לַן גִּיטֵּיךְ. תָּנוּ רַבָּנַן: שְׁנַיִם אוֹמְרִים: "נִתְקַדְּשָׁה" וּשְׁנַיִם אוֹמְרִים: "לֹא נִתְקַדְּשָׁה" — הֲרֵי זוֹ לֹא תִּנָּשֵׂא, וְאִם נִשֵּׂאת — לֹא תֵּצֵא. שְׁנַיִם אוֹמְרִים: "נִתְגָּרְשָׁה" וּשְׁנַיִם אוֹמְרִים: "לֹא נִתְגָּרְשָׁה" — הֲרֵי זוֹ לֹא תִּנָּשֵׂא, וְאִם נִשֵּׂאת — תֵּצֵא. מַאי

(תורה אור: משלי ד)

רש"י

*אֲמַתְלָא. מָשָׁל וְטַעַם לָמָּה אָמְרָה תְּחִלָּה מְקוּדֶּשֶׁת אֲנִי. **אם נתנה** אמתלא. הוֹאִיל וְנָתְנָה אֲמַתְלָא — נֶאֱמֶנֶת. **אמרה** טמאה אני. אָמְרָה לְבַעְלָהּ: נִדָּה אֲנִי. **טהורה אני.** לֹא הָיִיתִי נִדָּה. **לא עבד שמואל עובדא בנפשיה.** פַּעַם אַחַת אָמְרָה לוֹ אִשְׁתּוֹ כֵּן, וְנָתְנָה אֲמַתְלָא לִדְבָרֶיהָ — וּפֵירַשׁ הֵימֶנָּה עַד שֶׁטָּבְלָה. **לא תצא.** וּלְקַמֵּיהּ פָּרֵיךְ: תְּרֵי וּתְרֵי נִינְהוּ! **שֶׁבָּאוּ עדים.** שֶׁאָמְרוּ לֹא מֵת. **באשם תלוי.** דְּאַ עַל סְפֵק כָּרֵת. **לאחד מעדיה.** שֶׁאָמְרוּ מֵת. דְּאֵין אָשָׁם תָּלוּי אֶלָּא לְמִי שֶׁלִּבּוֹ נוֹקְפוֹ, וְזֶה אוֹמֵר בָּרִי לִי. **באומרת ברי לי.** אֵין לִבִּי נוֹקְפִי, שֶׁבָּרִי לִי אִילּוּ הָיָה קַיָּים — הָיָה בָּא. **תרגמה.** לְהָא דְּר' יוֹחָנָן. **בעד אחד.** וְלָאו שְׁנַיִם אִיתְמַר, אֶלָּא עֵד אוֹמֵר כו' וְעֵד אוֹמֵר כו'. **הימנוהו רבנן כבתרי.** לוֹמַר מֵת, כִּדְאָמְרִינַן בִּיבָמוֹת בְּ"הָאִשָּׁה": מִתּוֹךְ חוֹמֶר שֶׁהֶחְמַרְתָּ עָלֶיהָ בְּסוֹפָהּ — הֵקַלְתָּ עָלֶיהָ בִּתְחִלָּתָהּ. **אפי' לכתחלה** נמי. תִּינָּשֵׂא. **דרב אסי.** בִּיבָמוֹת, בְּפֶ' שֵׁנִי. **תרוייהו באשת איש קא מסהדי.** שְׁנֵיהֶן מְעִידִין שֶׁאֵשֶׁת אִישׁ הָיְתָה. **מיתה** אֵינָהּ יְכוֹלָה מַכְחַשְׁתּוֹ. אִם יָבֹא בַּעְלָהּ אֵינָהּ יְכוֹלָה לוֹמַר "מֵת אַתָּה", הִלְכָּךְ אִי לָאו דְּבָרִי לָהּ שֶׁמֵּת — מִירְתָּתָא וְלָא מִינַּסְבָא. **גירושין יכולה מכחשתו.** אִם יָבֹא וְיֹאמַר "לֹא גֵּירַשְׁתִּיךְ", הִיא תֹּאמַר "גֵּירַשְׁתַּנִי". הִלְכָּךְ, אִי שָׁרֵית לָהּ — סָמְכָה אַהַכְחָשָׁה, וּמִינַּסְבָא עַל פִּי עֵדִים הַלָּלוּ מִסָּפֵק, וְלָא מִירְתָּתָא לְמֵידַק שַׁפִּיר. **עכשיו** מת. הַיּוֹם. **ליכא לבירורה.** אִם אָמְרוּ טָבַע בַּמַּיִם, אוֹ אֲכָלוֹ אֲרִי — אֵין אָנוּ יְכוֹלִין לְבָרֵר הַדְּבָרִים. הִלְכָּךְ, לְכַתְּחִלָּה לֹא תִּינָּשֵׂא, וְאִם נִיסֵּת — לֹא תֵּצֵא, כְּרַבָּנַן, וּכְשֶׁנִּיסֵּת לְאֶחָד מֵעֵדֶיהָ. **אחוי גיטיך.** דִּבְשַׁעְתָּא פּוּרְתָּא לָא מְהֵימְנָא לְמֵימַר אִירְכַּס לִי. **הרי זו לא תנשא.** לְאַחֵר.

תרוייהו

תוספות

***חזרה** ואמרה טהורה אני מהו. פירוש: מועיל אמתלא או לא? אבל אין לפרש "מהו", אם צריכה אמתלא או לא, מדקאמר אף בזו אם נתנה כו'. **ואפילו** הכי לא עבד שמואל עובדא בנפשיה. ר"ח הביא ירושלמי: שמואל בעא לאזדקוקי לאתתיה, אמרה ליה: "טמאה אני", ולמחר אמרה: "טהורה אני", אמר לה: אתמול טמאה, יומא דין טהורה?! אמרה ליה: אתמול לא הוות בי חילא כי ההיא שעתא. אתא שאיל לרב, אמר ליה: אם נתנה אמתלא לדבריה — נאמנת.

הבא עליה באשם תלוי קאי. תימה: דבחטאת קאי, דהא מסקינן בפרק "ד' אחים" (יבמות דף לא. ושם) דתרי ותרי — ספיקא דרבנן, ומדאורייתא אוקמה אחזקה. ומאי משני נמי כשניסת לאחד מעדיה, הא עד נמי בחנק קאי. דאוקמה אחזקה! ואומר *ר"ת: דחזקה דאשה דייקא ומנסבא מרעה לה להך חזקה. דמהאי טעמא נמי שרינן לה כי ליכא עדים כלל, *אע"פ שהיא בחזקת אשת איש*). **באשם** תלוי. אפי' למאן דבעי חתיכה אחת משתי חתיכות — הכא לא בעינן שתי חתיכות. דמאן דמפרש בפרק "ספק אכל" (כריתות דף יז: ושם) טעמא דבעינן חתיכה משתי חתיכות — משום דאפשר לברר איסורו. פי': אפשר לברר על ידי בקי, שיכיר חתיכה הנשארת, אם חלב היא אם שומן היא. הכא נמי — אפשר לברר ע"י הזמה. ולמאן דמפרש משום דבשתי חתיכות אחת של חלב ואחת של שומן איקבע איסורא — ה"נ איקבע איסורא. שהיתה בחזקת אשת איש. אי נמי: לאו אשם תלוי ממש קאמר, אלא כלומר באיסור אשם תלוי. **כגון** שניסת לאחד מעדיה. והא דתנן בפ' שני דיבמות (דף כה. ושם): "הרגנוהו" — לא ישא את אשתו. לא ששנים מעידין כן, דבשום מקום אין שנים חשודין, כדמוכח לקמן, דאפילו למאן דחייש לגומלין, אם שנים מעידין על זה ושנים על זה — נאמנין. וכן מוכח נמי בפ"ב דיבמות (ג"ז שם:) דתנן התם: מיאנה או שחלצה בפניו — ישאנה, מפני שהוא ב"ד. ודייק בגמרא: טעמא דב"ד, הא בתרי — לא, מאי שנא מהא דתנן: עדים החתומים על שדה מקח או על גט אשה — לא חשו חכמים לדבר זה? היא גופה קמשמע לן, לאפוקי ממ"ד מיאון בשנים. אלא כלומר: שהרגו עם אנשים הרבה. **אי** הכי לכתחלה נמי. ומהא דתנן ב"האשה שלום" (יבמות דף קיז: ושם): עד אחד אומר מת ועד אחד אומר לא מת — הרי זו לא תנשא, ליכא לאקשויי לעולא. דהתם איירי בבת אחת, ואפילו אם ניסת תצא. ועולא איירי בזה אחר זה, כשבא עד אחד ואמר "מת" התירוה, ואח"כ בא אחר ואמר "לא מת", אם נשאת — לא תצא, אבל לכתחלה לא תנשא, משום דרב אסי, כדמסיק. ומרישא דהתם יש להוכיח שיש חילוק בין בבת אחת בין בזה אחר זה, דקתני: עד אחד אומר "מת" וניסת, ובא אחר ואמר "לא מת" — לא תצא. ומפרש בגמרא: דלא ניסת ממש, אלא התירוה לינשא אע"פ שלא ניסת, ולא תצא — היינו מהתירה הראשון. משמע: דווקא התירוה קודם שבא העד ואמר "לא מת", הא בא קודם שהתירוה — לא. ול"ע בפ' "מי שקינא" (סוטה דף לא:) דמשמע דאיירי עולא בכל ענין, בין בב"א בין בזה אחר זה. דתנן התם: עד אחד אומר "נטמאת" ועד אחד אומר "לא נטמאת" — היתה שותה. ודייק בגמ': טעמא דהאי מכחיש, אבל לא מכחיש — עד אחד נאמן, מנא ה"מ כו'. ופריך: כיון דמדאורייתא עד אחד נאמן — אידך היכי מצי מכחיש ליה? והאמר עולא: כל מקום שהאמינה כו'. אלא אמר עולא: תני לא היתה שותה, ור' חייא אומר: היתה שותה. לר' חייא קשיא דעולא? לא קשיא, כאן — בבת אחת, כאן — בזה אחר זה. משמע דעולא נמי איירי בבת אחת! ולכך צריך להגיה ולא משני כדמשני ר' חייא. ומיהו, איכא למימר דעולא לא מיירי אלא בזה אחר זה, אלא שנראה לו דוחק להעמיד המשנה בבת אחת, משום דמשמע ליה דמיירי בזה אחר זה. ועוד אומר ר"י: דאפילו איירי לעולא בכל ענין — הני מילי התם, דמדאורייתא עד אחד מהימן בסוטה, כדנפקא ליה התם מ"ועד אין בה", אבל הכא גבי אשה, דלא מהימן אלא מדרבנן — לא חשיב כשנים אלא בזה אחר זה. ואע"ג דיש חילוק בין דאורייתא לרבנן — מייתי מדעולא, דנראה לו דחשיב כשנים בזה אחר זה בדרבנן כמו בבת אחת בדאורייתא.

משום דרב אסי הסר ממך עקשות פה. פסוק הוא, אלא דרב אסי רגיל להביאו. וא"ת: והא דתנן ב"האשה שלום" (יבמות דף קיז: ושם): עד אחד אומר "מת" וניסת, ובא עד אחד ואמר "לא מת" — לא תצא. ופריך בגמרא: טעמא דניסת, הא לא ניסת — לא תנשא. והאמר עולא: כל מקום כו', ומאי פריך? והא עולא לא קאמר אלא בדיעבד, אבל לכתחלה מודה דלא תנשא, משום דרב אסי! ואומר ר"י: דהתם דייק: טעמא — דניסת, הא אם לא נשאת — לא תנשא, ואם נשאת — תצא. דהכי משמע מתניתין; דוקא נשאת ואחר כך בא העד לא תצא, הא בא העד קודם שנשאת ואחר כך ניסת — תצא, משום הכי פריך מדעולא. ואם תאמר: והיכי משני התם דה"ק: עד אחד אומר "מת" והתירוה לינשא, ובא אחר ואמר "לא מת" — לא תצא מהתירה הראשון, משמע ותנשא לכתחלה? וי"ל: דודאי לכתחלה לא תנשא, ולא תצא מהתירה הראשון — דלענין דאם נישאת לא תצא.

[תרווייהו באשת איש קמסהדי. תימה: דמה לנו לאותו עד שאומר לא נתגרשה? בלא איהו נמי תצא, דאין דבר שבערוה פחות משנים! דהא ליכא למימר שלא היינו יודעים שהיא א"א כי אם על פיהם, דא"כ להימניה להאי דאמר מגורשת, במיגו דאי בעי שתק. וי"ל: דאין זה מיגו, דשמא רוצה להעיד כדי לפוסלה מן הכהונה. ת"י].

*) [וע"ע תוס' לקמן כו: ד"ה אנן]

מאי

עין משפט נר מצוה

[שייך לע"א]

סה א ב ג מיי' פי"ב מהל' גירושין הל' כג טוש"ע אה"ע סימן יז סעיף מב:

סו ד מיי' שם הלכה ח טוש"ע אה"ע סימן קנב סעיף ג:

סז ה מיי' שם הלכה יח טוש"ע אה"ע סימן יז סעיף לז:

סח ו מיי' שם הלכה ט טוש"ע אה"ע סימן קנב סעיף ה:

[ביבמות פח: כתבו תוס' דבר זה בשם ר"י וע"ע תוס' ב"ב לב. ד"ה אנן]

ובשנים אומרים נתגרשה נמי דייקא כי ירלא שלא יוזמו עדיה אבל חזקה דאין אשה מעיזה ליכא כיון דאיכא עדים דקא מסייעי לה. ת"י עה"ג

סט ז מיי' שם הלכה ז ופ"ד מהל' איסורי ביאה הלכה יג סמג עשין סח טוש"ע אה"ע סימן יז סעיף ב:

ע ח ט מיי' פי"ב מהל' גירושין הל' ו ז טוש"ע אה"ע סי' קנב סעיף ב:

תוספות רי"ד

מספק ולא מירתתא למידק שפיר ומי מחצפי בי' והאמר ר"ה האשה שאמרה לבעלה גרשתני נאמנת דחזקתה אין אשה מעיזה פניה בפני בעלה ה"מ היכא דליכא עדים דמסייע לה אבל היכא דאיכא עדים דמסייע לה מעיזה ומעיזה ומדמקשינן ממילתא דר"ה ש"מ דהכי הל' שאין התלמוד מקשה אלא מהל' פסוקה כך העמדנו נמי בגיטין בריש פ' התקבל: ר"א אמר דאמרו עדים עכשיו מת פי' היום מת עכשיו גירשה מיתה ליכא לברורי פי' אם אמרו טבע בים או אכלו ארי אין אנו יכולים לברר הדברים הלכך לכתחלה לא תנשא מיד דהא צריכה להמתין שלשה חדשים ואם נשאת לא תצא כרבנן וכשנשאת לאחד מעידיה. גירושין איכא לברורינהו דאמרי לה אי איתא דהכי הוא אחוי גיטך פי' ולא תנשא מיד דהא צריכה להמתין ג' חדשים אלא כגון שהמתינה ג' חדשים ונשאת ואפ"ה כיון שעדים העידו שעכשיו גירשה אמרינן לה אי איתא כדאמרת הוה לך לאחזי גיטא דבשעתא פורתא לא מהימנא למימר אירכס לי א"ו שקרא מסהדי והני דאמרו לא גירשך הם נאמנים והלכך תצא ודוקא כשאמרו עכשיו גירשך דמוכחא מילתא דמשקרי אבל אם מעידים שגירשה זה כמה ימים לא תצא כרבנן וליתא לר' מנחם בר"י לא במיתה ולא בגירושין והלכה כר"א דהוא בתרא: ת"ר ב' אומרים נתקדשה וב' אומרים לא נתקדשה ה"ז ל"ת ואם נשאת ל"ת

מסורת הש"ס

[שייך לע"א עד ד"ה לא עבד שמואל כו']

[לקמן ג. וש"נ]

יבמות פח: כ"ב לא:

[שם ביבמות]

יבמות פח: קיז: סוטה לא: מז.

יבמות כד:

שם קטז. נדרים לא. גיטין סד: פט:

תרוייהו בפנויה קמסהדי. לדברי שניהם עד עכשיו בחזקת פנויה היתה, [קודם שנתקדשה]. איפוך. ברישא תני: אם ניסת – תלא, וסיפא: אם ניסת – לא תלא. דמגרשי בצנעא. ואפילו הכי, לכתחלה לא תנשא, משום לזות שפתים. ארישא. אם משניסת באו עדים שהיתה אשת איש, והיא ניסת על פי עצמה, שאמרה "גרושה אני". אסיפא. א"נשביתי וטהורה אני" והתירוה לינשא, ואח"כ באו עדים שנשבית. בשבויה הקילו. דאשה בעלמא הוא דאיכא, שמא נבעלה לגוי ונפסלה לכהונה. דרב המנונא. דאמר: האשה שאמרה לבעלה "גירשתני" – נאמנת. הלכך, הא דאמרה "גרושה אני" – מהימנא. ויש לי עדים. שהיו עמי תמיד, שלא נתייחדתי עם גוי. ואח"כ באו עדים. שנשבית. דהשתא לאו הפה שאסר הוא – אפי' הכי לא תלא. אפי' יש לה כמה בנים. מן הכהן הזה שנשאה. דאתיין לנהרדעא. להפדותן. אוקמינהו לשבויינהו אבראי. שלא יבואו לפני ב"ד, ולא ידעו ב"ד שהן שבויות אלא ע"פ עצמן, ויתירום. בנן דמוריין אינון. בנות אדם גדול ובעל הוראה הוא, שידעו לעשות כן. לרב שמן. כהן היה. איטפל בקרובותיך. שא אחת מהן, שהן קרובותיך. והא איכא סהדי במדינת הים. שראו שנשבו, ודלמא אתו לקמן למחר ולזומא אותן, לאסר שתנשא. השתא מיהא לא איתנהו. קודם נישואין, ומשום דלמא אתו לא אסרינן לה השתא. עדים בצד אסתן. בלד לפון ["מצפון זהב יאתה" (איוב לז) מתרגם: מדאיסתנא]. ותאסר. בתמיה. הא [לא] אתו קודם נישואין.

מתני'

תורה אור

מאי שנא רישא ומאי שנא סיפא? אמר אביי: תרגמה בעד אחד; [א] עד אחד אומר "נתקדשה" ועד אחד אומר "לא נתקדשה" – תרוייהו בפנויה קמסהדי, והאי דקאמר "נתקדשה" – הוה ליה חד ואין דבריו של אחד במקום שנים. סיפא, עד אחד אומר "נתגרשה" ועד אחד אומר "לא נתגרשה" – תרוייהו באשת איש קמסהדי, והאי דקאמר "נתגרשה" – הוה ליה חד, ואין דבריו של אחד במקום שנים. *רב אשי אמר: לעולם תרי ותרי, ואיפוך, [ב] שנים אומרים "ראינוה שנתקדשה", ושנים אומרים "לא ראינוה שנתקדשה" – הרי זו לא תנשא, ואם נשאת – תצא. פשיטא! *"לא ראינוה" אינה ראיה! לא צריכא, דדיירי בחצר אחד. מהו דתימא: אם איתא דנתקדשה – קלא אית לה למילתא, קא משמע לן: דעבדי אינשי דמקדשי בצנעא. סיפא, [ג] שנים אומרים "ראינוה שנתגרשה", ושנים אומרים "לא ראינוה שנתגרשה" – הרי זו לא תנשא, ואם נשאת – לא תצא. מאי קמ"ל – אע"ג דדיירי בחצר אחד. היינו הך! מהו דתימא: גבי קדושין הוא דעבידי אינשי דמקדשי בצנעא, אבל גבי גירושין, אם איתא דאיגרשא – קלא אית לה למילתא, קמ"ל דעבידי אינשי דמקדשי ודמגרשי בצנעא.§ ואם משנשאת באו עדים לא תצא כו'.§ רבי אושעיא *מתני לה ארישא, רבה בר אבין מתני לה אסיפא. מאן דמתני לה ארישא – כ"ש אסיפא, *דבשבויה הקילו. ומאן דמתני לה אסיפא, [ד] אבל ארישא – לא. לימא בדרב המנונא קמיפלגי, דמאן דמתני לה ארישא – אית ליה דרב המנונא, ומאן דמתני לה אסיפא – לית ליה דרב המנונא? לא, דכולי עלמא אית להו דרב המנונא. והכא בהא קמיפלגי; דמר סבר: כי איתמר דרב המנונא – בפניו, [ה] אבל שלא בפניו – מעיזה, ומר סבר: שלא בפניו נמי אינה מעיזה.§ ואם משנשאת באו עדים וכו'.§ אמר אבוה דשמואל: לא נשאת נשאת ממש, אלא [ו] כיון שהתירוה לינשא, אע"פ שלא נשאת. והא "לא תצא" קתני! לא תצא מהתירה הראשון. *ת"ר: אמרה [ז] "נשביתי וטהורה אני ויש לי עדים שטהורה אני". אין אומרים: נמתין עד שיבאו עדים, אלא מתירין אותה מיד. התירוה לינשא, ואחר כך באו עדים, ואמרו "לא ידענו" – הרי זו לא תצא. [ח] ואם באו עדי טומאה, אפי' יש לה כמה בנים – תצא. הנך שבוייתא דאתיין לנהרדעא. אותיב אבוה דשמואל נטורי בהדייהו. א"ל שמואל: ועד האידנא מאן נטרינהו? א"ל: אילו בנתך הוון, מי הוית מזלזל בהו כולי האי?! הואי °"כשגגה שיוצא מלפני השליט" ואישתביין בנתיה דמר שמואל, ואסקינהו לארעא דישראל. אוקמן לשבויינהו מאבראי, ועיילי לבי מדרשא דר' חנינא. הא אמרה: "נשביתי וטהורה אני", והא אמרה: "נשביתי וטהורה אני". °שרינהו. סוף עול אתו שבוינהו. אמר רבי חנינא: [ט] בנן דמוריין אינון. איגלאי מילתא דבנתיה דמר שמואל הוון. אמר ליה רבי חנינא לרב שמן בר אבא: פוק איטפל בקרובותיך – אמר ליה לרבי חנינא: והאיכא עדים במדינת הים! השתא מיהת ליתנהו קמן, עדים בצד *אסתן ותיאסר?! טעמא – דלא אתו עדים, הא אתו עדים מיתסרא? והאמר אבוה דשמואל: כיון שהתירוה לינשא – אף על פי שלא נשאת! אמר רב אשי: עדי טומאה איתמר.§

מתני'

מאי שנא רישא ומאי שנא סיפא. ואם תאמר: שנא ושנא, דרישא אית לן לאוקמה בחזקת פנויה, וסיפא בחזקת אשת איש! ויש לומר: דברישא, אע"ג דאית לן לאוקמה בחזקת פנויה – מ"מ תרי ותרי ספיקא דרבנן היא, כדמוכח בפרק "ד' אחין" (יבמות דף לא. ושם) והוה לן למימר תלא מדרבנן. וי"מ: כיון דלא מפליג בין באו עדים עד שלא ניסת – לבאו עדים משניסת – ש"מ דלאו רבי מנחם בר יוסי היא אלא רבנן, א"כ סיפא נמי אמאי תלא – הא שמעינן להו דאמרי לא תלא.

תרוייהו בפנויה קמסהדי. לא הוה לריך להא, דאפי' ליכא אלא ההוא דאמר נתקדשה – לא תלא, דאין דבר שבערוה פחות משנים. אבל תימה: אמאי לא תנשא לכתחלה? דהוה לן לאוקמה אחזקה! וי"ל: כגון שאנו יודעים שזרק לה קדושין, ומספקא לן אי קרוב לו או קרוב לה. והני ב' סהדי, חד אמר: קרוב לו, וחד אמר: קרוב לה, דכיון דודאי זרק לה הקדושין – לית לן למימר אוקמה אחזקה להתירה לכתחילה. אי נמי: כגון שהיו נרות דולקות ומטות מולעות, שהיה עומד לקדש, כדאמר בסוף "המגרש" (גיטין פט.), ועד אחד אומר נתקדשה ועד אחד אומר לא נתקדשה באותה שעה.

מאן דמתני לה ארישא כל שכן אסיפא. וא"ת: מנא ליה? דלמא אסיפא לא מלי קאי, דאפי' באו עדים ואחר כך נשאת – לא תלא! ולמאי דמפרש בסמוך לא ניסת ניסת ממש – אתי שפיר. אית ליה דרב המנונא. אע"ג °דרב המנונא איירי בפניו, מ"מ לענין ניסת ואח"כ באו עדים מהני שלא בפניו. לא תצא מהיתרה הראשון. פירוש: ותנשא [לכתחלה], דלא שייך לזות שפתים כלל. אבל אין לפרש כי ההיא דיבמות דלא תלא מהיתרה הראשון, לענין דאם נשאת לא תלא, אבל לכתחלה לא תינשא – כדמשמע גבי בנתיה דמר שמואל בסמוך שהתירן *לכתחילה.

באו עדים לא תצא. פירוש: לא תלא מהיתרה הראשון.

עד האידנא מאן נטרינהו. פי': דכבר נאסרו. והא איכא עדים במדינת הים. אין לפרש דלמא איכא עדים במדינת הים – דאם כן תיקשי ליה נמי אמתניתין. דקתני "נשביתי וטהורה אני" – נאמנת. ואמאי? דלמא איכא עדים! אלא הכי פירושה: הא יצא קול דאיכא עדים במדינת הים שיודעים שנשבית. ומיהו קשה לרשב"א: דהיכי סלקא דעתיה השתא דעדים היינו עדי שבויה – דא"כ מה הוה לריך למימר הא איכא עדים במדינת הים? הוה ליה למימר: הא איכא עדים קמן, דהא איכא שבויינהוא! עדי טומאה איתמר. והא איכא עדים במדינת הים דפריך לעיל – פירוש: והא יצא קול דאיכא התם עדי טומאה, כדפירשתי. הקשה ר"ת: בפרק קמא דקידושין (דף יב.) גבי ההוא גברא דקדיש באבנא דכוחלא, ויתיב רב חסדא וקא מעיין אי אית בה שוה פרוטה אי לא, ומסיק: לאו היינו דר' חנינא דאמר: עדים בלד אסתן ותאסר? וקאמר: אביי ורבא לא סבירא להו הא דרב חסדא, אם הקילו בשבויה – נקל באשת איש? והשתא למאי דמסיק דעדי טומאה איתמר, מה לי עדי שבויה מה לי עדי אשת איש? ורש"י *פירש שם: אם הקילו בשבויה דאיסור לאו. וקשה לרבינו תם: דבשבויה נמי איכא איסור סקילה, אם נשאת לכהן שישמש בנה על גבי מזבח בשבת. ומיהו, אית ספרים דגרסי התם: אם הקילו בשבויה – דמנוולה נפשה באפי שבויה כו', פירוש: ולא שכיח כולי האי שנטמאה, נקל באשת איש דשכיח דידעי אם אית בה שוה פרוטה. ובלאו הך גירסא איכא למימר דלא שכיח שיהו עדי טומאה, אבל עדים שידעו שוה פרוטה – שכיחנ).

א) [וי"ל דמחמת השבאים לא איתסרו דהא אינהו אתו בתר דשרינהו אבל הכא מחמת שבא הקול מקמי שריותא דידהו איכא למסרינהו וה"פ טעמא דלא אתו עדים הא אתו עדים מיתסרו כיון שנתגלה הקול שיש עדים מלפני היתר. ת"י עה"ג]. ב) [ולמאי דס"ד מעיקרא לעדי שבויה ניחא דהוי ספק ספיקא ספק אם נשבית אם לאו ואת"ל נשבית ספק לא נטמאה ובאשת איש ליכא אלא חדא ספיקא. ת"י עה"ג].

[לכתחלה דפריך טעמא דליכא עדים הא איכא עדים מתסרא ומאי פריך אי מתסרא לכתחלה. ת"י עה"ג]

עא א מיי' פ"ט מהל' איסורי ביאה הלכה לא טוש"ע אה"ע סימן מז סעיף ג:
עב ב מיי' שם הלכה ל טוש"ע שם סעיף ה:
עג ג מיי' פי"ב מהל' גירושין הלכה ח טוש"ע שם סימן קנב סעיף ז:
עד ד מיי' שם הלכה א טור טוש"ע שם סעיף ו:
עה ה מיי' שם הלכה ד טוש"ע שם סימן יז סעיף ב:
עו ו מיי' פי"ח מהל' איסורי ביאה הלכ' כב טוש"ע שם סי' ז סעיף [illegible]:
עז ז מיי' שם הלכה כג טור טוש"ע שם סעי' [illegible]:
עח ח ט מיי' שם טור טוש"ע שם סעיף ו:

ס"א רב אסי

[זבחים קג:]

גליון הש"ס

גמ' שריינהו. סוף עול אתו שבוינהו. עיין ב"ב קמנט ע"א תד"ה רב מרי. שבת קנב ע"א תד"ה ואמרי לה: תוס' ד"ה אית ליה. אע"ג דרב המנונא איירי בפניו. עיין יבמות קטז ע"ב תד"ה באותה שעה.

[לקמן כד.]

[לקמן כו: נא. קדושין יב: ב"ק קיד:]

[תוס' פ"ב]

[קהלת י]

קדושין יב: ב"ב קלה.

[לפנינו שם בכת"י לא נמצא ועי' תוס' שם ד"ה אם הקילו וכו' בתבו לבר זה בשם יש מפרשים]

תוספות רי"ד

מ"ש רישא ומ"ש סיפא פי' שאין לומר טעמא דרישא משום דאמרינן אוקי תרי לבהדי תרי ואוקי איתתא (אחזקה) [בחזקת פנויה] דתרי ותרי הן ספיקא דאורייתא ובספיקא דאורייתא לא אזלינן בתר חזקה אלא הבא עליה באשם תלוי קאי אמר (ר"פ) [אביי] תרגמה בע"א. ע"א אומר נתקדשה וע"א אומר לא נתקדשה תרוייהו בפנויה קמסהדי והאי דאמר נתקדשה הו"ל חד ואין דבריו של א' במקום ב'. ע"א אומר נתגרשה וע"א אומר לא נתגרשה תרוייהו באשת איש קמסהדי והאי דאמר נתגרשה הו"ל חד ואין דבריו של א' במקום שנים. ופי' לאו במוחזקת לפנינו שהיא א"א מיירי. דא"כ מה צורך להכחשת העד שאומר לא נתגרשה בלא הכחשתו נמי אינו נאמן ע"א בגירושין ואפי' לאביי דאמר ע"א נאמן באיסורין ואפילו באשה ה"מ לאסור כגון אשתו זינתה בע"א בפ' האומר [קדושין סו ע"ש] דאביי אמר ע"א נאמן בכל איסורין שבתורה ורבא אמר אין דבר שבערוה פחות משנים. ודוקא לאיסור היה אומר אביי דע"א נאמן אבל אשה שהוחזקה בא"א אין מי שיאמר שיהא ע"א נאמן לומר נתגרשה ולהוציאה מחזקת א"א דדוקא במת בעלך האמינו חכמים ע"א משום דמילתא דעבידי לגלויי לא משקרא והיא גופא דייקא ומנסבא. ומתוך חומר שהחמרת עליה בסופה הקלת עליה מתחלתה אבל בגירושין לא מהימן. עיין בהאשה רבה. ולא מתוקמא אלא באשה הבאה ממדה"י שלא ידענו מי היא ובאים אלה השנים ומעידים עליה כי א"א היתה אלא שא' אומר נתגרשה ואחד אומר לא נתגרשה. והלשון מוכיח כן שאומר תרווייהו בא"א קמסהדי. דמשמע שלא הוחזקה א"א אלא על פיהם. ואע"ג דאיהי נמי אמרה א"א הייתי וגרושה אני [מ"מ] כיון שיש עדים (שהיתה) [שאומרים] שא"א היתה אינה נאמנת. ועוד שהעד מכחישה ואומר לא נתגרשה. והלכך אם נשאת תצא אבל בודאי אם נשאת תחלה על פיה כשאמרה א"א הייתי וגרושה אני ואח"כ בא העד שאוסרה שאומר לא נתגרשה לא תצא. שאין מוציאין אשה מבעלה בע"א כדרבא דאמר אין דבר שבערוה פחות מב'. וכי היכי דבגירושין לא מתוקמא אלא בבאה ממדה"י שאין לה חזקה מה היא ה"נ עדות דקידושין לא מתוקם אלא בבאה ממדה"י שלא הוחזקה מה היא. והלשון מוכיח דקאמר תרווייהו בפנויה קמסהדי. דמשמע שלא הוחזקה פנויה אלא על פיהן. אבל אשה העומדת לפנינו בחזקת פנויה. ובא ע"א ואמר נתקדשה בפני פ' ופ' והלכו להן למדינת הים. אע"פ שאין עד אחר שיכחישנו. אינו נאמן לאוסרה עד שיבואו שנים כדרבא דאמר אין דבר שבערוה פחות מב'. ולכתחלה לא תנשא. ר"א אמר לעולם תרי ותרי ואיפוך פי' המורה ברישא תני תצא. ובסיפא תני לא תצא. ב' אומרים ראינוה שנתקדשה וב' אומרים לא ראינוה שנתקדשה ה"ז לא תנשא. פשיטא לא ראינו אינו ראיה. מ"ד איתא דקדיש קלא אית לה למילתא קמ"ל דעבידי אינשי דמקדשי בצנעא. ואי קשה תנינא דאמר' לא ראינוה שנתקדשה דלא ראינוה אינה ראיה אבל אי אמרי (בעיקר) [בבירור] דלא נתקדשה כגון דאמרו דאשה והמקדש הי' עמנו במקום פ' שמעידים עדות ברורה. ה"נ דאם נשאת לא תצא. ואמאי לא תצא. תרי ותרי נינהו והבא עלי' באשם תלוי קאי. ואי אמרת דר"א קסבר [illegible] אנו היינו כל היום עמהם באותו חצר ולא נתפרדנו מהם כלל ולא יתכן שנתקדשה באותו היום שאילו כך גם אנחנו היינו רואים המעשה. אלא שקר אתם מעידים. אין לומר כבאן תרי ותרי נינהו. שוואת היא הזמה.

א) ולפי מש"כ הר"ש כאן [illegible]

עט א מיי' פי"ח מהל' איסורי ביאה הלכ' יז סמג לאוין קכא טוש"ע אה"ע סימן ז סעיף א:
פ ב מיי' פ"כ שם הלכ' יג סמג לאוין קכב קכז טוש"ע שם סימן ג סעיף א:
פא ג מיי' שם הלכה יא טוש"ע שם סעיף ד:
פב ד מיי' שם הלכה ב:

מתני' שְׁתֵּי נָשִׁים שֶׁנִּשְׁבּוּ, זֹאת אוֹמֶרֶת: "נִשְׁבֵּיתִי וּטְהוֹרָה אֲנִי", וְזֹאת אוֹמֶרֶת: "נִשְׁבֵּיתִי וּטְהוֹרָה אֲנִי" — אֵינָן נֶאֱמָנוֹת. [א]וּבִזְמַן שֶׁהֵן מְעִידוֹת זוֹ אֶת זוֹ — הֲרֵי אֵלּוּ נֶאֱמָנוֹת.§ **גמ'** ת"ר: *"אֲנִי טְמֵאָה וַחֲבֶרְתִּי טְהוֹרָה" — נֶאֱמֶנֶת, "אֲנִי טְהוֹרָה וַחֲבֶרְתִּי טְמֵאָה" — אֵינָהּ נֶאֱמֶנֶת, "אֲנִי וַחֲבֶרְתִּי טְמֵאָה" נֶאֱמֶנֶת עַל עַצְמָהּ, וְאֵינָהּ נֶאֱמֶנֶת עַל חֲבֶרְתָּהּ, "אֲנִי וַחֲבֶרְתִּי טְהוֹרָה" — נֶאֱמֶנֶת עַל חֲבֶרְתָּהּ, וְאֵינָהּ נֶאֱמֶנֶת עַל עַצְמָהּ. אָמַר מָר: "אֲנִי טְהוֹרָה וַחֲבֶרְתִּי טְמֵאָה" — אֵינָהּ נֶאֱמֶנֶת. הֵיכִי דָּמֵי? אִי דְּלֵיכָּא עֵדִים — עַל עַצְמָהּ אַמַּאי לָא מְהֵימְנָא? "נִשְׁבֵּיתִי וּטְהוֹרָה אֲנִי" קָאָמְרָה! אֶלָּא פְּשִׁיטָא דְּאִיכָּא עֵדִים. אֵימָא מְצִיעֲתָא: "אֲנִי וַחֲבֶרְתִּי טְמֵאָה" — נֶאֱמֶנֶת עַל עַצְמָהּ וְאֵינָהּ נֶאֱמֶנֶת עַל חֲבֶרְתָּהּ. וְאִי דְּאִיכָּא עֵדִים אַמַּאי לָא מְהֵימְנָא? אֶלָּא פְּשִׁיטָא דְּלֵיכָּא עֵדִים. אֵימָא סֵיפָא: "אֲנִי וַחֲבֶרְתִּי טְהוֹרָה" — נֶאֱמֶנֶת עַל חֲבֶרְתָּהּ, וְאֵינָהּ נֶאֱמֶנֶת עַל עַצְמָהּ. וְאִי דְּלֵיכָּא עֵדִים — אַעַצְמָהּ אַמַּאי לָא מְהֵימְנָא? אֶלָּא פְּשִׁיטָא דְּאִיכָּא עֵדִים. רֵישָׁא וְסֵיפָא דְּאִיכָּא עֵדִים, מְצִיעֲתָא דְּלֵיכָּא עֵדִים?! אָמַר אַבַּיֵי: אִין, רֵישָׁא וְסֵיפָא — דְּאִיכָּא עֵדִים, מְצִיעֲתָא דְּלֵיכָּא עֵדִים. רַב פַּפָּא אָמַר: כּוּלָּהּ דְּאִיכָּא עֵדִים, וְאִיכָּא עֵד אֶחָד דְּקָא אַפֵּיךְ. אָמְרָה "אֲנִי טְמֵאָה וַחֲבֶרְתִּי טְהוֹרָה" וְאָמַר לָהּ עֵד אֶחָד "אַתְּ טְהוֹרָה וַחֲבֶרְתֵּךְ טְמֵאָה". אִיהִי — שַׁוְיָתָא לְנַפְשָׁהּ חֲתִיכָה דְּאִיסּוּרָא, חֲבֶרְתָּהּ — מִשְׁתַּרְיָא אַפּוּמָּא דִּידָהּ; "אֲנִי טְהוֹרָה וַחֲבֶרְתִּי טְמֵאָה" וְאָמַר לָהּ עֵד אֶחָד: "אַתְּ טְמֵאָה וַחֲבֶרְתֵּךְ טְהוֹרָה", "אִיהִי כֵּיוָן דְּאִיכָּא עֵדִים — לָאו כָּל כְּמִינַּהּ, חֲבֶרְתָּהּ — מִשְׁתַּרְיָא אַפּוּמָּא דְּעֵד; "אֲנִי וַחֲבֶרְתִּי טְמֵאָה" וְאָמַר לָהּ עֵד אֶחָד "אַתְּ וַחֲבֶרְתֵּךְ טְהוֹרָה", אִיהִי — שַׁוְיָתָא לְנַפְשָׁהּ חֲתִיכָה דְּאִיסּוּרָא, חֲבֶרְתָּא — מִשְׁתַּרְיָא אַפּוּמָּא דְּעֵד. הָא תּוּ לָמָּה לִי? הַיְינוּ רֵישָׁא! מַהוּ דְּתֵימָא: הָנֵי תַּרְוַיְיהוּ טְהוֹרוֹת נִינְהוּ, וְהַאי דְּקָאָמְרָה הָכִי — °"תָּמוֹת נַפְשִׁי עִם פְּלִשְׁתִּים" הִיא דְּקָא עָבְדָה, קמ"ל. "אֲנִי וַחֲבֶרְתִּי טְהוֹרָה" וְאָמַר לָהּ עֵד אֶחָד "אַתְּ וַחֲבֶרְתֵּךְ טְמֵאָה", אִיהִי, כֵּיוָן דְּאִיכָּא עֵדִים — לָאו כָּל כְּמִינַּהּ, חֲבֶרְתָּהּ — מִשְׁתַּרְיָא אַפּוּמָּא דִּידָהּ. הָא תּוּ לָמָּה לִי? הַיְינוּ רֵישָׁא דְּרֵישָׁא! מַהוּ דְּתֵימָא: כִּי מְהֵימְנָא — בְּמָקוֹם דְּפָסְלָה נַפְשָׁהּ, אֲבָל בְּמָקוֹם דְּמַכְשְׁרָא נַפְשָׁהּ אֵימָא לָא מְהֵימְנָא, קָא מַשְׁמַע לָן.§ **מתני'** [ב]וְכֵן שְׁנֵי אֲנָשִׁים, זֶה אוֹמֵר "כֹּהֵן אֲנִי" — וְזֶה אוֹמֵר "כֹּהֵן אֲנִי" — אֵינָן נֶאֱמָנִין, [ג]וּבִזְמַן שֶׁהֵן מְעִידִין זֶה אֶת זֶה — הֲרֵי אֵלּוּ נֶאֱמָנִין. [ד]רַבִּי יְהוּדָה אוֹמֵר: *אֵין מַעֲלִין לִכְהוּנָּה עַל פִּי עֵד אֶחָד. אָמַר רַבִּי אֶלְעָזָר: אֵימָתַי — בְּמָקוֹם שֶׁיֵּשׁ עוֹרְרִין. אֲבָל בְּמָקוֹם שֶׁאֵין עוֹרְרִין מַעֲלִין לִכְהוּנָּה עַל פִּי עֵד אֶחָד. רשב"ג אוֹמֵר מִשּׁוּם רַבִּי שִׁמְעוֹן בֶּן הַסְּגָן: מַעֲלִין לִכְהוּנָּה עַל פִּי עֵד אֶחָד.§ **גמ'** כָּל הָנֵי לָמָּה לִי? צְרִיכִי; דְּאִי תָּנָא מוֹדֶה רַבִּי יְהוֹשֻׁעַ — מִשּׁוּם דְּאִיכָּא דְּרָרָא דְּמָמוֹנָא, אֲבָל עֵדִים דְּלֵיכָּא דְּרָרָא דְּמָמוֹנָא — אֵימָא לָא. וְאִי תָּנָא עֵדִים — מִשּׁוּם דִּלְעָלְמָא, אֲבָל אִיהוּ, דִּלְנַפְשֵׁיהּ, אֵימָא

(שופטים טז)

שתי נשים שנשבו. אומר ר"י: דלא גרסינן זאת אומרת נשביתי וטהורה אני כו', אלא: זאת אומרת טהורה אני, דהא בדאיכא עדים שנשבו איירי. ומיהו יש לקיים הגירסא. דאיירי דאינהו לא ידעי דאיכא עדים, ואשמועינן דאפילו הכי לא מהימני.

אין רישא וסיפא דאיכא עדים ומציעתא דליכא עדים. השתא לא פריך הא תו למה לי, כדפריך אשנויא דרב פפא. דהשתא אצטריך כולהו: "אני טהורה וחברתי טמאה" אשמעינן: כיון דאיכא עדים – לא מהימנא אנפשה. ו"אני וחברתי טמאה" אשמעינן דלא מהימנא אחברתה היכא דליכא עדים, ומשתריא חברתה אפומא דנפשה. ו"אני וחברתי טהורה" אשמועינן: אע"ג דאיכא עדים – מהימנא אחברתה, דרישא דרישא איכא לאוקמי בדליכא עדים. ואין נראה: דאי בדליכא עדים – היינו מציעתא, אלא בדאיכא עדים איירי. ומ"מ איצטריך האי סיפא לאשמועינן דנאמנת אחברתה ואע"ג דלא פסלה נפשה, והיה לנו לחוש לגומלים – אפילו הכי מהימנא*. **הא** תו למה לי היינו רישא. וא"ת: ואמאי לא קאמר הכא מרישא דרישא, כדקאמר בסמוך? דהא שמעינן מרישא דרישא דאיהי שויתה לנפשה חתיכה דאיסורא, וחברתה משתריא אפומא דידה, וכ"ש דמשתריא אפומא דעד אחד! *וי"ל: דהכא ניחא ליה למנקט סתמא דהיינו רישא, משום דמרישא נמי שמעינן דחברתה משתריא אפומא דעד אחד, אבל בסמוך לא מצי פריך אלא מרישא דרישא. **דאיכא** דררא דממונא. פירש ר"ח: שהאומר הוא מוחזק בשדה, אבל העדים אין בידם כלום. **אבל** הכא דליכא דררא דממונא לא. קשה לרשב"א: הא איצטריך גבי עדים לאשמועינן דמהימני במגו לפסול השטר, דהא אע"ג דר' מאיר פליג אסיפא – מודה ברישא! נשביתי

[והיינו שיטיא דלקמן דלא פסלה נפשה והוה מצי למיפרך השתא ולשנויי ת"י]

[וי"ל דס"ד דהיא מהימנא טפי מעד אחד לפי שנשבית עמה יודעת יותר. ת"י]

מתני' שְׁתֵּי נָשִׁים שֶׁנִּשְׁבּוּ. שֶׁיֵּשׁ עֵדִים שֶׁנִּשְׁבּוּ. שֶׁמְּעִידוֹת זוֹ אֶת זוֹ. כָּל אַחַת אוֹמֶרֶת "חֲבֶרְתִּי טְהוֹרָה". הֲרֵי אֵלּוּ נֶאֱמָנוֹת. דִּבְשְׁבוּיָה הֵקִילּוּ לְהַאֲמִין עֵד אֶחָד, וַאֲפִילּוּ אִשָּׁה. **גמ'** נֶאֱמֶנֶת. עַל הַכֹּל. אֵינָהּ נֶאֱמֶנֶת. עַל כְּלוּם. וּלְקַמֵּיהּ מְפָרֵשׁ לָהּ לְכוּלָּהּ. **אִי דְּלֵיכָּא עֵדִים.** שֶׁנִּשְׁבּוּ. **אֶלָּא פְּשִׁיטָא דְּאִיכָּא עֵדִים.** הִלְכָּךְ, אַעַצְמָהּ אֵינָהּ נֶאֱמֶנֶת לְטַהֲרָהּ, וַחֲבֶרְתָּהּ נַמִי, אע"ג דַּאֲנַן אָמְרִינַן בְּחֶזְקַת טְמֵאָה קָיְימָא – הַהוּא לָאו מִשּׁוּם הֵימָנוּתָא דְּהָךְ הוּא, דִּבְלָאו סַהֲדוּתָא דִּידָהּ נַמִי בְּחֶזְקַת טוּמְאָה הִיא. **וְאֵינָהּ נֶאֱמֶנֶת עַל חֲבֶרְתָּהּ.** עַל כָּרְחָךְ מַשְׁמַע דַּחֲבֶרְתָּהּ בְּחֶזְקַת טְהוֹרָה קָיְימָא. דִּבִשְׁלָמָא אֵינָהּ נֶאֱמֶנֶת דְּרֵישָׁא, אע"ג דְּאַכּוּלָּהּ מִילְּתָא מַשְׁמַע – שַׁיָּיךְ לְמִיתְנְיֵיהּ מִשּׁוּם דִּידָהּ. אֶלָּא הָכָא, דִּבְהֶדְיָא תָּנָא אֵינָהּ נֶאֱמֶנֶת עַל חֲבֶרְתָּהּ – קָשֶׁה. **אֶלָּא פְּשִׁיטָא דְּלֵיכָּא עֵדִים.** וְאַדִּידָהּ מְהֵימְנָא, דְּשַׁוְיָתָהּ לְנַפְשָׁהּ חֲתִיכָה דְּאִיסּוּרָא. **דְּאַפֵּיךְ.** מֵיפַךְ אֶת כָּל דְּבָרֶיהָ. **חֲבֶרְתָּהּ מִשְׁתַּרְיָא אַפּוּמָּא דִּידָהּ.** דְּבִשְׁבוּיָה הֶאֱמִינוּ חֲכָמִים עֵד אֶחָד לְהָקֵל, וַאֲפִילּוּ עֶבֶד אוֹ שִׁפְחָה, כִּדְקָתָנֵי מַתְנִי' (לְקַמָּן דף כז.): אִם יֵשׁ לָהֶן עֵדִים אֲפִילּוּ עֶבֶד כו'. וְכָל מָקוֹם שֶׁנֶּאֱמָן בּוֹ עֵד אֶחָד – הֲרֵי הוּא כִּשְׁנַיִם, וְאֵין דִּבְרֵי אֶחָד שֶׁכְּנֶגְדּוֹ לְטַמֵּא עוֹמֵד בִּמְקוֹם שְׁנַיִם. הָכִי גָּרְסִינַן. **אִיהִי כֵּיוָן דְּאִיכָּא עֵדִים לָאו כָּל כְּמִינַּהּ.** וְאַעֲדֵי שְׁבוּיֵיהּ קָאֵי, דְּעֵד אֶחָד בְּטוּמְאָה אֵינוֹ כְּלוּם אֶלָּא בְּסוֹטָה בִּלְבָד, שֶׁרַגְלַיִם לַדָּבָר, שֶׁהֲרֵי קִינֵּא לָהּ וְנִסְתְּרָה. **שַׁוְיָתָהּ לְנַפְשָׁהּ חֲתִיכָה דְּאִיסּוּרָא.** לְפִיכָךְ אֵין הָעֵד נֶאֱמָן לְטַהֲרָהּ. **הַיְינוּ רֵישָׁא.** הָנֵי מִילֵּי תַּרְוַיְיהוּ אַשְׁמְעִינַן בְּרֵישָׁא: חֲתִיכָה דְּאִיסּוּרָא – מֵרֵישָׁא שָׁמְעִינַן, שָׁרְיוּתָא דַּחֲבֶרְתָּהּ אַפּוּמָּא דְּעֵד – מִסֵּיפָא דְּרֵישָׁא שָׁמְעִינַן. תַּרְתֵּי בָּבֵי קַמָּיְיתָא רֵישָׁא קָרֵי לְהוּ, דְּדָמְיָין לַהֲדָדֵי. וְתַרְתֵּי בָּבֵי בַּתְרָיְיתָא חֲדָא מִילְּתָא הִיא, דִּבְכָל חֲדָא תְּנַן מִילְּתָא וְחִילּוּפָהּ, בֵּין בְּרֵישָׁא בֵּין בְּסֵיפָא. **מַהוּ דְּתֵימָא כו'.** וּמִשּׁוּם נֶאֱמֶנֶת עַל עַצְמָהּ תָּנָא לֵיהּ. **אִיהִי, כֵּיוָן דְּאִיכָּא עֵדִים** גָּרְסִינַן. **הַיְינוּ רֵישָׁא דְּרֵישָׁא.** דְּהָא וַדַּאי מִשּׁוּם דְּאֵינָהּ נֶאֱמֶנֶת עַל עַצְמָהּ לָא אִצְטְרִיךְ לְמִיתְנְיֵיהּ, דְּהָא טוּבָא אַשְׁמוּעִינַן, דִּבְמָקוֹם עֵדֵי שְׁבוּיָה לָא מְהֵימְנָא לְמֵימַר טְהוֹרָה אֲנִי, וּמִשּׁוּם נֶאֱמֶנֶת עַל חֲבֶרְתָּהּ הוּא דְּאִצְטְרִיךְ, דְּאע"ג דְּעֵד קָא מַכְחִישׁ לָהּ – מְהֵימְנָא, וְהָא בְּרֵישָׁא דְּרֵישָׁא אַשְׁמְעִינַן. **בְּמָקוֹם דְּפָסְלָה לְנַפְשָׁהּ.** הָתָם הוּא דִּמְהֵימְנָא אַחֲבֶרְתָּהּ, מִשּׁוּם דְּקָאָמְרָה "טְמֵאָה אֲנִי". **אֲבָל הֵיכָא דְּמַכְשְׁרָא** נַמִי לְנַפְשָׁהּ. אֵימָא מִשּׁוּם דִּידָהּ הוּא דְּקָאָמְרָה, וְלָא אַחֲבֶרְתָּהּ. קמ"ל גָּרְסִינַן. ל"א גָּרְסִינַן: מַהוּ דְּתֵימָא כִּי מְהֵימְנָא בִּמְקוֹם עֵד פָּסוּל. כְּגוֹן דְּעֵד דְּקָא מַפִּיךְ הָוֵי אִשָּׁה, אֲבָל בִּמְקוֹם עֵד כָּשֵׁר – לָא, תָּנָא מִשְׁנָה יְתֵירָה דַּאֲפִי' בִּמְקוֹם עֵד כָּשֵׁר. **מתני'** וְכֵן שְׁנֵי אֲנָשִׁים. לָא גָּרְסִינַן שֶׁנִּשְׁבּוּ. **אֵין נֶאֱמָנִים.** לִיתֵּן לָהֶן תְּרוּמָה. **וּבִזְמַן שֶׁמְּעִידִין זֶה אֶת זֶה.** שֶׁכָּל אֶחָד אוֹמֵר "אֲנִי וַחֲבֵרִי כֹּהֵן". **רַבִּי יְהוּדָה אוֹמֵר אֵין מַעֲלִין לִכְהוּנָּה עַל פִּי עֵד אֶחָד.** וַאֲפִילּוּ הֵיכָא דְּלֵיכָּא גּוֹמְלִין, וְכָל שֶׁכֵּן הָכָא דְּאִיכָּא לְמֵיחַשׁ לְגוֹמְלִין: הָעֵד אַתָּה עָלַי וַאֲנִי עָלֶיךָ. **עוֹרְרִין.** שֶׁקּוֹרִין עָלָיו שֵׁשׁ פָּסוּל. **מַעֲלִין.** הֵיכָא דְּלֵיכָּא גּוֹמְלִין. וְהַיְינוּ דְּאִיכָּא בֵּין ר' אֶלְעָזָר לְתַנָּא קַמָּא דְּר' יְהוּדָה. **רַבָּן שִׁמְעוֹן כו'.** בַּגְּמָ' מְפָרֵשׁ מַאי בֵּינַיְיהוּ. **גמ' כָּל הָנֵי.** דְּתָנָא מַתְנִיתִין לְאַשְׁמוּעִינַן הַפֶּה שֶׁאָסַר הוּא הַפֶּה שֶׁהִתִּיר ל"ל? **מִשּׁוּם דְּאִיכָּא דְּרָרָא דְּמָמוֹנָא.** הִלְכָּךְ, אִי לָאו דִּפְשִׁיטָא מִלְּתָא שֶׁלְּקָחָהּ מֵאָבִיו – לָא הָיָה אוֹמֵר שֶׁל אָבִיךָ הָיְתָה, וְגוֹרֵם לְעַצְמוֹ הֶפְסֵד מָמוֹן. וּכְשֶׁאוֹמֵר תְּחִלַּת דְּבָרָיו – עַל שֵׁם סוֹפוֹ אֲמָרוֹ לִגְמוֹר בָּהֶן "וּלְקַחְתִּיהָ הֵימֶנּוּ". **אֲבָל עֵדִים.** שֶׁאָמְרוּ "כְּתַב יָדֵינוּ הוּא". **דְּלֵיכָּא דְּרָרָא דְּמָמוֹנָא.** לְגַבַּיְיהוּ, דְּלִימְטְיַיהוּ פְּסֵידָא בְּהַאי עֵדוּת. **אֵימָא לָא.** לִיתְהַמְנוּ לְמֵימַר "אֲנוּסִין הָיִינוּ". דְּמֵעִיקָּרָא כִּי אָמְרוּ "כְּתַב יָדֵינוּ הוּא" – אַדַּעְתָּא דְּסַהֲדוּתָא אָמְרוּ, וְלָאו לְמִיגְמַר בָּהּ "אֲנוּסִים הָיִינוּ", וַהֲדַר אִימְלִיכוּ לְמִיגְמַר בָּהּ הָכִי – קָמַשְׁמַע לָן. **דִּלְעָלְמָא.** אֵין הַדִּבּוּר הָאַחֲרוֹן מְהַנֵּי לְעַצְמוֹ אֶלָּא לַאֲחֵרִים, וּמִשּׁוּם אֲחֵרִים לָא הָווּ הָדְרֵי בְּמִלְּתַיְיהוּ. אֲבָל אִיהוּ גּוּפֵיהּ דִּלְנַפְשֵׁיהּ – מַהֲנֵי כִּי הָדַר וַאֲמַר "לְקַחְתִּיהָ".
מִשּׁוּם

[תוספתא פ"ב]

ב"ב לח:

גליון הש"ס
מתני' זה אומר כהן אני. עיין בהרא"ש פ"ה דגיטין סי' ח' בתום' ג':

תוספות רי"ד
הזמה גמורה. כיון שאומרי' להם והלא עמנו הייתם יחד במקום פ' כל היום כלו ואנו לא ראינו. ואתם האיך ראיתם ובהזמה האמינה התורה האחרונים ובטלי עדות הראשונים והלכך טעמא דאמרי לא ראינוה דאינה ראיה דתצא ול"א אי איתא דקדיש קלא אית לה ואכתי הזמה הוא. אבל אם העידו עדות ברורה כיון דמוזימים את הראשונים א) תנשא לכתחלה: סיפא ב' אומרים ראינוה שנתגרשה וב' אומרים לא ראינוה שנתגרשה ה"ז ל"ת. ואם נשאת לא תצא מאי קמ"ל אע"ג דדיירו בחצר א' היינו הך מ"ד גבי קידושין הוא דעבידי אינשי דמקדשי בצנעא אבל גירושין אי איתא דאינרשא קלא אית לי' למילתא קמ"ל דעבידי אינשי דמגרשי בצנעא פירוש ואפ"ה לכתחלה לא תנשא משום ולזות שפתים הרחק ממך: **מתני'** האשה שאמרה נשביתי וטהורה אני נאמנת שהפה שאסר הוא הפה שהתיר. ואם יש עדים שנשבית והיא אומרת טהורה אני אינה נאמנת ואם משנשאת באו עדים ה"ז ל"ת. פי' נשביתי לבין הגוים וטהורה אני שלא נבעלתי לגוי ואם משנשאת וכו'. בגמ' מפרש' אהיא קאי. ר"א מתני לה ארישא פי' האי ואם משנשאת באו עדים ארישא. האשה שאמרה א"א הייתי וגרושה אני. והכי קתני ואם משנשאת באו עדים שהיתה א"א. והיא נשאת ע"פ עצמה שאמרה גרושה אני ה"ז לא תצא. ורבא מתני לה אסיפא פי' אנשבית וטהורה אני והתירוה לינשא. ואח"כ באו עדים שנשבית. מאן דמתני' לה ארישא כ"ש אסיפא דבשבויה הקילו. פי' רחששא בעלמא הוא דאיכא שמא נבעלה לגוי ונפסלה לכהונה. ומאן דמתני לה אסיפא אבל ארישא לא. לימא בדר"ה קמיפלגי דאמר ר"ה האשה שאמרה לבעלה גרשתני נאמנת חזקה אין אשה מעיזה בפני בעלה. פי' דמאן דמתני לה ארישא אית ליה דר"ה ומאן דמתני לה אסיפא ל"ל דר"ה. לא דכ"ע א"ל דר"ה פי' ואע"ג דבחזקת (טומאה) [נשואה] קיימא דהלכתא כוותיה. מר סבר כי אתמר דר"ה בפניו אבל שלא בפניו מעיזה ב). פי' דוקא כשנשאת ואח"כ באו עדים סמכי' אחזקה אפילו שלא בפניו. אבל אם לא נשאת לא סמכי' אחזקה כי היכי דסמכי' עלה בפניו דלא דמי שלא בפניו כבפניו: ואם משנשאת באו עדים ה"ז ל"ת. אמר שמואל. לא נשאת ממש אלא כיון שהתירוה לינשא אע"פ שלא נשאת. והא ל"ת קתני. ל"ת מהתירא הראשון: ת"ר אמרה נשביתי וטהורה אני ויש לי עדים שטהורה אני פי' שהיו עמי תמיד שלא נתיחדתי עם גוי אין אומרים נמתין לה עד שיבואו עדים אלא מתירין אותה מיד. התירוה לינשא ואח"כ באו עדים ואמרו לא ידענו ה"ז ל"ת. פי' אע"פ שבאו אותם העדים שאמרה האשה ושאלנו אותן ואמרו לא ידענו. אין אומרים כיון שנמצאו דבריה שקר תצא. אלא ל"ת ואם באו עדי טומאה אפילו יש לה כמה בנים תצא. פי' דנבעלה לגוי הוי' לה זונה ובניה הם חללים: בנתי' דמר שמואל אשתביין. אסקינהו לארעא דישראל. אוקמינהו לשבוינהו אבראי. פי' שלא יבאו לפני ב"ד ולא ידעו ב"ד שהן שבויין אלא ע"פ עצמן ויתידום עיילו אינהו לבי מדרשא דר"ח. זו אומרת נשביתי וטהורה אני וזו אומרת נשביתי וטהורה אני. לסוף עול אתו שבוייהו. א"ר חנינא בנות מורין אינן. פי' בנות אדם גדול ובעל הוראה הן שידעו לעשות כך. ואיגלאי מילתא דבנתיה דמר שמואל אינון. א"ל ר"י לרשב"א כהנא פוק איטפל בקרובותיך. פי' [קח] א' מהן שהן קרובותיך. א"ל לר"ח והא איכא עדי טומאה שראוה כשנטמאה עם הגוים. ודילמא אתו לקמן למחר לאחר שתנשא. א"ל השתא מיהו ליתנהו פי' קודם נשואין. ומשום דלמא אתו לא (אהדרינן) [אסרינן] להו השתא עדים בצד אסתן ותאסר. פי' אסתן. צפון. כמו יומא דאיסתנא. מצפון תפתח הרעה. פי' העדים המכירים הן בבבל ואנחנו כאן וניחוש שמא יבואו ויעידו על הטומאה ולכולי האי לא חיישינן. ומותרות הן לכהונה אח"כ ודאי אם יבואו תצא ובניה חללים. אבל מסתמא לא חיישינן דאחזוקי איסורא לא מחזקינן ואלו הו' קרובים (לא) [לנו] היינו חוקרים אותם טרם שנתירם לינשא. עכשיו שהן רחוקים ממנו. לכולי האי לא חיישינן: **מתני'** שתי נשים שנשבו ז"א נשביתי וטהורה אני וז"א נשביתי וטהורה אני אינן נאמנות. ובזמן שמעידות זו ע"ז הרי אלו נאמנות פי' שנשבו בידוע כגון שיש עדים שנשבו הלכך אין נאמנות להעיד כל א' וא' בפ"ע. ובזמן שמעידות זו ע"ז שכל א' אומרת אני וחברתי טהורה הרי אלו נאמנות דבשבויה הקילו והאמינו בה אפילו ע"א ואפי' אשה ולא חיישינן לגומלין. ת"ר אני טמאה וחברתי טהורה נאמנת. אני טהורה וחברתי טמאה אינה נאמנת. פי' אינה נאמנת על כלום. אני וחברתי טמאות נאמנת לפסול א"ע. ואינה נאמנת לפסול חברתה. אני וחברתי טהורה נאמנת על חברתה. ואינה נאמנת ע"ע: אמר מר אני טהורה וחברתי טמאה אינה נאמנת. ה"ד אי דליכא עדים שנשבו אעצמה אמאי לא מהימנא נשביתי וטהורה אני קאמרה. פי' בשלמא אחברתה אינה נאמנת שכיון שאין עדים שנשבית הותרה חברתה וכאומרת נשביתי וטהורה אני. וזו שאומרת עליה כי נטמאת

א) הכי צ"ע דלאכתי איכא לאוקמי דהעידו עדות ברורה ומ"מ לא הויא הזמה כגון דאמרו דהמקדש היה עמנו במקום פלוני או דלאיתו דזכר הקדושין קרוב לו ולא היה קידושין כלל. ב) נ"ל ומר סבר דאפי' שלא בפניו נמי אינה מעיזה פי' דוקא.

פג א מיי' פי"ב מהל' מעשר הלכה י:

משום דבעי למיתני שתי נשים שנשבו. לאשמועינן דבזמן שמעידות זו את זו נאמנות. נאמן להאכילו בתרומה ואינו נאמן להשיאו אשה. מיוחסת, מעלה היא ביוחסין. למימרא כו'. קא ס"ד דטעמא דרבי יהודה משום גומלין. החמרים. סוחרי תבואה, ומוליכין ממקום הזול לכרכין. שלי חדש ושל חברי ישן שלי אינו מתוקן ושל חבירי מתוקן. משבח את של חבירו, ומזלזל את שלו. שלי אינו מעושר, של חבירי מעושר. שלי חדש ואינו יבש עדיין כל צורכו, [ושל חבירי ישן ויבש כל צורכו]. דסתם ישן טוב מן החדש בעת הגורן, כדאמרי' ב"איזהו נשך" (ב"מ עב:): היו חדשות מארבע וישנות משלש. אינו נאמן. הואיל ועם הארץ הוא, ואינו נאמן על המעשר. אע"פ שמעיד על שלו שאינו מתוקן, ועוד שמוסיף עם זו דברים אחרים לשבח את של חבירו – אינו נאמן להחזיק את של חבירו בחזקת מתוקן, שאינן אלא מערימין: אמור אתה כאן, ואני במקום אחר. בשכלי

נ"י כ"י [לעיל כג.] [ע"ז סא:] לקמן נו: דמאי פ"ד מ"ז שבת יג. כג. גיטין סא. לקמן נו: [כילה לה: יבמות קיז. מנחות לא.]

אימא לא. ואי אשמעינן הני תרתי – משום דממונא, אבל אשת איש דאיסורא – אימא לא. "נשביתי וטהורה אני" למה לי? משום דקא בעי למיתני "ואם משנשאת באו עדים הרי זו לא תצא". הניחא למאן *דמתני לה אסיפא, אלא למאן דמתני לה ארישא מאי איכא למימר? משום דקא בעי למיתני "שתי נשים שנשבו". ו"שתי נשים שנשבו" למה לי? מהו דתימא: ניחוש *לגומלין, קמשמע לן. "וכן שני אנשים" למה לי? משום דקא בעי למיתני פלוגתא דרבי יהודה ורבנן. ת"ר: "אני כהן וחברי כהן" – נאמן להאכילו בתרומה, ואינו נאמן להשיאו אשה, עד שיהו ג', שנים מעידין על זה ושנים מעידין על זה. רבי יהודה אומר: אף אינו נאמן להאכילו בתרומה עד שיהו שלשה, שנים מעידין על זה, ושנים מעידין על זה. למימרא דרבי יהודה חייש לגומלין ורבנן לא חיישי לגומלין? והא איפכא שמעינן להו, דתנן: *א החמרין שנכנסו לעיר, ואמר אחד מהן: "שלי חדש ושל חברי ישן", "שלי אינו מתוקן ושל חברי מתוקן" – אינו נאמן, רבי יהודה אומר: נאמן! אמר רב אדא בר אהבה אמר רב: מוחלפת השיטה. אביי אמר: לעולם לא תיפוך; *בדמאי הקילו, רוב עמי הארץ מעשרין הן, אמר רבא: דרבי יהודה אדרבי יהודה קשיא, דרבנן אדרבנן לא קשיא?! אלא, דרבי יהודה אדרבי יהודה לא קשיא – כדשנינן, דרבנן אדרבנן לא קשיא, כדאמר רבי חמא בר עוקבא: בשכלי אומנותו בידו, הכא

נשביתי וטהורה אני למה לי. וקשה לרשב"א: אמאי לא משני משום דבעי למיתני סיפא, אם יש עדים שנשבית ואמרה טהורה אני – אינה נאמנת! וי"ל: דמשום הא לא אצטריך, דמסיפא דמתני' שמעינן לה, דקתני סיפא: עיר שכבשוה כרכום – כל כהנות שנמצאו בתוכה פסולות, ואינה נאמנת לומר טהורה אני.

שתי נשים שנשבו למה לי. דאי לאשמעינן דאחת נאמנת על חברתה, הא בהדיא תנן (לקמן כז.) דאפי' עבד ושפחה נאמנים. **וכן** שני אנשים למה לי משום דבעי למיתני פלוגתא דרבי יהודה ורבנן. אבל בשתי נשים משמע דלא פליג רבי יהודה, משום דבשבויה הקילו. וקשה: דלקמן (דף כו.) אשכחן איפכא, דמסיח לפי תומו נאמן בתרומה אפי' על פי עצמו, כדאמר גבי יוחנן אוכל חלות דהעלהו רבי לכהונה על פיו, וגבי שבויה תני לקמן (דף כז:) הכל נאמנים להעידה, חוץ מבעלה, ומוקי לה במסיח לפי תומו! ומיהו, למאי דמוקמינן פלוגתייהו במעלין מתרומה ליוחסין – ניחא, דטעמא דמחמיר רבי יהודה טפי בתרומה מבשבויה, משום דמעלין מתרומה ליוחסין. אבל רבי, דמיקל טפי בתרומה במסיח לפי תומו – היינו משום דקסבר דאין מעלין מתרומה ליוחסין, כדאמר לקמן. אבל למאי דמוקי פלוגתייהו משום גומלים – קשה! וי"ל: דבתרומה דרבנן דוקא הוא דמתכשר במסיח לפי תומו, כדמשמע ב"הגוזל בתרא" (ב"ק קיד:) אבל בתרומה דאורייתא – לא.

אבל אינו נאמן להשיאו אשה. (א) פי' בקונטרס: משום חשש ממזרות ונתינות. וקשה: דלהכי ליכא למיחש כדאמרינן ב"החולץ" (יבמות מה. ושם) גבי גוי ועבד הבא על בת ישראל, דאמרינן ליה: זיל גלי, או נסיב בת מינך. משמע דאם ילך למקום שאין מכירים אותו – ישיאוהו בת ישראל, אע"פ שאין מכירים, ולא יסתפקו בו בנתין וממזר. וכן גבי ההוא דאתא לקמיה דרבי יהודה, וא"ל: נאמן אתה לפסול עצמך ואי אתה נאמן לפסול בניך. משמע שהוא ובניו היו בחזקת כשרים, אע"פ שלא היו מכירים בהם! ונראה לר"ת: דלהשיאו אשה דקאמר – היינו להשיאו בדוקה מד' אמהות, כדתנן ב"עשרה יוחסין" (קדושין דף עו. ושם): הנושא אשה צריך שיבדוק אחריה ד' אמהות, ואין נאמן אם ישא אשה בדוקה להכשיר בתו לכהן בלא בדיקה, אלא יצטרך לבדוק אחריו. וה"ה דמצי למימר ואינו נאמן להכשירו לעבודה. ואותה בדיקה היא משום חללות, דאין מכירין ישראל חללים שביניהם, ולא משום ספק ממזרות ונתינות – דלהא לא חיישינן, כדפי'. וכן משמע התם, דקאמר דהיא אינה בודקת בדידיה – דלא הוזהרו כשרות לינשא לפסולים, ואי משום ממזרות ונתינות הא ודאי הוזהרו, דהשוה הכתוב אשה לאיש לכל עונשין שבתורה! ואם תאמר: אי משום חללות בודקין – לא יבדקו אלא יחום אביה לבד, דאפילו היתה אמה חללה, כשרה היא ע"י אביה, דלכ"ע בני ישראל מקוה טהרה לחללות! ויש לומר: מאחר שהצריכו לבדוק את יחום האב משום חללות, אגב חללות הוצרכו לבדוק כל פסול שבה, גם של ממזרות ונתינות. וכולה הך שמעתין דמצרכי בדיקה להשיא בתו לכהן אתיא כרבי מאיר, דרבנן פליגי עליה התם, ולא מצרכי בדיקה, ואמרי: כל משפחות בחזקת כשרות הן עומדות, וא"נ אפילו עד אחד כדי להכשיר בתו לכהונה. ומיהו, להכשיר בנו או עצמו לעבודה צריך, דלאו בחזקת כהונה עומד. אי נמי, אפילו כרבנן – ובילא עליו ערער, כדקאמר התם במילתייהו דרבנן: בד"א – שלא יצא עליו ערער כו'. **שלי** חדש ושל חבירי ישן. בפרק "אע"פ" פי' בקונטרס: די"מ משום עומר. ולאו מילתא היא, דאם כן – מאי מתרץ בדמאי הקילו? התינח דמאי חדש, ישן מאי איכא למימר? ועוד: דלא מצינו בשום מקום שנחשדו עמי הארץ על החדש! ורשב"א פירש: דקאי אשביעית, וקאמר: שלי חדש וגדל בשביעית, ואסור להשהותו אחר הביעור, ושל חבירי ישן וגדל בשנה שעברה. ואשכחן דקרי לשביעית חדש, דתנן במסכת שביעית (פ"ז מ"ז): ורד חדש שכבשו בשמן ישן – ילקט את הורד. וכי משני בדמאי הקילו – בשביעית לא הוה לתרץ, דפשיטא ליה להתלמוד דרבי יהודה מיקל בשביעית, משום דבאתריה דרבי יהודה חמירא להו שביעית, כדאמר ב"הניזקין" (גיטין נד.). ואין נראה לר"ת, דסתם עמי הארץ לא נחשדו אשביעית, דתנן בפרק "עד כמה" (בכורות ל. ושם): החשוד על המעשר – אינו חשוד על השביעית, החשוד על השביעית – אינו חשוד על המעשר. אלמא דסתמא אינן חשודין בשביעית. ומעשר דקתני – היינו מעשר שני, דאמעשר ראשון חשודין הם. והא דתנן במסכת דמאי (פ"ג מ"ד) ומייתי לה ב"הניזקין" (גיטין סא:): המוליך חיטין לטוחן כותי או לטוחן עם הארץ – אינו חושש לא משום מעשר ולא משום שביעית, דמשמע דחשודים על השביעית – איכא למימר דמשום כותי נקט שביעית. אי נמי, בודאי חשוד איירי. וכן ההיא דמייתי בפרק קמא דחולין (דף ו. ושם): הנותן לשכנתו עיסה לאפות וקדירה לבשל – אינו חושש לשאור ותבלין שבה, לא משום מעשר ולא משום שביעית. ועוד קשה לר"ת: דאי באיסור חדש או שביעית מיירי, הוה ליה למימר של חברי אינו חדש, כדקאמר אינו מתוקן! ועוד הקשה ר"ת, דלעיל דההיא משנה דחמרין תנן במס' דמאי (פ"ג): הנכנס לעיר ואינו מכיר אדם שם, ואמר: מי כאן נאמן, מי כאן מעשר? ואמר לו אחד: אני איני נאמן איש פלוני נאמן, הלך ולקח הימנו, אמר ליה: מי כאן מוכר ישן? אמר ליה: מי ששלחך אצלי. אע"פ שהן כגומלין זה את זה – הרי אלו נאמנים. ואי ישן היינו דלית ביה איסור חדש או שביעית – היאך קונה ממי ששלחו אצלו, והלא הוא בעצמו אומר שאינו נאמן! ועוד: מדקא שאיל להיאך מי מוכר ישן – מכלל שמה שקנה ממנו כבר היה חדש או שביעית, והלא לא הלך אצלו אלא לפי שהוא נאמן! ופי' הקונטרס נראה לר"ת עיקר, דלהשביח קאמר. ולרבותא דרבי יהודה נקטיה, דאע"פ שמגרע את שלו ומשבח את של חבירו, ומיחזי טפי כגומלין – אפילו הכי נאמנין. ואם תאמר: א"כ מאי קשה ליה דרבנן אדרבנן? דלמא הכא הוא דחיישינן לגומלין, דדומה שהן גומלין, כדפי'! ויש לומר: דאי לאו דחיישינן לגומלים בעלמא – משום הכי לא הוו חיישינן טפי*. **אביי** אמר לעולם לא תיפוך בדמאי כו'. והא דאמר אביי בפרק "במה מדליקין" (שבת דף כג.): ספק דבריהם לא בעי ברכה. רבא אמר: רוב עמי הארץ מעשרין הן. וכן בפרק "אע"פ" (לקמן נו:) משני אביי: ודאי דבריהם – עשו חיזוק, ספק דבריהם – לא עשו חיזוק. רבא אמר: בדמאי הקילו. לא משום דלית ליה לאביי דרבא, דהא הכא אית ליה. ועוד דבשילהי "המביא" (בילה לה:) דייק ממתני' דרוב עמי הארץ מעשרין הן. אלא דאית ליה לאביי דכל ספק דבריהם, אע"ג דליכא רוב – לא בעי ברכה, וגם לא עשו חיזוק. ומיהו בפרק קמא דשבת (דף יג. ושם), אההיא דלא יאכל זב פרוש עם זב עם הארץ, מפרש אביי: שמא יאכילנו דברים שאינם מתוקנים. ולא סמיך ארוב עמי הארץ מעשרין, כדקאמר רבא! התם סבירא ליה דלהאי מלתא מחמירין, ולא סמכינן ארובא. וכן רבא בסוף "הניזקין" (גיטין סא. ושם) גבי משאלת אשה נפה כו' ולא בעי למיסמך ארוב עמי הארצות דמעשרין, לענין לסייע ידי עוברי עבירה, דנראה לו לענין זה להחמיר.
בשכלי

הגהות הב"ח

(א) תוס' ד"ה אבל כו' פי' בקונטרס. נ"ב ע"ל בפירושו סוף דף כ"ה:

[ועיין היטב תוס' בכורות לו: ד"ה הרי ועוד שם ל. ד"ה מתני' ותוס' סוכה לה: ד"ה במה]

תוספות רי"ד

טמאה אינה נאמנת דדוקא [להתיר] נאמן ע"א [משום] דבשבוי' הקילו ולא לאיסור כדרבא דאמר אין דבר שבערוה פחות מב'. שלא אעצמה אמאי לא מהימנא. אלא פשיטא דאיכא עדים פי' שנשבו ומ"ה אעצמה אינה נאמנת לומר נשביתי וטהורה אני וחברתה נמי אסורה בלא עדותה והא דקאמר אינה נאמנת כלומר בלא עדותה היא אסורה. אימא מציעתא אני וחברתי טמאות נאמנת ע"ע ואין נאמנת על חברתה. ואי דאיכא עידי שבויה אחברתה אמאי לא מהימנא והלא גם בלא עדותה אסורה המורה פי' ואינה נאמנת על חברתה ע"כ משמע חברתה בחזקת טהורה קיימא. דבשלמא אינה נאמנת דרישא אע"ג אכולה מילתא משמע שייך למתני [אינה נאמנת] משום היתר. אלא הכא דבהדי' תניא אינה נאמנת על חברתה קשה. אלא פשיטא דליכא עדים פי' מ"ה על עצמה נאמנת דשויתי' אנפשה חתיכה דאיסורא. אבל על חברתה אינה נאמנת דכיון דליכא עדי שבוי' חברתה משתריא באומר' נשביתי וטהורה אני וזו שמעידה עלי' כי טמאת אינה נאמנת כדרבא. שאין דבר שבערוה פחות מב'. אימא סיפא אני וחברתי טהורות נאמנת על חברתה ואינה נאמנת ע"ע. ואי דליכא עדים אעצמה אמאי לא מהימנא. אלא פשיטא דאיכא עדים. פי' ומ"ה אעצמה אינה נאמנת ואחברתה מהימנא שע"א נאמן בשבוי' רישא וסיפא דאיכא עדים ומציעתא דליכא עדים. אמר ר"פ כולה דאיכא עדים ואיכא ע"א דקמפיך פי' [דאיכא עדים] שמעידים שנשבו וע"א בא ומהפך כל הדברים. אני טמאה וחברתי טהורה וא"ל ע"א את טהורה וחברתך טמאה. איהי שויתה נפשה חתיכה דאיסורא וחברתה משתריא אפומא. פי' המורה. דבשבוי' האמינו חכמים ע"א להקל ואפי' עבד או שפחה. וכדקתני מתני' אם יש להן עדים אפילו עבד וכו' וכ"מ שנאמן ע"א הרי הוא כשנים ואין דברי א' שכנגדו לטמא עומד במקום שנים. ומשמע מפירושו. דאע"ג דלא נשאת וגם לא התירוה לינשא. ואינו נ"ל דכיון דאיכא עדות מכחשת לה היכי שריא לה לחברתה אפומא דידה. והתנן בפ' האשה רבה עד אומר מת ועד אומר לא מת ה"ז לא תנשא דכי מהימנינן ליה לע"א דאמר מת ולא מצי אידך למכחשי' ה"מ כשבאו בזה אח"ז וכבר התירוה ע"פ אותו העד (אמרת) [אמרינן] לא תצא מהתירא הראשון. אבל היכא דקימי תרווייהו ומכחשי להדדי אמרינן לא תנשא. והכא היכי אמרי' דהיא נאמנת אע"פ שהעד מכחישה. ובתוספתא דכתובות [בפ"ב] ברישא דהא מתני' תני הכי. עד אומר נשבית וטמאה היא. וע"א אומר נשבית וטהורה היא. אשה אומרת נשבית וטמאה היא ואשה אומרת נשבית וטהורה היא אין משיאין אותה. ואם נשאת ל"ת. וא"כ בע"כ מאי דתני הכא נאמנת הכי בעי' לפרושי כגון שהתירוה לינשא על פיה. ובתר הכי אתא ע"א ואמר נטמאת. אי נמי כגון שהלכה ונשאת דאמרינן ל"ת. אני טהורה וחברתי טמאה וא"ל עד אחד את טמאה וחברתך טהורה. איהי כיון דאיכא עדים לאו כל כמינה. פי' המורה ה"ג עדים וקאי אעידי שבוי' דע"א בטומאה אינו כלום אלא בסוטה בלבד שרגלים לדבר שהרי קינא לה ונסתרה חברתה משתריא אפומא דעד. פי' ה"נ כגון שנשאת. אני וחברתי טמאה. וא"ל עד את וחברתך טהורות איהי שויתי' נפשה חתיכה דאיסורא. פי' לפיכך אין העד נאמן לטהרה חברתה משתריא אפומא דעד כגון שנשאת. אני וחברתי טהורות ואמר לה עד את וחברתך טמאות. איהי כיון דאיכא עדים לאו כל כמינה. חברתה משתריא אפומה דידה פי' כגון שנשאת או התירוה לינשא כדפרי': **מתני'** וכן שני אנשים זה אומר כהן אני וז"א כהן אני אין נאמנים ובזמן שהן מעידים זע"ז הרי אלו נאמנים. ר"י אומר אין מעלין לכהונה ע"פ ע"א. אר"א אימתי בזמן שיש עוררים. אבל במקום שאין עוררים מעלין לכהונה ע"פ ע"א. רשב"ג אומר משום ר"ש בן הסגן מעלין לכהונה ע"פ ע"א. פי' ב' אנשים שבאו ממדה"י ולא ידענו מי הם ז"א כהן אני וז"א כהן אני. אין נאמנים ליתן להם תרומה ובזמן שמעידים זע"ז שז"א אני וחברי כהנים וכמו בן זה הרי אלו נאמנים שמעלין לכהונה ע"פ ע"א. ואפילו היכא דאיכא למיחש לגומלין. ר"י אומר אין וכו' ואפילו היכא דליכא גומלין וכ"ש היכא דאיכא גומלין. פי' העד אתה עלי ואני עליך. אר"א אימתי אין מעלין במקום שיש עוררים הבאים לפוסלו. אבל במקום שאין עוררין מעלין והוא דליכא גומלין רשב"ג אומר וכו'. לקמן מפרש מאי בינייהו: **ת"ר** זה אומר אני כהן וחבירי כהן (א). וז"א אני כהן וחבירי כהן נאמן להאכילו בתרומה ואינו נאמן להשיאו אשה עד שיהיה שלשה ב' מעידים ע"ז. וב' מעידים ע"ז. פי' המורה אינו נאמן להשיאו אשה מיוחסת ומעלה הוא בכהונה. (ולכך) [וכן] פי' גם ר"ח דאינו נאמן להשיאו אשה הראוה לכהונה. דחיישינן שמא חלל הוא. וק' לי א"כ איזה אשה יקח. דכשירה הראויה לכהונה אסרת לו ישא פסולה לכהונה אסור לו ליקח. דשויא אנפשיה חתיכה דאיסורא באומרו כהן אני. ותו אפילו אי בריירא לן

(א) גירסת רבינו וז"א אני כהן וחבירי כהן וכ"ה בתוספתא דמכילתין פ' ב' ע"ש.

הָכָא נַמִי – בְּשֶׁכְּלֵי אוּמָּנוּתוֹ בְּיָדוֹ. וְהֵיכָא אִתְּמַר דְּרַבִּי חָמָא בַּר עוּקְבָא – אַהָא, דִּתְנַן; *אהַקַּדָּר שֶׁהִנִּיחַ קְדֵירוֹתָיו וְיָרַד לִשְׁתּוֹת (*מַיִם מִן הַיְאוֹר) – הַפְּנִימִיּוֹת טְהוֹרוֹת וְהַחִיצוֹנוֹת טְמֵאוֹת. וְהָתַנְיָא: אֵלּוּ וְאֵלּוּ טְמֵאוֹת! אָמַר רַבִּי חָמָא בַּר עוּקְבָא: בבְּשֶׁכְּלֵי אוּמָּנוּתוֹ בְּיָדוֹ, מִפְּנֵי שֶׁיַּד הַכֹּל מְמַשְׁמֶשֶׁת בָּהֶן. וְהָתַנְיָא: אֵלּוּ וְאֵלּוּ טְהוֹרוֹת! א"ר חָמָא בַּר עוּקְבָא: גבְּשֶׁאֵין כְּלֵי אוּמָּנוּתוֹ בְּיָדוֹ. וְאֶלָּא הָא דִּתְנַן: הַפְּנִימִיּוֹת – טְהוֹרוֹת וְהַחִיצוֹנוֹת – טְמֵאוֹת. הֵיכִי מַשְׁכַּחַתְּ לַהּ? דדִּסְמִיכָא לִרְשׁוּת הָרַבִּים, וּמִשּׁוּם חִיפּוּפֵי רְשׁוּת הָרַבִּים. וְאִיבָּעֵית אֵימָא: ר' יְהוּדָה וְרַבָּנַן בְּמַעֲלִין מִתְּרוּמָה לְיוּחֲסִין קָמִיפַּלְגִי. אִיבַּעְיָא לְהוּ: מַהוּ לְהַעֲלוֹת מִשְּׁטָרוֹת לְיוּחֲסִין? הֵיכִי דָּמֵי? אִילֵימָא דִּכְתִיב בֵּיהּ "אֲנִי פְּלוֹנִי כֹּהֵן חָתַמְתִּי עֵד" – מַאן קָא מַסְהֵיד עִילָּוֵיהּ? לָא צְרִיכָא, דִּכְתִיב בֵּיהּ "אֲנִי פְּלוֹנִי כֹּהֵן לָוִיתִי מָנֶה מִפְּלוֹנִי" וַחֲתִימוּ סָהֲדֵי, מַאי? אַמָּנָה שֶׁבִּשְׁטָר קָא מַסְהֲדִי אוֹ דִּלְמָא אַכּוּלָּהּ מִילְּתָא קָא מַסְהֲדֵי? רַב הוּנָא וְרַב חִסְדָּא; חַד אָמַר: מַעֲלִין, וְחַד אָמַר: האֵין מַעֲלִין. אִיבַּעְיָא לְהוּ: מַהוּ לְהַעֲלוֹת מִנְּשִׂיאוּת כַּפַּיִם לְיוּחֲסִין? תִּיבָּעֵי לְמ"ד מַעֲלִין מִתְּרוּמָה לְיוּחֲסִין, וְתִיבָּעֵי לְמ"ד אֵין מַעֲלִין; תִּיבָּעֵי לְמ"ד מַעֲלִין: הָנֵי מִילֵּי – תְּרוּמָה, דַּעֲוֹן מִיתָה הִיא. אֲבָל נְשִׂיאוּת כַּפַּיִם, דְּאִיסּוּר עֲשֵׂה – לָא, אוֹ דִּלְמָא לָא שְׁנָא? תִּיבָּעֵי לְמ"ד אֵין מַעֲלִין: הָנֵי מִילֵּי – תְּרוּמָה דְּמִיתְאַכְלָא בִּצְנָעָא, אֲבָל נְשִׂיאוּת כַּפַּיִם דִּבְפַרְהֶסְיָא, אִי לָאו כֹּהֵן הוּא – כּוּלֵּי הַאי לָא מַחֲצִיף אֱינָשׁ נַפְשֵׁיהּ, אוֹ דִּלְמָא לָא שְׁנָא? רַב חִסְדָּא וְרַבִּי אָבִינָא: חַד אָמַר: מַעֲלִין, וְחַד אָמַר: ואֵין מַעֲלִין. א"ל רַב נַחְמָן בַּר יִצְחָק לְרָבָא: מַהוּ לְהַעֲלוֹת מִנְּשִׂיאוּת כַּפַּיִם לְיוּחֲסִין? א"ל: פְּלוּגְתָּא דְּרַב חִסְדָּא וְרַבִּי אָבִינָא. הִלְכְתָא מַאי? א"ל: אֲנָא מַתְנִיתָא יָדַעְנָא; דְּתַנְיָא, ר' יוֹסֵי אוֹמֵר: *גְּדוֹלָה חֲזָקָה, שֶׁנֶּאֱמַר: °"וּמִבְּנֵי הַכֹּהֲנִים בְּנֵי חֲבַיָּה בְּנֵי הַקּוֹץ בְּנֵי בַרְזִלַּי אֲשֶׁר לָקַח מִבְּנוֹת בַּרְזִלַּי הַגִּלְעָדִי אִשָּׁה וַיִּקָּרֵא עַל שְׁמָם. אֵלֶּה בִּקְשׁוּ כְתָבָם הַמִּתְיַחְשִׂים וְלֹא נִמְצָאוּ וַיְגֹאֲלוּ מִן הַכְּהֻנָּה. וַיֹּאמֶר הַתִּרְשָׁתָא לָהֶם אֲשֶׁר לֹא יֹאכְלוּ מִקֹּדֶשׁ הַקֳּדָשִׁים עַד עֲמֹד כֹּהֵן לְאוּרִים *וְתוּמִּים". אָמַר לָהֶם: הֲרֵי אַתֶּם בְּחֶזְקַתְכֶם, בַּמֶּה הֱיִיתֶם אוֹכְלִים בַּגּוֹלָה – בְּקָדְשֵׁי הַגְּבוּל, אַף כָּאן – בְּקָדְשֵׁי הַגְּבוּל. וְאִי סָלְקָא דַּעְתָּךְ מַעֲלִין מִנְּשִׂיאוּת כַּפַּיִם לְיוּחֲסִין, הָנֵי, כֵּיוָן דְּפָרְסֵי יְדַיְיהוּ – אָתֵי לְאַסּוֹקִינְהוּ! שָׁאנֵי הָכָא, דְּרִיעַ חֶזְקַיְיהוּ. דְּאִי לָא תֵּימָא הָכִי, לְמַאן דְּאָמַר מַעֲלִין מִתְּרוּמָה לְיוּחֲסִין, כֵּיוָן דְּאָכְלִי בִּתְרוּמָה – אָתֵי לְאַסּוֹקִינְהוּ! אֶלָּא לָאו – מִשּׁוּם דְּרִיעַ חֶזְקַיְיהוּ. וְאֶלָּא

תורה אור (עזרא ב)

בְּשֶׁכְּלֵי אוּמָּנוּתוֹ בְּיָדוֹ. חַמָּר הַמֵּבִיא תְּבוּאָה לִמְכּוֹר, הָיָה נוֹשֵׂא בְּיָדוֹ כְּלִי הֶיכֵּר שֶׁל מְכִירָה, כְּגוֹן מַחַק שֶׁמּוֹחֲקִין בּוֹ הַמִּדָּה. וְהַמְבִיאָהּ לְהַצְנִיעַ אֵינוֹ נוֹשֵׂא בְּיָדוֹ כְּלֵי אוּמָּנוּת מֶכֶר. וְהָכָא כְּגוֹן שֶׁכְּלֵי אוּמָּנוּתוֹ בְּיָדוֹ שֶׁל זֶה הַמְזַלְזֵל אֶת שֶׁלּוֹ, דְּאַתַּן סָהֲדֵי שֶׁלִּמְכּוֹר הֱבִיאָהּ. הִלְכָּךְ אֵין זֶה אֶלָּא גּוֹמֵל, וְזֶה יָעִיד עָלָיו כְּדֶרֶךְ שֶׁלִּפְנֵיהֶם. **הַקַּדָּר.** שֶׁהוּא חָבֵר. **הַפְּנִימִיּוֹת טְהוֹרוֹת.** כּוּלָּהּ מַתְנִיתָא וְאָזְלָא לְקַמֵּיהּ. **בְּשֶׁכְּלֵי אוּמָּנוּתוֹ בְּיָדוֹ.** לְהֶיכֵּר שֶׁהוּא נוֹשְׂאָן לְמוֹכְרָן. **מְמַשְׁמֶשֶׁת בָּהֶן.** לִבְדּוֹק וְלִיקַּח. **וּמִשּׁוּם חִיפּוּפֵי רְשׁוּת הָרַבִּים.** שֶׁנּוֹתְנִים בְּנֵי אָדָם אֲבָנִים גְּדוֹלוֹת אוֹ יְתֵדוֹת לְצִדֵּי רה"ר, לְהַרְחִיק הָעֲגָלוֹת מִלְּהַזִּיק אֶת הַכְּתָלִים, וּמִתּוֹךְ שֶׁהֵן דּוֹחֲקוֹת אֶת רה"ר וְזֶה הִנִּיחַ קְדֵירוֹתָיו אֶצְלָם – דָּחַק גַּם הוּא אֶת הַדֶּרֶךְ. וְהָעוֹבְרִין שָׁם מִתְחַכְּכִין בָּהֶן, וּבִגְדֵיהֶן עוֹבְרִין עַל פְּנֵי אֲוִירָן. וּבִגְדֵי עַם הָאָרֶץ טְמֵאִים הֵם, וּמְטַמְּאִים אֶת הַחִיצוֹנִיּוֹת. **בְּמַעֲלִין מִתְּרוּמָה לְיוּחֲסִין.** רַבִּי יְהוּדָה סָבַר: הָרוֹאֶה שֶׁמַּאֲכִילִין תְּרוּמָה לְאָדָם בְּחֶזְקַת כֹּהֵן – מֵעִיד עָלָיו בְּכָל מָקוֹם שֶׁהוּא כֹּהֵן, וּמַעֲלִין אוֹתוֹ לְיוּחֲסִין. הִלְכָּךְ, אִם תַּאֲכִילֵהוּ תְּרוּמָה – הֲרֵי אַתָּה מְבִיאוֹ לְהַשִּׂיאוֹ אִשָּׁה. וְטַעֲמֵיהּ לָאו מִשּׁוּם גּוֹמְלִין הוּא. וְרַבָּנַן סָבְרֵי: אֵין מַעֲלִין מִתְּרוּמָה לְיוּחֲסִין. **דְּאִיסּוּר מִיתָה.** אִם זָר הוּא – לֹא הָיָה אוֹכֵל תְּרוּמָה, שֶׁהוּא עֲוֹן מִיתָה. **דְּאִיסּוּר עֲשֵׂה.** "כֹּה תְבָרְכוּ" (במדבר ו) – אַתֶּם וְלֹא זָרִים, וְלָאו הַבָּא מִכְּלַל עֲשֵׂה – עֲשֵׂה. **גְּדוֹלָה חֲזָקָה.** שֶׁאֵין ב"ד יְכוֹלִין לְהוֹצִיא דָּבָר מֵחֶזְקָתוֹ. **בִּקְשׁוּ כְתָבָם הַמִּתְיַחְשִׂים.** שֶׁיְּהוּ כֹּהֲנִים כְּשֵׁרִים, לְפִי שֶׁהִתְחַתְּנוּ כֹּהֲנִים בַּגּוֹלָה בְּגוֹיֵי הָאָרֶץ וְיָלְדוּ לָהֶם בָּנִים, כִּדְכְתִיב בְּסֵפֶר עֶזְרָא, וְהֵם חֲלָלִים – הוּצְרְכוּ הַנּוֹלָדִים בַּגּוֹלָה לְהִתְיַחֵס, כְּשֶׁעָלוּ מִן הַגּוֹלָה לְשָׁרֵת בְּבִנְיָן שֵׁנִי. **וַיְגֹאֲלוּ.** נִפְסְלוּ, מִלְּשׁוֹן "לֶחֶם מְגוֹאָל" (מלאכי א). **הַתִּרְשָׁתָא.** הוּא נְחֶמְיָה בֶּן חֲכַלְיָה, וְכֵן כָּתוּב בְּסֵפֶר עֶזְרָא (נחמיה ח). **עַד עֲמוֹד כֹּהֵן לְאוּרִים וגו'.** כְּאָדָם (א) שֶׁאוֹמֵר לַחֲבֵירוֹ "עַד שֶׁיָּבֹא הַמָּשִׁיחַ". דְּאוּרִים וְתוּמִּים לֹא הֲווּ בְּמִקְדָּשׁ שֵׁנִי, שֶׁנֶּחְסְרוּ חֲמִשָּׁה דְּבָרִים, כִּדְאָמְרִינַן בְּסֵדֶר יוֹמָא (דף כא:). **מִקֹּדֶשׁ הַקֳּדָשִׁים.** דַּוְקָא מִקָּדְשֵׁי הַמִּקְדָּשׁ פְּסָלִינְהוּ, אֲבָל תְּרוּמָה שֶׁהָיוּ רְגִילִין בָּהּ בַּגּוֹלָה – לֹא אָסַר עֲלַיְיהוּ, מִשּׁוּם דְּהוּחְזְקוּ בָּהּ. **קָדְשֵׁי הַגְּבוּל.** תְּרוּמָה, שֶׁהִיא נוֹהֶגֶת בַּגְּבוּלִין, חוּץ לַמִּקְדָּשׁ וְלִירוּשָׁלַיִם. **אַף כָּאן בְּקָדְשֵׁי הַגְּבוּל.** וּמִדְּאָמַר רַבִּי יוֹסֵי גְּדוֹלָה חֲזָקָה – ש"מ נְשִׂיאוּת כַּפַּיִם נַמִּי לֹא אָסַר עֲלַיְיהוּ, שֶׁהֲרֵי הוּחְזְקוּ בָּהּ בַּגְּבוּלִין. **וְאִי סָלְקָא דַּעְתָּךְ כו' אָתוּ לְאַסּוֹקִינְהוּ.** וּמַה הוֹעִילוּ בְּתַקָּנָתָם. **שָׁאנֵי הָכָא.** דְּלֵיכָּא לְמֵיחַשׁ דְּלִיסּוֹקִינְהוּ, דְּהָא רִיעַ חֶזְקַיְיהוּ, שֶׁהֲרֵי הַכֹּל רוֹאִין שְׁאָר כֹּהֲנִים אוֹכְלִין קָדְשֵׁי הַמִּקְדָּשׁ, וְהֵם אֵינָן אוֹכְלִין – יֵשׁ כָּאן הֶיכֵּר גָּדוֹל שֶׁיֵּשׁ בָּהֶן צַד פְּסוּל. אֲבָל שְׁאָר בְּנֵי אָדָם, כְּגוֹן בַּזְּמַן הַזֶּה – לְעוֹלָם מַעֲלִין מִנְּשִׂיאוּת כַּפַּיִם לְיוּחֲסִין. [דְּאִי לָא תֵּימָא הָכִי. דְּעַל כָּרְחָךְ לָאו הַאי טַעְמָא, דְּהָא אִיכָּא דְּלֹא סָמֵיךְ, שֶׁיֵּשׁ בָּהֶן הֶיכֵּר תְּרוּמָה נַמִּי תִּקְשֵׁי, לְמ"ד מַעֲלִין מִתְּרוּמָה לְיוּחֲסִין]. וְאֶלָּא

בשכלי אומנותו בידו. פירש רבינו חננאל: זה שאומר עליו שהוא כהן – יש בידו כלים שמשמשין בהן בטהרה, כגון כלי גללים כלי אבנים כלי אדמה שאין מקבלין טומאה, שכל הרואה כלים הללו בידו מתרחק ממנו מלטמאותו, ודומה שהוא כהן, ולכך האמינוהו חכמים.

ואיבעית אימא רבי יהודה ורבנן במעלין מתרומה ליוחסין קמיפלגי. ולא אתא לשנויי אלא קשיא דרבי יהודה אדרבי יהודה, אבל דרבנן אדרבנן לעולם צריך לתרץ בשכלי אומנותו בידו. הקשה הר' שמואל מוורדין: ומעיקרא, היכי בעי למימר דטעמא דר"י משום גומלין? והא בלא גומלים ע"כ סבר רבי יהודה בשילהי פרקין (לקמן דף כח:) דמעלין מתרומה ליוחסין! ותירץ ר"י: דמעיקרא ס"ד דאי לאו טעמא משום גומלים – לא היינו מפסידים את הכהן מן התרומה כדי לומר מעלין, כיון דמן הדין ראוי לחלוק ע"פ חבירו. ואדרבה, קודם היינו אומרים אין מעלין, אע"ג דגבי עבד אמר לקמן לרבי יהודה דאין חולקין לו תרומה משום דמעלין – התם אין כל כך חששא בהפסד של עבד זה אם אין חולקין לו תרומה בלא רבו. וא"ת: ובאיזו סברא פליגי? לימרו תרוייהו דמעלין, ונצטרך שני עדים בתרומה, או לימרו תרוייהו דלא מעלין – ולא יצטרך אלא עד אחד בתרומה! וי"ל דבהא פליגי: דמר סבר חיישינן שמא יעלו מתרומה ליוחסין לפיכך הצריכו שני עדים, ומר סבר דלא חיישינן*.

אמנה שבשטר קמסהדי. וא"ת: ואי לאו אכולא מילתא קמסהדי, א"כ עדים חתמי אע"ג דלא ידעי אי כהן הוא אי לאו, ואם כן הא דתנן ב"גט פשוט" (ב"ב דף קעב.): שני יוסף בן שמעון הדרין בעיר אחת, אם היו משולשין – יכתבו כהן. ומה מועיל? כיון שעדים חותמין אע"פ שאין מכירים בו אם הוא כהן, והרי הוא יכול להעריס ולכתוב שטר אחר בשם חבירו כהן, ויוציא ממון מחבירו כהן! וי"ל: דהיכא דהוחזקו שני יוסף בן שמעון – ודאי אכולא מילתא קא מסהדי, כי אז הן צריכין לידע אם בן כהן הוא, והתם ודאי מעלין משטרות ליוחסין, והכא מיבעיא לן היכא דלא הוחזקו. **חד** אמר מעלין. ואם תאמר: ואמאי לא חשיב ליה בהדי הנך דתנן ב"עשרה יוחסין" (קדושין דף עו. ושם): אין בודקין מן המזבח ולמעלה, ולא מדוכן כו'? וי"ל: דהך דשטרות מלתא דפשיטא היא, דכיון דאכולא מלתא קמסהדי – א"כ הוי עדות גמור, ולכך לא קא חשיב עדים. וא"ת: ואמאי לא חשיב תרומה ונשיאות כפים למ"ד מעלין? ואור"ת: דתרומה בכלל מזבח, ונשיאות כפים בכלל דוכן. אע"ג דההוא דוכן היינו שיר, כדמשמע התם בגמרא, מ"ד מעלין – הוה מוקי לה נמי בדוכן כהנים שבגבולים. ומיהו, קשה: אמאי לא חשיב ס"ת שקרא בחזקת כהן כדלקמן? ויש לומר: דליכא למימר דתנא ושייר כולהו, ובספר הישר פירש ר"ת: דלאו בעבודת מזבח ממש איירי, אלא כגון הפסח וניתות, דברים הכשרים בזרים, דלא היו מניחין לעשות אותם אלא למיוחסין מן המשיאין לכהונה, אבל מילי דכהונה כגון תרומה ונשיאות כפים וס"ת – לא איצטריך למתני. **שאני** הכא דריע חזקייהו. פי' בקונטרס: שהכל רואים שאר כהנים אוכלין שאר קדשי מזבח, ואלו אין אוכלין. וק"ק: דמ"מ תיקשי למ"ד מעלין, אמאי לא אסקינהו לקדשי מזבח וליוחסין? ונראה לר"ת: דריע חזקייהו – היינו שהיו מיחסים אותם אחר בני ברזילי, שהיה ישראל. ועוד שלא מצאו כתבם. והיכא דאיתרע חזקה – אין מעלין לכ"ע. אבל קשה: דפריך מעיקרא אתי לאסוקינהו, הוה ליה למיפרך אמאי נגאלו כלל מן הכהונה? ויש לומר: דשפיר הוה ידע דריע חזקייהו, ומשום הכי לא אסקינהו, אלא דהוה ס"ד דאע"ג דריע חזקייהו – איכא למיחש דלמא אתי לאסוקינהו לבסוף, שלא ידעו שלא מצאו כתבם. ואלא

[ועוד רצה ר"י לפרש טעמא דמ"ד מעלין כדי שיהו עדים מצויין ליוחסין וחזר בו משום דלא משמע הכי בסמוך דקאמר ה"מ בתרומה דעון מיתה. ת"י עה"ג]

תוספות רי"ד

לן דחלל הוא. אמאי לא ישא אשה כשרה ואפי' בתו של כ"ג. והא קי"ל דלא הוזהרו כשרות להנשא לפסולים. ונ"ל לפרש דהאי דאמר להשיאו אשה לאו להשיאו לו אשה. אלא להשיא מנשיו לכהונה. כגון אלמנתו ובתו דמספקינן ליה בחלל. ובת חלל ואלמנות חלל הן פסולות לכהונה: איבעיא להו מהו להעלות משטרות ליוחסין. פי' אילימא דכתיב בי' אני פלוני כהן חתמתי עד מאן קמסהיד עלויה. לא צריכא דכתיב בי' אני פ' כהן לויתי מנה מפלוני וחתימו סהדי אמנה שבשטר קא מסהדי א"ד אכולה מילתא מסהדי. ר"ה ור"ח ח"א מעלין וח"א אין מעלין והלכתא כדברי המיקל. ואילו כתבו שני עדים פ' כהן לוה מפלוני דליכא מאן דפליג דודאי מעלין. דהא עדים מעידים כי הוא כהן א). איבעי' להו מהו להעלות מכהונה ליוחסין.

א) וכ"כ הר"נ כאן בשם הרא"ה ז"ל ע"ש ובזה מיושב קושית תוס' ד"ה אמנה מה שהקשו מפ' גט פשוט ודו"ק ועי' בש"ך חו"מ סי' מ"ט ס"ק ע"ו:

פד א ב ג ד מיי' פי"ב מהל' משכב ומושב הלכה כג:
פה ה מיי' פ"כ מהל' איסורי ביאה הלכ' ט טוש"ע אה"ע סי' ג סעיף ב:
פו ו מיי' שם הלכה ד והלכה יא:

טהרות פ"ז מ"א [במשנה ליתא]

הגהות הב"ח

(א) רש"י ד"ה עד עמוד כו' כאדם שאומר. נ"ב הוא בפ' עגלה ערופה דף מח ע"ב:

קדושין סט:

[נ"ל ולתומים]

נ"י כ

וְאֶלָּא מַאי גְּדוֹלָה חֲזָקָה? מֵעִיקָּרָא אֲכוּל בִּתְרוּמָה דְּרַבָּנַן, הָשְׁתָּא אֲכוּל בִּתְרוּמָה דְּאוֹרַיְיתָא. וְאִי בָּעֵית אֵימָא: [א]הָשְׁתָּא נַמִי בִּתְרוּמָה דְּרַבָּנַן אֲכוּל, בִּתְרוּמָה דְּאוֹרַיְיתָא לָא אֲכוּל. [ב]וְכִי מַסְּקִינַן מִתְּרוּמָה לְיוֹחֲסִין — בִּתְרוּמָה דְּאוֹרַיְיתָא, בִּתְרוּמָה דְּרַבָּנַן — לָא מַסְּקִינַן. וְאֶלָּא מַאי גְּדוֹלָה חֲזָקָה? דְּאע"ג דְּאִיכָּא לְמִיגְזַר מִשּׁוּם תְּרוּמָה דְּאוֹרַיְיתָא — לָא גָּזְרִינַן. וּבִתְרוּמָה דְּאוֹרַיְיתָא לָא אֲכוּל? וְהָא כְּתִיב: °"אֲשֶׁר לֹא יֹאכְלוּ מִקֹּדֶשׁ הַקֳּדָשִׁים", מִקֹּדֶשׁ הַקֳּדָשִׁים הוּא דְּלָא אֲכוּל, הָא בִּתְרוּמָה דְּאוֹרַיְיתָא אֲכוּל! ה"ק: לָא בְּמִידֵּי דְּאִיקְּרִי קֹדֶשׁ, דִּכְתִיב: °"וְכָל זָר לֹא יֹאכַל קֹדֶשׁ", וְלָא בְּמִידֵּי דְּאִיקְּרִי קֳדָשִׁים, דִּכְתִיב: °"וּבַת כֹּהֵן כִּי תִהְיֶה לְאִישׁ זָר הִיא בִּתְרוּמַת הַקֳּדָשִׁים לֹא תֹאכֵל". וְאָמַר מָר: *בַּמּוּרָם מִן הַקֳּדָשִׁים לֹא תֹאכֵל. ת"ש: חֲזָקָה לִכְהוּנָּה — נְשִׂיאוּת כַּפַּיִם בְּבָבֶל, וַאֲכִילַת חַלָּה בְּסוּרְיָא, *וְחִילּוּק מַתָּנוֹת בִּכְרַכִּין. קָתָנֵי מִיהַת נְשִׂיאוּת כַּפַּיִם, מַאי לָאו לְיוֹחֲסִין? [ג]לָא, לִתְרוּמָה. וְהָא דּוּמְיָא דַּאֲכִילַת חַלָּה קָתָנֵי, מָה אֲכִילַת חַלָּה לְיוֹחֲסִין — אַף נְשִׂיאוּת כַּפַּיִם לְיוֹחֲסִין! לָא, אֲכִילַת חַלָּה גּוּפָהּ לִתְרוּמָה. קָסָבַר: חַלָּה בַּזְּמַן הַזֶּה דְּרַבָּנַן, וּתְרוּמָה דְּאוֹרַיְיתָא, וּמַסְּקִינַן מֵחַלָּה דְּרַבָּנַן לִתְרוּמָה דְּאוֹרַיְיתָא. וְכִדְאַפֵּיךְ לְהוּ רַב הוּנָא בְּרֵיהּ דְּרַב יְהוֹשֻׁעַ לְרַבָּנַן. ת"ש: *חֲזָקָה לִכְהוּנָּה — נְשִׂיאוּת כַּפַּיִם וְחִילּוּק גְּרָנוֹת בְּא"י, וּבְסוּרְיָא וּבְכָל מָקוֹם שֶׁשְּׁלוּחֵי רֹאשׁ חוֹדֶשׁ מַגִּיעִין נְשִׂיאוּת כַּפַּיִם רְאָיָה, אֲבָל לֹא חִילּוּק גְּרָנוֹת. וּבָבֶל כְּסוּרְיָא, רשב"ג אוֹמֵר: אַף אֲלֶכְּסַנְדְּרִיָּא שֶׁל מִצְרַיִם בָּרִאשׁוֹנָה, מִפְּנֵי שֶׁבֵּית דִּין קְבוּעִין שָׁם. קָתָנֵי מִיהַת נְשִׂיאוּת כַּפַּיִם, מַאי לָאו לְיוֹחֲסִין? לָא, לְחַלָּה. הָא דּוּמְיָא דְּחִילּוּק גְּרָנוֹת קָתָנֵי, מַה חִילּוּק גְּרָנוֹת לְיוֹחֲסִין — אַף נְשִׂיאוּת כַּפַּיִם לְיוֹחֲסִין! לָא, חִילּוּק גְּרָנוֹת גּוּפָהּ לְחַלָּה. [ד]קָסָבַר: תְּרוּמָה בַּזְּמַן הַזֶּה דְּרַבָּנַן, וְחַלָּה דְּאוֹרַיְיתָא, וּמַסְּקִינַן מִתְּרוּמָה דְּרַבָּנַן לְחַלָּה דְּאוֹרַיְיתָא. וְכִדְאַשְׁכַּחִינְהוּ רַב הוּנָא בְּרֵיהּ דְּרַב יְהוֹשֻׁעַ לְרַבָּנַן. *דַּאֲמַר רַב הוּנָא בְּרֵיהּ דְּרַב יְהוֹשֻׁעַ: אַשְׁכַּחְתִּינְהוּ לְרַבָּנַן בְּבֵי רַב דְּיָתְבֵי וְקָאָמְרִי: אֲפִילּוּ לְמַאן דְּאָמַר תְּרוּמָה בַּזְּמַן הַזֶּה דְּרַבָּנַן — חַלָּה דְּאוֹרַיְיתָא, שֶׁהֲרֵי *ז' שֶׁכִּבְּשׁוּ וְז' שֶׁחִילְּקוּ נִתְחַיְּיבוּ בְּחַלָּה וְלֹא נִתְחַיְּיבוּ *בִּתְרוּמָה. וְאָמִינָא לְהוּ אֲנָא: אַדְּרַבָּה, אֲפִילּוּ לְמ"ד תְּרוּמָה בַּזְּמַן הַזֶּה דְּאוֹרַיְיתָא — חַלָּה [ה]דְּרַבָּנַן. דְּתַנְיָא: °"בְּבוֹאֲכֶם אֶל הָאָרֶץ", אִי *"בְּבוֹאֲכֶם" יָכוֹל מִשֶּׁנִּכְנְסוּ לָהּ שְׁנַיִם וּשְׁלֹשָׁה מְרַגְּלִים — ת"ל: "בְּבוֹאֲכֶם", בְּבִיאַת כּוּלְּכֶם אָמַרְתִּי, וְלֹא בְּבִיאַת מִקְצָתְכֶם. וְכִי אַסְּקִינְהוּ עֶזְרָא

לָאו

(Marginal source references beside the main text: עזרא ב | ויקרא כב | שם | במדבר טו; תורה אור)

רש"י

וְאֶלָּא מַאי גְּדוֹלָה חֲזָקָה. דְּקָאָמַר ר' יוֹסֵי, לָמָּה לָנוּ [לָחוּשׁ] לְהַשְׁבִּית חֶזְקָתָם, כִּי מַה יֵּשׁ לָחוּשׁ לְבַטָּלָה? בִּתְרוּמָה דְּרַבָּנַן. שֶׁהֲרֵי בַּגּוֹלָה הָיוּ, שֶׁאֵין שָׁם תְּרוּמָה מִן הַתּוֹרָה. דְּכָל מִצְוָה שֶׁהִיא תְּלוּיָה בָּאָרֶץ אֵינָהּ נוֹהֶגֶת אֶלָּא בָּאָרֶץ, כִּדְאָמְרִינַן בְּקִידּוּשִׁין (דף לו:). **וְאִיבָּעֵית אֵימָא הָשְׁתָּא נַמִי בִּתְרוּמָה דְּרַבָּנַן אֲכוּל.** תְּרוּמַת פֵּירוֹת הָאִילָן וְיָרָק. **דְּאוֹרַיְיתָא.** דָּגָן תִּירוֹשׁ וְיִצְהָר לָא אֲכוּל. ומש"ה לָא קַשְׁיָא לְמ"ד מַעֲלִין מִתְּרוּמָה לְיוֹחֲסִין, דְּכִי מַסְּקִינַן לְיוֹחֲסִין — מִתְּרוּמָה דְּאוֹרַיְיתָא כו'. **דְּאִיכָּא לְמִיגְזַר מִשּׁוּם תְּרוּמָה דְּאוֹרַיְיתָא.** שֶׁהֲרֵי לָאָרֶץ בָּאוּ, וּמְצוּיָה שָׁם תְּרוּמָה גְּמוּרָה דְּאוֹרַיְיתָא, מַה שֶּׁלֹּא הָיָה מָצוּי לָהֶם בַּגּוֹלָה, וְיֵשׁ לָחוּשׁ פֶּן יַאֲכִילוּם בָּהּ. **לָא בְּמִידֵּי דְּאִקְּרֵי קֹדֶשׁ.** וְהַיְינוּ תְּרוּמָה. **וְכָל זָר לֹא יֹאכַל קֹדֶשׁ.** בִּתְרוּמָה מִשְׁתָּעֵי, דִּכְתִיב בַּפָּרָשָׁה לְעֵיל מִינֵּיהּ "וּבָא הַשֶּׁמֶשׁ וְטָהֵר וְאַחַר יֹאכַל מִן הַקֳּדָשִׁים", וְאוֹקְמִינַן בִּתְרוּמָה, בִּיבָמוֹת בְּ"הֶעָרֵל" (דף עד:). **וְלָא בְּמִידֵּי דְּאִקְּרֵי קֳדָשִׁים.** אֲפִילּוּ חָזֶה וְשׁוֹק שֶׁל שְׁלָמִים הַנֶּאֱכָלִים לִנְשֵׁי כֹּהֲנִים וּלְעַבְדֵיהֶם. **וְאָמַר מָר.** בִּיבָמוֹת, בְּפֶרֶק "יֵשׁ מוּתָּרוֹת", בְּבַת כֹּהֵן שֶׁנִּישֵּׂאת לְיִשְׂרָאֵל וְנַעֲשֵׂית אַלְמָנָה וּגְרוּשָׁה וְזֶרַע אֵין לָהּ, שֶׁחוֹזֶרֶת לִתְרוּמַת אָבִיהָ וְאֵינָהּ חוֹזֶרֶת לְחָזֶה וְשׁוֹק. וְיָלֵיף לָהּ מֵהַאי קְרָא "כִּי תִהְיֶה לְאִישׁ זָר הִיא בִּתְרוּמַת הַקֳּדָשִׁים לֹא תֹאכֵל" עוֹד. **חֲזָקָה לִכְהוּנָּה.** לְהָעִיד עָלָיו שֶׁהוּא כֹּהֵן. **נְשִׂיאוּת כַּפַּיִם בְּבָבֶל.** הָרוֹאֵהוּ נוֹשֵׂא כַּפָּיו בְּבָבֶל מֵעִיד עָלָיו בְּכָל מָקוֹם שֶׁהוּא כֹּהֵן, וּמְקַבְּלִין הֵימֶנּוּ. לְפִי שֶׁיֵּשׁ שָׁם יְשִׁיבָה, וּב"ד קָבוּעַ בּוֹדְקִין אַחַר נוֹשְׂאֵי כַפַּיִם. אֲבָל אֲכִילַת חַלָּה וּתְרוּמָה אֵינָהּ חֲזָקָה, דְּחוּצָה לָאָרֶץ לָאו דְּאוֹרַיְיתָא תְּרוּמָה דִּילֵיהּ, וְלָא קָפְדִי כּוּלֵּי הַאי. **וַאֲכִילַת חַלָּה בְּסוּרְיָא.** הִיא אֲרַם צוֹבָה שֶׁכְּבָשָׁהּ דָּוִד וְחִיבְּרָהּ לְא"י. וְקָסָבַר הַאי תַּנָּא: כִּיבּוּשׁ יָחִיד שְׁמֵיהּ כִּיבּוּשׁ, וְחַלָּתָהּ וּתְרוּמָתָהּ דְּאוֹרַיְיתָא. וְקס"ד: תָּנָא חַלָּה, וְה"ה לִתְרוּמָה. **וְחִילּוּק מַתָּנוֹת.** דְּהַזְּרוֹעַ וְהַלְּחָיַיִם. **בִּכְרַכִּין.** וְאע"ג דְּאִיסּוּרָן אֵין אִיסּוּר לְזָרִים, הוֹאִיל וּכְרַכִּים מְקוֹם שְׁוָוקִין הֵן, וּמְצוּיִין בּוֹ עוֹבְרִים וְשָׁבִים הַמַּכִּירִין בּוֹ, אִי לָאו דְּכֹהֵן הֲוָה — לָא מַחְלִיף נַפְשֵׁיהּ. **לָא לִתְרוּמָה.** הָרוֹאֵהוּ נוֹשֵׂא כַּפָּיו בְּבָבֶל, אוֹ אוֹכֵל חַלָּה דַּוְוקָא בְּסוּרְיָא, וְהֵעִיד עָלָיו בְּא"י — מְקַבְּלִין עֵדוּתוֹ לְהַאֲכִילוֹ תְּרוּמָה, אֲבָל לֹא לְיוֹחֲסִין. **מָה אֲכִילַת חַלָּה.** עֵדוּת חֶזְקָתָהּ. **לְיוֹחֲסִין.** דְּאִי לִתְרוּמָה — פְּשִׁיטָא! הִיא גּוּפָהּ תְּרוּמָה הִיא, וּכְבָר הוּחְזַק בָּהּ. **וּמַסְּקִינַן מֵחַלָּה דְּרַבָּנַן כו'.** דְּאִי לָאו כֹּהֵן הוּא, לָא הֲווּ סָפוּ לֵיהּ חַלָּה, גְּזֵירָה מִשּׁוּם תְּרוּמָה. **וְכִדְאַפֵּיךְ.** לְקַמָּן מְפָרֵשׁ. **נְשִׂיאוּת כַּפַּיִם וְחִילּוּק גְּרָנוֹת.** דִּתְרוּמָה. **בְּא"י.** נוֹשְׂאֵי כַפַּיִם, דְּאִיכָּא ב"ד קְבוּעִין וּבָדְקִי. וְחִילּוּק גְּרָנוֹת קס"ד הַשְׁתָּא דִּתְרוּמָה בַּזְּמַן הַזֶּה דְּאוֹרַיְיתָא, וְכֵיוָן דַּעֲוֹן מִיתָה אִיכָּא — מַסְּקִינַן מִינֵּיהּ לְיוֹחֲסִין. **בְּסוּרְיָא וּבְכָל מָקוֹם שֶׁשְּׁלוּחֵי א"י מַגִּיעִין.** לְהוֹדִיעַ לַגּוֹלָה יוֹם שֶׁקִּידְּשׁוּ ב"ד אֶת הַחֹדֶשׁ לַעֲשׂוֹת פֶּסַח בִּזְמַנּוֹ, דְּהַיְינוּ הַיּוֹשְׁבִים בְּתוֹךְ מַהֲלַךְ חֲמִשָּׁה עָשָׂר יוֹם. **נְשִׂיאוּת כַּפַּיִם רְאָיָה.** לְפִי שֶׁב"ד קָבוּעַ שָׁם, שֶׁמְּקַבֵּל שְׁלִיחוּת הַחֹדֶשׁ שֶׁל ב"ד הַגָּדוֹל. **אֲבָל לֹא חִילּוּק גְּרָנוֹת.** דִּתְרוּמָה דִּידְהוּ לָאו דְּאוֹרַיְיתָא — וּבְסוּרְיָא נַמִי, הַאי תַּנָּא סָבַר: כִּיבּוּשׁ יָחִיד לָא שְׁמֵיהּ כִּיבּוּשׁ. וּפְלוּגְתָּא דְּתַנָּאֵי הִיא בְּהַךְ מִילְּתָא (ע"ז דף כא.). **בְּבֵי רַב.** בֵּית הַמִּדְרָשׁ קָרֵי בֵּי רַב. **נִתְחַיְּיבוּ בְּחַלָּה.** דִּכְתִיב "בְּבוֹאֲכֶם אֶל הָאָרֶץ", וְתַנְיָא בְּסִפְרֵי: ר' יִשְׁמָעֵאל אוֹמֵר: שִׁינָּה הַכָּתוּב בִּיאָה זוֹ מִכָּל בִּיאוֹת שֶׁבַּתּוֹרָה, שֶׁבְּכוּלָּן נֶאֱמַר "כִּי תָבֹאוּ" "כִּי יְבִיאֲךָ", וְכָאן "בְּבוֹאֲכֶם" — לְלַמֶּדְךָ שֶׁכֵּיוָן שֶׁנִּכְנְסוּ לָהּ נִתְחַיְּיבוּ. **וְלֹא נִתְחַיְּיבוּ בִּתְרוּמוֹת וּמַעַשְׂרוֹת.** דִּכְתִיב "דְּגָנְךָ" "תְּבוּאַת זַרְעֶךָ" — הַמְיוּחֶדֶת לָךְ. *וְעוֹד, שֶׁהֲרֵי תָּלָה הַכָּתוּב הַמַּעֲשֵׂר בְּמִנְיַן שְׁנוֹת הַשְּׁמִטָּה, דִּכְתִיב "בַּשָּׁנָה הַשְּׁלִישִׁית שְׁנַת הַמַּעֲשֵׂר", וּשְׁמִטּוֹת לֹא מָנוּ אֶלָּא מִשֶּׁכִּבְּשׁוּ וְחִילְּקוּ, כִּדְאָמְרִינַן בְּסֵדֶר עוֹלָם וּבְמַסֶּכֶת עֲרָכִין (דף יב:). הָכִי גָּרְסִינַן. **אִי בְּבוֹאֲכֶם יָכוֹל מִשֶּׁנִּכְנְסוּ לָהּ שְׁנַיִם וּשְׁלֹשָׁה מְרַגְּלִים תַּלְמוּד לוֹמַר בְּבוֹאֲכֶם בְּבִיאַת כּוּלְּכֶם כו'.** וְהָכִי פֵּירוּשׁוֹ: כֵּיוָן דְּשִׁינָּה הַכָּתוּב בִּיאָה זוֹ לִכְתּוֹב בָּהּ "בְּבוֹאֲכֶם" וְלָא כָּתַב "כִּי תָבֹאוּ", יָכוֹל מִשֶּׁנִּכְנְסוּ לָהּ מְרַגְּלִים, ת"ל כו'.

תוספות

ואלא מאי גדולה חזקה. בשלמא אי אין מעלין – ניחא הא דגדולה חזקה, אע"ג דאיכא למיחש לב"ד טועין שיעלו מן נשיאות כפים לקדשי קדשים. [ואע"ג דבלא חזקה, מעלין לתרומה ע"פ עד אחד ולא חיישינן לב"ד טועין שמא יעלו ליוחסין – השתא סבר המקשן דיוחסין חמירא, ולא אתו למיטעי, כמו לקדשי קדשים]. אבל השתא דאמרת טעמא דריע חזקייהו, ולא חיישינן דלמא אתי לאסוקי, כיון דלא אתי למטעי – מאי גדולה חזקה? (לעיל) **אן** דלמא אפילו למ"ד אין מעלין ה"מ תרומה דמתאכלא בצינעא כו'. תימה: מה תולה באכילה? והא פשיטא דלכ"ע אין מעלין מאכילת תרומה ליוחסין, דהא איכא למיחש דלמא עבד כהן, הוא אלא בחלוקת תרומה (א) בגורן הוא דפליגי אם מעלים ליוחסין אם לאו, ובמעלין מתרומה ליוחסין לא איפליגו בה תנאי בהדיא, אלא דתליא הא פלוגתא בפלוגתא אם חולקין תרומה לעבד בלא רבו אם לאו. למ"ד חולקין – אין מעלין, דדלמא עבד הוא. והכי איבעי ליה למימר הכא: אפילו למ"ד אין מעלין – ה"מ תרומה, דחולקין לעבד בלא רבו ואיכא למיחש דלמא עבד הוא, אבל נשיאו' כפים – לעולם אימא לך דמעלין, דאין עבד נושא כפיו! [נ"ל דספיר נקט דמתאכלא בצינעא, דלמ"ד מעלין – מאכילת תרומה נמי מעלין, ובעינן דליכא למיחש שהוא עבד, שילא מבית הספר. וטעמא, כיון דעון מיתה הוא – חיישינן שבא יעלוהו ליוחסין ולכך איצטריך שני עדים להאכילו בתרומה. ולכך נמי אין חולקין לעבד אלא א"כ רבו עמו. ומ"ד אין מעלין, אע"ג דעון מיתה הוא – לא חייש להכי שבא יעלוהו, כיון דבצנעא הויא אכילת תרומה וכן חלוקה. אבל נשיאות כפים דאיפרסם, איבעיא ליה אי חיישינן שמא יעלוהו. משום דאי לאו דכהן הוא – לא הוה מחלף כולי האי. ולא הוי מצי למנקט כמו שכתבו התוס' אפילו למ"ד אין מעלין, משום דאיכא למיחש דלמא עבד הוא. דלא תליא בהכי, דאפילו היכא דליכא למיחש דלמא עבד הוא אין מעלין, כמו ביוצא מבית הספר, או שמעידין עליו שאינו עבד. ואדרבה, הא דחולקין לו בלא רבו — הרינו משום דאין מעלין. ועיקר טעמא דפלוגתייהו משום מעלין ואין מעלין, דאי לאו הכי — קשה באיזה סברא פליגי, כמו שהקשו לעיל] (ת"י).

וכי מסקינן מתרומה ליוחסין ה"מ בדאורייתא כו'. רבינו יצחק בן רבינו מאיר לא גריס לה, דהא איבע"ת אימא רב נחמן קאמר לה, ואי גרסי' לה – א"כ היה סותר בעצמו רא"ה שהביא: דאי לא תימא הכי למ"ד מעלין מתרומה ליוחסין הא אתי לאסוקי! אלא טעמא משום דריע חזקייהו. ואין זו סוגיית התלמוד, אם לא יאמר "ולאו מילתא היא דאמרי". ובפ' "עשרה יוחסין" (קדושין סט:) גרסינן לה, ואגב שיטפא דהתם שיבשו לכותבה כאן. **לא** במידי דאיקרי קדש. וא"ת: תרומה נמי איקרי קדשים, דכתיב "ובא השמש וטהר ואחר יאכל מן הקדשים", וההוא קרא איירי בתרומה, דהעריב שמשו אוכל בתרומה! וי"ל: דודאי גבי טמא, תרומה מיקרי קדשים, אבל הכא אאכילת זר קאמר, דלא אשכחן קדשים גבי אכילת זר. **נשיאות** כפים בבבל. דוקא נשיאות כפים, ולא אכילת חלה. ואע"ג דבסוריא נמי הוי מדרבנן – אין מדקדקין בבבל כמו בסוריא. דסבר האי תנא כיבוש יחיד שמיה כיבוש. ואכילת חלה בסוריא ה"ה נשיאות כפים, כדמוכח לקמן. **לא** חילוק גרנות גופה לחלה וקסבר תרומה כו'. וי"ל דפליגי הנך ברייתות בפלוגתא דרב הונא בריה דרב יהושע ורבנן. דאי לאו הכי, בחד מהנך ברייתות ממה נפשך איכא למידק דמעלין מנשיאות כפים ליוחסין. ופליגי נמי, דלברייתא קמייתא אכילת חלה בסוריא חזקה לתרומה, וכל שכן דאכילת תרומה דאורייתא דהויא חזקה לאכילת חלה דרבנן. ובברייתא שניה קתני דחילוק גרנות, דהיינו תרומה בסוריא, לא הויא חזקה לחלה.

עדות

[עיין תוס' נדה מז. ד"ה ל"ג אילו נאמר]

ג"י כ"י

פז א מיי' פ"כ מהל' איסורי ביאה הלכה א ופ"ו מהל' תרומות ה"ב:
פח ב מיי' פ"כ מהל' איסורי ביאה הלכ' ז:
פט ג מיי' שם הלכה יא טוש"ע אה"ע סימן ג סעיף ב:
צ ד מיי' שם הלכה ג ופ"א מהל' תרומות ה"א סמג עשין מג טוש"ע י"ד סימן שלא סעיף ב:
צא ה מיי' פ"כ מהל' איסורי ביאה הלכה ג סמג עשין קמ טוש"ע י"ד סי' שכב סעיף ב:

הגהות הב"ח

(א) תד"ה או דלמא כו' אלא בחלוקת תרומה וכו'. נ"ב וכן פרש"י יבמות דף צט ע"ב:

יבמות סח: פז. קדושין סט:
[עיין תוס' שבת י: ד"ה יהבה]
[תוספתא פ"ג ותוספתא פאה פ"ד]
נדה מז.
[ב"מ פט.]
[בנדה מז. וכן בב"מ פט. איתא במעשר ועי' פרש"י דהכא דגרים תרווייהו]
[ועיין רש"י בנדה מז. וב"מ פט. מפרש בכל מקום טעם אחר]

צב א ב מיי' פ"כ מהל' איסורי ביאה הלכ' יא:
צג ג מיי' שם הלכה ה:

לָאו כּוּלְּהוּ סְלוּק. ת"ש: חֲזָקָה לִכְהוּנָּה — נְשִׂיאוּת כַּפַּיִם, וְחִילּוּק גְּרָנוֹת, וְעֵדוּת. עֵדוּת חֲזָקָה הִיא?! אֶלָּא לָאו הָכִי קָאָמַר: נְשִׂיאוּת כַּפַּיִם כִּי עֵדוּת, מָה עֵדוּת לְיוּחֲסִין אַף נְשִׂיאוּת כַּפַּיִם לְיוּחֲסִין. לָא, עֵדוּת הַבָּאָה מִכֹּחַ חֲזָקָה — כַּחֲזָקָה. [א]כִּי הַהוּא דַּאֲתָא לְקַמֵּיהּ דְּרַבִּי אַמִי, א"ל: מוּחְזְקַנִי בָּזֶה שֶׁהוּא כֹּהֵן. א"ל: מָה רָאִיתָ? אֲמַר לֵיהּ: שֶׁקָּרָא רִאשׁוֹן בְּבֵית הַכְּנֶסֶת. בְּחֶזְקַת שֶׁהוּא כֹּהֵן אוֹ בְּחֶזְקַת שֶׁהוּא גָּדוֹל? שֶׁקָּרָא אַחֲרָיו לֵוִי. וְהֶעֱלָהוּ ר' אַמִי לִכְהוּנָּה עַל פִּיו. הַהוּא דַּאֲתָא לְקַמֵּיהּ דְּרַבִּי יְהוֹשֻׁעַ בֶּן לֵוִי, אֲמַר לֵיהּ: [ב]מוּחְזְקַנִי בָּזֶה שֶׁהוּא לֵוִי. אֲמַר לֵיהּ: מָה רָאִיתָ? אֲמַר לֵיהּ: שֶׁקָּרָא שֵׁנִי בְּבֵית הַכְּנֶסֶת. בְּחֶזְקַת שֶׁהוּא לֵוִי, אוֹ בְּחֶזְקַת שֶׁהוּא גָּדוֹל? שֶׁקָּרָא לְפָנָיו כֹּהֵן. וְהֶעֱלָהוּ רַבִּי יְהוֹשֻׁעַ בֶּן לֵוִי לִלְוִיָּה עַל פִּיו. הַהוּא דַּאֲתָא לְקַמֵּיהּ דְּרֵישׁ לָקִישׁ, אֲמַר לֵיהּ: מוּחְזְקַנִי בָּזֶה שֶׁהוּא כֹּהֵן. א"ל: מָה רָאִיתָ? [א"ל:] שֶׁקָּרָא רִאשׁוֹן בְּבֵית הַכְּנֶסֶת. א"ל: רְאִיתִיו שֶׁחִילֵּק עַל הַגְּרָנוֹת? אָמַר לוֹ רַ' אֶלְעָזָר: וְאִם אֵין שָׁם גּוֹרֶן בָּטְלָה כְּהוּנָּה?! זִימְנִין הֲווּ יָתְבִי קַמֵּיהּ דְּרַ' יוֹחָנָן, אֲתָא כִּי הָא מַעֲשֶׂה לְקַמֵּיהּ. א"ל רֵישׁ לָקִישׁ: רְאִיתִיו שֶׁחִילֵּק עַל הַגּוֹרֶן? א"ל ר' יוֹחָנָן: וְאִם אֵין שָׁם גּוֹרֶן בָּטְלָה כְּהוּנָּה?! *הֲדַר חַזְיֵיהּ לְר"א בִּישׁוּת, אֲמַר: שָׁמְעַתְּ מִילֵּי *דְּבַר נַפָּחָא וְלָא אָמְרַתְּ לָן מִשְּׁמֵיהּ?! רַבִּי וְר' חִיָּיא, חַד הֶעֱלָה בֵּן ע"פ אָבִיו לִכְהוּנָּה, וְחַד הֶעֱלָה אָח ע"פ אָחִיו לִלְוִיָּה. תִּסְתַּיֵּים דְּרַ' הֶעֱלָה בֵּן ע"פ אָבִיו לִכְהוּנָּה, דְּתַנְיָא: [ג]הֲרֵי שֶׁבָּא וְאָמַר "בְּנִי זֶה, וְכֹהֵן הוּא" — נֶאֱמָן לְהַאֲכִילוֹ בִּתְרוּמָה, וְאֵינוֹ נֶאֱמָן לְהַשִּׂיאוֹ אִשָּׁה, דִּבְרֵי רַבִּי. אָמַר לוֹ ר' חִיָּיא: אִם אַתָּה מַאֲמִינוֹ לְהַאֲכִילוֹ בִּתְרוּמָה — תַּאֲמִינוֹ לְהַשִּׂיאוֹ אִשָּׁה, וְאִם אִי אַתָּה מַאֲמִינוֹ לְהַשִּׂיאוֹ אִשָּׁה — לֹא תַּאֲמִינוֹ לֶאֱכוֹל בִּתְרוּמָה! א"ל: אֲנִי מַאֲמִינוֹ לְהַאֲכִילוֹ בִּתְרוּמָה — שֶׁבְּיָדוֹ לְהַאֲכִילוֹ בִּתְרוּמָה, וְאֵינִי מַאֲמִינוֹ לְהַשִּׂיאוֹ אִשָּׁה — שֶׁאֵין בְּיָדוֹ לְהַשִּׂיאוֹ אִשָּׁה. תִּסְתַּיֵּים. וּמִדְּרַבִּי הֶעֱלָה בֵּן ע"פ אָבִיו לִכְהוּנָּה — ר' חִיָּיא הֶעֱלָה אָח ע"פ אָחִיו לִלְוִיָּה. וְרַבִּי חִיָּיא, מַאי שְׁנָא בֵּן דְּלָא, דְּקָרוֹב הוּא אֵצֶל אָבִיו — אָח נַמִּי קָרוֹב הוּא אֵצֶל אָחִיו?

בְּמֵסִיחַ

רש"י

לָאו כּוּלְּהוּ סְלוּק. רוּבָּן נִשְׁאֲרוּ בְּבָבֶל, דִּכְתִיב "כָּל הַקָּהָל כְּאֶחָד אַרְבַּע רִבּוֹא" (עזרא ב). **וְעֵדוּת.** אִם בָּאוּ עֵדִים שֶׁהוּא כֹּהֵן שֶׁמַּכִּירִין אֶת אָבִיו וְאֶת אִמּוֹ. **וְעֵדוּת חֲזָקָה הִיא.** בִּתְמִיָּה, וְכִי עֵדוּת חֲזָקָה קָרֵי לֵיהּ? **עֵדוּת הַבָּאָה מִכֹּחַ חֲזָקָה כַּחֲזָקָה.** הָעֵדוּת נְקַבֵּל, וְנַאֲכִילוֹ בִּתְרוּמָה כְּאִילּוּ רְאִינוּהָ אֲנַן לְאוֹתָהּ חֲזָקָה שֶׁזֶּה הֵעִיד. **אוֹ בְּחֶזְקַת שֶׁהוּא גָּדוֹל.** כִּדְאָמְרִינַן בְּעָלְמָא *(גיטין דף נט:): רַב קָרֵי בְּכָהֲנֵי, וְאַע"ג דְּלָאו כֹּהֵן הֲוָה. **שֶׁקָּרָא אַחֲרָיו לֵוִי.** וְאִי לָאו כֹּהֵן הוּא, אֵין לֵוִי קוֹרֵא אַחֲרָיו, דְּאָמְרִינַן בְּמַסֶּכֶת גִּיטִּין (שם): אִם אֵין שָׁם כֹּהֵן – נִתְפָּרְדָה חֲבִילָה. וּמְפָרְשִׁינַן: דְּאֵין לֵוִי קוֹרֵא בְּמָקוֹם שֶׁאֵין כֹּהֵן. וְיֵשׁ מְפָרְשִׁים: נִתְפָּרְדָה הַחֲבִילָה, שֶׁבְּמָקוֹם שֶׁאֵין כֹּהֵן, אִם רוֹצֶה יִשְׂרָאֵל לִקְרוֹת לִפְנֵי לֵוִי – קוֹרֵא. וְדַוְקָא דְּאֵין שָׁם כֹּהֵן, אֲבָל הֵיכָא דְּאִיכָּא כֹּהֵן – לֹא נִתְפָּרְדָה הַחֲבִילָה, וְלֹא יִקְרָא יִשְׂרָאֵל גָּדוֹל לִפְנֵי לֵוִי. וְהָכָא כֹּהֵן אַחֵר הֲוָה הָתָם, הִלְכָּךְ אִי לָאו דְּהַאי כֹּהֵן הֲוָה – לָא הֲוָה לֵוִי קָרֵי אַבַּתְרֵיהּ. **שֶׁקָּרָא לְפָנָיו כֹּהֵן.** וְאִי לָאו דְּהַאי לֵוִי הוּא – לֹא הָיָה קוֹרֵא שֵׁנִי אֶלָּא שְׁלִישִׁי, שְׁנֵיִם כֹּהֲנִים הָיוּ קוֹרִין לְפָנָיו וְהוּא שְׁלִישִׁי, דְּהָכִי אָמְרִינַן בְּמַסֶּכֶת גִּיטִּין: אִם אֵין שָׁם לֵוִי – קוֹרֵא כֹּהֵן בִּמְקוֹמוֹ. **לִלְוִיָּה.** לָתֵת לוֹ מַעֲשֵׂר רִאשׁוֹן. **וְאִם אֵין שָׁם גּוֹרֶן.** אִם אֵין שָׁם זוֹרְעֵי תְבוּאָה בִּמְקוֹמוֹ. **זִימְנִין.** פַּעַם אַחֶרֶת. **הֲדַר.** רֵישׁ לָקִישׁ. **חַזְיֵיהּ לְרַבִּי אֶלְעָזָר בִּישׁוּת.** הֶחֱזִיר פָּנָיו, וְנִסְתַּכֵּל בְּרַבִּי אֶלְעָזָר בְּעַיִן רָעָה. שֶׁהֵבִין שֶׁמִּפִּי ר' יוֹחָנָן שָׁמַע לָשׁוֹן זֶה, וּכְשֶׁאָמַר לָשׁוֹן זֶה לֹא אֲמָרָהּ בְּשֵׁם רַבִּי יוֹחָנָן, לְפִיכָךְ לֹא קִיבְּלָהּ הֵימֶנּוּ. **לְהַשִּׂיאוֹ אִשָּׁה.** שֶׁמָּא מַמְזֵר אוֹ נָתִין הוּא. **שֶׁיֵּשׁ בְּיָדוֹ לְהַאֲכִילוֹ תְּרוּמָה.** שֶׁהֲרֵי הוּא כֹּהֵן, וְהַכֹּל חוֹלְקִין לוֹ תְּרוּמָה.

וְהִטְבִּילוּנִי

[מגילה כב.]

[מכות ה:]

[פירושו תמצא ברש"י סנהדרין ט. ד"ה טבא וכו' אביו של ר"י וכו' על שם יפיו]

תוספות

עדות הבאה מכח חזקה. פי': שאנו יודעין שהוא כהן מחמת הקורא אחריו, שמוחזק לן שהוא לוי. **שקרא** אחריו לוי. לפירוש ר"י הלוי שפירש בגיטין (נט: ושם): אם אין שם כהן נתפרדה חבילה – שיקרא ישראל גדול לפני לוי, יש לפרש הכא שקרא אחריו לוי, קטן מישראל שקרא אחריו. **שקרא** לפניו כהן. פירוש: פעם אחת. **הרי** שאמר בני זה וכהן הוא. מדנקט "בני זה וכהן הוא" משמע שאינו ידוע לנו אם הוא בנו, והוא בא להעיד שהוא בנו ושהוא כהן שאינו בן גרושה. דאי ידוע לנו שהוא בנו – הוה ליה למינקט בני זה כהן, בלא וי"ו. ותימה: א"כ יהא נאמן לכולי עלמא לתרומה וליוחסין במגו דאי בעי אמר אינו בנו! וי"ל: דאע"ג דאיכא מגו לא מהימן, דלדבריו קרוב הוא, כדאמרינן ב"החולץ" (יבמות דף מז. ושם): לדבריך – כותי אתה ואין עדות לכותי. ואין אדם נאמן לפסול את בנו. ואע"ג דרבי קאמר בסמוך: אני מאמינו להאכילו בתרומה שהרי בידו להאכילו בתרומה, אלמא אע"ג דקרוב הוא לדבריו נאמן במגו – התם ודאי מהימנינן ליה, משום דאית ליה מגו אפי' ידעינן שהוא בנו. אבל האי מגו, אי הוה ידעינן שהוא בנו – ליכא מגו. **נאמן** להאכילו בתרומה. פירוש: אע"ג דליכא אלא הוא, שהוא קרוב. דקסבר רבי: אין מעלין מתרומה ליוחסין. ואין נאמן להשיאו אשה – פירוש: להצטרף עם אחר להשיאו אשה, כיון שהוא קרוב. והשתא אתי שפיר הא דאמר ר' חייא: אם אתה מאמינו יחידי להאכילו בתרומה, אע"פ שהוא קרוב – האמינהו עם אחר להשיאו אשה. אבל אין לפרש דאין נאמן יחידי להשיאו אשה, דפשיטא דאינו נאמן. ובהא לא הוה אמר רבי חייא האמינהו ליה, דלא מישתמיט שום תנא למימר דעד אחד כשר ליוחסין. ובהא נמי אין לפרש דנאמן עם אחר להאכילו בתרומה, דאי הוה צריך שני עדים בתרומה – א"כ הוה סבר דמעלין מתרומה ליוחסין, ואם כן היכי מכשיר קרוב, כיון דאינו נאמן להשיאו אשה. וא"ת: כיון דסבירא ליה דאין מעלין מתרומה ליוחסין, אם כן היכי מוקמינן ב"הגוזל בתרא" (ב"ק קיד:): ההיא דרבי דלקמן במסיח לפי תומו, ונאמן בתרומה דרבנן, אבל בתרומה דאורייתא לא מהימן, והא לרבי, כיון דס"ל דאין מעלין מתרומה ליוחסין – אם כן ס"ל דמעלין מתרומה דרבנן לתרומה דאורייתא, כדמשמע לעיל, דכל היכא דאכיל בתרומה דרבנן אכיל נמי בתרומה דאורייתא! וי"ל: דהאי דמצרכינן למימר דלעיל דמעלין מתרומה דרבנן לחלה דאורייתא או איפכא – היינו משום דלא תקשי למ"ד אין מעלין מנשיאות כפים ליוחסין. אבל רב אשי ב"הגוזל" אפשר דסבירא ליה כמ"ד מעלין. ועוד נראה: דלכולי עלמא, בין למאן דאמר מעלין מתרומה ליוחסין בין למאן דאמר אין מעלין – מעלין מתרומת דגן תירוש ויצהר של א"י, ואפי' היא דרבנן, לחלה דאורייתא, כיון שבזמן המקדש הויא דאורייתא. אבל תרומת פירות או תרומת חו"ל – אין מעלין לכ"ע, אפי' לתרומת דגן תירוש ויצהר של א"י דרבנן. דדוקא בתרומת א"י או חלה דאורייתא בסוריא אמר מעלין מדרבנן לדאורייתא, אבל לא בבבל, וההיא ד"הגוזל בתרא" איירי בתרומת פירות או חוצה לארץ. וכן מתני' דלקמן דנאמנים להעיד בגודלן מה שראו בקוטנן, ומוקי לה בתרומה דרבנן – היינו בתרומת פירות או חוצה לארץ. ולמ"ד מעלין מתרומה ליוחסין אפי' מתרומת דגן תירוש ויצהר דא"י, אפילו היא דרבנן, מעלין. דהא ר' יוסי ס"ל בפ' "יוצא דופן" (נדה מו:): תרומה בזמן הזה דרבנן, ודוקא משום דקסבר חולקין תרומה לעבד בלא רבו הוא דאית ליה דאין מעלין, הא אי הוה סבר דאין חולקין – הוה מודה דמעלין. והא דאמר לעיל מעיקרא אכול בתרומה דרבנן *ולבסוף אכול בתרומה דאורייתא – לא מכח שהיו אוכלין בגולה קדשי הגבול אוכלין בתרומה דאורייתא, אלא משום שהיו נושאים כפים בגולה, שמעלין מנשיאות כפים לתרומה דאורייתא. אע"ג דהרי אתם בחזקתכם במה הייתם אוכלין בגולה כו' משמע שמכח אכילה היה מתירו – אין לחוש בכך. ולההוא לישנא דקאמר בתרומה דרבנן אכול, בדאורייתא לא אכול, מה שלא העלם מנשיאות כפים לתרומה דאורייתא – היינו משום דריע חזקייהו. **נאמן** להאכילו בתרומה. הקשה ריב"ס: דתנן בפרק "עשרה יוחסין" (קדושין דף עט: ושם): מי שיצא הוא ואשתו למדינת הים, וכשחזר הביא עמו בנים, ומתה אשתו, צריך להביא ראיה על בניו, ואינו נאמן להאכילם בתרומה, כדמוכח התם בגמ', דתניא התם: הביא ראיה על הגדולים – א"צ ראיה על הקטנים. ואמר רשב"ל עלה: לא שנו אלא בקדשי הגבול, אבל ליוחסין – לא. והיכי קאמר רבי הכא דאב נאמן להאכילו בתרומה? ותירץ: דרבי תנא הוא ופליג. ור"ת אומר: דההיא דקדושין אתיא כר' יהודה, דאמר אין מעלין לכהונה ע"פ עד אחד. וקדשי הגבול דהתם היינו לכל דבר קדושה, כגון תרומה ונשיאות כפים ויוחסין. והא דקאמר התם* אבל ליוחסין לא – היינו יוחסין לקורבה, כגון לסקול ולשרוף על ידו. כדמסיק התם, ר' יוחנן אמר: אף ליוחסין, ואזדא ר' יוחנן לטעמיה: דאמר סוקלין על החזקות. א) [א"נ, הכא באשתו עמו, דאין צריך להביא ראיה, כדאמר התם]. **שבידו** להאכילו בתרומה. ב) תימה: איך נאמין אותו על תרומה בהאי מגו? הא אין בידו להאכילו אחר מיתה, וא"כ אין זה מגו! כמו שמצינו ב"יש נוחלין", (ב"ב קכז:) גבי בכור, ובפרק בתרא דקדושין (דף עח:) דתניא: "יכיר" יכירנו לאחרים, מכאן אמר רבי יהודה נאמן אדם לומר זה בני בכור כו'. למאי הלכתא? אי לתת לו פי שנים – אילו בעי למיתב ליה מתנה מי לא יהיב ליה? לא צריכא, בנכסים שנפלו לו כשהוא גוסס. אלמא, אי לאו קרא לא הוה נאמן, לפי שאין בידו! וי"ל: דלא דמי, דהכא כיון דנאמן להאכילו בחייו משום דבידו – סברא הוא דנאמן אפילו לאחר מיתה.

במסיח

א) ועיין היטב תוס' קדושין פ. ד"ה לא שנו] ב) [ועוד קשה לר"י דאין זה מיגו טוב שאם יוליכנו בגורן ויתן לו חלקו הרי יפסיד והשתא דקאמר שהוא כהן נוטל כל אחד חלקו ואין לפרש שבידו להאכילו בתרומה בשעה שהעיד שהיה יכול לומר אינו בני וכהן הוא דא"כ להשיאו אשה נמי נימא הכי. בתוס' לא תירץ והתירוץ שבפנים מצאתי]. ת"י

[ולפ"ז גרסינן לעיל שפיר כי מסקינן מתרומה ליוחסין הנ"מ בתרומה דאורייתא כו' ומ"מ אינו סותר ראייתו דהשתא נמי יכול לומר דאי לא תימא הכי היכי הוי פרסי ידייהו הא אתו לאסוקינהו לתרומה דאורייתא ועוד דהשתא להאי פירושא פשיטא ליה לתלמודא דאין מעלין מתרומה דרבנן דה"ל אפי' לדאורייתא וכ"ש ליוחסין לאב"א ע"כ אינו ראיה ואין חוזר מדבריו דמעיקרא לא הביא ראיה מתרומה אלא משום דאכיל מדאורייתא. ת"י]

[דליכא למימר ליוחסין להשיאו אשה דהא לרבי יהודה במקום שנאמן להאכילו תרומה נאמן גם להשיאו אשה דמעלין מתרומה ליוחסין. ת"י]

תוספות רי"ד

ת"ש חזקה לכהונה נשיאות כפים וחילוק גרנות ועדות. פי' המורה אם באו עדים ואומרים שהוא כהן וכגון שמכירים את אביו ואת אמו ועדות חזקה הוא בתמיה ה"ק עדות הבא מכח חזקה כחזקה. פי' כההוא דאתא לקמיה דר"א אמר מוחזקני בזה שהוא כהן א"ל מה ראית א"ל שקרא ראשון בבה"כ א"ל בחזקת שהוא כהן או בחזקת שהוא גדול פי' בחכמה כדאמרינן בעלמא רב קרי בכהני ואע"ג דלא הוה כהן א"ל שקרא אחריו לוי פי' דאי לאו דכהן הוא אין לוי קורא אחריו ואמרינן בהניזקין אין שם כהן נתפרדה החבילה כלומר איבד לוי את זכותו והעלהו ר"א לכהונה ע"פ: ההוא דאתא לקמיה דר"ל א"ל מוחזקני בזה שהוא כהן א"ל מה ראית [א"ל] שקרא ראשון בבה"כ. א"ל ראית שחלק על הגורן א"ל ר"א ואם אין שם גורן בטלה הכהונה. פי' המורה אם אין זורעים במקומו. (אר"י) תניא הרי שבא ואמר בני זה כהן הוא נאמן להאכילו בתרומה ואינו נאמן להשיאו אשה דברי רבי א"ל ר"ח אם אתה מאמינו להאכילו בתרומה האמינהו להשיאו אשה. ואם אינך מאמינו להשיאו אשה אל תאמינהו להאכילו בתרומה. א"ל רבי אני מאמינו להאכילו תרומה שכן בידו להאכילו תרומה. ואיני מאמינו להשיאו אשה שכן אין בידו להשיאו אשה:

במסיח לפי תומו, כי הא דאמר רב יהודה אמר שמואל: *[א]מעשה באדם אחד שהיה מסיח לפי תומו, ואמר: זכורני כשאני תינוק ומורכב על כתיפו של אבא, והוציאוני מבית הספר והפשיטוני את כותנתי, והטבילוני לאכול בתרומה לערב. ור' חייא מסיים בה: וחבירי בדילין ממני. והיו קורין אותי "יוחנן אוכל חלות", והעלהו רבי לכהונה על פיו. תניא, ר"ש בן אלעזר אומר: כשם שתרומה חזקה לכהונה — כך מעשר ראשון חזקה לכהונה, והחולק בבית דין — אינה חזקה. מעשר ראשון דלוי הוא! כר"א בן עזריה. דתניא: *[ב]תרומה לכהן, מעשר ראשון ללוי, דברי ר"ע. ר"א בן עזריה אומר: מעשר ראשון אף לכהן. אימור דאר"א בן עזריה אף לכהן, לכהן ולא ללוי מי אמר? [ג]אין, בתר דקנסינהו עזרא. ודלמא איקרו ויהבו ליה! אמר רב חסדא: הכא במאי עסקינן — [ד]כגון דמוחזק לן באבוה דהאי דכהן הוא, ונפק עליה קלא דבן גרושה ובן חלוצה הוא, וחלקו ליה לדידיה מעשר בבית הגרנות. לוי — דלאו לוי הוא, מאי איכא למימר — בן גרושה או בן חלוצה הוא, לא מיבעיא למאן דאמר: *מעשר ראשון אסור לזרים, דלא הוו יהבי ליה, אלא אפילו למ"ד: *מעשר ראשון מותר לזרים, הני מילי — למיספק להו, אבל בתורת חלוקה — לא יהבי ליה. "והחולק בבית דין אינה חזקה". — אי בבית דין לא הויא חזקה — היכא הויא חזקה?! אמר רב ששת, הכי קאמר: [ה]החולק תרומה בנכסי אביו עם אחיו בבית דין — אינה חזקה. פשיטא! מהו דתימא: מדהנך לאכילה האי נמי לאכילה, קמ"ל: הנך — לאכילה, האי — לזבוני.§ רבי יהודה אומר: אין מעלין לכהונה על פי עד אחד וכו'.§ רשב"ג היינו רבי אליעזר! וכי תימא: ערער חד איכא בינייהו: דרבי אליעזר סבר: ערער חד, ורשב"ג סבר ערער תרי. א]והאמר רבי יוחנן: דברי הכל *אין ערער פחות משנים! אלא, הכא במאי עסקינן דמוחזק לן באבוה דהאי דכהן הוא, ונפק עליה קלא דבן גרושה או בן חלוצה הוא, ואחתיניה, ואתא עד אחד ואמר: ידענא ביה דכהן הוא, ואסקיניה

רש"י

והטבילוני. מפני שמסתם תינוק מטפח באשפות, ושרצים מצויין שם. לערב. דצריך הערב שמש. והחולק בב"ד. קא ס"ד שעל פי ב"ד הקבוע בעיר היו חולקין לו תרומה בבית הגרנות. ולקמיה פריך: אי בב"ד לא הוי חזקה — היכא הויא חזקה? בתר דקנסינהו עזרא. ללוים, דלא ליתבו להו, כדאמרי' ביבמות בפ' "יש מותרות" (דף פו:). לוי דלאו לוי הוא. כלומר, בלוי ליכא לספוקי — דהא אביו כהן. למ"ד כו'. פלוגתא היא ביבמות (שם). בנכסי אביו כו' אינה חזקה. להשבית מעליו קול היוצא על אמו שהיא גרושה, והוא חלל. פשיטא. דהא אפי' הוא חלל יורש את אביו. רבן שמעון היינו רבי אליעזר. דהא ודאי במקום שיש עוררין לא אמר רבן שמעון דליהוי חד נאמן וכי אמר מעלין במקום שאין עוררין קאמר. דר"א סבר ערער חד. הוי ערער, ואין אחד נאמן עליו להכשירו. ונפק עליה קלא. קול בעלמא, ולא עדות. ואחתיניה. מן הכהונה עד שיבדקו את הדבר, שמעלה הוא לכהונה. ואסקיניה

תוספות

במסיח לפי תומו. וא"ת, ומנ"ל דהכי הוא? דלמא ר' חייא העלה בן על פי אביו במסיח לפי תומו, ורבי העלה אם ע"פ אחיו אפי' בלא מסיח! ואר"י: דמסתמא דבמאי דקתני בברייתא מילתא דרבי, עשה רבי מעשה. ועוד: דאי אפשר דרבי העלה את ע"פ אחיו ללויה אפילו בלא מסיח — דהתם אין שייך לומר שבידו להאכילו מעשר, למ"ד מעשר ראשון מותר לזרים. מבית הספר. נקט שלא לומר שהוא עבד, כדאמר בסוף פירקין (לקמן דף כח.). אין בתר דקנסינהו עזרא. ולר"ע דקודם קנסא הוי דוקא ללוי, בתר קנסא — אף לכהנים, אבל לר"א בן עזריה, דמקמי קנסא הוי אף לכהן — בתר קנסא הוי לכהן דוקא. והא דמעשר ראשון חזקה לכהונה — אתיא כר' אלעזר בן עזריה, ולא כר"ע. ויש שמוחקין אין, ומפרשים: דהא דקאמר בתר דקנסינהו עזרא — הוי אפי' לר"ע, דבתר קנסא הוי לכ"ע לכהן דוקא, והוי כמו "אלא". ושיבוש הוא בידם, דהא בכמה מקומות מוכיח דמעשר ראשון ללוי אף בתר קנסא, כדתנן בפ' "כל הגט" (גיטין דף ל.): המלוה מעות את הכהן ואת הלוי להיות מפריש עליהן כו'. וכן התם בגמרא: ישראל שאמר לבן לוי כור מעשר לאביך בידי, ובפ' "הזרוע" (חולין קלא: ושם) פריך: מעשר ראשון דלוי הוא! וכן בכמה מקומות, והיינו כר"ע. ועוד: דלמ"ד קנסא לעניים — היכי הוי חזקה לכהונה? דאליבא דר"כ פליגי בס"פ "יש מותרות" (יבמות פו: ושם) דאיכא למ"ד קנסא לכהנים, ואיכא למ"ד לעניים, דלר' אלעזר בן עזריה הוי דוקא לכהן, ואפי' לעשירים, כמו קודם קנסא. דלא קנס עזרא, שהרי עלו. ולמ"ד קנסא לעניים — משמע התם דוקא לעניים, ולא לכהנים עשירים אפי' בימי טומאה, דלית ליה דבימי טומאה עניים הוו, ועניים דהתם אין לפרש עניי לויים דוקא ולא עניי ישראל וכהנים — דא"כ נשתכרו עניי לויים במה שלא עלו. ועוד: דמשמע התם אילו הוו כהנים בימי טומאתם עניים — לכ"ע הוו שקלי, אע"ג דלענין חלוקת מעשר הוו כישראל, דללוי ולא לכהן קאמר. אלא לעניים — בין עניי כהנים בין עניי לויים, ולמ"ד מעשר ראשון מותר לזרים — שקלי אפילו עניי ישראל. אבל למ"ד אסור לזרים — אין נראה שינתן לעניי ישראל כדי למוכרו, דמילתא דאתי לידי תקלה לא אתקינו רבנן, דאיכא למיחש דלמא אתי למיכליה. [כדאמר בסמוך: לא מיבעיא לר"מ דאמר אסור לזרים כו']. ולר"ע לא הפקיע עזרא את הלויים מכל וכל להשוותן לישראל וכהנים שלא יטלו עשירים לויים אלא עניי לויים בתורת עניות, אלא ללויים — בין עניים בין עשירים היו חולקים לעולם, כדמוכח בכל הנהו שהבאתי, שהיו נוטלין בתורת לויות. ועוד: דר"ג בספינה שנתן מעשר ראשון לר' יהושע בן חנניא (מעשר שני פ"ה מ"ט) אי בתורת עניות יהיב ליה — אמאי לא יהב ליה נמי מעשר עני נתן לר"ע? שהרי מעשר עני נתן לר"ע? ומיהו, יש לדחות: דלעולם בתורת עניות נתן לו, ומה שלא נתן לו מעשר עני — לפי שהיו לו מאתים זוז, דאינו נוטל במעשר עני, כדתנן במסכת פאה (פ"ח מ"ח). אבל מעשר ראשון — יטול, אפי' יש לו מאתים זוז, דהא איכא למ"ד דאפי' כהנים עשירים בימי טומאה עניים נינהו. ועוד: דלא רצה ליתן כל מתנותיו לעני אחד. בתר דקנסינהו עזרא. לא אשכחן בהדיא בקרא דקנסינהו, רק מצינו בעזרא (נחמיה י) "והיה הכהן בן אהרן עם הלוים בעשר הלוים". ואיכא למימר דה"ק: כשיבאו הלוים לחלוק בבית הגרנות — יבאו הכהנים עמהם. ומיהו, לר"א בן עזריה דבתר קנסא דוקא לכהן — לא משמע מהאי קרא. דליכא למימר "עם הלוים" דקאמר קרא — היינו לקבל מהם מעשר ראשון משלהם — דהא משלהם לא קנסם עזרא כדמוכח בפרק "הזרוע" (חולין קלא:)! וי"ל דלר"א בן עזריה לא נמנעו הלוים מכל וכל מלילך לבית הגרנות לחלוק במעשר, כדאמר בסמוך: דלמא איקרי ויהיב ליה. כל שכן בימי עזרא, שעדיין לא פשט הקנס שהיו הולכים בבית הגרנות, ולכך נאמר שילכו הכהנים עם הלוים. ולמ"ד קנסא לעניים, הא דכתיב "והיה הכהן" — היינו בכהן עני. ומשום דכהנים עניים שכיחי טפי, לפי שאין כל כך עסוקים במלאכה אלא בעבודת בית המקדש, וגם אין להם קרקעות — נקט כהן. וה"ה עניי ישראל, למ"ד מעשר ראשון מותר לזרים. וה"ר יוסף פירש: מדכתיב (במלאכי ג) "הביאו את כל המעשר אל בית האוצר" דבית האוצר היה לשכה שתיקן עזרא לתת שם תרומת הכהנים, כדכתיב בעזרא (נחמיה י). וכיון שאומר להביא שם המעשר — א"כ של כהנים הוא. וקיימא לן (מגילה דף טו.) דמלאכי זה עזרא. ולמ"ד לעניים — נקט אל בית האוצר משום דכהנים עניים שכיחי טפי, כדפרישית. אי נמי: "אל בית האוצר" — לא ליתן לכהנים, אלא לחלק לעניים. וה"ר אלחנן הקשה: דבסוף עזרא משמע שהמעשר היה ללוים, דכתיב "ואדע כי מניות הלוים לא נתנה (להם) ויברחו איש לשדהו הלוים והמשוררים כו'" — משמע שהלוים והמשוררים היו חולקים! וצריך לומר דזה היה מקמי דקנסינהו עזרא. אך קראי לא מוכחי הכי. והאמר רבי יוחנן דברי הכל אין ערער כו'. נראה לר"י דר' יוחנן עיקר דבריו על משנתנו, ולהכי לא קא משני הכא: ה"מ — היכא דאיכא חזקה דכשרות כו', כדמשני בפרק "עשרה יוחסין" (קדושין דף עג:). ואם תאמר: והואיל ואמתני' קאי, היכי פריך מיניה התם, ובפרק קמא דגיטין (דף ט.) גבי גט? דלמא הא דקאמר ר' יוחנן דלא מהני ערער דחד — היינו היכא דאיכא עד אחד דמכשר, דקתני מעלין לכהונה על פי עד אחד! ויש לומר: דהתלמוד ידע דר' יוחנן אמסקנא דיבר, דבתחלה היה קול ואח"כ בא עד אחד להכשירו ולהסיר הקול, ואתו בי תרי ואמרי דבן גרושה ובן חלוצה הוא — דבכי האי גוונא א"ר יוחנן דבעינן שנים, אע"ג דהעד שהכשיר והקול כמאן דליתנהו דמי, שהרי העד גרוע מן הקול, אי לאו משום חזקה דמסייע ליה לבטל הקול, שהרי הקול פוסל והעד אינו פוסל לרבי יוחנן*. אין ערער פחות משנים. לאפוקי חד דלא הוי ערער. אבל קול נמי פוסל בתחלה בתרומה קודם שבא העד המכשיר. ואתא עד אחד ואמר ידענא ביה דכהן הוא. לא בעי למימר דפליגי אי מעלין ע"פ עד אחד כשהקול פוסל — דפשיטא ליה להתלמוד דלא פסיל קול לכ"ע, כיון דאיכא עד וחזקה. ועוד: דקול לא הוי קרי עוררין. ואסקיניה

עין משפט נר מצוה

צד א מיי' פ"כ מהל' איסורי ביאה הל' יד סמג לאוין קכב טוש"ע אה"ע סימן ג סעיף א:

צה ב מיי' פ"ו מהל' תרומות הלכה א סמג לאוין רכב:

צו ג מיי' פ"א מהל' מעשר הלכה ד:

צז ד מיי' פ"כ מהל' איסורי ביאה הלכה טז טוש"ע אה"ע סימן ג סעיף ו:

צח ה מיי' שם הלכה יב:

תוספות רי"ד

רשב"ג אומר וכו' רשב"ג היינו ת"ק פי' ר"א שאין לומר שבמקום עוררין קאמר רשב"ג דמעלין לכהונה ע"פ עד אחד אלא במקום שאין עוררין וה"ק נמי ר"א. ואסיק רב אשי דבמצטרפין לעדות קמיפלגי ובמקום שיש עוררין. והכא במאי עסקינן במוחזק לן באבוה דהאי דכהן הוא. ונפק עלי' [קלא] דבן גרושה ובן חלוצה הוא ואחתיני'. פי' עד שנבדוק הקול אם הוא אמת אם לאו ואתא עד אחד ואמר ידענא ביה

מסורת הש"ס

ב"ק קיז:

[כ"ב פח: יבמות פו. חולין קלא:]

[יבמות עד: פח: פו.]

[שם פו.]

כ"ב לב. קדושין עג: גיטין ט.

ת"י כ"י

[וע"ע תוס' שם וכ"ב לב.]

הגהות מהר"ב רנשבורג

א] גמ' והאמר ר' יוחנן דברי הכל אין ערער פחות משנים. עי' תוס' ד"ה והאמר ובחדושי הר"ן בחולין פא ע"א ד"ה וקשיא לן:

צט א מיי' פ"ד מהל' עדות הלכה ד סמג עשין קט טוש"ע ח"מ סימן ל סעיף ו:
ק ב מיי' שם ופ"כ מהלכ' איסורי ביאה הל' טז סמג שם טוש"ע ח"מ סי' ל סעיף ט וטוש"ע אה"ע סי' ג סעיף ז:
קא ג ד מיי' פי"ח מהל' איסורי ביאה הלכ' ל סמג לאוין קכא טוש"ע אה"ע סימן ז סעיף יא:

אי נמי אחתיניה לאו דוקא אלא שירד מעצמו. ת"י

ואסקיניה. *ואתו בי תרי ואמרי: בן גרושה ובן חלוצה הוא, ואחתיניה. ואתא עד אחד ואמר: ידענא ביה דכהן הוא. ודכולי עלמא מצטרפין לעדות, והכא — במיחש לזילותא דבי דינא קמיפלגי. תנא קמא סבר: כיון דאחתיניה — לא מסקינן ליה, חיישינן לזילותא דבי דינא. ורשב"ג סבר: אנן אחתינן ליה, ואנן מסקינן ליה, ולזילותא דבי דינא לא חיישינן. מתקיף לה רב אשי: אי הכי אפי' תרי ותרי נמי! אלא אמר רב אשי: במצטרפין לעדות קמיפלגי, *ובפלוגתא דהני תנאי. דתניא: אין עדותן מצטרפת עד שיראו שניהם כאחד, ר' יהושע בן קרחה אמר: [א]אפי' בזה אחר זה. ואין עדותן מתקיימת בב"ד עד שיעידו שניהם כאחד, ר' נתן אומר: [ב]שומעין דבריו של זה היום, וכשיבא חבירו למחר — שומעין דבריו.§

מתני' *[ג]האשה שנחבשה בידי גוים, על ידי ממון — מותרת לבעלה, על ידי נפשות — אסורה לבעלה.§

גמ' אמר רב שמואל בר רב יצחק אמר רב: [ד]לא שנו אלא שיד ישראל תקיפה על אומות העולם אבל יד אומות העולם תקיפה על עצמן — אפילו על ידי ממון אסורה לבעלה. מתיב רבא: *העיד רבי יוסי הכהן ור' זכריה בן הקצב על בת ישראל שהורהנה באשקלון, וריחקוה בני משפחתה, ועדיה מעידים אותה שלא נסתרה ושלא נטמאה. ואמרו להם חכמים: אם אתם מאמינים שהורהנה — האמינו שלא נסתרה ושלא נטמאה, ואם אי אתם מאמינים שלא נסתרה ושלא נטמאה — אל תאמינו שהורהנה. והא אשקלון, דיד אומות העולם תקיפה על עצמן, וקתני: הורהנה

ואסקיניה. דבמקום קול הוי חד מהימן. ודכולי עלמא. בין לר' אלעזר בין לר"ש. מצטרפין. שני עדים המעידים זה שלא בפני זה כשאר עדיות. דחיישינן לזילותא דבי דינא. שהורידוהו שני פעמים, ועכשיו יעלוהו, ויבטלו דבריהם. והיינו דקאמר ר' אלעזר: דמאחר שהורדנוהו ע"פ העוררין — אין מעלין ע"פ עד זה השני, אע"פ שיש לצרפו עם האחר. ואנן מסקינן ליה. ואי קשיא: תרי ותרי נינהו! אוקי תרי לבהדי תרי, ואוקמינן אחזקיה קמייתא, דאסקיניה ע"פ עד הראשון, שהוא נאמן, דהא אכתי אין עוררין. דקול לאו עוררין הוא. אפילו תרי. אתו בהדדי נמי בפעם שניה, לרבי אלעזר לא מסקינן ליה. עד שיראו שניהם כאחד. את העדות. לאפוקי אחד אומר: בפני הלווהו, ואחד אומר: בפני הודה לו עליו. ואין עדותן מתקיימת. להתקבל בב"ד, ואפי' ראו שניהן כאחד. ופלוגתא אחריתי היא, ולאו ר' יהושע בן קרחה קאמר לה. ורבי אלעזר ורבן שמעון בפלוגתא דרבי נתן ורבנן פליגי. מתני' ע"י ממון מותרת לבעלה. דמרתתי להפסיד ממונן, ואינן מפקירין אותה. ע"י נפשות. שהיתה נידונת למות. אסורה לבעלה. דהואיל ונוהגין בה הפקר — חוששין שמא נתרצתה באחד מהן. גמ' לא שנו. דע"י ממון מותרת לבעלה. אלא שיד ישראל תקיפה על אומות העולם. ויראים לעשות שלא כדין, שמא יפסידו ממונם. שהורהנה. נתמשכנה. ועדיה. אותן שהעידו שהורהנה. והא אשקלון. דארץ פלשתים היא, ועוד: כבר גלו ישראל.

הורהנה

ואסקיניה · וא"ת: ולמאן דחייש לזילותא דבי דינא היכי אסקוהו, כיון דאחתיניה מחמת הקול? וליכא למימר דליכא זילותא דבי דינא אלא היכא שהורידוהו שתי פעמים, כדמוכח ב"חזקת הבתים" (ב"ב דף לב.)! וי"ל: דליכא זילותא דבי דינא אלא היכא שהורידוהו ע"י עדות, אבל בהורדה שע"י הקול — ליכא זילותא דב"ד. ואע"ג דאמרינן (גיטין דף פא.) גבי גרושה לכהן דלא מבטלים קלא — היינו משום דלית ליה תקנתא, אבל הכא, דאי לא מסקינן ליה לעולם פסול — מבטלין. *אי נמי: בתרומה דרבנן הקילו. **אנן** אחתינן ליה אנן מסקינן ליה. פי' בקונטרס: אע"ג דתרי ותרי נינהו — אוקי תרי לבהדי תרי, ואוקי גברא אחזקתיה. וקשה לר"י: דבפרק "האומר" בקדושין (דף סו. ושם) קאמר גבי ינאי: היכי דמי? אילימא דתרי אמרי אשתבאי, ותרי אמרי לא אשתבאי — מאי חזית דסמכת אהני. פירוש: אהני דאמרו לא אשתבאי, סמוך אהני. ואמאי קאמר ויבוקש הדבר ולא נמצא? והתם פי' בקונטרס דלא אמרי' אוקי תרי בהדי תרי ואוקי גברא אחזקיה, דהא לא באו להעיד על אמו אלא על ינאי, ולו לא היה חזקת כשרות. ואין נראה לר"י: דחזקת האם מהניא גם לינאי, כדמשמע הכא! ואמרינן נמי לעיל בפ"ק (דף יג. ושם)? לדברי המכשיר בה — מכשיר בבתה. ואפילו מאן דפסל בבתה — היינו משום דמעלה עשו גבי זנות. וגם אין לומר כמו שתירץ ר"ת, דליכא למימר התם אוקמינן אחזקה לפי שכל הנשים היו בחזקת שבויות — דא"כ היכי מייתי מינה ראיה על אשתו שזינתה בעד אחד? דשאני התם, דכל הנשים בחזקת שבויות, אבל אשתו זינתה — היא בחזקת היתר! ונראה לר"י: דתרי ותרי ספיקא דרבנן הוא, ומדרבנן החמירו דלא מוקמינן לה אחזקה. והכא בתרומה דרבנן — הקילו ובפרק "בכל מערבין" (עירובין דף לה.) גבי תרומה ונטמאה כו', ספק — הרי זה חמר גמל, דברי ר"מ. ומוקי לה* רבה ורב (ושם:) יוסף בשתי כתי עדים. הא דלא מוקמינן לה אחזקתה דלא נטמאת, אע"ג דתרומה בזמן הזה דרבנן — היינו משום דערובי תחומין דאורייתא לר"מ. אי נמי: שאני התם דאיכא ריעותא דהרי נטמאת לפניך, ולא אמרינן השתא הוא דאיטמי, אע"ג דגבי מקוה אמרינן השתא הוא דחסר ואתאי (נדה דף ב:), הכא דאיכא שתי כתי עדים — לא אמרינן השתא הוא דאיטמי. ובשנים אומרים מת ושנים אומרים לא מת, דאמרינן לעיל (דף כב:): לא תנשא, ולא מוקמינן לה אחזקת אשת איש — היינו משום דחזקה דאשה דייקא ומנסבא מרעה לה לחזקת אשת איש. אע"ג דבשנים אומרים מת אמרינן ב"האשה רבה" (יבמות פז:) דמותרת לחזור לו, וכיון דליכא חומרא בסוף — לא דייקא, מ"מ, הכא כיון דמכחישין זה את זה איכא חומרא. ובשנים אומרים נתגרשה ושנים אומרים לא נתגרשה, דאמרינן נמי לא תנשא, אע"ג דלא דייקא, וליכא נמי חזקה דאין האשה מעיזה פניה, דשלא בפני בעלה מעיזה, וכ"ש היכא דמסייעין לה עדים! ויש לומר: דמכל מקום דייקא, לפי שיראה שיוזמו עדיה או יפסלו אותם בגזלנותא. וב"האשה רבה" (שם צג: ושם) גבי בעו מיניה מרב ששת עד אחד ביבמה מהו כו' אמר להו: תניתוה, אמרו לה מת בנך ואחר כך מת בעליך ונתייבמה, ואח"כ אמרו לה חילוף הדברים — תצא, והולד ראשון והאחרון ממזר. היכי דמי? אילימא תרי ותרי — מאי חזית דסמכת אהני דאסרי ליבם — סמוך אהני דשרו לה. וקשה: דמאי פריך? והא אית לן לאוקמי אחזקה דאסורה ליבם שמת בעלה תחלה כדאמרינן בפרק "ארבעה אחין" (שם דף לא. ושם) גבי נפל הבית עליו ועל בת אחיו כו'! ועוד: כיון דתרי ותרי ספיקא דרבנן הוא — יש לאוסרה כדאמרינן גבי ינאי. והתם לא דייקא, כדאמרינן התם: זימנין דרחמא ליה ליבם! וי"ל: דמ"מ מהני דיוקא דידה לענין דמרעה ליה לחזקת איסור ליבם. והא דפריך נמי התם כו' ועוד: ממזר — ספק ממזר הוא. אע"ג דבחזקת איסור ליבם היא — מ"מ לא הוי ממזר ודאי, דמהני דיוקא דידה כדפרשינן. ועוד: כיון דתרי ותרי ספיקא דרבנן — אין לנו להעמידה על חזקתה ולהתירו בממזרת. ורבינו יצחק בר ברוך פי': דלא אמרינן בכל הני אוקמא אחזקה, לפי שהשנים שמוציאים אותו מחזקתו של היתר — הם מעידים תחלה, ומיד כשהעידו יצא מחזקתו ע"י עדותן, ותו לא אמרינן אוקמא אחזקה. ולהכי פריך לעיל: מאי שנא רישא ומאי שנא סיפא? דשנים שאומרים נתקדשה העידו תחלה. ובשנים אומרים נתגרשה, אע"פ שהם העידו תחלה — מ"מ היתה בחזקת אשת איש. וכן ההיא ד"האשה רבה" ודינאי — שנים המוציאין אותו מחזקתו באו תחלה. ואין נראה לרבינו יצחק; דהא הכא בשמעתין מוקמינן ליה אחזקה אע"ג דכבר פסלוהו השנים והוציאוהו מחזקתו. ואין סברא שיועיל מה שעד אחד המכשיר העיד קודם. *ועוד: דרב אשי משמע דבעי למימר דאפילו אתו שניהם לבסוף, דמסקינן ליה: **על** ידי ממון מותרת לבעלה. נראה דמותרת אפילו לבעלה כהן, דלא חיישינן אפי' לאונסא, משום דמרתתי להפסיד ממונם, ולא דמי לשבויה, וכן מוכח בגמרא, דקאמר: לא שנו אלא שיד ישראל תקיפה על אומות העולם, אבל יד אומות העולם תקיפה על עצמן אפילו ע"י ממון אסורה לבעלה. ועל כרחן היינו לכהונה, מדקאמרי: אף אנן נמי תנינא, מההיא דריחקוה בני משפחתה. והא לא שייך אלא לכהונה, דבישראל לא שייך וריחקוה. בני משפחתה — דאינה אסורה אלא לבעלה. ועוד ראיה, דתנן בפ' שני דמסכת ע"ז (דף כב.): אין מעמידין בהמה בפונדקאות של גוים מפני שחשודים על הרביעה. ורמינהו לוקחין מהן בהמה לקרבן! לא קשיא הא לכתחלה והא דיעבד, ומנא תימרא דשני בין לכתחלה כו'. דתנן: לא תתייחד אשה עמהם, מפני שחשודים על העריות. ורמינהו: האשה שנחבשה ע"י גוים ע"י ממון — מותרת לבעלה. אלא ש"מ שני לן בין לכתחלה לדיעבד. משמע דאין לחוש כלל שנבעלה, דאי מותרת לבעלה ישראל קאמר, דלא חיישינן שמא נתרצת, אבל לבעלה *כהן אסורה. דחיישינן שמא נאנסה — א"כ לא הוה מייתי מידי. **ועל** ידי נפשות אסורה לבעלה. היינו אפילו לבעלה ישראל, דחיישינן שמא נתרצת כדי למצא חן שלא יהרגנה. דאי לבעלה כהן קאמר, ואסורה שמא נאנסה, א"כ הוה ליה למימר אסורה לכהונה. אלא ודאי אפילו לבעלה ישראל אסורה. וא"ת: לנועות ליסתרו, דקודש לכן מסרן נפשייהו. כדמשמע בריש מכילתין (דף ג:) גבי כל הנשאת ברביעי תיבעל להגמון תחלה! וצריך לומר: דהכא חיישינן על כל אחת שמא אינה לנועה, ואפילו נראית לנועה — שמא אינה.

כאן

ב"ב לב.
ג"ז שם ודף קסה: סנהדרין ל. גיטין לג: [תוספתא סנהדרין פ"ה]
ע"ז כב.
עדיות פ"ח מ"ב

[ואומר ריצב"א דרב אשי נמי מוקי לה כשבא עד אחד המכשיר קודם שנים הפוסלים אבל בבאו שנים הפוסלים תחלה ואח"כ באו שנים המכשירים בזה אחר זה לא בעי לאוקמי דהא לא הוי קרי במתני' ע"פ עד אחד דכיון דכי אתי עד אחר אין ממש בדבריו עד שבא האחר]. ת"י

[ונקט רישא לבעלה אגב סיפא ובגמ' נמי נקט לבעלה אגב מתני'. ת"י]

תוספות רי"ד

דכהן הוא ואסקיני' פי' דע"א נאמן להכחיש את הקול. ואתו בי תרי עוררים ואמרו בן גרושה ובן חלוצה הוא ואחתיני'. ואתא ע"א ואמר ידענא בי' דכהן הוא ר"א סבר הכא [כיון] דאיכא עוררים תרי דפסלו לי' אין מעלין לכהונה ע"פ ע"א שמכשירו ואע"ג דאיכא ע"א קמא שהכשירו כיון שלא העידו יחד בב"ד אין מצטרפים ורשב"ג סבר אע"פ שיש עוררים מעלין ע"פ ע"א זה שמכשירו שמצטרפים אותו עם הראשון ואמרי' אוקי תרי לבהדי תרי ואוקי גברא אחזקתיה. ואי קשיא והא אמרת לעיל דבתרי ותרי דהוא ספק תורה ל"א אוקי גברא אחזקתיה יש לתרץ ודאי באיסור תורה אמרינן הכי והכא בתרומה דרבנן והכי מוקמי' לה לקמן בשילהי פירקין והלכך מקילין בה ואמרי' אוקי תרי לבהדי תרי ואוקי גברא אחזקתיה. ובפלוגתא דתניא. אין עדיות מצטרפין עד שיראו שניהם כאחד (דברי ר"א) ר"י [בן קרחה] אומר אפילו בזה אח"ז פי' לאפוקי ז"א בפני הלוה לו וז"א בפני הודה לו שמה שראה זה לא ראה זה. ואע"ג דבמנה חד מסהדי לת"ק לא מצטרפי. ולר"י מצטרפי: ואין עדותן מתקיימת בב"ד עד שיעידו שניהם כאחד ר"נ אומר שומעין דבריו של זה היום ולכשיבוא חבירו למחר שומעין דבריו ואתי ר"א כת"ק ורשב"ג כר"נ וקי"ל דהלכה כר"י [בן קרחה] שעדותן מצטרפות אע"פ שלא ראו שניהן כאחד. והל' נמי כר"נ שעדותן מתקיימת בב"ד ואף על פי שלא העידו כאחד: **מתני'** האשה שנחבשה בידי גוים. ע"י ממון מותרת לבעלה ע"י נפשות אסורה. עיר שכבשוה כרכום כל כהנות שבתוכה פסולות. ואם יש להן עדים אפי' עבד אפי' שפחה הרי אלו נאמנין שאין אדם נאמן ע"י עצמו. א"ר זכריה בן הקצב המעון הזה לא זזה ידה מתוך ידי משעה שנכנסו גוים לירושלים ועד שיצאו א"ל אין אדם נאמן על ידי עצמו. פי' באשת כהן מיירי דאי באשת ישראל אפילו ע"י נפשות מותרת דאנוסה היא ומדסיפא בכהנות רישא נמי בכהנות הלכך ע"י ממון מותרת לבעלה דמירתתי דלמא מפסדי ממונא ולא אנסו לה אבל ע"י נפשות דלא מירתתי אנסו לה. והמורה פי' הואיל ונוהגים בה הפקר חוששים שמא נתרצת לא' מהן ומשמע שהיא אסורה לישראל ואינו נ"ל דא"כ גם בשבוי' נאמר כן ונאסור אותה על בעלה ישראל. והאיך מתנה אדם לאשתו אם תשתבאי אפרקינך ואותבינך לי לאינתו. א"ו אע"פ שמפקירים אותה לא חיישינן שמא מתרצת אלא הכל הוא באונס. וכך פי' גם ר"ח ז"ל אסורה לבעלה כהן: המעון הזה. פי' שבועה הוא. א"ר שמואל ברבי יצחק ל"ש פי' שע"י ממון מותרת אלא שיד ישראל תקיפה על אומות העולם פי' שיראים מישראל אבל יד אומות העולם תקיפה על ישראל אפילו על ידי ממון אסורה דלא מירתתי ומפקרי

הורהנה – אין, נחבשה – לא! הוא הדין אפילו נחבשה, *ומעשה שהיה – כך היה. איכא דאמרי, אמר רבא: אף אנן נמי תנינא: *העיד רבי יוסי הכהן ורבי זכריה בן הקצב על בת ישראל שהורהנה באשקלון וריחקוה בני משפחתה, ועדיה מעידים עליה שלא נסתרה ושלא נטמאה. ואמרו חכמים: אם אתם מאמינים שהורהנה – האמינו שלא נסתרה ושלא נטמאה, ואם אין אתם מאמינים שלא נסתרה ושלא נטמאה – אל תאמינו שהורהנה, והא אשקלון דעל ידי ממון הוה, וטעמא דעדים מעידין אותה, הא אין עדים מעידין אותה – לא, מאי לאו לא שנא הורהנה ולא שנא נחבשה! לא, הורהנה שאני. איכא דרמי לה מירמא, תנן: על ידי ממון – מותרת לבעלה. ורמינהו: העיד רבי יוסי כו', והא אשקלון דע"י ממון, וקתני טעמא דעדים מעידים אותה, הא אין עדים מעידין אותה – לא! ומשני: אמר רב שמואל בר רב יצחק: לא קשיא, כאן שיד ישראל תקיפה על אומות העולם, כאן שיד אומות העולם תקיפה על עצמן.§ על ידי נפשות אסורה וכו'.§ אמר רב: כגון (א) נשי גנבי. ולוי אמר: [א]כגון אשתו של בן דונאי. אמר חזקיה: והוא שנגמר דינן להריגה. ורבי יוחנן אמר: [ב]אע"פ שלא נגמר דינן להריגה.§ **מתני'** *[ג]עיר שכבשוה *כרכום – כל כהנות שנמצאו בתוכה פסולות. [ד]ואם יש להן עדים, אפילו עבד, אפי' שפחה – הרי אלו נאמנין. ואין נאמן אדם על ידי עצמו.§ **גמ'** ורמינהו: *[ה]בלשת שבאה לעיר; בשעת שלום, חביות פתוחות – אסורות, סתומות – מותרות. בשעת מלחמה – אלו ואלו מותרות, לפי שאין פנאי לנסך! אמר רב מרי: לבעול – יש פנאי, לנסך – אין פנאי. רבי יצחק בר אלעזר משמיה דחזקיה אמר: כאן – [ו]בכרכום של אותה מלכות, כאן – בכרכום של מלכות אחרת – של אותה מלכות נמי אי אפשר דלא (ב) ערק חד מינייהו! אמר רב יהודה אמר שמואל: כשמשמרות רואות זו את זו. אי אפשר דלא נייםא פורתא! אמר רבי לוי: [ז]כגון דמהדר לה למתא שושילתא וכלבא וגוווזא ואווזא. אמר רבי אבא בר זבדא: פליגי בה רבי יהודה נשיאה ורבנן, חד אמר: כאן בכרכום של אותה מלכות, כאן בכרכום של מלכות אחרת, ולא קשיא ליה ולא מידי וחד קשיא ליה כל הני, ומשני: כגון דמהדר ליה למתא שושילתא וכלבא וגוווזא ואווזא. אמר רב אידי בר אבין אמר ר' יצחק בר אשיאן: [ח]אם יש שם מחבואה אחת – מצלת על הכהנות כולן. בעי רבי ירמיה: אינה מחזקת אלא אחת, מהו? מי אמרינן: [ט]כל חדא וחדא – היינו הא. או דלמא לא אמרינן? ומאי שנא משני *שבילין, אחד טמא ואחד טהור, והלך באחד מהן ועשה טהרות, ובא חבירו והלך בשני ועשה טהרות, רבי יהודה אומר: אם נשאל זה בפני עצמו וזה בפני עצמו – טהורות, שניהם כאחת – טמאות. ר' יוסי אומר: בין כך ובין כך טמאין. ואמר רבא ואיתימא ר' יוחנן: [י]בבת אחת דברי הכל טמאין, בזה אחר זה דברי הכל טהורים. לא נחלקו אלא בבא לישאל עליו ועל חבירו, מר מדמי ליה לבבת אחת, ומר [כ]מדמי ליה לבזה אחר זה. והכא נמי, כיון דשרי להו לכולהו – כבת אחת דמי. הכי השתא?! התם – ודאי איכא טומאה, הכא – מי יימר דאיטמי! בעי רב אשי: אמרה "לא נחבאתי ולא נטמאתי" מהו? מי אמרינן: מה

רש"י

הורהנה. דמדעת. וכיון דהגיע זמן ולא נפדית – הרי היא של גוים בדיניהם, משום הכי בעינן עדים מעידין אותה שלא נסתרה. נחבשה. דאינה נחלטת להם – לא בעינן עדים, הואיל ועל ידי ממון הוא. ואיכא דרמי לה מרמא. לא מתני לה להא דרב שמואל בר רב יצחק אפירושא דמתניתין בלשון לא שנו, אלא רמי מירמא מתניתין וברייתא אהדדי, ועלה שני רב שמואל חילוק בין יד ישראל תקיפה ליד אומות העולם תקיפה. הני נשי דגנבי. שבעליהן ניתלין, ודרך המלכות להפקיר ביתם ונשיהן. בן דונאי. רוצח היה, ואלעזר שמו, כדאמרינן בפ' "עגלה ערופה" (סוטה מז.). אבל נשי דגנבי הגונבים ממון – לא מפקרי. **מתני'** כרכום. "מצור" מתרגמינן כרכומא (דברים כ). פסולות. אסורות לבעליהן, דאשת כהן אסורה באונס. **גמ'** בלשת. חיל. על שם שמחפשים כל המטמונים. לבעול יש פנאי. דתקיף להו יצרייהו. רבי יצחק בן אלעזר אמר. אף בבעילה פעמים שהן מותרות. כרכום של אותה מלכות. אינו רוצה להשחית את בני העיר, וכשכובש עיר הסמוך לממשלתו – שומרה, והיא לו למס עובד. משמרות. מקום מעמד השומרים שהעמיד המלך שלא יחבל אדם באנשי העיר. דמהדר למתא כו'. שמו סביבות העיר שלשלות ברזל שישמיעו קול בהכשל איש רץ עליהם, וכלבים ואווזים זועקין. וגוווזא. מקלות וקיסמין להכשל בהן. ולא קשיא ליה מידי. לא חייש למיעקר איניש יחידאה ולבעול, הואיל ואין הדבר הפקר. ומאי שנא משני שבילין. דכיון דבא לשאול עליו ועל חבירו – אמר רבי יוסי טמאין, הכא נמי – לכולהו שרינן כי הדדי. אחד טמא. שיש בו קברות מפסיק כל רחבו, ואין ידוע איזהו הטמא, אבל כך מוחזקים באחד מהן. ועשה טהרות. נגע בטהרות. טהורים. דכל חד כי אתי לקמן – תלינן ליה למימר בטהור הלך, דהוה ליה ספק טומאה ברה"ר, וספיקו טהור. טמאין. דהיכי נימא להו טהורים אתם? חד מינייהו ודאי בטמא אזל. בבת אחת. באו לשאול בבת אחת. הכא נמי כו'. ור' יהודה ור' יוסי הלכה כר' יוסי.

מה

תוספות

כאן בכרכום של אותה מלכות. פי': שיושבין בטח, לפי שאין אחריהן מחנה, ויש פנאי לנסך ולבעול. אבל בלשת של מלכות אחרת, שאימת מלכות שבאו בגבולה עליהם אין להן פנאי. וכן פי' ר"ח ור"ת, וכן מוכח בירושלמי. ופריך: כרכום של אותה מלכות אי אפשר דלא ערקא חדא מינייהו! והוה לן למשרינהו לכולהו ולמיתלי לקולא, דבשבויה הקילו, כדאמרינן בסמוך: אם יש מחבואה אחת – מצלת על כל הכהנות כולן. אע"ג דמספקא לן באינה מחזקת אלא אחת – הכא פשיטא לן דשרו, דהתם לא ודאי נחבאת, אבל הכא – ודאי ערקא. ולפי' הקונטרס קשה טובא, חדא: דפריך נתלי לחומרא, וגבי מחבואה תלינן לקולא! ועוד, דמה מתרץ דמהדר למתא כו' ואין אדם נכנס לשם, והא קתני בלשת שנכנסה לעיר! ועוד: כיון דאההיא דע"ז פריך – הוה ליה למימר: אי אפשר דלא ערק חד מינייהו ונסך! ועוד: דהתם מפרש טעמא לפי שאין פנאי לנסך, ולית ליה טעמא לפי שאין כרכום של אותה מלכות רוצה להשחית את בני העיר! [ועוד: מאי שנא שעת מלחמה משעת שלום]? ויש ליישב לפי שיטת הקונטרס דרבי יצחק בן אלעזר לא אתי לשנויי מתני' אההיא דע"ז, אלא אדת ליה שינויא דרב מרי, ומתניתין דהתם נמי בכרכום של מלכות אחרת, ולא בא אלא לפרושי מתניתין. וכן משמע בפרק בתרא דע"ז (דף עא.), דפריך התם ממתניתין דהכא אמתניתין דבלשת, ולא מייתי התם דרבי יצחק.

והלך באחד מהם ועשה טהרות. להכי נקט ועשה טהרות, דלענין האדם אנו מזקיקים שניהם לטבול ולהזות, פן יבואו לידי טומאה ודאי אם יגעו שניהם בככר אחד. לכך אומר להו: זילו טבילו, דהכי נהרא קמייכו. ועוד: דמשום דבעי למתני *סיפא: הזה וטבל – טהור, הלך בשני ועשה טהרות – הרי אלו טהורות, ואם קיימות הראשונים – אלו ואלו תלויות, ואם לא טהר בינתים, הראשונות תלויות, והשניות ישרפו*.

ואם נשאל זה בפני עצמו וזה בפני עצמו טהורות. לא שיאכלם אדם אחד, דאם כן יאכל ודאי טומאה, דהכי אמרינן בשבועות בפ"ב (דף יט.): הלך בראשון ולא נכנס, בשני ונכנס – חייב, דטמא הוא ממה נפשך.

בבא לישאל עליו ועל חברו. אין לפרש שבא לישאל בבת אחת, דהתם מודו כולי עלמא דטמאות – מכל שכן דבאו לישאל שניהם בבת אחת. אלא מיירי שנשאל על עצמו וטהרוהו, ואח"כ בא לישאל על חבירו, דמר מדמי ליה לבת אחת, כיון שנשאל על שניהם במעמד אחד, ומר מדמי ליה לזה אחר זה כיון שטיהרוהו קודם. והכא נמי, כיון דשרו לכולהו – כבת אחת דמי, אף על פי שאין בא לפנינו אלא על אחת, מ"מ הדבר ידוע לכל שהרבה כהנות היו, והוי כאילו בא לישאל על כולם בבת אחת, והכא מודו כ"ע. ובחנם דחק בקונטרס לפרש כר' יוסי.

לא

עין משפט נר מצוה

קב א ב מיי' (פ"ח) [פי"ח] מהל' איסורי ביאה הלכה ל טוש"ע אה"ע סימן ז סעיף יא בהג"ה:

קג ג מיי' פי"ח מהל' א"ב הלכה כו טור ש"ע שם סעיף י:

קד ד מיי' שם הל' יט טוש"ע שם סעיף א:

קה ה מיי' פי"ב מהל' מאכלות אסורות הלכה כד סמג לאוין קמח טוש"ע י"ד סי' קכט סעיף יב:

קו ו ז ח ט מיי' פי"ח מהל' איסורי ביאה הלכה כז כח כט טוש"ע אה"ע סי' ז סעיף י:

קז י כ מיי' פי"ט מהל' אבות הטומאה הלכה ב:

מסורת הש"ס

[עירובין סה: וש"נ]

עדיות פ"ח מ"ב

ע"ז עא.

[בערוך איתא ברקום בקו"ף]

שם ע: שבת מא. נדה יג.

טהרות פ"ה מ"ה פסחים י.

[למיתנא סיפא כריתא כל"ל מהרש"א]

[ועי' תוס' פסחים י. ד"ה הלך]

הגהות הב"ח

(א) גמ' כגון הני נשי דגנבי: (ב) שם דלא (ערק) תז"מ. ונ"ב ס"א עקר וכן משמע מפרש"י:

גליון הש"ס

רש"י ד"ה בלשת וכו' שמחפשין. כי בפסוק ויחפש ברלשית מ"ד התרגום ובלש:

תוספות רי"ד

ומפקרי לה. ה"ד ע"י נפשות א"ר כגון נשי דגנבי אמר חזקיה והוא שנגמר דינם להריגה פי' שבעליהן נתלו ודרך המלכות להפקיר טפם ונשיהם ור"י אמר אעפ"י שלא נגמר דינן להריגה והל' כחזקיה דהוא רביה דר' יוחנן: עיר שכבשוה כרכום. פי' חיל הצרים עליה. מצור תרגומו כרכום כל כהנות שבתוכה פסולו' לבעליהן פי' דבחזקת שנבעלו קיימו ואנוסה אסורה לכהן ואם יש להן עדים שלא נבעלו אפילו עבד אפילו שפחה הרי אלו נאמנים ואין אדם נאמן ע"י עצמו לא האשה להעיד על עצמה ולא הבעל להעיד על אשתו ורמינהו בולשת שנכנסה לעיר. פי' חיל ונקרא כן ע"ש שמחפשים את כל המטמוניות תרגום ויחפש ובלש בזמן שלום חביות פתוחות אסורות וסתומות מותרת בשעת מלחמה אלו ואלו מותרות לפי שאין פנאי לנסך. אמר ר"מ לנסך אין פנאי לבעול יש פנאי דיצרא דעבירה תקיף מיין נסך ר"י בן אלעזר משמיה דחזקי' אמר כאן בכרכום של אותה מלכות אינן יראים ויש להם פנאי לבעול ולנסך. אבל של מלכות אחרת יראים [שמא] יבוא חיל מאיזה מלכות לעזור להן וממהרים לשלול ולהבריח ואין להן פנאי לא לבעול ולא לנסך. א"ר אידי ב"א אר"י ב"א אם יש שם מחבואה א' [מצלת] על כל הכהנות ומותרות כלן: בעי ר"י אם אינה מחזקת אלא א' מהן מהו. מי אמרינן כל חדא וחדא היינו האי א"ד לא אמרינן ולא איפשטא

תורה אור

*מה לי לשקר, או דלמא לא אמרינן? ומאי שנא מההוא מעשה, דההוא גברא *דאגר ליה חמרא לחבריה, א"ל: לא תיזיל באורחא דנהר פקוד, דאיכא מיא, זיל באורחא דנרש דליכא מיא, ואזל איהו באורחא דנהר פקוד, ומית חמרא. אתא לקמיה דרבא. א"ל: אין, באורחא דנהר פקוד אזלי, מיהו לא הוו מיא. אמר *רבא: מה לי לשקר, אי בעי א"ל: באורחא דנרש אזלי. ואמר ליה אביי: *"מה לי לשקר" במקום עדים לא אמרינן! הכי השתא?! התם – ודאי איכא עדים דאיכא מיא, הכא – ודאי איטמי?! חששא הוא, ובמקום חששא – אמרינן.§ אם יש עדים אפילו עבד ואפילו שפחה נאמנין.§ ואפילו שפחה דידה מהימנא? ורמינהי: *לא תתייחד עמו אלא ע"פ עדים. ואפילו ע"פ עבד וע"פ שפחה, חוץ משפחתה, מפני שלבה גם בשפחתה! אמר רב פפי: *בשבויה הקילו. רב פפא אמר: הא בשפחה דידה, הא בשפחה דידיה. ושפחה דידה לא מהימנא? הא קתני: אין אדם מעיד על עצמו, הא שפחה דידה – מהימנא! שפחתה נמי כעצמה דמי. רב אשי אמר: הא והא בשפחה דידה, ושפחה מיחזא חזיא ושתקה. התם, דשתיקתה מתירתה – לא מהימנא, הכא דשתיקתה אוסרתה – מהימנא. השתא נמי אתיא ומשקרא! תרתי לא עבדה. *כי הא דמרי בר איסק, ואמרי לה חנא בר איסק, אתא ליה אחא מבי חוזאה. א"ל: פלוג לי בנכסי דאבא. א"ל: לא ידענא לך. אתא לקמיה דרב חסדא, א"ל: שפיר קאמר לך, דכתיב: "ויכר יוסף את אחיו והם לא הכירהו" (בראשית מב) *מלמד שיצא בלא חתימת זקן ובא בחתימת זקן. א"ל: זיל אייתי סהדי דאחוה את. א"ל: אית לי סהדי *ומסתפינו מיניה, דגברא אלמא הוא. א"ל לדידיה: זיל (א) אייתינהו את דלאו אחוך הוא. א"ל: דינא הכי?! המוציא מחבירו עליו הראיה! א"ל: הכי דאיננא לך ולכולהו אלמי חברך. השתא נמי אתו ומשקרי! תרתי לא עבדי. לימא כתנאי: זו עדות איש ואשה, תינוק ותינוקת, אביה ואמה ואחיה ואחותה, אבל לא בנה ובתה, לא עבדה ושפחתה. ותניא אידך: הכל נאמנין להעיד, חוץ מהימנה ובעלה. דרב פפי ודרב אשי – תנאי היא. דרב פפא [מי] לימא תנאי היא? אמר לך רב פפא: כי תניא ההיא – במסיחה לפי תומה. כי הא *דכי אתא רב דימי אמר, רב חנן קרטיגנאה משתעי: מעשה בא לפני רבי יהושע בן לוי, ואמרי לה רבי יהושע בן לוי מישתעי: מעשה בא לפני רבי באדם אחד שהיה מסיח לפי תומו, ואמר: אני ואמי נשבינו לבין הגוים, יצאתי לשאוב מים – דעתי על אמי, ללקט עצים – דעתי על אמי. והשיאה ר' לכהונה על פיו.§ **מתני'** אמר ר' זכריה בן הקצב: *המעון הזה! לא זזה ידה מתוך ידי משעה שנכנסו נכרים לירושלים ועד שיצאו. אמרו לו: אין אדם מעיד על עצמו.§ **גמ'** תנא: *ואעפ"כ יחד לה בית בחצרו, וכשהיא יוצאה – יוצאה בראש בניה, וכשהיא נכנסת – נכנסת בסוף בניה. בעי אביי: מהו לעשות בגרושה כן? התם הוא – דבשבויה הקילו, אבל הכא – לא, או דלמא לא שנא? ת"ש, דתניא: *המגרש את אשתו – לא תנשא בשכונתו, ואם

מה לי לשקר. אי בעיא אמרה נחבאתי. במקום עדים. דאכן סהדי דכל שעתא איכא מיא. ודאי איטמי. בתמיה. לא תתייחד עמו. במסכת גיטין היא: שכיב מרע שכתב ומסר גט לאשתו על מנת שאם מת יהא גט למפרע ולא תיזקק לחליצה – לא תתייחד עמו, שמא יבא עליה והוה ליה גט ישן, ותנן: בית הלל אוסרין לפטור בגט ישן. ואיזהו גט ישן – כל שנתייחד עמה מאחר שכתבו לה. וטעמא – גזירה שמא יאמרו: גיטה קודם לבנה. ואפילו על פי עבד. דייה בעבד שהיה עמה. שלבה גם בשפחתה. ותשמש בפניה. רב אשי אמר הא והא בשפחה דידה. והיינו טעמא דמתני' מהימנא והתם לא מהימנא, דשפחה דידה מיחזא חזיא בקילקול גבירתה ושתקה. התם. גבי גט. דשתיקותה מתירתה. שאינה צריכה שתעיד לומר לא שמשה, אלא שתאמר: אני הייתי עמה. לא מהימנא. להיות זו מותרת על ידה. דאי נמי חזיא – לא מסהדא. הכא. גבי שבויה. דשתיקותה. דשפחה. אוסרתה. לגבירתה, דכל כמה שאינה מעידה לומר טהורה היא – מחזקינן לה בטמאה. כי מסהדא ואמרה טהורה היא – מהימנא, דלשקורי לאו אורחא, אלא למשתק. השתא נמי. כיון (ב) דרחמא לה לגבירתה, או דדחלה מינה – אתיא ומשקרא, ואמרה: טהורה היא. תרתי לא עבדא. חדא למשתק בקלקולה, ועוד דאתיי ותשקר. אחא מבי חוזאה. שהלך אביו שם והוליכו עמו וגדלו שם, ומת אביו, וחזר לעירו ותבע חלקו בנכסי אביו. א"ל. רב חסדא להההוא אחא. שפיר קאמר לך. שאינו מכירך, לפי שיצאת בלא חתימת זקן [ובאת בחתימת זקן]. ויכר יוסף את אחיו. שכשפירש מהן כבר היו חתומי זקן. א"ל. רב חסדא למרי. זיל (ג) אייתינהו את. להנהו סהדי המכירין אותו, ויעידוך שאינו בן אביך. השתא נמי. כיון דדחלי מיניה אתו ומשקרי. תרתי לא עבדי. חדא דשתקי מלהעיד אמת, וחדא דמסהדי שיקרא. לימא כתנאי. שפחתה אי מהימנא אי לא. זו עדות. עדות זו של שבויה הכל כשרים בה, איש ואשה תינוק ותינוקת. חוץ מהימנה. היא עצמה. דרב פפי ורב אשי. דאמרו לעיל שפחה דידה מהימנה. ודאי תנאי היא. על כרחך יאמרו: תנן דאמרי' – כי מתניתא בתרייתא, מדקשיא להו קמייתא. דרב פפא. דאמר: לא מהימנה. מי לימא תנאי היא. כלומר, דחוק הוא לומר: תנא דאמרי כי מתניתא קמייתא. או יוכל לתרץ מתניתא בתרייתא נמי כוותיה, למימר: שפחתה כעצמה דמי, והרי היא בכלל חוץ מהימנה דקתני בה. או תירוצא אחרינא. אמר לך רב פפא כי תניא ההיא. דקתני הכל נאמנים ואפילו שפחה דידה – במסיחה לפי תומה. רב חנא קרטיגנאה משתעי. רב חנן דמן קרטיגי היה מספר מעשה זה. מתני' המעון הזה. שבועה היא. גמ' ואעפ"כ. שאסרו עליו, לפי שכהן היה. כשהיא יוצאה. והוא בחצר. יוצאה בראש בניה. שיהו הבנים עמהם, שלא יתייחדו. וכשהיא נכנסת, נכנסת בסוף בניה. כדי שלא יהא הוא והיא בחצר, והבנים מבחוץ. בגרושה. כהן שגירש את אשתו, מהו לדור עמו בחצר? לא תנשא בשכונתו. לפי שמכירה ברמיזותיו וקריצותיו, שמא יבואו לידי עבירה. ואם

לא תתיחד עמו אלא בעדים. פירוש בקונטרס: משום גט ישן. ולא פירש לטעמיה, דפירש בגיטין (דף עג.): דבמהיום אם מתי מגורשת למפרע משעת נתינה, ולא תתיחד עמו משום חשש קידושין. כמו המגרש אשתו ולנה עמו בפונדקי, בית הלל אומרים: צריכה הימנו גט שני (שם דף פא.) [ולא שייך גט ישן כלל לפירוש דהתם]. וכן משמע התם בגמרא. אבל לרבינו תם דמפרש מה היא באותן הימים קאי א"מהיום אם מתי", ונעשה כאומר "מעת שאני בעולם", שאין דעתו לגרשה, אע"פ שאומר "מהיום", אלא שעה אחת לפני מיתתו – הוי טעמא משום גט ישן, ובתוספתא משמע כפי' רבינו תם*.

שפיר קאמר לך דכתיב ויכר יוסף. זה שבא נולד כאן, והלך עם אביו למדינת הים, ועתה כשחזר ואמר לא ידענא לך – מיחזי כשיקרא, כי היה לו לידע אם הוא אחיו אם לאו, כיון שמכירו קודם, להכי קאמר רב חסדא דשפיר קאמר ליה שאינו מכירו, כדאשכחן ביוסף. **אמר** ליה אית לי סהדי ומסתפינו מיניה דאיניש אלמא הוא. נראה לר"י דמיירי שהביא עדים, ואומרים: אותו עדות שאתה שואל לא נאמר (ד) לך כלום עליו, דרגלים לדבר שהוא אלם. אמר ליה זיל כו', פי': לך הבא אותם עדים עצמם שיראים להעיד (ה) עליך, שיעידו שאינו אחיך, או שיאמרו שאינם יודעים אם הוא אחיך אם לאו. וקאמר: השתא נמי כיון שיראים ממנו – ישקרו לומר אינו אחיו, או שאינן יודעין אם הוא אחיו. אבל אם אין רגלים לדבר – אין נראה כלל שיהא נאמן לומר דגברא אלמא הוא, דאם לא כן כל אדם יאמר על חבירו שהוא גברא אלמא, ויביא הוא עדים, ואם לא יביא – יפסיד. ועוד: דקאמר השתא נמי אתו ומסהדי, אטו משום דמסתפו מיניה הני סהדי, מסתפו מיניה כולי עלמא?

תרתי לא עבדי. שישתקו ולא יעידו האמת, ועוד שיאמרו שקר. וכן גבי שפחה.

במסיחה לפי תומה. ואפילו הכי היא ובעלה אינן נאמנין. אע"ג דיוחנן אוכל חלות (לעיל דף כו.) היה נאמן על עצמו במסיח לפי תומו – הני מילי לתרומה, אבל הכא – מעלה עשו ביוחסין. [אומר ר"י: דמסיח לפי תומו אינו כשר אלא לעדות אשה א] דרבנן, כדאמר ביבמות והכא: בשבויה הקילו]*. ואם

בעילתן בעילת זנות. ואסיק ר"א הא והא בשפחה דידה ושפחתה מיחזא ושתקת התם דשתיקותא מתירתה לא מהימנא והכא דשתיקתה אוסרתה מהימנא השתא נמי אתיא ומשקרא תרתי לא עבדי. פי' חדא ששותקת מלהעיד האמת ועוד שתעיד שקר. תנא זו עדות כשר איש ואשה תינוק ותינוקת אביה ואמה אחיה ואחיותה אבל לא בתה ובנה. פי' זו עדות של שבויה כל אלו כשרין להעיד ואם הבן מסיח ל"ת ואומר אני ואמי נשבינו לבין עובדי כוכבים ויצאתי לשאוב מים וללקוט עצים ודעתי על אמי והשיאה ר' לכהונה על פיו. פי' מסיח ל"ת יקרא כ"ז שלא בא לפני ב"ד להעיד אלא מספר עם חבירו. והשומעים מפיו מגידים לב"ד וכ"מ שהעבד ואשה נאמנים גם הקטן נאמן ולגבי מת בעלך שעבד ואשה נאמנים כדתנן החזקנו לחיות משיאים עד מפי עד (עד) מפי שפחה הקטן נמי נאמן כדתנן התם ר"י אומר אפילו שמע מן התינוקות אומרים הרי אנו הולכים לספוד ולקבור את איש פ' והשתא השומע מן התינוקות מעיד תינוקות עצמן לא כ"ש: [מתני'] א"ר זכריה וכו'. תנא אע"פ. פי' אע"פ שאסורה לו לפי שהיה כהן יחד לה בית בחצירו כשהיא יוצאה יוצאה בראש בניה וכשהיא נכנסת נכנסת בסוף בניה. ופי' כדי שלא יתייחדו. בעי אביי מהו לעשות כן בגרושה. פי' לדור עמה בחצר התם בשבויה היקילו אבל הכא לא. א"ד ל"ש. ת"ש

עין משפט נר מצוה:

קח א מיי' פ"ד מהל' שכירות הלכה ג סמג עשין פט טוש"מ סימן סט:

קט ב מיי' פי"ח מהל' איסורי ביאה הלכ' כח טוש"ע אה"ע סי' קיט סעיף ז:

קי ג מיי' פ"ח מהל' גירושין הל' כ סמג עשין נ טוש"ע שם סימן קמח סעיף ב:

קיא ד מיי' פי"ח מהל' איסורי ביאה הלכ' יט סמג לאוין קלב טוש"ע שם סימן ז סעיף ב:

[ועיין היטיב תוס' גיטין עג. ד"ה לא]

קיב ה מיי' פ"ג מהל' עדות הלכה יב סמג עשין קט טוש"ע ח"מ סי' כח סעיף ה:

קיג ו מיי' פי"ח מהל' איסורי ביאה הל' יט טוש"ע אה"ע סי' ז סעיף ב:

קיד ז מיי' שם הלכה יח טוש"ע שם סעיף ו:

קטו ח מיי' שם הלכה יט טוש"ע שם סעיף ג:

קטז ט מיי' שם הלכה כה טוש"ע שם סעיף ט:

קיז י מיי' פכ"א שם הלכה כו סמג לאוין קכז טוש"ע אה"ע סי' ז סעיף ז ופי' קיט סעיף ז:

נ"ל ומסתפו. יעב"ץ

[כל זה מבואר בסוגיא ב"ק קיד:]

מסורת הש"ס:

[קדושין סה: וש"נ]

בכורות לו. ב"מ פא:

[נ"ל רבה ועי' תוס' בכורות לו. ד"ה ואמר] [ב"ב לב: קדושין סה: ושם נסמן]

גיטין עג.

[לעיל כג: וש"נ]

ב"מ לט: ע"ש

שם יבמות פח.

[פי' נקבע שבועה במקדש. ערוך וכן פי' רשב"ם בב"ב קסו.]

[שמחות פ"ב ע"ש]

הגהות הב"ח

(א) גמ' זיל אייתי את: (ב) רש"י ד"ה השתא (דרחמא לה לגבירתה או) תא"מ ונ"ב ס"א אין נ: (ג) ד"ה זיל אייתי את: (ד) תוס' ד"ה אמר וכו' לא נאמר כלום לרגלים כצ"ל ותי' לך ותי' עליו נמחק: (ה) באד"ה להעיד שיעידו כצ"ל ותי' עליך נמחק:

הגהות מהר"י לנדא

א] תוס' ד"ה במסיחה. אלא לעדות אשה כדאמר ביבמות והכא בשבויה הקילו לרבנן כצ"ל.

תוספות רי"ד

איפשיטא ולקולא עבדי' בעי ר"א לא נחבאתי ולא נטמאתי מהו מי אמרינן מה לי לשקר במקום חששא אי לא. ולא איפשיטא ולקולא עבדי. ואם יש להן עדים אפילו עבד ואפילו שפחה דידה מהימני ורמינהו לא תתיחד עמו אלא בעדים אפילו עבד ואפילו שפחה חוץ משפחתה מפני שלבה גם בשפחתה. פי' גבי שב"מ שנתן גט לאשתו דחיישינן שמא יבוא עליה והוה' צריכה גט שני שאין אדם עושה

וְאִם הָיָה כֹּהֵן — לֹא תָדוּר עִמּוֹ בְּמָבוֹי. אִם הָיָה כְּפָר קָטָן, זֶה הָיָה מַעֲשֶׂה, וְאָמְרוּ: כְּפָר קָטָן נִידּוֹן (א) כִּשְׁכוּנָה. מִי נִדְחֶה מִפְּנֵי מִי? ת"ש, דְּתַנְיָא: [א]הִיא נִדְחֵית מִפָּנָיו, וְאֵין הוּא נִדְחֶה מִפָּנֶיהָ. וְאִם הָיְתָה חָצֵר שֶׁלָּהּ — הוּא נִדְחֶה מִפָּנֶיהָ. אִיבַּעְיָא לְהוּ: הָיְתָה חָצֵר שֶׁל שְׁנֵיהֶם מַהוּ? ת"ש: הִיא נִדְחֵית מִפָּנָיו. בְּמַאי עָסְקִינַן? אִילֵימָא בְּחָצֵר שֶׁלּוֹ — פְּשִׁיטָא! וְאֶלָּא בְּחָצֵר שֶׁלָּהּ — וְהָתַנְיָא: אִם הָיְתָה חָצֵר שֶׁלָּהּ — הוּא נִדְחֶה מִפָּנֶיהָ. אֶלָּא לָאו — כִּי הַאי גַּוְונָא. [ב]דִּלְמָא דַּאֲגִיר מֵיגָר. מַאי הָוֵי עֲלָהּ? ת"ש: °"הִנֵּה ה' מְטַלְטֶלְךָ טַלְטֵלָה גָּבֶר" *וְאָמַר רַב: [ג]טִלְטוּלֵי דְּגַבְרָא קָשִׁין מִדְּאִיתְּתָא. ת"ר: [ד]לָוָה הֵימֶנָּה בְּנִכְסֵי אָבִיהָ — אֵינָהּ נִפְרַעַת אֶלָּא ע"י אַחֵר. אָמַר רַב שֵׁשֶׁת: וְאִי אָתוּ לְקַמָּן לְדִינָא לָא מִזְדַּקְקִינַן לְהוּ. רַב פַּפָּא אָמַר: [ה]שַׁמּוּתֵי מְשַׁמְּתִינַן לְהוּ. רַב הוּנָא בְּרֵיהּ דְּרַב יְהוֹשֻׁעַ אָמַר: [ו]נַגּוּדֵי (ב) נַמִּי מְנַגְּדִינַן לְהוּ. אָמַר רַב נַחְמָן: תָּנָא *בְּאֵבֶל רַבָּתִי: בד"א — שֶׁנִּתְגָּרְשָׁה מִן הַנִּשּׂוּאִין, [ז]אֲבָל כְּשֶׁנִּתְגָּרְשָׁה מִן הָאֵירוּסִין — נִפְרַעַת ע"י עַצְמָהּ, שֶׁאֵין לִבּוֹ גַּס בָּהּ. הַהוּא אָרוּס וַאֲרוּסָתוֹ דְּאָתוּ לְקַמֵּיהּ דְּרָבָא, יְתֵיב רַב אַדָּא בַּר מַתְנָא קַמֵּיהּ, אוֹקֵי רָבָא שְׁלוּחָא בֵּינָתַיְיהוּ. א"ל רַב אַדָּא בַּר מַתְנָא: וְהָאָמַר רַב נַחְמָן, תָּנָא בְּאֵבֶל רַבָּתִי כו'! א"ל: קָא חָזֵינַן דְּקָא גָּיְיסֵי בַּהֲדָדֵי. אִיכָּא דְּאָמְרִי: לָא אוֹקֵי רָבָא שָׁלִיחַ בֵּינָתַיְיהוּ. א"ל: רַב אַדָּא בַּר מַתְנָא: נֵיקוּם מָר שְׁלוּחָא בֵּינָתַיְיהוּ! א"ל: וְהָא [אָמַר] רַב נַחְמָן: תָּנָא בְּאֵבֶל רַבָּתִי כו'! א"ל: [ח]ה"מ — הֵיכָא דְּלָא גָּיְיסֵי בַּהֲדָדֵי, אֲבָל הָנֵי — קָא חָזֵינָא לְהוּ דְּגָיְיסֵי בַּהֲדָדֵי.§ **מתני'** וְאֵלּוּ נֶאֱמָנִין לְהָעִיד בְּגוֹדְלָן מַה שֶּׁרָאוּ בְּקוֹטְנָן: [ט]נֶאֱמָן אָדָם לוֹמַר "זֶה כְּתַב יָדוֹ שֶׁל אַבָּא" וְ"זֶה כְּתַב יָדוֹ שֶׁל רַבִּי" וְ"זֶה כְּתַב יָדוֹ שֶׁל אָחִי". "זָכוּר הָיִיתִי בִּפְלוֹנִית שֶׁיָּצְאָה בְּהִינוּמָא וְרֹאשָׁהּ פָּרוּעַ". וְ"שֶׁהָיָה אִישׁ פְּלוֹנִי יוֹצֵא מִבֵּית הַסֵּפֶר לִטְבּוֹל לֶאֱכוֹל בִּתְרוּמָה". וְ"שֶׁהָיָה חוֹלֵק עִמָּנוּ עַל הַגּוֹרֶן", וְ"הַמָּקוֹם הַזֶּה בֵּית הַפְּרָס". וְ"עַד כָּאן הָיִינוּ בָּאִין בְּשַׁבָּת". אֲבָל אֵין אָדָם נֶאֱמָן לוֹמַר "דֶּרֶךְ הָיָה לִפְלוֹנִי בַּמָּקוֹם הַזֶּה, מַעֲמָד *וּמִסְפֵּד הָיָה לִפְלוֹנִי בַּמָּקוֹם הַזֶּה".§ **גמ'** אָמַר רַב הוּנָא בְּרֵיהּ דְּרַב יְהוֹשֻׁעַ: [י]וְהוּא שֶׁיֵּשׁ גָּדוֹל עִמּוֹ. וּצְרִיכָא, דְּאִי אַשְׁמְעִינַן אָבִיו — מִשּׁוּם דִּשְׁכִיחַ גַּבֵּיהּ, אֲבָל רַבּוֹ — לָא. וְאִי אַשְׁמְעִינַן רַבּוֹ — מִשּׁוּם דְּאִית לֵיהּ אֵימְתֵיהּ דְּרַבֵּיהּ, אֲבָל אָבִיו — לָא. וְאִי אַשְׁמְעִינַן הָנֵי תַּרְתֵּי, אָבִיו — דִּשְׁכִיחַ גַּבֵּיהּ, וְרַבּוֹ — דְּאִית לֵיהּ אֵימְתֵיהּ, אֲבָל אָחִיו דְּלֵית לֵיהּ לָא הָא וְלָא הָא — אֵימָא לָא, קמ"ל: כֵּיוָן *דְּקִיּוּם שְׁטָרוֹת מִדְּרַבָּנַן — הֵימְנוּהוּ רַבָּנַן בִּדְרַבָּנַן.§ [כ]זָכוּר הָיִיתִי בִּפְלוֹנִית שֶׁיָּצְאָה בְּהִינוּמָא וְרֹאשָׁהּ פָּרוּעַ.§ מַאי טַעְמָא? *כֵּיוָן דְּרוֹב נָשִׁים בְּתוּלוֹת נִישָּׂאוֹת, גִּלּוּי מִלְּתָא בְּעָלְמָא הוּא.§ [ל]וְשֶׁהָיָה אִישׁ פְּלוֹנִי יוֹצֵא מִבֵּית הַסֵּפֶר לִטְבּוֹל לֶאֱכוֹל בִּתְרוּמָה.§ וְדִלְמָא עֶבֶד כֹּהֵן הוּא? מְסַיֵּיעַ לֵיהּ לְר' יְהוֹשֻׁעַ בֶּן לֵוִי. דְּאָמַר ר' יְהוֹשֻׁעַ בֶּן לֵוִי: [מ]אָסוּר לְאָדָם שֶׁיְּלַמֵּד אֶת עַבְדּוֹ תּוֹרָה. וְלָא? *[נ]וְהָתַנְיָא: לָוָה הֵימֶנּוּ רַבּוֹ, אוֹ שֶׁעֲשָׂאוֹ רַבּוֹ אַפּוֹטְרוֹפּוֹס

רש"י

וְאִם הָיָה כֹּהֵן. אֲפִילּוּ לֹא נִיסֵּת. לֹא תָּדוּר עִמּוֹ בְּמָבוֹי. שֶׁמָּא יָבֹא עָלֶיהָ, וְכֹהֵן אָסוּר בִּגְרוּשָׁה. אֲבָל יִשְׂרָאֵל, כָּל זְמַן שֶׁלֹּא נִיסֵּת — תָּדוּר בִּשְׁכוּנָתוֹ. וַאֲמַר רַב גָּרֵס, וּמֵהַאי קְרָא שָׁמְעִינַן לָהּ. לָוָה הֵימֶנָּה. בִּהְיוֹתָהּ תַּחְתָּיו. בְּנִכְסֵי אָבִיהָ. שֶׁהָיוּ בְּיָדָהּ נִכְסֵי מְלוֹג, וּבְכֹהֵן שֶׁגֵּירֵשׁ אֶת אִשְׁתּוֹ קָא מַיְירֵי. אֵינָהּ נִפְרַעַת. הֵימֶנּוּ ע"י עַצְמָהּ, שֶׁלֹּא יִקָּרְבוּ בִּדְבָרִים. בְּאֵבֶל רַבָּתִי. מַסֶּכְתָּא הִיא, וְקוֹרִין אוֹתָהּ שְׂמָחוֹת, וְזוֹ הִיא מִשְׁנָה רִאשׁוֹנָה שֶׁלָּהּ: הַגּוֹסֵס הֲרֵי הוּא כְּחַי לְכָל דְּבָרָיו. אָרוּס וַאֲרוּסָתוֹ. כֹּהֵן הָיָה. וְהָאֲמַר רַב נַחְמָן תָּנָא בְּאֵבֶל רַבָּתִי. דְּמִן הָאֵירוּסִין נִפְרַעַת עַל יְדֵי עַצְמָהּ. דְּגָיְיסֵי בַּהֲדָדֵי. מַכִּירִין זֶה אֶת זֶה בִּרְמִיזוֹת וּקְרִיצוֹת. בְּלַעַ"ז פריווי"ץ. **מתני'** זֶה כְּתַב יָדוֹ שֶׁל אַבָּא. וּמְקַיְּימִין הַשְּׁטָר עַל פִּיו, אע"פ שֶׁמֵּת אָבִיו בְּעוֹד זֶה קָטָן. שֶׁיָּצְאת בְּהִינוּמָא. וְהוּא סִימָן שֶׁנִּיסֵּת בְּתוּלָה וּכְתוּבָּתָהּ מָאתַיִם, כִּדְאָמְרִינַן בְּרֵישׁ פִּירְקִין. יוֹצֵא מִבֵּית הַסֵּפֶר. כְּשֶׁהָיִינוּ לְמֵידִין תִּינוֹקוֹת בְּבֵית רַבָּן. וּבְכוּלְּהוּ מְפָרֵשׁ טַעְמָא בַּגְּמָרָא. אֲבָל אֵין נֶאֱמָנִין כו'. דְּאַפּוּקֵי מָמוֹנָא הוּא, וּבָעֵינַן עֵדוּת מְעַלְּיָיתָא. וּכְתוּבָּה הַיְינוּ טַעְמָא — דְּרוֹב נָשִׁים בְּתוּלוֹת נִישָּׂאוֹת. מַעֲמָד וּמִסְפֵּד. מָקוֹם הָיָה לוֹ כָּאן לְהַסְפִּיד מֵתָיו כְּשֶׁמּוֹלִיכָן לְבֵית קְבָרוֹת שֶׁלּוֹ, וְלַעֲשׂוֹת שָׁם מַעֲמָדוֹת וּמוֹשָׁבוֹת שֶׁהָיוּ עוֹשִׂין שִׁבְעָה לְמֵת. רַבִּי יוֹחָנָן בֶּן בְּרוֹקָא אוֹמֵר נֶאֱמָנִים. לָא גָּרְסִינַן לֵיהּ בְּמַתְנִי', אֶלָּא בְּבָרַיְיתָא, וְלֹא אַדֶּרֶךְ מַעֲמָד וּמִסְפֵּד קָאֵי. **גמ'** דִּשְׁכִיחַ גַּבֵּיהּ. וְנָתַן עֵינָיו בְּקַטְנוּתוֹ בִּכְתַב יַד אָבִיו. קִיּוּם שְׁטָרוֹת מִדְּרַבָּנַן. דְּמִדְּאוֹרַיְיתָא לָא בָּעֵינַן קִיּוּם, דְּאָמַר ר"ל (לעיל דף יח:): עֵדִים הַחֲתוּמִים עַל הַשְּׁטָר נַעֲשָׂה כְּמִי שֶׁנֶּחְקְרָה עֵדוּתָן בְּב"ד. הֵימְנוּהוּ רַבָּנַן בִּדְרַבָּנַן. בְּדָבָר שֶׁהוּא מִדִּבְרֵיהֶם הֶאֱמִינוּ, וְאֵין זֶה עוֹקֵר דָּבָר מִן הַתּוֹרָה, הֵם אָמְרוּ וְהֵם אָמְרוּ. הֵם הִצְרִיכוּ קִיּוּם הָעֵדוּת, וְהֵם הִכְשִׁירוּ בּוֹ אֶת אֵלּוּ. גִּלּוּי מִלְּתָא בְּעָלְמָא הוּא. כְּלוֹמַר, אֵין הַדָּבָר צָרִיךְ עֵדוּת, אֶלָּא לְפַרְסֵם שֶׁיֵּצֵא הַדִּין לָאוֹר בְּלֹא גִּמְגּוּם.

תוספות

ואם היה כהן לא תדור עמו במבוי*. דכיון דפנויה היא — קיל ליה. אבל אם נישאת — אין צריך להרחיק אלא כדי שכונה, דהיינו ג' בתים. כדאמרינן בסוף פרק קמא דע"ז (דף כא.), דכיון דנישאת חמירא ליה, אפי' לכהן. **כפר** קטן נידון [ג] כשכונה. וטעמא לפי שאין בני אדם מצוין שם, ורגיל יותר לבא אצלה. ודווקא כפר קטן, אבל כפר בינוני לא. **רב** הונא אמר נגודי מנגדינן להו. נראה לר"ת דלרב הונא נמי משמתינן וגם מנגדין, שכל אחד מחמיר מחבירו. ואם הוא אומר דנגדינן ליה בלא שמתא — הוה מיקל טפי, כדאמרינן במועד קטן (דף יז.) ובפרק "מקום שנהגו" (פסחים נב.): במערבא, כי מחייב צורבא מרבנן — מימנו אנגידא ולא מימנו אשמתא. **אלו** נאמנין להעיד בגודלן מה שראו בקוטנן. משמע דבקוטנן לא מהימן, אפילו בדרבנן, דהא מוקי לה בגמרא בתרומה דרבנן, וקשה לריב"א, דאמר בפ"ק דפסחים (דף ד: ושם) דנאמנים על בדיקת חמץ אפי' נשים ועבדים וקטנים. ופריך: מידי משמא אית בהו? ומשני: הואיל ובדיקת חמץ דרבנן — הימנוהו רבנן בדרבנן! וי"ל: דהתם היינו טעמא משום דבדיקת חמץ הוא בידו, לכן נאמן אפילו קטן בדרבנן. אבל קשה: דהיכא דבידו, אפי' בדאורייתא, אשה מהימנא. דבפרק "המדיר" (לקמן דף עב. ושם) תנן: (ד) וקושה לה חלה, ובניקור מעשים בכל יום שאנו סומכין עליהן! וי"ל דבירושלמי מפרש דבדיקת חמץ הוא טורח, ונשים עצלניות הן, ולהכי אי לאו דבדיקת חמץ דרבנן — לא הוו מהימני.
והוא שיש גדול עמו. ⊕לא קאי אתרומה, דבתרומה סגי בלא. כיון דאין מעלין מתרומה דרבנן ליוחסין. דלהכי מוקי לה בתרומה דרבנן. דבתרומה דאורייתא, כיון דסבר תנא דידן דמעלין ממנה ליוחסין כדאמרינן לקמן, אינו נאמן, אפי' יש גדול עמו. הלכך, בתרומה סגי באיהו לחודיה. וכל היכא דבעינן תרי מדרבנן — סגי בהוא ואחר. **קיום** שטרות דרבנן. תימה: כיון דמדאורייתא אפילו אין עדים שיכירו חתימת העדים השטר כשר, א"כ כל אדם שירצה יזייף, ויכתוב ויחתום מה שירצה, ויגבה ממנו! והכא אור"י: *דאיכא למימר כגון שלוה מודה שכתבו, וטוען שהוא פרוע. וקסבר האי תנא: דמודה בשטר שכתבו — צריך לקיימו, והאי קיום הוי ודאי מדרבנן. אי נמי: כגון שנתקיים משדה אחת או משתי שדות, ויוצא מתחת ידי עצמו, דאמר לעיל (דף כ.) דחיישינן שמא זייף. ומיהו, בריש גיטין (דף ג. ושם) מוכח דאפילו היכא דאין מכירין החתימה כלל — הוי מדאורייתא כמי שנחקרה עדותן בב"ד.
ודלמא עבד כהן הוא. פי': ועכשיו נשתחרר, ונוטל שלא כדין. וקשה לרבינו יצחק: דבפ' "נושאין על האנוסה" (יבמות דף צט: ושם) מפרש התלמוד הא דאין חולקין תרומה לעבד — משום דלמא אתי לאסוקיה ליוחסין. מה צריך להאי טעמא? הוה ליה למימר דאין חולקין אפי' אין מעלין, שמא ישאל גם אחר שישתחרר, כדפריך הכא התלמוד! וכן מפרש התם התלמוד דאין חולקין לאשה בלא בעלה משום גרושה. ומאי טעמא נמי דמאן דאמר חולקין? וי"ל: דלא שכיחא כולי האי שישאל תרומה אחר שישתחרר, לא בתורת עבד ולא בתורת כהן, כי ירא פן יבדקוהו ויתברר שהוא עבד, ויוציאו עליו קול עבדות. ולא חיישינן נמי פן ימכרנו רבו לישראל וישאל תרומה — שהרי מזונותיו על רבו, ואין אדם חוטא ולא לו. וכולי האי לא חיישינן שמא יאמר לו רבו ישראל: צא מעשה ידיך במזונותיך.

סנהדרין כו.
[בערוך ערך עמד גורס ומושב]
[לעיל כח:]
[לעיל עז. ב"ב לב:]
גיטין מ.

הגהות הב"ח

(א) גמ' כפר קטן נידון כמבוי מי: (ב) שם נגודי מנגדינן כצ"ל ותיבת נמי נמחק: (ג) תום' ד"ה כפר קטן נידון כמבוי וטעמא: (ד) ד"ה אלו כו' דבפרק המדיר תנן ואינה קוצה לה:

גליון הש"ס

תום' ד"ה והוא וכו' לא קאי אתרומה. עי' עירובין דף נט ע"א תום' ד"ה אפילו עבד:

עין משפט נר מצוה

[ונראתי דאם רשות הרבים מפסיק מבית לבית שרי. ר"י]

קיח א ב ג מיי' פכ"א מהל' איסורי ביאה הלכה כז סמג לאוין קכז טוש"ע אה"ע סימן ו סעיף ז וסימן קיט סעיף יא:

קיט ד מיי' שם טוש"ע שם סי' קיט ס"ח:

קכ ה ו מיי' שם טוש"ע שם סעיף ט:

קכא ז ח מיי' שם טוש"ע שם סעיף י:

קכב ט י מיי' פי"ז מהל' עדות הלכ' א ופי"ד הלכה ג סמג לאוין רטו טוש"ע ח"מ סי' לה סעיף ד ה ו וסי' מו סעי' יז [וברב אלפס עוד ביבמות פ"ג דף י ע"ב]:

קכג כ מיי' פט"ז מהל' איסות הלכה כה סמג עשין מח טוש"ע אה"ע סי' נו סעיף טו:

קכד ל מיי' פ"כ מהל' איסורי ביאה הלכ' טו טוש"ע שם סי' ג' סעיף ה:

[מס' שמחות פ"ב]

קכה מ מיי' פ"ח מהל' עבדים הלכה יח טוש"ע י"ד סי' רסז סעיף עח:

קכו נ מיי' שם הלכה יז טוש"ע שם סעיף ע:

[עי' תוס' לעיל יט. ד"ה מודה]

תוספות רי"ד

ת"ש המגרש את אשתו לא תנשא בשכונתו. פי' לפי שמכרת ברמיזותו ובקריצותו ושמא יבואו לידי עבירה. ואם היה כהן לא תדור עמו במבוי. פי' שמא יבוא עליה וכהן אסור בגרושה [אם היה כפר קטן] זה היה מעשה ואמרו כפר קטן נידון כשכונה: איבעי' להו מי נדחה בפני מי ת"ש דתניא היא נדחת מפניו והוא אינו נדחה מפניה. ואם היתה חצר שלה הוא נדחה מפניה איבעיא להו היתה חצר של שניהם מהו. ת"ש

היא נדחות מפניו דטלטולא דגברא קשה מדאיתתא: ת"ר לוה ממנה בנכסי אביה. פי' בעודה תחתיו שהי' בידה נכסי מלוג ובכהן שגירש את אשתו מיירי ה"ז אינה נפרעת אלא על ידי שליח. פי' ולא ע"י עצמה שלא יתקרבו בדבריהם. א"ר ששת כי אתו לקמן לא מזדקקינן להו. ר"פ אמר שמותי משמתינן להו ר"ה ברי' דר"י אמר נגידי נמי מנגדינן להו. אמר ר"נ תנא באבל רבתי פי' מסכתא היא וקרי' אותה מס' שמחות ומשנה ראשונה שלה זו היא הגוסס הרי הוא כחי לכל דבריו בר"א בשנתגרשה מן הנשואין אבל נתגרשה מן האירוסין נפרעת ע"י עצמה שאין לבו גס בה. ההוא ארוס וארוסתו דאתו קמי' דרבא אוקי רבא שלוחא ביניהו. פי' בפניו היו הוה יתיב ר"א ב"מ קמי'. א"ל למה ליה למר כולי האי והאר"נ תנא באבל רבתא וכו'. א"ל ה"מ היכי דלא גיסי אהדדי הכא הא חזינא דגיסי אהדדי. פי' שמכירין זא"ז ברמזות ובקריצות: **מתני'** ואלו נאמנין להעיד בגודלן על מה שראו בקוטנן. פי' אע"ג דבעינן ראי' והגדה בכשרות הכא נאמנים על ראיית קטנותם משום דהוה מדרבנן ודוקא להעיד בגודלן על מה שראו בקוטנן אבל להעיד בקטנותם לא נאמנין הקטן זה כת"י של אבא אין משגיחין בדבריו אבל כשהגדיל ומעיד על ראיית קטנותו אמרי' אי לאו דקים לי' שפיר לא הוה מסהיד בגודלו. נאמן אדם לומר זה כת"י של אבא זה כת"י של אחי. פי' ומקיימים השטר על פיו. ואע"פ שמתו בעוד זה קטן. שנמצא שמעיד עכשיו כשהוא גדול על ראיית קטנותו נאמן הוא משום דקיום שטרות דרבנן. זכור אני באשת פ' שיצאת בהינומא וראשה פרוע פי' והוא סימן שנשאת בתולה וכתובתה מאתים כדאמרינן בריש פירקן. ושהיה איש פ' יוצא מבית הספר לטבול לתרומתו ושהיה חולק עמנו בגורן ושהמקום הזה הוא בית הפרס אבל אינו נאמן לאיש פלוני במקום הזה מעמד ומספד הי' לפלוני במקום הזה. פי' דאפוקי ממונא הוא ובעי' עדות מעלייתא והיינו טעמא דכתובה דרוב נשים בתולות נשאות: אמר ר"ה ברי' דר"י והוא שיש גדול עמו. צריך להעיד על חתימ' שהיא שלהן כדאמר לעיל דע"כ לא פליגי רבנן עלי' דר' אלא בז"א זה כתבי אבל זה כתב חבירי מודו רבנן דבעינן שנים עדים על כל חתימה וחתימה והכא אמר ר"ה דוקא ראיית קטנותו ולא ראיית שני קטנים שאם היו שניהם מעידין בגודלן על מה שראו בקוטנן אינן נאמנים אלא בעי' שיהא א' גדול מעיד על ראיית קטנותו. וצריכא דאי אשמעינן אביו משום דשכיח גבי' פי' ונתן עיניו יד אביו אבל רבו אימא לא ואי אשמועינן רבו משום דאית ליה אימתי' דרביה אבל אביו אימא לא ואי אשמיענן הני תרתי אביו משום דשכיח גבי' ורבו משום דא"ל אימתי' אבל אחיו דלא הא ולא הא אימא לא קמ"ל דקיום שטרות דרבנן. פי' דמדאורייתא לא בעי קיום דאר"ל עדים החתומים ע"ה נעשה כמי שנחקרה עדותן בב"ד הימנוה רבנן בדרבנן פי' בדבר שהוא מדבריהם האמינוהו. ואין זה עוקר דבר מן התורה הם אמרו והם אמרו. הם הצריכו העדות והם הכשירו בו את אלו ודוקא באלו שהוא רגיל בהן הוא נאמן אבל על כתב נכרים אינו נאמן להעיד על ראיות קטנותו דדילמא לא קים ליה שפיר ואפילו אמר אני בשטר זה אין ראיית הקטן עדות עד שיאמר כי אני מכיר בחתימתו ודוקא הקרוב מעיד על חתימת הקרוב ואין זה נוגע בעדותו שאין מגיע לקרובו שום הנאה והפסד אלא למלוה וללוה מגיעים. אבל לא עדות קרובים למלוה או ללוה או שהי' שניהם קרובים זל"ז אינן נאמנים להעיד על החתימה שאין מוציאין ממון ע"פ קרובים. ואע"ג דקיום שטרות דרבנן ראיית קטן הוא דהכשירו בהן חכמים. אבל לא עדות הייתי וכו' מ"ט כיון דרוב נשים בתולות נשאות גלוי מילתא בעלמא הוא לברר הדבר. פי' אע"ג דבמידי דממונא לאו מהימן דלאו עליה בלחוד סמכי אלא על הרוב. וה"ה דבעינן נמי הכא והוא שיש גדול עמו ששני עדים

אַפּוֹטְרוֹפּוֹס, *אוֹ שֶׁהִנִּיחַ תְּפִילִּין בִּפְנֵי רַבּוֹ, אוֹ שֶׁקָּרָא שְׁלֹשָׁה פְּסוּקִים בְּבֵית הַכְּנֶסֶת — הֲרֵי זֶה לֹא יָצָא לְחֵירוּת! הָתָם דְּאִיקְרִי עֶבֶד מִדַּעְתּוֹ, כִּי קָאָמְרִינַן — דְּקָא נָהֵיג בֵּיהּ מִנְהַג בָּנִים.§ לִטְבּוֹל לֶאֱכוֹל בִּתְרוּמָה.§ בִּתְרוּמָה דְּרַבָּנַן.§ וְשֶׁהָיָה חוֹלֵק עִמָּנוּ עַל הַגּוֹרֶן.§ וְדִלְמָא עֶבֶד כֹּהֵן הוּא? תְּנַן כְּמַאן דְּאָמַר: [א]אֵין חוֹלְקִין תְּרוּמָה לְעֶבֶד אֶלָּא אִם כֵּן רַבּוֹ עִמּוֹ. דְּתַנְיָא: *אֵין חוֹלְקִין תְּרוּמָה לְעֶבֶד אֶלָּא אִם כֵּן רַבּוֹ עִמּוֹ, דִּבְרֵי רַבִּי יְהוּדָה. רַבִּי יוֹסֵי אוֹמֵר: יָכוֹל הוּא שֶׁיֹּאמַר: אִם כֹּהֵן אֲנִי — תְּנוּ לִי בִּשְׁבִיל עַצְמִי, וְאִם עֶבֶד כֹּהֵן אֲנִי — תְּנוּ לִי בִּשְׁבִיל רַבִּי. בִּמְקוֹמוֹ שֶׁל רַבִּי יְהוּדָה °הָיוּ מַעֲלִין מִתְּרוּמָה לְיוֹחֲסִין, בִּמְקוֹמוֹ שֶׁל רַבִּי יוֹסֵי לֹא הָיוּ מַעֲלִין מִתְּרוּמָה לְיוֹחֲסִין. תַּנְיָא, *א"ר אֶלְעָזָר בְּרַבִּי יוֹסֵי: מִיָּמַי לֹא הֵעַדְתִּי, פַּעַם אַחַת הֵעַדְתִּי, וְהֶעֱלוּ עֶבֶד לִכְהוּנָּה עַל פִּי. הֶעֱלוּ סָלְקָא דַּעְתָּךְ?! *הַשְׁתָּא, וּמָה בְּהֶמְתָּן שֶׁל צַדִּיקִים *אֵין הקב"ה מֵבִיא תַּקָּלָה עַל יָדָם — צַדִּיקִים עַצְמָם לֹא כ"ש! אֶלָּא, בִּקְּשׁוּ לְהַעֲלוֹת עֶבֶד לִכְהוּנָּה עַל פִּי. חֲזָא בְּאַתְרֵיהּ דְּרַבִּי יוֹסֵי, וַאֲזַל וְאַסְהֵיד בְּאַתְרֵיהּ דְּרַבִּי יְהוּדָה.§ וְשֶׁהַמָּקוֹם הַזֶּה בֵּית הַפְּרָס הוּא.§ מ"ט? בֵּית הַפְּרָס דְּרַבָּנַן. *דְּאָמַר רַב יְהוּדָה אָמַר שְׁמוּאֵל: [ב]מְנַפֵּחַ אָדָם בֵּית הַפְּרָס וְהוֹלֵךְ. *וְרַב יְהוּדָה בַּר אַמִי מִשְּׁמֵיהּ דְּרַב יְהוּדָה אָמַר: [ג]בֵּית הַפְּרָס שֶׁנִּידַּשׁ — טָהוֹר. מַאי טַעְמָא — אִי אֶפְשָׁר לְעֶצֶם כִּשְׂעוֹרָה שֶׁלֹּא נִידַּשׁ בָּרֶגֶל.§ [ד]וְעַד כָּאן הָיִינוּ בָּאִין בְּשַׁבָּת.§ קָסָבַר: תְּחוּמִין דְּרַבָּנַן.§ וְאֵין נֶאֱמָן לוֹמַר דֶּרֶךְ הָיָה לִפְלוֹנִי בְּמָקוֹם הַזֶּה, מַעֲמָד וּמִסְפֵּד הָיָה לִפְלוֹנִי בְּמָקוֹם הַזֶּה.§ מַאי טַעְמָא? אַפּוֹקֵי מָמוֹנָא — לָא מַפְּקִינַן. תָּנוּ רַבָּנַן: *[ה]נֶאֱמָן הַתִּינוֹק לוֹמַר כָּךְ אָמַר לִי אַבָּא: "מִשְׁפָּחָה זוֹ טְהוֹרָה, מִשְׁפָּחָה זוֹ טְמֵאָה". טְהוֹרָה וּטְמֵאָה סָלְקָא דַּעְתָּךְ?! אֶלָּא, מִשְׁפָּחָה זוֹ כְּשֵׁרָה, וּמִשְׁפָּחָה זוֹ פְּסוּלָה. ו"שֶׁאָכַלְנוּ בִּקְצָצָה שֶׁל בַּת פְּלוֹנִי לִפְלוֹנִי". ו"שֶׁהָיִינוּ מוֹלִיכִים חַלָּה וּמַתָּנוֹת לִפְלוֹנִי כֹּהֵן". עַל יְדֵי עַצְמוֹ, אֲבָל לֹא עַל יְדֵי אַחֵר. [ו]וְכוּלָּן, אִם הָיָה גּוֹי וְנִתְגַּיֵּיר, עֶבֶד וְנִשְׁתַּחְרֵר — אֵין נֶאֱמָנִים. וְאֵין נֶאֱמָן לוֹמַר "דֶּרֶךְ הָיָה לִפְלוֹנִי בְּמָקוֹם הַזֶּה", "מַעֲמָד וּמִסְפֵּד הָיָה לִפְלוֹנִי בְּמָקוֹם הַזֶּה". רַבִּי יוֹחָנָן בֶּן בְּרוֹקָא אוֹמֵר: נֶאֱמָנִים. ר' יוֹחָנָן בֶּן בְּרוֹקָא אַהַיָּיא? אִילֵימָא אַסֵּיפָא — אַפּוֹקֵי מָמוֹנָא הוּא! אֶלָּא אַרֵישָׁא: וְכוּלָּם אִם הָיָה גּוֹי וְנִתְגַּיֵּיר, עֶבֶד וְנִשְׁתַּחְרֵר — אֵין נֶאֱמָנִין, ר' יוֹחָנָן בֶּן בְּרוֹקָא אוֹמֵר: נֶאֱמָנִין. בְּמַאי קָמִיפַּלְגִי? ת"ק סָבַר: כֵּיוָן דְּגוֹי הוּא — לָא הֲוָה דָּיֵיק, וְרַבִּי יוֹחָנָן בֶּן בְּרוֹקָא סָבַר: כֵּיוָן דְּדַעְתֵּיהּ לְאִיגַּיּוּרֵי — מֵידָק הֲוָה דָּיֵיק. מַאי קְצָצָה? דְּתָנוּ רַבָּנַן: כֵּיצַד קְצָצָה? [ז]אֶחָד מִן הָאַחִין שֶׁנָּשָׂא אִשָּׁה שֶׁאֵינָהּ הוֹגֶנֶת לוֹ, בָּאִין בְּנֵי מִשְׁפָּחָה וּמְבִיאִין חָבִית מְלֵאָה פֵּירוֹת, וְשׁוֹבְרִין אוֹתָהּ בְּאֶמְצַע רְחָבָה, וְאוֹמְרִים: אַחֵינוּ בֵּית יִשְׂרָאֵל, שִׁמְעוּ! אָחִינוּ פְּלוֹנִי נָשָׂא אִשָּׁה שֶׁאֵינָהּ הוֹגֶנֶת לוֹ, וּמִתְיָירְאִים אָנוּ שֶׁמָּא יִתְעָרֵב זַרְעוֹ בְּזַרְעֵינוּ, בּוֹאוּ וּקְחוּ לָכֶם דּוּגְמָא לְדוֹרוֹת, שֶׁלֹּא יִתְעָרֵב זַרְעוֹ בְּזַרְעֵינוּ. וְזוֹ הִיא קְצָצָה שֶׁהַתִּינוֹק נֶאֱמָן לְהָעִיד עָלֶיהָ.§

הדרן עלך האשה שנתארמלה

אַפּוֹטְרוֹפּוֹס. מָסַר נְכָסָיו בְּיָדוֹ לְהַכְנִיס וּלְהוֹצִיא לִסְחוֹרָה. הֲרֵי זֶה לֹא יָצָא לְחֵירוּת. וְלָא אָמְרִינַן: אִי לָאו דְּשַׁחְרְרֵיהּ, לָא הֲוָה יָזֵיף מִינֵּיהּ, וְלָא הֲוָה שָׁבֵיק לֵיהּ לִנְהוֹג מִנְהַג בֶּן חוֹרִין. וְשָׁמְעִינַן מִינָּהּ דְּיֵשׁ עֶבֶד שֶׁלּוֹמֵד תּוֹרָה. בִּתְרוּמָה דְּרַבָּנַן. כְּגוֹן תְּרוּמַת חוּצָה לָאָרֶץ, אוֹ פֵּירוֹת — הֵימְנִינְהוּ לְהָנֵי לְהַאֲכִילוֹ עַל פִּיהֶם. הָכִי גָּרְסִינַן. דְּתַנְיָא שֶׁאֵין חוֹלְקִין תְּרוּמָה לְעֶבֶד כו'. וְרֵישָׁא דְּבָרַיְיתָא: כֹּהֶנֶת שֶׁנִּתְעָרֵב וְלָדָהּ בִּוְלַד שִׁפְחָתָהּ — שְׁנֵיהֶן יוֹצְאִין לַגּוֹרֶן וְנוֹטְלִין חֵלֶק אֶחָד, שֶׁאֵין חוֹלְקִין תְּרוּמָה לְעֶבֶד כו'. הִלְכָּךְ, אִי אָזֵיל חַד מִינַּיְיהוּ לָא פָּלְגִינַן לֵיהּ, דִּלְמָא אָתֵי לְאַחֲזוּקֵי בְּכֹהֵן, וְדִלְמָא הַאי נִיהוּ הָעֶבֶד. בִּמְקוֹמוֹ שֶׁל ר' יְהוּדָה. מִשּׁוּם הָכִי אָמַר: אֵין חוֹלְקִין. בְּהֶמְתָּן שֶׁל צַדִּיקִים. חֲמוֹרוֹ שֶׁל רַבִּי פִּנְחָס בֶּן יָאִיר, בְּ"הַכֹּל שׁוֹחֲטִין" (חולין ז.). חֲזָא בְּאַתְרֵיהּ דְּרַבִּי יוֹסֵי. שֶׁחָלְקוּ לוֹ תְּרוּמָה בַּגּוֹרֶן. וְאַסְהֵיד בְּאַתְרֵיהּ דְּרַבִּי יְהוּדָה. וְשָׁם לֹא הָיוּ חוֹלְקִין תְּרוּמָה לְעַבְדֵי כֹהֲנִים. בֵּית הַפְּרָס. הַחוֹרֵשׁ אֶת הַקֶּבֶר — הֲרֵי זֶה עוֹשֶׂה בֵּית הַפְּרָס מֵאָה אַמָּה, שֶׁכָּךְ שִׁיעֲרוּ שֶׁהַמַּחֲרֵישָׁה מוֹלֶכֶת אֶת עַצְמוֹת הַמֵּת, וְדִלְמָא נָגַע אוֹ הֵסִיט הַמְהַלֵּךְ בּוֹ אֶת עֶצֶם כִּשְׂעוֹרָה, שֶׁמְּטַמֵּא בְּמַגָּע וּבְמַשָּׂא. מְנַפֵּחַ אָדָם בֵּית הַפְּרָס. וְסוֹמֵךְ עַל כָּךְ, שֶׁאִם יֵשׁ עֶצֶם — רוֹאֵהוּ. וְאַע"ג דְּמַאֲהִיל — לָא חָיְישִׁינַן, דְּאֵין עֶצֶם כִּשְׂעוֹרָה מְטַמֵּא בְּאֹהֶל עַד דְּאִיכָּא שִׁדְרָה אוֹ גּוּלְגּוֹלֶת שְׁלֵמָה, אוֹ רוֹב בִּנְיָן, אוֹ רוֹב מִנְיָן. שֶׁנִּידַּשׁ. דִּישָׁה רַבָּה, בְּרַגְלַיִם הַרְבֵּה. טָהוֹר. דְּתָלֵינַן לְקוּלָּא, וְאָמְרִינַן: כָּל הָעֲצָמוֹת נִכְתְּתוּ לְפָחוֹת מִכַּשִּׁיעוּר. אַלְמָא, חֲשָׁשָׁא דְּרַבָּנַן בְּעָלְמָא הוּא. נֶאֱמָן הַתִּינוֹק. לְהָעִיד בְּגוֹדְלוֹ מַה שֶּׁרָאָה בְּקוֹטְנוֹ. טְמֵאָה וּטְהוֹרָה סָלְקָא דַּעְתָּךְ. מַה טּוּמְאָה וְטָהֳרָה יֵשׁ לוֹמַר בְּמִשְׁפָּחוֹת? בִּקְצָצָה. לְקַמָּן מְפָרֵשׁ לָהּ. שֶׁל בַּת פְּלוֹנִי לִפְלוֹנִי. כְּשֶׁנָּשָׂא פְּלוֹנִי אֶת בַּת פְּלוֹנִי. וְשֶׁהָיִינוּ מוֹלִיכִין כו' עַל יְדֵי עַצְמוֹ. אִם כָּךְ הֵעִיד הַתִּינוֹק: עַל יָדַי הָיָה אַבָּא שׁוֹלֵחַ לוֹ חַלָּה וּמַתָּנוֹת. אִם הָיָה גּוֹי וְנִתְגַּיֵּיר. וְהֵעִיד מִשֶּׁנִּתְגַּיֵּיר שֶׁרָאָה אֶת אֵלֶּה בְּגֵיוּתוֹ — אֵינוֹ נֶאֱמָן. דּוּגְמָא. אוֹת וְסִימָן, זִכָּרוֹן לְדוֹרוֹת הַבָּאִים.

הדרן עלך האשה שנתארמלה

תנן כמאן דאמר אין חולקין לעבד כו'. ואם תאמר: והא לא קאמר רבי יהודה דאין חולקין אלא בתרומה דאורייתא, דמעלין ממנה ליוחסין, אבל מתני' דאוקמינן בתרומה דרבנן, דאין מעלין ממנה ליוחסין — מודה דחולקין לעבד בלא רבו. ואם כן, אכתי תקשי: ודלמא עבד כהן הוא! ולאו מלתא היא, דמתניתין איירי שפיר שמעיד שחלק לו תרומה דאורייתא, אלא שאינו נאמן להאכילו אלא בתרומה דרבנן.

ומה בהמתן של צדיקים. מפורש במקום אחר (גיטין דף ז.*).

ושהמקום הזה בית הפרס. ולא יותר, ובא לטהר.

***מנפח** · בדיעבד, אם עשה כבר טהרות, אבל בדיקה לכתחלה מפרש במשנה (אהלות פי"ח מ"ד) כילד בודקין*.

בית הפרס דרבנן. נראה דאפי' במקום הקבר מקילין כמו בשאר שדה, ואין לומר דמקום הקבר מטמא באהל. ומביא רבינו יצחק ראיה, מדתניא בפ"ק דמועד קטן (דף ה:): מצא שדה מצויינת ואינו יודע מה טיבה, יש בה אילנות בידוע שנחרש בה קבר, אין בה אילנות בידוע שאבד בה קבר. ומאי נפקא מינה, כיון שעתה אינו יודע מקום הקבר, בין נחרש בין אבד? אלא שמע מינה: דמקום הקבר טהור כשנחרש. ובית הפרס להכי הוי דרבנן, משום דהוי ספק טומאה ברשות הרבים. אע"ג דבעלמא טיהרו חכמים ספק טומאה ברה"ר — היינו, היכא שהטומאה מבוררת, ולא נולד הספק אלא באקראי, ופעם אחרת לא יטמא, כיון שמקום הטומאה ידוע. אבל הכא, שלעולם השדה בספק — לא רצו לטהר, אע"ג דמדאורייתא טהור.

הדרן עלך האשה שנתארמלה

תוספות רי"ד

עדי' צריך בעדות הינומא כדתנן אם יש עדים שיצאה בהינומא וראשה פרוע וכל היכא דבעי' שני עדים בעינן שיהא גדול עמו שלא יעידו שניהם על ראיית קטנותן: ושהיה איש פ' יוצא מבית הספר. פי' כשהיינו לומדים יחד עם תינוקות בבית רבן ומחזיקי' לכהונה בראיית קטנות ולא בעי' הכא גדול עומד עמו. שמעלים לכהונה ע"פ ע"א. ובגמרא מפרש בתרומה דרבנן כגון תרומות ח"ל או פירות והימנוהו רבנן בדרבנן. וה"נ בגודלו מעיד על מה שראה בקוטנו אבל הקטן אינו מעיד שאע"פ שמעלים בתרום' ע"פ ע"א דוקא גדול אבל קטן לא וכן עבד ואשה לא תנן שיהו נאמנים בכהונה כדתנן גבי שבוי' וא"א במת בעלה הלכך אין הקטן נאמן בכהונה והוא נאמן בשבוי' ומת בעלך ולא תימא כ"מ שע"א נאמן גם עבד ואשה נאמנים שהרי במת בעלך יש תנא שהיה מכשיר ע"א ולא היה מכשיר אשה וקרוב כדתנן בפ' בתרא דיבמו ר"א אומר אין משיאין את אשה ע"פ ע"א ר"ע אומר לא ע"פ אשה ולא ע"פ קרובים אלמא אע"ג דפליג ר"ע על ר"א ומכשיר בע"א. הא אמר לא ע"פ אשה ולא ע"פ קרובים א"כ אינו דין כלל להכשיר עבד ואשה במק שע"א נאמן אלא היכא דתנן תנן היכא דלא תנן לא תנן. ובמקום שעבד ואשה נאמנים גם הקטן נאמן. ומקשה דלמא עבד הוא מסייע ליה לריב"ל דאריב"ל אסור לו לאדם שילמוד את עבדו תורה מיתיבי לוה מט רבו או שעשאו רבו אפוטרופוס. פי' מסר כל נכסיו בידו להכנים ולהוציא בסחורה או שהניח תפילין בפני רבו או שקרא שלשה פסוקים בבה"כ ה"ז לא יצא לחירות. פי' לאו אומרים אי לאו דשחרריה לא הוה יז מיניה ולא הוי שביק ליה לנהוג [מנהג] ב"ח. ש"מ דיש עבד שלומד תורה התם דאיקרי עבד מדעתיה. וכי קאמרינן דקא נהוג בי' מנהג בנים: ושהיה חולק עמנו בגורן וליחוש דילמא עבד כהן הוא תנן אין חולקין תרומה לע אא"כ רבו עמו דברי ר' יהודה ר"י אומר יכול הוא שיאמר אם כהן אני תנו לי בשביל עצמי ואם אני עבד כהן תנו לי בשביל רבי ובמקומו של ר' יוסי לא היה מעלים מתרומה ליוחסים: ושהמקום הזה בית הפרס. פי' ה תנן בפ' בתרא דאהלות החורש את הקבר ה"ז עושה בית הפרס עד כמה הוא עושה מלא המענה ק' אמה בית ארבעת קבין. פי' החורש אנו חוששים שמא המחרישה פורה עצמות המת ועצם כשעורה ממנו מטמ במגע ובמשא אבל לא באהל פי' עד דאיכא שדרה או גולגולת שלמים או רוב מנין או רוב בנין ואנו חוששים שמא פורה שברי עצמות מן הקבר ועד ק' אמה שאם חרש מן הקבר לצד מזרח מונה מן הקבר ק' אמ ועושה אותה בית הפרס והנכנס טמא שמא נגע או היסט עצם כשעורה שהוא מכוסה בעפר ולאו אדעתיה ואלו ק' אמה המונה אותם מרובעין שהן ק' על ק' שיביאו ארבעת סאין. שהסאה הוא נ' על נ' ולמה אנו מחמיר כ"כ ולא נעשה אלא ק' אמה ברוחב הקבר שהמחרישה מוליכה את העצמות אלא אנו חוששים שמא הוליכה והחזירה ועוד הוליכה שדרך החורש לחרוש התלם ולחרוש עוד בצידו עד שיחרוש כל השדה לפיכך החמי והחזיקו חכמים כל ק' וק' במזרחו של קבר בבית הפרס ומפרש דבית הפרס דרבנן. פי' ומ"ה האמינו בו ראיית הקטן וכשמעיד להקל ולא להחמיר כגון שהיו יודעים השדה שנחרש בה קבר אבל לא היו מכירים מק הקבר שימדדו משם ק' אמה ובא זה והעיד שזה המקום הוא בית הפרס ולא יותר ומשום דבית הפרס הוא חששא בעלמא דרבנן. הימנוהו רבנן בדרבנן. ולא להחמיר שאם לא היו יודעים שהוא בית הפרס וזה מעיד א זוכר שהי' בית הפרס ומחזיקי' בחזקת טומאה למה תולה הטעם משום דבית הפרס דרבנן. השתא בדרבנן נאמן לאחזוקי איסורא כ"ש בדאורייתא. אלא לאו ש"מ להקל מעיד. וע"כ היינו באין בשבת קסבר תחומין דרבנן. ומ' האמינוהו ראיית הקטן: אבל אינו נאמן לומר דרך היה לפלוני במקום הזה שהיה הולך משם לשדהו. או מעמד ומספד הי' לפלוני במקום הזה שהיה מספיד שם את מתו ושהיה עושה שם מעמד ומושב למתו כשו חוזרים מבית הקברות. מ"ט אפוקי ממונא הוא ולא מפקי' ממונא ע"פ ראיית הקטן. עיין ברפ"ק דפסחים:

עין משפט נר מצוה

קכז א מיי' פי"ב מהל' תרומות הלכה כב:

קכח ב ג מיי' פ"ו מהל' קרבן פסח הל' ח:

קכט ד מיי' פכ"ח מהל' שבת הלכה יט טוש"ע א"ח סי' שצט סעי' יא:

[ד"ה השתא ותוס' שבת יב: ד"ה ר' נתן ותוס' חולין ה: ד"ה לצדיקים ותוס' פסחים קו: ד"ה אישתלאי]

קל ה מיי' פי"ד מהל' עדות הלכה ג סמג לאוין רט טוש"ע ח"מ סי' לה סעי' ו:

[ועי' היטב תוס' פסחים לב: ד"ה מאי בודקין ועוד תוס' בכורות כט. ד"ה היכי אזיל]

קלא ו מיי' שם הלכה ד וטוש"ע שם סעי' ז:

קלב ז מיי' שם הלכה ג טוש"ע אה"ע סי' ב סעי' א בהג"ה:

גיטין ז. חולין ה: ו. ז. [יבמות לט:]

[ברכות יט: ע"ש]

מסורת הש"ס

[עיין תוס' לקמן נו. ד"ה אבל]

יבמות לט.

[שם ע"ש]

[עיין תוס' יבמות שם ד"ה ס"ד השתא וכו']

ברכות יט: עירובין פסחים לב: מ"ק ה: חגיגה כה: בכורות כט. נדה נז

[תוספתא פ"ג]

גליון הש"ס

גמ' היו מעלין מתרומה ליוחסין. עיין ברכות טז ע"ב תוס' ד"ה עומדין:

אלו *א נערות שיש להן קנס: הבא על הממזרת, ועל הנתינה, ועל הכותית. הבא על הגיורת, ועל השבויה, ועל השפחה שנפדו ושנתגיירו ושנשתחררו פחותות מבנות שלש שנים ויום אחד. *הבא על אחותו ועל אחות אביו ועל אחות אמו ועל אחות אשתו ועל אשת אחיו ועל אשת אחי אביו ועל הנדה — יש להם קנס, אע"פ שהן בהכרת — אין בהן מיתת בית דין.§ **גמ'** הני נערות פסולות — אית להו קנס, כשירות — לא?! הכי קאמר: אלו נערות פסולות שיש להם קנס: הבא על הממזרת ועל הנתינה ועל הכותית.§ נערה — אין, קטנה — לא, מאן תנא? אמר רב יהודה אמר רב: רבי מאיר היא. דתניא*: ב קטנה, מבת יום אחד ועד שתביא שתי שערות — יש לה מכר *ואין לה קנס. ומשתביא שתי שערות ועד שתיבגר — יש לה קנס ואין לה מכר, דברי רבי מאיר. שהיה רבי מאיר אומר: כל מקום שיש מכר — אין קנס, וכל מקום שיש קנס — אין מכר. ג וחכמים אומרים: קטנה, מבת שלש שנים ויום אחד ועד שתיבגר — *יש לה קנס. קנס אין, מכר לא?! אימא: אף

אלו נערות. דווקא נערה, משתביא שתי שערות עד שתבגר, והם ששה חדשים שבין נערות לבגרות. אבל קטנה ובוגרת — אין להם קנס. שיש להן קנס. אם אנסה אדם — נותן לאביה חמשים כסף, כדכתיב "ונתן האיש השוכב" וגו' (דברים כב). הבא על הממזרת. בגמרא פריך: אבל כשירות לא? ומשני: פסולות איצטריכא ליה לאשמועינן. נתינה. מן הגבעונים, והיא אסורה לקהל, דדוד גזר עליהם, כדאמרינן ביבמות (ד' עח:). ועל שם "ויתנם יהושע חוטבי עצים ושואבי מים" וגו' (יהושע ט) קרי להו נתינים. כותית. קסבר: גירי אריות הן, וישנן בלאו "לא תתחתן בם" (דברים ז). ועל השבויה. ישראלית שנפדית פחותה מבת שלש שנים, דמוחזקת בתולה היא. שאפי' נבעלה בשביה — בתוליה חוזרים. ועל אשת אחיו. שנתקדשה לו לאחיו, וגירשה, שאין בה מיתה אלא כרת. ועל אשת אחי אביו. שנתקדשה לו וגירשה. אע"פ שהן בהכרת הרי אין בהם מיתת ב"ד. וכרת לא פטר ליה מן התשלומין. **גמ'** ר"מ היא. כדמייתי ברייתא לקמיה. יש לה מכר. יש לאביה בה זכייה למכרה לשפחות. ואין לה קנס. שהבא עליה אינו חייב קנס. ואין לה מכר. כדתניא (ערכין דף כט:): יכול ימכור אדם את בתו כשהיא נערה? אמרת ק"ו: מכורה — כבר יוצאה עכשיו; שאינה מכורה — אינו דין שלא תמכר? מבת ג' שנים ויום אחד. שהיא ראויה לביאה. מכר לא. בתמיה.
אף

אלו נערות. הבא על הנתינה. פי' בקונטרס: דדוד גזר עליהם שלא לבא בקהל, והיינו משום עבדות, כדאמרינן ב"הערל" (יבמות עח: ושם). ואין נראה לר"ת, דהא משמע בגמרא (ע"ב) דנתינה הויא דאורייתא, דקאמר: ממזרת ונתינה איכא בינייהו, למ"ד ראויה לקיימה כו' — משמע דהויא דאורייתא, דהא בקראי פליגי. ובריש "יש מותרות" (שם דף פה: ושם) אמרינן: ממזרת ונתינה איכא בינייהו, מ"ד דאורייתא — הא נמי דאורייתא! ועוד: דתנן (מכות דף יג.): אלו הן הלוקין, ממזרת ונתינה לישראל. משמע דלקי עלה מדאורייתא, דומיא דכל הנך דחשיב התם! ומיהו, איכא למימר דבכל הנהו נקט נתינה אגב ממזרת. וכן צריך לומר ע"כ לרבא, למאי דס"ד ב"הערל" (יבמות דף עו. ושם) דבגירותן לית להו איסור חתנות. ומ"מ אין נראה לר"ת פירוש, דהא מסיק רבא ב"הערל" (ג"ז שם) דבגירותן אית להו איסור חתנות, וכל היכא דחשיב נתינה בהדי ממזרת — איירי בגירות, כמו הכא. דבגויותה לית לה קנס, כדאמרינן לעיל בפ"ק (דף יא. ושם): יהבינן לה קנס ואזלה ואכלה בגויותה?! וכן בקדושין, בפרק "האומר" (דף סו:): תנן: כל מקום שיש קדושין ויש עבירה — כגון ממזרת ונתינה כו'. ועוד: לפירוש הקונטרס, כיון דעבדות ממש גזר עלייהו, שמתוך כך נאסרו לבוא בקהל משום "לא יהיה קדש" — א"כ אמאי יש לה קנס? הא תנן בהדיא במתניתין דשפחה אין לה קנס! ואי משום דנתינה מנטרא — נפשה הא אמרינן בירושלמי דשפחה אפילו משומרת אין לה קנס. ועוד: דתנן בפרק "עשרה יוחסין" (שם דף סט.) דחרורי ונתיני מותרים לבא זה בזה, ואמאי, והא חרורי אסירי בשפחה, כדתנן (גיטין דף מא.): לישא שפחה אינו יכול! ומיהו, הא י"ל: דלאו ממש ג"ר עלייהו עבדות לאסור ב"לא יהיה קדש". ונראה לר"ת: דנתינה אסורה דאורייתא משום "לא תתחתן", כדמסיק רבא ב"הערל" (יבמות דף עו. ושם). ודוד לא גזר עלייהו אלא שיעבוד, ולאו לאוסרן בבנות ישראל — דהא אסירי וקיימי מלאו ד"לא תתחתן", אלא כדי שלא יטמעו ישראל. והא דג"ר בהו טפי מבשאר פסולי קהל — משום דהוו אומה שלימה. והא דקאמר התם*: כל מי שיש בו שלשה סימנים הללו — ראוי לידבק בהן, לא ליבא מהן, אלא להיות בן חורין כמותן. וכן הא דקאמר התם*: בימי רבי בקשו להתיר נתינים, א"ר: אם חלקנו נתיר — חלק מזבח מי יתיר? לא שהיו רוצים להתירם לבא בקהל — דהא מדאורייתא אסירי, אלא בקשו לפטרן מעבדות, להיות בני חורין. ואמר להו רבי דאין יכולין להפקיע חלק מזבח. ואע"ג דקיימא לן* דהפקר ב"ד היה הפקר — היינו לצורך, אבל זה אינו צורך כל כך. ומיהו, בירושלמי משמע כפי' הקונט', בפ' "עשרה יוחסין" דקאמר התם: נתינים יהושע ריחקם. כלום ריחקם אלא משום פסול משפחה, דא"ת משום פסול עבדות — אלא מעתה הבא על הנתינה לא יהיה לה קנס? משמע משום דיהושע גזר עליהם נפסלו מלבא בקהל, וגזרת יהושע ודוד הכל גזירה אחת היא, כדמוכח ב"הערל" (שם דף עט.). ומיהו, בירושלמי איכא למימר דסבר כמו שהיה ס"ד דרבא מעיקרא ב"הערל", דבגירותן לית להו איסור חתנות. ועוד י"ל: דריחקן היינו שלא יטמעו בהן. והא דאמרינן ב"האומר" בקדושין (דף סח: ושם): גויה מנא לן דלא תפסי בה קדושין — דכתיב "לא תתחתן בם", אומר ר"ת: דאסיפיה דקרא סמיך "ובתו לא תקח לבנך". אבל רישיה דקרא — מיירי בגירות. וכענין זה מצינו ב"הערל" (יבמות דף עט.) דפריך גבי בני שאול: והכתיב "לא יומתו אבות על בנים", וע"כ לא פריך אלא מסיפא דקרא "איש בחטאו יומתו", דרישא דקרא מוקמינן ליה לפסול קרובים לעדות בפרק "החובל" (ב"ק דף פח.) ובפרק "זה בורר" (סנהדרין דף כז:)*. **ועל** הכותית. פירש בקונטרס: דקסבר כותים גירי אריות הן, וישנן בלאו ד"לא תתחתן" — וזהו לפי שיטתו, כדסלקא דעתין מעיקרא ב"הערל" (יבמות דף עו. ושם) דבגיותן אית להו איסור חתנות. ומה שפי' דקסבר כותים גירי אריות הן — ל"נ לרבינו יצחק בן רבינו מאיר, דא"כ גויה היא, וגויה אין לה קנס, כדפריך בפ"ק (לעיל יא.): יהבינן לה קנס ואזלה ואכלה בגויותה? ועוד: דבגמרא מוקי מתני' כר"מ, ור"מ אית ליה דגירי אמת הן, ואע"ג דכולה מתניתין לא אתיא כר"מ, דהא בתו אמר בגמרא דלא אתיא כוותיה — מ"מ בהא דסבר דגירי אמת הן אתיא כוותיה, דהא ב"שור שנגח ד' וה'" (ב"ק דף לח: ושם) מסקינן דשור ישראל שנגח שור של כותי פטור, משום דקנס הוא דקניס רבי מאיר בממונם, אע"ג דמן הדין חייב, דגירי אמת הם, ופריך ממתני' דהכא, דכותית יש לה קנס. ואי ס"ד דקנס הוא שקנס ר"מ בממונם — ה"נ לקנוס כו', אלמא דמתניתין דהכא סברה דגירי אמת הן! וא"ת: אם כן מאי קמ"ל? פשיטא דיש לה קנס, דישראלית גמורה היא! וי"ל: דס"ד דלא יהבינן לה קנס, שלא יטמעו בהן. *וא"ת: למ"ד בפרק "עשרה יוחסין" (קדושין דף עה:) דפסול כותים משום דעבד ושפחה נטמעו — בהן אמאי יש לה קנס? נימא לה: אייתי ראיה דלאו שפחה את, ושקילי. לשמואל דאמר (ב"ק דף מו:) אין הולכין בממון אחר הרוב. ואפילו לרב, אי דאזיל איהו גבה ה"ל קבוע, וכל קבוע כמחצה על מחצה דמי! ויש לומר: דכל אחת מוקמינן לה אחזקת אבהתא שהיו כותים. אע"ג דלענין פסול לא מוקמינן לה אחזקתה, לענין קנס — מוקמינן להו, שלא יהא חוטא נשכר. *ואם תאמר: *ואמאי לא חשיב נמי אלמנה לכ"ג, גרושה וחלוצה לכהן הדיוט? וי"ל: דבפסול כהונה לא קמיירי. והא דלא תני מצרי ואדומי — משום שיש להם היתר [א"נ לא חשיב אלא חייבי לאוין]. אבל קשה: דליתני מחזיר גרושתו משניסת ונבעלה שלא כדרכה, ואע"ג דאמרי' בפ' "עשרה יוחסין" (קדושין עח.) הכל מודים שאם בעל ולא קידש שאינו לוקה — מ"מ לר"ע, דאמר אין קדושין תופסין במחזיר גרושתו — ליתני! ועוד הוה מצי למיתני יבמה לשוק! [ועבד הבא על הכותית הולד ממזר ויש לה קנס. ת"י]! וי"ל: דתנא ושייר. ואע"ג דבפ"ק דקדושין (דף טז:) דייק: תנא תני "אלו", ואת אמרת תנא ושייר?! הכא דתני בסיפא ואלו שאין להם קנס — לא שייך למידק הכי, כדאשכחן בפרק "המזבח מקדש" (זבחים דף פד.), דקתני: ואלו פסולן בקדש ואלו שאין פסולן בקדש, ומשייר ברישא ובסיפא. *ועי"ל: דהכא לא חשיב אלא פסולי קהל. **והבא** על הגיורת. תימה, לתני חייבי לאוין לחודייהו, וגיורת ומשוחררת דכשירות הן לחודייהו, וחייבי כריתות לחודייהו, משום דבעי למיתני סיפא: "אע"פ שהם בהכרת כו'". אבל ב"אלו הן הלוקין" (מכות יג.) לא תני אלא הבא אחד על כולם. **ועל** אשת אחיו. פר"ח: דפריך בירושלמי: אשת אחיו! ולא יבמה היא לו, וזקוקה לו, ומה קנס וכרת שייך בה? ומשני: בשיש לו בנים מאשה אחרת, ואיירי במת מן האירוסין. והוא הדין דהוה מצי לאוקמה כשגירשה. וקשה לר"י ב"ר אברהם: לרב פפא דמוקי הך מתניתין במפותה, בפרק "בן סורר" (סנהדרין דף עד. ושם) תקשי: דהיכי מצי לאוקומי הכי? הא נתארסה ונתגרשה קנסה לעצמה (לקמן דף לח.), וכיון דלעצמה — מפותה אין לה קנס, כדאמרינן בגמרא (לקמן מ.) ובריש "נערה" משום דמדעתה עבדה! וכ"ת: דקסבר תנא דמתניתין כר"ע דברייתא, דקנסה לאביה הוי — אם כן אכתי *תיקשי ליה סיפא, דקתני (שם לו:): הבא על בתו — פטור. משום דקם ליה בדרבה מיניה, תיפוק ליה דקנסה לאביה הוי, דאי לעצמה — תיקשי ליה דמחלה, וממה נפשך תקשי סיפא! ומיהו, בירושלמי מוקי לה כשבא עליה עד שלא מת, ומת, והוא הדין עד שלא בגרה, ובגרה. ולמאי דאמר בירושלמי דמפותה אינו פטור אלא מבושת ופגם, אבל קנס אינה יכולה למחול — אתי שפיר. ומיהו, בתלמוד דידן משמע דאין לה אפי' קנס, דמוקי הא ד"אלו הן הלוקין" לקמן בגמ' (דף לב.) ביתומה ומפותה שאין לה קנס. **נערה** אין קטנה לא. תימה: מנא ליה? דלמא לא אתי למעוטי אלא בוגרת, דהא משמע* בס"פ "ארבע מיתות" (סנהדרין דף סו:) גבי הא דתנן אינו חייב אלא עד שתהא נערה בתולה מאורסה, דאי הוה תני אלא על נערה בתולה כו' הוה מוקמינן לה אפילו כרבנן ולא הוה אתי למעוטי קטנה אלא בוגרת! ותירץ ריצב"א: *דאסיפא דמתניתין סמיך, דתנן (לקמן דף מ:): כל מקום שיש מכר אין קנס.
נערה

עין משפט נר מצוה

א א מיי' פ"א מהל' נערה הלכה י סמג עשין נד טור אה"ע סי' קעז:

ב ב מיי' פ"ד מהל' עבדים הלכה א סמג עשין פה:

ג ג מיי' פ"א מהלכות נערה הלכה ח סמג עשין נד טוש"ע אה"ע סי' קעז סעיף א בהג"ה:

תוספות רי"ד

אלו נערות שיש להן קנס. פי' אנסה אדם נותן לאביה נ' כסף כדכתיב ונתן האיש וגו'. הבא על הממזרת ועל הנתינה ועל הכותית על הגיורת ועל השבויה. פי' ישראלית שנשבית. ועל השפחה. שנפדו ושנתגיירו ושנשתחררו פחותות מבנות ג"ש ויום אחד. הבא על אחותו ועל אחות אביו ועל אחות אמו ועל אחות אשתו ועל אשת אחיו ועל אשת אחי אביו ועל הנדה יש להן קנס. אע"פ שהן בכרת אין בהן מיתת ב"ד. פי' דוקא נערה ולא בוגרת וקטנה. שהבוגרת כלו בתוליה ואין להם קנס. וקטנה הויא כעין א) שמדמעת וחוזרת ומדמעת. ונערה היא מבת י"ב שנים ויום אחד אם הביאה ב' שערות וממתנת ששה חדשים אחר שהביאה ב' שערות והיא בוגרת שאין בין נערות לבוגרת אלא ו' חדשים בלבד. נתינה היא מן הגבעונים ע"ש ויתנם יהושע חוטבי עצים ושואבי מים. ומשום צד עבדות הן אסורות. והכותיות קסבר גירי אמת הן ומ"ה יש להן קנס. שאילו היו גירי אריות הויא לה גויה. ואין קנס לגויה אלא שהכותים פסולים כדתנן בעשרה יוחסין אלו הן הספיקות שתוקי ואסופי וכותי. והתם מפרש טעמא למה הן הכותים פסולין: ועל אשת אחיו. כגון שקידש את הבתולה וגירשה. א"נ שמת ויש לו בן מאשה אחרת דקיימי עליה בכרת אע"פ שהן בהכרת אין הכרת פוטרו מן התשלומין אלא מיתת ב"ד: נערה אין קטנה לא. דהיינו קודם שתביא ב' שערות. מאן תנא אר"י א"ר ר"מ הוא דתניא קטנה ב) מבת ג' שנים ויום אחד. פירוש שמזמן זה היא ראויה לביאה ועד שתביא ב' שערות יש לה מכר ואין לה קנס. ומשתביא ב' שערות ועד שתבגר יש לה קנס ואין לה מכר דברי ר"מ שהיה ר"מ אומר כ"מ שיש מכר אין קנס וכל מקום שיש קנס אין מכר. וחכ"א קטנה מבת ג' שנים ויום אחד עד שתבגר יש לה מכר ויש

א) דברי רבינו אינו מובן דהך סברא אמרינן בנדה (מ"ה) לענין קטנה פחותה מבת שלש דבתוליה חוזרין אבל מתני' הא ס"ל דאין קנס בקטנה כלל רק בנערה וצ"ע. ב) לפנינו בגמ' הגירסא בדברי ר"מ מבת יום אחד וגירסת רבינו צ"ע.

דפריך עד שתהא נערה אינו חייב אלא על נערה מבעי ליה. ת"י

מסורת הש"ס

לעיל יא. ב"ק לח:

סנהדרין עג:

[תוספתא פ"ג ע"ש] לקמן מ: חולין כו.

[לקמן לו.]

[לקמן לו.]

[דף עט.]

שם:

[שם פט:]

[ועי' תוס' יבמות עט. ד"ה ונתינים ותוס' ע"ז לו: ד"ה דכתיב]

א"כ היא גופא קמ"ל דגירי אמת הן. ת"י

[ועי' תוס' ב"ק לח: ד"ה ועל הכותית]

ועבד הבא על הכותית הולד ממזר ויש לה קנס. ת"י

[עי' תוס' יבמות פד: ד"ה אלא ותוס' זבחים פד. ד"ה הלן ותוס' שבועות לט. ד"ה ואלו נאמרין ותוס' שם מד: ד"ה כל הנשבעין ותוס' שבת עה: ד"ה חסר אחת]

אבל ליכא לאוקמי הבא על בתו אחר שנכנסה לחופה ולא נבעלה וגירשה דא"כ בלאו הכי אין לה קנס כיון דמוקי לה במפותה דמחלה וא"ל דסיפא בא על בתו לא איירי במפותה אלא באנוסה א"כ בתנס נקט בא על בתו דחייבי כריתות נמי אין לה קנס כיון דניתנה להצילה בנפשו דמשום הכי מוקי לה התם במפותה:

גליון הש"ס

תוס' ד"ה נערה וכו' דאסיפא דמתני' סמיך. עי' נדה מד ע"ב תוס' ד"ה שלשים יום:

עין משפט נר מצוה

ד א מיי׳ פ״א מהלכות נערה הל׳ טו סמג עשין נד טור אה״ע סי׳ קעז:
ה ב מיי׳ שם הל׳ א:
ו ג מיי׳ שם הל׳ ה:

אַף קְנָס בִּמְקוֹם מֶכֶר. וְהָנֵי בְּנֵי קְנָסָא נִינְהוּ? וְאַמַּאי? אִיקְּרֵי כָּאן: °"וְלוֹ *תִהְיֶה לְאִשָּׁה" — אִשָּׁה הָרְאוּיָה לוֹ! אָמַר רֵישׁ לָקִישׁ: °"נַעֲרָה", "נַעֲרָה", "הַנַּעֲרָה"; חַד — לְגוּפֵיהּ, וְחַד — לְאַתּוּיֵי חַיָּיבֵי לָאוִין, וְחַד — לְאַתּוּיֵי חַיָּיבֵי כָּרֵיתוֹת. רַב פָּפָּא אָמַר: °"בְּתוּלָה", "בְּתוּלֹת", "הַבְּתוּלֹת" חַד — לְגוּפֵיהּ, וְחַד — לְאַתּוּיֵי חַיָּיבֵי לָאוִין, וְחַד — לְאַתּוּיֵי חַיָּיבֵי כָּרֵיתוֹת. וְרַב פָּפָּא מ"ט לָא אָמַר כְּר"ל? הַהוּא מִיבְּעֵי לֵיהּ לְכִדְאַבָּיֵי. *דְּאָמַר אַבָּיֵי: ^א בָּא עָלֶיהָ וּמֵתָה — פָּטוּר, שֶׁנֶּאֱמַר: °"וְנָתַן לַאֲבִי הַנַּעֲרָה" — לַאֲבִי נַעֲרָה וְלֹא לַאֲבִי מֵתָה. וְרֵישׁ לָקִישׁ מ"ט לָא אָמַר כְּרַב פָּפָּא? הַהוּא מִיבְּעֵי לֵיהּ לִגְזֵירָה שָׁוָה. דְּתַנְיָא: *°"כֶּסֶף יִשְׁקוֹל כְּמוֹהַר הַבְּתוּלֹת" — ^ב שֶׁיְּהֵא זֶה כְּמוֹהַר הַבְּתוּלוֹת, וּמוֹהַר הַבְּתוּלוֹת כָּזֶה. וְרֵישׁ לָקִישׁ נַמִי, מִיבְּעֵי לֵיהּ לְכִדְאַבָּיֵי, וְרַב פָּפָּא נַמִי מִיבְּעֵי לֵיהּ לִגְזֵירָה שָׁוָה! אֶלָּא שִׁיתָּא קְרָאֵי כְּתִיבִי: "נַעֲרָה" "נַעֲרָה" "הַנַּעֲרָה" "בְּתוּלָה" "בְּתוּלֹת" "הַבְּתוּלֹת", תְּרֵי — לְגוּפַיְיהוּ, חַד — לְכִדְאַבָּיֵי, וְחַד — לִגְזֵירָה שָׁוָה. אִיַּיתְרוּ לֵיהּ תְּרֵי, חַד — לְאַתּוּיֵי חַיָּיבֵי לָאוִין, וְחַד — לְאַתּוּיֵי חַיָּיבֵי כָּרֵיתוֹת. וּלְאַפּוּקֵי מֵהַאי תַּנָּא; דְּתַנְיָא: "וְלוֹ תִהְיֶה לְאִשָּׁה", *שִׁמְעוֹן הַתִּימְנִי אוֹמֵר: אִשָּׁה שֶׁיֵּשׁ בָּהּ הֲוָיָה. רַבִּי שִׁמְעוֹן בֶּן מְנַסְיָא אוֹמֵר: ^ג אִשָּׁה הָרְאוּיָה לְקַיְּימָהּ. מַאי בֵּינַיְיהוּ? אָמַר ר' זֵירָא: מַמְזֶרֶת וּנְתִינָה אִיכָּא בֵּינַיְיהוּ. לְמַאן דְּאָמַר יֵשׁ בָּהּ הֲוָיָה — הָא נַמִי יֵשׁ בָּהּ הֲוָיָה, לְמַאן דְּאָמַר רְאוּיָה לְקַיְּימָהּ — הָא אֵינָהּ רְאוּיָה לְקַיְּימָהּ. וּלְרַבִּי עֲקִיבָא, דְּאָמַר: *אֵין קִידּוּשִׁין תּוֹפְסִין בְּחַיָּיבֵי לָאוִין, מַאי בֵּינַיְיהוּ? אִיכָּא בֵּינַיְיהוּ אַלְמָנָה לְכֹהֵן גָּדוֹל, כְּרַבִּי סִימַאי. דְּתַנְיָא, רַבִּי סִימַאי אוֹמֵר:* מִן הַכֹּל עוֹשֶׂה רַבִּי עֲקִיבָא מַמְזֵרִין, חוּץ מֵאַלְמָנָה לְכֹהֵן גָּדוֹל, שֶׁהֲרֵי אָמְרָה תּוֹרָה: °"לֹא יִקָּח" "וְלֹא יְחַלֵּל" — חִילּוּלִין הוּא עוֹשֶׂה, וְאֵין עוֹשֶׂה מַמְזֵרִין — וּלְרַבִּי יְשֵׁבָב, דְּאָמַר: בּוֹאוּ וְנִצְוַח עַל עֲקִיבָא בֶּן יוֹסֵף, שֶׁהָיָה אוֹמֵר: כָּל שֶׁאֵין לוֹ בִּיאָה בְּיִשְׂרָאֵל הַוָּלָד מַמְזֵר. מַאי בֵּינַיְיהוּ? אִיכָּא בֵּינַיְיהוּ חַיָּיבֵי

(דברים כב; שם; שמות כב; דברים כב; שמות כב; ויקרא כא)

וּמִשּׁוּם קְנָס נָקַט בַּת שָׁלֹשׁ. אֲבָל לְמֶכֶר — מִבַּת יוֹם אֶחָד וְעַד שֶׁתָּבִיא שְׁתֵּי שְׂעָרוֹת. וְאַמַּאי. יֵשׁ לָהֶן קְנָס לִנְעָרוֹת פְּסוּלוֹת? אִיקְּרֵי כָּאן כו׳. אַמַּתְנִי׳ מַקְשֵׁי: ה"ג. נַעֲרָה נַעֲרָה הַנַּעֲרָה. בְּאוֹנֵס כְּתִיב "כִּי יִמְצָא אִישׁ נַעֲרָה בְתוּלָה" וגו׳, וּכְתִיב בַּתְרֵיהּ "וְנָתַן הָאִישׁ הַשּׁוֹכֵב עִמָּהּ לַאֲבִי הַנַּעֲרָה", וְדָרְשִׁינַן "נַעֲרָה" יְתֵירָה, וְהֵ"א יְתֵירָה דְּ"הַנַּעֲרָה", דְּמָצֵי לְמִיכְתַּב "וְנָתַן לְאָבִיהָ". חַד לְגוּפֵיהּ. לִכְשֵׁרָה. בְּתוּלָה בְּתוּלוֹת הַבְּתוּלוֹת. בִּמְפַתֶּה כְּתִיב "וְכִי יְפַתֶּה אִישׁ בְּתוּלָה", וּקְרָא אַחֲרִינָא בַּתְרֵיהּ "כֶּסֶף יִשְׁקוֹל כְּמוֹהַר הַבְּתוּלוֹת". וּמָצֵי לְמִיכְתַּב "כְּמוֹהַר בְּתוּלוֹת", הָא תְּלָת, דְּדָרְשִׁינַן ה׳ יְתֵירָה וּ"בְתוּלוֹת", דְּמָצֵי לְמִיכְתַּב "כְּמוֹהַר" וְלִשְׁתּוֹק. הַהוּא מִיבְּעֵי לֵיהּ. הַהוּא "הַנַּעֲרָה", הָא דְּלָא כְּתִיב "וְנָתַן לְאָבִיהָ", מִיבְּעֵי לֵיהּ לְכִדְאַבָּיֵי, שֶׁאִם לֹא הִסְפִּיק הָאָב לְהַעֲמִידוֹ בַּדִּין עַד שֶׁמֵּתָה — פָּטוּר. לַאֲבִי הַנַּעֲרָה. מַשְׁמַע שֶׁהִיא קַיֶּימֶת. מִיבְּעֵי לֵיהּ לְג"ש. "בְּתוּלָה" דִּכְתִיב גַּבֵּי מְפַתֶּה — מִיבָּעֵי לֵיהּ לְג"ש, "בְּתוּלָה" "בְּתוּלָה" לְג"ש: מַה כֶּסֶף הָאָמוּר בְּאוֹנֵס חֲמִשִּׁים — אַף מְפַתֶּה חֲמִשִּׁים. וּמַה מְּפַתֶּה שְׁקָלִים, דִּכְתִיב בֵּיהּ "יִשְׁקוֹל" — אַף חֲמִשִּׁים שֶׁל אוֹנֵס — שְׁקָלִים קָאָמַר. כְּמוֹהַר הַבְּתוּלוֹת. חֲמִשִּׁים כֶּסֶף הַמְפוֹרָשִׁים בִּמְאַנֵּס אֶת הַבְּתוּלָה. שֶׁיְּהֵא זֶה. חֲמִשִּׁים כְּמוֹהַר הַבְּתוּלוֹת. וּמוֹהַר הַבְּתוּלוֹת. יִהְיוּ שְׁקָלִים כָּזֶה. וְחַד לְג"ש. וּתְהֵי מוּפְנָה מִצַּד אֶחָד, וּלְמֵידִים הֵימֶנָּה. וּלְאַפּוּקֵי מֵהַאי תַּנָּא. מַתְנִי׳ דְּקָתָנֵי יֵשׁ קְנָס לְמַמְזֶרֶת וְלַאֲחוֹתוֹ — לְאַפּוּקֵי מֵהַאי תַּנָּא. שֶׁיֵּשׁ בָּהּ הֲוָיָה. שֶׁקִּידּוּשִׁין תּוֹפְסִין לוֹ בָּהּ, פְּרָט לַאֲחוֹתוֹ וּלְכָל חַיָּיבֵי כָּרֵיתוֹת, דְּיָלְפִינַן בְּקִידּוּשִׁין שֶׁאֵין קִידּוּשִׁין תּוֹפְסִין בָּהֶן, בְּפֶרֶק שְׁלִישִׁי (דף סז:). וּמַשְׁמַע לֵיהּ "תִּהְיֶה" לְשׁוֹן הֲוָיַת קִידּוּשִׁין. וְר"ש בֶּן מְנַסְיָא מַשְׁמַע לֵיהּ "תִּהְיֶה" — לְשׁוֹן קִיּוּם. הָא נַמִי אִית בָּהּ הֲוָיָה. דְּקִידּוּשִׁין תּוֹפְסִין בְּחַיָּיבֵי לָאוִין, וְהָתָם יָלֵיף לָהּ. וּלְר"ע דְּאָמַר אֵין קִידּוּשִׁין תּוֹפְסִין בְּחַיָּיבֵי לָאוִין. בִּיבָמוֹת בְּ"הַחוֹלֵץ" (דף מד:) בְּבָרַיְיתָא: הַמַּחֲזִיר גְּרוּשָׁתוֹ, ר"ע אוֹמֵר: אֵין לוֹ בָּהּ קִידּוּשִׁין. מַאי בֵּינַיְיהוּ. מִשּׁוּם ר"ש בֶּן מְנַסְיָא קָא פָּרֵיךְ לָהּ. דְּאִילּוּ שִׁמְעוֹן הַתִּימְנִי שָׁמְעִינַן לֵיהּ בִּיבָמוֹת (דף מט.) דִּפְלֵיג עֲלֵיהּ דְּר"ע בְּהָא, דִּתְנַן: אֵיזֶהוּ מַמְזֵר — כָּל שְׁאֵר בָּשָׂר שֶׁהוּא בְּ"לֹא יָבֹא", דִּבְרֵי ר"ע. שִׁמְעוֹן הַתִּימְנִי אוֹמֵר: כָּל שֶׁחַיָּיבִין עָלָיו כָּרֵת בִּידֵי שָׁמַיִם. אֶלָּא לְר"ש בֶּן מְנַסְיָא קָא בָּעֵינַן לָהּ, אִי ס"ל כְּר"ע — מַאי אִיכָּא בֵּין מַשְׁמָעוּתָא דְּ"תִהְיֶה" לְשׁוֹן קִיּוּס, לְמַשְׁמָעוּת דְּשִׁמְעוֹן הַתִּימְנִי? אִי נַמִי, מַשְׁמַע לֵיהּ לְר"ש בֶּן מְנַסְיָא לְשׁוֹן הֲוָיָה אִימְעִיטָא לָהּ מַמְזֵר, וּמַה בֵּין רְאוּיָה לְקַיְּימָהּ לְיֵשׁ בָּהּ הֲוָיָה? אַלְמָנָה לְכֹהֵן גָּדוֹל. דְּמוֹדֶה בָּהּ ר"ע שֶׁקִּידּוּשִׁין תּוֹפְסִין לוֹ בָּהּ, וְאע"פ שֶׁהִיא בְּלָאו, וּכְרַבִּי סִימַאי. וְהוּא הַדִּין גְּרוּשָׁה לְהֶדְיוֹט. מִן הַכֹּל. כָּל הַנּוֹלָדִים מֵחַיָּיבֵי לָאוִין. לֹא יִקַּח. וּסְמִיךְ לֵיהּ "וְלֹא יְחַלֵּל זַרְעוֹ" — מִדִּין כְּהוּנָּה הוּא מְחַלְּלוֹ, וְלֹא שֵׁם מַמְזֵרִים עֲלֵיהֶם. בּוֹאוּ וְנִצְוַח עַל עֲקִיבָא בֶּן יוֹסֵף. שֶׁמַּרְבֶּה מַמְזֵרִים בְּיִשְׂרָאֵל חִנָּם. שֶׁהוּא אוֹמֵר כָּל שֶׁאֵין לוֹ בִּיאָה בְּיִשְׂרָאֵל. הַבָּא עַל אִשָּׁה שֶׁאֵין לוֹ בָּהּ הֶיתֵּר בִּיאָה — הַוָּלָד מַמְזֵר, אֲפִי׳ אַלְמָנָה לְכ"ג נַמִי.

נערה נערה הנערה. פי׳ רבינו חננאל: דמחד "נערה" דריש כולה מלתא, "נער" "נערה" "הנערה". ואין נראה לר"ת, דלא כתיב "נערה" מלא בה"א אלא ההוא דמוליא שם רע לחודיה, כדמוכח בסוף פרקין. ועוד הקשה רבינו יצחק: מה צריך חד לגופה? הא איכא "נערה" אחרינא בפרשה! אלא פי׳ הקונטרס עיקר.

בתולה בתולות הבתולות. כאן נמי פר"ח דמחד קרא נפקי כולהו. ואין נראה, דלא צריך חד לגופיה, דבתולה אחרינא כתיב.

וחד לאיתויי חייבי לאוין. הקשה ר"י בן רבינו מאיר, אכתי נימא: חד — לאתויי חייבי עשה, וחד — לאתויי חייבי לאוין, ואכתי חייבי כריתות מנא לן? ותירץ: דלחייבי לאוין ועשה לא צריך אלא חד קרא, דהא אי לאו דכתיב "ולו תהיה לאשה", דמשמע שיש בה הויה וראויה לקיימה, לא הוה צריך קרא לרבויינהו, הלכך מחד ריבויא מרבינן אין ראויה לקיימה, דהיינו חייבי עשה וחייבי לאוין, כיון דאית בהו הויה, ואידך ריבויא לחייבי כריתות. ולמאן דאמר אין קדושין תופסין בחייבי לאוין — הוי חד ריבויא לחייבי עשה, ואידך לחייבי לאוין וחייבי כריתות. וא"ת: ולשתוק מ"לו תהיה לאשה" ולא יצטרך להנך ריבויי? וי"ל: דאיצטריך למידרש "ולו תהיה לאשה" — מדעתה*.

[לקמן לט:]

אייתרו להו תרי כו׳. וחד ריבויא כתב באונס וחד במפתה. וא"ת: ומנא לן דחד לאתויי חייבי כריתות? אימא דתרוייהו אתו לרבויי חייבי לאוין, וחד לאונס וחד למפתה? וי"ל: דלהא לא צריך, דמגזרה שוה ילפינן אונס ומפתה מהדדי.

ת"י [ולאפוקי מהאי תנא. פי׳: תנא דברייתא, אבל מפיק מתרוייהו תנאי שמוזכרים בברייתא].

ולרבי עקיבא דאמר כו׳. ואף ע"ג דר"ש התימני פליג בהדיא אר׳ עקיבא ב"החולץ" (יבמות דף מד. ודף מט.) — הכא לר"ש בן מנסיא פריך, דאי סבר כר"ע — מאי בינייהו, פי׳: בינו לר"ש התימני? דמדנקט ראויה לקיימה ולא נקט שיש בה הויה — משמע דיש שאין ראויה לקיימה ויש בה הויה.

חילולין הוא עושה ואינו עושה ממזרים. משמע דהא בהא תליא, דכיון דלא הוי ממזר — קדושין תופסין. וכן משמע בפרק "החולץ" (שם דף מה:): מה אשת אב דלא תפסי בה קדושין והוולד ממזר כו׳, [ור"ע נמי, משום דיליף ב"החולץ" דיש ממזר מחייבי לאוין קאמר דאין קדושין תופסין בחייבי לאוין]. ותימה: דלרבי יהושע, אע"ג דאין ממזר מחייבי כריתות, כדיליף בשילהי "החולץ" (שם דף מט.) מודה דאין קדושין תופסין בחייבי כריתות, כדפריך ס"פ "ר"ג", ביבמות (דף נג. ושם): איצטריך לאשמעינן דאין קדושין תופסין בחייבי כריתות? ובפ׳ "החולץ" (שם דף מד: ושם) קאמר דלרבי יהושע פגוס מיהא הוי מחייבי כריתות, משום דעשאה זונה, וזונה לא הויא אלא מהנהו דלא תפסי בה קדושין, כדמוכח בתמורה (דף כט: ושם). וקאמרינן נמי ב"החולץ" (יבמות דף מד: ושם): הכל מודים בכותי ועבד הבא על בת ישראל הוולד ממזר. מאן הכל מודים — שמעון התימני, דאע"ג דאמר אין ממזר מחייבי לאוין — ה"מ חייבי לאוין דתפסי בהו קדושין, אבל כותי ועבד כו׳. ולא קאמר מאן הכל מודים ר׳ יהושע, דאע"ג דאמר אין ממזר מחייבי כריתות ה"מ חייבי כריתות דתפסי בהו קדושין כו׳. אלמא דלר׳ יהושע אין קדושין תופסין בחייבי כריתות, ואפ"ה לא הוי ממזר, ולהכי לא מצי למימר דמודה בכותי ועבד! ויש לומר: דלר"ש התימני ולר"ע ודאי הא בהא תליא, דליכא מידי דלא תפסי בה קדושין והוולד כשר, רק שהוא דומה לאשת אב. אבל לר׳ יהושע, אע"ג דאין קדושין תופסין בחייבי כריתות, כדילפי׳ בסוף "האומר" (קדושין סח. ושם) לא הוי ממזר אלא מחייבי מיתות ב"ד, כדיליף ר׳ יהושע בסוף "החולץ" (יבמות מט. ושם). אבל קשה: דא"כ לר׳ יהושע אין קדושין תופסין באלמנה לכ"ג לרבא, דאמר בפ"ק דתמורה (דף ד: ושם): כל דאמר רחמנא לא תעביד, אי עביד — לא מהני. דהתם* פריך ליה: והרי אלמנה לכ"ג דקאמר רחמנא "לא יקח" ותנן: כל מקום שיש קדושין ויש עבירה כגון אלמנה לכ"ג כו׳? ומשני: אמר לך רבא: שאני התם, דא"ק "לא יחלל" — חלולין הוא עושה, ואינו עושה ממזרים. ולר׳ יהושע ליכא לשנויי הכי. וא"ת: בקדושין בסוף "האומר" (דף סז: ושם) כי משכח דלא תפסי קדושין באשת אב, מאי פריך התם ואימא תרוייהו באשת אב הא לכתחלה הא דיעבד? אמאי לא יליף מינה דכל היכא דהוי ממזר לא תפסי בה קדושין, כיון דהא בהא תליא, כדפירשנו! וי"ל: דאכתי לא שמעינן ממזרות בשאר חייבי כריתות כל כמה דלא מייתי התם היקישא דר׳ יונה, דמ"לא יקח" ו"לא יגלה" דאיירי באשת אב ובשומרת יבם של אביו לא שמעינן מינה ממזרות באשת איש ובאחות אשה דיש היתר לאיסורן, וכל דכוותייהו. אבל לבסוף דמייתי היקישא דרבי יונה התם — איכא למילף בעלמא כדפירשנו.

[דף ה:]

כ"י [וכן משמע בפרק "ד׳ מיתות" דליכא מאן דפליג דבחייבי כריתות לא תפסי קידושין. וט"ו נשים דפוטרות צרותיהן מן החליצה, ואי קידושין תופסין בחייבי כריתות א"כ היו עולין לחליצה כמו חייבי לאוין, כדאמר התם בפ"ב: מסתברא חייבי לאוין תפסי בהו קידושין, ולכך עולין לחליצה. והאיך מתני׳ אתיא כר"ע, דהא קאמר עלה דבפלוגתא לא קא מיירי.

מאי בינייהו. תימה: אמאי לא קאמר איכא בינייהו סוטה שאירסה וזינתה תחתיו שלא כדרכה, וגירשה, דאית בה הויה לכ"ע, כדאמרינן בסוף "החולץ": הכל מודים בבא על הסוטה שאין הוולד ממזר].

תוספות רי"ד

לה קנס: ומקשינן אמתני׳ קרי כאן ולו תהיה לאשה אשה הראוי׳ לו. פי׳ באשה הראויה לו יתן קנס דמקיים בה ולו תהיה לאשה. אבל באשה שאינה ראויה לו דלא מקיים בה ולו תהיה לאשה גם מן הקנס יהא פטור. אר"ל נער נערה הנערה. חד לגופיה. פי׳ לכשירה. וחד לאתויי חייבי לאוין. וחד לאתויי חייבי כריתות. פי׳ גבי אונס כתיב וכי ימצא איש נערה בתולה. וכתיב בתרי׳ ונתן האיש השוכב עמה לאבי הנערה דהו"ל למיכתב לאביה וקרא יתירה הוא. ודרשי׳ נערה וה׳ דהנערה תרי קראי יתירי חד לרבויי חייבי לאוין וחד לאתויי חייבי כריתות. ואי קשיא והא בפ"ב דיבמות תנן כלל אמרו ביבמה כל שאיסורה איסור ערוה (קדושה) לא חולצת ולא מתיבמת עד אסור קדושה אלמנה לכ"ג גרושה וחלוצה לכהן הדיוט [חולצת ולא מתייבמת]. ומקשה בגמ׳ ואמאי אין מתייבמת ליתי עשה וידחה את ל"ת. ותירץ רבא גזירה ביאה ראשונה אטו ביאה שניה. ותנ"ה אם בעלו קנו בביאה ראשונה ואסור לקיימם בביאה שניה. ופי׳ אלא מוציא בגט שכבר פרחה מצות יבמה בביאה ראשונה. ואע"ג דמצי למיחלץ. אמרי׳ התם חליצה במקום ייבום אינה מצוה. והתם נמי כתיב ולקחה לו לאשה ויבמה. דאיכא למימר באשה הראויה לו. ואפ"ה אתי עשה ודחי את ל"ת וה"נ ליתי עשה דולו תהיה לאשה ולידחי את ל"ת ואע"פ שהיא ממזרת יקחנה לו לאשה דהאי ולו תהיה לאשה עשה הוא כדאמרי׳ בפ׳ אלו הן הלוקין בהלכה זר טמא שאכל את הקודש אונס שגירש. אם ישראל הוא מחזיר ואינו לוקה. והוי לאו שניתק לעשה דהאי ולו תהיה לאשה קאי אכל ימיו דכל ימיו בעמוד והחזר קאי. וכיון דעשה הוא ליתי ולדחי את ל"ת ואמאי דרשי׳ אשה הראויה לו. ולקמן בפירקין [דף מ ע"ב] מקשה לה ר"ב ומתרץ לה:

מסורת הש"ס

[לקמן לט.]
[לקמן לח:]
[לעיל י. לקמן לח:]
[לקמן לו.]
[יבמות י: ושם נסמן]
[יבמות סט.] קידושין סח.
[יבמות סח.]

חַיָּיבֵי עֲשֵׂה – מִצְרִי וַאֲדוֹמִי. הָנִיחָא לְר' יְשֵׁבָב, אִי לְאַפּוּקֵי מִטַּעֲמָא דְּר' סִימַאי קָאָתֵי – שַׁפִּיר. אֶלָּא אִי טַעֲמָא דְּנַפְשֵׁיהּ קָאָמַר, כָּל שֶׁאֵין לוֹ בִּיאָה בְּיִשְׂרָאֵל הַוָּלָד מַמְזֵר – וַאֲפִי' חַיָּיבֵי עֲשֵׂה, מַאי בֵּינַיְיהוּ? °אִיכָּא בֵּינַיְיהוּ בְּעוּלָה לְכ"ג. ומ"ש? דַּהֲוָה לֵיהּ עֲשֵׂה שֶׁאֵינוֹ שָׁוֶה בַּכֹּל. אָמַר רַב חִסְדָּא: הַכֹּל מוֹדִים בְּבָא עַל הַנִּדָּה שֶׁמְּשַׁלֵּם קְנָס. לְמ"ד יֵשׁ בָּהּ הֲוָיָה – הָא נַמִי יֵשׁ בָּהּ הֲוָיָה, לְמ"ד רְאוּיָה לְקַיְּימָהּ – הָא נַמִי רְאוּיָה לְקַיְּימָהּ. וּלְאַפּוּקֵי מִדְּרַבִּי נְחוּנְיָא בֶּן הַקָּנָה. דְּתַנְיָא: *רַבִּי נְחוּנְיָא בֶּן הַקָּנָה הָיָה עוֹשֶׂה אֶת יוֹם הַכִּפּוּרִים כְּשַׁבָּת לְתַשְׁלוּמִין; מַה שַּׁבָּת מִתְחַיֵּיב בְּנַפְשׁוֹ וּפָטוּר מִן הַתַּשְׁלוּמִין – אַף יוֹם הַכִּפּוּרִים מִתְחַיֵּיב בְּנַפְשׁוֹ וּפָטוּר מִן הַתַּשְׁלוּמִין. מ"ט דְּר' נְחוּנְיָא בֶּן הַקָּנָה? אָמַר אַבַּיֵי: נֶאֱמַר °"אָסוֹן" בִּידֵי אָדָם וְנֶאֱמַר °"אָסוֹן" בִּידֵי שָׁמַיִם, אמָה "אָסוֹן" הָאָמוּר בִּידֵי אָדָם פָּטוּר מִן הַתַּשְׁלוּמִין, אַף "אָסוֹן" הָאָמוּר בִּידֵי שָׁמַיִם פָּטוּר מִן הַתַּשְׁלוּמִין. מַתְקִיף לָהּ רַב אַדָּא בַּר אַהֲבָה: מִמַּאי דְּכִי קָא מַזְהַר לְהוּ יַעֲקֹב לְבָנֵיהּ עַל צִינִּים וּפַחִים, דְּבִידֵי שָׁמַיִם נִינְהוּ? דִּלְמָא עַל אַרְיָא וְגַנָּבֵי, דְּבִידֵי אָדָם נִינְהוּ! אַטּוּ יַעֲקֹב אַהָא אַזְהַר, אַהָא לָא אַזְהַר? יַעֲקֹב עַל כָּל מִילֵּי אַזְהַר. וְצִינִּים פַּחִים בִּידֵי שָׁמַיִם נִינְהוּ? וְהָתַנְיָא: *הַכֹּל בִּידֵי שָׁמַיִם חוּץ מִצִּינִּים פַּחִים, שֶׁנֶּאֱמַר: °"צִנִּים פַּחִים בְּדֶרֶךְ עִקֵּשׁ שׁוֹמֵר נַפְשׁוֹ יִרְחַק מֵהֶם"! וְתוּ: אַרְיָא וְגַנָּבֵי בִּידֵי אָדָם נִינְהוּ? *וְהָאָמַר רַב יוֹסֵף, וְכֵן תָּנֵי רַבִּי חִיָּיא: מִיּוֹם שֶׁחָרַב בֵּית הַמִּקְדָּשׁ, אַף עַל פִּי שֶׁבָּטְלוּ סַנְהֶדְרִין – אַרְבַּע מִיתוֹת לֹא בָּטְלוּ? לֹא בָּטְלוּ?! הָא בָּטְלוּ לְהוּ! אֶלָּא:
דִּין

[יבמות נט:] [שמות כא] [בראשית מב] [משלי כב]

חַיָּיבֵי עֲשֵׂה מִצְרִי וַאֲדוֹמִי. בְּתוֹךְ שְׁלֹשָׁה דּוֹרוֹת, דִּכְתִיב (דברים כג) "דּוֹר שְׁלִישִׁי יָבֹא לָהֶם", דּוֹר שֵׁנִי – לֹא, וְלָאו הַבָּא מִכְּלַל עֲשֵׂה – עֲשֵׂה. הָנִיחָא. אִי רַבִּי יְשֵׁבָב הַאי כָּל שֶׁאֵין לוֹ הֶיתֵּר בִּיאָה כְּלָלָא קָיֵיל, אֶלָּא לְאַפּוּקֵי מִדְּרַבִּי סִימַאי לְאוֹדוּיֵי אָתָא, וְאַחַיָּיבֵי לָאוִין הוּא דְּפָלֵיג, לְאוֹסוּפֵי חַיָּיבֵי לָאוִין *בִּכְהוּנָּה, אֲבָל שׁוּם חַיָּיבֵי עֲשֵׂה לֹא הוֹסִיף. שַׁפִּיר. מָלֵינוּ לְמֵימַר אִיכָּא בֵּינַיְיהוּ דְּשִׁמְעוֹן הַתִּימְנִי וְר"ש בֶּן מְנַסְיָא חַיָּיבֵי עֲשֵׂה. אֶלָּא. אִי לָאו אַדְּרַבִּי סִימַאי קָאֵי, וְטַעְמָא דְּנַפְשֵׁיהּ קָאָמַר בְּשֵׁם ר"ע, שֶׁכָּל שֶׁאֵין לוֹ הֶיתֵּר בִּיאָה בְּאִשָּׁה זוֹ הַוָּלָד מַמְזֵר – מַאי אִיכָּא לְמֵימַר? בְּעוּלָה לְכ"ג. שֶׁאֵין בָּהּ לָאו דְּאַלְמָנוּת וְגֵירוּשִׁין אֶלָּא עֲשֵׂה ד"בְתוּלָה יִקָּח" (ויקרא כא), וְלֹא בְּעוּלָה. וא"ת: יֵשׁ כָּאן לָאו דְּזוֹנָה! לָא אַשְׁכַּחַן תַּנָּא דְּאָמַר פָּנוּי הַבָּא עַל הַפְּנוּיָה עֲשָׂאָהּ זוֹנָה אֶלָּא ר' אֱלְעָזָר*, (א) וְלֵית הִלְכְתָא כְּוָתֵיהּ, וְאֵין זוֹנָה אֶלָּא הַנִּבְעֶלֶת לְפָסוּל לָהּ. וּבִבְעוּלָה שֶׁלֹּא כְּדַרְכָּהּ אַיְירֵי, דְּאִי כְּדַרְכָּהּ – תּוּ לֵיכָּא קְנָס. וּמַאי שְׁנָא. הַאי עֲשֵׂה מִשְּׁאָר עֲשֵׂה דְּמוֹדֶה בֵּיהּ ר"ע. דַּהֲוָה לֵיהּ עֲשֵׂה שֶׁאֵינוֹ שָׁוֶה בַּכֹּל. שֶׁאֵינוֹ נוֹהֵג אֶלָּא בְּכ"ג, אֲבָל עֲשֵׂה דְּמִצְרִי וַאֲדוֹמִי נוֹהֵג בְּכָל הַקָּהָל. הָא נַמִי יֵשׁ בָּהּ הֲוָיָה. הַמְקַדֵּשׁ אִשָּׁה בִּימֵי נִדּוּתָהּ מְקוּדֶּשֶׁת. וּלְאַפּוּקֵי מִדְּר' נְחוּנְיָא. מַתְנִי' דִּמְחַיֵּיב תַּשְׁלוּמִין לַבָּא עַל אֲחוֹתוֹ, וְאַע"פ שֶׁמִּתְחַיֵּיב כָּרֵת בְּבִיאָתוֹ – מַפְּקָא מִדְּר' נְחוּנְיָא. אֶת יוֹם הַכִּפּוּרִים כְּשַׁבָּת. לִפְטוֹר הַמַּדְלִיק אֶת הַגָּדִישׁ בְּיוֹם הַכִּפּוּרִים כְּאִילּוּ הִדְלִיקוֹ בְּשַׁבָּת. מַה שַּׁבָּת. שֶׁהוּא מִיתַת ב"ד. פָּטוּר מִן הַתַּשְׁלוּמִין. כִּדְתְנַן בְּמַתְנִי' גַּבֵּי בָּא עַל בִּתּוֹ, וְיָלֵיף לָהּ מִ"וְלֹא יִהְיֶה אָסוֹן עָנוֹשׁ יֵעָנֵשׁ". אַף יוֹם הַכִּפּוּרִים. שֶׁהוּא בְּכָרֵת, חִיּוּב נֶפֶשׁ הוּא זֶה – וּפָטוּר מִן הַתַּשְׁלוּמִין. אָסוֹן בִּידֵי אָדָם. "וְלֹא יִהְיֶה אָסוֹן" דְּמִשְׁתָּעֵי בְּמִיתַת ב"ד, לְמֵימַר דְּהֵיכָא דְּלֵיכָּא מִיתַת ב"ד – מְשַׁלֵּם דְּמֵי וְלָדוֹת. אָסוֹן בִּידֵי שָׁמַיִם. "וּקְרָאָהוּ אָסוֹן". צִינִּים פַּחִים. קוֹר וָחוֹם. בִּידֵי שָׁמַיִם. אִם בָּאִים פּוּרְעָנִיּוֹת עַל הָאָדָם – גְּזֵירַת הַמֶּלֶךְ הוּא. חוּץ מִצִּינִּים וּפַחִים. שֶׁפְּעָמִים שֶׁבָּאִין בִּפְשִׁיעָה. בִּידֵי אָדָם נִינְהוּ. שֶׁלֹּא מִגְּזֵירַת מֶלֶךְ.
דִּין

אי לאפוקי מדרבי סימאי קאתי. תימה, תיפשוט דרבי ישבב טעמא דנפשיה קאמר, אליבא דמ"ד בפ"ק דיבמות (דף יא. ושם): הבא על יבמתו וחזר ובא אחד מן האחים על צרתה – בעשה. דהא תנן בפרק "ר"ג" (יבמות דף נ.): ר"ג אומר דאין בעילה אחר בעילה, ע"כ רבי ישבב טעמא דנפשיה קאמר, והוי התם כר' ישבב דאין קידושין תופסין בחייבי עשה, ולהכי אין אחר בעילה כלום, כדאמר התם בגמרא*, אמתני' דאין אחר חליצה כלום, אמר רב הונא אמר רב: זו דברי ר"ע, דאמר דאין קידושין תופסין בחייבי לאוין. ומסתמא הכא אליבא דכ"ע מספקא ליה אי טעמא דנפשיה קאמר אי לאו! לכך נראה לר"ת דגרסי' בפ"ק דיבמות (דף יא.) חד אמר בלאו. ובלא זה מוכיח ר"ת בההיא שמעתא דל"ג "בעשה". וכן פר"ת דהיינו לאו שהלך לאחת, דאמר קרא "אשר לא יבנה" כיון שלא בנה שוב לא יבנה אחרת, ה"נ כיון שבנה שוב יבמה – לא יבנה אחרת.

איכא בינייהו בעולה לכ"ג. פי' בקונט': בעולה שלא כדרכה. וקשה: דפלוגתא דר"מ ורבי אלעזר היא בפרק "הבא על יבמתו" (יבמות דף נט. ושם) אי כשירה לכ"ג, וה"ל למימר: ולר"מ דאמר כשירה לכ"ג מאי איכא למימר? כדקאמר ולר"ע דאמר כו'! ואור"י: דמר"ע פריך שפיר טפי לאוקומי ר"ש בן מנסיא שהוא בתרא כר"ע שהיה רבו, אבל בהא לא חייש אי פליג ר"מ אר"ש בן מנסיא. ור"ח פי': דהכא לא מיירי בבעולה מאחר, אלא בכ"ג שאנס בתולה גמורה, ולא חשיבה ראויה לקיימה, אע"ג דאמר ב"הבא על יבמתו"*: אנוסת עצמו ומפותת עצמו לא ישא, ואם נשא – נשוי, מ"מ כיון דלכתחלה לא ישא – לא חשיבה ראויה לקיימה, דהאי "לא ישא" – הוי מן התורה, אף ע"ג דאם נשא נשוי. ה"נ אמר בוגרת ומוכת עץ לא ישא, ואם נשא – נשוי, אע"ג דהוי מן התורה, כדמוכח התם. ועוד דקאמר התם*: מתיב רבא "ולו תהיה לאשה" – באשה הראויה לו, פרט אלמנה לכ"ג. היכי דמי: אילימא בכדרכה – מאי איריא משום אלמנה, תיפוק ליה דהויא לה בעולה! משכב דבעולת עצמו אסורה לו מן התורה. ור"ת לא פירש כן.

הכל מודים בבא על הנדה שמשלם קנס. תימה לר"י: מנלן דר"ש בן מנסיא מודה בזה? דלמא כר' נחוניא בן הקנה ס"ל דחייבי כריתות פטורים מן התשלומין? ומיהו, ר"ש התימני ע"כ לית ליה דר' נחוניא, מדאיצטריך למעוטי חייבי כריתות מ"ולו תהיה לאשה" אשה שיש בה הויה. דע"כ לא איצטריך למעוטי אלא חייבי כריתות, דחייבי לאוין ס"ל בסוף "החולץ" (יבמות דף מט. ושם) דאית בהו הויה. אבל מר"ש בן מנסיא קשה: מנלן דלית ליה דר' נחוניא? ועוד, אפי' ר"ש התימני דלמא אית ליה דר' נחוניא, ואיצטריך למעוטי מ"ולו תהיה לאשה" יבמה לשוק, דאין קידושין תופסין בה לכ"ע, כדאמר ב"האשה רבה" (שם דף צב: ושם)! וי"ל: דרב חסדא ס"ל דאין שום תנא סובר כרבי נחוניא, ולה"ק ולאפוקי כו'. ובקונטר' פירש דאמתני' קאי דמפקא מדר' נחוניא. ותימה: מנ"ל דמפקא מיניה? דלמא מודה ר' נחוניא דחייבי כריתות. יש להן קנס דרבינהו קרא חד לחייבי לאוין וחד לחייבי כריתות ולר"ע ניחא דמפקא מתני' מדר' נחוניא דכיון דאין קידושין תופסין בחייבי לאוין – איכא לאוקומי הנך תרי ריבויי חד לחייבי עשה וחד לחייבי לאוין, אבל חייבי כריתות לר' נחוניא – לא. *ונראה לרשב"א לתרץ: *דע"כ מפקא מתני' מר' נחוניא, דלר' נחוניא אין חילוק בין חייבי כריתות לחייבי מיתות ב"ד, או מ"אסון" "אסון", או כדדריש רבא: כרת שלי כמיתה שלכם. ואם יש קנס לר' נחוניא בחייבי כריתות – יש ג"כ בחייבי מיתות ב"ד, ומתני' קתני: בא על בתו פטור. **הכל** בידי שמים חוץ מצינים פחים. והא דאמרי' (שבת דף לב.): לעולם אל יעמוד אדם במקום סכנה, אלמא יכול לשמור עצמו מן הפורענות! וכן קיר נטוי דאסור לעבור תחתיו! התם מן הפשיעה יכול לשמור עצמו, דהא ודאי שבידו להמית עצמו, אבל כשמביאין עליו מן השמים באונס – אי אפשר לו לשמור, אבל צינים פחים לעולם אל יבואו עליו באונס אם רוצה ליזהר. וא"ת: והא דרשינן (ב"מ דף קז:) "והסיר ה' ממך כל חולי" – זה צינה, אלמא דבידי שמים הוא! וי"ל: דהיינו שיתם הקב"ה עולמו, או יתן לו מלבושים, ולא יצטרך ליזהר. וא"ת: והא פחים בידי שמים הוא, כדאמרי' בבראשית רבה בפרשה ט"ו, א"ל אנטונינוס לרבי: צלי עלי. א"ל: רחמנא שיזבך מצינתא. א"ל: דא צלותא היא?! יתיר חד כסו וצינתא אזלא. א"ל: תשתזב משרבא. א"ל: הא כדו צלותא, דכתיב "אין נסתר מחמתו"! וי"ל דקרא כתיב בעוברי דרכים, או במלחמה, כדרך שהמלכים עושים, דבדרך אין אדם יכול ליזהר מן החום. אבל אם רוצה לישב בביתו – יכול להזהר שישב בבית של אבנים או יכנס במרתף. ויש מפרשים דלינים פחים חדא מילתא היא, כלומר: ליניס שהם פחים לאדם, לשון פח ומוקש. ואינו כן, דבפ"ק דמסכת ע"ז (דף ג: ושם) מייתי לה [אהא דכתיב "ותעשה אדם כדגי הים" מה] דגים שבים, כיון שקדרה עליהן חמה מיד מתים – [אף בני אדם כיון שקדרה עליהם חמה מיד מתים]. והא דאמר (ברכות דף לג:): הכל בידי שמים חוץ מיראת שמים – אין ענינו לכאן, דהתם קאי על הולד במעי אמו (נדה טז:), שגוזרין אם יהא עני או עשיר גבור או חלש טפש או חכם, אבל צדיק ורשע – לא, *והכא מיירי במאורעות הבאות על האדם*. **מיום** שחרב בית כו'. וא"ת: אמאי לא נקט מ' שנה קודם שחרב בהמ"ק? דמ' שנה קודם חורבן גלתה סנהדרין כו', שלא דנו דיני נפשות! וי"ל: דלפעמים לצורך שעה היו חוזרין סנהדרין ללשכת הגזית, ולהכי לא פסיקא ליה למיתני מ' שנה קודם חורבן. וא"ת: א"כ מאי פריך בפרק "היו בודקין" (סנהדרין דף מא.) גבי מעשה ובדק ר' יוחנן בן זכאי בעוקצי תאנים, ופריך: מי הוה בסנהדרין? והא תניא כל שנותיו של רבן יוחנן בן זכאי מאה ועשרים שנה, מ' עסק בפרקמטיא, ומ' למד ומ' לימד. ותניא: מ' שנה קודם חורבן גלתה סנהדרין כו'. והשתא מאי קשיא ליה? כיון דלפעמים היו חוזרין ודנין! וי"ל: דרבן יוחנן בן זכאי דבדק בעוקצי תאנה – אמעשה דרציחה היה, ומשום דיני נפשות דרציחה לא היו חוזרין לעולם, דעיקרם לא גלו אלא משום רציחה, דחזו דנפישי רוצחים, כדאמרינן בפ"ק דמסכת ע"ז (דף ח: ושם). וי"מ דלהכי נקט משחרב בהמ"ק, מש"ס דקודם לכן אע"פ שגלו היו בגדי כהונה מכפרים על מזיד דלא אתרו ביה, כדאמרינן בפרק יש בערכין (ערכין דף טז. ושם). ואין נראה, דהא בימי שמעון בן שטח היו בגדי כהונה, והיה דין ארבע מיתות, כדאמרינן בפרק "אחד דיני ממונות" (סנהדרין דף לז: ושם): א"ר שמעון בן שטח: אראה בנחמה אם לא ראיתי אחד שרץ אחר חברו לחורבה וכו' לא זז משם עד שנשכו נחש. ופריך: והאי בר נחש הוא? והא תני ר' חייא: אע"פ שבטלו סנהדרין כו'? ועוד אמר (מכות י:) "מרשעים יצא רשע כו'" *)והתם בזמן שבהמ"ק קיים איירי, מדקאמר: ונמצא זה מת וזה גולה**).
דין

*) [ומיהו אפשר לומר לפי שלפעמים היו מכפרים לא פסיקא ליה. ת"י] **) [וע"ע תוס' סוטה ח: וזבחים פח: ד"ה מכפרים]

ז א (מיי' פ"א מהלכות נערה הלכה יג ופ"ג מהלכות גניבה הלכה ב טוש"ע ח"מ סי' שנא):

תוספות רי"ד

מתני' דלא כר"נ בן הקנה. פירוש מתני' דמחייב קנס לבא על אחותו ואע"פ שמתחייב כרת בביאתו. דתניא ר"נ [בן הקנה] היה עושה יוה"כ כשבת לתשלומין. פי' לפטור המדליק את הגדיש ביוה"כ כאילו הדליקו בשבת מה שבת שהיא מיתת ב"ד פטור מתשלומין כדתנן מתני' לקמן בבא על בתו וילפי' לה מולא יהי' אסון. אף יוה"כ שהוא בכרת מתחייב בנפשו ופטור מן התשלומין. מ"ט דר"נ ב"ה. אמר אביי נאמר אסון בידי שמים. פי' וקראהו אסון ונאמר אסון בידי אדם ואם אסון יהיה מה אסון הנאמר בידי אדם פטור מן התשלומין. פי' דמשתעי במיתת ב"ד למימר היכא דליכא מיתת ב"ד משלם דמי וולדות. אף אסון האמור בידי שמים פטור מן התשלומין:

[יבמות דף נט:] [דף נט. ושם ד"ה אילימא]

[ומהר"מ אומר כי מצא בתוספתא פרק אלו נערות ר' נחוניא אומר הבא על אחותו ועל אחות אביו ועל אחות אמו אין להם קנס וכן היה עושה ר' נחוניא בן הקנה יוה"כ כשבת]

[והא דתנן (פ"ד דאבות) על כרחך אתה חי היינו שאין לך אדם שמניח להרוג עצמו ועוד נראה לר"י דע"כ אתה חי לא קאמר וגרסי' ע"כ אתה מת ועל כרחך אתה חי והיינו כמו המתים להחיות והחיים לידון. תו"י]

נ"ל דכהונה

[תוספתא ב"ק פ"ז] שבועות לג. מגילה ז: פסחים כט. לב. [תוספתא פ"ג תוספתא דמגילה פ"א]

הגהות הב"ח

(א) רש"י ד"ה בעולה וכו' אלא ר' אלעזר וליח. נ"ב וביבמות נ"ט ע"ב מסיק דאף אליבא דר"א משכחת לה כממאנת ע"ש:

ב"מ קז: ב"ב קמה: ע"ש ע"ז ג: ע"ש

סוטה ח: סנהדרין לז: ע"ש

גליון הש"ס

גמ' איכא בינייהו בעולה לכ"ג. עי' פסחים מא ע"ב תוד"ה אכל:

[ול"נ לתרץ דע"כ מפקא מתני' מר' נחוניא דלר' נחוניא איצטריך לאוקמי חד לחייבי לאוין ועשה וחד ללאו דיבמה לשוק אבל חייבי כריתות קים ליה בדרבה מיניה וכ"מ לקמן בפירקין אי כרבי נחוניא קשיא אחותו משמע דבחייבי כריתות לא מתוקמא כוותיה. ת"י]

[וע"ע תוס' מגילה כה. ד"ה הכל ותוס' נדה טז: ד"ה הכל]

ח א מיי' פ"ו מהלכות תרומות הל' ו סמג לאוין רכו:
ט ב מיי' פ"ב מהלכות גניבה הלכה ד סמג עשין עא טוש"ע ח"מ סימן שנ:

דִּין אַרְבַּע מִיתוֹת לֹא בָּטְלוּ: מִי שֶׁנִּתְחַיֵּיב סְקִילָה — אוֹ נוֹפֵל מִן הַגַּג, אוֹ חַיָּה דּוֹרַסְתּוֹ. וּמִי שֶׁנִּתְחַיֵּיב שְׂרֵיפָה — אוֹ נוֹפֵל בִּדְלֵיקָה, אוֹ נָחָשׁ מַכִּישׁוֹ. וּמִי שֶׁנִּתְחַיֵּיב הֲרִיגָה — אוֹ נִמְסָר לַמַּלְכוּת, אוֹ לִיסְטִים בָּאִין עָלָיו. וּמִי שֶׁנִּתְחַיֵּיב חֶנֶק — אוֹ טוֹבֵעַ בְּנָהָר, אוֹ מֵת בִּסְרוּנְכִי? אֶלָּא אֵיפוֹךְ: אַרְיָא וְגַנָּבֵי — בִּידֵי שָׁמַיִם, צִינִּים וּפַחִים — בִּידֵי אָדָם. רָבָא אָמַר: טַעֲמָא דְּרַבִּי נְחוּנְיָא בֶּן הַקָּנָה מֵהָכָא: °"וְאִם הַעְלֵם יַעְלִימוּ עַם הָאָרֶץ אֶת עֵינֵיהֶם מִן הָאִישׁ הַהוּא בְּתִתּוֹ מִזַּרְעוֹ לַמֹּלֶךְ וְשַׂמְתִּי אֲנִי אֶת פָּנַי בָּאִישׁ הַהוּא וּבְמִשְׁפַּחְתּוֹ וְהִכְרַתִּי אוֹתוֹ" אָמְרָה תּוֹרָה: כָּרֵת שֶׁלִּי כְּמִיתָה שֶׁלָּכֶם, מַה מִּיתָה שֶׁלָּכֶם — פָּטוּר מִן הַתַּשְׁלוּמִין, אַף כָּרֵת שֶׁלִּי — פָּטוּר מִן הַתַּשְׁלוּמִין. מַאי אִיכָּא בֵּין רָבָא לְאַבָּיֵי? אִיכָּא בֵּינַיְיהוּ זָר שֶׁאָכַל תְּרוּמָה. לְאַבָּיֵי [א]פָּטוּר, וּלְרָבָא חַיָּיב. וּלְאַבָּיֵי פָּטוּר?! וְהָאָמַר רַב חִסְדָּא: מוֹדֶה ר' נְחוּנְיָא בֶּן הַקָּנָה [ב]בְּגוֹנֵב חֶלְבּוֹ שֶׁל חֲבֵירוֹ וַאֲכָלוֹ — שֶׁהוּא חַיָּיב, שֶׁכְּבָר נִתְחַיֵּיב בִּגְנֵיבָה קוֹדֶם שֶׁבָּא לִידֵי אִיסּוּר חֵלֶב. אַלְמָא, דְּמֵעִידָּנָא דְּאַגְבְּהֵיהּ קַנְיֵיהּ, מִתְחַיֵּיב בְּנַפְשׁוֹ *לָא הֲוָה עַד דְּאָכֵיל לֵיהּ. הָכָא נַמִי, בְּעִידָּנָא דְּאַגְבְּהֵיהּ קַנְיֵיהּ, מִתְחַיֵּיב בְּנַפְשׁוֹ לָא הֲוֵי עַד דְּאָכֵיל לֵיהּ! הָכָא בְּמַאי עָסְקִינַן — כְּגוֹן שֶׁתָּחַב לוֹ חֲבֵירוֹ לְתוֹךְ פִּיו. סוֹף סוֹף, כֵּיוָן דְּלָעֲסֵיהּ — קַנְיֵיהּ, מִתְחַיֵּיב בְּנַפְשׁוֹ לָא הָוֵי עַד דְּבָלְעָהּ! כְּגוֹן *שֶׁתָּחַב לוֹ לְתוֹךְ בֵּית הַבְּלִיעָה. הֵיכִי דָּמֵי? אִי דְּמָצֵי לְאַהֲדוּרַהּ — נִיהֲדַר, אִי לָא מָצֵי לְאַהֲדוּרַהּ — אַמַּאי חַיָּיב? לָא צְרִיכָא, דְּמָצֵי לְאַהֲדוּרַהּ ע"י הַדְּחָק. רַב פַּפָּא אָמַר: כְּגוֹן שֶׁתָּחַב לוֹ חֲבֵירוֹ מַשְׁקִין שֶׁל תְּרוּמָה לְתוֹךְ פִּיו. רַב אַשִׁי אָמַר: בְּזָר שֶׁאָכַל תְּרוּמָה מִשֶּׁלּוֹ, וְקָרַע

תורה אור: ויקרא כ

רש"י

דִּין ד' מִיתוֹת. עוֹנֶשׁ דּוּגְמָתָם. נוֹפֵל מִן הַגַּג. דּוֹמֶה לְנִסְקָל, שֶׁדּוֹחֲפִין אוֹתוֹ מִבֵּית הַסְּקִילָה לָאָרֶץ. דְּגָבוֹהַּ ב' קוֹמוֹת הָיָה, כִּדְאָמְרִי' בְּ"נִגְמַר הַדִּין" (סנהדרין דף מה.). חַיָּה דּוֹרַסְתּוֹ. אֲרִי מַפִּילוֹ לָאָרֶץ וְהוֹרְגוֹ בִּדְרִיסָה. נָחָשׁ מַכִּישׁוֹ. וְהָאֶרֶס שׂוֹרְפוֹ. נִמְסָר לַמַּלְכוּת. וְהֵן מַתִּיזִין רֹאשׁוֹ בְּסַיִיף, כִּי כֵּן דֶּרֶךְ הַמּוּמָתִין עַל יְדֵיהֶן, וְזוֹ הִיא מִיתַת סַיִיף. סְרוּנְכִי. אַסְכָּרָא, וְהוּא בַּגָּרוֹן, מלנ"ט. מִן הָאִישׁ הַהוּא. שֶׁהוּא חַיָּיב מִיתַת ב"ד. וְשַׂמְתִּי אֲנִי אֶת פָּנַי וְהִכְרַתִּי. לָמַדְנוּ שֶׁהַכָּרֵת בִּמְקוֹם מִיתָה וְחִילּוּפָהּ. זָר שֶׁאָכַל תְּרוּמָה. בְּמֵזִיד, הוּא בְּמִיתָה בִּידֵי שָׁמַיִם וְלֹא בְּכָרֵת. כָּרֵת — הוּא וְזַרְעוֹ נֶעֱנָשִׁין, דִּכְתִיב (ויקרא כ) "עֲרִירִים יִהְיוּ". לְאַבָּיֵי פָּטוּר. מִתַּשְׁלוּמִין, דְּנָפְקָא לֵיהּ מֵאָסוֹן בִּידֵי שָׁמַיִם, וְכָל אָסוֹן בְּמַשְׁמַע, בֵּין בְּמִיתָה בֵּין בְּכָרֵת. וּלְאַבָּיֵי פָּטוּר. בִּתְמִיָּה; נְהִי נַמִי דְּמִיתָה בִּידֵי שָׁמַיִם פּוֹטֶרֶת מִתַּשְׁלוּמִין, אֲבָל הֵיכָא דְּאָכֵיל תְּרוּמָה דִּגְזוּלָה מִי מִיפְּטַר? הָא כֵּיוָן דְּאַגְבְּהָהּ קָנְיָהּ, וְחַיָּיב בְּתַשְׁלוּמִין, וַאֲפִילּוּ תִּישָּׂרֵף, וּמִתְחַיֵּיב בְּנַפְשׁוֹ לָא הָוֵי עַד דְּאָכֵיל לָהּ. שֶׁתָּחַב לוֹ חֲבֵרוֹ. דְּלָא אַגְבְּהָהּ וְלָא קָנְיָהּ וְלָא מִיחַיֵּיב בְּתַשְׁלוּמִין, אֶלָּא בִּבְלִיעָתוֹ מִתְחַיֵּיב דְּמֵי הֲנָיַית מֵעָיו, וְלֹא דְּמֵי כוּלָּהּ. וּבְהַהִיא שַׁעְתָּא חִיּוּב מִיתָה נַמִי אִיכָּא. אִיבָּעֵי לֵיהּ לְאַהֲדוּרַהּ. וְכִי לָא אַהַדְרַהּ — מֵהַהִיא שַׁעְתָּא אִיהוּ מַזִּיק לָהּ. דְּרִאשׁוֹן לָאו מִידֵי עֲבַד, וְלֹא נִתְחַיֵּיב לַכֹּהֵן כְּלוּם. וְאִי דְּלָא מָצֵי לְאַהֲדוּרַהּ אַמַּאי חַיָּיב. מִיתָה? אָנוּס הוּא! ע"י הַדְּחָק. דְּאִי נַמִי אַהַדְרַהּ — מִמְאֲסָהּ, וְלָא חַזְיָא לַבְּעָלִים. הִלְכָּךְ, מִגְזַל לָא גְּזָלָהּ. אַמַּאי קָא מְחַיְּיבַתְּ לֵיהּ בְּתַשְׁלוּמִין — אַהֲנָאַת גְּרוֹנוֹ וּמֵעָיו? הַהִיא שַׁעְתָּא חִיּוּב מִיתָה אִיכָּא! מַשְׁקִין שֶׁל תְּרוּמָה. וְלָא תִּדְחָקֵהּ לְשַׁנּוּיֵהּ בְּבֵית הַבְּלִיעָה, אֶלָּא מִכֵּיוָן שֶׁתְּחָבָהּ לְתוֹךְ פִּיו אִימְאֲסָא לָהּ, וְלָא מָטֵית לְאִיחַיּוּבֵי מִשּׁוּם גְּזֵילָה — דְּהָא לָא חַזְיָא לְמִידֵי, אֶלָּא אַהֲנָיַית גְּרוֹנוֹ וּמֵעָיו מִיחַיֵּיב, וּמִיתָה וְתַשְׁלוּמִין בָּאִים כְּאֶחָד. וְקָרַע

תוספות

דין ד' מיתות לא בטלו. וא"ת: והא אמר ב"השוכר את הפועלים" (ב"מ פג:) בההוא דזקפוהו, אע"פ שהיה חייב סקילה, שבעלו הוא ובנו נערה המאורסה! וי"ל: שבעל בנו תחלה ואח"כ הוא, דהוי בעולה, והרי הוא בחנק. אבל קשה: דחזינן כמה עבריינים ועובדי עבודה זרה שמתים על מטותם? ויש לומר דע"י תשובה הקב"ה מיקל, ולפעמים מוחל לגמרי, או זכות תולה לו ואינו נפרע ממנו בחייו. ובפ' "אחד דיני ממונות" (סנהדרין דף לז: ושם) דפריך: והא בר נחש הוא! לפי שהחמיר עליו יותר. **זר** שאכל תרומה לאביי פטור. ואוכל תרומה בשוגג והזיד במעילה, לרבי דאמר במיתה (פסחים דף לג.) דחייב — גזירת הכתוב הוא. וא"ת: לאביי דפטר חייבי מיתות בידי שמים, אי ר' נחוניא ס"ל כרבי דאמר הזיד במעילה במיתה — אמאי תניא בפרק "כל שעה" (פסחים דף כט. ושם): האוכל חמץ של הקדש במועד — יש אומרים לא מעל. ואמרינן: מאן י"א — רבי נחוניא בן הקנה. והא כיון דגלי רחמנא גבי הקדש, דלא שייך קים ליה (א), דאם לא כן אין לך אדם שמועל בהקדש — א"כ בפסח נמי, דאיכא כרת — ליחייב, ולא הוה לן למימר דקים ליה בדרבה מיניה! וכ"ת: במיתה דהקדש דוקא גלי רחמנא דלא אמרינן דקים ליה בדרבה מיניה, אבל התם דהוי בפסח דאיכא כרת לא גלי קרא — א"כ הא דתנן התם (שם דף לא:): האוכל תרומת חמץ בפסח, בשוגג — משלם קרן וחומש, במזיד — פטור מן התשלומין, ומפרש בגמ': במזיד פטור דקים ליה בדרבה מיניה, כרבי נחוניא. והשתא בשוגג נמי ליפטר משום כרת דפסח, דאפי' בשוגג אמרי' דקים ליה בדרבה מיניה, כדאמרינן לקמן בפירקין (דף לה.)! אלא ע"כ משום דגלי רחמנא במיתה דתרומה בשוגג, דלא אמרינן קים ליה בדרבה מיניה, וה"ה כי איכא כרת. ולא אמרינן דוקא במיתה דגלי גלי, אבל כי איכא כרת לא. וי"ל: דשאני שוגג דתרומה, משום דתשלומין דידיה כפרה ולא ממונא, כדאמרינן במסכת תרומות (פ"ו מ"א) דאם רצה כהן למחול — אינו יכול למחול, משום דלא הוי ממון אלא כפרה. ואפילו אוכל תרומת עצמו, דלא גזל מידי, משלם כפרה לעצמו וחומש לכהן. ולכך לא שייך קים ליה בדרבה מיניה לפוטרו מכפרה. אבל קרן וחומש של הקדש אינו משום כפרה, אלא משלם ממון שגזל הקדש. ותדע, דבתרומה חייב משום דכפרה הוא, ולא משום כיון דגלי גלי, דהא לרבא דלא פטר במיתה מטעם דקים ליה בדרבה מיניה — מאי טעמא לא מיפטר אוכל תרומת חמץ בפסח? אלא ודאי משום כפרה הוא*. וא"ת: והא דתנן בפרק "נושאין" (יבמות דף צט:): כהנת שנתערב ולדה בולד שפחתה, ושחררו זה את זה. וכן ספק בן תשעה לראשון או בן ז' לאחרון, דאמרינן אם אכלו בתרומה — אין משלמין קרן וחומש, ואמאי? כיון דכפרה הוא — ליחייבו מספק! וי"ל: דודאי צריכין להפריש אבל אין נותנין לכהן. ולפי זה צריך לומר שהכפרה תלויה בהפרשה, והא דאין הכהן יכול למחול — היינו לענין שלא יהיה צריך להפריש, אבל לאחר שהפריש — יכול למחול לו שיהא שלו. **ולאביי** פטור והאמר רב חסדא כו'. הכי נמי הוה מצי לאקשויי אמתניתין ד"כל שעה" (פסחים דף לא:) דקתני: פטור מן התשלומין, לפי מה דמוקמינן לה כרבי נחוניא בן הקנה. **אי** דמצי לאהדורה ניהדרה. וכי לא מיהדר — חייב, דמיתה לא פטרה ליה, דלא אתיא עד דבלע לגמרי. **ואי** דלא מצי לאהדורה אמאי חייב. פירש בקונטרס אמאי חייב מיתה. וקשה לר"י: דלוקי כגון שמרצונו מניח לו לתחוב, דהשתא ודאי חייב מיתה, אע"ג דלא מצי לאהדורה, וממון נמי לא מיחייב, כיון דלא מצי לאהדורה, אלא על הנאת גרונו ומעיו, וההיא שעתא קים ליה בדרבה מיניה! ונראה לר"י דה"פ: אמאי חייב ממון? והרי הוא לא גזלו, וההנאתו לא מיחייב, דאע"ג דאמרי' (ב"ק דף קיא:): גזל ולא נתייאשו הבעלים, ובא אחר ואכלו — רצה מזה גובה כו'. היינו דוקא לפי שהדבר הגזול ישנו בעולם בשעה שזה שני גוזלו, אבל הכא, דבשעה שזה נהנה ממנו כבר הוא אבוד מן העולם, שהוא במקום דלא אפשר לאהדוריה — אין לו על השני כלום. *וריב"א מפרש כשיטת רש"י. ופשיטא ליה להתלמוד דאיירי כשתוחב לו בע"כ, דכשתוחב לו מרצונו — מיד כשמשים בפיו ולא אהדרה — קנאה מיד להתחייב באונסין, ואין באין כאחד, דמסתמא מניחה בפיו, ואח"כ תוחב לו באצבעו או בכוש. ואת"ל שהוא ברא"ש הכוש מתחלתו ועד גמר בית הבליעה — מ"מ קונה אותו בפיו להתחייב באונסים, אע"ג דיכול לנתקו ולהביאו אצלו. °דדוקא לענין הגט אמרי' היכא דיכול לנתקו דלא הוי גט משום דבעינן כריתות, והא אגידא ביה. אבל לענין זכיה אשכחן בפ"ק דב"מ (דף ט. ושם) טלית, תליה על גבי קרקע ותליה על גבי העמוד, והגביה תליה שעל גבי קרקע — דלא קני, מטעם שיכול לנתקה ולהביאה אצלו. וכיון שאינו זוכה מטעם זה — ה"ה דאינו מגרע זכיית האחר, שהוא מונח בתוך ידו או בתוך פיו, מטעם זה. ועוד: דלכל הפחות קונה מחלה, כמו שנים שהגביהו מציאה. ולכך פשיטא ליה להתלמוד דבאונס איירי, וה"פ: אנוס הוא ופטור ממיתה וממון, דאנן סהדי דלא ניחא ליה באכילת איסור. **לא** צריכא דמצי לאהדורה על ידי הדחק. והשתא ליכא למימר דניהדרה, דאין מרויחין בעלים בכך, דכבר נמאסו. הלכך ליכא חיוב ממון אלא ע"י הנאת מעיו ואז באין כאחד. ואע"ג שחבירו גזלה, הואיל ויכול להחזירה הויא כמו שהיא בעין, והרי הוא בולעה ונהנה בה. ואם תאמר: והא אמרינן בפרק "בהמה המקשה" (חולין דף עא.) גבי טומאה בלועה [דלא מטמאה לא משום דלא חזיא, דנהי בפניו לא חזיא] שלא בפניו מיחזא חזיא, א"כ אי הוה מהדר לה הויא חזיא! וי"ל: כגון דמעיקרא לא הוי בה כי אם שוה פרוטה, או מעט יותר, ועתה, שנתקלקלה קצת, אינה שוה פרוטה. ואפילו אי זה נהנה וזה לא חסר פטור — °מ"מ כיון דשוין כל שהוא אז מיחייב בכל, כדאמרינן התם (ב"ק דף כ:): משום דא"ל את גרמת לי היזקא יתירתא מיחייב בכל הנאה, או משום שחרוריתא דאשיתא מיחייב לכולי עלמא בכל. וריב"א פי' דמיירי אפי' באוכלין דלא מאיסי, וכיון דתחב לו בבית הבליעה ובלע ונהנה מיד — חשוב באין כאחת אע"פ שאין כאחד ממש. כדאשכחן בסוף פרק "ד' אחין" (יבמות דף לג. ושם) דמפרש: בעל מום ששמש בטומאה דאתו בהדי הדדי, כגון שחתך אצבעו בסכין טמאה, אע"פ שאי אפשר שלא יגע בסכין קודם שיחתוך*. **רב** אשי אמר בזר שאכל תרומה משלו וקרע שיראים כו'. פ"ה דסבירא ליה לרב אשי דמיתה לזה ותשלומין לזה פטור, ופליג אדרבא דאמר בפרק קמא דסנהדרין (דף י. ושם): פלוני בא על בת פלוני והוזמו — נהרגין ומשלמין — ממון לזה ונפשות לזה. *פי': ממון לבת שרצו להפסיד לה כתובתה, ונפשות לזה שאומר שבא עליה. ואין נראה, **) דאי חשיב אכילת תרומה וקריעת שיראין ממון לזה ונפשות לזה — א"כ תקשי ליה לרבא הא דתנן ב"המניח את הכד" (ב"ק דף לד: ושם):

והוא

גליון הש"ס

תוס' ד"ה ואי וכו' לדוקא לענין הגט. תמוה לי הא להדיא איתא כן בב"מ ז ע"א ולנע"ג: **ד"ה** לא צריכא וכו' מ"מ כיון דשוין כל שהוא. עי' בב"ק דף כ ע"ב תוד"ה הא איתהנית:

[וא"ת כיון דלעס ליה נתקלקל והיאך חייב תו עלה כדאמר פ"ק דכריתות [דף ז.] כהן שסך שמן של תרומה בן בתו ישראל מתעגל בו ואינו חושש וי"ל דהתם ודאי נתקלקל שכבר נגמרה כל הנאתו אבל הכא לא נגמרה כל הנאתו בלעיסה לחודיה. ת"י]

[ועוד יש להוכיח דכפרה הוי מדפטרי' לאביי מזיד בתרומה ואע"ג דגלי רחמנא גבי שוגג דלא אמרינן קים ליה בדרבה מיניה במיתה דתרומה אלא ודאי משום כפרה הוא ויש לדחות דשאני שוגג דתרומה לפי שמצינו שהוא חמור שמשלם חומש. ת"י]

[פי' ריב"א לא יתחייב בממון דקאמר או בכי גתון ואכיל. ת"י]

[פי' ממון לאב שרצו להפסידו כתובה כנ"ל מהרש"א]

[עי' תוס' בבא קמא כ: ד"ה הא]

הגהות הב"ח

(א) תוס' ד"ה זר וכו' קים ליה בדרבה מיניה לאו:

[ור"ת פירש כיון שהוא במקום דלא מצי לאהדורי אלא ע"י הדחק כבר נהנה גרונו ובאין כאחד וא"ת והיאך יתחייב ממון כיון שנתחב בו כאונס וי"ל כיון דמצי לאהדורה ע"י הדחק ולא הדררה ניחא ליה בהנאה זו. ת"י]

**) [ועוד לאכתי מאי איכא בין רבא לאביי דאפי' אי הוי סבר רבא דילוף מאסון אסון הוי מיחייב כיון דהוי ממון לזה ונפשות לזה. ת"י]

וְקָרַע שִׁירָאִין שֶׁל חֲבֵירוֹ. גּוּפָא, אָמַר רַב חִסְדָּא: מוֹדֶה רַבִּי נְחוּנְיָא בֶּן הַקָּנָה בְּגוֹנֵב חֶלְבּוֹ שֶׁל חֲבֵירוֹ וַאֲכָלוֹ – שֶׁהוּא חַיָּיב שֶׁכְּבָר נִתְחַיֵּיב בִּגְנֵיבָה קוֹדֶם שֶׁיָּבֹא לִידֵי אִיסּוּר חֵלֶב. לֵימָא פְּלִיגָא דְּרַבִּי אָבִין, דְּאָמַר רַבִּי אָבִין: *[א]הַזּוֹרֵק חֵץ מִתְּחִילַּת אַרְבַּע לְסוֹף אַרְבַּע וְקָרַע שִׁירָאִין בַּהֲלִיכָתוֹ – פָּטוּר, שֶׁעֲקִירָה צוֹרֶךְ הַנָּחָה הִיא. הָכָא נַמִי – הַגְבָּהָה צוֹרֶךְ אֲכִילָה הִיא; הָכִי הָשְׁתָּא? הָתָם – אִי אֶפְשָׁר לְהַנָּחָה בְּלֹא עֲקִירָה, הָכָא אֶפְשָׁר לַאֲכִילָה בְּלֹא הַגְבָּהָה, דְּאִי בָּעֵי – *[ב]גָּחֵין וְאָכֵיל. אִי נַמִי: הָתָם, אִי בָּעֵי לְאַהֲדוּרָהּ לָא מָצֵי מַהֲדַר לָהּ, הָכָא – מָצֵי מַהֲדַר לָהּ. מַאי אִיכָּא בֵּין הַאי לִישָּׁנָא לְהַאי לִישָּׁנָא? אִיכָּא בֵּינַיְיהוּ הַמַּעֲבִיר סַכִּין בִּרה"ר, וְקָרַע שִׁירָאִין בַּהֲלִיכָתוֹ. לְהַךְ לִישָּׁנָא דְּאָמְרַתְּ אִי אֶפְשָׁר לְהַנָּחָה בְּלֹא עֲקִירָה – הָכָא נַמִי אִי אֶפְשָׁר לְהַנָּחָה בְּלֹא עֲקִירָה. לְהַךְ לִישָּׁנָא דְּאָמְרַתְּ לָא מָצֵי מַהֲדַר לָהּ – הָכָא מָצֵי מַהֲדַר לָהּ. גּוּפָא, אָמַר רַבִּי אָבִין: הַזּוֹרֵק חֵץ מִתְּחִילַּת אַרְבַּע לְסוֹף אַרְבַּע, וְקָרַע שִׁירָאִין בַּהֲלִיכָתוֹ – פָּטוּר, שֶׁעֲקִירָה צוֹרֶךְ הַנָּחָה הִיא. מְתִיב רַב בֵּיבַי בַּר אַבַּיֵי: *[ג]הַגּוֹנֵב כִּיס בְּשַׁבָּת – חַיָּיב, שֶׁכְּבָר נִתְחַיֵּיב בִּגְנֵיבָה קוֹדֶם שֶׁיָּבֹא לִידֵי אִיסּוּר סְקִילָה. [ג]הָיָה מְגָרֵר וְיוֹצֵא, מְגָרֵר וְיוֹצֵא – פָּטוּר, שֶׁהֲרֵי אִיסּוּר שַׁבָּת וּגְנֵיבָה בָּאִין כְּאֶחָד. וְאַמַּאי? הָכָא נַמִי לֵימָא הַגְבָּהָה צוֹרֶךְ הוֹצָאָה הִיא! הָכָא בְּמַאי עָסְקִינַן – כְּגוֹן שֶׁהִגְבִּיהוֹ עַל מְנָת לְהַצְנִיעוֹ וְנִמְלַךְ עָלָיו וְהוֹצִיאוֹ. וְכִי הַאי גַּוְונָא מִי חַיָּיב? וְהָאָמַר רַב סִימוֹן אָמַר רַבִּי אַמִּי אָמַר רַבִּי יוֹחָנָן: *[ד]הַמְפַנֶּה חֲפָצִים מִזָּוִית לְזָוִית, וְנִמְלַךְ עֲלֵיהֶם וְהוֹצִיאָן – פָּטוּר, שֶׁלֹּא הָיְתָה עֲקִירָה מִשָּׁעָה רִאשׁוֹנָה לְכָךְ! לָא תֵּימָא ע"מ לְהַצְנִיעוֹ, אֶלָּא אֵימָא ע"מ לְהוֹצִיאוֹ, הָכָא בְּמַאי עָסְקִינַן – [ה]כְּשֶׁעָמַד. עָמַד לְמַאי? אִי לְכַתֵּף – אוֹרְחֵיהּ הוּא! אֶלָּא בְּעוֹמֵד לָפוּשׁ, אֲבָל לְכַתֵּף מַאי –
פָּטוּר

רש"י

וְקָרַע שִׁירָאִים. בְּשָׁעָה שֶׁהוֹלְכָה. וְאע"ג דְּמִיתָה לָאו מִשּׁוּם מָמוֹנָא דְּנִיזָּק אָתְיָא לֵיהּ – מִיפְּטַר. וּסְבִירָא לֵיהּ לְרַב חִסְדָּא מִיתָה לָזֶה וְתַשְׁלוּמִין לָזֶה – פָּטוּר. שֶׁעֲקִירָה צוֹרֶךְ הַנָּחָה הִיא. הִלְכָּךְ, אע"ג דְּחִיּוּב מָמוֹן מִקַּמֵּי הַנָּחָה אָתְיָא לֵיהּ – פָּטוּר, הוֹאִיל וּבֵין עֲקִירָה וְהַנָּחָה אָתְיָא לֵיהּ, מִיתָה וְתַשְׁלוּמִין בָּאִין כְּאֶחָד, שֶׁעֲקִירָה צוֹרֶךְ הַנָּחָה הִיא, וּמֵהַהִיא שַׁעְתָּא אַתְחָלָה לָהּ מְלָאכָה. דְּאִי בָּעֵי גָּחֵין. לְמַטָּה מִג' טְפָחִים וְאָכֵיל. וּלְבַר מִג' לָאו הַגְבָּהָה הִיא. לָא מָצֵי לְאַהֲדוּרָהּ. מִשֶּׁנִּזְרַק אֶת הַחֵץ. הִלְכָּךְ מִשְּׁעַת עֲקִירָה סוֹפוֹ לִקְרוֹעַ לוֹ שִׁירָאִין. הָכָא מָצֵי מַהֲדַר לֵיהּ. הִלְכָּךְ לָא אָמְרִי' מִשְּׁעַת הַגְבָּהָה אַתְחָלָה לָהּ אֲכִילָה. הַמַּעֲבִיר סַכִּין. בְּיָדוֹ בַּהֲלִיכָה. הַגּוֹנֵב כִּיס בְּשַׁבָּת. הִגְבִּיהוֹ בִּרְשׁוּת הַבְּעָלִים, וְהוֹצִיאוֹ לִרה"ר. חַיָּיב. בְּתַשְׁלוּמִין, אַף עַל פִּי שֶׁנֶּהֱרַג. שֶׁכְּבָר נִתְחַיֵּיב בִּגְנֵיבָה. לְשַׁלֵּם, דְּהַגְבָּהָה קוֹנָה בְּכָל מָקוֹם וְקָמָה לָהּ בִּרְשׁוּתֵיהּ אַף לְהִתְחַיֵּיב בָּאוֹנָסִים. הָיָה מְגָרֵר וְיוֹצֵא. שֶׁלֹּא הִגְבִּיהוֹ בִּרְשׁוּת הַבְּעָלִים. וְלֹא קְנָאוֹ אֶלָּא בְּהוֹצָאָה מֵרְשׁוּת הַבְּעָלִים – פָּטוּר, שֶׁאִיסּוּר שַׁבָּת כו'. וְאַמַּאי. כִּי הִגְבִּיהוֹ בִּרְשׁוּת הַבְּעָלִים וּקְנָאוֹ אַמַּאי חַיָּיב? נֵימָא מִשְּׁעַת הַגְבָּהָה אַתְחָלָה לָהּ הוֹצָאָה. וּכה"ג מִי חַיָּיב. מִשּׁוּם שַׁבָּת. לְכָךְ. לְהוֹצִיאוֹ. לָא תֵּימָא בְּהִגְבִּיהוֹ ע"מ לְהַצְנִיעוֹ אֶלָּא הִגְבִּיהוֹ ע"מ לְהוֹצִיאוֹ. וּדְקַשְׁיָא לָךְ נֵימָא הַגְבָּהָה צוֹרֶךְ הוֹצָאָה הִיא. הָכָא בְּמַאי עָסְקִינַן כְּשֶׁעָמַד. וַעֲמִידָתוֹ הִיא הַנָּחָה לַעֲקִירָה רִאשׁוֹנָה, וְאֵין חִיּוּב שַׁבָּת בָּא לוֹ ע"י עֲקִירַת חֵפֶץ הָרִאשׁוֹנָה, אֶלָּא ע"י עֲקִירַת גּוּפוֹ שֶׁעוֹקֵר עַצְמוֹ אַחַר הָעֲמִידָה עַל מְנָת לְהוֹצִיא, וַעֲקִירַת גּוּפוֹ כַּעֲקִירַת חֵפֶץ. אוֹרְחֵיהּ הוּא. וְאֵין עֲמִידָתוֹ הַנָּחָה לְבַטֵּל עֲקִירָה רִאשׁוֹנָה מִמְּלֶאכֶת שַׁבָּת.
פָּטוּר

תוספות

והוא שהדליק את הגדיש בשבת פטור מפני שנידון בנפשו, והיינו מיתה לזה משום שבת, ותשלומין לזה משום גדיש. אלא על כרחך חשיב מיתה ותשלומין לאחד, הואיל ולא מתחייב מיתה בשביל אדם אלא לשמים. וה"נ אכילת תרומה וקריעת שיראין – הוי מיתה ותשלומין לאחד. ור"י רצה ליישב פי' הקונט' דחשיב הכא מיתה לזה ותשלומין לזה לפי שהן ב' מעשים, אכילת תרומה וקריעת שיראין. וכן פלוני בא על בתו של פלוני, הם ב' עדיות. שהיו יכולין להעיד עליו בלא הבת, ועל הבת בלא עליו: פלוני בא על נערה המאורסה, פלונית זינתה. אבל מדליק גדיש – הכל בא על מעשה אחד, ולכך חשיב מיתה ותשלומין לאחד. ואין נראה לרשב"א, דהא אמר רב יוסף בפ"ק דסנהדרין (דף ט: ושם): הביא הבעל עדים שזינתה, והביא האב עדים והזימום לעידי הבעל, עידי הבעל נהרגים ואין משלמין ממון. חזר והביא הבעל עדים והזימום לעידי האב, עדי האב נהרגין ומשלמין ממון. ממון לזה, פירוש: לבעל, שרצו להפסידו כתובה. ונפשות, לעדים. והתם על הזמה אחת בא להם הכל! ונראה לר"ת: דרבא דוקא גבי עדים זוממים אית ליה דממון לזה ונפשות לזה חייב, משום דבעינן שתתקיים הזמה בלפי כל אחד. ומיהו, ממון ונפשות בחד גברא – פטור, כיון דמתקיים בו קצת הזמה. אבל בעלמא מודה רבא דממון לזה ונפשות לזה פטור, דהא גדי סמוך לו ועבד כפות לו, דתנן פטור, ומוקמינן בפרק "כילד הרגל" (ב"ק דף כב: ושם) בגדי דחד ועבדא דחד. ועוד: דרבא גופיה אית ליה בפרק "בן סורר ומורה" (סנהדרין דף עד.) דרודף ששבר כלים, בין של נרדף בין של כל אדם, פטור, אע"ג דהוי מיתה לנרדף ותשלומין לבעל הכלים. ומיהו, התם גבי רודף רבה גרס, כדמוכח ב"הגוזל בתרא" (ב"ק דף קיז:) ובפ"ק דסנהדרין (דף י.) הוי רבא. ועוד אומר ר"ת: דע"כ נ"ע מיתה לזה ותשלומין לזה פטור, דהא קים ליה בדרבה מיניה דפטור – נפקא לן מ"לא יהיה אסון וגו'" והתם הוי מיתה לאשה ותשלומין לבעל שהולדות שלו. ואומר ר"י דאינה ראיה, דהתם כיון שהולדות הן בגוף האשה – חשיב מיתה ותשלומין לאחד. תדע, דבפרק "בן סורר ומורה" (שם דף עד.) בעי לחייב כשאין אסון באשה אף ע"ג דניתן להצילו בנפשו, דבמצות שבמיתה הכתוב מדבר, משום דהוי מיתה לזה שרצה להורגו, ותשלומין לבעל. ואפי' הכי כשיש אסון – פטור, והיינו משום דחשיב מיתה ותשלומין לאחד, לפי שהן בגוף האשה, כדפרישית. וריב"א אומר: דבכל מקום מיתה לזה ותשלומין לזה חייב, ועבד כפות לו ורודף שאני, דניתן להציל לכל אדם, וחייב מיתה לכל העולם, [אף לבעל העבד ולבעל הכלים], ולהכי חשיב מיתה ותשלומין לאחד. ואע"ג דמעיקרא בפרק "בן סורר" (ג"ז שם) חשיב רודף מיתה לזה ותשלומין לזה, לפי המסקנא דקאמר: אלא לא שנא – חזר בו מאותה סברא. וה"פ: אלא לא שנא משום דהוי מיתה ותשלומין לאחד [והכא חשיב מיתה ותשלומין לאחד. כמו במדליק גדיש].

שעקירה צורך הנחה היא. קשה: דאמרינן ב"מרובה" (ב"ק דף ע:) גבי גנב ומכר בשבת דפטור, כגון דאמר ליה זרוק גניבותיך לחצרי ותיקני לי חצירי גניבותיך. ופריך: מכי מטי לאויר חצירו קנה, ומתחייב בנפשו משום שבת לא הוי עד שתנוח! ומאי פריך? והא עקירה צורך הנחה היא, כדאמר הכא! ולפר"ת אתי שפיר. דפירש דאי אפשר לניסוך בלא הגבהה, ואפ"ה קאמר רב מנסך ממש ב"הניזקין" (גיטין דף נב: ושם). ולא קא מפטר משום דקים ליה בדרבה מיניה, כדרבי ירמיה, דמשעת הגבהה קונה, ומתחייב בנפשו לא הוי עד שעת ניסוך. והשתא רבי ירמיה לית ליה דהגבהה צורך ניסוך היא, וה"ה דלית ליה דעקירה צורך הנחה היא, ולא הוה מפליג בין מצי לאהדורי ללא מצי לאהדורי. תדע, ללישנא דאי אפשר להנחה בלא עקירה אמאי נקט רבי אבין זרק חץ? לינקוט מעביר! אלא ודאי כי הדדי נינהו. ומאן דפליג אמעביר – פליג נמי אזורק. ואליבא דרבי ירמיה פריך ב"מרובה" (ב"ק דף ע: ושם). אבל אם אפשר לניסוך בלא הגבהה – לא פליג רבי ירמיה אדרבי אבין, וב"הגוזל בתרא" (שם דף קיז.) משמע קצת דרבי ירמיה פליג אדרבי אבין, גבי חזרו לומר אף המנסך. דקאמר התם: מעיקרא סבור כדרבי אבין, ולבסוף סבור כדרבי ירמיה. [ומיהו יש לדחות: דמעיקרא סבור דדמיא לדרבי אבין, ולבסוף סבור דדמיא לדר' ירמיה]. **דאי** בעי גחין ואכיל. פי' בקונט': למטה מג' דלא הויא הגבהה. וקשה לר"י: דמה שייך הגבהה בדבר שהוא תופס בידו או בפיו? ד"ונתן בידה" אמר רחמנא, ואמרינן בגיטין (דף עח.) זרק לתוך קלתה – מגורשת, קשורה אע"פ שאינה תלויה, אע"ג דמיירי ברשות הבעל. ואפי' מאן דבעי התם תלויה – אינו מצריך שתהא גבוה ג'! אלא נראה לר"י *דה"פ: דאי בעי גחין ואכיל, אם הוא בראש קנה יכול הוא לשחות ולתוחבה עד בית בליעתו, אע"ג דהכי אכילה אינו עושה כן והויא הגבהה זו לצורך אכילה, מ"מ הואיל ויכול להתחייב בלא הגבהה – לאו צורך אכילה היא. וה"ה דה"מ למימר דאפשר לאכילה בלא הגבהה, כגון אם תחבה לו חבירו. **הכא** נמי נימא הגבהה צורך הוצאה היא. ללישנא דאי בעי לאהדורי לא מצי מיהדר [א]לא פריך מידי, אבל ללישנא דאי אפשר להנחה בלא עקירה פריך, דהכא נמי אי אפשר להנחה בלא הגבהה. אע"ג דאפשר בגרירה, כך לי עקירה זו כמו עקירה אחרת, דמ"מ האיסור מתחיל משעת הגבהה. דאם היה אחר עושה עקירה – לא היה מתחייב בהנחה, נמצא עקירה גורמת החיוב, ועד שעת הנחה מושך החיוב. **נימא** הגבהה צורך הוצאה היא. תימה: לפר"ת דהגבהה קונה פחות משלשה טפחים – *מאי פריך? והא כיון דקנאה קודם התחלת העקירה, דעקירה לא הויא עד שיגביה שלשה, דלמטה משלשה הוי כלבוד, כדאמרינן ב"המוציא" (שבת דף פ. ושם): העביר תאני גרוגרת דרך עליה – חייב. ואם כן דין הוא שיתחייב, כמו לבן עזאי, דאמר: מהלך כעומד דמי, דחייב לפי שקנאה קודם שהתחיל העקירה! ואומר רשב"א: דמשמע ליה בכל ענין גונב כיס אפילו מונח על גבי מקל שהוא גבוה שלשה טפחים, שבא הקנין והעקירה בבת אחת. **שהגביהו** על מנת להצניעו ונמלך להוציאו. ואם תאמר: וכיון דסלקא דעתיה השתא דמיחייב אהך הוצאה, אם כן הדרא קושיא לדוכתין, דלורך הוצאה היא! ויש לומר: דסלקא דעתין הא דנמלך והוציאו הוי עקירה שניה. **אבל** לכתף מאי פטור כו'. אפילו הוי לכתף חייב, הוי מצי למיפרך דליפלוג בדידיה, בין עמד ללא עמד כלל.

מהלך

עין משפט נר מצוה

י א מיי' פ"ג מהל' גניבה הלכה ב:

יא ב ג מיי' שם טוש"ע ח"מ סימן שנא:

יב ד ה מיי' פי"ג מהל' שבת הלכה יב:

תוספות רי"ד

א"ר אבין הזורק חץ מתחילת ד' לסוף ד' וקרע שיראין בהליכתו פטור שעקירה צורך הנחה היא. פי' ומההיא שעתא אתחלה לה מלאכה והלכך אע"ג דחיוב ממון מקמי הנחה אתיא ליה פטור הואיל א) וכן עקיר להנחה אתיא לה מיתה ותשלומין באין כאחד ולא תימא תשלומין קדמי למיתה: תניא הגונב כיס בשבת חייב. פי' חייב בתשלומין אע"פ שנהרג שכבר נתחייב בגניבה קודם שיבוא לידי איסור שבת פי' דמשעה דאגבהה קניא שהגבהה קונה בכ"מ אפילו ברה"ר. ופי' אף להתחייב באונסים מתחייב בנפשו לא הוי עד דמפיק ליה היה מגרר ויוצא פירוש שלא הגביהו ברשות הבעלים ולא קנאה אלא בהוצאה מרשות בעלים פטור. שהרי איסור שבת ואיסור גניבה באין כא'. בפ' בן סורר ומורה מוקי לה כגון דשדייה בנהרא שאין הכים בעין שאם הוא בעין א"י לזכות בו אלא בעל הכים בא ונוטלו.

א) נראה דצ"ל הואיל דהא דקא עקיר להנחה אתיא לה הוי לה מיתה ותשלומין וכו'.

[ועי"ע תוס' עירובין עט: ד"ה לריך ותוס' קדושין כו. ד"ה אי נמי ותוס' ב"ק כט: ד"ה אלא]

מסורת הש"ס

ב"ק קיז.

[מנחות ע.]

ב"ב פו. סנהדרין עב. שבת נה: תוספתא דב"ק פט

שבת ה: עירובין כ: ע"ש

גליון הש"ס

גמ' הגונב כיס בשבת. עיין ירושלמי ב"ק פ"ג הלכה ז:

הגהות מהר"ב רנשבורג

א] תוס' ד"ה הכא וכו' לא פריך מידי. עי' פ"י בשם הרא"ה דלהך לישנא נמי פריך ולדבריו צ"ל דרב ביבי בר אביי המותיב לית ליה איכא בינייהו דעביד הש"ס לעיל בסמוך. ועי' הרא"ה ושיטה מקובצת בשם הרמב"ן והרא"ה וקרובים דבריהם לדברי וזה ברור ודו"ק:

[וכן רואה לומר הספר המס מתחיל האיסור משעת עקירה הכא אין האיסור מתחיל אלא משעת אכילה דאי בעי גחין ואכיל או בלא הגבהה אבל כאן לא היה אפשר בלא הגבהה היה מתחיל האיסור משעת הגבהה. ת"י]

יג א מיי' פ"ד מהל' מכירה הלכה ד טוש"ע ח"מ סימן קלח סעיף יד:
יד ב מיי' פי"ג מהל' שבת הלכה (טו) [ב]:
[ביתר ביאור כתבו תוס' שבת ה: ד"ה בשלמא]
טו ג מיי' פ"ג מהל' גניבה הלכה ב טור ש"ע ח"מ סימן שנח:
טז ד ה מיי' פ"ב מהל' גניבה הל' טז סמג עשין עא טוש"ע ח"מ סי' שמח סעיף ד:
יז ו מיי' פי"ט מהל' סנהדרין הלכה א:

פָּטוּר, אַדִּתְנֵי הָיָה מְגָרֵר וְיוֹצֵא מְגָרֵר וְיוֹצֵא פָּטוּר, נִפְלוֹג וְנִיתְנֵי בְּדִידָהּ: בַּמֶּה דְּבָרִי' אֲמוּרִים בְּעוֹמֵד לָפוּשׁ, אֲבָל לְכַתֵּף — פָּטוּר! אֶלָּא הָא מַנִּי — *בֶּן עַזַּאי הִיא, דְּאָמַר: מְהַלֵּךְ כְּעוֹמֵד דָּמֵי. אֲבָל זוֹרֵק מַאי — פָּטוּר, נִיפְלוֹג [וְנִיתְנֵי] בְּדִידָהּ: בַּמֶּה דְּבָרִים אֲמוּרִים — בִּמְהַלֵּךְ, אֲבָל זוֹרֵק — פָּטוּר! מְגָרֵר וְיוֹצֵא אִיצְטְרִיכָא לֵיהּ, ס"ד אָמִינָא: אֵין דֶּרֶךְ הוֹצָאָה בְּכָךְ, קמ"ל. וּבְמַאי? אִי בְּרַבְרְבֵי — אוֹרְחֵיהּ הוּא, אִי בְּזוּטְרֵי — לָאו אוֹרְחֵיהּ הוּא! אֶלָּא, בְּמִיצְעֵי. וּדְאַפְּקֵיהּ לְהֵיכָא? אִי דְּאַפְּקֵיהּ לִרה"ר אִיסּוּר שַׁבָּת — אִיכָּא, אִיסּוּר גְּנֵיבָה — לֵיכָּא, אִי דְּאַפְּקֵיהּ לִרְשׁוּת הַיָּחִיד — אִיסּוּר גְּנֵיבָה אִיכָּא, אִיסּוּר שַׁבָּת — לֵיכָּא! לָא צְרִיכָא, דְּאַפְּקֵיהּ לְצִידֵּי רְשׁוּת הָרַבִּים. וּכְמַאן? אִי כְּר' אֱלִיעֶזֶר, דְּאָמַר: *צִידֵּי רה"ר כִּרה"ר דָּמוּ אִיסּוּר שַׁבָּת אִיכָּא אִיסּוּר גְּנֵיבָה לֵיכָּא, אִי כְּרַבָּנַן דְּאָמְרִי צִידֵּי רה"ר לָאו כִּרה"ר דָּמוּ — אִיסּוּר גְּנֵיבָה אִיכָּא, אִיסּוּר שַׁבָּת לֵיכָּא. לְעוֹלָם כְּר' אֱלִיעֶזֶר, וְכִי אָמַר ר"א צִידֵּי רה"ר כִּרה"ר דָּמוּ — הָנֵי מִילֵּי לְעִנְיַן חִיּוּבָא דְּשַׁבָּת, דְּזִימְנִין דְּדָחֲקֵי רַבִּים וְעָיְילֵי לְהָתָם, [א]אֲבָל לְעִנְיַן מִיקְנָא — קָנֵי, מ"ט — דְּהָא לָא שְׁכִיחִי רַבִּים. רַב אַשִׁי אָמַר: כְּגוֹן שֶׁצֵּירֵף יָדוֹ לְמַטָּה מִשְּׁלֹשָׁה וְקִיבְּלוֹ, כִּדְרָבָא. דְּאָמַר רָבָא: *[ב]יָדוֹ שֶׁל אָדָם חֲשׁוּבָה לוֹ כְּאַרְבָּעָה עַל אַרְבָּעָה. רַב אַחָא מַתְנֵי הָכִי. רָבִינָא מַתְנֵי: לְעוֹלָם דְּאַפְּקֵיהּ לִרה"ר [ג]וּבִרה"ר נַמִּי קָנָה. וְתַרְוַיְיהוּ בְּדִיוּקָא דְּהָא מַתְנִי' קָמִיפַּלְגִי, דִּתְנַן: *[ד]הָיָה מוֹשְׁכוֹ וְיוֹצֵא, וּמֵת בִּרְשׁוּת בְּעָלִים — פָּטוּר, הִגְבִּיהוֹ אוֹ שֶׁהוֹצִיאוֹ מֵרְשׁוּת בְּעָלִים וּמֵת — חַיָּיב. רָבִינָא דָּיֵיק מֵרֵישָׁא, רַב אַחָא דָּיֵיק מִסֵּיפָא. רָבִינָא דָּיֵיק מֵרֵישָׁא: הָיָה מוֹשְׁכוֹ וְיוֹצֵא, וּמֵת בִּרְשׁוּת בְּעָלִים — פָּטוּר. טַעְמָא — דְּמֵת בִּרְשׁוּת בְּעָלִים, [ה]הָא הוֹצִיאוֹ מֵרְשׁוּת בְּעָלִים וּמֵת — חַיָּיב. רַב אַחָא דָּיֵיק מִסֵּיפָא: הִגְבִּיהוֹ אוֹ שֶׁהוֹצִיאוֹ, הוֹצָאָה דּוּמְיָא דְּהַגְבָּהָה; מָה הַגְבָּהָה — דְּאָתֵי לִרְשׁוּתֵיהּ, אַף הוֹצָאָה נַמִּי — דְּאָתֵי לִרְשׁוּתֵיהּ. לְרַב אַחָא קַשְׁיָא רֵישָׁא, לְרָבִינָא קַשְׁיָא סֵיפָא! רֵישָׁא לְרַב אַחָא לָא קַשְׁיָא: כַּמָּה דְּלָא אָתֵי לִרְשׁוּתֵיהּ — רְשׁוּת בְּעָלִים קָרֵינָא בֵּיהּ. סֵיפָא לְרָבִינָא לָא קַשְׁיָא: הוֹצָאָה דּוּמְיָא דְּהַגְבָּהָה — לָא אָמְרִינַן.§ הַבָּא עַל אֲחוֹתוֹ וְעַל אֲחוֹת אָבִיו כו'.§ וּרְמִינְהוּ: *[ו]אֵלּוּ הֵן הַלּוֹקִין: הַבָּא עַל אֲחוֹתוֹ, וְעַל אֲחוֹת אָבִיו, וְעַל אֲחוֹת אִמּוֹ, וְעַל אֲחוֹת אִשְׁתּוֹ, וְעַל אֵשֶׁת אָחִיו, וְעַל אֵשֶׁת אֲחִי אָבִיו, וְעַל הַנִּדָּה. וְקַיְימָא

רש"י

פָּטוּר. מִתַּשְׁלוּמִין, דְּקָתֵי עֲלֵיהּ חִיּוּב שַׁבָּת מֵחֲמַת הַגְבָּהָה רִאשׁוֹנָה שֶׁבָּהּ נִקְנֶה לוֹ הַכִּיס, וּמִיתָה וְתַשְׁלוּמִין בָּאִין כְּאֶחָד. נִיפְלוֹג בְּדִידָהּ. בְּמַגְבִּיהַּ עַצְמוֹ יָכוֹל לִשְׁנוֹת בּוֹ חִיּוּב וּפְטוּר. אֶלָּא. לָא תּוֹקְמָהּ כְּשֶׁעָמַד, וַאֲפ"ה חִיּוּב שַׁבָּת דַּעֲקִירָה לָאו מֵחֲמַת עֲקִירָה רִאשׁוֹנָה דְּהַגְבָּהָה אָתְיָא לֵיהּ, אֶלָּא בַּעֲקִירַת גּוּפוֹ שֶׁל פְּסִיעָה אַחֲרוֹנָה כְּשֶׁיּוֹצֵא מִן הַבַּיִת, וּבֶן עַזַּאי הִיא. דְּאָמַר. בְּפ"ק דְּשַׁבָּת. מְהַלֵּךְ כְּעוֹמֵד דָּמֵי. וַעֲקִירַת כָּל פְּסִיעָה הָוְיָא עֲקִירָה, וְהַנָּחַת הָרֶגֶל הִיא הַנָּחָה, הִלְכָּךְ קָנְיֵהּ מִשְּׁעַת הַגְבָּהָה, וְחִיּוּב מִיתָה בִּפְסִיעָה בַּתְרַיְיתָא קָא אָתְיָא לֵיהּ. אֲבָל זוֹרֵק מַאי. הִגְבִּיהוֹ וּזְרָקוֹ. פָּטוּר. מִתַּשְׁלוּמִין, דְּאָתְיָא לֵיהּ חִיּוּב שַׁבָּת ע"י חִיּוּב הַגְבָּהָה, דְּתוּ לֵיתָא עֲקִירָה אַחֲרִיתִי. אֵין דֶּרֶךְ הוֹצָאָה בְּכָךְ. וְאֵין כָּאן חִיּוּב שַׁבָּת. וּבְמַאי. אִיצְטְרִיךְ לְאַשְׁמוּעִינַן דְּדֶרֶךְ הוֹצָאָה בְּכָךְ. אִי בְּרַבְרְבֵי. כִּיס גָּדוֹל שֶׁיֵּשׁ בּוֹ מַשּׂוֹי לְהַגְבִּיהוֹ. אוֹרְחֵיהּ הוּא. לְגָרְרוֹ, וּפְשִׁיטָא דְּהוֹצָאָה הִיא. לָאו אוֹרְחֵיהּ הוּא. וְאַמַּאי חַיָּיב מִשּׁוּם שַׁבָּת? אִיסּוּר גְּנֵיבָה לֵיכָּא. דִּמְשִׁיכָה בְּלָא הַגְבָּהָה, קס"ד דְּלָא קָנְיָא בִּרה"ר. לִרְשׁוּת הַיָּחִיד. לִרְשׁוּתוֹ, שֶׁהָיְתָה חֲצֵירוֹ סְמוּכָה לַחֲצַר הַבְּעָלִים. צִידֵּי רה"ר. סָמוּךְ לַבָּתִּים, שֶׁנּוֹתְנִין לְהַלָּן מִן הַבָּתִּים אֲבָנִים וּמַכְשׁוֹלִין לְהַרְחִיק חִיכּוּךְ הָעֲגָלוֹת. וּמֵאוֹתָן חִיפּוּפֵי וְלִפְנִים קָרֵי לֵיהּ צִידֵּי רה"ר. פְּלוּגְתָּא דְּרַבִּי אֱלִיעֶזֶר וְרַבָּנַן בְּעֵירוּבִין בְּפֶרֶק "כָּל גַּגּוֹת". דְּהָא לָא שְׁכִיחִי רַבִּים. וְהָוֵי לֵיהּ כְּסִימְטָא, דְּתִיקּוּן בָּהּ מְשִׁיכָה. רַב אַשִׁי אָמַר. מְגָרֵר וְיוֹצֵא דְּקָאָמַר פָּטוּר — לְעוֹלָם בִּרְשׁוּת הָרַבִּים, וּדְקַשְׁיָא לָךְ אִיסּוּר גְּנֵיבָה לֵיכָּא. כְּגוֹן שֶׁצֵּירַף יָדוֹ. הַשְּׁנִיָּה לִפְחוֹת מִשְּׁלֹשָׁה סָמוּךְ לַקַּרְקַע, וּבְיָדוֹ אַחַת גֵּירְרָהּ, וְנָפְלָה לְתוֹךְ חֲבֶרְתָּהּ, וְיָדוֹ קָנְיָא לֵיהּ. כִּדְרָבָא דְּאָמַר רָבָא יָדוֹ שֶׁל אָדָם חֲשׁוּבָה. לְעִנְיַן הַנָּחַת שַׁבָּת, כִּמְקוֹם אַרְבָּעָה עַל אַרְבָּעָה. וְכִי הֵיכִי דִּלְעִנְיַן שַׁבָּת חָשׁוּב מָקוֹם — לְעִנְיַן מִיקְנָא נַמִּי חָשׁוּב מָקוֹם לְמִיקְנֵי, כְּאִילּוּ הִגְבִּיהָהּ לְמַעְלָה מִשְּׁלֹשָׁה. וּמִיהוּ, בִּרְשׁוּת הַיָּחִיד לָא אַגְבָּהָהּ דְּתִיקְנֵי לֵיהּ מִקַּמֵּי דְּלֵיתֵי חִיּוּב שַׁבָּת עֲלֵיהּ, וּבִיאָתָהּ לִרה"ר וּקְנִיָּיתָהּ בָּאִין כְּאֶחָד. וּלְהָכִי מְשַׁנֵּי כְּשֶׁצֵּירַף, דְּלָא תֶּיהֱוֵי הַגְבָּהָה בִּרְשׁוּת הַיָּחִיד, כִּדְקָתָנֵי "מְגָרֵר וְיוֹצֵא". רַב אַחָא מַתְנֵי הָכִי. כְּדַאֲמַרַן, דִּמְשִׁיכָה בִּרְשׁוּת הָרַבִּים לָא קָנֵי, וּמוֹקִים לָהּ כְּשֶׁצֵּירַף יָדוֹ וְקִיבְּלָהּ לְתוֹכָהּ. הָיָה מוֹשְׁכוֹ. בְּגוֹנֵב בְּהֵמָה בִּרְשׁוּת בְּעָלִים קָאֵי, בְּפֶרֶק "מְרוּבֶּה". וּמֵת. הַשּׁוֹר. בִּרְשׁוּת הַבְּעָלִים פָּטוּר. הַגַּנָּב מִלְּשַׁלֵּם כְּלוּם, דְּלָא קָנֵי לְהִתְחַיֵּיב בְּאוֹנָסִין. הִגְבִּיהוֹ. אֲפִי' בִּרְשׁוּת הַבְּעָלִים. הָא הוֹצִיאוֹ. כָּל הֵיכָא דְּאַפְּקֵיהּ, וַאֲפִי' לִרה"ר. אֵלּוּ הֵן הַלּוֹקִין. אִם הִתְרוּ בָּהֶן. וְקַיְימָא לָן דְּאֵין לוֹקֶה וּמְשַׁלֵּם. דְּנָפְקָא לָן לְקַמָּן מִ"כְּדֵי רִשְׁעָתוֹ" — מִשּׁוּם רִשְׁעָה אַחַת אַתָּה מְחַיְּיבוֹ, וְאִי אַתָּה מְחַיְּיבוֹ מִשּׁוּם שְׁתֵּי רִשְׁעָיוֹת. מַתְנִי'

תוספות

מהלך כעומד דמי. ומעביר ארבע אמות דחייב ברה"ר — הלכתא גמירי לה, כדאמרינן ב"הזורק" (שבת דף צו:) ולא ילפינן מינה, דהתם מקום חיובא הוא. אבל בן עזאי מיירי במהלך מחנות לפלטיא דרך סטיו שהוא מקום פטור. ובירושלמי פריך: לבן עזאי היכי משכחת מעביר ד"א ברה"ר דמיחייב? ומשני: בקופץ*. אבל זורק מאי פטור ליפלוג וליתני בדידה. משום הכי חשיב זורק בדידה טפי ממגרר, משום דבמוליא ובזורק בשניהם בא בהגבהה הקנין, קודם שיבא חיוב הולאה. אבל במגרר — ההולאה והקנין באין כאחד. מגרר ויוצא איצטריך ליה. לעיל דפריך: דליפלוג בין לפוש ובין לכתף, לא בעי לשנויי הכי, משום דלכתף פטור נראה לו חידוש טפי מחידוש דמגרר. [ועוד, דהכא לא הוי לגמרי בדידה, אבל לעיל, דהוי ממש בדידה — לא שייך לשנויי הכי].

אי דאפקיה לרה"ר איסור גניבה ליכא. אף על גב דאיכא למ"ד בפ"ק דב"מ (דף י. ושם) דד' אמות קונות לו לאדם אפילו ברה"ר — ה"מ גבי מליאה, דלא ליתו לאנלויי, ובגט משום עיגונא. אבל לגנב — לא תקינו שיקנו לו ד' אמות. אלא במיצעי. תימה לר"י: דבפרק "הספינה" (ב"ב דף פו. ושם) גבי דברים שדרכן להגביהן אין נקנין במשיכה אלא בהגבהה, ופריך מהגונב כיס, דבר הגבהה הוא, ומשני: במידי דבעי מיתנא. משמע דאי הוה אמר דבר הגבהה נמי נקנה במשיכה — הוה אתי ליה שפיר אפילו בזוטרי, ואמאי? הא על כרחך לא מצי איירי בזוטרי, דא"כ היכי מיחייב לענין שבת בגרירה? דאין דרך הולאה בכך? וי"ל: דאפשר שיהא דרך הולאה בכך אפילו בזוטרי, כגון שמוליאו דרך מחתרת, דדרכו בגרירה, ואינו נקנה אלא בהגבהה. אי נמי: הוה מצי למימר ולטעמיך, ולא פריך. וכן דרך התלמוד בכמה מקומות. רב אשי אמר כגון שצירף ידו למטה מג' וקיבלה, וכדרבא. פירש בקונטרס, דקאי אמאי דפריך לעיל איסור גניבה ליכא, והשתא משני דאיכא נמי איסור גניבה, כדרבא. וקשה לר"י: חדא, דמה ענין חשיבות מקום ד' דלענין שבת לקנין? ועוד: דאין צריך שום ראיה להביא דקניא ליה ידו, דפשיטא ד"ונתן בידה" אמר רחמנא, כדפרישית לעיל. ועוד: *) דאמאי לא מוקי אפילו כשצירף ידו למעלה מג', כגון שהאסקופה גבוהה ג' דליכא הגבהה ברה"י, והוה מייתי מדרבא אקנין ואשבת! ונראה כגירסת הספר שמצא ר"י בן רבינו מאיר בספרי אשכנז דגרס: אי נמי כדרבא. וכולה מילתא אשבת קאי, כשצירף ידו למטה מג', דאע"ג דלא חשיבא לענין שבת הנחה אלא על גבי מקום ד', איכא הכא חיוב שבת כשצירף ידו למטה מג', דלמטה מג' לא בעינן מקום ד', דכלבוד דמי, *וכמונחת אארעא דמיא. אי נמי, אפי' צירף ידו למעלה מג', וכדרבא, דידו חשובה כד' על ד'. ור"ת ל"ג דאמר רבא ידו של אדם, אלא וכדרבא, ותו לא. ואתא לשנויי דמגרר ויולא אילטריך ליה לאשמועינן, דאגד יד לא שמיה אגד, והא מייתי כדרבא דאמר ב"המלניע" (שבת דף צב.) דאגד יד לא שמיה אגד. ומיירי כשהוא נשאר בפנים והוליא ידו אחת, ובאחרת מגרר לתוכה. ודוקא צירף למטה מג', דלמעלה משלשה שמיה אגד, דבתר גופו גרירא. [ולפי' קמא קשה: דלשנויא קמא לית ליה דרבא, וכולהו מתנייתא דשבת וכן ר' יוחנן (שבת ה.) אתו כרבא]. וברשות הרבים נמי קנה. והא דאמר ב"המוכר את הספינה" (ב"ב פד:) דאביי ורבא דאמרי תרוייהו דמשיכה לא קניא ברה"ר, אומר ר"י: דלא פליגי אדרבינא דהכא, דהא דקאמר דקני — היינו לענין להתחייב באונסין, אבל אינו קונה שיהא שלו לגמרי. וריב"א נראה לו דפליג, דהא ב"מרובה" (ב"ק דף עט. ושם) גבי נתנה לבכורות בנו דקתני סיפא, איכא נמי למידק כמו שמדקדק כאן. והתם לענין משיכה דקנין איירי, ללשון ראשון שפי' שם בקונט', ואפילו ללשון שני הא מוכח התם בגמ' (דף סה.) שאין לגנב להתחייב אלא במשיכה הראויה לקנין. ורמינהי אלו הן הלוקין הבא על אחותו. ארישא דמתניתין הוה מצי למיפרך, דקתני: הבא על הממזרת יש לה קנס, והתם קתני דלקי עלה, אלא נטר הכא עד "הבא על אחותו" למיפרך מרישא דמתניתין דהתם, דחייבי לאוין שנויין שם בתר חייבי כריתות והיה צריך להביא כל המשנה עד "הבא על הממזרת". וקיימא

*) [ור' אליהו פי' כגון שהאסקופה כרמלית ולהכי לריך כשלירף ידו למטה מג' מגב האסקופה דאי בתוך ג' לראשה הוי כרמלית כמו אסקופה עלמה ולא מחייב. ת"י]

תוספות רי"ד

ע"ש בפסקי: ובמאי. פי' ובמאי איצטריך לאשמועינן דדרך הוצאה בכך אי בגדול שיש בו משוי להגביה אורחיה הוא לגוררו ופשיטא דהוצאה היא ואי בזוטרא לאו אורחי' הוא ואמאי חייב משום שבת (איסור א) גניבה ליכא דמשיכה בלא הגבהה לא קניא ברה"ר) אלא במיצעי. פי' אם היה הכיס קטן שדרכו להוציאו בהגבהה והוציאו בגרירה פטור לענין שבת דהוצאה כלאחר יד הוא. וגם לענין קני' נמי אמרינן בפ' המוכר את הספינה דדברים שדרכן להגביהן אינן נקנים אלא בהגבהה לא במשיכה ומוקמי להא דתני היה מגרר ויוצא במידי דצריך מיתנא. ודאפקוה היכא אי דאפקי' לרה"ר איסור שבת איכא איסור גניבה ליכא פי' (אי) דמשיכה [אינה] קונה ברה"ר ואי דאפקה לרה"י איסור גניבה איכא איסור שבת ליכא ר"א אמר כגון שצירף ידו למטה מג' וקבלה. פי' מכי נפלה לתוך ידו איכא איסור גניבה שידו קונה לו ואיכא איסור שבת שכל פחות מג' כלבוד דמי וכאילו נחה ברשות הרבים דמי פי' המורה: לעולם הא דקתני מגרר ויוצא פטור לעולם דאפקה לרה"ר ודק' לך איסור גניבה ליכא איכא ודאי כגון שצירף ידו השנית לפחות מג' סמוך לקרקע ובידו הא' גוררה והפילה לתוך יד חברתה וידו של אדם קני' ליה כדרבא דאמר ידו של אדם חשובה לו כד' על ד'. פי' לענין הנחת שבת וכי היכי דלענין שבת חשיבא מקום לענין מיקנא נמי חשיב מקום למיקני' כאילו הגביה למעלה מג' מיהו ברה"י לא אגביה דתיקני לי' מקמי דליתי חיוב שבת עלי' ויציאתה וביאתה לרה"ר וקנייתה באין כא' ולהכי משני כשצירף דלא תהוי הגבהה ברשות היחיד כדקתני היה (מכנים) [מגרר] ויוצא. א"נ כדרבא ב) דאמר ידו של אדם חשובה לו כד' על ד'. פי' ואע"פ שהיתה למעלה מג' יש בה איסור שבת דידו של אדם פי' לענין שבת בעינן שיעשה הנחה ע"ג מקום חשוב שיש בו ד' על ד' והיד היא חשובה כד' על ד': רב אחא מתני הכי פי' כדאמרי' דמשיכ' ברה"ר לא קניא ומוקי לה כשצירף ידו וקבלה לתוכה. רבינא מתני לעולם דאפקיה לרה"ר וברה"ר נמי קני. פי' דמשיכה ברה"ר קונה. ואע"ג דקיי"ל דכל היכא דפליגי רב אחא ורבינא הלכתא כרבינא. הכא הלכתא כר"א משום דקיימו כוותיה אביי ורבא בפרק המוכר את הספינה ואמרי שאין משיכה קונה ברה"ר. ותלמודא נמי מקשה ממילתיה וקיי"ל שאין התלמוד מקשה אלא מהלכה פסוקה: הבא על אחותו וכו'. ורמינהו אלו הן הלוקין הבא על אחותו וכו' וקי"ל דאין לוקה ומשלם. פי' דנפקא לן מכדי רשעתו משום רשעה א' אתה מחיבו ולא משום ב' רשעיות. פי' המורה והא דאוקי מתני' דמכות בבוגרת ולא אוקי מתני' דהכא בשלא היתרו בו ש"מ אפילו איתרו ביה נמי ממונא משלם וכו':

א) מתיבת איסור גניבה ליכא עד ברה"ר שייך להלן. ב) גירסת רבינו א"נ כדרבא וכ"ה בתוס' בד"ה רב אשי בשם הריב"ס.

[שבת ה: עירובין לח.]

שבת ה.

שבת ו. עירובין לג.

ב"ק עט.

מכות יג.

גליון הש"ס

תוס' ד"ה רב אשי וכו' דקניא ליה ידו. עי' ב"ק כט ע"ב תוד"ה אלא אמר רב אשי:

[ורש"י פי' דלריך הגבהה הא דלאמרי בהמניח (דף כט:) כשהגביה פחות מג' וקאמר דקני הא פי' התם בקונט' משום דהוי הפקר ואיכא למ"ד הכי בהפקר קני ושיתופי מבואות לאמר שלריך שיגביה טפח התם נמי בעירוב הקולו. ת"י]

וקיימא לן דאינו לוקה ומשלם! אמר עולא: לא קשיא; כאן – באחותו נערה, כאן – באחותו בוגרת. אחותו בוגרת נמי, הא איכא [א]בושת ופגם! [ב]בשוטה. והא איכא [ג]צערא! במפותה. השתא דאתית להכי, אפי' תימא אחותו נערה – ביתומה ומפותה. אלמא קסבר עולא: כל היכא דאיכא ממון ומלקות – ממונא משלם, מילקא לא לקי. מנא ליה לעולא הא? גמר מחובל בחבירו: מה חובל בחבירו, דאיכא ממון ומלקות, ממונא משלם, מילקא לא לקי, אף כל היכא דאיכא ממון ומלקות, ממונא משלם, מילקא לא לקי. מה לחובל בחבירו – שכן חייב בחמשה דברים, ואי ממונא לקולא, שכן הותר מכללו בבית דין! אלא גמר מעדים זוממין, מה עדים זוממין דאיכא ממון ומלקות – ממונא משלם, מילקא לא לקי! אף כל היכא דאיכא ממון ומלקות – ממונא משלם, מילקא לא לקי! [ד]מה לעדים זוממין – שכן אינן צריכים התראה, ואי ממונא לקולא הוא – שכן לא עשו מעשה! אלא, גמר מתרוייהו; מה הצד השוה שבהן – דאיכא ממון ומלקות – ממונא משלם מילקא לא לקי, אף כל היכא דאיכא ממון ומלקות – ממונא משלם, מילקא לא לקי. מה להצד השוה שבהן – *שכן יש בהן צד חמור, ואי ממונא לקולא הוא – שכן יש בהן צד הקל!
אלא

רש"י

מתני' באחותו נערה. דאיכא קנס, וסבירא ליה דממונא משלם ולא לקי. והיא דמכות – בבוגרת, דאין לה קנס. בושת ופגם. דגבי קנס הוא דבעינן נערה, אבל בושת – ממונא הוא. ופגם. כאילו היא שפחה נמכרת בשוק, כמה פיחתה מדמיה להשיאה לעבד שיש לרבו קורת רוח הימנו, כדלקמן (דף מ:). והא בוגרת נמי איתא. בשוטה. שאין לה בושת, ודמים למכור בשוק נמי אין לה. והא איכא צערא. דהכי תנן במתניתין: המפתה נותן בושת ופגם וקנס. מוסיף עליו האונס, שנותן את הצער. במפותה. דאין לה צער, כדאמרי' לקמן בפירקין (ד' לט:): פקחות שבהן אומרות, מפותה אין לה צער. ביתומה. שקנסה ובושתה ופגמה שלה. ומפותה. כיון שהכל שלה – אין כאן חיוב ממון, דהא עבדא מדעתה, ואחולי אחלה גביה. שוטה לא גרסי', דבפקחת נמי אין שום חיוב ממון במפותה יתומה. קסבר עולא. דאוקי מתני' דמכות בבוגרת, ולא אוקמה למתני' דהכא בשלא התרו בו – שמעת מינה: אפי' אתרו ביה, נמי ממונא משלם ולא לקי. חובל בחבירו. איכא מלקות ד"לא יוסיף" (דברים כה), וממונא משלם, כדכתיב (שמות כא) "שבתו יתן". ואפילו אתרו ביה, נמי מרבי ליה לקמן בשמעתין בהדיא לתשלומין. מה לחובל בחבירו. דין הוא לידון בממון שהוא חמור ממלקות, שכן יש בו חומר אחר. שחייב בחמשה דברים. נזק צער ריפוי שבת ובושת. ואי ממונא לקולא הוא. וא"ת: ממון קל מן המלקות, ואין זו תשובה שהשבנו, דכ"ש בעלמא, מה זה שחמור להתחייב בחמשה דברים נדון בקלה שבשני חיובין שבהן – ק"ו לשאר חייבי ממון הקלין, שידונו בממון הקל, איכא למיפרך: מה לחובל בחבירו – שכן הותר מכללו בב"ד, דניתן רשות לב"ד להלקותו. תאמר בשאר חייבי ממון, כגון קנס דאונס ומפתה, שלא הותרו מכללן בב"ד. אלא גמר מעדים זוממים. במה מצינו. דאיכא ממון. ד"כאשר זמם". ומלקות. ד"לא תענה". ממונא משלם. לקמן יליף לה בשמעתין. שכן אין צריכין התראה. ונענשין במיתה או במלקות או בממון, ודין הוא שידונו בחמורה כי איכא תרתי. ואי ממונא קולא הוא. אשכחן בהן צד הקל, ודין הוא שידונו בקלה. שכן לא עשו מעשה. אלא בדיבורא בעלמא מיענשי. מתרוייהו. כי פרכת מה לחובל בחבירו שכן חייב בחמשה דברים – עדים זוממין יוכיחו, מה לעדים זוממין שכן אין צריכין התראה – חובל יוכיח; וחזר הדין.
תחת

[פסחים עז. סוטה כט: מכות ז:]

תוספות

וקיימא לן דאינו לוקה ומשלם. נראה לר"י דלא פריך *אמתני' דהתם אמאי לוקה, דהא פשיטא דמשכחת לה מלקות בלא קנס, כגון בוגרת ומפותה או בעולה, אלא אמתניתין קשיא ליה: אמאי משלם קנס כיון דאיכא מלקות? ואפילו בלא אתרו ביה, מצינן למימר דס"ד דמקשה דחייבי מלקיות שוגגים פטורים מן התשלומין. ומשני עולא דמתניתין אפילו בהתרו בו, דממונא משלם ולא לקי, ורבי יוחנן משני דמיירי בלא התרו בו. ואזיל לטעמיה דאית ליה דחייבי מלקיות שוגגים חייבין בתשלומין. דאין לוקה ומשלם. תימה דבפ"ק דמכות (דף ד: ושם) משמע דבקנס לוקה ומשלם. דקאמר אפלוגתא דר' מאיר ורבנן דמעידין אנו באיש פלוני שחייב לחברו מאתים זוז: בשלמא רבנן – כי טעמייהו, משום רשעה אחת כו'. אלא ר"מ מ"ט? גמר ממוציא שם רע. מה למוציא שם רע – שכן קנס! קסבר ר"מ עדים זוממין נמי קנסא. משמע דלרבנן לא ילפינן ממוציא שם רע, משום דסברי דעדים זוממין ממונא, אבל קנסא ילפינן שפיר ממוציא שם רע דלוקה ומשלם! ועולא גופיה דדחיק הכא לשנויי: כאן באחותו נערה – הוא דמסיק התם הכי. וליכא למימר דמבושת ופגם שהן ממון פריך, דהא מדמשני: כאן באחותו בוגרת, משמע דלאו מבושת ופגם פריך, דא"כ לא הוה משני מידי! וי"ל: כיון דלרבנן דר' מאיר עדים זוממין לאו קנסא הוא, ולכך לא ילפינן ממוציא שם רע, אלא אין לוקין ומשלמין מ"כדי רשעתו", דהשתא אית לן למילף בכל דוכתין מעדים זוממין ולא ממוציא שם רע, דכל מלקיות ילפינן ממלקות דעדים זוממין, דסמיך ליה לאו דחסימה, ד"ארבעים יכנו" בעדים זוממין כתיב, ולפי שמפורש בהן מלקות – ילפינן כולהו לאוי דליהוי דומין ללאו דחסימה דסמיך ליה. וכי היכי דעדים זוממין אין לוקין ומשלמין בכל ענין, בין בממון בין בקנס, דמקרא מלא דבר הכתוב "כדי רשעתו" – משום רשעה אחת אתה מחייבו כו', אפילו נתחייבו קנס כגון בשעה שהעידו טבחו או מכרו שור של גניבה, הם או אחרים בשבילם – הכי נמי בכל מלקיות. ועוד תירץ ריצב"א: דרבנן נמי מלו סברי דעדים זוממין קנסא, ומ"מ לא ילפינן ממוציא שם רע, משום ד"כדי רשעתו" משמע בממון ומלקות. אבל לר"מ, משום בנין אב דמוציא שם רע, מוקי "כדי רשעתו" למיתה ומלקות, ומפיק ליה ממשמעותיה. אי נמי, טעמא דרבנן כדמפרש בירושלמי דמוציא שם רע חידוש הוא, דבדיבור גרידא מיחייב. דאע"ג דעדים זוממין נמי בדיבורייהו מיחייבי – מ"מ לא הוי חידוש כולי האי, דע"י דבורם היה נפסד, אבל במוציא שם רע – לא איתעבד מעשה בדבורו, אלא ע"י עדים. וכן משמע לקמן (דף לה:): דאפילו עדים זוממין קנסא – אין לוקה ומשלם קנס, דאמר: ולרבה דאמר לר"מ חידוש הוא שחידשה תורה בקנס מתני' במאי מוקים להו? ואמאי לא מוקים לה כר' עקיבא, דס"ל בפ' קמא דב"ק (דף ה.): עדים זוממין קנסא הוא, דלדידיה לא שמעינן דאית ליה מת ומשלם! אלא משמע דאין שום תנא דסבר לוקה ומשלם, אלא רבי מאיר לחודיה. אלמא קסבר עולא כל היכא דאיכא ממון ומלקות ממונא משלם מילקא לא לקי. וא"ת מנא ליה להש"ס, דלמא בעלמא סבר דמילקא לקי וממונא לא משלם, והכא דוקא הוא דמשלם ממונא דגלי קרא, כדאמרינן לעיל (דף כט:): "נערה" "נערה" "הנערה"? ואין לומר כמו שפירש ר"ת דאי ס"ל דבעלמא מילקא לקי ולא משלם, הוה ליה לאוקומי מתני' דמכות (דף יג.) נמי באחותו נערה ובהתרו בו, ומתני' בשלא התרו בו, אלא ודאי סבר דבעלמא נמי ממונא משלם ולא לקי, ולהכי לא הוה מצי לאוקומי מתניתין דמכות באחותו נערה. דאין זה דיוק, דאיכא למימר דעולא סבר לה כריש לקיש דלא בעי לשנויי: כאן בהתרו בו, כאן שלא התרו בו, כדאמרינן לקמן, דאין חילוק לדידיה דאית ליה דחייבי מלקיות שוגגין פטורין מן התשלומין בין התרו בו בין לא התרו בו, ואי מרבינן לקנס מקרא בלא התרו ה"ה התרו. ונראה לר"י דע"כ ס"ל ממונא משלם מילקא לא לקי, מדמרבינן מחד קרא חייבי לאוין ומחד חייבי כריתות, דאי בעלמא מילקא לקי, דלמא חד לחייבי עשה וחד לחייבי לאוין אע"ג דבעלמא לוקה ואינו משלם, *אבל חייבי כריתות לא, משום דבעינן אשה שיש בה הויה, וכדרבנן דאמרי קדושין תופסין בחייבי לאוין.

[ועוד פי' ר"ת דדייק דממונא משלם, מדפריך: בוגרת, והא איכא בושת ופגם! ומשני, בשוטה. ולא משני דלוקה ואינו משלם, אלא ודאי סבר דבעלמא נמי ממונא משלם ולא לקי. וקשה, דאין נראה שיהא זה מדברי עולא אלא תלמודא הוא דקאמר ליה! ועוד, מדמסיק: אלא [עולא] "תחת" "תחת" גמר – משמע דבקנס גופיה בעי קרא דממונא משלם ואמאי לא שמעינן מ"נער" "נערה" "הנערה"?! ועוד, מאי קאמר "מנ"ל"? לעולא נימא דיליף בושת ופגם מקנס דרבי קרא! וכ"ת מקנס לא ילפינן, נילף מקנס וחובל ועדים זוממין! ועוד, כיון דאבושת ופגם קאי, מאי קאמר בסמוך: מה לחובל שכן חייב בד' דברים, אטו בושת לאו חובל הוא?! וכמה ענייני חבלות שאין בהן כל ה' דברים כדאמר ב"החובל"!. ומיהו ריב"ם פי' דהכי פריך: מה ללאו דחובל שכן פעמים יש בו כל ה' דברים, תאמר בלאו ד"ערות אחותך לא תגלה" שלעולם אין בו כל ה' דברים?! ופי' ר"י נראה עיקר].

ת"י כ"י

ואי ממונא קולא הוא. וא"ת איתגורי איתגור שנידון בקלה? דהכי פריך בפרק "הנשרפין" (סנהדרין דף פא.) גבי מי שנתחייב שתי מיתות! וי"ל: דשאני הכא דהס רחמנא אממונא של נחבל. שכן יש בהן צד חמור. קשה דא"כ לא נלמד עוד מהצד השוה בשום מקום, דאכולהו איכא למיפרך או צד חמור או צד קל! ונראה לר"י דהכא פריך הכי: שכן יש בהן צד חמור משונה, כי ההיא דבפרק "ד' מיתות" (שם דף סו.): מה להצד השוה שבהן שכן משונין, גבי דיין נשיא וחרש. דהכא חמשה דברים שאין צריכין התראה הוי צד חמור יותר משאר דברים, וצד הקל נמי הוי קולא יתירא בחובל – שהותר מכללו, שמותר לחבול. בחבירו וכן עדים זוממין לא עשו מעשה הוי קולא יתירא, ואפילו למ"ד עקימת שפתים הוי מעשה, הא אמרי' בסנהדרין (דף סה: ושם): שאני עדים זוממין הואיל וישנן בראיה. *ובפרק "כשם" (סוטה כט:) יש לפרש נמי דפריך גבי טבול יום וכלי חרש: מה להצד השוה שבהן שכן צד חמור! דקרי צד חמור משונה: כלי חרש שמטמא באוירו. וטבול יום נמי יש לפרש בדוחק שקורא צד חמור מה שנעשה אב הטומאה במגע, שלא היה נראה שיהיה שום דבר אב הטומאה אלא אם כן טומאה יוצאה מגופו. ועוד יש לומר דצד חמור דהתם, היינו: דאיכא למפרך שכן במינו אב הטומאה, דנהי דכלי חרש אינו נעשה אב מכל מקום
יש

הג"ה עיקר חיובא בא ע"י הראיה שמעידין שראו וראיה לית בה מעשה. לשון רש"י

עין משפט נר מצוה

[נראה איפכא דאמתני' לא קשיא ליה הא דמשלם דהא רבי קרא חייבי לאוין וכריתות דמשלמין אלא אההיא מתני' קשיא ליה אמאי לוקה דמשמע ליה דאיירי התם בנערה דומיא דמתני' ומיהו איכא למימר דפריך אמתני' אמאי משלם בחייבי כריתות כדפי' ר"י בסמוך. ת"י]

יח א מיי' פ"ב מהלכות נערה הלכה יא טור אה"ע סימן קעז:
יט ב מיי' פ"ג מהל' חובל ומזיק הל' ד ופ"ב מהל' נערה הל' יא טור שם טוש"ע ח"מ סי' תכ סעיף לז:
כ ג מיי' פ"א שם הלכה ב סמג עשין ע טור אה"ע שם:
כא ד מיי' פי"ח מהל' עדות הלכה ד סמג עשין קי טור ח"מ סי' לח:

תוספות רי"ד

אמר עולא ל"ק כאן באחותו נערה כאן באחותו בוגרת אחותו נערה דאיכא קנס משלם ולא לקי. בוגרת דליכא קנס לקי פי' המורה מתני' דהכא בנערה. ומתני' דמכות בבוגרת. אלמא קסבר עולא כל היכא דאיכא ממון ומלקות ממונא משלם מילקי לא לקי דגמיר לה מחובל בחבירו ומעדים זוממין דממונא משלם ומילקי לא לקי. פי' חובל בחבירו איכא מלקות בלא יוסיף פן יוסיף. וממונא משלם כדכתיב רק שבתו יתן ואפי' אתרו בי' נמי עדים זוממין נמי (במה) מצינו דאיכא ממון דכאשר זמם ומלקות מלא תענה:

[ורשב"ל נמי לא אוקמי כרבנן משום חייבי כריתות ולר"י דאמר מלקי לקי כר' דסבר ממונא קילא דאי חומרא וכי אתגורי אתגור והשתא א"ש דקאמר מנ"ל הא דע"כ מדמוקי חד לחייבי כריתות נפקא ליה בעלמא דממונא משלם ולא לקי ולפי המסקנא דגמר תחת אילטריך קרא לחייבי עשה דאי לאו ההוא קרא הוי דרשי תחת לדרשא אחריתי ואידך לחייבי כריתות. ת"י]

כב א מיי' פי"ט מהל' סנהדרין הל' ד סי' קלא טוש"ע ח"מ סימן תכ סעיף ב:
כג ב מיי' פ"ד מהל' חובל ומזיק הל' א סמג עשין ע טוש"ע ח"מ סימן תכ סעיף ב:
כד ג מיי' פי"ח מהל' עדות הל' א סמג עשין קי טור ח"מ סי' לח:

יש במינו אב הטומאה יותר מככר שהרי יש בו שום כלי שהוא אב הטומאה, כגון כלי עץ, אבל שום אוכל אינו נעשה אב הטומאה. ועל שני הפירושים קשה לרשב"א: דנימא, התם אוכל ראשון יוכיח שאין במינו אב הטומאה ומטמא תרומה, אף אני אביא שני! וכי תימא: מה לאוכל ראשון שכן עושה שני בחולין? טבול יום יוכיח. וליכא למיפרך נמי השתא שכן משונה, דאין כאן שום שינוי! ונראה לפרש צד חמור דהתם לפי שבאין מכח אב הטומאה, דטבול יום וכלי חרס ואוכל ראשון כולם נגעו באב הטומאה, מה שאין כן בשני דלא נגע אלא בראשון. ור"ת מפרש: דגבי עדים זוממין שייך צד חמור משום דאותו צד חמור של חובל יכול להיות בעדים זוממין, אם העידו על אחד שחבל בחבירו והוזמו, דמשלמין חמשה דברים מה שרצו לחייבו. וצד הקל יש לפרש, שכן לאו דבחובל ועדים זוממין אין בהן כרת אלא לאו גרידא, ולא נגמר מינייהו חייבי כריתות. וכן בפ"ק דמכות (דף ד:): דיליף ממוציא שם רע ועדים זוממין דלאו שאין בו מעשה לוקין עליו, ופריך: מה להצד השוה שבהם שכן צד חמור – יש לפרש כי הכא לרבינו תם ולרבינו יצחק. ובפרק "כיצד צולין" (פסחים דף עז.) גבי "במועדו" ואפילו בטומאה, דאמר: אי כתב בתמיד – שכן כליל, ואי כתב בפסח – שכן כרת, בתרוייהו – שכן יש בהן צד חמור! התם יש שום פירכא אחריתי דלא מצינו למילף במה הצד, ולא חש התלמוד לפרשה, ובטעם מועט מסתלק לומר דצריכי. **אלא** עולא תחת תחת גמר. מצינו למימר לפי מסקנא זו דלא קאמר עולא דממונא משלם ולא לקי – אלא בהנהו תלת דגלי בהו קרא. וליכא למימר דילפינן לעולא בכל דוכתא מ"תחת" "נתינה" "ישלם" "כסף", דמהאי גזירה שוה ילפינן* מיטב בכולהו. דדוקא לענין מיטב נתקבל, שהוא גוף התשלומין, דאם לא כן תקשי לר' יוחנן ולאביי דפליגי אעולא – דאטו מי לית להו גזירה שוה לענין מיטב? והכא לעולא אייתר ליה האי "תחת" למיפטר ממלקות מגזירה שוה דחובל בחברו. הלכך צריך לומר לקמן לעולא דנפקא ליה בושת ופגם מדרבנן.

אֶלָּא, עוּלָּא "תַּחַת" "תַּחַת" גָּמַר, כְּתִיב הָכָא: °"תַּחַת אֲשֶׁר עִנָּהּ", וּכְתִיב הָתָם: °"עַיִן תַּחַת עַיִן", מָה הָתָם, מָמוֹנָא מְשַׁלֵּם מִילְקָא לָא לָקֵי – אַף כָּל הֵיכָא דְּאִיכָּא מָמוֹנָא וּמַלְקוֹת – מָמוֹנָא מְשַׁלֵּם, מִילְקָא לָא לָקֵי. רַבִּי יוֹחָנָן אָמַר: אֲפִי' תֵּימָא אֲחוֹתוֹ נַעֲרָה. כָּאן – שֶׁהִתְרוּ בּוֹ, כָּאן – שֶׁלֹּא הִתְרוּ בּוֹ. אַלְמָא קָסָבַר רַבִּי יוֹחָנָן: כָּל הֵיכָא דְּאִיכָּא מָמוֹן וּמַלְקוֹת, וְאַתְרוּ בֵּיהּ, מִילְקָא לָקֵי, מָמוֹנָא לָא מְשַׁלֵּם. מְנָא לֵיהּ לְר' יוֹחָנָן הָא? אָמַר קְרָא: °"כְּדֵי רִשְׁעָתוֹ" – *"מִשּׁוּם רִשְׁעָה אַחַת אַתָּה מְחַיְּיבוֹ, וְאִי אַתָּה מְחַיְּיבוֹ מִשּׁוּם שְׁתֵּי רִשְׁעָיוֹת, וּסְמִיךְ לֵיהּ "אַרְבָּעִים יַכֶּנּוּ". וַהֲרֵי חוֹבֵל בַּחֲבֵירוֹ, דְּאִיכָּא מָמוֹן וּמַלְקוֹת – מָמוֹנָא מְשַׁלֵּם, מִילְקָא לָא לָקֵי! וְכִי תֵּימָא: הָנֵי מִילֵּי הֵיכָא דְּלָא אַתְרוּ בֵּיהּ, אֲבָל אַתְרוּ בֵּיהּ – מִילְקָא לָקֵי, מָמוֹנָא לָא מְשַׁלֵּם, *וְהָאָמַר ר' אַמִּי א"ר יוֹחָנָן: הִכָּהוּ אהַכָּאָה שֶׁאֵין בָּהּ שָׁוֶה פְּרוּטָה – לוֹקֶה. הֵיכִי דָּמֵי? אִי דְּלָא אַתְרוּ בֵּיהּ – אַמַּאי לוֹקֶה? אֶלָּא פְּשִׁיטָא. דְּאַתְרוּ בֵּיהּ, וְטַעֲמָא – דְּלֵית בָּהּ שָׁוֶה פְּרוּטָה, הָא אִית בָּהּ שָׁוֶה פְּרוּטָה – מָמוֹנָא מְשַׁלֵּם, מִילְקָא לָא לָקֵי! כִּדְאָמַר רַבִּי אֶילְעָא: בְּפֵירוּשׁ רִיבְּתָה תּוֹרָה עֵדִים זוֹמְמִין לְתַשְׁלוּמִין, בהָכָא נָמֵי, בְּפֵירוּשׁ רִיבְּתָה תּוֹרָה חוֹבֵל בַּחֲבֵירוֹ לְתַשְׁלוּמִין. וְהֵיכָא אִיתְּמַר דְּר' אֶילְעָא – אַהָא: *מְעִידִין אָנוּ אֶת אִישׁ פְּלוֹנִי שֶׁחַיָּיב לַחֲבֵירוֹ מָאתַיִם זוּז, וְנִמְצְאוּ זוֹמְמִין – לוֹקִין וּמְשַׁלְּמִין, שֶׁלֹּא הַשֵּׁם הַמְּבִיאָן לִידֵי מַכּוֹת מְבִיאָן לִידֵי תַּשְׁלוּמִין, דִּבְרֵי ר"מ, וַחֲכָמִים אוֹמְרִים: גכָּל הַמְשַׁלֵּם אֵינוֹ לוֹקֶה. וְנֵימָא: כָּל הַלּוֹקֶה אֵינוֹ מְשַׁלֵּם! א"ר אֶילְעָא: בְּפֵירוּשׁ רִיבְּתָה תּוֹרָה עֵדִים זוֹמְמִין לְתַשְׁלוּמִין. הֵיכָן רִיבְּתָה תּוֹרָה? מִכְּדִי כְּתִיב: °"וַעֲשִׂיתֶם לוֹ כַּאֲשֶׁר זָמַם לַעֲשׂוֹת לְאָחִיו". °"יָד בְּיָד" לָמָּה לִי – דָּבָר הַנִּיתָּן מִיָּד לְיָד. וּמַאי נִיהוּ – מָמוֹן. חוֹבֵל בַּחֲבֵירוֹ נָמֵי, מִכְּדִי כְּתִיב: °"כַּאֲשֶׁר עָשָׂה כֵּן יֵעָשֶׂה לּוֹ", "כֵּן יִנָּתֶן בּוֹ" לָמָּה לִי – דָּבָר שֶׁיֵּשׁ בּוֹ נְתִינָה, וּמַאי נִיהוּ – מָמוֹן. וְרַבִּי יוֹחָנָן, מ"ט לֹא אָמַר כְּעוּלָּא? אִם כֵּן בִּטַּלְתָּ °"עֶרְוַת אֲחוֹתְךָ לֹא תְגַלֶּה" חוֹבֵל

תַּחַת תַּחַת גָּמַר. וּגְזֵירָה שָׁוָה מוּפְנָה הִיא, וּלְמֵדִין וְאֵין מְשִׁיבִין. **אֲפִי' תֵּימָא.** הַהִיא דְּמַכּוֹת בַּאֲחוֹתוֹ נַעֲרָה, וּכְשֶׁהִתְרוּ בּוֹ – דְּאִיכָּא מָמוֹן וּמַלְקוֹת, וְאַשְׁמְעִינַן דְּלָקֵי וְלָא מְשַׁלֵּם. וּמַתְנִיתִין דִּכְתוּבּוֹת – בְּשֶׁלֹּא הִתְרוּ בּוֹ, דְּלֵיכָּא מַלְקוֹת. וּסְמִיךְ לֵיהּ אַרְבָּעִים יַכֶּנּוּ. דְּהֵיכָא דְּאִיכָּא שְׁתֵּי רְשָׁעִיוֹת נֶיעֱבַד בֵּיהּ הַכָּאָה. **בְּפֵירוּשׁ רִיבְּתָה.** לְקַמֵּיהּ מְפָרֵשׁ הֵיכָא. **שֶׁלֹּא הַשֵּׁם הַמְּבִיאוֹ** לִידֵי מַכּוֹת כו'. הַמִּקְרָא הַמְּבִיאוֹ לִידֵי מַלְקוֹת אֵינוֹ מְבִיאוֹ לְתַשְׁלוּמִין. מַלְקוֹת מִ"לֹּא תַעֲנֶה", תַּשְׁלוּמִין מִ"כַּאֲשֶׁר זָמַם", וְכֵיוָן דִּשְׁנֵי שֵׁמוֹת הֵן – חַיָּיב עַל שְׁנֵיהֶם. **נֵימָא** כָּל הַלּוֹקֶה אֵינוֹ מְשַׁלֵּם. וְנִידַיְינֵיהּ בְּמַלְקוֹת, מַאי שְׁנָא מָמוֹן דִּפְשִׁיטָא לְהוּ? **יָד בְּיָד.** דִּסְמִיךְ לֵיהּ "לֹא תָחוֹס עֵינֶךָ, נֶפֶשׁ בְּנֶפֶשׁ" וגו'. **כֵּן יִנָּתֶן.** "כַּאֲשֶׁר יִתֵּן מוּם בָּאָדָם" וגו'. **מַאי טַעְמָא לֹא אָמַר כְּעוּלָּא.** דְּגָמַר גְּזֵירָה שָׁוָה לְעוֹנְשׁוֹ מָמוֹן וְלֹא מַלְקוֹת לְכָל חַיָּיבֵי מָמוֹן וּמַלְקוֹת. **אִם כֵּן.** דְּפָטַרְתָּ בָּא עַל אֲחוֹתוֹ מִמַּלְקוֹת – בִּטַּלְתָּ לָאו שֶׁבָּהּ, שֶׁעוֹנֶשׁ לָאו בְּמַלְקוֹת. וּפָרְכִינַן

[מנא ליה לר"י הא. וא"ת: לעיל בעי מנא ליה לעולא דממונא משלם ולא לקי כו' והשתא בעי איפכא! וי"ל: דהכא משום ג"ש ד"תחת" "תחת" קאמר, מנ"ל לר"י דלא דרשינן ג"ש להכי? דג"ש זו נתקבלה לכ"ע בבכורות (דף יב.) לגבי בכור].

שלא השם המביאו לידי מלקות מביאו כו'. פירש בקונטרס: משום דממון ומלקות אתו מתרי קראי, מלקות מ"לא תענה" וממון מ"ועשיתם לו כאשר זמם". וקשה: דכ"ש דאי הוו כתיבי בחד קרא שילקה וישלם – שהיה לוקה ומשלם! ומיהו – שמא יש לפרש לפ"ה משום דממון ומלקות אתו מתרי קראי – אין לנו לבטל פסוק אחד לגמרי ולקיים האחר. אבל אם היו באים שניהם מ"ועשיתם לו כאשר זמם", כגון שהעידו על אחד שהוציא שם רע על אשתו, דבאין לחייבו ממון ומלקות – אין לוקין ומשלמין. ואין נראה לר"י: דלא מסתבר שלא יהו חייבין ממון ומלקות בכה"ג, כיון שרצו לחייבו שניהם! ונראה לר"י לפרש: שלא השם המביאו לידי מכות כו', כלומר שהתשלומין לא נכתבו בסמוך למלקות. דאם היה כתוב באותו פסוק עצמו "לא תענה ואם ענה ועשיתם לו כאשר זמם" – אז ודאי הוה אמינא דה"ל לאו שניתק לעשה, ולא ילקה עליו, אבל עתה שנכתב רחוק זה מזה – לא הוי ניתק לעשה. ולא דמי ללאו דגזילה דחשיב ליה ניתק לעשה בפ' בתרא דמכות (דף טז.) וב"שלוח הקן" (חולין קמא.) אע"ג דעשה ד"והשיב את הגזילה" לא כתיב אצל לאו ד"לא תגזול" – דהתם ודאי ע"כ הוא ניתק לעשה, שהרי עוקר גזילה מתחת ידו, אבל קרא ד"ועשיתם לו כאשר זמם" אינו עוקר הלאו ד"לא תענה", דעל ידי שאנו עושין לו "כאשר זמם" אינו נעקר עדותו, אלא ע"י שהוזם, הלכך לא חשבינן ליה ניתק לעשה, כיון שלא נכתב אחריו סמוך לו. והר"ר שלמה מדרוי"ש מפרש: שלא השם המביאו לידי מכות – דהיינו: "לא תענה", מביאו לידי תשלומין, פי': אינו בא להיות אזהרה לענוש תשלומין, כדאמרינן במכות, דממון לא בעי אזהרה. ועוד: דר' מאיר נפקא ליה אזהרה ל"כאשר זמם" מ"וכל ישראל ישמעו ויראו ולא יוסיפו" כדאמרינן בפ"ק דמכות (דף ד:), שאם היה צריך "לא תענה" לאזהרה ממון – אז לא היה לוקה עליו, דמחד לאו לא הוה ענשינן ליה ממון ומלקות.

[כדמשמע בפ"ק דמכות אהאיא דתנן: מעידין אנו באיש פלוני שחייב מלקות מ' – לוקים שמונים, א' מ"ועשיתם כאשר זמם" וא' מ"לא תענה". וחכ"א: אין סופג אלא מ'. ורבנן האי "לא תענה" מאי עבדי ליה? מיבעיא להו לאזהרת עדים זוממים. ור"מ אזהרה נפקא ליה מ"וכל ישראל וגו'". משמע דאי לאו קרא אחרינא לאזהרה, מ"לא תענה" לא הוה ענשינן ליה תרי מלקיות. ולרבנן, אע"ג ד"לא תענה" לא צריך לאזהרת ממון, מ"מ אינו לוקה ומשלם משום "כדי רשעתו", ולא לקי לרבנן אלא כשמעידים שהוא בן גרושה דליכא כאשר זמם. ואע"ג ד"לא תענה" לאו שאין בו מעשה, ועוד דניתן לאזהרת מיתת ב"ד, הכא גלי קרא דלקי מ"והיה אם בן הכות הרשע"].

מכדי כתיב ועשיתם לו כאשר זמם יד ביד למה לי. וליכא למימר דלמה לי "יד ביד" דמ"ועשיתם לו כאשר זמם" משמע בהדיא ממון, דכמו שהיה רוצה לחייבו ממון כן יתחייב לו ממון? דמצינו למימר ד"כאשר זמם" מיירי במיתה ומלקות אבל בממון – מילקא לקי ממונא לא משלם. ומיהו, קשה לישנא דמכדי כתיב "ועשיתם לו כו'" "יד ביד" למה לי, דמשמע דמייתורא דלא איצטריך לגופיה הוא דמפיק ליה, והא אפילו לא מייתר "יד ביד" משמע שפיר ממון, דליכא לפרושי יד ביד ממש כדנפקא לן ב"החובל" (ב"ק דף פג: ופד.) מ"עין תחת עין". ועוד, הא דקאמר גבי חובל בחבירו: "כן ינתן בו" למה לי, דבר הניתן מיד ליד, ומאי ניהו ממון. אימא הני מילי היכא דלא אתרו ביה דמ"כן ינתן בו" נפקא ב"החובל" נזק ולא מ"כאשר עשה", אבל היכא דאתרו ביה אימא דמילקא לקי? ונראה לר"י דהך סוגיא אתיא כמאן דמפיק התם "עין תחת עין" – ממון, מקרא ד"יד ביד", והיינו דקאמר: מכדי כתיב "ועשיתם לו כאשר זמם" ואי ס"ד *עין תחת עין ממש, א"כ "יד ביד" בעדים זוממין למה לי – מ"כאשר זמם" נפקא! אלא אייתר "יד ביד" למידרש דבר הניתן מיד ליד דהיינו ממון, אבל אי לא אייתר הוה אמינא יד ביד ממש. (א) **חובל** בחבירו מכדי כתיב כאשר עשה כן יעשה לו. דמשמע ממון, כדאוכחן מייתורא ד"יד ביד" כדפרישית. וא"כ "כן ינתן בו" למה לי? והא ליכא למימר דאתא להיכא דלא אתרו ביה, דמ"יד ביד" נפקא, אלא ע"כ לא איצטריך אלא היכא דאתרו ביה. ומיהו הא לא קשיא ליה אמאי איצטריך "כאשר עשה וגו'", דנשנה כאן לשום צורך, כדאמרינן: כל פרשה שנאמרה ונישנית כו'. אבל "כן ינתן בו" למה חזר ושנה שתי פעמים? אלא לומר לך דבר הניתן מיד ליד להיכא דאתרו ביה. והוא הדין דהוה מצי למימר מכדי כתיב "יד ביד" "כן ינתן בו" למה לי. **ורבי** יוחנן מ"ט לא אמר כעולא. והא ליכא למימר דלא שמיע ליה גזירה שוה ד"תחת" "תחת" – דהא ילפינן לה בבכורות* גבי בכור, ובכמה מקומות. **אם** כן בטלת ערות אחותך לא תגלה. וא"ת: כל לאו שאין בו מעשה ולאו הניתק לעשה ביטלנו הלאו כיון שאין לוקין עליו! הא לאו מילתא היא, דההיא לאו בר מלקות הוא, אבל הכא דשייך ביה מלקות, לית לן למידרש גזירה שוה לאפוקי מלקות מיניה, כיון דאיכא לאוקומי גז"ש אמילתא אחריתי.
אלא

תוספות רי"ד

ור"י אמר אפילו תימא באחותו נערה. כאן שהתרו בו כאן שלא התרו בו אלמא קסבר ר"י כל היכא דאיכא ממון ומלקות מילקא לקי ממונא לא משלם פי' המורה. אפילו תימא ההיא דמכות באחותו נערה וכשהתרו בו דאיכא ממון ומלקות דלקי ולא משלם. ומתני' דהכא בשלא אתרו בי' דליכא מלקות כ"א ממון.

הגהות הב"ח

(א) תוס' ד"ה מכדי וד"ה חובל בחבירו נמי מכדי הל"א:

דברים כב
שמות כא
דברים כה
לקמן לו. ב"ק פג: מכות ד: יג:
סנהדרין פה. מכות ע.
מכות ד.
דברים יט
שם
ויקרא כד
שם יח
[ב"ק ה.]
ת"י כ"י
ס"א יד תחת יד ממש
[דף יב. נז.]

חובל בחבירו נמי, א"כ, בטלת °"לא יוסיף פן יוסיף"! עדים זוממין נמי, א"כ, בטלת °"והיה אם בן הכות הרשע"! אלא עדים זוממין אפשר לקיומה בבן גרושה ובן חלוצה. — חובל בחבירו נמי, איכא לקיומה כגון שהכהו הכאה שאין בה שוה פרוטה. אחותו נמי, איכא לקיומה באחותו בוגרת! (א) אמר לך ר' יוחנן: האי "תחת אשר עינה" מיבעי ליה לכדאביי, *דאמר אביי: אמר קרא °"תחת אשר עינה", האי — "תחת אשר עינה", מכלל דאיכא בושת ופגם. ועולא נפקא ליה מדרבא. דאמר רבא: אמר קרא: °"ונתן האיש השוכב עמה לאבי הנערה חמשים כסף", הנאת שכיבה — חמשים, מכלל דאיכא בושת ופגם. רבי *אליעזר אומר: עדים זוממין ממונא משלמי ומילקא לא לקי, משום [א]דלאו בני התראה נינהו. אמר רבא: תדע, ניתרי בהו אימת? ניתרי בהו מעיקרא — [ב]אמרי אישתלין. ניתרי בהו בשעת מעשה — פרשי ולא מסהדי. ניתרי בהו לבסוף — מאי דהוה הוה. מתקיף לה אביי: וניתרי בהו בתוך כדי דבור! מתקיף לה רב אחא בריה דרב איקא: וניתרי בהו מעיקרא, ונרמז בהו רמוזי! הדר אמר אביי: לאו מילתא היא דאמרי: אי סלקא דעתך עדים זוממין צריכין התראה, כי לא מתרינן בהו לא קטלינן להו — מי איכא מידי דאינהו בעו קטיל בלא התראה, ואינהו בעו התראה? הא בעינן "ועשיתם לו כאשר זמם לעשות לאחיו" וליכא. מתקיף לה רב סמא בריה דרב ירמיה: אלא מעתה, בן גרושה ובן חלוצה, דלא מ"כאשר זמם" קא מיתרבי, ליבעי התראה! *אמר קרא: °"משפט אחד יהיה לכם", *משפט השוה לכולכם. רב שישא בריה דרב אידי אמר: חובל בחבירו נמי, ממונא משלם ומילקא לא לקי — מהכא: °"וכי ינצו אנשים ונגפו אשה הרה ויצאו ילדיה", ואמר רבי אלעזר: *במצות שבמיתה הכתוב מדבר, דכתיב: °"ואם אסון יהיה ונתתה נפש תחת נפש". היכי דמי? אי דלא אתרו ביה — אמאי מיקטיל, אלא פשיטא דאתרו ביה, *[ג]ומותרה לדבר חמור הוי מותרה לדבר הקל, ואמר רחמנא: "ולא יהיה אסון ענוש יענש". מתקיף לה רב אשי: ממאי דמותרה לדבר חמור הוי מותרה לדבר הקל, דלמא לא הוי? אם תמצא לומר הוי — ממאי דמיתה חמורה, דלמא

רש"י

ופרכינן. חובל בחבירו. דעל כרחך בממון נידון – תקשי: בטלת לאו ד"לא יוסיף פן יוסיף", שהוא אזהרה למכה את חבירו! והיה אם בן הכות. במסכת מכות (דף ב:) מוקמינן לה בעדים זוממין. אלא. על כרחך, כיון דרבייה קרא לתשלומין, איכא לאוקמא לעונש מלקות דלאו דידיה, במעידין אנו את איש פלוני כהן שהוא בן גרושה. דליכא לאוקמי "כאשר זמם" ולומר יהא הוא בן גרושה תחתיו, אלא סופג את הארבעים. והכי תנן במסכת מכות. וחובל בחבירו נמי מוקמינן ליה בשאין בה שוה פרוטה בכל המשה דברים שבה, כגון שלא פיחתו מכספו וממלאכתו, וריפוי לא הוצרך, ולא צער היה בה, ובשוטה שאין לה בושת. והכא נמי באחותו מצית לאוקמי מלקות דידה בבוגרת. אבל נערה – לישלם ולא לילקי, הואיל וריבתה גזירה שוה ד"תחת" "תחת" לתשלומין. לכדאביי. בשילהי פירקין, דפרכינן: ואימא חמשים אמר רחמנא מכל מילי? ושני אביי: חמשים *כסף נתחדשו תחת קנס העינוי, אבל בושת ופגם שהוא בשאר חובלים – לא כלל כאן. השוכב עמה. קרא יתירא הוא לדרשה, גימא: ונתן לאבי הנערה חמשים כסף. מכלל דבושת ופגם. דלאו מחמת הנאת שכיבה נינהו, שהרי ישנן בשאר חובלים – לא כיילינהו בגוייהו דהני. רבי אלעזר אומר עדים זוממין דממונא משלמי ולא לקו. לא צריכי קרא, דסברא היא דמלקות לא שייך בהו. דלאו בני התראה נינהו. קודם עדות, כדמפ' רבא ואזיל. הלכך, אי איכא למענשינהו – לא מענשינהו אלא ממון, דאין עונש הגוף בלא התראה. ואע"ג דגבי בן גרושה ובן חלוצה ענשינן להו מלקות בלא התראה – התם גזירת הכתוב, דאשכחן בהו מלקות בהדיא "והיה אם בן הכות", ומוקמינן לקרא במידי דלא מצית למענשינהו מ"כאשר זמם". אבל היכא דמצית למיעבד בהו הזמה – לא שייך בהו מלקות. תדע. שאי אפשר להתרות בהם. מעיקרא. יום או שעה קודם שיעידו העדות. אמרי אישתלין. שכחנו ההתראה, הרי שבטלה ההתראה. פרשי ולא מסהדי. אפילו אמת. הואיל ואנו חשודים בעיניכם, מה לנו ולצרה? לבסוף. לאחר שהעידו. מאי דהוה הוה. דכיון שהגיד אינו חוזר ומגיד, ואינן יכולין לחזור. וניתרי בהו בתוך כדי דבור. לאחר שהעידו, דתוך כדי דבור כדבור דמי, ויכולים לחזור. תוך כדי דבור. כדי שאילת שלום. ונרמז רמוזי. בשעת העדות נרמוז להם רמזים על ההתראה להזכירם, ובלשון רך, שלא יקפידו. לאו מילתא היא דאמרי. שיהו עדים זוממין צריכין התראה. ה"ג: דאינהו בעו למיקטל בלא התראה, ואינהו בעו התראה כו'. כאשר זמם. והם זממו להרוג את זה בעדותן שלא היה ולא נברא, ולא התרו בו ההתראה שהעידו עליה. אלא מעתה. דהאי דלא בעו התראה משום "כאשר זמם" הוא, מלקות של זוממי עדות בן גרושה ובן חלוצה. דלאו מכאשר זמם אתי. עונש דידהו, שהרי לא זממו להלקותו אלא לחללו. משפט השוה. וכיון דרוב זוממין לאו בני התראה נינהו, הני נמי לא בעו התראה. במצות שבמיתה. שמתכוין היה להורגו. הכתוב מדבר. דכתיב "אם אסון יהיה", שמתה האשה – "ונתתה נפש", ואע"פ שלא נתכוון אלא לחבירו. ואשמעינן: נתכוון להרוג את זה והרג את זה – חייב. אי דלא אתרו ביה. אם תמיתנו תהרג. לדבר חמור. מיתה. הוי מותרה לדבר הקל. שאם יכנו ולא ימות ילקה, ואפילו הכי אמר רחמנא דכי אין שם חיוב מיתה – יענש דמי ולדות, ואף על גב דאיכא התראה למלקות. אלמא: משלם ואינו לוקה.

נגהיה

תוספות

אלא אפשר לקיומי בבן גרושה או בבן חלוצה. ואם תאמר: אמאי לקו – אעדות דבן גרושה, הא הוי עדות שאין אתה יכול להזימה! ויש לומר: דלא חשיב עדות שאין אתה יכול להזימה אלא במעידין על הטרפה, דאי אפשר לקיומי בשום דבר, לא במיתה ולא במלקות, דגברא קטילא בעו למיקטל. אבל הכא נתקיימה הזמה במלקות*.

מיבעי ליה לכדאביי. ואם תאמר: כיון דאיצטריך "תחת" להך דרשה, א"כ מנא לן מיטב? וי"ל: דיליף מנתינה או מכסף.

ועולא נפקא ליה מדרבא. משמע דרבא סבר כעולא, דרבי יוחנן גופיה הוה דריש כעולא אי לאו משום דמיבעי ליה לכדאביי. וקשה לרשב"א: דבפרק "השוכר את הפועלים" (ב"מ צא. ושם) משמע בהדיא דסבר כרבי יוחנן גבי חוסם פרה ודש בה – לוקה ומשלם, דמוקי לה אביי כרבי מאיר. ורבא אמר לעולם כרבנן, ואתנן אסרה תורה אפי' בא על אמו. פירוש: ומשלם מאת ידי שמים. משמע דבדין לוקה ואינו משלם! ולמאי דפרישי' לעיל – דלמסקנא דווקא בהני תלת אית ליה לעולא דממונא משלם ולא לקי – אתי שפיר, דבעלמא סבר כרבי יוחנן דלוקה ואין משלם, כדדריש רבי יוחנן, וסמיך ליה "ארבעים יכנו".

ניתרי בהו מעיקרא וכו'. ואם תאמר: תיפוק ליה דהויא התראת ספק, דאין אנו יודעין אם מעידים שקר? ויש לומר: דהתראת ספק לא הויא אלא כגון אל תותיר, שאף למותרה עצמו הוא ספק, שסבור שעדיין יש שהות ביום, אבל הכא המותרין יודעין שמעידין שקר.

וניתרי בהו בתוך כדי דבור. ואם תאמר: היכי מצי הדרי בהו? והא בהתראה איכא טפי מכדי דבור, שהוא כדי שאילת שלום! ויש לומר: דכל זמן שעסוקים באותו דבר חשיב הכל תוך כדי דבור, כדאמרינן במכות (דף ו.) דאפי' מעידין מאה, כל אחד תוך כדי דבור של חבירו – חשובין כולן תוך כדי דבור של ראשון, ואם נמצא אחד מהן קרוב או פסול – עדותן בטילה.

אלא פשיטא דאתרו ביה. וא"ת: היכי משלם ממון אפי' כי אין אסון? הא כיון דמתכוין להרוג – הוי ליה רודף, ומתחייב בנפשו, וקים ליה בדרבה מיניה! וי"ל: בשיכולין להצילו באחד מאבריו. והכי אמרינן ב"בן סורר" (סנהדרין דף עד.).

ממאי דמותרה לדבר חמור הוי מותרה לדבר הקל דלמא לא הוי. אין לומר דטעמא משום דאהריגה הוא דקיבל התראה, דניחא ליה ליהרג על מנת שיהרוג שונאו, ד"תמות נפשי עם פלשתים" הוא דקאמר. אבל לא ניחא ליה להכות את חבירו על מנת שילקוהו. דהא אמתני' דפרק "הנשרפין" (סנהדרין ד' עט:) דקתני דחייבי מיתות שנתערבו ידונו בקלה, וקאמר בגמ' (שם דף פ:): ש"מ מותרה לדבר חמור הוי מותרה לדבר הקל. והתם פשיטא דכיון דהתרו בו לסקילה וקבל – כ"ש שאם התרו בו חנק על אותו דבר עצמו שהיה מקבל. ואפ"ה בעי למימר דמותרה לדבר חמור לא הוי מותרה לדבר הקל. אלא יש לומר דגזירת הכתוב הוא, דבעינן שיתיר עצמו לאותה מיתה, בין קלה בין חמורה.

ודלמא

מסורת הש"ס

לקמן מ:

ס"א כסף נתחייבו תחת

[ב"ק פג: פד. סנהדרין כח.]

סנהדרין עב. עט. [וע"ש על הגליון מ"ש בשם התוי"ט]

[סנהדרין פ:]

עין משפט נר מצוה

כה א מיי' פי"ח מהל' עדות הל' ד סמג עשין קי טור ח"מ סי' לח:

[ועיין תוס' מכות ב. ד"ה מעידין וכו' ביתר ביאור]

כו ב ג מיי' פי"ב מהל' סנהדרין הלכה ב [דין דמותרה לדבר חמור לא מצאתי במיי' שם מבואר רק כשהתרו בו בסתם מיתה פסק דהוי התראה והיינו דהוי כמקבל עליו בין מיתה חמורה כגון סקילה ובין קלה אבל כשהתרו בו בחמורה לבד לא נתבאר שם ועי' בתוספות דהכא סד"ה אמאי וכו' דגזירת הכתוב הוא וכו']

[נ"ל אלעזר]

הגהות הב"ח

(א) גמ' אמר לך ר"י נ"ב ס"א אלא ר' יוחנן:

גליון הש"ס

גמ' אמר קרא משפט אחד. עיין מכות דף ד ע"ב ברש"י ד"ה עדים זוממין א"צ התראה וצע"ק:

תורה אור

דִּלְמָא מַלְקוֹת חָמוּר? דְּאָמַר רַב: אִילְמָלֵי נַגְּדוּהּ לַחֲנַנְיָה מִישָׁאֵל וַעֲזַרְיָה – פָּלְחוּ לְצַלְמָא! א"ל רַב סַמָּא בְּרֵיהּ דְּרַב אַסִי לְרַב אַשִׁי, וְאָמְרִי לָהּ רַב סַמָּא בְּרֵיהּ דְּרַב אַשִׁי לְרַב אַשִׁי: וְלָא שָׁנֵי לָךְ בֵּין הַכָּאָה שֶׁיֵּשׁ לָהּ קִצְבָה לְהַכָּאָה שֶׁאֵין לָהּ קִצְבָה?! מַתְקִיף לָהּ רַב יַעֲקֹב מִנְּהַר פְּקוֹד: הָנִיחָא לְרַבָּנַן *דְּאָמְרִי נֶפֶשׁ מַמָּשׁ, אֶלָּא לְרַבִּי דְּאָמַר *מָמוֹן מַאי אִיכָּא לְמֵימַר? אֶלָּא אָמַר רַב יַעֲקֹב מִנְּהַר פְּקוֹד מִשְּׁמֵיהּ דְּרָבָא: מֵהָכָא: °"אִם יָקוּם וְהִתְהַלֵּךְ בַּחוּץ עַל מִשְׁעַנְתּוֹ וְנִקָּה הַמַּכֶּה". *וְכִי תַּעֲלֶה עַל דַּעְתְּךָ שֶׁזֶּה מְהַלֵּךְ בַּשּׁוּק וְזֶה נֶהֱרָג? [א]אֶלָּא מְלַמֵּד שֶׁחוֹבְשִׁין אוֹתוֹ, וְאִי מִית – קָטְלִינַן לֵיהּ, וְאִי לָא מִית – "שִׁבְתּוֹ יִתֵּן וְרַפֹּא יְרַפֵּא". הֵיכִי דָּמֵי? אִי דְּלָא אַתְרוּ בֵּיהּ – אַמַּאי מִיקְטִיל? אֶלָּא פְּשִׁיטָא – דְּאַתְרוּ בֵּיהּ, וּמוּתְרֶה לְדָבָר חָמוּר מוּתְרֶה לְדָבָר הַקַּל, וְאָמַר רַחֲמָנָא "שִׁבְתּוֹ יִתֵּן וְרַפֹּא יְרַפֵּא". מַתְקִיף לָהּ רַב אַשִׁי: מִמַּאי דְּמוּתְרֶה לְדָבָר חָמוּר הָוֵי מוּתְרֶה לְדָבָר הַקַּל? דִּלְמָא לָא הָוֵי, וְאִם תִּמְצָא לוֹמַר הָוֵי – מִמַּאי דְּמִיתָה חֲמוּרָה, דִּלְמָא מַלְקוֹת חָמוּר? דְּאָמַר רַב: אִילְמָלֵי נַגְּדוּהּ לַחֲנַנְיָה מִישָׁאֵל וַעֲזַרְיָה פָּלְחוּ לְצַלְמָא! א"ל רַב סַמָּא בְּרֵיהּ דְּרַב אַסִי לְרַב אַשִׁי, וְאָמְרִי לָהּ רַב סַמָּא בְּרֵיהּ דְּרַב אַשִׁי לְרַב אַשִׁי: וְלָא שָׁנֵי לָךְ בֵּין הַכָּאָה שֶׁיֵּשׁ לָהּ קִצְבָה לְהַכָּאָה שֶׁאֵין לָהּ קִצְבָה? מַתְקִיף לָהּ רַב מָרִי: מִמַּאי דִּבְמֵזִיד "וְנִקָּה" מִקְטָלָא, דִּלְמָא בְּשׁוֹגֵג "וְנִקָּה" מִגָּלוּת? קַשְׁיָא.§ רֵישׁ לָקִישׁ אָמַר: הָא מַנִּי – רַבִּי מֵאִיר הִיא, *דְּאָמַר: לוֹקֶה וּמְשַׁלֵּם. אִי רַבִּי מֵאִיר – אֲפִי' בִּתּוֹ נַמִּי! וְכִי תֵּימָא ר' מֵאִיר לוֹקֶה וּמְשַׁלֵּם אִית לֵיהּ, מֵת וּמְשַׁלֵּם – לֵית לֵיהּ, וְלָא? וְהָתַנְיָא: גָּנַב וְטָבַח בְּשַׁבָּת, גָּנַב וְטָבַח לַעֲבוֹדָה זָרָה, גָּנַב שׁוֹר הַנִּסְקָל וּטְבָחוֹ – (ב)מְשַׁלֵּם תַּשְׁלוּמֵי אַרְבָּעָה וַחֲמִשָּׁה, דִּבְרֵי רַבִּי מֵאִיר, וַחֲכָמִים פּוֹטְרִין. הָא אִיתְּמַר עֲלָהּ, אָמַר רַבִּי יַעֲקֹב א"ר יוֹחָנָן, וְאָמְרִי לָהּ אָמַר רַבִּי יִרְמְיָה אָמַר ר' שִׁמְעוֹן בֶּן לָקִישׁ: ר' אָבִין וְרַבִּי אֶלְעָא וְכָל חֲבוּרָתָא מִשְּׁמֵיהּ דְּרַבִּי יוֹחָנָן אָמְרִי: [ג]בְּטוֹבֵחַ עַל יְדֵי אַחֵר. וְכִי זֶה חוֹטֵא וְזֶה מִתְחַיֵּיב? אָמַר רָבָא, אָמַר רַחֲמָנָא: °"וּטְבָחוֹ אוֹ מְכָרוֹ" *[ד]מַה מְּכִירָה עַל יְדֵי אַחֵר – אַף טְבִיחָה עַל יְדֵי אַחֵר. דְּבֵי רַבִּי יִשְׁמָעֵאל תָּנָא: "אוֹ" – לְרַבּוֹת אֶת הַשָּׁלִיחַ. דְּבֵי חִזְקִיָּה תָּנָא: "תַּחַת" – לְרַבּוֹת אֶת הַשָּׁלִיחַ. *מַתְקִיף לָהּ מָר זוּטְרָא: מִי אִיכָּא מִידֵי דְּאִילּוּ עָבֵד אִיהוּ לָא מִיחַיַּיב, וְעָבֵיד שָׁלִיחַ וּמִחַיַּיב? אִיהוּ לָאו מִשּׁוּם דְּלָא מִיחַיַּיב, [ה]אֶלָּא מִשּׁוּם דְּקָם לֵיהּ בִּדְרַבָּה מִינֵּיהּ. אִי בְּטוֹבֵחַ עַל יְדֵי אַחֵר, מַאי טַעֲמַיְיהוּ דְּרַבָּנַן דְּפָטְרִי? *מַאן חֲכָמִים – רַבִּי

שמות כא | שם

רש"י

נַגְּדוּהּ. יִסּוּרִין. וְלָא שָׁנֵי לָךְ כו'. יִסּוּרֵי הַמַּלְכוּת – הַכָּאָה שֶׁאֵין לָהּ קִצְבָה הִיא. אֲבָל מַלְקוֹת יֵשׁ לָהּ קִצְבָה – אַרְבָּעִים. הָנִיחָא לְרַבָּנַן דְּאָמְרִי. בְּסַנְהֶדְרִין, בְּ"אֵלּוּ הֵן הַנִּשְׂרָפִים" (עט.): נִתְכַּוֵּון לַהֲרוֹג אֶת זֶה וְהָרַג אֶת זֶה – חַיָּיב, וְהַאי "וְנָתַתָּ נֶפֶשׁ" – מַמָּשׁ קָאָמַר, אִית לָן לְמֵידַק וְאוֹקְמֵי קְרָא בְּשֶׁהִתְרוּ בּוֹ, וּלְמֵילַף דְּאַע"ג דְּאִיכָּא הַתְרָאָה – יֵעָנֵשׁ מָמוֹן כְּשֶׁאֵין שָׁם מִיתָה. אֶלָּא לְרַבִּי דְּאָמַר. הָתָם: נִתְכַּוֵּון לַהֲרוֹג אֶת זֶה וְהָרַג אֶת זֶה – אֵינוֹ נֶהֱרָג, אֶלָּא מְשַׁלֵּם דְּמֵי הָאִשָּׁה לְיוֹרְשֶׁיהָ, אִם כֵּן אֶפְשָׁר לְאוֹקְמֵי קְרָא בְּשֶׁלֹּא הִתְרוּ בּוֹ, וּמִשּׁוּם הָכִי, כִּי אֵין אָסוֹן מְשַׁלֵּם דְּמֵי וְלָדוֹת, וְכִי יֵשׁ אָסוֹן מְשַׁלֵּם דְּמֵי אִשָּׁה. אֲבָל אַתְרוּ בֵּיהּ – אֵימָא לָךְ לוֹקֶה וְאֵינוֹ מְשַׁלֵּם. מַאי אִיכָּא לְמֵימַר. מֵהֵיכָא תֵּיתֵי חוֹבֵל בַּחֲבֵירוֹ לְתַשְׁלוּמִין, וְאַף כְּשֶׁהִתְרוּ בּוֹ? עַל מִשְׁעַנְתּוֹ. כִּדְמְתַרְגְּמִינַן: "עַל בּוּרְיוֹ", שֶׁשָּׁב לְכֹחוֹ וּלְאֵיתָנוֹ הָרִאשׁוֹן. אֶלָּא מְלַמֵּד שֶׁחוֹבְשִׁין אוֹתוֹ. לֹא נֶאֱמַר מִקְרָא זֶה אֶלָּא לְלַמֶּדְךָ דְּהֵיכָא דְּהִכָּהוּ וְלֹא מֵת וְנָפַל לְמִשְׁכָּב – יַחְבְּשׁוּ אֶת הַמַּכֶּה הַהוּא בְּבֵית הָאֲסוּרִין, עַד שֶׁנִּרְאֶה: "אִם יָקוּם וְהִתְהַלֵּךְ בַּחוּץ", אָז "וְנִקָּה הַמַּכֶּה". מִכְּלָל דְּעַד הַשְׁתָּא לֹא יָצָא מִידֵי בֵּית דִּין, אֶלָּא נֶחְבָּשׁ. וְאִי מָיֵית קָטְלִינַן לֵיהּ. [כֵּיוָן דְּאָמְרַתְּ חוֹבְשִׁין, מִכְּלָל דְּאִי מָיֵית נִיזָּק – קָטְלִינַן לֵיהּ לְהַאי. דְּאִי לָאו לְקַטְלָא, לְמַאי חָבְשִׁינַן לֵיהּ? לְדָבָר חָמוּר. מִיתָה. לְדָבָר הַקַּל. מַלְקוֹת דְּ"לֹא יוֹסִיף" דְּחוֹבֵל וְלֹא מֵת]. וְאָמַר רַחֲמָנָא. לְהֵיכָא דְּלֹא מֵת, דְּאִיכָּא מָמוֹן וּמַלְקוֹת – נִידּוֹן בְּמָמוֹן, דִּכְתִיב "שִׁבְתּוֹ יִתֵּן". מִמַּאי. דְּהַאי "וְהִכָּה אִישׁ אֶת רֵעֵהוּ" בְּמֵזִיד קָא מִשְׁתָּעֵי, וְהַאי "וְנִקָּה" דִּילְפִינַן מִינֵּיהּ חֲבִישָׁה – וְנִקָּה מִקְּטָלָא קָאָמַר, דְּתִשְׁמַע מִינֵּיהּ דְּאִי מָיֵית קָטְלִינַן לֵיהּ, וְעַל כָּרְחִין בְּהִתְרוּ בּוֹ. דִּלְמָא בְּשׁוֹגֵג. מִשְׁתָּעֵי, וְלֹא הִתְרוּ בּוֹ. וַחֲבִישָׁה לָאו לְקַטְלָא, "וְנִקָּה" נַמִּי לָאו לְקַטְלָא, אֶלָּא מִגָּלוּת דְּעָרֵי מִקְלָט. וַחֲבִישָׁה דִּילְפִינַן מִינָּהּ לְגָלוּת קָאָמַר, וּמִשּׁוּם הָכִי כִּי נִקָּה מִגָּלוּת – יְשַׁלֵּם מָמוֹן. אֲבָל הֵיכָא דְּאַתְרוּ בֵּיהּ, אֵימָא לָךְ דְּכִי לָא מָיֵית – לוֹקֶה וְאֵינוֹ מְשַׁלֵּם. רֵישׁ לָקִישׁ מְהַדַּר אַשִּׁינּוּיָא דְּרוּמְיָא דְּרָמֵינַן בְּרֵישׁ שְׁמַעְתִּין מַתְנִי' דְּמַכּוֹת אַדִּכְתוּבּוֹת. הָא מַנִּי. מַתְנִיתִין דְּקָתָנֵי בָּא עַל אֲחוֹתוֹ נוֹתֵן קְנָס – ר"מ הִיא דַּאֲמַר לְעֵיל לוֹקֶה וּמְשַׁלֵּם, שֶׁלֹּא הַשֵּׁם הַמְּבִיאוֹ לִידֵי מַכּוֹת מְבִיאוֹ לִידֵי תַּשְׁלוּמִין. אֲפִי' בִּתּוֹ נַמִּי. דְּמִיקְטִיל עֲלָהּ, לִישַׁלֵּם. דְּהָא לָא סְבִירָא לֵיהּ לְר"מ דְּפָטוּר מִשּׁוּם דְּרַבָּה מִינֵּיהּ, וְאַמַּאי תְּנַן מַתְנִי' הַבָּא עַל בִּתּוֹ פָּטוּר מִן הַקְּנָס? וְטָבַח בְּשַׁבָּת. אִיכָּא חִיּוּב מִיתָה, וְכֵן לַעֲבוֹדָה זָרָה. שׁוֹר הַנִּסְקָל. לְקַמָּן פָּרֵיךְ: הָא לֹא שָׁוֶה מִידֵי. בְּטוֹבֵחַ עַל יְדֵי אַחֵר. הַגַּנָּב נָוֶה לִשְׁלוּחוֹ לִשְׁחוֹט. וְכִי. שָׁלִיחַ חוֹטֵא, וְשׁוֹלֵחַ מִתְחַיֵּיב קְנָס דְּאַרְבָּעָה וַחֲמִשָּׁה? וְהָא קַיְימָא לָן בְּקִדּוּשִׁין (מב:): אֵין שָׁלִיחַ לִדְבַר עֲבֵירָה. מְכִירָה אִי אֶפְשָׁר אֶלָּא ע"י אַחֵר, שֶׁהַלּוֹקֵחַ לוֹקְחוֹ מִמֶּנּוּ. תַּחַת הַשּׁוֹר. מָלֵי לְמִכְתַּב "יְשַׁלֵּם בַּשּׁוֹר". עָבֵד אִיהוּ לָא מִיחַיַּיב. דְּהָא מִיקְטִיל. לָאו מִשּׁוּם דְּלָא מִיחַיַּיב הוּא. דְּחִיּוּבָא רָמְיָא עֲלֵיהּ, אֶלָּא מִשּׁוּם דְּקָם לֵיהּ בִּדְרַבָּה מִינֵּיהּ. רַבִּי

תוספות

ודלמא מלקות חמור. הוה מצי לשנויי: מסתברא מיתה חמורה שכן ניתנה לאנשי עיר הנידחת, כדאמרי' בפ' "ד מיתות" (סנהדרין נ.). **אילמלי** נגדוה לחנניה מישאל ועזריה הוו פלחי לצלמא. תימה מנא לן (א) דהא אמרי' בהרואה (ברכות סא:) כשהוציאו את ר"ע אמר כל ימי הייתי מצטער על פסוק זה אימתי יבא לידי ואקיימנו בכל נפשך אלמא משמע דבכל נפשך איירי אפי' היו מייסרין את האדם ביסורין קשין דומיא דר' עקיבא שהיו מסרקין בשרו במסרקי ברזל וכ"ש לנגודי ואור"ת דאותו צלם לא היה עבודה זרה ממש אלא היה עשוי לכבוד המלך ואעפ"כ היה בו קידוש השם ולכך מסרו עצמן למיתה, והיינו דכתיב (דניאל ג) "לאלהך לית אנן פלחין ולצלם דהבא די אקימת לא נסגוד" משמע שהצלם לא היה תופס באלהות. ומיהו, "פלחו לצלמא" משמע שהצלם היה עבודה זרה, מדקאמר "פלחו"*.

דלמא בשוגג ונקה מגלות. תימה לר"י: היכי שייך גלות אם מת אחר שחבשוהו ב' או שלשה ימים? הא אמרינן ב"מי שאחזו" (גיטין ע: ושם): שחט בו שנים או רוב שנים – הרי זה אינו גולה, דחיישינן שמא הרוח בלבלתו. וטעמא, דגבי גלות אשכחן מילי טובא דפטור, כגון דרך עלייה, דגבי מיתה אין חילוק בין דרך עלייה לדרך ירידה. הכי נמי גבי גלות בעינן שימות מיד, כדכתיב "ויפל עליו וימות" משמע מיד. ואע"ג דגבי מיתה נמי כתיב "מכה איש ומת" – וי"ל: דמשכחת לה בביאה דשישא, דלא חיישינן שמא הרוח בלבלתו, כדאמרינן התם. אי נמי: דוקא בשחט בו רוב שנים חיישינן שמא הרוח בלבלתו, דבקל הרוח מבלבלו, אבל בשאר חבלות – אין הרוח מזיק כל כך, שיכולין לשמור יפה מבלבול רוח, לכרוך על המכה שום דבר. וא"ת: היכי מיתוקם קרא בשוגג? הא כתיב שבת בקרא "רק שבתו יתן וגו'" ובשוגג לא מיחייב, כדאמרינן בס"פ "כיצד הרגל" (ב"ק כו: ושם) דמרבה מ"פצע תחת פצע" לחייב על השוגג כמזיד נזק, אבל לא ד' דברים! וי"ל: דמשכחת לה בהוסיף לו רצועה אחת, דאמר ב"המניח" (שם לב:) דגולה, ואם לא מת – חייב בד' דברים, ולא דמי לשאר שוגג. או כגון שנכנס לחנותו של נגר (שלא) ברשות, דמוכח התם לרב פפא דשייך ביה גלות וד' דברים. או נפל מן הגג ברוח מצויה דחייב בד' דברים כדאמרי' בסוף "כיצד הרגל" (שם כז.) ומסתברא דאם מת – דגולה. ועוד, דאפשר דהוי שוגג על המיתה ומזיד על החבלה*. **גנב** שור הנסקל וטבחו משלם תשלומי ד' וה'. תימה: דתיקשי מהכא לריש לקיש, דאמר בפ' "מרובה" (שם עו: ושם): כל היכא דליתיה במכירה ליתיה בטביחה, והכא שור הנסקל ליתיה במכירה! וי"ל: דהתם קדשים אמירי, דליתנהו כלל במכירה! אבל שור הנסקל, אם ימכרנו לגוי אין תופס דמיו. ולר"ת שאומר דאין שור הנסקל ⊕נאסר מחיים ניחא. **לאו** משום דלא מיחייב כו'. אע"ג דהכא אפי' לצאת ידי שמים אינו חייב, דדוקא בממון הוא דאמר רבא ב"השוכר את הפועלים" (ב"מ נא. ושם): אתנן אסרה תורה אפי' בא על אמו, דמיחייב בבא לצאת ידי שמים. אבל קנס לא מיחייב אלא ע"פ ב"ד, כדאמרי': "אשר ירשיעון אלהים" – פרט למרשיע עצמו. מ"מ ניחא, דכיון שהיה ראוי להתחייב אם לא היה מתחייב בנפשו – מתחייב נמי אממון ע"י שליח, כיון שאינו מתחייב בנפשו. רבי

עין משפט נר מצוה

כז א מיי' פ"ד מהל' רוצח ושמירת נפש הל' ג:

כח (ב) ג מיי' פ"ג מהל' גניבה הל' ו:

כט ד מיי' פ"ב שם הל' י:

ל ה מיי' פ"ג שם ה"ג

[וע"ע תוס' פסחים נג: ד"ה מה ראו ותוס' ע"ז ג. ד"ה שלא]

רש"א מ"ז

[וע"ע תוס' יבמות קכ: ד"ה אלא וד"ה חיישינן ותוס' גיטין ע: ובשבועות לג. ד"ה ע"פ]

הגהות הב"ח

(א) תוס' ד"ה אילמלי כו' מנא לן ועוד דהא:

מסורת הש"ס

[סנהדרין עט.]

[שם]

שם עח: [תוס' דב"ק פ"ט]

[לקמן לד: לז.] ב"ק ע: ב"מ לא.

קדושין מג. ב"ק עא. [ע"ע]

ב"ק עא.

[עירובין פג. וש"נ]

גליון הש"ס

תוס' ד"ה גנב וכו' נאסר מחיים ניחא. עי' זבחים דף עא ע"א תוס' ד"ה (בעמוד הקודם) אפי':

תורה אור

ר' שמעון היא, *דאמר: אשחיטה שאינה ראויה – לא שמה שחיטה. התינח עבודה זרה ושור הנסקל, אלא שחיטת שבת – שחיטה ראויה היא, דתנן: *בהשוחט בשבת וביום הכפורים, אע"פ שמתחייב בנפשו – שחיטתו כשרה! סבר לה כר' יוחנן הסנדלר, *דתניא: *המבשל בשבת, בשוגג – יאכל, במזיד – לא יאכל, דברי ר"מ. ר' יהודה אומר: גבשוגג – יאכל למוצאי שבת, במזיד – לא יאכל עולמית. רבי יוחנן הסנדלר אומר: בשוגג – יאכל למוצאי שבת לאחרים, ולא לו. במזיד – לא יאכל עולמית, לא לו ולא לאחרים. מאי טעמא דרבי יוחנן הסנדלר? כדדריש ר' חייא אפיתחא דבי נשיאה: °"ושמרתם את השבת כי קדש היא לכם". מה קודש אסור באכילה אף מעשה שבת אסורין באכילה. אי מה קודש אסור בהנאה אף מעשה שבת אסור בהנאה – ת"ל: "לכם", שלכם יהא. יכול אפילו בשוגג – ת"ל: "מחלליה מות יומת", במזיד אמרתי לך, ולא בשוגג. פליגי בה רב אחא ורבינא: חד אמר: מעשה שבת דאורייתא, וחד אמר: דרבנן, מאן דאמר דאורייתא – כדאמרן. מאן דאמר דרבנן – אמר קרא: "קדש היא" – *היא קודש, דואין מעשיה קודש. ולמאן דאמר דרבנן, מאי טעמייהו דרבנן דפטרי? כי קא פטרי רבנן – אשארא. טובח לעבודה זרה, *כיון דשחט ביה פורתא איתסר ליה, אידך כי קא טבח – לאו דמריה קא טבח! אמר רבא: *באומר "בגמר זביחה הוא עובדה". שור הנסקל – לאו דידיה הוא דקטבח! אמר רבה: הכא במאי עסקינן – כגון שמסרו לשומר, והזיק בבית שומר, ונגמר דינייה בבית שומר, וגנבו גנב מבית שומר. ורבי מאיר סבר לה כר' יעקב, וסבר לה כר"ש; סבר לה כר' יעקב – *דאמר: אף משנגמר דינו, החזירו שומר לבעליו – מוחזר. וסבר לה כר"ש, *דאמר: הדבר הגורם לממון כממון דמי. רבה אמר: לעולם בטובח על ידי עצמו, ור'

רש"י

רבי שמעון. בפרק "מרובה" וב"כסוי הדם" וב"אותו ואת בנו". התינח עבודה זרה. דזבחי מתים אסורים, וכן שור הנסקל, דמשנגמר דינו אסור בהנאה, כדאמרינן בב"ק (דף מא.) ובפסחים (דף כב:): ממשמע שנאמר "סקול יסקל" איני יודע שהוא נבילה, ונבילה סו'? בשוגג יאכל. אפי' בו ביום. במזיד לא יאכל. הוא לעולם, אבל אחרים ישראלים – אוכלים. ר' יהודה אומר בשוגג יאכל. הוא למוצאי שבת, ולא בו ביום. דקנסינן שוגג אטו מזיד. במזיד לא יאכל. הוא עולמית, אלא אחרים. כדרבי יוחנן הסנדלר גרסינן יאכל. לאחרים. לישראל. לא לו ולא לאחרים. ישראל, אבל מוכרו ונותנו לגוים. מ"ט דר' יוחנן הסנדלר. דאמר: מעשה שבת אסורין באכילה. יכול אפילו בשוגג. תאסר באכילה, אם שגג בבשול, שלא ידע שהוא שבת. מחלליה וגו'. היכא דאיכא חיוב מיתה אסירי באכילה כי קודש. במזיד אמרתי. שהוא אסור כקודש, דהא גבי חיוב מיתה כתיב, ולא בשוגג. מעשה שבת. במזיד אסורין מן התורה באכילה, לר' יוחנן הסנדלר. מ"ט דרבנן. דפליגי אדרבי מאיר, ופטרי מקנס ארבעה וחמשה, הואיל ובטובח על ידי אחר אוקימתא – הא שחיטה ראויה היא מדאורייתא. אשארא. אעבודה זרה ואשור הנסקל. כיון דשחט ביה פורתא איתסר ליה. דאמר מר (חולין דף מ.): השוחט בהמת חבירו רבולה לפני עבודה זרה, כיון ששחט בה סימן אחד – אסרה. לאו דמריה קא טבח. דהא איתסרא עליה. וחיובא דתשלומי ארבעה וחמשה "טביחה" כתיב בהו, ועד גמר שחיטה לא מיחייב. ומקמי דלמטי גמר שחיטה איתסרא בהנאה על בעליה, ומההיא שעתא אפסדה מיניה, דאי איתא – לא הדרא בעינא, ולאו דמריה היא. באומר בגמר זביחה הוא עובדה. לעבודה זרה, אינו עובד לעבודה זרה עד גמר זביחה. פלוגתא דר' יעקב בבבא קמא. החזירו שומר לבעליו מוחזר. דאמר ליה: תורא אשלמת לי – תורא אשלימית לך. בממון דמי. והאי נמי, אע"ג דלא שוי מידי – גורם לממון הוא, דכי ליתא בעי לשלומי ליה תורא מעליא. דר' שמעון בבבא קמא, בפרק "מרובה": קדשים שחייב באחריותן משלם ארבעה וחמשה, משום דגורם לממון הוא, ואע"ג דהקדש לאו ממון בעלים הוא, ובהקדש לא שייך קנס, ד"רעהו" כתיב. רבה גרסינן בכולהו. ותדע, מדאמר לקמן: א"ל רב פפא לאביי: לרבה דאמר חידוש הוא כו', ואם איתא דרבא גרסינן – הא רב פפא תלמידו של רבא היה, כדאמר לקמן: אמר ליה רב פפא לרבא: הי מכה? מאי שנא דשבקיה לרבא ולא שייליה [לתרולי שמעתיה], ושייליה לאביי [שמעתא דרבא]? אלא רבה גרסינן. ורב פפא לא היה בימיו, ושייל לאביי שהיה תלמידו של רבה. רבה אמר לעולם בטובח בעצמו ור'

תוספות

רבי שמעון היא דאמר שחיטה שאינה ראויה לא שמה שחיטה. תימה: דעד כאן לא פליגי רבנן התם גבי אותו ואת בנו אלא כדמפרש התם בחולין (דף פה.) טעמא: דנין שחיטה משחיטה, פירוש: משחוטי חוץ, ואין דנין שחיטה מטביחה. אבל הכא, גבי תשלומי ד' וה' דכתיב טביחה – אית לן למילף טביחה מטביחה, ולא שמה שחיטה! ואור"י: דאיכא למימר דנין דבר הנאמר בסיני, מדבר הנאמר בסיני ואין דנין דבר הנאמר בסיני מ"טבוח טבח והכן" שלא נאמר בסיני. והתם נמי, ה"מ למימר הכי, אלא דאית ליה שינויא אחרינא. א"נ י"ל: דצריך שינויא, דהתם דנין שחיטה משחיטה, דאי הוה כתיב טביחה גבי אותו ואת בנו – הוה ילפינן הכא והתם מ"טבוח טבח והכן" טביחה מטביחה, אע"ג דלא נאמרה בסיני, דהוי בדדמי, מדנילף טביחה משחיטה דלא דמי אע"ג דנאמרה בסיני. אבל השתא דכתיב שחיטה גבי אותו ואת בנו – דנין שחיטה משחיטה. וילפינן נמי השתא אטביחה דד' וה'. ואיפכא ליכא למימר דנין טביחה דתשלומי ד' וה' מטביחה, ולמילף מהתם אשחיטה דאותו ואת בנו, דכיון דשקולים הן, ואיכא למילף הכי ואיכא למילף הכי, אית לן למימר: דנין דבר הנאמר בסיני ממה שנאמר בסיני*.

המבשל בשבת בשוגג יאכל. פי': בו ביום, ואפילו הוא, כדמוכח בפ' "כירה" (שבת לח.) דבעו מרבי חייא בר אבא: שכח קדירה על גבי כירה ובשלה בשבת כו', עד המבשל בשבת כו' בשוגג יאכל. ולאותו שבת קא בעי התם, אי אסיר גזרה שלא יאמר "שוכח אני". במזיד לא יאכל – פירוש: בין הוא בין אחרים בו ביום, אבל במוצאי שבת – לדידיה נמי שרי, דהא בפ' קמא דחולין (דף טו. ושם) אההיא מתני' דהשוחט בשבת וביה"כ, אע"פ שמתחייב בנפשו – שחיטתו כשרה, פריך: ונוקמא במזיד ור' מאיר ומשני: לא סלקא דעתין, דקתני שבת דומיא דיה"כ, מה יה"כ לא שנא שוגג ול"ש מזיד. והשתא, אי לאחרים שרי בו ביום – לפרוך ממזיד גופיה: מה יוה"כ לא שנא לו ולא שנא לאחרים כו', ואי לדידיה אסור אף למוצאי שבת – הוה ליה למימר: שחיטתו כשרה קתני, ל"ש לו לא שנא לאחרים, כדקאמר התם על ר' יוחנן הסנדלר. ועוד: דא"כ היינו מזיד דר' יהודה, כמו שאפרש. ומדאצטריך לרבי יהודה לאפוקי מזיד במילתיה – משמע דפליג נמי אמזיד. בשוגג יאכל במוצאי שבת. שוגג דר' יהודה הוי כמו שפירשתי מזיד דר"מ. דהא מוקי התם מתני' דהשוחט בשבת כוותיה. במזיד לא יאכל עולמית. הוא, אבל אחרים אוכלים. דאי אחרים נמי לא יאכלו עולמית – היינו מזיד דרבי יוחנן הסנדלר. כללא דמילתא: מזיד דרבי מאיר – שוגג דרבי יהודה, מזיד דרבי יהודה – שוגג דרבי יוחנן הסנדלר. אמר קרא לכם. וא"ת ולא לכתוב לא קדש ולא לכם ואנא ידענא דאסירי באכילה מלא תאכל כל תועבה דכל שתעבתי לך הרי הוא בבל תאכל וי"ל דאי מהתם ה"א בין שוגג בין מזיד להכי איצטריך למכתב הכא למסמכיה למחלליה לומר במזיד אמרתי לך ולא בשוגג. היא קדש ואין מעשיה קודש. ואין להקשות דלא לכתוב לא היא ולא קדש דהוה אסורה באכילה מכל אשר תיעבתי לך והכי אמרי' בהדיא בפ' כל הבשר (חולין קטו. ושם). מאי טעמא דרבנן דפטרי. לא בעי למימר דלא דרשי "או" ו"תחת" לרבות את השליח – דלא ניחא ליה למימר דפליגי בשליח. כי קא פטרי רבנן אשארא. וא"ת: אמאי אצטריך למתני כלל טבח בשבת? דאפי' בשחיטה שאינה ראויה מחייב ר"מ, כ"ש הא דשחיטה ראויה היא! וי"ל: דזו אף זו קתני. וא"ת: כל טובח נמי, לאו דמריה קא טבח, דמכי שחט פורתא – קניא בשינוי? אלא ע"כ בהכי חייב רחמנא, והכא נמי לא שנא! ואור"י: דלא חשיב שינוי לקנותה בכך. סבר לה כר"ש דאמר דבר הגורם לממון כו'. וא"ת: ואמאי לא קאמר דר"מ לטעמיה דדאין דינא דגרמי (ב"ק ק.) גבי מקדש תבואת חבירו או שורף שטרות חבירו (שם צח:), וכ"ש דמחייב בדבר הגורם לממון, כדאמר התם ב"הגוזל" (שם צח:): דלמא עד כאן לא קאמר ר"ש אלא בדבר שעיקרו ממון, אבל שטר דאין גופו ממון – לא! וי"ל: דאיכא למימר נמי איפכא, דעד כאן לא קאמר ר"מ אלא בשורף שטרות של חבירו, או מקדש תבואת חבירו, שהוא ממון הראוי לכל העולם. אבל שור הנסקל – אין ראוי אלא לזה השומר, שיפטור עצמו. וי"מ: דמשום הכי קאמר ס"ל כר"ש מש"ס דר"ש קאמר דבר הגורם לממון הוי ממון לענין תשלומי ד' וה', דהכי תני ליה ב"מרובה" (שם עא:), ואילו ר' מאיר לא חזינא דמחייב בדינא דגרמי אלא קרן, אבל לחייב לשלם על ידו תשלומי ד' וה' – לא חזינא. ועוד אומר ריצב"א: דמשום דינא דגרמי לא מחייב אלא מדרבנן, כדמוכח בסוף "הכונס" (שם סב.)*.

ורבי

עין משפט נר מצוה

לא א מיי' (פ' יב הל' ה) ופי"ב מהל' שחיטה הל' י ופ"ב מהל' גניבה הל' ח סמג עשין סג ועשה ולאוין קמט טוש"ע י"ד סימן כח סעיף ט וסי' כח סעיף יז וטור ח"מ סימן שנ:

לב ב מיי' פ"א מהל' שחיטה הל' כג סמג עשין סג טוש"ע י"ד סי' יא סעיף ב:

לג ג ד מיי' פ"ו מהל' שבת הל' כג סמג לאוין סה טוש"ע א"ח סימן שיח סעיף א:

לד ה מיי' פ"ג מהל' חובל הל' ז טוש"ע ח"מ סי' שפו סעי' ב:

[ועי' תוס' ב"ק עא: ד"ה איסורא ותוס' חולין פה. ד"ה דנין]

[ופירש"י אפי' למ"ד ישנה לשחיטה מתחלה ועד סוף כדאמרי' במרובה ובעבודה כולו בעינן. ת"י עה:]

[ועי' תוס' ב"ק נב. ד"ה חמור ועוד שם עט: ד"ה ומכר]

מסורת הש"ס

קדושין נז. [ב"ק עא. חולין פ. פה. פה.]

חולין יד. ב"ק עא.

[משום פלוגתא דר"י ור"י הסנדלר דליתא במשנה שפיר גרסי' דתניא]

ב"ק עא. חולין טו. גיטין נג. כולה יז: תרומות פ"ב מ"ג שבת לח. [תוספתא דשבת פ"ג]

[חולין קטו.]

[ב"ק עא. ע"ז נד: חולין מ:]

ב"ק מה. עא. לח:

ב"ק סט פסחים כט: שבועות לב. נג. [ב"ק קה:]

וְר' מֵאִיר, *לוֹקֶה וּמְשַׁלֵּם אִית לֵיהּ, מֵת וּמְשַׁלֵּם לֵית לֵיהּ. וְשָׁאנֵי הָנֵי, דְּחִידּוּשׁ הוּא שֶׁחִידְּשָׁה תּוֹרָה בִּקְנָס, אע"ג דְּמִיקְטִיל — מְשַׁלֵּם. וְאָזְדָא רַבָּה לְטַעֲמֵיהּ, דְּאָמַר רַבָּה: הָיָה גְּדִי גָּנוּב לוֹ וּטְבָחוֹ בְּשַׁבָּת — חַיָּיב, שֶׁכְּבָר נִתְחַיֵּיב בִּגְנֵיבָה קוֹדֶם שֶׁיָּבֹא לִידֵי אִיסּוּר שַׁבָּת. גָּנַב וְטָבַח בְּשַׁבָּת — פָּטוּר, שֶׁאִם אֵין גְּנֵיבָה — אֵין טְבִיחָה וְאֵין מְכִירָה. וְאָמַר רַבָּה: הָיָה גְּדִי גָּנוּב לוֹ וּטְבָחוֹ בַּמַּחְתֶּרֶת — חַיָּיב, שֶׁכְּבָר נִתְחַיֵּיב בִּגְנֵיבָה קוֹדֶם שֶׁיָּבֹא לִידֵי אִיסּוּר מַחְתֶּרֶת. [א]גָּנַב וְטָבַח בַּמַּחְתֶּרֶת — פָּטוּר, שֶׁאִם אֵין גְּנֵיבָה — אֵין טְבִיחָה וְאֵין מְכִירָה. וּצְרִיכָא, דְּאִי אַשְׁמְעִינַן שַׁבָּת — מִשּׁוּם דְּאִיסּוּרָהּ אִיסּוּר עוֹלָם, אֲבָל מַחְתֶּרֶת דְּאִיסּוּר שָׁעָה הוּא — אֵימָא לָא; וְאִי אַשְׁמְעִינַן מַחְתֶּרֶת — מִשּׁוּם *דְּמַחְתַּרְתּוֹ זוֹ הִיא הַתְרָאָתוֹ, אֲבָל שַׁבָּת דְּבָעֲיָא הַתְרָאָה — אֵימָא לָא, צְרִיכָא. אָמַר רַב פַּפָּא: *הָיְתָה פָּרָה גְּנוּבָה לוֹ וּטְבָחָהּ בְּשַׁבָּת — חַיָּיב, שֶׁכְּבָר נִתְחַיֵּיב בִּגְנֵיבָה קוֹדֶם שֶׁיָּבֹא לִידֵי אִיסּוּר שַׁבָּת. [ב]הָיְתָה פָּרָה שְׁאוּלָה לוֹ, וּטְבָחָהּ בְּשַׁבָּת — פָּטוּר. אֲמַר לֵיהּ רַב אַחָא בְּרֵיהּ דְּרָבָא לְרַב אַשִׁי: רַב פַּפָּא פָּרָה אֲתָא לְאַשְׁמוּעִינַן?! אֲמַר לֵיהּ: רַב פַּפָּא שְׁאוּלָה אֲתָא לְאַשְׁמוּעִינַן; סָלְקָא דַּעְתָּךְ אָמִינָא. הוֹאִיל וְאָמַר רַב פַּפָּא: *[ג]מִשְׁעַת מְשִׁיכָה הוּא דְּאִתְחַיַּיב לֵיהּ בִּמְזוֹנוֹתֶיהָ, הָכָא נַמִי [ד]מִשְׁעַת שְׁאֵלָה אִתְחַיַּיב בְּאוֹנְסֶיהָ, קָא מַשְׁמַע לָן. *אָמַר רָבָא: [ה]הִנִּיחַ לָהֶן אֲבִיהֶן פָּרָה שְׁאוּלָה — מִשְׁתַּמְּשִׁין בָּהּ כָּל יְמֵי שְׁאֵלָתָהּ, מֵתָה — אֵין חַיָּיבִין בְּאוֹנְסָהּ. [ו]כִּסְבוּרִין שֶׁל אֲבִיהֶם הִיא וּטְבָחוּהָ וַאֲכָלוּהָ — [א] מְשַׁלְּמִין *דְּמֵי בָשָׂר בְּזוֹל. הִנִּיחַ לָהֶן אֲבִיהֶן אַחֲרָיוּת נְכָסִים — חַיָּיבִין לְשַׁלֵּם. אִיכָּא דְּמַתְנֵי לָהּ אַרֵישָׁא, וְאִיכָּא דְּמַתְנֵי לָהּ אַסֵּיפָא. מַאן דְּמַתְנֵי לָהּ אַרֵישָׁא — כׇּל שֶׁכֵּן אַסֵּיפָא, וּפְלִיגָא דְּרַב פַּפָּא, וּמַאן [ז]דְּמַתְנֵי לָהּ אַסֵּיפָא — אֲבָל אַרֵישָׁא לָא, וְהַיְינוּ דְּרַב פַּפָּא. בִּשְׁלָמָא ר' יוֹחָנָן לָא אָמַר כְּרֵישׁ לָקִישׁ — דְּקָא מוֹקִים לָהּ כְּרַבָּנַן. אֶלָּא רֵישׁ לָקִישׁ מ"ט לָא אָמַר כְּר' יוֹחָנָן? אָמַר לָךְ: כֵּיוָן דְּאִילּוּ אַתְרוּ בֵּיהּ — פָּטוּר, כִּי לָא אַתְרוּ בֵּיהּ — נַמִי פָּטוּר. *וְאָזְדוּ לְטַעֲמַיְיהוּ: דְּכִי אֲתָא רַב דִּימִי אֲמַר: חַיָּיבֵי מִיתוֹת שׁוֹגְגִין וְחַיָּיבֵי מַלְקִיּוֹת שׁוֹגְגִין וְדָבָר אַחֵר, ר' יוֹחָנָן אָמַר: חַיָּיב, וְרֵישׁ לָקִישׁ אָמַר: פָּטוּר. ר' יוֹחָנָן אָמַר: חַיָּיב, דְּהָא לָא אַתְרוּ בֵּיהּ. ר"ל אָמַר: פָּטוּר, כֵּיוָן דְּאִילּוּ אַתְרוּ בֵּיהּ — פָּטוּר, כִּי לָא אַתְרוּ בֵּיהּ נַמִי פָּטוּר. אֵיתִיבֵיהּ ר"ל לְרַבִּי יוֹחָנָן: "וְלֹא יִהְיֶה אָסוֹן עָנוֹשׁ יֵעָנֵשׁ" (שמות כא) מַאי

תורה אור

רש"י

ור' מאיר. בעלמא בתשלומי ממון לית ליה מת ומשלם, והכא תשלומי ארבעה וחמשה קנס הם, וכל משפט קנס חידוש הוא. הלכך, אע"ג דמיקטיל נמי לא מיפטר מיניה. ולקמן פריך: לרבה אליבא דרבי מאיר קשיא בתו, דמתניתין נמי קנס הוא, וקא פטר ליה אבתו. **היה גדי גנוב לו.** גנב גדי בחול ונתחייב הקרן וטבחו בשבת, דלא אתי עליה חיובא דממון באיסור שבת, אלא חיוב קנס. **חייב.** ד' וה'. דקנס חידוש הוא, ורבה סבירא ליה כרבי מאיר. **גנב וטבח בשבת.** דחיוב ממון דקרן אתא עליה באיסור שבת. **פטור.** דקיימא לן: אין מת ומשלם. וכיון דאקרן לא מיחייב — קנס נמי לא משלם, דתשלומי ד' וה' אמר רחמנא, ולא תשלומי שלשה וארבעה. ולא סבירא לן כרבי נתן דאמר (שבת דף לג.): חי נושא את עצמו. אי נמי: בכפות. **שאם אין גניבה.** כלומר, שמאחר שפטור על הקרן משום מיתה. **אין טביחה ואין מכירה.** אינו מחויב קנס, כדפירשתי, דתשלומי ארבעה וחמשה כתיב ולא תשלומי שלשה וארבעה. **מחתרת.** שחתר בית והוציאו. **וטבחו במחתרת.** עצמה, דההיא שעתא בר קטלא הוא אי הוה אשכחיה בעל הבית, כדכתיב (שמות כב) "אין לו דמים". **משום דאיסוריה איסור עולם.** כל זמן שיעידו עליו שחילל שבת ימיתוהו בית דין. הלכך חמירא מיתה דילה לפוטרו מממון. **דאיסור שעה.** אי לא משכח ליה ההיא שעתא — תו לא מיקטיל. **היתה פרה שאולה לו וטבחה בשבת פטור.** דההיא שעתא דקא טבח לה גזיל לה ממרה, ומיתה וממון באין כאחד. ולא גרסינן שאם אין גניבה אין טביחה ואין מכירה, דגבי שואל לא שייך לא כפל ולא ארבעה וחמשה, שהרי חייב בקרן לעולם, אפילו טוען טענת גנב. ואין קנס אלא או בגנב או בשומר חנם הפוטר עצמו בטוען טענת גנב, שאומר "נגנבה". **פרה אתא לאשמועינן.** בתמיה: מה למדנו ממנה שלא למדנו מגדי דקאמר רבה? **שאולה אתא לאשמועינן.** דטובחה בשבת פטור. **ס"ד אמינא הואיל ואמר רב פפא.** ב"השוכר את הפועלים". **הכא נמי.** נימא משעת שאלה רמיא עליה חיוב קרן, וכי טבחה בשבת ליחייב. קמ"ל. כיון דכל כמה דאיתא הדרא בעינא, ההיא שעתא דקא טבח לה — קא גזיל לה. **כל ימי שאלתה.** כל ימי משך הזמן ששאלה אביהן מן הבעלים. **אין חייבין באונסה.** דאינהו לאו שואלין נינהו עלה. **דמי בשר בזול.** כל זוזא חשבינן בארבעה דנקי. הכי אמרינן בפרק "מי שמת" (ב"ב קמו:) והעור יחזירו לבעלים. **אחריות נכסים.** קרקעות. **איכא דמתני ארישא.** להאי הניח להן אביהן אחריות נכסים חייבין לשלם, ואמרינן דחייבין באונסין, דאישתעבוד נכסים דאבוהון מחיים, משעת שאלה. **כ"ש אסיפא.** כשטבחוה ואכלוה. **ופליגא דרב פפא.** דאמר לעיל ההיא שעתא דמטו לה אונסין הוא דאתי חיובא עליה, ולא משעת שאלה. **ואיכא דמתני לה אסיפא.** היכא דטבחוה, אם הניח להן אביהן אחריות נכסים — משלמין תשלומי מעליא ולא בזול, דאיבעי להו למידק. **אבל ארישא.** אם מתה לא מיחייבי לשלומי, ולא אמרינן אישתעבוד נכסי דאבוהון משעת שאלה. **והיינו דרב פפא.** דאמר לעיל: לא אמרינן משעת שאלה רמו עליה תשלומין, אלא משעת אונסין ואילך, וההיא שעתא ליתיה לשואל דליחייב. **בשלמא רבי יוחנן.** דמוקי מתניתין בשלא התרו בו. **לא אמר כריש לקיש.** דאוקמיה כר' מאיר. **כי לא אתרו ביה נמי פטור.** הואיל ואיכא לד מלקות. **שוגגין.** שלא התרו בהן. **ודבר אחר.** ממון. ואכולה מילתא קאי, כלומר: חייבי מיתות שוגגין וממון, או חייבי מלקיות שוגגין וממון. **ר' יוחנן אומר חייב.** בתשלומין. **דהא לא אתרו ביה.** ואין אתה מחייבו אלא משום רשעה אחת דממון. **כי לא אתרו ביה נמי פטור.** ולקמן יליף טעמא. מאי

תוספות

ורבי מאיר לוקה ומשלם אית ליה מת ומשלם לית ליה ושאני הני. משמע דרבי מאיר אית ליה לוקה ומשלם אף בממון שאינו קנס, וכן משמע ב"השוכר את הפועלים" (ב"מ צ"א.) שהבאתי לעיל* ותימה: דבפ"ק דמכות (ד' ד:) קאמר עולא: טעמא דרבי מאיר דאמר עדים זוממין לוקין ומשלמין — משום דגמר ממוציא שם רע. ופריך: מה למוציא שם רע — שכן קנס. סבר לה כר' עקיבא, דאמר: עדים זוממין קנס הוא. משמע דבממון אינו לוקה ומשלם! ויש לומר: דודאי, אי עדים זוממין הוי ממונא — לא הוה גמר ממוציא ש"ר, שכן הוא קנס, אלא הוה דרשינן מ"כדי רשעתו" שאינו לוקה ומשלם, אבל השתא, דסבר עדים זוממין קנסא, וגמר ממוציא שם רע דלוקין ומשלמין — ע"כ מוקי "כדי רשעתו" במיתה ומלקות, כיון ד"כדי רשעתו" לא הוי במלקות וממון, מהשתא בכל דוכתא לוקה ומשלם, דמהיכא נמעיט שלא ילקה וישלם?

דאמר רבה היה גדי גנוב לו. אליבא דרבי מאיר קאמר ולא משום דסבר הכי.

משום דאיסורו איסור עולם כו'. שאם חלל שבת, לאחר השבת יעידו עליו ויהרגוהו. אבל מחתרת, אע"פ שמתחייב בנפשו בעודו במחתרת, מ"מ אחר שילא — תו לא הוי בר קטלא, ולא הוי דומיא ד"אם יהיה אסון".

אבל שבת דבעי התראה אימא לא. תימה: דעיקר קים ליה בדרבה מיניה ברליחה כתיב, דבעינן התראה? ועוד, דשבת ומחתרת תרווייהו תננהי, דבפרק "המניח" (ב"ק דף לד:) תנן: והוא שהדליק את הגדיש בשבת — פטור, מפני שנידון בנפשו. ומחתרת נמי תניא בפרק "בן סורר" (סנהדרין עב.): היה בא במחתרת ושיבר את החבית, אם אין לו דמים פטור! ונראה דהכא עביד צריכותא אמאי דקנס מיקטיל ומשלם. וה"ק: משום דחמיר איסוריה, והוה אמינא דהתם דווקא הוא דליחייב קנס עם המיתה, וכה"ג עביד צריכותא לקמן (דף לז.) גבי "לא יהיה אסון" ו"כדי רשעתו", דמשום דחמור הוי אמרינן דלעביד ביה תרתי. אבל קשה: למאי דפרישית דרבה אליבא דרבי מאיר קאמר, אם כן — היכי קאמר: אבל שבת דבעיא התראה — אימא לא מיקטיל ומשלם. והא עיקר מילתיה דרבי מאיר גבי שבת תניא לעיל! ומצינן למימר: דרבה אשמועינן דשייך קים ליה בדרבה מיניה, אע"ג דבשעה דמתחייב עדיין הממון בעין — לא הוה לן למימר קים לי' בדרבה מיניה. כדאמר רבה גופיה בפרק "בן סורר" (סנהדרין עב. ושם) אמר *רבה: מסתברא מילתיה דרב כששיבר — דליתנהו, אבל נטל — דאיתנהו — לא, אפ"ה, כיון דטבח אחרי כן — מיפטר על הגנבה. והא דפטור אגנבה אף על גב דאותה שעה הוי בעין עביד צריכותא.

מתה אין חייבין באונסין. אבל בגנבה ואבדה נראה לר"י שהן חייבין, דהואיל ונהנין, דמשתמשין בה, והכי (א) אמר ב"השואל" (ב"מ צו. ושם).

אבל ארישא לא והיינו דרב פפא. דלא אמרינן משעת שאלה חייב באונסין. וא"ת: אם כן, בסיפא נמי בשטבחוה, אמאי משלמין כשהניח להן אביהן אחריות נכסים? הא לא נתחייב בהן האב! וי"ל: דהתם פשע בה האב, שהיה לו לומר לבניו שאינה שלו, הלכך מחיים פשע בה, ונתחייב בה באותה שעה, ונשתעבדו נכסיו. מאי

עין משפט נר מצוה

לה א מיי' פ"ז מהל' גנבה הל' יג סג לאוין קס:

[דף לג. ד"ה ועולא]

לו ב מיי' פ"ג שם הל' ד סמג שם:

לז ג ד מיי' פ"א מהל' שאלה הל' ד סמג עשין פב טוש"ע ח"מ סימן שמ סעיף ד:

לח ה מיי' שם הל' ה וסמג שם טוש"ע שם סי' שמא סעיף ג:

לט ו ז מיי' שם טוש"ע שם סעי' ד:

תוספות רי"ד

אמר רבא הניח להן אביהם פרה שאולה משתמשין בה כל ימי שאלה. מתה אין חייבים באונסיה פי' שלא שאלו הן ולא קבלו עליהן אונסים. כסבורין של אביהן היא טבחוה ואכלוה משלמין דמי בשר בזול. פי' כל זוזי בארבע דנקא והעור יחזירו לבעלים. ואם הניח להן אביהן אחריות נכסים. פי' קרקעות חייבים לשלם משום דאישתעביד נכסיה. פי' נכסי דאבוהון מחיים משעת שאלה:

כי אתא רב דימי אמר חייבי מיתות שוגגין וד"א. פי' ממון או חייבי מלקות שוגגין וד"א ר"י אמר חייב בתשלומין ור"ל אמר פטור ר"י אמר חייב דהא לא התרו ביה פי' ואי אתה מחייבו אלא משום רשעה א' בממון ור"ל אמר פטור (א) כי אתרו בי' נמי פטור פי' הואיל ואיכא צד מלקות:

(א) נ"ל כיון דאילו אתרו ביה פטור כי לא אתרו ביה נמי פטור פי' וכו'.

הגהות הב"ח

(א) תוס' ד"ה מתה וכו' והכי אמרי' בהשואל דף פא ע"א:

הגהות מהר"ב רנשבורג

א] גמ' משלמין דמי בשר בזול. עי' רש"י ד"ה דמי בשר וכו' ורשב"ם בב"ב דף קמו ע"ב בד"ה ושמין להם וכו':

מסורת הש"ס

[לעיל לג: וש"נ]

[סנהדרין עב:]

ב"ק קיב.

ב"מ לח.

ב"ק קיב.

ב"ק שם [כ. ב"מ מב: ב"ב קמו:]

חולין פח:

[בסנהדרין שם איתא רבה]

מַאי לָאו אָסוֹן מַמָּשׁ? לֹא, דִּין אָסוֹן. אִיכָּא דְּאָמְרִי, אֵיתִיבֵיהּ רַבִּי יוֹחָנָן לְר"ל: "וְלֹא יִהְיֶה אָסוֹן עָנוֹשׁ יֵעָנֵשׁ" מַאי לָאו – דִּין אָסוֹן? לֹא, אָסוֹן מַמָּשׁ. אָמַר רָבָא: וּמִי אִיכָּא לְמ"ד חַיָּיבֵי מִיתוֹת שׁוֹגְגִין חַיָּיבִים? וְהָא תָּנָא *) דְּבֵי חִזְקִיָּה: מַכֵּה אָדָם וּמַכֵּה בְהֵמָה, מַה מַּכֵּה בְהֵמָה – לֹא חִילַּקְתָּ בּוֹ בֵּין בְּשׁוֹגֵג בֵּין בְּמֵזִיד, בֵּין מִתְכַּוֵּין לְשֶׁאֵין מִתְכַּוֵּין, בֵּין דֶּרֶךְ יְרִידָה לְדֶרֶךְ עֲלִיָּיה, לְפוֹטְרוֹ מָמוֹן אֶלָּא לְחַיְּיבוֹ מָמוֹן – אַף מַכֵּה אָדָם לֹא תַחֲלוֹק בּוֹ בֵּין בְּשׁוֹגֵג בֵּין בְּמֵזִיד, בֵּין מִתְכַּוֵּין לְשֶׁאֵין מִתְכַּוֵּין, בֵּין דֶּרֶךְ יְרִידָה לְדֶרֶךְ עֲלִיָּיה – לְחַיְּיבוֹ מָמוֹן, אֶלָּא לְפוֹטְרוֹ מָמוֹן. אֶלָּא, כִּי אֲתָא רָבִין אֲמַר: חַיָּיבֵי מִיתוֹת שׁוֹגְגִין כּוּלֵּי עָלְמָא לָא פְּלִיגִי דִּפְטוּרִין. כִּי פְּלִיגִי בְּחַיָּיבֵי מַלְקוּת שׁוֹגְגִין וְדָבָר אַחֵר. רַבִּי יוֹחָנָן אָמַר: חַיָּיב, חַיָּיבֵי מִיתוֹת אִיתְקוּשׁ, חַיָּיבֵי מַלְקִיּוֹת – לָא אִיתְקוּשׁ. רֵישׁ לָקִישׁ אָמַר: פָּטוּר, בְּפֵירוּשׁ רִיבְּתָה תּוֹרָה חַיָּיבֵי מַלְקִיּוֹת כְּחַיָּיבֵי מִיתוֹת. הֵיכָן רִיבְּתָה תּוֹרָה? *אָמַר אַבַּיֵי: אָתְיָא "רָשָׁע" "רָשָׁע". רָבָא אָמַר: אָתְיָא "מַכֵּה" "מַכֵּה". אֲמַר לֵיהּ רַב פָּפָּא לְרָבָא: *הֵי מַכֵּה? אִילֵימָא "וּמַכֵּה בְהֵמָה יְשַׁלְּמֶנָּה וּמַכֵּה אָדָם יוּמָת" – הַאי בְּקַטְלָא כְּתִיב! אֶלָּא הַאי "מַכֵּה": "מַכֵּה נֶפֶשׁ בְּהֵמָה יְשַׁלְּמֶנָּה נֶפֶשׁ תַּחַת נָפֶשׁ" וּסְמִיךְ לֵיהּ "וְאִישׁ כִּי יִתֵּן מוּם בַּעֲמִיתוֹ [כַּאֲשֶׁר עָשָׂה כֵּן יֵעָשֶׂה לּוֹ]". – וְהַאי לָאו "מַכֵּה" הִיא! אֲנַן הַכָּאָה הַכָּאָה קָאָמְרִינַן. וְהָא כִּי כְּתִיב – בְּחוֹבֵל בַּחֲבֵירוֹ הוּא דִּכְתִיב, וְחוֹבֵל בַּחֲבֵירוֹ בַּר תַּשְׁלוּמִין הוּא! אִם אֵינוֹ עִנְיָן לְהַכָּאָה שֶׁיֵּשׁ בָּהּ שָׁוֶה פְּרוּטָה – תְּנֵהוּ עִנְיָן לְהַכָּאָה שֶׁאֵין בָּהּ שָׁוֶה פְּרוּטָה.

סוף

*) לקמן לח. ב"ק לה. סנהדרין עט: פד:

תורה אור: שמות כא; במדבר לה; דברים כה; ויקרא כד; שם

רש"י

מַאי לָאו אָסוֹן מַמָּשׁ. אִם לֹא מֵתָה הָאִשָּׁה – יֵעָנֵשׁ הַנּוֹגֵף בִּדְמֵי וְלָדוֹת. הָא אִם מֵתָה – לֹא יֵעָנֵשׁ, וַאֲפִי' לֹא הִתְרוּ בוֹ, וְקַשְׁיָא לְר' יוֹחָנָן. לֹא דִּין אָסוֹן. הָכִי קָאָמַר קְרָא: אִם אֵין מִשְׁפַּט מָוֶת לַנּוֹגֵף, כְּגוֹן שֶׁלֹּא מֵתָה הָאִשָּׁה, אוֹ מֵתָה וְלֹא הִתְרוּ בוֹ – עָנוֹשׁ יֵעָנֵשׁ. מַכֵּה אָדָם וּמַכֵּה בְהֵמָה. מַכֵּה בְהֵמָה יְשַׁלְּמֶנָּה, וּמַכֵּה אָדָם לֹא יְשַׁלֵּם, אֶלָּא יוּמָת. הִקִּישׁ פְּטוּר מָמוֹן דְּמַכֵּה אָדָם לְחִיּוּב מָמוֹן דְּמַכֵּה בְהֵמָה: מַה מַּכֵּה בְהֵמָה אֵין לְךָ בּוֹ חִילּוּק *לְחִיּוּב, אַף מַכֵּה אָדָם אֵין לְךָ בּוֹ חִילּוּק *לִפְטוּר. מַכֵּה בְהֵמָה לְעוֹלָם חַיָּיב, דְּאָמְרִי' בְּב"ק (דף כו:): "פֶּצַע תַּחַת פָּצַע" – לְחַיֵּיב עַל הַשּׁוֹגֵג כְּמֵזִיד, וְאוֹנֶס כְּרָצוֹן. שֶׁאֵין מִתְכַּוֵּין. אֵין בּוֹ חִיּוּב מִיתָה בְּאָדָם. דֶּרֶךְ עֲלִיָּיה. שֶׁהִכָּהוּ בְּהַגְבָּהַת יָדוֹ, אוֹ שֶׁחֲתָכוֹ בְּחַרְבּוֹ מִלְּמַטָּה לְמַעְלָה. בֵּין דֶּרֶךְ יְרִידָה לְדֶרֶךְ עֲלִיָּיה. מִשּׁוּם דְּגַבֵּי גָלוּת דְּהוֹרֵג בְּשׁוֹגֵג אִיכָּא חִילּוּק בֵּין דֶּרֶךְ יְרִידָה לְדֶרֶךְ עֲלִיָּיה, כִּדְאָמְרִי' בְּמַכּוֹת (דף ז:): כָּל שֶׁבְּדֶרֶךְ יְרִידָתוֹ גּוֹלֶה, דִּכְתִיב "וַיַּפֵּל עָלָיו", עַד שֶׁיִּפּוֹל כְּדֶרֶךְ נְפִילָה. כּוּלֵּי עָלְמָא לָא פְּלִיגִי דִּפְטוּר. מִדְּתַנָּא דְּבֵי חִזְקִיָּה. חַיָּיבֵי מִיתוֹת אִיתְקוּשׁ. לְמַכֵּה בְהֵמָה. אָתְיָא רָשָׁע רָשָׁע. נֶאֱמַר בְּחַיָּיבֵי מִיתוֹת "אֲשֶׁר הוּא רָשָׁע לָמוּת", וְנֶאֱמַר בְּחַיָּיבֵי מַלְקוּת "וְהָיָה אִם בִּן הַכּוֹת הָרָשָׁע". רָבָא אָמַר אָתְיָא מַכֵּה מַכֵּה. דְּמַלְקוּת נַמִי אִיתְקוּשׁ לְמַכֵּה בְהֵמָה, וְלָאו מִגְּזֵרָה שָׁוָה דְּחַיָּיבֵי מִיתוֹת יָלְפִינַן. וְאִישׁ כִּי יִתֵּן מוּם בַּעֲמִיתוֹ כַּאֲשֶׁר עָשָׂה כֵּן יֵעָשֶׂה לוֹ. וְהַאי "יֵעָשֶׂה לּוֹ" – מַלְקוּת קָאָמַר. וּלְקַמָּן פָּרֵיךְ: וְהָא חוֹבֵל בַּחֲבֵירוֹ בְּתַשְׁלוּמִין, וְלֹא מַלְקוּת! וְהַאי. מַלְקוּת לָאו מַכֶּה כְּתִיב, אֶלָּא "כִּי יִתֵּן מוּם", וּמַאי אָתְיָא "מַכֵּה" "מַכֵּה" דְּקָאָמַר רָבָא? הַכָּאָה הַכָּאָה קָאָמְרִינַן. וּמוּם ע"י הַכָּאָה הוּא נִיתָּן. וְחוֹבֵל בַּחֲבֵירוֹ בַּר תַּשְׁלוּמִין הוּא. וְהֵיכִי מוֹקְמַתְּ לֵיהּ אַתְּ בְּמַלְקוּת וּפְטוּר מָמוֹן? אִם אֵינוֹ עִנְיָן. הַאי קְרָא. לְהַכָּאָה שֶׁיֵּשׁ בָּהּ שָׁוֶה פְּרוּטָה. וּלְתַשְׁלוּמִין, דְּהָא מִקְּרָא דְּבַתְרֵיהּ יָלְפִינַן, דִּכְתִיב בֵּיהּ "כֵּן יִנָּתֶן בּוֹ" – דָּבָר הַנִּיתָּן מִיָּד לְיָד. תְּנֵהוּ עִנְיָן. לְהַאי "כֵּן יֵעָשֶׂה לוֹ". לְהַכָּאָה שֶׁאֵין בָּהּ שָׁוֶה פְּרוּטָה. וּלְמַלְקוּת, וְאִיתְקִישׁ לְמַכֵּה בְהֵמָה שֶׁלֹּא תַּחֲלוֹק בּוֹ.

סוף

ס"א לפטור | ס"א לחיוב | [סנהדרין י: וש"נ] | ב"ק פג:

תוספות

מאי לאו אסון ממש. אע"ג דסיפיה דקרא ד"אם אסון יהיה" ע"כ היינו דין אסון, כדכתיב "ונתת נפש" וגו' – מ"מ "לא יהיה אסון" הוה משמע ליה אסון ממש. אי נמי: "אם אסון יהיה" נמי בעי למימר דהוי אסון ממש, ודריש "ונתת נפש" וגו' – היינו ממון. ומי איכא למאן דאמר חייבי מיתות שוגגין חייבין והא תנא דבי חזקיה וכו'. וא"ת: והא אמרינן בפ' "הנשרפין" (סנהדרין עט: ושם): תנא דבי חזקיה מפקא מדרבי, ומפקא מדרבנן. אלמא פליגי תנאי אתנא דבי חזקיה! וי"ל: דלענין ממון אחר אית להו לכולהו היקישא דתנא דבי חזקיה, ולא פליגי עליה *אלא במאי דקתני בין מתכוין לשאינו מתכוין, דמשמע בין מתכוין להרוג האשה בין אין מתכוין להורגה, אלא להרוג את חברו והרגה, דבכל ענין פטור מדמי האשה. דלענין ממון אחר כבר תנא דלא תחלוק בין שוגג בין מזיד, והיינו דמפקא מדרבי ומדרבנן, דלר' נתכוין להרוג את זה והרג את זה חייב ממון, ולרבנן חייב מיתה, ולתנא דבי חזקיה פטור ממיתה וממון. אבל קשה לרבינו יצחק: דבריש "הנחנקין" (שם פד:) אמרינן: הניחא למאן דאית ליה דתנא דבי חזקיה, אבל למאן דלית ליה כו'. משמע דאיכא תנא דפליג! ואומר רבינו יצחק: דהיינו רבי חגא מדרומא, דאייתי מתניתא בידיה. כדאמרינן בפרק "שור שנגח ארבעה וחמשה" (ב"ק מב. ושם) דשני אנשים כי נתכוונו זה לזה, אע"פ שיש אסון באשה – יענשו בדמי ולדות. אלמא לית ליה היקישא דבין שוגג למזיד. והא דקאמר מי איכא למאן דאמר כו' – היינו משום דתנא דבי חזקיה עיקר, שהיה שונה ברייתות של רבי חייא שהיה אביו, כדמוכח בסוף פרק "הבא על יבמתו" (יבמות סה:), והן עיקר, ומותבינן תיובתא מינייהו. ולרשב"א נראה: דמשום הכי קא פריך ליה מתנא דבי חזקיה – משום דרבי יוחנן מוקי מתניתין (לעיל לב:) בשלא התרו בו, וקתני סיפא דחייבי מיתות פטורין – *א"כ מתני' סברה דחייבי מיתות שוגגין פטורין. דלאו סיפא מיירי בשהתרו בו – ליפלוג בחייבי מלקיות גופייהו. והוה מצי למיפרך ממתני', אלא דלא מצי למיפרך אלא מדיוקא, ולהכי פריך ליה מתנא דבי חזקיה, ומתניתין סמיך. ולפי זה מצינן למימר דמפקא מדרבי ורבנן בכולה מילתא. ועוד אומר רשב"א: דר' ישמעאל בנו של רבי יוחנן בן ברוקה לקמן בפירקין (דף לז:) *הוא תנא דלית ליה דתנא דבי חזקיה. וצריך לומר דלתנא דבי חזקיה "לא יהיה אסון" – היינו אסון ממש, וקרא ד"אם אסון יהיה" – היינו דין אסון, כגון שנתכוין לאשה. דאם לא נתכוין לה – פטור ממיתה וממון לתנא דבי חזקיה. א"נ: לא קאי קרא דאסון אאשה, אלא אחברו שנתכוין לו, ולא איירי קרא שנתכוין להרוג את זה והרג את זה. ובפ' "הנשרפין" דדייק לר"ש דפטר נתכוין להרוג את זה והרג את זה היכי מפרש קראי – הוה מצי למימר כדפרישית, אלא אליבא דר"א, דאמר: קראי בנתכוין להרוג את זה והרג את זה דייק.

אף מכה אדם לא תחלוק בו כו'. וקרא ד"לא יהיה אסון" דאשמעינן דלא ישלם דמי ולדות בהדי מיתה, והא נמי דדרשינן בשילהי פרק "כיצד הרגל" (ב"ק כו.) עליו – ולא על האדם, דלא תשקול מיניה ממונא ותקטליה על הרציחה לחוד, וקרא ד"לא תקחו" דדרשינן מיניה דלא תשקול ממונא מיניה ונפטריה – אצטריכו כולהו, דלא מצי למילף מהיקישא דתנא דבי חזקיה, כדפירש בקונטרס לקמן (דף לח.) דמ"מכה בהמה" לא מצי למילף פטור ממון, דאדרבה חיוב היה לו למילף, דמכה בהמה חייב, להכי איצטריך למכתב כולהו. והכי ילפינן: מה מכה בהמה לא חלקת במה שכתוב בו, דהיינו חיוב, דבכל ענין חייב – אף מכה אדם כל עניני פטור ממון שכתוב בו – לא תחלוק בין שוגג בין מזיד, ובין דרך עלייה לדרך ירידה. ושוגג למזיד היינו ממון אחר בהדי מיתה, ודרך עלייה וירידה בכל ענין לא תשקול ממונא מיניה ונפטריה, כדאמרינן לקמן. ומתכוין לשאין מתכוין – לענין דמי האשה.

רבא אמר אתיא מכה מכה. תימה: לרבא לית ליה הכא גזרה שוה ד"רשע" "רשע", וכן ר' יוחנן. ולקמן (דף לז.) נמי מצרכינן חד קרא למיתה וממון; וחד למלקות וממון, ולא ילפינן מלקות וממון ממיתה וממון בגזרה שוה ד"רשע" "רשע", וסתמא דהתלמוד דריש ליה בפ"ק דמכות (דף ה:) גבי אין עדים זוממין נהרגין עד שיגמר הדין על פיהן, דאמרינן: חייבי מלקיות מנין? אתיא "רשע" "רשע". ובריית' נמי איכא בר"פ "אחד דיני ממונות" (סנהדרין לג: ושם) גבי דיני נפשות מחזירין לזכות אבל לא לחובה, דאמרינן: חייבי מלקיות מנין – אתיא "רשע" "רשע", תניא נמי הכי כו'. ור' יהודה נמי דריש ליה ב"החובל" (ב"ק פו: ושם) גבי וכן היה ר"י פוטרו, פירוש: את הסומא, מחייבי גליות ומחייבי מלקיות ומחייבי מיתות ב"ד. וגמר התם חייבי מיתות ב"ד מ"רוצח" "רוצח", וחייבי מלקיות אתיא "רשע" "רשע". ורבנן דפליגי עליה התם – לאו משום דלית להו "רשע" "רשע" אלא משום דמחייבי ליה כחייבי מיתות ב"ד! וי"ל: דרבא ור' יוחנן אית להו *בכ"מ גז"ש ד"רשע" "רשע" בדבר שהוא בגוף המלקות, אבל הכא לענין פטור ממון שהוא עם המלקות, וכן לקמן – לא ילפינן "רשע" "רשע". וטעמא – משום דקרא מוכח דרבע כתיב לענין מלקות "והיה אם בן הכות הרשע". והא דדריש "מכה" "מכה" – משום דמכה גבי תשלומין כתיב, שנאמר "מכה בהמה ישלמנה". ואביי אית ליה גזרה שוה ד"רשע" "רשע" בכ"מ. וסוגיא דלקמן כרבא ודלא כאביי. ואביי מוקי קרא במיתה ומלקות כר"מ, דלמלקות וממון לא צריך קרא, דאתיא "רשע" "רשע". ואם תאמר: ר' יוחנן אמאי לא דריש "מכה" "מכה", הא ברייתא היא בריש "החובל" (שם פג: ושם)! וי"ל: דסבר כאידך תנאי דהתם, דלא דרשי "מכה" "מכה" אלא ילפי מאידך קראי דלאו עין תחת עין ממש.

וכתיב ואיש כי יתן מום וגו'. אית דגרסי: וסמיך ליה, ולא מגזרה שוה יליף אלא מסמוכין. וכן משמע קצת, מדשביק קרא ד"מכה בהמה ישלמנה" ונקיט קרא אחרינא. ומיהו, מדפריך בריש "החובל" (שם פג:): מאי חזית דילפת ממכה בהמה, נילף ממכה אדם! משמע דגזרה שוה הוא, והא דהדר ביה מקרא קמא – משום דאיצטריך למהדר ממכה אדם ולאתויי "כי יתן מום בעמיתו", הדר ביה נמי מ"מכה בהמה ישלמנה" ומייתי "מכה נפש בהמה" דסמיך ליה. אי נמי משום דאיצטריך קרא קמא לכדתנא דבי חזקיה. ולמאן דלית ליה נמי איצטריך, מה מכה בהמה לרפואה פטור אף מכה אדם כו', כדאמרינן בריש "הנחנקין" (סנהדרין פד: ושם).

אכ

(ועיין לקמן תוס' לח. ד"ה אבל סימא]

עין משפט נר מצוה

מ א ב מיי' פ"א מהל' נערה בתולה הל' יג ופ"ד מהל' חובל הל' ז סמג עשין ע טוש"ע ח"מ סי' תכג סעיף ד:

מא ג מיי' פ"א מהל' נערה בתולה הל' יא ופ"ג מהל' גניבה הל' א סמג עשין נב:

מב ד מיי' פ"ד מהל' חובל הל' ט ופ"ה הל' ג סמג עשין ע טוש"ע ח"מ סי' תכ סעי' ב:

[וטעמא דרבי דדריש ונתת וגו' ממון ורבנן דרשי נפש ממש ולהכי לא מצי לאוקמי הקישא לאין מתכוין אבל לענין שוגג ומזיד כולהו אית להו הקישא. ת"י]

תוספות רי"ד

א"ר ומי איכא למ"ד חייבי מיתות שוגגין חייבין והתנא דבי חזקי' מכה אדם ומכה בהמה ישלמנה מה מכה בהמה לא חלקת בה בין בשוגג בין במזיד בין מתכוין לאינו מתכוין בין דרך ירידה לדרך עליה לפוטרו ממון אלא לחייבו ממון אף מכה אדם לא חלקת בו בין שוגג למזיד בין מתכוין לא"מ בין דרך ירידה לד"ע לחייבו ממון אלא לפוטרו ממון. פי' המורה (מכה אדם) מכה בהמה ישלמנה ומכה אדם לא ישלם אלא יומת הקיש פטור ממון דמכה אדם לחיוב ממון דמכה בהמה. מה מכה בהמה אין לך בו חילוק לפטור מלשלם דאדם מועד לעולם בין ער ובין ישן בין שוגג בין מזיד אף מכה אדם אין לך בו חילוק לחיובא ומכה בהמה לעולם חייב דאמרי' בב"ק פצע תחת פצע לחייב השוגג כמזיד ואונס כרצון פי' שאין מתכוין אין בו חיוב מיתה באדם פי' דרך עלי' שהכהו בהגבהת ידו או בחרבו ממטה למעלה פי' בין דרך עליה וכו' משום דגבי גלות דהורג בשוגג איכא חילוק בין דרך ירידה לדרך עלייה. כדאמרי' במס' מכות כל שבדרך ירידתו גולה דכתיב ויפל עליו עד שיפול בדרך נפילה: אלא כי אתא רבין אמר ח"מ שוגגין דכ"ע לא פליגי דפטירי פי' מדתנא דבי חזקי' כי פליגי בחייבי מלקות שוגגים וד"א ר"י אמר חייבי מיתות איתקוש [חייבי מלקות לא איתקוש] ור"ל אמר פטור בפירוש רבתה תורה חייבי מלקות כחייבי מיתות היכן ריבתה אביי אמר רשע רשע פי' נאמר בחייבי מיתות אשר הוא רשע למות ונאמר בח"מ והי' אם בן הכות הרשע. רבא אמר אתיא מכה מכה פי' דחייבי מלקות נמי איתקש למכה בהמה ולא מג"ש דח"מ ילפינן וקי"ל כר"י:

גליון הש"ס

תום' ד"ה ומי איכא וכו' א"כ מתני' סברה. כעין זה בב"מ דף ח ע"ב תום' ד"ה מנהיג לחודיה:

וכפ' קמא דסנהדרין דקאמר מ"ע דר' ישמעאל דאמר מלקות בכ"ג אביי אמר אתיא רשע רשע רבא אמר מלקות תחת מיתה עומדת לא משום דלית ליה כו' אלא משום דא"נ כדאמר בפ"ק דמכות גבי ואין משלשין במכות וגבי מחזירים לזכות לא בעי למימר דתחת מיתה עומדת דשמא במיתה דוקא משום דכתיב ושפטו העדה והצילו. ת"י עה"ג:

תורה אור

סוף סוף לאו בר תשלומין הוא! (א) לא צריכא, דבהדי דמחייה קרע שיראין דיליה. א"ל רב חייא לרבא: ולתנא דבי חזקיה, דאמר: "מכה אדם ומכה בהמה" ממאי דבחול כתיב, וליכא לאיפלוגי, דלמא בשבת כתיב, דבבהמה גופה איכא לאיפלוגי? לא ס"ד, דכתיב: °"ומכה בהמה ישלמנה ומכה אדם יומת" (ויקרא כד). היכי דמי? אי דלא אתרו ביה – מכה אדם אמאי יומת? אלא פשיטא – דאתרו ביה, ואי בשבת – מכה בהמה ישלמנה?! אלא לאו – בחול. א"ל רב פפא לאביי: *לרבה, דאמר: חידוש הוא שחידשה תורה בקנס, ואף על גב דמיקטיל משלם, מתניתין כמאן מוקים לה? אי כר"מ – קשיא בתו, אי כרבי נחוניא בן הקנה – קשיא אחותו, אי כר' יצחק – קשיא ממזרת! הניחא אי סבר לה כר' יוחנן – הוא נמי מתרץ לה כר' יוחנן, אלא אי סבר כר"ל – היכי מתרץ לה? על כרחך כר' יוחנן ס"ל. א"ל רב מתנא לאביי: לר"ל, דאמר: בפירוש ריבתה תורה חייבי מלקיות כחייבי מיתות, מאן תנא דפליג עליה דרבי נחוניא בן הקנה – אי ר"מ, אי רבי יצחק. § ת"ר: עריות ושניות לעריות אין להן לא קנס ולא פיתוי. [א]הממאנת אין לה לא קנס ולא פיתוי. איילונית אין לה לא קנס ולא פיתוי, והיוצאת משום שם רע אין לה לא קנס ולא פיתוי. מאי עריות ומאי שניות לעריות? אילימא עריות עריות

עריות

רש"י

סוף סוף. האי לא תחלוק בו לחייבו ממון, טעמא משום דאין בו כדי תשלומין, ולא משום היקישא. אבל היכא דיש בה שוה פרוטה – אימא תחלוק. לא צריכא. להכי איתקש. דבהדי דמחייה קרע שיראין וכו'. כלומר, ואשמועינן דלוקה משום חבלה, ופטור מתשלומי קריעה. לא שנא התרו בו, ולא שנא לא התרו, דלא לקי – פטור מתשלומין מהיקישא דלא תחלוק. ממאי דבחול כתיב. דפשיטא ליה דמכה בהמה בין שוגג בין מזיד חייב לשלם. דלמא בשבת כתיב. ועל כרחך אשוגג כתיב קרא, דאי במזיד – הו"ל מתחייב בנפשו, ופטור מן התשלומין. איכא לאיפלוגי. בין שוגג למזיד. לא ס"ד. דבשבת כתיב ובשוגג. ואי בשבת מכה בהמה ישלמנה. בתמיה. אלא לאו בחול. דליכא לפלוגי, ואיתקש לה מכה אדם, שלא תחלוק בו, ואפי' אינו חייב מיתה. לרבה דאמר. לרבי מאיר חדוש הוא כו'. מתניתין כמאן מוקים. לשנויי רומיא דרמינן עלה דאלו הן הלוקין, וקיימא לן דאין לוקה ומשלם. אי כר' מאיר. דאמר לוקה ומשלם, וכדשנינהו ריש לקיש. קשיא בתו. דבשלמא לריש לקיש דאוקמה להיא דגנב וטבח בשבת בטובח על ידי אחר, אבל בטובח על ידי עצמו – לא משלם, לא קשיא; דמת ומשלם לית ליה לר' מאיר אפי' בקנס. אלא לרבה קשיא בתו, דקנס הוא, וקתני מתניתין פטור. ואי כר' נחוניא בן הקנה. דאית ליה נמי לוקה ומשלם כר' מאיר, מדקאמר יום הכפורים כשבת. יה"כ הוא דפטור מתשלומין, ומשום כרת דאית ביה, ומג"ש ד"אסון" "אסון", אבל משום לאו ומלקות דאית ביה – לא פטר. ומתניתין נמי דאית ליה לוקה ומשלם – דידיה הוא, ומת ומשלם – לית ליה, אפי' בקנס. קשיא אחותו. נהי נמי דמשום מלקות לא פטר ליה, ליפטריה משום כרת. ואי כרבי יצחק. תוקמה, דאמר במסכת מכות (דף יד.): אין חייבי כריתות בכלל מלקות מ'. ולית ליה האי ד"אלו הן הלוקין": הבא על אחותו, ומשום הכי חייבין בתשלומין. קשיא ממזרת. דהכל מודים שהוא במלקות, וקתני: אית לה קנס. הניחא אי סבר. רבה כר' יוחנן, כשלא התרו בו, דמשלם, דחייבי מלקיות שוגגין ודבר אחר חייב. איהו נמי. מוקי למתני' בשלא התרו בו, כר' יוחנן. אלא אי סבר לה. בממון ומלקות דאפי' לא התרו בו פטור מממון, ופליג אדרבי יוחנן, וכל שכן אדעולא, דאמר אפילו התרו בו משלם ממון ואינו לוקה. היכי מתרץ לה. לא כר' יוחנן ולא כעולא ולא כריש לקיש. על כרחך. אי סבירא ליה בממון ומלקות דלוקה ואינו משלם – כרבי יוחנן סבירא ליה בשוגגים דמשלם ממון, ומוקי לה בשלא התרו בו. לריש לקיש דאמר בפירוש ריבתה תורה כו'. דחייבי מלקיות שוגגין פטורין מלשלם. מאן תנא דפליג אדר' נחוניא. ומחייב תשלומין בחייבי כריתות, כגון ההיא דשבועות: ושהדליק גדיש ביה"כ – חייבין, בפרק "שבועת העדות" (שבועות לג.), ומתני' דהכא דקנסה באחותו. ונהי נמי דלית ליה "אסון" "אסון" למיפטריה משום כרת – ליפטריה משום לאו, בין התרו בו בין לא התרו בו. דאין כרת בלא לאו חוץ מפסח ומילה. דבשלמא ר' יוחנן – מוקי לה אפילו כרבנן דפליגי עליה דרבי מאיר, דאמרי אין לוקה ומשלם, והני – בשלא התרו בו. אלא לריש לקיש כמאן מוקי לה? אי רבי מאיר. דאמר לוקה ומשלם. אי רבי יצחק. דאמר לא שייך מלקות בחייבי כריתות. וג"ש ד"אסון" "אסון" לית ליה, ובמאי ליפטר? הילכך מתניתין דהכא על כרחך ר"מ היא ולא רבי יצחק, משום דקשיא ממזרת. אבל ההיא דשבועות – בין כר"מ בין כרבי יצחק. עריות ושניות. לקמן מפרש להו. קנס. דאנוסה. פיתוי. דמפותה. הממאנת. בבעלה, כגון יתומה קטנה שהשיאתה אמה וממאנה בבעלה. אין לה קנס. שאינה בחזקת בתולה, הואיל וניסת. איילונית. שאין לה סימני נערות לעולם, ואינה יולדת. לשון איל זכר, דוכרניתא דלא ילדה (לעיל דף יא.). אין לה קנס. לפי שאין קנס אלא לנערה, וזו שלא תביא שערות לעולם – כל כ' שנה היא בחזקת קטנה, ומשם ואילך – בוגרת. והיוצאת משום שם רע. קס"ד שלא מצא לה בעלה בתולים. ולקמן פריך: בת סקילה היא!

עריות

תוספות

אם אינו ענין להכאה שיש בה שוה פרוטה. וא"ת: והא איצטריך להכי, דמהכא נפקא לן חובל בחברו לתשלומין בריש "החובל" (ב"ק פג: ושם)! וי"ל: דהך סוגיא כאידך תנאי דהתם, דמפקי החובל בחברו לתשלומין מקרא אחרינא: **דלמא** בשבת כתיב דבבהמה גופה כו'. וא"ת: א"כ היקישא למה ליה? וי"ל: דאתיא לבין דרך ירידה לדרך עלייה, דלא שייך לפלוגי גבי שבת. **אלא** לאו בחול. וא"ת: בחול נמי מצינן למימר, דבהדי דמחייה לבהמה הרג את האדם, ולא אתרו ביה משום אדם! ואפי' בשבת נמי מצינן למימר דאתרו ביה משום בהמה ולא אתרו בו משום שבת! וי"ל: דמ"מ ילפינן שפיר, דמה מכה בהמה לא חלקת בין שוגג בהכאתה למזיד בהכאתה – אף אדם לא תחלוק בו בין מזיד בהכאתו לשוגג בהכאתו. א"נ: הואיל ומכה אדם איירי באתרו ביה – מכה בהמה נמי איירי בכל ענין דאתרו ביה, ולהכי לא מצי איירי בשבת, ולא בהרג אדם עמה. **מתניתין** כמאן מוקי לה. *תימה: תיקשי ליה לרב פפא גופיה דאיהו סבר לעיל (דף לד:) כרבה, דאמר: היתה פרה גנובה לו כו'! ועוד קשה: דלישני כעולא, דמאי דפירש בקונ' דאי סבר כריש לקיש דחייבי מלקיות שוגגין פטורין כ"ש דפליג אדעולא – זה אינו נראה, דלמא בממון אחר סבר כריש לקיש, אבל בממונא דההוא מילתא גופיה – משלם ממון ומיפטר ממלקות מג"ש ד"תחת" "תחת"! *ונראה: דרב פפא, אפי' סבר כר"ל מצי לשנויי כדעולא, כדפרישית. אבל לאביי פריך שפיר, דלית ליה דעולא, דהא מוקי לעיל "תחת" לדרשא אחרינא. ולהכי קשיא ליה, אי ס"ל כר"ל מתני' כמאן מוקי לה. **אי** כר' נחוניא קשיא אחותו. לא מצי למימר קשיא ממזרת ואחותו, דע"כ כר"מ ס"ל, מדנקט: יום הכפורים כשבת, וה"ל למימר יו"ט כשבת וכ"ש יום הכפורים, אלא ודאי ס"ל או כר"מ דאמר לוקה ומשלם, או כר' יצחק דאמר אין מלקות בחייבי כריתות. הלכך לא נקט, יו"ט דמיניה לא הוה שמעינן יוה"כ שאין בו מלקות. וכיון דלא הוי כרבנן לא מוקמי ליה כרבי יצחק אלא כר"מ, ולא תיקשי ממזרת. **אי** כרבי יצחק קשיא ממזרת. לא הוצרך לומר אי כרבנן, דלדידהו קשיא ממזרת ואחותו. ולא מצי למימר נמי דמתני' כרבי עקיבא, דסבר עדים זוממין קנסא, ואית ליה לוקה ומשלם, ולית ליה מת ומשלם – דלרבי עקיבא מצינן למימר דלא גמר עדים זוממין ממוציא ש"ר, אע"ג דהוי קנסא מקנסא, כדפרי' לעיל (דף לג. ד"ה דאין). ואית ליה שפיר כרבנן דלוקה ואינו משלם. **מאן** תנא דפליג עליה דרבי נחוניא אי ר' מאיר אי רבי יצחק. תימה: דלריש לקיש בהדיא פליג ר"מ ארבי נחוניא, דהא מוקים מתני' כר"מ, וקתני דיש קנס בחייבי כריתות! וי"ל: דידע שפיר דר"מ פליג עליה, אלא דק"ל דרבנן לא מצינן למימר דפליגי עליה, אבל לר' יוחנן – אתי שפיר: **לא** קנס ולא פיתוי. אית דגרס: ולא אונס, משום דפיתוי נמי קנס הוא. ואומר ר"י: דגרסי' ליה, דשייך למיקרי לאונס קנס טפי מלפיתוי, משום דאונס שותה בעציצו (לקמן דף לט.).

הממאנת אין לה לא קנס. פירש בקונט': לפי שהיא בחזקת בעולה. וקשה לר"י: דא"כ הכי דייק לקמן: הא קטנה בעלמא אית לה, דלמא ה"ק: הממאנת אין לה קנס אם בא עליה כשהיא נערה, הא נערה בעלמא – אית לה! ומיהו, אין להקשות אמאי נקט ממאנת ה"ל למינקט כל אשה שניסת ונתגרשה, דהא איכא למ"ד לקמן (דף לח.) דאפי' אם נתארסה ונתגרשה אין לה קנס! ונראה לר"י דה"פ: אין לה לא קנס ולא פיתוי – אם אנסה בעלה או פיתה אותה, כשהיתה תחתיו קודם מיאון, אע"ג דכשמיאנה איגלאי מילתא שלא היתה אשתו. והשתא דייק שפיר לקמן: הא קטנה בעלמא אית לה. אבל קשה לר"י מהא דקאמר בסמוך: וכ"ת כולה ר"מ היא, וממאנת סבר לה כרבי יהודה. והשתא, כיון דאיירי שבא עליה בעלה כשהיא נערה שוב אינה יכולה למאן, דמודה רבי יהודה כשבעל, כדאמר בפרק "בא סימן" (נדה נב. ושם)! ותירץ ר"י: דמיירי כשפירש בהדיא שאינו בועל לשם קידושין. ועוד: דפיתוי ואונס לאו לשם קידושין הוא, דבההיא לא מודה רבי יהודה.

ולא פיתוי. קשה לרשב"א: אמאי נקט פיתוי, למאי דמוקי לה בסמוך בנערה? הא כל נערה מפותה אין לה קנס, דמחלה, אפי' נערה שאינה ממאנת! ויש לומר: דנקט אין לה פיתוי אגב דנקט באידך.

אבל

עין משפט נר מצוה

מג א מיי' פ"א מהל' נערה בתולה הל' ט סמג עשין כד טור אה"ע סי' קעז:

[לרב פפא לא שייך למיפרך דהא לא פריך לנפשיה משום דידע דסבר כר' יוחנן דלא דריש ג"ש דרשע ודמכה וכ"מ קאת דקאמר הי מכה. ת"י]

לפי' ר"י דלעיל אתי שפיר דרשב"ל מוקי לה כר"מ אבל רבה כמאן מוקי לה אי כר' נחוניא קשיא אחותו דלדידיה אחותו לית לה קנס דחד ריבויא מוקי לחייבי לאוין וחד ליבמה לשוק אי כדפי' רשב"א לעיל קשיא אחותו דאי נוקי חד קרא לחייבי כריתות א"כ חייבי מיתות נמי ולמה שהביא מהר"מ לעיל בתוס' אתי טפי שפיר אי ר' יצחק קשיא ממזרת דלדידיה מוקמינן חד לחייבי עשה וחד לחייבי כריתות הניחא אי סבר לה כר' יוחנן אלא אי סבר כרשב"ל דחייבי מלקות שוגגין פטורין א"כ איצטריך תרי ריבויי חד לחייבי עשה וחד לחייבי לאוין והא דלא קאמר אי כרבנן קשיא אחותו משום דעיקר קושיא כבר הקשה לרבנן לעיל והא קי"ל דאין לוקה ומשלם ולכך לא חזר והקשה. ת"י עה"ג:

מסורת הש"ס

[לעיל לד: לקמן לח.]

הגהות הב"ח

(א) גמ' תשלומין הוא (לא נריכא) תא"מ ונ"ב ס"א הא לא קשיא:

עֲרָיוֹת מַמָּשׁ, שְׁנִיּוֹת – מִדִּבְרֵי סוֹפְרִים, כֵּיוָן דְּמִדְּאוֹרַיְיתָא חַזְיָא לֵיהּ – אַמַּאי אֵין לָהֶן קְנָס? אֶלָּא: עֲרָיוֹת – [א]חַיָּיבֵי מִיתוֹת בֵּית דִּין, שְׁנִיּוֹת – חַיָּיבֵי כְרֵיתוֹת, אֲבָל חַיָּיבֵי לָאוִין – יֵשׁ לָהֶן קְנָס, וּמַנִּי – *שִׁמְעוֹן הַתִּימְנִי הִיא. אִיכָּא דְּאָמְרִי: עֲרָיוֹת – חַיָּיבֵי מִיתוֹת ב"ד וְחַיָּיבֵי כְרֵיתוֹת, שְׁנִיּוֹת – חַיָּיבֵי לָאוִין, מַנִּי – *ר"ש בֶּן מְנַסְיָא הִיא.§ הַמְמָאֶנֶת אֵין לָהּ לֹא קְנָס וְלֹא פִּיתּוּי. הָא קְטַנָּה בְּעָלְמָא – אִית לָהּ, מַנִּי – רַבָּנַן הִיא, דְּאָמְרִי: *קְטַנָּה יֵשׁ לָהּ קְנָס. אֵימָא סֵיפָא: אַיְילוֹנִית אֵין לָהּ לֹא קְנָס וְלֹא פִּיתּוּי. אֲתָא לְר"מ, דְּאָמַר: *קְטַנָּה אֵין לָהּ קְנָס, וְהָא – מִקַּטְנוּתָהּ יָצְתָה לְבֶגֶר. רֵישָׁא רַבָּנַן וְסֵיפָא ר"מ! וְכ"ת: כּוּלָּהּ ר"מ הִיא, וּבִמְמָאֶנֶת סָבַר לָהּ כְּרַבִּי יְהוּדָה; וּמִי סָבַר לָהּ?! וְהָתַנְיָא: *עַד מָתַי הַבַּת מְמָאֶנֶת? [ב]עַד שֶׁתָּבִיא שְׁתֵּי שְׂעָרוֹת, דִּבְרֵי ר"מ. *ר' יְהוּדָה אוֹמֵר: עַד שֶׁיִּרְבֶּה שָׁחוֹר עַל הַלָּבָן! אֶלָּא ר' יְהוּדָה הִיא, וּבִקְטַנָּה סָבַר לָהּ כְּר"מ. וּמִי סָבַר לָהּ? וְהָאָמַר רַב יְהוּדָה אָמַר רַב: *זוֹ דִּבְרֵי ר"מ. וְאִם אִיתָא, זוֹ דִּבְרֵי ר"מ וְר' יְהוּדָה מִיבָּעֵי לֵיהּ! הַאי תַּנָּא סָבַר לָהּ כְּר"מ בַּחֲדָא, וּפָלֵיג עֲלֵיהּ בַּחֲדָא. רַפְרָם אָמַר: מַאי מְמָאֶנֶת – הָרְאוּיָה לְמָאֵן. וְלִיתְנֵי קְטַנָּה! קַשְׁיָא.§ אַיְילוֹנִית אֵין לָהּ לֹא קְנָס וְלֹא פִּיתּוּי. וּרְמִינְהִי: הַחֵרֶשֶׁת וְהַשּׁוֹטָה וְהָאַיְילוֹנִית יֵשׁ לָהֶן קְנָס וְיֵשׁ לָהֶן טַעֲנַת בְּתוּלִים! וְהָא מַאי רוּמְיָא? הָא – ר"מ, הָא – רַבָּנַן. וּדְקָאָרֵי לָהּ מַאי קָאָרֵי לָהּ? מִשּׁוּם דְּאִית לֵיהּ לְמִירְמָא אַחֲרִיתִי עִילָּוֵיהּ: [ג]הַחֵרֶשֶׁת וְהַשּׁוֹטָה וְהַבּוֹגֶרֶת וּמוּכַּת עֵץ – אֵין לָהֶן טַעֲנַת בְּתוּלִים, [ד]הַסּוּמָא וְאַיְילוֹנִית – יֵשׁ לָהֶן טַעֲנַת בְּתוּלִים. סוּמָכוֹס אוֹמֵר מִשּׁוּם ר"מ: סוּמָא אֵין לָהּ טַעֲנַת בְּתוּלִים! אָמַר רַב שֵׁשֶׁת: לָא קַשְׁיָא; הָא – *רַבָּן גַּמְלִיאֵל, וְהָא – ר' יְהוֹשֻׁעַ. אֵימַר דְּשָׁמְעַתְּ לֵיהּ לְרַבָּן גַּמְלִיאֵל הֵיכָא דְּקָא טָעֲנָה אִיהִי, הֵיכָא דְּלָא קָא טָעֲנָה אִיהִי מִי שָׁמְעַתְּ לֵיהּ? אִין, כֵּיוָן דְּאָמַר ר"ג מְהֵימְנָא, *כְּגוֹן זוֹ °"פְּתַח פִּיךָ לְאִלֵּם" (משלי לא) הוּא.§ וְהַבּוֹגֶרֶת אֵין לָהּ טַעֲנַת בְּתוּלִים.§ וְהָאָמַר רַב: *[ה]בּוֹגֶרֶת נוֹתְנִין לָהּ לַיְלָה הָרִאשׁוֹן!

אִי

רש"י

עֲרָיוֹת מַמָּשׁ. הַמְפוֹרָשׁ בְּ"אַחֲרֵי מוֹת", וְהֵן בְּכָרֵיתוֹת. שְׁנִיּוֹת. שֶׁגָּזְרוּ חֲכָמִים עַל שְׁנִיּוֹת לָהֶן לְהַרְחִיק מִן הָעֲבֵירָה, כְּגוֹן אֵם אִמּוֹ וְאֵם אָבִיו, וּשְׁאָר עֲרָיוֹת הַשְּׁנוּיוֹת בְּפֶרֶק ב' דִּיבָמוֹת (דף כא.). כֵּיוָן דִּשְׁנִיּוֹת חֲזָיִין לֵיהּ מִדְּאוֹרַיְיתָא. קָרֵינַן בֵּיהּ "וְלוֹ תִהְיֶה לְאִשָּׁה". אַמַּאי אֵין לָהּ קְנָס. בִּשְׁלָמָא בַּעֲרָיוֹת אִיכָּא לְמֵימַר כְּשִׁמְעוֹן הַתִּימְנִי, דְּלֵית לֵיהּ "נַעֲרָה" "נַעֲרָה" "הַנַּעֲרָה". אֶלָּא שְׁנִיּוֹת קַשְׁיָא. שִׁמְעוֹן הַתִּימְנִי. בְּרֵישׁ פִּירְקִין, דְּאָמַר: אִשָּׁה שֶׁיֵּשׁ בָּהּ הֲוָיָה. ר"ש בֶּן מְנַסְיָא. דְּאָמַר: אִשָּׁה הָרְאוּיָה לְקַיְּימָהּ. רַבָּנַן הִיא. דִּפְלִיגִי אַדְּר"מ, בְּרֵישׁ פִּירְקִין. וּבִמְמָאֶנֶת סָבַר לָהּ כְּר' יְהוּדָה. דְּאָמַר נַעֲרָה מְמָאֶנֶת. וְהָכִי תֵּידוּק מִינָּהּ: נַעֲרָה מְמָאֶנֶת אֵין לָהּ קְנָס, הָא נַעֲרָה בְּעָלְמָא – יֵשׁ לָהּ קְנָס. עַד שֶׁתָּבִיא שְׁתֵּי שְׂעָרוֹת. וּמִשֶּׁהֵבִיאָה אֵינָהּ מְמָאֶנֶת, וַאֲפִילּוּ לֹא בָּעַל לְאַחַר מִיכָּן. רַבִּי יְהוּדָה אוֹמֵר. אִם לֹא בָּעַל לְאַחַר שֶׁגָּדְלָה – מְמָאֶנֶת. עַד שֶׁיִּרְבֶּה שָׁחוֹר עַל הַלָּבָן. וּבְנִדָּה מְפָרֵשׁ: שְׁתֵּי שְׂעָרוֹת שׁוֹכְבוֹת, וְנִרְאֶה כְּמוֹ שֶׁיִּרְבֶּה הַשָּׁחוֹר. אֶלָּא ר' יְהוּדָה הִיא. וּבִמְמָאֶנֶת נַעֲרָה אַשְׁמְעִינַן דְּאֵין לָהּ קְנָס, וְלָא תֵּידוּק הָא קְטַנָּה יֵשׁ לָהּ קְנָס. וְגַבֵּי אַיְלוֹנִית, דְּתָנָא נַמִי אֵין לָהּ קְנָס – מִשּׁוּם דִּבְקְטַנָּה סָבַר כְּר"מ, וְזוֹ מִקַּטְנוּתָהּ יָצְאת לְבֶגֶר. זוֹ דִּבְרֵי כו'. לְקַמָּן בְּפִרְקִין (דף מ:). סָבַר לָהּ כְּר' מֵאִיר. דִּקְטַנָּה אֵין לָהּ קְנָס, מִשּׁוּם הָכִי אֵין קְנָס בְּאַיְלוֹנִית. וּפָלֵיג עֲלֵיהּ. בִּמְמָאֶנֶת, וְאָמַר: עַד שֶׁיִּרְבֶּה הַשָּׁחוֹר. וְכִי תָּנָא הַמְמָאֶנֶת אֵין לָהּ קְנָס, הָא הָרְאוּיָה לְמָאֵן יֵשׁ לָהּ קְנָס, בְּנַעֲרָה קָאָמַר. מַאי מְמָאֶנֶת הָרְאוּיָה לְמָאֵן. כְּלוֹמַר, כָּל קְטַנָּה קָאָמַר, וְכוּלָּהּ ר"מ הִיא. וְיֵשׁ לָהֶן טַעֲנַת בְּתוּלִים. לְהַפְסִידָהּ כְּתוּבָּתָהּ. הָא ר"מ. דְּאָמַר: קְטַנָּה אֵין לָהּ קְנָס, וְאַיְלוֹנִית מִקַּטְנוּתָהּ יָצְתָה לְבֶגֶר. וּדְקָאָרֵי לָהּ מַאי קָאָרֵי לָהּ. מִי שֶׁהֵשִׁיב תְּשׁוּבָה זוֹ בְּבֵית הַמִּדְרָשׁ, מֶה עָלְתָה עַל רוּחוֹ, וְלָא סְבִירָא לֵיהּ דְּאִיכָּא לְאוֹקְמִינְהוּ כְּר"מ וְרַבָּנַן? מִשּׁוּם דְּאִית לֵיהּ לְמִירְמָא אַחֲרִיתָא עֲלֵיהּ. לֹא הֱבִיאָהּ לְבֵית הַמִּדְרָשׁ אֶלָּא לְפִי שֶׁיֵּשׁ לְהָשִׁיב אַחֶרֶת עַל זוֹ; חֵרֶשֶׁת וְשׁוֹטָה אַחֲרֶשֶׁת וְשׁוֹטָה. בּוֹגֶרֶת. בְּתוּלֶיהָ כָּלִים מֵאֵילֵיהֶן. הָא רַבָּן גַּמְלִיאֵל. דְּאָמַר בְּפ"ק (דף יב:): הִיא אוֹמֶרֶת "מִשֶּׁאֵירַסְתַּנִי נֶאֱנַסְתִּי" – נֶאֱמֶנֶת. הָכָא נַמִי אֵין לָהּ טַעֲנַת בְּתוּלִים לְהַפְסִידָהּ כְּתוּבָּתָהּ, דְּאָמְרִינַן: אִי הֲוָה פִּקַּחַת לִטְעוֹן – הֲוָה טָעֲנָה "מִשֶּׁאֵירַסְתַּנִי נֶאֱנַסְתִּי", וּמְהֵימְנָא. הָא רַבִּי יְהוֹשֻׁעַ. דְּאָמַר "לֹא מִפִּיהָ אָנוּ חַיִּין" – הָכָא יֵשׁ לָהּ טַעֲנַת בְּתוּלִים, דְּאִי נַמִי הֲוָה טָעֲנָה קַמָּן – לָא מְהֵימְנִינַן לָהּ. נוֹתְנִין לָהּ לַיְלָה הָרִאשׁוֹן. וּבוֹעֵל כַּמָּה בְּעִילוֹת, וְתָלֵינַן כָּל דָּמִים שֶׁל אוֹתוֹ הַלַּיְלָה בְּדַם בְּתוּלִים. אַלְמָא: אִית לָהּ דַּם בְּתוּלִים לְבוֹגֶרֶת. דְּאִי לָא – לָא הֲוָה בָּעֵי לְמֵיתַב לָהּ אֶלָּא בְּעִילַת מִצְוָה, וְכֵיוָן דְּאִית לָהּ בְּתוּלִים – הֵיכָא דְּבָעַל וְלֹא מָצָא דָּם תַּפְסִיד כְּתוּבָּתָהּ, דְּהָא כְּנָסָהּ בְּחֶזְקַת בְּתוּלָה וּמְצָאָהּ בְּעוּלָה.

ה"ג

תוספות

[אבל חייבי לאוין יש להן קנס ומני שמעון התימני היא. לא הוה מצי למימר מני רבי נחוניא היא, דלדידיה לא הוה קרי להו שניות, שהרי מבוה חייבי כריתות לחייבי מיתות ב"ד. והא דלא קאמר הא מני רבי עקיבא, ועריות – חייבי מיתות, ושניות – חייבי כריתות וחייבי לאוין – אלא דניחא ליה לאוקמי אפי' כרבנן, דאמרי קידושין תופסין. ועוד: משום דקאמר בלישנא קמא מני שמעון התימני היא, קאמר נמי באיכא דאמרי מני רבי שמעון בן מנסיא היא, דהוי בר פלוגתיה דשמעון התימני].

עד שירבה השחור כו'. א"ת דלא גרסי "על הלבן", משום דאמרינן בפרק "בא סימן" (נדה דף נב. ושם): לא שירבה ממש, אלא כדי שיהו שתי שערות שוכבות, ונראה כמו שירבה שחור. ו"על הלבן" משמע יותר מן הלבן. ור"ת פירש: על הלבן – שהשערות סמוך לבשר הם שחורים, ובראשם לבנים*. **זו** דברי ר"מ. למתניתין דלקמן (דף מ:) דכל מקום שיש מכר אין קנס, קאמר לה רב יהודה.

ואם איתא זו דברי ר"מ ורבי יהודה מיבעי ליה. ואע"ג דרבי יונתן ור' יאשיה סבירא להו כר"מ בס"פ "ד' מיתות" (סנהדרין סו: ושם) לפי' ר"ת, דפי': עד שיהיו שניהם שוין במיתה אחת. ואפי' לפ"ה דמפרש בני עונשין – מ"מ ר' יאשיה כר' מאיר סבירא ליה, דלית ליה הא דדרשי רבנן לקמן (דף מ:) כאן נערה כו', דהא פטר קטנה מאורסה. מ"מ לא קאמר זו דברי ר"מ ור' יאשיה, דלא פריך הכא: זו דברי ר"מ ורבי יהודה מיבעי ליה, אלא משום דרבי יהודה בר פלוגתיה דר"מ, והוי בכלל חכמים דפליגי עליה. ולהכי, אם איתא דלא פליג – ה"ל למימר זו דברי ר"מ ור' יהודה. אבל קשה: דה"ל למימר הא מני – ר' יאשיה היא, ובממאנת סבר לה כר' יהודה.

וליתני קטנה קשיא. אע"ג דהוי תני קטנה דאין לה קנס, מ"מ תני נמי אילונית. דה"א דוקא קטנה שיש לה נערות אין לה קנס. ותימה לר"י: אמאי לא משני דאגב אורחיה קמ"ל, דעד מתי הבת ממאנת – עד שתביא שתי שערות.

החרשת והשוטה כו' אין להן טענת בתולים. פי' בקונטרס: דאי הוה פקחת לטעון הוה טענה "משאירסתני נאנסתי". וקשה לר"י: דהיכי טענינן לה הכי מספק לאפוקי ממונא, כיון דאיהי לא טענה, חזקת גופה איתרעי, דהוי שור שחוט לפניך, אבל חזקת ממון לא איתרע! ומיהו, מביא ר"י ראיה לפי' הקונטרס: דאמר בפ' "המדיר" (לקמן עו: ושם): לא הוגלד פי המכה – המוציא מחבירו עליו הראיה. ומפרש דאפי' לא יהיב טבח דמי – על הטבח להביא ראיה שברשות המוכר נטרפה. והא דמפרש רב אשי למתני' ד"המדיר" דהיו בה מומין ועודה בבית אביה על האב להביא ראיה, רישא – מנה לאבא בידך, סיפא – מנה לי בידך. לא מטעם דברי ושמא ברי עדיף, כדמשמע לפום ריהטא – דא"כ הוה קשה דהיכי טענינן לה הכי? אלא כדפי' התם בקונטרס: רישא מנה לאבא בידך – דלגבי האב לא מהני חזקת הגוף דבתו, דהכתובה היא באירוסין של אב. סיפא מנה לי בידך, דלגבי דידה מהני חזקת הגוף דידה. וכן צריך לפרש, דאי מטעם ברי קאמר התם – אמאי קאמר דעודה בבית אביה על האב להביא ראיה דמשנתארסה נולדו בה מומין, אמאי צריך להביא ראיה, כיון דאמר ברי לי? דבכל ענין משמע דצריך להביא ראיה, אפילו אב אמר ברי לי. ולר"י נראה לפרש הכא: דאין להן טענת בתולים לפי שבחזקת מוכת עץ היא. ואע"ג דכולהו נמי חבוטי מחבטן – מ"מ שאר נשים יש להן טענת בתולים, מדלא קאמרי שהן מוכת עץ. אבל הנך, חרשת ושוטה, דלא מצי אמרי – בחזקת מוכת עץ נשאות. וכן נראה, דברוב ספרים ל"ג לעיל בברייתא אלא: החרשת והשוטה והאילונית יש להן קנס, ותו לא. ואין כתוב ברוב ספרים "ויש להן טענת בתולים". ולפר"י פריך שפיר, דמדקאמר יש להן קנס – אלמא לא חשבינן להו בחזקת מוכת עץ. אבל לפי' הקונטרס מאי קפריך? הכא נמי בחזקת בתולות חשבינן להו, דהא אמרינן התם* דמשנתארסה נארסה. ורשב"א א) הקשה לפר"י: דאמאי לא משני הא דקתני אין להן טענת בתולים כר"מ, דאמר בפ"ק (לעיל יג.): מוכת עץ, בין הכיר בה בין לא הכיר בה – מאתים. והא דקתני יש להן טענת בתולים – *כרבנן, דאמרי כתובתן מנה! וכי תימא משום דקתני חרשת דומיא דאילונית – הא ע"כ איילונית גופה לא הפסידה כתובתה לגמרי, דהא רב ששת דמשני הא ר"ג הא ר' יהושע סבירא ליה בפ"ק (דף יא:): כנסה בחזקת בתולה ונמצאת בעולה – יש לה כתובה מנה.

אי

א) [נראה דלא מצי למימר הא ר"מ דהא ר"מ פליג בסיפא א"כ תנא קמא בר פלוגתיה תנא אחרינא הוא. ת"י]

עין משפט נר מצוה

מד א מיי' פ"א מהל' נערה בתולה הל' יא יג סמג עשין כג טור אה"ע סי' קעז:

מה ב מיי' פ"א מהל' גירושין הל' ד סמג עשין נ טוש"ע אה"ע סי' קנה סעי' יב:

מו ג מיי' פ"א מהל' אישות הלכה ג ד ח סמג עשין מח טוש"ע שם סי' סז סעיף ה. [וברב אלפס פ"א דמכילתין דף סו.]

מז ד מיי' שם טוש"ע שם סעי' ו:

מח ה מיי' פ"ה מהל' איסורי ביאה הל' יט סמג לאוין קיא [וברב אלפס שם]:

[ועי' תוס' ב"ב קנו. ותוס' חולין כו: ד"ה עד]

תוספות רי"ד

תנו רבנן. החרשת והשוטה והבוגרת ומוכ"ע אין להם קנס וא"ל טענת בתולים פי' להפסידן כתובתן חרשת ושוטה לא דאמרי' אי הוו פקחות לטעון הוו טענו כל חדא וחדא משאירסתני נאנסתי ומהימן בוגרת נמי לא שבתולי' כלין מאליהן האיילונית והסומא יש להן ט"ב פי' א) ודוקא דקא טעין טענת פ"פ אבל אי טעין טענת דמים ל"ל דבוגרת כלין בתוליה. אבל פתח נעול יש לה (והרב אומר היפך טענות דמים יש לה טענות פ"פ אין לה):

א) הך פי' קאי אבוגרת ונראה דל"ל פי' ודווקא דקא טעין טענת דמים אבל אי טעין טענת פ"פ טענתו טענה דבוגרת כלו בתוליה וכו'.

[לעיל כט.] [שם] [שם] [לעיל כט. וש"נ] חולין כו: יבמות יב: ב"ב קנו: נדה נב. [לקמן מ:] [לעיל יב:] [ב"ב מא. גיטין לז:] נדה סד:

[ולכאורה נראה דלא מצי לשנויי קמייתא כרבנן דכתובתה מנה דמ"מ תקשי אמאי יש לה קנס כיון שהיא בחזקת מוכת עץ. ת"י]

[ולמאן דמפרש התם משום כאן נמצא וכאן היה ל"ל דהכא איירי כגון שיצא קול שמשנתארסה נאנסה דאי לאו הכי הוי לן למימר כיון שבבית אביה נאנסה שמעיקרא נאנסה כדאמר התם גבי מומין. ת"י]

אִי דְּקָא טָעֵין טַעֲנַת דָּמִים — הָכִי נַמִי, הָכָא בְּמַאי עָסְקִינַן — דְּקָטָעֵין טַעֲנַת פֶּתַח פָּתוּחַ.§ סוּמָכוֹס אוֹמֵר מִשּׁוּם ר"מ: סוּמָא אֵין לָהּ טַעֲנַת בְּתוּלִים.§ מ"ט דְּסוּמָכוֹס? א"ר זֵירָא: מִפְּנֵי שֶׁנֶּחְבֶּטֶת עַל גַּבֵּי קַרְקַע. כּוּלְּהוּ נַמִי חַבּוֹטֵי מִיחַבְּטִי! כּוּלְּהוּ רוֹאוֹת וּמַרְאוֹת לְאִמָּן, זוֹ אֵינָהּ רוֹאָה, וְאֵינָהּ מַרְאָה לְאִמָּהּ.§ וְהַיּוֹצֵאת מִשּׁוּם שֵׁם רַע אֵין לָהּ לֹא קְנָס וְלֹא פִּיתּוּי.§ הַיּוֹצֵאת מִשּׁוּם שֵׁם רַע בַּת סְקִילָה הִיא! אָמַר רַב שֵׁשֶׁת: הָכִי קָאָמַר: מִי שֶׁיָּצָא עָלֶיהָ שֵׁם רַע בְּיַלְדוּתָהּ — אֵין לָהּ לֹא קְנָס וְלֹא פִּיתּוּי. אָמַר רַב פַּפָּא: ש"מ, *הַאי שְׁטָרָא רִיעָא לָא מַגְבִּינַן בֵּיהּ. הֵיכִי דָּמֵי? אִילֵימָא דִּנְפַק קָלָא עֲלֵיהּ דִּשְׁטָרָא דְּזַיְיפָא הוּא, דִּכְוָותָהּ הָכָא — דִּנְפַק עֲלָהּ קָלָא דִּזְנַאי, וְהָא אָמַר רָבָא: *[א]יָצָא לָהּ שֵׁם מְזַנָּה בָּעִיר — אֵין חוֹשְׁשִׁין לָהּ! אֶלָּא, [ב]דְּאָתוּ בֵּי תְּרֵי וְאָמְרִי: לְדִידְהוּ תְּבַעֲתִנְהִי בְּאִיסּוּרָא. דִּכְוָותָהּ הָכָא — [ג]דְּאָתוּ בֵּי תְּרֵי וְאָמְרִי: לְדִידְהוּ אֲמַר לְהוּ "זַיְּיפוּ לִי". בִּשְׁלָמָא הָתָם — שְׁכִיחִי פְּרוּצִין, אֶלָּא הָכָא — *אִם הוּא הוּחְזַק — כָּל יִשְׂרָאֵל מִי הוּחְזְקוּ?! הָכָא נַמִי, כֵּיוָן דְּקָא מְהַדֵּר אַזִּיּוּפָא — אֵימַר זִיּוּפֵי זַיֵּיף וְכָתַב.§ **מתני'** [ד]וְאֵלּוּ שֶׁאֵין לָהֶן קְנָס: הַבָּא עַל הַגִּיּוֹרֶת, וְעַל הַשְּׁבוּיָה, וְעַל הַשִּׁפְחָה, שֶׁנִּפְדּוּ וְשֶׁנִּתְגַּיְּירוּ וְשֶׁנִּשְׁתַּחְרְרוּ יְתֵירוֹת עַל בְּנוֹת שָׁלֹשׁ שָׁנִים וְיוֹם אֶחָד. רַבִּי יְהוּדָה אוֹמֵר: שְׁבוּיָה שֶׁנִּפְדֵּית הֲרֵי הִיא בִּקְדוּשָּׁתָהּ, אע"פ שֶׁגְּדוֹלָה. *[ה]הַבָּא עַל בִּתּוֹ, עַל בַּת בִּתּוֹ, עַל בַּת בְּנוֹ, *עַל בַּת אִשְׁתּוֹ, עַל בַּת בְּנָהּ, עַל בַּת בִּתָּהּ — אֵין לָהֶן קְנָס, מִפְּנֵי שֶׁמִּתְחַיֵּיב בְּנַפְשׁוֹ, שֶׁמִּיתָתָן בִּידֵי בֵּית דִּין, וְכׇל הַמִּתְחַיֵּיב בְּנַפְשׁוֹ אֵין מְשַׁלֵּם מָמוֹן, שֶׁנֶּאֱמַר: °"וְאִם לֹא יִהְיֶה אָסוֹן עָנוֹשׁ יֵעָנֵשׁ" (שמות כא).§ **גמ'** א"ר יוֹחָנָן: רַבִּי יְהוּדָה וְרַבִּי דוֹסָא אָמְרוּ דָּבָר אֶחָד; רַבִּי יְהוּדָה — הָא דַּאֲמַרַן, רַבִּי דוֹסָא — *דְּתַנְיָא: *שְׁבוּיָה אוֹכֶלֶת בִּתְרוּמָה, דִּבְרֵי ר' דוֹסָא. אָמַר רַבִּי דוֹסָא: וְכִי מָה עָשָׂה לָהּ עַרְבִי הַלָּז? וְכִי מִפְּנֵי שֶׁמִּיעֵךְ לָהּ בֵּין דַּדֶּיהָ פְּסָלָהּ מִן הַכְּהוּנָּה? אָמַר *רַבָּה: דִּלְמָא לָא הִיא; עַד כָּאן לָא קָאָמַר ר' יְהוּדָה הָכָא אֶלָּא שֶׁלֹּא יְהֵא חוֹטֵא נִשְׂכָּר, אֲבָל הָתָם — [ו]כְּרַבָּנַן סְבִירָא לֵיהּ. אִי נַמִי: עַד כָּאן לָא קָאָמַר ר' דוֹסָא הָתָם — אֶלָּא בִּתְרוּמָה דְּרַבָּנַן, אֲבָל קְנָס דְּאוֹרָיְיתָא — כְּרַבָּנַן סְבִירָא לֵיהּ. אֲמַר לֵיהּ אַבָּיֵי: וְטַעְמֵיהּ דְּרַבִּי יְהוּדָה הָכָא שֶׁלֹּא יְהֵא חוֹטֵא נִשְׂכָּר הוּא? וְהָא תַּנְיָא, *ר' יְהוּדָה אוֹמֵר: *שְׁבוּיָה שֶׁנִּשְׁבֵּית הֲרֵי הִיא בִּקְדוּשָּׁתָהּ, אֲפִי' בַּת עֶשֶׂר שָׁנִים כְּתוּבָּתָהּ מָאתַיִם, וְהָתָם — מַאי שֶׁלֹּא יְהֵא חוֹטֵא נִשְׂכָּר אִיכָּא? הָתָם נַמִי, דִּלְמָא מִימְנְעִי וְלָא נָסְבִי לַהּ. וְסָבַר ר"י בִּקְדוּשָּׁתָהּ קַיְימָא? וְהָתַנְיָא: *הַפּוֹדֶה אֶת הַשְּׁבוּיָה יִשָּׂאֶנָּה; מֵעִיד בָּהּ — לֹא יִשָּׂאֶנָּה. ר' יְהוּדָה אוֹמֵר: בֵּין כָּךְ וּבֵין כָּךְ — לֹא יִשָּׂאֶנָּה! הָא גּוּפָהּ קַשְׁיָא; אָמְרַתְּ: הַפּוֹדֶה אֶת הַשְּׁבוּיָה יִשָּׂאֶנָּה, וַהֲדַר תָּנָא: מֵעִיד בָּהּ — לֹא יִשָּׂאֶנָּה, מִשּׁוּם דְּמֵעִיד בָּהּ לֹא יִשָּׂאֶנָּה?! הָא לָא קַשְׁיָא; הָכִי קָאָמַר: הַפּוֹדֶה אֶת הַשְּׁבוּיָה וּמֵעִיד בָּהּ — יִשָּׂאֶנָּה, מֵעִיד בָּהּ כְּדֵי — לֹא יִשָּׂאֶנָּה. מ"מ קַשְׁיָא לְר' יְהוּדָה! אָמַר רַב פַּפָּא: אֵימָא; רַבִּי יְהוּדָה אוֹמֵר בֵּין כָּךְ וּבֵין כָּךְ — יִשָּׂאֶנָּה. רַב הוּנָא בְּרֵיהּ דְּרַב יְהוֹשֻׁעַ אוֹמֵר: לְעוֹלָם כִּדְקָתָנֵי, ר' יְהוּדָה לְדִבְרֵיהֶם דְּרַבָּנַן קָאָמַר לְהוּ: לְדִידִי — בֵּין כָּךְ וּבֵין כָּךְ יִשָּׂאֶנָּה, אֶלָּא לְדִידְכוּ — בֵּין כָּךְ וּבֵין כָּךְ לֹא יִשָּׂאֶנָּה מִבָּעֵי לֵיהּ! וְרַבָּנַן? [ז]הַפּוֹדֶה אֶת הַשְּׁבוּיָה וּמֵעִיד בָּהּ יִשָּׂאֶנָּה — לָא שָׁדֵי אִינִישׁ זוּזֵי בְּכְדִי, [ח]מֵעִיד בָּהּ כְּדֵי לֹא יִשָּׂאֶנָּה — שֶׁמָּא עֵינָיו נָתַן בָּהּ. רָמֵי לֵיהּ רַב פַּפָּא בַּר שְׁמוּאֵל לְרַב יוֹסֵף:

וְסָבַר

ה"ג: אִי דְּקָא טָעֵין טַעֲנַת דָּמִים הָכִי נַמִי. הב"ע דְּקָטָעֵין טַעֲנַת פֶּתַח פָּתוּחַ. אִי דְּקָאָמַר בָּעַלְתִּי וְלֹא מָצָאתִי דָּם – וַדַּאי טַעֲנָה מַעַלְיְיתָא הִיא. וְהָכָא דְּקָתָנֵי אֵין לָהּ טַעֲנַת בְּתוּלִים – דְּקָטָעֵין וְאָמַר פֶּתַח פָּתוּחַ מָצָאתִי, וְדָם לֹא בָּדַקְתִּי אִם נִמְצָא בָּהּ אִם לָאו. בְּנַעֲרָה וּקְטַנָּה – טַעֲנָה הִיא, כִּדְאָמְרִינַן בְּפ"ק. וְאע"פ שֶׁאֵין יָכוֹל לְבָרֵר דְּבָרָיו בְּפָנֵינוּ – אָמְרִינַן: חֲזָקָה אֵין אָדָם טוֹרֵחַ בִּסְעוּדָה וּמַפְסִידָהּ. אֲבָל מִשֶּׁבָּגְרָה, אֵין רַחְמָהּ צַר כְּבַתְּחִילָּה, וְדוֹמֶה לוֹ כְּאִילּוּ פֶּתַח פָּתוּחַ. שֶׁנֶּחְבְּטָה. וּבְתוּלֶיהָ נוֹשְׁרִין. כּוּלְּהוּ רוֹאוֹת. אִם נָשְׁרוּ בְּתוּלֵיהֶן [רוֹאוֹת דָּם]. וּמַרְאוֹת לְאִמָּן. וּפוֹסְקוֹת עֲלֵיהֶן שֶׁאֵינָן בְּתוּלוֹת, וְאִם לֹא הוֹדִיעַתּוּ – הִטְעַתּוּ. וְזוֹ אֵינָהּ רוֹאָה וְאֵינָהּ מַרְאָה לְאִמָּהּ. וְזֶה שֶׁכְּנָסָהּ – בְּחֶזְקַת נֶחְבֶּטֶת כְּנָסָהּ, וְאֵין אָדָם פּוֹסֵק עָלֶיהָ, וְלָאו טָעוּת הוּא. רִיעָא. שֶׁיָּצָא עָלָיו שֵׁם זִיּוּף. אֵין חוֹשְׁשִׁין לָהּ. אֲפִי' לִכְהוּנָּה. אֶלָּא. יָצָא עָלֶיהָ שֵׁם רַע הֵיכִי דָּמֵי – כְּגוֹן בְּעֵדִים. וְלֹא שֶׁאָמְרוּ עָלֶיהָ שֶׁנִּבְעֲלָה – דְּא"כ מַאי לְמֵימְרָא? הָא לָאו בְּתוּלָה הִיא! אֶלָּא אָמְרִי: לְדִידְהוּ תְּבַעֲתִנְהוּ לְאִיסּוּרָא, הִפְקִירָה עַצְמָהּ לְכָךְ, וְלֹא שָׁמְעוּ לָהּ. בִּשְׁלָמָא הָתָם כו'. הֵיכִי גָּמַר רַב פַּפָּא מִינָּהּ דְּלָא מַגְבִּינַן בִּשְׁטָרָא כִּי הַאי? בִּשְׁלָמָא הָתָם – שְׁכִיחִי פְּרוּצִין, וְכֵיוָן שֶׁיֵּשׁ עֵדִים שֶׁהָיְתָה מְחַזֶּרֶת אַחַר הַזְּנוּת – הַרְבֵּה מָצְאָה לָהּ, מִשּׁוּם הָכִי אֵין לָהּ קְנָס לְאַחַר זְמַן, דְּלָאו בְּחֶזְקַת בְּתוּלָה הֲוַאי. אֶלָּא. לְגַבֵּי שְׁטָר. אִם הוּא הוּחְזַק. לַחֲזוֹר אַחַר עֵידֵי שֶׁקֶר. כָּל יִשְׂרָאֵל מִי הוּחְזְקוּ. לִהְיוֹת שׁוֹמְעִין לוֹ לְזַיֵּיף. אֵימַר זִיּוּפֵי זַיֵּיף. הוּא עַצְמוֹ לָמַד לְכַוֵּין כְּתָב הַדּוֹמֶה לִכְתַב יְדֵי עֵדִים שֶׁחָתַם בּוֹ. **מתני'** יְתֵירוֹת עַל בְּנוֹת שָׁלֹשׁ שָׁנִים. דְּכֵיוָן דִּרְאוּיוֹת לְבִיאָה – בְּחֶזְקַת הֶפְקֵר הֵן, וְנִבְעָלוֹת בְּגֵיוּתָן, וְהַשְּׁבוּיָה בְּשִׁבְיָיתָהּ. וְלֹא יִהְיֶה אָסוֹן עָנוֹשׁ יֵעָנֵשׁ. הָא אִם יִהְיֶה אָסוֹן – לֹא יֵעָנֵשׁ. **גמ'** שְׁבוּיָה. בַּת כֹּהֵן. אוֹכֶלֶת בִּתְרוּמָה. וְלָא מַחְזְקִינַן לָהּ בְּחֶזְקַת בְּעוּלָה לִפְסוֹל לָהּ הַמְחַלְּלָהּ בְּבִיאָתוֹ. מִפְּנֵי שֶׁמִּיעֵךְ לָהּ. כְּלוֹמַר, אֵין נוֹהֲגִין בָּהֶן הֶפְקֵר לְאוֹנְסָן בִּבְעִילָה, אֶלָּא לְשַׂחֵק עִמָּהֶן. [רַבָּנַן פְּלִיגֵי אַדְּרַבִּי דוֹסָא, וְאָמְרוּ: יֵשׁ שְׁבוּיָה אוֹכֶלֶת וְיֵשׁ שֶׁאֵינָהּ אוֹכֶלֶת. כֵּיצַד? הָאִשָּׁה שֶׁאָמְרָה נִשְׁבֵּיתִי וּטְהוֹרָה אֲנִי – אוֹכֶלֶת, וְאִם יֵשׁ עֵדִים שֶׁנִּשְׁבֵּית וְהִיא אוֹמֶרֶת טְהוֹרָה אֲנִי – אֵינָהּ אוֹכֶלֶת. בְּמַסֶּכֶת עֵדֻיּוֹת]. אֶלָּא בִּתְרוּמָה בַּזְּמַן הַזֶּה דְּרַבָּנַן. דְּכֵיוָן דַּאֲפִילּוּ נִבְעֲלָה, אִיסּוּרָא דְּרַבָּנַן בְּעָלְמָא הוּא – לֹא גָּזְרוּ עַל סְפֵיקָהּ. אֲבָל קְנָס, דְּאַפּוּקֵי מָמוֹנָא הוּא, אֵימָא לָךְ: סָפֵק בְּעוּלָה הִיא, וּמִסְּפֵיקָא לָא מַפְּקִינַן מָמוֹנָא. דִּלְמָא מִמְנְעֵי וְלָא נָסְבֵי לַהּ. אִי פָּחֲתַתְּ כְּתוּבָּתָהּ מְשַׁוֵּית לָהּ בְּחֶזְקַת בְּעוּלָה, וּמְרַחֲקֵי לָהּ אֲפִילּוּ יִשְׂרְאֵלִים. מֵעִיד בָּהּ. קָא סָלְקָא דַּעְתִּין דְּאַפּוֹדֶה קָאֵי, שֶׁאִם הָיָה מֵעִיד בָּהּ שֶׁלֹּא נִבְעֲלָה לְגוֹי – לֹא יִשָּׂאֶנָּה אִם כֹּהֵן הוּא. מִשּׁוּם דְּמֵעִיד בָּהּ וכו'. וְהָא אָמְרוּ: הַפּוֹדֶה אֶת הַשְּׁבוּיָה – יִשָּׂאֶנָּה. הַפּוֹדֶה אֶת הַשְּׁבוּיָה וּמֵעִיד בָּהּ יִשָּׂאֶנָּה. דְּאִי לָאו דְּקִיס לֵיהּ בְּגַוָּהּ – לָא שָׁדֵי זוּזֵי בְּכְדִי, שֶׁהֲרֵי לִישָּׂאֶנָּה פְּדָאָהּ. מֵעִיד בָּהּ כְּדֵי לֹא יִשָּׂאֶנָּה. שֶׁמָּא עֵינָיו נָתַן בָּהּ.

וְרָאֲתָה

אי דקא טעין טענת דמים ה"נ כו'. כך גרס בקונטרס. ור"ת גריס איפכא, *כמו שהיה כתוב בספרים: אי דקא טעין טענת פתח פתוח – ה"נ כו'. ולעיל בפ"ק (דף ט. ד"ה האומר) פירשתי. קצת קשה לפי' ר"ת, דמפרש דמוכת עץ אין לה דמים, אבל פתחה נעול – אם כן בחנם דחק לשנויי הא ר"ג והא רבי יהושע, דה"מ לשנויי: הא – דקא טעין פתח פתוח, הא – דקא טעין טענת דמים. ושמא לית ליה חזקה דאין אדם טורח בסעודה ומפסידה, ולא מהימן בפתח פתוח להפסידה כתובתה. אע"ג דקאמר אי דקא טעין פתח פתוח הכי נמי, דמשמע דנאמן – שמא היינו לאוסרה עליו. אבל ברייתא דלעיל משמע דיש להן טענת בתולים לענין כתובה, דומיא דקנס.

כולהו רואות ומראות לאמן. פירש הקונטרס: ופוסקות עליהן שהן בעולות, ואם לא הודיעתו – הטעתו. וקשה לפירושו: דהא אליבא דר"מ קיימינן, ור' מאיר אית לי' בפ"ק (דף יג.) דמוכת עץ, בין הכיר בה בין לא הכיר בה – מאתים! ונראה לר"י דה"פ: כולהו רואות ומראות לאמן, ויודעות שהן מוכת עץ, שאמותיהן מגידות להן. ולהכי [כשהוא אומר לא מצאתי לבתך בתולים, והיא אומרת בתולה הייתי – אין לנו לתלות במוכת עץ, שא"כ היתה אומרת: מוכת עץ אני]. וכי לא אמרה מוכת עץ אני – יש לה טענת בתולים. אבל סומא – תלינן שהיא מוכת עץ אע"ג דלא אמרה, דאינה יודעת, לפי שאינה רואה ואינה מראה לאמה, ואין אמה מגדת לה.

היוצאת משום שם רע *בת סקילה היא. ופשיטא דלאו בת קנס היא, דהא בעולה ודאי היא. אבל אין לפרש הואיל ויש חיוב סקילה לבא עליה פשיטא דאין לה קנס, דקם ליה בדרבה מיניה – דהא קתני במתניתין הבא על בתו, ולעיל נמי קתני עריות בברייתא.

ואלו שאין להן קנס הגיורת והשבויה כו'. אף על גב דמדאורייתא שבויה לא הויא בחזקת בעולה, כדאמרינן בכל דוכתי דבשבויה הקילו – מ"מ אין לה קנס, דמשום גזירה שלא תינשא לכהן, עשאוה כבעולה לכל דבריה.

וכי מה עשה לה ערבי זה. נקט ערבי לפי שהם שטופים בזימה, כדאמר בקדושין (דף מט:): עשרה קבין זימה ירדו לעולם ט' נטלו ערביים.

משום דמעיד בה לא ישאנה. קס"ד: הפודה את השבויה ישאנה, בלא עדות קאמר.

מכל מקום קשיא. אליבא דרבי יוחנן פריך. וכן כל הנך פירכי דלקמן. אבל לרבה, דאמר דטעמא דרבי יהודה שלא יהא חוטא נשכר – לא קשיא מידי.

וסבר

מט א מיי' פי"ז מהל' איסורי ביאה הל' כא טוש"ע אה"ע סי' ו סעיף טז:

נ ב מיי' פ"א מהל' נערה בתולה הל' ט סמג עשין נד טוש"ע שם סי' קעז ס"ד בהג"ה.

נא ג מיי' פכ"ב מהל' עדות הל' ה סמג עשין קי טוש"ע ח"מ סי' לא סעיף ד וסי' סג סעיף ח:

נב ד מיי' פ"א מהל' נערה בתולה הל' י סמג עשין נד טור אה"ע סי' קעז:

נג ה מיי' שם הל' יג יד:

נד ו מיי' פ"ו מהל' תרומות הל' יא סמג לאוין רנו:

נה ז ח מיי' פי"ח מהל' איסורי ביאה הל' כ טוש"ע אה"ע סי' ז ס"ג:

[וכן גירסת הערוך ערך פתח ע"ש]

גיטין פט.

ת"י כ"י

[נ"ל דמלינן לפרש בת סקילה הוא דקם ליה בדרבה מיניה ופשיטא דמדיוקא דברייתא ממעטי' לה. ת"י]

[משום סיומא דמילתא לאמר ר' דוסא וכי מה עשה לה כו' שהביאו הש"ס לחזק הענין שפיר גרסי' דתניא]

[תוספתא פ"ג]

[ע' היטב תוס' לקמן פה. ד"ה מרעגא ותוס' לקמן לב: ד"ה דינא ותוס' שבועות מב. ד"ה איפרע ותוס' יבמות קא: ד"ה מרעגא]

[מכות ה:]

[ע' תו' לקמן לז. ד"ה הבא]

[וע' תו' שם ד"ה ועל]

גיטין פח. עדיות פ"ג ומ"ו

[נ"ל רבא וע' בתוס' לעיל יח. בד"ה אביי לא אמר ועי' תוס' לקמן לז. ד"ה אמר רבה קסבר וכו' נע"ק]

[בתוספתא איתא קטנה]

[תוס' דיבמות פ"ד]

תוספות רי"ד

ת"ר יצא עליה ש"ר בילדותה אין לה לא אונס ולא פיתוי אמר ר"פ ש"מ האי שטרא ריעא לא מגבינן בי' פי' שיצא עלי' שם זיוף ה"ד אי נימא דנפיק עלי' קלא דשטר זייפא הוא דכוותה הכא נמי דנפיק עלי' קלא דונאי והא"ר יצא עליה שם מזנה בעיר אין חוששין לה אפי' לכהונה אלא דאתי בי תרי ואמרו לדידהו תבעתנהי באיסורא פי' אלא יצא עליה ש"ר ה"ד כגון בעדים לא שאמרו נבעלה דא"כ מאי למימרא הא לאו בתולה היא אלא אמרי לדידהו וכו' פירוש והפקירה עצמה לכך ולא שמעו לה דכותה התם דאתי בי תרי ואמרו לדידהו אמר זייפו לי. בשלמא הכא שכיחי פריצות פי' היכא גמר ר"פ מינה דלא מגבי' בשטרא כי האי התם שכיחי פרוצות וכיון שיש עדים שהיתה מחזרת אחר זנות הרבה מצאה לה מ"ה אין לה קנס לאחר זמן דלאו בחזקת בתולה הואי אלא התם אם הוא מוחזק כל ישראל מי הוחזקו פי' גבי שטר אם הוא מוחזק לחזר אחר עידי שקר כ"י מי הוחזקו להיות שומעי' לו לזייף. התם נמי כיון דמהדר אזייפא אימור זיופי' זייף וכתב פי' הוא עצמו למד לכוין כתב הדומה לכת"י העדים שחתום בו. והילכך אפי' יש עדים המכירים החתימה ואומרים שחתימות יד העדים הוא לא מגבי' ביה: **מתני'** ואלו שאין להן קנס. הבא על הגיורת ועל השבויה ועל השפחה שנפדו ושנתגיירו ושנשתחררו יתירות על בנות ג"ש ויום א'. פי' שכיון שראויה לביאה בחזקת הפקר הן ונבעלו בגיותם ר"י אומר שבויה שנשבית ה"ה בקדושתה אע"פ שגדולה. הבא על בתו ועל בת בנו ועל ב"א על בת בתה ועל בת בנה אין להם קנס מפני שנתחייב בנפשו שמיתתו ע"י ב"ד וכל המתחייב בנפשו אינו משלם ממון שנאמר ולא יהיה אסון ענוש יענש פי' הא אם יהיה אסון לא יענש ובגמרא פריך והא מהכא נפקא מהתם נפקא פי' מכדי רשעתו. משום רשעה אחת אתה מחייבו ולא משום ב' ומשני חדא במיתה וממון וחדא במלקות וממון וצריכי וכו' ואין הל' כר"י: ת"ר הפודה את השבויה ומעיד בה ישאנה דלא שדא איניש זוזי בכדי. מעיד בה כדי לא ישאנה פי' אם הוא כהן חיישינן שמא עיניו נתן בהו לעלמא שריא:

תורה אור

וְסָבַר רַבִּי יְהוּדָה בִּקְדוּשָּׁתָהּ קַיְימָא? וְהָתַנְיָא: הַגִּיּוֹרֶת שֶׁנִּתְגַּיְּירָה וְרָאֲתָה דָּם, ר' יְהוּדָה אוֹמֵר דַּיָּהּ שַׁעְתָּהּ, [א]ר' יוֹסֵי אוֹמֵר: הֲרֵי הִיא כְּכָל הַנָּשִׁים, וּמְטַמְּאָה מֵעֵת לְעֵת וּמִפְּקִידָה לִפְקִידָה, וּצְרִיכָה לְהַמְתִּין ג' חֳדָשִׁים, דִּבְרֵי ר' יְהוּדָה. ר' יוֹסֵי מַתִּיר לֵיאָרֵס וְלִינָּשֵׂא מִיָּד! א"ל: גִּיּוֹרֶת אַשְׁבוּיָה קָא רָמֵית?! גִּיּוֹרֶת – לָא מְנַטְּרָא נַפְשָׁהּ, שְׁבוּיָה – מְנַטְּרָא נַפְשָׁהּ. וְרָמֵי שְׁבוּיָה אַשְּׁבוּיָה; דְּתַנְיָא: *הַגִּיּוֹרֶת וְהַשְּׁבוּיָה וְהַשִּׁפְחָה שֶׁנִּפְדּוּ וְשֶׁנִּתְגַּיְּירוּ, וְשֶׁנִּשְׁתַּחְרְרוּ יְתֵירוֹת עַל בְּנוֹת ג' שָׁנִים וְיוֹם אֶחָד – [א]צְרִיכוֹת לְהַמְתִּין ג' חֳדָשִׁים, דִּבְרֵי ר' יְהוּדָה. ר' יוֹסֵי מַתִּיר לֵיאָרֵס וְלִינָּשֵׂא מִיָּד! אִשְׁתִּיק. א"ל: מִידֵי שְׁמִיעַ לָךְ בְּהָא? אֲמַר לֵיהּ, הָכִי אֲמַר רַב שֵׁשֶׁת: שֶׁרָאוּהָ שֶׁנִּבְעֲלָה. א"ה מַאי טַעֲמָא דְּר' יוֹסֵי? אָמַר רַבָּה: קָסָבַר ר' יוֹסֵי אִשָּׁה מְזַנָּה מְשַׁמֶּשֶׁת בְּמוֹךְ שֶׁלֹּא תִּתְעַבֵּר. בִּשְׁלָמָא גִּיּוֹרֶת, כֵּיוָן דְּדַעְתָּהּ לְאִיגַּיּוֹרֵי – מְנַטְּרָא נַפְשָׁהּ; שְׁבוּיָה נַמִי, דְּלָא יָדְעָה הֵיכָא מַמְטוּ לָהּ; שִׁפְחָה נַמִי, דְּשָׁמְעָה מִפִּי מָרָהּ; אֶלָּא יוֹצְאָה בְּשֵׁן וָעַיִן – מַאי אִיכָּא לְמֵימַר? וְכִי תֵּימָא כָּל מִמֵּילָא לֹא א"ר יוֹסֵי – הֲרֵי אֲנוּסָה *וּמְפוּתָּה, דְּמִמֵּילָא, וְתַנְיָא: אֲנוּסָה [ב]וּמְפוּתָּה צְרִיכוֹת לְהַמְתִּין ג' חֳדָשִׁים, דִּבְרֵי ר' יְהוּדָה, [ב]ר' יוֹסֵי מַתִּיר לֵיאָרֵס וְלִינָּשֵׂא מִיָּד! אֶלָּא אָמַר *רַבָּה: קָסָבַר ר' יוֹסֵי: [ג]אִשָּׁה מְזַנָּה מִתְהַפֶּכֶת כְּדֵי שֶׁלֹּא תִּתְעַבֵּר. וְאִידָךְ: חָיְישִׁי' שֶׁמָּא לֹא נֶהֶפְכָה יָפֶה יָפֶה.§ שֶׁנֶּאֱ': °"וְלֹא יִהְיֶה אָסוֹן עָנוֹשׁ יֵעָנֵשׁ" וכו'.§ וְהָא מֵהָכָא נָפְקָא? (שמות כא) מֵהָתָם נָפְקָא: °"כְּדֵי רִשְׁעָתוֹ" – *מִשּׁוּם רִשְׁעָה אַחַת אַתָּה מְחַיְּיבוֹ, וְאִי אַתָּה מְחַיְּיבוֹ מִשּׁוּם שְׁתֵּי רִשְׁעָיוֹת! (דברים כה) חֲדָא בְּמִיתָה וּמָמוֹן, וַחֲדָא בְּמַלְקוֹת וּמָמוֹן. וּצְרִיכָא: דְּאִי אַשְׁמְעִינַן מִיתָה וּמָמוֹן – מִשּׁוּם דְּאִיכָּא אִיבּוּד נְשָׁמָה, אֲבָל מַלְקוֹת וּמָמוֹן דְּלֵיכָּא אִיבּוּד נְשָׁמָה, אֵימָא לָא. וְאִי אַשְׁמְעִינַן מַלְקוֹת וּמָמוֹן – מִשּׁוּם דְּלָא חֲמִיר אִיסּוּרֵיהּ, אֲבָל מִיתָה וּמָמוֹן דַּחֲמִיר אִיסּוּרֵיהּ אֵימָא לָא, צְרִיכָא. וּלְרַבִּי מֵאִיר, *דְּאָמַר לוֹקֶה וּמְשַׁלֵּם, תַּרְתֵּי לָמָּה לִי? חֲדָא בְּמִיתָה וּמָמוֹן וַחֲדָא

רש"י

וְרָאֲתָה דָּם. בּוֹ בַּיּוֹם. דַּיָּהּ שַׁעְתָּהּ. וְלֹא גָּזְרוּ בָּהּ טוּמְאַת מֵעֵת לְעֵת לְטַמֵּא טְהָרוֹת שֶׁנָּגְעָה בָּהֶן מִשְּׁעַת טְבִילָה עַד שְׁעַת רְאִיָּיה. דְּהָא אֲפִי' יָצָא דָּם זֶה מֵאֶתְמוֹל, וְהֶעֱמִידוּהוּ כּוֹתְלֵי בֵּית הָרֶחֶם, שֶׁזֶּהוּ הַטַּעַם שֶׁל מֵעֵת לְעֵת בִּבְנוֹת יִשְׂרָאֵל – הֲלֹא דַּם גּוֹיָה כְּדַם בְּהֵמָה. וְאִם תֹּאמַר: נֵיחוּשׁ שֶׁמָּא מִשֶּׁטָּבְלָה נֶעֱקַר וְיָצָא מִיָּד? טוּמְאָה לְמַפְרֵעַ דְּרַבָּנַן הִיא, וְהֵיכָא דְּאִיכָּא לְמִיגְזַר מֵעֵת לְעֵת שָׁלֵם – גְּזוּר מִפְּקִידָה לִפְקִידָה, וְהֵיכָא דְּלָא גְּזוּר מֵעֵת לְעֵת° – לָא גְּזוּר מִפְּקִידָה לִפְקִידָה. וּצְרִיכָה לְהַמְתִּין ג' חֳדָשִׁים. שֶׁלֹּא תִּנָּשֵׂא, לְהַבְחִין בֵּין זֶרַע הַנִּזְרָע בִּקְדוּשָּׁה לְזֶרַע הַנִּזְרָע שֶׁלֹּא בִּקְדוּשָּׁה. רַבִּי יוֹסֵי מַתִּיר. לְקַמֵּיהּ מְפָרֵשׁ טַעְמָא. צְרִיכוֹת לְהַמְתִּין. וְאַף עַל פִּי שֶׁקְּטַנָּה אֵינָהּ מִתְעַבֶּרֶת, גְּזֵירָה קְטַנָּה אַטּוּ גְּדוֹלָה. מְשַׁמֶּשֶׁת בְּמוֹךְ. נוֹתֶנֶת מוֹךְ לְאַחַר בְּעִילָה, וְשׁוֹאֶבֶת הַזֶּרַע. מְנַטְּרָא נַפְשָׁהּ. וּמַזְמֶנֶת לָהּ מוֹךְ. דְּלָא יָדְעָה הֵיכָא מַמְטוּ לָהּ. שֶׁבָּאִים לְמוֹכְרָהּ, וְסָבְרָה דִּלְמָא מַמְטוּ לָהּ לְגַבֵּי יִשְׂרָאֵל וּפָרְקוּ לָהּ וּמְנַטְּרָא נַפְשָׁהּ לְשַׁמֵּשׁ בְּמוֹךְ. אֶלָּא יוֹצְאָה בְּשֵׁן וָעַיִן. שִׁפְחָה שֶׁסִּימֵּא אֲדוֹנֶיהָ אֶת עֵינָהּ וְיָצְאָה לְחֵירוּת, מְנָא הֲוַת יָדְעָה מֵעִיקָּרָא דְּתֵיפּוֹק לְחֵירוּת, דְּמִנַּטְרָא נַפְשָׁהּ לְזַמֵּן מוֹךְ לְשִׁימּוּשָׁהּ? כָּל מִמֵּילָא. מִידֵי דְּלֵיכָּא לְאִיזְדַּהוּרֵי בֵּיהּ מֵעִיקָּרָא דְּתֵיפּוֹק לְחֵירוּת – מוֹדֶה רַבִּי יוֹסֵי. הֲרֵי אֲנוּסָה דְּמִמֵּילָא. דְּלָא הֲוַת יָדְעָה דְּלִיסְלִיק בָּהּ הָכִי, וּתְזַמֵּן לָהּ מוֹךְ. מִתְהַפֶּכֶת. שֶׁיֵּצֵא הַזֶּרַע וְלֹא יִקְלוֹט. וְהָא אֲפִילּוּ בְּמִידֵי דְּמִמֵּילָא מָצוּ לְמֶיעֱבַד, וְכוּלָּן עוֹשׂוֹת כֵּן. מִשּׁוּם דְּאִיכָּא אִיבּוּד נְשָׁמָה. יֵשׁ כָּאן עוֹנֶשׁ חָמוּר, וְדַיּוֹ בְּכָךְ אִם עֲנַשְׁתּוֹ לְאַבֵּד נְשָׁמָה, לֵיהָרֵג. אֵימָא לָא. אֵין זֶה עוֹנֶשׁ יְתֵירָה, וְלִיעֲבִיד בֵּיהּ תַּרְתֵּי. דְּלָא חֲמִיר אִיסּוּרֵיהּ. לֹא עָבַר עֲבֵירָה חֲמוּרָה, וְדַיּוֹ שֶׁתַּעַנְשֵׁהוּ עוֹנֶשׁ אֶחָד. לא

תוספות

וסבר רבי יהודה בקדושתה קיימא והתניא הגיורת כו'. קשה: דהשתא דמדמה גיורת לשבויה – א"כ תיקשי ליה כתניתין גופה, דר' יהודה לא משוה גיורת לשבויה, דתנן: ר' יהודה אומר: שבויה שנפדית הרי היא בקדושתה, משמע דבהנך מודה לתנא קמא! ואמר ר"י: דמתני' אתי ליה שפיר, דמודה בגיורת שאין לה קנס, דודאי היא בחזקת בעולה, שנבעלה בעוד שלא היה דעתה להתגייר. ואפילו אם היה דעתה להתגייר משהיתה בת שלש שנים ויום אחד – מ"מ לא מנטרא נפשה, כיון דאינה ראויה להתעבר. אבל מהך דצריכה להמתין שלשה חדשים, אף על גב דדעתה לאיגיורי ומנטרא נפשה – אפילו הכי קאמר צריכה להמתין ג' חדשים, דאי אפשר לשמור עצמה מן הגוים, כ"ש שבויה שהיא מסורה בידם. **רבי** יהודה אומר דיה שעתה. פירש הקונטרס: כיון דליכא מעת לעת – מפקידה לפקידה נמי לא גזור רבנן. ורבי יוסי דקאמר ומטמאה מעת לעת – לאו דוקא מעת לעת, אלא כלומר: בתורת מעת לעת מטמאה משנתגיירה. **שבויה** מנטרא נפשה. וא"ת: והא בקטנה נמי איירי, דלא מנטרא נפשה, דהא אינה יודעת לשמור עצמה? וקאמר ר"י דבקדושתה קיימא, דקתני במתני', יתירה מבת ג' שנים ויום אחד! וי"ל: דקטנה לגמרי אינה מוסרת עצמה לביאה, וכשהיא מוסרת עצמה לביאה, קצת היא בת דעת, ויודעת לשמור עצמה. **צריכות** להמתין שלשה חדשים דברי ר' יהודה. משמע דאפי' בקטנה שאינה ראויה להתעבר קאמר רבי יהודה דצריכה להמתין, מדקאמר: יתירות מבנות ג' ויום אחד, דגזר קטנה אטו גדולה. וקשה לר"י ולרבינו תם: דתניא ב"החולץ" (יבמות דף מב: ושם): הרי שהיתה רדופה לילך לבית אביה או קטנה כו' – צריכה להמתין ג' חדשים, דברי ר"מ. ר' יהודה מתיר ליארס ולינשא מיד. אלמא לא גזר רבי יהודה קטנה אטו גדולה! וכ"ת: דוקא בגיורת ומשוחררת ושבויה גזר טפי, כדי להבחין בין זרע שנזרע בקדושה לשנזרע שלא בקדושה – זה אין נראה, דהא לרבא דמפרש התם לעיל *טעם דצריכות להמתין גזירה שמא ישא אחותו מאביו, וייבם אשת אחיו מן אמו כו' – טפי אית לן למיגזר בקטנה בת ישראל, דשייך בה כל הנהו דמפרש התם, אבל בגיורת ושבויה ומשוחררת לא שייך שמא ישא אחותו מאביו. ועוד: דשמואל אית ליה סברא איפכא מדר' יהודה, דהא שמואל קאמר בס"פ "ד' אחין" (שם דף לד: ושם) דכולן צריכות להמתין ג' חדשים חוץ מגיורת ומשוחררת קטנה, אבל קטנה בת ישראל – צריכה להמתין. אלמא בקטנה בת ישראל גזר קטנה אטו גדולה, ובגיורת ומשוחררת לא גזר, והיינו איפכא מדרבי יהודה. ועוד: לשמואל, בשלמא בקטנה בת ישראל סבר כר"מ, אלא בגיורת כמאן? לא כרבי יהודה ולא כר' יוסי. דלרבי יהודה – בין קטנה בין גדולה צריכה להמתין, ולרבי יוסי – אפי' גדולה אינה צריכה להמתין! ומיהו, למאי דמוקי להך דהכא בראוה שנבעלה – אתי שפיר כר' יהודה. ומצינן למימר דדוקא בראוה שנבעלה קאמר ר' יהודה, דגזר' קטנה אטו גדולה, אבל אותה שאינה ודאי בעולה – לא. ולפי לשון אחרון דהתם לא קשה כלל, אע"ג דשמואל איפכא מדרבי יהודה, כיון דאין הטעם משום *דגזרינן קטנה אטו גדולה. דאפילו בגדולה נמי שרי, לפי שמתהפכת. ואר"י: דבס"פ "ד' אחין" (ג"ז שם לה.) מייתי הך ברייתא דהכא, ול"ג בה יתירות מבנות ג' ויום אחד. ובתוספתא נמי ל"ג ליה. ולפי זה ניחא, דמיירי בגדולה, אבל בקטנה מודה דאין צריכה להמתין, כדקאמר בברייתא דרדופה. ואפשר דבגיורת קטנה מודה ר' מאיר דאין צריכה להמתין. והשתא שמואל בגיורת כר' יהודה, ובבת ישראל כרבי מאיר. ולגבי לשון אחרון דהתם, דאמר שמואל כולם צריכות להמתין חוץ מגיורת ומשוחררת גדולה, וקטנה בת ישראל אינה צריכה להמתין בזנות, משום דזנות דקטנה לא שכיח. אבל בנשואין גזר קטנה אטו גדולה, וסבר בגיורת כרבי יוסי, ובבת ישראל כר"מ, דגזר קטנה אטו גדולה, וס"ל דדוקא בנשואין גזר ר"מ, ושמא בנשואין מודה ר' יוסי לר"מ, ומיהו, בזנות ודאי פליג, דהא שרי אנוסה ומפותה אפילו גדולה. ולית דגרסי בברייתא דרדופה ר' יוסי במקום ר' יהודה, ושם פירשנו. **אי** הכי מ"ט דר' יוסי. תימה לר"י: דמשמע דמשום דאוקימנא בראוה שנבעלה הוא דקשיא ליה מאי טעמא, בלאו הכי נמי תיקשי ליה ברייתא דרבי יוסי, דמייתי לקמן דאנוסה ומפותה, ולפי הסוגיא נראה דזה המקשה עצמו הוא דמייתי לה? ומיהו, י"ס דגרסי בסמוך: א"ל אביי: בשלמא גיורת כיון דדעתה לאיגיורי כו', ולפי גירסא זו אתי שפיר, שזה המקשה לא ידע ברייתא דמייתי לקמן, דאביי הוא דמייתי לה. וכן הוא גירסא בשילהי "ד' אחין" (ג"ז שם).

אמר רבה קסבר רבי יוסי כו'. אליבא דרבי יוחנן משני, דלדידיה דמפרש טעמא דר' יהודה שלא יהא מוטא נשכר – לא קניא מידי [ומיהו, רבה לא קאמר אלא דלמא]. **אשה** מזנה מתהפכת. ומהשתא לא קשה אנוסה ומפותה. ומיהו, יוצאה בשן ועין מודה רבי יוסי דצריכה להמתין, דאותה למה תתהפך: ***הבא** על בתו. למאי דמוקי מתני' בפרק "בן סורר" (סנהדרין דף עג: ושם) במפותה – צריך לאוקמה בשבא עליה ובגרה, כדפרישית לעיל*: ***ועל** בת אשתו. הוה מצי למיתני אשת אביו וכלתו, דהא חשיב נמי עריות דעל ידי קדושין, אלא תנא ושייר. **חדא** במלקות וממון. לעיל* פירשתי למה לא יליף "רשע" "רשע". תימה: דבריש "החובל" (ב"ק דף פג:) פריך: הא מיבעי ליה קרא ד"לא תקחו כופר" דלא תשקול מיניה ממונא ותקטליה! ומשני: ההוא מ"כדי רשעתו" נפקא. הוה ליה למימר: ההוא מ"לא יהיה אסון" נפקא, ד"כדי רשעתו" אתא למלקות וממון! וי"ל: דהתם טעי כי היכי דטעי הכא מעיקרא לומר דמ"כדי רשעתו" נפקא מיתה וממון. [והא דלא פריך: האי במלקות וממון כתיב – לא חש להקשות משום דהוי מצי לשנויי מ"לא יהיה אסון" נפקא], אי נמי לסימנא בעלמא נקטיה התם. וחדא

נו א ב ג מיי' פי"א מהל' גירושין הל' כא כב סמג עשין נ טוש"ע אה"ע סימן יג סעיף ה ו:

גליון הש"ס

רש"י ד"ה דיה שעתה וכו' לא גזור מפקידה לפקידה. כדאיתא בנדה לו ע"א.

[אין לזה מובן וכן נראה מפירש"י ליתא]

[שם מב.]

הגהות מהר"ב רנשבורג

א] גמ' ר' יוסי אומר הרי היא ככל הנשים. עי' נדה דף לו ע"א תוד"ה דליכא שהות וכו'. והגאון מהרר"פ לא ציינו בתלמוד החדשים בהגהותיו:

[שייך לעיל במשנה לו:]

[ג"ז שייך שם]

[לה. ד"ה רבא]

יבמות לה. [כל הסוגיא ע"ש]

[שם איתא אביי]

ב"ק פג: מכות ד: יג: [לעיל לב:]

[לעיל לג: וש"נ]

[ולא גזרינן כצ"ל רש"ל]

[דף כט. ד"ה ועל אשת]

וַחֲדָא בְּמִיתָה וּמַלְקוֹת. וּצְרִיכָא; דְּאִי אַשְׁמְעִינַן מִיתָה וּמָמוֹן – מִשּׁוּם דַּחֲדָא בְּגוּפֵיהּ וַחֲדָא בְּמָמוֹנֵיהּ לָא עָבְדִינַן, אֲבָל בְּמִיתָה וּמַלְקוֹת דְּאִידִי וְאִידִי בְּגוּפֵיהּ – אֵימָא מִיתָה אֲרִיכְתָּא הִיא, וְנַעֲבֵיד בֵּיהּ. וְאִי אַשְׁמְעִינַן מִיתָה וּמַלְקוֹת – דְּתַרְתֵּי בְּגוּפֵיהּ לָא עָבְדִינַן, אֲבָל מִיתָה וּמָמוֹן דַּחֲדָא בְּגוּפֵיהּ וַחֲדָא בְּמָמוֹנֵיהּ – אֵימָא נַעֲבֵיד בֵּיהּ, צְרִיכָא. "°וְלֹא תִקְחוּ כֹפֶר לְנֶפֶשׁ רֹצֵחַ" (במדבר לה) לָמָּה לִי? *דְּאָמַר רַחֲמָנָא: [א]לָא תִּשְׁקוֹל מָמוֹנָא מִינֵּיהּ וְתִפְטְרֵיהּ מִקְּטָלָא. °"לֹא תִקְחוּ כֹפֶר לָנוּס אֶל עִיר מִקְלָטוֹ" (שם) *לָמָּה לִי? [ב]דְּאָמַר רַחֲמָנָא: לָא תִּשְׁקוֹל מָמוֹנָא מִינֵּיהּ וְתִפְטְרֵיהּ מִן גָּלוּת. וּתְרֵי קְרָאֵי לָמָּה לִי? חַד בְּשׁוֹגֵג וְחַד בְּמֵזִיד, וּצְרִיכִי; דְּאִי אַשְׁמְעִינַן מֵזִיד – מִשּׁוּם דַּחֲמִיר אִיסּוּרֵיהּ, אֲבָל שׁוֹגֵג דְּלָא חֲמִיר אִיסּוּרֵיהּ – אֵימָא לָא. וְאִי אַשְׁמְעִינַן שׁוֹגֵג – מִשּׁוּם דְּלֵיכָּא אִיבּוּד נְשָׁמָה, אֲבָל מֵזִיד דְּאִיכָּא אִיבּוּד נְשָׁמָה – אֵימָא לָא, צְרִיכָא. °"וְלָאָרֶץ לֹא יְכֻפַּר לַדָּם אֲשֶׁר שֻׁפַּךְ בָּהּ כִּי אִם בְּדַם שֹׁפְכוֹ" (שם) לָמָּה לִי? מִבָּעֵי לֵיהּ לִכְדְתַנְיָא: *מִנַּיִן [ג]שֶׁאִם נִתְעָרְפָה עֶגְלָה וְאַחַ"כ נִמְצָא הַהוֹרֵג, מִנַּיִן שֶׁאֵין פּוֹטְרִין אוֹתוֹ – שֶׁנֶּאֱמַר: "וְלָאָרֶץ לֹא יְכֻפַּר לַדָּם אֲשֶׁר שֻׁפַּךְ בָּהּ וגו'". °"וְאַתָּה תְּבַעֵר הַדָּם הַנָּקִי מִקִּרְבֶּךָ" (דברים כא) לָמָּה לִי? מִיבָּעֵי לֵיהּ לִכְדְתַנְיָא: *מִנַּיִן לַמּוּמָתִים בְּסַיִיף שֶׁהוּא מִן הַצַּוָּאר – ת"ל: "וְאַתָּה תְּבַעֵר הַדָּם הַנָּקִי מִקִּרְבֶּךָ", הוּקְשׁוּ כָּל שׁוֹפְכֵי דָמִים לְעֶגְלָה עֲרוּפָה, מַה לְּהַלָּן מִן הַצַּוָּאר – [ד]אַף שׁוֹפְכֵי דָמִים מִן הַצַּוָּאר. אִי מַה [ה]לְּהַלָּן בְּקוֹפִיץ, וּמִמּוּל עוֹרֶף, אַף כָּאן בְּקוֹפִיץ וּמִמּוּל עוֹרֶף? *אָמַר רַב נַחְמָן אָמַר רַבָּה בַּר אֲבוּהּ: אָמַר קְרָא °"וְאָהַבְתָּ לְרֵעֲךָ כָּמוֹךָ" (ויקרא יט) – בְּרוֹר לוֹ מִיתָה יָפָה. °"כָּל חֵרֶם אֲשֶׁר יָחֳרַם מִן הָאָדָם לֹא יִפָּדֶה" (שם כז) לָמָּה לִי? מִיבָּעֵי לֵיהּ לִכְדְתַנְיָא: *מִנַּיִן לַיּוֹצֵא לֵיהָרֵג וְאָמַר אֶחָד "עֶרְכּוֹ עָלַי", מִנַּיִן [ו]שֶׁלֹּא אָמַר כְּלוּם – שֶׁנֶּאֱמַר: "כָּל חֵרֶם אֲשֶׁר יָחֳרַם מִן הָאָדָם לֹא יִפָּדֶה". יָכוֹל אַף קוֹדֶם שֶׁנִּגְמַר דִּינוֹ כֵּן – ת"ל: "מִן הָאָדָם" – וְלֹא כָּל הָאָדָם. *וּלְרַבִּי חֲנַנְיָא בֶּן עֲקַבְיָא, דְּאָמַר: נֶעֱרָךְ, מִפְּנֵי שֶׁדָּמָיו קְצוּבִין, הַאי "כָּל חֵרֶם" מַאי עָבֵיד לֵיהּ? מִיבָּעֵי לֵיהּ לִכְדְתַנְיָא, *רַבִּי יִשְׁמָעֵאל בְּנוֹ שֶׁל ר' יוֹחָנָן בֶּן בְּרוֹקָה אוֹמֵר: [ז]לְפִי שֶׁמָּצִינוּ לַמּוּמָתִים בִּידֵי שָׁמַיִם שֶׁנּוֹתְנִין מָמוֹן וּמִתְכַּפֵּר לָהֶן, שֶׁנֶּאֱמַר: "°אִם כֹּפֶר יוּשַׁת עָלָיו" (שמות כא), יָכוֹל אַף בִּידֵי אָדָם כֵּן – ת"ל: "חֵרֶם מִן הָאָדָם לֹא יִפָּדֶה". וְאֵין לִי אֶלָּא מִיתוֹת חֲמוּרוֹת, שֶׁלֹּא נִיתְּנָה שִׁגְגָתָן לְכַפָּרָה, מִיתוֹת קַלּוֹת, שֶׁנִּיתְּנָה שִׁגְגָתָן לְכַפָּרָה מִנַּיִן – ת"ל: "כָּל חֵרֶם". וְלָא מִמֵּילָא, מִ"לֹּא תִקְחוּ כֹפֶר" שָׁמְעַתְּ מִינָּהּ: לָא תִּשְׁקוֹל מָמוֹנָא מִינֵּיהּ וְתִיפְטְרֵיהּ, "כָּל חֵרֶם" ל"ל? אָמַר רָמִי בַּר חָמָא: אִיצְטְרִיךְ; ס"ד אָמִינָא: הָנֵי

לֹא תִקְחוּ כוֹפֶר. מַשְׁמַע נַמִי: אִם תַּהַרְגֶנּוּ – לֹא תַעַנְשֶׁנּוּ מָמוֹן. דְּאָמַר רַחֲמָנָא. שִׁנּוּיָא הוּא דִּמְשַׁנֵּינַן: לָאו לְאַשְׁמְעִינַן דְּלָא תַּעֲבֵיד בֵּיהּ תַּרְתֵּי, אֶלָּא לְאַשְׁמוּעִינַן בְּחִיּוּב מִיתָה לְבַדָּהּ, שֶׁלֹּא יִפָּדֶה בְּמָמוֹן. לֹא תִקְחוּ כוֹפֶר לָנוּס. קָא ס"ד לָא תַּעֲבֵיד בֵּיהּ תַּרְתֵּי לַהוֹרֵג בְּשׁוֹגֵג, גָּלוּת וּמָמוֹן. וּצְרִיכִי דְּאִי אַשְׁמְעִינַן מֵזִיד. דְּלָא לִיפְרוֹק נַפְשֵׁיהּ בְּמָמוֹן, הֲוָה אָמֵינָא: מִשּׁוּם דַּחֲמִיר אִיסּוּרֵיהּ, אֲבָל בְּשׁוֹגֵג – לִיפְרוֹק נַפְשֵׁיהּ בְּמָמוֹן מִגָּלוּת. וְאִי אַשְׁמְעִינַן שׁוֹגֵג. דְּמִשּׁוּם דְּאֵין בְּגָלוּתוֹ אִיבּוּד נְשָׁמָה, לְהָכִי לָא לִפְטְרֵיהּ בְּמָמוֹן אֶלָּא לִיגְלֵי. אֲבָל מֵזִיד. מִשּׁוּם אִיבּוּד נְשָׁמָה אֵימוֹר נִישְׁקוֹל מָמוֹנָא, וּנְקַיֵּים נֶפֶשׁ בְּיִשְׂרָאֵל. כִּי אִם בְּדַם שׁוֹפְכוֹ. וְלֹא בְּפִדְיוֹן מָמוֹן, לָמָּה לִי? מִ"לֹּא תִקְחוּ כוֹפֶר" נָפְקָא. שֶׁאֵין פּוֹטְרִין אוֹתוֹ. לוֹמַר כְּבָר נִתְכַּפֵּר בְּעוֹדוֹ סָפֵק, שֶׁהָעֶגְלָה מְכַפֶּרֶת עַל הַסָּפֵק. וְאַתָּה תְּבַעֵר. בָּתַר עֲרִיפָה כְּתִיב. מִיתָה יָפָה. בְּסַיִיף, וּמִצַּד הַסִּימָנִים, שֶׁיָּמוּת מַהֵר. כָּל חֵרֶם וגו'. מַשְׁמַע לְשׁוֹן חַיָּיבֵי מִיתוֹת, כְּמוֹ "זוֹבֵחַ לָאֱלֹהִים יָחֳרָם" (שמות כב). עֶרְכּוֹ עָלַי. וְאע"פ שֶׁעֵרֶךְ אֵינוֹ לְפִי דָּמִים אֶלָּא לְפִי שָׁנִים – לֹא אָמַר כְּלוּם, דְּמַעֲטֵיהּ קְרָא הָכָא. וְהַאי "חֵרֶם" לְשׁוֹן הֶקְדֵּשׁ הוּא. שֶׁדָּמָיו קְצוּבִין. בַּתּוֹרָה, לְפִי שָׁנִים. וְלָא דָּמֵי לְאוֹמֵר "דָּמָיו עָלַי" – דְּדָמִים אֵין לוֹ, אֲבָל עֵרֶךְ יֵשׁ לוֹ. לַמּוּמָתִין בִּידֵי שָׁמַיִם. כְּגוֹן מִי שֶׁהָרַג שׁוֹרוֹ אֶת הַנֶּפֶשׁ, דִּכְתִיב בֵּיהּ "יוּמָת". וְלֹא מִיתַת בֵּית דִּין, דְּנָפְקָא לָן בְּסַנְהֶדְרִין (דף טו:) "מוֹת יוּמַת הַמַּכֶּה רוֹצֵחַ הוּא" – עַל רְצִיחָתוֹ אַתָּה הוֹרְגוֹ, וְאִי אַתָּה הוֹרְגוֹ עַל רְצִיחַת שׁוֹרוֹ. וְהַאי "יוּמַת" – בִּידֵי שָׁמַיִם. יָכוֹל אַף. חַיָּיבֵי מִיתוֹת ב"ד יִפָּדוּ בְּמָמוֹן. חֵרֶם מִן הָאָדָם. אָדָם שֶׁמְּחוּיָּיב חֵרֶם. אֶלָּא מִיתוֹת חֲמוּרוֹת שֶׁלֹּא נִיתְּנָה שִׁגְגָתָן לְכַפָּרָה. כֵּיוָן דִּקְרָא לָא פָּרֵישׁ כָּל מִיתוֹת, מִיסְתַּיֵּיךְ אִי שָׁדֵית הָךְ חוּמְרָא דְּאֵין מָמוֹנוֹ מַצִּילוֹ אַמִּיתוֹת חֲמוּרוֹת, וּמַאי נִינְהוּ – כְּגוֹן הָעוֹשֶׂה חַבּוּרָה בְּאָבִיו, אוֹ גּוֹנֵב נֶפֶשׁ מִיִּשְׂרָאֵל, שֶׁאֵין כַּפָּרָה כְּתוּבָה בְּשִׁגְגָתוֹ, שֶׁאֵין כָּרֵת בִּזְדוֹנוֹ דְּלִיחַיֵּיב חַטָּאת בְּשִׁגְגָתוֹ. מִיתוֹת קַלּוֹת. הַיְינוּ כָּל מִיתוֹת הַחֲמוּרוֹת בָּהֶן כָּרֵת עַל זְדוֹנוֹ בְּלֹא הַתְרָאָה – יֵשׁ כַּפָּרָה בְּשִׁגְגָתָהּ בְּחַטָּאת, כְּגוֹן עֲבוֹדָה זָרָה וְשַׁבָּת וַעֲרָיוֹת. א"נ, רוֹצֵחַ – שֶׁיֵּשׁ כַּפָּרָה לְשִׁגְגָתוֹ בְּגָלוּת. וְלָא מִמֵּילָא. שָׁמְעַתְּ לָהּ מִ"לֹּא תִקְחוּ כוֹפֶר" הָא גַּבֵּי רוֹצֵחַ כְּתִיבָא, וְנִיתְּנָה כַּפָּרָה לְשִׁגְגָתוֹ, וְאַשְׁמְעִינַן קְרָא שֶׁלֹּא יַצִּיל אֶת עַצְמוֹ בְּמָמוֹן. וְלָמָּה לִי תּוּ "כָּל חֵרֶם"? הָנֵי

וחדא במיתה ומלקות. ורבנן, מלקות וממון ומיתה ומלקות תרוייהו נפקי מ"כדי רשעתו" דמשמע: אם נתחייב בהדי מלקות מיתה או ממון – משום רשעה אחת אתה מחייבו. ואע"ג דסמיך ליה "ארבעים יכנו לא יוסיף" – מ"מ אין לנו לומר דילקה ולא ימות כמו שלוקה ואינו משלם – דאתגורי איתגור?! כדפריך ב"הנשרפים" (סנהדרין דף פא. ושם). ואע"ג דגבי ממון ומלקות אמרינן דנדון בממון, אפילו ממונא קולא – התם משום דחס רחמנא אנחבל*. **לא** תשקול ממונא מיניה ותפטריה מגלות. קשה לרשב"א: דל"ל קרא? מתנא דבי חזקיה נפקא דלא חילקת בין שוגג למזיד, וכי היכי דבמזיד לא תשקול מיניה ממונא ותפטריה מקטלא – אף שוגג לא תשקול מיניה ממונא ותפטריה מגלות! ואומר ר"י: דלא שייך לאקושי שוגג למזיד כי האי גוונא, כיון שאין פדיון שניהם שוה. דפדיון של מזיד לפוטרו ממיתה, ופדיון של שוגג לפוטרו מגלות.

ואח"כ נמצא ההורג. בפירוש החומש פ"ה הך דרשה מ"ואתה תבער דם הנקי" ולא עיין כאן. ומיהו, יש לקיים פירושו דהך סוגיא דשמעתא דמוקמי' "ואתה תבער" להקיש שופכי דמים לעגלה ערופה, אתיא כמאן דאמר חנק חמור, כדמוכח בפרק "ד' מיתות" (שם דף נב:), דלמאן דאמר חנק קל – יליף סייף ברוצח מ"נקום ינקם". הלכך לדידיה אייתר "ואתה תבער" לנערפה העגלה ואח"כ נמצא ההורג. וקרא ד"ולארץ לא יכופר" דרשינן ליה לכדרבא בפ' בתרא דכריתות (דף כו.) דמייתינן עגלה ערופה אע"פ שעבר יוה"כ עליה. **מה** להלן בקופיץ וממול עורף. וא"ת: ממול עורף מנלן? והא "וערפו" כתיב, דמשמע עורף ממש! ויש לומר: דבפ' "עגלה ערופה" (סוטה דף מו:) גמר "עריפה" "עריפה" מחטאת העוף. **הוקשו** שופכי דמים כו'. הוה מצי למימר: הניחא למ"ד חנק חמור אלא למ"ד חנק קל כו'. **ברור** לו מיתה יפה. ומהאי טעמא לא הוה שמעינן מן הצואר, דאם יתחב סכין בלבו – הוי נמי מיתה יפה. **לפי** שמצינו מומתים בידי שמים. דכתיב "וגם בעליו יומת" דע"כ לא בידי אדם קאמר דכתיב "מות יומת המכה רוצח הוא" וגו' על רציחתו אתה הורגו כו'. אלא ודאי בידי שמים. ואף על גב דדרשינן מיניה בפ"ק דסנהדרין (דף טו. ושם): כמיתת בעלים כך מיתת השור – היינו מדכתיב "יומת" ולא כתיב "ימות". וכ"ת כולה להכי הוא דאתא – אם כן ליכתוב השור יסקל כבעלים, ולישתוק. אי נמי: *וגם כבעליו יומת, הלכך שמע מינה תרתי. **יכול** אף בידי אדם כן. יש תימה: דהיכי בעי למימר מיתה בידי אדם ממיתה בידי שמים! [ותירץ מהר"ם: כיון דאיתקש מיתת שור למיתת בעלים – נקיש נמי מיתת בעלים בידי אדם למיתת בעלים שעל ידי שור]. **מיתות** קלות שניתן שגגתן לכפרה מנין. פי' בקונט': כגון עבודה זרה ושבת וגילוי עריות שניתן שגגתן לכפרה ע"י קרבן, וכן רוצח ניתנה שגגתו לכפרה ע"י גלות. וקשה: דא"כ למסקנא אמאי איצטריך "חרם" ו"כל חרם" ו"לא תקחו" ג' קראי? ב"לא תקחו כופר" וב"חרם" סגי, דחד לדרך עלייה וחד לדרך ירידה שניתן שגגתו לכפרה, דהיינו מיתות קלות לפ"ה! לכך נראה: דמיתות קלות לא חשיב אלא הנהו שניתן שגגתן לכפרה ע"י ממון, או ע"י קרבן. אבל רוצח – לא ניתן שגגתו לכפרה ע"י ממון, אלא על ידי גלות. וה"פ דברייתא: אין לי אלא מיתות חמורות שלא ניתן שגגתן לכפרה ע"י קרבן, דהיינו כל מיתות שאין בהן כרת, כגון מסית ומדיח, ונביא השקר, וזקן ממרא, ומכה אביו ואמו, ומקלל אביו ואמו, וגונב נפש, ומגדף, אליבא דרבנן דאמרי בכריתות (דף ג:) דאין מביא קרבן על שגגתו, דכתיב "לעושה בשגגה" – פרט למגדף שאין בו מעשה, ורוצח. ומיתות קלות – כגון עבודה זרה ושבת ועריות, דיש בהן כרת ומביא קרבן על שגגתן. ופריך: ולא ממילא שמעת מינה מ"לא תקחו כופר", ומהתם שמעינן כל מיתות חמורות – ולמה לי קרא למיתות חמורות? אבל למיתות קלות ודאי צריך קרא. ומשני: דאיצטריך תרי קראי למיתות חמורות, חד לדרך עלייה שלא ניתן שגגתו לכפרה כלל, וחד לדרך ירידה שניתן שגגתו לכפרה על ידי גלות. קשה לרשב"א: דמאי איצטריך קרא לחייבי מיתות קלות, כגון עבודה זרה ושבת ועריות, דמה שייך שם כופר, למ"ד כופר היינו דמי ניזק? ותירץ: דרבי ישמעאל בנו של רבי יוחנן בן ברוקה לטעמיה, דאמר בפרק "שור שנגח ד' וה'" (ב"ק דף מ.): "ונתן פדיון נפשו" – דמי מזיק. הני

נז א מיי' פ"א מהל' רוצח ושמירת נפש הלכה ד סמג לאוין קסח:
נח ב מיי' פ"ה שם הל' א סמג לאוין קסב:
נט ג מיי' פ"י שם הל' ח סמג עשין עח:
ס ד מיי' פט"ו מהל' סנהדרין הלכה ד סמג עשין קב:
[וע"ע תוס' לעיל לב. ד"ה ואי]
סא ה מיי' פ"ט מהל' רוצח הלכה ג סמג עשין עח:
סב ו מיי' פ"א מהל' ערכין הל' יג סמג עשין קכח:
סג ז מיי' פ"י מהלכות נזקי ממון הל' ד סמג עשין סז:
ס"א ליכתוב וגם בעליו יומת ותו לא.
ת"י כ"י

ב"ק פג.
[דנפקא לן מתנא דבי חזקיה דלא חילקת בין שוגג למזיד למאי דס"ד השתא דבעי למימר קרא לא תשקול מיניה ממונא ונחייביה. ת"י]
סוטה מז:
סנהדרין נב:
שם ודף מה. פסחים עה. [ב"ק נא. סוטה ח:]
ערכין ו:
[שם]
[שם]

הָנֵי מִילֵּי הֵיכָא דַּהֲרָגוֹ דֶּרֶךְ עֲלִיָּה, אשֶׁלֹּא נִיתְּנָה שִׁגְגָתוֹ לְכַפָּרָה. אֲבָל הֲרָגוֹ דֶּרֶךְ יְרִידָה, דְּנִיתְּנָה שִׁגְגָתוֹ לְכַפָּרָה, אֵימָא נִישְׁקוֹל מָמוֹנָא מִינֵּיהּ וְנִיפַּטְרֵיהּ, קמ"ל. א"ל רָבָא: הָא — מִדְּתַנָּא דְּבֵי חִזְקִיָּה נָפְקָא, *דְּתָנָא דְּבֵי חִזְקִיָּה: מַכֵּה אָדָם וּמַכֵּה בְהֵמָה, מַה מַּכֵּה בְהֵמָה לֹא חִלַּקְתָּ בּוֹ בֵּין שׁוֹגֵג לְמֵזִיד, בֵּין מִתְכַּוֵּין לְשֶׁאֵין מִתְכַּוֵּין, בֵּין דֶּרֶךְ יְרִידָה לְדֶרֶךְ עֲלִיָּה, לְפוֹטְרוֹ מָמוֹן אֶלָּא לְחַיְּיבוֹ מָמוֹן, אַף מַכֵּה אָדָם לֹא תַּחֲלוֹק בּוֹ בֵּין שׁוֹגֵג לְמֵזִיד, °בֵּין מִתְכַּוֵּין לְשֶׁאֵין מִתְכַּוֵּין, בֵּין דֶּרֶךְ יְרִידָה לְדֶרֶךְ עֲלִיָּה, לְחַיְּיבוֹ מָמוֹן אֶלָּא לְפוֹטְרוֹ מָמוֹן! אֶלָּא אָמַר רָמִי בַּר חָמָא: אִיצְטְרִיךְ; ס"ד אָמִינָא: ה"מ — הֵיכָא דְּסִימֵּא אֶת עֵינוֹ וַהֲרָגוֹ בָּהּ, אֲבָל הֵיכָא דְּסִימֵּא אֶת עֵינוֹ וַהֲרָגוֹ בְּדָבָר אַחֵר — אֵימָא נִישְׁקוֹל מָמוֹנָא מִינֵּיהּ. א"ל רָבָא: הָא נַמִי מֵאִידָךְ תָּנָא דְּבֵי חִזְקִיָּה נָפְקָא. *דְּתָנָא דְּבֵי חִזְקִיָּה: °"עַיִן תַּחַת עַיִן" (שמות כא) בוְלֹא עַיִן וְנֶפֶשׁ תַּחַת עַיִן! אֶלָּא אָמַר רַב אַשִׁי: אִיצְטְרִיךְ; ס"ד אָמִינָא: הוֹאִיל וְחִידּוּשׁ הוּא שֶׁחִידְּשָׁה תּוֹרָה בִּקְנָס, אע"ג דְּמִיקְטִיל מְשַׁלֵּם, קמ"ל. וּלְרַבָּה דְּאָמַר: *חִידּוּשׁ הוּא שֶׁחִידְּשָׁה תּוֹרָה בִּקְנָס, אע"ג דְּמִיקְטִיל מְשַׁלֵּם, הַאי "כָּל חֵרֶם" מַאי עָבֵיד לֵיהּ? סָבַר לָהּ כְּתַנָּא קַמָּא דְּר' חֲנַנְיָא בֶּן עֲקַבְיָא.§ **מתני'** נַעֲרָה שֶׁנִּתְאָרְסָה וְנִתְגָּרְשָׁה, רַבִּי יוֹסֵי הַגְּלִילִי אוֹמֵר: אֵין לָהּ קְנָס, ר"ע אוֹמֵר: *גיֵשׁ לָהּ קְנָס, וּקְנָסָהּ לְעַצְמָהּ.§ **גמ'** (דברים כב) מ"ט דְּר' יוֹסֵי הַגְּלִילִי? אָמַר קְרָא: °"אֲשֶׁר לֹא אוֹרָשָׂה", הָא אוֹרָסָה — אֵין לָהּ קְנָס. וְר"ע: "אֲשֶׁר לֹא אוֹרָשָׂה" — לְאָבִיהָ, הָא אוֹרָסָה — לְעַצְמָהּ. אֶלָּא מֵעַתָּה "נַעֲרָה" וְלֹא בוֹגֶרֶת, ה"נ דִּלְעַצְמָהּ? "בְּתוּלָה" וְלֹא בְעוּלָה, ה"נ דִּלְעַצְמָהּ? אֶלָּא, לְגַמְרֵי — הָכָא נַמִי לְגַמְרֵי! אָמַר לָךְ ר"ע: הַאי "לֹא אוֹרָשָׂה" מִיבָּעֵי לֵיהּ לְכִדְתַנְיָא: "אֲשֶׁר לֹא אוֹרָשָׂה" — פְּרָט לְנַעֲרָה שֶׁנִּתְאָרְסָה וְנִתְגָּרְשָׁה, שֶׁאֵין לָהּ קְנָס, דִּבְרֵי ר' יוֹסֵי הַגְּלִילִי. ר"ע אוֹמֵר: יֵשׁ לָהּ קְנָס, וּקְנָסָהּ לְאָבִיהָ. וְהַדִּין נוֹתֵן: הוֹאִיל וְאָבִיהָ זַכַּאי בְּכֶסֶף קִידּוּשֶׁיהָ, וְאָבִיהָ זַכַּאי בְּכֶסֶף קְנָסָהּ, דמַה כֶּסֶף קִידּוּשֶׁיהָ, אע"פ שֶׁנִּתְאָרְסָה וְנִתְגָּרְשָׁה — לְאָבִיהָ, אַף כֶּסֶף קְנָסָהּ, אע"פ שֶׁנִּתְאָרְסָה וְנִתְגָּרְשָׁה — לְאָבִיהָ. א"כ, מַה ת"ל: "אֲשֶׁר לֹא אוֹרָשָׂה" — מוּפְנֶה לְהַקִּישׁ לוֹ, וְלָדוּן הֵימֶנּוּ ג"ש: נֶאֱמַר כָּאן: "אֲשֶׁר לֹא אוֹרָשָׂה", וְנֶאֱמַר לְהַלָּן: °"אֲשֶׁר לֹא אוֹרָשָׂה" (שמות כב) מַה כָּאן נ' — אַף לְהַלָּן נ'; וּמַה לְהַלָּן שְׁקָלִים — אַף כָּאן שְׁקָלִים. וְר"ע, מַאי חָזֵית דַּ"אֲשֶׁר לֹא אוֹרָשָׂה" לִג"ש, וּ"בְתוּלָה" לְמַעוּטֵי בְּעוּלָה, אֵימָא

רש"י

הָנֵי מִילֵּי. דְּ"לֹא תִקְחוּ כוֹפֶר" לִפְטוֹר רוֹצֵחַ מֵזִיד מִקְּטָלָא. הֵיכָא דַּהֲרָגוֹ. בְּמֵזִיד, דֶּרֶךְ עֲלִיָּיה. בַּהֲנָפַת יָדוֹ הִכָּהוּ מֵאַחֲרָיו, דִּדְכַוָּותָהּ בְּשׁוֹגֵג לֹא נִיתַּן לְכַפָּרַת גָּלוּת, כְּדִכְתִיב "וַיַּפֵּל" — דֶּרֶךְ נְפִילָה. מִדְּתַנָּא דְּבֵי חִזְקִיָּה נָפְקָא. שֶׁאֵין חִילּוּק בֵּין דֶּרֶךְ עֲלִיָּיה לְדֶרֶךְ יְרִידָה. לְחַיְּיבוֹ מָמוֹן. וְהוּא הַדִּין לִפְדוּתוֹ. וְ"לֹא יִהְיֶה אָסוֹן" מִיהָא אִיצְטְרִיךְ, דְּאִי מֵהֶיקֵּישָׁא, הֲוָה אָמִינָא: אַדְּרַבָּה, לְאִידָּךְ גִּיסָא: מַה מַּכֵּה בְהֵמָה — לְעוֹלָם יְשַׁלֵּם, אַף מַכֵּה אָדָם — יְשַׁלֵּם. וְהַשְׁתָּא דְּנָפְקָא לָן פְּטוּר תַּשְׁלוּמִין לְמֵזִיד מִ"לֹּא יִהְיֶה אָסוֹן", עַל כָּרְחָךְ הֶיקֵּישָׁא לִפְטוֹר שׁוֹגֵג דֶּרֶךְ עֲלִיָּיה. הָכִי גָּרְסִינַן. אֶלָּא אֲמַר רָמִי בַּר חָמָא כו'. אִיצְטְרִיךְ חַד מֵהָנֵי קְרָאֵי, לְאַשְׁמוּעִינַן דְּלָא לִיעֲבִיד בֵּיהּ תַּרְתֵּי, וְאַף עַל גַּב דְּנָפְקָא לָן מִ"וְלֹא יִהְיֶה אָסוֹן". הָנֵי מִילֵּי. דְּלָא עָנְשִׁינַן לֵיהּ בְּתַרְתֵּי — הֵיכָא דְּסִימֵּא אֶת עֵינוֹ וַהֲרָגוֹ בָּהּ בְּאוֹתָהּ מַכָּה, וָמֵת. בְּדָבָר אַחֵר. בְּמַכָּה אַחֶרֶת וּבְבַת אַחַת. אֵימָא. נִיעַנְשֵׁיהּ דְּמֵי עַיִן, וּמִיתָה בִּשְׁבִיל הַהֲרִיגָה. הָא. דְּסִימֵּא עֵינוֹ וַהֲרָגוֹ בָּהּ. מֵאִידָךְ דְּבֵי חִזְקִיָּה נָפְקָא. דְּלָא תִּיעַנְשֵׁיהּ. וְלֹא עַיִן וָנֶפֶשׁ תַּחַת עַיִן. מִינֵּיהּ קַיְימָא לָן בְּ"הַחוֹבֵל" (ב"ק פד.), דְּ"עַיִן תַּחַת עַיִן" (שמות כא) מָמוֹן. דְּאִי אָמְרַתְּ מַמָּשׁ — דִּלְמָא בַּהֲדֵי דְּסַמֵּינַן לְעֵינֵיהּ מָיֵית, וְהָוֵה לֵיהּ עַיִן וָנֶפֶשׁ תַּחַת עַיִן. מִיהוּ, שָׁמְעִינַן מִינָּהּ דְּלָא תַּעֲבֵיד בֵּיהּ תַּרְתֵּי, לָא שְׁנָא מֵת בְּאוֹתָהּ מַכָּה לָא שְׁנָא לֹא מֵת. (לעיל לד: לה:) סָלְקָא דַּעְתָּךְ אָמִינָא חִידּוּשׁ הוּא שֶׁחִידְּשָׁה תוֹרָה. בְּכָל תַּשְׁלוּמֵי קְנָס, שֶׁאֵינוֹ דִּין אֶלָּא גְּזֵרַת מֶלֶךְ בְּעָלְמָא, וְכֵיוָן דְּחִידּוּשׁ הוּא וּגְזֵירַת חוֹק — אֵימָא אע"ג דְּאִיכָּא בַּהֲדֵיהּ מִיתָה — לְשַׁלֵּם. קמ"ל. (לקמן ע.) חַד מֵהָנָךְ קְרָאֵי יְתֵירָא שֶׁאֵינוֹ עִנְיָן לְמָמוֹן, תְּנֵיהוּ עִנְיָן לִקְנָס. (דברים כב) כְּתַנָּא קַמָּא. וְדָרֵישׁ לֵיהּ בְּאוֹמֵר "עֶרְכּוֹ שֶׁל יוֹצֵא לֵיהָרֵג עָלַי". **מתני'** שֶׁנִּתְאָרְסָה וְנִתְגָּרְשָׁה. דְּאִילּוּ אֲרוּסָה שֶׁלֹּא נִתְגָּרְשָׁה חַיָּיב מִיתָה, וְאֵין שָׁם קְנָס. אֵין לָהּ קְנָס. טַעְמָא מְפָרֵשׁ בַּגְּמָרָא. וְרֵישָׁא דְּקָתָנֵי אֵשֶׁת אָחִיו וְאֵשֶׁת אֲחִי אָבִיו דִּבְנִתְאָרְסָה וְנִתְגָּרְשָׁה עָסְקִינַן, וְקָתָנֵי יֵשׁ לָהֶן קְנָס — ר' עֲקִיבָא הִיא. **גמ'** אֶלָּא מֵעַתָּה. לְר' עֲקִיבָא, הָא דִּכְתִיב "נַעֲרָה" לְמַעוּטֵי בּוֹגֶרֶת, וּ"בְתוּלָה" לְמַעוּטֵי בְּעוּלָה. הָכִי נַמִי. דְּלָא מְמַעֵט לְגַמְרֵי, וְתִדְרוֹשׁ: נַעֲרָה — לְאָבִיהָ, הָא בּוֹגֶרֶת — לְעַצְמָהּ. הָא לָא אַשְׁכַּחַן דְּאִישְׁתַּמֵּיט תַּנָּא וּמַתְנֵי בּוֹגֶרֶת יֵשׁ לָהּ קְנָס, וְנֵימָא רַבִּי עֲקִיבָא הִיא. וּקְנָסָהּ לְאָבִיהָ. וּלְקַמָּן מַקְשִׁינַן דְּר"ע אַדְּר"ע. הוֹאִיל וְאָבִיהָ זַכַּאי בְּכֶסֶף קִידּוּשֶׁיהָ. שֶׁלּוֹ הוּא בְּנַעֲרוּתָהּ. וּלְקַמָּן יָלֵיף לָהּ בְּפֶרֶק "נַעֲרָה שֶׁנִּתְפַּתְּתָה" (דף מו:). מַה כֶּסֶף קִידּוּשֶׁיהָ אַף עַל פִּי שֶׁנִּתְאָרְסָה וְנִתְגָּרְשָׁה. מֵאַחֵר, כְּשֶׁחוֹזֶרֶת וּמִתְקַדֶּשֶׁת בְּתוֹךְ נַעֲרוּת. לְאָבִיהָ הָוֵי. דְּהָא כָּל קִידּוּשֵׁי נַעֲרוּת יָלְפִינַן לְאָבִיהָ, דְּגַבֵּי קִידּוּשִׁין לָא כְּתִיב מִיעוּטָא דַּ"אֲשֶׁר לֹא אוֹרָסָה" כִּי הָכָא. נֶאֱמַר כָּאן. בְּאוֹנֵס. לְהַלָּן. בִּמְפַתֶּה. מַה לְהַלָּן. בִּמְפַתֶּה, שְׁקָלִים, דִּכְתִיב "יִשְׁקוֹל". אֵימָא

תוספות

הני מילי היכא דהרגו דרך עלייה דלא ניתן שגגתו לכפרה. פירוש: לכפרה בידי אדם. אע"ג דדרך עלייה קיל טפי מדרך ירידה, כדמוכח בפרק "אלו הן הגולין" (מכות דף ז. ושם) גבי גר תושב. גולה ע"י גר תושב וכל חומרי דשמעתין לא תלי אלא במה שלא ניתן לכפרה, דאינו מקפיד התלמוד במה שסקילה ושריפה חמורין מהרג וחנק. **אבל** סימא את עינו והרגו בדבר אחר אימא נשקול מיניה ממונא ונקטליה. כך גרס ר"ת, דמ"לא יהיה אסון" לא נפקא לן אלא סימא את עינו והרגו בה, כי התם, שבהכאה אחת הרג את האשה וגם הולדות. אבל סימא את עינו והרגו בדבר אחר בבת אחת — לא, *להכי איצטריך "כל חרם" למיפטריה. קשה לרשב"א: דהא ר' ישמעאל בנו של ר' יוחנן בן ברוקה לא דריש קרא להכי דלא נשקול מיניה ממונא ונקטליה, אלא שלא יתן ממון ונפטריה! ושמא "אילו לא נאמר" קאמר, כדאשכחן ריש פרק "נגמר הדין" (סנהדרין דף מג. ושם) ובכמה דוכתי. ולרשב"א נראה: דהכא מסיק אליבא דתנא דבי חזקיה, אבל לרבי ישמעאל ודאי לית ליה הא דתנא דבי חזקיה. והא דאמר בריש "הנחנקין" (שם דף פד: ושם): הניחא למאן דאית ליה דתנא דבי חזקיה, אלא למאן דלית ליה — היקישא למה לי? תנא דלית ליה דבי חזקיה היינו רבי ישמעאל. ובסמוך דקאמר: ולרבה דאמר חידוש הוא שחידשה תורה בקנס כו' — סבר לה כת"ק דר' חנניא בן עקביא. הוה מצי למימר: ס"ל כרבי ישמעאל. **הא** נמי מאידך תנא דבי חזקיה נפקא. לאו מההיא דרשה גופה קאמר דנפקא לן, דהא ההיא דרשה לא שייכא כלל לסימא את עינו והרגו בדבר אחר, אלא הכי דייק: דכי היכי דדרשי' ולא עין ונפש תחת עין — ה"נ דרשינן נפש תחת נפש ולא עין ונפש תחת נפש. וסימא את עינו והרגו בד"א לא חשיב עין ונפש; אלא נפש גריד', דמה שסימא את עינו בשעת הריגה — לא חשיב כלום, דבלאו הכי היה מת, אלא שהמיתו בלער מרובה. וא"ת: *הא מילתא נמי מתנא דבי חזקיה דלעיל נפקא, דמה מכה בהמה לא חלקת בין סימא את עינה והרגה בה, להורגה בד"א כו'! וי"ל: דמכה אדם ומכה בהמה משמע ליה בהכאה אחת. וא"ת: סימא את עינו והרג בד"א, תיפוק ליה דפטור מדמי עין אפי' לא הרג, דבשעה שסימא את עינו היה רודף, וניתן להצילו בנפשו! וי"ל דמיירי בשיכול להצילו באחד מאיבריו — שלא ניתן להצילו בנפשו. **אמר** רב אשי איצטריך כו'. תימה: דמשמע דאם הרגו וקרע שיראין דידיה — דמחייב, דליכא למיפטריה לא מקרא ד"לא יהיה אסון" ולא מקרא ד"נפש תחת נפש", דהא הוי ממון ונפש תחת ממון ונפש, ולעיל (דף ל:) פטר *אביי זר שאכל תרומה משלו וקרע שיראין של חבירו! וי"ל: דלפי האמת נפקי כולהו מתנא דבי חזקיה. וה"פ: והא נמי מאידך תנא דבי חזקיה נפקא. כלומר: ע"כ לא איצטריך "כל חרם" להכי, אלא כולה נפקא לן מתנא דבי חזקיה דפטור. דאי הוה צריך קרא למפטריה בלא "כל חרס" הוה פטרינן ליה, מאידך תנא דבי חזקיה. וא"ת: ולישני דאיצטריך "כל חרס" להרג חבירו וקרע שיראין! וי"ל: ד"כל חרס לא יפדה" משמע ליה בממון שבא על ידי אותה חבלה שהמיתה באה על ידה.
סלקא דעתך אמינא חידוש הוא קמ"ל. אע"ג דבמתני' מייתי קרא ד"לא יהיה אסון" והכא מפיק קנס מ"כל חרס" — היינו משום דכייל מתניתין כל חייבי מיתות, דקתני: וכל המתחייב בנפשו כו'. אי נמי, מתניתין אתיא כתנא קמא דרבי חנניא בן עקיבא.
אימא

עין משפט נר מצוה

סד א מיי' פ"ו מהלכות רוצח ושמירת נפש הל' יב יג סמג עשין עה:
סה ב מיי' פ"א מהל' חובל הלכה ב ג ד סמג עשין ע:
סו ג מיי' פ"ב מהל' נערה הל' טז סמג עשין נד טור אה"ע סימן קעז:
סז ד מיי' פ"ג מהל' איסות הל' יא סמג עשין מח טוש"ע אה"ע סימן לז סעיף א:

[וליכא למימר דהכא לא קאי אקרא דכל חרס אלא אקרא דלא תקחו כופר דהא אמרי' בסמוך ולרבה דאמר חידוש כו'. ת"י]

תוספות רי"ד

מתני' נערה שנתארסה ונתגרשה ר"י הגלילי אומר אין לה קנס ר"ע אומר יש לה קנס וקנס' לעצמה. מ"ט דר' יוסי אמר קרא אשר לא אורסה הא אורסה אין לה קנס ור"ע אומר אשר לא אורסה לאביה הא אורסה לעצמה. וקי"ל הלכה כר"ע מחבירו. ומתני' דתני הבא על בתו אין לה קנס מפני שמתחייב בנפשו כר"ע אתיא. דהיכי דמי שיתחייב בבתו השתא אילו בא עליה אחר שקיל איהו קנס. השתא שבא עליה הוא לא כ"ש ובלא מיתה נמי פשיטא דלא משלם קנס. אלא ודאי מתני' בבתו נערה שנתארסה ונתגרשה עסקינן שקנסה לעצמה כר"ע ומפני שנתחייב בנפשו פטור ותדע דסתם מתני' כר"ע אתיא דהא אשת אחיו ואשת אחי אביו דתנן לעיל יש לה קנס לא אתיא אלא כר"ע דבע"כ גירשה או נתאלמנה שאל"כ הו"ל א"א ויש בהן מיתת ב"ד:

[ולפי האמת אע"ג דמלא יהיה אסון נפקי כולהו מדתנא דבי חזקיה איצטריך עין תחת עין לכדדרשינן ולא עין ונפש תחת עין אבל לא עין ונפש תחת נפש לא איצטריך למדרשי' ולאו קרא יתירא הוא אלא מפשטיה דקרא קדריש וליכא למימר לליפתוק מלא יהיה אסון ומנפש תחת נפש נפיק כולהו מכח הקישא דתנא דבי חזקיה דאכתי לא שמעי' מיניה ממון אחר בהדי מיתה דסימא את עינו והרגו בדבר אחר לא חשיב ממון ונפש אלא נפש גרידא כדמוכח בפנים להכי איצטריך לא יהיה אסון ומהשתא שמעי' מינה אפי' הרג וקרע שיראין מהקישא דתנא דבי חזקיה. ת"י]

צ"ל לה. ב"ק לה. סנהדרין עט: פד:
ב"ק פד.
[לעיל לד: לה:]
[לקמן ע.]

גליון הש"ס

מ' בין מתכוין לשאין מתכוין. עיין לקמן מ ע"א תוד"ה אחד כלרבה.

סח א מיי' פ"א מהל' נערה הלכה טו סמג עשין נד טור אה"ע סימן קעז:

אימא "בתולה" — לגזירה שוה ו"אשר לא אורסה" — פרט לנערה שנתארסה ונתגרשה! מסתברא "אשר לא אורסה" לגזירה שוה, שהרי אני קורא בה "נערה בתולה". אדרבה, "בתולה" לגזירה שוה, שהרי אני קורא בה "אשר לא אורסה"! מסתברא, *הא — אישתני גופה, והא — לא אישתני גופה. ורבי יוסי הגלילי האי סברא מנא ליה? נפקא ליה *מדתניא: °"כסף ישקול כמוהר הבתולות" (שמות כב) — שיהא זה כמוהר הבתולות, ומוהר הבתולות כזה. קשיא דר"ע אדר' עקיבא! תרי תנאי ואליבא דר"ע. בשלמא ר"ע דמתני' — לא אתיא ג"ש ומפקא ליה לקרא מפשטיה לגמרי, אלא לר"ע דברייתא — אתיא גזירה שוה ומפקא מפשטיה לגמרי! אמר רב נחמן בר יצחק: קרי ביה "אשר לא ארוסה". ארוסה בת סקילה היא! ס"ד אמינא: הואיל וחידוש הוא שחידשה תורה בקנס, אע"ג דמיקטיל — משלם. ולרבה, דאמר: *חידוש הוא שחידשה תורה בקנס, אע"ג דמיקטיל משלם — מאי איכא למימר? סבר לה כרבי עקיבא דמתניתין. תנו רבנן: קנסה למי — לאביה, וי"א אומרים: לעצמה. לעצמה אמאי? אמר רב חסדא: הכא בנערה שנתארסה ונתגרשה עסקינן, וקמיפלגי בפלוגתא דר"ע דמתניתין ורבי עקיבא דברייתא. *אמר אביי: א בא עליה ומתה — פטור, שנאמר: °"ונתן לאבי הנערה" (דברים כב) — ולא לאבי מתה. מלתא דפשיטא ליה לאביי, מיבעיא ליה לרבא. דבעי רבא: יש בגר בקבר או אין בגר בקבר? יש בגר בקבר — ודבנה הוי, או דלמא אין בגר בקבר — ודאביה הוי? ומי

אימא בתולה לגזירה שוה. ולאו למעוטי בעולה, ויהא קנס לבעולה. מסתברא אשר לא אורסה לגזירה שוה. ואפי' אורסה אית לה קנס. שהרי אני קורא בה נערה בתולה. אע"פ שנתארסה ונתגרשה, דהא נערה בתולה היא, כדכתיב קרא. אבל בעולה שאין אני קורא בה נערה בתולה — אין לה קנס. אדרבה בתולה לגזירה שוה. ולאו למעוטי בעולה בזנות, אלא יש לה קנס לבעולה בזנות, שהרי אני קורא אותה "נערה אשר לא אורסה". מסתברא. ארוסה יש לה קנס, ובעולה אין לה. דהא אישתני גופה. ופגמה אין רב כל כך. והא. דנתארסה ונתגרשה לא נשתנה גופה. הא סברא. דחמשים כסף דאונס שקלים הן, ו"כסף ישקול" דמפתה יהו חמשים. כמוהר הבתולות. מנין המפורש אצל אונס, דהיינו חמשים. ומוהר הבתולות. יהיו שקלים. כזה. שכתוב בו "ישקול". קשיא דרבי עקיבא. דברייתא, דאמר קנסה לאביה. אדרבי עקיבא. דמתני'. לא אתיא גזירה שוה ומפקא לקרא מפשטיה לגמרי. דאתא פשטיה לאשמועינן הא ארוסה לעצמה, וחד מתרוייהו לאפנויי. אי נמי לא מופני — ליכא למיפרך מידי. אלא לרבי עקיבא דברייתא וכי אתיא גזירה שוה ומפקא מפשטיה לגמרי. דלא דריש פשטא ד"אשר לא אורסה" כלל, ומשוי אורסה כלא אורסה, ואם כן מיעקר משמעותיה! קרי ביה. בפשטיה אשר לא ארוסה — למעוטי ארוסה. בת סקילה היא. ומ"לא יהיה אסון" נפקא פטורא מתשלומין. קנסה למי. קא סלקא דעתך בסתם ארוסה קאי. בא עליה ומתה. לא הספיק האב להעמידו בדין, עד שמתה. יש בגר בקבר. אם מתה בנערותה עד שלא עמדה בדין, והגיע זמן בגרותה בקבר, מי חשיב בגר או לא? ולקמיה מפרש ואזיל למאי הלכתא. יש בגר בקבר. וכי היכי דאם לא הספיקה לעמוד בדין עד שבגרה, תנן לקמן בפרק "נערה שנתפתתה" (דף מא:) דהרי הן לעצמה ולא לאביה, והשתא נמי בגר בקבר מפקיע כח האב, ובנה ירית לה, אם יש לה בן. ומי

[אימא: בתולה לג"ש. ולא נמעט בעולה, כדמשמע בסמוך. נראה דר"ע דריש ג"ש מקרא דלגופיה, דהיינו בתולה קמייתא, ודקנס ודמפתה, אבל "הבתולות" דריש לכתובת בתולות, ולא שייך למידרשיה לג"ש ולא לשום רבוי, ואייתר "נער" "נערה" "הנערה" וה' ד"הבתולות" חד לחייבי לאוין ועשה, וחד לחייבי לאוין וכריתות. ואיכא ג' רבויין; ה' ד"הבתולות", ו"נער" "נערה" "הנערה". חד לכדאביי, וחד לחייבי עשה, וחד — לחייבי לאוין וכריתות. דאי איכא לר"ע חד לגופיה בלא ג"ש — א"כ נמעוט בעולה מההוא דלגופיה. ואף על גב דבקנס ליכא אלא חד בתולה דלגופיה, מגזירה שוה דמפתה יליף בתולה ולא בעולה, כי היכי דיליף מפתה מאונס לענין נערה, דלא כתיב במפתה]. (ת"י כ"י).

אימא בתולה לג"ש. תימה: דתיקשי ליה: דאימא תרוייהו לגופייהו, ולא לג"ש! ונראה דהתלמוד קים ליה דחד מינייהו לגזירה שוה, הואיל והמקראות סתומים לענין שקלים וחמשים. הלכך פריך ואימא איפכא, ולא פריך ואימא תרוייהו לגופייהו. וכי האי גוונא איכא פ"ק דסנהדרין (דף טז.) דאמר: ולא את נביא השקר אלא בב"ד של ע' ואחד. מה"מ? א"ר יוסי בר חנינא: אתיא "הזדה" "הזדה" מזקן ממרא, ופריך: הא "הזדה" כי כתיב — בקטלא הוא דכתיב, וקטלא בכ"ג! אלא אמר ריש לקיש: גמר "דבר" "דבר" מהמראתו. והשתא היכי הוה בעי למילף ולמימר רבי יוסי ברבי חנינא דאתיא "הזדה" "הזדה". אלא דהוה קים ליה דאיכא ג"ש ולא הוה ידע במאי וקאמר מסברא דאתיא הזדה הזדה. **מי אתיא** גזרה שוה ומפקא ליה מפשטיה לגמרי. דדיוק הא אורסה הוי שקר. וקשה: דבריש "הערל" (יבמות ד' ע.) יליף דערל אסור בתרומה מגזירה שוה דתושב ושכיר מפסח, וכתיב "תושב ושכיר לא יאכל בו" גבי פסח משום גזירה שוה, אע"פ שאינו אמת, דהא תושב ושכיר אוכלין בפסח, כדאמרינן התם דלא קני ליה רביה, ומפקי' קרא מפשטיה טפי מהכא! ואומר ר"ת: דההוא תושב ושכיר מיירי בערלים, ולהכי לא יאכל. ומוכח דלאו תושב ישראל קאמר, דהא לא קני ליה רביה, אלא ודאי בערל, ומשום הפנאה כתביה*.

ארוסה בת סקילה היא. וא"ת: מאי קשיא ליה? הא השתא לא נפיק קרא ממשמעותיה. ואי לא איצטריך לגופיה כ"ש דניחא טפי, דג"ש מופנה! ואומר ר"י, דהכי פירושו: ארוסה בת סקילה היא, וכיון דלא איצטריך למידי אלא לגזירה שוה — הוה ליה למכתב "אשר לא ארוסה" בהדיא, ואמאי שני למכתב "אשר לא ארוסה" דאיכא למטעי ולמימר הא אורסה לעצמה? דבשלמא אי הוה בארוסה שום חידוש הוה אתי שפיר במה ששינה הלשון, דאמרינן האי דשנה וכתב "אורסה" — למדרש לגזירה שוה ואתא פשטיה לחידושא, אבל השתא למה לי?

לאבי הנערה ולא לאבי מתה. וא"ת: דבפרק "נערה" לקמן (דף מה:) גבי סרחה ולבסוף בגרה תידון בסקילה, דרשינן "הנערה" — שהיתה כבר! ויש לומר: דהתם מענינא דקרא, והכא מענינא דקרא. והתם ודאי אתיא לחייבה, דאי לפוטרה — לשתוק קרא מיניה ואנא ידענא דלא הויא בסקילה, דלאו נערה היא. והכא לחיובא דקנס לא אצטריך, דמסברא מחייב אשעת ביאה, ואי אפשר לפוטרו בולא כלום — הלכך אתא לפוטרו. **יש** בגר בקבר ודבנה הוי. וא"ת: היכי מצי למימר שתהא מורשת קנס לבנה? הא אין אדם מוריש קנס לבניו, כדאמרינן ריש פרק "נערה" לקמן (דף מב:), ובסמוך נמי אמר: יש בגר בקבר ופקע אב, ואי אדם מוריש קנס — כי יש בגר בקבר נמי לא פקע אב, ויהא לו מתורת ירושה! ומיהו, ההיא דבסמוך יש לדחות: דנפקא מינה אם היא חייבת לאחרים, דאם יש בגר בקבר — פקע אב, אע"ג דאדם מוריש קנס, דנוטלין בעלי חובות, אבל אם אין בגר בקבר — אין נוטלין בעלי חובות כלום, דלא פקע אב, והקנס הוא שלו ולא שלה. ויש לומר: *דהכא ה"מ לאקשויי והא אין מורשת קנס לבנה, אלא דעדיפא מיניה פריך. ור"י מוקי הך בעיא דהכא בבושת ופגם, דממונא הוי, ויכולה להוריש. ואע"ג דתנן בריש "נערה" (שם מא:): לא הספיקה לעמוד בדין עד שמת האב — הרי הן של עצמה, ואבושת ופגם נמי קאי, מדקתני הרי הן — משמע דאין יכול להוריש בושת ופגם! ואור"י: דלענין זה ודאי איתקוש בושת ופגם לקנס, דכתיב "תחת אשר ענה" מכלל דאיכא בושת ופגם, דלמי שזה ניתן — זה ניתן. אבל למילי אחריני — לא איתקוש. דהא בושת ופגם משלם ע"פ עצמו, וקנס אינו משלם ע"פ עצמו. אבל הקשה ריב"ס: דאמרינן ב"מרובה" (ב"ק דף עא: ושם): א"ל "חמשה בקר" אמר רחמנא, ולא חמשה חצאי בקר. איתיביה: גנב משל אביו וטבח ומכר, ואח"כ מת אביו — משלם תשלומי ד' וה'. והא הכא כיון דמת אביו זכה ליה במנתא דידיה, וקתני דמשלם תשלומי ד' וה'! ומשני: הב"ע — שעמד בדין. משמע דאי לאו משום דחמשה בקר ולא חמשה חצאי בקר — הוה אתי ליה שפיר, ולא הוה צריך לאוקומי בשעמד בדין, אלמא דאדם מוריש קנס לבניו! ומיהו, יש לדחות: דה"מ למימר וליטעמיך. אבל קשה: דמסיק לפרא א"ל "חמשה בקר" אמר רחמנא, ואפי' חמשה חצאי בקר. א"ל מאי שנא רישא ומאי שנא סיפא? פירוש: דקתני גנב משל אביו ומת, ואח"כ טבח ומכר פטור? א"ל: רישא קרינן ביה וטבחו כולו באיסורא, סיפא לא קרינן וטבחו כולו באיסורא. משמע דאי קרינן ביה וטבחו כולו באסורא — חייב, אע"ג דלא עמד בדין, דאדם מוריש קנס לבניו. דאי בעמד בדין לא מחייב קנס, דשלו הוא טובח ומוכר! ותי' ר"י: דמיירי דעמד בדין, ואמרו: חייב אתה ליתן לו. דאם הוא טובח אחרי כן — חייב, כדאמרינן ב"הגוזל" (שם דף קו: ושם). ור"י הלבן תירץ: דההיא דפרק "נערה" איירי לענין קרבן שבועה. והכי פירושו דסוגיא דהתם: מודינא לך לענין קרבן שבועה, דרחמנא פטריה מ"וכחש בעמיתו בפקדון" וכי קאמינא דממון הוי להורישו לבניו, שאם יתבעוהו לאחר מיתת אביהן קנס שהיה חייב לאביהן שהעמידו בדין ונתחייב וכפר ונשבע והודה, הואיל וכשנפל ליורשין — כבר היה ממון, שכבר עמד בדין, ולא היה יכול להודות ולהפטר — א"כ הוי דומיא דפקדון דקרא, ומחייב קרבן שבועה. איתיביה ר"ש אומר כו' דאחין הוא. ופירוש: שאם אינו לאחין — איך מתחייב הכופר קרבן שבועה על טענותם? והא לאו בעל דברים דידהו, הוא אלא ש"מ דאחין הוא. ומסיק: כי קאמר רבה דממון הוא להורישו לבניו — בשאר קנסות, לענין חיוב קרבן שבועה. ומסיק דאצטריך "וכחש" לעמדה בדין ובגרה ואחר כך מתה, דמינה קא ירית. מכל מקום עיקרו קנס מיקרי לגבי דידה ודידיה, ולא דמי לשאר קנסות דמוריש לבניו, דלגבי בניו לא הוה קנס כלל. ומיהו, לשון להורישו לבניו — לא משמע כפירוש זה. [ועיין תוספות בבא קמא עב. ד"ה סיפא].

שלש

תוספות רי"ד

אמר אביי בא עליה ומתה פטור שנאמר ונתן לאבי הנערה ולא לאבי מתה. פי' כגון שלא הספיק האב להעמידו בדין עד שמתה. אבל אם עמד עמו בדין ונתחייב לו אע"פ שמתה [אח"כ] נותן לאביה:

[ועי' תוס' לקמן מה. ד"ה דלמא ותוס' יבמות נט. ד"ה הא]

[לעיל לד: לה:]

לעיל כט:

לעיל י. [לעיל כט:]

[ועי' תוס' יבמות ע: ד"ה אלא]

נ"ל דהכא נמי

תורה אור

ומי מעברא? והתני רב ביבי קמיה דרב נחמן: *שלש נשים משמשות במוך, אלו הן: קטנה, ומעוברת, ומניקה; קטנה — שמא תתעבר ותמות, מעוברת — שמא תעשה עוברה סנדל, מניקה — שמא תגמול את בנה. ואיזוהי קטנה — מבת אחת עשרה שנה ויום אחד עד שתים עשרה שנה ויום אחד. פחות מיכן ויתר על כן — משמשת כדרכה והולכת, דברי ר"מ. וחכמים אומרים: אחת זו ואחת זו משמשת כדרכה והולכת, ומן השמים ירחמו, משום שנאמר: °"שומר פתאים ה'"! וכי תימא דאיעברא כשהיא נערה ואולידה כשהיא נערה, ובשיתא ירחי מי קא ילדה? והאמר שמואל: *אאין בין נערות לבגרות אלא ששה חדשים! וכי תימא: בציר הוא דליכא, הא טפי איכא — הא "אלא" קאמר! אלא הכי קמיבעיא ליה: יש בגר בקבר ופקע אב, או דלמא: אין בגר בקבר ולא פקע אב? מר בר רב אשי בעי לה הכי: מיתה עושה בגרות, או אין עושה בגרות? תיקו. בעי מיניה רבא מאביי: בא עליה ונתארסה מהו? א"ל: במי כתיב "ונתן לאבי הנערה אשר לא ארוסה"? ולטעמיך, הא דתניא: גבא עליה ונשאת — לעצמה, מי כתיב "ונתן לאבי הנערה אשר לא נשואה"? הכי השתא?! התם, הואיל ובגרות מוציאה מרשות אב, ונישואין מוציאין מרשות אב, מה בגרות, בא עליה ובגרה — לעצמה, אף נישואין, בא עליה ונשאת — לעצמה, אלא אירוסין — מי קא מפקי מרשותא דאב לגמרי? הא תנן: *דנערה המאורסה אביה ובעלה מפירין לה נדריה.§ **מתני'** *ההמפתה נותן שלשה דברים, והאונס ארבעה. המפתה נותן בושת ופגם וקנס, מוסיף עליו אונס שנותן את הצער. מה בין אונס למפתה? האונס — נותן את הצער, והמפתה — אינו נותן את הצער. האונס — נותן מיד, והמפתה — לכשיוציא. האונס — שותה בעציצו, והמפתה — אם רצה להוציא, מוציא. וכיצד שותה בעציצו — אפילו היא חיגרת, אפי' היא סומא, ואפילו היא מוכת שחין. זנמצא בה דבר ערוה, או שאינה ראויה לבא בישראל — אינו רשאי לקיימה, שנאמר: °*"ולו תהיה לאשה" — אשה הראויה לו.§ **גמ'** צער דמאי? אמר אבוה דשמואל: צער שחבטה על גבי קרקע. מתקיף לה רבי זירא: אלא מעתה, חבטה על גבי שיראין הכי נמי דפטור? וכי תימא הכי נמי — והתניא, ר' שמעון בן יהודה אומר משום רבי שמעון: *אונס אינו משלם את הצער מפני שסופה

תהלים קטז | דברים כב

ומי מעברא. בקטנות או בנערות כשהיא בת קנס שתלד בנערות. משמשות במוך. מותר להן לשמש במוך, ואינן כמשחיתות זרע. שמא יעשה עוברה סנדל. שאם תתעבר עובר שני, פוחת השני את צורת (א) הראשון, ודומה לסנדל שהוא דג שטוח. שמא תגמול את בנה. מפני שהחלב נעכר כשמתעברת, ואינו טוב ליונק, ותצטרך להעתיקו משדים, וימות. פחות מכאן. מבת אחת עשרה שנה משמשת כדרכה, לפי שלא תתעבר. ויתר על כן. על בת שתים עשרה שנה משמשת כדרכה, שאם תתעבר — לא תמות. אלמא: בקטנות לא מיעברא, שיבא לכלל לידה, דהא "ותמות" קתני. וכי תימא. מבת שתים עשרה ויום אחד שהגיעו ימי הנעורים נתעברה וילדה בנערות ומתה בנערות — הא נמי ליתא, דאמר שמואל: אין בין נערות לבגרות אלא ששה חדשים. משתביא שתי שערות — הויא נערה באותן שתביא משתים עשרה שנה והלאה, ומשתביאם עד שתבגור — ששה חדשים ותו לא. ומתניתא דקתני מבת שתים עשרה ואילך אי מעברא לא מתה — במביאה שתי שערות קודם שתתעבר קאמר. אבל כל זמן שלא הביאה — קטנה היא. והאי דנקט מנין שנים — משום דבגליר משתים עשרה ויום אחד, אפילו הביאה שערות אינו אלא שומא, כדאמרינן במסכת נדה ובקדושין. ופקע אב. פוקעה תביעת אב, וזכה הלה במה שבידו, שאין בעל דינו קיים. וקנס לאו ממון הוא להורישו לאחיה בתורת ירושה, כל כמה דלא גבתיה. או אין בגר בקבר. לאפקועי תביעת אב. מר בר רב אשי. לא בעי לה בעיא דרבא משום בגר בקבר, אלא אם מתה בנערותה מי פקעה כי בגרות דמחיים, או לא. ולהאי לישנא דמר בר רב אשי אליבא דרבא אמרו לעיל: מילתא דפשיטא ליה לאביי מיבעיא ליה לרבא. דאילו ללישנא קמא — מפשט פשיטא ליה לרבא דמיתה לא מפקעא, ודלא כאביי, כל זמן שלא בגרה. וכי קא מיבעיא ליה — בבגר בקבר קמבעיא ליה, אבל במיתה, כל זמן שלא בגרה פליג אדאביי ואמר: לא מפקעא, וחייב. מיתה עושה בגרות. עושה דין בגרות, דמפקעא כח אב כי בגרות. מהו. מי הוי לאביה או לעצמה. בגרות מוציאה מרשות אב. דלא מצינו שזיכתה לו תורה בבתו אלא מכר בקטנות, ושאר שבח כגון קנסה ומעשה ידיה בנערות, כדילפינן בפרק "נערה" (לקמן דף מו:), אבל בבגרות לא אשכחן. וכיון דלא זיכתה לו תורה — אנן מהיכא תיתי לן לזכותו בשלה. ונשואין מוציאין מרשות אב. כדאשכחן בהפרת נדרים, דכל זמן דלא ניסת — אביה מיפר, ומשניסת — אין יכול להפר. בא עליה. כשהיא נערה ובגרה. לעצמה. דכתיב "ונתן האיש השוכב עמה לאבי הנערה", אם נערה היא בשעת נתינה. אביה ובעלה. ואינו מופר עד שיפרו שניהם. **מתני'** בושת ופגם. במתני' לקמן מפרש להו. האונס נותן מיד. לאביה, אע"פ שכונסה. לכשיוציא. בגמרא פריך: הטו אשתו היא? ומפרש לה לכשלא יכנוס. דאם כנסה — אינו נותן קנס, כדכתיב "מהר ימהרנה לו, ואם מאן ימאן וגו' כסף ישקול". אבל אונס — כתיב "ונתן חמשים כסף ולו תהיה לאשה". שותה בעציצו. בכלי שבחר לו לשתות בו, כלומר: על כרחו ישאנה, כדכתיב "לא יוכל לשלחה" (דברים כב). **גמ'** שסופה

שלש נשים משמשות במוך. פי' בקונטרס: מותרות לשמש במוך, אע"ג דשאר נשים אסורות משום השחתת זרע. ואין נראה לר"ת: *דהא קטנה ואילונית מותר לשמש בהדייהו, ולא הוי השחתת זרע, כיון שהוא דרך תשמיש, ומפרש ר"ת: "משמשות" — צריכות לשמש במוך אחר תשמיש, ועלה טובה קמ"ל. ולר"י נראה לקיים פי' הקונט'. דבריש נדה (דף ג.) משמע שהמוך הוא במעיה כל שעה, והוי כמשמש על האבנים ועל העצים, ולא דמי למשמש קטנה ואילונית. ועוד: אפילו היתה נותנת מוך אחר תשמיש אסורה, *דאף על פי שאינה מצווה על פריה ורביה — מ"מ אסורה היא להשחית זרע, כדמשמע בנדה (דף יג.), דתנן: כל היד המרבה לבדוק בנשים — משובחת, באנשים — תיקצץ. ומפרש בגמרא משום דנשים לאו בנות הרגשה נינהו. משמע דאם היו בנות הרגשה — הוו אסירי. ויש לדחות: דלאו בנות איסור הרגשה נינהו קאמר. **וכי** תימא בצר הוא כו' והא בלבד קאמר. בקונטרס (בקדושין דף עט.) ל"ג ליה, דבלאו "בלבד" משמע טפי לא*. **בא** עליה ונתארסה מהו. לרבי עקיבא דמתני' קא מיבעיא ליה, דאמר נתארסה ונתגרשה קנסה לעצמה. דמי אמרינן: כיון שיצאה מרשות האב לענין קנס — יהא קנסה לעצמה, או דלמא, כיון דלענין שאר מילי לא נפקא מרשות האב — יהא קנסה לאביה. אבל לרבי עקיבא דברייתא — פשיטא דקנסה לאביה. ולר' יוסי הגלילי, נהי דאמר אין לה קנס — נמי לא מיבעיא ליה, דהא דאין לה קנס — לאו משום מיפק מרשותא דאב היא, אלא גזירת הכתוב הוא דאין לה קנס, ולא נפקא באירוסין כלל מרשות אביה, דאב זכאי בקידושיה ובמעשה ידיה אע"ג דנתארסה. והא דקא בעי לה סתם, ולא קאמר לרבי עקיבא בהדיא מהו — משום דהלכה כר' עקיבא מחבירו. **הואיל** ונישואין מוציאין מרשות אב. פי' בקונט' דילפינן מהפרת נדרים, ואע"ג דקי"ל דממונא מאיסורא לא ילפינן — ה"מ לאוקמה ברשות אב, הוא דלא ילפינן ממונא מאיסורא, אבל לאפוקי מרשות אב — ילפינן שפיר מהפרת נדרים, דבסברא מועטת יש להוציאה מרשות אב. ור"י ב"ר אברהם פי': כיון דגלי לן קרא דלאוקמה ברשות אב איסורא וממונא שוין — ה"ה לאפוקה. [ור"י מפרש: דנישואין מוציאין מרשות אב, מדדרשינן "איש אמו ואביו תיראו" איש סיפק כו' אשה אין סיפק בידה לעשות. ולא נהירא, דמעשה ידיה אינו לבעל מן התורה!]. **מה** בוגרת בא עליה ובגרה לעצמה. פירוש: דהא מלינו בוגרת שיוצאה מרשות אב לענין ממון. וקשה: דה"נ נישואין מוציאין מרשות אב לענין ממון, ואמאי צריך למילף מבוגרת? ונראה דבא עליה ובגרה לעצמה נפקא לן מ"ונתן לאבי הנערה", דדרשינן: לאבי נערה ולא לאבי בוגרת. **צער** דמאי. קשה לר"י: דמאי קא מיבעיא ליה, וכי לא ידע התלמוד שיש צער גדול לבתולה בביאה ראשונה, וכמה קטנות חולות מזה? וכ"ת דמאותו צער פשיטא ליה להתלמוד דפטור, שהרי סופה להצטער בכך תחת בעלה, והא איכא כמה תנאי ב"הכונס" (ב"ק דף נט. ושם) דלא חיישי לכחש גופנא, פירוש: דבר שסופו להיות כן. ונראה לר"י דצער בעילה משום תאות תשמיש אינו בא בשעת תשמיש אלא אחר כך, וכל צער החבלה דמחייב היינו אותו צער הבא לו בשעת חבלה, אבל מה שבא לו אחר כך מיפטר, דגרמא בעלמא הוא, הלכך בעי: צער דמאי? ורשב"א מפרש דפשיטא דצער של בתולים ליכא למימר, דע"כ תנא דמתני' חייב לכחש גופנא, מדמפתה פטור. אי

[עי' תוס' יבמות יב: ותוס' נדה יג.]

סט א מיי' פ"ב מהל' איסות הל' ב טור ש"ע יו"ד סימן רלד סעיף א בהג"ה:

ע ב מיי' פ"ב מהל' נערה הל' טז סמג עשין נד טור אה"ע סימן קעז:

עא ג מיי' שם הל' טו:

עב ד מיי' פי"א מהל' נדרים הל' ט סמג לאוין רמב טוש"ע י"ד סי' רלד סעיף ה:

עג ה מיי' פ"ב מהלכות נערה הל' ז סמג עשין נד טוש"ע אה"ע סי' קעז סעיף א:

עד ו מיי' פ"א שם הל' ג סמג שם טוש"ע שם סעיף ג:

עה ז מיי' שם הל' ה טוש"ע שם סעי' ד:

[ועי' תוס' נדה סה. ד"ה וכ"ת כו' מייתבין הגירסא]

תוספות רי"ד

תניא בא עליה ונשאת לעצמה הואיל ובגרות מוציאה מרשות אב. פי' שלא מצינו שזכתה לו תורה בבתו אלא מכר בקטנותה ושאר שבח ממון כגון קנסה ומעשה ידיה בנערות כדילפי' לקמן בפ' נערה ונשואין נמי מוציאין מרשות אב. פירוש כדאשכחן בהפרת נדרים דכ"ז שלא נשאת אביה מפר נדריה ומשנשאת אין יכול להפר. מה בוגרת בא עלי' ובגרה לעצמה דכתיב ונתן האיש השוכב עמה לאבי הנערה. אם היא נערה בשעת נתינה אף נשואין בא עליה ונשאת לעצמה: **מתני'** המפתה נותן ג' דברים והאונס ד' המפתה נותן בושת ופגם וקנס מוסיף עליו אונס שנותן את הצער מה בין אונס למפתה האונס נותן את הצער והמפתה אין נותן את הצער האונס נותן מיד והמפתה לכשיוציא האונס שותה בעציצו. פי' בכלי שבחר לו לשתות בו כלומר ע"כ ישאנה דכתיב לא יוכל לשלחה כל ימיו והמפתה אם רצה להוציא מוציא. פי' האונס נותן מיד ואע"פ שכונסה שנאמר ונתן האיש השוכב עמה לאבי הנערה חמשים כסף ולו תהיה לאשה. ודרשי' תו לו אתה כופה ולא לה:

יבמות יב: ק: נדה מה. נדרים לה: [תוספתא נדה פ"ב]

קדושין עט. נדה סה.

הגהות הב"ח

(א) רש"י ד"ה שמא יעשה עוברה וכו' צורת השני. נ"ב ותוספות פרק המפלת הביא בשם רש"י שולד אחרון ממעך צורת הראשון ע"ש בד"ה קמ"ל בדף כה מיהו ביבמות דף יב כתב רש"י ז"ל דוחק האחד את חברו ופוחת צורתו משמע לפעמים הראשון גובר ולפעמים השני גובר ופעם פי' כך ופעם פי' כך ואין כאן טעות:

נדרים סו: עב: יבמות כט: לקמן מו: קדושין ד. לקמן מב.

גליון הש"ס

תום' ד"ה שלש וכו' דאע"פ שאינה מצווה על פריה ורביה. עי' סנהדרין דף נט ע"ב תוד"ה והא:

[לעיל כט:]

ב"ק נט. ע"ש

[נ"ל דאמתניתא לא ה"מ כו'. מהרש"א]

ת"י כ"י

עו א מיי' פ"ב מהל' נערה הל' ז סמג עשין נד טור אה"ע סי' קעז:

עז ב מיי' פ"א שם הל' ג סמג וטור שם:

עח ג ד מיי' שם הל' ד:

ת"י כ"י

אי הכי מפותה נמי. יש לה לער פיסוק רגלים כמו אנוסה, ואמאי קאמר אין דומה נבעלת באונס לנבעלת ברצון? ואמר מורי הרב דודי ז"ל: *דאמתני' לא ה"מ למיפרך אמאי אונס חייב, כיון שסופה להצטער בכך תחת בעלה – דהא אפילו בעולה מצטערת בכך, ואע"ג דבא עליה עתה – סופה נמי להצטער ולא תרויח כלום. [קצת נראה דאמתני' פריך, אמאי מפותה פטור].

קרע שיראין שלי והפטר. ואע"ג דלא אמרה "על מנת לפטור" – איכא למימר דמחמת הנאת בעילה מחלה לגמרי.

[**לכשיוציא** אשתו היא. אפי' פיתה לשם אישות, מ"מ פריך: אשתו היא?! כיון דאינה צריכה גט].

בושת ופגם נותן מיד. אע"ג דאיתקש לקנס – היינו לענין שניתן זה למי שזה ניתן, אבל יש מקומות שפטור מקנס לגמרי, וחייב בבושת ופגם. **אין** לי אלא אביה היא עצמה מנין כו'. (ב) תימה לר"י: במאי מיירי? אי בקטנה או בנערה – היאך היא יכולה למאן, כיון שהאב רוצה, והוא יכול לקדשה בעל כרחה למי שירצה, וה"ה לזה. ואי בשאין לה אב או שבגרה אחר כך – מה צריך קרא? תיפוק ליה שיכולה לעכב, שלא יהא חוטא נשכר, כדקאמר אביי בסמוך. וכן אביה, אמאי צריך קרא לאביי? ואומר ר"י: דנהי שאינה יכולה לעכב על אביה שלא יקדשנה לו, מ"מ מועיל מיאונה לענין שישלם קנס, וכן במיאון אביה. והא דתניא הכא המפתה לכשלא יכנוס – צריך לפרש לכשלא יכנוס מדעתה. ומיהו קשה: דהכא דרשינן מ"אם מאן ימאן" – מ"מ, שהיא יכולה לעכב. ובפרק "נערה" (לקמן מד:) דרשינן מינה לרבות יתומה לקנס! וי"ל: דליכתוב או "מאן מאן" או "ימאן ימאן" מאי "מאן ימאן" – ש"מ תרתי. ובכה"ג אמרינן ב"מרובה" (ב"ק דף סה. ושם): גבי "אם המצא תמצא" וב"החובל" (שם דף פה.): גבי "ורפא ירפא". ועוד, נראה דלאו מיתורא דקרא דריש לה התם, דאם כן מאי פריך מינה לרבי יוסי בר' חנינא דפטר מוציא שם רע על היתומה, דשאני מפתה דרבי קרא. אלא כן הוא עיקר כמו שפירש בקונטרס לקמן, דלאו מריבוי דריש, אלא ה"פ: לרבות יתומה לקנס – דדרשינן שיש קנס כשהיא מעכבת. והוא הדין דה"מ למימר לרבות בוגרת לקנס כשהיא מעכבת, דדוקא בבוגרת או ביתומה יש קנס בעיכוב שלהן. אבל כל זמן שלא בגרה – תלוי באב. והשתא דייק התם שפיר, דשמעינן דסבר האי תנא שיש קנס ביתומה, ולא ממעטינן ליה מדכתיב "לאבי הנערה" אע"ג דליכא ריבוי ליתומה כדפירשתי, דאיכא לאוקמי קרא לבוגרת.

אלא אונס בשלמא איהי כו'. תימה: כיון דאונס ומפתה מיגמר גמירי מהדדי – להא מילתא נמי ליגמרו מהדדי, כדפריך בסמוך, ומאי קאמר אלא אביה מנלן? וי"ל: דלהאי מילתא לא גמרינן מהדדי, דהא מפתה יכול לעכב ואונס שותה בעציצו. וה"ה ה"נ אין אביה יכול לעכב, וה"נ קאמר אביי בסמוך. ורבא לא מסתבר ליה למימר הכי, כיון דאיכא ק"ו. וא"ת: ואיהי גבי אונס אמאי איצטריך למיכתב? נילף לאביי מסברא שלא יהא חוטא נשכר, ולרבא מק"ו! ויש לומר: ד"לו תהיה לאשה" אינו מיותר, [דאיצטריך לעשה ולדרשות דלעיל. מהר"ס. א"נ, אביי ורבא לא הוו משנו הכי אלא בתר דגלי קרא דהדיא]. **מפתה** דאיהו מצי מעכב. ואפי' פיתה לשם אישות יכול הוא לגרשה.

טעמא מאי תקינו לה רבנן כתובה שלא תהא קלה בעיניו להוציאה. אע"ג דבתולה יש לה כתובה מן התורה – זאת בעולה היא. ומיהו, תימה: דקא פסיק ותני דבכל ענין אין לה כתובה, אפילו בא עליה שלא כדרכה, ובתולה גמורה היא, ויש לה כתובה מן התורה. דהא אם בא עליה שני – יש לה קנס, ולא הוי טעמא שלא תהא קלה בעיניו להוציאה! תימה לר"י: כיון דטעמא שלא תהא קלה בעיניו להוציאה – אלמנה אמאי תקינו לה רבנן כתובה? לא היה להם לתקן אלא לגרושה בלבד! ואומר ר"י: דמתוך שהוצרכו לתקן בגרושה שלא תהא קלה בעיניו להוציאה – תקינו נמי לאלמנה, משום חינא. ומיהו, לכתחילה לא היו מתקנים משום חינא. קשה לרשב"א: הא דתניא ב"החובל" (ב"ק דף פט. ושם) וכן היא שחבלה בבעלה – לא הפסידה כתובתה. ופריך: אמאי? תזבין לכתובתה *בטובת הנאה, ותיתיב ליה בהאי חבלה! ומשני: הא מני – רבי מאיר היא, דאמר: אסור לאדם שישהא את אשתו בלא כתובה אפילו שעה אחת. והשתא כיון דטעמא שלא תהא קלה בעיניו להוציאה – תזבין כתובתה על מנת שאם תתאלמן, אבל אם יגרשנה – יהא לה כתובה, דהתם לא שייך משום חינא! ואומר ר"י: כיון דבשאר נשים שייך חינא, אף על גב דבזאת לא שייך – לא פלוג רבנן, ואסור להשהותה בלא כתובה לר"מ. וא"ת: ואמאי תני הכא יצא כסף קנסה בכתובתה? ליתני: מת – אין לה עליו כלום, דהא לא תקינו רבנן לאלמנה אלא משום גרושה, והכא מכח גרושה אין לתקן לזאת, דהא לא מצי לגרשה! ואור"י: דה"נ כיון דשייך בה חינא כמו בשאר אלמנות – אין לנו לשנותה משאר אלמנות, להכי איצטריך טעמא דיצא כסף קנסה בכתובתה, ולא חשו במה דאין לה כתובה.

מהר

תורה אור

שֶׁסּוֹפָהּ לְהִצְטַעֵר תַּחַת בַּעְלָהּ, אָמְרוּ לוֹ: אֵינוֹ דּוֹמֶה נִבְעֶלֶת בְּאוֹנֶס לְנִבְעֶלֶת בְּרָצוֹן! אֶלָּא אָמַר רַב נַחְמָן, אָמַר רַבָּה בַּר אֲבוּהּ: צַעַר שֶׁל פִּיסּוּק הָרַגְלַיִם. וְכֵן הוּא אוֹמֵר: °"וַתְּפַשְּׂקִי אֶת רַגְלַיִךְ לְכָל עוֹבֵר". אִי הָכִי מְפוּתָּה נַמִּי! אָמַר רַב נַחְמָן אָמַר רַבָּה בַּר אֲבוּהּ: מָשָׁל דִּמְפוּתָּה לְמָה הַדָּבָר דּוֹמֶה – לְאָדָם שֶׁאָמַר לַחֲבֵירוֹ: קְרַע שִׁירָאִין שֶׁלִּי וְהִפָּטֵר. שֶׁלִּי?! דַּאֲבוּהָ נִינְהוּ! אֶלָּא אָמַר רַב נַחְמָן אָמַר רַבָּה בַּר אֲבוּהּ: פִּקְחוֹת שֶׁבָּהֶן אוֹמְרוֹת: מְפוּתָּה אֵין לָהּ צַעַר. וְהָא קָא חָזֵינַן דְּאִית לַהּ! אָמַר אַבָּיֵי, *אָמְרָה לִי אֵם: כְּמַיָּא חֲמִימֵי עַל רֵישֵׁיהּ דְּקָרְחָא. רָבָא אָמַר: אָמְרָה לִי בַּת רַב חִסְדָּא: כִּי רִיבְדָּא דְּכוּסִילְתָּא. רַב פַּפָּא אָמַר: אָמְרָה לִי בַּת אַבָּא סוּרָאָה: כִּי נַהֲמָא אַקּוּשָׁא בְּחִינְכֵי.§ הָאוֹנֵס נוֹתֵן מִיָּד, הַמְפַתֶּה לִכְשֶׁיּוֹצִיא וכו'.§ לִכְשֶׁיּוֹצִיא, אִשְׁתּוֹ הִיא?! אָמַר אַבָּיֵי: אֵימָא לִכְשֶׁלֹּא יִכְנוֹס. תַּנְיָא נַמִּי הָכִי: אע"פ שֶׁאָמְרוּ [א]הַמְפַתֶּה נוֹתֵן לִכְשֶׁלֹּא יִכְנוֹס, בּוֹשֶׁת וּפְגָם – נוֹתֵן מִיָּד. וְאֶחָד [ב]הָאוֹנֵס וְאֶחָד הַמְפַתֶּה, בֵּין הִיא וּבֵין אָבִיהָ יְכוֹלִין לְעַכֵּב. בִּשְׁלָמָא מְפוּתָּה – כְּתִיב: °"אִם מָאֵן יְמָאֵן אָבִיהָ", *אֵין לִי אֶלָּא אָבִיהָ, הִיא עַצְמָהּ מִנַּיִן – תַּלְמוּד לוֹמַר: "יְמָאֵן", מִכׇּל מָקוֹם. אֶלָּא אוֹנֵס, בִּשְׁלָמָא אִיהִי – כְּתִיב: °"וְלוֹ תִהְיֶה" – מִדַּעְתָּהּ. אֶלָּא אָבִיהָ מְנָלַן? אָמַר אַבָּיֵי: *שֶׁלֹּא יְהֵא חוֹטֵא נִשְׂכָּר. רָבָא אָמַר: ק"ו: וּמָה מְפַתֶּה שֶׁלֹּא עָבַר אֶלָּא עַל דַּעַת אָבִיהָ בִּלְבַד, בֵּין הִיא וּבֵין אָבִיהָ יְכוֹלִין לְעַכֵּב, אוֹנֵס שֶׁעָבַר עַל דַּעַת אָבִיהָ וְעַל דַּעַת עַצְמָהּ – לֹא כׇּל שֶׁכֵּן. רָבָא לֹא אָמַר כְּאַבָּיֵי, כֵּיוָן דְּקָא מְשַׁלֵּם קְנָס – לָאו חוֹטֵא נִשְׂכָּר הוּא. אַבָּיֵי לֹא אָמַר כְּרָבָא, מְפַתֶּה דְּאִיהוּ מָצֵי מְעַכֵּב – אָבִיהָ נַמִּי מָצֵי מְעַכֵּב, אוֹנֵס דְּאִיהוּ לָא מָצֵי מְעַכֵּב – אָבִיהָ נַמִּי לָא מָצֵי מְעַכֵּב. תַּנְיָא אִידָךְ: אע"פ שֶׁאָמְרוּ אוֹנֵס נוֹתֵן מִיָּד, כְּשֶׁיּוֹצִיא הוּא – אֵין לָהּ עָלָיו כְּלוּם. כְּשֶׁיּוֹצִיא? מִי מָצֵי מַפֵּיק לַהּ?! אֵימָא: כְּשֶׁתֵּצֵא הִיא – אֵין לָהּ עָלָיו כְּלוּם. [ג]מֵת – *יָצָא כֶּסֶף קְנָסָהּ בִּכְתוּבָּתָהּ. רַבִּי יוֹסֵי בְּרַבִּי יְהוּדָה אוֹמֵר: יֵשׁ לָהּ כְּתוּבָּה מָנֶה. בְּמַאי קָמִיפַּלְגִי? רַבָּנַן סָבְרִי: *[ד]טַעְמָא מַאי תַּקִּינוּ רַבָּנַן כְּתוּבָּה – כְּדֵי שֶׁלֹּא תְּהֵא קַלָּה בְּעֵינָיו לְהוֹצִיאָהּ, וְהָא לָא מָצֵי מַפֵּיק לַהּ. וְרַבִּי יוֹסֵי בְּרַבִּי יְהוּדָה סָבַר: הָא נַמִּי מְצַעֵר לַהּ עַד דְּאָמְרָה הִיא "לָא בָּעֵינָא לָךְ".§ אוֹנֵס שׁוֹתֶה בַּעֲצִיצוֹ.§ אֲמַר לֵיהּ רָבָא מִפַּרְזְקִיָּא לְרַב אַשִׁי: מִכְּדִי, מִיגְמַר גָּמְרֵי מֵהֲדָדֵי

לְהָא

שֶׁסּוֹפָהּ לְהִצְטַעֵר כו'. וְאִי חִיבּוּט עַל גַּבֵּי קַרְקַע הוּא, וְכִי סוֹפָהּ לֵיחָבֵט עַל גַּבֵּי קַרְקַע תַּחַת בַּעְלָהּ? שֶׁלִּי. בִּתְמִיָּה. דַּאֲבוּהָ הוּא. דְּהָא כׇּל שְׁבַח נְעוּרִים יָלְפִינַן לְקַמָּן (דף מו:) לְאָבִיהָ, וְהֵיאָךְ הִיא יְכוֹלָה לִמְחוֹל? רִיבְדָּא דְּכוּסִילְתָּא. פולטווייר"א דפלמוא"ה בְּלַעַ"ז. רִיבְדָּא. נִיקּוּר. כּוּסִילְתָּא. כְּלִי אוּמָּן מַקִּיז. וְאִית דְּגָרְסִי: כִּי תַּרְפְּתָא דְּסִיכּוּרֵי, וְהִיא הִיא. אָמְרָה לִי אֵם. (א) אוֹמַנְתּוֹ הָיְתָה. בַּת רַב חִסְדָּא. אִשְׁתּוֹ שֶׁל רָבָא. בַּת אַבָּא סוּרָאָה. דְּבֵיתְהוּ דְּרַב פַּפָּא. נַהֲמָא אַקִּישָׁא בְּחִינְכֵי. כְּלֶחֶם קָשֶׁה שֶׁגּוֹרֵר אֶת הַחֵיךְ. אִשְׁתּוֹ הִיא. וְכִי אִשְׁתּוֹ הִיא כְּבָר דְּקָאָמַר "לִכְשֶׁיּוֹצִיא"? לִכְשֶׁלֹּא יִכְנוֹס. שֶׁתְּמָאֵן הִיא, אוֹ אָבִיהָ, אוֹ הַמְפַתֶּה עַצְמוֹ. יְכוֹלִין לְעַכֵּב. שֶׁלֹּא יַכְנִיסֶנָּה. תִּהְיֶה. מַשְׁמַע: הִיא מְהַוָּה אֶת עַצְמָהּ לוֹ. מָצֵי מְעַכֵּב. שֶׁאִם רָצָה אֵינוֹ כּוֹנֵס, כִּדְאָמְרִינַן לְקַמָּן: יְמַהֲרֶנָּה לוֹ – מִדַּעְתּוֹ. אָבִיהָ נַמִּי לָא מָצֵי מְעַכֵּב. אִי לָאו שֶׁלֹּא יְהֵא חוֹטֵא נִשְׂכָּר. אע"פ שֶׁאָמְרוּ אוֹנֵס נוֹתֵן מִיָּד כְּשֶׁיּוֹצִיאֶנָּה אֵין לָהּ עָלָיו כְּלוּם. וְלָא אָמְרִינַן אֵין קְנָסָהּ תַּחַת כְּתוּבָּתָהּ, שֶׁהֲרֵי לְאָבִיהָ נוֹתֵן מִיָּד. אֶלָּא כֶּסֶף קְנָסָהּ הוּא כְּתוּבָּתָהּ, וְכֵן אִם מֵת – יֵצֵא כֶּסֶף קְנָסָהּ בִּכְתוּבָּתָהּ. מִי מָצֵי מַפֵּיק לַהּ. "לֹא יוּכַל לְשַׁלְּחָהּ" כְּתִיב. כְּשֶׁתֵּצֵא הִיא. אִם יָצְתָה מֵאֵלֶיהָ, וְתָבְעָה הֵימֶנּוּ גֵּט. טַעְמָא מַאי תַּקִּינוּ רַבָּנַן כְּתוּבָּה. לִשְׁאָר נָשִׁים. מִיגְמַר גָּמְרֵי מֵהֲדָדֵי. אוֹנֵס מִמְּפַתֶּה לִשְׁקָלִים, וּמְפַתֶּה מֵאוֹנֵס לַחֲמִשִּׁים.

לְהָא

יחזקאל טז

שמות כב

[קדושין לה: וש"נ]

קדושין מו.

דברים כב

[לעיל יח. וש"נ]

לקמן נד.

[לעיל יח. לקמן נד. יבמו פט.]

ת"י כ"י

לבעלה בטובת הנאה כצ"ל מהרש"א

תוספות רי"ד

והמפתה לכשיוציא וכי אשתו היא. אמר אביי אימא לכשלא יכנום. פי' שתמאן הוא או היא או אבי' דדרשי' לו מדעתו. אבל אם כנסה אינו נותן כלום דכתיב גבי מפתה מהר ימהרנה לו לאשה ואם מאן ימאן אביה לתתה לו כסף ישקול. תנ"ה אע"פ שאמרו המפתה נותן לכשלא יכנום בושת ופגם נותן מיד אחד האונס ואחד. המפתה בין היא ובין אביה יכולין לעכב. פי' שלא יכנסנה. בשלמא מפותה כתיב אם מאן ימאן אביה אין לי אלא אביה היא עצמה מנין ת"ל מאן ימאן מ"מ. אלא אונס בשלמא איהי דכתיב ולו תהיה לאשה מדעתה אלא אביה מנלן. אביי אמר שלא יהא חוטא נשכר. רבא אמר (קנס) [ק"ו] הוא מה מפתה שלא עבר אלא ע"ד אביה בין היא בין אביה יכולין לעכב אונס שעבר על דעתה וע"ד אביה לא כ"ש. תניא אע"פ שאמרו האונס נותן מיד לכשהיא יוצאה. פי' כגון שנתרצו שניהן בגירושין אין לה עליו כלום. מת יצא כסף קנסה בכתובתה. ר' יוסי ברבי יהודה אומר יש לה כתובה מנה וקיי"ל כת"ק והמפתה אם רצה להוציא מוציא מ"ט אמר רב אשי א"ק מהר ימהרנה לו מדעתו פירוש ומאי דתנן אם רצה להוציא יוצא מתפרש אם רצה שלא יכנום לא יכנום כדפרישנא לכשיוציא דרישא:

הגהות הב"ח

(א) רש"י ד"ה אמרה וכו' אומנתו. נ"ב דילדתו אמ ומתה עי' קדושין דף ל ע"ב: (ב) תוס' ד"ה אי לי וכו' תימה. נ"ב עי' ב האיש מקדש דף מ ע"ב ובמ"ש התוס' לשם:

לְהָא מִילְּתָא נַמִי לִיגְמְרוּ מֵהֲדָדֵי! אָמַר קְרָא: °"מָהֹר יִמְהָרֶנָּה לּוֹ לְאִשָּׁה" לוֹ – מִדַּעְתּוֹ.§ כֵּיצַד שׁוֹתֶה בַּעֲצִיצוֹ כו'.§ אָמַר רַב כָּהֲנָא, אֲמַרִיתָא לִשְׁמַעְתָּא קַמֵּיהּ דְּרַב זְבִיד מִנְּהַרְדְּעָא: נֵיתֵי עֲשֵׂה וְנִדְחֶה לֹ"ת! אָמַר לִי: אהֵיכָא אָמְרִינַן *נֵיתֵי עֲשֵׂה וְנִידְחֵי לֹ"ת – כְּגוֹן מִילָה בְּצָרַעַת, דְּלָא אֶפְשָׁר לְקַיּוּמֵיהּ לַעֲשֵׂה. אֲבָל הָכָא, אִי אָמְרָה דְּלָא בָּעֵינָא מִי אִיתֵיהּ לַעֲשֵׂה כְּלָל?.§ **מתני'** יְתוֹמָה שֶׁנִּתְאָרְסָה וְנִתְגָּרְשָׁה, ר' אֱלִיעֶזֶר אוֹמֵר: הָאוֹנֵס חַיָּיב, וְהַמְפַתֶּה פָּטוּר.§ **גמ'** אָמַר רַבָּה בַּר בַּר חָנָה אָמַר ר' יוֹחָנָן: ר"א בְּשִׁיטַת ר"ע רַבּוֹ אֲמָרָהּ, דְּאָמַר: *יֵשׁ לָהּ קְנָס, וּקְנָסָהּ לְעַצְמָהּ. מִמַּאי – מִדְּקָתָנֵי: יְתוֹמָה, ר"א אוֹמֵר: הָאוֹנֵס חַיָּיב וְהַמְפַתֶּה פָּטוּר. יְתוֹמָה פְּשִׁיטָא! אֶלָּא הָא קמ"ל: דְּנַעֲרָה שֶׁנִּתְאָרְסָה וְנִתְגָּרְשָׁה כִּיתוֹמָה, מַה בִּיתוֹמָה לְעַצְמָהּ – אַף נַעֲרָה שֶׁנִּתְאָרְסָה וְנִתְגָּרְשָׁה לְעַצְמָהּ. א"ר זֵירָא אָמַר רַבָּה בַּר שֵׁילָא אָמַר רַב הַמְנוּנָא סָבָא א"ר אַדָּא בַּר אַהֲבָה אָמַר רַב: גהֲלָכָה כְּר' אֱלִיעֶזֶר. *קָרֵי רַב עֲלֵיהּ דְּרַבִּי אֱלִיעֶזֶר: טוּבִינָא דְּחַכִּימֵי.§ **מתני'** *אֵיזֶהוּ בּוֹשֶׁת? דהַכֹּל לְפִי הַמְבַיֵּישׁ וְהַמִּתְבַּיֵּישׁ. פְּגָם – רוֹאִין אוֹתָהּ כְּאִילּוּ הִיא שִׁפְחָה נִמְכֶּרֶת בַּשּׁוּק, כַּמָּה הָיְתָה יָפָה וְכַמָּה הִיא יָפָה. הקְנָס שָׁוֶה בְּכָל אָדָם. וְכָל שֶׁיֵּשׁ לוֹ קִצְבָּה מִן הַתּוֹרָה – שָׁוֶה בְּכָל אָדָם.§ **גמ'** וְאֵימָא *חֲמִשִּׁים סְלָעִים אָמַר רַחֲמָנָא, מִכָּל מִילֵּי! א"ר זֵירָא: יֹאמְרוּ בָּעַל בַּת מְלָכִים – חֲמִשִּׁים, בָּעַל בַּת הֶדְיוֹטוֹת – חֲמִשִּׁים?! א"ל אַבַּיֵי: אִי הָכִי, גַּבֵּי עֶבֶד נַמִי יֹאמְרוּ: עֶבֶד נוֹקֵב מַרְגָּלִיּוֹת – שְׁלֹשִׁים, עֶבֶד עוֹשֶׂה מַעֲשֶׂה

תורה אור: שמות כב

רש"י

לְהָא מִילְּתָא. שֶׁיְּהֵא מְפַתֶּה נוֹשְׂאָהּ עַל כָּרְחוֹ. עֲשֵׂה. "לוֹ תִהְיֶה לְאִשָּׁה". וְנִדְחֶה אֶת לֹא תַעֲשֶׂה. דְּאֵינָהּ רְאוּיָה לָבֹא בְּיִשְׂרָאֵל, כְּגוֹן מַמְזֶרֶת. מִי אִיתֵיהּ לַעֲשֵׂה כְּלָל. הַשְׁתָּא נַמִי, מְלַמְּדִין אוֹתָהּ לוֹמַר "אֵינִי רוֹצָה". **מתני'** יְתוֹמָה שֶׁנִּתְאָרְסָה וְנִתְגָּרְשָׁה הָאוֹנֵס חַיָּיב וְהַמְפַתֶּה פָּטוּר. דְּכֵיוָן דִּיתוֹמָה הִיא, וּקְנָס שֶׁלָּהּ הוּא, וְאַחִילְתֵּיהּ, דְּמִדַּעְתָּהּ נִתְפַּתְּתָה לוֹ – פָּטוּר. וּבַגְּמָרָא מְפָרֵשׁ דְּנִתְאָרְסָה וְנִתְגָּרְשָׁה מִילְּתָא אַחֲרִיתִי הִיא, וְלָאו אַיְּתוֹמָה קָאֵי. **גמ'** בְּשִׁיטַת ר"ע רַבּוֹ אֲמָרָהּ. דְּאָמַר בְּמַתְנִי': *נַעֲרָה שֶׁנִּתְאָרְסָה וְנִתְגָּרְשָׁה – קְנָסָהּ לְעַצְמָהּ. וְהָךְ נִתְאָרְסָה וְנִתְגָּרְשָׁה דְּר' אֱלִיעֶזֶר – כְּשֶׁאָבִיהָ קַיָּים, וְקָרֵי לָהּ יְתוֹמָה מִשּׁוּם דְּפָקַע זְכוּת אָב מִינָּהּ לְגַבֵּי קְנָסָא. מִמַּאי. דְּכְר"ע סְבִירָא לֵיהּ. מִדְּקָתָנֵי אוֹנֵס חַיָּיב וּמְפַתֶּה פָּטוּר. אַלְמָא יֵשׁ לָהּ קְנָס, וּלְעַצְמָהּ. הִלְכָּךְ מְפַתֶּה פָּטוּר – דְּמִדַּעְתָּהּ עֲבַד, וְאוֹנֵס חַיָּיב. וַאֲפִילּוּ אָבִיהָ קַיָּים. דְּאִי יְתוֹמָה כִּדְקָתָנֵי – פְּשִׁיטָא דִּמְפַתֶּה פָּטוּר, אֶלָּא הָא קמ"ל כו'. יְתוֹמָה פְּשִׁיטָא. מַסְקָנָא דְּמִילְּתָא דְּר' יוֹחָנָן הִיא. טוּבִינָא דְּחַכִּימֵי. מְאוּשָּׁר שֶׁבַּחֲכָמִים. "אַשְׁרֵי" מְתַרְגְּמִינַן טוּבַאי. ר' אֱלִיעֶזֶר הוּא ר' אֱלְעָזָר בֶּן שַׁמּוּעַ, וְתַלְמִידוֹ שֶׁל ר"ע הָיָה, כִּדְאָמְרִינַן בְּיָבָמוֹת בְּ"הַבָּא עַל יְבִמְתּוֹ" (דף סב:): וְהָיָה הָעוֹלָם שָׁמֵם עַד שֶׁבָּא ר"ע אֵצֶל רַבּוֹתֵינוּ שֶׁבַּדָּרוֹם וְשָׁנָה לָהֶם, ר"מ, וְר' יְהוּדָה, וְר' יוֹסֵי, וְר"ש, וְרַבִּי אֶלְעָזָר בֶּן שַׁמּוּעַ. **מתני'** הַכֹּל לְפִי הַמְבַיֵּישׁ. אָדָם בֵּינוֹנִי הַמְבַיֵּשׁ בָּשְׁתּוֹ קָשֶׁה מֵאָדָם זוֹלֵל וּמֵאָדָם חָשׁוּב. וְהַמִּתְבַּיֵּישׁ. לְפִי חֲשִׁיבוּתוֹ בָּשְׁתּוֹ. כְּאִילּוּ הִיא שִׁפְחָה. בַּגְּמָרָא מְפָרֵשׁ מַאי גְּרִיעוּתָא מֵחֲמַת בְּעִילָה. **גמ'** יֹאמְרוּ כו'. וְהֵיכָן הוּא חִילּוּק שֶׁבֵּינֵיהֶן אֵצֶל בּוֹשֶׁת? הִלְכָּךְ יָהֵיב בּוֹשֶׁת. גַּבֵּי עֶבֶד. שֶׁנְּגָחוֹ שׁוֹר, שֶׁנָּתְנָה תּוֹרָה קִצְבָּה ל' שְׁקָלִים.

תוספות

מהר ימהרנה לו מדעתו. וא"ת: "ולו תהיה לאשה" נידרוש נמי: "לו" – מדעתו. והא דכתיב "לא יוכל לשלחה" היינו היכא דכבר נשאה! וי"ל: דאין סברא שיהיה מדעתו, כיון שאם נשאה לא יוכל לשלחה. [ועוד "ולו תהיה" קאי אאשה, ולהכי בעינן מדעתה. אבל "מהר ימהרנה" קאי אגברא]. **ניתי** עשה ונדחה לא תעשה. לאו אמנלא בה דבר ערוה פריך, דהא אית בה לאו ועשה, כדאמרי' בפ"ק דיבמות (דף יא: ושם): "לא יוכל בעלה" וגו' – לרבות סוטה שנסתרה. והיינו לאו, ודרשינן (סוטה דף כז:): "ונטמאה" "ונטמאה" – חד לבעל וחד לבועל. אלא אשאינה ראויה לקהל פריך. וא"ת: ומאי פריך וליתי עשה ולידחי ל"ת? הא דריש מקרא בהדיא במשנה, דבעינן אשה הראויה לו! ולמאי דמשני דלא חשיב עשה – קשה, דמאי איצטריך קרא למעוטי שאינה ראויה לו? וי"ל: דלאו מיתורא דקרא מפיק ליה במתניתין, אלא ד"ולו תהיה לאשה" משמע מדעתה, ולהכי כמעט אשה שאינה ראויה לו, דהא אי אמרה לא בעינא ליה – מי איתא לעשה כלל, הלכך לא חשיב עשה, ולא דחי לא תעשה. ומ"מ ס"ד דפריך השתא היכא דאמרה בעינא ליה – ליתי עשה ולידחי ל"ת, ומסיק דאפילו אמרה בעינא ליה – לא חשיב עשה, דלא דמי למילה בצרעת. אי נמי מיתורא דקרא דריש, ופריך דליתי עשה וידחה ל"ת, ויתורא דקרא נוקי לחייבי כריתות. דאי לאו קרא – הוה שרינן אפי' חייבי כריתות, דהואיל ואיתרבו לקנס לעיל בריש פירקין, איתרבו נמי לנישואין. דקראי משתמעי שפיר דהיכא דאיכא קנס איכא נמי נישואין. אי נמי, יש לומר דהכי פריך: ניתי עשה ונידחי לא תעשה, וכי תימא שאני הכא דגלי קרא – א"כ ניגמר מהכא בכל דוכתא דלא דחי! ומשני: דלא חשיב עשה. ומ"מ איצטריך קרא, דאי לאו קרא – הוה חשבינן ליה דלא אפשר לקיים שניהם, וחשיב עשה, דעיקר מצוה היא ליבא, כי היכי דאמרינן בפרק ב' דיבמות (דף כא.), דחליצה במקום יבום לאו *כלום הוא.

כגון מילה בצרעת. *אומר ר"ת: דלסימנא בעלמא נקטיה. דהא בקוצץ בהרתו איכא עשה ולא תעשה, כדאמרינן בפרק "ר' אליעזר דמילה" (שבת דף קלב:) ללשון אחד הכתוב בספרים. ומהתם לא ילפינן בעלמא דליתי עשה ודחי לא תעשה ועשה, דמה למילה שכן נכרתו עליה י"ג בריתות. אלא עיקר מילתא מכלאים בציצית. וא"ת: והא כלאים בציצית אפשר לקיים שניהם, שיעשה בטלית למר חוטין של למר! ואומר ר"י: דבטלית של פשתן אי אפשר לקיים שניהם, דלא אפשר לקיים מצות תכלת אלא ע"י כלאים, דתכלת עמרא הוא. וזה אין לנו לומר שיהא אסור ללבוש טלית של פשתן משום דאפשר בשל למר – דאין זה חשוב אפשר. והא דאמרי' בפ' "התכלת" (מנחות דף מ. ושם): כל המטיל תכלת בסדין בירושלים אינו אלא מן המתמיהין. ומפרש בגמרא גזירה משום קלא אילן. ופריך: לא יהיה אלא לבן! ומשני: אפשר במינו, כדריש לקיש, דאמר: כל מקום שאתה כו'. התם ודאי, כיון דליכא תכלת אלא הכל לבן – מצות לבן אפשר לקיים במינו. וא"ת: והא אמר התם לעיל *חוטי למר פוטרין בשל פשתן, ושל פשתן פוטרין בשל למר, ואמאי פוטרין? והא אפשר לקיים שניהם, דלבן אפשר במינו! ואור"ת: דכל ד' חוטין לבן ודאי אסור, דאפשר במינו. אבל התם קאמר דשני חוטי למר לבן פוטרים בשל פשתן, דמגו דתכלת פטרה, שכבר נעשה כלאים ע"י תכלת שבו, לבן של למר נמי פטר. ומגו דשני חוטי לבן של למר פוטרים בשל פשתן – שני חוטי לבן של פשתן נמי פוטרין בשל למר, אע"ג דלא נעשה התם כלאים ע"י תכלת שבו. וצריך עיון אם שני חוטי לבן של פשתן ושני חוטי לבן של למר מותר לתת בטלית של למר או בטלית של פשתן, דשמא לא הותרו שני חוטי לבן אלא דווקא במקום תכלת, אבל שלא במקום תכלת – לא, או דלמא לא שנא, דהא שני חוטי לבן של פשתן פוטרים בשל למר, אע"ג דהתם תכלת לא מעלה ולא מוריד, דע"י אותו תכלת לא נעשה אכתי כלאים. ואין להקשות: אי שרו שני חוטי לבן בכלאים – אפי' אין תכלת עמהן – אמאי מטיל תכלת בסדין בירושלים אינו אלא מן המתמיהין? יטילו עמו שני חוטי לבן של פשתן, דאפילו הוי ההוא תכלת קלא אילן או לבן גמור – שרי! דאיכא למיגזר שמא יטילו עמו שני חוטי לבן של למר, ויסברו שאותן שני חוטין הצבועין הן תכלת, ויהיו כל ד' חוטין לבן של למר.

[**אי** אמרה לא בעינא מי איתיה לעשה כלל. הקשה הר"ר עזרא: אמאי איצטריך קרא בפ"ק דיבמות (דף ה:) דאין עשה דכיבוד דוחה שבת? הא ליכא עשה, דאי אמר לא בעינא לכיבוד – מי איתא לעשה כלל? וי"ל: דהתם מ"מ מיד כשצוה אב – הוי עשה לעשות מצותו. ול"נ: דהכא גבי דידה ליכא עשה, דהא אי בעיא אמרה לא בעינא ליה, הלכך אין לה לעבור בלאו משום עשה דידיה, דהיא מוזהרת כמותו, והשוה הכתוב אשה לאיש, כדאמרינן ב"יש מותרות" (יבמות דף פד:). תו"י כ"י].

הכי גרסינן: ממאי מדקתני האונס חייב והמפתה פטור יתומה פשיטה **אלא הא** קמ"ל כו'. כלומר, מדקתני האונס חייב והמפתה פטור – ש"מ דיש לה קנס, וקנסה לעצמה. דאי משום יתומה נקט מפתה פטור – פשיטא דפטור, דהא מחלה. אלא ע"כ לא נקט מפתה פטור אלא משום נערה שנתארסה ונתגרשה, ולא נקט יתומה במתני' אלא ליתן טעם אמאי מפתה פטור, והלא קנסה לאביה, ואשמעי' דהרי היא כיתומה, שקנסה לעצמה. וא"ת: ומנלן הא? אדרבה, אימא דנקט יתומה למידק: טעמא דהויא נמי יתומה, הא אינה יתומה – אפילו מפתה חייב, דקנסה לאביה! וי"ל: דלית לן למימר דלדיוקא אתא כל זמן דנוכל לומר דלגופיה אתא. ***אחד** כדרכה ואחד שלא כדרכה. שלא כדרכה ה"ל למינקט ברישא, אלא כן דרך התלמוד שאינו חושש, כדנקט לעיל (דף לה.) בתנא דבי חזקיה בין מתכוין לשאין מתכוין, דה"ל למינקט שאין מתכוין ברישא, כדקתני בין שוגג למזיד, אלא כן דרך התלמוד במקום שצריך לשנות הן ולאו*. **יאמרו** בעל שלימה חמשים. פירוש: הראשון שבא עליה שלא כדרכה, דמחייב קנס אפילו שלא כדרכה, כדאמרינן בפ"ק דקידושין (דף ט:): בא עליה י' ועדיין היא בתולה כו', פירוש: שלא כדרכה. וקאמר מודה רבי לענין קנס, דכולהו משלמי. ובפרק "הבא על יבמתו" (יבמות דף נט. ושם) גבי "ולו תהיה לאשה" – באשה הראויה לו, פרט לאלמנה לכ"ג כו'. ופריך: היכי דמי? אילימא כדרכה – תיפוק ליה דהויא לה בעולה, אלא לאו – שלא כדרכה. והכא הוה מצי למינקט שבאו עליה ב' שלא כדרכה, וכן בפרק "בן סורר" (סנהדרין עג:) דמוקי הסיא ד"אלו נערות שיש להן קנס" כגון שבא עליה שלא כדרכה, וחזר ובא עליה כדרכה – הוי מצי למינקט: וחזר ובא עליה שלא כדרכה. ומה שקשה על פירוש הקונטרס דהתם פירשנו ב"הבא על יבמתו" (יבמות דף נט.) ובפרק קמא דקידושין (דף ט:). ולימא

עין משפט נר מצוה

עט א מיי' פ"ג מהל' נערה הלכה ו:
פ ב מיי' פ"ב מהלכות נערה הלכה יד סמג עשין נג טור אה"ע סי' קנז:
פא ג מיי' פ"א שם הל' ט סמג וטור שם:
פב ד מיי' פ"ב שם הל' ד ומיי' פ"ב מהל' חובל ומזיק הל' א סמג שם ועשין ע טור שם וטוש"ע ח"מ סי' תכ סעיף לב:
פג ה מיי' פ"ב מהלכות נערה הל' ג סמג עשין נג טור אה"ע סי' קנז:

מסורת הש"ס

[לעיל לח.]
שבת קלב: כריתות ח.
[לעיל לח.]
גיטין כו: כריתות יג.
[ב"ק פג:]
ערכין יד:
ס"א מצוה היא
[ולספרים דלא גרסי הכא מילה בצרעת וכלאים בציצית אלא מילה בצרעת לחודיה הייו משום דבכלאים אינו פטור כל כך דאי אפשר לקיים שניהם. תו"י]
[לקמן לט:]
שייך לע"ב
[ועי' ארוכות תוספות כזה בפסחים פה. ועוד ביתר ביאור בסוכה כ. ד"ה אתא]

תוספות רי"ד

מתני' כיצד שותה בעציצו אפי' היא חיגרת ואפילו סומא אפי' מוכת שחין נמצא בה דבר זימה או שאינה ראויה לבוא בישראל אינו רשאי לקיימה שנאמר ולו תהיה לאשה אשה הראויה לו: וליתי עשה ולדחי את ל"ת היכא אמרי' דאתי עשה ודחי את ל"ת כגון מילה בצרעת דא"א לי' לקיומי לעשה אבל הכא אי אמרה לא בעינא ליה ליתא לעשה כלל. פי' המורה והשתא נמי מלמדים אותה לומר איני רוצה וקשה לי להאי פי' דא"כ גבי יבם אמאי אמרינן דאתי עשה ודחי ל"ת כיון דכתיב אם לא יחפוץ נלמדנו לומר איני רוצה ליבם ולא לידחי ואמאי אמרי' התם דדחי מ"ה נ"ל לפרש דמאי דאמר רחמנא גבי אונס ולו תהיה לאשה אינה אלא להפים דעתה ואי אמרה לא בעינא לי' ליתי' לעשה כלל הלכך לאו כלום הוא עשה למדחי את ל"ת כיון שלא ציוהו הבורא אלא להפים דעתה אבל מצות יבום רחמנא הוא דרמי עליה דאע"ג דאמרה אשה לא בעינא לא מיעקרא מצות יבום הלכך מצוה דרמי עליה רחמנא הוא ולהכי דחיא את ל"ת ואע"ג דמצי יבם למימר לא בעינא ליבומי כ"א למיחלץ הא אמרי' התם חליצה במקום יבום אינה מצוה: מתני' יתומה שנתארס' ונתגרשה ר"א אומר האונס חייב והמפתה פטור. פי' שתי נערות הן יתומות אע"פ שלא נתארסה שקנסה הוא לעצמה כיון שאין לה אב שאין אדם מוריש זכות בתו לבניו. וכן נערה שנתארס' ונתגרש' אע"פ שיש לה אב הוי קנסא לעצמה כר"ע. הלכך האונס חייב ליתן קנסא אבל המפתה פטור דאיהי אחילתי' גביה כיון שנתרצית לו: אמר רבה בב"ח אר"י ר"א בשיטת ר"ע אמרה דאמר נערה המאורסה יש לה קנס וקנסה לעצמה ממאי מדקתני יתומה פשיטא אלא הא קמ"ל דנערה שנתארס' ונתגרשה ה"ה כיתומה מה יתומה לעצמה אף נערה שנתארסה ונתגרשה לעצמה אמר ר"א ב"א אמר רב הלכתא כר"א וקרי ליה רב עליה דר"א טובינא דחכימא. פי' מאושר שבחכמים תרגום אשריך ישראל טובך ישראל: מתני' איזהו בושת הכל לפי המבייש והמתבייש. פי' אדם בינוני המבייש בושתו קשה מאדם זולל ומאדם חשוב והמתבייש פי' לפי חשיבותו בושתו: פגם רואים אותה כאילו היא שפחה נמכרת לשוק כמה היתה יפה וכמה היא יפה וקנס שוה בכל אדם וכל שיש לו קצבה מה"ת שוה בבכל אדם: ואימא נ' כסף אמר רחמנא מכל מילי. אמר

עין משפט נר מצוה

פד א מיי' פ"ב מהל' נערה הל' א סמג עשין נו טוש"ע אה"ע סי' קעז סעיף א:
פה ב מיי' שם הל' יד:
פו ג מיי' פ"ג מהלכות אישות הל' יא סמג עשין מח טוש"ע שם סי' לז סעיף א:
פז ד ה מיי' פ"ב מהל' נערה הל' ו ופ"א מהל' חובל ומזיק הל' ב סמג עשין נו ועי' טור אה"ע סימן קעז וטור ש"ע ח"מ סימן תכ סעיף טו:
פח ו מיי' פ"ג מהלכות נערה הל' ב סמג לאוין פז ועשין נה טור אה"ע סי' קעז:

[וע"ע תוס' יומא מט: סד"ה שאני ותוס' חולין עח: סד"ה זה בנה]

[כמו שהיה סבור המקשה וה"פ שאני בושת ופגם דלאביה נמי שייך פי' שמתבייש ומצטער כמותה ולא כמו שפי' שם בקונט' דאי בעי מסר לה למנוול ומוכה שחין דאכתי לא קיים ליה שיכול לקדשה. ת"י עה"ג]

גמרא

תורה אור

מעשה מחט שלשים?! אלא א"ר זירא: *אילו באו עליה שנים, אחד כדרכה ואחד שלא כדרכה, יאמרו: בעל שלימה חמשים, בעל פגומה — חמשים?! א"ל אביי: אי הכי, גבי עבד נמי יאמרו, עבד בריא — שלשים, עבד מוכה שחין — שלשים?! אלא *אמר אביי, אמר קרא: °"תחת אשר עינה" (דברים כב), הני — תחת אשר עינה, מכלל דאיכא בושת ופגם. רבא אמר, אמר קרא: °"ונתן האיש השוכב עמה לאבי הנערה חמשים כסף" (שם) [א]הנאת שכיבה — נ', מכלל דאיכא בושת ופגם. ואימא לדידה? א"ק: °"בנעוריה בית אביה" (במדבר ל) — [ב]כל שבח נעוריה לאביה. ואלא הא דאמר רב הונא אמר רב: *מנין שמעשה הבת לאביה? שנאמר: °"וכי ימכור איש את בתו לאמה" (שמות כא) מה אמה מעשה ידיה לרבה, [ג]אף בת מעשה ידיה לאביה — למה לי? תיפוק ליה מ"בנעוריה בית אביה"! אלא, ההיא בהפרת נדרים הוא דכתי'. וכי תימא: נילף מיניה — *ממונא מאיסורא לא ילפינן. וכי תימא: נילף מקנסא — ממונא מקנסא לא ילפינן. אלא מסתברא דאביה הוי, דאי בעי — מסר לה למנוול ומוכה שחין.§ [ד]פגם רואין אותה כאילו היא שפחה נמכרת.§ היכי שיימינן לה? אמר אבוה דשמואל: אומדין כמה אדם רוצה ליתן בין שפחה בתולה לשפחה בעולה לשמשו. שפחה בעולה לשמשו, מאי נפקא ליה מינה? אלא: בין שפחה בעולה לשפחה שאינה בעולה להשיאה לעבדו. ולעבדו מאי נפקא ליה מינה? [ה]בעבד שיש לו לרבו קורת רוח הימנו.§

מתני' *כל מקום שיש מכר — אין קנס, וכל מקום שיש קנס — אין מכר. קטנה — יש לה מכר ואין לה קנס, נערה — יש לה קנס ואין לה מכר. הבוגרת — אין לה לא מכר ולא קנס.§

גמ' *אמר רב יהודה אמר רב: זו דברי ר"מ, אבל חכמים אומרים: יש לה קנס במקום מכר. דתניא: *קטנה מבת יום אחד ועד שתביא שתי שערות — יש לה מכר ואין לה קנס, משתביא שתי שערות עד שתיבגר יש לה קנס ואין לה מכר, דברי ר"מ, שהיה ר"מ אומר: כ"מ שיש מכר — אין קנס, וכ"מ שיש קנס — אין מכר. וחכמים אומרים: קטנה מבת ג' שנים ויום אחד ועד שתיבגר — יש לה קנס. קנס אין, מכר לא?! אימא: אף קנס במקום מכר. א"ר חסדא: מ"ט דר"מ — א"ק: °"ולו תהיה לאשה" (דברים כב) — במהוה עצמה הכתוב מדבר. ורבנן? אמר ר"ל: א"ק (א)"נערה" — אפילו קטנה במשמע. שמעה רב פפא בריה דרב חנן מבי כלוחית, אזל אמרה קמיה דרב שימי בר אשי. א"ל: אתון אהא מתניתו לה, אנן אהא מתנינן לה: אמר ר"ל: *[ו]המוציא שם רע על הקטנה — פטור, שנא': °"ונתנו לאבי הנערה" (שם) — נערה מלא דיבר הכתוב. מתקיף לה רב אדא בר אהבה: טעמא דכתב רחמנא "נערה", הא לאו הכי — הוה אמינא אפילו קטנה? והא כתיב: °"ואם אמת היה הדבר הזה לא נמצאו בתולים לנערה (שם) והוציאו את הנערה אל פתח בית אביה וסקלוה" — וקטנה לאו בת עונשין היא! אלא: כאן — נערה, הא כל מקום שנאמר "נער" — אפילו קטנה במשמע.§

מתני'

רש"י

מעשה מחט. חייט, תופר. אלא אמר רבי זירא. מהכא מסתברא שאין בושת בכלל חמשים, דאם כן — אין הפרש בין בעל שלימה לבעל פגומה שנבעלה שלא כדרכה, והיכן הוא הפרש שביניהם? ש"מ גבי בושת, כיון שנפגמה כבר — אין בושתה רב כשלימה. תחת אשר עינה. גבי "חמשים כסף" כתיב. מכלל דבושת ופגם. שאינם משום עינוי, שהרי ישנן בשאר חובלין — אינו בכלל זה. פגם הוא נזק הנישום נמי בשאר חבלות. ואימא לדידה הוי. דבשלמא קנס כתיב ביה "ונתן לאבי הנערה", אלא הני — ליהוו לדידה. בנעוריה בית אביה. גבי נדרים כתיב. ומיהו, איכא למשמע מינה דימי נעוריה תלאה הכתוב בבית אביה. בתו לאמה. הקיש בת לאמה. תיפוק ליה כו'. אלא על כרחך מהתם לא מצי למילף, דההוא בהפרת נדרים כתיב. נילף מקנסא. מה קנסה לאביה — אף שאר שבח ממון נעורים לאביה. אלא מסתברא. דבושת ופגם דאב הויא, שהרי בידו לביישה בבושת בעילה, ולפוגמה בפגם בעילה. דאי בעי מסר לה. לקדשה ביאה. למנוול ומוכה שחין. כדתנן לקמן, האב זכאי בבתו בקידושיה, בכסף ובשטר ובביאה, וכיון דבידו ליטול ממון לפוגמה ולביישה בושה זו — השתא אפסדיה האי דפגמה: [מאי נפקא ליה. לכל אדם בבעילתה, אם בעולה היא, הואיל ולמלאכה קיימא]: ולעבדו מאי נפקא ליה. למריה מינה אם בעולה היא, מי קפיד מריה אלא שיהו להן ולדות. קורת רוח. שזהיר בעבודתו, ואף הוא רוצה לעשות לו נחת רוח, להטעימו טעם בתולה. **מתני'** כ"מ שיש מכר. לאב בבתו, דהיינו בקטנותה. אין לו בה קנס. דאין קנס לקטנה. כל מקום שיש קנס. משהיא נערה. אין מכר. דתניא (ערכין דף כט:): יכול ימכור אדם בתו כשהיא נערה — אמרת (ב) מכורה כבר יוצאה עכשיו, שאינה מכורה אינו דין שלא תימכר? **גמ'** זו דברי ר"מ. דאמר אין קנס לקטנה. מבת ג' שנים. שביאתה ביאה, ואין בתוליה חוזרין. מכר לא. בתמיה. אף קנס במקום מכר. משתהא ראויה לביאה עד שתביא שתי שערות הוו תרוייהו, ומשהביאה שערות עד שתבגר — קנס ולא מכר. מאי טעמא דר"מ. דאמר קטנה אין לה קנס. דאמר קרא. גבי קנס "ולו תהיה לאשה". במהוה עצמה. במי שיש בידה להקנות עצמה לאישות הכתוב מדבר. אהא מתניתו לה. להא דריש לקיש, דאמר כ"מ שנכתב "נער" בלא ה' וקרינן נערה — ללמד על הקטנה בא. שם רע. לא מצאתי לבתך בתולים. פטור. ד"וענשו אותו מאה כסף ונתנו לאבי הנערה" מלא כתיב. אלא כאן נערה. האי דכתיב "נערה" מלא, לאו לגלויי עליה אתא, אלא על כל מקום שנאמר "נער" חסר, ויליף הכי: כאן שאי אפשר אלא בנערה — כתיב "נערה" מלא, וללמדך דכל מקום שנאמר "נער" — אפילו קטנה במשמע.

תוספות

ואימא לדידה. אע"ג דפרישית לעיל (דף לח:), דבושת ופגם הוקשו לקנס, וניתן למי שקנס ניתן — היינו בתר דקים לן הכא דהוי הכל לאביה. **מסתברא** דאביה הוי דאי בעי כו'. וא"ת: אמאי לא קאמר דאביה הוי מדקא יהיב מפתה, כדאמר לקמן בריש "נערה" (דף מב.)! וי"ל: דלמא לא יהיב מפתה, דקראי דאביי ורבא באונס כתיבי. **דאי** בעי מסר לה למנוול ומוכה שחין. וממעשה ידיה ליכא למילף, דהא מיתזנא מיניה, כדאמרינן בפרק קמא דקדושין (דף ד. ושם). ולא מקדושין — דמעלמא קאתו לה. ומתרוייהו נמי לא, דהכא דגופה שאני. תימה: דהכא לא קים לן בושת ופגם דהוי לאביה אלא מכח שיכול לקדשה למנוול ומוכה שחין, ואם כן, היכי בעי למימר בריש קדושין (דף ג:) גבי קדושי כסף: מנא לן דמיקדשה בכסף וקידושין דאביה הן? וכי תימא נילף מבושת ופגם, הא בושת ופגם גופיה לא קים לן אלא מכח שיכול לקדשה! ואומר ר"י: דאורחיה דהתלמוד דבעי לדחויי אפילו קים לן דבושת ופגם הוי דאביה ממקום אחר. *א"נ: התם בעי למילף קדושי נערה מבושת ופגם של קטנה. ומקדושי קטנה הוה יליף להו, אי לאו דהוה אמינא: הני מילי — קטנה דלית לה יד ונערה אית לה יד, כדאמרינן התם לעיל. ולהכי קאמר: וכי תימא נילף מבושת ופגם דקטנה, אע"ג דלהכי אית לה יד כדאמרינן ב"החובל" (ב"ק דף פז:): יעשה לה סגולה, ואפ"ה הוי דאביה, ה"נ קדושי נערה. ואם *היינו מפרשים דלא קאי אקדושין הא דקאמר ונילף מבושת ופגם, אלא אמעשה ידיה דאייתי התם לעיל — הוה אתי שפיר, אבל לא משמע הכי. ועוד: דא"כ הכא נמי ה"ל לאסוקי וכ"ת נילף מבושת ופגם, כיון דאמעשה ידיה קאי. וכן לקמן בפרק "נערה" (דף מו:). **כמה** אדם רוצה ליתן כו' להשיא לעבדו. תימה: דמה שומא היא זו? וכי אשה חשובה ממשפחה גדולה אינה נפסדת בפגמה אלא שוה שפחה הניסת לעבד? וי"ל: דכל אשה שמין לפי מה שהיא בענין זה, כמה אדם רוצה ליתן בין בתולה לבעולה להשיא לעבדו אשה כזאת הנפגמת. והא דנקט שפחה — אורחא דמלתא נקט, דאין דרך להשיא לעבדו בת מלכים.

הא לאו הכי ה"א אפילו קטנה והכתיב אם אמת היה וכו'. תימה לר"י: מה בכך אם קרא איירי בבת עונשין; מ"מ מלינו למימר דה"ה קטנה. דהא בא על קטנה מאורסה הוי בסקילה לרבנן, בפרק "ד' מיתות" (סנהדרין דף סו:) אע"ג דההיא פרשה דנערה המאורסה בבת עונשין כתיבא [כדכתיב "ואת הנערה על דבר אשר לא צעקה"]! ותירץ: דהתם משום דמסקינן בסמוך: כאן "נערה" — הא כל מקום שנאמר "נער" — אפילו קטנה במשמע. הלכך מחייבין ליה התם, וכולהו עריות ילפי מינה. אי נמי: דוקא במוציא שם רע סברא הוא לומר דלא מחייב קנס ומלקות אלא בגדולה, כיון דקרא איירי בבת עונשין, ולא בעלמא, משום דמוציא שם רע על הקטנה סברא הוא דפטור, דפיתוי קטנה אונס הוא*, והוי כמוציא שם רע על הנערה שנאנסה דלא מחייב. אבל אין לומר דמסתבר ליה דדוקא בבת עונשין מחייב ליה, משום שבא להורגה — דבפרק קמא דסנהדרין (דף ח:) בשמעתא דחוששין ללעז, משמע דלאו משום דקא גריס לה קטלא מיחייב.

תוספות רי"ד

אמר אביי א"ק תחת אשר ענה הני תחת אשר ענה מכלל דאיכא בושת ופגם רבא אמר א"ק ונתן האיש השוכב עמה לאבי הנערה נ' כסף. הנאת שכיבה נ' כסף מכלל דאיכא בושת ופגם: ואימא לדידה. פי' דדוקא נ' כסף זכה רחמנא לאב אבל בושת ופגם להוי דידה. מסתברא דאבוה הוי מיגו דאי בעי מסר לה למנוול ומוכה שחין: פגם רואים אותה וכו'. היכי שיימינן לה אמר אבוה דשמואל אומדים כמה אדם רוצה ליתן בין שפחה בתולה לשפחה בעולה להשיאה לעבדו שיש לו קורת רוח ממנו: **מתני'** כל מקום שיש מכר אין קנס וכ"מ שיש קנס אין מכר קטנה יש לה מכר ואין לה קנס נערה יש לה קנס ואין לה מכר בוגרת לא קנס ולא מכר אר"י א"ר זו דברי רבי מאיר אבל חכמים אומרים יש קנס במקום מכר א"ר חסדא מ"ט דר"מ דאמר קרא ולו תהיה לאשה במהווה עצמה הכתוב מדבר ורבנן אמרי אמר קרא נערה ואפילו קטנה במשמע פי' נער כתיב וקרינן נערה מלא:

[כלאי' יבמות לג: וסא:]

הגהות הב"ח

(א) גמ' אמר ר"ל אמר קרא נערה: (ב) רש"י ד"ה אין מכר וכו' אמרת קל וחומר מכורה.

מסורת הש"ס

[ערכין טו.] | לעיל לג. | לקמן מו: מז. קדושין ג: | [ברכות יט: וש"נ] | נ"י כ"י | לעיל כט. חולין כו: | [לעיל ט. חולין כו:] | לעיל כט. חולין כו: [תוספתא פ"ג ע"ש]

וליתני

מתני' ^א האומר: "פתיתי את בתו של פלוני" – משלם בושת ופגם על פי עצמו, ואין משלם קנס. ^ב האומר "גנבתי" – *משלם את הקרן על פי עצמו, ואין משלם תשלומי כפל ותשלומי ארבעה וחמשה. *^ג "המית שורי את פלוני" או "שורו של פלוני" – הרי זה משלם על פי עצמו. "המית שורי עבדו של פלוני" – אין משלם ע"פ עצמו. ^ד זה הכלל: כל המשלם יתר על מה שהזיק – אינו משלם ע"פ עצמו.§ **גמ'** וליתני "אנסתי"! לא מבעיא קאמר; לא מבעיא "אנסתי" דלא קא פגים לה, דמשלם בושת ופגם על פי עצמו, אבל "פתיתי" דקא פגים לה – אימא לא משלם על פי עצמו – קא משמע לן. מתניתין דלא כי האי תנא; דתניא, רבי שמעון בן יהודה אומר משום ר' שמעון: אף בושת ופגם אינו משלם ע"פ עצמו, לא כל הימנו שיפגום בתו של פלוני. אמר ליה רב פפא לאביי: ניחא לה לדידה מאי? דלמא לא ניחא ליה לאביה. ניחא ליה לאביה מאי? דלמא לא ניחא להו לבני משפחה. ניחא להו לבני משפחה מאי? אי אפשר דליכא חד במדינת הים דלא ניחא ליה.§ האומר גנבתי משלם את הקרן וכו'.§ איתמר, פלגא ניזקא; *רב פפא אמר: פלגא ניזקא ממונא, רב הונא בריה דרב יהושע אמר: ^ה פלגא ניזקא קנסא. רב פפא אמר: פלגא ניזקא ממונא, קסבר: סתם שוורים לאו בחזקת שימור קיימי, ובדין הוא דמשלם כוליה, ורחמנא הוא דחייס עלויה, דאכתי לא איעד תורא. רב הונא בריה דרב יהושע אמר: פלגא ניזקא קנסא. קסבר: סתם שוורים בחזקת שימור קיימי, ובדין הוא דלא לישלם כלל, ורחמנא הוא דקנסיה, כי היכי דנינטריה לתוריה.§ סימן: היזיק מה והמית כלל.§ תנן: *הניזק והמזיק בתשלומין. בשלמא למאן דאמר פלגא ניזקא ממונא – היינו דשייך ניזק בתשלומין. אלא למ"ד פלגא ניזקא קנסא – השתא, דלאו דידיה קא שקיל, בתשלומין איתיה?! לא נצרכא אלא לפחת נבילה. פחת נבילה תנינא: תשלומי נזק ^ו מלמד שהבעלים מטפלין בנבילה. חדא בתם וחדא במועד. וצריכא, דאי אשמועינן תם – משום דאכתי לא איעד, אבל מועד דאיעד – אימא לא. ואי אשמועינן מועד – משום דקא משלם כוליה, אבל תם – אימא לא, צריכא. ת"ש: *מה בין תם למועד? ^ז שהתם משלם חצי נזק מגופו, ^ח ומועד משלם נזק שלם מן העלייה. *ולא קתני שהתם אינו משלם ע"פ עצמו ומועד משלם ע"פ עצמו! *)תנא ושייר. מאי שייר דהאי שייר? שייר ^ט חצי כופר. אי משום חצי כופר – לאו שיורא הוא, הא

*) [סוכה נג. וש"נ]

רש"י

מתני' פתיתי. בגמ' מפרש אמאי לא תנא "אנסתי". ואינו משלם קנס. בבבא קמא* נפקא לן מודה בקנס פטור מ"אשר ירשיעון אלהים" – פרט למרשיע את עצמו. המית שורי את פלוני. והריני חייב בכופר. הרי זה משלם ע"פ עצמו. קסבר כופרא ממונא. עבדו של פלוני. והריני חייב שלשים סלע. אינו משלם. דקנס נינהו, שאפי' אין יפה דינר נותן שלשים. **גמ'** דלא פגים לה. אין לעז של אנוסה גדול כלעז של מפותה, וכיון דלאו פגם דילה הוא – מהימנינן ליה למשקל מיניה בושת ופגם על פיו. אימא לא. נהימניה להחזיק את הלעז. לא כל הימנו. שיוציא עליה לעז מזנה בעיר. ניחא לה לדידה. לשאת את הלעז כדי להשתכר הממון. לא ניחא להו לבני משפחה. וב"ד אין עליהם לעשות דבר להחזיק בושתם. פלגא ניזקא. שחייבה תורה שור תם: [ממונא. ומשלם ע"פ עצמו]. לאו בחזקת שימור קיימי. אם לא ישמרום בעלים שלא יזיקו – [אינם בחזקת משתמרים מאליהם שלא יזיקו], אלא מזיקין אפי' ניזקא דלאו אורחיה, הלכך על מרייהו רמיא לנטורינהו, וזה שלא שמרו – בדין הוא דלישלם כולה, אלא דרחמנא חס עליה. ומיהו, מה שמשלם – בדין משלם. כי היכי דנינטריה. שיוסיף שמירה על שמירתו. תנן. בבבא קמא. הניזק והמזיק בתשלומין. שניהם מפסידין בדבר. ס"ד דהכי קאמר: תרוייהו מטי להו בהאי פסידא, דניזק מפסיד פלגא, ומזיק פלגא. היינו דשייך ניזק בתשלומין. דמפסיד פלגא בממוניה. דלאו דידיה שקיל. דמה שנוטל – בחנם נוטל. בתשלומין איתיה. בתמיה. לא נצרכא אלא לפחת נבילה. הא דקתני ניזק בתשלומין, לאו בפלגא דקא שביק קאמר, אלא בההוא פלגא ניזקא נמי דקני ליה רחמנא – מפסיד כל פחת שפחתה נבילה מדמיה משעת מיתה עד שעת העמדה בדין, ששמין את הנבילה כמה היה יפה השור בחייו וכמה היתה נבילה יפה בשעת מיתה, ומשלם החצי. אבל מה שהוזלו דמי נבילה משעת מיתה עד שעת מכירה – אין המזיק משלם כלום באותו פחת. ובבבא קמא (דף י:) יליף לה מקראי, ואשמעינן האי תנא דפחת נבילה דניזק הוי. תשלומי נזק מלמד שהבעלים מטפלין בנבילה. תנא דברייתא דריש לישנא דמתניתין, דתנן בבבא קמא: משלם תשלומי נזק במיטב הארץ. ותנא עלה בברייתא, דהאי דנקט תנא דמתני' תשלומי נזק, ולא תנא משלם את הנזק – לאשמועינן אתא, שהניזק נוטל את נבילתו ומטפל בה ומוכרה, והמזיק משלים עליה מה שחייבתו תורה, אם תם – חצי, ואם מועד – הכל. ותרתי למה ליה לרבי למיסתם במתני' דבעלים מטפלין בנבילה? דקא משלם כוליה. ודיו בהפסד זה. מגופו. אינו גובה אלא מגוף השור, ואם אין בו כדי חצי נזקו – יפסיד המותר. מן העלייה. מן המיטב שבנכסי מזיק. דגבי תם כתיב (שמות כא) "וחצו את כספו", מגופו, ובמועד כתיב (שם) "שלם ישלם שור". ואם איתא דפלגא ניזקא קנסא – ניתני נמי שהתם אינו משלם על פי עצמו, ומועד משלם על פי עצמו. דמועד ודאי בדין משלם, שהרי התרו והעידו בו לשמור שורו. שייר חצי כופר. לא שנה כל החילוקים שביניהם, שהרי אף יש חילוק זה ביניהם: שהמועד שהמית את האדם משלם כופר שלם, ותם שהמית – אפילו חצי כופר, כדינו בניזקין, לא משלם. דכתיב "בעל השור נקי", ודרשינן (ב"ק דף מא:): נקי מחצי כופר. הא

תוספות

וליתני אנסתי. דהוי חדוש טפי דפטור, אע"ג דמודה שעשה פריצות. **רבי** שמעון בן יהודה אומר אף בושת ופגם אינו משלם ע"פ עצמו. אור"י: דאי קאי ר"ש בן יהודה אמתניתין דהכא, הא דמשמע בריש "נערה" לקמן (דף מב.) דלר"ש, אי דקא תבע בושת ופגם – מחייב ליה קרבן שבועה – היינו משום דהתם תבעו האב תחלה, ואין שייך לומר לאו כל הימנו כו' כדקאמר הכא. ואין צריך לומר דתרי תנאי אליבא דר' שמעון. (א) ועוד אומר רשב"א: דההיא דלקמן איכא לאוקמי בבת גרים, וניחא לה לדידה ולאביה, דליכא למימר דלמא איכא חד במדינת הים דלא ניחא ליה. ומיהו, אי קאי ר' שמעון אמתניתין דשבועות, דמייתי לקמן בריש "נערה" (ג"ז שם) – ע"כ תרי תנאי אליבא דר' שמעון.

***האומר** גנבתי כו'. מוצא ש"ר, ויוצא בשן ועין דלא תנא – איכא למימר דאתיא בזה הכלל.

***זה** הכלל כל המשלם יותר על מה שהזיק כו'. ואפילו למ"ד בפרק "שור שנגח ארבעה וחמשה" (ב"ק דף מ.) דכופר היינו דמי המזיק, לא חשיב יותר ממה שהזיק, אע"פ שפעמים שוה מזיק יותר מניזק – דפדיון נפשו הוא נותן.

לא נצרכא אלא לפחת נבילה. אע"ג דלאו דידיה שקיל, מ"מ כיון דזכי ליה רחמנא חצי נזק – חשבינן ליה בתשלומין מה שפחתה הנבלה. והכא לא שייך למימר קרנא דתוך קבירא ביה, כדאמרי' ב"המניח" בסופו (ב"ק דף לד.), דהתם ודאי שלא נהרג השור, שייך לומר הכי, דאין לו למכור שורו בשביל כן, שסבור שישביח. אבל הכא, מיד כשנהרג – יש לו למוכרו, שידוע שתפחת הנבילה ותסריח.

תנינא תשלומי נזק מלמד שהבעלים מטפלים בנבילה כו'. הכי דייקא לה בבבא קמא (דף י:): מדתני בנזקו לא קתני, אלא בתשלומי נזקו כו'. **אי** משום חצי כופר לאו שיורא הוא וכו'. לאו פירכא היא, אלא שינויא הוא, דלא תיקשי למ"ד פלגא ניזקא ממונא מאי שייר – דשייר חצי כופר, ומשני: לא שייר כלום, וחצי כופר לאו שיורא הוא. וכן איכא בנזיר בפ' "ג' מינים" (דף לח: ושם) גבי אי משום "לא יחל" – לאו שיורא הוא, וכן בפרק "החליל" (סוכה דף נג. ושם). וההוא דהתם מגומגם טפי. הא

עין משפט נר מצוה

פט א מיי' פ"ב מהל' נערה הל' יב ופ"ה מהל' סנהדרין הל' יד:
צ ב מיי' פ"ג מהלכות גניבה הלכה ט סמג עשין עא טור ח"מ סי' שמח:
צא ג מיי' פ"ה מהלכות סנהדרין הלכה יד סמג עשין ע:
צב ד מיי' פ"ב מהל' נזקי ממון הל' ח.
צג ה מיי' פ"ב שם הל' ז ופ"ה מהלכות סנהדרין הלכה ט סמג עשין נו טוש"ע ח"מ סי' א סעי' א:
צד ו ז ח מיי' פ"א מהל' נזקי ממון הלכה ג סמג עשין סו טוש"ע ח"מ סי' שפט סעיף ב ג ד ט:
צה ט מיי' פ"י שם הל' ב סמג שם:

[שייך לעיל במתני']

[ג"ז שייך לעיל]

מסורת הש"ס

[דף עה.]

ס"א טבחתי ומכרתי

ב"ק טו: מג.

טו. [וכס כל הסוגיא ונזכר עוד שבועות לג.]

שם יד:

שם טו:

ס איתא ליתני נמי שהתם כו' כצ"ל רש"ל

הגהות הב"ח

(א) תוס' ד"ה ר' שמעון וכו' דתרי תנאי אליבא דר"ש ומיהו אי קאי אמתניתין וכו' ועוד אומר רשב"א וכו' דלא ניחא ליה כס"ד:

תוספות רי"ד

מתני' האומר פתיתי את בתו של פלוני משלם בושת ופגם ע"פ עצמו ואינו משלם קנס. האומר גנבתי משלם את הקרן ע"פ עצמו ואינו משלם לא תשלומי כפל ולא ד' וה'. המית שורי את פלוני או שורו של פלוני ה"ז משלם על פי עצמו. המית שורי עבדו של פלוני אינו משלם ע"פ עצמו. זה הכלל כל המשלם יתר ממה שהזיק אינו משלם ע"פ עצמו: וליתני אנסתי. לא מבעיא קאמר לא מבעיא אנסתי דלא פגים לה אבל פתיתי דפגים לה אימא לא משלם בושת ופגם ע"פ עצמו קמ"ל: ומתני' דלא כי האי תנא דתניא ר"ש בן יהודה אומר משום (רב הונא) [ר"ש] אף בושת ופגם אינו משלם ע"פ עצמו לא כל הימנו שיפגום בתו של פלוני. ואינו משלם קנס ע"פ עצמו כדנפקא לן מאשר ירשיעון אלהים פרט למרשיע את עצמו: ואי קשיא. הכא תנן דבושת הוי ממון ומשלם ע"פ עצמו ובריש פרק המניח אמרי' חסרא חסרא קנסא קמגבית בבבל וקרי התם לבושת קנס. תשובה לעולם בושת ממונא הוי לשלם ע"פ עצמו שאין בו שום יתירות אלא שמין לפי המבייש והמתבייש והתם קרי ליה קנסא לומר שאין גובין אותו בבבל דכל מידי דאית ביה חסרון כיס גבינן ליה בבבל אבל בושת דלית ביה חסרון כיס לא גבי' לי' בבבל כדאמרינן בפרק החובל: המית שורי את פלוני משלם ע"פ עצמו פי' דכופרא לאו קנסא הוא דכפי שוי' נזק משלם ואף למ"ד כפי שויה של מזיק כופרא ממונא הוי ומשלם ע"פ עצמו: המית שורי את עבדו וכו'. בפרק שור שנגח ד' וה' מוכיח שאפילו שויה של עבד אינו משלם ע"פ עצמו דכל ל' כסף הוו קנסא: זה הכלל וכו'. איתמר פלגא נזקא שחייבה תורה לשור תם. ר"פ אמר ממונא. פי' ומשלם ע"פ עצמו. רב הונא בריה דרב יהושע אמר פלגא נזקא קנסא רב פפא אמר ממונא סתם שורים לאו בחזקת שימור קיימי. פי' אם לא ישמרו בעלים שלא יזיקו אינן בחזקת משתמר מאיליהן שלא יזיקו אלא מזיקין אפילו נזקא דלאו אורחיה הלכך על מרייהו רמיא לנטורינהו וזה שלא שמרו בדין הוא דלשלם כולה. ורחמנא הוא דחס עליה דאכתי לא אייעד תורא. פי' ואיהו מה שמשלם בדין משלם. ורב הונא בריה דרב יהושע אמר פלגא נזקא קנסא קסבר סתם שוורים בחזקת שימור קיימי ובדין הוא דלא לשלם כלל ורחמנא הוא דקנסיה כי היכי דנטרינהו לתורי'. פי' שיוסיף

הָא מַנִּי – ר' יוֹסֵי הַגְּלִילִי הִיא, דְּאָמַר: תָּם מְשַׁלֵּם חֲצִי כּוֹפֶר. *ת"ש: "הֵמִית שׁוֹרִי אֶת פְּלוֹנִי", אוֹ "שׁוֹרוֹ שֶׁל פְּלוֹנִי" – הֲרֵי זֶה מְשַׁלֵּם עַל פִּי עַצְמוֹ. מַאי לָאו בְּתָם? לָא, בְּמוּעָד. אֲבָל בְּתָם מַאי – אֵינוֹ מְשַׁלֵּם עַל פִּי עַצְמוֹ. אַדְּתָנֵי סֵיפָא: "עַבְדּוֹ שֶׁל פְּלוֹנִי" אֵינוֹ מְשַׁלֵּם ע"פ עַצְמוֹ – נִיפְלוֹג וְנִיתְנֵי בְּדִידָהּ: בַּמֶּה דְּבָרִים אֲמוּרִים – בְּמוּעָד, *אֲבָל תָּם אֵינוֹ מְשַׁלֵּם עַל פִּי עַצְמוֹ! כּוּלָּהּ בְּמוּעָד קָמַיְירֵי. ת"ש, זֶה הַכְּלָל: כָּל הַמְשַׁלֵּם יָתֵר עַל מַה שֶּׁהִזִּיק אֵינוֹ מְשַׁלֵּם ע"פ עַצְמוֹ. הָא פָּחוֹת מִמַּה שֶּׁהִזִּיק – מְשַׁלֵּם ע"פ עַצְמוֹ! לָא תֵּימָא: הָא פָּחוֹת מִמַּה שֶּׁהִזִּיק, אֶלָּא אֵימָא: הָא כְּמָה שֶׁהִזִּיק – מְשַׁלֵּם ע"פ עַצְמוֹ. אֲבָל פָּחוֹת מַאי – אֵינוֹ מְשַׁלֵּם ע"פ עַצְמוֹ. לִיתְנֵי: זֶה הַכְּלָל: כָּל שֶׁאֵינוֹ מְשַׁלֵּם כְּמָה שֶׁהִזִּיק – אֵינוֹ מְשַׁלֵּם עַל פִּי עַצְמוֹ, דְּמַשְׁמַע פָּחוֹת וּמַשְׁמַע יָתֵר! תְּיוּבְתָּא. וְהִלְכְתָא: פַּלְגָּא נִיזְקָא קְנָסָא. *תְּיוּבְתָּא וְהִלְכְתָא?! אִין, טַעֲמָא מַאי אִיתּוֹתַב – מִשּׁוּם דְּלָא קָתָנֵי כְּמָה שֶׁהִזִּיק. לָא פְּסִיקָא לֵיהּ, כֵּיוָן דְּאִיכָּא [א]חֲצִי נֶזֶק צְרוֹרוֹת דְּהִלְכְתָא גְּמִירִי לָהּ דְּמָמוֹנָא הוּא – מִשּׁוּם הָכִי לָא קָתָנֵי. וְהָשְׁתָּא דְּאָמְרַתְּ פַּלְגָּא נִיזְקָא קְנָסָא, [ב]הַאי כַּלְבָּא דַּאֲכַל אִימְרֵי, וְשׁוּנְרָא דְּאָכֵיל תַּרְנְגוֹלֵי רַבְרְבֵי – מְשׁוּנֶּה הוּא, וְלָא מַגְבִּינַן בְּבָבֶל. אֲבָל זוּטְרֵי – אוֹרְחֵיהּ הוּא, וּמַגְבִּינַן. [ג]וְאִי תָּפַס – לָא מַפְּקִינַן מִינֵּיהּ. וְאִי אָמַר: אַקְבְּעוּ לִי זִמְנָא לְאֶרֶץ יִשְׂרָאֵל, מַקְבְּעִינַן לֵיהּ, וְאִי לָא אָזֵיל, מְשַׁמְּתִינַן לֵיהּ. בֵּין כָּךְ וּבֵין כָּךְ מְשַׁמְּתִינַן לֵיהּ. דְּאָמְרִינַן לֵיהּ: סַלֵּיק הֶיזֵּיקָךְ, *מִדְּרַבִּי נָתָן. דְּתַנְיָא, ר' נָתָן אוֹמֵר: [ד]מִנַּיִן שֶׁלֹּא יְגַדֵּל אָדָם כֶּלֶב רַע בְּתוֹךְ בֵּיתוֹ וְלֹא יַעֲמִיד סוּלָּם רָעוּעַ בְּתוֹךְ בֵּיתוֹ – שֶׁנֶּאֱמַר: °"וְלֹא תָשִׂים דָּמִים בְּבֵיתֶךָ". (דברים כב) §

הדרן עלך אלו נערות

נַעֲרָה [ה]שֶׁנִּתְפַּתְּתָה – בּוֹשְׁתָּהּ וּפְגָמָהּ וּקְנָסָהּ שֶׁל אָבִיהָ, וְהַצַּעַר בְּתְפוּסָה. [ו]עָמְדָה בַּדִּין עַד שֶׁלֹּא מֵת הָאָב – הֲרֵי הֵן שֶׁל אָב. מֵת הָאָב – הֲרֵי הֵן שֶׁל אַחִין. לֹא הִסְפִּיקָה לַעֲמוֹד בַּדִּין עַד שֶׁמֵּת הָאָב – הֲרֵי הֵן שֶׁל עַצְמָהּ, *עָמְדָה בַּדִּין עַד שֶׁלֹּא בָּגְרָה – הֲרֵי הֵן שֶׁל אָב. מֵת הָאָב – הֲרֵי הֵן שֶׁל אַחִין. לֹא הִסְפִּיקָה לַעֲמוֹד בַּדִּין עַד שֶׁבָּגְרָה – הֲרֵי הֵן שֶׁל עַצְמָהּ. רַבִּי שִׁמְעוֹן אוֹמֵר: אִם לֹא הִסְפִּיקָה לִגְבּוֹת עַד *שֶׁמֵּת הָאָב – הֲרֵי הֵן שֶׁל עַצְמָהּ.

מַעֲשֶׂה

רש"י

הָא מַנִּי ר' יוֹסֵי הַגְּלִילִי הִיא דְּאָמַר תָּם מְשַׁלֵּם חֲצִי כּוֹפֶר. דְּדָרֵישׁ לְהַאי "נָקִי" לִדְרָשָׁה אַחֲרִיתִי, לִדְמֵי וְלָדוֹת – אִם נָגַח אִשָּׁה וְיָצְאוּ יְלָדֶיהָ. הִלְכָּךְ לָא הֲוָה לֵיהּ לִפְלוּגֵי בֵּינַיְיהוּ בְּכוֹפֶר. וְכִי תֵּימָא: הֲוָה לֵיהּ לִפְלוּגֵי, דְּהַאי פַּלְגָּא וְהַאי כּוּלֵּיהּ – הַהִיא בִּכְלַל רֵישָׁא הִיא, דְּקָתָנֵי: תָּם מְשַׁלֵּם חֲצִי נֶזֶק וּמוּעָד נֶזֶק שָׁלֵם, וְתָנָא בִּנְזִיקִין, וְהוּא הַדִּין לְכוֹפֶר. מַאי לָאו בְּתָם. וְאִי מִשּׁוּם דְּקָתָנֵי בָּהּ "הֵמִית שׁוֹרִי אֶת פְּלוֹנִי" דְּחִיּוּבוֹ כּוֹפֶר, וְתָם לָאו בַּר כּוֹפֶר הוּא – הָא מַנִּי רַבִּי יוֹסֵי הַגְּלִילִי הִיא. אַדְּתָנֵי עַבְדּוֹ שֶׁל פְּלוֹנִי כו'. דְּלָא אַשְׁכַּח פָּטוּר עַל פִּי עַצְמוֹ אֶלָּא בְּעֶבֶד. נִיפְלוֹג בְּדִידָהּ. כְּבֶן חוֹרִין. וּבִבְהֵמָה נַמִי הֲוָה מָצֵי לְשַׁנּוּיֵי חִילּוּק, וּלְמִיתְנֵי דְּאִיכָּא דְּלָא מְשַׁלֵּם עַל פִּי עַצְמוֹ. בד"א. דִּמְשַׁלֵּם ע"פ עַצְמוֹ בְּמוּעָד כו'. כּוּלָּהּ בְּמוּעָד קָמַיְירֵי. בְּמוּעָד אָתָא לְאַשְׁמוּעִי', דְּאַף הוּא יֵשׁ בּוֹ חִילּוּק, דְּאִיכָּא בֵּיהּ מִידֵּי דְּלָא מְשַׁלֵּם עַל פִּי עַצְמוֹ, וּמַאי נִיהוּ – נְגִיחַת עֶבֶד. וְאִי הֲוָה תָּנֵי כִּדְקָאָמְרַתְּ – הֲוָה שָׁבֵיק נַמִי לְאוֹרְחֵיהּ, דְּרֵישָׁא אַיְירֵי בְּמוּעָד וְסֵיפָא נִיתְנֵי תָּם. וּמַה לִּי שְׁבַקֵיהּ תַּנָּא לְאוֹרְחֵיהּ גַּבֵּי נִיזָּק לְדַלֵּג מִבֶּן חוֹרִין לְעֶבֶד, מַה לִּי שְׁבַקֵיהּ בְּמַזִּיק וּלְדַלֵּג מִמּוּעָד לְתָם. יָתֵר עַל מַה שֶּׁהִזִּיק. כְּגוֹן נְגִיחַת עֶבֶד. וְכֵן אוֹנֵס, וּמְפַתֶּה, וּמוֹצִיא שֵׁם רַע, וְתַשְׁלוּמֵי כֵּפֶל, וְתַשְׁלוּמֵי אַרְבָּעָה וַחֲמִשָּׁה. הָא פָּחוֹת מִמַּה שֶּׁהִזִּיק. כְּגוֹן חֲצִי נֶזֶק דְּתָם. הָכִי גָּרְסִינַן: לִיתְנֵי כָּל שֶׁאֵינוֹ מְשַׁלֵּם כְּמָה שֶׁהִזִּיק אֵינוֹ מְשַׁלֵּם ע"פ עַצְמוֹ. וְהִלְכְתָא פַּלְגָּא נִיזְקָא קְנָסָא. דְּהוֹאִיל וְכָל חֲצִי נֶזֶק אֵינוֹ אֶלָּא בְּנִיזְקָא דְּלָאו אוֹרְחֵיהּ, לָאו עַל מָרֵיהּ הֲוָה רַמְיָא לְמִינְטְרֵיהּ בְּהָכִי, אֶלָּא קְנָסָא הוּא, כִּי הֵיכִי דְּלוֹסִיף בֵּיהּ נְטִירוּתָא. טַעֲמָא מַאי אִיתּוֹתַב. כְּלוֹמַר, תְּיוּבְתָּא מַאי הִיא? מִשּׁוּם דְּלָא קָתָנֵי כָּל שֶׁאֵינוֹ מְשַׁלֵּם כְּמָה שֶׁהִזִּיק אֵינוֹ מְשַׁלֵּם עַל פִּי עַצְמוֹ. דְּלִישְׁתַּמַּע מִינָּהּ נַמִי חֲצִי נֶזֶק – הָא לָאו תְּיוּבְתָּא הִיא. כֵּיוָן דְּאִיכָּא חֲצִי נֶזֶק. דְּמִשְׁתַּלֵּם בְּנִזְקֵי בְהֵמָה בְּמְהַלֶּכֶת וְהִתִּיזָה צְרוֹרוֹת מִתַּחַת רַגְלֶיהָ וְהִזִּיקָה, דִּתְנַן בְּבָבָא קַמָּא (דף יז.) דִּמְשַׁלֶּמֶת חֲצִי נֶזֶק. וּבְהַהוּא חֲצִי נֶזֶק קַיְימָא לָן בְּב"ק דְּהִלְכְתָא גְּמִירֵי לָהּ מִסִּינַי שֶׁהוּא תּוֹלָדָה שֶׁל רֶגֶל, וּפְטוּרָה בִּרה"ר כִּי רֶגֶל. וְנִזְקֵי רֶגֶל לָאו קְנָסָא נִינְהוּ אֶלָּא מָמוֹנָא, שֶׁהֲרֵי מוּעֶדֶת מִתְּחִילָּתָהּ, וְגַבֵּי צְרוֹרוֹת הוּא דְּאַקִּיל רַחֲמָנָא. וְכֵיוָן דְּמָמוֹנָא הוּא, מְשַׁלֵּם ע"פ עַצְמוֹ, מִשּׁוּם הָכִי לָא פְּסִיקָא לֵיהּ לְמִיתְנֵי כָּל שֶׁאֵינוֹ מְשַׁלֵּם כְּמָה שֶׁהִזִּיק, דְּהָא אִיכָּא הַאי. דַּאֲכִיל אִימְרֵי. שֶׁחָנַק טְלָאִים חַיִּים וַאֲכָלָם. מְשׁוּנֶּה הוּא. אֵין דַּרְכּוֹ בְּכָךְ, וְכָל נֶזֶק מְשׁוּנֶּה בִּבְהֵמָה הֲוֵי תּוֹלָדָה דְּקֶרֶן תַּמָּה, שֶׁאַף הִיא מְשׁוּנָּה, שֶׁאֵין דַּרְכָּהּ בְּכָךְ, וַחֲצִי נֶזֶק הוּא דִּמְשַׁלֵּם. וְכֵיוָן דִּקְנָסָא הוּא – לָא מַגְבִּינַן לֵיהּ בְּדַיָּינֵי בָּבֶל, שֶׁאֵין שָׁם סְמִיכָה בִּזְקֵנִים וְלָא מִקְרוּ מוּמְחִים, וְגַבֵּי קְנָס כְּתִיב (שמות כב) "יַרְשִׁיעוּן אֱלֹהִים". אוֹרְחֵיהּ הוּא. וְהָווּ לְהוּ נִזְקֵי דְשֵׁן, וְשֵׁן מְשַׁלֶּמֶת נֶזֶק שָׁלֵם, וּמָמוֹנָא הוּא וְגוֹבִין אוֹתוֹ בְּבָבֶל. וְאִי תָּפַס. נִיזָּק מָמוֹנָא דְּמַזִּיק גַּבֵּי קְנָסָא דַּחֲצִי נִזְקוֹ, דְּאֵין צָרִיךְ לִתְבּוֹעַ לְפָנֵינוּ. לָא מַפְּקִינַן מִינֵּיהּ. וְגַבֵּי פַּלְגָּא נִזְקֵיהּ. וְאִי. לָא תָּפֵיס, וְאָמַר קַמָּן: קִבְעוּ לִי זְמַנָּא בְּאַרְעָא דְּיִשְׂרָאֵל, הַשִּׂיאוּהוּ לֵילֵךְ עִמִּי לָדוּן לִפְנֵי דַּיָּינֵי אֶרֶץ יִשְׂרָאֵל – קָבְעִינַן לֵיהּ. בֵּין כָּךְ וּבֵין כָּךְ. בֵּין שֶׁרוֹצֶה נִיזָּק לֵילֵךְ לְאֶרֶץ יִשְׂרָאֵל, בֵּין שֶׁאֵינוֹ רוֹצֶה. מְשַׁמְּתִינַן לֵיהּ. לַמַּזִּיק, מִיהָא לַהֲרוֹג אוֹתוֹ כֶּלֶב וּלְסַלֵּק הֶיזֵּיקֵיהּ.

הדרן עלך אלו נערות

נַעֲרָה שֶׁנִּתְפַּתְּתָה. וְהַצַּעַר בִּתְפוּסָה. וְהַצַּעַר נַמִי לְאָבִיהָ, בַּאֲנוּסָה. בִּתְפוּסָה. לִישָּׁנָא דִּקְרָא "וּתְפָשָׂהּ וְשָׁכַב עִמָּהּ" (דברים כב). לֹא הִסְפִּיקָה לַעֲמוֹד בַּדִּין וכו'. כֵּיוָן דְּלָא עָמְדָה בַּדִּין לָאו מָמוֹן הוּא לְהוֹרִישׁוֹ לְבָנָיו. וְאָמְרִינַן לְקַמָּן (דף מג.): אֵין אָדָם מוֹרִישׁ לִבְנוֹ זְכוּת שֶׁזָּכְתָה לוֹ תּוֹרָה בְּבִתּוֹ, וְיָלֵיף לָהּ מִקְּרָא. מֵת הָאָב. מִשֶּׁעָמְדָה בַּדִּין בְּנַעֲרוּתֶיהָ, בֵּין בָּגְרָה קוֹדֶם מִיתָה בֵּין לֹא בָּגְרָה. הֲרֵי הֵן שֶׁל אַחִין. דְּכֵיוָן דְּעָמְדָה בַּדִּין זָכָה בָּהֶן אָב. ר"ש אוֹמֵר. אע"פ שֶׁעָמְדָה בַּדִּין לָא הָוֵי מָמוֹן דְּאָב לְהוֹרִישׁוֹ לְבָנָיו עַד דְּמָטֵי לִידֵיהּ, וּבַגְּמָרָא יָלֵיף טַעְמָא.

מַעֲשֶׂה

תוספות

הא מני רבי יוסי הגלילי היא דאמר תם משלם חצי כופר. וליכא שיורא, דאי משום דמועד משלם כופר שלם ותם אינו משלם אלא חצי כופר – הא לאו שיורא הוא, דהא תנן תם משלם חצי נזק ומועד נזק שלם, וכופר בכלל. וא"ת: אכתי ליתני דמועד אף כשהוא בסקילה משלם כופר, ותם כשהוא בסקילה אינו משלם כופר כלל, דהביאהו לב"ד וישלם לך, דהוא עצמו אינו משתלם אלא מגופו, כדאמרינן בפרק "שור שנגח ד' וה'" (ב"ק דף מג. ושם)! וי"ל: דהך נמי לא הוי שיור, דהוי בכלל הא דקתני תם מגופו ומועד מן העלייה. ומיהו תימה: דלא אשכחן בהדיא בשום מקום שהיה אומר ר' יוסי הגלילי דתם משלם חצי כופר. ואי משום דדריש רבי יוסי הגלילי בפרק "שור שנגח ד' וה'" (ג"ז שם) "נקי" מדמי ולדות, ולא דריש "נקי" מחצי כופר, מכלל דסבר דחייב – ודלמא לעולם סבר דפטור, וטעמא משום דפטור מחצי כופר לא איצטריך קרא, דכשהשור בסקילה לא שייך כופר, דהביאהו לב"ד וישלם לך. וכשאין השור בסקילה, כגון על פי עד אחד או על פי הבעלים, פטור מדרבה, דאמר התם (דף מג.) שור שהמית בן חורין שלא בכוונה – פטור, שנאמר "השור יסקל וגם בעליו יומת" – בזמן שהשור בסקילה בעלים משלמין כופר כו'! ונראה דה"פ: הא מני ר' יוסי הגלילי היא, דאמר תם משלם חצי כופר. פי': דלא ממעט חצי כופר מ"נקי", ולאו דוקא משלם קאמר, אלא היה משלם אם היה לו ממה להשתלם. ולשום תנא לא הוה חצי כופר שיור כי אם לרבי אלעזר, דדריש "נקי" מחצי כופר, ולית ליה דרבה. וכשאין השור בסקילה – מועד משלם, ותם אינו משלם. והא דנקט רבי יוסי הגלילי טפי מרבי עקיבא, דדריש "נקי" מדמי עבד, לדידיה נהי דחצי כופר לא הוי שיור – דמי עבד הוי שיור*. [ועי' תוס' ב"ק טו: ד"ה הא]

ואי תפס כו'. פר"ת דדוקא אי תפס את המזיק עצמו, אבל דבר אחר – לא, דלענין מזיק עצמו, הקילו חכמים, שיכול לתופסו, דאל"כ יתפוס כל אשר לו ולא נפיק מיניה, דאין דנין דיני קנסות, ואם נוציא המותר ונשאיר כדי נזק, הרי אנו דנין דיני קנסות, ודוחק.

הדרן עלך אלו נערות

נערה. לא הספיקה לעמוד בדין עד שמת האב הרי הן של עצמה. תימה: תינח קנס, אלא בושת ופגם דממונא הוא – דאחין בעי למיהוי! ושמא מקראי דלעיל דנפקי בושת ופגם איתקוש אהדדי כדפי' לעיל*).

*) [ד' לח: ד"ה יש]

לאביה

תוספות רי"ד

שויסף שמירה על שמירתו ת"ש כל המשלם יתר ממה שהזיק אינו משלם ע"פ עצמו. פי' כגון נגיחת העבד וכן אונס ומפתה ומוציא שם רע ותשלומי כפל ותשלומי ד' וה' הא פחות משלם פי' כגון חצי נזק דתם. לא תימא פחות ממה שהזיק אלא אימא הא כמה שהזיק משלם ע"פ עצמו א"ה ליתני זה הכלל כל שאינו משלם כל מה שהזיק משלם ע"פ עצמו דמשמע פחות ומשמע יותר תיובתא. ופסיק תלמודא והלכתא פלגא נזקא קנסא. פי' דהואיל וכל חצי נזק אינו אלא היזקא דלאו אורחיה לאו על מרא רמיא לנטורי בהכי אלא קנסא הוא כי היכי דלוסיף ביה נטירותא תיובתא והלכתא אין טעמא מאי איתותב. פי' תיובתיה מאי הוא משום דלא תני הכי פי' לא קתני כל שאינו משלם (כלו) [כמה שהזיק] ש"מ (נמי) חצי נזק [ממונא] הא לאו תיובתא הוא כיון דאיכא חצי נזק צרורות דהל' גמירי לה דממונא הוא ומשלם ע"פ עצמו שהן תולדה דרגל מש"ה לא קתני פי' משום כיון (דאין) [דאיכא] חצי נזק המשתלם [ע"פ עצמו] (כנזק) [כגון] בהמה המהלכת ותתיזה צרורות מתחת רגליה והזיקו דתנן בבבא קמא דמשלם חצי נזק והאי חצי נזק קי"ל דהל' גמירי לה דממונא הוא ומשלם ע"פ עצמו שהן תולדה דרגל ופטורים ברה"ר כרגל ונזקי רגל לאו קנסא נינהו אלא ממונא שהרי מועדת בתחלתה דגבי צרורות הוא דאקיל רחמנא. וכיון דממונא הוא משלם ע"פ עצמו מ"ה לא פסיקא ליה למיתני כל שאינו משלם דהא איכא האי. והשתא דאמרת פ"נ קנסא האי כלבא דאכיל אימרא ושונרא דאכיל תרנגולא רברבא משונה הוא. פי' אין דרכו בכך וכל נזק משונה בבהמה הוי תולדה דקרן תמה שאין דרכה בכך וחצי נזק הוא שמשלם. וכיון דקנסא הוא לא מגבי' בבבל. פי' בדייני בבל שאין שם סמיכה בזקנים ולא מיקרי אלהים מומחים ולגבי קנס כתיב אשר ירשיעון אלהים. ואי תפיש ניזק ממונו של מזיק גבי קנסא דחצי נזקו ולא מפקי' מיניה. ואי אמר אזמיניה בהדי לדינא בא"י מזמינן לי'. פי' ואי לאו תפיש ואמר קמן קבעי לי זמנא בא"י קבעי' לי' ואי לא אזיל משמתינן לי': בין כך ובין כך. פי' בין שרצה ניזק לילך בא"י בין לא. משמתינן ליה עד דמסלק הזיקיה מביתיה מר' נתן דתניא אר"נ מנין שלא יגדל אדם כלב רע בתוך ביתו ולא יעמיד סולם רעוע שנאמר ולא תשים דמים בביתך. ופי' וה"ה נמי לקנס דאונס ומפתה אע"ג דלא מגבי' ליה בבבל אי תפיש לא מפקי' מיניה אבל להזמינו לדין לא"י לא מזמינן ליה שאין עתה ישיבות קבועות שם כאשר היה אז. וראיתי בתשובות רב צמח גאון ז"ל אלו נערות שיש להן קנס ששאלת מהו להגבות שלא יהא חוטא נשכר כיוצא בזה אמרו חכמים אין מגבין קנס בבבל שלח לי' חסדא קנס קמגבית בבבל אלמא הלכתא רווחת היא שאין מגבין קנסות אלא בירושלים ובסנהדרין של כ"ג ותו קאמרי' א"ר נזקי שור בשור ונזקי שור באדם גובין אותן בבבל אבל אדם באדם ואדם בשור אין מגבין אותו בבבל (ולא) [אך] משום שלא יהא חוטא נשכר ושלא יהיו [בני אדם] פרוצים בניזקין שכיון שהם יודעים שאין מגבין קנסות בבבל שולחים יד זה בזה נהגו חכמים האחרונים לנדותו עד שהוא מפייסו בממון או שירבה עליו רעים ויפייסנו בדברים. ומעשה בא' שהפיל שינו של חבירו ובא לפני מר רב צמח גאון ז"ל וא"ל דבר קצוב אני חותך עליך ופייסהו או בממון או בדברים ועכשיו כל דיני קנסות בטלו ומנהג שהנהיג אדונינו מר רב צמח גאון ז"ל אנו נוהגים בו היום בבל קהילות הקודש:

פרק ד נערה שנתפתתה בושתה ופגמה וקנסה לאביה והצער בתפוסה. פי' המורה והצער נמי לאביה כלומר יתירה עליה אנוסה שכן יש לה צער ולישנא דקרא נקט ותפשה ושכב עמה עמדה בדין עד שלא מת האב ה"ה של אב מת האב ה"ה של אחין אם לא הספיקה לעמוד בדין עד שמת האב ה"ה של עצמה עמדה בדין עד שלא בגרה ה"ה של אב מת האב ה"ה של אחין אם לא הספיקה לעמוד בדין עד שבגרה ה"ה של עצמה רש"א אם לא הספיקה לגבות עד שמת האב ה"ה של עצמה מע"י ומציאתה אע"פ שלא גבתה מת האב ונתחייב בדין ליתן לאב הקנס ובושת ופגם ה"ה של אב ואע"פ שלא הספיק לגבות ואם מת האב ה"ה של אחין. פי' שכיון שנתחייב בב"ד ליתן לאב כבר זכה בהן האב אע"פ שלא גבה ואם מת עד שלא הספיק לגבות אותן דאחין הוו כלהו ואם לא הספיקה לעמוד בדין עד שמת האב ה"ה של עצמה לא של אחין שאין האב מוריש זכות בתו לבניו ואילו מתה היא אחר שמת האב אם עמדה בדין עמו ונתחייבו לה גם הקנס בב"ד מורישתו לאחים ואם לא עמדה בדין הקנס אינה מורשת אותם לאחים דהכי אמרי' בגמרא כיון דאילו מודה ביה מיפטר אינו ממון להורישו ליורשים אבל הבושת והפגם והצער שאין יכול להפטר מהן בהודאתו היא מורישתו לאחי'. וה"ה בכל חבלה דעלמא אע"פ שלא עמד עליהן בדין מורישן אדם לבניו שאם חבל ראובן בשמעון ולא הספיק לתובעו בדין עד שמת יורשיו תובעים אותו אבל אם גנב ראובן שורו של שמעון וטבח ומכר ולא הספיק לתובעו בדין עד שמת אין יורשיו יכולים לתובעו דכל קנסא דינן דאי

מודי

עין משפט נר מצוה

צו א מיי' פ"ב מהל' נזקי ממון הלכה ב ז סמג עשין סז טוש"ע ח"מ סימן א סעיף א וסי' שצ סעיף ג:

צז ב מיי' פ"ג שם הל' ז ופ"ה מהל' סנהדרין הל' ט סמג עשין נז טור ש"ע שם סי' א סעיף א וסי' שצא סעיף ו:

צח ג מיי' פ"ה מהל' סנהדרין הלכה יז סמג עשין נז טוש"ע שם סימן א סעיף ה:

צט ד מיי' פ"ה מהל' נזקי ממון הל' ט ופי"א מהל' רוצח הל' ד סמג עשין סו טוש"ע שם סי' תט סעיף ג וסימן תכז סעיף ח:

א ה מיי' פ"ב מהלכות נערה הלכה יד סמג עשין כל טור אה"ע סי' קעז:

ב ו מיי' שם הל' טו:

מסורת הש"ס

[ב"ק טו: מג.]

[קשה דלא מצי תני הכי דמשמע ע"פ עצמו אינו משלם אבל ע"פ עדים משלם ולמאי לא סבר כר' יוסי הגלילי אלא סבר לאפלוגי ע"פ עדים אינו משלם חצי כופר והוריך מהר"ס דמ"מ הוי ליה לפלוגי בדידיה בשור של פלוני גרידא ולא הוי ליה למינקט עבד. תו"ח]

[עירובין י. עז: ב"ק טו:]

גליון הש"ס

תוס' ד"ה הא מני וכו' ומיהו תימה. פי' תשובת מהרלב"ח סי' ס"ה.

ב"ק טו: מו.

נ"א ר"ש אומר אם לא הספיקה לגבות עד שמת האב הרי הן של עצמה

נ"א שבגרה

ג א מיי' פ"ח מהלכות שבועות הלכה ג:
ד ב מיי' שם ופ"ב מהל' נערה הל' יב:
ה ג מיי' פ"ח מהלכות שבועות הל' ב ג סמג לאוין רמח:

*מַעֲשֵׂה יָדֶיהָ וּמְצִיאָתָהּ, אע"פ שֶׁלֹּא גָּבְתָה, מֵת הָאָב – הֲרֵי הֵן שֶׁל אַחִין.§ **גמ'** מַאי קמ"ל? תָּנֵינָא: *הַמְפַתֶּה נוֹתֵן שְׁלֹשָׁה דְּבָרִים, וְהָאוֹנֵס אַרְבָּעָה, הַמְפַתֶּה נוֹתֵן בּוֹשֶׁת וּפְגָם וּקְנָס, מוֹסִיף עָלָיו אוֹנֵס שֶׁנּוֹתֵן אֶת הַצַּעַר! לְאָבִיהָ אִיצְטְרִיךְ לֵיהּ. לְאָבִיהָ נַמִּי פְּשִׁיטָא, מִדְּקָא יָהֵיב מְפַתֶּה. דְּאִי לְעַצְמָהּ – אַמַּאי יָהֵיב מְפַתֶּה? מִדַּעְתָּהּ עֲבַד! עָמְדָה בַּדִּין אִיצְטְרִיכָא לֵיהּ, פְּלוּגְתָּא דר"ש וְרַבָּנַן. תְּנַן הָתָם: *א"אָנַסְתָּ וּפִיתִּיתָ אֶת בִּתִּי", וְהוּא אוֹמֵר: "לֹא אָנַסְתִּי וְלֹא פִּיתִּיתִי". "מַשְׁבִּיעֲךָ אֲנִי", וְאָמַר: "אָמֵן", וְאח"כ הוֹדָה – חַיָּיב. ר"ש פּוֹטֵר, שֶׁאֵינוֹ מְשַׁלֵּם קְנָס ע"פ עַצְמוֹ. אָמְרוּ לוֹ: באע"פ שֶׁאֵינוֹ מְשַׁלֵּם קְנָס ע"פ עַצְמוֹ, אֲבָל מְשַׁלֵּם בּוֹשֶׁת וּפְגָם ע"פ עַצְמוֹ. °בְּעָא מִינֵּיהּ אַבָּיֵי מֵרַבָּה: הָאוֹמֵר לַחֲבֵירוֹ: "אָנַסְתָּ וּפִיתִּיתָ אֶת בִּתִּי וְהֶעֱמַדְתִּיךָ בַּדִּין וְנִתְחַיַּיבְתָּ לִי מָמוֹן", וְהוּא אוֹמֵר: "לֹא אָנַסְתִּי וְלֹא פִּיתִּיתִי וְלֹא הֶעֱמַדְתַּנִי בַּדִּין וְלֹא נִתְחַיַּיבְתִּי לְךָ מָמוֹן", וְנִשְׁבַּע, וְהוֹדָה, לְר' שִׁמְעוֹן מַאי? כֵּיוָן דְּעָמַד בַּדִּין – מָמוֹנָא הֲוַאי, וּמִיחַיַּיב עֲלֵיהּ קָרְבַּן שְׁבוּעָה, אוֹ דִּלְמָא: אע"ג דְּעָמַד בַּדִּין – קְנָס הָוֵי? א"ל: מָמוֹנָא הָוֵי, וּמִיחַיַּיב עֲלֵיהּ קָרְבַּן שְׁבוּעָה. אֵיתִיבֵיהּ: ר"ש אוֹמֵר: יָכוֹל הָאוֹמֵר לַחֲבֵירוֹ: "אָנַסְתָּ וּפִיתִּיתָ אֶת בִּתִּי", וְהוּא אוֹמֵר: "לֹא אָנַסְתִּי וְלֹא פִּיתִּיתִי". "הֵמִית שׁוֹרְךָ אֶת עַבְדִּי" וְהוּא אוֹמֵר: "לֹא הֵמִית". אוֹ שֶׁאָמַר לוֹ עַבְדּוֹ: "הִפַּלְתָּ אֶת שִׁנִּי וְסִימִּיתָ אֶת עֵינִי", וְהוּא אוֹמֵר: "לֹא הִפַּלְתִּי וְלֹא סִימִּיתִי", וְנִשְׁבַּע, וְהוֹדָה, יָכוֹל יְהֵא חַיָּיב – ת"ל: °"וְכִחֵשׁ בַּעֲמִיתוֹ בְּפִקָּדוֹן אוֹ בִתְשׂוּמֶת יָד אוֹ בְגָזֵל אוֹ עָשַׁק אֶת עֲמִיתוֹ אוֹ מָצָא אֲבֵידָה וְכִחֶשׁ בָּהּ וְנִשְׁבַּע עַל שָׁקֶר". גמָה אֵלּוּ מְיוּחָדִין – שֶׁהֵן מָמוֹן, אַף כָּל – שֶׁהֵן מָמוֹן, יָצְאוּ אֵלּוּ שֶׁהֵן קְנָס.
מַאי

[לקמן מג.] [לעיל לט.] [שבועות לו:] [ויקרא ה]

רש"י

מַעֲשֶׂה יָדֶיהָ. שֶׁעָשְׂתָה בְּחַיֵּי אָבִיהָ. אע"פ שֶׁלֹּא גָּבְתָה. כְּגוֹן שָׂכָר פְּעוּלָּה. מֵת הָאָב הֲרֵי הוּא שֶׁל אַחִים. דְּמִשֶּׁבָּא לָעוֹלָם זָכָה בּוֹ הָאָב. וְלָא דָּמֵי לִקְנָס, דְּלָא הָוֵי מָמוֹן עַד שֶׁעָמַד בַּדִּין וִיעִידוּהוּ, דְּהָא אִי מוֹדֶה מִיפְּטַר. מְצִיאָתָהּ. בַּגְּמָ' פָּרֵיךְ: מַאן גָּבְיָא? גמ' לְאָבִיהָ אִיצְטְרִיכָא לֵיהּ. דְּלָא תְּנַן. מִדְּקָא יָהֵיב מְפַתֶּה. תורה אור
קְנָס וּבוֹשֶׁת וּפְגָם – פְּשִׁיטָא דִּלְאָבִיהָ נִיתְּנוּ, דְּאִי לְדִידָהּ – הָא אַחֲלָה גַּבֵּיהּ. אָנַסְתָּ וּפִיתִּיתָ. אוֹ פִּיתִּיתָ. חַיָּיב. קֶרֶן וְחוֹמֶשׁ וְאָשָׁם, אִם הוֹדָה אַחֲרֵי כֵן, וְזֶהוּ אֲשַׁם גְּזֵילוֹת. שֶׁאֵינוֹ מְשַׁלֵּם קְנָס ע"פ עַצְמוֹ. אֶלָּא עַל פִּי עֵדִים. וְכֵיוָן דְּאִילּוּ אוֹדֵי לֵיהּ קַמָּן כְּשֶׁתְּבָעוֹ הֲוָה מִיפְּטַר, פִּי' כְּפָרֵיהּ, נַמִּי, אֵין זוֹ שְׁבוּעַת כְּפִירַת מָמוֹן. אֲבָל מְשַׁלֵּם בּוֹשֶׁת וּפְגָם. דְּמָמוֹנָא הוּא, וְאִשְׁתַּכַּח דְּמָמוֹנָא כְּפָרֵיהּ. וּלְקַמָּן מְפָרֵשׁ טַעְמָא דְּרַבָּנַן, דְּקָא סָבְרֵי: כֵּיוָן טוֹעֵן אָנַסְתָּ – לָא תְּבָעוֹ אֶלָּא בּוֹשֶׁת וּפְגָם, וְלָא נִשְׁבַּע זֶה עַל כְּפִירַת קְנָס. בְּעָא מִינֵּיהּ אַבָּיֵי מֵרַבָּה. בַּר נַחְמָנִי, דְּרַבֵּיהּ הֲוָה. כֵּיוָן דְּעָמַד בַּדִּין. כְּבָר. וְאִי הֲוָה מוֹדֵי לֵיהּ קַמָּן – הֲוָה מְשַׁלֵּם, שֶׁכְּבָר חִיְּיבוּהוּ ב"ד רִאשׁוֹן עַל פִּי עֵדִים, הַשְׁתָּא מָמוֹנָא כְּפָרֵיהּ – וְחַיָּיב. אוֹ דִּלְמָא אַף עַל גַּב דְּעָמַד בַּדִּין. וְאִי מוֹדֶה הֲוָה מִיחַיַּיב, אֲפִילּוּ הָכִי לָא מִיחַיַּיב בִּכְפִירָתוֹ קָרְבַּן שְׁבוּעָה, הוֹאִיל וְעִיקָּרוֹ קְנָס, וְלָא חִיְּיבָה תּוֹרָה קָרְבַּן שְׁבוּעָה אֶלָּא עַל פִּקָּדוֹן וּתְשׂוּמֶת יָד וְכַיּוֹצֵא בָּהֶן. הִפַּלְתָּ אֶת שִׁנִּי. נַמִּי קְנָסָא הוּא, שֶׁהֲרֵי מָמוֹנוֹ הוּא, כְּאֶחָד מִן הַחֲמוֹרִים.
מַאי

תוספות

לאביה נמי פשיטא מדקא יהיב מפתה. אע"ג דאיכא למימר דהא דמחייבין מפתה, היינו בקטנה דלא שייך בה מחילה, וכדרבנן דאמרי יש קנס במקום מכר, מ"מ משמע ליה דבנערה איירי, דפשטא דמתני' א"אלו נערות" דרישא קאי. **רבי** שמעון פוטר שאינו משלם קנס ע"פ עצמו. תימה לר"י: תיפוק ליה דאפי' בעושק והלואה גופייהו דכתיבי בקרא, לא מיחייב קרבן אלא כשייחד לו כלי להלואתו ולעושקו (ב"מ דף מח.), ובאן בקנס מה ייחוד שייך כאן? דמיירי שלא עמד בדין, דבעמד – איבעיא ליה לאביי בסמוך! ואומר ר"י: כגון שייחד לו כלי כך לכשיעמוד בדין בב"ד ויתחייב לו, יהא כלי זה מיוחד לו לגבות ממנו דמי אונסו. וא"ת: וכי נימא דסבר ר"ש דאדם מקנה דבר שלא בא לעולם? דאפי' את"ל דאם אמר: "כלי זה יהא שלך אם ירדו גשמים היום", דחשיב דבר בא לעולם – היינו משום דכלי שנותן לו הוא בעולם, חסר בו למפרע כשירדו גשמים. והא דקאמר "אם ירדו" – תנאה בעלמא הוא. אבל הכא – אין נותן לו הכלי מיד, אלא שמייחדו לו לגבות הימנו קנס אם יתחייב כשיעמוד בדין, והא לא בא לעולם הוא! וכ"ת ה"נ – א"כ נחשביה בהדי הנך תנאי דחשיב בפרק "האומר" בקדושין (דף סג: ושם) דסבירא להו אדם מקנה דבר שלא בא לעולם. דהא *פריך נמי התם: ונחשוב נמי ר"ע! ואור"י: דר"ש חדא ועוד קאמר, חדא – דייחוד אינו מועיל, דדשלב"ל הוא, דאינו מתחייב כלל אלא משעת העמדה בדין ואילך. ועוד, אפי' קונה בייחודו – אין כאן כפירת ממון, שאין משלם קנס ע"פ עצמו, ואי מודה – מיפטר. [ורבנן אית להו דאדם מקנה דשלב"ל, ולא חשיב התם אלא אותן תנאים שהוזכרו שם]. **ונשבע** והודה לר"ש מהו. ק"ק: דבהך מתניתין לא פליגי, אלא דלרבנן בושת ופגם קא תבע. ולר"ש קנס קא תבע אבל אם היה מפרש בהדיא דקנס קא תבע – היה פטור לרבנן כמו לר"ש. א"כ אמאי בעי אליבא דר"ש טפי מלרבנן? דה"נ הוה מצי למבעי לרבנן, אם פירש דקנס קא תבע, ואההיא ברייתא דמייתי בסמוך היה לו לקבוע בעייתו לר"ש. **או** דלמא אע"ג דעמד בדין קנסא הוא ומודה בקנס פטור. כן כתוב בכל הספרים. אבל בקונטרס פירש: או דלמא אע"ג דעמד בדין, ואי מודה ביה מיחייב, אפילו הכי לא מיחייב קרבן שבועה, כיון דעיקרו קנס, ולא הוי דומיא דפקדון דקרא. משמע מתוך פירושו דפשיטא ליה לאביי שהוא ממון לכל שאר דברים היכא דעמד בדין לשלם על פי עצמו, או להורישו לבניו, דמאי שנא? ולא מיבעיא ליה אלא לענין קרבן שבועה דווקא, משום דכתיב "וכחש", ובעינן דומיא דפקדון דעיקרו ממון, כדפי'. וההיא דלקמן דחקו לפרש כן, דפריך אביי בסוף הסוגיא אמתני' דר"ש פוטר כו', וקאמר: טעמא דלא עמד בדין, הא עמד בדין – דמשלם ע"פ עצמו כו'. משמע דפשיטא ליה לאביי היכא דעמד בדין דהוי ממונא. וקשה: שצריך למחוק הספרים! ועוד: דאדפריך ליה אביי לרבה ממתניתין לא הספיקה לגבות כו' ואי אמרת ממונא הוי להורישו לבניו כו' – תקשי ליה לנפשיה, דאביי גופיה מודה דהוי ממון לכל דבר, אלא דמבעיא ליה דווקא לענין קרבן שבועה, כדפי'! ועוד: אמאי איצטריך לשנויי: כי קאמר רבה – בשאר קנסות, נימא דבקנס דאונס נמי קאמר רבה דהוי ממון להתחייב בהודאתו כשעמד בדין, דהא אפי' בסוף הסוגיא פשיטא ליה לאביי דהוי ממון לענין שמתחייב בהודאה! והא נמי דפריך ליה אביי לרבה מר"ש פוטר, טעמא – דלא עמד בדין, הא עמד בדין – דמשלם ע"פ עצמו, מיחייב קרבן שבועה – ליקשי אביי לנפשיה, הואיל ופשיטא ליה בכולהו קנסות דהוי ממון להתחייב בהודאתו! *ונראה לפרש: דאביי מספקא ליה אליבא דר"ש, לפי שמצינו במשנתינו דלר"ש לא הוי ממון להורישו לבניו, להכי מבעיא ליה אי לא חשיב נמי לר' שמעון ממון לענין קרבן שבועה והודאה, אי לאו. ואתרווייהו מבעיא ליה, כדגרסינן בכל הספרים, דהא בהא תליא: דאי מיחייב בהודאתו – אם כן כפר ליה ממונא, ומיחייב קרבן שבועה. ואי מיפטר בהודאה – אם כן לאו מידי כפר ליה. ילכך הוצרך רבה לקמן לשנויי: כי קאמינא ממון הוי להורישו לבניו, דלא מצי למימר ממון הוי להתחייב בהודאה, דהא מדפטר ליה מקרבן שבועה – מכלל דאי מודה מיפטר. ולקמן דאמר אביי: הא עמד בדין דמשלם ע"פ עצמו – הכי פי': הא עמד בדין ובגרה ומתה, דמינה ירית, מיחייב קרבן שבועה. **אמר** ליה ממונא הוי ומיחייב עליה קרבן שבועה. וה"ה דאי מודה ביה מיחייב, דהא בהא תליא. ויש שמוחקין "ומיחייב עליה קרבן שבועה", דהא לקמן קאמר רבה: כי קאמינא ממונא הוי להורישו לבניו, *ולא גרסינן אלא: "ממונא הוי", ולא פי' עד לבסוף דלענין להורישו לבניו קאמר. ואומר רבינו יצחק: דאין למוחקו בשביל כך. דהא למאי דמסיק כי קאמר רבה בשאר קנסות – הדר ביה, דמעיקרא השיב לאביי דממונא הוי הקנס דאונס ופיתוי. ונראה לרבינו יצחק דרבה קיבל מרבותיו דממונא הוי; והשיב לו תחילה לענין קרבן שבועה, וכשסתר לו אביי – חזר בו, ואמר: לא לענין קרבן קבלתי דממון הוי, אלא לענין להורישו לבניו. וכן משמע, דכשהוב הקשה לו ממתני' אמאי קשו בה עשרים ותרתין שנין? הוה ליה לחזור מדבריו, אלא ודאי מרבותיו קבל. **הפלת** את שיני וסימית את עיני. וא"ת: מה ייחוד כלי שייך גבי עבד? דהא מיד כשהפיל את שינו – קנה העבד בעצמו, דגבי עבד גלי רחמנא שזוכה בעצמו מיד כשיפיל שינו, כדאמרי' ב"מרובה" (ב"ק דף עד. ושם). ותו לא הוי קנס! ואין לומר כגון שהפיל שינו וסימא את עינו, דיוצא בשינו ונותן לו דמי עינו, ומייחד לו כלי על זה, דהא מוכח בבבא קמא דמאן דאית ליה יוצא בשינו ונותן לו דמי עינו – סבר דאין צריך גט שחרור, ור"ש אית ליה בהדיא *דצריך גט שחרור! וי"ל: דסימא את עינו אין צריך ייחוד, דאין ייחוד גדול מזה, שהרי העבד תובע את גופו מרבו שישחררנו ויכתוב לו גט שחרור. ואם תאמר: פשיטא דלא מיחייב קרבן שבועה על העבד, דאפילו רבי אליעזר דדריש רבויי ומיעוטי, ומרבה קרקעות לשבועה – לענין קרבן שבועה פוטר בפרק "שבועת הפקדון" (שבועות לז:), דדריש "מכל" ולא כל, והוא הדין בעבדים! ויש לומר: דאע"ג דבקרקעות אין קרבן – בעבד יש קרבן, דהכי נמי אשכחן רבי מאיר דאית ליה דאין נשבעין על הקרקעות, ועל העבדים סבירא ליה דנשבעין, כדאמרינן ב"השואל" (בבא מציעא דף ק:).
מאי

[ומיהו י"ל דלא חשיב אלא הני דאמרי בהדיא דאדם מקנה אבל כר"ש לא אמר בהדיא אלא שיש לדקדק מדבריו לא חשיב ועוד דבלאו הכי צריך לתרץ אמאי לא חשיב ר"א כר"ש דהמוכר את הספינה. ת"י עה"ג]

[ומאי שייך למיבעי אמתני' דהכא אברייתא הוי ליה למיבעי אי רישא רבנן וסיפא ר"ש. ת"י עה"ג]

[וע"ע תוס' ב"ק עב. ד"ה סיפא וכו']

[קדושין כב: גיטין מב:]

גליון הש"ס

גמ' בעא מיניה אביי מרבה. עיין בתשובת מהרלב"ח סימן סז ובתשובת רשד"ם חא"ח וי"ד סימן רנ"ב שהאריכו בסוגיא זו:

תוספות רי"ד

מודי ביה מיפטר לא הוי ממון להורישו לבניו: עמדה בדין עד שלא בגרה ה"ה של האב וכיון שנתחייב ליתן לאב בעדים דתו לא מצי מודי ומיפטר ומת האב קודם שהספיקה לגבותן ה"ה של אחין ואם לא הספיקה לעמוד בדין עד שבגרה דפקע זכות האב דרחמנא אמר ונתן לאבי הנערה ולא לאבי הבוגרת ה"ה של עצמה ואם מתה רואים אם עמדה בדין ונתחייב לה גם הקנס ואח"כ מתה הכל הוא של אחים ואם לא הספיקה לעמוד בדין עד שמתה הקנס הוא שלו [דכיון] דאי מודה ביה מיפטר אינו ממון להורישן לירושין והרי הוא של מאנס אבל בושת ופגם וצער שהן ממון הן של אחין. רש"א וכו'. פי' ר"ש פליג בהכי על ת"ק ואמר אע"פ שעמדה בדין ונתחייב לתת לאב בב"ד ע"פ עדים ששוב אין יכול להודות ולהפטר עדיין לא זכי בהן האב ואף על גב דבכל קנסא דעלמא מודה ר' שמעון דמשעה שעמד עליו בדין ששוב א"י להפטר בהודאתו הוי ממון ומורישו לבניו הכא פליג משום דכתיב ונתן האיש השוכב עמה לאבי הנערה לא זכתה תורה לאב אלא משעת נתינה וכ"ז שלא באו ליד אב [הם] של בתו הכל הקנס והבושת והפגם והצער. ואם מת האב אינו של אחים אלא של עצמה ואין הל' כר"ש שהוא יחיד אלא כת"ק דמשעה שעמד עליהן בדין ונתחייב לו זכה בהן ואם מת האב הן של אחין: מעשה ידיה של אנוסה שמתבטלת מחמת הצער אע"פ שלא גבתה מן המאנס כשמת האב ה"ה של אב להורישו לאחים כבושת ופגם וממונא הוא פי' וה"ה נמי לרבנן אע"פ שלא עמדה בדין עליהם ומת האב ה"ה של אחים: שמשעה שבאו לעולם זכה בהן האב ומורישן לבניו. ופי' המורה ולא דמי לקנס דלא הוי ממון עד עמדו בדין ויעדוהו דהא אי מודי מיפטר ואינו נ"ל דבושת ופגם וצער אינו קנס ואפ"ה תנן במתני' שאם לא עמדה בדין עליהן לא זכה בהן האב ואע"ג דאילו מודה בהו לא מיפטר. וטעמא דמילתא נ"ל אע"פ שהן ממון כיון שצריך לעמוד עליהן בדין שהרי הן צריכין שומת ב"ד ובלא ב"ד לא יהיב ליה לא זכה בהן ולא יקראו ממונו עד עמדו בדין עליהם ועד שלא יעמוד בדין עליהם הן של בת אבל מעשה ידיה ומציאתה שאין צריך לעמוד בדין עליהן דמסתמא פרע לי' ולא כפר לי' זכה בהן האב מיד וה"נ אמרי' בפ"ה אמרי נהרדעא לא כתבינן אורכתא אמטלטלי דכפרי' וה"נ אמרי' לגבי הקדש דכל מטלטלי דכפריה אע"פ שהוא יכול להוציאו בדיינים אם הקדישו בעליו אינו מוקדש עד שלא יתחייב לו והלכך בושת ופגם נמי אע"פ שממון הן כיון דמסתמא לא יהיב ליה אלא ע"פ ב"ד והו"ל ממון שצריך להוציא בדיינים אינו ממון לא להורישו מבתו לבניו ולא לכתוב עליו הרשאה ולא להקדישו אבל האב מוריש חבלותיו לבניו וגם הבת לאחיה שהיורש הוא זוכה בכל זכותו של אב והרי הוא תחתי' חוץ מן הקנס שאינו חשוב ממון מפני שיכול להודות ולהפטר והבא שאינו מוריש האב לבניו משום (דקאמרה בת) דהדן שלה ואין אדם מוריש זכות בתו לבניו:

תורה אור

מַאי לָאו בְּשֶׁעָמַד בַּדִּין! לֹא, בְּשֶׁלֹּא עָמַד בַּדִּין. וְהָא מִדְּרֵישָׁא בְּשֶׁעָמַד בַּדִּין, סֵיפָא נַמִי בְּשֶׁעָמַד בַּדִּין! דְּקָתָנֵי רֵישָׁא: אֵין לִי אֶלָּא דְּבָרִים שֶׁמְּשַׁלְּמִין עֲלֵיהֶם אֶת הַקֶּרֶן, תַּשְׁלוּמֵי כֵפֶל, תַּשְׁלוּמֵי אַרְבָּעָה וַחֲמִשָּׁה, וְהָאוֹנֵס, וְהַמְפַתֶּה וּמוֹצִיא שֵׁם רַע – מִנַּיִן? ת"ל: °"וּמָעֲלָה (ויקרא ה) מַעַל", רִיבָּה. הֵיכִי דָּמֵי? אִי דְּלֹא עָמַד בַּדִּין – כְּפֵילָא מִי אִיכָּא? אֶלָּא פְּשִׁיטָא – בְּשֶׁעָמַד בַּדִּין, וּמִדְּרֵישָׁא בְּשֶׁעָמַד בַּדִּין – סֵיפָא נַמִי בְּשֶׁעָמַד בַּדִּין! א"ל: יָכֵילְנָא לְשַׁנּוּיֵי לָךְ: רֵישָׁא – בְּשֶׁעָמַד בַּדִּין, *וְסֵיפָא – בְּשֶׁלֹּא עָמַד בַּדִּין, וְכוּלָּהּ ר"ש הִיא, *וְשִׁינּוּיֵי דְּחִיקֵי לָא מְשַׁנֵּינַן לָךְ. דְּא"כ אָמְרַתְּ לִי: (א) לִיתְנֵי רֵישָׁא "ר"ש אוֹמֵר" אוֹ לִיתְנֵי סֵיפָא "דִּבְרֵי ר"ש". אֶלָּא, כּוּלָּהּ בְּשֶׁעָמַד בַּדִּין, וְרֵישָׁא רַבָּנַן וְסֵיפָא ר"ש, וּמוֹדֵינָא לָךְ לְעִנְיַן קָרְבַּן שְׁבוּעָה, דְּרַחֲמָנָא פְּטָרֵיהּ מִ"וְכִחֵשׁ". וְכִי קָאָמִינָא מָמוֹן הָוֵי – לְהוֹרִישׁוֹ לְבָנָיו. אֵיתִיבֵיהּ: ר"ש אוֹמֵר: אִם לֹא הִסְפִּיקָה לִגְבּוֹת עַד שֶׁמֵּת הָאָב – הֲרֵי הֵן שֶׁל עַצְמָהּ. וְאִי אָמְרַתְּ מָמוֹן הָוֵי לְהוֹרִישׁוֹ לְבָנָיו – לְעַצְמָהּ אַמַּאי? דְּאַחִין בָּעֵי מֵיהֱוֵי! אָמַר רָבָא? *הַאי מִילְּתָא קַשְׁיָא בָּהּ רַבָּה וְרַב יוֹסֵף עֶשְׂרִין וְתַרְתֵּין שְׁנִין, וְלָא אִיפְּרַק, עַד דְּיָתֵיב רַב יוֹסֵף בְּרֵישָׁא וּפֵירְקָהּ: שָׁאנֵי הָתָם דְּאָמַר קְרָא: °"וְנָתַן (דברים כב) הָאִישׁ הַשּׁוֹכֵב עִמָּהּ לַאֲבִי הַנַּעֲרָה חֲמִשִּׁים כָּסֶף" – לֹא זִיכְּתָה תּוֹרָה לָאָב אֶלָּא מִשְּׁעַת נְתִינָה. וְכִי קָאָמַר רַבָּה מָמוֹנָא הָוֵי לְהוֹרִישׁוֹ לְבָנָיו – בִּשְׁאָר קְנָסוֹת. אֶלָּא מֵעַתָּה, גַּבֵּי עֶבֶד, דִּכְתִיב: °"כֶּסֶף (שמות כא) שְׁלֹשִׁים שְׁקָלִים יִתֵּן לַאדוֹנָיו" הָכִי נַמִי לֹא זִיכְּתָה תּוֹרָה לָאָדוֹן אֶלָּא מִשְּׁעַת נְתִינָה!? "יִתֵּן" לְחוּד "וְנָתַן" לְחוּד. אִי הָכִי, ת"ל "וְכִחֵשׁ"? ת"ל "וְנָתַן" מִיבָּעֵי לֵיהּ! אָמַר רָבָא: כִּי אִיצְטְרִיךְ "וְכִחֵשׁ" – כְּגוֹן שֶׁעָמְדָה בַּדִּין, וּבָגְרָה וּמֵתָה. דְּהָתָם כִּי קָא יָרֵית אָבִיהָ – מִינָּהּ דִּידָהּ קָא יָרֵית. אִי הָכִי יָצְאוּ אֵלּוּ שֶׁהֵן קְנָס? מָמוֹן הוּא! אָמַר רַב נַחְמָן בַּר יִצְחָק: יָצְאוּ אֵלּוּ שֶׁעִיקָּרָן קְנָס. אֵיתִיבֵיהּ: ר"ש פּוֹטֵר, שֶׁאֵינוֹ מְשַׁלֵּם קְנָס עַל פִּי עַצְמוֹ. טַעֲמָא, דְּלֹא עָמַד בַּדִּין. הָא עָמַד בַּדִּין, דִּמְשַׁלֵּם עַל פִּי עַצְמוֹ – קָרְבַּן שְׁבוּעָה נַמִי מִיחַיַּיב! רַבִּי שִׁמְעוֹן לְדִבְרֵיהֶם דְּרַבָּנַן קָאָמַר לְהוּ: לְדִידִי, אע"ג דְּעָמַד בַּדִּין רַחֲמָנָא פְּטָרֵיהּ מִ"וְכִחֵשׁ". אֶלָּא לְדִידְכוּ, אוֹדוּ לִי מִיהַת הֵיכָא דְּלֹא עָמַד בַּדִּין, דְּכִי קָא תָּבַע – קְנָסָא קָא תָּבַע.

וּמוֹדֶה

מאי לאו בשעמד בדין. בב"ד אחד, ובאו עדים באותו ב"ד, וחייבוהו ב"ד על פיהם, ועכשיו זה תובעו מה שחייבוהו ב"ד, וחזר וכפר, וקתני: פטור. בשלא עמד בדין. ועדיין לא העידו עדים. והא מדרישא. מילתייהו דרבנן דאיפליגו עליה וחייבוהו קרבן שבועה איירי בשעמד בדין, מכלל דסיפא, כלומר ר"ש, דאתא לאיפלוגי עלייהו – בדכוותה איירי. אין לי. שיתחייב קרן וחומש ואשם. כפילא מי איכא. מי יימר דגנב, דתתבעיה כפילא? ועוד: דלמא מודי ומיפטר. אלא פשיטא בשעמד בדין. והא דקתני יצאו אלו שהן קנס – לקמן מפרש לה: שעיקרן קנס. או ליתני רישא. דכולה, "רבי שמעון אומר" או ליתני סיפא כו' מאי שנא דאיפסיק ותנא "רבי שמעון אומר" בי מילעי? ומודינא לך לענין קרבן שבועה. דלרבי שמעון אע"ג דעמד בדין לא מיחייב עליה קרבן שבועה. להורישו לבניו. משעמד בדין ומת עד שלא הספיק לגבות הרי הוא של אחיה ולא שלה. עשרין ותרתין שנין. הן היו ימי שררתו של רבה*, ומת, וישב רב יוסף בראש, וסייעוהו מן השמים לפרקה, להיות לו לשם. לפי שהיה רבה חריף, ולכך קראוהו "עוקר הרים", ורב יוסף היה בעל שמועות ומשנה וברייתא לכך קראוהו "סיני"*. וכי אמר רבה ממונא הוי להורישו. משעמד בדין בשאר קנסות ולא מיפטר בהודאה. יתן לחוד ונתן לחוד. "יתן" משמע לשון לווי, ולעולם. "ונתן" משמע דבר הנתון כבר. אי הכי. דשאני קנס דאונס ומפתה משאר קנסות, דאפילו עמד בדין נמי לאו ממונא הוא. ת"ל וכחש. בתמיה: כלומר, מאי איריא דנסיב לה הש"ס לפטורא מ"וכחש" כי היכי דיליף שאר קנסות, כלומר, מדלא דמי לתשומת יד למיהוי עיקר תחילתו ממון – תיפוק ליה דהשתא נמי לאו ממונא הוא, דרחמנא אמר "ונתן", דלא זיכתה לו תורה עד שעת נתינה. כי איצטריך וכחש. לקנס דאונס ופתוי, למילפינהו בהדי שאר קנסות לפטורא מ"וכחש" משום דעיקרן קנס, ולא מצי למילף מ"ונתן". כגון שעמדה בדין ובגרה. דלרבי שמעון דידה הוא. דכי היכי דפליג במתניתין בלא הספיקה לגבות עד שמת האב – הכי נמי פליג בלא הספיקה לגבות עד שבגרה, דקאמר ת"ק הרי הן של אב, ולרבי שמעון הרי הוא של עצמה. ואם מתה אחרי כן – ירית לה אביה מכח דידה. והוי ממון גמור, ואע"ג דלא מטא לידה. דלגבי דידה לא הוה שאני משאר קנסות, דמשעת העמדה בדין ממונא הוא, וכי מייתא – ירית הוא כל זכות שהיה לה בו. הלכך מ"ונתן" לא מצי למיפטריה, ונסיב תלמודא מ"וכחש", ומשום דעיקרו קנס. אי הכי. דבשעמד בדין אוקימתה, וכבר נעשה ממון – היכי קתני יצאו אלו שהן קנס? הא ממון נינהו! שאינו משלם קנס כו'. ואי הוה מודי הוה מיפטר. אלמא, טעמא דרבי שמעון משום דאי הוה מודי מיפטר הוא, והא ליתא אלא כשלא עמד בדין. ה"ג: והא עמד בדין דמשלם ע"פ עצמו קרבן שבועה נמי מיחייב. רחמנא פטריה. מקרבן שבועה. מוכחש בעמיתו. שלא פירש בו אלא דברים שעיקרן ממון.

ומודה

מאי לאו בשעמד בדין. וא"ת: בשלמא לרבי יוחנן דסגי ביחוד כלי, דסבירא ליה *דמעות קונות – אתי שפיר, דאע"ג דייחד לו כלי לקנס וקני ליה – מ"מ דין קנס עליו לענין קרבן שבועה, ולענין כמה דברים, עד שיבא לידו. אלא לר"ל, דלא מיחייב קרבן שבועה אלא כשנטלו ממנו וחזר והפקידו אצלו – אמאי פטר ר"ש הכא? הואיל ועמד בדין ונטלו הימנו – ממון גמור הוא! ואומר רשב"א: דלריש לקיש מצי למימר דמיירי שנתן לו כלי בתורת משכון לקנסו, וחזר והפקידו אצלו. דהואיל ולא נתן לו אלא בתורת משכון – לא חשיב ממון. אע"פ שהיה בידו. תימה לרבינו יצחק: בהפיל את שינו וסימא את עינו אמאי לא מיחייב קרבן שבועה? הא מתחייב בהודאתו, כיון שעמד בדין ופטרוהו ב"ד, ואין לו עליו כלום! ושמא כיון דאכתי מחוסר גט שחרור, אם היה מודה שסימא את עינו – לא היה יוצא לחירות.

לא בשלא עמד בדין. וא"ת: אי בלא עמד בדין – פשיטא דלא מיחייב קרבן שבועה, דלא מידי כפריה, דאי מודה מיפטר, ומה צריך קרא ד"וכחש" לכך? והו"ל לאקשויי: ת"ל "וכחש"? (ב) "אשר ירשיעון אלהים" מיבעי ליה! כדפריך לקמן: ת"ל "וכחש"? ת"ל "ונתן" מיבעי ליה! וי"ל: דהכא לא בעי לאקשויי הכי, דאיכא למימר אסמכתא בעלמא הוא. אבל לקמן פריך שפיר, כי היכי ד"וכחש" הוה לדרשא גמורה לענין שאר קנסות – הכי נמי הוה דרשא גמורה לענין אונס ופתוי.

[**תשלומי** כפל ותשלומי ד' וה'. ר"ש לא פליג אהא, דלא שביק איניש מידי דכי מודה מיחייב, ותבע מידי דכי מודה מיפטר, דהכא הכל קיין. מהר"מ ת"י כ"י.]

דאחין בעי למיהוי. בשלמא לדידי – הוא קנס לכל מילי, מדגלי רחמנא לענין קרבן שבועה. אלא לדידך, דאחין בעי למיהוי! תימה: וכי רבה לא ידע מתני'? ותירץ ר"י ברבי אברהם: דרבה דאמר דממון הוי להורישו לבניו – היינו כשאין הבת קיימת, אבל מתני' איירי כשהבת קיימת, דאז אין ראוי להורישו לבניו כל זמן שלא בא לידו, משום דאין אדם מוריש זכות בתו לבנו. ואביי דאקשי ליה – לא ניחא ליה לאיפלוגי בהאי, ורבה נמי הודה לו*.

ונתן לחוד. וגבי מוציא שם רע דכתי' "ונתנו לאבי הנערה" איכא למימ': "ונתן" לחוד; "ונתנו" לחוד.

אי הכי ת"ל "וכחש" ת"ל "ונתן" מיבעי ליה. בשלמא לדידי מ"ונתן" לא גמרי מידי, וכולה מילתא ילפינן מ"וכחש", דאף דלא הוי ממון להורישו לבניו – ילפינן מהתם, מדגלי רחמנא גבי קרבן שבועה. אלא לדידך דילפת מ"ונתן" דלא הוי ממונא עד שעת נתינה, ולא זכי אב אחר העמדה בדין כמו קודם, א"כ "ונתן" מיבעי ליה, ואין צריך קרא ד"וכחש" על כך, דפשיטא דכיון דאי מודה מיפטר – פטור נמי מקרבן שבועה.

כי אצטריך קרא כגון שעמדה בדין ובגרה ואח"כ מתה דכי ירית מינה דידה קא ירית. ואע"ג דהשתא ממון גמור הוא שלא בא לידו מכח קנס, ואי מודה – מיחייב, אפ"ה פטור מקרבן שבועה מ"וכחש". והיינו דפריך למאי דשני השתא: יצאו אלו שהן קנס? ממון הוא! אבל עד השתא הוה אתי ליה שפיר דקרי ליה קנס! הואיל ובא לידו מכח קנס, ואי מודה – מיפטר. אבל השתא, דמוקמינן לקרא בכי האי גוונא, כגון שעמדה בדין ומתה, שלא בא לידו מכח הקנס אלא מכח ירושה, ומלתא דפשיטא היא דאי מודה – מיחייב, אמאי קרי ליה קנס? ומשני: תני יצאו אלו שעיקרן קנס. והשתא כולהו קנסות משעמד בדין ממונא הוי ומיחייב בהודאתו, ואפי' הכי גזירת הכתוב היא מ"וכחש" דפטור מקרבן שבועה. והכי נמי אפילו לר' אלעזר דאמר *נשבעין על הקרקעות – גזירת הכתוב היא דפטור מקרבן שבועה, אע"ג דמיחייב בהודאתו.

הא עמד בדין דמשלם ע"פ עצמו כו'. ולדבריו דרבה קאמר לה: בשלמא לדידי, דסבירא לי דבכל קנסות אפילו עמד בדין אינו משלם ע"פ עצמו, ולעולם חשיב קנס לרבי שמעון עד שיגיע לידו, כדשמעינן מ"וכחש" – אתי שפיר, דכל היכא דמיחייב ע"פ עצמו – מיחייב נמי קרבן שבועה, כגון עמדה בדין ובגרה ומתה, דמינה ירית. אלא לדידך – הא כל קנסות שעמד בדין, או באונס ומפתה שעמדה בדין ובגרה ומתה, אף על גב דמיחייב בהודאתו פטור מקרבן שבועה – תיקשי.

רבי

[ב"מ מז:]

[עיין תוס' לעיל לח: בד"ה יש בגר וכו' ביאור בסוגיא דהכא]

[ומיהו לקמן פריך מאי למימרא דאע"פ שלא גבתה מוריש לבניו. ת"י]

[ב"ק מג. קו.]

[ברכות סד.]

[שם]

[ב"ק סו:]

[שבועות לז:]

הגהות הב"ח

(א) גמ' אמרת לי או ליתני רישא: (ב) תוס' ד"ה לא וכו' וכחש ת"ל אשר ירשיעון:

וּמוֹדֶה בִּקְנָס פָּטוּר. וְרַבָּנַן סָבְרִי: כִּי קָא תָבַע – בּוֹשֶׁת וּפְגָם קָא תָבַע. בְּמַאי קָא מִיפַּלְגִי? א"ר פַּפָּא: ר"ש סָבַר: *לָא שָׁבֵיק אִינִישׁ מִידֵי דְּקִיץ וְתָבַע מִידֵי דְּלָא קִיץ. וְרַבָּנַן סָבְרִי: לָא שָׁבֵיק אִינִישׁ מִידֵי דְּכִי מוֹדֵי בֵּיהּ לָא מִיפְּטַר, וְתָבַע מִידֵי דְּכִי מוֹדֶה בֵּיהּ מִיפְּטַר. בְּעָא מִינֵּיהּ רַבִּי אָבִינָא מֵרַב שֵׁשֶׁת: בַּת הַנִּיזּוֹנֶת מִן הָאַחִין מַעֲשֵׂה יָדֶיהָ לְמִי? בִּמְקוֹם אָב קַיְימֵי: מָה הָתָם – מַעֲשֵׂה יָדֶיהָ לָאָב, ה"נ – מַעֲשֵׂה יָדֶיהָ לָאַחִין. אוֹ דִּלְמָא, לָא דָּמֵי לָאָב: הָתָם – מִדִּידֵיהּ מִיתְזְנָא, הָכָא – לָאו מִדִּידְהוּ מִיתְזְנָא? א"ל: תְּנֵיתוּהָ: *[א]אַלְמָנָה נִיזּוֹנֶת מִנִּכְסֵי יְתוֹמִים, וּמַעֲשֵׂה יָדֶיהָ שֶׁלָּהֶן. מִי דָּמֵי? אַלְמָנְתוֹ – לָא נִיחָא לֵיהּ בְּהַרְוָוחָה, בִּתּוֹ – נִיחָא לֵיהּ בְּהַרְוָוחָה. לְמֵימְרָא דְּבִתּוֹ עֲדִיפָא לֵיהּ מֵאַלְמָנָתוֹ? וְהָאָמַר רַבִּי אַבָּא א"ר יוֹסֵי: *עָשׂוּ אַלְמָנָה אֵצֶל הַבַּת כְּבַת אֵצֶל אַחִין בִּנְכָסִין מוּעָטִין, מָה הַבַּת אֵצֶל אַחִין – [ב]הַבַּת נִיזּוֹנֶת וְהָאַחִין יִשְׁאֲלוּ עַל הַפְּתָחִים, אַף אַלְמָנָה אֵצֶל הַבַּת – [ג]אַלְמָנָה נִיזּוֹנֶת וְהַבַּת תִּשְׁאַל עַל הַפְּתָחִים! לְעִנְיַן זִילוּתָא – אַלְמָנְתוֹ עֲדִיפָא לֵיהּ, לְעִנְיַן הַרְוָוחָה – בִּתּוֹ עֲדִיפָא לֵיהּ. מְתִיב רַב יוֹסֵף: *מַעֲשֵׂה יָדֶיהָ וּמְצִיאָתָהּ, אע"פ שֶׁלֹּא גָּבְתָה, מֵת הָאָב – הֲרֵי הֵן שֶׁל אַחִין. טַעְמָא – דִּבְחַיֵּי הָאָב, הָא לְאַחַר מִיתַת הָאָב – לְעַצְמָהּ. מַאי לָאו – בְּנִיזּוֹנֶת? לֹא, בְּשֶׁאֵינָהּ נִיזּוֹנֶת. אִי בְּשֶׁאֵינָהּ נִיזּוֹנֶת מַאי לְמֵימְרָא? אֲפִילּוּ *לְמ"ד: יָכוֹל הָרַב לוֹמַר לָעֶבֶד "עֲשֵׂה עִמִּי וְאֵינִי זָנְךָ", [ד]ה"מ בְּעֶבֶד כְּנַעֲנִי, דְּלָא כְּתִיב בֵּיהּ "עִמָּךְ", אֲבָל עֶבֶד עִבְרִי דִּכְתִיב בֵּיהּ °"עִמָּךְ" לָא, כָּל שֶׁכֵּן בִּתּוֹ! אָמַר רַבָּה בַּר עוּלָּא: *לֹא נִצְרְכָה אֶלָּא לְהַעֲדָפָה. אָמַר רָבָא: *גַּבְרָא רַבָּה כְּרַב יוֹסֵף לָא יָדַע דְּאִיכָּא הַעֲדָפָה, וְקָמוֹתֵיב תְּיוּבְתָּא?! אֶלָּא אָמַר רָבָא: רַב יוֹסֵף מַתְנִי' גּוּפָא קַשְׁיָא לֵיהּ; דְּקָתָנֵי: מַעֲשֵׂה יָדֶיהָ וּמְצִיאָתָהּ, אע"פ שֶׁלֹּא גָּבְתָה. מְצִיאָתָהּ מִמַּאן גָּבְיָא? אֶלָּא לָאו – הָכִי קָאָמַר: מַעֲשֵׂה יָדֶיהָ כִּמְצִיאָתָהּ, מַה מְּצִיאָתָהּ – בְּחַיֵּי הָאָב לָאָב, [ה]לְאַחַר מִיתַת הָאָב לְעַצְמָהּ, אַף מַעֲשֵׂה יָדֶיהָ נַמִי, בְּחַיֵּי הָאָב לָאָב, לְאַחַר מִיתַת הָאָב לְעַצְמָהּ, ש"מ. אִיתְּמַר נַמִי, א"ר יְהוּדָה אָמַר רַב: [ו]בַּת הַנִּיזּוֹנֶת מִן הָאַחִין מַעֲשֵׂה יָדֶיהָ לְעַצְמָהּ. אָמַר רַב כָּהֲנָא: מ"ט – דִּכְתִיב: °"וְהִתְנַחַלְתֶּם אוֹתָם לִבְנֵיכֶם אַחֲרֵיכֶם", *אוֹתָם לִבְנֵיכֶם, וְלֹא בְּנוֹתֵיכֶם לִבְנֵיכֶם; מַגִּיד שֶׁאֵין אָדָם מוֹרִישׁ זְכוּת בִּתּוֹ לִבְנוֹ. מַתְקִיף לָהּ רַבָּה: וְאֵימָא בְּפִיתּוּי הַבַּת וּקְנָסוֹת וַחֲבָלוֹת הַכָּתוּב מְדַבֵּר? וְכֵן תָּנָא רַב חֲנִינָא: בְּפִתּוּי הַבַּת וּקְנָסוֹת וַחֲבָלוֹת הַכָּתוּב מְדַבֵּר. [ז]חֲבָלוֹת – צַעֲרָא דְּגוּפָא נִינְהוּ! *[ח]אָמַר רַבִּי יוֹסֵי בַּר חֲנִינָא: שֶׁפְּצָעָהּ

(דברים טו) (ויקרא כה)

רש"י

וּמוֹדֶה בִּקְנָס פָּטוּר. וַהֲרֵי לֹא תְּבָעוֹ אֶלָּא קְנָס לְבַדּוֹ, וְעָלָיו נִשְׁבַּע. וְכֵיוָן דְּאִי אוֹדֵי לֵיהּ קַמָּן לֹא מְשַׁלֵּם, כִּי כָּפְרֵיהּ נַמִי לָאו מָמוֹנָא כָּפְרֵיהּ. בַּת הַנִּיזּוֹנִית מִן הָאַחִין. שֶׁכָּךְ הוּא תְּנַאי כְּתוּבָּה בְּפִרְקִין (לקמן דף נג:): בְּנָן נוּקְבָן דְּיֶהֶוְיָין לִיכִי מִינַּאי, אִינּוּן יְהוֹן יָתְבָן בְּבֵיתִי וּמִיתְזְנָן מִנְּכָסַיי עַד דְּתִלָּקְחוּן לְגוּבְרִין. לָאו מִדִּידְהוּ. אֶלָּא מִתְּנַאי כְּתוּבַּת אִמָּן. אַלְמָנָה נִיזּוֹנֶת מִנִּכְסֵי יְתוֹמִים. דְּהַאי נַמִי תְּנַאי כְּתוּבָּה הוּא, בְּפִרְקִין: אַתְּ תְּהֵא יָתְבָא בְּבֵיתִי וּמִיתְזְנָא מִנְּכָסַי כָּל יְמֵי מֵיגַר אַרְמְלוּתִיךְ. וּמַעֲשֵׂה יָדֶיהָ שֶׁלָּהֶן. אַלְמָא בִּמְקוֹם אָב קַיְימֵי. בִּתּוֹ נִיחָא לֵיהּ בְּהַרְוָוחָה. שֶׁתַּרְוִיחַ מַעֲשֵׂה יָדֶיהָ (א) לְבַד מְפַרְנָסָתָהּ. אַלְמָנָה אֵצֶל הַבַּת. מִי שֶׁמֵּת וְהִנִּיחַ אַלְמָנָה וּבַת. בִּנְכָסִים מוּעָטִין. שֶׁאֵין בָּהֶן כְּדֵי פַּרְנָסַת שְׁנֵיהֶם עָשָׂר חוֹדֶשׁ, כִּדְאָמַר בְּפֶ' "מִי שֶׁמֵּת" בְּב"ב, וְקָתָנֵי: הַבָּנוֹת יִזּוֹנוּ וְהַבָּנִים יִשְׁאֲלוּ עַל הַפְּתָחִים. טַעְמָא דִּבְחַיֵּי הָאָב. עֲשָׂתָהּ, וְזָכָה בּוֹ הָאָב לְהוֹרִישׁוֹ לְבָנָיו. הָא לְאַחַר מִיתַת הָאָב. עֲשָׂתָהּ, הָוֵי לְעַצְמָהּ, מִדְּאִצְטְרִיךְ לְתַנָּא לְאַשְׁמוֹעִינַן. לֹא בְּשֶׁאֵינָהּ נִיזּוֹנֶת. כְּגוֹן שֶׁלֹּא הָיוּ נְכָסִים. מַאי לְמֵימְרָא. דְּיוּקָא לָא אִצְטְרִיךְ לְאַשְׁמוֹעִינַן דַּעֲשָׂתָהּ לְאַחַר מִיתַת הָאָב לְעַצְמָהּ, וְאִי לְאַשְׁמוֹעִינַן הִיא גּוּפָהּ דְּמַה שֶּׁעֲשָׂתָהּ בְּחַיֵּי הָאָב לָאַחִים – פְּשִׁיטָא, דְּהָא זָכָה בֵּיהּ אָב, דְּמָמוֹנָא הוּא וְלָאו קְנָסָא. אֲפִי' לְמַאן דְּאָמַר. בְּמַסֶּכֶת גִּיטִּין (יב.) פְּלוּגְתָּא. לְהַעֲדָפָה. לְעוֹלָם לְדִיוּקָא דִּילָהּ אִיצְטְרִיךְ, לְאַשְׁמוֹעִינַן דְּמַעֲשֵׂה יָדֶיהָ לְאַחַר מִיתַת אָב לְעַצְמָהּ, וּבְשֶׁאֵינָהּ נִיזּוֹנֶת. דְּלָא תֵּימָא זְכוּת שֶׁזִּיכְּתָה תּוֹרָה לָאָב בְּבִתּוֹ מָמוֹן הוּא לְהוֹרִישׁוֹ לַבָּנִים. וּדְקַשְׁיָא לָךְ, בְּמַאי תִּיתְזוֹן, הָא לָא גָּרְעָה מֵעֶבֶד עִבְרִי? כִּי אִצְטְרִיךְ לְאַשְׁמוֹעִינַן – לְהַעֲדָפָה, שֶׁמַּעֲשֵׂה יָדֶיהָ עוֹדֵף עַל מְזוֹנוֹתֶיהָ, אִצְטְרִיךְ לְאַשְׁמוֹעִינַן. אָמַר רָבָא וְכִי גַּבְרָא רַבָּה כְּרַב יוֹסֵף. דְּאוֹתְבַהּ לְהָא תְּיוּבְתָּא, לָא הֲוָה יָדַע דְּאִיכָּא הַעֲדָפָה, וּמָצֵי לְדַחוּיֵי וּלְשַׁנּוּיֵי בְּשֶׁאֵינָהּ נִיזּוֹנֶת וּלְהַעֲדָפָה, וְאַפְּ"ה אוֹתְבַהּ? אֶלָּא ע"כ רַב יוֹסֵף טַעְמָא יָדַע, דִּתְיוּבְתָּא מַעַלְיְיתָא הִיא, וְהָכִי קַשְׁיָא לֵיהּ מִמַּתְנִי' אַדְּרַב שֵׁשֶׁת. דְּקָתָנֵי. מַתְנִי' מְצִיאָתָהּ עִם מַעֲשֵׂה יָדֶיהָ, וְלָמָּה לִי לְמִתְנְיֵיהּ? וְהָא לָא שַׁיָּיךְ לְמִיתְנֵי אע"ג שֶׁלֹּא גָּבְתָה – דְּמִמַּאן גָּבְתָה? אֶלָּא לָאו ה"ק מַעֲשֵׂה יָדֶיהָ כִּמְצִיאָתָהּ. דְּמַה שֶׁעֲשָׂתָהּ בְּחַיֵּי הָאָב לָאָב וְלַיּוֹרְשִׁין, וּמַה שֶּׁעֲשָׂתָהּ לְאַחַר מִיתַת הָאָב – לְעַצְמָהּ. מַה מְּצִיאָתָהּ כו'. דִּמְצִיאָתָהּ פְּשִׁיטָא לָן דִּלְעַצְמָהּ, דְּהָא אֲפִי' בְּחַיֵּי הָאָב לָא זָכֵי בָּהֶן אָב אֶלָּא ע"כ סְמוּכָה עַל שֻׁלְחָנוֹ, כִּדְאָמְרִינַן בְּב"מ (דף יב:), וּמִשּׁוּם אֵיבָה, דְּכֵיוָן דְּאֵינוֹ חַיָּיב בִּמְזוֹנוֹתֶיהָ בְּחַיָּיו, כִּדְתְנַן בְּפִרְקִין*: הָאָב אֵינוֹ חַיָּיב בִּמְזוֹנוֹת בִּתּוֹ, וְאִי אָמְרַתְּ מְצִיאָתָהּ לְעַצְמָהּ – תּוּ לָא יָהֵיב לָהּ מְזוֹנוֹת. וּלְקַמָּן בְּפִירְקִין *נַמִי אָמְרִי': וְהַאי בִּמְצִיאָתָהּ מִשּׁוּם אֵיבָה. אֲבָל אַחִין – עַל כָּרְחַיְיהוּ מִתְזְנָא מִנִּכְסֵי הָאָב. דִּכְתִיב וְהִתְנַחַלְתֶּם אוֹתָם. עֲבָדִים כְּנַעֲנִים. זְכוּת בִּתּוֹ. זְכוּת שֶׁזִּיכְּתָה לוֹ תּוֹרָה בְּבִתּוֹ. וְאֵימָא בְּפִתּוּי הַבַּת וּקְנָסוֹת. דְּאוֹנֶס וַחֲבָלוֹת הַכָּתוּב מְדַבֵּר. אֲבָל מַעֲשֵׂה יָדֶיהָ, דְּמִידֵי דְּשָׁכִיחַ וְחַסְרֵי בֵּהּ מָמוֹנָא, דְּהָא מִיתְזְנָא מִינַּיְיהוּ – אֵימָא דִּידְהוּ הָוֵי. צַעֲרָא דְּגוּפָא הוּא. וְנַעֲרָה לָא זָכֵי לֵיהּ רַחֲמָנָא לָאָב, כִּדְתַנְיָא בְּ"הַחוֹבֵל" (ב"ק פז:): בְּבָנוֹ וּבְבִתּוֹ הַקְּטַנִּים – יַעֲשֶׂה לָהֶם סְגוּלָּה. שֶׁפְּצָעָהּ

(שבועות לח:) (לקמן פה. נה:) (ב"ב קמ: [ע"ש]) ([לעיל מב.]) ([ב"מ לג.] ב"ק פז: לקמן נח: גיטין יב.) (ב"ק פז:) ([זבחים מד. ק:]) (קדושין עז:) ([לקמן דף מט.]) (ב"ק פח.) ([דף מו:])

תוספות

[רבי שמעון סבר כו'. והשתא פליגי בתרתי, בעמד בדין ובדלא עמד בדין. אבל קשה: דסוף סוף, כיון דצריך לומר דפטור מקרבן אע"ג דאי מודה מיחייב – א"כ במנס דחק לחלק בין קנס זה לשאר קנסות, אלא הוה ליה למימר: כי קאמר רבה דממונא הוי – לענין הודאה! וע"ק: לאביי, אמאי תלי ר"ש קרבן שבועה בהודאה? אדרבה, הודאה תליא בקרבן שבועה! ועוד: היכי הוה בעי למילף הודאה מקרבן? הרי קרקעות, דפטור מקרבן, אע"ג דאי מודה מיחייב! ועוד: הא דאמר לקמן הא עמד בדין דמשלם כו' – משמע אאונס ומפתה, דקאי ביה, אם עמד בדין – חייב קרבן, אע"ג דלא נגרה ומתה! ומפרש ר"י: דאביי מיבעיא ליה כיון דאינו מוריש לבניו אפי' עמד בדין לר"ש במתני', משום דאין אדם מוריש זכות בתו לבנו, ותשיב זכות בתו כל זמן שלא בא לידו – ה"ה לענין שבועה, דראוי למעטו מ"וכחש" אע"פ שממון גמור הוא לענין הודאה, כשמודה כשעמד בדין – מ"מ שם קנס עליו, כיון דאם היה מודה באונס ופיתוי ולא היה מודה שעמד בדין – פטור. וסוף הסוגיא מ"מ לא יתיישב].

בת הניזונת מן האחין מעשה ידיה למי. מדאורייתא פשיטא ליה דהוי לעצמה, כדדרשינן לקמן מ"והתנחלתם", אלא מדרבנן בעי, מדתלי טעמא במזונות, ומדמייתי עלה מאלמנה. ומיבעיא ליה: כיון דניזונת משלהן, מי התקינו להו רבנן מעשה ידיה תחת מזונות, או לא? וכן משמע כל הסוגיא. ולקמן דבעי מ"ט דרב, ה"מ למיבעי נמי מ"ט דרב ששת, דמדאורייתא מודה דהוה לעצמה. אלא נקט רב משום דקאמר בהדיא דמעשה ידיה לעצמה, אף מדרבנן. וקלת מגמגם רשב"א: דהכא משמע דטפי הוו מעשה ידיה שלה, כיון שניזונת בעל כרחם בתנאי ב"ד, ממה שהיתה ניזונת מדעתם. ולקמן בריש "אלמנה" (דף נה:) גבי אלמנה משמע איפכא, דאדרבה: כיון שניזונת ע"י תנאי ב"ד – הוה מעשה ידיה שלהן טפי ממה שהיתה ניזונת מדעתם, וצ"ע. [ודוחק לחלק בין אלמנה לבת דניחא ליה בהרווחה, דמ"מ סברא הוי איפכא].

עשו אלמנה אצל הבת כבת אצל האחין. וא"ת: אלמנה אצל הבת אמאי קרי ליה נכסים מועטין? בשלמא גבי בת אצל אחין – מפרש בפ' "מי שמת" (ב"ב קלט: ושם): כדי שיזונו אלו ואלו עד שיבגרו. אבל הכא אין שייך אותו שיעור, שהאלמנה יש לה לעולם מזונות! ונראה לר"י: דדוקא כשיש אלמנה ובנים ובת תקנו לאלמנה ונתנו לה מה שהיה (ב) ליקח לבת, והיינו עד שתיבגר הבת. אבל כשאין אלא אלמנה ובנים, או אלמנה ובת, שהבת יורשת – לא עשו תקנה בשביל האלמנה. דמשום אלמנה לא רצו להפקיע כח הירושה אלא כשכבר הפקיעו בשביל הבת, ובשביל הבת הפקיעו טפי, לפי שהיא יורשת כשאין בנים. וכן משמע בירושלמי בפרק "מי שמת", דאמר התם: אין האלמנה דוחה את הבנות ולא הבנות דוחות את האלמנה, ופעמים שהאלמנה דוחה את הבנות על ידי בנים, ואת הבנים על ידי הבנות. **לא** בשאינה ניזונת. פירוש: מן האחים, אבל מן האב היתה ניזונת. ומשום הכי פריך: אי בשאינה ניזונת – מאי למימרא? דפשיטא דלאחר מיתת האב לעצמה. ומשום היא גופה – דמת האב הרי הן של אחין – נמי לא איצטריך, הואיל וניזונת היתה מן האב פשיטא דיורשין אותו. ואית ספרים דלא גרסי מאי למימרא, אלא גרסי: אי בשאינה ניזונת אפי' למ"ד כו', וכן עיקר. ומיירי בשאינה ניזונת לא מן האב ולא מן האחין, דאחר מיתת האב אית לן למידק דומיא דבחיי האב. ופריך אגופה: אמאי מת האב הרי הן של אחין? הא אפי' אב עצמו אין לו, כיון שאינה ניזונת ממנו. **ל"ג** "כי טוב לו", דבספרי (פ' ראה) לא מפיק ליה מהאי קרא, אלא דריש לה מ"כשכיר כתושב יהיה עמך" ומיותר הוא "עמך" דה"מ למכתב "כשכיר כתושב יהיה עד שנת היובל", אבל "כי טוב לו עמך" – אינו אלא סיפור דברים בעלמא*. **מגיד** שאין אדם מוריש זכות בתו לבנו. תימה: אמאי איצטריך קרא להכי? הא היא גופה לא נפקא לן דמעשה ידיה לאביה אלא מ"לאמה", מה אמה מעשה ידיה לרבה – אף בת מעשה ידיה לאביה, ואמה גופה אינה עובדת לא את הבן ולא את הבת, כדאמרי' בפ"ק דקידושין (דף יז:)! ונראה לרשב"א: דלא איצטריך האי קרא אלא משום קטנה. דהקישא לא איצטריך אלא לנערה, אבל לקטנה לא צריך הקישא, דהשתא זבוני מזבן לה – מעשה ידיה מיבעי. [א"נ: אי לאו האי קרא ה"א לאמה – לקטנה איצטריך לאשמועינן, דאין מעשה ידיה לאחין דומיא דאמה, ולא הוה ידעי' נערה. אבל תימה: דהשתא זבוני מזבן לה הוי ק"ו, וצ"ע דיו]. **חבלות** דידה נינהו. ואם תאמר: וכי אם קיצץ ידיה לא תהיה חבלה של אב? והלא מפסיד מעשה ידיה, ואמרינן ב"החובל" (ב"ק דף פז.) הקוצץ יד עבד עברי של חבירו (ג) – נותן דמי שבת גדולה לעבד, ודמי שבת קטנה לרבו. ורבנן אמרי: ינתן הכל לעבד, וילקח בהן קרקעות, *והוא אוכל פירות! ויש לומר: דפשיטא ליה דמיירי בחבלות קטנות, שאין בהן ביטול מלאכה, דאי יש בהם – הפסד מעשה ידיה אמאי אין מוריש לבנו כמו שמוריש מעשה ידיה?! להכי פריך דידה נינהו.

([ועיין עוד תוס' קדושין עז. ד"ה כי ובב"ק פז: ד"ה דכתב]) (ת"י כ"') ([נ"ל והרכב])

תוספות רי"ד

בעא מיניה רבינא מר"ש בת הניזונת מן האחין מעשה ידיה למי. אחים במקום אב קיימי מה התם מעשה ידיה לאב ה"נ מעשה ידיה לאחין. א"ד לא דמי [לאב] התם מדידיה מיתזנא הכא לאו מדידהו מיתזנא אלא מתנאי ב"ד קאכלי. פי' שכך כתבו לה בכתובתה בנין נוקבין דיהוי ליכי מינאי אנון מיתזנין וכו' א"ל תניתוה אלמנה ניזונת מנכסי יתומים ומעשה ידיה שלהן. פי' והאי נמי תנאי כתובה הוא שכך כותב לה ואת תהא יתבא בביתי ומיתזנא וכו' אלמא במקום אב קיימי מי דמי אלמנותו לא ניחא ליה בהרוחה בתו ניחא ליה בהרוחה. ור"י פשיט מדקתני מעשה ידיה ומציאתה אע"פ שלא גבתה מת האב הרי הן של אחין. בשלמא מעשה ידיה איכא גוביינא אלא מציאתה ממאן גביא אלא לאו הכי קאמר מעשה ידיה כמציאתה מה מציאתה בחיי האב לאב לאחר מיתת האב לעצמה פי' דמציאתה פשיטא לן דלעצמה דהא אפילו בחיי אביה לא זכי בהו האב אלא משום איבה שסמוכה על שלחנו ואינו חייב לזונה בחייו אבל אחין בע"כ יהבו לה מזוני א) בחיי אביה לפיכך אינם זוכים במציאתה אף מעשה ידיה בחיי אב לאב לאחר מיתת האב לעצמה. איתמר נמי אר"י א"ר בת הניזונת מן האחים מעשה ידיה לעצמה אמר (ר"ה) [רב כהנא] מ"ט דרב דכתיב והתנחלתם אותם לבניכם אחריכם אותם לבניכם ולא בנותיכם לבניכם. מגיד לך הכתוב שאין אדם מוריש זכות בתו לבנו:

א) נ"ל יהבי לה מזוני מנכסי אביה.

עין משפט נר מצוה

ו א מיי' פי"ח מהל' אישות הל"א סמג לאוין פ"א טוש"ע אה"ע סי' נה סעי' א:
ז ב מיי' פי"ט שם הל' טז ופ"ה מהל' נחלות הל"ב סמג שם טוש"ע שם סי' קיב סעי' יא:
ח ג מיי' פי"ט מהל' אישות הל' כא סמג שם טוש"ע שם סעי' טז וסי' נג סעי' ד:
ט ד מיי' פ"ט מהל' עבדים הל"ז טוש"ע יו"ד סי' רסז סעי' כ:
י ה ו מיי' פי"ט מהל' אישות הל"י ופ"ג מהל' עבדים הל' טו סמג עשין פג טוש"ע אה"ע סי' קיב סעי' ב:
יא ז ח מיי' פ"ד מהל' חובל הל' יד סמג עשין ב טוש"ע חו"מ סי' תכד סעי' ו:

הגהות הב"ח

(א) רש"י ד"ה בתו כו' לבד מפרנסתה. נ"ב כלומר נדונייתא: (ב) תד"ה עשו כו' שהיה לה ליקח: (ג) ד"ה חבלות כו' של חבירו אביי אמר נותן וכו' ורבא אמר ינתן:

יב א מיי' פ"ג מהל' אישות הל' א ופ"י הל' יא סמג עשין מח טוש"ע אה"ע סי' לז סעי' א:

יג ב מיי' פ"ג שם הל' יב סמג שם טוש"ע שם סי' לז סעי' ג (וסי' נה סעי' ז):

יד ג מיי' פכ"א מהל' איסורי ביאה הל' לא סמג לאוין קכו טוש"ע שם סי' ט סעי' א:

טו ד מיי' פ"י מהל' אישות הל' יא ופט"ז הל"י סמג עשין מח טוש"ע שם (סי' נה סעי' ו) וסי' ק סעי' יד:

שֶׁפְּצָעָהּ בְּפָנֶיהָ. אָמַר רַב זֵירָא אָמַר רַב מַתָּנָה אָמַר רַב, וְאָמְרִי לָהּ, אָמַר רַבִּי זֵירָא א"ר מַתָּנָה אָמַר רַב: בַּת הַנִּיזּוֹנֶת מִן הָאַחִין – מַעֲשֵׂה יָדֶיהָ לְעַצְמָהּ, דִּכְתִיב: °"וְהִתְנַחַלְתֶּם אוֹתָם לִבְנֵיכֶם אַחֲרֵיכֶם" אוֹתָם לִבְנֵיכֶם וְלֹא בְּנוֹתֵיכֶם לִבְנֵיכֶם, מַגִּיד שֶׁאֵין אָדָם מוֹרִישׁ זְכוּת בִּתּוֹ לִבְנוֹ. א"ל אֲבִימִי בַּר פַּפִּי: שָׁקוּד אֲמָרָהּ. שָׁקוּד מַנּוּ – שְׁמוּאֵל, הָא רַב אֲמָרָהּ! אֵימָא אַף שָׁקוּד אֲמָרָהּ. אָמַר מָר בַּר אַמֵימַר לְרַב אַשִׁי: הָכִי אָמְרִי נְהַרְדְּעֵי, הִלְכְתָא כְּוָותֵיהּ דְּרַב שֵׁשֶׁת. רַב אַשִׁי אָמַר: הִלְכְתָא כְּוָותֵיהּ דְּרַב. וְהִלְכְתָא כְּוָותֵיהּ דְּרַב.§ **מתני'** [א]הַמְאָרֵס אֶת בִּתּוֹ וְגֵרְשָׁהּ, אֵירְסָהּ וְנִתְאַרְמְלָה – כְּתוּבָּתָהּ שֶׁלּוֹ. הִשִּׂיאָהּ וְגֵרְשָׁהּ, הִשִּׂיאָהּ וְנִתְאַרְמְלָה – כְּתוּבָּתָהּ שֶׁלָּהּ. ר' יְהוּדָה אוֹמֵר: הָרִאשׁוֹנָה שֶׁל אָב. אָמְרוּ לוֹ: [ב]*(אִם) מִשֶּׁהִשִּׂיאָהּ – אֵין לְאָבִיהָ רְשׁוּת בָּהּ.§ **גמ'** טַעֲמָא – דְּהִשִּׂיאָהּ וְגֵרְשָׁהּ, הִשִּׂיאָהּ וְנִתְאַרְמְלָה, [ג]אֲבָל נִתְאַרְמְלָה תְּרֵי זִמְנֵי – תּוּ לָא חַזְיָא לְאִינְסוּבֵי. וְאַגַּב אוֹרְחֵיהּ קָא סָתֵים לָן תַּנָּא כְּרַבִּי, דְּאָמַר: *בִּתְרֵי זִמְנֵי הָוְיָא חֲזָקָה.§ רַבִּי יְהוּדָה אוֹמֵר: הָרִאשׁוֹנָה שֶׁל אָב.§ מ"ט דְּרַבִּי יְהוּדָה? רַבָּה וְרַב יוֹסֵף דְּאָמְרִי תַּרְוַיְיהוּ: הוֹאִיל וּמִשְּׁעַת אֵירוּסִין זָכָה בָּהֶן הָאָב. מְתִיב רָבָא: רַבִּי יְהוּדָה אוֹמֵר: הָרִאשׁוֹנָה שֶׁל אָב, וּמוֹדֶה רַבִּי יְהוּדָה בִּמְאָרֵס אֶת בִּתּוֹ כְּשֶׁהִיא קְטַנָּה, וּבָגְרָה, וְאח"כ נִשֵּׂאת – שֶׁאֵין לְאָבִיהָ רְשׁוּת בָּהּ. אַמַּאי? ה"נ לֵימָא: הוֹאִיל וּמִשְּׁעַת אֵירוּסִין זָכָה בָּהֶן הָאָב! אֶלָּא, אִי אִתְּמַר הָכִי אִתְּמַר: רַבָּה וְרַב יוֹסֵף דְּאָמְרִי תַּרְוַיְיהוּ: הוֹאִיל וּבִרְשׁוּתוֹ נִכְתָּבִין. וּמִיגְבָּא מֵאֵימַת גָּבְיָא? אָמַר רַב הוּנָא: מָנֶה, מָאתַיִם – מִן הָאֵירוּסִין, וְתוֹסֶפֶת – מִן הַנִּשּׂוּאִין. וְרַב אַסִּי אָמַר: [ד]אֶחָד זֶה וְאֶחָד זֶה – מִן הַנִּשּׂוּאִין. וּמִי אָמַר רַב הוּנָא הָכִי? וְהָאִתְּמַר: הוֹצִיאָה עָלָיו שְׁתֵּי כְתוּבּוֹת, אַחַת שֶׁל מָאתַיִם וְאַחַת שֶׁל שְׁלֹשׁ מֵאוֹת. וְאָמַר רַב הוּנָא: בָּאתָה לִגְבּוֹת מָאתַיִם – גּוֹבָה מִזְּמַן רִאשׁוֹן, שְׁלֹשׁ מֵאוֹת – גּוֹבָה מִזְּמַן שֵׁנִי. וְאִם אִיתָא – תִּיגְבֵּי מָאתַיִם מִזְּמַן רִאשׁוֹן, וּמֵאָה מִזְּמַן שֵׁנִי! וּלְטַעֲמִיךְ תִּיגְבֵּי חֲמֵשׁ מֵאוֹת כּוּלָּם, מָאתַיִם מִזְּמַן רִאשׁוֹן, תְּלַת מֵאָה מִזְּמַן שֵׁנִי! אֶלָּא: חֲמֵשׁ מֵאוֹת מ"ט לָא גָּבְיָא – כֵּיוָן דְּלָא כָּתַב לָהּ "צְבִיתִי וְאוֹסִיפִית לָךְ תְּלַת מֵאָה אַמָּאתַיִם", הָכִי קָאָמַר לָהּ: אִי מִזְּמַן רִאשׁוֹן גָּבְיַאתְּ – גָּבְיָא מָאתַיִם, אִי מִזְּמַן שֵׁנִי גָּבְיַאתְּ – גָּבְיָא תְּלַת מֵאָה. הָכָא

רש"י

שֶׁפְּצָעָהּ בְּפָנֶיהָ. דִּפְלַתָּהּ מִכַּסְפָּהּ. דְּאִי אִיתֵיהּ לְאָב – דִּילֵיהּ הוּא, דְּהָא יֵשׁ לוֹ בָּהּ מֶכֶר. אָמַר רַב זֵירָא וְאָמְרִי לָהּ אָמַר רַבִּי זֵירָא. הוּא רַבִּי זֵירָא הוּא *רַב זֵירָא. אֶלָּא, בְּבָבֶל מִקַּמֵּי דִּסְלִיק לְאַרְעָא דְיִשְׂרָאֵל לְקַמֵּיהּ דְּרַבִּי יוֹחָנָן, וְאֵין סְמִיכָה בְּבָבֶל – הֲווּ קָרוּ לֵיהּ רַב זֵירָא. וּבְהָא שְׁמַעְתָּא, אִיכָּא לְמ"ד מִקַּמֵּי דְּסָמְכוּהוּ אֲמָרָהּ, וְאִיכָּא לְמ"ד בָּתַר דְּסָמְכוּהוּ אֲמָרָהּ. שְׁמוּאֵל. הֲווּ קָרוּ לֵיהּ שָׁקוּד עַל שׁוּם דְּהִלְכְתָא כְּוָותֵיהּ בְּדִינֵי, וְשׁוֹקֵד עַל דְּבָרָיו לְאוֹמְרָם כְּהִלְכָתָא*. הָא רַב אֲמָרָהּ. לְעֵיל. כְּרַב שֵׁשֶׁת. דִּפְשִׁיט לְעֵיל בִּתּוֹ מֵאַלְמְנָתוֹ, וְאָמַר מַעֲשֵׂה יָדֶיהָ לָאַחִין. **מתני'** כְּתוּבָּתָהּ שֶׁל אָב. כְּתוּבָּה שֶׁהִיא גּוֹבָה מִשְּׁנֵי אֵרוּסִין הַלָּלוּ. וְקָסָבַר: יֵשׁ כְּתוּבָּה לַאֲרוּסָה, וּבִימֵי נַעֲרוּת וְקַטְנוּת קָאָמַר. כְּתוּבָּתָהּ שֶׁלָּהּ. דְּמִשֶּׁהִשִּׂיאָהּ פָּקְעָה רְשׁוּתוֹ, וּבָתַר גּוּבַיְינָא אָזְלִינַן, וְגוּבַיְינָא בָּתַר הָכִי הוּא. וְלָא אָזְלִינַן בָּתַר כְּתִיבָה, לוֹמַר: הוֹאִיל וְהָרִאשׁוֹנָה נִכְתְּבָה בְּעוֹדָהּ בִּרְשׁוּת הָאָב – תֶּיהֱוֵי דְּאָב. הָרִאשׁוֹנָה שֶׁל אָב. טַעְמָא מְפָרֵשׁ בַּגְּמָרָא. **גמ'** תּוּ לָא חַזְיָא לְאִינְסוּבֵי. דְּהָוְיָא חֲזָקָה לִהְיוֹת בְּעָלֶיהָ מֵתִים. וְדַק תַּנָּא בְּמִלְּתֵיהּ, דְּלָא לִינְקוֹט בְּדֶרֶךְ פּוּרְעָנוּת. וְאַגַּב אוֹרְחֵיהּ. דְּבָעֵי לְאַגְמוּרִינַן מִשְׁפַּט הַכְּתוּבָּה וּמַחְלוֹקֶת ר' יְהוּדָה וְרַבָּנַן, נָקַט לִישָּׁנָא דִּידֵיהּ לְמִסְתַּם לָן כְּרַבִּי דְּאָמַר בְּמַסֶּ' יְבָמוֹת (דף סד:): נִשֵּׂאת לָרִאשׁוֹן וּמֵת, לַשֵּׁנִי וּמֵת – לַשְּׁלִישִׁי לֹא תִּנָּשֵׂא. דִּבְתְרֵי זִמְנֵי הָוְיָא חֲזָקָה. דְּמִשְּׁעַת אֵירוּסִין. שֶׁל בַּעַל הָרִאשׁוֹן, נִתְחַיֵּיב לָהּ כְּתוּבָּה וְזָכָה בָּהּ אָב. אֲבָל בְּאֵירוּסִין שֵׁנִי לֹא זָכָה, דְּמִשֶּׁנִּשֵּׂאת לָרִאשׁוֹן – פָּקְעָה זְכוּתֵיהּ מִינָּהּ. הוֹאִיל וּבִרְשׁוּתוֹ נִכְתָּבִין. כְּתוּבָּה הָרִאשׁוֹנָה שֶׁהָיָה לִפְנֵי הַנִּשּׂוּאִין. וְהִלְכָּךְ, בָּגְרָה קוֹדֶם נִשּׂוּאִין – לֹא נִכְתַּב בִּרְשׁוּתוֹ. הָא דְּגָרְסִינַן "נִכְתָּבִים" לְשׁוֹן רַבִּים – הַמָּנֶה וּמָאתַיִם דִּכְתוּבָּה קָאֵי. וּמִגְבָּא מֵאֵימַת גָּבְיָא. כְּלוֹמַר, לְעִנְיַן זַכַּיָּיה דְּאָב, דְּהָא חָזֵינַן דְּלָאו בָּתַר אֵירוּסִין אָזְלִינַן אֲפִי' לְר"י, כִּדְקָתָנֵי: וּמוֹדֶה ר"י בִּמְאָרֵס אֶת בִּתּוֹ וּבָגְרָה כו'. אַלְמָא בָּתַר כְּתִיבָה אָזֵיל. לְעִנְיַן מִטְרַף לָקוֹחוֹת מֵאֵימַת טָרְפָא מִמְּשַׁעְבְּדֵי? מִשְּׁעַת אֵירוּסִין – דְּהָא מֵהַהִיא שַׁעְתָּא אִיחַיַּיב בְּתַקַּנְתָּא דְרַבָּנַן, אוֹ דִּלְמָא עַד שְׁעַת כְּתִיבָה, דְּהָוְיָא מִלְוֶה בִּשְׁטָר, לָא טָרְפָא. מָנֶה מָאתַיִם. דְּמִתַּקַּנְתָּא דְרַבָּנַן מְחַיַּיב – טָרְפָא מִזְּמַן אֵירוּסִין, אִם מֵת אוֹ גֵּרְשָׁהּ לְאַחַר נִשּׂוּאִין – טוֹרֶפֶת לָקוֹחוֹת שֶׁלָּקְחוּ מִנְּכָסָיו מִזְּמַן אֵירוּסִין וְאֵילָךְ, דְּמֵהַהִיא שַׁעְתָּא אִשְׁתַּעְבַּד. וְתוֹסֶפֶת. שֶׁמֵּעַצְמָהּ הִיא בָּאָה לָהּ – לֹא נִשְׁתַּעְבֵּד עַד זְמַן כְּתִיבַת הַכְּתוּבָּה, שֶׁקָּנוּ מִיָּדוֹ וְכָתַב. אֶחָד זֶה וְאֶחָד זֶה מִן הַנִּשּׂוּאִין. דְּהִיא גּוּפָהּ מָחֲלָה לְשִׁעְבּוּדָא קַמָּא, וְנִתְרַצְּתָה בִּזְמַן הַכָּתוּב בִּשְׁטַר הַכְּתוּבָּה בְּכָל הַמְּפוֹרָשׁ בָּהּ, בֵּין עִיקָּר בֵּין תּוֹסֶפֶת. אַחַת שֶׁל מָאתַיִם. וְהִיא מוּקְדֶּמֶת, דְּדַוְקָא כַּסֵּדֶר נָקַט. וְאָמַר רַב הוּנָא בָּאתָה לִגְבּוֹת מָאתַיִם כו'. כְּלוֹמַר, אֵין לָהּ אֶלָּא אֶחָד מֵהֶן, וְיָפֶה כֹּחָהּ לִגְבּוֹת אֵיזֶה שֶׁתִּרְצֶה. בָּאתָה לִגְבּוֹת מָאתַיִם, דְּנִיחָא לָהּ בְּהָכִי, וּכְגוֹן שֶׁמָּכַר נְכָסָיו בֵּין זְמַן רִאשׁוֹן לִזְמַן שֵׁנִי, דְּאִי מַפְקָא לְמִיגְבֵּי בְּשֶׁל שְׁלֹשׁ מֵאוֹת – נִמְצְאוּ שִׁטְרֵי הַלָּקוֹחוֹת קוֹדְמִין. גּוֹבָה. מָאתַיִם, וְטוֹרֶפֶת לָקוֹחוֹת מִזְּמַן הַכָּתוּב. וְאִם אִיתָא. דְּסָבַר רַב הוּנָא חוֹב רִאשׁוֹן מִזְּמַן רִאשׁוֹן, וְתוֹסֶפֶת מִזְּמַן שֵׁנִי – ה"נ תִּיגְבֵּי מָאתַיִם מִזְּמַן רִאשׁוֹן, וּמֵאָה מִזְּמַן שֵׁנִי! כֵּיוָן דְּלָא כְּתִיב בָּהּ. בִּכְתוּבָּה שְׁנִיָּה. צְבִיתִי וְאוֹסִיפִית לָךְ תְּלַת מֵאָה אַמָּאתַיִם. ש"מ לֹא לְהוֹסִיף עַל הָרִאשׁוֹנָה בָּא, וְלֹא תִּגְבֶּה הַשְּׁנִיָּה אא"כ הָרִאשׁוֹנָה בָּטְלָה. הָכָא

תוספות

שפצעה בפניה. ואם תאמר: תקשי הך ברייתא לרב וריש לקיש, דמשמע ב"החובל" (ב"ק דף פז: ושם) דפליגי ארבי יוחנן דאמר פלעה בפניה דהוי דאב! ויש לומר: דבפחת דעד הנערות – מודו כולי עלמא דהוי דאב, שמפסיד במה שהיה יכול למוכרה. והתם פליגי במה שהיא נפחתת גם מנערות ואילך. וסבר רבי יוחנן דכל הפחיתה הויא דאב, הואיל ונעשה לה בעוד שהיא ברשות אב. אי נמי: בפחיתת מכירה – מודו כולי עלמא דהויא דאב, והתם פליגי במה שנפחתה לקידושין. דסבירא להו לרב וריש לקיש דלא זכיא ליה רחמנא אלא קידושין ממש. [ורשב"א פירש: אע"ג דפליגי בפלעה בפניה, בקלן לה ידיה – מודו כולי עלמא דהוי דאב. ומוקמי הך ברייתא דהכא בחבלות גדולות, וסברי נמי דאין אדם מוריש מעשה ידיה לאחין].

טעמא דהשיאה וגרשה וכו'. משום מאן דאמר מעיין גורס (יבמות דף סד:) דייק לה מסיפא. ואם תאמר: ותקשי ליה מרישא, דמשמע דמזל גורס! ויש לומר: דמצי למימר דנקט רישא אגב סיפא. וריב"ן מוקי כולה מתניתין באשה אחת, ומפרש הכי: טעמא דהשיאה וגרשה אחר שאירסה, ונתארמלה. הא השיאה ונתארמלה – תו לא הוי מצי למימר השיאה שנית. ואין נראה לר"י: דאם כן לא הוה מצי מוכח אלא למאן דאמר מזל גורס. דלמאן דאמר מעיין גורס – אכתי הוי מצי למתני תו השיאה, ואם כן תקשי ליה ממתני' דהכא. **ומיגבא** מאימת גביא. פירש בקונטרס: אי משעת אירוסין, דהא מההיא שעתא איחייב ליה בתקנתא דרבנן, או דלמא עד שעת כתיבה דהויא מלוה בשטר, לא טרפא ממשעבדי. וקשה לר"י: דמאי שייכא הך בעיא הכא? ועוד: מדנקט מאימת גביא – משמע דבנשואה בעי מאיזה זמן טורפת. ואמאי? ליבעי אי כל ארוסות טרפי ממשעבדי או לא! ונראה לר"י: דדוקא בהך דמיירי רבי יהודה בה, במארס את בתו ובגרה ואחר כך ניסת, קא בעי. דאי טעמא דמודה משום דלא נכתבו ברשותו – הוי טעמא משום דבשעת כתיבה מחלה לשיעבודא, דלא תקינו ליה רבנן לאב אלא כשלא מחלה, ואם כן איהי גופה נמי לא גביא מידי. או דלמא טעמא דר' יהודה לאו משום דמחלה לשעבודא קמא קאמר, אלא משום דלא תקינו לאב זכיה בשלא נכתבה ברשותו. ומיהו, היכא דלא נכתבה כלל – פשיטא דהוי דאב, כגון שגירשה מן האירוסין, ואם כן גביא מזמן ראשון. ודוחק להעמיד כולה שמעתין אליבא דרבי יהודה. ונראה לרשב"א: דאליבא דרבנן בעי. ובעי טפי הכא מבעלמא היכא דליכא אב, דהכא אם נתאלמנה או נתגרשה מן האירוסין – היתה הכתובה של אב, וכי היכי דמפסיד כחו האב בשעת נשואין – מספקא ליה אם גם היא מפסדת. הכא

תוספות רי"ד

א"ל מר בר אמימר לרב אשי הכי אמרי נהרדעי הלכתא כוותיה דרב ששת פי' דפשיט לעיל בתו מאלמנותו ואמר שמעשה ידיה לאחין. ורב אשי אמר הלכתא כוותיה דרב. ומסיק תלמודא והלכתא כוותיה דרב: **מתני'** המארס את בתו וגירשה אירסה ונתארמלה כתובתה שלו השיאה וגירשה השיאה ונתאלמנה כתובתה שלה ר"י אומר הראשונה של אב. א"ל משהשיאה אין לאביה בה רשות. פי' כיון שביד האב לקדשה וזוכה בכסף קידושיה זוכה נמי בכסף כתובתה של שני האירוסין הללו כיון שלא נשאת ולא בגרה ואכתי לא נפקא מרשותי' ובעידן גוביינא נמי היא ברשותיה וקסבר האי תנא יש כתובה לארוסה. אבל אם השיאה וגירשה השיאה ונתאלמנה כתובתה שלה ואע"פ שנכתבה הראשונ' בעודה ארוסה בתר גוביינא אזלינן וכיון דנשאת כבר יצאה מרשות האב וכתובתה שלה ור"י פליג בראשונה ואמר שהוא של אב: מ"ט דר"י רבה ורב יוסף דאמרי תרוויהו הואיל וברשותו נכתבין פי' המאתים זוז הראשונים נכתבו בעודה ארוסה קודם שנשאת ולא אזיל ר"י בתר גוביינא: תניא מודה ר"י במארס בתו כשהיא קטנה ובגרה ואח"כ נשאת שאין לאביה רשות בה פי' כשנכתבה הכתובה הראשונה קודם נישואין בוגרת הות ולא נכתבו ברשותו ומכאן מוכיח שיש כתובה לארוסה בתנאי ב"ד ואע"ג דלא כתב לה. דאי בדכתב לה עסקינן אמאי מודה בהא ר"י והא בשעת אירוסין דכתב לה (ארוסה) [קטנה] הות ור"י אזיל בתר כתיבה אלא לאו ש"מ בדלא כתב לה עסקינן ויש כתובה לארוסה ואע"ג דלא כתב לה: השיאה וגירשה וכו' טעמא דהשיאה וגירשה השיאה ונתארמלה כלומר היינו טעמא דנקט נשואין בתרי גווני חד בגירושין וחד באלמנות ולא נקט תרוויהו באלמנות משום דלא ניחא ליה

לתנא לאשמעינן בקלקול ובאשה מקולקלת דכי נתאלמנה תרי זימני נקראת קטלנית ותו לא חזיא לאינסובי וסתם לן כרבי דאמר בפ' הבא על יבמתו נשאת לא' ומת לב' ומת לג' לא תנשא ואי הוה תני תרווייהו בגירושין א) לא סתם לן כוותיה אלא אורחיה דתלמודא הכי הוי למתני בגירושין תרי זימני אבל כי קתני חד בגירושין וחד בנשואין הא וודאי לאו אורחיה דתלמודא הוא ומשום דבעי למיסתם לן כרבי תני הכי אבל נתאלמנה תרי זימני תו לא חזיא לאנסובי ואגב אורחיה קסתים לן תנא כר' דאמר בתרי זימני הוי חזקה: ומיגבא מאימת גביא ב) פי' המורה לענין זכיה דאב חזינן דלאו בתר אירוסין אזלינן ואפי' לר"י כדקתני ומודה ר"י וכו' אלמא בתר כתיבה אזיל ולא פליגי ר"י וחכמים אלא בזכות האב אבל שיעבוד כתובה מאימת חיילא לא קמיירו והשתא איבעיא לן כל אשה שנשאת ונתאלמנה או נתגרשה ובאת לגבות כתובתה לטורפה ממשעבדי היינו מן הלקוחות מאיזה זמן טורפת מנה מאתים יש לה בתנאי ב"ד משעה שאירסה וכתובה כתב לה עכשיו בעת הנשואין מאתים זוז והתוספת ועכשיו מאיזה זמן היא טורפת מזמן אירוסין או מזמן כתיבת הכתובה שהיא בעת הנשואין אמר ר"ה מנה ומאתים מן האירוסין ותוספת מן הנשואין פי' מנה מאתים שנתחייב לה משעת אירוסין בתנאי ב"ד גביא משעת אירוסין ותוספת לא נשתעבד לה אלא משעת נשואין ורב אסי אמר אחד זה ואחד זה מן הנשואין דתנאי ב"ד הוא להיות כתובה לארוסה ה"מ אם נתאלמנה או נתגרשה מן האירוסין. אבל אשה שנשאת וכותב לה מאתים ותוספת בתר נשואין אזלי' ולא גביא להו אלא משעת נשואין דהכי הוי עיקר תנאי ב"ד מן הנשואין ג) דינו משנשאת. וגם מכאן מוכיח שיש כתובה לארוסה ואע"ג דלא כתב לה דאי כתב לה אמאי פליג ר"א למימר מן הנשואין והא כתב לה מן האירוסין ונשתעבדו לו נכסיו. ואמרינן לקמן מאי הוי עלה ת"ר י"א משום ר"א בר"ש מנה מאתים מן האירוסין ותוספת מן הנשואין וחכ"א אחד זה ואחד זה מן הנשואין ומסיק תלמודא והלכתא אחד זה ואחד זה מן הנשואין: אמר רב [הונא] הוציאה עליו ב' כתובות אחת של מאתים ואחת של ג' מאות באת לגבות מאתים גובה מזמן ראשון [באת לגבות] ג' מאות גובה מזמן שני וכלהו חמש מאות לא גביא דכיון דלא כתב לה צביתי ואוסיפת לך ג' מאות אמאתים הכי קא"ל אי מזמן ראשון גבית גבי מאתים ואי מזמן שני גבי ג' מאות פי' אם תרצה למחול שיעבודך שלא לטרוח לקוחות שקנו לאחר זמן ראשון עד זמן זה תיגבי ג' מאות וכיון שלא קרעה הראשונה ידה על העליונה או תגבה מאתים מזמן ראשון כגון שאין לה מה לטרוף מזמן שני

א) אולי צ"ל לא הוי ידעינן דסתם לן תנא כוותיה. ב) הוא פרש"י ז"ל. ג) אולי צ"ל דאם כבר נשאת שתגבה מן הנשואין.

[ובתוס' למנחות מ: הביאו בזה דר' זירא לאו היינו רב זירא]

[ובערוך ערך שקד א' איתא שהיה שוקד על דלתי תורה]

[במשנה שבמשניות ליתא]

ב"מ קו: [יבמות סו. סד: עירובין נז. סנהדרין פא: נדה י. סד.]

גליון הש"ס

רש"י ד"ה הואיל וברשותו וכו' נכתבים לשון רבים. עי' תוס' פ"ג מ"ו דכתובות:

הָכָא נַמִי הַיְינוּ טַעֲמָא דְּלָא גָּבְיָא, מִדְּלָא כָּתַב לָהּ "אוֹסִיפִית לָךְ מֵאָה אַמָּאתַיִם" – אַחוּלֵי אַחִילְתֵּיהּ לְשִׁעְבּוּדָא קַמָּא. אָמַר מָר: אִי בָּעֲיָא בְּהַאי – גָּבְיָא, אִי בָּעֲיָא בְּהַאי גָּבְיָא, לֵימָא פְּלִיגָא דְּרַב נַחְמָן, *דְּאָמַר רַב נַחְמָן: שְׁנֵי שְׁטָרוֹת הַיּוֹצְאִין בָּזֶה אַחַר זֶה – בִּיטֵּל שֵׁנִי אֶת הָרִאשׁוֹן! לָאו מִי אִיתְּמַר עֲלָהּ, אָמַר רַב פַּפָּא: וּמוֹדֶה ר"נ דְּאִי אוֹסֵיף בֵּיהּ דִּיקְלָא לְתוֹסֶפֶת כְּתָבֵיהּ – הָכָא נַמִי, הָא אוֹסֵיף לָהּ מִידֵּי. גּוּפָא, אָמַר רַב נַחְמָן: שְׁנֵי שְׁטָרוֹת הַיּוֹצְאִין בָּזֶה אַחַר זֶה – בִּיטֵּל שֵׁנִי אֶת הָרִאשׁוֹן. אָמַר רַב פַּפָּא: וּמוֹדֶה רַב נַחְמָן דְּאִי אוֹסֵיף בֵּיהּ דִּיקְלָא – לְתוֹסֶפֶת כְּתָבֵיהּ. פְּשִׁיטָא, רִאשׁוֹן בְּמֶכֶר וְשֵׁנִי בְּמַתָּנָה – לְיַפּוֹת כֹּחוֹ הוּא דִּכְתַב לֵיהּ, מִשּׁוּם דִּינָא דְּבַר מִצְרָא. וְכָל שֶׁכֵּן רִאשׁוֹן בְּמַתָּנָה וְשֵׁנִי בְּמֶכֶר, דְּאָמְרִינַן: מִשּׁוּם דִּינָא דְּבַעַל חוֹב הוּא דִּכְתַב כֵּן. אֶלָּא, אִי שְׁנֵיהֶם בְּמֶכֶר, שְׁנֵיהֶם בְּמַתָּנָה – בִּיטֵּל שֵׁנִי אֶת הָרִאשׁוֹן. מַאי טַעְמָא? רַפְרָם אָמַר: אֵימַר אוֹדוּיֵי אוֹדֵי לֵיהּ. רַב אַחָא אָמַר: אֵימַר אַחוּלֵי אַחְלֵיהּ לְשִׁיעְבּוּדֵיהּ. מַאי בֵּינַיְיהוּ? אִיכָּא בֵּינַיְיהוּ אוֹרוּעֵי סָהֲדֵי, וּלְשַׁלּוּמֵי פֵּירֵי, וּלְטַסְקָא. מַאי הָוֵי עֲלָהּ דִּכְתוּבָּה? ת"ש: דְּאָמַר רַב יְהוּדָה אָמַר שְׁמוּאֵל מִשּׁוּם ר"א בר"ש: מָנֶה מָאתַיִם – מִן הָאֵירוּסִין, וְתוֹסֶפֶת – מִן הַנִּישּׂוּאִין. וחכ"א: אֶחָד זֶה וְאֶחָד זֶה מִן הַנִּישּׂוּאִין. וְהִלְכְתָא: אֶחָד זֶה וְאֶחָד זֶה מִן הַנִּישּׂוּאִין.§

מתני' הַגִּיּוֹרֶת – שֶׁנִּתְגַּיְּירָה בִּתָּהּ עִמָּהּ וְזִינְּתָה – הֲרֵי זוֹ בְּחֶנֶק. אֵין לָהּ לֹא פֶּתַח בֵּית הָאָב, וְלֹא מֵאָה סֶלַע. הָיְתָה הוֹרָתָהּ שֶׁלֹּא בִּקְדוּשָּׁה וְלֵידָתָהּ בִּקְדוּשָּׁה – הֲרֵי זוֹ בִּסְקִילָה, וְאֵין לָהּ לֹא פֶּתַח בֵּית הָאָב, וְלֹא מֵאָה סֶלַע. הָיְתָה הוֹרָתָהּ וְלֵידָתָהּ בִּקְדוּשָּׁה – הֲרֵי הִיא כְּבַת יִשְׂרָאֵל לְכָל דְּבָרֶיהָ. יֵשׁ לָהּ אָב וְאֵין לָהּ פֶּתַח בֵּית הָאָב, יֵשׁ לָהּ פֶּתַח בֵּית הָאָב וְאֵין לָהּ אָב – הֲרֵי זוֹ בִּסְקִילָה, לֹא נֶאֱמַר "פֶּתַח בֵּית *אָב" (דברים כג) אֶלָּא לְמִצְוָה.§

גמ'

רש"י

הָכָא נַמִי. מִדְּלָא כָּתַב "וְאוֹסִיפִית לָהּ מֵאָה אַמָּאתַיִם קַמָּאֵי", אֶלָּא כָּתַב זְמַן שֵׁנִי לְכָל הַשָּׁלֹשׁ מֵאוֹת, וְלֹא בִּלְשׁוֹן מוֹסִיף עַל הַשְּׁטָר הָרִאשׁוֹן – ש"מ אַחִילְתֵּיהּ לְשִׁעְבּוּדָא קַמָּא. וְאִם בָּאתָ לִגְבּוֹת שְׁטָר הַשֵּׁנִי – תִּגְבֶּה מִזְּמַן שֵׁנִי. אֲבָל גַּבֵּי תוֹסֶפֶת, הַמּוֹסִיף בְּכָל כְּתוּבּוֹת עַל מָנֶה מָאתַיִם כּוֹתְבִין בּוֹ "וְאוֹסִיפִית לָהּ עַל מַאי דְּתַקּוּן רַבָּנַן", הִלְכָּךְ לָא אַחִילְתֵּיהּ לְשִׁעְבּוּדָא קַמָּא, וּכְדְקָאֵי קָאֵי. אָמַר מָר. אַדְּרַב הוּנָא קָאֵי, דְּאָמַר: אִם בָּאת לִגְבּוֹת מָאתַיִם כו'. שְׁנֵי שְׁטָרוֹת. שֶׁל שָׂדֶה אַחַת, שֶׁל מֶכֶר אוֹ מַתָּנָה, וּכְתָבָן רְאוּבֵן לְשִׁמְעוֹן, אֶחָד בְּנִיסָן וְאֶחָד בְּסִיוָן. בִּיטֵּל שֵׁנִי אֶת הָרִאשׁוֹן. וְאִם כָּתַב לוֹ אַחֲרָיוּת וּטְרָפוּהָ מִמֶּנּוּ – אֵין גּוֹבֶה אֶלָּא מִזְּמַן שֵׁנִי. וְה"נ, נֵימָא רִאשׁוֹן בְּטֵיל לֵיהּ, דְּאַחְלֵיהּ לְשִׁעְבּוּדֵיהּ קַמָּא. דְּאִי מוֹסִיף בָּהּ דִּיקְלָא. בִּשְׁטָר בַּתְרָא. לְתוֹסֶפֶת כְּתָבֵיהּ. וְלָא לְבַטּוּלֵי לְקַמָּא, אֶלָּא דְּאִי מִזְּמַן שֵׁנִי אָתֵי לְמִגְבֵּי – לִיקְנֵי עִיקָּר וְתוֹסֶפֶת, וְאִי נִיחָא לֵיהּ בְּקַמָּא מִשּׁוּם דְּקָדֵים – לָא לִיקְנֵי תּוֹסֶפֶת. וְה"נ הָא אוֹסֵיף לָהּ. דִּכְתַב לָהּ שְׁלֹשׁ מֵאוֹת. לְיַפּוֹת כֹּחוֹ כְּתָבֵיהּ. וְאִי נַמִי לָא אוֹסֵיף בֵּיהּ לָא בִּיטֵּל אֶת הָרִאשׁוֹן, אֶלָּא דְּלָא לֵיתוּ בְּנֵי מִצְרָא לְעַרְעוּרֵי עֲלֵיהּ. דְּקַיְימָא לָן: *מַתָּנָה לֵית בָּהּ מִשּׁוּם דִּינָא דְּבַר מִצְרָא. דִּינָא דְּבַעַל חוֹב. דְּאִי אָתֵי ב"ח וְטָרֵיף לֵיהּ מִינֵּיהּ – קִבֵּל עָלָיו אַחֲרָיוּת בִּשְׁטָר הַשֵּׁנִי, דְּנֶהְדַּר וְנִיגְבֵּי מִינֵּיהּ מָעוֹת הַכְּתוּבִים כָּאן. מַאי טַעְמָא. בִּיטֵּל. אוֹדֵי לֵיהּ. בַּעַל הַשְּׁטָר שֶׁהָרִאשׁוֹן מְזוּיָּף הָיָה, וְנִתְרַצָּה עַל הָאַחֵר לִגְבּוֹת מִזְּמַן שֵׁנִי. אוֹרוּעֵי סָהֲדֵי. הַחֲתוּמִים בָּרִאשׁוֹן. לְרַפְרָם – פְּסוּלִים, לְרַב אַחָא – כְּשֵׁרִים. וּלְשַׁלּוּמֵי פֵּירֵי. שֶׁאָכַל לוֹקֵחַ בֵּין זְמַן רִאשׁוֹן לִזְמַן שֵׁנִי, לְרַפְרָם מְשַׁלֵּם. וּלְטַסְקָא. לִפְרוֹעַ מַס הַקַּרְקַע לַמֶּלֶךְ מִזְּמַן רִאשׁוֹן לִזְמַן שֵׁנִי. לְרַפְרָם – עַל הַמּוֹכֵר לִפְרוֹעַ, לְרַב אַחָא – עַל הַלּוֹקֵחַ לִפְרוֹעַ. מַאי הָוֵי עֲלָהּ דִּכְתוּבָּה. מֵאֵימַת גָּבְיָא.

מתני' וְזִינְּתָה. בָּאֵירוּסִין, וְהִיא נַעֲרָה. הֲרֵי זוֹ בְּחֶנֶק. וַאֲפִי' נִתְגַּיְּירָה פְּחוּתָה מִבַּת ג' שָׁנִים, דְּמוּחְזֶקֶת בְּתוּלָה הִיא. דְּכִי כְּתִיבָא סְקִילָה בְּנַעֲרָה הַמְאוֹרָסָה – בְּיִשְׂרָאֵל כְּתִיבָא, דִּכְתִיב "כִּי עָשְׂתָה נְבָלָה בְּיִשְׂרָאֵל". אֵין לָהּ לֹא פֶּתַח בֵּית אָבִיהָ. א"צ לְהוֹצִיאָהּ אֶל פֶּתַח בֵּית אָבִיהָ. וְלֹא מֵאָה סֶלַע. אִם נִמְצָא בַּעַל שַׁקְרָן וְעֵדָיו זוֹמְמִין. דְּכוּלָּהּ פָּרָשָׁה בְּיִשְׂרָאֵל כְּתִיבָא. הֲרֵי זוֹ בִּסְקִילָה. בַּגְּמָרָא יָלֵיף לָהּ. הֲרֵי הִיא כְּבַת יִשְׂרָאֵל לְכָל דְּבָרֶיהָ. וְיֵשׁ לָהּ פֶּתַח בֵּית אָב וּמֵאָה סְלָעִים. יֵשׁ לָהּ אָב וְאֵין לָהּ פֶּתַח בֵּית אָב. כְּגוֹן שֶׁאֵין לוֹ בַּיִת. וּבְיִשְׂרְאֵלִית קָמַיְירֵי.

תוספות

הכא נמי בדאוסיף לה. פי': שכתב בכתובה שניה יותר מבראשונה. אבל אין לפרש שכתב ""לביתי ואוסיפית כך וכך" – דא"כ היתה גובה שתיהן, כדאמרינן לעיל. **משום** דינא דבר מצרא. ולניע אותו של מכר. דאם ירצה שניהם – אית בה דינא דבר מצרא. דאפילו מתנה שכתוב בה אחריות אית בה דינא דבר מצרא*. ונראה דאם הלוקח עצמו מצרן דלא שייך דינא דבר מצרא – דביטל שני את הראשון. ויש מפרשים: דלאו דוקא נקט משום דינא דבר מצרא, דאפילו לא שייך דינא דבר מצרא – לא ביטל שני את הראשון, דנפקא מינה לענין דרך, דאפי' למ"ד (ב"ב דף סד:) מוכר בעין רעה מוכר – נותן בעין יפה נותן. **אימר** אחולי אחליה לשיעבודא. תימה: מה אחליה לשיעבודא שייך גבי מתנה? ונראה לר"י: כגון שבין זמן הראשון לזמן שני קנה הנותן שדה אצל שדה הנית', והשתא אחליה מקבל מתנה לשיעבודא, ולא יוכל לטעון דינא דבר מצרא. ועוד אומר רשב"א: דנפקא מינה אם לוה נותן בין זמן הראשון לזמן שני שיטרפו בעלי חוביו מאותה שדה. [א"נ: אם יאכל הנותן פירות בין זמן ראשון לשני]. **איכא** בינייהו אורועי סהדי. תימה גדולה הוא מה שפירש בקונטרס לפסול העדים, דאין יכול לפסול העדים בענין זה! ונראה לר"י: דאם יש לזה מקבל מתנה שום שטר אחר, שהעדים אלו חתומים בו – מרעין ליה לשטרא, הואיל והוא מודה שהן פסולין. אי נמי – לפסול חתימתן קאמר, דאימר זיופי זייף, הואיל והוא מודה שהשטר הזה מזויף. **והלכתא** אחד זה ואחד זה מן הנשואין. תימה לרבינו יצחק: דהשתא מסקינן דאחד זה ואחד זה מן הנשואין, אע"ג דאוסיף לה, ופליגא אדרב נחמן דאמר לעיל אי אוסיף דיקלא לתוספת – אדעתא דתוספת כתביה, ולא ביטל שני את הראשון. וזהו תימה: דהלכתא כרב נחמן בדיני, ורפרם ורב אחא איפלגו אליביה, ודייקינן נמי בשילהי "הכותב" (לקמן דף פט: ושם) כוותיה! ואור"י: דהכא, אע"ג דאיכא תוספת – ביטל (א) את הראשון. וטעמא – משום דליכא שטר כתובה באירוסין אלא מתנאי ב"ד, הלכך נתבטל תנאי ראשון ע"י שטר. אבל לעיל, דאיכא שני שטרות, כשהוסיף בשני – לא ביטל את הראשון, הואיל והוא בידו עדיין. וא"ת: וכיון דאיירי מילתייהו דרב הונא ורב אסי בדלא כתב לה – א"כ תפשוט מהכא הא דבעי בפ"ק דב"מ (דף יז: ושם) אי ארוסה אית לה כתובה בדלא כתב לה? וי"ל: שאינו רוצה לפשוט אלא מן המשנה או מברייתא. ואע"ג דאיכא לאוכוחי ממילתא דר' אלעזר ב"ר שמעון ורבנן – הא נמי מימרא היא, דרב יהודה אמר שמואל אמרה משמיה, ואינה ברייתא. וממתניתין דהמארס את בתו ליכא לאוכוחי, דאיכא לאוקמה בדכתב לה. וא"ת: ותפשוט מהא דתניא לעיל מודה ר' יהודה במארס את בתו וגרשה ונשאת, שאין לאביה רשות בה! וע"כ בדלא כתב לה מיירי, דאי כתב לה – הויא שלו, הואיל וברשותו נכתבה, כדאמר לעיל. ואי ארוסה אין לה כתובה – פשיטא דאין לו בה כלום! ונראה לרשב"א: דלעולם איכא לאוקמה בדכתב לה. ומיירי כגון שהוסיף לה בשעת נשואין. דסלקא דעתא הואיל ומנה מאתים שלו – תוספת נמי שלו, קמ"ל*. **הגיורת** שנתגיירה בתה עמה. הא דלא נקט הגיורת שנתגיירה סתמא – משום דאיירי בפחותה מבת שלש, דאין דרכה להתגייר אלא עם אמה. ועוד: דאין סברא שיטבילוה על דעת ב"ד, שאין מטבילין גר קטן על דעת ב"ד אא"כ הוא תובע להתגייר, וזאת פחותה מבת ג' – אין בה דעת לתבוע. להכי נקט שנתגיירה בתה עמה, והטבילוה על דעת אמה. ועוד: משום דבעי למיתני היתה הורתה שלא בקדושה ולידתה בקדושה. **אין** לה פתח בית אב כו' הוי זו בסקילה. תימה: דתיקשי מהכא למ"ד בפ' "נגמר הדין" (סנהדרין דף מה:): נקטעה יד העדים – פטור, דבעינן קרא כדכתיבו! וי"ל: דשאני הכא, דגלי קרא "ומתה" – לרבות הורתה שלא בקדושה, והיינו נמי אין לה אב. אבל קשה: דתקשי ליה מברייתא דבעיר שרובה גוים סוקלין אותה על שער ב"ד, דדרש "בשעריך" – ולא בשערי גוים, ואמאי לא פטרינן לה לגמרי? וי"ל: דברוב גוים הוי "שעריך" שערי ב"ד, ולא שער העיר. מנא

[ועוד דאיכא למימר דהכא איירי בכתב לה ולא תקשי אדרב נחמן דהכא מיירי כשמחזרת לו כתובה ראשונה כשנותן לה השניה. ת"י כ"י]

תוספות רי"ד

שני. או אם יש לה מה לטרוף גובה ג' מאות מזמן שני: וא"ר נחמן שני שטרות היוצאים בזא"ז בטל שני את הראשון. פי' אם כתב לו שני שטרי מכר או שטרי מתנה על שדה אחת הא' כתב בניסן וא' כתב בתשרי בטל שני את הראשון פי' אם היה בו אחריות וטרפוהו ממנו אינו גובה אלא מזמן שני. אמר ר"פ ומודה ר"נ דאי אוסיף ביה דיקלא לתוספת כתביה. פי' אי אוסיף דיקלא בשטרא בתרא לא בטל שני את הראשון אלא ידו על העליונה דקא"ל אי מזמן ראשון בעית למיגבי גבי' במאי דכתיב ביה ואם תרצה למחול שיעבודך מזמן ראשון ולגבות מזמן שני תגבה כל התוספת הכתובה בשטר השני: פשיטא לי פי' בשני שטרות היוצאין בזא"ז שלא בטל שני את הראשון אי הוי ראשון במכר ושני במתנה דליפות כחו הוא דכתב ליה משום דינא דבר מצרא פי' כי במכר יכול בעל מצרא להוציא מידו אבל מתנה לית בה משום דינא דבר מצרא ולהכי הדר וכתב לה בלשון מתנה לשתק מעליו בר מצרא ולא לבטל את הראשון וכ"ש ראשון במתנה ושני במכר דמשום דינא דב"ח כתביה. פי' דבמתנה ליכא אחריות ובמכר איכא אחריות ואי אתי בע"ח וטריף לה מיניה הדר על המוכר ומ"ה הדר וכתב ליה ולא

עין משפט נר מצוה

טז א ב ג מיי' פט"ו מהל' אישות הל' ט"ע טוש"ע אה"ע סי' ק סעי' יד:

[כדאיתא ב"מ קח:]

יז ד ה ו ז ח מיי' פ"ה מהל' זכיה הל' ח ע סמג עשין פב טוש"ע חו"מ סי' רמ סעי' א ב:

יח ט מיי' פ"ג מהל' איסורי ביאה הל' ז סמג עשין נו:

יט י מיי' שם הל' יח:

כ כ מיי' פ"ג מהל' נערה הל' ח סמג עשין נה:

כא ל מיי' פ"ג מהל' איסורי ביאה הל' יח:

ת"י כ"י

מסורת הש"ס

לקמן פט:

ב"מ קח:

[ס"א אביה]

הגהות הב"ח

(א) תוס' ד"ה והלכתא וכו' דאיכא תוספת ביטל שני את הראשון:

גליון הש"ס

רש"י ד"ה לאורועי סהדי וכו' לרפרם פסולים. עי' מ"ל (פ"ג) [פי"א] מהל' שלוחין הל' כו: תוס' ד"ה אומר רשב"א דנ"מ. עי' בתשובת מהר"א ששון סי' קפה: ד"ה ויש לומר שאינו רוצה לפשוט. כעין זה בתוס' קדושין ד"ה אמרה משמיה ואינה ברייתא. עיין לקמן פו ע"א ברש"י ד"ה ול"ל:

רבינו חננאל

לבטל את הראשון. ודאי שניהם במכר שניהם במתנה בטל שני את הראשון מ"ט רפרם אמר אודויי אודי ליה. ר"א אמר אימור איחוליה אחליה לשיעבודיה קמא. פי' רפרם אמר הודה לו המקבל לנותן שהשטר הראשון נכתב בשקר ולא היה אמת לפיכך ביקש לו שיכתוב לו שטר שני ור"א סבר אין אנו מחזיקין את הראשון בפסול אלא אמרינן כשר היה ולמה כתב לו השני שפייסו המוכר ללוקח שימחול שיעבוד של זמן א' ויתפש מזמן שני מפני שהיה לו שום שדה למכור בין זמן הא' לזמן הב' ולא היה הלוקח רוצה לקנותו מפני שיעבודו של זה ולפיכך פייסו שימחול לו שעבוד דמזמן ראשון מ"ב א"ב אורועי סהדי לרפרם כיון שהודה לו שבשקר נכתב הא' העדים הם פסולים לו שאם יש לו שום שטר שהם חתומים בו הוא בטל דפיו כק' עדים והוא הודה שהם פסולים אבל לעלמא לא כל הימנו לפוסלם ומ"ה אמר לאורועי ול"א לפסול ולמ"ד אחולי אחליה וכו' נאמנים. א"נ לשלומי פירי לרפרם דאמר אודויי אודי ליה שהראשון היה פסול א"כ כל הפירות שאכל הלוקח בין זמן הא' לזמן הב' חייב להחזיר לבעלים ולר"א אינו חייב להחזיר לבעלים: א"נ לטסקא. פי' לפרוע מס המלך מזמן א' ועד זמן ב' לרפרם דאמר אודויי אודי ליה גם המוכר הודה ללוקח שהא' היה בטל והב' עיקר וא"כ מס הקרקע על המוכר לפרוע מניסן ועד תשרי ולר"א על הלוקח לפרוע ומסתברא כר"א דאחזוקי סהדי בשיקרא לא מחזקינן: **מתני'** הגיורת שנתגיירה בתה עמה וזנתה ה"ז בחנק אין לה פתח בית אב ולא ק' סלע. פי' שנתגיירה עמה כשהיא קטנה דעכשיו בתולה היא שבפ"ע אין לה לקטנה דעת להתגייר ואי בגדולה שנתגיירה שוב אינה בתולה. וזינתה מן האירוסין והיא נערה ה"ז בחנק. פי' אם נשאת והוציא עליה בעלה שם רע ע"פ עדים שזנתה באירוסין דאין לה דין מאורסה בת ישראל שנסקלין ע"י הוצאת שם רע. דכי כתב סקילה בנערה המאורסה בישראל כתיב. דכתיב כי עשתה נבלה בישראל. והאי לאו בת ישראל היא הואיל והיתה הורתה ולידתה שלא בקדושה אלא בחנק היא כשאר א"א דעלמא: אין לה פתח בית אב ובאותה מיתה דיהבינן לה [illegible] ונתעברה אמה בעודה יהודית עכשיו יש לה אב: יש לה אב ואין לה פתח בית אב וא"ל אב. הרי זו בסקילה לא נאמר פתח בית אב אלא למצוה:

גמ' מְנָא הָנֵי מִילֵּי? אָמַר ר"ל, דְּאָמַר קְרָא: °"וָמֵתָה" – לְרַבּוֹת הוֹרָתָהּ שֶׁלֹּא בִּקְדוּשָּׁה וְלֵידָתָהּ בִּקְדוּשָּׁה. אִי הָכִי, מִילְקָא נַמִי נִילְקֵי, וּמֵאָה סֶלַע נַמִי לְשַׁלֵּם! אָמַר קְרָא: "וָמֵתָה" – לְמִיתָה נִתְרַבְּתָה, וְלֹא לִקְנָס. וְאֵימָא: לְרַבּוֹת הוֹרָתָהּ וְלֵידָתָהּ בִּקְדוּשָּׁה! הַהִיא יִשְׂרְאֵלִית מַעַלְיְיתָא הִיא. וְאֵימָא לְרַבּוֹת הוֹרָתָהּ וְלֵידָתָהּ שֶׁלֹּא בִּקְדוּשָּׁה! א"כ "בְּיִשְׂרָאֵל" מַאי אַהֲנֵי לֵיהּ? אָמַר ר' יוֹסֵי בַּר חֲנִינָא: הַמּוֹצִיא שֵׁם רַע עַל הַיְתוֹמָה – פָּטוּר, שֶׁנֶּאֱמַר: °"וְנָתְנוּ לַאֲבִי הַנַּעֲרָה" – פְּרָט לָזוֹ שֶׁאֵין לָהּ אָב. מְתִיב ר' יוֹסֵי בַּר אָבִין, וְאִיתֵּימָא ר' יוֹסֵי בַּר זְבִידָא: °"וְאִם מָאֵן יְמָאֵן אָבִיהָ" – לְרַבּוֹת יְתוֹמָה לִקְנָס, דִּבְרֵי ר' יוֹסֵי הַגְּלִילִי. הוּא מוֹתִיב לָהּ וְהוּא מְפָרֵק לָהּ: בְּבָא עָלֶיהָ וְאח"כ נִתְיַתְּמָה. רָבָא אָמַר: [א]חַיָּיב. מִמַּאי – מִדְּתָנֵי אַמֵּי: "בְּתוּלַת יִשְׂרָאֵל" וְלֹא בְּתוּלַת גֵּרִים. אִי אָמְרַתְּ בִּשְׁלָמָא כִּי הַאי גַּוְונָא בְּיִשְׂרָאֵל מִיחַיַּיב – הַיְינוּ דְּאִיצְטְרִיךְ קְרָא לְמַעוּטֵי גֵּרִים, אֶלָּא אִי אָמְרַתְּ בְּיִשְׂרָאֵל כְּה"ג פָּטוּר, הַשְׁתָּא בְּיִשְׂרָאֵל פָּטוּר – בְּגֵרִים מִיבַּעְיָא?! *אָמַר רֵישׁ לָקִישׁ: [ב]הַמּוֹצִיא שֵׁם רַע עַל הַקְּטַנָּה – פָּטוּר, שֶׁנֶּאֱמַר: "וְנָתְנוּ לַאֲבִי הַנַּעֲרָה", נַעֲרָה מָלֵא דִּבֵּר הַכָּתוּב. מַתְקִיף לָהּ *רַב אַחָא בַּר אַבָּא: טַעְמָא דִּכְתִיב בָּהּ "הַנַּעֲרָה" הָא לָאו הָכִי – הֲוָה אָמִינָא אֲפִילּוּ קְטַנָּה, °הָא כְּתִיב: °"וְאִם אֱמֶת הָיָה הַדָּבָר הַזֶּה לֹא נִמְצְאוּ בְתוּלִים לַנַּעֲרָה וְהוֹצִיאוּ אֶת הַנַּעֲרָה אֶל פֶּתַח בֵּית אָבִיהָ וּסְקָלוּהָ" – וּקְטַנָּה לָאו בַּת עוֹנָשִׁין הִיא! אֶלָּא, כָּאן – נַעֲרָה, הָא כָּל מָקוֹם שֶׁנֶּאֱמַר "נַעַר" – אֲפִילּוּ קְטַנָּה בְּמַשְׁמָע. תָּנֵי שֵׁילָא: שָׁלֹשׁ מִדּוֹת בְּנַעֲרָה: [ג]בָּאוּ לָהּ עֵדִים בְּבֵית חָמִיהָ שֶׁזִּינְּתָה בְּבֵית אָבִיהָ – סוֹקְלִין

(דברים כב; שם; שמות כב; דברים כב)

גמ' מְנָא הָנֵי מִילֵּי. שֶׁהוֹרָתָהּ שֶׁלֹּא בִּקְדוּשָּׁה וְלֵידָתָהּ בִּקְדוּשָּׁה בִּסְקִילָה. **וָמֵתָה.** "וּסְקָלוּהָ כָּל אַנְשֵׁי עִירָהּ בָּאֲבָנִים וָמֵתָה", וְהַאי "וָמֵתָה" קְרָא יְתֵירָא הוּא. **בְּיִשְׂרָאֵל.** "כִּי עָשְׂתָה נְבָלָה בְּיִשְׂרָאֵל". **מָאֵן יְמָאֵן.** בִּמְפַתֶּה הַכָּתוּב מְדַבֵּר, דְּמָצֵי לְמִיכְתַּב "וְאִם יְמָאֵן", וּכְתַב "וְאִם מָאֵן יְמָאֵן" – בֵּין אָבִיהָ קַיָּים וּמְמָאֵן, בֵּין שֶׁאֵין אָבִיהָ קַיָּים וְהִיא מְמָאֶנֶת. אַלְמָא, אַע"ג דִּכְתִיב בְּאוֹנֵס "וְנָתַן לַאֲבִי הַנַּעֲרָה", וְאוֹנֵס וּמְפַתֶּה מֵהֲדָדֵי גָּמְרִי – מִיחַיַּיב קְנָס אַיְּתוֹמָה. וְכִי תֵּימָא שָׁאנֵי הָכָא דְּרַבֵּי רַחֲמָנָא, [אֲבָל לְגַבֵּי מוֹצִיא ש"ר לָא אִתְרַבַּאי] – הָכָא נַמִי לָאו יְתוֹמָה מַשְׁמַע מֵרִיבּוּי, אֶלָּא דְּבֵין הִיא וּבֵין אָבִיהָ יְכוֹלִין לְעַכֵּב, כִּדְאָמְרִינַן בְּ"אֵלּוּ נְעָרוֹת" (לעיל דף לט:). וִיתוֹמָה לָא אִתְרַבַּאי הָכָא, אֶלָּא דִּסְבִירָא לֵיהּ לְתַנָּא דְּ"אָבִיהָ" דְּקָאָמַר קְרָא – לָאו לְמַעוּטֵי יְתוֹמָה, אֶלָּא לְמֵימְרָא דִּקְנָסָהּ לְאָבִיהָ וְלֹא לְעַצְמָהּ, וְהוּא הַדִּין לְ"אָבִיהָ" הָאָמוּר בְּמוֹצִיא שֵׁם רָע. **הוּא מוֹתִיב** כו'. הָא יְתוֹמָה דְּקָאָמַר תַּנָּא. **בְּבָא עָלֶיהָ וְאח"כ נִתְיַתְּמָה.** וּלְעוֹלָם "אֲבִי הַנַּעֲרָה" לְמַעוּטֵי יְתוֹמָה, בֵּין בִּקְנָס בֵּין בְּהוֹצָאַת שֵׁם רָע. **רָבָא אָמַר חַיָּיב.** הַמּוֹצִיא שֵׁם רַע עַל הַיְתוֹמָה. **מִדְּתָנֵי אַמֵּי כִּי הוֹצִיא שֵׁם רַע עַל בְּתוּלַת יִשְׂרָאֵל וְלֹא בְּתוּלַת גֵּרִים.** וְהָא בְּתוּלַת גֵּרִים יְתוֹמָה הִיא, דְּרַחֲמָנָא אַפְקְרֵיהּ לְזַרְעֵיהּ דְּמִצְרִי כְּשֶׁל חֲמוֹר, דִּכְתִיב (יחזקאל כג) "וְזִרְמַת סוּסִים זִרְמָתָם". וְהוּא לְשׁוֹן שִׁכְבַת זֶרַע הַזּוֹרֵם כְּזֶרֶם מַיִם, וְאִצְטְרִיךְ קְרָא לְמַעוּטֵי. **אִי אָמְרַתְּ בִּשְׁלָמָא** כו'. **נַעֲרָה מָלֵא דִּבֵּר הַכָּתוּב.** בְּכָל מָקוֹם כְּתִיב "נַעֲרָ" וְכָאן כְּתִיב "נַעֲרָה" מָלֵא – לְהוֹצִיא אֶת הַקְּטַנָּה. **אֶלָּא כָּאן נַעֲרָה** כו'. אֶלָּא הַאי דִּכְתִיב מָלֵא – לֹא לְלַמֵּד עַל עַצְמוֹ בָּא וּלְהוֹצִיא אֶת הַקְּטַנָּה, דְּבְלָאו הָךְ דְּרָשָׁא אִמַּעִיטָא לָהּ קְטַנָּה, כִּדְאָמְרִינַן דְּלָאו בַּת עוֹנָשִׁין. אֶלָּא לְלַמֵּד בָּא עַל כָּל נַעֲרָה שֶׁבַּתּוֹרָה שֶׁכְּתוּבִין חָסֵר – לוֹמַר שֶׁאַף הַקְּטַנָּה בְּמַשְׁמַע. וְהָכִי יָלֵיף: כָּאן נַעֲרָה, כָּאן שֶׁאִי אֶפְשָׁר בִּקְטַנָּה – כְּתִיב מָלֵא, הָא לָמַדְתָּ שֶׁכָּל מָקוֹם שֶׁנִּכְתַּב חָסֵר – אַף הַקְּטַנָּה בְּמַשְׁמַע, כְּגוֹן בְּאוֹנֵס וּמְפַתֶּה. **שָׁלֹשׁ מִדּוֹת.** בְּמִיתַת נַעֲרָה הַמְאוֹרָסָה. **בָּאוּ לָהּ עֵדִים בְּבֵית חָמִיהָ.** לְאַחַר שֶׁנִּיסֵּת. **שֶׁזִּינְּתָה בְּבֵית אָבִיהָ.** בָּאֵירוּסִין.

סוֹקְלִין

מנא הני מילי. משום דכתיב "בישראל" קא בעי. **ואימא** לרבות הורתה ולידתה בקדושה ההיא ישראלית מעלייתא היא. תימה: דגבי חליצה, דדרשינן (יבמות דף קב.) מ"ונקרא שמו בישראל" דאין כשר לדין חליצה עד שיהא אביו ואמו מישראל, אלמא ממעטי מ"בישראל" אפי' הורתו ולידתו בקדושה! וכ"ת: דהתם משום דהורתו שלא בקדושה לא אצטריך למעוטי, ד"מקרב אחיך" ידעינן בכל דין דבעינן הורתו ולידתו בקדושה, ואייתר גבי דין חליצה "בישראל" עד שיהא אביו ואמו מישראל – אכתי איכא לאקשויי: אימא ד"בישראל" אתא למעוטי הורתו שלא בקדושה אפי' לחליצת בני גרים, ד"מקרב אחיך" לא דרשינן אלא למיפסליה לדין ישראל, אבל גר חבירו – מצי דיין, כדדרשינן התם: "עליך" הוא דבעינן "מקרב אחיך" כו'! ואור"י: כיון דהורתו ולידתו בקדושה – ישראל מעליא הוא, כדאמרינן הכא, אם כן הכי נמי בני גרים, כיון שהורתן ולידתן בקדושה – הוו ישראל מעלייתא, וקרינא בהו "עליך". והואיל וכן – בלא "ונקרא שמו בישראל" נפקא לן שפסול גר לחליצת בני גרים, דבעינן "מקרב אחיך" עד שתהא אמו מישראל. ולהכי אייתר "בישראל" לאצרוכי אביו מישראל*:

ואימא לרבות הורתה ולידתה שלא בקדושה. תימה: אדרבה, אית לן לאוקמי קרא בדדמי! וי"ל: כיון דמרבינן הורתה שלא בקדושה – אם כן גלי לן קרא ד"בישראל" לאו דוקא, וא"כ ממילא נרבה אפילו לידתה שלא בקדושה. **אם** כן בישראל מאי אהני ליה. תימה לרשב"א: דנימא אהני ליה שלא ילקה ולא ישלם מאה כסף! ואור"י: דסברא הוא שיהנה לכל הכתוב בפרשה. ועוד אור"י: דלענין מלקות ומאה כסף לא איצטריך למעוטי מ"בישראל", דמ"בתולת ישראל" ולא בתולת גרים ממעטינן להו. והשתא אתי שפיר דלא תיקשי: אמאי איצטריך בתולת ישראל ולא בתולת גרים, תיפוק ליה מ"בישראל", ואע"ג דלגבי מיתה כתיב – מ"מ גמרינן מינה קנס, כדמשמע בסמוך, דקאמר: טעמא דכתב רחמנא "נערה", הא לאו הכי ה"א אפי' קטנה, והכתיב "אם אמת וגו'", אלמא דילפינן קנס ממיתה; אלא ודאי, אי לא כתיב "בתולת ישראל" – ה"א דאפילו הורתה ולידתה שלא בקדושה הוה מרבינן מ"ומתה", ובישראל אהני שלא ילקה ולא ישלם מאה כסף. אבל השתא דשמעינן לה מ"בתולת ישראל" – ע"כ "בישראל" אתא למעוטי הורתה ולידתה שלא בקדושה*.

המוציא שם רע על היתומה פטור כו'. תימה: דתקשי ליה ממתני', דקתני הורתה שלא בקדושה ולידתה בקדושה – הרי זו בסקילה, ואין לה פתח בית אב, ולא מאה כסף, משמע: הא ישראלית גמורה דכוותה, שאין לה אב – יש לה מאה כסף. ולעיל נמי תנן דגיורת פחותה מבת ג' יש לה קנס, וי"ל דמוקי מתני'. אליבא דר"ע, דאמר לעיל (דף לח.) נערה שנתארסה ונתגרשה – קנסה לעצמה, ודריש: "אשר לא אורסה" – לאביה, הא אורסה – לעצמה. וה"נ דריש "לאבי הנערה", הא אין לה אב – לעצמה. אבל ר' יוסי בר' חנינא דהכא אליבא דר"י הגלילי קאמר דפטור. דכי היכי דדריש לעיל הא אורסה אין לה קנס – ה"נ דריש הכא "לאבי הנערה", הא אין לה אב – אין לה קנס. ורבא דפליג עליה סבר דאפי' לר"י הגלילי חייב, מדתני אמי, דדריש ליה מקרא, ומסתבר דלא פליג שום תנא אההיא דרשא. והשתא פריך הכא רבי יוסי בר אבין מדתני "אם מאן ימאן" לרבות יתומה לקנס, דברי ר"י הגלילי. וה"ג ר"ת. וכן במכילתא גרס: דברי ר' יוסי הגלילי. ופריך מר' יוסי הגלילי אר' יוסי בר' חנינא, דר' יוסי בר' חנינא אליבא דר' יוסי הגלילי קאמר לה, ומתני' כר"ע. ופריך נמי מלרבות יתומה לקנס דברי ר' יוסי הגלילי, ומשני נמי כדמשני הכא. אבל התם קאמר מילתיה אאונס ואמפתה, ולא אמוציא שם רע*. **בתולת** ישראל ולא בתולת גרים. וא"ת: אמאי איצטריך "אם מאן ימאן" לרבות יתומה, מ"בתולת ישראל" נפקא, מדממעט דווקא בת גרים! ולמאי דפ"ה דיתומה לאו מרבויא משתמעא – ניחא. ונראה לרשב"א: דאי לאו דמרבינן יתומה מ"מאן ימאן" – לא הוה דרשינן "בתולת ישראל" ולא בתולת גרים, אלא לדרשה אחריתי. כיון דמשום בת גרים לא צריך קרא דמ"ונתן לאבי הנערה" נפקא. ולא היה סברא לומר דלא איצטריך קרא אלא לדיוקא הא יתומה בת ישראל יש לה קנס, אבל השתא דמרבינן יתומה – לית לן למעוטי מ"לאבי הנערה" בת גרים, דדרשינן שפיר "בתולת ישראל" ולא בתולת גרים. **הא** לאו הכי ה"א אפילו קטנה והכתיב ואם אמת היה. נראה לר"י דלא בעי רב אחא למילף קנס ממיתה, דכל היכא דלא מחייב מיתה לא מחייב קנס. ולא בעי למימר נמי הואיל וקרא איירי בגדולה – כל דינין שבפרשה אין נוהגין אלא בגדולה. אלא הכי פריך: טעמא דכתב רחמנא "נערה" ב"הא", הא לאו הכי ה"א אפילו קטנה במשמע, והיינו משום דכיון דלא כתיב "הא" – ביטל משמעות נערה, דמשמע דווקא גדולה, והא כתיב "אם אמת וגו'" וקטנה לאו בת עונשין היא, ואפ"ה כתב "נערה" חסר – אלמא משום חסרון "הא" אינו מבוטל משמעות נערה דהוי גדולה. והשתא לא קשה מידי לרבנן* מנא להו דמחייבי סקילה בבא על הקטנה, והא קרא בבת עונשין איירי! דהא הכא לא בעי למעוטי קטנה מקנס משום דקרא בבת עונשין איירי, אלא כדפרישית. ולא תקשי נמי אמאי איצטריך "בתולת ישראל", תיפוק ליה מ"בישראל" דגבי סקילה – דהא לא ילפינן מהדדי. **הא** כל מקום שנאמר נער אפי' קטנה במשמע. ור"מ נמי הוה דריש הכי, אי לאו משום ד"לו תהיה לאשה" דדריש לעיל (דף מ:) במהוה עצמה. וא"ת: הואיל ומסתבר למדרש דכל מקום שנאמר "נער" אפילו קטנה במשמע, כרבנן, נימא לר"מ דווקא באונס ומפתה דגלי קרא גלי, אבל בכל מקום נדרוש דאפילו קטנה במשמע! ואור"י: דהיינו טעמא דר"מ, דאי דווקא לאונס ומפתה אתא קרא ד"ולו תהיה לאשה" – ליכתוב בהו "נערה" מלא, כמו במוציא שם רע, וה"א כאן נערה הא בכל מקום כו', ומדכתיב "לו תהיה לאשה" במהוה עצמה, בא ללמד דבכל מקום שנאמר "נער" כמו הכא – במהוה עצמה מיירי.

אמר

תוספות רי"ד

מנה"מ. פי' דהורתה שלא בקדושה ולידתה בקדושה שהיא בסקילה. אר"ל דא"ק ומתה. פי' מריבוי דקרא דסגי לה בהכי וסקלוה כל אנשי עירה באבנים ומתה קרא יתירה הוא למידרש ולרבות זו שהורתה שלא בקדושה ולידתה בקדושה: א"ה מילקי נמי לילקי ומאה סלע נמי לישלם. פי' כיון דמרבה ליה לסקילה לירבי ליה למלקות. שאם אינו אמת מלקין אותו כדכתיב ויסרו אותו דהיינו מלקות: א"ק ומתה למיתה נתרבתה ולא לקנס ואימא לרבות הו"ל בקדושה ההיא ישראלית מעלייתא היא ואימא לרבות הו"ל שלא בקדושה א"כ בישראל מאי מהני ליה. כלומר מאי ממעט: א"ר יוסי בר' חנינא המוציא ש"ר על היתומה פטור שנאמר ונתן לאבי הנערה פרט לזו שא"ל אב. ואי קשיא והאי נשואה היא ויצאת מרשות האב והיכי כתב רחמנא ונתן לאבי הנערה. י"ל לאו דליהוי דידיה אלא שיעשה מהן סגולה לבתו שלא יזכה בהן בעלה: מתיב ריב"א ואם מאן ימאן אביה לרבות יתומה לקנס דברי ר"י בר יהודה. פי' מדמצי למיכתב ואם ימאן אביה ורבה עכשיו וכתב ואם מאן ימאן. משמע בין אביה קיים וממאן בין שמת אביה והיא ממאנת שאינה רוצה להנשא לו כסף ישקול והאי דכ' ונתן לאבי הנערה לאו דוקא אלמא יש קנס ליתומה וה"ה גבי מוציא שם רע אביה לאו דוקא ואי קשיא והא האי קרא במפתה כתיב והיכי מצינן לרבויי יתומה לקנס. והתנן בפירקין דלעיל יתומה האונס חייב והמפתה פטור. דכיון דא"ל אב וקנסה לעצמה אוחלתיה גביה שנתרצית לו. י"ל האי דמרבה יתומה לקנס לאו במפתה דודאי אין קנס ליתומה מפותה ולא רבה אלא להיות דהיינו באנוסה ואע"ג דקרא במפותה כתיב הא גמרי מהדדי אונס ממפתה: הוא מותיב לה והוא מפרק לה. בבא עליה ואח"כ נתיתמה. פי' לעולם מוציא שם רע על היתומה פטור והאי דמרבה לה להאי יתומה בין בקנס בין בהוצאת שם רע ממאן ימאן בבא עליה בעוד שאביה קיים וקודם שעמד בדין נתיתמה והואיל והיה לה אב משעת ביאה אינה כשאר יתומות ויש לה קנס והכי נמי מפרשה יתומה דמתני' ואפ"ה המפתה פטור כיון דלדידה הוי ולא מכח אב קא ירתא דאילו הוו מכח אב הוו ירתין אחיה ולא היא: ורבא אמר חייב מדתני ר"א בתולות ישראל ולא בתולות גרים פי' כגון שהיתה הורתה שלא בקדושה ולידתה בקדושה והא בתולת גרים כיתומה היא. א"א בשלמא בישראל כה"ג מחייב ולאו דוקא אביה היינו דאיצטריך קרא למעוטי גרים. אלא אי אמרת בישראל פטורים גרים מיבעי' אלא לאו ש"מ בישראל חייב ואע"פ שבא עליה בעודה יתומה ואביה לאו דוקא כדרבינן ממאן ימאן: והלכתא כרבא ומתני' דתנן שהיתומה י"ל קנס והאונס חייב והמפתה פטור אע"פ שבא עליה בעודה יתומה:

כב א מיי' פ"ג מהל' נערה הל"א סמג עשין נה טור אה"ע סי' קעז:
כג ב מיי' שם הל' ב סמג עשין קא קב:
כד ג (מיי' שם הל"ט):

[ולפי' ל"ל דרב שמואל בר יהודה דהתם היתה אמו מישראל מדמייתי עלה קרא דבישראל והא לא איצטריך אלא לאמו מישראל. ת"י]

לעיל מ:

[לעיל מ: איתא רב אדא בר אהבה]

גליון הש"ס

גמ' הא כתיב ואם אמת. עי' תוס' סנהדרין ח ע"ב ד"ה והכיא:

[אבל ק"ק דכי פריך אי הכי מילקא נמי לילקי ומאה כסף לשלם הוי ליה לשנויי מיד דמבתולת ישראל נפקא כיון דהשתא אתא סמיך. ת"י]

[ומיהו לעיל משמע דלא דריש ר"ע הא אורסה לעצמה אלא משום דאשר לא אורסה אתיא לג"ש הא אי לאו הכי הוי דריש לה נמי הא אורסה אין לה. ת"י]

[בסנהדרין סו:]

סוקלין אותה על פתח בית אביה, כלומר: ראו גידולים שגידלתם. באו לה עדים בבית אביה שזינתה בבית אביה — סוקלין אותה על פתח שער העיר. *סרחה ולבסוף בגרה — תידון בחנק. למימרא דכל היכא דאישתני גופא אישתני קטלא? ורמינהי: [א]נערה המאורסה שזינתה, ומשבגרה הוציא עליה שם רע — הוא אינו לוקה ואינו נותן מאה סלע, *היא וזוממיה מקדימין לבית הסקילה. היא וזוממיה ס"ד?! [ב]אלא: או היא או זוממיה מקדימין לבית הסקילה! אמר רבא: מוציא שם רע קאמרת — [ג]שאני מוציא שם רע דחידוש הוא. דהא נכנסה לחופה ולא נבעלה בעלמא, וזינתה — בחנק, ואילו מוציא שם רע — בסקילה. אמר ליה רב הונא בריה דרב יהושע לרבא: דלמא כי חדית רחמנא — היכא דלא אישתני גופא, אבל היכא דאישתני גופא — לא חדית רחמנא! אלא אמר רב נחמן בר יצחק: אישתני ולא אישתני תנאי היא, דתנן: *[ד]חטאו עד שלא נתמנו, ונתמנו — הרי הן כהדיוטות. רבי שמעון אומר: אם נודע להם עד שלא נתמנו — חייבים, משנתמנו — פטורים. אימור

רש"י

סוקלין אותה על פתח בית אביה. דהכי כתיב "והוציאו את הנערה אל פתח בית אביה", והאי דבאו עדים בבית חמיה כתיב — דהא במוציא שם רע כתיב, דמפרש ביה קרא "ואקרב אליה", אלמא: כשנישאת. ראו גידולים שגידלתם. כלומר, מבית זה יצאת הנבלה, שבו זינתה. באו לה עדים בבית אביה. קודם שנישאת. סוקלין אותה על שער העיר. דכתיב "כי יהיה נערה בתולה מאורסה וגו' והוצאתם את שניהם אל שער העיר ההיא". תידון בחנק. כי היכי דאילו זנאי השתא לאו סקילה איכא אלא חנק, דכי כתיב סקילה — בזינתה נערה כתיב, שנאמר "כי יהיה נערה בתולה" וגו', השתא נמי בחנק, דכיון דאשתני גופא בין חטא להעמדה בדין — אשתני קטלא לכדהשתא. הוציא עליה שם רע. שכנסה משבגרה, ולא מצא לה בתולים, ובא לב"ד. הוא אינו לוקה. אם כיחש. ואינו נותן מאה סלע. דכי כתיב "ויסרו אותו" מלקות, "וענשו אותו" ממון — בנערה כתיב. וזה עקימת שפתיו גורמין לו ליענש, כדמתרץ לקמן, ועקימת שפתיו בבוגרת הואי. היא. אם אמת היה. וזוממיה. עדים שהיו מעידים על זנותה, ונמצאו זוממין. מקדימין לבית הסקילה. כלומר, ישכימו בבוקר לשם. כי אין להם נס והמלטה מן המיתה הזאת. היא וזוממיה ס"ד. אם אמת היה אין שקר. אלא או היא. אם אמת. או זוממיה. אם שקר. לבית הסקילה. אלמא, אע"ג דאשתני גופא, ואילו זנאי השתא בת חנק היא — לא אמרינן אישתני קטלא. מוציא שם רע קאמרת. לאתויי אסרחה ולבסוף בגרה, דתני תנא דאיירי בבאו לה עדים בבית אביה. שאני. מיתה הבאה על ידי הוצאת שם רע דבעל, משנישאת. דחידוש הוא. ולא אמרינן בה דמשום דאישתני (א) דינא, דאי זנאי השתא — בת חנק היא, נימא אישתני קטלא דהך דזנאי בנערות. דהא נכנסה לחופה ולא נבעלה בעלמא וזינתה בחנק כו'. (ב) ותדע, דהא בלא בגרה נמי, [בלא] הוצאת שם רע, ואפי' בנערות — אשתני דינא הוא. דאילו זנאי השתא חנק הוא דאיכא, הואיל ונכנסה לחופה אע"פ שלא נבעלה, כדתניא [לקמן] (דף מח:): "נערה" — ולא בוגרת, "בתולה" — ולא בעולה, "מאורסה" — ולא נשואה. מאי לא נשואה? אי נימא נשואה ממש — היינו ולא בעולה! אלא לאו, נכנסה לחופה ולא נבעלה. אלמא, אילו זנאי השתא — בת חנק היא. ואילו מוציא שם רע. עליה השתא, וזנאי קודם כניסה לחופה — בסקילה. אלמא, בהוצאת שם רע לא אמרינן דמשום דאישתני דינא, אילו זנאי השתא — לישתני קטלא הבא ע"י זנות דמעיקרא. והילכך, כי בגרה נמי וניסת — לא אמרינן במוציא שם רע דמשום דאישתני דינא דהשתא אישתני קטלא דמעיקרא. ודלמא כי חדית. כלומר, הא ראייה דמייתינן מתפס מוציא ש"ר לכאן — לאו ראייה היא לכאן. דהתם הוא דאף על גב דאישתני דינא, דאילו זנאי השתא לא אישתני קטלא דהא דזנאי מעיקרא — משום דלא אישתני גופא הוא, וחידוש שחידשה תורה, (ג) באישתני דינא — חדית, באישתני גופא — לא חדית. אבל בגרה — אישתני גופא היא, ואי באו לה עדים בבית אביה — אית לך למימר סרחה ולבסוף בגרה בחנק, במוציא שם רע נמי משבגרה הוה ליה למיתני חנק. אלא אמר רב נחמן בר יצחק. הא דתני שלא תידון בחנק, הואיל ואישתני גופא אישתני קטלא, ותניא אחריתא בסקילה, ואע"ג דאישתני גופא לא אישתני קטלא — תנאי היא. אישתני ולא אישתני. אי אמרינן אישתני קטלא או לא אישתני קטלא — תנאי היא. חטאו עד שלא נתמנו. נשיא ומשיח, שאין קרבנם כשל יחיד, שהנשיא מביא שעיר, ומשיח מביא פר. הרי הן כהדיוטות. בכשבה ושעירה, שאע"פ שנשתנה גופם — לא נשתנה קרבנם. אם נודע להם עד שלא נתמנו. דהוה ליה ידיעה וחטאה בחד גופא — חייבין כהדיוטות. משנתמנו. דהוה ליה חטאה בשעת קרבן יחיד, וידיעה בשעת קרבן נשיא. פטורין. לגמרי. אלמא, דמשום דאישתני גופא — אישתני קרבן.

תוספות

אמר רבא מוציא שם רע קאמרת שאני מוציא שם רע דחידוש הוא. נראה דמתחלה מקשה ממוציא שם רע, משום דס"ד דהתלמוד דמסברא אמרינן ביה דתידון בסקילה, ולא אמרינן הואיל ואישתני גופא אישתני קטלא. הילכך מקשה דגבי נערה המאורסה נמי לית לן למימר דאישתני קטלא. ומשני רבא: שאני מוציא שם רע דחידוש הוא. ולא מסברא אמרינן ביה הכי, אלא משום דאשכחן דחדית ביה רחמנא כי האי גוונא, דלא אמרינן הואיל ואישתני דינא אישתני קטלא. והא דנקט נכנסה לחופה ולא נבעלה — לאו דווקא, אלא הכי נמי דהוה מצי למנקט ונבעלה — למאן דמוקי מוציא שם רע דווקא בבעל, [אלא נקט למאן דמוקי אע"ג דלא בעל]. ולפי זה לא גרסינן "בעלמא", דאי גרסינן נכנסה לחופה ולא נבעלה בעלמא בחנק — משמע דהכא במוציא שם רע חייב סקילה אפילו זינתה אחר חופה — והא ליתא, דזינתה אחר חופה אפילו במוציא שם רע בחנק. ולפי זה, הא דקתני לעיל: באו לה עדים בבית חמיה שזינתה בבית אביה, בסקילה — צריך לדחוק לרבא דאיירי במוציא שם רע, דאי לא הוציא שם רע — הויא לרבא בחנק, דכיון דאישתני דינא אישתני קטלא. ובדין דהוה ליה לאסוקי לעיל ההיא ברייתא באו לה עדים בבית חמיה שזינתה בבית אביה, ולא הוציא ש"ר בחנק, דהשתא הוה מפליג בדידה, ולא ה"ל למנקט בסיפא סרחה ולבסוף בגרה — אלא משום דעיקר ברייתא אתא לאשמועינן דיני פתח בית אב, וכיון דקאי מגיעתא בנערה המאורסה בבאו לה עדים בבית אביה — מסיק נמי סרחה ולבסוף בגרה בבית אביה, במה שעומד בו השתא. [והא דקאמר: ואילו מוציא ש"ר, אע"ג דהכל איירי במוציא ש"ר — ה"פ: ואילו מוציא ש"ר על האירוסין, דאיירי ביה קרא — הוי בסקילה. אבל ק"ק: דתני בשמעתין (לקמן מו.) בא אמר לעדים בואו והעידוני, והן מעידין מאליהן — היא וזוממיה מקדימין לבית הסקילה. אלמא, אפי' בלא הוצאת ש"ר לא אמרינן הואיל ואישתני דינא אישתני קטלא! ומיהו, י"ל: דאע"ג דלא אמר לעדים — הרי הוציא ש"ר, וחדית ביה רחמנא]. ורבינו שמואל מפרש: שאני מוציא שם רע דחידוש הוא — שהרי נכנסה לחופה ולא נבעלה בעלמא בלא הוצאת שם רע, וזינתה אחר חופה — בחנק, ואילו מוציא שם רע כי האי גוונא, שזינתה אחר נישואין — בסקילה. דהכי משתמעי קראי, דכתיב "ואם אמת היה כו' ולא נמצאו בתולים לנערה וסקלוה", משמע דבכל ענין שלא נמצאו לה בתולים הויא בסקילה, ואפילו זינתה תחתיו. ואע"ג דכתיב "אל פתח בית אביה", ובזינתה תחתיו אין כאן פתח בית אביה — היינו משום דלא שייך לומר ראו גידולים שגידלתם, והוי כמו יש לה אב ואין לה פתח בית אב. או אין לה אב, דהויא בסקילה אע"ג דליכא פתח בית אביה. והיינו חידוש, דבעלמא בלא הוצאת שם רע זינתה אחר חופה — בחנק, כדדרשינן לקמן: מאורסה ולא נשואה, שנכנסה לחופה ולא נבעלה, ובמוציא ש"ר — בסקילה. והשתא אתי נמי שפיר הא דלא נקט בברייתא באו לה עדים בבית חמיה שזינתה בבית אביה בלא הוצאת שם רע תידון בחנק, דהא מודה רבא דלא אמרינן הואיל ואישתני דינא אישתני קטלא. אבל קשה לרבינו יצחק לפירוש זה: דהא לקמן (דף מח:) דרשינן "לזנות בית אביה" — פרט שמסר האב לשלוחי הבעל, וכל שכן היכא שנכנסה לחופה. וההוא קרא ד"לזנות בית אביה" במוציא ש"ר בהדיא כתיב. **דלמא** כי חדית רחמנא היכא דלא אישתני גופא. ואע"ג דלעיל ב"אלו נערות" (דף לח: ושם) קרי לבעולה אישתני גופא — הכא לא חשיב אישתני גופא, אפילו למאן דלא מחייב במוצ"ש שם רע אלא בבעל, דהא כבר היתה בעולה מן הנואף, ובבעילה דנואף לא חשיב לה שינוי הגוף, דלא איירי הכא אלא בשינוי הגוף אחר העבירה*. **תנאי** היא דתניא כו'. וא"ת: והא הכא ליכא אלא שינוי דינא, והיכי מייתי לאישתני גופא דלעיל? ויש לומר: דלא מפליג לעיל בין אישתני גופא לאישתני דינא, אלא לרבא דאמר מוצ"ש שם רע חידוש הוא, הילכך פריך ליה כיון דאמרת דחידוש הוא ואינה סברא — אם כן יש לנו להעמיד בפחות שנוכל, דהיינו לא אישתני גופא. אבל לרב נחמן דאית ליה דמסברא קאמר דלא אישתני קטלא, ולא מחידושא — לדידיה ליכא לפלוגי בין אישתני דינא לאישתני גופא, הילכך מייתי שפיר תנאי היא. אי נמי יש לומר: דלא מייתי אלא מדרבי שמעון, דכיון דסבר הואיל ואישתני דינא אישתני קרבן — כל שכן באישתני גופא. ואינו חושש אלא להביא תנא דסבר כברייתא דשילא. משום דברייתא דשילא לא מיתניא בי רבי חייא ורבי אושעיא. אבל לאידך ברייתא לא מייתי שום ראיה מדרבנן דרבי שמעון. ותדע, דהא במסקנא משבשינן להביא דשילא. אימור

עין משפט נר מצוה

כה א מיי' פ"ג מהל' נערה בתולה הל' ז סמג עשין נה:
כו ב מיי' שם ופ"ג מהל' איסורי ביאה הלכה י סמג שם:
כז ג מיי' פ"ג מהל' איסורי ביאה הל' ח:
כח ד מיי' פט"ו מהל' שגגות הל' י:

מסורת הש"ס

סנהדרין עט: | [לקמן מו.] | הוריות י. | ת"י כ"י | ת"י כ"י | [ועי' תוס' יבמות נט. ד"ה והא]

הגהות הב"ח

(א) רש"י ד"ה לחידוש הוא וכו' דאישתני גופא לאו זנאי: (ב) ד"ה דהא נכנסה וכו' בחנק כו' כלומר ותדע: (ג) ד"ה ודלמא וכו' שחידשה תורה (באישתני דינא חדית) תא"מ ונ"ב ס"א בלא אישתני גופא חדית:

אימור דשמעינן ליה לר"ש דאזיל אף בתר ידיעה, דאזיל בתר ידיעה ולא אזיל בתר חטאה – מי שמעת ליה? א"כ לייתי קרבן כי דהשתא, משוח – פר, ונשיא – שעיר! האמר *ליה ר' יוחנן לתנא: תני "תידון בסקילה". – ואמאי? נערה המאורסה אמר רחמנא, והא בוגרת היא! א"ר אילעא, אמר קרא: "הנערה" הנערה שהיתה כבר. א"ל רבי חנניא לרבי אילעא: אי הכי – מילקא נמי לילקי, ומאה סלע נמי לישלם! א"ל: *רחמנא ניצלן מהאי דעתא. אדרבה, רחמנא ניצלן מדעתא דידך. – וטעמא מאי? אמר רבי יצחק בר אבין, ואיתימא רבי יצחק בר אבא: זו – מעשיה גרמו לה, וזה – עקימת שפתיו גרמו לו. זו מעשיה גרמו לה, כשהיא זנאי – נערה זנאי. וזה עקימת שפתיו גרמו לו, אימת קא מיחייב – ההיא שעתא, וההיא שעתא – בוגרת הואי. ת"ר: *נערה המאורסה שזינתה – סוקלין אותה על פתח בית אביה. אין לה פתח בית האב – סוקלין אותה על פתח שער העיר ההיא. [א]ובעיר שרובה נכרים – סוקלין אותה על פתח בית דין. כיוצא בדבר אתה אומר: [ב]העובד עבודה זרה – סוקלין אותו על שער שעבד בו. ובעיר שרובה נכרים – סוקלין אותו על פתח בית דין. מנא הני מילי? דתנו רבנן: "שעריך" – זה שער שעבד בו. – אתה אומר שער שעבד בו, או אינו אלא שער שנידון בו? נאמר "שעריך" למטה, ונאמר "שעריך" למעלה, מה "שעריך" האמור למעלה – שער שעבד בו, אף "שעריך" האמור למטה – שער שעבד בו. דבר אחר: "שעריך" ולא שערי גוים. האי "שעריך" הא אפיקתיה! אם כן לימא קרא "שער", מאי "שעריך"? שמע מינה תרתי. אשכחן עבודה זרה, נערה המאורסה מנא לן? א"ר אבהו: גמר "פתח" מ"פתח", ו"פתח" מ"שער", ו"שער" מ"שעריך". תנו רבנן: המוציא שם רע – לוקה ונותן מאה סלע. רבי יהודה אומר: ללקות – לוקה מכל מקום. מאה סלע, בעל – נותן, לא בעל – אינו נותן. קא מיפלגי בפלוגתא דרבי אליעזר בן יעקב ורבנן. והכי קאמר: המוציא שם רע – לוקה ונותן מאה סלע, בין בעל בין שלא בעל, כרבנן. ר' יהודה אומר: ללקות – לוקה מ"מ. מאה סלע, בעל – נותן, לא בעל – אינו נותן, כר"א בן יעקב. איכא דאמרי: כולה כרבי אליעזר בן יעקב, והכי קאמר: [ג]המוציא שם רע – לוקה ונותן מאה סלע, והוא שבעל. רבי יהודה אומר: ללקות לוקה מ"מ. וסבר רבי יהודה ללקות לוקה מ"מ? והתניא, רבי יהודה אומר: בעל – לוקה, לא בעל – אינו לוקה! אמר רב נחמן בר יצחק: [ד]לוקה *מכת מרדות, מדרבנן.

רב

אימור דשמעינן ליה כו'. כלומר, ליכא למ"ד הכא איתני קרבן משום שינויא דגופא, מדלא מחייב להו ר"ש לנודע להם משנתמנו, לאיתויי כדהשתא. אלא פטורין לגמרי קאמר, וטעמא דידיה משום דבעי ידיעה וחטאה בחד גופה. דאזיל אף בתר ידיעה. כלומר, שעת החטא מחייבתו כשבה, ושעת ידיעה מחייבתו שעיר. לפיכך אין כאן אחד מכל הקרבנות שחייבתו תורה. דאזיל בתר ידיעה. דשינוי הגוף. ולא אזיל בתר חטאה. כי ההיא דתני שילא תידון בחנק, מי שמעת ליה? אם כן. דהכי שמעת ליה – לייתי כי השתא. האמר ליה כו'. שינויא הוא. לתנא. דתנא קמיה להא דתני שילא. הנערה. "והוציאו את הנערה", ולא כתב "והוציאוה". שהיתה כבר. ואע"פ שאינה עכשיו. רחמנא ניצלן מהאי דעתא. כיחד ממנו טעמו של דבר, מפני שתלוי בהבנת הלב, כדמפרש לקמן: זו מעשיה גרמו לה כו'. על פתח בית אביה. אם באו עדים משניסת. על שער העיר שעבד בה. ואפי' נידון בעיר אחרת. שעריך למעלה. "כי ימצא בקרבך באחד שעריך" וגו', דהא ודאי באותו שער שעבד בו עבירה. ונאמר שעריך למטה. "והוצאת את האיש ההוא אל שעריך" וגו'. שעריך. בעבודה זרה כתיב (דברים יז) "והוצאת את האיש ההוא או את האשה ההיא אשר עשו" וגו'. גמר פתח מפתח ופתח משער. אסמכתא דרבנן בעלמא, כתיב הכא "אל פתח בית אביה", וכתיב במשכן (במדבר ד) "מסך פתח שער החצר". מה פתח האמור במשכן – שער עמו, אף פתח האמור כאן – שער עמו. והדר גמר האי שער מ"שעריך" האמור בעבודה זרה. ללקות. מלקות במוציא שם רע, מ"ויסרו אותו". לוקה מ"מ. בין בעל ובא לב"ד והוציא שם רע ע"י בעילתו, ואמר לא מצאתי לבתך בתולים, בין לא בעל ובא לבית דין ואמר: באו לי עדים שזינתה בבית אביה, והרי היא לפניכם. פלוגתא דרבי אליעזר בן יעקב ורבנן. לקמן בשמעתין. כרבנן. דאמרי: פרשת מוציא שם רע בין בעל בין לא בעל, וכתיב ביה "ויסרו וענשו". כר' אליעזר בן יעקב. דאמר לקמן: לא נאמר פרשת מוציא שם רע אלא כשבעל. הלכך מאה סלע לא מחייבינן ליה אלא כשבעל. אבל מלקות, דמשום אזהרת "לא תלך רכיל" (ויקרא יט) הוא – לקי ואפילו לא בעל, דהא הלך רכיל. ואי משום דהוי לאו שאין בו מעשה – ר' יהודה לטעמיה, דאמר: לאו שאין בו מעשה לוקין עליו, במסכת מכות (דף ד:) וב"שחיטת חולין" (דף פג.). והוא שבעל. כר' אליעזר בן יעקב. וקסבר תנא קמא אליבא דר' אליעזר לאו שאין בו מעשה אין לוקין עליו. ומלקות דמוציא שם רע – חידוש הוא, ומ"ויסרו אותו" נפקא, וההוא קרא כשבעל כתיב. ר' יהודה אומר ללקות לוקה מכל מקום. דמלקות משום אזהרת "לא תלך רכיל" הוא, ולאו שאין בו מעשה לוקין עליו. אמר רב נחמן בר יצחק. לוקה מ"מ דקאמר – מכת מרדות, דרבנן.

רב

אימור דשמעינן לר"ש דאזיל אף בתר ידיעה. תימה לרשב"א: דמ"מ מייתי שפיר מדר"ש דתידון בחנק לכל הפחות, כיון דבחטאה מיחייבא בסקילה ובבגרות מיחייבא חנק. מידי דהוה *אנחנקין שנתערבו בנסקלין דנידון בחנק, כיון שאינו יכול לקיים בו מצות סקילה! ולא דמי לקרבן, כיון דלא ידע הי קרבן לאיתויי – פטור, דלא שייך למימר דיביא קרבן קטן שבהם, דאפי' יביא גדול לא יתכפר אם הוא מחוייב קטן, ונמצא מביא חולין לעזרה.

הנערה שהיתה כבר. ומהכא שמעינן דכל היכא דאיתני גופא לא איתני קטלא, דבתר מעיקרא אזלינן.

על פתח ב"ד. לאו דווקא על פתח ב"ד, אלא חוץ לב"ד כי היכי דלא ליתחזי ב"ד רוצחין, כדאמרינן בפרק "נגמר הדין" (סנהדרין דף מג: ושם*) אמילתא אחריתא. אבל קשה לר"י: כיון דמסתמא ב"ד לאו חוץ לשלש מחנות יתבי, היכי קאמר הכא סוקלין אותה על פתח בית דין? הא ילפינן התם ב"כל הנסקלין" מפרים הנשרפין, וצריכין ליסקל חוץ לג' מחנות! ותירץ ר"י: דהכא בעיר שרובה גוים – בטלה קדושת היקף חומה, ואין צריך להוציאה לחוץ לחומה, דחומה כמאן דליתא. דהא עיירות המוקפות חומה משתלחין מצורעים מהם, כדאמרינן במסכת כלים (פ"א מ"ז), וכשהיא רובה גוים – אין משתלחין, משום דבטלה קדושת חומה.

סוקלין אותה על פתח שער העיר ההיא. היינו עיר שסרחה בו, כדגמרינן לקמן מעבודה זרה שסוקלין אותו על פתח העיר שעבד בו.

המוציא ש"ר לוקה ונותן מאה סלע גרסינן, ותו לא. ולא גרסינן בין בעל בין לא בעל, דהא איכא דאמרי מוקי לה והוא שבעל.

רבי יהודה אומר ללקות לוקה מ"מ. פ"ה: משום "לא תלך רכיל", אע"ג דהוי לאו שאין בו מעשה – לוקין עליו. ואין נראה לר"ת, דלקמן בעי התלמוד: אזהרה למוציא ש"ר מנלן? ומסיק: מ"לא תלך רכיל". משמע דלא מהני אלא לאזהרה, אבל לא למילקי. ועוד: כל אדם שמחרף אשתו מזנות, לילקי מ"לא תלך רכיל"! ועוד הקשה ר"י: דאי לוקה מ"לא תלך רכיל" לרבי יהודה – אמאי צריך "ויסרו"? ומיהו, לרשב"א נראה דהא לאו פירכא היא, דאי לא כתיב "ויסרו" לא הוה מוקמינן "לא תלך רכיל" לאזהרה דמוציא ש"ר. אבל השתא דשמעינן דלקי מ"ויסרו" אנו צריכין למצוא אזהרה, מוקמינן (א) לאזהרה, דלא ענש אלא אם כן הזהיר. ונראה לר"ת: דלוקה – היינו מכת מרדות לכ"ע. והא דקאמר רב פפא מאי לוקה ממון – לא אתא לאיפלוגי אהא דמפרש דלוקה היינו מכת מרדות, אלא דאינו נראה לו להעמיד הסיפא דבעל לוקה ולא בעל אינו לוקה במלקות ממש, דאין לו לשנות אינו לוקה הואיל ומדרבנן מיהא לקי. ועוד: דאין נראה לו שינית התנא לשנות מאה סלעים דכתיב בהדיא בקרא, וישנה מלקות שאינו מפורש. דבכל הנהו מתניתין דלעיל לא קתני מלקות גרידא אלא בהדי מאה סלע. ואע"ג דלרבי יהודה בעלמא לאו שאין בו מעשה לוקין עליו, ואפ"ה לא לקי בלא בעל – הכא שאני, דגלי קרא דלא לקי אלא דווקא כשבעל. וא"ת: לר' יהודה דאמר לוקין על לאו שאין בו מעשה, אמאי איצטריך "והיה אם בן הכות הרשע"? דבפרק קמא דסנהדרין (ד' י.) ובמכות (ד' ד: ושם) פריך: ותיפוק ליה מ"לא תענה", ומשני: דהוה ליה לאו שאין בו מעשה! וי"ל: דלר' יהודה איכא לשנויי משום דהוי לאו שניתן לאזהרת מיתת ב"ד. ועוד: דהא דלוקין על לאו שאין בו מעשה – מהכא הוא דקיימא ליה לר' יהודה, כדאמרינן התם דר' יהודה גמר ממוציא שם רע ועדים זוממין.

אתיא

עין משפט נר מצוה

כט א מיי' פ"ג מהל' איסורי ביאה הל' יא:

ל ב מיי' פט"ו מהל' סנהדרין הל' ב:

לא ג ד מיי' פ"ג מהל' נערה בתולה הל' א סמג עשין לה טור אה"ע סי' קעז:

[סנהדרין עט:]

[ע"ש בתוס' ד"ה כי היכי וכו' כתבו באופן אחר]

מסורת הש"ס

[סנהדרין עח:]

[שבת פד: ב"ק סה:]

[תוספתא סנהדרין פ"י]

[שבת מ: יבמות נב. נזיר כג. חולין קמא.]

הגהות הב"ח

(א) תוס' ד"ה ר' יהודה וכו' מוקמינן ליה לאזהרה.

רַב פַּפָּא אָמַר: מַאי בָּעַל לוֹקֶה דְּקָתָנֵי הָתָם? מָמוֹן. וְקָרֵי לֵיהּ לְמָמוֹן מַלְקוֹת? אִין, וְהָא *תְּנַן: **א"הָאוֹמֵר חֲצִי עֶרְכִּי עָלַי" — נוֹתֵן חֲצִי עֶרְכּוֹ, רַבִּי יוֹסֵי בְּר' יְהוּדָה אוֹמֵר: לוֹקֶה וְנוֹתֵן עֵרֶךְ שָׁלֵם. לוֹקֶה אַמַּאי? אָמַר רַב פַּפָּא: לוֹקֶה בְּעֵרֶךְ שָׁלֵם. מַאי טַעֲמָא — גְּזֵירָה חֲצִי עֶרְכּוֹ אַטּוּ עֵרֶךְ חֶצְיוֹ, בוְעֵרֶךְ חֶצְיוֹ — הָוֵי לֵיהּ אֵבֶר שֶׁהַנְּשָׁמָה תְּלוּיָה בּוֹ. ת"ר: °"וְעָנְשׁוּ אוֹתוֹ" — זֶה מָמוֹן, °"וְיִסְּרוּ" — זֶה מַלְקוֹת. בִּשְׁלָמָא "וְעָנְשׁוּ" זֶה מָמוֹן — דִּכְתִיב: "וְעָנְשׁוּ אוֹתוֹ מֵאָה כֶסֶף וְנָתְנוּ לַאֲבִי הַנַּעֲרָה" אֶלָּא "וְיִסְּרוּ" זֶה מַלְקוֹת מְנָלַן? *א"ר אַבָּהוּ: לָמַדְנוּ "יִסְּרוּ" מִ"יִּסְּרוּ" וְ"יִסְּרוּ" מִ"בֵּן" וּ"בֵן" מִ"בִּן" — °"וְהָיָה אִם בִּן הַכּוֹת הָרָשָׁע". אַזְהָרָה לְמוֹצִיא שֵׁם רַע מְנָלַן? ר' אֶלְעָזָר אָמַר: °מִ"לֹּא תֵלֵךְ רָכִיל", רַבִּי נָתָן אוֹמֵר: °מִ"וְנִשְׁמַרְתָּ מִכֹּל דָּבָר רָע". וְרַבִּי אֶלְעָזָר מַאי טַעֲמָא לָא אָמַר מֵהַאי? הַהוּא מִיבָּעֵי לֵיהּ לְכִדְר' פִּנְחָס בֶּן יָאִיר. "וְנִשְׁמַרְתָּ מִכֹּל דָּבָר רָע" *מִכָּאן אָמַר ר' פִּנְחָס בֶּן יָאִיר: גאַל יְהַרְהֵר אָדָם בַּיּוֹם וְיָבֹא לִידֵי טוּמְאָה בַּלַּיְלָה. וְר' נָתָן, מַאי טַעֲמָא לָא אָמַר מֵהַאי? הַהוּא דאַזְהָרָה לְב"ד, שֶׁלֹּא יְהֵא רַךְ לָזֶה וְקָשֶׁה לָזֶה. *הלֹא אָמַר לָעֵדִים "בּוֹאוּ וַהֲעִידוּנִי" וְהֵן מְעִידִים אוֹתוֹ מֵאֲלֵיהֶן — הוּא אֵינוֹ לוֹקֶה וְאֵינוֹ נוֹתֵן מֵאָה סְלָעִים, *הִיא וְזוֹמְמֶיהָ מַקְדִּימִין לְבֵית הַסְּקִילָה. הִיא וְזוֹמְמֶיהָ סָלְקָא דַּעְתָּךְ?! אֶלָּא: אוֹ הִיא אוֹ זוֹמְמֶיהָ מַקְדִּימִין לְבֵית הַסְּקִילָה. טַעֲמָא — דְּלָא אֲמַר לְהוּ, הָא אֲמַר לְהוּ — אע"ג דְּלָא אַגְרִינְהוּ. לְאַפּוֹקֵי מִדְּר' יְהוּדָה, דְּתַנְיָא, רַבִּי יְהוּדָה אוֹמֵר: אֵינוֹ חַיָּב עַד שֶׁיִּשְׂכּוֹר עֵדִים. מ"ט דְּר' יְהוּדָה? אָמַר ר' אַבָּהוּ. אָתְיָא "שִׂימָה" "שִׂימָה"; כְּתִיב הָכָא: °"וְשָׂם לָהּ עֲלִילוֹת דְּבָרִים" וּכְתִיב הָתָם: °"לֹא תְשִׂימוּן עָלָיו נֶשֶׁךְ", מַה לְהַלָּן מָמוֹן — אַף כָּאן מָמוֹן. אָמַר רַב נַחְמָן בַּר יִצְחָק. וְכֵן תָּנֵי רַב יוֹסֵף צִידוֹנִי בֵּי רַבִּי שִׁמְעוֹן בֶּן יוֹחַאי: אָתְיָא "שִׂימָה" "שִׂימָה". בָּעֵי רַבִּי יִרְמְיָה: שְׂכָרָן בְּקַרְקַע מַהוּ. בְּפָחוֹת מִשָּׁוֶה פְּרוּטָה מַהוּ. שְׁנֵיהֶם בִּפְרוּטָה מַהוּ? בָּעֵי רַב אַשִׁי: והוֹצִיא שֵׁם רַע עַל הַנִּישּׂוּאִין הָרִאשׁוֹנִים מַהוּ, עַל נִשּׂוּאֵי אָחִיו מַהוּ? פְּשׁוֹט מִיהָא חֲדָא, *דְּתָנֵי ר' יוֹנָה: °"אֶת בִּתִּי נָתַתִּי לָאִישׁ הַזֶּה" זלָזֶה — וְלֹא לְיָבָם. מַאי רַבָּנַן וּמַאי ר' אֱלִיעֶזֶר בֶּן יַעֲקֹב? דְּתַנְיָא: *כֵּיצַד חהוֹצָאַת שֵׁם רַע? בָּא לְבֵית דִּין, וְאָמַר: "פְּלוֹנִי, לֹא מָצָאתִי לְבִתְּךָ בְּתוּלִים". אִם יֵשׁ עֵדִים שֶׁזִּינְּתָה תַּחְתָּיו — יֵשׁ לָהּ כְּתוּבָּה מָנֶה. אִם יֵשׁ עֵדִים שֶׁזִּינְּתָה תַּחְתָּיו יֵשׁ לָהּ כְּתוּבָּה מָנֶה?! בַּת סְקִילָה הִיא! הָכִי קָאָמַר: אִם יֵשׁ עֵדִים שֶׁזִּינְּתָה תַּחְתָּיו — בִּסְקִילָה, זִינְּתָה מֵעִיקָּרָא — יֵשׁ לָהּ כְּתוּבָּה מָנֶה. נִמְצָא שֶׁשֵּׁם רַע אֵינוֹ שֵׁם רַע — הוּא לוֹקֶה וְנוֹתֵן מֵאָה סֶלַע, בֵּין בָּעַל וּבֵין לֹא בָּעַל. רַבִּי אֱלִיעֶזֶר בֶּן יַעֲקֹב אוֹמֵר: לֹא נֶאֶמְרוּ דְּבָרִים הַלָּלוּ אֶלָּא כְּשֶׁבָּעַל. בִּשְׁלָמָא לְרַבִּי אֱלִיעֶזֶר בֶּן יַעֲקֹב — הַיְינוּ דִּכְתִיב: °"וּבָא אֵלֶיהָ" "וָאֶקְרַב אֵלֶיהָ". אֶלָּא לְרַבָּנַן — מַאי "וּבָא אֵלֶיהָ" "וָאֶקְרַב אֵלֶיהָ"? "וּבָא אֵלֶיהָ" — בַּעֲלִילוֹת, "וָאֶקְרַב אֵלֶיהָ" — בִּדְבָרִים. בִּשְׁלָמָא לְרַבִּי אֱלִיעֶזֶר בֶּן יַעֲקֹב — הַיְינוּ דִּכְתִיב: "לֹא מָצָאתִי לְבִתְּךָ בְּתוּלִים". אֶלָּא לְרַבָּנַן — מַאי "לֹא מָצָאתִי לְבִתְּךָ בְּתוּלִים"? לֹא מָצָאתִי לְבִתְּךָ כָּשְׁרֵי בְתוּלִים. בִּשְׁלָמָא לְרַבִּי אֱלִיעֶזֶר בֶּן יַעֲקֹב — הַיְינוּ דִּכְתִיב: "וְאֵלֶּה בְּתוּלֵי בִתִּי", אֶלָּא לְרַבָּנַן מַאי "וְאֵלֶּה בְּתוּלֵי בִתִּי"? טוְאֵלֶּה כָּשְׁרֵי בְתוּלֵי בִתִּי. בִּשְׁלָמָא לְר"א בֶּן יַעֲקֹב — הַיְינוּ דִּכְתִיב: "וּפָרְשׂוּ הַשִּׂמְלָה", אֶלָּא לְרַבָּנַן מַאי "וּפָרְשׂוּ הַשִּׂמְלָה"? אָמַר רַבִּי אַבָּהוּ: פֵּרְשׁוּ מַה שֶּׁשָּׂם לָהּ. כִּדְתַנְיָא: "וּפָרְשׂוּ הַשִּׂמְלָה". ימְלַמֵּד שֶׁבָּאִין עֵדִים שֶׁל זֶה וְעֵדִים שֶׁל זֶה, וּבוֹרְרִין אֶת הַדָּבָר כְּשִׂמְלָה חֲדָשָׁה. רַבִּי אֱלִיעֶזֶר בֶּן יַעֲקֹב אוֹמֵר: דְּבָרִים כִּכְתָבָן, שִׂמְלָה מַמָּשׁ. שְׁלַח רַבִּי יִצְחָק בַּר רַב יַעֲקֹב בַּר גִּיּוֹרֵי מִשְּׁמֵיהּ דְּרַבִּי יוֹחָנָן: אע"ג כשֶׁלֹּא מָצִינוּ בְּכָל הַתּוֹרָה כּוּלָּהּ שֶׁחִלֵּק הַכָּתוּב בֵּין בִּיאָה כְּדַרְכָּהּ לְבִיאָה שֶׁלֹּא כְּדַרְכָּהּ לְמַכּוֹת וּלְעוֹנָשִׁין, אֲבָל מוֹצִיא שֵׁם רַע — חִלֵּק: לאֵינוֹ חַיָּיב עַד שֶׁיִּבְעוֹל שֶׁלֹּא כְּדַרְכָּהּ, וְיוֹצִיא שֵׁם רַע כְּדַרְכָּהּ. כְּמַאן? אִי כְּרַבָּנַן — אַף עַל גַּב דְּלָא בָּעַל, אִי כְּר' אֱלִיעֶזֶר בֶּן יַעֲקֹב — אִידִי

רַב פַּפָּא אָמַר. לְעוֹלָם מַלְקוּת מַמָּשׁ, וּמַאי "בָּעַל לוֹקֶה" דְּקָאָמַר בְּהַךְ בָּרַיְיתָא — מָמוֹן דְּמֵאָה סֶלַע קָאָמַר. חֲצִי עֶרְכּוֹ. לְפִי שָׁנָיו. דְּעֵרֶךְ קָצוּב בַּפָּרָשָׁה לְפִי הַשָּׁנִים. גְּזֵירָה חֲצִי עֶרְכּוֹ. שֶׁקָּצוּב לוֹ לְפִי שָׁנִים. אַטּוּ עֵרֶךְ חֶצְיוֹ. דְּמַשְׁמַע חֲצִי עֵרֶךְ שָׁלֵם, "עָלַי". וְהָאוֹמֵר "עֵרֶךְ חֶלְיוֹ עָלַי" אוֹ "עֵרֶךְ רֹאשִׁי" אוֹ "לִבִּי עָלַי" — נוֹתֵן עֵרֶךְ שָׁלֵם. דְּהָוֵה לֵיהּ מַעֲרִיךְ אֵבֶר שֶׁהַנְּשָׁמָה תְּלוּיָה בּוֹ, וְגַבֵּי עֲרָכִין כְּתִיב (ויקרא כז) "בְּעֶרְכְּךָ נְפָשׁוֹת", שֶׁהַמַּעֲרִיךְ אֵבֶר שֶׁהַנְּשָׁמָה תְּלוּיָה בּוֹ — נוֹתֵן קִצְבָּה שֶׁנָּתְנָה בּוֹ תּוֹרָה. וְיִסְּרוּ מִוְּיִסְּרוּ וְיִסְּרוּ מִבֵּן. כְּתִיב הָכָא "וְיִסְּרוּ אוֹתוֹ", וּכְתִיב גַּבֵּי סוֹרֵר וּמוֹרֶה *"וְיִסְּרוּ". מַה לְהַלָּן בֵּן עִמּוֹ — אַף כָּאן בֵּן עִמּוֹ, וְהַיְינוּ "וְיִסְּרוּ" דְּהָכָא מִ"וְיִסְּרוּ" דְּהָתָם. וְהַהוּא "וְיִסְּרוּ" דְּהָתָם מִ"בֵּן" שֶׁעִמּוֹ, דִּלְגָמְרֵיהּ לְ"בֵן" שֶׁעִמּוֹ עַל "וְיִסְּרוּ" דְּהָכָא, וַהֲדַר יָלֵיף "בֵּן" דְּאַיְיתִינַן הָכָא מִ"בִּן" "וְהָיָה אִם בִּן הַכּוֹת", מַה הָתָם מַלְקוֹת — אַף הָכָא מַלְקוֹת. וְנִשְׁמַרְתָּ מִכֹּל דָּבָר רָע. וְכָל מָקוֹם שֶׁנֶּאֱמַר "הִשָּׁמֶר" "פֶּן" וְ"אַל" — אֵינוֹ אֶלָּא לֹא תַעֲשֶׂה. לְכִדְרַבִּי פִּנְחָס. בְּמַסֶּכֶת עֲבוֹדָה זָרָה. שֶׁלֹּא יְהַרְהֵר בַּיּוֹם וְיָבֹא לִידֵי טוּמְאָה בַּלַּיְלָה. דִּסְמִיךְ לֵיהּ "כִּי יִהְיֶה בְךָ אִישׁ" וגו'. רַךְ לָזֶה. וְרָכִיל, לָשׁוֹן: רַךְ לִי תִּהְיֶה. לֹא אָמַר לָעֵדִים. הַמְּעִידִים עַל זְנוּתָהּ. שְׂכָרָן בְּקַרְקַע. לְרַבִּי יְהוּדָה, מַהוּ? כֵּיוָן דְּמַרְבִּית גָּמַר — כֶּסֶף אוֹ אוֹכֶל בָּעֵינַן, דַּהֲווּ מִטַּלְטְלִין, כִּדְכְתִיב לְעִנְיַן רִבִּית, אוֹ דִּלְמָא לְמָמוֹן הוּא דְּגָמַר ג"ש, וַאֲפִי' מְקַרְקְעֵי. עַל נִשּׂוּאִין הָרִאשׁוֹנִים. כְּנָסָהּ וְלֹא הוֹצִיא ש"ר וְגֵרְשָׁהּ וְהֶחֱזִירָהּ, וְאַחַר כָּךְ מוֹצִיא שֵׁם רָע: לֹא מָצָאתִי בְּתוּלִים לְנִישּׂוּאִין קַמָּאֵי. וְלֹא לְיָבָם. אֵין יָבָם שֶׁהוֹצִיא שֵׁם רָע עַל נִישּׂוּאֵי אָחִיו בִּכְלַל פָּרָשָׁה זוֹ, לִטְעוֹן טַעֲנַת בְּתוּלִים. אִיפְּשִׁיטָא לֵיהּ בָּעְיָא בַּתְרַיְיתָא. זִינְּתָה מֵעִיקָּרָא יֵשׁ לָהּ כְּתוּבָּה מָנֶה. קָסָבַר: כְּנָסָהּ בְּחֶזְקַת בְּתוּלָה וְנִמְצֵאת בְּעוּלָה — יֵשׁ לָהּ כְּתוּבָּה מָנֶה. כָּשְׁרֵי בְתוּלִים. עֵדִים שֶׁיָּזִימוּ אוֹ יַכְחִישׁוּ אֶת אֵלּוּ, וְיַכְשִׁירוּ אֶת בִּתְּךָ לִבְתוּלָה גְּמוּרָה. כָּשְׁרֵי בְתוּלֵי בִתִּי. עֵדִים הַמְזִימִין אֶת עֵדָיו. שֶׁלֹּא מָצִינוּ שֶׁחִלֵּק הַכָּתוּב. "מִשְׁכְּבֵי אִשָּׁה כְּתִיב" שְׁנֵי מִשְׁכְּבוֹתֶיהָ שָׁוִין לְכָל מִשְׁפַּט עֲרָיוֹת. בְּמוֹצִיא שֵׁם רָע חִלֵּק. שֶׁאִם הֵבִיא עֵדִים שֶׁנִּבְעֲלָה אֲרוּסָתוֹ שֶׁלֹּא כְּדַרְכָּהּ, וְנִמְצְאוּ זוֹמְמִין — אֵינוֹ נוֹתֵן מֵאָה סֶלַע. דְּ"לֹא מָצָאתִי בְּתוּלִים" כְּתִיב, בִּמְקוֹם בְּתוּלִים. אֵינוֹ חַיָּיב עַד שֶׁיִּבְעוֹל שֶׁלֹּא כְּדַרְכָּהּ וְיוֹצִיא שֵׁם רָע בִּכְדַרְכָּהּ. כְּלוֹמַר כְּשֶׁבָּעַל נֶאֶמְרוּ דְּבָרִים, וּבְעִילָתוֹ אֲפִילּוּ הִיא שֶׁלֹּא כְּדַרְכָּהּ. כִּי הֵיכִי דְּלֹא חִלֵּק בִּשְׁאָר עוֹנָשִׁין. אֲבָל בִּיאָה שֶׁל זְנוּת שֶׁהוּא מוֹצִיא לַעַז עָלֶיהָ — צָרִיךְ שֶׁיֹּאמַר עַל בִּיאָה כְּדַרְכָּהּ, וּלְקַמָּן מְפָרֵשׁ לָהּ. אִידִי

אתיא שימה שימה. נראה דלאו ג"ש גמורה היא, מדבעי בסמוך שכרן בקרקע או בפחות משוה פרוטה מהו? אף ע"ג דאין רבית בקרקע, אלא דווקא דומיא דכסף ואוכל. ולא בפחות משוה פרוטה, מדאמר בריש "איזהו נשך" (ב"מ דף סא. ושם): למה לי דכתב רחמנא לאו בגזל, לאו ברבית, לאו באונאה? ואם יש רבית בפחות משוה פרוטה — הא איצטריך לאו ברבית לפחות משוה פרוטה. והנך נמי לא ילפינן מיניה, דמה לרבית — שכן ישנה בפחות משוה פרוטה. והא דאמר בערכין (דף לא. ושם) גבי בתי ערי חומה: רבית הוא, אלא שהתורה התירתו — התם חשיב רבית לפי שעומד בבית בשכר המתנת מעותיו. אבל אם אדם לוה שדה שאם שטפה נהר יפרע לו שדה ושלי, או עשר גפנים טעונות פגין או בוסר, בי"א — דלכ"לי עלמא כקרקע דמיא לשבועה ולכל דבר, שמא כי האי גוונא לא הוי רבית בקרקע.

בשלמא לר"א בן יעקב היינו דכתיב ופרשו השמלה. תימה: דע"כ בשיש עדים שזינתה איירי, דמשום שלא ימלאו על השמלה דם בתולים אין להורגה — א"כ מה תועלת יש בפריסת השמלה? דפשיטא דלא מיתכחשי עדים בשביל כך, דיש לתלות שהנואף הטה! וי"ל: דסבר דלא מיחייב, אלא אם כן העיז פניו לשנות הידוע, שמחליף להראות השמלה בלא בתולים לבית דין, ונמצא שקרן, שהיא מלאה דם.

דברים ששם לה. לא מלשון שמלה דריש, דהא מפרש בברייתא דמייתי "שמלה" כשמלה חדשה. אלא לישנא דקרא נקט "ושם לה עלילות דברים".

ואיתא

לב א ב מיי' פ"ב מהל' ערכין הל' ב סמג עשין קכח:

לג ג מיי' פכ"א מהל' איסורי ביאה הל' ה כא סמג לאוין קכו טוש"ע אה"ע סי' כג סעיף ג:

[נ"ל והא תניא פירוש בניחותא]

לד ד מיי' פכ"א מהל' סנהדרין הל' א סמג עשין קמ טוש"ע ח"מ סי' יז סעי' א:

לה ה מיי' פ"ג מהל' נערה בתולה הל' יא טואה"ע סי' קעז:

לו ו ז מיי' שם הל' ט:

לז ח ט י מיי' שם הל' ו יב:

לח כ מיי' פ"א מהל' איסורי ביאה הל' י טז יז סמג לאוין כ טוש"ע אה"ע סי' כ סעי' א בהגה"ה:

לט ל (מיי' פ"ג מהל' נערה הל' י):

ערכין כ. [תוס' ערכין פ"ג ע"ש]

[דברים כא]

סנהדרין עח:

ע"ז כ: ע"ש (שקלים ז.)

[תוספ' פ"א ע"ש]

[לעיל מה.]

לעיל כב.

לעיל יח:

מ א מיי' פ"ג מהל' נערה בתולה הל' י' סמג עשין נה טוש"ע אה"ע סי' קנז:

מא ב מיי' פ"ג מהל' אישות הלכה יא ופ' יז מהל' אבידה הלכה יג סמג עשין מח עד טוש"ע אה"ע סימן לז סעיף א וטוש"ע ח"מ סי' רע סעיף ב:

מב ג מיי' פי"א מהל' נדרים הל' ו סמג לאוין רמב טוש"ע י"ד סי' רלד סעי' א:

מג ד מיי' פ"ב מהל' גירושין הל' יח סמג עשין נ טוש"ע אה"ע סימן קמא סעיף ד:

מד ה מיי' פ"ד מהל' חובל הל' יט סמג עשין ע טוש"ע ח"מ סי' תכד סעיף ז:

מה ו מיי' פי"ב מהל' אישות הל' ג ופכ"ב הל' ז סמג עשין מח טוש"ע אה"ע סי' סט סעיף ג.

מו ז מיי' פי"ב שם הל' ב טוש"ע שם סעי' ב:

מז ח מיי' פי"ד שם הל' כג סמג לאוין פא טוש"ע שם סימן פט סעיף א:

תורה אור

אידי ואידי כדרכה בעינן! אלא שלח רב כהנא משמיה דרבי יוחנן: [א]אינו חייב עד שיבעול כדרכה, ויוציא שם רע בכדרכה.§ **מתני'** *[ב]האב זכאי בבתו בקידושיה בכסף, בשטר ובביאה. *זכאי במציאתה ובמעשה ידיה, [ג]ובהפרת נדריה, [ד]ומקבל את גיטה, [ה]ואינו אוכל פירות בחייה. נשאת – יתר עליו הבעל [ו]שאוכל פירות בחייה, [ז]וחייב במזונותיה ובפרקונה ובקבורתה. רבי יהודה אומר: [ח]אפי' עני שבישראל לא יפחות משני חלילין ומקוננת.§ **גמ'** *בכסף מנלן? אמר רב יהודה: אמר קרא °"ויצאה חנם אין כסף" (שמות כא) – אין כסף לאדון זה, ויש כסף לאדון אחר, ומנו – אביה. ואימא לדידה? השתא אביה מקבל קידושיה, דכתיב: °"את בתי נתתי לאיש הזה" (דברים כב), איהי שקלא כספא?! ואימא: הני מילי – קטנה, דלית לה יד, אבל נערה דאית לה יד – איהי תקדש נפשה, ואיהי תשקול כספא! אמר קרא: °"בנעוריה בית אביה" (במדבר ל) – כל שבח נעורים לאביה. ואלא, הא דא"ר הונא אמר רב: *מנין שמעשה הבת לאביה – שנאמר: °"וכי ימכור איש את בתו לאמה" (שמות כא), מה אמה מעשה ידיה לרבה, אף בת מעשה ידיה לאביה – למה לי, תיפוק ליה מ"בנעוריה בית אביה"? אלא, ההוא בהפרת נדרים הוא דכתיב. וכ"ת: ניליף מינה – *ממונא מאיסורא לא ילפינן. וכ"ת: ניליף מקנסא – ממונא מקנסא לא ילפינן. וכ"ת: ניליף מבושת ופגם – שאני בושת ופגם דאביה נמי שייך ביה. אלא, מסתברא דכי ממעט רחמנא – יציאה דכוותה קא ממעט. והא לא דמיא הא יציאה להא יציאה, התם גבי אדון – נפקא לה מרשותיה לגמרי, יציאה דאב – אכתי מחסרא מסירה לחופה! מהפרת נדרים מיהא נפקא לה מרשותיה. דתנן: *נערה המאורסה אביה ובעלה מפירין לה נדריה.§ "שטר וביאה".§ מנא לן? אמר קרא: °"והיתה לאיש אחר" (דברים כד) – *איתקוש הוויות להדדי.§ "זכאי במציאתה".§ משום

רש"י

אידי ואידי כדרכה בעינן. כיון דאמר דברים ככתבן, היאך אתה קורא "לא מצאתי לה בתולים"? אלא אם כן אמר בעלתיה כדרכה ומצאתיה בעולה. **מתני'** האב זכאי בבתו. בקטנות ובנערות. בקידושיה בכסף. שכסף קידושיה שלו. ובשטר. שאם קבל שטר אירוסין עליה – הרי זו מקודשת. בביאה. רשאי למוסרה לביאה לשם קידושין. ומקבל את גיטה. אם נתגרשה מן האירוסין, וקודם שבגרה. אבל בגרה או ניסת – שוב אין לו רשות בה. ואינו אוכל פירות בחייה. אם נפלו לה קרקעות בירושה מבית אמה – אין אביה אוכל פירותיהן, אלא עושין לה סגולה. בחייה. אלא אם כן מתה והוא יורשה. יתר עליו הבעל. שהוא זוכה גם בכל השנויים למעלה, ואוכל פירות מנכסים שנפלו לה בירושה משניסת לו. וחייב במזונותיה ובפרקונה. אם נשבית, שהוא תנאי ב"ד, כדתנן במתני'. בקבורתה. דאמרינן לקמן: קבורתה תחת כתובתה שהכניסה לו מבית אביה, והוא יורשה במיתתה. משני חלילין. להספד, קלמיל"ש. **גמ'** בכסף מנלן. דכסף קידושיה לאביה. אין כסף. באמה העבריה כתיב. ובקידושין פריך: האי מבעי ליה לגופיה! אין כסף לאדון זה. בצאתה מרשותו בסימני נערות, כדילפינן בקידושין דיוצאה בסימנים משמעי קרא. אבל יש כסף לאדון אחר. כשיוצאה מרשותו. ומנו אב. שאין אדון לבת ישראל אלא אביה, חוץ מזה שנמכרה לו. ואימא לדידה הוי. וקרא כי אתא לאשמועינן אתא, שהיא נקנית לבעל בקידושי כסף. והכי תדרשיה: אין כסף ביציאה זו, אבל יש כסף ביציאה אחרת. ולעולם דידה הוי. ואימא הני מילי. דאמרה תורה "את בתי נתתי" – שבידו נתינתה. קטנה דלית לה יד. לקדש עצמה. ואע"ג דגבי מוציא שם רע כתיב, והיא נערה הוה – דלמא הכי קאמר: את בתי נתתי בקטנותה, ועתה נערה. אלא ההיא בהפרת נדרים כתיב. מסקנא דקושיא היא, ולא שינויא הוא. וכי תימא ניליף. כסף קידושיה מקנסה שזיכתה תורה לאב. מבושת ופגם. דאמרינן ב"אלו נערות" (לעיל מ:) שהוא של אב. שייך בה. בידו ליטול ממון ולביישה בבושת זה, למוסרה לביאת קידושין למנוול ולמוכה שחין. אלא. כי פרכת אימא לדידה, הכי תשני: מסתברא כי קא ממעט קרא יציאתה מרשות אב בקידושין, מתורת יציאתה מרשות אדון בסימנין. יציאה דכוותה קא ממעט. מה כסף דיציאת אדון, אי הוה התם כסף, דאדון שהיא יוצאה ממנו בעי מהוי, כפדיון גרעונה, דמגרעת עמו ויוצאה, והמותר נותנת לו. אף כי קאמר נמי יש כסף ביציאה אחרת – דאדון שהיא יוצאה ממנו בעי למהוי, ולא לדידה. ואי אמרת לדידה הוה – לא קא ממעט יציאה דכוותה. כך מפורש בשאלתות דרב אחאי גאון. *ואני שמעתי יציאה דכוותה קא ממעט – מה התם נערה, אף הכא נערה. וקשיא לי: אכתי אימא לדידה! ובמסכת קידושין פירשתיה בלשון שמועתי, ובקושי. והא לא דמיא. יציאה דקידושין ליציאת אמה העבריה, ולא יציאה דכוותה היא. אכתי מיחסרא מסירה לחופה. ועדיין היא ברשות האב לירושתה ולמעשה ידיה. נפקא לה מרשותיה. דעד עכשיו היה מיפר לבדו, ועתה מיפר בשותפות עם בעלה. בשטר ובביאה מנלן. דביד אביה לקדשה ולמוסרה על כרחה. איתקוש הוויות להדדי. מה כסף ברשות אביה – אף קידושי שטר וביאה ביד אביה, וקידושי שטר וביאה דמקדשת בהו ילפינן בקידושין.
משום

תוספות

ואימא לדידה. תימה: היכי מצי למימר שיהא שלה? הא אמרינן בפרק קמא דקידושין (דף ד:): ואצטריך למכתב "כי יקח" ואצטריך למכתב "ויצאה חנם", דאי כתב רחמנא "כי יקח" הוי אמינא כספא דידה הוי, כתב רחמנא "ויצאה חנם"! ואומר ר"י: דהתם לפי מסקנא דשמעתין קאמר, דאמר: יציאה דכוותה קא ממעט. אבל אי לאו היה שום משמעות מ"ויצאה חנם" שיהא של אב – מייתורא לא הוה אמרינן שיהא שלו. **השתא** אביה מקבל קידושיה דכתיב את בתי נתתי וגו'. תימה: למאי דסלקא דעתין השתא, אמאי איצטריך "ויצאה חנם"? דמקדשה בכסף שמעינן מ"כי יקח", ומ"את בתי" שמעינן לה דלא הוי לדידה.

ואימא הני מילי קטנה. ואע"ג דקרא בבת עונשין איירי, ה"ק: בתי נתתי כשהיתה קטנה. וא"ת: הא לקטנה לא איצטריך קרא, השתא זבוני מזבין לה – כסף קידושיה מיבעיא? דבכה"ג קאמר בסמוך גבי מעשה ידיה! וי"ל: דגבי מעשה ידיה קאמר שפיר, דכיון שיש לו כח למכור מעשה ידיה לאחר – פשיטא שהם שלו. אבל מה ענין קידושין אצל מכירה? אע"ג דיכול האדון לייעדה בכסף קנייתה – היינו משום דגזירת הכתוב הוא דיכול לייעדה בכסף קנייתה, אבל שאר קידושין – אימא דאין האב זוכה בהן כלום. ועי"ל: דאמעשה ידיה פשיטא ליה שהם שלו כל זמן שיכול למוכרה, דהיינו עד נערות. אבל משום דמצי מזבן לה עד נערות – לא שמעינן שיהא שלו כסף קידושין שהיא מתקדשת בו לעולם. ועוד: ד"את בתי נתתי" אינו מיותר, ואיצטריך אפילו לקטנה, דאיצטריך לאשמעינן דאב נאמן לאסור את בתו*. ולפי המסקנא ע"כ לא אתא אלא להכי. והא דדרשינן השתא אביה מקבל קידושיה – היינו מפשטיה דקרא.

ממונא מאיסורא לא ילפינן. וא"ת: ניליף מהפרת נדרים, דאביה יכול לקדשה, דהיינו איסורא מאיסורא, וממילא שמעינן דכספא דאביה הוי, כדאמר לעיל: השתא אביה מקבל קידושיה – איהי שקלה כספא? וי"ל: דאיסורא דאית ביה ממונא מאיסורא דלית ביה ממונא – לא ילפי'.

יציאה דכוותה קא ממעט. פי' בקונטרס בלשון שני, וכן פירש רבינו חננאל: דכוותה – היינו מה התם בנערה, אף הכא נמי להאי אדון מרבינן כסף בנערה. ואין נראה, דאכתי תקשי: ואימא לדידה! אלא פירוש הקונטרס עיקר. והשתא, כיון דשמעינן מהאי קרא דכספא דאביה הוי – סברא הוא דאיהו נמי מקבל. דהשתא אביה שקיל כסף קדושיה ואיהי תקדוש נפשה?

לענין הפרת נדרים נפקא לה מרשותו. הכי נמי הוה מצי למימר דלענין אכילת תרומה נפקא לה מרשותו, דאם בת כהן לישראל היא – אינה אוכלת בתרומה, כדאמרינן ב"יש מותרות" (יבמות דף פז. ושם). אלא ניחא ליה למנקט הפרת נדרים, שהפסיד כחו שהיה לו בה להפר נדריה, דומיא דיציאת אדון שמפסיד מעשה ידיה.

זכאי במציאתה משום איבה. מדאורייתא ליכא למילף שתהא מציאתה לאביה כמו שקידושיה לאביה, דשאני קידושין דלא קטרחא בהו כלל, אבל מציאתה דקטרחא להגביה מציאתה. וכה"ג עביד צריכותא בריש קידושין (דף ד.) דלא גמרינן מעשה ידיה מקידושיה דלא קא טרחא בהו כלל. ואם תאמר: ניליף מתרוייהו, דהשתא ומה הנך דמחמת גופה קא אתו הוי דאב, מציאה לכ"ש! וי"ל: דמה להנך – שהאב נפסד על ידיהן, דעל ידי קידושין היא מפקעת עצמה ממנו, ומעשה ידיה משום דקא מיתזנא מיניה, כדאמרינן בריש קידושין (ג"ז שם).
משום

תוספות רי"ד

מתני' האב זכאי בבתו בקידושיה בכסף בשטר ובביאה. פי' האב זכאי לקדש את בתו בעודה קטנה או נערה בין בכסף בין בשטר. פי' כותב לו על הנייר בתך מקודשת לי והאב מקבל השטר ממנו ומקנה אותה לו בו וכן מקבל הכסף ממנו ומקנה אותה לו בו וכן בביאה יכול למוסרו לו לבא עליה לשם נשואין. ובפ"ק דקידושין מפרש להו דבכל הני מיקדשו כסף אתיא קיחה קיחה משדה עפרון שטר מקשי' יציאה להויה ביאה כי יקח איש אשה ובעלה: וזכאי במציאתה ובמעש' ידיה ובהפרת נדריה פי' שמפר נדרים שלה כל זמן שהיא נערה ומקבל את גיטה פי' אם נתגרשה מן האירוסין בעודה קטנה או נערה. אבל אם בגרה או נשאת אין לו רשות בה. ואינו אוכל פירות בחייה פי' אם נפלו לה פירות מבית אמה אינו אוכל פירותיהן אלא עושה מהן סגולה. נשאת יתר עליו הבעל שהוא אוכל פירות בחייה פי' זוכה במציאתה ובמעשה ידיה ובהפרת נדריה כאב יתר עליו הבעל שהוא אוכל פירות נכסיה בתקנת חכמים. וחייב במזונותיה פי' משא"כ האב חייב דהכי תנן לקמן בפירקין האב אינו חייב במזונות בתו. אלא תקנה הוא שתיקנו גאוני' הראשוני'. ובפירקונה פי' מפני שהוא תנאי ב"ד שכך כותב לה אם תשתבאי אפרקינך. ובקבורתה פי' אם מתה בחייו מפני שהוא יורש כתובתה ר"י אומר אפילו עני שבישראל לא יפחות לה מב' חלילים ומקוננת פי' חלילים שיספידוה בהן ומקוננת אחת שתקונן עליה: בקידושי' מנ"ל. דכתיב את בתי נתתי לאיש הזה. פי' אלמא ברשות אב לתתה לכל מי שיחפוץ ומנין שזוכה בכסף קידושין דכתיב ויצאה חנם אין כסף לאדון זה אבל יש כסף לאדון אחר ומנו אב. פי' ממשמע שנאמר ויצאה חנם איני יודע שאין כסף ומת"ל אין כסף וקרא יתירה הוא לדרשא אתא אין כסף לאדון זה פי' שהמוכר את בתו קטנה יוצאה בסימנים וכשתצא מרבה אינה נותנת לו כסף. אבל יש כסף לאדון אחר דכי נפקא מרשות אב לרשות בעל אית ליה כסף קידושין: ובמעשה ידיה מנלן אמר ר"ה א"ר מניין למעשה הבת שהן לאביה שנא' וכי ימכור איש את בתו לאמה מה אמה מעשה ידיה לרבה אף בת מעשה ידיה לאביה פי' מלאמה דהוא יתר קדריש:

מסורת הש"ס

קדושין ג: י. לקמן סה:
[נדה מז.]
[קדושין ג: כל הסוגיא ע"ש]
לעיל מ: קדושין ג: [לקמן מז.]
[ברכות יט: וש"נ]
נדרים סז. עד: יבמות כט: לעיל לט. קדושין ד:
[לקמן עד. קדושין ע:]
[פ' משפטים סי' כט]

מִשּׁוּם אֵיבָה.§ "בְּמַעֲשֵׂה יָדֶיהָ".§ מְנָלַן? *דְּאָמַר רַב הוּנָא אָמַר רַב: מִנַּיִן שֶׁמַּעֲשֵׂה הַבַּת לָאָב? שֶׁנֶּאֱמַר: °"וְכִי יִמְכּוֹר אִישׁ אֶת בִּתּוֹ לְאָמָה" – מָה אָמָה מַעֲשֵׂה יָדֶיהָ לְרַבָּהּ – אַף בַּת מַעֲשֵׂה יָדֶיהָ לְאָבִיהָ. – וְאֵימָא: הָנֵי מִילֵּי קְטַנָּה, דְּמָצֵי מְזַבֵּן לָהּ, אֲבָל נַעֲרָה, דְּלָא מָצֵי מְזַבֵּן לָהּ, מַעֲשֵׂה יָדֶיהָ דִּידָהּ הָווּ! מִסְתַּבְּרָא דְּאָבִיהָ הָווּ, דְּאִי ס"ד מַעֲשֵׂה יָדֶיהָ לָאו דְּאָבִיהָ, אֶלָּא הָא דְּזַכֵּי לֵיהּ רַחֲמָנָא לָאָב לְמִימְסְרָהּ לְחוּפָּה – הֵיכִי מָצֵי מָסַר לָהּ? הָא קָמְבַטֵּל לָהּ מִמַּעֲשֵׂה יָדֶיהָ! *פָּרֵיךְ רַב אַחַאי: אֵימָא דְּיָהֵיב לָהּ שְׂכַר פְּקַעְתָּהּ. אִי נַמִי: דְּמָסַר לָהּ בְּלֵילְיָא. אִי נַמִי: •דְּמָסַר לָהּ בְּשַׁבָּתוֹת וְיָמִים טוֹבִים! אֶלָּא, קְטַנָּה לָא צְרִיכָא קְרָא: הַשְׁתָּא זַבּוּנֵי מְזַבֵּין לָהּ, מַעֲשֵׂה יָדֶיהָ מִיבָּעֵי?! [אֶלָּא] כִּי אִיצְטְרִיךְ קְרָא – לְנַעֲרָה.§ בַּהֲפָרַת נְדָרֶיהָ.§ מְנָלַן? דִּכְתִיב: °"בִּנְעוּרֶיהָ בֵּית אָבִיהָ".§ וּמְקַבֵּל אֶת גִּיטָּהּ.§ מְנָלַן? דִּכְתִיב: °"וְיָצְאָה וְהָיְתָה" – *אִיתְקוּשׁ יְצִיאָה לַהֲוָיָה.§ וְאֵינוֹ אוֹכֵל פֵּירוֹת בְּחַיֶּיהָ.§ ת"ר: הָאָב אֵינוֹ אוֹכֵל פֵּירוֹת בְּחַיֵּי בִּתּוֹ. רַבִּי יוֹסֵי בְּרַבִּי יְהוּדָה אוֹמֵר: הָאָב אוֹכֵל פֵּירוֹת בְּחַיֵּי בִּתּוֹ. בְּמַאי קָמִיפַּלְגִי? ת"ק סָבַר: בִּשְׁלָמָא בַּעַל תַּקִּינוּ לֵיהּ רַבָּנַן פֵּירֵי, דְּא"כ מִימְנַע וְלָא פָּרֵיק, אֶלָּא אָב מַאי אִיכָּא לְמֵימַר – דְּמִימְנַע וְלָא פָּרֵיק? בְּלָאו הָכִי פָּרֵיק לָהּ! וְר' יוֹסֵי בַּר' יְהוּדָה סָבַר: אָב נַמִי מִימְנַע וְלָא פָּרֵיק. סָבַר: כִּיסָא נְקִיטָא עִילָּוָהּ, תֵּיזִיל וְתִפְרוֹק נַפְשָׁהּ.§ נִיסֵּת – יָתֵר עָלָיו הַבַּעַל שֶׁהוּא אוֹכֵל כו'.§ ת"ר: כָּתַב לָהּ פֵּירוֹת, כְּסוּת וְכֵלִים שֶׁיָּבוֹאוּ עִמָּהּ מִבֵּית אָבִיהָ לְבֵית בַּעְלָהּ. מֵתָה – לֹא זָכָה הַבַּעַל בַּדְּבָרִים הַלָּלוּ. מִשּׁוּם רַבִּי נָתָן אָמְרוּ: זָכָה הַבַּעַל בַּדְּבָרִים הַלָּלוּ. לֵימָא בִּפְלוּגְתָּא דְּרַבִּי אֶלְעָזָר בֶּן עֲזַרְיָה וְרַבָּנַן קָמִיפַּלְגִי. דִּתְנַן: *נִתְאַרְמְלָה אוֹ נִתְגָּרְשָׁה, בֵּין מִן הַנִּשּׂוּאִין בֵּין מִן הָאֵירוּסִין – גּוֹבָה אֶת הַכֹּל. ר"א ב"ע אוֹמֵר: מִן הַנִּשּׂוּאִין – גּוֹבָה אֶת הַכֹּל, וּמִן הָאֵירוּסִין – בְּתוּלָה גּוֹבָה מָאתַיִם, וְאַלְמָנָה מָנֶה, שֶׁלֹּא

תורה אור: שמות כא; במדבר ל; דברים כד

רש"י

מִשּׁוּם אֵיבָה. דְּכֵיוָן דְּאֵינוֹ חַיָּיב בִּמְזוֹנוֹתֶיהָ, אִי אָמְרַתְּ מְצִיאָתָהּ שֶׁלָּהּ – אִיכָּא אֵיבָה וְלָא זַיֵּין לָהּ תּוּ. הָא דְּזַכֵּי לֵיהּ רַחֲמָנָא לָאָב לְמִימְסְרָהּ לְחוּפָּה. כִּדְכְתִיב "אֶת בִּתִּי נָתַתִּי" – כָּל נְתִינוֹת שֶׁבָּהּ בְּמַשְׁמַע. וְאוֹתוֹ הַיּוֹם אֵינָהּ עוֹשָׂה מְלָאכָה, הֵיכִי מָצֵי כו'. פְּקַעְתָּהּ. בְּטֵילוּתָהּ. אֶלָּא קְטַנָּה לָא צְרִיכָא קְרָא. דְּקַשְׁיָא לָךְ לְעֵיל, אֵימָא ה"מ קְטַנָּה דְּמָצֵי מְזַבֵּן לָהּ – לָאו קוּשְׁיָא הִיא. כִּי אִיצְטְרִיךְ קְרָא לְנַעֲרָה. וְאַע"ג דְּעִיקַּר קְרָא בִּקְטַנָּה כְּתִיב, מִיהוּ קְרָא יְתֵירָא הוּא, דִּכְתִיב "לְאָמָה" – לְאַקּוּשֵׁי בַּת לְאָמָה, לְהֶיקֵּישָׁא דְּנַעֲרָה אָתְיָא. בִּנְעוּרֶיהָ. גַּבֵּי הֲפָרַת נְדָרִים כְּתִיב. וְהָכִי קָאָמַר: בִּנְעוּרֶיהָ – בִּרְשׁוּת אָבִיהָ הִיא. וְכִי תֵּימָא: הָא בְּהֶדְיָא כְּתִיב "כִּי הֵנִיא אָבִיהָ אוֹתָהּ"! אִי לָאו הַאי – הֲוָה אָמֵינָא בִּקְטַנָּה מִשְׁתָּעֵי. וּמִימְנַע וְלָא פָּרֵיק. לְפִיכָךְ תִּקְּנוּ לוֹ פֵּירוֹת, כִּדְאָמַר לְקַמָּן: וּפֵירְקוֹנָהּ תַּחַת פֵּירוֹת, דְּלֵיכְלִינְהוּ בַּעַל וְכָל פִּדְיוֹנָהּ יְהֵי עָלָיו, אִם רַב אִם מְעַט. דְּאִי אָמְרַתְּ לֵינְחִינְהוּ, וְיִפְדּוּהָ מֵהֶם אִם תִּהְיֶה שְׁבוּיָה – זִמְנִין דְּלָא מָלוּ. וְהַשְׁתָּא יָהֵיב מִדִּידֵיהּ. כִּיסָא נְקִיטָא. כִּיס מָלֵא מָעוֹת יֵשׁ לָהּ בִּסְגוּלָּה, וְעַד הֵנָּה לֹא נֶהֱנֵיתִי מֵהֶם – עַתָּה תִּפְדֶּה אֶת עַצְמָהּ, וְאִם יֶחְסַר – אֲנִי לֹא אַשְׁלִים. כָּתַב לָהּ פֵּירוֹת כְּסוּת וְכֵלִים. פָּסַק לָהּ הָאָב בִּנְדוּנְיָיתָהּ שֶׁמַּכְנִיס לְבַעְלָהּ מִטַּלְטְלִין, כְּגוֹן פֵּירוֹת תְּלוּשִׁין וּכְסוּת וְכֵלִים, וּכְתָבָן לָהּ מִן הָאֵירוּסִין. וּמֵתָה. בָּאֵירוּסִין – לֹא זָכָה כו'. לֵימָא בִּפְלוּגְתָּא כו'. דְּמ"ד בַּעְלָהּ יוֹרֵשׁ נְדוּנְיָיתָהּ מִן הָאֵירוּסִין – כְּרַבָּנַן, דְּאָמְרִי: אִם מֵת הוּא – גּוֹבָה אֶת הַכֹּל: מָנֶה, מָאתַיִם, וְתוֹסֶפֶת. אַלְמָא, כְּתוּבָּתָהּ קַיְימָא כְּאִילּוּ נִישֵּׂאת. אִם מֵתָה אִיהִי – נַמִי יָרֵית אִיהוּ נְדוּנְיָא, שֶׁאַף הִיא בְּתוֹךְ הַשְּׁטָר נִכְתְּבָה, דְּהָכִי כָּתְבִינַן: דָּא נְדוּנְיָא דְּהַנְעֲלַת לֵיהּ מִבֵּי אֲבוּהָ, כָּךְ וְכָךְ, וּצְבִי וְאוֹסִיף לָהּ מִדִּילֵיהּ כָּךְ וְכָךְ.

מ"ד

תוספות

משום איבה. פירש בקונטרס: כיון דאינו חייב במזונותיה, אי אמרת מציאתה לעצמה – איכא איבה, ולא זיין לה. ולר"י נראה. איבה דמציאתה – היינו שלא יקדשנה למנוול ומוכה שחין. והא דאמרינן בפ"ק דב"מ (דף יב: ושם) גבי מציאת בנו ובתו הקטנים: לא קטן קטן ממש, אלא גדול וסמוך על שולחן אביו זהו קטן, קטן ואינו סמוך על שולחן אביו זהו גדול – היינו דווקא בקטן, אבל בקטנה, אפילו אינה סמוכה על שולחן אביה – הרי מציאתה לאב משום איבה, שלא יקדשנה למנוול ומוכה שחין. ולשמואל דאמר התם: קטן קטן ממש אפי' אין סמוך על שולחן אביו, משום דבשעה שמוצאה מריצה אצל אביו – צ"ל לפ"ה *דמתני' דהתם לנדדין קתני: קטנה אפילו באינה סמוכה, נערה בסמוכה. וגדול הסמוך על שולחן אביו הוי מציאתו לעצמו, לשמואל, דליכא למיחש כולי האי לאיבה בבנים כמו בבנות, דזילא בהו מילתא לחזר על הפתחים. אבל קשה לפ"ה: דפשיטא ליה לעיל* דמציאתה לאחר מיתת האב לעצמה, אע"ג דניזונית מן האחין! ומה שפירש בקונטרס לעיל דלהכי פשיטא ליה דלעצמה דלא שייך בהו איבה, כיון דבעל כרחייהו מיתזנא – אין נראה לרשב"א, דשייך איבה אפילו היכא דקא מיתזנא בעל כרחייהו, שלא יטריחוה כל שעה לב"ד במזונות, כדמוכח לקמן בפרק "אלמנה" (דף נה: ושם) דאלמנה מעשה ידיה ליתומים, אע"ג דבעל כרחייהו מיתזנא, ומעשה ידיה אינן של בעל אלא משום איבה, כדאמר בפרק "אע"פ" (לקמן דף נח:): מזוני עיקר, ומעשה ידיה משום איבה. ולפי' ר"י ניחא. ואע"ג דמציאת אשה לבעלה אינה אלא משום איבה *ואמר בפרק "אלמנה" (לקמן דף נו.) דגבי יתומים תיהוי ליה איבה ואיבה, ההיא איבה לאו משום מזונות הוא, דלא דמיא למעשה ידיה, אלא איבה דקטטה, ובקטטה דידה ודיתומין והבת עם האחים – לא חיישינן, כיון דליכא איבה דמזונות. ועוד נראה לר"י: דמציאתה דומיא דקידושיה, דהוי דאב אפילו אינה סמוכה על שולחנו, ומעשה ידיה נמי אפילו אינה סמוכה – הויא העדפה דאב.

דזכי ליה רחמנא לאב למימסרה לחופה. פריש בקונטרס: דכתיב "את בתי נתתי". ואע"ג דקרא כשהיתה קטנה, כדפרישית לעיל, אלא דבלאו הכי פריך שפיר. ועי"ל: דהא דפריך לעיל ה"מ קטנה – משום דאכתי לא קים לן שיהא לאב שום כח בנערה, אבל השתא דכבר למד שיש לה כח לקדשה – תו לית לן לאוקמא קרא בקטנה דווקא. ולפ"ה דלעיל דזינתה אחר החופה לא הויא בסקילה – ע"כ חופה הויא בנערות, מדנסקלה על זנות בית אביה. ול"ע: אמאי לא גמרינן קידושין מחופה? **דמסר** לה בשבתות וי"ט. אע"ג דאמר במו"ק (דף ח: ושם) "ושמחת בחגך" ולא באשתך, דאין נושאים נשים בחולו של מועד, משום דאין מערבין שמחה בשמחה, ודרשה גמורה היא, כדאמר בחגיגה (דף ח: ושם) דהוי מדאורייתא – איכא למימר דהכא איירי שעה אחת לפני יו"ט, שהוא כיו"ט לענין מלאכה, דתוספת דאורייתא, ובטילה באותה שעה מן המלאכה. א"נ: כשמסרה האב לשלוחי הבעל, או נשואין בלא סעודה. אע"ג דאמר ב"החולץ" (יבמות דף מג: ושם) דנשואין בלא סעודה איכא שמחה – לא חשיבא שמחה כולי האי שיהא אסור לישא ביו"ט מטעם זה. **השתא** זבוני מזבן לה כו' כי איצטריך קרא לנערה. הקשה ה"ר יעקב מאורלינ"ש: דאמאי איצטריך בערכין (דף כט:) למילף מק"ו דאין אדם יכול למכור את בתו כשהיא נערה, דהשתא מכורה כבר יוצאה, שאינה מכורה אינו דין שלא תמכר – תיפוק ליה מהכא דאין יכול למוכרה מדאיצטריך "לאמה", דאי יכול למוכרה – מה צריך קרא? פשיטא דהשתא זבוני מזבן לה מעשה כו'! ושמעתי בשם מורי הר"ס: דמהכא נמי לא ידעינן אלא מכח ק"ו דהשתא זבוני מזבין לה. ולי נראה: דאי לאו ק"ו דהתם – ה"א דמצי מזבן לה, והוה דרשינן מ"לאמה" דמעשה ידיה לאביה, אפי' בבוגרת*. **כתב** לה פירות כסות וכלים. לאמי דמוקי בקונטרס הך ברייתא מן האירוסין, הא דקתני לקמן הלכו שלוחי האב עם שלוחי הבעל כו' מתה אביה יורשה – אתיא כרבנן. ומיהו, בנישואין כ"ע מודו, כדקתני בסיפא דההיא. ואין נראה לר"ת: דאי מן האירוסין – למה קבעה אמתני' דהכא דאיירי בנישאת? ועוד: אמאי זכה לרבי נתן? הא קתני שכתב (א) שיבואו עמה מבית אביה לבית בעלה, והא לא באו! ועוד: דמסיק אבל הכא משום איתתוני הוא, ואי באירוסין – אירוסין לא הוי קרי איתון, אלא איקרובי דעתא, כדלקמן בריש "אע"פ" (דף נו.). ואע"ג דבפרק "הנושא" (לקמן דף קב.) קאמר גבי כמה אתה נותן לבתך כך וכך וכו' דאיירי באירוסין: בההיא הנאה דאיתתני אהדדי גמרי ומקנו באמירה – יש לומר דה"פ: בההיא הנאה שיבואו לבסוף לידי איתון נשואין – גמרי ומקנו אהדדי אף בשעת אירוסין. ונראה לר"ת: דהך ברייתא בנשואין מיירי, וטעמא דלא זכה לתנא קמא – משום דאנן סהדי דאין דעת האב ליתן נדוניא זו אלא ע"מ שתהנה בתו ממנה כמו הבעל. ולרבי נתן לית ליה אומדנא, וזכה הבעל. וקאמר: לימא דבפלוגתא דרבי אלעזר ורבנן קמיפלגי, דמ"ד לא זכה – כרבי אלעזר, ואע"ג דההוא דר"א באירוסין והכא בנישואין – מכל מקום מדמה להו, כי היכי דאזיל ר' אלעזר בתר אומדנא, דלא כתב אלא על מנת לכונסה – ה"נ אזיל בתר אומדנא שלא כתב אלא על מנת שתהנה בתו. ולבתר הכי קאמר למ"ד זכה, דעד כאן לא קאמר ר"א אלא מדידיה לדידה, דלא אקני לה אלא ע"מ לכונסה – משום חיבת חופה, אבל מדידיה לדידיה אפי' ר"א מודה דדי לנו באומדנא של איתון נישואין, אע"ג דאיכא תו אומדנא אחרינא – די לנו באומדנא זו, כיון

דהוי

לעיל מ: [מו:] קדושין ג:
[קדושין יג. וש"נ]
[שם ה. וש"נ]
לקמן נג: פט: ב"מ יז:
[דף מג.]

גי' מהרש"א דמתני' דהתם הוי לנדדין וכצ"ל

[ובירושלמי אמר טעם אחר שלא תגנוב מכל בעלה ותאמר מאבא. ת"י]

הגהות הב"ח

(א) תוס' ד"ה כתב וכו' הא קתני שכתב לה שיבואו:

גליון הש"ס

גמ' דמסר לה בשבתות ויו"ט. קשה לי הא מ"מ שייך ביטול מלאכה דהא יכולה לעשות דברים המותרים לחתוך תלוש ולשמור פירות וכדומה דהא שכר שבת ליכא דרלה לאיסורא דאורייתא וצ"ע.

ובזה מיתרלא פירכא אחריתא דאמאי אילטריך אין כסף וילאה חנם חד לבוגרת וחד לנערות לכתוב חד וע"כ מוקמינן לנערות דאי לבוגרת אמאי אילטריך לאמה אלא ע"כ דהוי מוקמינן לה לבוגרת והוי דרשינן מלאמה למעשה ידיה דבוגרת לאב ויש מפרשים דאי לאו ק"ו דערכין ה"א דמצי מזבין לה ולאמה אילטריך לנערה שנתארסה ונתגרשה שאינו יכול למוכרה דכיון שפירש טליתו עליה דהייט קדושין שוב אינו יכול למוכרה והקשה ה"ר ידידיה מנירינבורק אמאי אילטריך ק"ו ע"כ לא מצי מזבן נערה דאי מצי מזבן אמאי אילטריך לאמה דע"כ לנערה אילטריך ולא לנתארסה ונתגרשה מדאילטריך בבגדו בה ומיהו אין זה כל כך פשוט לכך נקיט ק"ו דהתם בפשיטות:

תוספות רי"ד

זכאי במציאתה משום איבה. פי' ואע"ג דכל זכותא דמתני' יליף מקראי מציאתה אינה אלא תקנתא דרבנן ומבנעוריה לא מצי למילף דבפ' אלו נערות בעי למילף בושת ופגם וצער שהם של אב מבנעוריה בית אביה ואקשינן אלא הא דאמר ר"ה א"ר מניין שמעשה הבת לאב שנאמר וכי ימכור תיפוק ליה מבנעוריה בית אביה אלא ההיא בהפרת נדריה הוא דכתיב. וכ"ת ילפינן מיניה ממונא מאיסורא לא ילפינן ובשני' אוחזין תנן מציאות בנו ובתו הקטנים הרי אלו שלו ומציאות בנו ובתו הגדולים הרי אלו שלהן ואמרי' התם לא קטן קטן ממש ולא גדול גדול ממש אלא כל שסומך על שלחן אביו קורא קטן ואע"פ שהוא גדול בשנים וכל שאינו סמוך על שלחן אביו קורא גדול ואע"פ שהוא קטן בשנים: ואינו אוכל פירות וכו'. ת"ר האב אינו אוכל פירות בחיי בתו. ר"י בר"י אומר האב אוכל פירות בחיי בתו במאי קמיפלגי ת"ק סבר בשלמא בעל תקינו ליה רבנן פירות דאם תשתבי ממנע ולא פריק לה אלא אב מא"ל מימנע ולא פריק. בלא"ה נמי פריק לה. פי' רחם עלה ור"י בר"י סבר ה"מ היכא דל"ל אבל היכא דא"ל (מימנע ולא פריק לה) אב נמי מימנע ולא פריק לה אמר כיסא נקיטא לה תיזיל ותפרוק נפשה. פי' סגולה יש לה מן הנכנסים שנפלו לה והלכתא כת"ק: נשאת יותר וכו'. ת"ר כתב לה פירות כסות וכלים שיבואו עמה מבית אביה לבית בעלה ומתה לא זכה הבעל בדברים הללו. משום ר"נ אמרו זכה הבעל בדברים הללו. (והרב מפרש שאם מתה אחר שנשאת אע"פ שהנכנסים בבית אביה זכה בהן הבעל כדמוכח לקמן בהלכתין גבי מסר האב לשלוחי הבעל שאפי' מסרה להם ומתה זכה הבעל לירש נכסי נדוניתה ואפי' הן בבית אביה ולא באו ליד הבעל והכא מיירי כגון שמתה מן האירוסין ועדיין לא נשאת ומש"ה לא זכה בהן הבעל אליבא דת"ק) פי' דאביה כתב ליתן לה מטלטלים בנדוניא ולא הספיק לחתם לה עד שמתה וכבר נשאת אע"פ שהבעל יורש את אשתו וכל נכסי נדוניתה הן שלו כיון שעדיין לא הספיק האב ליתן לבתו ולא באו לידה עד שמתה אין הבעל יורשה דאדעתיה דהכי קיבל אנפשיה שיתנם לבתו ולא לבעלה ור"נ היה אומר זכה כיון שכתב עליו ליתנן ה"ה ככל נכסי נדוניתה והלכתא כת"ק ואילו זקפן עליו במלוה ולא כתב לשם מוהר אלא כתב לו שחייב כך וכך זכה בהן רכאילו נתנן לו דמי:

עין משפט
נר מצוה

מח א מיי׳ פכ״ג מהל׳ אישות טוש״ע אה״ע סי׳ נג סעי׳ ג בהג״ה:
מט ב מיי׳ פי״ב מהל׳ אישות הל׳ ב סמג עשין מח ולאוין פא טוש״ע שם סימן סט סעי׳ ב:

שֶׁלֹּא כָּתַב לָהּ אֶלָּא עַל מְנָת לְכוֹנְסָהּ. [א]לְמַאן דְּאָמַר לֹא זָכָה — כְּרַבִּי אֶלְעָזָר בֶּן עֲזַרְיָה, וּמַאן דְּאָמַר זָכָה — כְּרַבָּנַן. לֹא, דְּכוּלֵּי עָלְמָא כְּרַבִּי אֶלְעָזָר בֶּן עֲזַרְיָה. מַאן דְּאָמַר לֹא זָכָה — כְּרַבִּי אֶלְעָזָר בֶּן עֲזַרְיָה, וּמַאן דְּאָמַר זָכָה — עַד כָּאן לָא קָאָמַר רַבִּי אֶלְעָזָר בֶּן עֲזַרְיָה אֶלָּא מִדִּידֵיהּ לְדִידָהּ, שֶׁלֹּא כָּתַב לָהּ אֶלָּא עַל מְנָת לְכוֹנְסָהּ. אֲבָל מִדִּידָהּ לְדִידֵיהּ — אֲפִילּוּ ר׳ אֶלְעָזָר בֶּן עֲזַרְיָה מוֹדֵי דְּמִשּׁוּם אִיחַתּוּנֵי הוּא, וְהָא אִיחַתְּנֵי לְהוּ. § חַיָּיב בִּמְזוֹנוֹתֶיהָ וכו׳. § תָּנוּ רַבָּנַן: *תִּיקְּנוּ מְזוֹנוֹתֶיהָ תַּחַת מַעֲשֵׂה יָדֶיהָ, *וּקְבוּרָתָהּ תַּחַת כְּתוּבָּתָהּ. לְפִיכָךְ בַּעַל אוֹכֵל פֵּירוֹת. פֵּירוֹת מַאן דְּכַר שְׁמַיְיהוּ?! חַסּוֹרֵי מִחַסְּרָא, וְהָכִי קָתָנֵי: תִּיקְּנוּ מְזוֹנוֹתֶיהָ תַּחַת מַעֲשֵׂה יָדֶיהָ, וּפִירְקוֹנָהּ תַּחַת פֵּירוֹת, וּקְבוּרָתָהּ תַּחַת כְּתוּבָּתָהּ. לְפִיכָךְ בַּעַל אוֹכֵל פֵּירוֹת. מַאי לְפִיכָךְ? מַהוּ דְּתֵימָא: מֵיכַל לָא נִכְלִינְהוּ, אַנּוֹחֵי — נְנַחִינְהוּ, דְּאִם כֵּן מִימְנַע וְלָא פָּרֵיק, קמ״ל דְּהָא עֲדִיפָא, זִימְנִין דְּלָא מָלוּ וּפָרֵיק לָהּ מִדִּידֵיהּ. וְאֵיפוֹךְ אֲנָא! אָמַר אַבַּיֵי: תִּיקְּנוּ *מָצוּי לְמָצוּי, וְשֶׁאֵינוֹ מָצוּי לְשֶׁאֵינוֹ מָצוּי. אָמַר רָבָא: הַאי תַּנָּא סָבַר מְזוֹנוֹת מִדְּאוֹרַיְיתָא, דְּתַנְיָא: °״שְׁאֵרָהּ״ — [ב]אֵלּוּ מְזוֹנוֹת, וְכֵן הוּא אוֹמֵר: °״וַאֲשֶׁר אָכְלוּ שְׁאֵר עַמִּי״. ״כְּסוּתָהּ״ — כְּמַשְׁמָעוֹ. ״עוֹנָתָהּ״ — זוֹ עוֹנָה, הָאֲמוּרָה בַּתּוֹרָה, וְכֵן הוּא אוֹמֵר: °״אִם תְּעַנֶּה אֶת בְּנוֹתַי״. רַבִּי אֶלְעָזָר אוֹמֵר: ״שְׁאֵרָהּ״ — זוֹ עוֹנָה, וְכֵן הוּא אוֹמֵר: °״אִישׁ אִישׁ אֶל כָּל שְׁאֵר בְּשָׂרוֹ לֹא תִקְרְבוּ לְגַלּוֹת עֶרְוָה״. ״כְּסוּתָהּ״ — כְּמַשְׁמָעוֹ. ״עוֹנָתָהּ״ אֵלּוּ מְזוֹנוֹת, וְכֵן הוּא אוֹמֵר: °״וַיְעַנְּךָ וַיַּרְעִבֶךָ״.
רַבִּי

רש״י

מ״ד לֹא זָכָה כְּרַבִּי אֶלְעָזָר. דְּאָמַר: לֹא כָּתַב לָהּ כְּתוּבָּה אֶלָּא עַל מְנָת לְכוֹנְסָהּ. וּמָנֶה מָאתַיִם דְּתַקִּינוּ לָהּ רַבָּנַן הוּא דְּאִית לָהּ. אִיהִי נַמִי לָא כָּתְבָה לוֹ ״וְדָא נְדוּנְיָא דְּהַנְעֲלַת לֵיהּ״ אֶלָּא ע״מ חִיבַּת נִשּׂוּאִין. כ״ע כְּר״א בֶּן עֲזַרְיָה. תַּרְוַיְיהוּ הָנָךְ תַּנָּאֵי דִּלְעֵיל (תַּרְוַיְיהוּ) כְּר״א בֶּן עֲזַרְיָה, דְּפָסְקִינַן הִלְכְתָא כְּוָותֵיהּ לְקַמָּן. מִדִּידֵיהּ לְדִידָהּ. מַה שֶּׁחָתָן פּוֹסֵק לַכַּלָּה בִּכְתוּבָּתָהּ. תַּחַת כְּתוּבָּתָהּ. תַּחַת הַנְּדוּנְיָא שֶׁהִכְנִיסָה לוֹ, וְהִיא כְּתוּבָה בִּשְׁטַר הַכְּתוּבָּה, וְהוּא יוֹרֵשׁ. תַּחַת פֵּירוֹת. שֶׁהוּא אוֹכֵל מִנִּכְסֵי מְלוֹג שֶׁלָּהּ, כְּגוֹן נְכָסִים שֶׁנָּפְלוּ לָהּ מִשֶּׁנִּישֵּׂאת, אוֹ שֶׁהָיוּ לָהּ קוֹדֶם לָכֵן, שֶׁלֹּא שָׁמְּתָה לוֹ בִּנְדוּנְיַית כְּתוּבָּתָהּ. דְּלָא מָלוּ. לֹא יְהֵא בַּפֵּירוֹת כְּדֵי פִּרְקוֹנָהּ. וְהַשְׁתָּא, כִּי אַכְלִינְהוּ וְלָא יָדַע כַּמָּה הֲוָה — פָּרֵיק לָהּ מִדִּילֵיהּ, דְּהָכִי תִּיקּוּן, דְּאִיהוּ אָכֵיל בֵּין רַב בֵּין מְעַט, וְהוּא פָּרֵיק כָּל כַּמָּה דְּהָוֵי. וְאֵיפוֹךְ אֲנָא. מְזוֹנוֹת תַּחַת פֵּירוֹת, וּפִרְקוֹנָהּ תַּחַת מַעֲשֵׂה יָדֶיהָ. וְנָפְקָא מִינָּהּ, דְּאִי אָמְרָה אֵינִי נִיזּוֹנֵית וְאֵינִי עוֹשָׂה — לָא כְּלוּם קָאָמְרָה: מְזוֹנוֹת וּמַעֲשֵׂה יָדֶיהָ מְצוּיִן, שֶׁבְּכׇל יוֹם. וְאִשָּׁה שֶׁיֵּשׁ לָהּ נִכְסֵי מְלוֹג — לָא שְׁכִיחִי.
עוֹנָה

תוספות

דהוי מדידה לדידיה. ולא דמי להכיא דר״א דהוי מדידיה לדידה, ואי הוה שייך התם אומדנא אחרינא הוה אמדינן. ופסק רבינו תם, וכן רבינו חננאל כרבנן דרבי נתן, משום דמוקמינן להו כר״א בן עזריה, דפסקינן הילכתא כוותיה בפרק ״אע״פ״ (לקמן דף נו.). ואע״ג דדחי התלמוד: לא, דכולי עלמא כר׳ אלעזר — דיחויא בעלמא הוא, ואדיחויא לא סמכינן. והורה ר״ת הלכה למעשה בחתן אחד שמתה אשתו, והיה אבי הכלה מוחזק בנדוניא, ופסק לה דלא זכה הבעל, מכח שמעתין דהכא. ועוד תיקן, לא מכח ההלכה, שאפי׳ בעל מוחזק — שיחזיר אם מתה בתוך שנה. וחזר בו בסוף ימיו מאותה תקנה. והא דאמרינן בפ׳ ״מציאת האשה״ (לקמן דף סו.): הפוסק מעות לחתנו ומת חתנו — יכול הוא שיאמר: לאחיך הייתי רוצה ליתן, לך אי אפשי ליתן. ופריך בירושלמי: ולא דברים הניקנין באמירה הן? ומשני: כשפסק על מנת לכנוס, דמשמע הא אם כנס גופה אחיו — לא קשה מידי לפירוש רבינו תם, דהתם הרי בתו קיימת, והיבם רוצה ליבמה. והא דאמרינן בתורת כהנים: ״ותם לריק כחכם״ — זה שפוסק לבתו ממון מרובה ומתה בתוך שבעת ימי המשתה הרי הפסיד בתו והפסיד ממונו! ההיא אתיא כרבי נתן. א״נ כרבנן, ומיירי שהחתן מוחזק בה. וצריך עיון שלא יקשה לרבינו תם, דלקמן בריש ״אע״פ״ (דף נו.) מוכח דרבנן נמי אזלי בתר אומדנא דמימון. ועוד דחוק קצת לרבינו תם: דמה לו להזכיר מדידיה לדידה ומדידה לדידיה? הל״ל ע״כ לא קאמר רבי אלעזר אלא משום דלא נישאת, אבל הכא דנישאת — לא! ועוד: דכולהו אמוראי דלקמן משמע דאית להו דבעל יורשה משמסרה האב לשלוחי הבעל! ושמא היינו כשהכתובה ביד הבעל, וברייתא דקתני התם לקמן אע״פ שכתובתה בבית אביה בעלה יורשה — אתיא כרבי נתן*.

שלא כתב לה אלא על מנת לכונסה. אין לתמוה בסברא זאת, דבכמה מקומות בתלמוד מצינו כן. ואם תאמר: אם כן, כל אדם הלוקח פרה מחבירו, ונטרפה או מתה, אנן סהדי שלא על מנת כן לקחה! וי״ל: דהתם אנן סהדי שבאותו ספק היה רוצה ליכנס, ואפי׳ אם אומר לו אם תטרף יש לך לקבל הפסד — היה לוקחה. אבל הכא לא כתב כלל כי אם ע״מ לכונסה, ואין דעתו כלל להכניס עצמו בספק. וכן *ההוא דזבין ולא אידטריכו ליה זוזי. והא דפריך בסוף ״הגוזל קמא״ (ב״ק דף קי*:): (א) יבמה שנפלה לפני מוכה שחין תיפוק בלא חליצה, דאדעתא דהכי לא קידשה. אע״ג דבאותו ספק מסתמא היתה נכנסת בשעת קדושין! אומר רבינו יצחק: דלא פריך התם אלא משום דהוי דומיא דקאמר התם, נתן כסף לאנשי משמר ומת, שהוא שלהם. ומסיק התם: ש״מ כסף מכפר מחלה, דאי לא מכפר — לימא דאדעתא דהכי לא יהיב, דהואיל ואינו תלוי אלא בנותן יש לנו ללכת אחר דעתו, וכיון שבו תלוי — ודאי אינו רוצה ליכנס בשום ספק. ולא דמי ללוקח חפץ ואירע בו אונס, דלא אמרינן דאדעתא דהכי לא קנה ומבטל המקח — דאינו תלוי בדעת הקונה לבדו, דהא איכא נמי דעת מקנה שלא היה מקנה לו לדעתו אם לא יפרע, להכי פריך שפיר מיבמה שנפלה לפני מוכה שחין, משום דבדידה תלוין הקידושין, שברור לנו שהוא לא יעכב בשביל שום דבר שאירע אחר מיתתו — כי אינו חושש במה שאירע אחריו. ולהכי לא פריך מאשה שנעשה בעלה בעל מום: תיפוק בלא גט, דאדעתא דהכי לא קידשה נפשה! כיון דתלוי נמי בדעת המקדש. וכן כל הנהו דמייתי התם אין תלוי אלא בדעתו. **תיקנו** מזונות תחת מעשה ידיה. בפ׳ ״אע״פ״ (לקמן נח: ושם) דקאמר רב הונא: יכולה אשה שתאמר לבעלה איני ניזונית ואיני עושה, קסבר: כי תקינו רבנן מזוני עיקר כו׳. ופריך מהכא ומשני: אימא תקנו מעשה ידיה תחת מזונות. והשתא, ריש לקיש דפליג עליה התם ואמר מעשה ידיה עיקר, אינו מגיה ברייתא דהכא, אלא שונה: תיקנו מזונות תחת מעשה ידיה. ולכאורה, לדידיה יכול הבעל לומר לאשתו צאי מעשה ידיך למזונותיך ואע״ג דלא ספקה, כיון דקסבר דמעשה ידיה עיקר. אבל אי אפשר לומר כן, כדמוכח בריש ״המדיר״ (לקמן דף ע:) ובפ״ק דגיטין (דף יב.) דבלא ספקה חייב לזונה! וצ״ל: דלא אמר ריש לקיש דמעשה ידיה עיקר אלא לענין שאינה יכולה לומר ״איני ניזונית ואיני עושה״. **וקבורתה** תחת כתובתה. פירוש: נדונייתה. אבל אין לפרש תחת מנה ומאתים, דהא אמר לקמן (דף נג.*) דארוסה אין לה קבורה: **אנוחי** ננחינהו. פירוש: עד שלא יהא לו במה להתפרנס, ואז יקחם. אבל לא בעי למימר דלעולם לינחינהו, דא״כ מאי תחת פירות דקתני? הא אין לו פירות! **זימנין** דלא מלו ופריק לה מדידיה. אע״ג דעיקר תקנה בשביל דידה, כדמשמע הכא. וכן לעיל, דקאמר: בשלמא בעלה תקינו ליה פירי, דלמא אשתבאי וממנע ולא פריק לה, מ״מ אינה יכולה לומר איני נפדית ואיני נותנת פירות, דהא קתני בברייתא: פירקונה תחת פירות, משמע דאינה יכולה לומר. כי היכי דדייק לקמן דאינה יכולה אשה שתאמר איני ניזונת כו׳ מברייתא דלעיל, דקתני תיקנו מזונות תחת מעשה ידיה — אלמא דאין יכולה, והוצרך להגיה הברייתא בשביל כך. ועוד דב״חזקת הבתים״ (ב״ב דף מט. ושם) וב״הזורק״ בגיטין (דף עז. ושם) לא מצי לאשכוחי שיהא חצר לאשה בלא בעלה, דפריך: חצרה — מה שקנתה אשה קנה בעלה! ומוקי בכותב לה דין ודברים אין לי בנכסייך. וכי כתב לה מאי הוי, והתניא כו׳, ומשני: בכותב לה ועודה ארוסה. והשתא מאי דוחקין לאוקמא הכי? לימא כגון שאמרה ״איני נפדית ואיני נותנת פירות״! ואע״ג דהוה נמי מצי לאוקמא כגון שנתנו לה על מנת שאין לבעלה רשות בה, ולא קאמר — היינו משום דאין יורד לסברא זו, אבל כבר ירד לסברא שהבעל מסתלק מנכסים — א״כ לימא כגון שאמרה איני נפדית כו׳. אלא ודאי אינה יכולה לומר. ויש ליתן טעם, אע״ג דלרב הונא יכולה אשה שתאמר לבעלה איני ניזונית כו׳ — התם משום דאינה מפקעת לגמרי התקנה, שאם אמרה היום איני ניזונת ואיני עושה — למחר תעשה ותהא ניזונית. אבל אם אמרה איני נפדית ואיני נותנת פירות — הרי מפקעת לגמרי תקנת פירות, דהא פירות של כל ימיה הם תחת פרקונה. ואפילו את״ל דיכולה לומר איני ניזונית ואיני עושה לעולם — אכתי יש לומר דלא מצי אמרה איני נפדית — שלא תטמע בין הגוים. א״נ: שאני פירות, דידו כידה וזוכה בגוף הקרקע. אבל מעשה ידיה אינם בעין, דלא שייך למימר שיזכה בגוף הידים. **אם** תענה את בנותי. ואם תאמר: לאדרבה, מהאי קרא משמע דעונתה לאו היינו עונה של תשמיש, דבפרק בתרא דיומא (דף עז.) משמע ״אם תענה את בנותי״ — היינו שימנע מהן תשמיש, דמהאי קרא נפקא לן דמניעת תשמיש המטה קרוי עינוי! ויש לומר: דה״נ קאמר קרא, ״עונתה לא יגרע״ — דבר שהוא כעינוי כשמונעו ממנה, דהיינו תשמיש.
רבי

[לקמן נז.]
[ע״ש תוס׳ ד״ה לאדעתיה]

תוספות רי״ד
וחייב במזונותיה וכו׳: ת״ר תקנו מזונות תחת מעשה ידיה וקבורתה תחת כתובתה ופרקונה תחת פירות ואמר רבא האי תנא סבר מזונות דאורייתא דתניא שארה כסותה ועונתה לא יגרע שארה אלו מזונות וכה״א אשר אכלו שאר עמי כסות כמשמעה עונה זו עונה האמורה בתורה וכה״א אם תענה את בנותי:

מסורת הש״ס

תורה אור

לקמן נח: נט.
[בשאלתות איתא ופירקונה]
[ע׳ תוס׳ לקמן נב. ד״ה רלה]
שמות כא
מיכה ג
בראשית לא
ויקרא יח
דברים ח

ולריצב״א נראה מ[...] קושיות אלו דפי׳ הקונט[רס] עיקר והא דקבעי אמת[...] משום דלרבנן לא ז[...] משום דלא נשאת ו[...] דקתני שיבואו עמה [...] שכתוב בשטר כן א[...] נתינת טעם הוא למיל[...] דת״ק דטעם דלא זכה [...] שלא כתב אלא על מ[...] שיבואו עמה לבית בע[...] ולישנא דאחתוני הוי כ[...] הנושא דכתיב לא תתר[...] בה. גליון

[ושם ד״ה שאין]

הגהות הב״ח
(א) תום׳ ד״ה שלא [...] הגוזל קמא אלא מט[...] יבמה שנפלה:

גליון הש״ס
תום׳ ד״ה זמנין וכו׳ [...] שאני פירות. עיין גיטין ע״ב תד״ה ידה: ד״ה [...] וכו׳ וא״ת לאדרבה ו[...] עיין בדרשות הרא״נ״ח שמות:

רַבִּי אֱלִיעֶזֶר בֶּן יַעֲקֹב אוֹמֵר: "שְׁאֵרָהּ כְּסוּתָהּ" — לְפוּם שְׁאֵרָהּ תֵּן כְּסוּתָהּ. שֶׁלֹּא יִתֵּן לָהּ לֹא שֶׁל יַלְדָּה לִזְקֵנָה, וְלֹא שֶׁל זְקֵנָה לְיַלְדָּה. "כְּסוּתָהּ וְעוֹנָתָהּ" — לְפוּם עוֹנָתָהּ תֵּן כְּסוּתָהּ, [א]שֶׁלֹּא יִתֵּן חֲדָשִׁים בִּימוֹת הַחַמָּה וְלֹא שְׁחָקִים בִּימוֹת הַגְּשָׁמִים.§ תָּנֵי רַב יוֹסֵף: "שְׁאֵרָהּ" — זוֹ קֵרוּב בָּשָׂר, שֶׁלֹּא יִנְהַג בָּהּ מִנְהַג פַּרְסִיִּים, שֶׁמְּשַׁמְּשִׁין מִטּוֹתֵיהֶן בִּלְבוּשֵׁיהֶן. מְסַיֵּיעַ לֵיהּ לְרַב הוּנָא, דְּאָמַר רַב הוּנָא: [ב]הָאוֹמֵר "אִי אֶפְשִׁי אֶלָּא אֲנִי בְּבִגְדִי וְהִיא בְּבִגְדָהּ" — יוֹצִיא וְנוֹתֵן כְּתוּבָּה.§ רַבִּי יְהוּדָה אוֹמֵר: אֲפִילּוּ עָנִי שֶׁבְּיִשְׂרָאֵל וכו'.§ מִכְּלָל דְּת"ק סָבַר הָנֵי לָא. הֵיכִי דָּמֵי? אִי דְּאוֹרְחָהּ — מ"ט דְּת"ק דְּאָמַר לָא? וְאִי דְּלָאו אוֹרְחָהּ — מ"ט דְּר"י? לָא צְרִיכָא, *כְּגוֹן דְּאוֹרְחֵיהּ דִּידֵיהּ וְלָאו אוֹרְחָהּ דִּידָהּ. ת"ק סָבַר: כִּי אָמְרִינַן *עוֹלָה עִמּוֹ וְאֵינָהּ יוֹרֶדֶת עִמּוֹ — הָנֵי מִילֵּי מֵחַיִּים, אֲבָל לְאַחַר מִיתָה — לָא. וְרַבִּי יְהוּדָה סָבַר: אֲפִילּוּ לְאַחַר מִיתָה. אָמַר רַב חִסְדָּא אָמַר מָר עוּקְבָא: הֲלָכָה כְּרַבִּי יְהוּדָה. וְאָמַר רַב חִסְדָּא אָמַר מָר עוּקְבָא: [ג]מִי שֶׁנִּשְׁתַּטָּה — בֵּית דִּין יוֹרְדִין לִנְכָסָיו, וְזָנִין וּמְפַרְנְסִין אֶת אִשְׁתּוֹ [ד]וּבָנָיו וּבְנוֹתָיו וְדָבָר אַחֵר. א"ל רָבִינָא לְרַב אַשִׁי. מ"ש מֵהָא דְּתַנְיָא: *מִי שֶׁהָלַךְ לִמְדִינַת הַיָּם וְאִשְׁתּוֹ תּוֹבַעַת מְזוֹנוֹת — בֵּית דִּין יוֹרְדִין לִנְכָסָיו וְזָנִין וּמְפַרְנְסִין [ה]אֶת אִשְׁתּוֹ, אֲבָל לֹא בָּנָיו וּבְנוֹתָיו, וְלֹא דָּבָר אַחֵר! א"ל: וְלָא שָׁאנֵי לָךְ בֵּין יוֹצֵא לָדַעַת לְיוֹצֵא שֶׁלֹּא לָדַעַת? מַאי דָּבָר אַחֵר? רַב חִסְדָּא אָמַר: זֶה [ו]תַּכְשִׁיט. רַב יוֹסֵף אָמַר: [ז]צְדָקָה. מ"ד תַּכְשִׁיט — כ"ש צְדָקָה, מ"ד צְדָקָה — אֲבָל תַּכְשִׁיט יָהֲבִינַן לָהּ, דְּלָא נִיחָא לֵיהּ דְּתִתְנַוֵּול. אָמַר רַב חִיָּיא בַּר אָבִין אָמַר רַב הוּנָא: [ח]מִי שֶׁהָלַךְ לִמְדִינַת הַיָּם וּמֵתָה אִשְׁתּוֹ — ב"ד יוֹרְדִין לִנְכָסָיו, וְקוֹבְרִין אוֹתָהּ לְפִי כְּבוֹדוֹ. לְפִי כְּבוֹדוֹ וְלֹא לְפִי כְּבוֹדָהּ?! אֵימָא: [ט]אַף לְפִי כְּבוֹדוֹ. הָא קמ"ל: עוֹלָה עִמּוֹ וְאֵינָהּ יוֹרֶדֶת עִמּוֹ, וַאֲפִילּוּ לְאַחַר מִיתָה. אָמַר רַב מַתְּנָה: הָאוֹמֵר "אִם מֵתָה לֹא תִּקְבְּרוּהָ מִנְּכָסָיו" — שׁוֹמְעִין לוֹ. מ"ש כִּי אָמַר — דְּנָפְלֵי נִכְסֵי קַמֵּי יַתְמֵי, כִּי לָא אָמַר נַמִּי — נִכְסֵי קַמֵּי יַתְמֵי רָמוּ! אֶלָּא, [י]הָאוֹמֵר "אִם מֵת הוּא לֹא *תִּקְבְּרוּהוּ מִנְּכָסָיו" — אֵין שׁוֹמְעִין לוֹ, לָאו כָּל הֵימֶנּוּ שֶׁיַּעֲשִׁיר אֶת בָּנָיו, וְיַפִּיל עַצְמוֹ עַל הַצִּיבּוּר.§ **מתני'** לְעוֹלָם הִיא בִּרְשׁוּת הָאָב עַד שֶׁתִּכָּנֵס לִרְשׁוּת

רש"י

לעיל *עונה האמורה בתורה. כאן נאמרה עונת תשמיש. ולקמן (דף סא:) תנן אימת היא עונה. לפום שארה. זקינה קשה לה משאוי, ואינה יכולה לסבול בגדים רבים, וילדה צריכה בגדים רבים להתנאות בהם. לפום עונתה. לפי העת, אם חמה אם צנה. חדשים. חמים הם יותר מן השחקים. דאורחה. דרך בנות משפחתה בכך. מאי טעמא דתנא קמא. דאמר לא צריך. אורחיה. לבנות משפחתו עושין כן. עולה עמו ואינה יורדת עמו. מ"בעולת בעל" נפקא לן: בעלייתו של בעל, ולא בירידתו של בעל, בפרק "אף על פי" (שם). ה"מ מחיים. כגון: הוא אומר להניק את בנה והיא אומרת שלא להניק, ודרך בנות משפחתה להניק בניהם, ולא דרך משפחתו. ודבר אחר. לקמן מפרש. זנין. מזונות. מפרנסין. לבוש וכסות. אבל לא בניו ובנותיו. שאינו חייב במזונותיהן בחייו. ולא שאני לך כו'. יוצא מן המקום לדעת, היה בידו לצוות על מזונות בניו ובנותיו [לקמן סה.] ואשתו, ולא צוה – גילה דעתו שאינו [לקמן סא.] רוצה לזונן. הילכך, אשתו דמיחייב לה בתנאי כתובה – אשתעבוד ניכסיה; בניו ובנותיו – לא. אבל נשתטה, דיצא מן העולם שלא לדעת – מסתמא ניחא ליה שיזונו בניו ובנותיו משלו. תכשיט. בשמים של אבקת רוכל, שהנשים מתקשטות בהם. מ"ד תכשיט. לא יהבינן לאשתו, כ"ש שאין עלינו לעשות צדקה מנכסיו. [לקמן קז.] ואמתניתא קיימי. לא ניחא ליה דתיתנוול. אע"פ שלא צוה בלכתו – עבדינן. ולי נראה דאדמר עוקבא קיימי, דאמר: מי שנשתטה יורדין לנכסיו וזנין כו' וד"א. ואיפכא גרסינן: מ"ד צדקה – כ"ש תכשיט, ומ"ד תכשיט – אבל צדקה לא. התם היינו טעמא, דלא ניחא ליה דתיתנוול. לפי כבודו ולא לפי כבודה. בתמיה: מידי דאורחה ולאו אורחיה מי לא בעי למיעבד לה?! הא ודאי אינה יורדת עמו! ואפילו למאן דלית ליה עולה עמו לאחר מיתה – אינה יורדת אית ליה. האומר. בשעת מיתתו. אם מתה אשתו כו' שומעין לו. דכיון דהוא מת בחייה, והיא גובה כתובתה – אינו חייב לקוברה, דתנן (לקמן דף נה:): יורשיה, יורשי כתובתה, חייבין בקבורתה. נכסי קמי יתמי רמו. ופשיטא דאין קבורתה עליהם. [עיין תוס' בכורות נב: ד"ה כאן] אל תקברוהו מנכסיו. אלא מן הצדקה. **מתני'** לעולם היא ברשות האב. ואם בת ישראל מאורסה לכהן היא – אינה אוכלת בתרומה, וזכאי בה בכל זכות אב בבתו.

לרשות

תוספות

רבי אליעזר בן יעקב אומר שארה כסותה לפום שארה תן כסותה כו'. פירש רשב"ם: דרבי אליעזר בן יעקב סבר נמי דמזונות דאורייתא, דהכי מתניא סיפא דברייתא: מזונות מנין – אמרת ק"ו: ומה דברים שאין בהן קיום נפש כך, דברים שיש בהן קיום נפש, על אחת כמה וכמה. דרך ארץ מנין – אמרת קל וחומר: ומה דברים שלא נישאת עליהם לכתחילה, אינו רשאי למנוע ממנה, דברים שנישאת עליהם לכתחילה – אינו דין שאינו רשאי למנוע ממנה. ולפי זה תימה ברייתא דלעיל, דקתני: תיקנו מזונות תחת מעשה ידיה, דמשמע דמזונות דרבנן, כמאן אתיא! **דאורחיה** דידיה ולאו אורחה דידה. פי' בקונטרס: דאורחיה בבנות משפחתו, אבל אין דרך בבנות משפחתה. וקשה: דאמאי נקט שני חלילין ומקוננת אחת? הוה ליה למינקט לא יפחות לה מדרכו! ואומר רבינו תם: דאורחיה דידיה – היינו אפי' לעני שבישראל אין פוחתין משני חלילין ומקוננת. אבל לנקיבות – יש שפוחתין. וקאמר ר' יהודה לא יפחות משני חלילין, אע"ג דאם לא נישאת שמא היו פוחתין לה – כיון דנישאת לא יפחות לה, כמו שאין פוחתין לו. ומיהו, הלשון דחוק, דקאמר: כגון דאורחיה דידיה – משמע דאיכא דלאו אורחיה בהכי!

ולא שאני לך בין יוצא לדעת ליוצא שלא לדעת. לקמן בפ' בתרא (דף קז. ושם) דמוקי לה ההיא דמי שהלך למדינת הים כשהשרה אשתו ע"י שליש, אבל לא בניו ובנותיו, משמע דקודם שילא לא היה משרה אותם, אבל אם היה משרה אותם – גם אנו היינו זנין אותם, כיון דניחא ליה. ולפי זה צריך לומר, ההיא דמי שנשתטה דזנין בניו ובנותיו – אפי' לא היה משרה אותם מתחלה. ואין נראה לר"י: דאם לא השרה אותם מתחלה ע"י שליש ולא פירנסם – אמאי מפרנסין אותם? אלא ודאי איירי כשהיה מפרנסם קודם. וכן ההיא דמי שהלך למדינת הים, מדפריך מינה אההיא דנשתטה. ובפ' בתרא דמוקי לה במשרה אשתו על ידי שליש אבל לא בניו ובנותיו – היינו: בשעה שהלך הניח מעות ביד שליש לפרנס אשתו, ולא הניח לפרנס בניו. אבל קודם שהלך היו כולם ניזונין משלו. **הכי** גרסינן: מאי ולא דבר אחר. וגרסינן נמי: ומאן דאמר צדקה – אבל תכשיט יהבינן לה, דלא ניחא ליה דתינוול. לאההיא דמי שהלך איפליגו בה בהדיא בפרק בתרא (לקמן דף קז.). **תכשיט**. והא דאמר בפרק "המדיר" (לקמן דף עא:) פוסקין קישוטין לאשה – היינו כל זמן שהוא עמה, שלא תתגנה עליו. **מי** שהלך למדינת הים כו'. אית ספרים דגרסי: קוברין אותה לפי כבודה. לפי כבודה אין, לפי כבודו – לא?! אימא: אף לפי כבודה. ואין נראה: חדא, דאמאי נקט מי שהלך למדינת הים? אדרבה, טפי הוי רבותא דאפי' כשהוא אצלה דאינה יורדת עמו, וכ"ש כשאינו אצלה. ועוד: מאי אפי' לאחר מיתה דקאמר? אדרבה, טפי הוי רבותא בכחיים מלאחר מיתה! ועוד: דקאמר אימא אף לפי כבודה – אדרבה, לפי כבודו הוי רבותא טפי, דלא הוי אלא לר' יהודה. אבל לפי כבודה, דאינה יורדת עמו – לא הוי רבותא כולי האי! דהא לעיל פריך: אי דאורחה – מ"ט דת"ק? משמע דמילתא דפשיטא הוא! ונראה לר"ת דגרסינן: קוברין אותה לפי כבודו, לפי כבודו אין, לפי כבודה – לא?! אימא: אף לפי כבודו. אבל קשה לרשב"א: דאמאי קמתמה לפי כבודו ולא לפי כבודה? אמאי סלקא דעתיה דנקט לפי כבודו דוקא ולא לפי כבודה? **לעולם** היא ברשות האב עד שתכנס לחופה גרסינן. ול"ג עד שתכנס לרשות הבעל – דא"כ הוה משמע עד שימסור האב לשלוחי הבעל, כדמוכח בגמרא. דקאמר רב נחמן בר יצחק: אף אנן נמי תנינא הבא על אשת איש כו' לרשות הבעל בעלמא. ומתני' דהכא מוקמינן לה בגמרא לענין תרומה, לאפוקי ממשנה ראשונה. א"כ הויא תיובתא דרב, דאמר בגמרא: מסירתה לכל חוץ מלתרומה. ומיהו, י"ל: דהא דדייק רב נחמן בר יצחק בגמרא – היינו מדקתני כיון שנכנסה כו', לכך משמע ליה אפילו מסר. אבל הכא, דקתני: לעולם היא ברשות האב עד שתכנס לרשות הבעל, משמע שפיר דהיינו עד שתכנס לחופה.

לאפוקי

עין משפט נר מצוה

נ א מיי' פי"ג מהל' אישות הל' א סמג עשין מח טוש"ע אה"ע סי' עג סעי' א:

נא ב טוש"ע שם סי' עו סעי' יג:

נב ג מיי' פי"ב מהל' אישות הל' יז סמג לאוין פא טוש"ע שם סי' ע סעי' ו בהג"ה:

נג ד מיי' וסמ"ג שם טוש"ע שם סי' עא סעי' ג:

נד ה מיי' שם סמג שם טוש"ע שם סי' ע סעי' ה:

נה ו מיי' פי"ג מהל' אישות הל' ז טוש"ע שם סי' ע סעי' ה ו:

נו ז מיי' פי"א מהל' נחלות הל' יא טוש"ע חו"מ סי' רל סעי' טו:

נז ח ט מיי' פי"ד מהל' אישות הל' כד סמג לאוין קא טוש"ע אה"ע סי' פט סעי' ג:

נח י מיי' פי"א מהל' זכיה הל' כד סמג עשין פב טוש"ע יו"ד סי' שמח סעי' ב וטוש"ע חו"מ סי' רנג סעי' ל':

תוספות רי"ד

וראב"י אומר שארה כסותה לפום שארה תן כסותה שלא יתן של ילדה לזקנה ושל זקנה לילדה כסותה ועונתה לפום עונה תן כסותה שלא יתן לה חדשים בימות החמה שחקים בימות הגשמים: תני ר"י שארה זו קירוב בשר שלא ינהוג בה מנהג פרסיים שמשמשין מטותיהם בבגדיהם מסייע ליה לר"ה דאמר האומר א"א אלא אני בבגדי והיא בבגדה יוציא ויתן כתובה: ר"י אומר וכו'. מכלל דת"ק סבר הני לא ה"ד אי דאורחה. פי' שדרך בני משפחתה בכך מ"ט דת"ק דאמר לא ואי דלאו אורחה מ"ט דר"י ל"צ דאורחיה ולא אורחה ת"ק סבר כי אמרי' עולה עמו ה"מ מחיים פי' כגון הוא אומר להניק והיא אומרת שלא להניקו ודרך בנות משפחתה להניק בניהם ואינו דרך בני משפחתו. אבל לאחר מיתה לא. ור"י סבר אפילו לאחר מיתה: אמר ר"ח אמר מר עוקבא הל' כר"י. ואמר ר"ח אמר מ"ע. מי שנשתטה ב"ד יורדין לנכסיו וזנין ומפרנסין את אשתו ובניו ובני ביתו וד"א פי' תכשיטי נשים. א"ל רבינא לר"א ומ"ש מהא דתניא מי שהלך למדינת הים ואשתו תובעת מזונות. ב"ד יורדים לנכסיו וזנין ומפרנסין את אשתו אבל לא בניו ובנותיו ולא ד"א. פי' משום דבמזונות אשתו מחוייב בתנאי כתובה אבל במזונות בניו ובנותיו לא מחוייב. א"ל ולא שני לך בין יוצא לדעת ליוצא שלא לדעת פי' יוצא מן המקום לדעת היה בידו לצוות על מזונות בניו ובנותיו ומדלא צוה גלה דעתו שאינו חפץ לזון הילכך אשתו דמחייב לה בתנאי כתובה אישתעביד נכסיה אבל בניו ובנותיו לא. אבל נשתטה דכיוצא מן העולם שלא לדעת הוא אזלי' בתר רובא דעלמא ואמרי' דמסתמא ניחא ליה שיזון בניו ובנותיו משלו. מאי ד"א ר"ח אמר תכשיט פי' בשמים להתקשט ואע"ג דהיה צריך לעשות לה קצבה בקישוטי' כמה נותן לה בשבת כדמפרש לקמן בהמדיר. ה"מ כי איתיה בהדה דניחא ליה שתתקשט ונאותה לה ולא שתתנוול אבל הלך למד"ה כיון דליתה בהדה לא בעי למיתן לה ונשתטה נמי שאין לו דעת להתנאות א) אין אשתו מתקשטת משלו ר"י אמר צדקה פי' מ"ד תכשיט כ"ש צדקה פי' שאין לנו לעשות צדקה משלו ומ"ד צדקה אבל תכשיט [יהבינן לה דלא] ניחא ליה דתנוול: אמר ר"ח מי שהלך למד"ה ומתה אשתו ב"ד יורדים לנכסיו וקוברים אותה לפי כבודו. לפי כבודו ולא לפי כבודה. פי' בתמיה והרי אינה יורדת עמו. ואם דרכה שתקבר בשירין ואין דרכו אמאי לא קברה לא לפי כבודה ואפילו למ"ד דל"א עולה עמו לאחר מיתה. אימא אף לפי כבודו. וקמ"ל עולה עמו לאחר מיתה: אמר ר"מ האומר אם מתה אשתו אפילו לא תקברוה מנכסיו אין שומעין לו לפי' דכיון דהוא מת ברישא והיא גובה כתובתה אבל כיון שהיא מתה בחייו ולא גבתה כתובה ואין היורשים חייבים בקבורתה מ"ש כי אמר אפילו לא אמר נמי מסתמא נמי לא קבר' לה דנכסי קמי יתמי נפלו ואין היתומים חייבים בקבורת האלמנה. אלא האומר אם מת לא תקברוהו מנכסיו אין שומעין לו. לא כל הימנו להעשיר את בניו ויפיל את עצמו על הציבור: מתני' לעולם היא ברשות האב עד שתכנס לחופה. פי' לשם נשואין ואם היא בת ישראל מאורסה

לכהן

א) אינו מובן דהא גבי נשתטה תולה לטעמים לאשתו גם כן לכך אחר ואולי צ"ל אחרת סי' ט' כבאן וצ"ע.

תורה אור

לרשות הבעל לנשואין. מסר האב לשלוחי הבעל – הרי היא ברשות הבעל. הלך האב עם שלוחי הבעל, או שהלכו שלוחי האב עם שלוחי הבעל – הרי היא ברשות האב. מסרו שלוחי האב לשלוחי הבעל – הרי היא ברשות הבעל.§ **גמ'** מאי לעולם? לאפוקי ממשנה ראשונה. דתנן: *הגיע זמן ולא נישאו – אוכלות משלו ואוכלות בתרומה. קמ"ל: לעולם.§ מסר האב לשלוחי הבעל הרי היא ברשות הבעל וכו'.§ אמר רב: מסירתה לכל, חוץ מתרומה. ורב אסי אמר: אף לתרומה. איתיביה רב הונא לרב אסי, ואמרי לה חייא בר רב לרב אסי: לעולם היא ברשות האב, עד שתכנס לחופה! אמר להו רב: לאו אמינא לכו: *לא תיזלו בתר איפכא?! יכול לשנויי לכו: מסירתה זו היא כניסתה לחופה. ושמואל אמר: לירושתה. ר"ל אמר: לכתובתה. כתובתה מאי היא – דאי מתה ירית לה, היינו דשמואל! אמר רבינא: לומר כתובתה מאחר – מנה. רבי יוחנן ורבי חנינא דאמרי תרוייהו: מסירתה לכל, אף לתרומה. מיתיבי: *[א]הלך האב עם שלוחי הבעל, או שהלכו שלוחי האב עם שלוחי הבעל, או שהיתה לה חצר בדרך ונכנסה עמו ללין, אע"פ שכתובתה בבית בעלה, מתה – אביה יורשה. מסר האב לשלוחי הבעל, או שמסרו שלוחי האב לשלוחי הבעל, או שהיתה לו חצר בדרך ונכנסה עמו לשום נישואין, אע"פ שכתובתה בבית אביה, מתה – בעלה יורשה. בד"א – לירושתה. [ג]אבל לתרומה – *אין אשה אוכלת בתרומה עד שתכנס לחופה. תיובתא דכולהו! תיובתא. הא גופא קשיא: אמרת: נכנסה עמו ללין. טעמא דללין, הא סתמא – לשם נישואין; אימא סיפא: נכנסה עמו לשם נישואין, הא סתמא – ללין! אמר רב אשי: סתמי סתמי קתני; [ג]סתם חצר דידה – ללין, סתם חצר דידיה – לנשואין. תנא: [ד]מסר האב לשלוחי הבעל וזינתה – הרי זו בחנק. מנה"מ? א"ר אמי בר חמא: אמר קרא: °"לזנות בית אביה" – *פרט לשמסר האב לשלוחי הבעל. ואימא פרט שנכנסה לחופה ולא נבעלה! אמר רבא, אמר לי אמי: חופה בהדיא כתיבא °"כי יהיה נערה בתולה מאורשה לאיש", *[ה]"נערה" – ולא בוגרת, "בתולה" – ולא בעולה, "מאורשה" – ולא נשואה. מאי נשואה? אילימא נשואה ממש – היינו בתולה ולא בעולה. אלא לאו – שנכנסה לחופה ולא נבעלה.

ואימא

דברים כב | שם

לרשות הבעל לנשואין. כלומר, שתכנס לחופה לשם נשואין, שתהא מסורה לרשות הבעל. מסרו שלוחי האב. שהיה האב משלחה לו ע"י שלוחיו, ופגעו בשלוחי הבעל ומסרוה להם. **גמ'** ממשנה ראשונה. בפרק "אף על פי". הגיע זמן. שנים עשר חדש לבתולה, משתתבעה הבעל להכין עצמה לנשואין, ולאלמנה שלשים יום. ולא נישאו. כגון שעכב החתן, או אונס שלו. ואוכלות בתרומה. אם בת ישראל מאורסת לכהן היא. מסירתה לכל. ליורשה, וליטמא לה, ולמעשה ידיה, ולכל דבר איש באשה – קיימא מסירת שלוחים במקום חופה. חוץ מאכילת תרומה. דטעמא דידה משום סימפון, כדלקמן בפרק "אף על פי" (דף נז:). והכא נמי איכא למיחש להכי, שמא ימצאו בה מומין, ויהיו קידושיה ונישואיה טעות. ורב אסי אמר אף לתרומה. קסבר: הא דאמור רבנן ארוסה לא תאכל בתרומה – משום שמא ימזגו לה כוס בבית אביה ותשקה לאחיה ולאחיותיה, והשתא דאין אחיה ואחיותיה אצלה – שרי. לעולם היא ברשות האב. ואוקימנא דהאי לעולם משום אכילת תרומה נקט לה, וקתני: עד שתכנס לחופה. אמר להו רב. לתלמידו ובנו. לא תיזלו בתר איפכא. לא תשיבו בבית המדרש ממשנה הנהפכת לשני צדדים, שיוכל המתרץ לתרץ משמעה אחר דבריו. שמואל אמר לירושתה. הוא דמהניא מסירה, שאם מתה בדרך – בעל יורש נדונייתה. דאע"ג דאמר מר (לקמן דף נג.): אשתו ארוסה, מתה – אינו יורשה. הכא, כיון דמסרה – אחולי אחיל אב מהשתא, מחמת קירוב נישואין. אבל לתרומה, ולהפרת נדריה שלא בשותפות, ולמליאתה דאינה אלא משום איבה ואהכי ליכא למיחש להכי – לא מהניא מסירה כי חופה. לכתובתה. הוא דמהניא מסירה. והשתא קא בעי תלמודא למילתיה. מאי היא דאם מתה ירית. בעל את הנדוניא שפסק לה האב. לומר כתובתה מאחר מנה. לשוייה אלמנה מן הנשואין, שלא תיקנו לה חכמים אלא מנה מן הכונסה אחרי כן. הלך האב כו'. אין מסירתו מסירה. ונכנסה עמו. עם בעלה ללון, כשאר לינה בדרך בעלמא, ולא לשם נשואין. שכתובתה. מטלטלין שייחד אביה לנדונייתה. במה דברים אמורים. שמסירתה לשלוחים הוו נשואין. ליורשה. להא מילתא לחודא הוא דהויא נשואין. תיובתא דכולהו. הנך דפליגי אדשמואל. הא סתמא. אם נכנסה ושהתה עמו סתם, אמרינן: נשואין נינהו, וזו היא כניסת חופתה, ואע"פ שלא נבעלה – הוי נשואין. סתמי סתמי קתני. הא דקתני נכנסה עמו ללון – לא שפירשה "ללון אני נכנסת ולא לשם נשואין", והא דקתני נכנסה עמו לנשואין לא שפירשה "לנשואין אני נכנסת". אלא, זו וזו שנכנסה סתם. ותנא הוא דקאמר, דהיכא דחצר שלה – סתם כניסתה לא לנשואין הן אלא ללון, והיכא דחצר שלו – סתם כניסתה לשם נשואין. הרי זו בחנק. כנשואה, ולא בסקילה כארוסה. ואימא פרט לכשנכנסה לחופה ולא נבעלה. דייך אם מיעטת כגון זו, דלא תימא נערה בתולה כתיב גבי סקילה, והא אכתי בתולה הואי. אבל זו, שאף לחופה לא נכנסה – לא מיעטה הכתוב, ואכתי "בית אביה" קרינא ביה. חופה. בלא בעילה בהדיא כתיבא דלאו בסקילה היא, וכי אילטריך האי למסירה. אילימא נשואה ממש. שנכנסה לחופה ונבעלה.

הכי

לעיל ב. לקמן נז. ע: [נדרים עג]

[קדושין מו. כריתות יז:]

[תוספתא פ"ד]

לקמן נז: [קדושין יז:]

[סנהדרין סו: בבריתא ע"ש בפרש"י דאהך קרא קאי וע"ע]

[סנהדרין סו:]

לאפוקי ממשנה ראשונה. אע"ג דתנן בהדיא בפ' "אע"פ" (לקמן דף נז.): זו משנה ראשונה, ב"ד של אחריהם אמרו כו' – כן דרך התנאים להשמיענו בקולר אע"ג דכבר השמיענו במקום אחר. וכה"ג איכא בריש ברכות (דף ב*.). **רב** אסי אמר אף לתרומה. פי' בקונטרס: דקסבר רב אסי דטעמא דאין ארוסה בת ישראל אוכלת בתרומה – כדעולא, שמא ימזגו לה כוס. וכיון שמסרה – תו ליכא למיחש. וקשה לר"י: דאפי' עולא דמפרש טעמא דמשנה ראשונה שמא ימזגו לה כוס – למשנה אחרונה מודה דטעמא משום סימפון. וע"כ רב אסי איירי לפי משנה אחרונה, דאמתני' קאי, ומפקה מתני' ממשנה ראשונה, מדקתני "לעולם"! ועוד: דאיתותב מברייתא דלקמן, ולא משני ההיא כמשנה אחרונה! ונראה לר"י: דטעמא דרב אסי משום סימפון, ומשמסרה – תו ליכא למיחש, דמסתמא בדקי לה. וקשה: דרב אסי חייש לסימפון בהגעת זמן טפי מבמסר האב לשלוחי הבעל, ובפ' "אע"פ" (לקמן דף נח.) אמרי' איפכא, דקאמר: מאי בינייהו, בין למאן דאמר משום סימפון בין למ"ד משום שמא תשקה? איכא בינייהו קיבל מסר והלך. פירוש: מסר האב לשלוחי הבעל, דלמאן דאמר משום סימפון – איכא, אע"ג דבהגיע זמן לא חיישינן לסימפון למשנה ראשונה! ואור"י: דודאי סברא הוא דבמשנה אחרונה דחיישינן לסימפון בהגעת זמן – כל שכן במסר כדאמרינן התם. אבל הכא רב אסי מתניתין דחקתיה, דקתני "הרי היא ברשות הבעל" – דמשמע לגמרי, אפילו לתרומה. ועוד אור"י: דמצינו לפרש דאיכא בינייהו למאן דאמר סימפון ליכא, דבמסר לא חיישינן לסימפון, ולמאן דאמר שמא ימזגו – איכא, דחיישינן שמא תשקה לשלוחי הבעל. ובקונטרס – לא פירש התם כן*). **ושמואל** אמר לירושתה. לא אתא לאפוקי הפרת נדרים – דהא תנא דבי רבי ישמעאל בסמוך דהויא ברשות הבעל להפרת נדריה, ויצתה מרשות האב. ונראה דהוא הדין מיטמא לה, כיון דאפקה רחמנא מסקילה לחנק, דמהתם יליף לכל מילי. אלא למעוטי תרומה אתי. וירושתה נקט לרבותא דלא מיבעיא ליטמא לה ולהפרת נדריה דהויא מסירה כחופה, אלא אפילו ליורשה. דהוה ס"ד כיון דירושת הבעל תקנתא דרבנן היא, הכא במסר – לא תקון. אי נמי: ס"ד דאין האב מזכה לבתו עד שתכנס לחופה – אפ"ה יורשה. אי נמי: אף כתובה דריש לקיש אתא למעוטי. וריש לקיש נמי לא מיבעיא קאמר, ולא אתא למעוטי אלא תרומה. אי נמי: ממעט נמי ירושתה, מטעמא דפרישית. **תיובתא** דכולהו. לאו דווקא דכולהו, אלא להנהו דאמרי אף לתרומה. וכענין זה מצינו ב"יש נוחלין" (ב"ב דף קכט:) גבי מחלק נכסיו על פיו "תיובתא דכולהו", אע"ג דלא הוי תיובתא אלא לחד. **היינו** בתולה ולא בעולה. וא"ת: אימא ולא נשואה שנכנסה לחופה ונבעלה שלא כדרכה, דאכתי בתולה היא, כדאמרינן בפ"ק דקדושין (דף ט:): בא עליה עשרה ועדיין היא בתולה – כולן בסקילה! ויש לומר: דהא אמר התם דבעל עושה אותה בעולה שלא כדרכה.

ואימא

*) [וע' תוס' קדושין יח. ד"ה קבל]

[וע"ע תוס' מנחות נג. ד"ה הכל וכו' האריכו טפי]

נט א מיי' פכ"ב מהל' אישות הל"ב ופי"א מהל' נדרים הל' כב סמג עשין מח ולאוין פא ורמב טוש"ע יו"ד סי' רלד סעי' ח וטוש"ע אה"ע סי' נו:

ס ב מיי' פ"ו מהל' תרומות הל"ג ופ"ח הל' ז:

סא ג טוש"ע אה"ע סס בהג"ה:

סב ד ה מיי' פ"ג מהל' איסורי ביאה הל"ד סמג לאוין נו:

תוספות רי"ד

לכהן אינה אוכלת בתרומה דקנין כספו גמור בעינן מסר האב לרשות הבעל ה"ה ברשות הבעל הלכו שלוחי האב עם שלוחי הבעל ה"ה ברשות האב. מסרו שלוחי האב לשלוחי הבעל ה"ה ברשות הבעל: מאי לעולם לאפוקי ממשנה ראשונה. דקתני בפ' אע"פ נותנים לבתולה י"ב חודש ולאלמנה ל' יום משתבעה הבעל להנשא לפרנס א"ע. הגיע זמן ולא נשאו אוכלות משלו ואוכלות בתרומה פי' וקתני התם זו משנה ראשונה. אבל ב"ד שלאחריהם אמרו וכו' קמ"ל לעולם. פי' אע"פ דאמר ר' לאפוקי ממשנה ראשונה לא נתבטלה לענין מזונות שאם מעכב הבעל מלכנוס חייב במזונותיה והכי אזלא סוגיא דשמעתא קמייתא דמכילתין והכי תנן נמי בנדרים בפ' נערה המאורסה בוגרת. פי' בוגרת שיצאת כבר מרשות אביה אע"פ שלא נשאת הואיל ויצאת מרשות האב הבעל מפר נדריה ושהשתה י"ב חודש ר"א אומר הואיל ובעלה חייב במזונותיה יפר וחכ"א אין הבעל מיפר עד שתכנס לרשותו אלמא קים לן דחייב במזונותיה ואפילו רבנן לא פליגי אלא בנדרים דאע"ג דחייב במזונותיה א"י להפר עד שתכנס לרשותו דומיא דתרומה דלא אכלה עד שתכנס לחופה והאי דקאמר הכא לאפוקי הכי פירושו איצטריך לעולם היא ברשות אב לאפוקי ממשנה ראשונה דעביד לה כאשתו לכל דבר אפילו לתרומה וכ"ש למציאתה ולמעשה ידיה ולירושתה להכי תנן לעולם לומר לך שאינו זכאי במציאתה ובמעשה ידיה ובהפרת נדריה ואינו יורשה אע"פ שחייב במזונותיה: מסר האב וכו' א"ר מסירתה לכל חוץ לתרומה פי' לכל דבר ליורשה ולטמא לה ולזכות במציאתה ובמעשה ידיה דמסירה לשלוחים במקום חופה קיימא חוץ מאכילת תרומה דטעמיה דידיה משום סמפון כדלקמן ואיכא למיחש שמא ימצאו בה מומין ונמצא נשואיה וקידושיה טעות ורב אסי [אמר] אפילו לתרומה קסבר הא דאמרי רבנן ארוסה בת ישראל לא תאכל בתרומה שמא ימזגו לה כוס בבית (חמיה) [אביה] ותשקה לאחיה ולאחיותיה כיון שמסר תו ליכא למיחש למזיגת כוס. ושמואל אמר לירושתה פי' שאם מתה בדרך הוא יורשה ואע"ג דאמר מר אשתו ארוסה מתה אינה יורשה והכא כיון דמסרה אחוליה אחלי גביה מחמת קירוב נשואין. אבל לתרומה ולהפר נדריה לא מהני מסירה בלא חופה כחופה. ר"י ור"ח דאמרי תרווייהו מסירתה לכל אף לתרומה: מיתיבי הלך (הבעל) [האב] עם שלוחי הבעל או שהלכו שלוחי האב עם שלוחי הבעל או שהיתה לה חצר בדרך ונכנסה עמו סתמא ללין (הוי) אע"פ שכתובתה בבית בעלה מתה אביה יורשה מסר האב לשלוחי הבעל או שמסרו שלוחי האב לשלוחי הבעל או שהיה לו חצר בדרך ונכנסה עמו סתמא לשום נשואין אע"פ שכתובתה בבית אביה מתה בעלה יורשה בד"א לירושתה אבל לתרומה אין האשה אוכלת בתרומה עד שתכנס לחופה תיובתא דכלהו דאמרי אף לתרומה פי' שאין אשה אוכלת בתרומה עד שתכנס לחופה:

וְאֵימָא: הֵיכָא דְּהָדְרָא לְבֵי נָשָׂא — הָדְרָא לְמִילְּתָא קַמַּיְיתָא! אָמַר רָבָא: הַהוּא כְּבָר פְּסָקָהּ תַּנָּא דְּבֵי רַבִּי יִשְׁמָעֵאל. *דְּתָנָא דְּבֵי רַבִּי יִשְׁמָעֵאל: °"וְנֵדֶר אַלְמָנָה וּגְרוּשָׁה כֹּל אֲשֶׁר אָסְרָה עַל נַפְשָׁהּ יָקוּם עָלֶיהָ", מַה תַּלְמוּד לוֹמַר? וַהֲלֹא מוּצֵאת מִכְּלַל אָב וּמוּצֵאת מִכְּלַל בַּעַל! ^[א]אֶלָּא, הֲרֵי שֶׁמָּסַר הָאָב לִשְׁלוּחֵי הַבַּעַל, אוֹ שֶׁמָּסְרוּ שְׁלוּחֵי הָאָב לִשְׁלוּחֵי הַבַּעַל, וְנִתְאַרְמְלָה בַּדֶּרֶךְ אוֹ נִתְגָּרְשָׁה — הֵיאַךְ אֲנִי קוֹרֵא בָּהּ, בֵּית אָבִיהָ שֶׁל זוֹ אוֹ בֵּית בַּעְלָהּ שֶׁל זוֹ? אֶלָּא לוֹמַר לָךְ: כֵּיוָן שֶׁיָּצְאָה שָׁעָה אַחַת מֵרְשׁוּת הָאָב — שׁוּב אֵינוֹ יָכוֹל לְהָפֵר. אָמַר רַב פָּפָּא: אַף אֲנַן נַמִי תְּנֵינָא: *הַבָּא עַל נַעֲרָה הַמְאוֹרָסָה — אֵינוֹ חַיָּיב עַד שֶׁתְּהֵא נַעֲרָה בְּתוּלָה מְאוֹרָסָה, וְהִיא בְּבֵית אָבִיהָ. בִּשְׁלָמָא נַעֲרָה — וְלֹא בּוֹגֶרֶת, בְּתוּלָה — וְלֹא בְּעוּלָה, מְאוֹרָסָה — וְלֹא נְשׂוּאָה, "בְּבֵית אָבִיהָ" לְמַעוּטֵי מַאי — לָאו לְמַעוּטֵי מָסַר הָאָב לִשְׁלוּחֵי הַבַּעַל? אָמַר רַב נַחְמָן בַּר יִצְחָק: אַף אֲנַן נַמִי תְּנֵינָא: הַבָּא עַל אֵשֶׁת אִישׁ, כֵּיוָן שֶׁנִּכְנְסָה לִרְשׁוּת הַבַּעַל לְנִשּׂוּאִין, אַף עַל פִּי שֶׁלֹּא נִבְעֲלָה — הַבָּא עָלֶיהָ הֲרֵי זֶה בְּחֶנֶק. נִכְנְסָה לִרְשׁוּת הַבַּעַל בְּעָלְמָא — שְׁמַע מִינַּהּ.§

מתני' הָאָב אֵינוֹ חַיָּיב בִּמְזוֹנוֹת בִּתּוֹ. זֶה מִדְרָשׁ *דָּרַשׁ רַבִּי אֶלְעָזָר בֶּן עֲזַרְיָה לִפְנֵי חֲכָמִים בַּכֶּרֶם בְּיַבְנֶה: הַבָּנִים יִירְשׁוּ, וְהַבָּנוֹת יִזּוֹנוּ. מַה הַבָּנִים אֵינָן יוֹרְשִׁין — אֶלָּא לְאַחַר מִיתַת הָאָב, אַף הַבָּנוֹת אֵין נִיזּוֹנוֹת — אֶלָּא לְאַחַר מִיתַת אֲבִיהֶן.§

גמ' בִּמְזוֹנוֹת בִּתּוֹ — הוּא דְּאֵינוֹ חַיָּיב, הָא בִּמְזוֹנוֹת בְּנוֹ — חַיָּיב. בִּתּוֹ נַמִי, חוֹבָה הוּא דְּלֵיכָּא, הָא מִצְוָה — אִיכָּא, מַנִּי מַתְנִיתִין? לָא רַבִּי מֵאִיר, לָא רַבִּי יְהוּדָה, וְלָא רַבִּי יוֹחָנָן בֶּן בְּרוֹקָא. *דְּתַנְיָא: מִצְוָה לָזוּן אֶת הַבָּנוֹת, קַל וָחוֹמֶר לַבָּנִים, *דְּעָסְקֵי בַּתּוֹרָה, דִּבְרֵי רַבִּי מֵאִיר. רַבִּי יְהוּדָה אוֹמֵר: מִצְוָה לָזוּן אֶת הַבָּנִים, וְקַל וָחוֹמֶר לַבָּנוֹת, מִשּׁוּם זִילוּתָא. ר' יוֹחָנָן בֶּן בְּרוֹקָא אוֹמֵר: חוֹבָה לָזוּן אֶת הַבָּנוֹת לְאַחַר מִיתַת אֲבִיהֶן, אֲבָל בְּחַיֵּי אֲבִיהֶן — אֵלּוּ וְאֵלּוּ אֵינָן נִיזּוֹנִין. מַנִּי מַתְנִיתִין? אִי רַבִּי מֵאִיר — הָא אָמַר בָּנִים מִצְוָה, אִי רַבִּי יְהוּדָה — הָא אָמַר בָּנִים נַמִי מִצְוָה, אִי רַבִּי יוֹחָנָן בֶּן בְּרוֹקָא — אֲפִי' מִצְוָה נַמִי לֵיכָּא! אִיבָּעֵית אֵימָא רַבִּי מֵאִיר, אִיבָּעֵית אֵימָא ר' יְהוּדָה, אִיבָּעֵית אֵימָא רַבִּי יוֹחָנָן בֶּן בְּרוֹקָא. אִיבָּעֵית אֵימָא ר' מֵאִיר, וְהָכִי קָאָמַר: הָאָב אֵינוֹ חַיָּיב בִּמְזוֹנוֹת בִּתּוֹ, וְהוּא הַדִּין לִבְנוֹ. הָא מִצְוָה בְּבִתּוֹ — אִיכָּא, קַל וָחוֹמֶר לַבָּנִים. וְהַאי דְּקָתָנֵי בִּתּוֹ — הָא קמ"ל: דַּאֲפִילּוּ

תורה אור: במדבר ל

רש"י

הכי גרסינן. ואימא היכא דהדרא לבי נשא תהדר למילתא קמייתא. מי הויא כמי שלא נמסרה. דבעיא בעלמא היא, ואינה קושיא כל כך, אלא דקתני מתני' הרי היא ברשות הבעל, ומשמע ואפי' חזרה מן הדרך לבית אביה כבר יצאה מרשות האב, וכיון דלא נפקא לן מסירת שלוחין אלא מקרא יתירא ד"בית אביה", אימא היכא דהדרא – בית אביה קרינן ביה, ואם זינתה תהא בסקילה. כבר פסקה תנא דבי רבי ישמעאל. דלא הדרא למילתא קמייתא, למיהוי כמי שלא נמסרה. מה תלמוד לומר. למה הוצרך לכתוב "יקום עליה", וכי מי יפר לה? והלא לא נאמרו מפירים אלא אביה בבתו עד שלא ניסת, ובעלה משניסת. וזו שנתארמלה משניסת – מוצאת מכלל אב ומכלל בעל. אלא הרי שמסר כו'. כלומר, לא בא הכתוב לאלמנה ולגרושה מן נשואין – דהא כתיב בה "אם בית אישה נדרה אישה יפירנו" – והרי אין אישה קיים. אלא לאלמנה ע"י מסירת שלוחין. שעד עכשיו לא פירשו לך הכתובים אלא משפט נודרת בבית אביה ומשפט נודרת בבית אישה, וזו שנדרה בדרך משמסרוה לשלוחין – אין אני יודע היאך אני קורא בה, אם "בית אביה" אם "בית אישה", לפיכך בא כתוב זה ולמדך שלא תקרא לה "בית אביה" אלא "בית אישה", ולא נתרוקנה רשות לאב במיתתו של בעל, ושוב אינו יכול להפר. אלמא: לא הדרא למילתא קמייתא, דאילו נתארמלה מן האירוסין עד שלא נמסרה לשלוחין – תנן במסכת נדרים (דף ע.): מת הבעל – נתרוקנה רשות לאב. וילפינן לה מקראי. אף אנן נמי תנינא. במתניתין, כי ההיא ברייתא דתניא לעיל "הרי זו בחנק". מאורסה ולא נשואה. נכנסה לחופה, ואע"פ שלא נבעלה. דאי נבעלה – הא תנא ליה בתולה. נכנסה לרשות הבעל בעלמא. תנן, ולא תנן בה "נכנסה לחופה". מתני' האב אינו חייב במזונות בתו. בחייו. ובגמ' מפרש אמאי נקט בתו. זה מדרש דרש ר' אלעזר ב"ע. ביום שמינוהו נשיא. בכרם ביבנה. על שם שהיו יושבין שורות שורות ככרם. הבנים יירשו והבנות יזונו. שתי תקנות תקנו ב"ד בתנאי כתובה: הבנים יירשו כתובת בנין דכרין, דתנן במתניתין (לקמן דף נב:): "בנין דכרין דיהוויין ליכי מינאי, אינון ירתון כסף כתובתיך יתר על חולקהון דעם אחוהון". והיינו הבנים יירשו – כתובת בנין דכרין. ולקמן בשמעתין מפרשינן לה מאי היא. והבנות יזונו. "בנן נוקבן די יהוויין ליכי מינאי, אינון יהוויין יתבן בביתי ומיתזנן מנכסי עד דתיבגרון או עד דתלקחון לגוברין". מה הבנים אין יורשין. כתובה אמן אלא לאחר מיתת אביהן, דהא "אינון ירתון" תנן, והכי מפרש לה ב"יש נוחלין", דהאי הבנים יירשו – אכתובת בנין דכרין קאי. גמ' חובה לזון הבנות. תנאי כתובה הוא. אין נזונין. אפילו מצוה אין כאן. האמר בנים נמי מצוה. ולא חובה. אפילו מצוה ליכא. לא בבנים ולא בבנות. איבעית אימא רבי מאיר והכי קאמר כו'. כלומר, בתו דנקט לאו למידק הא בנו חייב, אלא משום דרבי מאיר עדיף ליה בנו, אי נקט "אינו חייב במזונות בנו" – הוה אמינא: בנו הוא דחובה ליכא מצוה איכא, אבל בתו אפילו מצוה ליכא. להכי תנא "אינו חייב בבתו" – למימרא דמצוה מיהא איכא. וה"ה לבנו – דחובה מיהא ליכא. דאפילו

תוספות

ואימא הני מילי היכא דלא הדרא לבי נשא. נראה לר"י דהכי פריך: מנ"ל דאייתר "בית אביה" למעוטי מסר האב לשלוחי הבעל? דלמא תרוייהו צריכי לנכנסה לחופה ולא נבעלה. דאי לא כתב אלא חד – ה"א ה"מ היכא דלא הדרא לבי נשא, אבל הדרא לבי נשא – אימא דתהדר למלתא קמייתא, להכי איצטריך קרא אחרינא, ואכתי מסר מנלן? ואע"ג דהיכא דנבעלה קים לן דלא הדרא – היינו משום דאשתני גופא, אבל לא נבעלה דאכתי בתולה היא – אימא דתהדר. אמר רבא: כבר פסקה תנא דבי רבי ישמעאל, ואשמועינן דלא הדרא. והיינו לכל הפחות כשנכנסה לחופה ולא נבעלה. וגלי קרא בנדרים – וה"ה בכל מקום. אם כן אייתר חד מהנך קראי למסר האב לשלוחי הבעל, למפטרה מסקילה, הואיל ואשכחנא דלא הדרא מדתנא דבי ר' ישמעאל – סברא הוא דלא הדרא בכל הנך דאמעיט מסקילה, כגון מסר. ולהכי נקט במלתיה דתנא דבי רבי ישמעאל "מסר". ומיהו, קשה לפי' זה: דהיכי ילפינן מנדרים דלא הדרא למילתא קמייתא? נהי דגבי נדרים לא הדרא – היינו משום דגלי לן קרא דכיון דיצאה מרשות האב שעה אחת – שוב אין לו כח בה, מ"מ לענין סקילה היכי שייך לומר דלא הדרא? דאף ע"פ שנכנסה לחופה, כיון שלא נבעלה ונתאלמנה או נתגרשה, וחזרה ונתארסה – למה לא תהיה בסקילה, כיון שהיא נערה בתולה מאורסה? ואע"ג דיצאה מרשות האב – מ"מ תהא כמו יתומה שאין לה אב, דהויא בסקילה. כדאשכחנא בגיורת דמתני'! ויש לומר: דהא פשיטא ליה דנשואה שאינה בעולה חשובה כבעולה, ואין חילוק כלל, דנשואין משוו לה כבעולה לכל דבר. וכי היכי דבעולה פשיטא דלא הדרא למילתא קמייתא לכל דבר – ה"נ שאינה בעולה. ולא איצטריך דרשה דתנא דבי רבי ישמעאל אלא לאשמועינן דלא נימא כיון דלא נבעלה ונתאלמנה או נתגרשה – בטלו להו שם נשואין מינה, והוי כלא נשאת מעולם. וכיון דגלי לן קרא בהפרת נדרים, דע"י אלמנות וגרושין לא נתבטלו הנשואין כאילו לא הוו – ה"ה לענין סקילה. וכיון דלא נתבטלו – פשיטא דלא הדרא למילתא קמייתא, דחשובה ממש כבעולה. ומה שפ"ה דל"ג ה"מ, דלאו קושיא היא, ופירש נמי דאמתניתין קא בעי קשה: דאי אמתני' קא בעי למה המתין כל כך? ובחנם מוחק הני מילי, דיש נמי לפרשו בלשון בעיא כמו ואימא.

היאך אני קורא בה. מתוך פירוש הקונטרס משמע דאיצטריך ליה למגמר אם היא ברשות האב אם לאו כשהיא בדרך. וקשה לר"י: דהא מ"לזנות בית אביה" נפקא, וגמרינן נדרים מהתם! ונראה דלענין חזרה כשנתארמלה או נתגרשה איצטריך למילף מהכא.

ונדר אלמנה וגרושה מה תלמוד לומר. תימה: דאיצטריך, לכדדרשינן בפרק בתרא דנדרים (דף פח:).

קל וחומר לבנים דעסקי באורייתא. ולקמן בפרק בתרא (דף קח: וסס), גבי אדמון דפריך: דעסיק באורייתא ירית, דלא עסיק באורייתא לא ירית? לענין ירושה דאורייתא – ודאי איכא למיפרך, דאין לנו לגזול לו מה שזיכתה לו תורה. אבל הכא קאמר דלא מחמרינן באותו שעוסק בתורה, ומפרנסינן ליה כדי שיעסוק בתורה.

כשהם

תוספות רי"ד

מתני' האב אינו חייב במזונות בתו זה מדרש דרש ראב"ע פי' ביום שמינהו נשיא בכרם שביבנה פי' בתוך הישיבה וע"ש שהיו יושבים שורות שורות נקראין כרם: הבנים יירשו והבנות יזונו מה הבנים אינן יורשים אלא לאחר מיתת אביהן אף הבנות אינן ניזונות אלא לאחר מיתת אביהן. פי' אע"ג דבתנאי כתובה כתוב סתם בנין נוקבין דיהווין ליכי מינאי יהוון יתבין בביתי ומיתזני מנכסיי עד דתינסבן לגוברין פי' ומשמע אפילו בחייו. אפ"ה לא הוי האי תנאה אלא לאחר מיתה וילוף לה ר"א מתנאי דבנים דמה תנאי דבנים אינו אלא לאחר מיתה דהא ירתון תנן. אף תנאי דבנות לא הוי אלא לאחר מיתה אבל בחייו לא מחייב ואין אשתו יכולה לכופו לזון

עין משפט נר מצוה

סג א מיי' פי"א מהל' נדרים הל' כב טוש"ע יו"ד סי' רלד סעי' יב:

מסורת הש"ס

יבמות פז.

סנהדרין סו:

כ"ב קלא:

[תוספתא פ"ד ע"ש] כ"ב קמא.

[...יעס זה דעסקי בתורה ...תא בתוספתא וכ"כ הרקב"ס בכ"ב בזה"ל שעסקי באורייתא ולא ...תלוי פירוש הוא ואינו מן הברייתא]

תורה אור

דַּאֲפִילּוּ בִּתּוֹ, חוֹבָה הוּא דְּלֵיכָּא, הָא מִצְוָה — אִיכָּא. וְאִיבָּעֵית אֵימָא ר' יְהוּדָה, וְהָכִי קָאָמַר: הָאָב אֵינוֹ חַיָּיב בִּמְזוֹנוֹת בִּתּוֹ, וְכׇל שֶׁכֵּן לִבְנוֹ. הָא מִצְוָה בִּבְנוֹ — אִיכָּא, וְקַל וָחוֹמֶר לַבָּנוֹת. וְהָא דְּקָתָנֵי בִּתּוֹ — הָא קָא מַשְׁמַע לַן: דַּאֲפִילּוּ בִּתּוֹ חוֹבָה לֵיכָּא. וְאִיבָּעֵית אֵימָא ר' יוֹחָנָן בֶּן בְּרוֹקָא, וְהָכִי קָאָמַר: אֵינוֹ חַיָּיב בִּמְזוֹנוֹת בִּתּוֹ, וְהוּא הַדִּין לִבְנוֹ. וְהוּא הַדִּין דַּאֲפִילּוּ מִצְוָה נַמִי לֵיכָּא, וְאַיְּידֵי דְּבָנוֹת לְאַחַר מִיתַת אֲבִיהֶן חוֹבָה — תָּנָא נַמִי אֵינוֹ חַיָּיב. אָמַר רַבִּי אֶילְעָא אָמַר רֵישׁ לָקִישׁ מִשּׁוּם רַבִּי *יְהוּדָה בַּר חֲנִינָא: [א]בְּאוּשָׁא הִתְקִינוּ שֶׁיְּהֵא אָדָם זָן אֶת בָּנָיו וְאֶת בְּנוֹתָיו כְּשֶׁהֵן קְטַנִּים. אִיבַּעְיָא לְהוּ: הִלְכְתָא כְּוָותֵיהּ אוֹ אֵין הִלְכְתָא כְּוָותֵיהּ? תָּא שְׁמַע: [ב]כִּי הֲוָה אָתוּ לְקַמֵּיהּ דְּרַב יְהוּדָה, אֲמַר לְהוּ: יָארוֹד יָלְדָה וְאַבְּנֵי מָתָא שַׁדְיָא?! כִּי הֲוָה אָתוּ לְקַמֵּיהּ דְּרַב חִסְדָּא, אֲמַר לְהוּ: כְּפוּ לֵיהּ אָסִיתָא בְּצִבּוּרָא, וְלֵיקוּם וְלֵימָא: עוֹרְבָא בָּעֵי בְּנֵיהּ, וְהַהוּא גַּבְרָא לָא בָּעֵי בְּנֵיהּ. וְעוֹרְבָא בָּעֵי בְּנֵיהּ? וְהָכְתִיב: °"לִבְנֵי עוֹרֵב אֲשֶׁר יִקְרָאוּ"! (תהלים קמז) לָא קַשְׁיָא, הָא — בְּחִיוָּרֵי, הָא — בְּאוּכָּמֵי. כִּי הֲוָה אָתֵי לְקַמֵּיהּ דְּרָבָא, אֲמַר לֵיהּ: נִיחָא לָךְ דְּמִיתַּזְנֵי בָּנֶיךָ מִצְּדָקָה? וְלָא אֲמַרַן אֶלָּא דְּלָא אֲמִיד, [ג]אֲבָל אֲמִיד — כָּפֵינַן לֵיהּ עַל כׇּרְחֵיהּ. *כִּי הָא דְּרָבָא כַּפְיֵיהּ לְרַב נָתָן בַּר אַמֵּי וְאַפֵּיק מִינֵּיהּ ד' מֵאָה זוּזֵי לִצְדָקָה. אָמַר רַבִּי אֶילְעָא אָמַר רֵישׁ לָקִישׁ: בְּאוּשָׁא הִתְקִינוּ: הַכּוֹתֵב כׇּל נְכָסָיו לְבָנָיו — הוּא וְאִשְׁתּוֹ נִזּוֹנִים מֵהֶם. מַתְקִיף לַהּ רַבִּי זֵירָא וְאִיתֵּימָא רַבִּי שְׁמוּאֵל בַּר נַחְמָנִי: גְּדוֹלָה מִזּוֹ אָמְרוּ: אַלְמְנָתוֹ נִזּוֹנֶת מִנְּכָסָיו, הוּא וְאִשְׁתּוֹ מִיבַּעְיָא?! *דְּשָׁלַח רָבִין בְּאִיגַּרְתֵּיהּ: מִי שֶׁמֵּת וְהִנִּיחַ אַלְמָנָה וּבַת — [ד]אַלְמְנָתוֹ נִיזּוֹנֶת מִנְּכָסָיו, נִישֵּׂאת הַבַּת — אַלְמְנָתוֹ נִיזּוֹנֶת מִנְּכָסָיו, מֵתָה הַבַּת, אָמַר *רַבִּי יְהוּדָה בֶּן אֲחוֹתוֹ שֶׁל רַבִּי יוֹסֵי בַּר חֲנִינָא: עַל יָדַי הָיָה מַעֲשֶׂה, [ה]וְאָמְרוּ: אַלְמְנָתוֹ נִיזּוֹנֶת מִנְּכָסָיו — הוּא וְאִשְׁתּוֹ מִיבַּעְיָא?! מַהוּ דְּתֵימָא: הָתָם הוּא דְּלֵיכָּא דְּטָרַח, אֲבָל הָכָא — נִטְרַח לְדִידֵיהּ וּלְדִידָהּ, קָא מַשְׁמַע לַן. אִיבַּעְיָא לְהוּ: הִלְכְתָא כְּוָותֵיהּ אוֹ לֵית הִלְכְתָא כְּוָותֵיהּ? ת"ש, דְּרַבִּי חֲנִינָא וְר' יוֹנָתָן הָווּ קָיְימִי, אֲתָא הַהוּא גַּבְרָא, גְּחִין וּנְשַׁקֵיהּ לְר' יוֹנָתָן אַכַּרְעֵיהּ. אֲמַר לֵיהּ ר' חֲנִינָא: מַאי הַאי? א"ל: כּוֹתֵב נְכָסָיו לְבָנָיו הוּא, וַעֲשִׂיתִינְהוּ

רש"י

דַּאֲפִי' בִּתּוֹ. דְּקִילָא, דְּלָא עָסְקָא בְּאוֹרַיְיתָא. וְאַיְּידֵי דְּתָנָא בָּנוֹת כו'. לָא גָּרְסִינַן דְּתָנָא, דְּהָא לָא תָּנֵי לֵיהּ בְּמַתְנִי'. אֶלָּא ה"ג: וְאַיְּידֵי דְּבָנוֹת לְאַחַר מִיתַת אֲבִיהֶן חוֹבָה כו'. בְּאוּשָׁא הִתְקִינוּ. כְּשֶׁיָּשְׁבוּ סַנְהֶדְרֵי גָּזִית בְּאוּשָׁא, שֶׁהִיא אַחַת מֵעֶשֶׂר גָּלֻיּוֹת שֶׁגָּלְתָה סַנְהֶדְרִין, כִּדְאָמַר בְּר"ה (דף לא.). כְּשֶׁהֵן קְטַנִּים. עַד שֶׁיָּבִיאוּ שְׂעָרוֹת. תָּא שְׁמַע. דְּלֵית הִלְכְתָא כְּוָותֵיהּ, אֶלָּא מֵימַר אָמְרִינַן לֵיהּ, וְאוּלַי יְכַלְכְּלֵם וְיָזוּן, אֲבָל מֵיכַף — לָא כָּיְיפִינַן. יָארוֹד. תַּנִּין. "מְעוֹן תַּנִּים" (ירמיהו ט) מְתַרְגְּמִינַן מְדוֹר יָארוֹדִין. וְהוּא אַכְזָרִי עַל בָּנָיו. יָארוֹד יָלְדָה וְאַבְּנֵי מָתָא שַׁדְיָא. הַתַּנִּין הוֹלִיד תּוֹלְדוֹתָיו, וְהִטִּיל פַּרְנָסָתָן עַל בְּנֵי הָעִיר. כְּפוּ לֵיהּ אָסִיתָא. כְּפוּ מַכְתֶּשֶׁת עַל פִּיהָ, וְיַעֲמוֹד זֶה עַל גַּב שׁוּלֶיהָ בְּגוֹבַהּ, שֶׁיִּשְׁמְעוּ קוֹלוֹ, וְיַכְרִיז עַל עַצְמוֹ שֶׁהוּא רַע מִן הָעוֹרְבִים, דְּעוֹרְבָא בָּעֵי בָּנֵי וְהַהוּא גַּבְרָא לָא בָּעֵי בָּנֵי. וְאִית דִּמְפָרְשֵׁי: שְׁלִיחַ לִבּוּר יַעֲמוֹד עָלֶיהָ וְיֹאמַר כֵּן עַל אוֹתוֹ הָאִישׁ. לִבְנֵי עוֹרֵב אֲשֶׁר יִקְרָאוּ. אַלְמָא לָא זַיֵּין לְהוּ. אוּכָּמֵי. כְּשֶׁגָּדֵל מַשְׁחִיר, וְהָאֵם וְהָאָב אוֹהֲבִין אוֹתָן. אֲבָל מִתְּחִילָּתָן — לְבָנִים, וְשׂוֹנְאִין אוֹתָן. וְלָא אֲמַרַן. דְּלָא כָּפֵינַן. אֶלָּא דְּלָא אֲמִיד. שֶׁאֵינוֹ עָשִׁיר. בְּעַל כׇּרְחוֹ. לֹא יְהֵא אֶלָּא לִצְדָקָה בְּעָלְמָא, וַאֲפִי' אֵינָן בָּנָיו. כִּי הָא דְּרָבָא כַּפְיֵיהּ. עַל הַצְּדָקָה. הוּא וְאִשְׁתּוֹ נִזּוֹנִין מֵהֶן. וַאֲפִילּוּ כְּתָבָן מֵעַכְשָׁיו. וְלֹא מִן הַדִּין, אֶלָּא תַּקָּנַת חֲכָמִים הִיא. גְּדוֹלָה מִזּוֹ אָמְרוּ. בִּגְדוֹלָה מִזּוֹ אָמְרוּ. כְּגוֹן אַלְמָנָה וּבַת, וְנִיסֵּת הַבַּת. שֶׁאַף עַל פִּי שֶׁהוּא מֵת, וְהַנְּכָסִים נִשְׁתַּעְבְּדוּ לַלּוֹקֵחַ דְּרַבָּנַן, כְּגוֹן בַּעַל בְּנִכְסֵי אִשְׁתּוֹ, וְקי"ל (גיטין דף מח:): אֵין מוֹצִיאִין לִמְזוֹן הָאִשָּׁה מִנְּכָסִים מְשׁוּעְבָּדִים — אֲפִי' הָכִי, הֵיכָא דְּלֵיכָּא לְמֵיחַשׁ לְתִיקּוּן הָעוֹלָם, כְּגוֹן כִּי הַאי לוֹקֵחַ שֶׁלֹּא הוֹצִיא מָעוֹת — שַׁוְיוּהוּ רַבָּנַן כְּיוֹרֵשׁ, וְאָמְרִי: תִּזּוֹן הָאַלְמָנָה מִנִּכְסֵי בַּעְלָהּ. כִּי הָא דְּשָׁלַח רָבִין בְּאִיגַּרְתֵּיהּ כו' נִיסֵּת הַבַּת. אע"ג דַּאֲמוּר רַבָּנַן בַּעַל בְּנִכְסֵי אִשְׁתּוֹ לוֹקֵחַ הָוֵי, וְקַיְימָא לַן: אֵין מוֹצִיאִין לִמְזוֹן הָאִשָּׁה מִנְּכָסִים מְשׁוּעְבָּדִים — הָכָא שַׁוְיוּהוּ רַבָּנַן כְּיוֹרֵשׁ, מִשּׁוּם פְּסֵידָא דְּאַלְמָנָה. וְהָכִי מְפוֹרָשׁ בְּ"יֵשׁ נוֹחֲלִין". הוּא וְאִשְׁתּוֹ. שֶׁהוּא קַיָּים, וְאֵלּוּ בָּנָיו הֵם, וְלֹא הוֹצִיאוּ מָעוֹת, אֶלָּא מַתָּנָה בְּעָלְמָא. מִיבַּעְיָא. וְאַע"ג דְּמַתָּנָה כְּמֶכֶר לְעִנְיַן שִׁעְבּוּד, הָתָם הוּא דְּאִי לָאו דַּעֲבִיד לֵיהּ נַיְחָא לְנַפְשֵׁיהּ — לָא יָהֵיב לֵיהּ מַתָּנָה. ⊕אֲבָל בְּנוֹ — לֵיכָּא לְמֵימַר הָכִי. מֵתָה הַבַּת. וּבַעְלָהּ יוֹרְשָׁהּ. אַלְמְנָתוֹ. שֶׁל אֲבִי הַבַּת. נִיזּוֹנֶת מִנְּכָסָיו. וְלָא אָמְרִינַן אִישׁ נׇכְרִי הוּא זֶה וְאֵינוֹ יוֹרְשׁוֹ שֶׁל אָב אֶלָּא שֶׁל אִשְׁתּוֹ וּכְלוֹקֵחַ בְּעָלְמָא דָּמֵי, וְאֵין מוֹצִיאִין לִמְזוֹן הָאִשָּׁה מִנְּכָסִים מְשׁוּעְבָּדִין. הָתָם הוּא דְּלֵיכָּא דְּטָרַח קַמַּהּ. שֶׁמֵּת בַּעְלָהּ, לְהָכִי עֲבוּד רַבָּנַן תַּקַּנְתָּא. אֲבָל הָכָא. דְּקָאֵי אִיהוּ, נִטְרַח לְדִידֵיהּ וּלְדִידָהּ, קמ"ל. הִלְכְתָא כְּוָותֵיהּ. אַדְּר' אֶילְעָא קָאֵי. אַכַּרְעֵיהּ. עַל רַגְלוֹ.

וַעֲשִׂיתִיהוּ

תוספות

כשהם קטנים. אבל קטני קטנים לכ"ע חייב, כדאמר בסוף "אע"פ" (לקמן דף סה: ושם). **הא** בחיוורי הא באוכמי. שני מיני עורבים יש, אחד לבן ואחד שחור, כדמוכח בפרק "אלו טריפות" (חולין דף סג.) גבי סימני עופות, דמרבה עורב העמקי, ומפרש: העמקי – כמראה החמה שעמוקה מן הצל, פי': לבן*.

אכפייה רבא כו'. וא"ת: היאך כפה אותו בשביל צדקה? והכתיב מתן שכרה בצדה, דכתיב "(*למען) יברכך", ואמרי' בפ' "כל הבשר" (חולין קי: ושם): כל מצות עשה שמתן שכרה בצדה – אין בית דין של מטה מוזהרין עליה! ויש לומר: דאכפייה בדברים. א"נ: קבלו ביניהן בני העיר לתת כך וכך לחדש, הלכך אכפייה, כדאמרינן בפרק קמא דבבא בתרא (דף ח: ושם) דרשאין בני העיר להסיע על קיצתן. ועוד: דבצדקה איכא תרתי לאוי: "לא תאמץ" ו"לא תקפוץ" (דברים טו). **הוא** ואשתו נזונים מהם. משמע: הא לאחר – אין נזונין, דמתנה הויא כמכר, כדפי' בקונטרס. דאי לא דעבד ליה ניחא לנפשיה – לא הוה יהיב ליה. ואין מוציאין למזון האשה והבנות מנכסים משועבדים, לפי שאין קצובין, או לפי שאין כתובין, כדאמר ב"הנזקין" (גיטין דף נ:). ומיהו, מהכא יש לדחות, דאיכא למימר דנקט בנו – משום דאיירי דנזונין אפי' ממטלטלין, אבל לאחר – לא היו נזונין ממטלטלין, כמו שאין אלמנה נזונת ממטלטלין דיורשין אי נמי: משום הוא, דאי כתב לאחר – לא היה ניזון הוא, אבל היא – לעולם אימא דנזונת ממתנה, אע"ג דלא טרפא מן הלקוחות. ומיהו, ב"יש נוחלין" (ב"ב דף קלג.) משמע דלא טרפא ממקבל מתנה, דקאמר: השתא ירושה דאורייתא אלמנתו ניזונת מנכסיו – מתנת שכיב מרע דרבנן לא כל שכן! משמע דממתנת בריא דאורייתא אינה ניזונת מנכסיו, אע"ג דמיתזנא מן היורשין. ואין לומר דממתנה דאורייתא, נהי דכ"ש לא הוי, ה"ה מיהא הוי, דלא אלים כח מתנה מכח יורשים. דעל כרחיך אלים כח מקבל מתנה מכח יורשים, דמסקינן בפ"ק דב"מ (דף יג. ושם) דשטר שיש בו אחריות נכסים – לא יחזיר, אפילו חייב מודה, דחיישינן לפרעון ולקנוניא. ושטר שאין בו אחריות נכסים – יחזיר, דלא גבי ממשעבדי. ואי גבי ממתנה – אמאי יחזיר? אלא ודאי דלא גבי. ואילו מן היורשין גבי, דהא פסקינן בסוף "גט פשוט" (ב"ב דף קעו.) הלכתא: מלוה על פה גובה מן היורשין. על כן נראה דאין חילוק בין מתנה למכר לענין זה, אע"ג דיש מקומות שסברא הוא לחלק בין מתנה למכר, כמו בעשה שורו אפותיקי ומכרו (ב"ב דף מד:) דנראה דווקא מכרו, אבל נתנו – בעל חובו גובה ממנו. וכן ב"הנזקין" (גיטין ד' נ: ושם) גבי אין נפרעין מנכסים משועבדין במקום שיש נכסים בני חורין ואפי' הן זיבורית, מבעיא לן במתנה היאך – דווקא להא מילתא הוא דאבעיא לן, אבל הכא אין לחלק. והא דאמרינן בפ' "מציאת האשה" (לקמן דף סט.): מכרו או משכנו – מוציאין לפרנסה, ואין מוציאין למזונות. ה"ה נתנו, והא דנקט מכרו – לאשמועינן דאפי' במכרו מוציאין לפרנסה. [ורבי חייא דמבעיא ליה במכרו או משכנו – היינו לפרנסה] אבל למזונות פשיטא ליה דאין מוציאין אפילו נתנו, כדתנן ב"הנזקין" (גיטין דף מח:): אין מוציאין למזון האשה והבנות מנכסים משועבדין. ולפי מה שתקנו הגאונים דאשה גובה כתובתה ומזונות ממטלטלי דיתמי, אע"ג דירושה הויא דאורייתא – כ"ש דגביא ממטלטלי דמתנת ש"מ דרבנן, דבכה"ג אמרי' ב"יש נוחלין" (ב"ב דף קלג.). אבל מטלטלי דמתנת בריא, דהויא דאורייתא – לא גביא כתובתה. ומזונות לא גביא אפילו ממקרקעי, כי היכי דלא גביא מלקוחות, כדפרשינן. ולא מבעיא נתן הוא, אלא אפילו נתנו יתומים, אע"ג שכבר משמת נשתעבדו הנכסים. **אלמנתו** נזונת מנכסיו **הוא ואשתו מבעיא.** אע"ג דלא דמי, דהתם אינן יכולין לירש אלא מה שהוא מוריש, ומזון אלמנה הוא חייב מקודם – מכל מקום מייתי הכי, הואיל ואלמוה רבנן לשעבודא דידה, שאף מן הבעל שאינו כיורש אלא כלוקח גובה, אע"ג דלא היתה גובה מלוקח אחר – הכי נמי אית לן לתקוני בכותב לבנו שיהא הוא ואשתו נזונין מהן.

עשיתינהו

עין משפט נר מצוה

סד א ב מיי' פי"ב מהל' אישות הל' יד סמג לאוין פא טוש"ע אה"ע סי' עא סעי' א:

[בחולין סג. איתא הכי להדיא עמקי חיוורא וכן הוא אומר ומראהו וכו' כמראה חמה וכו' ולכן ע"כ שלא היה מלת חיוורא כתוב בגרסת התוס']

[נ"ל בגלל הדבר הזה]

סה ג מיי' שם הלט"ו ופ"ז מהל' מתנות עניים הל"י סמג עשין קסב טוש"ע [שם וטוש"ע] יו"ד סי' רמח סעי' א:

סו ד ה מיי' פי"ט מהל' אישות הל' כא סמג לאוין פא טוש"ע אה"ע סי' צג סעי' ד:

תוספות רי"ד

את בנותיה בחיוו: א"ר אילא [אמר ר"ל] משום ר"ח באושא התקינו שיהא אדם זן את בניו ואת בנותיו כשהן קטנים. פי' כשישבו סנהדרין באושא והיא אחת מי' גליות שגלתה סנהדרין כדאמרי' בר"ה [דף לא]: הל' כוותיה או לית הל' כוותיה פי' כלום יש לסמוך על דברי ר' אילא שכך התקינו: ת"ש דלית הל' כוותיה דכי הוה אתו לקמיה דר"י א"ל יערוד ילדה ואבני מתא שדיא להו פי' יערוד תנין כדמתרגמינן מעון תנין (יערוד) [מדור] יערודין והוא עוף אכזרי על בניו. כך זה האיש אכזרי על בניו ומשליכם על הציבור והיה אומר לו כך אולי יבוש ויכלם ויפרנסם אבל לכוף לא הי' כופה אותו: כי אתו לקמיה דר"ח א"ל כפו לי' אסיתא בציבורא וליקום ולימא עורבא בעי בני והאי גברא לא בעי בני פי' כפו מכתשת על פיה ויעמוד עליה ויאמר אלו הדברים כדי שידעו הצבור וירחמו עליהם שהוא אינו מרחם עליהם. כי הוה אתי לקמיה דרבא א"ל ניחא לך דליתזני בניך מן הצדקה ול"א אלא דלא אמיד פי' עשיר אבל אמיד כייפי' ליה בע"כ לא יהא אלא אחר פי' לא יהא אלא צדקה ואפילו אינן בניו כי הא [דרבא] פי' כ"ש דכופין אותו לזון את בניו דרבא כפייה ליה לר"נ ב"א ואפיק מיניה ד' מאות זוז לצדקה (הרב פי' שעשוי אינה כפי' (אלא) [של] מלקות ויסורין כשאר עשוי דעלמא אלא כפי' של דברים ע"י הכלמות ופיתוים עד שנתפתה לזון אותם). ובשילהי פירקין דלקמן אמרי' דרש עולא רבה אפתחא דב"נ אע"פ שאמרו אין אדם זן את בניו ואת בנותיו כשהן קטנים אבל זן הוא אותן כשהן קטני קטנים ועד כמה עד בן שש: א"ר אילא אר"ל באושא התקינו הכותב נכסיו לבניו הוא ואשתו נזונין מהן פי' ואפי' כתבם מעכשיו ולא מן הדין אלא תקנת חכמים הוא. הל' כוותיה או לית הל' כוותיה ת"ש דר"ח ור' יוחנן הוו קיימו אתא ההוא גברא גחין ונשקי' לר"י אכרעי' א"ל ר"ח מאי האי א"ל כותב נכסיו לבניו הוה ועשיתינהו לבריה לזונם:

מסורת הש"ס

[נ"ל ר' יוסי וכ"א בריף וברא"ש]

ב"ב ח.

שם קלט.

[נ"ל רב יהודה וכ' הרשב"ם שהוא אמורא]

גליון הש"ס

רש"י ד"ה מיבעיא וכו' אבל בנו ליכא למימר הכי. עיין בהרש"ש לקמן נד ע"ב ד"ה דנייחא:

וַעֲשִׂיתִינְהוּ לְזָנֵיהּ. אִי אָמְרַתְּ בִּשְׁלָמָא לָאו דִּינָא — מִשּׁוּם הָכִי עַשְׂיֵינְהוּ, ^א^אֶלָּא אִי אָמְרַתְּ דִּינָא — עַשְׂיֵינְהוּ בָּעֵי?! *א"ר אֶילְעָא: ^ב^בְּאוּשָׁא הִתְקִינוּ: ^ג^הַמְבַזְבֵּז — אַל יְבַזְבֵּז יוֹתֵר מֵחוֹמֶשׁ. תַּנְיָא נַמִי הָכִי: הַמְבַזְבֵּז — אַל יְבַזְבֵּז יוֹתֵר מֵחוֹמֶשׁ, שֶׁמָּא יִצְטָרֵךְ לַבְּרִיּוֹת. וּמַעֲשֶׂה בְּאֶחָד שֶׁבִּקֵּשׁ לְבַזְבֵּז [יוֹתֵר מֵחוֹמֶשׁ], וְלֹא הִנִּיחַ לוֹ חֲבֵירוֹ, וּמַנּוּ — רַבִּי יְשֵׁבָב. וְאָמְרִי לָהּ: רַבִּי יְשֵׁבָב, וְלֹא הִנִּיחוֹ חֲבֵירוֹ, וּמַנּוּ — רַבִּי עֲקִיבָא. אָמַר רַב נַחְמָן, וְאִיתֵּימָא רַב אַחָא בַּר יַעֲקֹב: מַאי קְרָא — °"וְכֹל אֲשֶׁר תִּתֶּן לִי עַשֵּׂר אֲעַשְּׂרֶנּוּ לָךְ". (בראשית כח) וְהָא לָא דָּמֵי עִישּׂוּרָא בַּתְרָא לְעִישּׂוּרָא קַמָּא! אָמַר רַב אַשִׁי: "אֲעַשְּׂרֶנּוּ" לְבַתְרָא כִּי קַמָּא. אָמַר רַב שִׁימִי בַּר אַשִׁי: וּשְׁמוּעוֹת הַלָּלוּ מִתְמַעֲטוֹת וְהוֹלְכוֹת, וְסִימָנֵיךְ: קְטַנִּים כָּתְבוּ וּבִזְבְּזוּ. אָמַר רַב יִצְחָק: בְּאוּשָׁא הִתְקִינוּ ^ד^שֶׁיְּהֵא אָדָם מִתְגַּלְגֵּל עִם בְּנוֹ עַד שְׁתֵּים עֶשְׂרֵה שָׁנָה, מִכָּאן וְאֵילָךְ — יוֹרֵד עִמּוֹ לְחַיָּיו. אִינִי?! וְהָא *אָמַר לֵיהּ רַב לְרַב שְׁמוּאֵל בַּר שִׁילַת: ^ה^בְּצִיר מִבַּר שִׁית — לָא תְּקַבֵּיל, בַּר שִׁית — קַבֵּיל, וּסְפֵי לֵיהּ כְּתוֹרָא! אִין, סְפֵי לֵיהּ כְּתוֹרָא. מִיהוּ, אֵינוֹ יוֹרֵד עִמּוֹ לְחַיָּיו עַד לְאַחַר שְׁתֵּים עֶשְׂרֵה שָׁנָה. וְאִב"א, לָא קַשְׁיָא: הָא — לְמִקְרָא, הָא — לְמִשְׁנָה. דַּאֲמַר אַבָּיֵי: *אָמְרָה לִי אֵם: בַּר שִׁית — לְמִקְרָא, בַּר עֶשֶׂר — לְמִשְׁנָה, בַּר תְּלֵיסַר — לְתַעֲנִיתָא מֵעֵת לְעֵת, וּבְתִינוֹקֶת בַּת תְּרֵיסַר. אָמַר אַבָּיֵי: אָמְרָה לִי אֵם: הַאי בַּר שִׁית דְּטָרְקָא לֵיהּ עַקְרַבָּא בְּיוֹמָא דְּמִישְׁלַם שִׁית — לָא חָיֵי. מַאי אַסּוּתֵיהּ — מְרָרְתָּא דְּדַיְּה חִיוַּרְתָּא בְּשִׁיכְרָא, נִשַׁפְיֵיהּ וְנַשְׁקְיֵיהּ. הַאי בַּר שַׁתָּא דְּטָרֵיק לֵיהּ זִיבּוּרָא בְּיוֹמָא דְּמִישְׁלַם שַׁתָּא — לָא חָיֵי. מַאי אַסּוּתֵיהּ — אַצְוָתָא דְּדִיקְלָא בְּמַיָּא, נִשַׁפְיֵיהּ וְנַשְׁקְיֵיהּ. אָמַר רַב קְטִינָא: כָּל הַמַּכְנִיס אֶת בְּנוֹ פָּחוֹת מִבֶּן שֵׁשׁ — רָץ אַחֲרָיו וְאֵינוֹ מַגִּיעוֹ. אִיכָּא דְּאָמְרִי: חֲבֵירָיו רָצִין אַחֲרָיו וְאֵין מַגִּיעִין אוֹתוֹ. וְתַרְוַיְיהוּ אִיתְנְהוּ: חָלִישׁ וְנָמֵיר. אִיבָּעֵית אֵימָא: הָא — דִּכְחִישׁ, הָא — דְּבָרִיא. אָמַר רַבִּי יוֹסֵי בַּר חֲנִינָא: *בְּאוּשָׁא הִתְקִינוּ: ^ו^הָאִשָּׁה שֶׁמָּכְרָה בְּנִכְסֵי מְלוֹג בְּחַיֵּי בַעְלָהּ, וּמֵתָה — הַבַּעַל מוֹצִיא מִיַּד הַלָּקוֹחוֹת. אַשְׁכְּחֵיהּ רַב יִצְחָק בַּר יוֹסֵף לר' אַבָּהוּ דַּהֲוָה קָאֵי בְּאוּכְלוּסָא דְּאוּשָׁא. אֲמַר לֵיהּ: מַאן מָרֵיהּ דִּשְׁמַעְתָּא דְּאוּשָׁא? אֲמַר לֵיהּ: רַבִּי יוֹסֵי בַּר חֲנִינָא. *תְּנָא מִינֵּיהּ אַרְבְּעִין זִימְנִין, וְדָמֵי לֵיהּ כְּמַאן דְּמַנְּחָא לֵיהּ בְּכִיסְתֵּיהּ. °"אַשְׁרֵי שׁוֹמְרֵי מִשְׁפָּט עוֹשֵׂה צְדָקָה בְכָל עֵת" (תהלים קו) ^ז^וְכִי אֶפְשָׁר לַעֲשׂוֹת צְדָקָה בְּכָל עֵת? דָּרְשׁוּ רַבּוֹתֵינוּ שֶׁבְּיַבְנֶה, וְאָמְרִי לָהּ רַבִּי אֱלִיעֶזֶר: ^ח^זֶה הַזָּן בָּנָיו וּבְנוֹתָיו כְּשֶׁהֵן קְטַנִּים. רַבִּי שְׁמוּאֵל בַּר נַחְמָנִי אָמַר: זֶה הַמְגַדֵּל יָתוֹם וִיתוֹמָה בְּתוֹךְ בֵּיתוֹ וּמַשִּׂיאָן. °"הוֹן וָעֹשֶׁר בְּבֵיתוֹ וְצִדְקָתוֹ עֹמֶדֶת לָעַד" (שם קיב) רַב הוּנָא וְרַב חִסְדָּא; חַד אָמַר: זֶה הַלּוֹמֵד תּוֹרָה וּמְלַמְּדָהּ, וְחַד אָמַר: זֶה הַכּוֹתֵב תּוֹרָה, נְבִיאִים וּכְתוּבִים, וּמַשְׁאִילָן לַאֲחֵרִים. °"וּרְאֵה בָנִים לְבָנֶיךָ שָׁלוֹם עַל יִשְׂרָאֵל", (שם קכח) אָמַר רַבִּי יְהוֹשֻׁעַ בֶּן לֵוִי: כֵּיוָן שֶׁבָּנִים לְבָנֶיךָ — שָׁלוֹם עַל יִשְׂרָאֵל, דְּלָא אָתֵי לִידֵי חֲלִיצָה וְיִבּוּם. רַבִּי שְׁמוּאֵל בַּר נַחְמָנִי אָמַר: כֵּיוָן שֶׁבָּנִים לְבָנֶיךָ — שָׁלוֹם עַל דַּיָּינֵי יִשְׂרָאֵל, דְּלָא אָתֵי לְאִינְצוּיֵי.§ זֶה מִדְרָשׁ דָּרַשׁ ר"א לִפְנֵי חֲכָמִים כו'.§ יָתֵיב

רש"י

וַעֲשִׂיתִינְהוּ. כְּפִיתִי אוֹתָם בַּחֲזָקָה. וּמִפְּנֵי שֶׁטָּרַחְתִּי עָלָיו לִיכָּנֵס לוֹ לִפְנִים מִשּׁוּרַת הַדִּין — מְחַבְּבִינִי. וְאִי דִּינָא הוּא. אֵין כָּאן גְּמִילוּת טוֹבָה לְהַחֲזִיק לוֹ טוֹבָה, שֶׁעַל כָּרְחוֹ יִשְׁפּוֹט אֱמֶת. הַמְבַזְבֵּז. לַעֲנִיִּים. מֵחוֹמֶשׁ. שֶׁבִּנְכָסָיו, שֶׁלֹּא יִצְטָרֵךְ לַבְּרִיּוֹת. עַשֵּׂר אֲעַשְּׂרֶנּוּ. שְׁנֵי עִישּׂוּרִין, הָווּ לְהוּ חוֹמֶשׁ. וְהָא לָא דָּמֵי בַּתְרָא לְקַמָּא. דְּכִי שֶׁקָּלַתְּ לְקַמָּא פָּשׁוּ לְהוּ ט', וְכִי הָדְרַתְּ מַדְלֵית מַעֲשֵׂר דִּידְהוּ — לָאו כִּי קַמָּא הוּא, וְאֵין כָּאן חוֹמֶשׁ בִּשְׁנֵיהֶם. אֲעַשְּׂרֶנּוּ. מִדְּלָא כְּתִיב עַשֵּׂר אֲעַשֵּׂר לָךְ — הָכִי קָאָמַר: אֲעַשְּׂרֶנּוּ כָּרִאשׁוֹן, כְּלוֹמַר: מַעֲשֵׂר שֵׁנִי יְהֵא כָּרִאשׁוֹן. שְׁמוּעוֹת הַלָּלוּ. דְּרַבִּי אִילְעָא בְּתַקָּנַת אוּשָׁא. מִתְמַעֲטוֹת וְהוֹלְכוֹת. מֵאֲמוֹרָאִים. הָרִאשׁוֹנָה — א"ר אִילְעָא אָמַר ר"ל מִשּׁוּם דְּר"י בַּר חֲנִינָא. הַשְּׁנִיָּה — ר' אִילְעָא אָמַר ר"ל. שְׁלִישִׁית — ר' אִילְעָא לְחוּדֵיהּ. וְסִימָנֵיךְ. בְּסֵדֶר הַהֲלָכוֹת, וּבוֹ תֵּדַע סֵדֶר מִיעוּטָן. קְטַנִּים כָּתְבוּ וּבִזְבְּזוּ. בָּנָיו וּבְנוֹתָיו כְּשֶׁהֵן קְטַנִּים, כּוֹתֵב נְכָסָיו, הַמְבַזְבֵּז אַל יְבַזְבֵּז. וּמִעוּטָהּ לֹא תַּחֲלִיף בְּאֵיזוֹ שְׁלֹשָׁה וּבְאֵיזוֹ שְׁנַיִם וּבְאֵיזוֹ אֶחָד. מִתְגַּלְגֵּל עִם בְּנוֹ. אִם מְסָרֵב מִלִּלְמוֹד — יְגַלְגֵּל עִמּוֹ בְּנַחַת וּבִדְבָרִים רַכִּים. יוֹרֵד עִמּוֹ לְחַיָּיו. לִרְדּוֹתוֹ בִּרְצוּעָה וּבְחוֹסֶר לֶחֶם. רַב שְׁמוּאֵל בַּר שִׁילַת. מְלַמֵּד תִּינוֹקוֹת הָיָה. וּסְפֵי לֵיהּ כִּי תוֹרָא. הַלְעִיטֵהוּ תּוֹרָה, כְּשׁוֹר שֶׁאַתָּה מַלְעִיטוֹ וְאוֹבְסוֹ מַאֲכָל. לְתַעֲנִיתָא מֵעֵת לְעֵת. לְהִתְעַנּוֹת כָּל הַיּוֹם. וְחִינּוּכָא לְשָׁעוֹת, מִקּוֹדֶם לָכֵן שְׁנָתַיִים, כִּדְאָמְרִינַן בְּיוֹמָא (דף פב.). וּבְתִינוֹקֶת. שֶׁהִיא מְמַהֶרֶת לְהָבִיא כֹּחַ, שֶׁאֵינָהּ מַתֶּשֶׁת כֹּחַ בְּלִימּוּד תּוֹרָה. וְתַרְתֵּי סְרֵי דְּקָאָמַר — שְׁנַת שְׁתֵּים עֶשְׂרֵה גּוּפָא קָאָמַר. דְּאִי בַּת שְׁתֵּים עֶשְׂרֵה וְיוֹם אֶחָד — דְּאוֹרַיְיתָא הִיא, שֶׁמְּבִיאָה שְׁתֵּי שְׂעָרוֹת, וּבַת עוֹנָשִׁים, וְאֵין צָרִיךְ לָנוּ לִלְמוֹד מִמֵּינִיקְתּוֹ שֶׁל אַבָּיֵי. לָא חָיֵי. אִם לֹא בִּרְפוּאָה בְּדוּקָה. מְרָרְתָּא דְּדַיְּה. מָרָה שֶׁל דַּיָּה, שֶׁקּוֹרִין וושט"ו. נִשַׁפְיֵיהּ וְנַשְׁקְיֵיהּ. תִּמְשָׁחֶנּוּ מִמֶּנּוּ, וְתַשְׁקֶנּוּ מִמֶּנּוּ בְּשֵׁכָר. אַצְוָתָא דְּדִיקְלָא. סִיב שֶׁגָּדֵל סָבִיב דֶּקֶל תּוֹמֶר, כְּעֵין ווילד"ה שֶׁכּוֹרֵךְ אֶת עֵץ הַגֶּפֶן. הַמַּכְנִיס אֶת בְּנוֹ. לִלְמוֹד תּוֹרָה. רָץ אַחֲרָיו. לְהַבְרוֹתוֹ וּלְהַחֲיוֹתוֹ. וְאֵין מַגִּיעוֹ. מְסוּכָּן הוּא לָמוּת מֵרוֹב חוּלְשׁוֹ. חֲבֵירָיו רָצִין אַחֲרָיו. לִהְיוֹת פִּקְחִין בַּתּוֹרָה כְּמוֹתוֹ. הָא דִּכְחִישׁ. אַל יַכְנִיסֶנּוּ, שֶׁמְּסוּכָּן הוּא פֶּן יַחֲלִישׁ וְיָמוּת. דְּבָרִיא. יַכְנִיסֶנּוּ לְפִי שֶׁמִּתְפַּקֵּחַ. שֶׁמָּכְרָה בְּנִכְסֵי מְלוֹג. הַקֶּרֶן. הַבַּעַל מוֹצִיא. דְּשַׁוְיוּהוּ רַבָּנַן כְּלוֹקֵחַ, וְהוּא לוֹקֵחַ רִאשׁוֹן. [בְּאוּכְלוּסָא. אֲסִיפַת בְּנֵי אָדָם]. תְּנָא מִינֵּיהּ. דְּר' יוֹסֵי בַּר חֲנִינָא מָרֵיהּ הוּא. זֶה הַזָּן בָּנָיו וּבְנוֹתָיו קְטַנִּים. שֶׁתָּמִיד יוֹם וָלַיְלָה הֵן עָלָיו, וְהִיא צְדָקָה, שֶׁאֵינוֹ חִיּוּב עָלָיו בָּהֶם. הוֹן וָעוֹשֶׁר בְּבֵיתוֹ. שֶׁאֵין הַמָּמוֹן כָּלֶה, וְאעפ"כ — צִדְקָתוֹ עוֹמֶדֶת לָעַד. זֶה הַלּוֹמֵד תּוֹרָה וּמְלַמְּדָהּ. מִתְקַיֶּימֶת בּוֹ, הֲרֵי "הוֹן וָעוֹשֶׁר בְּבֵיתוֹ", "וְצִדְקָתוֹ עוֹמֶדֶת לָעַד" — עַל שֶׁטָּרַח לְלַמֵּד לְתַלְמִידִים. זֶה הַכּוֹתֵב כו'. הַסְּפָרִים קַיָּימִים לוֹ, שֶׁאֵינָם כָּלִים, וְצִדְקָתוֹ עוֹמֶדֶת לָעַד. לְאִינְצוּיֵי. מִי קָרוֹב וְקוֹדֵם בְּנַחֲלָה.

אֲוֵוש

תוספות

עשיתינהו בעי. הלי עשוי לריך לומר דהיינו בדברים, כי ההוא דלקמן (דף נג.): מעלאי דידי — היינו עשוי. והשתא אתי שפיר דקאמר "עשיתינהו בעי!" דאם מן הדין היה — מה היה לו לעשותם בדברים? היה לו להלקותם ולכופם עד שיזונו אותו. וכן פר"ת. ומיהו מלינו "עשוי" שלא בדברים, כגון: אין מעשין אלא לפסולות (לקמן דף עז.).

אל יבזבז יותר מחומש. מפרש בירושלמי שפעם ראשונה יכול לבזבז חומש, ומכאן ואילך בכל שנה ושנה יתן חומש הריות.

שיהא אדם מגלגל עם בנו עד י"ב שנה. והא דתנן במסכת אבות (פ"ה): בן עשר למשנה — לא שירד עמו, לחייו אלא לגלגל.

וספי ליה כי תורא. ולא ירד עמו לחייו עד י"ב. שנה והא דתנן במסכת אבות: בן חמש שנים למקרא — היינו לגלגל, ולא למיספי ליה.

בר שית למקרא. היינו בר שית ויום אחד, דומיא דבר עשר למשנה דהוי בר עשר ויום אחד, כי ההוא דמסכת אבות דהתם הוי בר עשר ויום אחד, דומיא דבן י"ג למצות. והשתא האי בר שית למקרא לא הוי דומיא דבן עשר למשנה, דבר שית למקרא — היינו למיספי ליה כי תורא, ובר עשר למשנה לא למיספי ליה, אלא לגלגל עד י"ב שנה.

ובת תריסר לתעניתא. פירש בקונטרס: שנת י"ב, ומשום חינוך. ולר"י נראה: דבת י"ב שנה ויום אחד קאמר, דומיא דבר עשר, כדפרישית. ואשמעינן דלית לן השלמה דרבנן, כר"י בפרק בתרא דיומא (דף פב.). והא דפי' נמי בקונט' בתינוקת שהיא ממהרת להביא כח — לא היה לריך לפרש כן, אלא שחינוך שלה שנה לפני גדלותה, דהיינו י"ב שנה ויום אחד, כמו תינוק שחינוכו שנה לפני גדלותו.

ומאי אסותיה. פר"ת: שלא ישכם. אבל אין נראה לפרש לאחר שנשכו, דהא אמר דלא חיי — משמע דאין רפואה מועלת לו.

הבעל מוציא מיד הלקוחות. אליבא דר"י דאמר: קנין פירות כקנין הגוף דמי — לא לריכא לתקנת אושא, אלא לריש לקיש. ואליבא דריש לקיש מסיק לה בפ' "החובל" (ב"ק ד' פח: ושם). אי נמי, לר"י נמי אלטריך, כגון נותן מתנה לאשתו שקנתה ואין הבעל אוכל פירות. א"נ, דכתב לה: דין ודברים *אין לי בפירות נכסייך. אבל אין לומר דכתב לה: דין ודברים אין לי בנכסייך ובפירותיהם — דהא תנן בפרק "הכותב" (לקמן דף פג.) דאם מכרה ונתנה — קיים*.

יתיב

עין משפט נר מצוה

סז א טור חו"מ סי' רנז בב"י:

סח ב מיי' (פ"ז מהל' מתנות עניים) ופ"ח מהל' ערכין הלי"ג סמג עשין קסב טוש"ע יו"ד סי' רמט סעי' א:

סט ג מיי' פ"א מהל' ת"ת הל' ו ופ"ב הל' ב סמג עשין יב טוש"ע שם סי' רמה סעי' ה:

ע ד טוש"ע שם סעי' ח:

עא ה מיי' פכ"ב מהל' אישות הל' ז סמג עשין פט טוש"ע אה"ע סי' צ סעיף ט:

עב ו מיי' פ"י מהל' מתנות עניים הל' טז טוש"ע יו"ד סי' רנא סעי' ג:

אין לי בנכסיך ובפירותיך אבל אם כתב לה דין ודברים אין לי בנכסיך אין לומר כו' כצ"ל רש"ל ועי' במהרש"א

[ועי' תוס' יבמות לו: ד"ה קנין ותוס' ב"ק פח: ד"ה באושא]

מסורת הש"ס

[לקמן סז: ערכין כח. ע"ש]

ב"ב כא.

[קדושין לה: וש"נ]

[לקמן עח: ב"ק פח: ב"מ לה. ודף לו: ב"ב נ. ודף קלט:]

[לעיל כב: ברכות כח. מגילה ז: פסחים עב.]

תורה אור

גליון הש"ס

גמ' באושא התקינו המבזבז. בירושלמי פ"א דפאה כך היתה הלכה בידם ושכחוה וחזרו ועמדו השניים והסכימו ע"ד הראשונים: **שם** וכי אפשר לעשות צדקה בכל עת. עי' מדרש רבה אסתר סי' קכל דף ל"ד ע"ד:

תוספות רי"ד

אא"ב לאו דינא הוא מש"ה עשינהו אלא אי אמרת דינא הוא עשינהו בעי פי' הא בחזקת אב עומדים הנכסים לגבי מזונות. א"ר אילא באושא התקינו המבזבז אל יבזבז יותר מחומש שמא יצטרך לבריות תנ"ה מעשה באחד שבקש לבזבז יותר מחומש ולא הניחו [חבירו] ומני ר"ע. אר"נ ב"י ואיתימא ר"א ב"י מאי קראה וכל אשר תתן לי עשר אעשרנו לך פי' משמע שנוטל שני עישורים והיינו חומש. א' מחמשה והא לא דמי עשורא קמא לעשורא בתרא פי' דקמא הוי חד מעשר ובתרא קשקיל מט' דאישתייר בציר ממאה ולא הוי בין תרווייהו חומש. אמר ר"א ה"ק אעשרנו לבתרא כקמא פי' מדלא כתיב אעשר לך: אר"י באושא התקינו שיהא אדם מתגלגל עם בנו בתלמוד תורה עד י"ב שנה פי' מתנהג עמו בפיוסים מכאן ואילך יורד עמו עד לחייו פי' לרדותו ברצועה ובחוסר לחם. איני והא"ל רב לר"ש בר שילת בציר משית לא תקביל מכאן ואילך קבל ואספי ליה כתורא פי' שמואל ב"ש מלמד תינוקות הוה ואספי פי' לשון ספו לי מאליה כלומר מלעיטו ד"ת כשור הלועט לגימות גדולות: ל"ק הא למשנה הא למקרא דאמר אביי אמרה ל' אם בר שית למקרא [בר עשר למשנה] בר תריסר לתעניתא מע"ל ובתינוקת [בת תריסר] פי' ישלים תעניתו כל היום ובתינוקת פי' לפי שממהרת להביא שנה א' קודם לאיש ומדאורייתא אינה מתענה כל היום כי אם בשנת י"ג אבל כל שנת י"ב כקטנה דמיא ומדרבנן מחנכין אותה להשלים התענית שנה א' קודם הזמן: א"ר קטינא כל המכנים את בנו פחות מבן שש רץ אחריו להברותו ואינו מגיעו פי' להברותו ואין מגיעו שחלש הוא יותר מדאי ורוצה לרפאותו ולא יועיל לו א"ד חביריו רצין אחריו ואין מגיעין אותו פי' מרוב חכמתו ותרווייהו איתנהו הא בכחיש והא בבריא פי' דכחיש שמסוכן הוא ופן יחלש וימות ולפיכך לא יכניסנו ואי בריא הוא מכניסו לתורה פחות מבן שש ואז חביריו רצין אחריו ואין מגיעים אותו אבל מיחלש לא חליש כולי האי כיון דבריא הוא. גרסי' בפ' מציאת האשה מעשה הוה ההוא עניא דהוה רגיל לשדורי ליה כל מעלי יומא דכיפורי ד' מאה זוזי. יומא חד שדריה נהליה ביד בריה אתא א"ל לא צריך א"ל מאי חזית א"ל חזאי דקמזלפי עליה יין ושמן אמר מפקנא כולי האי עיפינהו שדרינהו פי' כפליה כי קא ניחא נפשיה א"ל אייתי חשבוני דצדקה חזא דהוי כתיב ביה שבעה אלפי דינרי קיסרי פי' שם מקום אמר אורחא רחיקא זוודא קלילי פי' צדה קלה הכינותי לדרך שאני אבוא לה קם בזביה לפלגא דממונא והיכי עביד הכי והא א"ר אילא המבזבז וכו' ה"מ מחיים פי' שמא ירד מנכסיו אבל לאחר מיתה לית לן בה: אר"י ב"ח באושא התקינו האשה שמכרה בנכ"מ בחיי בעלה ומתה הבעל מוציא מיד הלקוחות פי' אע"פ שמן הדין יהא מכרה קיים שאין לבעל בחיי אשתו אלא פירות והגוף לאשה פי' הקרן וכשמתה בעלה יורש גם הגוף אבל עתה שקדמה ומכרה מכרה מכור דומיא דבן שיורש נכסי אביו ואם מכרן אביו בחייו הן מכורים שהיורש אינו יורש אלא מה שמוצא לאחר מיתה ובאושא התקינו שיוציא הבעל מיד הלקוחות בלא דמים שעשאוהו חז"ל כלוקח משעה שכנס את אשתו ולא כיורש וכיון שהוא לוקח ראשון מוציא מיד הלקוחות: אשרי שומרי משפט עושה צדקה בכל עת. רבותינו שביבנה ואמרי לה ר"א אומר זה הזן בניו ובנותיו כשהן קטנים ר"ש ב"נ אמר זה המגדל יתום ויתומה בתוך ביתו ומשיאן סמוך לפירקן: הון ועושר בביתו וצדקתו עומדת לעד. ר"ה ור"ח חד אמר זה המלמד תורה ומלמדה. וחד אמר זה הכותב תנ"ך ומשאילן לאחרים. זה מדרש דרש וכו':

יתיב רב יוסף קמיה דרב המנונא, ויתיב רב המנונא וקאמר: כשם שאין הבנים יורשין אלא מן הקרקע — כך אין הבנות ניזונות אלא מן הקרקע. אווש עליה כולי עלמא: דשביק ארעא — הוא דירתי ליה בניה, דלא שביק ארעא — לא ירתי ליה בניה?! אמר ליה רב יוסף: ודלמא [א]כתובת בנין דכרין קאמר מר? אמר ליה: *מר, דגברא רבא הוא, ידע מאי קאמינא. אמר רבי חייא בר יוסף: רב זן מחיטי דעלייה. איבעיא להו: פרנסה הויא, ומאי עלייה — מעילוייא דאב, וכדשמואל. *דאמר שמואל: [ב]לפרנסה שמין באב. או דלמא: מזוני ממש הוה, ומאי עלייה — מדברים טובים שנאמרו בעלייה. דאמר רב יצחק בר יוסף: בעלייה התקינו שיהו בנות ניזונות מן המטלטלין. תא שמע: בידיה דרבי בנאי, אחוה דרבי חייא בר אבא, הוו מטלטלין דיתמי, אתו לקמיה דשמואל, א"ל: זיל זון. מאי לאו למזוני, וכדרב יצחק בר יוסף סבירא ליה? לא, התם לפרנסה הואי. ושמואל לטעמיה, דאמר שמואל: לפרנסה שמין באב. הוה עובדא בנהרדעא, ודון דייני דנהרדעא, בפומבדיתא ואגבי רב חנא בר ביזנא. אמר להו רב נחמן: זילו אהדרו, ואי לא — מגבינא לכו לאפדנייכו מינייכו. רבי אמי ורבי אסי סבור למיזן ממטלטלי. אמר להו רבי יעקב בר אידי: מילתא דר' יוחנן ור"ל לא עבדו בה עובדא, אתון עבדין בה עובדא?! רבי אלעזר סבר למיזן ממטלטלין, אמר לפניו רבי שמעון בן אליקים: רבי, יודע אני בך שאין מדת הדין אתה עושה אלא מדת רחמנות, אלא, *שמא יראו התלמידים ויקבעו הלכה לדורות. ההוא דאתא לקמיה דרב יוסף, אמר להו: הבו לה מתמרי דעל בודיא. אמר ליה אביי: אילו בעל חוב הוה, כי האי גוונא מי הוה יהיב ליה מר? אמר ליה: דחזייא לבודיא קאמינא.

סוף

אווש עליה כולי עלמא. והוא לא פי' דבנים יורשין דקאמר, כתובת בנין דיכרין היא, וסבורים שסתם ירושה קאמר, שאין הבנים יורשין מטלטלין. דלמא כתובת בנין דיכרין קאמר מר. לפי ששתי תקנות הללו שתקנו חכמים בתנאי כתובה לומדות זו מזו, ובכתובת בנין דכרין תנן, בפרק "מי שהיה נשוי" (לקמן דף נא.), דאין נגבית מן המטלטלין. דתנן: ר' שמעון אומר, אפי' יש שם נכסים שאין להם אחריות — אינן כלום, עד שיהא שם נכסים שיש להן אחריות מותר על שתי הכתובות דינר. והתם מפרש *להילכתא כתובת בנין דיכרין. דתנן: מי שהיה נשוי שתי נשים ומתו, ואח"כ מת הוא, ויתומין של כל אחת מבקשין כתובת אמן, כגון שכתובת האחת מרובה, או אם שתיהן שוות — פעמים שבני האחת רבים ובני האחת מועטין, ואותן המועטין מבקשים כתובת אמן לחלקוה ביניהן, ובני השניה יחלקו את כתובת אמן ביניהן. ובאין עליהם מכח תנאי כתובת אמן, שכתוב בה: "כתובת בנין דכרין דיהוויין ליכי מינאי, אינון ירתון כסף כתובתיך" כו'. אם יש מותר דינר על שתי הכתובות, שמתקיים בו נחלה דאורייתא — אלו נוטלין כתובת אמן, ואלו נוטלין כתובת אמן; ואם לאו — חולקין בשוה למנין גולגלותם. דבמקום דמיעקרא נחלה דאורייתא — לא תקון רבנן. מר דגברא רבה הוא ידע. שאין ללמוד מזון בנות מירושת בנים, אלא מירושת כתובת בנין דכרין, שבאה מכח תנאי כתובה כמותה. רב זן מחיטי דעלייה. יתומות באו לפניו ותובעות מזונות מחיטי דאביהן, שלא היו שם קרקעות אלא מטלטלין, ונתן להם. פרנסה הואי. לא מזונות היו, אלא פרנסת נדוניא לינשא, והיא גביא ממטלטלי. וכדשמואל דאמר לפרנסה שמין באב. אומדין לפי וותרנותו של אב, או לפי קמצנותו; אם היה קיים — כך וכך היה נותן להם מנכסים הללו. וכיון דאומד דעתו שיימינן — מקרקעי ומטלטלי שוים בכך. מעילוייא דאב. לפי אומד עילוי דעת וותרנותו. או דלמא מזוני ממש. ואע"ג דתנאי כתובה ככתובה, ואין נגבית ממטלטלי, דכל אסמכתא דשטרי אקרקעות היא, לפי שעומדות בעין — רב סבר לה כתקנת עלייה, והיינו דקאמר מחיטי דעלייה. זיל זון. את הבנות. הוה עובדא ודון דייני. לזון מן המטלטלין. מתמרי דעל בודיא. שהן מטלטלין. בודיא. מחצלות שפותחין תחת הדקלין כשגודרין התמרים. אילו בעל חוב הוה. כלומר אפילו בעל חוב שייפה כחו לטרוף ממשועבדין, אינו גובה ממטלטלין של יתומים, וזו תגבה למזון הבנות שהורע כחן אצל משועבדים? דחזו לבודיא. הקרובות לגדור ועדיין מחוברות.

יתום

יתיב רב יוסף קמיה דרב המנונא. משמע דרב יוסף היה קטן מרב המנונא, ובפ"ק דקידושין (דף כה. ושם) משמע דרב המנונא תלמידו של רב חסדא היה, גבי ספי דנזייתא דלא אתו לפירקיה דרב חסדא, אמר ליה לרב המנונא: זיל לנעינהו. ורב יוסף חבירו של רב חסדא היה! אלא צ"ל דתרי רב המנונא הוו*.

ומאי עלייה מעילוייא דאב. לקמן בפרק "מציאת האשה" (דף סח.) פר"ת: דהא דאמר שמואל שמין באב — לא ליפות כח הבת, ליתן לה יותר מעשור נכסים אם האב היה וותרן — אלא לגרוע כחה, וליתן לה פחות מעשור נכסים, אם אנו יודעין שהוא עצרן. דלא מצינו שומא לעלויא, אלא לגריעותא, כדאמרי' בפ' "מציאת האשה" (ג"ז שם): מעשה ונתן לה רבי עד שנים עשר בנכסים, ולקמן (דף נג:) נמי משמע דדוקא עד עישור נכסים שרו רבנן, אבל טפי — איכא עבורי אחסנתא. דפריך: מי איכא מידי דרחמנא אמר ברא לירות ברתא לא תירות, ומתקני רבנן כו'? ומסיק עד כמה, משמע — עד כמה שרו רבנן אע"ג דדמי לעבורי אחסנתא — עד עישור נכסים. ומיהו, הכא משמע עלוייא דאב דשמואל לעלוייא קאמר. ויש לומר: דלענין מטלטלי דוקא הוי לעלויא. דכיון דשמין בדעת האב — גביא נמי ממטלטלי. אבל לענין כמה בדעת האב ליתן — הוי לגריעותא, שלא להוסיף על עישור, אלא לפחות. וא"ת: דבפרק "מציאת האשה" (ג"ז שם) תנן: רבי יהודה אומר: אם השיא בת הראשונה ינתן לשניה כדרך שנתן לראשונה. משמע, אפילו נתן לראשונה יותר מעישור נכסים, מדקא מהדרי ליה רבנן: פעמים שאדם עשיר והעני. פירוש: עשיר בדעת והעני בדעת, ולא יתן לזאת כמו שנתן לראשונה. אלא שמין את הנכסים, ועישור נכסים יתנו ולא יותר, ושמואל דאמר שמין באב — כר"י סבירא ליה! ואור"י: דלעולם לא קאמר רבי יהודה ינתן לשניה כדרך שנתן לראשונה, אלא דווקא כשנתן לראשונה עישור נכסים או פחות. ורבנן מהדרו ליה דאין ללכת אחר דעתו הראשונה, כיון שדעת האדם משתנה — הילכך לעולם יתנו עישור נכסים. ויש להביא ראיה, דרבי אית ליה בהדיא כר"י בפרק "מציאת האשה" (שם), וקאמר רבי בההיא שמעתא דפרנסה טרפא ממשעבדי ולא מזונות, לפי שמזונות אינן קצובים, כדאמרינן ב"הניזקין" (גיטין דף נא. ושם), ופרנסה מיקץ קייצא כדאמר התם. ואם איתא דלהוסיף על עישור נכסים נמי שמין באב, אם כן פרנסה נמי אינה קצובה? אבל אם אין שמין אלא לפחות מעישור נכסים — ניחא, אע"פ שאין לה קצבה למטה, כיון דלמעלה מיהא יש לה קצבה — יכולין הלקוחות ליזהר ולהניח מבני חרי כדי עישור נכסים. ומיהו אין ראיה, דאם כן — מהאי טעמא נמי יש קצבה למזונות כששיעבדו האחים, דהא יש קצבה למעלה עד בגר. ואין לומר דהתם איכא למימר שמא תלקה ותצטרך רפואה, ואמרינן בפרקין *דרפואה שאין לה קצבה היא בכלל מזונות — דהא חשיב ב"הניזקין" (ג"ז שם) פסק לזון ה' שנים בת אשתו — יש לה קצבה, דקתני: והיא ניזונת מנכסים משועבדים, אלא ודאי אע"פ שקצובים למעלה עד בגר, כיון שאין קצובין למטה, דאפשר שתנשא קודם — לא חשיבי קצובין. אבל פרנסה יש לה קצבה, שאפשר ללקוחות לברר הדברים ע"י ב"ד, ולשום דעתו של אב בין למעלה בין למטה. **ואמר** ליה זיל זון כו'. ואם תאמר: ומאי אולמיה הא דשמואל יותר מההיא דרב יצחק בר יוסף, דמבעיא לן אי סבר רב כוותיה? וי"ל: משום דשמואל עביד עובדא, מייתי מיניה. ולא מסתבר ליה דרב פליג אדשמואל, דהא בלאו הכי משמע דרב זן היינו מזונות, אלא דמבעיא ליה משום דלא ניחא ליה למימר שיחלוק רב על המשנה, דקתני דמזונות הבנות הוי כירושת בנין דיכרין, ומייתי ראייה משמואל דעביד עובדא, והכי נמי מצי סבר רב כדמשמע לישנא דזן רב. וסברי דאחרי כן שינו התקנה. וא"ת: והיכי משמע מילתא דשמואל דאמר "זיל זון" דמזונות ממש קאמר — יותר ממילתיה דרבי חייא בר יוסף דקאמר "רב זן"? וי"ל: דסברא הוא, בשעה שפוסק הוראה — יש לו לפסוק בלשון דליכא למיטעי, הילכך איכא למימר טפי דזיל זון ממש קאמר. אבל רבי חייא בר יוסף היה שונה קבלתו, ולא היה כל כך מדקדק בלשונו. **אמר** להו זילו אהדרו כו'. טועין בדבר משנה חשיב להו רב נחמן, והוא בעצמו היה יכול להחזיר הדין, אלא שבעלי דינין לא היו שומעין לו כמו לדיינין, לכך קאמר להו: זילו אהדרו.

סוף

עג א מיי' פט"ז מהל' אישות הל"ז טוש"ע אה"ע סי' קיא סעי' יד:
עד ב מיי' פ"כ שם הל' ג סמג לאוין פא טוש"ע שם סי' קיג סעי' א':

[וכ"כ תוס' בעירובין סג. ותוס' יבמות פג: וע' תוס' סנהדרין יז:]

תוספות רי"ד
יתיב ר"י קמיה דר"ה ויתיב ר"ה וקאמר כשם שאין (הבעל יורש) [הבנים יורשין] כתובת בנ"ד אלא מן הקרקע כך אין הבנות ניזונות אלא מן הקרקע:

ס"א לכתובת בנין. כן רש"ל

[זבחים סב.]

לקמן סח.

[ברכות יח.]

[לקמן נב:]

יָתוֹם וִיתוֹמָה. אָח וַאֲחוֹת וְנִכְסֵיהֶם בְּיַד אַפּוֹטְרוֹפּוֹס. הַעֲלוּ לַיָּתוֹם בִּשְׁבִיל יְתוֹמָה. הַעֲלוּ לַיָּתוֹם מְזוֹנוֹת יְתֵירִים, שֶׁתִּיזּוֹן אֲחוֹתוֹ עִמּוֹ. דְּאִיכָּא תַּרְתֵּי. אֲחוֹתוֹ, וּתְשַׁמְּשֶׁנּוּ. מוֹצִיאִין. מִן הַיְּתוֹמִים. מוֹצִיאִין לַבָּנוֹת מִן הַבָּנִים. לִמְזוֹנוֹת וּלְפַרְנָסָה. וְלַבָּנוֹת מִן הַבָּנוֹת. לַקְּטַנּוֹת מִן הַגְּדוֹלוֹת. אִם אֵין שָׁם אֶלָּא בָּנוֹת, וְהֶחֱזִיקוּ גְּדוֹלוֹת בַּנְּכָסִים – מוֹצִיאִין מִיָּדָם וְחוֹלְקוֹת בְּשָׁוֶה. וְהָכָא לֵיכָּא מְזוֹנֵי, שֶׁאֵין הַבָּנוֹת נִזּוֹנוֹת מִן הַבָּנוֹת, לְפִי שֶׁכּוּלָּן שָׁווֹת בִּירוּשָּׁה. וְלַבָּנִים מִן הַבָּנִים. לַקְּטַנִּים מִן הַגְּדוֹלִים לַחֲלוֹק בְּשָׁוֶה. אֲבָל לֹא לַבָּנִים מִן הַבָּנוֹת בִּנְכָסִים מוּעָטִין. שֶׁאֵין בָּהֶן כְּדֵי לָזוּן אֵלּוּ וָאֵלּוּ עַד שֶׁיִּבָּגְרוּ, דְּאָמְרִי רַבָּנַן: הַבָּנוֹת יִזּוֹנוּ, וְהַבָּנִים יִשְׁאֲלוּ עַל הַפְּתָחִים. לְפַרְנָסָה. לִנְדוּנְיָא. **מתני'** וְלֹא כָּתַב לָהּ כָּל נְכָסִים כו'. חַיָּיב לִהְיוֹת כָּל הַנְּכָסִים אַחֲרָאִין לָהּ, וְלֹא יָכוֹל לוֹמַר לָהּ: אֵין לִיךְ אֶלָּא שָׂדֶה הַכְּתוּבָה לָךְ בִּשְׁטַר כְּתוּבָּתֵיךְ. וּבְכֹהֶנֶת. שֶׁאֵינוֹ יָכוֹל לְקַיְּימָהּ מִשֶּׁנִּשְׁבֵּית, כּוֹתֵב לָהּ: אֶפְרְקִינֵךְ וְאַהַדְרִינָךְ לִמְדִינְתֵּךְ. לְפִי שֶׁאֵשֶׁת כֹּהֵן אֲסוּרָה לְבַעְלָהּ אִם נֶאֶנְסָה. אֵינוֹ רַשַּׁאי. שֶׁכְּבָר נִתְחַיֵּיב בְּפִדְיוֹנָהּ מִשֶּׁנִּשְׁבֵּית. חַיָּיב לְרַפְּאוֹתָהּ. שֶׁהָרְפוּאָה כִּמְזוֹנוֹת. רַשַּׁאי. שֶׁאֵין אָדָם חַיָּיב לָזוּן גְּרוּשָׁתוֹ. **גמ'** פְּלוּגְתָּא דְּרַבִּי מֵאִיר וְרַבִּי יְהוּדָה. בְּפֶרֶק "אַף עַל פִּי". וְהִיא כּוֹתֶבֶת הִתְקַבַּלְתִּי כו'. לְשׁוֹן שׁוֹבֵר, וַאֲפִי' לֹא נִתְקַבְּלָה. וּלְר' מֵאִיר אֵינָהּ יְכוֹלָה לִמְחוֹל בְּעוֹדָהּ תַּחְתָּיו. וּמַתְנִי' נַמִי, דְּקָתָנֵי לֹא כָּתַב לָהּ כְּתוּבָּה – גּוֹבָה כְּתוּבָּתָהּ שְׁלֵימָה, קָא סָלְקָא דַּעְתָּךְ וַאֲפִילּוּ מְחָלָה. אַחֲרָאִין לִכְתוּבָּתֵיךְ חַיָּיב. שֶׁנִּשְׁתַּעְבְּדוּ נְכָסָיו. וְקס"ד, נִשְׁתַּעְבְּדוּ בְּכָל דִּין שִׁעְבּוּד כְּאִילּוּ נִכְתַּב בְּתוֹךְ הַשְּׁטָר, וְאִם יִמְכּוֹר נְכָסָיו תִּטְרוֹף לָקוֹחוֹת. אֲתָאַן לְר' יְהוּדָה. דְּאָמַר: שְׁטָר שֶׁלֹּא נִכְתַּב בּוֹ אַחֲרָיוּת – לֹא מִדַּעַת הַמַּלְוֶה נַעֲשָׂה, אֶלָּא סוֹפֵר טָעָה, וַהֲרֵי הוּא כְּמִי שֶׁנִּכְתַּב, וְטוֹרֵף מִן הַמְּשׁוּעְבָּדִים.

סוֹף סוֹף, כָּל הָעוֹמֵד *לִגְזוֹז כְּגָזוּז דָּמֵי! דִּצְרִיכָא לְדִיקְלָא קָאמִינָא.§ הַהוּא יָתוֹם וִיתוֹמָה דְּאָתוּ לְקַמֵּיהּ דְּרָבָא, אֲמַר לְהוּ רָבָא: הַעֲלוּ לַיָּתוֹם בִּשְׁבִיל יְתוֹמָה. אָמְרִי לֵיהּ רַבָּנַן לְרָבָא: וְהָא מָר הוּא דַּאֲמַר: *מִמְּקַרְקְעֵי וְלָא מִמִּטַּלְטְלֵי, בֵּין לִמְזוֹנֵי, בֵּין לִכְתוּבָּה וּבֵין לְפַרְנָסָה! אֲמַר לְהוּ: אִילּוּ רָצָה שִׁפְחָה לְשַׁמְּשׁוֹ – מִי לָא יָהֲבִינַן לֵיהּ? כָּל שֶׁכֵּן הָכָא, דְּאִיכָּא תַּרְתֵּי.§ תָּנוּ רַבָּנַן: *[א]אֶחָד נְכָסִים שֶׁיֵּשׁ לָהֶן אַחֲרָיוּת וְאֶחָד נְכָסִים שֶׁאֵין לָהֶן אַחֲרָיוּת – מוֹצִיאִין לִמְזוֹן אִשָּׁה וְלַבָּנוֹת, דִּבְרֵי רַבִּי. רַבִּי שִׁמְעוֹן בֶּן אֶלְעָזָר אוֹמֵר: נְכָסִים שֶׁיֵּשׁ לָהֶן אַחֲרָיוּת – מוֹצִיאִין לַבָּנוֹת מִן הַבָּנִים, וְלַבָּנוֹת מִן הַבָּנוֹת, וְלַבָּנִים מִן הַבָּנִים. וְלַבָּנִים מִן הַבָּנוֹת בִּנְכָסִים מְרוּבִּין, אֲבָל לֹא לַבָּנִים מִן הַבָּנוֹת בִּנְכָסִים מוּעָטִין. נְכָסִים שֶׁאֵין לָהֶן אַחֲרָיוּת – מוֹצִיאִין לַבָּנִים מִן הַבָּנִים, וְלַבָּנוֹת מִן הַבָּנוֹת, [ו]וְלַבָּנִים מִן הַבָּנוֹת, אֲבָל לֹא לַבָּנוֹת מִן הַבָּנִים. אע"ג דְּקַיְימָא לָן *הֲלָכָה כְּרַבִּי מֵחֲבֵירוֹ – הָכָא הֲלָכָה כְּרַבִּי שִׁמְעוֹן בֶּן אֶלְעָזָר. דְּאָמַר רָבָא: *[ב]הִלְכְתָא; מִמְּקַרְקְעֵי וְלָא מִמִּטַּלְטְלֵי, בֵּין לִכְתוּבָּה בֵּין לִמְזוֹנֵי בֵּין לְפַרְנָסָה.§ **מתני'** [ג]לֹא כָּתַב לָהּ כְּתוּבָּה – בְּתוּלָה גּוֹבָה מָאתַיִם, וְאַלְמָנָה מָנֶה, מִפְּנֵי שֶׁהוּא תְּנַאי בֵּית דִּין. כָּתַב לָהּ שָׂדֶה שָׁוֶה מָנֶה תַּחַת מָאתַיִם זוּז. [ד]וְלֹא כָּתַב לָהּ "כָּל נְכָסִים דְּאִית לִי אַחֲרָאִין לִכְתוּבָּתֵיךְ" – חַיָּיב. שֶׁהוּא תְּנַאי בֵּית דִּין. [ה]לֹא כָּתַב לָהּ "אִם תִּשְׁתַּבַּאי אֶפְרְקִינֵךְ וְאוֹתְבִינֵךְ לִי לְאִינְתּוּ" *[ו]וּבְכֹהֶנֶת "אֲהַדְרִינָךְ לִמְדִינְתֵּךְ" – חַיָּיב, שֶׁהוּא תְּנַאי בֵּית דִּין. [ז]נִשְׁבֵּית – חַיָּיב לִפְדוֹתָהּ. [ח]וְאִם אָמַר: "הֲרֵי גִּיטָּהּ וּכְתוּבָּתָהּ, וְתִפְדֶּה אֶת עַצְמָהּ" – אֵינוֹ רַשַּׁאי. [ט]לָקְתָה – חַיָּיב לְרַפְּאוֹתָהּ. *[י]אָמַר "הֲרֵי גִּיטָּהּ וּכְתוּבָּתָהּ, תְּרַפֵּא אֶת עַצְמָהּ" – רַשַּׁאי.§

גמ' מַנִּי? רַבִּי מֵאִיר הִיא, דְּאָמַר: *[כ]כָּל הַפּוֹחֵת לִבְתוּלָה מִמָּאתַיִם וּלְאַלְמָנָה מִמָּנֶה – הֲרֵי זוֹ בְּעִילַת זְנוּת. דְּאִי רַבִּי יְהוּדָה – הָאָמַר: *רָצָה – כּוֹתֵב לִבְתוּלָה שְׁטָר שֶׁל מָאתַיִם, וְהִיא כּוֹתֶבֶת "הִתְקַבַּלְתִּי מִמְּךָ מָנֶה", וּלְאַלְמָנָה מָנֶה, וְהִיא כּוֹתֶבֶת "הִתְקַבַּלְתִּי מִמְּךָ חֲמִשִּׁים זוּז". אֵימָא סֵיפָא: כָּתַב לָהּ שָׂדֶה שָׁוֶה מָנֶה תַּחַת מָאתַיִם זוּז, וְלֹא כָּתַב לָהּ "כָּל נְכָסִים דְּאִית לִי אַחֲרָאִין לִכְתוּבָּתֵיךְ" – חַיָּיב, שֶׁהוּא תְּנַאי בֵּית דִּין. אֲתָאַן לְר"י, דְּאָמַר: אַחֲרָיוּת – טָעוּת סוֹפֵר הוּא. דְּאִי רַבִּי מֵאִיר – הָאָמַר: *אַחֲרָיוּת לָאו טָעוּת סוֹפֵר הוּא. דִּתְנַן: *מָצָא שִׁטְרֵי חוֹב, אִם יֵשׁ

יֵשׁ

סוף סוף כל העומד לגזוז כגזוז דמי. אע"ג דפלוגתא דר"מ ורבנן היא בפרק "שבועת הדיינין" (שבועות מג. ושם) בענבים העומדים ליבצר, דר"מ סבר כבצורות דמיין ורבנן סברי לאו כבצורות דמיין – מ"מ פריך הכא בפשיטות דכגזוז דמי, כמו שפר"ת דמהיא דפרק "הכונס" (ב"ק דף נט: ושם) קיימא לן הכי. דקאמר התם: רבי שמעון אומר אכלה פירות גמורין – משלמת פירות גמורין, אם סאה – סאה, אם סאתים – סאתים, דחשבינן להו כתלושים. ופסקינן התם הלכה כר"ש. אבל אין לומר דבהכהו דאי קיימי מכחשי מודו כ"ע דכבצורות דמיין, דב"השולח" (גיטין דף לט.) ובפרק קמא דסנהדרין (דף טו.) משמע דבהא נמי פליגי. **ממקרקעי** ולא ממטלטלי בין למזונות בין לפרנסה. וא"ת: קשיא דרבא אדרבא, דבפרק "מציאת האשה" (לקמן דף סח.) פסיק רבא הלכה כר"י, דאמר: ינתן לשניה כדרך שנתן לראשונה, ואמרינן התם דשמואל כר"י ס"ל. אלמא סבר רבא דשמין באב, וא"כ גביא ממטלטלי, כדאמרינן בשמעתין! וליכא למימר דהתם רבא משמיה דרב חסדא קאמר לה, וליה לא ס"ל, דהא התם בההיא סוגיא פריך מינה אמילתיה דרבא גופיה, ולא קא משני הכי! וי"ל: דהא דאמר רבא הכא ממקרקעי ולא ממטלטלי – היינו בדלא אמידניה. והא דסבר רבא התם כרבי יהודה ושמואל בדאמידניה, שדעתו שתגבה ממטלטלי. וכה"ג מפליג התלמוד התם. ונראה דבזמן הזה דכולהו גבי ממטלטלי, כתובה ומזונות מתקנת הגאונים, ופרנסה נמי אנן סהדי שכל בני אדם רגילים להשיא בנותיהם ממטלטלי, וחשיב כמו באמידניה דפסיק רבא כר"י. **מני** ר' מאיר היא דאמר כל הפוחת כו'. בפרק "אע"פ" (לקמן דף נו:) דייק: כל הפוחת – אפי' בתנאי, אלמא סבר דתנאו בטל, ואית לה. וכיון דאמר (א) לית לה – לא סמכה דעתה, והוי בעילתו בעילת זנות. ופריב"ן, דבכל מקום דאית לה ואין האשה בטוחה בו דלא סמכה דעתה – תקנו חכמים שיהא בעילתו בעילת זנות. אבל אם היה תנאו קיים, כיון דלית לה – אין בעילתו בעילת זנות. ואלמנה, אע"פ דלדרבנן תנאו קיים – הכא תנאו בטל, דכל דתקון רבנן – כעין דאורייתא תקון. וקשה לר"י: דבפרק "החובל" (ב"ק דף פט. ושם) משמע דאפי' היכא דלית לה הוי לר' מאיר בעילת זנות, משום שלא תהא קלה בעיניו להוציאה! דפריך התם התלמוד גבי אשה שחבלה בבעלה לא הפסידה כתובתה, ואמאי? תזבין לכתובתה בטובת הנאה לבעלה כו'! ומשני: הא מני – ר"מ היא, דאמר: אסור לאדם שישהא עם אשתו שעה אחת בלא כתובה, מ"ט – שלא תהא קלה בעיניו להוציאה, על כן נראה דר"מ לא מבעיא קאמר: לא מבעיא היכא דלית לה – דהויא בעילתו בעילת זנות, משום דקלה בעיניו להוציאה, אלא אפילו אית לה, כיון דלא סמכה דעתה – הויא בעילתו בעילת זנות. ודייק מדלא קתני כל בתולה שאין לה מאתים, ואלמנה שאין לה – מנה הרי היא בעילת זנות. אלא נקט: כל הפוחת, משמע שבא לומר: אע"ג דתנאו בטל ואית לה – הויא בעילת זנות. וקשה לר"י: דמנא לן דכל הפוחת ואפי' בתנאי? דלמא בתנאי מודה ר"מ דתנאו קיים, דכל הפוחת דמשמע דאפילו באותו ענין שיש לה, היינו בסוף ביאה, דאמרינן בפ' "אע"פ" (לקמן דף נו.) דאינה מוחלת! וי"ל: דלשון כל הפוחת – משמע שהוא פוחת לה, ובסוף ביאה אינו יכול לפחות לה, אלא היא פוחתת לעצמה, ולא שייך לשון פחת אלא בתנאה. א"נ, מדנקט "כל" קא דייק. וא"ת: דבפרק "אע"פ" (שם) אמר דבסוף ביאה לדברי הכל אינה מוחלת, וב"החובל" (ב"ק פט. ושם) משמע שיכולה למכור ולמחול! ויש לומר כדפירש הקונטרס לקמן: דדוקא בעל פה אינה מוחלת, דאמירתה לאו כלום היא, כיון דכבר זכתה, אלא אם כן כתבה שובר. ואם תאמר: ומאי קאמר: (ב) הא מני רבי מאיר היא, הא משמע בפרק "אע"פ" (לקמן שם) דלרבי יהודה נמי אינה יכולה למחול, דתנאו בטל. ודווקא בכותבת לו "התקבלתי" קאמר! ויש לומר: דהתם מיירי לפי המסקנא דשמעתין, דקאמר: ואי בעית אימא רבי יהודה, התם בכתבה ליה "התקבלתי". ואם תאמר: ומנא לן דלרבי מאיר אפילו בכתבה ליה "התקבלתי" לא מצי מחלה דקאמר מני ר' מאיר היא? דלמא ר"מ לא מבעיא ב"התקבלתי" קאמר דמצי מחלה, דהויא בעילת זנות. אלא אפי' בעל פה, דתנאו בטל – הויא בעילת זנות! וי"ל: דהשתא אין נראה לו לחלק בין כתבה ללא כתבה. **מני** רבי מאיר היא. השתא משמע ליה מתני' דלא כתב לה – היינו לפי שהתנה עמה. **אתאן** לר' יהודה דאמר אחריות טעות סופר הוא רישא ר"מ סיפא ר' יהודה. אסיפא בלא רישא ה"מ לדקדק: מני! אי רבי מאיר – הא אמר אחריות לאו טעות סופר הוא! אי רבי יהודה – כתב לה שדה שוה מנה במאתים אמאי חייב? והא לרבי יהודה יכולה למחול! אלא דרך הש"ס דמדקדק מרישא כל כמה דמצי למידק. וכענין זה יש בפרק "כירה" (שבת לט:) גבי מעשה שעשו אנשי טבריא, ובפרק קמא דעירובין (דף טז.) גבי נמצאת שלשה מדות במחילה. [וע"ע תוספות שבת לט: ד"ה אלא פניו וכו' ומש"ש על הגליון].

ממשה

תוספות רי"ד

א"ר הל' ממקרקעי ולא ממטלטלי בין למזונות בין לפרנסה. פי' פרנסה הוא נדוניתא. והאידנא תקינו רבנן בתראי דמיתזני אפי' ממטלטלי. עיין בפרק מציאת האשה: **מתני'** לא כתב לה כתובה בתולה גובה מאתים ואלמנה מנה מפני שהוא תנאי ב"ד כתב לה שדה שוה מנה תחת מאתים זוז ולא כתב לה כל נכסין דאית לי אחר אין לכתובתך חייב מפני שהוא תנאי ב"ד לא כתב לה אם תשתבאי אפרקינך ואותבינך לי לאנתו ובכהנת אהדרינך למדינתך חייב מפני שהוא תנאי ב"ד: נשבית חייב לפדותה אמר הרי גיטה וכתובתה תפדה א"ע אינו רשאי. פי' מפני שתנאי ב"ד הוא להתחייב בפרקונה. ואפילו נתן לה כתובה לאחר מכאן הואיל וכשנשבית היא תחתיו. לקתה חייב לרפאותה אמר הרי גיטה וכתובתה תרפא א"ע רשאי. פי' דרפואה דמיא למזונות. וכי היכי דכי יהיב לה גט וכתובה תו לא יהיב לה מזונות. רפואה נמי לא יהיב לה. פי' תנאי ב"ד. כל דבר שתיקנו ב"ד לא בעי כתיבה דתקנות ב"ד כמאן דנקט שטרי' בידיה דמי. כתב לה שדה שוה וכו' לא מבעיא היכא דלא כתב לה כתובה דלא מצי למיעקר תקנות ב"ד וחייב לתת לה מאתים. אלא אע"ג דכתב לה שדה שוה מנה תחת מאתים זוז וא"ל זה השדה יהיה לך לשיעבוד כתובתיך שעשה תחבול' שלא פיחת תנאי ב"ד אלא אוקיר לה שדהו שוה מאה במאתים ולא כתב לה כל נכסי דאית לי אחראין לכתובתך שנמצא עכשיו שאינה יכולה לטרוף היום או למחר אלא אותו השדה שאינו שוה אלא ק' גם זה לא הועיל לו כלום שכל נכסיו אחראין לכתובתה. ואע"ג דלא כתב לה מפני שהוא תנאי ב"ד שיכתוב אדם כך כדאמרי' לקמן בפ' האשה שמעון בן שטח תיקן שיכתוב כל אדם לאשתו כל נכסי אחראין לכתובתך. וכיון שתקנות ב"ד הוא אע"פ שלא כתב לה ככתוב דמי וה"ה נמי אם כתב לה שדה שוה מאתים לכתובתה כדי שיהי' נכסיו בנ"ח ויוכל למוכרן ולא תחזור האשה עליהן לא עשה כלום. מפני תנאו של שמעון בן שטח אלא תנא דמתני' אתא לאשמועינן שא"י לפחות ממאתים זוז בשום ענין ואם השדה שוה מאתים ולא פיחת כלום אך אם נשתדף אותו השדה טורפת משאר נכסיו. ואע"ג דלא כתב לה כל נכסי אחראין לכתובתך כתקנת שמעון בן שטח: ודייקו בגמרא מני מתני' ר"מ היא דאמר כל הפוחת לבתולה מר' ולאלמנה מק' ה"ז בעילת זנות. פי' ואפילו מחלה איהי לאו כל כמינה דאי ר"י האמר אם רצה כותב לבתולה ר' והיא כותבת לו שנתקבלתי ממך ק'. ולאלמנה ק והיא כותבת לו התקבלתי ממך נ' זוז פי' ובמתני' תני שאם כתב לה שדה שוה ק' תחת ר' זוז אע"פ שהאשה נתרצית בכך אין ממש במעשיו אלא מתני' דלא כר"י אימא סיפא כתב לה שדה שוה ק' תחת ר' זוז ולא כתב לה כל נכסי דאית לי אחראין לכתובתך חייב מפני שהוא תנאי ב"ד. פי' משמע דנביא ממשעבדי אע"ג דלא כתב לה שיעבוד נכסין. אתאן לר"י דאמר אחריות ט"ס הוא ואע"ג דלא כתוב ככתוב דמי דאי לר"מ נהי דנביא מב"ד משום שאינו רשאי לפחות לה

ג"י ערוך לגרוד כגרוד [וכן איתא בתוס' ב"ב מב: ד"ה שבת ובכתה"ש לקמן פ"ח סי' ז] אבל בתוס' ב"ק נט: ד"ה ופסק ושם לה: ד"ה שבת גרסו לגזוז כגזוז דמי וכן בתוס' דהכא]

[לקמן סח:]

[לעיל כח. וש"נ]

[לקמן סט:]

[עי' תוס' יבמות לה. ד"ה כתובות]

[עי' תוס' לקמן נב: ד"ה אמר הרי גיטה]

לקמן נד:

ג"ז שם

[ב"ק שם וש"נ] ב"מ יב:

הגהות הב"ח

(א) תוס' ד"ה מני וכו' וכיון דאמר להו ליה לך אלא מנה לא סמכה דעתה: (ב) בא"ד וא"ת ומאי קאמר הכא מני ר"מ:

גליון הש"ס

גמ' ולבנים מן הבנות. עיין לקמן דף נו ע"א תוס' ד"ה אלמנה שתפסה.

עה א ב מיי' פט"ו מהל' אישות הלכה ז טוש"ע אה"ע סי' קיב סעיף א וסי' קיג סעי' א:

עו ג מיי' פי"ב שם הל' ב סמג עשין מח טוש"ע שם סימן סו סעיף א:

עז ד מיי' פי"ז שם הל' י סמג שם טוש"ע שם סי' ק סעיף א:

עח ה מיי' פי"ד שם הלכה ה ופי"ב שם הלכה יח סמג שם טוש"ע שם סי' עח סעיף א:

עט ו מיי' פי"ד שם הלכה יח סמג שם טוש"ע שם סימן עח סעיף ז:

פ ז ח מיי' שם הל' יח יט טוש"ע שם סעיף ח:

פא ט מיי' שם הל' יז סמג שם טוש"ע שם סי' עט סעיף א:

פב י מיי' שם טוש"ע שם סעיף ב:

פג כ מיי' פ"ו שם הל' ב ופ"ו שם הל' ב סמג שם ואלוין עח טוש"ע שם סי' סו סעיף ט:

פד א מיי' פי"ח מהל' גזילה ואבידה הלכ' א סמג עשין מד טוש"ע ח"מ סי' סה סעיף ו:
פה ב מיי' פ"ט שם הל' ז סמג עשין עג טוש"ע שם סי' שעב סעיף א:
[ועי' תוס' יבמות ג: ד"ה למעוטי וכו' ומש"ש בס"ד על הגליון]
פו ג מיי' וסמג שם טוש"ע שם סימן שעג סעיף א:
פז ד מיי' פכ"ג מהל' אישות הלכ' יח סמג עשין מח טוש"ע אה"ע סי' קיד סעיף ד:
פח ה מיי' פכ"ד שם הלכ' יט ופ"א מהל' איסורי ביאה הלכה ט סמג עשין מח:
פט ו מיי' פכ"ד מהל' אישות הלכה יט [ופי"ח מהל' איסורי ביאה הלכה ח] טוש"ע אה"ע סי' ו סעיף יא:
צ ז מיי' פי"ח מהלכות איסורי ביאה הלכ' ח סמג לאוין קכה טוש"ע שם סי' ו סעיף י:
צא ח מיי' פ"ג שם הלכה ב:
צב ט מיי' פכ"ד מהל' אישות הלכה כ סמג עשין מח:

יש בהן אחריות נכסים – לא יחזיר, שבית דין נפרעין מהן. אין בהן אחריות נכסים – יחזיר, שאין בית דין נפרעין מהן, דברי רבי מאיר. [א]וחכמים אומרים: אחד זה ואחד זה לא יחזיר, שבית דין נפרעין מהן. רישא ר"מ וסיפא ר' יהודה! וכי תימא: כולה ר' מאיר היא, ושאני ליה לר"מ בין כתובה לשטרי – ומי שאני ליה? והתניא: *חמשה גובין מן המחוררין, ואלו הן: [ב]פירות, [ג]ושבח פירות, [ד]והמקבל עליו לזון את בן אשתו ובת אשתו, וגט חוב שאין בו אחריות, וכתובת אשה שאין בה אחריות, מאן שמעת ליה דאמר אחריות לאו טעות סופר הוא – רבי מאיר, וקתני: כתובת אשה! איבעית אימא ר' מאיר, ואיבעית אימא ר' יהודה; איבעית אימא ר' יהודה: התם – כתבה ליה "התקבלתי". הכא – לא כתבה ליה "התקבלתי". איבעית אימא ר' מאיר: מאי חייב דקתני – מן המחוררין.§ לא כתב לה וכו'.§ אמר אבוה דשמואל: אשת ישראל שנאנסה – אסורה לבעלה, חיישינן שמא תחלתה באונס וסופה ברצון. איתיביה רב לאבוה דשמואל: "אם תשתבאי אפרקינך ואותבינך לי לאינתו"! אישתיק. קרי רב עליה דאבוה דשמואל: °"שרים עצרו במלים וכף ישימו לפיהם" (איוב כט). מאי אית ליה למימר – *בשבויה הקילו. ולאבוה דשמואל, אונס דשריא רחמנא היכי משכחת לה? כגון דקאמרי עדים שצווחה מתחלה ועד סוף. ופליגא דרבא, דאמר רבא: [ה]כל שתחלתה באונס וסוף ברצון אפי' היא אומרת: הניחו לו, שאלמלא (*לא) נזקק לה היא שוכרתו – מותרת, מ"ט – °יצר אלבשה. תניא כוותיה דרבא: °"והיא לא נתפשה" (במדבר ה) – אסורה. [ו]הא נתפשה – מותרת. ויש לך אחרת שאע"פ שלא נתפשה – מותרת. *ואיזו – זו כל שתחלתה באונס וסופה ברצון. תניא אידך: *"והיא לא נתפשה" – אסורה, הא נתפשה – מותרת. ויש לך אחרת שאע"פ שנתפשה אסורה, ואיזו – [ז]זו אשת כהן. אמר רב יהודה אמר שמואל משום רבי ישמעאל: *"והיא לא נתפשה" – אסורה, הא נתפשה – מותרת, [ח]ויש לה אחרת שאע"פ שלא נתפשה מותרת, *ואיזו – זו שקידושיה קידושי טעות, שאפי' בנה מורכב על כתיפה ממאנת והולכת לה. אמר רב יהודה: [ט]הני נשי דגנבו גנבי – שריין לגוברייהו. אמרי ליה רבנן לרב יהודה: והא קא ממטיאן להו נהמא! מחמת יראה. והא קא משלחן להו גירי! מחמת יראה. ודאי, שבקינהו ואזלן מנפשייהו – אסירן. ת"ר: שבויי מלכות – הרי הן כשבויין, גנובי ליסטות – אינן כשבויין. והתניא איפכא! מלכות אמלכות לא קשיא; הא – במלכות אחשורוש, הא – במלכות בן נצר. ליסטות אליסטות לא קשיא; הא – בבן נצר, הא – בליסטים דעלמא. ובן נצר, התם קרי ליה מלך והכא קרי ליה לסטים! אין, גבי אחשורוש – לסטים הוא, גבי לסטים דעלמא – מלך הוא.§ ובכהנת אהדרינך למדינתך וכו'.§ אמר אביי: אלמנה לכ"ג – חייב לפדותה, שאני קורא בה "ובכהנת אהדרינך למדינתך".

ממזרת

רש"י

יש בהן אחריות נכסים. ששיעבד לוה נכסיו לאותה מלוה, לא יחזירנו מוצאו למלוה, ואפי' הלוה מודה שהוא חייב לו. ומפרש התם דחיישינן שמא פרעו, ומן הלוה נפל, וזה שהוא מודה – עצת קנוניא היא ביניהם לטרוף לקוחות, ויחלקו ביניהם. וחכ"א כו'. דאחריות טעות סופר הוא, וטריף ממשעבדי ומפסדי לקוחות, ובהא פלוגתייהו דר"מ ר"י הוה בהדייהו, שבדורו היה. ושאני ליה כו'. דבכתובה אית ליה: אחריות *ט"ס הוא. מן המחוררין. *)אם יש נכסים בני חורין אצל החייב – נגבין, ואם לאו – אין נגבין מן המשועבדין. פירות ושבח פירות. כדתנן במס' גיטין (מח:): אין מוציאין לאכילת פירות ולשבח קרקעות מנכסים משועבדים, מפני תיקון העולם. וב"שנים אוחזין בטלית" (ב"מ יד:) מפרש: לאכילת פירות ולשבח קרקעות כיצד? – הרי שגזל שדה מחבירו ומכרה לאחר והשביחה, והרי היא יוצאה בדין מתחת יד הלוקח עם שבחה שהשביח הלוקח בזבל ובניר ועם פירות שבה, שהנגזל טורפה ממנו, כשהוא חוזר על המוכר שמכרה לו באחריות – גובה קרן מנכסים משועבדין, ושבח מנכסים בני חורין ולא מן המשועבדין, מפני תיקון העולם, לפי שאין קצובין, ואין הלוקח יודע בכמה להזהר. והמקבל עליו לזון בן אשתו ובת אשתו. אף הוא אין גובה מן המשועבדים, לפי שאין קצובין ואין כתובים. והא דתנן ב"הנושא": והיא נזונית מנכסים משועבדין, מפני שהיא כבעל חוב – מוקמינן לה התם (דף קב:) כשקנו לה מידו, דסתם קנין לכתיבה עומד. וגט חוב. כל שטרות נקראין גט. הכא לא כתבה ליה התקבלתי. ואשמעינן מתני', דאע"פ שלא כתב לה כתובה, לא אמרינן מחלה לו עליה, אלא אמרינן: סמכה על תקנת ב"ד שהכל יודעין שהנושא אשה יש לה כתובה. מאי חייב נמי דקתני מן המחוררין. אע"פ שלא כתב לה אחריות, תנאי ב"ד הוא להיות כל נכסיו אחראין לה בעודם לפניו. אבל אם מכרם אינה טורפת לקוחות, הואיל ולא נכתב בשטר, ולא אמרינן אחריות טעות סופר הוא. תחלתה באונס. תחלתה של בעילה. וסופה. של בעילה. ולקמיה פריך: אונס דשריא רחמנא היכי משכחת לה? בשבויה הקילו. שלא ראינוה שנבעלה, וכי קאמר איהו בנבעלה. יצר אלבשה. וגם זה אונס. שבתחלת בעילה, שהיא באונס, הלבישה הבועל יצר. והיא. מיעוטא הוא. כלומר, בסתם אשה אמרתי לך טעם האיסור תלוי ב"לא נתפשה", הא נתפשה מותרת, ויש אשה שאע"פ שברצון – מותרת, ואיזו זו כו'. קידושי טעות. על תנאי, ולא נתקיים התנאי, אם זינתה תחתיו מותרת לו, לפי שאינה אשתו אלא פנויה בעלמא היא. הני נשי דגנבו גנבי. שלסטים גונבין מתחת בעליהן. שריין לגברייהו. לפי שבאונס הם באין עליהן. והא קא ממטין להו נהמא. והרי אנו רואים שבעודן אצלן מוליכות להן לאותן גנבים לחם ומזון, אלמא רצון הוא! ומשני: מחמת יראה הוא דעבוד. והא קא משלחן להו גירי. כשנלחמין, מזמנות ומושיטות להם חיצים לירות. ודאי אי שבקינהו. גנבים ללכת אל בעליהן, ואינהו אזלן מנפשייהו אל הגנבים – אסירן. שבויי מלכות. נשים ששבה המלך לתשמיש. הרי הן כשבויין. ומותרין לבעליהן, כדתנן: ואותבינך לי לאינתו. במלכות אחשורוש. הן כשבויין, לפי שמלך גדול הוא, ויודעת שלא ישאנה, ובעילתה באונס. בן נצר. לסטים היה, ולכד עיירות ומלך עליהם, ונעשה ראש לסטים. ובדידיה תנן: שבויי מלכות אינן כשבויין, ואסורות לבעליהן. דסברה: מינסב קא נסיב לה, ונבעלת ברצון. ליסטות אליסטות כו'. כבן נצר אסורות, כדאמרינן, דסברה: מינסב נסיב לי, והריני אשת מלך. ליסטים דעלמא. אפילו לקוחים שלו קשין לה, לפיכך אינה אלא אנוסה. לגבי אחשורוש לסטים הוא. הלכך מתני' קמייתא דמיירי במלכות אחשורוש – קרי לבן נצר גנובי ליסטות. וברייתא דתנן איפכא דגנובי ליסטות מיירי בליסטים דעלמא, קרי לבן נצר שבויי מלכות. אלמנה לכהן גדול. קיימא לן לקמן בפ' "אלמנה ניזונית" (דף ק:) יש לה כתובה ותנאי כתובה, דלמיקם קמיה, כגון מזונות ורפואה – אמרינן ביבמות דלית לה, בפרק "יש מותרות" (דף פה.). והכא אשמעינן אביי, דתנאי כתובה דפירקונה אית לה, דמעיקרא אישתעבד לה, שהרי אף לכשרה לא היה מתנה "ואותבינך לאינתו" אלא "אהדרינך למדינתך", והא נמי קרינן בה הכי. והאי תנא נמי למישקל ומיפק קאי.

ממזרת

תוספות

חמשה גובין מן המחוררין. אע"ג דקתני מניינא – תנא ושייר. הא דתנן בפרק "הניזקין" (גיטין דף מח: ושם*): אין מוציאין למזון האשה והבנות מנכסים משועבדים. והא דפריך בפרק קמא דקידושין (דף טז: ושם) גבי ארבעה מעניקין להם שלש באיש ושלש באשה כו': תנא תני ארבעה ואת אמרת תנא ושייר?! היינו משום דקתני: ואי אתה יכול לומר ארבעה באחד מהם*. וגט חוב שאין בו אחריות. וא"ת: תקשי מהכא לשמואל, דאמר בפרק קמא דב"מ (דף יג.): אומר היה רבי מאיר שטר שאין בו אחריות – אינו גובה לא מנכסים משועבדין ולא מנכסים בני חורין, והכא משמע בהדיא דגבי מבני חרי? ומיהו, בלאו הכי איתותב שמואל התם מברייתא. ורשב"א אומר: דמהכא הוה מצי למידחי, דגט חוב שאין בו אחריות – היינו שמפורש בו דלא למיגבי ביה ממשעבדי, וכעין זה מצינו בפרק "גט פשוט" (ב"ב דף קסח:) גבי מי שבא ואמר אבד שטר חובי. והא דמוקי לה הכא כרבי מאיר – היינו משום דלכאורה כוותיה אתיא, אבל אי הוה פריך מינה לשמואל – הוה מצי למידחי, כדפרישית. אסורה לבעלה. אין להקשות מאסתר דהות שריא למרדכי (מגילה דף יג:) – דלדקת גמורה היתה. אונס דשרי רחמנא היכי משכחת לה כו'. * אע"ג דאבוה דשמואל "חיישינן" קאמר, משמע ליה דמדאורייתא קאמר, דאי מדרבנן – לא הוי מוציאין אותה מבעלה על כך.

ממזרת

תוספות רי"ד

לה מכתובתה אבל ממשעבדי אמאי גביא והא ס"ל דאחריות לאו ט"ס הוא דתנן בב"מ פ"ק מצא שט"ח אם יש בו אחריות נכסים פי' ששיעבד לו כל קרקעותיו לא יחזיר למלוה דשמא פרוע הוא ומלוה נפל ויהיו ב"ד נפרעים שלא כדין. אין בהם אחריות נכסים יחזיר פי' א) למלוה לצור ע"פ צלוחיתו ונהדר ליה ללוה לצור ע"פ צלוחיתו דלוה קאמר להד"מ. שאין ב"ד נפרעין מהן דברי ר"מ ר"י אומר בין כך ובין כך לא יחזיר מפני שב"ד נפרעין מהן. פי' מן הלקוחות דס"ל אחריות ט"ס הוא ואפי' שטר שאין בו אחריות גובה מנכסים משועבדים הלכך אם אין החייב מודה לא יחזיר דחיישי' לפרעון ואם החייב מודה לא יחזיר דחיישינן לקנוניא ורבינו יצחק פוסק דהכי הלכתא. רישא ר"מ וסיפא ר"י וכ"ת כולה ר"מ ושאני ליה לר"מ בין כתובה לשטר פי' דדוקא בשטר קאמר דאחריות לאו ט"ס הוא אבל בכתובה מודה דט"ס הוא הואיל דהוא תנאי ב"ד ואי אמרת השתא בשט"ח דקיהיב מלוה זוזי דא"ל לא שדי איניש זוזי בבדי אר"מ דאחריות לאו ט"ס הוא כתובה דלא יהבה אשה כלום לא כ"ש י"ל דכתובה מודה ר"מ דאית ליה תקנות שמעון בן שטח. וכיון דתקנות ב"ד הוא אע"ג דלא כתב ככתוב דמי ומי שני ליה והתניא ה' גובין מן המחוררין. פי' ולא ממשועבדים כדתנן בגיטין אין מוציאין לאכילת פירות ולמזון האשה והבנות מפני תקון העולם ואלו הן פירות גזל שדה מלאה פירות ואכלן וחזר נגזל ולקחה מגזלן ובא לגבות פירותיו אינו גובה אותן ממשעבדי אלא מבנ"ח ושבח קרקעות פי' גזל שדה ומכרה לאחר והשביחה ובא נגזל וטורפה מלוקח ובא לוקח על גזלן לטרוף קרן ושבח הקרן גובה מנכסים משועבדים והשבח גובה מב"ח והמקבל עליו לזון בן אשתו ובת אשתו ושט"ח שאין בו אחריות וכתובת אשה שאין בה אחריות מאן שמעת ליה דאמר גבי שט"ח אחריות לאו ט"ס הוא ר"מ וקתני כתובת אשה שאין בה אחריות אלמא לית ליה לר"מ תקנות שמעון בן שטח. איבע"א ר"מ איבע"א ר"י איבע"א ר"מ מאי חייב דקתני מן המחוררין. פי' ולעולם לית ליה לר"מ תקנות שמעון בן שטח. והא דקתני בתולה גובה מאתים לא ממשעבדי אלא מבנ"ח כדקתני בברייתא ה' גובין מן המחוררין וכו'. איבע"א ר"י התם כתבה ליה התקבלתי. פי' אשה קמחלה ליה ויכולה היא למחול. אבל הכא לא כתבה ליה התקבלתי פי' במתני' הוא כתב לה שדה שוה מנה והיא לא מחלה לו הלכך לא עשה כלום: אם תשתבאי וכו' אמר אבוה דשמואל אשת ישראל שנאנסה אסורה לבעלה פי' מדרבנן. דאע"ג דמדאורייתא אונס בישראל שרי כדנפקא מהוא לא נתפשה א"נ מולנערה לא תעשה דבר חיישינן שמא תחילתה באונס וסופה ברצון ופליגא דרבא דאמר רבא כל שתחלתה באונס ובסוף היא אומרת הניחו לו שאלמלא לא נזקק עמי הייתי שוכרתו מותרת מ"ט יצר אלבשה פי' תחלת ביאה וסוף ביאה. תניא כוותיה דרבא והיא לא נתפשה אסורה הא נתפשה מותרת ויש לך אחרת שאע"פ שלא נתפשה מותרת ואיזו זו שתחלתה באונס וסופה ברצון: תניא אידך והיא לא נתפשה אסורה הא נתפשה מותרת ויש לך אחרת שאע"פ שנתפשה אסורה ואיזו זו אשת כהן גרס' ב) בהמדיר אר"י א"ש והיא לא נתפשה אסורה הא נתפשה מותרת ויש לך אחרת [שאע"פ] שלא נתפשה מותרת ואיזו זו שקידושיה קידושי טעות. פי' כגון שקידשה ע"מ שהוא כהן ונמצא לוי דהוא לגריעותא ג) וכ"ש ע"מ שהוא לוי ונמצא כהן דהוא לשבח שקידושי' קידושי טעות כדפסיק לית הל' כר"ש בפ"ב דקידושין. ואם זינתה אפילו ברצון מותרת לבעלה שהרי היא לו כפנויה ולא כאשתו שזינתה (לשום) [דהך] נשואין אינה כלום: ואפי' בנה מורכב על כתפה ממאנת והולכת לה. פי' לאו דווקא ממאנת אלא הרי היא מותרת לכל אדם בלא גט: אמר ר"י הני נשי דגנבו גנבי שריין לגברייהו ואע"ג דממטיין להו מיא ונהמא ומשלחי להו גירא שמחמת יראה הוא דקא עבדין פי' כשנלחמין מזמינין ומושיטין להן חיצים לירות שבקינהו ואזלי מנפשייהו ודאי אסורין: ת"ר שבויי מלכות ה"ה כשבוי' גנבים ולסטים אינן כשבוין והתניא איפכא לא ק' כאן במלכות אחשורוש כאן במלכות בן נצר גנבים אלסטים ל"ק הא בב"נ הא בלסטים דעלמא וב"נ הכא קרי ליה מלך והכא קרי ליה לסטים אין גבי אחשורוש ליסטים הוא גבי ליסטים דעלמא מלך הוא. פי' שבויי מלכות הרי הן כשבויין כמו מלכות אחשורוש שאנס הרבה נשים למשכבו ואותן הנשים הן כשבויים שהן אנוסין ומותרות לבעליהן שמסתמא לא נתרצות לו דמימר אמרה מלך גדול כזה לא ישימני גברת ולתאות יצרו הוא מתכוין והלכך אנוסה היא ושבויי ליסטים אינן כשבויים דתני התם הן כמו בן נצר שהי' ליסטים ושולל ונתגבר וכבש הרבה עיירות ומפני שלא היה מלך נכבד וחשוב האשה שהי'

אונס

א) היינו לאוקימתא דשמואל בב"מ (דף י"ג) וצ"ל והא דלא מהדרינן ליה ללוה לצור ע"פ צלוחיתו היינו משום דלוה הא אמר להד"מ. ב) מלשון רבינו שכתב גרסינן בהמדיר משמע שלא היה גורס בכאן למימרא דשמואל. ג) אינו מובן דמאי כ"ש הוא זה ואולי דצ"ל ואפילו ע"מ שהוא לוי וכו' ומה שמסיק כדפסיק לית הלכתא כר"ש. יש לעיין דהא בלשבח יותן גם ר"ש מודה וכדאמרינן התם:

מסורת הש"ס

ואע"ג דבשטרי אמרינן לאו טעות סופר הוא בכתובה מודה הואיל דתנאי ב"ד הוא. ס"א
*) מנכסי בני חורין לבד אם יש כו' כצ"ל. ס"א.
ב"ק נה.
[לעיל כג. וש"נ]
[עי' תוס' מגילה כח.]
[עי' תוס' יבמות נו. ד"ה ואיזו]
[יבמות נו:]
[לקמן עד. יבמות קי: נדה נב.]
[עי' תוס' יבמות נו: ושוד שם קי: ד"ה ואיזו כו' אסמכתא היא על סי']

גליון הש"ס

גמ' יצר אלבשה. עי' ב"ק דף מח ע"א תוס' ד"ה כמאן: תום' ד"ה אונס וכו' אע"ג דאבוה דשמואל וכו'. עיין שער המלך פ"ה מהלכות יסודי התורה ה"ג:

ממזרת ונתינה לישראל — אינו חייב לפדותה, שאין אני קורא בה "ואותבינך לי לאנתו". רבא אמר: [א] כל שאיסור שבייה גורם לה — חייב לפדותה, איסור דבר אחר גורם לה — אינו חייב לפדותה. לימא כתנאי: המדיר את אשתו ונשבית, רבי אליעזר אומר: פודה ונותן לה כתובתה, רבי יהושע אומר: [ב] נותן לה כתובתה, ואינו פודה. אמר רבי נתן, שאלתי את סומכוס: כשאמר רבי יהושע נותן לה כתובתה ואינו פודה — כשהדירה ולבסוף נשבית, או בנשבית ולבסוף הדירה? ואמר לי: לא שמעתי, ונראין דברים [ג] שהדירה ולבסוף נשבית. דאי אמרת נשבית ולבסוף הדירה — אתי לאיערומי. מאי לאו במדיר אשת כהן קמיפלגי, ואביי דאמר כרבי אליעזר, ורבא דאמר כרבי יהושע? לא, הכא במאי עסקינן — *כגון שנדרה איהי וקיים לה הוא. ר' אליעזר סבר: *[ד] הוא נותן אצבע בין שיניה, ורבי יהושע סבר: היא נתנה אצבע בין שיניה. אי היא נתנה אצבע בין שיניה — כתובה מאי עבידתה? ותו, אמר ר' נתן: שאלתי את סומכוס: כשאמר רבי יהושע נותן לה כתובתה ואינו פודה — כשהדירה ולבסוף נשבית, או בשנשבית ולבסוף הדירה? ואמר: לא שמעתי. ואי דנדרה איהי — מה לי הדירה ולבסוף נשבית, מה לי נשבית ולבסוף הדירה? אלא לעולם דאדרה איהו, ואביי מתרץ לטעמיה, ורבא מתרץ לטעמיה. אביי מתרץ לטעמיה: אלמנה לכהן גדול — כולי עלמא לא פליגי דחייב לפדותה, ממזרת ונתינה לישראל — כולי עלמא לא פליגי דאינו חייב לפדותה, מדיר אשת כהן נמי — כולי עלמא לא פליגי דחייב לפדותה, דהיינו אלמנה [לכ"ג]. כי פליגי — במדיר אשת ישראל. רבי אליעזר אזיל בתר מעיקרא, ורבי יהושע אזיל בתר בסוף. רבא מתרץ לטעמיה: אלמנה לכ"ג, ממזרת ונתינה לישראל — כולי עלמא לא פליגי דאינו חייב לפדותה, כי פליגי — במדיר בין אשת כהן ובין אשת ישראל. רבי אליעזר אזיל בתר מעיקרא, ורבי יהושע אזיל בתר בסוף.§ נשבית חייב לפדותה וכו'.§ ת"ר: נשבית בחיי בעלה ואח"כ מת בעלה, הכיר בה בעלה — יורשין חייבין לפדותה, לא הכיר בה בעלה — אין יורשין חייבין לפדותה. לוי סבר למיעבד עובדא כי הא מתניתא. א"ל רב: הכי אמר חביבי: לית הלכתא כי הא מתניתא, אלא כי הא דתניא: *[ה] נשבית לאחר מיתת בעלה — אין היתומין חייבין לפדותה. ולא עוד, אלא אפילו נשבית בחיי בעלה ואחר כך מת בעלה — אין היתומין חייבין לפדותה, שאין אני קורא בה "ואותבינך לאינתו". תנו רבנן: [ו] נשבית והיו מבקשין ממנו עד עשרה בדמיה, פעם ראשונה — פודה, מכאן ואילך, רצה — פודה, רצה — אינו פודה. רבן שמעון בן גמליאל אומר: אין

ממזרת ונתינה לישראל. אע"ג דאית לה כתובה ותנאי כתובה דלמשקל ומיפק, לית לה תנאי כתובה דפרקונה, דמעיקרא לא אשתעבד לה. שאין אני קורא בה ואותבינך לאינתו. שזהו תנאי כתובה לישראלית. רבא אמר כו'. בממזרת ונתינה כאביי סבירא ליה, דלא אשתעבד לה. אבל באלמנה לכ"ג פליג עליה, ואמר מעיקרא לא אשתעבד לכהנת "ואהדרינך למדינתך" אלא מחמת שאסרה השבויה עליו, אבל לנאסרה מחמת דבר אחר – לא נשתעבד, דתנאי כתובה דישראל וכהן שוין, אלא שהכהן מתנה עמה שאפי' תאסר עליו מחמת שבייתה – לא תפסיד כתובת פרקונה. המדיר את אשתו. מליהנות לו. פודה. ואע"פ שסופו לגרשה מחמת נדר. ואינו פודה. לקמן מפרש טעמיה. או בנשבית ולבסוף הדירה. [כלומר: או אפי' כשנשבית ולבסוף הדירה] נמי אמר, ואע"ג דאיכא למימר לא הדירה אלא להפטר מן הפדיון. מאי לאו במדיר אשת כהן. בכהן שהדיר את אשתו. דאי בישראל – לא אמר ר' אליעזר פודה, שהרי אין אני קורא בה תנאי כתובת ישראל "ואותבינך לי לאינתו". אלא בכהן קיימינן, ומשום שאני קורא בה "ואהדרינך למדינתך" קאמר ר' אליעזר פודה, ואע"ג דאיסור דבר אחר גרם לה [ליאסר עליו. ואביי כרבי אליעזר, ורבא כר' יהושע דאמר אינו פודה, הואיל ואיסור דבר אחר גרם לה]. הכא במאי עסקינן כו'. כלומר לעולם רבי אליעזר ורבי יהושע לאו בפלוגתא דאביי ורבא פליגי. ואי באיסור דבר אחר שלא על ידי נדר, אי נמי בכהנת ע"י נדר – דכולי עלמא אי כאביי אי כרבא. והכא כגון שנדרה היא וקיים לה הוא, שאמר "יתקיים", או החריש ולא הפר ביום שמעו, ובישראל פליגי. וטעמא דרבי יהושע, דקסבר: היא נתנה אצבע בין שיניה ונושכתו, כלומר: היא גרמה לעצמה לבטל תנאה, שאין אני יכול לקרות בישראל "ואותבינך לאינתו". ור' אליעזר סבר: הוא נתן אצבעו בין שיניה לינשך, שלא הפר לה. מה לי הדירה ולבסוף נשבית. הא לא הערים מידי, שהרי היא התחילה בנדר. ואביי מתרץ לטעמיה. למימר לאו תנאי היא, אלא דכ"ע כוותי קיימי. וכן רבא מתרץ לטעמיה. דחייב לפדותה. שהרי אני קורא בה בין בתחלת התנאי בין בסוף קיומו "ואהדרינך למדינתך", ואע"ג דאיסור דבר אחר גרם לה – אהדרינך למדינתך הוא. ממזרת ונתינה לישראל אין חייב לפדותה. שאין אני קורא בה לא בשעת התנאי ולא בסופו "ואותבינך לי לאינתו". מדיר אשת כהן נמי. כהן שהדיר את אשתו נמי, שתנאי הראשון "ואהדרינך למדינתך" הוא, ואפשר לו לחול בשעת התנאי ואפשר לו לקיימו בסופו – חייב לפדותה, היינו כאלמנה לכ"ג. כי פליגי בישראל שהדיר את אשתו. שתנאו הראשון "ואותבינך לאינתו" היה ראוי לחול, אבל בסופו אי אפשר לקיימו. ר' אליעזר אזל בתר מעיקרא כו'. דאינו חייב לפדותה. אלמנה שאין אני קורא בה "אהדרינך למדינתך" מחמת שבייה, אלא מחמת דבר אחר. וממזרת שאין אני קורא בה "ואותבינך לאינתו" לא בתחילה ולא בסוף. כי פליגי במדיר בין אשת כהן. דמעיקרא בשעת התנאי קרינן ביה "ואהדרינך" מחמת שבייה, ובסוף איכא איסור דבר אחר. וכן במדיר אשת ישראל, מעיקרא קרינן בה "ואותבינך לאינתו", ובסוף לא קרינן בה הכי. הכיר בה בעלה. עד שלא מת נודע לו שנשבית, ונתחייב בפרקונה בחייו. חביבי. רבי חייא, שהוא דודו אחי אביו. רצה אינו פודה. דלא תקינו בה רבנן אלא חד פדיון. מפני

[לקמן עא.]
[שם]
רש"ל
[תוספתא פ"ד]

ממזרת ונתינה לישראל אינו חייב לפדותה. וא"ת: בין לאביי בין לרבא, הא אמרינן בפ' "יש מותרות" (יבמות דף פה. ושם): אלמנה לכ"ג כו' ממזרת ונתינה לישראל – יש להן כתובה, פירות, ובלאות. ופירות – היינו פרקונה, דפרקונה תחת פירות! ואור"י: דהתם פי' בקונט' דיש להן פירות שאוכל הבעל משלהן, אבל אם לא מלו – לא פריק להו מדידיה. אבל שניות, דקתני התם דאין להם פירות – אפי' מה שאכל הבעל לא יחזיר, ואלמנה לכ"ג מפרש אביי דיש לה לגמרי דין פירות, שחייב לפדותה. אבל רבא מפרש פירות ממש, כמו שאכל. ואותן פירות עצמן לא יתן הבעל אא"כ נשבית. דאי אפילו לא נשבית – א"כ היתה נשכרת, וכל הנשים היו רוצות בכך שלא יפדו ויהיו הפירות שלהן, אע"ג דאמר לעיל דפרקונה עדיף לה טפי מפירות.

כגון שנדרה היא וקיים לה הוא. טפי הוה ליה למימר דפליגי דמר אזיל בתר מעיקרא ומר אזיל בתר בסוף, כדמסיק לקמן. אלא דניחא ליה לאוקומי פלוגתייהו בנותן אצבע בין שיניה, דאשכחן דפליגי בה תנאי בפרק "המדיר" (לקמן דף עא. ושם).

והיו מבקשין ממנה עד עשרה בדמיה פעם ראשונה פודה. וא"ת: והא דבעי בפ' "השולח" (גיטין דף מה. ושם) אהא דתנן אין פודין את השבויין יותר מכדי דמיהן מפני תיקון העולם, אי משום דוחקא דציבורא הוא, או משום דלא *ליגרו בהו טפי – תפשוט מהכא דמשום דוחקא דציבורא, דקתני דפודה עד עשרה בדמיה! וי"ל: דאפי' לטעמא דלא ליגרו וליתו טפי, לא תקינו שלא יוכל לפדות אדם את עצמו יותר מכדי דמיו, שהרי "עור בעד עור וכל אשר לאיש יתן בעד נפשו" (איוב ב) והכא אשתו כגופו. והא דבעי התם למיפשט מהא דלוי פרקיה לברתיה עד תליסר אלפי דינרי – היינו משום דאין בתו כגופו. **רצה** אינו פודה. פי' בקונטרס: דלא תקינו רבנן אלא חד פדיון. משמע מתוך פירושו דאם נשבית פעם שנית – דאינו פודה כלל אפילו בדמיה. וקשה, דלעיל (דף מז:) מסקינן: תקנו מלוי למלוי. דמשמע דפירות ופרקון מלווין יותר מכתובה וקבורה, לפי שאלו אינם אלא פעם אחת כל ימיה, אבל פירות ופרקון – אפשר להיות כמה פעמים! וצ"ל לפירושו דאדרבה, פירות ופרקון אינו מלוי, אבל קבורה חשיבא מלוי, לפי שהנשים ממהרות למות מן האנשים, כדאמר בירושלמי. וכן כתובה מלוי הוא. ור"ח פירש: דרצה אינו פודה – יותר מכדי דמיה, אבל כדי דמיה – פודה. ותימה לרשב"א: דא"כ לרבנן נמי תיקשי פרקון אפרקון שני, אע"ג דכדי דמיה – יוכר על כתובתה, וברייתא אחרת משמע דאין פודה יותר על כתובתה, וילטרך לשנויי תרי קולי אית להו בפרקון שני, ומשמע דלא צריך לשנויי הכי אלא לרשב"א.

גליון הש"ס

צג א מיי' פי"ד מהל' אישות הלכה כב סמג עשין מח טוש"ע אה"ע סי' עח סעיף ו:

צד ב ג מיי' שם הלכה כא טוש"ע שם סעיף ה:

צה ד מיי' פי"ב מהל' אישות הלכה כד סמג שם טוש"ע י"ד סי' רלה סעיף ג וטור אה"ע סי' עב:

צו ה מיי' פי"ח שם הלכה ה סמג לאוין פא טוש"ע אה"ע סי' עח סעיף ח:

צז ו מיי' פי"ד שם הלכה יט טור וב"י י"ד סי' רנב וטוש"ע אה"ע סי' עח סעיף ג בהג"ה:

תוספות רי"ד

אונס למשכבו סמכה דעתה שישימנה גבירה ומסתמא היא מתרצת לו ואין דינה כשבויין והיא אסורה לבעלה ישראל ולגבי אחשורוש קורא לבן נצר ליסטים שלא מלך כ"א בליסטיות ומאי שבויי ליסטים ה"ה כשבויין אלו הן ליסטים דעלמא והן כשבויי אנוסים ומותרת לבעליהן דמסתמא לא נתרצית לו ואין חפצה להיות אשתו שבויי מלכות אינן כשבויין והוא בן נצר שמלך ואינן כשבויין דמסתמא היא נתרצית לו כדאמרן ולגבי ליסטים דעלמא שלא מלכו קרי לבן נצר מלך מפני שמלך: ובכהנו' אהדרינך למדינתך פי' אוציאך מבית השבי ואשיבך לבית אביך בכ"מ שהוא: אמר אביי אלמנה לכ"ג גרושה וחלוצה לכ"ה חייב לפדותה שאני קורא בה ואהדרינך למדינתך פי' המורה קי"ל בפ' אלמנה נזונית יש לה כתובה ותנאי כתובה ההיא דלמשקל ולמיפק קאי אבל תנאי כתובה דלמיקם קמיה כגון מזוני ורפואה אמרינן [ביבמות] בפ' יש מותרות דלית לה. ואשמועינן אביי הכא דתנאי כתובה דפרקונה אית לה דמעיקרא אישתעביד לה שהרי אף לכשרה לא היה מתנה ואותבינך לאנתו אלא אהדרינך למדינה ובהא נמי קרינא בה הכי ואע"ג דאסירא ליה והוא תנאה דלמיפק הוא. ממזרת ונתינה לישראל אינו חייב לפדותה שאין אני קורא בה ואותבינך לי לאינתו. פי' אע"ג דאית לה כתובה ותנאי כתובה דלמישקל ולמיפק קאי. ל"ל תנאי כתובה דפרקונה דמעיקרא לא אישתעביד לה ואין אני קורא בה ואותבינך לי לאנתו. רבא אמר כל שאיסור שבוי' גורם לה פי' ליאסר על בעלה חייב לפדותה פי' דהכי משמע תנאה אי תשתבאית שמחמת שבוי' מיפסלת לי הריני מתנה לך דאפריקינך ואהדרינך למדינתך ומנה (דאומר פסלת לי) [דעל פסול שהיא פסולה ליה]

מחמת ד"א שלא מחמת שבויה לא מתנה בהדה למיפרקה הלכך אלמנה לכ"ג גרושה וחלוצה לכהן הדיוט ממזרת ונתינה לישראל מחמת ד"א הוא ופטור. וקי"ל הלכה כרבא: תניא המדיר את אשתו. פי' הדירה ואסורה עליו בהנאה ואח"כ נשבית. פי' שא"י להחזירה לו לאשה מפני נדרו ר"א אומר פודה אותה ונותן לה גט וכתובתה ר"י אומר נותן לה כתובתה ואינו פודה ואוקי פלוגתא הכי. באלמנה לכ"ג גרושה וחלוצה לכהן הדיוט וממזרת ונתינה לישראל כ"ע לא פליגי דאינו חייב לפדותה. פי' מפני שאיסור ד"א גורם לה כדאמרן כי פליגי במדיר שהוא גרם האיסור ופליגי בין באשת כהן בין באשת ישראל דר"א סבר בתר מעיקרא אזלי' כרנסבא וכתב לה תנאה ואז הות שריא ליה אע"ג דהשתא בשעת פריון היא אסורה לו כיון שהוא גרם לאיסור הזה שיבא חייב לפדותה ור"א כאביי ס"ל ור"י סבר אע"ג שהוא גורם לאיסור בתר לבסוף אזלי' דהיינו בשעת פרי'. ולא מיבעיא באשת ישראל שאינו יכול לקיים ואותבינך לי לאינתו שהרי סופו להוציאה משום הנדר פטור. פי' דאיסור ד"א גורם. אלא אפי' באשת כהן דמצי למיקם תנאי' היינו ואהדרינך למדינתך פטור משום דס"ל כרבא והלכתא כר"י: נשבית חייב לפדותה. ת"ר נשבית בחיי בעלה ואח"כ מת בעלה הכיר בה בעלה. פי' נודע לבעלה עד שלא מת יורשים חייבים לפדותה שכבר נתחייב בעלה לפדותה ונשתעבדו כל נכסיו בפרקונה. לא הכיר בה בעלה אין היורשים חייבים לפדותה ואין אני קורא בה ואותבינך לי לאינתו שהרי מת: לוי סבר למיעבד עובדא כי הא מתני'. פי' שאם הכיר בה בעלה היורשים חייבים לפדותה. א"ל רב הכי אמר חביבי פי' רבי חייא שהוא דודו כלומר אחי אביו לית הל' כי הא מתני' אלא כי הא דתנ"א נשבית לאחר מיתת בעלה אין היתומים חייבים לפדותה. ולא עוד אלא אפילו נשבית בחיי בעלה ואח"כ מת בעלה אין חייבים לפדותה שאין אני קורא בה ואותבינך לי לאינתו פי' שאעפ"י שהיבם מיבמה לא איקרי לי לאנתו שיבמה נקראת ולא אשה והא דכתיב ולקחה לו לאשה לדרשה [אתא] שיגרשנה בגט ומחזירה ככל אשה דעלמא אבל יבמתו נקראת וכדכתיב ויבמה וכ"ש אם היא פסולה שאינו רשאי ליקח אותה לאשה שאין חייב לפדותה ואפילו אם היתה אשת כהן דהל' כרבא שכל שבישראל אינו פודה כהן נמי אינו פודה. כיון שאין חייבים לפדותה ממילא אין להם פירות לא ליבם ולא ליורשים: ת"ר נשבית והיו מבקשים ממנו עד עשרה בדמיה פעם ראשונה פודה. פי' שחובה הוא המוטל עליו שכך כותב לה בכתובתה מכאן ואילך רצה פודה רצה אינו פודה. פי'

אין פודין את השבוין כו'. ארישא קאי: *__אמר__ הרי גיטה וכתובתה תרפא __עצמה__ רשאי. לפי שרפואה היא בכלל מזונות, והרי קבלה כנגד מעשה ידיה שעד עכשיו. אבל אינו רשאי לומר תקבל את גיטה ותפדה את עצמה – לפי שלא קבלה תשלום מפירות שאכל עד עכשיו.

ותגבה ממטלטלי ככתובה שויוה רבנן. והשתא שתקנו הגאונים שכתובה גובה ממטלטלי – כתובת בנין דכרין נמי גביא ממטלטלי, דהא ככתובה שויוה רבנן.

תטרוף ממשעבדי ירתון תנן. אף על פי שידע גם (ב) המקשה דירתון תנן, אלא שבלשון קצר משיבו. ור"ל דחכמים לא רצו לתת להם אלא דין ירושה, כיון דמכח ירושה קאתו. **ירתון** תנן. גבי בת בין הבנים לא בעי לשנויי בהא לישנא דירתון תנן, דאפילו למ"ד [יסבון] תנן, מודה דלגבי הכי כנחלה שויוה רבנן, כדמוכח ב"ב "יש נוחלין" (ב"ב דף קלא.). אבל לגבי ממשעבדי – איכא פלוגתא בינייהו, כדאמר התם ובריש "אע"פ" (לקמן דף נה.).

השתא

תורה אור

*[א] אֵין פּוֹדִין אֶת הַשְּׁבוּיִין יוֹתֵר עַל כְּדֵי דְמֵיהֶם, מִפְּנֵי תִּקּוּן הָעוֹלָם. [ב] הָא בִּכְדֵי דְמֵיהֶן – פּוֹדִין, אע"ג דְּפִרְקוֹנָהּ יוֹתֵר עַל כְּתוּבָּתָהּ. וּרְמִינְהִי: נִשְׁבֵּית, וְהָיוּ מְבַקְּשִׁין מִמֶּנּוּ עַד עֲשָׂרָה בִּכְתוּבָּתָהּ, [ג] פַּעַם רִאשׁוֹנָה – פּוֹדֶה, מִכָּאן וְאֵילָךְ רָצָה – פּוֹדֶה, רָצָה – אֵינוֹ פּוֹדֶה. ר"ש בֶּן גַּמְלִיאֵל אוֹמֵר: אִם הָיָה פִּרְקוֹנָהּ כְּנֶגֶד כְּתוּבָּתָהּ – פּוֹדֶה, אִם לָאו – אֵינוֹ פּוֹדֶה! רַבָּן שִׁמְעוֹן בֶּן גַּמְלִיאֵל תְּרֵי קוּלֵּי אִית לֵיהּ.§ לָקְתָה חַיָּיב לְרַפְּאוֹתָהּ.§ תָּנוּ רַבָּנַן: *אַלְמָנָה נִיזּוֹנֶת מִנִּכְסֵי יְתוֹמִין, וּצְרִיכָה רְפוּאָה – הֲרֵי הִיא כִּמְזוֹנוֹת. רַבָּן שִׁמְעוֹן בֶּן גַּמְלִיאֵל אוֹמֵר: [ד] רְפוּאָה שֶׁיֵּשׁ לָהּ קִצְבָה – נִתְרַפֵּאת מִכְּתוּבָּתָהּ, שֶׁאֵין לָהּ קִצְבָה – הֲרֵי הִיא כִּמְזוֹנוֹת. אָמַר רַבִּי יוֹחָנָן: עָשׂוּ הַקָּזַת דָּם בְּאֶרֶץ יִשְׂרָאֵל כִּרְפוּאָה שֶׁאֵין לָהּ קִצְבָה. קְרִיבֵיהּ דְּרַבִּי יוֹחָנָן הֲוָה לְהוּ אִיתַּת אַבָּא דַּהֲוַת צְרִיכָה רְפוּאָה כָּל יוֹמָא. אֲתוֹ לְקַמֵּיהּ דְּר' יוֹחָנָן, אֲמַר לְהוּ: [ה] אֵיזִילוּ קוּצוּ לֵיהּ מִידֵּי לְרוֹפֵא. אָמַר רַבִּי יוֹחָנָן: *עָשִׂינוּ עַצְמֵנוּ כְּעוֹרְכֵי הַדַּיָּינִין. מֵעִיקָּרָא מַאי סָבַר וּלְבַסּוֹף מַאי סָבַר? מֵעִיקָּרָא סָבַר: °"וּמִבְּשָׂרְךָ לֹא תִתְעַלָּם" וּלְבַסּוֹף סָבַר: *אָדָם חָשׁוּב שָׁאנֵי.§ (ישעיה נח)

מתני' *[ו] לֹא כָּתַב לָהּ [ז] "בְּנִין דִּכְרִין דְּיֶהֶווֹן לִיכִי מִינַּאי אִינּוּן יִרְתּוּן כֶּסֶף כְּתוּבְּתִיךְ יָתֵר עַל חוּלַקְהוֹן דְּעִם אֲחוּהוֹן" – חַיָּיב, שֶׁהוּא תְּנַאי ב"ד. *[ח] "בְּנָן נוּקְבָן דְּיֶהֶוְיָן לִיכִי מִינַּאי יֶהֶוְיָן יָתְבָן בְּבֵיתִי וּמִיתְזְנָן מִנִּכְסַי עַד דְּתִלָּקְחוּן לְגוּבְרִין" – חַיָּיב, שֶׁהוּא תְּנַאי בֵּית דִּין. *"אַתְּ [ט] תְּהֵא יָתְבָא בְּבֵיתִי וּמִיתְּזְנָא מִנִּכְסַי כָּל יְמֵי *מֵיגַר אַלְמְנוּתִיךְ בְּבֵיתִי" – חַיָּיב, שֶׁהוּא תְּנַאי בֵּית דִּין. כָּךְ הָיוּ אַנְשֵׁי יְרוּשָׁלַיִם כּוֹתְבִין. *אַנְשֵׁי גָּלִיל הָיוּ כּוֹתְבִין כְּאַנְשֵׁי יְרוּשָׁלַיִם. אַנְשֵׁי יְהוּדָה הָיוּ כּוֹתְבִין: עַד שֶׁיִּרְצוּ הַיּוֹרְשִׁין לִיתֵּן לָךְ כְּתוּבָּתֵיךְ. לְפִיכָךְ, אִם רָצוּ יוֹרְשִׁין – נוֹתְנִין לָהּ כְּתוּבָּתָהּ, וּפוֹטְרִין אוֹתָהּ.§ [לקמן קג.] [לקמן נה:]

גמ' אָמַר רַבִּי יוֹחָנָן מִשּׁוּם רַבִּי שִׁמְעוֹן בֶּן יוֹחַאי: מִפְּנֵי מָה הִתְקִינוּ כְּתוּבַּת בְּנִין דִּכְרִין – כְּדֵי שֶׁיִּקְפּוֹץ אָדָם וְיִכְתּוֹב לְבִתּוֹ כִּבְנוֹ. וּמִי אִיכָּא מִידֵּי דְּרַחֲמָנָא אָמַר בְּרָא – לֵירוּת, בְּרַתָּא – לָא תֵּירוּת, וַאֲתוּ רַבָּנַן וּמְתַקְּנֵי דְּתֵירוּת בְּרַתָּא? הָא נַמִּי דְּאוֹרַיְיתָא הוּא, דִּכְתִיב: °"קְחוּ נָשִׁים וְהוֹלִידוּ בָּנִים וּבָנוֹת וּקְחוּ לִבְנֵיכֶם נָשִׁים וְאֶת בְּנוֹתֵיכֶם תְּנוּ לַאֲנָשִׁים". *בִּשְׁלָמָא בָּנִים – בִּידֵיהּ קַיְימִי, אֶלָּא בְּנָתֵיהּ מִי קַיְימָן בִּידֵיהּ? הָא קָא מַשְׁמַע לָן: דְּנַלְבְּשַׁהּ, וְנִיכַסְּהּ, וְנֵיתִיב לָהּ מִידֵּי, כִּי הֵיכִי דְּקָפְצִי עֲלַהּ וַאֲתוּ נָסְבִי לַהּ. וְעַד כַּמָּה? אַבַּיֵּי וְרָבָא דְּאָמְרִי תַּרְוַיְיהוּ: [כ] עַד לְעִישּׂוּר נְכָסֵי. וְאֵימָא, דְּאָב – לֵירוּת, דְּבַעַל – לָא לֵירוּת! אִם כֵּן אָב נַמִּי מִימְנַע וְלָא כָּתַב. וְאֵימָא הֵיכָא דְּכָתַב אָב – (א) לִכְתּוֹב בַּעַל, הֵיכָא דְּלָא כָּתַב אָב – לָא לִכְתּוֹב בַּעַל! *לָא פְּלוּג רַבָּנַן. – בַּת בֵּין הַבָּנִים נַמִּי תֵּירוּת! כְּנַחֲלָה שַׁוְיוּהָ רַבָּנַן. בַּת בֵּין הַבָּנוֹת תֵּירוּת! לָא פְּלוּג רַבָּנַן. וְתִיגְבֵּי מִמִּטַּלְטְלֵי! כִּכְתוּבָּה שַׁוְיוּהָ רַבָּנַן. תִּטְרוֹף מִמְּשַׁעְבְּדֵי! *"יִרְתּוּן" תְּנַן. וְאֵימָא אַף עַל גַּב דְּלֵיכָּא *מוֹתַר דִּינָר! [ל] בִּמְקוֹם דְּקָא מֵיעַקְּרָא נַחֲלָה דְּאוֹרַיְיתָא – לָא תַּקִּינוּ רַבָּנַן. רַב פַּפָּא אִיעַסַּק לֵיהּ לִבְרֵיהּ בֵּי אַבָּא סוּרָאָה, אֲזַיל לְמִיכְתַּב לָהּ כְּתוּבָּתָהּ. שָׁמַע יְהוּדָה בַּר מָרֵימָר, נְפַק אֲתָא אִיתְחֲזֵי לֵיהּ. כִּי מָטוּ לְפִיתְחָא הֲוָה קָא מִפְּטַר מִינֵּיהּ. אֲמַר לֵיהּ: נֵיעוּל מָר בַּהֲדַאי! (ירמיה כט)

חַזְיֵיהּ

מִפְּנֵי תִיקּוּן הָעוֹלָם. שֶׁלֹּא יַרְגִּילוּ לְהַעֲלוֹת עַל דְּמֵיהֶן. **כְּנֶגֶד כְּתוּבָּתָהּ.** אֲבָל יוֹתֵר מִכְּתוּבָּתָהּ – לֹא, דְּלֹא יְהֵא טָפֵל חָמוּר מִן הָעִיקָּר – תְּנַאי כְּתוּבָּתָהּ יָתֵר עַל הַכְּתוּבָּה. **תְּרֵי קוּלֵּי.** לֹא יוֹתֵר עַל דָּמֶיהָ שֶׁהִיא רְאוּיָה לִימָּכֵר בַּשּׁוּק, וְלֹא יוֹתֵר עַל כְּתוּבָּתָהּ. **וּצְרִיכָה רְפוּאָה הֲרֵי הִיא כִּמְזוֹנוֹת.** וְאִם צְרִיכָה רְפוּאָה, הֲרֵי הָרְפוּאָה כִּמְזוֹנוֹת, דְּתַרְוַויְהוּ חִיּוּתָא נִינְהוּ. מְזוֹנוֹת אֵין לָהֶם קִצְבָה, הִלְכָּךְ רְפוּאָה שֶׁיֵּשׁ לָהּ קִצְבָה, שֶׁאֵינָהּ חוֹלָה תָּדִיר – אֵינָהּ בִּכְלַל מְזוֹנוֹת. **קוּצוּ לֵיהּ מִידֵּי לְרוֹפֵא.** שֶׁיְּקַבֵּל עָלָיו רְפוּאָתָהּ עוֹלָמִית בְּכָךְ וָכָךְ. **כְּעוֹרְכֵי הַדַּיָּינִין.** אוֹהֵב אֶחָד מִבַּעֲלֵי דִינִין, וּמַטְעִים זְכִיּוֹתָיו לַדַּיָּין, וְעוֹרֵךְ [הַדִּין לִפְנֵי] הַדַּיָּינִין לִזְכוּתוֹ – מִיקְּרֵי עוֹרְכֵי הַדַּיָּינִין, שֶׁעוֹרֵךְ אֶת הַדַּיָּינִין לַהֲפוֹךְ לִבָּם לְטוֹבָתוֹ שֶׁל זֶה. **מֵעִיקָּרָא.** כְּשֶׁהֵשִׂיא עֵצָה. **וּלְבַסּוֹף.** כְּשֶׁנִּתְחָרֵט. **מתני'** יָתֵר עַל חוּלַקְהוֹן **דְּעִם אֲחוּהוֹן.** בְּנֵי אִשָּׁה אַחֶרֶת. אִם תָּמוּתִי בְּחַיַּי וְאִירָשֵׁךְ – יִטְּלוּ בָּנַיִךְ כְּתוּבָּתֵיךְ. וְנַפְקָא מִינָּהּ, שֶׁמָּא מְרוּבָּה הִיא, אוֹ שֶׁמָּא יִהְיוּ בְּנֵי אִשָּׁה הָאַחֶרֶת מְרוּבִּים וּבָנַיִךְ מוּעָטִים, וְטוֹב לָהֶן שֶׁיִּטְּלוּ כְּתוּבַּת אִמָּן וְהַמְרוּבִּים כְּתוּבַּת אִמָּן, וַאֲפִי' הַכְּתוּבּוֹת שָׁווֹת. **כָּל יְמֵי מֵיגַר אַרְמְלוּתִיךְ.** כָּל יְמֵי מֶשֶׁךְ אַלְמָנוּתֵיךְ. **גמ'** מִפְּנֵי מָה תִּקְּנוּ כְּתוּבַּת בְּנִין דִּכְרִין. מֵאַחַר שֶׁהַבַּעַל יוֹרֵשׁ אֶת אִשְׁתּוֹ, לָמָּה תִּקְּנוּ שֶׁיּוֹרִישׁ לְבָנֶיהָ מַה שֶּׁיָּרַשׁ מִמֶּנָּה, דְּהַיְינוּ נְדוּנְיָא שֶׁלָּהּ? **וְיִתֵּן לְבִתּוֹ.** נְדוּנְיָא יָפֶה, דְּאִילּוּ מֵתָה יִירְשׁוּ בָּנֶיהָ. **דְּרַחֲמָנָא אָמַר בְּרָא לֵירוּת.** דִּכְתִיב (במדבר כז) "אִישׁ כִּי יָמוּת וּבֵן אֵין לוֹ" וגו', הָא יֵשׁ לוֹ – בְּנוֹ יוֹרְשׁוֹ, וְלֹא בִּתּוֹ. **וְתַקּוּן דְּתֵירוּת בְּרַתָּא.** שֶׁיִּתֵּן לָהּ הָאָב מָמוֹנוֹ שֶׁהָיוּ בָּנָיו רְאוּיִין לִירַשׁ. **בִּשְׁלָמָא בְּנוֹ בְּיָדוֹ.** לְבַקֵּשׁ לוֹ אִשָּׁה, שֶׁדַּרְכּוֹ שֶׁל אִישׁ לַחֲזֵר עַל אִשָּׁה. **אֶלָּא בִּתּוֹ מִי בְּיָדוֹ.** וְכִי דֶּרֶךְ אִשָּׁה לַחֲזֵר עַל אִישׁ? **וְאֵימָא דְּאָב לֵירוּת דְּבַעַל לָא לֵירוּת.** כֵּיוָן דְּטַעְמָא כְּדֵי שֶׁיִּקְפּוֹץ לִיתֵּן לְבִתּוֹ הוּא דְּתַקּוּן, נְדוּנְיָא דְּיָהַב אָב לְבִתּוֹ – לֵירְתוּן בָּנִים דִּילָהּ, אֲבָל שְׁאָר כְּתוּבּוֹת נִכְסֵי הַבַּעַל, כְּגוֹן מָנֶה מָאתַיִם וְתוֹסֶפֶת דְּבַעַל – לָא לֵירְתוּן. **אִם כֵּן.** דְּלָא יָרְתִי לִשְׁאָר הַכְּתוּבָּה. **אָב נַמִּי מִימְנַע וְלָא כָּתַב.** לְבִתּוֹ, אַחֲרֵי שֶׁזֶּה מַקְפִּיד עַל שֶׁלּוֹ מִלְּהוֹרִישׁ לִבְנֵי בִּתִּי – אַף אֲנִי אֶמְשׁוֹךְ יָדִי מִלְּהַרְבּוֹת לוֹ נְדוּנְיָא. **הֵיכָא דְּכָתַב אָב כו'.** כֵּיוָן דְּטַעְמָא מִשּׁוּם שֶׁיִּקְפּוֹץ אָב לָתֵת נְדוּנְיָא לְבִתּוֹ הִיא, הֵיכָא דְּכָתַב אָב נְדוּנְיָא לְבִתּוֹ – נִכְתּוֹב בַּעַל תְּנַאי כְּתוּבַּת בְּנִין דִּכְרִין, וְהֵיכָא דְּלֹא כָּתַב אָב נְדוּנְיָא לְבִתּוֹ – לֹא נִכְתּוֹב בַּעַל תְּנַאי כְּתוּבַּת בְּנִין דִּכְרִין. **לָא פְּלוּג רַבָּנַן.** לֹא חִלְּקוּ בֵּין כְּתוּבָּה לִכְתוּבָּה, אַחֲרֵי שֶׁרוֹב כְּתוּבּוֹת יֵשׁ בָּהֶן נְדוּנְיָא לֹא חִלְּקוּ. **בַּת בֵּין הַבָּנִים תֵּירוּת.** [כֵּיוָן דְּטַעְמָא מִשּׁוּם נְדוּנְיָא הוּא, הֵיכָא דְּאֵין לוֹ בָּנִים מִמֶּנָּה אֶלָּא] יֵשׁ לוֹ בַּת מִן אִשָּׁה אַחַת, וּבָנִים מִן הָאַחֶרֶת – תִּטּוֹל בַּת הַיְחִידָה כְּתוּבַּת אִמָּהּ לִירַשׁ נְדוּנְיָא שֶׁנָּתַן אֲבִי אִמָּהּ, מַאי שְׁנָא דְּתַקּוּן בְּנִין דִּכְרִין? **בְּנַחֲלָה שָׁוְיוּהָ רַבָּנַן.** ד"יִרְתּוּן" תְּנַן, וְאֵין בַּת יוֹרֶשֶׁת בֵּין הַבָּנִים. **בַּת בֵּין הַבָּנוֹת תֵּירוּת.** יֵשׁ לוֹ בַּת מִן אִשָּׁה אַחַת, וּבָנוֹת מִן הָאַחֶרֶת – תִּטּוֹל בַּת הַיְחִידָה כְּתוּבַּת אִמָּהּ לִירַשׁ נְדוּנְיַית אֲבִי אִמָּהּ. דְּהָא אַ"כ שָׁוְיוּהָ כְּנַחֲלָה – יֵשׁ מִשְׁפַּט נַחֲלָה לְבַת בֵּין הַבָּנוֹת. **לָא פְּלוּג רַבָּנַן.** בְּמִשְׁפַּט כְּתוּבַּת בְּנִין דִּכְרִין, דְּבַת בֵּין הַבָּנִים לֹא תִּשְׁקוֹל, וּבַת בֵּין הַבָּנוֹת תִּשְׁקוֹל. **וְתִגְבֵּי מִמִּטַּלְטְלֵי.** כֵּיוָן דְּטַעְמָא מִשּׁוּם נְדוּנְיַית אֲבִי הָאֵם הוּא, אַלְּמָה אָמְרִינַן לְעֵיל (דף נ:): כְּשֵׁם שֶׁאֵין הַבָּנִים יוֹרְשִׁין אֶלָּא מִקַּרְקַע, וְאוֹקִימְנָא בִּכְתוּבַּת בְּנִין דִּכְרִין. **כִּכְתוּבָּה שָׁוְיוּהָ רַבָּנַן.** וּמִטַּלְטְלֵי דְּיַתְמֵי לָא מִשְׁתַּעְבְּדֵי לִשְׁטָרָא. **תִּטְרוֹף מִמְּשַׁעְבְּדֵי.** אִי כִּכְתוּבָּה שָׁוְיוּהָ. וּלְקַמָּן פְּלִיגֵי בָּהּ בְּרֵישׁ פֶּרֶק "אַף עַל פִּי". **יִרְתּוּן תְּנַן.** וְאֵין יְרוּשָּׁה בִּמְשׁוּעְבָּדִין. **וְאֵימָא אַע"ג דְּלֵיכָּא מוֹתַר דִּינָר.** יָתֵר עַל שְׁתֵּי הַכְּתוּבּוֹת – יִטְּלוּ כְּתוּבַּת אִמָּם, כְּדִין כְּתוּבַּת בְּנִין דִּכְרִין. אַלְּמָה תְּנַן בְּפֶרֶק "מִי שֶׁהָיָה נָשׂוּי" (לקמן צא.): אֵין שָׁם אֶלָּא שְׁתֵּי כְתוּבּוֹת – חוֹלְקִין בְּשָׁוֶה. **מָקוֹם דְּמֵיעִקָּרָא נַחֲלָה דְּאוֹרַיְיתָא.** מִשּׁוּם נַחֲלָה דְּרַבָּנַן. **לָא תַּקּוּן רַבָּנַן.** נַחֲלָה דִּידְהוּ לַעֲקוֹר נַחֲלַת חֲלוּקָה שָׁוָה לְגַמְרֵי שֶׁהִיא מִן הַתּוֹרָה. הִלְכָּךְ, כִּי אִיכָּא מוֹתַר דִּינָר שֶׁיַּחַלְקוּהוּ בְּשָׁוֶה בְּנַחֲלָה דְּאוֹרַיְיתָא – יִטְּלוּ אֵלּוּ כְּתוּבַּת אִמָּן וְאֵלּוּ כְּתוּבַּת אִמָּן מִשּׁוּם נַחֲלָה דְּרַבָּנַן, וְאִי לָא – לָא. **בֵּי אַבָּא סוּרָאָה.** חָמִיו הָיָה, וְהִשִּׂיא רַב פַּפָּא לִבְנוֹ אֲחוֹת אִשְׁתּוֹ, כִּדְאָמְרִינַן בְּאֵלּוּ נְעָרוֹת (לעיל לט:): אָמְרָה לִי בַּת אַבָּא סוּרָאָה, כִּי נַהֲמָא אַקּוּשָׁא בְּחִינְכֵי. וּבְסַנְהֶדְרִין (דף יד:) נַמִּי אָמְרִינַן: אִישׁ וּשְׁתֵּי נָשִׁים שֶׁאֵין מַטִּילִין לְכִיס אֶחָד – כְּגוֹן רַב פַּפָּא וּבַת אַבָּא סוּרָאָה. **אָזִיל.** רַב פַּפָּא לְבֵית אֲבִי הַנַּעֲרָה לִכְתּוֹב כְּתוּבָּתָהּ, וְשָׁם יִפְסוֹק אָבִיהָ וְיִכְתּוֹב לָהּ בִּנְדוּנְיָיתָהּ מַה שֶּׁיִּכְתּוֹב. **כִּי מָטוּ לְפִתְחָא.** דְּאַבָּא סוּרָאָה. **הֲוָה מִיפְּטַר מִינֵּיהּ.** יְהוּדָה, נָטַל רְשׁוּת מֵרַב פַּפָּא לַחֲזוֹר לַאֲחוֹרָיו.

חָזָא

[שייך לעיל נא. במשנה]

צח א מיי' פ"ח מהל' מתנות עניים הלכה יב [ופי"ד מהל' אישות הלכה יט] טוש"ע י"ד סי' רנב סעיף ד [וטוש"ע אה"ע סי' עח סעיף ב]:
צט ב ג מיי' פי"ד מהל' אישות הלכה יט סמג לאוין פא טוש"ע אה"ע סי' עח סעיף ב:
ק ד מיי' פי"ח שם הל' ה סמג לאוין פה טוש"ע שם סימן עט סעיף א וסי' נד סעיף ג:
קא ה טוש"ע שם סימן עט סעיף א:
קב ו מיי' פי"ב שם הלכ' ב סמג עשין מח טוש"ע שם סימן סט סעיף א:
קג ז מיי' פ"ב שם ופי"ט שם הלכה א סמג עשין מח טוש"ע שם סימן סט סעיף ב וסי' קיא סעיף א:
קד ח מיי' פי"ט שם הלכ' ו ופי"ט הלכה י סמג שם טוש"ע שם סימן סט סעיף א ב וסימן קיב סעיף ט:
קה ט מיי' פי"ב שם הלכה א ב ופי"ח שם הלכה א סמג שם טוש"ע שם סי' א סעיף א ב וסימן נג סעיף ג וסי' נד סעיף א:
קו י מיי' פ"כ שם הלכ' ב סמג לאוין עה טוש"ע שם סימן נו סעיף א:
קז כ מיי' שם הלכה ג סמג שם טוש"ע שם סי' קיא סעיף א:
קח ל מיי' פי"ט שם הל' ג סמג שם עשין מח ולאוין עה טוש"ע שם סי' קיא סעיף ב:

גיטין מה. ע"ש | [תוספתא פ"ד] | לקמן סו. ע"ש | [ברכות יט. וש"נ] ב"ב קלא. | ג"ז שם | [במשנה שבמשניות איתא מיגר וישכנו מתניס ונגידו ע' תוי"ט] | קדושין ל: | [יבמות סו. קז. ב"מ נג:] | [לקמן נה. ב"ב קלא.] | [לקמן נא.] | נ"י כ"י

הגהות הב"ח

(א) גמ' היכא דכתב אב (לכתוב וכו' לא לכתוב בעל) תא"מ. ונ"ב ס"א לא גרסינן ליה: (ב) תוס' ד"ה תטרוף וכו' שידע גם המקשה. נ"ב עיין בפ' אע"פ דף נה:

תוספות רי"ד

פי' ואפילו בכדי דמיה דחד פדיון תקינו ליה רבנן ולא שנים רשב"ג אומר אין פודין את השבוין יותר על דמיהן מפני תקון העולם ופי' משנה הוא בסוף פרק השולח [דף מה] איבעיא להו מפני תקון עולם משום דוחקא דציבורא א"ד משום דלא (ניגרי) [לגרבו] וניתי טפי. ת"ש דלוי בר דרגא פרקה לברתיה בתריסר אלפא דינרי. אמר אביי מאן לימא לן שברצון חכמים עביד דלמא שלא ברצון חכמים עביד הלכך מפני תקון העולם הוא שלא יהא השבויים מעלין את השבאים לדמים יקרים. לפיכך אין מלמדים לפדות השבוים מיתר מכדי דמיהן: ת"ר נשבית והיו מבקשים בה עד עשרה בכתובתה פעם א' פודה מכאן ואילך רצה פודה רצה אינו פודה דברי ר' רשב"ג אומר אם היה פרקונה כנגד כתובתה פודה (הרב מפרש נגד כתובתה כנגד כל הכתוב בכתובה כגון מנה מאתים ותוספת ונדוניא וכל מה שהיה חייב לה ליתן אם בא לגרשה) ואם לאו אינו פודה. פי' שלא יהיה תנאי כתובה גדול מן הכתובה ופסק רבינו יצחק הל' כרבי ואינו נ"ל דקי"ל הל' כר' מחבירו ולא מרבו: לקתה בחלאים חייב לרפאותה אמר הרי גיטה וכתובתה תרפא א"ע רשאי פי' דרפואה כמזונות דמיא וכשם שיכול לפסוקי מזונותיה על גיטה וכתובה ה"נ יכול לפסוקי רפואתה ולא דמי רפואה לפדיון: ת"ר אלמנה נזונית מנכסי יתומים ואם צריכה רפואה ה"ה כמזונות. פי' דתרווייהו חיותא נינהו רשב"ג אומר רפואה שיש לו קצבה מרפאים אותה מכתובתה. פי' דכיון שיש לה קצבה כמה רופא לוקח עליה לא דמי למזוני דמזוני ל"ל קצבה ורפואה שאין לה קצבה ה"ה כמזונות: קריביה דר"י הוו להו איתת אבא דהוה צריכה רפואה כל יומא. פי' היה מפרנסין אשת אביהן אתו לקמי' דר"י א"ל זילי קיצי לה מידי לרפואה. פי' כדי שתהיה לה קצבה ותתרפא מכתובתה אר"י עשינו עצמינו כעורכי דיינין. פי' שאינן כשרים שמלמדים טענות לבעל דין. מעיקרא מאי סבר פי' כשהשיאן עצה ולבסוף מאי סבר פי' כשנתחרט מעיקרא סבר ומבשרך לא תתעלם ולבסוף סבר אדם חשוב שאני משום ולזות שפתים הרחק ממך. בעי מימנע נפשיה מליזותא ונ"ל דוקא יורשים שאין חייבים בפרקונה אין חייבים ברפואה שיש לה קצבה אבל בעל שחייב בפרקונה חייב אפי' ברפואה שיש לה קצבה: **מתני'** לא כתב לה בנין דכרין דיהוין ליכי מינאי אינון ירתין כסף כתובתך יתר על חולקיהון דעם אחוהון חייב מפני שהוא תנאי ב"ד בנן נוקבין דיהויין ליכי מינאי תהוין יתבן בביתי ומתזנן מנכסי עד דתלקחין לגוברין חייב מפני שהוא תנאי ב"ד. פי' בנ"ד הם יורשין כל הכתוב בשטר הכתובה בין נדוניא בין תוספת ובפ' י"ג [דף קלא] מקשה והא אין אדם מקנה דבר למי שלא בא לעולם ואפילו לר"מ דאמר אדם מקנה דבר שלא בא לעולם ה"מ למי שישנו בעולם אבל למי שאינו בעולם לא ומשני תנאי ב"ד שאני: אר"י משום רשב"י מפני מה תקינו כתובת בנ"ד. פי' המורה וכי מאחר שמה"ת בעל יורש את אשתו למה תקינו שיוריש לבנים מה שיורש הוא ממנה דהיינו נדוני' כדי שיקפוץ אדם ליתן לבתו כבנו. פי' שאלמלא לא תקנוהו יהא כאו"א דן בעצמו איך אני נותן נכסי לבתי שמא תמות בחיי בעלה וירשנה ותפול ירושתי ביד אחרים אבל עכשיו יתן לה (המה) [האב] ואומר אפי' תמות בתי בחיי בעלה יירשנה בנה וכך בתי חביבה עלי כבני: ועד כמה פי' זקוק לתת לה אביי ורבא דאמרי תרווייהו עד עישור נכסי. ואימא דאב לירות דהיינו הנדוניא דבעל לא לירות דהיינו מנה ומאתים ותוספת. פי' אחרי שהתקנה היא כדי שיקפוץ ניתקן נמי דנדוניא דאב לירות. א"כ פי' דלא ירתי לשאר כתובה מימנע אב ולא כתב לבתו. פי' יאמר כך אחרי שזה מקפיד על שלו מלהוריש לבני בתי גם אני אמשוך ידי מלהרבות נדוניא: ואימא. פי' כיון דטעם דניתקנה הוא כדי שיקפוץ היכא דכתב אב נדוניא לכתוב בעל להאי תנאה פי' בנ"ד היכא דלא כתב אב לא לכתוב בעל לא פלוג רבנן א) שלא יהא תנאי כתובה עדיף מכתובה עצמה והשתא דתקון רבנן דמתיבתא למיגבי כתובה ממטלטלי מיבעיא לי אי גביא נמי כתובת בנ"ד ממטלטלי אי לא ומסתמא דגביא דהא אי לאו דלא להוי תנאי כתובה עדיף מכתובה עצמה הוי מן דינא דליגבי ממטלטלי והשתא דכתובה עצמה גביא איהי נמי גביא: ותטרוף ממשעבדי. פי' אם ככתובה שוינהו כדרך שטורפת האשה דהא כבע"ח היא ונשתעבדו לה קודם לכן ולמה בפ' י"ג ובפ' אע"פ נמי בשמעתא קמייתא אמרי' לא טרפא ממשועבדים. ירתון תנן. פי' ואין ירושה ממשועבדים. פי' במה ששעבד האב אין הבנים יורשים: ואימא. פי' כיון שהטעם הוא כדי שיקפוץ אע"ג דליכא מותר דינר לחלוק

שאין

א) נ"ל דחסר כאן וצ"ל ותגבי ממטלטלי ככתובה שוויה רבנן שלא יהא תנאי כתובה וכו'.

חַזְיֵיהּ דְּלָא הֲוָה נִיחָא לֵיהּ. אֲמַר לֵיהּ: מַאי דַּעְתִּיךְ – מִשּׁוּם *דַּאֲמַר לֵיהּ שְׁמוּאֵל לְרַב יְהוּדָה: *שִׁינָּנָא, אלָא תֶּיהֱוֵי בְּעִבּוּרֵי אַחְסַנְתָּא אֲפִילּוּ מִבְּרָא בִּישָׁא לִבְרָא טָבָא, דְּלָא יְדִיעָ מַאי זַרְעָא נָפֵיק מִינֵּיהּ, וְכָל שֶׁכֵּן מִבְּרָא לִבְרַתָּא. הַאי נַמִי – תַּקַּנְתָּא דְּרַבָּנַן הִיא, דְּאָמַר רַבִּי יוֹחָנָן מִשּׁוּם ר' שִׁמְעוֹן בֶּן יוֹחַי. אֲמַר לֵיהּ: בה"מ – מִדַּעְתֵּיהּ, לְעַשּׂוּיֵיהּ נַמִי? א"ל: אַטּוּ מִי קָאָמִינָא לָךְ דְּעוּל וְעַשְּׂיֵיהּ? עוּל וְלָא תְּעַשְּׂיֵיהּ קָאָמִינָא. אֲמַר לֵיהּ: מַעֲלַאי דִּידִי הַיְינוּ עַשְּׂיֵיהּ. אַכְפְּיֵיהּ *וְעוּל. אִישְׁתִּיק וִיתֵיב. סָבַר (א) הַהוּא – מִירְתַּח רָתַח, כְּתָבֵיהּ לְכָל מַאי דַּהֲוָה לֵיהּ. לְסוֹף אֲמַר לֵיהּ: הַשְׁתָּא נַמִי לָא מִישְׁתַּעֵי מָר? חַיֵּי דְּמָר, לָא שְׁבִיקִי מִידֵּי לְנַפְשַׁאי. אֲמַר לֵיהּ: אִי מִינַּאי דִּידִי – אֲפִי' הַאי נַמִי דִּכְתַבְתְּ לָא נִיחָא לִי. א"ל: הַשְׁתָּא נַמִי אַהֲדַר בִּי! א"ל: שַׁוְיֵיהּ נַפְשָׁךְ הַדְּרָנָא – לָא קָאָמִינָא. בְּעָא מִינֵּיהּ רַב יֵימָר סָבָא מֵרַב נַחְמָן: מָכְרָה כְּתוּבָּתָהּ לְבַעְלָהּ, יֵשׁ לָהּ כְּתוּבַּת בְּנִין דִּכְרִין אוֹ אֵין לָהּ כְּתוּבַּת בְּנִין דִּכְרִין? א"ל רָבָא: וְתִבְּעֵי לָךְ מוֹחֶלֶת! אֲמַר לֵיהּ הַשְׁתָּא מוֹכֶרֶת קָמִיבַּעְיָא לִי, דְּאע"ג דְּאִיכָּא לְמֵימַר זוּזֵי אֲנָסוּהָ, דְּאָמִינָא כְּמַאן דְּקָא *מָחוּ לָהּ מֵאָה עוּכְלֵי בְּעוּכְלָא, מוֹחֶלֶת מִיבַּעְיָא?! אֲמַר רָבָא: פְּשִׁיטָא לִי: גמוֹכֶרֶת כְּתוּבָּתָהּ לַאֲחֵרִים – יֵשׁ לָהּ כְּתוּבַּת בְּנִין דִּכְרִין, מַאי טַעֲמָא – זוּזֵי אֲנָסוּהָ. דמוֹחֶלֶת כְּתוּבָּתָהּ לְבַעְלָהּ – אֵין לָהּ כְּתוּבַּת בְּנִין דִּכְרִין, מַאי טַעֲמָא – אַחוּלֵי אַחֵילְתָּא. בָּעֵי רָבָא: *מוֹכֶרֶת כְּתוּבָּתָהּ לְבַעְלָהּ כְּמוֹכֶרֶת לַאֲחֵרִים דָּמֵי, אוֹ כְּמוֹחֶלֶת לְבַעְלָהּ דָּמֵי? בָּתַר דִּבְעָיָא הֲדַר פַּשְׁטָא: המוֹכֶרֶת כְּתוּבָּה לְבַעְלָהּ כְּמוֹכֶרֶת לַאֲחֵרִים דָּמֵי. מְתִיב רַב אִידִי בַּר אָבִין: *ומֵתָה – אֵין יוֹרְשִׁין שֶׁל זֶה וְאֵין יוֹרְשִׁין שֶׁל זֶה יוֹרְשִׁין כְּתוּבָּתָהּ. וְהָוֵינַן בָּהּ: *כְּתוּבָּתָהּ מַאי עֲבִידְתָּהּ? וְאָמַר רַב פַּפָּא: זכְּתוּבַּת בְּנִין דִּכְרִין. וְאַמַּאי? הָכָא נַמִי לֵימָא: יֵצֶר אֲנָסָהּ! הָתָם קְנָסָא הוּא דִּקְנָסוּהָ רַבָּנַן. יְתֵיב רָבִין בַּר חֲנִינָא קַמֵּיהּ דְּרַב חִסְדָּא, וִיתֵיב וְקָאָמַר מִשְּׁמֵיהּ דְּרַבִּי אֶלְעָזָר: חמוֹחֶלֶת כְּתוּבָּתָהּ לְבַעְלָהּ – אֵין לָהּ מְזוֹנוֹת. אֲמַר לֵיהּ: אִי לָאו דְּקָאָמְרַתְּ לִי מִשְּׁמֵיהּ דְּגַבְרָא רַבָּא – הֲוָה אָמִינָא לָךְ: °"מֵשִׁיב רָעָה תַּחַת טוֹבָה לֹא תָמוּשׁ רָעָה מִבֵּיתוֹ". יְתֵיב ר"נ וְעוּלָּא וַאֲבִימִי בַּר רַב פַּפִּי, וִיתֵיב רַב חִיָּיא בַּר אַמִּי גַּבַּיְיהוּ. אֲתָא הַהוּא גַּבְרָא דִּשְׁכִיבָא אֲרוּסָתוֹ, אָמְרִי לֵיהּ: זִיל קְבַר, אוֹ הַב לָהּ כְּתוּבָּתָהּ. אֲמַר לְהוּ רַב חִיָּיא, תְּנֵינָא: *טאִשְׁתּוֹ אֲרוּסָה – לֹא אוֹנֵן וְלֹא מִיטַּמֵּא לָהּ, וְכֵן הִיא – לֹא אוֹנֶנֶת וְלֹא מִיטַּמְּאָה לוֹ, ימֵתָה – אֵינוֹ יוֹרְשָׁהּ, כמֵת הוּא – גּוֹבָה כְּתוּבָּתָהּ. טַעְמָא – דְּמֵת הוּא, להָא מֵתָה הִיא – אֵין לָהּ כְּתוּבָּה. מַאי טַעְמָא? אָמַר רַב הוֹשַׁעְיָא: שֶׁאֵין אֲנִי קוֹרֵא בָּהּ *"לִכְשֶׁתִּנָּשְׂאִי לְאַחֵר תִּטְּלִי מַה שֶּׁכָּתוּב לִיכִי". כִּי אֲתָא רָבִין אֲמַר רֵישׁ לָקִישׁ: אֲרוּסָה שֶׁמֵּתָה – אֵין לָהּ כְּתוּבָּה. אֲמַר לְהוּ אַבָּיֵי: זִילוּ אָמְרִי לֵיהּ: שְׁקִילָא

תורה אור — משלי יז

חֲזָא. רַב פַּפָּא דְּלָא נִיחָא לֵיהּ לִיהוּדָה לְמֵיעַל. וְכ"ש מִבְּרָא לִבְרַתָּא. וְהָכָא אִיעֲבוּרֵי אַחְסַנְתָּא הוּא, שֶׁזֶּה כּוֹתֵב לְבִתּוֹ מַה שֶּׁהָיָה רָאוּי לְהוֹרִישׁ לְבָנָיו. דא"ר יוֹחָנָן. לְעֵיל, שֶׁיִּקְפּוֹץ אָדָם וְיִתֵּן לְבִתּוֹ, וְיָלֵיף לָהּ מִקְּרָא. לְעַשּׂוּיֵיהּ נַמִי. בִּתְמִיָּה. מַעֲלַאי דִּידִי הַיְינוּ עַשּׂוּיֵי. כְּנִיסָתִי עִמְּךָ זֶהוּ עִשּׂוּי, שֶׁיִּרְצֶה לִפְסוֹק בִּשְׁבִיל כְּבוֹדִי. אַכְפְּיֵיהּ. רַב פַּפָּא לִיהוּדָה בִּדְבָרִים, וְעַל. סָבַר אִיהוּ. אַבָּא סוּרָא, הַאי דְּשָׁתֵיק יְהוּדָה – מִרְתַּח רָתַח, שֶׁאֵין הַנְּדוּנְיָא הוֹגֶנֶת בְּעֵינָיו. אִי מִינַּאי דִּידִי. אִם נָטַלְתָּ מִמֶּנִּי עֵצָה. אוֹ אֵין לָהּ. מִי אָמְרִינַן כֵּיוָן דְּמָכְרָה לְבַעְלָהּ פָּקְעָה לָהּ תּוֹרַת יְרוּשַּׁת אָבִיהָ מִלְּהוֹרִישׁ נְדוּנְיָא שֶׁלּוֹ לִבְנֵי בִתּוֹ, שֶׁהֲרֵי מְכָרָתָהּ, וְאֵין כָּל הַיְרוּשָּׁה בָּאָה מֵעַכְשָׁיו אֶלָּא מִכֹּחַ הַבַּעַל – וְיַחְלְקוּ כָּל בָּנָיו בְּשָׁוֶה בְּנֵי ב' נָשָׁיו. וְתִיבְּעֵי לָךְ מוֹחֶלֶת. שֶׁהוּא דָּבָר מָצוּי מִן הַמֶּכֶר. וְאִי מִשּׁוּם דְּלָא מְטָא הֲנָאָה לְיָדָהּ – מִכָּל מָקוֹם פָּקְעָה זְכוּתָהּ בְּחַיֶּיהָ. הַשְׁתָּא מוֹכֶרֶת מִבַּעְיָא לִי. כְּלוֹמַר, מִי סָבְרַתְּ דְּמִשּׁוּם הֲנָאָה דִּמְטָא לְיָדָהּ תִּיסַּק אַדַּעְתַּאי דְּפָקְעָה זְכוּתָהּ. הַשְׁתָּא מוֹכֶרֶת. דַּאֲנוּסָה הִיא, סָלְקָא אַדַּעְתַּאי דְּפָקְעָה זְכוּתָהּ וּמִיבַּעְיָא לִי, כָּל שֶׁכֵּן מוֹחֶלֶת דְּלָא אֲנוּסָה. מָחוּ לָהּ מֵאָה עוּכְלֵי בְּעוּכְלָא. מַכִּין אוֹתָהּ מֵאָה מַכּוֹת בִּרְלוּעָה שֶׁבְּרֹאשָׁהּ בַּרְזֶל, כְּמִין מִשְׁקוֹלֶת קְטַנָּה שֶׁשְּׁמָהּ עוּכְלָא. מוֹכֶרֶת כְּתוּבָּתָהּ לַאֲחֵרִים. בְּטוֹבַת הֲנָאָה, שֶׁאִם נִתְאַרְמְלָה אוֹ נִתְגָּרְשָׁה – יִטְּלוּהָ לָקוֹחוֹת, וְאִם מֵתָה – יִרָשֶׁנָּה בַּעְלָהּ וּמֵתָה וִירָשָׁהּ בַּעְלָהּ. יֵשׁ לְבָנֶיהָ כְּתוּבַּת בְּנִין דִּכְרִין. דְּהָא כִּי לָא זְבִינְתָּהּ נַמִי יָרֵית לָהּ בַּעַל, וְתַקִּין לָהּ רַבָּנַן. הָשְׁתָּא נַמִי לְגַבֵּי בַּעַל בְּמוֹכֶרֶת לֹא פָּקְעָה זְכוּתָהּ, וְאִי מִשּׁוּם דְּהוּקַל בְּעֵינֶיהָ לְמוֹכְרָהּ וּלְהַפְסִיד אֶת בָּנֶיהָ אִם נִתְאַרְמְלָה אוֹ נִתְגָּרְשָׁה – זוּזֵי אֲנָסוּהָ, שֶׁהוּצְרְכָה לָהֶם. אַחוּלֵי אַחֵילְתָּהּ. וְנָקֵל בְּעֵינֶיהָ לְהַפְסִיד בָּנֶיהָ מִכְּתוּבָּתָהּ חִנָּם. מוֹכֶרֶת לְבַעְלָהּ. נַמִי טוֹבַת הֲנָאָה בְּעָלְמָא דָּבָר מוּעָט, שֶׁהֲרֵי אִם מֵתָה – יוֹרְשָׁהּ, וְאֵינוֹ לוֹקֵחַ מִמֶּנָּה, אֶלָּא שֶׁאִם מֵת הוּא – לֹא תִּגְבֶּה. וַהֲרֵי לֹא מֵת, וּבָא לִידֵי יְרוּשָּׁה – הִלְכָּךְ כְּמוֹכֶרֶת לַאֲחֵרִים דָּמֵי. אוֹ כְּמוֹחֶלֶת לְבַעְלָהּ דָּמֵי. הוֹאִיל וּבְיָדוֹ הַכְּתוּבָּה, וְהוּקַל בְּעֵינֶיהָ לְהַחֲלִיטָהּ. אֵין יוֹרְשִׁין שֶׁל זֶה כו'. מִשְׁנָה הִיא בִּיבָמוֹת: הָאִשָּׁה שֶׁהָלַךְ בַּעְלָהּ לִמְדִינַת הַיָּם, וְאָמַר לָהּ עֵד אֶחָד "מֵת בַּעֲלֵיךְ", וְהִתִּירוּהָ לִינָּשֵׂא, וְנִישֵּׂאת, וְאַחַר כָּךְ בָּא בַּעְלָהּ – תֵּצֵא מִזֶּה וּמִזֶּה, וְאֵין לָהּ כְּתוּבָּה לֹא מִזֶּה וְלֹא מִזֶּה. וְאִם מֵתָה – אֵין יוֹרְשִׁין שֶׁל זֶה וָזֶה, בָּנִים שֶׁיֵּשׁ לָהּ מִזֶּה וּמִזֶּה יוֹרְשִׁין כְּתוּבָּתָהּ. וְהָוֵינַן בָּהּ כְּתוּבָּתָהּ מַאי עֲבִידְתָּהּ. הָא אָמְרַתְּ אֵין לָהּ כְּתוּבָּה. וְאָמַר רַב פַּפָּא כְּתוּבַּת בְּנִין דִּכְרִין. וְהָכִי קָאָמַר: מֵתָה הִיא בְּחַיֵּי שְׁנֵיהֶם וִירָשׁוּהָ הֵם – אֵין בָּנִים שֶׁיֵּשׁ לָהּ מִזֶּה וּמִזֶּה נוֹטְלִין כְּתוּבַּת אִמָּן כִּבְנִין דִּכְרִין, כְּשֶׁבָּאִין לַחֲלוֹק בְּנִכְסֵי אֲבִיהֶם, אֶלָּא חוֹלְקִין בְּשָׁוֶה. וְאַמַּאי. כֵּיוָן דְּאָמְרִינַן כִּי אֲנִיסָא לָא מַפְסְדָא כְּתוּבַּת בְּנִין דִּכְרִין. נֵימָא יֵצֶר אֲנָסָהּ. שֶׁהָיְתָה מִתְאַוָּה לְבַעַל. קְנָסָא. מִשּׁוּם דְּלָא דַּיְיקָא שַׁפִּיר שֶׁמֵּת בַּעְלָהּ, מִקַּמֵּי דְּתִינְּסֵב. אֵין לָהּ מְזוֹנוֹת. בְּאַלְמְנוּתָהּ, דִּתְנָאֵי כְּתוּבָּה כִּכְתוּבָּה. אוֹ הַב לָהּ כְּתוּבָּה. דְּתִקְּנוּ קְבוּרָתָהּ תַּחַת כְּתוּבָּתָהּ. וְסָבַר לְמֵימַר: תַּחַת מָנֶה מָאתַיִם שֶׁתִּקְּנוּ לָהּ חֲכָמִים. תְּנֵינָא. אֲנִי שׁוֹנֶה שֶׁאֵין לַאֲרוּסָה שֶׁמֵּתָה מִשְׁפַּט כְּתוּבָּה דְּהַיְינוּ קְבוּרָה. לֹא אוֹנֵן. לֵיאָסֵר בְּקָדָשִׁים. וְלֹא מִיטַּמֵּא לָהּ. אִם כֹּהֵן הוּא, דְּלָאו שְׁאֵרוֹ הִיא. וְלֹא מִיטַּמְּאָה לוֹ. אֵינָהּ חַיֶּיבֶת לִיטַּמֵּא לוֹ, וְאַע"פ שֶׁמִּצְוָה לְהִתְעַסֵּק *בְּשִׁשָּׁה מֵתֵי מִצְוָה הָאֲמוּרִים בְּפָרָשַׁת כֹּהֲנִים (ויקרא כא), דִּכְתִיב "לָהּ יִטַּמָּא" – מִצְוָה, זוֹ אֵינָהּ מֵהֶם, דְּלָאו שְׁאֵרוֹ הִיא. אֲבָל אִם רוֹצָה הִיא לִיטַּמֵּא – אֵינָהּ מוּזְהֶרֶת מִלִּיטַּמֵּא, אֲפִילּוּ כֹּהֶנֶת, דִּ"בְנֵי אַהֲרֹן" כְּתִיב, וְלֹא בְּנוֹת אַהֲרֹן. אֵינוֹ יוֹרְשָׁהּ. נְדוּנְיַית בֵּית אָבִיהָ. דְּלָא תִּקֵּן יְרוּשַּׁת הַבַּעַל עַד שֶׁתִּכָּנֵס לַחוּפָּה, אוֹ שֶׁתִּמָּסֵר לִשְׁלוּחִים. מֵת הוּא. בְּחַיֶּיהָ. גּוֹבָה כְּתוּבָּתָהּ. מָנֶה מָאתַיִם, וְתוֹסֶפֶת אִם כָּתַב לָהּ. אִי לָהּ כְּתוּבָּה. דִּין כְּתוּבָּה. וּקְבוּרָתָהּ תַּחַת כְּתוּבָּתָהּ דְּתַנְיָא לְעֵיל – בִּנְשׂוּאָה תַּנְיָא, וְתַחַת נְדוּנְיַית בֵּית אָבִיהָ שֶׁהוּא יוֹרְשָׁהּ. אֲבָל הָכָא, כֵּיוָן דְּכִי מֵתָה אֵינוֹ יוֹרְשָׁהּ – אַף הוּא לֹא נִתְחַיֵּיב לְקוֹבְרָהּ. מַאי טַעְמָא. דְּאָמְרִינַן כִּי מֵתָה בְּחַיָּיו אֵין לָהּ תְּבִיעַת כְּתוּבָּה, תִּקָּבֵר בִּשְׁבִיל מָנֶה מָאתַיִם שֶׁהוּא יוֹרֵשׁ. שֶׁאֵין אֲנִי קוֹרֵא כו'. וְכָךְ הָיוּ כּוֹתְבִין בִּשְׁטַר כְּתוּבָּתָהּ. הִלְכָּךְ, כָּל זְמַן שֶׁלֹּא מֵת וְלֹא נִתְגָּרְשָׁה – לֹא נִשְׁתַּעְבֵּד לָהּ, וְלֹא יוֹרֵשׁ מִמֶּנָּה כְּלוּם. שְׁקִילָא

השתא נמי אהדר בי. אע"ג דהן הן דברים הנקנים באמירה* – היינו היכא דעמדו וקדשו, והכא כשרצה לחזור עדיין לא קדשו. אי נמי: הכא כבר קידשו קודם לכן ואח"כ כתב, ולא אמרינן הן הן דברים הנקנים באמירה אלא כשקידשו אחר כך.

ותבעי לך מוחלת. נראה לר"י לפרש דהוה לך למנקט בעייתך במוחלת, דשכיח טפי, כדפירש בקונטרס. ומסיק, השתא מוכרת דאיכא למימר זוזי אנסוה, אפ"ה דעתי נוטה לומר הואיל ומכרה – הפסידה, מוחלת מיבעיא? דפשיטא דלית לה כתובת בנין דכרין. וכה"ג פר"ח בשילהי "המצניע" (שבת דף צה:) גבי ניקב בכדי טהרתו. **שאין** אני קורא בה לכשתנשאי לאחר תטלי מה שכתוב ליכי. והא דתניא לעיל (דף מז:): קבורתה תחת כתובתה – היינו נדוניית כתובתה, והיינו דוקא נשואה שהוא יורש נדונייתה. ומצינו שנקראת נדוניא כתובה, כדאמר לעיל (דף מח:): נכנסה עמו ללון אע"פ שכתובתה בבית בעלה. ואם תאמר: והא מדרש כתובה לא דרשי אלא בית שמאי, כדאמרינן בפרק "האשה שלום" (יבמות דף קטז: ושם), דתנן: האשה שאמרה מת בעלי, ב"ש אומרים תנשא ותטול כתובה, וב"ה אומרים: תנשא ולא תטול כתובה כו'. א"ל ב"ש לב"ה: והלא מספר כתובה נלמד, שהרי כותב לה לכשתנשאי לאחר כו'. ואע"ג דקתני התם: חזרו ב"ה להורות כב"ש – לא משום דאית להו מדרש כתובה הדרי בהו. אלא מק"ו, שאמרו להו ב"ש: התרתם הערוה החמורה, לא נתיר ממון הקל? דהא אמר בפרק "האשה שנפלו" (לקמן דף פא. ושם) מאן שמעת להו דאית להו מדרש כתובה – ב"ש משמע. דלא חזרו ב"ה משום מדרש כתובה, אלא מק"ו, כדפרי'. וא"כ היכי אתי הכא כב"ש? ותו, אביי ורבא דדרשי לעיל (דף נב.). ואהדריך למדינתך ואותבינך לאינתו, ושמואל דדריש נמי לשון השטר בפ"ק דב"מ (דף טו.), גבי הא דאמר בעל חוב גובה את השבח: תדע שכך כותב לו "ואנא איקום ואשפי כו'" אטו כולהו כב"ש? והא בית שמאי במקום בית הלל אינה משנה! ונראה, דבהא הלכה כב"ש, משום דאשכחנא כמה תנאי דקיימי

תוספות רי"ד

שאין שם אלא שתי כתובות מצומצמות ושקלו נמי בנין דקמייתא כתובת בנ"ד כדי שיקפוץ ואמאי תנן לקמן בפ' מי שהי' נשוי [דף לא] דאם אין שם מותר דינר על שתי כתובות אינן נוטלין כתובת בנ"ד אלא חולקין אותה בשוה וילפינן להא מלתא מעיקר תקנתא דכתוב יתר על חולקיהון דעם אחוהון: במקום דמיעקרא נחלה דאוריית' לא תיקון רבנן. פי' במקום דמיעקרא נחלה דאורייתא משום נחלה דרבנן לא תיקון רבנן נחלה דידהו לעקור נחלת חלוקת שוה לגמרי שהוא מן התורה הלכך כי איכא מותר דינר שיחלקוה בשוה כנחלה שהוא מן התורה אז יטלו אלו כתובות אמן ואלו כתוב' אמן משום נחלה דרבנן ואי לא לא: אמר רבא פשיטא לי מוכרת כתובתה לאחרים יש להן כתובת בנין דכרין. מ"ט זוזי אנסוה. פי' היא מכרה כתובתה לאחרים בטובת הנאה שנותנים ממונם על הספק שאם תתאלמן או תתגרש יזכו הלקוחות בכתובתה אבל אם תמות היא בעלה יורשה והלכך יש לה כתובת בנ"ד שהרי הבעל יורשה והיא כשמכרה לא נסתלקה מכל תנאי כתובתה שלא נסתלקה בכל לב אלא זוזי אנסוה: מוחלת כתובתה לבעלה אין לה כתובת בנ"ד מאי טעמא אחולי' אחילתא. פי' ואינה אנוסה ובכל לב נותנה לו ואין הבעל יורשה שיוריש עכשיו גם הוא לב"ד שכבר מחלה לו אפילו מחיים וא"צ עכשיו לירושה

הלכך אין לה כבנ"ד מכאן מוכח שראובן שאמר לשמעון קנה ממני בסודר שאתן ללוי חפץ פ' אם ירצה שמעון למחול מוחל (והרב אומר אם ירצה למחול א"י למחול ולהפסיד ללוי מה שקנה בשבילו ואינו דומה זה לזה ואין ללמוד זה מזה) ולא אמרינן זכותא דלוי הוא ולא כל הימנו של שמעון למחול דהא הכא זכותא דבני' היא ומשום דבעל לא אתני אלא בהדי אשה היא יכולה למחול. ודוקא כשלא אמר זכה בעבור פ' דודאי זכה ההוא פ' ואין ליה כח לעכב בידו ולמחול דזכין לאדם שלא בפניו: בעי רבא מוכרת כתובתה לבעלה. פי' בטובת הנאה בדבר מועט שאם תמות בחייו יורשה ואם ימות הוא לא תגבה והרי לא מת ובא לידי ירושה כמוכרת לאחרים דמי. או כמוחלת לבעלה דמי מי אמרינן כמו שהיה יורשה מתחילה גם עתה יורשה שאין האשה מוכרת אלא אם תתאלמן או תתגרש אבל אם תמות בעלה יורשה הלכך ירושה כדקימי קיימי ואית לה א"ד כיון שמכרה לו א"צ עכשיו לירושה שאפילו אם היו יורשיה יורשים אותה הוה הוא זוכה בכל נכסי' אחרי שמכרה לו וכיון שא"צ לירושתה [אינו] מוריש לבניה כתובתה בתר דאיבעיא הדר פשטי' מוכרת כתובתה לבעלה כמוכרת לאחרים דמי. ודוקא תנאי דבנ"ד לית לה למוחלת כתובתה דאתי מכח כתובתה וי"ל כיון דמחלה אין לה ירושת בנ"ד. אבל תנאי דבנין נוקבין שאינו תלוי בכתובתה אלא תנאי בפ"ע הוא שהתנה עליה אע"פ שמחלה כתובתה תנאו קיים ואע"ג דאר"א לקמן מוחלת כתובתה אין לה מזונות דלא דוקא מזונות דתלו בכתובתה שאינה ניזונית אלא עד שתגבה כתובתה וכיון דמחלה כתובתה כאילו גבאתה דמי ואין לה מזונות אבל מזונות הבנות דלא תלו בכתובתה קיים הוא: יתיב רבין ב"ח קמי' דר"ח ויתיב וקאמר משמיה דר"א מוחלת כתובתה לבעלה אין לה מזונות. פי' מן היתומים באלמנותה דכמאן דגביא לכתובתה דמיא הואיל ותנאי כתובה ככתובה ואמרי' לקמן דתובעת כתובתה מן היתומים א"ל מזונות: א"ל אי לאו דקאמרת לי משמיה דגברא רבא הוה אמינא לך משיב רעה תחת טובה לא תמוש רעה מביתו יתיב ר"נ ועולא ואבימי בר פפי ויתיב ר"ח ב"א גבייהו אתא האי גברא דשכיב ארוסתו א"ל זיל קבור או הב לה כתובה. פי' שיש כתובה לארוסה א"ל ר"ח ב"א תנינא. פי' המורה ברייתא אני שונה דאיכא למשמע מינה שאינו חייב בקבורה של ארוסתו דתני ר"ח ב"א אשתו ארוסה לא אונן לאסור עצמו בקדשים. ואפילו במעשר הקל דכתיב לא אכלתי באוני ממני. ואין אנינות אלא בלב ואין אנינות אלא יום א' כדגמרי' במועד קטן מואחריתה כיום מר ובשעה שמתו מוטל לפניו: ולא מטמא לה. פי' אם הוא כהן דכהן אינו מטמא אלא בו' מת מצוה האמורים בפ' כהנים ושארו היא א' מהן. דכתיב לה יטמא מצוה ואמרינן ביבמות שארו זו אשתו וארוסתו אינה שארו וכן היא לא אוננת לא מטמאה לו. פי' אם כהנת

עין משפט נר מצוה

[לקמן קב. ועי' עוד כתוס' לקמן קט. ד"ה תקבע]

קט א מיי' פי"ב מהל' נחלות הלכה יא סמג עשין עו טוש"ע ח"מ סי' רפב סעי' ח:

קי ב מיי' פי"ב מהל' אישות הלכ' א סמג לאוין עח טוש"ע אה"ע סי' עח סעיף א בהג"ה:

קיא ג ד ה מיי' פי"ט מהל' אישות הלכה יג סמג עשין מח טוש"ע שם סי' קיא סעיף טו:

קיב ו ז מיי' פי"ח מהל' גירושין הלכה ז סמג עשין נ טוש"ע שם סי' יז סעיף נו:

קיג ח מיי' פי"ב מהל' אישות הלכה יח ופי"ז הל' יט ופי"ח הל' כג סמג לאוין מח טוש"ע שם סי' נג סעיף ט וסי' קה סעיף ד:

קיד ט מיי' פ"ב מהל' אבל הלכה ז סמג לאוין רלב טוש"ע יו"ד סי' שעג סעיף ד וסי' שעד סעיף ד וטוש"ע אה"ע סי' נד סעיף ה:

קטו י מיי' פכ"ב מהל' אישות הלכה ב סמג עשין מח טוש"ע אה"ע סי' נה סעיף ו:

קטז כ מיי' פ"י שם הלכה יא סמג שם טוש"ע שם סימן נג סעיף ו:

קיז ל טוש"ע שם סעי' ה:

מסורת הש"ס

כ"ב קלג: | [לעיל יב: וש"נ ועמ"ש בס"ד על הגליון חגיגה טו:] | [נ"ל ועל וכן העתיקו תוס' ב"ב ח: ד"ה אכפיה וכ"א בשאלתות פרשה ויצא סי' כא] | [ב"ב פה:] | [עי' תוס' ב"ק פט: ד"ה אמר] | יבמות פז: | [שם נא.] | ב"מ יח. יבמות כט: מג: לקמן פט: סנהדרין כח: [ע"ש ונ"ע] | [יבמות קיז.] | [נ"ל בשבעה וכ"א ברש"י ב"מ יח. ד"ה ולא]

הגהות הב"ח

(א) גמ' סבר איהו מירתח רתח:

*שְׁקִילָא טִיבוּתָךְ שַׁדְיָא אַחִיזְרֵי, כְּבָר תַּרְגְּמָא רַב הוֹשַׁעְיָא לִשְׁמַעְתֵּי' בְּבָבֶל.§ בְּנָן נוּקְבָן דִּיהֶוְיָין לִיכִי מִינַּאי וכו'.§ רַב תָּנֵי: °עַד דְּתִלָּקְחָן לְגוּבְרִין, וְלֵוִי תָּנֵי: עַד דְּתִבָּגְרָן. לְרַב – אע"ג דְּבָגַר, וְלֵוִי – אע"ג דְּאִינְסִיב? אֶלָּא, [א]בָּגַר וְלָא אִינְסִיב, אִינְסִיב וְלָא בָּגַר – דְּכוּלֵּי עָלְמָא לָא פְּלִיגִי. כִּי פְּלִיגִי – בַּאֲרוּסָה וְלָא בָּגַר. וְכֵן תָּנֵי לֵוִי בְּמַתְנִיתֵיהּ: עַד דְּתִבָּגְרָן וְיִמְטֵי זִמְנֵיהוֹן דְּאִינַּסְבָן. תַּרְתֵּי?! אֶלָּא: אוֹ תִּבָּגְרָן, אוֹ יִמְטֵי זִמְנֵיהוֹן לְאִיתְנַסְבָא. כְּתַנָּאֵי: [ב]עַד מָתַי הַבַּת נִזּוֹנֵית – עַד שֶׁתֵּאָרֵס. מִשּׁוּם רַבִּי אֶלְעָזָר אָמְרוּ: עַד שֶׁתִּבָּגֵר. תָּנֵי רַב יוֹסֵף: עַד דְּיֶהֶוְיָין. אִיבַּעְיָא לְהוּ: הֲוָיָה דְּאֵירוּסִין, אוֹ הֲוָיָה דְּנִישּׂוּאִין? תֵּיקוּ. אֲמַר לֵיהּ רַב חִסְדָּא לְרַב יוֹסֵף: מִי שְׁמִיעַ לָךְ מִינֵּיהּ דְּרַב יְהוּדָה, אֲרוּסָה יֵשׁ לָהּ מְזוֹנוֹת אוֹ אֵין לָהּ מְזוֹנוֹת? אֲמַר לֵיהּ: מִשְׁמַע לָא שְׁמִיעַ לִי, אֶלָּא מִסְּבָרָא לֵית לָהּ. כֵּיוָן דְּאֵירְסָהּ – לָא נִיחָא לֵיהּ דְּתִיתְזִיל. אֲמַר לֵיהּ: אִם מִשְׁמַע לָא שְׁמִיעַ לָךְ – מִסְּבָרָא אִית לָהּ, כֵּיוָן דְּלָא קִים לֵיהּ בְּגַוַּהּ – לָא שָׁדֵי זוּזֵי בִּכְדִי. וְאִיכָּא דְּאָמְרִי, אֲמַר לֵיהּ: מִשְׁמַע לָא שְׁמִיעַ לִי, מִסְּבָרָא אִית לָהּ, כֵּיוָן דְּלָא קִים לֵיהּ בְּגַוַּהּ – לָא שָׁדֵי זוּזֵי בִּכְדִי. – אֲמַר לֵיהּ: [ג]אִי מִשְׁמַע לָא שְׁמִיעַ לָךְ – מִסְּבָרָא לֵית לָהּ, כֵּיוָן דְּאֵירְסָהּ – לָא נִיחָא לֵיהּ דְּתִיתְזִיל.§ סִימָן דְּגַבְרֵי: שק זרף, מאנה ויבמה שניה ארוסה ואנסה.§ בָּעוּ מִינֵּיהּ מֵרַב שֵׁשֶׁת: מְמָאֶנֶת יֵשׁ לָהּ מְזוֹנוֹת אוֹ אֵין לָהּ מְזוֹנוֹת? אֲמַר לְהוּ רַב שֵׁשֶׁת, תְּנֵיתוּהָ: [ד]אַלְמָנָה בְּבֵית אָבִיהָ, וּגְרוּשָׁה בְּבֵית אָבִיהָ, וְשׁוֹמֶרֶת יָבָם בְּבֵית אָבִיהָ – יֵשׁ לָהּ מְזוֹנוֹת. רַבִּי יְהוּדָה אוֹמֵר: עוֹדָהּ בְּבֵית אָבִיהָ – יֵשׁ לָהּ מְזוֹנוֹת, אֵינָהּ בְּבֵית אָבִיהָ – אֵין לָהּ מְזוֹנוֹת. רַבִּי יְהוּדָה הַיְינוּ ת"ק! אֶלָּא לָאו – מְמָאֶנֶת אִיכָּא בֵּינַיְיהוּ, דְּתַנָּא קַמָּא סָבַר: [ה]אִית לָהּ, וְרַבִּי יְהוּדָה סָבַר: לֵית לָהּ. בָּעֵי רֵישׁ לָקִישׁ: בַּת יְבָמָה יֵשׁ לָהּ מְזוֹנוֹת אוֹ אֵין לָהּ מְזוֹנוֹת? כֵּיוָן דְּאָמַר מָר: *[ו]כְּתוּבָּתָהּ עַל נִכְסֵי בַּעְלָהּ הָרִאשׁוֹן – לֵית לָהּ, אוֹ דִּלְמָא כֵּיוָן [ז]דְּאִי לֵית לָהּ מֵרִאשׁוֹן – תַּקִּינוּ לָהּ רַבָּנַן מִשֵּׁנִי, אִית לָהּ? תֵּיקוּ.§ בָּעֵי רַבִּי אֶלְעָזָר: בַּת שְׁנִיָּה יֵשׁ לָהּ מְזוֹנוֹת, אוֹ אֵין לָהּ מְזוֹנוֹת?

כֵּיוָן

רש"י

שְׁקִילָא טִיבוּתִיךְ. חִיזּוּק טוֹבוֹתֶיךָ, שֶׁאַתָּה סָבוּר שֶׁנַּחֲזִיק לְךָ טוֹבָה בָּזוֹ – נְטוּלָה הִיא מִמְּךָ וּמוּטֶּלֶת עַל הַחֲרוּלִּים. לְרַב אע"ג דְּבָגַר. בִּתְמִיָּה, וַהֲלֹא בַּגְּרוּת מוֹצִיאָהּ מֵרְשׁוּת אָב, וְלָמָּה תִּיזּוֹן מִבֵּיתוֹ? וּבֵין לְרַבִּי בֵּין לְר' אֶלְעָזָר בְּר' שִׁמְעוֹן שֶׁנֶּחְלְקוּ בַּדָּבָר בְּפֶרֶק "מְצִיאַת הָאִשָּׁה" (לקמן סח:) בְּעִישּׂוּר נְכָסִים, מוֹדִים בִּמְזוֹנוֹת, דְּבֵין נִשְּׂאוּ בֵּין בָּגְרוּ – אִבְּדוּ מְזוֹנוֹת. כִּי פְּלִיגִי בַּאֲרוּסָה. רַב אָמַר: "עַד דְּתִלָּקְחָן" – קִיחָה דְּאֵירוּסִין, וַאֲפִילּוּ לֹא בָּגַר. וּלְלֵוִי אוֹ תִּבָּגַרְן אוֹ יִנָּשְׂאוּ וְיֵצְאוּ מֵרְשׁוּת אָב לְגַמְרֵי כִּי בַּגְּרוּת. וְכֵן תָּנֵי לֵוִי בְּמַתְנִיתֵיהּ. דְּלֵוִי סִידֵּר בָּרַיְיתָא שִׁשָּׁה סְדָרִים, כְּר' חִיָּיא וּכְרַבִּי אוֹשַׁעְיָא. תַּרְתֵּי. בִּתְמִיָּה. וּמָטֵי זִמְנֵיהוֹן. הִגִּיעַ זְמַן שְׁנֵים עָשָׂר חוֹדֶשׁ לִבְתוּלָה, מִשֶּׁתְּבָעָהּ הַבַּעַל, כִּדְלְקַמָּן בְּ"אַף עַל פִּי" (דף נז.). אֲרוּסָה יֵשׁ לָהּ מְזוֹנוֹת. אֲרוּסָה יְתוֹמָה יֵשׁ לָהּ מְזוֹנוֹת מִן הָאַחִין, אוֹ לֹא: הָכִי גָּרְסִינַן: מִסְּבָרָא לֵית לָהּ כֵּיוָן דְּאֵירְסָהּ לָא נִיחָא לֵיהּ דְּתִיתְזִיל. מִסְּבָרָא אֲנִי אוֹמֵר שֶׁאֵין לָהּ מְזוֹנוֹת מִן הָאַחִין. דְּמַאי טַעְמָא תַּקּוּן רַבָּנַן מְזוֹנוֹת לְבַת מִנִּכְסֵי הָאָב – כִּי הֵיכִי דְּלָא תִּיתְזִיל עַל הַפְּתָחִים. הָכָא לֵיכָּא לְמֵיחַשׁ לְהָכִי. דְּכִי חָזֵי אָרוּס דְּמִתְזַלָּא – זָיֵין לָהּ אִיהוּ מִדִּידֵיהּ, וְאַע"פ שֶׁאֵינוֹ מְחוּיָּב לְזוּנָהּ. דְּכֵיוָן דְּאֵירְסָהּ – לָא נִיחָא לֵיהּ דְּתִיתְזִיל. אֲמַר לֵיהּ אִי מִשְׁמַע לָא שְׁמִיעַ לָךְ. בְּהֶדְיָא. מִסְּבָרָא אִית לָהּ. יֵשׁ לְךָ לוֹמַר שֶׁנִּזּוֹנֶת מִן הָאַחִים, דְּאָרוּס לָא זָיֵין לָהּ. כֵּיוָן דְּלָא קִים לֵיהּ בְּגַוַּהּ. אִם תִּינָּשֵׂא לוֹ, שֶׁמָּא יִמְצָא בָּהּ מוּם, לָא שָׁדֵי זוּזֵי בִּכְדִי. מְמָאֶנֶת. קְטַנָּה יְתוֹמָה שֶׁהִשִּׂיאוּהָ אַחֶיהָ, וּמֵיאֲנָה בְּבַעְלָהּ, וְחָזְרָה אֶצְלָם. יֵשׁ לָהּ מְזוֹנוֹת. עַד שֶׁתִּבָּגֵר, אוֹ לֹא? מִי אָמְרִינַן עֲקַרְתִּינְהוּ לְנִישּׂוּאֵי מֵעִיקָּרָן, וְהָוְיָא לָהּ כְּמִי שֶׁלֹּא נִיסֵּת, אוֹ דִּלְמָא הָא נִיסֵּת וְיָצְאָה מֵרְשׁוּת אָב. אַלְמָנָה בְּבֵית אָבִיהָ. כְּלוֹמַר, מִן הָאֵירוּסִין. דְּאִי מִן הַנִּשּׂוּאִין – לָא אָמְרִינַן יֵשׁ לָהּ מְזוֹנוֹת, דְּ"עַד דְּתִלָּקְחָן" תְּנַן, וַאֲפִילּוּ לְלֵוִי – בְּנִשּׂוּאִין מוֹדֶה. ת"ק סָבַר מְמָאֶנֶת אִית לָהּ. וְה"ק: אַלְמָנָה בְּבֵית אָבִיהָ כו' וְה"ה לִמְמָאֶנֶת, דְּאֵין כָּאן נִשּׂוּאִין, דְּהָא עֲקַרְתִּינְהוּ. וְאָתָא רַבִּי יְהוּדָה לְמֵימַר: עוֹדָהּ בְּבֵית אָבִיהָ בִּתְחִלָּתָהּ, שֶׁלֹּא יָצְתָה מִשָּׁם בְּנִשּׂוּאִין – יֵשׁ לָהּ מְזוֹנוֹת, אֲבָל מִשֶּׁיָּצְאָה בְּנִישּׂוּאִין – אֵין לָהּ. בַּת יְבָמָה. הַכּוֹנֵס אֶת יְבִמְתּוֹ וְיָלְדָה לוֹ בַּת – יֵשׁ לָהּ מְזוֹנוֹת לְאַחַר מִיתַת הָאָב, מִן הָאַחִין, מִנִּכְסֵי אָבִיהָ, אוֹ לֹא? כֵּיוָן דְּאָמַר מַר. כְּתוּבָּתָהּ אֵינָהּ עַל נִכְסֵי יָבָם, תְּנָאֵי כְתוּבָּה דִּלָהּ נַמִי לָאו עַל נְכָסָיו הוּא. אוֹ דִלְמָא. כֵּיוָן דְּאָמְרִינַן הָתָם: אִי לֵית לֵיהּ נְכָסִים לָרִאשׁוֹן – תַּקִּינוּ לָהּ רַבָּנַן מִשֵּׁנִי, כְּדֵי שֶׁלֹּא תְּהֵא קַלָּה בְּעֵינָיו לְהוֹצִיאָהּ. אית לה. נַמִי תְּנָאֵי כְתוּבָּה, לִהְיוֹת בִּתּוֹ נִזּוֹנֶת. בַּת שְׁנִיָּה. מִי שֶׁנָּשָׂא שְׁנִיָּה מִדִּבְרֵי סוֹפְרִים, דְּאָמְרֵי רַבָּנַן לְקַמָּן בְּפֶרֶק "אַלְמָנָה" (דף ק:): הַשְּׁנִיָּה אֵין לָהּ כְּתוּבָּה וְלֹא מְזוֹנוֹת. בִּתָּהּ שֶׁיָּלְדָה לוֹ וּמֵת. יֵשׁ לָהּ מְזוֹנוֹת. מִנְּכָסָיו, אוֹ לֹא?

כֵּיוָן

תוספות

דקיימי כוותיה בריש "המקבל" (ב"מ דף קד. ושם) דדרשי לשון הדיוט: רבי מאיר, ורבי יהודה, והלל הזקן, ורבי יהושע בן קרחה, ורבי יוסי. וכיון דדרשי לשון הדיוט שנהגו ההדיוטות לכתוב בשטרות, אע"פ שלא תקנו חכמים – כ"ש תנאי כתובה שהוא תקון חכמים. והתם ב"המקבל" (ג"ז שם) מוכח דהכי הלכתא. ומיהו, קשה מבית הלל אהלל הזקן! ושמא, *אע"ג דבית הלל הם תלמידי הלל הזקן – פליגי עליה. אי נמי: כי לית להו לבית הלל מדרש כתובה – היינו לגרע כחה, אבל לייפות כחה – אית להו. ולהכי חזרו בית הלל להודות לבית שמאי ביבמות, דהתם הוי ליפות כחה, ולא משום קל וחומר דהתם, כדמוכח מתניתין דהתם. והיא ד"המקבל" נמי לייפות כחה, דעל ידי שהיה כתוב בכתובת אמן "לכשתכנסי לחופה הוי לי לאינתו" – לא עשה בניה ממזרים. ובתר חזרה אמרה הלל הזקן, ומיהו, בית שמאי אית להו מדרש כתובה אפילו לגרע כחה, וקיימא לן כוותייהו, דהא הכא בשמעתין לגרע כחה הוא. **הויה** דאירוסין או הויה דנשואין. הכא ליכא למיפרך אי הויה דנשואין היא אע"ג דבגר, כדפריך לעיל לרב דתני "עד דתלקחן". דהתם פריך משום דמשמע דאתא לאפוקי מדלוי אבל הכא – רב יוסף תני ברייתא באפי נפשה, וקמשמע לן ניסאת כשהיא קטנה, והוא הדין לאיבגר ולא אינסיב. **ארוסה** יש לה מזונות או אין לה מזונות. לא שמיע ליה פלוגתא דתנאי דלעיל. אי נמי, שמיע ליה, ומבעיא ליה היכי הלכתא. **אלמנה** בבית אביה. פירש בקונטרס דהיינו מן האירוסין, דמן הנשואין – לכולי עלמא לית לה, דכיון שנפקעה שעה אחת ממזונות – שוב אין לה. אבל מן האירוסין לא פקעי, דקסבר: ארוסה יש לה מזונות. וא"ת: א"כ אמאי נקט אלמנה? כיון דאפילו לא נתאלמנה יש לה מזונות! ויש לומר: לאשמועינן אבל מן הנשואין, אפילו נתאלמנה – אין לה. אי נמי: לאשמועינן דוקא אלמנה מן האירוסין יש לה, מן הנשואין – אין לה, אבל ממאנת אע"ג דנשאת – אית לה. ואתי שפיר הא דאמר ממאנת איכא בינייהו. ואם תאמר: ובשומרת יבם מאי אתא לאשמועינן? דאי למידק דוקא מן האירוסין אבל מן הנישואין לא – מאי איריא שומרת יבם? אפילו אלמנה שאינה זקוקה ליבם נמי אין לה! ויש לומר: דנקט שומרת יבם לרבותא, דלא מיבעיא ארוסה דאכתי מיחסרא מסירה לחופה, אלא אפי' שומרת יבם דלא מיחסרא, שיכול לבא עליה בעל כרחה – אפי' הכי יש לה מזונות. ורבינו תם מפרש: אלמנה בבית אביה – שהיתה נשואה ונתאלמנה או נתגרשה בחיי אביה. והיינו בבית אביה יש לה מזונות – הואיל כשנתאלמנה או נתגרשה אכתי לא מת האב, ולא בא זמן חיוב מזונות, ולא מיפסיד מידי. ודייק דממאנת לת"ק מבית אביה נפקא, דמדאתא רבי יהודה לטפויי, למימר דעודה בבית אביה בעינן – מכלל דת"ק דבית אביה אפילו יצתה. והיינו בכה"ג דמיאנה, דעקרתינהו לנשואין קמאי והרי היא כאילו לא נשאת מעולם. ואין נראה, דכיון דנשאת – שוב אין לה מזונות. דאין לאב רשות בה. ופירוש הקונטרס נראה עיקר. **בת** יבמה יש לה מזונות או אין לה מזונות. נראה דיבמה עצמה פשיטא ליה דיש לה מזונות, דגבי דידה אמרינן תנאי כתובה ככתובה, וכי לית ליה לראשון – תקינו לה גם מזונות משני. אבל בת מיבעיא ליה, אי אלימא כמותה למהוי תנאי כתובה ככתובה. וכגון דלית ליה לראשון, דאי אית ליה – ממה נפשך גביא. ובכה"ג אזלה בעיא דבת שניה, דפשיטא ליה דשניה עצמה לית לה, דלגבי דידה הוי תנאי כתובה ככתובה, אבל גבי בת מיבעיא לן. וי"מ: דאף בדאית ליה לראשון קבעי, אע"ג דלדידה פשיטא דאית לה מזונות, בין אית ליה בין לית ליה כדפי', בבתו מיבעיא ליה. דמראשון ודאי לית לה, שהרי הוא לא כתב לה אלא "בנן נוקבן דיהויין ליכי מינאי אינון יתבין" והאי לאו מיניה היא. אבל מן השני – דלמא אית לה, כיון דאי לית לה מראשון – תקינו לה משני, דכל תנאי יהיו על השני מוטלין. ולענין מזונות הבת, אע"ג דאית ליה לראשון, כיון שאינה נזונת מהם – כמאן דלית ליה דמי, ותקינו לה רבנן משני, או דלמא משני נמי לית לה. וצריך עיון אי הוה מצי למיבעי נמי לענין כתובת בנין דכרין, דדלמא לית לה, דהא מאחיו ירית, או דלמא איכא למיחש דלמא מימנע האב ולא יהיב, דחייש דלמא נפלה לה קמיה יבם. ומיהו, אארוסה נראה דלא הוה מצי למיבעי לענין כתובת בנין דכרין, דהא לא יהיב לה אב מידי כל זמן שהיא ארוסה.

בת

עין משפט נר מצוה

קיח א ב מיי' פי"ט מהל' אישות הלכ' י סמג לאוין פא ועשין סח טוש"ע אה"ע סימן סט סעיף ב וסי' קיב סעיף א:

[עי' תוס' יבמות קיז. ד"ה ב"ה]

קיט ג מיי' שם הלכה טו טוש"ע שם סעיף ג:

קכ ד ה מיי' שם הלכ' טז טוש"ע שם סעיף ד

קכא ו ז מיי' שם הלכ' יד טוש"ע שם סעיף ה:

מסורת הש"ס

[שבת סג: וש"נ]

[יבמות פה. וש"נ]

גליון הש"ס

גמ' עד דתלקחן לגוברין. עיין לקמן דף ס"ח ע"ב תוס' ד"ה בין נשאו:

תוספות רי"ד

א) כהנת היא אינה צריכה להטמא לו שאינו חשוב בעלה מידו אם רצתה מטמאה לו דכהנות אינה מוזהרת על הטומאה דבני אהרן כתיב ולא בנות אהרן. מתה אינה יורשה. פי' נדוניית בית אביה דלא תקנו ירושת הבעל אלא עד שתכנס לחופה או תמסר לשלוחי הבעל: מת הוא אינה גובה כתובתה פי' מ"מ ותוספת אם כתב לה דטעמא דמית הוא הא מתה היא א"ל (כתובה) דין כתובה שהוא חייב לקוברה שאינו דהוא לעיל קבורתה תחת כתובתה בנשואה תנא שירש נדוני' וכל נכסי מלוג שלה. פי' מ"מ אין לה כתובה כי מתה היא בחייו אין לה תביעת כתובתה ותקבר בשביל שהוא יורש א"ר הושעיא שאין אני קורא בה לכשתנשאי לאחר תהוי לי מה שכתוב ליכי. פי' תנאי ב"ד הוא זה אפילו לא כתב לה הלכך כ"ז שלא מת ולא גירשה ולא נשתעבד לה אינו יורש ממנה כלום ואע"פ שזה הטעם יש ליתן גם בנשואה שמתה בחייו וא"כ נמצא שאינו יורש מ"מ ותוספת שהרי לא נתחייב לה לתתם לה אפ"ה מורישם לבנים זכרים כדאמרינן טעמא כדי שיקפוץ וכו': כי אתא רבין א"ל ארוסה שמתה א"ל כתובה א"ל אבי זילו אמרו לי' שקילא טיבותיך ושדי אחוריא כבר תרגמה לעיל רב אושעיא ולוי לשמעתי' בבבל: בנין נוקבין וכו'. רב תני עד דתלקחן ולוי תני עד דתבגרן בגר אף על פי דלא אנסוב אע"ג דלא איבגר דכ"ע לא אכלי. פי' שהרי נישאין ובגרות מוציאין מרשות אב לגמרי כ"ש מרשות אחים ופשיטא דאין לה מזונות כי פליגי בארוסה פי' בנערה שלא בגרה רב סבר לית לה דתני עד דתלקחן. פי' ולקיחה דאירוסין שמה קיחה ולא מחייב במזונות ולוי סבר אית לה דתני עד דתבגרן. פי' אבל נערה שנתארסה יש לה מזונות עד שתבגר או עד שתנשא: כתנאי עד מתי הבת ניזונית עד שתתארס משום ר"א אמרו עד שתבגר וקי"ל דאין הלכה כיחיד אלא כת"ק: בעו מיני' מר"ש ממאנת י"ל מזונות או אין לה מזונות. פי' הבת שהשיאוה בקטנותה אמה ואחי' ומיאנה בבעלה וחזרה אצל אחין יש לה מזונות מן האחין דאמרי' נשואין קמאי עקרי וה"ה כמי שלא נשאת ולא יצאת מבית אביה יצאת ונשאת וא"ל מזונות אבל באלמנה וגרושה אפי' קטנה פשיטא דל"ל דהא לא עקרה לנשואין א"ל ר"ש תניתוה אלמנה בבית אביה וגרושה בבית אבוה ושומרת יבם בבית אבי' י"ל מזונות. פי' שנתארסה ונתאלמנה ונתגרשה והיא בבית אבי' ר"י אומר עודה בבית אבי' י"ל מזונות אינה בבית אביה א"ל מזונות ר"י היינו ת"ק אלא ממאנת א"ב דת"ק סבר א"ל דעכשיו בבית אבי' חזרה ור"י סבר אין לה. כיון דיצא' מבית אביה והלכתא כת"ק: בעי ר"ל בת יבמה י"ל מזונות או א"ל מזונות. פי' ייבם את אשת אחיו והוליד ממנה בת אם יש לה מזונות אצל האחים בנכסי האב או אין לה כיון דאמר מר כתובתה ב) על נכסי הראשון אית לה פי' כדאמרן בהחולץ א"ד כיון דא"ל על השני כתובה תנאי כתובה נמי ל"ל כגון מזוני דתנאי כתובה ככתובה ואע"ג דמו שהרי קם הוא לנחלה אפ"ה אין על הבנים של יבם לזון את היבמה שהרי ראשון לא כתב לה אלא בנין נוקבין דיהוויין ליכי מינאי ולא מאחי א"ד כיון דאי לית לה מראשון כתובה. פי' כגון שיעור כתובתה תקינו לה רבנן משני כדמפרש בהחולץ כדי שלא תהא קלה בעיניו להוציאה הלכך תנאי כתובה נמי כגון מזון הבת י"ל על השני וי"ל מזונות אצל הבנים (והאי דלא מיבעי' ליה ביבמה גם דגבי יבמה פשיטא ליה דא"ל מזונות מנכסי יבם אצל הבנים שהרי מחמת נשואי ראשון נזקקה ליבם וכשמת היבם נתאלמנה זו מנשואי ראשון והרי היא אלמנת ראשון וקורא אני בה ומיתזנא מנכסי לפיכך מזונותי' על נכסי בעל הראשון ואם אין לו נכסים אין לה מזונות על נכסי שני) מאי תיקו: בעי ר"א בת שניה. פי' הבא על אם אמו והוליד ממנה בת (בן) ויש לו בנים מאשה אחרת ומת י"ל מזונות או לא

כיון

א) לא קמ"ל רבותא דאפי' אם היא כהנת מ"מ אם רצתה מיטמאה לו. ב) נראה דכן צ"ל על נכסי הראשון כדאמרינן בהחולץ לית לה פי' כיון דאין לה על השני כתובה תנאי כתובה נמי לית לה וכו'.

כֵּיוָן דְּלֵית לָהּ כְּתוּבָּה – [א]לֵית לָהּ מְזוֹנֵי, אוֹ דִּלְמָא: אִמָּהּ דַּעֲבָדָא אִיסּוּרָא – קְנָסוּהָ רַבָּנַן, אִיהִי דְּלָא עָבְדָא אִיסּוּרָא – לָא קְנָסוּהָ רַבָּנַן? תֵּיקוּ. בָּעֵי רָבָא: בַּת אֲרוּסָה, יֵשׁ לָהּ מְזוֹנוֹת אוֹ אֵין לָהּ מְזוֹנוֹת? כֵּיוָן דְּאִית לָהּ כְּתוּבָּה – אִית לָהּ, אוֹ דִּלְמָא: כֵּיוָן דְּלָא תַּקִּינוּ רַבָּנַן כְּתוּבָּה עַד שְׁעַת נִישּׂוּאִין – [ב]לֵית לָהּ? תֵּיקוּ. § בָּעֵי רַב פַּפָּא: בַּת אֲנוּסָה, יֵשׁ לָהּ מְזוֹנוֹת אוֹ אֵין לָהּ מְזוֹנוֹת? אַלִּיבָּא דְּרַבִּי יוֹסֵי בְּרַבִּי יְהוּדָה – לָא תִּיבָּעֵי לָךְ, דְּאָמַר:* יֵשׁ לָהּ כְּתוּבָּה מָנֶה. כִּי תִּיבָּעֵי לָךְ – אַלִּיבָּא דְּרַבָּנַן, דְּאָמְרִי: יָצָא כֶּסֶף קְנָסָהּ בִּכְתוּבָּתָהּ – מַאי? כֵּיוָן דְּלֵית לָהּ כְּתוּבָּה – [ג]לֵית לָהּ מְזוֹנֵי, אוֹ דִּלְמָא: כְּתוּבָּה *טַעְמָא מַאי? כְּדֵי שֶׁלֹּא תְּהֵא קַלָּה בְּעֵינָיו לְהוֹצִיאָהּ, וְהָא – לָא מָצֵי מַפֵּיק לָהּ? תֵּיקוּ. § אַתְּ תְּהֵא יָתְבָא בְּבֵיתִי וכו'. § תָּנֵי רַב יוֹסֵף: *בְּבֵיתִי וְלֹא בְּבִיקְתִי. אֲבָל מְזוֹנֵי – אִית לָהּ. מָר בַּר רַב אַשִׁי אָמַר: אֲפִילּוּ מְזוֹנֵי נַמִי לֵית לָהּ. וְלֵית הִלְכְתָא כְּמָר בַּר רַב אַשִׁי. אָמַר רַב נַחְמָן אָמַר שְׁמוּאֵל: תְּבָעוּהָ לְהִנָּשֵׂא וְנִתְפַּיְּיסָה – אֵין לָהּ מְזוֹנוֹת, הָא לֹא נִתְפַּיְּיסָה – יֵשׁ לָהּ מְזוֹנוֹת? אָמַר רַב עָנָן: לְדִידִי מְפָרְשָׁא לִי מִינֵּיהּ דְּמָר שְׁמוּאֵל: אָמְרָה "מֵחֲמַת פְּלוֹנִי בַּעְלִי" – יֵשׁ לָהּ מְזוֹנוֹת, "מֵחֲמַת בְּנֵי אָדָם שֶׁאֵינָן מְהוּגָּנִין לָהּ" – אֵין לָהּ מְזוֹנוֹת. אָמַר רַב חִסְדָּא: זִינְּתָה – אֵין לָהּ מְזוֹנוֹת. אָמַר רַב יוֹסֵף: כִּיחֲלָה וּפִירְכְּסָה – אֵין לָהּ מְזוֹנוֹת. מַאן דְּאָמַר זִינְּתָה – כׇּל שֶׁכֵּן כִּיחֲלָה וּפִירְכְּסָה. מַאן דְּאָמַר כִּיחֲלָה וּפִירְכְּסָה, אֲבָל זִינְּתָה – אִית לָהּ, מַאי טַעְמָא – יֵצֶר אֲנָסָהּ. וְלֵית הִלְכְתָא כְּכׇל הָנֵי שְׁמַעְתָּתָא, אֶלָּא כִּי הָא *דְּאָמַר רַב יְהוּדָה אָמַר שְׁמוּאֵל: [ד]הַתּוֹבַעַת כְּתוּבָּתָהּ בְּבֵית דִּין – אֵין לָהּ מְזוֹנוֹת. וְלָא? וְהָתַנְיָא: *[ה]מָכְרָה כְּתוּבָּתָהּ, וּמִשְׁכְּנָה כְּתוּבָּתָהּ, עָשְׂתָה כְּתוּבָּתָהּ אַפּוֹתִיקֵי לְאַחֵר – אֵין לָהּ מְזוֹנוֹת. הָנֵי – אִין, אֲבָל תּוֹבַעַת – לָא! הָנֵי – בֵּין בְּבֵית דִּין, בֵּין שֶׁלֹּא בְּבֵית דִּין. תּוֹבַעַת, בְּבֵית דִּין – אִין, שֶׁלֹּא בְּבֵ"ד – לָא. § וְכָךְ הָיוּ אַנְשֵׁי יְרוּשָׁלַיִם וכו'. § אִתְּמַר, רַב אָמַר: הֲלָכָה כְּאַנְשֵׁי יְהוּדָה, וּשְׁמוּאֵל אָמַר [ו]הֲלָכָה כְּאַנְשֵׁי גָלִיל. בָּבֶל וְכׇל פַּרְוָודָהָא נְהוּג כְּרַב, נְהַרְדְּעָא וְכׇל פַּרְוָודָהָא נְהוּג כִּשְׁמוּאֵל. הַהִיא בַּת מְחוֹזָא דַּהֲוַת נְסִיבָא לִנְהַרְדְּעָא, אָתוּ לְקַמֵּיהּ דְּרַב נַחְמָן, [ז]שְׁמָעָהּ לְקָלָהּ דְּבַת מְחוֹזָא הִיא. אֲמַר לְהוּ: בָּבֶל וְכׇל פַּרְוָודָהָא נְהוּג כְּרַב. אָמְרוּ לֵיהּ: וְהָא לִנְהַרְדְּעָא נְסִיבָא! אֲמַר לְהוּ: אִי הָכִי – נְהַרְדְּעָא וְכׇל פַּרְוָודָהָא נְהוּג כִּשְׁמוּאֵל. וְעַד הֵיכָא נְהַרְדְּעָא – עַד הֵיכָא דְּסָגֵי קַבָּא דִּנְהַרְדְּעָא. אִיתְּמַר: [ח]אַלְמָנָה, רַב אָמַר: [ט]שָׁמִין מַה שֶּׁעָלֶיהָ, וּשְׁמוּאֵל אָמַר: אֵין שָׁמִין מַה שֶּׁעָלֶיהָ. אָמַר רַב חִיָּיא בַּר אָבִין: וְחִילּוּפָהּ בְּלַקִּיט. רַב כָּהֲנָא מַתְנֵי: וְכֵן בְּלַקִּיט, וּמַנַּח בָּהּ סִימָנָא: "יַתְמָא וְאַרְמַלְתָּא שְׁלַח וּפוֹק". אָמַר רַב נַחְמָן: אע"ג דִּתְנַן בְּמַתְנִיתִין כְּוָותֵיהּ דִּשְׁמוּאֵל – הִלְכְתָא כְּוָותֵיהּ דְּרַב. דִּתְנַן: *אֶחָד [י]הַמַּקְדִּישׁ נְכָסָיו, וְאֶחָד הַמַּעֲרִיךְ אֶת עַצְמוֹ – אֵין לוֹ לֹא בִּכְסוּת אִשְׁתּוֹ, וְלֹא בִּכְסוּת בָּנָיו, וְלֹא בְּצֶבַע שֶׁצְּבָעוֹ לִשְׁמָן, וְלֹא בְּסַנְדָּלִים חֲדָשִׁים שֶׁלְּקָחָן לִשְׁמָן. אֲמַר לֵיהּ רָבָא לְרַב נַחְמָן: וְכִי מֵאַחַר דִּתְנַן מַתְנִיתִין כְּוָותֵיהּ דִּשְׁמוּאֵל, אַמַּאי הִלְכְתָא כְּוָותֵיהּ דְּרַב? אֲמַר לֵיהּ: *לִכְאוֹרָה כִּשְׁמוּאֵל רְהִיטָא, כִּי מְעַיְּינַתְּ בָּהּ – הִלְכְתָא כְּוָותֵיהּ דְּרַב. מַאי טַעְמָא? כִּי אַקְנֵי לַהּ – אַדַּעְתָּא לְמֵיקַם קַמֵּיהּ, אַדַּעְתָּא לְמִשְׁקַל וּלְמֵיפַּק – לָא אַקְנֵי לַהּ. § כַּלְּתָא דְּבֵי בַּר אֶלְיָשִׁיב הֲוָה קָא תָּבְעָה כְּתוּבָּתָהּ מִיַּתְמֵי. הֲוָה קָא מַמְטֵי לְהוּ לְבֵי דִינָא, אָמְרִי: זִילָא לַן מִילְּתָא דְּתֵיזְלֵי הָכִי. אָזְלָא לְבִישְׁתִּינְהוּ וְאִיכַּסְתִּינְהוּ לְכוּלֵּיהּ מָנָא. אָתוּ לְקַמֵּיהּ דְּרָבִינָא, אֲמַר לְהוּ: הִלְכְתָא כְּוָותֵיהּ דְּרַב, דְּאָמַר: אַלְמָנָה שָׁמִין מַה שֶּׁעָלֶיהָ. הַהוּא דַּאֲמַר לְהוּ: נְדוּנְיָא לִבְרַת. זַל נְדוּנְיָא. א"ר אִידִי בַּר אָבִין: [כ]פּוּרְנָא לְיַתְמֵי. [ל]הַהוּא דַּאֲמַר לְהוּ:

אַרְבַּע

כֵּיוָן דְּלֵית לָהּ כְּתוּבָּה. לְאֵם, לֵית לָהּ מְזוֹנֵי דְּבַת. דְּהָא תְּנַאי כְּתוּבָּה הוּא. בַּת אֲרוּסָה. הַבָּא עַל אֲרוּסָתוֹ וְיָלְדָה לוֹ, וּמֵת וְלוֹ בָּנִים, יֵשׁ לָהּ מְזוֹנוֹת מִנְּכָסָיו, אוֹ לָא? כֵּיוָן דְּאִית לָהּ כְּתוּבָּה. כְּגוֹן שֶׁכָּתַב לָהּ מִן הָאֵירוּסִין. אִי נַמִי, רַבָּנַן תַּקּוּן נַמִי לַאֲרוּסָה. אוֹ דִּלְמָא כֵּיוָן דְּלָא תַּקּוּן רַבָּנַן. לְמִכְתַּב עַד שְׁעַת נִשּׂוּאִין, תְּנַאי כְּתוּבָּה נַמִי מִקַּמֵּי הָכִי לָא חָיֵיל. בַּת אֲנוּסָה. אָנַס אֶת הַנַּעֲרָה וּנְשָׂאָהּ אַחֲרֵי כֵן, כְּדִכְתִיב "וְלוֹ תִהְיֶה לְאִשָּׁה", וְיָלְדָה לוֹ בַּת וּמֵת, יֵשׁ לָהּ מְזוֹנוֹת מִן הָאַחִין אוֹ לָא? יֵשׁ לָהּ כְּתוּבָּה. מִנְּכָסָיו. מָנֶה. אִם מֵת, וְאע"ג שֶׁכְּבָר נָתַן כֶּסֶף קְנָסָהּ לְאָבִיהָ. יָצָא כֶּסֶף קְנָסָהּ בִּכְתוּבָּתָהּ. וְאֵין לָהּ כְּתוּבָּה. מַאי. מְזוֹנוֹת הַבַּת שֶׁהֵן תְּנַאי כְּתוּבָּה פָּקְעִי בְּהָכִי, אוֹ לָא? מִי אָמְרִינַן: כֵּיוָן דְּלֵית לָהּ כו'. אוֹ דִּלְמָא כְּתוּבָּה הַיְינוּ טַעְמָא. דְּלָא תַּקּוּן לָהּ רַבָּנַן, מִשּׁוּם דְּכׇל כְּתוּבַּת אִשָּׁה מִשּׁוּם שֶׁלֹּא תְּהֵא קַלָּה בְּעֵינָיו לְהוֹצִיאָהּ תִּקְּנוּהָ. וְהָא לָא מָצֵי מַפֵּיק. כְּדִכְתִיב "לֹא יוּכַל שַׁלְּחָהּ". כְּתוּבָּה דְּמִשּׁוּם אַפּוּקֵי הוּא, דְּלָא תַּקּוּן דְּלֵיכָּא לְמֵיחַשׁ – לֵית לָהּ. אֲבָל שְׁאָר תְּנָאֵי כְּתוּבָּה, דְּלָאו מִשּׁוּם שֶׁלֹּא תְּהֵא קַלָּה אִיתְקַן – אִית לָהּ. בְּבֵיתִי וְלֹא בְּבִיקְתִי. אִם יֵשׁ לוֹ בַּיִת כּוֹפִין אֶת הַיּוֹרְשִׁין לָתֵת לָהּ מָדוֹר לְפִי כְּבוֹדָהּ, וְאֵין יְכוֹלִין לוֹמַר לָהּ: לְכִי לְבֵית אָבִיךְ וְאָנוּ זָנִין אוֹתָךְ שָׁם. אֲבָל אֵין לוֹ בַּיִת אֶלָּא בִּיקְתָא בְּעָלְמָא, צָרִיךְ צַר וְקָטָן. וּלְשׁוֹן בִּיקְתָא – בֵּי עַקְתָא (שבת דף עז:). יְכוֹלִין לוֹמַר: לְכִי מֵאֶצְלֵנוּ, ד"אַתְּ תְּהֵא יָתְבָא בְּבֵיתִי" כָּתַב לָךְ, וְלֹא בְּבִיקְתִי. אֲבָל מְזוֹנֵי אִית לָהּ. בְּבֵית אָבִיהָ מִנְּכָסָיו, וְלָא אָמְרִינַן כֵּיוָן דְּלָא קָרֵינַן בָּהּ "וְאַתְּ תְּהֵא יָתְבָא בְּבֵיתִי" לָא קָרֵינַן בָּהּ "וּמִתְזְנָא מִנְּכָסַי". וְרַב יוֹסֵף "בְּבֵיתִי" יְתֵירָא דָּרֵישׁ, דְּתַקּוּן לְמִכְתַּב "בְּבֵיתִי" תְּרֵי זִימְנֵי, "וְאַתְּ תְּהֵא יָתְבָא בְּבֵיתִי כׇּל יְמֵי מֵיגַר אַרְמְנוּתֵיךְ בְּבֵיתִי". [וְנִתְפַּיְּיסָה. תּוּ לָא קָרֵינַן בָּהּ "מֵיגַר אַלְמְנוּתֵיךְ"]. הָא לֹא נִתְפַּיְּיסָה יֵשׁ לָהּ. בִּתְמִיָּה, וַאֲפִילּוּ אֵין הָעַכָּבָה מֵחֲמַת כְּבוֹד בַּעְלָהּ, אֶלָּא שֶׁלֹּא הָיָה תּוֹבְעָהּ הָגוּן לָהּ? כִּיחֲלָה וּפִירְכְּסָה. גַּלְיָא דַּעְתָּהּ דְּלָא מֵחֲמַת כְּבוֹד בַּעְלָהּ מְעַכֶּבֶת לִינָּשֵׂא. עָשְׂתָה כְּתוּבָּתָהּ אַפּוֹתִיקֵי. קַרְקַע הַמְיוּחֶדֶת לִכְתוּבָּתָהּ, עֲשָׂאָהּ אַפּוֹתֵיקֵי לְבַעַל חוֹב שֶׁלָּהּ. הָנֵי אִין. לְפִי שֶׁהֵן גִּיבּוּי כְּתוּבָּה, אֲבָל תְּבִיעָה – לָא. פַּרְוָודָהָא. כְּרַכִּים הַסְּמוּכִים לָהּ. מְחוֹזָא. מִפַּרְוָודֵי בָבֶל. דְּסָגֵי קַבָּא דִּנְהַרְדְּעָא. כׇּל מָקוֹם שֶׁמּוֹדְדִין תְּבוּאָה בְּמִדַּת קַב נְהַרְדְּעָא. שָׁמִין מַה שֶּׁעָלֶיהָ. כְּשֶׁמַּגְבִּין לָהּ בֵּית דִּין כְּתוּבָּתָהּ, שָׁמִין בְּגָדֶיהָ בְּפֵרָעוֹן כְּתוּבָּה. בְּלַקִּיט. שָׂכִיר שֶׁגָּר בְּבֵית בַּעַל הַבַּיִת, וְלָקַח לוֹ בַּעַל הַבַּיִת בְּגָדִים, כְּשֶׁיּוֹצֵא מִמֶּנּוּ – שָׁם אוֹתָן בְּגָדִים בִּשְׂכָרוֹ לִשְׁמוּאֵל, וְרַב אָמַר: אֵין שָׁמִין. וְכֵן בְּלַקִּיט. לְרַב שָׁמִין, וְלִשְׁמוּאֵל אֵין שָׁמִין. וּמַנַּח בָּהּ. רַב סִימָנָא בְּמִילְּתֵיהּ. יַתְמָא וְאַרְמַלְתָּא שְׁלַח וּפוֹק. הַפְשֵׁט בִּגְדֵיהֶן וָצֵא. יַתְמָא. לַקִּיט. דִּתְנַן בְּמַתְנִיתִין. בְּסוֹף דַּעֲרָכִין. אֶחָד הַמַּקְדִּישׁ נְכָסָיו כו' וְאֶחָד הַמַּעֲרִיךְ עַצְמוֹ. וְהַגִּזְבָּר בָּא לְמַשְׁכְּנוֹ עַל עֶרְכּוֹ הַקָּצוּב בַּפָּרָשָׁה, אֵין לוֹ לַגִּזְבָּר לֹא בִּכְסוּת אִשְׁתּוֹ כו'. לִשְׁמָן. בְּגָדִים שֶׁצָּבַע לְשֵׁם אִשְׁתּוֹ וּלְשֵׁם בָּנָיו, וְאע"פ שֶׁלֹּא לְבָשׁוּם עֲדַיִין. אַלְמָא בְּגָדֶיהָ שֶׁלָּהּ, כִּשְׁמוּאֵל. לִכְאוֹרָה כִּשְׁמוּאֵל רִיהֲטָא. פִּתְאוֹם מְרוּלָא מַשְׁמָעוּת הַמִּשְׁנָה כִּשְׁמוּאֵל, אֲבָל כִּי מְעַיֵּינַתְּ בָּהּ – לָא מְסַיְּיעָא לִשְׁמוּאֵל. דְּהָא קַמֵּיהּ קָיְימָא, וְאֵינָהּ יוֹצְאָה מִבֵּיתוֹ, וְאַדַּעְתָּא דְּהָכִי מַקְנֵי לָהּ שֶׁיְּהוּ שֶׁלָּהּ כׇּל זְמַן שֶׁהִיא תַּחְתָּיו. הַהוּא דַּאֲמַר לְהוּ. נוֹטֶה שְׁכִיב מְרַע. נְדוּנְיָא לִבְרַת. קְלוּדִים הָיוּ תַּכְשִׁיטֵי הַבָּנוֹת, כָּךְ וְכָךְ לְבוּשִׁים. פּוּרְנָא לְיַתְמֵי. הָרֶיוַח לַיְתוֹמִים. וְלָא אָמְרִינַן: נֵיתִיב לָהּ דְּמֵי הַנְּדוּנְיָא כְּיוֹם הַצַּוָּאָה.

אַרְבַּע

בת אנוסה מהו. תימה: דאנוסה גופה תיבעי. בביתי ולא בביקתי. כשאין להן כי אם ביקתי – היא מפסדת, דלכולי עלמא יכולין לגרשה. ויש להם בתים טובים – היא מרווחת בהאי לישנא דביתי, שמשתמשת במדור כדרך שנשתמשה בחיי בעלה. כדאמרינן ב"הנושא" (לקמן דף קג.), ואין להחליף לה לגרוע ממנו, או שמא אפילו לכיוצא בו. לית הלכתא ככל הני שמעתתא. [אכולהו קאי], בר מתבעוה לינשא, דההוא עדיפא. דאי ככל הני דוקא, וקאי נמי אתבעוה לינשא – א"כ קשיא דשמואל אדשמואל לרב ענן, דאמר לעיל: לדידי מפרשא לי מיניה דמר שמואל כו'. וכה"ג איכא בפרק "תולין" (שבת דף קמ.): לית הלכתא ככל הני שמעתתא, דלאו דוקא*. ושמואל אמר הלכה כאנשי גליל. פר"ח: ובמקום שיש מנהג – ילכו אחר המנהג, ובמקום שאין מנהג – יעשו כשמואל, דהלכתא כוותיה. והא דבעי בסמוך עד היכן נהרדעא – לאו משום דאין הלכה כשמואל, אלא משום. דשאר בבל נהוג כרב. והא דקשה מההיא ד"אלמנה" (לקמן נה:), שם *אפרש בע"ה.

אדבע

עין משפט נר מצוה

קכב א ב ג מיי' פי"ט מהל' אישות הלכ' יד טוש"ע אה"ע סי' סט סעיף ה:
קכג ד מיי' פי"ח שם הלכה א סמג לאוין פא ועשין מח טוש"ע שם סימן צג סעיף ה:
קכד ה מיי' שם טוש"ע שם סעיף ח:
קכה ו ז מיי' שם טוש"ע שם סעיף ג:
קכו ח ט מיי' פט"ז שם הלכה ד סמג עשין מח טוש"ע שם סי' צט סעיף א:
קכז י מיי' פ"ג מהל' ערכין הלכה יד סמג עשין קלא:

[ועי' תוס' שבת כג: ד"ה ולית וכו' וכן הרא"ש דהכא סי' ל כתב דאיה זו]

קכח כ ל מיי' פי"א מהל' זכיה הלכה כב סמג עשין עב טוש"ע ח"מ סי' רנג סעיף טז:

[ד"ה ניזונת תנן]

לעיל לט:

[שם וש"נ]

לקמן קג.

גיטין לה. [ערכין כב.]

לקמן לג:

ב"ק קב: ערכין כד.

[ובערוך ערך באור פי' כשאלמנה פותחת קודם שתמטין בה תפלה על דעתך שהיה כשמואל ולכאורה לשון ארמי הוא]

תוספות רי"ד

כיון דל"ל לשני' כתובה פי' כדתנן בפ' אלמנה ניזונית [דף ק' ע"ב] השני' והאיילונית אין לה כתובה וא"ל מזונות וטעמא מפורש בפ' י"מ משום דאיהי מרגלא ליה וקנסוה רבנן הלכך תנאי כתובה נמי אין לה דבנין נוקבין. א"ד אימא דעבדא איסורא קנסוה רבנן אבל איהי דלא עבדא איסורא לא קנסוהו רבנן תיקו: בעי רבא בת ארוסה. פי' המורה ארום הבא על ארוסתו והוליד ממנה בת והי' לו בנים מאשה אחרת ומת הארום י"ל מזונות. פי' מן האחים בנכסי האב או לא כיון דאית לה לארוסה כתובה. פי' היינו מו"מ מן האירוסין כדאמרינן לקמן בשלהי הכותב תנאי כתובה נמי כגון מזוני דבנן נוקבן אית לה א"ד כיון דלא תקינו רבנן למכתב כתובה עד שעת נשואין ומקמי הכי לא חיילא לית לה נמי תנאי כתובה באירוסין תיקו. ומהכא נמי מוכח דאית כתובה לארוסה אע"ג דלא כתב לה דאי בדכתב לה מאי קמבעי' להו. אי דכתב לה תנאי דבנן נוקבין יש לה ואי דלא כתב לה תנאי דבנין נוקבין ומנה מאתים כתב לה פשיטא דכתובה אית לה תנאי דבנין נוקבין ל"ל ואמאי קמבעיא להו א"ו הכי סבר אע"ג דלא כתב לה כתובתה אית לה מנה ומאתים ומ"ה בעי אי אית לה נמי תנאי דב"נ אי לא וה"נ איכא למבעי על ארוסה גופא אי מתזנא לאחר מיתת הבעל מנכסיו או לא וטעם אחד להן. ובפ' האומר בקידושין מוכיח בפירוש שיש כתובה לארוסה אע"ג דלא כתב לה דתנן התם [היא אומרת] קידשתני והוא אומר לא קדשתיך היא אסורה בקרוביו והוא מותר בקרובותיה ואמרינן התם אם נתן גט מעצמו כופין אותו ליתן כתובה ואי בדכתב לה תיפוק ליה דהא כתב לה ותו האיך יכול לכפור ולומר לא קדשתיך א"ו בדלא כתב לה: בעי רבא בת אנוסה. פי' אנס את הנערה ונשאה אח"כ כדכתיב ולו תהיה לאשה והולידה לו בת ומת י"ל מזונות מן האחין מנכסיו או לא מזונות הבת שהן תנאי כתובה מיפקע בהכי או לא מי אמרינן כיון דל"ל כתובה ת"כ נמי ל"ל א"ד כתובה היינו טעמא דלא תיקון לה רבנן דכל כתובת אשה הוא משום שלא תהא קלה בעיניו להוציאה והאי לא מצי מפיק לה כדכתיב לא יוכל לשלחה כל ימיו והשתא כתובה דמשום אפוקי הוא דלא תקינו רבנן דליכא למיחש לה אבל שאר ת"כ דלא משום להוציאה איתקון אית לה תיקו: מתני' את תהא יתבא בביתי ומיתזנא מנכסי כל ימי מיגר אלמנותיך חייב מפני שהוא תנאי ב"ד. פי' מיגר משך או מיגר לשון דירה וכך היו אנשי ירושלים כותבין אנשי גליל הי' כותבין כאנשי ירושלים וביהודה היו כותבין עד שירצו היתומים ליתן לה כתובתה. לפיכך אם רצו היורשים נותנים לה כתובתה ופוטרים אותה: תני ר"י בביתי ולא בביקתי. פי' דוקא אם הניח בית גדול שראוי לה ולהם הן חייבים לתת לה מדור ואין יכולים לומר לה לכי לבית אביך ואנו זנין אותך שם. אבל אם הניח מדור צר ודחוק אין חייבים לתת לה מדור דמתני' תני תרי בביתי כדי לדיוקא בביתי ולא בביקת אלא זנים אותה בבית אביה מנכסיו ול"א כיון דלא קרינן ביה בביתי לא קרינא ביה נמי ומתזני מנכסי: מר בר"א אמר אפילו מזוני נמי ל"ל. פי' כיון דבטל התנאי דמדור בטל נמי תנאי דמזונות דיתבא בביתי אתני בהדי' וכיון דלא יתבה בביתיה לא מיתזנא. ומסיק תלמודא ולית הל' כמר בר"א דהאי דקתני בביתי שלא תוכל היא לומר תנו לי מזונות בבית אבי וא"א לדור עמכם דלא יהבי לה אא"כ יושבת וניזונית עמהן דברכת הבית ברובה אבל הכא דאינהו מעכבי מעלין לה מזונות בבית אביה: אר"נ א"ש תבעוה להנשא ונתפייסה א"ל מזונות. פי' דלא קרינן בה מיגר ארמלותיך בביתי הא לא נתפייסה י"ל מזונות. פי' ואע"פ שהעכבה היתה כחמת שלא הי' התובעה הגון לה לא מחמת כבוד בעלה: אר"ע לדידי מפרשא לי מיניה דמר שמואל אמרה מחמת פ' בעלי י"ל מזונות מחמת ב"א שאינן מהוגנים לי אין לה מזונות. פי' משמע דאי הוו מהוגנים הוה מינסבא להו: אר"ח זנתה אין לה מזונות אמר ר"י כחלה ופרכסה א"ל מזונות. פי' דגלי דעתא דלא משום כבוד בעלה מעכבא מ"ד זנתה כ"ש כחלה ופרכסה ומ"ד כחלה ופרכסה אבל זנתה י"ל מזונות מ"ט יצר אנסוה ומסיק תלמודא ולית הל' ככל הני [illegible] אין לה מזונות. פי' [אפותיקי] פה תהא קאי למיקם אמרה לבע"ח לא תבעה חובך אלא משדה זו [illegible] אע"פ

קכט א מיי' פי"ח מהל' אישות הלכ' יח טוש"ע אה"ע סי' נג סעיף טז:
א ב מיי' פ"י מהל' אישות הלכה ז ופט"ז הלכ' ג סמג עשין מח טוש"ע שם סי' סו סעיף ז:
ב ג מיי' פ"י שם הלכ' יא סמג שם טוש"ע שם סי' נל סעיף ו:
ג ד מיי' פ"י שם הלכה ז ופי"ב שם הל' ח סמג שם טוש"ע שם סי' סו סעיף ט:
ד ה מיי' פט"ז שם הל' ג סמג שם טוש"ע שם סעיף ז:
ה ו מיי' פי"ח שם הל' כח טוש"ע שם סי' נג סעיף י:
ו ז מיי' פי"ד שם הלכ' ח ט [ופט"ז הלכה יד] סמג לאוין פא טוש"ע שם סימן עז סעיף ב [וסי' נו סעיף ז]:
ז ח מיי' פי"ח שם הלכ' א טוש"ע שם סימן נג סעיף יא:
ח ט מיי' פכ"ד שם הל' טז סמג עשין מח טוש"ע שם סימן קטו סעיף ד ה:

אַרְבַּע מְאָה זוּזֵי מִן חַמְרָא לִבְרַת. אִייַּקַר חַמְרָא. אֲמַר רַב יוֹסֵף: רַוְוחָא לְיַתְמֵי. קְרִיבֵיהּ דְּרַבִּי יוֹחָנָן הֲוָה לְהוּ אִיתַּת אַבָּא דַּהֲוָה קָמַפְסְדָה מְזוֹנֵי. אֲתוֹ לְקַמֵּיהּ דְּרַבִּי יוֹחָנָן. אֲמַר לְהוּ: אֵיזִילוּ וְאִמְרוּ לֵיהּ לַאֲבוּכוֹן דְּנֵיְיחֵד לָהּ אַרְעָא לִמְזוֹנָהּ. אֲתוֹ לְקַמֵּיהּ דְּרֵישׁ לָקִישׁ, אֲמַר לְהוּ: כׇּל שֶׁכֵּן שֶׁרִיבָּה לָהּ מְזוֹנוֹת! אָמְרוּ לֵיהּ: וְהָא רַבִּי יוֹחָנָן לָא אֲמַר הָכִי! אֲמַר לְהוּ: זִילוּ הֲבוּ לָהּ, וְאִי לָא — מַפֵּיקְנָא לְכוּ רַבִּי יוֹחָנָן מֵאוּנַיְיכוּ. אֲתוֹ לְקַמֵּיהּ דְּרַבִּי יוֹחָנָן. אֲמַר לְהוּ:* מָה אֶעֱשֶׂה? שֶׁכְּנֶגְדִּי חָלוּק עָלַי. אָמַר רַבִּי אֲבָהוּ, לְדִידִי מְפָרְשָׁא לִי מִינֵּיהּ דְּרַבִּי יוֹחָנָן: אָמַר [א]"לִמְזוֹנוֹת" — רִיבָּה לָהּ מְזוֹנוֹת, אָמַר "בִּמְזוֹנוֹת" — קָצַץ לָהּ מְזוֹנוֹת.§

הדרן עלך נערה

אַף עַל פִּי שֶׁאָמְרוּ בְּתוּלָה גּוֹבָה מָאתַיִם וְאַלְמָנָה מָנֶה, [ב]אִם רָצָה לְהוֹסִיף, אֲפִי' מֵאָה מָנֶה — יוֹסִיף. *נִתְאַרְמְלָה אוֹ נִתְגָּרְשָׁה, בֵּין מִן הָאֵרוּסִין בֵּין מִן הַנִּשּׂוּאִין — גּוֹבָה אֶת הַכֹּל. רַבִּי אֶלְעָזָר בֶּן עֲזַרְיָה אוֹמֵר: [ג]מִן הַנִּשּׂוּאִין — גּוֹבָה אֶת הַכֹּל, מִן הָאֵירוּסִין, בְּתוּלָה — גּוֹבָה מָאתַיִם וְאַלְמָנָה מָנֶה, שֶׁלֹּא כָּתַב לָהּ אֶלָּא עַל מְנָת לְכוֹנְסָהּ. *רַבִּי יְהוּדָה אוֹמֵר: אִם רָצָה — כּוֹתֵב לִבְתוּלָה שְׁטָר שֶׁל מָאתַיִם, וְהִיא כּוֹתֶבֶת "הִתְקַבַּלְתִּי מִמְּךָ מָנֶה", וּלְאַלְמָנָה מָנֶה, וְהִיא כּוֹתֶבֶת "הִתְקַבַּלְתִּי מִמְּךָ חֲמִשִּׁים זוּז". רַבִּי מֵאִיר אוֹמֵר: [ד]כׇּל הַפּוֹחֵת לִבְתוּלָה מִמָּאתַיִם וּלְאַלְמָנָה מִמָּנֶה — הֲרֵי זוֹ בְּעִילַת זְנוּת.§ **גמ'** פְּשִׁיטָא! מַהוּ דְּתֵימָא: קִיצוּתָא עָבְדוּ רַבָּנַן, *שֶׁלֹּא לְבַיֵּישׁ אֶת מִי שֶׁאֵין לוֹ — קמ"ל.§ [אִם רָצָה לְהוֹסִיף כו'].§ "רָצָה לִכְתּוֹב לָהּ" — לָא קָתָנֵי, אֶלָּא "רָצָה לְהוֹסִיף". מְסַיַּיע לֵיהּ לְר' אִיבוֹ אָמַר רַבִּי יַנַּאי. *דְּאָמַר ר' אִיבוֹ אָמַר רַבִּי יַנַּאי: [ה]תְּנַאי כְּתוּבָּה כִּכְתוּבָּה דָּמֵי. נָפְקָא מִינַּהּ [ו]לְמוֹכֶרֶת, וּלְמוֹחֶלֶת, [ז]לְמוֹרֶדֶת, וּלְפוֹגֶמֶת, [ח]לְתוֹבַעַת, [ט]וּלְעוֹבֶרֶת עַל דָּת, לְשֶׁבַח

אַרְבַּע מְאָה זוּזֵי מִן חַמְרָא. מַשְׁמַע: אוֹתוֹ יַיִן יְהֵא מְשׁוּעְבָּד לְכָךְ, אֲבָל הַיַּיִן עַצְמוֹ לֹא אָמַר לִיתֵּן לָהּ כְּדָמָיו שֶׁל יוֹם הַצַּוָּואָה. מַפְסְדָה מְזוֹנֵי. מַרְבָּה לֶאֱכוֹל. דְּנֵייחֵד לָהּ. בְּצַוָּואַת שְׁכִיב מְרַע, וּבְעֵדִים, אוּלַי תְּקַבֵּל עָלֶיהָ. דַּאֲפִי' גַּבֵּי כְּתוּבָּה תְּנַן (פאה פ"ג מ"ז): הַכּוֹתֵב כׇּל נְכָסָיו לְבָנָיו וְכָתַב לְאִשְׁתּוֹ קַרְקַע כׇּל שֶׁהוּא — אִבְּדָה כְּתוּבָּתָהּ רַבִּי יוֹסֵי אוֹמֵר אִם קִבְּלָה עָלֶיהָ אע"פ שֶׁלֹּא כָּתַב לָהּ לִישָּׁנָא אַחֲרִינָא דַּהֲוֵי לֵיהּ כְּמְחַלֵּק נְכָסָיו עַל פִּיו וְנָתַן שְׁאָר הַנְּכָסִים לְבָנָיו וְהָוֵה לְהוּ מְשַׁעְבְּדֵי °וְאֵין הַבָּנוֹת וְהָאִשָּׁה נִיזּוֹנוֹת מִמְּשַׁעְבְּדֵי. כׇּל שֶׁכֵּן שֶׁרִיבָּה לָהּ מְזוֹנוֹת. אִם אָמַר קַרְקַע זוֹ לִמְזוֹנוֹתַיִךְ אֵין זֶה אֶלָּא אִם לֹא יִתְּנוּ לִיךְ מְזוֹנוֹת מְרוּוָחִים אֶלָּא מְלוּמְצָמִים טוֹלִי קַרְקַע זוֹ לְהַעֲדָפָה דְּאִי לְשַׁעְבְּדָהּ לִמְזוֹנוֹתֶיהָ הֲרֵי כׇּל נְכָסָיו מְשׁוּעְבָּדִים לְכָךְ. שֶׁכְּנֶגְדִּי. אֱנוֹשׁ כְּעֶרְכִּי וְרָאוּי לַחֲלוֹק עָלַי. בִּמְזוֹנוֹת. בְּחוֹב מְזוֹנוֹת שֶׁיֵּשׁ לִיךְ עָלַי מַשְׁמַע שֶׁזּוֹ תְּהֵא פֵּרָעוֹן לְכָךְ.

הדרן עלך נערה

אַף עַל פִּי. אִם רָצָה. בַּגְּמָרָא פָּרֵיךְ: פְּשִׁיטָא. שֶׁלֹּא כָּתַב לָהּ. תּוֹסֶפֶת דְּמִדַּעְתּוֹ, אֶלָּא עַל מְנָת לְכוֹנְסָהּ. וְהִיא כּוֹתֶבֶת. אע"פ שֶׁלֹּא נִתְקַבְּלָה, מוֹחֶלֶת, וְכוֹתֶבֶת בִּלְשׁוֹן שׁוֹבֵר. **גמ'** רָצָה לִכְתּוֹב לָא קָתָנֵי. אִי תָּנָא "לִכְתּוֹב", לָא הֲוָה שָׁמְעִינַן מִינָּהּ שֶׁיְּהֵא הַתּוֹסֶפֶת קָרוּי כְּתוּבָּה, אֶלָּא כְּמַתָּנָה מִדַּעְתּוֹ, וְאֵין שֵׁם כְּתוּבָּה עָלָיו. הָשְׁתָּא דִּתְנַן "לְהוֹסִיף" — מַשְׁמַע נוֹסָף עַל הַכְּתוּבָּה שֶׁתִּקְּנוּ חֲכָמִים, וְשֵׁם כְּתוּבָּה עָלָיו, גַּם הוּא מְסַיֵּיעַ לֵיהּ כו'. תְּנַאי כְּתוּבָּה. תּוֹסֶפֶת שֶׁהוּא מַתְנֶה לְהוֹסִיף לָהּ, וְכֵן מְזוֹנוֹת, וְכׇל הָנָךְ דִּתְנַן בְּפִרְקִין דִּלְעֵיל. לְמוֹכֶרֶת וּלְמוֹחֶלֶת. מוֹכֶרֶת כְּתוּבָּתָהּ אוֹ מוֹחֶלֶת כְּתוּבָּתָהּ — מָחֲלָה וּמָכְרָה אֶת הַכֹּל, לְפִי שֶׁהַכֹּל קָרוּי כְּתוּבָּה, וְלָא אָמְרִינַן לָא מִיקְרֵי כְּתוּבָּה אֶלָּא מָנֶה מָאתַיִם. לְמוֹרֶדֶת. דִּתְנַן בְּפִרְקִין (לקמן סג.). הַמּוֹרֶדֶת עַל בַּעְלָהּ — פּוֹחֲתִין לָהּ מִכְּתוּבָּתָהּ כו'. עַד מָתַי הוּא פּוֹחֵת — עַד כְּנֶגֶד כְּתוּבָּתָהּ. לָא תֵּימָא כְּנֶגֶד מָנֶה מָאתַיִם לְחוּדַיְיהוּ, אֶלָּא אַף הַתּוֹסֶפֶת פּוֹחֲתִין וְהוֹלְכִין. וּלְפוֹגֶמֶת. בְּפֶרֶק "הַכּוֹתֵב" (לקמן פז.) תְּנַן. הַפּוֹגֶמֶת כְּתוּבָּתָהּ — לֹא תִּפָּרַע אֶלָּא בִּשְׁבוּעָה. אִם פָּגְמָה תּוֹסֶפֶת נַמִי, שֶׁאָמְרָה לְשֵׁם פֵּרָעוֹן הַתּוֹסָפוֹת הִתְקַבַּלְתִּי דִּינָר — אַף זוֹ פּוֹגֶמֶת כְּתוּבָּתָהּ הִיא, וְאִם טוֹעֵן בַּעְלָהּ הִתְקַבַּלְתְּ כׇּל כְּתוּבָּתֵיךְ — לֹא תִּפָּרַע אֶלָּא בִּשְׁבוּעָה. לְתוֹבַעַת. הַתּוֹבַעַת כְּתוּבָּתָהּ בְּב"ד — אֵין לָהּ מְזוֹנוֹת. תּוֹבַעַת תּוֹסֶפֶת — נַמִי אֵין לָהּ מְזוֹנוֹת. עוֹבֶרֶת עַל דָּת. בְּפֶרֶק "הַמַּדִּיר" (לקמן עב.) שֶׁאָמְרוּ עָלֶיהָ. תֵּצֵא שֶׁלֹּא בִּכְתוּבָּה. לָא תֵּימָא כְּתוּבַּת מָנֶה מָאתַיִם, אֲבָל תּוֹסֶפֶת מַתָּנָה בְּעָלְמָא הוּא לֹא הִפְסִידָה. לְשֶׁבַח

ארבע מאה זוזי מן חמרא לברת. וא"ת: דבפרק "התקבל" (גיטין דף סה:) גבי גניבא יולא בקולר הוה, כי נפק אמר: הבו ארבע מאה זוזי לרבי אבינא מחמרא דהרפניא. וקאמר התם (דף סו.) דלא קנה רבי אבינא, דחמרא לא קאמר, דמי חמרא לא קאמר! אלא מחמרא קאמר! ואין סברא לחלק בין "מחמרא" ל"מן חמרא". ויש לומר: דהתם נמי מסיק מחמרא — לייפות את כחו. **דנייחד** לה ארעא למזונה. אע"ג דלעיל (נג:) נתחרט ר' יוחנן על מה שהשיאן עלה, הכא אין גנאי, כיון דבדעתה תלוי אם תרלה לקבל. **למזונות** ריבה לה מזונות כו'. תימה: דבפ' "המקבל" (ב"מ דף קד:) מסיק דלא שנא אמר "לכתובתה" ל"ש אמר "בכתובתה" — ארבע מאה זוזי דאינון מאתן, גבי "הבו לה ארבע מאה זוזי לברת"! ויש לומר: דהכא דווקא, לפי שהיא מוחזקת במזונות אמרינן: למזונות — ריבה לה מזונות. אבל התם — אין הבת מוחזקת. אי נמי: התם לא הוה ליה למימר אלא הבו לה ארבע מאה זוזי, ומדקאמר לכתובתה, משמע דעם של בעל קאמר דליהוי ארבע מאה זוזי, אבל הכא דלריך לפרש למזונות יש לחלק.

הדרן עלך נערה

אף על פי. אם רצה להוסיף אפי' מאה מנה מוסיף. תימה: דעכשיו נהגו שכותב חתן לכלה מאה ליטרין, אע"פ שאין לו שוה פרוטה דבשלמא כשיש לו — הוא משעבד נכסיו לזה החוב. והואיל ונתחייב, אפילו נאבדו אלו הנכסים וקנה אחרים — הם משתעבדים, אע"פ שאין אדם מקנה דבר שלא בא לעולם, מ"מ אדם משעבד דבר שלא בא לעולם, כיון דכתב "ודעתיד אנא למיקני" כדאמרינן ב"מי שמת" (ב"ב קנז. ושם). אבל אותו שאין לו — היאך ישתעבד נכסיו שיקנה אחרי כן? כיון שלא נתחייב לה — היינו דבר שלא בא לעולם! ושאל ר"י לרבי אליהו, והשיב לו: דמלינו כענין זה בפרק "השוכר את הפועלים" (ב"מ דף לד. ושם), דתניא: מתנה שומר חנם להיות כשואל. ופריך: במאי — בדברים? ומשני: בשקנו מידו. משמע בכל ענין, אע"פ שאין מקנה לו שום נכסים, אלא שמשעבד גופו לזה החוב מעתה, ולכשיהיו לו נכסים חל שעבודו מעתה. ואין זה קנין דברים בעלמא, דקנין דברים לא הוי אלא כההיא דריש בבא בתרא (דף ג.) שקנו מידם לחלוק חצר שאין בה דין חלוקה. אבל מה שמשעבד גופו להתחייב לדבר זה — משתעבד, ואין זה קנין דברים בעלמא. וי"מ: דכיון דכותב סתמא שיהיו כל נכסיו אחראין למה לא נתחייב? הרי הודה שיש לו נכסים! ואע"פ שאנו יודעים שאין לו — הודאת בעל דין כמאה עדים דמי. ומטעם זה אור"ת: שכותבין בהרשאות "והקניתי לו ארבע אמות קרקע בחצרי" אע"פ שאנו יודעים שאין לו קרקע, כיון דמודה שיש לו — הודאת בעל דין כמאה עדים דמי*. **למורדת**. אליבא דר' יוסי לא איצטריך, דאפי' לא הוי תנאי כתובה ככתובה — פוחת לה. דהא אמר לקמן במתני' לעולם פוחת והולך, שאם נפלה לה ירושה ממקום אחר חוזר וגובה ממנה. אלא לרבנן איצטריך, שאינו פוחת אלא כתובה. דתוספת נמי ככתובה. **ולפוגמת**. איצטריך, דאם פגמה כתובתה לא תגבה גם התוספת אלא בשבועה, אפי' היתה הכתובה בשטר אחד והתוספת בשטר אחר*. **ולתובעת**. פירש בקונטרס: שאם תבעה תוספת — שאין לה מזונות. ולא יתכן פירושו אליבא דרבנן, דאמרי לקמן בפרק אלמנה (דף נד:): משכנה או נתנה מקצת כתובתה — יש לה מזונות! אלא יש לפרש: ולתובעת — שאם תבעה מנה מאתים ושיירה תוספת, דיש לה מזונות, כיון דתנאי כתובה ככתובה — הרי לא תבעה כי אם מקצת כתובה. **ולעוברת** על דת. דהואיל והפסידה כתובתה — הפסידה נמי תוספת. ואף על גב דבממאנת ושניה ואיילונית אין להן כתובה ויש להן תוספת, התם היינו טעמא דמתחלה, כשכתב תוספת, לאו אדעתא דכתובה כתב לה, דהא יודע שאין לממאנת ושניה כתובה. הלכך, תוספת דכתב לה — מתנה בעלמא כתב לה, ולא שייכא לכתובה כלל. ואיילונית נמי, תוספת דכתב לה — מתנה בעלמא, מחמת חיבת לילה הראשונה, ואפילו תמלא איילונית, הואיל ולא פירש. אבל הכתובה עצמה, הואיל ואינה תלויה בכתיבתו — אין דעתו לכותבה אלא כמו שחייבוהו חכמים, אם אינה איילונית. אבל עוברת על דת, דמעיקרא תוספת אדעתא דכתובה כתב לה, כשקנסוה בכתובה — קנסוה גם בתוספת.

ולשבח

תוספות רי"ד

את עצמו פי' והגזבר בא למשכנו על ערכו הקצוב לו בפרשה לפי שניו אין לו לגזבר לא בכסות אשתו ולא בכסות בניו ולא בצבע שצבען לשמן ולא בסנדלים חדשים שלקח לשמן פי' אע"פ שלא לבשם עדיין כיון שלקחן או צבען לשמן קנו אותם במתנה אלמא אין שמין לכסות אשה כשמואל א"ל רבא לר"נ וכי מאחר דתנן מתני' כוותיה דשמואל אמאי הל' כוותיה דרב א"ל לכעורה כשמואל נקטה. פי' לאדם כיעור שאינו מעיין ומדקדק לפום ריהטא נראה לו כשמואל ס"ל מתני' דעירובין אבל כי מעיינת ביה שפיר הל' כרב מ"ט כי אקנו לה אדעתא למיקם קמיה פי' ומתכבד בהן לפיכך אין לו בכסות אשתו וכו'. אדעתא למשקל ומיפק לא אקני לה. פי' כגון אלמנה שהולכת ונשאת לאחר: כלתי' דר' אלישוב הוה תבעה כתובה מיתמי הות ממטיא לה לב"ד א"ל זילא מילתא דתיזלי הכי לבישתינהו וכיסיתינהו לכולהו אתו לקמיה דרבינא א"ל הל' כוותיה דרב דאמר אלמנה שמין מה שעליה: ההוא דאמר נדוניא לברת פי' שכ"מ היה וצוה שיתנו מנכסיו נדוניא לבתו והי' קצובים להן בגדי הנדוניא כמה מלבושים כמה קשרי הראש זול נדוניא פי' שבשעת צוואה היתה הנדוניא נקחת במאתים ועכשיו נקחו במנה: אר"א ב"א פורנא ליתמי. פי' הריוח ואע"ג דא"ל כי אמר אביה למיתב לה נדוניא מידע ידע דבמאתן מזבנא ומאתן זוזי שבק לה השתא נמי כי זל שיתנו לה מאתן זוזי אפ"ה ל"ל אלא נדוניא הנקחת במנה וה"ה נמי אם הוקרה הנדוניא שחייבים לקנות לה היקרים כפי מה שנמכרים עכשיו: ההוא דא"ל ד' מאות זוזי מן חמרא לברת איקר חמרא אמר ר"י (דניחא) [רווחא] ליתמי וימכרו היין ויתנו לה ד' מאות זוז ול"א כבר זכתה בשעת הצוואה היין שוה ד' מאות זוז ואם הוקיר הוקיר לבת: קריביה דר"י הוות להו אתת אבא דהות (קמרוחה) [קמפסדה] מזוני אתו לקמי' דר"י בעוד שהי' אביהן שכ"מ א"ל זילו אמרו ליה לאבוכון דליתיב לה ארעא למזונה אתו לקמיה דר"ל אחר שמת ועשה הצואה כר"י א"ל כ"ש שריבה לה מזונות דהכי קא"ל אם לא יתנו לך מזונות מרווחים כמו שאת רגילה עמי גבי מזונותיך מזו הקרקע: א"ר אבהו לדידי מפרשא ליה מיניה דר"י אמר למזונות ריבה לה. אמר במזונות קצץ לה מזונות ומכאן מוכח דר"י ס"ל כשמואל דאי כרב יתנו לה כתובתה ויסלקוה מעליהן: **הדרן עלך נערה**

אע"פ שאמרו בתולה גובה מאתים ואלמנה מנה אם רצה להוסיף אפילו מאה מנה יוסיף נתאלמנה או נתגרשה בין מן האירוסין בין מן הנשואין גובה את הכל ראב"ע אומר מן הנשואין גובה הכל מן האירוסין בתולה גובה מאתים ואלמנה מנה שלא כתב לה אלא ע"מ לכונסה. פי' נתאלמנה וכו' היכא דקדים וכ' לה תוספת מן האירוסין ומ"ה אמר ת"ק דגובה את הכל דכיון דכתב לה הכל לפי תנאו והא דאוקימנא לעיל הל' א' זה וא' זה מן הנשואין ה"מ לטרוף לקוחות מזמן נשואין שלא כתב לה אחריותא אלא משעת חופה ואילך אבל מן המחוררין גובה אף מן האירוסין ור"א פליג ואמר דמן האירוסין לא גביא אלא מנה מאתים ולא תוספת שלא כתב לה תוספת מן האירוסין אלא ע"מ לכונסה וזה שכתב לה מן האירוסין כדי להבטיחה שכך הוא עתיד להוסיף לה אבל מנה מאתים גביא בין אם נאמר שיש כתובה לארוסה בתנאי ב"ד אע"ג דלא כתב לה בין אם נאמר דוקא שכתב לה שאין לומר שם לא כתב לה אלא ע"מ לכונסה שהדבר ידוע שאם יכניסנה יש לה מנה מאתים ולמה כתב לה מקודם לכן אילולי שתגבה מן האירוסין אבל התוס' שאינו ידוע אלא אחר שיכנוס שהיא תלוי ברצון האיש אם ירצה יוסיף ואם לאו לא יוסיף. אמרינן לא כתב לה אלא ע"מ לכונסה והבטיחה מקודם לכן כמה יוסיף לה אם יכנוס: פשיטא פי' ובמאי דתנן בפ"ק ב"ד של כהנים היו גובין לבתולה ד' מאות זוז ולא מיחו בידם חכמים לא אמרינן פשיטא שהן היו כותבין לבתולה ד' מאות זוז והוא נראה שמוסיפים על דברי חכמים ואדרבה הי' ראוי למחות בידן אבל זה שאינו כותב לבתולה אלא מאתים כדברי חכמים אם רוצה להוסיף משלו פשיטא שהוא יכול להוסיף מ"ד קיצותא הוא דעבדי רבנן שלא לבייש את מי שאין לו קמ"ל. פי' מנה מאתים אין טפי לא שלא לבייש את מי שאין לו להוסיף קמ"ל אם רוצה להוסיף וכו': רצה לכתוב לא קתני אלא רצה להוסיף. פי' אי הוי תני לכתוב לא הוה שמעי' מינה שתהא התוס' קרויה כתובה אלא במתנה מדעתו ואין שם כתובה עליו השתא דתנא להוסיף משמע נוספת על הכתובה שתקנו חכמים ושם כתובה עליו גם הוא. מסייע ליה לר"א דאמר ר"א תנאי כתובה. פי' התוס' ככתובה דמי פי' דכי היכי דאמרת לעיל לא כתב לבתולה מאתים ולאלמנה מנה חייב תוספת נמי כיון דאמר הכי והכי אוסיפ' לה אע"פ שלא כתב לה חייב.

למאי

(גיטין סה:) ... [ולקמן פד:]
לעיל מז. לקמן פט: ב"מ יז:
לעיל נח.
[פסחים פב. וש"נ]
גירסת רש"ל
[לקמן קד:]
[ועי' תוס' ב"ק קד: ד"ה אגב ותוס' ב"ב מד: ד"ה דלא]
[אבל אם הכל בשטר א' אפי' אין תנאי כתובה ככתובה נגבית על הכל דהא בפוגם שטר שטרות נמי איכא שבועה. מ"ו]

גליון הש"ס

רש"י ד"ה דנייחד לה וכו' ואין הבנות והאשה ניזונות ממשעבדי. עיין לעיל דף מט ע"ב רש"י ד"ה מיבעיא וצ"ע:

א לְשֶׁבַח, ב לִשְׁבוּעָה, ג וְלַשְּׁבִיעִית, ד וְלַכּוֹתֵב כָּל נְכָסָיו לְבָנָיו, לִגְבּוֹת מִן הַקַּרְקַע, ה וּמִן הַזִּיבּוּרִית, ו וְכָל זְמַן שֶׁהִיא בְּבֵית אָבִיהָ, ז וְלִכְתוּבַּת בְּנִין דִּכְרִין. אִיתְּמַר: כְּתוּבַּת בְּנִין דִּכְרִין, פּוּמְבְּדִיתָא אָמְרִי: *לָא טָרְפָא מִמְּשַׁעְבְּדֵי, "יִרְתוּן" תְּנַן, בְּנֵי מָתָא מְחַסְיָא אָמְרִי: טָרְפָא מִמְּשַׁעְבְּדֵי, *"יִסְבוּן" תְּנַן. ח וְהִלְכְתָא: לָא טָרְפָא מִמְּשַׁעְבְּדֵי, *"יִרְתוּן" תְּנַן. ט מִטַּלְטְלֵי וְאִיתְנְהוּ בְּעֵינַיְיהוּ – בְּלָא שְׁבוּעָה. לֵיתְנְהוּ בְּעֵינַיְיהוּ, פּוּמְבְּדִיתָא אָמְרִי: בְּלָא שְׁבוּעָה, בְּנֵי מָתָא מְחַסְיָא אָמְרִי: בִּשְׁבוּעָה. וְהִלְכְתָא: י בְּלָא שְׁבוּעָה. יִיחֵד לָהּ אַרְעָא, בְּאַרְבָּעָה מִצְרָנָהָא – בְּלָא שְׁבוּעָה. בְּחַד מִצְרָא, פּוּמְבְּדִיתָא אָמְרִי: בְּלָא שְׁבוּעָה, בְּנֵי מָתָא מְחַסְיָא אָמְרִי: בִּשְׁבוּעָה. וְהִלְכְתָא: כ בְּלָא שְׁבוּעָה. ל אָמַר לְעֵדִים "כִּתְבוּ וְחִתְמוּ וַהֲבוּ לֵיהּ", קָנוּ מִינֵּיהּ – לָא צָרִיךְ אִימְּלוּכֵי בֵּיהּ, לֹא קָנוּ מִינֵּיהּ, פּוּמְבְּדִיתָא אָמְרִי: לָא צָרִיךְ אִימְּלוּכֵי בֵּיהּ, בְּנֵי מָתָא מְחַסְיָא אָמְרִי: צָרִיךְ אִימְּלוּכֵי בֵּיהּ. מ וְהִלְכְתָא: צָרִיךְ אִימְּלוּכֵי בֵּיהּ. § ר' אֶלְעָזָר בֶּן עֲזַרְיָה וכו'. § אִיתְּמַר, רַב וְרַבִּי נָתָן; חַד אָמַר: הֲלָכָה כְּרַבִּי אֶלְעָזָר בֶּן עֲזַרְיָה, וְחַד אָמַר: אֵין הֲלָכָה כְּר' אֶלְעָזָר בֶּן עֲזַרְיָה. תִּסְתַּיֵּים, דְּר' נָתָן הוּא דְּאָמַר הֲלָכָה כְּר' אֶלְעָזָר בֶּן עֲזַרְיָה, דְּשָׁמְעִי' לֵיהּ לְרַבִּי נָתָן דְּאָזֵיל בָּתַר אוּמְדָּנָא. *דְּאָמַר רַבִּי *נָתָן: הֲלָכָה כְּרַבִּי שִׁמְעוֹן שְׁזוּרִי נ בִּמְסוּכָּן,

וּבִתְרוּמַת

רש"י

לְשֶׁבַח. שֶׁאָמְרוּ בִּבְכוֹרוֹת (דף נב.). אֵין הַבְּכוֹר נוֹטֵל פִּי שְׁנַיִם בְּשֶׁבַח שֶׁשָּׁבְחוּ הַנְּכָסִים לְאַחַר מִיתַת אֲבִיהֶן, וְלֹא הָאִשָּׁה בִּכְתוּבָּתָהּ. וְתוֹסֶפֶת נַמִי לָא גָּבְיָא מִשֶּׁבַח שֶׁשָּׁבְחוּ נְכָסִים לְאַחַר מִיתַת בַּעְלָהּ. וְלִשְׁבוּעָה. לְכָל מִילֵּי דְּשַׁיְיכָא לִישָּׁבַע עַל הַכְּתוּבָּה, כְּגוֹן הַנִּפְרַעַת שֶׁלֹּא בְּפָנָיו, וְעֵד אֶחָד מְעִידָהּ שֶׁהִיא פְּרוּעָה, וְהַנִּפְרַעַת מִנְּכָסִים מְשׁוּעְבָּדִים וּמִנִּכְסֵי יְתוֹמִים, דִּתְנַן בְּפֶרֶק הַכּוֹתֵב (לקמן פז.) דְּבָעוּ שְׁבוּעָה – אַף תּוֹס' נַמִי בָּעֵי שְׁבוּעָה. וְאַע"ג דְּפוֹגֶמֶת בְּהַאי כְּלָלָא אִיתֵיהּ – אִיצְטְרִיךְ לְמִינְקְטֵיהּ בְּהֶדְיָא, לְאַשְׁמוּעִינַן דִּפְגִימַת תּוֹסֶפֶת מְהַנְיָא לְהַשְׁבִּיעָהּ כִּפְגִימַת כְּתוּבָּה. וְלַשְּׁבִיעִית. שֶׁאֵין שְׁבִיעִית מְשַׁמֶּטֶת כְּתוּבָּה, כִּשְׁאָר שְׁטָרוֹת, אֶלָּא אִם כֵּן פְּגָמָהּ וּזְקָפָהּ, כִּדְאָמְרִינַן בְּמַסֶּכֶת גִּיטִּין (דף יח.). וְתוֹסֶפֶת נַמִי לָא מְשַׁמֵּט. לְכוֹתֵב נְכָסָיו לְבָנָיו. וְכָתַב לְאִשְׁתּוֹ קַרְקַע כָּל שֶׁהוּא – אִבְּדָה כְּתוּבָּתָהּ, כִּדְאִיתָא בְּ"יֵשׁ נוֹחֲלִין" (ב"ב קלב.), וְתוֹסֶפֶת כִּכְתוּבָּה. אֵין כְּתוּבָּה נִגְבֵּית אֶלָּא מִן הַקַּרְקַע וּמִן הַזִּיבּוּרִית, כִּדְתְנַן בְּ"הַנִּיזָּקִין" (גיטין מח.), וְהֵן תּוֹסֶפֶת. כָּל זְמַן שֶׁהִיא בְּבֵית אָבִיהָ. תְּנַן בְּ"הַנּוֹשֵׂא" (לקמן קד.). כָּל זְמַן שֶׁהִיא בְּבֵית בַּעְלָהּ בְּמֶשֶׁךְ אַלְמְנוּתָהּ – גּוֹבָה כְּתוּבָּתָהּ לְעוֹלָם. וְכָל זְמַן שֶׁהִיא בְּבֵית אָבִיהָ, שֶׁלֹּא הָיוּ עוֹדְדִים אוֹתָהּ הַיְתוֹמִים וְלֹא זָנִין אוֹתָהּ – גּוֹבָה כְּתוּבָּתָהּ עַד כ"ה שָׁנִים. וְאִם שָׁתְקָה יָתֵר עַל כֵּן יוֹם אֶחָד – מְחַלְתָּהּ, וְכֵן תּוֹסֶפֶת. כְּתוּבַּת בְּנִין דִּכְרִין. כְּשֵׁם שֶׁנּוֹטְלִים נְדוּנְיַית אֲבִי אִמָּם וּמָנֶה מָאתַיִם, כָּךְ נוֹטְלִים תּוֹסֶפֶת. אִיתְּמַר גָּרַס, וְלֹא גָּרַס "דְּאִיתְּמַר". יִרְתוּן תְּנַן. "אִינּוּן יִרְתוּן כֶּסֶף כְּתוּבָּתִיךְ", וִירוּשָּׁה לָא טָרְפָא לָקוֹחוֹת. יִסְבוּן תְּנַן. לְשׁוֹן ב"ח. מִטַּלְטְלֵי וְאִיתְנְהוּ בְּעֵינַיְיהוּ. הַמְיַיחֵד מִטַּלְטְלִין לִכְתוּבַּת אִשְׁתּוֹ וּמֵת, וְהֵן בָּעַיִן, וְהִיא נִפְרַעַת מֵהֶן – נוֹטַלְתָּן שֶׁלֹּא בִּשְׁבוּעָה. דְּטַעְמָא מַאי אָמוּר רַבָּנַן מִנִּכְסֵי יְתוֹמִין לֹא תִּפָּרַע אֶלָּא בִּשְׁבוּעָה, דְּחָיְישִׁינַן דִּלְמָא צְרָרֵי אַתְפְּסָהּ, וְהָכָא הַיְינוּ צְרָרֵי דְּאַתְפְּסָהּ. לֵיתְנְהוּ בְּעֵינַיְיהוּ. כְּגוֹן שֶׁאָבְדוּ. בְּלָא שְׁבוּעָה. דְּכֵיוָן דַּאֲבוּד הָנֵי, לָא אַתְפְּסָהּ אַחֲרִינֵי, וְכָל נְכָסָיו אַחְרָאִין לִכְתוּבָּתָהּ, וְנִפְרַעַת מִן הַקַּרְקָעוֹת. בְּאַרְבָּעָה מִצְרָנָהָא. שֶׁיִּיחֵד לָהּ קַרְקַע וְכָתַב לָהּ בְּאַרְבָּעָה הַמְּצָרִים שֶׁלָּהּ בְּחַיָּיו, לַעֲשׂוֹתָהּ אַפּוֹתֵיקֵי לִכְתוּבָּתָהּ, וּמֵת – נִפְרַעַת הֵימֶנָּה בְּלֹא שְׁבוּעָה, דְּוַדַּאי תּוּ לָא מַתְפִּיס לָהּ צְרָרֵי אַחֲרִינֵי. בִּשְׁבוּעָה. דְּכֵיוָן דְּלֹא כָּתַב לָהּ אַרְבָּעָה הַמְּצָרִים – אֵין זוֹ סְמִיכָה לִסְמוֹךְ עָלֶיהָ, וַהֲרֵי הִיא כְּמִי שֶׁלֹּא יִיחֵד, וְאִיכָּא לְמֵיחַשׁ לִצְרָרֵי. אָמַר לְעֵדִים כִּתְבוּ וְחִתְמוּ. כְּגוֹן מַתְּנַת קַרְקַע. לָא צָרִיךְ לְאִימְּלוּכֵי בֵּיהּ. אִם עֲדַיִין עוֹמֵד בְּדִבּוּרוֹ שֶׁיִּכְתְּבוּ לוֹ, דְּכֵיוָן דְּקָנוּ מִמֶּנּוּ – סְתָם קִנְיָן לִכְתִיבָה עוֹמֵד. בָּתַר אוּמְדָּנָא. אוֹמֶד הַדַּעַת. בְּדָבָר שֶׁאֵינוֹ מְפוֹרָשׁ אוֹמְדִין בֵּית דִּין, וְאוֹמְרִים: סְתָם אִינִישׁ לְהָכִי אִיכַּוֵּון, דְּלֹא כּוֹתֵב לָהּ מָמוֹנוֹ חִנָּם אֶלָּא לְחִיבַּת בִּיאָה. בִּמְסוּכָּן. בְּמַסֶּכֶת גִּיטִּין (דף סה.). הַמְפָרֵשׁ וְהַיּוֹצֵא בְּשַׁיָּירָא וְאוֹמֵר "כִּתְבוּ גֵּט לְאִשְׁתִּי", אע"פ שֶׁלֹּא אָמַר "תְּנוּ" – הֲרֵי אֵלּוּ יִכְתְּבוּ וְיִתְּנוּ. דְּמֵחֲמַת טִרְדָּתוֹ, שֶׁהוּא בָּהוּל עַל נַפְשׁוֹ, לֹא הִסְפִּיק לִגְמוֹר דְּבָרָיו, וּמֵעִיקָּרָא לְכִתְבוּ וּתְנוּ נִתְכַּוֵּון. ר"ש שְׁזוּרִי אוֹמֵר. אַף הַמְסוּכָּן, הַגּוֹסֵס. וְהַיְינוּ בָּתַר אוּמְדָּן דַּעְתָּא, דְּאָמְרִינַן לֹא אָמַר כִּתְבוּ אֶלָּא שֶׁיִּתְּנוּ, הוֹאִיל וּמְסוּכָּן הוּא – לֹא נִתְכַּוֵּון לְצַחֵק בָּהּ.

וּבִתְרוּמַת

תוספות

ולשבח · תוספת היא ככתובה, שלא תגבה השבח, אבל אי לאו הוי תנאי כתובה ככתובה – היתה גובה תוספת מן השבח, כמו בעל חוב דגבי אפי' משבח שהשביחו יתומים. ואע"ג דאין להם על מי לחזור, והוי כמקבל מתנה, דאמרינן בפרק קמא דבבא מליעא (דף טו.) דלא גבי בעל חוב שבח מיניה – משום דאין לו על מי לחזור, מכל מקום מן היורשין גבי, דלא דמו למקבל מתנה – שעליהם מוטל יותר לפרוע חוב אביהם. וכן משמע* בפרק "יש בכור" (בכורות דף נא: ושם) דתנן: אין הבכור נוטל פי שנים מן השבח, ולא האשה בכתובתה, ולא הבנות במזונותיהן. ופריך בגמרא, והאמר שמואל: בעל חוב גובה את השבח! ומשני: מקולי כתובה שנו כאן, והתם בשבח שהשביחו יתומים איירי, ולא בשבח של לקוחות, מדקתני: ולא הבנות במזונותיהן. ואי מלקוחות – מאי איריא שבח? הא קרקע נמי לא גבו, דאין מוציאין למזון הבנות מנכסים משועבדים. והא דאמר ב"המקבל" (ב"מ דף קי. ושם): יתומים אומרים, אנו השבחנו, ובעל חוב אומר, אביכם השביח, על מי להביא ראיה? משמע דאי יתומים השביחו – לא היה נוטל בעל חוב שבח! התם מיירי כגון שעשאו אביהן לו אותה קרקע אפותיקי, ואמר: אם לא אפרעך עד זמן פלוני – יהיה קרקע זה קנוי לך מעכשיו. דהתם ודאי השבח של יתומים, דהוי כיורד לתוך שדה חבירו שלא ברשות, דשמין לו וידו על התחתונה. ותדע, דהא קאמר התם דעל היתומים להביא ראיה. מאי טעמא – דארעא כיון דלגובינא קיימא כמאן דגביא דמיא. ואי דלא עשאה אפותיקי – אמאי חשיב לה בחזקת ב"ח? אדרבה, הוה בחזקת יתמי, דהא מצי לסלוקי ליה בזוזי, וב"ח ניתי ראיה. ולשבועה · פ"ה: לענין עד אחד מעידה שהיא פרועה, ונפרעת שלא בפניו כו'. ולא אתי שפיר למאן דמשוה שאר שטרות לכתובה! ונראה לר"י, דה"פ: ולשבועה, שאם נשבעה כל הכתובה – נשבעת נמי על התוספת, דכשבאה לגבות תוספת איכה צריכה לחזור ולישבע. ולשביעית · תימה: דבסוף מסכת שביעית פליגי בהקפת חנות ובשכר שכיר, דאיכא למ"ד דאין משמטין, ור' יוסי פליג ואמר: כל מלאכה שפוסקת בשביעית – משמטת. ולדידיה ניחא, דה"ה דמשמט הקפת החנות, וכל מילי אפילו דלאו הלואה. ואי לאו דתוספת ככתובה – הוי משמט. אבל לרבנן, דאית להו אין משמטו אלא מלוה – אם כן אפי' אם אין התוספת ככתובה אינו משמט, דלאו הלואה היא! ואור"י: דלמ"ד בפ"ב דגיטין (יח. ושם) פגמה אע"פ שלא זקפה גבי כתובה דמשמט, נפקא מיניה אם פגמה הכתובה הוי כאילו פגמה התוספת. וכן למ"ד עד שתפגום ותזקוף, אם פגמה וזקפה הכתובה – כאילו פגמה וזקפה התוספת. יסבון תנן. ואם תאמר: תקשי ליה מתניתין ד"מי שהיה נשוי" (לקמן דף צ.) דתנן: שניה ויורשיה קודמין ליורשי ראשונה! וי"ל: דהתם דחי לה לעולם ארת בחייו ואחת במותו אין לה כתובת בנין דכרין, ומאי קודמין – קודמין לנחלה. נראה כפי' ר"ח דגרים ברישא "ייחד לה ארעא בארבע מצרנהא" ואח"כ גרים "מטלטלי ואיתנהו בעינייהו". והשתא אתי שפיר דלא הזכיר יחוד גבי מטלטלי, משום דכבר הזכיר יחוד גבי ארעא, ועלה קאי. אבל לספרים דגרסי "מטלטלי ואיתנהו בעינייהו" ברישא, תימה דלא קאמר "ייחד לה מטלטלי", כיון דלא דיבר כלום ביחוד! כתובו וחתומו והבו ליה קנו מיניה לא צריך לאמלוכי ביה. וה"ה אפי' לא אמר כתובו וחתומו, כיון דקנו מיניה – לא צריך לאמלוכי ביה, דסתם קנין לכתיבה עומד, כדאמרינן ב"חזקת הבתים" *(ב"ב דף מ. ושם). ולא נקט כתובו וחתומו אלא משום סיפא, דאפילו הכי צריך לאמלוכי ביה. וטעמא, כיון דבעין יפה נותן, שמקנה לו מיד ואינו רוצה להמתין עד שילך ויזכה בשדה – יש לנו לומר דייפה כחו נמי לענין כתיבה, דסתם קנין שבתלמוד היינו קנין חליפין. ומיהו, למ"ד אחריות לאו טעות סופר הוא – צריך לאמלוכי ביה לכתוב בו אחריות, כדאמר שמואל בפרק קמא דב"מ (דף יד.): שעבוד צריך לימלך. אבל למ"ד טעות סופר הוא – אין צריך לימלך. ומיהו, אם רוצה יכול לחזור בו, כדאמרינן ב"המוכר הספינה" (ב"ב דף עז. ושם): "זכו בשדה זו לפלוני וכתבו לו את השטר" – חוזר בשטר, ואינו חוזר בשדה. ופר"י ב"ר מרדכי בשם ריב"א: דדוקא בשטר מכר חוזר, שאינו רוצה שיהיה עליו שעבוד בשטר, דשטר מכר טריף ממשעבדי. אבל במתנה, שאין השטר אלא לראיה – אף בשטר אינו יכול לחזור, דעבדינן תקנתא לרמאה. דמוכחא מילתא שרוצה לחזור ממתנה. ור"ת מפרש: דאף במתנה חוזר בשטר, משום דלא ניחא ליה דליפשו שטרי עילויה, שיסברו העולם שהוא שטר מכר, שיש שעבוד, ונמנעים מלהלוות לו, וזיילי נמי נכסיה כשילא קול שמכר קרקעות או נתן. ואע"ג דתנן בפרק "גט פשוט" (ב"ב דף קסח.): מי שנמחק שטר חובו, שבא לב"ד ועושין לו שטר אחר, ולא חיישינן שמא יסברו שזהו שיעבוד חדש מה שכותבין לו עתה – דמשום הך חשש אין לנו להפסיד לזה זכותו שכבר היה לו שטר. [וע"ע תוס' סנהדרין כט: ד"ה הודה].

ובתרומת

עין משפט נר מצוה

ט א מיי' פט"ז מהל' אישות הלכה ה סמג עשין מח טוש"ע אה"ע סי' לה סעיף ז וסי' ק סעיף ב:

י ב מיי' שם הלכה ד סמג שם טוש"ע שם סי' צו סעיף א:

יא ג מיי' פ"ט מהל' שמיטה הלכה יג טוש"ע שם סימן קא סעיף א:

[ויש לדחות הכוא דסתמא קאמר התם דאין האשה גובה ולהכי פריך והאמר שמואל בעל חוב גובה את השבח מלוקח ומשני מקולי כתובה שנו כאן דאפי' מלוקח לא גבית. ת"י]

יב ד מיי' פ"ו מהלכ' זכיה הלכה ט סמג עשין פב טוש"ע שם סי' קו סעיף א:

יג ה מיי' פט"ז מהל' אישות הלכה ג סמג עשין מח טוש"ע שם סי' ק סעיף ב:

יד ו מיי' שם הלכה כג טוש"ע שם סימן קא סעי' א:

טו ז מיי' פי"ט שם הלכ' א סמג שם טוש"ע שם סימן קיא סעיף א:

טז ח מיי' שם הלכה ט טוש"ע שם סעי' יג:

יז ט י כ מיי' פט"ז שם הלכה (ז) [יג] טוש"ע שם סי' צו סעיף א:

יח ל מיי' פי"א מהל' מלוה ולוה הלכ' א סמג עשין נד טוש"ע ח"מ סי' לט סעיף ב ג:

יט נ מיי' פ"ב מהל' גירושין הלכה יב סמג עשין נ טוש"ע אה"ע סי' קמא סעיף טז [וברב אלפס גיטין פ"ו דף קטה ע"ב]:

תוספות רי"ד

למאי נ"מ למוכרת ולמוחלת ולפוגמת ולתובעת ולעוברת על דת ולשבח ולשבועה ולשביעית ולכותב כל נכסיו [לבניו] ולגבות מן הקרקעות ומן הזיבורית. וכ"ז שהיא בבית אביה ולכתובת בנ"ד. פי' למוכרת שהמוכרת כתובה לבעלה או מוחלת כתובתה לבעלה מחלה ומכרה את הכל לפי שהכל קרוי כתובה ולא אמרינן דלא איקרי כתובה אלא מנה ומאתים. ולמורדת דתנן לקמן בפירקין המורדת על בעלה פוחתין מכתובתה עד כמה הוא פוחת עד כנגד כתובתה ול"ת עד כנגד מו"מ לחודייהו אלא גם התוס' פוחתין והולכין. ולפוגמת בפ' הכותב תנן הפוגמת כתובתה לא תפרע אלא בשבועה שאם פגמה תוספת נמי כגון שאמר' התקבלתי מן תוס' דינר אף זו פוגמת כתובתה היא ואם טוען בעלה כל כתובתך התקבלת לא תגבה אלא בשבועה. ולתובעת בפירקן דלעיל אמרינן התובעת כתובתה בב"ד א"ל מזונות וה"ה אם תבעה תוס' ולא כתובה. ולעוברת על דת דאמרינן בהמדיר אלו יוצאין שלא בכתובה ועוברת א' מהן ולא תימא דוקא כתובת מו"מ אבל תוס' מתנה בעלמא הוא ולא הפסידה. ולשבח דאמרי' בבכורות אין הבכור נוטל פי שנים בשבח ששבחו נכסים לאחר מיתת אביהן ואין האשה גובה כתובתה מן השבח שהשביחו הנכסים לאחר מיתת הבעל כלומר אם אין הנכסים שהניח הבעל כדי כתובה ולאחר מכאן השביחו לא תטול אלא במה שהניח לה הבעל והשבח ליתומים ומקולי כתובה שנו כאן אבל בע"ח גובה את השבח ותוספת נמי דינו ככתובה לא כבע"ח. ולשבועה שהבא ליפרע מנכסי יתומים לא יפרע אלא בשבועה דלא אתפשה בעלה צררי. ואע"ג דלא ניתנה כתובת לגבות מחיים אפ"ה חיישינן דלמא צררי אתפסה. והנפרעת נמי שלא בפניו לא תפרע לה בשבועה א) אבל שט"ח שלא הגיע זמנו ליפרע גובה מן היתומים בלא שבועה חזקה אין אדם פורע אלא בזמנו ותוס' לא דמיא לחוב אלא לכתובה. ולשביעית שאין שביעית משמטת את הכתובה כשאר חובות שהיא משמטת אא"כ פגמה וזקפה השאר במלוה דהוויא להו כהלואה דעלמא כדאמרינן במס' גיטין ותוס' נמי לא משמטה. ולכותב כל נכסיו דאמרי' בי"נ הכותב כל נכסיו לבניו וכתב לאשתו קרקע כ"ש איבדה כתובתה ומוקי לה התם במחלק לפניה והיא שותקת דכיון דשתקה סמכא אההוא פורתא ואדולי' אוחלתיה ואבדה נמי גם התוס'. ולגבות מן הקרקע. פי' לא מיתמי קאמר שה"ה לכל שט"ח דמטלטלי דיתמי לבע"ח לא משתעבדי אלא מינה כדאמרינן לקמן בפ' הכותב דכתובה לא גביא אפילו מיניה אם גירשה אלא מן הקרקע אבל בע"ח אפי' מגלימא דעל כתפי' ותוס' ככתובה דמיא. ומן הזיבורית אפי' מיניה ואילו ב"ד דינו בבינונית. וכ"ז שהיא בבית אביה. בפ' הנושא תנן כ"ז שהיא בבית בעלה במשך אלמנותה גובה כתובתה לעולם וכ"ז שהיא בבית אביה שלא היו עובדים אותה היתומים ולא זנין אותה גובה כתובתה עד כ"ה שנים ואם שתקה יותר מכן מחלה ובן התום'. ולכתובת בנ"ד כשם שנוטלת מו"מ כן נוטלת גם התוס': איתמר כתובת בנ"ד פומבדיתאי אומרים לא טרפא ממשעבדי פי' מן הלקוחות שקנו אחר שנכתב כתובת אמן: ירתון רנן בפירקן דלעיל. בני מתא

מחסיא

א) אינו מובן דגבי נפרע שלא בפניו אין נ"מ בין כתובה לשט"ח ואולי לאם הוא כתוך זמנו יש חילוק.

[לקמן ל:]

[ב"ב קלא.]

[שם ולעיל נב:]

חולין עה: ע"ש מנחות ל:

[בחולין איתא ר' יונתן ובמנחות איתא ר' יוחנן]

וי"מ דהכותב לחזקת הבנים קאי אהודאה דלעיל מיניה דקאמר הודאה בפני שנים לריך כתובו קנין בפני שנים א"ל לומר כתובו דכיון דבכבר הודאה למה הכל זו וכמו אם לא סי שיכתבו א"כ התם איירי במתנה לכולה שעבוד והתם הוי סתם קנין לכתיבה אבל הכא בתוספת כתובה לא לגמרי והכי לה הכלך אע"ג דקנו מיניה לריך לאמלוכי ביה דלמא לא ניחא ליה לשעבודי נכסי משעבדי ת"י. ע"ש. ואין נראה דסתם קנין לכתיבה משמע בכל דבר אע"ג דטריף ממשעבדי:

כ א מיי' פי"ב מהל' מעשר הלכה ד סמג עשין קלה:
כא ב מיי' פ"ח מהל' זכיה הלכה י סמג עשין פב טוש"ע ח"מ סימן רנ סעיף ט:

א וּבִתְרוּמַת מַעֲשֵׂר שֶׁל דְּמַאי. וְרַב לָא אָזֵיל בָּתַר אוּמְדָּנָא? וְהָא *אִיתְּמַר, מַתְּנַת שְׁכִיב מְרַע שֶׁכָּתוּב בָּהּ קִנְיָן, בְּבֵי רַב מִשְּׁמֵיהּ דְּרַב אָמְרִי: אַרְכְּבֵיהּ אַתְּרֵי רִכְשֵׁי, וּשְׁמוּאֵל אָמַר: לָא יָדַעְנָא מַאי אֵידוּן בָּהּ, בְּבֵי רַב מִשְּׁמֵיהּ דְּרַב אָמְרִי: אַרְכְּבֵיהּ אַתְּרֵי רִכְשֵׁי, הֲרֵי הִיא כְּמַתְּנַת בָּרִיא, וַהֲרֵי הִיא כְּמַתְּנַת שְׁכִיב מְרַע. הֲרֵי הִיא כְּמַתְּנַת בָּרִיא – דְּאִם עָמַד אֵינוֹ יָכוֹל לַחֲזוֹר בּוֹ, הֲרֵי הִיא כְּמַתְּנַת שְׁכִיב מְרַע – *שֶׁאִם אָמַר "הַלְוָאָתִי לִפְלוֹנִי" – הַלְוָאָתוֹ לִפְלוֹנִי. וּשְׁמוּאֵל אָמַר: לָא יָדַעְנָא מַאי אֵידוּן בָּהּ – ב שֶׁמָּא לֹא גָּמַר לְהַקְנוֹתוֹ אֶלָּא בִּשְׁטָר, וְאֵין שְׁטָר לְאַחַר מִיתָה. אֶלָּא

רש"י:

וּבִתְרוּמַת מַעֲשֵׂר שֶׁל דְּמַאי. מִשְׁנָה הִיא בְּמַסֶּכֶת דְּמַאי (פ"ד מ"א). תְּרוּמַת מַעֲשֵׂר שֶׁל דְּמַאי שֶׁחָזְרָה לִמְקוֹמָהּ, וְאָסְרָה אֶת הַחוּלִּין מִשּׁוּם מְדוּמָּע. ר"ש שְׁזוּרִי אוֹמֵר. אַף בַּחוֹל שׁוֹאֲלוֹ לְעַם הָאָרֶץ שֶׁלָּקַח הֵימֶנּוּ הַפֵּירוֹת הַלָּלוּ, וְאוֹכְלָן עַל פִּיו. אִם אָמַר הִפְרַשְׁתִּי מַעַשְׂרוֹתָיו כָּרָאוּי עַד שֶׁלֹּא מְכַרְתִּים לְךָ – סוֹמֵךְ עָלָיו, דְּהוֹאִיל וּמִדְּרַבָּנַן הוּא – הֵימְנוּהוּ רַבָּנַן בִּמְקוֹם פְּסֵידָא כִּי הָכָא, שֶׁאֵין לוֹ תַּקָּנָה לַחֲזוֹר וּלְהַפְרִישׁ, אֶלָּא לְמוֹכְרָהּ לְכֹהֲנִים בִּדְמֵי תְרוּמָה, וְהֶפְסֵד הוּא לוֹ. הַאי דְּנָקַט אַף בַּחוֹל – מִשּׁוּם דְּקָתָנֵי הָתָם מִילְּתָא אַחֲרִיתִי. וְיֵשׁ בָּהּ חִילּוּק, דִּבְשַׁבָּת שׁוֹאֲלוֹ וְאוֹכְלוֹ עַל פִּיו מִפְּנֵי עוֹנֶג שַׁבָּת, וּלְמוֹ"ש לֹא יֹאכַל עַד שֶׁיְּעַשֵּׂר. מַתְּנַת שְׁכִיב מְרַע. אֵינָהּ צְרִיכָה קִנְיָן, שֶׁתִּקְּנוּ חֲכָמִים שֶׁדְּבָרָיו כִּכְתוּבִים וְכִמְסוּרִים, שֶׁלֹּא תִּטָּרֵף דַּעְתּוֹ עָלָיו. וְאִם כָּתוּב בָּהּ קִנְיָן – אָמַר רַב. אַרְכְּבֵיהּ אַתְּרֵי רִכְשֵׁי, כְּמוֹ "רוֹכְבֵי הָרֶכֶשׁ" (אסתר ח). כְּלוֹמַר, נָתַן בָּהּ שְׁתֵּי כֹחוֹת. עַל יְדֵי שֶׁכָּתוּב בָּהּ "כִּדְקָלִיר וּרְמֵי בְּעַרְסֵיהּ" וְכָל לְשׁוֹן שְׁכִיב מְרַע – נָתַן בָּהּ כֹּחַ שְׁכִיב מְרַע, וְעַל יְדֵי קִנְיָן שֶׁכָּתוּב בָּהּ, שֶׁאֵינוֹ נוֹהֵג אֶלָּא בְּבָרִיא – נָתַן בָּהּ כֹּחַ בָּרִיא. וְהַשְׁתָּא מְפָרֵשׁ לְהוּ. כֹּחַ מַתְּנַת בָּרִיא – שֶׁאִם עָמַד מֵחוֹלְיוֹ אֵינוֹ חוֹזֵר מִמַּתְּנָתוֹ, מַשֶּׁא"כ בְּשׁ"מ. וַהֲרֵי הִיא כְּמַתְּנַת ש"מ שֶׁאֵין בְּמַתְּנַת בָּרִיא אֲפִי' בְּקִנְיָן, שֶׁאִם כָּתַב בְּמַתָּנָה זוֹ "הַלְוָאָתִי שֶׁהִלְוֵיתִי לִפְלוֹנִי נְתוּנָה לִפְלוֹנִי זֶה" – הַלְוָאָתוֹ לִפְלוֹנִי, וְאִילּוּ גַּבֵּי בָרִיא מִשּׁוּם קִנְיָן לָא קָנֵי בֵּיהּ, שֶׁאֵין מַטְבֵּעַ נִקְנֶה בַּחֲלִיפִין אֶלָּא אַגַּב קַרְקַע, כִּדְאָמְרִינַן בְּ"הַזָּהָב" (ב"מ מו.). וְזֶה קָנָה אִם מֵת, לֹא מֵחֲמַת קִנְיָן אֶלָּא מֵחֲמַת דִּבְרֵי ש"מ. שֶׁמָּא לֹא גָּמַר בְּלִבּוֹ לְהַקְנוֹתוֹ [אֶלָּא בִּשְׁטָר. שֶׁמָּא לְהָכִי כָּתַב בָּהּ קִנְיָן, דְּלֹא גָּמַר לְהַקְנוֹתוֹ] מַתָּנָה זוֹ עַל יְדֵי דִּבְרֵי שְׁכִיב מְרַע שֶׁהֵן כִּכְתוּבִים וּמְסוּרִים דָּמֵי, אֶלָּא עַל יְדֵי כְּתִיבָה וְקִנְיָן, כְּבָרִיא. דִּסְתָם קִנְיָן לִכְתִיבָה עוֹמֵד, וּשְׁטָר שְׁכִיב מְרַע אֵינוֹ קוֹנֶה מֵחַיִּים, שֶׁהֲרֵי אֵין דַּעְתּוֹ לִיתֵּן כְּלוּם אֶלָּא לְאַחַר מִיתָה. וַאֲפִילּוּ לְרַבִּי יוֹסֵי דְּאָמַר (גיטין דף עב.). זְמַנּוֹ שֶׁל שְׁטָר מוֹכִיחַ עָלָיו – הָנֵי מִילֵּי בְּבָרִיא הַכּוֹתֵב נְכָסָיו לִבְנוֹ לְאַחַר מוֹתוֹ, דְּדַעְתּוֹ לְאַקְנוּיֵי גּוּף הַקַּרְקַע מֵהַיּוֹם, וּפֵירוֹת לְאַחַר מִיתָה. אֲבָל זֶה – אֵין דַּעְתּוֹ לִיתֵּן בְּחַיָּיו כְּלוּם, וְכֵיוָן דְּמִית – תּוּ לָא מָצֵי לְאַקְנוּיֵי מִידֵי, דְּהָא לֵיתֵיהּ דְּלִיקְנֵי נִיהֲלֵיהּ. וְשָׁמְעִינַן מִיהַת דְּרַב בָּתַר אוּמְדָּנָא אָזֵיל, שֶׁאוֹמֵד דַּעְתּוֹ שֶׁל זֶה דְּלַאֲרְכְּבֵיהּ אַתְּרֵי רִכְשֵׁי עֲבַד, וְאַף עַל פִּי שֶׁלֹּא פֵּירֵשׁ – מַפִּיק רַב מִמּוֹנָא בְּהָכִי. אֶלָּא

ב"ב קנב. | שם קמח.

תוספות:

ובתרומת מעשר כו'. רישא דמתניתין הכי במסכת דמאי (פ"ד מ"א): הלוקח פירות דמאי ממי שאינו נאמן, בשבת – שואלו ואוכל על פיו. חשכה מו"ש – לא יאכל עד שיעשר. פי': אף על מה שהעיד ביום לא יאכל בלילה, דלא שרו ליה רבנן אלא בשבת, שאינו יכול לתקן. וטעמא דרבנן לא משום עונג שבת, כדפירש בקונטרס, דמשום עונג שבת לא שרינן ליה לאכול דמאי, אלא משום אימת שבת, כדמשמע בירושלמי, דקאמר להו ר"ש שזורי לרבנן: כשם שאימת שבת על עם הארץ – כך אימת תרומה על עם הארץ. פי': עם הארץ ירא לשקר בשבת בדבר שאינו מעושר, משום דשבת קובעת למעשר. סבר ר"ש דכמו כן אימת תרומה עליו, דנהי דאינו ירא מאיסור טבל – ירא הוא מאיסור תרומה, כשתרם וחזרה למקומה. ורבנן פליגי עליה בהא, אע"ג דלית ליה תקנתא. מתנת שכיב מרע שכתוב בה קנין, רב אמר ארכביה אתרי רכשי. *נראה דוקא שכתב בה קנין בתוך השטר, דהוי לרב כמתנת בריא, דאלומי אלמיה לפי שכתב כן בתוך השטר. אבל אם כתב כל נכסיו, וקנו מידו, ולא נכתב הקנין בתוך השטר – לא הוי לרב כמתנת בריא, ואם עמד – חוזר. ואם מת – קנה, כדין מתנת ש"מ, כמו שפירש ר"י ב"ר מרדכי. כדמוכח מתני' ד"מי שמת" (ב"ב דף קמו:), דתנן: ש"מ שכתב כל נכסיו, שייר קרקע כל שהוא – מתנתו מתנה, לא שייר קרקע כל שהוא – אין מתנתו מתנה. והתם בקנין איירי. דאי בלא קנין, אפילו שייר – נמי אין מתנתו מתנה, כדפסק התם הלכתא, דבמקצת בלא קנין – לא קנה, ואפי' מת, אלא דווקא בקנין. וקתני היכא דלא שייר – אין מתנתו מתנה, ואם עמד – חוזר. ובהדיא דייקינן הכי בפרק "מי שמת" (שם דף קנא:) דרישא וסיפא בקנין. ושמואל דאמר שמא לא גמר להקנותו אלא בשטר, ואין שטר לאחר מיתה, כיון דמגרע שמואל כח מתנה מחמת הקנין שהוא כתוב בשטר – כ"ש כשאינו כתוב בשטר. וכן משמע בפרק "מי שמת" (שם קנג.), דפריך התם אהא דקאמר שמואל דאין שטר לאחר מיתה, מההיא דאמר שמואל: ש"מ שכתב כל נכסיו לאחרים, אע"פ שקנו מידו, אם עמד – חוזר. משמע ואם מת – קנה. ומאי קושיא? התם ודאי קנה, לפי שלא נכתב הקנין בשטר. אלא ודאי בכל ענין קאמר שמואל, דאין שטר לאחר מיתה, בין בכתוב בו קנין בין לא כתוב. וכי פריך מדשמואל אדשמואל – הוה מצי למיפרך ליה ממתני' דהתם, דלא מגרע כח מתנה מחמת הקנין,◉ אלא דניחא ליה למיפרך דשמואל אדשמואל. ואיכא לשנויי מתניתין במייפה את כחו, דכתב, "וקנינא מיניה מוסף על מתנתא דא" דמודה שמואל דקנה לאחר מיתה, כיון שמוכיח שהקנין ליפוי כח בא. והכי מוקמינן התם מילתיה דשמואל גופיה. ורבינו יצחק בר אברהם נראה לו כפירוש רבינו שמואל: דרב ושמואל פליגי אפי' אין כתוב הקנין בשטר. ואין שטר לאחר מיתה דקאמר שמואל – אפילו אין כאן שטר כלל, משום דסתם קנין לכתיבה עומד – יש לחוש שמא לא רצה שיגמר הקנין אלא בכתיבת השטר ובמסירתו ליד מקבל מתנה, ועקר מיניה כח מתנת ש"מ שקונה באמירה בעלמא, ואין רוצה שיקנה אלא לאחר מיתה, ואז פקע כחו. ומתני' דלא שייר קרקע כל שהוא – מוקמי בין לרב בין לשמואל, דקנו מיניה בחזקה, שאינו עומד לכתיבה כמו קנין חליפין. ולא הוי לרב כמו מתנת בריא, ולשמואל קניא כדין מתנת שכיב מרע. והא דפריך התם מהא דאמר שמואל: ש"מ שכתב כל נכסיו, אע"פ שקנו מידו, אם עמד – חוזר. אין נראה לו להעמיד בקנין חזקה, דקנו מידו משמע טפי קנין חליפין, שהן מיד ליד. אבל קנו מיניה – משמע שפיר חזקה. ועוד: דעיקר מילתיה דשמואל משמע דאתא לאפוקי דלא נימא דארכביה אתרי רכשי, והיינו בחליפין דווקא. והשתא אתי שפיר כי פריך מהא דשלח ר"א לגולה כו' :ומשני הא – דקנו מיניה. הא – דלא קנו מיניה. דמשמע, דאי קנו מיניה אע"ג דלא נכתב הקנין בתוך השטר – הוי כמתנת בריא. והשתא אתי נמי שפיר הא דקשיא ליה מדשמואל דאמר כותבין ונותנין, דאי בקנין קאמר משום דלכתיבה עומד לא ידענא מה אידון בה – כ"ש בכתבו ותנו מנה לפלוני ומת, שלא יקנה כי אם בכתיבה. ולמאי דקי"ל כשמואל יש תימה מה שתיקנו הגאונים לכתוב במתנת ש"מ "ואמר לנו הוו עלי עדים וקנו ממני בכל לשון של זכות", ולא כתבו שום ייפוי כח. ועוד, דכרב נמי לא הוי, דלדידיה הויא כמתנת בריא! וי"ל: ד"כל לשון של זכות" חשוב ייפוי כח. וטוב שיכתבו "וקנינא מיניה מוסיף על מתנתא דא" או יכתבו בתחלה "ואף קנו ממנו בכל לשון של זכות" דומיא דאף כתבו וחתמו והבו ליה ד"יש נוחלין" (שם דף קנו. ושם).

ואין שטר לאחר מיתה. פי': ואין קנין לאחר מיתה, כדפרשינן לעיל ויש לגמגם על הלשון "דלאחר מיתה", דמשמע אם הקנה לו לאחר ל' יום – קנה אם הוא חי, בקנין סודר דהשתא, וב"האשה רבה" (יבמות דף לג. ושם) וכן ב"האשה שנפלו" (לקמן דף פב. שם) לא משמע הכי, כדפרישית ביבמות*. שאם אמר הלוואתי לפלוני כו'. פי' בקונטרס: דאילו גבי בריא – לא זכה בה משום קנין, דאין מטבע נקנה בחליפין אלא אגב קרקע. וקשה: דאם כן לא ה"ל למימר הלוואתו, אלא מעותיו לפלוני, הואיל וטעמא משום מטבע הוא. ועוד: דאפילו אגב קרקע, דמטבע נקנה – אין הלואה נקנית, כדאמרינן ב"מי שמת" (ב"ב דף קמז: ושם): למימרא דמילתא דאיתא בבריא איתא בש"מ, דליתא בבריא כו', והא הלוואתו לפלוני – דליתא בבריא ואיתיה בש"מ! ומשני: הא נמי איתיה בבריא, הואיל ויורש יורשו. אי נמי, במעמד שלשתן. ואם יכול להקנותה אגב קרקע – הל"ל דאיתיה נמי בבריא על ידי קרקע, ולא ה"ל לדחוקי בכי האי גוונא. אלא ודאי לא מהני בה קנין. וסברא הוא, דהיאך יהנה קנין לדבר שאינו בעין? ואף על גב דמהני לענין הרשאה, כדמוכח ב"הגוזל קמא" (ב"ק דף קד: ושם) בשמעתין דאין משלחין מעות בדיוקני – היינו משום דפסקינן דשליח שוויה, ולענין שליחות שיהא מורשה במקומו – מהני הקנין, אבל לענין להיות שלו – לא. ואם תאמר: והואיל ולא הוי מורשה אלא להיות שליח, אם מת המרשה – פקע שליחות, ויכולין היתומים לתבוע מן הנפקד, והתם משמע דאין יכולין! וי"ל: כיון דאם היה נפקד בא לפני ב"ד היו אומרין לו לתת ליד המורשה, שהרי יש להחזיק המרשה בחזקת חי, אע"ג דאיגלי מילתא לבסוף דמת המרשה קודם שהגיע הפקדון ליד המורשה – אין יכולין לתבוע מן הנפקד כלום, שהרי ברשות ב"ד נתנם. והשתא משמע ליה דרב אזיל בתר אומדנא, מדקאמר: הרי היא כמתנת ש"מ, דאי לא אזיל – הל"ל הרי היא כמתנת בריא לבד. אע"ג דכתוב בשטר "כדקליר ורמי על ערסיה" – היינו משום דהכי הוה מעשה, ולאו משום דליבעי הנותן שתהא מתנת ש"מ, ומדקאמר הרי היא כמתנת ש"מ – אלמא אזיל בתר אומדנא. ואע"ג דשמואל נמי אזיל בתר אומדנא – לאו לאפוקי מדשמואל אתי, דהא בסמוך פסק שמואל כרבי אלעזר ב"ע. ועי"ל: דפריך מהא דרב אית ליה אומדנא אפילו להוציא ממון, אע"ג דשמואל לית ליה כהאי גוונא. אע"ג דגבי שודא שמעינן להו איפכא (לקמן לד.) דשמואל אית ליה שודא, ולרב חלוקה ולא שודא – מלינו למימר כמו שמפר"ת: דשודא לאו אומדנא הוא, כמו שפירש בקונטרס, אלא יתנו ב"ד למי שירצו*. אמר

[דף לג.

ועוד נראה דכשכתב השטר בלשון מתנה ולא בלשון צוואה חשיב מסירת השטר כקנין וצריך יפוי כח לשמואל לכתוב אף כתבו וחתמו מדפריך התם רבה לרב נחמן גבי מתנת שכיב מרע ממתני' דשייר קרקע כל שהוא כו' ומשני כגון שקנו מידו אי דקנו מיניה אימא סיפא ואמאי לא מוקי רישא וסיפא דלא קני אלא שמסר השטר דבמקצת קני דהוי כמתנת בריא וכי לא שייר לא קני אלא ודאי המסירה הוי כקנין ורבא דפריך הוי מוקמי מתני' בלשון צוואה וכן הא דמשמע ביש נוחלין דלא צריך לכתוב אף כתבו וחתמו אלא כשלא בא השטר לידו מחיים היינו בשטר שכתוב בלשון צוואה [ועיין בהרא"ש שם במי שמת סי' לא ת"י]

גליון הש"ס

תוס' ד"ה מתנת ש"מ וכו' אלא דניחא ליה למיפרך דשמואל אדשמואל. עי' יבמות דף כז ע"ב תוס' ד"ה ורב וחולין דף קנז ע"ב תוס' ד"ה ומי אמר ודף קכה ע"ב תוס' ד"ה ומי אמר ויומא דף לו ע"ב תוס' ד"ה הנ"מ:

ועוד יש לומר שהתלמוד נראה לו לדמות אומדנא דרב לאומדנא דר' אלעזר בן עזריה. ת"י

תוספות רי"ד

מחסיא אמרי טרפי ממשעבדי יסבון תנן לשון ב"ח והל' לא טרפי משעבדי דירתון תנן: מטלטלין ואיתנהו בעינייהו בלא שבועה ליתנהו בעינייהו. פומבדיתאי אמרי בלא שבועה בני מתא מחסיא אמרי בשבועה והל' בלא שבועה. פי' המורה המיחד מטלטלי לכתובת אשתו ומת והן בעין והיא נפרעת מהן נוטלן בלא שבועה דטעמא מאי אמרי רבנן הבא ליפרע מנכסי יתומים לא יפרע אלא בשבועה דחיישינן לצררי הכא כיון דיחד לה מקום לגבות הימנו לא פרע לה ממקום אחר כלומר היינו צררי דאתפסה. ואינו נ"ל דכי היכי דאמרי' לקמן ייחד לה קרקע בר' מצרנאה אמאי לא אמרינן נמי ייחד לה מטלטלי ורב משה גאון ור"ח ז"ל פירשו מטלטלי דכתיבי בכתובתה בין דהנעל' ליה בין דכתב לה איהו וליתנהו בעינייהו עכשיו כגון דחליפינון וידוע מילתא דהני מטלטלי מחמת מטלטלי קמאי ניגהו הלכך גביא להו בלא שבועה וזה הפתרון נ"ל. ייחד לה שדה בר' מצרנאה בלא שבועה וחד מצרא פומבדיתאי אמרי בלא שבועה בני מתא מחסיא אמרי בשבועה והל' בלא שבועה. פי' ייחד לה קרקע וכתב לה ד' מצרים שלה בחייו לעשותה אפותיקי בכתובתה ומת נפרעת ממנו בלא שבועה היכא דלא אתפסה צררי אחריני. אמר לעדים כתבו וחתמו והבו ליה קנו מיניה לא צריך לאמלוכי בי'. פי' כשבאים עדים לכותבה א"צ לראות אם בלב שלם ובנפש חפיצה רוצה שיכתבו לו שהרי קנו מידו בקנין וסתם קנין לכתיבה עומד ולא חיישינן דלמא הדר דאפי' אי הדר בי' תו לא חיישינן ליה. לא קנו מיני' פומבדיתאי אמרי לא צריך לאמלוכי בי' בני מתא מחסיא אמרי צריך לאמלוכי ביה. פי' המורה דהיא מתנת קרקע. משמע מפירושו דמ"ה צריך לאמלוכי ביה דכל כמה דלא מטא שטרא לידי' דמקבל מצינן ביה למיהדר אבל באודיתא אמרינן דצ"ל כתובו ומפיו אמר לעדים כתובו וקיבל עליו שתהא מלוה בשטר תו לא צריך לאמלוכי בי' אלא כתבו שטרא ויהיבי ליה למלוה משום דבשעת הלואה אישתעבדו נכסיו וכיון דקיבל עליו [לעשות] מלוה בשטר תו לא צריך לאמלוכי ביה וכ"כ גם רבינו יוסף הלוי ז"ל ואינו נ"ל לחלק בין שטר אודיתא לשטר מתנה אע"פ שהמעות בידו כיון שבשעת ההלואה לא קבלה ע"ד מלוה בשטר אלא הוא רוצה עכשיו לעשותה מלוה בשטר [כל זמן] שלא הגיע השטר ליד המלוה יכול לחזור בו אע"פ שאמר כתובו וצריך לאמלוכי ביה דבאודיתא נמי פליגי ולא קשה מאי דאמרי' בפ' חז"ה ובפ' דיני ממונות בתרא הודאה בפני שנים וצ"ל כתובו דמשמע מכי אמר כתובו די לנו ולא צריך לאמלוכי בי' א) והאי דנקיט צ"ל

א) אולי צ"ל י"ל דה"ה נמי דצריך לאמלוכי ביה והאי דנקיט וכו'.

אלא תרוייהו. רב ורבי נתן. משום רבינו. רב. והלכה למעשה כו'. התלמוד קא פסיק שכך נמנו וגמרו בני הישיבה. מהו. לרבי אלעזר בן עזריה. ופירסה נדה. ופירש ממנה ומת. יחליף. יכתוב שטר אחר כדי חוב הנשאר, ויקרע הראשון. ולא יכתוב שובר להרע כח הלוה, שילטרך לשמור שוברו מן העכברים. רבי יוסי אומר יכתוב שובר. ולא יחליף, להרע כח המלוה למחול שעבודו מזמן ראשון. כששוברתה בתוכה. בתוך הכתובה עלמה יכתוב השובר. והיא אמרה בפנינו התקבלתי חליה. דטעמא מאי אמר רבי יהודה אין כותבין שובר – משום דלא ילטרך לוה לשומרו מן העכברים, דאי מרקב – הדר האי וגבי שטריה כוליה, הכא ליכא למיחש להכי. אפי' תימא כו'. דבהאי שובר לא חייש רבי יהודה לעכברים כי התם, דאילו התם מיפרע פרעיה דלמא כו'. הכא ודאי יהב לה. בתמיה. אבל על פה. דהוה ליה תנאה בעלמא – לא הוי תנאה, דמתנה על מה שכתוב בתורה הוא. בדבר שבממון. שאר וכסות. והרי פירות. דנכסי מלוג. דרבנן. האי דבעל אוכלן – תקנתא דרבנן היא, ולא עבוד רבנן חיזוק שיהא תנאו בטל, אם התנה למחול אכילתו. פירי פירות. אם כתב לה. "דין ודברים אין לי בנכסיך ובפירותיהן" – אוכל הוא פירי פירות, מוכר פירות ולוקח קרקע שיהא לה קרן, והוא אוכל פירות. וקיימא

אמר רב יצחק בר אבדימי משום רבינו. פירש בקונטרס: רבינו – רב. וקשה: דא"כ תקשי מהכא, תסתייס דרב הוא דאמר כר"א בן עזריה! לכך נראה דרבינו היינו רבי, ורב יצחק בר אבדימי דהכא הוא רב יצחק בר אבדימי הקדמון, שהיה תלמידו של רבי, כדאמרינן בפרק "כירה" (שבת דף מ:): אמר רב יצחק בר אבדימי פעם אחת נכנסתי אחר רבי לבית המרחץ. והוא היה רבו של רב דאתנייה לרב כחל, בפרק "כל הבשר" (חולין דף קי. ושם), ומדות, בפרק "המוכר את הספינה" (ב"ב דף פז. ושם). **רבי** יוסי אומר יכתוב שובר. פירש הקונטרס: משום דלא מרעינן כח המלוה לגבות מזמן שני. ולא פירש לפי המסקנא ד"גט פשוט" (שם דף קעא.) דקאמר התם דטעמא דרבי יוסי כדי שיכוף לפורעו.

כששוברתה מתוכה. וא"ת: ולרבי יוחנן, דאמר: *הטוען אחר מעשה ב"ד – לא אמר כלום, מה תועלת יש במה שנכתב השובר בתוך הכתובה? היא תטמין הכתובה, ומפקא עידי הינומא וגביא מאתים! וי"ל: כגון שהביאה עמה נדוניא והיא כפולה בכתובה, דאז לא תטמין הכתובה, דא"כ היתה מפסדת יותר. ועוד י"ל: דבמקום שכותבין כתובה, או אפילו במקום שאין כותבין, ויש עדים שכתב לה – אינה יכולה לגבות כלום, אפילו כודה שלא פרע לה, עד שתביא כתובה. כיון דסבר דאין כותבין שובר, הואיל ויכול לבא לידי הפסד אם יפסיד שוברו. וכ"ת: היא תשרוף הכתובה בפני עדים! דא"כ אותן עדים ידעו מה היה כתוב בה, דאל"כ – היאך יעידו שנשרפה כתובתה, מה יודעין אם כתובתה היתה, אם לא ראו מה היה כתוב בה.

טעמא דכתבה ליה הא על פה לא. וליכא למימר: מאי כותבת – אומרת, כדאמר בסמוך: מאי כותב אומר – דע"כ דווקא כותבת נקט, דהא פליג ארבי יוסי דאמר רשאי, בברייתא דלקמן. **הרי** זו מקודשת ותנאו בטל. ע"כ בדכפליה לתנאיה איירי, דאמר לה: אם אין ליך עלי שאר כסות ועונה – הרי את מקודשת, ואם לאו – אל תהי מקודשת. מדקאמר לקמן דטעמא דר' מאיר דתנאו בטל – משום דמתנה על מה שכתוב בתורה. ואי לא כפיל לתנאה – תיפוק ליה דתנאו בטל לרבי מאיר משום דבעי תנאי כפול, כדאמר ב"האומר" (קדושין דף סא. ושם). *ותימה: אם כן אמאי היא מקודשת? הרי התנה בפירוש שאם יהא לה עליו שאר כסות ועונה – שאינה מקודשת! ואין לומר דלכך מקודשת לפי שמקדשה ע"מ שתמחול לו והרי מחלה, אלא דאין מחילתה מחילה – דהא תניא בפרק ב' דנזיר (דף יא. ושם): הריני נזיר ע"מ שאשתה יין ואטמא למתים – הרי זה נזיר, ואסור בכולן, מפני שהתנה על מה שכתוב בתורה. והתם לא שייך לשנויי הכי! ואור"י: דאי לאו דילפינן מתנאי בני גד ובני ראובן – ה"א דשום תנאי אינו מבטל את המעשה, ואפילו לא יתקיים בסוף – המעשה קיים. והשתא דילפינן מהתם דמהני תנאי לבטל המעשה, אמרינן דדוקא כשאינו מתנה על מה שכתוב בתורה, דומיא דבני גד ובני ראובן, שלא התנו על מה שכתוב בתורה. וא"ת: הא דתנן בפרק בתרא דמנחות (דף קט.): "הריני נזיר ע"מ שאגלח בבית חוניו" יגלח בבית המקדש, ואם גלח בבית חוניו יצא. ומפרש בגמרא היינו טעמא דהאי גברא לצעורי נפשיה קא מכוין, אמר: אם סגי בבית חוניו – טרחנא. פירוש, הלכך אם רצה לגלח במקדש – חל עליו נזירות, ואם אינו יכול או אם אינו רוצה לטרוח – אדעתא דהכי לא נדר, אגלוי מלתא דלא הוי נזיר. והיינו פירוש יצא – כלומר, שלא חלה עליו הנזירות. והשתא אמאי? והא מתנה על מה שכתוב בתורה הוא, דאין גילוח אלא במקדש! ואר"י: דלא אמרינן מתנה על מה שכתוב בתורה תנאו בטל אלא היכא שמתכוין לעקור מה שכתוב בתורה, אבל התם – סבור הוא שיש מלוה בבית חוניו כמו בבית המקדש, ואין מתכוין לעקור, אית לן למילף מתנאי דבני גד ובני ראובן. וא"ת: כיון דשייך מתנה על מה שכתוב בתורה אפילו גבי ממון, א"כ לא יוכל אדם למחול חובו לעולם על ידי תנאי, שאם יאמר עשה עמי היום ומובך מחול לך – יהא מתנה על מה שכתוב בתורה. מיהו, מלוה לא חשבינן כתובה בתורה דאפילו למאן דאמר (קדושין דף יג:): מלוה הכתובה בתורה ככתובה בשטר דמי – היינו דוקא כגון נזקין וערכין ופדיון הבן, דמסברא לא הוה מחייבינן להו אם לא שחייבתו תורה בפירוש. אבל מלוה – כולי עלמא מודו דלא טרפא ממשעבדי, דאינה באה מכח התורה, דסברא הוא שיש לו לשלם מה שלוה ממנו. אבל קשה: דלענין ניזקין

אלא, תרוייהו ^[א] אזלי בתר אומדנא. מאן דאמר הלכה – שפיר, מאן דאמר אין הלכה – הכא נמי אומדן דעתא הוא: משום איקרובי דעתא הוא, והא איקרבא ליה דעתא. יתיב רב חנינא (א) קמיה דרבי ינאי, וקאמר: הלכה כרבי אלעזר בן עזריה. אמר ליה: *פוק קרי קראך לברא! אין הלכה כרבי אלעזר בן עזריה. אמר רב יצחק בר אבדימי משום רבינו: הלכה כרבי אלעזר בן עזריה. אמר רב נחמן אמר שמואל: הלכה כרבי אלעזר בן עזריה. ורב נחמן דידיה אמר: אין הלכה כרבי אלעזר בן עזריה. ונהרדעי משמיה דרב נחמן אמרי: הלכה כרבי אלעזר בן עזריה. ואע"ג דלט רב נחמן, ואמר: כל דיינא דדאין כרבי אלעזר בן עזריה – הכי והכי תיהוי, אפילו הכי הלכה כרבי אלעזר בן עזריה. ^[ב] והלכה למעשה – כרבי אלעזר בן עזריה.§ בעי רבין: נכנסה לחופה ולא נבעלה מהו? חיבת חופה קונה או חיבת ביאה קונה? תא שמע, דתני רב יוסף: שלא כתב לה אלא על חיבת לילה הראשון. אי אמרת בשלמא חיבת חופה קונה – היינו דאמר לילה הראשון, אלא אי אמרת חיבת ביאה קונה – ביאה בלילה הראשון איתא, מכאן ואילך ליתא?! ואלא מאי – חופה, חופה בלילה איתא, ביממא ליתא? ולטעמיך, ביאה בלילה איתא, ביממא ליתא? הא *אמר רבא: ^[ג] אם היה בבית אפל – מותר! הא לא קשיא, אורח ארעא קא משמע לן, דביאה בלילה. אלא חופה קשיא! חופה נמי לא קשיא: כיון דסתם חופה לביאה קיימא – אורח ארעא קא משמע לן, דבלילה. בעי רב אשי: נכנסה לחופה ופירסה נידה מהו? אם תימצי לומר ^[ד] חיבת חופה קונה – חופה דחזיא לביאה, ^[ה] אבל חופה דלא חזיא לביאה – לא, או דלמא לא שנא? תיקו.§ רבי יהודה אומר: רצה – כותב לבתולה וכו'.§ וסבר רבי יהודה דכותבין שובר? והתנן: *מי שפרע מקצת חובו, רבי יהודה אומר: ^[ו] יחליף, רבי יוסי אומר: ^[ז] יכתוב לו *שובר! אמר רבי ירמיה: כששוברתה מתוכה. אביי אמר: אפילו תימא בשאין שוברתה מתוכה, בשלמא התם – ודאי פרעיה, דלמא מירכס תברתא, ומפיק ליה לשטרא, והדר גבי זימנא אחרינא. הכא – ודאי יהב לה? מילתא בעלמא היא דאמרה ליה, אי נטריה – נטריה. אי לא נטריה – איהו הוא דאפסיד אנפשיה. בשלמא אביי לא אמר כרבי ירמיה לא קתני שוברתה מתוכה, אלא ר' ירמיה מ"ט לא אמר כאביי? גזירה שובר דהכא אטו שובר דעלמא. טעמא – דכתבה ליה, אבל על פה – לא. אמאי? דבר שבממון הוא, ושמעינן ליה לר' יהודה דאמר: דבר שבממון – תנאו קיים! דתניא, *האומר לאשה: הרי את מקודשת לי על מנת שאין ליך עלי שאר כסות ועונה – הרי זו מקודשת, ותנאו בטל, דברי רבי מאיר. ר' יהודה אומר: ^[ח] בדבר שבממון – תנאו קיים. קסבר רבי יהודה: ^[ט] כתובה דרבנן, *^[י] וחכמים עשו חיזוק לדבריהם יותר משל תורה. הרי פירות דרבנן, ולא עבדו להו רבנן חיזוק! דתנן, *רבי יהודה אומר: ^[כ] לעולם הוא אוכל פירי פירות, עד שיכתוב לה "דין ודברים אין לי בנכסיך ובפירותיהן ובפירות פירותיהן עד עולם". וקיימא

מתני' ר"י אומר אם רוצה כותב לבתולה שטר של מאתים והיא כותבת לו התקבלתי ממך מנה ולאלמנה מנה והיא כותבת לו התקבלתי ממך ג' וכו' ר"מ אומר כל הפוחת לבתולה ממאתים ולאלמנה ממנה הרי זה בעילת זנות קסבר ר"י דבהדיא אסור לפחות לבתולה ממאתים כדי שלא יעבור על תנאי ב"ד אבל בענין זה ע"י תחבולה מותר שכותב לה מאתים זוז והיא כותבת לו שובר שהתקבלה מנה ור"מ סבר אפי' ע"י תחבולה אסור לפחות:

עין משפט נר מצוה

כב א מיי' פ"ו מהלכ' זכיה הלכ' א סמג עשין כב טוש"ע ח"מ סי' רמו סעיף א:

כג ב מיי' פ"י מהלכ' אישות הל' יא סמג עשין מח טוש"ע אה"ע סי' נה סעיף ו:

כד ג מיי' פכ"א מהלכ' איסורי ביאה הלכה י סמג לאוין קכו טוש"ע א"ח סי' רמ סעיף יא:

כה ד ה מיי' פ"י מהלכ' אישות הל' ב סמג עשין מח טוש"ע אה"ע סי' סא סעי' א:

כו ו ז מיי' פכ"ג מהלכ' מלוה ולוה הלכ' טו סמג עשין כב טוש"ע ח"מ סי' נד סעי' א:

[ב"מ יז.]

כז ח מיי' פ"ו מהלכ' אישות הלכה ט י ופ' יב הלכה ו סמג עשין מח טוש"ע אה"ע סי' לח סעי' ה וסי' סט סעי' ו:

כח ט מיי' פ"י שם הלכ' ז ופי"א הלכה יד ופי"ב הלכה ב:

כט י מיי' פי"ב שם הלכה ט:

ל כ מיי' פכ"ג שם הלכ' ז סמג שם טוש"ע שם סימן צב סעי' ה.

ואר"ת דהוי מפליג בדברים ואין זה תנאי כלל שיתקיים התנאי למאן דאמר מתנה על מה שכתוב בתורה תנאו בטל והוי כמו על מנת שתעלי לרקיע דבהשוכר את הפועלים. ת"י

תוספות רי"ד

צריך לומר כתובו משום דבקנין ובהודה בפני ג' אין צ"ל כתובו אבל מיהו ה"ה נמי דצריך לאמלוכי בי' כדאמרינן הכא: ראב"ע [וכו']. אמר ר"נ א"ש הל' כראב"ע ואע"ג דר"נ לייט דאמר כל דיין דדאין כראב"ע כו': בעי רבין נכנסה לחופה ולא נבעלה מהו חיבת חופה קונה או חיבת ביאה קונה. בעי ר"א נכנסה לחופה ופרסה נדה מהו מי אמרינן חיבת חופה קונה חופה דחזיא לביאה אבל חופה דלא חזיא לביאה לא א"ד ל"ש תיקו ומספיקא אינה קונה:

מסורת הש"ס

[ברכות לו: יבמות מ.]

לקמן סה: שבת פו. נדה יז.

ב"ב קע:

[לעיל עז: וש"נ]

ב"מ נא. לד. קדושין יט: ב"ב קכו:

[יבמות לו: וש"נ]

לקמן פג.

הגהות הב"ח

(א) גמ' יתיב ר' חנינא קלא קמיה דר' ינאי. נ"ב הכי איתא פ"ק תפלת השחר דף ל ע"ב:

וְקַיְימָא לָן: *מַאי כּוֹתֵב — אוֹמֵר! אָמַר אַבַּיֵי: לַכֹּל יֵשׁ כְּתוּבָּה, וְלֹא לַכֹּל יֵשׁ פֵּירוֹת?! *מִילְּתָא דִּשְׁכִיחָא עָבְדוּ בָּהּ רַבָּנַן חִיזּוּק, מִילְּתָא דְּלָא שְׁכִיחָא — לָא עָבְדוּ בָּהּ רַבָּנַן חִיזּוּק. הֲרֵי חַמָּרִים דִּשְׁכִיחִי, וְלָא עָבְדוּ לָהּ רַבָּנַן חִיזּוּק! דִּתְנַן: *הַחַמָּרִין שֶׁנִּכְנְסוּ לָעִיר, וְאָמַר אֶחָד מֵהֶן: שֶׁלִּי חָדָשׁ, וְשֶׁל חֲבֵרִי יָשָׁן, שֶׁלִּי אֵינוֹ מְתוּקָּן וְשֶׁל חֲבֵרִי מְתוּקָּן, אֵין נֶאֱמָנִים. רַבִּי יְהוּדָה אוֹמֵר: נֶאֱמָנִים. אָמַר אַבַּיֵי: וַדַּאי דְּדִבְרֵיהֶם עָבְדוּ רַבָּנַן חִיזּוּק, סְפֵק דְּדִבְרֵיהֶם — לָא עָבְדוּ רַבָּנַן חִיזּוּק. רָבָא אָמַר: *בִּדְמַאי הֵקִילּוּ.§ ר' מֵאִיר אוֹמֵר: כָּל הַפּוֹחֵת וכו'.§ כָּל הַפּוֹחֵת — *[א]אֲפִי' בִּתְנָאָה. אַלְמָא קָסָבַר: תְּנָאוֹ בָּטֵל, וְאִית לָהּ. וְכֵיוָן דְּאָמַר לָהּ "לֵית לִיךְ אֶלָּא מָנֶה" — לָא סָמְכָא דַּעְתָּהּ, וְהָוְיָא לָהּ בְּעִילָתוֹ בְּעִילַת זְנוּת. וְהָא שָׁמְעִינַן לֵיהּ לְרַבִּי מֵאִיר, דְּאָמַר: כָּל הַמַּתְנֶה עַל מַה שֶּׁכָּתוּב בַּתּוֹרָה — תְּנָאוֹ בָּטֵל, הָא בִּדְרַבָּנַן — תְּנָאוֹ קַיָּים! קָסָבַר ר' מֵאִיר *כְּתוּבָּה דְּאוֹרַיְיתָא.§ תַּנְיָא, רַבִּי מֵאִיר אוֹמֵר: כָּל הַפּוֹחֵת לִבְתוּלָה מִמָּאתַיִם, וּלְאַלְמָנָה מִמָּנֶה — הֲרֵי זוֹ בְּעִילַת זְנוּת. רַבִּי יוֹסֵי אוֹמֵר: רַשַּׁאי. רַבִּי יְהוּדָה אוֹמֵר: רָצָה, כּוֹתֵב לִבְתוּלָה שְׁטָר שֶׁל מָאתַיִם, וְהִיא כּוֹתֶבֶת לוֹ "הִתְקַבַּלְתִּי מִמְּךָ מָנֶה". וּלְאַלְמָנָה מָנֶה, וְהִיא כּוֹתֶבֶת לוֹ "הִתְקַבַּלְתִּי מִמְּךָ חֲמִשִּׁים זוּז". וְסָבַר רַבִּי יוֹסֵי רַשַּׁאי? וּרְמִינְהִי: אֵין עוֹשִׂין כְּתוּבַּת אִשָּׁה מִטַּלְטְלִין מִפְּנֵי תִּיקּוּן הָעוֹלָם. אָמַר רַבִּי יוֹסֵי: וְכִי מַה תִּיקּוּן הָעוֹלָם יֵשׁ בְּזוֹ? וַהֲלֹא אֵין קְצוּבִין, וּפוֹחֲתִין! תַּנָּא קַמָּא נַמִי "אֵין עוֹשִׂין" קָאָמַר! אֶלָּא לָאו — הָכִי קָאָמַר: [ב]בַּמֶּה דְּבָרִים אֲמוּרִים — בְּשֶׁלֹּא קִבֵּל עָלָיו אַחֲרָיוּת. אֲבָל קִבֵּל עָלָיו אַחֲרָיוּת — עוֹשִׂין. וַאֲתָא רַבִּי יוֹסֵי לְמֵימַר: כִּי קִיבֵּל עָלָיו אַחֲרָיוּת — אַמַּאי עוֹשִׂין? וַהֲלֹא אֵין קְצוּבִין וּפוֹחֲתִין. הַשְׁתָּא, וּמָה הָתָם דִּדְלְמָא פָּחֲתֵי — חָיֵישׁ רַבִּי יוֹסֵי, הָכָא דְּוַדַּאי קָא פָּחֲתָה — לֹא כָּל שֶׁכֵּן?! הָכִי הַשְׁתָּא? הָתָם — לָא יָדְעָה דְּתָחֵיל, הָכָא — יָדְעָה וְקָא מָחֲלָה. אַחְתֵיהּ דְּרָמֵי בַּר חָמָא הֲוַת נְסִיבָא לְרַב אָוְיָא, אִירְכַּס

וְקַיְימָא לָן. בְּ"הַכּוֹתֵב"*. מַאי כּוֹתֵב אוֹמֵר. אַלְמָא. תְּנָאֵיהּ תְּנָאָה. וַהֲרֵי חַמָּרִים. גַּבֵּי דְּמַאי דְּרַבָּנַן הוּא, וְלָא עֲבַדוּ בְּהוּ חִיזּוּק, לְמֵיחַשׁ לְגוֹמְלִין לְרַבִּי יְהוּדָה. שֶׁלִּי חָדָשׁ. וְהַיָּשָׁן טוֹב מִמֶּנּוּ. שֶׁהֶחָדָשׁ עֲדַיִין אֵינוֹ יָבֵשׁ כָּל צָרְכּוֹ. וְהָכִי נַמִי אָמְרִינַן בְּ"אֵיזֶהוּ נֶשֶׁךְ" (ב"מ עב.). הָיוּ חֲדָשׁוֹת מֵאַרְבַּע וִישָׁנוֹת מִשָּׁלֹשׁ כו'. וְיֵשׁ מְפָרְשִׁים מִשּׁוּם עוֹמֶר. וְלָאו מִילְּתָא הִיא, דְּא"כ דִּמְתָרֵץ בִּדְמַאי הֵקִילּוּ — הָתֵינַח דְּמַאי, (א) חָדָשׁ מַאי אִיכָּא לְמֵימַר? וְעוֹד: לֹא מָצִינוּ שֶׁנֶּחְשְׁדוּ עַמֵּי הָאָרֶץ עַל אִיסּוּר חָדָשׁ. וְלָא נָקַט לָהּ אֶלָּא מִשּׁוּם אֵין נֶאֱמָנִים דִּדְמַאי. וּרְבוּתָא אַשְׁמוּעִינַן, דְּאַע"ג דְּמַשְׁבַּח לָהּ לְחַבְרֵיהּ נַמִי בְּמִילֵּי אַחֲרָנְיָיתָא — אֵינוֹ נֶאֱמָן עַל הַדְּמַאי, דְּחָיְישִׁינַן לְגוֹמְלִין. בִּדְמַאי הֵקִילּוּ. מִשּׁוּם סְפֵק דְּדִבְרֵיהֶם. וַאֲפִילּוּ סָפֵק לֵיתֵיהּ, דְּרוֹב עַמֵּי הָאָרֶץ מְעַשְּׂרִין הֵן. כָּל הַפּוֹחֵת אֲפִילּוּ בִּתְנָאָה. מִדְּלָא תָּנָא כָּל בְּתוּלָה (ב) שֶׁאֵין לָהּ מָאתַיִם וְאַלְמָנָה שֶׁאֵין לָהּ מָנֶה הֲרֵי זוֹ בְּעִילַת זְנוּת, ש"מ דְּהָכִי אַשְׁמוּעִינַן: שֶׁאַע"פ שֶׁהִיא גּוֹבָה לְבַסּוֹף, דְּאֵין תְּנָאוֹ קַיָּים — אֲפִילּוּ הָכִי, כֵּיוָן דִּמֵעִיקָּרָא אַתְנֵי — קָרֵי לָהּ בְּעִילַת זְנוּת, מִשּׁוּם דְּמַשְׁמַעַת בִּיאָה לָא הֲוָה סָמְכָא דַּעְתָּהּ אַכְּתוּבָּה. אַלְמָא קָסָבַר תְּנָאוֹ בָּטֵל. דְּבְלָאו הָכִי (ג) לָאו רְבוּתָא הִיא דְּנָקַט "כָּל הַפּוֹחֵת". וְהָא שָׁמְעִינַן לֵיהּ. לְעֵיל. ר' יוֹסֵי אוֹמֵר רַשַּׁאי. וַאֲפִילּוּ עַל פֶּה נַמִי תְּנָאוֹ קַיָּים. וַאֲתָא ר' יְהוּדָה לְמֵימַר נַמִי רַשַּׁאי, כְּר' יוֹסֵי. מִיהוּ, עַל פֶּה — תְּנָאוֹ בָּטֵל, כִּדְאָמְרִינַן לְעֵיל: חֲכָמִים עָשׂוּ חִיזּוּק לְדִבְרֵיהֶם יוֹתֵר מִשֶּׁל תּוֹרָה. אֲבָל בָּאת לִמְחוֹל — תִּכְתּוֹב שׁוֹבֵר. אֵין עוֹשִׂין כְּתוּבָּה מִטַּלְטְלִין. אֵין מְיַיחֲדִין מִטַּלְטְלִין לִכְתוּבָּה. מִפְּנֵי תִּיקּוּן הָעוֹלָם. שֶׁמָּא יֹאבְדוּ, אוֹ יִפְחֲתוּ דְּמֵיהֶן. אֵין קְצוּבִין. אֵין דְּמֵיהֶן קְלוּבִין עוֹלָמִית, דְּמוֹקְרֵי וּמוֹזְלֵי, הִלְכָּךְ פְּעָמִים שֶׁפּוֹחֲתִין מִכְּדֵי מַה שֶּׁשָּׁמָאוּם. אֵין עוֹשִׂין קָאָמַר. וּפְחִיתָה נַמִי, בִּכְלַל תִּיקּוּן הָעוֹלָם הִיא. שֶׁלֹּא קִבֵּל עָלָיו אַחֲרָיוּת. הַבַּעַל, אִם יֹאבְדוּ. וּפָרֵישׁ לֵיהּ תַּנָּא דְּלָא חָיֵישׁ לְזוֹלָא אֶלָּא לְאוֹנְסָא, וְקָאָמַר לֵיהּ רַבִּי יוֹסֵי: וְכִי קִבֵּל עָלָיו אַחֲרָיוּת נַמִי, מַה נִּתְקַן הָעוֹלָם בְּכָךְ? וַהֲלֹא אַף כְּשֶׁהֵן קַיָּימִין, אֵין קְלוּבִין וּפוֹחֲתִין. אִירְכַּס

*נזקין (וערכין) נימא שלא יוכל למחול, דמתנה הוא על מה שכתוב בתורה. וכי תימא ה"נ – והתנן ב"החובל" (ב"ק דף צב.): קרע את כסותי ושבר כדי, על מנת לפטור – פטור! *ותירץ ה"ר אלחנן: דהתם נמי, אם היה אומר קרע ושבר ע"מ שאין לי עליך דין נזק – הוי חשיב מתנה על מה שכתוב בתורה. אבל למחול יכול.
וכן הכא, גבי שאר כסות ועונה – דוקא כשאמר על מנת שאין ליך עלי דין שאר כסות ועונה – הוי מתנה על מה שכתוב בתורה, אבל ע"מ שתפטרי אותי משאר כו' – פטור. וכן על מנת שאין לך עלי אונאה – על מנת שאין לך עלי דין אונאה. וכן על מנת שלא תשמיטנו שביעית. ועי"ל: דנזקין לא דמו לקדושין. דהכא היינו טעמא – דאין קדושין לחצאין. דאין לך קדושין שאין לה עליו שאר כסות ועונה. וכן גבי נזיר – *אין נזיר לחצאין. אבל גבי נזקין – לא שייך למימר הכי. וא"ת: א"כ היכי מדמה בפרק "המגרש" (גיטין פד.): הרי את מגורשת ע"מ שתאכלי בשר חזיר, למתנה על מה שכתוב בתורה. והא בתנאי זה לא הוי גרושין לחצאין? וי"ל: דגבי ממון דניתן למחילה, דוקא אמרינן טעמא משום דלחצאין. אבל גבי איסורא – לא בעינן האי טעמא. והא דתנן ב"יש נוחלין" (ב"ב דף קל.): האומר פלוני יירש במקום שיש בת, בתי תירש במקום שיש בן – לא אמר כלום, שהתנה על מה שכתוב בתורה! התם היינו טעמא דאין יכול לומר פלוני יירש והוא אינו יורש, אבל במתנה – יכול ליתן. והא דמפרש התם בגמרא (דף קכו:) הכא מי מחל – לרווחא דמלתא נקט. וא"ת: והא דתנן ב"השוכר את הפועלים" (ב"מ דף צד. ושם) מתנה שומר חנם להיות פטור משבועה, ופריך בגמרא: והא מתנה על מה שכתוב בתורה הוא כו'! ומסיק: אפילו תימא רבי מאיר, שאני הכא דמעיקרא לא שיעבד נפשיה. ומאי משני? והא הכא נמי לא קידשה על מנת כן, ולא שיעבד נפשיה! וי"ל: דשאני התם, כיון דריבתה תורה שומרים הרבה, שומר חנם והשואל נושא שכר כו' – יכול נמי כל אחד להיות לפי תנאו. א"נ: שאני התם דחייבתו תורה; שומר שכר על שלוקח שכר, ושואל לפי שכל הנאה שלו, ומשעבדים עצמם לכל הכתוב בפרשה. הלכך, במקום שאין משעבדים עצמם – פטורים. ובקונטרס פירש שם דהכא מקודשת – משום דכי יהיב לה קדושיה אקדשה. ותנאה דבתר הכי – לאו כלום הוא, שכבר היא אשתו, אבל שומר חנם – מתנה קודם שמשך. ואין נראה, דהא כל תנאי לרבי מאיר תנאי קודם למעשה הוא. **כל** הפוחת אפילו בתנאה. פירשתי לעיל (דף נו.). **ושמעינן** ליה לרבי מאיר דאמר מתנה על מה שכתוב בתורה תנאו בטל הא בדרבנן תנאו קיים. פירש בקונטרס: דשמעינן ליה בברייתא דלעיל. וא"ת: מנא ליה למידק הא בדרבנן תנאו קיים? דלמא כל שכן, דבדרבנן דעבוד חיזוק טפי ותנאו בטל, כמו לרבי יהודה! וי"ל: דדייק מדלא קתני לעיל על מנת שאין לך עלי שאר כסות ועונה וכתובה, כיון דאיכא מ"ד דלא עשו חכמים חיזוק לדבריהם אפילו בשל תורה, אע"ג דרבי יהודה מודה בכתובה – מ"מ הוה ליה לשנות. כי היכי דקתני עונה, אע"ג דמודה בה רבי יהודה. **הא** בדרבנן תנאו קיים. תימה: הא שמעינן ליה לרבי מאיר בפרק "הזהב" (ב"מ דף נה:) דהאוכל תרומת מעשר של דמאי דמוסיף חומש, דעשו חכמים חיזוק לדבריהם כשל תורה. ובריש "החולץ" (יבמות דף לו: ושם) גבי מעוברת חבירו ומינקת חבירו שמעינן ליה דעשו חיזוק לדבריהם אף יותר משל תורה! וי"ל: דההיא דיבמות משום דקנסא הוא – עשו חיזוק לדבריהם יותר, וההיא ד"הזהב" גבי תרומה, וכן גבי גט דמייתי התם, דאיסורא הוא – התם עשו חיזוק כשל תורה. והכא, גבי כתובה, שאינו לא איסור ולא קנס אלא ממונא בעלמא – לא עשו חיזוק כלל. **קסבר** רבי מאיר כתובה דאורייתא. אע"ג דכתובת אלמנה דרבנן, מ"מ עיקר כתובה דאורייתא היא. וכעין זה אמרינן בסוף "הערל" (יבמות דף פא. ושם): אמר ליה רבי יוחנן לר"ל: מי סברת תרומה בזמן הזה דרבנן? א"ל: אין, שאני אומר עיגול בעיגולין עולה. פירוש: ואי תרומה בזמן הזה דאורייתא – לא היא עולה, אף על גב דתרומת תאנים דרבנן, כיון דעיקר תרומה מיהא דאורייתא. וא"ת: דתנן לקמן ב"הכותב" (דף פג: ושם): כתב לה דין ודברים אין לי בנכסיך בחייך ובמותך כו', רבן שמעון בן גמליאל אומר ירשנה כו'. ומסיק אליבא דרב דירושת הבעל דרבנן, וחכמים עשו חיזוק לדבריהם כשל תורה. ומה צריך להאי טעמא? אפילו לא עשו חיזוק לדבריהם – תיפוק ליה משום דעיקר ירושה דאורייתא! וי"ל: דלא דמיא ירושת הבעל לשאר ירושות שבאות מחמת קורבה. **אין** עושין כתובת אשה מטלטלין. והא דאמרינן בפ"ק (לעיל דף ז.) אמר להו אתפסוה מטלטלי – כשקבל עליו אחריות אם יאבדו או יוזלו. **אבל** קבל עליו אחריות עושין. וליכא למיחש שמא יאמר לה טלי כתובתיך ולאי, כדאמרינן בסוף "האשה שנפלו" (לקמן דף פב: ושם). דדוקא בדלא קיבל עליו אחריות איכא למיחש להכי, הואיל ואינו יכול ליהנות מן המטלטלין לעשות בהן סחורה ולהשתכר בהן, שהאשה לא תתן לו, הואיל ואין אחריות עליו. אבל היכא דכתב לה כל נכסי אחראין וערבאין – יכול לייחד, ואין לחוש שתאמר לה טלי כתובתיך ולאי, כיון שיכול ליהנות, מהן שלא תקפיד האשה אם יעשה בהן שום סחורה. והיינו טעמא דאמר בפרק "נערה" (לעיל דף נא.) [דתנן: כתב שוה מנה תחת מאתים זוז, ולא כתב לה נכסים דאית לי אחראין, משמע] שיכול לייחד שדה לכתובתה בלא שום אחריות, דכיון שיש לו הנאת אכילת פירות – ודאי לא יאמר לה.

[נזקין ופדיון הבן נימא כו' כצ"ל מהרש"א]

אבל קשה דגבי כתובה משמע שאינה יכולה למחול כלל לרבי יהודה בעל פה אלא דוקא בכותבת לו התקבלתי ושמא בכתובה דרבנן עשו חיזוק טפי לר' יהודה מלר' מאיר דאמר דאורייתא ואין יכולה למחול אלא בכתיבה. ת"י

לא א מיי' פי"ב מהלכ' אישות הלכה ח סמג עשין מח טוש"ע אה"ע סי' סו סעיף ט וסי' סט סעיף ו:

לב ב סמג עשין מח טוש"ע שם סימן סו סעיף ב:

[ואתיא כרבי שמעון דאמר דאינו נזיר עד שידור מכולן. ת"י]

הגהות הב"ח

(א) רש"י ד"ה שלי חדש וכו' חדש מאי איכא למימר. נ"ב עיין ברטנורה שמתרץ זה: (ב) ד"ה כל הפוחת וכו' שאין לה. נ"ב זהו כפר"י ולא כפריב"ן לעיל בתוס' דף נו בד"ה מני: (ג) ד"ה אלמא וכו' לאו רבותא. נ"ב זהו נוסחא אחרת מפי' הקונטרס וגם פי' זה ע"ל שיטת פר"י ולא כפריב"ן:

[דף פג.]

[לקמן פג.]

[עירובין סג: וש"נ]

לעיל כד. דמאי פ"ד מ"ז

[לעיל כד. וש"נ]

[ועי' תוס' ב"ק פט. ד"ה טעמא וכו' פירוש כסוגיא דהכא]

[לעיל ו.]

אִירְכַּס כְּתוּבָּתָהּ. אָתוּ לְקַמֵּיהּ דְּרַב יוֹסֵף, אֲמַר לְהוּ: הָכִי אָמַר רַב יְהוּדָה אָמַר שְׁמוּאֵל: זוֹ *דִּבְרֵי ר' מֵאִיר, אֲבָל חֲכָמִים אוֹמְרִים: מַשְׁהֶא אָדָם אֶת אִשְׁתּוֹ שְׁתַּיִם וְשָׁלֹשׁ שָׁנִים בְּלֹא כְּתוּבָּה. אֲמַר לֵיהּ אַבַּיֵי: וְהָא אָמַר *רַב נַחְמָן אָמַר שְׁמוּאֵל: הֲלָכָה כְּרַבִּי מֵאִיר בִּגְזֵירוֹתָיו! אִי הָכִי, [א]זִיל כְּתוֹב לָהּ. כִּי אֲתָא רַב דִּימִי אָמַר רַבִּי שִׁמְעוֹן בֶּן פָּזִי אָמַר רַבִּי יְהוֹשֻׁעַ בֶּן לֵוִי מִשּׁוּם בַּר קַפָּרָא: מַחֲלוֹקֶת בַּתְּחִלָּה, אֲבָל בַּסּוֹף — לְדִבְרֵי הַכֹּל אֵינָהּ מוֹחֶלֶת. וְרַבִּי יוֹחָנָן אָמַר: בֵּין בְּזוֹ וּבֵין בְּזוֹ מַחֲלוֹקֶת. אָמַר רַבִּי אַבָּהוּ, לְדִידִי מִפָּרְשָׁא לִי מִינֵּיהּ דְּרַבִּי יוֹחָנָן: דַּאֲנָא וְרַבִּי יְהוֹשֻׁעַ בֶּן לֵוִי לָא פְּלִיגִינַן אַהֲדָדֵי. מַאי 'בַּתְּחִלָּה' דְּקָאָמַר רַבִּי יְהוֹשֻׁעַ בֶּן לֵוִי — תְּחִלַּת חוּפָּה, וּמַאי סוֹף — סוֹף בִּיאָה. וְכִי קָאָמִינָא אֲנָא בֵּין בְּזוֹ וּבֵין בְּזוֹ מַחֲלוֹקֶת — תְּחִלַּת חוּפָּה וְסוֹף חוּפָּה, דְּהִיא תְּחִילַּת בִּיאָה. כִּי אֲתָא רָבִין אָמַר רַבִּי שִׁמְעוֹן בֶּן פָּזִי אָמַר רַבִּי יְהוֹשֻׁעַ בֶּן לֵוִי מִשּׁוּם בַּר קַפָּרָא: מַחֲלוֹקֶת לְבַסּוֹף, אֲבָל בַּתְּחִלָּה — דִּבְרֵי הַכֹּל מוֹחֶלֶת. וְרַבִּי יוֹחָנָן אָמַר: בֵּין בְּזוֹ וּבֵין בְּזוֹ מַחֲלוֹקֶת. אָמַר רַבִּי אַבָּהוּ: לְדִידִי מִפָּרְשָׁא לִי מִינֵּיהּ דְּרַבִּי יוֹחָנָן: דַּאֲנָא וְרַבִּי יְהוֹשֻׁעַ בֶּן לֵוִי לָא פְּלִיגִינַן אַהֲדָדֵי, מַאי 'לְבַסּוֹף' דְּאָמַר רַבִּי יְהוֹשֻׁעַ בֶּן לֵוִי — סוֹף חוּפָּה, וּמַאי תְּחִלָּה — תְּחִלַּת חוּפָּה. וְכִי קָאָמִינָא אֲנָא בֵּין בְּזוֹ בֵּין בְּזוֹ מַחֲלוֹקֶת — תְּחִלַּת בִּיאָה וְסוֹף בִּיאָה. אָמַר רַב פַּפָּא: אִי לָאו דַּאֲמַר רַבִּי אַבָּהוּ: לְדִידִי מִפָּרְשָׁא לִי מִינֵּיהּ דְּרַבִּי יוֹחָנָן דַּאֲנָא וְרַבִּי יְהוֹשֻׁעַ בֶּן לֵוִי לָא פְּלִיגִינַן אַהֲדָדֵי, הֲוָה אָמִינָא: רַבִּי יוֹחָנָן וְרַבִּי יְהוֹשֻׁעַ בֶּן לֵוִי — פְּלִיגִי, רַב דִּימִי וְרָבִין — לָא פְּלִיגִי, מַאי סוֹף דְּקָאָמַר רָבִין — סוֹף חוּפָּה, וּמַאי תְּחִלָּה דְּקָאָמַר רַב דִּימִי — תְּחִלַּת בִּיאָה. מַאי קמ"ל? הָא קמ"ל: דִּפְלִיגִי תְּרֵי אֲמוֹרָאֵי אַטַּעְמָא דְּנַפְשַׁיְיהוּ, וְלָא פְּלִיגִי תְּרֵי אֲמוֹרָאֵי אַלִּיבָּא דְּחַד אָמוֹרָא.§

מתני' *[ב]נוֹתְנִין לִבְתוּלָה שְׁנֵים עָשָׂר חוֹדֶשׁ מִשֶּׁתְּבָעָהּ הַבַּעַל לְפַרְנֵס אֶת עַצְמָהּ, [ג]וּכְשֵׁם שֶׁנּוֹתְנִין לָאִשָּׁה — כָּךְ נוֹתְנִין לָאִישׁ לְפַרְנֵס אֶת עַצְמוֹ. [ד]וּלְאַלְמָנָה שְׁלֹשִׁים יוֹם. *[ה]הִגִּיעַ זְמַן וְלֹא נִישְּׂאוּ — אוֹכְלוֹת מִשֶּׁלּוֹ וְאוֹכְלוֹת בִּתְרוּמָה. רַבִּי טַרְפוֹן אוֹמֵר: נוֹתְנִין לָהּ הַכֹּל תְּרוּמָה. רַבִּי עֲקִיבָא אוֹמֵר: [א] מֶחֱצָה חוּלִּין וּמֶחֱצָה תְּרוּמָה. [ו]הַיָּבָם אֵינוֹ מַאֲכִיל בִּתְרוּמָה. עָשְׂתָה שִׁשָּׁה חֳדָשִׁים בִּפְנֵי הַבַּעַל, וְשִׁשָּׁה חֳדָשִׁים בִּפְנֵי הַיָּבָם, *וַאֲפִילּוּ כּוּלָּן בִּפְנֵי הַבַּעַל חָסֵר יוֹם אֶחָד בִּפְנֵי הַיָּבָם, אוֹ כּוּלָּן בִּפְנֵי הַיָּבָם חָסֵר יוֹם אֶחָד בִּפְנֵי הַבַּעַל — אֵינָהּ אוֹכֶלֶת בִּתְרוּמָה. זוֹ מִשְׁנָה רִאשׁוֹנָה. בֵּית דִּין שֶׁל אַחֲרֵיהֶן אָמְרוּ:

אֵין

רש"י

אִירְכַּס כְּתוּבָּתָהּ. שְׁטַר כְּתוּבָּתָהּ. זוֹ דִּבְרֵי ר"מ. דַּאֲמַר לְעֵיל: כָּל הַפּוֹחֵת לִבְתוּלָה מִמָּאתַיִם, וַאֲפִי' בִּתְנָאָה, וְהַתְּנַאי בָּטֵל — קָרֵי לָהּ בְּעִילַת זְנוּת, מִשּׁוּם דְּלָא סָמְכָא דַּעְתָּהּ. וְהָכָא נַמִי, לר"מ הוּא דְּאָסוּר לְשַׁהוֹת אִשָּׁה שֶׁאִבְּדָה שְׁטַר כְּתוּבָּתָהּ, וַאֲפִי' אִית לַהּ, דְּלָא מַפְסְדָא בְּהָכִי, דְּגָבְיָא בִּתְנַאי ב"ד מִיהָא לָא סָמְכָא דַּעְתָּהּ, דְּאָמְרָה: כִּי תָּבַעְנָא לֵיהּ אָמַר "פְּרַעְתִּיךְ", הִלְכָּךְ בְּעִילַת זְנוּת הִיא. אֲבָל חֲכָמִים אוֹמְרִים כו'. דְּלֵית לָן לְמֵיחַשׁ מִשּׁוּם מִסְמַךְ דַּעְתָּא, דְּתֶיהֱוֵי בְּעִילַת זְנוּת. בִּגְזֵירוֹתָיו. בְּדָבָר שֶׁהוּא מַחְמִיר עַל דְּבַר תּוֹרָה בְּאִיסּוּר וְהֶיתֵּר, עַל יְדֵי גְּזֵירַת דִּבְרֵיהֶם. אִי הָכִי זִיל כְּתוֹב לָהּ. כְּתוּבָּה אַחֲרִיתִי. וְהָא דְּאָמְרִינַן לְעֵיל (דף נו.): לֹא כָּתַב לָהּ כְּתוּבָּה — בְּתוּלָה גּוֹבָה מָאתַיִם, וְאוֹקְמִינַן כר"מ — הָתָם בְּמָקוֹם שֶׁאֵין כּוֹתְבִין כְּתוּבָּה, דְּכוּלְּהוּ אַתְּנַאי קָא סָמְכֵי. אִי נַמִי: בְּמָקוֹם שֶׁכּוֹתְבִין, וְגוֹבָה לר"מ. מִיהוּ, בְּעִילַת זְנוּת בְּאִיסּוּר הִיא. מַחֲלוֹקֶת. דְּרַבִּי יְהוּדָה וְר' יוֹסֵי, דְּאָמַר ר' יְהוּדָה עַל פֶּה — לָאו תְּנָאָה הוּא, וְר' יוֹסֵי סָבַר: תְּנָאָה קַיָּים. בַּתְּחִלָּה. מְפָרֵשׁ לְקַמָּן תְּחִלַּת מַאי. דִּבְרֵי הַכֹּל אֵינָהּ מוֹחֶלֶת. שֶׁכְּבָר זָכְתָה, וַאֲמִירָתָהּ לָאו כְּלוּם, אֶלָּא א"כ כָּתְבָה שׁוֹבֵר "הִתְקַבַּלְתִּי". תְּחִלַּת חוּפָּה וּמַאי סוֹף סוֹף בִּיאָה. וה"ק: מִתְּחִלַּת חוּפָּה וְעַד סוֹף חוּפָּה פְּלִיגִי בָּהּ רַבִּי יְהוּדָה וְר' יוֹסֵי, אֲבָל מִשֶּׁבָּא עָלֶיהָ מוֹדֶה ר' יוֹסֵי דְּאֵין בִּדְבָרָיו כְּלוּם. וְכִי אָמִינָא אֲנָא בֵּין בְּזוֹ בֵּין בְּזוֹ מַחֲלוֹקֶת. לָאו אַסּוֹף דְּרַבִּי יְהוֹשֻׁעַ קָאָמִינָא, אֶלָּא אַסּוֹף חוּפָּה, דְּהִיא קוֹדֶם בִּיאָה. אָמַר רַב פַּפָּא אִי לָאו דַּאֲמַר כו'. אֲנָא לָא הֲוָה נִיחָא לִי לְפָרוּשֵׁי מִילְּתַיְיהוּ הָכִי, דְּרַבִּי יוֹחָנָן וְר' יְהוֹשֻׁעַ לָא לִיפְלְגוּ, וְרַב דִּימִי וְרָבִין נִיפְלְגוּ בִּדְרַבִּי יְהוֹשֻׁעַ. אֶלָּא הָכִי הֲוָה אָמִינָא: רַבִּי יוֹחָנָן וְר' יְהוֹשֻׁעַ בֶּן לֵוִי פְּלִיגִי, דְּאַהַהוּא סוֹף דְּקָאָמַר רַבִּי יְהוֹשֻׁעַ בֶּן לֵוִי — דִּבְרֵי הַכֹּל אֵינָהּ מוֹחֶלֶת, אָתָא רַבִּי יוֹחָנָן לְמֵימַר אַף בְּזוֹ מַחֲלוֹקֶת. וְרַב דִּימִי וְרָבִין לָא פְּלִיגִי בִּדְרַבִּי יְהוֹשֻׁעַ, וְהָכִי הֲוָה מְפָרֵישְׁנָא לִדְרַב דִּימִי: אָמַר רַבִּי יְהוֹשֻׁעַ מַחֲלוֹקֶת בִּתְחִלַּת בִּיאָה, דְּהִיא סוֹף חוּפָּה, אֲבָל בְּסוֹף בִּיאָה — דִּבְרֵי הַכֹּל אֵינָהּ מוֹחֶלֶת. וְרַבִּי יוֹחָנָן פָּלֵיג עֲלֵיהּ דַּאֲפִילּוּ בְּסוֹף בִּיאָה נַמִי פְּלִיגִי. וְכִי אָתָא רָבִין אָמַר רַבִּי יְהוֹשֻׁעַ בֶּן לֵוִי: מַחֲלוֹקֶת בְּסוֹף חוּפָּה, וְהִיא תְּחִלַּת בִּיאָה דְּקָאָמַר נַמִי רַב דִּימִי, אֲבָל בִּתְחִלַּת חוּפָּה — דִּבְרֵי הַכֹּל מוֹחֶלֶת. אֲבָל הַשְׁתָּא דְּפָרֵישׁ רַבִּי אַבָּהוּ לִדְרַב דִּימִי, דְּבֵין לְרַבִּי יוֹחָנָן וּבֵין לְרַבִּי יְהוֹשֻׁעַ בֶּן לֵוִי פְּלִיגִי רַבִּי יוֹסֵי וְרַבִּי יְהוּדָה בִּתְחִלַּת חוּפָּה וּבְסוֹף חוּפָּה, עַל כָּרְחָךְ פְּלִיגָא דְּרָבִין אַדְּרַב דִּימִי, דְּהָא אָמַר רָבִין בִּתְחִלַּת חוּפָּה ד"ה מוֹחֶלֶת. מַאי קמ"ל. בְּהָא דַּאֲמַר אִי לָאו דְּקָאָמַר רַבִּי אַבָּהוּ כו' הָאָמַר רַבִּי אַבָּהוּ וְאִיהוּ לָא בָּעֵי לְאִיפְלוּגֵי עֲלֵיהּ, וּלְמַאי הִלְכְתָא אַשְׁמוּעִינַן? דְּאִי לָא אֲמָרָהּ רַבִּי אַבָּהוּ הֲוָה נִיחָא לֵיהּ לְדִידֵיהּ לְפָרוּשֵׁי בְּעִנְיָן אַחֵר. הָא קמ"ל. דְּהֵיכָא דְּאַשְׁכְּחַן אֲמוֹרָאֵי דִּפְלִיגֵי אַהֲדָדֵי, כָּל חַד אַלִּיבָּא דְּנַפְשֵׁיהּ, וּתְרֵי אֲמוֹרָאֵי אַחֲרִינֵי דִּפְלִיגֵי בִּפְלוּגְתָּא דְּהָנָךְ אֲמוֹרָאֵי, וְאִית לָן לְפָרוּשֵׁי מִילְּתָא בִּתְרֵי לִישָּׁנֵי, חֲדָא מִינַּיְיהוּ מִיפַּלְגֵי תְּרֵי אֲמוֹרָאֵי אַלִּיבָּא דְּנַפְשַׁיְיהוּ, שֶׁכָּל אֶחָד אוֹמֵר סְבָרָא שֶׁלּוֹ, כְּגוֹן רַבִּי יוֹחָנָן וְרַבִּי יְהוֹשֻׁעַ, וְאִיכָּא תְּרֵי אֲמוֹרָאֵי [אַלִּיבָּא דְּחַד] לָא מִיפַּלְגֵי, אֶלָּא אָמְרֵי חֲדָא מִלְּתָא. וַחֲדָא מִן לִישָּׁנָא מִיפַּלְגֵי תְּרֵי אֲמוֹרָאֵי אַלִּיבָּא דְּחַד, כְּגוֹן רַב דִּימִי וְרָבִין, וּמְשַׁוְּיָא מִלְּתָא דִּתְרֵי אֲמוֹרָאֵי קַמָּאֵי חֲדָא מִלְּתָא — שָׁבְקִינַן הַהִיא לִישָּׁנָא דְּמִיפַּלְגֵי תְּרֵי אֲמוֹרָאֵי אַלִּיבָּא דְּחַד, וְנָקְטִינַן הַהִיא דְּמִיפַּלְגֵי תְּרֵי אֲמוֹרָאֵי אַלִּיבָּא דְּנַפְשַׁיְיהוּ. דְּכִי פְּלִיגִי תְּרֵי אַלִּיבָּא דְּחַד, מַר אָמַר: הָכִי אָמַר פְּלוֹנִי, וּמַר אָמַר: הָכִי אָמַר פְּלוֹנִי — חַד מִינַּיְיהוּ מְשַׁקֵּר. אֲבָל כִּי פְּלִיגִי תְּרֵי אֲמוֹרָאֵי בְּדִין אוֹ בְּאִיסּוּר וְהֶיתֵּר, כָּל חַד אָמַר: הָכִי מִיסְתַּבַּר טַעְמָא — אֵין כָּאן שֶׁקֶר, כָּל חַד וְחַד סְבָרָא דִּידֵיהּ קָאָמַר, מַר יָהֵיב טַעְמָא לְהֶיתֵּירָא, וּמַר יָהֵיב טַעְמָא לְאִיסּוּרָא. מַר מְדַמֵּי מִילְּתָא לְמִילְּתָא הָכִי, וּמַר מְדַמֵּי לֵיהּ בְּעִנְיָינָא אַחֲרִינָא. ואִיכָּא לְמֵימַר: אֵלּוּ וָאֵלּוּ דִּבְרֵי אֱלֹהִים חַיִּים הֵם, זִימְנִין דְּשַׁיָּיךְ הַאי טַעְמָא וְזִימְנִין דְּשַׁיָּיךְ הַאי טַעְמָא, שֶׁהַטַּעַם מִתְהַפֵּךְ לְפִי שִׁינּוּי הַדְּבָרִים בְּשִׁינּוּי מוּעָט.

מתני' נוֹתְנִין לִבְתוּלָה. זְמַן לִכְנִיסָתָהּ לַחוּפָּה מִיּוֹם שֶׁתְּבָעָהּ הַבַּעַל, לְאַחַר שֶׁקִּידְּשָׁהּ, לְהַזְהִירָהּ עַל. עִסְקֵי חוּפָּה, לְהָכִין תַּכְשִׁיטֶיהָ. לְפַרְנֵס עַצְמָהּ. בְּתַכְשִׁיטִין. לְפַרְנֵס עַצְמוֹ. בְּצָרְכֵי סְעוּדָה וְחוּפָּה. וּלְאַלְמָנָה ל' יוֹם. שֶׁאֵינָהּ טוֹרַחַת כָּל כָּךְ בְּתַכְשִׁיטִין, שֶׁכְּבָר יֵשׁ בְּיָדָהּ. וְלֹא נִישְּׂאוּ. שֶׁהַבְּעָלִים מְעַכְּבִין. וְאַיְּידֵי דְּתָנָא *רֵישָׁא בְּדִידְהִי — תָּנָא סֵיפָא נַמִי בְּדִידְהִי. וְאוֹכֶלֶת בִּתְרוּמָה. אִם כֹּהֵן הוּא וְהִיא יִשְׂרְאֵלִית, שֶׁמִּשָּׁעָה שֶׁקִּידְּשָׁהּ אוֹכֶלֶת בִּתְרוּמָה מִן הַתּוֹרָה כִּדְמְפָרֵשׁ בַּגְּמָרָא, וְרַבָּנַן גְּזוּר עַד שֶׁתִּכָּנֵס. נוֹתְנִין לָהּ הַכֹּל תְּרוּמָה. אִם יִרְצֶה. וּכְשֶׁיַּגִּיעוּ יְמֵי טוּמְאָתָהּ — תִּמְכְּרֶנָּה וְתִקַּח חוּלִּין. מֶחֱצָה חוּלִּין. לֶאֱכוֹל בִּימֵי טוּמְאָתָהּ. הַיָּבָם אֵינוֹ מַאֲכִיל בִּתְרוּמָה. בְּעוֹדָהּ שׁוֹמֶרֶת יָבָם. וְטַעְמָא יָלֵיף בַּגְּמָרָא. עָשְׂתָה שִׁשָּׁה חֳדָשִׁים בִּפְנֵי הַבַּעַל. מֵהָנָךְ שְׁנֵים עָשָׂר חֹדֶשׁ הַקְּבוּעִים לָהּ מִשֶּׁתְּבָעָהּ הַבַּעַל. אוֹ אֲפִילּוּ כּוּלָּם בִּפְנֵי הַבַּעַל וְאֶחָד בִּפְנֵי הַיָּבָם. אע"ג דְּרוּבָּא בִּפְנֵי הַבַּעַל — סוֹף לֹא נִתְחַיֵּיב בִּמְזוֹנוֹתֶיהָ בְּחַיָּיו, וְהוּא הַדִּין נַמִי אִם נִתְחַיֵּיב בְּחַיָּיו לֹא אָכְלָה מִשֶּׁמֵּת, דְּקִנְיַין הַבַּעַל פָּקַע. אֶלָּא דְּאִי כּוּלָּם בִּפְנֵי הַבַּעַל — הֲוָה אָכְלָה מִיהָא בְּחַיָּיו. אוֹ כּוּלָּן בִּפְנֵי הַיָּבָם. בַּגְּמָרָא פָּרֵיךְ עֲלָהּ: לְמַאי תַּנְיָא? זוֹ מִשְׁנָה רִאשׁוֹנָה. דְּמִשֶּׁהִגִּיעַ זְמַן אוֹכֶלֶת בִּתְרוּמָה.

אֵין

תוספות

שתים ושלש שנים. אין לדקדק כאן: השתא שלש מותר, שתים מיבעיא? דדלמא שתים ושלש ואפי' טובא, כדאמרי אינשי. כדמשני בפרק "מפנין" (שבת קכז.). ואין להאריך כאן*. **ולא** פליגי תרי גברי אליבא דחד גברא. וא"ת: ומאי נפקא מינה? דהשתא נמי פליגי ר' יוחנן ור' יהושע ב"ל אליבא דחד תנא, ומה לי תרי אמוראי אליבא דחד אמורא ומה לי אליבא דחד תנא? וי"ל: דאי פליגי ר' יוחנן ור' יהושע בן לוי אליבא דחד תנא — לא חיישינן, דבסברא הוא דפליגי, ולא טעו בשמועתם. אבל אי פליגי רבין ורב דימי בדברי רבי יוחנן ורבי יהושע בן לוי, שזה אומר: כך אמר, וזה אומר: כך אמר — אחד מהם טעה בשמועתו.

ואין

תוספות רי"ד

אחתא דרמי בר פפא הוה נסיבא ליה לרב אויא. אירכס כתובתה אתא לקמיה דר"י א"ל מאי לשהויי. א"ל הכי אמר ר"י א"ש זו דברי ר"מ אבל חכמים אומרים משהא אדם את אשתו ב' ג' שנים בלא כתובה. פי' זו דברי ר"מ דאמר לעיל דבפחות מר' הוי בעילת זנות וכ"ש אי לית לה כתובה לגמרי דהא הוא דאמר אסור לאדם לשהות את אשתו שעה אחת בלא כתובה ואפילו בתנאה מ"ט דלא סמכא דעתא ואע"ג דקי"ל דאי לא כתב ככתוב דמי דתנאי ב"ד כמאן דנקט שטריה בידיה הוא אפ"ה לא סמכא דעתא ומש"ה אמר ר"מ דהוי בעילת זנות אבל חכמים דלא חיישי להכי מותר להשהותה בלא כתובה. א"ל אביי והאר"נ א"ש הלכה כר"מ בגזירותיו פי' בחומרותיו בדבר שהוא מחמיר בד"ת באיסור והיתר ע"י גזירת דבריהם: א"ל א"ה זיל כתוב לה פי' כתובה אחריתי והא דתנן לעיל לא כתב לה כתובה בתולה גובה וכו'. ואוקימנא כר"מ התם במקום שאין כותבין כתובות דכלהו סמכי אתנאי ב"ד א"נ במקום שכותבין מיהו הבעילה באיסור הוא: **מתני'** נותנין לבתולה י"ב חודש משתבעה הבעל לפרנס א"ע כשם שנותנים לאשה כך נותנים לאיש לפרנס א"ע ולאלמנה שלשים יום הגיע זמן ולא נשאו או שמתו בעליהן אוכלת משלו ואוכלת בתרומה ר"ט אומר נותנים לה הכל תרומה ר"ע אומר מחצה חולין ומחצה תרומה היבם אינו מאכיל בתרומה עשתה ו' חדשים בפני הבעל ו' חדשים בפני היבם ואפילו כלן בפני הבעל חסר יום א' או כלן בפני היבם אינה אוכלת בתרומה זו משנה ראשונה אבל ב"ד של אחריהן אמרו אין האשה אוכלת בתרומה עד שתכנס לחופה. פי' נותנים לבתולה זמן מיום שתבעה הבעל לאחר שקידשה להזהירה על עסקי חופה ולזמן תכשיטיה לפרנס א"ע בתכשיטין ואם הגיע זמן זה ואינה חפיצה להנשא הויא לה מורדת לפחות לה כתובתה כדאמרינן לקמן (דף ס"ד) כותבין אגרת מרד על ארוסה א' ארוסה ואחת נשואה דאלמא ארוסה נמי דין מורדת יש לה: כשם שנותנים וכו'. לפרנס א"ע בצרכי חופה. ולאלמנה שאינה טורחת כ"כ בתכשיטין שכבר יש בידה הכל ל' יום: הגיע זמן ולא נישאו. פי' שהבעלים מעכבים והם בחיים אוכלת משלו ואוכלת בתרומה (א"ר חייא) [אם היא] בת ישראל נשאת לכהן שמשעה שקדשה אוכלת בתרומה מה"ת ומדרבנן הוא דגזור כדאמרינן לקמן ובהגיע הזמן ולא נשאו אכלה או אם הגיע הזמן ומתו בעליהן אוכלת משלו מן היורשים הם אוכלת בתרומה וגם אם היא זקוקה ליבם אוכלת בתרומה שכ"ז שנתחייב הבעל במזונותי' ואוכלת א) כגון תרומה היבם. ר"ט וכו' ור"ע אומר מחצה וכו'. כדי שתאכל בימי טומאתה. היבם אינו מאכיל בתרומה אהגיע זמן קאי שאע"פ שנתנו לו זמן לכנוס והגיע הזמן ולא כנס אינו מאכיל בתרומה כיון דלא אכלה בחיי בעלה כדמפרש טעמא לקמן מוכחן כי יקנה נפש קנין כספו והאי כסף אחיו הוא אבל משכנסה הרי היא כאשתו לכל דבר דכתיב ולקחה לו לאשה כדאמרינן ביבמות דקניא בביאה וכי היכי דקידושי ביאה מאכילין בתרומה דאיתקש הוויות להדדי. כך מאכילין ביבמה: עשתה ששה חדשים בפני הבעל מהנך י"ב חודש הקבועים לה משתבעה הבעל או אפילו כלם בפני הבעל חסר יום א' לפני היבם כיון דאכתי לא אכלה בחיי בעלה אין היבם מאכילה אבל אי עשתה כולן בפני הבעל דאכלה בחייו ה"נ היבם מאכילה דהיבם במקום בעל קיימי: או כלן בפני היבם נפרש לקמן. זו משנה ראשונה

דמשהגיע

עין משפט נר מצוה

[ועי' תוספות שבת ס. ד"ה השתא ובמה שמצויין שם על הגליון]

לג א מיי' פ"י מהלכ' אישות הלכ' י ופ"ד מהל' חובל הלכה יח סמג עשין מח טוש"ע אה"ע סי' סו סעיף ג וטוש"ע ח"מ סי' תכד סעיף י:

לד ב מיי' פ"י מהל' אישות הלכה יז סמג שם טוש"ע אה"ע סי' ט סעיף א:

לה ג מיי' שם הלכה יח טוש"ע שם סעי' ב:

לו ד מיי' שם הלכה יז טוש"ע שם סעי' א:

לז ה מיי' שם הלכ' יט טוש"ע שם סעיף ג:

לז [ה] [מיי' פי"ב מהל' אישות הלכה יג]:

לח ו מיי' פ"ח מהל' תרומות הלכה ה:

מסורת הש"ס

[מפורש בב"ק פט.]

[לקמן ס: עירובין מז.]

נדרים עג:

נדרים שם לעיל ב. מח: ע:

[עי' תוס' לקמן נח. ד"ה ואפי']

גליון הש"ס

רש"י ד"ה הא קמ"ל וכו' ואיכא למימר אלו ואלו דברי אלהים חיים. עירובין דף יג ע"ב:

א) נ"ל ואוכלת בתרומה גם היבם מאכילה.

אין האשה אוכלת בתרומה עד שתכנס לחופה.§ **גמ'** מנא הני מילי? אמר רב חסדא, דאמר קרא: °"ויאמר אחיה ואמה תשב הנערה אתנו ימים או עשור". מאי "ימים"? אילימא תרי יומי – משתעי איניש הכי? אמרו ליה: תרי יומי – אמר להו: לא. אמרו ליה עשרה יומי?! אלא מאי "ימים" – שנה, דכתיב: °"ימים תהיה גאולתו". ואימא חדש, דכתיב: °"עד חדש ימים"? אמרי: דנין "ימים" סתם מ"ימים" סתם, ואין דנין "ימים" סתם מ"ימים" שנאמר בהן "חדש". אמר רבי זירא, תנא: *קטנה, בין היא ובין אביה יכולין לעכב. בשלמא איהי – מצי מעכבא, אלא אביה, אי איהי ניחא לה – אביה מאי נפקא ליה מינה? סבר: השתא לא ידעה, למחר מימרדא ונפקא, ואתיא ונפלה עילואי. אמר רבי אבא בר לוי: אין פוסקין על הקטנה להשיאה כשהיא קטנה, אבל פוסקין על הקטנה להשיאה כשהיא גדולה. פשיטא! מהו דתימא: ליחוש דלמא מעיילא פחדא מהשתא וחלשה, קא משמע לן. אמר רב הונא: בגרה יום אחד ונתקדשה – נותנין לה שלשים יום כאלמנה. מיתיבי: בגרה – הרי היא כתבועה, מאי לאו – כתבועה דבתולה? לא, כתבועה דאלמנה. תא שמע: *בוגרת ששהתה שנים עשר חדש, רבי אליעזר אומר: הואיל וחייב בעלה במזונותיה – יפר! אימא: בוגרת וששהתה שנים עשר חודש, רבי אליעזר אומר: הואיל ובעלה חייב במזונותיה – יפר. תא שמע: המארס את הבתולה, בין שתבעה הבעל והיא מעכבת, ובין שתבעה היא ובעל מעכב – נותנין לה שנים עשר חדש משעת תביעה, אבל לא משעת אירוסין. ובגרה הרי היא כתבועה. כיצד? בגרה יום אחד ונתקדשה – נותנין לה שנים עשר חדש, ולארוסה שלשים יום. תיובתא דרב הונא! תיובתא. מאי ולארוסה שלשים יום? אמר רב פפא, הכי קאמר: בוגרת שעברו עליה שנים עשר חדש בבגרות, ונתקדשה – נותנין לה שלשים יום כאלמנה.§ הגיע זמן ולא נישאו.§ *אמר עולא: דבר תורה, ארוסה בת ישראל אוכלת בתרומה, שנאמר: °"וכהן כי יקנה נפש, *קנין כספו" – והאי נמי קנין כספו הוא. מה טעם אמרו אינה אוכלת – שמא ימזגו לה כוס בבית אביה, ותשקה לאחיה ולאחותה. אי הכי, הגיע זמן ולא נישאו נמי! התם דוכתא מייחד לה. אלא מעתה לקיט כהן לישראל לא ליכול בתרומה, דלמא אתו למיכל בהדיה! השתא מדידהו ספו ליה, מדידיה אכלי?! רב שמואל בר *רב יהודה אמר: משום סימפון. אי הכי נכנסה לחופה ולא נבעלה נמי! התם מיבדק בדיק לה, והדר מעייל. אלא מעתה, עבד כהן שלקחו מישראל לא ליכול בתרומה משום סימפון! *סימפון בעבדים ליכא; דאי דאבראי – הא קחזי ליה, ואי דגואי – למלאכה קא בעי, ושבסתר – לא איכפת ליה. *נמצא גנב או קוביוסטוס

רש"י

אין האשה אוכלת כו'. טעמא מפרש בגמרא: **גמ'** ואימא. מאי ימים – חודש, ועשור – עשרה ימים. יכולין לעכב. מלינקא עד שתגדל. מימרדא ונפקא. תמרוד בבעלה, שלא תוכל לסבול, ותלא ותבא אלי עד שתגדל, ונמצאתי צריך לתכשיטין אחרים. להשיאה כשהיא קטנה. שטורח הוא לה. אבל פוסקין כו'. ודוקא בלא קידושין. אבל קידושין בקטנות – לא, עד שתגדל ותאמר בפלוני אני רוצה. נותנין לה שלשים יום כאלמנה. משעת אירוסין. שכיון שבגרה היא מכינה תכשיטין קודם בגרות, שאינה רוצה לשהות עוד. כתבועה. כאילו תבעה להכין עצמה לנישואין. דבתולה. שנים עשר חודש משעת אירוסין. יפר. נדריה בלא שותפות דאב. שמעינן מינה דבוגרת נמי אינו חייב במזונותיה עד שתשהה י"ב חודש. וששהתה. והכי קאמר: בוגרת לסוף שלשים, והנערה ששהתה שנים עשר חודש. בעל נמי יהבו ליה רבנן זימנא. כדתנן במתני': לפרנס עצמו בצרכי חופה. ולארוסה שלשים יום. ויש ארוסה שאין נותנים לה אלא שלשים יום. ולקמן מפרש לה. נותנין לה שלשים יום. משעת אירוסין. שמא ימזגו לה כוס. של תרומה. בבית אביה גרסינן. דוכתא מייחד לה. מאחר שהוא זן אותה תמיד, מוליאה מבית אביה ומייחד לה מקום, שלא תפסיד מזונותיו לחלקם לקרוביה. לקיט. ששוכרו ללקוט תבואתו. לקיט כהן. לקיט שהוא כהן, ונשכר לישראל. משום סימפון. הוא דאמר ארוסה לא תאכל תרומה עד שיגיע זמן שחייב במזונותיה. ולשון סימפון הוא ביטול, כגון שובר המבטל שטר קרוי סימפון, ומום באשה או בבהמה שמבטל המקח קרוי סימפון. והכא גזור בה שמא ימצא בה מום, ונמצאו קידושי טעות ובטלים, ונמצא שאכלה זרה בתרומה. אי הכי נכנסה לחופה ולא נבעלה. קס"ד שעדיין אינו מכיר במומין שבה, ואמאי תני מתני', אפילו למשנה אחרונה, עד שתכנס לחופה? וכ"ש דקשיא משהגיע זמן דמשנה ראשונה. מיבדק בדיק לה. ע"י קרובותיו. סימפון בעבדים ליכא. אין מומין מבטל מקח.

קוביוסטוס

תוספות

ואין דנין ימים סתם מימים שנאמר בהם "חדש". והא דכתיב "ובכתה את אביה ואת אמה ירח ימים" ודרשינן בשילהי "החולץ" (יבמות דף מח:): "ירח" – שלשים, "ימים" – שלשים, ולא אמר התם ימים שנים עשר חודש – משום דכתיב אצל "ירח". **אי** איהי ניחא לה אביה מאי נפקא ליה מינה. משמע כיון דלא נפקא ליה מינה הוי מרידה, ופוחתין מכתובתה. ותימה: דאטו משום דאין האב רוצה, נקנוס הקטנה בכתובתה? היא מה פשעה! וי"ל: דהוה לן למימר יגרשנה בלא כתובה, שהרי כתובתה לאב. **בגרה** יום אחד ונתקדשה כו'. וא"ת: ומתני' דקתני דמשתבעה נותנין לה י"ב חודש, היכי משכחת לה? כיון דאין נותנין לעולם אלא ל' יום בבגרות, דמסתמא איירי בנתקדשה כשהיא נערה, כמו שדרך בני אדם, דאסור לקדש את בתו קטנה, ואין פוסקין נמי על הקטנה להשיאה! וי"ל: דדוקא בבגרה ואח"כ נתקדשה קאמר רב הונא דאין לה אלא ל' יום, אבל נתקדשה קודם בגרות – יש לה י"ב חודש משעת תביעה. וטעמא, דכשבגרה קודם שנתקדשה אין לה י"ב חודש – דמסתמא הכינה כל תכשיטיה, שאם ימלא לה בעל יהא הכל מוכן. אבל נתקדשה קודם בגרות – אינה מקפדת, שכבר היא מקודשת. **מאי** לאו כתבועה דבתולה. ולא מצי לשנויי: אין, כתבועה דבתולה, ובשקידשה ואח"כ בגרה. דפשיטא ליה דאז לא הוי בגר כתבועה. ור"ת מפרש: דסתם האי לישנא דבגרה משמע שנתקדשה (א) בבגר, ולא קודם. **תיובתא** דרב הונא תיובתא. תימה: דהכא קאי בתיובתא, ובפ' "נערה המאורסה" (נדרים דף ע:) אתיא סוגיא סתמא דהתלמוד כוותיה, דקאמר אמילתיה דרבי אליעזר [ההיא דבוגרת ששהתה י"ב חודש] דמייתי לעיל – בוגרת בל' יום סגי – אימא בוגרת וששהתה, והיינו כרב הונא! ונראה לפרש דה"ק: בוגרת בל' יום סגי. והיכי קתני במתני' בוגרת ששהתה שנים עשר חודש, דמשמע דבוגרת לא סגי לה בשום ענין בלא שנים עשר חודש, בל' יום סגי, כגון שקידשה לאחר ששהתה י"ב חודש בבגרות. ומשני: תני בוגרת וששהתה. והשתא קתני סתם בוגרת בהדי נערה ששהתה שנים עשר חודש, ובהדי אלמנה ששהתה שלשים יום, משום דיש בוגרת שדינה כנערה בשנים עשר חודש, כגון בגרה יום אחד ונתקדשה. ויש בוגרת שדינה כאלמנה כגון עמדה י"ב חודש בבגרותה ונתקדשה. והשתא אתיא דלא כרב הונא. ובפירוש דסוגיא דהתם אין להאריך כאן. **לקיט** כהן כו'. מעשיר לא פריך, דלא שכיח שיאכל בבית ישראל, וגם אין רגילין להוליך תרומה עמהם, אבל לקוטות – רגילין להשתכר עם ישראל, ופעמים מתפרנסים משל עצמם. **השתא** מדידהו ספו ליה כו'. ולקיט ישראל בבית כהן לא חיישינן כלל. דדוקא מלקיט כהן בבית ישראל הוא דפריך, לפי שדרך האכסנאי להשקות לבני הבית כדי למצוא חן בעיניהם. וכשהוא מושיט להם – אינו מדקדק מה הוא נותן. אבל ללקיט ישראל בבית כהן, כשפרנסתו עליו בשעת אכילה – מדקדק היטב מה הוא נותן לו.

קוביוסטוס

תוספות רי"ד

דמשהגיע זמן אוכלת בתרומה אבל ב"ד וכו'. כדמפרש טעמא לקמן משום גזירה דעולא: נותנין לבתולה י"ב חודש וכו' מנה"מ אר"ח דאמר קרא תשב הנערה אתנו ימים או עשור מאי ימים אי נימא תרי יומא מישתעי אינשי הכי דאמרי תרי יומא ואי לא עשרה יומא אלא מאי ימים שנה דכתיב ימים תהיה גאולתו ואימא ימים דחודש דכתיב עד חודש ימים דנין ימים סתם מימים סתם ואין דנין ימים סתם מימים שנאמר בהן חודש: אר"ז קטנה בין היא בין אביה יכולין לעכב פי' שאם נתארסה יכולים לעכב יותר מי"ב חודש שלא להשיאה לו עד שתגדיל בשלמא איהי מצי מעכבא ע"י שקטנה היא ותשמיש קשה לה ואם תנשא לו היום ולמחר כשאינה יכולה לסבול תשמיש וטורח הבית תמרוד בו עד שיגרשנה ותחזור לביתה ונמצאת צריך תכשיטין אחרים ומפני טענה זו יש בידה לעכב אלא אביה אי איהי ניחא לה אביה מאי נפקא ליה מיניה סבר השתא לא ידעא למחר מימרדא ואתיא ונפלה עלי: א"ר [אבא] בר לוי תנא אין פוסקים על הקטנה להשיאה כשהיא קטנה. פי' משום טעמא דאמרן אבל פוסקין על הקטנה להשיאה כשהיא גדולה פשיטא מ"ד ניחוש דלמא מעיילא בלבה פחד (או חלשא) [מהשתא וחלשא] קמ"ל. פי' מעכשיו נותנין אל לבה פחד תשמיש וטורח הבית הואיל ומזכירה לה בקוטנה ואימא דאין פוסקין קמ"ל דפוסקין: ת"ר המארס את הבתולה בין שתבעה היא והבעל מעכב בין שתבע הבעל והיא מעכבת נותנים לה י"ב חודש משעת תביעה אבל לא משעת האירוסין ובגר ה"ה כתביעה כיצד בגרה יום א' ונתקדשה נותנים לה י"ב חודש. פי' כבתולה: ולארוסה ל' יום מאי ולארוסה ל' יום אמר ר"פ ה"[ק] (ארוסה) בוגרת שעברו עליה י"ב חודש בבגרותה ונתקדשה נותנים לה ל' יום כאלמנה. א) פי' אפי' לא בגרה אלא יום א' נותנים לה ל' יום כאלמנה וא"צ להמתין עד י"ב חודש לפרנסה שמאחר שבגרה אין רצויה לשה[ות] עוד ומשעה שקירב זמנה לעמוד על פירקה זמנה תכשיטיה. לפיכך נותנים לה ל' יום שהוא זמן מועט כדי לתקן שאר דברים קטנים: הגיע זמן ולא נישאו וכו' אמר עולא ארוסה בת ישראל ד"ת אוכלת בתרומה שנא' וכהן כי יקנה נפש קנין כספו ומ"ט אמרו אינה אוכלת גזירה שמא ימזגו לה כוס בבית חמי' הואיל ומה"ת אוכלת פי' ותשקה לאחי' ולאחיות' ע' פתרון זה בשמעתא קמייתא דקידושין א"ה אפילו הגיע זמן ולא נשאו נ[מי] התם

א) אולי צ"ל פי' ולא כרב הונא דאמר דאפילו לא בגרה וכו'.

עין משפט נר מצוה

לט א מיי' פ"ו מהל' תרומות הלכה ג ופ"ח הלכה ז:

מ ב מיי' פ"י מהל' אישות הלכה טז סמג עשין מח טוש"ע אה"ע סי' נה סעיף ד:

מא ג מיי' פ"ג מהל' אישות הלכה יט ופי"א מהל' גירושין הלכ' א סמג עשין נ טוש"ע שם סימן לז סעיף ח:

מב ד ה מיי' פ"י מהל' אישות הלכה יז סמג שם טוש"ע שם סימן נה סעיף א:

מג ו מיי' פ"ו מהל' תרומות הלכה ג:

מד ז ח מיי' פט"ו מהל' מכירה הלכה יב יג סמג לאוין קע טוש"ע ח"מ סי' רלב סעיף י:

הגהות הב"ח

(א) תוס' ד"ה מאי לא וכו' שנתקדשה בבגר. נ"[ב] וכן מוכח ממאי דפריך בסמוך מהא דתניא בוגרת ששהתה י"ב חודש ר"[א] אומר יפר כו' דקשה נמ[י] דלמא איירי כשנתקדש[ה] קודם שתתבגר:

מסורת הש"ס

[לעיל מח: קדושין י:] [תוספתא רפ"ה] נדרים ע: עג: קדושין ה. י: [יבמות סח.] [מלת רב נראה מיותר ועי' רש"י ריש נח: ד"ה אלא לרב שמואל בר יהודה וכו'] [קדושין יא. ע"ש [illegible] ועי' תוס' גיטין פו. ד"ה עד] [תוספתא דב"ב פ"ד]

בראשית כד; ויקרא כה; במדבר יא; ויקרא כב

*קוביוסטוס – הגיעו. מאי איכא – לסטים מזויין או מוכתב למלכות – הנהו קלא אית להו. מכדי, בין למר ובין למר לא אכלה. מאי בינייהו? איכא בינייהו: קבל, *מסר, והלך.§ רבי טרפון אומר: נותנין לה הכל תרומה וכו'.§ אמר אביי: מחלוקת בבת כהן לכהן, אבל בבת ישראל לכהן – דברי הכל מחצה חולין ומחצה תרומה. ואמר אביי: מחלוקת בארוסה, אבל בנשואה – דברי הכל מחצה חולין ומחצה תרומה. תניא נמי הכי, *רבי טרפון אומר: נותנין לה הכל תרומה. ר"ע אומר: [א]מחצה חולין ומחצה תרומה. במה דברים אמורים – בבת כהן לכהן, אבל בת ישראל לכהן – דברי הכל מחצה חולין ומחצה תרומה. במה דברים אמורים – בארוסה, אבל בנשואה – דברי הכל מחצה חולין ומחצה תרומה. רבי יהודה בן בתירא אומר: נותנין לה שתי ידות של תרומה, ואחת של חולין. רבי יהודה אומר: נותן לה הכל תרומה, והיא מוכרת ולוקחת בדמים חולין. רבן שמעון בן גמליאל אומר: כל מקום שהוזכרה תרומה – נותנין לה כפלים בחולין. מאי בינייהו? איכא בינייהו טירחא.§ היבם אינו מאכיל בתרומה.§ מאי טעמא? *"קנין כספו" אמר רחמנא, והאי – קנין דאחיו הוא.§ עשתה ששה חדשים בפני הבעל.§ השתא בפני הבעל אמרת – לא, בפני היבם מיבעיא?! *זו ואין צריך לומר זו קתני.§ זו משנה ראשונה כו'.§ מאי טעמא? אמר עולא ואיתימא רב שמואל בר יהודה: משום סימפון. בשלמא לעולא, קמייתא – שמא ימזגו לה כוס בבית אביה, ובתרייתא – משום סימפון. אלא

ויקרא כב

רש"י

קוביוסטוס. גונב נפשות. הגיעו. ללוקח, ואין המקח בטל. וברייתא היא בב"ב ב"המוכר פירות": המוכר עבד לחבירו ונמצא גנב או קוביוסטוס – הגיעו, שסתמן גנבים הן. לסטים מזוין. אין דרכו בכך. מוכתב למלכות. חטא למלכות, עד שצוה לגזור עליו שיהרגוהו כל מוצאו. קלא אית להו. וסבר וקביל. תורה אור

קבל מסר והלך. קיבל עליו בעל את המומין, לסימפון – ליכא למיחש, לשמא תשקה לאחיה ולאחותה – איכא למיחש. מסר. האב לשלוחי הבעל, או שהלכו שלוחי האב עם שלוחי הבעל – ליכא למיחש שמא תשקה לאחיה ולאחותה, דהא ליתנהו גבה, *ואיכא למיחש לסימפון. בת כהן בקיאה היא בשמירת תרומה, ולמוכרה בימי טומאתה. בת ישראל אינה בקיאה בכך. בארוסה. ובת כהן, דהואיל והיא בבית אביה – טרח אביה למכור תרומה בחולין לימי טומאה, לפי שהוא רגיל בכך. אבל בנשואה. שנותן לה בעלה מזונות בביתה, כגון משרה אשתו על ידי שליש, דתנן במתניתין (לקמן דף סד:). מחצה חולין. לפי שכל כבודה בת מלך פנימה, ואביה ואחיה אינן אצלה שיתעסקו בצרכיה. רבי יהודה אומר נותנין לה הכל תרומה כו'. בין רבי יהודה לרבי טרפון איכא, דאילו ר' טרפון סבר נותנין לה תרומה כדי מזונותיה, ואע"פ שהיא צריכה לחולין, ובאה למכור תרומה – אין דמי תרומה מגיעין ליקח בהן חולין, שהרי יקרים הם מן התרומה, שהכל קופצים עליהן. ולרבי יהודה נותנין לה תרומה כשיעור שהיא באה ליקח ממנה חולין לא תפחות מן דמי מחצית חולין, אבל טורח מכירה – מוטל עליה למכור, לתתה תחת חולין. נותנין לה תרומה כפלים בחולין. קסבר: לא מטרחינן לה למוכרה בשוייה, אלא נותן לה תרומה הרבה כדי שתתננה בזול, ותמצא לוקחין הרבה. איכא בינייהו טירחא. בין רבי יהודה לרבן שמעון. והאי קנין אחיו הוא. וכי מיית ליה פקע ליה קנינו. אבל כנסה – הרי היא אשתו לכל דבר, והכתוב קראה אשתו, דכתיב (דברים כה) "ולקחה לו לאשה" – דקנייה בביאה. וכי היכי דקידושי ביאה מאכילין בארוסה, דאיתקוש הוויות להדדי – כך מאכילין ביבמה. השתא בפני הבעל. חוץ מיום אחד אמרת לא אכלה. כולם בפני היבם, דבעל ידו אין לה לאכול, דלאו קנינו היא – מיבעיא ליה למימר דלא אכלה? קמייתא. משנה ראשונה שאוסרת משעת אירוסין, שהתורה התירתה והם גזרו עד שיגיע זמן – לא גזור מפני סימפון, אלא שמא תשקה, הלכך, משנתחייב לזונה, דמייחד לה דוכתא, וליכא למיחש לשמא תשקה – שריוה. ובתרייתא. משנה אחרונה, שחזרו וגזרו עד שתכנס לחופה – חשו לסימפון. אלא

תוספות

קוביוסטוס · פירש בקונטרס: גונב נפשות. ולא משמע הכי בפרק קמא דבכורות (דף ה. ושם), *דקא אמר ליה קיסר לרבן גמליאל: משה רבכם גנב היה או קוביוסטוס היה, או שאינו בקי בחשבונות היה. והתם אממון קאי, דאשאילה ראשונה, דבכלן של לוים אתה מוצא כו' ככר השיבו. ועוד, ד"הגיעו" מפרש בקונטרס דרובם הכי איתנהו', ואין נראה שיהיו רוב העבדים גונבי נפשות! ונראה כפירוש רבינו חננאל, דמפרש: קוביוסטוס – משחק בקוביא. והא דאמרי' (חולין דף נא:): "ויאמר שלחני כי עלה השחר" אמר ליה יעקב: וכי גנב אתה או קוביוסטוס אתה שאתה מתיירא מן השחר? לפירוש הקונטרס אתי שפיר. ולפירוש רבינו חננאל נמי י"ל שדרך משחקין בקוביא שנושין בהן, ודרכן להטמין מפני אדם. **הנהו** קלא אית להו. פירש בקונטרס: וסבר וקביל. וקשה לר"ת: דבריש "המוכר פירות" (ב"ב דף צג: ושם) אמר בהדיא: ליסטים מזויין או מוכתב למלכות – אומר לו: הרי שלך לפניך. ועוד, אמרי' בפרק "האומנין" (ב"מ דף פ. ושם): בפחה זו שוטה היא, נכפית היא כו' – הרי זה מקח טעות. אם כן בהנך מומי ניחוש לסימפון! ומפר"ת: קלא אית להו, ולא שכיחי, ולא חיישינן בהו לסימפון כיון דלא שכיחי. והנהו נמי דפרק "האומנין", לא שכיחי. והא דאמרינן בפרק "המגרש" (גיטין דף פו. ושם) דאתקין רב יהודה בשטרא דעבדי "עבדא דנן מולדק לעבדות, ופטיר ועטיר מן ערורי מלכא ומלכתא" – לא משום שהיה צריך להתנות, כדפי' דבשתמא נמי הוי מקח טעות, אלא משום שופרא דשטרא. ורבינו אליהו היה מקיים פירוש הקונטרס, דהיכא דקיבל המוכר מעות אמרי' מדלא בדק הלוקח קודם נתינת מעות הני מומין דאית להו קלא – א"כ סבר וקיבל. והא דאומר לו הרי שלך לפניך – מיירי קודם שנתן הלוקח מעות. וקצת משמע כן בפרק "המוכר פירות" (ב"ב דף צג:) דפריך [שם: הגיעו, לאו משום דרובא הכי איתנהו, וש"מ דאזלינן בתר רובא. ומאי פריך? דלמא] המוציא מחבירו עליו הראיה. אלמא מיירי שהלוקח מוחזק. *ואפילו כולן בפני הבעל חוץ מיום אחד אינה אוכלת. פירש בקונטרס: דהוא הדין אפילו כולם בפני הבעל לא אכלה משמת, דקנין כספו פקע ליה. אלא דאי כולן בפני הבעל – הוה אכלה מיהא בחייו. ולר"ת נראה: דהך דרשא דדריש בגמרא: קנין כספו אמר רחמנא, והאי קנין דאחיו הוא – אסמכתא בעלמא הוא. דמדאורייתא מיכל אכלה, ולפי משנה ראשונה היכא דאכלה בחיי הבעל – אוכלת נמי בזיקת היבם, מדקתני: ואפי' כולם בפני הבעל חוץ מיום אחד. משמע, הא כולן בפני הבעל – אוכלת. ועוד: דתנן בפרקין בסדר משנת ירושלמית: הגיע זמן ולא נשאו, או שמתו בעליהן – אוכלות משלו ואוכלות בתרומה. משמע כשמתו בעליהן – שהיבם מאכילן בלא ביאה, דומיא דהגעת זמן, דמיירי בלא נשאו, דאי אחר ביאה – פשיטא, דאשתו גמורה היא. ועוד מביא ראיה, מדתניא בתוספתא: זו משנה ראשונה, רבותינו אמרו: אין האשה אוכלת בתרומה עד שתכנס לחופה, ולא היבמה עד שתיבעל. והיינו טעמא דמשנה ראשונה, דכשלא אכלה בחיי הבעל אינה אוכלת – דהא איכא למיחש לסימפון, ולשמא תשקה. דהא כיון דלא הגיע זמן בחיי הבעל – לא בדק לה, דאינו חייב במזונותיה אלא א"כ עמד בדין וברח, כדאמרינן ב"החולץ" (יבמות דף מא:), ולא מייחד לה דוכתא. וטעמא משום שאין דרך לאחר, אלא מיד הוא רגיל או לחלוץ או לייבם, לכך לא תקנו לה מזונות מיבם כמו שתקנו מזונות בהגעת זמן דבעל. אבל כשאכלה בחיי הבעל – תו ליכא למיחש לסימפון, ולשמא תשקה נמי ליכא למיחש, דכיון דהגיע זמן – מייחד לה דוכתא בבית אביה, מסתמא אוכלת שם בכל שעה ואינה זזה ממקומה. וא"ת: ומאחר דמדאורייתא אכלה כשנפלה מן הנשואין, למה אסורה למשנה אחרונה עד שתיבעל? הא ליכא למיחש לסימפון, שכבר נבדקה בדיקת פנים! ויש לומר: דמאחר שאסרו ארוסה שהגיע זמנה – אסרו נמי ביבמה, משום דמיחלפא בה, ששתיהן זמן כניסתן לאלתר. אבל ק"ק: אי חשיבא יבמה קנין כספו דיבם – הא דקאמר ביבמות בפרק "אלמנה" (דף סז: ושם) גבי הא דתנן היבם פוסל ואינו מאכיל: אי בת כהן לישראל – היא פסיל לה "ושבה אל בית אביה כו'" ה"ל למימר דהא קנייה, כדקאמר התם גבי אירוסין! ויש לומר: ד"ושבה אל בית אביה" אתא למיפסל בת כהן לישראל, למידק: הא מעיקרא לא אכלה, כדאמר התם (דף סח.). א"כ לא אייתר לשומרת יבם, אלא הכי קאמר: "ושבה" כתיב, כלומר: דווקא אותה ששבה אל בית אביה. אבל זאת שזקוקה ליבם – אינה שבה, שהרי חשובה כאילו קנויה לו. **השתא** בפני הבעל אמרת לא, בפני היבם מיבעיא. ה"ג: [לא] זו אף זו קתני. לא מיבעיא ששה חדשים בפני הבעל וששה בפני היבם דלא אכלה, אלא אפילו כולם בפני הבעל חוץ מיום אחד לא אכלה. וכן מוכיח בירושלמי, דמפרש כולה מתניתין [בלא] זו אף זו.

מאי

תוספות רי"ד

התם דוכתא מייחד לה. פי' מאחר שהוא זן אותה תמיד מוציאה מבית אביה ומייחד לה מקום שלא תפסיד מזונותיו. פי' כי היכי דלא ליכול אינש בהדה: ר"ט אומר וכו' אמר אביי מחלוקת בבת כהן לכהן אבל בת ישראל לכהן דברי הכל מחצה חולין ומחצה תרומה פי' בת כהן אם תטמא יחליף לה אביה חולין בתרומה וחזיא לה ולא תצטרך למוכרה לכהנים בזול ולקנות חולין ביוקר אבל בת ישראל לכהן אין מי שיחליף לה ותצטרך למכור להם בזול הלכך נותנים לה מחצה חולין: ואמר אביי מחלוקת בארוסה פי' ובת כהן. אבל בנשואה ד"ה מחצה חולין ומחצה תרומה: היבם אינו מאכיל בתרומה מ"ט קנין כספו אמר רחמנא והאי קנין דאחיו הוא פי' והלכך אין לו כח להאכילה בגינו אך אם אכלה בחיי הבעל אוכלת דיבם במקום בעל קאי ומכח בעלה קאכלה: או כלם וכו' השתא כלם בפני הבעל חוץ מיום א אמרת לא אכלה כלן בפני היבם דע"י אין לה לאכול דלא קנינו הוא לא מיבעיא זו ואצ"ל זו קתני: זו משנה ראשונה וכו'. תניא בתוספתא ולא היבמה עד שתבעל. פי' זו רבנן שאמרו הגיע זמן ולא נשאו שהיא אוכלת בתרומה הוא משנה ראשונה אבל ב"ד של אחריהם אמרו אין האשה אוכלת בתרומה עד שתכנס לחופה וכן היבמה עד שתבעל ואע"ג דאכלה בחיי בעלה מ"ט אמר עולא ואיתימא ר"ש ב"י משום סימפון

מסורת הש"ס

כ"ב לג: קדושין יח.

[הא דחיישינן הכא לסימפון במסר היינו כרב דאמר לעיל מסירתה לכל חוץ מתרומה. גי' ת"י] [ועי' תוס' דלעיל מח: שילהי ד"ה רב אסי]

[תוספתא רפ"ה]

[יבמות סז:]

[עירובין טו. וש"נ]

[עי' בכורות ה. איתא בנוסחא אחרת ועי' רש"י בחולין נא: ד"ה ועוד שאלו]

גי' רש"ל

שייך לעיל דף נז ע"א על המשנה

עין משפט נר מצוה

מה א מיי' פי"ב מהל' אישות הלכה יג:

מו א ב מיי' פ"ו מהל' ערכין הלכה כח סמג עשין קלב טוש"ע אה"ע סי' פא סעיף א:
מז ג ד מיי' פי"ב מהלכ' אישות הלכה ד סמג עשין מח טוש"ע אה"ע סי' סט סעיף ד וסי' פ סעיף טו בהג"ה וסימן פא סעיף א בהג"ה:
מח ה מיי' פ"ט מהל' עבדים הלכ' ז סמג עשין עב טוש"ע י"ד סי' רסז סעיף כ:
[ב"ק ח: ב"ב מט: גיטין עז:] לקמן ע. פג: קז:
מט ו מיי' פכ"א מהל' אישות הלכה י סמג לאוין פא טוש"ע אה"ע סי' פ סעיף טו:
נ ז ח מיי' פ"ו מהל' ערכין הלכה כח סמג עשין קלב טוש"ע שם סי' פא סעיף א:

תורה אור

אֶלָּא לְרַב שְׁמוּאֵל בַּר יְהוּדָה, קַמַּיְיתָא מִשּׁוּם סִימְפּוֹן וּבַתְרַיְיתָא מִשּׁוּם סִימְפּוֹן?! מַאי בֵּינַיְיהוּ? אִיכָּא בֵּינַיְיהוּ בְּדִיקַת חוּץ. מָר סָבַר: בְּדִיקַת חוּץ — שְׁמָהּ בְּדִיקָה, וּמָר סָבַר: בְּדִיקַת חוּץ לָא שְׁמָהּ בְּדִיקָה.§ **מתני'** *אהַמַּקְדִּישׁ מַעֲשֵׂה יְדֵי אִשְׁתּוֹ — הֲרֵי זוֹ עוֹשָׂה וְאוֹכֶלֶת. הַמּוֹתָר, רַבִּי מֵאִיר אוֹמֵר: הֶקְדֵּשׁ, רַבִּי יוֹחָנָן הַסַּנְדְּלָר אוֹמֵר: בחוּלִּין.§ **גמ'** *אָמַר רַב הוּנָא *אָמַר רַב: גיְכוֹלָה אִשָּׁה לוֹמַר לְבַעְלָהּ "אֵינִי נִיזּוֹנֶת וְאֵינִי עוֹשָׂה". קָסָבַר: כִּי תַּקִּינוּ רַבָּנַן מְזוֹנֵי — עִיקָּר, וּמַעֲשֵׂה יָדֶיהָ — מִשּׁוּם אֵיבָה. וְכִי אָמְרָה "אֵינִי נִיזּוֹנֶת וְאֵינִי עוֹשָׂה" — הָרְשׁוּת בְּיָדָהּ. מֵיתִיבֵי: *תִּקְּנוּ מְזוֹנוֹת תַּחַת מַעֲשֵׂה יָדֶיהָ! אֵימָא: דתִּקְּנוּ מַעֲשֵׂה יָדֶיהָ תַּחַת מְזוֹנוֹת. לֵימָא מְסַיֵּיעַ לֵיהּ: הַמַּקְדִּישׁ מַעֲשֵׂה יְדֵי אִשְׁתּוֹ — הֲרֵי הִיא עוֹשָׂה וְאוֹכֶלֶת. מַאי לָאו — בְּנִיזּוֹנֶת? לָא, בְּשֶׁאֵינָהּ נִיזּוֹנֶת. אִי בְּשֶׁאֵינָהּ נִיזּוֹנֶת — מַאי לְמֵימְרָא? אֲפִי' *לְמַאן דְּאָמַר יָכוֹל הָרַב לוֹמַר לָעֶבֶד "עֲשֵׂה עִמִּי וְאֵינִי זָנְךָ", הָנֵי מִילֵּי — הבְּעֶבֶד כְּנַעֲנִי, דְּלָא כְּתִיב בֵּיהּ "עִמָּךְ". אֲבָל עֶבֶד עִבְרִי דִּכְתִיב בֵּיהּ °"עִמָּךְ" — לָא, וְכׇל שֶׁכֵּן אִשְׁתּוֹ! [דברים טו] סֵיפָא אִיצְטְרִיךְ לֵיהּ; מוֹתָר, רַבִּי מֵאִיר אוֹמֵר: הֶקְדֵּשׁ, רַבִּי יוֹחָנָן הַסַּנְדְּלָר אוֹמֵר: חוּלִּין. וּפְלִיגָא דְּרֵישׁ לָקִישׁ. דְּאָמַר רֵישׁ לָקִישׁ: *לָא תֵּימָא טַעֲמָא דְּרַבִּי מֵאִיר מִשּׁוּם דְּקָסָבַר אָדָם מַקְדִּישׁ דָּבָר שֶׁלֹּא בָּא לָעוֹלָם, אֶלָּא טַעֲמָא דְּרַבִּי מֵאִיר: מִתּוֹךְ ושֶׁיָּכוֹל לְכוֹפָהּ לְמַעֲשֵׂה יָדֶיהָ — נַעֲשָׂה כְּאוֹמֵר לָהּ ז"יִקָּדְשׁוּ יָדַיִךְ לְעוֹשֵׂיהֶם". *חוְהָא לָא אָמַר לָהּ הָכִי! כֵּיוָן דִּשְׁמַעִינַן לֵיהּ לְר"מ דְּאָמַר: *אֵין אָדָם מוֹצִיא דְּבָרָיו לְבַטָּלָה — נַעֲשָׂה כְּאוֹמֵר לָהּ "יִקָּדְשׁוּ יָדַיִךְ לְעוֹשֵׂיהֶם". וְסָבַר רַבִּי מֵאִיר: אֵין אָדָם מַקְדִּישׁ דָּבָר שֶׁלֹּא בָּא לָעוֹלָם? וְהָתַנְיָא: *הָאוֹמֵר לְאִשָּׁה "הֲרֵי אַתְּ מְקוּדֶּשֶׁת לִי לְאַחַר שֶׁאֶתְגַּיֵּיר" אוֹ "לְאַחַר שֶׁתִּתְגַּיְּירִי", "לְאַחַר שֶׁאֶשְׁתַּחְרֵר", "לְאַחַר שֶׁתִּשְׁתַּחְרְרִי", "לְאַחַר שֶׁיָּמוּת בַּעֲלֵיךְ" אוֹ "שֶׁתָּמוּת אֲחוֹתֵיךְ" אוֹ "לְאַחַר שֶׁיַּחֲלוֹץ לִיךְ יְבָמֵיךְ", רַבִּי מֵאִיר אוֹמֵר: מְקוּדֶּשֶׁת. ◦מֵהַהִיא — אִין, מֵהָא לֵיכָּא לְמִשְׁמַע מִינָּהּ.§ הַמּוֹתָר, רַבִּי מֵאִיר אוֹמֵר: הֶקְדֵּשׁ.§ אֵימַת קָדוֹשׁ? רַב וּשְׁמוּאֵל דְּאָמְרִי תַּרְוַיְיהוּ: מוֹתָר לְאַחַר מִיתָה קָדוֹשׁ. רַב אַדָּא בַּר אַהֲבָה אָמַר: מוֹתָר מֵחַיִּים קָדוֹשׁ. הָוֵי בָּהּ רַב פַּפָּא: בְּמַאי? אִילֵימָא בְּמַעֲלֶה לָהּ מְזוֹנוֹת, וּמַעֲלֶה לָהּ מָעָה כֶּסֶף לְצׇרְכֶיהָ — מ"ט דְּמ"ד לְאַחַר מִיתָה קָדוֹשׁ? וְאֶלָּא כְּשֶׁאֵין מַעֲלֶה לָהּ מְזוֹנוֹת, וְלָא מַעֲלֶה לָהּ מָעָה כֶּסֶף לְצׇרְכֶיהָ — מ"ט דְּמַאן דְּאָמַר מֵחַיִּים קָדוֹשׁ? לְעוֹלָם בְּמַעֲלֶה לָהּ מְזוֹנוֹת וְאֵינוֹ מַעֲלֶה לָהּ מָעָה כֶּסֶף לְצׇרְכֶיהָ. רַב וּשְׁמוּאֵל סָבְרִי: תִּקְּנוּ מְזוֹנוֹת

רש"י

אֶלָּא לְרַב שְׁמוּאֵל בַּר יְהוּדָה. דְּאָמַר לְעֵיל נַמִי טַעַם מִשְׁנָה רִאשׁוֹנָה מִשּׁוּם סִימְפּוֹן, וְהָשְׁתָּא נַמִי מוֹקֵי טַעַם ב"ד שֶׁל אַחֲרֵיהֶם מִשּׁוּם סִימְפּוֹן. מַאי בֵּינַיְיהוּ. כְּלוֹמַר, מָה רָאוּ רִאשׁוֹנִים לְהַתִּירָהּ מֵהַגִּיעַ זְמַן וְאֵילָךְ, וּמָה רָאוּ אַחֲרוֹנִים לוֹמַר עַד שֶׁתִּכָּנֵס לַחוּפָּה? מָר סָבַר. מִשְׁנָה רִאשׁוֹנָה. בְּדִיקַת חוּץ. שֶׁבְּדָקָהּ בְּיַד קְרוֹבוֹתָיו. שְׁמָהּ בְּדִיקָה. וְקוֹדֶם שֶׁיּוֹלִיא מָעוֹתָיו בִּמְזוֹנוֹתֶיהָ כְּבָר בְּדָקָהּ. הִלְכָּךְ, תּוּ לָא חָיְישִׁינַן לְסִימְפּוֹן. וּב"ד שֶׁל אַחֲרֵיהֶם סָבְרִי: אֵינָהּ בְּדִיקָה עַד שֶׁמִּתְיַיחֵד עִמָּהּ הוּא עַצְמוֹ וּבוֹדְקָהּ. **מתני'** מַעֲשֵׂה יְדֵי אִשְׁתּוֹ. בְּמַתְנִי' (לקמן דף סד:) מְפָרֵשׁ: מַה הִיא עוֹשָׂה לוֹ — מִשְׁקַל חָמֵשׁ סְלָעִים כו'. הֲרֵי זוֹ עוֹשָׂה וְאוֹכֶלֶת. אֵין מַעֲשֵׂה יָדֶיהָ קָדוֹשׁ עַל פִּיו. וּבַגְּמָרָא מְפָרֵשׁ לָהּ. הַמּוֹתָר. הִקְדִּישׁ אֶת מוֹתַר מַעֲשֵׂה יְדֵי אִשְׁתּוֹ מַה שֶּׁהִיא עוֹשָׂה לוֹ יוֹתֵר עַל הָרָאוּי שֶׁפָּסְקוּ חֲכָמִים, וְלֹא הִקְדִּישׁ מַעֲשֵׂה יָדֶיהָ עַצְמָן. וְהַמּוֹתָר קָנוּי לוֹ בְּמָעָה כֶּסֶף שֶׁתִּקְּנוּ לָהּ חֲכָמִים שֶׁיִּתֵּן לָהּ בְּכׇל שַׁבָּת מָעָה כֶּסֶף לְצׇרְכֶיהָ, לְבַד הַמְּזוֹנוֹת, כְּדִתְנַן בְּמַתְנִיתִין. רַבִּי מֵאִיר אוֹמֵר הֶקְדֵּשׁ כו'. מְפָרֵשׁ בַּגְּמָרָא. **גמ'** אֵינִי נִיזּוֹנֵית. מִשֶּׁלְּךָ. וְאֵינִי עוֹשָׂה. לְךָ כְּלוּם, אֶלָּא לְעַצְמִי. מְזוֹנֵי עִיקָּר. תְּחִילַּת תַּקָּנָתָא לְטוֹבָתָהּ תִּקְנוּהָ, מִשּׁוּם דִּזְמְנִין דְּלָא סַפְקָה בְּמַעֲשֵׂה יָדֶיהָ לִמְזוֹנוֹת, וְתִקְּנוּ תְּחִילָּה עִיקַּר תַּקָּנָתָא שֶׁיָּזוּן אֶת אִשְׁתּוֹ, וַהֲדַר תַּקּוּן לוֹ מַעֲשֵׂה יָדֶיהָ מִשּׁוּם אֵיבָה. וְכֵיוָן דְּעִיקַּר תַּקָּנְתָּא לְטוֹבָתָהּ, וּמִשּׁוּם דִּידָהּ הֲוַאי, כִּי אָמְרָה לָא נִיחָא לִי בְּהַאי טִיבוּתָא — שׁוֹמְעִין לָהּ. מַאי לָאו בְּנִיזּוֹנֶת. שֶׁיֵּשׁ לוֹ נְכָסִים, וּמְבַקֵּשׁ לְזוּנָהּ. וַאֲפִי' הָכִי תְּנַן: אֵין מַעֲשֵׂה יָדֶיהָ בִּרְשׁוּתוֹ לְהַקְדִּישָׁן. בְּשֶׁאֵינָהּ נִיזּוֹנֶת. שֶׁאֵין לוֹ בַּמֶּה לְזוּנָהּ. אֲפִי' לְמַאן דְּאָמַר כו'. פְּלוּגְתָּא בְּמַסֶּכֶת גִּיטִּין. סֵיפָא אִיצְטְרִיךְ לֵיהּ. לְאַשְׁמוּעִינַן פְּלוּגְתָּא בַּמּוֹתָר, דְּלָא שַׁיָּיךְ בַּמְּזוֹנוֹת. וְאַע"ג דְּאֵינָהּ נִזּוֹנֶת אִיכָּא לְמ"ד קָדוֹשׁ לְאַחַר מִיתָה כְּשֶׁיִּרָשֶׁנָּה, וּכְדִלְקַמָּן. וּפְלִיגָא. דְּרַב הוּנָא אַר"ש בֶּן לָקִישׁ. דָּבָר שֶׁלֹּא בָּא לָעוֹלָם. כְּגוֹן מַעֲשֵׂה יָדֶיהָ, שֶׁהִקְדִּישָׁן עַד שֶׁלֹּא עֲשָׂאָתָן. לְעוֹשֵׂיהֶן. לַמִּי שֶׁבְּרָאָן, וְיָדַיִם אִיתְנְהוּ בָּעוֹלָם. אַלְמָא: קָסָבַר יָכוֹל לְכוֹפָהּ, וְאֵינָהּ יְכוֹלָה לוֹמַר: אֵינִי נִיזּוֹנֵית וְאֵינִי עוֹשָׂה. וְהָא לָא אֲמַר. יִקָּדְשׁוּ יָדַיִךְ, אֶלָּא "מַעֲשֵׂה יָדַיִךְ". שָׁמְעִינַן לֵיהּ לְרַבִּי מֵאִיר. בְּמַסֶּכֶת עֲרָכִין (דף ה.), דְּאָמַר: אֵין אָדָם מוֹצִיא דְּבָרָיו לְבַטָּלָה. דִּתְנַן: הַמַּעֲרִיךְ פָּחוֹת מִבֶּן חֹדֶשׁ, ר"מ אוֹמֵר: נוֹתֵן דָּמָיו, דְּאָדָם יוֹדֵעַ שֶׁאֵין עֵרֶךְ לְפָחוֹת מִבֶּן חֹדֶשׁ, וְגָמַר וְאָמַר לְשֵׁם דָּמִים. הָכָא נַמִי, אָדָם יוֹדֵעַ שֶׁאֵין אָדָם מַקְדִּישׁ דָּבָר שֶׁלֹּא בָּא לָעוֹלָם, וְגָמַר וְאָמַר לְשֵׁם יָדַיִם עַצְמָן. לְאַחַר מִיתָה. כְּשֶׁתָּמוּת הִיא, וְיִירָשֶׁנָּה. מֵחַיִּים. כְּשֶׁתַּעֲשֶׂנּוּ. לְעוֹלָם בְּמַעֲלֶה לָהּ מְזוֹנוֹת כו'. וְה"ה נַמִי דְּמָצֵי לְאוֹקְמָא כְּשֶׁאֵין מַעֲלֶה לָהּ מְזוֹנוֹת וּמַעֲלֶה לָהּ מָעָה, אֶלָּא מִשּׁוּם רַב דְּאִית לֵיהּ יְכוֹלָה אִשָּׁה שֶׁתֹּאמַר "אֵינִי נִיזּוֹנֵית וְאֵינִי עוֹשָׂה". וְאוֹקֵי רֵישָׁא דְּמַתְנִי' דְּתָנֵי "עוֹשָׂה וְאוֹכֶלֶת" בְּנִיזּוֹנֶת, לְהָכִי אוֹקֵי סֵיפָא בְּנִיזּוֹנֶת. מְזוֹנוֹת

תוספות

מאי לאו בניזונת. לא כשהוא זן אותה קאמר, דאם כן - יקדשו מעשה ידיה, ואמאי עושה ואוכלת. כדקאמר לקמן: אי במעלה לה מזונות — מאי טעמא דמאן דאמר לאחר מיתה קדוש, פירוש: גם מחיים יהא קדוש! אלא בניזונת, כלומר: שהוא חפץ לזונה והיא אינה רוצה:

מתוך שיכול לכופה למעשה ידיה כו'. ומתני' דקתני עושה ואוכלת מוקי לה כרב אדא בר אהבה דבסמוך במעלה לה מזונות ואינו מעלה לה מעה כסף.

יקדשו ידיך לעושיהן. פירוש: להקב"ה שעשאן. אבל אין לפרש למלאכתן — דא"כ הל"ל למעשיהן, כדאמרינן בסוף פ"ק דנדרים (דף יג:).

לאחר שאתגייר. וא"ת: דבסוף פ"ק דגיטין (דף יג:) אמרינן: דאפילו לרבי מאיר דאמר אדם מקנה דבר שלא בא לעולם — ה"מ לדבר שהוא בעולם. אבל לדבר שלא בא לעולם — לא. והא "לאחר שאתגייר" הוי לדבר שלא בא לעולם! ואומר ר"י: ד"לאחר שאתגייר" לא חשיב כל כך דבר שלא בא לעולם, כיון שהגוף בעולם, אלא שמחוסר גירות ולא דמי לנולדים — דהתם לא באו לעולם כלל. וכעין זה תירץ ה"ר אליעזר משנז"א מה שמקשין אהא דאמר בריש "המפקיד" (ב"מ דף לג:) אימור דאמר ר"מ אדם מקנה דבר שלא בא לעולם — כגון פירות דקל דעבידי דאתו כו', והא כל הנהו דהכא לא עבידי דאתו! אלא הכא, כיון שהגוף בעולם — לא בעינן עבידי דאתו. וא"ת: אם כן מאי פריך הכא, וקאמר נמי מההיא אין, הא מההיא נמי לא שמעינן מעשה ידיה שאינם בעולם כלל, ואכתי מלי למימר דלא קדשי מעשה ידיה, אלא דנעשה כאומר יקדשו ידיך לעושיהן! וי"ל: כיון דבמקלת סבר רבי מאיר כרבי אליעזר בן יעקב — אית לן למימר דאף בדבר שלא בא לעולם כלל סבר כוותיה, דאית ליה ב"האשה רבה" (יבמות נג: ושם) וב"האומר" (קידושין דף סב:) דאדם מקנה. ועוד מתרץ: דכל הני דהכא איכא לאוקמא בדעבידי דאתו, כגון ששמע מרבו שישחררנו. ו"לאחר שימות בעליך ואחותיך" — כגון בגוססת, ו"לאחר שיחלוץ ליך יבמיך", באין דעתו של יבם. לייבם ומיהו ק"ק מותר דקדוש לאחר מיתה, אע"ג דלא עביד דאתי, דליכא לאוקמא בגוססת — דהא עושה מלאכה*. **אי** במעלה לה מזונות ומעלה לה מעה כסף מ"ט דמ"ד לאחר מיתה הוא קדוש. גם למ"ד מחיים הוא קדוש ה"מ למיפרך: כיון דמעלה מזונות ומעה כסף אמאי עושה ואוכלת? אלא משום דבעי למימר אי אין מעלה לה מזונות ולא מעה כסף — מ"ט דמאן דאמר מחיים הוא קדוש, נקט נמי הכא מ"ט דמ"ד לאחר מיתה הוא קדוש.

א) **במעלה** לה מזונות ואין מעלה לה מעה כסף. אליבא דרב אדא בר אהבה מוקי לה הכי. אבל רב ושמואל לא מלי מוקמי לה במעלה לה מזונות, דכיון דסברי דתיקנו מזונות תחת מעשה ידיה — א"כ אמאי עושה ואוכלת? אלא רב ושמואל מוקמי מתניתין בשאין מעלה לה מזונות ולא מעה כסף. ואם תאמר: ומאי דוחקיה דרב לאוקמא מתני' לאחר מיתה? לוקמה מחיים, וכגון דמעלה לה מעה כסף ואין מעלה לה מזונות! ויש לומר: דאין רגילות שיעלה לה מעה כסף ולא יעלה לה מזונות.

א) לרב ושמואל איכא לאוקמי מתני' במעלה לה מזונות והיא אינה רוצה דבהכי מיתוקמא מתני' לכולהו לרב ושמואל באינה רוצה ולרב אדא בר אהבה בניזונת ממנו. ת"י

[מיהו יש להעמיד בזקנה ועוד יש מפרשים דכל היכא דליכא אלא חד מי יימר חשיב עבידא דאתי ודוקא התם בהמפקיד גבי כפילא לא חשיב עבידא דאתי משום דאיכא מי יימר טובא מי יימר דמיגנבא ואת"ל דמיגנבא מי יימר דמשתכח גנבא כו'. ת"י]

תוספות רי"ד

סימפון שמא ימצא בה מומין שבסתר ויהיה קידושיו קידושי טעות. ודבר המבטל יקרא סמפון ולפיכך נקרא השובר סימפון: **מתני'** המקדיש מעשה ידי אשתו ה"ז עושה ואוכלת והמותר ר"מ אומר הקדש ור"י הסנדלר אומר חולין. פי' אפי' למ"ד שאין האשה יכולה לומר לבעלה איני ניזונת ואיני עושה אתיא מתני' וטעמא דמילתא מפני שיכול להערים ולומר איני רוצה לזונך והיא זקוקה להתפרנס ממעשה ידיה הלכך ה"ז עושה ואוכלת ואין ההקדש על מע"י חל מפני שהוא שלה. שאם תתפרנס היא ממנו והמותר מה שעשת יתר על מזונותיה של בעל [והכי תניא בתוספתא המקדיש מע"י אשתו ה"ז מעלה לה מתוכן פרנסה והשאר הקדש] ר"מ אומר הקדש דקסבר אדם מקדיש דבר שלא בא לעולם. יכולה אשה שתאמר לבעלה איני ניזונת ואיני עושה. פי' להאי סברא אפי' אותו המותר שעושה יתר על מזונותי' הוא שלה דאל"ה מאי מרווחת האשה בכך. א"ו הכל שלה ומפני שעושה יתר על מזונותי' מפני איני ניזונת ואיני עושה: ואי קשיא והאמרינן לקמן קונם שאני עושה לפיך א"צ להפר אלמא שמעשה ידיה הוא משועבד לבעל ואין הנדר חל עליו ואי אמרת יכולה אשה לומר לבעלה איני ניזונת ואיני עושה תשובה אע"ג דמציא למימר כ"ז שלא אמרה משועבד הוא מע"י לבעל והילכך א"צ להפר מיתיבי תיקנו מזונות תחת מע"י א) וקסבר מזוני עיקר ומע"י משום איבה וכך הלכה דהכי פסיק תלמודא כר"ה א"ר שתאמר וכו'. נימא מסייע ליה המקדיש ידי אשתו ה"ז עושה ואוכלת מאי לאו דניזונית. פי' שהבעל חפץ לזונה ואפ"ה היא עושה ואוכלת וטעמא דמילתא משום דמצי למימר א"נ וא"ע וכל מע"י שלה ואין ואפילו המותר שלה כדפי' והאי והמותר ר"מ אומר הקדש (שהוא) [היינו] לאחר מיתה שמה שנשאר לה ממע"י יורשה הבעל לאחר מיתתה והלכך ההקדש חל עליו שאדם מקדיש דשלב"ל: לא כשאינה ניזונת תסייע ולעולם לא מצי למימר הכי וטעמא דמערים ואינה רוצה לזונו והלכך ניזונית ממע"י. ולא חייל הקדש עילווי' כדפרישית והמותר שעשת יותר על מזונותיה הוא של בעל וקדוש מחיים אליבא דר"מ: מתני'

[נדרים פה.]
[בכ"ק פז: איתא אמר רב הונא יכולה וכו' ועי' תוס' לקמן סג. ד"ה רב הונא]
לעיל מז: [לקמן נט.]
ב"ק פז: [ב"מ נג.] לעיל מג. גיטין יב.
[עי' תוס' לעיל מז: ד"ה תקנו]
[ועי' תוס' לקמן ע: ד"ה נטשה]
[תמורה כו: ערכין ה וש"נ]
יבמות נג: ב"מ טז: קדושין סג.

גליון הש"ס

גמ' מההיא אין. עירובין דף לה ע"א שבועות דף לב ע"ב:

מזונות תחת מעשה ידיה, ומעה כסף תחת מותר. וכיון דלא קא יהיב לה מעה כסף — מותר דידה הוי. רב אדא בר אהבה סבר: תקנו מזונות תחת מותר, ומעה כסף תחת מעשה ידיה. וכיון דקא יהיב לה מזוני — מותר דידיה הוי. במאי קמיפלגי? מר סבר: מידי דשכיח ממידי דשכיח, ומר סבר: מידי דקייץ ממידי דקייץ. מיתיבי: *תקנו מזונות תחת מעשה ידיה! אימא, תחת מותר מעשה ידיה. תא שמע: *אם אינו נותן לה מעה כסף לצורכיה — מעשה ידיה שלה! אימא, מותר מעשה ידיה שלה. והא עלה קתני: מה היא עושה לו — משקל חמש סלעים שתי ביהודה! הכי קאמר: מעשה ידיה כמה הוי, דלידע מותר דידה כמה — משקל חמש סלעים שתי ביהודה, שהן עשר סלעים בגליל. *אמר שמואל: הלכה כרבי יוחנן הסנדלר. ומי אמר שמואל הכי? והתנן: *"קונם שאני עושה לפיך" — אינו צריך להפר. רבי עקיבא אומר; יפר, שמא תעדיף עליו יתר מן הראוי לו. רבי יוחנן בן נורי אמר: [א]יפר, שמא יגרשנה ותהא אסורה לחזור. ואמר שמואל: הלכה כרבי יוחנן בן נורי! כי אמר שמואל הלכה כרבי יוחנן בן נורי — להעדפה. ולימא: הלכה כרבי יוחנן בן נורי להעדפה, אי נמי: אין הלכה כתנא קמא, אי נמי: הלכה כרבי עקיבא! אלא אמר רב יוסף: קונמות קאמרת? שאני קונמות, מתוך שאדם אוסר פירות חבירו עליו — אדם מקדיש דבר שלא בא לעולם. אמר ליה אביי: בשלמא אדם אוסר פירות חבירו עליו — שכן אדם אוסר פירותיו על חבירו, יאסר דבר שלא בא לעולם על חבירו, שכן *אין אדם אוסר פירות חבירו על חבירו? *אלא אמר רב הונא בריה דרב יהושע: [ב]באומרת "יקדשו ידי לעושיהם" דידים איתנהו בעולם. וכי קאמרה הכי מי מקדש'? הא משעבדא ליה! דאמרה "לכי מיגרשה". ומי איכא מידי, דאילו השתא — לא קדיש, ולקמיה קדיש? אמר רבי אלעאי: אלמה לא? אילו [ג]האומר לחבירו "שדה זו שאני מוכר לך, לכשאקחנה ממך תיקדש" מי לא קדשה? מתקיף לה רבי ירמיה: מי דמי? התם — בידו להקדישה, הכא — אין בידה לגרש את עצמה. הא לא דמיא אלא לאומר לחבירו [ד]"שדה זו שמכרתי לך לכשאקחנה ממך תיקדש" — דלא קדשה! מתקיף לה רב פפא: מי דמי? התם — גופא ופירות בידא דלוקח, הכא — גופה בידה הוא! הא לא דמיא אלא [ה]לאומר לחבירו

שדה

רש"י

מזונות שביחי ומעשה ידיה שביח ומותר לא שביח. מעה כסף קייץ, ומעשה ידיה קייץ, כדתנן (לקמן דף סד:): מה היא עושה, משקל חמש סלעים. והא עלה קתני. במתני'. ומה היא עושה לו. ומדפריש בתר מעשה ידיה "ומה היא עושה לו" — מכלל דרישא במעשה ידיה איירי, ולא במותר. שתי. קשה לטוותו יותר מן הערב. הכי קאמר. [לעולם במותר איירי ברישא, והכי קאמר] סיפא: ומה היא עושה לו עיקר, דנדע מותר מאי ניהו. משקל חמש סלעים. סלע של יהודה כפליים במשקל סלע של גליל. מי אמר שמואל הכי. והאמר שמואל לעיל: במותר לאחר מיתה פליגי, ועלה א"ר יוחנן הסנדלר: חולין. ואע"פ דקספקא דידיה הוא. אלמא, טעמא דר' יוחנן משום דבר שלא בא לעולם הוא, שעדיין לא מתה, ואין לו רשות במותר, הואיל ואינו מעלה לה מעה כסף, והא אמר שמואל הלכה! והתנן קונם שאני עושה לפיך. מה שאני עושה יהיה קונם לפיך — יהי עליך כהקדש מליהנות לו. אינו צריך להפר. נדר זה, שאין בה כח להקדישו, לפי שהוא שלו. שמא תעדיף עליו. יותר ממה שפסקו לה חכמים, משקל חמש סלעים. דמותר זה אינו שלו, ויכולה להקדישו. ר' יוחנן בן נורי אומר. אף עיקר מעשה ידיה צריך הפרה. שמא יגרשנה. ויהא הנדר חל. שמשגרשה אינה משועבדת לו למעשה ידיה. ותהא אסורה לחזור לו. לפי שנאסר מעשה ידיה עליו, ואי אפשר לו ליזהר שלא תטחון ולא תאפה, וכל שאר מלאכות השנויות במשנתנו, שהאשה עושה לבעלה. ואמר שמואל הלכה כו'. אלמא, לכשיגרשנה חל הנדר. אלמא, אדם מקדיש דבר שלא בא לעולם, שעדיין לא גירשה. כי אמר שמואל הלכה כר' יוחנן בן נורי להעדפה. קאמר. כלומר, הלכה דיפר ולאו מטעמיה, דאילו לר' יוחנן — עיקר מעשה ידיה צריך הפרה, ולשמואל משום העדפה, שמא תעדיף על הראוי, הוא דאמר יפר. והשתא נמי הוה מצי לאקשויי: סוף סוף לא בא לעולם, דהא לא נעשה! אלא אקשי ליה קושיא אחריתא. אין הלכה כת"ק. דאמר אין צריך להפר, אלא יפר. אלא אמר רב יוסף. לעולם הלכה ומטעמיה קאמר, ומשום שמא יגרשנה. ושאני קונמות. הקדש, שאינו הקדש לכל אלא על אדם אחד, בלשון קונם. מתוך. שהוא תופס במקום שאין סתם הקדש תופס. שאדם אוסר פירות חבירו עליו, ואומר: קונם פירות פלוני עלי. ובסתם הקדש אין אדם מקדיש דבר שאינו שלו. הלכך, אדם אוסר עליו נמי דבר שלא בא לעולם. אבל מתני' — במקדיש הקדש גמור איירי, ואינו ממהר לתפוס בקונם. אמר ליה אביי. ומה ראיה פירות חבירו עליו לכאן? שהן פירות חבירו על חבירו, דעכשיו היא משועבדת לו למעשה ידיה, ואינה ראויה להתפיסו בקונם. ולכשיגרשנה קאמר דחייל. ועוד, שעדיין לא נעשית המלאכה עד לאחר גירושין וחזרה. בשלמא אדם אוסר פירות חבירו עליו. בקונם, שהרי אדם אוסר פירותיו על חבירו, בין בלשון קונם לחבירו לבדו, בין שהקדישו סתם הקדש גמור. יאסר דבר כו'. בתמיה. דבר שלא בא לעולם. לא המלאכה באה, ולא הרשות באה לידה להתפיס, עד שתתגרש. שכן אין אדם כו'. שממקום שבאת אין אתה יכול ללמוד איסור, שהרי אף בקונם אין אוסר פירות חבירו על חבירו לומר: קונם פירותיך עליך. באומרת יקדשו ידי כו'. שהמלאכה כמי שבאת לעולם. ועל הגירושין שלא באו קא מסיק ואזיל, ומתניתין באומר מעשה ידיך הקדש. ומי איכא מידי כו'. כלומר, תירצת לא בא לעולם דמלאכה, לא בא לעולם דגירושין לא תירצת. דאילו השתא לית לה רשותא לאקדושיה, והיכי קדיש לקמיה? אלמה לא. בתמיה. מי לא קדשה. אם מכרה וחזר ולקחה. בידו להקדישה. שהרי עכשיו שלו, וכי היכי דאילו מקדשה השתא — קדשה, כי אמר נמי תיקדוש לקמיה — קדשה. הא לא דמיא. מסקנא דקושיא היא. התם. גבי מכרתי לך, אין לו עכשיו בה לא גוף ולא פירות, ואין אדם מקדיש דבר שאינו שלו. הכא גופה בידה הוא. והרי יקדשו ידי אמרה. הא לא דמיא. מסקנא דאתקפתיה היא.

לא

תוספות

קונם שאני עושה לפיך. אפילו גרסי' "שאיני" לא הוי דבר שאין בו ממש, דהא תנן בפ' בתרא דנדרים (דף פה:): קונם שלא אתן תבן לפני בקרך — אינו יכול להפר:

אינו צריך להפר. במעלה לה מזונות ומעה כסף איירי. ולכך אינו צריך להפר, שהמותר הכל שלו. ואם משום העדפה שעל ידי הדחק — גם היא שלו. ואין לפרש טעם דאין צריך להפר משום דאין אדם מקדיש דבר שלא בא לעולם — דאם כן בחנם נקט "מה שאני עושה לפיך", דליתני "מקדיש ידי עצמו". **רבי** עקיבא אומר יפר. דקסבר דהעדפה שעל ידי הדחק הוי דאשה, כדאמרינן בריש "מציאת האשה" (לקמן סו. ושם). וא"ת: והיאך יכול להפר? והא אין זה מדברים שבינו לבינה! וי"ל: דחשיב בינו לבינה, לפי שאינו יכול ליזהר וליקח ממש בצמצום את הראוי לו, ולהניח שאינו ראוי לו. א"נ: גם חלקה משועבד לו שילקח בהם קרקע והוא יאכל פירות. וא"ת: אם כן, איך יכולה להדירו כיון דמשועבדת ליה? דאלמוה רבנן לשעבודיה דבעל, כדאמר בנסמך! וי"ל: דדוקא בעיקר מעשה ידיה הוא דאלמוה, שהם לבעל לגמרי. אבל הכא, דלאו דידיה ניהו אלא לפירות בעלמא — לא אלמוה.

שמא יגרשנה כו'. ואם תאמר: ולרב, דאמר: יכולה אשה שתאמר לבעלה איני ניזונת ואיני עושה, למה לי למנקט שמא יגרשנה? לימא: שמא תאמר "איני ניזונת ואיני עושה"? וי"ל: דהא לא שכיח שתהא אומרת כן. **כי** אמר שמואל הלכה כרבי יוחנן בן נורי להעדפה. פירוש הקונטרס מגומגם, כמו שפירש בעצמו. ונראה לר"ת דהכי פירושו: להעדפה, דסבר לה שמואל כרבי יוחנן בן נורי בהא דהעדפה לבעל. ובתר הכי גרים: ונימא הלכה כתנא קמא, אי נמי אין הלכה כרבי עקיבא. וכן פירש ר"ח.

בשלמא אדם אוסר פירות חבירו עליו שכן אוסר פירותיו על חבירו. פירוש: דהתם אוסר משום דאחד מהן ברשותו, יאסור דבר שלא בא לעולם על חבירו, שאין לא זה ולא זה ברשותו, שכן אין אדם אוסר פירות חבירו — על חבירו לפי ששניהן אינם ברשותו.

לכשאקחנה ממך כו'. ואע"ג דהתם קאמר "לכשאקחנה" והכא לא קאמרה "לכשאתגרש" — אין נראה לו לחלק.

הכא אין בידה לגרש עצמה. תימה: דהא בידה לומר איני ניזונת ואיני עושה! ויש לומר: דרוצה ליישב גם אליבא דריש לקיש.

שדה

עין משפט נר מצוה

נא א ב מיי' פי"ב מהל' נדרים הל' י סמג לאוין רמב טוש"ע י"ד סי' רלד סעי' עא וטוש"ע אה"ע סי' פא סעי' ב:
נב ג מיי' פ"ו מהל' ערכין הל' כט:
נג ד מיי' שם הל' כז:
נד ה מיי' שם הל' כט:

מסורת הש"ס

[לעיל מז: נח:]
לקמן סד:
תוס' יבמות סז. ד"ה [זו]
[קידושין סג. יבמות נג.] לקמן סו. ע. נדרים פה.
[נדרים מז.]
תוס' נדה מו: ד"ה ...ב פנחס כו' דלא גרסי אלא

נה א מיי' פ"ז מהל' ערכין הל' יד ופי"ח מהל' מלוה ולוה הל' ו ז סמג עשין לד טוש"ע ח"מ סי' קיז סעיף ז.
נו ב מיי' פ"ח מהלכות עבדים הל' טז סמג עשין פו טוש"ע שם סעי' ו וטוש"ע י"ד סי' רסז סעיף סח:
נז ג מיי' פכ"א מהל' אישות הל' ה סמג לאוין פא טוש"ע אה"ע סי' פ סעי' ו [וע"ש במ"מ]:
נח ד מיי' שם הל' ג טוש"ע שם סעי' ד:
נט ה מיי' שם הל' א טוש"ע שם סעיף א:
ס ו מיי' שם הל' ו טוש"ע שם סעי' ז:
סא ז ח מיי' שם טוש"ע שם סעיף ח:
סב ט מיי' שם הל' ב טוש"ע שם סעיף ב:
סג י מיי' שם הל' ג טוש"ע שם סעיף ג:
סד כ ל מיי' שם הל' ה טוש"ע שם סעי' ו:
סה מיי' שם הל' יג טוש"ע שם סימן פב סעי' א:
סו נ ס מיי' שם הל' טז טוש"ע שם סעי' ה:

"שָׂדֶה זוֹ שֶׁמִּשְׁכַּנְתִּי לְךָ, לִכְשֶׁאֶפְדֶּנָּה מִמְּךָ — תִּיקָּדֵשׁ" — דְּקָדְשָׁה. מַתְקִיף לָהּ רַב שִׁישָׁא בְּרֵיהּ דְּרַב אִידִי: מִי דָּמֵי? הָתָם בְּיָדוֹ לִפְדוֹתָהּ, הָכָא — אֵין בְּיָדָהּ לְגָרֵשׁ עַצְמָהּ. הָא לָא דָּמְיָא אֶלָּא לָאוֹמֵר לַחֲבֵירוֹ "שָׂדֶה זוֹ שֶׁמִּשְׁכַּנְתִּי לְךָ לְעֶשֶׂר שָׁנִים, לִכְשֶׁאֶפְדֶּנָּה מִמְּךָ — תִּיקָּדֵשׁ" דְּקָדְשָׁה. מַתְקִיף לָהּ רַב אַשִׁי: מִי דָּמֵי? הָתָם — לְעֶשֶׂר שָׁנִים מִיהָא בְּיָדוֹ לִפְדוֹתָהּ, הָכָא — אֵין בְּיָדָהּ לְגָרֵשׁ עַצְמָהּ לְעוֹלָם. אֶלָּא אָמַר רַב אַשִׁי: קוֹנָמוֹת קָא אָמְרַתְּ? שָׁאנֵי קוֹנָמוֹת דִּקְדוּשַּׁת הַגּוּף נִינְהוּ, וְכִדְרָבָא. *דְּאָמַר רָבָא: אהֶקְדֵּשׁ, חָמֵץ, בוְשִׁחְרוּר — מַפְקִיעִין מִידֵי שִׁיעְבּוּד. וְנִקְדְּשׁוּ מֵהָשְׁתָּא! אַלְמוּהָ רַבָּנַן לְשִׁיעְבּוּדֵיהּ דְּבַעַל, כִּי הֵיכִי דְּלָא תִּיקָּדֵשׁ מֵהָשְׁתָּא.§

מתני' גוְאֵלּוּ מְלָאכוֹת שֶׁהָאִשָּׁה עוֹשָׂה לְבַעְלָהּ: טוֹחֶנֶת, וְאוֹפָה, וּמְכַבֶּסֶת, מְבַשֶּׁלֶת, וּמֵינִיקָה אֶת בְּנָהּ, דמַצַּעַת לוֹ הַמִּטָּה, הוְעוֹשָׂה בַּצֶּמֶר. והִכְנִיסָה לוֹ שִׁפְחָה אַחַת — לֹא טוֹחֶנֶת וְלֹא אוֹפָה וְלֹא מְכַבֶּסֶת. זשְׁתַּיִם — אֵין מְבַשֶּׁלֶת וְאֵין מֵינִיקָה אֶת בְּנָהּ. חשָׁלֹשׁ — אֵין מַצַּעַת לוֹ הַמִּטָּה, וְאֵין עוֹשָׂה בַּצֶּמֶר. אַרְבַּע — יוֹשֶׁבֶת בְּקַתֶּדְרָא. רַבִּי אֱלִיעֶזֶר אוֹמֵר: טאֲפִי' הִכְנִיסָה לוֹ מֵאָה שְׁפָחוֹת — כּוֹפָהּ לַעֲשׂוֹת בַּצֶּמֶר, שֶׁהַבַּטָּלָה מְבִיאָה לִידֵי זִימָּה. רשב"ג אוֹמֵר: יאַף הַמַּדִּיר אֶת אִשְׁתּוֹ מִלַּעֲשׂוֹת מְלָאכָה — יוֹצִיא וְיִתֵּן כְּתוּבָּה, שֶׁהַבַּטָּלָה מְבִיאָה לִידֵי שִׁיעֲמוּם.§

גמ' טוֹחֶנֶת ס"ד? אֶלָּא אֵימָא: כמַטְחֶנֶת. וְאִיבָּעֵית אֵימָא: לבְּרֵיחַיָּא דִּידָא. מַתְנִי' דְּלָא כְּר' חִיָּיא. דְּתָנֵי ר' חִיָּיא: *אֵין אִשָּׁה אֶלָּא לְיוֹפִי, אֵין אִשָּׁה אֶלָּא לְבָנִים, וְתָנֵי ר' חִיָּיא: אֵין אִשָּׁה אֶלָּא לְתַכְשִׁיטֵי אִשָּׁה. וְתָנֵי ר' חִיָּיא: הָרוֹצֶה שֶׁיְּעַדֵּן אֶת אִשְׁתּוֹ — יַלְבִּישֶׁנָּה כְּלֵי פִשְׁתָּן, הָרוֹצֶה שֶׁיַּלְבִּין אֶת בִּתּוֹ — יַאֲכִילֶנָּה אֶפְרוֹחִים, וְיַשְׁקֶנָּה חָלָב סָמוּךְ לְפִירְקָהּ.§ וּמֵינִיקָה אֶת בְּנָהּ.§ לֵימָא מַתְנִיתִין דְּלָא כְּבֵית שַׁמַּאי, דְּתַנְיָא: *נָדְרָה שֶׁלֹּא לְהָנִיק אֶת בְּנָהּ, בש"א: שׁוֹמֶטֶת דַּד מִפִּיו, בה"א: מכּוֹפָהּ וּמְנִיקָתוֹ. נִנִתְגָּרְשָׁה — אֵינוֹ כּוֹפָהּ. סוְאִם הָיָה מַכִּירָהּ — נוֹתֵן לָהּ שְׂכָרָהּ, וְכוֹפָהּ וּמְנִיקָתוֹ, מִפְּנֵי הַסַּכָּנָה. אֲפִי' תֵּימָא ב"ש, *הָכָא בְּמַאי עָסְקִינַן — כְּגוֹן שֶׁנְּדָרָה הִיא וְקִיֵּים לָהּ הוּא. וְקָסָבְרִי ב"ש: *הוּא נוֹתֵן אֶצְבַּע בֵּין שִׁינֶּיהָ. וּב"ה סָבְרִי: הִיא נָתְנָה אֶצְבַּע בֵּין שִׁינֶּיהָ. וְנִפְלְגוּ בִּכְתוּבָּה בְּעָלְמָא! וְעוֹד, תַּנְיָא, בש"א: אֵינָהּ מֵינִיקָה. אֶלָּא מְחַוַּורְתָּא, מַתְנִיתִין דְּלָא כְּב"ש.§ אִם הָיָה מַכִּירָהּ.§

עַד

רש"י

לָא דָּמְיָא אֶלָּא לְהָא. לֹא דָּמֵי לְשָׂדֶה זוֹ שֶׁמִּשְׁכַּנְתִּי לְךָ סְתָם, אֶלָּא לְאוֹמֵר "שָׂדֶה זוֹ שֶׁמִּשְׁכַּנְתִּי לְעֶשֶׂר שָׁנִים", דְּאֵין בְּיָדוֹ לִפְדוֹתָהּ וּלְהַקְדִּישָׁהּ עַכְשָׁיו. דְּקָדְשָׁה. דְּהָא שֶׁלּוֹ הִיא. דִּקְדוּשַּׁת הַגּוּף נִינְהוּ. כִּקְדוּשַּׁת מִזְבֵּחַ, שֶׁאֵין לָהֶן פִּדְיוֹן — כָּךְ אֵין פִּדְיוֹן לְקוֹנָם לִהְיוֹת נִיתָּר לְמִי שֶׁנֶּאֱסַר עָלָיו. שֶׁהֲרֵי אֵינוֹ הֶקְדֵּשׁ גָּמוּר לִתְפּוֹס פִּדְיוֹנוֹ, אֶלָּא אָסוּר עַל אָדָם אֶחָד. וְכֵיוָן דִּקְדוּשַּׁת הַגּוּף הוּא — מַפְקִיעַ מִידֵי שִׁעְבּוּד שֶׁהָיְתָה מְשׁוּעְבֶּדֶת לְבַעְלָהּ, וְחָיֵיל. וּלְקַמָּן פָּרֵיךְ: א"כ מַאי אִירְיָא שֶׁמָּא יְגָרְשֶׁנָּה? מֵהָשְׁתָּא חָיֵיל! הֶקְדֵּשׁ. כְּגוֹן שֶׁשִּׁיעְבֵּד שׁוֹרוֹ לְבַעַל חוֹב, וְחָזַר וְהִקְדִּישׁוֹ — מַפְקִיעַ שִׁעְבּוּד הַמַּלְוֶה, וְגוֹבֶה חוֹבוֹ מִמָּקוֹם אַחֵר. וְזֶה כָּשֵׁר לְקָרְבָּן, וְאֵינוֹ גָּזוּל. דְּלָא הֲוָה קָנֵי לֵיהּ אֶלָּא לְגוּבַיְינָא בְּעָלְמָא. וְדַוְקָא קְדוּשַּׁת הַגּוּף, אֲבָל קְדוּשַּׁת דָּמִים דְּבֶדֶק הַבַּיִת — לֹא מַפְקִיעַ שִׁעְבּוּד, כִּדְתְנַן בַּעֲרָכִין (דף כג:): מוֹסִיף עוֹד דִּינָר, וּפוֹדֶה אֶת הַנְּכָסִים הַלָּלוּ כו'. חָמֵץ. עָשָׂה חֲמֵצוֹ אַפּוֹתֵיקִי לְגוֹי, וְהִגִּיעַ הַפֶּסַח — אִיסּוּר חָמֵץ מַפְקִיעוֹ מִשִּׁעְבּוּד הַגּוֹי, וְנֶאֱסָר בַּהֲנָאָה. וְהָא דִּתְנַן (פסחים דף ל:): גּוֹי שֶׁהִלְוָה לְיִשְׂרָאֵל עַל חֲמֵצוֹ, אַחַר הַפֶּסַח מוּתָּר בַּהֲנָאָה, אוֹקְמִינַן לָהּ הָתָם כְּשֶׁהִרְהִינוֹ אֶצְלוֹ, שֶׁמְּסָרוֹ בְּיָדוֹ מַשְׁכּוֹן. וְשִׁחְרוּר. עָשָׂה עַבְדּוֹ אַפּוֹתֵיקִי וְשִׁחְרְרוֹ הַלֹּוֶה — מְשׁוּחְרָר, וְזֶה גּוֹבֶה חוֹבוֹ מִמָּקוֹם אַחֵר. וְנִקְדְּשׁוּ מֵהָשְׁתָּא. מַאי אִירְיָא דְּקָתָנֵי שֶׁמָּא יְגָרְשֶׁנָּה? מֵהָשְׁתָּא נָמֵי קָדֵישׁ. אַלְמוּהָ רַבָּנַן לְשִׁעְבּוּדֵיהּ דְּבַעַל. בְּעוֹדָהּ תַּחְתָּיו, דְּשַׁוְיוּהוּ רַבָּנַן כְּלוֹקֵחַ גָּמוּר, וְלֹא כְּמַלְוֶה.

מתני' אוֹפָה. פַּת. שְׁתַּיִם אֵינָהּ מְבַשֶּׁלֶת כו'. בַּגְּמָרָא פָּרֵיךְ: אַמַּאי לָא אִיפַּטְרָה מִכּוּלְּהוּ בַּחֲדָא שִׁפְחָה שֶׁהִכְנִיסָה בִּמְקוֹמָהּ? יוֹשֶׁבֶת בְּקַתֶּדְרָא. לֹא תִּטְרַח בִּשְׁבִילוֹ לֵילֵךְ בִּשְׁלִיחוּת לְהָבִיא לוֹ חֵפֶץ מִבַּיִת לַעֲלִיָּה. שִׁעֲמוּם. שִׁיגָּעוֹן.

גמ' טוֹחֶנֶת ס"ד. הַמַּיִם מְגַלְגְּלִין הָאוֹפַן, וְטוֹחֵן. מַטְחֶנֶת. מְכִינָה צוֹרְכֵי טְחִינָה, נוֹתַנְתּוֹ בָּאֲפַרְכֶּסֶת וְקוֹלֶטֶת הַקֶּמַח. וְאִיבָּעֵית אֵימָא. לְעוֹלָם טוֹחֶנֶת הִיא עַצְמָהּ. דִּידָא. רֵחַיִם שֶׁל יָד. לְתַכְשִׁיטֵי אִשָּׁה. שֶׁיִּקְנוּ לָהּ תַּכְשִׁיטִין לְהִתְנָאוֹת בָּהֶן. שֶׁיְּעַדֵּן. אֶת זִיוָהּ, אישקלוייר בְּלַעַ"ז. לְפִירְקָהּ. יְמֵי הַנְּעוּרִים. שׁוֹמֶטֶת דַּד מִפִּיו. לֹא תְּנִיקֶנּוּ, שֶׁחָל הַנֶּדֶר. אַלְמָא: לָא מְשַׁעְבְּדָא לֵיהּ. כּוֹפָהּ וּמֵינִיקָהּ. דִּמְשַׁעְבְּדָא לֵיהּ, וְלֹא חָל הַנֶּדֶר. אִם הָיָה מַכִּירָהּ. שֶׁאֵינוֹ רוֹצֶה לִינַק מֵאַחֶרֶת. הָכָא בְּמַאי עָסְקִינַן. בְּרַיְיתָא. וְנִפְלְגוּ בִּכְתוּבָּה בְּעָלְמָא. נָדְרָה מִלֵּיהָנוֹת לוֹ וְקִיֵּים לָהּ, בש"א: תֵּצֵא וְתִטּוֹל כְּתוּבָּה, וּבה"א: תֵּצֵא בְּלֹא כְּתוּבָּה. וְעוֹד תַּנְיָא. גַּבֵּי נֶדֶר. אֵינָהּ מֵינִיקָה. אִם אֵינָהּ רוֹצָה.

עַד

תוספות

שדה זו שמשכנתי לך לכשאפדנה ממך תיקדש. משמע דבעודה ממושכנת אינו יכול להקדיש, דאין כח להקדש לבטל כח המלוה שהיא ממושכנת בידו. ותימה: דאמרי' בסוף "איזהו נשך" (ב"מ עג:): רב מרי בר רחל משכן ליה גוי ההוא ביתא, אזל גוי זבניה לרבא, נטר תריסר ירחי שתא ושקל אגר ביתא ואמטיה לרבא כו'. אלמא הפקיע המכר כחו של רב מרי, שהיה לו לדור בבית חנס, שהיתה ממושכנת בידו, והפקיע המכר כחו והוצרך להעלות לו שכר לרבא! וי"ל: דאין זה הפקעת כח. אלא לפי שהיה סבור רב מרי שהיה רבא חייב לו דמי המשכנתא במקום הגוי, ולא רצה לדור במכירו חנס משום רבית. וא"ל רבא: כדיניהם עבידנא לך, דרבא לא מיחייב ליה מידי אלא הגוי. וא"ת: והא דאמר בפ' "האומר משקלי עלי" (ערכין כא. ושם): הקדישו משכיר — הדר בו מעלה שכר להקדש. ופריך: היכי דייר ביה? הא במעילה קאי! דמשמע שבזמן השכירות יכול להקדישה! וי"ל: דכה שיש לשוכר אינו יכול להקדיש, אלא הוא והקדש שותפין בו, וימכר הבית ויקח זה דמי שכירות הבית, והמותר להקדש. אבל הכא מיירי שמקדיש כל השדה, אף מה שאינו יכול להקדיש עכשיו. אי נמי, בהקדש ממש היה חל על שדה הממושכנת אף קודם שתפדה, והכא מיירי שאוסר בקונם על המלוה לכשיפדנה. דיכול להיות דבשדה ממושכנת אינו יכול לאוסרה בקונם, אף על פי שיכול להקדישה, *כדמוכח בערכין דיכול להקדיש יותר ממה שיכול לאסור בקונם. ומתרצא בהכי האי דפריך לעיל: ומי איכא מידי דאילו השתא לא קדיש, ולקמיה קדיש. ומאי קשיא ליה: דלמה לא תוכל להקדיש מעשה ידיה לאחר שתתגרש? מאי שנא מנכסי מלוג, שיכולה למכור עכשיו לכשתתאלמן או תתגרש? אלא ודאי, אע"פ שיכולה להקדיש, מידי דהוי אמכר — לא תוכל לאסור. ועוד, יכול להיות דאפילו היתה מקדשת ידיה לשמים לגמרי לא היה ראוי לחול הקדש כמו על שדה. משום דבשדה חל ההקדש על גוף השדה בעודה ברשות המלוה, וממילא יקדשו הפירות כשילא הגוף מרשותו. אבל ידיה, אפי' הקדישו לשמים — אין נתפסות בהקדש. ואפילו בעבד אמר רב דגופיה לא קדיש, ובבן חורין מודו כ"ע. ולכך, אפי' הקדישו לגמרי — אין להקדש לחול יותר מאוסר למלוה בקונם שדה הממושכן לו.

קונמות קאמרת כו'. וא"ת: א"כ כל אדם יפקיע כל ממונו מבעל חובו על ידי קונם*! וי"ל: דלאו דווקא שעבוד דבעל אלמוה רבנן, אלא ה"נ דאלמוה לשעבודא דב"ח, כדמוכח בריש "המדיר" (לקמן ע.), דפריך: וכיון דמשועבד לה — היכי מצי מדיר לה? ולימא דמפקע שעבודה ע"י קונם, אלא ודאי דאלמוה נמי לשעבודא דאשה. וא"ת בפ' "אלמנה" ביבמות (דף סו: ושם) גבי אלטלא דפרסוה אמיתנא, אמאי קאמר רבא קנייה מיתנא? הא אלמוה רבנן לשעבודא דאשה! וי"ל: דדוקא בקונמות אלמוה, שלא יפקיע חובו. אבל ההיא דפ' "אלמנה" דנאסר לכל העולם — ליכא למיחש להכי, ומפקיע מידי שעבוד כמו הקדש. והא דאמר ב"החובל" (ב"ק דף צ. ושם) דעבדי מלוג אין יוצאין בשן ועין לא לאיש ולא לאשה, דאלמוה רבנן לשעבודא דבעל, אע"ג דשחרור דמי להקדש — סבירא ליה לרבא בפרק "אלמנה" (יבמות דף סו:) כמ"ד לאשה אבל לא לאיש. א"נ: ידו עדיפא מידה, כיון דאכיל פירות בחייה, כדאמרינן ב"הכותב" (לקמן דף פג.). **הקדש** חמץ ושחרור. כתבתי ב"השולח" (גיטין מ: ושם).

ארבע יושבת בקתדרא. אע"ג דבשלש נמי אינה עושה מכל מלאכות שהוזכרו במשנה, מכל מקום עושה מלאכות קטנות שבבית שלא הוזכרו במשנה. ואיכא נמי ארחי ופרחי דבגמרא. וכי הכניסה לו ד' — אינה עושה כלום. **טוחנת** ס"ד. הא דתנן ב"הניזקין" (גיטין סא:) אשת חבר טוחנת עם אשת עם הארץ לא פריך טוחנת ס"ד? דדוקא הכא פריך, דאתא לאשמועינן אלו מלאכות שהאשה עושה דקאי אעיקר מלאכה. **תני** רבי חייא אין אשה אלא ליופי. לא פליג אלא אטוחנת ואופה ומניקה את בנה וכיוצא בהן, שמכחישות יופיה, אבל אעושה בצמר — לא פליג, דמעשה ידיה תחת מזונות. **כגון** שנדרה היא וקיים לה הוא. שאסרה הנאת הנקה על עצמה, שהיא נהנית בהנקה, כדאמר לקמן: הוא אומר שלא להניק והיא אומרת להניק — שומעין לה, משום צערא דידה. וכי ההיא *דשוחה עליו ומניקתו מפני הסכנה. אבל ליכא למימר דאסרה הנאת יניקתה עליו, כיון דמשעבדא ליה אין הנדר חל. והשתא פליגי, דב"ש סברי: דהוא נתן אצבע בין שיניה, הלכך אינו כופה להניק. פי': להשכיר מינקת. וב"ה סברי: היא נתנה אצבע בין שיניה, וכופה להניק, שתשכיר לו מינקת, או תצא בלא כתובה.

רבי

[וכן משמע לעיל דקאמר בשלמא אדם אוסר פירות חבירו עליו שכן אדם אוסר פירותיו על חבירו ומה כח הוא זה שיכול להקדיש אלא אע"ג דיכול להקדישם לא היה לו לאוסרם על חבירו שאינו ברשותו אפ"ה אוסר ה"ה דאוסר פירות חבירו עליו. ת"י].

תוספות רי"ד

מתני' אלו מלאכות שהאשה עושה לבעלה טוחנת ואופה ומכבסת ומבשלת ומניקה את בנה ומצעת לו את המטה ועושה בצמר הכניסה לו שפחה א' לא טוחנת ולא אופה ולא מכבסת שתים אינה מבשלת ואינה מניקה את בנה שלש אינה מצעת לו את המטה ארבע יושבת בקתדרא ר"א אומר אפי' הכניסה לו ק' שפחות כופה לעשות בצמר שהבטלה מביאה לידי זימה רשב"ג אומר אף המדיר את אשתו מלעשות מלאכה יוציא ויתן כתובה שהבטלה מביאה לידי שיעמום. טוחנת ס"ד פי' דמשמע שהיא תגלגל הרחים ואם הם רחיים של מים או של בהמה למה תגלגל היא את הרחיים דטריחא לה מילתא טובא אלא אימא מטחנת פי' להזמין החטין וללקט הקמח א"נ ברחייא דידא פי' שיש מקומות שטוחנין ברחיים קטנים של יד: ומניקה את בנה מתני' דלא כב"ש דתניא נדרה שלא להניק את בנה בש"א שומטת דד מפיה ובה"א כופה ומניקתה נתגרשה אין כופה אותה להניק ואם הי' מכירה כופה ומניקתה מפני הסכנה ומעלה לה שכרה ודוקא גרושה אבל אלמנה חייבת להניק את בנה בלי שכר כמו שהיתה עושה בחיי בעלה ומ"ה אסורה להנשא עד כ"ד חדש והיתומים כופין אותה להניק (ומעלה) [ואין מעלין] לה שכר הנקה כ"א ניזונית מהן מזונות מרווחים ופותחין לה ממעשה ידיה כדין מניקה בחיי בעלה שאותו השיעבוד שהי' מוטל עלי' להניק את בנה בחיי בעלה מוטל עלי' אף לאחר מיתתו. ורב צמח גאון ז"ל כתב שגם האלמנה מעלין לה שכר הנקה ואינו נ"ל. אבל כשגירשה פקע שיעבודו מעלי' ואינו כופה אותה אך אם הוא מכירה [כופה] ובשכר וגרושה מניקה כיון שאין מוטל עלי' להניק את בנה ראשי היא להנשא מיד וא"צ להמתין כ"א ג"ח אף אם הי' מכירה כלל אמרו המשועבדת לינק אינה רשאי להנשא עד כ"ד חודש ושאינה משועבדת לינק היא רשאי להנשא מיד. ומ"ה אמרי' לקמן מניקה שמת בעלה בתוך כ"ד חודש ולא קתני מניקה סתם למימר דוקא שמת בעלה אבל אם נתגרשה א"צ להמתין. ובפ' החולץ דאמרי' התם לא ישא אדם מעוברת חבירו ומינקת חבירו דמשמע אפי' גרושה הא אמרי' התם ותיתי ותבעינהו ליורשין דאלמא לא מיירי אלא באלמנה אבל בגרושה כיון שהיא יכולה להשליך בנה לבעלה למה היא צריכה להמתין אך אם הי' מכירה כופין אותה מפני סכנות הולד (והרב אומר אע"ג דמכירה נמי יכולה להנשא הגרושה אחר ג' חדשים):

ועד

ב"ק פט: יבמות מו. סו: גיטין מ: נדרים פו:
תענית לא.
[תוספתא פ"ה]
לעיל נב. [לקמן עה.]
[שם]
[וי"ל שמלוה בעל חובו מאחרים והוא יפרע להם בעל כרחו ואש"ע שגם על אחרים יכול לאוסרו זה ודאי מופרש מכל אדם וכו' המדיר דקאמר היכי מדיר לה לא בעי למימר ע"י קונם דמשמע דמסתברא דאלמוה לשעבודה ה"נ אלמוה לשעבודא לאשה. ת"י]
גיטין
שבת קלה.

עד כמה? אמר רבא אמר רב ירמיה בר אבא אמר רב: שלשה חדשים, ושמואל אמר: שלשים יום, ורבי יצחק אמר ר' יוחנן: חמשים יום, אמר רב שימי בר אביי: הלכה כרבי יצחק שאמר משום רבי יוחנן. בשלמא רב ורבי יוחנן – *כל חד וחד כי חורפיה. אלא לשמואל, כי האי גוונא מי משכחת לה? °כי אתא רמי בר יחזקאל אמר: לא תציתינהו להני כללי דכייל יהודה אחי משמיה דשמואל. הכי אמר שמואל: [א]כל זמן שמכירה. ההיא דאתאי לקמיה דשמואל. אמר ליה לרב דימי בר יוסף: זיל בדקה. אזל, אותבה בדרי דנשי, ושקליה לברה וקמהדר ליה עלייהו. כי מטא לגבה – הוות קא מסוי לאפה, כבשתנהי לעינה מיניה. אמר לה: נטף עיניך, קום דרי בריך. [ב]סומא מנא ידע? אמר רב אשי: בריחא ובטעמא.§ תנו רבנן: *יונק תינוק והולך עד עשרים וארבעה חדש, מכאן ואילך – כיונק שקץ, דברי רבי אליעזר. רבי יהושע אומר: [ג]אפילו ארבע וחמש שנים, פירש לאחר עשרים וארבעה חדש, וחזר – כיונק שקץ. אמר מר: מכאן ואילך כיונק שקץ. ורמינהי: *יכול יהא חלב מהלכי שתים טמא, ודין הוא: ומה בהמה, שהקלת במגעה, החמרת בחלבה – אדם, שהחמרת במגעו – אינו דין שתחמיר בחלבו? תלמוד לומר: (ויקרא יא) °"את הגמל כי מעלה גרה הוא" – הוא טמא, ואין חלב מהלכי שתים טמא, אלא טהור. יכול אוציא את החלב שאינו שוה בכל, ולא אוציא את הדם שהוא שוה בכל – תלמוד לומר: "הוא" הוא טמא, ואין דם מהלכי שתים טמא, אלא טהור. ואמר רב ששת: אפילו מצות פרישה אין בו! לא קשיא; [ד]הא – דפריש, הא – דלא פריש. [ה]וחלופא בדם. *כדתניא: [ו]דם שעל גבי ככר – גוררו ואוכלו, שבין השינים – מוצצו ואינו חושש. אמר מר, רבי יהושע אומר: אפילו ארבע וחמש שנים. והתניא, ר' יהושע אומר: אפילו חבילתו על כתיפיו! אידי ואידי חד שיעורא הוא. אמר רב יוסף: הלכה כרבי יהושע.§ תניא, רבי מרינוס אומר: [ז]גונח יונק חלב בשבת. מאי טעמא – יונק מפרק כלאחר יד, ובמקום צערא – לא גזרו רבנן. אמר רב יוסף: הלכה כרבי מרינוס. תניא, נחום איש גליא אומר: [ח]צינור שעלו בו קשקשין – ממעיכן ברגלו בצנעא בשבת ואינו חושש. מאי טעמא – מתקן כלאחר יד הוא, ובמקום פסידא לא גזרו בה רבנן. אמר רב יוסף: הלכה כנחום איש גליא.§ פירש לאחר עשרים וארבעה חדש, וחזר – כיונק שקץ.§ וכמה? אמר רב יהודה בר חביבא אמר שמואל: [ט]שלשה ימים. איכא דאמרי, תני רב יהודה בר חביבא קמיה דשמואל: שלשה ימים. תנו רבנן: *מינקת שמת בעלה בתוך עשרים וארבעה חדש – °הרי זו לא *תתארס, ולא תינשא, עד

רש"י

עד כמה. כמה חדשים אית לן למימר שיודע להכירה מלינק מאשה אחרת. כל חד לפום חורפיה. יש תינוק חריף ומכירה בחמשים יום, ויש שאינו מכירה עד שלשה חדשים. כל זמן שמכירה. אין שיעור לדבר, אלא בבדיקה הדבר תלוי, אם אנו רואים שמכירה – כופה ומניקתו בשכר, [ואפי' גירשה]. ההיא דאתאי. גרושה, ולא היתה רוצה להניק. זיל בדקה. אם מכירה. אותבה בדרא דנשי. הושיבה בשורה של נשים. מסוי. מביט. נטוף עיניך. זקוף עיניך. כמו: דשפיל ואזיל בר אוווא ועינוהי מטייפי דב"ק (דף נב:). דרי בריך. שאי בנך. כיונק שקץ. כאילו יונק דבר משוקץ. חלב מהלכי שתים. חלב של אשה, המהלכת בשתי רגלים. טמא. אסור. שהקלת במגעה. שאינה מטמאה מחיים. החמרת בחלבה. כדאמרינן בבכורות (דף ו:) "גמל" "גמל" שני פעמים – חד לאסור חלבו. אדם שהחמרת במגעו. נדה. שאינו שוה בכל. שהרי בטהורה טהור. הוא טמא. מחד קרא נפקא ליה. ל"א: "זה" זה טמא כו', דכתיב ברישיה דקרא "אך את זה לא תאכלו", "זה" – מיעוטא הוא. ואמר רב ששת גרסי'. אפי' מצות פרישה. מדרבנן. אין בו. דמדאורייתא שרי. ורבנן נמי לא גזור ביה, דאמרי': חלב מהלכי שתים טהור. הא דפריש. הא דקתני מותר – כשפירש מדדי האשה לכלי, והיונק מן הדד כיונק שקץ מדרבנן. וחילופא בדם. דמדפריש – אסור מדרבנן, דמיחלף בדם בהמה, ואתי למימר: דם בהמה אכל. דם שעל גבי ככר. כגון שנשכו וניכר בו דם השינים. גוררו. לדם. מוצצו. דהא ליכא דחזי ליה. גונח. המיילל מכאב לבו, פליינדרי"א. יונק חלב. משום רפואה, ורפואתו חלב עז. מפרק. הנותק דבר ממקום שגדל בו, ולא מן המחובר אלא מן התלוש, ותולדה דדש הוא, שמפרק תבואה מקשיה (שבת דף עג:). כלאחר יד. שאין דרך בני אדם לינק, אלא לחלוב ביד. ובמקום צערא. שמצטער מכאבו. צנור. המקלח מים מן הגג. קשקשים. קשים ועשבים שסותמים ומעכבים את קלוחו, ומימיו יוצאים ומתפשטים לגג, ודולפין לבית. כלאחר יד. ע"י שינוי, ברגלו. ומשום דאמר רב יוסף הלכה כוותיהו, נקט לה הכא. וכמה. היא פרישה. איכא דאמרי תני רב יהודה. מתניתא ולא שמעתא. בתוך עשרים וארבעה חדש. שנולד בנה.

[גיטין נט.] | [תוספתא נדה פ"ב] | כריתות כב. [ע"ש ול"ע] | שם כא: | ויקרא יא | [תוספתא נדה פ"ב] | [עי' תוס' יבמות לו: ד"ה ולא וכו' שינוי נוסחאות בזה]

תוספות

רבי יהושע אומר אפילו ארבע וחמש שנים. אע"ג דהכא ליכא למימר ארבע וחמש שנים, כדאמרי אינשי °ואפי' טובא, דמשמע דוקא נקט עד חמש, מדפריך מחבילתו על כתיפיו, ומשני: אידי ואידי חד שיעורא הוא. מ"מ, ליכא למיפרך השתא חמש שרי ארבע מבעיא? דנקט ארבע לבריא וחמש לכחוש*.

החמרת בחלבה. כדדרשינן בבכורות (דף ו:) מ"ואת הגמל". יכול יהא חלב מהלכי שתים טמא ודם מהלכי שתים טמא. בת"כ גרסי' בשר במקום דם. וקאמר: ת"ל "זה" אוציא חלב שאינו נוהג בכל. פירוש: דחלב בהמה טהורה מותר, ולא אוציא את הבשר שהוא נוהג בכל, שאף בבהמה טהורה אסור בשר מן החי – ת"ל "זה טמא" – זה בלא תעשה על אכילתו, ואין בשר מהלכי שתים כו'. ואור"י: דבין לפי ספרים שלנו דדריש מ"הוא" היתר חלב ודם, ובין לת"כ דדריש מ"זה" אתי שפיר, דמצי למעוטי חלב בשר ודם כולהו מחד קרא. כמו שמצינו בכמה מקומות דממעטין מחד קרא כמה דברים, כדאשכחן בפרק "הנהנה מן ההקדש" (מעילה יח:) דכמה פעמים קאמר "תמעול מעל" ריבה. ופליגא השתא אברייתא דפרק "דם שחיטה" (כריתות כ: ושם) דממעט דם מהלכי שתים מדכתיב "לעוף ולבהמה" ויש ספרים דממעטין חלב מדכתיב :הוא", ודם מדכתיב "זה". ותימה לר"י: דמנא לן לאוקמא אדם? דסברא הוא יותר לאוקמא אבשר, ולהתיר בשר מדם, דאין איסור בשר נוהג בכל אלא מחיים, אבל דם – איסורו נוהג בכל, בין מחיים בין לאחר מיתה! ואור"י: דאי הוה גרים בשמעתין בשר במקום דם – הוה אתי שפיר, דמ"זה" ומ"הוא" ממעטינן חלב ובשר, ומההוא קרא דכריתות ממעטינן דם. וא"ת: וכיון דממעטינן דם מההוא קרא דכריתות – אמאי איצטריך קרא למישרי חלב? השתא דם מותר – חלב לא כ"ש! וי"ל: דמההוא קרא דכריתות לא מצי למישרי דם לגמרי, דלא ממעטינן ליה אלא מאיסור דם, אבל מאיסור טמא – לא ממעטינן ליה. והואיל ונתמעט מאיסור דם – השתא דם וחלב שוין.

גונח יונק חלב בשבת כו'. לאו בשיש בו סכנה איירי, דא"כ – מאי איריא משום דהוי מפרק כלאחר יד? אפי' הוי מלאכה דאורייתא שרי במקום סכנה. וקשה לר"ת מהא דאמר בפרק "חרש" (יבמות קיד.): אבא שאול אומר יונקים היינו מבהמה טהורה בי"ט. ופריך: אי דאיכא סכנה – אפילו בשבת נמי, ואי דליכא סכנה כו', ומשני: לא צריכא דאיכא צערא, ומפרק כלאחר יד הוא. שבת דאיסור סקילה – גזרו רבנן, י"ט דאיסור לאו – לא גזרו רבנן! ותירץ: דהתם מיירי בצער של רעב, והכא בצער של חולי, שהוא קרוב לסכנה, ובשבת לא גזרו. וקשה לר"י: הא דפריך התם אי דאיכא סכנה אפילו בשבת נמי, הוי ליה לאקשויי: אפי' אי ליכא סכנה, אי דחולה הוא – אפילו בשבת נמי! על כן נראה דברייתא דהתם פליגא אהך דהכא, וכן משמע, מדקאמר הכא הלכה כרבי מרינוס – מכלל דפליגי עליה. מפרק כלאחר יד הוא. וא"ת: אפילו לא הוי כלאחר יד נמי. דהא אין דישה אלא בגידולי קרקע, כדאמר בפרק "כלל גדול" (שבת עה.) גבי פולע חלזון! וכי תימא אע"ג דחלזון לא חשיב גידולי קרקע – בהמה חשיבא גדולי קרקע, כדאמרינן בריש "בכל מערבין" (עירובין דף כז:) דממעט דגים מדכתיב בקרא "בקר וצאן", מה הפרט מפורש גידולי קרקע כו' – זה אין לומר. דנהי דחשיבא בהמה גידולי קרקע, מכל מקום כיון דגמרי מסממנין – בעינן ממש שיהיה גדל מן הקרקע, כמו סממנין. דלגבי סממנין לא חשיבא בהמה גדולי קרקע, כדמוכח ב"השוכר את הפועלים" (ב"מ דף פט. ושם) דתניא: דיש, מה דיש מיוחד דבשעת מלאכה כו' יצא החולב והמגבן והמחבץ שאינם גדולי קרקע, ואין פועל אוכל בו. אלמא, לגבי דבר הגדל ממש מן הארץ – לא חשיבא בהמה גדולי קרקע! ויש לומר: דאיצטריך טעמא דהכא דמפרק כלאחר יד הוא משום דרבי יהודה, דסבר דיש דישה שלא בגדולי קרקע, דמחייב בפולע חלזון נמי משום דש: [ועיין תוספות שבת עג: ד"ה מפרק].

ממעכן ברגלו בצינעא בשבת. והא דאמר: כל מקום שאסרו חכמים מפני מראית העין אפי' בחדרי חדרים אסור – היינו דווקא באיסור מלאכה דאורייתא, כמו שוטחן בחמה אבל לא כנגד העם (שבת דף סה.), שאם יראו יסברו שכבסן בשבת, אבל הכא – לא יראו אלא מלאכה כלאחר יד, דהויא דרבנן, ולא גזרי רבנן לאסור בחדרי חדרים: [וע"ע תוס' מ"ק ח: ד"ה ומנסרן]:

אפי'

סז א ב מיי' פכ"א מהל' איסורי ביאה הל' טז טוש"ע אה"ע סי' פב סעיף ה:

[ועי' תוס' שבת ס: ד"ה בשתא וכמה שנויתי שם]

סח ג ד מיי' פ"ג מהל' מאכלות אסורות הל' ה סמג לאוין קלה טוש"ע י"ד סי' פא סעי' ז:

סט ה ו מיי' פ"ו שם הל' ב סמג לאוין קטו טוש"ע שם סי' סו סעיף י [וסי' ו סעיף טו]:

ע ז מיי' פכ"א מהל' שבת הל' יד סמג לאוין סה טוש"ע א"ח סי' שכח סעיף לג:

עא ח טוש"ע א"ח סי' שלו סעיף ט:

עב ט מיי' פ"ג מהל' מאכלות אסורות הל' ה סמג לאוין קלב טוש"ע י"ד סי' פא סעי' ז:

תוספות רי"ד

[א]עד כמה יהא מכירה אמר עולא ואיתימא ר"י א"ר עד ג"ח ושמואל אמר עד ל' יום ור"י אמר משום ר"י עד נ' יום אמר ר"ש ב"א הל' כר"י משום ר"י ומכירה פי' המורה שאינו רוצה לינוק מאשה אחרת. ואינו נ"ל דא"כ אמאי בעי ועד כמה ופליגי אמוראי בשיעורא. לכשנראה שאינו חפץ מאשה אחרת אז נכוף אותה. ועוד ההיא דאותבה בדרא דנשי כדאמרי' לקמן מה צורך בבדיקה זו נבדוק ונראה אם יונק מאשה אחרת ומש"ה נ"ל לפרש שאע"פ שהוא יונק מאשה אחרת אם הוא מכיר את אמו כופין אותה שכיון שהוא מכירה אם תניחנו תקשה לו פרידתה ויסתכן ומש"ה בעי ועד כמה שכמה זמן יכול התינוק להכיר את אמו שיסתכן בפרידתה וגם בבדיקה (חוזרת) [שמחזירים] הנער על כל הנשים לראות אם יכיר את אמו ואילו כפתרון המורה כיון שלא הי' יונק מאשה אחרת מה צורך לו לומר הוי קמסוה לאפה א"ו יונק הי' מהן ואפ"ה מפני שהי' מכיר את אמו כפו אותה והלשון מוכיח דקאמר ואם הי' מכירה ולא קאמר ואם אינו יונק אלא ממנה: ההיא גרושה דאתאי לקמי' דמר שמואל הוה יתיב ר"ד ב"י קמי' א"ל זיל בדקה אזל אותבה בדרא דנשי. שקילי' לבני' וקמהדר עלוייהו כי מטא לגבה הוי קמסוה לאפה כבשיתנהו לעינה מניה אמר לה שיף עיניך קום דרי בניך סומא מנא ידע אמר ר"א בריחא ובטעמא: ת"ר תינוק יונק והולך עד כ"ד חודש מכאן ואילך כיונק שקץ דברי ר"א ר"י אומר אפילו עד ד' וה' שנים פי' לאחר כ"ד חודש וחזר ה"ה כיונק שקץ: אמר ר"י הל' כר' יהושע: אמר מר מכאן ואילך כיונק שקץ ורמינהו יכול חלב מהלכי ב' טמא פי' אסור ודין הוא ומה בהמה טמאה שהקלת במגעה פי' שאינה מטמאה בחיים החמרת בחלבה כדילפי' בבכורות מגמל גמל תרי זימני חד לגופי' וחד לאיסור חלבו אדם שהחמרת במגעו א"ד שתחמיר בחלבו ת"ל א) וזה טמא זה טמא ואין חלב מהלכי ב' טמא אלא טהור יכול ארציא את החלב שאינו שוה בכל ב) ת"ל הוא הוא טמא ואין חלב מהלכי ב' טמא אלא טהור וא"ר ש אפילו מצות פרוש אין בו. ל"ק הא דפריש והא דלא פריש פי' אם פריש מדדי אשה הוא אסור מדרבנן וחילופא בדם דתניא דם על (הככר) [הכבד] ושל בין השינים מוצץ ואוכלו ואינו חושש פי' דם שפירש ממהלכי ב' אסור משום דמיחלף בדם בהמה: תניא ר' מרינוס אומר גונח יונק חלב בשבת ואינו חושש מ"ט מפרק כלאחר יד הוא ובמקום צערא לא גזרו רבנן פי' יונק חלב עז משום רפואה והוי מפרק חלבו ממקום גידולו כלאחר יד שאינו עושה בידו אלא בפיו והלכך במקום צערא שרו ליה רבנן אר"י הל' כר' מרינוס עיין מ"ש בפסקי בפ' חרש דפליג ר' מרינוס אדאבא שאול דלא שרי התם אלא ביו"ט ולא בשבת: תניא נחום איש גליא אומר צינור שעלו בו קשקשים ממעכן ברגלו בצנעא בשבת ואינו חושש פי' עלו בו עשבים המעכבים קלוח המים ומתוך כך המים מתפשטים ודולף בבית מאי טעמא מתקן כלא"י הוא ובמקום פסידא לא גזרי רבנן אמר ר"י הל' כנחום איש גליא: פירש וחזר ה"ה כיונק שקץ וכמה אר"י ב"ח ג' ימים: ת"ר מניקה שמת בעלה בתוך כ"ד חודש ה"ז ל"ת ולא תתארס

עד

גליון הש"ס

גמ' כי אתא רמי בר יחזקאל. לעיל דף כא ע"א לקמן דף עו ע"ב חולין דף מד ע"א: שם הרי זו לא תתארס. ע' יבמות דף לו ע"ב תוס' ד"ה ולא קתני: תוס' ד"ה רבי יהושע וכו' ואפי' טובא. כדאמרינן שבת דף קכז ע"א:

א) גירסת רבינו דנפק"ל מזה וכמה שפרש"י בל"א וכ"ה באמת בתו' בפ' שמיני וכ"ה ג"כ בכריתות. ב) ולא אוציא את הדם ת"ל הוא הוא טמא ואין דם מהלכי כו' כצ"ל.

אפילו ביעתא בכותחא. מפרש בערוך *דלאו בסתם ביצים איירי, דאין לך עם הארץ שלא ידע שהן מותרות בחלב. אלא בשוחט תרנגולת ומצא בה ביצים גמורות איירי, שמותר לאוכלן בחלב, כדתניא בפ"ק דביצה (דף ו: ושם). וא"ת: ולמאי מותר לאכלן בחלב? מאי שנא מבילת נבלה דאסרי בית הלל אפי' כמוה נמכרת בשוק, כדתנן במסכת עדיות (פ"א מ"ה)! ותירץ בהלכות גדולות: דגבי איסור נבילה החמירו, דהוי דאורייתא. אבל גבי בשר עוף בחלב, דרבנן – הקילו. וא"ת: ומאי אפי', דקאמר אפילו ביעתא בכותחא, הא איכא מאן דאמר (חולין דף קיג.): בשר עוף בחלב דאורייתא, ולדידיה אסורה כמו בילת נבילה! וי"ל: דמ"מ קאמר אפי', שכל העולם נהגו בו היתר. ולר"ת אתי שפיר, שתירץ דבבילת נבילה החמירו משום דנבלה דבר איסור הוא, אבל בבשר בחלב – לא החמירו, דהוי היתר, דכל חד וחד באפי נפשיה שרי*.

כי אפקירותא. ונפקא מיניה שהיכא שהרב מוחל על כבודו – דשרי, ואפ"ה אל יורה, דלא מסתייע מילתא, הואיל ורבו אצלו.

ואמר ר"נ אמר שמואל הלכה כר"מ בגזירותיו. א] אין לפרש דגזרינן מת אטו לא מת, ונתנה בנה להניק אטו לא נתנה, וגמלתו אטו לא גמלתו – דא"כ היכי שרא ר"נ לבי ריש גלותא! אלא י"ל: דגזרינן במת שמא תהרגנו, ונתנה בנה להניק שמא תחזור בה, וגמלתו אטו שמא תגמלנו ועדיין הוא צריך לינק. **והלכתא** מת מותר גמלתו אסור. רבינו שמשון הזקן אומר דגרושה מותרת לינשא, דלא משעבדא להניק, כדתניא לעיל (דף נט:): נתגרשה – אינו כופה, משום דלא משעבדא לי'. ור"ת אומר דאסורה לינשא, דתניא בפ' "החולץ" (יבמות מב. ושם): מעוברת חבירו ומינקת חבירו לא ישא. וקא פסיק ותני: לא שנא נתאלמנה ולא שנא נתגרשה. ועוד, דמפרש טעמא התם דסתם מעוברת למניקה קיימא, דמשמע: דהיינו טעמא דמניקה, היינו טעמא דמעוברת. ולמאי דהוה מפרש מעיקרא טעמא דמעוברת שייך בגרושה כמו באלמנה אע"ג דהדר בי' מההוא טעמא – מגופא דמילתא לא הדר ביה, דמיירי אפי' בגרושה. ועוד: דאלמנה נמי לא משעבדא מכי תבעה כתובתה או רוצה לינשא*.

עד עשרים וארבעה חדש. שמא תתעבר ותצטרך לגמול את בנה, ובעל זה אינו אביו שיקנה לו ביצים וחלב. שמונה עשר חדש. דיו לתינוק לינק בכך. אפקירותא. חוצפא. דלא מיסתייעא מילתא. שיורה כהלכה. נתנה בנה למינקת. זו שמת בעלה, או גמלתו בתוך זמנו או מת. לבי ריש גלותא. אלמנות שהיו בהן מיניקות, ונתנו בניהם למיניקה, והתירום לינשא. דלא הדרי בהו. מיניקה שפסקה להניק בניהם יראה לחזור בה, לפי שבני אדם מאויימים הם. אבל באינשי אחריני – דלמא הדרא בה המיניקה, וחוזר הבן אצל האם ומסתכן. לא תסברוה מהא. אי לא אמרה לכו סבתא מתמי' דר"נ לא הייתם יודעים ללמוד מתוך משנה זו שאסור? הרי שהיתה רדופה. רוב ימיה להיות בבית אביה כו'. כל אלו אין דרכן להתעבר. שאינה ראויה לילד. שנעקר בית הריון שלה. בגזירותיו. בכל מקום שהוא מחמיר מדרבנן. אלמא, אע"ג דאין כאן להבחין בין זרעו של ראשון לשל שני, דהא לא מיעברא – לא פלוג רבנן בתקנת גזירות שלהם בין אשה לאשה, וגזרו סתם שממתין כל אשה שלשה חדשים. והכי נמי, לא פלוג רבנן במינקת שמת בעלה, בין שהיא מניקתו בין שאינה מניקתו. גמלתו אסור. שגמלתו מחמת שרוצה לינשא. פסקה קימעא. פסקו ליתן לה מזונות מועטים. אוכלת הרבה. משלה, כדי שיהיה לה חלב הרבה ולא תמיתנו. כשות. הומלו"ן. חזיז. עשבים של זרע תבואה. חבושא. קורליי"ה. קורא. רך הגדל בדקל, מה שנוסף על הענף בשנה זו. כופרא. תמרים בקטנותן. כמכא. כותח. והרסנא. דגים מטוגנין בקמח ולייר ושומן שלהן. מינייהו פסקי חלבא. יש בדברים הללו שפוסקין חלב האשה, ויש בהן שאין מפסיקין אלא עוכרין. בני נכפי. ולדות שמתעברות שם נופלים מחולי שמו פיסיאו"ן. שמוטי. ארוכי צואר, והוא מום. גירדני. פי': אדם שנמרט שערות ראשו, או בעל גרב. זלזלני. רעבתנין. דולפני. עיניהם זולפות מים תמיד. מוניני. הורגלה לאכול דגים קטנים. מציצי עינא. עיניו פורחות ונעות תמיד. גרגושתא. אדמה, ארזילא"ה בלע"ז.

עד עשרים וארבעה חדש, דברי רבי מאיר. ור' יהודה מתיר *בשמונה עשר חדש. אמר רבי *נתן בר יוסף: הן הן דברי בית שמאי, הן הן דברי בית הלל. שבית שמאי אומרים: עשרים וארבעה חדש, ובית הלל אומרים: שמונה עשר חדש. אמר רבן שמעון בן גמליאל: אני *אכריע; לדברי האומר עשרים וארבעה חדש – מותרת לינשא בעשרים ואחד חדש, לדברי האומר בשמונה עשר חדש – מותרת להנשא בחמשה עשר חדש, לפי שאין החלב נעכר אלא לאחר שלשה חדשים. אמר עולא: הלכה כרבי יהודה. ואמר מר עוקבא: לי התיר רבי חנינא לשאת לאחר חמשה עשר חדש. אריסיה דאביי אתא לקמיה דאביי, אמר ליה: מהו ליארס בחמשה עשר חדש? אמר ליה: חדא – דר"מ ורבי יהודה *הלכה כרבי יהודה, ועוד: בית שמאי ובית הלל – הלכה כבית הלל, ואמר עולא: הלכה כרבי יהודה, ואמר מר עוקבא: לי התיר רבי חנינא לשאת לאחר חמשה עשר חדש, כל שכן דאת ליארס. כי אתא לקמיה דרב יוסף א"ל: *רב ושמואל דאמרי תרווייהו: א צריכה להמתין עשרים וארבעה חדש, חוץ מיום שנולד בו וחוץ מיום שנתארסה בו. *רהט בתריה תלתא פרסי, ואמרי לה: פרסא בחלא, ולא אדרכיה. אמר אביי: האי מילתא דאמור רבנן: *אפילו ב ביעתא בכותחא לא לישרי איניש במקום רביה – לא משום דמיחזי כאפקירותא, ג אלא משום דלא מסתייעא מילתא למימרא. דהא אנא הוה גמירנא ליה להא דרב ושמואל, אפי' הכי – לא מסתייעא לי מילתא למימר. ת"ר: נתנה בנה למינקת, או גמלתו, או מת – מותרת לינשא מיד. רב פפא ורב הונא בריה דרב יהושע סבור למיעבד עובדא כי הא מתניתא. אמרה להו ההיא סבתא: בדידי הוה עובדא, ד ואסר לי רב נחמן. איני?! והא רב נחמן שרא להו לבי ריש גלותא! שאני בי ריש גלותא, דלא הדרי בהו. אמר להו רב פפי: ואתון לא תסברוה מהא דתניא: *הרי שהיתה רדופה לילך לבית אביה, או שהיה לה כעס בבית בעלה, או שהיה בעלה חבוש בבית האסורין, או שהלך בעלה למדינת הים, או שהיה בעלה זקן או חולה, או שהיתה עקרה, וזקנה, איילונית, וקטנה, והמפלת אחר מיתת בעלה, ושאינה ראויה לילד – ה כולן צריכות להמתין שלשה חדשים, דברי ר"מ. רבי יוסי מתיר ליארס ולינשא מיד. *ואמר רב נחמן אמר שמואל: הלכה כרבי מאיר בגזירותיו! אמרי ליה: *לאו אדעתין. והלכתא: ו מת – מותר, גמלתו – אסור. מר בר רב אשי אמר: אפילו מת נמי אסור, דלמא קטלה ליה, ואזלא ומינסבא. הוה עובדא וחנקתיה. ז ולא היא, ההיא שוטה הואי, דלא עבדי נשי דחנקן בנייהו.§ תנו רבנן: ח הרי שנתנו לה בן להניק – הרי זו לא תניק עמו לא בנה ולא בן חברתה. ט פסקה קימעא – אוכלת הרבה, י לא תאכל עמו דברים הרעים לחלב. השתא בנה אמרת לא, בן חברתה מיבעיא?! מהו דתימא: בנה הוא דחיים עילויה – ממציא ליה טפי, אבל בן חברתה, אי לאו דהוה לה מותר – לא הוה ממציא ליה, קא משמע לן. פסקה קימעא אוכלת הרבה, מהיכא? אמר רב ששת: כ משלה. לא תאכל עמו דברים הרעים. מאי נינהו? א"ר כהנא: כגון כשות, וחזיז, ודגים קטנים, ואדמה. אביי אמר: אפילו קרא וחבושא. רב פפא אמר: אפילו קרא וכופרא. רב אשי אמר: אפי' כמכא והרסנא. מינייהו פסקי חלבא, מינייהו עכרי חלבא.§ דמשמשא בי ריחיא – הוו לה בני נכפי, דמשמשא על ארעא – הוו לה בני שמוטי, דדרכא על *רמא דחמרא – הוו לה בני גירדני, דאכלה חרדלא – הוו לה בני זלזלני, דאכלה תחלי – הוו לה בני דולפני, דאכלה מוניני – הוו לה בני *)מציצי עינא, דאכלה גרגושתא – הוו לה בני מכוערי, דשתיא שיכרא – הוו לה בני אוכמי, דאכלה בישרא ושתיא חמרא – הוו לה בני בריי

*) [בערוך ערך מן פירק קטני עינים]

תוספות רי"ד

עד כ"ד חודש דברי ר"מ ור"י מתיר בי"ח חודש: אר"נ ב"י הן הן דברי ב"ש והן הן דברי ב"ה. שבש"א כ"ד חודש ובה"א י"ח חודש. רשבג"א אני אכריע לדברי האומר כ"ד חודש מותרת להנשא בכ"א חודש ולדברי האומר בי"ח חודש מותרת להנשא בט"ו חודש לפי שאין החלב נעכר אלא לאחר ג' חדשים: אמר עולא הל' כר"י ואמר מר עוקבא התיר ר"ח לישא בט"ו חודש כר"י: אריסי' דאביי אתא לקמי' דאביי א"ל מהו ליארס בחמשה עשר חודש א"ל חדא דר"מ ור"י הל' כר"י וב"ש וב"ה הל' כב"ה ואמר עולא הל' כר"י ואמר מר עוקבא לי התיר ר"ח לאחר ט"ו וכ"ש את דליארס כי אתא אביי לקמי' דר"י א"ל רב ושמואל דאמרי תרווייהו צריכה להמתין כ"ד חודש חוץ מיום שנולד בו וחוץ מיום שנתארסה בו רהיט בתרי' תלתא פרסי וא"ל פרסא בחלא ולא אדרכי' אמר אביי הא מילתא דאמר רבנן א) אפי' בשעתא דדוחקא לא לישרי איניש במקום רבי' לא משום דמחזי כאפקירותא ותו לא אלא משום דלא מסתייע נמי מילתא דהא אנא הוה גמירא להא דרב ושמואל עשרים וארבע שנין ואפ"ה במקום רבי' לא מסתייע מילתא ובההיא שעתא איעלמא מיני': ת"ר נתנה בנה למניקה גמלתו או מת מותרת להנשא מיד ר"פ ור"ה ברי' דר"י סבור למיעבד עובדא כי הא מתני' א"ל ההיא סבתא בדידי הוה עבודא ואסר לי ר"נ איני והא ר"נ שרא להו לבי ריש גלותא שאני דבי ר"נ דמכי יהבי בנייהו למניקה תו לא הדרי בהו ומסיק תלמודא מת מותר גמלתו אסור מר בר"א אמר אפי' מת נמי אסור דילמא קטלה ליה ואזלא ומינסבא הוה עובדא וחנקתי'. ולא היא. ההיא כותית הוה: ת"ר הרי שנתנו לה בן להניק ה"ז לא תניק עמו לא בנה ולא בן חברתה. פסקה קמעא אוכלת הרבה ולא תאכל דברים הרעים לחלב. אוכלת הרבה מהיכא משלה:

א) נראה דט"ס הוא וצ"ל אפילו ביעתא בכותחא לא לישרי איניש וכו'

הגהות מהר"ב רנשבורג

א] תוס' ד"ה ואמר רב נחמן וכו' אין לפרש דגזרינן מת אטו לא מת.

[גי' הערוך בערך גרגן דמא ובערך גרגן איתא דמה ובראשית חכמה בפ' לדך ארץ שער ד' העתיק דדרכא אדמא דחמרא פי' דם החמור]

אמר

ברייי, דאכלה ביעי – הוו לה בני עינני, דאכלה כוורי – הוו לה בני חינני, דאכלה כרפסא – הוו לה בני *זיותני, דאכלה כוסברתא – הוו לה בני *בישרני, דאכלה אתרוגא – הוו לה בני ריחני. ברתיה דשבור מלכא אכלה בה אמה אתרוגא, והוו מסקי לה לקמיה אבוה בריש ריחני. אמר *רב הונא: *בדק לן רב הונא בר חיננא: א היא אומרת להניק והוא אומר שלא להניק – שומעין לה, צערא דידה הוא. הוא אומר להניק והיא אומרת שלא להניק – מהו? ב כל היכא דלאו אורחה – שומעין לה, היא אורחה והוא לאו אורחיה – מאי? בתר דידיה אזלינן או בתר דידה אזלינן? ופשיטנא ליה מהא: *ג עולה עמו ואינה יורדת עמו. אמר רב הונא: מאי קראה? °"והיא בעולת בעל" [בראשית כ] – בעלייתו של בעל, ולא בירידתו של בעל. ר' אלעזר אמר מהכא: °"כי היא היתה אם כל חי" [שם ג] – לחיים ניתנה, ולא לצער ניתנה.§ הכניסה לו שפחה וכו'.§ הא שארא – עבדא. ותימא ליה: עיילית לך איתתא *בחריקאי! משום דאמר לה: הא טרחא לדידי ולדידה, קמי דידך מאן טרח?§ שתים אינה מבשלת ואינה מניקה וכו'.§ הא שארא – עבדא. ותימא ליה: עיילית לך איתתא אחריתי דטרחה לדידי ולדידה, וחדא לדידך ולדידה! משום דאמר לה: קמי אורחי ופרחי מאן טרח?§ שלש אינה מצעת המטה.§ הא שארא – עבדא. ותימא ליה: עיילית לך אחריתי לאורחי ופרחי! משום דאמר לה: נפיש בני ביתא – נפיש אורחי ופרחי. אי הכי, אפי' ארבע נמי! ארבע, כיון דנפישי להו מסייען אהדדי. א"ר חנא ואיתימא ר' שמואל בר נחמני: לא הכניסה לו ממש, אלא ד כיון שראויה להכנים, אע"פ שלא הכניסה. תנא: אחד שהכניסה לו, ואחד שצמצמה לו משלה.§ ארבע יושבת בקתדרא.§ אמר רב יצחק בר חנניא אמר רב הונא: אע"פ שאמרו יושבת בקתדרא – ה אבל מוזגת לו כוס, ומצעת לו את המטה, ומרחצת לו פניו ידיו ורגליו. *אמר רב יצחק בר חנניא *אמר רב הונא: ו כל מלאכות שהאשה עושה לבעלה – נדה עושה לבעלה, חוץ ממזיגת הכוס, והצעת המטה, והרחצת פניו ידיו ורגליו. והצעת המטה – אמר רבא: ז לא אמרן אלא בפניו, אבל שלא בפניו לית לן בה.§ ומזיגת הכוס – ח שמואל מחלפא ליה דביתהו בידא דשמאלא, אביי מנחא ליה אפומא דכובא. רבא אבי סדיא, רב פפא אשרשיפא. *אמר רב יצחק בר חנניא אמר רב הונא: הכל משהין בפני השמש, חוץ מבשר ויין. אמר רב חסדא: בשר שמן ויין ישן. אמר רבא: בשר שמן – כל השנה כולה, יין ישן – בתקופת תמוז. אמר רב ענן בר תחליפא: הוה קאימנא קמיה דמר שמואל, ואייתו ליה תבשילא דארדי, ואי לאו דיהב לי – איסתכני. אמר רב אשי: הוה קאימנא קמיה דרב כהנא, ואייתו ליה גרגלידי דליפתא בחלא, ואי לאו דיהב לי – איסתכני. רב פפא אמר: אפילו תמרתא דהנוניתא. כללא דמילתא: ט כל דאית ליה ריחא ואית ליה קיוהא. אבוה בר איהי, ומנימין בר איהי, י חד ספי מכל מינא ומינא, וחד ספי מחד מינא. מר – משתעי אליהו בהדיה, ומר – לא משתעי אליהו בהדיה. הנהו תרתין חסידי, ואמרי לה רב מרי ורב פנחס בני רב חסדא, כ מר קדים ספי ומר מאחר ספי, דקדים ספי – אליהו משתעי בהדיה, דמאחר ספי – לא משתעי אליהו בהדיה. אמימר ומר זוטרא ורב אשי הוו קא יתבי אפיתחא דבי אזגור מלכא, חליף ואזיל אטורנגא דמלכא. חזייה רב אשי למר זוטרא דחוור

דחוור

רש"י

ברייי. בריאים. עינני. עיניהם גדולות. חינני. בעלי חן. כרפסא. אפי"א. כוסברתא. אליינדר"א בלע"ז. צערא דידה הוא. החלב רב בדדיה, ומצערה. דלאו אורחה. אין דרך משפחתה להניק. בחריקאי. במקומי. ולי נראה *לשון חידקי – קרן, כלומר לשון פקידת מקום, כפקד מקומי ובפגמי. אורחי. אורחים המשתהים שבת או חדש. פרחי. עוברים לדרכם. לפי שבמקום שיש בני בית רבים נוהגים להתארח עוברי דרך. הא שארא. כגון דברים קטנים. שראויה להכנים. שהכניסה נדוניא רבה, ויש כדאי למביאה נדוניא זו לקנות ממקצתה שפחות להכנים ולשמשה. אבל מוזגת לו כוס ומצעת לו מטה. לפרוס סדין ולבדין, דבר שאינו טורח. ומשום דמילי דחיבה נינהו, כדי שתתחבב עליו. ולא דמי למצעת דמתני' דהוי דבר של טורח. ובכפייה הני לא כפי לה, אלא חכמים השיאוה עצה טובה להנהיג זאת בישראל. חוץ ממזיגת כוס. כל שהוא דברים של קירוב וחיבה, ומביאין לידי הרגל דבר. מיחלפא ליה. בימי ליבונה. אבי סדיא. מראשותיו. אשרשיפא. ספסל. הכל משהין לפני שמש. המשמש בסעודה, ואוכלין בפניו, ושוהין מלהאכילו עד שיקומו הקרואים. חוץ מבשר שמן כו'. שמתאוה להם, ומצטער. בתקופת תמוז. שריחו חזק, וחום היום מחרחר בו *כארס. תבשילא דארדי. מין כמהין ופטריות. איסתכני. הייתי מסוכן לאחזני בולמוס, מחמת תאוות רעבוני. גרגלידי. חתיכות דקות ועגולות, מריר"א בלע"ז. תמרתא דהנוניתא. תמרה שמינה, כמו: קריב לגבי דהינא ואידהן (שבועות דף מז:). קיוהא. קיהיון שיניים, איגרו"ר בלע"ז. כל דאית ליה ריחא או קיוהא. מזיק את מי שאוכלין לפניו ואינו אוכל. חד ספי. מאכיל את השמש מכל מין ומין. וחד ספי ליה ממין אחד. בתחלת סעודה לשובע, ומשהה המינין משהוא עד שיגמור סעודתו. קדים ספי. קודם שיתן לפניו. מאחר ספי. מכל מין ומין, לאחר שנתן לפניו ולפני האורחין. דקדים ספי משתעי אליהו בהדיה. לפי שכשנותן לפניהן והוא רואה ומתאוה ומצטער, ופעמים שיש אורחין הרבה. אזגור. שם מלך פרס. אטורנגא דמלכא. *מושיב המנות לפני השרים, ובלשונינו שינישקלאקו"ש. דחוור

תוספות

הכניסה לו שפחה אחת. קשה תימה: אם הוא זן אותה, א"כ מה מרויח הבעל? דבלא שפחה היא היתה עושה הכל, ולא היה זן אלא אותה לבדה, ועתה זן אותה ואת שפחתה.

ואחת שצמצמה לו משלה גרסי'. פירוש: שמצמה לו ממה שהוא חייב ליתן לה, כמו קופה של בשמים ושאר דברים, ומצמה כל כך שיכול לקנות מזה כמה שפחות, רבינו תם. ויש גורסין: שמצאה לו משלו, כלומר: שהוא עשיר, שיכול לקנות הרבה שפחות כפי צרכה.

אבל מוזגת לו את הכוס ומצעת לו המטה. והא דתנן שלש אינה מצעת – כתבתי בריש מכילתין (דף ד:) [דלא הוי כמו הצעת המטה דמתני'].

מחלפא דביתהו בידא דשמאלא. במחזור ויטרי פי' הרב ר' שמעיה שהיה נזהר רש"י אפי' שלא ליתן מפתח מידו לידה. ומכאן אין ראיה, דשאני מזיגת כוס שהוא דבר של חיבה, ואסורה אפילו להביא לפניו על השולחן, אלא למר מנחא ליה אבי סדיא, ולמר אפומא דכובא. ומסדר אליהו דקתני גבי ההוא עובדא דמייתי בפ"ק דשבת (דף יג: ושם) במעשה באדם אחד שקרא הרבה ושנה הרבה כו' ששאל אליהו לאשתו: שמא הבאת לו את הפך, שמא הבאת לו את השמן? ואמרה לו: חס ושלום, אפי' באצבע קטנה לא נגע בי – נמי אין ראיה. דמצינן לפרש דשלא על הבאת הפך היה מקפיד, אלא הכי קאמר: שמא בשעת הבאת הפך לא נזהרת ונגע ביך. וכן משמע, שהשיבתו: אפילו באצבע קטנה לא נגע בי. אבל שלא הביאה לו – לא קאמרה. ומה שפירש דמחלפא ליה בידא דשמאלא בימי לבונה, דמשמע שיש להקל בימי לבונה מבימי נדותה, וכן מצינו בפרק קמא דשבת (שם) בההוא עובדא שהבאתי לעיל, דקאמר: בימי נדותיך מהו אצלך, בימי לבוניך מהו אצלך – נראה דהיו רגילין לטבול אחר שבעה לראיה כשפוסקת, דלא אסירא השתא אלא מדרבנן. אבל בזמן הזה, שאין רגילות לטבול כי אם אחר שבעה נקיים – אין חילוק בין ימי נדות לימי לבון, כדאמרינן במסכת שבת (דף סד:): "תהיה בנדתה" – בהווייתה תהא, עד שתבא במים.

לא

עין משפט נר מצוה

פ א מיי' פכ"א מהלכות אישות הל' יג סמג לאוין פא טוש"ע אה"ע סימן פב סע"ב:

פא ב מיי' שם הל' יד סמג שם טוש"ע אה"ע סי' פ סעיף א וסעיף י:

פב ג מיי' וסמג שם טוש"ע אה"ע סי' פב סעיף ג:

[פי' בעלי בשר ר"ח]

פג ד מיי' שם הל' ו סמג שם טוש"ע אה"ע סי' פ סעיף ח:

פד ה מיי' שם הל' ג טור ש"ע שם סעי' ד ה:

פה ו ז ח מיי' פכ"א מהל' אישות הל' ה ומיי' פי"א מהל' איסורי ביאה הל' יט סמג לאוין קיא טור אה"ע סימן פ וטוש"ע י"ד סימן קנה סעי' י:

פו ט י כ מיי' פ"ז מהל' ברכות הל' ז ומיי' פ"ט מהל' עבדים הל' ח סמג עשין כז טוש"ע א"ח סימן קסט סעי' א וטוש"ע י"ד סימן רסז סעי' יז:

תוספות רי"ד

אמר ר"פ בדיק לן ר"ה ב"ח היא אומרת להניק והוא אומר שלא להניק שומעים לה דצערא דידה הוא. הוא אומר להניק והיא אומר' שלא להניק מהו כל היכא דלאו אורחא לה שומעים אורחא ולאו אורחא מאי בתר דידיה אזלינן או בתר דידה אזלינן. ופשיטנא לי' עולה עמו ואינה יורדת. אמר ר"ה והיא בעולת בעל בעליתו של בעל ולא בירידתו של בעל: הכניסה לו שפחה א'. א"ר חנא ואיתימא רשב"נ לא שהכניסה לו ממש אלא כיון שראויה להכניסה אע"פ שלא הכניסה פירוש כיון שהכניסה לו כספים לקנותה ממקצתן. תניא אחד שהכניסה לו א) וא' שמצאתה לו בתוך ביתו. ארבע יושבת בקתדרא. אר"י ב"ח אמר ר"ה אע"פ שאמרו ד' יושבת בקתדרא אבל מוזגת לו את הכוס ומצעת לו את המטה ומרחצת פניו ידיו ורגליו (פי' הרב שאינו דומה הצעה זו להצעה דמתני' והצעה דמתני' מתפרש לקמן המטה והכרים והכסתות ויש שם טורח יותר אבל הצעה דהכא הוא לפרוש הסדינין על המטה שהוא לקירוב וחבה דומיא דמזיגת הכוס) ואר"י ב"ח אר"ה כל מלאכות שהאשה עושה לבעלה נדה עושה לבעלה חוץ ממז"ה והצעת המטה והרחצת פניו ידיו ורגליו: א"ר והצעת המטה ל"א אלא בפניו אבל שלא בפניו ל"ל בה: מזיגת הכוס. דביתהו דשמואל מחלפא ליה בידא דשמאלא דאביי מנחה פומא דכובא דרבא אבי סדיא דר"פ אשרשיפא פי' המורה בימי ליבונה וכך פי' ר"ח ז"ל ואינו נ"ל דאטו קילי ימי ליבונה מימי נדותה טרם שלא תטבול בברת קיימא ואדרבה בימי ליבונה שכבר פסקה מראות יש לה חק יותר ויותר. ומכאן מוכח שלא היו אוכלין בטהרה חולין. והדין נותן שמה טהרה יכולין לעשות בח"ל ב) שהוא מטמאה בקברות: ואר"י ב"ח אר"ה. הכל משהין בפני שמש חוץ מבשר ויין ואר"ח בשר שמן ויין ישן רבא בשר שמן כל השנה ויין ישן בתקופת תמוז. אמר רב ענן בר"ת הוה קאימנא קמי' דמ"ש ואייתו לי' תבשילא דארדי ואי לא דיהבי לי מיני' איסתכני ר"פ אמר אפי' תמרי דאווניתא כללא דמילתא כל דאית ליה ריחא ואית

א) גי' הרי"ף וכ"ה בתוס' ד"ה ואחת בשם יש גורסין. ב) נראה לנ"ל שהיא טמאה בטומאת קברות.

מסורת הש"ס

[תורה אור]
[בראשית כ] [שם ג]
היוצא פרש"י לקמן קס. ד"ה בחריקאי]
[בעלי זוו והדר ערוך ז' זוו. פי' יפים ונאים פירוש לראשית חכמה]
[גי' הרא"ש רב פפא] [עירובין נח. וש"נ]
[לעיל מח.]
[הערוך בערך הרק בחריקאי]
ס"א כאלם
[נ"ל ואמר]
לעיל ד:
[המזון לפני השרים כצ"ל רש"ל]
[נ"ל ואמר]

דְּחָוַור אַפֵּיהּ, שָׁקַל בְּאֶצְבְּעָתֵיהּ, אַנַּח לֵיהּ בְּפוּמֵּיהּ. א"ל: אַפְסַדְתְּ לִסְעוּדָתָא דְּמַלְכָּא. אֲמַרוּ לֵיהּ: אַמַּאי תֵּיעֲבִיד הָכִי? אֲמַר לְהוּ: מַאן דְּעָבֵיד הָכִי – פָּסֵיל לְמֵאֲכַל דְּמַלְכָּא. אָמְרוּ לֵיהּ: אַמַּאי? אֲמַר לְהוּ: דָּבָר אַחֵר חֲזַאי בֵּיהּ. בָּדְקוּ וְלָא אַשְׁכְּחוּ. שָׁקַל אֶצְבְּעָתֵיהּ אַנַּח עֲלֵיהּ אֲמַר לְהוּ: הָכָא מִי בְּדַקִיתוּ? בָּדְקוּ אַשְׁכַּחוּ. אָמְרוּ לֵיהּ רַבָּנַן: מ"ט סָמְכַתְּ אַנִּיסָּא? אֲמַר לְהוּ: חֲזַאי רוּחַ צָרַעַת דְּקָא פָּרְחָה עִילָּוֵיהּ.§ הַהוּא רוֹמָאָה דַּאֲמַר לָהּ לְהַהִיא אִיתְּתָא: מִינַּסְבַּתְּ לִי? אָמְרָה לֵיהּ: לָא. אָזֵיל אַיְיתֵי רִימָּנֵי, פָּלֵי וַאֲכַל קַמַּהּ, כָּל מַיָּא דְּצָעֲרֵי לָהּ – בַּלַּעְתֵּיהּ, וְלָא הַב לָהּ, עַד דְּזָג לָהּ. לְסוֹף אֲמַר לָהּ: אִי מָסֵינָא לָךְ מִינַּסְבַּתְּ לִי? אָמְרָה לֵיהּ: אִין. אָזֵיל אַיְיתֵי רִימָּנֵי, פָּלֵי וַאֲכַל קַמַּהּ. אֲמַר לָהּ: כָּל מַיָּא דְּצָעֲרֵי לָךְ – תּוּף שְׁדַאי, תּוּף שְׁדַאי. עַד דְּנָפְקָא מִינָּהּ כִּי הוּצָא יָרְקָא, וְאִתַּסִּיאַת.§ וְעוֹשָׂה בַּצֶּמֶר.§ בַּצֶּמֶר – אִין, בְּפִשְׁתִּים – לָא. מַתְנִי' מַנִּי – ר' יְהוּדָה הִיא. דְּתַנְיָא: [א]אֵינוֹ כּוֹפָה לֹא לַעֲמוֹד לִפְנֵי אָבִיו, וְלֹא לַעֲמוֹד לִפְנֵי בְּנוֹ, [ב]וְלֹא לִיתֵּן תֶּבֶן לִפְנֵי בְּהֶמְתּוֹ. אֲבָל כּוֹפָה לִיתֵּן תֶּבֶן לִפְנֵי בְּקָרוֹ. רַבִּי יְהוּדָה אוֹמֵר: [ג]אַף אֵינוֹ כּוֹפָה לַעֲשׂוֹת בְּפִשְׁתָּן, מִפְּנֵי שֶׁפִּשְׁתָּן מַסְרִיחַ אֶת הַפֶּה וּמְשַׁרְבֵּט אֶת הַשְּׂפָתַיִם. וְהָנֵי מִילֵּי – בְּכִיתָּנָא רוֹמָאָה.§ ר' אֱלִיעֶזֶר אוֹמֵר: אֲפִילּוּ הִכְנִיסָה לוֹ מֵאָה שְׁפָחוֹת.§ אָמַר רַב מַלְכִּיוּ אָמַר רַב אַדָּא בַּר אַהֲבָה: הֲלָכָה כְּרַבִּי אֱלִיעֶזֶר. אָמַר רַבִּי חֲנִינָא בְּרֵיהּ דְּרַב אִיקָא: *שְׁפוּד, שְׁפָחוֹת וְגוּמוֹת – רַב מַלְכִּיוּ, בְּלוֹרִית, אֵפֶר מִקְלֶה וּגְבִינָה – רַב מַלְכִּיָא. רַב פַּפָּא אָמַר: מַתְנִיתִין וּמַתְנִיתָא – רַב מַלְכִּיָא, שְׁמַעְתָּתָא – רַב מַלְכִּיוּ. וְסִימָנָךְ: מַתְנִיתָא מַלְכְּתָא. מַאי בֵּינַיְיהוּ? אִיכָּא בֵּינַיְיהוּ שְׁפָחוֹת.§ רשב"ג אוֹמֵר וכו'.§ הַיְינוּ תַּנָּא קַמָּא! אִיכָּא בֵּינַיְיהוּ דְּמִיטַּלְּלָא בְּגוּרְיָיתָא קִיטַנְיָיתָא (א) וְנַדְרַשִׁיר.§

מתני' *הַמַּדִּיר אֶת אִשְׁתּוֹ מִתַּשְׁמִישׁ הַמִּטָּה, ב"ש אוֹמְרִים: שְׁתֵּי שַׁבָּתוֹת, [ד]בֵּית הִלֵּל אוֹמְרִים: שַׁבָּת אַחַת. הַתַּלְמִידִים יוֹצְאִין לְתַלְמוּד תּוֹרָה שֶׁלֹּא בִּרְשׁוּת שְׁלֹשִׁים יוֹם, הַפּוֹעֲלִים שַׁבָּת אַחַת. הָעוֹנָה הָאֲמוּרָה בַּתּוֹרָה: הַטַּיָּילִין – בְּכָל יוֹם, הַפּוֹעֲלִים – שְׁתַּיִם בְּשַׁבָּת, הַחַמָּרִים – אַחַת בְּשַׁבָּת, הַגַּמָּלִים – אַחַת לִשְׁלֹשִׁים יוֹם, הַסַּפָּנִים – אַחַת לְשִׁשָּׁה חֳדָשִׁים, דִּבְרֵי רַבִּי אֱלִיעֶזֶר. **גמ'** מ"ט דב"ש? גָּמְרִי מִיּוֹלֶדֶת נְקֵבָה. וּבֵית הִלֵּל? גָּמְרִי מִיּוֹלֶדֶת זָכָר. וּב"ה נַמִי נִגְמְרוּ מִיּוֹלֶדֶת נְקֵבָה! אִי מִיּוֹלֶדֶת גָּמְרִי לָהּ – הָכִי נַמִי, אֶלָּא ב"ה מִנִּדָּה גָּמְרֵי לָהּ. בְּמַאי קָמִיפַּלְגִי? מָר סָבַר: מִידֵּי דִּשְׁכִיחַ מִמִּידֵּי דִּשְׁכִיחַ, וּמָר סָבַר: מִידֵּי דְּהוּא גָּרֵים לָהּ מִמִּידֵּי דְּהוּא גָּרֵים לָהּ. *אָמַר רַב: מַחֲלוֹקֶת בִּמְפָרֵשׁ, אֲבָל בִּסְתָם – דִּבְרֵי הַכֹּל יוֹצִיא לְאַלְתַּר, וְיִתֵּן כְּתוּבָּה. וּשְׁמוּאֵל אָמַר: [ה]אֲפִי' בִּסְתָם נַמִי יַמְתִּין, שֶׁמָּא יִמְצָא פֶּתַח לְנִדְרוֹ. הָא פְּלִיגִי בַּהּ חֲדָא זִימְנָא, דִּתְנַן: *הַמַּדִּיר אֶת אִשְׁתּוֹ מִלֵּיהָנוֹת לוֹ, עַד שְׁלֹשִׁים יוֹם – יַעֲמִיד פַּרְנָס, יוֹתֵר מִכָּאן – יוֹצִיא וְיִתֵּן כְּתוּבָּה. וְאָמַר רַב: לֹא שָׁנוּ אֶלָּא בִּמְפָרֵשׁ, אֲבָל בִּסְתָם – יוֹצִיא לְאַלְתַּר וְיִתֵּן כְּתוּבָּה. וּשְׁמוּאֵל אָמַר: אֲפִי' בִּסְתָם נַמִי יַמְתִּין, שֶׁמָּא יִמְצָא פֶּתַח לְנִדְרוֹ! צְרִיכָא, *דְּאִי אִיתְּמַר בְּהָא – בְּהָא קָאָמַר רַב, מִשּׁוּם דְּלָא אֶפְשָׁר בְּפַרְנָס. אֲבָל בְּהַהִיא, דְּאֶפְשָׁר בְּפַרְנָס – אֵימָא מוֹדֵי לֵיהּ לִשְׁמוּאֵל. וְאִי אִיתְּמַר בְּהַהִיא – בְּהַהִיא קָאָמַר שְׁמוּאֵל, אֲבָל בְּהָא – אֵימָא מוֹדֵי לֵיהּ לְרַב, צְרִיכָא.§ הַתַּלְמִידִים יוֹצְאִין לְתַלְמוּד וכו'.§ בִּרְשׁוּת כַּמָּה? [ו]כַּמָּה דְּבָעֵי.

אוֹרְחָא

רש"י

דְּחָוַור אַפֵּיהּ. פָּנָיו זוֹעֲפִים, שֶׁנִּתְאַוָּה לְמַאֲכָל. א"ל. אַטוּרַנְגָּא לְרַב אַשִׁי. אַפְסַדְתָּא לִסְעוּדָתָא. לֹא יֹאכַל הַמֶּלֶךְ מֵעַתָּה. אָמְרוּ לוֹ. שׁוֹטְרֵי הַמֶּלֶךְ: אַמַּאי תַּעֲבֵיד הָכִי? אָמַר לְהוּ. רַב אַשִׁי. דְּעָבֵיד הָכִי פָּסֵיל לְמֵיכַל לְמַלְכָּא. הָעוֹשֶׂה מַאֲכָל כָּזֶה – אֵין רָאוּי שֶׁיֹּאכַל הַמֶּלֶךְ מַאֲכָל מִיָּדוֹ. דָּבָר אַחֵר חֲזַאי בֵּיהּ. בָּשָׂר שֶׁל חֲזִיר מְצוֹרָע, וּבִלְשׁוֹן לַעַז קוֹרִין לוֹ סורשמי"ן. שָׁקַל אֶצְבְּעָתֵיהּ. רַב אַשִׁי שָׁקַל אֶצְבָּעָתֵיהּ דְּקַפִּילָא. אַנַּח עֲלֵיהּ. עַל אַחַת הַחֲתִיכוֹת: אַנְחִירֵיהּ לָא גָּרְסִי'. הָכָא מִי בְּדַקִיתוּ. כְּלוֹמַר, בְּדַקְתֶּם אֶת חֲתִיכָה הַזּוֹ? בָּדְקוּ אַשְׁכְּחוּ. נֵס נַעֲשָׂה לוֹ. דְּפָרְחָה עִילָּוֵיהּ. דְּמַר זוּטְרָא. פָּלֵי. מְבַקֵּעַ. וְהַרְבֵּה יֵשׁ לוֹ דּוֹמִים בְּמַסֶּכֶת נִדָּה (דף כא:): דְּפָלֵי פַּלּוּיֵי. מַיָּא דְּצָעֲרֵי. רוֹק שֶׁגָּדֵל בְּתוֹךְ הַפֶּה מֵחֲמַת קִיּוּהָא דָּבָר הַנֶּאֱכָל בְּפָנָיו, וְאֵינוֹ אוֹכֵל מִמֶּנּוּ. עַד דְּזָג. נָפְחוּ פָּנֶיהָ וּכְרֵיסָהּ, וְנַעֲשׂוּ כִּזְכוּכִית, שֶׁכֵּן דַּרְכֵי הַנְּפוּחִים. תּוּף שְׁדַאי. רְקוֹקִי וְהַשְׁלִיכִי. לַעֲמוֹד. לְשָׁרֵת. בְּהֶמְתּוֹ. סוּס וַחֲמוֹר, שֶׁהֵן מְזוּיָּינִין וְגוֹהֲלִים לִרְבִיעָה. אֲבָל בָּקָר אֵינוֹ לָהוּט אַחַר רְבִיעַת אִשָּׁה, וְאֵין יִצְרוֹ נִיכָּר כָּל כָּךְ, לְפִיכָךְ אֵין אִשָּׁה נִסֵּית לוֹ. וַאֲנִי שָׁמַעְתִּי: בְּקָרוֹ – נְקֵבוֹת, בְּהֶמְתּוֹ – זְכָרִים (ג). מְשַׁרְבֵּט. פּוֹשְׁטָן כְּמִין שַׁרְבִיט עַד שֶׁנַּעֲשִׂין גְּדוֹלוֹת. וּבִלְשׁוֹנֵינוּ נִקְרָא אשא"ש. ע"י שֶׁהִיא צְרִיכָה לִשְׁרוֹת הַחוּט תָּמִיד בְּרוֹק. שְׁפוּד שְׁפָחוֹת וְגוּמוֹת. סִימָנֵי הֲלָכוֹת הֵן: שְׁפוּד – בְּמַסֶּכֶת בֵּיצָה, שְׁפָחוֹת – כָּאן, גּוּמוֹת – בְּמַסֶּכֶת נִדָּה. בְּלוֹרִית – בְּמַסֶּכֶת עֲבוֹדָה זָרָה, אֵפֶר מִקְלֶה – בְּמַסֶּכֶת מַכּוֹת, גְּבִינָה – בְּמַסֶּכֶת עֲבוֹדָה זָרָה. תְּלָת מִנַּיְיהוּ מַתְנִי' – שְׁפָחוֹת וּבְלוֹרִי' וּגְבִינָה, וּתְלָת מִנַּיְיהוּ שְׁמַעְתְּתָא, וּפָרְשִׁינְהוּ רַב מַלְכִּיוּ וְרַב מַלְכִּיָּא. רַב פַּפָּא. אַסִּימָנָא דְּרַב מַלְכִּיוּ פָּלֵיג, דְּקָאָמַר: שְׁפָחוֹת רַב מַלְכִּיוּ, דְּכָל מַתְנִי' וּמַתְנִיתָא דְּהָכָא – רַב מַלְכִּיָּא פָּרְשִׁינְהוּ. אֲבָל שְׁמַעְתְּתָא דְּאָמַר רַב מַלְכִּיוּ – מוֹדֵינָא לָךְ. וְסִימָנָיךְ. שֶׁלֹּא תַּחֲלִיף בִּגְירְסָא. מַתְנִיתָא מַלְכְּתָא. לְגַבֵּי שְׁמַעְתָּא הָוְיָא מַתְנִיתָא מַלְכְּתָא, דְּהָא מִינָּהּ מוֹתְבִינַן תְּיוּבְתָּא לִשְׁמַעְתָּא. וְסִימָנֵיךְ – מַלְכִּיָּא, לְשׁוֹן נְקֵבָה. אֲבָל מַלְכִּיוּ – לְשׁוֹן זָכָר. הַיְינוּ ת"ק. רַבִּי אֱלִיעֶזֶר, מַה לִּי לִידֵי שִׁעֲמוּם מַה לִּי לִידֵי זִימָּה? דְּמִיטַּלְּלָא בְּגוּרְיָיתָא קִיטַנְיָיתָא וְנַדְרַשִׁיר. מְשַׂחֶקֶת בִּכְלָבִים דַּקִּים, וּשְׂחוֹק שֶׁקּוֹרִין אישקקי"ש. לִידֵי זִימָּה לֵיכָּא, לִידֵי שִׁעֲמוּם – לֵיכָּא, דְּאֵין שִׁעֲמוּם אֶלָּא בְּיוֹשֵׁב וְתוֹהֶא וּבָטֵל לְגַמְרֵי. **מתני'** הַמַּדִּיר אֶת אִשְׁתּוֹ. כְּגוֹן דְּקָאָמַר: יֵאָסֵר הֲנָאַת תַּשְׁמִישֵׁךְ עָלַי. אֲבָל הֲנָאַת תַּשְׁמִישִׁי עָלַיִךְ – לָא מִיתַּסְרָא, דְּהָא מְשׁוּעְבָּד לָהּ, דִּכְתִיב "וְעוֹנָתָהּ לֹא יִגְרָע". וְהָכִי מוֹקְמִינַן בִּנְדָרִים בְּפֶרֶק "וְאֵלּוּ נְדָרִים" (דף פא:). ב"ש אוֹמְרִים שְׁתֵּי שַׁבָּתוֹת. אִם הִדִּירָהּ ב' שַׁבָּתוֹת – תַּמְתִּין, וְאִם יוֹתֵר – יוֹצִיא וְיִתֵּן כְּתוּבָּה. הַטַּיָּילִין. מְפָרֵשׁ בַּגְּמָרָא. הַחַמָּרִים. שֶׁיּוֹצְאִין לַכְּפָרִים לְהָבִיא תְּבוּאָה לִמְכּוֹר בַּשּׁוּק. הַגַּמָּלִין. סוֹחֲרֵי חֲבִילוֹת, וּמְבִיאִין עַל הַגְּמַלִּים מִמָּקוֹם רָחוֹק. הַסַּפָּנִים. פּוֹרְשִׁין לַיָּם הַגָּדוֹל לְקַצְוֵי אֶרֶץ. **גמ'** מִיּוֹלֶדֶת נְקֵבָה. שֶׁשּׁוֹפָא שְׁבוּעַיִים מִתַּשְׁמִישׁ. נִגְמְרוּ מִיּוֹלֶדֶת נְקֵבָה. כֵּיוָן דְּאַשְׁכְּחַן אוֹרַח אַרְעָא לִשְׁהוֹת כָּל כָּךְ – אֵין לָנוּ לְכוֹפוֹ לְהוֹצִיא. ה"ג: אִי מִיּוֹלֶדֶת גָּמְרִי הָכִי נַמִי. מִידֵּי דִּשְׁכִיחַ. כַּעַס, שֶׁכּוֹעֵס עַל אִשְׁתּוֹ וּמַדִּירָהּ. מִמִּידֵּי דִּשְׁכִיחַ. נִדּוּת, לְאַפּוּקֵי לֵידָה דְּלָא שְׁכִיחַ כּוּלֵּי הַאי. מִידֵּי דְּהוּא גָּרֵים לֵהּ. נֶדֶר הָאִישׁ גּוֹרֵם לָהּ לִשְׁהוֹת, וְכֵן לֵידָה עַל יָדוֹ בָּאָה לָהּ, לְאַפּוּקֵי נִדָּה דְּמִמֵּילָא. וְיֵשׁ לָנוּ לִלְמוֹד מִן הַדּוֹמֶה [אֲפִילּוּ לָא שְׁכִיחַ כּוּלֵּי הַאי]. אֲפִי' בִּסְתָם נַמִי יַמְתִּין. לְב"ש שְׁתֵּי שַׁבָּתוֹת וּלְב"ה שַׁבָּת אַחַת. שֶׁמָּא. בְּתוֹךְ הַזְּמַן יִלְמוֹד לִמְצוֹא פֶּתַח חֲרָטָה, לוֹמַר: אַדַּעְתָּא דְּהָכִי לָא נָדְרִי, וְיַתִּיר לוֹ חָכָם נִדְרוֹ. מִלֵּיהָנוֹת לוֹ עַד ל' יוֹם. קוֹנָם אַתְּ נֶהֱנֵית לִי עַד ל' יוֹם, וְלֹא הִדִּירָהּ מֵהֲנָאַת תַּשְׁמִישׁ, דְּהָא לָא חָיֵיל, מִשּׁוּם דִּמְשׁוּעְבָּד לָהּ. וּבְגַבֵּי מְזוֹנוֹת נַמִי מוֹקְמִינַן לֵיהּ לְקַמָּן (ד' עא.) בְּאוֹמֵר לָהּ "אֵין מַעֲשֵׂה יָדַיִךְ לִמְזוֹנוֹתַיִךְ". וּפַרְנָס – מִשּׁוּם דְּלָא סַפְקָא. וְאִית דְּמוֹקְמָא כְּגוֹן שֶׁהוּא מִן הַגַּמָּלִ' אוֹ מִן הַסַּפָּנִים, שֶׁאֵין לְכוֹפוֹ בִּשְׁבִיל תַּשְׁמִישׁ. וְלָאו מִילְּתָא הִיא, דְּהָא מוֹקְמָא לְקַמָּן אַכּוּלְּהוּ קָתָנֵי מַתְנִי' לְעִנְיַן מַדִּיר – שָׁבוּעַ אַחַת. יַעֲמִיד פַּרְנָס. שֶׁיָּזוּן אוֹתָהּ. וְהָתָם פָּרֵיךְ: וְאַטּוּ פַּרְנָס לָאו שְׁלִיחוּתֵיהּ עָבֵיד? תַּשְׁמִישׁ. לֹא אֶפְשָׁר בְּפַרְנָס. וְאִי אִתְּמַר בְּהָא. (ג) מִלֵּיהָנוֹת לוֹ. בְּהָא אָמַר שְׁמוּאֵל. מִשּׁוּם דְּאֶפְשָׁר בְּפַרְנָס.

אוֹרְחָא

תוספות

לא ליתן תבן לפני בהמתו ולא ליתן תבן לפני בקרו. דשניהם אינה מחויינת, כדתניא בפרק בתרא דנדרים (דף פא:): דברים שבינה לבין אחרים – אינו מיפר. כיצד? קונם שאני עושה לפי אבא, לפי אביך, לפי אחי, לפי אחיך, שלא אתן תבן לפני בהמתך, שלא אתן תבן לפני בקרך – אינו יכול להפר.

וה"מ בכיתנא רומאה. והא דדייקינן אמתני'; בצמר – אין, בפשתים – לא, בכיתנא רומאה.

הלכה כר"א. והא דקי"ל *בכ"מ ששנה רשב"ג במשנתנו הלכה כמותו – אין זה אותו שהיה בימי ר"א. **איכא** בינייהו שפחות. אומר רשב"ם: שפחות ושכנגדה, דהיינו אפר מקלה, שהוא מימרא, דתרווייהו בינייהו נינהו. ור"ת פי': דהא דקאמר מתני' ומתניתא רב מלכיא – לא אתא לאפלוגי על מימרא של רב מלכיא, אלא אתא למימר דכל מתני' ומתניתא רב מלכיא ולא רב מלכיו. אבל [שמעתתא – יש מהם רב מלכיו ויש מהם] נמי רב מלכיא. וכן מוכח, דקאמר: וסימניך מתניתא מלכתא. אבל משמעתתא לא נותן סימן. **התלמידים** יוצאין שלא ברשות ל' יום והפועלים שבת אחת. פי' ר"י: דאתא לאשמועינן דאף על גב דמנהגם היה ללמוד ולעשות מלאכה בעירם, ועונה האמורה בתור' לתלמיד מע"ש לע"ש, כדאמרי' בגמ'. ולפועלים שתים בשבת, כדקתני סיפא. אפ"ה יכולים לשנות ממנהגם וללאת, תלמידים ל' יום ופועלים שבת אחת.

אלא

פז א מיי' פכ"א מהל' אישות הל' ג סמג לאוין עא טוש"ע אה"ע סי' פ סעי' ז:

פח ב מיי' שם הל' ה טוש"ע שם סע"ו:

פט ג מיי' שם הל' א טור שו"ע שם סעי' א:

[לקמן עז.]

צ ד ה מיי' פי"ד שם הל' ו סמג לאוין פא טור ש"ע י"ד סימן רלה סעי' א וטוש"ע אה"ע סי' עו סעי' ט:

צא ו מיי' פט"ו שם הל' א סמג עשין מט טוש"ע אה"ע סי' עו סעי' ו:

תוספות רי"ד

ואית לי' קיוהא. אבוה בר איהי ומנימין בר איהי חד ספא מכל מינא ומינא וחד ספא (מכל) [מחד] מינא מר משתעי אליהו בהדיה ומר לא משתעי אליהו בהדיה: ועושה בצמר. צמר אין פשתן לא מתני' מני ר"י היא דתניא אינו כופה לא לעמוד בפני אביו ולא לעמוד בפני א) אמו ולא ליתן תבן לפני בקרו פי' שורים שחורש בהן דטריחא מילתא וזילה לה אבל בהמתו או סוס או חמור שרוכב עלי' ולית בה טרחא יתירה ולא זילותא כופה ר"י אומר אינה כופה לעשות בפשתן מפני שהפשתן מסריח את הפה ומשרטט את שפתים. אמר אביי ובכיתנא דרומאי: ר"א אומר וכו' אמר רב מלכי' אמר ר"א ב"א הל' כר"א: **מתני'** המדיר את אשתו מתשמיש המטה בש"א שתי שבתות ובה"א שבת אחת. התלמידים יוצאים לת"ת שלא ברשות ל' יום מכאן לעונה האמורה בתורה הטיילים בכל יום הפועלים שתים בשבת החמרים אחד בשבת הגמלים אחד לל' יום הספנים א' לו' חדשים דברי ר"א **המדיר** כגון דאמר תיאסר הנאת תשמישך עלי אבל אם אמר הנאת תשמישי עליך לא מיתסרא דהא משועבד לה דכתיב ועונתה לא יגרע והכי מוקמי לה בנדרים בפ' אלו מותרים: בש"א ב' שבתות: מ"ט דב"ש גמרי מיולדת נקבה וב"ה גמרי מידי דשכיח ממידי דשכיח: אמר רב מחלוקת במפרש אבל בסתם יוציא ויתן כתובה לאלתר ושמואל אמר אפילו בסתם לא יוציא שמא ימצא פתח לנדרו וקי"ל כשמואל

א) נראה שצ"ל בנו וכמו לאיתא בגמ'.

מכות כא. ביצה כח: כט. נדה נב.

עדיות פ"ד מ"י [לקמן כ

לקמן עא.

[לקמן ע.]

[שם עא. ע"ש]

הגהות הב"ח

(א) גמ' ונדרשיר נ"ב בערוך נדרשיר מין בקסמים: (ב) רש"י בהמתו כו' זכרים. וקשה לאיתא בתוס' תס' דף ט. תמירים מן הן וכו' מן זכרים על כו' דכתיב בהמה והכל כו' ושמא לשון תורה כו' ולשון גמרא לחוד: (ג) ואי אתמר בהא מליהנות:

אורחא דמילתא. דרך ארץ, שלא ישא עליו חטא, ואפי' הוא יכול לפתותה שתתן לו רשות. **לכל דבר המחלקות הבאה והיוצאת חדש בחדש.** בדברי הימים במחלקות שהיו עובדים את דוד כל מחלקות חדש. ואע"ג דמשמעותא דעניינא משמע שלא היה פורש מביתו אלא חדש אחד בשנה, ואין ללמוד משם אלא חדש כאן וי"א חדשים בביתו – רב קרא יתירא דהבאה והיוצאת דריש, דהוה ליה למכתב: "המשרתים את המלך לכל דבר מחלקות חדשי השנה", וכתב "דבר המחלקות הבאה והיוצאת חדש בחדש לכל חדשי השנה", משמע שהיו שתי מחלקות נכנים ומשרתים, שמשרתים עם השכר, זו ו' חדשים בדילוג וזו ו' חדשים בדילוג. זו באה וזו יוצאה מדי חדש בחדש, הרי חדש בבית המלך וחדש בביתו. ואף כאן – חדש בבית רבו וחדש בביתו. **ושנים חדשים בביתו.** האיש בביתו. שהרי ל' אלף איש היה המס, "וישלחם לבנונה עשרת אלפים בחדש", כשמחליפים אלו הולכין עשרת אלפים אחרים, ובחדש השלישי עשרת אלפים שלישי'. נמצא שעמדו הראשונים בביתם ב' חדשים. וכן כולם בחלופיהם כך. **שאפשר ע"י אחרים.** לפי מנין החליפות כך היו עולים. **שאני התם דאית ליה הרווחה.** שהיו נהנים מבית המלך, ואיכא רווח ביתא, לפיכך מקבלת עליה שיהי' בבית המלך [חדש] אחד משני חדשים, שכיון שיש לו שכר יש לה מזונות מרווחים ותכשיטין. אבל ת"ת – מצוה דיליה הוא. **אנחה שוברת כו'.** איידי דאיפלגו בה רב ורבי יוחנן בדרשא דקרא, נקט לה נמי הכא. **מתנים.** באמצע הגוף. **דשנן בה.** הורגלנו בה, כמו "כיון דדש דש" (גיטין דף נו:). **דמלפא תכלי לא בהתה.** אשה הלימודת לשכל בניה לקוברם אינה תמיהא ומפחדת במות א' מהם, שכבר לימודת. **בני פירקי.** תלמידים שהרב מלוי להם בעירן, ושונים פרקם, ולנים בביתם. **מאן דכתיב בהן.** בשבילם נאמר לבעלי אומניות. **שוא לכם משכימי קום מאחרי שבת.** למלאכת הרשות, אוכלי לחמם בעצב – כן יתן הקב"ה לידידו שנא – למי שמנדד לכבודו ולמצותו שינה. **מנדדות שינה.** ממתינות את בעליהן שהן בבית רבם ושונים פרקם. **אלמא,** בשעת שינה עודן בבית רבן. ואת אמרת יש להן פנאי לעונה בכל לילה?! **רב שמואל בר שילת.** מלמד תינוקות היה, ומתפרנס מהן, כדאמרי' ב"נערה שנתפתתה" (לעיל נ.). **ולא חליף פריסתקא דמלכא אבביה.** אין שליח מלך פרס עובר על פתחו לשאול לו עבודת המלך. שאין עין המלך עליו, שאינו עשיר בעיניהם. **מפנקי דמערבא.** בני ארץ ישראל מעונגים במאכל ומשתה, לכך הם בריאים ובעלי כח לתשמיש. **איפחית בי באני.** תחת המרחצאות יש חלל שהמים נופלים שם. **אסקינהו.** העלה את העבדים בידו אחת, ובשניה היה מטפס ועולה בעמוד. **מאחר דהכי.** שבעל כח אתה. **אם כן.** שאחיש את כחי, ולא יסמכוני. **מה אניח.** כח בעלמי להשתמש בו לעת זקנה. **בעירם.** **שתים בשבת.** **איכפל תנא לאשמועינן טייל ופועל.** תנא דקתם לעיל: המדיר את אשתו, בית הלל אומרים שבת אחת – אין לו לומר זאת לא בספן ולא בגמל ולא בחמר ולא בתלמידי חכמים, שהרי [אף החמר] עונתו אחת בשבת, ובשביל יום אחד יוציא ויתן כתובה? הרי עונתו משבעה לשבעה, וכ"ש גמל וספן! אין בכלל הזה אלא טייל ופועל העושה מלאכה בעירו, שדרכו לשמש שתים בשבת. אכולהו

אלא אורחא דמילתא כמה. פי' בקונטרס שלא ישא עליו חטא ואפי' הוא יכול לפתותה. וא"ת: והיאך יצא ר"ע וכל הנהו דלקמן? וי"ל: דהתם בלא פתוי היו שמחות שהיו בעליהן הולכין ללמוד תורה. ולהיות תלמידי חכמים. ואדרבה, אדעתא דהכי נשאו שילכו ללמוד תורה. ונראה לר"י דאפועלים קאי, ולא אתלמידים. דהא אפי' שלא ברשות יוצאין לעולם ל' יום ויחזור לביתו יום אחד. והכא קרא קאמר חדש בביתו או ב' חדשים למ"ד דאע"פ שהוא ברשות. אלא אפועלים קאי, וקרא נמי דמייתי בפועלים איירי. וא"ת: והיכי קאמר בסמוך שאני התם דאית להו רווחא, פועלים דמתני' נמי אית להו רווחא! וי"ל: רווחא דהתם דמלאכת המלך, נפיש. **שאני** שמועת בית המקדש דתקיפא טובא. וא"ת: והא האי קרא ד"ואתה בן אדם האנח בשברון מתנים" גבי בהמ"ק כתיב, דכתיב בתרי' "והיה כי יאמרו אליך על מה אתה נאנח ואמרת (להם) אל שמועה כי באה ונמס כל לב"! וי"ל: דההוא קרא קודם חורבן כתיב. וכן היה אומר נביא לישראל שהיה נאנח על שמועת בהמ"ק שעתיד ליחרב, ואז "ונמס כל לב" מתוך האנחה שתהי' אחר החורבן על שמועת בית המקדש.

טיילין. על שם שדרכם בטולא דאפדנייהו:

מנדדות שינה מעיניהם. בתלמידים הלומדים בעירם קאי, דאי בעיר אחרת – אמאי מנדדות שינה? הא אין דרך ליכנס בעיר בלילה. **והתניא** הפועלים אחת בשבת. מרישא דקתני הפועלים שבת אחת לא מצי למיפרך. דרישא לאו בדין עונה מיירי, אלא אדרבה, אשמועינן דשרי לשנות ולבטל עונה ממה שהיה מנהגם תחלה. אבל מברייתא פריך שפיר, דאיירי בדין עונה האמורה בתורה ולא ביציאה שלא ברשות, מדקתני: אחת בשבת, ולא קתני שבת אחת כמו במתני'. ומשני: דבעושה מלאכה בעיר אחרת איירי, והיה דרכם ומנהגם כך. וא"ת: מאי איריא כשמנהגם כך? אפי' לשנות יכולין שבת אחת כדפרישית במתני'! וי"ל: דברייתא קמ"ל דאע"פ שמנהגם כך לעשות מלאכה בעיר אחרת, אם רוצי' לשנות ולשהות יותר – אין הרשות בידם. ור"י בר' ברוך היה אומר דג' מדות בפועלי', דהעושין מלאכה בעירן – שתים בשבת, כדתנן במתני', וברייתא בעושין מלאכה בעיר אחרת וחוזרין בכל יום לביתם אחת בשבת, לפי שיש להם טורח הדרך. אבל אותם שאין חוזרין לביתם, בין היה מנהגם בין לא היה, כמו רישא דמתני' דקתני יוצאין שבת אחת – משמע שהן כל ז' בחוץ וחוזרין בכל יום שמיני. אבל ר"י לא פירש אלא ב' מדות שתים בשבת, ואחת בשבת כדפרישנא.

תורה אור

אורחא דמילתא כמה? אמר רב: חדש כאן וחדש בבית, שנאמר: °"לכל דבר המחלקות הבאה והיוצאת חדש בחדש לכל חדשי השנה". (דה"א כז) ור' יוחנן אמר: חדש כאן ושנים בביתו, שנאמר: °"חדש יהיו בלבנון שנים חדשים בביתו". (מ"א ה) ורב נמי: מ"ט לא אמר מההיא? שאני בנין בית המקדש, דאפשר ע"י אחרים. ור' יוחנן, מ"ט לא אמר מההיא? שאני התם, דאית ליה הרווחה. *אמר רב: אנחה שוברת חצי גופו של אדם, שנאמר: °"ואתה בן אדם האנח בשברון מתנים ובמרירות תאנח". (יחזקאל כא) ורבי יוחנן אמר: אף כל גופו של אדם, שנאמר: °"והיה כי יאמרו אליך על מה אתה נאנח ואמרת אל שמועה כי באה ונמס כל לב ורפו כל ידים וכהתה כל רוח וכל ברכים תלכנה מים". (שם) ורבי יוחנן נמי, הכתיב: "בשברון מתנים"! ההיא דכי מתחלא – ממתנים מתחלא. ורב נמי, הכתי': "ונמס כל לב ורפו כל ידים וכהתה כל רוח"! שאני שמועה דבית המקדש, דתקיפא טובא. ההוא ישראל וגוי דהוו קאזלי באורחא בהדי הדדי, לא אימצי גוי לסגויי בהדי ישראל. אדכריה חורבן בית המקדש, נגיד ואיתנח, ואפ"ה לא אימצי גוי לסגויי בהדיה. א"ל: לאו אמריתו אנחה שוברת חצי גופו של אדם? א"ל: ה"מ מילתא חדתי אבל הא דשנן בה – לא, דאמרי אינשי: דמלפי תכלי לא *בהתה.§ [א]הטיילין בכל יום.§ מאי טיילין? אמר רבא: בני פירקי. א"ל אביי: מאן דכתיב בהו: °"שוא לכם משכימי קום מאחרי שבת אוכלי לחם העצבים כן יתן לידידו שנא". (תהלים קכז) *ואמר רב יצחק: אלו נשותיהן של ת"ח שמנדדות שינה מעיניהם בעוה"ז, ובאות לחיי העוה"ב. ואת אמרת בני פירקי? אלא, אמר אביי: כדרב, דאמר רב: כגון רב שמואל בר שילת, דאכיל מדידיה ושתי מדידיה, וגני בטולא דאפדניה, ולא חליף *פריסתקא דמלכא אבביה. כי אתא רבין אמר: [ב]כגון מפנקי דמערבא. ר' אבהו הוה קאי בי באני, הוו סמכי ליה תרי עבדי. איפחית בי באני מתותיה, איתרמי ליה עמודא, סליק ואסקינהו. ר' יוחנן הוה קסליק בדרגא, הוו סמכי ליה רב אמי ורב אסי. איפחתא דרגא תותיה, סליק ואסקינהו. אמרי ליה רבנן: וכי *מאחר דהכי – למה ליה למיסמכיה? אמר להו: א"כ מה אניח לעת זקנה?§ והפועלים שתים בשבת.§ והתניא: הפועלים אחת בשבת! א"ר יוסי ברבי חנינא, לא קשיא: כאן – בעושין מלאכה בעירן, כאן – בעושין מלאכה בעיר אחרת. תניא נמי הכי: [ג]"הפועלים שתים בשבת, במה דברים אמורים – בעושין מלאכה בעירן, אבל בעושין מלאכה בעיר אחרת – אחת בשבת.§ החמרים אחת בשבת.§ אמר ליה רבה בר רב חנן לאביי: איכפל תנא לאשמועינן טייל ופועל? אמר ליה: לא, רוצה אכולהו

צב א ב מיי' פי"ד מהל' אישות הל' א סמג לאוין פא טוש"ע אה"ע סימן עו סעי' א:
צג ג מיי' שם טוש"ע שם סעי' ב:

תוספות רי"ד

בדיני: הטיילים וכו'. כי אתא רב דימי אמר כגון מפנקי דמערבא: הפועלים וכו'. אמר ר"פ לאביי איכפל תנא לאשמועינן במדיר את אשתו טייל ופועל פי' דלא מתוקמא מתני' דקתני שבת א' אלא בטיילים ופועל דאי חמרין א' בשבת וכ"ש ספנין וגמלין ות"ח נמי א' בשבת א"ל

ברכות נח:

[עי' פירושו בערוך ערך תכל ב']

[בע"י הגדה ליומא סי' סו וביומא עז.]

[גי' הערוך בערך חל ח' וכי מאחר דחיליה דמר כולי האי ל"ל למר למיסמכיה. יש לאל ידי תרגום אית חילא בידי]

[גי' הערוך דרוקא פי' חול של מלך]

צד א מיי' פי"ד מהל' אישות הל' ו טור ש"ע אה"ע סי' עו סעי' ט:
צה ב ג מיי' שם הל' ב טוש"ע שם סעי' ה:
צו ד מיי' שם הלכה א טור ש"ע שם סעי' ב:

[כלתנן פ"ח מ"ז דפאה]

אַכּוּלְּהוּ. וְהָא שִׁשָּׁה חֳדָשִׁים קָאָמַר! *אֵינוֹ
דּוֹמֶה מִי שֶׁיֵּשׁ לוֹ פַּת בְּסַלּוֹ, לְמִי שֶׁאֵין לוֹ פַּת
בְּסַלּוֹ. א"ל *רַבָּה בַּר רַב חָנָן לְאַבַּיֵי: חַמָּר
וְנַעֲשָׂה גַּמָּל מַאי? א"ל: *ב רוֹצָה אִשָּׁה בְּקַב
וְתִיפְלוּת *מֵעֲשָׂרָה קַבִּין וּפְרִישׁוּת.§ הַסַּפָּנִים
אַחַת לְשִׁשָּׁה חֳדָשִׁים דִּבְרֵי ר' אֱלִיעֶזֶר.§ אָמַר רַב
*בְּרוֹנָא אָמַר *רַב: הֲלָכָה כְּר"א. אָמַר רַב אַדָּא
בַּר אַהֲבָה אָמַר רַב: זוֹ דִּבְרֵי ר' אֱלִיעֶזֶר, אֲבָל
חֲכָמִים אוֹמְרִים: ג הַתַּלְמִידִים יוֹצְאִין לְת"ת ב'
וְג' שָׁנִים שֶׁלֹּא בִּרְשׁוּת. אָמַר רָבָא: סָמְכוּ רַבָּנַן
אַדְּרַב אַדָּא בַּר אַהֲבָה וְעָבְדֵי עוּבְדָא בְּנַפְשַׁיְיהוּ.
כִּי הָא דְּרַב רְחוּמִי הֲוָה שְׁכִיחַ קַמֵּיהּ דְּרָבָא
*בְּמָחוֹזָא. הֲוָה רָגִיל דַּהֲוָה אָתֵי לְבֵיתֵיהּ כָּל
מַעֲלֵי יוֹמָא דְּכִיפּוּרֵי. יוֹמָא חַד מְשַׁכְתֵּיהּ
שְׁמַעְתָּא, הֲוָה מְסַכְּיָא דְּבֵיתְהוּ: הָשְׁתָּא אָתֵי,
הָשְׁתָּא אָתֵי. לָא אֲתָא. חֲלַשׁ דַּעְתָּהּ, אַחֵית
דִּמְעֲתָא מֵעֵינָהּ. הֲוָה יָתֵיב בְּאִיגְּרָא — אִפְּחִית
אִיגְּרָא מִתּוּתֵיהּ, וְנָח נַפְשֵׁיהּ. עוֹנָה שֶׁל תַּלְמִידֵי
חֲכָמִים אֵימַת? אָמַר רַב יְהוּדָה אָמַר שְׁמוּאֵל:
ד מֵעֶ"שׁ לְעֶ"שׁ. °"אֲשֶׁר פִּרְיוֹ יִתֵּן בְּעִתּוֹ" *אָמַר רַב (תהלים א)
יְהוּדָה וְאִיתֵּימָא רַב הוּנָא וְאִיתֵּימָא רַב נַחְמָן:
זֶה הַמְשַׁמֵּשׁ מִטָּתוֹ מֵעֶ"שׁ לְעֶ"שׁ. יְהוּדָה בְּרֵיהּ
דְּר' חִיָּיא חַתְנֵיהּ דְּר' יַנַּאי הֲוָה אָזֵיל וְיָתֵיב בְּבֵי
רַב, וְכָל בֵּי *שִׁמְשֵׁי הֲוָה אָתֵי לְבֵיתֵיהּ. וְכִי הֲוָה
אָתֵי — הֲוָה קָא חָזֵי קַמֵּיהּ עַמּוּדָא דְּנוּרָא. יוֹמָא חַד
מְשַׁכְתֵּיהּ שְׁמַעְתָּא. כֵּיוָן דְּלָא חָזֵי הַהוּא סִימָנָא — אֲמַר לְהוּ רַבִּי יַנַּאי: כְּפוּ מִטָּתוֹ,
שֶׁאִילְמָלֵי יְהוּדָה קַיָּים — לֹא בִּיטֵּל עוֹנָתוֹ. הֲוַאי °"כִּשְׁגָגָה שֶׁיּוֹצָא מִלִּפְנֵי הַשַּׁלִּיט" (קהלת י)
וְנָח נַפְשֵׁיהּ. רַבִּי אִיעֲסַק לֵיהּ לִבְרֵיהּ בֵּי רַבִּי חִיָּיא. כִּי מְטָא לְמִיכְתַּב כְּתוּבָּה נָח
נַפְשָׁהּ דְּרִבִיתָא. אָמַר רַבִּי: ח"ו פְּסוּלָא אִיכָּא? יָתִיבוּ וְעַיְינוּ בְּמִשְׁפָּחוֹת: ה רַבִּי אָתֵי
מִשְּׁפַטְיָה בֶּן אֲבִיטַל, וְרַבִּי חִיָּיא אָתֵי מִשִּׁמְעִי אֲחִי דָּוִד. אָזֵיל אִיעֲסַק לֵיהּ לִבְרֵיהּ
בֵּי ר' יוֹסֵי בֶּן זִימְרָא. פָּסְקוּ לֵיהּ תַּרְתֵּי סְרֵי שְׁנִין לְמֵיזַל בְּבֵי רַב. אַחְלְפוּהָ קַמֵּיהּ,
אֲמַר לְהוּ: נֶיהֱווּ שִׁית שְׁנִין. אַחְלְפוּהָ קַמֵּיהּ, אֲמַר לְהוּ: אִיכְנִיס, וַהֲדַר אֵיזִיל. הֲוָה קָא
מְכַסִּיף מֵאֲבוּהּ. א"ל: בְּנִי, דַּעַת קוֹנְךָ יֵשׁ בְּךָ. מֵעִיקָּרָא כְּתִיב: °"תְּבִיאֵמוֹ וְתִטָּעֵמוֹ", (שמות טו)
וּלְבַסּוֹף כְּתִיב: °"וְעָשׂוּ לִי מִקְדָּשׁ וְשָׁכַנְתִּי בְּתוֹכָם". אָזֵיל יָתֵיב תַּרְתֵּי סְרֵי שְׁנֵי (א)בְּבֵי (שם כה)
רַב, עַד דַּאֲתָא אִיעַקְּרָא דְּבֵיתְהוּ. אֲמַר רַבִּי: הֵיכִי נַעֲבֵיד? נְגָרְשַׁהּ — יֹאמְרוּ: עֲנִיָּיה
זוֹ לַשָּׁוְא שִׁימְּרָה. נִינְסֵיב אִיתְּתָא אַחֲרִיתֵי — יֹאמְרוּ: זוֹ אִשְׁתּוֹ, וְזוֹ זוֹנָתוֹ. בָּעֵי עֲלָהּ
רַחֲמֵי וְאִיתַּסִּיאַת.§ רַבִּי חֲנַנְיָה בֶּן חֲכִינַאי הֲוָה קָאָזֵיל לְבֵי רַב בְּשִׁילְהֵי הִלּוּלֵיהּ
דְּר"שׁ בֶּן יוֹחַאי. א"ל: אִיעַכַּב לִי עַד דְּאָתֵי בַּהֲדָךְ. לָא אִיעַכְּבָא לֵיהּ. אֲזַל יְתֵיב
תְּרֵי סְרֵי שְׁנֵי בְּבֵי רַב. עַד דְּאָתֵי — אִישְׁתַּנּוּ שְׁבִילֵי דְּמָתָא, וְלָא יָדַע לְמֵיזַל לְבֵיתֵיהּ.
אֲזַל יְתֵיב אַגּוּדָּא דְּנַהֲרָא. שְׁמַע לְהַהִיא רְבִיתָא דַּהֲווּ קָרוּ לָהּ: בַּת חֲכִינַאי,
בַּת חֲכִינַאי, מְלִי קוּלְתִּיךְ וְתָא נֵיזִיל. אֲמַר: ש"מ, הַאי רְבִיתָא דִּידַן. אֲזַל בַּתְרָהּ,
הֲוָה יְתִיבָא דְּבֵיתְהוּ קָא נָהֲלָה קִמְחָא. דָּל עֵינָהּ, חֲזִיתֵיהּ, סָוֵי לִבָּהּ, פָּרַח רוּחָהּ.
אָמַר לְפָנָיו: רבש"ע, עֲנִיָּיה זוֹ, זֶה שְׂכָרָהּ?! בְּעָא רַחֲמֵי עֲלָהּ וַחֲיַיה. רַבִּי חָמָא בַּר בִּיסָא
אָזֵיל יָתֵיב תְּרֵי סְרֵי שְׁנֵי בְּבֵי מִדְרְשָׁא. כִּי אֲתָא, אֲמַר: לָא אִיעֲבֵיד כִּדְעֲבֵיד בֶּן
חֲכִינַאי. עָיֵיל יָתֵיב בְּמִדְרְשָׁא, שְׁלַח לְבֵיתֵיהּ. אֲתָא ר' אוֹשַׁעְיָא בְּרֵיהּ, יָתֵיב קַמֵּיהּ.
הֲוָה קָא מַשְׁאֵיל לֵיהּ שְׁמַעְתָּא, חֲזָא דְּקָא מִתְחַדְּדֵי שְׁמַעְתֵּיהּ, חָלַשׁ דַּעְתֵּיהּ, אֲמַר:
אִי הֲוַאי הָכָא — הֲוָה לִי זֶרַע כִּי הַאי. עָל לְבֵיתֵיהּ. עָל בְּרֵיהּ, קָם קַמֵּיהּ. הוּא סָבַר — לְמִשְׁאֲלֵיהּ שְׁמַעְתְּתָא
קָא בָּעֵי. אָמְרָה לֵיהּ דְּבֵיתְהוּ: מִי אִיכָּא אַבָּא דְּקָאֵים מִקַּמֵּי בְּרָא? *קָרֵי עֲלֵיהּ רָמֵי בַּר חָמָא: °"הַחוּט (קהלת ד)
הַמְשׁוּלָּשׁ לֹא בִמְהֵרָה יִנָּתֵק" — זֶה ר' אוֹשַׁעְיָא, בְּנוֹ שֶׁל רַבִּי חָמָא בַּר בִּיסָא. ר"ע רַעְיָא דְּבֶן כַּלְבָּא שָׂבוּעַ
הֲוָה. חֲזִיתֵיהּ בְּרַתֵּיהּ דַּהֲוָה צְנִיעַ וּמַעֲלֵי, אָמְרָה לֵיהּ: אִי מִקַּדְּשְׁנָא לָךְ אָזְלַתְּ לְבֵי רַב? אֲמַר לָהּ: אִין. אִיקַּדְּשָׁא
לֵיהּ בְּצִינְעָה, וּשְׁדַרְתֵּיהּ. *שְׁמַע אֲבוּהָ אַפְּקַהּ, מִבֵּיתֵיהּ אַדְּרַהּ הֲנָאָה מִנִּכְסֵיהּ. אָזֵיל יָתֵיב תְּרֵי סְרֵי שְׁנִין (נדרים נ. [ע"ש כל שינויים])
בְּבֵי רַב, כִּי אֲתָא — אַיְיתֵי בַּהֲדֵיהּ תְּרֵי סְרֵי אַלְפֵי תַּלְמִידֵי. שְׁמַעֵיהּ לְהַהוּא סָבָא דְּקָאָמַר לָהּ: עַד כַּמָּה
קָא

רוצה אשה בקב ותיפלות כו'. תימה: דאמרינן לעיל: שאני התם דאית להו רווחא! ושמא עבודת המלך איכא רווחא טפי.
מתשעה קבין ופרישות גרסי' דהמשרה אשתו ע"י שליש תנן (לקמן סד:) דנותן לה שני קבין, ואינו פורש מתשמיש.

והמורד על אשתו מתשמיש — מוסיפין על כתובתה ג' דינר (לקמן סג.). ולפי חשבון ד' סאין בסלע הוי ג' דינר י"ח קבין*, א] כן פי' בערוך*.
החוט המשולש לא במהרה ינתק. לפי שלשתן ראו זה את זה. כדאמרי' בעלמא (בב"ב נט.) שאמר ר' אושעיא דבר, ואתו ושאלו לר' ביסא. לכך קרי עלייהו "החוט המשולש לא במהרה ינתק", כלומר: לא ינתק מזרעו לעולם, כדאמרי' בעלמא (ב"מ דף פה.): כיון שאדם לומד הוא ובנו ובן בנו, מכאן ואילך תורה חוזרת על אכסניא שלה, ודריש מ"ואני זאת בריתי וגו'".
[וע"ע תוספות ב"ב נט. ד"ה החוט].
דהוה צניע ומעלי. והא דאמר ב"אלו עוברין" (פסחים מט:): אמר ר"ע: כשהייתי עם הארץ הייתי אומר: מי יתן לי תלמיד חכם ואנשכנו כחמור. משמע דלא הוה מעלי! איכא למימר דהתם לאו משום שהיה שונא תלמידי חכמים, אלא משום שהי' סבור שמתגאין על עמי הארץ מפני תורתן, והיו תלמידי חכמים שונאים אותם. וגם משום שלא היו מניחין אותם ליגע בהם, כדאמרינן (חגיגה דף יח:): בגדי עם הארץ מדרס לפרושים. אבל מכל מקום שומר מצות היה — רבינו תם.
אדעתא

אכולהו. נַמִי קָאָמַר, דְּע"י נֶדֶר יָתֵר מִשַּׁבָּת אַחַת — לֹא. וְהָא. בְּלֹא נֶדֶר, שִׁשָּׁה חֳדָשִׁים קָאָמַר בְּסַפָּנִים. אֵינוֹ דּוֹמֶה. לְעִנְיַן תַּעֲנִית מִי שֶׁיֵּשׁ לוֹ כו' — אַף כָּאן, בְּלֹא נֶדֶר דַּעְתָּהּ נוֹחָה לְבַעְלָהּ, שֶׁמָּא יָבֹא בְּתוֹךְ הַזְּמַן. אֲבָל זוֹ, מִשֶּׁהִדִּירָהּ הֲרֵי הִיא כְּמִי שֶׁאֵינָהּ מְצַפָּה לְבַעַל. חַמָּר וְנַעֲשָׂה גַּמָּל מַאי. נִישֵּׂאת לוֹ כְּשֶׁהוּא חַמָּר, מַהוּ לֵיעָשׂוֹת גַּמָּל שֶׁלֹּא בִּרְשׁוּת? הַרְוָוחָה עֲדִיפָא לָהּ, שֶׁיִּתְעַשֵּׁר, אוֹ עוֹנָה עֲדִיפָא לָהּ? בְּקַב וְתִיפְלוּת. לִהְיוֹת בַּעְלָהּ עִמָּהּ. מֵעֲשָׂרָה קַבִּין. לְהִתְעַשֵּׁר. דִּבְרֵי ר"א. אַמַּתְנִי' קָאֵי. וְסֵיפָא דְּמַתְנִי' נָקֵיט. זוֹ דִּבְרֵי ר"א. הָנָךְ עוֹנוֹת וִילִיאוֹת שֶׁלֹּא בִּרְשׁוּת דְּמַתְנִי', דְּקָתָנֵי: הַתַּלְמִידִים יוֹצְאִים לְת"ת שֶׁלֹּא בִּרְשׁוּת שְׁלֹשִׁים יוֹם. סָמְכוּ רַבָּנַן. תַּלְמִידִים שֶׁבְּדוֹרֵנוּ סוֹמְכִים עַל דְּבָרָיו, וְיוֹצְאִין שֶׁלֹּא בִּרְשׁוּת. וְעָבְדִי עוּבְדָא. כְּוָותֵיהּ. בְּנַפְשַׁיְיהוּ. וְהוּא בָּא לָהֶם לִיטּוֹל מֵהֶם נְפָשׁוֹת, שֶׁנֶּעֱנָשִׁים וּמֵתִים. מְסַכְּיָא. תַּרְגּוּם שֶׁל מְצַפָּה. מֵעֶ"שׁ כו'. שֶׁהוּא לֵיל תַּעֲנוּג, וּשְׁבִיתָה, וַהֲנָאַת הַגּוּף. כְּפוּ מִטָּתוֹ. כְּדַת הַמִּתְאַבְּלִים, דְּחַיָּיבִין בִּכְפִיַּית הַמִּטָּה. אִיעֲסַק לִבְרֵיהּ. לְהַשִּׂיא בִּתּוֹ שֶׁל רַבִּי חִיָּיא. אִיכָּא פְּסוּלָא. שֶׁלֹּא הָיוּ מְהוּגָּנִים לְזוּג אֶחָד. שְׁפַטְיָה בֶּן אֲבִיטַל. בֶּן דָּוִד הָיָה, אֲבִיטַל שֵׁם אֵשֶׁת דָּוִד. וְר' חִיָּיא אָתֵי מִשִּׁמְעִי, וְזֶהוּ הַפְּסוּל: שֶׁר' הָיָה מִבֵּית דָּוִד, וְלֹא הָיְתָה בַּת הַבָּאָה מִשִּׁמְעִי הוֹגֶנֶת לִבְנוֹ, שֶׁלֹּא הָיְתָה בַּת מְלָכִים. פָּסְקוּ לֵיהּ תַּרְתֵּי סְרֵי שְׁנִין. קוֹדֶם שֶׁיִּכְנוֹס. אַחְלְפוּהָ קַמֵּיהּ. הֶעֱבִירוּ הַנַּעֲרָה לִפְנֵי הֶחָתָן. דַּעַת קוֹנְךָ יֵשׁ בְּךָ. שֶׁאָמַר לְהַרְחִיק זְמַן חוּפָּתוֹ, וְחָזַר וְקֵרְבָהּ מֵרוֹב חִיבַּת כַּלָּתוֹ. מֵעִיקָּרָא כְּתִיב תְּבִיאֵמוֹ וְתִטָּעֵמוֹ בְּהַר נַחֲלָתְךָ מָכוֹן לְשִׁבְתְּךָ. שֶׁיָּבֹאוּ לָאָרֶץ וְאַחַ"כ יִבְנוּ לוֹ מִקְדָּשׁ. וּלְבַסּוֹף אָמַר וְעָשׂוּ לִי מִקְדָּשׁ. בַּמִּדְבָּר. אִיעַקְּרָא. נַעֲשֵׂית עֲקָרָה. כֵּן דֶּרֶךְ הָעוֹמְדוֹת עֶשֶׂר שָׁנִים בְּלֹא בַּעַל*. בְּשִׁילְהֵי הִלּוּלֵיהּ דְּר' שִׁמְעוֹן. סוֹף יְמֵי חוּפָּתוֹ. אִיעַכַּב לִי. הַמְתֵּן לִי עַד שֶׁיִּכְלוּ יְמֵי חוּפָּתִי, וְאֵלֵךְ עִמְּךָ לְבֵי רַב. אִישְׁתַּנּוּ שְׁבִילֵי דְּמָתָא. שֶׁנִּבְנוּ בָּעִיר בִּנְיָנִים חֲדָשִׁים, וְנִסְתְּמוּ בָּהּ מְבוֹאוֹת. לְהַהִיא רְבִיתָא. נַעֲרָה. סָוֵי לִבָּהּ. רָאָה לִבָּהּ, כְּלוֹמַר: נִדְמָה לְלִבָּהּ פִּתְאוֹם שֶׁזֶּה בַּעְלָהּ. לָא אִיעֲבִיד כִּדְעֲבַד בַּר חֲכִינַאי. שֶׁנִּכְנַס לְבֵיתוֹ פִּתְאוֹם. יָתֵיב קַמֵּיהּ. וְלֹא הָיָה הָאָב מַכִּירוֹ. חַזְיָא. לִבְרֵיהּ דְּמִחַדְּדָן שְׁמַעְתְּתֵיהּ. אִי הֲוַאי הָכָא. אִילּוּ הָיִיתִי כָּאן כְּשֶׁהִנַּחְתִּי בְּנִי קָטָן וְהָלַכְתִּי — הָיִיתִי מְלַמְּדוֹ תּוֹרָה, וְהָיָה חָכָם כָּזֶה. כַּלְבָּא שָׂבוּעַ. שֵׁם א' מֵעֲשִׁירֵי יְרוּשָׁלַיִם, שֶׁכָּל הַנִּכְנָס לְבֵיתוֹ רָעֵב כְּכֶלֶב הָיָה יוֹצֵא שָׂבֵעַ.
קָא

תורה אור

תוספות רי"ד

אכולהו והא ספנים ו' חדשים קתני אינו דומה מי שיש לו פת בסלו למי שאין לו. פי' בלא נדר דעתיה עילוי' ומצפה לו תדיר שמא יבא משא"כ במדיר: הגמלים א' וכו'. א"ל רבא בר ר"ח לאביי חמר ונעשה גמל מאי א"ל רוצה אשה בקב ותיפלות מט' קבין ופרישות דברי ר"א: אמר ר"ב א"ר הל' כר"א: אמר ראב"א זו דברי ר"א אבל חכ"א יוצא אדם לת"ת ב' וג' שנים שלא ברשות א"ר סמכי רבנן אהא ועבדי עובדא בנפשייהו למימרא דלא שרי למיעבד הכי כי הא דר' רחומי הוה שכיח במחוזא קמי' דרבא הוה רגיל למיתי' לביתי' כל מעלי יומא דכיפורא יומא חדא משכתיה שמעתא ולא אתא הות (קמהויא) [קמסכיא] דביתהו השתא אתי א) ותחלש דעתה אחתא דמעא מעיני' הות יתבא באגרא איפחת איגרא מתותי' ונח נפשיה. (כ"ז הוא לצאת שלא ברשות אבל אם יוצא ועומד ברשות אשתו אפי' הרבה שנים יכול לעמוד ואינו נענש כדאמרי' בגמרא שעמד ר"ע כ"ד שנה ברשות אשתו ולא נענש והרב פי' שאם התנה עם אשתו לילך ולשנות ורוצה האשה לחזור מתנאה התנאי בטל לפי שתנאי זה הוא תנאי לבטל מ"ש בתורה דהיינו למעט העונה והמתנה עמש"כ בתורה תנאו בטל) עונת ת"ח עד כמה אמר ר"י א"ש מע"ש לע"ש:

א) לפי הגי' בגמ' צ"ל חלש דעתה אחית דמעתא מעינה הוה יתיב באיגרא וכו' ואולי לרבינו היה לו גי' אחרת וצ"ע:

הגהות הב"ח

(א) גמ' בבי רב. ע' מ"ר סדר אחרי מות פ' כא:

ב"ב נט.

גליון הש"ס

גמ' רבי אתי משפטיה עי' כנה"ג חו"מ סימן ג' בהגהותיו להב"י אות ו:

מסורת הש"ס

יומא יח: סז. עד: יבמות לז: [לקמן סג.]
[ברא"ש איתא רבא]
סוטה כ. כא:
נ"א מתשעה
[גי' הרי"ף רב מתנא]
[גי' הרא"ש רבא]
[עי' רש"י עירובין סג ד"ה מחוזא]
ב"ק פב. ע"ש
[עי' רש"י לקמן קג. ד"ה בי שימשי]
[כדאיתא יבמות לז:]

הגהות מהר"ב רנשבורג

א] תום' ד"ה מתשעה וכו' ולפי חשבון ארבע סאה בסלע הוי שלשה דינר י"ח קבין. דבריהם מבוארים יותר בסוטה ד' כא ע"ש בד"ה רוצה וכו' והגהת מהרי"ף לא לייט כאן:

קָא מְדַבְּרַתְּ. אַתְּ מִתְנַהֶגֶת. שִׁיבָבָתָא. הַשְּׁכֵינוֹת. שֶׁלִּי וְשֶׁלָּכֶם שֶׁלָּהּ הוּא. תּוֹרָה שֶׁלָּמַדְתִּי אֲנִי וְשֶׁלְּמַדְתֶּם אַתֶּם – עַל יָדָהּ הוּא. שְׁקַל מָנָא. כְּלִי זַיִן, כְּאִילּוּ בָּא לְהִלָּחֵם. אִיטְרוּד. בְּאוֹתָהּ מְרִיבָה. לָא מָר אִיפְסִיק וְלָא מָר אִיפְסִיק. לֹא אָכְלוּ סְעוּדַּת יוֹם הַכִּפּוּרִים שֶׁמַּפְסִיקִין בָּהּ אֲכִילָה לְהִתְעַנּוֹת. סְעוּדָּה אַחֲרוֹנָה שֶׁל עֶרֶב ט' בְּאָב וְיוה"כ קְרֵי סְעוּדָּה הַמַּפְסֶקֶת, שֶׁמַּפְסִיקִים בָּהּ, בְּמַסֶּ' תַּעֲנִית (דף ל.). מתני' הַמּוֹרֶדֶת עַל בַּעְלָהּ. בַּגְּמָ' מְפָרֵשׁ מִמַּאי. טְרַפָּעִיקִין. בַּגְּמָרָא מְפָרֵשׁ. עַד כְּדֵי כְתוּבָּתָהּ. וְאַחַר כָּךְ נוֹתֵן לָהּ גֵּט, וְיוֹצְאָה בְּלֹא כְּתוּבָּה. אֲבָל אֵינוֹ מַשְׁהָהּ לִפְסוֹק עַל הַנְּכָסִים שֶׁנָּפְלוּ לָהּ מִבֵּית אָבִיהָ וּלְהַפְסִידָהּ מִמֶּנָּה. שְׁלֹשָׁה דִּינָרִים. בַּגְּמָרָא מְפָרֵשׁ מַאי שְׁנָא הוּא מִינָּהּ דִּידָהּ. גמ' בְּאוֹמֵר אֵינִי זָן. דְּהַיְינוּ תַּחַת מְלָאכָה. וְהָאָמַר רַב יוֹצִיא. וּמַתְנִיתִין מוֹסִיפִין תְּנַן, וְאֵינוֹ מוֹצִיאָהּ לְאַלְתַּר. וְלָאו אִימְלוּכֵי בֵּיהּ בָּעֵי. שֶׁמָּא יַחֲזוֹר בּוֹ. וּבְתוֹךְ זְמַן שֶׁאָנוּ נִמְלָכִין בּוֹ, וּמַחֲזִירִין עָלָיו שֶׁיַּחֲזוֹר בּוֹ – מוֹסִיפִין עַל כְּתוּבָּתָהּ. אַחַת לִי. כּוּלָּן שָׁווֹת בְּתוֹרַת מֶרֶד, וַאֲפִילּוּ שֶׁהִיא נִדָּה אוֹ חוֹלָה וְהִיא מוֹרֶדֶת. אֲרוּסָה. שֶׁאָמְרָה לֹא אֶנָּשֵׂא. ה"ג: בִּשְׁלָמָא לְמ"ד מִתַּשְׁמִישׁ – שַׁפִּיר. אֶלָּא לְמ"ד מִשּׁוּם מְלָאכָה, חוֹלָה בַּת מְלָאכָה הִיא? בִּשְׁלָמָא לְמ"ד מִתַּשְׁמִישׁ – שַׁפִּיר, וְאִי מִשּׁוּם נִדָּה דְּלָאו בַּת תַּשְׁמִישׁ הִיא – אֵינוֹ דּוֹמֶה מִי שֶׁיֵּשׁ לוֹ פַּת בְּסַלּוֹ כו', כִּדְלְקַמָּן. אֶלָּא לְמַאן דְּאָמַר כו'.

אֶלָּא

תורה אור

קָא מְדַבְּרַתְּ אַלְמָנוּת חַיִּים. אָמְרָה לֵיהּ: אִי לְדִידִי צָיְיתַתְּ — יָתֵיב תְּרֵי סְרֵי שְׁנֵי אַחֲרִינֵי. אֲמַר: בִּרְשׁוּת קָא עָבֵידְנָא. הֲדַר אֲזַל וְיָתֵיב תְּרֵי סְרֵי שְׁנֵי אַחֲרִינֵי בְּבֵי רַב. כִּי אֲתָא, אַיְיתֵי בַּהֲדֵיהּ עֶשְׂרִין וְאַרְבְּעָה אַלְפֵי תַּלְמִידֵי. שָׁמְעָה דְּבֵיתְהוּ, הֲוַת קָא נָפְקָא לְאַפֵּיהּ. אָמְרוּ לָהּ שִׁיבָבָתָא: (משלי יב) שְׁאִילִי מָאנֵי לְבוּשׁ וְאִיכַּסַּאי! אָמְרָה לְהוּ: °"יוֹדֵעַ צַדִּיק נֶפֶשׁ בְּהֶמְתּוֹ". כִּי מְטָא לְגַבֵּיהּ — נָפְלָה עַל אַפָּהּ, קָא מְנַשְּׁקָא לֵיהּ לְכַרְעֵיהּ. הָווּ קָא מַדְחֲפֵי לָהּ שַׁמָּעֵיהּ. אֲמַר לְהוּ: שִׁבְקוּהָ, שֶׁלִּי וְשֶׁלָּכֶם — שֶׁלָּהּ הוּא. שְׁמַע אֲבוּהּ דְּאָתָא גַּבְרָא רַבָּה לְמָתָא, אֲמַר: אֵיזִיל לְגַבֵּיהּ אֶפְשָׁר דְּמֵפֵר נִדְרַאי. אֲתָא לְגַבֵּיהּ, א"ל: אַדַּעְתָּא דְּגַבְרָא רַבָּה מִי נָדְרַתְּ? א"ל: אֲפִילּוּ פֶּרֶק אֶחָד וַאֲפִי' הֲלָכָה אַחַת. אֲמַר לֵיהּ: אֲנָא הוּא. נָפַל עַל אַפֵּיהּ, וּנְשַׁקֵיהּ עַל כַּרְעֵיהּ, וְיָהֵיב לֵיהּ פַּלְגָא מָמוֹנֵיהּ. בְּרַתֵּיהּ דְּר"ע עָבְדָא לֵיהּ לְבֶן עַזַּאי הָכִי. וְהַיְינוּ דְּאָמְרִי אֱינָשֵׁי: רְחֵילָא בָּתַר רְחֵילָא אָזְלָא, כְּעוֹבָדֵי אִמָּהּ כָּךְ עוֹבָדֵי בְּרַתָּא. רַב יוֹסֵף בְּרֵיהּ דְּרָבָא שַׁדְרֵיהּ אֲבוּהִי לְבֵי רַב לְקַמֵּיהּ דְּרַב יוֹסֵף. פָּסְקוּ לֵיהּ שִׁית שְׁנֵי. כִּי הֲוָה תְּלָת שְׁנֵי מְטָא מַעֲלֵי יוֹמָא דְּכִפּוּרֵי, אֲמַר: אֵיזִיל וְאֶיחֱזֵינְהוּ לֶאֱינָשֵׁי בֵּיתִי. שְׁמַע אֲבוּהִי, שְׁקַל מָנָא וּנְפַק לְאַפֵּיהּ. אֲמַר לֵיהּ: *זוֹנָתְךָ נִזְכַּרְתָּ? אִיכָּא דְּאָמְרִי, אֲמַר לֵיהּ: יוֹנָתְךָ נִזְכַּרְתָּ? אִיטְרוּד, לָא מָר אִיפְסִיק וְלָא מָר אִיפְסִיק.§ [בע"י הגי' זונתך ועי' רש"א שם] **מתני'** הַמּוֹרֶדֶת עַל בַּעְלָהּ — פּוֹחֲתִין לָהּ מִכְּתוּבָּתָהּ *שִׁבְעָה דִּינָרִין בְּשַׁבָּת, ר' יְהוּדָה אוֹמֵר: שִׁבְעָה טְרַפָּעִיקִין. עַד מָתַי הוּא פּוֹחֵת — עַד כְּנֶגֶד כְּתוּבָּתָהּ. ר' יוֹסֵי אוֹמֵר: לְעוֹלָם הוּא פּוֹחֵת *וְהוֹלֵךְ, עַד שֶׁאִם תִּפּוֹל לָהּ יְרוּשָּׁה מִמָּקוֹם אַחֵר גּוֹבֶה הֵימֶנָּה. [במ"כ סדר ויקרא פ' נב מפרש למה שבעה דינרין דוקא וכן לשלשה דינרין דבסמוך] וְכֵן הַמּוֹרֵד עַל אִשְׁתּוֹ — [א]מוֹסִיפִין עַל כְּתוּבָּתָהּ שְׁלֹשָׁה דִּינָרִין בְּשַׁבָּת, ר' יְהוּדָה אוֹמֵר: שְׁלֹשָׁה טְרַפָּעִיקִין.§ **גמ'** מוֹרֶדֶת מִמַּאי? רַב הוּנָא אָמַר: [ב]מִתַּשְׁמִישׁ הַמִּטָּה, ר' יוֹסֵי בְּרַבִּי חֲנִינָא אָמַר: מִמְּלָאכָה. תְּנַן: וְכֵן הַמּוֹרֵד עַל אִשְׁתּוֹ, בִּשְׁלָמָא לְמ"ד מִתַּשְׁמִישׁ — לְחַיֵּי, אֶלָּא לְמַאן דְּאָמַר מִמְּלָאכָה — מִי מְשׁוּעְבָּד לָהּ? אִין, בְּאוֹמֵר "אֵינִי זָן וְאֵינִי מְפַרְנֵס". *וְהָאָמַר רַב: הָאוֹמֵר "אֵינִי זָן וְאֵינִי מְפַרְנֵס" — יוֹצִיא וְיִתֵּן כְּתוּבָּה! וְלָאו לְאִמְלוּכֵי בֵּיהּ בָּעֵי?§ (לקמן עז.) מֵיתִבֵי: *[ג]אַחַת לִי אֲרוּסָה וּנְשׂוּאָה, וַאֲפִי' נִדָּה, וַאֲפִילּוּ חוֹלָה, [ד]וַאֲפִי' שׁוֹמֶרֶת יָבָם. [לקמן סד.] (בִּשְׁלָמָא לְמַאן דְּאָמַר מִמְּלָאכָה — שַׁפִּיר. אֶלָּא לְמַאן דְּאָמַר מִתַּשְׁמִישׁ — נִדָּה בַּת תַּשְׁמִישׁ הִיא? אָמַר לָךְ: *אֵינוֹ דּוֹמֶה מִי שֶׁיֵּשׁ לוֹ פַּת בְּסַלּוֹ לְמִי שֶׁאֵין לוֹ. [ס"א ל"ג] [לעיל סב: וש"נ] אִיכָּא דְּאָמְרִי:) בִּשְׁלָמָא לְמַאן דְּאָמַר מִתַּשְׁמִישׁ — *הַיְינוּ דְּקָתָנֵי חוֹלָה, [ס"א שפיר]

אֶלָּא

אדעתא דגברא רבה מי נדרת. וא"ת: והלא אסור לפתוח בנולד, דאמרינן בנדרים בפ' "ר' אליעזר" (דף סד.): כיצד, אמר קונם שאיני נהנה לפלוני, ונעשה סופר כו'! וי"ל: דהכא לא חשיב נולד, כיון שהלך לבי רב. דדרך הוא בהולך ללמוד שנעשה אדם גדול. אי נמי, כגון דתלה נדרו בדבר, שפירש בשעה שנדר על דעת אם לא יעשה סופר. דבענין זה לא הוה נולד, כדתנן בפרק "רבי אליעזר" (שם דף סה.): קונם שאיני נושא את פלונית שאביה רע, אמרו לו מת, או עשה תשובה כו'. ופריך בגמ': מת נולד הוא! וה"ה עשה תשובה. ומשני, אמר רב הונא: נעשה כתולה נדרו בדבר. ורבי יוחנן דמשני התם בענין אחר – לאו משום דפליג אתולה נדרו בדבר, אלא דלא חשיב ליה כתולה נדרו בדבר. **ברתיה** דר' עקיבא עבדא ליה לבן עזאי הכי. וא"ת: והא בפ' קמא דסוטה (דף ד:) פריך: והא איכא בן עזאי דלא נסיב? ולההוא לישנא דמשני נסיב ופירש – אכי שפיר. ויש לומר: דאע"ג דקאמר הכא דעבדא הכי לבן עזאי – מ"מ לא נשאה, אלא באירוסין. **פוחתין** לה ז' דינרין. בירושלמי מפרש: כנגד שבע מלאכות שהאשה עושה לבעלה. וגבי המורד דמוסיפין שלשה דינרין מפרש: כנגד שארה כסותה ועונתה. והתלמוד שלנו (א) אין סובר כן, דהא בעי בגמרא מה בין מורד למורדת, ומפרש טעמא אחרינא. **רב** הונא אמר מתשמיש. אבל ממלאכה לא הוה מורדת. דרב הונא לטעמיה, דאמר לעיל (דף נח:): יכולה אשה שתאמר לבעלה איני ניזונית ואיני עושה. ור' יוסי בר חנינא סבר כר"ל. וליכא למימר דקסבר כרב הונא, דאמר שיכולה אשה שתאמר לבעלה כו', ומורדת ממלאכה היינו מזיגת הכוס והצעת המטה והרחצת פניו ידיו ורגליו, דמסתברא דחייבת אפילו אמרה איני ניזונית ואיני עושה, מידי דהוה איושבת בקתדרא דחייבת בהן. דאין נראה שתהא מורדת אלא מהמלאכות המפורשות במתני'. ועוד. מדקאמר בסמוך חולה בת מלאכה היא? ואותן מלאכות – אפילו חולה יכולה לעשות, דאינה חולה כל כך, כיון שיכולה לסבול תשמיש. ואי הוה אמרינן דכי אמרה איני ניזונת ואיני עושה לא מפקעת עצמה אלא מעשיית לגמר, שהוא עיקר מעשה ידיה, אבל שאר מלאכות כגון טוחנת ואופה כי' עבדא – הו"מ שפיר סבר כרב הונא. וכן משמע קצת, דקרי לעיל (דף נט.) מעשה ידיה מידי דקיין, ובשאר מלאכות כגון טוחנת ואופה לא שייך קילותא. אבל אין נראה, אלא כי אמרה איני ניזונת ואיני עושה פטורה מכל ז' מלאכות, וכי עבדא שאר מלאכות – פוחתין לה מעשיית בגמר, כדתנן במתניתין (לקמן סד:): ואם היתה מינקת פוחתין לה ממעשה ידיה, ונראה דהוא הדין טוחנת ואופה. והא דנקט מינקת – משום דאיירי במסרה אותה על ידי שלים, דאינה יכולה לעשות לו מלאכה אחרת, כיון דאינה עמו בבית. ומיהו, יש לדחות: דאיכא למימר דדווקא נקט מניקה, ומשום דטורח ממעט חלב – פוחתין לה ממעשה ידיה. אבל מכל מקום נראה דכי אמרה איני ניזונת ואיני עושה – דפטורה מכל המלאכות. שאם תעשה לו מלאכות אחרות – אם כן לעולם לא תעשה לעצמה, ובמאי תהא ניזונת? ואם תאמר: מורדת ממלאכה אמאי פוחתין לה מכתובתה? לינקוט *פיזרא וליתיב, דהא יכול לכופה למעשה ידיה כריש לקיש! וי"ל: כיון דאינה רוצה לעשות אלא ע"י כפייה – חשיבא מורדת, ופוחתין, דאין אדם דר עם נחש בכפיפה אחת. **באומר** איני זן ואיני מפרנס. מכאן מוכיח רבינו אליהו שחייב אדם להשכיר עצמו ללמד תינוקת, או לעשות מלאכה אחרת, כדי לזון את אשתו. דאם לא כן – מה ענין זה אצל מורד ממלאכה? ומיהו, בקונטרס פירש משום דזן ומפרנס הוא כנגד מלאכה של אשה. ועוד הביא ראיה: מדכתבינן בכתובה "ואנא אפלח כו'". ומיהו, גם זה יש לדחות, כמו שמפרש ר"ת: דאפלח – היינו עבודת הקרקע, פירוש: אחרוש ואכנש ואעדור את השדה ואביא מזונות לבית, אבל להשכיר עצמו – אינו חייב. **והאמר** רב האומר איני זן ואיני מפרנס יוציא ויתן כתובה. משמע דפליג עליה דרב "בסוף המדיר" (לקמן דף עז.), דקאמר: עד שכופין אותו להוציא – יכפוהו לזון, לא מצי למפרך. דלדידיה אתי שפיר דאע"פ שכופין אותו על כרחו לזונה – מכל מקום מוסיפין, כיון דאינו רוצה לזונה אלא על ידי כפיה, דאין אדם דר עם נחש בכפיפה אחת. אבל לרב שכופין אותו לגרשה מיד – מה שייך תוספת? ואם תאמר: למאן דאמר מתשמיש – נמי תקשי, דכל כרחך מורד מתשמיש נמי כופין להוציא, דאטו לעולם יוסיפו על כתובתה ותתעגן כל ימיה? ויש לומר: דהוה מצי למימר ולטעמיך.

אבל

צז א ב מיי' פי"ד מהל' אישות הלכה טו סמג לאוין פא טוש"ע אה"ע סימן עז סעיף א:
צח ג מיי' שם הלכה יב טור ש"ע שם סעיף ב:
צט ד מיי' וסמג שם ומיי' פ"ב מהל' יבום וחליצה הלכה י סמג עשין נא טוש"ע שם וסי' קסה סעיף א:

הגהות הב"ח

(א) תד"ה פוחתין כו'. נ"ב ותימה דהא האי ש"ס שלנו אינו אלא במורדת מתשמיש ובירושלמי לא קאמר אלא למורדת ממלאכה:

ס"א והולך שמא [ודע לגירסת תוספות לעיל נד: ד"ה למורדת כו' לעולם פוחת והולך שאם נפלה לה ירושה כו']

[לקמן עז.] [פירוש מקל]

תוספות רי"ד

מתני' המורדת על בעלה פוחתין לה מכתובתה ז' דינרים בשבת ר"י אומר שבעה טרפעיקין ועד כמה הוא פוחת והולך עד כנגד כתובתה ר"י אומר לעולם הוא פוחת והולך שמא תפול לה ירושה ממקום אחר ויחזור ויגבה ממנה. וכן המורד על אשתו מוסיפין לה על כתובתה ג' דינרים בשבת ר"י אומר שלשה טרפעיקין פי' המורדת על בעלה מתשמיש שאינה רוצה להזקק לו קנסוה חכמים לפחות מכתובתה ז' דינרים בשבת ומרויח הבעל שאפי' אם תתרצה אחר מיכן לעמוד בשלום [עמו] אלו ז' דינרים הרויחן הבעל בכל שבת ושבת ופוחתת מכתובתה ואם קדם הבעל ונתן לה גט בתוך ימי מרדה נותן לה כל כתובתה חוץ מפחת זה שאינה מפסדת במרדה אלא ז' דינרים בשבת ותו לא וכגון שאינה תובעת גירושין אלא שמתכוונת לצערו כדאמרינן לקמן אבל אם תובעת גירושין נותן לה גט ומפסדת כל כתובתה מיד והוא שיתרו בה ויודיעוה כי תפסיד כל כתובתה מפני שתובעת גט ואם חזרה בה הרי טוב ואם לאו נותן לה גיטא ומפסדת כל כתובתה אלא מתני' מיירי כגון דלא תבעה גט אלא מכוונת לצערו מפני שכעוסה עליו. עד כמה פוחת וכו' פי' כתובתה יקרא מו"מ ותוס' (קורא) כל נכסי נדוניתה ופחתו וכלו או אבדו אבל אותן שהן בעין מיבעי לן לקמן אם הפסידה במורדה ואם לאו ודוקא כנגד כתובתה פוחת והולך אבל כנגד נ"מ שלה לא שאינה מפסדת נ"מ שלה במרדה כ"א כ"ש בשטר כתובתה ואחרי שכלתה כל כתובתה אם רוצה פוטרה בגט ואם לאו אינו פוטרה אלא מעגנה לעולם שאין האיש מוציא אלא לרצונו ואם תתרצה להשלים עמו כבר הפסידה כל כתובתה והרויחה הבעל בימי מרדה אלא כותב לה כאדם הנושא את בעולה וכ"ו שהבעל מתרצה לתת לה גט בתוך ימי מרדה אינו מרויח אלא ז' דינרים בכל שבת והשאר נותן לה: ר"י אומר לעולם וכו' פי' לא מיבעי' נ"מ שיש לה שהיא מפסדת אם שהתה במרדה אלא אפילו מה שעתידין ליפול לה תפסיד הלכך מונין לה בכל שבת ז' דינרים שאם תפול לה ירושה ממקום אחר יגבה מהן הבעל וכן המורד על אשתו ומעגנה מתשמיש ואינו פוטרה בגט שאם היה רוצה לפוטרה בגט היה מגרשה ונותן לה כל כתובתה אלא שמעגנה מחמת שהוא כעוס עליה מוסיפים לה על כתובתה ג' דינרים בכל שבת והאשה מרוחת אותן שאפילו אם יתרצה להשלים עמה אלו הדינרים הרויחה וניזונת ממעשה ידיה ואי לא ספקא שקלה מבעלה קשה אמאי גבי נדר לא יהבינן ליה אלא שבת אחד ואם שהה יותר יוציא ויתן כתובה והכא משהינן ליה משום דהתם נדר וא"א בפיוס אבל הכא בלא נדר דלמא מפייס אבל ודאי אי אמרה אשה לא מצינא לשהויי

או

אֶלָּא לְמַאן דְּאָמַר מִמְּלָאכָה – חוֹלָה בַּת מְלָאכָה הִיא? אֶלָּא, מִתַּשְׁמִישׁ כּוּלֵּי עָלְמָא לָא פְּלִיגִי דְּהָוְיָא מוֹרֶדֶת. כִּי פְּלִיגִי – מִמְּלָאכָה. מָר סָבַר: [א]מִמְּלָאכָה לָא הָוְיָא מוֹרֶדֶת, וּמָר סָבַר: מִמְּלָאכָה נַמִּי הָוְיָא מוֹרֶדֶת.§ גּוּפָא: הַמּוֹרֶדֶת עַל בַּעְלָהּ פּוֹחֲתִין לָהּ מִכְּתוּבָּתָהּ שִׁבְעָה דִּינָרִים בְּשַׁבָּת, רַבִּי יְהוּדָה אוֹמֵר: שִׁבְעָה טַרְפָּעִיקִין. *רַבּוֹתֵינוּ חָזְרוּ וְנִמְנוּ [ב]שֶׁיְּהוּ מַכְרִיזִין עָלֶיהָ אַרְבַּע שַׁבָּתוֹת זוֹ אַחַר זוֹ, וְשׁוֹלְחִין לָהּ ב"ד: הֱוִי יוֹדַעַת שֶׁאֲפִי' כְּתוּבָּתֵיךְ מֵאָה מָנֶה הִפְסַדְתְּ. אַחַת לִי אֲרוּסָה וּנְשׂוּאָה אֲפִילּוּ נִדָּה, אֲפִי' חוֹלָה, וַאֲפִי' שׁוֹמֶרֶת יָבָם. אֲמַר לֵיהּ ר' חִיָּיא בַּר יוֹסֵף לִשְׁמוּאֵל: נִדָּה בַּת תַּשְׁמִישׁ הִיא? אֲמַר לֵיהּ: אֵינוֹ דּוֹמֶה *מִי שֶׁיֵּשׁ לוֹ פַּת בְּסַלּוֹ לְמִי שֶׁאֵין לוֹ פַּת בְּסַלּוֹ. אָמַר רָמִי בַּר חָמָא: [ג]אֵין מַכְרִיזִין עָלֶיהָ אֶלָּא בְּבָתֵּי כְנֵסִיּוֹת וּבְבָתֵּי מִדְרָשׁוֹת. אָמַר רָבָא: דַּיְקָא נַמִי, דְּקָתָנֵי: אַרְבַּע שַׁבָּתוֹת זוֹ אַחַר זוֹ – ש"מ. אָמַר רָמִי בַּר חָמָא: [ד]פְּעָמִים שׁוֹלְחִין לָהּ מִבֵּית דִּין; אַחַת קוֹדֶם הַכְרָזָה וְאַחַת לְאַחַר הַכְרָזָה. דָּרַשׁ רַב נַחְמָן בַּר רַב חִסְדָּא: הֲלָכָה כְּרַבּוֹתֵינוּ. אֲמַר רָבָא: *הַאי בּוּרְכָא. אֲמַר לֵיהּ רַב נַחְמָן בַּר יִצְחָק: מַאי בּוּרְכָתֵיהּ? אֲנָא אֲמַרִיתָהּ נִיהֲלֵיהּ, וּמִשְּׁמֵיהּ דְּגַבְרָא רַבָּה אֲמַרִיתָהּ נִיהֲלֵיהּ, וּמַנּוּ – רַבִּי יוֹסֵי בְּר' חֲנִינָא. וְאִיהוּ כְּמַאן סָבַר? כִּי הָא דְּאִתְּמַר, רָבָא אָמַר רַב שֵׁשֶׁת: [ה]הֲלָכָה נִמְלָכִין בָּהּ. רַב הוּנָא בַּר יְהוּדָה אָמַר רַב שֵׁשֶׁת: הֲלָכָה, אֵין נִמְלָכִין בָּהּ. הֵיכִי דָּמְיָא מוֹרֶדֶת? אָמַר אַמֵימָר: [ו]דְּאָמְרָה "בָּעֵינָא לֵיהּ וּמְצַעַרְנָא לֵיהּ", [ז]אֲבָל אָמְרָה "מְאִיס עָלַי" – לָא כָּיְיפִינַן לָהּ. מָר זוּטְרָא אָמַר: כָּיְיפִינַן לָהּ. הֲוָה עוּבְדָא, וְאַכְפַּהּ מָר זוּטְרָא, וּנְפַק מִינֵּיהּ רַבִּי חֲנִינָא מִסּוּרָא. וְלָא הִיא, הָתָם סִיַּיעְתָּא דִּשְׁמַיָּא הֲוָה. °כַּלָּתֵיהּ דְּרַב זְבִיד אִימְּרְדָא. הֲוָה תְּפִיסָא חַד שִׁירָא, יָתֵיב אַמֵימָר וּמָר זוּטְרָא וְרַב אַשִׁי, וְיָתֵיב רַב גַּמְדָּא גַּבַּיְיהוּ. יָתְבִי וְקָאָמְרִי: מָרְדָה – הִפְסִידָה בְּלָאוֹתֶיהָ קַיָּימִין. אֲמַר לְהוּ רַב גַּמְדָּא: מִשּׁוּם דְּרַב זְבִיד גַּבְרָא רַבָּה מַחֲנִיפִיתוּ לֵיהּ? וְהָאָמַר רַב כָּהֲנָא: מִיבַּעְיָא בְּעֵי רָבָא וְלָא פְּשֵׁיט. אִיכָּא דְּאָמְרִי, יָתְבִי וְקָאָמְרִי: [ח]מָרְדָה – לֹא הִפְסִידָה בְּלָאוֹתֶיהָ קַיָּימִין, אֲמַר לְהוּ רַב גַּמְדָּא: מִשּׁוּם

רש"י

אלא מתשמיש דכולי עלמא לא פליגי דהויא מורדת. והך מתניתא במורדת מתשמיש. חזרו ונמנו. שלא ישהו אותה לפחות מעט מעט, אלא יפסידוה כל כתובתה לאחר ארבע שבתות של הכרזה. דיקא נמי דקתני ארבע שבתות. ימים שאינם של מלאכה, והכל מצוין בבתי כנסיות ובבתי מדרשות. בורכא. דבר שאינו הגון. ואיהו כמאן סבר. רבא דאמר בורכא היא, כמאן סבר? נמלכין בה. משהין את גיטה ומחזירין עליה שתחזור בה, ובתוך כך פוחתין מכתובתה שבעה דינרין בשבת. היכי דמיא מורדת. דכופין אותה, דמשהין גיטה ופוחתין כתובתה. דאמרה בעינא ליה כו'. שיש לכופה על ידי פחיתת כתובתה. אבל אמרה מאים עלי. לא הוא ולא כתובתו בעינא. לא כייפינן לה. להשהותה, אלא נותן לה גט, ויוצאה בלא כתובתה. כלתיה דרב זביד אימרידא. ואמרה מאים עלי. הוה תפיסא חדא שירא. מעיל אחד שהכניסה לו בכתובה. הפסידה בלאותיה קיימין. אפילו בגדיה שהכניסה לו בנדונייתה ושמאום עליו בכתובתה, ועדיין הבלאות קיימין תפסיד אותם. מיבעיא בעי. אם הפסידה בלאותיה אם לאו. משום

תוספות

אלא למאן דאמר מתשמיש נדה בת תשמיש היא. וא"ת: למאן דאמר ממלאכה מאי אפילו דקתני "ואפי' נדה"? ויש לומר: דהוי רבותא, משום דסתם נדות חולות קצת. אי נמי, דאינה בת מלאכה כמו שאר נשים, דאינה מוזגת לו הכוס כו'. אינו דומה מי שיש לו פת בסלו כו'. ולעיל דגמר מדיר מנדה – משום דמדיר הוי טפי פת בסלו ממורד, שמא ימצא פתח לנדרו. תדע דבמורד מוסיפין אבל לא במדיר.

דיקא נמי דקתני ד' שבתות. דליכא למימר שמכריזין ד' שבתות בכל יום, דבהדיא תני בתוספ' דפעם אחת בשבת מכריזין.

ואינהו כמאן סברוה. רש"י גריס: ואיהו כמאן סבר. פירוש: רבא דאמר בורכא. ור"ל דלרבא אין הלכה כרבותינו, אלא כמתני' דפוחתין לה עד כלות כתובתה. ונמלכין בה – היינו נמי דפוחתין, ולא תפסיד מיד אחר ארבע שבתות. ור"ת מפרש: דרמי בר חמא בא להוסיף על דברי רבותינו. אע"ג דלא קתני דשולחין לה אלא אחר הכרזה, קאמר רמי בר חמא דה"נ היו אומרים דשולחין לה נמי קודם הכרזה, דרש רב נחמן בר רב חסדא: הלכה כרבותינו, כלומר: ממש כדבריהם, דלא קתני שליחות של קודם הכרזה. ופליג ארמי בר חמא. אמר רבא האי בורכא, אלא הלכה כרמי בר חמא, דפעמים שולחין לה. וגרסינן: אינהו כמאן סברוה. וכן כתוב בספרים ישנים ובה"ג, ולא קאי ארב נחמן בר יצחק (א) ור"נ בר רב חסדא, דאינהו סברי כרבי יוסי ברבי חנינא, שהיה גדול הרבה מרב ששת, אלא ארמי בר חמא ורבא קאי. הלכה נמלכין בה – פירוש: קודם הכרזה. והלכה אין נמלכין בה – נמי, היינו קודם הכרזה. אבל אחר הכרזה – מודה, כדתניא בהדיא בדברי רבותנו, וכן משמע מתוך פר"ת, דפסק דאע"ג דאמר ר"נ בר רב חסדא הלכה כדברי רבותינו – הלכה כרבא דאמר משמיה דרב ששת הלכה נמלכין בה. דהא רמי בר חמא דאמר פעמים שולחין לה מסייע ליה. ומיהו, מסקנא דשמעתין דמשהינן לה תריסר ירחי שתא אגיטא, ולית לה מזוני – אמורדת דהכא קאי, ולא אאומרת מאיס עלי, כמו שמפרש ר"ת. דהא כיון שמכניס חפצים בגירושין, כמו שנפרש – למה נשהא אותה מלהתגרש? אלא אמורדת דהכא קאי. ומצא רבינו יהודה בכתב רב שרירא, שתקנו בימיו לתת גט לאשה לאלתר, דלא כשמעתין דכלתיה דרב זביד. וכתב נמי רבינו יהודה דרבנן סבוראי תקנו למישקל מינה מאי דתפיסא, ומייתי לה גיטא לאלתר*. אבל אמרה מאים עלי לא כייפינן לה. פי' בקונטרס לא כייפינן לה לעמוד תחתיו אלא יתן גט ויוצאה בלא כתובה °וי"מ דכופין אותו להוציא ואין נראה לר"ת דניחוש שמא עיניה נתנה באחר כי ההיא דתנן בפרק בתרא דנדרים (דף צ:) גבי שלש נשים יוצאות ונוטלות כתובה ויש לדחות דהתם נוטלות כתובה דוקא איכא למיחש שמא עיניה נתנה באחר אבל הכא דיוצאה בלא כתובה לא ולהכי נמי לא קתני לה עם אותן שכופין להוציא דהתם נותן כתובה וכן בפרק המגרש (גיטין דף פח:) דתנן: גט מעושה ביד גוים פסול, שלא תהא אשה תולה עצמה ביד גוי, ומפקעת עצמה מבעלה. אין להקשות אם באומרת מאים עלי כופין אותו להוציא – א"כ מה הועילו חכמים בתקנתם? הא יכולה להפקיע עצמה מבעלה בטענת מאים עלי, דהא במאים עלי אין לה כתובה. ולא תפקיע עצמה להפסיד כתובתה! ועוד הקשה ר"ת: דבריש "הנזקין" (שם דף מט:) אמר: וכ"ת כי נפקא איהי נתקנו ליה כתובה מינה – ת"ש: האיש אינו מוציא אלא לרצונו. ואמאי? אי כופין במאים עלי להוציא – א"כ נתקנו ליה כתובה מינה! ומיהו, יש לדחות דלא מציא למימר מאים עלי אלא היכא דיש רגלים לדבר שהבעל אינו מתקבל לה. ובשביל אותן נשים – לא רצו לתקן כתובה לאיש, כיון דלא שייך לתקן ברוב נשים. ויהודית דביתהו דרבי חייא דהויא לה צער לידה דאמרינן בפ"ק דקדושין (דף יב:) דאמרה: אמרה לי אם דאביה קיבל בה קדושין כי זוטרא – לא רצתה לומר מאים עלי. ועוד: לפי מה דפרישית אתי שפיר. וזה נמי אין להקשות במתני' לר' יוסי: אמאי פוחת לה מירושה שנפלה לה? תטעון מאים עלי! דקודם כלות הכתובה אינה טוענת ברצון מאים עלי, כי היא בטוחה שלא ירצה להמתין ולהיות מעוגן עד כלות הכתובה, דכל זמן דאגידא ביה (ב) לא יהבינן ליה אחרינא, ויגרשנה ויתן לה כתובה. אבל אחר שכבר הפסידה כל הכתובה – לא תטעון, דהא כיון דהמתינה ולא טענה עד שפיחתו כל כתובתה, דברים ניכרים דאיערומי קא מערמא. ועוד קשה: מאלהי נדרים (דף נא:) מההוא נואף דהוה מיהרזק בביתא הוא ואינתתא, אתא מריה דביתא, פרטיה נואף להוצא וערק. אמר רבא: איתתא שריא, דאם איתא דעבד איסורא – אירכוסי הוה מירכס. משמע דאי הוה מירכס – הוה אסירא. א"כ לכאורה נראה דבאומרת טמאה אני לך איירי, דאי לאו הכי – אמאי הוות מיתסרא? הא אין אשה נאסרת על בעלה עד שיראו כדרך המנאפים, וכיון דבאומרת טמאה אני לך מיירי – א"כ רוצה להפסיד כתובתה, דהא מסתמא ברצון הוה, דבביתה היה. ועוד: דלא נוותא. אפילו הכי, כי לא מירכס – שריא, דאית לן למימר דעיניה נתנה באחר, כיון דלא מירכס, ואמאי? תהא נאמנת במגו דאי בעיא אמרה מאים עלי! וי"ל: דלעולם לא מיירי באומרת טמאה אני לך, ואיתתא שריא דקאמר – היינו לבועל, אם גירשה הבעל או מת, אבל אי הוה מירכס – הוה אסירא לבועל, כדאמרינן בפ' שני דיבמות (דף כד: ושם): הואיל ומכוער הדבר – תצא. ומפרש ר"ת: דתצא מרוכל. וכן נראה דבאומרת טמאה אני לך – אין נראה כלל להתירה מטעם דאירכוסי הוה מירכס, כיון דשוייה נפשה חתיכה דאיסורא. וכ"ש לפי השאלות *) דמפרש דהיכא דאיכא עדים בדבר מכוער – תצא אף מן הבעל, דאתי שפיר, ואין להקשות משם כלל. ועוד י"ל: דהתם איירי כגון שבתחלה כששאלוה שתקה, ולאחר שעה אמרה דאינה טמאה, ונותנת טעם על שתיקותה. ועוד מקשה רבינו תם: דבכל השמועה אינו מזכיר כפיית הבעל, אלא כפיית האשה? ונראה

*) [פרכם בלה סימן קלד]

עין משפט נר מצוה

ק א מיי' פכ"א מהלכות אישות הלכה י סמג לאוין פא טוש"ע אה"ע סימן פ סעיף טו:

קא ב ג ד ה ו ז ח מיי' פי"ד שם הלכה ט י יא יג סמג שם טוש"ע שם סי' עז סעיף ב וסעיף ג:

תוספות רי"ד

או ישלים עמה או יוציא ויתן כתובה בודאי שהדין עמה ומיהו בתוך ימי מרדו היא מרוחת ג' דינרים בכל שבת. מורדת ממאי ר"ה אמר מתשמיש ר"י אומר ממלאכה מתשמיש כו"ע לא פליגי דהויא מורדת כי פליגי ממלאכה מר סבר מתשמיש אין ממלאכה לא ומר סבר אפי' ממלאכה. פי' ר"ה לטעמיה דאמר לעיל יכולה אשה ש"ל א"נ וא"ע הלכך ממלאכה לא הויא מורדת אלא מתשמיש ור"י ב"ח ל"ל דר"ה וקסבר אין האשה י"ל לבעלה א"נ וא"ע ואי אמרה הוי מורדת א"נ דכו"ע יכולה אשה לומר לבעלה א"נ וכו' מיהו דוקא במעשה ידיה המפורשין במשנה דתנן וכמה היא עושה לו משקל ה' סלעים וכו' שתחת מע"י תקנו המזונות אבל שאר מלאכות המפורשות במשנה כגון טוחנת ואופה וכו' א"י להפטר מהן הלכך אם מרדה שלא לעשותן הוי מורדת ופסקי' רבואתא הלכה כר"ה (והרב אומר דלר"ה לא הוה מורדת לעולם אלא מתשמיש לבדו שהוא עיקר האישות) תנן המורד על אשתו וכו' בשלמא למ"ד מתשמיש שפיר דכי היכי דאיהי משעבדא ליה לדידיה איהו נמי משועבד לה לדידה אלא למאן דאמר ממלאכה מלאכה מי משעבד לה אין באומר איני זן ואיני מפרנס פי' והמזונות הן תחת המלאכה והא"ר האומר איני זן ואיני מפרנס יוציא ויתן כתובה פי' והיכי תנן מוסיפין לה ג' דינרים ותו לא ומהדר ולאו לאימלוכי ביה בעי פי' ואע"ג דא"ר יוציא ויתן כתובה [אינו] מיד אלא נמלכים בו ומתרים בו שאם לא יתרצה חייב להוציא וליתן כתובה ומאי דתנן מוסיפין לה על כתובתה באותן הימים שנמלכים לפתותו שאע"פ שנתפיים נותן לה בכל שבת ג' דינר כל הימים שעמד במרדו ומכאן מוכח שאם טוענת האשה ואומרת א"א בתום' זה או תתרצה ותשלים עמי או תן לי גיטי וכתובתי שהדין עמה כדכתיב לעיל. אבל אם הבעל אומר לאשה כשהיא מורדת א"א לעמוד בתוספת שא"א לעמוד בלא אשה או תתרצה עמי או צאי בלא כתובה אין שומעין לו שאין דומה האיש לאשה שעיגון האשה גדול משל

מסורת הש"ס

[תוספתא פ"ה ע"ש]

[לעיל סב: וש"נ]

[שבועות יב: חולין פח: ובחולין פרש"י שהוא מלשון בור וכ"כ בערוך ערך בכך ה' כלומר דבר בורות הוא ובור הוא מי שאומר דבר זה ועי' פירוש רש"י בשבועות יב: בענין אחר]

הגהות הב"ח

(א) תד"ה ואינהו כו' ורב נחמן בר רב חסדא כו'. נ"ב פירוש וקאמר דאינהו סברי כרב ששת וכמאן דאמר הלכה אין נמלכין בה קאמר: (ב) ד"ה אבל כו' לא יהבו ליה אחריתא:

גליון הש"ס

גמ' כלתיה דרב זביד אימרדא. בפרש"י אות לט יח הגי' כאן אמריא: תד"ה אבל כו'. וי"מ דכופין וכו'. עי' גיטין פד ע"א תוס' ד"ה הכא (בידה) [בידיה].

ומורי הרב ר' אביגדור ז"ל כתב דבמורדת האומרת בעינא ליה ומצערנא ליה דפוחתין לה ז' דינרין עד כלות כתובתה כמתני' ובמאים עלי להשהותה י"ב חודש ואז תצא בלא כתובה וזה כדברי ר"ת כמ"ש בתוספותיו וכתב כמו כן שלא פסק מ"ש ברב אלפס דלא קנסינן לה בדידה מה שהביאה עמו אלא מפסדת הכל ומהר"ם כתב כרב אלפס. ת"י

תוספות רי"ד

אחת ארוסה שאינה חפצה להנשא מפסדת מאתים וזו שיש לה מן האירוסין בתנאי ב"ד וגם שומרת יבם נמי שאינה רוצה להתייבם היא בכלל מורדת. אר"ח בר יוסף לשמואל נדה בת תשמיש היא א"ל אינו דומה מי שיש לו פת בסלו. אמר רמב"ח כשמכריזין עליה אין מכריזין עליה אלא בב"כ ובב"מ. א"ר דיקא נמי דקתני ד' שבתות זא"ז ש"מ: אמר רמב"ח פעמים שולחים לה מב"ד אחת קודם הכרזה ואחת לאחר הכרזה דרש רנב"ר"ח הלכה כרבותינו אמר רבא הא בורכתא א"ל רנב"י ומאי בורכתא אנא אמריתה ניהליה ומשמיה דגברא רבה אמריתה ניהליה ומנו ר' יוסי ב"ר חנינא וכו' מר זוטרא ונפק מיני' ר"ח מסורא

משום דרב זביד גברא רבה הוא אפכיתו ליה לדינא עילויה? האמר רב כהנא: מיבעיא בעי לה רבא ולא פשיט! השתא דלא אתמר לא הכי ולא הכי, [א]תפסה – לא מפקינן מינה, לא תפסה – לא יהבינן לה. [ב]ומשהינן לה תריסר ירחי שתא אגיטא, ובהנך תריסר ירחי שתא לית לה מזוני מבעל. אמר רב טובי בר קיסנא אמר שמואל: כותבין אגרת מרד על ארוסה, ואין כותבין אגרת מרד על שומרת יבם. מיתיבי: *אחת לי ארוסה ונשואה, אפילו נדה, אפילו חולה, ואפילו שומרת יבם! לא קשיא; כאן – שתבע הוא, כאן – שתבעה היא. דאמר רב תחליפא בר אבימי אמר שמואל: [ג]תבע הוא – נזקקין לו, תבעה היא – אין נזקקין לה. במאי אוקימתא להא דשמואל – בשתבעה היא, האי כותבין אגרת מרד על ארוסה? לארוסה מיבעי ליה! הא לא קשיא, תני: לארוסה. מאי שנא שומרת יבם דלא – דאמרינן לה: זיל, לא מפקדת. ארוסה נמי – נימא לה: זיל, לא מפקדת! אלא בבאה מחמת טענה, דאמרה: בעינא *חוטרא לידא ומרה לקבורה – ה"נ שומרת יבם – בבאה מחמת טענה! אלא, אידי ואידי שתבע הוא, ולא קשיא; [ד]כאן – לחלוץ, וכאן – לייבם. דאמר ר' פדת אמר ר' יוחנן: תבע לחלוץ – נזקקין לו, תבע לייבם – אין נזקקין לו. מאי שנא לייבם דלא – דאמרינן ליה: זיל ונסיב איתתא אחריתי. לחלוץ נמי, נימא ליה: זיל ונסיב איתתא אחריתי! אלא, [ה]דאמר כיון דאגידא בי – לא קא יהבו לי אחריתי. הכא נמי כיון דאגידא בי – לא קא יהבו לי אחריתי! אלא, אידי ואידי שתבע לייבם. ולא קשיא; כאן – כמשנה ראשונה, כאן – כמשנה אחרונה, דתנן: *[ו]מצות יבום קודמת למצות חליצה. בראשונה, שהיו מתכוונין לשום מצוה. עכשיו שאין מתכוונין לשום מצוה – [ז]אמרו: מצות חליצה קודמת למצות יבום. § עד מתי הוא פוחת וכו'. § מאי *טרפעיקין? אמר רב ששת: אסתירא. וכמה אסתירא? *פלגא דזוזא. תניא נמי הכי, ר' יהודה אומר: שלשה טרפעיקין, שהן תשע מעין, מעה וחצי לכל יום. אמר ליה רבי חייא בר יוסף לשמואל: מאי שנא איהו דיהבינן ליה דשבת, ומאי שנא איהי דלא יהבינן לה דשבת? איהי דמיפחת קא פחית – לא מיחזי כשכר שבת, איהו דאוסופי קא מוספא – מיחזי

[לעיל סג.] [יבמות סה:] [שם לט:] בכורות יג. [גיטין מה:] [קדושין יח: וש"נ]

רש"י

משום דרב זביד גברא רבה הוא. ולא יערער על דברינו, מחמת ענוותנותו. מפכיתו דינא. לחובתו. ומשהינן לה. אולי תחזור בה. תריסר ירחי שתא. ותו לא. שתבע הוא. והיא מורדת. תבעה היא. והוא מורד. אין נזקקין לה. לכתוב לה אגרת מרד להוסיף על כתובתה. ולקמן מפיק פירושא ואזיל: משום דלא מפקדא אפריה ורביה. לארוסה מבעי ליה. וכותבין אגרת על הבעל. דלא מפקדת. בפריה ורביה, כדאמרינן ביבמות (דף סה:). חוטרא לידא. רוצה אני שיהא לי בן שיחזיק בידי בזקנותי ואשען עליו, וביום מותי יקברני. תבע לחלוץ. והיא אינה רוצה אלא להתייבם – נזקקין לו לכתוב אגרת מרד עליה. אין נזקקין לו. לפי שאין מתכוין לשם מצוה. וכמשנה אחרונה. ואמרינן ליה: זיל נסיב אחריתי. אסתירא. סלע מדינה. פלגא דזוזא. זוז צורי, שהוא שש מעה כסף, נמצא טרפעיק שלשה מעות. מעה וחצי ליום. לששת ימי המעשה, ומשבת לא יהבינן לה, כדאמר לקמן. מאי שנא איהו דיהבינן ליה דשבת. כשהיא מורדת עליו, דהא שבעה טרפעיקים, טרפעיק ליום. כשכר שבת. [כמו שמשתכר בשבת], גזרה משום מקח וממכר ושכירות.

תוספות

ונראה לר"ת דהכי פירושו: בעינא ליה, ואינה רוצה להתגרש בלא כתובה, ומצערנא ליה עד שיגרשנה ויתן לה כתובה. אבל אמרה מאיס עלי, ולא בעינא ליה לא הוא ולא כתובתו – לא כייפינן לה שתחזור בה ע"י שנאמר שלא תועיל מחילה, משום דהוי מחילה בטעות, דאגב צערה קא אמרה הכי, ומתוך כך – לא יגרשנה בעלה, שאינו רוצה ליתן כתובה. אלא מחילה גמורה היא, ומתוך כך יעלה בדעתו לגרשה. מר זוטרא אמר: כייפינן לה, דהויא כמחילה בטעות. והיינו כפיה – דעל ידי כך תשאר תחת בעלה שלא ברצונה, כי בעלה לא יגרשנה, כיון שחייב ליתן כתובתה. ואין חילוק למר זוטרא בין מורדת דבעינא ליה ומצערנא ליה, בין אומרת מאיס עלי. ור"ח נמי פירש דאין כופין הבעל ליתן גט. וגם בקונט' לא פי' שיכופו הבעל ליתן גט. **משום** דרב זביד גברא רבה הוא אפכיתו לדינא עילויה. וא"ת: כיון דלא פשיט – המע"ה, וכיון דתפסה – לא מפקינן מינה! וי"ל: דהאי נמי שיראי טובא דלא הות תפיסה. ובלישנא קמא קאמר משום דרב זביד גברא רבה אחנפיתו ליה, משום הך שירא דהות תפיסה. ובאיכא דאמרי קאמר – משום הנך שיראי דלא הות תפיסה, אלא הבעל היה תפוס. **תבע** לחלוץ נזקקין לו. פי' בקונט': והיא אינה רוצה אלא להתיבם. וכן תבע לייבם – פירוש: והיא אינה רוצה אלא לחלוץ. ותימה: דמאי קא פריך לייבם נמי, כיון דאגידא ביה לא יהבי ליה איתתא אחריתא, ויחלוץ לה! וי"ל: שאינו רוצה לחלוץ, שלא יצטרך ליתן כתובה. ועי"ל: תבע לחלוץ והיא אינה רוצה לא לחלוץ ולא לייבם, וכן תבע לייבם. וכן הא דאמר כאן שתבעה היא והוא אינו רוצה לא לחלוץ ולא לייבם. ואין להקשות א"כ מאי פריך שומרת יבם נמי בבאה מחמת טענה, מאי איריא בבאה מחמת טענה? אפילו אינה באה נמי תיקשי ליה, מדתנן ב"החולץ" (יבמות לט.): חוזרין אצל גדול, ואומרים לו: עליך המצוה, או כנוס או פטור. וקאמר בגמ': דחוזרין אצל גדול למיכפייה, אלמא בתבעה היא נמי כייפינן ליה, אפילו אינה באה מחמת טענה! דאיכא למימר דכייפינן ליה, אבל אין נזקקין לכתוב עליו איגרת מרד, להוסיף על כתובתה. אי נמי, משום דהיא גופה איכא לפרושי בבאה מחמת טענה. לכך נקט למיפרך מהאי טעמא. **מאי** שנא לייבם דלא. וא"ת: *אי מילתיה דר' יוחנן לפי משנה אחרונה, כדמשמע פשטא דמילתא – א"כ מאי פריך לייבם נמי כיון דאגידא ביה לא יהבי ליה איתתא אחריתא, והא לייבם לא יוכל לכוף אותה לפי משנה אחרונה! ואי לחלוץ – והלא הוא אינו רוצה לחלוץ אלא לייבם, ומאי שייך לכופה לדבר שאינו תובע הוא! וי"ל: דמעיקרא ס"ד מילתיה דרבי יוחנן לפי משנה ראשונה, ומשום הכי פריך דאפילו לייבם נמי נוכל לכופה. ולבסוף דמשני כאן כמשנה ראשונה כאן כמשנה אחרונה – מילתיה דר' יוחנן נמי לפי משנה אחרונה נזקקין לחלוץ ואין נזקקין לייבם. וה"ה דאכתי הוה מצי לשנויי כאן לחלוץ כאן לייבם כרבי יוחנן, ואידי ואידי לפי משנה אחרונה, אלא דניחא ליה לאוקמא תרווייהו כשתבע לייבם, דדומיא דארוסה קתני שתובע לכנוס והיא מורדת. ר"ת. וק"ק: דאיך תיסק אדעתין למימר דאתי לפי משנה ראשונה אדרבה לפי משנה ראשונה איפכא מסתברא: לייבם – נזקקין לו, לחלוץ – אין נזקקין לו! וי"ל: דאפי' לפי משנה ראשונה נזקקין לו לחלוץ, משום דבדידיה תלי רחמנא "אם לא יחפוץ האיש" כדאמרינן ב"החולץ" (יבמות דף לט. ושם). אבל לייבם – ס"ד שאין מוסרין אותה לייבם על כרחה. אי נמי, י"ל: תבע אף לחלוץ – נזקקין לו, תבע לייבם דווקא – אין נזקקין לו. **ודיני** חליצה ויבום פירש בקונטרס ב"החולץ" (ג"ז שם) גבי הא דמייתי התם מתניתין דבכורות (דף יג. ושם) משנה ראשונה ואחרונה דמייתי הכא, ואמר רב עלה דאין כופין. ופירש בקונטרס: דאפילו למשנה אחרונה דמצות חליצה קודמת – אין כופין אותו לחלוץ היכא דניחא לתרווייהו ליבומי, דנימא תרווייהו לאו למצוה מכווני ופגע בערוה, אלא אי בעי – מייבם, אע"ג דמצות חליצה קודמת. ומיהו, היכא דלדהו בעי ליבומי, ואיהי אמרה לא בעינא ליה, ואמרה דברים ניכרים, אי מצינן לאטעויי – מטעינן ליה, לא מצינן לאטעויי – כייפינן ליה לחלוץ. ואמר רב ששת בפ"ק דיבמות (דף ד.): מנין ליבמה שנפלה לפני מוכה שחין שאין חוסמין אותה לפניו כו'. ולא תימא מוכה שחין דווקא, אלא כל אמתלא שתתן לדבריה, דתנן ב"המדיר" (לקמן דף עז.): מעשה בצידון בבורסי שמת ולו אח בורסי, ואמרו חכמים: יכולה היא שתאמר: לאחיך הייתי יכולה לקבל ולך איני יכולה לקבל. ועוד פסקינן: והלכתא, כותבין אגרת מרד על ארוסה ואין כותבין אגרת מרד על שומרת יבם. מכל הני טעמי כייפינן ליה לחלוץ ושקלה כתובתה. וכל הני אין כופין דהכא – היכא דניחא להו לתרווייהו, עכ"ל. ואור"י: דמה שהביא מוכה שחין ומבורסי – אינה ראיה. דדוקא מוכה שחין ובורסי דהוו מהנך דכופין אותו להוציא. ומה שהביא נמי מאין כותבין אגרת מרד על שומרת יבם – לאו ראיה היא, (א) דהתם אין כותבין אפילו בלא אמתלא, משום דמצות חליצה קודמת. וא"כ, לדבריו אפילו בלא אמתלא הוה לן למימר דכופין. ואדרבה, יש להוכיח משם דאין כופין. דאי בר כפייה הוא – למה ליה למימר דאין כותבין אגרת מרד? עדיפא מינה ה"ל למימר, דכופין אותו לחלוץ! ואמרינן נמי בשמעתין: תבע לייבם – אין נזקקין לו, משמע אין נזקקין לו לכתוב אגרת מרד, אדרבה נזקקין לה וכייפינן ליה! ולהכי נראה לר"י: דרב איירי בכל ענין, דודאי בכל ענין אין כופין. ואף לפי' ר"ת, דמפרש דאמר רב אין כופין קאי אמשנה ראשונה, דאין כופין לייבם אע"פ שמצות יבום קודמת, וה"מ בזמן הזה היכא שידוע לנו שמתכוונין למצוה, כגון אותן שבאין לחלוץ, דאותן ודאי אין מתכוונין לא לשום נוי ולא לשום אישות. אבל היכא דלא ברור לן שמתכוונין למצוה – כופין במילי, ומרחיקין אותן מן היבום, דקי"ל כאבא שאול, כמו שפירשנו ביבמות (דף לט: ד"ה אמר רב). וגם לפירושו, אם תבע לייבם – לא כייפינן ליה לחלוץ, אלא מטעינן ליה אם אינה חפצה, אבל אם (ב) אינו רוצה לא לייבם ולא לחלוץ – נראה דכופין.

מיחזי

[ואי לפי משנה ראשונה היאך יתיישבו דבריו לפי המסקנא. ת"י]

עין משפט נר מצוה

קב א מיי' פי"ד מהל' אישות הל' יג טור שו"ע אה"ע סימן עז סעיף ג:

קג ב מיי' שם הלכה י טור שו"ע שם סע"ב:

קד ג ד ה מיי' פ"ב מהל' יבום וחליצה הלכה י סמג עשין נא טוש"ע שם סימן קסה סעיף א ג:

קה ו מיי' פ"א שם הל' ב ופ"ב הלכה ז סמג עשין נב טוש"ע שם סעיף א:

קו ז טור שו"ע שם סעיף א ובהג"ה:

הגהות הב"ח

(א) תד"ה ודיני כו' לאו ראיה היא דא"כ לדבריו אפילו בלא אמתלא הוה לן למימר דכופין דהתם אין כותבין אפילו בלא אמתלא משום דמצות חליצה קודמת ואדרבה יש להוכיח כו' כצ"ל: (ב) בא"ד אבל אם אינו רוצה. נ"ב פי' היכא דהיא חפצה אותו והוא אינו רוצה לא לייבם ולא לחלוץ:

תוספות רי"ד

שאינה מתרצה בדבר אין ב"ד נזקקים לכופה דשמא אנוסה היא ושמא גם היא עציבה בדבר שבעלה מאוס בעיניה ואי משום עיגון הבעל יכול לישא אשה אחרת עד שלא יפטור לזו ויוציא זו ויתן לה כתובתה שאין בית דין יכולין לקונסה בכתובתה מאחר שהיא טוענת טענת אונס וזה הפתרון הוא נכון שאין לזוז ממנו. ולפי"ז הפתרון היכא שאומרת מאיס עלי לא הוי מורדת וא"כ כשבא לגרשה נותן לה כתובה ותוספת שהרי התוספת כותב אדם לאשתו בעבור חיבת ביאה וכבר בא עליה ואימתי אין לה תוספת כשמגרשה משום מורדת שכך היא תקנות הגאונים שתוספת אין לה אבל כתובה יש לה אבל עכשיו שמגרשה משום טענה ולא הוי מורדת אפילו תוספת יש לה שהרי אינו מגרשה כתקנות הגאוני' שנאמר כתובה יש לה תוספת אין לה): כלתי' דר"ז אימרדא הות תפישה חד שיראי יתיב אמימר ומ"ז ור"א ויתיב ר"ג גבייהו וקאמר מרדה הפסידה בלאותי' קיימים א"ל ר"ג משום דר"ז גברא רבא הוא מחניפיתו ליה והאמר ר"כ מיבעי בעי ליה לרבא ולא איפשטא ומאי דתנן עד כנגד כתובתה כל הכתוב בשטר הכתובה משמע ואפילו נכסי נדוניתה אלא קא מבעי ליה די"ל דוקא מידי דמיחסר גוביינא כגון שנאבדו או שבלו שאינו משלם לה הפחת שלהן אבל מה שהן קיימים דקיימו בעיני' ולא מיחסרא גוביינא לא הפסידה א"ד כתובתה קאמר ואע"פ שהן קיימים. איכא דאמרי יתבי וקאמרי מרדה לא הפסידה בלאותיה קיימים א"ל ר"ג משום דר"ז גברא רבא הוא אכפיתוהו לדינא עלוי' והאמר ר"כ מיבעי' בעי ליה רבא ולא איפשטא ליה ומסיק תלמודא והשתא דל"א הלכתא לא כמר ולא כמר תפשה לא שקלי' מינה לא תפשה לא יהבין לה ומשהינן לה תריסר ירחי שתא אגיטא וזהו דין המורדת מכח ההלכה כמו שאמרנו וראיתי כתוב לר' שרירא גאון ז"ל וששאלתם אשה היושבת תחת בעלה ואמרה לו גרשני איני רוצה לשבת עמך מסורא ומסיק תלמודא ולא היא סייעתא דשמיא הואי פי' ואין ללמוד מאותו מעשה אלא כיון שתובעת גירושין לא כייפי' לה (אבל הרב פי' דאדרבה להקל באו עליה ולא להחמיר וכך היא משמעות הדברים: ה"ד מורדת שכופין אותה על הפסד כתובתה לרבנן כדאית להו ולרבותינו כדאית להו דאמרה בעינא ליה ומצערנא ליה שאין בעלה מאוס בעיניה בין תובעת גירושין בין אינה תובעת גירושין הואיל ואין בעלה מאים בעיניה ודאי כופין אותה ע"י הפסד כתובתה כדי שתתפיים עם בעלה אבל אמרה מאים עלי שבעלה מאים בעיניה לא כייפינן לה ע"י הפסד כתובתה אלא מניחין אותה במרדה דכיון דבעלה מאים בעיניה אנוסה היא בדבר ולא מדעתה עושה כן ואפילו אשה כשרה אי אפשר להבעל לשנאוי לה ואע"פ שאין שום מום ניכר בו הרבה פעמים אשה מואסת בבעל ואע"פ שאין שום מום ניכר בו וזה דומה לאדם שאין יכול לאכול מאכל השנאוי לו ונתעב עליו ואין שום דרך כאן לכפויה כ"א לעשות דרך בקשה ולפתותה אולי תחשוק בו ואדרבה אם היינו יודעים בוודאי שטעמה אמת שהוא מאוס בעיניה ולא נתנה עיניה באחר היינו כופין הבעל להוציא כי הך דתנן לקמן בפרק המדיר ואלו שכופין אותן להוציא מפני שהוא מאוס בעיניה ואין האשה יכולה לסבול שתבעל לו אלא משום דהכא אנו מסופקים בטענתה שכיון שאין אנו רואים בבעלה באותן המומים י"ל שמא עיניה נתנה באחר (שהיא) [ומשום זה היא] אומרת כך לפיכך אין כופין הבעל להוציא אבל מ"מ גם היא נמי אין כופין להפסיד כתובתה דשמא טענתה אמת דלב יודע מרת נפשו אלא מפתין אותה שמא תחשוק (בה) [בו] ואם רואין חייב לה כלום מכתובתה או לא וכגון זו אי הוה מורדת אי לא. כך ראינו ששורת הדין היתה מעיקרא שאין מחייבים את הבעל לגרש את אשתו אם תבעה גירושין חוץ מאותן שאמרו רבותינו מהו שכופין אותן להוציא וכשהאשה נמנעת מן התשמיש ומן המלאכות שחייבת לעשותן לו זו היא המורדת שפוחתין לה מכתובתה בכל שבת ושבת וצריכה התראה ואח"כ תקנו תקנה אחרת שיכריזו עליה ד' שבתות זא"ז ושולחין לה מב"ד הוי יודע שאפילו כתובתך ק' מנה הפסדת ואמרינן עלה ארמב"ח פעמים שולחים לה א' קודם הכרזה וא' אחר הכרזה כל אלה לענין מה ששם לה בעלה על עצמו ואינו מצוי בעינו או מה שבלה ואבד מנדוניתה ומתכשיטי' שהן נצ"ב שצריך הבעל לשלם לה דמיהן מפני שאחריות עליו היו פוחתין מאשה על האיש

ז'

קז א מיי' פי"ב מהלכות אישות הלכה י טוש"ע אה"ע סימן ע סעיף ג:
קח ב מיי' פי"ג שם הלכה ג סמג לאוין פא טוש"ע שם סימן עג סעיף א:
קט ג מיי' פי"ב שם הלכה י טוש"ע שם סימן ע סעיף ג:
קי ד מיי' שם הלכה יב טוש"ע שם סעיף ב:
קיא ה מיי' פכ"א שם הלכה יא טוש"ע שם סימן פ סעיף יא:
קיב ו מיי' פי"ב שם הל' יא ופי"ג שם הל' ה סמג עשין מח ולאוין פא טוש"ע שם סימן ע סעיף ג וסימן עג סעיף ד:
קיג ז מיי' פ"א מהל' עירובין הלכה ט ופ"ו הלכה ז סמג עשין דרבנן א טוש"ע א"ח סימן שפו סעיף ו [וסי' תט סעיף ז]:
קיד ח מיי' פט"ז מהל' טומאת צרעת הל' ו סמג עשין רלט:
קטו ט מיי' פ"ד מהל' טומאת אוכלין הלכה א ג:
קטז י מיי' שם הל' א:
קיז כ מיי' פ"ל מהלכות שבת הלכה ט סמג עשין ל טוש"ע א"ח סימן רלא סעיף א:

ס"א כלל רש"י

לעיל נט:

עירובין פב: כלים פי"ז מי"א

[לקמן סה:]

עירובין פב:

שבת קיז:

[לאורחי ועיין פרש"י לעיל סא. ד"ה ארחי וד"ה פרחי]

מיחזי כשכר שבת. אמר ליה ר' חייא בר יוסף לשמואל: מה בין מורד למורדת? אמר ליה: צא ולמד משוק של זונות. מי שוכר את מי? דבר אחר: זה – יצרו מבחוץ, וזו – יצרה מבפנים.§ **מתני'** [א]המשרה את אשתו על ידי שליש – לא יפחות לה משני קבין חטין, או מארבעה קבין שעורין. אמר רבי יוסי: לא פסק לה שעורין אלא ר' ישמעאל, שהיה סמוך לאדום. ונותן לה חצי קב קיטנית, וחצי לוג שמן, וקב גרוגרות, או מנה דבילה. ואם אין לו – פוסק לעומתן פירות ממקום אחר. [ב]ונותן לה מטה, מפץ ומחצלת, ונותן לה כפה לראשה וחגור למתניה, ומנעלים ממועד למועד, וכלים של חמשים זוז משנה לשנה. ואין נותנין לה לא חדשים בימות החמה, ולא שחקים בימות הגשמים. אלא נותן לה כלים של חמשים זוז בימות הגשמים, והיא מתכסה בבלאותיהן בימות החמה, והשחקים שלה. [ג]נותן לה מעה כסף לצורכה, [ד]ואוכלת עמו מלילי שבת ללילי שבת. *ואם אין נותן לה מעה כסף לצורכה – מעשה ידיה שלה. ומה היא עושה לו – משקל חמש סלעים שתי ביהודה, שהן עשר סלעים בגליל. או משקל עשר סלעים ערב ביהודה, שהן עשרים סלעים בגליל. [ה]ואם היתה מניקה – פוחתין לה ממעשה ידיה, ומוסיפין לה על מזונותיה. [ו]במה דברים אמורים – בעני שבישראל, אבל במכובד – הכל לפי כבודו.§ **גמ'** מני מתניתין? לא רבי יוחנן בן ברוקא, ולא ר"ש. *דתנן: [ז]וכמה שיעורו – מזון שתי סעודות לכל אחד ואחד, מזונו לחול ולא לשבת, דברי ר"מ. רבי יהודה אומר: לשבת ולא לחול, וזה וזה מתכוונין להקל. ר' יוחנן בן ברוקא אומר: ככר הלקוח בפונדיון. מארבע סאין לסלע. ר"ש אומר: שתי ידות לככר, משלש ככרות לקב. [ח]חציה – לבית המנוגע, [ט]וחצי חציה – לפסול את הגויה, [י]וחצי חצי חציה – לקבל טומאת אוכלין. מני? אי רבי יוחנן בן ברוקא – תמני הויין, ואי ר"ש – תמני סרי הויין! לעולם ר' יוחנן בן ברוקא, וכדאמר רב חסדא: צא מהן שליש לחנווני. הכא נמי – אייתי תילתא שדי עלייהו. אכתי תרתי סרי הויין! אוכלת עמו לילי שבת. הניחא למאן דאמר *אכילה ממש, אלא למאן דאמר אכילה תשמיש – מאי איכא למימר? ועוד: תליסר הויין! אלא, כדאמר רב חסדא: צא מהן *מחצה לחנווני, ה"נ אתיא פלגא ושדי עלייהו. קשיא דרב חסדא אדרב חסדא! לא קשיא; הא – באתרא דיהבי ציבי, הא – באתרא דלא יהבי ציבי. אי הכי שיתסרי הויין? כמאן – כרבי חידקא, דאמר: *ארבע סעודות חייב אדם לאכול בשבת? אפילו תימא [כ]רבנן, דל חדא *לארחי ופרחי. השתא דאתית להכי – אפילו תימא ר' שמעון. לרבנן – דל תלת לארחי ופרחי, לרבי חידקא – דל תרתי לארחי ופרחי.§ אמר רבי יוסי לא פסק שעורין וכו'.§ אלא באדום הוא דאכלין שעורים, בכולי עלמא לא אכלי?! ה"ק: לא פסק שעורים כפלים בחטין אלא רבי ישמעאל, שהיה סמוך לאדום, מפני ששעורין אדומיות רעות הן.§ ונותן לה חצי קב קיטנית.§ ואילו יין – לא קתני. מסייע ליה לר' אלעזר, דאמר ר' אלעזר:
אין

רש"י

מיחזי כשכר שבת. וא"ת: והא שכר שבת על ידי הבלעה מותר, כדאמרינן בפרק "הזהב" (ב"מ דף נח.): אם היה שכיר שבת שכיר חדש שכיר שנה – נותנין לו שכר שבת! וי"ל: דהכא אסור משום דלא הוי כמו הבלעה, דאין מוסיפין לכל שבת יחד אלא מה שעולה בכל יום ויום. שאם יתפייס היום או למחר באמצע השבוע – אין מצטרפין כל ימי השבוע זה עם זה. **וחצי** חצייה לפסול את הגוייה. הך פסול גוייה אין זה אותה גזרה די"ח דבר דהאוכל אוכל ראשון כו' כמו שפירשנו בפרק "כיצד משתתפין" (עירובין דף פב: ושם).
כמאן כרבי חידקא כו'. וא"ת: לדידיה נמי לא ניחא ליה, למאן דאמר אוכלת עמו לילי שבת אוכלת ממש. ושמא היה יכול לומר ולטעמיך. ולפי המסקנא אתי שפיר, דכל היתרון הוי לארחי ופרחי.
אחרי

מה בין מורד למורדת. מאי שנא כשהוא מורד אינו נותן אלא חצי טרפעיק ליום, וכשהיא מורדת נוטלת טרפעיק? מי שוכר את מי. הוי אומר האיש שוכר את האשה, ש"מ – שיצרו מרובה. ויצרו מבחוץ. קשויו ניכר, ומתבייש. **מתני'** המשרה את אשתו על ידי שליש. שנותן לה מזונותיה בבית אפוטרופוס, ואינה מתגלגלת עמו. המשרה. המכרה. "ויכרה להם כירה" מתרגמינן שירותא (מ"ב ו). לא יפחות לה. בשבת. לא פסק שעורים* כו'. בגמ' מפרש לה. גרוגרות. תאנים יבשין. דבילה. תאנים דרוסות בעיגול, ונמכרות במשקל. מפץ. רך ממחצלת. כפה. נעיף אחד משנה לשנה. ממועד למועד. המנעלים קאי, מנעלים חדשים לכל שלשת רגלים. חדשים. קשים לה בימות החמה, לפי שהם חמים, ויפים לה בימות הגשמים. אלא נותן לה כלים. חדשים, של חמשים זוז בימות הגשמים כו'. והשחקים שלה. אף כשיקנה לה חדשים. ובגמרא מפרש למאי מיבעי לה. ונותן לה מעה כסף. לכל שבת לדברים קטנים. מעשה ידיה. אוקימנן לעיל (דף נח.) מותר מעשה ידיה. ואוכלת עמו לילי שבת. שהוא ליל עונה. שתי. קשה לטוותו כפלים כשל ערב. משקל של יהודה כפלים כשל גליל. **גמ'** ה"ג: מני מתני' לא רבי יוחנן בן ברוקא ולא ר"ש. כמה הוא שיעורו. של עירובי תחומין. מתכוונין להקל. ר' מאיר היה רגיל לאכול פת בשבת יותר מבחול, שהיה ממשיך פת לכל מינים הבאין לפניו. ור"י היה אוכל פת בחול יותר מבשבת, שהיה שבע במיני מעדנים. ר' יוחנן בן ברוקא. נתן שיעור קלוב: ככר הלקוח בפונדיון, כשלוקחין ד' סאין בסלע, הן שתי סעודות. וקס"ד חצי קב, שהרי הסלע מ"ח פונדיונין, שש מעה כסף דינר, ומעה שני פונדיונין – הרי י"ב לדינר, וד' דינר לסלע – הרי מ"ח. וד' סאין כ"ד, קבין מ"ח חצאי קבין, נמצא לר' יוחנן לחצי קב שתי סעודות. רבי שמעון אומר. ג' סעודות הן שתי ידות של ככר משלש ככרות לקב, ונמצא הקב ט' סעודות, שלש סעודות לככר ושלש ככרות לקב. חציה. של ככר. לבית המנוגע. השוהה בבית המנוגע כדי אכילת פרס – חצי ככר – מטמא בגדים, כדכתיב: "והאוכל בבית יכבס בגדיו", כששוהה שיעור אכילה הכתוב מדבר, כדתניא בתורת כהנים. ואע"ג דגבי סעודת עירוב אמרנו ג' סעודות בככר – אין בו אלא ב' סעודות בינוניות, ושל עירוב שיעורו להקל, ובמלומצמות. והיינו דאמרינן אכילת פרס בכל שיעור שהיית סעודה, לפי ששיערוהו בחצי הככר. וחצי חציה לפסול את הגויה. האוכל שיעור חצי פרס אוכלים טמאים נפסל גופו מלאכול בתרומה עד שיטבול. והוא ג' ביצים. שהככר של ג' לקב ח' ביצים הוא, שהקב כ"ד ביצים, ד' לוגין. חציה של ככר ד' ביצים, חצי חציה – ב' ביצים. תמני סעודות הויין. קביים חטים דמתני', וארבעה עשרה סעודות היא צריכה לשבת. ואי ר"ש. דאמר ט' סעודות לקב. שמונה עשר הויין. והיא אינה צריכה אלא י"ד. רבי יוחנן לא שיער בחצי קב אלא בככר הלקוח בפונדיון מן החנווני, והוא לקח ארבע סאין חטין בסלע, ומשתכר שליש בטורח, נמצאו בחצי קב שלש סעודות. השתא הוא מוכר בפונדיון שמנן, והג' משתכר. אכתי. קביים דמתניתין תרתי סרי הויין. ומשנינן: אוכלת עמו לילי שבת. כדתנן במתני'. הניחא כו'. פלוגתא לקמיה בשמעתין. באתרא דיהיב ציבי. מי שמוכר חטים לחנווני לעשות ככרות ולמכור בשוק, במקום שהוא נותן לחנווני עצים לאפות – אינו משתכר אלא שליש, ובמקום שאינו נותן עצים – מעכב לעצמו מחצה, שממעט הככרות למכור ביוקר כדי יציאת העצים. כמאן כר' חידקא. בתמיה: נימא כר' חידקא סתם לה מתני', דאמר ב"כל כתבי הקדש" ארבעה סעודות לשבת? ר"ש. דאמר תמני סרי הויין. ואי כרבנן סבירא ליה לתנא דידן בסעודות שבת, דל תלת יתירתא לארחי ופרחי.
אין

תוספות רי"ד

ז' דינרים בשבת לסוף התקינו שמכריזין עליה ד' שבתות ומפסדת כולן ואעפ"כ לא היו מחייבים את הבעל לכתוב לה גט ואם מת נפטרו יורשיו מכתובה מאשר הוא כתובה עליו אבל הנמצא בעין בין מן נדוניתה בין מתכשיטיה דתפשא לא מפקינן מינה ודלא תפשא לא מפקינן מיניה והתקינו שמשהין אותה בלא גירושין י"ב חודש שמא תתפייס ולאחר יב"ח כופין את הבעל וכותב לה גט ואח"כ רבנן סבוראי בראותם שבנות ישראל הולכות ונתלות לעובדי כוכבים ליטול להן גיטין באונס מבעליהן וישראל כותבין גיטין באונס ומסתפק לגט מעושה שלא כדין וקנפיק מיני' חורבא תקנו בימי רבה בר מר ר"ה נימוס למורדת ותובעת גירושין שכל נצ"ב שהכניסה לו משלה ישלם ואפילו מה שכלה ואבד ישלם לה. ומ"ש לה ע"ע מה שאינו מצוי לא ישלם לה ומה שמצוי נמי אע"ג דתפשה לה מפקינן מינה ומהדרי' ליה לבעל וכופין אותו וכותב לה גט לאלתר ויש לה מו"מ ובואו אנו מתנהגים היום כשלש מאות שנה ויותר אף אתם עשו כן. ועיין מ"ש בפרק בתרא דגיטין בהל' גט מעושה שכתבתי שם שכופין הבעל עד שיאמר רוצה אני כתב ר"י ז"ל ולד"ה כל מאן דכפינן לאפוקי בין מעיקרא דדינא כדתנן אלו שכופים אותן להוציא ומאי דדמי להון ופי' מעיקר תקנתא אי מתה לה איתתא מקמי' דתיפוק מיניה דבעל בגט בעל ירית לה ולא מיפקעא ירושה דבעל אלא בגירושין גמורים והל' הכי. ונ"ל דדווקא המורדת על בעלה וכן אותן שכופין להוציא ירית לה בעל אבל אם הוא הדיר את אשתו או אם הוא מורד בה ואינו רוצה להתפיים עמה אלא רוצה לגרשה ומת אשתו קודם גירושי' אינו מן הדין שיירשנה שהרי אינו נוהג בה מנהג בעל א) אבל זה שנוהג בה מנהג בעל אינו מן הדין שיגרשנה: אמר ר"ט ב"ק כותבין אגרת מרד על ארוסה וא"כ אגרת מרד על שומרת יבם ואותבינן ליה ממאי דתניא אחת היא לי ארוסה ונשואה ואפילו נדה ואפילו ש"י ושקלינן וטרינן ואסיקנא אידי ואידי שתבע ליבם ולא קשיא כאן כמשנ"ר כאן כמשנ"א דתנן מצות יבום קודמת למצות חליצה בראשונה שהיו מתכוונים לשם מצוה עכשיו שאין מתכוונים לשם מצוה אמרינן מצות חליצה קודמת למצות יבום (והרב פוסק מצות חליצה קודם למצות יבום כמשנה אחרונה): וכיון דאמרי' בפ' החולץ אר"י ב"א חזרו לומר מצות יבום קודמת למצות חליצה עד ולבסוף סברוה כרבנן דאמרי יבמה יבא עליה מ"מ בטלה לה למשנ"א ובטלה לה למימרא דשמואל דסבר כמשנ"א וכותבים אגרת מרד אף על ש"י כדתניא בברייתא ונ"ל שהתובעת יבום גם מבעלה בעודו שכ"מ כדי שלא תהיה זקוקה ליבם כדין מורדת משוינן לה שהרי אוסרת עצמה על יבם ואין לבעל לעכבה בגט עד שתמחול לו כתובתה וזה מדין התלמוד עיין למטה בפ' דיני בהל' הפוסקים אבל תיקון הגאונים כיון שבמורדת תקנו ליתן גט כ"ש בש"י שעדיין אינה אשתו מיהו ה"מ דשקולי בגוונא דאמרן ובתוספת לא שכל דינה דומה לדין המורדת: ר"י אומר וכו'. מאי טרעפיקין אמר ר"ש איסתרא ובכמה איסתרא פלגי דזוזא תנ"ה ר"י אומר ג' טרעפיקין שהן ט' מעות מעה וחצי בכל יום א"ל ר"ח ב"י לשמואל מ"ש איהו דיהבינן ליה שכר שבת ומ"ש איהי דלא יהבינן לה שכר שבת א"ל איהי דמפחת קא פחית לא מחזי כשכר שבת איהי דאוספא קא מוסיפי מיחזי כש"ש. א"ל ר"ח לשמואל מה בין מורד
למורדת

תוספות רי"ד

למורדת א"ל צא ולמד משוק של זונות מי שוכר את מי ד"א זו יצרה מבפנים וזה יצרו בחוץ פי' שהוא תובע בפה והאשה אינה תובעת בפה הלכך של איש קשה משל אשה: **מתני'** המשרה את אשתו ע"י שליש לא יפחות לה מקביים חטים ומד' קבין שעורים אר"י לא פסק [לה] שעורים אלא ר"י שהוא סמוך לאדום ונותנים לה חצי קב קטנית וחצי לוג שמן קב גרוגרות או מנה דבילה ואם אין לו פוסק לעומתן פירות ממקום אחר ונותן לה מטה ומפץ ב) ואם אין לו מפץ מחצלת ונותן לה כפה לראשה וחגור למתניה ומנעלים לרגליה ממועד למועד וכלים של נ' זוז משנה לשנה ואינו נותן לה לא ג) שחקים בימות החמה ולא חדשים בימות הגשמים והיא מתכסה בכל אותן בימות החמה והשחקים שלה ונותן לה מעה כסף לצרכיה והיא אוכלת עמו מליל שבת לליל שבת ואם אין נותן לה מעה כסף לצרכיה מעשה ידיה שלה. ומה היא עושה לו משקל ה"ס שתי ביהודה שהן (ט"ז) [עשר] סלעים בגליל או משקל י' סלעים ערב ביהודה שהן כ' שקלים בגליל. ואם היתה מניקה פוחת' לה ממעשה ידיה ומוסיפים לה על מזונותיה בד"א בעני שבישראל אבל במכובד הכל לפי כבודו פי' המשרה אשתו ע"י שליש כגון שהוא עבד ונשכר לאחרים ואוכל עמהן כדרך הפועלים שאוכלים במקום שעושים מלאכתן ואומר לב"ד שיפרנסו את אשתו משכר פעולתו ומשרה הוא לשון ויכרה להם כירה גדולה דמתרגמינן שירותא לא יפחות מקביין חטין אי קשיא היאך יספיק לה קביים בשבוע והרי העומר היה מאכל כל איש ואיש ליום שנמצא כ"ו סעודות לעומר והעומר הוא מ"ג ביצים וחומש ביצה קרוב ב' קבים שב' קבים הן מ"ח ביצים מצאתי ששאלה זו נשאלה למר רב שלום ז"ל והשיב כל מדות חכמים כך הם כל דבר ודבר יתנו בו שיעור למטה ושיעור למעלה וכו' עד אף כאן לענין משרה את אשתו זו שיעור קטן למטה כדי קיום נשמה ולא לכל אדם פוסקים כך אלא לעני שכך שנינו בד"א בעני מישראל אבל במכובד כו' ועד כמה עד ז' רביעית ועוד שהן מ"ג ביצים וחומש ביצה: א"ר יוסי לא (פחות) [פסק] שעורים וכו' אטו באדום הוא דאכלינן שעורים וכ"ע ל"א שעורים אלא ה"ק לא פסק שעורים כפל כחטים אלא ר"י שהיה סמוך לאדום. ששעורים של אדום רעות הן: ונותן לה קב גרוגרות פי' תאנים יבשים או מנה דבילה (תני) [פי'] דרוסין ועושין מהן עגולין ונמכרים במשקל. ואם אין לו מפץ מחצלת פי' המפץ הוא יותר יקר מן המחצלת: תניא בתוספתא בפרק הבוגרות המשרה את אשתו ע"י שליש וכו' וכולן במדת איטלקי אפילו נדה אפילו שומרת יבם נותנים לה כוס חבית פך נר ופתילה יין שאין ד) נשותיהן של עניים יושבות על הכר. ואמרינן ואילו יין לא קתני מסייע ליה לרבי אלעזר דאמר רבי אלעזר אין פוסקין יינות לאשה:
מיתיבי

א) נראה דחסר כאן ואולי צ"ל שדין ירושת הבעל אינו אלא אם נוהג בה מנהג בעל אבל זה שאינו נוהג בה מנהג בעל אינו בדין שירשנה. ב) נ"ל ואם אין לו מפץ נותן לה מחצלת וכ"ה גירסת הרי"ף והרמב"ם ז"ל וכ"מ גם מפרש"י ד"ה מפץ. ג) נ"ל לא חדשים בימות החמה ולא שחקים בימות הגשמים אלא נותן לה כלים של חמשים זוז בימות הגשמים והיא כו'. ד) נראה דחסר כאן ואולי צ"ל יין אין לה שאין נשותיהן של עניים שותות יין כר אין לה שאין נשותיהן של עניים ישנות על כרים וכ"ה בתוספתא שם.

אֵין פּוֹסְקִין יֵינוֹת לְאִשָּׁה. וְאִם תֹּאמַר: °"אֵלְכָה אַחֲרֵי מְאַהֲבַי נוֹתְנֵי לַחְמִי וּמֵימַי צַמְרִי וּפִשְׁתִּי שַׁמְנִי וְשִׁקּוּיָי" – דְּבָרִים שֶׁהָאִשָּׁה מִשְׁתּוֹקֶקֶת עֲלֵיהֶן, וּמַאי נִינְהוּ – תַּכְשִׁיטִין. דָּרַשׁ רַבִּי יְהוּדָה אִישׁ כְּפַר *גְּבִירַיָא, וְאָמְרִי לָהּ אִישׁ כְּפַר נְפוֹר חַיִל: מִנַּיִן שֶׁאֵין פּוֹסְקִין יֵינוֹת לְאִשָּׁה – שֶׁנֶּאֱמַר: °"וַתָּקָם חַנָּה אַחֲרֵי אָכְלָה בְשִׁלֹה וְאַחֲרֵי שָׁתֹה". "שָׁתֹה" וְלֹא שָׁתַת. אֶלָּא מֵעַתָּה "אָכְלָה" וְלֹא אָכַל הָכִי נַמִי?! אֲנַן מִדְּשַׁנֵּי קְרָא בְּדִבּוּרֵיהּ קָאָמְרִינַן, מִכְּדִי בְּגַוַּהּ קָא עָסֵיק וְאָתֵי, מַאי טַעְמָא שַׁנֵּי? ש"מ: "שָׁתֹה" – וְלֹא שָׁתַת. מֵיתִיבֵי: רְגִילָה נוֹתְנִין לָהּ! רְגִילָה שָׁאנֵי. דְּאָמַר רַב חִינָּנָא בַּר כָּהֲנָא אָמַר שְׁמוּאֵל: רְגִילָה – נוֹתְנִין לָהּ כּוֹס אֶחָד, שֶׁאֵינָהּ רְגִילָה – נוֹתְנִין לָהּ שְׁנֵי כוֹסוֹת. מַאי קָאָמַר? אָמַר אַבָּיֵי, הָכִי קָאָמַר: רְגִילָה – בִּפְנֵי בַעְלָהּ שְׁנֵי כוֹסוֹת, שֶׁלֹּא בִּפְנֵי בַעְלָהּ – נוֹתְנִין לָהּ כּוֹס אֶחָד. אֵינָהּ רְגִילָה – בִּפְנֵי בַעְלָהּ אֶלָּא כּוֹס אֶחָד, שֶׁלֹּא בִּפְנֵי בַעְלָהּ – אֵין נוֹתְנִין לָהּ כָּל עִיקָּר. וְאִי בָּעֵית אֵימָא: רְגִילָה – נוֹתְנִין לָהּ לְצִיקֵי קְדֵירָה. דְּא"ר אַבָּהוּ א"ר יוֹחָנָן: מַעֲשֶׂה בְּכַלָּתוֹ שֶׁל נַקְדִּימוֹן בֶּן גּוּרְיוֹן שֶׁפָּסְקוּ לָהּ חֲכָמִים סָאתַיִם יַיִן לְצִיקֵי קְדֵירָה מֵעֶרֶב שַׁבָּת לְע"ש. *אָמְרָה לָהֶן: כָּךְ תִּפְסְקוּ לִבְנוֹתֵיכֶם. תָּנָא: שׁוֹמֶרֶת יָבָם הָיְתָה, וְלֹא עָנוּ אַחֲרֶיהָ אָמֵן. תָּנָא: כּוֹס אֶחָד – יָפֶה לְאִשָּׁה, שְׁנַיִם – נִיווּל הוּא, שְׁלֹשָׁה – תּוֹבַעַת בַּפֶּה, אַרְבָּעָה – אֲפִילּוּ חֲמוֹר תּוֹבַעַת בַּשּׁוּק, וְאֵינָהּ מַקְפֶּדֶת. אָמַר רָבָא: לֹא שָׁנוּ אֶלָּא שֶׁאֵין בַּעְלָהּ עִמָּהּ, אֲבָל בַּעְלָהּ עִמָּהּ – לֵית לָן בָּהּ. וְהָא חַנָּה דְּבַעְלָהּ עִמָּהּ הֲוַאי! אַכְסַנַאי שָׁאנֵי. דְּאָמַר רַב הוּנָא: [א]מִנַּיִן לְאַכְסְנַאי שֶׁאָסוּר בְּתַשְׁמִישׁ הַמִּטָּה – שֶׁנֶּאֱמַר: °"וַיַּשְׁכִּימוּ בַבֹּקֶר וַיִּשְׁתַּחֲווּ לִפְנֵי ה' וַיָּשֻׁבוּ וַיָּבֹאוּ אֶל בֵּיתָם הָרָמָתָה וַיֵּדַע אֶלְקָנָה אֶת חַנָּה אִשְׁתּוֹ וַיִּזְכְּרֶהָ ה'". הַשְׁתָּא – אִין, מֵעִיקָּרָא – לָא. *חוֹמָא דְּבֵיתְהוּ דְּאַבָּיֵי אֲתַאי לְקַמֵּיהּ דְּרָבָא. אָמְרָה לֵיהּ: פְּסוֹק לִי מְזוֹנֵי! פְּסַק לָהּ. פְּסוֹק לִי חַמְרָא! א"ל: יָדַעְנָא בֵּיהּ בְּנַחְמָנִי, דְּלָא הֲוָה שָׁתֵי חַמְרָא. אָמְרָה לֵיהּ: חַיֵּי דְמָר, דַּהֲוֵי מַשְׁקֵי לֵיהּ בְּשׁוּפְרָזֵי כִּי הַאי. בַּהֲדֵי דְּקָא מַחְוְיָא לֵיהּ אִיגַּלֵּי דַּרְעָא, נָפַל נְהוֹרָא בְּבֵי דִּינָא. קָם רָבָא, עָל לְבֵיתֵיהּ, תַּבְעָהּ לְבַת רַב חִסְדָּא. אָמְרָה לֵיהּ בַּת רַב חִסְדָּא: מַאן הֲוֵי הָאִידָּנָא בְּבֵי דִינָא? אָמַר לָהּ: *חוֹמָא דְּבֵיתְהוּ דְּאַבָּיֵי. נָפְקָא אַבַּתְרָהּ, מַחְתָא לָהּ בְּקוּלְפֵי דְשִׁידָּא עַד דְּאַפְּקָהּ לָהּ מִכּוּלֵּי מְחוֹזָא. אָמְרָה לָהּ: קְטַלְתְּ לֵיךְ תְּלָתָא, וַאֲתַתְּ לְמִיקְטַל אַחֲרִינָא?! דְּבֵיתְהוּ דְּרַב יוֹסֵף בְּרֵיהּ דְּרָבָא אֲתַאי לְקַמֵּיהּ דְּרַב נְחֶמְיָה בְּרֵיהּ דְּרַב יוֹסֵף. אָמְרָה לֵיהּ: פְּסוֹק לִי מְזוֹנֵי! פְּסַק לָהּ. פְּסוֹק לִי חַמְרָא! פָּסַק לָהּ. אֲמַר לָהּ: [ב]יָדַעְנָא בְּהוּ בִּבְנֵי מְחוֹזָא דְּשָׁתוּ חַמְרָא. דְּבֵיתְהוּ דְּרַב יוֹסֵף בְּרֵיהּ דְּרַב מְנַשְּׁיָא מִדְּוִיל אֲתַאי לְקַמֵּיהּ דְּרַב יוֹסֵף, א"ל: פְּסוֹק לִי מְזוֹנֵי! פָּסַק לָהּ. פְּסוֹק לִי חַמְרָא! פָּסַק לָהּ. פְּסוֹק לִי שִׁירָאֵי! אֲמַר לָהּ: שִׁירָאֵי לָמָּה? אָמְרָה לֵיהּ: לָךְ, וּלְחַבְרָךְ, וּלְחַבְרוּתָךְ. § וְנוֹתֵן לָהּ מִטָּה וּמַפָּץ וכו'. § מַפָּץ וּמַחְצֶלֶת לָמָּה לָהּ דְּיָהֵב לָהּ? אָמַר רַב פַּפָּא: בְּאַתְרָא דְּנָהִיגִי דְּמָלוּ פּוּרְיָא בְּחַבְלֵי, דִּמְבַגַּר לָהּ. ת"ר: אֵין נוֹתְנִין לָהּ כַּר וָכֶסֶת. מִשּׁוּם ר' נָתָן אָמְרוּ: נוֹתְנִין לָהּ כַּר וָכֶסֶת. הֵיכִי דָּמֵי? אִי דְּאוֹרְחָהּ – מַאי טַעְמָא דְּת"ק? וְאִי דְּלָאו אוֹרְחָהּ – מ"ט דְּרַבִּי נָתָן? לָא צְרִיכָא, *כְּגוֹן דְּאוֹרְחֵיהּ דִּידֵיהּ וְלָאו אוֹרְחָהּ דִּידָהּ. תַּנָּא קַמָּא סָבַר: אָמַר לָהּ: כִּי אָזֵילְנָא – שָׁקֵילְנָא לְהוּ, וְכִי אָתֵינָא – מַיְיתֵינָא לְהוּ בַּהֲדַאי. וְרַבִּי נָתָן סָבַר: אָמְרָה לֵיהּ: זִימְנִין דְּמִיתְרְמֵי בֵּין הַשְּׁמָשׁוֹת וְלָא מָצֵית מַיְיתֵי לְהוּ, וְשָׁקְלַתְּ לְהוּ לְדִידִי, וּמַגְנֵית לִי עַל אַרְעָא. § וְנוֹתֵן לָהּ כְּפָה. § אֲמַר לֵיהּ רַב פַּפָּא לְאַבָּיֵי: הַאי

רש"י

אֵין ב"ד פּוֹסְקִין יֵינוֹת לְאִשָּׁה. שֶׁהַיַּיִן מַרְגִּילָהּ לְתַאֲוַת תַּשְׁמִישׁ. רְגִילָה שָׁאנֵי. כֵּיוָן דְּאֵינוֹ חִידּוּשׁ לָהּ, כְּבָר דָּשָׁה בּוֹ וְאֵינוֹ מֵזִיחַ לִבָּהּ. לְצִיקֵי קְדֵירָה. לְהַטְעִים תַּבְשִׁיל. תּוֹבַעַת בַּפֶּה. תַּשְׁמִישׁ. וַיָּבֹאוּ אֶל בֵּיתָם. וַהֲדַר "וַיֵּדַע אֶלְקָנָה אֶת חַנָּה". חוֹמָא. זֶה שְׁמָהּ. שׁוּפְרָזֵי. גְּבִיעִים אֲרוּכִּים שֶׁקּוֹרִין מדירני"ש [פליידרי"ן]. כִּי הַאי. כְּמִדַּת אַמָּתִי וּזְרוֹעִי. תַּבְעָהּ לְבַת רַב חִסְדָּא. תָּבַע אֶת אִשְׁתּוֹ לְתַשְׁמִישׁ. בְּקוּלְפֵי דְּשִׁידָּה. בְּמַנְעוּל שֶׁל אַרְגָּז. קְטַלְתְּ לָךְ תְּלָת. שֶׁכְּבָר נִישֵּׂאת לְג' וּמֵתוּ, כִּדְאָמַר בִּיבָמוֹת בְּפֶ' "הַבָּא עַל יְבִמְתּוֹ" (דף סד:). לְמִיקְטַל אַחֲרִינָא. שֶׁבָּאת לְהַרְאוֹת יׇפְיֵךְ, שֶׁיִּקָּפוֹץ אִישׁ עָלַיִךְ. לְחַבְרָךְ וּלְחַבְרוּתָךְ. שֶׁלֹּא אֶתְבַּזֶּה עַל הַבְּרִיּוֹת מִכְּבוֹדִי הָרִאשׁוֹן, לֹא בְּפָנֶיךָ וְלֹא בִּפְנֵי חֲבֵירֶיךָ. מַפָּץ וּמַחְצֶלֶת לָמָּה לָהּ. הֲרֵי עוֹר שָׁטוּחַ עַל מִטָּה טוֹב מִן הַמַּפָּץ! וּמְשַׁנֵּי: בְּאַתְרָא דְּמָלוּ פּוּרְיָא בְּחַבְלֵי – בְּמָקוֹם שֶׁאֵין רְגִילִין לַעֲשׂוֹת שְׁטִיחַ עוֹר לְמַטָּה, אֶלָּא סֵירוּגֵי חֲבָלִים. וּמְבַגַּר לָהּ. מְצַעֲרֵי לָהּ וּמַזִּיקִין אוֹתָהּ, לְשׁוֹן בּוֹגֶרֶת. אִי דְּאוֹרְחָהּ. דֶּרֶךְ בְּנוֹת מִשְׁפַּחְתָּהּ. אוֹרְחֵיהּ. דַּרְכּוֹ לִישַׁן עַל כָּרִים וּכְסָתוֹת. וַאֲנַן קַיְימָא לָן: *עוֹלָה עִמּוֹ. כִּי אָזֵילְנָא. וַאֲנִי מַשְׂרֶה אוֹתָךְ עַל יְדֵי שָׁלִישׁ, שָׁקֵילְנָא לְהוּ בַּהֲדַאי. וְכִי אָתֵינָא. וְתִשְׁכְּבִי עִמִּי, מַיְיתֵינָא לְהוּ. וְשָׁקְלַתְּ לְדִידִי. מַפָּץ שֶׁלִּי, אוֹ אִם אֶקְנֶה כַּר וָכֶסֶת מִשֶּׁלִּי. הַאי

תוספות

אחרי אכלה. כמו אחרי אָכְלָהּ, מפיק הֵ' משמע. ואף על פי שלא אכלה. כדכתיב "ותבכה ולא תאכל" – מ"מ אית לן למידרש הכי "ותקם חנה אחרי" – שעת אכילתה שהיה לה לאכול, "ואחרי שתה" אלקנה וביתו חוץ ממנה, שלא היה לה לשתות. ולכך "ויחשבה עלי לשכורה".

שתה ולא שתת. מדלא קאמר ואחרי שתותה דומיא דאכילה שתלה בה. אי נמי; "אחרי אכול ואחרי שתה", כדכתיב (משלי כג) "אכול ושתה יאמר לך". ומדשני קרא בדבריה דריש הכי, כדמפרש לקמן. **אכלה** ולא אכל. בתמיה: וכי תדרוש ככה כן שאין פוסקים מזונות לאיש? **מכדי** בגוה קא עסיק קרא. דהא כתיב חנה בקרא, וכתיב נמי אכלה. אם כן לכתוב נמי שתותה, או לא לכתוב קרא בגוה, ולכתוב אכל ושתה. **רגילה** שאני דאמר ר' חיננא כו'. וא"ת: ומאי ראיה צריך על זה? דברייתא גופה קתני רגילה, משמע – דווקא רגילה! ויש לומר: דר' אלעזר נמי איירי ברגילה. דאי בשאינה רגילה כלל, בפני בעלה פשיטא דאין פוסקין, דאטו יש לנו ליתן לה שאין בעלה נותן לה כשהיתה עמו?! לכך צריך לאתויי מדרבי חיננא, שיש רגילה שנותנים לה, כגון שרגילה שני כוסות. **אינה** רגילה בפני בעלה אלא כוס אחד כו'. וזהו פירוש דברי שמואל: רגילה נותנין לה כוס אחד – היינו שרגילה בשני כוסות. ודקאמר שאינה רגילה נותנין לה שני כוסות – היינו שאינה רגילה שהיו נותנין לה שני כוסות אלא כוס אחד, אין נותנין לה כלל שלא בפני בעלה.

לציקי קדרה. אברייתא קאי, כלומר: מברייתא לא תקשי. אבל מילתא דשמואל לא מיפרשא אלא כדשנינן. ***ונותנין** לה מטה ומפץ. אע"ג דלגבי סדור אמרינן ב"המקבל" (ב"מ דף קיג: ושם) דנותנין לו מטה ומטה ומפץ – משום דשמא גבי אשה לא* הטריחוהו חכמים כ"כ, דאפשר לה שתלך ד' אמות אחר אכילה*). **מפץ** ומחצלת למה לה. ר"ת לא גרס מפץ ומחצלת. אלא: ומחצלת למה. דמפץ הוא רך, וראוי גם לסמיכה. ונהי דלשכיבה אין צריך, דהא אית לה מטה – *לסמיכה מיהא צריכה. **ושקלת** להו לדידי כו'. פירש בקונטרס: ושקלת לדידי – מפץ שלי. ואין להקשות: א"כ תסגי לה בשני מפלין! דשמא מתוך שהוא מעונג, שעד עתה הורגל לשכב על כר – יטול שני מפלין לעצמו. ורבינו יצחק בן רבי מאיר ז"ל לא גרים ושקלת לדידי. ואינה מתרעמת, אלא שרוצה לעלות עמו ולשכב על כר. אע"פ שלעצמו אין לו עכשיו. וכן משמע, דלסתור טענה דקא טעין בעלה אליבא דרבנן קא אתי.

*) [בב"מ תירצו באופן אחר]

רב

עין משפט נר מצוה

קיח א מיי' פכ"א מהל' איסורי ביאה הלכה טו סמג עשין מח טור ש"ע א"ח סימן רמ סעיף יג וטוש"ע אה"ע סימן כה סעיף ז:

קיט ב מיי' פי"ב מהל' אישות הלכה י יא סמג עשין מח ולאוין פח טוש"ע אה"ע סימן ע סעיף ג:

תוספות רי"ד

מיתיבי רגילה נותנים לה כוס א' רגילה שאני תני כוס א' יפה לאשה שנים (שוו) [ניוול] הוא לה ג' תובעת בפה ד' אפי' חמור תבעה אינה מקפדת א"ר לא אמרן אלא שאין בעלה עמה אבל בעלה עמה בעלה משמרה. אר"י מנין לאכסנאי שאסו' בתשמיש המטה שנאמר וישכימו בבקר וגו' וידע אלקנה את אשתו השתא אין מעיקרא לא: (הימא) [חומא] דביתהו דאביי אתיא לקמיה דרבא אמרה פסיקי לי מזונות פסיק לה פסיקי לי חמרא אמר לה ידענא ביה בנחמני א) דלא הוי משקה בשופריזי [כי הא] לך חמרא א"ל בחיי דמר דהוה משקה לי בשופריזי כי האי פי' בגביעות (מרובים) [גדולים] כזרוע: דביתהו דר"י בריה דרבא אתיא לקמיה דר"נ בריה דר"י א"ל פסוקי לי מזוני פסק לה פסיקי לי חמרא פסק לה א"ל ידענא בהו בבני מחוזא דרגילו דשתו חמרא: דביתהו דר"י בריה דר"מ מדויל אתיא לדינא קמיה דר"י א"ל פסוק לי מזוני פסק לה פסוק לי חמרא פסק לה פסוק לי שיראי א"ל שיראי למה לך א"ל לחברך ולחברותך פי' (להנאתן) [להתנאות בהן] בפני הבריות ולא אתבזה מכבודי הראשון ומכאן מוכח וגם ממאי דאמרי' לקמן מותר בלאות אלמנה ליורשים שחייבים

א) גירסת רבינו בכאן אינו מדוקדק ואולי דטס"ה וצ"ל כמו דאיתא בגמ'.

וכן מוכח בפ' המקבל קיג: דקאמר דנותנין מטה ומפץ ואמאי יתנו כר או כסת או מחצלת הראוי לשכיבה אלא דנותנין לו מפץ משום דראוי גם לסמיכה. ת"י.

[נ"ל גבוריא ואמרי לה איש כפר גבור חיל כך איתא במגילה יח.]

[לעיל מח. סא.]

[לקמן סו:]

ש"א א

[נ"ל חומה בס"א וכ"א ביבמות סד: וכ"א להדיא בש"ע אה"ע סימן קכט סעיף לד]

[נ"ל חומה רש"ל]

[לעיל מח.]

[נ"ל מנחם בן מדויל]

[נ"ל חומה]

רב אשי אמר תשמיש. אפילו גמל וספן, הואיל ומשרה אותה על ידי שליש. **אבל** זן קטני קטנים. וכייפינן ליה, והא דקאמר בפ' "נערה" (לעיל דף מט: ושם): כפו ליה אסיתא – היינו יתריס על שם.

הדרן עלך אף על פי

האי תנא שליח ערטילאי ורמי מסאני. מופשט וערום, שאין לו חליפות בגדים אלא משנה לשנה, ומנעלים קאמר ממועד למועד. ושאר בגדים לא תחליף במועד. "והפשיט" מתרגמינן "וישלח" (ויקרא א). זוזי פשיטי. זוזי מדינה, שהן שמינית שבזוזי צורי. כל כסף מדינה אחד משמונה בכסף צורי, כדאמרי' לעיל סלע מדינה פלגא דזוזא, שהוא אחד משמונה בסלע. מותר מזונות. כגון אשה שמזונות האמורים במשנתנו עודפין לה, שאינה רעבתנית. שלא תתגנה על בעלה. בימי טהרתה, בלובשת בגדים שלבשה בימי נדות. מותר בלאות. אלמנה הניזונת מנכסי יתומים, ועליהן ליתן לה כלים של חמשים זוז משנה לשנה. יוצא בעירוב אמו. ערבה אמו לצפון ואביו לדרום – אמו מוליכתו אצלה, ואין אביו מוליכו אצלו. שעדיין הוא צריך לאמו, ובתרה שדיוהו רבנן. אלמא: עד שש צריך סיוע מאמו, וכשם שהבעל זן אותה – כך זן אותו עמה.

הדרן עלך אף על פי

מציאת האשה. וירושתה. אם נפלה לה ירושה, הוא אוכל פירות בחייה והקרן שלה. לישנא אחרינא: ואם מתה בחייו – יורשה. ופגמה. נזק חבלה אם יחבלו בה. ובזמן שבגלוי. שהבושת שלו, ועוד: שנמאסת עליו והוא סובל. ילקח בהן קרקע. שהרי זה כשאר נכסים הנופלים לה, שהן מלוג. אוכל פירות בחייה. והקרן שלה, אם יגרשנה או ימות. ואם תמות היא – יורשה. **גמ'** תנינא. בפ' "נערה". יתר עליו הבעל. אלמא בעל זכאי בכולן. העדפה. אם תעשה מלאכה יותר ממה שפסקו לה חכמים.

תורה אור

*האי תנא – שליח ערטלאי ורמי מסאני! אמר ליה: תנא במקום הרים קאי, דלא סגיא בלא תלתא זוגי מסאני. ואגב אורחיה קא משמע לן דניתבינהו ניהלה במועד, כי היכי דניהוי לה שמחה בגווייהו.§ וכלים של חמשים זוז.§ אמר אביי: *חמשים זוזי פשיטי. ממאי? מדקתני: במה דברים אמורים – בעני שבישראל, אבל במכובד – הכל לפי כבודו. ואי ס"ד חמשים זוז ממש, עני חמשים זוז מנא ליה? אלא ש"מ – חמשים זוזי פשיטי.§ ואין נותנין לה לא חדשים וכו'.§ ת"ר: [א]מותר מזונות – לבעל, [ב]מותר בלאות – לאשה. מותר בלאות לאשה למה לה? אמר רחבה: שמתכסה בהן בימי נדתה, כדי שלא תתגנה על בעלה. אמר אביי, נקטינן: [ג]מותר בלאות אלמנה – ליורשיו. התם הוא דלא תתגני באפיה, הכא – תתגני ותתגני.§ נותן לה מעה כסף וכו'.§ מאי אוכלת? רב נחמן אמר: *[ד]אוכלת ממש. רב אשי אמר: תשמיש. תנן: אוכלת עמו לילי שבת. בשלמא למ"ד אכילה – היינו דקתני "אוכלת", אלא למאן דאמר תשמיש – (א) מאי "אוכלת"? *לישנא מעליא, כדכתיב: °"אכלה ומחתה פיה ואמרה לא פעלתי און". מיתיבי, רשב"ג אומר: אוכלת בלילי שבת ושבת. בשלמא למ"ד אכילה – היינו דקתני "ושבת". אלא למאן דאמר תשמיש – תשמיש בשבת מי איכא? *והאמר רב הונא: ישראל קדושים הן, ואין משמשין מטותיהן ביום! *האמר רבא: בבית אפל – מותר.§ ואם היתה מניקה.§ דרש רבי עולא רבה אפיתחא דבי נשיאה: [ה]אע"פ שאמרו אין אדם זן את בניו ובנותיו כשהן קטנים, אבל זן קטני קטנים. עד כמה – [ו]עד בן שש. כדרב אסי, *דאמר רב אסי: [ז]קטן בן שש יוצא בעירוב אמו. ממאי – מדקתני: היתה מניקה – פוחתין לה ממעשה ידיה, ומוסיפין לה על מזונותיה. מ"ט? לאו משום דבעי למיכל בהדה? ודלמא משום דחולה היא. אם כן ליתני "אם היתה חולה", מאי "אם היתה מניקה"? ודלמא הא קא משמע לן: דסתם מניקות חולות נינהו. איתמר, (ב) אמר רבי יהושע בן לוי: [ח]מוסיפין לה יין, שהיין יפה לחלב.§

הדרן עלך אף על פי

מציאת [ט]האשה [י]ומעשה ידיה – לבעלה, [כ]וירושתה – הוא אוכל פירות בחייה. בושתה ופגמה – שלה. רבי יהודה בן בתירא אומר: [ל]בזמן שבסתר – לה שני חלקים, ולו אחד. ובזמן שבגלוי – לו שני חלקים ולה אחד. שלו – ינתן מיד, ושלה – ילקח בהן קרקע, והוא אוכל פירות.§ **גמ'** מאי קא משמע לן? תנינא: *האב זכאי בבתו בקידושיה: בכסף, בשטר ובביאה. *)זכאי במציאתה ובמעשה ידיה ובהפרת נדריה. מקבל את גיטה ואינו אוכל פירות בחייה, נישאת – יתר עליו הבעל שהוא אוכל פירות בחייה! בושתה ופגמה איצטריכא ליה, פלוגתא דרבי יהודה בן בתירא ורבנן.§ תני תנא קמיה דרבא: מציאת האשה לעצמה, רבי עקיבא אומר: לבעלה. אמר ליה: השתא, ומה העדפה דמעשה

*) [נדה מז.]

מציאת האשה. בקונטרס גרס "המדיר" אחר "אע"פ", אגב דתנא ב"אע"פ" (לעיל דף סד:): המשרה אשתו על ידי שליש – קתני: המדיר אשתו שלשים יום יעמיד פרנס, שהוא כעין שליש. ואחר ששנה "המדיר" חוזר לענין ראשון. אבל בפירוש ר"ת, ובירושלמי, ובתוספתא, וברוב ספרים גרסינן "מציאת" האשה אחר "אע"פ", איידי דסליק: אם היתה מניקה פוחתין לה ממעשה ידיה, ואיידי דתנא בסוף מתניתין: המשליש מעות לבתו – תנא בתריה "המדיר", דקתני: יעמיד פרנס, דהוי כעין שליש. **וירושתה** הוא אוכל פירות בחייה. נראה לר"ת פירוש ראשון שבקונטרס עיקר. דפי': ירושתה – שנפלו לה נכסים ממקום אחר, הוא אוכל פירות בחייה. דאי כלשון אחרון שפי': ירושתה – שהוא יורשה לאחר מיתה, אמאי אצטריך למימר בגמרא: "בושתה ופגמה איצטריכא ליה" הו"ל למימר דקמ"ל שהוא יורשה, לאחר מיתה. דממתניתין ד"יתר עליו הבעל" לא שמעינן לה! דאע"ג דאביה יורשה, וקתני "יתר עליו הבעל" – היינו כשאין לה בנים, אבל יש לה בנים – לא שמעינן מהתם. ומיהו, איכא למימר דלא מלי למימר דיורשה איצטריכא ליה – דהא שמעינן לה ממתניתין ד"הכותב" (לקמן דף פג.) ומפרק "יש נוחלין" (ב"ב דף קח.). **ה"ג** בושתה ופגמה שלה. ור"ת הגיה בספרו: שלו. ולפי זה הא דבעי בפרק "המניח" (ב"ק דף לב.): המזיק אשתו בתשמיש המטה מהו – מלער קא בעי, אבל מבושת ופגם – פשיטא דפטור, דאפילו חבלו בה אחריני הוי שלו. ומיהו, אין נראה. דא"כ הו"ל למיתני לעיל (דף מו:) דהאב אינו זכאי בבתו בבושת ופגם של חבלה, אלא דווקא באונס ומפתה, כדאמרינן ב"החובל" (שם דף פז: ושם): לא זיכתה תורה לאב אלא שבח נעורים בלבד! ולעיל בריש "נערה" (דף מג.) נמי פריך: חבלות דידה נינהו. יתר עליו הבעל שהוא זכאי בבושת ופגם! אלא ודאי בושתה ופגמה שלה גרסינן. ור"ת עצמו חזר בו, וכן גריס בירושלמי. וכן משמע בגמרא, מדקאמר: בושתה ופגמה איצטריכא ליה פלוגתא דרבי יהודה בן בתירא ורבנן. דלא הוה ליה למימר טפי אלא בושתה ופגמה איצטריכא ליה, דאגב דבעי למיתני בושתה ופגמה שהוא שלו – תנא נמי מציאתה ומעשה ידיה שהן שלו. אבל אי גרסינן שלה – אתי שפיר, דמשום רבנן לא איצטריך למיתני כלל מציאתה ומעשה ידיה, דמה ענין זה אצל זה? דהאי הוי שלו, והאי הוי שלה. ולא איצטריך למיתני אלא משום רבי יהודה בן בתירא, דאליביה שייך בהו בעל. **שלה** • למ"ד ב"החובל" (ב"ק דף פו.) בקוטע יד עבד עברי של חבירו – ינתן הכל לעבד, וילקח בהן קרקע והוא אוכל פירות – אתי שפיר, דהכא נמי, הכל לאשה וילקח בהן קרקע והוא אוכל פירות. אבל למאן דאמר: ינתן שבח גדולה לעבד, ושבח קטנה לרב – צריך לחלק בין עבד לאשה. **בזמן** שבסתר. פגם שבסתר במקום שאין בני אדם יכולין לראות. שבגלוי – שפלעה בפניה, במקום שנראה לכל, ונפגם הוא עצמו עמה. בושת שבסתר – שביישה בינו לבינה, שבגלוי – שביישה בפני כל אדם. והא

קכב א מיי' פי"ב מהל' אישות הלכה יג טור ש"ע אה"ע סימן ע סעיף ג בהגה"ה:
קכבא ב מיי' שם הלכה ד סמג עשין מח ולאוין פא טור אה"ע סימן עג:
קכבב ג מיי' פי"ח שם הלכה ד סמג שם טוש"ע שם סימן לה סעיף ה:
קכבג ד מיי' פי"ב שם הלכה יב סמג לאוין פא טוש"ע שם סימן עו סעיף ב:
קכבד ה ו מיי' שם הל' יד סמג שם טוש"ע שם סימן עא סעיף א:
קכבה ז מיי' פ"ו מהלכות עירובין הלכה ח סמג עשין דרבנן א טוש"ע א"ח סימן תיד סעיף ב:
קכבו ח מיי' פכ"א מהל' אישות הלכה יא סמג לאוין פא טוש"ע אה"ע סימן פ סעיף יא:
א ט מיי' פ"ב שם הל' א ג ופכ"ב שם הל' א סמג שם טוש"ע שם סימן סט סעיף א:
ב י מיי' וסמג וטוש"ע שם סעיף ב:
ג כ מיי' פי"ב שם הלכה א ג ופכ"ב הלכה ז סמג שם טוש"ע שם סימן פה סעיף א ג וסי' פה סעיף א וסימן ל סעיף א:
ד ל מיי' פ"ד מהל' חובל ומזיק הלכה יז סמג עשין ע וטוש"ע ח"מ סי' תכד סעיף יא:

סוטה ח.
[לקמן סז.]
[לעיל סד:]
[לעיל יג. פסחים ג. וש"נ]
משלי ל
שבת פו. נדה יז.
לעיל נו.
עירובין פב.
לעיל מו: קדושין ג: י. [תוספתא דסוטה פ"ב]

הגהות הב"ח

(א) גמ' למ"ד תשמיש אמאי נקט אוכלת לישנא מעליא: (ב) שם איתמר מה הוא מוסיף לה אמר ר' יהושע בן לוי:

גליון הש"ס

גמ' ת"ר מותר מזונות. עי' נזיר דף כד ע"ב תוס' ד"ה שקמלתה:

תוספות רי"ד

היורשים להלביש את אלמנה כשם שחייבים לזונה והנ"ג אמרינן בפירקין שלפניו על הבנות הניזונות מן האחין שהן חייבין להלבישן: ונותן לה כפה לראשה פי' צעיף אחת לשנה וכן חגור למתניה ומנעל לרגליה ממועד למועד פי' בכל מועד ומועד יקנה לה מנעלים חדשים. וכלים שוים נ' זוז יעשה לה משנה לשנה: אמר אביי נ' זוז פשיטי פי' זוזי מדינה שהן ח' בזוז צורי דאי ס"ד נ' זוז ממש עני נ' זוז מנ"ל אלא ש"מ נ' זוזי פשיטי: ת"ר מותר מזונות לבעל מותר בלאות לאשה פי' אם נתן לה מזונות מרובים כדתנן בד"א בעני אבל במכובד הכל וכו' אבל מותר הבלאות שנשארו לה כשעשו לה חדשים הן לאשה כדתנן והשחקים שלה ואמרינן בלאות למה לה כיון שהוא עושה לה חדשים א"ר מתכסה בהן בימי נדותה כדי שלא תתבזה על בעלה פי' שלא תהא זקוקה ללבוש בגדים בימי נדותה: א"ר נקטינן מותר בלאות אלמנה ליורשים התם שלא תתגנה על בעלה הכא תתגנה ותתגנה: ונותן לה מעה כסף לצרכה פי' בכל שבת יתן לה מעה כסף שהוא ששית דינר לצרכי' קטנים שיש לה וגם היא אוכלת עמו מליל שבת לליל שבת שהוא זמן העונה [ואם] אינו נותן לה מעה כסף לצרכיה מותר מע"י שלה הכי אמרן לעיל בפירקין רב ושמואל דאמרי תרווייהו תקנו מזונות תחת מע"י ומעה כסף תיקנו תחת המותר והיכי תיקנו ומה היא עושה לו כדי שתהא מותר מע"י כמה הוו משקל ה' סלעים שתי ביהודה שהששתי שוייתו דקה וק' משל ערב כפלים שהן עשר סלעים בגליל שהסלע שביהודה היה גדול כפלים דסלע שבגליל או משקל י' סלעים ערב ביהודה שהן כ' סלעים בגליל: מאי אוכלת ר"נ אמר אוכלת ממש ור"א [אמר] תשמיש כדכתיב אכלה ומחתה פיה ואמרה לא פעלתי און וק"ל כר"נ דתניא רשב"ג אומר אוכלת עמו כל ליל שבת ושבת א): ואם היתה מניקה וכו' אריב"ל מוסיפין יין שהיין יפה לחלב: דרש רב עולא רבא אפיתחא דבי נשיאה אע"פ שאמרו אין אדם זן בניו ובנותיו כשהן קטנים אבל זן הוא קטני קטנים עד כמה עד בן שש: יוצא בעירוב אמו פי' אם ערבה אמו לצפון ואביו ערב לדרום עם אמו יוצא ולא עם אביו שאינו יכול להפרד מאמו והלכך כשם שחייב לזון את אשתו כך חייב לזון בנים קטנים התלויין עליו: **הדרן עלך פרק אף על פי**

מציאת האשה ומע"י לבעלה וירושתה הוא אוכל פירות בחייה בושתה ופגמה שלה ריב"ב אומר בזמן שבסתר לה ב' חלקים ולו חלק א' ובזמן שבגלוי לו ב' חלקים ולה חלק א' שלו נותנים מיד ושלה ילקח בהן קרקע והוא אוכל פירות וירושתה פי' שאם מתה בעלה יורשה הכל ואפילו נכסי מלוג שלה ובעודה בחיי' עמו הוא אוכל פירותיהן: בושתה ופגמה פי' נזק חבלתה הוא שלה כנכסי מלוג תני תנא קמיה דרבא מציאת האשה לעצמה פי' קסבר שלא תקנו מציאת האשה לבעלה אלא מע"י שלא תהא אלא אמה עבריה שקנאה בדמים שמע"י לרבה ומציאתה שלה ור"ע אומר לבעלה קסבר אע"ג דדינא הכי מ"מ תהוי לבעלה משום איבה כדאמרינן בפרק נערה שהאב זכאי במציאת בתו מ"ט משום איבה וכדאמרינן בפרק האשה רבה לא זה וזה זכאין במציאתה טעמא מאי אמור רבנן מציאות אשה לבעלה משום איבה הני תהוי להו איבה א"ל השתא ומה העדפה דמעשה

א) לכאורה הא אדחייה לה לאיה זו בגמ' ואמנם הרי"ף והרא"ש כתבו הטעם משום דהלכתא כר"נ בדיני.